The 2000

ESPN

Information Please®

Sports Almanac

With Year in Review Commentary from
ESPN anchors and analysts:

David Aldridge
on Pro Basketball

Chris Berman
on Pro Football

Al Bernstein
on Boxing

John Clayton
on Pro Football

Linda Cohn
on Women's Golf and
The 21st Century

Lee Corso
on College Football

Steve Cyphers
on College Sports

Rece Davis
on Auto Racing

Mike Durbin
on Bowling

Jack Edwards
on International Sports
and Soccer

Rich Eisen
on the Top 20 Moments

Chris Fowler
on College Basketball and
College Football

Hank Goldberg
on Horse Racing

Mimi Griffin
on Women's College Basketball

Steve Levy
on Pro Hockey

Bob Ley
on The Sports Century

Kenny Mayne
on the Top 20 Personalities

Sal Paolantonio
on Tennis

Dan Patrick
on the Top 20 Personalities

Karl Ravech
on Ballparks and Arenas
and Baseball

Jimmy Roberts
on Golf

Dave Ryan
on College Baseball

Stuart Scott
on the Top 20 Moments

Bob Stevens
on Business

Dick Vitale
on College Basketball

YEAR IN REVIEW

BASEBALL

COLLEGE FOOTBALL

PRO FOOTBALL

COLLEGE BASKETBALL

PRO BASKETBALL

HOCKEY

COLLEGE SPORTS

HALLS OF FAME AND AWARDS

WHO'S WHO

The Champions of 1999

Auto Racing

NASCAR Circuit
Daytona 500 . . . . .Jeff Gordon
Winston 500 . . . . .Dale Earnhardt
Coca-Cola 600 . . . . .Jeff Burton
Southern 500 . . . . .Jeff Burton
Winston Cup Points Title . . . . .Dale Jarrett, 4772 pts
(through Oct. 24)   Bobby Labonte, 4526 pts
CART Circuit
U.S. 500 . . . . .Tony Kanaan
PPG Cup Championship . . . . . .Dario Franchitti, 209 pts
(through Oct. 28)   Juan Montoya, 200 pts
Indy Racing League Circuit
Indianapolis 500 . . . . .Kenny Brack
Points Championship . . . . .Greg Ray
Formula One Circuit
World Driving Championship . . . . . . .Eddie Irvine, 70 pts
(through Oct. 31)   Mika Hakkinen, 66 pts

Baseball

World Series . . . . . .New York def. Atlanta, 4 games to 0
MVP . . . . .Mariano Rivera, NY, P
All-Star Game . . . . .AL 4, NL 1 in Boston
MVP . . . . .Pedro Martinez, Bos., P
College World Series . . . . .Miami 6, Florida St. 5
MVP . . . . .Marshall McDougall, FSU, 2B

College Basketball

Men's NCAA Final Four
Championship . . . . .Connecticut 77, Duke 74
MVP . . . . .Richard Hamilton, Connecticut, F
Women's NCAA Final Four
Championship . . . . .Purdue 62, Duke 45
MVP . . . . .Ukari Figgs, Purdue, G

Pro Basketball

NBA Finals . . .San Antonio def. New York, 4 games to 1
MVP . . . . .Tim Duncan, San Antonio, F
Eastern Final . . . . .New York def. Indiana, 4 games to 2
Western Final . .San Antonio def. Portland, 4 games to 0

Bowling

Men's Major Championships
Tournament of Champions (1998) . . . . .Bryan Goebel
PBA National . . . . .Tim Criss
ABC Masters . . . . .Brian Boghosian
BPAA U.S. Open .Bob Learn Jr.
Women's Major Championships
Sam's Town Invitational (1998) . . . . .Julie Gardner
WIBC Queens . . . . .Leanne Barrette
BPAA U.S. Open . . . . .Kim Adler
AMF Gold Cup . . . . .Dana Miller-Mackie

College Football (1998)

National Champions
AP . . . . .Tennessee (12-0)
ESPN/USA Today Coaches' . . . . .Tennessee (12-0)
Major Bowls
Orange . . . . .Florida 31, Syracuse 10
Rose . . . . .Wisconsin 38, UCLA 31
Sugar . . . . .Ohio St. 24, Texas A&M 14
Fiesta . . . . .Tennessee 23, Florida St. 16
Heisman Trophy . . . . .Ricky Williams, Texas, RB

Pro Football (1998)

Super Bowl XXXIII . . . . .Denver 34, Atlanta 19
MVP . . . . .John Elway, Denver, QB
AFC Championship . . . . .Denver 23, NY Jets 10
NFC Championship . . . . .Atlanta 30, Minnesota 27

Pro Bowl . . . . .AFC 23, NFC 10
MVP . . . .Ty Law, NE, CB & Keyshawn Johnson, NYJ, WR
CFL Grey Cup Final . . . . .Calgary 26, Hamilton 24
MVP . . . . .Jeff Garcia, Calgary, QB

Golf

Men's Major Championships
Masters .Jose Maria Olazabal
U.S. Open . . . . .Payne Stewart
British Open . . . . .Paul Lawrie
PGA Championship . . . . .Tiger Woods
Seniors Major Championships
The Tradition . . . . .Graham Marsh
PGA Seniors . . . . .Allen Doyle
U.S. Senior Open . . . . .Dave Eichelberger
Senior Players Championship . . . . .Hale Irwin
Women's Major Championships
Nabisco Dinah Shore . . . . .Dottie Pepper
LPGA Championship .Juli Inkster
U.S. Women's Open .Juli Inkster
du Maurier Classic .Karrie Webb
National Team Competition
Ryder Cup . . . . .United States 14½, Europe 13½

Hockey

Stanley Cup . . . . .Dallas def. Buffalo, 4 games to 2
MVP . . . . .Joe Nieuwendyk, Dallas, C
Western Final . . . . . .Dallas def. Colorado, 4 games to 3
Eastern Final . . . . .Buffalo def. Toronto, 4 games to 1
All-Star Game . . . . .North America 8, World 6 in Tampa
MVP . . . . .Wayne Gretzky, North America, C
NCAA Div. 1 Final . . . . .Maine 3, New Hamphire 2 (OT)
MVP . . . . .Alfie Michaud, Maine, G

Horse Racing

Triple Crown Champions
Kentucky Derby . . . . .Charismatic (Chris Antley)
Preakness . . . . .Charismatic (Chris Antley)
Belmont . . . . .Lemon Drop Kid (Jose Santos)
Harness Racing
Hambletonian . . . . .Self Possessed (Mike Lachance)
Little Brown Jug . . . . .Blissful Hall (Ron Pierce) .

Soccer

Women's World Cup . .United States 0, China 0, U.S. wins
5-4 on Shootout
MVP . . . . .Sun Wen, China, F
World Youth Championship . . . . .Spain 4, Japan 0

Tennis

Men's Grand Slam Championships
Australian Open . . . . .Yevgeny Kafelnikov
French Open . . . . .Andre Agassi
Wimbledon . . . . .Pete Sampras
U.S. Open . . . . .Andre Agassi
Women's Grand Slam Championships
Australian Open . . . . .Martina Hingis
French Open . . . . .Steffi Graf
Wimbledon .Lindsay Davenport
U.S. Open . . . . .Serena Williams
National Team Competition
Davis Cup (1998) . . . . .Sweden 4, Italy 1
Fed Cup (Women) . . . . .United States 4, Russia 1

Miscellaneous Champions

Little League World Series . . . . .Osaka, Japan
Tour de France . . . . .Lance Armstrong (USA)
Iditarod . . . . .Doug Swingley

THE 2000
ESPN INFORMATION PLEASE®
SPORTS ALMANAC

Gerry Brown
Michael Morrison
EDITORS

Information Please
www.infoplease.com

HYPERION
ESPN®
BOOKS

Editors
Gerry Brown, Michael Morrison
Assistant Editor
John Gettings
Reporter
Jason Peers
Production Editor
Elaine Rho
Database/Production Manager
Susan Hyde
Graphics
Barbara Pennucci
Technical Support
Karl DeBisschop
Fact Checking
Larry Schwartz

Comments and suggestions from readers are invited. Because of the many letters received, however, it is not possible to respond personally to every correspondent. Nevertheless, all letters are welcome and each will be carefully considered. The **2000 ESPN Information Please Sports Almanac** does not rule on bets or wagers. Address all correspondence to: Sports, Information Please, 20 Park Plaza, Boston, MA 02116.
Email: ipsa@infoplease.com.

ISBN 0-7868-8472-X

FIRST EDITION

10 9 8 7 6 5 4 3 2 1

CONTENTS 5

EDITORS' NOTE................................7
WHO PLAYS WHERE 8
THE SPORTS CENTURY
  Essay by Bob Ley 9
  A Look at the 21st Century by Linda Cohn .15
COMING ATTRACTIONS 18
THE YEAR IN REVIEW—1998-1999
  Top 20 Personalities by Dan Patrick
  and Kenny Mayne..........................19
  Top 20 Moments by Rich Eisen
  and Stuart Scott..............................27
  Month by Month Calendar..................39
  2000 Preview 64
BASEBALL
  Year in Review by Karl Ravech............65
  1999 Statistics...............................71
    Final Major League Standings 71
    Regular Season Leaders...................72
    1999 All-Star Game.......................77
    Team by Team Statistics...................78
    World Series and Playoffs................87
    College Baseball 96
  Through the Years...........................101
    The World Series..........................101
    Reg. Season League & Div. Winners 106
    The All-Star Game 108
    Major League Franchise Origins 110
    Annual Leaders 112
    No Hitters 123
    All-Time Leaders..........................125
    All-Time Winningest Managers..........133
    Annual Awards 134
    College Baseball..........................138
COLLEGE FOOTBALL
  Year in Review by Chris Fowler
  and Lee Corso 141
  1998 Season Statistics 147
    Final AP Top 25 Poll 147
    NCAA Division 1-A Final Standings.....152
    NCAA Division 1-A Leaders..............153
    Final NCAA Div. 1-AA Standings 157
    NCAA Division 1-AA Leaders 159
  Through the Years...........................162
    National Champions, 1869-1998 162
    AP Final Polls, 1936-98 166
    Bowl Games 181
    All-Time Winningest Div. 1-A Teams 189
    Major Conference Champions 190
    Annual NCAA Division 1-A Leaders 196
    All-Time NCAA Division 1-A Leaders....199
    Annual Awards 203
    All-Time Winningest Div. 1-A Coaches ..207
PRO FOOTBALL
  Year in Review by Chris Berman
  and John Clayton 213
  1998 Season Statistics 219
    Final NFL Standings.......................219
    Regular Season Individual Leaders 220
    Team by Team Statistics...................224
    NFL Playoffs and Super Bowl XXXIII 232

PRO FOOTBALL (CONT.)
    NFL College Draft.........................237
    Canadian Football League 238
  Through the Years...........................242
    The Super Bowl 242
    Super Bowl Playoffs, 1966-98 246
    NFL-NFC Championship Game 252
    AFL-AFC Championship Game 253
    NFL Divisional Champions...............254
    NFL Franchise Origins 258
    Annual NFL Leaders 260
    All-Time NFL Leaders.....................264
    Number One Draft Choices 270
    All-Time Winningest NFL Coaches 271
    Annual Awards 272
    Canadian Football League 276
COLLEGE BASKETBALL
  Year in Review by Chris Fowler
  and Dick Vitale..............................279
  1998-99 Statistics 285
    Final Regular Season AP Men's Top 25 .285
    1999 NCAA Men's Div. 1 Tournament .286
    Final NCAA Men's Div. 1 Standings 289
    1999 NCAA Women's Div. 1 Tourn.....301
  Through the Years...........................304
    National Champions, 1901-99 304
    NCAA Final Four, 1939-99 306
    All-Time NCAA Div. 1 Tourn. Leaders ...309
    Associated Press Final Polls, 1949-99 ..313
    Annual NCAA Div. 1 Leaders 327
    All-Time NCAA Div. 1 Indiv. Leaders 328
    Annual Awards 331
    All-Time Winningest Div. 1 Coaches 333
    Women's Basketball 337
PRO BASKETBALL
  Year in Review by David Aldridge 343
  1998-99 Statistics 349
    Final NBA Standings 349
    Regular Season Individual Leaders 351
    Team by Team Statistics...................353
    NBA Playoffs..............................359
    Annual Awards 362
    NBA Draft.................................363
  Through the Years...........................367
    The NBA Finals, 1947-99 367
    NBA Franchise Origins 371
    Annual NBA Leaders 373
    All-Time NBA Regular Season Leaders ..375
    All-Time Winningest NBA Coaches ..378
    Annual Awards 379
    Number One Draft Choices, 1966-99 ..380
    American Basketball Association........383
HOCKEY
  Year in Review by Steve Levy..............385
  1998-99 Statistics 391
    Final NHL Standings 391
    Regular Season Individual Leaders 394
    Team by Team Statistics...................396
    Stanley Cup Playoffs 403
    NHL Draft 408

6　　　　　　　　　　　**CONTENTS**

HOCKEY (CONT.)
College Hockey 408
Through the Years 413
　Stanley Cup Champions, 1893-1999...413
　All-Time Playoff Leaders 415
　NHL Franchise Origins 419
　Annual NHL Leaders 421
　All-Time NHL Regular Season Leaders...424
　All-Time Winningest NHL Coaches 428
　Annual Awards 429
　Number One Draft Choices 432
　World Hockey Association 433
　College Hockey 436

COLLEGE SPORTS
Year in Review by Steve Cyphers 439
　Div. 1 Basketball Schools 445
　Div. 1-A Football Schools 450
　Div. 1-AA Football Schools 452
　1998-99 NCAA Team Champions 458
　Annual NCAA Div. 1 Team Champions ..463

HALLS OF FAME & AWARDS
Halls of Fame 471
Retired Numbers 505
Awards 509
Trophy Case 515

WHO'S WHO
Sports Personalities 519

BALLPARKS & ARENAS
Year in Review by Karl Ravech 549
　Coming Attractions 555
　Sport-by-Sport 557

BUSINESS
Year in Review by Bob Stevens............579
　Media Statistics and Awards 585
　Directory of Organizations 596

OLYMPIC GAMES
Summer Games Through the Years 624
　Event-by-Event 661
　All-Time Leading Medal Winners 680
Winter Games Through the Years 684
　Event-by-Event 685
　All-Time Leading Medal Winners 694

INTERNATIONAL SPORTS
Year in Review by Jack Edwards 697
1999 Statistics 703
　Track & Field World Records 704
　Swimming World Records 710
Through the Years 717

SOCCER
Year in Review by Jack Edwards 729
　Women's World Cup '99 735
　1999 Major League Soccer 743
　College Soccer 749
Through the Years 751
　The World Cup, 1930-98 751
　Other Competition 756

BOWLING
Year in Review by Mike Durbin............765
1998-99 Statistics 771
Through the Years 774

HORSE RACING
Year in Review by Hank Goldberg 779
1998-99 Statistics 785
　Thoroughbred Racing 785
　Harness Racing 789
Through the Years 791
　Thoroughbred Racing 791
　Harness Racing 807

TENNIS
Year in Review by Sal Paolantonio 811
1998-99 Statistics 817
　Men's and Women's Tournaments 817
　Singles Rankings 821
Through the Years 823
　Grand Slam Championships 823
　Annual Number One Players 832
　Annual Top 10 World Rankings 833
　National Team Competition 838
　Colleges..................................839

GOLF
Year in Review by Jimmy Roberts..........841
1998-99 Statistics 847
　PGA, Seniors and LPGA Tournaments...847
　Women's Year in Review by
　Linda Cohn 853
Through the Years 856
　Major Championships 856
　National Team Competition 875
　Colleges..................................876

AUTO RACING
Year in Review by Rece Davis 877
1998-99 Statistics 883
　NASCAR Results 883
　CART Results 886
　Indy Racing League Results 888
　Formula One Results 889
　NHRA Results 891
Through the Years 892
　NASCAR Circuit 892
　CART Circuit 895
　IRL Circuit................................896
　Formula One 898
　NHRA 902

BOXING
Year in Review by Al Bernstein 903
　Current Champions 909
　Major Bouts, 1998-99 910
Through the Years 918
　Major Hvywgt. Championship Fights ...918
　Major Titleholders 925

MISCELLANEOUS SPORTS
1998-99 Statistics 933

DEATHS 949

BIBLIOGRAPHY 957

It's almost time to call it a century. Yeah, we know it doesn't technically end until Jan. 2001 but humor us, OK?

This past year, Mark and Sammy were at it again, the U.S. Ryder Cup team mounted a miracle comeback at Brookline and the U.S. Women's World Cup team took us on a mid-summer thrill ride. But it was a bittersweet year for fans around the country as it seemed like every other week a sports legend was calling it a career. From the "Big Three" of Jordan, Gretzky and Elway (see front cover) right down a list that included Barry Sanders, Reggie White, Steffi Graf, John Thompson and soon will include Dominik Hasek.

Maybe they were a step ahead like they were on the field of competition, getting out before the dreaded Y2K bug hit. As we sit here putting the finishing touches on the book you are now holding we are hoping that the Y2K bug spares us so that we might see the next Jordan, Gretzky, Elway or a Red Sox World Series win, if they ever happen to arrive in our lifetimes.

The completion of this, the 11th edition of the sports almanac took the hard work and dedication of many throughout the year. First of all, much thanks goes out to Assistant Editor John Gettings. JG's a drummer and listens to weird music but we still like him and his detailed eye and work ethic were instrumental in making the project a success.

Thanks to reporter Jason Peers. His tenacity at tracking down information made him a key player, even when he let the music take over from time to time. Thanks as always to the Information Please production crew, starting with Production Editor Elaine Rho and Database/Production Manager Susan Hyde. Elaine and Susan were dedicated team players and their contributions were immeasurable. As if putting a 960-page book together wasn't enough, Elaine also found the time to welcome a new son to her family.

We are also much obliged to the InfoPlease band of renown. Barbara Pennucci handled our graphics with aplomb, Paul Evenson, Ben Snowden and Ricco Siasoco worked their magic on the web and as usual the technical staff of Boris Goldowsky, Jim Dubinsky, Kate Wrigley and Karl DeBisschop handled the computer "stuff" so we don't have to.

Also a special thanks to Christian DelPrete, a member of the team who we lost in 1999. We considered Christian not only a colleague but a friend, and his love of life and sports gave us all a charge.

Thanks must also go out to our other Information Please brethren: Liz Kubik for her leadership, Jim Bryant and Scott Beatty (Go Browns!) for making everything possible, Borgna Brunner, Pam Greene, Nicole Guest, Dan Arel and Dan (Stan) Shafto for their individual and unique contributions.

There are many people at ESPN and our publisher Hyperion that deserve a large tip of the cap. At ESPN, Sharyn Taymor gave us a quality start, Kil-Jae Hong came in in middle relief for the hold and John Hassan took control in the bottom of the ninth for the save. As former editor of the almanac, we couldn't think of a better closer than John. Thanks also go out to all the ESPN essay contributors. For a full roster check out page one. Further appreciation goes to ESPN football guru Russell Baxter and to bowling aficionado Debbie Durbin who helped us in their own special ways.

At Hyperion, Gretchen Young, Jennifer Morgan and David Lott all were a crucial part of the process. JoAnn DeMeo at Command Web also successfully and happily dealt with any curveballs we threw her way.

We also leaned on many individuals while tracking down the numerous stats that grace these pages. Rick Campbell and Gary Johnson at the NCAA, Barbara Zidovsky at Nielsen Media Research, Bill Magrath at the Sports Business Daily, Larry Barber of the MEAC, Frank Mahon of the Utica Mullions and Larry Schwartz are just some of the many who made our lives a little easier. And thanks to the illustrious Carolyn McMahon at AP, our pipeline to the hundreds of great pictures you'll find in the book.

Thanks as well to founding editor Mike Meserole who stays in touch even though he now plays for another team. And perhaps most importantly, thanks to our families and friends. You know who you are.

Gerry Brown and Michael Morrison
Boston
October 19, 1999

Major League Cities & Teams

As of Oct. 31, 1999, there were 130 major league teams playing or scheduled to play baseball, basketball, NFL football, hockey and soccer in 49 cities in the United States and Canada. Listed below are the cities and the teams that play there.

Anaheim
AL	Angels
NHL	Mighty Ducks of Anaheim

Atlanta
NL	Braves
NBA	Hawks
NFL	Falcons
NHL	Thrashers

Baltimore
AL	Orioles
NFL	Ravens

Boston
AL	Red Sox
NBA	Celtics
NFL	N.E. Patriots (Foxboro)
NHL	Bruins
MLS	N.E. Revolution (Foxboro)

Buffalo
NFL	Bills (Orchard Park)
NHL	Sabres

Calgary
NHL	Flames

Charlotte
NBA	Hornets
NFL	Carolina Panthers

Chicago
AL	White Sox
NL	Cubs
NBA	Bulls
NFL	Bears
NHL	Blackhawks
MLS	Fire

Cincinnati
NL	Reds
NFL	Bengals

Cleveland
AL	Indians
NBA	Cavaliers
NFL	Browns

Columbus
MLS	Crew

Dallas
AL	Texas Rangers (Arlington)
NBA	Mavericks
NFL	Cowboys (Irving)
NHL	Stars
MLS	Burn

Denver
NL	Colorado Rockies
NBA	Nuggets
NFL	Broncos
NHL	Colorado Avalanche
MLS	Colorado Rapids

Detroit
AL	Tigers
NBA	Pistons (Auburn Hills)
NFL	Lions (Pontiac)
NHL	Red Wings

East Rutherford
NBA	New Jersey Nets
NFL	New York Giants
NFL	New York Jets
NHL	New Jersey Devils
MLS	NY/NJ Metrostars

Edmonton
NHL	Oilers

Green Bay
NFL	Packers

Houston
NL	Astros
NBA	Rockets

Indianapolis
NBA	Indiana Pacers
NFL	Colts

Jacksonville
NFL	Jaguars

Kansas City
AL	Royals
NFL	Chiefs
MLS	Wizards

Los Angeles
NL	Dodgers
NBA	Clippers
NBA	Lakers
NHL	Kings
MLS	Galaxy

Miami
NL	Florida Marlins
NBA	Heat
NFL	Dolphins
NHL	Florida Panthers (Sunrise)
MLS	Fusion (Ft. Lauderdale)

Milwaukee
NL	Brewers
NBA	Bucks

Minneapolis
AL	Minn. Twins
NBA	Minn. Timberwolves
NFL	Minn. Vikings

Montreal
NL	Expos
NHL	Canadiens

Nashville
NFL	Tennessee Titans
NHL	Predators

New Orleans
NFL	Saints

New York
AL	Yankees
NL	Mets (Flushing)
NBA	Knicks
NHL	Rangers
NHL	Islanders (Uniondale)

Oakland
AL	Athletics
NBA	Golden St. Warriors
NFL	Raiders

Orlando
NBA	Magic

Ottawa
NHL	Senators (Kanata)

Philadelphia
NL	Phillies
NBA	76ers
NFL	Eagles
NHL	Flyers

Phoenix
NBA	Suns
NFL	Arizona Cardinals (Tempe)
NL	Arizona Diamondbacks
NHL	Coyotes

Pittsburgh
NL	Pirates
NFL	Steelers
NHL	Penguins

Portland
NBA	Trail Blazers

Raleigh
NHL	Carolina Hurricanes

Sacramento
NBA	Kings

St. Louis
NL	Cardinals
NFL	Rams
NHL	Blues

Salt Lake City
NBA	Utah Jazz

San Antonio
NBA	Spurs

San Diego
NL	Padres
NFL	Chargers

San Francisco
NL	Giants
NFL	49ers

San Jose
NHL	Sharks
MLS	Clash

Seattle
AL	Mariners
NBA	SuperSonics
NFL	Seahawks

Tampa
NFL	T.B. Buccaneers
NHL	T.B. Lightning
AL	T.B. Devil Rays (St. Petersburg)
MLS	T.B. Mutiny

Toronto
AL	Blue Jays
NBA	Raptors
NHL	Maple Leafs

Vancouver
NBA	Grizzlies
NHL	Canucks

Washington
NBA	Wizards
NFL	Redskins (Raljon, Md.)
NHL	Capitals
MLS	D.C. United

Century

The sale of **Babe Ruth** to the New York Yankees was the most famous transaction of the century and has some convinced that the Boston Red Sox have played under a curse since he left Beantown in January of 1920.

AP/Wide World Photos

Signs of the Times

A look at those people and events responsible for guiding sports along a winding road this century.

by
Bob Ley

The hardest part of a fan's life at the turn of the millennium is hacking your way through the innumerable choices in the multi-billion dollar jungle of the sporting culture. Past thousands of web sites, through hundreds of satellite television channels, and scores of leagues, to wear officially licensed gear and purchase star-endorsed kitsch. With our favorite team's credit card, of course.

What hath sports wrought? Consider the choices a hundred years ago when "wrought" was in the vocabulary, and ACL simply a random collection of letters. There was baseball. And boxing. And that ruffian endeavor, football. And perhaps

tomorrow's newspaper to tell you about it.

Since then, we've seen a rollicking explosion of the sporting life, a cultural and economic revolution with these significant signposts pointing the way from then to now.

❧   ❧   ❧

Sports owners eternally plead poverty, but Red Sox owner Harry Frazee was cash-poor and the script of "No No Nannette" had his eye. A mere $125 thousand later, in January 1920, the wanna-be producer sold his stellar pitcher/slugger Babe Ruth to the New York Yankees. So began sports' modern era. Long before chicks dug the long ball, Ruth turned it from occasional curiosity to bombastic starmaking statement. He also transformed his club into an institution, and himself

---

Bob Ley has been a *SportsCenter* anchor since 1979.

AP/Wide World Photos

Heavyweight champion Cassius Clay, standing over fallen challenger Sonny Liston after flooring him on May 25, 1965, certainly seemed to have had a big impact on Liston's jaw that day. But it was two years later, when Clay changed his named to **Muhammad Ali** and refused induction into the U.S. Army, that he made his largest impact on American society.

into America's first sporting icon. The birth of radio, Ruth's outsized persona, and the Yankees' perennial dominance combined to unite the country in following his exploits, and with them, this national pastime.

&ampa;&ampa;&ampa;

With each passing year fewer people can personally recall the character of Jackie Robinson's courage, and the depth of the hatred he faced. To be sure, there was a pragmatic side to Branch Rickey's decision to sign Robinson. The Negro Leagues were rich with vibrant baseball talent, and there was a major league advantage to be gained. But Rickey, who quoted Scripture in everyday speech and worked beneath a picture of Lincoln, surely acted on what is often missing

in latter day sports—principle. One moment crystallized Robinson's epochal stand early in his 1947 rookie season. Having already endured taunts and threats, and with a possible boycott brewing, Robinson was the target of ugly on-field abuse in Cincinnati, when in the sixth inning, Pee Wee Reese called time. The Dodger shortstop—a son of the South from nearby Louisville—trotted over and placed his hand on Robinson's shoulder. The simple gesture quieted the stands and the dugout, and sent a signal resonating through the game: this man is my teammate, and he belongs.

&ampa;&ampa;&ampa;

Sports' neat and quaint geography—the world of train rides and familiar datelines—had existed for over a half-century while the country beyond it exploded in size and possibilities. Walter O'Malley knew this, sitting in Brooklyn. He also knew that, even with his 1955 World Series title, Dodgers' attendance was trending down. O'Malley's departure for the West Coast spawned equal measures of anger and romance back East, but it ended an era when a trip to St. Louis was both a Southern AND Western swing. More significantly, the Dodgers' arrival in Los Angeles, and the Giants' move to San Francisco ignited an era of new markets, new stadia, and new horizons for all sports. And it proved, back in Flatbush, and on Coogan's Bluff, that fan loyalty was not always repaid.

The bravery of **Jackie Robinson** went a long way toward improving society in 1947, not just major league baseball.

By the end of the 50's the NFL had, indeed, seen its greatest game—the Colts' 1958 overtime championship win over the Giants—but this was still a league before the dawn. The NFL's office was in Philadelphia, in Commissioner Bert Bell's basement. Choosing Bell's replacement took 24 ballots in early 1960. The choice of 34-year-old Pete Rozelle changed the modern business of sports. Within a year he saw Congress give the NFL the necessary protection to sell television rights as a single entity. And what Rozelle had inherited, a 12-team league with franchises worth $2 million, began to grow exponentially. He fought the AFL until peace made more sense, and centralized and unified the interests of his sport. And, like Pope Gregory XIII, he shaped the calendar, imbuing Sunday afternoons and Monday nights with cultural import.

On paper, Major League Baseball players did have a union since the late 1940's. But against the entrenched interests of the owners, this group was reduced to diddling around the margins. When a committee of baseball players hired Marvin Miller in 1965, the average major league player made less than $20,000 a year. Miller's arrival is the point from where all athletes measure their economic emancipation. Soft spoken and deliberate, Miller embarked on a strategy to not only improve pay scales, but change the rules by which pay was determined. Curt Flood's principled and courageous stand in 1970 cost him his career, but set the stage five years later for the death of the reserve clause and the birth of free agency. Miller's legacy is also the strikes, stoppages and litigation that litter recent sports history. But in today's players' contracts we count not just the dollars, but the number of digits. And we accept what used to be revolutionary: that athletes have rights, and a voice, one given to them by Miller.

🙚   🙚   🙚

Sports at the millennium is consumed with principal. But there are rare and incandescent moments when it is a stage for principle. Never more tellingly than when Muhammad Ali refused to take his step forward in 1967 and accept induction into the U.S. Army. In the broiling social revolution of the 60's, with race exploding into the angry national dialogue, Ali had already alienated the Establishment by changing his religion and his name. Now this loud black man took a stand on the divisive war in Vietnam. This was a year before the Olympic boycott, and the memorable protest of John Carlos and Tommie Smith. Ali was stripped of his title, and with it three prime years in the ring, along with untold millions and a deeper hold on boxing history. The Supreme Court eventually ruled in his favor, and Ali twice regained his title. What he truly gained was icon status for his principle, a courage standing in stark contrast in the age of *principal*.

🙚   🙚   🙚

Those under the age of 30 might dismiss as cruel fiction the fan's electronic landscape two decades ago. Televised sports existed basically two days a week, for several hours a day,

Archive Photos

Commissioner **Pete Rozelle** made the NFL what it is today, the center of America's sports consciousness, with his foresight and leadership.

on three networks. Then, Sept. 7, 1979, ESPN signed on. From that unremarkable evening sprung a competitive array of national networks, regional services, satellite channels, and now, the internet—where sports is a leading product. This daily injection of sports stars, news, images and highlights—from all sources—into America's sightlines has transformed sports from a sidelight into a central part of the national culture, and a multi-billion dollar industry. For some, suffocating overkill; for others, a democracy of choices.

🙚   🙚   🙚

It was the perfect convergence of a moment that transfixed the entire country, and a hero who appreciated his role and rare opportunity. Mark McGwire rose to the occasion, not merely with his bat, but also his heart.

His 1998 home run battle with Sammy Sosa highlighted a friendly mutual respect that helped rehabilitate the image of all pro athletes. And McGwire's near-mythic power brought casual fans back into baseball's tent, completing the repairs to the bonds between the game and its fans so badly frayed by the strike that claimed the World Series of 1994. McGwire touched all the right buttons, with grace and humility. Celebrating with his son, Matt. Hitting his 61st home run on his father's 61st birthday. Embracing the Maris family in the emotional moments following his historic 62nd homer. And closing with a ferocious barrage to punctuate his season at an unfathomable 70. He was a physical Superman, and emotional Everyman, especially after he confided to America, "Sometimes I amaze myself."

AP/Wide World Photos

St. Louis slugger **Mark McGwire** reached legendary status with his once-in-a-century season in 1998.

&a &a &a

Women's sports stars have grown from curiosities to mainstream figures, especially after the landmark Title IX legislation in 1972. But what happened in 1999 captured patriotic and sporting magic in a bottle, and begs questions for the next century. The United States Women's National Soccer Team had already won a World Cup, but that was eight years earlier, in virtual obscurity in China. Here in the States, beginning with a world-record crowd at Giants Stadium, an emotional momentum began to carry the American women through this tournament, with interest and attendance building from match to match. It crested with the championship at a sold-out Rose Bowl, in the gut-wrenching tension of a penalty kick shootout, as the United States defeated China with television ratings akin to the NBA Finals. Gender, flag and sport were all parts of this sudden explosion. It may be years before we learn how much of each.

&a &a &a

In the same century that men learned to walk on the moon while conceiving diabolically more productive ways to kill each other, sports grew from a genteel diversion to a socially seminal industry. At their finest, these games reflect the best in ourselves and our culture. The challenge in these superheated commercial times is to recognize those moments of redemption, and celebrate them. Even if they prove to be increasingly rare. ∎

The 21st Century

We've already seen glimpses of the technological and social changes that lie ahead for sports in the next century. Some are for the better and some aren't.

AP/Wide World Photos

Y2K Bugs

A list of things we hope to see disappear sometime in the next 100 years. Sooner, rather than later.

by
Linda Cohn

- **Fighting in the NHL.** We've come a long way since the 1970's and 80's, when stick-swinging and bench-clearing brawls marred the game. But more needs to be done.

- **Artificial turf.** All it took was the destruction of the 1999 Jets' season to finally make Meadowlands officials make the switch to grass. The artificial stuff served its purpose for the Astrodome a few decades ago but it has no place in the future. When it comes to grass, just say "yes."

- **Inconsistent umpiring.** The strike zone should *not* change depending on who happens to be working behind the plate. And not to be *too* rough on the men in blue (they've had a tough enough year already), but why is it that baseball is the only sport where umpires don't confer with each other on controversial calls? It makes no sense.

- **Cell phones at sporting events.** It's the newest fad. Bring a cell phone to the game, call a friend and wait until they see you on TV. That's your cue to scream and wave like an idiot. Please stop.

- **Big market advantages.** Sure the A's and Reds made a run at it this year, but did they honestly stand any chance at all against the Yankees or Braves? It's time baseball stopped using the Pirates, Expos and Twins as minor league systems for the big boys.

- **Work stoppages.** I'm not saying you shouldn't make a stand for what you believe in. But players and owners should both know that any strike or lockout really punches a hole in the hearts of all sports fans.

Linda Cohn is an anchor/reporter for ESPN's *SportsCenter*.

AP/Wide World Photos

No, these two aren't actually talking to each other. But as cell phones become more and more popular in the business world, they seem to be popping up in stadiums all over the country. Let's hope the trend goes away.

AP/Wide World Photos

It really doesn't seem like the money's affected him much at all, does it? When **Shaquille O'Neal** left Orlando for Los Angeles, the deal made him one of the highest paid players in NBA history and also helped to, gulp, further his movie career.

- **NBA teams scoring under 80 points.** With all the clutching and grabbing and an overall focus on style over substance, point totals have plummeted. The trend toward teams averaging below 100 points per game was bad enough. But these 75-68 stinkers have to go.

- **Four hour baseball games.** When no one under the age of 14 can stay up late enough to watch a League Championship Game, something's wrong.

- **Players saying it's not about the money.** Mo Vaughn left Boston for Anaheim for $80 million and a last-place finish, but it's not about the money. Alexei Yashin staged a holdout from the Ottawa Senators until he was treated with the respect he deserved. The huge raise he also asked for was secondary. Of course it's about the money!

- **Locker room interviews.** It doesn't even matter if you're male or female. It's a stupid, archaic thing to do. They're never good interviews anyway. Is it really going to kill us to wait another ten minutes to hear someone say, "we're just gonna take things one day at a time."

- **Endless debates over No. 1.** The Bowl Championship Series is a step in the right direction, but there's only one way to insure an undisputed national title game. College football needs a legitimate I-A playoff system. ■

Olympics
Winter Games

Year	No.	Host City	Dates
2002	XIX	Salt Lake City, Utah	Feb. 8-24
2006	XX	Turin, Italy	TBA

Summer Games

Year	No.	Host City	Dates
2000	XXVII	Sydney, Australia	Sept. 15-Oct. 1
2004	XXVIII	Athens, Greece	Aug. 13-29

All-Star Games
Baseball

Year	Site	Date
2000	Turner Field, Atlanta	July 11
2001	SAFECO Field, Seattle	TBA
2002	Miller Park, Milwaukee	TBA

NBA Basketball

Year	Site	Date
2000	Arena in Oakland	Feb. 13

NFL Pro Bowl

Year	Site	Date
2000	Aloha Stadium, Honolulu	Feb. 6
2001	Aloha Stadium, Honolulu	Feb. 4

NHL Hockey

Year	Site	Date
2000	Air Canada Center, Toronto	Feb. 6

Auto Racing

The Daytona 500 stock car race is usually held on the Sunday before the third Monday in February, while the Indianapolis 500 is usually held on the Sunday of Memorial Day weekend in May. The following dates are tentative.

Year	Daytona 500	Indianapolis 500
2000	Feb. 20	May 28
2001	Feb. 18	May 27
2002	Feb. 17	May 26

NCAA Basketball
Men's Final Four

Year	Site	Date
2000	RCA Dome, Indianapolis	April 1-3
2001	Metrodome, Minneapolis	Mar. 31-Apr. 2
2002	Georgia Dome, Atlanta	Mar. 30-Apr. 1
2003	Louisiana Superdome, New Orleans	April 5-7
2004	Alamodome, San Antonio	April 3-5

Women's Final Four

Year	Site	Date
2000	First Union Center, Philadelphia	Mar. 31-Apr. 2
2001	Kiel Center, St. Louis	Mar. 30-Apr. 1
2002	Alamodome, San Antonio	March 29-31
2003	Georgia Dome, Atlanta	April 4-6
2004	New Orleans Sports Arena	April 2-4

NFL Football
Super Bowl

No.	Site	Date
XXXIV	Georgia Dome, Atlanta	Jan. 30, 2000
XXXV	Raymond James Stadium, Tampa	Jan. 28, 2001
XXXVI	Louisiana Superdome, New Orleans	Jan. 27, 2002
XXXVII	Qualcomm Stadium, San Diego	Jan. 26, 2003

Golf
The Masters

Year	Site	Date
2000	Augusta National Ga.	April 6-9
2001	Augusta National Ga.	April 5-8
2002	Augusta National Ga.	April 11-14

U.S. Open

Year	Site	Date
2000	Pebble Beach (Calif.) Golf Links	June 15-18
2001	Southern Hills, Tulsa, Okla.	June 14-17
2002	Bethpage St. Park (Farmingdale, N.Y.)	June 13-16
2003	Olympia Fields (Ill.) Country Club	June 12-15

U.S. Women's Open

Year	Site	Date
2000	Merit Club, Libertyville, Ill.	July 20-23
2001	Pine Needles, Southern Pines N.C.	May 31-June 3
2002	Prairie Dunes CC, Hutchinson, Kan.	July 4-7

U.S. Senior Open

Year	Site	Date
2000	Saucon Valley GC, Bethlehem, Pa.	June 29-July 2
2001	Salem CC, Peabody Mass.	June 28-July 1
2002	Caves Valley GC, Owing Mills, Md.	June 27-30

PGA Championship

Year	Site	Date
2000	Valhalla GC, Louisville, Ky.	Aug. 17-20
2001	Atlanta Athletic Club, Duluth, Ga.	TBA
2002	Hazeltine National CC, Chaska, Minn.	TBA
2003	Oak Hill CC, Rochester, N.Y.	TBA

British Open

Year	Site	Date
2000	St. Andrews, Scotland	July 20-23
2001	Royal Lytham, England	July 19-22
2002	Muirfield, Scotland	July 18-21

Ryder Cup

Year	Site	Date
2001	The Belfrey, England	Sept. 28-30
2003	Oakland Hills CC, Bloomfield Hills, Mich.	TBA
2005	Kildare Hotel and CC, Dublin, Ireland	TBA
2007	Valhalla GC, Louisville, Ky.	TBA

Horse Racing
Triple Crown

The Kentucky Derby is always held at Churchill Downs in Louisville on the first Saturday in May, followed two weeks later by the Preakness Stakes at Pimlico Race Course in Baltimore and three weeks after that by the Belmont Stakes at Belmont Park in Elmont, N.Y.

Year	Ky Derby	Preakness	Belmont
2000	May 6	May 20	June 10
2001	May 5	May 19	June 9
2002	May 4	May 18	June 8

Tennis
U.S. Open

Usually held from the last Monday in August through the second Sunday in September, with Labor Day weekend the midway point in the tournament.

Year	Site	Date
2000	Arthur Ashe Stadium, NYC	Aug. 28-Sept. 10
2001	Arthur Ashe Stadium, NYC	Aug. 27-Sept. 9
2002	Arthur Ashe Stadium, NYC	Aug. 26-Sept. 8

Personalities

Tiger Woods won his second major championship in 1999 and capped off the year by earning a much-needed point for the Americans and captain Ben Crenshaw in their stunning Ryder Cup Sunday comeback.

Top 20 Sports Personalities of 1999

Dan and Kenny take a look back and choose their top newsmakers of the year.

by
Dan Patrick and Kenny Mayne

Once again, Kenny and Dan flipped a coin to see who got to list their selections first. An NFL official was brought in this year to flip the coin. Dan chose heads. The official heard tails. The coin landed on heads. Despite protests from Dan, Kenny goes first.

Dale Jarrett

I'm told he likes in on the action so we considered inviting him to throw in five bucks for our Daytona 500 pool, but we didn't want to get NASCAR involved. For his two Daytona 500 wins, and for the fact that he's one of the favorites to win each week, it has been even money for years that he'd finally get his season championship. And after his extraordi-

narily consistent 1999, the smart money says he's not done winning titles.

Team USA Soccer

It was the summer of 1998 and a World Cup goalie had skinned his butt diving for a ball. He lifted his shorts and sprayed some quick-freeze solution. This reminded me: Women's World Cup was less than a year away. Yeah, they were something to look at. But by that I mean the play, mostly. And more inspiring still was the way a good part of the nation watched, in awe.

Julie Krone

Once the bettor has made his scientific discovery as to which animal will win a race, he asks only that his jockey give an honest effort. Julie

---

Dan Patrick and Kenny Mayne are anchors of ESPN's *SportsCenter*.

AP/Wide World Photos

U.S. soccer team captain **Carla Overbeck** holds the Women's World Cup soccer trophy after the Americans' 5-4 overtime penalty shootout win over China at the Rose Bowl in July.

Krone did that often enough to make her the winningest female rider of all-time. Then she got real honest. Everyday, she said, she woke up with sore legs, sore knees, sore everything. So she put her career to bed. With three winners on her final day.

Kurt Warner

The game seems a bit preposterous when a quarterback can throw the ball the length of the field. But once in a while, look closer and you'll find a quarterback who can throw in any arena. The guys who opt for the CFL or NFL Europe or just opt out, know well about that fine line separating those who are invited and those who are turned away. Kurt Warner will never know just how many guys he really plays for.

Orlando Hernandez

In newspapers, corrections and omissions are noted daily. In magazines, once a week. This is a yearly publication and I blew it in these pages last year. It wasn't his 12-4 regular-season record and World Series win that stood out last year, and it's not his 17-9 record that rates inclusion this year.

The man risked his life to escape Cuba on a raft! How I missed noting

21

The sports world received a scare on June 13 as one of the good guys, **Larry Dierker**, suffered a grand mal seizure during the eighth inning of the Astros-Padres game. The Astros manager underwent brain surgery two days later and returned to the field on July 15.

it last time is regrettable. So is the way we often minimize that part of his story now.

Larry Dierker

So when his Astros stumble and find a way to complicate simple things, Larry Dierker can tell them, "It's not brain surgery" and really know of what he speaks. The Astrodome went silent (for baseball) after the 1999 season. It got that way in an unscheduled way in the eighth inning on June 13. But Dierker wasn't gone long. He got right back to doing life's simple things, like baseball.

Charismatic

We took some abuse as a company for putting Secretariat on the top 50 athletes of the century list. The uproar should be less severe here. When this 3-year-old finally got his proper respect from the public, it was as if some kind of racing karma intervened to punish all those who had disbelieved so long. But even with broken bones Charismatic was a game third in the Belmont.

Squall Watch

If you thought Charismatic was a long shot, try his half brother, Squall Watch. He was a long shot to live. He was once a $70,000 yearling but by age five was out of racing. Out of racing in the "let's-sell-his-flesh-for-food" kind of way. But then along came some good people from a group

AP/Wide World Photos

Maurice Greene is seriously pumped after crossing the finish line, breaking the 100 meter world record with a time of 9.79 on June 16 in Athens, Greece.

called Lost and Found Horse Rescue in Pennsylvania. And now Squall Watch can be seen as a polo pony.

Ricky Williams

I'm all for whatever the market will bear economically and I've never turned down a pay raise. I'm also one of those who thought Ricky Williams probably got hammered on that tackle football contract he signed with the Saints. But that way of thinking is relative only to current pro sports money. I don't agree with those who think Ricky was outsmarted. I believe he thinks it is a stupid thing that people are given money before they've earned it.

Maurice Greene

Yeah he was juiced up, but Ben Johnson did run 9.79 that day in Seoul. And though the time and medal were taken away, the guy really did go 9.79. So all along as the 100 meter mark was reduced (way up into the 9.8's), the ill-gotten mark from 1988 was still out there to match. And this year Maurice Greene pulled it off. Cleanly. Wind OK. Blood OK. Greene OK to shave off some more time.

Thanks Kenny. My ups.

Brett Hull

After so many years as the big, brash goal scorer who never won a championship, Hull goes to Dallas and

AP/Wide World Photos

Ricky Williams signed a risky, incentive-laden contract to play football for the New Orleans Saints. Mike Ditka's hoping he becomes the highest-paid running back in the league.

plays a different role: more defense, more leadership. Whatever the team needed. It just so happened that his team needed a Stanley Cup-winning goal. Hull obliged.

Tim Duncan

In his second year as a pro, Duncan led the San Antonio Spurs to the first post-Jordan NBA championship. Which is fitting because Duncan is his own man and is not interested in following in anybody's footsteps. I've met few athletes with such a confident sense of self.

Bobby Valentine

The mercurial and controversial Mets manager became a national story as his team threatened an historic September collapse. Many media outlets suggested Valentine was the most hated man in baseball. But the Mets hung on and Valentine got to manage his first postseason game after over 1,700 games on a big league bench.

Barry Sanders

Just as he did on the football field, Sanders eluded us all and walked away from the game. I think he'll be back. And I hope he gives us a chance to give him the farewell a hall of famer deserves.

Mark McGwire and Sammy Sosa

Yes, it was an encore. But while Sosa and McGwire hit more than 60

AP/Wide World Photos

San Antonio Spurs star **Tim Duncan** had quite a year in 1999. Just a year removed from being named Rookie of the Year, the seven-foot center led the Spurs to their first world championship and took home the award for Finals MVP.

home runs for the second year in a row, no one else in baseball even reached 50. It was just a little reminder that it isn't necessarily the ball, the ballparks or the pitching. It's Mac and Sammy.

Pedro Martinez

In the era of inflated ERA's, Pedro Martinez turned in one of the best years a pitcher has ever had, leading the A.L. in wins, ERA and strikeouts by unheard-of margins. His slight frame held up through September and October as he took the Red Sox further than anyone expected with dominating performances against the Indians and Yankees.

Steffi Graf

She never had Chris Evert's charm or Martina Navratilova's athleticism. She slipped onto the scene, won consistently but never seemed to capture us. Now, 22 Grand Slam singles victories later, she's leaving. Her legacy is still to be decided but in 1988 she won all four majors and an Olympic gold medal. No athlete ever had a better year. Few have had better careers.

Tiger Woods

Can you be over-rated at 21 and under-rated at 23? Tiger removed all doubts about his talent and determination in 1999 by winning his second major at the PGA and playing a key

Boston pitcher **Pedro Martinez** was as close to unbeatable as any pitcher in recent memory. His 23 wins, 2.07 ERA and 313 whiffs were all American League bests, and then he followed that performance by shutting down the Indians and Yankees in the postseason. If only he could pitch every day...

role on Ben Crenshaw's victorious USA Ryder Cup team.

Wilt Chamberlain

A 100-point game. Fifty points-per-game one year. Led the league in assists. Seven straight scoring titles and two championships. Yet even though he was over seven feet tall, Wilt never seemed to measure up to the expectations of other people. Anything he achieved was deemed inevitable. Any time he failed, it was a shame, a waste. Reactions to his untimely death, however, revealed that Wilt was much more than some Goliath. If you knew him, it seems, he was easy to root for.

Also Considered
(in alphabetical order)

Andre Agassi

Lance Armstrong

Ben Crenshaw

Richard Hamilton

Juli Inkster

Jaromir Jagr

Mario Lemieux

Justin Leonard

Tee Martin

John Thompson

Felix Trinidad

Serena Williams

Moments

American **Lance Armstrong** came back from cancer to win the 1999 Tour de France in one of the top moments of the year.

AP/Wide World Photos

Top 20 Sports Moments of 1999

Stuart and Rich team up once again to deliver the magic moments of the year in sports.

by
Rich Eisen and Stuart Scott

For the last two years, my partner Rich Eisen and I have joked about who gets to go first and leave the leftovers for the other guy. Well, with ten moments to pick from a load of phat moments, I can go first and still leave Rich with a bevy of choices. Rich, you can thank me later. So, in no particular order . . .

John Elway and Broncos repeat
Why not? He'd been best friend to Super Bowl misery so many times only to finally win the big one the year before. So as if to prove a point, he throws for 336 yards, and leads the Broncos to a 34-19 throttling of the

Atlanta Falcons in Super Bowl XXXIII. John Elway, who had engineered more fourth quarter, come-from-behind wins, and more wins overall, than any NFL quarterback, won his second straight Super Bowl and his first Super Bowl MVP award. A final exclamation point to a great career.

Farewell to Three Kings
This one is really three moments that just can't be separated. Jordan (Jan. 13), Gretzky (Apr. 16) and Elway (May 2). Three men who ruled their sports with statistics and championships but mostly with the steely resolve of their minds. In a five-month span they all said, "So long." Retired. Needless to say, we'll miss them.

Rich Eisen and Stuart Scott are anchor/reporters on ESPN's *SportsCenter*.

Venus and **Serena Williams** served notice that they will be a force to be reckoned with for the foreseeable future on the WTA Tour with their performances at the 1999 U.S. Open. Not only did younger sister Serena win the singles title but the siblings captured the women's doubles title as well.

"Soft" Spurs win hard fought title

They had been called soft, and no one really figured they could win an NBA championship. They were led by an aging admiral and a young gun who showed no emotion on the court. And they had a devoutly Christian point guard that everybody thought talked funny. But you know what? The unselfish David Robinson, Finals MVP Tim Duncan and Avery Johnson, who sank the series-clinching jump shot, led the so-called soft San Antonio Spurs over the big, bad New York Knicks in five games for their first NBA championship.

Williams sisters hit it big in NYC

A few years ago, rising women's tennis star Venus Williams bragged that her younger sister Serena would be her toughest opponent on the WTA tour. Everyone laughed then but no one was laughing at the 1999 U.S. Open. Not only did Serena make a prophet out of her sister but their father Richard also was proved to have made a decent prediction himself when he forecasted an all-Williams final at the Open. Big sis didn't quite make it, losing in the semis to the best in the sport, Martina Hingis, but little sis did and she avenged her sister's

29

Apparently, no one told home run kings **Mark McGwire** and **Sammy Sosa** that they were supposed to cool off some after their red-hot 1998 season because they were back hitting homer after homer in 1999.

loss against Hingis, 6-3, 7-6, who looked strong after redefining her game after a mid-year slump.

Tiger snares Second Major

Tiger Woods won the Masters with a bang in 1997, beating the course and the field like no one had ever done at Augusta. Despite, what was for him, an off year in 1998, he kept saying his game was getting better. Well, in 1999 he proved it. He won more than anyone else all summer and got his second major win at the PGA Championship in Medinah, Ill., which was more relief than victory after his narrow, one-shot win over Sergio Garcia.

Armstrong takes Tour

No one ever had a comeback like this one. This wasn't a career-threatening injury or an overwhelming late-game deficit. Lance Armstrong had cancer. Doctors had told him he would not live, much less ride again. Not only did he live, he rode. And not only did he ride, he shocked everyone by dominating the world's premier bike race, the Tour de France. With the stunning victory, Armstrong joined living legend Greg LeMond as the only Americans ever to win cycling's biggest prize. Then he went on a grueling marathon media tour to remind people that cancer doesn't win every time.

Fernando has grand outing in one inning

You figured if anybody could hit two grand slams in an inning, it would be that big guy from St. Louis. Well, it was a guy from St. Louis but he isn't very big and it wasn't Mark McGwire. On April 23, Fernando Tatis (5-10, 170 pounds) shocked the baseball world by becoming the first player in major league history to hit two grand slams in one inning (the third). Tatis' two blasts came off the Dodgers' Chan Ho Park in a 12-5 Cardinals win. Fernando also set the record for RBIs in one inning with eight and stole the St. Louis spotlight from Big Mac, for one night anyway.

McGwire and Sosa II

Again, this one is not about one moment but about two guys who delivered big moments all season. As phat as 1998 was for Mark McGwire and Sammy Sosa, nobody really thought they would come back and do it again in 1999. But with 65 and 63 homers, respectively, McGwire and Sosa beat Roger Maris again and this time nobody else in baseball even got 50. McGwire won the title with another big finish but they both proved to be in a class by themselves.

Fiesta Bowl is Tee's Party

Peyton Manning, their all-everything quarterback, had gone to the NFL. He had a nice season, set many big rookie passing records and was the only QB in the league to take every snap for his team. What were the Tennessee Volunteers going to do without him? Well, a few things that they never did with Peyton. They beat Steve Spurrier and the Florida Gators. They went undefeated. They won the national championship with a 23-16 Fiesta Bowl victory over Florida State. No offense, but Peyton who? Give it up for quarterback Tee Martin who stepped in for Manning and took his team all the way.

Triple Threat

It had been 21 years since horse racing had a Triple Crown winner. But in 1999, for the third straight year, a horse won the first two legs only to be nipped at the Belmont Stakes. This time the horse threatening to put himself up there with the all-time greats was Charismatic and the Belmont spoiler was Lemon Drop Kid. It reminded us of the great battles between the last Triple Crown winner Affirmed and his runner-up in all three races, Alydar. And it further illustrated just how tough the Triple Crown is to win. Maybe that's the reason it's only been done 11 times in 125 years.

Those are my ten. Now Rich can weigh in with a list worthy of going first as well.

      ❧   ❧   ❧

Stuart's top 10 moments were quite compelling, leaving me no choice but to bring my "A-game" in fashioning together my top 10 moments of the year, in NO specific order.

Anyway, here goes...

Mets third baseman **Robin Ventura** hit the world's loudest single in the 15th-inning of Game 5 of the NLCS against the Braves. Ventura hit the ball over the right field fence for an apparent grand slam but was mobbed by his teammates and Mets manager Bobby Valentine (#2) before he could reach second base.

Game 5 NLCS, Braves at Mets

Fifteen innings. Five hours, 46 minutes. Fifteen pitchers used, 45 players used, 126 plate appearances, 24 hits, 31 men left on base, 482 pitches thrown. The late-afternoon game finally came to an end on a rainy Queens night when Robin Ventura belted the only grand slam single you'll probably ever see. The Braves had taken a 3-2 lead in the top of the 15th, standing three outs away from the National League pennant. But the Mets tied the game with a bases loaded walk, scored by Todd Pratt, whose own walk-off home run provided the improbable ending to the divisional series against the Diamondbacks. Then, Ventura smacked one out of the park...only to be mobbed by his own teammates at second base. He never touched them all. So, in the end, the final score was 4-3, Mets, with Ventura credited with a single, not a home run. When asked if he should go back on the diamond and run the bases officially, Ventura said, "I've had enough."

1999 Ryder Cup

Who could have thought Colin Montgomerie could be the life of any party? But, he and the rest of Team Europe were the life of the Boston Tee Party at The Country Club in Brookline, Mass...for the first two days. On Sunday, the third day, the Americans stopped resting on their laurels. Down 10 points to 6, the

AP/Wide World Photos

U.S. Ryder Cup captain **Ben Crenshaw** gets a champagne shower following his team's miraculous comeback at The Country Club in Brookline, Mass. While Sunday's final round was a memorable moment for American golf fans, for European golf fans it was a moment they would rather forget.

American charge began from the first group, led by Tom Lehman. Then Hal Sutton, easily the Most Valuable American in the tournament. Phil Mickelson. Davis Love III. Tiger Woods. David Duval, who dismantled Jesper Parnevik. Steve Pate. Jim Furyk, who finally took down Sergio Garcia. Suddenly, the Americans had the LEAD. All the while, the supposedly cash-conscious players were firing up the crowd in fist-pumping fashion. It all came down to a man who Johnny Miller, in all too harsh, but accurate, terms, said on Saturday should be watching at home: Justin Leonard. He came back from four-down with eight to play to dormie on 17 thanks to a putt for the ages.

Milestone week in Major League Baseball

Mark McGwire hit his 500th home run on Thursday. Tony Gwynn belted his 3,000th hit on Friday. On Saturday, Wade Boggs became the first man to reach the 3,000-hit plateau by homering. Had even one of these remarkable players reached their milestones at any point during the season, it would have been thrilling enough. But to see them all accomplish their feats in the same season ON SUCCESSIVE DAYS is something akin to the stuff of which dreams are made. The week began with a celebration of all things Gwynn and McGwire as the two played a four-game set, bringing about

Tampa Bay third baseman **Wade Boggs** prepares to cross home plate after becoming the first player in major league history to get his 3,000th hit on a home run. Nearby, security guards subdue an overzealous fan who ran on the field to honor the occasion.

the possibility of the duo doing something unprecedented: setting their respective records in the SAME GAME. Alas, Gwynn came up one hit shy on the night McGwire not only hit 500, but 501 for good measure. That was OK, though. Gwynn just got his 3,000th hit the next night...on his mother's birthday.

McGwire's Home Run Derby

As he showed on his milestone night, McGwire has that Jordan-esque ability to come through when it's most expected. He certainly lived up to the hype in this year's home run derby at Fenway Park, out-monstering the Green Monster. First one titanic blast. Then another. And another. And another. San Diego coach Tim Flannery dealt McGwire another batting practice pitch and — SWAK — McGwire swatted yet another Ruthian blast, after which Big Mac turned to the catcher, Ray Fagnant, a Red Sox scout and dejectedly said, "I just cracked my bat." Big Mac then hit another eight home runs with a broken bat, including the final blast, which not only set a record for most home runs in one home run derby appearance, but also went 488 feet.

AP/Wide World Photos

All-Century Team nominees from left: Bob Feller, background partially obscured, Roger Clemens (in a Yankees cap!), Rollie Fingers, Bob Gibson, Juan Marichal and Robin Roberts line up on the field before the 1999 All-Star Game at Boston's Fenway Park.

All Star Pre-Game Ceremony

McGwire's home run festival was just the appetizer of All-Star week at Fenway Park. Ted Williams throwing out the first ball of the actual All-Star game was the main course and dessert. Because it wasn't just any, old ceremony. Prior to Teddy Ballgame's appearance in front of his adoring Red Sox Nation, about three dozen nominees for baseball's All-Century team strolled out from behind a curtain in center field and walked to the infield, lining up from third to second base and from second to first. Tom Seaver. Mike Schmidt. Roger Clemens (wearing a Yankee cap). Bob Feller. Harmon Killebrew. Joe Morgan. Hank Aaron. Willie Mays. Carl Yastrzemski (thunderous applause).

Then came the introduction of the 1999 All-Stars, who took their traditional positions from home plate up the third and first base lines. So, with the greatest constellation of baseball stars lined up in a literal diamond, Williams emerged on a golf cart from centerfield and eventually arrived at the mound. At that point, in most spontaneous fashion, the other stars broke ranks and huddled around Williams, who burst into tears. So did Mike Piazza. Ken Griffey Jr. stood with Mays. McGwire with Stan Musial. Stars of the past, present and future watched Williams, steadied by Tony Gwynn, throw a perfect strike to Carlton Fisk. Goosebumps. Bedlam. Unforgettable.

Playoff MVP **Joe Nieuwendyk** hoists the Texas-sized Stanley Cup during a parade in honor of the NHL champion Dallas Stars. The Stars beat the Buffalo Sabres in triple-overtime of Game 6 to capture the Cup.

Barry's final juke?

For one day, July 28, 1999, all eyes in the sports world read *The Wichita Eagle* website. For it was through his hometown newspaper that Barry Sanders, one of the greatest running backs of all time, announced his retirement from football at the age of 31, just 1,458 yards shy of Walter Payton's all-time rushing record.

"My desire to exit the game is greater than my desire to remain in it," Sanders wrote shortly before bolting by himself on a vacation to England. "I have searched my heart through and through and feel comfortable with this decision." Did he make this decision because he was sick and tired of losing with Detroit? Because he was trying to force a trade? Because he didn't want to break Payton's record in deference to Sweetness? We'll find out next year, if Sanders returns. What we do know now is how much we miss him.

Lord Stanley, Texan

Normally, in June, sports fans in Dallas wonder how things are shaping up for Cowboys mini-camp in the next month. Not in 1999. Big D became home to Lord Stanley's Cup as the Dallas Stars conquered the hockey world by beating the Sabres and Dominik Hasek in six games. It took three overtimes for the Stars to wrap up Game 6 and not without controversy. Brett Hull scored the game winner and thus had a hand in sealing the deal. The Sabres believe he also had a foot involved, too. Replays clearly showed Hull's skate in the crease as he popped in the series clincher. Even worse, media folks streamed on the ice to capture the celebration, further confusing matters had the Sabres requested a replay.

"That's the worst nightmare," Sabres coach Lindy Ruff said afterward. "His skate was in the crease. You can't explain that to me. Everybody saw it. Once you've got 200 people on the ice, they aren't going to review it." The folks in Dallas couldn't care less. They can hoist the Stanley Cup. Yeeee-hah!

Women's World Cup

Team USA, comprised of college students, soccer moms, ESPN analysts and international superstars, beat Denmark, 3-0, in the Meadowlands, Nigeria, 7-1, in Soldier Field, Korea, 3-0, in Foxboro, Germany, 3-2, in Jack Kent Cooke Stadium and Brazil, 2-0, in Stanford Stadium, all the way picking up more and more fans of all shapes, sizes and sexes. So, the ladies drew a wild, adoring, frenzied women's sports record throng of 90,185 to the Rose Bowl for the World Cup final match with China, which, back in April, had ended the American's 3-year-old, 50-game domestic unbeaten streak.

Fittingly, after 120 minutes of intense, scoreless soccer, the game went to penalty kicks. Both teams bur-

ied its first two shots, but China's third shot, by Liu Ying, was to the right side of the goal and Briana Scurry, all 5-foot, 8-inches of her, smacked it away safely. The Rose Bowl, including the President, who was in attendance, went nuts, a reaction topped only by Brandi Chastain banging home the Cup clinching goal. Her ripping off her shirt and baring her sports bra is an image that will forever be shown on sports highlight programs and in men's magazines.

Ricky Williams has himself a year

For a full calendar year, Ricky Williams captured the fancy of football fans everywhere. Would Ricky break the all-time NCAA rushing record? Would Ricky win the Heisman? Was that Ricky hitting the buffet on the awards circuit? Would Ricky lose the weight? Will Ricky be taken Number 1 overall? How cool is Ricky? Why did Ricky fire his agent and hire Master P? Why did the Eagles take Donovan McNabb instead of Ricky? Why did the Colts take Edgerrin James over Ricky? Did Mike Ditka really give up his entire draft for Ricky? Did Ricky get ripped off by signing such an incentive-laden contract? How badly did Ricky sprain his ankle in training camp? Would Ricky start the season? How much of Ricky's playing through pain has to do with getting paid? Why does Ricky conduct interviews with his helmet on?

For the second straight year a New York Yankees pitcher named David makes an appearance in the Top Moments of the Year for throwing a perfect game. Last year David Wells made history. This year it was **David Cone** who made his mark in the record books when he set down 27 straight Montreal Expos for Major League Baseball's 16th perfect game.

Coney's Island

In other words, the pitchers mound at Yankee Stadium on July 18, when David Cone achieved baseball immortality by tossing a perfect game against the Montreal Expos. 27 up, 27 down. 10 strikeouts. The man did not go to a three-ball count all afternoon. That would have been special in itself, but Cone decided to pitch his perfecto on New York Yankees Old-Timers day, with folks like Phil Rizzuto, Whitey Ford and Ron Guidry in attendance. And, of all people, Don Larsen and Yogi Berra, who re-enacted the last out of their 1956 World Series perfect game (when Larsen fanned Brooklyn's Dale Mitchell) in tossing out and catching the ceremonial first pitch. Berra caught Larsen's lob toss with Joe Girardi's glove, which Girardi, of course, went out and used to catch Cone's perfect game. Now, what could have been more perfectly scripted than that? ∎

Calendar

David Cone's perfect game on July 18 gave his New York Yankees teammates another reason to look up to him.

AP/Wide World Photos

NOV '98

Sun	Mon	Tue	Wed	Thu	Fri	Sat
1	2	3	4	5	6	7
8	9	10	11	12	13	14
15	16	17	18	19	20	21
22	23	24	25	26	27	28
29	30					

Unranked and Upset

When Michigan State defeated Ohio State on Nov. 7 it marked the 37th time since 1936 an unranked college football team beat or tied a No. 1 ranked team. Here are the schools that have pulled off the stunning upsets more than once.

Unranked Team	Upsets	Last Defeat of No. 1
Purdue	4	1976 beat Michigan
Michigan St.	**3**	**1998 beat Ohio St.**
Stanford	2	1990 beat Notre Dame
Georgia Tech	2	1980 tied Notre Dame
Minnesota	2	1977 beat Michigan

Tennessee Winnings

Three time defending NCAA women's basketball national champion Tennessee had its 46-game winning streak snapped by Purdue on Nov. 15, but not before the streak could become the second longest in women's hoop history.

Games	Team	Seasons
54	Louisiana Tech	1980-82
46	**Tennessee**	**1997-98**
40	Texas	1985-87
35	Connecticut	1994-96
33	Connecticut	1996-97

Hey Ref, Keep Your Day Job!

The botched overtime coin toss in Detroit on Thanksgiving Day began one of the strongest campaigns in recent history for an overhaul of NFL officiating. Should any officials be let go, here are a few of the more interesting weekday jobs held by the league's 113 officials.

Name	No.	Occupation
Walt Anderson	66	Dentist
Ron Blum	7	Professional golfer
Ed Fiffick	57	Foot doctor
Pete Morelli	135	High school principal
Bob Waggoner	25	Probation officer

1 **Jeff Gordon wraps up** his third Winston Cup Series title with a victory at the ACDelco 400.

Bobby Rahal ends his 17-year auto racing career after 24 wins and three CART championships with an 11th place finish at the Marlboro 500.

Kenyan John Kagwe captures his second consecutive New York City Marathon, while Franca Fiacconi becomes the first Italian woman to win the 29-year-old race.

2 **The Ontario Hockey League hands out** one of the harshest penalties in junior hockey history, banning Windsor Spitfires forward Jeff Kugel, 18, from the league for life for leaving the bench and slugging Juri Golicic on Oct. 25.

A work stoppage by ABC's off-camera employees forces the cancellation of the Monday Night Football pregame show. A backup crew of cameramen and graphics operators are used to broadcast the Dallas-Philadelphia game.

3 **Mark McGwire's 50th** home run ball is sold at auction for $46,000.

5 **WNBA players vote** 56-24 in favor of unionizing and having the National Basketball Players Association represent them.

Philadelphia Phillies outfielder Lenny Dykstra announces his retirement.

The American Basketball League tips off its third season with the New England Blizzard defeating the Philadelphia Rage 72-63 at the Hartford Civic Center.

7 **Veteran jockey Pat Day rides** Awesome Again to victory, ahead of one of the best fields ever, at the Breeders' Cup Classic.

Unranked Michigan State upsets No. 1 Ohio State 28-24 in college football, ruining the Buckeyes' perfect season.

8 **Senior golfer Hale Irwin cards** seven birdies en route to a final round 65 and captures his first Senior Tour Championship in three tries.

Steffi Graf captures her 105th career singles title at the Leipzig Open and breaks Martina Navratilova's record for career earnings with $20,445,842.

9 **The New York Post reports** Hall of Famer pitcher Jim "Catfish" Hunter has the fatal neuromuscular ailment known as Lou Gehrig's disease.

Chicago Cubs pitcher Kerry Wood is named NL Rookie of the Year.

10 **Oakland A's outfielder** Ben Grieve is named AL Rookie of the Year.

Oscar De La Hoya's fight with Ike Quartey is postponed until Feb. 13 because De La Hoya says he injured his eyelid during sparring.

11 **Utah Jazz All-Star forward** Karl Malone tells a radio audience he'll demand to be traded when the NBA lockout ends.

13 **Colts fullback Craig "Ironhead" Heyward** undergoes more than 12 hours of surgery to remove a benign tumor at the base of his skull.

A fire erupts high atop the frame of the American Airlines Arena, which is being built in downtown Miami as the future home of the Heat.

14 **After 29 years of losing** to Nebraska, Kansas State gets 442 yards of total offense from quarterback Michael Bishop and beats the Cornhuskers for the first time since 1968, 40-30, at Manhattan, Kan.

Tennessee Oilers owner Bud Adams announces that his team will change its name to the Titans in 1999.

AP/Wide World Photos

Undefeated thoroughbred **Awesome Again** (right) was simply that in his run at the $5.12 million Breeders' Cup Classic on Nov. 7, holding off an all-star field at Churchill Downs that included Silver Charm (center), and Swain (left) en route to his sixth victory of the year.

15 **Three-time defending women's** basketball national champion Tennessee Volunteers have their 46-game victory streak stopped by Purdue 78-68 in the Women's Tipoff Classic.

16 **Toronto pitcher Roger Clemens wins** an unprecedented fifth AL Cy Young Award.

17 **University of Kentucky football player** Jason Watts, the driver in a car accident that left two friends dead, is charged with two counts of second-degree manslaughter after a blood test reveals that he was legally drunk.

Atlanta pitcher Tom Glavine wins his second NL Cy Young Award.

18 **Rangers DH Juan Gonzalez captures** his second AL Most Valuable Player Award.

LSU's men's basketball program is given three years probation and a one-year ban from the NCAA Tournament because of recruiting violations.

19 **Sammy Sosa easily wins** the NL MVP Award over Mark McGwire, tallying 30 of the 32 total first-place votes.

The New England Patriots reach an agreement to build a new $350 million stadium and move the team to Hartford, Conn. in 2001.

20 **Golfers Mark O'Meara and Hale Irwin** take home Player of the Year honors in the PGA and Senior PGA respectively.

Two-time Indianapolis 500 winner Arie Luyendyk announces he'll retire after the 1999 Indy 500.

22 **John Elway joins Dan Marino as** the only two NFL quarterbacks to pass for more than 50,000 yards in a career after the Broncos QB throws for 197 yards in a 40-14 rout of Oakland.

Martina Hingis ends a six-month stretch without a title by beating Lindsay Davenport in the finals of the Chase Championships.

24 **All-Star 2B Roberto Alomar joins** his brother Sandy as a member of the Cleveland Indians after agreeing to a four-year, $32 million contract with the AL Central Division champs.

Former NBA player Orlando Woolridge has the interim tag removed from his title as head coach of the WNBA's Los Angeles Sparks.

25 **Yankees outfielder Bernie Williams re-signs** with the team for $87.5 million over seven years while former Red Sox 1B Mo Vaughn agrees to sign with the Angels for $80 million over six years.

Pittsburgh finally trades holdout Petr Nedved, sending him along with center Sean Pronger and defenseman Chris Tamer to the Rangers for Alexei Kovalev, center Harry York and future considerations.

26 **Confusion during the overtime coin flip** as to whether or not Pittsburgh's Jerome Bettis calls "heads" or "tails" ends with the Lions receiving the ball first, which helps set up a Jason Hanson game-winning field goal and a 19-16 Thanksgiving Day victory.

Marcelo Rios pulls out of the ATP Tour World Championship, which means Pete Sampras will end the season ranked number one for a record sixth straight year.

29 **Chicago White Sox outfielder Albert Belle agrees** to a five-year, $65 million contract with the Baltimore Orioles.

30 **Houston pitcher Randy Johnson signs** a four-year, $35 million deal to ace the Arizona Diamondbacks staff.

DEC '98

Sun	Mon	Tue	Wed	Thu	Fri	Sat
		1	2	3	4	5
6	7	8	9	10	11	12
13	14	15	16	17	18	19
20	21	22	23	24	25	26
27	28	29	30	31		

Oh Ricky, You're So Fine...

Texas running back Ricky Williams' 2,124 yards in 1998 was the fourth best total ever by a Heisman Trophy winner.

Heisman Winner	Year	Att	Yds	Yds/Gm
Barry Sanders, Ok. St.	1988	344	**2,628**	238.9
Marcus Allen, USC	1981	403	**2,342**	212.9
Mike Rozier, Neb.	1983	275	**2,148**	179.0
Ricky Williams, Texas	1998	361	**2,124**	193.1

Maruyama For President

By winning all five of his matches, Japan's Shigeki Maruyama led the International Team to its first victory over the United States in three Presidents Cup tournaments. Maruyama, who joins Mark O'Meara (in 1996) as the only golfers to win all five of their matches, cracks the International Team's list of all-time win leaders thanks to his clutch performance.

United States Golfer	Wins	International Golfer	Wins
Fred Couples	8	Steve Elkington	8
Davis Love III	8	Vijay Singh	8
Mark O'Meara	7	Ernie Els	6
Scott Hoch	7	Greg Norman	6
David Duval	4	Craig Parry	6
Phil Mickelson	3	Frank Nobilo	5
Corey Pavin	3	**Shigeki Maruyama**	**5**

Making Their Points

The Minnesota Vikings scored an NFL-record 556 points in 1998. Here's each major league sport's record holder for points scored by a team in a season.

League	Team	Year	Points	Per Game
NBA	Denver	1981-82	10,371	126.5
NFL	Minnesota	1998	556	34.8
NL	Boston	1894	1,220*	9.2
AL	New York	1931	1,067*	6.9
NHL	Edmonton	1983-84	446†	5.6

* total runs scored
† total goals scored

1 First baseman **Rafael Palmeiro** agrees to a five-year, $45 million contract that returns him to the Texas Rangers.

4 Former **Fighting Irish coach** Lou Holtz is introduced as the new head coach at the University of South Carolina.

5 Swiss doubles teammates Jonas Bjorkman and Nicklas Kulti rally to victory over Italy's Diego Nargiso and Davide Sanguinetti, clinching the third Davis Cup title in the last five years for Switzerland.

6 Despite being outshot 21-6, Florida's women's soccer team defeats 14-time national champion North Carolina 1-0 in the NCAA title game.

7 Lou's son Skip Holtz leaves his head coaching job at Connecticut and jumps on board his dad's new staff at South Carolina.

The WNBA announces its expansion franchise in Minnesota will be known as the Lynx.

8 The NBA All-Star Game becomes the latest casualty of the 160-day-old lockout.

Former heavyweight champion Mike Tyson announces he will fight Francois Botha on Jan. 16 in his first match since being suspended in 1997.

9 A judge orders the father of gymnast Dominique Moceanu to stay away from his daughter and forbids him from contacting her in any way after hearing testimony that he had used violence against her in the past.

The Little League World Series announces it is doubling its field of qualifiers to 16, starting with the 2001 season.

10 Relief pitcher Dennis Eckersley, third on the all-time saves list with 390, retires from baseball.

San Diego Chargers interim coach June Jones is hired to coach his alma mater, the 0-12 University of Hawaii Rainbow Warriors, at the conclusion of the 1998 season.

12 Texas running back Ricky Williams wraps his arms around the Heisman Trophy, exactly 50 years after one of his heroes – the late Doak Walker – won the award.

The Los Angeles Dodgers sign free agent pitcher Kevin Brown to a seven-year, $105 million contract.

Former vice president and current executive board member Marc Holder of Switzerland aims serious accusations of vote-buying at Salt Lake City 2002 Olympics organizers and the International Olympic Committee.

Pneumonia halts Montreal right wing Mark Recchi's consecutive regular season games played streak at 570, the NHL's longest current streak.

13 Japanese golfer Shigeki Maruyama leads the way for the International Team with five victories helping them to a 20½-11½ upset victory over the U.S. in the Presidents Cup competition in Australia.

Carolina Panthers LB Kevin Greene has to be restrained by teammates after fighting with position coach Kevin Steele on the sideline during the team's loss to the Redskins.

Indiana's men's soccer team defeats Stanford 3-1 to avenge last year's triple overtime loss to UCLA in the semifinals and capture its fourth national championship.

14 Atlanta Falcons coach Dan Reeves undergoes four hours of emergency quadruple bypass heart surgery one day after leading his team to a victory over New Orleans.

Midfielder Cobi Jones of the U.S. national men's soccer team and the Los Angeles Galaxy of the MLS is named U.S. National Player of the Year.

AP/Wide World Photos

Fans look down towards the artificial turf at Philadelphia's **Veterans Stadium** where nine Army cadets and prep school students lie injured after a railing at the 28-year-old stadium gave way during the fourth quarter of the Army-Navy football game on Dec. 5.

15 During a conference call organized by the NFL's competition committee, a proposal to institute instant replay for playoff games is defeated 7-1.

The WNBA announces its expansion franchise in Orlando will be named the Miracle.

17 After months of squabbling the Islanders sign holdout Zigmund Palffy to a five-year, $25 million contract.

Former NY Giants linebacker Lawrence Taylor turns himself in to police to face charges of possession of narcotics and narcotics paraphernalia.

19 Miami Heat guard Tim Hardaway scores 33 points and is named MVP of an exhibition game organized by locked out NBA players.

Eleventh-seeded Massachusetts shocks Georgia Southern 55-43 to capture its first Div. I-AA football championship.

Veteran QB Vinny Testaverde leads the NY Jets to their first AFC East Division title by tossing two touchdown passes in the Jets 17-10 victory over the Buffalo Bills.

Future Hall of Famer Ray Bourque has three assists in a Bruins victory over the Red Wings, moving him into third place on the all-time assists list.

21 French World Cup-winning playmaker Zinedine Zidane is named 1998 European Footballer of the Year.

22 The ABL announces it has halted operations for the season and has filed for Chapter 11 bankruptcy protection.

Second-ranked Duke defeats Kentucky 71-60 in a rare non-NCAA tournament battle between the two most successful men's college basketball teams of the decade.

Longtime boxing referee Mills Lane announces his retirement.

23 NBA Commissioner David Stern sets a "drop-dead" date of Jan. 7 for cancellation of the 1998-99 season if an agreement cannot be reached.

Toronto pitcher Roger Clemens rescinds his demand to be traded and says he'll report to spring training with the Blue Jays this February.

27 Arizona kicker Chris Jacke's last-second 52-yard field goal gives the Cardinals a 16-13 victory over San Diego and sends them to the playoffs for the first time since 1982.

Denver RB Terrell Davis rushes for 178 yards in the Broncos season finale against Seattle, giving him 2,008 for the season and the third highest single-season total in NFL history.

Two sailors are reported dead and several missing after being swept overboard in high seas during the Sydney-to-Hobart yacht race off the coast of Australia. (The final death toll from the accident was six.)

28 It's "Black Monday" in the NFL as five coaches are fired by their teams.

29 Former Senate Majority Leader George Mitchell, who is heading a five-member special commission, opens the investigation into the scandal surrounding Salt Lake City's successful bid for the 2002 Winter Games.

JAN '99

Sun	Mon	Tue	Wed	Thu	Fri	Sat
					1	2
3	4	5	6	7	8	9
10	11	12	13	14	15	16
17	18	19	20	21	22	23
24/31	25	26	27	28	29	30

A Long Road Back

The national champion Tennessee Volunteers took over the number-one ranking in the Associated Press poll on Jan. 9, 1999. The last time they were ranked number one in the AP poll was the week of Nov. 13, 1956. Current head coach Phillip Fulmer was six years old.

Orange You Glad He's Gone

When Georgetown's John Thompson resigned on Jan. 8 it meant the end of a terrific Big East coaching rivalry with Syracuse's Jim Boeheim. In 46 Big East regular season and tournament meetings, 33 of their games had been decided by 10 points or less and 25 by five points or less. Here's the breakdown through Jan. 8, 1999.

The Series	Georgetown	Syracuse
Big East Regular Season Wins	19	18
Big East Tournament Wins	5	4
Other	**Thompson**	**Boeheim**
Career Record	596-239	539-184
Big East Tournament Titles	6	3
NCAA Tourn. Appearances	20	18
NCAA Tourn. Wins	34	29
NBA 1st Round Picks	7	9

Rushing Roulette

Football experts will insist that you can't win the Super Bowl if you don't win the ground game. Usually they are right. But six times in Super Bowl history the losing team has rushed for more net yards than the eventual champion.

Bowl	Winner (yds)	Loser (yds)
III	New York Jets (142)	Baltimore (143)
V	Baltimore (69)	Dallas (102)
XIII	Pittsburgh (66)	Dallas (154)
XIV	Pittsburgh (84)	Los Angeles Rams (107)
XXX	Dallas (56)	Pittsburgh (103)
XXXIII	**Denver (121)**	**Atlanta (131)**

1 In Bowl Championship Series action, Wisconsin upsets UCLA 38-31 in the Rose Bowl and Ohio State holds off Texas A&M 24-14 in the Sugar Bowl.

4 Tennessee WR Peerless Price catches his second touchdown pass of more than 70 yards in the game early in the fourth quarter, helping the Volunteers to a 23-16 Fiesta Bowl victory and the school's first football national championship in 47 years.

NHL Commissioner Gary Bettman slaps the St. Louis Blues with a record $1.5 million fine and other sanctions for tampering with New Jersey free agent Scott Stevens in 1994.

Former 49ers coach George Seifert is hired to coach the Carolina Panthers.

5 Fresno State men's basketball coach Jerry Tarkanian records his 700th career victory.

6 The NBA and its player's union end their six-month labor dispute by agreeing on a six-year collective bargaining agreement in the eleventh hour.

Bowler Walter Ray Williams Jr. is named Professional Bowlers Association Player of the Year for the fifth time in his career.

7 Oregon State football coach Mike Riley signs a guaranteed five-year contract to coach the San Diego Chargers.

8 Georgetown men's basketball coach John Thompson resigns midway through his 27th season as coach of the team, citing personal reasons.

Former Green Bay coach Mike Holmgren signs an eight-year contract to be coach and general manager of the Seattle Seahawks for $4 million a year, making him the NFL's highest-paid coach.

10 Keyshawn Johnson's two touchdowns help the New York Jets advance to the AFC championship game for the first time since 1983. The Vikings beat Arizona to move into its first NFC title game in 11 seasons.

L.A. Kings left winger Luc Robitaille becomes the 27th player in NHL history to score 500 goals in a career.

11 Chiefs head coach Marty Schottenheimer quits after watching his team finish with a disappointing 7-9 record in 1998.

The NFL coaching carousel spins off former Eagles coach Ray Rhodes in Green Bay while former Packers quarterbacks coach Andy Reid replaces Rhodes in Philadelphia.

12 The baseball Mark McGwire hit into the stands at Busch Stadium for his 70th home run is sold at auction in New York City for $2.7 million plus a $305,000 commission fee.

In a television interview with WWOR's Russ Salzberg, Mike Tyson explodes into a series of embarrassing, expletive-filled answers to Salzberg's questions.

13 Chicago Bulls legend Michael Jordan retires from the NBA for the second (and apparently final) time.

Chris Ford is named as the new head coach of the Los Angeles Clippers.

14 Major League Baseball owners approve the sale of the Florida Marlins to commodities trader John Henry for a reported $150 million plus another $8 million to refurbish Pro Player Stadium.

Dolphins coach Jimmy Johnson announces he was close a day earlier, but after rethinking his decision, will not step down as coach of the team.

16 Heavyweight Mike Tyson registers a fifth-round knockout of Frans Botha in his first boxing match since his 1997 suspension.

AP/ Wide World Photos

It was announced on Jan. 6 that for the first time since Babe Ruth was chosen, three first-time candidates were elected to the National Baseball Hall of Fame. Shown here are **Robin Yount**, **Nolan Ryan** and **George Brett** posing with their rookie cards and searching for a bike with really big spokes.

17 **"Russian Rocket" Pavel Bure is dealt** as part of a seven-player deal from Vancouver to Florida, ending the All-Star's season-long holdout.

19 **Vikings offensive coordinator Brian Billick is** named the new head coach of the Baltimore Ravens.

20 **Former San Francisco coach Bill Walsh** is hired to fill the role of general manager of the team while former UCLA coach Terry Donahue is named director of player personnel.

Utah state officials announce they will open the fifth ongoing investigation into whether local organizers made improper payments to acquire the 2002 Olympic Winter Games.

Northwestern football coach Gary Barnett whose resurrection of the Big 10 team culminated with a 1996 Rose Bowl appearance, is hired to coach at Colorado.

21 **All the details of the NBA's** new collective bargaining agreement are finalized, and the league officially opens for business at 2 p.m. EST.

The NBA is thrilled to learn Latrell Sprewell is back in the league via Golden State's trade with the NY Knicks for three players, including guard John Starks.

Bulls star forward Scottie Pippen signs a five-year, $67 million deal with Houston after being traded to the Rockets for Roy Rogers and a 1999 or 2000 second-round draft pick.

The new Cleveland Browns hire former Jacksonville offensive coordinator Chris Palmer to be their new coach.

22 **Kansas City Chiefs defensive coordinator** Gunther Cunningham is introduced as the replacement for Marty Schottenheimer.

24 **Golfer David Duval records** 11 birdies and an 18th-hole eagle en route to a PGA record-tying final-round 59 and a victory at the Bob Hope Chrysler Classic.

Vancouver Canucks coach Mike Keenan is fired and former Colorado Avalanche coach Marc Crawford is hired to replace him.

Jaguars defensive coordinator Dick Jauron is hired as the new head coach of the Chicago Bears.

26 **An emotional Buck Williams** announces his retirement from the NBA after 17 seasons as a player and active member of the Players Association.

27 **Golfer Jack Nicklaus undergoes** successful hip replacement surgery which will keep him on the mend for at least three months and force him to miss his first Masters in 40 years.

29 **Baltimore pitcher Jimmy Key** announces his retirement from baseball.

30 **Less than 24 hours before Super Bowl XXXIII**, Miami police arrest Atlanta Falcons defensive back Eugene Robinson on a charge of soliciting. Robinson allegedly approached an undercover police woman who was posing as a prostitute and offered her $40 for oral sex.

31 **Denver quarterback John Elway** throws for 336 yards and a touchdown and rushes for another to lead the Broncos to a successful defense of their Super Bowl title 34-19 over the Atlanta Falcons.

FEB '99

Sun	Mon	Tue	Wed	Thu	Fri	Sat
	1	2	3	4	5	6
7	8	9	10	11	12	13
14	15	16	17	18	19	20
21	22	23	24	25	26	27
28						

A Season for Change?

The Sacramento Kings have labored through 15 straight losing seasons. Perhaps the lockout-shortened NBA season will change the fortunes of the Kings – and these other teams with active losing streaks.

Team	Years	Winning Pct.	Avg. GB
Sacramento (1982-83)	15	.370	27
Dallas (1989-90)	8	.274	36
Milwaukee (1990-91)	7	.361	33
Philadelphia (1990-91)	7	.315	31
L.A. Clippers (1992-93)	5	.307	36
Boston (1992-93)	5	.368	28

Note: Each team is shown with its last winning season, years since last .500+ season, winning percentage during the streak and the average number of games behind the division leader they've finished during the streak each year (based on regular season final standings).

Redemption Bowl

On Feb. 13, Bolingbrook, Ill. native Steve Jaros rolled the 13th televised 300 game in PBA history at the Chattanooga Open, obviously tying him for the highest score for a televised game. Hopefully this eased the pain for Jaros who also holds the distinction of owning the lowest televised score ever–192–at the Brunswick Memorial World Open in 1992.

Official Six-Pack of Daytona

With his exciting victory at the 1999 Daytona 500, Jeff Gordon became just the sixth driver to win the race from the pole position in the race's 41-year history.

Driver	Year(s)
Glen "Fireball" Roberts	1962
Richard Petty	1966
Cale Yarborough	1968 & 1984
Buddy Baker	1980
Bill Elliot	1985 & 1987
Jeff Gordon	1999

2 Former Chicago Bears running back Walter Payton tells the media he's been diagnosed with a rare liver disease (primary sclerosing cholangitis) and is awaiting a liver transplant.

San Diego's Greg Vaughn, who hit 50 home runs in 1998, is involved in a five-player trade that sends him to the Cincinnati Reds.

4 ABC Monday Night Football announcer Dan Dierdorf is fired by the network after 12 seasons with the nationally televised game.

5 The lockout-delayed 1998-99 NBA regular season opens.

Former heavyweight champion Mike Tyson is sentenced to two years in prison (with one suspended) after pleading no-contest to two counts of misdemeanor assault, stemming from a confrontation after a traffic accident in August.

New England Patriots running back Robert Edwards dislocates his left knee during a flag-football game on the beach during the NFL Pro Bowl weekend and requires emergency surgery.

6 Baseball's winningest Latin-American pitcher of all-time, Dennis Martinez, announces his retirement after 22 seasons in the major leagues.

7 AFC East stars Keyshawn Johnson and Ty Law are named co-MVPs and lead the AFC to its third straight Pro Bowl victory, 23-10, over the NFC.

8 Atlanta Falcons WR Tony Martin is named in a federal indictment out of Miami which alleges he helped a friend launder drug money.

Boston University's men's hockey team wins its fifth straight Beanpot tournament title and eighth of the decade.

Charlotte Motor Speedway changes its name to Lowe's Motor Speedway, after it announces it has sold its naming rights to the home improvement company for the next decade.

Comic-book creator Todd McFarlane identifies himself as the buyer of Mark McGwire's 70th home run ball, which was auctioned off in January for over $3 million.

9 The Cleveland Browns select 37 players in an NFL expansion draft created to fill out the new team's roster.

11 Former U.S. Senate candidate Mitt Romney, son of the late Michigan Gov. George Romney, is appointed president and CEO of the Salt Lake City Olympic Organizing Committee.

12 Country music star Garth Brooks, 37, is invited to spring training as a non-roster player by the San Diego Padres.

Four-time NBA All-Star Mark Price announces his retirement from basketball after 12 seasons in which he became the all-time leader in free-throw percentage.

13 The Chicago Blackhawks skate to a 6-2 victory over the Toronto Maple Leafs in the final game at Toronto's Maple Leaf Gardens, closing the doors to the last of the NHL's "Original Six" arenas.

Welterweight champion Oscar De La Hoya punches his way to a strong final round, leading him to a split-decision victory over Ike Quartey.

Michelle Kwan easily wins her third straight U.S. Figure Skating title, while Michael Weiss captures his first men's title.

14 In a dramatic finish separated by 0.128 seconds, Jeff Gordon holds off defending champion Dale Earnhardt to win his second Daytona 500 in three years.

Spawn comic book creator **Todd McFarlane** has a lot of these, considering that his final two purchases at an auction of sports memorabilia in January — Sammy Sosa's 66th home run ball (left hand) and Mark McGwire's 70th (right hand) — brought the number of 1998 home run balls in his personal collection to nine. A fact he revealed to the world Feb. 8.

Tiger Woods ends a nine-month victory drought by carding an eagle on the 72nd hole of the Buick Invitational for a two-stroke win over Billy Ray Brown.

15 The Washington Redskins acquire Minnesota QB Brad Johnson in exchange for three draft picks, including first and third round selections in 1999.

Former Detroit Lions lineman Mike Utley takes his first steps, seven years after doctors said he would never walk again because of a hit during a NFL game that left him paralyzed.

Former NBC broadcaster Marv Albert signs a multi-year deal with Turner Sports to call NBA games on cable stations TNT and TBS.

16 Skip Away wins the Eclipse Award for 1998 Horse of the Year.

18 Toronto pitcher Roger Clemens is traded to the defending world champion N.Y. Yankees in exchange for pitchers David Wells and Graeme Lloyd and second baseman Homer Bush.

Medical tests reveal a cancerous tumor in the lower back of Atlanta Braves first baseman Andres Galarraga, meaning the All-Star will likely miss the entire 1999 season.

Detroit Red Wings star Sergei Fedorov announces he's donating all of last season's salary to help establish a foundation bearing his name that will work with Orchards Children's Services, a nonprofit child welfare agency in the Detroit community.

20 Incarcerated Mike Tyson throws a television in his jail cell during a violent tantrum, landing him in solitary confinement.

IBF welterweight champion Felix Trinidad wins a unanimous 12-round decision over Pernell Whitaker at Madison Square Garden.

22 Houston Comets guard Kim Perrot, 32, reveals at an emotional news conference that she has developed a brain tumor as a result of the spread of lung cancer.

23 Media darling Dennis Rodman signs a contract to play for the Los Angeles Lakers.

The U.S. Supreme Court rules that the NCAA may not be sued under a 1972 law banning sexual discrimination because, although it receives dues from its member schools, that does not suffice to render the NCAA a recipient of federal funds.

24 LA Lakers head coach Del Harris is fired after leading the team to a 6-6 record to start the 1999 season.

26 The Los Angeles Lakers name assistant coach Kurt Rambis the team's new head coach.

28 Longtime Calgary Flames star Theo Fleury is traded to Colorado for left wing Rene Corbet, defenseman Wade Belak and future considerations.

PGA veteran Jeff Maggert holes a 20-foot chip shot on the second sudden-death hole to beat Andrew Magee in the Match Play Championship and claim the $1 million first prize – the Tour's biggest official payday ever.

WTA teenagers Serena and Venus Williams become the first sisters to win singles titles on the same day when Venus captures the IGA Superthrift Tennis Classic hours after Serena's victory at the Open Gaz de France earlier in the day.

MAR '99

Sun	Mon	Tue	Wed	Thu	Fri	Sat
	1	2	3	4	5	6
7	8	9	10	11	12	13
14	15	16	17	18	19	20
21	22	23	24	25	26	27
28	29	30	31			

Madness for Advertisers

A look at TV ratings for the NCAA men's basketball championship game at the beginning of the decade and the end (all games shown on CBS):

Year	Game	Rating*
1990	UNLV vs. Duke	20.0
1991	Duke vs. Kansas	19.4
1992	Duke vs. Michigan	22.7
1997	Arizona vs. Kentucky	18.9
1998	Kentucky vs. Utah	17.8
1999	UConn vs. Duke	17.2

* The estimated percent of all TV households tuned in.

Swinging for No Fences

During his tryout with the San Diego Padres, country music star Garth Brooks had 70 major leaguers sign up for his charity the "Touch 'em All Foundation." His on-the-field stats, however, were not as impressive.

G	AB	H	BB	K	AVG	RBI	E
15	22	1	1	4	.045	1	1

All-Cuban Team

As a tribute to the Baltimore Orioles-Cuban national team exhibition baseball game on March 28, we offer up our all-time Cuban-born All-Star team:

Pos		HR	RBI	AVG
C	Paul Casanova, 1965-74	50	252	.225
1B	Rafael Palmeiro, 1986—	314	1079	.294
2B	Cookie Rojas, 1962-77	54	593	.263
SS	Bert Campaneris, 1964-83	79	646	.259
3B	Tony Perez, 1964-86	79	379	.279
OF	Tony Oliva, 1962-76	220	947	.304
OF	Martin Dihigo, 1923-36*	—	—	.319
OF	Minnie Minoso, 1949-80	186	1023	.298
DH	Jose Canseco, 1985—	397	1214	.266
		W	ERA	K
P	Luis Tiant, 1964-82	229	3.30	2416

* A star at several positions in the Negro Leagues, Dihigo's career stats are incomplete.

1 New York Jets QB Vinny Testaverde is rewarded for leading the team to its first division title, signing what is reported to be a three-year contract worth $20 million plus a rare four-year club option.

2 Atlanta Falcons safety Eugene Robinson agrees to have an AIDS test and complete an AIDS awareness course as part of a pretrial arrangement. In turn, the solicitation charges filed against him during Super Bowl weekend are dropped.

3 Detroit Pistons owner William Davidson buys the Tampa Bay Lightning for a reported $100 million, $17 million less than Art Williams paid for the team less than 10 months earlier.

Houston Astros outfielder Moises Alou undergoes surgery to repair the ACL in his left knee which will sideline him for five to six months.

6 Last place Illinois knocks off its third nationally ranked team in as many days in the Big Ten Conference men's basketball tournament, stunning 12th-ranked Ohio State in the semifinals 79-77.

Unbeaten junior middleweight David Reid (12-0), the lone American boxer to win a gold medal at the 1996 Summer Games, captures the WBA title with a 12-round decision over Laurent Boudouani.

7 Major League Baseball officials confirm that an exhibition baseball game between the Cuban national team and the Baltimore Orioles is scheduled for March 28.

Charlotte Hornets coach Dave Cowens, who openly complained about his league-low salary, resigns after his team's 4-11 start.

Formula One driver Eddie Irvine wins the Australian Grand Prix, his first victory in 81 career starts.

8 Baseball legend Joe DiMaggio, 84, dies at his home in Hollywood, Fla.

Charlotte Hornets assistant Paul Silas replaces Dave Cowens as the team's head coach.

9 Quarterbacks coach Ray Sherman is named Vikings offensive coordinator, replacing Chip Myers who held the position for a month before dying of a heart attack in February.

New York Yankees manager Joe Torre is diagnosed with prostate cancer and leaves the team immediately to seek treatment.

A blockbuster trade in the NBA sends Glen Rice, J.R. Reid, and B.J. Armstrong from Charlotte to the L.A. Lakers for All-Star guard Eddie Jones and Elden Campbell.

10 Minnesota point guard Stephon Marbury is the centerpiece of an eight player deal that sends him from the Timberwolves to the New Jersey Nets.

12 FIFA's Executive Committee refuses to accept Mexico's bid to host the 2006 World Cup because it says the paperwork arrived one month late.

Donald Trump announces he and Bill France Jr. of International Speedway Corporation will build a 100,000-seat facility to be called "Trump Superspeedway" in an attempt to lure stock car racing to the New York metropolitan area.

13 The long-awaited heavyweight title unification fight between Evander Holyfield and Lennox Lewis ends in a controversial draw after 12 rounds despite a widespread belief from reporters and boxing fans alike that Lewis was the true winner of the bout.

Tenth-seeded Gonzaga upsets 1998 Final Four participant Stanford (#2 seed) 82-74 in the second round of the NCAA Tournament.

Reigning French Open champion Carlos Moya jumps from fourth to first in the world tennis rankings, bumping Pete Sampras out of the top spot.

AP/Wide World Photos

Country music fans who had mistakenly thought they had scored really cheap tickets to see **Garth Brooks** live, all seemed to agree on one thing after taking in his spring training tryout with the San Diego Padres: "too much bunting, not enough singing."

14 Newly acquired forward Dennis Rodman takes an unexplained and indefinite leave of absence from his new team the Los Angeles Lakers.

Kenyan Simon Bor sets a course record (2:09:25) in winning the Los Angeles Marathon, beating the mark set 11 years ago by almost one minute.

15 New Jersey Nets coach John Calipari is fired after leading the team to a dismal 3-17 start.

16 NL rookie of the year Kerry Wood, who complained of elbow soreness during his first spring training start (Mar. 14), opts to undergo "Tommy John" surgery and miss the entire 1999 season.

By an overwhelming 29-2 margin NFL owners vote to place the league's 32nd franchise in Los Angeles, possibly returning professional football to the nation's second-largest television market.

17 National Football League owners approve a new instant replay system to be used next season on a one-year trial basis.

The International Olympic Committee expels six members for their role in the Salt Lake City corruption scandal.

Blue Jays manager Tim Johnson, unable to put lies about his Vietnam military experience behind him, is fired and replaced by Jim Fregosi.

18 Yankees manager Joe Torre undergoes 2½ hours of surgery for prostate cancer and is expected to be out for three months.

22 Duke's women's basketball team upsets three-time defending national champion Tennessee 69-63 in the East Regional final.

27 Russian figure skater Maria Butyrskaya, 26, becomes the oldest women's world champion ever and completes Russia's sweep of major titles at the 1999 Figure Skating World Championships.

28 Baltimore beats Cuba's national baseball team 3-2 in Havana, Cuba when Harold Baines hits a single in the 11th inning to drive home the winning run.

Purdue's women's basketball team defeats Duke to capture its first national title ever.

Colorado goalie Patrick Roy makes 26 saves against the L.A. Kings and records his 506th career victory, moving him ahead of Jacques Plante and into first place on the all-time list.

Venus Williams defeats her younger sister Serena 6-1, 4-6, 6-4 in the first meeting of sisters in a WTA Tour final in more than 30 years.

For the first time ever a father and his son both win professional golf tournaments on the same day. David Duval claims his third PGA Tour title of the year, while 400 miles away his father Bob, wins the Emerald Coast Classic on the Senior Tour.

29 The University of Connecticut ends the madness and upsets heavily favored Duke to win its first NCAA men's basketball championship.

31 Rhode Island's Jim Harrick, coach of the men's basketball team, announces he's leaving to take the job at Georgia.

Former University of Kentucky football player Jason Watts pleads guilty to two counts of reckless homicide for his role in a truck crash that killed two men on Nov. 16.

APR '99

Sun	Mon	Tue	Wed	Thu	Fri	Sat
				1	2	3
4	5	6	7	8	9	10
11	12	13	14	15	16	17
18	19	20	21	22	23	24
25	26	27	28	29	30	

Gretzky vs. NHL

Here are the top 10 teams Wayne Gretzky victimized most often in his 20 NHL seasons.

Team	GM	G	A	PTS
1. Vancouver	117	76	163	239
2. Calgary	117	69	161	230
a-Phoenix	105	79	151	230
4. Los Angeles	69	60	119	179
5. Toronto	63	55	95	150
6. Detroit	62	37	108	145
7. Colorado	51	38	94	132
8. Pittsburgh	57	44	80	124
9. New Jersey	67	32	91	123
10. b-Carolina	57	36	73	109

a– Winnipeg Jets prior to 1996-97 season.
b– Hartford Whalers prior to the 1997-98 season.

History Lesson

Of the five quarterbacks taken in the first round of the 1999 NFL draft, three of them — Donovan McNabb, Akili Smith and Daunte Culpepper — are African-Americans. The three black quarterbacks selected are as many as have ever been taken in the first round during the previous 63 NFL drafts. They were:

Name (pick)	Team	Year
Doug Williams (#17)	Tampa Bay	1978
Andre Ware (#7)	Detroit	1990
Steve McNair (#3)	Tennessee	1995

Jose, Can't You See?

Hindsight is always 20/20 but someone looking at the numbers could have predicted who would win the 1999 Masters. No player who has logged between 25-49 Masters' rounds had a better scoring average than this year's winner, Jose Maria Olazabal.

Average	Player	Rounds	Best
71.78	Jose Maria Olazabal	40	66
71.96	Jerry Pate	28	67
72.00	Steve Elkington	28	67
72.03	John Huston	36	66
72.09	Mark Calcavecchia	46	65

1 **Missouri men's basketball coach** Norm Stewart announces his retirement after 32 seasons.

N.Y. Yankees owner George Steinbrenner calls Japanese pitcher Hideki Irabu a "fat . . . toad" after the bulky right-hander forgets to cover first base during a spring training game.

4 **The Colorado Rockies beat** the San Diego Padres 8-2 in Monterrey, Mexico in the first Major League Baseball season opener in a country other than the U.S. or Canada.

Snow in Scottsdale, Ariz. forces Senior PGA officials to call off The Tradition golf tournament after 36 holes and award the title to Graham Marsh.

5 **Washington Wizards coach** Bernie Bickerstaff is the fourth coach to lose his job this season. Replacing him on an interim basis is assistant Jim Brovelli.

Former Oakland QB Jeff George reaches a one-year $400,000 contract agreement with the Minnesota Vikings to backup Randall Cunningham.

6 **Actress Carmen Electra files** divorce papers in Los Angeles, ending "the bliss" that was her six-month marriage to L.A. Lakers forward Dennis Rodman.

7 **New York real estate developer** Howard Milstein's group withdraws its $803 million bid to buy the Redskins after it fails to gain a recommendation from the NFL's finance committee amid questions of the structuring of the would-be-record deal.

8 **Home run king Hank Aaron is honored** by the Atlanta Braves before their game, commemorating the 25th anniversary of his historic 715th home run.

Thoroughbred racing's winningest female jockey Julie Krone announces her retirement after 18 years and $80 million in purses.

11 **Spaniard Jose Maria Olazabal shoots** an 8-under-par 280 and holds off Greg Norman and Davis Love III in the final round to capture his second Masters green jacket.

12 **Former Olympic long distance runner** Mary Decker Slaney files a lawsuit against the IAAF and the USOC, claiming their negligence and fraud in the handling of her 1996 doping case and seeks unspecified damages.

13 **The *New York Post* reports** that NHL legend Wayne Gretzky will announce his retirement this week and play his final NHL game on Sunday.

All-Star center Peter Forsberg re-signs with Colorado for three years and $30 million, making him the NHL's highest paid player in terms of average annual salary.

14 **Duke sophomore Elton Brand becomes** the first underclassman in Mike Krzyzewski's 19-year tenure to leave school early for the NBA draft.

Tampa Bay slugger Jose Canseco becomes Major League Baseball's 28th player to hit 400 home runs in a career.

15 **Colorado Rockies coach Jim Leyland** becomes one of four active managers with 1,000 wins, joining Bobby Cox of Atlanta, Joe Torre of the New York Yankees and Tony La Russa of St. Louis.

Three-time Pro Bowler Marshall Faulk is traded from the Indianapolis Colts to the St. Louis Rams for undisclosed draft picks.

Lightning defenseman Kjell Samuelsson – in the most poorly timed announcement ever – tells the media (pre-occupied with Gretzky's retirement) that he will retire following the season.

UConn hoops star Khalid El-Amin pleads guilty to a marijuana possession charge (from Apr. 13) and is sentenced to six hours of community service.

AP/Wide World Photos

Saints head coach **Mike Ditka** (right) couldn't wait to show Heisman Trophy winner **Ricky Williams** "the steals" he found at the thrift store on his way to the 1999 NFL draft. Both the wig and the Hawaiian shirt reportedly cost him much less than the seven draft picks it took New Orleans to move up and draft Williams with the fifth pick overall.

16 The Great One makes it official at a news conference at Madison Square Garden, telling a huge media throng that Sunday will be his final game.

17 Kentucky quarterback Tim Couch is picked first overall by the Cleveland Browns to kickoff the 1999 NFL draft.

18 Former teammates and fans help pay tribute to Wayne Gretzky, who records one final assist in his last NHL game.

19 Kenya's Joseph Chebet wins the men's division of the 103rd Boston Marathon and Ethiopia's Fatuma Roba becomes the second woman ever to win the race three straight years.

L.A. Kings coach Larry Robinson, who has not won a playoff game in four years with the club, is fired.

20 Back pain lands ironman Cal Ripken on the 15-day disabled list for the first time in his career.

Cincinnati Reds owner Marge Schott announces she has agreed to sell control of the team to a partnership headed by businessman Carl Linder for $67 million.

Former University of Kentucky football player Jason Watts is sentenced to 10 years in prison for his role as the driver in a crash that killed two men last November.

21 NY Yankees pitcher Roger Clemens ties an American League record by winning his 17th consecutive decision.

23 Three-time Olympic champion Katja Seizinger, 26, announces her retirement from professional alpine skiing.

Cardinals 3B Fernando Tatis becomes the first player ever to hit two grand slams in one inning.

25 The New York Yankees give Joe DiMaggio their highest honor, unveiling a monument for the Hall of Famer beyond Yankee Stadium's left field in Monument Park.

26 The trustees of the Washington Redskins agree to sell the team to a group headed by communications executive Daniel Snyder for $800 million.

The IAAF finds Mary Decker Slaney guilty of a doping offense three years after she tested positive at the 1996 U.S. Trials.

27 Thoroughbred trainer D. Wayne Lukas is elected to the National Thoroughbred Racing Hall of Fame.

29 The WNBA and its new players union agree on the league's first collective-bargaining agreement, preventing a lockout and paving the way for the WNBA draft to be held on May 4.

30 New England Patriots owner Bob Kraft calls off his team's move to Connecticut over concerns that the new stadium in Hartford would not be finished in time for the 2002 season as promised.

Former NY Islanders player Butch Goring is hired as the team's new head coach.

Several thousand fans wearing t-shirts that read "share the wealth" to protest high baseball salaries, fill the left-field seats at Kauffman Stadium in Kansas City. They turn their backs when the Yankees bat and then leave in the top of the fourth inning.

MAY '99

Sun	Mon	Tue	Wed	Thu	Fri	Sat
						1
2	3	4	5	6	7	8
9	10	11	12	13	14	15
16	17	18	19	20	21	22
23	24	25	26	27	28	29
30	31					

Princess Mia

In a galaxy far, far away there may be a women's soccer player better than Mia Hamm. But not in this one. The 27-year-old U.S. national soccer team star scored her 108th goal in Orlando on May 22 and became the world record holder for international goals scored in a career – male or female. Here is a list of the 25 countries in this galaxy she scored goals against on her way to 108.

Canada	10	Sweden	3
Australia	8	Taiwan	3
China	8	Finland	3
Denmark	7	Netherlands	3
Germany	7	Argentina	2
Norway	7	Iceland	2
Brazil	6	Martinique	2
Trinidad & Tobago	6	Portugal	2
France	5	Russia	2
England	4	USSR	2
Mexico	4	Bulgaria	1
South Korea	4	TOTAL	108
Italy	4	source: USA TODAY	
Japan	3		

"Let's Race Two"

Winston Cup Rookie of the Year candidate Tony Stewart became the first driver ever to compete in a NASCAR event and the Indianapolis 500 in the same day on May 31. By the end of the Coca-Cola 600, Stewart had posted some impressive numbers and had driven the equivalent of a trip between L.A. and Denver.

Finish at Indianapolis 500: 9th
Finish at Coca-Cola 600: 4th
Driving Time: 7 hours, 15 minutes
Laps completed: 596
Miles driven: 1,090
Left turns: 2,384

1 Trainer D. Wayne Lukas earns his fourth Kentucky Derby victory when 31-1 longshot Charismatic captures the 125th running of the Derby by a neck.

Three spectators are killed when a wheel flies into the stands after a crash on the 62nd lap of an IRL race at Lowe's Motor Speedway in Concord, N.C.

2 Reigning Super Bowl MVP John Elway announces his retirement from the NFL after 16 thrilling seasons with the Denver Broncos.

3 Carolina Hurricanes defenseman Steve Chiasson is killed in the early morning when he is thrown from his pickup truck in a one-vehicle accident in North Carolina while traveling home from Carolina's playoff loss to Boston.

Cuba's national baseball team gets revenge on the Baltimore Orioles, defeating them 12-6 at Camden Yards in front of a sellout crowd peppered with anti-Castro demonstrators.

Detroit pitcher Brian Moehler is suspended 10 days by the American League after being caught (May 1) doctoring a baseball with sandpaper during a game against Tampa Bay.

4 ESPN files suit in federal court seeking to prevent Major League Baseball from canceling its $40 million-per-year deal because of the network's plan to switch September baseball games to ESPN2 to make way for higher-rated NFL football games.

Two time AP Player of the Year Chamique Holdsclaw is selected first overall by the Washington Mystics at the WNBA draft which saw 35 former ABL players and just 12 college seniors selected.

7 Yankees pitcher Hideki Irabu outduels Seattle's Mac Suzuki in the first-ever matchup of Japanese starting pitchers in Major League Baseball history.

8 *The Dallas Morning News* reports that former Dallas Cowboys coach Tom Landry began a 30-day treatment for leukemia May 4 at a local hospital.

Retired NBA star Michael Jordan breaks off negotiations to buy a 50 percent stake in the Charlotte Hornets, citing a struggle while deciding who would hold more sway in operations decisions about the team.

10 Boston Red Sox SS Nomar Garciaparra becomes just the 11th player in major league history to hit two grand slams in a game and homers three times, collecting 10 RBI in a 12-4 romp of Seattle.

13 Cleveland Indians owner Richard Jacobs stuns Indians fans by announcing he is putting the team up for sale.

Golfer Annika Sorenstam fires an 11-under-par 61, the best score in LPGA history on a par-72 course, during the opening round of the Sara Lee Classic in Nashville.

15 Charismatic wins the Preakness Stakes despite going off at 8-1 odds, the second-highest odds for a Kentucky Derby winner ever.

Colombian driver Juan Montoya sets a CART record by becoming the first rookie driver to win three straight races after a victory in the Rio 200.

18 The Colorado Avalanche dethrone two-time defending Stanley Cup champion Detroit Red Wings and reach the Western Conference finals.

Yankees manager Joe Torre returns to the dugout exactly two months after undergoing surgery for prostate cancer.

19 The *Chicago Tribune* announces that it will not cover the legendary Indianapolis 500 auto race (on May 30) after *Sports Illustrated* staffer Ed Hinton, who wrote about a deadly crash earlier this month, is denied credentials to report on the race.

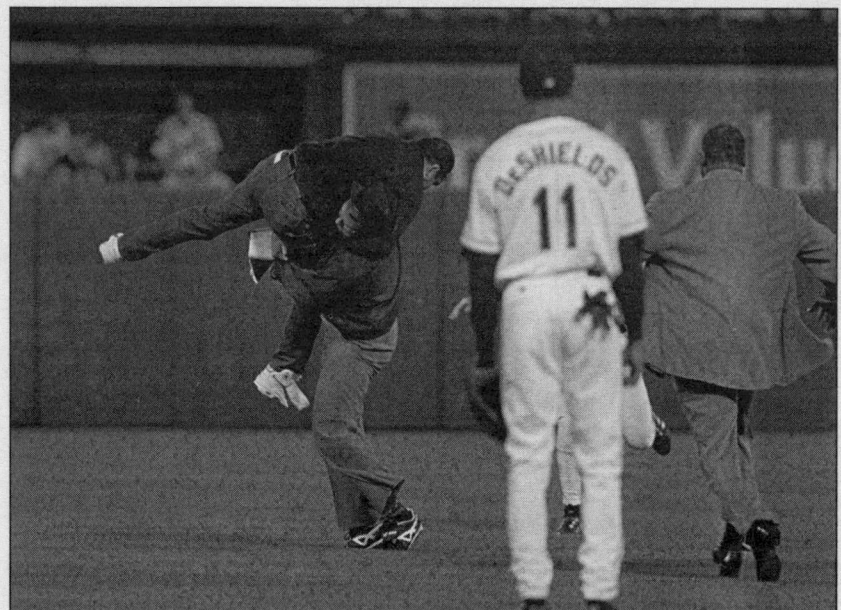

AP/Wide World Photos

Score two points for second base umpire **Cesar Valdez** whose takedown of a protester during the Cuban national team's 12-6 victory over the Baltimore Orioles at Camden Yards was mesmerizing for Orioles second baseman Delino DeShields and a problem solved for security (right).

Arizona outfielder Luis Gonzalez fails to get a hit in an afternoon game against the San Francisco Giants, ending his league-leading hitting streak at 30 games.

21 Relief pitcher Rick Aguilera and left-hander Scott Downs are traded from the Minnesota Twins to the Chicago Cubs for a pair of minor league pitchers.

22 Less than a year after winning their sixth NBA title in eight years, the Chicago Bulls win the top overall pick in the 1999 NBA draft lottery.

Yankees pitcher Roger Clemens sets a new American League record by earning his 18th straight victory.

U.S. women's soccer captain Mia Hamm scores her 108th career goal in a 3-0 victory over Brazil in Orlando, making her the world-record holder for goals scored in a career.

23 Pro wrestler Owen Hart is killed during a World Wrestling Federation pay-per-view event when he falls 70 feet in a pre-match stunt that goes awry at Kemper Arena in Kansas City.

24 Former heavyweight champion Mike Tyson walks out of a Maryland jail after signing parole papers that ended his 108-day jail stay more than eight months short of the one-year sentence he received for assaulting two motorists.

Two-time Norris Trophy winner Brian Leetch signs a four-year $35 million contract to stay with the New York Rangers, making him the league's highest-paid defenseman.

Phoenix Coyotes coach Jim Schoenfeld is fired by the team after it fails yet again to win its first playoff series since 1987.

25 NFL owners unanimously approve the sale of the Washington Redskins to communications executive Daniel Snyder for $800 million.

Orlando Magic coach Chuck Daly announces his retirement from coaching, ending a magnificent 14-year career that included two championships in Detroit and more playoff career victories than all but four coaches in NBA history.

26 Manchester United soccer team caps a magical season by scoring twice during injury time to beat Germany's Bayern Munich 2-1 and capture the Champions League title, the most coveted prize in international club soccer.

Tampa Bay pitcher Tony Saunders breaks his arm while throwing a pitch during an 8-6 victory over Texas and must be taken off the field by stretcher.

29 NY Islanders captain Trevor Linden is acquired by the Montreal Canadiens in exchange for the 10th pick in the 1999 NHL draft.

30 Reigning IRL champ Kenny Brack of Sweden cruises to a 6.5-second victory over Robby Gordon, who runs out of fuel with one lap to go, in the 83rd running of the Indianapolis 500.

PGA Tour rookie Rich Breem leads the Kemper Open from wire-to-wire and fires a 10-under-par 274 to win his first tour title after never finishing better than 45th in any other tournament.

31 Umpiring crew chief Frank Pulli ignites a controversy when he uses video replay to take away a home run from Florida's Cliff Floyd during the St. Louis Cardinals' 5-2 victory over the Marlins at Pro Player Stadium. Pulli's actions, and the game, were protested by the Marlins.

JUNE '99

Sun	Mon	Tue	Wed	Thu	Fri	Sat
		1	2	3	4	5
6	7	8	9	10	11	12
13	14	15	16	17	18	19
20	21	22	23	24	25	26
27	28	29	30			

Charmed Life

Silver Charm, the gray colt who came three-quarters of a length from winning the Triple Crown in 1997, was retired to stud on June 13. On his way to becoming thoroughbred racing's third-richest horse ever, here's a look at the first 12 of Silver Charm's 24 career starts. Notice two things: 1. They're all close. 2. He never finished worse than 2nd.

Date	Race (Grade)	Place	Margin
9/11/96	Del Mar Futurity (II)	1	Head
2/8/97	San Vincente Stakes (III)	1	1¾
3/16/97	San Felipe Stakes (II)	2	¼
4/5/97	Santa Anita Derby (I)	2	Head
5/3/97	Kentucky Derby (I)	1	Head
5/17/97	Preakness Stakes (I)	1	Head
6/7/97	Belmont Stakes (I)	2	¾
12/26/97	Malibu Stakes (I)	2	½
1/17/98	San Fernando BC (II)	1	1
2/7/98	Strub Stakes (II)	1	4
3/28/98	Dubai World Cup (I)	1	Nose
6/13/98	Stephen Foster (II)	2	1

Great Expectations to Phil

Immediately after Phil Jackson was named coach of the Los Angeles Lakers, talk of a championship began in La-La Land. But no NBA coach has ever won championships with two different franchises. In fact only six have made it back to the NBA Finals with another team.

Coach	Teams	App.	(W-L)
Red Auerbach	Washington	1	(0-1)
	Boston	10	(9-1)
Bill Fitch	Boston	1	(1-0)
	Houston	1	(0-1)
Alex Hannum	St. Louis	1	(0-1)
	San Francisco	1	(0-1)
K.C. Jones	Washington	1	(0-1)
	Boston	4	(2-2)
Pat Riley	Los Angeles	7	(4-3)
	New York	1	(0-1)
Bill Sharman	San Francisco	1	(0-1)
	Los Angeles	2	(1-1)

1 Former *"Czar of the Telestrator"* Mike Fratello is fired as head coach of the Cleveland Cavaliers and his boss, GM Wayne Embry, resigns, causing a shake-up of the team's leadership.

NL president Leonard S. Coleman says umpire Frank Pulli, who used instant replay to take a home run from Florida's Cliff Floyd on May 31, was acting in good faith, but use of video replay is not "an acceptable practice."

2 **Patrick Ewing's doctor examines** the Achilles tendon he tore in warm-ups the day before and announces he will be unavailable to the NY Knicks for the rest of the playoffs.

Place-kicker Eddie Murray, who is seventh on the all-time NFL scoring list, signs with the Detroit Lions and then retires as a member of his original NFL team.

3 **Utah Jazz power forward Karl Malone** is named the NBA's Most Valuable Player for the second time in three years.

5 **Longshot Lemon Drop Kid rallies** down the stretch to pass Charismatic, then holds off the fast-closing Vision and Verse to win the 131st Belmont Stakes and deny the Triple Crown bid by Charismatic who breaks his leg at the end of the race.

Steffi Graf beats Martina Hingis to win her sixth French Open crown and 22nd Grand Slam singles title.

6 **The San Antonio Spurs storm** into the NBA Finals for the first time in franchise history, completing a four-game sweep of the Portland Trail Blazers with a 94-80 road victory.

Andre Agassi stages a gritty comeback to beat Andrei Medvedev, capturing his first French Open title and becoming just the fifth tennis player to win all four Grand Slam singles titles in a career.

Barcelona running back Lawrence Phillips caps the greatest comeback in NFL Europe history with a 72-yard touchdown run with 1:50 left to lead the Barcelona Dragons, who trailed the Scottish Claymores 28-3 in the first half, to a 42-35 victory.

7 **Edmonton Oilers head coach Ron Low steps** down after rejecting a contract he deemed unacceptable "for a coach who took his team to the playoffs."

Former NBA guard Doc Rivers is named to succeed Chuck Daly as the Orlando Magic's head coach.

The WNBA announces it will expand by four teams in 2000, doubling its original size to 16 clubs by adding franchises in Indiana, Miami, Portland and Seattle.

8 **Irish swimmer Michelle Smith deBruin**, who won three gold medals at the 1996 Summer Games, announces her retirement after her appeal of a four-year ban from competitive swimming was rejected a day earlier.

9 **Mets manager Bobby Valentine** is ejected in the 12th inning of a 4-3 victory over the Blue Jays and surreptitiously returns to the dugout wearing fake glasses and a mustache as a disguise.

Officials at the University of Nevada announce that the school will leave the Big West Conference and join the Western Athletic Conference for the 2000-01 season.

13 **Houston Astros manager Larry Dierker** collapses in the dugout and suffers a grand mal seizure in the eighth inning of the team's game at the Astrodome against the San Diego Padres.

Five-year-old thoroughbred Silver Charm is retired by owners Bob and Beverly Lewis, finishing his career third all-time in money won.

AP/Wide World Photos

As if straight out of one of those silly soda commercials, giant in-line skater **Brandon Waring** appears to be using the San Francisco-Oakland Bay Bridge as a rail to practice his routine before the Aggressive In-line Street Competition at the fifth annual Summer X Games in San Francisco.

14 Stanford University's athletic department captures the Sears Directors' Cup Trophy for all-around athletic achievement in Division I for the fifth consecutive year.

15 Recently retired Joe Dumars joins the Detroit Pistons front office, accepting the position of vice president of player personnel.

Milwaukee Brewers pitcher Jim Abbott, who was born without a right hand, gets his first major league hit—a fifth-inning single to left field against the Cubs.

16 U.S. sprinter Maurice Greene demolishes the 100-meter world record in Athens, setting the new mark at 9.79 seconds.

Former Chicago Bulls coach Phil Jackson is announced as the new head coach of the L.A. Lakers.

British Formula One driver Damon Hill announces that he will retire at the end of the 1999 season.

NFL Hall of Famer Jim Brown is arrested and charged with a felony count of making terroristic threats towards his wife.

19 Dallas Stars winger Brett Hull ends the second-longest Stanley Cup Finals game ever with a controversial goal from the crease that earns the Stars their first Stanley Cup in franchise history.

U.S. women's soccer star Mia Hamm scores one goal and sets up another, helping her team defeat Denmark in the opening match of the Women's World Cup at the Meadowlands.

The IOC names Turin, Italy as host of the 2006 Olympic Winter Games.

20 Sophomore 1B Kevin Brown knocks in four runs, sparking the Miami Hurricanes to a 6-5 victory over Florida State in the finals of the College World Series.

N.Y. Islanders RW Ziggy Palffy is traded to the Los Angeles Kings as part of an eight-player deal.

Spain's Alex Criville wins the Catalan Grand Prix in Barcelona and becomes the first European motorcycle rider in nearly three decades to win four 500cc races in a row.

22 Top-ranked Martina Hingis is eliminated after her first round match at Wimbledon by 16-year-old Jelena Dokic of Australia who shocks Hingis 6-2, 6-0.

23 Former Boston Celtics forward Kevin McHale and Georgetown coach John Thompson highlight the Pro Basketball Hall of Fame's Class of 1999 which will be inducted on Oct. 1.

24 Pittsburgh Penguins winger Jaromir Jagr wins his first NHL MVP award, ending the two-year reign of Buffalo goalie Dominik Hasek.

The U.S. women's soccer team scores six first-half goals in a 7-1 first-round victory over Nigeria in front of a sellout crowd at Soldier Field in Chicago.

NHL Hall of Famer Mario Lemieux is granted ownership of his former team—the Pittsburgh Penguins—allowing the franchise to stay in the Steel City.

26 The expansion Atlanta Thrashers make Czech center Patrik Stefan the first European to be drafted first overall at the NHL draft since Roman Hamrlik in 1992.

27 Skateboarder Tony Hawk pulls off the first ever "front-side 900" (which is an aerial summersault off the lip of a halfpipe where he spins 2½ times with the board at his feet) during the X Games Best Trick competition in San Francisco.

29 NBC Sports chairman Dick Ebersol announces that the network has rehired basketball broadcaster Marv Albert to work games next fall.

JULY '99

Sun	Mon	Tue	Wed	Thu	Fri	Sat
				1	2	3
4	5	6	7	8	9	10
11	12	13	14	15	16	17
18	19	20	21	22	23	24
25	26	27	28	29	30	31

Strong Finishers

Detroit Lions RB Barry Sanders, who called it quits on July 28, isn't the first athlete to abruptly end a career. Here are some more Hall of Famers who left their respective games while still on top. It includes the player's age at retirement, selected final season statistics, (year of retirement) and reason for leaving.

Barry Sanders, 30: rushed for 1,491 yards on a team record 343 carries; earned a 10th straight Pro Bowl selection. (1999) After not showing up for training camp, he released a letter saying that his desire to exit the game is greater than his desire to stay in it.

Michael Jordan, 35: led the NBA in scoring for the third straight year; the final jumpshot of his career earned his team its sixth championship and helped cement his third straight NBA Finals MVP award. (1999) He announced at a United Center press conference that he was mentally exhausted and he wanted to spend more time with his family.

Bjorn Borg, 27: won the French Open and reached the finals at Wimbledon and the U.S. Open; ranked #4 in the world. (1983) He sat out the 1982 season after refusing to commit himself to playing the tour's required number of tournaments, opting instead for his annual four-month vacation from the tour. He retired the next year.

Jim Brown, 30: rushed for 1,544 yards; scored 21 touchdowns; named NFL's most valuable player for the second time. (1966) While on the set of "The Dirty Dozen" he annouced he wanted to devote more of his time to movie making and race relations.

Rocky Marciano, 32: registered a victory over Don Cockell and a ninth-round knockout of Archie Moore; improved his career record to 49-0-0, 43 by knockout. (1956) He said at a press conference that he wanted to spend more time with his family, but like many other athletes of that generation, he was worried about not making enough money in the sport, considering he had beaten all the top fighters of his day.

Wilma Rudolph, 21: won Sullivan Award and second straight AP Female Athlete of the Year Award; set world records in 60, 70 and 100-yard dashes. (1962) She left to focus time on her classes at Tennessee State University and her marriage.

Note: You may need to scribble Dominik Hasek's name in the margin next year. The Sabres goalie announced July 29 that the 1999-2000 NHL season will be his last.

2 **Umpire Tom Hallion is suspended** for three days without pay by the National League for appearing to bump a Chicago player and coach during an infield dispute, which may be the first time an umpire has been suspended for an onfield dispute.

4 **Czech decathalete Tomas Dvorak** smashes Dan O'Brien's decathlon record by 103 points at a European Cup event in Prague.

Eighteen-year-old Casey Atwood becomes the youngest driver to win in the NASCAR Busch Series, winning the DieHard 250 at The Milwaukee Mile.

5 **Boston's Nomar Garciaparra becomes** the first Red Sox shortstop to be voted a starter in the All-Star Game after he jumps two places in five days to lead all A.L. shortstops in fan voting.

7 **Italy's Mario Cipollini sets** a new Tour de France record by averaging 31.290 m.p.h. during his victory in the race's fourth stage.

Morroccan Hicham El Guerrouj shatters the mile record by 1.26 seconds, wowing the crowd in Rome with a time of 3:43.13.

Longtime Minnesota assistant Randy Wittman is named head coach of the Cleveland Cavaliers.

8 **Free agent RW Theo Fleury signs** a three-year $21-million contract with the New York Rangers.

10 **Brandi Chastain's blast gives** the U.S. women's soccer team a 5-4 advantage in penalty kicks and the 1999 World Cup title after the tournament's final game against China ended in a 0-0 tie.

11 **Two-time Formula One series champion** Michael Schumacher breaks his right leg in two places and is hospitalized after a crash into a tire wall during the first lap of the British GP, apparently ending his 1999 season. He returned Oct. 17.

Arizona Diamondbacks SS Jay Bell's sixth inning grand slam is predicted before the game by fan and radio-contest winner Gylene Holye who wins $1 million for her pick.

Eight-time NHRA Winston Funny Car champion John Force earns the crown of professional drag racing's king by winning the inaugural NHRA Winston Showdown at Bristol Dragway, the first drag race to feature Top Fuel dragsters against Funny Cars.

12 **The fact that Seattle's Ken Griffey Jr.** outdueled Milwaukee outfielder Jeremy Burnitz to win his second Home Run Derby title, is overshadowed by Mark McGwire's contest-record 13 home runs over Fenway Park's Green Monster in the first round.

The U.S. men's basketball team wraps up its sixth straight World University Games gold medal and 40th straight win—both records—by routing Yugoslavia 79-65. The women are upset by Spain in the finals.

13 **Boston Red Sox pitcher Pedro Martinez** strikes out five of the first six batters of the game, leading the A.L. to a 4-1 victory at the All-Star Game.

14 **Three construction workers are killed** and another is seriously injured when a 480-foot crane falls while trying to lift a section of Miller Park's (future home of the Brewers) retractable roof.

Umpire union leader Richie Phillips announces that after a meeting in Philadelphia, 57 of Major League Baseball's 66 umpires have decided to resign from their jobs effective Sept. 2.

Lisa Leslie and Sheryl Swoopes lead the Western Conference to a 79-61 victory over the East in the first-ever WNBA All-Star Game at sold-out Madison Square Garden.

The NHL's Atlanta Thrashers announce their first coach will be Curt Fraser who has been coach of the Orlando Solar Bears of the International Hockey League the last four seasons.

One of the year's most memorable moments occurred prior to baseball's 70th All-Star Game at Fenway Park on July 13, when nominees for baseball's "All-Century Team" gathered around Red Sox legend **Ted Williams** (right) to talk baseball. Ken Griffey Jr., Cal Ripken Jr. and Juan Marichal got in a couple of words before officials broke up the fun to get the game started.

15 **Houston Astros manager Larry Dierker returns** to the dugout after a month-long recovery from a grand mal seizure and leads his team to a 8-6 come-from-behind victory over Detroit.

Seattle relief pitcher Jose Mesa blows a save opportunity in the ninth inning, handing the Mariners a loss in their first game at SAFECO Field.

18 **N.Y. Yankees pitcher David Cone**, 36, becomes the oldest pitcher since Cy Young in 1904 to throw a perfect game, when he blanks the Montreal Expos 6-0 at Yankee Stadium.

France's Jean Van de Velde triple-bogies the British Open's 72nd hole to force a playoff with Justin Leonard and Paul Lawrie, which Lawrie wins, completing his amazing 10-stroke, final-round comeback.

21 **San Antonio Spurs forward Sean Elliott admits** that he's been keeping secret a serious medical condition that requires he get a kidney transplant soon and puts his playing career in jeopardy.

22 **Orel Hershiser becomes** the league's third active pitcher to win 200 games (Clemens, Maddux), allowing six hits in seven innings of work during a 7-4 victory over the Montreal Expos.

23 **Some 5,000 athletes from 42 countries** participate in opening ceremonies for the 13th Pan American Games in Winnipeg, Manitoba, Canada.

24 **Gonzaga's Dan Monson is hired** as men's basketball coach at Minnesota, a month after the school bought out the contract of former coach Clem Haskins following an academic fraud scandal.

Cleveland's Tracy Henderson is suspended for two games and four Detroit players are disciplined for their roles in a fight during the Rockers-Shock WNBA game the night before.

25 **American cyclist Lance Armstrong wins** the Tour de France by 7 minutes, 37 seconds, concluding the amazing story of the rider who was diagnosed with cancer in 1996.

PGA Tour golfer J.L. Lewis captures his first tour victory after scoring a birdie on the fifth hole of a sudden death playoff against Mike Brisky at the John Deere Classic.

26 **Top NBA draft pick Elton Brand signs** a three-year contract with the Chicago Bulls.

Former Tampa Bay and Notre Dame linebacker Demetrius DuBose is fatally shot by police who chased him down after he fled a burglary scene.

27 **The major league umpires' walkout** goes down in flames as all of the umps withdraw their resignations.

28 **Legendary Detroit Lions running back** Barry Sanders retires from football via a written statement.

Legally blind runner Marla Runyan wins a photo finish in the women's 1,500-meter race at the Pan American Games

29 **Buffalo goalie Dominik Hasek announces** that the 1999-2000 NHL season will be his last, insisting that he wants to return to the Czech Republic to raise his children.

Washington Capitals center Dale Hunter retires from the NHL after 19 penalty-filled seasons.

31 **Kansas City ace Kevin Appier**, the subject of trade rumors since spring training, is traded to the Oakland Athletics for three young pitchers.

Notre Dame football coach Bob Davie signs a contract extension to coach the Irish through the 2003 season.

AUG '99

Sun	Mon	Tue	Wed	Thu	Fri	Sat
1	2	3	4	5	6	7
8	9	10	11	12	13	14
15	16	17	18	19	20	21
22	23	24	25	26	27	28
29	30	31				

Statistically Streaking

Montreal outfielder Vladimir Guerrero had Major League Baseball's longest consecutive-game hitting streak in 12 years snapped on Aug. 27. But the 31-game streak easily set the Expos team record, making it one of five team records set or tied in 1999.

NATIONAL LEAGUE

Team	Player	Year	Streak
ARI	**Luis Gonzalez**	**1999**	**30**
ATL	Tommy Holmes	1945	37
CHI	Jerome Walton	1989	30
CIN	Pete Rose	1978	44
COL	Dante Bichette	1995	23
FLA	**Luis Castillo**	**1999**	**22**
	Edgar Renteria	1996	22
HOU	Art Howe	1981	23
	Luis Gonzalez	1997	23
LA	Willie Davis	1969	31
MIL	Paul Molitor	1987	39
MON	**Vladimir Guerrero**	**1999**	**31**
NY	**Mike Piazza**	**1999**	**24**
	Hubie Brooks	1984	24
PHI	Chuck Klein	1930	26*
PIT	Danny O'Connell	1953	26
STL	Rogers Hornsby	1922	33
SD	Benito Santiago	1987	34
SF	Jack Clark	1978	26

*Klein had two 26-game streaks during the 1930 season.

AMERICAN LEAGUE

Team	Player	Year	Streak
ANA	Garrett Anderson	1998	28
BAL	Eric Davis	1998	30
BOS	Dom DiMaggio	1949	34
CHI	Luke Appling	1936	27
	Albert Belle	1997	27
CLE	Sandy Alomar Jr.	1997	30
DET	Ty Cobb	1911	40
KC	George Brett	1980	30
MIN	Ken Landreaux	1980	31
NY	Joe DiMaggio	1941	56
OAK	Jason Giambi	1997	25
SEA	Joey Cora	1997	24
TB	Quinton McCracken	1998	18
TEX	Mickey Rivers	1980	24
TOR	**Shawn Green**	**1999**	**28**

1 **Senior golfer Al Geiberger** is brought to tears during his final round when he gets word that son Brent has won his first PGA Tour title at the Greater Hartford Open.

2 **Under floodlights** at Sherwood Country Club, Tiger Woods holds off David Duval 2&1 to win the first nationally televised primetime broadcast of a golf match ever.

Minnesota Vikings rookie Dimitrius Underwood, the 29th overall draft pick, disappears before the afternoon practice, mystifying team officials.

After trading point guard Mookie Blaylock the day before the draft, the Hawks complete a much-rumored purge of their backcourt, dealing Steve Smith to Portland for guards Isaiah Rider and Jim Jackson.

3 **Businessman David E. Simmons pleads** guilty to misdemeanor tax fraud after admitting he set up a fake job to help the son of a powerful International Olympic Committee member from South Korea obtain lawful permanent resident status. It's the first criminal case to arise out of the Salt Lake City 2000 scandal.

The Orlando Magic trade Nick Anderson, the only remaining member of the original expansion team, to the Sacramento Kings for Tariq Abdul-Wahad and a future first-round draft pick.

The umpires' union files an unfair labor practice charge against the American and National leagues, while the owners in turn file a grievance against the umpires, saying their mass resignations violated their labor contract.

4 **Cuban high jump great** Javier Sotomayor is stripped of his gold medal at the Pan American Games after testing positive for cocaine.

5 **Orlando point guard Penny Hardaway** is dealt to the Phoenix Suns for Danny Manning, Pat Garrity and two first-round draft picks.

Cardinals slugger Mark McGwire becomes the fastest player to hit 500 home runs in a career, then blasts his second homer of the game (#501) off the left-field scoreboard in a 10-3 loss to the San Diego Padres.

6 **Padres All-Star Tony Gwynn** goes 4-for-5, singling in his first at-bat to become the 22nd major leaguer to reach 3,000 hits.

Oakland Athletics OF Tim Raines, one of baseball's top career base stealers and leadoff batters, announces he is suffering from Lupus (a disease where the body acts as if it's allergic to its own tissues) and will miss the rest of the season.

7 **Tampa Bay 3B Wade Boggs** caps a third-straight day of milestone hits by becoming the first baseball player to have his 3,000th major league hit be a home run, in a 15-10 loss to Cleveland.

9 **A 27-year-old man is stabbed** and seriously injured during a game between MLS teams D.C. United and Tampa Bay Mutiny at RFK stadium, marking the second time this season violence has marred a game between the two teams.

10 **The umpire's union withdraws** its lawsuit against baseball, leaving a National Labor Relations Board meeting next month to decide the future of the 22 umps who want their jobs back.

11 **Vikings rookie lineman** Dimitrius Underwood decides he doesn't want to play football, and Minnesota announces a financial settlement with the first-round pick.

14 **Rangers catcher Ivan Rodriguez** swipes second base in the third inning of a game against the White Sox and becomes the first catcher in major league history to hit 20 homers and steal 20 bases in the same season.

AP/Wide World Photos

Venezuelan gymnast **Nadia Garcia** performs in the hoop portion of the individual all-around competition in rhythmic gymnastics at the 1999 Pan American Games in Winnipeg, Manitoba, Canada. Please don't try this at home.

15 **Tiger Woods staves off** 19-year-old Sergio Garcia with a clutch par save on the 17th hole to win the PGA Championship, his second career major.

16 **San Antonio Spurs forward Sean Elliot** undergoes a successful kidney transplant from his brother, Noel, and doctors announce that it will be at least two to three months before they will know if he can continue to play basketball.

Three Arizona Cardinals linemen are seriously injured in a one-car accident during a rain storm 25 miles south of the team's training camp.

Green Bay wide receiver Antonio Freeman becomes the richest man at his position in the NFL, signing a seven-year, $42 million contract.

17 **Baltimore Orioles reliever** Jesse Orosco sets a major league record by pitching in his 1,072nd game.

19 **San Diego Chargers QB Ryan Leaf** has to be forced away from a verbal confrontation with a fan whose heckling included singing lyrics from the song "Lonesome Loser" by the Little River Band during a combined workout with the Miami Dolphins.

21 **Actress Geena Davis finishes** 24th out of 28 competitors at the U.S. Olympic archery trial semifinals, missing a bid for the 2000 Summer Games.

24 **College coaching legend Don Haskins** retires as coach of the Texas-El Paso (UTEP) men's basketball team after 38 seasons at the helm.

Chargers coach Mike Riley confirms that quarterback Ryan Leaf has asked to be traded if the team puts him on injured reserve as a result of his shoulder surgery on July 26.

26 **Sprinter Michael Johnson breaks** the 400-meter world record at the Track and Field World Championships, clipping .11 seconds off of Butch Reynolds' record of 43.29 set in 1988.

Miami Dolphins receiver Tony Martin is acquitted of all charges in a case that involved his friend Rickey Brownlee, who was found guilty on five money laundering charges and two other drug-related charges.

27 **Montreal Expos outfielder Vladimir Guerrero** ends baseball's longest hitting streak in 12 years at 31 games after he goes 0-for-2 with an intentional walk against Cincinnati's Ron Villone.

Former Los Angeles Dodgers manager Tommy Lasorda returns to the dugout to lead the Class A Vero Beach Dodgers to a 1-0 win in a Florida State League game against the St. Lucie Mets, subbing for Vero Beach manager Alvaro Espinoza, whose wife recently had a baby.

28 **Winston Cup fan-favorite Dale Earnhardt** is showered with boos at Bristol Motor Speedway after he spins out Goody's 500 leader Terry Labonte on the final lap and takes the checkered flag for himself.

29 **Dallas Cowboys owner Jerry Jones** is arrested after he drives away with his family before a police officer can finish writing a speeding ticket.

30 **Mets 2B Edgardo Alfonzo goes** 6-for-6, hitting three home runs, scoring a team-record six times and driving in five runs in a 17-1 road victory over the Houston Astros.

College officials are startled by the release of a national survey by Alfred University (N.Y.) which reports that 80 percent of college athletes are hazed.

31 **NHL veteran Dino Ciccarelli**, one of just 10 players in NHL history to score 600 goals, announces his retirement after deciding his ailing back couldn't take the punishment anymore.

SEPT '99

Sun	Mon	Tue	Wed	Thu	Fri	Sat
			1	2	3	4
5	6	7	8	9	10	11
12	13	14	15	16	17	18
19	20	21	22	23	24	25
26	27	28	29	30		

Big Feat for Little Sister

Seventeen-year-old Serena Williams became the fifth woman in the Open Era (since 1968) to win both the singles and doubles titles at the U.S. Open as she teamed with her sister, Venus, to defeat fellow American Chanda Rubin and Sandrine Testud of France. Here is the complete list of champions to win both titles in the same year:

Serena Williams	w/ Venus Williams	1999
A. Sanchez Vicario	w/ Jana Novotna	1994
Martina Navratilova	w/ Pam Shriver	1983, 84, 86, 87
Billie Jean King	w/ Rosemary Casales	1974
Margaret Court	w/ Virginia Wade ('73) w/ Judy Tegart Dalton ('70)	1970, 73

Capture the Flag

NASCAR driver Joe Nemechek ended a winless streak that saw him make 180 Winston Cup circuit starts without recording a victory. Here are the other drivers with at least 100 starts but still waiting to bring home their first checkered flag (through September 1999).

Driver	Starts
Michael Waltrip	422
Rick Mast	303
Dick Trickle	292
Hut Stricklin	277
Ted Musgrave	275
Wally Dallenbach	189
Chad Little	183
Kenny Wallace	179
Robert Pressley	131
Ricky Craven	124
Johnny Benson	122
Mike Skinner	104

1 **Cancer survivor Darryl Strawberry** rejoins the New York Yankees after completing his suspension for cocaine possession.

2 **The absence of 22 veteran umpires** who lost their jobs is hardly noticed on the field as many of their replacements work their first games as permanent members of the majors.

Beer giant Molson Inc. announces that it wants to sell the Molson Centre, a 21,273-seat arena built for its Montreal Canadiens franchise in 1996.

Orioles 3B Cal Ripken Jr. becomes the 29th major league batter to hit 400 home runs, when he connects in the third inning off of Tampa Bay's Rolando Arrojo.

3 **A tearful Terry Collins resigns** as the Anaheim Angels' manager, less than three months after the last-place team gave him a two-year contract extension.

Former Pittsburgh Penguins forward Mario Lemieux becomes the first retired player ever to own a major league sports team for which he played, and immediately lowers ticket prices on 3,500 seats at the Civic Arena.

4 **N.Y. Liberty guard Teresa Weatherspoon** hits a 3-pointer from beyond midcourt at the buzzer to give New York a 68-67 victory over the Houston in Game 2 of the WNBA Finals, forcing a third and deciding game.

The Cincinnati Reds set an N.L. record with nine homers against Philadelphia, breaking a record they shared with three other teams.

Veteran goalie Grant Fuhr is traded to Calgary by St. Louis in exchange for a third-round draft pick in 2000.

5 **Houston Comets forward Cynthia Cooper** scores 24 points in the biggest game her team has had to play without the late Kim Perrot, sparking the Comets to an emotional 54-49 victory over the New York Liberty and their third consecutive WNBA title.

6 **The St. Louis Blues announce** that Wal-Mart heirs Bill and Nancy Laurie have purchased the team and their home, the Kiel Center, six months after the couple failed in their attempt to buy Denver's Avalanche and Nuggets.

A New Jersey man files a $35 million lawsuit against the Oriole Bird, claiming he got roughed up by the team mascot during a game.

10 **A jury acquits football Hall of Famer** Jim Brown of a charge that he made a terrorist threat to kill his wife by snapping her neck, but convicts him of a lesser charge of vandalizing her car.

11 **Serena Williams finishes the job** that big sister Venus couldn't (in the semifinals), beating Martina Hingis to capture the U.S. Open women's singles title at age 17 in only her second year as a pro.

Minnesota pitcher Eric Milton tosses a no-hitter in a 7-0 home victory over the Anaheim Angels.

12 **French Open champ Andre Agassi captures** his second Grand Slam event of the year at the U.S. Open, defeating Todd Martin in a grueling five-set match.

15 **Indiana Pacers coach Larry Bird** tells the media during a publicity tour for his new book that he has a minor heart defect and he will step down after the 1999-2000 season.

16 **Former UConn star Jennifer Rizzotti** accepts a job as head women's basketball coach at the University of Hartford.

17 **Seattle Mariners GM Woody Woodward** announces that he's stepping down after 11 years of running the team's baseball operations.

AP/Wide World Photos

For some players, like San Francisco Giants pitcher **Rich Rodriguez**, letting go isn't so easy. Three days after closing Tiger Stadium, Major League Baseball said goodbye to 3Com Park (formerly Candlestick Park) on Sept. 30 and Rodriguez grabbed some dirt from the pitcher's mound before he left.

18 Chicago Cubs outfielder Sammy Sosa becomes the first player in Major League Baseball history to hit 60 home runs in a season twice.

IBF welterweight champion Felix Trinidad wins a disputed 12-round majority decision over WBC champion Oscar De La Hoya, handing the former Olympic gold medallist his first loss as a professional.

Tampa Bay pitcher Jim Morris, a 35-year-old left-hander, becomes the oldest rookie in the majors in 29 years, and he strikes out Royce Clayton in the eighth inning of a 6-1 loss to Texas.

19 Winston Cup driver Joe Nemechek passes Terry Labonte on the 230th lap and goes on to win the Dura Lube 300. It is his first victory in 180 starts.

20 Atlanta RB Jamal Anderson, who led the NFC in rushing last year, tears the ACL in his right knee midway through the first quarter of a Monday night game against Dallas, ending his season.

21 The mother of Florence Griffith Joyner files a wrongful death lawsuit against her son-in-law, Al Joyner, for the death of her daughter last year.

22 Orioles 3B Cal Ripken Jr. decides to undergo back surgery and says he'll miss the rest of the season, leaving him nine hits shy of 3,000 for his career.

23 Wal-Mart heirs Bill and Nancy Laurie, who own the NHL Blues and the Kiel Center in St. Louis, agree to buy the Vancouver Grizzlies for $200 million, and give no assurance to the media that they won't try to move the team.

24 A fan jumps onto the field along the right field line and attacks Houston Astros right fielder Bill Spiers during a home game against Milwaukee. Then the fan is pummeled by Spiers's teammate Mike Hampton and the rest of the Astros team.

Kansas City closer Jeff Montgomery, one of 11 players to save 300 games in his career, announces that he will retire at the end of the season.

26 Heavily favored USA erases a four point deficit and beats 14½-13½ Europe in the 33rd Ryder Cup tournament.

LPGA golfer Juli Inkster earns her fifth tournament victory of the year at the Safeway Championship and becomes the 17th member of the LPGA Hall of Fame.

27 Detroit's Robert Fick hits his first career grand slam, helping Detroit close Tiger Stadium with an 8-2 victory over the Kansas City Royals on Monday.

Dimitrius Underwood's saga takes another bizarre turn when police find him lying on a sidewalk in Lansing, Mich. suffering from what police say was a self-inflicted knife wound in the neck.

The Seattle Seahawks withdraw their $35 million contract offer to Joey Galloway and tell their holdout wide receiver he must play under terms of his existing pact if he wants to play at all.

29 Houston Rockets forward Scottie Pippen unleashes a torrent of criticism at teammate Charles Barkley, calling Barkley "selfish" and "fat" and saying he doesn't have the desire to win an NBA championship.

Giants Stadium officials announce that the stadium will have a permanent natural grass field beginning in 2000.

30 The largest regular-season crowd in Candlestick Park (now 3Com Park) history is on hand to watch the Dodgers beat the Giants, 9-4, in the stadium's final game on a balmy, sunny day in San Francisco.

OCT '99

Sun	Mon	Tue	Wed	Thu	Fri	Sat
					1	2
3	4	5	6	7	8	9
10	11	12	13	14	15	16
17	18	19	20	21	22	23
24/31	25	26	27	28	29	30

Distancing Himself

On his first attempt from scrimmage on Oct. 17, Miami Dolphins quarterback Dan Marino hit Tony Martin with an eight-yard completion, giving him 60,001 career yards. Marino is the first quarterback to reach the 60,000-yard milestone. To put that in perspective, consider the following chart.

	Miles
60,000 yards	34.1
Length of Manhattan Island	13
Grand Canyon at widest point	18
10 laps at Indianapolis Motor Speedway	25
Olympic marathon	26.2
Boat trip through Panama Canal	27
Length of Chunnel (English Channel)	31
21 round trips across Golden Gate Bridge	33.4

source: NFL.com

14th Inning Stretch?

Kudos to the fans who stayed, despite a steady rain from the sixth inning on, for all 15 innings of the Mets victory over the Braves in Game 5 of the NLCS. Robin Ventura's "grand-slam single" slapped an exclamation point on the end of a legendary game that none of us will soon forget. Here's a closer look at some of the game's most important numbers:

5:46*	Time the game took to play
482	Pitches thrown by both teams
126	Plate appearances
45	Total players used (LCS record)
31	Runners left on base
19	Number of Braves left on base (LCS record)
15*	Pitchers used by both teams
13	Pitches during Shawon Dunston's final AB
9*	Mets pitchers used
1	Bases Ventura touched before being mobbed by teammates

*Major League Baseball postseason record.

1 Wayne Gretzky's No. 99 jersey is retired by the Edmonton Oilers and raised to the rafters in a ceremony at Skyreach Centre before their season-opening game with the New York Rangers.

2 Seven-time All-Star Scottie Pippen is traded from the Houston Rockets to Portland in exchange for six Trailblazers.

3 Reigning NFL MVP Terrell Davis tears ligaments and cartilage in his right knee while making a tackle, ending his 1999 season.

New crew chief Brian Whitesell, who replaced Ray Evernham as pit crew chief, helps guide Jeff Gordon to victory at the NAPA AutoCare 500 at Martinsville Speedway.

Retiring Colorado manager Jim Leyland watches his team put together a ninth-inning comeback to beat San Francisco, 9-8, in his final game on the bench.

4 Cubs manager Jim Riggleman is fired after a five-year run as manager after a horrendous season that saw the Cubs go from 90 wins and the playoffs to 95 losses and last place.

5 Two-time Indianapolis 500 champion Al Unser Jr. will leave CART and join the Indy Racing League next season, reports *Autoweek* magazine.

6 NFL owners award Houston with the league's 32nd franchise after hearing a proposal by billionaire businessman Bob McNair.

Winston Cup driver Jeff Gordon agrees to a contract with Hendrick Motorsports for the remainder of his career, giving him an undisclosed ownership stake in his No. 24 car team.

7 Florida State receiver Peter Warrick is suspended following his arrest on a felony grand theft charge, stemming from a department store scam where he and a former teammate allegedly bought more than $400 worth of designer clothes (Sept. 29) at a Dillard's department store for $21.40.

F1 World Motor Sports Council announces that the Indianapolis Motor Speedway will host the United States' first Formula One race in nine years (U.S. Grand Prix) on Sept. 24, 2000.

9 Michigan State QB Bill Burke passes for a school-record 400 yards and two touchdowns, and Plaxico Burress catches 10 passes for a school-record 255 yards and a score as the No. 11 Spartans hold off the third-ranked Wolverines 34-31.

10 Red Sox 3B John Valentin hits two homers, a double and has seven RBIs as Boston scores the most runs ever in a postseason game, shocking the Cleveland Indians 23-7 and forcing a deciding fifth game in their first round A.L. playoff series.

Cowboys receiver Michael Irvin is temporarily paralyzed after injuring his neck in a fall during Dallas' 13-10 loss to the Philadelphia Eagles.

11 Conference USA presidents unanimously approve the addition of TCU to the league in all sports beginning in 2001.

12 Basketball legend Wilt Chamberlain is found dead in his Bel Air, Calif. home after suffering congestive heart failure.

Longtime Phoenix Suns guard Kevin Johnson, who sat out the 1999 season, announces his retirement from the NBA.

The Toronto Blue Jays hire former manager Cito Gaston as a batting coach for next season.

15 Indians manager Mike Hargrove is fired by the team four days after losing its first round playoff series against Boston and missing out on another World Series title.

Ferrari Formula One driver **Michael Schumacher** trades in horsepower for lawnmower-power and holds off team test driver Luca Badoer in a go-cart race in Sepang, Malaysia five days before the Malaysian Grand Prix on Oct. 17.

16 **Red Sox pitcher Pedro Martinez leads** Boston past Roger Clemens and the N.Y. Yankees 13-1 in Game 3 of the ALCS, one of the most anticipated pitching match-ups in Fenway Park's 87-year history.

17 **N.Y. Mets 3B Robin Ventura hits** a "grand slam single" in the bottom of the 15th inning, giving the Mets a 4-3 victory over Atlanta in Game 5 of the NLCS, one of the greatest playoff games in history.

IRL driver Greg Ray wins the Mall.com 500 and clinches the 1999 Indy Racing League series championship. But on the way home he is pulled over by a Trophy Club, Texas police officer and given a $140 speeding ticket for going 72 mph in a 55 mph zone.

New Orleans Saints coach Mike Ditka makes an obscene gesture to the crowd after they booed his team during the halftime break.

18 **Figure skater Tonya Harding falls** twice during her first pro competition since being implicated in the attack on Nancy Kerrigan in 1994.

20 **Former Detroit manager Buddy Bell** who managed the Detroit Tigers from 1996-98, becomes the third manager in the Rockies' seven-year history, succeeding Jim Leyland, who retired after this season.

21 **The Indiana Dept. of Natural Resources** says that Indiana basketball coach Bob Knight accidentally shot a friend while hunting grouse without a license on Oct. 12, but failed to report the mishap.

22 **Florida State receiver Peter Warrick** pleads guilty to misdemeanor petty theft in connection with a department store scam and avoids jail time, meaning he can play in FSU's game the next day.

Two-time U.S. Open champion Curtis Strange is selected as the next captain of the U.S. Ryder Cup team that will try to retain the cup in 2001 at The Belfry in England.

23 **Luc Van Lierde of Belgium assumes** the lead just after the start of the marathon and steadily extends it en route to claiming the 23rd Ironman Triathlon World Championship by more than five minutes.

24 **Houston Rockets forward Charles Barkley** formally announces his pending retirement at the end of the season in the Birmingham (Ala.) Civic Center, just a half-hour drive from his hometown of Leeds.

Banned baseball legend Pete Rose gets a 55-second ovation before Game 2 of the World Series after he appears on the field at Turner Field as a member of baseball's "All-Century Team."

Nike Tour golfer Casey Martin's 37th-place finish in the final event of the season, drops him to 14th on the money list, but it's still good enough for the disabled golfer to finally earn his PGA Tour card.

25 **PGA Tour veteran Payne Stewart** is killed when the jet he and five others were traveling on flies uncontrolled for hours across the country before crashing in a field two miles west of Mina, S.D.

Former Toronto and Baltimore GM Pat Gillick, who retired after the 1998 season, is appointed the new executive vice president and general manager of the Seattle Mariners, replacing Woody Woodward.

26 **PGA Tour officials announce** that play will be suspended on Friday (Oct. 29) because of a memorial service for Payne Stewart.

NBC reporter Jim Gray apologizes to baseball fans for his contentious interview with Pete Rose before Game 2 of the World Series.

27 **N.Y. Yankees starter Roger Clemens** shuts down the Atlanta Braves 4-1 in Game 4 of the World Series, earning the Yankees their second straight world championship and 25th overall.

JANUARY

1 Major bowl games: Rose (Pasadena) and Orange (Miami)
2 Fiesta Bowl (Tempe, Ariz.)
4 Sugar Bowl, National Title Game (New Orleans)
8 NCAA Convention begins (San Diego)
8 NFL Playoffs (2): AFC/NFC Wildcard games
9 NFL Playoffs (2): AFC/NFC Wildcard games
15 NFL Playoffs (2): AFC/NFC semifinals games
16 NFL Playoffs (2): AFC/NFC semifinals games
17 Australian Open Tennis begins (Melbourne)
23 NFL playoffs (2): AFC/NFC championship games
30 Super Bowl XXXIV (Atlanta)

FEBRUARY

3 Winter X Games begin (Mt. Snow, Vt.)
4 Davis Cup Tennis First Round begins (various sites)
6 NFL Pro Bowl (Honolulu)
6 NHL All-Star Game (Toronto)
6 U.S. Figure Skating Champs. begin (Cleveland)
9 America's Cup Finals begin (New Zealand)
13 NBA All-Star Game (Oakland)
13 PBA National Championship begins (Toledo)
14 ESPY Awards (New York City)
14 Westminster Dog Show begins (New York City)
20 Daytona 500 (Daytona Beach, Fla.)

MARCH

4 Iditarod Trail Sled Dog race begins (Anchorage)
10 NCAA Indoor Track & Field Champs. begin (Fayetteville, Ark.)
12 NCAA Men's and Women's Basketball Tournament Selections
16 NCAA Men's Division I Basketball tournament begins
17 NCAA Women's Division I Basketball tournament begins
23 LPGA Nabisco Championship Golf begins (Rancho Mirage, Calif.)
23 NCAA Women's Div. I Swimming & Diving Champs. begin (Minneapolis)
25 NCAA Men's Div. I Swimming & Diving Championships begin (Indianapolis)
26 World Figure Skating Champs. begin (Nice, FRA)
29 Baseball Opening Day (Cubs vs. Mets in Tokyo)
31 NCAA Women's Basketball Final Four begins (Philadelphia)

APRIL

1 NCAA Men's Basketball Final Four begins (Indianapolis)
6 Masters Golf begins (Augusta, Ga.)
7 Davis Cup Tennis Second Round begins (various sites)
7 NCAA Division I Hockey Final Four begins (Providence)
9 NHL Regular Season ends
12 NHL Stanley Cup Playoffs begin
15 NFL Draft begins (New York City)
17 Boston Marathon
19 NBA Regular Season ends
22 NBA Playoffs begin
28 Women's Fed Cup Tennis First Round begins (various sites)

MAY

6 Kentucky Derby (Louisville)
20 Preakness Stakes (Baltimore)
21 NBA Draft Lottery
21 WIBC Queens women's bowling tournament begins (Reno)
25 NCAA Women's Softball Champs. begin (Oklahoma City)
27 NCAA Men's Lacrosse Final Four begins (College Park, Md.)
28 Indianapolis 500
29 French Open begins (Paris)
31 NCAA Men's and Women's Track & Field Champs. begin (Durham, N.C.)
    * tentative dates

JUNE

9 NCAA Div. I College World Series begins (Omaha, Neb.)
10 Belmont Stakes (Belmont, N.Y.)
12 ABC Masters Bowling tournament begins (Albuquerque, N.M.)
15 U.S. Open Golf begins (Pebble Beach, Calif.)
22 McDonald's LPGA Championship begins (Wilmington, Del.)
23 Summer X Games begin (San Francisco)
23 NHL Expansion Draft (Calgary)
24 NHL Entry Draft begins (Calgary)
26 Wimbledon Tennis begins
28 NBA Draft (Minneapolis)
29 Senior U.S. Open Golf begins (Bethlehem, Pa.)

JULY

1 Tour de France Cycling begins
11 Baseball All-Star Game (Atlanta)
13 MLS All-Star Game (Columbus)
14 Davis Cup Semifinals begin (various sites)
20 British Open Golf begins (St. Andrews)
20 B.A.S.S. Masters Classic begins (Chicago)
20 U.S. Open Women's Golf begins (Libertyville, Ill.)

AUGUST

10 LPGA du Maurier Classic Golf begins (Ottawa, CAN)
11 All-American Soap Box Derby begins (Akron, Ohio)*
14 PGA Championship begins (Louisville, Ky.)
15 U.S. Gymnastics Olympic trials begin (Boston)
21 U.S. Amateur Golf (Springfield, N.J.)
25 Little League World Series begins (Williamsport, Pa.)*
28 U.S. Open Tennis begins (Flushing Meadows, N.Y.)

SEPTEMBER

3 NFL Regular Season begins*
15 Summer Olympics begin (Sydney, AUS)
24 U.S. Grand Prix (Indianapolis)
26 Baseball Regular Season ends
29 Baseball Playoffs begin*

OCTOBER

1 Summer Olympics end (Sydney, AUS)
6 Solheim Cup Golf begins (Glasgow, SCOT)
14 College Football: Oklahoma at Texas
21 World Series begins (in city of AL champion)*
21 Ironman Triathlon Championship (Hawaii)
22 MLS Cup Final (TBD)*

NOVEMBER

4 Breeders' Cup Horse Racing (Lexington, Ky.)
4 Sam's Town Invitational Women's Bowling tournament begins (Las Vegas)
5 New York City Marathon
5 CFL Grey Cup (Calgary)
13 WTA Tour Tennis Championships begin
18 College Football: Michigan at Ohio St.; Auburn at Alabama; UCLA vs. USC and Yale at Harvard
24 Women's Fed Cup Tennis Finals begin
27 ATP Tour Tennis Championships begin

DECEMBER

1 National Finals Rodeo begin (Las Vegas)
1 NCAA Women's Soccer Final Four begins (San Jose)
2 College Football: Big 12 Championship Game (TBD); SEC Championship Game (Atlanta); Army vs. Navy (Philadelphia)
8 Davis Cup Final begins
8 NCAA Men's Soccer Final Four begins (Charlotte, N.C.)
9 Heisman Trophy winner announced (New York City)
16 NCAA Div. I-AA Football Championship (Chattanooga, Tenn.)
18 NFL Regular Season ends*
    * tentative dates

Baseball

New York Yankees closer **Mariano Rivera** and catcher **Jorge Posada** erupt into celebration after sweeping the Atlanta Braves for the Yankees' third World Series title in four years.

AP/Wide World Photos

New York, New York

The Yankees record their second consecutive World Series sweep and stake their claim as baseball's team of the 1990's.

by
Karl Ravech

The stage was set for disappointment. Major League Baseball was coming off a season unlike any it had ever seen before. In 1998, Mark McGwire and Sammy Sosa lifted the game into the consciousness of babies, baby boomers, housewives, business executives and anyone else with a pulse. Actually, their home run race and McGwire's final tally of 70 seemed to reincarnate Roger Maris himself. What could the nation's pastime do to ensure that the wave of positive vibes continued to roll?

Mexico. That was the answer. For the first time in history, baseball began its season outside the United States or Canada. The Colorado Rockies beat the San Diego Padres, 8-2. The significance of such a move in the short term was to increase ticket sales for Padres home games. In the long term, it reinforced baseball's continuing effort to globalize the game. It will not be long, perhaps by the year 2002 or 2003, that we will see a true *World* Series.

As for the 1999 World Series, it was a repeat of the '96 meeting between the New York Yankees and Atlanta Braves. It was a battle over bragging rights for the "team of the decade" moniker. The Braves were making their fifth appearance in the fall classic in the 90's, with their lone championship coming in 1995. The Yankees were after their third crown in the last four years. Better said, the Yankees were the team of the second half of the decade while the Braves' consistency gave them the nod inside baseball circles as the team of the

---

Karl Ravech is the host of ESPN's *Baseball Tonight*.

AP/Wide World Photos

Not everything was rosy for the Yankees in 1999. They endured the deaths of three players' fathers during the year and manager **Joe Torre**, left, missed the early part of the year due to his own battle with prostate cancer. But for the third time in the last four years, owner **George Steinbrenner** walked away with the World Series Trophy.

90's. Yet inside the minds of every other baseball fan, it was George Steinbrenner's team that not only claimed the 90's crown, but is clearly the team of the century.

The Yankees had set such lofty expectations the year prior by winning 125 games and their 24th World Series title, that their "paltry" 98 regular-season wins in 1999 had some people wondering what was wrong. As the Braves found out in a four-game sweep, absolutely nothing was wrong. Everything about Joe Torre's team was right. Incredible starting pitching, brilliant fielding, a deep bench and reliable relievers combined with a mix of personalities to produce one of the most proficient postseason machines of the modern era. After riding Roger Clemens' rejuvenated

spirit to a Game 4 win, the Yankees had claimed a record-tying 12 straight World Series games. The fact that the big spenders made it to the finals surprised few. However, that is not to say that they were the only teams successful in 1999.

The small market Cincinnati Reds and Oakland A's both found themselves in wildcard races until the final week, the Reds, in fact, to the final day before losing to the Mets in a one-game playoff. Out West, the Arizona Diamondbacks left everyone else in the desert dust. They spent wisely and benefited from breakdowns in Los Angeles and San Francisco. Texas, Cleveland and Houston won their respective divisions, and Boston won the American League wildcard race, ultimately setting up an A.L.C.S.

From left, **Wade Boggs** watches his 3000th hit sail over the right field fence, **Tony Gwynn** smacks a single for his 3,000th, and **Mark McGwire** stands in his familiar pose as he sees his 500th home run clear the wall in St. Louis. All three milestones amazingly occurred on three successive days from Aug. 5-7.

showdown with the Yankees that rekindled one of the greatest rivalries in sports.

Red Sox ace Pedro Martinez lit a fire under the "should a pitcher win the MVP award?" debate with 23 wins, 313 strikeouts and a 2.07 ERA. Offensively, both Tony Gwynn and Wade Boggs reached the career 3,000-hit plateau, while McGwire broke the 500-home run mark. And on July 18, the Yankees' David Cone pitched the 16th perfect game in Major League history, beating the Expos, 6-0.

As we turn the page to the year 2000, some 97 years removed from the first World Series, baseball can be proud of its rich past and its promising future. McGwire followed up his 70 home runs with 65, and the Yankees repeated as World Series champions. We, as fans, stood and cheered after 1998, begging baseball to return to the stage for another set. The encore left us wanting more. ∎

The Top Ten Highlights of the 1999 Baseball Season.

10. **Baltimore vs. Cuba** — The Baltimore Orioles met a group of Cuban All-Stars in a home and away series and the Americans, for the most part, were outplayed. While the Orioles payroll is a bit over $78 million, the Cubans make just about $2,250, combined.

9. **Closing Time** — Fans and players alike mourned the closing of a couple of baseball's beloved green cathedrals. The final outs were recorded at Detroit's Tiger Stadium and San Francisco's Candlestick (3Com) Park in 1999 and although gorgeous new parks will open in 2000, people couldn't help but get nostalgic at the end of an era in those two towns.

8. **All-Century Team** — It was literally a team a century in the making. Before Game 2 of the World Series, Major League Baseball officially unveiled the All-Century team. Just 30 players from the over 15,000 to play major league ball in the 20th century were on the team, including banned all-time hit leader Pete Rose.

This is one sight that hitters simply wanted no part of this season. Boston's **Pedro Martinez** won the pitching "Triple Crown" in 1999 by leading the league in wins, strikeouts and ERA. He also took home All-Star Game MVP honors by striking out five of the six batters he faced in the AL's 4-1 win.

7. **Tatis' Big Inning** — The Cardinals' little-known third baseman needed just one inning to truly make a name for himself on April 23, blasting two grand slams in the third inning off Chan Ho Park and the Los Angeles Dodgers. He drove in a record eight runs in the inning as the Cardinals won 12-5.

6. **Mark and Sammy's Encore** — Mark McGwire and Sammy Sosa brought their big bats back to parks across Major League Baseball. After a record setting homer race in '98, the two were doing it again in '99. This time there was much less fanfare but both still exceeded the once unreachable Maris mark for the second straight season.

5. **All-Star Magic** — You aren't a real baseball fan if you didn't feel a lump in your throat while watching the legendary Ted Williams come home to Fenway Park before the 70th All-Star Game. Watching him transform the surrounding major league legends back into wide-eyed sandlot kids was refreshing and touching. It was a climactic moment that was only partially eclipsed by the performance of A.L. starter Pedro Martinez, who started the game by striking out five of the six batters he faced.

4. **Cone's Perfect Game** — It would have been tough to script it any better. Before the game, Don Larsen threw out the first pitch to

catcher Yogi Berra in a re-enactment of Larsen's 1956 World Series perfect game. Berra borrowed Yankees catcher Joe Girardi's glove to receive the pitch, then handed it back to him so he could catch Cone's masterpiece.

3. **Milestone Week** — On Thursday Mark McGwire launched his 500th career home run. On Friday the classy Tony Gwynn collected his 3000th hit. And on Saturday Wade Boggs combined the two, becoming the first player to have his 3000th hit be a home run. No doubt it made things easier for the crew editing highlight tapes at the hall of fame.

2. **Ventura's Grand Slam Single** — They just wouldn't go away. Every time you thought the Mets were finished, someone came through. In Game 5 of the N.L.C.S. against Atlanta, that someone was Robin Ventura. After knocking the game-winning grand slam over the fence in right, he was mobbed by teammates before he could reach second. He was credited with just a single, but it didn't matter. They stayed alive.

1. **Yanks' Sweep-peat** — The Yankees found a way to improve on their 11-2 postseason record in 1998 by going on an 11-1 march through the playoffs in 1999. Consecutive World Series sweeps extended the team's winning streak to 12 games and earned them credentials as one of the sport's best teams ever. And don't consider it impossible that this team will be the first in more than 25 years to win three in a row next season. ∎

THE INSIDE NUMBERS

YANKEE CLIPPERS

With their four-game sweep of the Atlanta Braves in the World Series, the New York Yankees have sailed into a tie for the longest World Series game winning streak in history. The Yankees, which have won World Series titles in 1996, 1998 and 1999, have not lost a World Series game since Game 2 of the 1996 Series. Here are the longest consecutive game winning streaks in World Series history.

Years	Team	Streak
1996, 98, 99	**New York Yankees**	**12 (active)**
1927, 28, 32	New York Yankees	12
1938, 39, 41	New York Yankees	10
1975, 76, 90	Cincinnati Reds	9 (active)

90'S BASEBALL TRIVIA

Who has the most hits in the decade of the 1990's? Who played in the most games? Which team won the most games? Some of the answers to these questions may surprise you. Here's a look at the regular season leaders in those categories and others.

Hits	Mark Grace	1,754
Games	Rafael Palmeiro	1,526
Home Runs	Mark McGwire	405
RBIs	Albert Belle	1,099
Team Wins	Atlanta	925

∎

THE 2000

ESPN INFORMATION PLEASE SPORTS ALMANAC

BASEBALL
STATISTICS

THE SEASON IN REVIEW
1999
LEAGUE LEADERS • POSTSEASON

SEC A

PAGE 71

Final Major League Standings

Division champions (*) and Wild Card (†) winners are noted. Number of seasons listed after each manager refers to current tenure with club.

American League

East Division

	W	L	Pct	GB	Home	Road
*New York	98	64	.605	–	48-33	50-31
†Boston	94	68	.580	4	49-32	45-36
Toronto	84	78	.519	14	40-41	44-37
Baltimore	78	84	.481	20	41-40	37-44
Tampa Bay	69	93	.426	29	33-48	36-45

1999 Managers: NY– Joe Torre (4th season); **Bos**– Jimy Williams (3rd); **Tor**– Jim Fregosi (1st); **Bal**– Ray Miller (2nd); **TB**–Larry Rothschild (2nd).

1998 Standings: 1. New York (114-48); 2. Boston (92-70); 3. Toronto (88-74); 4. Baltimore (79-83); 5. Tampa Bay (63-99).

Central Division

	W	L	Pct	GB	Home	Road
*Cleveland	97	65	.599	–	47-34	50-31
Chicago	75	86	.466	21½	38-42	37-44
Detroit	69	92	.429	27½	38-43	31-49
Kansas City	64	97	.398	32½	33-47	31-50
Minnesota	63	97	.394	33	31-50	32-47

1999 Managers: Cle– Mike Hargrove (9th season); **Chi**– Jerry Manuel (2nd); **Det**– Larry Parrish (2nd); **KC**– Tony Muser (3rd); **Min**– Tom Kelly (14th).

1998 Standings: 1. Cleveland (89-73); 2. Chicago (80-82); 3. Kansas City (72-89); 4. Minnesota (70-92); 5. Detroit (65-97).

West Division

	W	L	Pct	GB	Home	Road
*Texas	95	67	.586	–	51-30	44-37
Oakland	87	75	.537	8	52-29	35-46
Seattle	79	83	.488	16	43-38	36-45
Anaheim	70	92	.432	25	37-44	33-48

1999 Managers: Tex– Johnny Oates (5th season); **Oak**– Art Howe (4th); **Sea**– Lou Piniella (7th); **Ana**– Terry Collins (3rd, 51-82) resigned on Sept. 3 and was replaced by bench coach Joe Maddon (19-10).

1998 Standings: 1. Texas (88-74); 2. Anaheim (85-77); 3. Seattle (76-85); 4. Oakland (74-88).

National League

East Division

	W	L	Pct	GB	Home	Road
*Atlanta	103	59	.636	–	56-25	47-34
†New York	97	66	.595	6½	49-32	48-34
Philadelphia	77	85	.475	26	41-40	36-45
Montreal	68	94	.420	35	35-46	33-48
Florida	64	98	.395	39	35-45	29-53

1999 Managers: Atl– Bobby Cox (10th season); **NY**– Bobby Valentine (4th); **Phi**– Terry Francona (3rd); **Mon**– Felipe Alou (8th); **Fla**– John Boles (1st).

1998 Standings: 1. Atlanta (106-56); 2. New York (88-74); 3. Philadelphia (75-87); 4. Montreal (65-97); 5. Florida (54-108).

Central Division

	W	L	Pct	GB	Home	Road
*Houston	97	65	.599	–	50-32	47-33
Cincinnati	96	67	.589	1½	45-37	51-30
Pittsburgh	78	83	.484	18½	45-36	33-47
St. Louis	75	86	.466	21½	38-42	37-44
Milwaukee	74	87	.460	22½	32-48	42-39
Chicago	67	95	.414	30	34-47	33-48

1999 Managers: Hou– Larry Dierker (3rd season); **Cin**– Jack McKeon (3rd); **Pit**– Gene Lamont (3rd); **St.L**– Tony La Russa (4th); **Mil**– Phil Garner (8th, 52-60) was fired on Aug. 12 and replaced by Jim Lefebvre (22-27); **Chi**– Jim Riggleman (5th).

1998 Standings: 1. Houston (102-60); 2. Chicago (90-73); 3. St. Louis (83-79); 4. Cincinnati (77-85); 5. Milwaukee (74-88); 6. Pittsburgh (69-93).

West Division

	W	L	Pct	GB	Home	Road
*Arizona	100	62	.617	–	52-29	48-33
San Francisco	86	76	.531	14	49-32	37-44
Los Angeles	77	85	.475	23	37-44	40-41
San Diego	74	88	.457	26	46-35	28-53
Colorado	72	90	.444	28	39-42	33-48

1999 Managers: Ari– Buck Showalter (2nd season); **SF**– Dusty Baker (7th); **LA**– Davey Johnson (1st); **SD**– Bruce Bochy (5th); **Col**– Jim Leyland (1st).

1998 Standings: 1. San Diego (98-64); 2. San Francisco (89-74); 3. Los Angeles (83-79); 4. Colorado (77-85); 5. Arizona (65-97).

Wild Card Playoff Game

On October 4, 1999, the New York Mets and Cincinnati Reds, each with a regular-season record of 96-66, staged a playoff game to determine the winner of the National League wild card spot. It was the tenth time in baseball history that an extra game was needed as a tie-breaker, and the second time in history that a tiebreaker was needed to determine the wild card winner (see p. 106 for details).

The game was played at Cinergy Field in Cincinnati due to a coin toss and the Mets went on to defeat the Reds 5-0 behind a two-hitter by pitcher Al Leiter to advance to the Division Series against Arizona.

Boston Red Sox
Nomar Garciaparra
Batting Avg.

Seattle Mariners
Ken Griffey
Home Runs

Cleveland Indians
Manny Ramirez
RBI, Slugging

Boston Red Sox
Pedro Martinez
ERA, Wins, K's, Opp. BA

American League Leaders

Batting

	Bat	Gm	AB	R	H	Avg	TB	2B	3B	HR	RBI	BB	Int BB	SO	SB	Slg Pct	OBP
Nomar Garciaparra, Bos	.R	135	532	103	190	**.357**	321	42	2	27	104	51	7	39	14	.603	.418
Derek Jeter, NY	.R	158	627	134	219	**.349**	346	37	9	24	102	91	5	116	19	.552	.438
Bernie Williams, NY	.S	158	591	116	202	**.342**	317	28	6	25	115	100	17	95	9	.536	.435
Edgar Martinez, Sea	.R	142	502	86	169	**.337**	274	35	1	24	86	97	5	99	7	.554	.447
Manny Ramirez, Cle	.R	147	522	131	174	**.333**	346	34	3	44	165	96	8	131	2	**.663**	.442
Omar Vizquel, Cle	.S	144	574	112	191	**.333**	243	36	4	5	66	65	0	50	42	.436	.397
Ivan Rodriguez, Tex	.R	144	600	116	199	**.332**	335	29	1	35	113	24	2	64	25	.558	.356
Tony Fernandez, Tor	.S	142	485	73	159	**.328**	214	41	0	6	75	77	11	62	6	.449	.427
Juan Gonzalez, Tex	.R	144	562	114	183	**.326**	338	36	1	39	128	51	7	105	3	.601	.378
Rafael Palmeiro, Tex	.L	158	565	96	183	**.324**	356	30	1	47	148	97	14	69	2	.630	.420
Roberto Alomar, Cle	.S	159	563	138	182	**.323**	299	40	3	24	120	99	3	96	37	.533	.422
Mike Sweeney, KC	.R	150	575	101	185	**.322**	297	44	2	22	102	54	0	48	6	.520	.387
Homer Bush, Tor	.R	128	485	69	155	**.320**	201	26	4	5	55	21	0	82	32	.421	.353
Randy Velarde, Ana-Oak	.R	156	631	105	200	**.317**	278	25	7	16	76	70	2	98	24	.455	.390
Jason Giambi, Oak	.L	158	575	115	181	**.315**	318	36	1	33	123	105	4	106	1	.553	.422

Home Runs

Griffey, Sea	48
Palmeiro, Tex	47
Delgado, Tor	44
Ramirez, Cle	44
Green, Tor	42
A. Rodriguez, Sea	42
Gonzalez, Tex	39
Palmer, Det	38
Stairs, Oak	38
Belle, Bal	37
Jaha, Oak	35
Rodriguez, Tex	35
Canseco, TB	34

Triples

Offerman, Bos	11
Damon, KC	9
Febles*, KC	9
Jeter, NY	9
Durham, Chi	8
Dye, KC	8
Polonia, Det	8
Randa, KC	8

On Base Pct.

Martinez, Sea	.447
Ramirez, Cle	.442
Jeter, NY	.438
Williams, NY	.435
Fernandez, Tor	.427
Thome, Cle	.426
R. Alomar, Cle	.422

Runs Batted In

Ramirez, Cle	165
Palmeiro, Tex	148
Delgado, Tor	134
Griffey, Sea	134
Gonzalez, Tex	128
Giambi, Oak	123
Green, Tor	123
R. Alomar, Cle	120
Dye, KC	119
Ordonez, Chi	117
Belle, Bal	117
Sexson, Cle	116
Williams, NY	115

Doubles

Green, Tor	45
Dye, KC	44
Sweeney, KC	44
Garciaparra, Bos	42
Fernandez, Tor	41
Greer, Tex	41
Zeile, Tex	41
R. Alomar, Cle	40

Slugging Pct.

Ramirez, Cle	.663
Palmeiro, Tex	.630
Garciaparra, Bos	.603
Gonzalez, Tex	.601
Green, Tor	.588
Rodriguez, Sea	.586
Griffey, Sea	.576

Hits

Jeter, NY	219
Surhoff, Bal	207
Williams, NY	202
Velarde, Ana-Oak	200
Rodriguez, Tex	199
Randa, KC	197
Beltran*, KC	194
Vizquel, Cle	191
Garciaparra, Bos	190
Green, Tor	190

Runs

R. Alomar, Cle	138
Green, Tor	134
Jeter, NY	134
Ramirez, Cle	131
Griffey, Sea	123
Knoblauch, NY	120
Rodriguez, Tex	116
Williams, NY	116
Giambi, Oak	115

Walks

Thome, Cle	127
Giambi, Oak	105
Belle, Bal	101
Jaha, Oak	101
Williams, NY	100
R. Alomar, Cle	99
Martinez, Sea	97
Palmeiro, Tex	97

Stolen Bases

	SB	CS
Hunter, Det-Sea	44	8
Vizquel, Cle	42	9
Goodwin, Tex	39	11
R. Alomar, Cle	37	6
Stewart, Tor	37	14
Anderson, Bal	36	6
Damon, KC	36	7
Durham, Chi	34	11
Encarnacion, Det	33	12
Bush, Tor	32	8
Knoblauch, NY	28	9
Beltran*, KC	27	8
Lawton, Min	26	4
Rodriguez, Tex	25	12
Lofton, Cle	25	6

Total Bases

Green, Tor	361
Palmeiro, Tex	356
Griffey, Sea	349
Jeter, NY	346
Ramirez, Cle	346
Gonzalez, Tex	338
Rodriguez, Tex	335
Surhoff, Bal	331
Belle, Bal	330
Delgado, Tor	327
Garciaparra, Bos	321
Dye, KC	320
Giambi, Oak	318
Ordonez, Chi	318

Strikeouts

Thome, Cle 171	Clark, Det 133
Palmer, Det 153	Stevens, Tex..........132
Glaus, Ana 143	Ramirez, Cle 131
Delgado, Tor 141	Jaha, Oak 129
Canseco, TB 135	Vaughn, Ana.........127

Hit By Pitch

Anderson, Bal 24	Ramirez, Cle 13
Knoblauch, NY 21	Jeter, NY.............12
Easley, Det 19	Green, Tor 11
Delgado, Tor 15	Vaughn, Ana........11
Saenz*, Oak.........15	Stanley, Bos 11
Ausmus, Det...........14	

Pitching

	Arm	W	L	ERA	Gm	GS	CG	ShO	Sv	IP	H	R	ER	HR	HB	BB	SO	WP
Pedro Martinez, Bos	R	23	4	2.07	31	29	5	1	0	213.1	160	56	49	9	9	37	313	6
David Cone, NY	R	12	9	3.44	31	31	1	1	0	193.1	164	84	74	21	11	90	177	7
Mike Mussina, Bal	R	18	7	3.50	31	31	4	0	0	203.1	207	88	79	16	1	52	172	2
Brad Radke, Min	R	12	14	3.75	33	33	4	0	0	218.2	239	97	91	28	1	44	121	4
Jose Rosado, KC	L	10	14	3.85	33	33	5	0	0	208.0	197	103	89	24	5	72	141	9
Jamie Moyer, Sea	L	14	8	3.87	32	32	4	0	0	228.0	235	108	98	23	9	48	137	3
Bartolo Colon, Cle	R	18	5	3.95	32	32	1	1	0	205.0	185	97	90	24	7	76	161	4
Mike Sirotka, Chi	L	11	13	4.00	32	32	3	1	0	209.0	236	108	93	24	3	57	125	4
Freddy Garcia*, Sea	R	17	8	4.07	33	33	2	1	0	201.1	205	96	91	18	10	90	170	12
Orlando Hernandez, NY	R	17	9	4.12	33	33	2	1	0	214.1	187	108	98	24	8	87	157	4
Omar Olivares, Ana-Oak	R	15	11	4.16	32	32	4	0	0	205.2	217	105	95	19	9	81	85	6
John Halama*, Sea	L	11	10	4.22	38	24	1	1	0	179.0	193	88	84	20	7	56	105	4
Dave Burba, Cle	R	15	9	4.25	34	34	1	0	0	220.0	211	113	104	30	8	96	174	13
Joe Mays*, Min	R	6	11	4.37	49	20	2	1	0	171.0	179	92	83	24	2	67	115	6
Chuck Finley, Ana	L	12	11	4.43	33	33	1	0	0	213.1	197	117	105	23	8	94	200	15

Wins

Martinez, Bos........23-4
Colon, Cle 18-5
Mussina, Bal.......18-7
Sele, Tex 18-9
Garcia*, Sea.......17-8
Hernandez, NY 17-9
Wells, Tor..........17-10
Nagy, Cle..........17-11
Appier, KC-Oak.....16-14
Olivares, Ana-Oak ...15-11
Burba, Cle 15-9
Erickson, Bal 15-12

Losses

Moehler, Det 10-16
Witt, Tam 7-15
Parque, Chi 9-15
Rosado, KC 10-14
Radke, Min.......12-14
Hawkins, Min.......10-14
Appier, KC-Oak......16-14
Fassero, Sea-Tex 16-14
Mlicki, LA-Det.......14-13
Baldwin, Chi 12-13
Sirotka, Chi 11-13
Navarro, Chi 8-13

Holds

Groom, Oak 27
Zimmerman*, Tex......24
Brocail, Det 23
Lloyd, Tor 22
Foulke, Chi 22
Lowe, Bos............22
Stanton, NY 21

HRs Given Up

Helling, Tex 41
Ponson, Bal 35
Fassero, Sea-Tex 35
Baldwin, Chi 34
Wells, Tor 32
Hentgen, Tor 32
Burba, Cle 30
Blair, Det............29
Navarro, Chi..........29
Hawkins, Min 29

Strikeouts

Martinez, Bos 313
Finley, Ana 200
Sele, Tex.............186
Cone, NY 177
Burba, Cle 174
Mussina, Bal 172
Garcia*, Sea 170
Wells, Tor...........169
Clemens, NY.........163
Milton, Min 163
Colon, Cle 161
Hernandez, NY 157
Rosado, KC 141
Moyer, Sea 137
Irabu, NY............133
Hudson*, Oak 132

Appearances

Wells, Min 76
Groom, Oak 76
Trombley, Min 75
Lloyd, Tor 74
Lowe, Bos...........74
Stanton, NY 73
Jackson, Cle..........72
Hernandez, TB 72
Shuey, Cle 72

Innings

Wells, Tor 231.2
Erickson, Bal 230.1
Moyer, Sea 228.0
Burba, Cle 220.0
Helling, Tex 219.1
Radke, Min 218.2
Hernandez, NY......214.1
Martinez, Bos 213.1
Finley, Ana.........213.1
Ponson, Bal 210.0

Wild Pitches

Finley, Ana...........15
Burba, Cle 13
Candiotti, Oak-Cle 13
Garcia*, Sea..........12
Suzuki, Sea-KC.......11
Baldwin, Chi 11
Snyder, Chi 11

Opp. Batting Average

Martinez, Bos....... .205
Cone, NY 229
Hernandez, NY .... .233
Colon, Cle 242
Milton, Min....... .243
Finley, Ana......... .246
Rosado, KC .... .248
Burba, Cle .... .254
Clemens, NY .... .261
Garcia*, Sea....... .263

Complete Games

Wells, Tor 7
Erickson, Bal...........6
Ponson, Bal............6
Rosado, KC 5
Martinez, Bos..........5

Saves

	SV	BS
Rivera, NY 45		4
Hernandez, TB ...43		4
Wetteland, Tex ...43		7
Jackson, Cle 39		4
Mesa, Sea 33		5
Koch*, Tor 31		4
Percival, Ana......31		8
Jones, Det 30		5
Howry, Chi 28		6
Timlin, Bal 27		9

Walks

Erickson, Bal 99
Witt, TB 96
Burba, Cle 96
Finley, Ana...........94
Garcia*, Sea.........90
Clemens, NY 90
Cone, NY 90

Shutouts

Erickson, Bal............3
Milton, Min.............2
Moehler, Det............2
Sele, Tex 2
Witt, TB 2

Stolen Bases

Wells, Tor 37
Wakefield, Bos 35
Gooden, Cle 27
Rapp, Bos............27
Garcia*, Sea..........26

Colorado Rockies
Larry Walker
Batting Avg., OBP, SLG

St. Louis Cardinals
Mark McGwire
HR, RBI

Arizona Diamondbacks
Tony Womack
Stolen Bases

Arizona Diamondbacks
Randy Johnson
ERA, Complete Games,
Inn., Strikeouts

National League Leaders

Batting

	Bat	Gm	AB	R	H	Avg	TB	2B	3B	HR	RBI	BB	Int BB	SO	SB	Slg Pct	OBP
Larry Walker, Col	L	127	438	108	166	**.379**	311	26	4	37	115	57	8	52	11	.710	.458
Luis Gonzalez, Ari	L	153	614	112	206	**.336**	337	45	4	26	111	66	6	63	9	.549	.403
Bob Abreu, Phi	L	152	546	118	183	**.335**	300	35	11	20	93	109	8	113	27	.549	.446
Sean Casey, Cin	L	151	594	103	197	**.332**	320	42	3	25	99	61	13	88	0	.539	.399
Jeff Cirillo, Mil	R	157	607	98	198	**.326**	280	35	1	15	88	75	4	83	7	.461	.401
Mark Grudzielanek, LA	R	123	488	72	159	**.326**	213	23	5	7	46	31	1	65	6	.436	.376
Carl Everett, Hou	S	123	464	86	151	**.325**	265	33	3	25	108	50	5	94	27	.571	.398
Doug Glanville, Phi	R	150	628	101	204	**.325**	287	38	6	11	73	48	1	82	34	.457	.376
Todd Helton, Col	L	159	578	114	185	**.320**	339	39	5	35	113	68	6	77	7	.587	.395
Chipper Jones, Atl	S	157	567	116	181	**.319**	359	41	1	45	110	126	18	94	25	.633	.441
Vladimir Guerrero, Mon	R	160	610	102	193	**.316**	366	37	5	42	131	55	14	62	14	.600	.378
Darryl Hamilton, Col-NY	L	146	505	82	159	**.315**	213	19	4	9	45	57	0	39	6	.422	.386
Brian Giles, Pit	L	141	521	109	164	**.315**	320	33	3	39	115	95	7	80	6	.614	.418
Rondell White, Mon	R	138	539	83	168	**.312**	272	26	6	22	64	32	2	85	10	.505	.359
Mark Grace, Chi	L	161	593	107	183	**.309**	285	44	5	16	91	83	4	44	3	.481	.390

Home Runs

McGwire, St.L.	65
Sosa, Chi	63
C. Jones, Atl.	45
Vaughn, Chi	45
Bagwell, Hou	42
V. Guerrero, Mon	42
Piazza, NY	40
Giles, Pit.	39
Bell, Ari.	38
Walker, Col	37
Williams, Ari	35
Helton, Col.	35

Triples

Abreu, Phi	11
Perez, Col	11
Finley, Ari	10
Womack, Ari	10
Cameron, Cin	9
Kotsay, Fla	9
Gonzalez*, Fla	8
Martin, Pit	8

On Base Pct.

Walker, Col	.458
Bagwell, Hou	.454
Abreu, Phi	.446
C. Jones, Atl.	.441
Olerud, NY	.427
McGwire, St.L	.424
Henderson, NY	.423

Runs Batted In

McGwire, St.L.	147
Williams, Ari	142
Sosa, Chi	141
Bichette, Col	133
V. Guerrero, Mon	131
Bagwell, Hou	126
Piazza, NY	124
Ventura, NY	120
Vaughn, Cin	118

Doubles

Biggio, Hou	56
Gonzalez, Ari	45
Vidro, Mon	45
Grace, Chi	44
Jenkins, Mil	43
Casey, Cin	42
Alfonzo, NY	41
C. Jones, Atl.	41
Young, Pit	41

Slugging Pct.

Walker, Col	.710
McGwire, St.L	.697
Sosa, Chi	.635
C. Jones, Atl	.633
Giles, Pit	.614
V. Guerrero, Mon	.600
Bagwell, Hou	.454
Helton, Col.	.587
Piazza, NY	.575

Hits

Gonzalez, Ari	206
Glanville, Phi	204
Cirillo, Mil	198
Casey, Cin	197
V. Guerrero, Mon	193
Perez, Col	193
Alfonzo, NY	191
Williams, Ari	190
Biggio, Hou	188

Runs

Bagwell, Hou	143
Bell, Ari	132
Alfonzo, NY	123
Biggio, Hou	123
Abreu, Phi	118
McGwire, St.L	118
C. Jones, Atl	116
Helton, Col	114

Walks

Bagwell, Hou	149
McGwire, St.L.	133
C. Jones, Atl	126
Olerud, NY	125
Abreu, Phi	109
Sheffield, LA	101
Giles, Pit	95
Larkin, Cin	93
Burnitz, Mil	91
Biggio, Hou	88

Stolen Bases

	SB	CS
Womack, Ari	72	13
Cedeno, NY	66	17
Young, LA	51	22
Castillo, Fla	50	17
Cameron, Cin	38	12
Reese, Cin	38	7
Henderson, NY	37	14
Renteria, St.L	37	8
Mondesi, LA	36	9
Sanders, SD	36	13

Total Bases

Sosa, Chi	397
V. Guerrero, Mon	366
McGwire, St.L.	363
C. Jones, Atl	359
Helton, Col	339
Gonzalez, Ari	337
Williams, Ari	336
Bagwell, Hou	332

Strikeouts

Sosa, Chi	171
Wilson*, Fla	156
Cameron, Cin	145
Hernandez, Chi-Atl.	145
Rivera, SD	143
McGwire, St.L.	141
Vaughn, Cin	137
Mondesi, Cin	134

Pitching

	Arm	W	L	ERA	Gm	GS	CG	ShO	Sv	IP	H	R	ER	HR	HB	BB	SO	WP
Randy Johnson, Ari L		17	9	2.48	35	35	12	2	0	271.2	207	86	75	30	9	70	364	4
Kevin Millwood, Atl.......R		18	7	2.68	34	34	2	2	0	228.0	168	80	68	24	4	59	205	5
Mike Hampton, Hou L		22	4	2.90	34	34	3	2	0	239.0	206	86	77	12	5	101	177	9
Kevin Brown, SD ....R		18	9	3.00	35	35	5	1	0	252.1	210	99	84	19	7	59	221	4
John Smoltz, Atl.........R		11	8	3.19	29	29	1	1	0	186.1	168	70	66	14	4	40	156	2
Todd Ritchie, Pit.........R		15	9	3.49	28	26	2	0	0	172.2	169	79	67	17	4	54	107	7
Curt Schilling, Phi........R		15	6	3.54	24	24	8	1	0	180.0	159	74	71	25	5	44	152	4
Greg Maddux, Atl........R		19	9	3.57	33	33	4	0	0	219.1	258	103	87	16	4	37	136	1
Jose Lima, Hou..........R		21	10	3.58	35	35	3	0	0	246.1	256	108	98	30	2	44	187	8
Omar Daal, Ari L		16	9	3.65	32	32	2	1	0	214.2	188	92	87	21	7	79	148	3
Pete Harnisch, Cin.......R		16	10	3.68	33	33	2	2	0	198.1	190	86	81	25	5	57	120	3
Andy Ashby, SD.........R		14	10	3.80	31	31	4	3	0	206.0	204	95	87	26	7	54	132	6
Russ Ortiz, SF...........R		18	9	3.81	33	33	3	0	0	207.2	189	109	88	24	6	125	164	13
Shane Reynolds, Hou.....R		16	14	3.85	35	35	4	2	0	231.2	250	108	99	23	1	37	197	4
Kent Bottenfield, St.L.....R		18	7	3.97	31	31	0	0	0	190.1	197	91	84	21	5	89	124	1
Ismael Valdes, LA........R		9	14	3.98	32	32	2	1	0	203.1	213	97	90	32	6	58	143	6
Jon Lieber, Chi..........R		10	11	4.07	31	31	3	1	0	203.1	226	107	92	28	1	46	186	2

Wins
Hampton, Hou 22-4
Lima, Hou..........21-10
Maddux, Atl 19-9
Bottenfield, St.L......18-7
Millwood, Atl 18-7
Brown, LA 18-9
Ortiz, SF 18-9
Johnson, Ari 17-9
Astacio, Col........17-11

Appearances
Kline, Mon 82
Wendell, NY 80
Sullivan, Cin 79
Telford, Mon 79
Benitez, NY 77
Graves, Cin 75
Rocker, Atl 74
Four tied with 73 each.

Complete Games
Johnson, Ari............12
Schilling, Phi...........8
Astacio, Col...........7
Brown, LA............5
Ashby, SD.............4
Maddux, Atl...........4
Reynolds, Hou........4
Trachsel, Chi 4

Losses
Trachsel, Chi.........8-18
Springer, Fla.........6-16
Meadows, Fla 11-15
Valdes, LA...........9-14
Jimenez*, St.L.......5-14
Benson, Pit 11-14
Hermanson, Mon......9-14
Hitchcock, SD 12-14
Reynolds, Hou 16-14

Innings
Johnson, Ari........271.2
Brown, LA 252.1
Lima, Hou..........246.1
Hampton, Hou......239.0
Glavine, Atl 234.0
Astacio, Col.........232.0
Reynolds, Hou......231.2
Millwood, Atl.......228.0
Maddux, Atl.........219.1
Hermanson, Mon ...216.1

Shutouts
Ashby, SD..............3
Hampton, Hou........2
Harnisch, Cin.........2
Jimenez*, St.L.........2
Johnson, Ari..........2
Reynolds, Hou........2
Springer, Fla...........2

Saves
	SV	BS
Urbina, Mon 41		9
Hoffman, SD 40		3
Wagner, Hou......39		3
Rocker, Atl 38		7
Nen, SF 37		9
Wickman, Mil 37		8
Shaw, LA 34		5
Mantei, Fla-Ari ...32		5
Veres, Col 31		8
Graves, Cin 27		9

HRs Given Up
Astacio, Col...........38
Ogea, Phi.............36
Benes, Ari............34
Byrd, Phi.............34
Kile, Col.............33
Williams, SD.........33
Trachsel, Chi.........32
Valdes, LA 32

Wild Pitches
Hitchcock, SD 15
Estes, SF..............15
Kile, Col..............13
Williamson*, Cin 13
Ortiz, SF..............13
Clement, SD...........11
Byrd, Phi..............11
Park, LA 11
Three tied with 10 each.

Walks
Ortiz, SF 125
Estes, SF..............112
Kile, Col..............109
Hampton, Hou 101
Park, LA 100
Leiter, NY..............93
Dempster, Fla..........93
Bohanon, Col 92

Strikeouts
Johnson, Ari...........364
Brown, LA 221
Astacio, Col...........210
Millwood, Atl..........205
Reynolds, Hou........197
Hitchcock, SD 194
Lima, Hou.............187
Lieber, Chi............186
Hampton, Hou 177
Park, LA 174
Ortiz, SF 164
Leiter, NY..............162
Nomo, Mil.............161
Estes, SF..............159
Smoltz, Atl 156
Schilling, Phi 152
Trachsel, Chi 149
Daal, Ari 148
Schmidt, Pit 148

Holds
Johnstone, SF..........28
Embree, SF............22
Wendell, NY 21
Remlinger, Atl 21
Cook, NY..............19
Swindell, SD...........19
Telford, Mon 18
Mills, LA...............18
Seanez, Atl............18
Wall, SD...............18
Benitez, NY 17
Plunk, Mil.............17
Powell, Hou 16
Kline, Mon 16

Opp. Batting Average
Millwood, Atl....... .202
Johnson, Ari .... .208
Brown, LA........ .222
Daal, Ari.......... .236
Schilling, Phi ...... .237
Hampton, Hou .... .241
Ortiz, SF.......... .244
Smoltz, Atl .... .245
Benson, Pit .... .249
Harnisch, Cin...... .252
Hitchcock, SD ..... .254
Nomo, Mil........ .256
Ashby, SD......... .258
Ritchie, Pit........ .259

Stolen Bases
Johnson, Ari...........42
Nomo, Mil............41
Leiter, NY.............28
Valdes, LA 26
Bohanon, Col 26
Ortiz, SF..............25
Thurman, Mon........25
Astacio, Col...........25
Ashby, SD 24

American League Team Leaders

Batting

Team	Avg	AB	R	H	HR	RBI	SB
Texas	.293	5651	945	1653	230	897	111
Cleveland	.289	5634	1009	1629	209	960	147
Kansas City	.282	5624	856	1584	151	800	127
New York	.282	5568	900	1568	193	855	104
Toronto	.280	5642	883	1580	212	856	119
Baltimore	.279	5637	851	1572	203	804	107
Boston	.278	5579	836	1551	176	808	67
Chicago	.277	5644	777	1563	162	742	110
Tampa Bay	.274	5586	772	1531	145	728	73
Seattle	.269	5572	859	1499	244	825	130
Minnesota	.264	5495	686	1450	105	643	118
Detroit	.261	5481	747	1433	212	704	108
Oakland	.259	5519	893	1430	235	845	70
Anaheim	.256	5494	711	1404	158	625	71

Pitching

Team	ERA	W	Sv	CG	ShO	HR	BB	SO
Boston	4.00	94	50	6	12	160	469	1131
New York	4.13	98	50	6	10	158	581	1111
Oakland	4.69	87	48	6	5	160	569	967
Baltimore	4.77	78	33	17	11	198	647	983
Anaheim	4.79	70	37	4	7	177	624	877
Cleveland	4.89	97	46	3	6	197	634	1120
Chicago	4.92	75	39	6	3	210	596	968
Toronto	4.92	84	39	14	9	191	575	1009
Minnesota	5.00	63	34	13	8	208	487	927
Tampa Bay	5.06	69	45	6	5	172	695	1055
Texas	5.07	95	47	6	9	186	509	979
Detroit	5.17	69	33	4	6	209	583	976
Seattle	5.24	79	40	7	6	191	684	980
Kansas City	5.35	64	29	11	3	202	643	831

National League Team Leaders

Batting

Team	Avg	AB	R	H	HR	RBI	SB
Colorado	.288	5717	906	1644	223	863	70
New York	.279	5572	853	1553	181	814	150
Arizona	.277	5658	908	1566	216	865	137
Philadelphia	.275	5598	841	1539	161	797	125
Milwaukee	.273	5582	815	1524	165	777	81
Cincinnati	.272	5649	865	1536	209	820	164
S. Francisco	.271	5563	872	1507	188	828	109
Houston	.267	5485	823	1463	168	784	166
Los Angeles	.266	5567	793	1480	187	761	167
Atlanta	.266	5569	840	1481	197	791	148
Montreal	.265	5559	718	1473	163	680	70
Florida	.263	5478	691	1465	128	655	92
St. Louis	.262	5570	809	1461	194	763	134
Pittsburgh	.259	5468	775	1417	171	735	112
Chicago	.257	5482	747	1411	189	717	60
San Diego	.252	5394	710	1360	153	671	174

Pitching

Team	ERA	W	Sv	CG	ShO	HR	BB	SO
Atlanta	3.63	103	45	9	9	142	507	1197
Arizona	3.77	100	42	16	9	176	543	1198
Houston	3.83	97	48	12	8	128	478	1204
Cincinnati	3.98	96	55	6	11	190	636	1081
New York	4.27	97	49	5	7	167	617	1172
Pittsburgh	4.33	78	34	8	3	160	633	1083
Los Angeles	4.45	77	37	8	6	192	594	1077
San Diego	4.47	74	43	5	6	193	529	1078
Montreal	4.69	68	44	6	4	152	572	1043
S. Francisco	4.71	86	42	6	3	194	655	1076
St. Louis	4.74	75	38	5	3	161	667	1025
Florida	4.90	64	33	6	5	171	655	943
Philadelphia	4.92	77	32	11	6	212	627	1030
Milwaukee	5.07	74	40	2	5	213	616	987
Chicago	5.27	67	32	11	6	221	529	980
Colorado	6.01	72	35	12	2	237	737	1032

Home Attendance

Overall 1999 regular season attendance in Major League Baseball was 70,120,362 in 2,401 games for an average per game crowd of 29,205; numbers in parentheses indicate ranking in 1998; HD indicates home dates; Attendance is based on tickets sold.

American League

	Attendance	HD	Average
1 Baltimore (1)	3,432,099	80	42,901
2 Cleveland (2)	3,468,436	81	42,820
3 New York (3)	3,293,659	81	40,662
4 Seattle (5)	2,915,908	81	35,999
5 Texas (4)	2,774,501	80	34,681
6 Boston (9)	2,446,277	81	30,201
7 Anaheim (6)	2,253,040	81	27,815
8 Toronto (8)	2,163,486	81	26,710
9 Detroit (11)	2,026,491	81	25,018
10 Tampa Bay (7)	1,650,361	78	21,158
11 Kansas City (10)	1,506,068	78	19,309
12 Oakland (13)	1,434,632	81	17,712
13 Chicago (12)	1,349,151	77	17,521
14 Minnesota (14)	1,202,829	81	14,850
TOTALS	31,916,938	1,122	28,446

National League

	Attendance	HD	Average
1 Colorado (1)	3,481,065	81	42,976
2 St. Louis (4)	3,235,833	79	40,960
3 Atlanta (3)	3,284,901	81	40,554
4 Los Angeles (5)	3,098,042	81	38,247
5 Arizona (2)	2,887,170	78	37,015
6 Chicago (6)	2,813,854	78	36,075
7 New York (9)	2,726,008	79	34,506
8 Houston (8)	2,706,017	81	33,408
9 San Diego (7)	2,523,538	81	31,155
10 San Francisco (10)	2,078,365	81	25,659
11 Cincinnati (13)	2,061,324	82	25,138
12 Philadelphia (14)	1,825,337	80	22,817
13 Milwaukee (11)	1,701,790	78	21,818
14 Pittsburgh (15)	1,638,023	80	20,475
15 Florida (12)	1,369,420	78	17,557
16 Montreal (16)	772,737	81	9,540
TOTALS	38,203,424	1,279	29,870

1999 All-Star Game

70th Baseball All-Star Game. **Date:** July 13 at Fenway Park, Boston, Mass.; **Managers:** Joe Torre, New York (AL) and Bruce Bochy, San Diego (NL); **Most Valuable Player:** P Pedro Martinez, Boston (AL): struck out five of the six batters he faced.

National League

	AB	R	H	BI	BB	SO	Avg
Barry Larkin, Cin, ss	3	0	1	1	0	1	.333
Alex Gonzalez, Fla, ss	1	0	0	0	0	0	.000
Larry Walker, Col, rf	2	0	0	0	0	1	.000
Luis Gonzalez, Ari, lf	2	0	1	0	0	0	.500
Sammy Sosa, Chi, cf	3	0	0	0	0	2	.000
Vladimir Guerrero, Mon, rf	1	0	0	0	0	0	.000
Mark McGwire, St.L, 1b	2	0	0	0	1	2	.000
Sean Casey, Cin, 1b	1	0	0	0	0	0	.000
Matt Williams, Ari, 3b	3	0	1	0	0	1	.333
Ed Sprague, Pit, 3b	1	0	0	0	0	0	.000
Jeff Bagwell, Hou, dh	3	0	1	0	0	2	.333
Gary Sheffield, LA, dh	1	0	0	0	0	0	.000
Mike Piazza, LA, c	2	0	1	0	0	1	.500
Mike Lieberthal, Phi, c	1	0	0	0	0	0	.000
Dave Nilsson, Mil, c	1	0	0	0	0	1	.000
Jeromy Burnitz, Mil, lf-rf	2	1	1	0	0	0	.500
Brian Jordan, Atl, cf	1	0	1	0	0	0	1.000
Jay Bell, Ari, 2b	1	0	0	0	1	1	.000
Jeff Kent, SF, 2b	1	0	0	0	1	0	.000
TOTALS	32	1	7	1	4	12	

American League

	AB	R	H	BI	BB	SO	Avg
Kenny Lofton, Cle, lf-cf	3	1	1	0	0	1	.333
Bernie Williams, NY, cf	1	0	0	0	0	1	.000
Nomar Garciaparra, Bos, ss	2	0	0	0	0	0	.000
Derek Jeter, NY, ss	1	0	0	0	0	1	.000
Omar Vizquel, Cle, ss	1	0	0	0	0	0	.000
Ken Griffey, Sea, cf	2	0	0	0	0	1	.000
B.J. Surhoff, Bal, lf	2	0	0	0	0	0	.000
Manny Ramirez, Cle, rf	1	1	0	0	1	1	.000
Shawn Green, Tor, rf	1	0	1	0	0	0	1.000
Magglio Ordonez, Chi, rf	1	0	0	0	0	0	.000
Jim Thome, Cle, 1b	2	1	1	1	1	0	.500
Ron Coomer, Min, 1b	1	0	0	0	0	1	.000
Cal Ripken Jr., Bal, 3b	1	1	1	1	0	0	1.000
Tony Fernandez, Tor, 3b	2	0	0	0	0	1	.000
Rafael Palmeiro, Tex, dh	2	0	1	1	0	0	.500
Harold Baines, Bal, dh	1	0	1	0	0	0	1.000
John Jaha, Oak, dh	1	0	0	0	0	1	.000
Ivan Rodriguez, Tex, c	2	0	0	0	0	1	.000
Brad Ausmus, Det, c	1	0	0	0	0	0	.000
Roberto Alomar, Cle, 2b	2	0	0	1	0	1	.000
Jose Offerman, Bos, 2b	1	0	0	0	0	0	.000
TOTALS	31	4	6	4	2	10	

	1	2	3	4	5	6	7	8	9		R	H	E
National League	0	0	1	0	0	0	0	0	0	–	1	7	1
American League	2	0	0	2	0	0	0	0	x	–	4	6	2

E— Williams (NL), Alomar and Offerman (AL). **LOB**— National 8, American 6. **2B**—Burnitz and Gonzalez (NL). **SB**—Lofton (AL, 2nd base off Schilling/Piazza). **CS**— Williams and Jordan (NL). **GIDP**—Lieberthal and Kent (NL).

NL Pitching	IP	H	R	ER	BB	SO	NP
Curt Schilling, Phi, (L)	2.0	3	2	2	1	3	37
Randy Johnson, Ari	1.0	0	0	0	0	1	9
Kent Bottenfield, St.L	1.0	1	2	2	1	2	30
Jose Lima, Hou	1.0	1	0	0	0	0	12
Kevin Millwood, Atl	1.0	1	0	0	0	1	25
Andy Ashby, SD	0.1	0	0	0	0	0	5
Mike Hampton, Hou	0.2	0	0	0	0	0	4
Trevor Hoffman, SD	0.1	0	0	0	0	1	5
Billy Wagner, Hou	0.2	0	0	0	0	2	10

AL Pitching	IP	H	R	ER	BB	SO	NP
Pedro Martinez, Bos (W)	2.0	0	0	0	0	5	28
David Cone, NY	2.0	4	1	1	1	3	39
Mike Mussina, Bal	1.0	1	0	0	1	2	21
Jose Rosado, KC	1.0	1	0	0	0	1	15
Jeff Zimmerman, Tex	1.0	0	0	0	2	0	20
Roberto Hernandez, TB	1.0	0	0	0	0	0	7
John Wetteland, Tex (S)	1.0	1	0	0	0	1	19

Umpires—Jim Evans (plate); Terry Tata (1b); Dale Ford (2b); Angel Hernandez (3b); Mark Johnson (lf); Larry Vanover (rf). **Attendance**—34,187. **Time**— 2:53. **TV Rating**—12/22 share (FOX).

Home Run Derby

Results of the All-Star Home Run Derby at Fenway Park, Boston, Mass. on July 12. **Avg**. refers to the average distance traveled by the home runs, in feet.

First Round

	No.	Avg.
Mark McGwire, St.Louis	13	437.8
Jeromy Burnitz, Milwaukee	6	393.3
Jeff Bagwell, Houston	5	380.0
Ken Griffey, Seattle	3	415.7
B.J. Surhoff, Baltimore	2	407.0
Larry Walker, Colorado	2	395.0
Nomar Garciaparra, Boston	2	389.5
Shawn Green, Toronto	2	435.5
John Jaha, Oakland	1	418.0
Sammy Sosa, Chi. Cubs	1	371.0

Semifinals

	No.	Avg.
Griffey, Seattle	10	419.1
Burnitz, Milwaukee	6	409.3
McGwire, St. Louis	3	439.0
Bagwell, Houston	1	373.0

Finals

	No.	Avg.
Griffey, Seattle	3	427.7
Burnitz, Milwaukee	2	410.5

Top 5 Homers by Distance

McGwire, 488 feet
McGwire, 486 feet
McGwire, 473 feet
McGwire, 471 feet
McGwire, 470 feet

AL Team by Team Statistics

At least 135 at bats or 40 innings pitched during the regular season, unless otherwise indicated. Players who competed for more than one AL team are listed with their final club. Players traded from the NL are listed with AL team only if they have 135 AB or 40 IP. Note that (*) indicates rookie and PTBN indicates player to be named.

Anaheim Angels

Batting (135 AB)	Avg	AB	R	H	HR	RBI	SB
Garret Anderson	.303	620	88	188	21	80	3
Mo Vaughn	.281	524	63	147	33	108	0
Orlando Palmeiro	.278	317	46	88	1	23	5
Tim Salmon	.266	353	60	94	17	69	4
Jeff Huson	.262	225	21	59	0	18	10
Darin Erstad	.253	585	84	148	13	53	13
Jim Edmonds	.250	204	34	51	5	23	5
Todd Greene	.243	321	36	78	14	42	1
Matt Walbeck	.240	288	26	69	3	22	2
Troy Glaus	.240	551	85	132	29	79	5
Gary DiSarcina	.229	271	32	62	1	29	2
Andy Sheets	.197	244	22	48	3	29	1

Pitching (40 IP)	ERA	W-L	Gm	IP	BB	SO
Mike Magnante	3.38	5-2	53	69.1	29	44
Al Levine	3.39	1-1	50	85.0	29	37
Mark Petkovsek	3.47	10-4	64	83.0	21	43
Troy Percival	3.79	4-6	60	57.0	22	58
Chuck Finley	4.43	12-11	33	213.1	94	200
Ken Hill	4.77	4-11	26	128.1	76	76
Shigetoshi Hasegawa	4.91	4-6	64	77.0	34	44
Mike Fyhrie*	5.05	0-4	16	51.2	21	26
Jarrod Washburn	5.25	4-5	16	61.2	26	39
Steve Sparks	5.42	5-11	28	147.2	82	73
Ramon Ortiz*	6.52	2-3	9	48.1	25	44
Tim Belcher	6.73	6-8	24	132.1	46	52

Saves: Percival (31); Lou Pote (1); Hasegawa (2); Petkovsek (1).
Complete games: Finley (1). **Shutouts:** none.

Baltimore Orioles

Batting (135 AB)	Avg	AB	R	H	HR	RBI	SB
Cal Ripken Jr.	.340	332	51	113	18	57	0
B.J. Surhoff	.308	673	104	207	28	107	5
Will Clark	.303	251	40	76	10	29	2
Albert Belle	.297	610	108	181	37	117	17
Jeff Conine	.291	444	54	129	13	75	0
Brady Anderson	.282	564	109	159	24	81	36
Rich Amaral	.277	137	21	38	0	11	9
Mike Bordick	.277	631	93	175	10	77	14
Jerry Hairston Jr.*	.269	175	26	47	4	17	9
Delino DeShields	.264	330	46	87	6	34	11
Charles Johnson	.251	426	58	107	16	54	0
Jeff Reboulet	.162	154	25	25	0	4	1

Traded: P Guzman and cash to Cin. for P B.J. Ryan and P Jacobo Sequea (Jul. 31).

Pitching (40 IP)	ERA	W-L	Gm	IP	BB	SO
Mike Mussina	3.50	18-7	31	203.1	52	172
Mike Timlin	3.57	3-9	62	63.0	23	50
Juan Guzman	4.18	5-9	21	122.2	65	95
Doug Johns	4.47	6-4	32	86.2	25	50
Sidney Ponson	4.71	12-12	32	210.0	80	112
Scott Erickson	4.81	15-12	34	230.1	99	106
Scott Kamieniecki	4.95	2-4	43	56.1	29	39
Arthur Rhodes	5.43	3-4	43	53.0	45	59
Jason Johnson	5.46	8-7	22	115.1	55	71
Doug Linton	5.95	1-4	14	59.0	25	32
Ricky Bones	5.98	3-8	43	43.2	19	26

Saves: Timlin (27); Rhodes (3); Kamieniecki (2); Jesse Orosco (1). **Complete games:** Erickson and Ponson (6); Mussina (4); Guzman (1). **Shutouts:** Erickson (3); Guzman (1).

Boston Red Sox

Batting (135 AB)	Avg	AB	R	H	HR	RBI	SB
Nomar Garciaparra	.357	532	103	190	27	104	14
Brian Daubach*	.294	381	61	112	21	73	0
Jose Offerman	.294	586	107	172	8	69	18
Butch Huskey	.282	386	62	109	22	77	3
Mike Stanley	.281	427	59	120	19	72	0
Troy O'Leary	.280	596	84	167	28	103	1
Reggie Jefferson	.277	206	21	57	5	17	0
Trot Nixon*	.270	381	67	103	15	52	3
Jason Varitek	.269	483	70	130	20	76	1
John Valentin	.253	450	58	114	12	70	0
Damon Buford	.242	297	39	72	6	38	9
Darren Lewis	.240	470	63	113	2	40	16

Acquired: P Santana from TB for PTBN (Jul. 16); OF Huskey from Sea. for P Robert Ramsay (Jul. 26); P Florie from Det. for P Mike Maroth (Jul. 31).
Traded: P Guthrie and IF Cole Liniak to ChC for P Rod Beck (Aug. 31).

Pitching (40 IP)	ERA	W-L	Gm	IP	BB	SO
Rich Garces	1.55	5-1	30	40.2	18	33
Pedro Martinez	2.07	23-4	31	213.1	37	313
Derek Lowe	2.63	6-3	74	109.1	25	80
Bret Saberhagen	2.95	10-6	22	119.0	11	81
Rheal Cormier	3.69	2-0	60	63.1	18	39
John Wasdin	4.12	8-3	45	74.1	18	57
Pat Rapp	4.12	6-7	37	146.1	69	90
Bryce Florie	4.65	4-1	41	81.1	35	65
Brian Rose*	4.87	7-6	22	98.0	29	51
Tim Wakefield	5.08	6-11	49	140.0	72	104
Mark Portugal	5.51	7-12	31	150.1	41	79
Mark Guthrie	5.83	1-1	46	46.1	20	36
Julio Santana	7.32	1-4	22	55.1	32	34

Saves: Lowe and Wakefield (15); Gordon (11); Beck (3); Garces, Guthrie and Wasdin (2). **Complete games:** Martinez (5); Portugal (1). **Shutouts:** Martinez (1).

Chicago White Sox

Batting (135 AB)	Avg	AB	R	H	HR	RBI	SB
Frank Thomas	.305	486	74	148	15	77	3
Magglio Ordonez	.301	624	100	188	30	117	13
Chris Singleton*	.300	496	72	149	17	72	20
Brook Fordyce	.297	333	36	99	9	49	2
Ray Durham	.296	612	109	181	13	60	34
Paul Konerko	.294	513	71	151	24	81	1
Carlos Lee*	.293	492	66	144	16	84	4
Darrin Jackson	.275	149	22	41	4	16	4
Greg Norton	.255	436	62	111	16	50	4
Mike Caruso	.250	529	60	132	2	35	12
Craig Wilson*	.238	252	28	60	4	26	1
Mark Johnson	.227	207	27	47	4	16	3

Pitching (40 IP)	ERA	W-L	Gm	IP	BB	SO
Keith Foulke	2.22	3-3	67	105.1	21	123
Bob Howry	3.59	5-3	69	67.2	38	80
Sean Lowe*	3.67	4-1	64	95.2	46	62
Bill Simas	3.75	6-3	70	72.0	32	41
Mike Sirotka	4.00	11-13	32	209.0	57	125
James Baldwin	5.10	12-13	35	199.1	81	123
Jim Parque	5.13	9-15	31	173.2	79	111
Carlos Castillo	5.71	2-2	18	41.0	14	23
Jaime Navarro	6.09	8-13	32	159.2	71	74
John Snyder	6.68	9-12	25	129.1	49	67

Saves: Howry (28); Foulke (9); Simas (2). **Complete games:** Sirotka (3); Baldwin, Parque and Snyder (1). **Shutouts:** Sirotka (1).

Cleveland Indians

Batting (135 AB)	Avg	AB	R	H	HR	RBI	SB
Manny Ramirez	.333	522	131	174	44	165	2
Omar Vizquel	.333	574	112	191	5	66	42
Roberto Alomar	.323	563	138	182	24	120	37
Harold Baines	.312	430	62	134	25	103	1
Sandy Alomar Jr.	.307	137	19	42	6	25	0
Kenny Lofton	.301	465	110	140	7	39	25
Wil Cordero	.299	194	35	58	8	32	2
David Justice	.287	429	75	123	21	88	1
Einar Diaz*	.281	392	43	110	3	32	11
Jim Thome	.277	494	101	137	33	108	0
Enrique Wilson	.262	332	41	87	2	24	5
Richie Sexson	.255	479	72	122	31	116	3
Travis Fryman	.255	322	45	82	10	48	2
David Roberts*	.238	143	26	34	2	12	11

Acquired: DH Baines from Bal. for P Juan Aracena and P Jimmy Hamilton (Aug. 27).
Signed: P Haney (Apr. 6); P Candiotti (Jun. 29).

Pitching (40 IP)	ERA	W-L	Gm	IP	BB	SO
Steve Karsay	2.97	10-2	69	78.2	30	68
Paul Shuey	3.53	8-5	72	81.2	40	103
Bartolo Colon	3.95	18-5	32	205.0	76	161
Mike Jackson	4.06	3-4	72	68.2	26	55
Steve Reed	4.23	3-2	61	61.2	20	44
Dave Burba	4.25	15-9	34	220.0	96	174
Ricky Rincon	4.43	2-3	59	44.2	24	30
Chris Haney	4.69	0-2	13	40.1	16	22
Charles Nagy	4.95	17-11	33	202.0	59	126
Mark Langston	5.25	1-2	25	61.2	29	43
Jaret Wright	6.06	8-10	26	133.2	77	91
Dwight Gooden	6.26	3-4	26	115.0	67	88
Tom Candiotti	7.32	4-6	18	71.1	30	41

Saves: Jackson (39); Shuey (6); Karsay (1). **Complete games:** Colon, Nagy and Burba (1). **Shutouts:** Colon (1).

Detroit Tigers

Batting (135 AB)	Avg	AB	R	H	HR	RBI	SB
Luis Polonia	.324	333	46	108	10	32	17
Deivi Cruz	.284	518	64	147	13	58	1
Tony Clark	.280	536	74	150	31	99	2
Frank Catalanotto	.276	286	41	79	11	35	3
Brad Ausmus	.275	458	62	126	9	54	12
Bill Haselman	.273	143	13	39	4	14	2
Damion Easley	.266	549	83	146	20	65	11
Dean Palmer	.263	560	92	147	38	100	3
Juan Encarnacion	.255	509	62	130	19	74	33
Gabe Kapler*	.245	416	60	102	18	49	11
Karim Garcia	.240	288	38	69	14	32	2
Bob Higginson	.239	377	51	90	12	46	4
Gregg Jefferies	.200	205	22	41	6	18	3

Acquired: P Mlicki, P Mel Rojas and cash from LA for P Rick Roberts, P Robinson Checo and P Apostol Garcia (Apr. 16).

Pitching (40 IP)	ERA	W-L	Gm	IP	BB	SO
Doug Brocail	2.52	4-4	70	82.0	25	78
Todd Jones	3.80	4-4	65	66.1	35	64
C.J. Nitkowski	4.30	4-5	68	81.2	45	66
Dave Mlicki	4.60	14-12	31	191.2	70	119
Brian Moehler	5.04	10-16	32	196.1	59	106
Justin Thompson	5.11	9-11	24	142.2	59	83
Jeff Weaver*	5.55	9-12	30	163.2	56	114
Nelson Cruz*	5.67	2-5	29	66.2	23	46
Dave Borkowski*	6.10	2-6	17	76.2	40	50
Masao Kida*	6.26	1-0	49	64.2	30	50
Willie Blair	6.85	3-11	39	134.0	44	82

Saves: Jones (30); Brocail (2); Kida (1). **Complete games:** Mlicki and Moehler (2). **Shutouts:** Moehler (2).

Kansas City Royals

Batting (135 AB)	Avg	AB	R	H	HR	RBI	SB
Mike Sweeney	.322	575	101	185	22	102	6
Joe Randa	.314	628	92	197	16	84	5
Johnny Damon	.307	583	101	179	14	77	36
Jermaine Dye	.294	608	96	179	27	119	2
Rey Sanchez	.294	479	66	141	2	56	11
Carlos Beltran*	.293	663	112	194	22	108	27
Jeremy Giambi*	.285	288	34	82	3	34	0
Scott Pose*	.285	137	27	39	0	12	6
Carlos Febles*	.256	453	71	116	10	53	20
Chad Kreuter	.225	324	31	73	5	35	0
Tim Spehr	.206	155	26	32	9	26	1

Acquired: P Stein, P Rigby and P Jeff D'Amico from Oak. for P Kevin Appier (Jul. 31).
Claimed: P Suzuki off waivers from NYM (Jun. 22).

Pitching (40 IP)	ERA	W-L	Gm	IP	BB	SO
Jose Santiago*	3.42	3-4	34	47.1	14	15
Jose Rosado	3.85	10-14	33	208.0	72	141
Alvin Morman	4.05	2-4	49	53.1	23	31
Jeff Suppan	4.53	10-12	32	208.2	62	103
Blake Stein	4.56	1-2	13	73.0	47	47
Brad Rigby	5.06	4-6	49	83.2	31	36
Jay Witasick*	5.57	9-12	32	158.1	83	102
Scott Service	6.09	5-5	68	75.1	42	68
Makoto Suzuki	6.79	2-5	38	110.0	64	68
Jeff Montgomery	6.84	1-4	49	51.1	21	27
Chris Fussell*	7.39	0-5	17	56.0	36	37

Saves: Montgomery (12); Service (8); Santiago and Fussell (2); Morman, Terry Mathews, Matt Whisenant, Tim Byrdak and Brian Barber (1). **Complete games:** Rosado (5); Suppan (4); Witasick (1). **Shutouts:** Suppan and Witasick (1).

Minnesota Twins

Batting (135 AB)	Avg	AB	R	H	HR	RBI	SB
Corey Koskie*	.310	342	42	106	11	58	4
Jacque Jones*	.289	322	54	93	9	44	3
Marty Cordova	.285	425	62	121	14	70	13
Terry Steinbach	.284	338	35	96	4	42	2
Todd Walker	.279	531	62	148	6	46	18
Chad Allen*	.277	481	69	133	10	46	14
Denny Hocking	.267	386	47	103	7	41	11
Ron Coomer	.263	467	53	123	16	65	2
Matt Lawton	.259	406	58	105	7	54	26
Torii Hunter*	.255	384	52	98	9	35	10
Brent Gates	.255	306	40	78	3	38	1
Javier Valentin	.248	218	22	54	5	28	0
Doug Mientkiewicz*	.229	327	34	75	2	32	1
Cristian Guzman*	.226	420	47	95	1	26	9

Acquired: P Ryan and P Kyle Lohse from ChC for P Rick Aguilera and P Scott Downs (May 21).

Pitching (40 IP)	ERA	W-L	Gm	IP	BB	SO
Travis Miller	2.72	2-2	52	49.2	16	40
Brad Radke	3.75	12-14	33	218.2	44	121
Bob Wells	3.81	8-3	76	87.1	28	44
Mike Trombley	4.33	2-8	75	87.1	28	82
Joe Mays*	4.37	6-11	49	171.0	67	115
Eric Milton	4.49		34	206.1	63	163
Eddie Guardado	4.50	2-5	63	48.0	25	50
Jason Ryan*	4.87	1-4	8	40.2	17	15
Hector Carrasco	4.96	2-3	39	49.0	18	35
Dan Perkins*	6.54	1-7	29	86.2	43	44
LaTroy Hawkins	6.66	10-14	33	174.1	60	103
Mike Lincoln*	6.84	3-10	18	76.1	26	27
Benj Sampson*	8.11	3-2	30	71.0	34	45

Saves: Trombley (24); Rick Aguilera (6); Guardado (2); Wells and Carrasco (1). **Complete games:** Milton (5); Radke (4); Mays (2); Ryan and Hawkins (1). **Shutouts:** Milton (2); Mays (1).

New York Yankees

Batting (135 AB)	Avg	AB	R	H	HR	RBI	SB
Derek Jeter	.349	627	134	219	24	102	19
Bernie Williams	.342	591	116	202	25	115	9
Chuck Knoblauch	.292	603	120	176	18	68	28
Paul O'Neill	.285	597	70	170	19	110	11
Ricky Ledee	.276	250	45	69	9	40	4
Chili Davis	.269	476	59	128	19	78	4
Tino Martinez	.263	589	95	155	28	105	3
Chad Curtis	.262	195	37	51	5	24	8
Scott Brosius	.247	473	64	117	17	71	9
Jorge Posada	.245	379	50	93	12	57	1
Joe Girardi	.239	209	23	50	2	27	3
Shane Spencer*	.234	205	25	48	8	20	0

Pitching (40 IP)	ERA	W-L	Gm	IP	BB	SO
Mariano Rivera	1.83	4-3	66	69.0	18	52
David Cone	3.44	12-9	31	193.1	90	177
Jason Grimsley	3.60	7-2	55	75.0	40	49
Orlando Hernandez	4.12	17-9	33	214.1	87	157
Ramiro Mendoza	4.29	9-9	53	123.2	27	80
Mike Stanton	4.33	2-2	73	62.1	18	59
Dan Naulty	4.38	1-0	33	49.1	22	25
Roger Clemens	4.60	14-10	30	187.2	90	163
Andy Pettitte	4.70	14-11	31	191.2	89	121
Hideki Irabu	4.84	11-7	32	169.1	46	133

Saves: Rivera (45); Mendoza (3); Grimsley and Jeff Nelson (1). **Complete games:** Hernandez and Irabu (2); Cone and Clemens (1). **Shutouts:** Cone, Hernandez, Clemens and Irabu (1).

Seattle Mariners

Batting (135 AB)	Avg	AB	R	H	HR	RBI	SB
Edgar Martinez	.337	502	86	169	24	86	7
Tom Lampkin	.291	206	29	60	9	34	1
Ken Griffey Jr.	.285	606	123	173	48	134	24
Alex Rodriguez	.285	502	110	143	42	111	21
David Bell	.268	597	92	160	21	78	7
Dan Wilson	.266	414	46	110	7	38	5
Raul Ibanez	.258	209	23	54	9	27	5
Russ Davis	.245	432	55	106	21	59	3
John Mabry	.244	262	34	64	9	33	2
Brian L. Hunter	.232	539	79	125	4	34	44
Jay Buhner	.222	266	37	59	14	38	0

Acquired: OF Hunter from Det. for two PTBN (Apr. 28); P Davey and P Steve Sinclair from Tor. for IF David Segui (Jul. 28).

Pitching (40 IP)	ERA	W-L	Gm	IP	BB	SO
Paul Abbott	3.10	6-2	25	72.2	32	68
Jamie Moyer	3.87	14-8	32	228.0	48	137
Jose Paniagua	4.06	6-11	59	77.2	52	74
Freddy Garcia*	4.07	17-8	33	201.1	90	170
John Halama*	4.22	11-10	38	179.0	56	105
Tom Davey*	4.71	2-1	45	65.0	40	59
Gil Meche*	4.73	8-4	16	85.2	57	47
Jose Mesa	4.98	3-6	68	68.2	40	42
Frank Rodriguez	5.65	2-4	28	73.1	30	47
Ken Cloude	7.96	4-4	31	72.1	46	35

Saves: Mesa (33); Paniagua and Rodriguez (3); Davey and Cloude (1). **Complete games:** Moyer (4); Garcia (2); Halama (1). **Shutouts:** Garcia and Halama (1).

Oakland Athletics

Batting (135 AB)	Avg	AB	R	H	HR	RBI	SB
Randy Velarde	.317	631	105	200	16	76	24
Jason Giambi	.315	575	115	181	33	123	1
Ramon Hernandez*	.279	136	13	38	3	21	1
John Jaha	.276	457	93	126	35	111	2
Olmedo Saenz*	.275	255	41	70	11	41	1
Ben Grieve	.265	486	80	129	28	86	4
Matt Stairs	.258	531	94	137	38	102	2
Miguel Tejada	.251	593	93	149	21	84	8
Eric Chavez*	.247	356	47	88	13	50	1
Tony Phillips	.244	406	76	99	15	49	11
Mike Macfarlane	.243	226	24	55	4	31	0
Scott Spiezio	.243	247	31	60	8	33	0
Tim Raines	.215	135	20	29	4	17	4
A.J. Hinch	.215	205	26	44	7	24	6
Ryan Christenson	.209	268	41	56	4	24	7
Jason McDonald	.209	187	26	39	3	8	6

Acquired: IF Velarde and P Olivares from Ana. for three minor leaguers (Jul. 29); P Appier from KC for P Blake Stein, P Brad Rigby and P Jeff D'Amico (Jul. 31). **Traded:** P Rogers to NYM for OF Terrence Long and P Leoner Vasquez (Jul. 23); P Taylor to NYM for P Jason Isringhausen and P Greg McMichael (Jul. 31).

Pitching (40 IP)	ERA	W-L	Gm	IP	BB	SO
Tim Hudson*	3.23	11-2	21	136.1	62	132
Doug Jones	3.55	5-5	70	104.0	24	63
T.J. Mathews	3.81	9-5	50	59.0	20	42
Billy Taylor	3.98	1-5	43	43.0	14	38
Tim Worrell	4.15	2-2	53	69.1	34	62
Omar Olivares	4.16	15-11	32	205.2	81	85
Kenny Rogers	4.30	5-3	19	119.1	41	68
Gil Heredia	4.81	13-8	33	200.1	34	117
Buddy Groom	5.09	3-2	76	46.0	18	32
Kevin Appier	5.17	16-14	34	209.0	84	131
Mike Oquist	5.37	9-10	28	140.2	64	89
Jimmy Haynes	6.34	7-12	30	142.0	80	93

Saves: Taylor (26); Jones (10); Jason Isringhausen (8); Mathews (3); Ron Mahay (1). **Complete games:** Olivares (4); Rogers (3); Hudson, Heredia and Appier (1). **Shutouts:** none.

Tampa Bay Devil Rays

Batting (135 AB)	Avg	AB	R	H	HR	RBI	SB
Fred McGriff	.310	529	75	164	32	104	1
Mike DiFelice	.307	179	21	55	6	27	0
Wade Boggs	.301	292	40	88	2	29	1
Kevin Stocker	.299	254	39	76	1	27	9
Miguel Cairo	.295	465	61	137	3	36	22
Bubba Trammell	.290	283	49	82	14	39	0
Dave Martinez	.284	514	79	146	6	66	13
Jose Canseco	.279	430	75	120	34	95	3
John Flaherty	.278	446	53	124	14	71	0
Randy Winn	.267	303	44	81	2	24	9
Aaron Ledesma	.265	294	32	78	0	30	1
Terrell Lowery*	.259	185	25	48	2	17	0
Herbert Perry	.254	209	29	53	6	32	0
Quinton McCracken	.250	148	20	37	1	18	6
Jose Guillen	.244	168	24	41	2	13	0
Paul Sorrento	.235	294	40	69	11	42	1
Bobby Smith	.181	199	18	36	3	19	4

Acquired: OF Guillen and P Jeff Sparks from Pit. for C Joe Oliver and C Humberto Cota (Jul. 23).

Pitching (40 IP)	ERA	W-L	Gm	IP	BB	SO
Roberto Hernandez	3.07	2-3	72	73.1	33	69
Mike Duvall*	4.05	1-1	40	40.0	27	18
Rick White	4.08	5-3	63	108.0	38	81
Wilson Alvarez	4.22	9-9	28	160.0	79	128
Norm Charlton	4.44	2-3	42	50.2	36	45
Ryan Rupe*	4.55	8-9	24	142.1	57	97
Albie Lopez	4.64	3-2	51	64.0	24	37
Rolando Arrojo	5.18	7-12	24	140.2	60	107
Dave Eiland	5.60	4-8	21	80.1	27	53
Bryan Rekar	5.80	6-6	27	94.2	41	55
Bobby Witt	5.84	7-15	32	180.1	96	123
Esteban Yan	5.90	3-4	50	61.0	32	46
Tony Saunders	6.43	3-3	9	42.0	29	30

Saves: Hernandez (43); Lopez and Jeff Sparks (1). **Complete games:** Witt (3); Arrojo (2); Alvarez (1). **Shutouts:** Witt (2).

Texas Rangers

Batting (140 AB)

	Avg	AB	R	H	HR	RBI	SB
Ivan Rodriguez	.332	600	116	199	35	113	25
Juan Gonzalez	.326	562	114	183	39	128	3
Rafael Palmeiro	.324	565	96	183	47	148	2
Rusty Greer	.300	556	107	167	20	101	2
Roberto Kelly	.300	290	41	87	8	37	6
Todd Zeile	.293	588	80	172	24	98	1
Royce Clayton	.288	465	69	134	14	52	8
Lee Stevens	.282	517	76	146	24	81	2
Mark McLemore	.274	566	105	155	6	45	16
Tom Goodwin	.259	405	63	105	3	33	39
Luis Alicea	.201	164	33	33	3	17	2

Acquired: P Fassero from Sea. for PTBN (Aug. 27).

Pitching (40 IP)

	ERA	W-L	Gm	IP	BB	SO
Jeff Zimmerman*	2.36	9-3	65	87.2	23	67
Mike Venafro*	3.29	3-2	65	68.1	22	37
Tim Crabtree	3.46	5-1	68	65.0	18	54
John Wetteland	3.68	4-4	62	66.0	19	60
Mike Munoz	3.93	2-1	56	52.2	18	27
Esteban Loaiza	4.56	9-5	30	120.1	40	77
Aaron Sele	4.79	18-9	33	205.0	70	186
Rick Helling	4.84	13-11	35	219.1	85	131
John Burkett	5.62	9-8	30	147.1	46	96
Danny Patterson	5.67	2-0	53	60.1	19	43
Mike Morgan	6.24	13-10	34	140.0	48	61
Jeff Fassero	7.20	5-14	37	156.1	83	114
Ryan Glynn*	7.24	2-4	13	54.2	35	39
Mark Clark	8.60	3-7	15	74.1	34	44

Saves: Wetteland (43); Zimmerman (3); Munoz (1). **Complete games:** Helling (3); Sele (2); Morgan (1). **Shutouts:** Sele (2).

Toronto Blue Jays

Batting (180 AB)

	Avg	AB	R	H	HR	RBI	SB
Tony Fernandez	.328	485	73	159	6	75	6
Homer Bush	.320	485	69	155	5	55	32
Shawn Green	.309	614	134	190	42	123	20
Shannon Stewart	.304	608	102	185	11	67	37
David Segui	.298	440	57	131	14	52	1
Darrin Fletcher	.291	412	48	120	18	80	0
Tony Batista	.285	375	61	107	26	79	2
Carlos Delgado	.272	573	113	156	44	134	1
Jose Cruz Jr.	.241	349	63	84	14	45	14
Willis Otanez*	.237	207	28	49	7	24	0
Willie Greene	.204	226	22	46	12	41	0

Acquired: P Spoljaric from Phi. for P Robert Person (May 5); IF Batista and P John Frascatore from Ari. for P Dan Plesac (Jun. 12); IF Segui from Sea. for P Tom Davey and P Steve Sinclair (Jul. 28). **Claimed:** IF Otanez off waivers from Bal. (May 28).

Pitching (40 IP)

	ERA	W-L	Gm	IP	BB	SO
Paul Quantrill	3.33	3-2	41	48.2	17	28
Billy Koch*	3.39	0-5	56	63.2	30	57
Graeme Lloyd	3.63	5-3	74	72.0	23	47
Roy Halladay*	3.92	8-7	36	149.1	79	82
Chris Carpenter	4.38	9-8	24	150.0	48	106
Paul Spoljaric	4.65	2-2	37	62.0	32	63
Pat Hentgen	4.79	11-12	34	199.0	65	118
David Wells	4.82	17-10	34	231.2	62	169
Kelvim Escobar	5.69	14-11	33	174.0	81	129
Peter Munro*	6.02	0-2	31	55.1	23	38
Joey Hamilton	6.52	7-8	22	98.0	39	56

Saves: Koch (31); Lloyd (3); Robert Person (2); Halladay and John Frascatore (1). **Complete games:** Wells (7); Carpenter (4); Halladay, Hentgen and Escobar (1). **Shutouts:** Halladay, Carpenter and Wells (1).

Two Grannys

St. Louis Cardinals

Fernando Tatis

Became the first player in major league history to smack two grand slams in the same inning...hit both shots off Dodgers starter Chan Ho Park in the third inning of the Cardinals' 12-5 victory on April 23...his eight RBI in one inning also set a major league mark...they were the first two grand slams of his career.

Perfection

New York Yankees

David Cone

Pitched the 16th perfect game in major league history in a 6-0 Yankees win over the Montreal Expos on July 18 at Yankee Stadium (for other perfect games, see page 122)...struck out 10 batters...performed the feat in front of Yankees' greats Don Larsen and Yogi Berra, on hand to celebrate their World Series gem in 1956.

3,000 Hits

San Diego Padres

Tony Gwynn

Became the 22nd member of the 3,000-hit club on Aug. 6 with a first-inning single off Montreal's Dan Smith in a 12-10 Padres win at Olympic Stadium...in typical Gwynn fashion, he stroked four hits in the night...it was his 2,284th game...only two players (Ty Cobb and Nap Lajoie) have reached 3,000 in fewer games.

3,000 Hits

Tampa Bay Devil Rays

Wade Boggs

Blasted a sixth-inning home run to right field off Cleveland's Chris Haney in a 15-10 Indians win on Aug. 7 to become the 23rd member of the 3,000-hit club, just one night after Gwynn ...he was the first player ever to reach the mark with a home run...it was the 118th home run of his career.

NL Team by Team Statistics

At least 135 at bats or 40 innings pitched during the regular season unless otherwise indicated. Players who competed for more than one NL team are listed with their final club. Players traded from the AL are listed with NL team only if they have 135 AB or 40 IP. Note that (*) indicates rookie and PTBN indicates player to be named.

Arizona Diamondbacks

Batting (160 AB)	Avg	AB	R	H	HR	RBI	SB
Luis Gonzalez	.336	614	112	206	26	111	9
Lenny Harris	.310	187	17	58	1	20	2
Matt Williams	.303	627	98	190	35	142	2
Bernard Gilkey	.294	204	28	60	8	39	2
Jay Bell	.289	589	132	170	38	112	7
Tony Womack	.277	614	111	170	4	41	72
Damian Miller	.270	296	35	80	11	47	0
Steve Finley	.264	590	100	156	34	103	8
Andy Fox	.255	274	34	70	6	33	4
Travis Lee	.237	375	57	89	9	50	17
Kelly Stinnett	.232	284	36	66	14	38	2

Acquired: P Mantei from Fla. for P Vladimir Nunez, P Brad Penny and PTBN (Jul. 9); IF Harris from Col. for IF Belvani Martinez (Aug. 31).

Pitching (50 IP)	ERA	W-L	Gm	IP	BB	SO
Randy Johnson	2.48	17-9	35	271.2	70	364
Greg Swindell	2.51	4-0	63	64.2	21	51
Matt Mantei	2.76	1-3	65	65.1	44	99
Omar Daal	3.65	16-9	32	214.2	79	148
Gregg Olson	3.71	9-4	61	60.2	25	45
Todd Stottlemyre	4.09	6-3	17	101.1	40	74
Armando Reynoso	4.37	10-6	31	167.0	67	79
Brian Anderson	4.57	8-2	31	130.0	28	75
Andy Benes	4.81	13-12	33	198.1	82	141

Saves: Mantei (32); Olson (14); Swindell, Bobby Chouinard, Dan Plesac, Anderson and Byung-Hyun Kim (1). **Complete games:** Johnson (12); Daal and Anderson (2). **Shutouts:** Johnson (2); Daal and Anderson (1).

Atlanta Braves

Batting (190 AB)	Avg	AB	R	H	HR	RBI	SB
Chipper Jones	.319	567	116	181	45	110	25
Javy Lopez	.317	246	34	78	11	45	0
Randall Simon*	.317	218	26	69	5	25	2
Ryan Klesko	.297	404	55	120	21	80	5
Brian Jordan	.283	576	100	163	23	115	13
Andruw Jones	.275	592	97	163	26	84	24
Gerald Williams	.275	422	76	116	17	68	19
Jose Hernandez	.266	508	79	135	19	62	11
Greg Myers	.265	200	19	53	5	24	0
Bret Boone	.252	608	102	153	20	63	14
Eddie Perez	.249	309	30	77	7	30	0
Ozzie Guillen	.241	232	21	56	1	20	4
Walt Weiss	.226	279	38	63	2	29	7
Jorge Fabregas	.199	231	20	46	3	21	0

Acquired: C Myers from SD for P Doug Dent (Jul. 26); IF Hernandez and P Mulholland from ChC for P Micah Bowie, P Ruben Quevedo and PTBN (Jul. 31). **Signed:** C Fabregas (Aug. 31); P Bergman (Sept. 5).

Pitching (60 IP)	ERA	W-L	Gm	IP	BB	SO
Mike Remlinger	2.37	10-1	73	83.2	35	81
John Rocker	2.49	4-5	74	72.1	37	104
Kevin Millwood	2.68	18-7	33	228.0	59	205
Kevin McGlinchy*	2.82	7-3	64	70.1	30	67
John Smoltz	3.19	11-8	29	186.1	40	156
Greg Maddux	3.57	19-9	33	219.1	37	136
Tom Glavine	4.12	14-11	35	234.0	83	138
Terry Mulholland	4.39	10-8	42	170.1	45	83
Sean Bergman	5.21	5-6	25	105.1	29	44
Odalis Perez	6.00	4-6	18	93.0	53	82

Saves: Rocker (38); Rudy Seanez (3); Remlinger, Russ Springer, Mulholland and Derrin Ebert (1). **Complete games:** Maddux (4); Millwood, Glavine and Bergman (2); Smoltz (1). **Shutouts:** Smoltz and Bergman (1).

Chicago Cubs

Batting (190 AB)	Avg	AB	R	H	HR	RBI	SB
Mark Grace	.309	593	107	183	16	91	3
Henry Rodriguez	.304	447	72	136	26	87	2
Glenallen Hill	.300	253	43	76	20	55	5
Sammy Sosa	.288	625	114	180	63	141	7
Lance Johnson	.260	335	46	87	1	21	13
Jeff Reed	.258	256	29	66	3	28	1
Benito Santiago	.249	350	28	87	7	36	1
Mickey Morandini	.241	456	60	110	4	37	6
Jeff Blauser	.240	200	41	48	9	26	2
Tyler Houston	.233	249	26	58	9	27	1
Gary Gaetti	.204	280	22	57	9	46	0
Shane Andrews	.195	348	41	68	16	51	1

Acquired: P Aguilera and P Scott Downs from Min. for P Jason Ryan and P Kyle Lohse (May 21); P Bowie, P Ruben Quevedo and PTBN from Atl. for IF Jose Hernandez and P Terry Mulholland (Jul. 31). **Claimed:** C Reed off waivers from Col. (Jul. 8). **Signed:** P Ayala (Sept. 3); IF Andrews (Sept. 9). **Traded:** IF Houston to Cle. for P Richard Negrette (Aug. 31).

Pitching (40 IP)	ERA	W-L	Gm	IP	BB	SO
Bobby Ayala	3.51	1-7	66	82.0	39	79
Rick Aguilera	3.69	6-3	44	46.1	10	32
Terry Adams	4.02	6-3	52	65.0	28	57
Jon Lieber	4.07	10-11	31	203.1	46	186
Rodney Myers	4.38	3-1	46	63.2	25	41
Kevin Tapani	4.83	6-12	23	136.0	33	72
Felix Heredia	4.85	3-1	69	52.0	25	50
Kyle Farnsworth*	5.05	5-9	27	130.0	52	70
Scott Sanders	5.52	4-7	67	104.1	53	89
Andrew Lorraine	5.55	2-5	11	61.2	22	40
Steve Trachsel	5.56	8-18	34	205.2	64	149
Dan Serafini	6.93	3-2	42	62.1	32	17
Micah Bowie*	10.24	2-7	14	51.0	34	41

Saves: Adams (13); Aguilera (8); Rod Beck (7); Sanders (2); Heredia and Serafini (1). **Complete games:** Trachsel (4); Lieber (3); Lorraine (2); Tapani and Farnsworth (1). **Shutouts:** Lieber, Farnsworth and Lorraine (1).

Cincinnati Reds

Batting (180 AB)	Avg	AB	R	H	HR	RBI	SB
Sean Casey	.332	594	103	197	25	99	0
Eddie Taubensee	.311	424	58	132	21	87	0
Dmitri Young	.300	373	63	112	14	56	3
Barry Larkin	.293	583	108	171	12	75	30
Pokey Reese	.285	585	85	167	10	52	38
Aaron Boone	.280	472	56	132	14	72	17
Jeffrey Hammonds	.279	262	43	73	17	41	3
Mike Cameron	.256	542	93	139	21	66	38
Michael Tucker	.253	296	55	75	11	44	11
Greg Vaughn	.245	550	104	135	45	118	15

Acquired: P Guzman and cash from Bal. for P B.J. Ryan and P Jacobo Sequea (Jul. 31).

Pitching (70 IP)	ERA	W-L	Gm	IP	BB	SO
Scott Williamson*	2.41	12-7	62	93.1	43	107
Scott Sullivan	3.01	5-4	79	113.2	47	78
Juan Guzman	3.03	6-3	12	77.1	21	60
Danny Graves	3.08	8-7	75	111.0	49	69
Steve Parris	3.50	11-4	22	128.2	52	86
Pete Harnisch	3.68	16-10	33	198.1	57	120
Ron Villone	4.23	9-7	29	142.2	73	97
Denny Neagle	4.27	9-5	20	111.2	40	76
Brett Tomko	4.92	5-7	33	172.0	60	132
Steve Avery	5.16	6-7	19	96.0	78	51

Saves: Graves (27); Williamson (19); Sullivan (3); Dennys Reyes, Villone and Stan Belinda (2). **Complete games:** Parris and Harnisch (2); Guzman and Tomko (1). **Shutouts:** Harnisch (2); Parris (1).

Colorado Rockies

Batting (135 AB)

	Avg	AB	R	H	HR	RBI	SB
Larry Walker	.379	438	108	166	37	115	11
Terry Shumpert	.347	262	58	91	10	37	14
Todd Helton	.320	578	114	185	35	113	7
Mike Lansing	.310	145	24	45	4	15	2
Kirt Manwaring	.299	137	17	41	2	14	0
Dante Bichette	.298	593	104	177	34	133	6
Angel Echevarria	.293	191	28	56	11	35	1
Neifi Perez	.280	690	108	193	12	70	13
Vinny Castilla	.275	615	83	169	33	102	2
Kurt Abbott	.273	286	41	78	8	41	3
Jeff Barry	.268	168	19	45	5	26	0
Edgard Clemente*	.253	162	24	41	8	25	0
Henry Blanco*	.232	263	30	61	6	28	1
Brian McRae	.224	321	36	72	9	37	2

Acquired: OF McRae, P Beltran and OF Thomas Johnson from NYM for OF Darryl Hamilton and P Chuck McElroy (Jul. 31).
Traded: OF McRae to Tor. for P Pat Lynch (Aug. 9).

Pitching (40 IP)

	ERA	W-L	Gm	IP	BB	SO
David Lee*	3.67	3-2	36	49.0	29	38
Jerry Dipoto	4.26	4-5	63	86.2	44	69
Rigo Beltran	4.50	1-1	33	42.0	19	50
Jamey Wright	4.87	4-3	16	94.1	54	49
Pedro Astacio	5.04	17-11	34	232.0	75	210
Curt Leskanic	5.08	6-2	63	85.0	49	77
Dave Veres	5.14	4-8	73	77.0	37	71
Brian Bohanon	6.20	12-12	33	197.1	92	120
Bobby M. Jones	6.33	6-10	30	112.1	77	74
Darryl Kile	6.61	8-13	32	190.2	109	116
John Thomson	8.04	1-10	14	62.2	36	34
Roberto Ramirez*	8.26	1-5	32	40.1	22	32
Mike DeJean	8.41	2-4	56	61.0	32	31

Saves: Veres (31); Dipoto and Ramirez (1). **Complete games:** Astacio (7); Bohanon (3); Kile and Thomson (1). **Shutouts:** Bohanon (1).

Florida Marlins

Batting (135 AB)

	Avg	AB	R	H	HR	RBI	SB
Cliff Floyd	.303	251	37	76	11	49	5
Luis Castillo	.302	487	76	147	0	28	50
Mike Redmond	.302	242	22	73	1	27	0
Bruce Aven*	.289	381	57	110	12	70	3
Danny Bautista	.288	205	32	59	5	24	3
Dave Berg	.286	304	42	87	3	25	2
Kevin Millar*	.285	351	48	100	9	67	1
Preston Wilson*	.280	482	67	135	26	71	11
Alex Gonzalez*	.277	560	81	155	14	59	3
Mark Kotsay	.271	495	57	134	8	50	7
Kevin Orie	.254	240	26	61	6	29	1
Mike Lowell*	.253	308	32	78	12	47	0
Todd Dunwoody	.220	186	20	41	2	20	3
Derrek Lee	.206	218	21	45	5	20	2

Acquired: P Nunez, P Brad Penny and PTBN from Ari. for P Matt Mantei (Jul. 9).

Pitching (40 IP)

	ERA	W-L	Gm	IP	BB	SO
Antonio Alfonseca	3.24	4-5	73	77.2	29	46
Alex Fernandez	3.38	7-8	24	141.0	41	91
A.J. Burnett*	3.48	4-2	7	41.1	25	33
Braden Looper*	3.80	3-3	72	83.0	31	50
Vladimir Nunez*	4.06	7-10	44	108.2	54	86
Ryan Dempster	4.71	7-8	25	147.0	93	126
Dennis Springer	4.86	6-16	38	196.1	64	83
Brian Meadows	5.60	11-15	31	178.1	57	72
Brian Edmondson	5.84	5-8	68	94.0	44	58
Jesus Sanchez	6.01	5-7	59	76.1	60	62

Saves: Alfonseca (21); Nunez, Springer and Edmondson (1). **Complete games:** Springer (3); Fernandez (1). **Shutouts:** Springer (2).

Houston Astros

Batting (135 AB)

	Avg	AB	R	H	HR	RBI	SB
Carl Everett	.325	464	86	151	25	108	27
Jeff Bagwell	.304	562	143	171	42	126	30
Craig Biggio	.294	639	123	188	16	73	28
Bill Spiers	.288	393	56	113	4	39	10
Ken Caminiti	.286	273	45	78	13	56	6
Stan Javier	.285	397	61	113	3	34	16
Russ Johnson*	.282	156	24	44	5	23	2
Daryle Ward*	.273	150	11	41	8	30	0
Tony Eusebio	.272	323	31	88	4	33	0
Ricky Gutierrez	.261	268	33	70	1	25	2
Paul Bako	.256	215	16	55	2	17	1
Tim Bogar	.239	309	44	74	4	31	3
Derek Bell	.236	509	61	120	12	66	18
Richard Hidalgo	.227	383	49	87	15	56	8

Acquired: OF Javier from SF for P Joe Messman (Aug. 31).

Pitchers (40 IP)

	ERA	W-L	Gm	IP	BB	SO
Billy Wagner	1.57	4-1	66	74.2	23	124
Mike Hampton	2.90	22-4	34	239.0	101	177
Scott Elarton	3.48	9-5	42	124.0	43	121
Jose Lima	3.58	21-10	35	246.1	44	187
Shane Reynolds	3.85	16-14	35	231.2	37	197
Jay Powell	4.32	5-4	67	75.0	40	77
Brian Williams	4.41	2-1	50	67.1	35	53
Doug Henry	4.65	2-3	35	40.2	24	36
Chris Holt	4.66	5-13	32	164.0	57	115
Trever Miller	5.07	3-2	47	49.2	29	37

Saves: Wagner (39); Powell (4); Henry (2); Elarton, Holt and Miller (1). **Complete games:** Reynolds (4); Hampton and Lima (3). **Shutouts:** Hampton and Reynolds (2).

Los Angeles Dodgers

Batting (135 AB)

	Avg	AB	R	H	HR	RBI	SB
Mark Grudzielanek	.326	488	72	159	7	46	6
Eric Karros	.304	578	74	176	34	112	8
Gary Sheffield	.301	549	103	165	34	101	11
Todd Hollandsworth	.284	261	39	74	9	32	5
Eric Young	.281	456	73	128	2	41	51
Adrian Beltre	.275	538	84	148	15	67	18
Devon White	.268	484	60	127	14	68	19
Raul Mondesi	.253	601	98	152	33	99	36
Jose Vizcaino	.252	266	27	67	1	29	2
Craig Counsell	.218	174	24	38	0	11	1
Todd Hundley	.207	376	49	78	24	55	3

Acquired: IF Counsell from Fla. for P Ryan Moskau (Jun. 15).
Signed: P Maddux (Apr. 25).

Pitching (40 IP)

	ERA	W-L	Gm	IP	BB	SO
Jeff Shaw	2.78	2-4	64	68.0	15	43
Kevin Brown	3.00	18-9	35	252.1	59	221
Alan Mills	3.73	3-4	68	72.1	43	49
Mike Maddux	3.77	1-1	53	59.2	22	45
Ismael Valdes	3.98	9-14	32	203.1	58	143
Pedro Borbon	4.09	4-3	70	50.2	29	33
Onan Masaoka*	4.32	2-4	54	66.2	47	61
Darren Dreifort	4.79	13-13	30	178.2	76	140
Chan Ho Park	5.23	13-11	33	194.1	100	174
Jamie Arnold*	5.48	2-4	36	69.0	34	26
Carlos Perez	7.43	2-10	17	89.2	39	40

Saves: Shaw (34); Borbon, Masaoka and Arnold (1). **Complete games:** Brown (5); Valdes (2); Dreifort (1). **Shutouts:** Brown, Valdes and Dreifort (1).

Milwaukee Brewers

Batting (135 AB)	Avg	AB	R	H	HR	RBI	SB
Jeff Cirillo	.326	607	98	198	15	88	7
Geoff Jenkins	.313	447	70	140	21	82	5
Dave Nilsson	.309	343	56	106	21	62	1
Alex Ochoa	.300	277	47	83	8	40	6
Ron Belliard*	.295	457	60	135	8	58	4
Mark Loretta	.290	587	93	170	5	67	4
Jeromy Burnitz	.270	467	87	126	33	103	7
Marquis Grissom	.267	603	92	161	20	83	24
Fernando Vina	.266	154	17	41	1	16	5
Lou Collier	.259	135	18	35	2	21	3
Rich Becker	.252	139	15	35	5	16	5
Brian Banks	.242	219	34	53	5	22	6
Sean Berry	.228	259	26	59	2	23	0
Jose Valentin	.227	256	45	58	10	38	3

Signed: P Nomo (Apr. 29); Bere (Aug. 19).
Released: P Abbott (Jul. 23).
Traded: OF Becker to Oak. for P Carl Dale (Aug. 18).

Pitching (40 IP)	ERA	W-L	Gm	IP	BB	SO
Bob Wickman	3.39	3-8	71	74.1	38	60
Steve Woodard	4.52	11-8	31	185.0	36	119
Hideo Nomo	4.54	12-8	28	176.1	78	161
Kyle Peterson*	4.56	4-7	17	77.0	25	34
Dave Weathers	4.65	7-4	63	93.0	38	74
Scott Karl	4.78	11-11	33	197.2	69	74
Eric Plunk	5.02	4-4	68	75.1	43	63
Mike Myers	5.23	2-1	71	41.1	13	35
Rafael Roque*	5.34	1-6	43	84.1	42	66
Bill Pulsipher	5.98	5-6	19	87.1	36	42
Jason Bere	6.08	5-0	17	66.2	50	47
Jim Abbott	6.91	2-8	20	82.0	42	37
Cal Eldred	7.79	2-8	20	82.0	46	60

Saves: Wickman (37); Weathers (2); Roque (1). **Complete games:** Woodard (2). **Shutouts:** none.

Montreal Expos

Batting (135 AB)	Avg	AB	R	H	HR	RBI	SB
Vladimir Guerrero	.316	610	102	193	42	131	14
Rondell White	.312	539	83	168	22	64	10
Jose Vidro	.304	494	67	150	12	59	0
Michael Barrett*	.293	433	53	127	8	52	0
Wilton Guerrero	.292	315	42	92	2	31	7
Brad Fullmer	.277	347	38	96	9	47	2
Orlando Merced	.268	194	25	52	8	26	2
Chris Widger	.264	383	42	101	14	56	1
Orlando Cabrera	.254	382	48	97	8	39	2
Manny Martinez	.245	331	48	81	2	26	19
Mike Mordecai	.235	226	29	53	5	25	2
Ryan McGuire	.221	140	17	31	2	18	1

Pitching (40 IP)	ERA	W-L	Gm	IP	BB	SO
Guillermo Mota*	2.93	2-4	51	55.1	25	27
Ugueth Urbina	3.69	6-6	71	75.2	36	100
Steve Kline	3.75	7-4	82	69.2	33	69
Anthony Telford	3.94	5-4	79	96.0	38	69
Mike Thurman	4.05	7-11	29	146.2	52	85
Dustin Hermanson	4.20	9-14	34	216.1	69	145
Jeremy Powell*	4.73	4-8	17	97.0	44	44
Miguel Batista	4.88	8-7	39	134.2	58	95
Javier Vazquez	5.00	9-8	26	154.2	52	113
J.D. Smart*	5.02	0-1	29	52.0	17	21
Carl Pavano	5.63	6-8	19	104.0	35	70
Dan Smith*	6.02	4-9	20	89.2	39	72

Saves: Urbina (41); Telford (2); Batista (1). **Complete games:** Vazquez (3); Batista (2); Pavano (1). **Shutouts:** Batista, Vazquez and Pavano (1).

New York Mets

Batting (135 AB)	Avg	AB	R	H	HR	RBI	SB
Shawon Dunston	.321	243	35	78	5	41	10
Rickey Henderson	.315	438	89	138	12	42	37
Darryl Hamilton	.315	505	82	159	9	45	6
Roger Cedeno	.313	453	90	142	4	36	66
Edgardo Alfonzo	.304	628	123	191	27	108	9
Mike Piazza	.303	534	100	162	40	124	2
Robin Ventura	.301	588	88	177	32	120	1
John Olerud	.298	581	107	173	19	96	3
Todd Pratt	.293	140	18	41	3	21	2
Benny Agbayani*	.286	276	42	79	14	42	6
Rey Ordonez	.258	520	49	134	1	60	8

Acquired: P Rogers from Oak. for OF Terrence Long and P Leoner Vasquez (Jul. 23); OF Hamilton and P McElroy from Col. for OF Brian McRae, P Rigo Beltran and OF Thomas Johnson (Jul. 31); OF Dunston from St.L for IF Craig Paquette (Jul. 31).

Pitching (40 IP)	ERA	W-L	Gm	IP	BB	SO
Armando Benitez	1.85	4-3	77	78.0	41	128
John Franco	2.88	0-2	46	40.2	19	41
Turk Wendell	3.05	5-4	80	85.2	37	77
Pat Mahomes	3.68	8-0	39	63.2	37	51
Dennis Cook	3.86	10-5	71	63.0	27	68
Kenny Rogers	4.03	5-1	12	76.0	28	58
Al Leiter	4.23	13-12	32	213.0	93	162
Masato Yoshii	4.40	12-8	31	174.0	58	105
Orel Hershiser	4.58	13-12	32	179.0	77	89
Rick Reed	4.58	11-5	26	149.1	47	104
Octavio Dotel*	5.38	8-3	19	85.1	49	85
Chuck McElroy	5.50	3-1	56	54.0	36	44
Bobby Jones	5.61	3-3	12	59.1	11	31

Saves: Benitez (22); Franco (19); Wendell and Cook (3); Allen Watson and Jason Isringhausen (1). **Complete games:** Rogers (2); Leiter, Yoshii and Reed (1). **Shutouts:** Rogers, Leiter and Reed (1).

Philadelphia Phillies

Batting (135 AB)	Avg	AB	R	H	HR	RBI	SB
Bobby Abreu	.335	546	118	183	20	93	27
Doug Glanville	.325	628	101	204	11	73	34
Alex Arias	.303	347	43	105	4	48	2
Mike Lieberthal	.300	510	84	153	31	96	0
Kevin Jordan	.285	347	36	99	4	51	0
Rico Brogna	.278	619	90	172	24	102	8
Kevin Sefcik	.278	209	28	58	1	19	9
Scott Rolen	.268	421	74	113	26	77	12
Rob Ducey	.261	188	29	49	8	33	2
Ron Gant	.260	516	107	134	17	77	13
Marlon Anderson*	.252	452	48	114	5	54	13
Desi Relaford	.242	211	31	51	1	26	4

Acquired: P Person from Tor. for P Paul Spoljaric (May 5).
Claimed: P Telemaco off waivers from Ari. (Jun. 8).

Pitchers (40 IP)	ERA	W-L	Gm	IP	BB	SO
Steve Montgomery*	3.34	1-5	53	64.2	31	55
Curt Schilling	3.54	15-6	24	180.1	44	152
Wayne Gomes	4.26	5-5	73	74.0	56	58
Robert Person	4.27	10-5	31	137.0	70	127
Steve Schrenk*	4.29	1-3	32	50.1	14	36
Paul Byrd	4.60	15-11	32	199.2	70	106
Carlton Loewer	5.12	2-6	20	89.2	26	48
Randy Wolf*	5.55	6-9	22	121.2	67	116
Chad Ogea	5.63	6-12	36	168.0	61	77
Amaury Telemaco	5.77	4-0	49	53.0	26	43
Mike Grace	7.69	1-4	27	55.0	30	28

Saves: Gomes (19); Jeff Brantley (5); Montgomery (3); Billy Brewer (2); Scott Aldred, Schrenk, and Jim Poole (1). **Complete games:** Schilling (8); Loewer (2); Byrd (1). **Shutouts:** Schilling and Loewer (1).

Pittsburgh Pirates

Batting (135 AB)	Avg	AB	R	H	HR	RBI	SB
Jason Kendall........	.332	280	61	93	8	41	22
Brian Giles	.315	521	109	164	39	115	6
Kevin Young.........	.298	584	103	174	26	106	22
Warren Morris*	.288	511	65	147	15	73	3
Al Martin	.277	541	97	150	24	63	20
Adrian Brown	.270	226	34	61	4	17	5
Ed Sprague	.267	490	71	131	22	81	3
Mike Benjamin......	.247	368	42	91	1	37	10
Brant Brown........	.232	341	49	79	16	58	3
Abraham Nunez*....	.220	259	25	57	0	17	9
Keith Osik..........	.186	167	12	31	2	13	0

Pitching (40 IP)	ERA	W-L	Gm	IP	BB	SO
Scott Sauerbeck* ...	2.00	4-1	65	67.2	38	55
Brad Clontz	2.74	1-3	56	49.1	24	40
Todd Ritchie	3.49	15-9	28	172.2	54	107
Kris Benson*	4.07	11-14	31	196.2	83	139
Jason Schmidt	4.19	13-11	33	212.2	85	148
Marc Wilkins	4.24	2-3	46	51.0	26	44
Francisco Cordova ...	4.43	8-10	27	160.2	59	98
Mike Williams	5.09	3-4	58	58.1	37	76
Pete Schourek	5.34	4-7	30	113.0	49	94
Jose Silva	5.73	2-8	34	97.1	39	77
Chris Peters	6.59	5-4	19	71.0	27	46

Saves: Williams (23); Silva (4); Jason Christiansen (3); Sauerbeck and Clontz (2). **Complete games:** Ritchie, Benson, Schmidt and Cordova (2). **Shutouts:** none.

St. Louis Cardinals

Batting (135 AB)	Avg	AB	R	H	HR	RBI	SB
Ray Lankford	.306	422	77	129	15	63	14
Fernando Tatis	.298	537	104	160	34	107	21
Thomas Howard	.292	195	16	57	6	28	1
Craig Paquette.......	.287	157	21	45	10	37	1
Mark McGwire	.278	521	118	145	65	147	0
Placido Polanco......	.277	220	24	61	1	19	1
Edgar Renteria	.275	585	92	161	11	63	37
Joe McEwing*	.275	513	65	141	9	44	7
Alberto Castillo	.263	255	21	67	4	31	0
Darren Bragg	.260	273	38	71	6	26	3
Eric Davis	.257	191	27	49	5	30	5
Willie McGee	.251	271	25	68	0	20	7
J.D. Drew*.........	.242	368	72	89	13	39	19
Eli Marrero	.192	317	32	61	6	34	11

Acquired: IF Paquette from NYM for OF Shawon Dunston (Jul. 31).
Traded: P Mercker to Bos. for C David Benham and P Mike Matthews (Aug. 24).
Signed: P Slocumb (May 15).

Pitching (40 IP)	ERA	W-L	Gm	IP	BB	SO
Heathcliff Slocumb ..	2.36	3-2	40	53.1	30	48
Kent Bottenfield	3.97	18-7	31	190.1	89	124
Rich Croushore	4.14	3-7	59	71.2	43	88
Garrett Stephenson ..	4.22	6-3	18	85.1	29	59
Darren Oliver	4.26	9-9	30	196.1	74	119
Mike Mohler	4.38	1-1	48	49.1	23	31
Lance Painter	4.83	4-5	56	63.1	25	56
Ricky Bottalico	4.91	3-7	68	73.1	49	66
Kent Mercker	5.12	6-5	25	103.2	51	64
Larry Luebbers	5.12	3-3	8	45.2	16	16
Manny Aybar	5.47	4-5	65	97.0	36	74
Jose Jimenez*	5.85	5-14	29	163.0	71	113
Juan Acevedo	5.89	6-8	50	102.1	48	52

Saves: Bottalico (20); Acevedo (4); Croushore, Aybar and Scott Radinsky (3); Slocumb (2); Mohler, Painter and Rich Ankiel (1). **Complete games:** Oliver and Jimenez (2); Luebbers (1). **Shutouts:** Jimenez (2); Oliver (1).

San Diego Padres

Batting (135 AB)	Avg	AB	R	H	HR	RBI	SB
Tony Gwynn.........	.338	411	59	139	10	62	7
Reggie Sanders......	.285	478	92	136	26	72	36
Quilvio Veras	.280	475	95	133	6	41	30
Dave Magadan.......	.274	248	20	68	2	30	1
John Vander Wal.....	.272	246	26	67	6	41	2
Phil Nevin...........	.269	383	52	103	24	85	1
Eric Owens	.266	440	55	117	9	61	33
Chris Gomez	.252	234	20	59	1	15	1
Wally Joyner........	.248	323	34	80	5	43	0
Ben Davis*..........	.244	266	29	65	5	30	2
George Arias*	.244	164	20	40	7	20	0
Damian Jackson*.....	.224	388	56	87	9	39	34
Ruben Rivera	.195	411	65	80	23	48	18

Pitching (40 IP)	ERA	W-L	Gm	IP	BB	SO
Trevor Hoffman	2.14	2-3	64	67.1	15	73
Donne Wall	3.07	7-4	55	70.1	23	53
Brian Boehringer.....	3.24	6-5	33	94.1	35	64
Carlos Reyes	3.72	2-4	65	77.1	24	57
Andy Ashby.........	3.80	14-10	31	206.0	54	132
Sterling Hitchcock	4.11	12-14	33	205.2	76	194
Woody Williams	4.41	12-12	33	208.1	73	137
Dan Miceli	4.46	4-5	66	68.2	36	59
Matt Clement*	4.48	10-12	31	180.2	86	135
Heath Murray*	5.76	0-4	22	50.0	26	25

Saves: Hoffman (40); Miceli (2); Reyes (1). **Complete games:** Ashby (4); Hitchcock (1). **Shutouts:** Ashby (3).

San Francisco Giants

Batting (135 AB)	Avg	AB	R	H	HR	RBI	SB
Armando Rios*	.327	150	32	49	7	29	7
Brent Mayne	.301	322	39	97	2	39	2
Marvin Benard	.290	562	100	163	16	64	27
Bill Mueller.........	.290	414	61	120	2	36	4
Jeff Kent	.290	511	86	148	23	101	13
Ellis Burks	.282	390	73	110	31	96	7
Rich Aurilia	.281	558	68	157	22	80	2
J.T. Snow	.274	580	93	156	24	98	0
Scott Servais	.273	198	21	54	5	21	0
Ramon Martinez*	.264	144	21	38	5	19	1
Barry Bonds	.262	355	91	93	34	83	15
F.P. Santangelo	.260	254	49	66	3	26	12
Charlie Hayes	.205	264	33	54	6	48	3

Acquired: P Spradlin from Cle. for OF Dan McKinley and PTBN (Apr. 23); P Hernandez from Fla. for P Jason Grilli and P Nathan Bump (Jul. 24).

Pitching (40 IP)	ERA	W-L	Gm	IP	BB	SO
John Johnstone........	2.60	4-6	62	65.2	20	56
Alan Embree	3.38	3-2	68	58.2	26	53
Felix Rodriguez	3.80	2-3	47	66.1	29	55
Russ Ortiz	3.81	18-9	33	207.2	125	164
Robb Nen	3.98	3-8	72	72.1	27	77
Joe Nathan*	4.18	7-4	19	90.1	46	54
Jerry Spradlin	4.19	3-1	59	58.0	29	52
Livan Hernandez	4.64	8-12	30	199.2	76	144
Shawn Estes..........	4.92	11-11	32	203.0	112	159
Rich Rodriguez	5.24	3-0	62	56.2	28	44
Kirk Rueter	5.41	15-10	33	184.2	55	94
Chris Brock..........	5.48	6-8	19	106.2	41	76
Julian Tavarez	5.93	2-0	47	54.2	25	33
Mark Gardner	6.47	5-11	29	139.0	57	86

Saves: Nen (37); Johnstone (3); Nathan and Bronswell Patrick (1). **Complete games:** Ortiz (3); Hernandez (2); Estes, Rueter and Gardner (1). **Shutouts:** Estes (1).

Players Who Played in Both Leagues in 1999

While all individual major league statistics count on career records, players cannot transfer their stats from one league to the other if they are traded during the regular season. Here are the combined stats for batters with 150 at bats and pitchers with 50 innings pitched, who played in both leagues in 1999.

Batters (150 AB)

	Avg	AB	R	H	HR	RBI	SB
Carlos Baerga	.241	137	10	33	3	10	2
SD	.250	80	6	20	2	5	1
CLE	.228	57	4	13	1	5	1
Tony Batista	.277	519	77	144	31	100	4
ARI	.257	144	16	37	5	21	2
TOR	.285	375	61	107	26	79	2
Rich Becker	.258	264	36	68	6	26	8
MIL	.252	139	15	35	5	16	5
OAK	.264	125	21	33	1	10	3
Jacob Brumfield	.241	187	29	45	2	20	1
LA	.294	17	4	5	0	1	0
TOR	.235	170	25	40	2	19	1
Curtis Goodwin	.230	165	15	38	0	9	2
CHI (NL)	.242	157	15	38	0	9	2
TOR	.000	8	0	0	0	0	0
Jose Guillen	.253	288	42	73	3	31	1
PIT	.267	120	18	32	1	18	1
TB	.244	168	24	41	2	13	0
Tyler Houston	.225	276	28	62	10	30	1
CHI (NL)	.233	249	26	58	9	27	1
CLE	.148	27	2	4	1	3	0
Jim Leyritz	.235	200	25	47	8	26	0
SD	.239	134	17	32	8	21	0
NY (AL)	.227	66	8	15	0	5	0
Brian McRae	.218	403	47	88	12	48	2
NY (NL)	.221	298	35	66	8	36	2
COL	.261	23	1	6	1	1	0
TOR	.195	82	11	16	3	11	0
Matt Mieske	.307	150	24	46	9	29	0
SEA	.366	41	11	15	4	7	0
HOU	.284	109	13	31	5	22	0

Pitchers (50 IP)

	ERA	W-L	Gm	IP	BB	SO
Rick Aguilera	2.93	9-4	61	67.2	12	45
MIN	1.27	3-1	17	21.1	2	13
CHI (NL)	3.69	6-3	44	46.1	10	32
Scott Aldred	4.45	4-3	66	56.2	29	41
TB	5.18	3-2	37	24.1	14	22
PHI	3.90	1-1	29	32.1	15	19
Rocky Coppinger	5.40	5-4	40	58.1	42	56
BAL	8.31	0-1	11	21.2	19	17
MIL	3.68	5-3	29	36.2	23	39
John Frascatore	3.73	8-5	59	70.0	21	37
ARI	4.09	1-4	26	33.0	12	15
TOR	3.41	7-1	33	37.0	9	22
Mark Guthrie	5.37	1-3	57	58.2	24	45
BOS	5.83	1-1	46	46.1	20	36
CHI (NL)	3.65	0-2	11	12.1	4	9
Juan Guzman	3.74	11-12	33	200.0	86	155
BAL	4.18	5-9	21	122.2	65	95
CIN	3.03	6-3	12	77.1	21	60
Jason Isringhausen	4.73	1-4	33	64.2	34	51
NY (NL)	6.41	1-3	13	39.1	22	31
OAK	2.13	0-1	20	25.1	12	20
Kent Mercker	4.80	8-5	30	129.1	64	81
ST.L	5.12	6-5	25	103.2	51	64
BOS	3.51	2-0	5	25.2	13	17
Dave Mlicki	4.61	14-13	33	199.0	72	120
LA	4.91	0-1	2	7.1	2	1
DET	4.60	14-12	31	191.2	70	119
Robert Person	4.68	10-7	42	148.0	85	139
TOR	9.82	0-2	11	11.0	15	12
PHI	4.27	10-5	31	137.0	70	127
Al Reyes	4.52	4-3	53	65.2	41	67
MIL	4.25	2-0	26	36.0	25	39
BAL	4.85	2-3	27	29.2	16	28
Kenny Rogers	4.19	10-4	31	195.1	69	126
OAK	4.30	5-3	19	119.1	41	68
NY (NL)	4.03	5-1	12	76.0	28	58
Heathcliff Slocumb	3.77	3-2	50	62.0	39	60
BAL	12.46	0-0	10	8.2	9	12
ST.L	2.36	3-2	40	53.1	30	48
Paul Spoljaric	6.26	2-5	42	73.1	39	73
PHI	15.09	0-3	5	11.1	7	10
TOR	4.65	2-2	37	62.0	32	63
Jerry Spradlin	4.87	3-1	63	61.0	32	54
CLE	18.00	0-0	4	3.0	3	2
SF	4.19	3-1	59	58.0	29	52
Billy Taylor	4.95	1-6	61	56.1	23	52
OAK	3.98	1-5	43	43.0	14	38
NY (NL)	8.10	0-1	18	13.1	9	14
Allen Watson	3.51	6-3	38	77.0	35	64
NY (NL)	4.08	2-2	14	39.2	22	32
SEA	12.00	0-1	3	3.0	3	2
NY (AL)	2.10	4-0	21	34.1	10	30
Matt Whisenant	5.63	4-5	67	54.1	36	37
KC	6.35	4-4	48	39.2	26	27
SD	3.68	0-1	19	14.2	10	10

All-Century Team

Major League Baseball presented its All-Century Team before Game 2 of the World Series at Atlanta's Turner Field on Oct. 24, 1999. A 25-man roster was selected by fan vote, and five more players were added by a special panel of baseball executives, media and historians. Those five are noted by a (*). Players are listed by position and then in order of their votes received.

Pitchers
Nolan Ryan
Sandy Koufax
Cy Young
Roger Clemens
Bob Gibson
Walter Johnson
Lefty Grove
Warren Spahn*
Christy Mathewson*

Outfielders
Babe Ruth
Hank Aaron
Ted Williams
Willie Mays
Joe DiMaggio
Mickey Mantle
Ty Cobb
Ken Griffey Jr.
Pete Rose
Stan Musial*

Catchers
Johnny Bench
Yogi Berra

First Basemen
Lou Gehrig
Mark McGwire

Second Basemen
Jackie Robinson
Rogers Hornsby

Shortstops
Cal Ripken Jr.
Ernie Banks
Honus Wagner*

Third Basemen
Mike Schmidt
Brooks Robinson

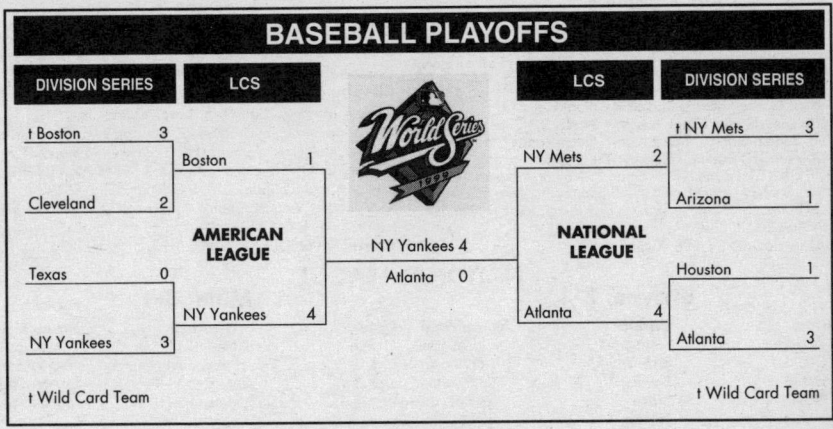

BASEBALL PLAYOFFS

DIVISION SERIES	LCS		LCS	DIVISION SERIES

t Boston 3

Boston 1

Cleveland 2

AMERICAN LEAGUE

Texas 0

NY Yankees 4

NY Yankees 3

NY Yankees 4
Atlanta 0

t NY Mets 3

NY Mets 2

Arizona 1

NATIONAL LEAGUE

Houston 1

Atlanta 4

Atlanta 3

t Wild Card Team   t Wild Card Team

Divisional Series Summaries
AMERICAN LEAGUE

Yankees, 3-0

Date	Winner	Home Field
Oct. 5	Yankees, 8-0	at New York
Oct. 7	Yankees, 3-1	at New York
Oct. 9	Yankees, 3-0	at Texas

Game 1
Tuesday, Oct. 5, at New York

	1 2 3	4 5 6	7 8 9	R H E
Texas	0 0 0	0 0 0	0 0 0 -	0 2 1
New York	0 1 0	0 2 4	0 1 x -	8 10 0

Win: Hernandez, NY (1-0). **Loss:** Sele, Tex. (0-1).
2B: Texas— Rodriguez; New York— Ledee, Williams, Posada. **HR:** New York— Williams (1). **RBI:** New York— Ledee, Williams 6.
Attendance: 57,099. **Time:** 3:37.

Game 2
Thursday, Oct. 7, at New York

	1 2 3	4 5 6	7 8 9	R H E
Texas	0 0 0	1 0 0	0 0 0 -	1 7 0
New York	0 0 0	0 1 0	1 1 x -	3 7 2

Win: Pettitte, NY (1-0). **Loss:** Helling, Tex. (0-1). **Save:** Rivera, NY (1).
2B: Texas— Stevens; New York— Jeter, Brosius, Ledee. **HR:** Texas— Gonzalez (1). **RBI:** Texas— Gonzalez; New York— Brosius, Ledee, Leyritz.
Attendance: 57,485. **Time:** 3:32.

Game 3
Saturday, Oct. 9, at Texas

	1 2 3	4 5 6	7 8 9	R H E
New York	3 0 0	0 0 0	0 0 0 -	3 6 1
Texas	0 0 0	0 0 0	0 0 0 -	0 5 1

Win: Clemens, NY (1-0). **Loss:** Loaiza, Tex. (0-1). **Save:** Rivera (2).
3B: New York— Jeter. **HR:** New York— Strawberry (1).
RBI: New York— Strawberry 3.
Attendance: 50,269. **Time:** 3:00.

Red Sox, 3-2

Date	Winner	Home Field
Oct. 6	Indians, 3-2	at Cleveland
Oct. 7	Indians, 11-1	at Cleveland
Oct. 9	Red Sox, 9-3	at Boston
Oct. 10	Red Sox, 23-7	at Boston
Oct. 11	Red Sox, 12-8	at Cleveland

Game 1
Wednesday, Oct. 6, at Cleveland

	1 2 3	4 5 6	7 8 9	R H E
Boston	0 1 0	1 0 0	0 0 0 -	2 5 1
Cleveland	0 0 0	0 0 2	0 0 1 -	3 6 1

Win: Shuey, Cle. (1-0). **Loss:** Lowe, Bos. (0-1).
2B: Boston— Garciaparra. **HR:** Boston— Garciaparra (1); Cleveland— Thome (1). **RBI:** Boston— Garciaparra, Stanley; Cleveland— Thome 2, Fryman. **SB:** Cleveland— R. Alomar (1).
Attendance: 45,182. **Time:** 2:53.

Game 2
Thursday, Oct. 7, at Cleveland

	1 2 3	4 5 6	7 8 9	R H E
Boston	0 0 1	0 0 0	0 0 0 -	1 6 0
Cleveland	0 0 6	5 0 0	0 0 x -	11 8 0

Win: Nagy, Cle. (1-0). **Loss:** Saberhagen, Bos. (0-1).
2B: Boston— Nixon, Stanley; Cleveland— R. Alomar 2. **3B:** Cleveland— Vizquel. **HR:** Cleveland— Baines (1), Thome (2). **RBI:** Boston— Offerman; Cleveland— Vizquel 2, R. Alomar 2, Baines 3, Thome 4. **SB:** Cleveland— Fryman (1).
Attendance: 45,184. **Time:** 2:47.

Game 3
Saturday, Oct. 9, at Boston

	1 2 3	4 5 6	7 8 9	R H E
Cleveland	0 0 0	1 0 1	1 0 0 -	3 9 1
Boston	0 0 0	0 2 1	6 0 x -	9 11 2

Win: Lowe, Bos. (1-1). **Loss:** Wright, Cle. (0-1).
2B: Cleveland— R. Alomar; Boston— Varitek, Valentin, Offerman. **HR:** Boston— Valentin (1), Daubach (1). **RBI:** Cleveland— Justice, Baines; Boston— Lewis, Nixon, Valentin 3, Daubach 3, Merloni. **SB:** Cleveland— Lofton (1).
Attendance: 33,539. **Time:** 3:08.

Game 4
Sunday, Oct. 10, at Boston

	1 2 3	4 5 6	7 8 9	R H E
Cleveland	1 1 0	0 4 0	0 0 1	- 7 8 0
Boston	2 5 3	5 3 0	3 2 x	-23 24 0

Win: Garces, Bos. (1-0). **Loss:** Colon, Cle. (0-1). **2B:** Cleveland— Lofton; Boston— Nixon 2, Varitek 2, Valentin, Sadler, Stanley. **3B:** Boston— Stanley. **HR:** Cleveland— Cordero (1); Boston— Valentin 2 (3), Offerman (1), Varitek (1). **RBI:** Cleveland— R. Alomar, S. Alomar, Cordero 2, Sexson, Fryman, Lofton; Boston— Valentin 7, Lewis, Nixon 5, Offerman 5, Varitek 3, Stanley, Hatteberg. **SB:** Cleveland— R. Alomar (2); Boston— Lewis (1). **Attendance:** 33,898. **Time:** 3:49.

Game 5
Monday, Oct. 11, at Cleveland

	1 2 3	4 5 6	7 8 9	R H E
Boston	2 0 5	1 0 0	3 0 1	-12 10 0
Cleveland	3 2 3	0 0 0	0 0 0	- 8 7 1

Win: P. Martinez, Bos. (1-0). **Loss:** Shuey, Cle. (1-1). **2B:** Boston— Daubach 2, Lewis, Garciaparra; Cleveland— Vizquel, R. Alomar, Ramirez. **HR:** Boston— Garciaparra (2), O'Leary 2 (2); Cleveland— Thome 2 (4), Fryman (1). **RBI:** Boston— Garciaparra 3, Valentin 2, O'Leary 7; Cleveland— Vizquel, Thome 4, Fryman 2, Ramirez. **SB:** Cleveland— Lofton (2). **Attendance:** 45,114. **Time:** 3:12.

NATIONAL LEAGUE

Braves, 3-1

Date	Winner	Home Field
Oct. 5	Astros, 6-1	at Atlanta
Oct. 6	Braves, 5-1	at Atlanta
Oct. 8	Braves, 5-3 (12 inn.)	at Houston
Oct. 9	Braves, 7-5	at Houston

Mets, 3-1

Date	Winner	Home Field
Oct. 5	Mets, 8-4	at Arizona
Oct. 6	Diamondbacks, 7-1	at Arizona
Oct. 8	Mets, 9-2	at New York
Oct. 9	Mets, 4-3 (10 inn.)	at New York

Game 1
Tuesday, Oct. 5, at Atlanta

	1 2 3	4 5 6	7 8 9	R H E
Houston	0 0 0	0 0 1	0 0 4	- 6 13 0
Atlanta	0 0 0	0 1 0	0 0 0	- 1 7 0

Win: Reynolds, Hou. (1-0). **Loss:** Maddux, Atl. (0-1). **HR:** Houston— Ward (1), Caminiti (1); Atlanta— Williams. **RBI:** Houston— Eusebio, Ward, Everett, Caminiti 3; Atlanta— Williams. **SB:** Houston— Spiers (1); Atlanta— Jo. Hernandez (1). **Attendance:** 39,119. **Time:** 3:03.

Game 2
Wednesday, Oct. 6, at Atlanta

	1 2 3	4 5 6	7 8 9	R H E
Houston	0 1 0	0 0 0	0 0 0	- 1 1 1
Atlanta	1 0 0	0 0 1	3 0 x	- 5 11 1

Win: Millwood, Atl. (1-0). **Loss:** Lima, Hou. (0-1). **2B:** Houston— A. Jones, Boone. **HR:** Houston— Caminiti (2). **RBI:** Houston— Caminiti; Atlanta— Jordan 2, Perez, Klesko, A. Jones. **SB:** Atlanta— Williams (1). **Attendance:** 41,913. **Time:** 2:13.

Game 3
Friday, Oct. 8, at Houston

	1 2 3 4 5 6 7 8 9 10 11 12	R H E
Atlanta	0 0 0 0 0 3 0 0 0 0 0 2	- 5 12 0
Houston	2 0 0 1 0 0 0 0 0 0 0 0	- 3 9 2

Win: Rocker, Atl. (1-0). **Loss:** Powell, Hou. (0-1). **Save:** Millwood, Atl. (1). **2B:** Atlanta— Jordan; Houston— Johnson. **HR:** Atlanta— Jordan (1). **RBI:** Atlanta— Jordan 5; Houston— Caminiti, Eusebio, Spiers. **SB:** Atlanta— Nixon (1); Houston— Barker (1). **Attendance:** 48,625. **Time:** 4:19.

Game 4
Saturday, Oct. 9, at Houston

	1 2 3	4 5 6	7 8 9	R H E
Atlanta	1 0 1	0 0 5	0 0 0	- 7 15 1
Houston	0 0 0	0 0 0	1 4 0	- 5 8 1

Win: Smoltz, Atl. (1-0). **Loss:** Reynolds, Hou. (1-1). **Save:** Rocker, Atl. (1). **2B:** Atlanta— Williams, Smoltz; Houston— Bogar. **HR:** Houston— Eusebio (1), Caminiti (3). **RBI:** Atlanta— C. Jones, Boone, A. Jones, Perez 2, Williams 2; Houston— Eusebio, Caminiti 3, Bogar. **SB:** Atlanta— Boone (1); Houston— Everett (1). **Attendance:** 48,553. **Time:** 3:12.

Game 1
Tuesday, Oct. 5, at Arizona

	1 2 3	4 5 6	7 8 9	R H E
New York	1 0 2	1 0 0	0 0 4	- 8 10 0
Arizona	0 0 1	0 0 2	0 0 0	- 4 7 0

Win: Wendell, NY (1-0). **Loss:** Johnson, Ariz. (0-1). **2B:** New York— Ventura; Arizona— Gonzalez, Johnson. **3B:** Arizona— Womack. **HR:** New York— Alfonzo 2 (2), Olerud (1); Arizona— Durazo (1), Gonzalez (1). **RBI:** New York— Alfonzo 5, Olerud 2, Ordonez; Arizona— Bell, Durazo, Gonzalez 2. **SB:** New York— Henderson 2 (2). **Attendance:** 49,584. **Time:** 2:53.

Game 2
Wednesday, Oct. 6, at Arizona

	1 2 3	4 5 6	7 8 9	R H E
New York	0 0 1	0 0 0	0 0 0	- 1 5 0
Arizona	0 0 3	0 2 0	2 0 x	- 7 9 1

Win: Stottlemyre, Ariz. (1-0). **Loss:** Rogers, NY (0-1). **2B:** New York— Ordonez; Arizona— Colbrunn, Finley, Williams. **RBI:** New York— Olerud; Arizona— Colbrunn, Finley 5, Ward. **SB:** New York— Henderson 3 (5), Ordonez (1). **Attendance:** 49,328. **Time:** 3:13.

Game 3
Friday, Oct. 8, at New York

	1 2 3	4 5 6	7 8 9	R H E
Arizona	0 0 0	0 0 2	0 0 0	- 2 5 3
New York	0 1 2	0 0 6	0 0 x	- 9 11 0

Win: Reed, NY (1-0). **Loss:** Daal, Ariz. (0-1). **2B:** Arizona— Stinnett; New York— Alfonzo. **HR:** Arizona— Ward (1). **RBI:** Arizona— Ward 2; New York— Ordonez, Olerud 3, Ventura, Henderson, Cedeno, Hamilton 2. **SB:** New York— Henderson (6). **Attendance:** 56,180. **Time:** 3:05.

Game 4
Saturday, Oct. 9, at New York

	1 2 3	4 5 6	7 8 9 10	R H E
Arizona	0 0 0	0 1 0	0 2 0 0	- 3 5 1
New York	0 0 0	1 0 1	0 1 0 1	- 4 8 0

Win: Franco, NY (1-0). **Loss:** Mantei, Ariz. (0-1). **2B:** Arizona— Bell; New York— Ventura, Agbayani. **HR:** Arizona— Colbrunn (1); New York— Alfonzo (3), Pratt (1). **RBI:** Arizona— Colbrunn, Bell 2; New York— Alfonzo, Agbayani, Cedeno, Pratt. **Attendance:** 56,177. **Time:** 3:23.

American League Championship Series
Yankees, 4-1

Date	Winner	Home Field
Oct. 13	Yankees, 4-3 (10 inn.)	at New York
Oct. 14	Yankees, 3-2	at New York
Oct. 16	Red Sox, 13-1	at Boston
Oct. 17	Yankees, 9-2	at Boston
Oct. 18	Yankees, 6-1	at Boston

Game 1
Wednesday, Oct. 13, at New York

```
               1 2 3  4 5 6  7 8 910   R H E
Boston........2 1 0  0 0 0  0 0 0 0 - 3 8 3
New York .....0 2 0  0 0 0  1 0 0 1 - 410 1
```

Win: Rivera, NY (1-0). **Loss:** Beck, Bos. (0-1).
2B: Boston— Valentin; New York— Jeter. **3B:** New York—
Brosius. **HR:** New York— Brosius (1), Williams (2). **RBI:**
Boston— Daubach, Offerman; New York— Brosius 2, Jeter,
Williams. **SB:** Boston— Lewis (2); New York— Williams (1).
Attendance: 57,181. **Time:** 3:39.

Game 2
Thursday, Oct. 14, at New York

```
              1 2 3  4 5 6  7 8 9   R H E
Boston.......0 0 0  0 2 0  0 0 0 - 2 10 0
New York ...0 0 0  1 0 0  2 0 x - 3  7 0
```

Win: Cone, NY (1-0). **Loss:** R. Martinez, Bos. (0-1). **Save:**
Rivera, NY (3).
2B: Boston— Varitek, O'Leary; New York— Knoblauch. **3B:**
Boston— Varitek. **HR:** Boston— Garciaparra (3); New
York— Martinez (1). **RBI:** Boston— Garciaparra 2; New
York— Martinez, Knoblauch, O'Neill. **SB:** Boston— Offer-
man (1); New York— Knoblauch (1).
Attendance: 57,180. **Time:** 3:46.

Most Valuable Player

Orlando Hernandez, New York, P

ERA	W-L	IP	H	ER	BB	SO	HR
1.80	1-0	15.0	12	3	6	13	1

Game 3
Saturday, Oct. 16, at Boston

```
             1 2 3  4 5 6  7 8 9   R H E
New York ...0 0 0  0 0 0  0 1 0 - 1 3 3
Boston ......2 2 2  0 2 1  4 0 x - 13 21 1
```

Win: P. Martinez, Bos. (2-0). **Loss:** Clemens, NY (1-1).
2B: Boston— Nixon 2, Garciaparra, Daubach, Lewis,
O'Leary. **3B:** Boston— Offerman. **HR:** New York— Brosius
(2); Boston— Valentin (4), Daubach (2), Garciaparra (4).
RBI: New York— Brosius; Boston— Valentin 5, Garciaparra
3, Daubach 2, Lewis, Stanley.
Attendance: 33,190. **Time:** 3:14.

Game 4
Sunday, Oct. 17, at Boston

```
             1 2 3  4 5 6  7 8 9   R H E
New York .....0 1 0  2 0 0  0 0 6 - 9 11 0
Boston .......0 1 1  0 0 0  0 2 0 - 2 10 4
```

Win: Pettitte, NY (2-0). **Loss:** Saberhagen, Bos. (0-2).
Save: Rivera, NY (4).
2B: New York—Martinez, Williams; Boston— Huskey, Val-
entin, O'Leary. **HR:** New York— Strawberry (2), Ledee (1).
RBI: New York— Strawberry, Martinez, Williams, Ledee 4;
Boston— O'Leary, Offerman. **SB:** Boston— Buford (1).
Attendance: 33,586. **Time:** 3:39.

Game 5
Monday, Oct. 18, at Boston

```
             1 2 3  4 5 6  7 8 9   R H E
New York .....2 0 0  0 0 0  2 0 2 - 6 11 1
Boston .......0 0 0  0 0 0  0 1 0 - 1 5 2
```

Win: Hernandez, NY (2-0). **Loss:** Mercker, Bos. (0-1).
Save: Mendoza, NY (1).
2B: Boston— Garciaparra. **HR:** New York— Jeter (1),
Posada (1); Boston— Varitek (2). **RBI:** New York— Jeter 2,
Davis, Martinez, Posada 2; Boston— Varitek. **SB:** New
York— Curtis (1); Boston— Garciaparra (1).
Attendance: 33,589. **Time:** 4:09.

ALCS Composite Box Score
Boston Red Sox

Batting	Avg	AB	R	H	HR	RBI	BB	SO	Avg	AB	R	H	HR	RBI	BB	SO
		LCS vs. New York								Overall AL Playoffs						
Jose Offerman, 2b	.458	24	4	11	0	2	1	3	.429	42	8	18	1	8	8	3
Damon Buford, cf-ph	.400	5	1	2	0	0	0	2	.250	8	1	2	0	0	0	3
Nomar Garciaparra, ss	.400	20	2	8	2	5	2	2	.406	32	8	13	4	9	5	5
Troy O'Leary, lf	.350	20	2	7	0	1	2	5	.275	40	6	11	2	8	4	8
John Valentin, 3b	.348	23	3	8	1	5	2	4	.333	45	9	15	4	17	2	8
Trot Nixon, rf	.286	14	2	4	0	0	1	5	.250	28	7	7	0	6	5	10
Mike Stanley, 1b	.222	18	1	4	0	1	2	4	.368	38	5	14	0	3	4	7
Butch Huskey, ph-dh	.200	5	1	1	0	0	1	1	.200	10	1	2	0	0	1	2
Jason Varitek, c	.200	20	1	4	1	1	1	4	.220	41	8	9	2	4	1	8
Brian Daubach, dh-1b	.176	17	2	3	1	4	1	4	.212	33	5	7	2	6	1	11
Darren Lewis, cf	.118	17	2	2	0	1	1	3	.242	33	7	8	0	3	1	5
Scott Hatteberg, c-ph	.000	1	0	0	0	0	0	1	.500	2	1	1	0	1	0	1
Lou Merloni, ph	—	0	0	0	0	0	1	0	.333	6	1	2	0	1	2	1
Donnie Sadler, dh-rf	—	0	0	0	0	0	0	0	.500	2	1	1	0	0	0	1
TOTALS	.293	184	21	54	5	19	15	38	.306	360	68	110	15	66	34	73

Pitching	ERA	W-L	SV	Gm	IP	H	BB	SO	ERA	W-L	Sv	Gm	IP	H	BB	SO
Pedro Martinez	0.00	1-0	0	1	7.0	2	2	12	0.00	2-0	0	3	17.0	5	6	23
Rheal Cormier	0.00	0-0	0	4	3.2	3	3	4	0.00	0-0	0	6	7.2	5	4	8
Pat Rapp	0.00	0-0	0	1	1.0	0	1	0	0.00	0-0	0	1	1.0	0	1	0
Derek Lowe	1.42	0-0	0	3	6.1	6	2	7	3.07	1-1	0	6	14.2	12	3	14
Bret Saberhagen	1.50	0-1	0	1	6.0	5	1	5	11.17	0-2	0	3	9.2	14	5	7
Ramon Martinez	4.05	0-1	0	1	6.2	6	3	5	3.65	0-1	0	2	12.1	11	6	11
Kent Mercker	4.70	0-1	0	2	7.2	12	4	5	5.79	0-1	0	3	9.1	15	7	6
Rich Garces	12.00	0-0	0	2	3.0	3	1	2	8.44	1-0	0	4	5.1	5	4	4
Tom Gordon	13.50	0-0	0	3	2.0	3	1	3	9.00	0-0	0	5	4.0	4	2	6
Rod Beck	27.00	0-1	0	2	0.2	2	0	1	6.75	0-1	0	4	2.2	4	0	3
TOTALS	3.68	1-4	0	5	44.0	42	18	44	4.84	4-6	0	10	87.1	80	46	87

Wild Pitches— LCS (none); OVERALL (none). **Hit Batters—** LCS (Mercker); OVERALL (Mercker).

New York Yankees

Batting		LCS vs Boston								Overall AL Playoffs						
Batting	Avg	AB	R	H	HR	RBI	BB	SO	Avg	AB	R	H	HR	RBI	BB	SO
Derek Jeter, ss	.350	20	3	7	1	3	2	3	.387	31	6	12	1	3	4	6
Chuck Knoblauch, 2b	.333	18	3	6	0	1	3	0	.267	30	4	8	0	1	4	3
Darryl Strawberry, dh-ph	.333	6	1	2	1	1	1	2	.333	12	3	4	2	4	2	2
Paul O'Neill, rf	.286	21	2	6	0	1	1	5	.276	29	4	8	0	1	2	6
Tino Martinez, 1b	.263	19	3	5	1	3	2	4	.233	30	5	7	1	3	4	6
Joe Girardi, c	.250	8	0	2	0	0	0	2	.143	14	0	2	0	0	0	3
Ricky Ledee, lf-dh	.250	8	2	2	1	4	1	4	.263	19	3	5	1	6	2	9
Bernie Williams, cf	.250	20	3	5	1	2	2	5	.290	31	5	9	2	8	3	7
Scott Brosius, 3b	.222	18	3	4	2	3	1	4	.179	28	3	5	2	4	1	4
Shane Spencer, lf	.111	9	1	1	0	0	1	6	.111	9	1	1	0	0	1	6
Jorge Posada, c	.100	10	1	1	1	2	1	2	.143	14	1	2	1	2	1	2
Chili Davis, ph-dh	.091	11	0	1	0	1	3	4	.143	14	0	2	0	1	3	6
Clay Bellinger, ss-dh	.000	1	0	0	0	0	0	0	.000	1	0	0	0	0	0	0
Chad Curtis, lf-cf-dh	.000	6	1	0	0	0	0	2	.000	9	2	0	0	0	0	2
Luis Sojo, ph-2b	.000	1	0	0	0	0	0	0	.000	1	0	0	0	0	0	0
Jim Leyritz, dh	—	0	0	0	0	0	0	0	.000	2	0	0	0	0	1	0
TOTALS	.239	176	23	42	8	21	18	44	.237	274	37	65	10	34	28	63

Pitching	ERA	W-L	Sv	Gm	IP	H	BB	SO	ERA	W-L	Sv	Gm	IP	H	BB	SO
Mariano Rivera	0.00	1-0	2	3	4.2	5	0	3	0.00	1-0	4	5	7.2	6	0	6
Ramiro Mendoza	0.00	0-0	1	2	2.1	0	0	2	0.00	0-0	1	3	2.1	0	0	2
Allen Watson	0.00	0-0	0	3	1.0	2	2	1	0.00	0-0	0	3	1.0	2	2	1
Jeff Nelson	0.00	0-0	0	2	0.2	0	0	0	0.00	0-0	0	5	2.1	1	1	3
Mike Stanton	0.00	0-0	0	3	0.1	1	1	0	0.00	0-0	0	3	0.1	1	1	0
Orlando Hernandez	1.80	1-0	0	2	15.0	12	6	13	1.17	2-0	0	3	23.0	14	12	17
Andy Pettitte	2.45	1-0	0	1	7.1	8	1	5	1.84	2-0	0	2	14.2	15	1	10
David Cone	2.57	1-0	0	1	7.0	7	3	9	2.57	1-0	0	1	7.0	7	3	9
Hideki Irabu	13.50	0-0	0	1	4.2	13	0	3	13.50	0-0	0	1	4.2	13	0	3
Roger Clemens	22.50	0-1	0	1	2.0	6	2	2	5.00	1-1	0	2	9.0	9	4	4
TOTALS	3.80	4-1	3	5	45.0	54	15	38	2.50	7-1	5	8	72.0	68	24	55

Wild Pitches— LCS (none); OVERALL (Rivera). **Hit Batters—** LCS (Nelson); OVERALL (Nelson).

Score by Innings

	1	2	3	4	5	6	7	8	9	10		R	H	E
Boston	4	4	3	0	4	1	4	1	0	0	-	21	54	10
New York	2	3	0	3	0	0	5	1	8	1	-	23	42	5

E: Boston— Garciaparra 4, Offerman 2, Lewis, Saberhagen, Varitek and Stanley; New York— Jeter 2, Knoblauch, Ledee and Posada. **DP:** Boston 0, New York 7. **2B:** Boston— O'Leary 3, Garciaparra, Valentin 2, Nixon 2, Huskey, Varitek, Daubach and Lewis; New York— Jeter, Knoblauch, Martinez and Williams. **3B:** Boston— Offerman and Varitek; New York— Brosius. **SB:** Boston— Offerman, Buford, Garciaparra and Lewis; New York— Knoblauch, Williams and Curtis. **CS:** Boston— Lewis; New York— Ledee. **S:** Boston— Varitek; New York— Brosius and Knoblauch. **SF:** none. **HBP:** by Nelson (Stanley), by Mercker (Martinez).
Umpires: Tim McClelland, Dan Morrison, Rick Reed, Al Clark, Dale Scott and Tim Tschida.

National League Championship Series

Braves, 4-2

Date	Winner	Home Field
Oct. 12	Braves, 4-2	at Atlanta
Oct. 13	Braves, 4-3	at Atlanta
Oct. 15	Braves, 1-0	at New York
Oct. 16	Mets, 3-2	at New York
Oct. 17	Mets, 4-3 (15 inn.)	at New York
Oct. 19	Braves, 10-9 (11 inn.)	at Atlanta

Most Valuable Player

Eddie Perez, Atlanta, C

Avg	AB	R	H	HR	RBI	BB	SO
.500	20	2	10	2	5	1	3

Game 1

Tuesday, Oct. 12, at Atlanta

```
            1 2 3   4 5 6   7 8 9     R H E
New York ...0 0 0   1 0 0   0 0 1  -  2 6 2
Atlanta .....1 0 0   0 1 1   0 1 x  -  4 8 2
```

Win: Maddux, Atl. (1-1). **Loss:** Yoshii, NY (0-1). **Save:** Rocker, Atl. (2).
2B: New York— Cedeno, Alfonzo 2; Atlanta— Perez, Weiss. **HR:** Atlanta— Perez (1). **RBI:** New York— Piazza, Pratt; Atlanta— Boone, Williams, Perez, Weiss. **SB:** Atlanta— Williams (2), C. Jones (1), Weiss (1).
Attendance: 44,172. **Time:** 3:09.

Game 2

Wednesday, Oct. 13, at Atlanta

```
            1 2 3   4 5 6   7 8 9     R H E
New York ...0 1 0   0 1 0   0 1 0  -  3 5 1
Atlanta .....0 0 0   0 0 4   0 0 x  -  4 9 1
```

Win: Millwood, Atl. (2-0). **Loss:** Rogers, NY (0-2). **Save:** Smoltz, Atl. (1).
2B: New York— Alfonzo. **HR:** New York— Mora (1); Atlanta— Jordan (2), Perez (2). **RBI:** New York— Cedeno, Mora, Alfonzo; Atlanta— Jordan 2, Perez 2.
Attendance: 44,624. **Time:** 2:42.

Game 3

Friday, Oct. 15, at New York

```
            1 2 3   4 5 6   7 8 9     R H E
Atlanta .....1 0 0   0 0 0   0 0 0  -  1 3 1
New York ...0 0 0   0 0 0   0 0 0  -  0 7 2
```

Win: Glavine, Atl. (1-0). **Loss:** Leiter, NY (0-1). **Save:** Rocker, Atl. (3).
SB: Atlanta— Boone (2), Williams (3).
Attendance: 55,911. **Time:** 3:04.

Game 4

Saturday, Oct. 16, at New York

```
            1 2 3   4 5 6   7 8 9     R H E
Atlanta .......0 0 0   0 0 0   0 2 0  -  2 3 0
New York ...0 0 0   0 0 1   0 2 x  -  3 5 0
```

Win: Wendell, NY (2-0). **Loss:** Remlinger, Atl. (0-1). **Save:** Benitez, NY (1).
HR: Atlanta— Jordan (3); Klesko (1); New York— Olerud (2). **RBI:** Atlanta— Jordan, Klesko; New York— Olerud 3. **SB:** New York— Cedeno 2 (3), Mora (1).
Attendance: 55,872. **Time:** 2:20.

Game 5

Sunday, Oct. 17, at New York

```
               1 2 3    4 5 6    7 8 9
Atlanta .........0 0 0    2 0 0    0 0 0
New York .....2 0 0    0 0 0    0 0 0

            10 11 12   13 14 15      R H E
Atlanta .......0  0  0    0  0  1  -  3 13 2
New York ...0  0  0    0  0  2  -  4 11 1
```

Win: Dotel, NY (1-0). **Loss:** McGlinchy, Atl. (0-1).
2B: Atlanta— Perez, Boone, C. Jones 2, Williams, Weiss; New York— Hamilton. **3B:** Atlanta— Lockhart. **HR:** New York— Olerud (3). **RBI:** Atlanta— C. Jones, Jordan, Lockhart; New York— Olerud 2, Pratt, Ventura. **SB:** Atlanta— Nixon (2), Battle (1), Weiss (2); New York— Agbayani (1), Dunston (1).
Attendance: 55,723. **Time:** 5:46.

Game 6

Tuesday, Oct. 19, at Atlanta

```
            1 2 3 4 5 6 7 8 9 10 11    R H E
New York ..0 0 0 0 0 3 4 1 0 1  0  -  9 15 2
Atlanta .....5 0 0 0 2 0 1 0 1 1  1  - 10 10 1
```

Win: Springer, Atl. (1-0). **Loss:** Rogers, NY (0-3).
2B: New York— Alfonzo, Ventura, Franco, Henderson; Atlanta— Williams. **HR:** New York— Piazza (1). **RBI:** New York— Piazza 3, Hamilton 2, Henderson, Olerud, Mora, Pratt; Atlanta— Jordan, Perez 2, Hunter 2, Hernandez 2, Guillen, A. Jones. **SB:** New York— Henderson (7), Mora (2); Atlanta— Boone (3), Williams (4), C. Jones 2 (3), Hunter (1), Nixon (3).
Attendance: 52,335. **Time:** 4:25.

NLCS Composite Box Score

New York Mets

Batting	Avg	LCS vs Atlanta							Overall NL Playoffs							
		AB	R	H	HR	RBI	BB	SO	Avg	AB	R	H	HR	RBI	BB	SO
Roger Cedeno, rf-pr	.500	12	2	6	0	1	1	1	.421	19	3	8	0	3	1	2
Matt Franco, ph	.500	2	1	1	0	0	1	0	.500	2	1	1	0	0	2	0
Todd Pratt, ph-c	.500	2	0	1	0	3	1	1	.200	10	2	2	1	4	3	2
Melvin Mora, ph-of	.429	14	3	6	1	2	3	2	.400	15	4	6	1	2	3	2
Darryl Hamilton, cf	.353	17	0	6	0	2	0	4	.280	25	0	7	0	4	2	4
Bobby Bonilla, ph	.333	3	0	1	0	0	0	2	.250	4	1	1	0	0	1	2
John Olerud, 1b	.296	27	4	8	3	6	2	3	.349	43	7	15	3	12	5	5
Edgardo Alfonzo, 2b	.222	27	2	6	0	1	2	9	.233	43	8	10	3	7	4	11
Rickey Henderson, lf	.174	23	2	4	0	1	0	5	.263	38	7	10	0	2	3	6
Mike Piazza, c	.167	24	1	4	1	4	1	10	.182	33	1	6	1	4	1	10
Shawon Dunston, ph-cf	.143	7	2	1	0	0	0	2	.154	13	2	2	0	0	0	3
Benny Agbayani, rf-lf	.143	7	2	1	0	0	4	2	.235	17	3	4	0	1	4	5
Robin Ventura, 3b	.120	25	2	3	0	1	1	5	.154	39	3	6	0	2	6	7
Rey Ordonez, ss	.042	24	0	1	0	0	0	2	.132	38	1	5	0	2	0	7
Masato Yoshii, p	.000	3	0	0	0	0	0	1	.000	5	0	0	0	0	0	2
Al Leiter, p	.000	2	0	0	0	0	0	0	.000	5	0	0	0	0	0	3
Pat Mahomes, p	.000	2	0	0	0	0	0	0	.000	2	0	0	0	0	0	0
Rick Reed, p	.000	2	0	0	0	0	0	0	.000	3	0	0	0	0	0	1
Kenny Rogers, p	.000	1	0	0	0	0	0	1	.000	3	0	0	0	0	0	2
Orel Hershiser, p	.000	1	0	0	0	0	0	0	.000	1	0	0	0	0	0	0
Turk Wendell, p	—	0	0	0	0	0	0	0	.000	0	0	0	0	0	0	1
TOTALS	.218	225	21	49	4	21	15	49	.231	359	43	83	9	43	35	77

Pitching	ERA	W-L	Sv	Gm	IP	H	BB	SO	ERA	W-L	Sv	Gm	IP	H	BB	SO
Orel Hershiser	0.00	0-0	0	2	4.1	1	3	5	0.00	0-0	0	3	5.1	1	3	6
Dennis Cook	0.00	0-0	0	3	1.1	1	2	1	0.00	0-0	0	4	3.0	2	3	2
Armando Benitez	1.35	0-0	1	5	6.2	3	2	9	1.00	0-0	1	7	9.0	5	3	11
Pat Mahomes	1.42	0-0	0	3	6.1	4	3	3	2.25	0-0	0	4	8.0	7	3	4
Rick Reed	2.57	0-0	0	1	7.0	3	0	5	2.77	1-0	0	2	13.0	7	3	7
Octavio Dotel	3.00	1-0	0	1	3.0	4	2	5	8.10	1-0	0	2	3.1	5	4	5
John Franco	3.38	0-0	0	3	2.2	3	1	3	1.42	1-0	0	6	6.1	4	1	5
Masato Yoshii	4.70	0-1	0	2	7.2	9	3	4	5.54	0-1	0	3	13.0	15	3	7
Turk Wendell	4.76	1-0	0	5	5.2	2	4	5	3.52	2-0	0	7	7.2	2	6	5
Kenny Rogers	5.87	0-2	0	3	7.2	11	7	2	6.75	0-3	0	4	12.0	16	9	8
Al Leiter	6.43	0-1	0	2	7.0	5	4	5	4.91	0-1	0	3	14.2	8	7	9
TOTALS	3.49	2-4	1	6	59.1	46	31	47	3.68	5-5	1	10	95.1	72	45	69

Wild Pitches— LCS (Leiter); OVERALL (Leiter and Reed). **Hit Batters—** LCS (Leiter 2, Hershiser, Wendell); OVERALL (Leiter 3, Hershiser, Wendell, Rogers and Dotel).

Atlanta Braves

	LCS vs New York								Overall NL Playoffs							
Batting	Avg	AB	R	H	HR	RBI	BB	SO	Avg	AB	R	H	HR	RBI	BB	SO
Eddie Perez, c	.500	20	2	10	2	5	1	3	.389	36	3	14	2	8	1	6
Jose Hernandez, ph	.500	2	0	1	0	2	0	1	.154	13	1	2	0	2	1	4
Keith Lockhart, ph-2b	.400	5	0	2	0	1	0	2	.333	6	0	2	0	1	0	3
Ozzie Guillen, ss-ph	.333	3	0	1	0	1	0	0	.250	4	0	1	0	1	0	0
Walt Weiss, ss	.286	21	2	6	0	1	2	4	.259	27	3	7	0	1	2	6
Chipper Jones, 3b	.263	19	3	5	0	1	9	7	.250	32	5	8	0	2	14	9
Andruw Jones, cf	.217	23	5	5	0	1	4	3	.220	41	6	9	0	3	5	5
Brian Jordan, rf	.200	25	3	5	2	5	3	5	.310	42	5	13	3	12	4	7
Bret Boone, 2b	.182	22	2	4	0	1	1	7	.317	41	5	13	0	2	1	11
Gerald Williams, lf	.179	28	4	5	0	1	2	2	.261	46	6	12	0	4	2	5
Ryan Klesko, 1b	.125	8	1	1	1	1	2	1	.250	20	4	5	1	2	3	5
Brian Hunter, 1b-ph	.100	10	1	1	0	2	5	2	.071	14	1	1	0	2	6	5
Greg Maddux, p	.000	5	0	0	0	0	0	4	.000	6	0	0	0	0	0	4
Kevin Millwood, p	.000	4	0	0	0	0	0	2	.125	8	0	1	0	0	1	3
Howard Battle, ph-1b	.000	2	0	0	0	0	0	0	.400	5	1	2	0	0	0	0
John Smoltz, p	.000	2	0	0	0	0	0	1	.000	2	0	0	0	0	0	1
Jorge Fabregas, ph	.000	2	0	0	0	0	1	1	.000	2	0	0	0	0	1	1
Greg Myers, c	.000	2	0	0	0	0	0	1	.000	2	0	0	0	0	0	2
Tom Glavine, p	.000	2	0	0	0	0	0	1	.000	4	0	0	0	0	1	0
Kevin McGlinchy, p	.000	1	0	0	0	0	0	1	.000	1	0	0	0	0	1	0
John Rocker, p	—	0	0	0	0	0	0	0	—	0	0	0	0	0	0	0
Otis Nixon, pr-lf	—	0	0	0	0	0	0	0	1.000	1	2	1	0	0	0	0
TOTALS	.223	206	24	46	5	22	31	47	.257	354	42	91	6	40	42	82

Pitching	ERA	W-L	Sv	Gm	IP	H	BB	SO	ERA	W-L	Sv	Gm	IP	H	BB	SO
Tom Glavine	0.00	1-0	0	1	7.0	7	1	8	1.38	1-0	0	2	13.0	12	4	14
John Rocker	0.00	0-0	1	6	6.2	3	2	9	0.00	0-0	3	8	10.0	3	4	14
Terry Mulholland	0.00	0-0	0	2	2.2	1	1	2	5.40	0-0	0	4	3.1	4	1	2
Russ Springer	0.00	1-0	0	2	2.0	0	1	1	0.00	1-0	0	3	3.0	2	2	2
Greg Maddux	1.93	1-0	0	2	14.0	12	1	7	2.14	1-1	0	4	21.0	22	6	12
Mike Remlinger	3.18	0-1	0	5	5.2	3	3	4	5.79	0-1	0	7	9.1	7	6	8
Kevin Millwood	3.55	1-0	0	2	12.2	13	1	9	2.38	2-0	1	4	22.2	14	1	18
John Smoltz	6.23	0-1	0	3	8.2	8	0	9	5.74	0-1	1	4	15.2	14	3	11
Kevin McGlinchy	18.00	0-1	0	1	1.0	2	4	1	13.50	0-1	0	2	1.1	2	4	1
TOTALS	2.69	4-2	2	6	60.1	49	14	49	2.99	7-3	5	10	99.1	80	31	82

Wild Pitches— LCS (Rocker); OVERALL (Rocker 2). **Hit Batters—** LCS (none); OVERALL (Glavine and Smoltz).

Score by Innings

	1	2	3	4	5	6	7	8	9	10	11	12	13	14	15	R	H	E
New York	2	1	0	1	1	4	4	4	1	1	0	0	0	0	2	21	49	8
Atlanta	7	0	0	2	1	7	0	4	0	1	1	0	0	0	1	24	46	7

E: New York— Piazza 3, Olerud 2, Leiter, Alfonzo and Henderson; Atlanta— Klesko 2, C. Jones 2, Hunter, Williams and Weiss. **DP:** New York 9, Atlanta 4. **2B:** New York— Alfonzo 4, Cedeno, M. Franco, Hamilton and Henderson; Atlanta— Perez 2, Weiss 2, C. Jones 2, Williams 2 and Boone. **3B:** Atlanta— Lockhart. **SB:** New York— Cedeno 2, Mora 2, Henderson, Agbayani and Dunston; Atlanta— Williams 3, C. Jones 3, Weiss 2, Boone 2, Nixon 2, Battle and Hunter. **CS:** New York— Agbayani, Dunston and Cedeno; Atlanta— Williams, A. Jones and Boone. **S:** New York— Ordonez, Alfonzo and Rogers; Atlanta— Perez 2, Boone, Weiss, A. Jones, Maddux and Glavine. **SF:** New York— Pratt and Piazza; Atlanta— Hunter.
Umpires: Ed Montague, Jerry Crawford, Jerry Layne, Charles Reliford, Ed Rapuano and Jeffrey Kellogg.

WORLD SERIES

New York, 4-0

Date	Winner	Home Field
Oct. 23	Yankees, 4-1	at Atlanta
Oct. 24	Yankees, 7-2	at Atlanta
Oct. 26	Yankees, 6-5 (10 inn.)	at New York
Oct. 27	Yankees, 4-1	at New York

Most Valuable Player

Mariano Rivera, New York, P

IP	H	ER	BB	SO	SV	ERA
4²/₃	3	0	1	3	2	0.00

Game 1
Saturday, Oct. 23, at Atlanta

	1 2 3	4 5 6	7 8 9	R H E
New York.....	0 0 0	0 0 0	0 4 0 —	4 6 0
Atlanta	0 0 0	1 0 0	0 0 0 —	1 2 2

New York	AB	R	H	BB	SO
Knoblauch, 2b.................	4	1	0	0	0
Jeter, ss.....................	4	1	2	1	1
O'Neill, rf...................	4	0	1	0	1
B. Williams, cf...............	2	0	0	2	1
Martinez, 1b..................	3	0	0	1	2
Posada, c....................	4	0	0	0	1
Ledee, lf....................	3	0	0	0	1
Leyritz, ph.................	0	0	0	1	0
Nelson, p..................	0	0	0	0	0
Stanton, p.................	0	0	0	0	0
Rivera, p.................	0	0	0	0	0
Brosius, 3b..................	4	1	3	0	1
O. Hernandez, p.............	1	0	0	0	0
Strawberry, ph.............	0	0	0	1	0
Curtis, pr-lf.............	1	1	0	0	0
TOTALS.....................	30	4	6	6	8

Atlanta	AB	R	H	BB	SO
G. Williams, lf..............	4	0	0	0	2
Boone, 2b..................	4	0	1	0	2
C. Jones, 3b..............	2	1	1	2	1
Jordan, rf.................	4	0	0	0	1
Klesko, 1b.................	3	0	0	0	0
Hunter, 1b...............	0	0	0	0	0
Myers, ph...............	1	0	0	0	0
A. Jones, cf.............	2	0	0	1	0
Perez, c.................	2	0	0	1	2
Weiss, ss.................	2	0	0	0	1
Guillen, ss.............	0	0	0	0	0
J. Hernandez, ph-ss.......	1	0	0	0	1
Maddux, p.................	2	0	0	0	2
Rocker, p...............	0	0	0	0	0
Battle, ph.............	0	0	0	0	0
Lockhart, ph.............	1	0	0	0	0
Remlinger, p.............	0	0	0	0	0
TOTALS.................	28	1	2	4	13

New York	IP	H	ER	BB	SO
O. Hernandez (W, 1-0)	7	1	1	2	10
Nelson (H, 1)...................	⅓	0	0	1	1
Stanton (H, 1).................	⅓	0	0	0	1
Rivera (S, 1)..................	1⅓	1	0	1	1

Atlanta	IP	H	ER	BB	SO
Maddux (L, 0-1)................	7	5	2	3	5
Rocker......................	1	1	0	2	3
Remlinger....................	1	0	0	1	0

HR: Atlanta— C. Jones (1). **RBI:** New York— Jeter, O'Neill 2, Leyritz; Atlanta— C. Jones. **S:** New York— O. Hernandez, Knoblauch. **SB:** New York— Jeter (1), B. Williams (1). **CS:** New York—Jeter; Atlanta— C. Jones. **Attendance:** 51,342. **Time:** 2:57.

Game 2
Sunday, Oct. 24, at Atlanta

	1 2 3	4 5 6	7 8 9	R H E
New York.....	3 0 2	1 1 0	0 0 0 —	7 14 1
Atlanta	0 0 0	0 0 0	0 0 2 —	2 5 1

New York	AB	R	H	BB	SO
Knoblauch, 2b.................	4	1	2	1	1
Jeter, ss.....................	5	2	2	0	1
O'Neill, rf...................	4	0	1	1	0
B. Williams, cf...............	4	1	3	1	0
Martinez, 1b..................	5	2	2	0	0
Ledee, lf....................	4	0	2	1	2
Brosius, 3b..................	5	1	2	0	2
Girardi, c...................	4	0	0	0	0
Cone, p.....................	4	0	0	0	0
Mendoza, p..................	1	0	0	0	0
Nelson, p.................	0	0	0	0	0
TOTALS....................	40	7	14	4	8

Atlanta	AB	R	H	BB	SO
G. Williams, lf..............	4	0	0	0	1
Guillen, ss..................	4	0	0	0	0
C. Jones, 3b.................	3	1	1	1	0
Jordan, rf...................	3	0	0	1	0
Klesko, 1b...................	4	0	0	0	1
Lockhart, 2b.................	2	1	0	2	0
Myers, c....................	3	0	2	1	0
A. Jones, cf.................	3	0	0	0	1
McGlinchy, p.................	0	0	0	0	0
Boone, ph...................	1	0	0	0	0
Millwood, p..................	0	0	0	0	0
Mulholland, p................	0	0	0	1	0
Fabregas, ph.................	1	0	0	0	0
Springer, p..................	0	0	0	0	0
Nixon, cf....................	2	0	1	0	0
TOTALS......................	30	2	5	6	4

New York	IP	H	ER	BB	SO
Cone (W, 1-0)	7	1	0	5	4
Mendoza	1⅔	3	2	1	0
Nelson	⅓	1	0	0	0

Atlanta	IP	H	ER	BB	SO
Millwood (L, 0-1).............	2	8	4	2	2
Mulholland	3	3	2	1	3
Springer	2	1	0	0	1
McGlinchy	2	2	0	1	2

2B: New York— Ledee, Jeter, Brosius; Atlanta—Boone. **RBI:** New York— O'Neill, Martinez 2, Brosius, Ledee, Knoblauch; Atlanta— Myers, Boone. **S:** New York—Girardi. **SB:** Knoblauch (1). **Attendance:** 51,226. **Time:** 3:14.

Game 3
Tuesday, Oct. 26 at New York

	1	2	3	4	5	6	7	8	9	10	R	H	E
Atlanta	1	0	3	1	0	0	0	0	0	0	5	14	1
New York	1	0	0	0	1	0	1	2	0	1	6	9	0

Atlanta	AB	R	H	BB	SO
G. Williams, lf	5	2	2	0	0
Boone, 2b	5	1	4	0	0
Nixon, pr	0	0	0	0	0
Lockhart, 2b	0	0	0	0	0
C. Jones, 3b	4	0	1	1	1
Jordan, rf	3	1	1	2	0
A. Jones, cf	5	1	1	0	0
J. Hernandez, dh	4	0	1	0	1
Guillen, ph-dh	1	0	0	0	0
Perez, c	4	0	1	0	1
Klesko, ph-1b	1	0	1	0	0
Hunter, 1b	4	0	1	0	1
Myers, ph-c	1	0	0	0	0
Weiss, ss	4	0	1	0	0
TOTALS	41	5	14	3	5

New York	AB	R	H	BB	SO
Knoblauch, 2b	4	2	2	0	0
Jeter, ss	4	0	1	0	1
O'Neill, rf	4	0	1	0	0
B. Williams, cf	4	0	0	0	0
Davis, dh	4	0	0	0	2
Martinez, 1b	4	1	1	0	0
Brosius, 3b	4	0	0	0	0
Curtis, lf	4	2	2	0	0
Girardi, c	3	1	2	0	0
TOTALS	35	6	9	0	4

Atlanta	IP	H	ER	BB	SO
Glavine	7	7	4	0	3
Rocker	2	1	0	0	1
Remlinger (L, 0-1)	0	1	1	0	0

New York	IP	H	ER	BB	SO
Pettitte	3⅔	10	5	1	1
Grimsley	2⅓	2	0	2	0
Nelson	2	0	0	0	2
Rivera (W, 1-0)	2	2	0	0	2

2B: Atlanta— Boone 3, J. Hernandez; New York— Knoblauch. **3B:** Atlanta— G. Williams. **HR:** New York— Curtis 2 (2), Martinez (1), Knoblauch (1). **RBI:** Atlanta— C. Jones, Jordan, J. Hernandez 2, Boone; New York— O'Neill, Curtis 2, Martinez, Knoblauch 2. **SB:** Atlanta— J. Hernandez (1) **CS:** Atlanta—Boone, Nixon. **Attendance:** 56,794. **Time:** 3:16.

Game 4
Wednesday, Oct. 27, at New York

	1	2	3	4	5	6	7	8	9	R	H	E
Atlanta	0	0	0	0	0	0	0	1	0	1	5	0
New York	0	0	3	0	0	0	0	1	x	4	8	0

Atlanta	AB	R	H	BB	SO
G. Williams, lf	4	0	1	0	1
Boone, 2b	3	0	1	1	1
C. Jones, 3b	4	0	0	1	1
Jordan, rf	3	0	0	1	1
Klesko, 1b	4	0	1	0	0
Lockhart, dh	4	0	0	0	0
Perez, c	2	0	0	0	0
Myers, c	1	0	0	0	0
A. Jones, cf	3	0	0	0	1
Weiss, ss	3	1	1	0	0
TOTALS	31	1	5	2	4

New York	AB	R	H	BB	SO
Knoblauch, 2b	4	1	1	0	2
Sojo, 2b	0	0	0	0	0
Jeter, ss	4	1	1	0	0
O'Neill, rf	3	0	0	1	1
B. Williams, cf	3	1	0	1	1
Martinez, 1b	3	0	1	1	1
Strawberry, dh	3	0	1	0	2
Leyritz, dh	1	1	1	0	0
Posada, c	4	0	2	0	1
Ledee, lf	3	0	0	0	1
Curtis, lf	1	0	0	0	0
Brosius, 3b	3	0	1	0	1
TOTALS	32	4	8	3	11

Atlanta	IP	H	ER	BB	SO
Smoltz (L, 0-1)	7	6	3	3	11
Mulholland	⅔	2	1	0	0
Springer	⅓	0	0	0	0

New York	IP	H	ER	BB	SO
Clemens (W, 1-0)	7⅔	4	1	2	4
Nelson (H, 2)	0	1	0	0	0
Rivera (S, 2)	1⅓	0	0	0	0

2B: New York— Posada. **HR:** New York— Leyritz (1). **RBI:** Atlanta— Boone; New York— Martinez 2, Posada, Leyritz. **SB:** New York— Jeter 2 (3). **Attendance:** 56,752. **Time:** 2:58.

World Series Composite Box Score
Atlanta Braves

Batting	WS vs New York								Overall Playoffs						
	Avg	AB	R	H	HR	RBI	BB	SO	Avg	AB	R	H	HR	RBI	BB	SO
Bret Boone, 2b-ph	.538	13	1	7	0	3	1	3	.370	54	6	20	0	5	2	14
Otis Nixon, cf-pr	.500	2	0	1	0	0	0	0	.667	3	2	2	0	0	0	0
Greg Myers, ph-c	.333	6	0	2	0	1	1	0	.250	8	0	2	0	1	2	1
Brian Hunter, 1b	.250	4	0	1	0	0	0	1	.111	18	1	2	0	2	6	6
Chipper Jones, 3b	.231	13	2	3	1	2	4	2	.244	45	7	11	1	4	18	11
Walt Weiss, ss	.222	9	1	2	0	0	0	1	.250	36	4	9	0	1	2	7
Jose Hernandez, ph-ss-dh	.200	5	0	1	0	2	0	2	.167	18	1	3	0	4	1	6
Gerald Williams, lf	.176	17	2	3	0	0	0	1	.238	63	8	15	0	4	2	9
Ryan Klesko, 1b-ph	.167	12	0	2	0	1	0	0	.219	32	4	7	1	2	3	6
Keith Lockhart, 2b-dh	.143	7	1	1	0	0	2	0	.231	13	1	3	0	1	2	3
Eddie Perez, c	.125	8	0	1	0	0	1	3	.341	44	3	15	2	8	2	9
Andruw Jones, cf	.077	13	1	1	0	0	1	3	.185	54	7	10	0	3	6	9
Brian Jordan, rf	.077	13	1	1	0	1	4	2	.255	55	6	14	3	13	8	9
Ozzie Guillen, ph-ss-dh	.000	5	0	0	0	0	0	1	.111	9	0	1	0	1	0	1
Greg Maddux, p	.000	2	0	0	0	0	0	0	.000	8	0	0	0	0	0	6
Jorge Fabregas, ph	.000	1	0	0	0	0	0	0	.000	3	0	0	0	0	0	2
Howard Battle, ph	—	0	0	0	0	0	0	0	.000	3	0	0	0	0	0	2

Atlanta

Batting	WS vs New York								Overall Playoffs							
	Avg	AB	R	H	HR	RBI	BB	SO	Avg	AB	R	H	HR	RBI	BB	SO
Tom Glavine, p	—	0	0	0	0	0	0	0	.000	4	0	0	0	0	0	2
Kevin McGlinchy, p	—	0	0	0	0	0	0	0	.000	1	0	0	0	0	0	1
Kevin Millwood, p	—	0	0	0	0	0	0	0	.125	8	0	1	0	0	1	3
Terry Mulholland, p	—	0	0	0	0	0	1	0	—	0	0	0	0	0	1	0
John Smoltz, p	—	0	0	0	0	0	0	0	.400	5	1	2	0	0	0	1
TOTALS	.200	130	9	26	1	9	15	26	.242	484	51	117	7	49	56	108

Pitching	ERA	W-L	Sv	Gm	IP	H	BB	SO	ERA	W-L	Sv	Gm	IP	H	BB	SO
John Rocker	0.00	0-0	0	2	3.0	2	2	4	0.00	1-0	3	10	13.0	5	6	18
Russ Springer	0.00	0-0	0	1	2.1	1	0	1	0.00	1-0	0	5	5.1	3	2	3
Kevin McGlinchy	0.00	0-0	0	1	2.0	2	1	2	5.40	0-1	0	3	3.1	4	5	3
Greg Maddux	2.57	0-1	0	1	7.0	5	3	5	2.25	1-2	0	5	28.0	27	9	17
John Smoltz	3.86	0-1	0	1	7.0	6	3	11	5.16	1-1	1	5	22.2	20	6	22
Tom Glavine	5.14	0-0	0	1	7.0	7	0	3	2.70	1-0	0	3	20.0	19	4	17
Terry Mulholland	7.36	0-0	0	2	3.2	5	1	3	6.43	0-0	0	6	7.0	9	2	5
Mike Remlinger	9.00	0-1	0	1	1.0	1	1	0	6.10	0-2	0	9	10.1	8	7	8
Kevin Millwood	18.00	0-1	0	1	2.0	8	2	2	3.65	2-1	0	5	24.2	22	3	20
TOTALS	4.37	0-4	0	4	35.0	37	13	31	3.35	7-7	5	14	134.1	117	44	113

Wild Pitches—WS (none); OVERALL (Rocker 2). **Hit Batters**—WS (none); OVERALL (Glavine and Smoltz).

New York Yankees

Batting	WS vs Atlanta								Overall Playoffs							
	Avg	AB	R	H	HR	RBI	BB	SO	Avg	AB	R	H	HR	RBI	BB	SO
Jim Leyritz, ph-dh	1.000	1	1	1	1	2	1	0	.333	3	1	1	1	3	2	0
Scott Brosius, 3b	.375	16	2	6	0	1	0	5	.250	44	5	11	2	5	1	9
Derek Jeter, ss	.353	17	4	6	0	1	1	3	.375	48	10	18	1	4	5	9
Chad Curtis, pr-lf-ph	.333	6	3	2	2	2	0	0	.133	15	5	2	2	2	0	2
Darryl Strawberry, ph-dh	.333	3	0	1	0	0	1	2	.333	15	3	5	2	4	3	4
Chuck Knoblauch, 2b	.313	16	5	5	1	3	1	3	.283	46	9	13	1	4	5	6
Joe Girardi, c	.286	7	1	2	0	0	0	1	.190	21	1	4	0	0	1	5
Tino Martinez, 1b	.267	15	3	4	1	5	2	4	.244	45	8	11	2	8	6	10
Jorge Posada, c	.250	8	0	2	0	1	0	3	.182	22	1	4	1	3	1	5
Bernie Williams, cf	.231	13	2	3	0	0	4	2	.273	44	7	12	0	8	7	9
Paul O'Neill, rf	.200	15	0	3	0	4	2	2	.250	44	4	11	0	5	4	8
Ricky Ledee, lf	.200	10	0	2	0	0	1	4	.241	29	3	7	1	7	3	13
David Cone, p	.000	4	0	0	0	0	0	0	.000	4	0	0	0	0	0	0
Chili Davis, dh	.000	4	0	0	0	0	0	2	.111	18	0	2	0	1	3	8
Orlando Hernandez, p	.000	1	0	0	0	0	0	0	.000	1	0	0	0	0	0	0
Ramiro Mendoza, p	.000	1	0	0	0	0	0	0	.000	1	0	0	0	0	0	0
Luis Sojo, 2b	—	0	0	0	0	0	0	0	.000	1	0	0	0	0	0	0
Clay Bellinger, ph	—	0	0	0	0	0	0	0	.000	1	0	0	0	0	0	1
Shane Spencer, lf	—	0	0	0	0	0	0	0	.111	9	1	1	0	0	1	6
TOTALS	.270	137	21	37	5	20	13	31	.248	411	58	102	15	54	41	94

Pitching	ERA	W-L	Sv	Gm	IP	H	BB	SO	ERA	W-L	Sv	Gm	IP	H	BB	SO
David Cone	0.00	1-0	0	1	7.0	1	5	4	1.29	2-0	0	2	14.0	8	8	13
Mariano Rivera	0.00	1-0	2	3	4.2	3	1	3	0.00	2-0	6	8	12.1	9	1	9
Jeff Nelson	0.00	0-0	0	4	2.2	2	1	3	0.00	0-0	0	9	5.0	3	2	6
Jason Grimsley	0.00	0-0	0	1	2.1	2	2	0	0.00	0-0	0	1	2.1	2	2	0
Mike Stanton	0.00	0-0	0	1	0.1	0	0	1	0.00	0-0	0	4	0.2	1	1	1
Roger Clemens	1.17	1-0	0	1	7.2	4	2	4	3.24	2-1	0	3	16.2	13	6	8
Orlando Hernandez	1.29	1-0	0	1	7.0	1	2	10	1.20	3-0	0	4	30.0	15	14	27
Ramiro Mendoza	10.80	0-0	0	1	1.2	3	1	1	4.50	0-0	1	3	4.0	3	1	2
Andy Pettitte	12.27	0-0	0	1	3.2	10	1	1	3.93	2-0	0	3	18.1	25	2	11
Hideki Irabu	—	0-0	0	0	0.0	0	0	0	13.50	0-0	0	1	4.2	13	0	3
Allen Watson	—	0-0	0	0	0.0	0	0	0	0.00	0-0	0	3	1.0	2	2	1
TOTALS	2.19	4-0	2	4	37.0	26	15	26	2.39	11-1	7	12	109.0	94	39	81

Wild Pitches—WS (Pettitte); OVERALL (Pettitte and Rivera). **Hit Batters**—WS (none); OVERALL (Nelson).

Score by Innings

	1	2	3	4	5	6	7	8	9	10		R	H	E
Atlanta	1	0	3	2	0	0	0	1	2	0	—	9	26	4
New York	4	0	5	1	2	0	1	7	0	1	—	21	37	1

E: Atlanta— Hunter 2, Jordan and Guillen; New York— Cone. **DP:** Atlanta 4, New York 5. **LOB:** Atlanta 25, New York 27. **2B:** Atlanta— Boone and J. Hernandez; New York— Brosius, Jeter, Knoblauch, Posada and Ledee. **3B:** Atlanta— G. Williams. **SB:** Atlanta— J. Hernandez; New York— Jeter. **CS:** Atlanta— C. Jones, Boone and Nixon; New York— Jeter. **S:** New York— Girardi, Knoblauch and O. Hernandez. **IBB:** New York— off Rocker (B. Williams), off Mulholland (B. Williams), off Smoltz (B. Williams).
Umpires: Randy Marsh, Rocky Roe, Steve Rippley, Derryl Cousins, Gerry Davis and Jim Joyce.

COLLEGE

Final *Baseball America* Top 25

Final 1999 Division I Top 25, voted on by the editors of *Baseball America* and released after the NCAA College World Series. Given are final records (excluding ties) and winning percentage (including all postseason games); records in College World Series and team eliminated by (DNP indicates team did not play in tourney); head coach (career years and Division I record including 1999 postseason); preseason ranking and rank before start of CWS.

		Record	Pct	CWS Recap	Head Coach	Preseason Rank	Rank before CWS
1	Miami-FL	.50-13	.794	4-0	Jim Morris (18 yrs: 803-332-1)	3	2
2	Florida St.	.57-14	.803	4-2 (Miami)	Mike Martin (20 yrs: 1079-364-3)	4	3
3	Stanford	.50-15	.769	2-2 (Fla. St.)	Mark Marquess (23 yrs: 945-482-5)	7	1
4	Alabama	.53-16	.768	2-2 (Miami)	Jim Wells (10 yrs: 439-179)	13	7
5	Rice	.59-15	.797	1-2 (Alabama)	Wayne Graham (8 yrs: 336-155)	6	4
6	CS-Fullerton	.50-14	.781	1-2 (Fla. St.)	George Horton (3 yrs: 136-55-1)	14	6
7	Texas A&M	.52-18	.743	0-2 (CS-Full.)	Mark Johnson (15 yrs: 668-279-2)	11	5
8	Baylor	.50-15	.769	DNP	Steve Smith (5 yrs: 180-112-1)	NR	8
9	Oklahoma St.	.46-21	.687	0-2 (Rice)	Tom Holliday (3 yrs: 132-61)	21	9
10	USC	.36-26	.581	DNP	Mike Gillespie (13 yrs: 519-293-2)	1	10
11	Wake Forest	.47-16	.746	DNP	George Greer (18 yrs: 536-396-6)	17	11
12	Ohio St.	.50-14	.781	DNP	Bob Todd (16 yrs: 613-319-1)	NR	12
13	Auburn	.46-19	.708	DNP	Hal Baird (20 yrs: 738-374)	18	13
14	Wichita St.	.59-14	.808	DNP	Gene Stephenson (22 yrs: 1224-360-3)	5	14
15	Tulane	.48-17	.738	DNP	Rick Jones (6 yrs: 252-123)	NR	15
16	Louisiana St.	.41-24	.631	DNP	Skip Bertman (16 yrs: 774-288-2)	8	16
17	Clemson	.42-27	.609	DNP	Jack Leggett (20 yrs: 665-402)	15	17
18	Pepperdine	.46-16	.742	DNP	Frank Sanchez (3 yrs: 112-63)	NR	18
19	East Carolina	.46-16	.742	DNP	Keith LeClair (8 yrs: 305-180-1)	NR	19
20	Southwestern La.	.42-24	.636	DNP	Tony Robichaux (12 yrs: 413-269)	NR	20
21	Florida Atlantic	.54-9	.857	DNP	Kevin Cooney (12 yrs: 394-282-4)	NR	21
22	Providence	.49-16	.754	DNP	Charlie Hickey (3 yrs: 106-61-1)	NR	22
23	Arkansas	.42-23	.646	DNP	Norm DeBriyn (30 yrs: 1075-565-6)	22	23
24	Houston	.40-24	.625	DNP	Rayner Noble (5 yrs: 169-129)	24	24
25	Nebraska	.42-18	.700	DNP	Dave Van Horn (5 yrs: 172-103)	NR	25

College World Series

CWS Seeds: 1. Miami-FL (46-13); **2.** Florida St. (53-12); **3.** CS-Fullerton (49-12); **4.** Oklahoma St. (46-19); **5.** Alabama (51-14); **6.** Stanford (48-13); **7.** Texas A&M (52-16); **8.** Rice (58-13).

Bracket One

June 11—Alabama 11 ....Oklahoma St. 3
June 11—Miami-FL 8 ....Rice 4
June 13—Miami-FL 8 ....Alabama 1
June 13—Rice 7 ....Oklahoma St. 2 (out)
June 16—Alabama 6 ....Rice 5 (out)
June 17—Miami-FL 5 ....Alabama 2 (out)

Bracket Two

June 12—Florida St. 7 ....Texas A&M 3
June 12—Stanford 9 ....CS-Fullerton 2
June 14—Stanford 10 ....Florida St. 6
June 14—CS-Fullerton 4 ....Texas A&M 2 (out)
June 16—Florida St. 7 ....CS-Fullerton 2 (out)
June 17—Florida St. 8 ....Stanford 6
June 18—Florida St. 14 ....Stanford 11, 13-inn (out)

CWS Championship Game

Saturday, June 19, at Rosenblatt Stadium in Omaha.

	1 2 3	4 5 6	7 8 9	R H E
Florida St.	0 1 1	0 0 0	2 1 0	—5 7 1
Miami-FL	0 1 0	0 5 0	0 0 X	—6 8 2

Win: UM– Alex Santos (13-3). **Loss:** FSU– Blair Varnes (11-2). **Save:** UM– Michael Neu (16). **Starters:** UM– Santos; FSU– Varnes. **Strikeouts:** UM– Santos 4, Vince Vazquez and Neu 2; FSU– Chris Whidden 2, Varnes 1.
2B: UM– Kevin Brown. **3B:** FSU– Ryan Barthelemy. **HR:** UM– Brown (22); FSU– Sam Scott (12). **SB:** UM– Bobby Hill (52).
Attendance: 23,563. **Time:** 2:50.

Most Outstanding Player

Marshall McDougall, Florida St., 2B

Avg	AB	R	H	HR	RBI
.385	26	6	10	3	8

All-Tournament Team

C– Jeremiah Klosterman, Florida St.; **1B–** John Gall, Stanford; **2B–** Marshall McDougall, Florida St.; **3B–** Lale Esquivel, Miami; **SS–** Bobby Hill, Miami; **OF–** Matt Diaz, Florida St.; G.W. Keller, Alabama; Manny Crespo, Miami; **DH–** Sam Scott, Florida St.; **P–** Chris Chavez, Florida St.; Michael Neu, Miami.

Annual Awards

Chosen by *Baseball America*, *Collegiate Baseball*, National Collegiate Baseball Writers Association and the American Baseball Coaches Association. The Rotary Smith award is chosen by college sports information directors.

Player of the Year

Jason Jennings, Baylor ....*BA*, *CB*, ABCA, Smith, Howser (NCBWA)

Coaches of the Year

Jim Morris, Miami ....ABCA, *CB*
Wayne Graham, Rice ....*BA*

Consensus All-America Team

NCAA Division I players cited most frequently by the following four selectors: the American Baseball Coaches Assn. (ABCA), *Baseball America, Collegiate Baseball* and the National Collegiate Baseball Writers Assn. (NCBWA).

First Team

Pos		Cl	Avg	HR	RBI
C	Josh Bard, Texas Tech	Jr.	.353	13	92
1B	Ken Harvey, Nebraska	Jr.	.478	23	86
2B	Marshall McDougall, Fla. St.	Jr.	.419	28	106
SS	Willie Bloomquist, Arizona St.	Jr.	.394	10	84
3B	Xavier Nady, California	So.	.374	23	62
OF	Matt Cepicky, SW Mo. St.	Jr.	.414	30	100
OF	Keith Reed, Providence	Jr.	.398	17	79
OF	Spencer Oborn, CS-Fullerton	Jr.	.395	14	82
UT	Jason Jennings, Baylor	Jr.	.386	17	68

		Cl	W-L	Sv	ERA
P	Ben Sheets, NE Louisiana	Jr.	14-1	2	3.11
P	Barry Zito, USC	Jr.	12-3	0	3.28
P	Mario Ramos, Rice	Jr.	13-3	2	2.51
P	Jay Gehrke, Pepperdine	Jr.	1-1	18	0.86
P	Todd Moser, Fla. Atlantic	Sr.	15-1	0	2.34
P	Jason Young, Stanford	So.	12-3	0	3.43

Second Team

Pos		Cl	Avg	HR	RBI
C	Casey Dunn, Auburn	Sr.	.379	16	86
1B	Ben Broussard, McNeese St.	Sr.	.427	27	91
2B	James Jurries, Tulane	Fr.	.374	20	79
SS	Andy Phillips, Alabama	Sr.	.393	22	66
3B	Taggert Bozied, San Francisco	So.	.412	30	82
OF	Daylan Holt, Texas A&M	So.	.341	34	105
OF	Larry Bigbie, Ball St.	Jr.	.419	17	54
OF	Lamont Matthews, Oklahoma St.	Jr.	.384	30	105
UT	Mike Dwyer, Richmond	Sr.	.412	21	78

		Cl	W-L	Sv	ERA
P	Phil Devey, SW Louisiana	Jr.	10-1	0	3.14
P	Brent Schoening, Auburn	Jr.	13-1	0	3.32
P	Mike MacDougal, W. Forest	Jr.	13-3	0	2.62
P	Nick Stocks, Florida St.	So.	13-2	0	3.25
P	Michael Neu, Miami-FL	Jr.	3-1	16	2.94
P	Marc DesRoches, Providence	Sr.	14-2	1	2.86
P	Justin Fry, Ohio St.	Sr.	11-2	0	3.70

NCAA Division I Leaders

Batting
Average

(At least 75 AB)	Cl	Gm	AB	H	Avg
Ken Harvey, Nebraska	Jr.	57	224	107	.478
Hunter Bledsoe, Vanderbilt	Sr.	54	207	95	.459
B.J. Barns, Duquesne	Jr.	56	195	89	.456
Jim Sweeney, Holy Cross	So.	30	116	52	.448
Joe Zeccardi, LIU-Brooklyn	Sr.	43	153	68	.444
David Lohman, Hofstra	Sr.	34	113	50	.442
Steve Tomshack, UMBC	Jr.	35	132	58	.439
Joe Francisco, Wagner	Sr.	42	163	71	.436
Brian Thrash, UMBC	Sr.	35	124	54	.435
Ben Johnstone, Yale	Jr.	40	151	65	.430
Sean McGowan, BC	Sr.	47	179	77	.430

Home Runs (per game)

(At least 15 HR)	Cl	Gm	HR	Avg
Taggert Bozied, San Fran.	So.	56	30	0.54
Matt Cepicky, SW Mo. St.	Jr.	56	30	0.54
Sean McGowan, BC	Sr.	47	25	0.53
Daylan Holt, Texas A&M.	So.	70	34	0.49
Ben Broussard, McNeese St.	Sr.	56	27	0.48
Kelly Eddlemon, Sam Houston	Jr.	55	26	0.47
Don Price, Nevada	Jr.	58	27	0.47
Bill Scott, UCLA	So.	61	28	0.46
Lamont Matthews, Okla. St.	Jr.	67	30	0.45
Jon Hale, SW Mo. St.	Sr.	56	25	0.45

Runs Batted In (per game)

(At least 50 RBI)	Cl	Gm	RBI	Avg
Matt Cepicky, SW Mo. St.	Jr.	56	100	1.79
Kelly Eddlemon, Sam Houston	Jr.	55	95	1.73
Jon Weber, Texas Tech	Jr.	50	84	1.68
Ben Broussard, McNeese St.	Sr.	56	91	1.63
Josh Bard, Texas Tech	Jr.	58	92	1.59
Lamont Matthews, Okla. St.	Jr.	67	105	1.57
Don Price, Nevada	Jr.	58	89	1.53
Lyle Overbay, Nevada	Sr.	58	88	1.52
Ken Harvey, Nebraska	Jr.	57	86	1.51
Daylan Holt, Texas A&M	So.	70	105	1.50

Stolen Bases

(At least 25)	Cl	Gm	SB	SBA	Avg
Brian Roberts, S. Carolina	Jr.	58	67	79	1.16
T Riley, James Madison	Jr.	51	54	61	1.06
Tony Coleman, Grambling	Sr.	42	39	45	0.93
Chris Morris, Citadel	So.	59	52	63	0.88
Tim Boeth, Central Fla.	Sr.	53	45	54	0.85
Billy Colome, Coll. of Charles.	Sr.	55	46	56	0.84
Bobby Hill, Miami-FL	Jr.	63	52	67	0.83
Jeff Stallings, Oral Roberts	Jr.	61	49	55	0.80
Shawn Pearson, Old Dominion	Sr.	54	43	49	0.80
Rich Thompson, James Madison	So.	44	35	42	0.80

Pitching
Earned Run Avg.

(At least 50 inn.)	Cl	Gm	IP	ERA
Derrick DePriest, N. Carolina	Jr.	36	73.2	1.71
Jeremy Sanders, Eastern Ill.	Jr.	34	71.2	1.76
Brian Gismonde, Monmouth	So.	26	55.0	1.96
Greg Montalbano, Northeastern	Jr.	11	64.2	2.09
Chris Chavez, Florida St.	Sr.	36	87.0	2.17
Mark Short, Pacific	Jr.	31	77.2	2.20
David Mittauer, Fla. Int'l	So.	17	88.1	2.24
Kenny Baugh, Rice	So.	20	111.2	2.26
Adam Poturnicki, Cent. Conn.	Sr.	18	89.0	2.33
Todd Moser, Fla. Atlantic	Sr.	19	103.2	2.34

Wins

	Cl	Gm	IP	W-L
Todd Moser, Fla. Atlantic	Sr.	19	103.2	15-1
Jeff Nichols, Rice	Jr.	25	137.2	15-4
Ben Sheets, Northeast La.	Jr.	18	115.2	14-1
Marc DesRoches, Providence	Sr.	17	103.2	14-2
Brent Schoening, Auburn	Jr.	21	138.1	13-1
Ron Deubel, Coastal Car.	Sr.	23	130.2	13-2
Jason Jennings, Baylor	Jr.	22	146.2	13-2
Nick Stocks, Florida St.	So.	21	127.1	13-2
Jared Berkowitz, Tulane	Jr.	19	123.2	13-3
Mario Ramos, Rice	Jr.	25	154.0	13-3
Alex Santos, Miami-FL	Jr.	20	122.0	13-3
Mike MacDougal, Wake Forest	Jr.	17	120.1	13-3
Kurt Ainsworth, LSU	So.	22	130.1	13-6
Hayden Gliemmo, Auburn	So.	21	123.1	13-7

Strikeouts (per 9 inn.)

(At least 50 inn.)	Cl	IP	SO	Avg
Michael Neu, Miami-FL	Jr.	67.1	110	14.7
Brian Wiley, Citadel	Sr.	93.1	150	14.5
Harold Eckert, Fla. Int'l	Sr.	74.2	112	13.5
Rick Cercy, Morehead St.	Sr.	63.1	92	13.1
Barry Zito, USC	Jr.	112.2	154	12.3
Ben Sheets, Northeast La.	Jr.	115.2	158	12.3
Scott Martin, Cent. Conn.	Sr.	76.2	103	12.1
Dan Jackson, Fla. Atlantic	Jr.	95.2	126	11.9
Jesse Kurtz-Nicholl, Rice	Sr.	76.0	100	11.8
Casey Burns, Richmond	Jr.	95.1	124	11.7

Saves

	Cl	IP	ERA	Saves
Jay Gehrke, Pepperdine	Jr.	31.1	0.86	18
Marc Bluma, Wichita St.	Sr.	37.0	1.70	17
Brandon Belanger, Tulane	Jr.	66.0	2.45	16
Michael Neu, Miami-FL	Jr.	67.1	2.94	16
Dan Adams, Kent	Jr.	31.2	1.99	15
Mark Squire, Wright St.	Sr.	36.1	3.22	15
Steve Kent, Florida Int'l	Jr.	26.0	0.69	13
Kit Kadlec, Coastal Car.	Jr.	45.0	2.53	13
Brian Gismonde, Monmouth	So.	55.0	1.96	12
Five tied with 11 each.				

Other College World Series

Participants' final records in parentheses.

NCAA Div. II
at Montgomery, Ala. (May 22-29)

Participants: Adelphi, N.Y. (31-15); Ashland, Ohio (45-14); Cal State-Chico (46-17); Carson-Newman, Tenn. (42-12-2); Kennesaw St., Ga. (46-12); North Alabama (44-10); Rockhurst, Mo. (34-16); West Virginia St. (33-9).

Championship: Cal State-Chico def. Kennesaw St., 11-5.

NCAA Div. III
at Salem, Va. (May 28-June 1)

Participants: Aurora, Ill. (38-6); Brandeis, Mass. (33-4); California Lutheran (31-12); Cortland St., N.Y. (35-8); Marietta, Ohio (49-6); N.C. Wesleyan (37-9); St. Thomas, Minn. (39-5); William Paterson, N.J. (29-12).

Championship: N.C. Wesleyan def. St. Thomas, 1-0.

NAIA
at Jupiter, Fla. (May 24-31)

Participants: Albertson, Idaho (45-17); Bellevue, Neb. (60-9); Birmingham Southern (48-16); Culver-Stockton, Mo. (35-17); Dallas Baptist (46-18); Dominican, N.Y. (36-20); Embry-Riddle, Fla. (44-11-1); Indiana Tech. (50-21); Lewis-Clark, Idaho (53-13); Oklahoma City (56-13).

Championship: Lewis-Clark def. Albertson, 7-2.

NJCAA Div. I
at Grand Junction, Colo. (May 29-June 4)

Participants: Briarcliffe, N.Y. (31-19); Central Arizona (45-17); Garden City CC, Kan. (32-24); Grayson County, Tex. (50-13); Manatee CC, Fla. (51-8); Muscatine CC, Iowa (39-16); San Jacinto, Tex. (42-11); Seminole St., Okla. (56-6); Volunteer St. CC, Tenn. (52-11); Wallace St. CC, Al., (45-15).

Championship: Grayson County def. San Jacinto, 12-7.

MLB Amateur Draft

First round selections at the 35th Amateur Draft held June 2-3, 1999 in New York.

First Round

No		Pos
1	Tampa Bay . Josh Hamilton, Athens Drive HS, Raleigh, N.C.	OF-LHP
2	Florida . . . . Josh Beckett, Spring (Tex.) HS	RHP
3	Detroit . . . . .Eric Munson, USC	C
4	Arizona . . . . . . .Corey Myers, Desert Vista HS, Scottsdale, Ariz.	SS
5	Minnesota . . . . . .Brandon Garbe, Moses Lake (Wash.) HS	OF
6	Montreal . . . . . .Josh Girdley, Jasper (Tex.) HS	LHP
7	Kansas City . . . . .Kyle Snyder, UNC	RHP
8	Pittsburgh . . .Robert Bradley, Wellington (Fla.) Comm. HS	RHP
9	Oakland . . . . .Barry Zito, USC	LHP
10	Milwaukee . . . . .Ben Sheets, NE Louisiana	RHP
11	Seattle . . . . . .Ryan Christianson, Arlington HS, Riverside, Calif.	C
12	Philadelphia . . . . .Brett Myers, Englewood HS, Jacksonville, Fla.	RHP
13	Baltimore . . . . .Mike Paradis, Clemson	RHP
14	Cincinnati . . .Ty Howington, Hudson's Bay HS Vancouver, Wash.	LHP
15	Chicago-AL . . . . Jason Stumm, Centralia (Wash.) HS	RHP

No		Pos
16	Colorado . . . . .Jason Jennings, Baylor	RHP
17	a-Boston . . .Eric Asadoorian, Northbridge HS Whitinsville, Mass.	OF
18	b-Baltimore . . . . . . .Richard Stahl, Newton HS Covington, Ga.	LHP
19	Toronto . . . . .Alexis Rios, San Pedro Martin HS Guaynabo, Puerto Rico	3B
20	c-San Diego .Vince Faison, Toombs County HS Lyons, Ga.	OF
21	d-Baltimore . . . . .Larry Bigbie, Ball St.	OF
22	e-Chicago-AL . . . . .Matt Ginter, Mississippi St.	RHP
23	f-Baltimore . . . . .Keith Reed, Providence	OF
24	San Francisco . . . . .Kurt Ainsworth, LSU	RHP
25	g-Kansas City .Mike MacDougal, Wake Forest	RHP
26	Chicago-NL . . . . .Ben Christensen, Wichita St.	RHP
27	New York-AL . . . . .David Walling, Arkansas	RHP
28	San Diego . . . . . . .Gerik Baxter, Woodway HS Edmonds, Wash.	RHP
29	h-San Diego . . . . . .Omar Ortiz, Texas Pan-Am	RHP
30	i-St. Louis . . . . .Chance Caple, Texas A&M	RHP

Acquired picks: a–from Anaheim for signing Mo Vaughn; **b**–from St. Louis for signing Eric Davis; **c**–from Los Angeles for signing Kevin Brown; **d**–from Texas for signing Rafael Palmeiro; **e**–from N.Y. Mets for signing Robin Ventura; **f**–from Cleveland for signing Roberto Alomar; **g**–from Boston for signing Jose Offerman; **h**–from Houston for signing Ken Caminiti; **i**–from Atlanta for signing Brian Jordan.

Omaha: The Old and New

by Dave Ryan

History and the College World Series go hand in hand. This year marked the Golden Anniversary of the CWS in Nebraska, 50 years of memories celebrating some of the sport's all-time great players and teams.

The College World Series belongs to the people of Omaha and the NCAA responded to their loyalties by signing a new, richly deserved multi-year contract extension. In turn, the city stepped up to the plate and continued to fix up Rosenblatt Stadium. The newly renovated $4.5 million entrance plaza is a perfect indication that Omaha had no intentions of losing the event. A new majestic statue called "The Road to Omaha" now greets you at the entrance of the stadium and perfectly symbolizes the Series, aptly depicting a team celebrating a run being scored. The expression on the players' faces is priceless, describing the sheer joy of winning in Omaha.

For the first time in Jim Morris' six years at the helm of Miami's super power, it was the Hurricanes who had that look of the players in the statue, that of national champions. Morris has led Miami to the World Series in each of his six seasons but emerged as champion for the first time this year after a thrilling 6-5 victory over Florida St.

Along the way, many more fascinating stories came into play. Cal State Fullerton, cheered on by alum Kevin Costner, overcame the suspension of four key players during the Super Regionals and an exhausting road trip but still managed to have a good showing in Omaha. The Titans spent just one night at home out of 25 but were still one of the final six teams.

Rice University had never won a College World Series game in school history but, led by veteran coach Wayne Graham, the Owls took care of that with a 7-2 win over Oklahoma St., before finally bowing out to Alabama in a gut wrenching extra inning homer fest. The team's shortstop and emotional leader Damon Thames turned down the New York Yankees after being drafted last year.

"All I wanted was a chance to come here, to play at Rosenblatt," said Thames. "That's why I came back to Rice." His decision paid off as he belted two homers in that loss to 'Bama, including a three-run shot in the eighth off the left field foul pole to briefly give the Owls the lead. Despite the loss, Thames said after the game, "You see? It was all worth it. These are memories I'll have with me forever."

Injury is defined as any hurt or harm, physical or moral. But there's something about the opportunity to play in Omaha that makes players forget about the hurt. Stanford's Edmund Muth overcame a severe bout with viral meningitis, which caused him to be hospitalized four times during the season, to lead the Cardinal as the team's starting center fielder in the CWS.

No one in Omaha will forget Alabama's classy shortstop Andy Phillips. Badly hobbled by torn ligaments in his knee, Phillips gutted out the Series, keeping a 36-game htting streak until his final game, and running the bases as if he were 100 percent.

And, of course, there was Florida State freshman pitcher Blair Varnes. Varnes was supposed to be a starter in Omaha but after his team beat Auburn to advance to the CWS, he piled on to celebrate, and in the process, tore his left ACL. But when FSU edged Stanford in a dramatic extra inning slugfest for a birth in the finals, coach Mike Martin had no where else to turn. All of his starters and most of his bullpen were spent, and the championship game was the next day against powerful and well-rested Miami.

Varnes answered the call with six gutsy innings that Saturday afternoon. He gave up six earned runs and the Noles lost the title game, but that wasn't the point. Facing reconstructive surgery exactly five days later, Varnes went to the mound and pitched with everything he had. He was reaching for the feeling those fictional players on the statue will forever have. He will go down in CWS history as one of the all-time great heroes, making Omaha and the College World Series once again an unforgettable experience. ∎

Dave Ryan is an in-the-stands reporter for ESPN's college baseball coverage.

Minor League Triple-A Final Standings
International League

North Division	W	L	Pct	GB
Scranton-WB (Phillies)	78	66	.542	—
Pawtucket (Red Sox)	76	68	.528	2
Syracuse (Blue Jays)	73	71	.507	5
Buffalo (Indians)	72	72	.500	6
Rochester (Orioles)	61	83	.424	17
Ottawa (Expos)	59	85	.410	19

South Division	W	L	Pct	GB
Durham (Devil Rays)	83	60	.580	—
Charlotte (White Sox)	82	62	.569	1½
Norfolk (Mets)	77	63	.550	4½
Richmond (Braves)	64	78	.451	18½

West Division	W	L	Pct	GB
Columbus (Yankees)	83	58	.589	—
Indianapolis (Reds)	75	69	.521	9½
Louisville (Brewers)	63	81	.438	21½
Toledo (Tigers)	57	87	.396	27½

Playoffs
Division Finals (Best-of-Five)

Charlotte 3 .... Scranton-WB 2
Durham 3 .... Columbus 0

Championship (Best-of-Five)

Charlotte vs. Durham

Sept. 13	Durham, 3-1	at Durham
Sept. 14	Charlotte, 7-3	at Durham
Sept. 16	Charlotte, 6-3	at Charlotte
Sept. 17	Charlotte, 2-1	at Charlotte

Charlotte wins series, 3-1

Pacific Coast League

American Conference

East Division	W	L	Pct	GB
Oklahoma (Rangers)	83	59	.585	—
Nashville (Pirates)	80	60	.571	2
Memphis (Cardinals)	74	64	.536	7
New Orleans (Astros)	55	85	.393	27

Central Division	W	L	Pct	GB
Omaha (Royals)	81	60	.574	—
Colorado Springs (Rockies)	66	73	.475	14
Albuquerque (Dodgers)	65	74	.468	15
Iowa (Cubs)	65	76	.461	16

Pacific Conference

North Division	W	L	Pct	GB
Vancouver (Athletics)	84	58	.592	—
Tacoma (Mariners)	69	70	.496	13½
Edmonton (Angels)	65	74	.468	17½
Calgary (Marlins)	57	82	.410	25½

South Division	W	L	Pct	GB
Salt Lake (Twins)	73	68	.518	—
Fresno (Giants)	73	69	.514	½
Las Vegas (Padres)	67	75	.472	6½
Tucson (D'Backs)	66	76	.465	7½

Playoffs
Division Finals (Best-of-Five)

Vancouver 3 .... Salt Lake 2
Oklahoma 3 .... Omaha 1

Championship (Best-of-Five)

Vancouver vs. Oklahoma

Sept. 14	Vancouver, 2-0	at Oklahoma
Sept. 15	Oklahoma, 1-0	at Oklahoma
Sept. 16	Vancouver, 5-4	at Vancouver
Sept. 17	Vancouver, 5-3	at Vancouver

Vancouver wins series, 3-1

1999 Minor League All-Star Team

As presented by *Baseball America* and covering all Minor League levels.

Pos.	Name, Team (Major Affiliate)
C	Ben Petrick, Colorado Springs (Rockies)
1B	Steve Cox, Durham (Devil Rays)
2B	Adam Kennedy, Memphis (Cardinals)
3B	Adam Piatt, Midland (Athletics)
SS	Rafael Furcal, Myrtle (Braves)
OF	Ching-Feng Chen, San Bern. (Dodgers)
OF	Corey Patterson, Lansing (Cubs)
OF	Vernon Wells, Syracuse (Blue Jays)
DH	Jack Cust, High Desert (D'Backs)
SP	Rich Ankiel*, Memphis (Cardinals)
SP	Eric Gagne, San Antonio (Dodgers)
SP	Tomokazu Ohka, Pawtucket (Red Sox)
SP	Matt Riley, Bowie (Orioles)
RP	Francisco Cordero, Jacksonville (Tigers)

*Player of the Year

Triple-A World Series

The Triple-A World Series was introduced in 1998 and will continue at least through the year 2000. Played between the champions of the International and Pacific Coast leagues, it is the first time in history that there is a single Triple-A champion on a continuing basis. All games are played at Cashman Field in Las Vegas.

Vancouver vs. Charlotte
(Best-of-Five)

Sept. 20	Charlotte, 6-5
Sept. 21	Vancouver, 5-4
Sept. 23	Charlotte, 4-2
Sept. 24	Vancouver, 9-7
Sept. 25	Vancouver, 16-2

Vancouver wins series, 3-2

MVP: Terrance Long, OF, Vancouver

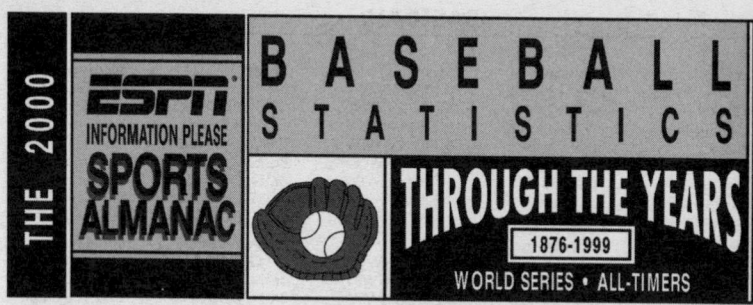

THE 2000 ESPN INFORMATION PLEASE SPORTS ALMANAC

BASEBALL STATISTICS

THROUGH THE YEARS
1876-1999
WORLD SERIES • ALL-TIMERS

SEC B

PAGE 101

The World Series

The World Series began in 1903 when Pittsburgh of the older National League (founded in 1876) invited Boston of the American League (founded in 1901) to play a best-of-9 game series to determine which of the two league champions was the best. Boston was the surprise winner, 5 games to 3. The 1904 NL champion New York Giants refused to play Boston the following year, so there was no Series. Giants' owner John T. Brush and his manager John McGraw both despised AL president Ban Johnson and considered the junior circuit to be a minor league. By the following year, however, Brush and Johnson had smoothed out their differences and the Giants agreed to play Philadelphia in a best-of-7 game series. Since then the World Series has been a best-of-7 format, except from 1919-21 when it returned to best-of-9.

After surviving two world wars and an earthquake in 1989, the World Series was cancelled for only the second time in 1994 when the players went out on strike Aug. 12 to protest the owners' call for revenue sharing and a salary cap. On Sept. 14, with no hope of reaching a labor agreement to end the 34-day strike, the owners called off the remainder of the regular season and the entire postseason. The strike ended after 232 days on Mar. 31, 1995.

In the chart below, the National League teams are listed in CAPITAL letters. Also, each World Series champion's wins and losses are noted in parentheses after the Series score in games.

Multiple champions: New York Yankees (25); Philadelphia-Oakland A's and St. Louis Cardinals (9); Brooklyn-Los Angeles Dodgers (6); Boston Red Sox, Cincinnati Reds, New York-San Francisco Giants and Pittsburgh Pirates (5); Detroit Tigers (4); Baltimore Orioles, Boston-Milwaukee-Atlanta Braves and Washington Senators-Minnesota Twins (3); Chicago Cubs, Chicago White Sox, Cleveland Indians, New York Mets and Toronto Blue Jays (2).

Year	Winner	Manager	Series	Loser	Manager
1903	Boston Red Sox	Jimmy Collins	5-3 (LWLLWWWW)	PITTSBURGH	Fred Clarke
1904	Not held				
1905	NY GIANTS	John McGraw	4-1 (WLWWW)	Philadelphia A's	Connie Mack
1906	Chicago White Sox	Fielder Jones	4-2 (WLWLWW)	CHICAGO CUBS	Frank Chance
1907	CHICAGO CUBS	Frank Chance	4-0-1 (TWWWW)	Detroit	Hughie Jennings
1908	CHICAGO CUBS	Frank Chance	4-1 (WWLWW)	Detroit	Hughie Jennings
1909	PITTSBURGH	Fred Clarke	4-3 (WLWLWLW)	Detroit	Hughie Jennings
1910	Philadelphia A's	Connie Mack	4-1 (WWWLW)	CHICAGO CUBS	Frank Chance
1911	Philadelphia A's	Connie Mack	4-2 (LWWWLW)	NY GIANTS	John McGraw
1912	Boston Red Sox	Jake Stahl	4-3-1 (WTLWWLLW)	NY GIANTS	John McGraw
1913	Philadelphia A's	Connie Mack	4-1 (WLWWW)	NY GIANTS	John McGraw
1914	BOSTON BRAVES	George Stallings	4-0	Philadelphia A's	Connie Mack
1915	Boston Red Sox	Bill Carrigan	4-1 (LWWWW)	PHILA. PHILLIES	Pat Moran
1916	Boston Red Sox	Bill Carrigan	4-1 (WWLWW)	BROOKLYN	Wilbert Robinson
1917	Chicago White Sox	Pants Rowland	4-2 (WWLLWW)	NY GIANTS	John McGraw
1918	Boston Red Sox	Ed Barrow	4-2 (WLWWLW)	CHICAGO CUBS	Fred Mitchell
1919	CINCINNATI	Pat Moran	5-3 (WWLWWLLW)	Chicago White Sox	Kid Gleason
1920	Cleveland	Tris Speaker	5-2 (WLLWWWW)	BROOKLYN	Wilbert Robinson
1921	NY GIANTS	John McGraw	5-3 (LLWWLWWW)	NY Yankees	Miller Huggins
1922	NY GIANTS	John McGraw	4-0-1 (WTWWW)	NY Yankees	Miller Huggins
1923	NY Yankees	Miller Huggins	4-2 (LWLWWW)	NY GIANTS	John McGraw
1924	Washington	Bucky Harris	4-3 (LWLWWLW)	NY GIANTS	John McGraw
1925	PITTSBURGH	Bill McKechnie	4-3 (LWLLWWW)	Washington	Bucky Harris
1926	ST.L. CARDINALS	Rogers Hornsby	4-3 (LWWLLWW)	NY Yankees	Miller Huggins
1927	NY Yankees	Miller Huggins	4-0	PITTSBURGH	Donie Bush
1928	NY Yankees	Miller Huggins	4-0	ST.L. CARDINALS	Bill McKechnie
1929	Philadelphia A's	Connie Mack	4-1 (WWLWW)	CHICAGO CUBS	Joe McCarthy
1930	Philadelphia A's	Connie Mack	4-2 (WWLLWW)	ST.L. CARDINALS	Gabby Street
1931	ST.L. CARDINALS	Gabby Street	4-3 (LWWLWLW)	Philadelphia A's	Connie Mack
1932	NY Yankees	Joe McCarthy	4-0	CHICAGO CUBS	Charlie Grimm
1933	NY GIANTS	Bill Terry	4-1 (WWLWW)	Washington	Joe Cronin
1934	ST.L. CARDINALS	Frankie Frisch	4-3 (WLWLLWW)	Detroit	Mickey Cochrane
1935	Detroit	Mickey Cochrane	4-2 (LWWWLW)	CHICAGO CUBS	Charlie Grimm
1936	NY Yankees	Joe McCarthy	4-2 (WLWWLW)	NY GIANTS	Bill Terry
1937	NY Yankees	Joe McCarthy	4-1 (WWWLW)	NY GIANTS	Bill Terry
1938	NY Yankees	Joe McCarthy	4-0	CHICAGO CUBS	Gabby Hartnett
1939	NY Yankees	Joe McCarthy	4-0	CINCINNATI	Bill McKechnie
1940	CINCINNATI	Bill McKechnie	4-3 (LWLWLWW)	Detroit	Del Baker
1941	NY Yankees	Joe McCarthy	4-1 (WLWWW)	BKLN. DODGERS	Leo Durocher

Year	Winner	Manager	Series	Loser	Manager
1942	ST.L. CARDINALS	Billy Southworth	4-1 (LWWWW)	NY Yankees	Joe McCarthy
1943	NY Yankees	Joe McCarthy	4-1 (WLWWW)	ST.L. CARDINALS	Billy Southworth
1944	ST.L. CARDINALS	Billy Southworth	4-2 (LWLWWW)	St. Louis Browns	Luke Sewell
1945	Detroit	Steve O'Neill	4-3 (LWLWWLW)	CHICAGO CUBS	Charlie Grimm
1946	ST.L. CARDINALS	Eddie Dyer	4-3 (LWLWLWW)	Boston Red Sox	Joe Cronin
1947	NY Yankees	Bucky Harris	4-3 (WWLLWLW)	BKLN. DODGERS	Burt Shotton
1948	Cleveland	Lou Boudreau	4-2 (LWWWLW)	BOSTON BRAVES	Billy Southworth
1949	NY Yankees	Casey Stengel	4-1 (WLWWW)	BKLN. DODGERS	Burt Shotton
1950	NY Yankees	Casey Stengel	4-0	PHILA. PHILLIES	Eddie Sawyer
1951	NY Yankees	Casey Stengel	4-2 (LWWLWW)	NY GIANTS	Leo Durocher
1952	NY Yankees	Casey Stengel	4-3 (LWLWLWW)	BKLN. DODGERS	Charlie Dressen
1953	NY Yankees	Casey Stengel	4-2 (WWLLWW)	BKLN. DODGERS	Charlie Dressen
1954	NY GIANTS	Leo Durocher	4-0	Cleveland	Al Lopez
1955	BKLN. DODGERS	Walter Alston	4-3 (LLWWWLW)	NY Yankees	Casey Stengel
1956	NY Yankees	Casey Stengel	4-3 (LLWWWLW)	BKLN. DODGERS	Walter Alston
1957	MILW. BRAVES	Fred Haney	4-3 (LWWWLLW)	NY Yankees	Casey Stengel
1958	NY Yankees	Casey Stengel	4-3 (LLWLWWW)	MILW. BRAVES	Fred Haney
1959	LA DODGERS	Walter Alston	4-2 (LWWWLW)	Chicago White Sox	Al Lopez
1960	PITTSBURGH	Danny Murtaugh	4-3 (WLLWWLW)	NY Yankees	Casey Stengel
1961	NY Yankees	Ralph Houk	4-1 (WLWWW)	CINCINNATI	Fred Hutchinson
1962	NY Yankees	Ralph Houk	4-3 (WLWLWLW)	SF GIANTS	Alvin Dark
1963	LA DODGERS	Walter Alston	4-0	NY Yankees	Ralph Houk
1964	ST.L. CARDINALS	Johnny Keane	4-3 (WLLWWLW)	NY Yankees	Yogi Berra
1965	LA DODGERS	Walter Alston	4-3 (LLWWWLW)	Minnesota	Sam Mele
1966	Baltimore	Hank Bauer	4-0	LA DODGERS	Walter Alston
1967	ST.L. CARDINALS	Red Schoendienst	4-3 (WLWWLLW)	Boston Red Sox	Dick Williams
1968	Detroit	Mayo Smith	4-3 (LWLLWWW)	ST.L. CARDINALS	Red Schoendienst
1969	NY METS	Gil Hodges	4-1 (LWWWW)	Baltimore	Earl Weaver
1970	Baltimore	Earl Weaver	4-1 (WWWLW)	CINCINNATI	Sparky Anderson
1971	PITTSBURGH	Danny Murtaugh	4-3 (LLWWWLW)	Baltimore	Earl Weaver
1972	Oakland A's	Dick Williams	4-3 (WWLWLLW)	CINCINNATI	Sparky Anderson
1973	Oakland A's	Dick Williams	4-3 (WLWLWLW)	NY METS	Yogi Berra
1974	Oakland A's	Alvin Dark	4-1 (WLWWW)	LA DODGERS	Walter Alston
1975	CINCINNATI	Sparky Anderson	4-3 (LWWLWLW)	Boston Red Sox	Darrell Johnson
1976	CINCINNATI	Sparky Anderson	4-0	NY Yankees	Billy Martin
1977	NY Yankees	Billy Martin	4-2 (WLWLW)	LA DODGERS	Tommy Lasorda
1978	NY Yankees	Bob Lemon	4-2 (LLWWWW)	LA DODGERS	Tommy Lasorda
1979	PITTSBURGH	Chuck Tanner	4-3 (LWLLWWW)	Baltimore	Earl Weaver
1980	PHILA. PHILLIES	Dallas Green	4-2 (WWLLWW)	Kansas City	Jim Frey
1981	LA DODGERS	Tommy Lasorda	4-2 (LLWWWW)	NY Yankees	Bob Lemon
1982	ST.L. CARDINALS	Whitey Herzog	4-3 (LWWLLWW)	Milwaukee Brewers	Harvey Kuenn
1983	Baltimore	Joe Altobelli	4-1 (LWWWW)	PHILA. PHILLIES	Paul Owens
1984	Detroit	Sparky Anderson	4-1 (WWLWW)	SAN DIEGO	Dick Williams
1985	Kansas City	Dick Howser	4-3 (LLWLWWW)	ST.L. CARDINALS	Whitey Herzog
1986	NY METS	Davey Johnson	4-3 (LLWWLWW)	Boston Red Sox	John McNamara
1987	Minnesota	Tom Kelly	4-3 (WWLLLWW)	ST.L. CARDINALS	Whitey Herzog
1988	LA DODGERS	Tommy Lasorda	4-1 (WWLWW)	Oakland A's	Tony La Russa
1989	Oakland A's	Tony La Russa	4-0	SF GIANTS	Roger Craig
1990	CINCINNATI	Lou Piniella	4-0	Oakland A's	Tony La Russa
1991	Minnesota	Tom Kelly	4-3 (WWLLLWW)	ATLANTA BRAVES	Bobby Cox
1992	Toronto	Cito Gaston	4-2 (WLWWLW)	ATLANTA BRAVES	Bobby Cox
1993	Toronto	Cito Gaston	4-2 (WLWWLW)	PHILA. PHILLIES	Jim Fregosi
1994	Not held				
1995	ATLANTA BRAVES	Bobby Cox	4-2 (WWWLW)	Cleveland	Mike Hargrove
1996	New York Yankees	Joe Torre	4-2 (LLWWWW)	ATLANTA BRAVES	Bobby Cox
1997	FLORIDA MARLINS	Jim Leyland	4-3 (WLWLWLW)	Cleveland	Mike Hargrove
1998	New York Yankees	Joe Torre	4-0	SAN DIEGO	Bruce Bochy
1999	New York Yankees	Joe Torre	4-0	ATLANTA BRAVES	Bobby Cox

Most Valuable Players

Currently selected by media panel made up of representatives of CBS Sports, CBS Radio, AP, UPI, and World Series official scorers. Presented by *Sport* magazine from 1955-88 and by Major League Baseball since 1989. Winner who did not play for World Series champions is in **bold** type.

Multiple winners: Bob Gibson, Reggie Jackson and Sandy Koufax (2).

Year	Year	Year
1955 Johnny Podres, Bklyn, P	1960 **Bobby Richardson**, NY, 2B	1965 Sandy Koufax, LA, P
1956 Don Larsen, NY, P	1961 Whitey Ford, NY, P	1966 Frank Robinson, Bal., OF
1957 Lew Burdette, Mil., P	1962 Ralph Terry, NY, P	1967 Bob Gibson, St.L., P
1958 Bob Turley, NY, P	1963 Sandy Koufax, LA, P	1968 Mickey Lolich, Det., P
1959 Larry Sherry, LA, P	1964 Bob Gibson, St.L., P	1969 Donn Clendenon, NY, 1B

Year		Year		Year	
1970	Brooks Robinson, Bal., 3B	1981	Pedro Guerrero, LA, OF;	1990	Jose Rijo, Cin., P
1971	Roberto Clemente, Pit., OF		Ron Cey, LA, 3B;	1991	Jack Morris, Min., P
1972	Gene Tenace, Oak., C		& Steve Yeager, LA, C	1992	Pat Borders, Tor., C
1973	Reggie Jackson, Oak., OF	1982	Darrell Porter, St.L., C	1993	Paul Molitor, Tor., DH/1B/3B
1974	Rollie Fingers, Oak., P	1983	Rick Dempsey, Bal., C	1994	Series not held.
1975	Pete Rose, Cin., 3B	1984	Alan Trammell, Det., SS	1995	Tom Glavine, Atl., P
1976	Johnny Bench, Cin., C	1985	Bret Saberhagen, KC, P	1996	John Wetteland, NY, P
1977	Reggie Jackson, NY, OF	1986	Ray Knight, NY, 3B	1997	Livan Hernandez, Fla., P
1978	Bucky Dent, NY, SS	1987	Frank Viola, Min., P	1998	Scott Brosius, NY, 3B
1979	Willie Stargell, Pit., 1B	1988	Orel Hershiser, LA, P	1999	Mariano Rivera, NY, P
1980	Mike Schmidt, Phi., 3B	1989	Dave Stewart, Oak., P		

All-Time World Series Leaders
CAREER

World Series leaders through 1999. Years listed indicate number of World Series appearances.

Hitting

Games
	Yrs	Gm
Yogi Berra, NY Yankees	14	75
Mickey Mantle, NY Yankees	12	65
Elston Howard, NY Yankees-Boston	10	54
Hank Bauer, NY Yankees	9	53
Gil McDougald, NY Yankees	8	53

At Bats
	Yrs	AB
Yogi Berra, NY Yankees	14	259
Mickey Mantle, NY Yankees	12	230
Joe DiMaggio, NY Yankees	10	199
Frankie Frisch, NY Giants-St.L. Cards	8	197
Gil McDougald, NY Yankees	8	190

Batting Avg. (minimum 50 AB)
	AB	H	Avg
Pepper Martin, St.L. Cards	55	23	.418
Paul Molitor, Mil. Brewers-Tor. Blue Jays	55	23	.418
Lou Brock, St. Louis	87	34	.391
Marquis Grissom, Atl-Cle.	77	30	.390
Thurman Munson, NY Yankees	67	25	.373
George Brett, Kansas City	51	19	.373
Hank Aaron, Milw. Braves	55	20	.364

Hits
	AB	H	Avg
Yogi Berra, NY Yankees	259	71	.274
Mickey Mantle, NY Yankees	230	59	.257
Frankie Frisch, NYG-St.L. Cards	197	58	.294
Joe DiMaggio, NY Yankees	199	54	.271
Hank Bauer, NY Yankees	188	46	.245
Pee Wee Reese, Brooklyn	169	46	.272

Runs
	Gm	R
Mickey Mantle, NY Yankees	65	42
Yogi Berra, NY Yankees	75	41
Babe Ruth, Boston Red Sox-NY Yankees	41	37
Lou Gehrig, NY Yankees	34	30
Joe DiMaggio, NY Yankees	51	27

Home Runs
	AB	HR
Mickey Mantle, NY Yankees	230	18
Babe Ruth, Boston Red Sox-NY Yankees	129	15
Yogi Berra, NY Yankees	259	12
Duke Snider, Brooklyn-LA	133	11
Lou Gehrig, NY Yankees	119	10
Reggie Jackson, Oakland-NY Yankees	98	10

Runs Batted In
	Gm	RBI
Mickey Mantle, NY Yankees	65	40
Yogi Berra, NY Yankees	75	39
Lou Gehrig, NY Yankees	34	35
Babe Ruth, Boston Red Sox-NY Yankees	41	33
Joe DiMaggio, NY Yankees	51	30

World Series Appearances

In the 95 years that the World Series has been contested, American League teams have won 56 championships while National League teams have won 39.

The following teams are ranked by number of appearances through the 1999 World Series; (*) indicates AL teams.

	App	W	L	Pct.	Last Series	Last Title
NY Yankees*	36	25	11	.694	1999	1999
Bklyn/LA Dodgers	18	6	12	.333	1988	1988
NY/SF Giants	16	5	11	.313	1989	1954
St.L. Cardinals	15	9	6	.600	1987	1982
Phi/KC/Oak.A's*	14	9	5	.643	1990	1989
Chicago Cubs	10	2	8	.200	1945	1908
Boston Red Sox*	9	5	4	.556	1986	1918
Cincinnati Reds	9	5	4	.556	1990	1990
Detroit Tigers*	9	4	5	.444	1984	1984
Bos/Mil/Atl.Braves	9	3	6	.333	1999	1995
Pittsburgh Pirates	7	5	2	.714	1979	1979
St.L/Bal.Orioles*	7	3	4	.429	1983	1983
Wash/Min.Twins*	6	3	3	.500	1991	1991
Cle.Indians*	5	2	3	.400	1997	1948
Phi.Phillies	5	1	4	.200	1993	1980
Chi.White Sox*	4	2	2	.500	1959	1917
NY Mets	3	2	1	.667	1986	1986
Tor. Blue Jays*	2	2	0	1.000	1993	1993
KC Royals*	2	1	1	.500	1985	1985
SD Padres	2	0	2	.000	1998	—
Fla. Marlins	1	1	0	1.000	1997	1997
Sea/Mil.Brewers*	1	0	1	.000	1982	—

Stolen Bases
	Gm	SB
Lou Brock, St. Louis	21	14
Eddie Collins, Phi. A's-Chisox	34	14
Frank Chance, Chi. Cubs	20	10
Davey Lopes, Los Angeles	23	10
Phil Rizzuto, NY Yankees	52	10

Total Bases
	Gm	TB
Mickey Mantle, NY Yankees	65	123
Yogi Berra, NY Yankees	75	117
Babe Ruth, Boston Red Sox-NY Yankees	41	96
Lou Gehrig, NY Yankees	34	87
Joe DiMaggio, NY Yankees	51	84

Slugging Pct. (minimum 50 AB)
	AB	Pct
Reggie Jackson, Oakland-NY Yankees	98	.755
Babe Ruth, Boston Red Sox-NY Yankees	129	.744
Lou Gehrig, NY Yankees	119	.731
Al Simmons, Phi. A's-Cincinnati	73	.658
Lou Brock, St. Louis	87	.655

Pitching

Games

	Yrs	Gm
Whitey Ford, NY Yankees	11	22
Rollie Fingers, Oakland	3	16
Allie Reynolds, NY Yankees	6	15
Bob Turley, NY Yankees	5	15
Clay Carroll, Cincinnati	3	14

Wins

	Gm	W-L
Whitey Ford, NY Yankees	22	10-8
Bob Gibson, St. Louis	9	7-2
Allie Reynolds, NY Yankees	15	7-2
Red Ruffing, NY Yankees	10	7-2
Lefty Gomez, NY Yankees	7	6-0
Chief Bender, Philadelphia A's	10	6-4
Waite Hoyt, NY Yankees-Phi. A's	12	6-4

ERA (minimum 25 IP)

	Gm	IP	ERA
Jack Billingham, Cincinnati	7	25.1	0.36
Harry Brecheen, St. Louis	7	32.2	0.83
Babe Ruth, Boston Red Sox	3	31.0	0.87
Sherry Smith, Brooklyn	3	30.1	0.89
Sandy Koufax, Los Angeles	8	57.0	0.95

Saves

	Gm	IP	Sv
Rollie Fingers, Oakland	16	33.1	6
Mariano Rivera, NY Yankees	10	14.2	5
Allie Reynolds, NY Yankees	15	77.1	4
Johnny Murphy, NY Yankees	8	16.1	4
John Wetteland, NY Yankees	5	4.1	4
Eight pitchers tied with 3 each.			

Shutouts

	GS	CG	ShO
Christy Mathewson, NY Giants	11	10	4
Three Finger Brown, Chi. Cubs	7	5	3
Whitey Ford, NY Yankees	22	7	3
Seven pitchers tied with 2 each.			

Innings Pitched

	Gm	IP
Whitey Ford, NY Yankees	22	146.0
Christy Mathewson, NY Giants	11	101.2
Red Ruffing, NY Yankees	10	85.2
Chief Bender, Philadelphia A's	10	85.0
Waite Hoyt, NY Yankees-Phi. A's	12	83.2

Complete Games

	GS	CG	W-L
Christy Mathewson, NY Giants	11	10	5-5
Chief Bender, Philadelphia A's	10	9	6-4
Bob Gibson, St. Louis	9	8	7-2
Whitey Ford, NY Yankees	22	7	10-8
Red Ruffing, NY Yankees	10	7	7-2

Strikeouts

	Gm	IP	SO
Whitey Ford, NY Yankees	22	146.0	94
Bob Gibson, St. Louis	9	81.0	92
Allie Reynolds, NY Yankees	15	77.1	62
Sandy Koufax, Los Angeles	8	57.0	61
Red Ruffing, NY Yankees	10	85.2	61

Bases on Balls

	Gm	IP	BB
Whitey Ford, NY Yankees	22	146.0	34
Allie Reynolds, NY Yankees	15	77.1	32
Art Nehf, NY Giants-Chi. Cubs	12	79.0	32
Jim Palmer, Baltimore	9	64.2	31
Bob Turley, NY Yankees	15	54.0	29

Losses

	Gm	W-L
Whitey Ford, NY Yankees	22	10-8
Christy Mathewson, NY Giants	11	5-5
Joe Bush, Phi. A's-Bosox-NY Yankees	9	2-5
Rube Marquard, NY Giants-Brooklyn	11	2-5
Eddie Plank, Philadelphia A's	7	2-5
Schoolboy Rowe, Detroit	8	2-5

League Championship Series

Division play came to the major leagues in 1969 when both the American and National Leagues expanded to 12 teams. With an East and West Division in each league, League Championship Series (LCS) became necessary to determine the NL and AL pennant winners. In 1994, teams were realigned into three divisions, the East, Central, and West with division winners and one wildcard team playing a best of five series to determine the LCS competitors. In the charts below, the East Division champions are noted by the letter E, the Central division champions by C and the West Division champions by W. A wildcard winner is noted by WC. Also, each playoff winner's wins and losses are noted in parentheses after the series score. The LCS changed from best-of-5 to best-of-7 in 1985. Each league's LCS was cancelled in 1994 due to the players' strike.

National League

Multiple champions: Atlanta, Cincinnati and LA Dodgers (5); NY Mets, Philadelphia and St. Louis (3); Pittsburgh and San Diego (2).

Year	Winner	Manager	Series	Loser	Manager
1969	E- New York	Gil Hodges	3-0	W- Atlanta	Lum Harris
1970	W- Cincinnati	Sparky Anderson	3-0	E- Pittsburgh	Danny Murtaugh
1971	E- Pittsburgh	Danny Murtaugh	3-1 (LWWW)	W- San Francisco	Charlie Fox
1972	W- Cincinnati	Sparky Anderson	3-2 (LWLWW)	E- Pittsburgh	Bill Virdon
1973	E- New York	Yogi Berra	3-2 (LWWLW)	W- Cincinnati	Sparky Anderson
1974	W- Los Angeles	Walter Alston	3-1 (WWLW)	E- Pittsburgh	Danny Murtaugh
1975	W- Cincinnati	Sparky Anderson	3-0	E- Pittsburgh	Danny Murtaugh
1976	W- Cincinnati	Sparky Anderson	3-0	E- Philadelphia	Danny Ozark
1977	W- Los Angeles	Tommy Lasorda	3-1 (LWWW)	E- Philadelphia	Danny Ozark
1978	W- Los Angeles	Tommy Lasorda	3-1 (WWLW)	E- Philadelphia	Danny Ozark
1979	E- Pittsburgh	Chuck Tanner	3-0	W- Cincinnati	John McNamara
1980	E- Philadelphia	Dallas Green	3-2 (WLLWW)	W- Houston	Bill Virdon
1981	W- Los Angeles	Tommy Lasorda	3-2 (WLLWW)	E- Montreal	Jim Fanning
1982	E- St. Louis	Whitey Herzog	3-0	W- Atlanta	Joe Torre
1983	E- Philadelphia	Paul Owens	3-1 (WLWW)	W- Los Angeles	Tommy Lasorda
1984	W- San Diego	Dick Williams	3-2 (LLWWW)	E- Chicago	Jim Frey
1985	E- St. Louis	Whitey Herzog	4-2 (LLWWWW)	W- Los Angeles	Tommy Lasorda
1986	E- New York	Davey Johnson	4-2 (LWWLWW)	W- Houston	Hal Lanier
1987	E- St. Louis	Whitey Herzog	4-3 (WLWLLWW)	W- San Francisco	Roger Craig
1988	W- Los Angeles	Tommy Lasorda	4-3 (LWLWWLW)	E- New York	Davey Johnson
1989	W- San Francisco	Roger Craig	4-1 (WLWWW)	E- Chicago	Don Zimmer

Year	Winner	Manager	Series	Loser	Manager
1990	W- Cincinnati	Lou Piniella	4-2 (LWWWLW)	E- Pittsburgh	Jim Leyland
1991	W- Atlanta	Bobby Cox	4-3 (LWWLLWW)	E- Pittsburgh	Jim Leyland
1992	W- Atlanta	Bobby Cox	4-3 (WWLWLLW)	E- Pittsburgh	Jim Leyland
1993	E- Philadelphia	Jim Fregosi	4-2 (WLLWWW)	W- Atlanta	Bobby Cox
1994	Not held				
1995	E- Atlanta	Bobby Cox	4-0	C- Cincinnati	Davey Johnson
1996	E- Atlanta	Bobby Cox	4-3 (WLLLWWW)	C- St. Louis	Tony LaRussa
1997	WC-Florida	Jim Leyland	4-2 (WLWLWW)	E-Atlanta	Bobby Cox
1998	W-San Diego	Bruce Bochy	4-2 (WLWWLL)	E-Atlanta	Bobby Cox
1999	E-Atlanta	Bobby Cox	4-2 (WWWLLW)	WC-New York	Bobby Valentine

NLCS Most Valuable Players

Winners who did not play for NLCS champions are in **bold** type.

Multiple winner: Steve Garvey (2).

Year	Year	Year
1977 Dusty Baker, LA, OF	1985 Ozzie Smith, St.L., SS	1992 John Smoltz, Atl., P
1978 Steve Garvey, LA, 1B	1986 **Mike Scott**, Hou., P	1993 Curt Schilling, Phi., P
1979 Willie Stargell, Pit., 1B	1987 **Jeff Leonard**, SF, OF	1994 LCS not held.
1980 Manny Trillo, Phi., 2B	1988 Orel Hershiser, LA, P	1995 Mike Devereaux, Atl., OF
1981 Burt Hooton, LA, P	1989 Will Clark, SF, 1B	1996 Javy Lopez, Atl., C
1982 Darrell Porter, St.L., C	1990 Rob Dibble, Cin., P	1997 Livan Hernandez, Fla., P
1983 Gary Matthews, Phi., OF	& Randy Myers, Cin., P	1998 Sterling Hitchcock, SD, P
1984 Steve Garvey, SD, 1B	1991 Steve Avery, Atl., P	1999 Eddie Perez, Atl., C

American League

Multiple champions: NY Yankees (7); Oakland (6); Baltimore (5); Boston, Cleveland, Kansas City, Minnesota and Toronto (2).

Year	Winner	Manager	Series	Loser	Manager
1969	E- Baltimore	Earl Weaver	3-0	W- Minnesota	Billy Martin
1970	E- Baltimore	Earl Weaver	3-0	W- Minnesota	Bill Rigney
1971	E- Baltimore	Earl Weaver	3-0	W- Oakland	Dick Williams
1972	W- Oakland	Dick Williams	3-2 (WWLLW)	E- Detroit	Billy Martin
1973	W- Oakland	Dick Williams	3-2 (LWWLW)	E- Baltimore	Earl Weaver
1974	W- Oakland	Alvin Dark	3-1 (LWWW)	E- Baltimore	Earl Weaver
1975	E- Boston	Darrell Johnson	3-0	W- Oakland	Alvin Dark
1976	E- New York	Billy Martin	3-2 (WLWLW)	W- Kansas City	Whitey Herzog
1977	E- New York	Billy Martin	3-2 (LWLWW)	W- Kansas City	Whitey Herzog
1978	E- New York	Bob Lemon	3-1 (WLWW)	W- Kansas City	Whitey Herzog
1979	E- Baltimore	Earl Weaver	3-1 (WWLW)	W- California	Jim Fregosi
1980	W- Kansas City	Jim Frey	3-0	E- New York	Dick Howser
1981	E- New York	Bob Lemon	3-0	W- Oakland	Billy Martin
1982	E- Milwaukee	Harvey Kuenn	3-2 (LLWWW)	W- California	Gene Mauch
1983	E- Baltimore	Joe Altobelli	3-1 (LWWW)	W- Chicago	Tony La Russa
1984	E- Detroit	Sparky Anderson	3-0	W- Kansas City	Dick Howser
1985	W- Kansas City	Dick Howser	4-3 (LLWLWWW)	E- Toronto	Bobby Cox
1986	E- Boston	John McNamara	4-3 (LWLLWWW)	W- California	Gene Mauch
1987	W- Minnesota	Tom Kelly	4-1 (WWLWW)	E- Detroit	Sparky Anderson
1988	W- Oakland	Tony La Russa	4-0	E- Boston	Joe Morgan
1989	W- Oakland	Tony La Russa	4-1 (WWLWW)	E- Toronto	Cito Gaston
1990	W- Oakland	Tony La Russa	4-0	E- Boston	Joe Morgan
1991	W- Minnesota	Tom Kelly	4-1 (WLWWW)	E- Toronto	Cito Gaston
1992	E- Toronto	Cito Gaston	4-2 (LWWWLW)	W- Oakland	Tony La Russa
1993	E- Toronto	Cito Gaston	4-2 (WWLLWW)	W- Chicago	Gene Lamont
1994	Not held				
1995	C- Cleveland	Mike Hargrove	4-2 (LWLWWW)	W- Seattle	Lou Piniella
1996	E- New York	Joe Torre	4-1 (WLWWW)	WC- Baltimore	Davey Johnson
1997	C- Cleveland	Mike Hargrove	4-2 (LWWWLW)	E- Baltimore	Davey Johnson
1998	E- New York	Joe Torre	4-2 (WWWLLW)	C- Cleveland	Mike Hargrove
1999	E- New York	Joe Torre	4-1 (WWLWW)	WC- Boston	Jimy Williams

ALCS Most Valuable Players

Winner who did not play for ALCS champions is in **bold** type.

Multiple winner: Dave Stewart (2).

Year	Year	Year
1980 Frank White, KC, 2B	1987 Gary Gaetti, Min., 3B	1994 LCS not held.
1981 Graig Nettles, NY, 3B	1988 Dennis Eckersley, Oak., P	1995 Orel Hershiser, Cle., P
1982 **Fred Lynn**, Cal., OF	1989 Rickey Henderson, Oak., OF	1996 Bernie Williams, NY, OF
1983 Mike Boddicker, Bal., P	1990 Dave Stewart, Oak., P	1997 Marquis Grissom, Cle., OF
1984 Kirk Gibson, Det., OF	1991 Kirby Puckett, Min., OF	1998 David Wells, NY, P
1985 George Brett, KC, 3B	1992 Roberto Alomar, Tor., 2B	1999 Orlando Hernandez, NY, P
1986 Marty Barrett, Bos., 2B	1993 Dave Stewart, Tor., P	

Other Playoffs

Ten times since 1946, playoffs have been necessary to decide league or division championships or wild card berths when two teams were tied at the end of the regular season. Additionally, in the strike year of 1981 there were playoffs between the first and second half-season champions in both leagues.

National League

Year	NL	W	L	Manager	Year	NL East	W	L	Manager
1946	Brooklyn	96	58	Leo Durocher	1981	(1st Half) Philadelphia	34	21	Dallas Green
	St. Louis	96	58	Eddie Dyer		(2nd Half) Montreal	30	23	Jim Fanning
	Playoff: (Best-of-3) St. Louis, 2-0					Playoff: (Best-of-5) Montreal, 3-2 (WWLLW)			

Year	NL	W	L	Manager	Year	NL West	W	L	Manager
1951	Brooklyn	96	58	Charlie Dressen	1981	(1st Half) Los Angeles	36	21	Tommy Lasorda
	New York	96	58	Leo Durocher		(2nd Half) Houston	33	20	Bill Virdon
	Playoff: (Best-of-3) New York, 2-1 (WLW)					Playoff: (Best-of-5) Los Angeles, 3-2 (LLWWW)			

Year	NL	W	L	Manager	Year	NL Wild Card	W	L	Manager
1959	Milwaukee	86	68	Fred Haney	1998	Chicago	89	73	Jim Riggleman
	Los Angeles	86	68	Walter Alston		San Francisco	89	73	Dusty Baker
	Playoff: (Best-of-3) Los Angeles, 2-0					Playoff: (1 game) Chicago, 5-3 (at Chicago)			

Year	NL	W	L	Manager	Year	NL Wild Card	W	L	Manager
1962	Los Angeles	101	61	Walter Alston	1999	Cincinnati	96	66	Jack McKeon
	San Francisco	101	61	Alvin Dark		New York	96	66	Bobby Valentine
	Playoff: (Best-of-3) San Francisco, 2-1 (WLW)					Playoff: (1 game) New York, 5-0 (at Cincinnati)			

Year	NL West	W	L	Manager
1980	Houston	92	70	Bill Virdon
	Los Angeles	92	70	Tommy Lasorda
	Playoff: (1 game) Houston, 7-1 (at LA)			

American League

Year	AL	W	L	Manager	Year	AL West	W	L	Manager
1948	Boston	96	58	Joe McCarthy	1981	(1st Half) Oakland	37	23	Billy Martin
	Cleveland	96	58	Lou Boudreau		(2nd Half) Kan. City	30	23	Jim Frey
	Playoff: (1 game) Cleveland, 8-3 (at Boston)					Playoff: (Best-of-5), Oakland, 3-0			

Year	AL East	W	L	Manager	Year	AL West	W	L	Manager
1978	Boston	99	63	Don Zimmer	1995	Seattle	78	66	Lou Piniella
	New York	99	63	Bob Lemon		California	78	66	M. Lachemann
	Playoff: (1 game) New York, 5-4 (at Boston)					Playoff: (1 game) Seattle, 9-1 (at Seattle)			

Year	AL East	W	L	Manager
1981	(1st Half) N.Y.	34	22	Bob Lemon
	(2nd Half) Milw.	31	22	Buck Rodgers
	Playoff: (Best-of-5) New York, 3-2 (WWLLW)			

Regular Season League & Division Winners

Regular season National and American League pennant winners from 1900-68, as well as West and East divisional champions from 1969-93. In 1994, both leagues went to three divisions, West, Central and East, and each league also sent a wild card (WC) team to the playoffs.

Due to the 1994 players' strike that resulted in the cancelling of the season after games played on Aug. 11, division leaders at the time of the strike are not considered official champions by either league. Note that (*) indicates 1994 divisional champion is unofficial and that GA column indicates games ahead of the second place club. See National League Pennant Winners from 1876-99 for NL Pennant winners before 1900.

National League

Year		W	L	Pct	GA	Year		W	L	Pct	GA
1900	Brooklyn	82	54	.603	4½	1922	New York	93	61	.604	7
1901	Pittsburgh	90	49	.647	7½	1923	New York	95	58	.621	4½
1902	Pittsburgh	103	36	.741	27½	1924	New York	93	60	.608	1½
1903	Pittsburgh	91	49	.650	6½	1925	Pittsburgh	95	58	.621	8½
1904	New York	106	47	.693	13	1926	St. Louis	89	65	.578	2
1905	New York	105	48	.686	9	1927	Pittsburgh	94	60	.610	1½
1906	Chicago	116	36	.763	20	1928	St. Louis	95	59	.617	2
1907	Chicago	107	45	.704	17	1929	Chicago	98	54	.645	10½
1908	Chicago	99	55	.643	1	1930	St. Louis	92	62	.597	2
1909	Pittsburgh	110	42	.724	6½	1931	St. Louis	101	53	.656	13
1910	Chicago	104	50	.675	13	1932	Chicago	90	64	.584	4
1911	New York	99	54	.647	7½	1933	New York	91	61	.599	5
1912	New York	103	48	.682	10	1934	St. Louis	95	58	.621	2
1913	New York	101	51	.664	12½	1935	Chicago	100	54	.649	4
1914	Boston	94	59	.614	10½	1936	New York	92	62	.597	5
1915	Philadelphia	90	62	.592	7	1937	New York	95	57	.625	3
1916	Brooklyn	94	60	.610	2½	1938	Chicago	89	63	.586	2
1917	New York	98	56	.636	10	1939	Cincinnati	97	57	.630	4½
1918	Chicago	84	45	.651	10½	1940	Cincinnati	100	53	.654	12
1919	Cincinnati	96	44	.686	9	1941	Brooklyn	100	54	.649	2½
1920	Brooklyn	93	61	.604	7	1942	St. Louis	106	48	.688	2
1921	New York	94	59	.614	4	1943	St. Louis	105	49	.682	18

Year		W	L	Pct	GA	Year		W	L	Pct	GA
1944	St. Louis	105	49	.682	14½	1981	West—Los Angeles$	63	47	.573	—
1945	Chicago	98	56	.636	3		East—Montreal$	60	48	.556	—
1946	St. Louis†	98	58	.628	2	1982	West—Atlanta	89	73	.549	1
1947	Brooklyn	94	60	.610	5		East—St. Louis	92	70	.568	3
1948	Boston	91	62	.595	6½	1983	West—Los Angeles	91	71	.562	3
1949	Brooklyn	97	57	.630	1		East—Philadelphia	90	72	.556	6
1950	Philadelphia	91	63	.591	2	1984	West—San Diego	92	70	.568	12
1951	New York†	98	59	.624	1		East—Chicago	96	65	.596	6½
1952	Brooklyn	96	57	.627	4½	1985	West—Los Angeles	95	67	.586	5½
1953	Brooklyn	105	49	.682	13		East—St. Louis	101	61	.623	3
1954	New York	97	57	.630	5	1986	West—Houston	96	66	.593	10
1955	Brooklyn	98	55	.641	13½		East—N.Y. Mets	108	54	.667	21½
1956	Brooklyn	93	61	.604	1	1987	West—San Francisco	90	72	.556	6
1957	Milwaukee	95	59	.617	8		East—St. Louis	95	67	.586	3
1958	Milwaukee	92	62	.597	8	1988	West—Los Angeles	94	67	.584	7
1959	Los Angeles†	88	68	.564	2		East—N.Y. Mets	100	60	.625	15
1960	Pittsburgh	95	59	.617	7	1989	West—San Francisco	92	70	.568	3
1961	Cincinnati	93	61	.604	4		East—Chicago	93	69	.574	6
1962	San Francisco†	103	62	.624	1	1990	West—Cincinnati	91	71	.562	5
1963	Los Angeles	99	63	.611	6		East—Pittsburgh	95	67	.586	4
1964	St. Louis	93	69	.574	1	1991	West—Atlanta	94	68	.580	1
1965	Los Angeles	97	65	.599	2		East—Pittsburgh	98	64	.605	14
1966	Los Angeles	95	67	.586	1½	1992	West—Atlanta	98	64	.605	8
1967	St. Louis	101	60	.627	10½		East—Pittsburgh	96	66	.593	9
1968	St. Louis	97	65	.599	9	1993	West—Atlanta	104	58	.642	1
1969	West—Atlanta	93	69	.574	3		East—Philadelphia	97	65	.599	3
	East—N.Y. Mets	100	62	.617	8	1994	West—Los Angeles*	58	56	.509	3½
1970	West—Cincinnati	102	60	.630	14½		Central—Cincinnati*	66	48	.579	½
	East—Pittsburgh	89	73	.549	5		East—Montreal*	74	40	.649	6
1971	West—San Francisco	90	72	.556	1	1995	West—Los Angeles	78	66	.542	1
	East—Pittsburgh	97	65	.599	7		Central—Cincinnati	85	59	.590	9
1972	West—Cincinnati	95	59	.617	10½		East—Atlanta	90	54	.625	21
	East—Pittsburgh	96	59	.619	11		WC—Colorado	77	67	.535	—
1973	West—Cincinnati	99	63	.611	3½	1996	West—San Diego	91	71	.562	1
	East—N.Y. Mets	82	79	.509	1½		Central—St. Louis	88	74	.543	6
1974	West—Los Angeles	102	60	.630	4		East—Atlanta	96	66	.593	8
	East—Pittsburgh	88	74	.543	1½		WC—Los Angeles	90	72	.556	—
1975	West—Cincinnati	108	54	.667	20	1997	West—San Francisco	90	72	.556	2
	East—Pittsburgh	92	69	.571	6½		Central—Houston	84	78	.519	5
1976	West—Cincinnati	102	60	.630	10		East—Atlanta	101	61	.623	9
	East—Philadelphia	101	61	.623	9		WC—Florida	92	70	.568	—
1977	West—Los Angeles	98	64	.605	10	1998	West—San Diego	98	64	.605	9½
	East—Philadelphia	101	61	.623	5		Central—Houston	102	60	.630	12½
1978	West—Los Angeles	95	67	.586	2½		East—Atlanta	106	56	.654	18
	East—Philadelphia	90	72	.556	1½		WC—Chicago†	90	73	.552	—
1979	West—Cincinnati	90	71	.559	1½	1999	West—Arizona	100	62	.617	14
	East—Pittsburgh	98	64	.605	2		Central—Houston	97	65	.599	1½
1980	West—Houston †	93	70	.571	1		East—Atlanta	103	59	.636	6½
	East—Philadelphia	91	71	.562	1		WC—N.Y. Mets†	97	66	.595	

†**Regular season playoffs:** See "Other Playoffs" on page 106 for details.
$**Divsional playoffs:** See "Other Playoffs" on page 106 for details.

American League

Year		W	L	Pct	GA	Year		W	L	Pct	GA
1901	Chicago	83	53	.610	4	1918	Boston	75	51	.595	2½
1902	Philadelphia	83	53	.610	5	1919	Chicago	88	52	.629	3½
1903	Boston	91	47	.659	14½	1920	Cleveland	98	56	.636	2
1904	Boston	95	59	.617	1½	1921	New York	98	55	.641	4½
1905	Philadelphia	92	56	.622	2	1922	New York	94	60	.610	1
1906	Chicago	93	58	.616	3	1923	New York	98	54	.645	16
1907	Detroit	92	58	.613	1½	1924	Washington	92	62	.597	2
1908	Detroit	90	63	.588	½	1925	Washington	96	55	.636	8½
1909	Detroit	98	54	.645	3½	1926	New York	91	63	.591	3
1910	Philadelphia	102	48	.680	14½	1927	New York	110	44	.714	19
1911	Philadelphia	101	50	.669	13½	1928	New York	101	53	.656	2½
1912	Boston	105	47	.691	14	1929	Philadelphia	104	46	.693	18
1913	Philadelphia	96	57	.627	6½	1930	Philadelphia	102	52	.662	8
1914	Philadelphia	99	53	.651	8½	1931	Philadelphia	107	45	.704	13½
1915	Boston	101	50	.669	2½	1932	New York	107	47	.695	13
1916	Boston	91	63	.591	2	1933	Washington	99	53	.651	7
1917	Chicago	100	54	.649	9	1934	Detroit	101	53	.656	7

Year		W	L	Pct	GA	Year		W	L	Pct	GA
1935	Detroit	93	58	.616	3	1979	West—California	88	74	.543	3
1936	New York	102	51	.667	19½		East—Baltimore	102	57	.642	8
1937	New York	102	52	.662	13	1980	West—Kansas City	97	65	.599	14
1938	New York	99	53	.651	9½		East—New York	103	59	.636	3
1939	New York	106	45	.702	17	1981	West—Oakland$	64	45	.587	—
1940	Detroit	90	64	.584	1		East—New York$	59	48	.551	—
1941	New York	101	53	.656	17	1982	West—California	93	69	.574	3
1942	New York	103	51	.669	9		East—Milwaukee	95	67	.586	1
1943	New York	98	56	.636	13½	1983	West—Chicago	99	63	.611	20
1944	St. Louis	89	65	.578	1		East—Baltimore	98	64	.605	6
1945	Detroit	88	65	.575	1½	1984	West—Kansas City	84	78	.519	3
1946	Boston	104	50	.675	12		East—Detroit	104	58	.642	15
1947	New York	97	57	.630	12	1985	West—Kansas City	91	71	.562	1
1948	Cleveland†	97	58	.626	1		East—Toronto	99	62	.615	2
1949	New York	97	57	.630	1	1986	West—California	92	70	.568	5
1950	New York	98	56	.636	3		East—Boston	95	66	.590	5½
1951	New York	98	56	.636	5	1987	West—Minnesota	85	77	.525	2
1952	New York	95	59	.617	2		East—Detroit	98	64	.605	2
1953	New York	99	52	.656	8½	1988	West—Oakland	104	58	.642	13
1954	Cleveland	111	43	.721	8		East—Boston	89	73	.549	1
1955	New York	96	58	.623	3	1989	West—Oakland	99	63	.611	7
1956	New York	97	57	.630	9		East—Toronto	89	73	.549	2
1957	New York	98	56	.636	8	1990	West—Oakland	103	59	.636	9
1958	New York	92	62	.597	10		East—Boston	88	74	.543	2
1959	Chicago	94	60	.610	5	1991	West—Minnesota	95	67	.586	8
1960	New York	97	57	.630	8		East—Toronto	91	71	.562	7
1961	New York	109	53	.673	8	1992	West—Oakland	96	66	.593	6
1962	New York	96	66	.593	5		East—Toronto	96	66	.593	4
1963	New York	104	57	.646	10½	1993	West—Chicago	94	68	.580	8
1964	New York	99	63	.611	1		East—Toronto	95	67	.586	7
1965	Minnesota	102	60	.630	7	1994	West—Texas*	52	62	.456	1
1966	Baltimore	97	63	.606	9		Central—Chicago*	67	46	.593	1
1967	Boston	92	70	.568	1		East—New York*	70	43	.619	6½
1968	Detroit	103	59	.636	12	1995	West—Seattle†	79	66	.545	1
1969	West—Minnesota	97	65	.599	9		Central—Cleveland	100	44	.694	30
	East—Baltimore	109	53	.673	19		East—Boston	86	58	.597	7
1970	West—Minnesota	98	64	.605	9		WC—New York	79	65	.549	—
	East—Baltimore	108	54	.667	15	1996	West—Texas	90	72	.556	4½
1971	West—Oakland	101	60	.627	16		Central—Cleveland	99	62	.615	14½
	East—Baltimore	101	57	.639	12		East—New York	92	70	.568	4
1972	West—Oakland	93	62	.600	5½		WC—Baltimore	88	74	.543	—
	East—Detroit	86	70	.551	½	1997	West—Seattle	90	72	.556	6
1973	West—Oakland	94	68	.580	6		Central—Cleveland	86	75	.534	6
	East—Baltimore	97	65	.599	8		East—Baltimore	98	64	.605	2
1974	West—Oakland	90	72	.556	5		WC—New York	96	66	.593	—
	East—Baltimore	91	71	.562	2	1998	West—Texas	88	74	.543	3
1975	West—Oakland	98	64	.605	7		Central—Cleveland	89	73	.549	9
	East—Boston	95	65	.594	4½		East—New York	114	48	.704	22
1976	West—Kansas City	90	72	.556	2½		WC—Boston	92	70	.568	—
	East—New York	97	62	.610	10½	1999	West—Texas	95	67	.586	8
1977	West—Kansas City	102	60	.630	8		Central—Cleveland	97	65	.599	21½
	East—New York	100	62	.617	2½		East—New York	98	64	.605	4
1978	West—Kansas City	92	70	.568	5		WC—Boston	94	68	.580	—
	East—New York†	100	63	.613	1						

†Regular season playoffs: See "Other Playoffs" on page 106 for details.
$Divisional playoffs: See "Other Playoffs" on page 106 for details.

The All-Star Game

Baseball's first All-Star Game was held on July 6, 1933, before 47,595 at Comiskey Park in Chicago. From that year on, the All-Star Game has matched the best players in the American League against the best in the National. From 1959-62, two All-Star Games were played. The only year an All-Star Game wasn't played was 1945, when World War II travel restrictions made it necessary to cancel the meeting. The NL leads the series, 40-29-1. In the chart below, the American League is listed in **bold** type.

The All-Star Game MVP Award is named after Arch Ward, the *Chicago Tribune* sports editor who founded the game in 1933. First given at the two All-Star games in 1962, the name of the award was changed to the Commissioner's Trophy in 1970 and back to the Ward Memorial Award in 1985.

Multiple winners: Gary Carter, Steve Garvey and Willie Mays (2).

Year	Host	Host	AL Manager	NL Manager	MVP
1933	**American,** 4-2	Chicago (AL)	Connie Mack	John McGraw	No award
1934	**American,** 9-7	New York (NL)	Joe Cronin	Bill Terry	No award
1935	**American,** 4-1	Cleveland	Mickey Cochrane	Frankie Frisch	No award

Year		Host	AL Manager	NL Manager	MVP
1936	National, 4-3	Boston (NL)	Joe McCarthy	Charlie Grimm	No award
1937	**American,** 8-3	Washington	Joe McCarthy	Bill Terry	No award
1938	National, 4-1	Cincinnati	Joe McCarthy	Bill Terry	No award
1939	**American,** 3-1	New York (AL)	Joe McCarthy	Gabby Hartnett	No award
1940	National, 4-0	St. Louis (NL)	Joe Cronin	Bill McKechnie	No award
1941	**American,** 7-5	Detroit	Del Baker	Bill McKechnie	No award
1942	**American,** 3-1	New York (NL)	Joe McCarthy	Leo Durocher	No award
1943	**American,** 5-3	Philadelphia (AL)	Joe McCarthy	Billy Southworth	No award
1944	National, 7-1	Pittsburgh	Joe McCarthy	Billy Southworth	No award
1945	Not held				
1946	**American,** 12-0	Boston (AL)	Steve O'Neill	Charlie Grimm	No award
1947	**American,** 2-1	Chicago (NL)	Joe Cronin	Eddie Dyer	No award
1948	**American,** 5-2	St. Louis (AL)	Bucky Harris	Leo Durocher	No award
1949	**American,** 11-7	Brooklyn	Lou Boudreau	Billy Southworth	No award
1950	National, 4-3 (14)	Chicago (AL)	Casey Stengel	Burt Shotton	No award
1951	National, 8-3	Detroit	Casey Stengel	Eddie Sawyer	No award
1952	National, 3-2 (5, rain)	Philadelphia (NL)	Casey Stengel	Leo Durocher	No award
1953	National, 5-1	Cincinnati	Casey Stengel	Charlie Dressen	No award
1954	**American,** 11-9	Cleveland	Casey Stengel	Walter Alston	No award
1955	National, 6-5 (12)	Milwaukee	Al Lopez	Leo Durocher	No award
1956	National, 7-3	Washington	Casey Stengel	Walter Alston	No award
1957	**American,** 6-5	St. Louis	Casey Stengel	Walter Alston	No award
1958	**American,** 4-3	Baltimore	Casey Stengel	Fred Haney	No award
1959-a	National, 5-4	Pittsburgh	Casey Stengel	Fred Haney	No award
1959-b	**American,** 5-3	Los Angeles	Casey Stengel	Fred Haney	No award
1960-a	National, 5-3	Kansas City	Al Lopez	Walter Alston	No award
1960-b	National, 6-0	New York	Al Lopez	Walter Alston	No award
1961-a	National, 5-4 (10)	San Francisco	Paul Richards	Danny Murtaugh	No award
1961-b	TIE, 1-1 (9, rain)	Boston	Paul Richards	Danny Murtaugh	No award
1962-a	National, 3-1	Washington	Ralph Houk	Fred Hutchinson	Maury Wills, LA (NL), SS
1962-b	**American,** 9-4	Chicago (NL)	Ralph Houk	Fred Hutchinson	Leon Wagner, LA (AL), OF
1963	National, 5-3	Cleveland	Ralph Houk	Alvin Dark	Willie Mays, SF, OF
1964	National, 7-4	New York (NL)	Al Lopez	Walter Alston	Johnny Callison, Phi., OF
1965	National, 6-5	Minnesota	Al Lopez	Gene Mauch	Juan Marichal, SF, P
1966	National, 2-1 (10)	St. Louis	Sam Mele	Walter Alston	Brooks Robinson, Bal., 3B
1967	National, 2-1 (15)	California	Hank Bauer	Walter Alston	Tony Perez, Cin., 3B
1968	National, 1-0	Houston	Dick Williams	Red Schoendienst	Willie Mays, SF, OF
1969	National, 9-3	Washington	Mayo Smith	Red Schoendienst	Willie McCovey, SF, 1B
1970	National, 5-4 (12)	Cincinnati	Earl Weaver	Gil Hodges	Carl Yastrzemski, Bos., OF-1B
1971	**American,** 6-4	Detroit	Earl Weaver	Sparky Anderson	Frank Robinson, Bal., OF
1972	National, 4-3 (10)	Atlanta	Earl Weaver	Danny Murtaugh	Joe Morgan, Con., 2B
1973	National, 7-1	Kansas	Dick Williams	Sparky Anderson	Bobby Bonds, SF, OF
1974	National, 7-2	Pittsburgh	Dick Williams	Yogi Berra	Steve Garvey, LA, 1B
1975	National, 6-3	Milwaukee	Alvin Dark	Walter Alston	Bill Madlock, Chi. (NL), 3B & Jon Matlack, NY (NL), P
1976	National, 7-1	Philadelphia	Darrell Johnson	Sparky Anderson	George Foster, Cin., OF
1977	National, 7-5	New York (AL)	Billy Martin	Sparky Anderson	Don Sutton, LA, P
1978	National, 7-3	San Diego	Billy Martin	Tommy Lasorda	Steve Garvey, LA, 1B
1979	National, 7-6	Seattle	Bob Lemon	Tommy Lasorda	Dave Parker, Pit, OF
1980	National, 4-2	Los Angeles	Earl Weaver	Chuck Tanner	Ken Griffey, Cin., OF
1981	National, 5-4	Cleveland	Jim Frey	Dallas Green	Gary Carter, Mon., C
1982	National, 4-1	Montreal	Billy Martin	Tommy Lasorda	Dave Concepcion, Cin., SS
1983	**American,** 13-3	Chicago (AL)	Harvey Kuenn	Whitey Herzog	Fred Lynn, Cal., OF
1984	National, 3-1	San Francisco	Joe Altobelli	Paul Owens	Gary Carter, Mon., C
1985	National, 6-1	Minnesota	Sparky Anderson	Dick Williams	LaMarr Hoyt, SD, P
1986	**American,** 3-2	Houston	Dick Howser	Whitey Herzog	Roger Clemens, Bos., P
1987	National, 2-0 (13)	Oakland	John McNamara	Davey Johnson	Tim Raines, Mon., OF
1988	**American,** 2-1	Cincinnati	Tom Kelly	Whitey Herzog	Terry Steinbach, Oak., C
1989	**American,** 5-3	California	Tony La Russa	Tommy Lasorda	Bo Jackson, KC, OF
1990	**American,** 2-0	Chicago (NL)	Tony La Russa	Roger Craig	Julio Franco, Tex., 2B
1991	**American,** 4-2	Toronto	Tony La Russa	Lou Piniella	Cal Ripken Jr., Bal., SS
1992	**American,** 13-6	San Diego	Tom Kelly	Bobby Cox	Ken Griffey Jr., Sea., OF
1993	**American,** 9-3	Baltimore	Cito Gaston	Bobby Cox	Kirby Puckett, Min., OF
1994	National, 8-7 (10)	Pittsburgh	Cito Gaston	Jim Fregosi	Fred McGriff, Atl., 1B
1995	National, 3-2	Texas	Buck Showalter	Felipe Alou	Jeff Conine, Fla., PH
1996	National, 6-0	Philadelphia	Mike Hargrove	Bobby Cox	Mike Piazza, LA, C
1997	**American,** 3-1	Cleveland	Joe Torre	Bobby Cox	Sandy Alomar Jr., Cle., C
1998	**American,** 13-8	Colorado	Mike Hargrove	Jim Leyland	Roberto Alomar, Bal., 2B
1999	**American,** 4-1	Boston	Joe Torre	Bruce Bochy	Pedro Martinez, Bos., P

Major League Franchise Origins

Here is what the current 30 teams in Major League Baseball have to show for the years they have put in as members of the National League (NL) and American League (AL). Pennants and World Series championships are since 1901.

National League

	1st Year	Pennants & World Series	Franchise Stops
Arizona Diamondbacks	1998	None	• Phoenix (1998—)

Atlanta Braves	1876	9 NL (1914,48,57-58,91-92,95,96,99)
		3 WS (1914,57,95)
			• Boston (1876-1952)
			  Milwaukee (1953-65)
			  Atlanta (1966—)

Chicago Cubs	1876	10 NL (1906-08,10,18,29,32,35,38,45) 2 WS (1907-08)	• Chicago (1876—)
Cincinnati Reds	1876	9 NL (1919,39-40,61,70,72,75-76,90) 5 WS (1919,40,75-76,90)	• Cincinnati (1876-80) Cincinnati (1890—)
Colorado Rockies	1993	None	• Denver (1993—)
Florida Marlins	1993	1 NL (1997) 1 WS (1997)	• Miami (1993—)
Houston Astros	1962	None	• Houston (1962—)
Los Angeles Dodgers	1890	18 NL (1916,20,41,47,49,52-53,55-56, 59,63, 65-66,74,77-78, 81,88) 6 WS (1955,59,63,65,81,88)	• Brooklyn (1890-1957) Los Angeles (1958—)
Milwaukee Brewers	1969	1 AL (1982)	• Seattle (1969) Milwaukee (1970—)
Montreal Expos	1969	None	• Montreal (1969—)
New York Mets	1962	3 NL (1969,73,86) 2 WS (1969,86)	• New York (1962—)
Philadelphia Phillies	1883	5 NL (1915,50,80,83,93) 1 WS (1980)	• Philadelphia (1883—)
Pittsburgh Pirates	1887	7 NL (1903,09,25,27,60,71,79) 5 WS (1909,25,60,71,79)	• Pittsburgh (1887—)
St. Louis Cardinals	1892	15 NL (1926,28,30-31,34,42-44,46,64, 67-68,82,85,87) 9 WS (1926,31,34,42,44,46,64,67,82)	• St. Louis (1892—)
San Diego Padres	1969	2 NL (1984,98)	• San Diego (1969—)
San Francisco Giants	1883	16 NL (1905,11-13,17,21-24,33,36-37,51, 54,62,89) 5 WS (1905,21-22,33,54)	• New York (1883-1957) San Francisco (1958—)

American League

	1st Year	Pennants & World Series	Franchise Stops
Anaheim Angels	1961	None	• Los Angeles (1961-65) Anaheim, CA (1966—)

Baltimore Orioles	1901	7 AL (1944,66,69-71,79,83)
		3 WS (1966,70,83)
			• Milwaukee (1901)
			  St. Louis (1902-53)
			  Baltimore (1954—)

Boston Red Sox	1901	9 AL (1903,12,15-16,18,46,67,75,86) 5 WS (1903,12,15-16,18)	• Boston (1901—)
Chicago White Sox	1901	4 AL (1906,17,19,59) 2 WS (1906,17)	• Chicago (1901—)
Cleveland Indians	1901	5 AL (1920,48,54,95,97) 2 WS (1920,48)	• Cleveland (1901—)
Detroit Tigers	1901	9 AL (1907-09,34-35,40,45,68,84) 4 WS (1935,45,68,84)	• Detroit (1901—)
Kansas City Royals	1969	2 AL (1980,85) 1 WS (1985)	• Kansas City (1969—)

Minnesota Twins	1901	6 AL (1924-25,33,65,87,91)
		3 WS (1924,87,91)
			• Washington, DC (1901-60)
			  Bloomington, MN (1961-81)
			  Minneapolis (1982—)

New York Yankees	1901	36 AL (1921-23,26-28,32,36-39,41-43,47, 49-53,55-58,60-64,76-78,81,96,98-99) 25 WS (1923,27-28,32,36-39,41,43,47, 49-53,56,58,61-62,77-78,96,98-99)	• Baltimore (1901-02) New York (1903—)

Oakland Athletics	1901	14 AL (1905,10-11,13-14,29-31,72-74,
		88-90) 9 WS (1910-11,13,29-30,72-74,89)
			• Philadelphia (1901-54)
			  Kansas City (1955-67)
			  Oakland (1968—)

Seattle Mariners	1977	None	• Seattle (1977—)
Tampa Bay Devil Rays	1998	None	• Tampa Bay (1998—)
Texas Rangers	1961	None	• Washington, DC (1961-71) Arlington, TX (1972—)
Toronto Blue Jays	1977	2 AL (1992-93) 2 WS (1992-93)	• Toronto (1977—)

The Growth of Major League Baseball

The National League (founded in 1876) and the American League (founded in 1901) were both eight-team circuits at the turn of the century and remained that way until expansion finally came to Major League Baseball in the 1960s. The AL added two teams in 1961 and the NL did the same a year later. Both leagues went to 12 teams and split into two divisions in 1969. The AL then grew by two more teams in 1977, but the NL didn't follow suit until adding its 13th and 14th clubs in 1993. The NL added two teams in 1998 when the expansion Arizona Diamondbacks entered the league and the Milwaukee Brewers moved over from the AL.

Expansion Timetable (Since 1901)

1961—Los Angeles Angels (now Anaheim) and Washington Senators (now Texas Rangers) join AL; **1962**—Houston Colt .45s (now Astros) and New York Mets join NL; **1969**—Kansas City Royals and Seattle Pilots (now Milwaukee Brewers) join AL, while Montreal Expos and San Diego Padres join NL; **1977**—Seattle Mariners and Toronto Blue Jays join AL; **1993**—Colorado Rockies and Florida Marlins join NL; **1998**—Arizona Diamondbacks join NL and Tampa Bay Devil Rays join AL.

City and Nickname Changes
National League

1953—Boston Braves move to Milwaukee; **1958**—Brooklyn Dodgers move to Los Angeles and New York Giants move to San Francisco; **1965**—Houston Colt .45s renamed Astros; **1966**—Milwaukee Braves move to Atlanta.

Other nicknames: Boston (Beaneaters and Doves through 1908, and Bees from 1936-40); **Brooklyn** (Superbas through 1926, then Robins from 1927-31; then Dodgers from 1932-57); **Cincinnati** (Red Legs from 1944-45, then Redlegs from 1954-60, then Reds since 1961); **Philadelphia** (Blue Jays from 1943-44).

American League

1902—Milwaukee Brewers move to St. Louis and become Browns; **1903**—Baltimore Orioles move to New York and become Highlanders; **1913**—NY Highlanders renamed Yankees; **1954**—St. Louis Browns move to Baltimore and become Orioles; **1955**—Philadelphia Athletics move to Kansas City; **1961**—Washington Senators move to Bloomington, Minn., and become Minnesota Twins; **1965**—LA Angels renamed California Angels; **1966**—California Angels move to Anaheim; **1968**—KC Athletics move to Oakland and become A's; **1970**—Seattle Pilots move to Milwaukee and become Brewers; **1972**—Washington Senators move to Arlington, Texas, and become Rangers; **1982**—Minnesota Twins move to Minneapolis; **1987**—Oakland A's renamed Athletics; **1997**—California Angels renamed Anaheim Angels.

Other nicknames: Boston (Pilgrims, Puritans, Plymouth Rocks and Somersets through 1906); **Cleveland** (Broncos, Blues, Naps and Molly McGuires through 1914); **Washington** (Senators through 1904, then Nationals from 1905-44, then Senators again from 1945-60).

National League Pennant Winners from 1876-99

Founded in 1876, the National League played 24 seasons before the turn of the century and its eventual rivalry with the younger American League.

Multiple winners: Boston (8); Chicago (6); Baltimore (3); Brooklyn, New York and Providence (2).

Year		Year		Year		Year	
1876	Chicago	1882	Chicago	1888	New York	1894	Baltimore
1877	Boston	1883	Boston	1889	New York	1895	Baltimore
1878	Boston	1884	Providence	1890	Brooklyn	1896	Baltimore
1879	Providence	1885	Chicago	1891	Boston	1897	Boston
1880	Chicago	1886	Chicago	1892	Boston	1898	Boston
1881	Chicago	1887	Detroit	1893	Boston	1899	Brooklyn

Champions of Leagues That No Longer Exist

A Special Baseball Records Committee appointed by the commissioner found in 1968 that four extinct leagues qualified for major league status—the American Association (1882-91), the Union Association (1884), the Players' League (1890) and the Federal League (1914-15). The first years of the American League (1900) and Federal League (1913) were not recognized.

American Association

Year	Champion	Manager	Year	Champion	Manager	Year	Champion	Manager
1882	Cincinnati	Pop Snyder	1886	St. Louis	Charlie Comiskey	1890	Louisville	Jack Chapman
1883	Philadelphia	Lew Simmons	1887	St. Louis	Charlie Comiskey	1891	Boston	Arthur Irwin
1884	New York	Jim Mutrie	1888	St. Louis	Charlie Comiskey			
1885	St. Louis	Charlie Comiskey	1889	Brooklyn	Bill McGunnigle			

Union Association

Year	Champion	Manager
1884	St. Louis	Henry Lucas

Players' League

Year	Champion	Manager
1890	Boston	King Kelly

Federal League

Year	Champion	Manager
1914	Indianapolis	Bill Phillips
1915	Chicago	Joe Tinker

Annual Batting Leaders (since 1900)
Batting Average
National League

Multiple winners: Tony Gwynn and Honus Wagner (8); Rogers Hornsby and Stan Musial (7); Roberto Clemente and Bill Madlock (4); Pete Rose and Paul Waner (3); Hank Aaron, Richie Ashburn, Jake Daubert, Tommy Davis, Ernie Lombardi, Willie McGee, Lefty O'Doul, Dave Parker, Edd Roush and Larry Walker (2).

Year		Avg	Year		Avg	Year		Avg
1900	Honus Wagner, Pit	.381	1934	Paul Waner, Pit	.362	1968	Pete Rose, Cin	.335
1901	Jesse Burkett, St.L	.382	1935	Arky Vaughan, Pit	.385	1969	Pete Rose, Cin	.348
1902	Ginger Beaumont, Pit	.357	1936	Paul Waner, Pit	.373	1970	Rico Carty, Atl	.366
1903	Honus Wagner, Pit	.355	1937	Joe Medwick, St.L	.374	1971	Joe Torre, St.L	.363
1904	Honus Wagner, Pit	.349	1938	Ernie Lombardi, Cin	.342	1972	Billy Williams, Chi	.333
1905	Cy Seymour, Cin	.377	1939	Johnny Mize, St.L	.349	1973	Pete Rose, Cin	.338
1906	Honus Wagner, Pit	.339	1940	Debs Garms, Pit	.355	1974	Ralph Garr, Atl	.353
1907	Honus Wagner, Pit	.350	1941	Pete Reiser, Bklyn	.343	1975	Bill Madlock, Chi	.354
1908	Honus Wagner, Pit	.354	1942	Ernie Lombardi, Bos	.330	1976	Bill Madlock, Chi	.339
1909	Honus Wagner, Pit	.339	1943	Stan Musial, St.L	.357	1977	Dave Parker, Pit	.338
1910	Sherry Magee, Phi	.331	1944	Dixie Walker, Bklyn	.357	1978	Dave Parker, Pit	.334
1911	Honus Wagner, Pit	.334	1945	Phil Cavarretta, Chi	.355	1979	Keith Hernandez, St.L	.344
1912	Heinie Zimmerman, Chi	.372	1946	Stan Musial, St.L	.365	1980	Bill Buckner, Chi	.324
1913	Jake Daubert, Bklyn	.350	1947	Harry Walker, St.L-Phi	.363	1981	Bill Madlock, Pit	.341
1914	Jake Daubert, Bklyn	.329	1948	Stan Musial, St.L	.376	1982	Al Oliver, Mon	.331
1915	Larry Doyle, NY	.320	1949	Jackie Robinson, Bklyn	.342	1983	Bill Madlock, Pit	.323
1916	Hal Chase, Cin	.339	1950	Stan Musial, St.L	.346	1984	Tony Gwynn, SD	.351
1917	Edd Roush, Cin	.341	1951	Stan Musial, St.L	.355	1985	Willie McGee, St.L	.353
1918	Zack Wheat, Bklyn	.335	1952	Stan Musial, St.L	.336	1986	Tim Raines, Mon	.334
1919	Edd Roush, Cin	.321	1953	Carl Furillo, Bklyn	.344	1987	Tony Gwynn, SD	.370
1920	Rogers Hornsby, St.L	.370	1954	Willie Mays, NY	.345	1988	Tony Gwynn, SD	.313
1921	Rogers Hornsby, St.L	.397	1955	Richie Ashburn, Phi	.338	1989	Tony Gwynn, SD	.336
1922	Rogers Hornsby, St.L	.401	1956	Hank Aaron, Mil	.328	1990	Willie McGee, St.L	.335
1923	Rogers Hornsby, St.L	.384	1957	Stan Musial, St.L	.351	1991	Terry Pendleton, Atl	.319
1924	Rogers Hornsby, St.L	.424	1958	Richie Ashburn, Phi	.350	1992	Gary Sheffield, SD	.330
1925	Rogers Hornsby, St.L	.403	1959	Hank Aaron, Mil	.355	1993	Andres Galarraga, Col	.370
1926	Bubbles Hargrave, Cin	.353	1960	Dick Groat, Pit	.325	1994	Tony Gwynn, SD	.394
1927	Paul Waner, Pit	.380	1961	Roberto Clemente, Pit	.351	1995	Tony Gwynn, SD	.368
1928	Rogers Hornsby, Bos	.387	1962	Tommy Davis, LA	.346	1996	Tony Gwynn, SD	.353
1929	Lefty O'Doul, Phi	.398	1963	Tommy Davis, LA	.326	1997	Tony Gwynn, SD	.372
1930	Bill Terry, NY	.401	1964	Roberto Clemente, Pit	.339	1998	Larry Walker, Col.	.363
1931	Chick Hafey, St.L	.349	1965	Roberto Clemente, Pit	.329	1999	Larry Walker, Col.	.379
1932	Lefty O'Doul, Bklyn	.368	1966	Matty Alou, Pit	.342			
1933	Chuck Klein, Phi	.368	1967	Roberto Clemente, Pit	.357			

American League

Multiple winners: Ty Cobb (12); Rod Carew (7); Ted Williams (6); Wade Boggs (5); Harry Heilmann (4); George Brett, Nap Lajoie, Tony Oliva and Carl Yastrzemski (3); Luke Appling, Joe DiMaggio, Ferris Fain, Jimmie Foxx, Edgar Martinez, Pete Runnels, Al Simmons, George Sisler and Mickey Vernon (2).

Year		Avg	Year		Avg	Year		Avg
1901	Nap Lajoie, Phi.	.422	1924	Babe Ruth, NY	.378	1947	Ted Williams, Bos	.343
1902	Ed Delahanty, Wash.	.376	1925	Harry Heilmann, Det	.393	1948	Ted Williams, Bos	.369
1903	Nap Lajoie, Cle	.355	1926	Heinie Manush, Det	.378	1949	George Kell, Det.	.343
1904	Nap Lajoie, Cle	.381	1927	Harry Heilmann, Det	.398	1950	Billy Goodman, Bos	.354
1905	Elmer Flick, Cle	.306	1928	Goose Goslin, Wash	.379	1951	Ferris Fain, Phi	.344
1906	George Stone, St.L	.358	1929	Lew Fonseca, Cle	.369	1952	Ferris Fain, Phi	.327
1907	Ty Cobb, Det	.350	1930	Al Simmons, Phi	.381	1953	Mickey Vernon, Wash	.337
1908	Ty Cobb, Det	.324	1931	Al Simmons, Phi	.390	1954	Bobby Avila, Clev	.341
1909	Ty Cobb, Det	.377	1932	Dale Alexander, Det-Bos	.367	1955	Al Kaline, Det	.340
1910	Ty Cobb, Det	.385	1933	Jimmie Foxx, Phi	.356	1956	Mickey Mantle, NY	.353
1911	Ty Cobb, Det	.420	1934	Lou Gehrig, NY.	.363	1957	Ted Williams, Bos	.388
1912	Ty Cobb, Det	.410	1935	Buddy Myer, Wash	.349	1958	Ted Williams, Bos	.328
1913	Ty Cobb, Det	.390	1936	Luke Appling, Chi	.388	1959	Harvey Kuenn, Det	.353
1914	Ty Cobb, Det	.368	1937	Charlie Gehringer, Det	.371	1960	Pete Runnels, Bos	.320
1915	Ty Cobb, Det	.369	1938	Jimmie Foxx, Bos.	.349	1961	Norm Cash, Det	.361*
1916	Tris Speaker, Cle	.386	1939	Joe DiMaggio, NY	.381	1962	Pete Runnels, Bos	.326
1917	Ty Cobb, Det	.383	1940	Joe DiMaggio, NY	.352	1963	Carl Yastrzemski, Bos	.321
1918	Ty Cobb, Det	.382	1941	Ted Williams, Bos	.406	1964	Tony Oliva, Min	.323
1919	Ty Cobb, Det	.384	1942	Ted Williams, Bos	.356	1965	Tony Oliva, Min	.321
1920	George Sisler, St.L	.407	1943	Luke Appling, Chi	.328	1966	Frank Robinson, Bal	.316
1921	Harry Heilmann, Det	.394	1944	Lou Boudreau, Clev	.327	1967	Carl Yastrzemski, Bos	.326
1922	George Sisler, St.L	.420	1945	Snuffy Stirnweiss, NY	.309	1968	Carl Yastrzemski, Bos	.301
1923	Harry Heilmann, Det	.403	1946	Mickey Vernon, Wash	.353	1969	Rod Carew, Min	.332

Year		Avg	Year		Avg	Year		Avg
1970	Alex Johnson, Cal	.329	1981	Carney Lansford, Bos	.336	1992	Edgar Martinez, Sea	.343
1971	Tony Oliva, Min	.337	1982	Willie Wilson, KC	.332	1993	John Olerud, Tor	.363
1972	Rod Carew, Min	.318	1983	Wade Boggs, Bos	.361	1994	Paul O'Neill, NY	.359
1973	Rod Carew, Min	.350	1984	Don Mattingly, NY	.343	1995	Edgar Martinez, Sea	.356
1974	Rod Carew, Min	.364	1985	Wade Boggs, Bos	.368	1996	Alex Rodriguez, Sea	.358
1975	Rod Carew, Min	.359	1986	Wade Boggs, Bos	.357	1997	Frank Thomas, Chi	.347
1976	George Brett, KC	.333	1987	Wade Boggs, Bos	.363	1998	Bernie Williams, NY	.339
1977	Rod Carew, Min	.388	1988	Wade Boggs, Bos	.366	1999	Nomar Garciaparra, Bos	.357
1978	Rod Carew, Min	.333	1989	Kirby Puckett, Min	.339			
1979	Fred Lynn, Bos	.333	1990	George Brett, KC	.329			
1980	George Brett, KC	.390	1991	Julio Franco, Tex	.341			

*Norm Cash later admitted to using a corked bat the entire season. He played 16 other seasons and never hit better than .286.

Home Runs
National League

Multiple winners: Mike Schmidt (8); Ralph Kiner (7); Gavvy Cravath and Mel Ott (6); Hank Aaron, Chuck Klein, Willie Mays, Johnny Mize, Cy Williams and Hack Wilson (4); Willie McCovey (3); Ernie Banks, Johnny Bench, George Foster, Rogers Hornsby, Tim Jordan, Dave Kingman, Eddie Mathews, Mark McGwire, Dale Murphy, Bill Nicholson, Dave Robertson, Wildfire Schulte and Willie Stargell (2).

Year		HR	Year		HR	Year		HR
1900	Herman Long, Bos	12	1933	Chuck Klein, Phi	28	1966	Hank Aaron, Atl	44
1901	Sam Crawford, Cin	16	1934	Rip Collins, St.L	35	1967	Hank Aaron, Atl	39
1902	Tommy Leach, Pit	6		& Mel Ott, NY	35	1968	Willie McCovey, SF	36
1903	Jimmy Sheckard, Bklyn	9	1935	Wally Berger, Bos	34	1969	Willie McCovey, SF	45
1904	Harry Lumley, Bklyn	9	1936	Mel Ott, NY	33			
1905	Fred Odwell, Cin	9	1937	Joe Medwick, St.L	31	1970	Johnny Bench, Cin	45
1906	Tim Jordan, Bklyn	12		& Mel Ott, NY	31	1971	Willie Stargell, Pit	48
1907	Dave Brain, Bos	10	1938	Mel Ott, NY	36	1972	Johnny Bench, Cin	40
1908	Tim Jordan, Bklyn	12	1939	Johnny Mize, St.L	28	1973	Willie Stargell, Pit	44
1909	Red Murray, NY	7	1940	Johnny Mize, St.L	43	1974	Mike Schmidt, Phi	36
1910	Fred Beck, Bos	10	1941	Dolf Camilli, Bklyn	34	1975	Mike Schmidt, Phi	38
	& Wildfire Schulte, Chi	10	1942	Mel Ott, NY	30	1976	Mike Schmidt, Phi	38
1911	Wildfire Schulte, Chi	21	1943	Bill Nicholson, Chi	29	1977	George Foster, Cin	52
1912	Heinie Zimmerman, Chi	14	1944	Bill Nicholson, Chi	33	1978	George Foster, Cin	40
1913	Gavvy Cravath, Phi	19	1945	Tommy Holmes, Bos	28	1979	Dave Kingman, Chi	48
1914	Gavvy Cravath, Phi	19	1946	Ralph Kiner, Pit	23	1980	Mike Schmidt, Phi	48
1915	Gavvy Cravath, Phi	24	1947	Ralph Kiner, Pit	51	1981	Mike Schmidt, Phi	31
1916	Cy Williams, Chi	12		& Johnny Mize, NY	51	1982	Dave Kingman, NY	37
	& Dave Robertson, NY	12	1948	Ralph Kiner, Pit	40	1983	Mike Schmidt, Phi	40
1917	Gavvy Cravath, Phi	12		& Johnny Mize, NY	40	1984	Dale Murphy, Atl	36
	& Dave Robertson, NY	12	1949	Ralph Kiner, Pit	54		& Mike Schmidt, Phi	36
1918	Gavvy Cravath, Phi	8	1950	Ralph Kiner, Pit	47	1985	Dale Murphy, Atl	37
1919	Gavvy Cravath, Phi	12	1951	Ralph Kiner, Pit	42	1986	Mike Schmidt, Phi	37
1920	Cy Williams, Phi	15	1952	Ralph Kiner, Pit	37	1987	Andre Dawson, Chi	49
1921	George Kelly, NY	23		& Hank Sauer, Chi	37	1988	Darryl Strawberry, NY	39
1922	Rogers Hornsby, St.L	42	1953	Eddie Mathews, Mil	47	1989	Kevin Mitchell, SF	47
1923	Cy Williams, Phi	41	1954	Ted Kluszewski, Cin	49	1990	Ryne Sandberg, Chi	40
1924	Jack Fournier, Bklyn	27	1955	Willie Mays, NY	51	1991	Howard Johnson, NY	38
1925	Rogers Hornsby, St.L	39	1956	Duke Snider, Bklyn	43	1992	Fred McGriff, SD	35
1926	Hack Wilson, Chi	21	1957	Hank Aaron, Mil	44	1993	Barry Bonds, SF	46
1927	Cy Williams, Phi	30	1958	Ernie Banks, Chi	47	1994	Matt Williams, SF	43
	& Hack Wilson, Chi	30	1959	Eddie Mathews, Mil	46	1995	Dante Bichette, Col	40
1928	Jim Bottomley, St.L	31	1960	Ernie Banks, Chi	41	1996	Andres Galarraga, Col	47
	& Hack Wilson, Chi	31	1961	Orlando Cepeda, SF	46	1997	Larry Walker, Col	49
1929	Chuck Klein, Phi	43	1962	Willie Mays, SF	49	1998	Mark McGwire, St.L	70
1930	Hack Wilson, Chi	56	1963	Hank Aaron, Mil	44	1999	Mark McGwire, St.L	65
1931	Chuck Klein, Phi	31		& Willie McCovey, SF	44			
1932	Chuck Klein, Phi	38	1964	Willie Mays, SF	47			
	& Mel Ott, NY	38	1965	Willie Mays, SF	52			

Note: In 1997 Mark McGwire hit 58 home runs but hit 34 of them in the AL with Oakland before getting traded to St. Louis.

American League

Multiple winners: Babe Ruth (12); Harmon Killebrew (6); Home Run Baker, Harry Davis, Jimmie Foxx, Hank Greenberg, Ken Griffey Jr., Reggie Jackson, Mickey Mantle and Ted Williams (4); Lou Gehrig and Jim Rice (3); Dick Allen, Tony Armas, Jose Canseco, Joe DiMaggio, Larry Doby, Cecil Fielder, Juan Gonzalez, Mark McGwire, Wally Pipp, Al Rosen and Gorman Thomas (2).

Year		HR	Year		HR	Year		HR
1901	Nap Lajoie, Phi	14	1904	Harry Davis, Phi	10	1907	Harry Davis, Phi	8
1902	Socks Seybold, Phi	16	1905	Harry Davis, Phi	8	1908	Sam Crawford, Det	7
1903	Buck Freeman, Bos	13	1906	Harry Davis, Phi	12	1909	Ty Cobb, Det	9

Year		HR
1910	Jake Stahl, Bos	10
1911	Home Run Baker, Phi	11
1912	Home Run Baker, Phi	10
	& Tris Speaker, Bos.	10
1913	Home Run Baker, Phi	12
1914	Home Run Baker, Phi	9
1915	Braggo Roth, Chi-Cle	7
1916	Wally Pipp, NY	12
1917	Wally Pipp, NY	9
1918	Babe Ruth, Bos	11
	& Tilly Walker, Phi	11
1919	Babe Ruth, Bos	29
1920	Babe Ruth, NY	54
1921	Babe Ruth, NY	59
1922	Ken Williams, St.L.	39
1923	Babe Ruth, NY	41
1924	Babe Ruth, NY	46
1925	Bob Meusel, NY	33
1926	Babe Ruth, NY	47
1927	Babe Ruth, NY	60
1928	Babe Ruth, NY	54
1929	Babe Ruth, NY	46
1930	Babe Ruth, NY	49
1931	Lou Gehrig, NY.	46
	& Babe Ruth, NY	46
1932	Jimmie Foxx, Phi	58
1933	Jimmie Foxx, Phi	48
1934	Lou Gehrig, NY.	49
1935	Jimmie Foxx, Phi	36
	& Hank Greenberg, Det.	36
1936	Lou Gehrig, NY.	49
1937	Joe DiMaggio, NY	46
1938	Hank Greenberg, Det.	58
1939	Jimmie Foxx, Bos.	35
1940	Hank Greenberg, Det.	41
1941	Ted Williams, Bos	37

Year		HR
1942	Ted Williams, Bos	36
1943	Rudy York, Det.	34
1944	Nick Etten, NY	22
1945	Vern Stephens, St.L	24
1946	Hank Greenberg, Det.	44
1947	Ted Williams, Bos	32
1948	Joe DiMaggio, NY	39
1949	Ted Williams, Bos	43
1950	Al Rosen, Cle	37
1951	Gus Zernial, Chi-Phi	33
1952	Larry Doby, Cle	32
1953	Al Rosen, Cle	43
1954	Larry Doby, Cle	32
1955	Mickey Mantle, NY	37
1956	Mickey Mantle, NY	52
1957	Roy Sievers, Wash	42
1958	Mickey Mantle, NY	42
1959	Rocky Colavito, Cle	42
	& Harmon Killebrew, Wash	42
1960	Mickey Mantle, NY	40
1961	Roger Maris, NY.	61
1962	Harmon Killebrew, Min	48
1963	Harmon Killebrew, Min	45
1964	Harmon Killebrew, Min	49
1965	Tony Conigliaro, Bos	32
1966	Frank Robinson, Bal	49
1967	Harmon Killebrew, Min	44
	& Carl Yastrzemski, Bos.	44
1968	Frank Howard, Wash.	44
1969	Harmon Killebrew, Min	49
1970	Frank Howard, Wash.	44
1971	Bill Melton, Chi	33
1972	Dick Allen, Chi	37
1973	Reggie Jackson, Oak	32
1974	Dick Allen, Chi	32

Year		HR
1975	Reggie Jackson, Oak	36
	& George Scott, Mil	36
1976	Graig Nettles, NY	32
1977	Jim Rice, Bos	39
1978	Jim Rice, Bos	46
1979	Gorman Thomas, Mil	45
1980	Reggie Jackson, NY	41
	& Ben Oglivie, Mil	41
1981	Tony Armas, Oak	22
	Dwight Evans, Bos	22
	Bobby Grich, Cal	22
	& Eddie Murray, Bal	22
1982	Reggie Jackson, Cal	39
	& Gorman Thomas, Mil	39
1983	Jim Rice, Bos	39
1984	Tony Armas, Bos	43
1985	Darrell Evans, Det	40
1986	Jesse Barfield, Tor	40
1987	Mark McGwire, Oak	49
1988	Jose Canseco, Oak	42
1989	Fred McGriff, Tor	36
1990	Cecil Fielder, Det	51
1991	Jose Canseco, Oak	44
	& Cecil Fielder, Det	44
1992	Juan Gonzalez, Tex	43
1993	Juan Gonzalez, Tex	46
1994	Ken Griffey Jr., Sea	40
1995	Albert Belle, Cle	50
1996	Mark McGwire, Oak	52
1997	Ken Griffey Jr., Sea	56
1998	Ken Griffey Jr., Sea	56
1999	Ken Griffey Jr., Sea	48

Note: In 1997 Mark McGwire hit 58 home runs but hit 24 of them in the NL with St. Louis after getting traded from Oakland.

Runs Batted In
National League

Multiple winners: Hank Aaron, Rogers Hornsby, Sherry Magee, Mike Schmidt and Honus Wagner (4); Johnny Bench, George Foster, Joe Medwick, Johnny Mize and Heinie Zimmerman (3); Ernie Banks, Jim Bottomley, Orlando Cepeda, Gavvy Cravath, Andres Galarraga, George Kelly, Chuck Klein, Willie McCovey, Dale Murphy, Stan Musial, Bill Nicholson and Hack Wilson (2).

Year		RBI
1900	Elmer Flick, Phi	110
1901	Honus Wagner, Pit	126
1902	Honus Wagner, Pit	91
1903	Sam Mertes, NY	104
1904	Bill Dahlen, NY	80
1905	Cy Seymour, Cin	121
1906	Jim Nealon, Pit	83
	& Harry Steinfeldt, Chi.	83
1907	Sherry Magee, Phi.	85
1908	Honus Wagner, Pit	109
1909	Honus Wagner, Pit	100
1910	Sherry Magee, Phi	123
1911	Wildfire Schulte, Chi	121
1912	Heinie Zimmerman, Chi	103
1913	Gavvy Cravath, Phi	128
1914	Sherry Magee, Phi	103
1915	Gavvy Cravath, Phi	115
1916	Heinie Zimmerman, Chi-NY	83
1917	Heinie Zimmerman, NY.	102
1918	Sherry Magee, Cin.	76
1919	Hy Myers, Bklyn	73
1920	Rogers Hornsby, St.L.	94
	& George Kelly, NY	94
1921	Rogers Hornsby, St.L	126
1922	Rogers Hornsby, St.L	152

Year		RBI
1923	Irish Meusel, NY	125
1924	George Kelly, NY	136
1925	Rogers Hornsby, St.L	143
1926	Jim Bottomley, St.L	120
1927	Paul Waner, Pit	131
1928	Jim Bottomley, St.L	136
1929	Hack Wilson, Chi	159
1930	Hack Wilson, Chi	191
1931	Chuck Klein, Phi	121
1932	Don Hurst, Phi	143
1933	Chuck Klein, Phi	120
1934	Mel Ott, NY	135
1935	Wally Berger, Bos	130
1936	Joe Medwick, St.L	138
1937	Joe Medwick, St.L	154
1938	Joe Medwick, St.L	122
1939	Frank McCormick, Cin	128
1940	Johnny Mize, St.L	137
1941	Dolph Camilli, Bklyn	120
1942	Johnny Mize, NY	110
1943	Bill Nicholson, Chi	128
1944	Bill Nicholson, Chi	122
1945	Dixie Walker, Bklyn	124
1946	Enos Slaughter, St.L	130
1947	Johnny Mize, NY	138

Year		RBI
1948	Stan Musial, St.L.	131
1949	Ralph Kiner, Pit	127
1950	Del Ennis, Phi	126
1951	Monte Irvin, NY	121
1952	Hank Sauer, Chi	121
1953	Roy Campanella, Bklyn	142
1954	Ted Kluszewski, Cin	141
1955	Duke Snider, Bklyn	136
1956	Stan Musial, St.L.	109
1957	Hank Aaron, Mil	132
1958	Ernie Banks, Chi	129
1959	Ernie Banks, Chi	143
1960	Hank Aaron, Mil	126
1961	Orlando Cepeda, SF	142
1962	Tommy Davis, LA	153
1963	Hank Aaron, Mil	130
1964	Ken Boyer, St.L	119
1965	Deron Johnson, Cin	130
1966	Hank Aaron, Atl	127
1967	Orlando Cepeda, St.L.	111
1968	Willie McCovey, SF	105
1969	Willie McCovey, SF	126
1970	Johnny Bench, Cin	148
1971	Joe Torre, St.L.	137

Year	RBI	Year	RBI	Year	RBI
1972 Johnny Bench, Cin	125	1982 Dale Murphy, Atl	109	1990 Matt Williams, SF.	122
1973 Willie Stargell, Pit.	119	& Al Oliver, Mon	109	1991 Howard Johnson, NY	117
1974 Johnny Bench, Cin	129	1983 Dale Murphy, Atl	121	1992 Darren Daulton, Phi	109
1975 Greg Luzinski, Phi	120	1984 Gary Carter, Mon	106	1993 Barry Bonds, SF	123
1976 George Foster, Cin.	121	& Mike Schmidt, Phi.	106	1994 Jeff Bagwell, Hou	116
1977 George Foster, Cin.	149	1985 Dave Parker, Cin	125	1995 Dante Bichette, Col	128
1978 George Foster, Cin.	120	1986 Mike Schmidt, Phi.	119	1996 Andres Galarraga, Col	150
1979 Dave Winfield, SD	118	1987 Andre Dawson, Chi	137	1997 Andres Galarraga, Col	140
1980 Mike Schmidt, Phi.	121	1988 Will Clark, SF.	109	1998 Sammy Sosa, Chi.	158
1981 Mike Schmidt, Phi.	91	1989 Kevin Mitchell, SF.	125	1999 Mark McGwire, St.L.	147

American League

Multiple winners: Babe Ruth (6); Lou Gehrig (5); Ty Cobb, Hank Greenberg and Ted Williams (4); Albert Belle, Sam Crawford, Cecil Fielder, Jimmie Foxx, Jackie Jensen, Harmon Killebrew, Vern Stephens and Bobby Veach (3); Home Run Baker, Cecil Cooper, Harry Davis, Joe DiMaggio, Buck Freeman, Nap Lajoie, Roger Maris, Jim Rice, Al Rosen, and Bobby Veach (2).

Year	RBI	Year	RBI	Year	RBI
1901 Nap Lajoie, Phi.	125	1935 Hank Greenberg, Det	170	1968 Ken Harrelson, Bos	109
1902 Buck Freeman, Bos	121	1936 Hal Trosky, Cle	162	1969 Harmon Killebrew, Min	140
1903 Buck Freeman, Bos	104	1937 Hank Greenberg, Det	183	1970 Frank Howard, Wash	126
1904 Nap Lajoie, Cle	102	1938 Jimmie Foxx, Bos	175	1971 Harmon Killebrew, Min	119
1905 Harry Davis, Phi	83	1939 Ted Williams, Bos.	145	1972 Dick Allen, Chi	113
1906 Harry Davis, Phi	96	1940 Hank Greenberg, Det	150	1973 Reggie Jackson, Oak	117
1907 Ty Cobb, Det.	116	1941 Joe DiMaggio, NY	125	1974 Jeff Burroughs, Tex	118
1908 Ty Cobb, Det.	108	1942 Ted Williams, Bos.	137	1975 George Scott, Mil.	109
1909 Ty Cobb, Det.	107	1943 Rudy York, Det	118	1976 Lee May, Bal	109
1910 Sam Crawford, Det	120	1944 Vern Stephens, St.L.	109	1977 Larry Hisle, Min	119
1911 Ty Cobb, Det.	144	1945 Nick Etten, NY	111	1978 Jim Rice, Bos.	139
1912 Home Run Baker, Phi	133	1946 Hank Greenberg, Det	127	1979 Don Baylor, Cal	139
1913 Home Run Baker, Phi	126	1947 Ted Williams, Bos.	114	1980 Cecil Cooper, Mil.	122
1914 Sam Crawford, Det	104	1948 Joe DiMaggio, NY	155	1981 Eddie Murray, Bal.	78
1915 Sam Crawford, Det	112	1949 Ted Williams, Bos.	159	1982 Hal McRae, KC.	133
& Bobby Veach, Det	112	& Vern Stephens, Bos.	159	1983 Cecil Cooper, Mil.	126
1916 Del Pratt, St.L.	103	1950 Walt Dropo, Bos.	144	& Jim Rice, Bos.	126
1917 Bobby Veach, Det	103	& Vern Stephens, Bos.	144	1984 Tony Armas, Bos.	123
1918 Bobby Veach, Det	78	1951 Gus Zernial, Chi-Phi.	129	1985 Don Mattingly, NY	145
1919 Babe Ruth, Bos	114	1952 Al Rosen, Cle	105	1986 Joe Carter, Cle	121
1920 Babe Ruth, NY	137	1953 Al Rosen, Cle	145	1987 George Bell, Tor	134
1921 Babe Ruth, NY	171	1954 Larry Doby, Cle.	126	1988 Jose Canseco, Oak	124
1922 Ken Williams, St.L	155	1955 Ray Boone, Det.	116	1989 Ruben Sierra, Tex	119
1923 Babe Ruth, NY	131	& Jackie Jensen, Bos	116	1990 Cecil Fielder, Det	132
1924 Goose Goslin, Wash	129	1956 Mickey Mantle, NY	130	1991 Cecil Fielder, Det	133
1925 Bob Meusel, NY	138	1957 Roy Sievers, Wash	114	1992 Cecil Fielder, Det	124
1926 Babe Ruth, NY	145	1958 Jackie Jensen, Bos	122	1993 Albert Belle, Cle.	129
1927 Lou Gehrig, NY	175	1959 Jackie Jensen, Bos	112	1994 Kirby Puckett, Min	112
1928 Lou Gehrig, NY	142	1960 Roger Maris, NY	112	1995 Albert Belle, Cle.	126
& Babe Ruth, NY	142	1961 Roger Maris, NY	142	& Mo Vaughn, Bos.	126
1929 Al Simmons, Phi	157	1962 Harmon Killebrew, Min	126	1996 Albert Belle, Cle.	148
1930 Lou Gehrig, NY	174	1963 Dick Stuart, Bos	118	1997 Ken Griffey Jr., Sea	147
1931 Lou Gehrig, NY	184	1964 Brooks Robinson, Bal	118	1998 Juan Gonzalez, Tex	157
1932 Jimmie Foxx, Phi	169	1965 Rocky Colavito, Cle	108	1999 Manny Ramirez, Cle	165
1933 Jimmie Foxx, Phi	163	1966 Frank Robinson, Bal	122		
1934 Lou Gehrig, NY	165	1967 Carl Yastrzemski, Bos	121		

Batting Triple Crown Winners

Players who led either league in Batting Average, Home Runs and Runs Batted In over a single season.

National League

	Year	Avg	HR	RBI
Paul Hines, Providence	1878	.358	4	50
Hugh Duffy, Boston	1894	.438	18	145
Heinie Zimmerman, Chicago	1912	.372	14	103
Rogers Hornsby, St. Louis	1922	.401	42	152
Rogers Hornsby, St. Louis	1925	.403	39	143
Chuck Klein, Philadelphia	1933	.368	28	120
Joe Medwick, St. Louis	1937	.374	31*	154

*Tied for league lead in HRs with Mel Ott, NY.

American League

	Year	Avg	HR	RBI
Nap Lajoie, Philadelphia	1901	.422	14	125
Ty Cobb, Detroit	1909	.377	9	115
Jimmie Foxx, Philadelphia	1933	.356	48	163
Lou Gehrig, New York	1934	.363	49	165
Ted Williams, Boston	1942	.356	36	137
Ted Williams, Boston	1947	.343	32	114
Mickey Mantle, New York	1956	.353	52	130
Frank Robinson, Baltimore	1966	.316	49	122
Carl Yastrzemski, Boston	1967	.326	44*	121

*Tied for league lead in HRs with Harmon Killebrew, Min.

Stolen Bases
National League

Multiple winners: Max Carey (10); Lou Brock (8); Vince Coleman and Maury Wills (6); Honus Wagner (5); Bob Bescher, Kiki Cuyler, Willie Mays and Tim Raines (4); Bill Bruton, Frankie Frisch, Pepper Martin and Tony Womack (3); George Burns, Frank Chance, Augie Galan, Marquis Grissom, Stan Hack, Sam Jethroe, Davey Lopes, Omar Moreno, Pete Reiser and Jackie Robinson (2).

Year	Player	SB	Year	Player	SB	Year	Player	SB
1900	Patsy Donovan, St.L.	.45	1934	Pepper Martin, St.L.	.23	1970	Bobby Tolan, Cin	.57
	& George Van Haltren, NY	.45	1935	Augie Galan, Chi	.22	1971	Lou Brock, St.L.	.64
1901	Honus Wagner, Pit	.49	1936	Pepper Martin, St.L.	.23	1972	Lou Brock, St.L.	.63
1902	Honus Wagner, Pit	.42	1937	Augie Galan, Chi	.23	1973	Lou Brock, St.L.	.70
1903	Frank Chance, Chi	.67	1938	Stan Hack, Chi	.16	1974	Lou Brock, St.L.	.118
	& Jimmy Sheckard, Bklyn.	.67	1939	Stan Hack, Chi	.17	1975	Davey Lopes, LA	.77
1904	Honus Wagner, Pit	.53		& Lee Handley, Pit	.17	1976	Davey Lopes, LA	.63
1905	Art Devlin, NY	.59	1940	Lonny Frey, Cin	.22	1977	Frank Taveras, Pit	.70
	& Billy Maloney, Chi	.59	1941	Danny Murtaugh, Phi	.18	1978	Omar Moreno, Pit.	.71
1906	Frank Chance, Chi	.57	1942	Pete Reiser, Bklyn	.20	1979	Omar Moreno, Pit.	.77
1907	Honus Wagner, Pit	.61	1943	Arky Vaughan, Bklyn	.20	1980	Ron LeFlore, Mon	.97
1908	Honus Wagner, Pit	.53	1944	Johnny Barrett, Pit	.28	1981	Tim Raines, Mon	.71
1909	Bob Bescher, Cin	.54	1945	Red Schoendienst, St.L.	.26	1982	Tim Raines, Mon	.78
1910	Bob Bescher, Cin	.70	1946	Pete Reiser, Bklyn	.34	1983	Tim Raines, Mon	.90
1911	Bob Bescher, Cin	.81	1947	Jackie Robinson, Bklyn.	.29	1984	Tim Raines, Mon	.75
1912	Bob Bescher, Cin	.67	1948	Richie Ashburn, Phi.	.32	1985	Vince Coleman, St.L.	.110
1913	Max Carey, Pit	.61	1949	Jackie Robinson, Bklyn.	.37	1986	Vince Coleman, St.L.	.107
1914	George Burns, NY	.62	1950	Sam Jethroe, Bos.	.35	1987	Vince Coleman, St.L.	.109
1915	Max Carey, Pit	.36	1951	Sam Jethroe, Bos.	.35	1988	Vince Coleman, St.L.	.81
1916	Max Carey, Pit	.63	1952	Pee Wee Reese, Bklyn	.30	1989	Vince Coleman, St.L.	.65
1917	Max Carey, Pit	.46	1953	Bill Bruton, Mil.	.26	1990	Vince Coleman, St.L.	.77
1918	Max Carey, Pit	.58	1954	Bill Bruton, Mil.	.34	1991	Marquis Grissom, Mon	.76
1919	George Burns, NY	.40	1955	Bill Bruton, Mil.	.25	1992	Marquis Grissom, Mon	.78
1920	Max Carey, Pit	.52	1956	Willie Mays, NY	.40	1993	Chuck Carr, Fla	.58
1921	Frankie Frisch, NY	.49	1957	Willie Mays, NY	.38	1994	Craig Biggio, Hou	.39
1922	Max Carey, Pit	.51	1958	Willie Mays, SF	.31	1995	Quilvio Veras, Fla	.56
1923	Max Carey, Pit	.51	1959	Willie Mays, SF	.27	1996	Eric Young, Col	.53
1924	Max Carey, Pit	.49	1960	Maury Wills, LA	.50	1997	Tony Womack, Pit	.60
1925	Max Carey, Pit	.46	1961	Maury Wills, LA	.35	1998	Tony Womack, Pit	.58
1926	Kiki Cuyler, Pit.	.35	1962	Maury Wills, LA	.104	1999	Tony Womack, Ari	.72
1927	Frankie Frisch, St.L	.48	1963	Maury Wills, LA	.40			
1928	Kiki Cuyler, Chi.	.37	1964	Maury Wills, LA	.53			
1929	Kiki Cuyler, Chi.	.43	1965	Maury Wills, LA	.94			
1930	Kiki Cuyler, Chi.	.37	1966	Lou Brock, St.L.	.74			
1931	Frankie Frisch, St.L	.28	1967	Lou Brock, St.L.	.52			
1932	Chuck Klein, Phi	.20	1968	Lou Brock, St.L.	.62			
1933	Pepper Martin, St.L.	.26	1969	Lou Brock, St.L.	.53			

30 Homers & 30 Stolen Bases in One Season
National League

Player	Year	Gm	HR	SB
Willie Mays, NY Giants	1956	152	36	40
Willie Mays, NY Giants	1957	152	35	38
Hank Aaron, Milwaukee	1963	161	44	31
Bobby Bonds, San Francisco	1969	158	32	45
Bobby Bonds, San Francisco	1973	160	39	43
Dale Murphy, Atlanta	1983	162	36	30
Eric Davis, Cincinnati	1987	129	37	50
Howard Johnson, NY Mets	1987	157	36	32
Darryl Strawberry, NY Mets	1987	154	39	36
Howard Johnson, NY Mets	1989	153	36	41
Ron Gant, Atlanta	1990	152	32	33
Barry Bonds, Pittsburgh	1990	151	33	52
Ron Gant, Atlanta	1991	154	32	34
Howard Johnson, NY Mets	1991	156	38	30
Barry Bonds, Pittsburgh	1992	140	34	39
Sammy Sosa, Chicago	1993	159	33	36
Barry Bonds, San Francisco	1995	144	33	31
Sammy Sosa, Chicago	1995	144	36	34
Barry Bonds, San Francisco	1996	158	42	40
Ellis Burks, Colorado	1996	156	40	32

Player	Year	Gm	HR	SB
Dante Bichette, Colorado	1996	159	31	31
Larry Walker, Colorado	1997	153	49	33
Barry Bonds, San Francisco	1997	159	40	37
Raul Mondesi, Los Angeles	1997	159	30	32
Jeff Bagwell, Houston	1997	162	43	31
Jeff Bagwell, Houston	1999	162	42	30
Raul Mondesi, Los Angeles	1999	159	33	36

American League

Player	Year	Gm	HR	SB
Kenny Williams, St. Louis	1922	153	39	37
Tommy Harper, Milwaukee	1970	154	31	38
Bobby Bonds, New York	1975	145	32	30
Bobby Bonds, California	1977	158	37	41
Bobby Bonds, Chicago-Texas	1978	156	31	43
Joe Carter, Cleveland	1987	149	32	31
Jose Canseco, Oakland	1988	158	42	40
Alex Rodriguez, Seattle	1998	161	42	46
Shawn Green, Toronto	1998	158	35	35

American League

Multiple winners: Rickey Henderson (12); Luis Aparicio (9); Bert Campaneris, George Case and Ty Cobb (6); Kenny Lofton (5); Ben Chapman, Eddie Collins and George Sisler (4); Bob Dillinger, Minnie Minoso and Bill Werber (3); Elmer Flick, Tommy Harper, Brian Hunter, Clyde Milan, Johnny Mostil, Bill North and Snuffy Stirnweiss (2).

Year		SB	Year		SB	Year		SB
1901	Frank Isbell, Chi	52	1934	Bill Werber, Bos	40	1967	Bert Campaneris, KC	55
1902	Topsy Hartsel, Phi	47	1935	Bill Werber, Bos	29	1968	Bert Campaneris, Oak	62
1903	Harry Bay, Cle	45	1936	Lyn Lary, St.L	37	1969	Tommy Harper, Sea	73
1904	Elmer Flick, Cle	42	1937	Ben Chapman, Wash-Bos	35	1970	Bert Campaneris, Oak	42
1905	Danny Hoffman, Phi	46		& Bill Werber, Phi	35	1971	Amos Otis, KC	52
1906	John Anderson, Wash	39	1938	Frank Crosetti, NY	27	1972	Bert Campaneris, Oak	52
	& Elmer Flick, Cle	39	1939	George Case, Wash	51	1973	Tommy Harper, Bos	54
1907	Ty Cobb, Det	49	1940	George Case, Wash	35	1974	Bill North, Oak	54
1908	Patsy Dougherty, Chi	47	1941	George Case, Wash	33	1975	Mickey Rivers, CA	70
1909	Ty Cobb, Det	76	1942	George Case, Wash	44	1976	Bill North, Oak	75
1910	Eddie Collins, Phi	81	1943	George Case, Wash	61	1977	Freddie Patek, KC	53
1911	Ty Cobb, Det	83	1944	Snuffy Stirnweiss, NY	55	1978	Ron LeFlore, Det	68
1912	Clyde Milan, Wash	88	1945	Snuffy Stirnweiss, NY	33	1979	Willie Wilson, KC	83
1913	Clyde Milan, Wash	75	1946	George Case, Cle	28	1980	Rickey Henderson, Oak	100
1914	Fritz Maisel, NY	74	1947	Bob Dillinger, St.L	34	1981	Rickey Henderson, Oak	56
1915	Ty Cobb, Det	96	1948	Bob Dillinger, St.L	28	1982	Rickey Henderson, Oak	130
1916	Ty Cobb, Det	68	1949	Bob Dillinger, St.L	20	1983	Rickey Henderson, Oak	108
1917	Ty Cobb, Det	55	1950	Dom DiMaggio, Bos	15	1984	Rickey Henderson, Oak	66
1918	George Sisler, St.L	45	1951	Minnie Minoso, Cle-Chi	31	1985	Rickey Henderson, NY	80
1919	Eddie Collins, Chi	33	1952	Minnie Minoso, Chi	22	1986	Rickey Henderson, NY	87
1920	Sam Rice, Wash	63	1953	Minnie Minoso, Chi	25	1987	Harold Reynolds, Sea	60
1921	George Sisler, St.L	35	1954	Jackie Jensen, Bos	22	1988	Rickey Henderson, NY	93
1922	George Sisler, St.L	51	1955	Jim Rivera, Chi	25	1989	R. Henderson, NY-Oak	77
1923	Eddie Collins, Chi	47	1956	Luis Aparicio, Chi	21	1990	Rickey Henderson, Oak	65
1924	Eddie Collins, Chi	42	1957	Luis Aparicio, Chi	28	1991	Rickey Henderson, Oak	58
1925	Johnny Mostil, Chi	43	1958	Luis Aparicio, Chi	29	1992	Kenny Lofton, Cle	66
1926	Johnny Mostil, Chi	35	1959	Luis Aparicio, Chi	56	1993	Kenny Lofton, Cle	70
1927	George Sisler, St.L	27	1960	Luis Aparicio, Chi	51	1994	Kenny Lofton, Cle	60
1928	Buddy Myer, Bos	30	1961	Luis Aparicio, Chi	53	1995	Kenny Lofton, Cle	54
1929	Charlie Gehringer, Det	28	1962	Luis Aparicio, Chi	31	1996	Kenny Lofton, Cle	75
1930	Marty McManus, Det	23	1963	Luis Aparicio, Bal	40	1997	Brian Hunter, Det	74
1931	Ben Chapman, NY	61	1964	Luis Aparicio, Bal	57	1998	Rickey Henderson, Oak	66
1932	Ben Chapman, NY	38	1965	Bert Campaneris, KC	51	1999	Brian Hunter, Det-Sea	44
1933	Ben Chapman, NY	27	1966	Bert Campaneris, KC	52			

Consecutive Game Streaks

Regular season games through 1999.

Games Played

Gm		Dates of Streak
2632	Cal Ripken Jr., Bal	5/30/82 to 9/19/98
2130	Lou Gehrig, NY	6/1/25 to 4/30/39
1307	Everett Scott, Bos-NY	6/20/16 to 5/5/25
1207	Steve Garvey, LA-SD	9/3/75 to 7/29/83
1117	Billy Williams, Cubs	9/22/63 to 9/2/70
1103	Joe Sewell, Cle	9/13/22 to 4/30/30
895	Stan Musial, St.L	4/15/52 to 8/23/57
829	Eddie Yost, Wash	4/30/49 to 5/11/55
822	Gus Suhr, Pit	9/11/31 to 6/4/37
798	Nellie Fox, Chisox	8/8/55 to 9/3/60
745	Pete Rose, Cin-Phi	9/2/78 to 8/23/83
740	Dale Murphy, Atl	9/26/81 to 7/8/86
730	Richie Ashburn, Phi	6/7/50 to 4/13/55
717	Ernie Banks, Cubs	8/28/56 to 6/22/61
678	Pete Rose, Cin	9/28/73 to 5/7/78

Others

Gm		Gm	
673	Earl Averill	565	Aaron Ward
652	Frank McCormick	540	Candy LaChance
648	Sandy Alomar Sr.	535	Buck Freeman
618	Eddie Brown	533	Fred Luderus
585	Roy McMillan	511	Clyde Milan
577	George Pinckney	511	Charlie Gehringer
574	Steve Brodie	508	Vada Pinson

Hitting

	Gm	Year
Joe DiMaggio, New York (AL)	56	1941
Willie Keeler, Baltimore (NL)	44	1897
Pete Rose, Cincinnati (NL)	44	1978
Bill Dahlen, Chicago (NL)	42	1894
George Sisler, St. Louis (AL)	41	1922
Ty Cobb, Detroit (AL)	40	1911
Paul Molitor, Milwaukee (AL)	39	1987
Tommy Holmes, Boston (NL)	37	1945
Billy Hamilton, Philadelphia (NL)	36	1894
Fred Clarke, Louisville (NL)	35	1895
Ty Cobb, Detroit (AL)	35	1917
Ty Cobb, Detroit (AL)	34	1912
George Sisler, St. Louis (AL)	34	1925
George McQuinn, St. Louis (AL)	34	1938
Dom DiMaggio, Boston (AL)	34	1949
Benito Santiago, San Diego (NL)	34	1987
George Davis, New York (NL)	33	1893
Hal Chase, New York (AL)	33	1907
Rogers Hornsby, St. Louis (NL)	33	1922
Heinie Manush, Washington (AL)	33	1933
Ed Delahanty, Philadelphia (NL)	31	1899
Nap Lajoie, Cleveland (AL)	31	1906
Sam Rice, Washington, (AL)	31	1924
Willie Davis, Los Angeles (NL)	31	1969
Rico Carty, Atlanta (NL)	31	1970
Ken Landreaux, Minnesota (AL)	31	1980
Vladimir Guerrero, Montreal (NL)	31	1999

Annual Pitching Leaders (since 1900)
Winning Percentage
At least 15 wins, except in strike years of 1981 and 1994 (when the minimum was 10).

National League
Multiple winners: Ed Reulbach and Tom Seaver (3); Larry Benton, Harry Brecheen, Jack Chesbro, Paul Derringer, Freddie Fitzsimmons, Don Gullett, Claude Hendrix, Carl Hubbell, Sandy Koufax, Bill Lee, Greg Maddux, Christy Mathewson, Don Newcombe, Preacher Roe and John Smoltz (2).

Year		W-L	Pct	Year		W-L	Pct
1900	Jesse Tannehill, Pittsburgh	20-6	.769	1950	Sal Maglie, New York	18-4	.818
1901	Jack Chesbro, Pittsburgh	21-10	.677	1951	Preacher Roe, Brooklyn	22-3	.880
1902	Jack Chesbro, Pittsburgh	28-6	.824	1952	Hoyt Wilhelm, New York	15-3	.833
1903	Sam Leever, Pittsburgh	25-7	.781	1953	Carl Erskine, Brooklyn	20-6	.769
1904	Joe McGinnity, New York	35-8	.814	1954	Johnny Antonelli, New York	21-7	.750
1905	Christy Mathewson, New York	31-8	.795	1955	Don Newcombe, Brooklyn	20-5	.800
1906	Ed Reulbach, Chicago	19-4	.826	1956	Don Newcombe, Brooklyn	27-7	.794
1907	Ed Reulbach, Chicago	17-4	.810	1957	Bob Buhl, Milwaukee	18-7	.720
1908	Ed Reulbach, Chicago	24-7	.774	1958	Warren Spahn, Milwaukee	22-11	.667
1909	Howie Camnitz, Pittsburgh	25-6	.806		& Lew Burdette, Milwaukee	20-10	.667
	& Christy Mathewson, New York	25-6	.806	1959	Roy Face, Pittsburgh	18-1	.947
1910	King Cole, Chicago	20-4	.833	1960	Ernie Broglio, St. Louis	21-9	.700
1911	Rube Marquard, New York	24-7	.774	1961	Johnny Podres, Los Angeles	18-5	.783
1912	Claude Hendrix, Pittsburgh	24-9	.727	1962	Bob Purkey, Cincinnati	23-5	.821
1913	Bert Humphries, Chicago	16-4	.800	1963	Ron Perranoski, Los Angeles	16-3	.842
1914	Bill James, Boston	26-7	.788	1964	Sandy Koufax, Los Angeles	19-5	.792
1915	Grover Alexander, Phila.	31-10	.756	1965	Sandy Koufax, Los Angeles	26-8	.765
1916	Tom Hughes, Boston	16-3	.842	1966	Juan Marichal, San Francisco	25-6	.806
1917	Ferdie Schupp, New York	21-7	.750	1967	Dick Hughes, St. Louis	16-6	.727
1918	Claude Hendrix, Chicago	19-7	.731	1968	Steve Blass, Pittsburgh	18-6	.750
1919	Dutch Ruether, Cincinnati	19-6	.760	1969	Tom Seaver, New York	25-7	.781
1920	Burleigh Grimes, Brooklyn	23-11	.676	1970	Bob Gibson, St. Louis	23-7	.767
1921	Bill Doak, St. Louis	15-6	.714	1971	Don Gullett, Cincinnati	16-6	.727
1922	Pete Donohue, Cincinnati	18-9	.667	1972	Gary Nolan, Cincinnati	15-5	.750
1923	Dolf Luque, Cincinnati	27-8	.771	1973	Tommy John, Los Angeles	16-7	.696
1924	Emil Yde, Pittsburgh	16-3	.842	1974	Andy Messersmith, Los Angeles	20-6	.769
1925	Bill Sherdel, St. Louis	15-6	.714	1975	Don Gullett, Cincinnati	15-4	.789
1926	Ray Kremer, Pittsburgh	20-6	.769	1976	Steve Carlton, Philadelphia	20-7	.741
1927	Larry Benton, Boston-NY	17-7	.708	1977	John Candelaria, Pittsburgh	20-5	.800
1928	Larry Benton, New York	25-9	.735	1978	Gaylord Perry, San Diego	21-6	.778
1929	Charlie Root, Chicago	19-6	.760	1979	Tom Seaver, Cincinnati	16-6	.727
1930	Freddie Fitzsimmons, NY	19-7	.731	1980	Jim Bibby, Pittsburgh	19-6	.760
1931	Paul Derringer, St. Louis	18-8	.692	1981	Tom Seaver, Cincinnati	14-2	.875
1932	Lon Warneke, Chicago	22-6	.786	1982	Phil Niekro, Atlanta	17-4	.810
1933	Ben Cantwell, Boston	20-10	.667	1983	John Denny, Philadelphia	19-6	.760
1934	Dizzy Dean, St. Louis	30-7	.811	1984	Rick Sutcliffe, Chicago	16-1	.941
1935	Bill Lee, Chicago	20-6	.769	1985	Orel Hershiser, Los Angeles	19-3	.864
1936	Carl Hubbell, New York	26-6	.813	1986	Bob Ojeda, New York	18-5	.783
1937	Carl Hubbell, New York	22-8	.733	1987	Dwight Gooden, New York	15-7	.682
1938	Bill Lee, Chicago	22-9	.710	1988	David Cone, New York	20-3	.870
1939	Paul Derringer, Cincinnati	25-7	.781	1989	Mike Bielecki, Chicago	18-7	.720
1940	Freddie Fitzsimmons, Bklyn	16-2	.889	1990	Doug Drabek, Pittsburgh	22-6	.786
1941	Elmer Riddle, Cincinnati	19-4	.826	1991	John Smiley, Pittsburgh	20-8	.714
1942	Larry French, Brooklyn	15-4	.789		& Jose Rijo, Cincinnati	15-6	.714
1943	Mort Cooper, St. Louis	21-8	.724	1992	Bob Tewksbury, St. Louis	16-5	.762
1944	Ted Wilks, St. Louis	17-4	.810	1993	Mark Portugal, Houston	18-4	.818
1945	Harry Brecheen, St. Louis	14-4	.778	1994	Marvin Freeman, Colorado	10-2	.833
1946	Murray Dickson, St. Louis	15-6	.714	1995	Greg Maddux, Atlanta	19-2	.905
1947	Larry Jansen, New York	21-5	.808	1996	John Smoltz, Atlanta	24-8	.750
1948	Harry Brecheen, St. Louis	20-7	.741	1997	Greg Maddux, Atlanta	19-4	.826
1949	Preacher Roe, Brooklyn	15-6	.714	1998	John Smoltz, Atlanta	17-3	.850
				1999	Mike Hampton, Houston	22-4	.846

Note: In 1984, Sutcliffe was also 4-5 with Cleveland for a combined AL-NL record of 20-6 (.769).

American League
Multiple winners: Lefty Grove (5); Chief Bender and Whitey Ford (3); Johnny Allen, Eddie Cicotte, Roger Clemens, Mike Cuellar, Lefty Gomez, Catfish Hunter, Randy Johnson, Walter Johnson, Jim Palmer, Pete Vuckovich and Smokey Joe Wood (2).

Year		W-L	Pct	Year		W-L	Pct
1901	Clark Griffith, Chicago	24-7	.774	1904	Jack Chesbro, New York	41-12	.774
1902	Bill Bernhard, Phila-Cleve	18-5	.783	1905	Andy Coakley, Philadelphia	20-7	.741
1903	Cy Young, Boston	28-9	.757	1906	Eddie Plank, Philadelphia	19-6	.760

Year		W-L	Pct	Year		W-L	Pct
1907	Wild Bill Donovan, Detroit	25-4	.862	1955	Tommy Byrne, New York	16-5	.762
1908	Ed Walsh, Chicago	40-15	.727	1956	Whitey Ford, New York	19-6	.760
1909	George Mullin, Detroit	29-8	.784	1957	Dick Donovan, Chicago	16-6	.727
					& Tom Sturdivant, New York	16-6	.727
1910	Chief Bender, Philadelphia	23-5	.821	1958	Bob Turley, New York	21-7	.750
1911	Chief Bender, Philadelphia	17-5	.773	1959	Bob Shaw, Chicago	18-6	.750
1912	Smokey Joe Wood, Boston	34-5	.872				
1913	Walter Johnson, Washington	36-7	.837	1960	Jim Perry, Cleveland	18-10	.643
1914	Chief Bender, Philadelphia	17-3	.850	1961	Whitey Ford, New York	25-4	.862
1915	Smokey Joe Wood, Boston	15-5	.750	1962	Ray Herbert, Chicago	20-9	.690
1916	Eddie Cicotte, Chicago	15-7	.682	1963	Whitey Ford, New York	24-7	.774
1917	Reb Russell, Chicago	15-5	.750	1964	Wally Bunker, Baltimore	19-5	.792
1918	Sad Sam Jones, Boston	16-5	.762	1965	Mudcat Grant, Minnesota	21-7	.750
1919	Eddie Cicotte, Chicago	29-7	.806	1966	Sonny Siebert, Cleveland	16-8	.667
				1967	Joe Horlen, Chicago	19-7	.731
1920	Jim Bagby, Cleveland	31-12	.721	1968	Denny McLain, Detroit	31-6	.838
1921	Carl Mays, New York	27-9	.750	1969	Jim Palmer, Baltimore	16-4	.800
1922	Joe Bush, New York	26-7	.788				
1923	Herb Pennock, New York	19-6	.760	1970	Mike Cuellar, Baltimore	24-8	.750
1924	Walter Johnson, Washington	23-7	.767	1971	Dave McNally, Baltimore	21-5	.808
1925	Stan Coveleski, Washington	20-5	.800	1972	Catfish Hunter, Oakland	21-7	.750
1926	George Uhle, Cleveland	27-11	.711	1973	Catfish Hunter, Oakland	21-5	.808
1927	Waite Hoyt, New York	22-7	.759	1974	Mike Cuellar, Baltimore	22-10	.688
1928	General Crowder, St. Louis	21-5	.808	1975	Mike Torrez, Baltimore	20-9	.690
1929	Lefty Grove, Philadelphia	20-6	.769	1976	Bill Campbell, Minnesota	17-5	.773
				1977	Paul Splittorff, Kansas City	16-6	.727
1930	Lefty Grove, Philadelphia	28-5	.848	1978	Ron Guidry, New York	25-3	.893
1931	Lefty Grove, Philadelphia	31-4	.886	1979	Mike Caldwell, Milwaukee	16-6	.727
1932	Johnny Allen, New York	17-4	.810				
1933	Lefty Grove, Philadelphia	24-8	.750	1980	Steve Stone, Baltimore	25-7	.781
1934	Lefty Gomez, New York	26-5	.839	1981	Pete Vuckovich, Milwaukee	14-4	.778
1935	Eldon Auker, Detroit	18-7	.720	1982	Pete Vuckovich, Milwaukee	18-6	.750
1936	Monte Pearson, New York	19-7	.731		& Jim Palmer, Baltimore	15-5	.750
1937	Johnny Allen, Cleveland	15-1	.938	1983	Rich Dotson, Chicago	22-7	.759
1938	Red Ruffing, New York	21-7	.750	1984	Doyle Alexander, Toronto	17-6	.739
1939	Lefty Grove, Boston	15-4	.789	1985	Ron Guidry, New York	22-6	.786
				1986	Roger Clemens, Boston	24-4	.857
1940	Schoolboy Rowe, Detroit	16-3	.842	1987	Roger Clemens, Boston	20-9	.690
1941	Lefty Gomez, New York	15-5	.750	1988	Frank Viola, Minnesota	24-7	.774
1942	Ernie Bonham, New York	21-5	.808	1989	Bret Saberhagen, Kansas City	23-6	.793
1943	Spud Chandler, New York	20-4	.833				
1944	Tex Hughson, Boston	18-5	.783	1990	Bob Welch, Oakland	27-6	.818
1945	Hal Newhouser, Detroit	25-9	.735	1991	Scott Erickson, Minnesota	20-8	.714
1946	Boo Ferriss, Boston	25-6	.806	1992	Mike Mussina, Baltimore	18-5	.783
1947	Allie Reynolds, New York	19-8	.704	1993	Jimmy Key, New York	18-6	.750
1948	Jack Kramer, Boston	18-5	.783	1994	Jason Bere, Chicago	12-2	.857
1949	Ellis Kinder, Boston	23-6	.793	1995	Randy Johnson, Seattle	18-2	.900
				1996	Charles Nagy, Cleveland	17-5	.773
1950	Vic Raschi, New York	21-8	.724	1997	Randy Johnson, Seattle	20-4	.833
1951	Bob Feller, Cleveland	22-8	.733	1998	David Wells, New York	18-4	.818
1952	Bobby Shantz, Philadelphia	24-7	.774	1999	Pedro Martinez, Boston	23-4	.852
1953	Ed Lopat, New York	16-4	.800				
1954	Sandy Consuegra, Chicago	16-3	.842				

Earned Run Average

Earned Run Averages were based on at least 10 complete games pitched (1900-49), at least 154 innings pitched (1950-60), and at least 162 innings pitched since 1961 in the AL and 1962 in the NL. In the strike years of 1981, '94 and '95, qualifiers had to pitch at least as many innings as the total number of games their team played that season.

National League

Multiple winners: Grover Alexander, Sandy Koufax and Christy Mathewson (5); Greg Maddux (4); Carl Hubbell, Tom Seaver, Warren Spahn and Dazzy Vance (3); Bill Doak, Ray Kremer, Dolf Luque, Howie Pollet, Nolan Ryan, Bill Walker and Bucky Walters (2).

Year		ERA	Year		ERA	Year		ERA
1900	Rube Waddell, Pit	2.37	1908	Christy Mathewson, NY	1.43	1916	Grover Alexander, Phi	1.55
1901	Jesse Tannehill, Pit	2.18	1909	Christy Mathewson, NY	1.14	1917	Grover Alexander, Phi	1.86
1902	Jack Taylor, Chi	1.33	1910	George McQuillan, Phi	1.60	1918	Hippo Vaughn, Chi.	1.74
1903	Sam Leever, Pit	2.06	1911	Christy Mathewson, NY	1.99	1919	Grover Alexander, Chi.	1.72
1904	Joe McGinnity, NY	1.61	1912	Jeff Tesreau, NY	1.96	1920	Grover Alexander, Chi.	1.91
1905	Christy Mathewson, NY	1.27	1913	Christy Mathewson, NY	2.06	1921	Bill Doak, St.L	2.59
1906	Three Finger Brown, Chi	1.04	1914	Bill Doak, St.L	1.72	1922	Rosy Ryan, NY	3.01
1907	Jack Pfiester, Chi	1.15	1915	Grover Alexander, Phi	1.22	1923	Dolf Luque, Cin	1.93

Year		ERA
1924	Dazzy Vance, Bklyn	2.16
1925	Dolf Luque, Cin	2.63
1926	Ray Kremer, Pit	2.61
1927	Ray Kremer, Pit	2.47
1928	Dazzy Vance, Bklyn	2.09
1929	Bill Walker, NY	3.09
1930	Dazzy Vance, Bklyn	2.61
1931	Bill Walker, NY	2.26
1932	Lon Warneke, Chi	2.37
1933	Carl Hubbell, NY	1.66
1934	Carl Hubbell, NY	2.30
1935	Cy Blanton, Pit	2.58
1936	Carl Hubbell, NY	2.31
1937	Jim Turner, Bos	2.38
1938	Bill Lee, Chi	2.66
1939	Bucky Walters, Cin	2.29
1940	Bucky Walters, Cin	2.48
1941	Elmer Riddle, Cin	2.24
1942	Mort Cooper, St.L	1.78
1943	Howie Pollet, St.L	1.75
1944	Ed Heusser, Cin	2.38
1945	Hank Borowy, Chi	2.13
1946	Howie Pollet, St.L	2.10
1947	Warren Spahn, Bos	2.33
1948	Harry Brecheen, St.L	2.24
1949	Dave Koslo, NY	2.50
1950	Jim Hearn, St.L-NY	2.49
1951	Chet Nichols, Bos	2.88
1952	Hoyt Wilhelm, NY	2.43
1953	Warren Spahn, Mil	2.10
1954	Johnny Antonelli, NY	2.30
1955	Bob Friend, Pit	2.83
1956	Lew Burdette, Mil	2.70
1957	Johnny Podres, Bklyn	2.66
1958	Stu Miller, SF	2.47
1959	Sam Jones, SF	2.83
1960	Mike McCormick, SF	2.70
1961	Warren Spahn, Mil	3.02
1962	Sandy Koufax, LA	2.54
1963	Sandy Koufax, LA	1.88
1964	Sandy Koufax, LA	1.74
1965	Sandy Koufax, LA	2.04
1966	Sandy Koufax, LA	1.73
1967	Phil Niekro, Atl	1.87
1968	Bob Gibson, St.L	1.12
1969	Juan Marichal, SF	2.10
1970	Tom Seaver, NY	2.81
1971	Tom Seaver, NY	1.76
1972	Steve Carlton, Phi	1.97
1973	Tom Seaver, NY	2.08
1974	Buzz Capra, Atl	2.28
1975	Randy Jones, SD	2.24
1976	John Denny, St.L	2.52
1977	John Candelaria, Pit	2.34
1978	Craig Swan, NY	2.43
1979	J.R. Richard, Hou	2.71
1980	Don Sutton, LA	2.21
1981	Nolan Ryan, Hou	1.69
1982	Steve Rogers, Mon	2.40
1983	Atlee Hammaker, SF	2.25
1984	Alejandro Peña, LA	2.48
1985	Dwight Gooden, NY	1.53
1986	Mike Scott, Hou	2.22
1987	Nolan Ryan, Hou	2.76
1988	Joe Magrane, St.L	2.18
1989	Scott Garrelts, SF	2.28
1990	Danny Darwin, Hou	2.21
1991	Dennis Martinez, Mon	2.39
1992	Bill Swift, SF	2.08
1993	Greg Maddux, Atl	2.36
1994	Greg Maddux, Atl	1.56
1995	Greg Maddux, Atl	1.63
1996	Kevin Brown, Fla	1.89
1997	Pedro Martinez, Mon	1.90
1998	Greg Maddux, Atl	2.22
1999	Randy Johnson, Ari	2.48

Note: In 1945, Borowy had a 3.13 ERA in 18 games with New York (AL) for a combined ERA of 2.65.

American League

Multiple winners: Lefty Grove (9); Roger Clemens (6); Walter Johnson (5); Spud Chandler, Stan Coveleski, Red Faber, Whitey Ford, Lefty Gomez, Ron Guidry, Addie Joss, Hal Newhouser, Jim Palmer, Gary Peters, Luis Tiant and Ed Walsh (2).

Year		ERA
1901	Cy Young, Bos	1.62
1902	Ed Siever, Det	1.91
1903	Earl Moore, Cle	1.77
1904	Addie Joss, Cle	1.59
1905	Rube Waddell, Phi	1.48
1906	Doc White, Chi	1.52
1907	Ed Walsh, Chi	1.60
1908	Addie Joss, Cle	1.16
1909	Harry Krause, Phi	1.39
1910	Ed Walsh, Chi	1.27
1911	Vean Gregg, Cle	1.81
1912	Walter Johnson, Wash	1.39
1913	Walter Johnson, Wash	1.09
1914	Dutch Leonard, Bos	1.01
1915	Smokey Joe Wood, Bos	1.49
1916	Babe Ruth, Bos	1.75
1917	Eddie Cicotte, Chi	1.53
1918	Walter Johnson, Wash	1.27
1919	Walter Johnson, Wash	1.49
1920	Bob Shawkey, NY	2.45
1921	Red Faber, Chi	2.48
1922	Red Faber, Chi	2.80
1923	Stan Coveleski, Cle	2.76
1924	Walter Johnson, Wash	2.72
1925	Stan Coveleski, Wash	2.84
1926	Lefty Grove, Phi	2.51
1927	Wilcy Moore, NY	2.28
1928	Garland Braxton, Wash	2.51
1929	Lefty Grove, Phi	2.81
1930	Lefty Grove, Phi	2.54
1931	Lefty Grove, Phi	2.06
1932	Lefty Grove, Phi	2.84
1933	Monte Pearson, Cle	2.33
1934	Lefty Gomez, NY	2.33
1935	Lefty Grove, Bos	2.70
1936	Lefty Grove, Bos	2.81
1937	Lefty Gomez, NY	2.33
1938	Lefty Grove, Bos	3.08
1939	Lefty Grove, Bos	2.54
1940	Ernie Bonham, NY	1.90
1941	Thornton Lee, Chi	2.37
1942	Ted Lyons, Chi	2.10
1943	Spud Chandler, NY	1.64
1944	Dizzy Trout, Det	2.12
1945	Hal Newhouser, Det	1.81
1946	Hal Newhouser, Det	1.94
1947	Spud Chandler, NY	2.46
1948	Gene Bearden, Cle	2.43
1949	Mel Parnell, Bos	2.77
1950	Early Wynn, Cle	3.20
1951	Saul Rogovin, Det-Chi	2.78
1952	Allie Reynolds, NY	2.06
1953	Ed Lopat, NY	2.42
1954	Mike Garcia, Cle	2.64
1955	Billy Pierce, Chi	1.97
1956	Whitey Ford, NY	2.47
1957	Bobby Shantz, NY	2.45
1958	Whitey Ford, NY	2.01
1959	Hoyt Wilhelm, Bal	2.19
1960	Frank Baumann, Chi	2.67
1961	Dick Donovan, Wash	2.40
1962	Hank Aguirre, Det	2.21
1963	Gary Peters, Chi	2.33
1964	Dean Chance, LA	1.65
1965	Sam McDowell, Cle	2.18
1966	Gary Peters, Chi	1.98
1967	Joe Horlen, Chi	2.06
1968	Luis Tiant, Cle	1.60
1969	Dick Bosman, Wash	2.19
1970	Diego Segui, Oak	2.56
1971	Vida Blue, Oak	1.82
1972	Luis Tiant, Bos	1.91
1973	Jim Palmer, Bal	2.40
1974	Catfish Hunter, Oak	2.49
1975	Jim Palmer, Bal	2.09
1976	Mark Fidrych, Det	2.34
1977	Frank Tanana, Cal	2.54
1978	Ron Guidry, NY	1.74
1979	Ron Guidry, NY	2.78
1980	Rudy May, NY	2.47
1981	Steve McCatty, Oak	2.32
1982	Rick Sutcliffe, Cle	2.96
1983	Rick Honeycutt, Tex	2.42
1984	Mike Boddicker, Bal	2.79
1985	Dave Stieb, Tor	2.48
1986	Roger Clemens, Bos	2.48
1987	Jimmy Key, Tor	2.76
1988	Allan Anderson, Min	2.45
1989	Bret Saberhagen, KC	2.16
1990	Roger Clemens, Bos	1.93
1991	Roger Clemens, Bos	2.62
1992	Roger Clemens, Bos	2.41
1993	Kevin Appier, KC	2.56
1994	Steve Ontiveros, Oak	2.65
1995	Randy Johnson, Sea	2.48
1996	Juan Guzman, Tor	2.93
1997	Roger Clemens, Tor	2.05
1998	Roger Clemens, Tor	2.65
1999	Pedro Martinez, Bos	2.07

Strikeouts
National League

Multiple winners: Dazzy Vance (7); Grover Alexander (6); Steve Carlton, Christy Mathewson and Tom Seaver (5); Dizzy Dean, Sandy Koufax and Warren Spahn (4); Don Drysdale, Sam Jones and Johnny Vander Meer (3); David Cone, Dwight Gooden, Bill Hallahan, J.R. Richard, Robin Roberts, Nolan Ryan, Curt Schilling, John Smoltz and Hippo Vaughn (2).

Year	SO	Year	SO	Year	SO
1900 Rube Waddell, Pit	130	1934 Dizzy Dean, St.L	195	1966 Sandy Koufax, LA	317
1901 Noodles Hahn, Cin	239	1935 Dizzy Dean, St.L	190	1967 Jim Bunning, Phi	253
1902 Vic Willis, Bos	225	1936 Van Lingle Mungo, Bklyn	238	1968 Bob Gibson, St.L	268
1903 Christy Mathewson, NY	267	1937 Carl Hubbell, NY	159	1969 Ferguson Jenkins, Chi	273
1904 Christy Mathewson, NY	212	1938 Clay Bryant, Chi	135		
1905 Christy Mathewson, NY	206	1939 Claude Passeau, Phi-Chi	137	1970 Tom Seaver, NY	283
1906 Fred Beebe, Chi-St.L	171	& Bucky Walters, Cin	137	1971 Tom Seaver, NY	289
1907 Christy Mathewson, NY	178			1972 Steve Carlton, Phi	310
1908 Christy Mathewson, NY	259	1940 Kirby Higbe, Phi	137	1973 Tom Seaver, NY	251
1909 Orval Overall, Chi	205	1941 John Vander Meer, Cin	202	1974 Steve Carlton, Phi	240
		1942 John Vander Meer, Cin	186	1975 Tom Seaver, NY	243
1910 Earl Moore, Phi	185	1943 John Vander Meer, Cin	174	1976 Tom Seaver, NY	235
1911 Rube Marquard, NY	237	1944 Bill Voiselle, NY	161	1977 Phil Niekro, Atl	262
1912 Grover Alexander, Phi	195	1945 Preacher Roe, Pit	148	1978 J.R. Richard, Hou	303
1913 Tom Seaton, Phi	168	1946 Johnny Schmitz, Chi	135	1979 J.R. Richard, Hou	313
1914 Grover Alexander, Phi	214	1947 Ewell Blackwell, Cin	193		
1915 Grover Alexander, Phi	241	1948 Harry Brecheen, St.L	149	1980 Steve Carlton, Phi	286
1916 Grover Alexander, Phi	167	1949 Warren Spahn, Bos	151	1981 F. Valenzuela, LA	180
1917 Grover Alexander, Phi	201			1982 Steve Carlton, Phi	286
1918 Hippo Vaughn, Chi	148	1950 Warren Spahn, Bos	191	1983 Steve Carlton, Phi	275
1919 Hippo Vaughn, Chi	141	1951 Don Newcombe, Bklyn	164	1984 Dwight Gooden, NY	276
		& Warren Spahn, Bos	164	1985 Dwight Gooden, NY	268
1920 Grover Alexander, Chi	173	1952 Warren Spahn, Bos	183	1986 Mike Scott, Hou	306
1921 Burleigh Grimes, Bklyn	136	1953 Robin Roberts, Phi	198	1987 Nolan Ryan, Hou	270
1922 Dazzy Vance, Bklyn	134	1954 Robin Roberts, Phi	185	1988 Nolan Ryan, Hou	228
1923 Dazzy Vance, Bklyn	197	1955 Sam Jones, Chi	198	1989 Jose DeLeon, St.L	201
1924 Dazzy Vance, Bklyn	262	1956 Sam Jones, Chi	176		
1925 Dazzy Vance, Bklyn	221	1957 Jack Sanford, Phi	188	1990 David Cone, NY	233
1926 Dazzy Vance, Bklyn	140	1958 Sam Jones, St.L	225	1991 David Cone, NY	241
1927 Dazzy Vance, Bklyn	184	1959 Don Drysdale, LA	242	1992 John Smoltz, Atl	215
1928 Dazzy Vance, Bklyn	200			1993 Jose Rijo, Cin	227
1929 Pat Malone, Chi	166	1960 Don Drysdale, LA	246	1994 Andy Benes, SD	189
		1961 Sandy Koufax, LA	269	1995 Hideo Nomo, LA	236
1930 Bill Hallahan, St.L	177	1962 Don Drysdale, LA	232	1996 John Smoltz, Atl	276
1931 Bill Hallahan, St.L	159	1963 Sandy Koufax, LA	306	1997 Curt Schilling, Phi	319
1932 Dizzy Dean, St.L	191	1964 Bob Veale, Pit	250	1998 Curt Schilling, Phi	300
1933 Dizzy Dean, St.L	199	1965 Sandy Koufax, LA	382	1999 Randy Johnson, Ari	364

Pitching Triple Crown Winners

Pitchers who led either league in Earned Run Average, Wins and Strikeouts over a single season.

National League

	Year	ERA	W-L	SO
Tommy Bond, Bos	1877	2.11	40-17	170
Hoss Radbourne, Prov	1884	1.38	60-12	441
Tim Keefe, NY	1888	1.74	35-12	333
John Clarkson, Bos	1889	2.73	49-19	284
Amos Rusie, NY	1894	2.78	36-13	195
Christy Mathewson, NY	1905	1.27	31-8	206
Christy Mathewson, NY	1908	1.43	37-11	259
Grover Alexander, Phi	1915	1.22	31-10	241
Grover Alexander, Phi	1916	1.55	33-12	167
Grover Alexander, Phi	1917	1.86	30-13	201
Hippo Vaughn, Chi	1918	1.74	22-10	148
Grover Alexander, Chi	1920	1.91	27-14	173
Dazzy Vance, Bklyn	1924	2.16	28-6	262
Bucky Walters, Cin	1939	2.29	27-11	137
Sandy Koufax, LA	1963	1.88	25-5	306
Sandy Koufax, LA	1965	2.04	26-8	382
Sandy Koufax, LA	1966	1.73	27-9	317
Steve Carlton, Phi	1972	1.97	27-10	310
Dwight Gooden, NY	1985	1.53	24-4	268

Ties: In 1894, Rusie tied for league lead in wins with Jouett Meekin, NY (36-10); in 1939, Walters tied for league lead in strikeouts with Claude Passeau, Phi-Chi; in 1963, Koufax tied for the league lead in wins with Juan Marichal, SF.

American League

	Year	ERA	W-L	SO
Cy Young, Bos	1901	1.62	33-10	158
Rube Waddell, Phi	1905	1.48	26-11	287
Walter Johnson, Wash	1913	1.09	36-7	243
Walter Johnson, Wash	1918	1.27	23-13	162
Walter Johnson, Wash	1924	2.72	23-7	158
Lefty Grove, Phi	1930	2.54	28-5	209
Lefty Grove, Phi	1931	2.06	31-4	175
Lefty Gomez, NY	1934	2.33	26-5	158
Lefty Gomez, NY	1937	2.33	21-11	194
Hal Newhouser, Det	1945	1.81	25-9	212
Roger Clemens, Tor	1997	2.05	21-7	292
Roger Clemens, Tor	1998	2.65	20-6	271
Pedro Martinez, Bos	1999	2.07	23-4	313

Ties: In 1998, Clemens tied for league lead in wins with David Cone, NY (20-7) and Rick Helling, Tex (20-7).

American League

Multiple winners: Walter Johnson (12); Nolan Ryan (9); Bob Feller and Lefty Grove (7); Rube Waddell (6); Roger Clemens and Sam McDowell (5); Randy Johnson (4); Lefty Gomez, Mark Langston and Camilo Pascual (3); Len Barker, Tommy Bridges, Jim Bunning, Hal Newhouser, Allie Reynolds, Herb Score, Ed Walsh and Early Wynn (2).

Year		SO
1901	Cy Young, Bos	158
1902	Rube Waddell, Phi	210
1903	Rube Waddell, Phi	302
1904	Rube Waddell, Phi	349
1905	Rube Waddell, Phi	287
1906	Rube Waddell, Phi	196
1907	Rube Waddell, Phi	232
1908	Ed Walsh, Chi	269
1909	Frank Smith, Chi	177
1910	Walter Johnson, Wash.	313
1911	Ed Walsh, Chi	255
1912	Walter Johnson, Wash.	303
1913	Walter Johnson, Wash.	243
1914	Walter Johnson, Wash.	225
1915	Walter Johnson, Wash.	203
1916	Walter Johnson, Wash.	228
1917	Walter Johnson, Wash.	188
1918	Walter Johnson, Wash.	162
1919	Walter Johnson, Wash.	147
1920	Stan Coveleski, Cle	133
1921	Walter Johnson, Wash.	143
1922	Urban Shocker, St.L	149
1923	Walter Johnson, Wash.	130
1924	Walter Johnson, Wash.	158
1925	Lefty Grove, Phi	116
1926	Lefty Grove, Phi	194
1927	Lefty Grove, Phi	174
1928	Lefty Grove, Phi	183
1929	Lefty Grove, Phi	170
1930	Lefty Grove, Phi	209
1931	Lefty Grove, Phi	175
1932	Red Ruffing, NY	190
1933	Lefty Gomez, NY	163
1934	Lefty Gomez, NY	158

Year		SO
1935	Tommy Bridges, Det	163
1936	Tommy Bridges, Det	175
1937	Lefty Gomez, NY	194
1938	Bob Feller, Cle	240
1939	Bob Feller, Cle	246
1940	Bob Feller, Cle	261
1941	Bob Feller, Cle	260
1942	Tex Hughson, Bos	113
	& Bobo Newsom, Wash	113
1943	Allie Reynolds, Cle	151
1944	Hal Newhouser, Det	187
1945	Hal Newhouser, Det	212
1946	Bob Feller, Cle	348
1947	Bob Feller, Cle	196
1948	Bob Feller, Cle	164
1949	Virgil Trucks, Det	153
1950	Bob Lemon, Cle	170
1951	Vic Raschi, NY	164
1952	Allie Reynolds, NY	160
1953	Billy Pierce, Chi	186
1954	Bob Turley, Bal	185
1955	Herb Score, Cle	245
1956	Herb Score, Cle	263
1957	Early Wynn, Cle	184
1958	Early Wynn, Chi	179
1959	Jim Bunning, Det	201
1960	Jim Bunning, Det	201
1961	Camilo Pascual, Min	221
1962	Camilo Pascual, Min	206
1963	Camilo Pascual, Min	202
1964	Al Downing, NY	217
1965	Sam McDowell, Cle	325
1966	Sam McDowell, Cle	225
1967	Jim Lonborg, Bos	246

Year		SO
1968	Sam McDowell, Cle	283
1969	Sam McDowell, Cle	279
1970	Sam McDowell, Cle	304
1971	Mickey Lolich, Det	308
1972	Nolan Ryan, Cal	329
1973	Nolan Ryan, Cal	383
1974	Nolan Ryan, Cal	367
1975	Frank Tanana, Cal	269
1976	Nolan Ryan, Cal	327
1977	Nolan Ryan, Cal	341
1978	Nolan Ryan, Cal	260
1979	Nolan Ryan, Cal	223
1980	Len Barker, Cle	187
1981	Len Barker, Cle	127
1982	Floyd Bannister, Sea	209
1983	Jack Morris, Det	232
1984	Mark Langston, Sea	204
1985	Bert Blyleven, Cle-Min	206
1986	Mark Langston, Sea	245
1987	Mark Langston, Sea	262
1988	Roger Clemens, Bos	291
1989	Nolan Ryan, Tex	301
1990	Nolan Ryan, Tex	232
1991	Roger Clemens, Bos	241
1992	Randy Johnson, Sea	241
1993	Randy Johnson, Sea	308
1994	Randy Johnson, Sea	204
1995	Randy Johnson, Sea	294
1996	Roger Clemens, Bos	257
1997	Roger Clemens, Tor	292
1998	Roger Clemens, Tor	271
1999	Pedro Martinez, Bos	313

Perfect Games

Eighteen pitchers have thrown perfect games (27 up, 27 down) in major league history. However, the games pitched by Harvey Haddix and Ernie Shore are not considered to be official.

National League

	Game	Date	Score
Lee Richmond	Wor. vs Cle.	6/12/1880	1-0
Monte Ward	Prov. vs Bos.	6/17/1880	5-0
Harvey Haddix	Pit. at Mil.	5/26/1959	0-1*
Jim Bunning	Phi. at NY	6/21/1964	6-0
Sandy Koufax	LA vs Chi.	9/9/1965	1-0
Tom Browning	Cin. vs LA	9/16/1988	1-0
Dennis Martinez	Mon. at LA	7/28/1991	2-0

*Haddix pitched 12 perfect innings before losing in the 13th. Braves' lead-off batter Felix Mantilla reached on a throwing error by Pirates 3B Don Hoak, Eddie Mathews sacrificed Mantilla to 2nd, Hank Aaron was walked intentionally, and Joe Adcock hit a 3-run HR. Adcock, however, passed Aaron on the bases and was only credited with a 1-run double.

American League

	Game	Date	Score
Cy Young	Bos. vs Phi.	5/5/1904	3-0
Addie Joss	Cle. vs Chi.	10/2/1908	1-0
Ernie Shore	Bos. vs Wash.	6/23/1917	4-0*
Charlie Robertson	Chi. at Det.	4/30/1922	2-0
Catfish Hunter	Oak. vs Min.	5/8/1968	4-0
Len Barker	Cle. vs Tor.	5/15/1981	3-0
Mike Witt	Cal. at Tex.	9/30/1984	1-0
Kenny Rogers	Tex. vs Cal.	7/28/1994	4-0
David Wells	NY vs Min.	5/17/1998	4-0
David Cone	NY vs Mon.	7/18/1999	6-0

*Babe Ruth started for Boston, walking Senators' lead-off batter Ray Morgan, then was thrown out of game by umpire Brick Owens for arguing the call. Shore came on in relief. Morgan was caught stealing and Shore retired the next 26 batters in a row. While technically not a perfect game—since he didn't start—Shore gets credit anyway.

World Series

Pitcher	Game	Date	Score
Don Larsen	NY vs Bklyn	10/8/1956	2-0

No-Hit Games

Nine innings or more, including perfect games, since 1876. Losing pitchers in **bold** type. **Multiple no-hitters:** Nolan Ryan (7); Sandy Koufax (4); Larry Cocoran, Bob Feller and Cy Young (3); Jim Bunning, Steve Busby, Carl Erskine, Bob Forsch, Pud Galvin, Ken Holtzman, Addie Joss, Hub Leonard, Jim Maloney, Christy Mathewson, Allie Reynolds, Warren Spahn, Bill Stoneham, Virgil Trucks, Johnny Vander Meer and Don Wilson (2).

National League

Year	Date	Pitcher	Result	Year	Date	Pitcher	Result
1876	7/15	George Bradley	St.L vs Har, 2-0	1956	5/12	Carl Erskine	Bklyn vs NY, 3-0
1880	6/12	Lee Richmond	Wor vs Cle, 1-0		9/25	Sal Maglie	Bklyn vs Phi, 5-0
			(perfect game)	1960	5/15	Don Cardwell	Chi vs St.L, 4-0
	6/17	Monte Ward	Prov vs Buf, 5-0		8/18	Lew Burdette	Mil vs Phi, 1-0
			(perfect game)		9/16	Warren Spahn	Mil vs Phi, 4-0
	8/19	Larry Corcoran	Chi vs Bos, 6-0	1961	4/28	Warren Spahn	Mil vs SF, 1-0
	8/20	Pud Galvin	Buf at Wor, 1-0	1962	6/30	Sandy Koufax	LA vs NY, 5-0
1882	9/20	Larry Corcoran	Chi vs Wor, 1-0	1963	5/11	Sandy Koufax	LA vs SF, 1-0
1883	7/25	Old Hoss Rad-	Prov at Cle, 8-0		5/17	Don Nottebart	Hou vs Phi, 4-1
		bourne			6/15	Juan Marichal	SF vs Hou, 1-0
	9/13	Hugh Daily	Cle at Phi, 1-0	1964	4/23	**Ken Johnson**	Hou vs Cin, 0-1
1884	6/27	Larry Cocoran	Chi vs Prov, 6-0		6/4	Sandy Koufax	LA at Phi, 3-0
	8/4	Pud Galvin	Buf at Det, 18-0		6/21	Jim Bunning	Phi at NY, 6-0
1885	7/27	John Clarkson	Chi vs Prov, 6-0				(perfect game)
	8/29	Charlie Ferguson	Phi vs Prov, 1-0	1965	8/19	Jim Maloney	Cin at Chi, 1-0 (10)
1891	6/22	Tom Lovett	Bklyn vs NY, 4-0		9/9	Sandy Koufax	LA vs Chi, 1-0
	7/31	Amos Rusie	NY vs Bklyn, 11-0				(perfect game)
1892	8/6	John Stivetts	Bos vs Bklyn, 11-0	1967	6/18	Don Wilson	Hou vs Atl, 2-0
	8/22	Ben Sanders	Lou vs Bal, 6-2	1968	7/29	George Culver	Cin at Phi, 6-1
	10/22	Bumpus Jones	Cin vs Pit, 7-1		9/17	Gaylord Perry	SF vs St.L, 1-0
			(1st major league game)		9/18	Ray Washburn	St.L at SF, 2-0
1893	8/16	Bill Hawke	Bal vs Wash, 5-0				(next day, same park)
1897	9/18	Cy Young	Cle vs Cin, 6-0	1969	4/17	Bill Stoneman	Mon at Phi, 7-0
1898	4/22	Ted Breitenstein	Cin vs Pit, 11-0		4/30	Jim Maloney	Cin vs Hou, 10-0
	4/22	Jim Hughes	Bal vs Bos, 8-0		5/1	Don Wilson	Hou at Cin, 4-0
	7/8	Frank Donahue	Phi vs Bos, 5-0		8/19	Ken Holtzman	Chi vs Atl, 3-0
	8/21	Walter Thornton	Chi vs Bklyn, 2-0		9/20	Bob Moose	Pit at NY, 4-0
1899	5/25	Deacon Phillippe	Lou vs NY, 7-0	1970	6/12	Dock Ellis	Pit at SD, 2-0
1900	7/12	Noodles Hahn	Cin vs Phi, 4-0		7/20	Bill Singer	LA vs Phi, 5-0
1901	7/15	Christy Mathewson	NY vs St.L, 5-0	1971	6/3	Ken Holtzman	Chi at Cin, 1-0
1903	9/18	Chick Fraser	Phi at Chi, 10-0		6/23	Rick Wise	Phi at Cin, 4-0
1905	6/13	Christy Mathewson	NY at Chi, 1-0		8/14	Bob Gibson	St.L at Pit, 11-0
1906	5/1	John Lush	Phi at Bklyn, 1-0	1972	4/16	Burt Hooton	Chi vs Phi, 4-0
	7/20	Mal Eason	Bklyn at St.L, 2-0		9/2	Milt Pappas	Chi vs SD, 8-0
1907	5/8	Frank Pfeffer	Bos vs Cin, 6-0		10/2	Bill Stoneman	Mon vs NY, 7-0
	9/20	Nick Maddox	Pit vs Bkn, 2-1	1973	8/5	Phil Niekro	Atl vs SD, 9-0
1908	7/4	Hooks Wiltse	NY vs Phi, 1-0 (10)	1975	8/24	Ed Halicki	SF vs NY, 6-0
	9/5	Nap Rucker	Bklyn vs Bos, 6-0	1976	7/9	Larry Dierker	Hou vs Mon, 6-0
1912	9/6	Jeff Tesreau	NY at Phi, 3-0		8/9	John Candelaria	Pit vs LA, 2-0
1914	9/9	George Davis	Bos vs Phi, 7-0		9/29	John Montefusco	SF vs Atl, 9-0
1915	4/15	Rube Marquard	NY vs Bklyn, 2-0	1978	4/16	Bob Forsch	St.L vs Phi, 5-0
	8/31	Jimmy Lavender	Chi at N.Y, 2-0		6/16	Tom Seaver	Cin vs St.L, 4-0
1916	6/16	Tom Hughes	Bos vs. Pit, 2-0	1979	4/7	Ken Forsch	Hou vs Atl, 6-0
1917	5/2	Fred Toney	Cin at Chi, 1-0 (10)	1980	6/27	Jerry Reuss	LA at SF, 4-0
1919	5/11	Hod Eller	Cin at St.L, 6-0	1981	5/10	Charlie Lea	Mon vs SF, 4-0
1922	5/7	Jesse Barnes	NY vs Phi, 6-0		9/26	Nolan Ryan	Hou vs LA, 5-0
1924	7/17	Jesse Haines	St.L vs Bos, 5-0	1983	9/26	Bob Forsch	St.L vs Mon, 3-0
1925	9/17	Dazzy Vance	Bklyn vs Phi, 10-1	1986	9/25	Mike Scott	Hou vs SF, 2-0
1929	5/8	Carl Hubbell	NY vs Pit, 2-0	1988	9/16	Tom Browning	Cin vs LA, 1-0
1934	9/21	Paul Dean	St.L vs Bkyn, 3-0				(perfect game)
1938	6/11	Johnny Vander Meer	Cin vs Bos, 3-0	1990	6/29	Fernando Valenzuela	LA vs St.L, 6-0
	6/15	Johnny Vander Meer	Cin at Bklyn, 6-0		8/15	Terry Mulholland	Phi vs SF, 6-0
			(consecutive starts)	1991	5/23	Tommy Greene	Phi at Mon, 2-0
1940	4/30	Tex Carleton	Bklyn at Cin, 3-0		7/28	Dennis Martinez	Mon at LA, 2-0
1941	8/30	Lon Warneke	St.L at Cin, 2-0				(perfect game)
1944	4/27	Jim Tobin	Bos vs Bklyn, 2-0		9/11	Kent Mercker (6),	Atl vs SD, 1-0
	5/15	Clyde Shoun	Cin vs Bos, 1-0			Mark Wohlers (2)	(combined no-hitter)
1946	4/23	Ed Head	Bklyn at NY, 2-0			& Alejandro Peña (1)	
1947	6/18	Ewell Blackwell	Cin vs Bos, 6-0	1992	8/17	Kevin Gross	LA vs SF, 2-0
1948	9/9	Rex Barney	Bklyn at NY, 2-0	1993	9/8	Darryl Kile	Hou vs NY, 7-1
1950	8/11	Vern Bickford	Bos vs Bklyn, 7-0	1994	4/8	Kent Mercker	Atl at LA, 6-0
1951	5/6	Cliff Chambers	Pit at Bos, 3-0	1995	7/14	Ramon Martinez	LA vs Fla, 7-0
1952	6/19	Carl Erskine	Bklyn vs Chi, 5-0	1996	5/11	Al Leiter	Fla vs Col, 11-0
1954	6/12	Jim Wilson	Mil vs Phi, 2-0		9/17	Hideo Nomo	LA at Col, 9-0
1955	5/12	Sam Jones	Chi vs Pit, 4-0				

Year	Date	Pitcher	Result
1997	6/10	Kevin Brown	Fla at SF, 9-0
	7/12	Francisco Cordova (9)	Pit vs. Hou, 3-0 (10 inn.)
		Ricardo Rincon (1)	(combined no-hitter)

Year	Date	Pitcher	Result
1999	6/25	Jose Jimenez	St.L vs Ari, 1-0

American League

Year	Date	Pitcher	Result
1902	9/20	Jimmy Callahan	Chi vs Det, 3-0
1904	5/5	Cy Young	Bos vs Phi, 3-0
			(perfect game)
	8/17	Jesse Tannehill	Bos vs Chi, 6-0
1905	7/22	Weldon Henley	Phi at St. L, 6-0
	9/6	Frank Smith	Chi at Det, 15-0
	9/27	Bill Dinneen	Bos vs Chi, 2-0
1908	6/30	Cy Young	Bos at NY, 8-0
	9/18	Dusty Rhoades	Cle vs Bos, 2-1
	9/20	Frank Smith	Chi vs Phi, 1-0
	10/2	Addie Joss	Cle vs Chi, 1-0
			(perfect game)
1910	4/20	Addie Joss	Cle at Chi, 1-0
	5/12	Chief Bender	Phi vs Cle, 4-0
1911	7/19	Smokey Joe Wood	Bos vs St. L, 5-0
	8/27	Ed Walsh	Chi vs Bos, 5-0
1912	7/4	George Mullin	Det vs St. L, 7-0
	8/30	Earl Hamilton	St. L at Det, 5-1
1914	5/31	Joe Benz	Chi vs Cle, 6-1
1916	6/16	Rube Foster	Bos vs NY, 2-0
	8/26	Joe Bush	Phi vs Cle, 5-0
	8/30	Hub Leonard	Bos vs St. L, 4-0
1917	4/14	Ed Cicotte	Chi at St. L, 11-0
	4/24	George Mogridge	NY at Bos, 2-1
	5/5	Ernie Koob	St. L vs Chi, 1-0
	5/6	Bob Groom	St. L vs Chi, 3-0
	6/23	Babe Ruth (0)	Bos vs Wash, 4-0
		& Ernie Shore (9)	(combined no-hitter)
1918	6/3	Hub Leonard	Bos at Det, 5-0
1919	9/10	Ray Caldwell	Cle at NY, 3-0
1920	7/1	Walter Johnson	Wash at Bos, 1-0
1922	4/30	Charlie Robertson	Chi at Det, 2-0
			(perfect game)
1923	9/4	Sam Jones	NY at Phi, 2-0
	9/7	Howard Ehmke	Bos at Phi, 4-0
1926	8/21	Ted Lyons	Chi at Bos, 6-0
1931	4/29	Wes Ferrell	Cle vs St. L, 9-0
	8/8	Bob Burke	Wash vs Bos, 5-0
1935	8/31	Vern Kennedy	Chi vs Cle, 5-0
1937	6/1	Bill Dietrich	Chi vs St. L, 8-0
1938	8/27	Monte Pearson	NY vs Cle, 13-0
1940	4/16	Bob Feller	Cle at Chi, 1-0
			(Opening Day)
1945	9/9	Dick Fowler	Phi vs St. L, 1-0
1946	4/30	Bob Feller	Cle vs NY, 1-0
1947	7/10	Don Black	Cle vs Phi, 3-0
	9/3	Bill McCahan	Phi vs Wash, 3-0
1948	6/30	Bob Lemon	Cle at Det, 2-0
1951	7/1	Bob Feller	Cle vs Det, 2-1
	7/12	Allie Reynolds	NY vs Cle, 1-0
	9/28	Allie Reynolds	NY vs Bos, 8-0
1952	5/15	Virgil Trucks	Det vs Wash, 1-0
	8/25	Virgil Trucks	Det at NY, 1-0
1953	5/6	Bobo Holloman	St. L vs Phi, 6-0
			(first major league start)
1956	7/14	Mel Parnell	Bos vs Chi, 4-0
	10/8	Don Larsen	NY vs Bklyn, 2-0
			(perfect W. Series game)
1957	8/20	Bob Keegan	Chi vs Wash, 6-0
1958	7/20	Jim Bunning	Det at Bos, 3-0
	9/2	Hoyt Wilhelm	Bal vs NY, 1-0
1962	5/5	Bo Belinsky	LA vs Bal, 2-0
	6/26	Earl Wilson	Bos vs LA, 2-0
	8/1	Bill Monbouquette	Bos at Chi, 1-0

Year	Date	Pitcher	Result
	8/26	Jack Kralick	Min vs KC, 1-0
1965	9/16	Dave Morehead	Bos vs Cle, 2-0
1966	6/10	Sonny Siebert	Cle vs Wash, 2-0
1967	4/30	**Steve Barber** (8⅔)	Bal vs Det, 1-2
		& Stu Miller (⅓)	(combined no-hitter)
	8/25	Dean Chance	Min at Cle, 2-1
	9/10	Joel Horlen	Chi vs Det, 6-0
1968	4/27	Tom Phoebus	Bal vs Bos, 6-0
	5/8	Catfish Hunter	Oak vs Min, 4-0
			(perfect game)
1969	8/13	Jim Palmer	Bal vs Oak, 8-0
1970	7/3	Clyde Wright	Cal vs Oak, 4-0
	9/21	Vida Blue	Oak vs Min, 6-0
1973	4/27	Steve Busby	KC at Det, 3-0
	5/15	Nolan Ryan	Cal at KC, 3-0
	7/15	Nolan Ryan	Cal at Det, 6-0
	7/30	Jim Bibby	Tex at Oak, 6-0
1974	6/19	Steve Busby	KC at Mil, 2-0
	7/19	Dick Bosman	Cle at Oak, 4-0
	9/28	Nolan Ryan	Cal at Min, 4-0
1975	6/1	Nolan Ryan	Cal vs Bal, 1-0
	9/28	Vida Blue (5),	Oak vs Cal, 5-0
		Glenn Abbott (1),	(combined no-hitter)
		Paul Lindblad (1),	
		& Rollie Fingers (2)	
1976	7/28	John Odom (5) &	Chi at Oak, 2-1
		Francisco Barrios (4)	(combined no-hitter)
1977	5/14	Jim Colborn	KC vs Tex, 6-0
	5/30	Dennis Eckersley	Cle vs Cal, 1-0
	9/22	Bert Blyleven	Tex at Cal, 6-0
1981	5/15	Len Barker	Cle vs Tor, 3-0
			(perfect game)
1983	7/4	Dave Righetti	NY vs Bos, 4-0
	9/29	Mike Warren	Oak vs Chi, 3-0
1984	4/7	Jack Morris	Det at Chi, 4-0
	9/30	Mike Witt	Cal at Tex, 1-0
			(perfect game)
1986	9/19	Joe Cowley	Chi at Cal, 7-1
1987	4/15	Juan Nieves	Mil at Bal, 7-0
1990	4/11	Mark Langston (7)	Cal vs Sea, 1-0
		& Mike Witt (2)	(combined no-hitter)
	6/2	Randy Johnson	Sea vs Det, 2-0
	6/11	Nolan Ryan	Tex at Oak, 5-0
	6/29	Dave Stewart	Oak at Tor, 5-0
	9/2	Dave Stieb	Tor at Cle, 3-0
1991	5/1	Nolan Ryan	Tex vs Tor, 3-0
	7/13	Bob Milacki (6),	Bal at Oak, 2-0
		Mike Flanagan (1),	(combined no-hitter)
		Mark Williamson (1)	
		& Gregg Olson (1)	
	8/11	Wilson Alvarez	Chi at Bal, 7-0
	8/26	Bret Saberhagen	KC vs Chi, 7-0
1993	4/22	Chris Bosio	Sea vs Bos, 7-0
	9/4	Jim Abbott	NY vs Cle, 4-0
1994	4/27	Scott Erickson	Min vs Mil, 6-0
	7/28	Kenny Rogers	Tex vs Cal, 4-0
			(perfect game)
1996	5/14	Dwight Gooden	NY vs Sea, 2-0
1998	5/17	David Wells	NY vs Min, 4-0
			(perfect game)
1999	7/18	David Cone	NY vs Mon, 6-0
			(perfect game)
	9/11	Eric Milton	Min vs Ana, 7-0

All-Time Major League Leaders

Based on statistics compiled by *The Baseball Encyclopedia* (9th ed.); through 1999 regular season.

CAREER

Players active in 1999 in **bold** type.

Batting

Note that (*) indicates left-handed hitter and (†) indicates switch-hitter.

Batting Average

		Yrs	AB	H	Avg
1	Ty Cobb*	24	11,429	4191	.367
2	Rogers Hornsby	23	8,137	2930	.358
3	Joe Jackson*	13	4,981	1774	.356
4	Ed Delahanty	16	7,509	2597	.346
5	Tris Speaker*	22	10,197	3514	.345
6	Ted Williams*	19	7,706	2654	.344
7	Billy Hamilton*	14	6,284	2163	.344
8	Willie Keeler*	19	8,585	2947	.343
9	Dan Brouthers*	19	6,711	2296	.342
10	Babe Ruth*	22	8,399	2873	.342
11	Harry Heilmann	17	7,787	2660	.342
12	Pete Browning	13	4,820	1646	.341
13	Bill Terry*	14	6,428	2193	.341
14	George Sisler*	15	8,267	2812	.340
15	Lou Gehrig*	17	8,001	2721	.340
16	Jesse Burkett*	16	8,413	2853	.339
17	**Tony Gwynn***	18	9,059	3067	.339
18	Nap Lajoie	21	9,592	3244	.338
19	Riggs Stephenson	14	4,508	1515	.336
20	Al Simmons	20	8,761	2927	.334
21	Paul Waner*	20	9,459	3152	.333
22	Eddie Collins*	25	9,951	3313	.333
23	Stan Musial*	22	10,972	3630	.331
24	Sam Thompson*	14	6,005	1986	.331
25	Heinie Manush*	17	7,654	2524	.330

Hits

		Yrs	AB	H	Avg
1	Pete Rose†	24	14,053	**4256**	.303
2	Ty Cobb*	24	11,429	**4191**	.367
3	Hank Aaron	23	12,364	**3771**	.305
4	Stan Musial*	22	10,972	**3630**	.331
5	Tris Speaker*	22	10,197	**3514**	.345
6	Carl Yastrzemski*	23	11,988	**3419**	.285
7	Honus Wagner	21	10,443	**3418**	.327
8	Paul Molitor	21	10,835	**3319**	.306
9	Eddie Collins*	25	9,951	**3313**	.333
10	Willie Mays	22	10,881	**3283**	.302
11	Eddie Murray†	21	11,336	**3255**	.287
12	Nap Lajoie	21	9,592	**3244**	.338
13	George Brett*	21	10,349	**3154**	.305
14	Paul Waner*	20	9,459	**3152**	.333
15	Robin Yount	20	11,008	**3142**	.285
16	Dave Winfield	22	11,003	**3110**	.283
17	**Tony Gwynn***	18	9,059	**3067**	.339
18	Rod Carew*	19	9,315	**3053**	.328
19	Lou Brock*	19	10,332	**3023**	.293
20	**Wade Boggs***	18	9,180	**3010**	.328
21	Al Kaline	22	10,116	**3007**	.297
22	Cap Anson	22	9,108	**3000**	.329
	Roberto Clemente	18	9,454	**3000**	.317
24	**Cal Ripken Jr.**	19	10,765	**2991**	.278
25	Sam Rice*	20	9,269	**2987**	.322

Players Active in 1999

(Minimum 3000 AB)

		Yrs	AB	H	Avg
1	Tony Gwynn*	18	9,059	3067	.339
2	Mike Piazza	8	3,653	1200	.328
3	Wade Boggs*	18	9,180	3010	.328
4	Frank Thomas	10	4,892	1564	.320
5	Edgar Martinez	13	4,876	1558	.320
6	Larry Walker*	11	4,592	1431	.312
7	Mark Grace*	12	6,646	2058	.310
8	Kenny Lofton*	9	4,379	1356	.310
9	Manny Ramirez	7	3,031	932	.307
10	Hal Morris*	12	3,829	1169	.305
11	Jeff Bagwell	9	4,759	1447	.304
12	Bernie Williams†	9	4,269	1298	.304
13	Roberto Alomar†	12	6,611	2007	.304

Players Active in 1999

		Yrs	AB	H	Avg
1	Tony Gwynn*	18	9,059	**3067**	.339
2	Wade Boggs*	18	9,180	**3010**	.328
3	Cal Ripken Jr.	19	10,765	**2991**	.278
4	Rickey Henderson	21	9,911	**2816**	.284
5	Harold Baines*	20	9,541	**2783**	.292
6	Tim Raines†	21	8,694	**2561**	.295
7	Chili Davis†	19	8,673	**2380**	.274
8	Gary Gaetti	19	8,941	**2280**	.255
9	Willie McGee†	18	7,649	**2254**	.295
10	Tony Fernandez†	16	7,788	**2240**	.288
11	Julio Franco	16	7,274	**2177**	.301
12	Rafael Palmeiro*	14	7,281	**2158**	.296
13	Mark Grace*	12	6,646	**2058**	.310

Games Played

1	Pete Rose	3562
2	Carl Yastrzemski	3308
3	Hank Aaron	3298
4	Ty Cobb	3034
5	Stan Musial	3026
	Eddie Murray	3026
7	Willie Mays	2992
8	Dave Winfield	2973
9	Rusty Staub	2951
10	Brooks Robinson	2896
11	Robin Yount	2856
12	Al Kaline	2834
13	Eddie Collins	2826
14	Reggie Jackson	2820
15	Frank Robinson	2808
16	**Cal Ripken Jr.**	2790
17	Tris Speaker	2789
	Honus Wagner	2789
19	Tony Perez	2777
20	**Rickey Henderson**	2733

At Bats

1	Pete Rose	14,053
2	Hank Aaron	12,364
3	Carl Yastrzemski	11,988
4	Ty Cobb	11,429
5	Eddie Murray	11,336
6	Robin Yount	11,008
7	Dave Winfield	11,003
8	Stan Musial	10,972
9	Willie Mays	10,881
10	Paul Molitor	10,835
11	**Cal Ripken Jr.**	10,765
12	Brooks Robinson	10,654
13	Honus Wagner	10,441
14	George Brett	10,349
15	Lou Brock	10,332
16	Luis Aparicio	10,230
17	Tris Speaker	10,197
18	Al Kaline	10,116
19	Rabbit Maranville	10,078
20	Frank Robinson	10,006

Total Bases

1	Hank Aaron	6856
2	Stan Musial	6134
3	Willie Mays	6066
4	Ty Cobb	5863
5	Babe Ruth	5793
6	Pete Rose	5752
7	Carl Yastrzemski	5539
8	Eddie Murray	5397
9	Frank Robinson	5373
10	Dave Winfield	5221
11	Tris Speaker	5103
12	Lou Gehrig	5059
13	George Brett	5044
14	Mel Ott	5041
15	Jimmie Foxx	4956
16	Ted Williams	4884
17	Honus Wagner	4868
18	**Cal Ripken Jr.**	4856
19	**Paul Molitor**	4854
20	Al Kaline	4852

Home Runs

		Yrs	AB	HR	AB/HR
1	Hank Aaron	23	12,364	755	16.4
2	Babe Ruth*	22	8,399	714	11.8
3	Willie Mays	22	10,881	660	16.5
4	Frank Robinson	21	10,006	586	17.1
5	Harmon Killebrew	22	8,147	573	14.2
6	Reggie Jackson*	21	9,864	563	17.5
7	Mike Schmidt	18	8,352	548	15.2
8	Mickey Mantle†	18	8,102	536	15.1
9	Jimmie Foxx	20	8,134	534	15.2
10	**Mark McGwire**	14	5,652	522	10.8
11	Ted Williams*	19	7,706	521	14.8
	Willie McCovey*	22	8,197	521	15.7
13	Eddie Mathews*	17	8,537	512	16.7
	Ernie Banks	19	9,421	512	18.4
15	Mel Ott*	22	9,456	511	18.5
16	Eddie Murray†	21	11,336	504	22.5
17	Lou Gehrig*	17	8,001	493	16.2
18	Willie Stargell*	21	7,927	475	16.7
	Stan Musial*	22	10,972	475	23.1
20	Dave Winfield	22	11,003	465	23.7
21	Carl Yastrzemski*	23	11,988	452	26.5
22	**Barry Bonds***	14	6,976	445	15.7
23	Dave Kingman	16	6,677	442	15.1
24	Andre Dawson	21	9,927	438	22.7
25	**Jose Canseco**	15	6,472	431	15.0

Runs Batted In

		Yrs	Gm	RBI	P/G
1	Hank Aaron	23	3298	2297	.70
2	Babe Ruth*	22	2503	2211	.88
3	Lou Gehrig*	17	2164	1990	.92
4	Ty Cobb*	24	3034	1961	.65
5	Stan Musial*	22	3026	1951	.64
6	Jimmie Foxx	20	2317	1921	.83
7	Eddie Murray†	21	2980	1917	.64
8	Willie Mays	22	2992	1903	.64
9	Mel Ott*	22	2732	1861	.68
10	Carl Yastrzemski*	23	3308	1844	.56
11	Ted Williams*	19	2292	1839	.80
12	Dave Winfield	22	2973	1833	.62
13	Al Simmons	20	2215	1827	.82
14	Frank Robinson	21	2808	1812	.65
15	Honus Wagner	21	2786	1732	.62
16	Cap Anson	22	2276	1715	.75
17	Reggie Jackson*	21	2820	1702	.60
18	Tony Perez	23	2777	1652	.59
19	Ernie Banks	19	2528	1636	.65
20	Goose Goslin*	18	2287	1609	.70
21	Nap Lajoie	21	2475	1599	.65
22	Mike Schmidt	18	2404	1595	.66
	George Brett*	21	2707	1595	.59
24	Andre Dawson	21	2627	1591	.61
25	Rogers Hornsby*	23	2259	1584	.70
	Harmon Killebrew	22	2435	1584	.65

Players Active in 1999

		Yrs	AB	HR	AB/HR
1	Mark McGwire	14	5,652	522	10.8
2	Barry Bonds*	14	6,976	445	15.7
3	Jose Canseco	15	6,472	431	15.0
4	Cal Ripken Jr.	19	10,765	402	26.8
5	Ken Griffey Jr.*	11	5,832	398	14.7
6	Fred McGriff*	14	6,786	390	17.4
7	Harold Baines*	20	9,541	373	25.6
8	Rafael Palmeiro*	14	7,281	361	20.2
9	Gary Gaetti	19	8,941	360	24.8
10	Albert Belle	11	5,294	358	14.8
11	Chili Davis†	19	8,673	350	24.8
12	Juan Gonzalez	11	4,831	340	14.2
13	Sammy Sosa	11	5,289	336	15.7
14	Darryl Strawberry*	17	5,418	335	16.2
15	Matt Williams	13	5,872	334	17.6

Players Active in 1999

		Yrs	Gm	RBI	P/G
1	Harold Baines*	20	2702	1583	.59
2	Cal Ripken Jr.	19	2790	1571	.56
3	Chili Davis†	19	2436	1372	.56
4	Gary Gaetti	19	2502	1340	.54
5	Jose Canseco	15	1713	1309	.76
6	Barry Bonds*	14	2000	1299	.65
7	Mark McGwire	14	1688	1277	.76
8	Rafael Palmeiro*	14	1940	1227	.63
9	Fred McGriff*	14	1897	1192	.63
10	Andres Galarraga	14	1774	1172	.66
11	Ken Griffey Jr.*	11	1535	1152	.75
12	Albert Belle	11	1398	1136	.81
13	Will Clark*	14	1846	1135	.61
14	Bobby Bonilla†	14	1906	1124	.59
15	Tony Gwynn*	18	2333	1104	.47

Runs

1	Ty Cobb	2245
2	Babe Ruth	2174
	Hank Aaron	2174
4	Pete Rose	2165
5	**Rickey Henderson**	2103
6	Willie Mays	2062
7	Stan Musial	1949
8	Lou Gehrig	1888
9	Tris Speaker	1881
10	Mel Ott	1859
11	Frank Robinson	1829
12	Eddie Collins	1820
13	Carl Yastrzemski	1816
14	Ted Williams	1798
15	Paul Molitor	1782
16	Charlie Gehringer	1774
17	Jimmie Foxx	1751
18	Honus Wagner	1735
19	Willie Keeler	1727
20	Cap Anson	1719

Extra Base Hits

1	Hank Aaron	1477
2	Stan Musial	1377
3	Babe Ruth	1356
4	Willie Mays	1323
5	Lou Gehrig	1190
6	Frank Robinson	1186
7	Carl Yastrzemski	1157
8	Ty Cobb	1139
9	Tris Speaker	1132
10	George Brett	1119
11	Ted Williams	1117
	Jimmie Foxx	1117
13	Eddie Murray	1099
14	Dave Winfield	1093
15	Reggie Jackson	1075
16	Mel Ott	1071
17	Pete Rose	1041
18	Andre Dawson	1039
19	**Cal Ripken Jr.**	1017
20	Mike Schmidt	1015

Slugging Percentage

1	Babe Ruth	.690
2	Ted Williams	.634
3	Lou Gehrig	.632
4	Jimmie Foxx	.609
5	Hank Greenberg	.605
6	**Mark McGwire**	.587
7	Joe DiMaggio	.579
8	Rogers Hornsby	.577
9	**Manny Ramirez**	.576
10	**Mike Piazza**	.575
11	**Albert Belle**	.573
12	**Frank Thomas**	.573
13	**Juan Gonzalez**	.572
14	**Ken Griffey Jr.**	.569
15	**Larry Walker**	.567
16	Johnny Mize	.562
17	Stan Musial	.559
18	**Barry Bonds**	.559
19	Willie Mays	.557
20	Mickey Mantle	.557

Stolen Bases

1	**Rickey Henderson**	1334
2	Lou Brock	938
3	Billy Hamilton	937
4	Ty Cobb	892
5	**Tim Raines**	807
6	Vince Coleman	752
7	Eddie Collins	743
8	Max Carey	738
9	Honus Wagner	720
10	Joe Morgan	689
11	Arlie Latham	679
12	Willie Wilson	668
13	Bert Campaneris	649
14	Tom Brown	627
15	**Otis Nixon**	620
16	George Davis	615
17	Dummy Hoy	597
18	Maury Wills	586
19	Hugh Duffy	583
	George Van Haltren	583

Walks

1	Babe Ruth	2062
2	Ted Williams	2019
3	**Rickey Henderson**	1972
4	Joe Morgan	1865
5	Carl Yastrzemski	1845
6	Mickey Mantle	1734
7	Mel Ott	1708
8	Eddie Yost	1614
9	Darrell Evans	1605
10	Stan Musial	1599
11	Pete Rose	1566
12	Harmon Killebrew	1559
13	Lou Gehrig	1508
14	Mike Schmidt	1507
15	Eddie Collins	1503
16	Willie Mays	1463
17	Jimmie Foxx	1452
18	Eddie Mathews	1444
19	**Barry Bonds**	1430
20	Frank Robinson	1420

Strikeouts

1	Reggie Jackson	2597
2	Willie Stargell	1936
3	Mike Schmidt	1883
4	Tony Perez	1867
5	Dave Kingman	1816
6	**Jose Canseco**	1765
7	Bobby Bonds	1757
8	Dale Murphy	1748
9	Lou Brock	1730
10	Mickey Mantle	1710
11	Harmon Killebrew	1699
12	**Chili Davis**	1698
13	Dwight Evans	1697
14	Dave Winfield	1686
15	**Andres Galarraga**	1615
16	**Gary Gaetti**	1599
17	Lee May	1570
18	Dick Allen	1556
19	Willie McCovey	1550
20	Dave Parker	1537

Pitching

Note that (*) indicates left-handed pitcher. Active pitching leaders are listed for wins and strikeouts.

Wins

		Yrs	GS	W	L	Pct
1	Cy Young	22	815	**511**	316	.618
2	Walter Johnson	21	666	**417**	279	.599
3	Christy Mathewson	17	551	**373**	188	.665
	Grover Alexander	20	598	**373**	208	.642
5	Warren Spahn*	21	665	**363**	245	.597
6	Kid Nichols	15	561	**361**	208	.634
	Pud Galvin	14	682	**361**	308	.540
8	Tim Keefe	14	594	**342**	225	.603
9	Steve Carlton*	24	709	**329**	244	.574
10	Eddie Plank*	17	527	**327**	193	.629
11	John Clarkson	12	518	**326**	177	.648
12	Don Sutton	23	756	**324**	256	.559
	Nolan Ryan	27	773	**324**	292	.526
14	Phil Niekro	24	716	**318**	274	.537
15	Gaylord Perry	22	690	**314**	265	.542
16	Old Hoss Radbourn	12	503	**311**	194	.616
	Tom Seaver	20	647	**311**	205	.603
18	Mickey Welch	13	549	**308**	209	.596
19	Lefty Grove*	17	456	**300**	141	.680
	Early Wynn	23	612	**300**	244	.551
21	Tommy John*	26	700	**288**	231	.555
22	Bert Blyleven	22	685	**287**	250	.534
23	Robin Roberts	19	609	**286**	245	.539
24	Tony Mullane	13	505	**285**	220	.564
25	Ferguson Jenkins	19	594	**284**	226	.557
26	Jim Kaat*	25	625	**283**	237	.544
27	Red Ruffing	22	536	**273**	225	.548
28	Burleigh Grimes	19	495	**270**	212	.560
29	Jim Palmer	19	521	**268**	152	.638
30	Bob Feller	18	484	**266**	162	.621

Strikeouts

		Yrs	IP	SO	P/9
1	Nolan Ryan	27	5387.0	**5714**	9.54
2	Steve Carlton*	24	5217.1	**4136**	7.13
3	Bert Blyleven	22	4970.1	**3701**	6.70
4	Tom Seaver	20	4782.2	**3640**	6.85
5	Don Sutton	23	5282.1	**3574**	6.09
6	Gaylord Perry	22	5350.1	**3534**	5.94
7	Walter Johnson	21	5923.2	**3508**	5.33
8	Phil Niekro	24	5404.1	**3342**	5.57
9	**Roger Clemens**	16	3462.1	**3316**	8.62
10	Ferguson Jenkins	19	4500.2	**3192**	6.38
11	Bob Gibson	17	3884.1	**3117**	7.22
12	Jim Bunning	17	3760.1	**2855**	6.83
13	Mickey Lolich*	16	3638.1	**2832**	7.01
14	Cy Young	22	7354.2	**2796**	3.42
15	Frank Tanana*	21	4186.2	**2773**	5.96
16	**Randy Johnson***	12	2250.0	**2693**	10.77
17	Warren Spahn*	21	5243.2	**2583**	4.43
18	Bob Feller	18	3827.0	**2581**	6.07
19	Jerry Koosman*	19	3839.1	**2556**	5.99
20	Tim Keefe	14	5061.1	**2527**	4.50
21	Christy Mathewson	17	4781.0	**2502**	4.71
22	Don Drysdale	14	3432.0	**2486**	6.52
23	Jack Morris	18	3824.2	**2478**	5.83
24	**Mark Langston***	16	2962.2	**2464**	7.49
25	Jim Kaat*	25	4530.1	**2461**	4.89
26	Sam McDowell*	15	2492.1	**2453**	8.86
27	**David Cone**	14	2590.0	**2420**	8.41
28	Luis Tiant	19	3486.1	**2416**	6.24
29	Dennis Eckersley	24	3285.2	**2401**	6.58
30	Sandy Koufax*	12	2324.1	**2396**	9.28

Pitchers Active in 1999

		Yrs	GS	W	L	Pct
1	Roger Clemens	16	480	**247**	134	.648
2	Greg Maddux	14	432	**221**	126	.637
3	Orel Hershiser	17	460	**203**	145	.583
4	Dwight Gooden	15	396	**188**	107	.637
5	Tom Glavine*	13	399	**187**	116	.617
6	David Cone	14	361	**180**	102	.638
7	Mark Langston*	16	428	**179**	158	.531
8	Bret Saberhagen	15	368	**166**	115	.591
9	Chuck Finley*	14	379	**165**	140	.541
10	Randy Johnson*	12	322	**160**	88	.645

Pitchers Active in 1999

		Yrs	IP	SO	P/9
1	Roger Clemens	16	3462.1	**3316**	8.62
2	Randy Johnson*	12	2250.0	**2693**	10.77
3	Mark Langston*	16	2962.2	**2464**	7.49
4	David Cone	14	2590.0	**2420**	8.41
5	Dwight Gooden	15	2695.2	**2238**	7.47
6	Greg Maddux	14	3068.2	**2160**	6.33
7	Chuck Finley*	14	2675.0	**2151**	7.24
8	John Smoltz	12	2414.1	**2098**	7.82
9	Orel Hershiser	17	3105.2	**2001**	5.80
10	Bobby Witt	14	2406.1	**1918**	7.17

Winning Pct.

		Yrs	W-L	Pct
1	Bob Caruthers	9	218-97	.692
2	Dave Foutz	11	147-66	.690
3	Whitey Ford*	16	236-106	.690
4	**Pedro Martinez**	8	107-50	.682
5	Lefty Grove*	17	300-141	.680
6	**Mike Mussina**	9	136-66	.673
7	Vic Raschi	10	132-66	.667
8	Christy Mathewson	17	373-188	.665
9	Larry Corcoran	8	177-90	.663
10	Sam Leever	13	194-101	.658
11	Sal Maglie	10	119-62	.657
12	Sandy Koufax*	12	165-87	.655
13	Johnny Allen	13	142-75	.654
14	Ron Guidry*	14	170-91	.651
15	Lefty Gomez*	14	189-102	.649

Losses

		Yrs	GS	W	L	Pct
1	Cy Young	22	815	511	**316**	.618
2	Pud Galvin	14	682	361	**308**	.540
3	Nolan Ryan	27	773	324	**292**	.526
4	Walter Johnson	21	666	417	**279**	.599
5	Phil Niekro	24	716	318	**274**	.537
6	Gaylord Perry	22	690	314	**265**	.542
7	Jack Powell	16	517	245	**256**	.489
	Don Sutton	23	756	324	**256**	.559
9	Eppa Rixey*	21	552	266	**251**	.515
10	Bert Blyleven	22	685	287	**250**	.534
11	Robin Roberts	19	609	286	**245**	.539
	Warren Spahn*	21	665	363	**245**	.597
13	Early Wynn	23	612	300	**244**	.551
	Steve Carlton*	24	709	329	**244**	.574
15	Jim Kaat*	25	625	283	**237**	.544

Appearances

1	**Jesse Orosco**	1090
2	Dennis Eckersley	1071
3	Hoyt Wilhelm	1070
4	Kent Tekulve	1050
5	Lee Smith	1022
6	Rich Gossage	1002
7	Lindy McDaniel	987
8	Rollie Fingers	944
9	Gene Garber	931
10	Cy Young	906
11	Sparky Lyle	899
12	Jim Kaat	898
13	**Paul Assenmacher**	884
14	Jeff Reardon	880
15	**John Franco**	878

Innings Pitched

1	Cy Young	7356.0
2	Pud Galvin	5941.1
3	Walter Johnson	5923.2
4	Phil Niekro	5403.1
5	Nolan Ryan	5387.0
6	Gaylord Perry	5350.1
7	Don Sutton	5280.1
8	Warren Spahn	5243.2
9	Steve Carlton	5217.1
10	Grover Alexander	5189.2
11	Kid Nichols	5084.0
12	Tim Keefe	5061.1
13	Bert Blyleven	4970.1
14	Mickey Welch	4802.0
15	Tom Seaver	4782.2

Earned Run Avg.

1	Ed Walsh	1.82
2	Addie Joss	1.88
3	Three Finger Brown	2.06
4	Monte Ward	2.10
5	Christy Mathewson	2.13
6	Rube Waddell	2.16
7	Walter Johnson	2.17
8	Orval Overall	2.24
9	Tommy Bond	2.25
10	Will White	2.28
11	Ed Reulbach	2.28
12	Jim Scott	2.32
13	Eddie Plank	2.34
14	Larry Corcoran	2.36
15	Eddie Cicotte	2.37

Shutouts

1	Walter Johnson	110
2	Grover Alexander	90
3	Christy Mathewson	80
4	Cy Young	76
5	Eddie Plank	69
6	Warren Spahn	63
7	Nolan Ryan	61
	Tom Seaver	61
9	Bert Blyleven	60
10	Don Sutton	58
11	Three Finger Brown	57
	Pud Galvin	57
	Ed Walsh	57
14	Bob Gibson	56
15	Steve Carlton	55

Walks Allowed

1	Nolan Ryan	2795
2	Steve Carlton	1833
3	Phil Niekro	1809
4	Early Wynn	1775
5	Bob Feller	1764
6	Bobo Newsom	1732
7	Amos Rusie	1704
8	Charlie Hough	1665
9	Gus Weyhing	1566
10	Red Ruffing	1541
11	Bump Hadley	1442
12	Warren Spahn	1434
13	Earl Whitehill	1431
14	Tony Mullane	1409
15	Sad Sam Jones	1396

HRs Allowed

1	Robin Roberts	505
2	Ferguson Jenkins	484
3	Phil Niekro	482
4	Don Sutton	472
5	Frank Tanana	448
6	Warren Spahn	434
7	Bert Blyleven	430
8	Steve Carlton	414
9	Gaylord Perry	399
10	Jim Kaat	395
11	Jack Morris	389
12	Charlie Hough	383
13	Tom Seaver	380
14	Catfish Hunter	374
15	Jim Bunning	372
	Dennis Martinez	372

Saves

1	Lee Smith	478	11	Bruce Sutter	300
2	**John Franco**	416	12	**John Wetteland**	296
3	Dennis Eckersley	390	13	**Rick Aguilera**	289
4	Jeff Reardon	367	14	**Rod Beck**	260
5	**Randy Myers**	347	15	Todd Worrell	256
6	Rollie Fingers	341	16	Dave Righetti	252
7	Tom Henke	311	17	Dan Quisenberry	244
8	Rich Gossage	310	18	Sparky Lyle	238
9	**Jeff Montgomery**	304	19	**Roberto Hernandez**	234
10	**Doug Jones**	301	20	**Trevor Hoffman**	228

21	Hoyt Wilhelm	227
22	Gene Garber	218
23	**Gregg Olson**	217
24	Dave Smith	216
25	Bobby Thigpen	201
26	Roy Face	193
	Mike Henneman	193
28	Mitch Williams	192
29	Jeff Russell	186
30	**Robb Nen**	185

SINGLE SEASON
Through 1999 regular season.
Batting

Home Runs

		Year	Gm	AB	HR
1	Mark McGwire, St.L	1998	155	509	70
2	Sammy Sosa, Chi-NL	1998	159	643	66
3	**Mark McGwire**, St.L	1999	153	521	65
4	**Sammy Sosa**, Chi-NL	1999	162	625	63
5	Roger Maris, NY-AL	1961	162	590	61
6	Babe Ruth, NY-AL	1927	151	540	60
7	Babe Ruth, NY-AL	1921	152	540	59
8	Mark McGwire, Oak-St.L	1997	156	540	58
	Hank Greenberg, Det	1938	155	556	58
	Jimmie Foxx, Phi-AL	1932	154	585	58
11	Hack Wilson, Chi-NL	1930	155	585	56
	Ken Griffey Jr., Sea	1997	157	608	56
	Ken Griffey Jr., Sea	1998	161	633	56
14	Babe Ruth, NY-AL	1920	142	458	54
	Mickey Mantle, NY-AL	1961	153	514	54
	Babe Ruth, NY-AL	1928	154	536	54
	Ralph Kiner, Pit	1949	152	549	54
18	Mickey Mantle, NY-AL	1956	150	533	52
	Willie Mays, SF	1965	157	558	52
	George Foster, Cin	1977	158	615	52
	Mark McGwire, Oak	1996	130	423	52

Hits

		Year	AB	H	Avg
1	George Sisler, StL-AL	1920	631	**257**	.407
2	Bill Terry, NY-NL	1930	633	**254**	.401
	Lefty O'Doul, Phi-NL	1929	638	**254**	.398
4	Al Simmons, Phi-AL	1925	658	**253**	.384
5	Rogers Hornsby, StL-NL	1922	623	**250**	.401
6	Chuck Klein, Phi-NL	1930	648	**250**	.386
7	Ty Cobb, Det	1911	591	**248**	.420
8	George Sisler, StL-AL	1922	586	**246**	.420
9	Babe Herman, Bklyn	1930	614	**241**	.393
	Heinie Manush, StL-AL	1928	638	**241**	.378
11	Wade Boggs, Bos	1985	653	**240**	.368
12	Rod Carew, Min	1977	616	**239**	.388
13	Don Mattingly, NY-AL	1986	677	**238**	.352
14	Harry Heilmann, Det	1921	602	**237**	.394
	Paul Waner, Pit	1927	623	**237**	.380
	Joe Medwick, StL-NL	1937	633	**237**	.374
17	Jack Tobin, StL-AL	1921	671	**236**	.352
18	Rogers Hornsby, StL-NL	1921	592	**235**	.397
19	Lloyd Waner, Pit	1929	662	**234**	.353
	Kirby Puckett, Min	1988	657	**234**	.356

Batting Average

From 1900-49

		Year	AB	H	Avg
1	Rogers Hornsby, StL-NL	1924	536	227	.424
2	Nap Lajoie, Phi-AL	1901	543	229	.422
3	George Sisler, StL-AL	1922	586	246	.420
4	Ty Cobb, Det	1911	591	248	.420
5	Ty Cobb, Det	1912	533	227	.410
6	Joe Jackson, Cle	1911	571	233	.408
7	George Sisler, StL-AL	1920	631	257	.407
8	Ted Williams, Bos-AL	1941	456	185	.406
9	Rogers Hornsby, StL-NL	1925	504	203	.403
10	Harry Heilmann, Det	1923	524	211	.403

Since 1950

		Year	AB	H	Avg
1	Tony Gwynn, SD	1994	419	175	.394
2	George Brett, KC	1980	449	175	.390
3	Ted Williams, Bos	1957	420	163	.388
4	Rod Carew, Min	1977	616	239	.388
5	**Larry Walker**, Col	1999	438	166	.379
6	Tony Gwynn, SD	1997	592	220	.372
7	Andres Galarraga, Col	1993	470	174	.370
8	Tony Gwynn, SD	1987	589	218	.370
9	Tony Gwynn, SD	1995	535	197	.368
10	Wade Boggs, Bos	1985	653	240	.368

Total Bases

From 1900-49

		Year	TB
1	Babe Ruth, New York-AL	1921	457
2	Rogers Hornsby, St. Louis-NL	1922	450
3	Lou Gehrig, New York-AL	1927	447
4	Chuck Klein, Philadelphia-NL	1930	445
5	Jimmie Foxx, Philadelphia-AL	1932	438
6	Stan Musial, St. Louis-NL	1948	429
7	Hack Wilson, Chicago-NL	1930	423
8	Chuck Klein, Philadelphia-NL	1932	420
9	Lou Gehrig, New York-AL	1930	419
10	Joe DiMaggio, New York-AL	1937	418

Since 1950

		Year	TB
1	Sammy Sosa, Chi-NL	1998	416
2	Larry Walker, Colorado	1997	409
3	Jim Rice, Boston	1978	406
4	Hank Aaron, Milwaukee	1959	400
5	Albert Belle, Chi-AL	1998	399
6	**Sammy Sosa**, Chi-NL	1999	397
7	Ken Griffey Jr., Seattle	1997	393
8	Ellis Burks, Colorado	1996	392
9	George Foster, Cincinnati	1977	388
	Don Mattingly, New York-AL	1986	388

Runs Batted In

From 1900-49

		Year	Avg	HR	RBI
1	Hack Wilson, Chi-NL	1930	.356	56	191
2	Lou Gehrig, NY-AL	1931	.341	46	184
3	Hank Greenberg, Det	1937	.337	40	183
4	Lou Gehrig, NY-AL	1927	.373	47	175
	Jimmie Foxx, Bos-AL	1938	.349	50	175
6	Lou Gehrig, NY-AL	1930	.379	41	174
7	Babe Ruth, NY-AL	1921	.378	59	171
8	Chuck Klein, NY-AL	1930	.386	40	170
	Hank Greenberg, Det	1935	.328	36	170
10	Jimmie Foxx, Phi-AL	1932	.364	58	169

Since 1950

		Year	Avg	HR	RBI
1	**Manny Ramirez**, Cle	1999	.333	44	165
2	Sammy Sosa, Chi-NL	1998	.308	66	158
3	Juan Gonzalez, Tex	1998	.318	45	157
4	Tommy Davis, LA-NL	1962	.346	27	153
5	Albert Belle, Chi-AL	1998	.328	49	152
6	Andres Galarraga, Col	1996	.304	47	150
7	George Foster, Cin	1977	.320	52	149
8	**Rafael Palmeiro**, Tex	1999	.324	47	148
	Johnny Bench, Cin	1970	.293	45	148
	Albert Belle, Cle	1996	.311	48	148

Runs

		Year	Runs
1	Babe Ruth, New York-AL	1921	177
2	Lou Gehrig, New York-AL	1936	167
3	Babe Ruth, New York-AL	1928	163
	Lou Gehrig, New York-AL	1931	163
5	Babe Ruth, New York-AL	1920	158
	Babe Ruth, New York-AL	1927	158
	Chuck Klein, Philadelphia-NL	1930	158
8	Rogers Hornsby, Chicago-NL	1929	156
9	Kiki Cuyler, Chicago-NL	1930	155
10	Lefty O'Doul, Philadelphia-NL	1929	152
	Woody English, Chicago-NL	1930	152
	Al Simmons, Philadelphia-AL	1930	152
	Chuck Klein, Philadelphia-NL	1932	152
14	Babe Ruth, New York-AL	1923	151
	Jimmie Foxx, Philadelphia-AL	1932	151
	Joe DiMaggio, New York-AL	1937	151
17	Babe Ruth, New York-AL	1930	150
	Ted Williams, Boston-AL	1940	150
19	Lou Gehrig, New York-AL	1927	149
	Babe Ruth, New York-AL	1931	149

Walks

		Year	BB
1	Babe Ruth, New York-AL	1923	170
2	Ted Williams, Boston-AL	1947	162
	Ted Williams, Boston-AL	1949	162
	Mark McGwire, St. Louis	1998	162
5	Ted Williams, Boston-AL	1946	156
6	Barry Bonds, San Francisco	1996	151
	Eddie Yost, Washington	1956	151
8	**Jeff Bagwell**, Houston	1999	149
	Eddie Joost, Philadelphia-AL	1949	149
10	Babe Ruth, New York-AL	1920	148
	Eddie Stanky, Brooklyn	1945	148
	Jimmy Wynn, Houston	1969	148

Extra Base Hits

		Year	EBH
1	Babe Ruth, New York-AL	1921	119
2	Lou Gehrig, New York-AL	1927	117
3	Chuck Klein, Philadelphia-NL	1930	107
4	Chuck Klein, Philadelphia-NL	1932	103
	Hank Greenberg, Detroit	1937	103
	Stan Musial, St. Louis-NL	1948	103
	Albert Belle, Cleveland	1995	103
8	Rogers Hornsby, St. Louis-NL	1922	102
9	Lou Gehrig, New York-AL	1930	100
	Jimmie Foxx, Philadelphia-AL	1933	100

Slugging Percentage
From 1900-49

		Year	Pct
1	Babe Ruth, New York-AL	1920	.847
2	Babe Ruth, New York-AL	1921	.846
3	Babe Ruth, New York-AL	1927	.772
4	Lou Gehrig, New York-AL	1927	.765
5	Babe Ruth, New York-AL	1923	.764
6	Rogers Hornsby, St. Louis-NL	1925	.756
7	Jimmie Foxx, Philadelphia-AL	1932	.749
8	Babe Ruth, New York-AL	1924	.739
9	Babe Ruth, New York-AL	1926	.737
10	Ted Williams, Boston-AL	1941	.735

Since 1950

		Year	Pct
1	Mark McGwire, St. Louis	1998	.752
2	Jeff Bagwell, Houston	1994	.750
3	Ted Williams, Boston	1957	.731
4	Mark McGwire, Oakland	1996	.730
5	Frank Thomas, Chicago-AL	1994	.729
6	Larry Walker, Colorado	1997	.720

Stolen Bases

		Year	SB
1	Rickey Henderson, Oakland	1982	130
2	Lou Brock, St. Louis	1974	118
3	Vince Coleman, St. Louis	1985	110
4	Vince Coleman, St. Louis	1987	109
5	Rickey Henderson, Oakland	1983	108
6	Vince Coleman, St. Louis	1986	107
7	Maury Wills, Los Angeles-NL	1962	104
8	Rickey Henderson, Oakland	1980	100
9	Ron LeFlore, Montreal	1980	97
10	Ty Cobb, Detroit	1915	96
	Omar Moreno, Pittsburgh	1980	96
12	Maury Wills, Los Angeles	1965	94
13	Rickey Henderson, New York-AL	1988	93
14	Tim Raines, Montreal	1983	90
15	Clyde Milan, Washington	1912	88
16	Rickey Henderson, New York-AL	1986	87
17	Ty Cobb, Detroit	1911	83
	Willie Wilson, Kansas City	1979	83
19	Bob Bescher, Cincinnati	1911	81
	Eddie Collins, Philadelphia-AL	1910	81
	Vince Coleman, St. Louis	1988	81

Strikeouts

		Year	SO
1	Bobby Bonds, San Francisco	1970	189
2	Bobby Bonds, San Francisco	1969	187
3	Rob Deer, Milwaukee	1987	186
4	Pete Incaviglia, Texas	1986	185
5	Cecil Fielder, Detroit	1990	182
6	Mike Schmidt, Philadelphia	1975	180
7	Rob Deer, Milwaukee	1986	179
8	Dave Nicholson, Chicago-AL	1963	175
	Gorman Thomas, Milwaukee	1979	175
	Jose Canseco, Oakland	1986	175
	Rob Deer, Detroit	1991	175
	Jay Buhner, Seattle	1997	175

Pinch Hits
Career pinch hits in parentheses.

		Year	PH	
1	John Vander Wal, Colorado	1995	28	(90)
2	Jose Morales, Montreal	1976	25	(123)
3	Dave Philley, Baltimore	1961	24	(93)
	Vic Davalillo, St. Louis	1970	24	(95)
	Rusty Staub, New York-NL	1983	24	(100)
	Four tied with 22 each.			

Note: The all-time career pinch hit leader is Manny Mota (150).

Four Home Runs in One Game
National League

	Date	H/A	Inn
Bobby Lowe, Boston	5/30/1894	H	9
Ed Delahanty, Philadelphia	7/13/1896	A	9
Chuck Klein, Philadelphia	7/10/1936	A	10
Gil Hodges, Brooklyn	8/31/1950	H	9
Joe Adcock, Milwaukee	7/31/1954	A	9
Willie Mays, San Francisco	4/30/1961	A	9
Mike Schmidt, Philadelphia	4/17/1976	A	10
Bob Horner, Atlanta	7/6/1986	H	9
Mark Whiten, St. Louis	9/7/1993	A	9

American League

	Date	H/A	Inn
Lou Gehrig, New York	6/3/1932	A	9
Pat Seerey, Chicago	7/18/1948	A	11
Rocky Colavito, Cleveland	6/10/1959	A	9

Pitching
Wins

From 1900-49

		Year	W	L	Pct
1	Jack Chesbro, NY-AL	1904	41	12	.774
2	Ed Walsh, Chi-AL	1908	40	15	.727
3	Christy Mathewson, NY-NL	1908	37	11	.771
4	Walter Johnson, Wash	1913	36	7	.837
5	Joe McGinnity, NY-NL	1904	35	8	.814
6	Smokey Joe Wood, Bos-AL	1912	34	5	.872
7	Cy Young, Bos-AL	1901	33	10	.767
	Grover Alexander, Phi-NL	1916	33	12	.733
	Christy Mathewson, NY-NL	1904	33	12	.733
10	Cy Young, Bos-AL	1902	32	11	.744

Since 1950

		Year	W	L	Pct
1	Denny McLain, Det.	1968	31	6	.838
2	Robin Roberts, Phi-NL	1952	28	7	.800
3	Bob Welch, Oak	1990	27	6	.818
	Don Newcombe, Bklyn	1956	27	7	.794
	Sandy Koufax, LA	1966	27	9	.750
	Steve Carlton, Phi.	1972	27	10	.730
7	Sandy Koufax, LA	1965	26	8	.765
	Juan Marichal, SF	1968	26	9	.743

Note: 11 pitchers tied with 25 wins, including Marichal twice.

Earned Run Average

From 1900-49

		Year	ShO	ERA
1	Dutch Leonard, Bos-AL	1914	7	1.01
2	Three Finger Brown, Chi-NL	1906	10	1.04
3	Walter Johnson, Wash	1913	11	1.09
4	Christy Mathewson, NY-NL	1909	8	1.14
5	Jack Pfiester, Chi-NL	1907	3	1.15
6	Addie Joss, Cle	1908	9	1.16
7	Carl Lundgren, Chi-NL	1907	7	1.17
8	Grover Alexander, Phi-NL	1915	12	1.22
9	Cy Young, Bos-AL	1908	3	1.26
10	Three pitchers tied at 1.27			

Since 1950

		Year	ShO	ERA
1	Bob Gibson, St.L	1968	13	1.12
2	Dwight Gooden, NY-NL	1985	8	1.53
3	Greg Maddux, Atl.	1994	3	1.56
4	Luis Tiant, Cle	1968	9	1.60
5	Greg Maddux, Atl	1995	3	1.63
6	Dean Chance, LA-AL	1964	11	1.65
7	Nolan Ryan, Cal	1981	3	1.69
8	Sandy Koufax, LA	1966	5	1.73
9	Sandy Koufax, LA	1964	7	1.74
10	Ron Guidry, NY-AL	1978	9	1.74

Winning Pct.

		Year	W-L	Pct
1	Roy Face, Pit	1959	18-1	.947
2	Rick Sutcliffe, Chi-NL*	1984	16-1	.941
3	Johnny Allen, Cle	1937	15-1	.938
4	Greg Maddux, Atl	1995	19-2	.904
5	Randy Johnson, Sea	1995	18-2	.900
6	Ron Guidry, NY-AL	1978	25-3	.893
7	Freddie Fitzsimmons, Bklyn.	1940	16-2	.889
8	Lefty Grove, Phi-AL	1931	31-4	.886
9	Bob Stanley, Bos.	1978	15-2	.882
10	Preacher Roe, Bklyn	1951	22-3	.880
11	Tom Seaver, Cin	1981	14-2	.875
12	Smokey Joe Wood, Bos-AL	1912	34-5	.872

*Sutcliffe began 1984 with Cleveland and was 4-5 before being traded to the Cubs; his overall winning pct. was .769 (20-6).

Strikeouts

		Year	SO	P/G
1	Nolan Ryan, Cal	1973	383	10.57
2	Sandy Koufax, LA	1965	382	10.24
3	Nolan Ryan, Cal	1974	367	9.92
4	**Randy Johnson**, Ari	1999	364	10.40
5	Rube Waddell, Phi-AL	1904	349	8.12
6	Bob Feller, Cle	1946	348	8.45
7	Nolan Ryan, Cal	1977	341	10.26
8	Nolan Ryan, Cal	1972	329	10.43
	Randy Johnson, Sea-Hou	1998	329	9.68
10	Nolan Ryan, Cal	1976	327	10.36

Appearances

		Year	App	Sv
1	Mike Marshall, LA	1974	106	21
2	Kent Tekulve, Pit	1979	94	31
3	Mike Marshall, LA	1973	92	31
4	Kent Tekulve, Pit	1978	91	31
5	Wayne Granger, Cin	1969	90	27
	Mike Marshall, Min	1979	90	32
	Kent Tekulve, Phi.	1987	90	3

Saves

		Year	App	Sv
1	Bobby Thigpen, Chi-AL	1990	77	57
2	Randy Myers, Chi-NL	1993	73	53
	Trevor Hoffman, SD	1998	66	53
4	Dennis Eckersley, Oak	1992	69	51
	Rod Beck, Chi-NL	1998	81	51
6	Dennis Eckersley, Oak	1990	63	48
	Rod Beck, SF	1993	76	48
	Jeff Shaw, Cin-LA	1998	73	48
9	Lee Smith, St.L	1991	67	47

Innings Pitched *(since 1920)*

		Year	IP	W-L
1	Wilbur Wood, Chi-AL	1972	377	24-17
2	Mickey Lolich, Det	1971	376	25-14
3	Bob Feller, Cle	1946	371	26-15
4	Grover Alexander, Chi-NL	1920	363	27-14
5	Wilbur Wood, Chi-AL	1973	359	24-20

Shutouts

		Year	ShO	ERA
1	Grover Alexander, Phi-NL	1916	16	1.55
2	Jack Coombs, Phi-AL	1910	13	1.30
	Bob Gibson, St.L	1968	13	1.12
4	Christy Mathewson, NY-NL	1908	12	1.43
	Grover Alexander, Phi-NL	1915	12	1.22

Walks Allowed

		Year	BB	SO
1	Bob Feller, Cle	1938	208	240
2	Nolan Ryan, Cal	1977	204	341
3	Nolan Ryan, Cal	1974	202	367
4	Bob Feller, Cle	1941	194	260
5	Bobo Newsom, St.L-AL	1938	192	226

Home Runs Allowed

		Year	HRs
1	Bert Blyleven, Minnesota	1986	50
2	Robin Roberts, Philadelphia	1956	46
	Bert Blyleven, Minnesota	1987	46
4	Pedro Ramos, Washington	1957	43
5	Denny McLain, Detroit	1966	42

Home Run in First Major League At bat
* on first pitch

A.L.

Luke Stuart, St. Louis, August 8, 1921.
Earl Averill, Cleveland, April 16, 1929.
Ace Parker, Philadelphia, April 30, 1937.
Gene Hasson, Philadelphia, September 9, 1937, first game.
Bill Lefebvre, Boston, June 10, 1938.*
Hack Miller, Detroit, April 23, 1944, second game.
Eddie Pellagrini, Boston, April 22, 1946.
George Vico, Detroit, April 20, 1948.*
Bob Nieman, St. Louis, September 14, 1951.
Bob Tillman, Boston, May 19, 1962.
John Kennedy, Washington, September 5, 1962, first game.
Buster Narum, Baltimore, May 3, 1963.
Gates Brown, Detroit, June 19, 1963.
Bert Campaneris, Kansas City, July 23, 1964.*
Bill Roman, Detroit, September 30, 1964, second game.
Brant Alyea, Washington, September 12, 1965.*
John Miller, New York, September 11, 1966.
Rick Renick, Minnesota, July 11, 1968.
Joe Keough, Oakland, August 7, 1968, second game.
Gene Lamont, Detroit, September 2, 1970, second game.
Don Rose, California, May 24, 1972.*
Reggie Sanders, Detroit, September 1, 1974.
Dave McKay, Minnesota, August 22, 1975.
Al Woods, Toronto, April 7, 1977.
Dave Machemer, California, June 21, 1978.
Gary Gaetti, Minnesota, September 20, 1981.
Andre David, Minnesota, June 29, 1984, first game.
Terry Steinbach, Oakland, September 12, 1986.
Jay Bell, Cleveland, September 29, 1986.*
Junior Felix, Toronto, May 4, 1989.*
Jon Nunnally, Kansas City, April 29, 1995.
Carlos Lee, Chicago, May 7, 1999.
Total number of players: 32

N.L.

Joe Harrington, Boston, September 10, 1895.
Bill Duggleby, Philadelphia, April 21, 1898.
Johnny Bates, Boston, April 12, 1906.
Walter Mueller, Pittsburgh, May 7, 1922.
Clise Dudley, Brooklyn, April 27, 1929.*
Gordon Slade, Brooklyn, May 24, 1930.
Eddie Morgan, St. Louis, April 14, 1936.*
Ernie Koy, Brooklyn, April 19, 1938.
Emmett Mueller, Philadelphia, April 19, 1938.
Clyde Vollmer, Cincinnati, May 31, 1942, second game.*
Paul Gillespie, Chicago, September 11, 1942.
Buddy Kerr, New York, September 8, 1943.
Whitey Lockman, New York, July 5, 1945.
Dan Bankhead, Brooklyn, August 26, 1947.
Les Layton, New York, May 21, 1948.
Ed Sanicki, Philadelphia, September 14, 1949.
Ted Tappe, Cincinnati, September 14, 1950, first game.
Hoyt Wilhelm, New York, April 23, 1952.
Wally Moon, St. Louis, April 13, 1954.
Chuck Tanner, Milwaukee, April 12, 1955.*
Bill White, New York, May 7, 1956.
Frank Ernaga, Chicago, May 24, 1957.
Don Leppert, Pittsburgh, June 18, 1961, first game.
Cuno Barragan, Chicago, September 1, 1961.
Benny Ayala, New York, August 27, 1974.
John Montefusco, San Francisco, September 3, 1974.
Jose Sosa, Houston, July 30, 1975.
Johnnie LeMaster, San Francisco, September 2, 1975.
Tim Wallach, Montreal, September 6, 1980.
Carmelo Martinez, Chicago, August 22, 1983.
Mike Fitzgerald, New York, September 13, 1983.
Will Clark, San Francisco, April 8, 1986.
Ricky Jordan, Philadelphia, July 17, 1988.
Jose Offerman, Los Angeles, August 19, 1990.
Dave Eiland, San Diego, April 10, 1992.
Jim Bullinger, Chicago, June 8, 1992, first game.
Jay Gainer, Colorado, May 14, 1993.*
Mitch Lyden, Florida, June 16, 1993.
Garey Ingram, Los Angeles, May 19, 1994.
Jermaine Dye, Atlanta, May 17, 1996.
Dustin Hermanson, Montreal, April 16, 1997.
Brad Fullmer, Montreal, Sept. 2, 1997.
Marlon Anderson, Philadelphia, Sept. 8, 1998.
Total number of players: 43

Unassisted Triple Plays

The unassisted triple play is one of the rarest feats in baseball. So much so, in fact, that it has been accomplished only 11 times in major league history. Ironically, in what can only be described as a statistic anomaly, the trick was turned twice in two days in May of 1927.

Player, Position, Team	Date	Opponent
Paul Hines, OF, Providence	May 8, 1878	Boston-NL
Neal Ball, SS, Cleveland	July 19, 1909	Boston-AL
Bill Wambganss, 2B, Cleveland*	Oct. 10, 1920	Brooklyn
George Burns, 1B, Boston-AL	Sept. 14, 1923	Cleveland
Ernie Padgett, SS, Boston-NL	Oct. 6, 1923	Philadelphia
Glenn Wright, SS, Pittsburgh	May 7, 1925	St.Louis-NL
Jimmy Cooney, SS, Chicago-NL	May 30, 1927	Pittsburgh
Johnny Neun, 1B, Detroit	May 31, 1927	Cleveland
Ron Hansen, SS, Washington	July 30, 1968	Cleveland
Mickey Morandini, 2B, Philadelphia	Sept. 20, 1992	Pittsburgh
John Valentin, SS, Boston	July 8, 1994	Seattle

*World Series game

All-Time Winningest Managers

Top 20 Major League career victories through the 1999 season. Career, regular season and postseason (playoffs and World Series) records are noted along with AL and NL pennants and World Series titles won. Managers active during 1999 season in **bold** type.

		Yrs	Career W	L	Pct	Regular Season W	L	Pct	Postseason W	L	Pct	Titles
1	Connie Mack	53	**3755**	3967	.486	3731	3948	.486	24	19	.558	9 AL, 5 WS
2	John McGraw	33	**2866**	2012	.588	2840	1984	.589	26	28	.482	10 NL, 3 WS
3	Sparky Anderson	26	**2228**	1855	.547	2194	1834	.545	34	21	.618	4 NL, 1 AL, 3 WS
4	Bucky Harris	29	**2168**	2228	.493	2157	2218	.493	11	10	.524	3 AL, 2 WS
5	Joe McCarthy	24	**2155**	1346	.616	2125	1333	.615	30	13	.698	1 NL, 8 AL, 7 WS
6	Walter Alston	23	**2063**	1634	.558	2040	1613	.558	23	21	.523	7 NL, 4 WS
7	Leo Durocher	24	**2015**	1717	.540	2008	1709	.540	7	8	.467	3 NL, 1 WS
8	Casey Stengel	25	**1942**	1868	.510	1905	1842	.508	37	26	.587	10 AL, 7 WS
9	Gene Mauch	26	**1907**	2044	.483	1902	2037	.483	5	7	.417	—None—
10	Bill McKechnie	25	**1904**	1737	.523	1896	1723	.524	8	14	.364	4 NL, 2 WS
11	**Tony La Russa**	21	**1665**	1531	.521	1639	1511	.520	26	20	.565	3 AL, 1 WS
12	Tommy Lasorda	21	**1630**	1469	.526	1599	1439	.526	31	30	.508	4 NL, 2 WS
13	Ralph Houk	20	**1627**	1539	.514	1619	1531	.514	8	8	.500	3 AL, 2 WS
14	Fred Clarke	19	**1609**	1189	.575	1602	1181	.576	7	8	.467	4 NL, 1 WS
15	Dick Williams	21	**1592**	1474	.519	1571	1451	.520	21	23	.477	3 AL, 1 NL, 2 WS
16	**Bobby Cox**	18	**1571**	1247	.557	1521	1204	.558	50	43	.538	5 NL, 1 WS
17	Earl Weaver	17	**1506**	1080	.582	1480	1060	.583	26	20	.565	4 AL, 1 WS
18	Clark Griffith	20	**1491**	1367	.522	1491	1367	.522	0	0	.000	1 AL (1901)
19	Miller Huggins	17	**1431**	1149	.555	1413	1134	.555	18	15	.545	6 AL, 3 WS
20	Al Lopez	17	**1412**	1012	.583	1410	1004	.584	2	8	.200	2 AL

Notes: John McGraw's postseason record also includes two World Series tie games (1912,'22); Miller Huggins postseason record also includes one World Series tie game (1922).

Where They Managed

Alston—Brooklyn/Los Angeles NL (1954-76); **Anderson**—Cincinnati NL (1970-78), Detroit AL (1979-95); **Clarke**—Louisville NL (1897-99), Pittsburgh NL (1900-15); **Cox**—Atlanta (1978-81, 1990-), Toronto (1982-85); **Durocher**—Brooklyn NL (1939-46,48), New York NL (1948-55), Chicago NL (1966-72), Houston NL (1972-73); **Griffith**—Chicago AL (1901-02), New York AL (1903-08), Cincinnati NL (1909-11), Washington AL (1912-20); **Harris**—Washington AL (1924-28,35-42,50-54), Detroit AL (1929-33,55-56), Boston AL (1934), Philadelphia NL (1943), New York AL (1947-48); **Houk**—New York AL (1961-63,66-73), Detroit AL (1974-78), Boston AL (1981-84); **Huggins**—St. Louis NL (1913-17), New York AL (1918-29); **La Russa**—Chicago AL (1979-86), Oakland (1986-95), St. Louis (1996-); **Lasorda**—Los Angeles NL (1976-96); **Lopez**—Cleveland AL (1951-56), Chicago AL (1957-65,68-69); **Mack**—Pittsburgh NL (1894-96), Philadelphia AL (1901-50); **Mauch**—Philadelphia NL (1960-68), Montreal NL (1969-75), Minnesota AL (1976-80), California AL (1981-82,85-87); **McCarthy**—Chicago NL (1926-30), New York AL (1931-46), Boston AL (1948-50); **McGraw**—Baltimore NL (1899), Baltimore AL (1901-02), New York NL (1902-32); **McKechnie**—Newark FL (1915), Pittsburgh NL (1922-26), St. Louis NL (1928-29), Boston NL (1930-37), Cincinnati NL (1938-46); **Stengel**—Brooklyn NL (1934-36), Boston NL (1938-43), New York AL (1949-60), New York NL (1962-65); **Weaver**—Baltimore AL (1968-82,85-86); **Williams**—Boston AL (1967-69), Oakland AL (1971-73), California AL (1974-76), Montreal NL (1977-81), San Diego NL (1982-85), Seattle AL (1986-88).

Regular Season Winning Pct.

Minimum of 750 victories.

		Yrs	W	L	Pct	Pen
1	Joe McCarthy	24	2125	1333	**.615**	9
2	Charlie Comiskey	12	838	541	**.608**	4
3	Frank Selee	16	1284	862	**.598**	5
4	Billy Southworth	13	1044	704	**.597**	4
5	Frank Chance	11	946	648	**.593**	4
6	John McGraw	33	2784	1959	**.587**	10
7	Al Lopez	17	1410	1004	**.584**	2
8	Earl Weaver	17	1480	1060	**.583**	4
9	Cap Anson	20	1296	947	**.578**	5
10	Fred Clarke	19	1602	1181	**.576**	4
11	**Davey Johnson**	13	1062	812	**.567**	1
12	Steve O'Neill	14	1040	821	**.559**	1
13	Walter Alston	23	2040	1613	**.558**	7
14	**Bobby Cox**	18	1521	1204	**.558**	5
15	Bill Terry	10	823	661	**.555**	3
16	Miller Huggins	17	1413	1134	**.555**	6
17	Billy Martin	16	1253	1013	**.553**	2
18	Harry Wright	18	1000	825	**.548**	3
19	Charlie Grimm	19	1287	1067	**.547**	3
20	Sparky Anderson	26	2194	1834	**.545**	5

World Series Victories

		App	W	L	T	Pct	WS
1	Casey Stengel	10	**37**	26	0	.587	7
2	Joe McCarthy	9	**30**	13	0	.698	7
3	John McGraw	9	**26**	28	2	.482	3
4	Connie Mack	8	**24**	19	0	.558	5
5	Walter Alston	7	**20**	20	0	.500	4
6	Miller Huggins	6	**18**	15	1	.544	3
7	Sparky Anderson	5	**16**	12	0	.571	3
8	**Joe Torre**	3	**12**	2	0	.857	3
	Tommy Lasorda	4	**12**	11	0	.522	2
	Dick Williams	4	**12**	14	0	.462	2
11	Frank Chance	4	**11**	9	1	.548	2
	Bucky Harris	3	**11**	10	0	.524	2
	Billy Southworth	4	**11**	11	0	.500	2
	Earl Weaver	4	**11**	13	0	.458	1
	Bobby Cox	5	**11**	18	0	.379	1
16	Whitey Herzog	3	**10**	11	0	.476	1
17	Bill Carrigan	2	**8**	2	0	.800	2
	Danny Murtaugh	2	**8**	6	0	.571	2
	Ralph Houk	3	**8**	8	0	.500	2
	Bill McKechnie	4	**8**	14	0	.364	2
	Tom Kelly	2	**8**	6	0	.571	2

Active Managers' Records
Regular season games only; through 1999.

National League

		Yrs	W	L	Pct
1	Tony La Russa, St.L	21	**1639**	1511	.520
2	Bobby Cox, Atl	18	**1521**	1204	.558
3	Davey Johnson, LA	13	**1062**	812	.567
4	Bobby Valentine, NY	12	**866**	838	.508
5	Jack McKeon, Cin	11	**685**	656	.511
6	Felipe Alou, Mon.	8	**603**	590	.505
7	Dusty Baker, SF	7	**558**	512	.521
8	Gene Lamont, Pit.	7	**484**	469	.508
9	Buck Showalter, Ari.	6	**478**	427	.528
10	Bruce Bochy, SD	5	**409**	383	.516
11	Larry Dierker, Hou.	3	**283**	203	.582
12	Terry Francona, Phi	3	**220**	266	.453
13	Buddy Bell, Col	3	**184**	277	.399
14	John Boles, Fla	2	**104**	133	.439
	Chicago				
	Milwaukee				

American League

		Yrs	W	L	Pct
1	Joe Torre, NY	18	**1294**	1251	.508
2	Lou Piniella, Sea.	13	**1019**	949	.518
3	Tom Kelly, Min.	14	**986**	1074	.479
4	Jim Fregosi, Tor	14	**945**	1016	.482
5	Johnny Oates, Tex.	8	**715**	638	.528
6	Art Howe, Oak.	9	**696**	762	.477
7	Phil Garner, Det.	8	**563**	617	.477
8	Jimy Williams, Bos	7	**545**	463	.541
9	Tony Muser, KC	3	**167**	234	.416
10	Jerry Manuel, Chi.	2	**155**	168	.480
11	Larry Rothschild, TB	2	**132**	192	.407
	Anaheim				
	Baltimore				
	Cleveland				

Annual Awards

MOST VALUABLE PLAYER

There have been three different Most Valuable Player awards in baseball since 1911—the Chalmers Award (1911-14), presented by the Detroit-based automobile company; the League Award (1922-29), presented by the National and American Leagues; and the Baseball Writers' Award (since 1931), presented by the Baseball Writers' Association of America. Statistics for winning players are provided below. Stats for winning pitchers before advent of Cy Young Award are in MVP Pitchers' Statistics table.

Multiple winners: NL—Barry Bonds, Roy Campanella, Stan Musial and Mike Schmidt (3); Ernie Banks, Johnny Bench, Rogers Hornsby, Carl Hubbell, Willie Mays, Joe Morgan and Dale Murphy (2). **AL**—Yogi Berra, Joe DiMaggio, Jimmie Foxx and Mickey Mantle (3); Mickey Cochrane, Lou Gehrig, Juan Gonzalez, Hank Greenberg, Walter Johnson, Roger Maris, Hal Newhouser, Cal Ripken Jr., Frank Thomas, Ted Williams and Robin Yount (2). **NL & AL**—Frank Robinson (2, one in each).

Chalmers Award

National League

Year		Pos	HR	RBI	Avg
1911	Wildfire Schulte, Chi	OF	21	121	.300
1912	Larry Doyle, NY	2B	10	90	.330
1913	Jake Daubert, Bklyn	1B	2	52	.350
1914	Johnny Evers, Bos	2B	1	40	.279

American League

Year		Pos	HR	RBI	Avg
1911	Ty Cobb, Det	OF	8	144	.420
1912	Tris Speaker, Bos	OF	10	98	.383
1913	Walter Johnson, Wash	P	—	—	—
1914	Eddie Collins, Phi	2B	2	85	.344

League Award

National League

Year		Pos	HR	RBI	Avg
1922	No selection				
1923	No selection				
1924	Dazzy Vance, Bklyn	P			
1925	Rogers Hornsby, St.L	2B-Mgr	39	143	.403
1926	Bob O'Farrell, St.L	C	7	68	.293
1927	Paul Waner, Pit	OF	9	131	.380
1928	Jim Bottomley, St.L	1B	31	136	.325
1929	Rogers Hornsby, Chi	2B	39	149	.380

American League

Year		Pos	HR	RBI	Avg
1922	George Sisler, St.L	1B	8	105	.420
1923	Babe Ruth, NY	OF	41	131	.393
1924	Walter Johnson, Wash	P	—	—	—
1925	Roger Peckinpaugh, Wash.	SS	4	64	.294
1926	George Burns, Cle	1B	4	114	.358
1927	Lou Gehrig, NY	1B	47	175	.373
1928	Mickey Cochrane, Phi	C	10	57	.293
1929	No selection				

Most Valuable Player

National League

Year		Pos	HR	RBI	Avg	Year		Pos	HR	RBI	Avg
1931	Frankie Frisch, St.L	2B	4	82	.311	1943	Stan Musial, St.L	OF	13	81	.357
1932	Chuck Klein, Phi	OF	38	137	.348	1944	Marty Marion, St.L	SS	6	63	.267
1933	Carl Hubbell, NY	P	—	—	—	1945	Phil Cavarretta, Chi	1B	6	97	.355
1934	Dizzy Dean, St.L	P	—	—	—	1946	Stan Musial, St.L	1B-OF	16	103	.365
1935	Gabby Hartnett, Chi	C	13	91	.344	1947	Bob Elliott, Bos	3B	22	113	.317
1936	Carl Hubbell, NY	P	—	—	—	1948	Stan Musial, St.L	OF	39	131	.376
1937	Joe Medwick, St.L	OF	31	154	.374	1949	Jackie Robinson, Bklyn	2B	16	124	.342
1938	Ernie Lombardi, Cin	C	19	95	.342						
1939	Bucky Walters, Cin	P	—	—	—	1950	Jim Konstanty, Phi	P	—	—	—
						1951	Roy Campanella, Bklyn	C	33	108	.325
1940	Frank McCormick, Cin	1B	19	127	.309	1952	Hank Sauer, Chi	OF	37	121	.270
1941	Dolf Camilli, Bklyn	1B	34	120	.285	1953	Roy Campanella, Bklyn	C	41	142	.312
1942	Mort Cooper, St.L	P	—	—	—	1954	Willie Mays, NY	OF	41	110	.345

Year		Pos	HR	RBI	Avg
1955	Roy Campanella, Bklyn	C	32	107	.318
1956	Don Newcombe, Bklyn	P	—	—	—
1957	Hank Aaron, Mil	OF	44	132	.322
1958	Ernie Banks, Chi	SS	47	129	.313
1959	Ernie Banks, Chi	SS	45	143	.304
1960	Dick Groat, Pit	SS	2	50	.325
1961	Frank Robinson, Cin	OF	37	124	.323
1962	Maury Wills, LA	SS	6	48	.299
1963	Sandy Koufax, LA	P	—	—	—
1964	Ken Boyer, St.L	3B	24	119	.295
1965	Willie Mays, SF	OF	52	112	.317
1966	Roberto Clemente, Pit	OF	29	119	.317
1967	Orlando Cepeda, St.L	1B	25	111	.325
1968	Bob Gibson, St.L	P	—	—	—
1969	Willie McCovey, SF	1B	45	126	.320
1970	Johnny Bench, Cin	C	45	148	.293
1971	Joe Torre, St.L	3B	24	137	.363
1972	Johnny Bench, Cin	C	40	125	.270
1973	Pete Rose, Cin	OF	5	64	.338
1974	Steve Garvey, LA	1B	21	111	.312
1975	Joe Morgan, Cin	2B	17	94	.327
1976	Joe Morgan, Cin	2B	27	111	.320
1977	George Foster, Cin	OF	52	149	.320
1978	Dave Parker, Pit	OF	30	117	.334
1979	Keith Hernandez, St.L	1B	11	105	.344
	Willie Stargell, Pit	1B	32	82	.281
1980	Mike Schmidt, Phi	3B	48	121	.286
1981	Mike Schmidt, Phi	3B	31	91	.316
1982	Dale Murphy, Atl	OF	36	109	.281
1983	Dale Murphy, Atl	OF	36	121	.302
1984	Ryne Sandberg, Chi	2B	19	84	.314
1985	Willie McGee, St.L	OF	10	82	.353
1986	Mike Schmidt, Phi	3B	37	119	.290
1987	Andre Dawson, Chi	OF	49	137	.287
1988	Kirk Gibson, LA	OF	25	76	.290
1989	Kevin Mitchell, SF	OF	47	125	.291
1990	Barry Bonds, Pit	OF	33	114	.301
1991	Terry Pendleton, Atl	3B	22	86	.319
1992	Barry Bonds, Pit	OF	34	103	.311
1993	Barry Bonds, SF	OF	46	123	.336
1994	Jeff Bagwell, Hou	1B	39	116	.368
1995	Barry Larkin, Cin	SS	15	66	.319
1996	Ken Caminiti, SD	3B	40	130	.326
1997	Larry Walker, Col	OF	49	130	.366
1998	Sammy Sosa, Chi	OF	66	158	.308

American League

Year		Pos	HR	RBI	Avg
1931	Lefty Grove, Phi	P	—	—	—
1932	Jimmie Foxx, Phi	1B	58	169	.364
1933	Jimmie Foxx, Phi	1B	48	163	.356
1934	Mickey Cochrane, Det	C-Mgr	2	76	.320
1935	Hank Greenberg, Det	1B	36	170	.328
1936	Lou Gehrig, NY	1B	49	152	.354
1937	Charlie Gehringer, Det	2B	14	96	.371
1938	Jimmie Foxx, Bos	1B	50	175	.349
1939	Joe DiMaggio, NY	OF	30	126	.381
1940	Hank Greenberg, Det	OF	41	150	.340

Year		Pos	HR	RBI	Avg
1941	Joe DiMaggio, NY	OF	30	125	.357
1942	Joe Gordon, NY	2B	18	103	.322
1943	Spud Chandler, NY	P	—	—	—
1944	Hal Newhouser, Det	P	—	—	—
1945	Hal Newhouser, Det	P	—	—	—
1946	Ted Williams, Bos	OF	38	123	.342
1947	Joe DiMaggio, NY	OF	20	97	.315
1948	Lou Boudreau, Cle	SS-Mgr	18	106	.355
1949	Ted Williams, Bos	OF	43	159	.343
1950	Phil Rizzuto, NY	SS	7	66	.324
1951	Yogi Berra, NY	C	27	88	.294
1952	Bobby Shantz, Phi	P	—	—	—
1953	Al Rosen, Cle	3B	43	145	.336
1954	Yogi Berra, NY	C	22	125	.307
1955	Yogi Berra, NY	C	27	108	.272
1956	Mickey Mantle, NY	OF	52	130	.353
1957	Mickey Mantle, NY	OF	34	94	.365
1958	Jackie Jensen, Bos	OF	35	122	.286
1959	Nellie Fox, Chi	2B	2	70	.306
1960	Roger Maris, NY	OF	39	112	.283
1961	Roger Maris, NY	OF	61	142	.269
1962	Mickey Mantle, NY	OF	30	89	.321
1963	Elston Howard, NY	C	28	85	.287
1964	Brooks Robinson, Bal	3B	28	118	.317
1965	Zoilo Versalles, Min	SS	19	77	.273
1966	Frank Robinson, Bal	OF	49	122	.316
1967	Carl Yastrzemski, Bos	OF	44	121	.326
1968	Denny McLain, Det	P	—	—	—
1969	Harmon Killebrew, Min	3B-1B	49	140	.276
1970	Boog Powell, Bal	1B	35	114	.297
1971	Vida Blue, Oak	P	—	—	—
1972	Dick Allen, Chi	1B	37	113	.308
1973	Reggie Jackson, Oak	OF	32	117	.293
1974	Jeff Burroughs, Tex	OF	25	118	.301
1975	Fred Lynn, Bos	OF	21	105	.331
1976	Thurman Munson, NY	C	17	105	.302
1977	Rod Carew, Min	1B	14	100	.388
1978	Jim Rice, Bos	OF-DH	46	139	.315
1979	Don Baylor, Cal	OF-DH	36	139	.296
1980	George Brett, KC	3B	24	118	.390
1981	Rollie Fingers, Mil	P	—	—	—
1982	Robin Yount, Mil	SS	29	114	.331
1983	Cal Ripken Jr., Bal	SS	27	102	.318
1984	Willie Hernandez, Det	P	—	—	—
1985	Don Mattingly, NY	1B	35	145	.324
1986	Roger Clemens, Bos	P	—	—	—
1987	George Bell, Tor	OF	47	134	.308
1988	Jose Canseco, Oak	OF	42	124	.307
1989	Robin Yount, Mil	OF	21	103	.318
1990	Rickey Henderson, Oak	OF	28	61	.325
1991	Cal Ripken Jr., Bal	SS	34	114	.323
1992	Dennis Eckersley, Oak	P	—	—	—
1993	Frank Thomas, Chi	1B	41	128	.317
1994	Frank Thomas, Chi	1B	38	101	.353
1995	Mo Vaughn, Bos	1B	39	126	.300
1996	Juan Gonzalez, Tex	OF-DH	47	144	.314
1997	Ken Griffey Jr., Sea	OF	56	147	.304
1998	Juan Gonzalez, Tex	OF	45	157	.318

MVP Pitchers' Statistics

Pitchers have been named Most Valuable Player on 23 occasions, 10 times in the NL and 13 in the AL. Four have been relief pitchers—Jim Konstanty, Rollie Fingers, Willie Hernandez and Dennis Eckersley.

National League

Year		Gm	W-L	SV	ERA
1924	Dazzy Vance, Bklyn	35	28-6	2	2.16
1933	Carl Hubbell, NY	45	23-12	5	1.66
1934	Dizzy Dean, St.L	50	30-7	7	2.66
1936	Carl Hubbell, NY	42	26-6	3	2.31
1939	Bucky Walters, Cin	39	27-11	0	2.29
1942	Mort Cooper, St.L	37	22-7	0	1.78
1950	Jim Konstanty, Phi	74	16-7	22	2.66

American League

Year		Gm	W-L	SV	ERA
1913	Walter Johnson, Wash	47	36-7	2	1.09
1924	Walter Johnson, Wash	38	23-7	0	2.72
1931	Lefty Grove, Phi	41	31-4	5	2.06
1943	Spud Chandler, NY	30	20-4	0	1.64
1944	Hal Newhouser, Det	47	29-9	2	2.22
1945	Hal Newhouser, Det	40	25-9	2	1.81
1952	Bobby Shantz, Phi	33	24-7	0	2.48

CY YOUNG AWARD

Voted on by the Baseball Writers Association of America. One award was presented from 1956-66, two since 1967. Pitchers who won the MVP and Cy Young awards in the same season are in **bold** type.

Multiple winners: NL—Steve Carlton and Greg Maddux (4); Sandy Koufax and Tom Seaver (3); Bob Gibson and Tom Glavine (2). **AL**—Roger Clemens (5); Jim Palmer (3); Denny McLain (2). **NL & AL**—Gaylord Perry (2, one in each).

NL and AL Combined

Year	National League	Gm	W-L	SV	ERA	Year	National League	Gm	W-L	SV	ERA
1956	**Don Newcombe**, Bklyn	38	27-7	0	3.06	1966	Sandy Koufax, LA	41	27-9	0	1.73
1957	Warren Spahn, Mil.	39	21-11	3	2.69						
1960	Vernon Law, Pit	35	20-9	0	3.08	**Year**	**American League**	**Gm**	**W-L**	**SV**	**ERA**
1962	Don Drysdale, LA	43	25-9	1	2.83	1958	Bob Turley, NY	33	21-7	1	2.97
1963	**Sandy Koufax**, LA	40	25-5	0	1.88	1959	Early Wynn, Chi	37	22-10	0	3.17
1965	Sandy Koufax, LA	43	26-8	2	2.04	1961	Whitey Ford, NY	39	25-4	0	3.21
						1964	Dean Chance, LA	46	20-9	4	1.65

Separate League Awards

National League						American League				
Year		**Gm**	**W-L**	**SV**	**ERA**	**Year**		**Gm**	**W-L**	**SV** **ERA**
1967	Mike McCormick, SF	40	22-10	0	2.85	1967	Jim Lonborg, Bos	39	22-9	0 3.16
1968	**Bob Gibson**, St.L	34	22-9	0	1.12	1968	**Denny McLain**, Det	41	31-6	0 1.96
1969	Tom Seaver, NY	36	25-7	0	2.21	1969	Denny McLain, Det	42	24-9	0 2.80
1970	Bob Gibson, St.L	34	23-7	0	3.12		Mike Cuellar, Bal	39	23-11	0 2.38
1971	Ferguson Jenkins, Chi	39	24-13	0	2.77	1970	Jim Perry, Min	40	24-12	0 3.03
1972	Steve Carlton, Phi	41	27-10	0	1.97	1971	**Vida Blue**, Oak	39	24-8	0 1.82
1973	Tom Seaver, NY	36	19-10	0	2.08	1972	Gaylord Perry, Cle	41	24-16	1 1.92
1974	Mike Marshall, LA	106	15-12	21	2.42	1973	Jim Palmer, Bal	38	22-9	1 2.40
1975	Tom Seaver, NY	36	22-9	0	2.38	1974	Catfish Hunter, Oak	41	25-12	0 2.49
1976	Randy Jones, SD	40	22-14	0	2.74	1975	Jim Palmer, Bal	39	23-11	1 2.09
1977	Steve Carlton, Phi	36	23-10	0	2.64	1976	Jim Palmer, Bal	40	22-13	0 2.51
1978	Gaylord Perry, SD	37	21-6	0	2.72	1977	Sparky Lyle, NY	72	13-5	26 2.17
1979	Bruce Sutter, Chi	62	6-6	37	2.23	1978	Ron Guidry, NY	35	25-3	0 1.74
1980	Steve Carlton, Phi	38	24-9	0	2.34	1979	Mike Flanagan, Bal	39	23-9	0 3.08
1981	Fernando Valenzuela, LA	25	13-7	0	2.48	1980	Steve Stone, Bal	37	25-7	0 3.23
1982	Steve Carlton, Phi	38	23-11	0	3.10	1981	**Rollie Fingers**, Mil	47	6-3	28 1.04
1983	John Denny, Phi	36	19-6	0	2.37	1982	Pete Vuckovich, Mil	30	18-6	0 3.34
1984	Rick Sutcliffe, Chi	20*	16-1	0	2.69	1983	LaMarr Hoyt, Chi	36	24-10	0 3.66
1985	Dwight Gooden, NY	35	24-4	0	1.53	1984	**Willie Hernandez**, Det	80	9-3	32 1.92
1986	Mike Scott, Hou	37	18-10	0	2.22	1985	Bret Saberhagen, KC	32	20-6	0 2.87
1987	Steve Bedrosian, Phi	65	5-3	40	2.83	1986	**Roger Clemens**, Bos	33	24-4	0 2.48
1988	Orel Hershiser, LA	35	23-8	1	2.26	1987	Roger Clemens, Bos	36	20-9	0 2.97
1989	Mark Davis, SD	70	4-3	44	1.85	1988	Frank Viola, Min	35	24-7	0 2.64
1990	Doug Drabek, Pit	33	22-6	0	2.76	1989	Bret Saberhagen, KC	36	23-6	0 2.16
1991	Tom Glavine, Atl	34	20-11	0	2.55	1990	Bob Welch, Oak	35	27-6	0 2.95
1992	Greg Maddux, Chi	35	20-11	0	2.18	1991	Roger Clemens, Bos	35	18-10	0 2.62
1993	Greg Maddux, Atl	36	20-10	0	2.36	1992	**Dennis Eckersley**, Oak	69	7-1	51 1.91
1994	Greg Maddux, Atl	25	16-6	0	1.56	1993	Jack McDowell, Chi	34	22-10	0 3.37
1995	Greg Maddux, Atl	28	19-2	0	1.63	1994	David Cone, KC	23	16-5	0 2.94
1996	John Smoltz, Atl	35	24-8	0	2.94	1995	Randy Johnson, Sea	30	18-2	0 2.48
1997	Pedro Martinez, Mon	31	17-8	0	1.90	1996	Pat Hentgen, Tor	35	20-10	0 3.22
1998	Tom Glavine, Atl	33	20-6	0	2.47	1997	Roger Clemens, Tor	34	21-7	0 2.05
						1998	Roger Clemens, Tor	33	20-6	0 2.65

*NL games only, Sutcliffe pitched 15 games with Cleveland before being traded to the Cubs.

ROOKIE OF THE YEAR

Voted on by the Baseball Writers Assn. of America. One award was presented from 1947-48. Two awards (one for each league) have been presented since 1949. Winner who was also named MVP is in **bold** type.

NL and AL Combined

Year		Pos	Year		Pos
1947	Jackie Robinson, Brooklyn	1B	1948	Alvin Dark, Boston-NL	SS

National League

Year		Pos	Year		Pos	Year		Pos
1949	Don Newcombe, Bklyn	P	1958	Orlando Cepeda, SF	1B	1967	Tom Seaver, NY	P
			1959	Willie McCovey, SF	1B	1968	Johnny Bench, Cin	C
1950	Sam Jethroe, Bos	OF				1969	Ted Sizemore, LA	2B
1951	Willie Mays, NY	OF	1960	Frank Howard, LA	OF			
1952	Joe Black, Bklyn	P	1961	Billy Williams, Chi	OF	1970	Carl Morton, Mon	P
1953	Jim Gilliam, Bklyn	2B	1962	Ken Hubbs, Chi	2B	1971	Earl Williams, Atl	C
1954	Wally Moon, St.L	OF	1963	Pete Rose, Cin	2B	1972	Jon Matlack, NY	P
1955	Bill Virdon, St.L	OF	1964	Richie Allen, Phi	3B	1973	Gary Matthews, SF	OF
1956	Frank Robinson, Cin	OF	1965	Jim Lefebvre, LA	2B	1974	Bake McBride, St.L	OF
1957	Jack Sanford, Phi	P	1966	Tommy Helms, Cin	3B	1975	John Montefusco, SF	P

Year	Pos	Year	Pos	Year	Pos
1976 Butch Metzger, SD	P	1983 Darryl Strawberry, NY	OF	1991 Jeff Bagwell, Hou	1B
& Pat Zachry, Cin	P	1984 Dwight Gooden, NY	P	1992 Eric Karros, LA	1B
1977 Andre Dawson, Mon	OF	1985 Vince Coleman, St.L	OF	1993 Mike Piazza, LA	C
1978 Bob Horner, Atl	3B	1986 Todd Worrell, St.L	P	1994 Raul Mondesi, LA	OF
1979 Rick Sutcliffe, LA	P	1987 Benito Santiago, SD	C	1995 Hideo Nomo, LA	P
		1988 Chris Sabo, Cin	3B	1996 Todd Hollandsworth, LA	OF
1980 Steve Howe, LA	P	1989 Jerome Walton, Chi	OF	1997 Scott Rolen, Phi	3B
1981 Fernando Valenzuela, LA	P			1998 Kerry Wood, Chi	P
1982 Steve Sax, LA	2B	1990 David Justice, Atl	OF		

American League

Year	Pos	Year	Pos	Year	Pos
1949 Roy Sievers, St.L	OF	1966 Tommie Agee, Chi	OF	1982 Cal Ripken Jr., Bal	SS-3B
		1967 Rod Carew, Min	2B	1983 Ron Kittle, Chi	OF
1950 Walt Dropo, Bos	1B	1968 Stan Bahnsen, NY	P	1984 Alvin Davis, Sea	1B
1951 Gil McDougald, NY	3B	1969 Lou Piniella, KC	OF	1985 Ozzie Guillen, Chi	SS
1952 Harry Byrd, Phi	P			1986 Jose Canseco, Oak	OF
1953 Harvey Kuenn, Det	SS	1970 Thurman Munson, NY	C	1987 Mark McGwire, Oak	1B
1954 Bob Grim, NY	P	1971 Chris Chambliss, Cle	1B	1988 Walt Weiss, Oak	SS
1955 Herb Score, Cle	P	1972 Carlton Fisk, Bos	C	1989 Gregg Olson, Bal	P
1956 Luis Aparicio, Chi	SS	1973 Al Bumbry, Bal	OF		
1957 Tony Kubek, NY	INF-OF	1974 Mike Hargrove, Tex	1B	1990 Sandy Alomar Jr., Cle	C
1958 Albie Pearson, Wash	OF	1975 **Fred Lynn**, Bos	OF	1991 Chuck Knoblauch, Min	2B
1959 Bob Allison, Wash	OF	1976 Mark Fidrych, Det	P	1992 Pat Listach, Mil	SS
		1977 Eddie Murray, Bal	DH-1B	1993 Tim Salmon, Cal	OF
1960 Ron Hansen, Bal	SS	1978 Lou Whitaker, Det	2B	1994 Bob Hamelin, KC	DH
1961 Don Schwall, Bos	P	1979 John Castino, Min	3B	1995 Marty Cordova, Min	OF
1962 Tom Tresh, NY	SS-OF	& Alfredo Griffin, Tor	SS	1996 Derek Jeter, NY	SS
1963 Gary Peters, Chi	P			1997 Nomar Garciaparra, Bos	SS
1964 Tony Oliva, Min	OF	1980 Joe Charboneau, Cle	OF-DH	1998 Ben Grieve, Oak	OF
1965 Curt Blefary, Bal	OF	1981 Dave Righetti, NY	P		

MANAGER OF THE YEAR

Voted on by the Baseball Writers Association of America. Two awards (one for each league) presented since 1983. Note that (*) indicates manager's team won division championship and (†) indicates unofficial division won in 1994.

Multiple winners: Tony La Russa (3); Sparky Anderson, Dusty Baker, Bobby Cox, Tommy Lasorda, Jim Leyland and Joe Torre (2).

National League

Year	Improvement		
1983 Tommy Lasorda, LA	88-74	to	91-71*
1984 Jim Frey, Chi	71-91	to	96-75*
1985 Whitey Herzog, St. L	84-78	to	101-61*
1986 Hal Lanier, Hou	83-79	to	96-66*
1987 Buck Rodgers, Mon	78-83	to	91-71
1988 Tommy Lasorda, LA	73-89	to	94-67*
1989 Don Zimmer, Chi	77-85	to	93-69*
1990 Jim Leyland, Pit	74-88	to	95-67*
1991 Bobby Cox, Atl	65-97	to	94-68*
1992 Jim Leyland, Pit	98-64*	to	96-66*
1993 Dusty Baker, SF	72-90	to	103-59
1994 Felipe Alou, Mon	94-68	to	74-40†
1995 Don Baylor, Col	53-64	to	77-67
1996 Bruce Bochy, SD	70-74	to	91-71
1997 Dusty Baker, SF	68-94	to	90-72
1998 Larry Dierker	84-78	to	102-60*

American League

Year	Improvement		
1983 Tony La Russa, Chi	87-75	to	99-63*
1984 Sparky Anderson, Det	92-70	to	104-58*
1985 Bobby Cox, Tor	89-73	to	99-62*
1986 John McNamara, Bos	81-81	to	95-66*
1987 Sparky Anderson, Det	87-75	to	98-64*
1988 Tony La Russa, Oak	81-81	to	104-58*
1989 Frank Robinson, Bal	54-107	to	87-75
1990 Jeff Torborg, Chi	69-92	to	94-68
1991 Tom Kelly, Min	74-88	to	95-67*
1992 Tony La Russa, Oak	84-78	to	96-66*
1993 Gene Lamont, Chi	86-76	to	94-68*
1994 Buck Showalter, NY	88-74	to	70-43†
1995 Lou Piniella, Sea	49-63	to	79-66*
1996 Joe Torre, NY	79-65	to	92-70
& Johnny Oates, Tex	74-70	to	90-72
1997 Davey Johnson, Bal	88-74	to	98-64
1998 Joe Torre, NY	96-66	to	114-48*

HANK AARON AWARD

The inaugural award was presented in 1999 to the best "complete" hitter in both the American and National leagues. In 1999, hitters received one point for every hit, home run and RBI. In subsequent years, winners will be selected more subjectively by a panel.

National League

Year	H	HR	RBI	Pts
1999 Sammy Sosa, Chi-NL	180	63	141	384

American League

Year	H	HR	RBI	Pts
1999 Manny Ramirez, Cle	174	44	165	383

COLLEGE BASEBALL

College World Series

The NCAA Division I College World Series has been held in Kalamazoo, Mich. (1947-48), Wichita, Kan. (1949) and Omaha, Neb. (since 1950).

Multiple winners: USC (12); Arizona St. (5); LSU and Texas (4); Arizona, CS-Fullerton, Miami-FL and Minnesota (3); California, Michigan, Oklahoma and Stanford (2).

Year	Winner	Coach	Score	Runner-up	Year	Winner	Coach	Score	Runner-up
1947	California	Clint Evans	8-7	Yale	1974	USC	Rod Dedeaux	7-3	Miami-FL
1948	USC	Sam Barry	9-2	Yale	1975	Texas	Cliff Gustafson	5-1	S. Carolina
1949	Texas	Bibb Falk	10-3	W. Forest	1976	Arizona	Jerry Kindall	7-1	E. Michigan
					1977	Arizona St.	Jim Brock	2-1	S. Carolina
1950	Texas	Bibb Falk	3-0	Wash. St.	1978	USC	Rod Dedeaux	10-3	Ariz. St.
1951	Oklahoma	Jack Baer	3-2	Tennessee	1979	CS-Fullerton	Augie Garrido	2-1	Arkansas
1952	Holy Cross	Jack Baer	8-4	Missouri					
1953	Michigan	Ray Fisher	7-5	Texas	1980	Arizona	Jerry Kindall	5-3	Hawaii
1954	Missouri	Hi Simmons	4-1	Rollins	1981	Arizona St.	Jim Brock	7-4	Okla. St.
1955	Wake Forest	Taylor Sanford	7-6	W. Mich.	1982	Miami-FL	Ron Fraser	9-3	Wichita St.
1956	Minnesota	Dick Siebert	12-1	Arizona	1983	Texas	Cliff Gustafson	4-3	Alabama
1957	California	Geo. Wolfman	1-0	Penn St.	1984	CS-Fullerton	Augie Garrido	3-1	Texas
1958	USC	Rod Dedeaux	8-7	Missouri	1985	Miami-FL	Ron Fraser	10-6	Texas
1959	Oklahoma St.	Toby Greene	5-3	Arizona	1986	Arizona	Jerry Kindall	10-2	Fla. St.
					1987	Stanford	M. Marquess	9-5	Okla. St.
1960	Minnesota	Dick Siebert	2-1	USC	1988	Stanford	M. Marquess	9-4	Ariz. St.
1961	USC	Rod Dedeaux	1-0	Okla. St.	1989	Wichita St.	G.Stephenson	5-3	Texas
1962	Michigan	Don Lund	5-4	S. Clara					
1963	USC	Rod Dedeaux	5-2	Arizona	1990	Georgia	Steve Webber	2-1	Okla. St.
1964	Minnesota	Dick Siebert	5-1	Missouri	1991	LSU	Skip Bertman	6-3	Wichita St.
1965	Arizona St.	Bobby Winkles	2-1	Ohio St.	1992	Pepperdine	Andy Lopez	3-2	CS-Fullerton
1966	Ohio St.	Marty Karow	8-2	Okla. St.	1993	LSU	Skip Bertman	8-0	Wichita St.
1967	Arizona St.	Bobby Winkles	11-2	Houston	1994	Oklahoma	Larry Cochell	13-5	Ga. Tech
1968	USC	Rod Dedeaux	4-3	So. Ill.	1995	CS-Fullerton	Augie Garrido	11-5	USC
1969	Arizona St.	Bobby Winkles	10-1	Tulsa	1996	LSU	Skip Bertman	9-8	Miami-FL
					1997	LSU	Skip Bertman	13-6	Alabama
1970	USC	Rod Dedeaux	2-1	Fla. St.	1998	USC	Mike Gillespie	21-14	Arizona St.
1971	USC	Rod Dedeaux	7-2	So. Ill.	1999	Miami-FL	Jim Morris	6-5	Fla. St.
1972	USC	Rod Dedeaux	1-0	Ariz. St.					
1973	USC	Rod Dedeaux	4-3	Ariz. St.					

Most Outstanding Player

The Most Outstanding Player has been selected every year of the College World Series since 1949. Winners who did not play for the CWS champion are listed in **bold** type. No player has won the award more than once.

Year	Year	Year
1949 **Charles Teague,** W. Forest, 2B	1966 Steve Arlin, Ohio St., P	1983 Calvin Schiraldi, Texas, P
1950 **Ray VanCleef,** Rutgers, CF	1967 Ron Davini, Ariz. St., C	1984 John Fishel, CS-Fullerton, LF
1951 **Sidney Hatfield,** Tenn., P-1B	1968 Bill Seinsoth, USC, 1B	1985 Greg Ellena, Miami-FL, LF
1952 James O'Neill, Holy Cross, P	1969 John Dolinsek, Ariz. St., LF	1986 Mike Senne, Arizona, DH
1953 **J.L. Smith,** Texas, P	1970 **Gene Ammann,** Fla. St., P	1987 Paul Carey, Stanford, RF
1954 **Tom Yewcic,** Mich. St., C	1971 **Jerry Tabb,** Tulsa, 1B	1988 Lee Plemel, Stanford, P
1955 **Tom Borland,** Okla. St., P	1972 Russ McQueen, USC, P	1989 Greg Brummett, Wich. St., P
1956 Jerry Thomas, Minn., P	1973 **Dave Winfield,** Minn., P-OF	1990 Mike Rebhan, Georgia, P
1957 **Cal Emery,** Penn St., P-1B	1974 George Milke, USC, P	1991 Gary Hymel, LSU, C
1958 Bill Thom, USC, P	1975 Mickey Reichenbach, Texas, 1B	1992 **Phil Nevin,** CS-Fullerton, 3B
1959 Jim Dobson, Okla. St., 3B	1976 Steve Powers, Arizona, P-DH	1993 Todd Walker, LSU, 2B
1960 John Erickson, Minn., 2B	1977 Bob Horner, Ariz. St., 3B	1994 Chip Glass, Oklahoma, OF
1961 **Littleton Fowler,** Okla. St., P	1978 Rod Boxberger, USC, P	1995 Mark Kotsay, CS-Fullerton, OF
1962 **Bob Garibaldi,** Santa Clara, P	1979 Tony Hudson, CS-Fullerton, P	1996 **Pat Burrell,** Miami-FL, 3B
1963 Bud Hollowell, USC, C	1980 Terry Francona, Arizona, LF	1997 Brandon Larson, LSU, SS
1964 **Joe Ferris,** Maine, P	1981 Stan Holmes, Ariz. St., LF	1998 Wes Rachels, USC, 2B
1965 Sal Bando, Ariz. St., 3B	1982 Dan Smith, Miami-FL, P	1999 **Marshall McDougall,** Fla. St., 2B

Annual Awards
Golden Spikes Award

First presented in 1978 by USA Baseball, honoring the nation's best amateur player. Alex Fernandez, the 1990 winner, has been the only junior college player chosen.

Year	Year	Year
1978 Bob Horner, Ariz. St, 2B	1985 Will Clark, Miss. St., 1B	1992 Phil Nevin, CS-Fullerton, 3B
1979 Tim Wallach, CS-Fullerton, 1B	1986 Mike Loynd, Fla. St., P	1993 Darren Dreifort, Wichita St., P
1980 Terry Francona, Arizona, OF	1987 Jim Abbott, Michigan, P	1994 Jason Varitek, Ga. Tech, C
1981 Mike Fuentes, Fla. St., OF	1988 Robin Ventura, Okla. St., 3B	1995 Mark Kotsay, CS-Fullerton, OF
1982 Augie Schmidt, N. Orleans, SS	1989 Ben McDonald, LSU, P	1996 Travis Lee, San Diego St., 1B
1983 Dave Magadan, Alabama, 1B	1990 Alex Fernandez, Miami-Dade, P	1997 J.D. Drew, Florida St., OF
1984 Oddibe McDowell, Ariz. St., OF	1991 Mike Kelly, Ariz. St., OF	1998 Pat Burrell, Miami-FL, 3B

Baseball America Player of the Year

Presented to the College Player of the Year since 1981 by *Baseball America*.

Year
1981 Mike Sodders, Ariz. St., 3B
1982 Jeff Ledbetter, Fla. St., OF/P
1983 Dave Magadan, Alabama, 1B
1984 Oddibe McDowell, Ariz. St., OF
1985 Pete Incaviglia, Okla. St., OF
1986 Casey Close, Michigan, OF
1987 Robin Ventura, Okla. St., 3B

Year
1988 John Olerud, Wash. St., 1B/P
1989 Ben McDonald, LSU, P
1990 Mike Kelly, Ariz. St., OF
1991 David McCarty, Stanford, 1B
1992 Phil Nevin, CS-Fullerton, 3B
1993 Brooks Kieschnick, Texas, DH/P
1994 Jason Varitek, Ga. Tech, C

Year
1995 Todd Helton, Tenn., 1B/P
1996 Kris Benson, Clemson, P
1997 J.D. Drew, Florida St., OF
1998 Jeff Austin, Stanford, RHP
1999 Jason Jennings, Baylor, DH/P

Dick Howser Trophy

Presented to the College Player of the Year since 1987, by the American Baseball Coaches Association (ABCA) from 1987-98 and the National Collegiate Baseball Writers Association (NCBWA) beginning in 1999. Named after the late two-time All-America shortstop and college coach at Florida State. Howser was also a major league manager with Kansas City and the New York Yankees.
Multiple winner: Brooks Kieschnick (2).

Year
1987 Mike Fiore, Miami-FL, OF
1988 Robin Ventura, Okla. St., 3B
1989 Scott Bryant, Texas, DH
1990 Paul Ellis, UCLA, C
1991 Bobby Jones, Fresno St., P

Year
1992 Brooks Kieschnick, Texas, DH/P
1993 Brooks Kieschnick, Texas, DH/P
1994 Jason Varitek, Ga. Tech, C
1995 Todd Helton, Tenn., 1B/P
1996 Kris Benson, Clemson, P

Year
1997 J.D. Drew, Florida St., OF
1998 Eddie Furniss, LSU, 1B
1999 Jason Jennings, Baylor, DH/P

Baseball America Coach of the Year

Presented to the College Coach of the Year since 1981 by *Baseball America*.
Multiple winners: Skip Bertman, Dave Snow and Gene Stephenson (2).

Year
1981 Ron Fraser, Miami-FL
1982 Gene Stephenson, Wichita St.
1983 Barry Shollenberger, Alabama
1984 Augie Garrido, CS-Fullerton
1985 Ron Polk, Mississippi St.
1986 Skip Bertman, LSU
    & Dave Snow, Loyola-CA

Year
1987 Mark Marquess, Stanford
1988 Jim Brock, Arizona St.
1989 Dave Snow, Long Beach St.
1990 Steve Webber, Georgia
1991 Jim Hendry, Creighton
1992 Andy Lopez, Pepperdine
1993 Gene Stephenson, Wichita St.

Year
1994 Jim Morris, Miami-FL
1995 Rob Delmonico, Tennessee
1996 Skip Bertman, LSU
1997 Jim Wells, Alabama
1998 Pat Murphy, Arizona St.
1999 Wayne Graham, Rice

All-Time Winningest Coaches

Coaches active in 1999 are in **bold** type. Records given are for four-year colleges only. For winning percentage, a minimum 10 years in Division I is required.

Top 25 Winning Percentage

		Yrs	W	L	T	Pct
1	John Barry	40	619	147	6	.806
2	W.J. Disch	29	465	115	0	.802
3	Cliff Gustafson	29	1427	373	2	.792
4	Harry Carlson	17	143	41	0	.777
5	**Gene Stephenson**	22	1224	360	3	.772
6	Gary Ward	19	953	313	1	.753
7	George Jacobs	11	76	25	0	.752
8	Bobby Winkles	13	524	173	0	.752
9	**Mike Martin**	20	1079	364	3	.747
10	Frank Sancet	23	831	283	8	.744
11	Ron Fraser	30	1271	438	9	.742
12	Bob Wren	23	464	160	4	.742
13	Bibb Falk	25	435	152	0	.741
14	**Skip Bertman**	16	774	291	2	.726
15	Bud Middaugh	22	821	319	1	.720
16	J.F. "Pop" McKale	30	302	118	7	.715
17	Jim Brock	28	1100	440	0	.714
18	**Jim Wells**	10	439	179	0	.710
19	**Jim Morris**	18	803	332	1	.707
20	Toby Green	21	318	132	0	.707
21	Joe Arnold	18	750	313	2	.705
22	**Mark Johnson**	15	668	279	2	.705
23	Joe Bedenk	32	380	159	3	.701
24	Rod Dedeaux	45	1332	571	11	.699
25	**Rick Jones**	11	426	184	0	.698

Top 25 Victories

		Yrs	W	L	T	Pct
1	Cliff Gustafson	29	1427	373	2	.792
2	Rod Dedeaux	45	1332	571	11	.699
3	Ron Fraser	30	1271	438	9	.742
4	**Jack Stallings**	39	1258	796	5	.612
5	**Chuck Hartman**	40	1242	626	5	.664
6	**Augie Garrido**	31	1238	604	8	.671
7	**Gene Stephenson**	22	1224	360	3	.772
8	Al Ogletree	41	1217	713	1	.631
9	**Larry Hays**	29	1199	640	2	.652
10	**Bob Bennett**	31	1190	685	8	.634
11	Chuck Brayton	33	1162	523	8	.689
12	Bill Wilhelm	36	1161	536	10	.683
13	**Larry Cochell**	33	1145	656	2	.636
14	**Jim Dietz**	28	1120	673	18	.623
15	Jim Brock	23	1100	440	0	.714
16	**Mike Martin**	20	1079	364	3	.747
17	**Norm DeBriyn**	30	1075	565	6	.655
18	**Richard Jones**	33	1056	600	5	.637
19	**Les Murakami**	29	1051	542	4	.659
20	Ron Polk	26	1043	486	0	.682
21	**Bob Hannah**	36	1016	444	6	.695
22	**Gary Adams**	30	1015	744	12	.577
23	Gary Ward	19	953	313	1	.753
24	**Mark Marquess**	23	945	482	5	.662
25	John Winkin	42	934	670	11	.582

Other NCAA Champions
Division II

Multiple winners: Florida Southern (8); Cal Poly Pomona and Tampa (3); CS-Chico, CS-Northridge, Jacksonville St., Troy St., UC-Irvine and UC-Riverside (2).

Year		Year		Year		Year	
1968	Chapman, CA	1976	Cal Poly Pomona	1984	CS-Northridge	1992	Tampa
1969	Illinois St.	1977	UC-Riverside	1985	Florida Southern	1993	Tampa
1970	CS-Northridge	1978	Florida Southern	1986	Troy St., AL	1994	Central Missouri St.
1971	Florida Southern	1979	Valdosta St., GA	1987	Troy St., AL	1995	Florida Southern
1972	Florida Southern	1980	Cal Poly Pomona	1988	Florida Southern	1996	Kennesaw St., GA
1973	UC-Irvine	1981	Florida Southern	1989	Cal Poly SLO	1997	CS-Chico
1974	UC-Irvine	1982	UC-Riverside	1990	Jacksonville St., AL	1998	Tampa
1975	Florida Southern	1983	Cal Poly Pomona	1991	Jacksonville St., AL	1999	CS-Chico

Division III

Multiple winners: Eastern Conn. St. and Marietta (3); CS-Stanislaus, Glassboro St., Ithaca, Montclair St., NC-Wesleyan, Southern Maine and Wm. Paterson, NJ (2).

Year		Year		Year		Year	
1976	CS-Stanislaus	1982	Eastern Conn. St.	1989	NC-Wesleyan	1996	Wm. Paterson, NJ
1977	CS-Stanislaus	1983	Marietta, OH	1990	Eastern Conn. St.	1997	Southern Maine
1978	Glassboro St., NJ	1984	Ramapo, NJ	1991	Southern Maine	1998	Eastern Conn. St.
1979	Glassboro St., NJ	1985	Wisconsin-Oshkosh	1992	Wm. Paterson, NJ	1999	NC-Wesleyan
1980	Ithaca, NY	1986	Marietta, OH	1993	Montclair St., NJ		
1981	Marietta, OH	1987	Monclair St., NJ	1994	Wisconsin-Oshkosh		
		1988	Ithaca, NY	1995	La Verne, CA		

Major League Number One Draft Picks

The Major League First-Year Player Draft has been held every year since 1965. Clubs select in reverse order of their won-loss records from the previous regular season with National League and American League teams alternating. AL teams select first in odd-numbered years while NL teams go first in even-numbered years. The pool of draftees consists of graduated high school players, junior or senior college players, Junior college players and anyone over the age of 21. Listed are the top selections from each draft.

Year		Pos	Team	Year		Pos	Team
1965	Rick Monday	OF	Kansas City Athletics	1983	Tim Belcher	P	Minnesota Twins
1966	Steve Chilcott	C	New York Mets	1984	Shawn Abner	OF	New York Mets
1967	Rom Blomberg	1B	New York Yankees	1985	B.J. Surhoff	C	Milwaukee Brewers
1968	Tim Foli	IF	New York Mets	1986	Jeff King	IF	Pittsburgh Pirates
1969	Jeff Burroughs	OF	Washington Senators	1987	Ken Griffey Jr.	OF	Seattle Mariners
1970	Mike Ivie	C	San Diego Padres	1988	Andy Benes	P	San Diego Padres
1971	Danny Goodwin	C	Chicago White Sox	1989	Ben McDonald	P	Baltimore Orioles
1972	Dave Roberts	IF	San Diego Padres	1990	Chipper Jones	SS	Atlanta Braves
1973	David Clyde	P	Texas Rangers	1991	Brien Taylor	P	New York Yankees
1974	Bill Almon	IF	San Diego Padres	1992	Phil Nevin	3B	Houston Astros
1975	Danny Goodwin	C	California Angels	1993	Alex Rodriguez	SS	Seattle Mariners
1976	Floyd Bannister	P	Houston Astros	1994	Paul Wilson	P	New York Mets
1977	Harold Baines	OF	Chicago White Sox	1995	Darin Erstad	OF/P	California Angels
1978	Bob Horner	3B	Atlanta Braves	1996	Kris Benson	P	Pittsburgh Pirates
1979	Al Chambers	OF	Seattle Mariners	1997	Matt Anderson	P	Detroit Tigers
1980	Darryl Strawberry	OF	New York Mets	1998	Pat Burrell	3B	Philadelphia Phillies
1981	Mike Moore	P	Seattle Mariners	1999	Josh Hamilton	OF	T.B. Devil Rays
1982	Shawon Dunston	SS	Chicago Cubs				

Straight to the Majors

Since Major League baseball began its free agent draft in 1965, 17 selections have advanced directly to the major leagues without first playing in the minors

Draft		Pos	Team	Draft		Pos	Team
1967	Mike Adamson, South Carolina	P	Baltimore	1978	Tim Conroy, Gateway HS (Pa.)	P	Oakland
1969	Steve Dunning, Stanford	P	Cleveland		Bob Horner, Arizona St.	IF	Atlanta
1971	Pete Broberg, Dartmouth	P	Washington		Brian Milner, Southwest HS (Tex.)	C	Toronto
	Rob Ellis, Michigan St.	IF	Milwaukee		Mike Morgan, Valley HS (Nev.)	P	Oakland
	Burt Hooton, Texas	P	Chicago	1985	Pete Incaviglia, Oklahoma St.	OF	Montreal
1972	Dave Roberts, Oregon	IF	San Diego	1988	Jim Abbott, Michigan	P	California
1973	Dick Ruthven, Fresno St.	P	Philadelphia	1989	John Olerud, Washington St.	IF	Toronto
1973	David Clyde, Westchester HS (Tex.)	P	Texas				
	Dave Winfield, Minnesota	OF	San Diego				
	Eddie Bane, Arizona St.	P	Minnesota				

College Football

Tennessee's **Phil Fulmer** takes a gander at the national championship trophy following the Vols' 23-16 win over Florida St. in the Fiesta Bowl.

AP/Wide World Photos

Saturday Night Special for BCS

Late season upsets help the Bowl Championship Series work out after all.

by
Chris Fowler

Covering college football sure can make you feel foolish sometimes.

We were obsessed all season with the new math. The subject we should have been studying was recent history.

In Year One of the new Bowl Championship Series' rankings, Steve Spurrier was quoted less than computer guru Jeff Sagarin. Quarterbacks got less ink than "quartiles"—part of the complex rating system used to match the nation's top two teams in a Fiesta Bowl showdown.

I spent maybe a hundred hours chewing on strength of schedule data, margins of victory, and poll fluctuations. A dozen more engaged in high decibel debates on decimal points.

In the end, it was much hullabaloo about nothing.

Because in a nationally televised tripleheader on the season's final Saturday, 10 scintillating, stunning hours shook up the season, rendered the math meaningless and deflated a blimp-full of bowl speculation hot air.

From chaos came order. The BCS brass was rescued from embarrassment. The matchup of lone unbeaten Tennessee and consensus #2 Florida State made sense to most everybody.

Here are some snapshots from Dec. 5, 1998, a Shakeup Saturday for the ages.

The drama started with yet another epic in the relic that is the Orange Bowl. It was the rescheduled "Hurricane Bowl," pushed back from September into the only acceptable slot for both teams—a quirk of fate that only heightened its already huge impact on the title chase.

UCLA jumped to a big lead, ripping off huge yardage at will on a Miami

---

Chris Fowler is the host of ESPN's *College GameDay*.

After a UCLA loss earlier in the day, Kansas St. was ready to play Tennessee for the national championship. But the Wildcats were knocked from Fiesta Bowl consideration by a devastating loss in the Big 12 Championship against Texas A&M.

defense that had surrendered 66 points to Syracuse seven days earlier. They looked equally powerless against Cade McNown's wizardry. It was a laugher. At least Bruin Brendon Ayanbadejo thought so. After leaving the game with a first half shoulder injury, he later emerged from the visitors tunnel and as he made his way back to the UCLA bench, chuckled at and taunted Canes fans by striking bodybuilder poses!

I recall thinking that no one associated with UCLA's defense had earned the right to "flex." And in the oppressive mugginess of that Miami afternoon, the porous unit that for three months had put intense pressure on McNown and Co. to outscore folks finally melted as Miami roared back.

The Canes' Edgerrin James made more than 300 yards and probably three million bucks—his draft stock skyrocketing in the thorough shredding of a whipped and helpless Bruins defense.

When a final incompletion ended UCLA's title dreams, old school Miami mayhem broke out. As delirious fans collided with aggressive cops all around him, Bruin receiver Brian Poli-Dixon stood frozen at the 20-yard line, wearing a thousand-yard stare. I've rarely seen a stronger image of despair, at least on a football field.

A few hours later, Kansas State felt the same pain. A fumble by the brilliant Michael Bishop keyed a Wildcat collapse. A Texas A&M offense, known for anything but comeback fireworks, had rallied against KSU's stout defense from two touchdowns down to steal the Big 12 crown.

143

AP/Wide World Photos

All-American running back **Ricky Williams** of Texas made his mark in 1998, winning the Heisman Trophy and a spot atop the NCAA career list for rushing yards.

Only Tennessee among the three unbeatens at the start of the day navigated the upset minefield, and only after some very tense moments against Mississippi State in the SEC title game.

When the smoke cleared at around midnight, all the new math was meaningless. The Vols' "behind-the-woodshed" beating of QB-challenged FSU in Tempe was the same title game matchup we would have had under the old system.

History held the answers all along. Having a defense as poor as UCLA's eventually catches up to you. Apparent mismatches in conference championship games are fertile ground for upsets. Three teams do not go unbeaten into the Bowls ranked 1-2-3. That hasn't happened in decades. So, to the BCS architects...you were right all along fellas. You said it would all

work out. All it took was two teams with 21 wins between them blowing big leads to big underdogs within six hours.

So, here's hoping it keeps working out. Math was never my best subject. I don't want Sagarin to be bigger than Spurrier. And I'd rather not see the BCS boys wearing self-satisfied smiles. Because what the drama of Dec. 5, 1998 illustrated better than anything was how much fun a college football playoff system would be. ■

Lee Corso's Ten Biggest Moments of the Year in College Football

10. **Arkansas returns** to the ranks of college football's elite teams under first-year coach Houston Nutt.

9. **Miami-FL returns** to national prominence by ending UCLA's

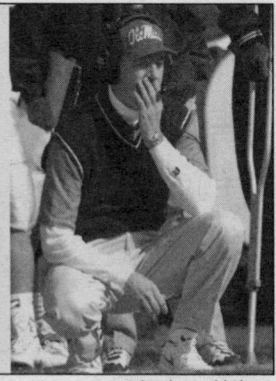

Auburn had a game of musical chairs in the office of head football coach this year. **Terry Bowden** started the season before quitting after a 1-5 start. Defensive Coordinator **Bill Oliver** stepped up to fill the void on an interim basis but was replaced at season's end with **Tommy Tuberville**, who was hired away from Ole Miss.

school-record 20-game winning streak and costing the Bruins a shot at the national championship.

8. **Washington fires** Coach Jim Lambright a month after giving him a vote of confidence. The school hires Rick Neuheisel from Colorado who promptly gets in hot water over some recruiting violations.

7. **Tulane goes 12-0**, the first perfect record in school history but loses coach Tommy Bowden to Clemson.

6. **Lou Holtz** (South Carolina), **Dennis Erickson** (Oregon State) and **John Robinson** (UNLV) all return to the college coaching ranks.

5. **Penn State's Joe Paterno** becomes the sixth coach in college football history at any level to win 300 games. He needs seven more to catch Amos Alonzo Stagg for third all-time.

4. **Frank Solich succeeds** Tom Osborne at Nebraska and the Cornhuskers stretch their streak of

nine-win seasons to 30, but lose four games for the first time since 1968.

3. **Texas's Ricky Williams** rumbles to an NCAA major-college career rushing record and wins the Heisman Trophy.

2. **The Auburn mess**. Coach Terry Bowden resigns—or was he pushed?—in mid-season. Bill Oliver takes over on an interim basis. Auburn then hires Tommy Tuberville away from Ole Miss shortly after he says the only way he'd leave Oxford is "in a pine box." Tennessee assistant David Cutcliffe takes over at Ole Miss and beats Texas Tech in the Independence Bowl.

1. **The Bowl Championship Series**. Everyone except Kansas State says it worked. Question for BCS pooh-bahs: Why did K-State's last-second loss to Texas A&M on Dec. 5 carry more weight than Florida State's convincing loss to North Carolina State on Sept. 12?

Despite the loss, FSU's dynasty rolls on with its 12th straight 10-win season. ■

THE **NUMBERS**

INSIDE

AT LEAST THEY'RE CONSISTENT

First year Nebraska head coach Frank Solich may have a long way to go before he matches his predecessor. The team lost four games for the first time in 30 years but the Cornhuskers did add to their streak of consecutive nine-win seasons and consecutive seasons without a losing record. The Huskers have now gone 37 years without a losing season, currently the longest such streak in the nation. Here is a look at how Nebraska's run stacks up against college football's longest ever.

Seasons		When
42	Notre Dame	1889-1934*
38	Alabama	1911-50†
37	Nebraska	1962—
29	Oklahoma	1966-94

*Notre Dame did not field teams in 1890-91.
†Alabama did not field teams in 1918 and 1943.

ONE YEAR **WONDER**

Texas running back Ricky Williams rewrote the NCAA record books in 1998, topping the Division I career lists in several categories, including rushing yards and touchdowns. But his time atop the charts could be short-lived. Two seniors will make a run for his records in 1999. Wisconsin's Ron Dayne and Miami of Ohio's Travis Prentice are threatening to knock Williams from the top just a year after the Heisman Trophy winner left campus. Below is where Dayne and Prentice stood at the conclusion of the 1998 season and their projected pace if both play in all 11 of their team's games in 1999.

NCAA record	Williams	Prentice/pace
Overall TDs	75	57/76
Rushing TDs	72	56/75
Points	452	342/456
	Williams	**Dayne/pace**
Rushing yards	6279	4563/6132

COALITION HISTORY

The Bowl Championship Series was designed to guarantee what the previous Bowl Coalitions and Bowl Alliances couldn't—a "national championship game" between the #1 and #2 teams in the country at the end of the season. It worked out just fine in its debut despite concerns to the contrary. Below is a rundown of the previous attempts (since the idea first took shape in 1992) to try to end the "who's #1?" controversy and when it worked out with a matchup between the two top-ranked teams and when it didn't.

Season	Bowl	Results
1992	Sugar	#2 Alabama 34, #1 Miami 13
1993	Orange	#1 FSU 18, #2 Nebraska 16
1994	Orange	#1 Nebraska 24, #3 Miami-FL 17
	Rose	#2 Penn St. 38, #12 Oregon 20
1995	Fiesta	#1 Nebraska 62, #2 Florida 24
1996	Sugar	#3 Florida 52, #1 Florida St. 20
	Rose	#2 Arizona St. 20, #4 Ohio St. 17
1997	Rose	#1 Michigan 21, #8 Wash. St. 16
	Orange	#2 Nebraska 42, #3 Tennessee 17
1998	Fiesta	#1 Tennessee 23, #2 Fla. St. 16

■

COLLEGE FOOTBALL
S T A T I S T I C S

THE SEASON IN REVIEW
1998-1999
TOP 25 • BOWLS • STANDINGS

SEC A

PAGE 147

THE 2000

Final AP Top 25 Poll

Voted on by panel of 70 sportswriters & broadcasters and released on Jan. 5, 1999, following the Fiesta Bowl: winning team receives the Bear Bryant Trophy, given since 1983; first place votes in parentheses, records, total points (based on 25 for 1st, 24 for 2nd, etc.) bowl game result, head coach and career record, preseason rank (released on Aug. 16, 1998) and final regular season rank (released Dec. 6, 1998).

	Final Record	Points	Bowl Game	Head Coach	Aug. 16 Rank	Dec. 6 Rank
1 Tennessee (70)	13-0	1750	won Fiesta	Phillip Fulmer (7 yrs: 67-11-0)	10	1
2 Ohio St.	11-1	1673	won Sugar	John Cooper (22 yrs: 178-74-6)	1	3
3 Florida St.	11-2	1574	lost Fiesta	Bobby Bowden (33 yrs: 292-85-4)	2	2
4 Arizona	12-1	1535	won Holiday	Dick Tomey (22 yrs: 147-98-7)	24	5
5 Florida	10-2	1463	won Orange	Steve Spurrier (12 yrs: 113-31-2)	3	7
6 Wisconsin	11-1	1427	won Rose	Barry Alvarez (9 yrs: 60-42-4)	20	9
7 Tulane	12-0	1252	won Liberty	Tommy Bowden (2 yrs: 19-4-0)	NR	10
8 UCLA	10-2	1123	lost Rose	Bob Toledo (9 yrs: 54-46-0)	7	6
9 Georgia Tech	10-2	1122	won Gator	George O'Leary (4 yrs: 28-21-0)	NR	12
10 Kansas St.	11-2	1086	lost Alamo	Bill Snyder (10 yrs: 77-39-1)	6	4
11 Texas A&M	11-3	1071	lost Sugar	R.C. Slocum (10 yrs: 94-28-2)	14	8
12 Michigan	10-3	1052	won Florida Citrus	Lloyd Carr (4 yrs: 39-11-0)	5	15
13 Air Force	12-1	980	won Oahu	Fisher DeBerry (15 yrs: 120-64-1)	NR	16
14 Georgia	9-3	785	won Peach	Jim Donnan (9 yrs: 88-32-0)	19	19
15 Texas	9-3	740	won Cotton	Mack Brown (15 yrs: 96-77-1)	NR	20
16 Arkansas	9-3	621	lost Florida Citrus	Houston Nutt (6 yrs: 44-26-0)	NR	11
17 Penn St.	9-3	619	won Outback	Joe Paterno (33 yrs: 307-80-3)	13	22
18 Virginia	9-3	544	lost Peach	George Welsh (26 yrs: 176-121-4)	16	13
19 Nebraska	9-4	454	lost Holiday	Frank Solich (1 yr: 9-4-0)	4	14
20 Miami-FL	9-3	426	won Micron PC	Butch Davis (4 yrs: 31-15-0)	NR	24
21 Missouri	8-4	335	won Insight.com	Larry Smith (22 yrs: 136-111-7)	NR	23
22 Notre Dame	9-3	315	lost Gator	Bob Davie (2 yrs: 16-9-0)	22	17
23 Virginia Tech	9-3	256	won Music City	Frank Beamer (18 yrs: 119-82-4)	NR	NR
24 Purdue	9-4	236	won Alamo	Joe Tiller (8 yrs: 57-37-1)	NR	NR
25 Syracuse	8-4	161	lost Orange	Paul Pasqualoni (13 yrs: 102-43-1)	17	18

Other teams receiving votes: 26. **Colorado** (8-4, 46 points, won Aloha); 27. **Marshall** (12-1, 45 pts, won Motor City); 28. **Oregon** (8-4, 28 pts, lost Aloha); 29. **Mississippi St.** (8-5, 10 pts, lost Cotton); 30. **Miami-OH** (10-1, 9 pts, no bowl); 31. **West Virginia** (8-4, 6 pts, lost Insight.com); 32. **Idaho** (9-3, 2 pts, won Humanitarian) and **TCU** (7-5, 2 pts, won Sun); 34. **Mississippi** (7-5, 1 pt, won Independence) and **USC** (8-5, 1 pt, lost Sun).

AP Preseason and Final Regular Season Polls
First place votes in parentheses.

Top 25
(Aug. 16, 1998)

	Pts			Pts
1 Ohio St. (30)	1668		14 Texas A&M	760
2 Florida St. (22)	1663		15 Colorado St.	631
3 Florida (5)	1547		16 Virginia	620
4 Nebraska (4)	1534		17 Syracuse	608
5 Michigan (4)	1475		18 Washington	494
6 Kansas St. (2)	1335		19 Georgia	480
7 UCLA (1)	1331		20 Wisconsin	444
8 Arizona St. (2)	1256		21 Southern Miss.	341
9 LSU	1237		22 Notre Dame	291
10 Tennessee	1094		23 Michigan St.	211
11 West Virginia	985		24 Arizona	208
12 North Carolina	864		25 Auburn	201
13 Penn St.	804			

Top 25
(Dec. 6, 1998)

	Pts			Pts
1 Tennessee (70)	1750		14 Nebraska	815
2 Florida St.	1671		15 Michigan	793
3 Ohio St.	1602		16 Air Force	689
4 Kansas St.	1476		17 Notre Dame	665
5 Arizona	1412		18 Syracuse	610
6 UCLA	1398		19 Georgia	478
7 Florida	1337		20 Texas	442
8 Texas A&M	1310		21 Oregon	322
9 Wisconsin	1176		22 Penn St.	293
10 Tulane	1067		23 Missouri	206
11 Arkansas	960		24 Miami	190
12 Georgia Tech	874		25 Mississippi St.	159
13 Virginia	817			

1998-99 Bowl Games

Listed by bowls matching highest-ranked teams as of final regular season AP poll (released Dec. 6, 1998). Attendance figures indicate tickets sold.

Bowl	Winner	Regular Season		Loser	Regular Season	Score	Date	Attendance
Fiesta ....#1	Tennessee	12-0	#2	Florida St.	11-1	23-16	Jan. 4	80,470
Sugar ....#3	Ohio St.	10-1	#8	Texas A&M	11-2	24-14	Jan. 1	76,503
Alamo	Purdue	8-4	#4	Kansas St.	11-1	37-34	Dec. 29	60,780
Holiday...............#5	Arizona	11-1	#14	Nebraska	9-3	23-20	Dec. 30	65,354
Rose ....#9	Wisconsin	10-1	#6	UCLA	10-1	38-31	Jan. 1	93,872
Orange...............#7	Florida	9-2	#18	Syracuse	8-3	31-10	Jan. 2	67,919
Liberty...............#10	Tulane	11-0		BYU	9-4	41-27	Dec. 31	52,192
Citrus ....#15	Michigan	9-3	#11	Arkansas	9-2	45-31	Jan. 1	63,584
Gator ....#12	Georgia Tech	9-2	#17	Notre Dame	9-2	35-28	Jan. 1	70,791
Peach ....#19	Georgia	8-3	#13	Virginia	8-3	35-33	Dec. 31	72,876
Oahu ....#16	Air Force	11-1		Washington	6-5	45-25	Dec. 25	46,451*
Cotton ....#20	Texas	8-3	#25	Mississippi St.	8-4	38-11	Jan. 1	72,611
Aloha..................	Colorado	7-4	#21	Oregon	8-3	51-43	Dec. 25	46,451*
Outback ....#22	Penn St.	8-3		Kentucky	7-4	26-14	Jan. 1	66,005
Insight.com ....#23	Missouri	7-4		West Virginia	8-3	34-31	Dec. 26	36,147
Micron PC..........#24	Miami-FL	8-3		N.C. State	7-4	46-23	Dec. 29	44,387
Independence...........	Mississippi	6-5		Texas Tech	7-4	35-18	Dec. 31	46,862
Sun.................	TCU	6-5		USC	8-4	28-19	Dec. 31	46,612
Humanitarian	Idaho	8-3		Southern Miss.	7-4	42-35	Dec. 30	19,664
Music City............	Virginia Tech	8-3		Alabama	7-4	38-7	Dec. 29	41,248
Motor City............	Marshall	11-1		Louisville	7-4	48-29	Dec. 23	32,206
Las Vegas	North Carolina	6-5		San Diego St.	7-4	20-13	Dec. 19	21,429

*The Oahu and Aloha Bowls were held as a single-admission doubleheader.

FAVORITES:

Fiesta (Florida St. by 5½); **Sugar** (Ohio St. by 12½); **Alamo** (Kansas St. by 13); **Holiday** (Nebraska by 3); **Rose** (UCLA by 9); **Orange** (Florida by 7); **Liberty** (Tulane by 7); **Citrus** (Michigan by 3); **Gator** (Georgia Tech by 2½); **Peach** (Virginia by 2); **Oahu** (Air Force by 3½); **Cotton** (Texas by 6½); **Aloha** (Oregon by 5½); **Outback** (Penn St. by 7); **Insight-.com** (Missouri by 3½); **Micron PC** (Miami by 7); **Independence** (Texas Tech by 9½); **Sun** (USC by 16); **Humanitarian** (Southern Mississippi by 17); **Music City** (Virginia Tech by 5); **Motor City** (Louisville by 3½); **Las Vegas** (North Carolina by 7).

PER TEAM PAYOUTS:

Tostitos Fiesta, Rose, FedEx Orange and **Nokia Sugar** ($12.5 million); **CompUSA Florida Citrus** ($3.6 million); **Southwestern Bell Cotton** ($2.5 million); **Culligan Holiday** and **Outback** ($1.8 million); **Chick-fil-A Peach** ($3 million); **Toyota Gator** ($1.4 million); **Builders Square Alamo** and **AXA/Equitable Liberty** ($1.1 million); **Sanford Independence** and **Norwest Sun** ($1 million); **Insight.com** ($850,000); **Las Vegas, Jeep/Eagle Aloha** and **Jeep/Eagle Oahu** ($800,000); **Micron PC, Ford Motor City, American General Music City** and **Sports Humanitarian** ($750,000).

Final BCS Rankings

The Bowl Championship Series rankings were used for the first time during the 1998 season to determine BCS bowl match-ups. The final rankings were released Dec. 6, 1998. Note that Q-rank refers to Quartile rank and L refers to games lost.

		Polls		Computer Rankings							
	AP	ESPN	Avg.	Sea. Times	Sagarin	NY Times	Avg.	Sched.	Q-rank	L	Total
1 Tennessee 1	1	1	1	2		2	1.67	20	0.80	0	3.47
2 Florida St......2	2	2	2	2.25 (3)		1	1.75	4	0.16	1	4.91
3 Kansas St......4	4	4	4	1	4 (5)		3.00	49	1.96	1	9.96
4 Ohio St. 3	3	3	3	6.75 (7)	6	3	5.25	28	1.12	1	10.37
5 UCLA 6	5	5.5	5	4		5.25 (6)	4.08	8	0.32	1	10.90
6 Texas A&M 8	9	8.5	6	5		4	5.00	5	0.20	2	15.70
7 Arizona 5	6	5.5	5	9	9		7.67	58	2.32	1	16.49
8 Florida.......7	7	7	10	8	11		9.67	32	1.28	2	19.95
9 Wisconsin 9	8	8.5	9	10	10		9.67	61	2.44	1	21.61
10 Tulane 10	10	10	8	14	16.5 (23)		12.83	96	3.84	0	26.67
11 Nebraska 14	16	15	11	7	13.5 (15)		10.50	14	0.56	3	29.06
12 Virginia 13	12	12.5	13	18	17		16.00	43	1.72	2	32.22
13 Arkansas 11	11	11.0	17	12	21.75 (22)		16.92	59	2.36	2	32.28
14 Georgia Tech .12	14	13.0	16	20	12		16.00	44	1.76	2	32.76
15 Syracuse 18	17	17.5	17 25 (24)	16	7		13.42	22	0.88	3	34.80

Explanation Key

Poll Average—The average of the Associated Press media poll and the USA Today/ESPN coaches' poll. Others receiving votes are calculated in order received.

Computer Average—The average of The Hester & Anderson/Seattle Times, Jeff Sagarin's rankings and The New York Times rankings. In order to prevent differences in individual formulas, a maximum adjusted deviation of no greater than 50 percent of the average of the two lowest computer rankings is utilized. That number appears in parenthesis.

Quartile Rank—Rank of schedule strength compared to other Division I-A teams divided by 25. This component is calculated by determining the cumulative won/loss records of the team's opponents (66.6 percent) and the cumulative won/loss record of the team's opponents' opponents (33.3 percent).

Losses—One point for each loss during the season.

National Championship Game

Tennessee and Florida State were ranked first and second, respectively, in the final Bowl Championship Series rankings (released Dec. 6) and according to the BCS plan met in the so-called National Championship game at the Fiesta Bowl on Jan. 4. Opponents' records and AP rank listed below are day of game.

Tennessee Volunteers (12-0)

Date	AP Rank	Opponent	Result
Sept. 5	#10	at #17 Syracuse (0-0)	34-33
Sept. 19	#4	#2 Florida (2-0)	20-17
Sept. 26	#4	Houston (0-3)	42-7
Oct. 3	#4	at Auburn (1-2)	17-9
Oct. 10	#4	at #12 Georgia (4-0)	22-3
Oct. 24	#3	Alabama (4-2)	35-18
Oct. 31	#3	at South Carolina (1-7)	49-14
Nov. 7	#2	Alabama-Birmingham (2-6)	37-13
Nov. 14	#1	#10 Arkansas (8-0)	28-24
Nov. 21	#1	Kentucky (7-3)	59-21
Nov. 28	#1	at Vanderbilt (2-8)	41-0
Dec. 5	#1	#23 Mississippi St. (8-3)	24-14

Final Statistics

Passing (5 Att)

	Att	Cmp	Pct.	Yds	TD	Rate
Tee Martin	267	153	57.3	2164	19	180.3
Burney Veazey	7	4	57.1	86	1	14.3

Interceptions: Martin 6, Veazey 1.

Top Receivers

	No	Yds	Avg	Long	TD
Peerless Price	61	920	15.1	71-td	10
Cedrick Wilson	33	558	16.9	55-td	6
Jeremaine Copeland	28	438	15.1	35	1
Shawn Bryson	19	167	8.8	63-td	1
John Finlayson	4	47	11.8	21-td	1
Travis Henry	4	31	7.8	20	0
David Martin	3	59	19.7	29	0

Top Rushers

	Car	Yds	Avg	Long	TD
Travis Henry	176	970	5.5	36	7
Jamal Lewis	73	497	6.8	67-td	3
T. Stephens	107	477	4.5	30	4
Tee Martin	103	287	2.8	55	7
Shawn Bryson	21	200	9.5	58-td	4
Phillip Crosby	16	53	3.3	20	2
W. Bartholomew	7	34	4.9	14	0
Peerless Price	3	25	8.3	12	0
Tyrone Graham	2	-3	-1.5	1	0

Most Touchdowns

	TD	Run	Rec	Ret	Pts
Peerless Price	11	0	10	1	66
Travis Henry	7	7	0	0	42
Tee Martin	7	7	0	0	42
Cedrick Wilson	6	0	6	0	36
Shawn Bryson	5	4	1	0	30
Jamal Lewis	4	3	1	0	24
Travis Stephens	4	4	0	0	24
Philip Crosby	2	2	0	0	12

Kicking

	FG/Att	Lg	PAT/Att	Pts
Jeff Hall	19/24	47	47/47	104

Punting

	No	Yds	Long	Blk	Avg
D. Leaverton	55	2150	61	0	39.1

Most Interceptions

Deon Grant 5
D. Goodrich 3
D. Edmonds 2
six tied at 1 each.

Most Sacks

Corey Terry 17
Darwin Walker 4
Al Wilson 3
R. Thompson 3
seven tied at 1 each.

Florida State Seminoles (11-1)

Date	AP Rank	Opponent	Result
Aug. 31	#2	#14 Texas A&M* (0-0)	23-14
Sept. 12	#2	at N.C. State (1-0)	7-24
Sept. 20	#11	Duke (2-0)	62-13
Sept. 26	#10	#18 USC (3-0)	30-10
Oct. 3	#9	at Maryland (2-2)	24-10
Oct. 10	#8	at Miami (3-1)	26-14
Oct. 17	#6	Clemson (2-4)	48-0
Oct. 24	#6	at #20 Georgia Tech (5-1)	34-7
Oct. 31	#5	North Carolina (3-3)	39-13
Nov. 7	#6	#12 Virginia (7-1)	45-14
Nov. 14	#5	at Wake Forest (3-6)	24-7
Nov. 21	#5	#4 Florida (9-1)	23-12

*(at East Rutherford, N.J.)

Final Statistics

Passing (5 Att)

	Att	Cmp	Pct.	Yds	TD	Rate
Chris Weinke	286	145	50.7	2487	19	141.5
Marcus Outzen	60	36	60.0	464	1	123.8
Jared Jones	6	2	33.3	8	0	11.2

Interceptions: Weinke 6, Outzen 2, Jones 1.

Top Receivers

	No	Yds	Avg	Long	TD
Peter Warrick	61	1232	20.2	79-td	12
Ron Dugans	38	616	16.2	46-td	3
Marvin Minnis	22	338	15.4	43	2
Travis Minor	21	189	9.0	31	1
L. Coles	19	397	20.9	62	3
Dee Feaster	7	63	9.0	28	0

Top Rushers

	Car	Yds	Avg	Long	TD
Travis Minor	191	857	4.5	38	6
Jeff Chaney	120	573	4.8	41-td	5
Laveranues Coles	15	128	8.5	60-td	1
Peter Warrick	13	85	6.5	19	1
Raymont Skaggs	20	81	4.1	18-td	1
William McCray	22	73	3.3	30	2
Dee Feaster	21	70	3.3	12	0
Marcus Outzen	48	66	1.4	16	2
Lamarr Glenn	15	41	2.7	9	1
Billy Rhodes	2	3	1.5	3	0

Most Touchdowns

	TD	Run	Rec	Ret	Pts
Peter Warrick	13	1	12	0	78
Travis Minor	7	6	1	0	42
Jeff Chaney	5	5	0	0	30
Laveranues Coles	5	1	3	1	30
Ron Dugans	3	0	3	0	18
Marvin Minnis	3	1	2	0	18
Marcus Outzen	2	2	0	0	12
William McCray	2	2	0	0	12

Kicking

	FG/Att	Lg	PAT/Att	Pts
Sebastian Janikowski	27/32	53	42/43	123

Punting

	No	Yds	Long	Blk	Avg
Keith Cotrell	62	2558	69	1	41.3

Most Interceptions

Mario Edwards 6
Tay Cody 1
Derrick Gibson 1

Most Sacks

Tony Bryant 7
Corey Simon 5

Fiesta Bowl
Monday, Jan. 4, 1999 at Sun Devil Stadium in Tempe, Ariz.

#2 **Florida St.** (ACC) 0   9   0   7 — **16**
#1 **Tennessee** (SEC) . . . . .0 14   0   9 — **23**

2nd; 14:05; **Tennessee**—Shawn Bryson 4-yd pass from Tee Martin (Jeff Hall kick). Drive: 6 plays, 88 yards, 2:02.
2nd; 13:40; **Tennessee**—Dwayne Goodrich 54-yd interception return (Hall kick).
2nd; 08:59; **Florida St.**—William McCray 1-yd run (Sebastian Janikowski kick failed). Drive: 3 plays, 3 yards, 1:18.
2nd; 01:17; **Florida St.**—Janikowski 34-yd Field Goal. Drive: 10 plays, 10 yards, 4:33.
4th; 09:17; **Tennessee**—Peerless Price 79-yd pass from Martin (kick blocked). Drive: 3 plays, 80 yards, 1:24.
4th; 06:01; **Tennessee**—Hall 23-yd Field Goal. Drive: 6 plays, 22 yards, 2:55.
4th; 03:42; **Florida St.**—Marcus Outzen 7-yd run (Janikowski kick). Drive: 5 plays, 49 yards, 2:19.

Favorite: Florida St. by 5½   **Attendance:** 84,470
Field: Grass   **Time:** 3:46
Weather: 61 degrees and clear

MVP: Peerless Price, UT, 4 receptions, 199 yards, 1 TD

Team Statistics

	FSU	UT
Touchdowns	2	3
Rushing	2	0
Passing	0	2
Kick returns	0	0
Interception returns	0	1
Safeties	0	0
Time of possession	28:50	31:10
First downs	13	16
Rushing	9	4
Passing	4	8
Penalties	0	4
3rd down efficiency	4 of 15	1 of 12
4th down efficiency	1 of 1	1 of 1
Total offense (net yards)	253	392
Plays	63	64
Average gain	4.0	6.1
Carries/yards (includ. sacks)	41/108	42/114
Passing yards	145	278
Completions/attempts	9/22	11/19
Times sacked/yards lost	4/31	1/3
Return yardage	172	151
Punt returns/yards	2/51	4/34
Kickoff returns/yards	4/52	3/43
Interceptions/yards	2/69	2/74
Fumbles/lost	4/1	3/2
Penalties/yards	12/110	9/55
Punts/average	9/39.8	5/38.0

INDIVIDUAL STATISTICS
Florida State Seminoles

Passing (5 Att)	Att	Cmp	Pct.	Yds	TD	Int
Marcus Outzen	22	9	40.9	145	0	2

Rushing	Car	Yds	Avg	Long	TD
Travis Minor	15	83	5.5	23	0
Peter Warrick	1	11	11.0	11	0
William McCray	4	9	2.3	7	1
Laveranues Coles	2	4	2.0	10	0
Lamarr Glenn	1	2	2.0	2	0
Marcus Outzen	18	-1	-1.0	10	1
TOTAL	41	108	2.6	23	2

Receiving	No	Yds	Avg	Long	TD
Ron Dugans	6	135	22.5	39	0
William McCray	1	11	11.0	11	0
Peter Warrick	1	7	7.0	7	0
Travis Minor	1	-8	-8.0	-8	0
TOTAL	9	145	16.1	39	0

Field Goals	20-29	30-39	40-49	50-59	Total
Sebastian Janikowski	0-0	1-1	0-0	0-0	1-1

Punting	No	Yds	Long	Blk	Avg
Keith Cottrell	9	358	60	0	39.8

Punt Returns	FC	Ret	Yds	Lg	TD
Peter Warrick	0	1	51	51	0
Reggie Durden	0	1	0	0	0
TOTAL	0	2	51	51	0

Kickoff Returns	No	Yds	Long	Avg	TD
Reggie Durden	3	44	24	14.7	0
William McCray	1	8	8	8.0	0
TOTAL	4	52	24	13.0	0

Sacks		**Interceptions**	
Brian Allen	1	Derrick Gibson	1

Tennessee Volunteers

Passing (5 Att)	Att	Cmp	Pct.	Yds	TD	Int
Tee Martin	18	11	61.1	278	2	2
Travis Henry	1	0	0	0	0	0

Rushing	Car	Yds	Avg	Long	TD
Travis Stephens	13	60	4.6	18	0
Travis Henry	19	28	1.5	9	0
Tee Martin	10	19	1.9	20	0
Shawn Bryson	3	7	2.3	4	0
TOTAL	45	114	2.5	20	0

Receiving	No	Yds	Avg	Long	TD
Peerless Price	4	199	49.8	79	1
Shawn Bryson	3	34	11.3	22	1
Jeremaine Copeland	1	15	15.0	15	0
John Finlayson	1	14	14.0	14	0
Travis Henry	1	9	9.0	9	0
Cedrick Wilson	1	7	7.0	7	0
TOTAL	11	278	25.3	79	2

Field Goals	20-29	30-39	40-49	50-59	Total
Jeff Hall	1-1	0-1	0-0	0-0	1-2

Punting	No	Yds	Long	Blk	Avg
David Leaverton	5	190	47	0	38.0

Punt Returns	FC	Ret	Yds	Lg	TD
Eric Parker	0	4	34	17	0

Kickoff Returns	No	Yds	Long	Avg	TD
Peerless Price	2	43	22	21.5	0

Sacks		**Interceptions**	
Eric Westmoreland	1	Dwayne Goodrich	1
Raynoch Thompson	1		
Darwin Walker	1		
Billy Ratliff	1		

Other Final Division I-A Polls

USA Today/ESPN Coaches' Poll

Voted on by panel of 62 Division I-A head coaches; winning team receives the Sears Trophy (originally the McDonald's Trophy, 1991-93); first place votes in parentheses with total points (based on 25 for 1st, 24 for 2nd, etc.).

	Pts			Pts
1 Tennessee (62)	...1550		14 Georgia	677
2 Ohio St.	1473		15 Penn St.	640
3 Florida St.	1376		16 Texas	577
4 Arizona	1347		17 Arkansas	566
5 Wisconsin	1289		18 Virginia	485
6 Florida	1282		19 Virginia Tech	471
7 Tulane	1117		20 Nebraska	321
8 UCLA	998		21 Miami-FL	291
9 Kansas St.	991		22 Notre Dame	256
10 Air Force	971		23 Purdue	233
11 Georgia Tech	932		24 Syracuse	192
12 Michigan	863		25 Missouri	171
13 Texas A&M	839			

Other teams receiving votes: Mississippi St. (50 pts); Marshall (49); Colorado (38); Oregon (37); West Virginia (18); Kentucky (15); TCU (11); Mississippi (8); Miami-OH (7); Wyoming (6); Idaho (2); North Carolina (1).

NY Times Computer Ratings

Based on an analysis of each team's scores with emphasis on three factors: who won, by what margin, and against what quality of opposition. Computer balances lop-sided scores, notes home field advantage and gives late-season games more weight than those played earlier in the schedule.

The top team is assigned a rating of 1.000, ratings of all other teams reflect their strength relative to strength of No. 1 team. Rankings include all regular season games.

	Rating			Rating
1 Tennessee	..... 1.000		14 Texas A&M	.... .811
2 Ohio St.	.... .962		15 UCLA	.... .804
3 Florida St.	...... .937		16 Miami-FL	...... .801
4 Florida	.... .888		17 Syracuse	.... .795
4 Wisconsin	..... .888		18 Tulane	.... .771
6 Air Force	...... .881		19 Virginia Tech	... .766
7 Georgia Tech	.. .858		20 Missouri	...... .758
8 Arizona	.... .852		21 Georgia	.... .748
8 Purdue	.... .852		22 Nebraska	..... .743
10 Michigan	...... .850		23 West Virginia	.. .717
11 Penn St.	...... .830		24 Virginia	...... .716
12 Texas	.... .828		25 Wyoming	..... .714
13 Kansas St.	...... .823			

FWAA Poll

Voted on by a five-man panel comprised of Tony Barnhart of the *Atlanta Journal-Constitution*, Mark Blaudschun of the *Boston Globe*, Chris Dufresne of *The Los Angeles Times*, Ivan Maisel of CNN-*Sports Illustrated* and Steve Weiberg of *USA Today*. Each selector voted for one team.

Winning team receives the Grantland Rice Award, given since 1954.

Tennessee (5)

NFF's MacArthur Bowl

Voted on by panel of 62 members of the National Football Foundation and College Hall of Fame; winning team receives the NFF's MacArthur Bowl, given since 1959; The McArthur Bowl was the gift of an anonymous donor in the name of General Douglas MacArthur who served for several years as chairman of the Foundation's National Advisory Board. Almost 400 ounces of silver went into the bowl which represents a huge stadium with rows of seats carved in relief.

Tennessee

Winningest Teams of the 1990s

Division I-A schools with the best overall winning percentage from 1990-98, through the Jan. 4, 1999, bowl games.

National champions: 1990—Colorado (AP, FWAA, NFF) and Georgia Tech (UPI); 1991—Miami-FL (AP) and Washington (FWAA, NFF, USA Today/CNN); 1992—Alabama; 1993—Florida St; 1994—Nebraska; 1995—Nebraska; 1996—Florida; 1997—Michigan (AP, NFF) and Nebraska (USA Today/ESPN); 1998—Tennessee.

	Overall Record	Bowls W-L-T	Overall Win Pct.
1 Florida St.	97-13-1	7-2-0	.878
2 Nebraska	96-15-1	4-5-0	.862
3 Florida	93-18-1	5-3-0	.835
4 Tennessee	90-19-2	6-3-0	.820
5 Marshall†	101-25-0	1-1-0	.802
6 Penn St.	87-23-0	6-3-0	.791
7 Miami-FL	83-23-0	4-3-0	.783
8 Ohio St.	85-23-3	3-6-0	.779
9 Texas A&M	86-24-2	2-5-0	.777
10 Michigan	83-24-3	6-3-0	.768
11 Colorado	80-24-4	6-2-0	.759
12 Notre Dame	79-28-2	3-5-0	.734
13 Kansas St.	76-29-1	3-3-0	.722
14 Nevada†	77-31-0	1-2-0	.713
15 Washington	75-30-1	3-4-0	.712
16 Syracuse	75-30-3	5-2-0	.708
17 North Carolina	75-31-1	5-2-0	.706
18 BYU	78-35-2	2-4-1	.687
19 Virginia	71-35-1	2-4-0	.668
20 Alabama	73-37-0	5-2-0	.664
21 Toledo	66-33-3	1-0-0	.662
22 Auburn	67-34-3	3-1-0	.659
23 Air Force	72-39-0	7-7-1	.649
24 Virginia Tech	66-38-1	3-3-0	.633
25 UCLA	65-39-0	2-3-0	.625
26 Texas	65-39-2	2-3-0	.623
27 Georgia	64-39-1	4-1-0	.620
28 Arizona	65-40-1	3-3-0	.618
29 Central Florida†	63-39-0	0-0-0	.618
30 Colorado St.	66-42-0	2-3-0	.611

†Joined I-A as follows: Marshall (1997), Central Florida (1996) and Nevada (1992).

NCAA Division I-A Final Standings

Standings based on conference games only; overall records include postseason games.

Atlantic Coast Conference

	Conference				Overall			
	W	L	PF	PA	W	L	PF	PA
*Florida St.	7	1	283	88	11	2	401	161
*Georgia Tech	7	1	297	200	10	2	426	295
*Virginia	6	2	218	166	9	3	358	247
*N.C. State	5	3	241	225	7	5	366	352
*North Carolina	5	3	195	210	7	5	288	283
Duke	2	6	128	263	4	7	229	319
Wake Forest	2	6	182	249	3	8	235	335
Clemson	1	7	157	216	3	8	218	272
Maryland	1	7	129	213	3	8	202	290

*Bowls (2-3): Florida St. (lost Fiesta); Georgia Tech (won Gator); Virginia (lost Peach); N.C. State (lost Micron PC); N. Carolina (won Las Vegas).

Big East Conference

	Conference				Overall			
	W	L	PF	PA	W	L	PF	PA
*Syracuse	6	1	317	148	8	4	478	300
*Miami-FL	5	2	235	175	9	3	448	298
*Virginia Tech	5	2	195	103	9	3	381	149
*West Virginia	5	2	231	134	8	4	410	267
Boston College	3	4	147	165	4	7	273	311
Rutgers	2	5	112	270	5	6	206	376
Temple	2	5	100	226	2	9	198	360
Pittsburgh	0	7	128	244	2	9	234	334

*Bowls (2-2): Syracuse (lost Orange); Miami-FL (won Micron PC); Virginia Tech (won Music City); West Virginia (lost Insight.com).

Big Ten Conference

	Conference				Overall			
	W	L	PF	PA	W	L	PF	PA
*Ohio St.	7	1	288	99	11	1	430	144
*Wisconsin	7	1	221	91	11	1	382	143
*Michigan	7	1	159	93	10	3	359	235
*Purdue	6	2	304	158	9	4	444	276
*Penn St.	5	3	189	147	9	3	317	183
Michigan St.	4	4	223	193	6	6	336	294
Minnesota	2	6	157	214	5	6	229	249
Indiana	2	6	125	230	4	7	245	305
Illinois	2	6	79	251	3	8	149	326
Iowa	2	6	114	225	3	8	172	287
Northwestern	0	8	93	251	3	9	214	337

*Bowls (5-0): Ohio St. (won Sugar); Wisconsin (won Rose); Michigan (won Florida Citrus); Purdue (won Alamo); Penn St. (won Outback).

Big 12 Conference

North	Conference				Overall			
	W	L	PF	PA	W	L	PF	PA
*Kansas St.	8	1	375	146	11	2	610	197
*Nebraska	5	3	210	139	9	4	403	206
*Missouri	5	3	214	156	8	4	334	236
*Colorado	4	4	155	169	8	4	302	253
Kansas	1	7	155	269	4	7	280	341
Iowa St.	1	7	135	288	3	8	221	328

South	Conference				Overall			
	W	L	PF	PA	W	L	PF	PA
*Texas A&M.	8	1	227	145	11	3	335	214
*Texas	6	2	243	220	9	3	437	337
*Texas Tech	4	4	198	189	7	5	315	255
Oklahoma	3	5	125	198	5	6	184	229
Oklahoma St.	3	5	197	218	5	6	303	296
Baylor	1	7	142	239	2	9	195	323

Big 12 championship game: Texas A&M beat Kansas St., 36-33 (Dec. 5).

*Bowls (3-4): Kansas St. (lost Alamo); Nebraska (lost Holiday); Missouri (won Insight.com); Colorado (won Aloha); Texas A&M (lost Sugar); Texas (won Cotton); Texas Tech (lost Independence).

Big West Conference

	Conference				Overall			
	W	L	PF	PA	W	L	PF	PA
*Idaho	4	1	162	162	9	3	392	317
Nevada	3	2	202	143	6	5	371	316
North Texas	3	2	117	114	3	8	173	297
Boise St.	3	2	157	176	6	5	339	350
Utah St.	2	3	108	135	3	8	237	309
New Mexico St.	1	4	168	184	3	8	331	424

*Bowl (1-0): Idaho (won Humanitarian).

Conference USA

	Conference				Overall			
	W	L	PF	PA	W	L	PF	PA
*Tulane	6	0	239	149	12	0	540	295
*Southern Miss	5	1	207	80	7	5	384	238
*Louisville	4	2	238	203	7	5	473	435
East Carolina	3	3	171	215	6	5	274	297
Army	2	4	171	199	3	8	257	325
Houston	2	4	175	196	3	8	254	317
Cincinnati	1	5	161	259	2	9	259	456
Memphis	1	5	152	213	2	9	226	340

*Bowls (1-2): Tulane (won Liberty); Southern Miss. (lost Humanitarian); Louisville (lost Motor City).

Mid-American Conference

Eastern	Conference				Overall			
	W	L	PF	PA	W	L	PF	PA
*Marshall	8	1	262	147	12	1	405	236
Miami-OH	7	1	249	119	10	1	317	142
Bowling Green	5	3	258	189	5	6	292	312
Ohio	5	3	224	203	5	6	269	303
Akron	3	6	230	236	4	7	265	299
Kent	0	8	112	336	0	11	149	454

Western	Conference				Overall			
	W	L	PF	PA	W	L	PF	PA
Toledo	6	3	181	124	7	5	229	216
Western Michigan	5	3	276	229	7	4	360	312
Central Michigan	5	3	187	163	6	5	229	253
Eastern Michigan	3	6	186	237	3	8	216	309
Northern Illinois	2	6	126	194	2	9	160	329
Ball St.	1	7	116	230	1	10	150	343

*Bowl (1-0): Marshall (won Motor City).

Conference Bowling Results

Postseason records for 1998 season.

	W-L
Big Ten	5-0
SEC	4-4
Big 12	3-4
WAC	2-2
Big East	2-2
ACC	2-3
Mid-American	1-0
Big West	1-0
Conference USA	1-2
Pac-10	1-4

Pacific 10 Conference

	Conference				Overall		
	W	L	PF	PA	W	L	PF	PA
*UCLA	8	0	309	198	10	2	476	340
*Arizona	7	1	274	176	12	1	439	236
*Oregon	5	3	291	234	8	4	473	328
*USC	5	3	245	160	8	5	346	241
*Washington	4	4	198	221	6	6	303	343
Arizona St.	4	4	284	269	5	6	333	338
California	3	5	153	205	5	6	183	251
Oregon St.	2	6	191	252	5	6	286	291
Stanford	2	6	184	261	3	8	261	365
Washington St.	0	8	146	299	3	8	223	349

Bowls (1-4): UCLA (lost Rose); Arizona (won Holiday); Oregon (lost Aloha); USC (lost Sun), Washington (lost Oahu).

Southeastern Conference

	Conference				Overall		
Eastern	W	L	PF	PA	W	L	PF	PA
*Tennessee	9	0	295	120	13	0	431	189
*Florida	7	1	246	112	10	2	380	165
*Georgia	6	2	166	156	9	3	292	222
*Kentucky	4	4	266	281	7	5	431	375
Vanderbilt	1	7	66	290	2	9	142	369
South Carolina	0	8	129	258	1	10	207	330

	Conference				Overall		
Western	W	L	PF	PA	W	L	PF	PA
*Arkansas	6	2	254	139	9	3	390	227
*Mississippi St.	6	3	249	164	8	5	350	256
*Alabama	4	4	153	176	7	5	251	287
*Mississippi	3	5	137	188	7	5	280	274
LSU	2	6	206	214	4	7	337	279
Auburn	1	7	124	193	3	8	166	235

SEC championship game: Tennessee beat Mississippi St., 24-14 (Dec. 5).

Bowls (4-4): Tennessee (won Fiesta); Florida (won Orange); Georgia (won Peach); Kentucky (lost Outback); Arkansas (lost Florida Citrus); Mississippi St. (lost Cotton); Alabama (lost Music City); Mississippi (won Independence).

Western Athletic Conference

	Conference				Overall		
Pacific	W	L	PF	PA	W	L	PF	PA
*San Diego St.	7	1	194	128	7	5	243	244
*BYU	7	2	265	176	9	5	402	290
Utah	5	3	246	162	7	4	339	227
Fresno St.	5	3	192	135	5	6	265	225
San Jose St.	3	5	210	235	4	8	274	385
UTEP	3	5	173	204	3	8	226	305
New Mexico	1	7	164	286	3	9	274	397
Hawaii	0	8	105	280	0	12	149	422

	Conference				Overall		
Mountain	W	L	PF	PA	W	L	PF	PA
*Air Force	8	1	297	146	12	1	468	185
Wyoming	6	2	165	171	8	3	222	215
Colorado St.	5	3	235	163	8	4	345	263
Rice	5	3	181	154	5	6	235	257
*TCU	4	4	180	169	7	5	267	235
SMU	4	4	122	114	5	7	225	248
Tulsa	2	6	117	180	4	7	222	258
UNLV	0	8	122	265	0	11	156	389

WAC championship game: Air Force beat BYU, 20-13 (Dec. 5).

Bowls (2-2): San Diego St. (lost Las Vegas); BYU (lost Liberty); Air Force (won Oahu); TCU (won Sun).

I-A Independents

	W	L	PF	PA
Central Florida	9	3	256	209
*Notre Dame	9	3	328	248
Louisiana Tech	6	6	493	402
NE Louisiana	5	6	227	322
Ala.-Birmingham	4	7	237	308
Arkansas St.	4	8	216	385
Navy	3	8	255	376
SW Louisiana	2	9	199	453

Bowl (0-1): Notre Dame (lost Gator).

NCAA Division I-A Individual Leaders
REGULAR SEASON
Total Offense

		Rushing				Passing		Total Offense			
	Cl	Car	Gain	Loss	Net	Att	Yds	Plays	Yds	YdsPP	TDR*	YdsPG
Tim Rattay, La. Tech	Jr.	43	91	194	-103	559	4943	602	4840	8.04	47	403.33
Chris Redman, Louisville	Jr.	40	85	118	-33	473	4042	513	4009	7.81	31	400.90
Daunte Culpepper, C. Florida	Sr.	141	684	221	463	402	3690	543	4153	7.65	40	377.55
Tim Couch, Kentucky	Jr.	64	105	229	-124	553	4275	617	4151	6.73	37	377.36
David Neill, Nevada	Fr.	65	274	172	102	344	3249	409	3351	8.19	31	372.33
Shaun King, Tulane	Sr.	140	689	157	532	328	3232	468	3764	8.04	46	342.18
Drew Brees, Purdue	So.	59	283	115	168	516	3753	575	3921	6.82	39	326.75
Akili Smith, Oregon	Sr.	74	336	153	183	325	3307	399	3490	8.75	33	317.27
Cade McNown, UCLA	Sr.	63	260	93	167	323	3130	386	3297	8.54	26	299.73
Michael Bishop, Kansas St.	Sr.	177	899	151	748	295	2844	472	3592	7.61	37	299.33

*Touchdowns responsible for include TD passes and TDs scored.

All-Purpose Yards

	Cl	Gm	Rush	Rec	PR	KOR	Total Yds	YdsPG
Troy Edwards, La. Tech	Sr.	12	227	1996	235	326	2784	232.00
Ricky Williams, Texas	Sr.	11	2124	262	0	0	2386	216.91
Kevin Faulk, LSU	Sr.	11	1279	287	265	278	2109	191.73
Torry Holt, N.C. State	Sr.	11	102	1604	273	0	1979	179.91
Jaime Kimbrough, Fresno St.	Sr.	11	1168	391	0	393	1952	177.45
Amos Zereoue, W. Virginia	Jr.	10	1430	175	0	168	1773	177.30
Mike Cloud, Boston College	Sr.	11	1726	198	0	0	1924	174.91
Travis Prentice, Miami-OH	Jr.	11	1787	107	0	0	1894	172.18
Craig Yeast, Kentucky	Sr.	11	87	1311	33	410	1841	167.36
Kevin Johnson, Syracuse	Sr.	11	105	894	145	690	1834	166.73

Tulane	Louisiana Tech	Kansas St.	Texas
Shaun King	**Troy Edwards**	**David Allen**	**Ricky Williams**
Passing Efficiency	All-Purpose, Receptions, Scoring	Punt Returns	Rushing

Passing Efficiency

(Minimum 15 attempts per game)

	Cl	Gm	Att	Cmp	Cmp Pct	Int	Int Pct	Yds	Yds/ Att	TD	TD Pct	Rating Points
Shaun King, Tulane	Sr.	11	328	223	67.99	6	1.83	3232	9.85	36	10.98	183.3
Akili Smith, Oregon	Sr.	11	325	191	58.77	7	2.15	3307	10.18	30	9.23	170.4
Daunte Culpepper, C. Florida	Sr.	11	402	296	73.63	7	1.74	3690	9.18	28	6.97	170.2
Tim Rattay, Louisiana Tech	Jr.	12	559	380	67.98	13	2.33	4943	8.84	46	8.23	164.8
David Neill, Nevada	Fr.	9	344	199	57.85	9	2.62	3249	9.44	29	8.43	159.8
Michael Bishop, Kansas St.	Sr.	12	295	164	55.59	4	1.36	2844	9.64	23	7.80	159.6
Donovan McNabb, Syracuse	Sr.	11	251	157	62.55	5	1.99	2134	8.50	22	8.76	158.9
Marc Bulger, West Virginia	Jr.	11	369	240	65.04	8	2.17	3178	8.61	27	7.32	157.2
Cade McNown, UCLA	Sr.	11	323	188	58.20	10	3.10	3130	9.69	23	7.12	156.9
Joe Germaine, Ohio St.	Sr.	11	346	209	60.40	7	2.02	3108	8.98	24	6.94	154.7
Tim Couch, Kentucky	Jr.	11	553	400	72.33	15	2.71	4275	7.73	36	6.51	153.3
Chris Redman, Louisville	Jr.	10	473	309	65.33	15	3.17	4042	8.55	29	6.13	151.0
Jarious Jackson, Notre Dame	Sr.	10	188	104	55.32	6	3.19	1740	9.26	13	6.91	149.5

Rushing

	Cl	Car	Yds	TD	YdsPG
Ricky Williams, Texas	Sr.	361	2124	27	193.09
Travis Prentice, Miami-OH	Jr.	365	1787	19	162.45
Mike Cloud, Boston Coll.	Sr.	308	1726	14	156.91
Ricky Williams, Texas Tech	So.	306	1582	13	143.82
Devin West, Missouri	Sr.	283	1578	17	143.45
Amos Zereoue, West Va.	Jr.	261	1430	13	143.00
Denvis Manns, N. Mexico St.	Sr.	269	1469	6	133.55
Edgerrin James, Miami-FL	Jr.	242	1416	17	128.73
Ron Dayne, Wisconsin	Jr.	268	1279	11	127.90
Steve Hookfin, Ohio	Sr.	273	1315	11	119.55
Thomas Jones, Virginia	Jr.	238	1303	13	118.45
Eric Flowers, C. Michigan	Jr.	292	1302	16	118.36

Games: All played 11, except Zereoue and Dayne (10).

Receptions

	Cl	No	Yds	TD	P/Gm
Troy Edwards, La. Tech	Sr.	140	1996	27	11.67
Dameane Douglas, California	Sr.	100	1150	4	9.09
Geoff Noisy, Nevada	Sr.	94	1405	7	8.55
Arnold Jackson, Louisville	Jr.	90	1165	10	8.18
Torry Holt, N.C. State	Sr.	88	1604	11	8.00
Siaha Burley, C. Florida	Sr.	88	1142	8	8.00
Craig Yeast, Kentucky	Sr.	85	1311	14	7.73
Jerrian James, Houston	Jr.	80	931	5	7.27
Anthony White, Kentucky	Jr.	78	582	1	7.09
D'wayne Bates, Northwestern	Sr.	83	1245	9	6.92
Marty Booker, Northeast La.	Sr.	75	1168	11	6.82
David Boston, Ohio St.	Jr.	74	1330	13	6.73

Games: All played 11, except Edwards and Bates (12).

Scoring

Non-Kickers

	Cl	TD	Pts	P/Gm
Troy Edwards, La. Tech	Sr.	31	188*	15.67
Ricky Williams, Texas	Sr.	28	168	15.27
Travis Prentice, Miami-OH	Jr.	20	120	10.91
Leroy Collins, Louisville	Jr.	19	116*	10.55
Edgerrin James, Miami-FL	Jr.	19	114	10.36
Devin West, Missouri	Sr.	18	108	9.82
Kevin Faulk, LSU	Sr.	17	102	9.27
Shaun Alexander, Alabama	Jr.	17	102	9.27
Joe Thomas, Idaho	Sr.	16	102**	9.27
Doug Champman, Marshall	Jr.	18	110*	9.17
Eric Flowers, C. Michigan	Jr.	16	96	8.73

*Includes one 2-point conversion. **Includes three 2-point conversions.

Games: All played 11, except Edwards and Chapman (12).

Kickers

	FG/Att	PAT/Att	Pts	P/Gm
Martin Gramatica, Kansas St.	22/31	69/69	135	11.25
Sebastian Janikowski, Fla. St.	27/32	42/43	123	10.25
Nathan Villegas, Oregon	20/22	52/52	112	10.18
Shayne Graham, Va. Tech	22/32	37/37	103	9.36
Todd Latourette, Arkansas	17/24	41/41	92	9.20
Jeff Hall, Tennessee	19/24	47/47	104	8.67
Paul Edinger, Michigan St.	22/26	28/31	94	8.55
Nathan Trout, Syracuse	12/16	58/58	94	8.55
Brad Selent, W. Michigan	18/26	40/40	94	8.55
Kris Stockton, Texas	16/21	46/46	94	8.55

Games: All played 11, except Gramatica, Janikowski and Hall (12); Latourette (10).

Field Goals

	Cl	FG/Att	Pct	Lg
Sebastian Janikowski, Fla. St.	So.	27/32	.844	53
Brad Bohn, Utah St.	So.	24/28	.857	51
Paul Edinger, Michigan St.	Jr.	22/26	.846	49
Shayne Graham, Virginia Tech	Jr.	22/32	.688	53
Derek Franz, Colorado St.	Sr.	21/26	.808	46
Martin Gramatica, Kansas St.	Sr.	22/31	.710	65
Nathan Villegas, Oregon	Jr.	20/22	.909	49
Travis Forney, Penn St.	Jr.	20/29	.690	50

Games: All played 11, except Janikowski and Gramatica (12).
Longest FG of season: 65 yards, Martin Gramatica, Kansas St. vs. Northern Illinois (9/12).

Interceptions

	Cl	No	Yds	TD	Lg
Pat Dennis, NE Louisiana	So.	7	196	2	100-td
Lloyd Harrison, N.C. State	Jr.	7	51	0	35
Jamar Fletcher, Wisconsin	Fr.	6	99	2	52-td
Hank Poteat, Pittsburgh	Jr.	6	53	0	34
Wade Perkins, Missouri	Sr.	6	129	1	61-td
David Macklin, Penn St.	Jr.	6	120	1	55-td
Tim Smith, Stanford	Sr.	6	69	0	28
Chris Claiborne, USC	Jr.	6	159	2	66
Daninelle Derricott, Marshall	Jr.	6	118	0	49
Mario Edwards, Florida St.	Fr.	6	109	0	49
Chappell Mitchell, Arkansas St.	Sr.	6	41	0	18
Jason Walker, Brigham Young	Sr.	6	46	0	24

Games: All played 11 except, Fletcher (9), Poteat (10), Claiborne, Derricott, Edwards, Mitchell (12) and Walker (13).
Note: Perkins had two 61-yard interception returns but only one of them was for a touchdown.

Punting
(Minimum of 3.6 per game)

	Cl	No	Yds	Avg
Joe Kristosik, UNLV	Sr.	76	3509	46.17
Josh Bidwell, Oregon	Sr.	47	2153	45.81
Stephen Baker, Arizona St.	Fr.	56	2561	45.73
Dave Zastudil, Ohio	Fr.	50	2266	45.32
Bill Lafleur, Nebraska	Sr.	52	2337	44.94
Andy Pollock, Bowling Green	Sr.	50	2243	44.86
Deone Horinek, Colorado St.	Jr.	52	2331	44.83

Punt Returns
(Minimum of 1.2 per game)

	Cl	No	Yds	TD	Avg
David Allen, Kansas St.	So.	33	730	4	22.12
Damon Gourdine, S. Diego St.	Jr.	16	294	2	18.38
Nick Davis, Wisconsin	Fr.	27	424	2	15.70
David Boston, Ohio St.	Jr.	18	268	1	14.89
Payton Williams, Fresno St.	Jr.	24	343	1	14.29
Charlie Rogers, Ga. Tech	Sr.	30	425	2	14.17
Siaha Burley, C. Florida	Sr.	21	293	1	13.95
Peter Warrick, Florida St.	Jr.	15	208	0	13.87
Gari Scott, Michigan St.	Jr.	32	440	0	13.75
J.R. Redmond, Arizona St.	Jr.	18	246	1	13.67

Kickoff Returns
(Minimum of 1.2 per game)

	Cl	No	Yds	TD	Avg
Broderick McGrew, N. Texas	Jr.	18	587	1	32.61
Dee Moronkola, Washington St.	Sr.	16	504	2	31.50
Kevin Johnson, Syracuse	Sr.	23	690	2	30.00
Tim Alexander, Oregon St.	Sr.	27	799	1	29.59
Craig Yeast, Kentucky	Sr.	14	410	1	29.29
Toure Butler, Washington	So.	22	626	1	28.45
Deltha O'Neal, California	Jr.	22	624	0	28.36
Sam Simmons, Northwestern	Fr.	22	607	0	27.59
Russell Harvey, Illinois	Fr.	15	406	0	27.07
Antwan Edwards, Clemson	Sr.	13	350	0	26.92

NCAA Division I-A Team Leaders
REGULAR SEASON

Scoring Offense

	Gm	Record	Pts	Avg
Kansas St.	12	11-1	576	48.0
Tulane	11	11-0	499	45.4
Syracuse	11	8-3	468	42.5
Louisiana Tech	12	6-6	493	41.1
UCLA	11	10-1	445	40.5
Louisville	11	7-4	444	40.4
Oregon	11	8-3	430	39.1
Kentucky	11	7-4	417	37.9
Ohio St.	11	10-1	406	36.9
Miami-FL	11	8-3	402	36.5

Scoring Defense

	Gm	Record	Pts	Avg
Wisconsin	11	10-1	112	10.2
Florida St.	12	11-1	138	11.5
Ohio St.	11	10-1	130	11.8
Miami-OH	11	10-1	142	12.9
Virginia Tech	11	8-3	142	12.9
Kansas St.	12	11-1	160	13.3
Air Force	12	11-1	160	13.3
Florida	11	9-2	155	14.1
Tennessee	12	12-0	173	14.4
Texas A&M	13	11-2	190	14.6

Total Offense

	Gm	Plays	Yds	Avg	TD	YdsPG
Louisville	11	883	6156	7.0	62	559.64
Louisiana Tech	12	894	6479	7.2	66	539.92
Kentucky	11	911	5876	6.5	50	534.18
Tulane	11	816	5578	6.8	64	507.09
Nevada	11	869	5577	6.4	49	507.00
Ohio St.	11	853	5539	6.5	46	503.55
C. Florida	11	789	5365	6.8	50	487.73
UCLA	11	785	5309	6.8	56	482.64
Kansas St.	12	887	5742	6.5	65	478.50
Oregon	11	785	5260	6.7	49	478.18

Note: Touchdowns scored by rushing and passing only.

Total Defense

	Gm	Plays	Yds	Avg	TD	YdsPG
Florida St.	12	747	2578	3.5	14	214.8
Ohio St.	11	762	2835	3.7	12	257.7
Kansas St.	12	759	3220	4.2	18	268.3
Wisconsin	11	714	2973	4.2	9	270.3
BYU	13	830	3561	4.3	29	273.9
Oklahoma	11	694	3067	4.4	24	278.8
Virginia Tech	11	710	3134	4.4	18	284.9
Texas Tech	11	710	3135	4.4	21	285.0
Florida	11	773	3153	4.1	15	286.6
Texas A&M	13	871	3761	4.3	21	289.3

Note: Opponents' TDs scored by rushing and passing only.

Single Game Highs
INDIVIDUAL

Rushing Yards
Yds
350 Ricky Williams, Texas vs. Iowa St. (Oct. 3)

Total Offense
Yds
582 David Neill, Nevada vs. New Mexico St. (Oct. 10)

Points Scored
Att
36 Ricky Williams, Texas vs. Rice (Sept. 26)

Rushing TDs
Att
6 Ricky Williams, Texas vs. Rice (Sept. 26)

Passing TDs
Att
7 Tim Rattay, La. Tech vs. Boise St. (Oct. 3)
7 Tim Rattay, La. Tech vs. Arkansas St. (Nov. 7)

Receptions
No
18 Randall Lane, Purdue vs. Wisconsin (Oct. 10)

Receiving Yards
Yds
405 Troy Edwards, La. Tech vs. Nebraska (Aug. 29)

Passing Yards
Yds
611 David Neill, Nevada vs. New Mexico St. (Oct. 10)

Passes Completed
No
55 Drew Brees, Purdue vs. Wisconsin (Oct. 10)

Annual Awards

Player of the Year
Ricky Williams, Texas . . . . AP, Camp, Heisman, Maxwell

Position Players of the Year
O'Brien Award (Quarterback) . . . . .Michael Bishop, Kansas St.
Walker Award (Running Back) . . . . .Ricky Williams, Texas
Biletnikoff Award (Receiver). . . . . .Troy Edwards, La. Tech
Groza Award (Kicker). . . . . .Sebastian Janikowski, Fla. St.
Outland Trophy (Interior Lineman) . . . . . . .Kris Farris, UCLA, OT
Lombardi Award (Lineman) . . . . .Dat Nguyen, Texas A&M
Butkus Award (Linebacker) . . . . .Chris Claiborne, USC
Thorpe Award (Defensive Back) . . . .Antoine Winfield, Ohio St.
Nagurski Award (Defensive Player). . . .Champ Bailey, Georgia
Bednarik Award (Defensive Player) . . .Dat Nguyen, Texas A&M
Payton Award (IAA Player of the Year)Jerry Azumah, UNH, RB
Hill Trophy (Div. II Player of the Year). . . . . .Brian Shay,
Emporia St., RB

Coach of the Year
Phillip Fulmer, Tennessee .AFCA, FWAA, *The Sporting News*
Bill Snyder, Kansas St. .Camp, Dodd

Heisman Trophy Vote
Presented since 1935 by the Downtown Athletic Club of New York City and named after former college coach and DAC athletic director John W. Heisman. Voting done by national media and former Heisman winners. Each ballot allows for three names (points based on 3 for 1st, 2 for 2nd and 1 for 3rd).

Top 10 Vote-Getters

	Pos	1st	2nd	3rd	Pts
Ricky Williams, Texas	RB	714	91	31	2335
Michael Bishop, Kansas St. .	QB	41	250	169	792
Cade McNown, UCLA	QB	28	217	178	696
Tim Couch, Kentucky	QB	26	153	143	527
Donovan McNabb, Syracuse	QB	13	54	85	232
Daunte Culpepper, C. Fla. .	QB	5	11	30	67
Champ Bailey, Georgia	WR	6	8	21	55
Torry Holt, N.C. State	WR	2	8	22	44
Joe Germaine, Ohio St.	QB	2	11	15	43
Shaun King, Tulane	QB	1	11	13	38

Consensus All-America Team
NCAA Division I-A players cited most frequently by the following four selectors: AFCA, AP, *The Sporting News*, and Walter Camp Foundation. Holdover from 1997 All-America team is in **bold** type; (*) indicates unanimous selection.

Offense

	Player	Class	Ht	Wt
WR	Torry Holt*, N.C. State.	Sr.	6-1	188
WR	Peter Warrick, FSU.	Jr.	6-0	190
TE	Rufus French*, Mississippi	Jr.	6-4	245
OL	Matt Stinchcomb, Georgia.	Sr.	6-6	291
OL	Aaron Gibson, Wisconsin	Sr.	6-7	372
OL	Kris Farris, UCLA	Jr.	6-9	310
C	Craig Page, Georgia Tech.	Sr.	6-3	300
QB	Cade McNown, UCLA	Sr.	6-1	210
RB	**Ricky Williams***, Texas	Sr.	6-0	225
RB	Mike Cloud, Boston College	Sr.	5-11	200
K	Sebastian Janikowski, Fla. St..	So.	6-2	255

Defense

	Player	Class	Ht	Wt
DL	Jared DeVries, Iowa	Sr.	6-4	284
DL	Tom Burke*, Wisconsin	Sr.	6-4	250
DL	Montae Reagor*, Texas Tech.	Sr.	6-4	270
LB	Jeff Kelly, Kansas St.	Sr.	6-0	250
LB	Dat Nguyen*, Texas A&M.	Sr.	6-0	230
LB	Chris Claiborne*, USC	Jr.	6-3	250
LB	Al Wilson, Tennessee	Sr.	6-0	226
DB	Champ Bailey, Georgia	Jr.	6-1	180
DB	Chris McAllister*, Arizona.	Sr.	6-2	185
DB	Antoine Winfield, Ohio St.	Sr.	5-9	180
DB	Anthony Poindexter, Virginia.	Sr.	6-1	220
P	Joe Kristosik, UNLV	Sr.	6-3	220

Underclassmen who declared for the 1999 NFL Draft

Thirty-two players forfeited the remainder of their college eligibility and declared for the NFL draft in 1999. NFL teams drafted 25 underclassmen. Players listed in alphabetical order; first round selections in **bold** type.

	Pos	Drafted by	Overall pick
Rahim Abdullah, Clemson	LB	Cleveland	45
Champ Bailey, Georgia	CB/WR	Washington	7
Dre' Bly, North Carolina	DB	St. Louis	41
David Boston, Ohio St.	WR	Arizona	8
Chris Claiborne, USC	LB	Detroit	9
Cecil Collins, McNeese St.	RB	Miami	134
Leroy Collins, Louisville	RB	not drafted	
Tim Couch, Kentucky	QB	Cleveland	1
Kris Farris, UCLA	OG	Pittsburgh	74
Rufus French, Mississippi	TE	not drafted	
Charlie Higgins, Tulsa	RB	not drafted	
Brock Huard, Washington	QB	Seattle	77
Corey Hulsey, Clemson	G	not drafted	
Sedrick Irvin, Michigan St.	RB	Detroit	103
Edgerrin James, Miami-FL	RB	Indianapolis	4
Andy Katzenmoyer, Ohio St.	LB	New England	28
Jevon Kearse, Florida	LB	Tennessee	16
Torin Kirtsey, Mid. Tenn. St.	RB	not drafted	
Reggie McGrew, Florida	DT	San Francisco	24
Mike McKenzie, Memphis	DT	Green Bay	87
Robert Newkirk, Michigan St.	DT	not drafted	
Solomon Page, West Virginia	OT	Dallas	55
De'Mond Parker, Oklahoma	RB	Green Bay	159
Yusuf Scott, Arizona	G	Arizona	168
Brian Smith, Ala-Birmingham	LB	not drafted	
Larry Smith, Florida St.	DT	Jacksonville	56
John Tait, BYU	OT	Kansas City	14
Dimitrius Underwood, MSU	DE	Minnesota	29
Brad Ware, Auburn	S	Tennessee	114
Damien Woody, Boston Coll.	C	New England	17
Kenny Wright, NW Louisiana	DB	Minnesota	120
Amos Zereoue, West Virginia	RB	Pittsburgh	95

NCAA Division I-AA Final Standings

Standings based on conference games only; overall records include postseason games.

Atlantic 10 Conference

	Conference				Overall			
New England	W	L	PF	PA	W	L	PF	PA
*Connecticut	6	2	241	253	10	3	461	413
*Massachusetts	6	2	259	214	12	3	524	423
Maine	3	5	251	242	6	5	315	272
New Hampshire	3	5	166	201	4	7	287	274
Rhode Island	2	6	128	169	3	8	219	257

	Conference				Overall			
Mid-Atlantic	W	L	PF	PA	W	L	PF	PA
*Richmond	7	1	236	113	9	3	321	175
Delaware	4	4	254	228	7	4	359	299
Wm. & Mary	4	4	211	243	7	4	346	315
Villanova	4	4	207	240	6	5	358	340
Northeastern	3	5	173	183	5	6	252	227
James Madison	2	6	175	215	3	8	233	287

*Playoffs (5-2): Massachusetts (4-0), Connecticut (1-1), Richmond (0-1).

Big Sky Conference

	Conference				Overall			
	W	L	PF	PA	W	L	PF	PA
*Montana	6	2	209	162	8	4	339	315
CS-Northridge	5	3	234	189	7	4	333	270
Montana St.	5	3	253	216	7	4	348	254
Weber St.	4	4	148	150	6	5	240	193
Eastern Wash.	4	4	239	204	5	6	316	297
Portland St.	4	4	255	234	6	5	347	353
Northern Arizona	3	5	166	202	6	5	241	227
CS-Sacramento	3	5	225	239	5	6	289	300
Idaho St.	2	6	159	292	3	8	221	415

*Playoffs (0-1): Montana (0-1).

Best Conference Playoff Records

Postseason records for 1998 season.

	W-L
Atlantic 10	5-2
Southern	4-2
Gateway Athletic	2-2
Southland	2-2
Patriot	1-1

Gateway Athletic Conference

	Conference				Overall			
	W	L	PF	PA	W	L	PF	PA
*Western Ill.	5	1	116	45	11	3	332	175
*Illinois St.	4	2	203	181	8	4	425	341
Northern Iowa	3	3	147	137	7	4	288	191
Youngstown St.	3	3	106	156	6	5	250	261
SW Missouri St.	3	3	145	144	5	6	318	285
Indiana St.	2	4	122	136	5	6	261	275
Southern Ill.	1	5	123	188	3	8	259	296

*Playoffs (2-2): Western Ill. (2-1); Illinois St. (0-1).

Ivy League

	Conference				Overall			
	W	L	PF	PA	W	L	PF	PA
Pennsylvania	6	1	225	138	8	2	297	213
Brown	5	2	188	149	7	3	265	241
Yale	5	2	175	154	6	4	228	259
Princeton	4	3	156	111	5	5	225	162
Columbia	3	4	87	111	4	6	146	175
Harvard	3	4	85	142	4	6	136	211
Cornell	1	6	85	141	4	6	159	200
Dartmouth	1	6	102	157	2	8	142	226

Playoffs: League does not play postseason games.

Metro-Atlantic Conference

	Conference				Overall			
	W	L	PF	PA	W	L	PF	PA
Fairfield	6	1	274	92	9	2	346	131
Georgetown	6	1	255	92	9	2	325	163
Duquesne	5	2	239	109	8	3	347	186
Marist	5	2	194	97	7	3	294	129
St. John's	3	4	115	127	6	5	193	150
Canisius	2	5	87	210	3	7	120	284
Siena	1	6	64	195	4	6	146	261
†Iona	0	0	0	0	4	6	224	283
St. Peters	0	7	19	260	0	10	47	354

†The MAAC ruled before the season that Iona was ineligible to claim the league title because the school violated a league financial aid policy.

Playoffs: No teams invited.

Mid-Eastern Athletic Conference

	Conference				Overall			
	W	L	PF	PA	W	L	PF	PA
*Florida A&M	7	1	420	169	11	2	594	288
*Hampton	7	1	270	103	9	3	387	201
†Bethune-Cookman	6	2	249	205	8	3	328	297
N. Carolina A&T	5	3	180	171	8	3	277	213
Howard	5	3	311	246	7	4	373	304
South Carolina St.	3	5	170	171	5	6	220	205
Norfolk St.	2	6	210	402	2	9	252	494
Morgan St.	1	7	129	307	1	10	168	370
Delaware St.	0	8	153	324	0	11	189	482

*Playoffs (1-2): Florida A&M (1-1); Hampton (0-1).
†Heritage Bowl: Bethune-Cookman lost to SWAC entrant Southern-BR, 28-2 (Dec. 26).

Northeast Conference

	Conference				Overall			
	W	L	PF	PA	W	L	PF	PA
Monmouth (N.J.)	4	1	178	84	5	5	303	218
Robert Morris	4	1	189	71	4	5	274	171
Wagner	3	2	143	129	7	3	300	249
Central Conn.	3	2	101	107	4	6	155	258
Sacred Heart	1	4	63	186	2	8	134	318
St. Francis (Pa.)	0	5	38	135	0	10	66	271

Playoffs: No teams invited.

Ohio Valley Conference

	Conference				Overall			
	W	L	PF	PA	W	L	PF	PA
*Tennessee St.	6	1	287	142	9	3	461	277
Murray St.	5	2	217	175	7	4	313	328
Mid. Tenn. St.	5	2	206	172	5	5	250	256
Eastern Ill.	4	3	205	196	6	5	275	297
Eastern Ky.	4	3	193	174	6	5	270	274
Tennessee Tech	2	5	132	179	4	7	219	245
SE Missouri St.	2	5	150	177	3	8	204	295
Tenn.-Martin	0	7	170	345	0	11	214	502

*Playoffs (0-1): Tennessee St. (0-1).

Patriot League

	Conference				Overall			
	W	L	PF	PA	W	L	PF	PA
*Lehigh	6	0	231	63	12	1	396	189
Colgate	5	1	207	137	8	4	419	328
Bucknell	3	3	154	156	6	5	278	243
Lafayette	3	3	138	150	3	8	190	271
Fordham	2	4	113	162	4	7	252	336
Towson	1	5	100	228	5	6	243	336
Holy Cross	1	5	100	147	2	9	168	234

Playoffs (1-1): Lehigh (1-1).

Pioneer League

	Conference				Overall			
	W	L	PF	PA	W	L	PF	PA
Drake	4	0	139	59	7	3	291	182
Dayton	3	1	110	98	4	4	279	262
Valparaiso	2	2	82	73	5	6	233	222
Butler	1	3	73	116	4	6	222	273
San Diego	0	4	74	132	2	8	184	259

Playoffs: No teams invited.

Southern Conference

	Conference				Overall			
	W	L	PF	PA	W	L	PF	PA
*Ga. Southern	8	0	358	164	14	1	654	363
*Appalachian St.	6	2	214	114	10	3	356	222
W. Carolina	5	3	169	152	6	5	195	200
Tenn.-Chatt.	4	4	180	152	6	6	209	219
The Citadel	4	4	175	172	5	6	223	296
Furman	3	5	206	207	5	6	267	283
E. Tenn St.	3	5	205	192	4	7	269	340
Wofford	3	5	156	222	4	7	203	277
VMI	0	8	83	371	1	10	147	468

*Playoffs (4-2): Georgia Southern (3-1), Appalachian St. (1-1).

Southland Conference

	Conference				Overall			
	W	L	PF	PA	W	L	PF	PA
*Northwestern St.	6	1	236	120	11	3	465	280
*McNeese St.	5	2	175	92	9	3	388	157
Troy St.	5	2	130	105	8	4	235	203
Jacksonville St.	4	3	164	196	7	4	246	267
Nicholls St.	3	4	164	178	4	7	259	321
SW Texas St.	2	5	120	179	4	7	186	269
Stephen F. Austin	1	5	127	126	3	8	217	213
Sam Houston St.	1	6	120	240	3	8	191	335

*Playoffs (2-2): Northwestern St. (2-1), McNeese St. (0-1).

Southwestern Athletic Conference

	Conference				Overall			
	W	L	PF	PA	W	L	PF	PA
†Southern-BR	8	0	238	145	9	3	348	258
Jackson St.	7	1	367	214	7	4	403	326
Ark.-Pine Bluff	6	2	254	166	8	3	325	217
Texas Southern	4	4	216	189	6	5	309	236
Grambling	4	4	224	248	5	6	287	318
Alabama St.	3	5	200	219	5	6	261	280
Alcorn St.	3	5	181	233	6	5	250	291
Miss. Valley St.	1	7	143	253	1	10	190	351
‡Alabama A&M	0	0	0	0	5	6	220	246
Prairie View	0	8	134	290	1	10	175	340

†Heritage Bowl: Southern-BR beat MEAC entrant Bethune-Cookman, 28-2 (Dec. 26).
‡Alabama A&M was an affiliate member of the SWAC in 1998. Its games did not count in the SWAC standings.

NCAA I-AA Independents

	W	L	PF	PA
Morehead St.	9	2	430	306
Davidson	8	2	221	104
Hofstra	8	3	426	297
South Florida	8	3	402	178
Western Ky.	7	4	396	310
Samford	6	5	203	203
Elon College	5	6	289	214
Liberty	5	6	287	277
Southern Utah	5	6	313	347
Jacksonville	4	5	271	252
Austin Peay	4	7	199	326
Buffalo	4	7	315	340
LaSalle	3	6	171	267
Cal Poly-SLO	3	8	226	329
Charleston Southern	3	8	245	278
St. Mary's (Ca.)	2	8	154	270

Playoffs: No teams invited.

Villanova
Brian Westbrook
Scoring

CS-Sacramento
Charles Roberts
Rushing

Portland St.
Jim Blanchard
Passing Efficiency

Florida A&M
Patrick Bonner
Total Offense

NCAA Division I-AA Regular Season Leaders
INDIVIDUAL
Passing Efficiency
(Minimum 15 attempts per game)

	Cl	Gm	Att	Cmp	Cmp Pct	Int	Int Pct	Yds	Yds/ Att	TD	TD Pct	Rating Points
Jim Blanchard, Portland St.	So.	9	169	112	66.27	1	.59	1512	8.95	14	8.28	167.6
Matt Nagy, Delaware	So.	11	298	182	61.07	12	4.03	2916	9.79	20	6.71	157.4
Chad Barnhardt, South Florida	Sr.	10	193	114	59.07	9	4.66	1776	9.20	17	8.81	156.1
Patrick Bonner, Florida A&M	Sr.	11	426	265	62.21	7	1.64	3473	8.15	37	8.69	156.1
Ryan Vena, Colgate	Jr.	10	230	134	58.26	11	4.78	2298	9.99	16	6.96	155.6
Mike Cook, Wm. & Mary	Sr.	11	370	246	66.49	7	1.89	3028	8.18	26	7.03	154.6
Ted White, Howard	Sr.	11	383	219	57.18	7	1.83	3263	8.52	31	8.09	151.8
Mark Washington, Jackson St.	Jr.	11	257	134	52.14	9	3.50	2232	8.68	26	10.12	151.5
Marcus Brady, CS-Northridge	Fr.	11	376	255	67.82	11	2.93	2974	7.91	25	6.65	150.4
Steve O'Hare, Fordham	Sr.	9	265	161	60.75	6	2.26	2216	8.36	19	7.17	150.1

Total Offense

	Cl	Rush	Pass	Yds	YdsPG
Patrick Bonner, Fla. A&M	Sr.	29	3473	3568	324.36
James Perry, Brown	Jr.	-63	3165	3102	310.20
Ryan Vena, Colgate	Jr.	736	2298	3034	303.40
Brian Ah Yat, Montana	Sr.	-8	2952	2944	294.40
Ted White, Howard	Sr.	-48	3263	3215	292.27
Giovanni Carmazzi, Hofstra	Jr.	443	2751	3194	290.36
Mike Cook, Wm. & Mary	Sr.	29	3028	3057	277.91
Leon Murray, Tennessee St.	Jr.	54	3002	3056	277.82
Kevin Glenn, Illinois St.	So.	187	2818	3005	273.18
Phil Stambaugh, Lehigh	Jr.	-122	3121	2999	272.64

Rushing

	Cl	Car	Yds	TD	YdsPG
Charles Roberts, CS-Sac.	So.	386	2260	19	205.45
Jerry Azumah, UNH	Sr.	342	2195	22	199.55
Marcel Shipp, UMass	So.	319	1949	13	177.18
Adrian Peterson, Ga. So.	Fr.	257	1932	25	175.64
Karlton Carpenter, So. Ill.	Jr.	323	1892	16	172.00
J.J. Allen, Marist	Sr.	279	1646	21	164.60
Brad Hoover, W. Carolina	Jr.	331	1663	13	151.18
Morgan Welch, Weber St.	Jr.	305	1629	13	148.09
James Finn, Pennsylvania	Jr.	323	1450	17	145.00
Charles Dunn, Portland St.	So.	291	1561	9	141.91

Games: All played 11, except Allen and Finn (10).

Receptions

	Cl	No	Yds	TD	P/Gm
Jacquay Nunnally, Fla. A&M	So.	93	1316	12	8.45
Sean Morey, Brown	Sr.	83	1023	10	8.30
Eddie Conti, Delaware	Sr.	91	1712	10	8.27
Brian Westbrook, Villanova	So.	89	1144	15	8.09
Mike Furrey, Northern Iowa	Jr.	86	1074	10	7.82
Damon Hodge, Alabama St.	Jr.	83	1022	9	7.55
Earnest Payton, J. Madison	So.	82	921	3	7.45
Cainon Lamb, Fla. A&M	So.	74	1131	12	6.73
Rickey Garrett, Illinois St.	Jr.	72	1154	13	6.55
Tyrone Butterfield, Tenn. St.	Sr.	72	1129	11	6.55

Games: All played 11, except Morey (10).

Interceptions

	Cl	No	Yds	TD	LG
Ken Krapf, St. John's (N.Y.)	Jr.	9	144	2	68-td
Eric Kenesie, Valparaiso	Jr.	9	88	0	45
Clif Henry, Davidson	Sr.	7	145	0	34
Eric Sloan, Troy St.	Jr.	7	137	1	82-td
Ron Iannotti, Rhode Island	Sr.	7	131	0	32

Fifteen tied with six each.

Games: All played 11, except Henry (10).

Scoring
Non-Kickers

	Cl	TD	XPt	Pts	P/Gm
Brian Westbrook, Villanova	So.	26	4	160	14.55
Adrian Peterson, Ga. So.	Fr.	26	0	156	14.18
Chris Reed, Monmouth	Sr.	22	0	132	13.20
Jerry Azumah, UNH	Sr.	23	2	140	12.73
Jessie Burton, McNeese St.	Fr.	19	0	114	12.67
J.J. Allen, Marist	Sr.	21	0	126	12.60

Games: All played 11, except Reed and Allen (10); Burton (9).

Kickers

	Cl	FG/Att	PAT/Att	Pts
Juan Toro, Florida A&M	Sr.	14/15	56/59	98
Bill Gramatica, S. Florida	So.	16/24	46/47	94
Chad Johnson, Hofstra	So.	16/27	46/51	94
Chris Chambers, Ga. So.	Jr.	12/14	57/60	93
Shonz LaFrenz, McNeese St.	Jr.	14/17	43/46	85

Games: All played 11.

Field Goals

	Cl	FG/Att	Pct	LG
Mike Goldstein, N. Arizona	Sr.	16/23	.696	53
Scott Shields, Weber St.	Sr.	16/23	.696	55
Bill Gramatica, S. Florida	So.	16/24	.667	44
Chad Johnson, Hofstra	So.	16/27	.593	44
Joe Lopez, Western Ill.	So.	16/28	.571	55
Greg Miller, Murray St.	Fr.	15/19	.789	43
Kyle Leisher, Nicholls St.	So.	13/18	.722	46

Games: All played 11, except Leisher (10).
Longest FG of season: Three players tied with 55 yards each.

Punt/Kickoff Leaders

Punting	Cl	No	Yds	Avg
Chad Stanley, S. F. Austin	Sr.	58	2703	46.60

Punt Returns	Cl	No	Yds	TD	Avg
Bashir Levingston, E. Wash.	Sr.	16	333	3	20.81

Kickoff Returns	Cl	No	Yds	TD	Avg
Ryan Zimpleman, Butler	So.	28	972	4	34.71

TEAM
Scoring Offense

	Gm	Record	Pts	Avg		Gm	Record	Pts	Avg
Florida A&M	11	10-1	546	49.6	Colgate	11	8-3	391	35.5
Ga. Southern	11	11-0	468	42.5	Connecticut	11	9-2	389	35.4
Morehead St.	11	9-2	430	39.1	Massachusetts	11	8-3	380	34.5
Tennessee St.	11	9-2	430	39.1	Howard	11	7-4	373	33.9
Hofstra	11	8-3	426	38.7	McNeese St.	11	9-2	369	33.5
Jackson St.	11	7-4	403	36.6	Delaware	11	7-4	359	32.6
South Florida	11	8-3	402	36.5	Bethune-Cookman	10	8-2	326	32.6
Illinois St.	11	8-3	397	36.1	Villanova	11	6-5	358	32.5
Western Kentucky	11	7-4	396	36.0	Northwestern St.	11	9-2	355	32.3

Scoring Defense

	Gm	Record	Pts	Avg		Gm	Record	Pts	Avg
Western Ill.	11	10-1	103	9.4	Appalachian St.	11	9-2	160	14.5
Davidson	10	8-2	104	10.4	Georgetown	11	9-2	163	14.8
Fairfield	11	9-2	131	11.9	Troy St.	11	8-3	176	16.0
McNeese St.	11	9-2	136	12.4	South Florida	11	8-3	178	16.2
Lehigh	11	10-1	139	12.6	Princeton	10	5-5	162	16.2
Marist	10	7-3	129	12.9	Duquesne	11	8-3	186	16.9
St. John's (N.Y.)	11	6-5	150	13.6	Northwestern St.	11	9-2	191	17.4
Richmond	11	9-2	151	13.7	Northern Iowa	11	7-4	191	17.4
Hampton	11	9-2	159	14.5	Columbia	10	4-6	175	17.5

Total Offense

	Record	Plays	Yds	Avg		Record	Plays	Yds	Avg
Florida A&M	10-1	855	5893	535.73	Fairfield	9-2	632	2352	213.8
Ga. Southern	11-0	749	5419	492.64	Marist	7-3	626	2196	219.6
Massachusetts	8-3	882	5310	482.73	McNeese St.	9-2	704	2499	227.2
Colgate	8-3	808	5252	477.45	Davidson	8-2	656	2319	231.9
Morehead St.	9-2	776	5237	476.09	St. John's (N.Y.)	6-5	704	2579	234.5
Jackson St.	7-4	806	5184	471.27	Duquesne	8-3	756	2801	254.6
Lehigh	10-1	814	5182	471.09	Tennessee Tech	4-7	720	2909	264.5
Southern Utah	5-6	839	5141	467.36	Weber St.	6-5	728	3011	273.7
Tennessee St.	9-2	777	5139	467.18	Appalachian St.	9-2	709	3044	276.7
Portland St.	5-6	798	5111	464.64	Western Carolina	6-5	675	3086	280.5
Hofstra	8-3	762	5024	456.73	South Florida	8-3	694	3101	281.9
Howard	7-4	776	4915	446.82	Monmouth (N.J.)	5-5	589	2832	283.2
New Hampshire	4-7	796	4845	440.45	Bethune-Cookman	8-2	705	2866	286.6
Illinois St.	8-3	821	4829	439.00	Georgetown	9-2	763	3164	287.6
Brown	7-3	770	4338	433.80	Troy St.	8-3	668	3179	289.0

Total Defense

NCAA Playoffs

Division I-AA
First Round (Nov. 28)

at Georgia Southern 49 .Colgate 28
at Connecticut 42 . . . . .Hampton 34
at Florida A&M 27 . . . . .Troy State 17
at Westen Illinois 52 . . . . .Montana 9
Lehigh 24 . . . . .at Richmond 23
Massachusetts 21 . . . . .at McNeese St. 19
at Appalachian St. 45 . . . . .Tennessee St. 31
at Northwestern St. 48 . . . . .Illinois St. 28

Quarterfinals (Dec. 5)

at Georgia Southern 52 . . . . .Connecticut 30
at Massachusetts 27 . . . . .Lehigh 21
at Western Illinois 24 . . . . .Florida A&M 21
at Northwestern St. 31 . . . . .Appalachian St. 20

Semifinals (Dec. 12)

at Georgia Southern 42 . . . . .Western Illinois 14
Massachusetts 41 . . . . .at Northwestern St. 31

Championship Game
Dec. 19 at Chattanooga, Tenn. (Att: 17,501)

Massachusetts 55 . . . . .Georgia Southern 43
(12-3)   (14-1)

Division II
First Round (Nov. 21)

at Carson-Newman (Tenn.) 30 . . . . .West Georgia 20
Fort Valley St. (Ga.) 21 . . . . .at Delta St. (Miss.) 14
at Slippery Rock (Pa.) 37 . . . . . .Grand Valley St. (Mich.) 14
Shepherd (W. Va.) 9 . . . . .at Indiana (Pa.) 6
at NW Missouri St. 28 . . . . .Nebraska-Omaha 14
at Northern Colorado 52 . . . . .North Dakota 24
at Central Oklahoma 21 . . . . .Chadron St. (Neb.) 19
Texas A&M-Kingsville 54 . . . . .at UC-Davis 21

Quarterfinals (Nov. 28)

at Carson-Newman 38 . . . . .OT. . . . . .Fort Valley St. 31
at Slippery Rock 31 . . . . .Shepherd College 20
at NW Missouri St. 42 . . . . .Northern Colorado 17
Texas A&M-Kingsville 24 . . .OT. . .at Central Oklahoma 21

Semifinals (Dec. 5)

at Carson-Newman 47 . . . . .Slippery Rock 21
at NW Missouri St. 49 . . . . .Texas A&M-Kingsville 34

Championship Game
Dec. 12 at Florence, Ala. (Att: 6,149)

NW Missouri St. 24 . . . . .Carson-Newman 6
(15-0)   (12-2)

Division III
First Round (Nov. 21)

at Mount Union (Ohio) 21 . . . . .Albion (Mich.) 19
at Wittenberg (Ohio) 13 . . . . .Millikin (Ill.) 10
at Lycoming (Pa.) 49 . . . . .Catholic (D.C.) 14
at Trinity (Tex.) 30 . . . . .Western Maryland 20
Wisconsin-Eau Claire 28 . . . . .at Central (Iowa) 21
at St. John's (Minn.) 33 . . . . .Pacific Lutheran (Wash.) 20
Buffalo St. (N.Y.) 38 . . . . .at Springfield (Mass.) 35
Rowan (N.J.) 26 . . . . .at Coll. of New Jersey 2

Quarterfinals (Nov. 28)

at Mount Union 21 . . . . .Wittenberg 19
Trinity (Tex.) 37 . . . . .at Lycoming 21
Wisconsin-Eau Claire 10 . . . . .at St. John's 7
at Rowan 19 . . . . .Buffalo St. 17

Semifinals (Dec. 5)

at Mt. Union 34 . . . . .Trinity 29
at Rowan 22 . . . . .Wisconsin-Eau Claire 19

Amos Alonzo Stagg Bowl
Dec. 12 at Salem, Va. (Att: 5,145)

Mount Union 44 . . . . .Rowan 24
(14-0)   (10-3)

NAIA Playoffs
Division I

NAIA returned to a single division playoff for its football championship in 1998.

First Round (Nov. 21)

Olivet Nazarene (Ill.) 32 . . . . . .at Hastings Col. (Neb.) 26
at Georgetown Coll. 46 . . . . .Malone (Ohio) 41
at Sioux Falls (S.D.) 29 . . . . .Univ. of Mary (N.D.) 25
at Southwestern (Kan.) 12 . . . . .Lindenwood (Mo.) 10
Tri-State (Ind.) 33 . . . . .at Benedicine (Kan.) 28
Huron (S.D.) 61 . . . . .at Jamestown (N.D.) 19
Central Washington 41 . . . .OT. . .at Rocky Mtn. (Mont.) 38
at Azusa Pacific (Calif.) 31 . . . . .Taylor (Ind.) 28

Quarterfinals (Nov. 28)

Tri-State 37 . . . . .at Georgetown 23
Olivet Nazarene 37 . . . . .at Sioux Falls 34
at Huron 52 . . . . .Southwestern 6
at Azusa Pacific 35 . . . . .Central Washington 28

Semifinals (Dec. 5)

at Olivet Nazarene 33 . . . . .Tri-State 28
at Azusa Pacific 26 . . . . .Huron 24

Championship
Dec. 19 at Savannah, Tenn. (Att: 5,000 est.)

Azusa Pacific 17 . . . . .Olivet Nazarene 14
(12-2)   (11-3)

COLLEGE FOOTBALL
S T A T I S T I C S

THROUGH THE YEARS
1869-1999

BOWLS • ALL-TIME LEADERS

SEC **B** PAGE 162

National Champions

Over the last 129 years, there have been 25 major selectors of national champions by way of polls (11), mathematical rating systems (10) and historical research (4). The best-known and most widely circulated of these surveys, the Associated Press poll of sportswriters and broadcasters, first appeared during the 1936 season. Champions prior to 1936 have been determined by retro polls, ratings, and historical research.

The Early Years (1869-1935)

National champions based on the Dickinson mathematical system (DS) and three historical retro polls taken by the College Football Researchers Association (CFRA), the National Championship Foundation (NCF) and the Helms Athletic Foundation (HF). The CFRA and NCF polls start in 1869, college football's inaugural year, while the Helms poll begins in 1883, the first season the game adopted a point system for scoring. Frank Dickinson, an economics professor at Illinois, introduced his system in 1926 and retro-picked winners in 1924 and '25. Bowl game results were counted in the Helms selections, but not in the other three.

Multiple champions: Yale (18); Princeton (17); Harvard (9); Michigan (7); Notre Dame and Penn (4); Alabama, California, Cornell, Illinois, Pittsburgh and USC (3); Georgia Tech, Minnesota and Penn St. (2).

Year		Record	Year		Record	Year		Record
1869	**Princeton**	1-1-0	1880	**Yale** (CFRA)	4-0-1	1891	**Yale**	13-0-0
1870	**Princeton**	1-0-0		& **Princeton** (NCF)	4-0-1	1892	**Yale**	13-0-0
1871	No games played		1881	**Yale**	5-0-1	1893	**Princeton**	11-0-0
1872	**Princeton**	1-0-0	1882	**Yale**	8-0-0	1894	**Yale**	16-0-0
1873	**Princeton**	1-0-0	1883	**Yale**	8-0-0	1895	**Penn**	14-0-0
1874	**Yale**	3-0-0	1884	**Yale**	8-0-1	1896	**Princeton** (CFRA)	10-0-1
1875	**Princeton** (CFRA)	2-0-0	1885	**Princeton**	9-0-0		& **Lafayette** (NCF)	11-0-1
	& **Harvard** (NCF)	4-0-0	1886	**Yale**	9-0-1	1897	**Penn**	15-0-0
1876	**Yale**	3-0-0	1887	**Yale**	9-0-0	1898	**Harvard**	11-0-0
1877	**Yale**	3-0-1	1888	**Yale**	13-0-0	1899	**Princeton** (CFRA)	12-1-0
1878	**Princeton**	6-0-0	1889	**Princeton**	10-0-0		& **Harvard** (NCF, HF)	10-0-1
1879	**Princeton**	4-0-1	1890	**Harvard**	11-0-0			

Year		Record	Bowl Game	Head Coach	Outstanding Player
1900	**Yale**	12-0-0	No bowl	Malcolm McBride	Perry Hale, HB
1901	**Harvard** (CFRA)	12-0-0	No bowl	Bill Reid	Bob Kernan, HB
	& **Michigan** (NCF, HF)	11-0-0	Won Rose	Hurry Up Yost	Neil Snow, E
1902	**Michigan**	11-0-0	No bowl	Hurry Up Yost	Boss Weeks, QB
1903	**Princeton**	11-0-0	No bowl	Art Hillebrand	John DeWitt, G
1904	**Penn** (CFRA, HF)	12-0-0	No bowl	Carl Williams	Andy Smith, FB
	& **Michigan** (NCF)	10-0-0	No bowl	Hurry Up Yost	Willie Heston, HB
1905	**Chicago**	10-0-0	No bowl	Amos Alonzo Stagg	Walter Eckersall, QB
1906	**Princeton**	9-0-1	No bowl	Bill Roper	Cap Wister, E
1907	**Yale**	9-0-1	No bowl	Bill Knox	Tad Jones, HB
1908	**Penn** (CFRA, HF)	11-0-1	No bowl	Sol Metzger	Hunter Scarlett, E
	& **LSU** (NCF)	10-0-0	No bowl	Edgar Wingard	Doc Fenton, QB
1909	**Yale**	12-1-0	No bowl	Howard Jones	Ted Coy, FB
1910	**Harvard** (CFRA, HF)	8-0-1	No bowl	Percy Haughton	Percy Wendell, HB
	& **Pittsburgh** (NCF)	9-0-0	No bowl	Joe Thompson	Ralph Galvin, C
1911	**Princeton** (CFRA, HF)	8-0-2	No bowl	Bill Roper	Sam White, E
	& **Penn St.** (NCF)	8-0-1	No bowl	Bill Hollenback	Dexter Very, E
1912	**Harvard** (CFRA, HF)	9-0-0	No bowl	Percy Haughton	Charley Brickley, HB
	& **Penn St.** (NCF)	8-0-0	No bowl	Bill Hollenback	Dexter Very, E
1913	**Harvard**	9-0-0	No bowl	Percy Haughton	Eddie Mahan, FB
1914	**Army**	9-0-0	No bowl	Charley Daly	John McEwan, C
1915	**Cornell**	9-0-0	No bowl	Al Sharpe	Charley Barrett, QB
1916	**Pittsburgh**	8-0-0	No bowl	Pop Warner	Bob Peck, C
1917	**Georgia Tech**	9-0-0	No bowl	John Heisman	Ev Strupper, HB
1918	**Pittsburgh** (CFRA, HF)	4-1-0	No bowl	Pop Warner	Tom Davies, HB
	& **Michigan** (NCF)	5-0-0	No bowl	Hurry Up Yost	Frank Steketee, FB
1919	**Harvard** (CFRA-tie, HF)	9-0-1	Won Rose	Bob Fisher	Eddie Casey, HB
	Illinois (CFRA-tie)	6-1-0	No bowl	Bob Zuppke	Chuck Carney, E
	& **Notre Dame** (NCF)	9-0-0	No bowl	Knute Rockne	George Gipp, HB
1920	**California**	9-0-0	Won Rose	Andy Smith	Dan McMillan, T

Year		Record	Bowl Game	Head Coach	Outstanding Player
1921	**California** (CFRA)	9-0-1	Tied Rose	Andy Smith	Brick Muller, E
	& Cornell (NCF, HF)	8-0-0	No bowl	Gil Dobie	Eddie Kaw, HB
1922	**Princeton** (CFRA)	8-0-0	No bowl	Bill Roper	Herb Treat, T
	California (NCF)	9-0-0	No bowl	Andy Smith	Brick Muller, E
	& Cornell (HF)	8-0-0	No bowl	Gil Dobie	Eddie Kaw, HB
1923	**Illinois** (CFRA, HF)	8-0-0	No bowl	Bob Zuppke	Red Grange, HB
	& Michigan (NCF)	8-0-0	No bowl	Hurry Up Yost	Jack Blott, C
1924	**Notre Dame**	10-0-0	Won Rose	Knute Rochne	"The Four Horsemen"*
1925	**Alabama** (CFRA, HF)	10-0-0	Won Rose	Wallace Wade	Johnny Mack Brown, HB
	& Dartmouth (DS)	8-0-0	No bowl	Jesse Hawley	Swede Oberlander, HB
1926	**Alabama** (CFRA, HF)	9-0-1	Tied Rose	Wallace Wade	Hoyt Winslett, E
	& Stanford (DS)	10-0-1	Tied Rose	Pop Warner	Ted Shipkey, E
1927	**Yale** (CFRA)	7-1-0	No bowl	Tad Jones	Bill Webster, G
	& Illinois (NCF, HF, DS)	7-0-1	No bowl	Bob Zuppke	Bob Reitsch, C
1928	**Georgia Tech** (CFRA, NCF, HF)	10-0-0	Won Rose	Bill Alexander	Pete Pund, C
	& USC (DS)	9-0-1	No bowl	Howard Jones	Jesse Hibbs, T
1929	**Notre Dame**	9-0-0	No bowl	Knute Rockne	Frank Carideo, QB
1930	**Alabama** (CFRA)	10-0-0	Won Rose	Wallace Wade	Fred Sington, T
	& Notre Dame (NCF, HF, DS)	10-0-0	No bowl	Knute Rockne	Marchy Schwartz, HB
1931	**USC**	10-1-0	Won Rose	Howard Jones	John Baker, G
1932	**USC** (CFRA, NCF, HF)	10-0-0	Won Rose	Howard Jones	Ernie Smith, T
	& Michigan (DS)	8-0-0	No bowl	Harry Kipke	Harry Newman, QB
1933	**Michigan**	8-0-0	No bowl	Harry Kipke	Chuck Bernard, C
1934	**Minnesota**	8-0-0	No bowl	Bernie Bierman	Pug Lund, HB
1935	**Minnesota** (CFRA, NCF, HF)	8-0-0	No bowl	Bernie Bierman	Dick Smith, T
	& SMU (DS)	12-1-0	Lost Rose	Matty Bell	Bobby Wilson, HB

*Notre Dame's Four Horsemen were Harry Stuhldreher (QB), Jim Crowley (HB), Don Miller (HB-P) and Elmer Layden (FB).

The Media Poll Years (since 1936)

National champions according to seven media and coaches' polls: Associated Press (since 1936), United Press (1950-57), International News Service (1952-57), United Press International (1958-92), Football Writers Association of America (since 1954), National Football Foundation and Hall of Fame (since 1959) and USA Today/CNN (since 1991). In 1991, the American Football Coaches Association switched outlets for its poll from UPI to USA Today/CNN and then to USA Today/ESPN in 1997.

After 29 years of releasing its final Top 20 poll in early December, AP named its 1965 national champion following that season's bowl games. AP returned to a pre-bowls final vote in 1966 and '67, but has polled its writers and broadcasters after the bowl games since the 1968 season. The FWAA has selected its champion after the bowl games since the 1955 season, the NFF-Hall of Fame since 1971, UPI after 1974, USA Today/CNN 1991-96, and USA Today/ESPN since 1997.

The Associated Press changed the name of its national championship award from the AP trophy to the Bear Bryant Trophy after the legendary Alabama coach's death in 1983. The Football Writers' trophy is called the Grantland Rice Award (after the celebrated sportswriter) and the NFF-Hall of Fame trophy is called the MacArthur Bowl (in honor of Gen. Douglas MacArthur).

Multiple champions: Notre Dame (9); Alabama (7); Ohio St. and Oklahoma (6); USC and Nebraska (5); Miami-FL and Minnesota (4); Michigan St. and Texas (3); Army, Georgia Tech, Michigan, Penn St., Pittsburgh and Tennessee (2).

Year		Record	Bowl Game	Head Coach	Outstanding Player
1936	**Minnesota**	7-1-0	No bowl	Bernie Bierman	Ed Widseth, T
1937	**Pittsburgh**	9-0-1	No bowl	Jock Sutherland	Marshall Goldberg, HB
1938	**TCU**	11-0-0	Won Sugar	Dutch Meyer	Davey O'Brien, QB
1939	**Texas A&M**	11-0-0	Won Sugar	Homer Norton	John Kimbrough, FB
1940	**Minnesota**	8-0-0	No Bowl	Bernie Bierman	George Franck, HB
1941	**Minnesota**	8-0-0	No bowl	Bernie Bierman	Bruce Smith, HB
1942	**Ohio St.**	9-1-0	No bowl	Paul Brown	Gene Fekete, FB
1943	**Notre Dame**	9-1-0	No bowl	Frank Leahy	Angelo Bertelli, QB
1944	**Army**	9-0-0	No bowl	Red Blaik	Glenn Davis, HB
1945	**Army**	9-0-0	No bowl	Red Blaik	Doc Blanchard, FB
1946	**Notre Dame**	8-0-1	No bowl	Frank Leahy	Johnny Lujack, QB
1947	**Notre Dame**	9-0-0	No bowl	Frank Leahy	Johnny Lujack, QB
1948	**Michigan**	9-0-0	No bowl	Bennie Oosterbaan	Dick Rifenburg, E
1949	**Notre Dame**	10-0-0	No bowl	Frank Leahy	Leon Hart, E
1950	**Oklahoma**	10-1-0	Lost Sugar	Bud Wilkinson	Leon Heath, FB
1951	**Tennessee**	10-0-0	Lost Sugar	Bob Neyland	Hank Lauricella, TB
1952	**Michigan St.** (AP, UP)	9-0-0	No bowl	Biggie Munn	Don McAuliffe, HB
	& Georgia Tech (INS)	12-0-0	Won Sugar	Bobby Dodd	Hal Miller, T
1953	**Maryland**	10-1-0	Lost Orange	Jim Tatum	Bernie Faloney, QB
1954	**Ohio St.** (AP, INS)	10-0-0	Won Rose	Woody Hayes	Howard Cassady, HB
	& UCLA (UP, FW)	9-0-0	No bowl	Red Sanders	Jack Ellena, T
1955	**Oklahoma**	11-0-0	Won Orange	Bud Wilkinson	Jerry Tubbs, C
1956	**Oklahoma**	10-0-0	No bowl	Bud Wilkinson	Tommy McDonald, HB
1957	**Auburn** (AP)	10-0-0	No bowl	Shug Jordan	Jimmy Phillips, E
	& Ohio St. (UP, FW, INS)	9-1-0	Won Rose	Woody Hayes	Bob White, FB
1958	**LSU** (AP, UPI)	11-0-0	Won Sugar	Paul Dietzel	Billy Cannon, HB
	& Iowa (FW)	8-1-1	Won Rose	Forest Evashevski	Randy Duncan, QB

National Champions (Cont.)

Year		Record	Bowl Game	Head Coach	Outstanding Player
1959	Syracuse................11-0-0		Won Cotton	Ben Schwartzwalder	Ernie Davis, HB
1960	**Minnesota** (AP, UPI, NFF) 8-2-0		Lost Rose	Murray Warmath	Tom Brown, G
	& **Mississippi** (FW)..............10-0-1		Won Sugar	Johnny Vaught	Jake Gibbs, QB
1961	**Alabama** (AP, UPI, NFF)........11-0-0		Won Sugar	Bear Bryant	Billy Neighbors, T
	& **Ohio St.** (FW) 8-0-1		No bowl	Woody Hayes	Bob Ferguson, HB
1962	**USC** 11-0-0		Won Rose	John McKay	Hal Bedsole, E
1963	**Texas** 11-0-0		Won Cotton	Darrell Royal	Scott Appleton, T
1964	**Alabama** (AP, UPI)...............10-1-0		Lost Orange	Bear Bryant	Joe Namath, QB
	Arkansas (FW) 11-0-0		Won Cotton	Frank Broyles	Ronnie Caveness, LB
	& **Notre Dame** (NFF) 9-1-0		No bowl	Ara Parseghian	John Huarte, QB
1965	**Alabama** (AP, FW-tie).............9-1-1		Won Orange	Bear Bryant	Paul Crane, C
	& **Michigan St.** (UPI, NFF, FW-tie) ..10-1-0		Lost Rose	Duffy Daugherty	George Webster, LB
1966	**Notre Dame** (AP, UPI, FW, NFF-tie) ..9-0-1		No bowl	Ara Parseghian	Jim Lynch, LB
	& **Michigan St.** (NFF-tie)..........9-0-1		No bowl	Duffy Daugherty	Bubba Smith, DE
1967	**USC** 10-1-0		Won Rose	John McKay	O.J. Simpson, HB
1968	**Ohio St.**........................10-0-0		Won Rose	Woody Hayes	Rex Kern, QB
1969	**Texas** 11-0-0		Won Cotton	Darrell Royal	James Street, QB
1970	**Nebraska** (AP, FW) 11-0-1		Won Orange	Bob Devaney	Jerry Tagge, QB
	Texas (UPI, NFF-tie)............10-1-0		Lost Cotton	Darrell Royal	Steve Worster, RB
	& **Ohio St.** (NFF-tie)............9-1-0		Lost Rose	Woody Hayes	Jim Stillwagon, MG
1971	**Nebraska**........................13-0-0		Won Orange	Bob Devaney	Johnny Rodgers, WR
1972	**USC** 12-0-0		Won Rose	John McKay	Charles Young, TE
1973	**Notre Dame** (AP, FW, NFF) 11-0-0		Won Sugar	Ara Parseghian	Mike Townsend, DB
	& **Alabama** (UPI).................11-1-0		Lost Sugar	Bear Bryant	Buddy Brown, OT
1974	**Oklahoma** (AP)...................11-0-0		No bowl	Barry Switzer	Joe Washington, RB
	& **USC** (UPI, FW, NFF)............10-1-1		Won Rose	John McKay	Anthony Davis, RB
1975	**Oklahoma** 11-1-0		Won Orange	Barry Switzer	Lee Roy Selmon, DT
1976	**Pittsburgh** 12-0-0		Won Sugar	Johnny Majors	Tony Dorsett, RB
1977	**Notre Dame** 11-1-0		Won Cotton	Dan Devine	Ross Browner, DE
1978	**Alabama** (AP, FW, NFF).........11-1-0		Won Sugar	Bear Bryant	Marty Lyons, DT
	& **USC** (UPI)....................12-1-0		Won Rose	John Robinson	Charles White, RB
1979	**Alabama** 12-0-0		Won Sugar	Bear Bryant	Jim Bunch, OT
1980	**Georgia** 12-0-0		Won Sugar	Vince Dooley	Herschel Walker, RB
1981	**Clemson**........................12-0-0		Won Orange	Danny Ford	Jeff Davis, LB
1982	**Penn St.**.......................11-1-0		Won Sugar	Joe Paterno	Todd Blackledge, QB
1983	**Miami-FL**.......................11-1-0		Won Orange	H. Schnellenberger	Bernie Kosar, QB
1984	**BYU** 13-0-0		Won Holiday	LaVell Edwards	Robbie Bosco, QB
1985	**Oklahoma**.......................11-1-0		Won Orange	Barry Switzer	Brian Bosworth, LB
1986	**Penn St.**.......................12-0-0		Won Fiesta	Joe Paterno	D.J. Dozier, RB
1987	**Miami-FL**.......................12-0-0		Won Orange	Jimmy Johnson	Steve Walsh, QB
1988	**Notre Dame** 12-0-0		Won Fiesta	Lou Holtz	Tony Rice, QB
1989	**Miami-FL**.......................11-1-0		Won Sugar	Dennis Erickson	Craig Erickson, QB
1990	**Colorado** (AP, FW, NFF)..........11-1-1		Won Orange	Bill McCartney	Eric Bieniemy, RB
	& **Georgia Tech** (UPI)............11-0-1		Won Citrus	Bobby Ross	Shawn Jones, QB
1991	**Miami-FL** (AP) 12-0-0		Won Orange	Dennis Erickson	Gino Torretta, QB
	& **Washington** (USA, FW, NFF)....12-0-0		Won Rose	Don James	Steve Emtman, DT
1992	**Alabama** 13-0-0		Won Sugar	Gene Stallings	Eric Curry, DE
1993	**Florida St.**.....................12-1-0		Won Orange	Bobby Bowden	Charlie Ward, QB
1994	**Nebraska**.......................13-0-0		Won Orange	Tom Osborne	Zach Wiegert, OT
1995	**Nebraska**.......................12-0-0		Won Fiesta	Tom Osborne	Tommie Frazier, QB
1996	**Florida** 12-1*		Won Sugar	Steve Spurrier	Danny Wuerffel, QB
1997	**Michigan** (AP) 12-0		Won Rose	Lloyd Carr	Charles Woodson, DB
	& **Nebraska** (ESPN/USA)..........13-0		Won Orange	Tom Osborne	Ahman Green, RB
1998	**Tennessee** 13-0		Won Fiesta	Phillip Fulmer	Peerless Price, WR

*The NCAA instituted overtime for regular season games in 1996.

Number 1 vs. Number 2

Since the Associated Press writers poll started keeping track of such things in 1936, the No. 1 and No. 2 ranked teams in the country have met 32 times; 20 during the regular season and 12 in bowl games. Since the first showdown in 1943, the No. 1 team has beaten the No. 2 team 20 times, lost 10 and there have been two ties. Each showdown is listed below with the date, the match-up, each team's record going into the game, the final score, the stadium and site.

Date	Match-up	Stadium	Date	Match-up	Stadium
Oct. 9 1943	#1 Notre Dame (2-0) ......35 #2 Michigan (3-0).........12	Michigan (Ann Arbor)	1944	#2 Navy (6-2) 7	(Baltimore)
Nov. 20 1943	#1 Notre Dame (8-0) ....14 #2 Iowa Pre-Flight (8-0) 13	Notre Dame (South Bend)	Nov. 10 1945	#1 Army (6-0) ....48 #2 Notre Dame (5-0-1)......0	Yankee (New York)
Dec. 2	#1 Army (8-0) 23	Municipal	Dec. 1 1945	#1 Army (8-0) ....32 #2 Navy (7-0-1) 13	Municipal (Philadelphia)

Date	Match-up		Stadium
Nov. 9	#1 Army (7-0)	0	Yankee
1946	#2 Notre Dame (5-0)	0	(New York)
Jan. 1	#1 USC (10-0)	42	ROSE BOWL
1963	#2 Wisconsin (8-1)	37	(Pasadena)
Oct. 12	#2 Texas (3-0)	28	Cotton Bowl
1963	#1 Oklahoma (2-0)	7	(Dallas)
Jan. 1	#1 Texas (10-0)	28	COTTON BOWL
1964	#2 Navy (9-1)	6	(Dallas)
Nov. 19	#1 Notre Dame (8-0)	10	Spartan
1966	#2 Michigan St. (9-0)	10	(East Lansing)
Sept. 28	#1 Purdue (1-0)	37	Notre Dame
1968	#2 Notre Dame (1-0)	22	(South Bend)
Jan. 1	#1 Ohio St. (9-0)	27	ROSE BOWL
1969	#2 USC (9-0-1)	16	(Pasadena)
Dec. 6	#1 Texas (9-0)	15	Razorback
1969	#2 Arkansas (9-0)	14	(Fayetteville)
Nov. 25	#1 Nebraska (10-0)	35	Owen Field
1971	#2 Oklahoma (9-0)	31	(Norman)
Jan. 1	#1 Nebraska (12-0)	38	ORANGE BOWL
1972	#2 Alabama (11-0)	6	(Miami)
Jan. 1	#1 Alabama (10-1)	14	SUGAR BOWL
1979	#1 Penn St. (11-0)	7	(New Orleans)
Sept. 26	#1 USC (2-0)	28	Coliseum
1981	#2 Oklahoma (1-0)	24	(Los Angeles)
Jan. 1	#1 Penn St. (10-1)	27	SUGAR BOWL
1983	#1 Georgia (11-0)	23	(New Orleans)
Oct. 19	#1 Iowa (5-0)	12	Kinnick
1985	#2 Michigan (5-0)	10	(Iowa City)

Date	Match-up		Stadium
Sept. 27	#2 Miami-FL (3-0)	28	Orange Bowl
1986	#1 Oklahoma (2-0)	16	(Miami)
Jan. 2	#2 Penn St. (11-0)	14	FIESTA BOWL
1987	#1 Miami-FL (11-0)	10	(Tempe)
Nov. 21	#2 Oklahoma (10-0)	17	Memorial
1987	#1 Nebraska (10-0)	7	(Lincoln)
Jan. 1	#2 Miami-FL (11-0)	20	ORANGE BOWL
1988	#1 Oklahoma (11-0)	14	(Miami)
Nov. 26	#1 Notre Dame (10-0)	27	Coliseum
1988	#2 USC (10-0)	10	(Los Angeles)
Sept. 16	#1 Notre Dame (1-0)	24	Michigan
1989	#2 Michigan (0-0)	19	(Ann Arbor)
Nov. 16	#2 Miami-FL (8-0)	17	Doak Campbell
1991	#1 Florida St. (10-0)	16	(Tallahassee)
Jan. 1	#2 Alabama (12-0)	34	SUGAR BOWL
1993	#1 Miama-FL (11-0)	13	(New Orleans)
Nov. 13	#2 Notre Dame (9-0)	31	Notre Dame
1993	#1 Florida St. (9-0)	24	(South Bend)
Jan. 1	#1 Florida St. (11-1)	18	ORANGE BOWL
1994	#2 Nebraska (11-0)	16	(Miami)
Jan. 2	#1 Nebraska (11-0)	62	FIESTA BOWL
1996	#2 Florida (12-0)	24	(Tempe)
Nov. 30	#2 Florida St. (10-0)	24	Doak Campbell
1996	#1 Florida (10-1)	21	(Tallahassee)
Jan. 4	#1 Tennessee (12-0)	23	FIESTA BOWL
1999	#2 Florida St. (11-1)	16	(Tempe)

Top 50 Rivalries

Top Division I-A and I-AA series records, including games through the 1998 season. All rivalries listed below are renewed annually with the following exceptions. **LSU-Tulane** stopped playing in 1996 but have made plans to renew rivalry no later than 2001. **Nebraska-Oklahoma** now play only when matched up as part of the rotating Big 12 schedule.

RECENTLY DISCONTINUED SERIES: **Baylor vs TCU** in 1995 after 102 games (Baylor ahead 48-47-7); **Florida vs Miami-FL** in 1991 after 49 games (Florida ahead, 25-24); **Miami-FL vs Notre Dame** in 1990 after 23 games (ND ahead, 15-7-1).

	Gm	Series Leader		Gm	Series Leader
Air Force-Army	33	Air Force (20-12-1)	**Michigan-Notre Dame**	28	Michigan (16-11-1)
Air Force-Navy	31	Air Force (21-10-0)	**Michigan-Ohio St.**	95	Michigan (54-35-6)
Alabama-Auburn	63	Alabama (36-26-1)	**Minnesota-Wisconsin**	108	Minnesota (57-43-8)
Alabama-Tennessee	81	Alabama (42-32-7)	**Mississippi-Miss. St.**	95	Ole Miss (54-35-6)
Arizona-Arizona St.	72	Arizona (42-29-1)	**Missouri-Kansas**	107	Missouri (50-48-9)
Army-Navy	99	Army (48-44-7)	**Nebraska-Oklahoma**	78	Oklahoma (39-36-3)
Auburn-Georgia	102	Auburn (48-46-8)	**N. Mexico-N. Mexico St**	88	New Mexico (57-26-5)
California-Stanford	101	Stanford (51-39-11)	**N. Carolina-N.C. State**	88	N. Carolina (58-24-6)
The Citadel-VMI	58	Tied (28-28-2)	**Notre Dame-Purdue**	70	Notre Dame (46-22-2)
Clemson-S. Carolina	96	Clemson (57-35-4)	**Notre Dame-USC**	70	Notre Dame (39-26-5)
Colorado-Nebraska	57	Nebraska (41-14-2)	**Oklahoma-Okla. St.**	93	Oklahoma (72-14-7)
Colo. St.-Wyoming	88	Colorado St. (45-38-5)	**Oregon-Oregon St**	102	Oregon (51-41-10)
Duke-N. Carolina	84	N. Carolina (45-35-4)	**Penn-Cornell**	105	Penn (60-40-5)
Florida-Florida St.	43	Florida (26-15-2)	**Penn St.-Pittsburgh**	94	Penn St.(49-41-4)
Florida-Georgia	77	Georgia (46-29-2)	**Pittsburgh-West Va**	91	Pitt (56-32-3)
Florida St.-Miami,FL	42	Miami (23-19-0)	**Princeton-Yale**	121	Yale (65-46-10)
Georgia-Georgia Tech	93	Georgia (52-36-5)	**Purdue-Indiana**	101	Purdue (61-34-6)
Grambling-Southern	47	Southern (24-23-0)	**Richmond-Wm.& Mary**	108	Wm. & Mary (55-48-5)
Harvard-Yale	115	Yale (62-45-8)	**Tennessee-Vanderbilt**	92	Tennessee (61-26-5)
Kansas-Kansas St.	96	Kansas (61-30-5)	**Texas-Oklahoma**	93	Texas (54-34-5)
Kentucky-Tennessee	94	Tennessee (62-23-9)	**Texas-Texas A&M**	105	Texas (67-33-5)
Lafayette-Lehigh	134	Lafayette (71-58-5)	**UCLA-USC**	68	USC (34-27-7)
LSU-Tulane	93	LSU (64-22-7)*	**Utah-BYU**	74	Utah (44-26-4)
Miami,OH-Cincinnati	103	Miami (55-41-7)	**Utah-Utah St**	96	Utah (63-29-4)
Michigan-Michigan St	91	Michigan (60-26-5)	**Washington-Wash. St.**	91	Washington (59-26-6)

*Disputed series record: Tulane claims LSU leads 61-23-7

Associated Press Final Polls

The Associated Press introduced its weekly college football poll of sportswriters (later, sportswriters and broadcasters) in 1936. The final AP poll was released at the end of the regular season until 1965, when bowl results were included for one year. After a two-year return to regular season games only, the final poll has come out after the bowls since 1968. Starting in 1989, the AP Poll has ranked 25 teams but due to space constraints we are unable to list the complete polls for those years.

1936

Final poll released Nov. 30. Top 20 regular season results after that: **Dec. 5**–#8 Notre Dame tied USC, 13-13; #17 Tennessee tied Ole Miss, 0-0; #18 Arkansas over Texas, 6-0. **Dec. 12**–#16 TCU over #6 Santa Clara, 9-0.

			After
	As of Nov. 30	**Head Coach**	**Bowls**
1	Minnesota 7-1-0	Bernie Bierman	same
2	LSU 9-0-1	Bernie Moore	9-1-1
3	Pittsburgh 7-1-1	Jock Sutherland	8-1-1
4	Alabama 8-0-1	Frank Thomas	same
5	Washington 7-1-1	Jimmy Phelan	7-2-1
6	Santa Clara 7-0-0	Buck Shaw	8-1-0
7	Northwestern 7-1-0	Pappy Waldorf	same
8	Notre Dame 6-2-0	Elmer Layden	6-2-1
9	Nebraska 7-2-0	Dana X. Bible	same
10	Penn 7-1-0	Harvey Harman	same
11	Duke 9-1-0	Wallace Wade	same
12	Yale 7-1-0	Ducky Pond	same
13	Dartmouth 7-1-1	Red Blaik	same
14	Duquesne 7-2-0	John Smith	8-2-0
15	Fordham 5-1-2	Jim Crowley	same
16	TCU 7-2-2	Dutch Meyer	9-2-2
17	Tennessee 6-2-1	Bob Neyland	6-2-2
18	Arkansas 6-3-0	Fred Thomsen	7-3-0
	Navy 6-3-0	Tom Hamilton	same
20	Marquette 7-1-0	Frank Murray	7-2-0

Key Bowl Games

Sugar–#6 Santa Clara over #2 LSU, 21-14; **Rose**–#3 Pitt over #5 Washington, 21-0; **Orange**–#14 Duquesne over Mississippi St., 13-12; **Cotton**–#16 TCU over #20 Marquette, 16-6.

1937

Final poll released Nov. 29. Top 20 regular season results after that: **Dec. 4**–#18 Rice over SMU, 15-7.

			After
	As of Nov. 29	**Head Coach**	**Bowls**
1	Pittsburgh 9-0-1	Jock Sutherland	same
2	California 9-0-1	Stub Allison	10-0-1
3	Fordham 7-0-1	Jim Crowley	same
4	Alabama 9-0-0	Frank Thomas	9-1-0
5	Minnesota 6-2-0	Bernie Bierman	same
6	Villanova 8-0-1	Clipper Smith	same
7	Dartmouth 7-0-2	Red Blaik	same
8	LSU 9-1-0	Bernie Moore	9-2-0
9	Notre Dame 6-2-1	Elmer Layden	same
	Santa Clara 8-0-0	Buck Shaw	9-0-0
11	Nebraska 6-1-2	Biff Jones	same
12	Yale 6-1-1	Ducky Pond	same
13	Ohio St. 6-2-0	Francis Schmidt	same
14	Holy Cross 8-0-2	Eddie Anderson	same
	Arkansas 6-2-2	Fred Thomsen	same
16	TCU 4-2-2	Dutch Meyer	same
17	Colorado 8-0-0	Bunnie Oakes	8-1-0
18	Rice 4-3-2	Jimmy Kitts	6-3-2
19	North Carolina . . .7-1-1	Ray Wolf	same
20	Duke 7-2-1	Wallace Wade	same

Key Bowl Games

Rose–#2 Cal over #4 Alabama, 13-0; **Sugar**–#9 Santa Clara over #8 LSU, 6-0; **Cotton**–#18 Rice over #17 Colorado, 28-14; **Orange**–Auburn over Michigan St., 6-0.

1938

Final poll released Dec. 5. Top 20 regular season results after that: **Dec. 26**–#14 Cal over Georgia Tech, 13-7.

			After
	As of Dec. 5	**Head Coach**	**Bowls**
1	TCU 10-0-0	Dutch Meyer	11-0-0
2	Tennessee 10-0-0	Bob Neyland	11-0-0
3	Duke 9-0-0	Wallace Wade	9-1-0
4	Oklahoma 10-0-0	Tom Stidham	10-1-0
5	Notre Dame 8-1-0	Elmer Layden	same
6	Carnegie Tech 7-1-0	Bill Kern	7-2-0
7	USC 8-2-0	Howard Jones	9-2-0
8	Pittsburgh 8-2-0	Jock Sutherland	same
9	Holy Cross 8-1-0	Eddie Anderson	same
10	Minnesota 6-2-0	Bernie Bierman	same
11	Texas Tech 10-0-0	Pete Cawthon	10-1-0
12	Cornell 5-1-1	Carl Snavely	same
13	Alabama 7-1-1	Frank Thomas	same
14	California 9-1-0	Stub Allison	10-1-0
15	Fordham 6-1-2	Jim Crowley	same
16	Michigan 6-1-1	Fritz Crisler	same
17	Northwestern 4-2-2	Pappy Waldorf	same
18	Villanova 8-0-1	Clipper Smith	same
19	Tulane 7-2-1	Red Dawson	same
20	Dartmouth 7-2-0	Red Blaik	same

Key Bowl Games

Sugar–#1 TCU over #6 Carnegie Tech, 15-7; **Orange**–#2 Tennessee over #4 Oklahoma, 17-0; **Rose**–#7 USC over #3 Duke, 7-3; **Cotton**–St. Mary's over #11 Texas Tech 20-13.

1939

Final poll released Dec. 11. Top 20 regular season results after that: None.

			After
	As of Dec. 11	**Head Coach**	**Bowls**
1	Texas A&M 10-0-0	Homer Norton	11-0-0
2	Tennessee 10-0-0	Bob Neyland	10-1-0
3	USC 7-0-2	Howard Jones	8-0-2
4	Cornell 8-0-0	Carl Snavely	same
5	Tulane 8-0-1	Red Dawson	8-1-1
6	Missouri 8-1-0	Don Faurot	8-2-0
7	UCLA 6-0-4	Babe Horrell	same
8	Duke 8-1-0	Wallace Wade	same
9	Iowa 6-1-1	Eddie Anderson	same
10	Duquesne 8-0-1	Buff Donelli	same
11	Boston College . . .9-1-0	Frank Leahy	9-2-0
12	Clemson 8-1-0	Jess Neely	9-1-0
13	Notre Dame 7-2-0	Elmer Layden	same
14	Santa Clara 5-1-3	Buck Shaw	same
15	Ohio St. 6-2-0	Francis Schmidt	same
16	Georgia Tech 7-2-0	Bill Alexander	8-2-0
17	Fordham 6-2-0	Jim Crowley	same
18	Nebraska 7-1-1	Biff Jones	same
19	Oklahoma 6-2-1	Tom Stidham	same
20	Michigan 6-2-0	Fritz Crisler	same

Key Bowl Games

Sugar–#1 Texas A&M over #5 Tulane, 14-13; **Rose** –#3 USC over #2 Tennessee, 14-0; **Orange**–#16 Georgia Tech over #6 Missouri, 21-7; **Cotton**–#12 Clemson over #11 Boston College, 6-3.

1940

Final poll released Dec. 2. Top 20 regular season results after that: **Dec. 7**–#16 SMU over Rice, 7-6.

		As of Dec. 2	Head Coach	After Bowls
1	Minnesota	8-0-0	Bernie Bierman	same
2	Stanford	9-0-0	Clark Shaughnessy	10-0-0
3	Michigan	7-1-0	Fritz Crisler	same
4	Tennessee	10-0-0	Bob Neyland	10-1-0
5	Boston College	10-0-0	Frank Leahy	11-0-0
6	Texas A&M	8-1-0	Homer Norton	9-1-0
7	Nebraska	8-1-0	Biff Jones	8-2-0
8	Northwestern	6-2-0	Pappy Waldorf	same
9	Mississippi St.	9-0-1	Allyn McKeen	10-0-1
10	Washington	7-2-0	Jimmy Phelan	same
11	Santa Clara	6-1-0	Buck Shaw	same
12	Fordham	7-1-0	Jim Crowley	7-2-0
13	Georgetown	8-1-0	Jack Hagerty	8-2-0
14	Penn	6-1-0	George Munger	same
15	Cornell	6-2-0	Carl Snavely	same
16	SMU	7-1-1	Matty Bell	8-1-1
17	Hardin-Simmons	9-0-0	Warren Woodson	same
18	Duke	7-2-0	Wallace Wade	same
19	Lafayette	9-0-0	Hooks Mylin	same
20	–			

Note: Only 19 teams ranked.

Key Bowl Games

Rose–#2 Stanford over #7 Nebraska, 21-13; **Sugar**– #5 Boston College over #4 Tennessee, 19-13; **Cotton**–#6 Texas A&M over #12 Fordham, 13-12; **Orange**–#9 Mississippi St. over #13 Georgetown, 14-7.

1941

Final poll released Dec. 1. Top 20 regular season results after that: **Dec. 6**–#4 Texas over Oregon, 71-7; #9 Texas A&M over #19 Washington St., 7-0; #16 Mississippi St. over San Francisco, 26-13.

		As of Dec. 1	Head Coach	After Bowls
1	Minnesota	8-0-0	Bernie Bierman	same
2	Duke	9-0-0	Wallace Wade	9-1-0
3	Notre Dame	8-0-1	Frank Leahy	same
4	Texas	7-1-1	Dana X. Bible	8-1-1
5	Michigan	6-1-1	Fritz Crisler	same
6	Fordham	7-1-0	Jim Crowley	8-1-0
7	Missouri	8-1-0	Don Faurot	8-2-0
8	Duquesne	8-0-0	Buff Donelli	same
9	Texas A&M	8-1-0	Homer Norton	9-2-0
10	Navy	7-1-1	Swede Larson	same
11	Northwestern	5-3-0	Pappy Waldorf	same
12	Oregon St.	7-2-0	Lon Stiner	8-2-0
13	Ohio St.	6-1-1	Paul Brown	same
14	Georgia	8-1-1	Wally Butts	9-1-1
15	Penn	7-1-1	George Munger	same
16	Mississippi St.	7-1-1	Allyn McKeen	8-1-1
17	Mississippi	6-2-1	Harry Mehre	same
18	Tennessee	8-2-0	John Barnhill	same
19	Washington St.	6-3-0	Babe Hollingbery	6-4-0
20	Alabama	8-2-0	Frank Thomas	9-2-0

Note: 1942 Rose Bowl moved to Durham, N.C., for one year after outbreak of World War II.

Key Bowl Games

Rose–#12 Oregon St. over #2 Duke, 20-16; **Sugar**– #6 Fordham over #7 Missouri, 2-0; **Cotton**–#20 Alabama over #9 Texas A&M, 29-21; **Orange**–#14 Georgia over TCU, 40-26.

1942

Final poll released Nov. 30. Top 20 regular season results after that: **Dec. 5**–#6 Notre Dame tied Great Lakes Naval Station, 13-13; #13 UCLA over Idaho, 40-13; #14 William & Mary over Oklahoma, 14-7; #17 Washington St. lost to Texas A&M, 21-0; #18 Mississippi St. over San Francisco, 19-7. **Dec. 12**–#13 UCLA over USC, 14-7.

		As of Nov. 30	Head Coach	After Bowls
1	Ohio St.	9-1-0	Paul Brown	same
2	Georgia	10-1-0	Wally Butts	11-1-0
3	Wisconsin	8-1-1	Harry Stuhldreher	same
4	Tulsa	10-0-0	Henry Frnka	10-1-0
5	Georgia Tech	9-1-0	Bill Alexander	9-2-0
6	Notre Dame	7-2-1	Frank Leahy	7-2-2
7	Tennessee	8-1-1	John Barnhill	9-1-1
8	Boston College	8-1-0	Denny Myers	8-2-0
9	Michigan	7-3-0	Fritz Crisler	same
10	Alabama	7-3-0	Frank Thomas	8-3-0
11	Texas	8-2-0	Dana X. Bible	9-2-0
12	Stanford	6-4-0	Marchie Schwartz	same
13	UCLA	5-3-0	Babe Horrell	7-4-0
14	William & Mary	8-1-1	Carl Voyles	9-1-1
15	Santa Clara	7-2-0	Buck Shaw	same
16	Auburn	6-4-1	Jack Meagher	same
17	Washington St.	6-1-2	Babe Hollingbery	6-2-2
18	Mississippi St.	7-2-0	Allyn McKeen	8-2-0
19	Minnesota	5-4-0	George Hauser	same
	Holy Cross	5-4-1	Ank Scanlon	same
	Penn St.	6-1-1	Bob Higgins	same

Key Bowl Games

Rose–#2 Georgia over #13 UCLA, 9-0; **Sugar**–#7 Tennessee over #4 Tulsa, 14-7; **Cotton**–#11 Texas over #5 Georgia Tech, 14-7; **Orange**–#10 Alabama over #8 Boston College, 37-21.

1943

Final poll released Nov. 29. Top 20 regular season results after that: **Dec. 11**–#10 March Field over #19 Pacific, 19-0.

		As of Nov. 29	Head Coach	After Bowls
1	Notre Dame	9-1-0	Frank Leahy	same
2	Iowa Pre-Flight	9-1-0	Don Faurot	same
3	Michigan	8-1-0	Fritz Crisler	same
4	Navy	8-1-0	Billick Whelchel	same
5	Purdue	9-0-0	Elmer Burnham	same
6	Great Lakes Naval Station	10-2-0	Tony Hinkle	same
7	Duke	8-1-0	Eddie Cameron	same
8	DelMonte Pre-Flight	7-1-0	Bill Kern	same
9	Northwestern	6-2-0	Pappy Waldorf	same
10	March Field	8-1-0	Paul Schissler	9-1-0
11	Army	7-2-1	Red Blaik	same
12	Washington	4-0-0	Ralph Welch	4-1-0
13	Georgia Tech	7-3-0	Bill Alexander	8-3-0
14	Texas	7-1-0	Dana X. Bible	7-1-1
15	Tulsa	6-0-1	Henry Frnka	6-1-1
16	Dartmouth	6-1-0	Earl Brown	same
17	Bainbridge Navy Training School	7-0-0	Joe Maniaci	same
18	Colorado College	7-0-0	Hal White	same
19	Pacific	7-1-0	Amos A. Stagg	7-2-0
20	Penn	6-2-1	George Munger	same

Key Bowl Games

Rose–USC over #12 Washington, 29-0; **Sugar**–#13 Georgia Tech over #15 Tulsa, 20-18; **Cotton**–#14 Texas tied Randolph Field, 7-7; **Orange**–LSU over Texas A&M, 19-14.

Associated Press Final Polls (Cont.)

1944

Final poll released Dec. 4. Top 20 regular season results after that: **Dec. 10**—#3 Randolph Field over #10 March Field, 20-7; #18 Fort Pierce over Kessler Field, 34-7; Morris Field over #20 Second Air Force, 14-7.

	As of Dec. 4	Head Coach	After Bowls
1	Army 9-0-0	Red Blaik	same
2	Ohio St. 9-0-0	Carroll Widdoes	same
3	Randolph Field 10-0-0	Frank Tritico	12-0-0
4	Navy 6-3-0	Oscar Hagberg	same
5	Bainbridge Navy Training School ... 10-0-0	Joe Maniaci	same
6	Iowa Pre-Flight 10-1-0	Jack Meagher	same
7	USC 7-0-2	Jeff Cravath	8-0-2
8	Michigan 8-2-0	Fritz Crisler	same
9	Notre Dame 8-2-0	Ed McKeever	same
10	March Field 7-0-2	Paul Schissler	7-1-2
11	Duke 5-4-0	Eddie Cameron	6-4-0
12	Tennessee 7-0-1	John Barnhill	7-1-1
13	Georgia Tech 8-2-0	Bill Alexander	8-3-0
14	Norman Pre-Flight .. 6-0-0	John Gregg	same
15	Illinois 5-4-1	Ray Eliot	same
16	El Toro Marines 8-1-0	Dick Hanley	same
17	Great Lakes Naval Station 9-2-1	Paul Brown	same
18	Fort Pierce 8-0-0	Hamp Pool	9-0-0
19	St. Mary's Pre-Flight . .4-4-0	Jules Sikes	same
20	Second Air Force ... 10-2-1	Bill Reese	10-4-1

Key Bowl Games

Treasury—#3 Randolph Field over #20 Second Air Force, 13-6; **Rose**—#7 USC over #12 Tennessee, 25-0; **Sugar**—#11 Duke over #8 Alabama, 29-26; **Orange**—Tulsa over #13 Georgia Tech, 26-12; **Cotton**—Oklahoma A&M over TCU, 34-0.

1945

Final poll released Dec. 3. Top 20 regular season results after that: None.

	As of Dec. 3	Head Coach	After Bowls
1	Army 9-0-0	Red Blaik	same
2	Alabama 9-0-0	Frank Thomas	10-0-0
3	Navy 7-1-1	Oscar Hagberg	same
4	Indiana 9-0-1	Bo McMillan	same
5	Oklahoma A&M ... 8-0-0	Jim Lookabaugh	9-0-0
6	Michigan 7-3-0	Fritz Crisler	same
7	St. Mary's-CA 7-1-0	Jimmy Phelan	7-2-0
8	Penn 6-2-0	George Munger	same
9	Notre Dame 7-2-1	Hugh Devore	same
10	Texas 9-1-0	Dana X. Bible	10-1-0
11	USC 7-3-0	Jeff Cravath	7-4-0
12	Ohio St. 7-2-0	Carroll Widdoes	same
13	Duke 6-2-0	Eddie Cameron	same
14	Tennessee 8-1-0	John Barnhill	same
15	LSU 7-2-0	Bernie Moore	same
16	Holy Cross 8-1-0	John DeGrosa	8-2-0
17	Tulsa 8-2-0	Henry Frnka	8-3-0
18	Georgia 8-2-0	Wally Butts	9-2-0
19	Wake Forest 4-3-1	Peahead Walker	5-3-1
20	Columbia 8-1-0	Lou Little	same

Key Bowl Games

Rose—#2 Alabama over #11 USC, 34-14; **Sugar**— #5 Oklahoma A&M over #7 St. Mary's, 33-13; **Cotton**—#10 Texas over Missouri, 40-27; **Orange**—Miami-FL over #16 Holy Cross, 13-6.

1946

Final poll released Dec. 2. Top 20 regular season results after that: None.

	As of Dec. 2	Head Coach	After Bowls
1	Notre Dame 8-0-1	Frank Leahy	same
2	Army 9-0-1	Red Blaik	same
3	Georgia 10-0-0	Wally Butts	11-0-0
4	UCLA 10-0-0	Bert LaBrucherie	10-1-0
5	Illinois 7-2-0	Ray Eliot	8-2-0
6	Michigan 6-2-1	Fritz Crisler	same
7	Tennessee 9-1-0	Bob Neyland	9-2-0
8	LSU 9-1-0	Bernie Moore	9-1-1
9	North Carolina ... 8-1-1	Carl Snavely	8-2-1
10	Rice 8-2-0	Jess Neely	9-2-0
11	Georgia Tech 8-2-0	Bobby Dodd	9-2-0
12	Yale 7-1-1	Howard Odell	same
13	Penn 6-2-0	George Munger	same
14	Oklahoma 7-3-0	Jim Tatum	8-3-0
15	Texas 8-2-0	Dana X. Bible	same
16	Arkansas 6-3-1	John Barnhill	6-3-2
17	Tulsa 9-1-0	J.O. Brothers	same
18	N.C. State 8-2-0	Beattie Feathers	8-3-0
19	Delaware 9-0-0	Bill Murray	10-0-0
20	Indiana 6-3-0	Bo McMillan	same

Key Bowl Games

Sugar—#3 Georgia over #9 N. Carolina, 20-10; **Rose**— #5 Illinois over #4 UCLA, 45-14; **Orange**—#10 Rice over #7 Tennessee, 8-0; **Cotton**—#8 LSU tied #16 Arkansas, 0-0.

1947

Final poll released Dec. 8. Top 20 regular season results after that: None.

	As of Dec. 8	Head Coach	After Bowls
1	Notre Dame 9-0-0	Frank Leahy	same
2	Michigan 9-0-0	Fritz Crisler	10-0-0
3	SMU 9-0-1	Matty Bell	9-0-2
4	Penn St. 9-0-0	Bob Higgins	9-0-1
5	Texas 9-1-0	Blair Cherry	10-1-0
6	Alabama 8-2-0	Red Drew	8-3-0
7	Penn 7-0-1	George Munger	same
8	USC 7-1-1	Jeff Cravath	7-2-1
9	North Carolina ... 8-2-0	Carl Snavely	same
10	Georgia Tech 9-1-0	Bobby Dodd	10-1-0
11	Army 5-2-2	Red Blaik	same
12	Kansas 8-0-2	George Sauer	8-1-2
13	Mississippi 8-2-0	Johnny Vaught	9-2-0
14	William & Mary .. 9-1-0	Rube McCray	9-2-0
15	California 9-1-0	Pappy Waldorf	same
16	Oklahoma 7-2-1	Bud Wilkinson	same
17	N.C. State 5-3-1	Beattie Feathers	same
18	Rice 6-3-1	Jess Neely	same
19	Duke 4-3-2	Wallace Wade	same
20	Columbia 7-2-0	Lou Little	same

Key Bowl Games

Rose—#2 Michigan over #8 USC, 49-0; **Cotton**—#3 SMU tied #4 Penn St., 13-13; **Sugar**—#5 Texas over #6 Alabama, 27-7; **Orange**—#10 Georgia Tech over #12 Kansas, 20-14.

Note: An unprecedented "Who's No. 1?" poll was conducted by AP after the Rose Bowl game, pitting Notre Dame against Michigan. The Wolverines won the vote, 226-119, but AP ruled that the Irish would be the No. 1 team of record.

1948

Final poll released Nov. 29. Top 20 regular season results after that: **Dec. 3**–#12 Vanderbilt over Miami-FL, 33-6. **Dec. 4**–#2 Notre Dame tied USC, 14-14; #11 Clemson over The Citadel, 20-0.

		As of Nov. 29	Head Coach	After Bowls
1	Michigan	9-0-0	Bennie Oosterbaan	same
2	Notre Dame	9-0-0	Frank Leahy	9-0-1
3	North Carolina	9-0-1	Carl Snavely	9-1-1
4	California	10-0-0	Pappy Waldorf	10-1-0
5	Oklahoma	9-1-0	Bud Wilkinson	10-1-0
6	Army	8-0-1	Red Blaik	same
7	Northwestern	7-2-0	Bob Voigts	8-2-0
8	Georgia	9-1-0	Wally Butts	9-2-0
9	Oregon	9-1-0	Jim Aiken	9-2-0
10	SMU	8-1-1	Matty Bell	9-1-1
11	Clemson	9-0-0	Frank Howard	11-0-0
12	Vanderbilt	7-2-1	Red Sanders	8-2-1
13	Tulane	9-1-0	Henry Frnka	same
14	Michigan St.	6-2-2	Biggie Munn	same
15	Mississippi	8-1-0	Johnny Vaught	same
16	Minnesota	7-2-0	Bernie Bierman	same
17	William & Mary	6-2-2	Rube McCray	7-2-2
18	Penn St.	7-1-1	Bob Higgins	same
19	Cornell	8-1-0	Lefty James	same
20	Wake Forest	6-3-0	Peahead Walker	6-4-0

Note: Big Nine "no-repeat" rule kept Michigan from Rose Bowl.

Key Bowl Games

Sugar–#5 Oklahoma over #3 North Carolina, 14-6; **Rose**–#7 Northwestern over #4 Cal, 20-14; **Orange**–Texas over #8 Georgia, 41-28; **Cotton**–#10 SMU over #9 Oregon, 21-13.

1949

Final poll released Nov. 28. Top 20 regular season results after that: **Dec. 2**–#14 Maryland over Miami-FL, 13-0. **Dec. 3**–#1 Notre Dame over SMU, 27-20; #10 Pacific over Hawaii, 75-0.

		As of Nov. 28	Head Coach	After Bowls
1	Notre Dame	9-0-0	Frank Leahy	10-0-0
2	Oklahoma	10-0-0	Bud Wilkinson	11-0-0
3	California	10-0-0	Pappy Waldorf	10-1-0
4	Army	9-0-0	Red Blaik	same
5	Rice	9-1-0	Jess Neely	10-1-0
6	Ohio St.	6-1-2	Wes Fesler	7-1-2
7	Michigan	6-2-1	Bennie Oosterbaan	same
8	Minnesota	7-2-0	Bernie Bierman	same
9	LSU	8-2-0	Gaynell Tinsley	8-3-0
10	Pacific	10-0-0	Larry Siemering	11-0-0
11	Kentucky	9-2-0	Bear Bryant	9-3-0
12	Cornell	8-1-0	Lefty James	same
13	Villanova	8-1-0	Jim Leonard	same
14	Maryland	7-1-0	Jim Tatum	9-1-0
15	Santa Clara	7-2-1	Len Casanova	8-2-1
16	North Carolina	7-3-0	Carl Snavely	7-4-0
17	Tennessee	7-2-1	Bob Neyland	same
18	Princeton	6-3-0	Charlie Caldwell	same
19	Michigan St.	6-3-0	Biggie Munn	same
20	Missouri	7-3-0	Don Faurot	7-4-0
	Baylor	8-2-0	Bob Woodruff	same

Key Bowl Games

Sugar–#2 Oklahoma over #9 LSU, 35-0; **Rose**–#6 Ohio St. over #3 Cal, 17-14; **Cotton**–#5 Rice over #16 North Carolina, 27-13; **Orange**–#15 Santa Clara over #11 Kentucky, 21-13.

1950

Final poll released Nov. 27. Top 20 regular season results after that: **Nov. 30**–#3 Texas over Texas A&M, 17-0. **Dec. 1**–#15 Miami-FL over Missouri, 27–9. **Dec. 2**–#1 Oklahoma over Okla. A&M, 41-14; Navy over #2 Army, 14-2; #4 Tennessee over Vanderbilt, 43-0; #16 Alabama over Auburn, 34-0; #19 Tulsa over Houston, 28-21; #20 Tulane tied LSU, 14-14. **Dec. 9**–#3 Texas over LSU, 21-6.

		As of Nov. 27	Head Coach	After Bowls
1	Oklahoma	9-0-0	Bud Wilkinson	10-1-0
2	Army	8-0-0	Red Blaik	8-1-0
3	Texas	7-1-0	Blair Cherry	9-2-0
4	Tennessee	9-1-0	Bob Neyland	11-1-0
5	California	9-0-1	Pappy Waldorf	9-1-1
6	Princeton	9-0-0	Charlie Caldwell	same
7	Kentucky	10-1-0	Bear Bryant	11-1-0
8	Michigan St.	8-1-0	Biggie Munn	same
9	Michigan	5-3-1	Bennie Oosterbaan	6-3-1
10	Clemson	8-0-1	Frank Howard	9-0-1
11	Washington	8-2-0	Howard Odell	same
12	Wyoming	9-0-0	Bowden Wyatt	10-0-0
13	Illinois	7-2-0	Ray Eliot	same
14	Ohio St.	6-3-0	Wes Fesler	same
15	Miami-FL	8-0-1	Andy Gustafson	9-1-1
16	Alabama	8-2-0	Red Drew	9-2-0
17	Nebraska	6-2-1	Bill Glassford	same
18	Wash. & Lee	8-2-0	George Barclay	8-3-0
19	Tulsa	8-1-1	J.O. Brothers	9-1-1
20	Tulane	6-2-0	Henry Frnka	6-2-1

Key Bowl Games

Sugar–#7 Kentucky over #1 Oklahoma, 13-7; **Cotton**–#4 Tennessee over #3 Texas, 20-14; **Rose**–#9 Michigan over #5 Cal, 14-6; **Orange**–#10 Clemson over #15 Miami-FL, 15-14.

1951

Final poll released Dec. 3. Top 20 regular season results after that: None.

		As of Dec. 3	Head Coach	After Bowls
1	Tennessee	10-0-0	Bob Neyland	10-1-0
2	Michigan St.	9-0-0	Biggie Munn	same
3	Maryland	9-0-0	Jim Tatum	10-0-0
4	Illinois	8-0-1	Ray Eliot	9-0-1
5	Georgia Tech	10-0-1	Bobby Dodd	11-0-1
6	Princeton	9-0-0	Charlie Caldwell	same
7	Stanford	9-1-0	Chuck Taylor	9-2-0
8	Wisconsin	7-1-1	Ivy Williamson	same
9	Baylor	8-1-1	George Sauer	8-2-1
10	Oklahoma	8-2-0	Bud Wilkinson	same
11	TCU	6-4-0	Dutch Meyer	6-5-0
12	California	8-2-0	Pappy Waldorf	same
13	Virginia	8-1-0	Art Guepe	same
14	San Francisco	9-0-0	Joe Kuharich	same
15	Kentucky	7-4-0	Bear Bryant	8-4-0
16	Boston Univ.	6-4-0	Buff Donelli	same
17	UCLA	5-3-1	Red Sanders	same
18	Washington St.	7-3-0	Forest Evashevski	same
19	Holy Cross	8-2-0	Eddie Anderson	same
	Clemson	7-2-0	Frank Howard	7-3-0

Key Bowl Games

Sugar–#3 Maryland over #1 Tennessee, 28-13; **Rose**– #4 Illinois over #7 Stanford, 40-7; **Orange**–#5 Georgia Tech over #9 Baylor, 17-14; **Cotton**–#15 Kentucky over #11 TCU, 20-7.

Associated Press Final Polls (Cont.)

1952

Final poll released Dec. 1. Top 20 regular season results after that: **Dec. 6**–#15 Florida over #20 Kentucky, 27-20.

		As of Dec. 1	Head Coach	After Bowls
1	Michigan St.	9-0-0	Biggie Munn	same
2	Georgia Tech	11-0-0	Bobby Dodd	12-0-0
3	Notre Dame	7-2-1	Frank Leahy	same
4	Oklahoma	8-1-1	Bud Wilkinson	same
5	USC	9-1-0	Jess Hill	10-1-0
6	UCLA	8-1-0	Red Sanders	same
7	Mississippi	8-0-2	Johnny Vaught	8-1-2
8	Tennessee	8-1-1	Bob Neyland	8-2-1
9	Alabama	9-2-0	Red Drew	10-2-0
10	Texas	8-2-0	Ed Price	9-2-0
11	Wisconsin	6-2-1	Ivy Williamson	6-3-1
12	Tulsa	8-1-1	J.O. Brothers	8-2-1
13	Maryland	7-2-0	Jim Tatum	same
14	Syracuse	7-2-0	Ben Schwartzwalder	7-3-0
15	Florida	6-3-0	Bob Woodruff	8-3-0
16	Duke	8-2-0	Bill Murray	same
17	Ohio St.	6-3-0	Woody Hayes	same
18	Purdue	4-3-2	Stu Holcomb	same
19	Princeton	8-1-0	Charlie Caldwell	same
20	Kentucky	5-3-2	Bear Bryant	5-4-2

Note: Michigan St. would officially join Big Ten in 1953.

Key Bowl Games

Sugar–#2 Georgia Tech over #7 Ole Miss, 24-7; **Rose**–#5 USC over #11 Wisconsin, 7-0; **Cotton**–#10 Texas over #8 Tennessee, 16-0; **Orange**–#9 Alabama over #14 Syracuse, 61-6.

1953

Final poll released Nov. 30. Top 20 regular season results after that: **Dec. 5**–#2 Notre Dame over SMU, 40-14.

		As of Nov. 30	Head Coach	After Bowls
1	Maryland	10-0-0	Jim Tatum	10-1-0
2	Notre Dame	8-0-1	Frank Leahy	9-0-1
3	Michigan St.	8-1-0	Biggie Munn	9-1-0
4	Oklahoma	8-1-1	Bud Wilkinson	9-1-1
5	UCLA	8-1-0	Red Sanders	8-2-0
6	Rice	8-2-0	Jess Neely	9-2-0
7	Illinois	7-1-1	Ray Eliot	same
8	Georgia Tech	8-2-1	Bobby Dodd	9-2-1
9	Iowa	5-3-1	Forest Evashevski	same
10	West Virginia	8-1-0	Art Lewis	8-2-0
11	Texas	7-3-0	Ed Price	same
12	Texas Tech	10-1-0	DeWitt Weaver	11-1-0
13	Alabama	6-2-3	Red Drew	6-3-3
14	Army	7-1-1	Red Blaik	same
15	Wisconsin	6-2-1	Ivy Williamson	same
16	Kentucky	7-2-1	Bear Bryant	same
17	Auburn	7-2-1	Shug Jordan	7-3-1
18	Duke	7-2-1	Bill Murray	same
19	Stanford	6-3-1	Chuck Taylor	same
20	Michigan	6-3-0	Bennie Oosterbaan	same

Key Bowl Games

Orange–#4 Oklahoma over #1 Maryland, 7-0; **Rose**–#3 Michigan St. over #5 UCLA, 28-20; **Cotton**–#6 Rice over #13 Alabama, 28-6; **Sugar**–#8 Georgia Tech over #10 West Virginia, 42-19.

1954

Final poll released Nov. 29. Top 20 regular season results after that: **Dec. 4**–#4 Notre Dame over SMU, 26-14.

		As of Nov. 29	Head Coach	After Bowls
1	Ohio St.	9-0-0	Woody Hayes	10-0-0
2	UCLA	9-0-0	Red Sanders	same
3	Oklahoma	10-0-0	Bud Wilkinson	same
4	Notre Dame	8-1-0	Terry Brennan	9-1-0
5	Navy	7-2-0	Eddie Erdelatz	8-2-0
6	Mississippi	9-1-0	Johnny Vaught	9-2-0
7	Army	7-2-0	Red Blaik	same
8	Maryland	7-2-1	Jim Tatum	same
9	Wisconsin	7-2-0	Ivy Williamson	same
10	Arkansas	8-2-0	Bowden Wyatt	8-3-0
11	Miami-FL	8-1-0	Andy Gustafson	same
12	West Virginia	8-1-0	Art Lewis	same
13	Auburn	7-3-0	Shug Jordan	8-3-0
14	Duke	7-2-1	Bill Murray	8-2-1
15	Michigan	6-3-0	Bennie Oosterbaan	same
16	Virginia Tech	8-0-1	Frank Moseley	same
17	USC	8-3-0	Jess Hill	8-4-0
18	Baylor	7-3-0	George Sauer	7-4-0
19	Rice	7-3-0	Jess Neely	same
20	Penn St.	7-2-0	Rip Engle	same

Note: PCC and Big Seven "no-repeat" rules kept UCLA and Oklahoma from Rose and Orange bowls, respectively.

Key Bowl Games

Rose–#1 Ohio St. over #17 USC, 20-7; **Sugar**–#5 Navy over #6 Ole Miss, 21-0; **Cotton**–Georgia Tech over #10 Arkansas, 14-6; **Orange**–#14 Duke over Nebraska, 34-7.

1955

Final poll released Nov. 28. Top 20 regular season results after that: None.

		As of Nov. 28	Head Coach	After Bowls
1	Oklahoma	10-0-0	Bud Wilkinson	11-0-0
2	Michigan St.	8-1-0	Duffy Daugherty	9-1-0
3	Maryland	10-0-0	Jim Tatum	10-1-0
4	UCLA	9-1-0	Red Sanders	9-2-0
5	Ohio St.	7-2-0	Woody Hayes	same
6	TCU	9-1-0	Abe Martin	9-2-0
7	Georgia Tech	8-1-1	Bobby Dodd	9-1-1
8	Auburn	8-1-1	Shug Jordan	8-2-1
9	Notre Dame	8-2-0	Terry Brennan	same
10	Mississippi	9-1-0	Johnny Vaught	10-1-0
11	Pittsburgh	7-3-0	John Michelosen	7-4-0
12	Michigan	7-2-0	Bennie Oosterbaan	same
13	USC	6-4-0	Jess Hill	same
14	Miami-FL	6-3-0	Andy Gustafson	same
15	Miami-OH	9-0-0	Ara Parseghian	same
16	Stanford	6-3-1	Chuck Taylor	same
17	Texas A&M	7-2-1	Bear Bryant	same
18	Navy	6-2-1	Eddie Erdelatz	same
19	West Virginia	8-2-0	Art Lewis	same
20	Army	6-3-0	Red Blaik	same

Note: Big Ten "no-repeat" rule kept Ohio St. from Rose Bowl.

Key Bowl Games

Orange–#1 Oklahoma over #3 Maryland, 20-6; **Rose**–#2 Michigan St. over #4 UCLA, 17-14; **Cotton**–#10 Ole Miss over #6 TCU, 14-13; **Sugar**–#7 Georgia Tech over #11 Pitt, 7-0; **Gator**–Vanderbilt over #8 Auburn, 25-13.

1956

Final poll released Dec. 3. Top 20 regular season results after that: **Dec. 8**–#13 Pitt over #6 Miami-FL, 14-7.

		As of Dec. 3	Head Coach	After Bowls
1	Oklahoma	10-0-0	Bud Wilkinson	same
2	Tennessee	10-0-0	Bowden Wyatt	10-1-0
3	Iowa	8-1-0	Forest Evashevski	9-1-0
4	Georgia Tech	9-1-0	Bobby Dodd	10-1-0
5	Texas A&M	9-0-1	Bear Bryant	same
6	Miami-FL	8-0-1	Andy Gustafson	8-1-1
7	Michigan	7-2-0	Bennie Oosterbaan	same
8	Syracuse	7-1-0	Ben Schwartzwalder	7-2-0
9	Michigan St.	7-2-0	Duffy Daugherty	same
10	Oregon St.	7-2-1	Tommy Prothro	7-3-1
11	Baylor	8-2-0	Sam Boyd	9-2-0
12	Minnesota	6-1-2	Murray Warmath	same
13	Pittsburgh	6-2-1	John Michelosen	7-3-1
14	TCU	7-3-0	Abe Martin	8-3-0
15	Ohio St.	6-3-0	Woody Hayes	same
16	Navy	6-1-2	Eddie Erdelatz	same
17	G. Washington	7-1-1	Gene Sherman	8-1-1
18	USC	8-2-0	Jess Hill	same
19	Clemson	7-1-2	Frank Howard	7-2-2
20	Colorado	7-2-1	Dallas Ward	8-2-1

Note: Big Seven "no-repeat" rule kept Oklahoma from Orange Bowl and Texas A&M was on probation.

Key Bowl Games
Sugar–#11 Baylor over #2 Tennessee, 13-7; **Rose**– #3 Iowa over #10 Oregon St., 35-19; **Gator**–#4 Georgia Tech over #13 Pitt, 21-14; **Cotton**–#14 TCU over #8 Syracuse, 28-27; **Orange**–#20 Colorado over #19 Clemson, 27-21.

1957

Final poll released Dec. 2. Top 20 regular season results after that: **Dec. 7**–#10 Notre Dame over SMU, 54-21.

		As of Dec. 2	Head Coach	After Bowls
1	Auburn	10-0-0	Shug Jordan	same
2	Ohio St.	8-1-0	Woody Hayes	9-1-0
3	Michigan St.	8-1-0	Duffy Daugherty	same
4	Oklahoma	9-1-0	Bud Wilkinson	10-1-0
5	Navy	8-1-1	Eddie Erdelatz	9-1-1
6	Iowa	7-1-1	Forest Evashevski	same
7	Mississippi	8-1-1	Johnny Vaught	9-1-1
8	Rice	7-3-0	Jess Neely	7-4-0
9	Texas A&M	8-2-0	Bear Bryant	8-3-0
10	Notre Dame	6-3-0	Terry Brennan	7-3-0
11	Texas	6-3-1	Darrell Royal	6-4-1
12	Arizona St.	10-0-0	Dan Devine	same
13	Tennessee	7-3-0	Bowden Wyatt	8-3-0
14	Mississippi St.	6-2-1	Wade Walker	same
15	N.C. State	7-1-2	Earle Edwards	same
16	Duke	6-2-2	Bill Murray	6-3-2
17	Florida	6-2-1	Bob Woodruff	same
18	Army	7-2-0	Red Blaik	same
19	Wisconsin	6-3-0	Milt Bruhn	same
20	VMI	9-0-1	John McKenna	same

Note: Auburn on probation, ineligible for bowl game.

Key Bowl Games
Rose–#2 Ohio St. over Oregon, 10-7; **Orange**–#4 Oklahoma over #6 Duke, 48-21; **Cotton**–#5 Navy over #8 Rice, 20-7; **Sugar**–#7 Ole Miss over #11 Texas, 39-7; **Gator**–#13 Tennessee over #9 Texas A&M, 3-0.

1958

Final poll released Dec. 1. Top 20 regular season results after that: None.

		As of Dec. 1	Head Coach	After Bowls
1	LSU	10-0-0	Paul Dietzel	11-0-0
2	Iowa	7-1-1	Forest Evashevski	8-1-1
3	Army	8-0-1	Red Blaik	same
4	Auburn	9-0-1	Shug Jordan	same
5	Oklahoma	9-1-0	Bud Wilkinson	10-1-0
6	Air Force	9-0-1	Ben Martin	9-0-2
7	Wisconsin	7-1-1	Milt Bruhn	same
8	Ohio St.	6-1-2	Woody Hayes	same
9	Syracuse	8-1-0	Ben Schwartzwalder	8-2-0
10	TCU	8-2-0	Abe Martin	8-2-1
11	Mississippi	8-2-0	Johnny Vaught	9-2-0
12	Clemson	8-2-0	Frank Howard	8-3-0
13	Purdue	6-1-2	Jack Mollenkopf	same
14	Florida	6-3-1	Bob Woodruff	6-4-1
15	South Carolina	7-3-0	Warren Giese	same
16	California	7-3-0	Pete Elliott	7-4-0
17	Notre Dame	6-4-0	Terry Brennan	same
18	SMU	6-4-0	Bill Meek	same
19	Oklahoma St.	7-3-0	Cliff Speegle	8-3-0
20	Rutgers	8-1-0	John Stiegman	same

Key Bowl Games
Sugar–#1 LSU over #12 Clemson, 7-0; **Rose**–#2 Iowa over #16 Cal, 38-12; **Orange**–#5 Oklahoma over #9 Syracuse, 21-6; **Cotton**–#6 Air Force tied #10 TCU, 0-0.

1959

Final poll released Dec. 7. Top 20 regular season results after that: None.

		As of Dec. 7	Head Coach	After Bowls
1	Syracuse	10-0-0	Ben Schwartzwalder	11-0-0
2	Mississippi	9-1-0	Johnny Vaught	10-1-0
3	LSU	9-1-0	Paul Dietzel	9-2-0
4	Texas	9-1-0	Darrell Royal	9-2-0
5	Georgia	9-1-0	Wally Butts	10-1-0
6	Wisconsin	7-2-0	Milt Bruhn	7-3-0
7	TCU	8-2-0	Abe Martin	8-3-0
8	Washington	9-1-0	Jim Owens	10-1-0
9	Arkansas	8-2-0	Frank Broyles	9-2-0
10	Alabama	7-1-2	Bear Bryant	7-2-2
11	Clemson	8-2-0	Frank Howard	9-2-0
12	Penn St.	8-2-0	Rip Engle	9-2-0
13	Illinois	5-3-1	Ray Eliot	same
14	USC	8-2-0	Don Clark	same
15	Oklahoma	7-3-0	Bud Wilkinson	same
16	Wyoming	9-1-0	Bob Devaney	same
17	Notre Dame	5-5-0	Joe Kuharich	same
18	Missouri	6-4-0	Dan Devine	6-5-0
19	Florida	5-4-1	Bob Woodruff	same
20	Pittsburgh	6-4-0	John Michelosen	same

Note: Big Seven "no-repeat" rule kept Oklahoma from Orange Bowl.

Key Bowl Games
Cotton–#1 Syracuse over #4 Texas, 23-14; **Sugar**– #2 Ole Miss over #3 LSU, 21-0; **Orange**–#5 Georgia over #18 Missouri, 14-0; **Rose**–#8 Washington over #6 Wisconsin, 44-8; **Bluebonnet**–#11 Clemson over #7 TCU, 23-7; **Gator**–#9 Arkansas over Georgia Tech, 14-7; **Liberty**–#12 Penn St. over #10 Alabama, 7-0.

The Special Election That Didn't Count

There was one No. 1 vs No. 2 confrontation not noted in the Number 1 vs. Number 2 table on pages 164-5. It came in a special election or re-vote of AP selectors following the 1948 Rose Bowl. Here's what happened: Unbeaten Notre Dame was declared 1947 national champion by AP on Dec. 8, two days after closing out an undefeated season with a 38-7 rout of then third-ranked USC in Los Angeles. Twenty-four days later, however, unbeaten Michigan, AP's final No. 2 team, clobbered now 8th-ranked USC, 49-0, in the Rose Bowl. An immediate cry went up for an unprecedented two-team, "Who's No. 1" ballot and AP gave in. Michigan won the election, 226-119, with 12 voters calling it even. However, AP ruled that the Dec. 8 final poll won by Notre Dame would be the vote of record.

Associated Press Final Polls (Cont.)

1960

Final poll released Nov. 28. Top 20 regular season results after that: **Dec. 3**–UCLA over #10 Duke, 27-6.

		As of Nov. 28	Head Coach	After Bowls
1	Minnesota	8-1-0	Murray Warmath	8-2-0
2	Mississippi	9-0-1	Johnny Vaught	10-0-1
3	Iowa	8-1-0	Forest Evashevski	same
4	Navy	9-1-0	Wayne Hardin	9-2-0
5	Missouri	9-1-0	Dan Devine	10-1-0
6	Washington	9-1-0	Jim Owens	10-1-0
7	Arkansas	8-2-0	Frank Broyles	8-3-0
8	Ohio St.	7-2-0	Woody Hayes	same
9	Alabama	8-1-1	Bear Bryant	8-1-2
10	Duke	7-2-0	Bill Murray	8-3-0
11	Kansas	7-2-1	Jack Mitchell	same
12	Baylor	8-2-0	John Bridgers	8-3-0
13	Auburn	8-2-0	Shug Jordan	same
14	Yale	9-0-0	Jordan Olivar	same
15	Michigan St.	6-2-1	Duffy Daugherty	same
16	Penn St.	6-3-0	Rip Engle	7-3-0
17	New Mexico St.	10-0-0	Warren Woodson	11-0-0
18	Florida	8-2-0	Ray Graves	9-2-0
19	Syracuse	7-2-0	Ben Schwartzwalder	same
	Purdue	4-4-1	Jack Mollenkopf	same

Key Bowl Games

Rose–#6 Washington over #1 Minnesota, 17-7; **Sugar**–#2 Ole Miss over Rice, 14-6; **Orange**–#5 Missouri over #4 Navy, 21-14; **Cotton**–#10 Duke over #7 Arkansas, 7-6; **Bluebonnet**–#9 Alabama tied Texas, 3-3.

1961

Final poll released Dec. 4. Top 20 regular season results after that: None.

		As of Dec. 4	Head Coach	After Bowls
1	Alabama	10-0-0	Bear Bryant	11-0-0
2	Ohio St.	8-0-1	Woody Hayes	same
3	Texas	9-1-0	Darrell Royal	10-1-0
4	LSU	9-1-0	Paul Dietzel	10-1-0
5	Mississippi	9-1-0	Johnny Vaught	9-2-0
6	Minnesota	7-2-0	Murray Warmath	8-2-0
7	Colorado	9-1-0	Sonny Grandelius	9-2-0
8	Michigan St.	7-2-0	Duffy Daugherty	same
9	Arkansas	8-2-0	Frank Broyles	8-3-0
10	Utah St.	9-0-1	John Ralston	9-1-1
11	Missouri	7-2-1	Dan Devine	same
12	Purdue	6-3-0	Jack Mollenkopf	same
13	Georgia Tech	7-3-0	Bobby Dodd	7-4-0
14	Syracuse	7-3-0	Ben Schwartzwalder	8-3-0
15	Rutgers	9-0-0	John Bateman	same
16	UCLA	7-3-0	Bill Barnes	7-4-0
17	Rice	7-3-0	Jess Neely	7-4-0
	Penn St.	7-3-0	Rip Engle	8-3-0
	Arizona	8-1-1	Jim LaRue	same
20	Duke	7-3-0	Bill Murray	same

Note: Ohio St. faculty council turned down Rose Bowl invitation citing concern with OSU's overemphasis on sports.

Key Bowl Games

Sugar–#1 Alabama over #9 Arkansas, 10-3; **Cotton**–#3 Texas over #5 Ole Miss, 12-7; **Orange**–#4 LSU over #7 Colorado, 25-7; **Rose**–#6 Minnesota over #16 UCLA, 21-3; **Gotham**–Baylor over #10 Utah St., 24-9.

1962

Final poll released Dec. 3. Top 10 regular season results after that: None.

		As of Dec. 3	Head Coach	After Bowls
1	USC	10-0-0	John McKay	11-0-0
2	Wisconsin	8-1-0	Milt Bruhn	8-2-0
3	Mississippi	9-0-0	Johnny Vaught	10-0-0
4	Texas	9-0-1	Darrell Royal	9-1-1
5	Alabama	9-1-0	Bear Bryant	10-1-0
6	Arkansas	9-1-0	Frank Broyles	9-2-0
7	LSU	8-1-1	Charlie McClendon	9-1-1
8	Oklahoma	8-2-0	Bud Wilkinson	8-3-0
9	Penn St.	9-1-0	Rip Engle	9-2-0
10	Minnesota	6-2-1	Murray Warmath	same

Key Bowl Games

Rose–#1 USC over #2 Wisconsin, 42-37; **Sugar**–#3 Ole Miss over #6 Arkansas, 17-13; **Cotton**–#7 LSU over #4 Texas, 13-0; **Orange**–#5 Alabama over #8 Oklahoma, 17-0; **Gator**–Florida over #9 Penn St.,17-7.

1963

Final poll released Dec. 9. Top 10 regular season results after that: **Dec.14**–#8 Alabama over Miami-FL, 17-12.

		As of Dec. 9	Head Coach	After Bowls
1	Texas	10-0-0	Darrell Royal	11-0-0
2	Navy	9-1-0	Wayne Hardin	9-2-0
3	Illinois	7-1-1	Pete Elliott	8-1-1
4	Pittsburgh	9-1-0	John Michelosen	same
5	Auburn	9-1-0	Shug Jordan	9-2-0
6	Nebraska	9-1-0	Bob Devaney	10-1-0
7	Mississippi	7-0-2	Johnny Vaught	7-1-2
8	Alabama	7-2-0	Bear Bryant	9-2-0
9	Michigan St.	6-2-1	Duffy Daugherty	same
10	Oklahoma	8-2-0	Bud Wilkinson	same

Key Bowl Games

Cotton–#1 Texas over #2 Navy, 28-6; **Rose**–#3 Illinois over Washington, 17-7; **Orange**–#6 Nebraska over #5 Auburn, 13-7; **Sugar**–#8 Alabama over #7 Ole Miss, 12-7.

1964

Final poll released Nov. 30. Top 10 regular season results after that: **Dec. 5**–Florida over #7 LSU, 20-6.

		As of Nov. 30	Head Coach	After Bowls
1	Alabama	10-0-0	Bear Bryant	10-1-0
2	Arkansas	10-0-0	Frank Broyles	11-0-0
3	Notre Dame	9-1-0	Ara Parseghian	same
4	Michigan	8-1-0	Bump Elliott	9-1-0
5	Texas	9-1-0	Darrell Royal	10-1-0
6	Nebraska	9-1-0	Bob Devaney	9-2-0
7	LSU	7-1-1	Charlie McClendon	8-2-1
8	Oregon St.	8-2-0	Tommy Prothro	8-3-0
9	Ohio St.	7-2-0	Woody Hayes	same
10	USC	7-3-0	John McKay	same

Key Bowl Games

Orange–#5 Texas over #1 Alabama, 21-17; **Cotton**–#2 Arkansas over #6 Nebraska, 10-7; **Rose**– #4 Michigan over #8 Oregon St., 34-7; **Sugar**–#7 LSU over Syracuse, 13-10.

1965

Final poll taken after bowl games for the first time.

	After Bowls	Head Coach	Regular Season
1 Alabama	9-1-1	Bear Bryant	8-1-1
2 Michigan St.	10-1-0	Duffy Daugherty	10-0-0
3 Arkansas	10-1-0	Frank Broyles	10-0-0
4 UCLA	8-2-1	Tommy Prothro	7-1-1
5 Nebraska	10-1-0	Bob Devaney	10-0-0
6 Missouri	8-2-1	Dan Devine	7-2-1
7 Tennessee	8-1-2	Doug Dickey	6-1-2
8 LSU	8-3-0	Charlie McClendon	7-3-0
9 Notre Dame	7-2-1	Ara Parseghian	same
10 USC	7-2-1	John McKay	same

Key Bowl Games

Rankings below reflect final regular season poll, released Nov. 29. No bowls for then #8 USC or #9 Notre Dame. **Rose**–#5 UCLA over #1 Michigan St., 14-12; **Cotton**–LSU over #2 Arkansas, 14-7; **Orange**–#4 Alabama over #3 Nebraska, 39-28; **Sugar**–#6 Missouri over Florida, 20-18; **Bluebonnet**–#7 Tennessee over Tulsa, 27-6; **Gator**–Georgia Tech over #10 Texas Tech, 31-21.

1966

Final poll released Dec. 5, returning to pre-bowl status. Top 10 regular season results after that: None.

	As of Dec. 5	Head Coach	After Bowls
1 Notre Dame	9-0-1	Ara Parseghian	same
2 Michigan St.	9-0-1	Duffy Daugherty	same
3 Alabama	10-0-0	Bear Bryant	11-0-0
4 Georgia	9-1-0	Vince Dooley	10-1-0
5 UCLA	9-1-0	Tommy Prothro	same
6 Nebraska	9-1-0	Bob Devaney	9-2-0
7 Purdue	8-2-0	Jack Mollenkopf	9-2-0
8 Georgia Tech	9-1-0	Bobby Dodd	9-2-0
9 Miami-FL	7-2-1	Charlie Tate	8-2-1
10 SMU	8-2-0	Hayden Fry	8-3-0

Key Bowl Games

Sugar–#3 Alabama over #6 Nebraska, 34-7; **Cotton**–#4 Georgia over #10 SMU, 24-9; **Rose**–#7 Purdue over USC, 14-13; **Orange**–Florida over #8 Georgia Tech, 27-12; **Liberty**–#9 Miami-FL over Virginia Tech, 14-7.

1967

Final poll released Nov. 27. Top 10 regular season results after that: **Dec. 2**–#2 Tennessee over Vanderbilt, 41-14; #3 Oklahoma over Oklahoma St., 38-14; #8 Alabama over Auburn, 7-3.

	As of Nov. 27	Head Coach	After Bowls
1 USC	9-1-0	John McKay	10-1-0
2 Tennessee	8-1-0	Doug Dickey	9-2-0
3 Oklahoma	8-1-0	Chuck Fairbanks	10-1-0
4 Indiana	9-1-0	John Pont	9-2-0
5 Notre Dame	8-2-0	Ara Parseghian	same
6 Wyoming	10-0-0	Lloyd Eaton	10-1-0
7 Oregon St.	7-2-1	Dee Andros	same
8 Alabama	7-1-1	Bear Bryant	8-2-1
9 Purdue	8-2-0	Jack Mollenkopf	8-2-1
10 Penn St.	8-2-0	Joe Paterno	8-2-1

Key Bowl Games

Rose–#1 USC over #4 Indiana, 14-3; **Orange**–#3 Oklahoma over #2 Tennessee, 26-24; **Sugar**–LSU over #6 Wyoming, 20-13; **Cotton**–Texas A&M over #8 Alabama, 20-16; **Gator**–#10 Penn St. tied Florida St. 17-17.

1968

Final poll taken after bowl games for first time since close of 1965 season.

	After Bowls	Head Coach	Regular Season
1 Ohio St.	10-0-0	Woody Hayes	9-0-0
2 Penn St.	11-0-0	Joe Paterno	10-0-0
3 Texas	9-1-1	Darrell Royal	8-1-1
4 USC	9-1-1	John McKay	9-0-1
5 Notre Dame	7-2-1	Ara Parseghian	same
6 Arkansas	10-1-0	Frank Broyles	9-1-0
7 Kansas	9-2-0	Pepper Rodgers	9-1-0
8 Georgia	8-1-2	Vince Dooley	8-0-2
9 Missouri	8-3-0	Dan Devine	7-3-0
10 Purdue	8-2-0	Jack Mollenkopf	same
11 Oklahoma	7-4-0	Chuck Fairbanks	7-3-0
12 Michigan	8-2-0	Bump Elliott	same
13 Tennessee	8-2-1	Doug Dickey	8-1-1
14 SMU	8-3-0	Hayden Fry	7-3-0
15 Oregon St.	7-3-0	Dee Andros	same
16 Auburn	7-4-0	Shug Jordan	6-4-0
17 Alabama	8-3-0	Bear Bryant	8-2-0
18 Houston	6-2-2	Bill Yeoman	same
19 LSU	8-3-0	Charlie McClendon	7-3-0
20 Ohio Univ.	10-1-0	Bill Hess	10-0-0

Key Bowl Games

Rankings below reflect final regular season poll, released Dec. 2. No bowls for then #7 Notre Dame and #11 Purdue. **Rose**–#1 Ohio St. over #2 USC, 27-16; **Orange**–#3 Penn St. over #6 Kansas, 15-14; **Sugar**–#9 Arkansas over #4 Georgia, 16-2; **Cotton**–#5 Texas over #8 Tennessee, 36-13; **Bluebonnet**–#20 SMU over #10 Oklahoma, 28-27; **Gator**–#16 Missouri over #12 Alabama, 35-10.

1969

Final poll taken after bowl games.

	After Bowls	Head Coach	Regular Season
1 Texas	11-0-0	Darrell Royal	10-0-0
2 Penn St.	11-0-0	Joe Paterno	10-0-0
3 USC	10-0-1	John McKay	9-0-1
4 Ohio St.	8-1-0	Woody Hayes	same
5 Notre Dame	8-2-1	Ara Parseghian	8-1-1
6 Missouri	9-2-0	Dan Devine	9-1-0
7 Arkansas	9-2-0	Frank Broyles	9-1-0
8 Mississippi	8-3-0	Johnny Vaught	7-3-0
9 Michigan	8-3-0	Bo Schembechler	8-2-0
10 LSU	9-1-0	Charlie McClendon	same
11 Nebraska	9-2-0	Bob Devaney	8-2-0
12 Houston	9-2-0	Bill Yeoman	8-2-0
13 UCLA	8-1-1	Tommy Prothro	same
14 Florida	9-1-1	Ray Graves	8-1-1
15 Tennessee	9-2-0	Doug Dickey	9-1-0
16 Colorado	8-3-0	Eddie Crowder	7-3-0
17 West Virginia	10-1-0	Jim Carlen	9-1-0
18 Purdue	8-2-0	Jack Mollenkopf	same
19 Stanford	7-2-1	John Ralston	same
20 Auburn	8-3-0	Shug Jordan	8-2-0

Key Bowl Games

Rankings below reflect final regular season poll, released Dec. 8. No bowls for then #4 Ohio St., #8 LSU and #10 UCLA.

Cotton–#1 Texas over #9 Notre Dame, 21-17; **Orange**–#2 Penn St. over #6 Missouri, 10-3; **Sugar**–#13 Ole Miss over #3 Arkansas, 27-22; **Rose**–#5 USC over #7 Michigan, 10-3.

Associated Press Final Polls (Cont.)

1970

	After Bowls	Head Coach	Regular Season
1	Nebraska.......11-0-1	Bob Devaney	10-0-1
2	Notre Dame 10-1-0	Ara Parseghian	9-0-1
3	Texas 10-1-0	Darrell Royal	10-0-0
4	Tennessee.......11-1-0	Bill Battle	10-1-0
5	Ohio St. 9-1-0	Woody Hayes	9-0-0
6	Arizona St. 11-0-0	Frank Kush	10-0-0
7	LSU 9-3-0	Charlie McClendon	9-2-0
8	Stanford 9-3-0	John Ralston	8-3-0
9	Michigan 9-1-0	Bo Schembechler	same
10	Auburn 9-2-0	Shug Jordan	8-2-0
11	Arkansas 9-2-0	Frank Broyles	same
12	Toledo 12-0-0	Frank Lauterbur	11-0-0
13	Georgia Tech.....9-3-0	Bud Carson	8-3-0
14	Dartmouth 9-0-0	Bob Blackman	same
15	USC 6-4-1	John McKay	same
16	Air Force 9-3-0	Ben Martin	9-2-0
17	Tulane 8-4-0	Jim Pittman	7-4-0
18	Penn St. 7-3-0	Joe Paterno	same
19	Houston 8-3-0	Bill Yeoman	same
20	Oklahoma 7-4-1	Chuck Fairbanks	7-4-0
	Mississippi 7-4-0	Johnny Vaught	7-3-0

Key Bowl Games

Rankings below reflect final regular season poll, released Dec. 7. No bowls for then #4 Arkansas and #7 Michigan.
Cotton–#6 Notre Dame over #1 Texas, 24-11; **Rose**– #12 Stanford over #2 Ohio St., 27-17; **Orange**–#3 Nebraska over #8 LSU, 17-12; **Sugar**– #5 Tennessee over #11 Air Force, 34-13; **Peach**–#9 Ariz. St. over N. Carolina, 48-26.

1971

	After Bowls	Head Coach	Regular Season
1	Nebraska.......13-0-0	Bob Devaney	12-0-0
2	Oklahoma 11-1-0	Chuck Fairbanks	10-1-0
3	Colorado 10-2-0	Eddie Crowder	9-2-0
4	Alabama 11-1-0	Bear Bryant	11-0-0
5	Penn St. 11-1-0	Joe Paterno	10-1-0
6	Michigan 11-1-0	Bo Schembechler	11-0-0
7	Georgia 11-1-0	Vince Dooley	10-1-0
8	Arizona St. 11-1-0	Frank Kush	10-1-0
9	Tennessee 10-2-0	Bill Battle	9-2-0
10	Stanford 9-3-0	John Ralston	8-3-0
11	LSU 9-3-0	Charlie McClendon	8-3-0
12	Auburn 9-2-0	Shug Jordan	9-1-0
13	Notre Dame......8-2-0	Ara Parseghian	same
14	Toledo 12-0-0	John Murphy	11-0-0
15	Mississippi 10-2-0	Billy Kinard	9-2-0
16	Arkansas 8-3-1	Frank Broyles	8-2-1
17	Houston 9-3-0	Bill Yeoman	9-2-0
18	Texas...........8-3-0	Darrell Royal	8-2-0
19	Washington 8-3-0	Jim Owens	same
20	USC 6-4-1	John McKay	same

Key Bowl Games

Rankings below reflect final regular season poll, released Dec. 6.
Orange–#1 Nebraska over #2 Alabama, 38-6; **Sugar**–#3 Oklahoma over #5 Auburn, 40-22; **Rose**–#16 Stanford over #4 Michigan, 13-12; **Gator**–#6 Georgia over N. Carolina, 7-3; **Bluebonnet**–#7 Colorado over #15 Houston, 29-17; **Fiesta**–#8 Ariz. St. over Florida St., 45-38; **Cotton**–#10 Penn St. over #12 Texas, 30-6.

1972

	After Bowls	Head Coach	Regular Season
1	USC 12-0-0	John McKay	11-0-0
2	Oklahoma 11-1-0	Chuck Fairbanks	10-1-0
3	Texas 10-1-0	Darrell Royal	9-1-0
4	Nebraska........9-2-1	Bob Devaney	8-2-1
5	Auburn 10-1-0	Shug Jordan	9-1-0
6	Michigan 10-1-0	Bo Schembechler	same
7	Alabama 10-2-0	Bear Bryant	10-1-0
8	Tennessee 10-2-0	Bill Battle	9-2-0
9	Ohio St. 9-2-0	Woody Hayes	9-1-0
10	Penn St. 10-2-0	Joe Paterno	10-1-0
11	LSU 9-2-1	Charlie McClendon	9-1-1
12	North Carolina ..11-1-0	Bill Dooley	10-1-0
13	Arizona St. 10-2-0	Frank Kush	9-2-0
14	Notre Dame......8-3-0	Ara Parseghian	8-2-0
15	UCLA 8-3-0	Pepper Rodgers	same
16	Colorado 8-4-0	Eddie Crowder	8-3-0
17	N.C. State 8-3-1	Lou Holtz	7-3-1
18	Louisville........9-1-0	Lee Corso	same
19	Washington St....7-4-0	Jim Sweeney	same
20	Georgia Tech.....7-4-1	Bill Fulcher	6-4-1

Key Bowl Games

Rankings below reflect final regular season poll, released Dec. 4. No bowl for then #8 Michigan.
Rose–#1 USC over #3 Ohio St., 42-17; **Sugar**–#2 Oklahoma over #5 Penn St., 14-0; **Cotton**–#7 Texas over #4 Alabama, 17-13; **Orange**–#9 Nebraska over #12 Notre Dame, 40-6; **Gator**–#6 Auburn over #13 Colorado, 24-3; **Bluebonnet**–#11 Tennessee over #10 LSU, 24-17.

1973

	After Bowls	Head Coach	Regular Season
1	Notre Dame 11-0-0	Ara Parseghian	10-0-0
2	Ohio St.........10-0-1	Woody Hayes	9-0-1
3	Oklahoma 10-0-1	Barry Switzer	same
4	Alabama 11-1-0	Bear Bryant	11-0-0
5	Penn St. 12-0-0	Joe Paterno	11-0-0
6	Michigan 10-0-1	Bo Schembechler	same
7	Nebraska........9-2-1	Tom Osborne	8-2-1
8	USC 9-2-1	John McKay	9-1-1
9	Arizona St. 11-1-0	Frank Kush	10-1-0
	Houston 11-1-0	Bill Yeoman	10-1-0
11	Texas Tech 11-1-0	Jim Carlen	10-1-0
12	UCLA 9-2-0	Pepper Rodgers	same
13	LSU 9-3-0	Charlie McClendon	9-2-0
14	Texas...........8-3-0	Darrell Royal	8-2-0
15	Miami-OH 11-0-0	Bill Mallory	10-0-0
16	N.C. State 9-3-0	Lou Holtz	8-3-0
17	Missouri 8-4-0	Al Onofrio	7-4-0
18	Kansas 7-4-1	Don Fambrough	7-3-1
19	Tennessee.......8-4-0	Bill Battle	8-3-0
20	Maryland........8-4-0	Jerry Claiborne	8-3-0
	Tulane..........9-3-0	Bennie Ellender	9-2-0

Key Bowl Games

Rankings below reflect final regular season poll, released Dec. 3. No bowls for then #2 Oklahoma (probation), #5 Michigan and #9 UCLA.
Sugar–#3 Notre Dame over #1 Alabama, 24-23; **Rose**–#4 Ohio St. over #7 USC, 42-21; **Orange**–#6 Penn St. over #13 LSU, 16-9; **Cotton**–#12 Nebraska over #8 Texas, 19-3; **Fiesta**–#10 Ariz. St. over Pitt, 28-7; **Bluebonnet**–#14 Houston over #17 Tulane, 47-7.

1974

		After Bowls	Head Coach	Regular Season
1	Oklahoma	11-0-0	Barry Switzer	same
2	USC	10-1-1	John McKay	9-1-1
3	Michigan	10-1-0	Bo Schembechler	same
4	Ohio St.	10-2-0	Woody Hayes	10-1-0
5	Alabama	11-1-0	Bear Bryant	11-0-0
6	Notre Dame	10-2-0	Ara Parseghian	9-2-0
7	Penn St.	10-2-0	Joe Paterno	9-2-0
8	Auburn	10-2-0	Shug Jordan	9-2-0
9	Nebraska	9-3-0	Tom Osborne	8-3-0
10	Miami-OH	10-0-1	Dick Crum	9-0-1
11	N.C. State	9-2-1	Lou Holtz	9-2-0
12	Michigan St.	7-3-1	Denny Stolz	same
13	Maryland	8-4-0	Jerry Claiborne	8-3-0
14	Baylor	8-4-0	Grant Teaff	8-3-0
15	Florida	8-4-0	Doug Dickey	8-3-0
16	Texas A&M	8-3-0	Emory Ballard	same
17	Mississippi St.	9-3-0	Bob Tyler	8-3-0
	Texas	8-4-0	Darrell Royal	8-3-0
19	Houston	8-3-1	Bill Yeoman	8-3-0
20	Tennessee	7-3-2	Bill Battle	6-3-2

Key Bowl Games

Rankings below reflect final regular season poll, released Dec. 2. No bowls for #1 Oklahoma (probation) and then #4 Michigan.

Orange–#9 Notre Dame over #2 Alabama, 13-11; **Rose**–#5 USC over #3 Ohio St., 18-17; **Gator**–#6 Auburn over #11 Texas, 27-3; **Cotton**–#7 Penn St. over #12 Baylor, 41-20; **Sugar**–#8 Nebraska over #18 Florida, 13-10; **Liberty**–Tennessee over #10 Maryland, 7-3.

1975

		After Bowls	Head Coach	Regular Season
1	Oklahoma	11-1-0	Barry Switzer	10-1-0
2	Arizona St.	12-0-0	Frank Kush	11-0-0
3	Alabama	11-1-0	Bear Bryant	10-1-0
4	Ohio St.	11-1-0	Woody Hayes	11-0-0
5	UCLA	9-2-1	Dick Vermeil	8-2-1
6	Texas	10-2-0	Darrell Royal	9-2-0
7	Arkansas	10-2-0	Frank Broyles	9-2-0
8	Michigan	8-2-2	Bo Schembechler	8-1-2
9	Nebraska	10-2-0	Tom Osborne	10-1-0
10	Penn St.	9-3-0	Joe Paterno	9-2-0
11	Texas A&M	10-2-0	Emory Bellard	10-1-0
12	Miami-OH	11-1-0	Dick Crum	10-1-0
13	Maryland	9-2-1	Jerry Claiborne	8-2-1
14	California	8-3-0	Mike White	same
15	Pittsburgh	8-4-0	Johnny Majors	7-4-0
16	Colorado	9-3-0	Bill Mallory	9-2-0
17	USC	8-4-0	John McKay	7-4-0
18	Arizona	9-2-0	Jim Young	same
19	Georgia	9-3-0	Vince Dooley	9-2-0
20	West Virginia	9-3-0	Bobby Bowden	8-3-0

Key Bowl Games

Rankings below reflect final regular season poll, released Dec. 1. Texas A&M was unbeaten and ranked 2nd in that poll, but lost to #18 Arkansas, 31-6, in its final regular season game on Dec.6.

Rose–#11 UCLA over #1 Ohio St., 23-10; **Liberty**–#17 USC over #2 Texas A&M, 20-0; **Orange**–#3 Oklahoma over #5 Michigan, 14-6; **Sugar**–#4 Alabama over #8 Penn St., 13-6; **Fiesta**–#7 Ariz. St. over #6 Nebraska, 17-14; **Bluebonnet**–#9 Texas over #10 Colorado, 38-21; **Cotton**–#18 Arkansas over #12 Georgia, 31-10.

1976

		After Bowls	Head Coach	Regular Season
1	Pittsburgh	12-0-0	Johnny Majors	11-0-0
2	USC	11-1-0	John Robinson	10-1-0
3	Michigan	10-2-0	Bo Schembechler	10-1-0
4	Houston	10-2-0	Bill Yeoman	9-2-0
5	Oklahoma	9-2-1	Barry Switzer	8-2-1
6	Ohio St.	9-2-1	Woody Hayes	8-2-1
7	Texas A&M	10-2-0	Emory Bellard	9-2-0
8	Maryland	11-1-0	Jerry Claiborne	11-0-0
9	Nebraska	9-3-1	Tom Osborne	8-3-1
10	Georgia	10-2-0	Vince Dooley	10-1-0
11	Alabama	9-3-0	Bear Bryant	8-3-0
12	Notre Dame	9-3-0	Dan Devine	8-3-0
13	Texas Tech	10-2-0	Steve Sloan	10-1-0
14	Oklahoma St.	9-3-0	Jim Stanley	8-3-0
15	UCLA	9-2-1	Terry Donahue	9-1-1
16	Colorado	8-4-0	Bill Mallory	8-3-0
17	Rutgers	11-0-0	Frank Burns	same
18	Kentucky	8-4-0	Fran Curci	7-4-0
19	Iowa St.	8-3-0	Earle Bruce	same
20	Mississippi St.	9-2-0	Bob Tyler	same

Key Bowl Games

Rankings below reflect final regular season poll, released Nov. 29. No bowl for then #20 Miss. St. (probation).

Sugar–#1 Pitt over #5 Georgia, 27-3; **Rose**–#3 USC over #2 Michigan, 14-6; **Cotton**–#6 Houston over #4 Maryland, 30-21; **Liberty**–#16 Alabama over #7 UCLA, 36-6; **Fiesta**–#8 Oklahoma over Wyoming, 41-7; **Bluebonnet**–#13 Nebraska over #9 Texas Tech, 27-24; **Sun**–#10 Texas A&M over Florida, 37-14; **Orange**–#11 Ohio St. over #12 Colorado, 27-10.

1977

		After Bowls	Head Coach	Regular Season
1	Notre Dame	11-1-0	Dan Devine	10-1-0
2	Alabama	11-1-0	Bear Bryant	10-1-0
3	Arkansas	11-1-0	Lou Holtz	10-1-0
4	Texas	11-1-0	Fred Akers	11-0-0
5	Penn St.	11-1-0	Joe Paterno	10-1-0
6	Kentucky	10-1-0	Fran Curci	same
7	Oklahoma	10-2-0	Barry Switzer	10-1-0
8	Pittsburgh	9-2-1	Jackie Sherrill	8-2-1
9	Michigan	10-2-0	Bo Schembechler	10-1-0
10	Washington	8-4-0	Don James	7-4-0
11	Ohio St.	9-3-0	Woody Hayes	9-2-0
12	Nebraska	9-3-0	Tom Osborne	8-3-0
13	USC	8-4-0	John Robinson	7-4-0
14	Florida St.	10-2-0	Bobby Bowden	9-2-0
15	Stanford	9-3-0	Bill Walsh	8-3-0
16	San Diego St.	10-1-0	Claude Gilbert	same
17	North Carolina	8-3-1	Bill Dooley	8-2-1
18	Arizona St.	9-3-0	Frank Kush	9-2-0
19	Clemson	8-3-1	Charley Pell	8-2-1
20	BYU	9-2-0	LaVell Edwards	same

Key Bowl Games

Rankings below reflect final regular season poll, released Nov. 28. No bowl for then #7 Kentucky (probation).

Cotton–#5 Notre Dame over #1 Texas, 38-10; **Orange**–#6 Arkansas over #2 Oklahoma, 31-6; **Sugar**–#3 Alabama over #9 Ohio St., 35-6; **Rose**–#13 Washington over #4 Michigan, 27-20; **Fiesta**–#8 Penn St. over #15 Ariz. St., 42-30; **Gator**–#10 Pitt over #11 Clemson, 34-3.

Associated Press Final Polls (Cont.)

1978

		After Bowls	Head Coach	Regular Season
1	Alabama	11-1-0	Bear Bryant	10-1-0
2	USC	12-1-0	John Robinson	11-1-0
3	Oklahoma	11-1-0	Barry Switzer	10-1-0
4	Penn St.	11-1-0	Joe Paterno	11-0-0
5	Michigan	10-2-0	Bo Schembechler	10-1-0
6	Clemson	11-1-0	Charley Pell	10-1-0
7	Notre Dame	9-3-0	Dan Devine	8-3-0
8	Nebraska	9-3-0	Tom Osborne	9-2-0
9	Texas	9-3-0	Fred Akers	8-3-0
10	Houston	9-3-0	Bill Yeoman	9-2-0
11	Arkansas	9-2-1	Lou Holtz	9-2-0
12	Michigan St.	8-3-0	Darryl Rogers	same
13	Purdue	9-2-1	Jim Young	8-2-1
14	UCLA	8-3-1	Terry Donahue	8-3-0
15	Missouri	8-4-0	Warren Powers	7-4-0
16	Georgia	9-2-1	Vince Dooley	9-1-1
17	Stanford	8-4-0	Bill Walsh	7-4-0
18	N.C. State	9-3-0	Bo Rein	8-3-0
19	Texas A&M	8-4-0	Emory Bellard (4-2) & Tom Wilson (4-2)	7-4-0
20	Maryland	9-3-0	Jerry Claiborne	9-2-0

Key Bowl Games

Rankings below reflect final regular season poll, released Dec. 4. No bowl for then #12 Michigan St. (probation).
Sugar–#2 Alabama over #1 Penn St., 14-7; **Rose**–#3 USC over #5 Michigan, 17-10; **Orange**–#4 Oklahoma over #6 Nebraska, 31-24; **Gator**–#7 Clemson over #20 Ohio St., 17-15; **Fiesta**–#8 Arkansas tied #15 UCLA, 10-10; **Cotton**–#10 Notre Dame over #9 Houston, 35-34.

1979

		After Bowls	Head Coach	Regular Season
1	Alabama	12-0-0	Bear Bryant	11-0-0
2	USC	11-0-1	John Robinson	10-0-1
3	Oklahoma	11-1-0	Barry Switzer	10-1-0
4	Ohio St.	11-1-0	Earle Bruce	11-0-0
5	Houston	11-1-0	Bill Yeoman	10-1-0
6	Florida St.	11-1-0	Bobby Bowden	11-0-0
7	Pittsburgh	11-1-0	Jackie Sherrill	10-1-0
8	Arkansas	10-2-0	Lou Holtz	10-1-0
9	Nebraska	10-2-0	Tom Osborne	10-1-0
10	Purdue	10-2-0	Jim Young	9-2-0
11	Washington	9-3-0	Don James	8-3-0
12	Texas	9-3-0	Fred Akers	9-2-0
13	BYU	11-1-0	LaVell Edwards	11-0-0
14	Baylor	8-4-0	Grant Teaff	7-4-0
15	North Carolina	8-3-1	Dick Crum	7-3-1
16	Auburn	8-3-0	Doug Barfield	same
17	Temple	10-2-0	Wayne Hardin	9-2-0
18	Michigan	8-4-0	Bo Schembechler	8-3-0
19	Indiana	8-4-0	Lee Corso	7-4-0
20	Penn St.	8-4-0	Joe Paterno	7-4-0

Key Bowl Games

Rankings below reflect final regular season poll, released Dec. 3. No bowl for then #17 Auburn (probation).
Sugar–#2 Alabama over #6 Arkansas, 24-9; **Rose**–#3 USC over #1 Ohio St., 17-16; **Orange**–#5 Oklahoma over #4 Florida St., 24-7; **Sun**–#13 Washington over #11 Texas, 14-7; **Cotton**–#8 Houston over #7 Nebraska, 17-14; **Fiesta**–#10 Pitt over Arizona, 16-10.

1980

		After Bowls	Head Coach	Regular Season
1	Georgia	12-0-0	Vince Dooley	11-0-0
2	Pittsburgh	11-1-0	Jackie Sherrill	10-1-0
3	Oklahoma	10-2-0	Barry Switzer	9-2-0
4	Michigan	10-2-0	Bo Schembechler	9-2-0
5	Florida St.	10-2-0	Bobby Bowden	10-1-0
6	Alabama	10-2-0	Bear Bryant	9-2-0
7	Nebraska	10-2-0	Tom Osborne	9-2-0
8	Penn St.	10-2-0	Joe Paterno	9-2-0
9	Notre Dame	9-2-1	Dan Devine	9-1-1
10	North Carolina	11-1-0	Dick Crum	10-1-0
11	USC	8-2-1	John Robinson	same
12	BYU	12-1-0	LaVell Edwards	11-1-0
13	UCLA	9-2-0	Terry Donahue	same
14	Baylor	10-2-0	Grant Teaff	10-1-0
15	Ohio St.	9-3-0	Earle Bruce	9-2-0
16	Washington	9-3-0	Don James	9-2-0
17	Purdue	9-3-0	Jim Young	8-3-0
18	Miami-FL	9-3-0	H. Schnellenberger	8-3-0
19	Mississippi St.	9-3-0	Emory Bellard	9-2-0
20	SMU	8-4-0	Ron Meyer	8-3-0

Key Bowl Games

Rankings below reflect final regular season poll, released Dec. 8.
Sugar–#1 Georgia over #7 Notre Dame, 17-10; **Orange**–#4 Oklahoma over #2 Florida St., 18-17; **Gator**–#3 Pitt over #18 S. Carolina, 37-9; **Rose**–#5 Michigan over #16 Washington, 23-6; **Cotton**–#9 Alabama over #6 Baylor, 30-2; **Sun**–#8 Nebraska over #17 Miss. St., 31-17; **Fiesta**–#10 Penn St. over #11 Ohio St., 31-19; **Bluebonnet**–#13 N. Carolina over Texas, 16-7.

1981

		After Bowls	Head Coach	Regular Season
1	Clemson	12-0-0	Danny Ford	11-0-0
2	Texas	10-1-1	Fred Akers	9-1-1
3	Penn St.	10-2-0	Joe Paterno	9-2-0
4	Pittsburgh	11-1-0	Jackie Sherrill	10-1-0
5	SMU	10-1-0	Ron Meyer	same
6	Georgia	10-2-0	Vince Dooley	10-1-0
7	Alabama	9-2-1	Bear Bryant	9-1-1
8	Miami-FL	9-2-0	H. Schnellenberger	same
9	North Carolina	10-2-0	Dick Crum	9-2-0
10	Washington	10-2-0	Don James	9-2-0
11	Nebraska	9-3-0	Tom Osborne	9-2-0
12	Michigan	9-3-0	Bo Schembechler	8-3-0
13	BYU	11-2-0	LaVell Edwards	10-2-0
14	USC	9-3-0	John Robinson	9-2-0
15	Ohio St.	9-3-0	Earle Bruce	8-3-0
16	Arizona St.	9-2-0	Darryl Rogers	same
17	West Virginia	9-3-0	Don Nehlen	8-3-0
18	Iowa	8-4-0	Hayden Fry	8-3-0
19	Missouri	8-4-0	Warren Powers	7-4-0
20	Oklahoma	7-4-1	Barry Switzer	6-4-1

Key Bowl Games

Rankings below reflect final regular season poll, released Nov. 30. No bowl for then #5 SMU (probation), #9 Miami-FL (probation), and #17 Ariz. St. (probation).
Orange–#1 Clemson over #4 Nebraska, 22-15; **Sugar**–#10 Pitt over #2 Georgia, 24-20; **Cotton**–#6 Texas over #3 Alabama, 14-12; **Fiesta**–#7 Penn St. over #8 USC, 26-10; **Gator**–#11 N. Carolina over Arkansas, 31-27; **Rose**–#12 Washington over #13 Iowa, 28-0.

1982

		After Bowls	Head Coach	Regular Season
1	Penn St.	11-1-0	Joe Paterno	10-1-0
2	SMU	11-0-1	Bobby Collins	10-0-1
3	Nebraska	12-1-0	Tom Osborne	11-1-0
4	Georgia	11-1-0	Vince Dooley	11-0-0
5	UCLA	10-1-1	Terry Donahue	9-1-1
6	Arizona St.	10-2-0	Darryl Rogers	9-2-0
7	Washington	10-2-0	Don James	9-2-0
8	Clemson	9-1-1	Danny Ford	same
9	Arkansas	9-2-1	Lou Holtz	8-2-1
10	Pittsburgh	9-3-0	Foge Fazio	9-2-0
11	LSU	8-3-1	Jerry Stovall	8-2-1
12	Ohio St.	9-3-0	Earle Bruce	8-3-0
13	Florida St.	9-3-0	Bobby Bowden	8-3-0
14	Auburn	9-3-0	Pat Dye	8-3-0
15	USC	8-3-0	John Robinson	same
16	Oklahoma	8-4-0	Barry Switzer	8-3-0
17	Texas	9-3-0	Fred Akers	9-2-0
18	North Carolina	8-4-0	Dick Crum	7-4-0
19	West Virginia	9-3-0	Don Nehlen	9-2-0
20	Maryland	8-4-0	Bobby Ross	8-3-0

Key Bowl Games

Rankings below reflect final regular season poll, released Dec. 6. No bowl for then #7 Clemson (probation) and #15 USC (probation).
Sugar–#2 Penn St. over #1 Georgia, 27-23; **Orange**–#3 Nebraska over #13 LSU, 21-20; **Cotton**–#4 SMU over #6 Pitt, 7-3; **Rose**–#5 UCLA over #19 Michigan, 24-14; **Aloha**–#9 Washington over #16 Maryland, 21-20; **Fiesta**–#11 Ariz. St. over #12 Oklahoma, 32-21; **Bluebonnet**–#14 Arkansas over Florida, 28-24.

1984

		After Bowls	Head Coach	Regular Season
1	BYU	13-0-0	LaVell Edwards	12-0-0
2	Washington	11-1-0	Don James	10-1-0
3	Florida	9-1-1	Charley Pell (0-1-1) & Galen Hall (9-0)	same
4	Nebraska	10-2-0	Tom Osborne	9-2-0
5	Boston College	10-2-0	Jack Bicknell	9-2-0
6	Oklahoma	9-2-1	Barry Switzer	9-1-1
7	Oklahoma St.	10-2-0	Pat Jones	9-2-0
8	SMU	10-2-0	Bobby Collins	9-2-0
9	UCLA	9-3-0	Terry Donahue	8-3-0
10	USC	9-3-0	Ted Tollner	8-3-0
11	South Carolina	10-2-0	Joe Morrison	10-1-0
12	Maryland	9-3-0	Bobby Ross	8-3-0
13	Ohio St.	9-3-0	Earle Bruce	9-2-0
14	Auburn	9-4-0	Pat Dye	8-4-0
15	LSU	8-3-1	Bill Arnsparger	8-2-1
16	Iowa	8-4-1	Hayden Fry	7-4-1
17	Florida St.	7-3-2	Bobby Bowden	7-3-1
18	Miami-FL	8-5-0	Jimmy Johnson	8-4-0
19	Kentucky	9-3-0	Jerry Claiborne	8-3-0
20	Virginia	8-2-2	George Welsh	7-2-2

Key Bowl Games

Rankings below reflect final regular season poll, released Dec. 3. No bowl for then #3 Florida (probation).
Holiday–#1 BYU over Michigan, 24-17;
Orange–#4 Washington over #2 Oklahoma, 28-17; **Sugar**–#5 Nebraska over #11 LSU, 28-10; **Rose**–#18 USC over #6 Ohio St., 20-17; **Gator**–#9 Okla. St. over #7 S. Carolina, 21-14; **Cotton**–#8 BC over Houston, 45-28; **Aloha**–#10 SMU over #17 Notre Dame, 27-20.

1983

		After Bowls	Head Coach	Regular Season
1	Miami-FL	11-1-0	H. Schnellenberger	10-1-0
2	Nebraska	12-1-0	Tom Osborne	12-0-0
3	Auburn	11-1-0	Pat Dye	10-1-0
4	Georgia	10-1-1	Vince Dooley	9-1-1
5	Texas	11-1-0	Fred Akers	11-0-0
6	Florida	9-2-1	Charley Pell	8-2-1
7	BYU	11-1-0	LaVell Edwards	10-1-0
8	Michigan	9-3-0	Bo Schembechler	9-2-0
9	Ohio St.	9-3-0	Earle Bruce	8-3-0
10	Illinois	10-2-0	Mike White	10-1-0
11	Clemson	9-1-1	Danny Ford	same
12	SMU	10-2-0	Bobby Collins	10-1-0
13	Air Force	10-2-0	Ken Hatfield	9-2-0
14	Iowa	9-3-0	Hayden Fry	9-2-0
15	Alabama	8-4-0	Ray Perkins	7-4-0
16	West Virginia	9-3-0	Don Nehlen	8-3-0
17	UCLA	7-4-1	Terry Donahue	6-4-1
18	Pittsburgh	8-3-1	Foge Fazio	8-2-1
19	Boston College	9-3-0	Jack Bicknell	9-2-0
20	East Carolina	8-3-0	Ed Emory	same

Key Bowl Games

Rankings below reflect final regular season poll, released Dec. 5. No bowl for then #12 Clemson (probation).
Orange–#5 Miami-FL over #1 Nebraska, 31-30; **Cotton**–#7 Georgia over #2 Texas, 10-9; **Sugar**– #3 Auburn over #8 Michigan, 9-7; **Rose**–UCLA over #4 Illinois, 45-9; **Holiday**–#9 BYU over Missouri, 21-17; **Gator**–#11 Florida over #10 Iowa, 14-6; **Fiesta**–#14 Ohio St. over #15 Pitt, 28-23.

1985

		After Bowls	Head Coach	Regular Season
1	Oklahoma	11-1-0	Barry Switzer	10-1-0
2	Michigan	10-1-1	Bo Schembechler	9-1-1
3	Penn St.	11-1-0	Joe Paterno	11-0-0
4	Tennessee	9-1-2	Johnny Majors	8-1-2
5	Florida	9-1-1	Galen Hall	same
6	Texas A&M	10-2-0	Jackie Sherrill	9-2-0
7	UCLA	9-2-1	Terry Donahue	8-2-1
8	Air Force	12-1-0	Fisher DeBerry	11-1-0
9	Miami-FL	10-2-0	Jimmy Johnson	10-1-0
10	Iowa	10-2-0	Hayden Fry	10-1-0
11	Nebraska	9-3-0	Tom Osborne	9-2-0
12	Arkansas	10-2-0	Ken Hatfield	9-2-0
13	Alabama	9-2-1	Ray Perkins	8-2-1
14	Ohio St.	9-3-0	Earle Bruce	8-3-0
15	Florida St.	9-3-0	Bobby Bowden	8-3-0
16	BYU	11-3-0	LaVell Edwards	11-2-0
17	Baylor	9-3-0	Grant Teaff	8-3-0
18	Maryland	9-3-0	Bobby Ross	8-3-0
19	Georgia Tech	9-2-1	Bill Curry	8-2-1
20	LSU	9-2-1	Bill Arnsparger	9-1-1

Key Bowl Games

Rankings below reflect final regular season poll, released Dec. 9. No bowl for then #6 Florida (probation).
Orange–#3 Oklahoma over #1 Penn St., 25-10; **Sugar**–#8 Tennessee over #2 Miami-FL, 35-7; **Rose**–#13 UCLA over #4 Iowa, 45-28; **Fiesta**–#5 Michigan over #7 Nebraska, 27-23; **Bluebonnet**–#10 Air Force over Texas, 24-16; **Cotton**–#11 Texas A&M over #16 Auburn, 36-16.

Associated Press Final Polls (Cont.)

1986

		After Bowls	Head Coach	Regular Season
1	Penn St.	12-0-0	Joe Paterno	11-0-0
2	Miami-FL	11-1-0	Jimmy Johnson	11-0-0
3	Oklahoma	11-1-0	Barry Switzer	10-1-0
4	Arizona St.	10-1-1	John Cooper	9-1-1
5	Nebraska	10-2-0	Tom Osborne	9-2-0
6	Auburn	10-2-0	Pat Dye	9-2-0
7	Ohio St.	10-3-0	Earle Bruce	9-3-0
8	Michigan	11-2-0	Bo Schembechler	11-1-0
9	Alabama	10-3-0	Ray Perkins	9-3-0
10	LSU	9-3-0	Bill Arnsparger	9-2-0
11	Arizona	9-3-0	Larry Smith	8-3-0
12	Baylor	9-3-0	Grant Teaff	8-3-0
13	Texas A&M	9-3-0	Jackie Sherrill	9-2-0
14	UCLA	8-3-1	Terry Donahue	7-3-1
15	Arkansas	9-3-0	Ken Hatfield	9-2-0
16	Iowa	9-3-0	Hayden Fry	8-3-0
17	Clemson	8-2-2	Danny Ford	7-2-2
18	Washington	8-3-1	Don James	8-2-1
19	Boston College	9-3-0	Jack Bicknell	8-3-0
20	Virginia Tech	9-2-1	Bill Dooley	8-2-1

Key Bowl Games

Rankings below reflect final regular season poll, released Dec. 1.

Fiesta–#2 Penn St. over #1 Miami-FL, 14-10; **Orange**–#3 Oklahoma over #9 Arkansas, 42-8; **Rose**– #7 Ariz. St. over #4 Michigan, 22-15; **Sugar**–#6 Nebraska over #5 LSU, 30-15; **Cotton**–#11 Ohio St. over #8 Texas A&M, 28-12; **Citrus**–#10 Auburn over USC, 16-7; **Sun**–#13 Alabama over #12 Washington, 28-6.

1987

		After Bowls	Head Coach	Regular Season
1	Miami-FL	12-0-0	Jimmy Johnson	11-0-0
2	Florida St.	11-1-0	Bobby Bowden	10-1-0
3	Oklahoma	11-1-0	Barry Switzer	11-0-0
4	Syracuse	11-0-1	Dick MacPherson	11-0-0
5	LSU	10-1-1	Mike Archer	9-1-1
6	Nebraska	10-2-0	Tom Osborne	10-1-0
7	Auburn	9-1-2	Pat Dye	9-1-1
8	Michigan St.	9-2-1	George Perles	8-2-1
9	UCLA	10-2-0	Terry Donahue	9-2-0
10	Texas A&M	10-2-0	Jackie Sherrill	9-2-0
11	Oklahoma St.	10-2-0	Pat Jones	9-2-0
12	Clemson	10-2-0	Danny Ford	9-2-0
13	Georgia	9-3-0	Vince Dooley	8-3-0
14	Tennessee	10-2-1	Johnny Majors	9-2-1
15	South Carolina	8-4-0	Joe Morrison	8-3-0
16	Iowa	10-3-0	Hayden Fry	9-3-0
17	Notre Dame	8-4-0	Lou Holtz	8-3-0
18	USC	8-4-0	Larry Smith	8-3-0
19	Michigan	8-4-0	Bo Schembechler	7-4-0
20	Arizona St.	7-4-1	John Cooper	6-4-1

Key Bowl Games

Rankings below reflect final regular season poll, released Dec. 7.

Orange–#2 Miami-FL over #1 Oklahoma, 20-14; **Fiesta**–#3 Florida St. over #5 Nebraska, 31-28; **Sugar**–#4 Syracuse tied #6 Auburn, 16-16; **Gator**–#7 LSU over #9 S. Carolina, 30-13; **Rose**–#8 Mich. St. over #16 USC, 20-17; **Aloha**–#10 UCLA over Florida, 20-16; **Cotton**–#13 Texas A&M over #12 Notre Dame, 35-10.

1988

		After Bowls	Head Coach	Regular Season
1	Notre Dame	12-0-0	Lou Holtz	11-0-0
2	Miami-FL	11-1-0	Jimmy Johnson	10-1-0
3	Florida St.	11-1-0	Bobby Bowden	10-1-0
4	Michigan	9-2-1	Bo Schembechler	8-2-1
5	West Virginia	11-1-0	Don Nehlen	11-0-0
6	UCLA	10-2-0	Terry Donahue	9-2-0
7	USC	10-2-0	Larry Smith	10-1-0
8	Auburn	10-2-0	Pat Dye	10-1-0
9	Clemson	10-2-0	Danny Ford	9-2-0
10	Nebraska	11-2-0	Tom Osborne	11-1-0
11	Oklahoma St.	10-2-0	Pat Jones	9-2-0
12	Arkansas	10-2-0	Ken Hatfield	10-1-0
13	Syracuse	10-2-0	Dick MacPherson	9-2-0
14	Oklahoma	9-3-0	Barry Switzer	9-2-0
15	Georgia	9-3-0	Vince Dooley	8-3-0
16	Washington St.	9-3-0	Dennis Erickson	8-3-0
17	Alabama	9-3-0	Bill Curry	8-3-0
18	Houston	9-3-0	Jack Pardee	9-2-0
19	LSU	8-4-0	Mike Archer	8-3-0
20	Indiana	8-3-1	Bill Mallory	7-3-1

Key Bowl Games

Rankings below reflect final regular season poll, released Dec. 5.

Fiesta–#1 Notre Dame over #3 West Va., 34-21; **Orange**–#2 Miami-FL over #6 Nebraska, 23-3; **Sugar**–#4 Florida St. over #7 Auburn, 13-7; **Rose**–#11 Michigan over #5 USC, 22-14; **Cotton**–#9 UCLA over #8 Arkansas, 17-3; **Citrus**–#13 Clemson over #10 Oklahoma, 13-6.

1989

		After Bowls	Head Coach	Regular Season
1	Miami-FL	11-1-0	Dennis Erickson	10-1-0
2	Notre Dame	12-1-0	Lou Holtz	11-1-0
3	Florida St.	10-2-0	Bobby Bowden	9-2-0
4	Colorado	11-1-0	Bill McCartney	11-0-0
5	Tennessee	11-1-0	Johnny Majors	10-1-0
6	Auburn	10-2-0	Pat Dye	9-2-0
7	Michigan	10-2-0	Bo Schembechler	10-1-0
8	USC	9-2-1	Larry Smith	8-2-1
9	Alabama	10-2-0	Bill Curry	10-1-0
10	Illinois	10-2-0	John Mackovic	9-2-0
11	Nebraska	10-2-0	Tom Osborne	10-1-0
12	Clemson	10-2-0	Danny Ford	9-2-0
13	Arkansas	10-2-0	Ken Hatfield	10-1-0
14	Houston	9-2-0	Jack Pardee	same
15	Penn St.	8-3-1	Joe Paterno	7-3-1
16	Michigan St.	8-4-0	George Perles	7-4-0
17	Pittsburgh	8-3-1	Mike Gottfried (7-3-1) & Paul Hackett (1-0)	7-3-1
18	Virginia	10-3-0	George Welsh	10-2-0
19	Texas Tech	9-3-0	Spike Dykes	8-3-0
20	Texas A&M	8-4-0	R.C. Slocum	8-3-0

Key Bowl Games

Rankings below reflect final regular season poll, released Dec. 11. No bowl for then #13 Houston (probation).

Orange–#4 Notre Dame over #1 Colorado, 21-6; **Sugar**–#2 Miami-FL over #7 Alabama, 33-25; **Rose**– #12 USC over #3 Michigan, 17-10; **Fiesta**–#5 Florida St. over #6 Nebraska, 41-17; **Cotton**–#8 Tennessee over #10 Arkansas, 31-27; **Hall of Fame**–#9 Auburn over #21 Ohio St., 31-14; **Citrus**–#11 Illinois over #15 Virginia, 31-21.

1990

	After Bowls	Head Coach	Regular Season
1	Colorado 11-1-1	Bill McCartney	10-1-1
2	Georgia Tech 11-0-1	Bobby Ross	10-0-1
3	Miami-FL 10-2-0	Dennis Erickson	9-2-0
4	Florida St. 10-2-0	Bobby Bowden	9-2-0
5	Washington 10-2-0	Don James	9-2-0
6	Notre Dame 9-3-0	Lou Holtz	9-2-0
7	Michigan 9-3-0	Gary Moeller	8-3-0
8	Tennessee 9-2-2	Johnny Majors	8-2-2
9	Clemson 10-2-0	Ken Hatfield	9-2-0
10	Houston 10-1-0	John Jenkins	same
11	Penn St. 9-3-0	Joe Paterno	9-2-0
12	Texas 10-2-0	David McWilliams	10-1-0
13	Florida 9-2-0	Steve Spurrier	same
14	Louisville 10-1-1	H. Schnellenberger	9-1-1
15	Texas A&M 9-3-1	R.C. Slocum	8-3-1
16	Michigan St. 8-3-1	George Perles	7-3-1
17	Oklahoma 8-3-0	Gary Gibbs	same
18	Iowa 8-4-0	Hayden Fry	8-3-0
19	Auburn 8-3-1	Pat Dye	7-3-1
20	USC 8-4-1	Larry Smith	8-3-1

Key Bowl Games

Rankings below reflect final regular season poll, released Dec. 3. No bowl for then #9 Houston (probation), #11 Florida (probation) and #20 Oklahoma (probation).

Orange–#1 Colorado over #5 Notre Dame, 10-9; **Citrus**–#2 Ga. Tech over #19 Nebraska, 45-21; **Cotton**–#4 Miami-FL over #3 Texas, 46-3; **Blockbuster**–#6 Florida St. over #7 Penn St., 24-17; **Rose**–#8 Washington over #17 Iowa, 46-34; **Sugar**–#10 Tennessee over Virginia, 23-22; **Gator**–#12 Michigan over #15 Ole Miss, 35-3.

1991

	After Bowls	Head Coach	Regular Season
1	Miami-FL 12-0-0	Dennis Erickson	11-0-0
2	Washington 12-0-0	Don James	11-0-0
3	Penn St. 11-2-0	Joe Paterno	10-2-0
4	Florida St. 11-2-0	Bobby Bowden	10-2-0
5	Alabama 11-1-0	Gene Stallings	10-1-0
6	Michigan 10-2-0	Gary Moeller	10-1-0
7	Florida 10-2-0	Steve Spurrier	10-1-0
8	California 10-2-0	Bruce Snyder	9-2-0
9	East Carolina 11-1-0	Bill Lewis	10-1-0
10	Iowa 10-1-1	Hayden Fry	10-1-0
11	Syracuse 10-2-0	Paul Pasqualoni	9-2-0
12	Texas A&M 10-2-0	R.C. Slocum	10-1-0
13	Notre Dame 10-3-0	Lou Holtz	9-3-0
14	Tennessee 9-3-0	Johnny Majors	9-2-0
15	Nebraska 9-2-1	Tom Osborne	9-1-1
16	Oklahoma 9-3-0	Gary Gibbs	8-3-0
17	Georgia 9-3-0	Ray Goff	8-3-0
18	Clemson 9-2-1	Ken Hatfield	9-1-1
19	UCLA 9-3-0	Terry Donahue	8-3-0
20	Colorado 8-3-1	Bill McCartney	8-2-1

Key Bowl Games

Rankings below reflect final regular season poll, taken Dec. 2.

Orange–#1 Miami-FL over #11 Nebraska, 22-0; **Rose**–#2 Washington over #4 Michigan, 34-14; **Sugar**–#18 Notre Dame over #3 Florida, 39-28; **Cotton**–#5 Florida St. over #9 Texas A&M, 10-2; **Fiesta**–#6 Penn St. over #10 Tennessee, 42-17; **Holiday**–#7 Iowa tied BYU, 13-13; **Blockbuster**–#8 Alabama over #15 Colorado, 30-25; **Citrus**–#14 California over #13 Clemson, 37-13; **Peach**–#12 East Carolina over #21 N.C. State, 37-34.

1992

	After Bowls	Head Coach	Regular Season
1	Alabama 13-0-0	Gene Stallings	12-0-0
2	Florida St. 11-1-0	Bobby Bowden	10-1-0
3	Miami-FL 11-1-0	Dennis Erickson	11-0-0
4	Notre Dame 10-1-1	Lou Holtz	9-1-1
5	Michigan 9-0-3	Gary Moeller	8-0-3
6	Syracuse 10-2-0	Paul Pasqualoni	9-2-0
7	Texas A&M 12-1-0	R.C. Slocum	12-0-0
8	Georgia 10-2-0	Ray Goff	9-2-0
9	Stanford 10-3-0	Bill Walsh	9-3-0
10	Florida 9-4-0	Steve Spurrier	8-4-0
11	Washington 9-3-0	Don James	9-3-0
12	Tennessee 9-3-0	Johnny Majors (5-3) & Phillip Fulmer (4-0)	8-3-0
13	Colorado 9-2-1	Bill McCartney	9-1-1
14	Nebraska 9-3-0	Tom Osborne	9-2-0
15	Washington St. 9-3-0	Mike Price	8-3-0
16	Mississippi 9-3-0	Billy Brewer	8-3-0
17	N.C. State 9-3-1	Dick Sheridan	9-2-1
18	Ohio St. 8-3-1	John Cooper	8-2-1
19	North Carolina 9-3-0	Mack Brown	8-3-0
20	Hawaii 11-2-0	Bob Wagner	10-2-0

Key Bowl Games

Rankings below reflect final regular season poll, taken Dec. 5.

Sugar–#2 Alabama over #1 Miami-FL, 34-13; **Orange**–#3 Florida St. over #11 Nebraska, 27-14; **Cotton**–#5 Notre Dame over #4 Texas A&M, 28-3; **Fiesta**–#6 Syracuse over #10 Colorado, 26-22; **Rose**–#7 Michigan over #9 Washington, 38-31; **Citrus**–#8 Georgia over #15 Ohio St., 21-14.

1993

	After Bowls	Head Coach	Regular Season
1	Florida St 12-1-0	Bobby Bowden	11-1-0
2	Notre Dame 11-1-0	Lou Holtz	10-1-0
3	Nebraska 11-1-0	Tom Osborne	11-0-0
4	Auburn 11-0-0	Terry Bowden	11-0-0
5	Florida 11-2-0	Steve Spurrier	10-2-0
6	Wisconsin 10-1-1	Barry Alvarez	9-1-1
7	West Virginia 11-1-0	Don Nehlen	11-0-0
8	Penn St 10-2-0	Joe Paterno	9-2-0
9	Texas A&M 10-2-0	R.C. Slocum	10-1-0
10	Arizona 10-2-0	Dick Tomey	9-2-0
11	Ohio St 10-1-1	John Cooper	9-1-1
12	Tennessee 9-2-1	Phillip Fulmer	9-1-1
13	Boston College 9-3-0	Tom Coughlin	8-3-0
14	Alabama 9-3-1	Gene Stallings	8-3-1
15	Miami-FL 9-3-0	Dennis Erickson	9-2-0
16	Colorado 8-3-1	Bill McCartney	7-3-1
17	Oklahoma 9-3-0	Gary Gibbs	8-3-0
18	UCLA 8-4-0	Terry Donahue	8-3-0
19	North Carolina 10-3-0	Mack Brown	10-2-0
20	Kansas St 9-2-1	Bill Snyder	8-2-1

Key Bowl Games

Rankings below reflect final regular season poll, taken Dec. 5. No bowl for then #5 Auburn (probation).

Orange–#1 Florida St. over #2 Nebraska, 18-16; **Sugar**–#8 Florida over #3 West Virginia, 41-7; **Cotton**–#4 Notre Dame over #7 Texas A&M, 24-21; **Citrus**–#13 Penn St. over #6 Tennessee, 31-13; **Rose**–#9 Wisconsin over #14 UCLA, 21-16; **Fiesta**–#16 Arizona over #10 Miami-FL, 29-0; **Holiday**–#11 Ohio St. over BYU, 28-21; **Gator**–#18 Alabama over #12 North Carolina, 24-10; **Carquest**–#15 Boston College over Virginia, 31-13.

Associated Press Final Polls (Cont.)

1994

			After Bowls	Head Coach	Regular Season
1	Nebraska		13-0-0	Tom Osborne	12-0-0
2	Penn St.		12-0-0	Joe Paterno	11-0-0
3	Colorado		11-1-0	Bill McCartney	10-1-0
4	Florida St.		10-1-1	Bobby Bowden	9-1-1
5	Alabama		12-1-0	Gene Stallings	11-1-0
6	Miami-FL		10-2-0	Dennis Erickson	10-1-0
7	Florida		10-2-1	Steve Spurrier	10-1-1
8	Texas A&M		10-0-1	R.C. Slocum	same
9	Auburn		9-1-1	Terry Bowden	same
10	Utah		10-2-0	Ron McBride	9-2-0
11	Oregon		9-4-0	Rich Brooks	9-3-0
12	Michigan		8-4-0	Gary Moeller	7-4-0
13	USC		8-3-1	John Robinson	7-3-1
14	Ohio St.		9-4-0	John Cooper	9-3-0
15	Virginia		9-3-0	George Welsh	8-3-0
16	Colorado St.		10-2-0	Sonny Lubick	10-1-0
17	N.C. State		9-3-0	Mike O'Cain	8-3-0
18	BYU		10-3-0	LaVell Edwards	9-3-0
19	Kansas St		9-3-0	Bill Snyder	9-2-0
20	Arizona		8-4-0	Dick Tomey	8-3-0

Key Bowl Games

Rankings below reflect final regular season poll, taken Dec. 4. No bowls for then #8 Texas A&M (probation) and #9 Auburn (probation).

Orange– #1 Nebraska over #3 Miami-FL, 24-17; **Rose–** #2 Penn St. over #12 Oregon, 38-20; **Fiesta–** #4 Colorado over Notre Dame, 41-24; **Sugar–** #7 Florida St. over #5 Florida, 23-17; **Citrus–** #6 Alabama over #13 Ohio St., 24-17; **Freedom–** #14 Utah over #15 Arizona, 16-13.

1995

			After Bowls	Head Coach	Regular Season
1	Nebraska		12-0-0	Tom Osborne	11-0-0
2	Florida		12-1-0	Steve Spurrier	12-0-0
3	Tennessee		11-1-0	Phillip Fulmer	10-1-0
4	Florida St		10-2-0	Bobby Bowden	9-2-0
5	Colorado		10-2-0	Rick Neuheisel	9-2-0
6	Ohio St.		11-2-0	John Cooper	11-1-0
7	Kansas St.		10-2-0	Bill Snyder	9-2-0
8	Northwestern		10-2-0	Gary Barnett	10-1-0
9	Kansas		10-2-0	Glen Mason	9-2-0
10	Va. Tech		10-2-0	Frank Beamer	9-2-0
11	Notre Dame		9-3-0	Lou Holtz	9-2-0
12	USC		9-2-1	John Robinson	8-2-1
13	Penn St.		9-3-0	Joe Paterno	8-3-0
14	Texas		10-2-1	John Mackovic	10-1-1
15	Texas A&M		9-3-0	R.C. Slocum	8-3-0
16	Virginia		9-4-0	George Welsh	8-4-0
17	Michigan		9-4-0	Lloyd Carr	9-3-0
18	Oregon		9-3-0	Mike Bellotti	9-2-0
19	Syracuse		9-3-0	Paul Pasqualoni	8-3-0
20	Miami-FL		8-3-0	Butch Davis	same

Key Bowl Games

Rankings below reflect final regular season poll, taken Dec. 3. No bowl for then #22 Miami-FL (probation).

Fiesta– #1 Nebraska over #2 Florida, 62-24; **Rose–** #17 USC over #3 Northwestern, 41-32; **Citrus–** #4 (tie) Tennessee over #4 (tie) Ohio St., 20-14; **Orange–** #8 Florida St. over #6 Notre Dame, 31-26; **Cotton–** #7 Colorado over #12 Oregon, 38-6; **Sugar–** #13 Va. Tech over #9 Texas, 28-10; **Holiday–** #10 Kansas St. over Colo. St., 54-21; **Aloha–** #11 Kansas over UCLA, 51-30; **Alamo–** #14 Texas A&M over #14 Michigan, 22-20; **Outback–** #15 Penn St. over #16 Auburn, 43-14; **Peach–** #18 Virginia over Georgia, 34-27; **Gator–** Syracuse over #23 Clemson, 41-0.

1996

			After Bowls	Head Coach	Regular Season
1	Florida		12-1	Steve Spurrier	11-1
2	Ohio St.		11-1	John Cooper	10-1
3	Florida St		11-1	Bobby Bowden	11-0
4	Arizona St.		11-1	Bruce Snyder	11-0
5	BYU		14-1	LaVell Edwards	13-1
6	Nebraska		11-2	Tom Osborne	10-2
7	Penn St.		11-2	Joe Paterno	10-2
8	Colorado		10-2	Rick Neuheisel	9-2
9	Tennessee		10-2	Phillip Fulmer	9-2
10	North Carolina		10-2	Mack Brown	9-2
11	Alabama		10-3	Gene Stallings	9-3
12	LSU		10-2	Gerry DiNardo	9-2
13	Virginia Tech		10-2	Frank Beamer	10-1
14	Miami-FL		9-3	Butch Davis	8-3
15	Northwestern		9-3	Gary Barnett	9-2
16	Washington		9-3	Jim Lambright	9-2
17	Kansas St.		9-3	Bill Snyder	9-2
18	Iowa		9-3	Hayden Fry	8-3
19	Notre Dame		8-3	Lou Holtz	same
20	Michigan		8-4	Lloyd Carr	8-3

Key Bowl Games

Rankings below reflect final regular season poll, taken Dec. 8. No bowl for then #18 Notre Dame and #22 Wyoming.

Sugar– #3 Florida over #1 Florida St., 52-20; **Rose–** #4 Ohio St. over #2 Arizona St., 20-17; **Fiesta–** #7 Penn St. over #20 Texas, 38-15; **Cotton–** #5 BYU over #14 Kansas St., 19-15; **Citrus–** #9 Tennessee over #11 Northwestern, 48-28; **Orange–** #6 Nebraska over #10 Virginia Tech, 41-21; **Gator–** #12 North Carolina over #25 West Virginia, 20-13; **Outback–** #16 Alabama over #15 Michigan, 17-14. **Carquest–** #19 Miami over Virginia, 31-21.

1997

			After Bowls	Head Coach	Regular Season
1	Michigan		12-0	Lloyd Carr	11-0
2	Nebraska		13-0	Tom Osborne	12-0
3	Florida St		11-1	Bobby Bowden	10-1
4	Florida		10-2	Steve Spurrier	9-2
5	UCLA		10-2	Bob Toledo	9-2
6	North Carolina		11-1	Mack Brown (10-1) & Carl Torbush (1-0)	10-1
7	Tennessee		11-2	Phillip Fulmer	11-1
8	Kansas St.		11-1	Bill Snyder	10-1
9	Washington St.		10-2	Mike Price	10-1
10	Georgia		10-2	Jim Donnan	9-2
11	Auburn		10-3	Terry Bowden	9-3
12	Ohio St.		10-3	John Cooper	10-2
13	LSU		9-3	Gerry DiNardo	8-3
14	Arizona St.		9-3	Bruce Snyder	7-3
15	Purdue		9-3	Joe Tiller	8-3
16	Penn St.		9-3	Joe Paterno	9-2
17	Colorado St.		11-2	Sonny Lubick	10-2
18	Washington		8-4	Jim Lambright	7-4
19	So. Mississippi		9-3	Jeff Bower	8-3
20	Texas A&M		9-4	R.C. Slocum	9-3

Key Bowl Games

Rankings below reflect final regular season poll, taken Dec. 7.

Rose– #1 Michigan over #7 Washington St., 21-16; **Orange–** #2 Nebraska over #3 Tennessee, 42-17; **Sugar–** #4 Florida St. over #10 Ohio St., 31-14; **Gator–** #5 North Carolina over Virginia Tech, 42-3; **Cotton–** #6 UCLA over #19 Texas A&M, 29-23; **Citrus–** #8 Florida over #12 Penn St., 21-6; **Fiesta–** #9 Kansas St. over #14 Syracuse, 35-18; **Outback–** #11 Georgia over Wisconsin, 33-6; **Peach–** #13 Auburn over Clemson, 21-17; **Independence–** #15 LSU over Notre Dame, 27-9; **Alamo–** #17 Purdue over #24 Oklahoma St., 33-20; **Holiday–** #17 Colorado St. over #20 Missouri, 35-24.

1998

	After Bowls	Head Coach	Regular Season
1	Tennessee 13-0	Phillip Fulmer	12-0
2	Ohio St............11-1	John Cooper	10-1
3	Florida St...........11-1	Bobby Bowden	11-1
4	Arizona 12-1	Dick Tomey	11-1
5	Florida............10-2	Steve Spurrier	9-2
6	Wisconsin 11-1	Barry Alvarez	10-1
7	Tulane 12-0	Tommy Bowden	11-0
8	UCLA 10-2	Bob Toledo	10-1
9	Georgia Tech 10-2	George O'Leary	9-2
10	Kansas St..........11-2	Bill Snyder	11-1
11	Texas A&M 11-3	R.C. Slocum	11-2
12	Michigan 10-3	Lloyd Carr	9-3
13	Air Force..........12-1	Fisher DeBerry	11-1
14	Georgia............9-3	Jim Donnan	8-3
15	Texas 9-3	Mack Brown	8-3
16	Arkansas 9-3	Houston Nutt	9-2
17	Penn St.............9-3	Joe Paterno	8-3
18	Virginia 9-3	George Welsh	9-2
19	Nebraska 9-4	Frank Solich	9-3
20	Miami-FL 9-3	Butch Davis	8-3

Key Bowl Games

Rankings below reflect final regular season poll, taken Dec. 6. **Fiesta–** #1 Tennessee over #2 Florida St., 23-16; **Sugar–** #3 Ohio St. over #8 Texas A&M, 24-14; **Orange–** #7 Florida over #18 Syracuse, 31-10; **Rose–** #9 Wisconsin over #6 UCLA, 38-31; **Holiday–** #5 Arizona over #14 Nebraska, 23-20; **Citrus–** #15 Michigan over #11 Arkansas, 45-31; **Gator–** #12 Georgia Tech over #17 Notre Dame, 35-28; **Cotton–** #20 Texas over #9 Mississippi St., 38-11; **Peach–** #19 Georgia over #13 Virginia, 35-33; **Alamo–** Purdue over #4 Kansas St., 37-34; **Outback–** #22 Penn St. over Kentucky, 26-14.

All-Time AP Top 20

The composite AP Top 20 from the 1936 season through the 1998 season, based on the final rankings of each year. The final AP poll has been taken after the bowl games in 1965 and since 1968. Team point totals are based on 20 points for all 1st place finishes, 19 for each 2nd, etc. Also listed are the number of times each team has been named national champion by AP and times ranked in the final Top 10 and Top 20.

Final AP

		Pts	No.1	Top 10	Top 20
1	Notre Dame......626		8	34	44
2	Michigan 575		2	33	46
3	Oklahoma 558		6	29	41
4	Alabama 551		6	30	41
5	Ohio St..........518		3	24	41
6	Nebraska 502		4	27	38
7	Tennessee 421		2	21	35
8	USC 414		3	20	36
9	Texas 406		2	19	32
10	Penn St..........393		2	21	34
11	UCLA 322		0	16	29
12	Auburn 281		1	14	26
13	LSU 277		1	14	25
14	Florida St 272		1	14	18
15	Miami-FL........265		4	13	22
16	Arkansas 263		0	13	24
17	Georgia 256		1	14	22
18	Michigan St......238		1	12	19
19	Florida 219		1	11	19
20	Texas A&M 216		1	11	22

Bowl Games

From Jan. 1, 1902 through Jan. 4, 1999. Corporate title sponsors and automatic berths updated through Jan. 1, 1999. Please note that the Bowl selection process is now dominated by the recently-inaugurated Bowl Championship Series (which includes the Fiesta, Orange, Rose and Sugar Bowls) and the following non-BCS bowls' so called "automatic berths" are contingent upon several factors, including the leftovers from the BCS, Notre Dame's record and the record of their designated choices.

Rose Bowl

City: Pasadena, Calif. **Stadium:** Rose Bowl. **Capacity:** 102,083. **Playing surface:** Grass. **First game:** Jan. 1, 1902. **Playing sites:** Tournament Park (1902, 1916-22), Rose Bowl (1923-41 and since 1943) and Duke Stadium in Durham, N.C. (1942, due to wartime restrictions following Japan's attack on Pearl Harbor on Dec. 7, 1941). **Corporate sponsor:** AT&T (since 1998).

Automatic berths: Pacific Coast Conference champion vs. opponent selected by PCC (1924-45 seasons); Big Ten champion vs. Pac-10 champion (1946-97); Bowl Championship Series: Big Ten champion vs. Pac-10 champion, if available (1998-2000 seasons) and #1 vs. #2 on Jan. 3, 2002.

Multiple wins: USC (20); Michigan (8); Ohio St. and Washington (6); Stanford and UCLA (5); Alabama (4); Illinois and Michigan St. (3); California, Iowa and Wisconsin (2).

Year		Year		Year	
1902*	Michigan 49, Stanford 0	1934	Columbia 7, Stanford 0	1953	USC 7, Wisconsin 0
1916	Washington St. 14, Brown 0	1935	Alabama 29, Stanford 13	1954	Michigan St. 28, UCLA 20
1917	Oregon 14, Penn 0	1936	Stanford 7, SMU 0	1955	Ohio St. 20, USC 7
1918	Mare Island 19, Camp Lewis 7	1937	Pittsburgh 21, Washington 0	1956	Michigan St. 17, UCLA 14
1919	Great Lakes 17, Mare Island 0	1938	California 13, Alabama 0	1957	Iowa 35, Oregon St. 19
		1939	USC 7, Duke 3	1958	Ohio St. 10, Oregon 7
1920	Harvard 7, Oregon 6			1959	Iowa 38, California 12
1921	California 28, Ohio St. 0	1940	USC 14, Tennessee 0		
1922	0-0, California vs Wash. & Jeff.	1941	Stanford 21, Nebraska 13	1960	Washington 44, Wisconsin 8
1923	USC 14, Penn St. 0	1942	Oregon St. 20, Duke 16	1961	Washington 17, Minnesota 7
1924	14-14, Navy vs Washington	1943	Georgia 9, UCLA 0	1962	Minnesota 21, UCLA 3
1925	Notre Dame 27, Stanford 10	1944	USC 29, Washington 0	1963	USC 42, Wisconsin 37
1926	Alabama 20, Washington 19	1945	USC 25, Tennessee 0	1964	Illinois 17, Washington 7
1927	7-7, Alabama vs Stanford	1946	Alabama 34, USC 14	1965	Michigan 34, Oregon St. 7
1928	Stanford 7, Pittsburgh 6	1947	Illinois 45, UCLA 14	1966	UCLA 14, Michigan St. 12
1929	Georgia Tech 8, California 7	1948	Michigan 49, USC 0	1967	Purdue 14, USC 13
		1949	Northwestern 20, California 14	1968	USC 14, Indiana 3
1930	USC 47, Pittsburgh 14			1969	Ohio St. 27, USC 16
1931	Alabama 24, Washington St. 0	1950	Ohio St. 17, California 14		
1932	USC 21, Tulane 12	1951	Michigan 14, California 6	1970	USC 10, Michigan 3
1933	USC 35, Pittsburgh 0	1952	Illinois 40, Stanford 7	1971	Stanford 27, Ohio St. 17

Bowl Games (Cont.)

Year		Year		Year	
1972	Stanford 13, Michigan 12	1981	Michigan 23, Washington 6	1990	USC 17, Michigan 10
1973	USC 42, Ohio St. 17	1982	Washington 28, Iowa 0	1991	Washington 46, Iowa 34
1974	Ohio St. 42, USC 21	1983	UCLA 24, Michigan 14	1992	Washington 34, Michigan 14
1975	USC 18, Ohio St. 17	1984	UCLA 45, Illinois 9	1993	Michigan 38, Washington 31
1976	UCLA 23, Ohio St. 10	1985	USC 20, Ohio St. 17	1994	Wisconsin 21, UCLA 16
1977	USC 14, Michigan 6	1986	UCLA 45, Iowa 28	1995	Penn St. 38, Oregon 20
1978	Washington 27, Michigan 20	1987	Arizona St. 22, Michigan 15	1996	USC 41, Northwestern 32
1979	USC 17, Michigan 10	1988	Michigan St. 20, USC 17	1997	Ohio St. 20, Arizona St. 17
1980	USC 17, Ohio St. 16	1989	Michigan 22, USC 14	1998	Michigan 21, Washington St. 16
				1999	Wisconsin 38, UCLA 31
				*January game since 1902.	

Fiesta Bowl

City: Tempe, Ariz. **Stadium:** Sun Devil. **Capacity:** 73,656. **Playing surface:** Grass. **First game:** Dec. 27, 1971. **Playing site:** Sun Devil Stadium (since 1971). **Corporate title sponsors:** Sunkist Citrus Growers (1986-91), IBM OS/2 (1993-95) and Frito-Lay Tostitos chips (since 1996).

Automatic berths: Western Athletic Conference champion vs. at-large opponent (1971-79 seasons); Two of first five picks from 8-team Bowl Coalition pool (1992-94). Bowl Alliance (#1 vs. #2 on Jan. 2, 1996; #3 vs. #5 on Jan. 1, 1997; and #4 vs. #6 on Dec. 31, 1997); Big 12 champion vs. next best team in pool (New Bowl Alliance 1995-1997 seasons); Bowl Championship Series: #1 vs. #2 on Jan. 4, 1999 and Big 12 champion, if available, vs. at-large (1999-2001 seasons).

Multiple wins: Penn St. (6); Arizona St. (5); Florida St. (2).

Year		Year		Year	
1971†	Arizona St. 45, Florida St. 38	1983	Arizona St. 32, Oklahoma 21	1994	Arizona 29, Miami-FL 0
1972	Arizona St. 49, Missouri 35	1984	Ohio St. 28, Pittsburgh 23	1995	Colorado 41, Notre Dame 24
1973	Arizona St. 28, Pittsburgh 7	1985	UCLA 39, Miami-FL 37	1996	Nebraska 62, Florida 24
1974	Oklahoma St. 16, BYU 6	1986	Michigan 27, Nebraska 23	1997	Penn St. 38, Texas 15
1975	Arizona St. 17, Nebraska 14	1987	Penn St. 14, Miami-FL 10	1997†	Kansas St. 35, Syracuse 18
1976	Oklahoma 41, Wyoming 7	1988	Florida St. 31, Nebraska 28	1999	Tennessee 23, Florida St. 16
1977	Penn St. 42, Arizona St. 30	1989	Notre Dame 34, West Va. 21	†December game from 1971-80 and	
1978	10-10, Arkansas vs UCLA			in '97.	
1979	Pittsburgh 16, Arizona 10	1990	Florida St. 41, Nebraska 17	* January game since 1982.	
		1991	Louisville 34, Alabama 7		
1980	Penn St. 31, Ohio St. 19	1992	Penn St. 42, Tennessee 17		
1982*	Penn St. 26, USC 10	1993	Syracuse 26, Colorado 22		

Sugar Bowl

City: New Orleans, La. **Stadium:** Louisiana Superdome. **Capacity:** 77,446. **Playing surface:** AstroTurf. **First game:** Jan. 1, 1935. **Playing sites:** Tulane Stadium (1935-74) and Superdome (since 1975). **Corporate title sponsors:** USF&G Financial Services (1987-95) and Nokia cellular telephones of Finland (starting in 1995).

Automatic berths: SEC champion vs. at-large opponent (1976-91 seasons); SEC champion vs. one of first five picks from 8-team Bowl Coalition pool (1992-94 seasons); #4 vs. #6 on Dec. 31, 1995; #1 vs. #2 on Jan. 2, 1997; and #3 vs. #5 on Jan. 1, 1998; Bowl Championship Series: SEC champion, if available, vs. at-large (1998-99, 2000 seasons) and #1 vs. #2 on Jan. 4, 2000.

Multiple wins: Alabama (8); Mississippi (5); Georgia Tech, Oklahoma and Tennessee (4); Florida St., LSU and Nebraska (3); Florida, Georgia, Notre Dame, Pittsburgh, Santa Clara and TCU (2).

Year		Year		Year	
1935*	Tulane 20, Temple 14	1958	Mississippi 39, Texas 7	1980	Alabama 24, Arkansas 9
1936	TCU 3, LSU 2	1959	LSU 7, Clemson 0	1981	Georgia 17, Notre Dame 10
1937	Santa Clara 21, LSU 14			1982	Pittsburgh 24, Georgia 20
1938	Santa Clara 6, LSU 0	1960	Mississippi 21, LSU 0	1983	Penn St. 27, Georgia 23
1939	TCU 15, Carnegie Tech 7	1961	Mississippi 14, Rice 6	1984	Auburn 9, Michigan 7
		1962	Alabama 10, Arkansas 3	1985	Nebraska 28, LSU 10
1940	Texas A&M 14, Tulane 13	1963	Mississippi 17, Arkansas 13	1986	Tennessee 35, Miami-FL 7
1941	Boston College 19, Tennessee 13	1964	Alabama 12, Mississippi 7	1987	Nebraska 30, LSU 15
1942	Fordham 2, Missouri 0	1965	LSU 13, Syracuse 10	1988	16-16, Syracuse vs Auburn
1943	Tennessee 14, Tulsa 7	1966	Missouri 20, Florida 18	1989	Florida St. 13, Auburn 7
1944	Georgia Tech 20, Tulsa 18	1967	Alabama 34, Nebraska 7		
1945	Duke 29, Alabama 26	1968	LSU 20, Wyoming 13	1990	Miami-FL 33, Alabama 25
1946	Okla. A&M 33, St.Mary's 13	1969	Arkansas 16, Georgia 2	1991	Tennessee 23, Virginia 22
1947	Georgia 20, N. Carolina 10			1992	Notre Dame 39, Florida 28
1948	Texas 27, Alabama 7	1970	Mississippi 27, Arkansas 22	1993	Alabama 34, Miami-FL 13
1949	Oklahoma 14, N. Carolina 6	1971	Tennessee 34, Air Force 13	1994	Florida 41, West Va. 7
		1972	Oklahoma 40, Auburn 22	1995	Florida St. 23, Florida 17
1950	Oklahoma 35, LSU 0	1972†	Oklahoma 14, Penn St. 0	1995†	Va. Tech 28, Texas 10
1951	Kentucky 13, Oklahoma 7	1973	Notre Dame 24, Alabama 23	1997	Florida 52, Florida St. 20
1952	Maryland 28, Tennessee 13	1974	Nebraska 13, Florida 10	1998	Florida St. 31, Ohio St. 14
1953	Georgia Tech 24, Mississippi 7	1975	Alabama 13, Penn St. 6	1999	Ohio St. 24, Texas A&M 14
1954	Georgia Tech 42, West Va. 19	1977*	Pittsburgh 27, Georgia 3	*January game from 1935-72 and	
1955	Navy 21, Mississippi 0	1978	Alabama 35, Ohio St. 6	since 1987 (except in 1995).	
1956	Georgia Tech 7, Pittsburgh 0	1979	Alabama 14, Penn St. 7	†Game played on Dec. 31 from	
1957	Baylor 13, Tennessee 7			1972-75 and in 1995.	

Orange Bowl

City: Miami, Fla. **Stadium:** Pro Player. **Capacity:** 74,916. **Playing surface:** Grass. **First game:** Jan. 1, 1935. **Playing sites:** Orange Bowl (1935-95); Pro Player Stadium (since 1996). **Corporate title sponsor:** Federal Express (since 1989).

Automatic berths: Big 8 champion vs. Atlantic Coast Conference champion (1953-57 seasons); Big 8 champion vs. at-large opponent (1958-63 seasons and 1975-91 seasons); Big 8 champion vs. one of first five picks from 8-team Bowl Coalition pool (1992-94 seasons); #3 vs. #5 on Jan. 1, 1996; #4 vs. #6 on Dec. 31, 1996; and #1 vs. #2 on Jan. 2, 1998 (New Bowl Alliance 1995-97 seasons); Bowl Championship Series: Big East or ACC champion, if available, vs. at-large (1998-99, 2001 seasons) and #1 vs. #2 Jan. 3, 2001.

Multiple wins: Oklahoma (11); Nebraska (8); Miami-FL (5); Alabama (4); Florida State, Georgia Tech and Penn St. (3); Clemson, Colorado, Florida, Georgia, LSU, Notre Dame and Texas (2).

Year		Year		Year	
1935*	Bucknell 26, Miami-FL 0	1958	Oklahoma 48, Duke 21	1981	Oklahoma 18, Florida St. 17
1936	Catholic U. 20, Mississippi 19	1959	Oklahoma 21, Syracuse 6	1982	Clemson 22, Nebraska 15
1937	Duquesne 13, Mississippi St. 12	1960	Georgia 14, Missouri 0	1983	Nebraska 21, LSU 20
1938	Auburn 6, Michigan St. 0	1961	Missouri 21, Navy 14	1984	Miami-FL 31, Nebraska 30
1939	Tennessee 17, Oklahoma 0	1962	LSU 25, Colorado 7	1985	Washington 28, Oklahoma 17
1940	Georgia Tech 21, Missouri 7	1963	Alabama 17, Oklahoma 0	1986	Oklahoma 25, Penn St. 10
1941	Mississippi St. 14, Georgetown 7	1964	Nebraska 13, Auburn 7	1987	Oklahoma 42, Arkansas 8
1942	Georgia 40, TCU 26	1965†	Texas 21, Alabama 17	1988	Miami-FL 20, Oklahoma 14
1943	Alabama 37, Boston College 21	1966	Alabama 39, Nebraska 28	1989	Miami-FL 23, Nebraska 3
1944	LSU 19, Texas A&M 14	1967	Florida 27, Georgia Tech 12	1990	Notre Dame, 21, Colorado 6
1945	Tulsa 26, Georgia Tech 12	1968	Oklahoma 26, Tennessee 24	1991	Colorado 10, Notre Dame 9
1946	Miami-FL 13, Holy Cross 6	1969	Penn St. 15, Kansas 14	1992	Miami-FL 22, Nebraska 0
1947	Rice 8, Tennessee 0	1970	Penn St. 10, Missouri 3	1993	Florida St. 27, Nebraska 14
1948	Georgia Tech 20, Kansas 14	1971	Nebraska 17, LSU 12	1994	Florida St. 18, Nebraska 16
1949	Texas 41, Georgia 28	1972	Nebraska 38, Alabama 6	1995	Nebraska 24, Miami-FL 17
1950	Santa Clara 21, Kentucky 13	1973	Nebraska 40, Notre Dame 6	1996	Florida St. 31, Notre Dame 26
1951	Clemson 15, Miami-FL 14	1974	Penn St. 16, LSU 9	1996**	Nebraska 41, Virginia Tech 21
1952	Georgia Tech 17, Baylor 14	1975	Notre Dame 13, Alabama 11	1998*	Nebraska 42, Tennessee 17
1953	Alabama 61, Syracuse 6	1976	Oklahoma 14, Michigan 6	1999	Florida 31, Syracuse 10
1954	Oklahoma 7, Maryland 0	1977	Ohio St. 27, Colorado 10	*January game 1935-1996 and '98.
1955	Duke 34, Nebraska 7	1978	Arkansas 31, Oklahoma 6	**December game in 1996
1956	Oklahoma 20, Maryland 6	1979	Oklahoma 31, Nebraska 24	†Night game since 1965.
1957	Colorado 27, Clemson 21	1980	Oklahoma 24, Florida St. 7	

Cotton Bowl

City: Dallas, Tex. **Stadium:** Cotton Bowl. **Capacity:** 68,252. **Playing surface:** Grass. **First game:** Jan 1, 1937. **Playing sites:** Fair Park Stadium (1937) and Cotton Bowl (since 1938). **Corporate title sponsor:** Mobil Corporation (1988-95), Southwestern Bell (since 1997).

Automatic berths: SWC champion vs. at-large opponent (1941-91 seasons); SWC champion vs. one of first five picks from 8-team Bowl Coalition pool (1992-1994 seasons); second pick from Big 12 vs. first choice of WAC champion or second pick from Pac-10 (1995-97 seasons); Big 12 vs. SEC (since 1998).

Multiple wins: Texas (10); Notre Dame (5); Texas A&M (4); Rice (3); Alabama, Arkansas, Georgia, Houston, LSU, Penn St., SMU, Tennessee, TCU and UCLA (2).

Year		Year		Year	
1937*	TCU 16, Marquette 6	1959	0-0, TCU vs Air Force	1981	Alabama 30, Baylor 2
1938	Rice 28, Colorado 14	1960	Syracuse 23, Texas 14	1982	Texas 14, Alabama 12
1939	St. Mary's 20, Texas Tech 13	1961	Duke 7, Arkansas 6	1983	SMU 7, Pittsburgh 3
1940	Clemson 6, Boston College 3	1962	Texas 12, Mississippi 7	1984	Georgia 10, Texas 9
1941	Texas A&M 13, Fordham 12	1963	LSU 13, Texas 0	1985	Boston College 45, Houston 28
1942	Alabama 29, Texas A&M 21	1964	Texas 28, Navy 6	1986	Texas A&M 36, Auburn 16
1943	Texas 14, Georgia Tech 7	1965	Arkansas 10, Nebraska 7	1987	Ohio St. 28, Texas A&M 12
1944	7-7, Texas vs Randolph Field	1966	LSU 14, Arkansas 7	1988	Texas A&M 35, Notre Dame 10
1945	Oklahoma A&M 34, TCU 0	1966†	Georgia 24, SMU 9	1989	UCLA 17, Arkansas 3
1946	Texas 40, Missouri 27	1968*	Texas A&M 20, Alabama 16	1990	Tennessee 31, Arkansas 27
1947	0-0, Arkansas vs LSU	1969	Texas 36, Tennessee 13	1991	Miami-FL 46, Texas 3
1948	13-13, SMU vs Penn St.	1970	Texas 21, Notre Dame 17	1992	Florida St. 10, Texas A&M 2
1949	SMU 21, Oregon 13	1971	Notre Dame 24, Texas 11	1993	Notre Dame 28, Texas A&M 3
1950	Rice 27, N. Carolina 13	1972	Penn St. 30, Texas 6	1994	Notre Dame 24, Texas A&M 21
1951	Tennessee 20, Texas 14	1973	Texas 17, Alabama 13	1995	USC 55, Texas Tech 14
1952	Kentucky 20, TCU 7	1974	Nebraska 19, Texas 3	1996	Colorado 38, Oregon 6
1953	Texas 16, Tennessee 0	1975	Penn St. 41, Baylor 20	1997	BYU 19, Kansas St. 15
1954	Rice 28, Alabama 6	1976	Arkansas 31, Georgia 10	1998	UCLA 29, Texas A&M 23
1955	Georgia Tech 14, Arkansas 6	1977	Houston 30, Maryland 21	1999	Texas 38, Mississippi St. 11
1956	Mississippi 14, TCU 13	1978	Notre Dame 38, Texas 10	*January game from 1937-66 and since 1968.
1957	TCU 28, Syracuse 27	1979	Notre Dame 35, Houston 34	
1958	Navy 20, Rice 7	1980	Houston 17, Nebraska 14	†Game played on Dec. 31, 1966.

Bowl Games (Cont.)
Florida Citrus Bowl

City: Orlando, Fla. **Stadium:** Florida Citrus Bowl. **Capacity:** 70,188. **Playing surface:** Grass. **First game:** Jan. 1, 1947. **Name change:** Tangerine Bowl (1947-82) and Florida Citrus Bowl (since 1983). **Playing sites:** Tangerine Bowl (1947-72, 1974-82), Florida Field in Gainesville (1973), Orlando Stadium (1983-85) and Florida Citrus Bowl (since 1986). The Tangerine Bowl, Orlando Stadium and Florida Citrus Bowl are all the same stadium. **Corporate title sponsors:** Florida Department of Citrus (since 1983) and CompUSA (since 1992).

Automatic berths: Championship game of Atlantic Coast Regional Conference (1964-67 seasons); Mid-American Conference champion vs. Southern Conference champion (1968-71 seasons); ACC champion vs. at-large opponent (1988-91 seasons); second pick from SEC, if available, vs. second pick from Big 10, if available (since 1992 season).

Multiple wins: East Texas St., Miami-OH, Tennessee and Toledo (3); Auburn, Catawba, Clemson, East Carolina and Florida (2).

Year		Year		Year	
1947*	Catawba 31, Maryville 6	1965	E. Carolina 31, Maine 0	1984	17-17, Florida St. vs Georgia
1948	Catawba 7, Marshall 0	1966	Morgan St. 14, West Chester 6	1985	Ohio St. 10, BYU 7
1949	21-21, Murray St. vs Sul Ross St.	1967	Tenn-Martin 25, West Chester 8	1987*	Auburn 16, USC 7
1950	St. Vincent 7, Emory & Henry 6	1968	Richmond 49, Ohio U. 42	1988	Clemson 35, Penn St. 10
1951	M. Harvey 35, Emory & Henry 14	1969	Toledo 56, Davidson 33	1989	Clemson 13, Oklahoma 6
1952	Stetson 35, Arkansas St. 20	1970	Toledo 40, Wm. & Mary 12	1990	Illinois 31, Virginia 21
1953	E. Texas St. 33, Tenn. Tech 0	1971	Toledo 28, Richmond 3	1991	Georgia Tech 45, Nebraska 21
1954	7-7, E. Texas St. vs Arkansas St.	1972	Tampa 21, Kent St. 18	1992	California 37, Clemson 13
1955	Neb.-Omaha 7, Eastern Ky. 6	1973	Miami-OH 16, Florida 7	1993	Georgia 21, Ohio St. 14
1956	6-6, Juniata vs Missouri Valley	1974	Miami-OH 21, Georgia 10	1994	Penn St. 31, Tennessee 13
1957	W. Texas St. 20, So. Miss. 13	1975	Miami-OH 20, S. Carolina 7	1995	Alabama 24, Ohio St. 17
1958	E. Texas St. 10, So. Miss. 9	1976	Oklahoma 49, BYU 21	1996	Tennessee 20, Ohio St. 14
1958†	E. Texas St. 26, Mo. Valley 7	1977	Florida St. 40, Texas Tech 17	1997	Tennessee 48, Northwestern 28
		1978	N.C. State 30, Pittsburgh 17	1998	Florida 21, Penn St. 6
1960*	Mid. Tenn. 21, Presbyterian 12	1979	LSU 34, Wake Forest 10	1999	Michigan 45, Arkansas 31
1960†	Citadel 27, Tenn. Tech 0			*January game from 1947-58, in 1960 and since 1987.	
1961	Lamar 21, Middle Tenn. 14	1980	Florida 35, Maryland 20		
1962	Houston 49, Miami-OH 21	1981	Missouri 19, Southern Miss. 17	†December game in 1958 and 1960-85.	
1963	Western Ky. 27, Coast Guard 0	1982	Auburn 33, Boston College 26		
1964	E. Carolina 14, Massachusetts 13	1983	Tennessee 30, Maryland 23		

Gator Bowl

City: Jacksonville, Fla. **Stadium:** ALLTEL Stadium. **Capacity:** 73,000. **Playing surface:** Grass. **First game:** Jan. 1, 1946. **Playing sites:** Gator Bowl (1946-93), Florida Field in Gainesville (1994) and New Gator Bowl (since 1995). Name was changed to ALLTEL Stadium in 1997. **Corporate title sponsors:** Mazda Motors of America, Inc. (1986-91), Outback Steakhouse, Inc. (1992-94) and Toyota Motor Co. (since 1995).

Automatic berths: Third pick from SEC vs. sixth pick from 8-team Bowl Coalition pool (1992-94 seasons); second pick from ACC, if available, vs. second pick from Big East, if available (since 1995 season).

Multiple wins: Florida (6); North Carolina (5); Auburn and Clemson (4); Florida St., Georgia Tech and Tennessee (3); Georgia, Maryland, Oklahoma, Pittsburgh, and Texas Tech (2).

Year		Year		Year	
1946*	Wake Forest 26, S. Carolina 14	1965†	Georgia Tech 31, Texas Tech 21	1985	Florida St. 34, Oklahoma St. 23
1947	Oklahoma 34, N.C. State 13	1966	Tennessee 18, Syracuse 12	1986	Clemson 27, Stanford 21
1948	20-20, Maryland vs Georgia	1967	17-17, Florida St. vs Penn St.	1987	LSU 30, S. Carolina 13
1949	Clemson 24, Missouri 23	1968	Missouri 35, Alabama 10	1989*	Georgia 34, Michigan St. 27
1950	Maryland 20, Missouri 7	1969	Florida 14, Tennessee 13	1989†	Clemson 27, West Va. 7
1951	Wyoming 20, Wash. & Lee 7	1971*	Auburn 35, Mississippi 28	1991*	Michigan 35, Mississippi 3
1952	Miami-FL 14, Clemson 0	1971†	Georgia 7, N. Carolina 3	1991†	Oklahoma 48, Virginia 14
1953	Florida 14, Tulsa 13	1972	Auburn 24, Colorado 3	1992	Florida 27, N.C. State 10
1954	Texas Tech 35, Auburn 13	1973	Texas Tech 28, Tennessee 19	1993	Alabama 24, N. Carolina 10
1954†	Auburn 33, Baylor 13	1974	Auburn 27, Texas 3	1994	Tennessee 45, Va. Tech 23
1955	Vanderbilt 25, Auburn 13	1975	Maryland 13, Florida 0	1996*	Syracuse 41, Clemson 0
1956	Georgia Tech 21, Pittsburgh 14	1976	Notre Dame 20, Penn St. 9	1997	N. Carolina 20, West Va. 13
1957	Tennessee 3, Texas A&M 0	1977	Pittsburgh 34, Clemson 3	1998	N. Carolina 42, Va. Tech 3
1958	Mississippi 7, Florida 3	1978	Clemson 17, Ohio St. 15	1999	Ga. Tech 35, Notre Dame 28
1960*	Arkansas 14, Georgia Tech 7	1979	N. Carolina 17, Michigan 15	*January game from 1946-54, 1960, 1965, 1971, 1989, 1991 and since 1996.	
1960†	Florida 13, Baylor 12	1980	Pittsburgh 37, S. Carolina 9		
1961	Penn St. 30, Georgia Tech 15	1981	N. Carolina 31, Arkansas 27	†December game from 1954-58, 1960-63, 1965-69, 1971-87, 1989 and 1991-94.	
1962	Florida 17, Penn St. 7	1982	Florida St. 31, West Va. 12		
1963	N. Carolina 35, Air Force 0	1983	Florida 14, Iowa 6		
1965*	Florida St. 36, Oklahoma 19	1984	Oklahoma St. 21, S. Carolina 14		

Holiday Bowl

City: San Diego, Calif. **Stadium:** Qualcomm. **Capacity:** 71,000. **Playing surface:** Grass. **First game:** Dec. 22, 1978. **Playing site:** San Diego/Jack Murphy Stadium (since 1978). Name changed to Qualcomm Stadium in 1997. **Corporate title sponsors:** Sea World (1986-90), Thrifty Car Rental (1991-94), Chrysler-Plymouth Division of Chrysler Corp. (1995-97) and U.S. Filter/Culligan Water Tech. (since 1998).

Automatic berths: WAC champion vs. at-large opponent (1978-84, 1986-90 seasons); WAC champ vs. second pick from Big 10 (1991 season); WAC champ vs. third pick from Big 10 (1992-94 seasons); choice of WAC champion, if available, or second pick from Pac-10, if available vs. third pick from Big 12, if available (since 1995 season).

Multiple wins: BYU (4); Iowa and Ohio St. (2).

Year		Year		Year	
1978†	Navy 23, BYU 16	1986	Iowa 39, San Diego St. 38	1994	Michigan 24, Colo. St. 14
1979	Indiana 38, BYU 37	1987	Iowa 20, Wyoming 19	1995	Kansas St. 54, Colorado St. 21
		1988	Oklahoma St. 62, Wyoming 14	1996	Colorado 33, Washington 21
1980	BYU 46, SMU 45	1989	Penn St. 50, BYU 39	1997	Colorado St. 35, Missouri 24
1981	BYU 38, Washington St. 36			1998	Arizona 23, Nebraska 20
1982	Ohio St. 47, BYU 17	1990	Texas A&M 65, BYU 14	†December game since 1978.	
1983	BYU 21, Missouri 17	1991	13-13, Iowa vs BYU		
1984	BYU 24, Michigan 17	1992	Hawaii 27, Illinois 17		
1985	Arkansas 18, Arizona St. 17	1993	Ohio St. 28, BYU 21		

Outback Bowl

City: Tampa, Fla. **Stadium:** Raymond James. **Capacity:** 66,005. **Playing surface:** Grass. **First game:** Dec. 23, 1986. **Name change:** Hall of Fame Bowl (1986-95) and Outback Bowl (since 1995). **Playing sites:** Tampa Stadium (since 1986). Name changed to Houlihan's Stadium in 1996, Raymond James Stadium (since 1999). **Corporate title sponsor:** Outback Steakhouse, Inc. (since 1995).

Automatic berths: Fourth pick from ACC vs. fourth pick from Big 10 (1993-94 seasons); third pick from Big 10, if available, vs. third pick from SEC, if available (since 1995 season).

Multiple wins: Michigan, Penn St. and Syracuse (2).

Year		Year		Year	
1986†	Boston College 27, Georgia 24	1992	Syracuse 24, Ohio St. 17	1997	Alabama 17, Michigan 14
1988*	Michigan 28, Alabama 24	1993	Tennessee 38, Boston Col. 23	1998	Georgia 33, Wisconsin 6
1989	Syracuse 23, LSU 10	1994	Michigan 42, N.C. State 7	1999	Penn St. 26, Kentucky 14
		1995	Wisconsin 34, Duke 20	†December game in 1986.	
1990	Auburn 31, Ohio St. 14	1996	Penn St. 43, Auburn 14	*January game since 1988.	
1991	Clemson 30, Illinois 0				

Peach Bowl

City: Atlanta, Ga. **Stadium:** Georgia Dome. **Capacity:** 71,228. **Playing surface:** AstroTurf. **First game:** Dec. 30, 1968. **Playing sites:** Grant Field (1968-70), Atlanta-Fulton County Stadium (1971-92) and Georgia Dome (since 1993). **Corporate title sponsor:** Chick-fil-A (since 1998).

Automatic berths: Third pick from ACC vs. at-large opponent (1992 season); third pick from ACC vs. fourth pick from SEC (1993-94 seasons); third pick from ACC, if available, vs. fourth pick from SEC, if available (since 1995 season).

Multiple wins: N.C. State (4); West Virginia (3); Auburn, Georgia, LSU and Virginia (2).

Year		Year		Year	
1968†	LSU 31, Florida St. 27	1981*	Miami-FL 20, Va. Tech 10	1993	N. Carolina 21, Miss. St. 17
1969	West Va. 14, S. Carolina 3	1981†	West Va. 26, Florida 6	1993†	Clemson 14, Kentucky 13
		1982	Iowa 28, Tennessee 22	1995*	N.C. State 24, Miss. St. 24
1970	Arizona St. 48, N. Carolina 26	1983	Florida St. 28, N. Carolina 3	1995†	Virginia 34, Georgia 27
1971	Mississippi 41, Georgia Tech 18	1984	Virginia 27, Purdue 24	1996	LSU 10, Clemson 7
1972	N.C. State 49, West Va. 13	1985	Army 31, Illinois 29	1998*	Auburn 21, Clemson 17
1973	Georgia 17, Maryland 16	1986	Va. Tech 25, N.C. State 24	1998†	Georgia 35, Virginia 33
1974	6-6, Vanderbilt vs Texas Tech	1988*	Tennessee 27, Indiana 22	†December game from 1968-79,	
1975	West Va. 13, N.C. State 10	1988†	N.C. State 28, Iowa 23	1981-86, 1988-90, 1993, 1995,	
1976	Kentucky 21, N. Carolina 0	1989	Syracuse 19, Georgia 18	1996 and 1998.	
1977	N.C. State 24, Iowa St. 14			*January game in 1981, 1988, 1992-	
1978	Purdue 41, Georgia Tech 21	1990	Auburn 27, Indiana 23	93, 1995 and 1998.	
1979	Baylor 24, Clemson 18	1992*	E. Carolina 37, N.C. State 34		

Alamo Bowl

City: San Antonio, Tex. **Stadium:** Alamodome. **Capacity:** 65,000. **Playing surface:** AstroTurf. **First game:** Dec. 31, 1993. **Playing site:** Alamodome (since 1993). **Corporate title sponsor:** Builders Square (since 1993).

Automatic berths: third pick from SWC vs. fourth pick from Pac-10 (1993-94 seasons); fourth pick from Big 10, if available vs. fourth pick from Big 12, if available (since 1995 season).

Multiple wins: Purdue (2).

Year		Year		Year	
1993†	California 37, Iowa 3	1996	Iowa 27, Texas Tech 0	1998	Purdue 37, Kansas St. 34
1994	Washington St. 10, Baylor 3	1997	Purdue 33, Oklahoma St. 20	†December game since 1993.	
1995	Texas A&M 22, Michigan 20				

Bowl Games (Cont.)
Sun Bowl

City: El Paso, Tex. **Stadium:** Sun Bowl. **Capacity:** 52,000. **Playing surface:** AstroTurf. **First game:** Jan. 1, 1936. **Name changes:** Sun Bowl (1936-85), John Hancock Sun Bowl (1986-88), John Hancock Bowl (1989-93) and Sun Bowl (since 1994). **Playing sites:** Kidd Field (1936-62) and Sun Bowl (since 1963). **Corporate title sponsors:** John Hancock Financial Services (1986-93), Norwest Bank (1996-98), Wells Fargo (since 1999).

    Automatic berths: Eighth pick from 8-team Bowl Coalition pool vs. at-large opponent (1992); Seventh and eighth picks from 8-team Bowl Coalition pool (1993-94 seasons); third pick from Pac-10, if available, vs. fifth pick from Big 10, if available (since 1995 season).

    Multiple wins: Texas Western/UTEP (5); Alabama and Wyoming (3); Nebraska, New Mexico St., North Carolina, Oklahoma, Pittsburgh, SW Texas, Stanford, Texas, West Texas St. and West Virginia (2).

Year		Year		Year	
1936*	14-14, Hardin-Simmons vs New Mexico St.	1957	Geo. Wash. 13, Tex. Western 0	1979	Washington 14, Texas 7
1937	Hardin-Simmons 34, Texas Mines 6	1958*	Louisville 34, Drake 20	1980	Nebraska 31, Miss. St. 17
1938	West Va. 7, Texas Tech 6	1958†	Wyoming 14, Hardin-Simmons 6	1981	Oklahoma 40, Houston 14
1939	Utah 26, New Mexico 0	1959	New Mexico St. 28, N. Texas 8	1982	N. Carolina 26, Texas 10
		1960	New Mexico St. 20, Utah St. 13	1983	Alabama 28, SMU 7
1940	0-0, Catholic U. vs Arizona St.	1961	Villanova 17, Wichita 9	1984	Maryland 28, Tennessee 27
1941	W. Reserve 26, Arizona St. 13	1962	West Texas 15, Ohio U. 14	1985	13-13, Georgia vs Arizona
1942	Tulsa 6, Texas Tech 0	1963	Oregon 21, SMU 14	1986	Alabama 28, Washington 6
1943	Second Air Force 13, Hardin-Simmons 7	1964	Georgia 7, Texas Tech 0	1987	Oklahoma St. 35, West Va. 33
		1965	Texas Western 13, TCU 12	1988	Alabama 29, Army 28
1944	SW Texas 7, New Mexico 0	1966	Wyoming 28, Florida St. 20	1989	Pittsburgh 31, Texas A&M 28
1945	SW Texas 35, U. of Mexico 0	1967	UTEP 14, Mississippi 7		
1946	New Mexico 34, Denver 24	1968	Auburn 34, Arizona 10	1990	Michigan St. 17, USC 16
1947	Cincinnati 18, Va. Tech 6	1969	Nebraska 45, Georgia 6	1991	UCLA 6, Illinois 3
1948	Miami-OH 13, Texas Tech 12			1992	Baylor 20, Arizona 15
1949	West Va. 21, Texas Mines 12	1970	Georgia Tech 17, Texas Tech 9	1993	Oklahoma 41, Texas Tech 10
		1971	LSU 33, Iowa St. 15	1994	Texas 35, N. Carolina 31
1950	Tex. Western 33, Georgetown 20	1972	N. Carolina 32, Texas Tech 28	1995	Iowa 38, Washington 18
1951	West Texas 14, Cincinnati 13	1973	Missouri 34, Auburn 17	1996	Stanford 38, Michigan St. 0
1952	Texas Tech 25, Pacific 14	1974	Miss. St. 26, N. Carolina 24	1997	Arizona St. 17, Iowa 7
1953	Pacific 26, Southern Miss. 7	1975	Pittsburgh 33, Kansas 19	1998	TCU 28, USC 19
1954	Tex. Western 37, So. Miss. 14	1977*	Texas A&M 37, Florida 14	*January game from 1936-58 and in 1977.	
1955	Tex. Western 47, Florida St. 20	1977†	Stanford 24, LSU 14	†December game from 1958-75 and since 1977.	
1956	Wyoming 21, Texas Tech 14	1978	Texas 42, Maryland 0		

Insight.com Bowl

City: Tucson, Ariz. **Stadium:** Arizona. **Capacity:** 57,803. **Playing surface:** Grass. **First game:** Dec. 31, 1989. **Name change:** Copper Bowl (1989-1996), Insight.com Bowl (since 1997). **Playing site:** Arizona Stadium (since 1989). **Corporate title sponsors:** Domino's Pizza (1990-91), Weiser Lock (1992-1996) and Insight Enterprises (since 1997).

    Automatic berths: Third pick from WAC vs. at-large opponent (1992 season); third pick from WAC vs. fourth pick from Big Eight (1993-94 seasons); second pick from WAC vs. sixth pick from Big 12 (1995-97); third pick from Big East, if available vs. fifth pick from Big 12, if available (since 1998 season).

    Multiple wins: Arizona (2).

Year		Year		Year	
1989†	Arizona 17, N.C. State 10	1993	Kansas St. 52, Wyoming 17	1997	Arizona 20, New Mexico 14
1990	California 17, Wyoming 15	1994	BYU 31, Oklahoma 6	1998	Missouri 34, W. Virginia 31
1991	Indiana 24, Baylor 0	1995	Texas Tech 55, Air Force 41	†December game since 1989.	
1992	Washington St. 31, Utah 28	1996	Wisconsin 38, Utah 10		

Bowl Matchups of Unbeaten Teams

Date	Bowl	Winner	Head Coach	Score	Loser	Head Coach
1/1/21	Rose	California (8-0)	Andy Smith	28-0	Ohio St. (7-0)	John Wilce
1/2/22	Rose	Wash. & Jeff. (10-0)	Greasy Neale	0-0	California (9-0)	Andy Smith
1/1/27	Rose	Stanford (10-0)	Pop Warner	7-7	Alabama (9-0)	Wallace Wade
1/1/31	Rose	Alabama (9-0)	Wallace Wade	24-0	Washington St. (9-0)	Babe Hollingbery
1/2/39	Orange	Tennessee (10-0)	Bob Neyland	17-0	Oklahoma (10-0)	Tom Stidham
1/1/41	Sugar	Boston College (10-0)	Frank Leahy	19-13	Tennessee (10-0)	Bob Neyland
1/1/52	Sugar	Maryland (9-0)	Jim Tatum	28-13	Tennessee (10-0)	Bob Neyland
1/2/56	Orange	Oklahoma (10-0)	Bud Wilkinson	20-6	Maryland (10-0)	Jim Tatum
1/1/72	Orange	Nebraska (12-0)	Bob Devaney	38-6	Alabama (11-0)	Bear Bryant
12/31/73	Sugar	Notre Dame (10-0)	Ara Parseghian	24-23	Alabama (11-0)	Bear Bryant
1/2/87	Fiesta	Penn St. (11-0)	Joe Paterno	14-10	Miami-FL (11-0)	Jimmy Johnson
1/1/88	Orange	Miami-FL (11-0)	Jimmy Johnson	20-14	Oklahoma (11-0)	Barry Switzer
1/2/89	Fiesta	Notre Dame (11-0)	Lou Holtz	34-21	West Va. (11-0)	Don Nehlen
1/1/93	Sugar	Alabama (12-0)	Gene Stallings	34-13	Miami-FL. (11-0)	Dennis Erickson
1/2/96	Fiesta	Nebraska (11-0)	Tom Osborne	62-24	Florida (12-0)	Steve Spurrier

Liberty Bowl

City: Memphis, Tenn. **Stadium:** Liberty Bowl Memorial. **Capacity:** 62,380. **Playing surface:** Grass. **First game:** Dec. 19, 1959. **Playing sites:** Municipal Stadium in Philadelphia (1959-63), Convention Hall in Atlantic City, N.J. (1964), Memphis Memorial Stadium (1965-75) and Liberty Bowl Memorial Stadium (since 1976). Memphis Memorial Stadium renamed Liberty Bowl Memorial in 1976. **Corporate title sponsors:** St. Jude's Hospital (since 1993), AXA/Equitable (since 1997).

Automatic berths: Commander-in-Chief's Trophy winner (Army, Navy or Air Force) vs. at-large opponent (1989-92 seasons); none (1993 season); first pick from independent group of Cincinnati, East Carolina, Memphis, Southern Miss. and Tulane vs. at-large opponent (for 1994 and '95 seasons); Conference USA champion vs. fourth pick from the Big East (1996-97 seasons); Conference USA champion, if available, vs. fifth, sixth or seventh pick or at-large from SEC (since 1998 season).

Multiple wins: Mississippi (4); Penn St. and Tennessee (3); Air Force, Alabama, N.C. State, Syracuse and Tulane (2).

Year		Year		Year	
1959†	Penn St. 7, Alabama 0	1973	N.C. State 31, Kansas 18	1987	Georgia 20, Arkansas 17
1960	Penn St. 41, Oregon 12	1974	Tennessee 7, Maryland 3	1988	Indiana 34, S. Carolina 10
1961	Syracuse 15, Miami-FL 14	1975	USC 20, Texas A&M 0	1989	Mississippi 42, Air Force 29
1962	Oregon St. 6, Villanova 0	1976	Alabama 36, UCLA 6		
1963	Mississippi St. 16, N.C. State 12	1977	Nebraska 21, N. Carolina 17	1990	Air Force 23, Ohio St. 11
1964	Utah 32, West Virginia 6	1978	Missouri 20, LSU 15	1991	Air Force 38, Mississippi St. 15
1965	Mississippi 13, Auburn 7	1979	Penn St. 9, Tulane 6	1992	Mississippi 13, Air Force 0
1966	Miami-FL 14, Virginia Tech 7			1993	Louisville 18, Michigan St. 7
1967	N.C. State 14, Georgia 7	1980	Purdue 28, Missouri 25	1994	Illinois 30, E. Carolina 0
1968	Mississippi 34, Virginia Tech 17	1981	Ohio St. 31, Navy 28	1995	E. Carolina 19, Stanford 13
1969	Colorado 47, Alabama 33	1982	Alabama 21, Illinois 15	1996	Syracuse 30, Houston 17
		1983	Notre Dame 19, Boston Col. 18	1997	Southern Miss. 41, Pittsburgh 7
1970	Tulane 17, Colorado 3	1984	Auburn 21, Arkansas 15	1998	Tulane 41, BYU 27
1971	Tennessee 14, Arkansas 13	1985	Baylor 21, LSU 7		†December game since 1959.
1972	Georgia Tech 31, Iowa St. 30	1986	Tennessee 21, Minnesota 14		

Micron PC Bowl

City: Miami, Fla. **Stadium:** Pro Player. **Capacity:** 74,915. **Playing surface:** Grass. **First game:** Dec. 28, 1990. **Name change:** Blockbuster Bowl (1990-93), Carquest Bowl (1994-97) and Micron PC Bowl (since 1998). The game was called the Sunshine Football Classic for a short time in the offseason after Carquest Auto Parts dropped its sponsorship and before Micron signed on. **Playing site:** Joe Robbie Stadium (since 1990). Name changed to Pro Player Stadium in 1996. **Corporate title sponsors:** Blockbuster Video (1990-93), Carquest Auto Parts (1993-97) and Micron Electronics (since 1998).

Automatic berths: Penn St. vs. seventh pick from 8-team Bowl Coalition pool (1992 season); third pick from Big East vs. fifth pick from SEC (1993-94 seasons); third pick from Big East vs. fifth pick from SEC (1995 season); third pick from Big East vs. fourth pick from ACC (1996-97 season); sixth pick from Big Ten, if available, vs. fourth pick from ACC, if available (since 1998 season).

Multiple wins: Miami-FL (2).

Year		Year		Year	
1990†	Florida St. 24, Penn St. 17	1995	S. Carolina 24, West Va. 21	1998	Miami-FL 46, N.C. State 23
1991	Alabama 30, Colorado 25	1995†	N. Carolina 20, Arkansas 10		†December game from 1990-91 and
1993*	Stanford 24, Penn St. 3	1996	Miami-FL 31, Virginia 21		since 1995.
1994	Boston College 31, Virginia 13	1997	Ga. Tech 35, W. Virginia 30		*January game 1993-95.

Aloha Bowl

City: Honolulu, Hawaii. **Stadium:** Aloha. **Capacity:** 50,000. **Playing surface:** AstroTurf. **First game:** Dec. 25, 1982. **Playing site:** Aloha Stadium (since 1982). **Corporate title sponsor:** Jeep Eagle Division of Chrysler (since 1987).

Automatic berths: Second pick from WAC vs. third pick from Big Eight (1992-93 seasons); third pick from Big Eight vs. at-large (1994 season); fifth pick from Big 12 vs. fourth pick from Pac-10 (1995-97 season); fourth pick from Pac-10, if available vs. at-large (since 1998 season).

Multiple wins: Colorado, Kansas and Washington (2).

Year		Year		Year	
1982†	Washington 21, Maryland 20	1988	Washington St. 24, Houston 22	1994	Boston Col. 12, Kansas St. 7
1983	Penn St. 13, Washington 10	1989	Michigan St. 33, Hawaii 13	1995	Kansas 51, UCLA 30
1984	SMU 27, Notre Dame 20	1990	Syracuse 28, Arizona 0	1996	Navy 42, California 38
1985	Alabama 24, USC 3	1991	Georgia Tech 18, Stanford 17	1997	Washington 51, Michigan St. 23
1986	Arizona 30, N. Carolina 21	1992	Kansas 23, BYU 20	1998	Colorado 51, Oregon 43
1987	UCLA 20, Florida 16	1993	Colorado 41, Fresno St. 30		†December game since 1982.

Oahu Bowl

City: Honolulu, Hawaii. **Stadium:** Aloha. **Capacity:** 50,000. **Playing surface:** AstroTurf. **First game:** Dec. 25, 1998. **Playing site:** Aloha Stadium (since 1998). **Corporate title sponsor:** Jeep Eagle Division of Chrysler (since 1998).

Automatic berths: second or third pick from WAC, if available, vs. fifth pick from Pac-10, if available (since 1998 season).

Year
1998† Air Force 45, Washington 25
†December game since 1998.

Humanitarian Bowl

City: Boise, Idaho. **Stadium:** Bronco. **Capacity:** 30,000. **Playing surface:** AstroTurf. **First game:** Dec. 29, 1997. **Playing sites:** Bronco Stadium (since 1997). **Corporate title sponsor:** World Sports Humanitarian Hall of Fame (since 1997).

Automatic berths: Big West champion, if available, vs. at-large (since 1997 season).

Year			
1997†	Cincinnati 35, Utah St. 19	1998 Idaho 42, Southern Miss. 35	†December game since 1997.

Bowl Games (Cont.)
Las Vegas Bowl

City: Las Vegas, Nev. **Stadium:** Sam Boyd. **Capacity:** 40,000. **Playing surface:** AstroTurf. **First game:** Dec. 18, 1992. **Playing site:** Sam Boyd Stadium (since 1992).

Automatic berths: Mid-American champion vs. Big West champion (1992-96 season); none (1997 season); second or third pick from WAC, if available vs. at-large (since 1998 season).

Note: The MAC and Big West champs met in a bowl game from 1981 to 1996, originally in Fresno at the California Bowl (1981-88, 1992) and California Raisin Bowl (1989-91). The results from 1981-91 are included below.

Multiple wins: Fresno St. (4); Bowling Green, San Jose St. and Toledo (2).

Year		Year		Year	
1981†	Toledo 27, San Jose St. 25	1989	Fresno St. 27, Ball St. 6	1997	Oregon 41, Air Force 13
1982	Fresno St. 29, Bowling Green 28	1990	San Jose St. 48, C. Michigan 24	1998	N. Carolina 20, San Diego St. 13
1983	Northern Ill. 20, CS-Fullerton 13	1991	Bowling Green 28, Fresno St. 21	†December game since 1981.
1984*	UNLV 30, Toledo 13	1992	Bowling Green 35, Nevada 34	* Toledo later ruled winner of 1984
1985	Fresno St. 51, Bowling Green 7	1993	Utah St. 42, Ball St. 33	game by forfeit because UNLV used
1986	San Jose St. 37, Miami-OH 7	1994	UNLV 52, C. Michigan 24	ineligible players.
1987	E. Michigan 30, San Jose St. 27	1995	Toledo 40, Nevada 37 (OT)	
1988	Fresno St. 35, W. Michigan 30	1996	Nevada 18, Ball St. 15	

Independence Bowl

City: Shreveport, La. **Stadium:** Independence. **Capacity:** 50,832. **Playing surface:** Grass. **First game:** Dec. 13, 1976. **Playing site:** Independence Stadium (since 1976). **Corporate title sponsors:** Poulan/Weed Eater (1990-97) and Sanford (since 1998).

Automatic berths: Southland Conference champion vs. at-large opponent (1976-81 seasons); none (1982-95 seasons); fifth pick from SEC, if available, vs. at-large (1995-97 season); fifth, sixth or seventh pick from SEC, if available, vs. at-large (since 1998 season).

Multiple wins: Air Force, LSU, Mississippi and Southern Miss (2).

Year		Year		Year	
1976†	McNeese St. 20, Tulsa 16	1984	Air Force 23, Va. Tech 7	1992	Wake Forest 39, Oregon 35
1977	La. Tech 24, Louisville 14	1985	Minnesota 20, Clemson 13	1993	Va. Tech 45, Indiana 20
1978	E. Carolina 35, La. Tech 13	1986	Mississippi 20, Texas Tech 17	1994	Virginia 20, TCU 10
1979	Syracuse 31, McNeese St. 7	1987	Washington 24, Tulane 12	1995	LSU 45, Michigan St. 26
		1988	Southern Miss 38, UTEP 18	1996	Auburn 32, Army 29
1980	Southern Miss 16, McNeese St. 14	1989	Oregon 27, Tulsa 24	1997	LSU 27, Notre Dame 9
1981	Texas A&M 33, Oklahoma St. 16			1998	Mississippi 35, Texas Tech 18
1982	Wisconsin 14, Kansas St. 3	1990	34-34, La. Tech vs Maryland	†December game since 1976.
1983	Air Force 9, Mississippi 3	1991	Georgia 24, Arkansas 15	

Bowl Championship Series

Division I-A football remains the only NCAA sport on any level that does not have a sanctioned national champion. To that end, the Bowl Coalition was formed in 1992 and was updated and renamed the Bowl Alliance in 1995 in an attempt to keep the bowl system intact while forcing an annual championship game between the regular season's two top-ranked teams.

The Bowl Championship Series is the organizers' latest attempt to finally guarantee that the teams ranked #1 and #2 will play each other in a "national title game" come January. The key difference from the 1992-97 Bowl Coalition/Bowl Alliance is that the Bowl Championship Series will include the Big 10 and Pac-10 champions. These teams, which were originally locked into playing in the Rose Bowl, will be allowed under the new system to move to another bowl game in order to create a match-up featuring the #1 and #2 teams.

The bowls (the Fiesta, Orange, and Sugar) which made up the old Bowl Alliance kept their spots in this new four-bowl alliance. The Fiesta Bowl held the first national championship (#1 vs. #2) game under the Bowl Championship Series contract on Jan. 4, 1999, and it will be followed by the Sugar (Jan. 4, 2000), the Orange (Jan. 3, 2001) and Rose (Jan. 3, 2002). ABC will pay the alliance $525 million over seven years in rights fees for the four "title" games, with the final three years part of an option clause.

The 1992 Coalition, which lasted three seasons, consolidated the resources of four major bowl games (the Cotton, Fiesta, Orange and Sugar), the champions of five major conferences (the ACC, Big East, Big Eight, Southeastern and Southwest) and the national following of independent Notre Dame. It worked two out of three years with #1 vs. #2 show-downs in the 1993 Sugar Bowl (#2 Alabama over #1 Miami-FL) and 1994 Orange Bowl (#1 Florida St. over #2 Nebraska). The 1995 Orange Bowl had to settle for #1 Nebraska beating #3 Miami-FL because #2 Penn St., the Big Ten champion, was obligated to play in the Rose Bowl.

The Bowl Alliance, which ended a three-year run after the 1997 season, was an updated version of the Coalition.

Non-BCS matchups: ALAMO (fourth pick from Big 12 vs. fourth pick from Pac-10 vs. at-large); ALOHA (fourth pick from Pac-10 vs. at-large); CITRUS (second pick from Big 10 vs. second pick from SEC); COTTON (first choice of either WAC champ or second pick from Pac-10 vs. second pick from Big 12); OUTBACK (third pick from Big 10 vs. third pick from SEC); GATOR (second pick from ACC vs. second pick from Big East); HOLIDAY (second choice of either WAC champ or second pick from Pac-10 vs. third pick from Big 12); HUMANITARIAN (Big West champ vs. at-large); INDEPENDENCE (fifth, sixth or seventh pick from SEC vs. at-large); INSIGHT.COM (third pick from Big East vs. fifth pick from Big 12); LAS VEGAS (second or third pick from WAC vs. at-large); LIBERTY (Conference USA champ vs. at-large); MICRON PC (sixth pick from Big 10 vs. fourth pick from ACC); MOTOR CITY (MAC champ vs. at-large); MUSIC CITY (sixth pick from SEC vs. at-large); OAHU (second pick from WAC vs. fifth pick from Pac-10); PEACH (third pick from ACC vs. fourth pick from SEC); SUN (third pick from Pac-10 vs. fifth pick from Big 10). Note that eight teams have left the WAC to form the Mountain West Conference and that should force changes in the current scenarios for non-BCS bowl matchups.

Motor City Bowl

City: Pontiac, Mich. **Stadium:** Pontiac Silverdome. **Capacity:** 80,368. **Playing surface:** Turf. **First game:** Dec. 26, 1997. **Playing site:** Pontiac Silverdome (since 1997). **Corporate title sponsor:** Ford Division of Ford Motor Company (since 1997).

Automatic berths: Mid-American champions vs at-large (since 1997 season).

Year		Year		
1997†	Mississippi 34, Marshall 31	1998	Marshall 48, Louisville 29	†December game since 1997.

Music City Bowl

City: Nashville, Tenn. **Stadium:** Adelphia Coliseum **Capacity:** 67,000. **Playing surface:** Grass. **First game:** Dec. 29, 1998. **Playing sites:** Vanderbilt Stadium (1998) and Adelphia Coliseum (1999–). **Corporate title sponsors:** American General (1998) and HomePoint.com (since 1999).

Automatic berths: sixth choice from the SEC, if available, vs. at-large (since 1998 season).

Year		
1998	Va. Tech 38, Alabama 7	†December game since 1998.

All-Time Winningest Division I-A Teams

Schools classified as Division I-A for at least 10 years; through 1998 season (including bowl games).

Top 25 Winning Percentage

		Yrs	Gm	W	L	T	Pct	Bowls App	Bowls Record	1998 Season Bowl	1998 Season Record
1	Notre Dame	110	1035	762	231	42	.757	23	13-10-0	Lost Gator	9-3
2	Michigan	119	1079	786	257	36	.745	30	15-15-0	Won Citrus	10-3
3	Alabama*	104	1032	724	265	43	.722	49	28-18-3	Lost Music City	7-5
4	Ohio St.	109	1040	711	276	53	.709	31	14-17-0	Won Sugar	11-1
5	Texas	106	1053	726	294	33	.705	38	18-18-2	Won Cotton	9-3
6	Nebraska	109	1067	731	296	40	.704	37	18-19-0	Lost Holiday	9-4
7	Oklahoma	104	1008	682	273	53	.703	32	20-11-1	None	5-6
8	Penn St.	112	1067	724	302	41	.698	35	22-11-2	Won Outback	9-3
9	Tennessee*	102	1027	690	285	52	.697	39	22-17-0	Won Fiesta	13-0
10	USC	106	996	667	275	54	.697	39	25-14-0	Lost Sun	8-5
11	Florida St.*	52	569	369	183	17	.663	27	16-9-2	Lost Fiesta	11-2
12	Miami-OH*	110	951	584	323	44	.637	7	5-2-0	None	10-1
13	Washington*	109	980	599	331	50	.637	25	13-11-1	Lost Oahu	6-6
14	Central Michigan	98	827	506	285	36	.634	5	0-2-0	None	6-5
15	Georgia	105	1033	625	354	54	.631	34	17-14-3	Won Peach	9-3
16	LSU*	105	1002	607	348	47	.629	31	14-16-1	None	4-7
17	Arizona St.	86	780	478	278	24	.628	17	10-6-1	None	5-6
18	Army	109	1021	614	356	51	.626	4	2-2-0	None	3-8
19	Auburn*	106	998	596	355	47	.621	26	14-10-2	None	3-8
20	Colorado*	109	1000	601	363	36	.619	22	10-12-0	Won Aloha	8-4
21	Miami-FL	72	748	452	277	19	.617	23	12-11-0	Won Micron PC	9-3
22	Florida	92	925	545	340	40	.611	26	13-13-0	Won Orange	10-2
23	UCLA	80	812	474	301	37	.607	22	11-10-1	Lost Rose	10-2
24	Texas A&M	104	1019	594	377	48	.606	24	12-12-0	Lost Sugar	11-3
25	Syracuse	109	1075	625	401	49	.604	19	10-8-1	Lost Orange	8-4

*Includes games forfeited following rulings by the NCAA Executive Council and/or the Committee on Infractions.

Top 50 Victories

	Wins		Wins		Wins
1 Michigan	786	18 Texas A&M	594	35 Missouri	533
2 Notre Dame	762	19 West Virginia	592	36 Maryland	525
3 Nebraska	731	20 North Carolina	591	37 Boston College	521
4 Texas	726	21 Pittsburgh	584	38 Vanderbilt	517
5 Alabama	724	Georgia Tech	584	39 Wisconsin	516
Penn St.	724	Miami-OH	584	40 Illinois	513
7 Ohio St.	711	24 Arkansas	580	41 Utah	511
8 Tennessee	690	25 Navy	573	Kentucky	511
9 Oklahoma	682	Minnesota	573	43 Kansas	506
10 USC	667	27 Virginia Tech	557	Central Michigan	506
11 Syracuse	625	28 Clemson	556	45 Stanford	505
Georgia	625	29 California	551	46 Purdue	501
13 Army	614	30 Rutgers	546	47 Iowa	497
14 LSU	607	Michigan St	546	Arizona	497
15 Colorado	601	32 Florida	545	49 Tulsa	491
16 Washington	599	33 Mississippi	544	50 Baylor	490
17 Auburn	596	34 Virginia	542		

Top 30 Bowl Appearances

		App	Record			App	Record			App	Record
1	Alabama	49	28-18-3	12	Arkansas	29	9-17-3		North Carolina	23	11-12-0
2	USC	39	25-14-0	13	Georgia Tech	27	19-8-0	24	Clemson	22	12-10-0
	Tennessee	39	22-17-0		Florida St	27	16-9-2		Colorado	22	10-12-0
4	Texas	38	18-18-2		Mississippi	27	16-11-0		UCLA	22	11-10-1
5	Nebraska	37	18-19-0	16	Auburn	26	14-10-2	27	BYU	21	7-13-1
6	Penn St	35	22-11-2		Florida	26	13-13-0		Missouri	21	9-12-0
7	Georgia	34	17-14-3	18	Washington	25	13-11-1	29	West Va.	20	8-12-0
8	Oklahoma	32	20-11-1	19	Texas A&M	24	12-12-0	30	Syracuse	19	10-8-1
9	LSU	31	14-16-1	20	Miami-FL	23	12-11-0		Pittsburgh	19	8-11-0
	Ohio St	31	14-17-0		Texas Tech	23	5-17-1				
11	Michigan	30	15-15-0		Notre Dame	23	13-10-0				

Note: Alabama, Georgia, Georgia Tech, Notre Dame, Ohio State and Penn State are the only schools that have won all four of the traditional major bowl games—the Rose, Orange, Sugar and Cotton. Penn State and Notre Dame are the only schools to have won those four and the recently prestigious Fiesta bowl.

Major Conference Champions

Atlantic Coast Conference

Founded in 1953 when charter members all left Southern Conference to form ACC. **Charter members** (7): Clemson, Duke, Maryland, North Carolina, N.C. State, South Carolina and Wake Forest. **Admitted later** (3): Virginia in 1953 (began play in '54), Georgia Tech in 1979 (began play in '83); Florida St. in 1990 (began play in '92). **Withdrew later** (1): South Carolina in 1971 (became an independent after '70 season).

1999 playing membership (9): Clemson, Duke, Florida St., Georgia Tech, Maryland, North Carolina, N.C. State, Virginia and Wake Forest.

Multiple titles: Clemson (13); Maryland (8); Duke, Florida St. and N.C. State (7); North Carolina (5); Georgia Tech & Virginia (2).

Year		Year		Year		Year	
1953	Duke (4-0)	1964	N.C. State (5-2)	1977	North Carolina (5-0-1)	1989	Virginia (6-1)
	& Maryland (3-0)	1965	Clemson (5-2)	1978	Clemson (6-0)		& Duke (6-1)
1954	Duke (4-0)		& N.C. State (5-2)	1979	N.C. State (5-1)	1990	Georgia Tech (6-0-1)
1955	Maryland (4-0)	1966	Clemson (6-1)	1980	North Carolina (6-0)	1991	Clemson (6-0-1)
	& Duke (4-0)	1967	Clemson (6-0)	1981	Clemson (6-0)	1992	Florida St. (8-0)
1956	Clemson (4-0-1)	1968	N.C. State (6-1)	1982	Clemson (6-0)	1993	Florida St. (8-0)
1957	N.C. State (5-0-1)	1969	South Carolina (6-0)	1983	Clemson (7-0) †	1994	Florida St. (8-0)
1958	Clemson (5-1)				& Maryland (5-0)	1995	Virginia (7-1)
1959	Clemson (6-1)	1970	Wake Forest (5-1)	1984	Maryland (5-0)		& Florida St. (7-1)
		1971	North Carolina (6-0)	1985	Maryland (6-0)	1996	Florida St. (8-0)
1960	Duke (5-1)	1972	North Carolina (6-0)	1986	Clemson (5-1-1)	1997	Florida St. (8-0)
1961	Duke (5-1)	1973	N.C. State (6-0)	1987	Clemson (6-1)	1998	Florida St. (7-1)
1962	Duke (6-0)	1974	Maryland (6-0)	1988	Clemson (6-1)		& Georgia Tech (7-1)
1963	North Carolina (6-1)	1975	Maryland (5-0)				
	& N.C. State (6-1)	1976	Maryland (5-0)				† On probation, ineligible for championship.

Big East Conference

Founded in 1991 when charter members gave up independent football status to form Big East. **Charter members** (8): Boston College, Miami-FL, Pittsburgh, Rutgers, Syracuse, Temple, Virginia Tech and West Virginia. **Note:** Temple and Virginia Tech are Big East members in football only.

1999 playing membership (8): Boston College, Miami-FL, Pittsburgh, Rutgers, Syracuse, Temple, Virginia Tech and West Virginia.

Conference champion: Member schools needed two years to adjust their regular season schedules in order to begin round-robin conference play in 1993. In the meantime, the 1991 and '92 Big East titles went to the highest-ranked member in the final regular season *USA Today*/CNN coaches' poll.

Multiple titles: Miami-FL (5); Syracuse (4); Virginia Tech (2).

Year		Year		Year		Year	
1991	Miami-FL (2-0, #1)	1994	Miami-FL (7-0)	1996	Virginia Tech (6-1),	1997	Syracuse (6-1)
	& Syracuse (5-0, #16)	1995	Virginia Tech (6-1)		Miami-FL (6-1)	1998	Syracuse (6-1)
1992	Miami-FL (4-0, #1)		& Miami-FL (6-1)		& Syracuse (6-1)		
1993	West Virginia (7-0)						

Big Ten Conference

Originally founded in 1895 as the Intercollegiate Conference of Faculty Representatives, better known as the Western Conference. **Charter members** (7): Chicago, Illinois, Michigan, Minnesota, Northwestern, Purdue and Wisconsin. **Admitted later** (5): Indiana and Iowa in 1899; Ohio St. in 1912; Michigan St. in 1950 (began play in '53); Penn St. in 1990 (began play in '93). **Withdrew later** (2): Michigan in 1907 (rejoined in '17); Chicago in 1940 (dropped football after '39 season). **Note:** Iowa belonged to both the Western and Missouri Valley conferences from 1907-10.

Unofficially called the **Big Ten** from 1912 until Chicago's withdrawal in 1939, then the **Big Nine** from 1940 until Michigan St. began conference play in 1953. Formally named the **Big Ten** in 1984 and has kept the name even after adding Penn St. as its 11th member.

1999 playing membership (11): Illinois, Indiana, Iowa, Michigan, Michigan St., Minnesota, Northwestern, Ohio St., Penn St., Purdue, and Wisconsin.

Multiple titles: Michigan (39); Ohio St. (28); Minnesota (18); Illinois (14); Wisconsin (10); Iowa (9); Purdue and Northwestern (7); Chicago and Michigan St. (6); Indiana (2).

Year		Year		Year		Year	
1896	Wisconsin (2-0-1)	1922	Iowa (5-0) & Michigan (4-0)	1948	Michigan (6-0)	1975	Ohio St. (8-0)
1897	Wisconsin (3-0)	1923	Illinois (5-0) & Michigan (4-0)	1949	Ohio St. (4-1-1) & Michigan (4-1-1)	1976	Michigan (7-1) & Ohio St. (7-1)
1898	Michigan (3-0)	1924	Chicago (3-0-3)	1950	Michigan (4-1-1)	1977	Michigan (7-1) & Ohio St. (7-1)
1899	Chicago (4-0)	1925	Michigan (5-1)	1951	Illinois (5-0-1)		
1900	Iowa (3-0-1) & Minnesota (3-0-1)	1926	Michigan (5-0) & Northwestern (5-0)	1952	Wisconsin (4-1-1) & Purdue (4-1-1)	1978	Michigan (7-1) & Michigan St. (7-1)
1901	Michigan (4-0) & Wisconsin (2-0)	1927	Illinois (5-0) & Minnesota (3-0-1)	1953	Michigan St. (5-1) & Illinois (5-1)	1979	Ohio St. (8-0)
1902	Michigan (5-0)	1928	Illinois (4-1)	1954	Ohio St. (7-0)	1980	Michigan (8-0)
1903	Michigan (3-0-1), Minnesota (3-0-1) & Northwestern (1-0-2)	1929	Purdue (5-0)	1955	Ohio St. (6-0)	1981	Iowa (6-2) & Ohio St. (6-2)
		1930	Michigan (5-0) & Northwestern (5-0)	1956	Iowa (5-1)	1982	Michigan (8-1)
1904	Minnesota (3-0) & Michigan (2-0)	1931	Purdue (5-1), Michigan (5-1) & Northwestern (5-1)	1957	Ohio St. (7-0)	1983	Illinois (9-0)
1905	Chicago (7-0)			1958	Iowa (5-1)	1984	Ohio St. (7-2)
1906	Wisconsin (3-0), Minnesota (2-0) & Michigan (1-0)	1932	Michigan (6-0) & Purdue (5-0-1)	1959	Wisconsin (5-2)	1985	Iowa (7-1)
1907	Chicago (4-0)	1933	Michigan (5-0-1) & Minnesota (2-0-4)	1960	Minnesota (5-1) & Iowa (5-1)	1986	Michigan (7-1) & Ohio St. (7-1)
1908	Chicago (5-0)	1934	Minnesota (5-0)	1961	Ohio St. (6-0)	1987	Michigan St. (7-0-1)
1909	Minnesota (3-0)	1935	Minnesota (5-0) & Ohio St. (5-0)	1962	Wisconsin (6-1)	1988	Michigan (7-0-1)
1910	Illinois (4-0) & Minnesota (2-0)	1936	Northwestern (6-0)	1963	Illinois (5-1-1)	1989	Michigan (8-0)
1911	Minnesota (3-0-1)	1937	Minnesota (5-0)	1964	Michigan (6-1)	1990	Iowa (6-2), Michigan (6-2), Michigan St. (6-2) & Illinois (6-2)
1912	Wisconsin (6-0)	1938	Minnesota (4-1)	1965	Michigan St. (7-0)		
1913	Chicago (7-0)	1939	Ohio St. (5-1)	1966	Michigan St. (7-0)		
1914	Illinois (6-0)	1940	Minnesota (6-0)	1967	Indiana (6-1), Purdue (6-1) & Minnesota (6-1)	1991	Michigan (8-0)
1915	Minnesota (3-0-1) & Illinois (3-0-2)	1941	Minnesota (5-0)			1992	Michigan (6-0-2)
1916	Ohio St. (4-0)	1942	Ohio St. (5-1)	1968	Ohio St. (7-0)	1993	Wisconsin (6-1-1) & Ohio St. (6-1-1)
1917	Ohio St. (4-0)	1943	Purdue (6-0) & Michigan (6-0)	1969	Ohio St. (6-1) & Michigan (6-1)	1994	Penn St. (8-0)
1918	Illinois (4-0), Michigan (2-0) & Purdue (1-0)	1944	Ohio St. (6-0)	1970	Ohio St. (7-0)	1995	Northwestern (8-0)
		1945	Indiana (5-0-1)	1971	Michigan (8-0)	1996	Ohio St. (7-1) & Northwestern (7-1)
1919	Illinois (6-1)	1946	Illinois (6-1)	1972	Ohio St. (7-1) & Michigan (7-1)	1997	Michigan (8-0)
1920	Ohio St. (5-0)	1947	Michigan (6-0)	1973	Ohio St. (7-0-1) & Michigan (7-0-1)	1998	Ohio St. (7-1), Wisconsin (7-1) & Michigan (7-1)
1921	Iowa (5-0)			1974	Ohio St. (7-1) & Michigan (7-1)		

Big 12 Conference

Originally founded in 1907 as the Missouri Valley Intercollegiate Athletic Assn. **Charter members** (5): Iowa, Kansas, Missouri, Nebraska and Washington University of St. Louis. **Admitted later** (11): Drake and Iowa St. (then Ames College) in 1908; Kansas St. (then Kansas College of Applied Science and Agriculture) in 1913; Grinnell (Iowa) College in 1919; Oklahoma in 1920; Oklahoma A&M (now Oklahoma St.) in 1925; Colorado in 1947 (began play in '48); Baylor, Texas, Texas A&M and Texas Tech in 1994 (all four began play in '96).

Withdrew later (1): Iowa in 1911 (left for Big Ten after 1910 season); **Excluded later** (4): Drake, Grinnell, Oklahoma A&M and Washington-MO (left out when MVIAA cut membership to six teams in 1928.

Streamlined MVIAA unofficially called **Big Six** from 1928-47 with surviving members Iowa St., Kansas, Kansas St., Missouri, Nebraska and Oklahoma. Became the **Big Seven** after 1947 season when Colorado came over from the Skyline Conference, and then the **Big Eight** with the return of Oklahoma A&M in 1957. A&M, which resumed conference play in '60, became Oklahoma St. on July 10, 1957. The MVIAA was officially renamed the Big Eight in 1964 and became the **Big 12** after the 1995-96 academic year with the arrival of Baylor, Texas, Texas A&M and Texas Tech from the defunct Southwest Conference.

1999 playing membership (12): Baylor, Colorado, Iowa St., Kansas, Kansas St., Missouri, Nebraska, Oklahoma, Oklahoma St., Texas, Texas A&M and Texas Tech.

Multiple titles: Nebraska (42); Oklahoma (33); Missouri (12); Colorado and Kansas (5); Iowa St. and Oklahoma St. (2).

Year		Year		Year		Year	
1907	Iowa (1-0) & Nebraska (1-0)	1915	Nebraska (4-0)	1926	Okla. A&M (3-0-1)	1938	Oklahoma (5-0)
1908	Kansas (4-0)	1916	Nebraska (3-1)	1927	Missouri (5-1)	1939	Missouri (5-0)
1909	Missouri (4-0-1)	1917	Nebraska (4-0)	1928	Nebraska (4-0)	1940	Nebraska (5-0)
		1918	Vacant (WW I)	1929	Nebraska (3-0-2)	1941	Missouri (5-0)
1910	Nebraska (2-0)	1919	Missouri (4-0-1)				
1911	Iowa St. (2-0-1) & Nebraska (2-0-1)	1920	Oklahoma (4-0-1)	1930	Kansas (4-1)	1942	Missouri (4-0-1)
		1921	Nebraska (3-0)	1931	Nebraska (5-0)	1943	Oklahoma (5-0)
1912	Iowa St. (2-0) & Nebraska (2-0)	1922	Nebraska (5-0)	1932	Nebraska (5-0)	1944	Oklahoma (4-0-1)
		1923	Nebraska (3-0-2) & Kansas (3-0-3)	1933	Nebraska (5-0)	1945	Missouri (5-0)
1913	Missouri (4-0) & Nebraska (3-0)			1934	Kansas St. (5-0)	1946	Oklahoma (4-1) & Kansas (4-1)
		1924	Missouri (5-1)	1935	Nebraska (4-0-1)		
1914	Nebraska (3-0)	1925	Missouri (5-1)	1936	Nebraska (5-0)	1947	Kansas (4-0-1) & Oklahoma (4-0-1)
				1937	Nebraska (3-0-2)		

Major Conference Champions (Cont.)

Year		Year		Year		Year	
1948	Oklahoma (5-0)	1962	Oklahoma (7-0)	1974	Oklahoma (7-0)	1984	Oklahoma (6-1)
1949	Oklahoma (5-0)	1963	Nebraska (7-0)	1975	Nebraska (6-1)		& Nebraska (6-1)
1950	Oklahoma (6-0)	1964	Nebraska (6-1)		& Oklahoma (6-1)	1985	Oklahoma (7-0)
1951	Oklahoma (6-0)	1965	Nebraska (7-0)	1976	Colorado (5-2),	1986	Oklahoma (7-0)
1952	Oklahoma (5-0-1)	1966	Nebraska (6-1)		Oklahoma (5-2)	1987	Oklahoma (7-0)
1953	Oklahoma (6-0)	1967	Oklahoma (7-0)		& Oklahoma St. (5-2)	1988	Nebraska (7-0)
1954	Oklahoma (6-0)	1968	Kansas (6-1)	1977	Oklahoma (7-0)	1989	Colorado (7-0)
1955	Oklahoma (6-0)		& Oklahoma (6-1)	1978	Nebraska (6-1)		
1956	Oklahoma (6-0)	1969	Missouri (6-1)		& Oklahoma (6-1)	1990	Colorado (7-0)
1957	Oklahoma (6-0)		& Nebraska (6-1)	1979	Oklahoma (7-0)	1991	Nebraska (6-0-1)
1958	Oklahoma (6-0)	1970	Nebraska (7-0)	1980	Oklahoma (7-0)		& Colorado (6-0-1)
1959	Oklahoma (5-1)	1971	Nebraska (7-0)	1981	Nebraska (7-0)	1992	Nebraska (6-1)
		1972	Nebraska (5-1-1)*	1982	Nebraska (7-0)	1993	Nebraska (7-0)
1960	Missouri (7-0)	1973	Oklahoma (7-0)	1983	Nebraska (7-0)	1994	Nebraska (7-0)
1961	Colorado (7-0)					1995	Nebraska (7-0)

*Oklahoma (6-1) forfeited title in 1972.

Big 12 Championship Game

After expanding to 12 teams and splitting into two divisions in 1996, the Big 12 (formerly the Big Eight) now stages a conference championship game between the two division winners on the first Saturday in December. The game has been played at the Trans World Dome in St. Louis (1996, 1998) and the Alamodome in San Antonio (1997, 1999). The divisions: NORTH— Colorado, Iowa St., Kansas, Kansas St., Missouri and Nebraska; SOUTH— Baylor, Oklahoma, Oklahoma St., Texas, Texas A&M and Texas Tech.

Year	Year	Year
1996 Texas 37, Nebraska 27	1997 Nebraska 54, Texas A&M 15	1998 Texas A&M 36, Kansas St. 33

Big West Conference

Originally founded in 1969 as Pacific Coast Athletic Assn. **Charter members** (7): CS-Los Angeles, Fresno St., Long Beach St., Pacific, San Diego St., San Jose St. and UC-Santa Barbara. **Admitted later** (12): CS-Fullerton in 1974; Utah St. in 1977 (began play in '78); UNLV in 1982; New Mexico St. in 1983 (began play in '84); Nevada in 1991 (began play in '92); Arkansas St., Louisiana Tech, Northern Illinois and SW Louisiana in 1992 (all four began play in football only in '93); Boise St., Idaho and North Texas in 1994 (all three began play in '96); Arkansas St. rejoined in 1999 (in football only). **Withdrew later** (13): CS-Los Angeles and UC-Santa Barbara in 1972 (both dropped football after '71 season); San Diego St. in 1975 (became an independent after '75 season); Fresno St. in 1991 (left for WAC after '91 season); Long Beach St. in 1991 (dropped football after '91 season); CS-Fullerton in 1992 (dropped football after '92 season); San Jose St. and UNLV in 1994 (left for WAC after '95 season); Pacific in 1995 (dropped football after '95 season); Arkansas St., Louisiana Tech, Northern Illinois and SW Louisiana in 1995 (all four returned to independent football status after '95 season). **Conference renamed** Big West in 1988.

1999 playing membership (7): Arkansas St., Boise St., Idaho, Nevada, New Mexico St., North Texas and Utah St.

Multiple titles: San Jose St. (8); Fresno St. (6); Nevada, San Diego St. and Utah St. (5); Long Beach St. (3); CS-Fullerton and SW Louisiana (2).

Year		Year		Year		Year	
1969	San Diego St. (6-0)		& Utah St. (4-1)	1989	Fresno St. (7-0)	1996	Nevada (4-1)
1970	Long Beach St. (5-1)	1979	Utah St. (4-0-1)*	1990	San Jose St. (7-0)		& Utah St. (4-1)
	& San Diego St. (5-1)	1980	Long Beach St. (5-0)	1991	Fresno St. (6-1)	1997	Utah St. (4-1)
1971	Long Beach St. (5-1)	1981	San Jose St. (5-0)		& San Jose St. (6-1)		& Nevada (4-1)
1972	San Diego St. (4-0)	1982	Fresno St. (6-0)	1992	Nevada (5-1)	1998	Idaho (4-1)
1973	San Diego St. (3-0-1)	1983	CS-Fullerton (5-1)	1993	Utah St. (5-1)	*San Jose St. (4-0-1) forfeited share of title in 1979.
1974	San Diego St. (4-0)	1984	CS-Fullerton (6-1)†		& SW Louisiana (5-1)	†UNLV (7-0) forfeited title in 1984.
1975	San Jose St. (5-0)	1985	Fresno St. (7-0)	1994	UNLV (5-1),	
1976	San Jose St. (4-0)	1986	San Jose St. (7-0)		Nevada (5-1),	
1977	Fresno St. (4-0)	1987	San Jose St. (7-0)		& SW Louisiana (5-1)	
1978	San Jose St. (4-1)	1988	Fresno St. (7-0)	1995	Nevada (6-0)	

Conference USA

Founded in 1994 by six independent football schools which began play as a conference in 1996. **Charter members** (6): Cincinnati, Houston, Louisville, Memphis, Southern Mississippi and Tulane. **Admitted later** (2): East Carolina in 1997, Army in 1998 and Univ. of Alabama-Birmingham in 1999; **1999 playing members** (9): Alabama-Birmingham, Army, Cincinnati, East Carolina, Houston, Louisville, Memphis, Southern Mississippi and Tulane.

Multiple titles: Southern Mississippi (2).

Year	Year	Year
1996 Southern Mississippi (4-1) & Houston (4-1)	1997 Southern Mississippi (6-0)	1998 Tulane (6-0)

Ivy League

First called the "Ivy League" in 1937 by sportswriter Caswell Adams of the *New York Herald Tribune*. Unofficial conference of 10 eastern teams was occasionally referred to as the "Old 10" and included: Army, Brown, Columbia, Cornell, Dartmouth, Harvard, Navy, Pennsylvania, Princeton and Yale. Army and Navy were dropped from the group after 1940. **League formalized** in 1954 for play beginning in 1956. **Charter members** (8): Brown, Columbia, Cornell, Dartmouth, Harvard, Pennsylvania, Princeton, and Yale. League downgraded from Division I to Division I-AA after 1977 season. **1998 playing membership:** the same.

Multiple titles: Dartmouth (17); Yale (12); Penn (10); Harvard (9); Princeton (8); Cornell (3).

Year		Year		Year		Year	
1956	Yale (7-0)	1968	Harvard (6-0-1)	1978	Dartmouth (6-1)	1989	Princeton (6-1)
1957	Princeton (6-1)		& Yale (6-0-1)	1979	Yale (6-1)		& Yale (6-1)
1958	Dartmouth (6-1)	1969	Dartmouth (6-1),	1980	Yale (6-1)	1990	Cornell (6-1)
1959	Penn (6-1)		Yale (6-1)	1981	Yale (6-1)		& Dartmouth (6-1)
1960	Yale (7-0)		& Princeton (6-1)		& Dartmouth (6-1)	1991	Dartmouth (6-0-1)
1961	Columbia (6-1)	1970	Dartmouth (7-0)	1982	Harvard (5-2),	1992	Dartmouth (6-1)
	& Harvard (6-1)	1971	Cornell (6-1)		Penn (5-2)		& Princeton (6-1)
1962	Dartmouth (7-0)		& Dartmouth (6-1)		& Dartmouth (5-2)	1993	Penn (7-0)
1963	Dartmouth (5-2)	1972	Dartmouth (5-1-1)	1983	Harvard (5-1-1)	1994	Penn (7-0)
	& Princeton (5-2)	1973	Dartmouth (6-1)		& Penn (5-1-1)	1995	Princeton (5-1-1)
1964	Princeton (7-0)	1974	Harvard (6-1)	1984	Penn (7-0)	1996	Dartmouth (7-0)
1965	Dartmouth (7-0)		& Yale (6-1)	1985	Penn (6-1)	1997	Harvard (7-0)
1966	Dartmouth (6-1),	1975	Harvard (6-1)	1986	Penn (7-0)	1998	Penn (6-1)
	Harvard (6-1)	1976	Brown (6-1)	1987	Harvard (6-1)		
	& Princeton (6-1)		& Yale (6-1)	1988	Penn (6-1)		
1967	Yale (7-0)	1977	Yale (6-1)		& Cornell (6-1)		

Mid-American Conference

Founded in 1946. **Charter members** (6): Butler, Cincinnati, Miami-OH, Ohio University, Western Michigan and Western Reserve (Miami and WMU began play in '48). **Admitted later** (12): Kent St. (now Kent) and Toledo in 1951 (Toledo began play in '52); Bowling Green in 1952; Marshall in 1954; Central and Eastern Michigan in 1972 (CMU began play in '75 and EMU in '76); Ball St. and Northern Illinois in 1973 (both began play in '75); Akron in 1991 (began play in '92); Marshall and Northern Illinois in 1995 (both resumed play in '97); Buffalo in 1995 (will begin play in '99). **Withdrew later** (5): Butler in 1950 (left for the Indiana Collegiate Conference); Cincinnati in 1953 (went independent); Western Reserve (now Case Western) in 1955 (left for President's Athletic Conference); Marshall in 1969 (went independent); and Northern Illinois in 1986 (went independent).

1999 playing membership (12): Akron, Ball St., Bowling Green, Central Michigan, Eastern Michigan, Kent, Marshall, Miami-OH, Northern Illinois, Ohio University, Toledo and Western Michigan.

Multiple titles: Miami-OH (13); Bowling Green (10); Toledo (8); Ball St. and Ohio University (5); Central Michigan and Cincinnati (4); Marshall and Western Michigan (2).

Year		Year		Year		Year	
1947	Cincinnati (3-1)	1960	Ohio Univ. (6-0)	1972	Kent St. (4-1)	1987	Eastern Mich. (7-1)
1948	Miami-OH (4-0)	1961	Bowling Green (5-1)	1973	Miami-OH (5-0)	1988	Western Mich. (7-1)
1949	Cincinnati (4-0)	1962	Bowling Green (5-0-1)	1974	Miami-OH (5-0)	1989	Ball St. (6-1-1)
1950	Miami-OH (4-0)	1963	Ohio Univ. (5-1)	1975	Miami-OH (6-0)	1990	Central Mich. (7-1)
1951	Cincinnati (3-0)	1964	Bowling Green (5-1)	1976	Ball St. (4-1)		& Toledo (7-1)
1952	Cincinnati (3-0)	1965	Bowling Green (5-1)	1977	Miami-OH (5-0)	1991	Bowling Green (8-0)
1953	Ohio Univ. (5-0-1)		& Miami-OH (5-1)	1978	Ball St. (8-0)	1992	Bowling Green (8-0)
	& Miami-OH (3-0-1)	1966	Miami-OH (5-1)	1979	Central Mich. (8-0-1)	1993	Ball St. (7-0-1)
1954	Miami-OH (4-0)		& Western Mich. (5-1)	1980	Central Mich. (7-2)	1994	Central Mich. (8-1)
1955	Miami-OH (5-0)	1967	Toledo (5-1)	1981	Toledo (8-1)	1995	Toledo (7-0-1)
1956	Bowling Green (5-0-1)		& Ohio Univ. (5-1)	1982	Bowling Green (7-2)	1996	Ball St. (7-1)
	& Miami-OH (4-0-1)	1968	Ohio Univ. (6-0)	1983	Northern Ill. (8-1)	1997	Marshall (8-1)
1957	Miami-OH (5-0)	1969	Toledo (5-0)	1984	Toledo (7-1-1)	1998	Marshall (8-1)
1958	Miami-OH (5-0)	1970	Toledo (5-0)	1985	Bowling Green (9-0)		
1959	Bowling Green (6-0)	1971	Toledo (5-0)	1986	Miami-OH (6-2)		

Pacific-10 Conference

Originally founded in 1915 as Pacific Coast Conference. **Charter members** (4): California, Oregon, Oregon St. and Washington. **Admitted later** (6): Washington St. in 1917; Stanford in 1918; Idaho and USC (Southern Cal) in 1922; Montana in 1924; and UCLA in 1928. **Withdrew later** (1): Montana in 1950 (left for the Mountain States Conf.).

The **PCC** dissolved in 1959 and the **AAWU** (Athletic Assn. of Western Universities) was founded. **Charter members** (5): California, Stanford, UCLA, USC and Washington. **Admitted later** (5): Washington St. in 1962; Oregon and Oregon St. in 1964; Arizona and Arizona St. in 1978. **Conference renamed** Pacific-8 in 1968 and Pacific-10 in 1978.

1999 playing membership (10): Arizona, Arizona St., California, Oregon, Oregon St., Stanford, UCLA, USC, Washington and Washington St.

Multiple titles: USC (31); UCLA (17); Washington (14); California (13); Stanford (11); Oregon (5); Oregon St. (4); Washington St. (3); Arizona St. (2).

Year		Year		Year		Year	
1916	Washington (3-0-1)	1918	California (3-0)		& Washington (2-1)	1921	California (5-0)
1917	Washington St. (3-0)	1919	Oregon (2-1)	1920	California (3-0)	1922	California (3-0)

Major Conference Champions (Cont.)

Year		Year		Year		Year	
1923	California (5-0)	1941	Oregon St. (7-2)	1961	UCLA (3-1)	1983	UCLA (6-1-1)
1924	Stanford (3-0-1)	1942	UCLA (6-1)	1962	USC (4-0)	1984	USC (7-1)
1925	Washington (5-0)	1943	USC (4-0)	1963	Washington (4-1)	1985	UCLA (6-2)
1926	Stanford (4-0)	1944	USC (3-0-2)	1964	Oregon St. (3-1)	1986	Arizona St. (5-1-1)
1927	USC (4-0-1)	1945	USC (5-1)		& USC (3-1)	1987	USC (7-1)
	& Stanford (4-0-1)	1946	UCLA (7-0)	1965	UCLA (4-0)		& UCLA (7-1)
1928	USC (4-0-1)	1947	USC (6-0)	1966	USC (4-1)	1988	USC (8-0)
1929	USC (6-1)	1948	California (6-0)	1967	USC (6-1)	1989	USC (6-0-1)
1930	Washington St. (6-0)		& Oregon (6-0)	1968	USC (6-0)	1990	Washington (7-1)
1931	USC (7-0)	1949	California (7-0)	1969	USC (6-0)	1991	Washington (8-0)
1932	USC (6-0)	1950	California (5-0-1)	1970	Stanford (6-1)	1992	Washington (6-2)
1933	Oregon (4-1)	1951	Stanford (6-1)	1971	Stanford (6-1)		& Stanford (6-2)
	& Stanford (4-1)	1952	USC (6-0)	1972	USC (7-0)	1993	UCLA (6-2),
1934	Stanford (5-0)	1953	UCLA (6-1)	1973	USC (7-0)		Arizona (6-2)
1935	California (4-1),	1954	UCLA (6-0)	1974	USC (6-0-1)		& USC (6-2)
	Stanford (4-1)	1955	UCLA (6-0)	1975	UCLA (6-1)	1994	Oregon (7-1)
	& UCLA (4-1)	1956	Oregon St. (6-1-1)		& California (6-1)	1995	USC (6-1-1)
1936	Washington (6-0-1)	1957	Oregon (6-2)	1976	USC (7-0)		& Washington (6-1-1)
1937	California (6-0-1)		& Oregon St. (6-2)	1977	Washington (6-1)	1996	Arizona St. (8-0)
1938	USC (6-1)	1958	California (6-1)	1978	USC (6-1)	1997	Washington St. (7-1)
	& California (6-1)	1959	Washington (3-1),	1979	USC (6-0-1)		& UCLA (7-1)
1939	USC (5-0-2)		USC (3-1)	1980	Washington (6-1)	1998	UCLA (8-0)
	& UCLA (5-0-3)		& UCLA (3-1)	1981	Washington (6-2)		
1940	Stanford (7-0)	1960	Washington (4-0)	1982	UCLA (5-1-1)		

Southeastern Conference

Founded in 1933 when charter members all left Southern Conference to form SEC. **Charter members** (13): Alabama, Auburn, Florida, Georgia, Georgia Tech, Kentucky, LSU (Louisiana St.), Mississippi, Mississippi St., Sewanee, Tennessee, Tulane and Vanderbilt. **Admitted later** (2): Arkansas and South Carolina in 1990 (both began play in '92). **Withdrew later** (3): Sewanee in 1940; Georgia Tech in 1964; and Tulane in 1966.

1999 playing membership (12): Alabama, Arkansas, Auburn, Florida, Georgia, Kentucky, LSU, Mississippi, Mississippi St., South Carolina, Tennessee and Vanderbilt. **Note:** Conference title decided by championship game between Western and Eastern division winners since 1992.

Multiple titles: Alabama (20); Tennessee (13); Georgia (10); Florida (8); LSU (7); Mississippi (6); Auburn and Georgia Tech (5); Kentucky and Tulane (3).

Year		Year		Year		Year	
1933	Alabama (5-0-1)	1948	Georgia (6-0)	1965	Alabama (6-1-1)	1981	Georgia (6-0)
1934	Tulane (8-0)	1949	Tulane (5-1)	1966	Alabama (6-0)		& Alabama (6-0)
	& Alabama (7-0)	1950	Kentucky (5-1)		& Georgia (6-0)	1982	Georgia (6-0)
1935	LSU (5-0)	1951	Georgia Tech (7-0)	1967	Tennessee (6-0)	1983	Auburn (6-0)
1936	LSU (6-0)		& Tennessee (5-0)	1968	Georgia (5-0-1)	1984	Florida (5-0-1)*
1937	Alabama (6-0)	1952	Georgia Tech (6-0)	1969	Tennessee (5-1)	1985	Florida (5-1)†
1938	Tennessee (7-0)	1953	Alabama (4-0-3)	1970	LSU (5-0)		& Tennessee (5-1)
1939	Tennessee (6-0),	1954	Mississippi (5-1)	1971	Alabama (7-0)	1986	LSU (5-1)
	Georgia Tech (6-0)	1955	Mississippi (5-1)	1972	Alabama (7-1)	1987	Auburn (5-0-1)
	& Tulane (5-0)	1956	Tennessee (6-0)	1973	Alabama (8-0)	1988	Auburn (6-1)
1940	Tennessee (5-0)	1957	Auburn (7-0)	1974	Alabama (6-0)		& LSU (6-1)
1941	Mississippi St. (4-0-1)	1958	LSU (6-0)	1975	Alabama (6-0)	1989	Alabama (6-1),
1942	Georgia (6-1)	1959	Georgia (7-0)	1976	Georgia (5-1)		Tennessee (6-1)
1943	Georgia Tech (3-0)	1960	Mississippi (5-0-1)		& Kentucky (5-1)		& Auburn (6-1)
1944	Georgia Tech (4-0)	1961	Alabama (7-0)	1977	Alabama (7-0)	1990	Florida (6-1)†
1945	Alabama (6-0)		& LSU (6-0)		& Kentucky (6-0)		& Tennessee (5-1-1)
1946	Georgia (5-0)	1962	Mississippi (6-0)	1978	Alabama (6-0)	1991	Florida (7-0)
	& Tennessee (5-0)	1963	Mississippi (5-0-1)	1979	Alabama (6-0)	*Title vacated.	
1947	Mississippi (6-1)	1964	Alabama (8-0)	1980	Georgia (6-0)	†On probation, ineligible for championship.	

SEC Championship Game

Since expanding to 12 teams and splitting into two divisions in 1992, the SEC has staged a conference championship game between the two division winners on the first Saturday in December. The game has been played at Legion Field in Birmingham, Ala., (1992-93) and the Georgia Dome in Atlanta (since 1994). The divisions: EAST— Florida, Georgia, Kentucky, South Carolina, Tennessee and Vanderbilt; WEST— Alabama, Arkansas, Auburn, LSU, Mississippi and Mississippi St.

Year	Year	Year
1992 Alabama 28, Florida 21	1995 Florida 34, Arkansas 3	1998 Tennessee 24, Miss. St. 14
1993 Florida 28, Alabama 23	1996 Florida 45, Alabama 30	
1994 Florida 24, Alabama 23	1997 Tennessee 30, Auburn 29	

Southwest Conference (1914-95)

Founded in 1914 as Southwest Intercollegiate Athletic Conference. **Charter members** (8): Arkansas, Baylor, Oklahoma, Oklahoma A&M (now Oklahoma St.), Rice, Southwestern, Texas and Texas A&M. **Admitted later** (5): SMU (Southern Methodist) in 1918; Phillips University in 1920; TCU (Texas Christian) in 1923; Texas Tech in 1956 (began play in '60); Houston in 1971 (began play in '76). **Withdrew later** (9): Southwestern in 1917 (went independent); Oklahoma in 1920 (left for Missouri Valley after '19 season); Phillips in 1921; Oklahoma A&M (now Oklahoma St.) in 1925 (left for Big Six); Arkansas in 1990 (left for SEC after '91 season); Baylor, Texas, Texas A&M and Texas Tech in 1994 (all four left for Big 12 after '95 season); Rice, SMU and TCU in 1994 (all three left for WAC after '95 season); Houston in 1994 (left for Conference USA after '95 season).

1997 playing membership: Conference folded on June 30, 1996.

Multiple titles: Texas (25); Texas A&M (17); Arkansas (13); SMU (9); TCU (9); Rice (7); Baylor (5); Houston (4); Texas Tech (2).

Year		Year		Year		Year	
1914	No champion	1940	Texas A&M (5-1)	1961	Texas (6-1)	1981	SMU (7-1)
1915	Oklahoma (3-0)	1941	Texas A&M (5-1)		& Arkansas (6-1)	1982	SMU (7-0-1)
1916	No champion	1942	Texas (5-1)	1962	Texas (6-0-1)	1983	Texas (8-0)
1917	Texas A&M (2-0)	1943	Texas (5-0)	1963	Texas (7-0)	1984	SMU (6-2)
1918	No champion	1944	TCU (3-1-1)	1964	Arkansas (7-0)		& Houston (6-2)
1919	Texas A&M (4-0)	1945	Texas (5-1)	1965	Arkansas (7-0)	1985	Texas A&M (7-1)
1920	Texas (5-0)	1946	Rice (5-1)	1966	SMU (6-1)	1986	Texas A&M (7-1)
1921	Texas A&M (3-0-2)		& Arkansas (5-1)	1967	Texas A&M (6-1)	1987	Texas A&M (6-1)
1922	Baylor (5-0)	1947	SMU (5-0-1)	1968	Arkansas (6-1)	1988	Arkansas (7-0)
1923	SMU (5-0)	1948	SMU (5-0-1)		& Texas (6-1)	1989	Arkansas (7-1)
1924	Baylor (4-0-1)	1949	Rice (6-0)	1969	Texas (7-0)	1990	Texas (8-0)
1925	Texas A&M (4-1)	1950	Texas (6-0)	1970	Texas (7-0)	1991	Texas A&M (8-0)
1926	SMU (5-0)	1951	TCU (5-1)	1971	Texas (6-1)	1992	Texas A&M (7-0)
1927	Texas A&M (4-0-1)	1952	Texas (6-0)	1972	Texas (7-0)	1993	Texas A&M (7-0)
1928	Texas (5-1)	1953	Rice (5-1)	1973	Texas (7-0)	1994	Baylor, Rice, TCU,
1929	TCU (4-0-1)		& Texas (5-1)	1974	Baylor (6-1)		Texas and Texas Tech†
1930	Texas (4-1)	1954	Arkansas (5-1)	1975	Arkansas (6-1),		(4-3)
1931	SMU (5-0-1)	1955	TCU (5-1)		Texas (6-1)	1995	Texas (7-0)
1932	TCU (6-0)	1956	Texas A&M (6-0)		& Texas A&M (6-1)		
1933	Arkansas (4-1)*ı	1957	Rice (5-1)	1976	Houston (7-1)	*Arkansas (4-1) forced to
1934	Rice (5-1)	1958	TCU (5-1)		& Texas Tech (7-1)	vacate 1933 title for use of
1935	SMU (6-0)	1959	Texas (5-1),	1977	Texas (8-0)	ineligible player.
1936	Arkansas (5-1)		TCU (5-1)	1978	Houston (7-1)	†Texas A&M had the best
1937	Rice (4-1-1)		& Arkansas (5-1)	1979	Houston (7-1)	record (6-0-1) in 1994 but
1938	TCU (6-0)	1960	Arkansas (6-1)		& Arkansas (7-1)	was on probation and there-
1939	Texas A&M (6-0)			1980	Baylor (8-0)	fore ineligible for the South-
						west championship.	

Western Athletic Conference

Founded in 1962 when charter members left the Skyline and Border conferences to form the WAC. **Charter members** (6): Arizona and Arizona St. from Border; BYU (Brigham Young), New Mexico, Utah and Wyoming from Skyline. **Admitted later** (12): Colorado St. and UTEP (Texas-El Paso) in 1967 (both began play in '68); San Diego St. in 1978; Hawaii in 1979; Air Force in 1980; Fresno St. in 1991 (began play in '92); Rice, San Jose St., SMU (Southern Methodist), TCU (Texas Christian), Tulsa and UNLV (Nevada-Las Vegas) in 1994 (all began play in '96); Nevada set to join in 2000. **Withdrew later** (10): Arizona and Arizona St. in 1978 (left for Pac-10 after '77 season); Air Force, BYU, Colorado St., New Mexico, San Diego St., UNLV, Utah and Wyoming (left to form Mountain West conference in '99).

1999 playing membership (8): Fresno St., Hawaii, Rice, San Jose St., SMU, TCU, Tulsa and UTEP.

Multiple titles: BYU (19); Arizona St. and Wyoming (7); Air Force, New Mexico and Colorado St. (3); Arizona, Fresno St. and Utah (2).

Year		Year		Year		Year	
1962	New Mexico (2-1-1)	1972	Arizona St. (5-1)	1981	BYU (7-1)	1992	Hawaii (6-2),
1963	New Mexico (3-1)	1973	Arizona St. (6-1)	1982	BYU (7-1)		BYU (6-2)
1964	Utah (3-1),		& Arizona (6-1)	1983	BYU (7-0)		& Fresno St. (6-2)
	New Mexico (3-1)	1974	BYU (6-0-1)	1984	BYU (8-0)	1993	BYU (6-2),
	& Arizona (3-1)	1975	Arizona St. (7-0)	1985	Air Force (7-1)		Fresno St. (6-2)
1965	BYU (4-1)	1976	BYU (6-1)		& BYU (7-1)		& Wyoming (6-2)
1966	Wyoming (5-0)		& Wyoming (6-1)	1986	San Diego St. (7-1)	1994	Colorado St. (7-1)
1967	Wyoming (5-0)	1977	Arizona St. (6-1)	1987	Wyoming (8-0)	1995	Colorado St. (6-2),
1968	Wyoming (6-1)		& BYU (6-1)	1988	Wyoming (8-0)		Air Force (6-2),
1969	Arizona St. (6-1)	1978	BYU (5-1)	1989	BYU (7-1)		BYU (6-2)
1970	Arizona St. (7-0)	1979	BYU (7-0)	1990	BYU (7-1)		& Utah (6-2)
1971	Arizona St. (7-0)	1980	BYU (6-1)	1991	BYU (7-0-1)		

WAC Championship Game

In addition to expanding to 16 teams and splitting into two divisions in 1996, the WAC now stages a conference championship game between the two division winners on the first Saturday in December at Sam Boyd Stadium in Las Vegas. The divisions: Pacific Division—BYU, Fresno St., Hawaii, New Mexico, San Diego St., San Jose St., UTEP, Utah; Mountain Division—Air Force, Colorado St., Rice, SMU, TCU, Tulsa, UNLV, Wyoming.

Year		Year		Year	
1996	BYU 28, Wyoming 25 (OT)	1997	Colorado St. 41, New Mexico 13	1998	Air Force 20, BYU 13

Longest Division I Streaks

Winning Streaks
(Including bowl games)

No		Seasons	Spoiler	Score
47	Oklahoma 1953-57		Notre Dame	7-0
39	Washington. . . .1908-14		Oregon St.	0-0
37	Yale 1890-93		Princeton	6-0
37	Yale 1887-89		Princeton	10-0
35	Toledo 1969-71		Tampa	21-0
34	Penn 1894-96		Lafayette	6-4
31	Oklahoma 1948-50		Kentucky	13-7*
31	Pittsburgh 1914-18		Cleve. Naval	10-9
31	Penn 1896-98		Harvard	10-0
30	Texas 1968-70		Notre Dame	24-11*
29	Miami-FL 1990-93		Alabama	34-13
29	Michigan 1901-03		Minnesota	6-6
28	Alabama† 1991-93		Tennessee	17-17
28	Alabama 1978-80		Mississippi St.	6-3
28	Oklahoma 1973-75		Kansas	23-3
28	Michigan St. . . .1950-53		Purdue	6-0
27	Nebraska. 1901-04		Colorado	6-0
26	Nebraska. 1994-96		Arizona St.	19-0
26	Cornell. 1921-24		Williams	14-7
26	Michigan 1903-05		Chicago	2-0
25	BYU 1983-85		UCLA	27-24
25	San Diego St. . .1965-67		Utah St.	31-25
25	Michigan 1946-49		Army	21-7
25	Army 1944-46		Notre Dame	0-0
25	USC 1931-33		Oregon St.	0-0

*Note: Kentucky beat Oklahoma in 1951 Sugar Bowl and Notre Dame beat Texas in 1971 Cotton Bowl.

†Note: Alabama was forced to forfeit eight victories and one tie in 1993 by the NCAA Committee on Infractions.

Unbeaten Streaks
(Including bowl games)

No	W-T	Seasons	Spoiler	Score
63	59-4	Washington. . .1907-17	California	27-0
56	55-1	Michigan 1901-05	Chicago	2-0
50	46-4	California 1920-25	Olympic Club	15-0
48	47-1	Oklahoma 1953-57	N. Dame	7-0
48	47-1	Yale 1885-89	Princeton	10-0
47	42-5	Yale 1879-85	Princeton	6-5
44	42-2	Yale 1894-96	Princeton	24-6
42	39-3	Yale 1904-08	Harvard	4-0
39	37-2	N. Dame 1946-50	Purdue	28-14
37	36-1	Oklahoma 1972-75	Kansas	23-3
37	37-0	Yale 1890-93	Princeton	6-0
35	35-0	Toledo 1967-71	Tampa	21-0
35	34-1	Minnesota 1903-05	Wisconsin	16-12

Losing Streaks

No		Seasons	Victim	Score
80	Prairie View. 1989-98		Langston	14-12
44	Columbia. 1983-88		Princeton	16-14
34	Northwestern . . .1979-82		No. Illinois	31-6
28	Virginia 1958-60		Wm. & Mary	21-6
28	Kansas St. 1944-48		Arkansas St.	37-6
27	Eastern Mich. 1980-82		Kent St.	9-7
27	New Mexico St. . .1988-90		CS-Fullerton	43-9

Note: Virginia ended its losing streak in the opening game of the 1961 season.

Annual NCAA Division I-A Leaders

Note that Oklahoma A&M is now Oklahoma St. and Texas Mines is now UTEP.

Rushing

Individual championship decided on Rushing Yards (1937-69), and on Yards Per Game (since 1970).

Multiple winners: Troy Davis, Marshall Faulk, Art Luppino, Ed Marinaro, Rudy Mobley, Jim Pilot, O.J. Simpson and Ricky Williams (2).

Year		Car	Yards
1937	Byron (Whizzer) White, Colorado	181	1121
1938	Len Eshmont, Fordham	132	831
1939	John Polanski, Wake Forest	137	882
1940	Al Ghesquiere, Detroit	146	957
1941	Frank Sinkwich, Georgia	209	1103
1942	Rudy Mobley, Hardin-Simmons	187	1281
1943	Creighton Miller, Notre Dame	151	911
1944	Red Williams, Minnesota	136	911
1945	Bob Fenimore, Oklahoma A&M	142	1048
1946	Rudy Mobley, Hardin-Simmons	227	1262
1947	Wilton Davis, Hardin-Simmons	193	1173
1948	Fred Wendt, Texas Mines	184	1570
1949	John Dottley, Ole Miss	208	1312
1950	Wilford White, Arizona St.	199	1502
1951	Ollie Matson, San Francisco	245	1566
1952	Howie Waugh, Tulsa	164	1372
1953	J.C. Caroline, Illinois	194	1256
1954	Art Luppino, Arizona	179	1359
1955	Art Luppino, Arizona	209	1313
1956	Jim Crawford, Wyoming	200	1104
1957	Leon Burton, Arizona St.	117	1126
1958	Dick Bass, Pacific	205	1361
1959	Pervis Atkins, New Mexico St.	130	971
1960	Bob Gaiters, New Mexico St	197	1338
1961	Jim Pilot, New Mexico St.	191	1278
1962	Jim Pilot, New Mexico St.	208	1247
1963	Dave Casinelli, Memphis St	219	1016
1964	Brian Piccolo, Wake Forest	252	1044
1965	Mike Garrett, USC	267	1440
1966	Ray McDonald, Idaho	259	1329
1967	O.J. Simpson, USC	266	1415
1968	O.J. Simpson, USC	355	1709

Year		Car	Yards	
1969	Steve Owens, Oklahoma	358	1523	

Year		Car	Yards	P/Gm
1970	Ed Marinaro, Cornell	285	1425	158.3
1971	Ed Marinaro, Cornell	356	1881	209.0
1972	Pete VanValkenburg, BYU	232	1386	138.6
1973	Mark Kellar, Northern Ill	291	1719	156.3
1974	Louie Giammona, Utah St.	329	1534	153.4
1975	Ricky Bell, USC	357	1875	170.5
1976	Tony Dorsett, Pittsburgh	338	1948	177.1
1977	Earl Campbell, Texas	267	1744	158.5
1978	Billy Sims, Oklahoma	231	1762	160.2
1979	Charles White, USC	293	1803	180.3
1980	George Rogers, S. Carolina	297	1781	161.9
1981	Marcus Allen, USC	403	2342	212.9
1982	Ernest Anderson, Okla. St.	353	1877	170.6
1983	Mike Rozier, Nebraska	275	2148	179.0
1984	Keith Byars, Ohio St.	313	1655	150.5
1985	Lorenzo White, Mich. St.	386	1908	173.5
1986	Paul Palmer, Temple	346	1866	169.6
1987	Ickey Woods, UNLV	259	1658	150.7
1988	Barry Sanders, Okla. St.	344	2628	238.9
1989	Anthony Thompson, Ind	358	1793	163.0
1990	Gerald Hudson, Okla. St.	279	1642	149.3
1991	Marshall Faulk, S. Diego St.	201	1429	158.8
1992	Marshall Faulk, S. Diego St.	265	1630	163.0
1993	LeShon Johnson, No. Ill.	327	1976	179.6
1994	Rashaan Salaam, Colorado . . .	298	2055	186.8
1995	Troy Davis, Iowa St.	345	2010	182.7
1996	Troy Davis, Iowa St.	402	2185	198.6
1997	Ricky Williams, Texas	279	1893	172.1
1998	Ricky Williams, Texas	361	2124	193.1

All-Purpose Yardage

Multiple winners: Marcus Allen, Pervis Atkins, Ryan Benjamin, Troy Davis, Troy Edwards, Louie Giammona, Tom Harmon, Art Luppino, Napolean McCallum, O.J. Simpson, Charles White and Gary Wood (2).

Year		Yards	P/Gm
1937	Byron (Whizzer) White, Colorado	1970	246.3
1938	Parker Hall, Ole Miss	1420	129.1
1939	Tom Harmon, Michigan	1208	151.0
1940	Tom Harmon, Michigan	1312	164.0
1941	Bill Dudley, Virginia	1674	186.0
1942	Complete records not available		
1943	Stan Koslowski, Holy Cross	1411	176.4
1944	Red Williams, Minnesota	1467	163.0
1945	Bob Fenimore, Oklahoma A&M	1577	197.1
1946	Rudy Mobley, Hardin-Simmons	1765	176.5
1947	Wilton Davis, Hardin-Simmons	1798	179.8
1948	Lou Kusserow, Columbia	1737	193.0
1949	Johnny Papit, Virginia	1611	179.0
1950	Wilford White, Arizona St.	2065	206.5
1951	Ollie Matson, San Francisco	2037	226.3
1952	Billy Vessels, Oklahoma	1512	151.2
1953	J.C. Caroline, Illinois	1470	163.3
1954	Art Luppino, Arizona	2193	219.3
1955	Jim Swink, TCU	1702	170.2
	& Art Luppino, Arizona	1702	170.2
1956	Jack Hill, Utah St	1691	169.1
1957	Overton Curtis, Utah St	1608	160.8
1958	Dick Bass, Pacific	1878	187.8
1959	Pervis Atkins, New Mexico St	1800	180.0
1960	Pervis Atkins, New Mexico St	1613	161.3
1961	Jim Pilot, New Mexico St	1606	160.6
1962	Gary Wood, Cornell	1395	155.0
1963	Gary Wood, Cornell	1508	167.6
1964	Donny Anderson, Texas Tech	1710	171.0
1965	Floyd Little, Syracuse	1990	199.0
1966	Frank Quayle, Virginia	1616	161.6
1967	O.J. Simpson, USC	1700	188.9
1968	O.J. Simpson, USC	1966	196.6
1969	Lynn Moore, Army	1795	179.5
1970	Don McCauley, North Carolina	2021	183.7
1971	Ed Marinaro, Cornell	1932	214.7
1972	Howard Stevens, Louisville	2132	213.2
1973	Willard Harrell, Pacific	1777	177.7
1974	Louie Giammona, Utah St	1984	198.4
1975	Louie Giammona, Utah St	2045	185.9
1976	Tony Dorsett, Pittsburgh	2021	183.7
1977	Earl Campbell, Texas	1855	168.6
1978	Charles White, USC	2096	174.7
1979	Charles White, USC	1941	194.1
1980	Marcus Allen, USC	1794	179.4
1981	Marcus Allen, USC	2559	232.6
1982	Carl Monroe, Utah	2036	185.1
1983	Napolean McCallum, Navy	2385	216.8
1984	Keith Byars, Ohio St	2284	207.6
1985	Napolean McCallum, Navy	2330	211.8
1986	Paul Palmer, Temple	2633	239.4
1987	Eric Wilkerson, Kent St	2074	188.6
1988	Barry Sanders, Oklahoma St	3250	295.5
1989	Mike Pringle, CS-Fullerton	2690	244.6
1990	Glyn Milburn, Stanford	2222	202.0
1991	Ryan Benjamin, Pacific	2995	249.6
1992	Ryan Benjamin, Pacific	2597	236.1
1993	LeShon Johnson, Northern Ill.	2082	189.3
1994	Rashaan Salaam, Colorado	2349	213.5
1995	Troy Davis, Iowa St.	2466	224.2
1996	Troy Davis, Iowa St.	2364	214.9
1997	Troy Edwards, La. Tech	2144	194.9
1998	Troy Edwards, La. Tech	2784	232.0

Total Offense

Individual championship decided on Total Yards (1937-69) and on Yards Per Game (since 1970).

Multiple winners: Johnny Bright, Bob Fenimore, Mike Maxwell, Jim McMahon and Tim Rattay (2).

Year		Plays	Yards	P/Gm
1937	Byron (Whizzer) White, Colorado	224	1596	
1938	Davey O'Brien, TCU	291	1847	
1939	Kenny Washington, UCLA	259	1370	
1940	Johnny Knolla, Creighton	298	1420	
1941	Bud Schwenk, Washington-MO	354	1928	
1942	Frank Sinkwich, Georgia	341	2187	
1943	Bob Hoernschemeyer, Indiana	355	1648	
1944	Bob Fenimore, Oklahoma A&M	241	1758	
1945	Bob Fenimore, Oklahoma A&M	203	1641	
1946	Travis Bidwell, Auburn	339	1715	
1947	Fred Enke, Arizona	329	1941	
1948	Stan Heath, Nevada-Reno	233	1992	
1949	Johnny Bright, Drake	275	1950	
1950	Johnny Bright, Drake	320	2400	
1951	Dick Kazmaier, Princeton	272	1827	
1952	Ted Marchibroda, Detroit	305	1813	
1953	Paul Larson, California	262	1572	
1954	George Shaw, Oregon	276	1536	
1955	George Welsh, Navy	203	1348	
1956	John Brodie, Stanford	295	1642	
1957	Bob Newman, Washington St	263	1444	
1958	Dick Bass, Pacific	218	1440	
1959	Dick Norman, Stanford	319	2018	
1960	Billy Kilmer, UCLA	292	1889	
1961	Dave Hoppmann, Iowa St	320	1638	
1962	Terry Baker, Oregon St	318	2276	
1963	George Mira, Miami-FL	394	2318	
1964	Jerry Rhome, Tulsa	470	3128	
1965	Bill Anderson, Tulsa	580	3343	
1966	Virgil Carter, BYU	388	2545	
1967	Sal Olivas, New Mexico St.	368	2184	
1968	Greg Cook Cincinnati	507	3210	
1969	Dennis Shaw, San Diego St	388	3197	
1970	Pat Sullivan, Auburn	333	2856	285.6
1971	Gary Huff, Florida St	386	2653	241.2
1972	Don Strock, Va. Tech	480	3170	288.2
1973	Jesse Freitas, San Diego St	410	2901	263.7
1974	Steve Joachim, Temple	331	2227	222.7
1975	Gene Swick, Toledo	490	2706	246.0
1976	Tommy Kramer, Rice	562	3272	297.5
1977	Doug Williams, Gambling	377	3229	293.5
1978	Mike Ford, SMU	459	2957	268.8
1979	Marc Wilson, BYU	488	3580	325.5
1980	Jim McMahon, BYU	540	4627	385.6
1981	Jim McMahon, BYU	487	3458	345.8
1982	Todd Dillon, Long Beach St	585	3587	326.1
1983	Steve Young, BYU	531	4346	395.1
1984	Robbie Bosco, BYU	543	3932	327.7
1985	Jim Everett, Purdue	518	3589	326.3
1986	Mike Perez, San Jose St	425	2969	329.9
1987	Todd Santos, San Diego St.	562	3688	307.3
1988	Scott Mitchell, Utah	589	4299	390.8
1989	Andre Ware, Houston	628	4661	423.7
1990	David Klingler, Houston	704	5221	474.6
1991	Ty Detmer, BYU	478	4001	333.4
1992	Jimmy Klingler, Houston	544	3768	342.6
1993	Chris Vargas, Nevada	535	4332	393.8
1994	Mike Maxwell, Nevada	477	3498	318.0
1995	Mike Maxwell, Nevada	443	3623	402.6
1996	Josh Wallwork, Wyoming	525	4209	350.8
1997	Tim Rattay, La. Tech	541	3968	360.7
1998	Tim Rattay, La. Tech	602	4840	403.3

Annual NCAA Division I-A Leaders (Cont.)
Passing

Individual championship decided on Completions (1937-69), on Completions Per Game (1970-78) and on Passing Efficiency rating points (since 1979).

Multiple winners: Elvis Grbac, Don Heinrich, Jim McMahon, Davey O'Brien and Don Trull (2).

Year		Cmp	Pct	TD	Yds
1937	Davey O'Brien, TCU	.94	.402	–	969
1938	Davey O'Brien, TCU	.93	.557	–	1457
1939	Kay Eakin, Arkansas	.78	.404	–	962
1940	Billy Sewell, Wash. St.	.86	.494	–	1023
1941	Bud Schwenk, Wash.-MO	.114	.487	–	1457
1942	Ray Evans, Kansas	.101	.505	–	1117
1943	Johnny Cook, Georgia	.73	.465	–	1007
1944	Paul Rickards, Pittsburgh	.84	.472	–	997
1945	Al Dekdebrun, Cornell	.90	.464	–	1227
1946	Travis Tidwell, Auburn	.79	.500	5	943
1947	Charlie Conerly, Ole Miss	.133	.571	18	1367
1948	Stan Heath, Nev-Reno	.126	.568	22	2005
1949	Adrian Burk, Baylor	.110	.576	14	1428
1950	Don Heinrich, Washington	.134	.606	14	1846
1951	Don Klosterman, Loyola-CA	.159	.505	9	1843
1952	Don Heinrich, Washington	.137	.507	13	1647
1953	Bob Garrett, Stanford	.118	.576	17	1637
1954	Paul Larson, California	.125	.641	10	1537
1955	George Welsh, Navy	.94	.627	8	1319
1956	John Brodie, Stanford	.139	.579	12	1633
1957	Ken Ford, H-Simmons	.115	.561	14	1254
1958	Buddy Humphrey, Baylor	.112	.574	7	1316
1959	Dick Norman, Stanford	.152	.578	11	1963
1960	Harold Stephens, H-Simm.	.145	.566	3	1254
1961	Chon Gallegos, S. Jose St.	.117	.594	14	1480
1962	Don Trull, Baylor	.125	.546	11	1627
1963	Don Trull, Baylor	.174	.565	12	2157
1964	Jerry Rhome, Tulsa	.224	.687	32	2870
1965	Bill Anderson, Tulsa	.296	.582	30	3464
1966	John Eckman, Wichita St.	.195	.426	7	2339
1967	Terry Stone, N. Mexico	.160	.476	9	1946
1968	Chuck Hixson, SMU	.265	.566	21	3103
1969	John Reaves, Florida	.222	.561	24	2896

Year		Cmp	P/Gm	TD	Yds
1970	Sonny Sixkiller, Wash	.186	18.6	15	2303
1971	Brian Sipe, S. Diego St.	.196	17.8	17	2532
1972	Don Strock, Va. Tech	.228	20.7	16	3243
1973	Jesse Freitas, S. Diego St.	.227	20.6	21	2993
1974	Steve Bartkowski, Cal	.182	16.5	12	2580
1975	Craig Penrose, S. Diego St.	.198	18.0	15	2660
1976	Tommy Kramer, Rice	.269	24.5	21	3317
1977	Guy Benjamin, Stanford	.208	20.8	19	2521
1978	Steve Dils, Stanford	.247	22.5	22	2943

Year		Cmp	TD	Yds	Rating
1979	Turk Schonert, Stanford	.148	19	1922	163.0
1980	Jim McMahon, BYU	.284	47	4571	176.9
1981	Jim McMahon, BYU	.272	30	3555	155.0
1982	Tom Ramsey, UCLA	.191	21	2824	153.5
1983	Steve Young, BYU	.306	33	3902	168.5
1984	Doug Flutie, BC	.233	27	3454	152.9
1985	Jim Harbaugh, Michigan	.139	18	1913	163.7
1986	Vinny Testaverde, Miami-FL	.175	26	2557	165.8
1987	Don McPherson, Syracuse	.129	22	2341	164.3
1988	Timm Rosenbach, Wash. St.	.199	23	2791	162.0
1989	Ty Detmer, BYU	.265	32	4560	175.6
1990	Shawn Moore, Virginia	.144	21	2262	160.7
1991	Elvis Grbac, Michigan	.152	24	1955	169.0
1992	Elvis Grbac, Michigan	.112	15	1465	154.2
1993	Trent Dilfer, Fresno St.	.217	28	3276	173.1
1994	Kerry Collins, Penn St.	.176	21	2679	172.9
1995	Danny Wuerffel, Florida	.210	35	3266	178.4
1996	Steve Sarkisian, BYU	.278	33	4027	173.6
1997	Cade McNown, UCLA	.173	22	2877	168.6
1998	Shaun King, Tulane	.223	36	3232	183.3

Receptions

Championship decided on Passes Caught (1937-69) and on Catches Per Game (since 1970). Touchdown totals unavailable in 1939 and 1941-45.

Multiple winners: Neil Armstrong, Hugh Campell, Manny Hazard, Reid Moseley, Jason Phillips, Howard Twilley and Alex Van Dyke (2).

Year		No	TD	Yds
1937	Jim Benton, Arkansas	.47	7	754
1938	Sam Boyd, Baylor	.32	5	537
1939	Ken Kavanaugh, LSU	.30	–	467
1940	Eddie Bryant, Virginia	.30	2	222
1941	Hank Stanton, Arizona	.50	–	820
1942	Bill Rogers, Texas A&M	.39	–	432
1943	Neil Armstrong, Okla. A&M	.39	–	317
1944	Reid Moseley, Georgia	.32	–	506
1945	Reid Moseley, Georgia	.31	–	662
1946	Neil Armstrong, Okla. A&M	.32	1	479
1947	Barney Poole, Ole Miss	.52	8	513
1948	Red O'Quinn, Wake Forest	.39	7	605
1949	Art Weiner, N. Carolina	.52	7	762
1950	Gordon Cooper, Denver	.46	8	569
1951	Dewey McConnell, Wyoming	.47	9	725
1952	Ed Brown, Fordham	.57	6	774
1953	John Carson, Georgia	.45	4	663
1954	Jim Hanifan, California	.44	4	569
1955	Hank Burnine, Missouri	.44	2	594
1956	Art Powell, San Jose St.	.40	5	583
1957	Stuart Vaughan, Utah	.53	5	756
1958	Dave Hibbert, Arizona	.61	4	606
1959	Chris Burford, Stanford	.61	6	756
1960	Hugh Campbell, Wash. St.	.66	10	881
1961	Hugh Campbell, Wash. St.	.53	5	723

Year		No	TD	Yds
1962	Vern Burke, Oregon St	.69	10	1007
1963	Lawrence Elkins, Baylor	.70	8	873
1964	Howard Twilley, Tulsa	.95	13	1178
1965	Howard Twilley, Tulsa	.134	16	1779
1966	Glenn Meltzer, Wichita St	.91	4	1115
1967	Bob Goodridge, Vanderbilt	.79	6	1114
1968	Ron Sellers, Florida St	.86	12	1496
1969	Jerry Hendren, Idaho	.95	12	1452

Year		No	P/Gm	TD	Yds
1970	Mike Mikolayunas, Davidson	.87	8.7	8	1128
1971	Tom Reynolds, San Diego St	.67	6.7	7	1070
1972	Tom Forzani, Utah St	.85	7.7	8	1169
1973	Jay Miller, BYU	.100	9.1	8	1181
1974	D. McDonald, San Diego St	.86	7.8	7	1157
1975	Bob Farnham, Brown	.56	6.2	2	701
1976	Billy Ryckman, La. Tech	.77	7.0	10	1382
1977	W. Tolleson, W. Carolina	.73	6.6	7	1101
1978	Dave Petzke, Northern Ill	.91	8.3	11	1217
1979	Rick Beasley, Appalach. St	.74	6.7	12	1205
1980	Dave Young, Purdue	.67	6.1	8	917
1981	Pete Harvey, N. Texas St	.57	6.3	3	743
1982	Vincent White, Stanford	.68	6.8	8	677
1983	Keith Edwards, Vanderbilt	.97	8.8	8	909
1984	David Williams, Illinois	.101	9.2	8	1278
1985	Rodney Carter, Purdue	.98	8.9	4	1099

Year	No	P/Gm	TD	Yds
1986 Mark Templeton, L. Beach St	99	9.0	2	688
1987 Jason Phillips, Houston	99	9.0	3	875
1988 Jason Phillips, Houston	108	9.8	15	1444
1989 Manny Hazard, Houston	142	12.9	22	1689
1990 Manny Hazard, Houston	78	7.8	9	946
1991 Fred Gilbert, Houston	106	9.6	7	957
1992 Sherman Smith, Houston	103	9.4	6	923

Year	No	P/Gm	TD	Yds
1993 Chris Penn, Tulsa	105	9.6	12	1578
1994 Alex Van Dyke, Nevada	98	8.9	10	1246
1995 Alex Van Dyke, Nevada	129	11.7	16	1854
1996 Damond Wilkins, Nevada	114	10.4	4	1121
1997 Eugene Baker, Kent	103	9.4	18	1549
1998 Troy Edwards, La. Tech	140	11.7	27	1996

Scoring

Championship decided on Total Points (1937-69) and on Points Per Game (since 1970).

Multiple winners: Tom Harmon and Billy Sims (2).

Year	TD	XP	FG	Pts
1937 Byron (Whizzer) White, Colo	16	23	1	122
1938 Parker Hall, Ole Miss	11	7	0	73
1939 Tom Harmon, Michigan	14	15	1	102
1940 Tom Harmon, Michigan	16	18	1	117
1941 Bill Dudley, Virginia	18	23	1	134
1942 Bob Steuber, Missouri	18	13	0	121
1943 Steve Van Buren, LSU	14	14	0	98
1944 Glenn Davis, Army	20	0	0	120
1945 Doc Blanchard, Army	19	1	0	115
1946 Gene Roberts, Tenn-Chatt.	18	9	0	117
1947 Lou Gambino, Maryland	16	0	0	96
1948 Fred Wendt, Texas Mines	20	32	0	152
1949 George Thomas, Oklahoma	19	3	0	117
1950 Bobby Reynolds, Nebraska	22	25	0	157
1951 Ollie Matson, San Francisco	21	0	0	126
1952 Jackie Parker, Miss. St.	16	24	0	120
1953 Earl Lindley, Utah St.	13	3	0	81
1954 Art Luppino, Arizona	24	22	0	166
1955 Jim Swink, TCU	20	5	0	125
1956 Clendon Thomas, Oklahoma	18	0	0	108
1957 Leon Burton, Ariz. St.	16	0	0	96
1958 Dick Bass, Pacific	18	8	0	116
1959 Pervis Atkins, N. Mexico St.	17	5	0	107
1960 Bob Gaiters, N. Mexico St.	23	7	0	145
1961 Jim Pilot, N. Mexico St.	21	12	0	138
1962 Jerry Logan, W. Texas St.	13	32	0	110
1963 Cosmo Iacavazzi, Princeton	14	0	0	84
& Dave Casinelli, Memphis St.	14	0	0	84
1964 Brian Piccolo, Wake Forest	17	9	0	111
1965 Howard Twilley, Tulsa	16	31	0	127
1966 Ken Hebert, Houston	11	41	2	113
1967 Leroy Keyes, Purdue	19	0	0	114
1968 Jim O'Brien, Cincinnati	12	31	13	142

Year	TD	XP	FG	Pts
1969 Steve Owens, Oklahoma	23	0	0	138

Year	TD	XP	FG	Pts	P/Gm
1970 Brian Bream, Air Force	20	0	0	120	12.0
& Gary Kosins, Dayton	18	0	0	108	12.0
1971 Ed Marinaro, Cornell	24	4	0	148	16.4
1972 Harold Henson, Ohio St	20	0	0	120	12.0
1973 Jim Jennings, Rutgers	21	2	0	128	11.6
1974 Bill Marek, Wisconsin	19	0	0	114	12.7
1975 Pete Johnson, Ohio St.	25	0	0	150	13.6
1976 Tony Dorsett, Pitt	22	2	0	134	12.2
1977 Earl Campbell, Texas	19	0	0	114	10.4
1978 Billy Sims, Oklahoma	20	0	0	120	10.9
1979 Billy Sims, Oklahoma	22	0	0	132	12.0
1980 Sammy Winder, So. Miss	20	0	0	120	10.9
1981 Marcus Allen, USC	23	0	0	138	12.5
1982 Greg Allen, Fla. St	21	0	0	126	11.5
1983 Mike Rozier, Nebraska	29	0	0	174	14.5
1984 Keith Byars, Ohio St	24	0	0	144	13.1
1985 Bernard White, B. Green	19	0	0	114	10.4
1986 Steve Bartalo, Colo. St	19	0	0	114	10.4
1987 Paul Hewitt, S. Diego St.	24	0	0	144	12.0
1988 Barry Sanders, Okla.St.	39	0	0	234	21.3
1989 Anthony Thompson, Ind	25	4	0	154	14.0
1990 Stacey Robinson, No. Ill.	19	6	0	120	10.9
1991 Marshall Faulk, S.D. St.	23	2	0	140	15.6
1992 Garrison Hearst, Georgia	21	0	0	126	11.5
1993 Bam Morris, Texas Tech	22	2	0	134	12.2
1994 Rashaan Salaam, Colo	24	0	0	144	13.1
1995 Eddie George, Ohio St.	24	0	0	144	12.0
1996 Corey Dillon, Washington	23	0	0	138	12.6
1997 Ricky Williams, Texas	25	2	0	152	13.8
1998 Troy Edwards, La. Tech	31	2	0	188	15.7

All-Time NCAA Division I-A Leaders

Through the 1998 regular season. The NCAA does not recognize active players among career Per Game leaders.

CAREER

Passing
(Minimum 500 Completions)

Passing Efficiency

		Years	Rating
1	Danny Wuerffel, Florida	1993-96	163.6
2	Ty Detmer, BYU	1988-91	162.7
3	Steve Sarkisian, BYU	1995-96	162.0
4	Billy Blanton, San Diego St.	1993-96	157.1
5	Jim McMahon, BYU	1977-78, 80-81	156.9

Yards Gained

		Years	Yards
1	Ty Detmer, BYU	1988-91	15,031
2	Todd Santos, San Diego St	1984-87	11,425
3	Peyton Manning, Tennessee	1994-97	11,201
4	Eric Zeier, Georgia	1991-94	11,153
5	Alex Van Pelt, Pittsburgh	1989-92	10,913

Completions

		Years	No
1	Ty Detmer, BYU	1988-91	958
2	Todd Santos, San Diego St	1984-87	910
3	Brian McClure, Bowling Green	1982-85	900
4	Erik Wilhelm, Oregon St.	1985-88	870
5	Alex Van Pelt, Pittsburgh	1989-92	845

Receptions

Catches

		Years	No
1	Geoff Noisy, Nevada	1995-98	295
2	Troy Edwards, La. Tech	1996-98	280
3	Aaron Turner, Pacific	1989-92	266
4	Chad Mackey, La. Tech	1993-96	264
5	Terance Mathis, New Mexico	1985-87, 89	263

Catches Per Game

		Years	No	P/Gm
1	Manny Hazard, Houston	1989-90	220	10.5
2	Alex Van Dyke, Nevada	1994-95	227	10.3
3	Howard Twilley, Tulsa	1963-65	261	10.0
4	Jason Phillips, Houston	1987-88	207	9.4
5	Troy Edwards, La. Tech	1996-98	280	8.2

Yards Gained

		Years	No	Yards
1	Marcus Harris, Wyoming	1993-96	259	4518
2	Ryan Yarborough, Wyoming	1990-93	229	4357
3	Troy Edwards, La. Tech	1996-98	280	4352
4	Aaron Turner, Pacific	1989-92	266	4345
5	Terance Mathis, N. Mexico	1985-87, 89	263	4254

All-Time NCAA Division I-A Leaders (Cont.)

Rushing

Yards Gained

		Years	Yards
1	Ricky Williams, Texas	1995-98	6279
2	Tony Dorsett, Pittsburgh	1973-76	6082
3	Charles White, USC	1976-79	5598
4	Herschel Walker, Georgia	1980-82	5259
5	Archie Griffin, Ohio St	1972-75	5177

Yards Per Game

		Years	Yards	P/Gm
1	Ed Marinaro, Cornell	1969-71	4715	174.6
2	O.J. Simpson, USC	1967-68	3124	164.4
3	Herschel Walker, Georgia	1980-82	5259	159.4
4	LeShon Johnson, No. Ill.	1992-93	3314	150.6
5	Marshall Faulk, S. Diego St.	1991-93	4589	148.0

Total Offense

Yards Gained

		Years	Yards
1	Ty Detmer, BYU	1988-91	14,665
2	Doug Flutie, Boston College	1981-84	11,317
3	Peyton Manning, Tennessee	1994-97	11,020
4	Eric Zeier, Georgia	1991-94	10,841
5	Alex Van Pelt, Pittsburgh	1989-92	10,814

Yards Per Game

		Years	Yards	P/Gm
1	Chris Vargas, Nevada	1992-93	6,417	320.9
2	Ty Detmer, BYU	1988-91	14,665	318.8
3	Dante Culpepper*, C. Fla.	1996-98	10,344	313.5
4	Mike Perez, San Jose St	1986-87	6,182	309.1
5	Josh Wallwork, Wyoming	1995-96	6,753	307.0

*Culpepper played I-AA with Central Florida in 1995.

All-Purpose Yardage

Yards Gained

		Years	Yards
1	Ricky Williams, Texas	1995-98	7206
2	Napoleon McCallum, Navy	1981-85	7172
3	Darrin Nelson, Stanford	1977-78, 80-81	6885
4	Kevin Faulk, LSU	1995-98	6833
5	Terance Mathis, N. Mexico	1985-87, 89	6691

		Years	Yards	P/Gm
1	Ryan Benjamin, Pacific	1990-92	5706	237.8
2	Sheldon Canley, S. Jose St.	1988-90	5146	205.8
3	Howard Stevens, Louisville	1971-72	3873	193.7
4	O.J. Simpson, USC	1967-68	3666	192.9
5	Alex Van Dyke, Nevada	1994-95	4146	188.5

Miscellaneous

Interceptions

		Years	No
1	Al Brosky, Illinois	1950-52	29
2	John Provost, Holy Cross	1972-74	27
	Martin Bayless, Bowling Green	1980-83	27
4	Tom Curtis, Michigan	1967-69	25
	Tony Thurman, Boston College	1981-84	25
	Tracy Saul, Texas Tech.	1989-92	25

Punting Average*

		Years	Avg
1	Todd Sauerbrun, West Va.	1991-94	46.3
2	Reggie Roby, Iowa	1979-82	45.6
3	Greg Montgomery, Mich. St.	1985-87	45.4
4	Tom Tupa, Ohio St.	1984-87	45.2
5	Barry Helton, Colorado	1984-87	44.9

*At least 150 punts.

Punt Return Average*

		Years	Avg
1	Jack Mitchell, Oklahoma	1946-48	23.6
2	Gene Gibson, Cincinnati	1949-50	20.5
3	Eddie Macon, Pacific.	1949-51	18.9
4	Jackie Robinson, UCLA	1939-40	18.8
	Two tied at 17.7 each.		

*Minimum 1.2 punt returns per game and 30 career returns.

Kickoff Return Average*

		Years	Avg
1	Anthony Davis, USC	1972-74	35.1
2	Eric Booth, So. Miss.	1994-97	32.4
3	Overton Curtis, Utah St	1957-58	31.0
4	Fred Montgomery, New Mexico St.	1991-92	30.5
5	Allie Taylor, Utah St.	1966-68	29.3

*Minimum 1.2 kickoff returns per game and 30 career returns.

Scoring
Non-kickers

Points

		Years	TD	Xpt	FG	Pts
1	Ricky Williams, Texas	1995-98	75	2	0	452
2	Anthony Thompson, Ind.	1986-89	65	4	0	394
3	Marshall Faulk, S.D. St.	1991-93	62	4	0	376
4	Tony Dorsett, Pittsburgh	1973-76	59	2	0	356
5	Glenn Davis, Army	1943-46	59	0	0	354

Points Per Game

		Years	Pts	P/Gm
1	Marshall Faulk, S. Diego St.	1991-93	376	12.1
2	Ed Marinaro, Cornell	1969-71	318	11.8
3	Bill Burnett, Arkansas	1968-70	294	11.3
4	Steve Owens, Oklahoma	1967-69	336	11.2
5	Eddie Talboom, Wyoming	1948-50	303	10.8

Touchdowns Rushing

		Years	No
1	Ricky Williams, Texas	1995-98	72
2	Anthony Thompson, Indiana	1986-89	64
3	Marshall Faulk, S. Diego St.	1991-93	57
4	Steve Owens, Oklahoma	1967-69	56
5	Tony Dorsett, Pittsburgh	1973-76	55

Touchdowns Passing

		Years	No
1	Ty Detmer, BYU	1988-91	121
2	Danny Wuerffel, Florida	1993-96	114
3	David Klingler, Houston	1988-91	91
4	Peyton Manning, Tennessee	1994-97	89
5	Troy Kopp, Pacific	1989-92	87

Touchdown Catches

		Years	No
1	Troy Edwards, La. Tech	1996-98	50
2	Aaron Turner, Pacific	1989-92	43
3	Ryan Yarborough, Wyoming	1990-93	42
4	Clarkston Hines, Duke	1986-89	38
	Marcus Harris, Wyoming	1993-96	38

Kickers

Points

		Years	FG	XP	Pts
1	Roman Anderson, Hou	1988-91	70	213	423
2	Carlos Huerta, Mia-FL	1988-91	73	178	397
3	Jason Elam, Hawaii	1988-89, 91-92	79	158	395
4	Derek Schmidt, Fla. St	1984-87	73	174	393
5	Kris Brown, Nebraska	1995-98	57	217	388
6	Jeff Hall, Tennessee	1995-98	61	188	371
7	Luis Zendejas, Ariz. St.	1981-84	78	134	368
8	Jeff Jaeger, Wash.	1983-86	80	118	358
9	John Lee, UCLA	1982-85	79	116	353
	Max Zendejas, Arizona	1982-85	77	122	353
	Kevin Butler, Georgia	1981-84	77	122	353

Field Goals

		Years	No
1	Jeff Jaeger, Washington	1983-86	80
2	John Lee, UCLA	1982-85	79
	Jason Elam, Hawaii	1988-89, 91-92	79
4	Philip Doyle, Alabama	1987-90	78
	Luis Zendejas, Arizona St	1981-84	78

SINGLE SEASON
Rushing

Yards Gained	Year	Gm	Car	Yards
Barry Sanders, Okla. St	1988	11	344	2628
Marcus Allen, USC	1981	11	403	2342
Troy Davis, Iowa St.	1996	11	402	2185
Mike Rozier, Nebraska	1983	12	275	2148
Ricky Williams, Texas	1998	11	361	2124

Yards Per Game	Year	Gm	Yards	P/Gm
Barry Sanders, Okla. St	1988	11	2628	238.9
Marcus Allen, USC	1981	11	2342	212.9
Ed Marinaro, Cornell	1971	9	1881	209.0
Troy Davis, Iowa St.	1996	11	2185	198.6
Ricky Williams, Texas	1998	11	2124	193.1

Passing
(Minimum 15 Attempts Per Game)

Passing Efficiency	Year	Rating
Shaun King, Tulane	1998	183.3
Danny Wuerffel, Florida	1995	178.4
Jim McMahon, BYU	1980	176.9
Ty Detmer, BYU	1989	175.6
Steve Sarkisian, BYU	1996	173.6

Yards Gained	Year	Yards
Ty Detmer, BYU	1990	5188
David Klingler, Houston	1990	5140
Tim Rattay, La. Tech	1998	4943
Andre Ware, Houston	1989	4699
Jim McMahon, BYU	1980	4571

Completions	Year	Att	No
Tim Rattay, La. Tech	1998	559	380
David Klingler, Houston	1990	643	374
Andre Ware, Houston	1989	578	365
Tim Couch, Kentucky	1997	547	363
Ty Detmer, BYU	1990	562	361

Total Offense

Yards Gained	Year	Gm	Plays	Yards
David Klingler, Houston	1990	11	704	5221
Ty Detmer, BYU	1990	12	635	5022
Tim Rattay, La. Tech	1998	12	602	4840
Andre Ware, Houston	1989	11	628	4661
Jim McMahon, BYU	1980	12	540	4627

Yards Per Game	Year	Gm	Yards	P/Gm
David Klingler, Houston	1990	11	5221	474.6
Andre Ware, Houston	1989	11	4661	423.7
Ty Detmer, BYU	1990	12	5022	418.5
Tim Rattay, La. Tech	1998	12	4840	403.3
Mike Maxwell, Nevada	1995	9	3623	402.6

Scoring

Points	Year	TD	Xpt	FG	Pts
Barry Sanders, Okla. St	1988	39	0	0	234
Troy Edwards, La. Tech	1998	31	2	0	188
Mike Rozier, Nebraska	1983	29	0	0	174
Lydell Mitchell, Penn St	1971	29	0	0	174
Art Luppino, Arizona	1954	24	22	0	166

Points Per Game	Year	Pts	P/Gm
Barry Sanders, Okla. St	1988	234	21.3
Bobby Reynolds, Nebraska	1950	157	17.4
Art Luppino, Arizona	1954	166	16.6
Ed Marinaro, Cornell	1971	148	16.4
Lydell Mitchell, Penn St	1971	174	15.8

Touchdowns Rushing	Year	No
Barry Sanders, Okla. St	1988	37
Mike Rozier, Nebraska	1983	29
Ricky Williams, Texas	1998	27
Ricky Williams, Texas	1997	25
Travis Prentice, Miami-OH	1997	25

Receptions

Catches	Year	Gm	No
Manny Hazard, Houston	1989	11	142
Troy Edwards, La. Tech	1998	12	140
Howard Twilley, Tulsa	1965	10	134
Alex Van Dyke, Nevada	1995	11	129
Damond Wilkins, Nevada	1996	11	114

Catches Per Game	Year	No	P/Gm
Howard Twilley, Tulsa	1965	134	13.4
Manny Hazard, Houston	1989	142	12.9
Alex Van Dyke, Nevada	1995	129	11.7
Troy Edwards, La. Tech	1998	140	11.7
Damond Wilkins, Nevada	1996	114	10.4

Yards Gained	Year	No	Yards
Troy Edwards, La. Tech	1998	140	1996
Alex Van Dyke, Nevada	1995	129	1854
Howard Twilley, Tulsa	1965	134	1779
Troy Edwards, La. Tech	1997	102	1707
Manny Hazard, Houston	1989	142	1689

All-Purpose Yardage

Yards Gained	Year	Yards
Barry Sanders, Okla. St	1988	3250
Ryan Benjamin, Pacific	1991	2995
Troy Edwards, La. Tech	1998	2784
Mike Pringle, CS-Fullerton	1989	2690
Paul Palmer, Temple	1986	2633

Yards Per Game	Year	Yards	P/Gm
Barry Sanders, Okla. St	1988	3250	295.5
Ryan Benjamin, Pacific	1991	2995	249.6
Byron (Whizzer) White, Colo	1937	1970	246.3
Mike Pringle, CS-Fullerton	1989	2690	244.6
Paul Palmer, Temple	1986	2633	239.4

Touchdowns Passing	Year	No
David Klingler, Houston	1990	54
Jim McMahon, BYU	1980	47
Andre Ware, Houston	1989	46
Tim Rattay, La. Tech	1998	46
Ty Detmer, BYU	1990	41

Touchdown Catches	Year	No
Troy Edwards, La. Tech	1998	27
Randy Moss, Marshall	1997	25
Manny Hazard, Houston	1989	22
Desmond Howard, Michigan	1991	19
Five tied with 18 each.		

Field Goals	Year	No
John Lee, UCLA	1984	29
Paul Woodside, West Virginia	1982	28
Luis Zendejas, Arizona St	1983	28
Fuad Reveiz, Tennessee	1982	27
Sebastian Janikowski, FSU	1998	27
Three tied with 25 each.		

All-Time NCAA Division I-A Leaders (Cont.)
Miscellaneous

Interceptions	Year	No
Al Worley, Washington	1968	14
George Shaw, Oregon	1951	13
Eight tied with 12 each.		

Punting Average*	Year	Avg
Chad Kessler, LSU	1997	50.3
Reggie Roby, Iowa	1981	49.8
Kirk Wilson, UCLA	1956	49.3
Todd Sauerbrun, West Virginia	1994	48.4
Zack Jordan, Colorado	1950	48.2
*Qualifiers for championship.		

Punt Return Average*	Year	Avg
Bill Blackstock, Tennessee	1951	25.9
George Sims, Baylor	1948	25.0
Gene Derricotte, Michigan	1947	24.8
*At least 1.2 returns per game.		

Kickoff Return Average*	Year	Avg
Paul Allen, BYU	1961	40.1
Tremain Mack, Miami-FL	1996	39.5
Leeland McElroy, Texas A&M	1993	39.3
Forrest Hall, San Francisco	1946	38.2
Tony Ball, Tenn-Chattanooga	1977	36.4
*At least 1.2 kickoff returns per game.		

SINGLE GAME

Rushing

Yards Gained	Opponent	Year	Yds
Tony Sands, Kansas	Missouri	1991	396
Marshall Faulk, San Diego St	Pacific	1991	386
Troy Davis, Iowa St.	Missouri	1996	378
Anthony Thompson, Indiana	Wisconsin	1989	377
Astron Whatley, Kent	E. Michigan	1997	373

Passing

Yards Gained	Opponent	Year	Yds
David Klingler, Houston	Arizona St.	1990	716
Matt Vogler, TCU	Houston	1990	690
Scott Mitchell, Utah	Air Force	1988	631
Jeremy Leach, New Mexico	Utah	1989	622
Dave Wilson, Illinois	Ohio St.	1980	621

Completions	Opponent	Year	No
Drew Brees, Purdue	Wisconsin	1998	55
Rusty LaRue, Wake Forest	Duke	1995	55
David Klingler, Houston	SMU	1990	48
Tim Couch, Kentucky	Arkansas	1998	47
Jimmy Klingler, Houston	Rice	1992	46
Tim Rattay, La. Tech	Nebraska	1998	46
Sandy Schwab, Northwestern	Michigan	1982	45

Total Offense

Yards Gained	Opponent	Year	Yds
David Klingler, Houston	Arizona St.	1990	732
Matt Vogler, TCU	Houston	1990	696
David Klingler, Houston	TCU	1990	625
Scott Mitchell, Utah	Air Force	1988	625
Jimmy Klingler, Houston	Rice	1992	612

Receptions

Catches	Opponent	Year	No
Randy Gatewood, UNLV	Idaho	1994	23
Jay Miller, BYU	New Mexico	1973	22
Troy Edwards, La. Tech	Nebraska	1998	21
Rick Eber, Tulsa	Idaho St.	1967	20
Howard Twilley, Tulsa	Colo. St.	1965	19
Ron Fair, Arizona St	Wash. St.	1989	19
Manny Hazard, Houston	TCU	1989	19
Manny Hazard, Houston	Texas	1989	19

Yards Gained	Opponent	Year	Yds
Troy Edwards, La. Tech	Nebraska	1998	405
Randy Gatewood, UNLV	Idaho	1994	363
Chuck Hughes, UTEP*	N. Texas St.	1965	349
Rick Eber, Tulsa	Idaho St.	1967	322
Harry Wood, Tulsa	Idaho St.	1967	318
*UTEP was Texas Western in 1965.			

Scoring

Points	Opponent	Year	Pts
Howard Griffith, Illinois	So. Ill.	1990	48
Marshall Faulk, S. Diego St.	Pacific	1991	44
Jim Brown, Syracuse	Colgate	1956	43
Showboat Boykin, Ole Miss	Miss. St.	1951	42
Fred Wendt, UTEP*	N. Mex. St.	1948	42
*UTEP was Texas Mines in 1948.			

Touchdowns Rushing	Opponent	Year	No
Howard Griffith, Illinois	So. Ill	1990	8
Showboat Boykin, Ole Miss	Miss. St.	1951	7
Note: Griffith's TD runs (5-51-7-41-5-18-5-3).			

Touchdowns Passing	Opponent	Year	No
David Klingler, Houston	E. Wash.	1990	11
Dennis Shaw, San Diego St	N. Mex. St.	1969	9
Note: Klingler's TD passes (5-48-29-7-3-7-40-8-7-8-51).			

Touchdown Catches	Opponent	Year	No
Tim Delaney, S. Diego St	N. Mex. St.	1969	6
Note: Delaney's TD catches (2-22-34-31-30-9).			

Field Goals	Opponent	Year	No
Dale Klein, Nebraska	Missouri	1985	7
Mike Prindle, W. Mich	Marshall	1984	7
Note: Klein's FGs (32-22-43-44-29-43-43); Prindle's FGs (32-44-42-23-48-41-27).			

Extra Points (Kick)	Opponent	Year	No
Terry Leiweke, Houston	Tulsa	1968	13
Derek Mahoney, Fresno St	New Mexico	1991	13

Longest Plays (since 1941)

Rushing	Opponent	Year	Yds
Gale Sayers, Kansas	Nebraska	1963	99
Max Anderson, Ariz. St	Wyoming	1967	99
Ralph Thompson, W. Texas St	Wich. St.	1970	99
Kelsey Finch, Tennessee	Florida	1977	99
Eric Vann, Kansas	Oklahoma	1997	99
Eleven tied at 98 each.			

Passing	Opponent	Year	Yds
Fred Owens to Jack Ford, Portland	St. Mary's	1947	99
Bo Burris to Warren McVea, Houston	Wash. St.	1966	99
Colin Clapton to Eddie Jenkins, Holy Cross	Boston U.	1970	99
Terry Peel to Robert Ford, Houston	Syracuse	1970	99
Terry Peel to Robert Ford, Houston	S. Diego St.	1972	99

Passing	Opponent	Year	Yds
Cris Collinsworth to Derrick Gaffney, Florida	Rice	1977	99
Scott Ankrom to James Maness, TCU	Rice	1984	99
Gino Torretta to Horace Copeland, Miami-FL.	Ark.	1991	99
John Paci to Thomas Lewis, Indiana	Penn St.	1993	99

Field Goals	Opponent	Year	Yds
Steve Little, Arkansas	Texas	1977	67
Russell Erxleben, Texas	Rice	1977	67
Joe Williams, Wichita St	So. Ill.	1978	67
Tony Franklin, Tex. A&M	Baylor	1976	65
Martin Gramatica, Kan. St.	No. Ill.	1998	65

Annual Awards

Heisman Trophy

Originally presented in 1935 as the DAC Trophy by the Downtown Athletic Club of New York City to the best college football player east of the Mississippi. In 1936, players across the country were eligible and the award was renamed the Heisman Trophy following the death of former college coach and DAC athletic director John W. Heisman.

Multiple winner: Archie Griffin (2).

Winners in junior year (13): Doc Blanchard (1945), Ty Detmer (1990); Archie Griffin (1974), Desmond Howard (1991), Vic Janowicz (1950), Rashaan Salaam (1994), Barry Sanders (1988), Billy Sims (1978), Roger Staubach (1963), Doak Walker (1948), Herschel Walker (1982), Andre Ware (1989) and Charles Woodson (1997).

Winners on AP national champions (10): Angelo Bertelli (Notre Dame, 1943); Doc Blanchard (Army, 1945); Tony Dorsett (Pittsburgh, 1976); Leon Hart (Notre Dame, 1949); Johnny Lujack (Notre Dame, 1947); Davey O'Brien (TCU, 1938); Bruce Smith (Minnesota, 1941); Charlie Ward (Florida St., 1993); Danny Wuerffel (Florida, 1996); and Charles Woodson (Michigan, 1997).

Year		Points
1935	**Jay Berwanger,** Chicago, HB	84
	2nd–Monk Meyer, Army, HB	29
	3rd–Bill Shakespeare, Notre Dame, HB	23
	4th–Pepper Constable, Princeton, FB	20
1936	**Larry Kelley,** Yale, E	219
	2nd–Sam Francis, Nebraska, FB	47
	3rd–Ray Buivid, Marquette, HB	43
	4th–Sammy Baugh, TCU, HB	39
1937	**Clint Frank,** Yale, HB	524
	2nd–Byron (Whizzer) White, Colo., HB	264
	3rd–Marshall Goldberg, Pitt, HB	211
	4th–Alex Wojciechowicz, Fordham, C	85
1938	**Davey O'Brien,** TCU, QB	519
	2nd–Marshall Goldberg, Pitt, HB	294
	3rd–Sid Luckman, Columbia, QB	154
	4th–Bob MacLeod, Dartmouth, HB	78
1939	**Nile Kinnick,** Iowa, HB	651
	2nd–Tom Harmon, Michigan, HB	405
	3rd–Paul Christman, Missouri, QB	391
	4th–George Cafego, Tennessee, QB	296
1940	**Tom Harmon,** Michigan, HB	1303
	2nd–John Kimbrough, Texas A&M, FB	841
	3rd–George Franck, Minnesota, HB	102
	4th–Frankie Albert, Stanford, QB	90
1941	**Bruce Smith,** Minnesota, HB	554
	2nd–Angelo Bertelli, Notre Dame, QB	345
	3rd–Frankie Albert, Stanford, QB	336
	4th–Frank Sinkwich, Georgia, HB	249
1942	**Frank Sinkwich,** Georgia, TB	1059
	2nd–Paul Governali, Columbia, QB	218
	3rd–Clint Castleberry, Ga. Tech, HB	99
	4th–Mike Holovak, Boston College, FB	95
1943	**Angelo Bertelli,** Notre Dame, QB	648
	2nd–Bob Odell, Penn, HB	177
	3rd–Otto Graham, Northwestern, QB	140
	4th–Creighton Miller, Notre Dame, HB	134
1944	**Les Horvath,** Ohio St., TB-QB	412
	2nd–Glenn Davis, Army, HB	287
	3rd–Doc Blanchard, Army, FB	237
	4th–Don Whitmire, Navy, T	115
1945	**Doc Blanchard,** Army, FB	860
	2nd–Glenn Davis, Army, HB	638
	3rd–Bob Fenimore, Oklahoma A&M, HB	187
	4th–Herman Wedemeyer, St. Mary's, HB	152
1946	**Glenn Davis,** Army, HB	792
	2nd–Charlie Trippi, Georgia, HB	435
	3rd–Johnny Lujack, Notre Dame, QB	379
	4th–Doc Blanchard, Army, FB	267

Year		Points
1947	**Johnny Lujack,** Notre Dame, QB	742
	2nd–Bob Chappuis, Michigan, HB	555
	3rd–Doak Walker, SMU, HB	196
	4th–Charlie Conerly, Mississippi, QB	186
1948	**Doak Walker,** SMU, HB	778
	2nd–Charlie Justice, N. Carolina, HB	443
	3rd–Chuck Bednarik, Penn, C	336
	4th–Jackie Jensen, California, HB	143
1949	**Leon Hart,** Notre Dame, E	995
	2nd–Charlie Justice, N. Carolina, HB	272
	3rd–Doak Walker, SMU, HB	229
	4th–Arnold Galiffa, Army QB	196
1950	**Vic Janowicz,** Ohio St., HB	633
	2nd–Kyle Rote, SMU, HB	280
	3rd–Reds Bagnell, Penn, HB	231
	4th–Babe Parilli, Kentucky, QB	214
1951	**Dick Kazmaier,** Princeton, TB	1777
	2nd–Hank Lauricella, Tennessee, HB	424
	3rd–Babe Parilli, Kentucky, QB	344
	4th–Bill McColl, Stanford, E	313
1952	**Billy Vessels,** Oklahoma, HB	525
	2nd–Jack Scarbath, Maryland, QB	367
	3rd–Paul Giel, Minnesota, HB	329
	4th–Donn Moomaw, UCLA, C	257
1953	**Johnny Lattner,** Notre Dame, HB	1850
	2nd–Paul Giel, Minnesota, HB	1794
	3rd–Paul Cameron, UCLA, HB	444
	4th–Bernie Faloney, Maryland, QB	258
1954	**Alan Ameche,** Wisconsin, FB	1068
	2nd–Kurt Burris, Oklahoma, C	838
	3rd–Howard Cassady, Ohio St., HB	810
	4th–Ralph Guglielmi, Notre Dame, QB	691
1955	**Howard Cassady,** Ohio St., HB	2219
	2nd–Jim Swink, TCU, HB	742
	3rd–George Welsh, Navy, QB	383
	4th–Earl Morrall, Michigan St., QB	323
1956	**Paul Hornung,** Notre Dame, QB	1066
	2nd–Johnny Majors, Tennessee, HB	994
	3rd–Tommy McDonald, Oklahoma, HB	973
	4th–Jerry Tubbs, Oklahoma, C	724
1957	**John David Crow,** Texas A&M, HB	1183
	2nd–Alex Karras, Iowa, T	693
	3rd–Walt Kowalczyk, Mich. St., HB	630
	4th–Lou Michaels, Kentucky, T	330
1958	**Pete Dawkins,** Army, HB	1394
	2nd–Randy Duncan, Iowa, QB	1021
	3rd–Billy Cannon, LSU, HB	975
	4th–Bob White, Ohio St., FB	365

Annual Awards (Cont.)

Year	Points	Year	Points
1959 **Billy Cannon,** LSU, HB.....1929		1976 **Tony Dorsett,** Pittsburgh, RB.....2357	
2nd–Richie Lucas, Penn St., QB.....613		2nd–Ricky Bell, USC, RB.....1346	
3rd–Don Meredith, SMU, QB.....286		3rd–Rob Lytle, Michigan, RB.....413	
4th–Bill Burrell, Illinois, G.....196		4th–Terry Miller, Oklahoma St., RB.....197	
1960 **Joe Bellino,** Navy, HB.....1793		1977 **Earl Campbell,** Texas, RB.....1547	
2nd–Tom Brown, Minnesota, G.....731		2nd–Terry Miller, Oklahoma St., RB.....812	
3rd–Jake Gibbs, Mississippi, QB.....453		3rd–Ken MacAfee, Notre Dame, TE.....343	
4th–Ed Dyas, Auburn, HB.....319		4th–Doug Williams, Grambling, QB.....266	
1961 **Ernie Davis,** Syracuse, HB.....824		1978 **Billy Sims,** Oklahoma, RB.....827	
2nd–Bob Ferguson, Ohio St., HB.....771		2nd–Chuck Fusina, Penn St., QB.....750	
3rd–Jimmy Saxton, Texas, HB.....551		3rd–Rick Leach, Michigan, QB.....435	
4th–Sandy Stephens, Minnesota, QB.....543		4th–Charles White, USC, RB.....354	
1962 **Terry Baker,** Oregon St., QB.....707		1979 **Charles White,** USC, RB.....1695	
2nd–Jerry Stovall, LSU, HB.....618		2nd–Billy Sims, Oklahoma, RB.....773	
3rd–Bobby Bell, Minnesota, T.....429		3rd–Marc Wilson, BYU, QB.....589	
4th–Lee Roy Jordan, Alabama, C.....321		4th–Art Schlichter, Ohio St., QB.....251	
1963 **Roger Staubach,** Navy, QB.....1860		1980 **George Rogers,** South Carolina, RB.....1128	
2nd–Billy Lothridge, Ga. Tech, QB.....504		2nd–Hugh Green, Pittsburgh, DE.....861	
3rd–Sherman Lewis, Mich. St., HB.....369		3rd–Herschel Walker, Georgia, RB.....683	
4th–Don Trull, Baylor, QB.....253		4th–Mark Herrmann, Purdue, QB.....405	
1964 **John Huarte,** Notre Dame, QB.....1026		1981 **Marcus Allen,** USC, RB.....1797	
2nd–Jerry Rhome, Tulsa, QB.....952		2nd–Herschel Walker, Georgia, RB.....1199	
3rd–Dick Butkus, Illinois, C.....505		3rd–Jim McMahon, BYU, QB.....706	
4th–Bob Timberlake, Michigan, QB.....361		4th–Dan Marino, Pitt, QB.....256	
1965 **Mike Garrett,** USC, HB.....926		1982 **Herschel Walker,** Georgia, RB.....1926	
2nd–Howard Twilley, Tulsa, E.....528		2nd–John Elway, Stanford, QB.....1231	
3rd–Jim Grabowski, Illinois, FB.....481		3rd–Eric Dickerson, SMU, RB.....465	
4th–Donny Anderson, Texas Tech, HB.....408		4th–Anthony Carter, Michigan, WR.....142	
1966 **Steve Spurrier,** Florida, QB.....1679		1983 **Mike Rozier,** Nebraska, RB.....1801	
2nd–Bob Griese, Purdue, QB.....816		2nd–Steve Young, BYU, QB.....1172	
3rd–Nick Eddy, Notre Dame, HB.....456		3rd–Doug Flutie, Boston College, QB.....253	
4th–Gary Beban, UCLA, QB.....318		4th–Turner Gill, Nebraska, QB.....190	
1967 **Gary Beban,** UCLA, QB.....1968		1984 **Doug Flutie,** Boston College, QB.....2240	
2nd–O.J. Simpson, USC, HB.....1722		2nd–Keith Byars, Ohio St., RB.....1251	
3rd–Leroy Keyes, Purdue, HB.....1366		3rd–Robbie Bosco, BYU, QB.....443	
4th–Larry Csonka, Syracuse, FB.....136		4th–Bernie Kosar, Miami-FL, QB.....320	
1968 **O.J. Simpson,** USC, HB.....2853		1985 **Bo Jackson,** Auburn, RB.....1509	
2nd–Leroy Keyes, Purdue, HB.....1103		2nd–Chuck Long, Iowa, QB.....1464	
3rd–Terry Hanratty, Notre Dame, QB.....387		3rd–Robbie Bosco, BYU, QB.....459	
4th–Ted Kwalick, Penn St., TE.....254		4th–Lorenzo White, Michigan St., RB.....391	
1969 **Steve Owens,** Oklahoma, HB.....1488		1986 **Vinny Testaverde,** Miami-FL, QB.....2213	
2nd–Mike Phipps, Purdue, QB.....1344		2nd–Paul Palmer, Temple, RB.....672	
3rd–Rex Kern, Ohio St., QB.....856		3rd–Jim Harbaugh, Michigan, QB.....458	
4th–Archie Manning, Mississippi, QB.....582		4th–Brian Bosworth, Oklahoma, LB.....395	
1970 **Jim Plunkett,** Stanford, QB.....2229		1987 **Tim Brown,** Notre Dame, WR.....1442	
2nd–Joe Theismann, Notre Dame, QB.....1410		2nd–Don McPherson, Syracuse, QB.....831	
3rd–Archie Manning, Mississippi, QB.....849		3rd–Gordie Lockbaum, Holy Cross, WR-DB.....657	
4th–Steve Worster, Texas, RB.....398		4th–Lorenzo White, Michigan St., RB.....632	
1971 **Pat Sullivan,** Auburn, QB.....1597		1988 **Barry Sanders,** Oklahoma St., RB.....1878	
2nd–Ed Marinaro, Cornell, RB.....1445		2nd–Rodney Peete, USC, QB.....912	
3rd–Greg Pruitt, Oklahoma, RB.....586		3rd–Troy Aikman, UCLA, QB.....582	
4th–Johnny Musso, Alabama, RB.....365		4th–Steve Walsh, Miami-FL, QB.....341	
1972 **Johnny Rodgers,** Nebraska, FL.....1310		1989 **Andre Ware,** Houston, QB.....1073	
2nd–Greg Pruitt, Oklahoma, RB.....966		2nd–Anthony Thompson, Ind., RB.....1003	
3rd–Rich Glover, Nebraska, MG.....652		3rd–Major Harris, West Va., QB.....709	
4th–Bert Jones, LSU, QB.....351		4th–Tony Rice, Notre Dame, QB.....523	
1973 **John Cappelletti,** Penn St., RB.....1057		1990 **Ty Detmer,** BYU, QB.....1482	
2nd–John Hicks, Ohio St., OT.....524		2nd–Rocket Ismail, Notre Dame, FL.....1177	
3rd–Roosevelt Leaks, Texas, RB.....482		3rd–Eric Bieniemy, Colorado, RB.....798	
4th–David Jaynes, Kansas, QB.....394		4th–Shawn Moore, Virginia, QB.....465	
1974 **Archie Griffin,** Ohio St., RB.....1920		1991 **Desmond Howard,** Michigan, WR.....2077	
2nd–Anthony Davis, USC, RB.....819		2nd–Casey Weldon, Florida St., QB.....503	
3rd–Joe Washington, Oklahoma, RB.....661		3rd–Ty Detmer, BYU, QB.....445	
4th–Tom Clements, Notre Dame, QB.....244		4th–Steve Emtman, Washington, DT.....357	
1975 **Archie Griffin,** Ohio St., RB.....1800		1992 **Gino Torretta,** Miami-FL, QB.....1400	
2nd–Chuck Muncie, California, RB.....730		2nd–Marshall Faulk, San Diego St., RB.....1080	
3rd–Ricky Bell, USC, RB.....708		3rd–Garrison Hearst, Georgia, RB.....982	
4th–Tony Dorsett, Pitt, RB.....616		4th–Marvin Jones, Florida St., LB.....392	

Year	Points
1993 **Charlie Ward,** Florida St., QB	.2310
2nd–Heath Shuler, Tennessee, QB	.688
3rd–David Palmer, Alabama, RB	.292
4th–Marshall Faulk, S. Diego St., RB	.250
1994 **Rashaan Salaam,** Colorado, RB	.1743
2nd–Ki-Jana Carter, Penn St., RB	.901
3rd–Steve McNair, Alcorn St., QB	.655
4th–Kerry Collins, Penn St., QB	.639
1995 **Eddie George,** Ohio St., RB	.1460
2nd–Tommie Frazier, Nebraska, QB	.1196
3rd–Danny Wuerffel, Florida, QB	.987
4th–Darnell Autry, Northwestern, RB	.535

Year	Points
1996 **Danny Wuerffel,** Florida, QB	.1363
2nd–Troy Davis, Iowa St., RB	.1174
3rd–Jake Plummer, Arizona St., QB	.685
4th–Orlando Pace, Ohio St., OT	.599
1997 **Charles Woodson,** Michigan, DB-WR	.1815
2nd–Peyton Manning, Tennessee, QB	.1543
3rd–Ryan Leaf, Washington St., QB	.861
4th–Randy Moss, Marshall, WR	.253
1998 **Ricky Williams,** Texas, RB	.2355
2nd–Michael Bishop, Kansas St., QB	.792
3rd–Cade McNown, UCLA, QB	.696
4th–Tim Couch, Kentucky, QB	.527

Maxwell Award

First presented in 1937 by the Maxwell Memorial Football Club of Philadelphia, the award is named after Robert (Tiny) Maxwell, a Philadelphia native who was a standout lineman at the University of Chicago at the turn of the century. Like the Heisman, the Maxwell is given to the outstanding college player in the nation. Both awards have gone to the same player in the same season 33 times. Those players are preceded by (#). Glenn Davis of Army and Doak Walker of SMU won both but in different years.

Multiple winner: Johnny Lattner (2).

Year	Year	Year
1937 #Clint Frank, Yale, HB	1958 #Pete Dawkins, Army, HB	1979 #Charles White, USC, RB
1938 #Davey O'Brien, TCU, QB	1959 Rich Lucas, Penn St., QB	
1939 #Nile Kinnick, Iowa, HB		1980 Hugh Green, Pitt, DE
1940 #Tom Harmon, Michigan, HB	1960 #Joe Bellino, Navy, HB	1981 #Marcus Allen, USC, RB
1941 Bill Dudley, Virginia, HB	1961 Bob Ferguson, Ohio St., HB	1982 #Herschel Walker, Georgia, RB
1942 Paul Governali, Columbia, QB	1962 #Terry Baker, Oregon St., QB	1983 #Mike Rozier, Nebraska, RB
1943 Bob Odell, Penn, HB	1963 #Roger Staubach, Navy, QB	1984 #Doug Flutie, Boston Col., QB
1944 Glenn Davis, Army, HB	1964 Glenn Ressler, Penn St., G	1985 Chuck Long, Iowa, QB
1945 #Doc Blanchard, Army, FB	1965 Tommy Nobis, Texas, LB	1986 #V. Testaverde, Miami-FL, QB
1946 Charley Trippi, Georgia, HB	1966 Jim Lynch, Notre Dame, LB	1987 Don McPherson, Syracuse, QB
1947 Doak Walker, SMU, HB	1967 #Gary Beban, UCLA, QB	1988 #Barry Sanders, Okla. St., RB
1948 Chuck Bednarik, Penn, C	1968 #O.J. Simpson, USC, RB	1989 Anthony Thompson, Indiana, RB
1949 #Leon Hart, Notre Dame, E	1969 Mike Reid, Penn St., DT	
		1990 #Ty Detmer, BYU, QB
1950 Reds Bagnell, Penn, HB	1970 #Jim Plunkett, Stanford, QB	1991 #Desmond Howard, Mich., WR
1951 #Dick Kazmaier, Princeton, TB	1971 Ed Marinaro, Cornell, RB	1992 #Gino Torretta, Miami-FL, QB
1952 Johnny Lattner, Notre Dame, HB	1972 Brad Van Pelt, Michigan St., DB	1993 #Charlie Ward, Florida St., QB
1953 #Johnny Lattner, N. Dame, HB	1973 #John Cappelletti, Penn St., RB	1994 Kerry Collins, Penn St., QB
1954 Ron Beagle, Navy, E	1974 Steve Joachim, Temple, QB	1995 #Eddie George, Ohio St., RB
1955 #Howard Cassady, Ohio St., HB	1975 #Archie Griffin, Ohio St., RB	1996 Danny Wuerffel, Florida, QB
1956 Tommy McDonald, Okla., HB	1976 #Tony Dorsett, Pitt, RB	1997 Peyton Manning, Tennessee, QB
1957 Bob Reifsnyder, Navy, T	1977 Ross Browner, Notre Dame, DE	1998 #Ricky Williams, Texas, RB
	1978 Chuck Fusina, Penn St., QB	

Outland Trophy

First presented in 1946 by the Football Writers Association of America, honoring the nation's outstanding interior lineman. The award is named after its benefactor, Dr. John H. Outland (Kansas, Class of 1898). Players listed in **bold** type helped lead their team to a national championship (according to AP).

Multiple winner: Dave Rimington (2). **Winners in junior year:** Ross Browner (1976), Steve Emtman (1991), Orlando Pace (1996) and Rimington (1981).

Year	Year	Year
1946 **George Connor**, N. Dame, T	1964 Steve DeLong, Tennessee, T	1982 Dave Rimington, Nebraska, C
1947 Joe Steffy, Army, G	1965 Tommy Nobis, Texas, G	1983 Dean Steinkuhler, Nebraska, G
1948 Bill Fischer, Notre Dame, G	1966 Loyd Phillips, Arkansas, T	1984 Bruce Smith, Virginia Tech, DT
1949 Ed Bagdon, Michigan St., G	1967 **Ron Yary**, USC, T	1985 Mike Ruth, Boston College, NG
	1968 Bill Stanfill, Georgia, T	1986 Jason Buck, BYU, DT
1950 Bob Gain, Kentucky, T	1969 Mike Reid, Penn St., DT	1987 Chad Hennings, Air Force, DT
1951 Jim Weatherall, Oklahoma, T		1988 Tracy Rocker, Auburn, DT
1952 Dick Modzelewski, Maryland, T	1970 Jim Stillwagon, Ohio St., MG	1989 Mohammed Elewonibi, BYU, G
1953 J.D. Roberts, Oklahoma, G	1971 **Larry Jacobson**, Neb., DT	
1954 Bill Brooks, Arkansas, G	1972 Rich Glover, Nebraska, MG	1990 Russell Maryland, Miami-FL, NT
1955 Calvin Jones, Iowa, G	1973 John Hicks, Ohio St., OT	1991 Steve Emtman, Washington, DT
1956 Jim Parker, Ohio St., G	1974 Randy White, Maryland, DT	1992 Will Shields, Nebraska, G
1957 Alex Karras, Iowa, T	1975 **Lee Roy Selmon**, Okla., DT	1993 Rob Waldrop, Arizona, NG
1958 Zeke Smith, Auburn, G	1976 Ross Browner, Notre Dame, DE	1994 **Zach Wiegert**, Nebraska, OT
1959 Mike McGee, Duke, T	1977 Brad Shearer, Texas, DT	1995 Jonathan Ogden, UCLA, OT
	1978 Greg Roberts, Oklahoma, G	1996 Orlando Pace, Ohio St., OT
1960 **Tom Brown**, Minnesota, G	1979 Jim Richter, N.C. State, C	1997 Aaron Taylor, Nebraska, G
1961 Merlin Olsen, Utah St., T		1998 Kris Farris, UCLA, OT
1962 Bobby Bell, Minnesota, T	1980 Mark May, Pittsburgh, OT	
1963 **Scott Appleton**, Texas, T	1981 Dave Rimington, Nebraska, C	

Annual Awards (Cont.)
Butkus Award

First presented in 1985 by the Downtown Athletic Club of Orlando, Fla., to honor the nation's outstanding linebacker. The award is named after Dick Butkus, two-time consensus All-America at Illinois and six-time All-Pro with the Chicago Bears.

Multiple winner: Brian Bosworth (2).

Year	Year	Year
1985 Brian Bosworth, Oklahoma	1990 Alfred Williams, Colorado	1995 Kevin Hardy, Illinois
1986 Brian Bosworth, Oklahoma	1991 Erick Anderson, Michigan	1996 Matt Russell, Colorado
1987 Paul McGowan, Florida St.	1992 Marvin Jones, Florida St.	1997 Andy Katzenmoyer, Ohio St.
1988 Derrick Thomas, Alabama	1993 Trev Alberts, Nebraska	1998 Chris Claiborne, USC
1989 Percy Snow, Michigan St.	1994 Dana Howard, Illinois	

Lombardi Award

First presented in 1970 by the Rotary Club of Houston, honoring the nation's best lineman. The award is named after pro football coach Vince Lombardi, who, as a guard, was a member of the famous "Seven Blocks of Granite" at Fordham in the 1930s. The Lombardi and Outland awards have gone to the same player in the same year ten times. Those players are preceded by (#). Ross Browner of Notre Dame won both, but in different years.

Multiple winner: Orlando Pace (2).

Year	Year	Year
1970 #Jim Stillwagon, Ohio St., MG	1980 Hugh Green, Pitt, DE	1990 Chris Zorich, Notre Dame, NT
1971 Walt Patulski, Notre Dame, DE	1981 Kenneth Sims, Texas, DT	1991 #Steve Emtman, Wash., DT
1972 #Rich Glover, Nebraska, MG	1982 #Dave Rimington, Neb., C	1992 Marvin Jones, Florida St., LB
1973 #John Hicks, Ohio St., OT	1983 #Dean Steinkuhler, Neb., G	1993 Aaron Taylor, Notre Dame, OT
1974 #Randy White, Maryland, DT	1984 Tony Degrate, Texas, DT	1994 Warren Sapp, Miami-FL, DT
1975 #Lee Roy Selmon, Okla., DT	1985 Tony Casillas, Oklahoma, NG	1995 Orlando Pace, Ohio St., OT
1976 Wilson Whitley, Houston, DT	1986 Cornelius Bennett, Alabama, LB	1996 #Orlando Pace, Ohio St., OT
1977 Ross Browner, Notre Dame, DE	1987 Chris Spielman, Ohio St., LB	1997 Grant Wistrom, Nebraska, DE
1978 Bruce Clark, Penn St., DT	1988 #Tracy Rocker, Auburn, DT	1998 Dat Nguyen, Tex. A&M, LB
1979 Brad Budde, USC, G	1989 Percy Snow, Michigan St., LB	

O'Brien Quarterback Award

First presented in 1977 as the O'Brien Memorial Trophy, the award went to the outstanding player in the Southwest. In 1981, however, the Davey O'Brien Educational and Charitable Trust of Ft. Worth renamed the prize the O'Brien National Quarterback Award and now honors the nation's best quarterback. The award is named after 1938 Heisman Trophy-winning QB Davey O'Brien of Texas Christian.

Multiple winners: Ty Detmer, Mike Singletary and Danny Wuerffel (2).

Memorial Trophy

Year	Year	Year
1977 Earl Campbell, Texas, RB	1979 Mike Singletary, Baylor, LB	1980 Mike Singletary, Baylor, LB
1978 Billy Sims, Oklahoma, RB		

National QB Award

Year	Year	Year
1981 Jim McMahon, BYU	1987 Don McPherson, Syracuse	1993 Charlie Ward, Florida St.
1982 Todd Blackledge, Penn St.	1988 Troy Aikman, UCLA	1994 Kerry Collins, Penn St.
1983 Steve Young, BYU	1989 Andre Ware, Houston	1995 Danny Wuerffel, Florida
1984 Doug Flutie, Boston College	1990 Ty Detmer, BYU	1996 Danny Wuerffel, Florida
1985 Chuck Long, Iowa	1991 Ty Detmer, BYU	1997 Peyton Manning, Tennessee
1986 Vinny Testaverde, Miami, FL	1992 Gino Torretta, Miami-FL	1998 Michael Bishop, Kansas St.

Thorpe Award

First presented in 1986 by the Jim Thorpe Athletic Club of Oklahoma City to honor the nation's outstanding defensive back. The award is named after Jim Thorpe–Olympic champion and two-time consensus All-America halfback at Carlisle.

Year	Year	Year
1986 Thomas Everett, Baylor	1990 Darryl Lewis, Arizona	1995 Greg Myers, Colorado St.
1987 Bennie Blades, Miami-FL	1991 Terrell Buckley, Florida St.	1996 Lawrence Wright, Florida
& Rickey Dixon, Oklahoma	1992 Deon Figures, Colorado	1997 Charles Woodson, Michigan
1988 Deion Sanders, Florida St.	1993 Antonio Langham, Alabama	1998 Antoine Winfield, Ohio St.
1989 Mike Carrier, USC	1994 Chris Hudson, Colorado	

Payton Award

First presented in 1987 by the Sports Network and Division I-AA sports information directors to honor the nation's outstanding Division I-AA player. The award is named after Walter Payton, the NFL's all-time leading rusher who was an All-America running back at Jackson St.

Year	Year	Year
1987 Kenny Gamble, Colgate, RB	1991 Jamie Martin, Weber St., QB	1995 Dave Dickenson, Montana, QB
1988 Dave Meggett, Towson St., RB	1992 Michael Payton, Marshall, QB	1996 Archie Amerson, N. Arizona, RB
1989 John Friesz, Idaho, QB	1993 Doug Nussmeier, Idaho, QB	1997 Brian Finneran, Villanova, WR
1990 Walter Dean, Grambling, RB	1994 Steve McNair, Alcorn St., QB	1998 Jerry Azumah, N. Hampshire, RB

Hill Trophy

First presented in 1986 by the Harlon Hill Awards Committee in Florence, AL, to honor the nation's outstanding Division II player. The award is named after three-time NFL All-Pro Harlon Hill, who played college ball at North Alabama.

Multiple winner: Johnny Bailey (3).

Year	Year	Year
1986 Jeff Bentrim, N. Dakota St., QB	1991 Ronnie West, Pittsburg St., WR	1996 Jarrett Anderson, Truman St., RB
1987 Johnny Bailey, Texas A&I, RB	1992 Ronald Moore, Pittsburg St., RB	1997 Irv Sigler, Bloomsburg, RB
1988 Johnny Bailey, Texas A&I, RB	1993 Roger Graham, New Haven, RB	1998 Brian Shay, Emporia St., RB
1989 Johnny Bailey, Texas A&I, RB	1994 Chris Hatcher, Valdosta St., QB	
1990 Chris Simdorn, N. Dakota St., QB	1995 Ronald McKinnon, N. Alabama, LB	

All-Time Winningest Division I-A Coaches

Minimum of 10 years in Division I-A through 1998 season. Regular season and bowl games included. Coaches active in 1998 in **bold** type.

Top 25 Winning Percentage

		Yrs	W	L	T	Pct
1	Knute Rockne	13	105	12	5	.881
2	Frank Leahy	13	107	13	9	.864
3	George Woodruff	12	142	25	2	.846
4	Barry Switzer	16	157	29	4	.837
5	Tom Osborne	25	255	49	3	.836
6	Percy Haughton	13	96	17	6	.832
7	Bob Neyland	21	173	31	12	.829
8	Hurry Up Yost	29	196	36	12	.828
9	Bud Wilkinson	17	145	29	4	.826
10	Jock Sutherland	20	144	28	14	.812
11	Bob Devaney	16	136	30	7	.806
12	Frank Thomas	19	141	33	9	.795
13	**Joe Paterno**	33	307	80	3	.791
14	Henry Williams	23	141	34	12	.786
15	Gil Dobie	33	180	45	15	.781
16	**Steve Spurrier**	12	113	31	2	.781
17	Bear Bryant	38	323	85	17	.780
18	Fred Folsom	19	106	28	6	.779
19	Bo Schembechler	27	234	65	8	.775
20	**Bobby Bowden**	33	292	85	4	.772
21	Fritz Crisler	18	116	32	9	.768
22	Charley Moran	18	122	33	12	.766
23	**R.C. Slocum**	10	94	28	2	.766
24	Wallace Wade	24	171	49	10	.765
25	Frank Kush	22	176	54	1	.764

Top 25 Victories

		Yrs	W	L	T	Pct
1	Bear Bryant	38	323	85	17	.780
2	Pop Warner	44	319	106	32	.733
3	Amos Alonzo Stagg	57	314	199	35	.605
4	**Joe Paterno**	33	307	80	3	.791
5	**Bobby Bowden**	33	292	85	4	.772
6	Tom Osborne	25	255	49	3	.836
7	**LaVell Edwards**	27	243	91	3	.726
8	Woody Hayes	33	238	72	10	.759
9	Bo Schembechler	27	234	65	8	.775
10	**Hayden Fry**	37	232	178	10	.564
11	Lou Holtz	27	216	95	7	.690
12	Jess Neely	40	207	176	19	.539
13	Warren Woodson	31	203	95	14	.673
14	Vince Dooley	25	201	77	10	.715
	Eddie Anderson	39	201	128	15	.606
16	Jim Sweeney	32	200	154	4	.564
17	Dana X. Bible	33	198	72	23	.715
18	Dan McGugin	30	197	55	19	.762
19	Hurry Up Yost	29	196	36	12	.828
20	Howard Jones	29	194	64	21	.733
21	**Don Nehlen**	28	191	116	8	.619
22	Johnny Vaught	25	190	61	12	.745
23	John Heisman	36	185	70	17	.711
	Johnny Majors	29	185	137	10	.572
25	Darrell Royal	23	184	60	5	.749

Note: Eddie Robinson of Division I-AA Grambling St. (1941-42, 1945-97) is the all-time NCAA leader in coaching wins with a 408-165-15 record and .708 winning pct. over 55 seasons.

Where They Coached

Anderson–Loras (1922-24), DePaul (1925-31), Holy Cross (1933-38), Iowa (1939-42), Holy Cross (1950-64); **Bible**–Mississippi College (1913-15), LSU (1916), Texas A&M (1917,1919,28), Nebraska (1929-36), Texas (1937-46); **Bowden**–Samford (1959-62), West Virginia (1970-75), Florida St. (1976–); **Bryant**–Maryland (1945), Kentucky (1946-53), Texas A&M (1954-57), Alabama (1958-82); **Crisler**–Minnesota (1930-31), Princeton (1932-37), Michigan (1938-47); **Devaney**–Wyoming (1957-61), Nebraska (1962-72); **V. Dooley**–Georgia (1964-88); **Edwards**–BYU (1972–); **Folsom**–Colorado (1895-99, 1901-02), Dartmouth (1903-06), Colorado (1908-15).

Fry–SMU (1962-72), North Texas (1973-78), Iowa (1979-98); **Haughton**–Cornell (1899-1900), Harvard (1908-16), Columbia (1923-24); **Hayes**–Denison (1946-48), Miami-OH (1949-50), Ohio St. (1951-78); **Heisman**–Oberlin (1892), Akron (1893), Oberlin (1894), Auburn (1895-99), Clemson (1900-03), Georgia Tech (1904-19), Penn (1920-22), Washington & Jefferson (1923), Rice (1924-27); **Holtz**–William & Mary (1969-71), N.C. State (1972-75), Arkansas (1977-83), Minnesota (1984-85), Notre Dame (1986-96), South Carolina (1999–); **Jones**–Syracuse (1908), Yale (1909), Ohio St. (1910), Yale (1913), Iowa (1916-23), Duke (1924), USC (1925-40); **Kush**–Arizona St. (1958-79); **Leahy**–Boston College (1939-40), Notre Dame (1941-43, 1946-53); **Majors**–Iowa St. (1968-72), Pittsburgh (1973-76, 93-96), Tennessee (1977-92); **Moran**–Texas A&M (1909-14), Centre (1919-23), Bucknell (1924-26), Catawba (1930-33).

Neely–Rhodes (1924-27), Clemson (1931-39), Rice (1940-66); **Nehlen**–Bowling Green (1968-76), West Virginia (1980–); **Neyland**–Tennessee (1926-34, 1936-40, 1946-52); **Osborne**–Nebraska (1973-97); **Paterno**–Penn St. (1966–); **Rockne**–Notre Dame (1918-30); **Royal**–Mississippi St. (1954-55), Washington (1956), Texas (1957-76); **Schembechler**–Miami-OH (1963-68), Michigan (1969-89); **Slocum**–Texas A&M (1989–); **Spurrier**–Duke (1987-89), Florida (1990–); **Stagg**–Springfield College (1890-91), Chicago (1892-1932), Pacific (1933-46); **Sutherland**–Lafayette (1919-23), Pittsburgh (1924-38); **Sweeney**–Montana St. (1963-67), Washington St. (1968-75), Fresno St. (1976-96); **Switzer**–Oklahoma (1973-88).

Thomas–Chattanooga (1925-28), Alabama (1931-42, 1944-46); **Vaught**–Mississippi (1947-70); **Wade**–Alabama (1923-30), Duke (1931-41, 1946-50); **Warner**–Georgia (1895-96), Cornell (1897-98), Carlisle (1899-1903), Cornell (1904-06), Carlisle (1907-13), Pittsburgh (1915-23), Stanford (1924-32), Temple (1933-38); **Wilkinson**–Oklahoma (1947-63); **Williams**–Army (1891), Minnesota (1900-21); **Woodruff**–Penn (1892-1901), Illinois (1903), Carlisle (1905); **Woodson**–Central Arkansas (1935-39), Hardin-Simmons (1941-42, 1946-51), Arizona (1952-56), New Mexico St. (1958-67), Trinity-TX (1972-73); **Yost**–Ohio Wesleyan (1897), Nebraska (1898), Kansas (1899), Stanford (1900), Michigan (1901-23, 1925-26).

All-Time Winningest Division I-A Coaches (Cont.)

All-Time Bowl Appearances
Coaches active in 1998 in **bold** type.

Active Coaches' Victories
(Minimum 5 years in Division I-A.)

		Overall						Yrs	W	L	T	Pct
		App	W	L	T							
1	Bear Bryant	29	15	12	2	1	Joe Paterno, Penn St.	33	**307**	80	3	.791
	Joe Paterno	29	19	9	1	2	Bobby Bowden, Fla. St.	33	**292**	85	4	.772
3	Tom Osborne	25	12	13	0	3	LaVell Edwards, BYU	27	**243**	91	3	.726
4	**Bobby Bowden**	22	16	5	1	4	Lou Holtz, South Carolina	27	**216**	95	7	.690
5	LaVell Edwards	21	7	13	1	5	Don Nehlen, West Va.	28	**191**	116	8	.619
6	Lou Holtz	20	10	8	2	6	John Cooper, Ohio St.	22	**178**	74	6	.702
	Vince Dooley	20	8	10	2	7	George Welsh, Virginia	26	**176**	121	4	.591
8	Johnny Vaught	18	10	8	0	8	Jackie Sherrill, Miss. St.	21	**154**	87	4	.637
9	**Hayden Fry**	17	7	9	1	9	Dick Tomey, Arizona	22	**147**	98	7	.597
	Bo Schembechler	17	5	12	0	10	Ken Hatfield, Rice	20	**139**	90	4	.605
11	Johnny Majors	16	9	7	0	11	Larry Smith, Missouri	22	**136**	111	7	.549
	Darrell Royal	16	8	7	1	12	Dennis Franchione, TCU	16	**120**	60	2	.665
13	Don James	15	10	5	0		Fisher DeBerry, Air Force	15	**120**	64	1	.651
14	Bobby Dodd	13	9	4	0	14	Frank Beamer, Va. Tech	18	**119**	82	4	.590
	Terry Donahue	13	8	4	1	15	Steve Spurrier, Florida	12	**113**	31	2	.781
	Barry Switzer	13	8	5	0		Dennis Erickson, Oregon St.	13	**113**	40	1	.737
	Charlie McClendon	13	7	6	0	17	Bruce Snyder, Arizona St.	19	**112**	95	6	.540
	George Welsh	13	5	8	0	18	John Robinson, UNLV	12	**104**	35	4	.741
19	Earle Bruce	12	7	5	0	19	Mike Price, Wash. St.	18	**102**	101	0	.502
	Woody Hayes	12	6	6	0		Paul Pasqualoni, Syracuse	13	**102**	43	1	.702
	Shug Jordan	12	5	7	0							

Note: Only four coaches— **Bill Alexander** of Georgia Tech (1920–44); **Bob Neyland** of Tennessee (1926–34, 36–40, 46–52); **Frank Thomas** of Alabama (1931–42, 44–46) and **Joe Paterno** of Penn State (1966–)— have taken teams to the Rose, Orange, Sugar and Cotton Bowls. Paterno has won all four, while Alexander and Thomas won three and Neyland two.

AFCA Coach of the Year
First presented in 1935 by the American Football Coaches Association.

Multiple winners: Joe Paterno (4), Bear Bryant (3), John McKay and Darrell Royal (2).

Years

1935 Pappy Waldorf, Northwestern	1957 Woody Hayes, Ohio St.	1977 Don James, Washington
1936 Dick Harlow, Harvard	1958 Paul Dietzel, LSU	1978 Joe Paterno, Penn St.
1937 Hooks Mylin, Lafayette	1959 Ben Schwartzwalder, Syracuse	1979 Earle Bruce, Ohio St.
1938 Bill Kern, Carnegie Tech	1960 Murray Warmath, Minnesota	1980 Vince Dooley, Georgia
1939 Eddie Anderson, Iowa	1961 Bear Bryant, Alabama	1981 Danny Ford, Clemson
1940 Clark Shaughnessy, Stanford	1962 John McKay, USC	1982 Joe Paterno, Penn St.
1941 Frank Leahy, Notre Dame	1963 Darrell Royal, Texas	1983 Ken Hatfield, Air Force
1942 Bill Alexander, Georgia Tech	1964 Frank Broyles, Arkansas	1984 LaVell Edwards, BYU
1943 Amos Alonzo Stagg, Pacific	& Ara Parseghian, Notre Dame	1985 Fisher DeBerry, Air Force
1944 Carroll Widdoes, Ohio St.	1965 Tommy Prothro, UCLA	1986 Joe Paterno, Penn St.
1945 Bo McMillin, Indiana	1966 Tom Cahill, Army	1987 Dick MacPherson, Syracuse
1946 Red Blaik, Army	1967 John Pont, Indiana	1988 Don Nehlen, West Virginia
1947 Fritz Crisler, Michigan	1968 Joe Paterno, Penn St.	1989 Bill McCartney, Colorado
1948 Bennie Oosterbaan, Michigan	1969 Bo Schembechler, Michigan	1990 Bobby Ross, Georgia Tech
1949 Bud Wilkinson, Oklahoma	1970 Charlie McClendon, LSU	1991 Bill Lewis, East Carolina
1950 Charlie Caldwell, Princeton	& Darrell Royal, Texas	1992 Gene Stallings, Alabama
1951 Chuck Taylor, Stanford	1971 Bear Bryant, Alabama	1993 Barry Alvarez, Wisconsin
1952 Biggie Munn, Michigan St.	1972 John McKay, USC	1994 Tom Osborne, Nebraska
1953 Jim Tatum, Maryland	1973 Bear Bryant, Alabama	1995 Gary Barnett, Northwestern
1954 Red Sanders, UCLA	1974 Grant Teaff, Baylor	1996 Bruce Snyder, Arizona St.
1955 Duffy Daugherty, Michigan St.	1975 Frank Kush, Arizona St.	1997 Lloyd Carr, Michigan
1956 Bowden Wyatt, Tennessee	1976 Johnny Majors, Pittsburgh	1998 Phillip Fulmer, Tennessee

FWAA Coach of the Year
First presented in 1957 by the Football Writers Association of America. The FWAA and AFCA awards have both gone to the same coach in the same season 28 times. Those double winners are preceded by (#).

Multiple winners: Woody Hayes and Joe Paterno (3); Lou Holtz, Johnny Majors and John McKay (2).

Year

1957 #Woody Hayes, Ohio St.	1965 Duffy Daugherty, Michigan St.	1973 Johnny Majors, Pitt
1958 #Paul Dietzel, LSU	1966 #Tom Cahill, Army	1974 #Grant Teaff, Baylor
1959 #Ben Schwartzwalder, Syracuse	1967 #John Pont, Indiana	1975 Woody Hayes, Ohio St.
1960 #Murray Warmath, Minnesota	1968 Woody Hayes, Ohio St.	1976 #Johnny Majors, Pitt
1961 Darrell Royal, Texas	1969 #Bo Schembechler, Michigan	1977 Lou Holtz, Arkansas
1962 #John McKay, USC	1970 Alex Agase, Northwestern	1978 #Joe Paterno, Penn St.
1963 #Darrell Royal, Texas	1971 Bob Devaney, Nebraska	1979 #Earle Bruce, Ohio St.
1964 #Ara Parseghian, Notre Dame	1972 #John McKay, USC	1980 #Vince Dooley, Georgia

Year	Year	Year
1981 #Danny Ford, Clemson	1988 Lou Holtz, Notre Dame	1995 #Gary Barnett, Northwestern
1982 #Joe Paterno, Penn St.	1989 #Bill McCartney, Colorado	1996 #Bruce Snyder, Arizona St.
1983 Howard Schnellenberger, Miami-FL	1990 #Bobby Ross, Georgia Tech	1997 Mike Price, Washington St.
1984 #LaVell Edwards, BYU	1991 Don James, Washington	1998 #Phillip Fulmer, Tennessee
1985 #Fisher DeBerry, Air Force	1992 #Gene Stallings, Alabama	
1986 #Joe Paterno, Penn St.	1993 Terry Bowden, Auburn	
1987 #Dick MacPherson, Syracuse	1994 Rich Brooks, Oregon	

All-Time NCAA Division I-AA Leaders
CAREER

Total Offense

Yards Gained

		Years	Yards
1	Steve McNair, Alcorn St.	1991-94	16,823
2	Willie Totten, Miss. Valley	1982-85	13,007
3	Jamie Martin, Weber St.	1989-92	12,287
4	Doug Nussmeier, Idaho	1990-93	12,054
5	Neil Lomax, Portland St.	1978-80	11,647

Yards per Game

		Years	Yards	P/Gm
1	Steve McNair, Alcorn St.	1991-94	16,823	400.5
2	Neil Lomax, Portland St.	1978-80	11,647	352.9
3	Dave Dickenson, Montana	1992-95	11,523	329.2
4	Willie Totten, Miss. Valley	1982-85	13,007	325.2
5	Tom Ehrhardt, Rhode Island	1984-85	6,492	309.1

Rushing

Yards Gained

		Years	Yards
1	Jerry Azumah, N. Hampshire	1995-98	6193
2	Thomas Haskins, VMI	1993-96	5355
3	Frank Hawkins, Nevada	1977-80	5333
4	Kenny Gamble, Colgate	1984-87	5220
5	Markus Thomas, Eastern Ky.	1989-92	5149

Yards per Game

		Years	Yards	P/Gm
1	Arnold Mickens, Butler	1994-95	3813	190.7
2	Aaron Stecker, W. Ill.	1997-98	3081	151.1
3	Tim Hall, Robert Morris	1994-95	2908	153.1
4	Jerry Azumah, N. Hampshire	1995-98	6193	151.0
5	Archie Amerson, N. Ariz.	1995-96	3196	145.3

Passing
(Minimum 500 Completions)

Passing Efficiency

		Years	Rating
1	Shawn Knight, William & Mary	1991-94	170.8
2	Dave Dickenson, Montana	1992-95	166.3
3	Doug Nussmeier, Idaho	1990-93	154.4
4	Mike Simpson, E. Illinois	1996-97	148.9
5	Jay Johnson, Northern Iowa	1989-92	148.9

Yards Gained

		Years	Yards
1	Steve McNair, Alcorn St.	1991-94	14,496
2	Willie Totten, Miss. Valley	1982-85	12,711
3	Jamie Martin, Weber St.	1989-92	12,207
4	Neil Lomax, Portland St.	1978-80	11,550
5	Dave Dickenson, Montana	1992-95	11,080

Miscellaneous

Interceptions

		Years	No
1	Dave Murphy, Holy Cross	1986-89	28
2	Cedric Walker, S.F. Austin	1990-93	25
3	Issiac Holt, Alcorn St.	1981-84	24
	Bill McGovern, Holy Cross	1981-84	24
	Darren Sharper, Wm. & Mary	1993-96	24

Punting Average

		Years	Avg
1	Pumpy Tudors, Tenn.-Chatt.	1989-91	44.4
2	Case de Brujin, Idaho St.	1978-81	43.7
3	Terry Belden, Northern Ariz.	1990-93	43.4
4	Chad Stanley, SF Austin	1996-98	43.3
5	George Cimadevilla, East Tenn. St.	1983-86	43.0

Punt Return Average*

		Years	Avg
1	Willie Ware, Miss. Valley	1982-85	16.4
2	Buck Phillips, Western Ill.	1994-95	16.4
3	Tim Egerton, Delaware St.	1986-89	16.1
4	Mark Orlando, Towson St.	1991-94	15.7
5	Joey Jamison, TX-Southern	1997-98	14.8

Receiving

Catches

		Years	No
1	Jerry Rice, Miss. Valley	1981-84	301
2	Kasey Dunn, Idaho	1988-91	268
3	Sean Morey, Brown	1995-98	251
4	Brian Forster, Rhode Island	1983-85,87	245
5	Mark Didio, Connecticut	1988-91	239

Yards Gained

		Years	No	Yards
1	Jerry Rice, Miss. Valley	1981-84	301	4693
2	Kasey Dunn, Idaho	1988-91	268	3847
3	Sean Morey, Brown	1995-98	251	3850
4	Rennie Benn, Lehigh	1982-85	237	3662
5	David Rhodes, Central Fla.	1991-94	213	3618

Kickoff Return Average*

		Years	Avg
1	Troy Brown, Marshall	1991-92	29.7
2	Charles Swann, Indiana St.	1989-91	29.3
3	Craig Richardson, Eastern Wash.	1983-86	28.5
4	Kenyatta Sparks, Southern-BR	1992-95	28.2
5	Kerry Hayes, Western Caro.	1991-94	28.2

*(Minimum 1.2 returns per game)

Scoring
NON-KICKERS

Points

		Years	TD	XP	Pts
1	Jerry Azumah, N. Hampshire	1995-98	69	4	418
2	Sherriden May, Idaho	1991-94	61	0	366
3	Charvez Foger, Nevada	1985-88	60	2	362
4	Kenny Gamble, Colgate	1984-87	57	0	342
5	Rene Ingoglia, U Mass	1992-95	55	2	332

Touchdowns Rushing

		Years	No
1	Jerry Azumah, N. Hampshire	1995-98	60
2	Kenny Gamble, Colgate	1984-87	55
3	Rene Ingoglia, UMass	1992-95	54
4	Charvez Foger, Nevada	1985-88	52
5	Markus Thomas, Eastern Ky.	1989-92	51

Touchdowns Passing

		Years	No
1	Willie Totten, Miss. Valley	1982-85	139
2	Steve McNair, Alcorn St.	1991-94	119
3	Dave Dickenson, Montana	1992-95	96
4	Ted White, Howard	1995-98	92
5	Doug Nussmeier, Idaho	1990-93	91

Touchdown Catches

		Years	No
1	Jerry Rice, Miss. Valley	1981-84	50
2	Rennie Benn, Lehigh	1982-85	44
3	Dedric Ward, N. Iowa	1993-96	41
4	Sean Morey, Brown	1995-98	39
5	Roy Banks, Eastern Ill.	1983-86	38
	Mike Jones, Tennessee St.	1979-92	38

All-Time NCAA Division I-AA Leaders (Cont.)
KICKERS

	Points	Years	FG	XP	Pts		Field Goals	Years	No
1	Marty Zendejas, Nevada	1984-87	72	169	385	1	Marty Zendejas, Nevada	1984-87	72
2	B. Mitchell, Marshall/N. Iowa	1987,89-91	64	130	322	2	Kirk Roach, Western Carolina	1984-87	71
	Scott Shields, Weber St.	1995-98	67	109	322	3	Tony Zendejas, Nevada	1981-83	70
4	Thayne Doyle, Idaho	1988-91	49	160	307	4	Scott Shields, Weber St.	1995-98	67
5	Jose Larios, McNeese St.	1992-95	57	133	304	5	B. Mitchell, Marshall/N. Iowa	1987,89-91	64

All-Time Winningest Division I-AA Teams
Includes record at a senior college only, minimum of 20 seasons of competition. Bowl and playoff games are included.

Top 25 Winning Percentage

		Yrs	Gm	W	L	T	Pct.	Playoffs W-L-T
1	Yale	126	1141	790	296	55	.716	0-0-0
2	Florida A&M	66	666	464	184	18	.710	3-5-1
3	Grambling St.	56	599	413	171	15	.702	9-7-0
4	Tennessee St.	71	660	447	183	30	.700	8-3-1
5	Princeton	129	1094	734	310	50	.694	0-0-0
6	Harvard	124	1123	724	349	50	.667	1-0-0
7	Jackson St.	53	543	346	184	13	.649	1-11-1
8	Fordham	100	1115	686	376	53	.639	2-3-0
9	Dartmouth	117	1010	622	342	46	.639	0-0-0
10	Eastern Kentucky	75	745	457	267	27	.632	17-17-0
11	Southern	77	746	458	263	25	.631	6-0-0
12	Pennsylvania	122	1195	730	424	42	.628	0-1-0
13	S. Carolina St.	71	656	394	235	27	.621	6-5-0
14	Dayton	91	860	519	315	26	.619	16-11-0
15	Georgia Southern	30	333	206	120	7	.629	27-6-0
16	Hofstra	58	543	336	206	11	.629	2-9-0
17	McNeese St.	48	518	312	192	14	.616	11-10-0
18	Appalachian St.	69	722	429	264	29	.614	6-12-0
19	Mid. Tennessee St.	82	787	458	301	28	.600	8-9-0
20	Delaware	107	957	552	362	43	.599	22-13-0
21	Georgetown	87	737	424	282	31	.596	0-2-0
22	Youngstown St.	58	586	340	229	17	.595	23-7-0
23	Western Kentucky	80	756	434	291	31	.595	8-5-0
24	Northern Iowa	100	889	505	337	47	.594	8-10-0
25	Alcorn St.	75	657	369	249	39	.591	1-4-0

Top 50 Victories

		Wins			Wins			Wins
1	Yale	790	18	Drake	482	35	Georgetown	424
2	Princeton	734	19	Villanova	476	36	Howard	423
3	Pennsylvania	730	20	Furman	464	37	Maine	418
4	Harvard	724		Florida A&M	464	38	SW Texas St.	415
5	Fordham	686	22	William & Mary	463	39	Grambling St.	413
6	Dartmouth	622	23	Massachusetts	459		Richmond	413
7	Lafayette	584	24	Mid. Tenn. St.	458		Western Ill.	413
8	Cornell	573		Southern-BR	458	42	Citadel	412
9	Delaware	552	26	E. Kentucky	457	43	Connecticut	406
10	Lehigh	543	27	Tennessee St.	447	44	Montana	402
11	Holy Cross	534	28	Hampton	439	45	Idaho St.	399
12	Dayton	519	29	Tenn-Chat	438	46	S. Carolina St.	394
13	Bucknell	510	30	W. Kentucky	434		Eastern Ill.	394
14	Brown	505	31	Northwestern St.	431	48	Murray St.	392
	N. Iowa	505	32	New Hampshire	430	49	SW Missouri St.	386
16	Colgate	504	33	Appalachian St.	429	50	E. Washington	385
17	Butler	495	34	VMI	427			

Top 10 Playoff Game Appearances
Ranked by NCAA playoff games played from 1978-1998. CH refers to championships won.

		Years	Games	Record	CH			Years	Games	Record	CH
1	Georgia Southern	10	32	26-6	4	7	Furman	8	18	11-7	1
2	Eastern Ky.	17	31	16-15	2		Northern Iowa	9	18	9-9	0
3	Marshall*	8	29	23-6	2	9	Idaho*	11	17	6-11	0
4	Youngstown St.	8	24	20-4	4	10	Nevada*	7	16	9-7	0
5	Delaware	10	19	9-10	0						
	Montana	9	19	11-8	1						

*Marshall (1997), Idaho (1996), Nevada (1992) and Boise St. (1996) have all moved up to I-A.

Active Division I-AA Coaches
Minimum of 5 years as a Division I-A and/or Division I-AA through 1998 season.

Top 10 Winning Percentage

		Yrs	W	L	T	Pct
1	Mike Kelly, Dayton	18	171	32	1	.841
2	Al Bagnoli, Pennsylvania	17	133	41	0	.764
3	Pete Richardson, Southern	11	96	30	1	.760
4	Larry Blakeney, Troy St.	8	71	25	1	.737
5	Walt Hamelin, Wagner	18	136	51	2	.725
6	Roy Kidd, Eastern Ky.	35	286	108	8	.721
7	Tubby Raymond, Delaware	33	277	107	3	.720
8	Joe Gardi, Hofstra	9	70	27	3	.715
9	Greg Gattuso, Duquesne	6	45	18	0	.714
10	Billy Joe, Florida A&M	25	195	78	4	.711

Top 10 Victories

		Yrs	W	L	T	Pct
1	Roy Kidd, Eastern Ky	35	286	108	8	.721
2	Tubby Raymond, Delaware	33	277	107	3	.720
3	Billy Joe, Florida A&M	25	195	78	4	.711
4	Ron Randleman, Sam Houston St.	30	178	136	6	.566
5	Bill Bowes, New Hampshire	27	175	106	5	.621
6	Mike Kelly, Dayton	18	171	32	1	.841
7	Willie Jeffries, S. Carolina St.	26	166	113	6	.593
8	Bill Hayes, N. Carolina A&T	23	164	88	2	.650
9	Boots Donnelly, Mid. Tenn. St.	22	154	94	1	.620
10	Walt Hamelin, Wagner	18	136	51	2	.725

Note: Eddie Robinson of Grambling St. (1941-42, 1945-97) retired following the 1997 season as the all-time NCAA leader in coaching wins with a 408-165-15 record and a .707 winning pct. over 55 seasons.

Division I-AA Coach of the Year
First presented in 1983 by the American Football Coaches Association.
Multiple winners: Mark Duffner and Erk Russell (2).

Year		Year		Year	
1983	Rey Dempsey, Southern Ill.	1989	Erk Russell, Ga. Southern	1995	Don Read, Montana
1984	Dave Arnold, Montana St.	1990	Tim Stowers, Ga. Southern	1996	Ray Tellier, Columbia
1985	Dick Sheridan, Furman	1991	Mark Duffner, Holy Cross	1997	Andy Talley, Villanova
1986	Erk Russell, Ga. Southern	1992	Charlie Taafe, Citadel	1998	Mark Whipple, Massachusetts
1987	Mark Duffner, Holy Cross	1993	Dan Allen, Boston Univ.		
1988	Jimmy Satterfield, Furman	1994	Jim Tressel, Youngstown St.		

NCAA Playoffs

Division I-AA
Established in 1978 as a four-team playoff. Tournament field increased to eight teams in 1981, 12 teams in 1982 and 16 teams in 1986. Automatic berths have been awarded to champions of the Big Sky, Gateway, Ohio Valley, Southern, Southland and Atlantic 10 (formerly Yankee) conferences since 1992.
Multiple winners: Georgia Southern and Youngstown St. (4); Eastern Kentucky and Marshall (2).

Year	Winner	Score	Loser	Year	Winner	Score	Loser
1978	Florida A&M	35-28	Massachusetts	1989	Georgia Southern	37-34	S.F. Austin St.
1979	Eastern Kentucky	30-7	Lehigh, PA	1990	Georgia Southern	36-13	Nevada-Reno
1980	Boise St., ID	31-29	Eastern Kentucky	1991	Youngstown St., OH	25-17	Marshall
1981	Idaho St.	34-23	Eastern Kentucky	1992	Marshall	31-28	Youngstown St.
1982	Eastern Kentucky	17-14	Delaware	1993	Youngstown St.	17-5	Marshall
1983	Southern Illinois	43-7	Western Carolina	1994	Youngstown St.	28-14	Boise St.
1984	Montana St.	19-6	Louisiana Tech	1995	Montana	22-20	Marshall
1985	Georgia Southern	44-42	Furman, SC	1996	Marshall	49-29	Montana
1986	Georgia Southern	48-21	Arkansas St.	1997	Youngstown St.	10-9	McNeese St.
1987	NE Louisiana	43-42	Marshall, WV	1998	Massachusetts	55-43	Georgia Southern
1988	Furman, SC	17-12	Georgia Southern				

Division II
Established in 1973 as an eight-team playoff. Tournament field increased to 16 teams in 1988. From 1964-72, eight qualifying NCAA College Division member institutions competed in four regional bowl games, but there was no tournament and no national championship until 1973.
Multiple winners: North Dakota St. (5); North Alabama (3); Northern Colorado, Southwest Texas St. and Troy St. (2).

Year	Winner	Score	Loser	Year	Winner	Score	Loser
1973	Louisiana Tech	34-0	Western Kentucky	1986	North Dakota St.	27-7	South Dakota
1974	Central Michigan	54-14	Delaware	1987	Troy St., AL	31-17	Portland St., OR
1975	Northern Michigan	16-14	Western Kentucky	1988	North Dakota St.	35-21	Portland St., OR
1976	Montana St.	24-13	Akron, OH	1989	Mississippi Col.	3-0	Jacksonville St., AL
1977	Lehigh, PA	33-0	Jacksonville St., AL				
1978	Eastern Illinois	10-9	Delaware	1990	North Dakota St.	51-11	Indiana, PA
1979	Delaware	38-21	Youngstown St., OH	1991	Pittsburg St., KS	23-6	Jacksonville St., AL
				1992	Jacksonville St., AL	17-13	Pittsburg St., KS
1980	Cal Poly-SLO	21-13	Eastern Illinois	1993	North Alabama	41-34	Indiana, PA
1981	SW Texas St.	42-13	North Dakota St.	1994	North Alabama	16-10	Tex. A&M (Kings.)
1982	SW Texas St.	34-9	UC-Davis	1995	North Alabama	22-7	Pittsburg St., KS
1983	North Dakota St.	41-21	Central St., OH	1996	Northern Colorado	23-14	Carson-Newman
1984	Troy St., AL	18-17	North Dakota St.	1997	Northern Colorado	51-0	New Haven
1985	North Dakota St.	35-7	North Alabama	1998	NW Missouri St.	24-6	Carson-Newman

Division III

Established in 1973 as a four-team playoff. Tournament field increased to eight teams in 1975 and 16 teams in 1985. From 1969-72, four qualifying NCAA College Division member institutions competed in two regional bowl games, but there was no tournament and no national championship until 1973.

Multiple winners: Augustana and Mt. Union (4); Ithaca (3); Dayton, Widener, WI-La Crosse and Wittenberg (2).

Year	Winner	Score	Loser	Year	Winner	Score	Loser
1973	Wittenberg, OH	41-0	Juniata, PA	1987	Wagner, NY	19-3	Dayton
1974	Central, IA	10-8	Ithaca, NY	1988	Ithaca	39-24	Central, IA
1975	Wittenberg	28-0	Ithaca	1989	Dayton	17-7	Union
1976	St. John's, MN	31-28	Towson St., MD	1990	Allegheny, PA*	21-14	Lycoming, PA
1977	Widener, PA	39-36	Wabash, IN	1991	Ithaca	34-20	Dayton
1978	Baldwin-Wallace	24-10	Wittenberg	1992	WI-La Crosse	16-12	Wash. & Jeff., PA
1979	Ithaca, NY	14-10	Wittenberg	1993	Mt. Union, OH	34-24	Rowan, NJ
1980	Dayton, OH	63-0	Ithaca	1994	Albion, MI	38-15	Wash. & Jeff.
1981	Widener, PA	17-10	Dayton, OH	1995	WI-La Crosse	36-7	Rowan
1982	West Georgia	14-0	Augustana, IL	1996	Mt. Union	56-24	Rowan
1983	Augustana	21-17	Union, NY	1997	Mt. Union	61-12	Lycoming
1984	Augustana	21-12	Central, IA	1998	Mt. Union	44-24	Rowan
1985	Augustana	20-7	Ithaca	*Overtime			
1986	Augustana	31-3	Salisbury St., MD				

NAIA Playoffs

Division I

Established in 1956 as two-team playoff. Tournament field increased to four teams in 1958, eight teams in 1978 and 16 teams in 1987 before cutting back to eight teams in 1989. NAIA went back to a single division 16-team playoff in 1997. The title game has ended in a tie four times (1956, '64, '84 and '85).

Multiple winners: Texas A&I (7); Carson-Newman (5); Central Arkansas and Central St., OH (3); Abilene Christian, Central St-OK, Elon, Pittsburg St. and St. John's-MN (2).

Year	Winner	Score	Loser	Year	Winner	Score	Loser
1956	Montana St.	0-0	St. Joseph's, IN	1978	Angelo St., TX	34-14	Elon, NC
1957	Pittsburg St., KS	27-26	Hillsdale, MI	1979	Texas A&I	20-14	Central St., OK
1958	NE Oklahoma	19-13	Northern Arizona	1980	Elon, NC	17-10	NE Oklahoma
1959	Texas A&I	20-7	Lenoir-Rhyne, NC	1981	Elon, NC	3-0	Pittsburg St., KS
1960	Lenoir-Rhyne, NC	15-14	Humboldt St., CA	1982	Central St., OK	14-11	Mesa, CO
1961	Pittsburg St., KS	12-7	Linfield, OR	1983	Car-Newman, TN	36-28	Mesa, CO
1962	Central St., OK	28-13	Lenoir-Rhyne, NC	1984	Car-Newman, TN	19-19	Central Arkansas
1963	St. John's, MN	33-27	Prairie View, TX	1985	Hillsdale, MI	10-10	Central Arkansas
1964	Concordia, MN	7-7	Sam Houston, TX	1986	Car-Newman, TN	17-0	Cameron, OK
1965	St. John's, MN	33-0	Linfield, OR	1987	Cameron, OK	30-2	Car-Newman, TN
1966	Waynesburg, PA	42-21	WI-Whitewater	1988	Car-Newman, TN	56-21	Adams St., CO
1967	Fairmont St., WV	28-21	Eastern Wash.	1989	Car-Newman, TN	34-20	Emporia St., KS
1968	Troy St., AL	43-35	Texas A&I	1990	Central St., OH	38-16	Mesa, CO
1969	Texas A&I	32-7	Concordia, MN	1991	Central Arkansas	19-16	Central St., OH
1970	Texas A&I	48-7	Wofford, SC	1992	Central St., OH	19-16	Gardner-Webb, NC
1971	Livingston, AL	14-12	Arkansas Tech	1993	E. Central, OK	49-35	Glenville St., WV
1972	East Texas St.	21-18	Car-Newman, TN	1994	N'eastern St., OK	13-12	Ark-Pine Bluff
1973	Abilene Christian	42-14	Elon, NC	1995	Central St., OH	37-7	N'eastern St., OK
1974	Texas A&I	34-23	Henderson St., AR	1996	SW Oklahoma St.	33-31	Montana Tech
1975	Texas A&I	37-0	Salem, WV	1997	Findlay, OH	14-7	Willamette, ORE
1976	Texas A&I	26-0	Central Arkansas	1998	Azusa Pacific, CA	17-14	Olivet Nazarene, IL
1977	Abilene Christian	24-7	SW Oklahoma				

Division II

Established in 1970 as four-team playoff. Tournament field increased to eight teams in 1978 and 16 teams in 1987. NAIA went back to a single division playoff in 1997. The title game has ended in a tie twice (1981 and '87).

Multiple winners: Westminster (6); Findlay, Linfield and Pacific Lutheran (3); Concordia-MN, Northwestern-IA and Texas Lutheran (2).

Year	Winner	Score	Loser	Year	Winner	Score	Loser
1970	Westminster, PA	21-16	Anderson, IN	1984	Linfield, OR	33-22	Northwestern, IA
1971	Calif. Lutheran	20-14	Westminster, PA	1985	WI-La Crosse	24-7	Pacific Lutheran
1972	Missouri Southern	21-14	Northwestern, IA	1986	Linfield, OR	17-0	Baker, KS
1973	Northwestern, IA	10-3	Glenville St., WV	1987	Pacific Lutheran	16-16	WI-Stevens Pt.*
1974	Texas Lutheran	42-0	Missouri Valley	1988	Westminster, PA	21-14	WI-La Crosse
1975	Texas Lutheran	34-8	Calif. Lutheran	1989	Westminster, PA	51-30	WI-La Crosse
1976	Westminster, PA	20-13	Redlands, CA	1990	Peru St., NE	17-7	Westminster, PA
1977	Westminster, PA	17-9	Calif. Lutheran	1991	Georgetown-KY	28-20	Pacific Lutheran
1978	Concordia, MN	7-0	Findlay, OH	1992	Findlay, OH	26-13	Linfield, OR
1979	Findlay, OH	51-6	Northwestern, IA	1993	Pacific Lutheran	50-20	Westminster, PA
1980	Pacific Lutheran	38-10	Wilmington, OH	1994	Westminster, PA	27-7	Pacific Lutheran
1981	Austin College, TX	24-24	Concordia, MN	1995	Findlay, OH	21-21	Central Wash.
1982	Linfield, OR	33-15	Wm. Jewell, MO	1996	Sioux Falls, S.D.	47-25	W. Washington
1983	Northwestern, IA	25-21	Pacific Lutheran	1997	discontinued		

*Wisconsin-Stevens Point forfeited its entire 1987 schedule due to its use of an ineligible player.

Pro Football

Denver quarterback **John Elway** reacts to a fourth quarter Broncos touchdown, something he became quite good at over his 16-year career.

AP/Wide World Photos

Out with a Bang

Elway leads the Broncos to the promised land once again, then says goodbye.

by
Chris Berman

One may be an accident. Two is definitely a trend. The Denver Broncos, long ridiculed for their Super Bowl failures, are making this NFL championship thing quite a habit.

While that stunning upset of the Packers in Super Bowl XXXII in San Diego surprised many, there was little doubt in '98 that Mike Shanahan's club was the league's best team as John Elway and company capped off another title campaign by humbling the upstart Atlanta Falcons, 34-19, in Super Bowl XXXIII in Miami.

The Broncos not only picked up where they left off the previous January, but threatened the most fabled of the NFL's team records by winning their first 13 games, doing it sometimes without Elway but never minus All-Pro runner Terrell Davis. Davis, the NFL Most Valuable Player, made a serious run at the single-season rushing record, and when it was all said

Chris Berman is the host of ESPN's *NFL Prime Time.*

and done finished with 2,008 yards—the third-best rushing performance in league history.

While the 16-2 Broncos arrived in Miami as defending champions, the 16-2 Falcons were one of the league's bigger Cinderella stories of recent years, spearheaded by their own workhorse running back Jamal Anderson (who set an NFL record with 410 carries) and resilient quarterback Chris Chandler. More importantly, Atlanta's success was a direct reflection of head coach Dan Reeves, who showed us all just how human he was, overcoming heart surgery late in the season to lead his team to the brink of a championship.

The Falcons' appearance in Super Bowl XXXIII was a major surprise considering most "experts" expected the high-flying Minnesota Vikings to make the trip to sunny Florida. Thanks in part to rejuvenated passer Randall Cunningham and an offensive attack led by the receiving combo of veteran Cris Carter and rookie phenomenon Randy Moss, Dennis

AP/Wide World Photos

John Elway waves goodbye to fans and reporters as he leaves an NFL field for the final time after winning his second consecutive Super Bowl, 34-19, over Atlanta.

Green's talent-laden squad had lost just once all season and set an NFL record by scoring an amazing 556 points. But the Vikings' defense couldn't stop Chandler and company in the final minutes of the NFC title game, and Morten Andersen's 38-yard field goal in overtime won it, 30-27, silencing the Metrodome and sending the Falcons to Miami.

While the 1998 NFL season was still a game for the Young (as in Steve, who threw a career-best 36 touchdown passes), youth (with the exception of rookies Peyton Manning and Charlie Batch) was not served at quarterback as veterans such as Elway, Chandler and Cunningham took their teams to the NFL's version of the Final Four. And who could forget the return of Doug Flutie, who brought new meaning to the term "Comeback Player of the Year" by

returning to the NFL for the first time since 1989 and helping the Bills rebound from an 0-3 start to make the playoffs.

While the NFL is surely happy to have Flutie back in the league, it also saw the departure of its share of high-profile players. Future Hall of Famer Reggie White, "The Minister of Defense," called it quits after the season and went out as the NFL's all-time sack leader. He didn't exactly go out with a whimper, earning Defensive Player of the Year honors in his final season. Later we were all crushed to learn that Detroit's Barry Sanders, one of the most magical running backs in the history of the sport, would no longer dazzle us with his brilliance. No one wanted to believe it.

The 1998 season also brought us the long-awaited resurgence of the

215

To the shock and disappointment of many, Detroit running back **Barry Sanders** called it quits after the 1998 season, less than 1,500 yards away from breaking Walter Payton's all-time rushing record.

J-E-T-S, another team led by a veteran quarterback (Vinny Testaverde) as the Green and White captured their first-ever AFC East title and then led in the third quarter at Denver in the AFC Championship Game before falling, 23-10. The Jacksonville Jaguars also won their first division championship, while the long-dormant Arizona Cardinals not only went to the playoffs for the first time in 16 seasons but won a postseason game for the first time since 1947. And for sheer excitement, it was hard to top San Francisco's rousing 30-27 win over Green Bay in the NFC Wild Card Game as Young's last-second, thread-the-needle pass to Terrell Owens dethroned the two-time NFC champions.

But in the end, the season belonged to the Broncos and Elway. The savvy signal-caller wrapped up his amazing 16-year career by capturing MVP honors in Super Bowl XXXIII. The next stop is Canton, Ohio, where Elway will go all the way to the Pro Football Hall of Fame. ∎

John Clayton's Top Ten Highlights of the 1998 NFL season

10. **Peyton Manning earns** his NFL stripes on Nov. 15, driving the Indianapolis Colts on a 15-play, 80-yard drive in the final three minutes to upset the 7-2 New York Jets, 24-23. He establishes NFL season rookie records for attempts, completions, yards and touchdown tosses and sets the stage for the rebuilding of the Colts.

9. **Bills owner Ralph Wilson**, a noted traditionalist and replay opponent, fumes about a 25-21 loss

AP/Wide World Photos

Minnesota's draft day gamble on troubled receiver **Randy Moss**, right, paid huge dividends in 1998 as he led the NFC with 17 touchdowns and helped rejuvenate the career of **Randall Cunningham**.

to New England that shouldn't have been, after officials allow a 10-yard Shawn Jefferson completion on a fourth-and-nine when he was clearly out of bounds. Wilson changes his stance and unofficially sets the stage for the return of replay officiating in 1999.

8. **Jason Elam makes history.** Broncos coach Mike Shanahan, thoroughly enjoying a 37-24 blasting of Jacksonville, urged Elam to stay on the field despite a delay-of-game penalty prior to a 58-yard field goal attempt before the half. Undaunted, Elam, who attempts 65-yarders in pre-game, booms a 63-yarder that ties Tom Dempsey's long-standing record.

7. **Aging CFL star Doug Flutie** not only turns the Bills' 0-3 start into a playoff season, but he makes his personal cereal, Flutie Flakes, the most popular breakfast food in the Northeast. Only a goal-line stand by the Miami Dolphins in a 24-17 playoff victory prevents the Bills from moving past the first round.

6. **Who said, "You can't go home again?"** Former Giants coach Bill Parcells returns to the Meadowlands and quarterback Vinny Testaverde, signed in June to be Glenn Foley's backup, returns home to lead the New York Jets to the AFC title game. The Parcells-Testaverde combination gave a final NFL thrill to owner Leon Hess, who passed away after the season.

5. Thanks to **Randall Cunningham's miraculous rebound** from retirement and the emergence of rookie superstar Randy Moss, the Minnesota Vikings enjoy a 15-1 regular-season record and an NFL record 556 points.

4. **The Arizona Cardinals "snake"** their way to a 20-7 Jake Plummer-led victory over the Dallas Cowboys in the NFC playoffs. Thanks to Plummer's fourth-quarter tenacity, the Cards make their first playoff appearance since 1982 and record nine come-from-behind fourth quarter victories in two seasons.

3. **Terrell Owens catches** a 25-yard touchdown pass from Steve Young with three seconds remaining in a frantic NFC playoff game to end the Green Bay Packers two-year

217

NFC Championship reign, 30-27. The game marks the end of Reggie White's career and Mike Holmgren's tenure as Packers head coach.

2. **Cinderella is a Falcon.** Riding Jamal Anderson's 1,846-yard season and Chris Chandler's great deep throwing, the Falcons zip through a 14-2 season that propels them to a 20-18 home playoff victory over San Francisco and a stunning upset over powerful Minnesota, 30-27, in overtime at the Metrodome.

1. **Terrell Davis slips** through the arms of Falcon defenders en route to an easy 34-19 Super Bowl victory. It completes a season in which Davis takes the torch from John Elway as the franchise player for the two-time Super Bowl champion Broncos. Elway waits three months after the game to officially announce his retirement and the end of an era that started in 1983. Davis is the rushing star in a season that featured 20 1,000-yard rushers and 144 100-yard games. ■

MARSHALL LAW

Perhaps no player was more vital to any one team in 1998 than running back Marshall Faulk was to Indianapolis. Faulk was a busy man last season, accounting for 43.5 percent of the entire Colts offense, by far the highest percentage of any one player.

	Rush	Rec	Total	Pct.
Marshall Faulk, Ind.	1319	908	2227	**43.5**
Jamal Anderson, Atl.	1846	319	2165	**39.5**
Terrell Davis, Den.	2008	217	2225	**36.5**
Duce Staley, Phi.	1065	432	1497	**35.7**
Barry Sanders, Det.	1491	289	1780	**35.0**
Ricky Watters, Sea.	1239	373	1612	**34.8**
Fred Taylor, Jax.	1223	421	1644	**31.5**
Garrison Hearst, SF	1570	535	2105	**31.0**
Eddie George, Ten.	1294	310	1604	**30.5**
Curtis Martin, NYJ	1287	365	1652	**28.9**

AND STAY OUT!

Retired Lions' running back Barry Sanders will be sorely missed by his team, the league and fans alike. But not everyone is sad to see him go. Below are the top five defenses Barry abused throughout his career, ranked by rushing yards per game.

	Gm	Yds	Yds/Gm
Indianapolis	2	395	**197.5**
Cincinnati	3	450	**150.0**
Denver	1	147	**147.0**
NY Jets	3	425	**141.7**
New England	2	279	**139.5**

BARRY AT HIS BEST

Over his ten-year career, Barry Sanders broke the 100-yard mark 76 times (2nd place all-time) and the 200-yard mark four times. Below are his top five performances, the opponent and the date it happened.

Yards	Opponent	Date
237	Tampa Bay	11/13/94
220	at Minnesota	11/24/91
216	Indianapolis	11/23/97
215	at Tampa Bay	10/12/97
194	at Dallas	9/19/94

■

THE **NUMBERS**

INSIDE

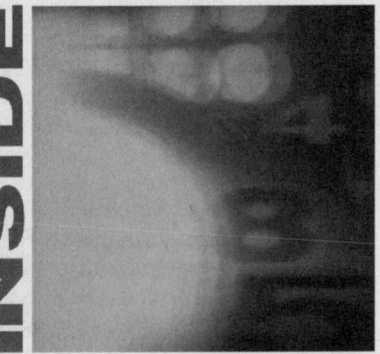

THE 2000

ESPN INFORMATION PLEASE SPORTS ALMANAC

PRO FOOTBALL
S T A T I S T I C S

THE SEASON IN REVIEW
1998-1999
STANDINGS • PLAYOFFS • DRAFTS

SEC
A

PAGE
219

Final NFL Standings

Division champions (*) and Wild Card playoff qualifiers (†) are noted; division champions with two best records received first round byes. Number of seasons listed after each head coach refers to latest tenure with club through 1998 season.

American Football Conference

Eastern Division

	W	L	T	PF	PA	vs Div	vs AFC
*NY Jets	12	4	0	416	266	7-1-0	10-2-0
†Miami	10	6	0	321	265	4-4-0	7-5-0
†Buffalo	10	6	0	400	333	4-4-0	7-5-0
†New England	9	7	0	337	329	4-4-0	7-5-0
Indianapolis	3	13	0	310	444	1-7-0	3-9-0

1998 Head coaches: NY—Bill Parcells (2nd season); **Buf**—Wade Phillips (1st); **Mia**—Jimmy Johnson (3rd); **NE**—Pete Carroll (2nd); **Ind**—Jim Mora (1st).
1997 Standings: 1. New England (10-6); 2. Miami (9-7); 3. NY Jets (9-7); 4. Buffalo (6-10); 5. Indianapolis (3-13).

Central Division

	W	L	T	PF	PA	vs Div	vs AFC
*Jacksonville	11	5	0	392	338	6-2-0	8-4-0
Tennessee	8	8	0	330	320	7-1-0	7-5-0
Pittsburgh	7	9	0	263	303	3-5-0	5-7-0
Baltimore	6	10	0	269	335	2-6-0	5-7-0
Cincinnati	3	13	0	268	452	2-6-0	2-10-0

1998 Head coaches: Jax—Tom Coughlin (4th season); **Ten**—Jeff Fisher (5th); **Pit**—Bill Cowher (7th); **Bal**—Ted Marchibroda (3rd); **Cin**—Bruce Coslet (3rd).
1997 Standings: 1. Pittsburgh (11-5); 2. Jacksonville (11-5); 3. Tennessee (8-8); 4. Cincinnati (7-9); 5. Baltimore (6-9-1).

Western Division

	W	L	T	PF	PA	vs Div	vs AFC
*Denver	14	2	0	501	309	8-0-0	11-1-0
Oakland	8	8	0	288	356	4-4-0	5-7-0
Seattle	8	8	0	372	310	3-5-0	5-7-0
Kansas City	7	9	0	327	363	4-4-0	4-8-0
San Diego	5	11	0	241	342	1-7-0	4-8-0

1998 Head coaches: Den—Mike Shanahan (4th season); **Sea**—Dennis Erickson (4th); **Oak**—Jon Gruden (1st); **KC**—Marty Schottenheimer (10th); **SD**—replaced Kevin Gilbride (3rd, 2-4) on Oct. 13 with June Jones (3-7).
1997 Standings: 1. Kansas City (13-3); 2. Denver (12-4); 3. Seattle (8-8); 4. Oakland (4-12); 5. San Diego (4-12).

National Football Conference

Eastern Division

	W	L	T	PF	PA	vs Div	vs NFC
*Dallas	10	6	0	381	275	8-0-0	9-3-0
†Arizona	9	7	0	325	378	4-4-0	8-4-0
NY Giants	8	8	0	287	309	5-3-0	5-7-0
Washington	6	10	0	319	421	2-6-0	4-8-0
Philadelphia	3	13	0	161	344	1-7-0	3-9-0

1998 Head coaches: Dal—Chan Gailey (1st season); **Ariz**—Vince Tobin (3rd); **NY**—Jim Fassel (2nd); **Wash**—Norv Turner (5th); **Phi**—Ray Rhodes (4th).
1997 Standings: 1. NY Giants (10-5-1); 2. Washington (8-7-1); 3. Philadelphia (6-9-1); 4. Dallas (6-10); 5. Arizona (4-12).

Central Division

	W	L	T	PF	PA	vs Div	vs NFC
*Minnesota	15	1	0	556	296	7-1-0	11-1-0
†Green Bay	11	5	0	408	319	4-4-0	8-4-0
Tampa Bay	8	8	0	314	295	4-4-0	6-6-0
Detroit	5	11	0	306	378	4-4-0	4-8-0
Chicago	4	12	0	276	368	1-7-0	2-10-0

1998 Head Coaches: Min—Dennis Green (7th season); **GB**—Mike Holmgren (7th); **TB**—Tony Dungy (3rd); **Det**—Bobby Ross (2nd); **Chi**—Dave Wannstedt (6th).
1997 Standings: 1. Green Bay (13-3); 2. Tampa Bay (10-6); 3. Detroit (9-7); 4. Minnesota (9-7); 5. Chicago (4-12).

Western Division

	W	L	T	PF	PA	vs Div	vs NFC
*Atlanta	14	2	0	442	289	7-1-0	11-1-0
†San Francisco	12	4	0	479	328	7-1-0	10-2-0
New Orleans	6	10	0	305	359	3-5-0	5-7-0
Carolina	4	12	0	336	413	3-5-0	3-9-0
St. Louis	4	12	0	285	378	0-8-0	1-11-0

1998 Head Coaches: Atl—Dan Reeves (2nd season); **SF**—Steve Mariucci (2nd); **NO**—Mike Ditka (2nd); **Car**—Dom Capers (4th); **St.L**—Dick Vermeil (2nd).
1997 Standings: 1. San Francisco (13-3); 2. Carolina (7-9); 3. Atlanta (7-9); 4. New Orleans (6-10); 5. St. Louis (5-11).

Playoff Tiebreakers

Home field priority—AFC: Miami (10-6) and Buffalo (10-6) each earned wild card berths, but Miami was awarded home field advantage in their game because they had more net points in division games than Buffalo. This was the fifth possible tiebreaker. The teams were still even after the first four.

NFL Regular Season Individual Leaders
(* indicates rookies)
Passing Efficiency
(Minimum of 224 attempts)

AFC	Att	Cmp	Cmp Pct	Yds	Yds/Att	TD	Long	Int	Sack/Lost	Rating Points
Vinny Testaverde, NYJ	421	259	61.5	3256	7.73	29	82-td	7	19/140	101.6
John Elway, Den.	356	210	59.0	2806	7.88	22	58	10	18/135	93.0
Neil O'Donnell, Cin.	343	212	61.8	2216	6.46	15	76-td	4	30/217	90.2
Mark Brunell, Jax.	354	208	58.8	2601	7.35	20	78-td	9	28/172	89.9
Doug Flutie, Buf.	354	202	57.1	2711	7.66	20	84-td	11	12/78	87.4
Drew Bledsoe, NE	481	263	54.7	3633	7.55	20	86-td	14	36/295	80.9
Steve McNair, Ten.	492	289	58.7	3228	6.56	15	47	10	33/176	80.1
Rich Gannon, KC	354	206	58.2	2305	6.51	10	80-td	6	25/155	80.1
Dan Marino, Mia.	537	310	57.7	3497	6.51	23	61-td	15	23/178	80.0
Warren Moon, Sea.	258	145	56.2	1632	6.33	11	45	8	22/140	76.6
Jim Harbaugh, Bal.	293	164	56.0	1839	6.28	12	66-td	11	23/145	72.9
Peyton Manning*, Ind.	575	326	56.7	3739	6.50	26	78-td	28	22/109	71.2
Kordell Stewart, Pit.	458	252	55.0	2560	5.59	11	55-td	18	33/211	62.9
Donald Hollas, Oak.	260	135	51.9	1754	6.75	10	47	16	36/207	60.6
Craig Whelihan, SD	320	149	46.6	1803	5.63	8	55	19	15/111	48.0

NFC	Att	Cmp	Cmp Pct	Yds	Yds/Att	TD	Long	Int	Sack/Lost	Rating Points
Randall Cunningham, Min.	425	259	60.9	3704	8.72	34	67-td	10	20/132	106.0
Steve Young, SF	517	322	62.3	4170	8.07	36	81-td	12	48/234	101.1
Chris Chandler, Atl.	327	190	58.1	3154	9.65	25	78-td	12	45/283	100.9
Troy Aikman, Dal.	315	187	59.4	2330	7.40	12	67-td	5	9/58	88.5
Steve Beuerlein, Car.	343	216	63.0	2613	7.62	17	68-td	12	44/251	88.2
Brett Favre, GB	551	347	63.0	4212	7.64	31	84-td	23	38/223	87.8
Charlie Batch*, Det.	303	173	57.1	2178	7.19	11	98-td	6	37/222	83.5
Erik Kramer, Chi.	250	151	60.4	1823	7.29	9	79-td	7	10/71	83.1
Trent Green, Was.	509	278	54.6	3441	6.76	23	75-td	11	49/338	81.8
Jake Plummer, Ari.	547	324	59.2	3737	6.83	17	57	20	49/280	75.0
Trent Dilfer, TB	429	225	52.4	2729	6.36	21	79-td	15	27/172	74.0
Tony Banks, St.L	408	241	59.1	2535	6.21	7	80-td	14	41/237	68.6
Danny Kanell, NYG	299	160	53.5	1603	5.36	11	46	10	22/172	67.3
Kerry Collins, Car.-NO	353	170	48.2	2213	6.27	12	89-td	15	31/191	62.0
Bobby Hoying, Phi.	224	114	50.9	961	4.29	0	38	9	35/185	45.6

Receptions

AFC	No	Yds	Avg	Long	TD
O.J. McDuffie, Mia.	90	1050	11.7	61-td	7
Rod Smith, Den.	86	1222	14.2	58	6
Marshall Faulk, Ind.	86	908	10.6	78-td	4
Keyshawn Johnson, NYJ	83	1131	13.6	41-td	10
Carl Pickens, Cin.	82	1023	12.5	67-td	5
Tim Brown, Oak.	81	1012	12.5	49	9
Jimmy Smith, Jax.	78	1182	15.2	72-td	8
Wayne Chrebet, NYJ	75	1083	14.4	63-td	8
Frank Wycheck, Ten.	70	768	11.0	38	2
Eric Moulds, Buf.	67	1368	20.4	84-td	9
Ben Coates, NE.	67	668	10.0	33	6
Courtney Hawkins, Pit.	66	751	11.4	53	1
Joey Galloway, Sea.	65	1047	16.1	81-td	10
Charles Johnson, Pit.	65	815	12.5	55-td	7

NFC	No	Yds	Avg	Long	TD
Frank Sanders, Ari.	89	1145	12.9	42	3
Antonio Freeman, GB	84	1424	17.0	84-td	14
Herman Moore, Det.	82	983	12.0	36	5
Jerry Rice, SF	82	1157	14.1	75-td	9
Cris Carter, Min.	78	1011	13.0	54-td	12
Michael Irvin, Dal.	74	1057	14.3	51	1
Larry Centers, Ari.	69	559	8.1	54	2
Raghib Ismail, Car.	69	1024	14.8	62	8
Johnnie Morton, Det.	69	1028	14.9	98-td	2
Randy Moss*, Min.	69	1313	19.0	61-td	17
Mushin Muhammad, Car.	68	941	13.8	72-td	6
Rob Moore, Ari.	67	982	14.7	57	5
Terrell Owens, SF	67	1097	16.4	79-td	14
Tony Martin, Atl.	66	1181	17.9	62	6

Rushing

AFC	Att	Yards	Avg	Long	TD
Terrell Davis, Den.	392	2008	5.1	70	21
Marshall Faulk, Ind.	324	1319	4.1	68-td	6
Eddie George, Ten.	348	1294	3.7	37-td	5
Curtis Martin, NYJ	369	1287	3.5	60-td	8
Ricky Watters, Sea.	319	1239	3.9	39-td	9
Fred Taylor*, Jax.	264	1223	4.6	77-td	14
Jerome Bettis, Pit.	316	1185	3.8	42	3
Corey Dillon, Cin.	262	1130	4.3	66	4
Antowain Smith, Buf.	300	1124	3.7	30	8
Robert Edwards*, NE	291	1115	3.8	53	9
Priest Holmes, Bal.	233	1008	4.3	56	7
Karim Abdul-Jabbar, Mia.	270	960	3.6	45	6
Napoleon Kaufman, Oak.	217	921	4.2	80-td	2
Natrone Means, SD	212	883	4.2	72-td	5

NFC	Att	Yards	Avg	Long	TD
Jamal Anderson, Atl.	410	1846	4.5	48	14
Garrison Hearst, SF	310	1570	5.1	96-td	7
Barry Sanders, Det.	343	1491	4.3	73-td	4
Emmitt Smith, Dal.	319	1332	4.2	32	13
Robert Smith, Min.	249	1187	4.8	74-td	6
Duce Staley, Phi.	258	1065	4.1	64-td	5
Gary Brown, NYG	247	1063	4.3	45	5
Adrian Murrell, Ari.	274	1042	3.8	32	5
Warrick Dunn, TB	245	1026	4.2	50	2
Mike Alstott, TB	215	846	3.9	37	8
Fred Lane, Car.	205	717	3.5	31	5
Terry Allen, Was.	148	700	4.7	45	2
Edgar Bennett, Chi.	173	611	3.5	43	2
Curtis Enis*, Chi.	133	497	3.7	29	0

Minnesota Vikings	Denver Broncos	Minnesota Vikings	New England Patriots
Randall Cunningham	**Terrell Davis**	**Gary Anderson**	**Ty Law**
Passing Efficiency	Rushing, Touchdowns	Scoring	Interceptions

All-Purpose Yardage

AFC	Rush	Rec	Ret	Total	NFC	Rush	Rec	Ret	Total
Marshall Faulk, Ind.	1319	908	0	2227	Brian Mitchell, Was.	208	306	1843	2357
Terrell Davis, Den.	2008	217	0	2225	Jamal Anderson, Atl.	1846	319	0	2165
Kevin Williams, Buf.	46	392	1428	1866	Garrison Hearst, SF	1570	535	0	2105
John Avery*, Mia.	503	67	1085	1655	Roell Preston, GB	0	23	1895	1918
Curtis Martin, NYJ	1287	365	0	1652	Glyn Milburn, Chi.	8	37	1841	1886
Fred Taylor*, Jax.	1223	421	0	1644	Reidel Anthony, TB	43	708	1118	1869
Ricky Watters, Sea.	1239	373	0	1612	Eric Metcalf, Ari.	0	324	1513	1837
Eddie George, Ten.	1294	310	0	1604	Barry Sanders, Det.	1491	289	0	1780
Desmond Howard, Oak.	0	16	1581	1597	David Palmer, Min.	52	185	1465	1702
Reggie Barlow, Jax.	0	168	1302	1470	Terry Fair*, Det.	0	0	1617	1617
Robert Edwards*, NE	1115	331	0	1446	Duce Staley, Phi.	1065	432	19	1516
Eric Moulds, Buf.	0	1368	0	1368	Emmitt Smith, Dal.	1332	175	0	1507

Ret column indicates all kickoff, punt, fumble and interception returns.

Scoring

Touchdowns

AFC	TD	Rush	Rec	Ret	Pts
Terrell Davis, Den.	23	21	2	0	138
Fred Taylor*, Jax.	17	14	3	0	102
Robert Edwards*, NE	12	9	3	0	72
Joey Galloway, Sea.	12	0	10	2	72
Keyshawn Johnson, NYJ	11	1	10	0	66
Ed McCaffrey, Den.	10	0	10	0	62†
Marshall Faulk, Ind.	10	6	4	0	60
Shannon Sharpe, Den.	10	0	10	0	60
Ricky Watters, Sea.	9	9	0	0	56†
Tim Brown, Oak.	9	0	9	0	54
Curtis Martin, NYJ	9	8	1	0	54
Eric Moulds, Buf.	9	0	9	0	54

Five tied with 8 each for 48 pts.

NFC	TD	Rush	Rec	Ret	Pts
Randy Moss*, Min.	17	0	17	0	106#
Jamal Anderson, Atl.	16	14	2	0	98†
Terrell Owens, SF	15	1	14	0	92†
Emmitt Smith, Dal.	15	13	2	0	90
Antonio Freeman, GB	14	0	14	0	86†
Cris Carter, Min.	12	0	12	0	72
Terance Mathis, Atl.	11	0	11	0	66
Leroy Hoard, Min.	10	9	1	0	60
Adrian Murrell, Ari.	10	8	2	0	60
Jerry Rice, SF	9	0	9	0	58#
Garrison Hearst, SF	9	7	2	0	56†
Leslie Shepherd, Was.	9	1	8	0	56†
Mike Alstott, TB	9	8	1	0	54

Four tied with 8 each for 48 pts.

† Includes one 2-point conversion.
# Includes two 2-point conversions.

Kickers

AFC	PAT	FG	Long	Pts
Steve Christie, Buf.	41/41	33/41	52	140
Al Del Greco, Ten.	28/28	36/39	48	136
Jason Elam, Den.	58/58	23/27	63	127
Adam Vinatieri, NE	32/32	31/39	55	127
John Hall, NYJ	45/46	25/35	54	120
Pete Stoyanovich, KC	34/34	27/32	53	115
Mike Hollis, Jax.	45/45	21/26	47	108
Mike Vanderjagt*, Ind.	23/23	27/31	53	104
Norm Johnson, Pit.	21/21	26/31	49	99
Olindo Mare, Mia.	33/34	22/27	48	99
Todd Peterson, Sea.	41/41	19/24	51	98
John Carney, SD	19/19	26/30	54	97
Matt Stover, Bal.	24/24	21/28	48	87
Greg Davis, Oak.	31/31	17/27	51	82
Doug Pelfrey, Cin.	21/21	19/27	51	78

NFC	PAT	FG	Long	Pts
Gary Anderson, Min.	59/59	35/35	53	164
Ryan Longwell, GB	41/43	29/33	45	128
Richie Cunningham, Dal.	40/40	29/35	54	127
Morten Andersen, Atl.	51/52	23/28	53	120
Jason Hanson, Det.	27/29	29/33	51	114
Wade Richey*, SF	49/51	18/27	46	103
Brad Daluiso, NYG	32/32	21/27	51	95
Michael Husted, TB	29/30	21/28	52	92
John Kasay, Car.	35/37	19/26	56	92
Doug Brien, NO	31/31	20/22	56	91
Jeff Jaeger, Chi.	27/28	21/26	52	90
Jeff Wilkins, St.L.	25/26	20/26	57	85
Joe Nedney, Ari.	30/30	13/19	53	69
Cary Blanchard, Was.	30/31	11/17	54	63
Chris Boniol, Phi.	15/17	14/21	50	57

Interceptions

AFC	No	Yds	Long	TD
Ty Law, NE	9	133	59-td	1
Terrell Buckley, Mia.	8	157	61	1
Sam Madison, Mia.	8	114	35	0
Shawn Springs, Sea.	7	142	56-td	2
Five tied with 6 each.				

NFC	No	Yds	Long	TD
Kwamie Lassiter, Ari.	8	80	29	0
Jimmy Hitchcock, Min.	7	242	79-td	3
Ray Buchanan, Atl.	7	102	34	0
Sammy Knight, NO.	6	171	91-td	2
Six tied with 5 each.				

Sacks

AFC	No
Michael Sinclair, Sea.	16.5
Michael McCrary, Bal.	14.5
Derrick Thomas, KC	12.0
Jason Gildon, Pit.	11.0
Lance Johnstone, Oak.	11.0

NFC	No
Reggie White, GB	16.0
Chris Doleman, SF	15.0
Kevin Greene, Car.	15.0
Mike Strahan, NYG	15.0
Hugh Douglas, Phi.	12.5

Punting

AFC	No	Yds	Lg	Avg	In20
Craig Hentrich, Ten.	69	3258	71	47.2	18
Tom Rouen, Den.	66	3097	76	46.9	14
Chris Gardocki, Ind.	79	3583	62	45.4	23
Bryan Barker, Jax.	85	3824	65	45.0	28
Lee Johnson, Cin.	69	3083	69	44.7	14

NFC	No	Yds	Lg	Avg	In20
Mark Royals, NO	88	4017	64	45.6	26
Brad Maynard, NYG	101	4566	63	45.2	33
Mitch Berger, Min.	55	2458	67	44.7	17
Rick Tuten, St.L	95	4202	64	44.2	16
Matt Turk, Was.	93	4103	69	44.1	33

Punt Returns

(Minimum of 20 returns)

AFC	No	FC	Yards	Avg	Long	TD
Reggie Barlow, Jax.	43	14	555	12.9	85-td	1
Jermaine Lewis, Bal.	32	10	405	12.7	87-td	2
Terrell Buckley, Mia.	29	3	354	12.2	35	0
Latario Rachal, SD	32	8	387	12.1	56	0
Desmond Howard, Oak.	45	13	541	12.0	75-td	0

NFC	No	FC	Yds	Avg	Long	TD
Deion Sanders, Dal.	24	8	375	15.6	69-td	2
Jacquez Green*, TB	30	9	453	15.1	95-td	1
Andre Hastings, NO	22	17	307	14.0	76	0
Glyn Milburn, Chi.	25	15	291	11.6	93-td	1
Brian Mitchell, Was.	44	18	506	11.5	47	0

Kickoff Returns

(Minimum of 20 returns)

AFC	No	Yards	Avg	Long	TD
Corey Harris, Bal.	35	965	27.6	95-td	1
Steve Broussard, Sea.	29	781	26.9	90-td	1
Vaughn Hebron, Den.	46	1216	26.4	95-td	1
Tremain Mack, Cin.	45	1165	25.9	97-td	1
John Avery*, Mia.	43	1085	25.2	55	0

NFC	No	Yards	Avg	Long	TD
Terry Fair*, Det.	51	1428	28.0	105-td	2
Tim Dwight*, Atl.	36	973	27.0	93-td	1
Roell Preston, GB	57	1497	26.3	101-td	2
Michael Bates, Car.	58	1467	25.3	99-td	1
Glyn Milburn, Chi.	62	1550	25.0	94-td	2

Single Game Highs

(†) indicates overtime game.

Passing

AFC	Att/Cmp	Yds	TD
Drew Bledsoe, NE vs. Mia. (11/23)	28/54	423	2
Vinny Testaverde, NYJ vs. Sea. (12/6)	42/63	418	2
Glenn Foley, NYJ vs. SF (9/6)†	30/58	415	3
John Elway, Den. vs. KC (12/6)	22/32	400	2
Mark Brunell, Jax. vs. Bal. (9/20)	25/34	376	2

NFC	Att/Cmp	Yds	TD
Jake Plummer, Ari. vs. Dal. (11/15)	31/56	465	3
Troy Aikman, Dal. vs. Min. (11/26)	34/57	455	1
Randall Cunningham, Min. vs. GB (10/5)	20/32	442	4
Jake Plummer, Ari. vs. NO (12/20)	32/44	394	0
Brett Favre, GB vs. Car. (9/27)	27/45	388	5

Rushing

AFC	Car	Yds	TD
Priest Holmes, Bal. vs. Cin. (11/22)	36	227	1
Terrell Davis, Den. vs. Sea. (10/11)	30	208	1
Robert Edwards*, NE vs. St.L (12/13)	24	196	0
Marshall Faulk, Ind. vs. Bal. (11/29)	17	192	1
Terrell Davis, Den. vs. Dal. (9/13)	23	191	3

NFC	Car	Yds	TD
Garrison Hearst, SF vs. Det. (12/14)	24	198	1
Jamal Anderson, Atl. vs. St.L (11/29)	31	188	1
Garrison Hearst, SF vs. NYJ (9/6)†	20	187	2
Barry Sanders, Det. vs. Cin. (9/13)†	26	185	3
Robert Smith, Min. vs. St.L (9/13)	23	179	2

Receiving Yards

AFC	Ct	Yds	TD
Carl Pickens, Cin. vs. Pit. (10/11)	13	204	1
Eric Moulds, Buf. vs. Cin. (12/6)	6	196	2
Terry Glenn, NE vs. Pit. (12/6)	9	193	1
Eric Moulds, Buf. vs. NE (11/29)	8	177	1
Derrick Alexander, KC vs. SD (11/22)	5	173	1

NFC	Ct	Yds	TD
Terance Mathis, Atl. vs. NO (12/13)	6	198	2
Antonio Freeman, GB vs. SF (11/1)	7	193	2
Mushin Muhammad, Car. vs. NO (9/13)	9	192	1
Isaac Bruce, St.L vs. Min. (9/13)	11	192	1
Frank Sanders, Ari. vs. Dal. (11/15)	11	190	1

NFL Bests

Longest Field Goal
63 yds .... Jason Elam, Den. vs. Jax. (10/25)

Longest Run from Scrimmage
96 yds .... Garrison Hearst, SF vs. NYJ (9/6), TD

Longest Pass Play
98 yds .... Charlie Batch* to Johnnie Morton, Det. vs. Chi. (10/4) TD

Longest Interception Return
94 yds .... Eric Turner, Oak. vs. Den. (9/20), TD

Longest Punt Return
95 yds .... Jacquez Green*, TB vs. GB (9/13), TD

Longest Kickoff Return
105 yds .... Terry Fair, Det. vs. TB (9/28), TD

NFL Regular Season Team Leaders
Offensive Downs

AFC	Tot	First Downs Rush	Pass	Pen	3rd Downs Made	Att	Pct	4th Downs Made	Att	Pct
Denver	347	135	186	26	90	207	43.5	4	10	40.0
NY Jets	338	99	207	32	103	224	46.0	9	16	56.3
Buffalo	319	115	176	28	97	219	44.3	3	8	37.5
Tennessee	308	118	171	19	84	210	40.0	4	11	36.4
Indianapolis	298	77	190	31	71	202	35.1	4	10	40.0
Kansas City	289	103	153	33	70	220	31.8	13	25	52.0
Jacksonville	287	111	153	23	94	220	42.7	4	8	50.0
New England	281	68	184	29	90	237	38.0	10	21	47.6
Oakland	273	89	156	28	71	225	31.6	6	13	46.2
San Diego	272	95	146	31	78	237	32.9	8	17	47.1
Cincinnati	271	92	148	31	76	224	33.9	11	29	37.9
Miami	269	73	176	20	81	226	35.8	6	12	50.0
Pittsburgh	268	106	135	27	87	224	38.8	3	15	20.0
Seattle	267	92	144	31	54	195	27.7	6	17	35.3
Baltimore	243	86	140	17	64	207	30.9	6	15	40.0

NFC	Tot	First Downs Rush	Pass	Pen	3rd Downs Made	Att	Pct	4th Downs Made	Att	Pct
San Francisco	381	129	223	29	96	211	45.5	4	9	44.4
Minnesota	335	98	210	27	107	208	51.4	3	3	100.0
Green Bay	329	93	210	26	99	218	45.4	5	13	38.5
Atlanta	319	111	175	33	83	199	41.7	1	3	33.3
Arizona	315	98	179	38	76	218	34.9	10	18	55.6
Dallas	308	125	154	29	76	206	36.9	8	12	66.7
Washington	295	84	186	25	68	215	31.6	5	15	33.3
St. Louis	281	81	164	36	77	222	34.7	9	16	56.3
Detroit	278	94	160	24	72	211	34.1	10	20	50.0
Chicago	264	89	154	21	75	215	34.9	11	25	44.0
NY Giants	263	104	129	30	70	229	30.6	8	18	44.4
Tampa Bay	262	111	139	12	93	230	40.4	6	14	42.9
Carolina	261	68	171	22	80	216	37.0	10	21	47.6
Philadelphia	259	86	141	32	80	240	33.3	7	23	30.4
New Orleans	258	67	165	26	77	215	35.8	6	17	35.3

Overall Club Rankings

Combined AFC and NFC rankings by yards gained on offense and yards given up on defense. Teams are ranked by offense with AFC teams in italics.

	Offense Rush	Pass	Rank	Defense Rush	Pass	Rank
San Francisco	1	2	1	10	29	23
Minnesota	11	1	2	11	19	13
Denver	2	7	3	3	26	11
NY Jets	13	4	4	14	9	7
Green Bay	25	3	5	4	10	4
Buffalo	3	12	6	5	14	6
Atlanta	6	11	7	2	21	8
Dallas	8	9	8	12	22	18
Tennessee	9	15	9	9	20	16
Jacksonville	5	20	10	22	23	25
New England	27	5	11	7	25	20
Indianapolis	26	6	12	29	16	29
Arizona	21	8	13	20	17	21
Detroit	10	19	14	25	8	15
Washington	18	13	15	28	5	24
Miami	24	10	16	6	6	3
Cincinnati	19	17	17	30	12	28
Oakland	16	21	18	15	4	5
Kansas City	23	16	19	18	7	9
Carolina	28	14	20	26	28	30
Chicago	17	23	21	19	15	14
Tampa Bay	4	27	22	8	2	2
Seattle	22	24	23	21	27	27
San Diego	15	26	24	1	11	1
Pittsburgh	7	29	25	13	18	12
Baltimore	20	25	26	17	24	22
St. Louis	29	22	27	24	3	10
New Orleans	30	18	28	16	30	26
NY Giants	12	28	29	23	13	19
Philadelphia	14	30	30	27	1	17

Takeaways/Giveaways

AFC	Takeaways Int	Fum	Total	Giveaways Int	Fum	Total	Net Diff
Buffalo	18	13	31	14	6	20	+11
Denver	19	11	30	14	6	20	+10
Jacksonville	13	17	30	12	8	20	+10
Miami	29	7	36	16	12	28	+8
Seattle	24	18	42	18	16	34	+8
New England	24	7	31	17	7	24	+7
NY Jets	21	9	30	13	11	24	+6
Kansas City	13	20	33	18	14	32	+1
Tennessee	12	7	19	10	9	19	0
Cincinnati	13	7	20	12	10	22	-2
Pittsburgh	16	13	29	20	12	32	-3
Baltimore	17	6	23	15	15	30	-7
Oakland	21	14	35	25	18	43	-8
Indianapolis	8	11	19	28	5	33	-14
San Diego	20	7	27	34	17	51	-24

NFC	Takeaways Int	Fum	Total	Giveaways Int	Fum	Total	Net Diff
Atlanta	19	25	44	15	9	24	+20
Minnesota	19	15	34	16	4	20	+14
Dallas	14	12	26	8	7	15	+11
Arizona	20	19	39	20	16	36	+3
San Francisco	21	12	33	15	15	30	+3
NY Giants	19	7	26	15	9	24	+2
New Orleans	21	11	32	19	14	33	-1
Carolina	19	14	33	18	17	35	-2
Detroit	12	9	21	13	12	25	-4
Tampa Bay	12	14	26	18	13	31	-5
Chicago	14	14	28	13	21	34	-6
Washington	13	8	21	14	15	29	-8
Philadelphia	9	8	17	18	8	26	-9
St. Louis	16	7	23	18	15	33	-10
Green Bay	13	10	23	23	11	34	-11

AFC Team by Team Statistics

Players with more than one team during the regular season are listed with club they ended season with; (*) indicates rookies.

Baltimore Ravens

Passing (5 Att)	Att	Cmp	Pct	Yds	TD	Rate
Jim Harbaugh	293	164	56.0	1839	12	72.9
Eric Zeier	181	107	59.1	1312	4	82.0

Interceptions: Harbaugh 11, Zeier 3.

Top Receivers	No	Yds	Avg	Long	TD
Priest Holmes	43	260	6.0	25	0
Jermaine Lewis	41	784	19.1	73-td	6
Michael Jackson	38	477	12.6	53	0
Eric Green	34	422	12.4	56	1
Floyd Turner	32	512	16.0	66-td	5
Roosevelt Potts	30	168	5.6	18	2

Top Rushers	Car	Yds	Avg	Long	TD
Priest Holmes	233	1008	4.3	56	7
Errict Rhett	44	180	4.1	46	0
Jim Harbaugh	39	172	4.4	15	0
Roosevelt Potts	36	115	3.2	33	0
Jay Graham	35	109	3.1	12	0

Most Touchdowns	TD	Run	Rec	Ret	Pts
Jermaine Lewis	8	0	6	2	48
Priest Holmes	7	7	0	0	42
Floyd Turner	5	0	5	0	34

Three tied with two each.

2-Pt. Conversions: (2-5) Turner 2.

Kicking	PAT/Att	FG/Att	Lg	Pts
Matt Stover	24/24	21/28	48	87

Punts (10 or more)	No	Yds	Long	Avg	In20
Kyle Richardson	90	3948	67	43.9	

Most Interceptions		Most Sacks	
Rod Woodson	6	Michael McCrary	14½

Buffalo Bills

Passing (5 Att)	Att	Cmp	Pct	Yds	TD	Rate
Doug Flutie	354	202	57.1	2711	20	87.4
Rob Johnson	107	67	62.6	910	8	102.9

Interceptions: Flutie 11, Johnson 3.

Top Receivers	No	Yds	Avg	Long	TD
Eric Moulds	67	1368	20.4	84-td	9
Andre Reed	63	795	12.6	67-td	5
Kevin Williams	29	392	13.5	55	1
Thurman Thomas	26	220	8.5	26	1
Jay Riemersma	25	288	11.5	28	6
Quinn Early	19	217	11.4	37	1
Sam Gash	19	165	8.7	20	3

Top Rushers	Car	Yds	Avg	Long	TD
Antowain Smith	300	1124	3.7	30	8
Thurman Thomas	93	381	4.1	17-td	2
Doug Flutie	48	248	5.2	23	1
Jonathan Linton*	45	195	4.3	20	1
Rob Johnson	23	137	6.0	32	1

Most Touchdowns	TD	Run	Rec	Ret	Pts
Eric Moulds	9	0	9	0	54
Antowain Smith	8	8	0	0	48
Jay Riemersma	6	0	6	0	36
Andre Reed	5	0	5	0	30
Sam Gash	3	0	3	0	18
Thurman Thomas	3	2	1	0	18

2-Pt. Conversions: (0-2).

Kicking	PAT/Att	FG/Att	Lg	Pts
Steve Christie	41/41	33/41	52	140

Punts (10 or more)	No	Yds	Long	Avg	In20
Chris Mohr	69	2882	57	41.8	18

Most Interceptions		Most Sacks	
Kurt Schulz	6	Bruce Smith	10

Cincinnati Bengals

Passing (5 Att)	Att	Cmp	Pct	Yds	TD	Rate
Neil O'Donnell	343	212	61.8	2216	15	90.2
Jeff Blake	93	51	54.8	739	3	78.2
Paul Justin	63	34	54.0	426	1	60.7
Eric Kresser	21	10	47.6	164	1	50.6

Interceptions: O'Donnell 4, Blake 3, Justin 3, Kresser 2.

Top Receivers	No	Yds	Avg	Long	TD
Carl Pickens	82	1023	12.5	67-td	5
Darnay Scott	51	817	16.0	70-td	7
Corey Dillon	28	178	6.4	41	1
Eric Bieniemy	27	153	5.7	15	0

Top Rushers	Car	Yds	Avg	Long	TD
Corey Dillon	262	1130	4.3	66	4
Brandon Bennett	77	243	3.2	17	2
Ray Zellars	56	162	2.9	15-td	1
NO	56	162	2.9	15-td	1
CIN	0	0	0.0	0	0

Signed: Zellars on Dec. 9 (waived by New Orleans, Dec. 8).

Most Touchdowns	TD	Run	Rec	Ret	Pts
Darnay Scott	7	0	7	0	42
Carl Pickens	5	0	5	0	32
Corey Dillon	5	4	1	0	30
Damon Gibson*	4	0	3	1	24

2-Pt. Conversion: (2-9) Justin, Pickens.

Kicking	PAT/Att	FG/Att	Lg	Pts
Doug Pelfrey	21/21	19/27	51	78

Punts (10 or more)	No	Yds	Long	Avg	In20
Lee Johnson	69	3083	69	44.7	14
Brad Costello*	10	495	73	49.5	0

Waived: Johnson on Dec. 7.

Most Interceptions		Most Sacks	
Artrell Hawkins*	3	Reinard Wilson	6
Sam Shade	3		

Denver Broncos

Passing (5 Att)	Att	Cmp	Pct	Yds	TD	Rate
John Elway	356	210	59.0	2806	22	93.0
Bubby Brister	131	78	59.5	986	10	99.0

Interceptions: Elway 10, Brister 3.

Top Receivers	No	Yds	Avg	Long	TD
Rod Smith	86	1222	14.2	58	6
Ed McCaffrey	64	1053	16.5	48	10
Shannon Sharpe	64	768	12.0	38-td	10
Terrell Davis	25	217	8.7	35	2

Top Rushers	Car	Yds	Avg	Long	TD
Terrell Davis	392	2008	5.1	70	21
Derek Loville	53	161	3.0	12	2
Bubby Brister	19	102	5.4	38-td	1
John Elway	37	94	2.5	16	1

Most Touchdowns	TD	Run	Rec	Ret	Pts
Terrell Davis	23	21	2	0	138
Ed McCaffrey	10	0	10	0	62
Shannon Sharpe	10	0	10	0	60
Rod Smith	7	0	6	1	42

2-Pt. Conversions: (1-3) McCaffrey.

Kicking	PAT/Att	FG/Att	Lg	Pts
Jason Elam	58/58	23/27	63	127

Punts (10 or more)	No	Yds	Long	Avg	In20
Tom Rouen	66	3097	76	46.9	14

Most Interceptions		Most Sacks	
Darrien Gordon	4	Trevor Pryce	8½
		Maa Tanuvasa	8½

Indianapolis Colts

Passing (5 Att)	**Att**	**Cmp**	**Pct**	**Yds**	**TD**	**Rate**
Peyton Manning*	...575	326	56.7	3739	26	71.2

Interceptions: Manning 28.

Top Receivers	**No**	**Yds**	**Avg**	**Long**	**TD**
Marshall Faulk	86	908	10.6	78-td	4
Marvin Harrison	59	776	13.2	61-td	7
Jerome Pathon*	50	511	10.2	45	1
Torrance Small	45	681	15.1	53	7
Ken Dilger	31	303	9.8	27	1
Marcus Pollard	24	309	12.9	44-td	4
E.G. Green*	15	177	11.8	25	1

Top Rushers	**Car**	**Yds**	**Avg**	**Long**	**TD**
Marshall Faulk	324	1319	4.1	68-td	6
Peyton Manning*	15	62	4.1	15	0
Lamont Warren	25	61	2.4	14	1
Keith Elias	8	24	3.0	8	0

Most Touchdowns	**TD**	**Run**	**Rec**	**Ret**	**Pts**
Marshall Faulk	10	6	4	0	60
Marvin Harrison	7	0	7	0	44
Torrance Small	7	0	7	0	42
Marcus Pollard	4	0	4	0	28
Lamont Warren	2	1	1	0	12

2-Pt. Conversions: (4-10) Pollard 2, Dilger, Harrison.

Kicking	**PAT/Att**	**FG/Att**	**Lg**	**Pts**
Mike Vanderjagt*	....23/23	27/31	53	104

Punts (10 or more)	**No**	**Yds**	**Long**	**Avg**	**In20**
Chris Gardocki	79	3583	62	45.4	23

Most Interceptions   **Most Sacks**
Eight tied with 1 each.   Ellis Johnson 8

Jacksonville Jaguars

Passing (5 Att)	**Att**	**Cmp**	**Pct**	**Yds**	**TD**	**Rate**
Mark Brunell	354	208	58.8	2601	20	89.9
Jonathan Quinn*	64	34	53.1	387	2	62.4
Jamie Martin	45	27	60.0	355	2	99.8

Interceptions: Brunell 9, Quinn 3.

Top Receivers	**No**	**Yds**	**Avg**	**Long**	**TD**
Jimmy Smith	78	1182	15.2	72-td	8
Keenan McCardell	64	892	13.9	67-td	6
Fred Taylor*	44	421	9.6	78-td	3
Pete Mitchell	38	363	9.6	38	2
Reggie Barlow	11	168	15.3	31	0
Daimon Shelton	10	79	7.9	19	0
Damon Jones	8	90	11.3	31-td	4

Top Rushers	**Car**	**Yds**	**Avg**	**Long**	**TD**
Fred Taylor*	264	1223	4.6	77-td	14
James Stewart	53	217	4.1	30	2
Mark Brunell	49	192	3.9	18	0
Tavian Banks*	26	140	5.4	51	1
George Jones	39	121	3.1	21	0

Signed: Jones on Sept. 23.

Most Touchdowns	**TD**	**Run**	**Rec**	**Ret**	**Pts**
Fred Taylor*	17	14	3	0	102
Jimmy Smith	8	0	8	0	48
Keenan McCardell	6	0	6	0	38
Damon Jones	4	0	4	0	24
James Stewart	3	2	1	0	18

2-Pt. Conversions: (1-2) McCardell.

Kicking	**PAT/Att**	**FG/Att**	**Lg**	**Pts**
Mike Hollis	..............45/45	21/26	47	108

Punts (10 or more)	**No**	**Yds**	**Long**	**Avg**	**In20**
Bryan Barker	85	3824	65	45.0	28

Most Interceptions   **Most Sacks**
Aaron Beasley 3   Joel Smeenge 7½
Chris Hudson 3

Kansas City Chiefs

Passing (5 Att)	**Att**	**Cmp**	**Pct**	**Yds**	**TD**	**Rate**
Rich Gannon	354	206	58.2	2305	10	80.1
Elvis Grbac	188	98	52.1	1142	5	53.1

Interceptions: Grbac 12, Gannon 6.

Top Receivers	**No**	**Yds**	**Avg**	**Long**	**TD**
Kimble Anders	64	462	7.2	29	2
Tony Gonzalez	59	621	10.5	32	2
Derrick Alexander	54	992	18.4	65	4
Andre Rison	40	542	13.6	80-td	5
Kevin Lockett	19	281	14.8	38	0
Donnell Bennett	16	91	5.7	14	1

Top Rushers	**Car**	**Yds**	**Avg**	**Long**	**TD**
Donnell Bennett	..148	527	3.6	26	5
Bam Morris	132	489	3.7	38	8
CHI	3	8	2.7	6	0
KC	129	481	3.7	38	8
Kimble Anders	58	230	4.0	20	1
Rich Gannon	44	168	3.8	21	3

Acquired: Morris from Chicago for 1999 draft pick (Oct. 13).

Most Touchdowns	**TD**	**Run**	**Rec**	**Ret**	**Pts**
Bam Morris	8	8	0	0	48
CHI	0	0	0	0	0
KC	8	8	0	0	48
Donnell Bennett	6	5	1	0	36
Andre Rison	5	0	5	0	30
Derrick Alexander	4	0	4	0	24

2-Pt. Conversions: (0-1).

Kicking	**PAT/Att**	**FG/Att**	**Lg**	**Pts**
Pete Stoyanovich	.........34/34	27/32	53	115

Punts (10 or more)	**No**	**Yds**	**Long**	**Avg**	**In20**
Louie Aguiar	75	3226	59	43.0	20

Most Interceptions   **Most Sacks**
James Hasty 4   Derrick Thomas 12

Miami Dolphins

Passing (5 Att)	**Att**	**Cmp**	**Pct**	**Yds**	**TD**	**Rate**
Dan Marino	537	310	57.7	3497	23	80.0
Damon Huard	9	6	66.7	85	0	57.4

Interceptions: Marino 15, Huard 1.

Top Receivers	**No**	**Yds**	**Avg**	**Long**	**TD**
O.J. McDuffie	90	1050	11.7	61-td	7
Oronde Gadsden	48	713	14.9	50	7
Lamar Thomas	43	603	14.0	56-td	5
Troy Drayton	30	334	11.1	35	3
Ed Perry	25	255	10.2	46	0

Top Rushers	**Car**	**Yds**	**Avg**	**Long**	**TD**
Karim Abdul-Jabbar	...270	960	3.6	45	6
John Avery*	143	503	3.5	44	2
Bernie Parmalee	8	20	2.5	10	0
Stanley Pritchett	6	19	3.2	11	1

Most Touchdowns	**TD**	**Run**	**Rec**	**Ret**	**Pts**
Oronde Gadsden	7	0	7	0	42
O.J. McDuffie	7	0	7	0	42
Karim Abdul-Jabbar	6	6	0	0	36
Lamar Thomas	5	0	5	0	30

2-Pt. Conversions: (0-3).

Kicking	**PAT/Att**	**FG/Att**	**Lg**	**Pts**
Olindo Mare	.............33/34	22/27	48	99

Punts (10 or more)	**No**	**Yds**	**Long**	**Avg**	**In20**
Klaus Wilmsmeyer	93	3949	57	42.5	23

Most Interceptions   **Most Sacks**
Terrell Buckley | 8   Trace Armstrong 10½
Sam Madison 8

New England Patriots

Passing (5 Att)	Att	Cmp	Pct	Yds	TD	Rate
Drew Bledsoe	.481	263	54.7	3633	20	80.9
Scott Zolak	.75	32	42.7	371	3	54.9

Interceptions: Bledsoe 14, Zolak 3.

Top Receivers	No	Yds	Avg	Long	TD
Ben Coates	.67	668	10.0	33	6
Terry Glenn	.50	792	15.8	86-td	3
Robert Edwards*	.35	331	9.5	46	3
Shawn Jefferson	.34	771	22.7	61-td	2
Tony Simmons*	.23	474	20.6	63-td	3
Troy Brown	.23	346	15.0	52	1

Top Rushers	Car	Yds	Avg	Long	TD
Robert Edwards*	.291	1115	3.8	53	9
Sedrick Shaw	.48	236	4.9	71	0
Derrick Cullors	.18	48	2.7	15	0
Drew Bledsoe	.28	44	1.6	10	0

Most Touchdowns	TD	Run	Rec	Ret	Pts
Robert Edwards*	.12	9	3	0	72
Ben Coates	.6	0	6	0	36
Terry Glenn	.3	0	3	0	18
Tony Simmons*	.3	0	3	0	18

Three tied with two each.

2-Pt. Conversions: (1-3) Adam Vinatieri.

Kicking	PAT/Att	FG/Att	Lg	Pts
Adam Vinatieri	.32/32	31/39	55	127

Punts (10 or more)	No	Yds	Long	Avg	In20
Tom Tupa	.74	3294	64	44.5	13

Most Interceptions		Most Sacks	
Ty Law	.9	Henry Thomas	6½

New York Jets

Passing (5 Att)	Att	Cmp	Pct	Yds	TD	Rate
Vinny Testaverde	.421	259	61.5	3256	29	101.6
Glenn Foley	.108	58	53.7	749	4	64.9

Interceptions: Testaverde 7, Foley 6.

Top Receivers	No	Yds	Avg	Long	TD
Keyshawn Johnson	.83	1131	13.6	41-td	10
Wayne Chrebet	.75	1083	14.4	43-td	8
Curtis Martin	.43	365	8.5	23	1
Kyle Brady	.30	315	10.5	35	5
Keith Byars	.26	258	9.9	29	3
Dedric Ward	.25	477	19.1	71-td	4

Top Rushers	No	Yds	Avg	Long	TD
Curtis Martin	.369	1287	3.5	60-td	8
Leon Johnson	.41	185	4.5	40	2
Jerald Sowell	.40	164	4.1	33	0

Most Touchdowns	TD	Run	Rec	Ret	Pts
Keyshawn Johnson	.11	1	10	0	66
Curtis Martin	.9	8	1	0	54
Wayne Chrebet	.8	0	8	0	48
Kyle Brady	.5	0	5	0	30

2-Pt. Conversions: (0-3)

Kicking	PAT/Att	FG/Att	Lg	Pts
John Hall	.45/46	25/35	54	120

Punts (10 or more)	No	Yds	Long	Avg	In20
John Kidd	41	1686	57	41.1	9
DET.	13	520	54	40.0	1
NYJ	28	1166	57	41.6	8
Brian Hansen	31	1233	62	39.8	6

Signed: Hansen on Sept. 13; Kidd on Nov. 3 (released by Detroit, Oct. 25).
Waived: Hansen on Nov. 3.

Most Interceptions		Most Sacks	
Aaron Glenn	.6	Mo Lewis	7

Oakland Raiders

Passing (5 Att)	Att	Cmp	Pct	Yds	TD	Rate
Donald Hollas	.260	135	51.9	1754	10	60.6
Jeff George	.169	93	55.0	1186	4	72.7
Wade Wilson	.88	52	59.1	568	7	85.8

Interceptions: Hollas 16, George 5, Wilson 4.

Top Receivers	No	Yds	Avg	Long	TD
Tim Brown	.81	1012	12.5	49	9
James Jett	.45	882	19.6	75-td	6
Rickey Dudley	.36	549	15.3	32	5
John Ritchie*	.29	225	7.8	31	0
Harvey Williams	.26	173	6.7	15	0
Napoleon Kaufman	.25	191	7.6	39	0
Terry Mickens	.24	346	14.4	32	1

Top Rushers	Car	Yds	Avg	Long	TD
Napoleon Kaufman	.217	921	4.2	80-td	2
Harvey Williams	.128	496	3.9	25-td	2
Randy Jordan	.47	159	3.4	23	1
Donald Hollas	.29	120	4.1	14	1

Most Touchdowns	TD	Run	Rec	Ret	Pts
Tim Brown	.9	0	9	0	54
James Jett	.6	0	6	0	36
Rickey Dudley	.5	0	5	0	32

Three tied with two each.

2-Pt. Conversions: (1-3) Dudley.

Kicking	PAT/Att	FG/Att	Lg	Pts
Greg Davis	.31/31	17/27	51	82

Punts (10 or more)	No	Yds	Long	Avg	In20
Leo Araguz	.98	4256	64	43.4	29

Most Interceptions		Most Sacks	
Charles Woodson*	.5	Lance Johnstone	11
Eric Allen	.5		

Pittsburgh Steelers

Passing (5 Att)	Att	Cmp	Pct	Yds	TD	Rate
Kordell Stewart	.458	252	55.0	2560	11	62.9
Mike Tomczak	.30	21	70.0	204	2	83.2

Interceptions: Stewart 18, Tomczak 2.

Top Receivers	No	Yds	Avg	Long	TD
Courtney Hawkins	.66	751	11.4	53	1
Charles Johnson	.65	815	12.5	55-td	7
Will Blackwell	.32	297	9.3	24-td	1
Mark Bruener	.19	157	8.3	20	2
Jerome Bettis	.16	90	5.6	26	0
Hines Ward*	.15	246	16.4	45	0
Jon Witman	.13	74	5.7	15	0

Top Rushers	Car	Yds	Avg	Long	TD
Jerome Bettis	.316	1185	3.8	42	3
Kordell Stewart	.81	406	5.0	56	2
Richard Huntley	.55	242	4.4	48	1
Fred McAfee	.18	111	6.2	14	0

Most Touchdowns	TD	Run	Rec	Ret	Pts
Charles Johnson	.7	0	7	0	46
Jerome Bettis	.3	3	0	0	18
C. Fuamatu-Ma'afala*	.3	2	1	0	18

Three tied with two each.

2-Pt. Conversions: (3-3) C. Johnson 2, Blackwell.

Kicking	PAT/Att	FG/Att	Lg	Pts
Norm Johnson	.21/21	26/31	49	99
Matt George*	.2/2	0/1	—	2

Punts (10 or more)	No	Yds	Long	Avg	In20
Josh Miller	.81	3530	73	43.6	34

Most Interceptions		Most Sacks	
Dewayne Washington	.5	Jason Gildon	11

San Diego Chargers

Passing (5 Att)

	Att	Cmp	Pct	Yds	TD	Rate
Craig Whelihan	320	149	46.6	1803	8	48.0
Ryan Leaf*	245	111	45.3	1289	2	39.0

Interceptions: Whelihan 19, Leaf 15.

Top Receivers	No	Yds	Avg	Long	TD
Freddie Jones	57	602	10.6	28	3
Charlie Jones	46	699	15.2	56	3
Bryan Still	43	605	14.1	67	2
Mikhael Ricks*	30	450	15.0	39-td	2
Terrell Fletcher	30	188	6.3	22	0
Ryan Thelwell*	16	268	16.8	55	1
Natrone Means	16	91	5.7	22	0

Top Rushers	No	Yds	Avg	Long	TD
Natrone Means	212	883	4.2	72-td	5
Terrell Fletcher	153	543	3.5	21	5
Tremayne Stephens*	35	122	3.5	12	1
Ryan Leaf*	27	80	3.0	20	0

Most Touchdowns	TD	Run	Rec	Ret	Pts
Terrell Fletcher	5	5	0	0	30
Natrone Means	5	5	0	0	30
Freddie Jones	3	0	3	0	20
Charlie Jones	3	0	3	0	18

2-Pt. Conversions: (2-4) F. Jones, Whelihan.

Kicking	PAT/Att	FG/Att	Lg	Pts
John Carney	19/19	26/30	54	97

Punts (10 or more)	No	Yds	Long	Avg	In20
Darren Bennett	95	4174	65	43.9	27

Most Interceptions
Greg Jackson 6

Most Sacks
Norman Hand 6

Seattle Seahawks

Passing (5 Att)

	Att	Cmp	Pct	Yds	TD	Rate
Warren Moon	258	145	56.2	1632	11	76.6
Jon Kitna	172	98	57.0	1177	7	72.3
John Friesz	49	29	59.2	409	2	82.8

Interceptions: Moon and Kitna 8, Friesz 2.

Top Receivers	No	Yds	Avg	Long	TD
Joey Galloway	65	1047	16.1	81-td	10
Mike Pritchard	58	742	12.8	50-td	3
Ricky Watters	52	373	7.2	24	0
Christian Fauria	37	377	10.2	25	1
James McKnight	21	346	16.5	59-td	2
Brian Blades	15	184	12.3	47	0

Top Rushers	Car	Yds	Avg	Long	TD
Ricky Watters	319	1239	3.9	39-td	9
Ahman Green*	35	209	6.0	64	1
Jon Kitna	20	67	3.4	21	1
Mack Strong	15	47	3.1	9	0

Most Touchdowns	TD	Run	Rec	Ret	Pts
Joey Galloway	12	0	10	2	72
Ricky Watters	9	9	0	0	56
Mike Pritchard	3	0	3	0	20
Shawn Springs	3	0	0	3	18

2-Pt. Conversions: (2-4) Watters, Pritchard.

Kicking	PAT/Att	FG/Att	Lg	Pts
Todd Peterson	41/41	19/24	51	98

Punts (10 or more)	No	Yds	Lg	Avg	In20
Jeff Feagles	81	3568	59	44.0	27

Most Interceptions
Shawn Springs 7

Most Sacks
Michael Sinclair 16½

Tennessee Oilers

Passing (5 Att)

	Att	Cmp	Pct	Yds	TD	Rate
Steve McNair	492	289	58.7	3228	15	80.1
Dave Krieg	21	12	57.1	199	0	89.2

Interceptions: McNair 10.

Top Receivers	No	Yds	Avg	Long	TD
Frank Wycheck	70	768	11.0	38	2
Jackie Harris	43	412	9.6	32	2
Yancey Thigpen	38	493	13.0	55	3
Eddie George	37	310	8.4	29	1
Willie Davis	32	461	14.4	38	3
Derrick Mason	25	333	13.3	47	3
Kevin Dyson*	21	263	12.5	45-td	2

Top Rushers	Car	Yds	Avg	Long	TD
Eddie George	348	1294	3.7	37-td	5
Steve McNair	77	559	7.3	71-td	4
Rodney Thomas	24	100	4.2	21	2

Most Touchdowns	TD	Run	Rec	Ret	Pts
Eddie George	6	5	1	0	38
Steve McNair	4	4	0	0	24
Willie Davis	3	0	3	0	18
Derrick Mason	3	0	3	0	18
Yancey Thigpen	3	0	3	0	18

2-Pt. Conversions: (1-4) George.

Kicking	PAT/Att	FG/Att	Lg	Pts
Al Del Greco	28/28	36/39	48	136

Punts (10 or more)	No	Yds	Long	Avg	In20
Craig Hentrich	69	3258	71	47.2	18

Most Interceptions
Darryll Lewis 4

Most Sacks
Lonnie Marts 4

AFC Team Leaders

Offense

	Points		Yardage			
	For	Avg	Rush	Pass	Total	Avg
Denver	501	31.3	2468	3624	6092	380.8
NY Jets	416	26.0	1879	3836	5715	357.2
Buffalo	400	25.0	2161	3380	5541	346.3
Tennessee	330	20.6	1970	3291	5261	328.8
Jacksonville	392	24.5	2102	3112	5214	325.9
New England	337	21.1	1480	3660	5140	321.3
Indianapolis	310	19.4	1486	3630	5116	319.8
Miami	321	20.1	1535	3395	4930	308.1
Cincinnati	268	16.8	1639	3185	4824	301.5
Oakland	288	18.0	1727	3088	4815	300.9
Kansas City	327	20.4	1548	3260	4806	300.5
Seattle	372	23.3	1626	3000	4626	289.1
San Diego	241	15.1	1728	2864	4592	287.0
Pittsburgh	263	16.4	2034	2552	4586	286.6
Baltimore	269	16.8	1629	2869	4498	281.1

Defense

	Points		Yardage			
	Opp	Avg	Rush	Pass	Total	Avg
San Diego	342	21.4	1140	3068	4208	263.0
Miami	265	16.6	1511	2924	4435	277.2
Oakland	356	22.3	1674	2876	4550	284.4
Buffalo	333	20.8	1493	3198	4691	293.2
NY Jets	266	16.6	1659	3040	4699	293.7
Kansas City	363	22.7	1869	2985	4854	303.4
Denver	309	19.3	1287	3648	4935	308.4
Pittsburgh	303	18.9	1642	3321	4963	310.2
Tennessee	320	20.0	1610	3511	5121	320.1
New England	329	20.6	1547	3635	5182	323.9
Baltimore	335	20.9	1705	3592	5297	331.1
Jacksonville	338	21.1	2000	3559	5559	347.4
Seattle	310	19.4	1999	3690	5689	355.6
Cincinnati	452	28.3	2612	3151	5763	360.2
Indianapolis	444	27.8	2570	3266	5836	364.8

NFC Team by Team Statistics

Players with more than one team during the regular season are listed with club they ended season with; (*) indicates rookies.

Arizona Cardinals

Passing (5 Att)	**Att**	**Cmp**	**Pct**	**Yds**	**TD**	**Rate**
Jake Plummer......547	324	59.2	3737	17	75.0
Dave Brown.........5	2	40.0	31	0	61.3

Interceptions: Plummer 20.

Top Receivers	**No**	**Yds**	**Avg**	**Long**	**TD**
Frank Sanders.........89	1145	12.9	42	3
Larry Centers.........69	559	8.1	54	2
Rob Moore............67	982	14.7	57	5
Eric Metcalf..........31	324	10.5	29	0
Johnny McWilliams.....26	284	10.9	26	4
Chris Gedney.........22	271	12.3	32	1

Top Rushers	**Car**	**Yds**	**Avg**	**Long**	**TD**
Adrian Murrell......274	1042	3.8	32	8
Jake Plummer.........51	217	4.3	27	4
Mario Bates..........60	165	2.8	15	6
Larry Centers.........31	110	3.5	14	0
Michael Pittman*......29	91	3.1	11	0

Most Touchdowns	**TD**	**Run**	**Rec**	**Ret**	**Pts**
Adrian Murrell..............10	8	2	0	60
Mario Bates..............6	6	0	0	36
Rob Moore.................5	0	5	0	30
Johnny McWilliams..........4	0	4	0	24
Jake Plummer.............4	4	0	0	24

2-Pt. Conversions (0-0).

Kicking	**PAT/Att**	**FG/Att**	**Lg**	**Pts**
Joe Nedney...........30/30	13/19	53	69
Chris Jacke 6/6	10/14	52	36

Punts (10 or more)	**No**	**Yds**	**Long**	**Avg**	**In20**
Scott Player 81	3378	67	41.7	12

Most Interceptions	**Most Sacks**
Kwamie Lassiter 8	Simeon Rice...........10

Atlanta Falcons

Passing (5 Att)	**Att**	**Cmp**	**Pct**	**Yds**	**TD**	**Rate**
Chris Chandler 327	190	58.1	3154	25	100.9
Steve DeBerg 59	30	50.8	369	3	80.4
Tony Graziani 33	16	48.5	199	0	42.4

Interceptions: Chandler 12, Graziani 2, DeBerg 1.

Top Receivers	**No**	**Yds**	**Avg**	**Long**	**TD**
Tony Martin 66	1181	17.9	62	6
Terance Mathis 64	1136	17.8	78-td	11
O.J. Santiago 27	428	15.9	62-td	5
Jamal Anderson 27	319	11.8	27	2
Bob Christian..........19	214	11.3	39	1
Todd Kinchen..........11	157	14.3	32	1

Top Rushers	**Car**	**Yds**	**Avg**	**Long**	**TD**
Jamal Anderson 410	1846	4.5	48	14
Chris Chandler 36	121	3.4	19	2
Ken Oxendine*......18	50	2.8	21	0
Harold Green 20	37	1.9	6	0

Most Touchdowns	**TD**	**Run**	**Rec**	**Ret**	**Pts**
Jamal Anderson..............16	14	2	0	98
Terance Mathis............11	0	11	0	66
Tony Martin 6	0	6	0	36
O.J. Santiago................5	0	5	0	30

2-Pt. Conversions (1-1) Anderson.

Kicking	**PAT/Att**	**FG/Att**	**Lg**	**Pts**
Morten Anderson.....51/52	23/28	53	120

Punts (10 or more)	**No**	**Yds**	**Long**	**Avg**	**In20**
Dan Stryzinski.........74	2963	55	40.0	25

Most Interceptions	**Most Sacks**
Ray Buchanan 7	Lester Archambeau 10

Carolina Panthers

Passing (5 Att)	**Att**	**Cmp**	**Pct**	**Yds**	**TD**	**Rate**
Steve Beuerlein 343	216	63.0	2613	17	88.2

Interceptions: Beuerlein 12.
Waived: Kerry Collins on Oct. 13 (see New Orleans).

Top Receivers	**No**	**Yds**	**Avg**	**Long**	**TD**
Raghib Ismail 69	1024	14.8	62	8
Mushin Muhammad ...68	941	13.8	72-td	6
Wesley Walls..........49	506	10.3	30	5
Anthony Johnson 27	242	9.0	38-td	1
William Floyd 24	123	5.1	20	1
Mark Carrier 19	301	15.8	42	2

Top Rushers	**Car**	**Yds**	**Avg**	**Long**	**TD**
Fred Lane...........205	717	3.5	31	5
Tim Biakabutuka 101	427	4.2	41	3
Anthony Johnson 36	135	3.8	21	0
William Floyd 28	71	2.5	7	3

Most Touchdowns	**TD**	**Run**	**Rec**	**Ret**	**Pts**
Raghib Ismail 8	0	8	0	48
Mushin Muhammad 6	0	6	0	38
Fred Lane.............5	5	0	0	30
Wesley Walls.........5	0	5	0	30

Two tied with four each.

2-Pt. Conversions: (2-3) Muhammad, Collins.

Kicking	**PAT/Att**	**FG/Att**	**Lg**	**Pts**
John Kasay 35/37	19/26	56	92

Punts (10 or more)	**No**	**Yds**	**Long**	**Avg**	**In20**
Ken Walter............77	3131	59	40.7	20

Most Interceptions	**Most Sacks**
Eric Davis 5	Kevin Greene..........15

Chicago Bears

Passing (5 Att)	**Att**	**Cmp**	**Pct**	**Yds**	**TD**	**Rate**
Erik Kramer 250	151	60.4	1823	9	83.1
Steve Stenstrom ...196	112	57.1	1252	4	70.4
Moses Moreno* 43	19	44.2	166	1	62.7

Interceptions: Kramer 7, Stenstrom 6.

Top Receivers	**No**	**Yds**	**Avg**	**Long**	**TD**
Bobby Engram...64	987	15.4	79-td	5
Curtis Conway 54	733	13.6	47	3
Chris Penn 31	448	14.5	37	3
Edgar Bennett 28	209	7.5	31	0
Ty Hallock 25	166	6.6	16	0
Ryan Wetnight 23	168	7.3	30	2

Top Rushers	**Car**	**Yds**	**Avg**	**Long**	**TD**
Edgar Bennett 173	611	3.5	43	2
Curtis Enis* 133	497	3.7	29	0
James Allen 58	270	4.7	57	1

Most Touchdowns	**TD**	**Run**	**Rec**	**Ret**	**Pts**
Bobby Engram...............5	0	5	0	30
Chris Penn 3	0	3	0	20
Curtis Conway 3	0	3	0	18
Glyn Milburn............3	0	0	3	18

2-Pt. Conversions: (1-2) Penn.

Kicking	**PAT/Att**	**FG/Att**	**Lg**	**Pts**
Jeff Jaeger...............27/28	21/26	52	90

Punts (10 or more)	**No**	**Yds**	**Long**	**Avg**	**In20**
Mike Horan 64	2643	57	41.3	12
Todd Sauerbrun........15	741	71	49.4	6

Signed: Horan on Sept. 23.

Most Interceptions	**Most Sacks**
Walt Harris............4	Jim Flanigan..........8½

Dallas Cowboys

Passing (5 Att)	Att	Cmp	Pct	Yds	TD	Rate
Troy Aikman	315	187	59.4	2330	12	88.5
Jason Garrett	158	91	57.6	1206	5	84.5

Interceptions: Aikman 5, Garrett 3.

Top Receivers	No	Yds	Avg	Long	TD
Michael Irvin	74	1057	14.3	51	1
Billy Davis	39	691	17.7	80-td	3
Ernie Mills	28	479	17.1	43-td	4
Emmitt Smith	27	175	6.5	24	2
David LaFleur	20	176	8.8	24	2
Patrick Jeffers	18	330	18.3	67-td	2
Daryl Johnston	18	60	3.3	9	1

Top Rushers	Car	Yds	Avg	Long	TD
Emmitt Smith	319	1332	4.2	32	13
Chris Warren	59	291	4.9	49	4
Sherman Williams	64	220	3.4	24	1
Troy Aikman	22	69	3.1	23	2

Most Touchdowns	TD	Run	Rec	Ret	Pts
Emmitt Smith	15	13	2	0	90
Chris Warren	5	4	1	0	30
Ernie Mills	4	0	4	0	24
Billy Davis	3	0	3	0	18
Deion Sanders	3	0	0	3	18

2-Pt. Conversion: (0-2).

Kicking	PAT/Att	FG/Att	Lg	Pts
Richie Cunningham	40/40	29/35	54	127

Punts (10 or more)	No	Yds	Long	Avg	In20
Toby Gowin	77	3342	65	43.4	31

Most Interceptions		Most Sacks	
Deion Sanders	5	Kavika Pittman	6

Detroit Lions

Passing (5 Att)	Att	Cmp	Pct	Yds	TD	Rate
Charlie Batch*	303	173	57.1	2178	11	83.5
Frank Reich	110	63	57.3	768	5	78.9
Scott Mitchell	75	38	50.7	452	1	57.2

Interceptions: Batch 6, Reich 4, Mitchell 3.

Top Receivers	No	Yds	Avg	Long	TD
Herman Moore	82	983	12.0	36	5
Johnnie Morton	69	1028	14.9	98-td	2
Barry Sanders	37	289	7.8	44	0
Germane Crowell*	25	464	18.6	68-td	3
Walter Rasby	15	119	7.9	17	1
Tommy Vardell	14	143	10.2	31	1
David Sloan	11	146	13.3	33	1

Top Rushers	Car	Yds	Avg	Long	TD
Barry Sanders	343	1491	4.3	73-td	4
Charlie Batch*	41	229	5.6	17	1
Ron Rivers	19	102	5.4	36-td	1
Tommy Vardell	18	37	2.1	17	6

Most Touchdowns	TD	Run	Rec	Ret	Pts
Tommy Vardell	7	6	1	0	42
Herman Moore	5	0	5	0	30
Barry Sanders	4	4	0	0	24
Germane Crowell*	3	0	3	0	18

Three tied with 2 each.

2-Pt. Conversion: (0-3).

Kicking	PAT/Att	FG/Att	Lg	Pts
Jason Hanson	27/29	29/33	51	114

Punts (10 or more)	No	Yds	Long	Avg	In20
John Jett	66	2892	60	43.8	17

Signed: John Kidd on Oct. 1.
Released: Kidd on Oct. 25 (see NY Jets).

Green Bay Packers

Passing (5 Att)	Att	Cmp	Pct	Yds	TD	Rate
Brett Favre	551	347	63.0	4212	31	87.8
Doug Pederson	24	14	58.3	128	2	100.7

Interceptions: Favre 23.

Top Receivers	No	Yds	Avg	Long	TD
Antonio Freeman	84	1424	17.0	84-td	14
Mark Chmura	47	554	11.8	25-td	4
William Henderson	37	241	6.5	15	1
Bill Schroeder	31	452	14.6	46	1
Robert Brooks	31	420	13.5	30-td	3

Top Rushers	Car	Yds	Avg	Long	TD
Darick Holmes	95	394	4.1	13	1
BUF	2	8	4.0	5	0
GB	93	386	4.2	13	1
Dorsey Levens	115	378	3.3	50	1
Travis Jervey	83	325	3.9	16	1
Raymont Harris	79	228	2.9	14	1

Acquired: Holmes from Buffalo for 1999 draft pick (Sept. 29).
Waived: Harris on Dec. 8.

Most Touchdowns	TD	Run	Rec	Ret	Pts
Antonio Freeman	14	0	14	0	86
Tyrone Davis	7	0	7	0	42
Mark Chmura	4	0	4	0	24

2-Pt. Conversion: (1-3) Freeman.

Kicking	PAT/Att	FG/Att	Lg	Pts
Ryan Longwell	41/43	29/33	45	128

Punts (10 or more)	No	Yds	Long	Avg	In20
Sean Landeta	65	2788	72	42.9	30

Most Interceptions		Most Sacks	
Tyrone Williams	5	Reggie White	16

Minnesota Vikings

Passing (5 Att)	Att	Cmp	Pct	Yds	TD	Rate
Randall Cunningham	425	259	60.9	3704	34	106.0
Brad Johnson	101	65	64.4	747	7	89.0
Jay Fiedler	7	3	42.9	41	0	22.6

Interceptions: Cunningham 10, Johnson 5, Fiedler 1.
Signed: Fiedler on Sept. 16.

Top Receivers	No	Yds	Avg	Long	TD
Cris Carter	78	1011	13.0	54-td	12
Randy Moss*	69	1313	19.0	61-td	17
Andrew Glover	35	522	14.9	36	5
Jake Reed	34	474	13.9	56-td	4
Robert Smith	28	291	10.4	67-td	2

Top Rushers	Car	Yds	Avg	Long	TD
Robert Smith	249	1187	4.8	74-td	6
Leroy Hoard	115	479	4.2	50-td	9
Randall Cunningham	32	132	4.1	22	1
Chuck Evans	23	67	2.9	12	1

Most Touchdowns	TD	Run	Rec	Ret	Pts
Randy Moss*	17	0	17	0	106
Cris Carter	12	0	12	0	72
Leroy Hoard	10	9	1	0	60
Robert Smith	8	6	2	0	48
Andrew Glover	5	0	5	0	30
Jake Reed	4	0	4	0	24

2-Pt. Conversion: (3-5) Moss 2, Cunningham.

Kicking	PAT/Att	FG/Att	Lg	Pts
Gary Anderson	59/59	35/35	53	164

Punts (10 or more)	No	Yds	Long	Avg	In20
Mitch Berger	55	2458	67	44.7	17

Most Interceptions		Most Sacks	
Jimmy Hitchcock	7	John Randle	10½

New Orleans Saints

Passing (5 Att)	Att	Cmp	Pct	Yds	TD	Rate
Kerry Collins	353	170	48.2	2213	12	62.0
CAR	162	76	46.9	1011	8	70.8
NO	191	94	49.2	1202	4	54.5
Billy Joe Tolliver	198	110	55.6	1427	8	83.5
Danny Wuerffel	119	62	52.1	695	5	66.3
Billy Joe Hobert	23	11	47.8	170	1	87.2

Interceptions: Collins 15, Wuerffel 5, Tolliver 4.
Claimed: Collins on Oct. 14 (waived by Carolina, Oct. 13).

Top Receivers	No	Yds	Avg	Long	TD
Cameron Cleeland	54	684	12.7	53	6
Sean Dawkins	53	823	15.5	64-td	1
Andre Hastings	35	455	13.0	89-td	3
Aaron Craver	33	214	6.5	49	2
Keith Poole	24	509	21.2	82-td	2
Lamar Smith	24	249	10.4	35-td	2

Top Rushers	Car	Yds	Avg	Long	TD
Lamar Smith	138	457	3.3	33	1
Aaron Craver	45	180	4.0	25	2
Kerry Collins	30	153	5.1	20	1
CAR	7	40	5.7	16	0
NO	23	113	4.9	20	1

Waived: Ray Zellars on Dec. 8 (see Cincinnati).

Most Touchdowns	TD	Run	Rec	Ret	Pts
Cameron Cleeland*	6	0	6	0	36
Aaron Craver	5	2	2	1	30

Three tied with three each.

2-Pt. Conversions: (0-3) Collins with Carolina.

Kicking	PAT/Att	FG/Att	Lg	Pts
Doug Brien	31/31	20/22	56	91

Punts (10 or more)	No	Yds	Long	Avg	In20
Mark Royals	88	4017	64	45.6	26

Most Interceptions
Sammy Knight 6

Most Sacks
La'Roi Glover 10

New York Giants

Passing (5 Att)	Att	Cmp	Pct	Yds	TD	Rate
Danny Kanell	299	160	53.5	1603	11	67.3
Kent Graham	205	105	51.2	1219	7	70.8

Interceptions: Kanell 10, Graham 5.

Top Receivers	No	Yds	Avg	Long	TD
Chris Calloway	62	812	13.1	36	6
Ike Hilliard	51	715	14.0	50	2
Tiki Barber	42	348	8.3	87-td	3
Charles Way	31	131	4.2	16	1
Amani Toomer	27	360	13.3	37-td	2

Top Rushers	Car	Yds	Avg	Long	TD
Gary Brown	247	1063	4.3	45	5
Charles Way	113	432	3.8	21	3
Tiki Barber	52	166	3.2	23	0
Kent Graham	27	138	5.1	23	2

Most Touchdowns	TD	Run	Rec	Ret	Pts
Chris Calloway	6	0	6	0	36
Gary Brown	5	5	0	0	30
Amani Toomer	5	0	5	0	30
Charles Way	4	3	1	0	24
Tiki Barber	3	0	3	0	18

2-Pt. Conversions: (0-0).

Kicking	PAT/Att	FG/Att	Lg	Pts
Brad Daluiso	32/32	21/27	51	95

Punts (10 or more)	No	Yds	Long	Avg	In20
Brad Maynard	101	4566	63	45.2	33

Most Interceptions
Percy Ellsworth 5

Most Sacks
Michael Strahan 15

Philadelphia Eagles

Passing (5 Att)	Att	Cmp	Pct	Yds	TD	Rate
Bobby Hoying	224	114	50.9	961	0	45.6
Koy Detmer	181	97	53.6	1011	5	67.7
Rodney Peete	129	71	55.0	758	2	64.7

Interceptions: Hoying 9, Detmer 5, Peete 4.

Top Receivers	No	Yds	Avg	Long	TD
Duce Staley	57	432	7.6	33	1
Irving Fryar	48	556	11.6	61-td	2
Jeff Graham	47	600	12.8	45	2
Kevin Turner	34	232	6.8	18	0
Freddie Solomon	21	198	9.4	20	1

Top Rushers	Car	Yds	Avg	Long	TD
Duce Staley	258	1065	4.1	64-td	5
Charlie Garner	96	381	4.0	40	4
Kevin Turner	20	94	4.7	19	0
Bobby Hoying	22	84	3.8	11	0

Most Touchdowns	TD	Run	Rec	Ret	Pts
Duce Staley	6	5	1	0	36
Charlie Garner	4	4	0	0	24
Irving Fryar	2	0	2	0	12
Jeff Graham	2	0	2	0	12

2-Pt. Conversions: (0-0).

Kicking	PAT/Att	FG/Att	Lg	Pts
Chris Boniol	15/17	14/21	50	57

Punts (10 or more)	No	Yds	Long	Avg	In20
Tom Hutton	104	4339	61	41.7	21

Most Interceptions
Brian Dawkins 2
Troy Vincent 2
Mike Zordich 2

Most Sacks
Hugh Douglas 12½

St. Louis Rams

Passing (5 Att)	Att	Cmp	Pct	Yds	TD	Rate
Tony Banks	408	241	59.1	2535	7	68.6
Steve Bono	136	69	50.7	807	5	69.1
Kurt Warner	11	4	36.4	39	0	47.2

Interceptions: Banks 14, Bono 4.

Top Receivers	No	Yds	Avg	Long	TD
Amp Lee	64	667	10.4	44	2
Ricky Proehl	60	771	12.9	47	3
June Henley	35	252	7.2	43	0
Isaac Bruce	32	457	14.3	80-td	1
J.T. Thomas	20	287	14.4	42	0
Az-zahir Hakim*	20	247	12.4	22	1

Top Rushers	Car	Yds	Avg	Long	TD
June Henley	88	313	3.6	22	3
Greg Hill	40	240	6.0	46	4
Robert Holcombe*	98	230	2.3	12	2
Amp Lee	44	175	4.0	38	2
Tony Banks	40	156	3.9	19	3

Most Touchdowns	TD	Run	Rec	Ret	PTS
Amp Lee	4	2	2	0	26
Greg Hill	4	4	0	0	24
Tony Banks	3	3	0	0	20
Ricky Proehl	3	0	3	0	20
June Henley	3	3	0	0	18

2-Pt. Conversions: (4-6) Banks, Bono, Lee, Proehl.

Kicking	PAT/Att	FG/Att	Lg	Pts
Jeff Wilkins	25/26	20/26	57	85

Punts (10 or more)	No	Yds	Long	Avg	In20
Rick Tuten	95	4202	64	44.2	16

Most Interceptions
Todd Lyght 3
Keith Lyle 3

Most Sacks
Kevin Carter 12

San Francisco 49ers

Passing (5 Att)	Att	Cmp	Pct	Yds	TD	Rate
Steve Young	517	322	62.3	4170	36	101.1
Ty Detmer	38	24	63.2	312	4	91.1

Interceptions: Young 12, Detmer 3.

Top Receivers	No	Yds	Avg	Long	TD
Jerry Rice	82	1157	14.1	75-td	9
Terrell Owens	67	1097	16.4	79-td	14
J.J. Stokes	63	770	12.2	33-td	8
Garrison Hearst	39	535	13.7	81-td	2
Irv Smith	25	266	10.6	25-td	5
Marc Edwards	22	218	9.9	47-td	2

Top Rushers	Car	Yds	Avg	Long	TD
Garrison Hearst	310	1570	5.1	96-td	7
Steve Young	70	454	6.5	24	6
Terry Kirby	48	258	5.4	31-td	3
Chuck Levy	25	112	4.5	21-td	1
Marc Edwards	22	94	4.3	32	1

Most Touchdowns	TD	Run	Rec	Ret	Pts
Terrell Owens	15	1	14	0	92
Jerry Rice	9	0	9	0	58
Garrison Hearst	9	7	2	0	56
J.J. Stokes	8	0	8	0	48
Steve Young	6	6	0	0	36
Irv Smith	5	0	5	0	30

2-Pt. Conversions: (5-9) Rice 2, Greg Clark, Hearst, Owens.

Kicking	PAT/Att	FG/Att	Lg	Pts
Wade Richey*	49/51	18/27	46	103

Punts (10 or more)	No	Yds	Long	Avg	In20
Reggie Roby	60	2511	66	41.9	14

Signed: Roby on Sept. 22.

Most Interceptions	Most Sacks
Four tied with 4 each.	Chris Doleman 15

Tampa Bay Buccaneers

Passing (5 Att)	Att	Cmp	Pct	Yds	TD	Rate
Trent Dilfer	429	225	52.4	2729	21	74.0
Steve Walsh	19	9	47.4	58	0	14.7

Interceptions: Dilfer 15, Walsh 3.

Top Receivers	No	Yds	Avg	Long	TD
Reidel Anthony	51	708	13.9	79-td	7
Warrick Dunn	44	344	7.8	31	0
Bert Emanuel	41	636	15.5	62-td	2
Dave Moore	24	255	10.6	44-td	4
Mike Alstott	22	152	6.9	26	1
Karl Williams	21	252	12.0	29-td	1
Jacquez Green*	14	251	17.9	64-td	2

Top Rushers	Car	Yds	Avg	Long	TD
Warrick Dunn	245	1026	4.2	50	2
Mike Alstott	215	846	3.9	37	8
Trent Dilfer	40	141	3.5	17	2

Most Touchdowns	TD	Run	Rec	Ret	Pts
Mike Alstott	9	8	1	0	54
Reidel Anthony	7	0	7	0	44
Dave Moore	4	0	4	0	24
Jacquez Green*	3	0	2	1	18

2-Pt. Conversions: (3-6) Anthony, Patrick Hape, Brice Hunter.

Kicking	PAT/Att	FG/Att	Lg	Pts
Michael Husted	29/30	21/28	52	92

Punts (10 or more)	No	Yds	Long	Avg	In20
Tommy Barnhardt	81	3340	55	41.2	19

Most Interceptions	Most Sacks
Charles Mincy 4	Brad Culpepper 9

Washington Redskins

Passing (5 Att)	Att	Cmp	Pct	Yds	TD	Rate
Trent Green	509	278	54.6	3441	23	81.8
Gus Frerotte	54	25	46.3	283	1	45.5

Interceptions: Green 11, Frerotte 3.

Top Receivers	No	Yds	Avg	Long	TD
Michael Westbrook	44	736	16.7	75-td	6
Brian Mitchell	44	306	7.0	24	0
Leslie Shepherd	43	712	16.6	43-td	8
Stephen Alexander*	37	383	10.4	33	4

Top Rushers	Car	Yds	Avg	Long	TD
Terry Allen	148	700	4.7	45	2
Skip Hicks*	122	433	3.5	28	8
Brian Mitchell	39	208	5.3	22	2

Most Touchdowns	TD	Run	Rec	Ret	Pts
Leslie Shepherd	9	1	8	0	56
Skip Hicks*	8	8	0	0	48
Michael Westbrook	6	0	6	0	36
Stephen Alexander*	4	0	4	0	24

2-Pt. Conversions: (1-3) Shepherd.

Kicking	PAT/Att	FG/Att	Lg	Pts
Cary Blanchard	30/31	11/17	54	63
Scott Blanton	4/4	2/4	46	10
David Akers*	2/2	0/2	—	2

Signed: Blanchard on Sept. 22.
Waived: Blanton on Sept. 15; Akers on Sept. 22.

Punts (10 or more)	No	Yds	Long	Avg	In20
Matt Turk	93	4103	69	44.1	33

Most Interceptions	Most Sacks
Leomont Evans 3	Dan Wilkinson 7½
Darrell Green 3	

NFC Team Leaders

Offense

	Points		Yardage		
	For	Avg	Rush	Pass	Total	Avg
---	---	---	---	---	---	---
San Francisco	479	29.9	2544	4256	6800	425.0
Minnesota	556	34.8	1936	4328	6264	391.5
Green Bay	408	25.5	1526	4110	5636	352.3
Atlanta	442	27.6	2101	3386	5487	342.9
Dallas	381	23.8	2014	3436	5450	340.6
Arizona	325	20.3	1627	3482	5109	319.3
Detroit	306	19.1	1955	3130	5085	317.8
Washington	319	19.9	1685	3325	5010	313.1
Carolina	336	21.0	1458	3322	4780	298.8
Chicago	276	17.3	1713	3053	4766	297.9
Tampa Bay	314	19.6	2148	2606	4754	297.1
St. Louis	285	17.8	1385	3087	4472	279.5
New Orleans	305	19.1	1325	3138	4463	278.9
NY Giants	287	17.9	1889	2566	4455	278.4
Philadelphia	161	10.1	1775	2413	4188	261.8

Defense

	Points		Yardage		
	Opp	Avg	Rush	Pass	Total	Avg
---	---	---	---	---	---	---
Tampa Bay	295	18.4	1583	2762	4345	271.6
Green Bay	319	19.9	1464	4507	281.7	
Atlanta	289	18.1	1203	3531	4734	295.9
St. Louis	378	23.6	2049	2831	4880	305.0
Minnesota	296	18.5	1614	3452	5066	316.6
Chicago	368	23.0	1875	3228	5103	318.9
Detroit	378	23.6	2102	3015	5117	319.8
Philadelphia	344	21.5	2416	2720	5136	321.0
Dallas	275	17.2	1619	3545	5164	322.8
NY Giants	309	19.3	2004	3167	5171	323.2
Arizona	378	23.6	1989	3276	5265	329.1
San Francisco	328	20.5	1610	3733	5343	333.9
Washington	421	26.3	2436	2918	5354	334.6
New Orleans	359	22.4	1700	3968	5668	354.3
Carolina	413	25.8	2133	3709	5842	365.1

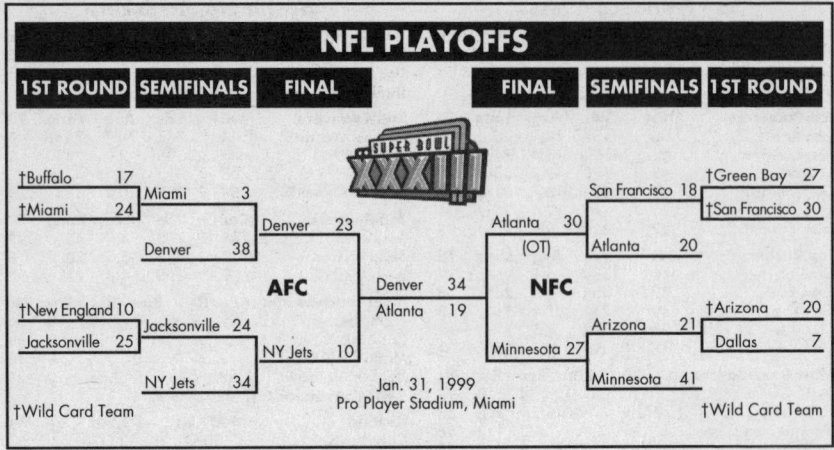

Playoff Game Summaries

Team records listed in parentheses indicate records before game.

WILD CARD ROUND

AFC

🏈 **Dolphins, 24-17**

Buffalo (10-6)	0	7	7	3—	**17**
Miami (10-6)	3	3	8	10—	**24**

Date—Jan. 2. **Att**—72,698. **Time**—3:17.

1st Quarter: MIA—Olindo Mare 31-yd FG, 6:07.

2nd Quarter: MIA—Mare 40-yd FG, 10:36; BUF—Thurman Thomas 1-yd run (Steve Christie kick), 8:54.

3rd Quarter: MIA—Karim Abdul-Jabbar 3-yd run (Stanley Pritchett, run), 2:32; BUF—Eric Moulds 32-yd pass from Doug Flutie (Christie kick), 0:48.

4th Quarter: MIA—Mare 23-yd FG, 9:45; MIA—Lamar Thomas 11-yd pass from Dan Marino (Mare kick), 3:42; BUF—Christie 33-yd FG, 1:33.

🏈 **Jaguars, 25-10**

New England (9-7)	0	0	7	3—	**10**
Jacksonville (11-5)	6	6	0	13—	**25**

Date—Jan. 3. **Att**—71,139. **Time**—3:22.

1st Quarter: JAX—Mike Hollis 35-yd FG, 8:57; JAX—Hollis 24-yd FG, 2:01.

2nd Quarter: JAX—Fred Taylor 13-yd run (two-pt attempt failed); 5:58.

3rd Quarter: NE—Robert Edwards 1-yd run (Adam Vinatieri kick), 4:27.

4th Quarter: NE—Vinatieri 27-yd FG, 14:48; JAX—Jimmy Smith 37-yd pass from Mark Brunell (Hollis kick), 12:24; JAX—Hollis 34-yd FG, 5:52; JAX—Hollis 21-yd FG, 1:44.

NFC

🏈 **Cardinals, 20-7**

Arizona (9-7)	7	3	7	3—	**20**
Dallas (10-6)	0	0	0	7—	**7**

Date—Jan. 2. **Att**—62,969. **Time**—3:10.

1st Quarter: ARI—Adrian Murrell 12-yd pass from Jake Plummer (Chris Jacke kick), 2:47.

2nd Quarter: ARI—Jacke 37-yd FG, 0:19.

3rd Quarter: ARI—Larry Centers 3-yd pass from Plummer (Jacke kick), 13:44.

4th Quarter: ARI—Jacke 46-yd FG, 12:55; DAL—Billy Davis 6-yd pass from Troy Aikman (Richie Cunningham kick), 3:33.

🏈 **49ers, 30-27**

Green Bay (11-5)	3	14	0	10—	**27**
San Francisco (12-4)	7	3	10	10—	**30**

Date—Jan. 3. **Att**—66,506. **Time**—3:05.

1st Quarter: GB—Ryan Longwell 23-yd FG, 9:26; SF—Greg Clark 1-yd pass from Steve Young (Wade Richey kick), 4:10.

2nd Quarter: GB—Antonio Freeman 2-yd pass from Brett Favre (Longwell kick), 14:56; SF—Richey 34-yd FG, 6:53; GB—Dorsey Levens 2-yd run (Longwell kick), 0:31.

3rd Quarter: SF—Clark 8-yd pass from Young (Richey kick), 9:02; SF—Richey 48-yd FG, 2:12.

4th Quarter: GB— Longwell 37-yd FG, 11:51; SF—Richey 40-yd FG, 6:12; GB—Freeman 15-yd pass from Favre (Longwell kick), 1:56; SF—Terrell Owens 25-yd pass from Young (Richey kick), 0:03.

DIVISIONAL SEMIFINALS

AFC

● Broncos, 38-3

Miami (11-6) 0   3   0   0— **3**
Denver (14-2) 14   7   3 14— **38**
Date—Jan. 9. **Att**—75,729. **Time**—2:48.

1st Quarter: DEN—Terrell Davis 1-yd run (Jason Elam kick), 5:55; DEN—Davis 20-yd run (Elam kick), 1:02.

2nd Quarter: MIA—Olindo Mare 22-yd FG, 10:07; DEN—Derek Loville 11-yd run (Elam kick), 4:39.

3rd Quarter: DEN—Jason Elam 32-yd FG, 11:52.

4th Quarter: DEN—Rod Smith 28-yd pass from John Elway (Elam kick), 13:23; DEN—Neil Smith 79-yd fumble return (Elam kick), 9:49.

● Jets, 34-24

Jacksonville (12-5) 0   7   7 10— **24**
NY Jets (12-4) ....7 10 14   3— **34**
Date—Jan. 10. **Att**—78,817. **Time**—3:07.

1st Quarter: NYJ—Keyshawn Johnson 21-yd pass from Vinny Testaverde (John Hall kick), 10:26.

2nd Quarter: NYJ—Hall 52-yd FG, 10:35; NYJ—Johnson 10-yd run (Hall kick), 0:33; JAX—Jimmy Smith 52-yd pass from Mark Brunell (Mike Hollis kick), 0:00.

3rd Quarter: NYJ—Curtis Martin 1-yd run (Hall kick), 9:13; JAX—Keenan McCardell 3-yd pass from Brunell (Hollis kick), 8:08; NYJ—Martin 1-yd run (Hall kick), 2:16.

4th Quarter: JAX—Smith 19-yd pass from Brunell (Hollis kick), 9:58; JAX—Hollis 37-yd FG, 6:38; NYJ—Hall 30-yd FG, 0:24.

NFC

● Falcons, 20-18

San Francisco (13-4) ....0 10   0   8— **18**
Atlanta (14-2) 7   7   3   3— **20**
Date—Jan. 9. **Att**—70,262. **Time**—2:57.

1st Quarter: ATL—Jamal Anderson 2-yd run (Morten Andersen kick), 6:25.

2nd Quarter: ATL—Anderson 34-yd run (Andersen kick), 3:12; SF—Jerry Rice 17-yd pass from Steve Young (Wade Richey kick), 1:10; SF—Richey 36-yd FG, 0:00.

3rd Quarter: ATL—Andersen 29-yd FG, 1:16.

4th Quarter: ATL—Andersen 32-yd FG, 10:33; SF—Young 8-yd run (Greg Clark pass from Ty Detmer), 2:57.

● Vikings, 41-21

Arizona (10-7) 0   7   7   7— **21**
Minnesota (15-1) ....7 17 10   7— **41**
Date—Jan. 10. **Att**—63,760. **Time**—3:08.

1st Quarter: MIN—Leroy Hoard 1-yd run (Gary Anderson kick), 7:40.

2nd Quarter: MIN—Andrew Glover 15-yd pass from Randall Cunningham (Anderson kick), 12:45; MIN—Anderson 34-yd FG, 11:24; ARI—Mario Bates 1-yd run (Chris Jacke kick), 11:24; MIN—Hoard 16-yd pass from Cunningham (Anderson kick), 0:24.

3rd Quarter: ARI—Bates 1-yd run (Jacke kick), 7:25; MIN—Anderson 20-yd FG, 3:59; MIN—Randy Moss 2-yd pass from Cunningham (Anderson kick), 1:31.

4th Quarter: ARI—Bates 1-yd run (Jacke kick), 11:45; MIN—Hoard 6-yd run (Anderson kick), 4:33.

CONFERENCE CHAMPIONSHIPS

AFC

● Broncos, 23-10

NY Jets (13-4) 0   3   7   0— **10**
Denver (15-2) 0   0 20   3— **23**
Date—Jan. 17. **Att**—75,482. **Time**—3:16.

2nd Quarter: NYJ—John Hall 32-yd FG, 0:00.

3nd Quarter: NYJ—Curtis Martin 1-yd run (Hall kick), 11:56; DEN—Howard Griffith 11-yd pass from John Elway (Jason Elam kick), 10:18; DEN—Elam 44-yd FG, 8:23; DEN—Elam 48-yd FG, 2:58; DEN—Terrell Davis 31-yd run (Elam kick), 0:18.

4th Quarter: DEN—Elam 35-yd FG, 3:40.

NFC

● Falcons, 30-27 (OT)

Atlanta (15-2) 7   7   3 10   3— **30**
Minnesota (16-1) ....7 13   0   7   0— **27**
Date—Jan. 17. **Att**—64,060. **Time**—3:43.

1st Quarter: ATL—Jamal Anderson 5-yd pass from Chris Chandler (Morten Andersen kick), 8:21; MIN—Randy Moss 31-yd pass from Randall Cunningham (Gary Anderson kick), 5:33.

2nd Quarter: MIN—Anderson 29-yd FG, 9:52; MIN—Cunningham 1-yd run (Anderson kick), 5:53; MIN—Anderson 35-yd FG, 2:45; ATL—Terance Mathis 14-yd pass from Chandler (Andersen kick), 0:56.

3rd Quarter: ATL—Andersen 27-yd FG, 5:36.

4th Quarter: MIN—Matt Hatchette 5-yd pass from Cunningham (Anderson kick), 13:41; ATL—Andersen 24-yd FG, 11:02; ATL—Mathis 16-yd pass from Chandler (Andersen kick), 0:49.

Overtime: ATL—Andersen 38-yd FG, 3:08.

Super Bowl XXXIII
Sunday, Jan. 31 at Pro Player Stadium, Miami, Fla.

Denver (16-2) ....7 10   0 17— **34**
Atlanta (16-2) 3   3   0 13— **19**

1st: ATL—Morten Andersen 32-yd FG, 9:35. Drive: 48 yards in 10 plays. Key play: 25-yd pass interference on Ray Crockett to DEN 21. DEN—Howard Griffith 1-yd run (Jason Elam kick), 3:55. Drive: 80 yards in 10 plays. Key play: John Elway 41-yd pass to Rod Smith on 3rd-and-7 to ATL 24.

2nd: DEN—Elam 26-yd FG, 9:17. Drive: 63 yards in 11 plays. Key play: Elway 18-yd pass to Smith to ATL 27. DEN—Smith 80-yd pass from Elway (Elam kick), 4:54. Drive: 80 yards in 1 play. ATL—Andersen 28-yd FG, 2:25. Drive: 38 yards in 7 plays. Key play: Tim Dwight 42-yd kick-off return to DEN 49.

4th: DEN—Griffith 1-yd run (Elam kick), 14:56. Drive: 24 yards in 5 plays. Key play: Darrien Gordon 58-yd interception return to ATL 24. DEN—Elway 3-yd run (Elam kick), 11:20. Drive: 48 yards in 3 plays. Key play: Gordon 50-yd interception return to ATL 24. ATL—Dwight 94-yd kickoff return (Andersen kick), 11:01. DEN—Elam 37-yd FG, 7:08. Drive: 36 yards in 7 plays. Key play: Byron Chamberlain recovers onside kick at DEN 46. ATL—Terance Mathis 3-yd pass from Chris Chandler (2-pt attempt failed), 2:04. Drive: 76 yards in 16 plays. Key play: Chandler 17-yd pass to Tony Martin on 3rd-and 4 to ATL 47.

Favorite: Broncos by 7½ **Attendance:** 74,803
Field: Grass   **Time:** 3:18
Start time: 6:25 EST **TV Rating:** 40.2/61 share (FOX)
MVP—John Elway, Denver QB (18-29 for 336 yds, 1 TD, 1 INT)

Officials: Bernie Kukar (referee); Jim Daopoulos (umpire); Ron Baynes (LJ); Gary Lane (SJ); Sanford Rivers (HL); Don Hakes (BJ); Tim Millis (FJ).

Team Statistics

	Broncos	Falcons
Touchdowns	4	2
Rushing	3	0
Passing	1	1
Returns	0	1
Field Goals made/attempted	2/4	2/3
Time of possession	31:23	28:37
First downs	22	21
Rushing	8	8
Passing	14	12
Penalty	0	1
3rd down efficiency	6/13	5/11
4th down efficiency	0/1	1/2
Total offense (net yards)	457	337
Plays	65	60
Average gain	7.0	5.6
Carries/yards	36/121	23/131
Yards per carry	3.4	5.7
Passing yards	336	206
Completions/attempts	18/29	19/35
Yards per pass	11.6	5.6
Times intercepted	1	3
Times sacked/yards lost	0/0	2/13
Return yardage	180	228
Punt returns/yards	0/0	0/0
Kickoff returns/yards	3/44	7/227
Interceptions/yards	3/136	1/1
Fumbles/lost	0/0	1/1
Penalties/yards	4/61	0/0
Punts/average	1/35.0	1/39.0
Punts blocked	0	0

Individual Statistics

Denver Broncos

Passing	Att	Cmp	Pct.	Yds	TD	Int
John Elway	29	18	62.1	336	1	1

Receiving	No	Yds	Avg	Long	TD
Rod Smith	5	152	30.4	80-td	1
Ed McCaffrey	5	72	14.4	25	0
Byron Chamberlain	3	29	9.7	13	0
Terrell Davis	2	50	25.0	39	0
Shannon Sharpe	2	26	13.0	14	0
Howard Griffith	1	7	7.0	7	0
TOTAL	18	336	18.7	80-td	1

Rushing	Car	Yds	Avg	Long	TD
Terrell Davis	25	102	4.1	15	0
Howard Griffith	4	9	2.3	4	2
Derek Loville	2	8	4.0	6	0
John Elway	3	2	0.7	3	1
Rod Smith	1	1	1.0	1	0
Bubby Brister	1	-1	-1.0	-1	0
TOTAL	36	121	3.4	15	3

Field Goals	20-29	30-39	40-49	50-59	Total
Jason Elam	1-1	1-2	0-1	0-0	2-4

Punting	No	Yds	Long	Avg	In 20	TB
Tom Rouen	1	35	35	35.0	1	0

Kickoff Returns	No	Yds	Long	Avg	TD
Vaughn Hebron	2	42	26	21.0	0
Byron Chamberlain	1	2	2	2.0	0

Interceptions	No	Yds	Long	Avg	TD
Darrien Gordon	2	108	58	54.0	0
Darrius Johnson	1	28	28	28.0	0

Sacks
Bill Romanowski 1.0
John Mobley 1.0

Most Tackles
Ray Crockett 5
Three tied with four each.

Atlanta Falcons

Passing	Att	Cmp	Pct.	Yds	TD	Int
Chris Chandler	35	19	54.3	219	1	3

Receiving	No	Yds	Avg	Long	TD
Terance Mathis	7	85	12.1	30	1
Tony Martin	5	79	15.8	23	0
Jamal Anderson	3	16	5.3	9	0
Ronnie Harris	2	21	10.5	13	0
O.J. Santiago	1	13	13.0	13	0
Brian Kozlowski	1	5	5.0	5	0
TOTAL	19	219	11.5	30	1

Rushing	Car	Yds	Avg	Long	TD
Jamal Anderson	18	96	5.3	15	0
Chris Chandler	4	30	7.5	12	0
Tim Dwight	1	5	5.0	5	0
TOTAL	23	131	5.7	15	0

Field Goals	20-29	30-39	40-49	50-59	Total
Morten Andersen 1-2	1-1	0-0	0-0	2-3

Punting	No	Yds	Long	Avg	In 20	TB
Dan Stryzinski	1	39	39	39.0	0	0

Punt Returns	FC	Ret	Yds	Long	Avg	TD
Tim Dwight	1	0	0	0	0	0

Kickoff Returns	No	Yds	Long	Avg	TD
Tim Dwight	5	210	94-td	42.0	1
Brian Kozlowski	2	17	16	8.5	0
TOTAL	7	227	94-td	32.4	1

Interceptions	No	Yds	Long	Avg	TD
Ronnie Bradford	1	1	1	1.0	0

Sacks
none

Most Tackles
William White 9

Super Bowl Finalists' Playoff Statistics

Denver (3-0)

Passing	Att	Cmp	Pct.	Yds	TD	Rating
John Elway	86	45	52.3	691	3	85.9

Interceptions: Elway 1.

Receiving	No	Yds	Avg	Long	TD
Rod Smith	12	260	21.7	80-td	2
Ed McCaffrey	11	190	17.3	47	0
Shannon Sharpe	9	78	8.7	14	0
Byron Chamberlain	5	55	11.0	16	0
Terrell Davis	4	69	17.3	39	0
Howard Griffith	3	32	10.7	14	1
Dwayne Carswell	1	7	7.0	7	0
TOTAL	45	691	15.4	80-td	3

Rushing	Car	Yds	Avg	Long	TD
Terrell Davis	78	468	6.0	62	3
Derek Loville	12	49	4.1	11-td	1
John Elway	9	34	3.8	11	1
Howard Griffith	4	9	2.3	4	2
Rod Smith	1	1	1.0	1	0
Bubby Brister	7	-3	-0.4	2	0
Tom Rouen	1	-9	-9.0	-9	0
TOTAL	112	549	4.9	62	7

Touchdowns	TD	Run	Rec	Ret	Pts
Terrell Davis	3	3	0	0	18
Howard Griffith	3	2	1	0	18
Rod Smith	2	0	2	0	12
John Elway	1	1	0	0	6
Derek Loville	1	1	0	0	6
Neil Smith	1	0	0	1	6
TOTAL	11	7	3	1	66

Kicking		PAT/Att	FG/Att	Lg	Pts
Jason Elam		11/11	6/8	48	29

Punts	No	Yds	Long	Avg	In20
Tom Rouen	10	449	59	44.9	4

Interceptions		Sacks	
Darrien Gordon	4	John Mobley	1
Darrius Johnson	2	Bill Romanowski	1
Bill Romanowski	1	Marvin Washington	1

Broncos' 1998 Schedule

Date	Regular Season (14-2)	Result	W-L
Sept. 7*	New England (0-0)	W, 27-21	1-0
Sept. 13	Dallas (1-0)	W, 42-23	2-0
Sept. 20	at Oakland (1-1)	W, 34-17	3-0
Sept. 27	at Washington (0-3)	W, 38-16	4-0
Oct. 4	Philadelphia (0-4)	W, 41-16	5-0
Oct. 11	at Seattle (3-2)	W, 21-16	6-0
Oct. 18	OPEN DATE	—	—
Oct. 25	Jacksonville (5-1)	W, 37-24	7-0
Nov. 1	at Cincinnati (2-5)	W, 33-26	8-0
Nov. 8	San Diego (3-5)	W, 27-10	9-0
Nov. 16*	at Kansas City (4-5)	W, 30-7	10-0
Nov. 22	Oakland (7-3)	W, 40-14	11-0
Nov. 29	at San Diego (5-6)	W, 31-16	12-0
Dec. 6	Kansas City (5-7)	W, 35-31	13-0
Dec. 13	NY Giants (5-8)	L, 16-20	13-1
Dec. 21*	Miami (9-5)	L, 21-31	13-2
Dec. 27	Seattle (8-7)	W, 28-21	14-2

Date	Playoffs (3-0)	Result	W-L
Jan. 3	Bye	—	—
Jan. 9†	Miami (11-6)	W, 38-3	15-2
Jan. 17	NY Jets (13-4)	W, 23-10	16-2
Jan. 31	at Atlanta (16-2)	W, 34-19	17-2

*Monday; †Saturday.

Atlanta (2-1)

Passing	Att	Cmp	Pct.	Yds	TD	Rate
Chris Chandler	97	59	60.8	728	4	80.6

Interceptions: Chandler 4.

Receiving	No	Yds	Avg	Long	TD
Terance Mathis	18	229	12.7	30	3
Tony Martin	14	271	19.4	70	0
Jamal Anderson	10	59	5.9	11	1
Brian Kozlowski	6	19	3.2	5	0
Ronnie Harris	4	72	18.0	29	0
O.J. Santiago	4	67	16.8	26	0
Harold Green	2	9	4.5	8	0
Ed Smith	1	2	2.0	2	0
TOTAL	59	728	12.3	70	4

Rushing	Car	Yds	Avg	Long	TD
Jamal Anderson	70	276	3.9	34-td	2
Chris Chandler	9	52	5.8	12	0
Tim Dwight	4	33	8.3	21	0
Gary Downs	1	16	16.0	16	0
Ken Oxendine	1	0	0.0	0	0
TOTAL	85	377	4.4	34-td	2

Touchdowns	TD	Run	Rec	Ret	Pts
Jamal Anderson	3	2	1	0	18
Terance Mathis	3	0	3	0	18
Tim Dwight	1	0	0	1	6
TOTAL	7	2	4	1	42

Kicking		PAT/Att	FG/Att	Lg	Pts
Morten Andersen		6/6	7/8	38	27

Punts	No	Yds	Long	Avg	In20
Dan Stryzinski	8	341	56	42.6	4

Interceptions		Sacks	
William White	2	Lester Archambeau	1
Eugene Robinson	1	Randy Fuller	1
Ronnie Bradford	1	Chuck Smith	1
		Esera Tuaolo	1

Falcons' 1998 Schedule

Date	Regular Season (14-2)	Results	W-L
Sept. 6	at Carolina (0-0)	W, 19-14	1-0
Sept. 13	Philadelphia (0-1)	W, 17-12	2-0
Sept. 20	OPEN DATE	—	—
Sept. 27	at San Francisco (2-0)	L, 20-31	2-1
Oct. 4	Carolina (0-3)	W, 51-23	3-1
Oct. 11	at NY Giants (2-3)	W, 34-20	4-1
Oct. 18	New Orleans (3-2)	W, 31-23	5-1
Oct. 25	NY Jets (3-3)	L, 3-28	5-2
Nov. 1	St. Louis (2-5)	W, 37-15	6-2
Nov. 8	at New England (5-3)	W, 41-10	7-2
Nov. 15	San Francisco (7-2)	W, 31-19	8-2
Nov. 22	Chicago (3-7)	W, 20-13	9-2
Nov. 29	at St. Louis (3-8)	W, 21-10	10-2
Dec. 6	Indianapolis (2-10)	W, 28-21	11-2
Dec. 13	at New Orleans (6-7)	W, 27-17	12-2
Dec. 20	at Detroit (5-9)	W, 24-17	13-2
Dec. 27	Miami (10-5)	W, 38-16	14-2

Date	Playoffs (2-1)	Result	W-L
Jan. 3	Bye	—	—
Jan. 9†	San Francisco (13-4)	W, 20-18	15-2
Jan. 17	at Minnesota (16-1)	W, 30-27 (OT)	16-2
Jan. 31	Denver (16-2)	L, 19-34	16-3

*Monday; †Saturday.

NFL Pro Bowl

49th NFL Pro Bowl Game and 29th AFC-NFC contest (NFC leads series, 15-14). **Date:** Feb. 7 at Aloha Stadium in Honolulu. **Coaches:** Bill Belichick, NYJ, replacing Bill Parcells (AFC) and Dennis Green, Min. (NFC). **Players of the Game:** WR Keyshawn Johnson of the NY Jets who had 7 catches for 87 yards, and DB Ty Law of New England who returned an interception 67 yards for a TD.

NFC	3	0	7	0—	**10**
AFC	7	3	10	3—	**23**

1st: AFC—Sam Gash 3-yd pass from John Elway (Jason Elam kick), 10:51; NFC—Gary Anderson 23-yd FG, 5:49.

2nd: AFC—Elam 23-yd FG, 3:29.

3rd: AFC—Ty Law 67-yd interception return (Elam kick), 9:42; NFC—Emmitt Smith 3-yd run (Anderson kick), 6:31; AFC—Elam 46-yd FG, 2:22.

4th: AFC—Elam 26-yd FG, 13:58.

Attendance— 50,075. **TV Rating**— 8.1/13 share (ABC). **Time**— 3:16.

STARTING LINEUPS

As voted on by NFL players and coaches.

American Conference

Pos	Offense	Pos	Defense
WR	Jimmy Smith, Jax.	E	Michael McCrary, Bal.
WR	Ed McCaffrey, Den.	E	Bruce Smith, Buf.
TE	Shannon Sharpe*, Den.	T	Darrell Russell, Oak.
T	Tony Boselli, Jax.	T	Tim Bowens*, Mia.
T	Jonathan Ogden, Bal.	LB	Chad Brown, Sea.
G	Ruben Brown, Buf.	LB	Mo Lewis, NYJ
G	Bruce Matthews*, Ten.	LB	Junior Seau, SD
C	Dermontti Dawson, Pit.	CB	Ty Law, NE
QB	John Elway, Den.	CB	Aaron Glenn*, NYJ
RB	Terrell Davis, Den.	S	Rodney Harrison, SD
RB	Marshall Faulk, Ind.	S	Steve Atwater, Den.
FB	Sam Gash, Buf.	P	Craig Hentrich, Ten.
K	Jason Elam, Den.	ST	Bennie Thompson, Bal.
KR	Jermaine Lewis, Bal.		

* injured and unable to play.

Reserves

Offense: WR—Eric Moulds, Buf. and Keyshawn Johnson, NYJ; **TE**—Ben Coates, NE; **T**—Tony Jones, Den.; **G**—Will Shields, KC; **C**—Tom Nalen, Den.; **QB**—Vinny Testaverde, NYJ and Doug Flutie, Buf.; **RB**—Eddie George, Tenn.

Defense: E—Michael Sinclair, Sea.; **T**—Ted Washington, Buf.; **LB**—Bill Romanowski, Den. and Ray Lewis, Bal.; **CB**—Shawn Springs, Sea.; **S**—Lawyer Milloy, NE.

Replacements: OFFENSE—G Mark Schlereth, Den. for Matthews; TE Frank Wycheck, Ten. for Sharpe. DEFENSE—T Cortez Kennedy, Sea. for Bowens; CB Charles Woodson, Oak. for Glenn. NEED PLAYER—Peter Boulware, Bal., LB.

National Conference

Pos	Offense	Pos	Defense
WR	Randy Moss, Min.	E	Reggie White, GB
WR	Antonio Freeman, GB	E	Michael Strahan, NYG
TE	Mark Chmura, GB	T	John Randle, Min.
T	Larry Allen, Dal.	T	Warren Sapp, TB
T	William Roaf*, NO	LB	Derrick Brooks, TB
G	Randall McDaniel, Min.	LB	Kevin Greene, Car.
G	Kevin Gogan, SF	LB	Jessie Tuggle, Atl.
C	Jeff Christy, Min.	CB	Deion Sanders, Dal.
QB	Steve Young, SF	CB	Ray Buchanan, Atl.
RB	Barry Sanders*, Det.	S	LeRoy Butler, GB
RB	Jamal Anderson, Atl.	S	Eugene Robinson, Atl.
FB	Mike Alstott, TB	P	Matt Turk, Was.
K	Gary Anderson, Min.	ST	Michael Bates, Car.
KR	Roell Preston, GB		

* injured and unable to play.

Reserves

Offense: WR—Cris Carter, Min. and Jerry Rice, SF; **TE**—Wesley Walls, Car.; **T**— Todd Steussie, Min.; **G**—Nate Newton, Dal.; **C**— Tony Mayberry, TB; **QB**—Randall Cunningham, Min. and Chris Chandler, Atl.; **RB**—Garrison Hearst*, SF.

Defense: E—Joe Johnson, NO; **T**—Leon Lett, Dal.; **LB**—Jessie Armstead, NYG and Ed McDaniel*, Min.; **CB**—Aeneas Williams, Ari.; **S**—Darren Woodson, Dal.

Replacements: OFFENSE—T Bob Whitfield, Atl. for Roaf; RB Emmitt Smith, Dal. for Hearst; RB Robert Smith, Min. for Sanders. DEFENSE—LB Hardy Nickerson, TB for McDaniel. NEED PLAYER—Winfred Tubbs, SF, LB.

Annual Awards

The NFL does not sanction any of the major postseason awards for players and coaches, but many are given out. Among the presenters for the 1998 regular season were AP, The Maxwell Football Club of Philadelphia, *The Sporting News* and the Pro Football Writers of America.

Most Valuable Player

NFL Terrell Davis, Denver, RB ....AP, PFWA, *TSN*
& Randall Cunningham, Min, QB ......Miller Lite/NFL

Offensive Player of the Year

NFL Terrell Davis, Denver, RB ....AP, PFWA

Defensive Player of the Year

NFL Reggie White, Green Bay, DE ....AP, PFWA

Rookies of the Year

NFL Randy Moss, Minnesota, WR ....*TSN*, PFWA, Progressive/NFL
Offense Randy Moss, Minnesota, WR ....AP, PFWA
Defense Charles Woodson, Oakland, CB ....AP, PFWA

Coach of the Year

NFL Dan Reeves, Atlanta ....AP, *TSN*, PFWA, Staples/NFL

1998 All-NFL Team

The 1998 All-NFL team combining the All-Pro selections of the Associated Press, *The Sporting News (TSN)* and the Pro Football Writers of America (PFWA). Holdovers from the 1997 All-NFL Team in **bold** type.

Offense

Pos		Selectors
WR—	Randy Moss, Minnesota	AP, PFWA, *TSN*
WR—	Antonio Freeman, Green Bay	AP, PFWA, *TSN*
TE—	**Shannon Sharpe**, Denver	AP, PFWA, *TSN*
T—	**Tony Boselli**, Jacksonville	AP, PFWA, *TSN*
T—	**Larry Allen**, Dallas	AP, PFWA, *TSN*
G—	**Randall McDaniel**, Minnesota	AP, PFWA, *TSN*
G—	Bruce Matthews, Tennessee	AP, PFWA, *TSN*
C—	**Dermontti Dawson**, Pittsburgh	AP, PFWA, *TSN*
QB—	Randall Cunningham, Minnesota	AP, PFWA
QB—	Steve Young, San Francisco	*TSN*
RB—	**Terrell Davis**, Denver	AP, PFWA, *TSN*
RB—	Jamal Anderson, Atlanta	AP, PFWA, *TSN*
FB—	**Mike Alstott**, Tampa Bay	AP

Defense

Pos		Selectors
DE—	Reggie White, Green Bay	AP, PFWA, *TSN*
DE—	**Michael Strahan**, NY Giants	AP, PFWA
DE—	Michael McCrary, Baltimore	*TSN*
DT—	**John Randle**, Minnesota	AP, PFWA, *TSN*
DT—	Darrell Russell, Oakland	AP, PFWA
DT—	Bryant Young, San Francisco	*TSN*
LB—	Chad Brown, Seattle	AP, PFWA, *TSN*
LB—	Mo Lewis, NY Jets	AP, PFWA, *TSN*
LB—	Junior Seau, San Diego	AP, PFWA, *TSN*
CB—	Ty Law, New England	AP, PFWA, *TSN*
CB—	**Deion Sanders**, Dallas	AP, PFWA, *TSN*
S—	**LeRoy Butler**, Green Bay	AP, PFWA, *TSN*
S—	Rodney Harrison, San Diego	AP, PFWA, *TSN*
S—	Robert Griffith, Minnesota	*TSN*
S—	Darren Woodson, Dallas	*TSN*

Specialists

Pos		Selectors
PK—	Gary Anderson, Minnesota	AP, PFWA, *TSN*
P—	Craig Hentrich, Tennessee	AP, PFWA, *TSN*
KR—	Jermaine Lewis, Baltimore	AP
KR—	Terry Fair, Detroit	PFWA, *TSN*

Pos		Selectors
KR—	Roell Preston, Green Bay	PFWA
PR—	Deion Sanders, Dallas	PFWA
PR—	Jermaine Lewis, Baltimore	*TSN*
ST—	Bennie Thompson, Baltimore	PFWA

1999 College Draft

First and second round selections at the 64th annual NFL College Draft held April 17-18, 1999, in New York City. Fifteen underclassmen were among the first 61 players chosen and are listed in capital LETTERS.

First Round

No	Team		Pos
1	Cleveland	TIM COUCH, Kentucky	QB
2	Philadelphia	Donovan McNabb, Syracuse	QB
3	Cincinnati	Akili Smith, Oregon	QB
4	Indianapolis	EDGERRIN JAMES, Miami-FL	RB
5	New Orleans	Ricky Williams, Texas	RB
6	St. Louis	Torry Holt, N.C. State	WR
7	Washington	CHAMP BAILEY, Georgia	CB
8	Arizona	DAVID BOSTON, Ohio St.	WR
9	Detroit	CHRIS CLAIBORNE, USC	LB
10	Baltimore	Chris McAlister, Arizona	CB
11	Minnesota	Daunte Culpepper, Central Fla.	QB
12	Chicago	Cade McNown, UCLA	QB
13	Pittsburgh	Troy Edwards, La. Tech	WR
14	Kansas City	JOHN TAIT, BYU	OT
15	Tampa Bay	Anthony McFarland, LSU	DT
16	Tennessee	JEVON KEARSE, Florida	LB
17	New England	DAMIEN WOODY, Boston Col.	C
18	Oakland	Matt Stinchcomb, Georgia	OT
19	NY Giants	Luke Petitgout, Notre Dame	OT
20	Dallas	Ebenezer Ekuban, North Carolina	DE
21	Arizona	L.J. Shelton, Eastern Michigan	OT
22	Seattle	Lamar King, Saginaw Valley St.	DE
23	Buffalo	Antoine Winfield, Ohio St.	CB
24	San Francisco	REGGIE MCGREW, Florida	DT
25	Green Bay	Antwan Edwards, Clemson	CB
26	Jacksonville	Fernando Bryant, Alabama	CB
27	Detroit	Aaron Gibson, Wisconsin	G
28	New England	ANDY KATZENMOYER, Ohio St.	LB
29	Minnesota	DIMITRIUS UNDERWOOD, Mich. St.	DE
30	Atlanta	Patrick Kerney, Virginia	DE
31	Denver	Al Wilson, Tennessee	LB

Second Round

No	Team		Pos
32	Cleveland	Kevin Johnson, Syracuse	WR
33	Cincinnati	Charles Fisher, W. Virginia	CB
34	Carolina	Chris Terry, Georgia	OT
35	Philadelphia	Barry Gardner, Northwestern	LB
36	Indianapolis	Mike Peterson, Florida	LB
37	Washington	Jon Jansen, Michigan	OT
38	Carolina	Mike Rucker, Nebraska	DE
39	Miami	James Johnson, Mississippi St.	RB
40	Oakland	Tony Bryant, Florida St.	DE
41	St. Louis	DRE' BLY, North Carolina	CB
42	Atlanta	Reginald Kelly, Mississippi St.	TE
43	Miami	Rob Konrad, Syracuse	RB
44	Minnesota	Jim Kleinsasser, N. Dakota	TE
45	Cleveland	RAHIM ABDULLAH, Clemson	LB
46	New England	Kevin Faulk, LSU	RB
47	Green Bay	Fred Vinson, Vanderbilt	CB
48	Chicago	Russell Davis, North Carolina	DT
49	NY Giants	Joe Montgomery, Ohio St.	RB
50	Tampa Bay	Shaun King, Tulane	QB
51	Arizona	Johnny Rutledge, Florida	LB
52	Tennessee	John Thornton, W. Virginia	DT
53	Buffalo	Peerless Price, Tennessee	WR
54	Kansas City	Mike Cloud, Boston College	RB
55	Dallas	SOLOMON PAGE, W. Virginia	OL
56	Jacksonville	LARRY SMITH, Florida St.	DT
57	NY Jets	Randy Thomas, Mississippi St.	G
58	Denver	Montae Reagor, Texas Tech	DE
59	Pittsburgh	Scott Shields, Weber St.	S
60	San Diego	Jermaine Fazande, Oklahoma	RB
61	Denver	Lennie Friedman, Duke	C

NFL Head Coaching Changes For 1999

As of March 1, 1999, nine new head coaches were in place for the start of the '99 regular season.

AFC	Old Coach	Why Left?	New Coach	Hired	Old Job
Baltimore	Ted Marchibroda	Fired (Dec. 28)	Brian Billick	Jan. 19	Off. Coord., NFL Vikings
Cleveland	—	—	Chris Palmer	Jan. 21	Off. Coord., NFL Jaguars
Kansas City	Marty Schottenheimer	Resigned (Jan. 11)	Gunther Cunningham	Jan. 22	Def. Coord., NFL Chiefs
San Diego	June Jones	to U. Hawaii (Dec. 10)	Mike Riley	Jan. 7	Head Coach, Oregon St.
Seattle	Dennis Erickson	Fired (Dec. 28)	Mike Holmgren	Jan. 8	Head Coach, NFL Packers

NFC	Old Coach	Why Left?	New Coach	Hired	Old Job
Carolina	Dom Capers	Fired (Dec. 28)	George Seifert	Jan. 4	CBS TV Analyst
Chicago	Dave Wannstedt	Fired (Dec. 28)	Dick Jauron	Jan. 24	Def. Coord., NFL Jaguars
Green Bay	Mike Holmgren	to Seattle (Jan. 8)	Ray Rhodes	Jan. 11	Head Coach, NFL Eagles
Philadelphia	Ray Rhodes	Fired (Dec. 28)	Andy Reid	Jan. 11	Quarterbacks Coach, NFL Packers

Canadian Football League
Final 1998 Standings

Division champions (*) and other playoff qualifiers (†) are noted. Number of seasons listed after each head coach refers to latest tenure with club through 1998 season.

East Division

	W	L	T	Pts	PF	PA	Pct
*Hamilton	12	5	1	25	503	351	.706
†Montreal	12	5	1	25	470	435	.706
†Toronto	9	9	0	18	452	410	.500
Winnipeg	3	15	0	6	399	588	.167

1998 Head Coaches: Ham—Ron Lancaster (1st season); **Mon**—Dave Ritchie (2nd); **Tor**—Don Matthews (3rd); **Win**—Jeff Reinebold (2nd, 2-12) was replaced on Oct. 8 by interim coach Gary Hoffman (1-3).

1997 East Div. standings: 1. Toronto (15-3); 2. Montreal (13-5); 3. Winnipeg (4-14); 4. Hamilton (2-16).

West Division

	W	L	T	Pts	PF	PA	Pct
*Calgary	12	6	0	24	558	397	.667
†Edmonton	9	9	0	18	396	450	.500
†Brit. Columbia	9	9	0	18	394	427	.500
Saskatchewan	5	13	0	10	411	525	.278

1998 Head Coaches: Calg—Wally Buono (9th season); **Edm**—Kay Stephenson (1st); **BC**—Adam Rita (2nd, 3-6) was replaced on Sept. 1 by interim coach Greg Mohns (6-3); **Sask**—Jim Daley (3rd).

1997 West Div. standings: 1. Edmonton (12-6); 2. Calgary (10-8); 3. Saskatchewan (8-10); 4. British Columbia (8-10).

All-CFL Team

The All-CFL team as selected by a Football Reporters of Canada panel. Holdovers from the 1997 team are in **bold** type.

Offense
WR Terry Vaughn, Calg.
WR Don Narcisse, Sask.
T **Uzooma Okeke**, Mon.
T Moe Elewonibi, B.C.
G **Fred Childress**, Calg.
G **Pierre Vercheval**, Mon.
C Carl Coulter, Ham.
QB Jeff Garcia, Calg.
RB Kelvin Anderson, Calg.
RB **Mike Pringle**, Mon.
SB Allen Pitts, Calg.
SB **Derrell Mitchell**, Tor.

Defense
E Joe Montford, Ham.
E **Elfrid Payton**, Mon.
T Johnny Scott, B.C.
T Joe Fleming, Win.
LB Alondra Johnson, Calg.
LB Calvin Tiggle, Ham.
LB **Willie Pless**, Edm.
CB Eric Carter, Ham.
CB Steve Muhammad, B.C.
DB Orlondo Steinauer, Ham.
DB Gerald Vaughn, Ham.
S Dale Joseph, B.C.

Specialists
PK—Paul Osbaldiston, Ham.
P—Tony Martino, Calg.
Special Teams—Eric Blount, Win.

CFL Playoffs
Division Semifinals
(Nov. 8)

East: at Montreal 41 ....Toronto 28
West: at Edmonton 40 .....................B.C. 33

Division Championships
(Nov. 15)

East: at Hamilton 22 ....Montreal 20
West: at Calgary 33 ....Edmonton 10

86th Grey Cup Championship
Sun., Nov. 22, 1998 at Winnipeg Stadium, Winnipeg, Manitoba (Att: 34,157)

Hamilton (13-5-1)	3	13	2	6—	**24**
Calgary (13-6)	4	6	7	9—	**26**

Passing: HAM— Danny McManus 20-39-1-288; CALG— Jeff Garcia 22-32-0-260, Dave Dickenson 0-1-0-0.

Rushing: HAM— Ronald Williams 12-42, Trevor Shaw 1-20, Danny McManus 3-14; CALG— Kelvin Anderson 18-105, Jeff Garcia 11-47.

Receiving: HAM— Ronald Williams 5-78, Mike Morreale 4-62, Darren Flutie 4-50, Andrew Grigg 4-43, Archie Amerson 2-56, Bobby Olive 1-minus 1; CALG— Vince Danielsen 6-82, Allen Pitts 5-74, Travis Moore 3-35, Kelvin Anderson 3-27, Terry Vaughn 3-24, Aubrey Cummings 2-18.

Most Outstanding Player: Jeff Garcia, Calgary, QB (Passing— 22 for 32, 260 yds; 0 TD, 0 Int; Rushing—11 carries for 47 yds, 1 TD).

Most Outstanding Canadian: Vince Danielsen, Calgary, SB (6 catches for 82 yards).

Most Outstanding Awards

Player	Mike Pringle, Montreal, RB
Canadian	Mike Morreale, Hamilton, WR
Offensive Lineman	Fred Childress, Calgary, G
Defensive Player	Joe Montford, Hamilton, DE
Rookie	Steve Muhammad, B.C., CB
Tom Pate Award (Sportsmanship)	Glen Scrivener, Winnipeg, DT
Coach	Ron Lancaster, Hamilton

Regular Season Individual Leaders
Passing Efficiency
(Minimum of 200 attempts)

	Att	Cmp	Cmp Pct	Yds	Yds/ Att	Tds	TD Pct	Long	Int	Int Pct	Rating
Kerwin Bell, Tor.	567	381	67.2	4983	8.8	27	4.8	66	14	2.5	100.3
Jeff Garcia, Calg.	554	348	62.8	4276	7.7	28	5.1	62	15	2.7	92.2
Reggie Slack, Sask.	463	287	62.0	3721	8.0	19	4.1	73	16	3.5	86.5
Tracy Ham, Mon.	326	178	54.6	2511	7.7	21	6.4	75	12	3.7	85.8
Danny McManus, Ham.	584	333	57.0	4864	8.3	24	4.1	92	19	3.3	84.4
David Archer, Edm.	362	202	55.8	2860	7.9	8	2.2	48	8	2.2	79.7
Damon Allen, B.C.	479	282	58.9	3519	7.3	16	3.3	85	16	3.3	79.0
T.J. Rubley, Win.	257	148	57.6	1575	6.1	4	1.6	71	12	4.7	61.3

Rushing

	Car	Yds	Avg	Long	TD
Mike Pringle, Mon.	347	2064	5.9	56	9
Kelvin Anderson, Calg.	236	1325	5.6	44	9
Juan Johnson, B.C.	156	973	6.2	54	6
Mike Saunders, Sask.	160	897	5.6	46	5
Troy Mills, Edm.	177	813	4.6	23	2
Ronald Williams, Ham.	154	807	5.2	66	13
Damon Allen, B.C.	115	782	6.8	29	2
Archie Amerson, Ham.	160	703	4.4	69	3
Robert Drummond, B.C.	138	690	5.0	66	3
Reggie Slack, Sask.	87	650	7.5	44	9
Mike Clemons, Tor.	148	610	4.1	25	3
Jeff Garcia, Calg.	94	575	6.1	46	6
Eric Blount, Win.	123	544	4.4	28	3
Deland McCullough, Win.	94	429	4.6	26	4
Sean Millington, Win.	82	424	5.2	40	3

Receiving

	Rec	Yds	Avg	Long	TD
Derrell Mitchell, Tor.	160	2004	12.5	46	10
Darren Flutie, Ham.	98	1386	14.1	73	5
Allen Pitts, Calg.	96	1372	14.3	62	11
Donald Narcisse, Sask.	95	1215	12.8	44	7
Chris Armstrong, Mon.	67	1162	17.3	43	6
Donald Blair, Edm.	64	1091	17.0	51	6
Mike Morreale, Ham.	67	1076	16.1	92	6
Nigel Williams, Tor.	61	1057	17.3	78	5
Terry Vaughn, Calg.	81	1045	12.9	49	5
Vince Danielsen, Calg.	83	1039	12.5	49	6
Mike Clemons, Tor.	93	995	10.7	41	6
Paul Masotti, Tor.	66	897	13.6	66	2
Andrew Grigg, Ham.	51	889	17.4	62	4
Travis Moore, Calg.	61	818	13.6	89	7
Rod Harris, B.C.	48	799	16.6	85	5

Touchdowns

	TD	Rush	Rec	Ret	Pts
Kelvin Anderson, Calg.	16	9	7	0	96
Ronald Williams, Ham.	13	13	0	0	78
Allen Pitts, Calg.	11	0	11	0	66
Mike Saunders, Sask.	11	5	6	0	66
Derrell Mitchell, Tor.	10	0	10	0	60
Mike Clemons, Tor.	9	3	6	0	54
Reggie Slack, Sask.	9	9	0	0	54
Mike Pringle, Mon.	9	9	0	0	54
Archie Amerson, Ham.	8	3	5	0	48
Five tied with seven each.					

Kicking

	PAT	FG	S*	Pts
Terry Baker, Mon.	43/43	47/66	19	203
Lui Passaglia, B.C.	30/30	52/66	11	197
Paul Osbaldiston, Ham.	50/50	41/50	15	188
Mark McLoughlin, Calg.	56/58	35/54	14	175
Sean Fleming, Edm.	37/37	34/40	9	148
Troy Westwood, Win.	30/30	36/54	6	144
Paul McCallum, Sask.	42/42	28/39	11	137
Arek Bigos, Tor.	32/32	23/36	10	111

*Singles (or Rouges)

Punting
(Minimum of 50 attempts)

	No	Yds	Lg	Avg
Anthony Martino, Calg.	113	5451	81	48.2
Noel Prefontaine, Tor.	132	6169	86	46.7
Terry Baker, Mon.	125	5718	72	45.7
Robert Cameron, Win.	139	6266	70	45.1
Lui Passaglia, B.C.	130	5736	75	44.1
Paul Osbaldiston, Ham.	140	6055	73	43.3
Sean Fleming, Edm.	146	5993	69	41.0
Paul McCallum, Sask.	100	4073	59	40.7

Sacks

	Sacks
Joe Montford, Ham.	21
Elfrid Payton, Mon.	16
Joe Flemming, Win.	15
Malvin Hunter, Edm.	13
Johnny Scott, B.C.	13
Dave Chaytors, B.C.	10
Dewayne Patterson, Sask.	10
Daved Benefield, B.C.	9
Swift Burch, Mon.	9

Interceptions

	No	Yds	Lg	TD
Steve Muhammad, B.C.	10	165	49	0
Orlondo Steinauer, Ham.	8	138	52	1
Jackie Kellogg, Calg.	8	72	56	1
Glenn Rogers, B.C.	6	82	23	0
Gerald Vaughn, Ham.	6	143	60	1
Barron Miles, Mon.	6	82	35	0
Dwayne Provo, Edm.	6	139	49	2
Lester Smith, Tor.	6	57	40	0
Maurice Kelly, Win.	5	121	90	1
Eric Carter, Ham.	5	85	48	2

NFL Europe

Final 1999 Standings

	W	L	T	Pct.	PF	PA
*Barcelona	7	3	0	.700	263	246
*Frankfurt	6	4	0	.600	239	223
Rhein	6	4	0	.600	286	149
Amsterdam	4	6	0	.400	236	243
Scotland	4	6	0	.400	270	298
Berlin	3	7	0	.300	173	308

*World Bowl participants

Note: The teams with the top two records after the regular season advance directly to the World Bowl. Frankfurt and Rhein finished the season with the same record but Frankfurt was 2-0 in head-to-head meetings so it was awarded the berth.

World Bowl '99

June 27, 1999 at Rheinstadion in Dusseldorf, Germany (Att: 39,643)

Frankfurt (6-4)	3	14	7	14	—	38
Barcelona (7-3)	10	0	7	7	—	24

MVP: Andy McCullough, Frankfurt, WR (6 catches for 151 yards and 3 TDs.)

Regular Season Individual Leaders
Passing Efficiency
(Min. 140 pass attempts)

	Att	Cmp	Cmp Pct	Yds	Yds/ Att	TD	TD Pct	Long	Int	Int Pct	Rating
Jim Arellanes, Rhe	151	80	53.0	1325	8.77	15	9.9	96-td	4	2.6	104.9
Jake Delhomme, Fra	202	136	67.3	1410	6.98	12	5.9	47	5	2.5	96.8
Dameyune Craig, Sco	339	198	58.4	2932	8.65	21	6.2	86-td	12	3.5	92.7
Pat Barnes, Fra	164	94	57.3	1468	8.95	12	7.3	73-td	8	4.9	91.2
Todd Bouman, Bar	324	170	52.5	2296	7.09	16	4.9	71	11	3.4	77.7

Scoring

Touchdowns	TD	Rus	Rec	Ret	Pts
Lawrence Phillips, Bar	14	14	0	0	84
Jesse Haynes, Sco	11	7	4	0	66
Andy McCullough, Fra	10	0	10	0	60
Brian Finneran, Bar	8	0	8	0	48
Mario Bailey, Fran	8	0	8	0	48

Kicking	PAT	FG/FGA	Lg	Pts
Manfred Burgsmuller, Rhe	32/33	12/15	31	68
Ralf Kleinmann, Fra	23/25	11/19	52	57
Rob Hart, Sco	32/32	8/12	42	56
Jesus Angoy, Bar	28/30	9/14	49	55
Silvio Diliberto, Ams	21/24	9/15	41	48

Rushing

	Car	Yards	Avg	Long	TD
Lawrence Phillips, Bar	194	1021	5.3	72-td	14
Kenny Bynum, Rhe	194	960	4.9	51	5
Derrick Clark, Rhe	104	521	5.0	29-td	3
David Thompson, Ams	114	503	4.4	62	3
Edwin Watson, Ber	117	503	4.3	33	3

Punting

	No	Yards	Avg	Long	In20
Chris Dolan, Sco	36	1655	46.0	59	12
Jeff Beckley, Bar	40	1820	45.5	59	13
Barry Cantrell, Fra	39	1602	41.1	58	12
F. Biancamono, Ams	46	1821	39.6	60	13
Charlie Pierce, Ber	47	1840	39.1	61	15
Marcus Williams, Rhe	40	1538	38.5	53	10

Receptions

	No	Yards	Avg	Long	TD
Mario Bailey, Fra	63	850	13.5	51-td	8
Donald Sellers, Sco	58	931	16.1	71	7
Brian Finneran, Bar	54	844	15.6	67-td	8
Andy McCullough, Fra	48	883	18.4	73-td	10
Yo Murphy, Sco	45	752	16.7	75-td	4

Sacks

	No
Tyrone Williams, Rhe	9
Shane Doyle, Ams	6½
Chris Wing, Ams	5½
Brandon Noble, Bar	5
Reginald Lowe, Rhe	5
Barry Mitchell, Bar	5

Interceptions

	No	Yards	Long	TD
Greg Williams, Ams	6	87	34	0
Dell McGee, Rhe	4	72	46	0
Mike Maslowski, Bar	4	56	30-td	1
Joey Eloms, Sco	3	98	90-td	1
Gregoire Malo, Bar	3	75	49	0
Tristan Moss, Bar	3	43	16	0
Cedric Donaldson, Rhe	3	27	27	0

All-NFL Europe League Team

The All-NFL Europe League Team as selected by members of the NFL Europe media and by fan vote.

Pos	Offense	Pos	Defense
QB	Dameyune Craig, Sco	DE	Shane Doyle, Ams
RB	Lawrence Phillips, Bar	DE	Reginald Lowe, Rhe
RB	Kenny Bynum, Rhe	DT	Tyrone Williams, Rhe
WR	Mario Bailey, Fra	DT	Brandon Noble, Bar
WR	Brian Finneran, Bar	LB	Matt Finkes, Sco
TE	Cory Geason, Ams	LB	Mike Maslowski, Bar
G	Steve Scifres, Fra	LB	Whit Marshall, Fra
G	Mike Halapin, Rhe	CB	Ricky Bell, Sco
C	Jason McEndoo, Ber	CB	Dell McGee, Rhe
T	Barry Stokes, Sco	S	Tristan Moss, Bar
T	Deron Thorp, Bar	S	Greg Williams, Ams

Pos	Special Teams
K	Ralf Kleinmann, Fra
P	Chris Dolan, Sco
Spec.	Yo Murphy, Sco

Annual Awards

Offensive MVP . . . . . . Lawrence Phillips, Barcelona, RB
Defensive MVP . . . . Mike Maslowski, Barcelona, LB
Coach of the Year . . . . Dick Curl, Frankfurt

Arena Football
Final 1999 Standings

Division champions (*) and playoff qualifiers (†) are noted; top eight seeds advance to the playoffs.

American Conference
Central Division

	W	L	T	Pct.	PF	PA
*Iowa	11	3	0	.786	750	643
†Grand Rapids	8	6	0	.571	726	654
†Milwaukee	7	7	0	.500	621	721
Houston	4	10	0	.286	742	815

Western Division

	W	L	T	Pct.	PF	PA
*Arizona	10	4	0	.714	749	639
Portland	7	7	0	.500	613	597
San Jose	6	8	0	.429	712	746

National Conference
Eastern Division

	W	L	T	Pct.	PF	PA
*Albany	11	3	0	.786	822	674
New Jersey	6	8	0	.429	583	666
New England	5	9	0	.357	647	723
Buffalo	1	13	0	.071	467	642

Southern Division

	W	L	T	Pct.	PF	PA
*Tampa Bay	11	3	0	.786	690	488
†Nashville	8	6	0	.571	754	710
†Orlando	7	7	0	.500	634	646
Florida	3	11	0	.214	555	701

Playoffs
First Round

Arizona 34	Nashville 30
Albany 55	Grand Rapids 45
Orlando 41	Tampa Bay 19
Iowa 66	Milwaukee 34

Semifinals

Orlando 48	Iowa 41
Albany 73	Arizona 47

ArenaBowl XIII

August 21, 1999 at the Pepsi Arena in Albany
(Att: 13,652)

Orlando	14	7	13	14	—	**48**
Albany	21	17	0	21	—	**59**

MVP: Eddie Brown, Albany, offensive specialist (12 catches for 185 yards and 4 TDs.)

Regular Season Individual Leaders
Passing Efficiency

	Att	Cmp	Cmp Pct	Yds	Yds/ Att	TD	TD Pct	Int	Int Pct	Rating
Mike Pawlawski, Alb	442	294	66.5	3864	8.74	79	17.9	7	1.6	126.9
Chad May, Ari	150	94	62.7	1157	7.71	23	15.3	0	0.0	126.0
Craig Kusick, GR	458	306	66.8	3529	7.71	68	14.8	8	1.7	122.2
Andy Kelly, Nash	501	324	64.7	3609	7.20	67	13.4	11	2.2	116.4
Clint Dolezel, Hou	556	374	67.3	4336	7.80	80	14.4	19	3.4	116.0

Scoring

Touchdowns	TD	Rus	Rec	Ret	PAT	Pts
Eddie Brown, Alb	49	3	45	1	0	294
Barry Wagner, Orl	39	3	30	6	2	238
Thomas Bailey, GR	37	2	33	2	1	224
Robert Hall, Hou	34	2	32	0	2	208
Kevin Swayne, Iowa	34	0	32	2	1	206
Cory Fleming, Nash	34	0	31	3	1	206

Kicking	PAT	2PAT	FG/FGA	Pts
Daron Alcorn, Por	57/72	0/3	32/54	153
Carlos Huerta, SJ	88/90	0/0	18/38	142
Mike Black, NE	75/77	0/0	22/45	141
Steve McLaughlin, Nash	85/93	0/0	17/35	136
Kenny Stucker, Mil	70/76	0/0	21/50	133

Rushing

	Car	Yards	Avg	TD
Bob McMillen, Ari	43	180	4.2	8
Rick Hamilton, Orl	51	147	2.9	4
Tony Burse, Buf	54	146	2.7	10
Tim Brown, Alb	47	145	3.1	6
Les Barley, TB	63	142	2.3	11

Receptions

	No	Yards	Avg	TD
Eddie Brown, Alb	138	1858	13.5	45
Thomas Bailey, GR	133	1578	11.9	33
Curtis Ceaser, Fla	118	1586	13.4	31
Cory Fleming, Nash	111	1227	11.1	31
Alvin Ashley, NJ	109	1352	12.4	26

Annual Awards

Tinactin Ironman of the Year . . . . . Hunkie Cooper, Ari.
Offensive Player of the Year . . . . . . Eddie Brown, Alb.
Defensive Player of the Year . . . . . James Baron, Nash.

All-Arena First Team

Pos	
QB	Mike Pawlawski, Albany
FB/LB	Andre Bowden, Tampa Bay
WR/DB	Carlos James, Iowa
WR/DB	Darryl Hammond, Nashville
WR/LB	Gary Compton, Milwaukee
OS	Eddie Brown, Albany
OL/DL	Joe Jacobs, Albany
OL/DL	James Baron, Nashville
OL/DL	Robert Stewart, New Jersey
DS	Cecil Doggette, Arizona
DS	Derek Stingley, Albany
K	Mike Black, New England

PRO FOOTBALL
STATISTICS

THROUGH THE YEARS
1920-1999
BOWLS • ALL-TIME LEADERS

THE 2000 ESPN INFORMATION PLEASE SPORTS ALMANAC

SEC B

PAGE 242

The Super Bowl

The first AFL-NFL World Championship Game, as it was originally called, was played seven months after the two leagues agreed to merge in June of 1966. It became the Super Bowl (complete with roman numerals) by the third game in 1969. The Super Bowl winner has been presented the Vince Lombardi Trophy since 1971. Lombardi, whose Green Bay teams won the first two title games, died in 1970. NFL champions (1966-69) and NFC champions (since 1970) are listed in CAPITAL letters.

Multiple winners: Dallas and San Francisco (5); Pittsburgh (4); Green Bay, Oakland-LA Raiders and Washington (3); Denver, Miami and NY Giants (2).

Bowl	Date	Winner	Head Coach	Score	Loser	Head Coach	Site
I	1/15/67	GREEN BAY	Vince Lombardi	35-10	Kansas City	Hank Stram	Los Angeles
II	1/14/68	GREEN BAY	Vince Lombardi	33-14	Oakland	John Rauch	Miami
III	1/12/69	NY Jets	Weeb Ewbank	16-7	BALTIMORE	Don Shula	Miami
IV	1/11/70	Kansas City	Hank Stram	23-7	MINNESOTA	Bud Grant	New Orleans
V	1/17/71	Baltimore	Don McCafferty	16-13	DALLAS	Tom Landry	Miami
VI	1/16/72	DALLAS	Tom Landry	24-3	Miami	Don Shula	New Orleans
VII	1/14/73	Miami	Don Shula	14-7	WASHINGTON	George Allen	Los Angeles
VIII	1/13/74	Miami	Don Shula	24-7	MINNESOTA	Bud Grant	Houston
IX	1/12/75	Pittsburgh	Chuck Noll	16-6	MINNESOTA	Bud Grant	New Orleans
X	1/18/76	Pittsburgh	Chuck Noll	21-17	DALLAS	Tom Landry	Miami
XI	1/9/77	Oakland	John Madden	32-14	MINNESOTA	Bud Grant	Pasadena
XII	1/15/78	DALLAS	Tom Landry	27-10	Denver	Red Miller	New Orleans
XIII	1/21/79	Pittsburgh	Chuck Noll	35-31	DALLAS	Tom Landry	Miami
XIV	1/20/80	Pittsburgh	Chuck Noll	31-19	LA RAMS	Ray Malavasi	Pasadena
XV	1/25/81	Oakland	Tom Flores	27-10	PHILADELPHIA	Dick Vermeil	New Orleans
XVI	1/24/82	SAN FRANCISCO	Bill Walsh	26-21	Cincinnati	Forrest Gregg	Pontiac, MI
XVII	1/30/83	WASHINGTON	Joe Gibbs	27-17	Miami	Don Shula	Pasadena
XVIII	1/22/84	LA Raiders	Tom Flores	38-9	WASHINGTON	Joe Gibbs	Tampa
XIX	1/20/85	SAN FRANCISCO	Bill Walsh	38-16	Miami	Don Shula	Stanford
XX	1/26/86	CHICAGO	Mike Ditka	46-10	New England	Raymond Berry	New Orleans
XXI	1/25/87	NY GIANTS	Bill Parcells	39-20	Denver	Dan Reeves	Pasadena
XXII	1/31/88	WASHINGTON	Joe Gibbs	42-10	Denver	Dan Reeves	San Diego
XXIII	1/22/89	SAN FRANCISCO	Bill Walsh	20-16	Cincinnati	Sam Wyche	Miami
XXIV	1/28/90	SAN FRANCISCO	George Seifert	55-10	Denver	Dan Reeves	New Orleans
XXV	1/27/91	NY GIANTS	Bill Parcells	20-19	Buffalo	Marv Levy	Tampa
XXVI	1/26/92	WASHINGTON	Joe Gibbs	37-24	Buffalo	Marv Levy	Minneapolis
XXVII	1/31/93	DALLAS	Jimmy Johnson	52-17	Buffalo	Marv Levy	Pasadena
XXVIII	1/30/94	DALLAS	Jimmy Johnson	30-13	Buffalo	Marv Levy	Atlanta
XXIX	1/29/95	SAN FRANCISCO	George Seifert	49-26	San Diego	Bobby Ross	Miami
XXX	1/28/96	DALLAS	Barry Switzer	27-17	Pittsburgh	Bill Cowher	Tempe, AZ
XXXI	1/26/97	GREEN BAY	Mike Holmgren	35-21	New England	Bill Parcells	New Orleans
XXXII	1/25/98	Denver	Mike Shanahan	31-24	GREEN BAY	Mike Holmgren	San Diego
XXXIII	1/31/99	Denver	Mike Shanahan	34-19	ATLANTA	Dan Reeves	Miami

Pete Rozelle Award (MVP)

The Most Valuable Player in the Super Bowl. Currently selected by an 11-member panel made up of national pro football writers and broadcasters chosen by the NFL. Presented by *Sport* magazine from 1967-89 and by the NFL since 1990. Named after former NFL commissioner Pete Rozelle in 1990. Winner who did not play for Super Bowl champion is in **bold** type.

Multiple winners: Joe Montana (3); Terry Bradshaw and Bart Starr (2).

Bowl		Bowl		Bowl	
I	Bart Starr, Green Bay, QB	XII	Harvey Martin, Dallas, DE	XXIII	Jerry Rice, San Francisco, WR
II	Bart Starr, Green Bay, QB		& Randy White, Dallas, DT	XXIV	Joe Montana, San Francisco, QB
III	Joe Namath, NY Jets, QB	XIII	Terry Bradshaw, Pittsburgh, QB	XXV	Ottis Anderson, NY Giants, RB
IV	Len Dawson, Kansas City, QB	XIV	Terry Bradshaw, Pittsburgh, QB	XXVI	Mark Rypien, Washington, QB
V	**Chuck Howley**, Dallas, LB	XV	Jim Plunkett, Oakland, QB	XXVII	Troy Aikman, Dallas, QB
VI	Roger Staubach, Dallas, QB	XVI	Joe Montana, San Francisco, QB	XXVIII	Emmitt Smith, Dallas, RB
VII	Jake Scott, Miami, S	XVII	John Riggins, Washington, RB	XXIX	Steve Young, San Francisco, QB
VIII	Larry Csonka, Miami, RB	XVIII	Marcus Allen, LA Raiders, RB	XXX	Larry Brown, Dallas, CB
IX	Franco Harris, Pittsburgh, RB	XIX	Joe Montana, San Francisco, QB	XXXI	Desmond Howard, Green Bay, KR
X	Lynn Swann, Pittsburgh, WR	XX	Richard Dent, Chicago, DE	XXXII	Terrell Davis, Denver, RB
XI	Fred Biletnikoff, Oakland, WR	XXI	Phil Simms, NY Giants, QB	XXXIII	John Elway, Denver, QB
		XXII	Doug Williams, Washington, QB		

All-Time Super Bowl Leaders

Through 1999; participants in Super Bowl XXXIII in **bold** type.

CAREER

Passing Efficiency

		Gm	Att	Cmp	Cmp%	Yards	Avg Gain	TD	TD%	Int	Int%	Rating
1	Phil Simms, NYG	1	25	22	88.0	268	10.72	3	12.0	0	0.0	150.9
2	Steve Young, SF	2	39	26	66.7	345	8.85	6	15.4	0	0.0	134.1
3	Doug Williams, Wash.	1	29	18	62.1	340	11.72	4	13.8	1	3.4	128.1
4	Joe Montana, SF	4	122	83	68.0	1142	9.36	11	9.0	0	0.0	127.8
5	Jim Plunkett, Raiders	2	46	29	63.0	433	9.41	4	8.7	0	0.0	122.8
6	Terry Bradshaw, Pit	4	84	49	58.3	932	11.10	9	10.7	4	4.8	112.8
7	Troy Aikman, Dal.	3	80	56	70.0	689	8.61	5	6.3	1	1.3	111.9
8	Bart Starr, GB.	2	47	29	61.7	452	9.62	3	6.4	1	2.1	106.0
9	Brett Favre, GB	2	69	39	56.5	502	7.28	5	7.2	1	1.4	97.6
10	Roger Staubach, Dal.	4	98	61	62.2	734	7.49	8	8.2	4	4.1	95.4

Ratings based on performance standards established for completion percentage, average gain, touchdown percentage and interception percentage. Quarterbacks are allocated points according to how their statistics measure up to those standards. Minimum 25 passing attempts.

Passing Yards

		Gm	Att	Cmp	Pct	Yds
1	Joe Montana, SF	4	122	83	68.0	1142
2	**John Elway**, Den	5	152	76	50.0	1128
3	Terry Bradshaw, Pit	4	84	49	58.3	932
4	Jim Kelly, Buf	4	145	81	55.9	829
5	Roger Staubach, Dal.	4	98	61	62.2	734
6	Troy Aikman, Dal.	3	80	56	70.0	689
7	Brett Favre, GB	2	69	39	56.5	502
8	Fran Tarkenton, Min	3	89	46	51.7	489
9	Bart Starr, GB	2	47	29	61.7	452
10	Jim Plunkett, Raiders	2	46	29	63.0	433
11	Joe Theismann, Wash.	2	58	31	53.4	386
12	Len Dawson, KC	2	44	28	63.6	353
13	Steve Young, SF	2	26	39	66.7	345
14	Doug Williams, Wash.	1	29	18	62.1	340
15	Dan Marino, Mia	1	50	29	58.0	318

Receptions

		Gm	No	Yds	Avg	TD
1	Jerry Rice, SF	3	28	512	18.3	7
2	Andre Reed, Buf	4	27	323	12.0	0
3	Roger Craig, SF	3	20	212	10.6	3
	Thurman Thomas, Buf	4	20	144	7.2	0
5	Jay Novacek, Dal	3	17	148	8.7	2
6	Lynn Swann, Pit	4	16	364	22.8	3
7	Michael Irvin, Dal	3	16	256	16.0	2
8	Chuck Foreman, Min.	3	15	139	9.3	0
9	Cliff Branch, Raiders	3	14	181	12.9	3
10	Don Beebe, Buf	3	12	171	14.3	2
	Preston Pearson, Bal-Pit-Dal	5	12	105	8.8	0
	Kenneth Davis, Buf	4	12	72	6.0	0
	Antonio Freeman, GB	2	12	231	19.3	3
14	John Stallworth, Pit	4	11	268	24.4	3
	Dan Ross, Cin	1	11	104	9.5	2

Super Bowl Appearances

Through Super Bowl XXXIII, 10 NFL teams have yet to play for the Vince Lombardi Trophy. In alphabetical order, they are: Arizona, Baltimore Ravens, Carolina, Cleveland, Detroit, Jacksonville, New Orleans, Seattle, Tampa Bay and Tennessee. Of the 21 teams that have participated, Dallas has the most appearances (8) and, along with San Francisco, has the most titles (5).

App		W	L	Pct	PF	PA
8	Dallas	5	3	.625	221	132
6	Denver	2	4	.333	115	206
5	San Francisco	5	0	1.000	188	89
5	Pittsburgh	4	1	.800	120	100
5	Washington	3	2	.600	122	103
5	Miami	2	3	.400	74	103
4	Green Bay	3	1	.750	127	76
4	Oak/LA Raiders	3	1	.750	111	66
4	Buffalo	0	4	.000	73	139
4	Minnesota	0	4	.000	34	95
2	NY Giants	2	0	1.000	59	39
2	Baltimore Colts	1	1	.500	23	29
2	Kansas City	1	1	.500	33	42
2	Cincinnati	0	2	.000	37	46
2	New England	0	2	.000	31	81
1	Chicago	1	0	1.000	46	10
1	NY Jets	1	0	1.000	16	7
1	Atlanta	0	1	.000	19	34
1	LA Rams	0	1	.000	19	31
1	Philadelphia	0	1	.000	10	27
1	San Diego	0	1	.000	26	49

Rushing

		Gm	Car	Yds	Avg	TD
1	Franco Harris, Pit.	4	101	354	3.5	4
2	Larry Csonka, Mia.	3	57	297	5.2	2
3	Emmitt Smith, Dal.	3	70	289	4.1	5
4	**Terrell Davis**, Den	2	55	259	4.7	3
5	John Riggins, Wash.	2	64	230	3.6	2
6	Timmy Smith, Wash.	1	22	204	9.3	2
	Thurman Thomas, Buf	4	52	204	3.9	4
8	Roger Craig, SF	3	52	201	3.9	2
9	Marcus Allen, Raiders	1	20	191	9.5	2
10	Tony Dorsett, Dal	2	31	162	5.2	1
11	Mark van Eeghen, Raiders	2	37	153	4.1	0
12	Dorsey Levens, GB	2	33	151	4.6	0
13	Kenneth Davis, Buf	4	30	145	4.8	0
14	Rocky Bleier, Pit	4	44	144	3.3	0
15	Walt Garrison, Dal	2	26	139	5.3	0

All-Purpose Yards

		Gm	Rush	Rec	Ret	Total
1	Jerry Rice, SF	3	15	512	0	527
2	Franco Harris, Pit	4	354	114	0	468
3	Roger Craig, SF	3	201	212	0	413
4	Lynn Swann, Pit	4	-7	364	34	391
5	Thurman Thomas, Buf	4	204	144	0	348
6	Emmitt Smith, Dal.	3	289	56	0	345
7	Antonio Freeman, GB	2	0	231	104	335
8	Andre Reed, Buf	3	0	323	0	323
9	**Terrell Davis**, Den	2	259	58	0	317
10	Larry Csonka, Mia.	3	297	17	0	314

Scoring

Points

		Gm	TD	FG	PAT	Pts
1	Jerry Rice, SF	3	7	0	0	42
2	Emmitt Smith, Dal.	3	5	0	0	30
3	Roger Craig, SF	3	4	0	0	24
	Franco Harris, Pit.	4	4	0	0	24
	Thurman Thomas, Buf	4	4	0	0	24
	John Elway, Den	5	4	0	0	24
7	Ray Wersching, SF	2	0	5	7	22
8	Don Chandler, GB	2	0	4	8	20
9	Cliff Branch, Raiders	3	3	0	0	18
	John Stallworth, Pit	4	3	0	0	18
	Lynn Swann, Pit	4	3	0	0	18
	Ricky Watters, SF	1	3	0	0	18
	Terrell Davis, Den	2	3	0	0	18
	Antonio Freeman, GB	2	3	0	0	18
15	Chris Bahr, Raiders	2	0	3	8	17
	Jason Elam, Den	2	0	3	8	17

Punting

(Minimum 10 Punts)

		Gm	No	Yds	Avg.
1	Jerrel Wilson, KC	2	11	511	46.5
2	Ray Guy, Raiders	3	14	587	41.9
3	Larry Seiple, Mia	3	15	620	41.3
4	Mike Eischeid, Raiders-Min	4	17	698	41.1
5	Danny White, Dal	2	10	406	40.6

Punt Returns

(Minimum 4 returns)

		Gm	No	Yds	Avg.	TD
1	John Taylor, SF	3	6	94	15.7	0
2	Desmond Howard, GB	1	6	90	15.0	0
3	Neal Colzie, Raiders	1	4	43	10.8	0
4	Dana McLemore, SF	1	5	51	10.2	0
5	Mike Fuller, Cin	1	4	35	8.8	0

Kickoff Returns

(Minimum 4 returns)

		Gm	No	Yds	Avg.	TD
1	**Tim Dwight**, Atl	1	5	210	42.0	1
2	Desmond Howard, GB	1	4	154	38.5	1
3	Fulton Walker, Mia	2	8	283	35.4	1
4	Andre Coleman, SD	1	8	242	30.3	1
5	Larry Anderson, Pit	2	8	207	25.9	0

Touchdowns

		Gm	Rush	Rec	Ret	TD
1	Jerry Rice, SF	3	0	7	0	7
2	Emmitt Smith, Dal.	3	5	0	0	5
3	Roger Craig, SF	3	2	2	0	4
	Franco Harris, Pit.	4	4	0	0	4
	Thurman Thomas, Buf	4	4	0	0	4
	John Elway, Den	5	4	0	0	4
7	Cliff Branch, Raiders	3	0	3	0	3
	John Stallworth, Pit	4	0	3	0	3
	Lynn Swann, Pit	4	0	3	0	3
	Ricky Watters, SF	1	1	2	0	3
	Terrell Davis, Den	1	3	0	0	3
	Antonio Freeman, GB	2	0	3	0	3
13	Twenty-three tied with 2 TDs each:					

Marcus Allen, Raiders; Ottis Anderson, NYG; Pete Banaszak, Raiders; Don Beebe, Buf.; Gary Clark, Wash.; Larry Csonka, Mia.; **Howard Griffith**, Den.; Michael Irvin, Dal.; Butch Johnson, Dal.; Jim Kiick, Mia.; Max McGee, GB; Jim McMahon, Chi.; Bill Miller, Raiders; Joe Montana, SF; Elijah Pitts, GB; Tom Rathman, SF; John Riggins, Wash.; Gerald Riggs, Wash.; Dan Ross, Cin.; Ricky Sanders, Wash.; Timmy Smith, Wash.; John Taylor, SF and Duane Thomas, Dal.

Interceptions

		Gm	No	Yds	TD
1	Larry Brown, Dal	2	3	77	0
	Chuck Howley, Dal	2	3	63	0
	Rod Martin, Raiders	2	3	44	0
4	Randy Beverly, NYJ	1	2	0	0
	Mel Blount, Pit	4	2	23	0
	Brad Edwards, Wash	1	2	56	0
	Thomas Everett, Dal.	2	2	22	0
	Darrien Gordon, Den.	3	2	108	0
	Jake Scott, Mia	3	2	63	0
	Mike Wagner, Pit.	3	2	45	0
	James Washington, Dal	2	2	25	0
	Barry Wilburn, Wash	1	2	11	0
	Eric Wright, SF.	4	2	25	0

Sacks

		Gm	No
1	Charles Haley, SF-Dal	5	4½
2	Reggie White, GB	2	3
	Leonard Marshall, NYG	2	3
	Danny Stubbs, SF	2	3
	Jeff Wright, Buf	4	3

Four or More Super Bowl Wins

Dallas Cowboys (5)

Year	Bowl	Head Coach	Quarterback	MVP	Opponent	Score	Site
1972	VI	Tom Landry	Roger Staubach	Staubach	Miami	24-3	New Orleans
1978	XII	Tom Landry	Roger Staubach	Harvey Martin & Randy White	Denver	27-10	New Orleans
1993	XXVII	Jimmy Johnson	Troy Aikman	Aikman	Buffalo	52-17	Pasadena
1994	XXVIII	Jimmy Johnson	Troy Aikman	Emmitt Smith	Buffalo	30-13	Atlanta
1996	XXX	Barry Switzer	Troy Aikman	Larry Brown	Pittsburgh	27-17	Tempe

San Francisco 49ers (5)

Year	Bowl	Head Coach	Quarterback	MVP	Opponent	Score	Site
1982	XVI	Bill Walsh	Joe Montana	Montana	Cincinnati	26-21	Pontiac
1985	XIX	Bill Walsh	Joe Montana	Montana	Miami	38-16	Stanford
1989	XXIII	Bill Walsh	Joe Montana	Jerry Rice	Cincinnati	20-16	Miami
1990	XXIV	George Seifert	Joe Montana	Montana	Denver	55-10	New Orleans
1995	XXIX	George Seifert	Steve Young	Young	San Diego	49-26	Miami

Pittsburgh Steelers (4)

Year	Bowl	Head Coach	Quarterback	MVP	Opponent	Score	Site
1975	IX	Chuck Noll	Terry Bradshaw	Franco Harris	Minnesota	16-6	New Orleans
1976	X	Chuck Noll	Terry Bradshaw	Lynn Swann	Dallas	21-17	Miami
1979	XIII	Chuck Noll	Terry Bradshaw	Bradshaw	Dallas	35-31	Miami
1980	XIV	Chuck Noll	Terry Bradshaw	Bradshaw	LA Rams	31-19	Pasadena

SINGLE GAME

Passing

Yards Gained

		Year	Att/Cmp	Yds
1	Joe Montana, SF vs Cin	1989	36/23	357
2	Doug Williams, Wash vs Den	1988	29/18	340
3	**John Elway**, Den vs Atl	1999	29/18	336
4	Joe Montana, SF vs Mia	1985	35/24	331
5	Steve Young, SF vs SD	1995	36/24	325
6	Terry Bradshaw, Pit vs Dal	1979	30/17	318
	Dan Marino, Mia vs SF	1985	50/29	318
8	Terry Bradshaw, Pit vs Rams	1980	21/14	309
9	John Elway, Den vs NYG	1987	37/22	304
10	Ken Anderson, Cin vs SF	1982	34/25	300

Touchdown Passes

		Year	TD	Int
1	Steve Young, SF vs SD	1995	6	0
2	Joe Montana, SF vs Den	1990	5	0
3	Terry Bradshaw, Pit vs Dal	1979	4	1
	Doug Williams, Wash vs Den	1988	4	1
	Troy Aikman, Dal vs Buf	1993	4	0
6	Roger Staubach, Dal vs Pit	1979	3	1
	Jim Plunkett, Raiders vs Phi	1981	3	0
	Joe Montana, SF vs Mia	1985	3	0
	Phil Simms, NYG vs Den	1987	3	0
	Brett Favre, GB vs Den	1998	3	1

Rushing

Yards Gained

		Year	Car	Yds	TD
1	Timmy Smith, Wash vs Den	1988	22	204	2
2	Marcus Allen, Raiders vs Wash	1984	20	191	2
3	John Riggins, Wash vs Mia	1983	38	166	1
4	Franco Harris, Pit vs Min	1975	34	158	1
5	Terrell Davis, Den vs GB	1998	30	157	3
6	Larry Csonka, Mia vs Min	1974	33	145	2
7	Clarence Davis, Raiders vs Min.	1977	16	137	0
8	Thurman Thomas, Buf vs NYG	1991	15	135	1
9	Emmitt Smith, Dal vs Buf	1994	30	132	2
10	Matt Snell, NYJ vs Bal	1969	30	121	1
11	Tom Matte, Bal vs NYJ	1969	11	116	0
12	Larry Csonka, Mia vs Wash	1973	15	112	1
13	Emmitt Smith, Dal vs Buf	1993	22	108	1
14	Ottis Anderson, NYG vs Buf	1991	21	102	1
	Terrell Davis, Den vs Atl	1999	25	102	0

Scoring

Points

		Year	TD	FG	PAT	Pts
1	Roger Craig, SF vs Mia	1985	3	0	0	18
	Jerry Rice, SF vs Den	1990	3	0	0	18
	Jerry Rice, SF vs SD	1995	3	0	0	18
	Ricky Watters, SF vs SD	1995	3	0	0	18
	Terrell Davis, Den vs GB	1998	3	0	0	18
6	Don Chandler, GB vs Raiders	1968	0	4	3	15

Touchdowns

		Year	TD	Rush	Rec
1	Roger Craig, SF vs Mia	1985	3	1	2
	Jerry Rice, SF vs Den	1990	3	0	3
	Jerry Rice, SF vs SD	1995	3	0	3
	Ricky Watters, SF vs SD	1995	3	1	2
	Terrell Davis, Den vs GB	1998	3	3	0

6 Nineteen tied with 2 TDs each:
(In order of occurrence) Max McGee, GB; Elijah Pitts, GB; Bill Miller, Raiders; Larry Csonka, Mia.; Pete Banaszak, Raiders; John Stallworth, Pit.; Franco Harris, Pit.; Cliff Branch, Oak.; Dan Ross, Cin.; Marcus Allen, Raiders; Jim McMahon, Chi.; Ricky Sanders, Wash.; Timmy Smith, Wash.; Tom Rathman, SF; Gerald Riggs, Wash.; Michael Irvin, Dal.; Emmitt Smith, Dal. (twice); Antonio Freeman, GB; **Howard Griffith**, Den.

Receiving

Catches

		Year	No	Yds	TD
1	Dan Ross, Cin vs SF	1982	11	104	2
	Jerry Rice, SF vs Cin	1989	11	215	1
3	Tony Nathan, Mia vs SF	1985	10	83	0
	Jerry Rice, SF vs SD	1995	10	149	3
	Andre Hastings, Pit vs Dal	1996	10	98	0
6	Ricky Sanders, Wash vs Den	1988	9	193	2
	Antonio Freeman, GB vs Den	1998	9	126	2
8	Five tied with eight each, including twice by Andre Reed.				

Yards Gained

		Year	No	Yds	TD
1	Jerry Rice, SF vs Cin	1989	11	215	1
2	Ricky Sanders, Wash vs Den	1988	9	193	2
3	Lynn Swann, Pit vs Dal	1976	4	161	1
4	Andre Reed, Buf vs Dal	1993	8	152	0
	Rod Smith, Den vs Atl	1999	5	152	1
6	Jerry Rice, SF vs SD	1995	10	149	3
7	Jerry Rice, SF vs Den	1990	7	148	3
8	Max McGee, GB vs KC	1967	7	138	2
9	George Sauer, NYJ vs Bal	1969	8	133	0
10	Willie Gault, Chi vs NE	1986	4	129	0

All-Purpose Yards

Yards Gained

		Year	Run	Rec	Tot
1	Desmond Howard, GB vs NE	1997	0	0	244
2	Andre Coleman, SD vs SF	1995	0	0	242
3	Ricky Sanders, Wash vs Den	1988	193	-4	235
4	Antonio Freeman, GB vs Den	1998	0	126	230
5	Jerry Rice, SF vs Cin	1989	215	5	220
6	**Tim Dwight**, Atl vs Den	1999	5	0	215
7	Timmy Smith, Wash vs Den	1988	204	9	213
8	Marcus Allen, Raiders vs Wash	1984	191	18	209
9	Stephen Starring, NE vs Chi	1986	0	39	192
10	Fulton Walker, Mia vs Wash	1983	0	0	190
	Thurman Thomas, Buf vs NYG	1991	135	55	190

Return Yardage: Howard 244, Coleman 242, Sanders 46, Freeman 104, Dwight 210, Starring 153, Walker 190.

Interceptions

		Year	No	Yds	TD
1	Rod Martin, Raiders vs Phi	1981	3	44	0
2	Seven tied with two each.				

Punting
(Minimum 4 punts)

		Year	No	Yds	Avg
1	Bryan Wagner, SD vs SF	1995	4	195	48.8
2	Jerrel Wilson, KC vs Min	1970	4	194	48.5
3	Jim Miller, SF vs Cin	1982	4	185	46.3

Punt Returns
(Minimum 3 returns)

		Year	No	Yds	Avg
1	John Taylor, SF vs Cin	1989	3	56	18.7
2	Desmond Howard, SF vs NE	1997	6	90	15.0
3	John Taylor, SF vs Den	1990	3	38	12.7
4	Kelvin Martin, Dal vs Buf	1993	3	35	11.7

Kickoff Returns
(Minimum 3 returns)

		Year	No	Yds	Avg
1	Fulton Walker, Mia vs Wash	1983	4	190	47.5
2	**Tim Dwight**, Atl vs Den	1999	5	210	42.0
3	Desmond Howard, GB vs NE	1997	4	154	38.5
4	Larry Anderson, Pit vs Rams	1980	5	162	32.4
5	Rick Upchurch, Den vs Dal	1978	3	94	31.3

Super Bowl Playoffs

The Super Bowl forced the NFL to set up pro football's first guaranteed multiple-game playoff format. Over the years, the NFL-AFL merger, the creation of two conferences comprised of three divisions each and the proliferation of wild card entries has seen the postseason field grow from four teams (1966), to six (1967-68), to eight (1969-77), to 10 (1978-81, 1983-89), to the present 12 (since 1990).

In 1968, there was a special playoff between Oakland and Kansas City which were both 12–2 and tied for first in the AFL's Western Division. In 1982, when a 57-day players' strike shortened the regular season to just nine games, playoff berths were extended to 16 teams (eight from each conference) and a 15-game tournament was played.

Note that in the following year-by-year summary, records of finalists include all games leading up to the Super Bowl; (*) indicates non-division winners or wild card teams.

1966 Season

AFL Playoffs

Championship . . . . Kansas City 31, at Buffalo 7

NFL Playoffs

Championship . . . . Green Bay 34, at Dallas 27

Super Bowl I

Jan. 15, 1967
Memorial Coliseum, Los Angeles
Favorite: Packers by 14   Attendance: 61,946

Kansas City (12-2-1)	0	10	0	0	**−10**
Green Bay (13-2)	7	7	14	7	**−35**

MVP: Green Bay QB Bart Starr (16 for 23, 250 yds, 2 TD, 1 Int)

1967 Season

AFL Playoffs

Championship . . . . at Oakland 40, Houston 7

NFL Playoffs

Eastern Conference . . . . at Dallas 52, Cleveland 14
Western Conference . . . . at Green Bay 28, LA Rams 7
Championship . . . . at Green Bay 21, Dallas 17

Super Bowl II

Jan. 14, 1968
Orange Bowl, Miami
Favorite: Packers by 13½   Attendance: 75,546

Green Bay (11-4-1)	3	13	10	7	**−33**
Oakland (14-1)	0	7	0	7	**−14**

MVP: Green Bay QB Bart Starr (13 for 24, 202 yds, 1 TD)

1968 Season

AFL Playoffs

Western Div. Playoff . . . . at Oakland 41, Kansas City 6
AFL Championship . . . . at NY Jets 27, Oakland 23

NFL Playoffs

Eastern Conference . . . . at Cleveland 31, Dallas 20
Western Conference . . . . . . at Baltimore 24, Minnesota 14
NFL Championship . . . . Baltimore 34, at Cleveland 0

Super Bowl III

Jan. 12, 1969
Orange Bowl, Miami
Favorite: Colts by 18   Attendance: 75,389

NY Jets (12-3)	0	7	6	3	**−16**
Baltimore (15-1)	0	0	0	7	**−7**

MVP: NY Jets QB Joe Namath (17 for 28, 206 yds)

1969 Season

AFL Playoffs

Inter-Division . . . . *Kansas City 13, at NY Jets 6
at Oakland 56, *Houston 7
AFL Championship . . . . Kansas City 17, at Oakland 7

NFL Playoffs

Eastern Conference . . . . Cleveland 38, at Dallas 14
Western Conference . . . . at Minnesota 23, LA Rams 20
NFL Championship . . . . at Minnesota 27, Cleveland 7

Super Bowl IV

Jan. 11, 1970
Tulane Stadium, New Orleans
Favorite: Vikings by 12   Attendance: 80,562

Minnesota (14-2)	0	0	7	0	**−7**
Kansas City (13-3)	3	13	7	0	**−23**

MVP: KC QB Len Dawson (12 for 17, 142 yds, 1 TD, 1 Int)

1970 Season

AFC Playoffs

First Round . . . . at Baltimore 17, Cincinnati 0
at Oakland 21, *Miami 14
Championship . . . . at Baltimore 27, Oakland 17

NFC Playoffs

First Round. . . . . at Dallas 5, *Detroit 0
San Francisco 17, at Minnesota 14
Championship . . . . Dallas 17, at San Francisco 10

Super Bowl V

Jan. 17, 1971
Orange Bowl, Miami
Favorite: Cowboys by 2½   Attendance: 79,204

Baltimore (13-2-1)	0	6	0	10	**−16**
Dallas (12-4)	3	10	0	0	**−13**

MVP: Dallas LB Chuck Howley (2 interceptions for 22 yds)

1971 Season

AFC Playoffs

First Round. . . . . Miami 27, at Kansas City 24 (OT)
*Baltimore 20, at Cleveland 3
Championship . . . . at Miami 21, Baltimore 0

NFC Playoffs

First Round . . . . Dallas 20, at Minnesota 12
at San Francisco 24, *Washington 20
Championship . . . . at Dallas 14, San Francisco 3

Super Bowl VI

Jan. 16, 1972
Tulane Stadium, New Orleans
Favorite: Cowboys by 6   Attendance: 81,023

Dallas (13-3)	3	7	7	7	**−24**
Miami (12-3-1)	0	3	0	0	**−3**

MVP: Dallas QB Roger Staubach (12 for 19, 119 yds, 2 TD)

1972 Season

AFC Playoffs

First Round . . . . .at Pittsburgh 13, Oakland 7
at Miami 20, *Cleveland 14
Championship . . . . .Miami 21, at Pittsburgh 17

NFC Playoffs

First Round . . . .*Dallas 30, at San Francisco 28
at Washington 16, Green Bay 3
Championship . . . . .at Washington 26, Dallas 3

Super Bowl VII

Jan. 14, 1973
Memorial Coliseum, Los Angeles
Favorite: Redskins by 1½   Attendance: 90,182

Miami (16-0) 7   7   0   0   —**14**
Washington (13-3) 0   0   0   7   —**7**
MVP: Miami safety Jake Scott (2 Interceptions for 63 yds)

1973 Season

AFC Playoffs

First Round . . . . .at Oakland 33, *Pittsburgh 14
at Miami 34, Cincinnati 16
Championship . . . . .at Miami 27, Oakland 10

NFC Playoffs

First Round . . . . .at Minnesota 27, *Washington 20
at Dallas 27, LA Rams 16
Championship . . . . .Minnesota 27, at Dallas 10

Super Bowl VIII

Jan. 13, 1974
Rice Stadium, Houston
Favorite: Dolphins by 6½   Attendance: 71,882

Minnesota (14-2) 0   0   0   7   —**7**
Miami (12-4) 14   3   7   0   —**24**
MVP: Miami FB Larry Csonka (33 carries, 145 yds, 2 TD)

1974 Season

AFC Playoffs

First Round . . . . .at Oakland 28, Miami 26
at Pittsburgh 32, *Buffalo 14
Championship . . . . .Pittsburgh 24, at Oakland 13

NFC Playoffs

First Round . . . . .at Minnesota 30, St.Louis 14
at LA Rams 19, *Washington 10
Championship . . . . .at Minnesota 14, LA Rams 10

Super Bowl IX

Jan. 12, 1975
Tulane Stadium, New Orleans
Favorite: Steelers by 3   Attendance: 80,997

Pittsburgh (12-3-1) 0   2   7   7   —**16**
Minnesota (12-4) 0   0   0   6   —**6**
MVP: Pittsburgh RB Franco Harris (34 carries, 158 yds, 1 TD)

1975 Season

AFC Playoffs

First Round . . . . .at Pittsburgh 28, Baltimore 10
at Oakland 31, *Cincinnati 28
Championship . . . . .at Pittsburgh 16, Oakland 10

NFC Playoffs

First Round . . . . .at LA Rams 35, St. Louis 23
*Dallas 17, at Minnesota 14
Championship . . . . .Dallas 37, at LA Rams 7

Super Bowl X

Jan. 18, 1976
Orange Bowl, Miami
Favorite: Steelers by 6½   Attendance: 80,187

Dallas (12-4) 7   3   0   7   —**17**
Pittsburgh (14-2) 7   0   0   14   —**21**
MVP: Pittsburgh WR Lynn Swann (4 catches, 161 yds, 1 TD)

1976 Season

AFC Playoffs

First Round . . . . .at Oakland 24, *New England 21
Pittsburgh 40, at Baltimore 14
Championship . . . . .at Oakland 24, Pittsburgh 7

NFC Playoffs

First Round . . . . .at Minnesota 35, *Washington 20
LA Rams 14, at Dallas 12
Championship . . . . .at Minnesota 24, LA Rams 13

Super Bowl XI

Jan. 9, 1977
Rose Bowl, Pasadena
Favorite: Raiders by 4½   Attendance: 103,438

Oakland (15-1) 0   16   3   13   —**32**
Minnesota (13-2-1) 0   0   7   7   —**14**
MVP: Oakland WR Fred Biletnikoff (4 catches, 79 yds)

1977 Season

AFC Playoffs

First Round . . . . .at Denver 34, Pittsburgh 21
*Oakland 37, at Baltimore 31 (OT)
Championship . . . . .at Denver 20, Oakland 17

NFC Playoffs

First Round . . . . .at Dallas 37, *Chicago 7
Minnesota 14, at LA Rams 7
Championship . . . . .at Dallas 23, Minnesota 6

Super Bowl XII

Jan. 15, 1978
Louisiana Superdome, New Orleans
Favorite: Cowboys by 6   Attendance: 75,583

Dallas (14-2) 10   3   7   7   —**27**
Denver (14-2) 0   0   10   0   —**10**
MVPs: Dallas DE Harvey Martin and DT Randy White
(Cowboys' defense forced 8 turnovers)

A Year Later . . .

Super Bowl champions who did not qualify for the playoffs the following season.

Season		Record	Finish	Season		Record	Finish
1968	Green Bay	6-7-1	3rd in NFL Central	1982	San Francisco	3-6-0*	11th in overall NFC
1970	Kansas City	7-5-2	2nd in AFC West	1987	NY Giants	6-9-0*	5th in NFC East
1980	Pittsburgh	9-7-0	3rd in AFC Central	1988	Washington	7-9-0	3rd in NFC East
1981	Oakland	7-9-0	4th in AFC West	1991	NY Giants	8-8-0	4th in NFC East

* Seasons when player strikes interrupted schedule.

Super Bowl Playoffs (Cont.)

1978 Season

AFC Playoffs

First Round . . . . *Houston 17, at *Miami 9
Second Round . . . . .Houston 31, at New England 14
at Pittsburgh 33, Denver 10
Championship . . . . .at Pittsburgh 34, Houston 5

NFC Playoffs

First Round . . . . .at *Atlanta 14, *Philadelphia 13
Second Round . . . . .at Dallas 27, Atlanta 20
at LA Rams 34, Minnesota 10
Championship . . . . .Dallas 28, at LA Rams 0

Super Bowl XIII

Jan. 21, 1979
Orange Bowl, Miami
Favorite: Steelers by 4   Attendance: 79,484

Pittsburgh (16-2) 7	14	0	14	**—35**	
Dallas (14-4) 7	7	3	14	**—31**	

MVP: Pittsburgh QB Terry Bradshaw (17 for 30, 318 yds, 4 TD, 1 Int)

1979 Season

AFC Playoffs

First Round . . . . .at *Houston 13, *Denver 7
Second Round . . . . .Houston 17, at San Diego 14
at Pittsburgh 34, Miami 14
Championship . . . . .at Pittsburgh 27, Houston 13

NFC Playoffs

First Round . . . . .at *Philadelphia 27, *Chicago 17
Second Round . . . . .at Tampa Bay 24, Philadelphia 17
LA Rams 21, at Dallas 19
Championship . . . . .LA Rams 9, at Tampa Bay 0

Super Bowl XIV

Jan. 20, 1980
Rose Bowl, Pasadena
Favorite: Steelers by 10½   Attendance: 103,985

LA Rams (11-7) 7	6	6	0	**—19**	
Pittsburgh (14-4) 3	7	7	14	**—31**	

MVP: Pittsburgh QB Terry Bradshaw (14 for 21, 309 yds, 2 TD, 3 Int)

1980 Season

AFC Playoffs

First Round . . . . .at *Oakland 27, *Houston 7
Second Round . . . . .at San Diego 20, Buffalo 14
Oakland 14, at Cleveland 12
Championship . . . . .Oakland 34, at San Diego 27

NFC Playoffs

First Round . . . . .at *Dallas 34, *LA Rams 13
Second Round . . . . .at Philadelphia 31, Minnesota 16
Dallas 30, at Atlanta 27
Championship . . . . .at Philadelphia 20, Dallas 7

Super Bowl XV

Jan. 25, 1981
Louisiana Superdome, New Orleans
Favorite: Eagles by 3   Attendance: 76,135

Oakland (14-5) 14	0	10	3	**—27**	
Philadelphia (14-4) 0	3	0	7	**—10**	

MVP: Oakland QB Jim Plunkett (13 for 21, 261 yds, 3 TD)

1981 Season

AFC Playoffs

First Round . . . .*Buffalo 31, at *NY Jets 27
Second Round . . . . .San Diego 41, at Miami 38 (OT)
at Cincinnati 28, Buffalo 21
Championship . . . . .at Cincinnati 27, San Diego 7

NFC Playoffs

First Round . . . .*NY Giants 27, at *Philadelphia 21
Second Round . . . . .at Dallas 38, Tampa Bay 0
at San Francisco 38, NY Giants 24
Championship . . . . .at San Francisco 28, Dallas 27

Super Bowl XVI

Jan. 24, 1982
Pontiac Silverdome, Pontiac, Mich.
Favorite: Pick'em   Attendance: 81,270

San Francisco (15-3) 7	13	0	6	**—26**	
Cincinnati (14-4) 0	0	7	14	**—21**	

MVP: San Francisco QB Joe Montana (14 for 22, 157 yds, 1 TD; 6 carries, 18 yds, 1 TD)

1982 Season

A 57-day players' strike shortened the regular season from 16 games to nine. The playoff format was changed to a 16-team tournament open to the top eight teams in each conference.

AFC Playoffs

First Round . . . . .at LA Raiders 27, Cleveland 10
at Miami 28, New England 3
NY Jets 44, at Cincinnati 17
San Diego 31, at Pittsburgh 28
Second Round . . . . .NY Jets 17, at LA Raiders 14
at Miami 34, San Diego 13
Championship . . . . .at Miami 14, NY Jets 0

NFC Playoffs

First Round . . . . .at Washington 31, Detroit 7
at Dallas 30, Tampa Bay 17
at Green Bay 41, St. Louis 16
at Minnesota 30, Atlanta 24
Second Round . . . . .at Washington 21, Minnesota 7
at Dallas 37, Green Bay 26
Championship . . . . .at Washington 31, Dallas 17

Super Bowl XVII

Jan. 30, 1983
Rose Bowl, Pasadena
Favorite: Dolphins by 3   Attendance: 103,667

Miami (10-2) 7	10	0	0	**—17**	
Washington (11-1) 0	10	3	14	**—27**	

MVP: Washington RB John Riggins (38 carries, 166 yds, 1 TD; 1 catch, 15 yds)

Most Popular Playing Sites

Stadiums hosting more than one Super Bowl.

No		Years
5	Orange Bowl (Miami)	1968-69, 71, 76, 79
5	Rose Bowl (Pasadena)	1977, 80, 83, 87, 93
5	Superdome (N. Orleans)	1978, 81, 86, 90, 97
3	Tulane Stadium (N. Orleans)	1970, 72, 75
3	Joe Robbie/Pro Player Stadium (Miami)	1989, 95, 99
2	LA Memorial Coliseum	1967, 73
2	Tampa Stadium	1984, 91
2	Jack Murphy/Qualcomm Stadium (San Diego)	1988, 98

1983 Season

AFC Playoffs

First Round.....................at *Seattle 31, *Denver 7
Second Round ....Seattle 27, at Miami 20
at LA Raiders 38, Pittsburgh 10
Championship..............at LA Raiders 30, Seattle 14

NFC Playoffs

First Round..................*LA Rams 24, at *Dallas 17
Second Round............at San Francisco 24, Detroit 23
at Washington 51, LA Rams 7
Championship ....at Washington 24, San Francisco 21

Super Bowl XVIII

Jan. 22, 1984
Tampa Stadium, Tampa
Favorite: Redskins by 3   Attendance: 72,920

Washington (16-2)	0	3	6	0	**—9**
LA Raiders (14-4)	7	14	14	3	**—38**

MVP: LA Raiders RB Marcus Allen (20 carries, 191 yds, 2 TD; 2 catches, 18 yds)

1984 Season

AFC Playoffs

First Round.................at *Seattle 13, *LA Raiders 7
Second Round ....at Miami 31, Seattle 10
Pittsburgh 24, at Denver 17
Championship................at Miami 45, Pittsburgh 28

NFC Playoffs

First Round..............*NY Giants 16, at *LA Rams 13
Second Round.........at San Francisco 21, NY Giants 0
Chicago 23, at Washington 19
Championship..........at San Francisco 23, Chicago 0

Super Bowl XIX

Jan. 20, 1985
Stanford Stadium, Stanford, Calif.
Favorite: 49ers by 3   Attendance: 84,059

Miami (16-2)	10	6	0	0	**—16**
San Francisco (17-1)	7	21	10	0	**—38**

MVP: San Francisco QB Joe Montana (24 for 35, 331 yds, 2 TD; 5 carries, 59 yards, 1 TD)

1985 Season

AFC Playoffs

First Round ....*New England 26, at *NY Jets 14
Second Round................at Miami 24, Cleveland 21
New England 27, at LA Raiders 20
Championship............New England 31, at Miami 14

NFC Playoffs

First Round ....at *NY Giants 17, *San Francisco 3
Second Round ....at LA Rams 20, Dallas 0
at Chicago 21, NY Giants 0
Championship................at Chicago 24, LA Rams 0

Super Bowl XX

Jan. 26, 1986
Louisiana Superdome, New Orleans
Favorite: Bears by 10   Attendance: 73,818

Chicago Bears (17-1)	13	10	21	2	**—46**
New England (14-5)	3	0	0	7	**—10**

MVP: Chicago DE Richard Dent (Bears defense: 7 sacks, 6 turnovers, 1 safety and gave up just 123 total yards)

1986 Season

AFC Playoffs

First Round..............at *NY Jets 35, *Kansas City 15
Second Round ....at Cleveland 23, NY Jets 20 (OT)
at Denver 22, New England 17
Championship ....Denver 23, at Cleveland 20 (OT)

NFC Playoffs

First Round ....at *Washington 19, *LA Rams 7
Second Round............Washington 27, at Chicago 13
at NY Giants 49, San Francisco 3
Championship ....at NY Giants 17, Washington 0

Super Bowl XXI

Jan. 25, 1987
Rose Bowl, Pasadena
Favorite: Giants by 9½   Attendance: 101,063

Denver (13-5)	10	0	0	10	**—20**
NY Giants (16-2)	7	2	17	13	**—39**

MVP: NY Giants QB Phil Simms (22 for 25, 268 yds, 3 TD; 3 carries, 25 yds)

1987 Season

A 24-day players' strike shortened the regular season to 15 games with replacement teams playing for three weeks.

AFC Playoffs

First Round ....at *Houston 23, *Seattle 20 (OT)
Second Round ....at Cleveland 38, Indianapolis 21
at Denver 34, Houston 10
Championship................at Denver 38, Cleveland 33

NFC Playoffs

First Round.........*Minnesota 44, at *New Orleans 10
Second Round........Minnesota 36, at San Francisco 24
Washington 21, at Chicago 17
Championship ....at Washington 17, Minnesota 10

Super Bowl XXII

Jan. 31, 1988
San Diego/Jack Murphy Stadium
Favorite: Broncos by 3½   Attendance: 73,302

Washington (13-4)	0	35	0	7	**—42**
Denver (12-4-1)	10	0	0	0	**—10**

MVP: Washington QB Doug Williams (18 for 29, 340 yds, 4 TD, 1 Int)

1988 Season

AFC Playoffs

First Round................*Houston 24, at *Cleveland 23
Second Round.................at Buffalo 17, Houston 10
at Cincinnati 21, Seattle 13
Championship...............at Cincinnati 21, Buffalo 10

NFC Playoffs

First Round ....at *Minnesota 28, *LA Rams 17
Second Round.........at San Francisco 34, Minnesota 9
at Chicago 20, Philadelphia 12
Championship ....San Francisco 28, at Chicago 3

Super Bowl XXIII

Jan. 22, 1989
Joe Robbie Stadium, Miami
Favorite: 49ers by 7   Attendance: 75,129

Cincinnati (14-4)	0	3	10	3	**—16**
San Francisco (12-6)	3	0	3	14	**—20**

MVP: San Francisco WR Jerry Rice (11 catches, 215 yds, 1 TD; 1 carry, 5 yds)

Super Bowl Playoffs (Cont.)

1989 Season

AFC Playoffs

First Round . . . . *Pittsburgh 26, at *Houston 23
Second Round . . . . at Cleveland 34, Buffalo 30
     at Denver 24, Pittsburgh 23
Championship . . . . at Denver 37, Cleveland 21

NFC Playoffs

First Round . . . . *LA Rams 21, at *Philadelphia 7
Second Round . . . . LA Rams 19, NY Giants 13 (OT)
     at San Francisco 41, Minnesota 13
Championship . . . . at San Francisco 30, LA Rams 3

Super Bowl XXIV
Jan. 28, 1990
Louisiana Superdome, New Orleans
Favorite: 49ers by 12½   Attendance: 72,919

San Francisco (17-2)	13	14	14	14	**—55**
Denver (13-6)	3	0	7	0	**—10**

MVP: San Francisco QB Joe Montana (22 for 29, 297 yds, 5 TD)

1990 Season

AFC Playoffs

First Round . . . . at *Miami 17, *Kansas City 16
     at Cincinnati 41, *Houston 14
Second Round . . . . at Buffalo 44, Miami 34
     at LA Raiders 20, Cincinnati 10
Championship . . . . at Buffalo 51, LA Raiders 3

NFC Playoffs

First Round . . . . *Washington 20, at *Philadelphia 6
     at Chicago 16, *New Orleans 6
Second Round . . . . at San Francisco 28, Washington 10
     at NY Giants 31, Chicago 3
Championship . . . . NY Giants 15, at San Francisco 13

Super Bowl XXV
Jan. 27, 1991
Tampa Stadium, Tampa
Favorite: Bills by 7   Attendance: 73,813

Buffalo (15-4)	3	9	0	7	**—19**
NY Giants (16-3)	3	7	7	3	**—20**

MVP: NY Giants RB Ottis Anderson (21 carries, 102 yds, 1 TD; 1 catch, 7 yds)

1991 Season

AFC Playoffs

First Round . . . . at *Kansas City 10, *LA Raiders 6
     at Houston 17, *NY Jets 10
Second Round . . . . at Denver 26, Houston 24
     at Buffalo 37, Kansas City 14
Championship . . . . at Buffalo 10, Denver 7

NFC Playoffs

First Round . . . . *Atlanta 27, at New Orleans 20
     *Dallas 17, at *Chicago 13
Second Round . . . . at Washington 24, Atlanta 7
     at Detroit 38, Dallas 6
Championship . . . . at Washington 41, Detroit 10

Super Bowl XXVI
Jan. 26, 1992
Hubert Humphrey Metrodome, Minneapolis
Favorite: Redskins by 7   Attendance: 63,130

Washington (16-2)	0	17	14	6	**—37**
Buffalo (15-3)	0	0	10	14	**—24**

MVP: Washington QB Mark Rypien (18 for 33, 292 yds, 2 TD, 1 Int)

1992 Season

AFC Playoffs

First Round . . . . at *Buffalo 41, *Houston 38 (OT)
     at San Diego 17, *Kansas City 0
Second Round . . . . Buffalo 24, at Pittsburgh 3
     at Miami 31, San Diego 0
Championship . . . . Buffalo 29, at Miami 10

NFC Playoffs

First Round . . . . *Washington 24, at Minnesota 7
     *Philadelphia 36, at *New Orleans 20
Second Round . . . . at San Francisco 20, Washington 13
     at Dallas 34, Philadelphia 10
Championship . . . . Dallas 30, at San Francisco 20

Super Bowl XXVII
Jan. 31, 1993
Rose Bowl, Pasadena
Favorite: Cowboys by 7   Attendance: 98,374

Buffalo (14-5)	7	3	7	0	**—17**
Dallas (15-3)	14	14	3	21	**—52**

MVP: Dallas QB Troy Aikman (22 for 30, 273 yds, 4 TD)

1993 Season

AFC Playoffs

First Round . . . . at Kansas City 27, *Pittsburgh 24 (OT)
     at *LA Raiders 42, *Denver 24
Second Round . . . . at Buffalo 29, LA Raiders 23
     Kansas City 28, at Houston 20
Championship . . . . at Buffalo 30, Kansas City 13

NFC Playoffs

First Round . . . . *Green Bay 28, at Detroit 24
     at *NY Giants 17, *Minnesota 10
Second Round . . . . at San Francisco 44, NY Giants 3
     at Dallas 27, Green Bay 17
Championship . . . . at Dallas 38, San Francisco 21

Super Bowl XXVIII
Jan. 30, 1994
Georgia Dome, Atlanta
Favorite: Cowboys by 10½   Attendance: 72,817

Dallas (15-4)	6	0	14	10	**—30**
Buffalo (14-5)	3	10	0	0	**—13**

MVP: Dallas RB Emmitt Smith (30 carries, 132 yds, 2 TDs; 4 catches, 26 yds)

1994 Season

AFC Playoffs

First Round . . . . at Miami 27, *Kansas City 17
     at *Cleveland 20, *New England 13
Second Round . . . . at Pittsburgh 29, Cleveland 9
     at San Diego 22, Miami 21
Championship . . . . San Diego 17, at Pittsburgh 13

NFC Playoffs

First Round . . . . at *Green Bay 16, *Detroit 12
     *Chicago 25, at Minnesota 18
Second Round . . . . at San Francisco 44, Chicago 15
     at Dallas 35, Green Bay 9
Championship . . . . at San Francisco 38, Dallas 28

Super Bowl XXIX
Jan. 29, 1995
Joe Robbie Stadium, Miami
Favorite: 49ers by 18   Attendance: 74,107

San Diego (13-5)	7	3	8	8	**—26**
San Francisco (15-3)	14	14	14	7	**—49**

MVP: San Francisco QB Steve Young (24 for 36, 325 yds, 6 TD)

1995 Season

AFC Playoffs

First Round . . . . .at Buffalo 37, *Miami 22
*Indianapolis 35, at *San Diego 20
Second Round . . . . .at Pittsburgh 40, Buffalo 21
*Indianapolis 10, at Kansas City 7
Championship. . . . . .at Pittsburgh 20, *Indianapolis 16

NFC Playoffs

First Round . . . . at *Philadelphia 58, *Detroit 37
at Green Bay 37, *Atlanta 20
Second Round . . . . Green Bay 27, at San Francisco 17
at Dallas 30, *Philadelphia 11
Championship . . . . at Dallas 38, Green Bay 27

Super Bowl XXX
Jan. 28, 1996
Sun Devil Stadium, Tempe, Ariz.
Favorite: Cowboys by 13½ Attendance: 76,347

Dallas (14-4)	. . . .	10	3	7	7	—27
Pittsburgh (13-5)	. . . .	0	7	0	10	—17

MVP: Dallas CB Larry Brown (2 interceptions for 77 yds)

1996 Season

AFC Playoffs

First Round . . . .*Jacksonville 30, at *Buffalo 27
at Pittsburgh 42, *Indianapolis 14
Second Round . . . .*Jacksonville 30, at Denver 27
at New England 28, Pittsburgh 3
Championship. . . . . . . .at New England 20, *Jacksonville 6

NFC Playoffs

First Round. . . . . at Dallas 40, *Minnesota 15
at *San Francisco 14, *Philadelphia 0
Second Round . . . . . . at Green Bay 35, *San Francisco 14
at Carolina 26, Dallas 17
Championship . . . . at Green Bay 30, Carolina 13

Super Bowl XXXI
Jan. 26, 1997
Louisiana Superdome, New Orleans
Favorite: Packers by 14 Attendance: 72,301

New England (13-5)	. . . .	14	0	7	0	—21
Green Bay (15-3)	. . . .	10	17	8	0	—35

MVP: Green Bay KR Desmond Howard (4 kickoff returns for 154 yds and 1 TD, also 6 punt returns for 90 yds)

1997 Season

AFC Playoffs

First Round . . . . .at *Denver 42, *Jacksonville 17
at New England 17, *Miami 3
Second Round . . . . .at Pittsburgh 7, New England 6
*Denver 14, at Kansas City 10
Championship . . . . *Denver 24, at Pittsburgh 21

NFC Playoffs

First Round . . . .*Minnesota 23, at NY Giants 22
at *Tampa Bay 20, *Detroit 10
Second Round . . . . . . .at San Francisco 38, *Minnesota 22
at Green Bay 21, *Tampa Bay 7
Championship . . . . . . .Green Bay 23, at San Francisco 10

Super Bowl XXXII
Jan. 25, 1998
Qualcomm Stadium, San Diego
Favorite: Packers by 11½ Attendance: 68,912

Green Bay (15-3)	. . . .	7	7	3	7	—24
Denver (15-4)	. . . .	7	10	7	7	—31

MVP: Denver RB Terrell Davis (30 carries, 157 yds, 3 TDs; 2 catches, 8 yds)

1998 Season

AFC Playoffs

First Round . . . . .at *Miami 24, *Buffalo 17
at Jacksonville 25, *New England 10
Second Round . . . . .at NY Jets 34, Jacksonville 24
at Denver 38, *Miami 3
Championship. . . . . at Denver 23, NY Jets 10

NFC Playoffs

First Round . . . . .at *San Francisco 30, *Green Bay 27
*Arizona 20, at Dallas 7
Second Round . . . . .at Atlanta 20, *San Francisco 18
at Minnesota 41, *Arizona 21
Championship . . . . .Atlanta 30, at Minnesota 27 (OT)

Super Bowl XXXIII
Jan. 31, 1999
Pro Player Stadium, Miami
Favorite: Broncos by 7½ Attendance: 74,803

Denver (16-2)	. . . .	7	10	0	17	—34
Atlanta (16-2)	. . . .	3	3	0	13	—19

MVP: Denver QB John Elway (18 for 29, 336 yds, 1 TD, 1 Int and 1 rushing TD)

Before the Super Bowl

The first NFL champion was the Akron Pros in 1920, when the league was called the American Professional Football Association (APFA) and the title went to the team with the best regular season record. The APFA changed its name to the National Football League in 1922.

The first playoff game with the championship at stake came in 1932, when the Chicago Bears (6-1-6) and Portsmouth (Ohio) Spartans (6-1-4) ended the regular season tied for first place. The Bears won the subsequent playoff, 9-0. Due to a snowstorm and cold weather, the game was moved from Wrigley Field to an improvised 80-yard dirt field at Chicago Stadium, making it the first indoor title game as well.

The NFL Championship Game decided the league title until the NFL merged with the AFL and the first Super Bowl was played following the 1966 season.

NFL Champions, 1920-32
Winning player-coaches noted by position.
Multiple winners: Canton-Cleveland Bulldogs and Green Bay (3); Chicago Staleys/Bears (2).

Year	Champion	Head Coach	Year	Champion	Head Coach
1920	Akron Pros	Fritz Pollard, HB & Elgie Tobin, QB	1927	New York Giants	Earl Potteiger, QB
1921	Chicago Staleys	George Halas, E	1928	Providence Steam Roller	Jimmy Conzelman, HB
1922	Canton Bulldogs	Guy Chamberlin, E	1929	Green Bay Packers	Curly Lambeau, QB
1923	Canton Bulldogs	Guy Chamberlin, E	1930	Green Bay Packers	Curly Lambeau
1924	Cleveland Bulldogs	Guy Chamberlin, E	1931	Green Bay Packers	Curly Lambeau
1925	Chicago Cardinals	Norm Barry	1932	Chicago Bears	Ralph Jones
1926	Frankford Yellow Jackets	Guy Chamberlin, E	(Bears beat Portsmouth-OH in playoff, 9-0)		

NFL-NFC Championship Game

NFL Championship games from 1933-69 and NFC Championship games since the completion of the NFL-AFL merger following the 1969 season.

Multiple winners: Green Bay (10); Dallas (8); Chicago Bears and Washington (7); NY Giants and San Francisco (5); Cleveland Browns, Detroit, Minnesota, and Philadelphia (4); Baltimore (3); Cleveland-LA Rams (2).

Season	Winner	Head Coach	Score	Loser	Head Coach	Site
1933	Chicago Bears	George Halas	23-21	New York	Steve Owen	Chicago
1934	New York	Steve Owen	30-13	Chicago Bears	George Halas	New York
1935	Detroit	Potsy Clark	26-7	New York	Steve Owen	Detroit
1936	Green Bay	Curly Lambeau	21-6	Boston Redskins	Ray Flaherty	New York
1937	Washington Redskins	Ray Flaherty	28-21	Chicago Bears	George Halas	Chicago
1938	New York	Steve Owen	23-17	Green Bay	Curly Lambeau	New York
1939	Green Bay	Curly Lambeau	27-0	New York	Steve Owen	Milwaukee
1940	Chicago Bears	George Halas	73-0	Washington	Ray Flaherty	Washington
1941	Chicago Bears	George Halas	37-9	New York	Steve Owen	Chicago
1942	Washington	Ray Flaherty	14-6	Chicago Bears	Hunk Anderson & Luke Johnsos	Washington
1943	Chicago Bears	Hunk Anderson & Luke Johnsos	41-21	Washington	Arthur Bergman	Chicago
1944	Green Bay	Curly Lambeau	14-7	New York	Steve Owen	New York
1945	Cleveland Rams	Adam Walsh	15-14	Washington	Dudley DeGroot	Cleveland
1946	Chicago Bears	George Halas	24-14	New York	Steve Owen	New York
1947	Chicago Cardinals	Jimmy Conzelman	28-21	Philadelphia	Greasy Neale	Chicago
1948	Philadelphia	Greasy Neale	7-0	Chicago Cardinals	Jimmy Conzelman	Philadelphia
1949	Philadelphia	Greasy Neale	14-0	Los Angeles Rams	Clark Shaughnessy	Los Angeles
1950	Cleveland Browns	Paul Brown	30-28	Los Angeles	Joe Stydahar	Cleveland
1951	Los Angeles	Joe Stydahar	24-17	Cleveland	Paul Brown	Los Angeles
1952	Detroit	Buddy Parker	17-7	Cleveland	Paul Brown	Cleveland
1953	Detroit	Buddy Parker	17-16	Cleveland	Paul Brown	Detroit
1954	Cleveland	Paul Brown	56-10	Detroit	Buddy Parker	Cleveland
1955	Cleveland	Paul Brown	38-14	Los Angeles	Sid Gillman	Los Angeles
1956	New York	Jim Lee Howell	47-7	Chicago Bears	Paddy Driscoll	New York
1957	Detroit	George Wilson	59-14	Cleveland	Paul Brown	Detroit
1958	Baltimore	Weeb Ewbank	23-17*	New York	Jim Lee Howell	New York
1959	Baltimore	Weeb Ewbank	31-16	New York	Jim Lee Howell	Baltimore
1960	Philadelphia	Buck Shaw	17-13	Green Bay	Vince Lombardi	Philadelphia
1961	Green Bay	Vince Lombardi	37-0	New York	Allie Sherman	Green Bay
1962	Green Bay	Vince Lombardi	16-7	New York	Allie Sherman	New York
1963	Chicago	George Halas	14-10	New York	Allie Sherman	Chicago
1964	Cleveland	Blanton Collier	27-0	Baltimore	Don Shula	Cleveland
1965	Green Bay	Vince Lombardi	23-12	Cleveland	Blanton Collier	Green Bay
1966	Green Bay	Vince Lombardi	34-27	Dallas	Tom Landry	Dallas
1967	Green Bay	Vince Lombardi	21-17	Dallas	Tom Landry	Green Bay
1968	Baltimore	Don Shula	34-0	Cleveland	Blanton Collier	Cleveland
1969	Minnesota	Bud Grant	27-7	Cleveland	Blanton Collier	Minnesota
1970	Dallas	Tom Landry	17-10	San Francisco	Dick Nolan	San Francisco
1971	Dallas	Tom Landry	14-3	San Francisco	Dick Nolan	Dallas
1972	Washington	George Allen	26-3	Dallas	Tom Landry	Washington
1973	Minnesota	Bud Grant	27-10	Dallas	Tom Landry	Dallas
1974	Minnesota	Bud Grant	14-10	Los Angeles	Chuck Knox	Minnesota
1975	Dallas	Tom Landry	37-7	Los Angeles	Chuck Knox	Los Angeles
1976	Minnesota	Bud Grant	24-13	Los Angeles	Chuck Knox	Minnesota
1977	Dallas	Tom Landry	23-6	Minnesota	Bud Grant	Dallas
1978	Dallas	Tom Landry	28-0	Los Angeles	Ray Malavasi	Los Angeles
1979	Los Angeles	Ray Malavasi	9-0	Tampa Bay	John McKay	Tampa Bay
1980	Philadelphia	Dick Vermeil	20-7	Dallas	Tom Landry	Philadelphia
1981	San Francisco	Bill Walsh	28-27	Dallas	Tom Landry	San Francisco
1982	Washington	Joe Gibbs	31-17	Dallas	Tom Landry	Washington
1983	Washington	Joe Gibbs	24-21	San Francisco	Bill Walsh	Washington
1984	San Francisco	Bill Walsh	23-0	Chicago	Mike Ditka	San Francisco
1985	Chicago	Mike Ditka	24-0	Los Angeles	John Robinson	Chicago
1986	New York	Bill Parcells	17-0	Washington	Joe Gibbs	New York
1987	Washington	Joe Gibbs	17-10	Minnesota	Jerry Burns	Washington
1988	San Francisco	Bill Walsh	28-3	Chicago	Mike Ditka	Chicago
1989	San Francisco	George Seifert	30-3	Los Angeles	John Robinson	San Francisco
1990	New York	Bill Parcells	15-13	San Francisco	George Seifert	San Francisco
1991	Washington	Joe Gibbs	41-10	Detroit	Wayne Fontes	Washington
1992	Dallas	Jimmy Johnson	30-20	San Francisco	George Seifert	San Francisco
1993	Dallas	Jimmy Johnson	38-21	San Francisco	George Seifert	Dallas
1994	San Francisco	George Seifert	38-28	Dallas	Barry Switzer	San Francisco
1995	Dallas	Barry Switzer	38-27	Green Bay	Mike Holmgren	Dallas
1996	Green Bay	Mike Holmgren	30-13	Carolina	Dom Capers	Green Bay
1997	Green Bay	Mike Holmgren	23-10	San Francisco	Steve Mariucci	San Francisco
1998	Atlanta	Dan Reeves	30-27*	Minnesota	Dennis Green	Minnesota

*Sudden death overtime

NFL-NFC Championship Game Appearances

App		W	L	Pct	PF	PA	App		W	L	Pct	PF	PA
16	Dallas Cowboys	8	8	.500	361	319	7	Minnesota	4	3	.571	135	110
16	NY Giants	5	11	.313	240	322	6	Detroit	4	2	.667	139	141
13	Green Bay Packers	10	3	.769	303	177	5	Philadelphia	4	1	.800	79	48
13	Chicago Bears	7	6	.538	286	245	4	Baltimore Colts	3	1	.750	88	60
12	Boston-Wash.Redskins	7	5	.583	222	255	2	Chicago Cardinals	1	1	.500	28	28
12	San Francisco	5	7	.417	245	222	1	Atlanta	1	0	1.000	30	27
12	Cleveland-LA Rams	3	9	.250	123	270	1	Carolina	0	1	.000	13	30
11	Cleveland Browns	4	7	.364	224	253	1	Tampa Bay	0	1	.000	0	9

AFL-AFC Championship Game

AFL Championship games from 1960-69 and AFC Championship games since the completion of the NFL-AFL merger following the 1969 season.

Multiple winners: Buffalo and Denver (6); Miami and Pittsburgh (5); Oakland-LA Raiders (4); Dallas Texans-KC Chiefs (3); Cincinnati, Houston, New England and San Diego (2).

Season	Winner	Head Coach	Score	Loser	Head Coach	Site
1960	Houston	Lou Rymkus	24-16	LA Chargers	Sid Gillman	Houston
1961	Houston	Wally Lemm	10-3	SD Chargers	Sid Gillman	San Diego
1962	Dallas	Hank Stram	20-17*	Houston	Pop Ivy	Houston
1963	San Diego	Sid Gillman	51-10	Boston Patriots	Mike Holovak	San Diego
1964	Buffalo	Lou Saban	20-7	San Diego	Sid Gillman	Buffalo
1965	Buffalo	Lou Saban	23-0	San Diego	Sid Gillman	San Diego
1966	Kansas City	Hank Stram	31-7	Buffalo	Joel Collier	Buffalo
1967	Oakland	John Rauch	40-7	Houston	Wally Lemm	Oakland
1968	NY Jets	Weeb Ewbank	27-23	Oakland	John Rauch	New York
1969	Kansas City	Hank Stram	17-7	Oakland	John Madden	Oakland
1970	Baltimore	Don McCafferty	27-17	Oakland	John Madden	Baltimore
1971	Miami	Don Shula	21-0	Baltimore	Don McCafferty	Miami
1972	Miami	Don Shula	21-17	Pittsburgh	Chuck Noll	Pittsburgh
1973	Miami	Don Shula	27-10	Oakland	John Madden	Miami
1974	Pittsburgh	Chuck Noll	24-13	Oakland	John Madden	Oakland
1975	Pittsburgh	Chuck Noll	16-10	Oakland	John Madden	Pittsburgh
1976	Oakland	John Madden	24-7	Pittsburgh	Chuck Noll	Oakland
1977	Denver	Red Miller	20-17	Oakland	John Madden	Denver
1978	Pittsburgh	Chuck Noll	34-5	Houston	Bum Phillips	Pittsburgh
1979	Pittsburgh	Chuck Noll	27-13	Houston	Bum Phillips	Pittsburgh
1980	Oakland	Tom Flores	34-27	San Diego	Don Coryell	San Diego
1981	Cincinnati	Forrest Gregg	27-7	San Diego	Don Coryell	Cincinnati
1982	Miami	Don Shula	14-0	NY Jets	Walt Michaels	Miami
1983	LA Raiders	Tom Flores	30-14	Seattle	Chuck Knox	Los Angeles
1984	Miami	Don Shula	45-28	Pittsburgh	Chuck Noll	Miami
1985	New England	Raymond Berry	31-14	Miami	Don Shula	Miami
1986	Denver	Dan Reeves	23-20*	Cleveland	Marty Schottenheimer	Cleveland
1987	Denver	Dan Reeves	38-33	Cleveland	Marty Schottenheimer	Denver
1988	Cincinnati	Sam Wyche	21-10	Buffalo	Marv Levy	Cincinnati
1989	Denver	Dan Reeves	37-21	Cleveland	Bud Carson	Denver
1990	Buffalo	Marv Levy	51-3	LA Raiders	Art Shell	Buffalo
1991	Buffalo	Marv Levy	10-7	Denver	Dan Reeves	Buffalo
1992	Buffalo	Marv Levy	29-10	Miami	Don Shula	Miami
1993	Buffalo	Marv Levy	30-13	Kansas City	Marty Schottenheimer	Buffalo
1994	San Diego	Bobby Ross	17-13	Pittsburgh	Bill Cowher	Pittsburgh
1995	Pittsburgh	Bill Cowher	20-16	Indianapolis	Ted Marchibroda	Pittsburgh
1996	New England	Bill Parcells	20-6	Jacksonville	Tom Coughlin	New England
1997	Denver	Mike Shanahan	24-21	Pittsburgh	Bill Cowher	Pittsburgh
1998	Denver	Mike Shanahan	23-10	NY Jets	Bill Parcells	Denver

*Sudden death overtime

AFL-AFC Championship Game Appearances

App		W	L	Pct	PF	PA	App		W	L	Pct	PF	PA
12	Oakland-LA Raiders	4	8	.333	228	264	3	Boston-NE Patriots	2	1	.750	61	71
10	Pittsburgh	5	5	.500	207	188	3	Baltimore-Indy Colts	1	2	.333	43	58
8	Buffalo	6	2	.750	180	92	3	NY Jets	1	2	.333	37	60
8	LA-San Diego Chargers	2	6	.250	128	161	3	Cleveland	0	3	.000	74	98
7	Denver	6	1	.857	172	132	2	Cincinnati	2	0	1.000	48	17
7	Miami	5	2	.714	152	115	1	Seattle	0	1	.000	14	30
6	Houston	2	4	.333	76	140	1	Jacksonville	0	1	.000	6	20
4	Dallas Texans/KC Chiefs	3	1	.750	81	61							

NFL Divisional Champions

The NFL adopted divisional play for the first time in 1967, splitting both conferences into two four-team divisions—the Capitol and Century divisions in the East and the Central and Coastal divisions in the West. Merger with the AFL in 1970 increased NFL membership to 26 teams and made it necessary for realignment. Two 13-team conferences—the AFC and NFC—were formed by moving established NFL clubs in Baltimore, Cleveland and Pittsburgh to the AFC and rearranging both conferences into Eastern, Central and Western divisions. Expansion has since increased the league to 31 teams with 16 teams in the AFC and 15 in the NFC. The AFC Central currently has six teams and all others have five.

Division champions are listed below; teams that went on to win the Super Bowl are in **bold** type. Note that in the 1980 season, Oakland won the Super Bowl as a wild card team, as did Denver in 1997; and in 1982, the players' strike shortened the regular season to nine games and eliminated divisional play for one season.

Multiple champions (since 1970): **AFC**—Pittsburgh (14); Miami (11); Denver and Oakland-LA Raiders (9); Buffalo (7); Cleveland (6); Baltimore-Indianapolis Colts, Cincinnati and San Diego (5); Kansas City and New England (4); Houston (2). **NFC**—San Francisco (16); Dallas (15); Minnesota (13); LA Rams (8); Chicago (6); Washington (5); Green Bay and NY Giants (4); Detroit (3); Atlanta, Philadelphia, St. Louis Cardinals and Tampa Bay (2).

American Football League

Season	East	West		Season	East		West	
1966	Buffalo	Kansas City		1966	Dallas		**Green Bay**	

Season	East	West		Season	Capitol	Century	Central	Coastal
1967	Houston	Oakland		1967	Dallas	Cleveland	**Green Bay**	LA Rams
1968	**NY Jets**	Oakland		1968	Dallas	Cleveland	Minnesota	Baltimore
1969	NY Jets	Oakland		1969	Dallas	Cleveland	Minnesota	LA Rams

Note: Kansas City, an AFL second-place team, won the Super Bowl in the 1969 season.

American Football Conference / National Football Conference

Season	East	Central	West		Season	East	Central	West
1970	**Baltimore**	Cincinnati	Oakland		1970	Dallas	Minnesota	San Francisco
1971	Miami	Cleveland	Kansas City		1971	**Dallas**	Minnesota	San Francisco
1972	**Miami**	Pittsburgh	Oakland		1972	Washington	Green Bay	San Francisco
1973	**Miami**	Cincinnati	Oakland		1973	Dallas	Minnesota	LA Rams
1974	Miami	**Pittsburgh**	Oakland		1974	St. Louis	Minnesota	LA Rams
1975	Baltimore	**Pittsburgh**	Oakland		1975	St. Louis	Minnesota	LA Rams
1976	Baltimore	Pittsburgh	**Oakland**		1976	Dallas	Minnesota	LA Rams
1977	Baltimore	Pittsburgh	Denver		1977	**Dallas**	Minnesota	LA Rams
1978	New England	**Pittsburgh**	Denver		1978	Dallas	Minnesota	LA Rams
1979	Miami	**Pittsburgh**	San Diego		1979	Dallas	Tampa Bay	LA Rams
1980	Buffalo	Cleveland	San Diego		1980	Philadelphia	Minnesota	Atlanta
1981	Miami	Cincinnati	San Diego		1981	Dallas	Tampa Bay	**San Francisco**
1982	—	—	—		1982	—	—	—
1983	Miami	Pittsburgh	**LA Raiders**		1983	Washington	Detroit	San Francisco
1984	Miami	Pittsburgh	Denver		1984	Washington	Chicago	**San Francisco**
1985	Miami	Cleveland	LA Raiders		1985	Dallas	**Chicago**	LA Rams
1986	New England	Cleveland	Denver		1986	**NY Giants**	Chicago	San Francisco
1987	Indianapolis	Cleveland	Denver		1987	**Washington**	Chicago	San Francisco
1988	Buffalo	Cincinnati	Seattle		1988	Philadelphia	Chicago	**San Francisco**
1989	Buffalo	Cleveland	Denver		1989	NY Giants	Minnesota	**San Francisco**
1990	Buffalo	Cincinnati	LA Raiders		1990	**NY Giants**	Chicago	San Francisco
1991	Buffalo	Houston	Denver		1991	**Washington**	Detroit	New Orleans
1992	Miami	Pittsburgh	San Diego		1992	**Dallas**	Minnesota	San Francisco
1993	Buffalo	Houston	Kansas City		1993	**Dallas**	Detroit	San Francisco
1994	Miami	Pittsburgh	San Diego		1994	Dallas	Minnesota	**San Francisco**
1995	Buffalo	Pittsburgh	Kansas City		1995	**Dallas**	Green Bay	San Francisco
1996	New England	Pittsburgh	Denver		1996	Dallas	**Green Bay**	Carolina
1997	New England	Pittsburgh	Kansas City		1997	NY Giants	Green Bay	San Francisco
1998	NY Jets	Jacksonville	**Denver**		1998	Dallas	Minnesota	Atlanta

Overall Postseason Games

The postseason records of all NFL teams, ranked by number of playoff games participated in from 1933 through the 1998 season.

Gm		W	L	Pct	PF	PA	Gm		W	L	Pct	PF	PA
52	Dallas Cowboys	32	20	.615	1261	952	20	Balt-Indianapolis Colts	10	10	.500	360	389
39	San Francisco 49ers	24	15	.615	984	759	20	Philadelphia Eagles	9	11	.450	356	369
36	Oakland-LA Raiders	21	15	.583	855	659	19	Dallas Texans/KC Chiefs	8	11	.421	301	384
36	Pittsburgh Steelers	21	15	.583	801	707	18	LA-San Diego Chargers	7	11	.389	332	428
36	Minnesota Vikings	15	21	.417	681	797	17	Boston-NE Patriots	7	10	.412	310	357
35	Boston-Wash. Redskins	21	14	.600	738	625	16	Detroit Lions	7	9	.438	352	377
34	Miami Dolphins	18	16	.529	727	705	13	New York Jets	6	7	.462	260	247
33	New York Giants	14	19	.424	551	616	12	Cincinnati Bengals	5	7	.417	246	257
33	Cleveland-LA Rams	13	20	.394	501	697	10	Atlanta Falcons	4	6	.400	208	260
32	Green Bay Packers	22	10	.688	772	558	7	Seattle Seahawks	3	4	.429	128	139
30	Cleveland Browns	11	19	.367	596	702	7	Chi-St.L.-Ari. Cardinals	2	5	.286	122	182
28	Buffalo Bills	14	14	.500	665	636	6	Jacksonville Jaguars	3	3	.500	132	160
28	Chicago Bears	14	14	.500	579	552	6	Tampa Bay Buccaneers	2	4	.333	68	125
27	Denver Broncos	16	11	.593	613	636	4	New Orleans Saints	0	4	.000	56	123
22	Houston Oilers	9	13	.409	371	533	2	Carolina Panthers	1	1	.500	39	47

All-Time Postseason Leaders

Through Super Bowl XXXIII in 1999; participants in 1998 season playoffs in **bold** type.

CAREER

Passing Efficiency

Ratings based on performance standards established for completion percentage, average gain, touchdown percentage and interception percentage. Minimum 150 passing attempts.

		Gm	Cmp%	Yds	TD	Int	Rtg
1	Bart Starr	10	61.0	1753	15	3	104.8
2	Joe Montana	23	62.7	5772	45	21	95.6
3	Kenny Anderson	6	66.3	1321	9	6	93.5
4	Joe Theismann	10	60.7	1782	11	7	91.4
5	**Brett Favre**	14	60.1	3390	25	12	91.1
6	**Troy Aikman**	15	64.2	3563	22	16	89.8
7	**Steve Young**	22	62.0	3325	20	13	85.8
8	Warren Moon	10	64.3	2870	17	14	84.9
9	Ken Stabler	13	57.8	2641	19	13	84.2
10	Bernie Kosar	10	56.3	1953	16	10	83.5

Passing

	Attempts	Gm	Att
1	Joe Montana, S.F.-KC	23	734
2	**John Elway**, Denver	22	651
3	**Dan Marino**, Miami	16	632

	Completions	Gm	Cmp
1	Joe Montana, SF-KC	23	460
2	**Dan Marino**, Miami	16	357
3	**John Elway**, Denver	22	355

	Yards Gained	Gm	Yds
1	Joe Montana, SF-KC	23	5772
2	**John Elway**, Denver	22	4964
3	**Dan Marino**, Miami	16	4219
4	Jim Kelly, Buffalo	17	3863
5	Terry Bradshaw, Pittsburgh	19	3833

Games

	Played	Gm
1	D.D. Lewis, Dallas	27
2	Larry Cole, Dallas	26
3	Charlie Waters, Dallas	25

	Coached	Gm
1	Tom Landry, Dallas	36
	Don Shula, Baltimore-Miami	36
3	Chuck Noll, Pittsburgh	24

Rushing

	Yards Gained	Gm	Car	Yds	Avg
1	Franco Harris	19	400	1556	3.89
2	**Emmitt Smith**	16	334	1487	4.45
3	**Thurman Thomas**	20	334	1432	4.29
4	Tony Dorsett	17	302	1383	4.58
5	Marcus Allen	16	267	1347	5.04

	Attempts	Gm	Att
1	Franco Harris, Pittsburgh	19	400
2	**Emmitt Smith**, Dallas	16	334
	Thurman Thomas, Buffalo	20	334

Receiving

	Catches	Gm	No	Yds	Avg
1	**Jerry Rice**, San Francisco	23	124	1811	14.6
2	**Michael Irvin**, Dallas	16	87	1315	15.1
3	**Andre Reed**, Buffalo	20	85	1229	14.5

	Yards Gained	Gm	Yds
1	**Jerry Rice**, San Francisco	23	1811
2	**Michael Irvin**, Dallas	16	1315
3	Cliff Branch, Oakland-LA	22	1289
4	**Andre Reed**, Buffalo	20	1229
5	Fred Biletnikoff, Oakland	19	1167

	Average Gain (min. 20 rec.)	Gm	Avg
1	Alvin Harper, Dallas	10	27.3
2	Willie Gault, Chicago-LA	12	23.7
3	Harold Jackson, LA-NE-Minn-Sea	14	22.8

Scoring

	Points	Gm	TD	FG	PAT	Pts
1	**Thurman Thomas**	20	21	0	0	126
2	**Emmitt Smith**	16	20	0	0	120
3	George Blanda	19	0	22	49	115

	Touchdowns	Gm	Run	Rec	Ret	No
1	**Thurman Thomas**	20	16	5	0	21
2	**Emmitt Smith**	16	18	2	0	20
3	**Jerry Rice**	23	0	19	0	19

	Field Goals	Gm	Att	FG	Pct
1	**Gary Anderson**	17	32	25	.781
2	George Blanda	19	39	22	.564
3	**Steve Christie**	11	24	21	.875
	Matt Bahr	14	25	21	.840

SINGLE GAME

Scoring

	Points Scored	Season	Pts
1	Ricky Watters, SF vs. NYG	1993	30
2	Pat Harder, Det. vs. LA	1952	19
	Paul Hornung, GB vs. NYG	1961	19

	Field Goals	Season	FG
1	Chuck Nelson, Min. vs. SF	1987	5
	Matt Bahr, NYG vs. SF	1990	5
	Steve Christie, Buf. vs. Mia	1992	5
	Brad Daluiso, NYG vs Min	1997	5

Rushing

	Yards Gained	Season	Yds
1	Eric Dickerson, LA Rams vs. Dal.	1985	248
2	Keith Lincoln, SD vs. Bos.	1963	206
3	Timmy Smith, Wash. vs. Den.	1987	204

	Most Attempts	Season	Att
1	Ricky Bell, T.B. vs. Phi	1979	38
	John Riggins, Wash. vs. Mia.	1982	38
3	Lawrence McCutcheon, LA vs. St. L	1975	37
	John Riggins, Wash. vs. Minn.	1982	37

Passing

	Attempts	Season	Att
1	Steve Young, SF vs. GB	1995	65
2	Bernie Kosar, Cle. vs. NYJ	1986	64
	Dan Marino, Mia. vs. Buf.	1995	64

	Completions	Season	Cmp
1	Warren Moon, Hou. vs. Buf.	1992	36
2	Dan Fouts, SD vs. Mia.	1981	33
	Bernie Kosar, Cle. vs. NYJ	1986	33
	Dan Marino, Mia. vs. Buf.	1995	33

	Yards Gained	Season	Yds
1	Bernie Kosar, Cle. vs. NYJ	1986	489
2	Dan Fouts, SD vs. Mia.	1981	433
3	Dan Marino, Mia. vs. Buf.	1995	422

Receiving

	Catches	Season	Rec
1	Kellen Winslow, SD vs. Mia	1981	13
	Thurman Thomas, Buf. vs. Cle.	1989	13
	Shannon Sharpe, Den. vs. LA Raiders	1993	13

	Yards Gained	Season	Yds
1	**Eric Moulds**, Buf. vs Mia.	1998	240
2	Anthony Carter, Min. vs. SF	1987	227
3	Jerry Rice, SF vs. Cin.	1988	215

Champions of Leagues That No Longer Exist

No professional league in American sports has had to contend with more pretenders to the throne than the NFL. Seven times in as many decades a rival league has risen up to challenge the NFL and six of them went under in less than five seasons. Only the fourth American Football League (1960-69) succeeded, forcing the older league to sue for peace and a full partnership in 1966.

Of the six leagues that didn't make it, only the All-America Football Conference (1946-49) lives on—the Cleveland Browns and San Francisco 49ers joined the NFL after the AAFC folded in 1949. The champions of leagues past are listed below.

American Football League I

Year		Head Coach
1926	Philadelphia Quakers (8-2)	Bob Folwell

Note: Philadelphia was challenged to a postseason game by the 7th place New York Giants (8-4-1) of the NFL. The Giants won, 31-0, in a snowstorm.

American Football League II

Year		Head Coach
1936	Boston Shamrocks (8-3)	George Kenneally
1937	Los Angeles Bulldogs (9-0)	Gus Henderson

Note: Boston was scheduled to play 2nd place Cleveland (5-2-2) in the '36 championship game, but the Shamrock players refused to participate because they were owed pay for past games.

American Football League III

Year		Head Coach
1940	Columbus Bullies (8-1-1)	Phil Bucklew
1941	Columbus Bullies (5-1-2)	Phil Bucklew

All-America Football Conference

Year	Winner	Head Coach	Score	Loser	Head Coach	Site
1946	Cleveland Browns	Paul Brown	14-9	NY Yankees	Ray Flaherty	Cleveland
1947	Cleveland Browns	Paul Brown	14-3	NY Yankees	Ray Flaherty	New York
1948	Cleveland Browns	Paul Brown	49-7	Buffalo Bills	Red Dawson	Cleveland
1949	Cleveland Browns	Paul Brown	21-7	S.F. 49ers	Buck Shaw	Cleveland

World Football League

Year	Winner	Head Coach	Score	Loser	Head Coach	Site
1974	Birmingham Americans	Jack Gotta	22-21	Florida Blazers	Jack Pardee	Birmingham
1975	WFL folded Oct. 22.					

United States Football League

Year	Winner	Head Coach	Score	Loser	Head Coach	Site
1983	Michigan Panthers	Jim Stanley	24-22	Philadelphia Stars	Jim Mora	Denver
1984	Philadelphia Stars	Jim Mora	23-3	Arizona Wranglers	George Allen	Tampa
1985	Baltimore Stars	Jim Mora	28-24	Oakland Invaders	Charlie Sumner	E. Rutherford

---

Defunct Leagues

AFL I (1926): Boston Bulldogs, Brooklyn Horseman, Chicago Bulls, Cleveland Panthers, Los Angeles Wildcats, New York Yankees, Newark Bears, Philadelphia Quakers, Rock Island Independents.

AFL II (1936-37): Boston Shamrocks (1936-37); Brooklyn Tigers (1936); Cincinnati Bengals (1937); Cleveland Rams (1936); Los Angeles Bulldogs (1937); New York Yankees (1936-37); Pittsburgh Americans (1936-37); Rochester Tigers (1936-37).

AFL III (1940-41): Boston Bears (1940); Buffalo Indians (1940-41); Cincinnati Bengals (1940-41); Columbus Bullies (1940-41); Milwaukee Chiefs (1940-41); New York Yankees (1940) renamed Americans (1941).

AAFC (1946-49): Brooklyn Dodgers (1946-48) merged to become Brooklyn-New York Yankees (1949); Buffalo Bisons (1946) renamed Bills (1947-49); Chicago Rockets (1946-48) renamed Hornets (1949); Cleveland Browns (1946-49); Los Angeles Dons (1946-49); Miami Seahawks (1946) became Baltimore Colts (1947-49); New York Yankees (1946-48) merged to become Brooklyn-New York Yankees (1949); San Francisco 49ers (1946-49).

WFL (1974-75): Birmingham Americans (1974) renamed Vulcans (1975); Chicago Fire (1974) renamed Winds (1975); Detroit Wheels (1974); Florida Blazers (1974) became San Antonio Wings (1975); The Hawaiians (1974-75); Houston Texans (1974) became Shreveport (La.) Steamer (1974-75); Jacksonville Sharks (1974) renamed Express (1975); Memphis Southmen (1974) also known as Grizzlies (1975); New York Stars (1974) became Charlotte Hornets (1974-75); Philadelphia Bell (1974-75); Portland Storm (1974) renamed Thunder (1975); Southern California Sun (1974-75).

USFL (1983-85): Arizona Wranglers (1983-84) merged with Oklahoma to become Arizona Outlaws (1985); Birmingham Stallions (1983-85); Boston Breakers (1983) became New Orleans Breakers (1984) and then Portland Breakers (1985); Chicago Blitz (1983-84); Denver Gold (1983-85); Houston Gamblers (1984-85); Jacksonville Bulls (1984-85); Los Angeles Express (1983-85); Memphis Showboats (1984-85).

Michigan Panthers (1983-84) merged with Oakland (1985); New Jersey Generals (1983-85); Oakland Invaders (1983-85); Oklahoma Outlaws (1984) merged with Arizona to become Arizona Outlaws (1985); Philadelphia Stars (1983-84) became Baltimore Stars (1985); Pittsburgh Maulers (1984); San Antonio Gunslingers (1984-85); Tampa Bay Bandits (1983-85); Washington Federals (1983-84) became Orlando Renegades (1985).

NFL Pro Bowl

A postseason All-Star game between the new league champion and a team of professional all-stars was added to the NFL schedule in 1939. In the first game at Wrigley Field in Los Angeles, the NY Giants beat a team made up of players from NFL teams and two independent clubs in Los Angeles (the LA Bulldogs and Hollywood Stars). An all-NFL All-Star team provided the opposition over the next four seasons, but the game was cancelled in 1943.

The Pro Bowl was revived in 1951 as a contest between conference all-star teams: American vs National (1951-53), Eastern vs Western (1954-70), and AFC vs NFC (since 1971). The NFC leads the current series with the AFC, 15-14.

The MVP trophy was named the Dan McGuire Award in 1984 after the late SF 49ers publicist and *Honolulu Advertiser* sports columnist.

Year	Winner	Score	Loser	Year	Winner	MVP
1939	NY Giants	13-10	All-Stars			Line—Merlin Olsen, LA
1940	Green Bay	16-7	All-Stars	1970	West, 16-13	Back—Gale Sayers, Chi.
1940	Chicago Bears	28-14	All-Stars			Line—George Andrie, Dal.
1942	Chicago Bears	35-24	All-Stars	1971	NFC, 27-6	Back—Mel Renfro, Dal.
1942	All-Stars	17-14	Washington			Line—Fred Carr, GB
1943-50	No game			1972	AFC, 26-13	Off—Jan Stenerud, KC
						Def—Willie Lanier, KC

Year	Winner	MVP		Year	Winner	MVP
1951	American, 28-27	Otto Graham, Cle., QB		1973	AFC, 33-28	O.J. Simpson, Buf., RB
1952	National, 30-13	Dan Towler, LA, HB		1974	AFC, 15-13	Garo Yepremian, Mia., PK
1953	National, 27-7	Don Doll, Det., DB		1975	NFC, 17-10	James Harris, LA Rams, QB
1954	East, 20-9	Chuck Bednarik, Phi., LB		1976	NFC, 23-20	Billy Johnson, Hou., KR
1955	West, 26-19	Billy Wilson, SF, E		1977	AFC, 24-14	Mel Blount, Pit., CB
1956	East, 31-30	Ollie Matson, Cards, HB		1978	NFC, 14-13	Walter Payton, Chi., RB
1957	West, 19-10	Back—Bert Rechichar, Bal.		1979	NFC, 13-7	Ahmad Rashad, Min., WR
		Line—Ernie Stautner, Pit.		1980	NFC, 37-27	Chuck Muncie, NO, RB
1958	West, 26-7	Back—Hugh McElhenny, SF		1981	NFC, 21-7	Eddie Murray, Det., PK
		Line—Gene Brito, Wash.		1982	AFC, 16-13	Kellen Winslow, SD, WR
1959	East, 28-21	Back—Frank Gifford, NY				& Lee Roy Selmon, TB, DE
		Line—Doug Atkins, Chi.		1983	NFC, 20-19	Dan Fouts, SD, QB
1960	West, 38-21	Back—Johnny Unitas, Bal.				& John Jefferson, GB, WR
		Line—Big Daddy Lipscomb, Pit.		1984	NFC, 45-3	Joe Theismann, Wash., QB
1961	West, 35-31	Back—Johnny Unitas, Bal.		1985	AFC, 22-14	Mark Gastineau, NYJ, DE
		Line—Sam Huff, NY		1986	NFC, 28-24	Phil Simms, NYG, QB
1962	West, 31-30	Back—Jim Brown, Cle.		1987	AFC, 10-6	Reggie White, Phi., DE
		Line—Henry Jordan, GB		1988	AFC, 15-6	Bruce Smith, Buf., DE
1963	East, 30-20	Back—Jim Brown, Cle.		1989	NFC, 34-3	Randall Cunningham, Phi., QB
		Line—Big Daddy Lipscomb, Pit.		1990	NFC, 27-21	Jerry Gray, LA Rams, CB
1964	West, 31-17	Back—Johnny Unitas, Bal.		1991	AFC, 23-21	Jim Kelly, Buf., QB
		Line—Gino Marchetti, Bal.		1992	NFC, 21-15	Michael Irvin, Dal., WR
1965	West, 34-14	Back—Fran Tarkenton, Min.		1993	AFC, 23-20 (OT)	Steve Tasker, Buf., Sp. Teams
		Line—Terry Barr, Det.		1994	NFC, 17-3	Andre Rison, Atl., WR
1966	East, 36-7	Back—Jim Brown, Cle.		1995	AFC, 41-13	Marshall Faulk, Ind., RB
		Line—Dale Meinhart, St. L.		1996	NFC, 20-13	Jerry Rice, SF, WR
1967	East, 20-10	Back—Gale Sayers, Chi.		1997	AFC, 26-23 (OT)	Mark Brunell, Jax, QB
		Line—Floyd Peters, Phi.		1998	AFC, 29-24	Warren Moon, Sea., QB
1968	West, 38-20	Back—Gale Sayers, Chi.		1999	AFC, 23-10	Ty Law, NE, CB
		Line—Dave Robinson, GB				& Keyshawn Johnson, NYJ, WR
1969	West, 10-7	Back—Roman Gabriel, LA				

Playing sites: Wrigley Field in Los Angeles (1939); Gilmore Stadium in Los Angeles (1940–both games); Polo Grounds in New York (Jan., 1942); Shibe Park in Philadelphia (Dec., 1942); Memorial Coliseum in Los Angeles (1951-72 and 1979); Texas Stadium in Irving, TX (1973); Arrowhead Stadium in Kansas City (1974); Orange Bowl in Miami (1975); Superdome in New Orleans (1976); Kingdome in Seattle (1977); Tampa Stadium in Tampa (1978) and Aloha Stadium in Honolulu (since 1980).

AFL All-Star Game

The AFL did not play an All-Star game after its first season in 1960 but did stage All-Star games from 1962-70. All-Star teams from the Eastern and Western divisions played each other every year except 1966 with the West winning the series, 6-2. In 1966, the league champion Buffalo Bills met an elite squad made up of the best players from the league's other eight clubs and lost, 30-19.

Year	Winner	MVP	Year	Winner	MVP
1962	West, 47-27	Cotton Davidson, Oak., QB	1967	East, 30-23	Off—Babe Parilli, Bos.
1963	West, 21-14	Off—Curtis McClinton, Dal.			Def—Verlon Biggs, NY
		Def—Earl Faison, SD	1968	East, 25-24	Off—Joe Namath, NY
1964	West, 27-24	Off—Keith Lincoln, SD			& Don Maynard, NY
		Def—Archie Matsos, Oak.			Def—Speedy Duncan, SD
1965	West, 38-14	Off—Keith Lincoln, SD	1969	West, 38-25	Off—Len Dawson, KC
		Def—Willie Brown, Den.			Def—George Webster, Hou.
1966	All-Stars 30	Off—Joe Namath, NY	1970	West, 26-3	John Hadl, SD, QB
	Buffalo 19	Def—Frank Buncom, SD			

Playing sites: Balboa Stadium in San Diego (1962-64); Jeppesen Stadium in Houston (1965); Rice Stadium in Houston (1966); Oakland Coliseum (1967); Gator Bowl in Jacksonville (1968-69) and Astrodome in Houston (1970).

NFL Franchise Origins

Here is what the current 31 teams in the National Football League have to show for the years they have put in as members of the American Professional Football Association (APFA), the NFL, the All-America Football Conference (AAFC) and the American Football League (AFL). Years given for league titles indicate seasons championships were won.

American Football Conference

	First Season	League Titles	Franchise Stops
Baltimore Ravens	1996 (NFL)	None	• Baltimore (1996—)
Buffalo Bills	1960 (AFL)	2 AFL (1964-65)	• Buffalo (1960-72) Orchard Park, NY (1973—)
Cincinnati Bengals	1968 (AFL)	None	• Cincinnati (1968—)
Cleveland Browns	1946 (AAFC)	4 AAFC (1946-49) 4 NFL (1950,54-55,64)	• Cleveland (1946-95, 99—)
Denver Broncos	1960 (AFL)	2 Super Bowls (1997-98)	• Denver (1960—)
Indianapolis Colts	1953 (NFL)	3 NFL (1958-59,68) 1 Super Bowl (1970)	• Baltimore (1953-83) Indianapolis (1984—)
Jacksonville Jaguars	1995 (NFL)	None	• Jacksonville, FL (1995—)
Kansas City Chiefs	1960 (AFL)	3 AFL (1962,66,69) 1 Super Bowl (1969)	• Dallas (1960-62) Kansas City (1963—)
Miami Dolphins	1966 (AFL)	2 Super Bowls (1972-73)	• Miami (1966—)
New England Patriots	1960 (AFL)	None	• Boston (1960-70) Foxboro, MA (1971—)
New York Jets	1960 (AFL)	1 AFL (1968) 1 Super Bowl (1968)	• New York (1960-83) E. Rutherford, NJ (1984—)
Oakland Raiders	1960 (AFL)	1 AFL (1967) 3 Super Bowls (1976,80,83)	• Oakland (1960-81, 1995—) Los Angeles (1982-94)
Pittsburgh Steelers	1933 (NFL)	4 Super Bowls (1974-75,78-79)	• Pittsburgh (1933—)
San Diego Chargers	1960 (AFL)	1 AFL (1963)	• Los Angeles (1960) San Diego (1961—)
Seattle Seahawks	1976 (NFL)	None	• Seattle (1976—)
Tennessee Titans	1960 (AFL)	2 AFL (1960-61)	• Houston (1960-96) Memphis (1997) Nashville (1998—)

National Football Conference

	First Season	League Titles	Franchise Stops
Arizona Cardinals	1920 (APFA)	2 NFL (1925,47)	• Chicago (1920-59) St. Louis (1960-87) Tempe, AZ (1988—)
Atlanta Falcons	1966 (NFL)	None	• Atlanta (1966—)
Carolina Panthers	1995 (NFL)	None	• Clemson, SC (1995) Charlotte, NC (1996—)
Chicago Bears	1920 (APFA)	8 NFL (1921, 32-33,40-41,43, 46,63) 1 Super Bowl (1985)	• Decatur, IL (1920) Chicago (1921—)
Dallas Cowboys	1960 (NFL)	5 Super Bowls (1971,77,92-93,95)	• Dallas (1960-70) Irving, TX (1971—)
Detroit Lions	1930 (NFL)	4 NFL (1935,52-53,57)	• Portsmouth, OH (1930-33) Detroit (1934-74) Pontiac, MI (1975—)
Green Bay Packers	1921 (APFA)	11 NFL (1929-31,36,39,44,61-62,65-67) 3 Super Bowls (1966-67,96)	• Green Bay (1921—)
Minnesota Vikings	1961 (NFL)	1 NFL (1969)	• Bloomington, MN (1961-81) Minneapolis, MN (1982—)
New Orleans Saints	1967 (NFL)	None	• New Orleans (1967—)
New York Giants	1925 (NFL)	4 NFL (1927,34,38,56) 2 Super Bowls (1986,90)	• New York (1925-73,75) New Haven, CT (1973-74) E. Rutherford, NJ (1976—)
Philadelphia Eagles	1933 (NFL)	3 NFL (1948-49,60)	• Philadelphia (1933—)
St. Louis Rams	1937 (NFL)	2 NFL (1945,51)	• Cleveland (1936-45) Los Angeles (1946-79) Anaheim (1980-94) St. Louis (1995—)
San Francisco 49ers	1946 (AAFC)	5 Super Bowls (1981,84,88-89,94)	• San Francisco (1946—)
Tampa Bay Buccaneers	1976 (NFL)	None	• Tampa, FL (1976—)
Washington Redskins	1932 (NFL)	2 NFL (1937, 42) 3 Super Bowls (1982, 87, 91)	• Boston (1932-36) Washington, DC (1937-96) Raljon, MD (1997—)

The Growth of the NFL

Of the 14 franchises that comprised the American Professional Football Association in 1920, only two remain—the Arizona Cardinals (then the Chicago Cardinals) and the Chicago Bears (originally the Decatur-IL Staleys). Green Bay joined the APFC in 1921 and the league changed its name to the NFL in 1922. Since then, 54 NFL clubs have come and gone, five rival leagues have expired and two other leagues have been swallowed up.

The NFL merged with the **All-America Football Conference** (1946-49) following the 1949 season and adopted three of its seven clubs—the Baltimore Colts, Cleveland Browns and San Francisco 49ers. The four remaining AAFC teams—the Brooklyn/NY Yankees, Buffalo Bills, Chicago Hornets and Los Angeles Dons—did not survive. After the 1950 season, the financially troubled Colts were sold back to the NFL. The league folded the team and added its players to the 1951 college draft pool. A new Baltimore franchise, also named the Colts, joined the NFL in 1953.

The formation of the **American Football League** (1960-69) was announced in 1959 with ownership lined up in eight cities—Boston, Buffalo, Dallas, Denver, Houston, Los Angeles, Minneapolis and New York. Set to begin play in the autumn of 1960, the AFL was stunned early that year when Minneapolis withdrew to accept an offer to join the NFL as an expansion team in 1961. The new league responded by choosing Oakland to replace Minneapolis and inherit the departed team's draft picks. Since no AFL team actually played in Minneapolis, it is not considered the original home of the Oakland Raiders.

In 1966, the NFL and AFL agreed to a merger that resulted in the first Super Bowl (originally called the AFL-NFL World Championship Game) following the '66 league playoffs. In 1970, the now 10-member AFL officially joined the NFL, forming a 26-team league made up of two conferences of three divisions each.

Expansion/Merger Timetable
For teams currently in NFL.

1921–Green Bay Packers; **1925**–New York Giants; **1930**–Portsmouth-OH Spartans (now Detroit Lions); **1932**–Boston Braves (now Washington Redskins); **1933**–Philadelphia Eagles and Pittsburgh Pirates (now Steelers); **1937**–Cleveland Rams (now St. Louis); **1950**–added AAFC's Cleveland Browns and San Francisco 49ers; **1953**–Baltimore Colts (now Indianapolis).

1960–Dallas Cowboys; **1961**–Minnesota Vikings; **1966**–Atlanta Falcons; **1967**–New Orleans Saints; **1970**–added AFL's Boston Patriots (now New England), Buffalo Bills, Cincinnati Bengals (1968 expansion team), Denver Broncos, Houston Oilers, Kansas City Chiefs, Miami Dolphins (1966 expansion team), New York Jets, Oakland Raiders and San Diego Chargers (the AFL-NFL merger divided the league into two 13-team conferences with old-line NFL clubs Baltimore, Cleveland and Pittsburgh moving to the AFC); **1976**–Seattle Seahawks and Tampa Bay Buccaneers (Seattle was originally in the NFC West and Tampa Bay in the AFC West, but were switched to their current divisions in 1977); **1995**–Carolina Panthers and Jacksonville Jaguars; **1996**—Cleveland Browns move to Baltimore and become Ravens. City of Cleveland retains rights to team name, colors and all memorabilia; **1999**–Cleveland Browns return to the NFL.

City and Nickname Changes

1921—Decatur Staleys move to Chicago; **1922**—Chicago Staleys renamed Bears; **1933**—Boston Braves renamed Redskins; **1937**—Boston Redskins move to Washington; **1934**—Portsmouth (Ohio) Spartans move to Detroit and become Lions; **1941**—Pittsburgh Pirates renamed Steelers; **1943**—Philadelphia and Pittsburgh merge for one season and become Phil-Pitt, or the "Steagles"; **1944**—Chicago Cardinals and Pittsburgh merge for one season and become Card-Pitt; **1946**—Cleveland Rams move to Los Angeles.

1960—Chicago Cardinals move to St. Louis; **1961**—Los Angeles Chargers (AFL) move to San Diego; **1963**—New York Titans (AFL) renamed Jets and Dallas Texans (AFL) move to Kansas City and become Chiefs; **1971**—Boston Patriots become New England Patriots; **1982**—Oakland Raiders move to Los Angeles; **1984**—Baltimore Colts move to Indianapolis; **1988**—St. Louis Cardinals move to Phoenix; **1994**—Phoenix Cardinals become Arizona Cardinals; **1995**—L.A. Rams move to St. Louis and L.A. Raiders move back to Oakland; **1996**—Cleveland Browns move to Baltimore and become Ravens. City of Cleveland retains rights to team name, colors and all memorabilia; **1997**—Houston Oilers move to Memphis and become Tennessee Oilers; **1998**— Tennessee Oilers move to Nashville; **1999**— Tennessee Oilers renamed Titans.

Defunct NFL Teams

Teams that once played in the APFA and NFL, but no longer exist.

Akron-OH–Pros (1920-25) and Indians (1926); **Baltimore**–Colts (1950); **Boston**–Bulldogs (1926) and Yanks (1944-48); **Brooklyn**–Lions (1926), Dodgers (1930-43) and Tigers (1944); **Buffalo**–All-Americans (1921-23), Bisons (1924-25), Rangers (1926), Bisons (1927,1929); **Canton-OH**–Bulldogs (1920-23,1925-26); **Chicago**–Tigers (1920); **Cincinnati**–Celts (1921) and Reds (1933-34); **Cleveland**–Tigers (1920), Indians (1921), Indians (1923), Bulldogs (1924-25,1927) and Indians (1931); **Columbus-OH**–Panhandles (1920-22) and Tigers (1923-26); **Dallas**–Texans (1952); **Dayton-OH**–Triangles (1920-29).

Detroit–Heralds (1920-21), Panthers (1925-26) and Wolverines (1928); **Duluth-MN**–Kelleys (1923-25) and Eskimos (1926-27); **Evansville-IN**–Crimson Giants (1921-22); **Frankford-PA**–Yellow Jackets (1924-31); **Hammond-IN**–Pros (1920-26); **Hartford**–Blues (1926); **Kansas City**–Blues (1924) and Cowboys (1925-26); **Kenosha-WI**–Maroons (1924); **Los Angeles**–Buccaneers (1926); **Louisville**–Brecks (1921-23) and Colonels (1926); **Marion-OH**–Oorang Indians (1922-23); **Milwaukee**–Badgers (1922-26); **Minneapolis**–Marines (1922-24) and Red Jackets (1929-30); **Muncie-IN**–Flyers (1920-21).

New York–Giants (1921), Yankees (1927-28), Bulldogs (1949) and Yankees (1950-51); **Newark-NJ**–Tornadoes (1930); **Orange-NJ**–Tornadoes (1929); **Pottsville-PA**–Maroons (1925-28); **Providence-RI**–Steam Roller (1925-31); **Racine-WI**–Legion (1922-24) and Tornadoes (1926); **Rochester-NY**–Jeffersons (1920-25); **Rock Island-IL**–Independents (1920-26); **Staten Island-NY**–Stapletons (1929-32); **St. Louis**–All-Stars (1923) and Gunners (1934); **Toledo-OH**–Maroons (1922-23); **Tonawanda-NY**–Kardex (1921), also called Lumbermen; **Washington**–Senators (1921).

Annual NFL Leaders

Individual leaders in NFL (1932-69), NFC (since 1970), AFL (1960-69) and AFC (since 1970).

Passing

Since 1932, the NFL has used several formulas to determine passing leadership, from Total Yards alone (1932-37), to the current rating system—adopted in 1973—that takes Completions, Completion Percentage, Yards Gained, TD Passes, Interceptions, Interception Percentage and other factors into account. The quarterbacks listed below all led the league according to the system in use at the time.

Multiple winners: Sammy Baugh and Steve Young (6); Joe Montana and Roger Staubach (5); Arnie Herber, Sonny Jurgensen, Bart Starr and Norm Van Brocklin (3); Ed Danowski, Otto Graham, Cecil Isbell, Milt Plum and Bob Waterfield (2).

NFL-NFC

Year		Att	Cmp	Yds	TD	Year		Att	Cmp	Yds	TD
1932	Arnie Herber, GB	101	37	639	9	1965	Rudy Bukich, Chi	312	176	2641	20
1933	Harry Newman, NY	136	53	973	11	1966	Bart Starr, GB	251	156	2257	14
1934	Arnie Herber, GB	115	42	799	8	1967	Sonny Jurgensen, Wash	508	288	3747	31
1935	Ed Danowski, NY	113	57	794	10	1968	Earl Morrall, Bal	317	182	2909	26
1936	Arnie Herber, GB	173	77	1239	11	1969	Sonny Jurgensen, Wash	442	274	3102	22
1937	Sammy Baugh, Wash	171	81	1127	8	1970	John Brodie, SF	378	223	2941	24
1938	Ed Danowski, NY	129	70	848	7	1971	Roger Staubach, Dal	211	126	1882	15
1939	Parker Hall, Cle. Rams	208	106	1227	9	1972	Norm Snead, NY	325	196	2307	17
1940	Sammy Baugh, Wash	177	111	1367	12	1973	Roger Staubach, Dal	286	179	2428	23
1941	Cecil Isbell, GB	206	117	1479	15	1974	Sonny Jurgensen, Wash	167	107	1185	11
1942	Cecil Isbell, GB	268	146	2021	24	1975	Fran Tarkenton, Min	425	273	2994	25
1943	Sammy Baugh, Wash	239	133	1754	23	1976	James Harris, LA	158	91	1460	8
1944	Frank Filchock, Wash.	147	84	1139	13	1977	Roger Staubach, Dal	361	210	2620	18
1945	Sammy Baugh, Wash	182	128	1669	11	1978	Roger Staubach, Dal	413	231	3190	25
	& Sid Luckman, Chi. Bears	217	117	1725	14	1979	Roger Staubach, Dal	461	267	3586	27
1946	Bob Waterfield, LA	251	127	1747	18	1980	Ron Jaworski, Phi	451	257	3529	27
1947	Sammy Baugh, Wash	354	210	2938	25	1981	Joe Montana, SF	488	311	3565	19
1948	Tommy Thompson, Phi	246	141	1965	25	1982	Joe Theismann, Wash	252	161	2033	13
1949	Sammy Baugh, Wash	255	145	1903	18	1983	Steve Bartkowski, Atl	432	274	3167	22
1950	Norm Van Brocklin, LA	233	127	2061	18	1984	Joe Montana, SF	432	279	3630	28
1951	Bob Waterfield, LA	176	88	1566	13	1985	Joe Montana, SF	494	303	3653	27
1952	Norm Van Brocklin, LA	205	113	1736	14	1986	Tommy Kramer, Min	372	208	3000	24
1953	Otto Graham, Cle	258	167	2722	11	1987	Joe Montana, SF	398	266	3054	31
1954	Norm Van Brocklin, LA	260	139	2637	13	1988	Wade Wilson, Min	332	204	2746	15
1955	Otto Graham, Cle	185	98	1721	15	1989	Don Majkowski, GB	599	353	4318	27
1956	Ed Brown, Chi. Bears	168	96	1667	11	1990	Joe Montana, SF	520	321	3944	26
1957	Tommy O'Connell, Cle	110	63	1229	9	1991	Steve Young, SF	279	180	2517	17
1958	Eddie LeBaron, Wash	145	79	1365	11	1992	Steve Young, SF	402	268	3465	25
1959	Charlie Conerly, NY	194	113	1706	14	1993	Steve Young, SF	462	314	4023	29
1960	Milt Plum, Cle	250	151	2297	21	1994	Steve Young, SF	461	324	3969	35
1961	Milt Plum, Cle	302	177	2416	16	1995	Brett Favre, GB	570	359	4413	38
1962	Bart Starr, GB	285	178	2438	12	1996	Steve Young, SF	316	214	2410	14
1963	Y.A. Tittle, NY	367	221	3145	36	1997	Steve Young, SF	356	241	3029	19
1964	Bart Starr, GB	272	163	2144	15	1998	Randall Cunningham, Min	425	259	3704	34

Note: In 1945, Sammy Baugh and Sid Luckman tied with 8 points on an inverse rating system.

AFL-AFC

Multiple winners: Dan Marino (5); Ken Anderson and Len Dawson (4); Bob Griese, Daryle Lamonica, Warren Moon and Ken Stabler (2).

Year		Att	Cmp	Yds	TD	Year		Att	Cmp	Yds	TD
1960	Jack Kemp, LA	406	211	3018	20	1980	Brian Sipe, Cle	554	337	4132	30
1961	George Blanda, Hou	362	187	3330	36	1981	Ken Anderson, Cin	479	300	3753	29
1962	Len Dawson, Dal	310	189	2759	29	1982	Ken Anderson, Cin	309	218	2495	12
1963	Tobin Rote, SD	286	170	2510	20	1983	Dan Marino, Mia	296	173	2210	20
1964	Len Dawson, KC	354	199	2879	30	1984	Dan Marino, Mia	564	362	5084	48
1965	John Hadl, SD	348	174	2798	20	1985	Ken O'Brien, NY	488	297	3888	25
1966	Len Dawson, KC	284	159	2527	26	1986	Dan Marino, Mia	623	378	4746	44
1967	Daryle Lamonica, Oak	425	220	3228	30	1987	Bernie Kosar, Cle	389	241	3033	22
1968	Len Dawson, KC	224	131	2109	17	1988	Boomer Esiason, Cin	388	223	3572	28
1969	Greg Cook, Cin	197	106	1854	15	1989	Dan Marino, Mia	550	308	3997	24
1970	Daryle Lamonica, Oak	356	179	2516	22	1990	Warren Moon, Hou	584	362	4689	33
1971	Bob Griese, Mia	263	145	2089	19	1991	Jim Kelly, Buf	474	304	3844	33
1972	Earl Morrall, Mia	150	83	1360	11	1992	Warren Moon, Hou	346	224	2521	18
1973	Ken Stabler, Oak	260	163	1997	14	1993	John Elway, Den	551	348	4030	25
1974	Ken Anderson, Cin	328	213	2667	18	1994	Dan Marino, Mia	615	385	4453	30
1975	Ken Anderson, Cin	377	228	3169	21	1995	Jim Harbaugh, Ind	314	200	2575	17
1976	Ken Stabler, Oak	291	194	2737	27	1996	John Elway, Den	466	287	3328	26
1977	Bob Griese, Mia	307	180	2252	22	1997	Mark Brunell, Jax	435	264	3281	18
1978	Terry Bradshaw, Pit	368	207	2915	28	1998	Vinny Testaverde, NYJ	421	259	3256	29
1979	Dan Fouts, SD	530	332	4082	24						

Receptions
NFL-NFC

Multiple winners: Don Hutson (8); Raymond Berry, Tom Fears, Pete Pihos, Jerry Rice, Sterling Sharpe and Billy Wilson (3); Dwight Clark, Herman Moore, Ahmad Rashad and Charley Taylor (2).

Year		No	Yds	Avg	TD	Year		No	Yds	Avg	TD
1932	Ray Flaherty, NY	21	350	16.7	3	1965	Dave Parks, SF	80	1344	16.8	12
1933	Shipwreck Kelly, Bklyn	22	246	11.2	3	1966	Charley Taylor, Wash	72	1119	15.5	12
1934	Joe Carter, Phi	16	238	14.9	4	1967	Charley Taylor, Wash	70	990	14.1	9
	& Red Badgro, NY	16	206	12.9	1	1968	Clifton McNeil, SF	71	994	14.0	7
1935	Tod Goodwin, NY	26	432	16.6	4	1969	Dan Abramowicz, NO	73	1015	13.9	7
1936	Don Hutson, GB	34	536	15.8	8	1970	Dick Gordon, Chi.	71	1026	14.5	13
1937	Don Hutson, GB	41	552	13.5	7	1971	Bob Tucker, NY	59	791	13.4	4
1938	Gaynell Tinsley, Chi. Cards	41	516	12.6	1	1972	Harold Jackson, Phi	62	1048	16.9	4
1939	Don Hutson, GB	34	846	24.9	6	1973	Harold Carmichael, Phi.	67	1116	16.7	9
1940	Don Looney, Phi.	58	707	12.2	4	1974	Charles Young, Phi.	63	696	11.0	3
1941	Don Hutson, GB	58	739	12.7	10	1975	Chuck Foreman, Min	73	691	9.5	9
1942	Don Hutson, GB	74	1211	16.4	17	1976	Drew Pearson, Dal	58	806	13.9	6
1943	Don Hutson, GB	47	776	16.5	11	1977	Ahmad Rashad, Min	51	681	13.4	2
1944	Don Hutson, GB	58	866	14.9	9	1978	Rickey Young, Min	88	704	8.0	5
1945	Don Hutson, GB	47	834	17.7	9	1979	Ahmad Rashad, Min	80	1156	14.5	9
1946	Jim Benton, LA	63	981	15.6	6	1980	Earl Cooper, SF	83	567	6.8	4
1947	Jim Keane, Chi. Bears	64	910	14.2	10	1981	Dwight Clark, SF	85	1105	13.0	4
1948	Tom Fears, LA	51	698	13.7	4	1982	Dwight Clark, SF	60	913	12.2	5
1949	Tom Fears, LA	77	1013	13.2	9	1983	Roy Green, St. L	78	1227	15.7	14
1950	Tom Fears, LA	84	1116	13.3	7		Charlie Brown, Wash	78	1225	15.7	8
1951	Elroy Hirsch, LA	66	1495	22.7	17		& Earnest Gray, NY	78	1139	14.6	5
1952	Mac Speedie, Cle	62	911	14.7	5	1984	Art Monk, Wash	106	1372	12.9	7
1953	Pete Pihos, Phi	63	1049	16.7	10	1985	Roger Craig, SF	92	1016	11.0	6
1954	Pete Pihos, Phi	60	872	14.5	10	1986	Jerry Rice, SF	86	1570	18.3	15
	& Billy Wilson, SF	60	830	13.8	5	1987	J.T. Smith, St. L	91	1117	12.3	8
1955	Pete Pihos, Phi	62	864	13.9	7	1988	Henry Ellard, LA	86	1414	16.4	10
1956	Billy Wilson, SF	60	889	14.8	5	1989	Sterling Sharpe, GB	90	1423	15.8	12
1957	Billy Wilson, SF	52	757	14.6	6	1990	Jerry Rice, SF	100	1502	15.0	13
1958	Raymond Berry, Bal	56	794	14.2	9	1991	Michael Irvin, Dal	93	1523	16.4	8
	& Pete Retzlaff, Phi	56	766	13.7	2	1992	Sterling Sharpe, GB	108	1461	13.5	13
1959	Raymond Berry, Bal	66	959	14.5	14	1993	Sterling Sharpe, GB	112	1274	11.4	11
1960	Raymond Berry, Bal	74	1298	17.5	10	1994	Cris Carter, Min	122	1256	10.3	7
1961	Red Phillips, LA	78	1092	14.0	5	1995	Herman Moore, Det	123	1686	13.7	14
1962	Bobby Mitchell, Wash	72	1384	19.2	11	1996	Jerry Rice, SF	108	1254	11.6	8
1963	Bobby Joe Conrad, St. L	73	967	13.2	10	1997	Herman Moore, Det	104	1293	12.4	8
1964	Johnny Morris, Chi. Bears	93	1200	12.9	10	1998	Frank Sanders, Ari	89	1145	12.9	3

AFL-AFC

Multiple winners: Lionel Taylor (5); Lance Alworth, Haywood Jeffires, Lydell Mitchell and Kellen Winslow (3); Fred Biletnikoff, Todd Christensen, Carl Pickens and Al Toon (2).

Year		No	Yds	Avg	TD	Year		No	Yds	Avg	TD
1960	Lionel Taylor, Den	92	1235	13.4	12	1980	Kellen Winslow, SD	89	1290	14.5	9
1961	Lionel Taylor, Den	100	1176	11.8	4	1981	Kellen Winslow, SD	88	1075	12.2	10
1962	Lionel Taylor, Den	77	908	11.8	4	1982	Kellen Winslow, SD	54	721	13.4	6
1963	Lionel Taylor, Den	78	1101	14.1	10	1983	Todd Christensen, LA	92	1247	13.6	12
1964	Charley Hennigan, Hou	101	1546	15.3	8	1984	Ozzie Newsome, Cle	89	1001	11.2	5
1965	Lionel Taylor, Den	85	1131	13.3	6	1985	Lionel James, SD	86	1027	11.9	6
1966	Lance Alworth, SD	73	1383	18.9	13	1986	Todd Christensen, LA	95	1153	12.1	8
1967	George Sauer, NY	75	1189	15.9	6	1987	Al Toon, NY	68	976	14.4	5
1968	Lance Alworth, SD	68	1312	19.3	10	1988	Al Toon, NY	93	1067	11.5	5
1969	Lance Alworth, SD	64	1003	15.7	4	1989	Andre Reed, Buf	88	1312	14.9	9
1970	Marlin Briscoe, Buf	57	1036	18.2	8	1990	Haywood Jeffires, Hou	74	1048	14.2	8
1971	Fred Biletnikoff, Oak	61	929	15.2	9		& Drew Hill, Hou	74	1019	13.8	5
1972	Fred Biletnikoff, Oak	58	802	13.8	7	1991	Haywood Jeffires, Hou	100	1181	11.8	7
1973	Fred Willis, Hou	57	371	6.5	1	1992	Haywood Jeffires, Hou	90	913	10.1	9
1974	Lydell Mitchell, Bal	72	544	7.6	2	1993	Reggie Langhorne, Ind	85	1038	12.2	3
1975	Reggie Rucker, Cle	60	770	12.8	3	1994	Ben Coates, NE	96	1174	12.2	7
	& Lydell Mitchell, Bal	60	544	9.1	4	1995	Carl Pickens, Cin	99	1234	12.5	17
1976	MacArthur Lane, KC	66	686	10.4	1	1996	Carl Pickens, Cin	100	1180	11.8	12
1977	Lydell Mitchell, Bal	71	620	8.7	4	1997	Tim Brown, Oak	104	1408	13.5	5
1978	Steve Largent, Sea	71	1168	16.5	8	1998	O.J. McDuffie, Mia	90	1050	11.7	7
1979	Joe Washington, Bal	82	750	9.1	3						

Annual NFL Leaders (Cont.)
Rushing

NFL-NFC

Multiple winners: Jim Brown (8); Walter Payton and Barry Sanders (5); Emmitt Smith and Steve Van Buren (4); Eric Dickerson (3); Cliff Battles, John Brockington, Larry Brown, Bill Dudley, Leroy Kelly, Bill Paschal, Joe Perry, Gale Sayers and Whizzer White (2).

Year		Car	Yds	Avg	TD	Year		Car	Yds	Avg	TD
1932	Cliff Battles, Bos	148	576	3.9	3	1966	Gale Sayers, Chi	229	1231	5.4	8
1933	Jim Musick, Bos	173	809	4.7	5	1967	Leroy Kelly, Cle	235	1205	5.1	11
1934	Beattie Feathers, Chi. Bears	119	1004	8.4	8	1968	Leroy Kelly, Cle	248	1239	5.0	16
1935	Doug Russell, Chi. Cards	140	499	3.6	0	1969	Gale Sayers, Chi	236	1032	4.4	8
1936	Tuffy Leemans, NY	206	830	4.0	2	1970	Larry Brown, Wash	237	1125	4.7	5
1937	Cliff Battles, Wash	216	874	4.0	5	1971	John Brockington, GB	216	1105	5.1	4
1938	Whizzer White, Pit	152	567	3.7	4	1972	Larry Brown, Wash	285	1216	4.3	8
1939	Bill Osmanski, Chi. Bears	121	699	5.8	7	1973	John Brockington, GB	265	1144	4.3	3
1940	Whizzer White, Det	146	514	3.5	5	1974	Lawrence McCutcheon, LA	236	1109	4.7	3
1941	Pug Manders, Bklyn	111	486	4.4	5	1975	Jim Otis, St. L	269	1076	4.0	5
1942	Bill Dudley, Pit	162	696	4.3	5	1976	Walter Payton, Chi	311	1390	4.5	13
1943	Bill Paschal, NY	147	572	3.9	10	1977	Walter Payton, Chi	339	1852	5.5	14
1944	Bill Paschal, NY	196	737	3.8	9	1978	Walter Payton, Chi	333	1395	4.2	11
1945	Steve Van Buren, Phi	143	832	5.8	15	1979	Walter Payton, Chi	369	1610	4.4	14
1946	Bill Dudley, Pit	146	604	4.1	3	1980	Walter Payton, Chi	317	1460	4.6	6
1947	Steve Van Buren, Phi	217	1008	4.6	13	1981	George Rogers, NO	378	1674	4.4	13
1948	Steve Van Buren, Phi	201	945	4.7	10	1982	Tony Dorsett, Dal	177	745	4.2	5
1949	Steve Van Buren, Phi	263	1146	4.4	11	1983	Eric Dickerson, LA	390	1808	4.6	18
1950	Marion Motley, Cle	140	810	5.8	3	1984	Eric Dickerson, LA	379	2105	5.6	14
1951	Eddie Price, NY Giants	271	971	3.6	7	1985	Gerald Riggs, Atl	397	1719	4.3	10
1952	Dan Towler, LA	156	894	5.7	10	1986	Eric Dickerson, LA	404	1821	4.5	11
1953	Joe Perry, SF	192	1018	5.3	10	1987	Charles White, LA	324	1374	4.2	11
1954	Joe Perry, SF	173	1049	6.1	8	1988	Herschel Walker, Dal	361	1514	4.2	5
1955	Alan Ameche, Bal	213	961	4.5	9	1989	Barry Sanders, Det	280	1470	5.3	14
1956	Rick Casares, Chi. Bears	234	1126	4.8	12	1990	Barry Sanders, Det	255	1304	5.1	13
1957	Jim Brown, Cle	202	942	4.7	9	1991	Emmitt Smith, Dal	365	1563	4.3	12
1958	Jim Brown, Cle	257	1527	5.9	17	1992	Emmitt Smith, Dal	373	1713	4.6	18
1959	Jim Brown, Cle	290	1329	4.6	14	1993	Emmitt Smith, Dal	283	1486	5.3	9
1960	Jim Brown, Cle	215	1257	5.8	9	1994	Barry Sanders, Det	331	1883	5.7	7
1961	Jim Brown, Cle	305	1408	4.6	8	1995	Emmitt Smith, Dal	377	1773	4.7	25
1962	Jim Taylor, GB	272	1474	5.4	19	1996	Barry Sanders, Det	307	1553	5.1	11
1963	Jim Brown, Cle	291	1863	6.4	12	1997	Barry Sanders, Det	335	2053	6.1	11
1964	Jim Brown, Cle	280	1446	5.2	7	1998	Jamal Anderson, Atl	410	1846	4.5	14
1965	Jim Brown, Cle	289	1544	5.3	17						

Note: Jim Brown led the NFL in rushing eight of his nine years in the league. The one season he didn't win (1962) he finished fourth (996 yds) behind Jim Taylor, John Henry Johnson of Pittsburgh (1,141 yds) and Dick Bass of the LA Rams (1,033 yds).

AFL-AFC

Multiple winners: Earl Campbell and O.J. Simpson (4); Terrell Davis and Thurman Thomas (3); Eric Dickerson, Cookie Gilchrist, Floyd Little, Jim Nance and Curt Warner (2).

Year		Car	Yds	Avg	TD	Year		Car	Yds	Avg	TD
1960	Abner Haynes, Dal	157	875	5.6	9	1980	Earl Campbell, Hou	373	1934	5.2	13
1961	Billy Cannon, Hou	200	948	4.7	6	1981	Earl Campbell, Hou	361	1376	3.8	10
1962	Cookie Gilchrist, Buf	214	1096	5.1	13	1982	Freeman McNeil, NY	151	786	5.2	6
1963	Clem Daniels, Oak	215	1099	5.1	3	1983	Curt Warner, Sea	335	1449	4.3	13
1964	Cookie Gilchrist, Buf	230	981	4.3	6	1984	Earnest Jackson, SD	296	1179	4.0	8
1965	Paul Lowe, SD	222	1121	5.0	7	1985	Marcus Allen, LA	380	1759	4.6	11
1966	Jim Nance, Bos	299	1458	4.9	11	1986	Curt Warner, Sea	319	1481	4.6	13
1967	Jim Nance, Bos	269	1216	4.5	7	1987	Eric Dickerson, Ind	223	1011	4.5	5
1968	Paul Robinson, Cin	238	1023	4.3	8	1988	Eric Dickerson, Ind	388	1659	4.3	14
1969	Dickie Post, SD	182	873	4.8	6	1989	Christian Okoye, KC	370	1480	4.0	12
1970	Floyd Little, Den	209	901	4.3	3	1990	Thurman Thomas, Buf	271	1297	4.8	11
1971	Floyd Little, Den	284	1133	4.0	6	1991	Thurman Thomas, Buf	288	1407	4.9	7
1972	O.J. Simpson, Buf	292	1251	4.3	6	1992	Barry Foster, Pit	390	1690	4.3	11
1973	O.J. Simpson, Buf	332	2003	6.0	12	1993	Thurman Thomas, Buf	355	1315	3.7	6
1974	Otis Armstrong, Den	263	1407	5.3	9	1994	Chris Warren, Sea	333	1545	4.6	9
1975	O.J. Simpson, Buf	329	1817	5.5	16	1995	Curtis Martin, NE	368	1487	4.0	14
1976	O.J. Simpson, Buf	290	1503	5.2	8	1996	Terrell Davis, Den	345	1538	4.5	13
1977	Mark van Eeghen, Oak	324	1273	3.9	7	1997	Terrell Davis, Den	369	1750	4.7	15
1978	Earl Campbell, Hou	302	1450	4.8	13	1998	Terrell Davis, Den	392	2008	5.1	21
1979	Earl Campbell, Hou	368	1697	4.6	19						

Note: Eric Dickerson was traded to Indianapolis from the NFC's LA Rams during the 1987 season. In three games with the Rams, he carried the ball 60 times for 277 yds, a 4.6 avg and 1 TD. His official AFC statistics above came in nine games with the Colts.

Scoring
NFL-NFC

Multiple winners: Don Hutson (5); Dutch Clark, Pat Harder, Paul Hornung, Chip Lohmiller and Mark Moseley (3); Kevin Butler, Mike Cofer, Fred Cox, Jack Manders, Chester Marcol, Eddie Murray, Emmitt Smith, Gordy Soltau and Doak Walker (2).

Year		TD	FG	PAT	Pts	Year		TD	FG	PAT	Pts
1932	Dutch Clark, Portsmouth	6	3	10	55	1966	Bruce Gossett, LA	0	28	29	113
1933	Glenn Presnell, Portsmouth	6	6	10	64	1967	Jim Bakken, St.L	0	27	36	117
	& Ken Strong, NY	6	5	13	64	1968	Leroy Kelly, Cle	20	0	0	120
1934	Jack Manders, Chi. Bears	3	10	31	79	1969	Fred Cox, Min	0	26	43	121
1935	Dutch Clark, Det	6	1	16	55	1970	Fred Cox, Min	0	30	35	125
1936	Dutch Clark, Det	7	4	19	73	1971	Curt Knight, Wash	0	29	27	114
1937	Jack Manders, Chi. Bears	5	8	15	69	1972	Chester Marcol, GB	0	33	29	128
1938	Clarke Hinkle, GB	7	3	7	58	1973	David Ray, LA	0	30	40	130
1939	Andy Farkas, Wash	11	0	2	68	1974	Chester Marcol, GB	0	25	19	94
1940	Don Hutson, GB	7	0	15	57	1975	Chuck Foreman, Min	22	0	0	132
1941	Don Hutson, GB	12	1	20	95	1976	Mark Moseley, Wash	0	22	31	97
1942	Don Hutson, GB	17	1	33	138	1977	Walter Payton, Chi	16	0	0	96
1943	Don Hutson, GB	12	3	26	117	1978	Frank Corral, LA	0	29	31	118
1944	Don Hutson, GB	9	0	31	85	1979	Mark Moseley, Wash	0	25	39	114
1945	Steve Van Buren, Phi	18	0	2	110	1980	Eddie Murray, Det	0	27	35	116
1946	Ted Fritsch, GB	10	9	13	100	1981	Rafael Septien, Dal	0	27	40	121
1947	Pat Harder, Chi. Cards	7	7	39	102		& Eddie Murray, Det	0	25	46	121
1948	Pat Harder, Chi. Cards	6	7	53	110	1982	Wendell Tyler, LA	13	0	0	78
1949	Gene Roberts, NY Giants	17	0	0	102	1983	Mark Moseley, Wash	0	33	62	161
	& Pat Harder, Chi. Cards	8	3	45	102	1984	Ray Wersching, SF	0	25	56	131
1950	Doak Walker, Det	11	8	38	128	1985	Kevin Butler, Chi	0	31	51	144
1951	Elroy Hirsch, LA	17	0	0	102	1986	Kevin Butler, Chi	0	28	36	120
1952	Gordy Soltau, SF	7	6	34	94	1987	Jerry Rice, SF	23	0	0	138
1953	Gordy Soltau, SF	6	10	48	114	1988	Mike Cofer, SF	0	27	40	121
1954	Bobby Walston, Phi	11	4	36	114	1989	Mike Cofer, SF	0	29	49	136
1955	Doak Walker, Det	7	9	27	96	1990	Chip Lohmiller, Wash	0	30	41	131
1956	Bobby Layne, Det	5	12	33	99	1991	Chip Lohmiller, Wash	0	31	56	149
1957	Sam Baker, Wash	1	14	29	77	1992	Chip Lohmiller, Wash	0	30	30	120
	& Lou Groza, Cle	0	15	32	77		& Morten Andersen, NO	0	29	33	120
1958	Jim Brown, Cle	18	0	0	108	1993	Jason Hanson, Det	0	34	28	130
1959	Paul Hornung, GB	7	7	31	94	1994	Emmitt Smith, Dal	22	0	0	132
1960	Paul Hornung, GB	15	15	41	176		& Fuad Reveiz, Min	0	34	30	132
1961	Paul Hornung, GB	10	15	41	146	1995	Emmitt Smith, Dal	25	0	0	150
1962	Jim Taylor, GB	19	0	0	114	1996	John Kasay, Car	0	37	34	145
1963	Don Chandler, NY	0	18	52	106	1997	Richie Cunningham, Dal	0	34	24	126
1964	Lenny Moore, Bal	20	0	0	120	1998	Gary Anderson, Min	0	35	59	164
1965	Gale Sayers, Chi	22	0	0	132						

AFL-AFC

Multiple winners: Gino Cappelletti (5); Gary Anderson (3); Jim Breech, Roy Gerela, Gene Mingo, Nick Lowery, John Smith, Pete Stoyanovich and Jim Turner (2).

Year		TD	FG	PAT	Pts	Year		TD	FG	PAT	Pts
1960	Gene Mingo, Den	6	18	33	123	1980	John Smith, NE	0	26	51	129
1961	Gino Cappelletti, Bos	8	17	48	147	1981	Nick Lowery, KC	0	26	37	115
1962	Gene Mingo, Den	4	27	32	137		& Jim Breech, Cin	0	22	49	115
1963	Gino Cappelletti, Bos	2	22	35	113	1982	Marcus Allen, LA	14	0	0	84
1964	Gino Cappelletti, Bos	7	25	36	155	1983	Gary Anderson, Pit	0	27	38	119
1965	Gino Cappelletti, Bos	9	17	27	132	1984	Gary Anderson, Pit	0	24	45	117
1966	Gino Cappelletti, Bos	6	16	35	119	1985	Gary Anderson, Pit	0	33	40	139
1967	George Blanda, Oak	0	20	56	116	1986	Tony Franklin, NE	0	32	44	140
1968	Jim Turner, NY	0	34	43	145	1987	Jim Breech, Cin	0	24	25	97
1969	Jim Turner, NY	0	32	33	129	1988	Scott Norwood, Buf	0	32	33	129
1970	Jan Stenerud, KC	0	30	26	116	1989	David Treadwell, Den	0	27	39	120
1971	Garo Yepremian, Mia	0	28	33	117	1990	Nick Lowery, KC	0	34	37	139
1972	Bobby Howfield, NY	0	27	40	121	1991	Pete Stoyanovich, Mia	0	31	28	121
1973	Roy Gerela, Pit	0	29	36	123	1992	Pete Stoyanovich, Mia	0	30	34	124
1974	Roy Gerela, Pit	0	20	33	93	1993	Jeff Jaeger, LA	0	35	27	132
1975	O.J. Simpson, Buf	23	0	0	138	1994	John Carney, SD	0	34	33	135
1976	Toni Linhart, Bal	0	20	49	109	1995	Norm Johnson, Pit	0	34	39	141
1977	Errol Mann, Oak	0	20	39	99	1996	Cary Blanchard, Ind	0	36	27	135
1978	Pat Leahy, NY	0	22	41	107	1997	Mike Hollis, Jax	0	31	41	134
1979	John Smith, NE	0	23	46	115	1998	Steve Christie, Buf	0	33	41	140

All-Time NFL Leaders

Through 1998 regular season.

CAREER

Players active in 1998 in **bold** type.

Passing Efficiency

Ratings based on performance standards established for completion percentage, average gain, touchdown percentage and interception percentage. Quarterbacks are allocated points according to how their statistics measure up to those standards. Minimum 1500 passing attempts.

		Yrs	Att	Cmp	Cmp%	Yards	Avg Gain	TD	TD%	Int	Int%	Rating
1	**Steve Young**	14	4065	2622	64.5	32,678	8.04	229	5.6	103	2.5	97.6
2	Joe Montana	15	5391	3409	63.2	40,551	7.52	273	5.1	139	2.6	92.3
3	**Brett Favre**	8	3757	2318	61.7	26,803	7.13	213	5.7	118	3.1	89.0
4	**Dan Marino**	16	7989	4763	59.6	58,913	7.37	408	5.1	235	2.9	87.3
5	**Mark Brunell**	6	1719	1038	60.4	12,512	7.28	72	4.2	43	2.5	86.3
6	Jim Kelly	11	4779	2874	60.1	35,467	7.42	237	5.0	175	3.7	84.4
7	Roger Staubach	11	2958	1685	57.0	22,700	7.67	153	5.2	109	3.7	83.4
8	**Troy Aikman**	10	4011	2479	61.8	28,346	7.07	141	3.5	115	2.9	82.8
9	Neil Lomax	8	3153	1817	57.6	22,771	7.22	136	4.3	90	2.9	82.7
10	Sonny Jurgensen	18	4262	2433	57.1	32,224	7.56	255	6.0	189	4.4	82.625
11	Len Dawson	19	3741	2136	57.1	28,711	7.67	239	6.4	183	4.9	82.555
12	Ken Anderson	16	4475	2654	59.3	32,838	7.34	197	4.4	160	3.6	81.9
13	Bernie Kosar	12	3365	1994	59.3	23,301	6.92	124	3.7	87	2.6	81.8
14	Danny White	13	2950	1761	59.7	21,959	7.44	155	5.3	132	4.5	81.7
15	**Neil O'Donnell**	9	2862	1650	57.7	19,026	6.65	104	3.6	57	2.0	81.640
16	**Randall Cunningham**	13	3875	2177	56.2	27,082	6.99	190	4.9	119	3.1	81.569
17	**Dave Krieg**	19	5311	3105	58.5	38,147	7.18	261	4.9	199	3.7	81.5
18	Boomer Esiason	14	5205	2969	57.0	37,920	7.29	247	4.7	184	3.5	81.1
19	**Warren Moon**	15	6786	3972	58.5	49,097	7.24	290	4.3	232	3.4	81.0
20	**Chris Chandler**	11	2587	1494	57.8	18,526	7.16	119	4.6	90	3.5	80.9
21	Jeff Hostetler	12	2338	1357	58.0	16,430	7.03	94	4.0	71	3.0	80.480
22	Bart Starr	16	3149	1808	57.4	24,718	7.85	152	4.8	138	4.4	80.465
23	Ken O'Brien	10	3602	2110	58.6	25,094	6.97	128	3.6	98	2.7	80.436
24	Fran Tarkenton	18	6467	3686	57.0	47,003	7.27	342	5.3	266	4.1	80.354
25	Dan Fouts	15	5604	3297	58.8	43,040	7.68	254	4.5	242	4.3	80.2

Note: The NFL does not recognize records from the All-American Football Conference (1946-49). If it did, **Otto Graham** would rank 5th (after Marino) with the following stats: 10 Yrs; 2,626 Att; 1,464 Comp; 55.8 Comp Pct; 23,584 Yards; 8.98 Avg Gain; 174 TD; 6.6 TD Pct; 135 Int; 5.1 Int Pct; and 86.6 Rating Pts.

Touchdown Passes

		No			No			No
1	**Dan Marino**	408	16	John Brodie	214	31	Bob Griese	192
2	Fran Tarkenton	342	17	**Brett Favre**	213	32	**Randall Cunningham**	190
3	**John Elway**	300	18	Terry Bradshaw	212	33	Sammy Baugh	187
4	Johnny Unitas	290		Y.A. Tittle	212	34	Craig Morton	183
	Warren Moon	290	20	Jim Hart	209	35	Steve Grogan	182
6	Joe Montana	273	21	**Vinny Testaverde**	204	36	Ron Jaworski	179
7	**Dave Krieg**	261	22	Jim Everett	203	37	Babe Parilli	178
8	Sonny Jurgensen	255	23	Roman Gabriel	201	38	Charlie Conerly	173
9	Dan Fouts	254	24	Phil Simms	199		Joe Namath	173
10	Boomer Esiason	247	25	Ken Anderson	197		Norm Van Brocklin	173
11	John Hadl	244	26	Joe Ferguson	196	41	Charley Johnson	170
12	Len Dawson	239		Bobby Layne	196	42	Daryle Lamonica	164
13	Jim Kelly	237		**Steve DeBerg**	196		Jim Plunkett	164
14	George Blanda	236		Norm Snead	196	44	Earl Morrall	161
15	**Steve Young**	229	30	Ken Stabler	194	45	Joe Theismann	160

Note: The NFL does not recognize records from the All-American Football Conference (1946-49). If it did, **Y.A. Tittle** would move up from 18th to 12th (after Hadl) with 242 TDs and **Otto Graham** would rank 38th (after Parilli) with 174 TDs.

Passes Intercepted

		No			No			No
1	George Blanda	277	10	**Warren Moon**	232	19	Steve Grogan	208
2	John Hadl	268	11	**John Elway**	226	20	**Steve DeBerg**	204
3	Fran Tarkenton	266	12	John Brodie	224	21	Sammy Baugh	203
4	Norm Snead	257	13	Ken Stabler	222	22	**Dave Krieg**	199
5	Johnny Unitas	253	14	Y.A. Tittle	221	23	Jim Plunkett	198
6	Jim Hart	247	15	Joe Namath	220	24	Tobin Rote	191
7	Bobby Layne	245		Babe Parilli	220	25	**Vinny Testaverde**	190
8	Dan Fouts	242	17	Terry Bradshaw	210			
9	**Dan Marino**	235	18	Joe Ferguson	209			

Passing Yards

		Yrs	Att	Comp	Pct	Yards
1	**Dan Marino**	16	7989	4763	59.6	58,913
2	**John Elway**	16	7250	4123	56.9	51,475
3	**Warren Moon**	15	6786	3972	58.5	49,097
4	Fran Tarkenton	18	6467	3686	57.0	47,003
5	Dan Fouts	15	5604	3297	58.8	43,040
6	Joe Montana	15	5391	3409	63.2	40,551
7	Johnny Unitas	18	5186	2830	54.6	40,239
8	**Dave Krieg**	19	5311	3105	58.5	38,147
9	Boomer Esiason	14	5205	2969	57.0	37,920
10	Jim Kelly	11	4779	2874	60.1	35,467
11	Jim Everett	12	4923	2841	57.7	34,837
12	Jim Hart	19	5076	2593	51.1	34,665
13	**Steve DeBerg**	17	5024	2874	57.2	34,241
14	John Hadl	16	4687	2363	50.4	33,503
15	Phil Simms	14	4647	2576	55.4	33,462
16	Ken Anderson	16	4475	2654	59.3	32,838
17	**Steve Young**	14	4065	2622	64.5	32,678
18	**Vinny Testaverde**	12	4598	2559	55.7	32,479
19	Sonny Jurgensen	18	4262	2433	57.1	32,224
20	John Brodie	17	4491	2469	55.0	31,548
21	Norm Snead	15	4353	2276	52.3	30,797
22	Joe Ferguson	18	4519	2369	52.4	29,817
23	Roman Gabriel	16	4498	2366	52.6	29,444
24	Len Dawson	19	3741	2136	57.1	28,711
25	**Troy Aikman**	10	4011	2479	61.8	28,346

Note: The NFL does not recognize records from the All-American Football Conference (1946-49). If it did, **Y.A. Tittle** would rank 16th (after Simms) with the following stats: 17 Yrs; 4,395 Att; 2,427 Comp; 55.2 Pct; and 33,070 Yards.

Receptions

		Yrs	No	Yards	Avg	TD
1	**Jerry Rice**	14	1139	17,612	15.5	164
2	Art Monk	16	940	12,721	13.5	68
3	**Andre Reed**	14	889	12,559	14.1	85
4	**Cris Carter**	12	834	10,447	12.5	101
5	Steve Largent	14	819	13,089	16.0	100
6	**Henry Ellard**	16	814	13,777	16.9	65
7	**Irving Fryar**	15	784	11,983	15.3	77
8	James Lofton	16	764	14,004	18.3	75
9	Charlie Joiner	18	750	12,146	16.2	65
10	**Michael Irvin**	11	740	11,737	15.9	62
11	Gary Clark	11	699	10,856	15.5	65
12	**Andre Rison**	10	681	9,381	13.8	78
13	**Tim Brown**	11	680	9,600	14.1	69
14	Ozzie Newsome	13	662	7,980	12.1	47
15	Charley Taylor	13	649	9,110	14.0	79
16	Drew Hill	15	634	9,831	15.5	60
17	Don Maynard	15	633	11,834	18.7	88
18	Raymond Berry	13	631	9,275	14.7	68
19	**Keith Byars**	13	610	5,661	9.3	31
	Herman Moore	8	610	8,467	13.9	57
21	Sterling Sharpe	7	595	8,134	13.7	65
	Anthony Miller	10	595	9,148	15.4	63
23	**Rob Moore**	9	591	8,747	14.8	44
24	Harold Carmichael	14	590	8,985	15.2	79
25	Fred Biletnikoff	14	589	8,974	15.2	76

Rushing

		Yrs	Car	Yards	Avg	TD
1	Walter Payton	13	3838	16,726	4.4	110
2	**Barry Sanders**	10	3062	15,269	5.0	99
3	Eric Dickerson	11	2996	13,259	4.4	90
4	Tony Dorsett	12	2936	12,739	4.3	77
5	**Emmitt Smith**	9	2914	12,566	4.3	125
6	Jim Brown	9	2359	12,312	5.2	106
7	Marcus Allen	16	3022	12,243	4.1	123
8	Franco Harris	13	2949	12,120	4.1	91
9	**Thurman Thomas**	11	2813	11,786	4.2	65
10	John Riggins	14	2916	11,352	3.9	104
11	O.J. Simpson	11	2404	11,236	4.7	61
12	Ottis Anderson	14	2562	10,273	4.0	81
13	Earl Campbell	8	2187	9,407	4.3	74
14	Jim Taylor	10	1941	8,597	4.4	83
15	Joe Perry	14	1737	8,378	4.8	53
16	Ernest Byner	14	2095	8,261	3.9	56
17	Herschel Walker	12	1954	8,225	4.2	61
18	Roger Craig	11	1991	8,189	4.1	56
19	Gerald Riggs	11	1989	8,188	4.1	69
20	Larry Csonka	11	1891	8,081	4.3	64
21	Freeman McNeil	12	1798	8,074	4.5	38
22	James Brooks	13	1685	7,962	4.7	49
23	**Ricky Watters**	7	1947	7,873	4.0	65
24	Mike Pruitt	11	1844	7,378	4.0	51
25	**Jerome Bettis**	6	1807	7,372	4.1	34

Note: The NFL does not recognize records from the All-American Football Conference (1946-49). If it did, **Joe Perry** would move up from 15th to 13th (after Anderson) with the following stats: 16 Yrs; 1,929 Att; 9,723 Yards; 5.0 Avg; and 71 TD.

All-Purpose Yards

		Rush	Rec	Ret	Total
1	Walter Payton	16,726	4,538	539	21,803
2	**Barry Sanders**	15,269	2,921	118	18,308
3	**Jerry Rice**	614	17,612	6	18,232
4	Herschel Walker	8,225	4,859	5,084	18,168
5	Marcus Allen	12,243	5,411	-6	17,648
6	Tony Dorsett	12,739	3,554	33	16,326
7	**Eric Metcalf**	2,365	5,420	8,495	16,280
8	**Thurman Thomas**	11,786	4,304	0	16,090
9	**Henry Ellard**	50	13,777	1,891	15,718
10	Jim Brown	12,312	2,499	648	15,459
11	Eric Dickerson	13,259	2,137	15	15,411
12	**Emmitt Smith**	12,566	2,609	0	15,175
13	**Brian Mitchell**	1,531	1,782	11,837	15,150
14	James Brooks	7,962	3,621	3,327	14,910
15	**Irving Fryar**	226	11,983	2,567	14,776
16	Franco Harris	12,120	2,287	215	14,622
17	O.J. Simpson	11,236	2,142	990	14,368
18	James Lofton	246	14,004	27	14,277
19	Bobby Mitchell	2,735	7,954	3,389	14,078
20	**Tim Brown**	116	9,600	4,344	14,060
21	**Dave Meggett**	1,684	3,038	9,274	13,996
22	Earnest Byner	8,261	4,605	631	13,497
23	John Riggins	11,352	2,090	-7	13,435
24	Steve Largent	83	13,089	224	13,396
25	Ottis Anderson	10,273	3,062	29	13,364

Years played: Allen (16), Anderson (14), Brooks (13), J. Brown (9), T. Brown (11), Byner (14), Dickerson (11), Dorsett (12), Ellard (16), Fryar (15), Harris (13), Largent (14), Lofton (16), Meggett (10), Metcalf (10), Bri. Mitchell (9), Bo. Mitchell (11), Payton (13), Rice (14), Riggins (14), Sanders (10), Simpson (11), Smith (9), Thomas (11) and Walker (12).

All-Time NFL Leaders (Cont.)
Scoring

Points

		Yrs	TD	FG	PAT	Total
1	George Blanda	26	9	335	943	2002
2	**Gary Anderson**	17	0	420	585	1845
3	**Morten Andersen**	17	0	401	558	1761
4	Nick Lowery	18	0	383	562	1711
5	Jan Stenerud	19	0	373	580	1699
6	**Norm Johnson**	17	0	348	613	1657
7	Eddie Murray	17	0	337	521	1532
8	Pat Leahy	18	0	304	558	1470
9	Jim Turner	16	1	304	521	1439
10	Matt Bahr	17	0	300	522	1422
11	Mark Moseley	16	0	300	482	1382
12	Jim Bakken	17	0	282	534	1380
13	Fred Cox	15	0	282	519	1365
14	**Al Del Greco**	17	0	299	463	1360
15	Lou Groza	17	1	234	641	1349
16	Jim Breech	14	0	243	517	1246
17	Chris Bahr	14	0	241	490	1213
18	Kevin Butler	13	0	265	413	1208
19	Gino Cappelletti	11	42	176	350	1130†
20	Ray Wersching	15	0	222	456	1122
21	**Pete Stoyanovich**	10	0	246	349	1087
22	Don Cockroft	13	0	216	432	1080
23	Garo Yepremian	14	0	210	444	1074
24	**Jerry Rice**	14	175	0	0	1058†
25	Bruce Gossett	11	0	219	374	1031

Touchdowns

		Yrs	Rush	Rec	Ret	Total
1	**Jerry Rice**	14	10	164	1	175
2	Marcus Allen	16	123	21	1	145
3	**Emmitt Smith**	9	125	9	0	134
4	Jim Brown	9	106	20	0	126
5	Walter Payton	13	110	15	0	125
6	John Riggins	14	104	12	0	116
7	Lenny Moore	12	63	48	2	113
8	**Barry Sanders**	10	99	10	0	109
9	Don Hutson	11	3	99	3	105
10	**Cris Carter**	12	0	101	1	102
11	Steve Largent	14	1	100	0	101
12	Franco Harris	13	91	9	0	100
13	Eric Dickerson	11	90	6	0	96
14	Jim Taylor	10	83	10	0	93
15	Tony Dorsett	12	77	13	1	91
	Bobby Mitchell	11	18	65	8	91
17	Leroy Kelly	10	74	13	3	90
	Charley Taylor	13	11	79	0	90
19	Don Maynard	15	0	88	0	88
20	Lance Alworth	11	2	85	0	87
21	Ottis Anderson	14	81	5	0	86
	Paul Warfield	13	1	85	0	86
	Andre Reed	14	1	85	0	86
	Thurman Thomas	11	65	21	0	86
25	Mark Clayton	11	0	84	1	85
	Tommy McDonald	12	0	84	1	85

† Cappelletti's total and Rice's total both include four 2-point conversions.

Note: The NFL does not recognize records from the All-American Football Conference (1946-49). If it did, **Lou Groza** would move up from 15th to 7th (after N. Johnson) with the following stats: 21 Yrs; 1 TD; 264 FG, 810 PAT; 1,608 Pts.

Interceptions

		Yrs	No	Yards	TD
1	Paul Krause	16	81	1185	3
2	Emlen Tunnell	14	79	1282	4
3	Dick (Night Train) Lane	14	68	1207	5
4	Ken Riley	15	65	596	5
5	Ronnie Lott	14	63	730	5

Sacks

		Yrs	No
1	**Reggie White**	14	192½
2	**Bruce Smith**	14	164
3	**Kevin Greene**	14	148
4	**Chris Doleman**	14	142½
5	Richard Dent	13	137½

Note: The NFL did not begin officially compiling sacks until 1982. Deacon Jones, who played with the Rams, Chargers and Redskins from 1961-74, is often credited with 173½ sacks. Jack Youngblood (150½) and Alan Page (148) would also make an unofficial top five. Also, Lawrence Taylor has 142 career sacks if you count his rookie year of 1981, the year before sacks became an official stat.

Safeties

		Yrs	No
1	Ted Hendricks	15	4
	Doug English	10	4

Fifteen players tied with three.

Kickoff Returns
Minimum 75 returns.

		Yrs	No	Yards	Avg	TD
1	Gale Sayers	7	91	2781	30.6	6
2	Lynn Chandnois	7	92	2720	29.6	3
3	Abe Woodson	9	193	5538	28.7	5
4	Buddy Young	6	90	2514	27.9	2
5	Travis Williams	5	102	2801	27.5	6

Punting
Minimum 300 punts.

		Yrs	No	Yards	Avg
1	Sammy Baugh	16	338	15,245	45.1
2	**Darren Bennett**	4	343	15,334	44.7
3	Tommy Davis	11	511	22,833	44.7
4	Yale Lary	11	503	22,279	44.3
5	**Matt Turk**	4	326	14,417	44.2

Punt Returns
Minimum 75 returns.

		Yrs	No	Yards	Avg	TD
1	**Darrien Gordon**	5	177	2329	13.2	6
2	George McAfee	8	112	1431	12.8	2
3	Jack Christiansen	8	85	1084	12.8	8
4	Claude Gibson	5	110	1381	12.6	3
5	**Jermaine Lewis**	3	96	1181	12.3	4

Long-Playing Records

Seasons

		No
1	George Blanda, QB-K	26
2	Earl Morrall, QB	21
3	Jim Marshall, DE	20
	Jackie Slater, OL	20

Games

		No
1	George Blanda, QB-K	340
2	Jim Marshall, DE	282
3	Clay Matthews, LB	278

Consecutive Games

		No
1	Jim Marshall, DE	282
2	Mick Tingelhoff, C	240
3	Jim Bakken, K	234

SINGLE SEASON
Passing

Yards Gained	Year	Att	Cmp	Pct	Yds	Efficiency	Year	Att/Cmp	TD	Rtg
Dan Marino, Mia	1984	564	362	64.2	5084	Steve Young, SF	1994	461/324	35	112.8
Dan Fouts, SD	1981	609	360	59.1	4802	Joe Montana, SF	1989	386/271	26	112.4
Dan Marino, Mia	1986	623	378	60.7	4746	Milt Plum, Cle	1960	250/151	21	110.4
Dan Fouts, SD	1980	589	348	59.1	4715	Sammy Baugh, Wash	1945	182/128	11	109.9
Warren Moon, Hou	1991	655	404	61.7	4690	Dan Marino, Mia	1984	564/362	48	108.9
Warren Moon, Hou	1990	584	362	62.0	4689	Sid Luckman, Bears	1943	202/110	28	107.5
Neil Lomax, St.L	1984	560	345	61.6	4614	Steve Young, SF	1992	402/268	25	107.0
Drew Bledsoe, NE	1994	691	400	57.9	4555	Randall Cunningham, Min	1998	425/259	34	106.0
Lynn Dickey, GB	1983	484	286	59.7	4458	Bart Starr, GB	1966	251/156	14	105.0
Brett Favre, GB	1995	570	359	63.0	4413	Roger Staubach, Dal	1971	211/126	15	104.8

Receptions

Catches	Year	No	Yds
Herman Moore, Det	1995	123	1686
Jerry Rice, SF	1995	122	1848
Cris Carter, Min	1995	122	1371
Cris Carter, Min	1994	122	1256
Isaac Bruce, St. L	1995	119	1781
Jerry Rice, SF	1994	112	1499
Sterling Sharpe, GB	1993	112	1274
Michael Irvin, Dal	1995	111	1603
Terance Mathis, Atl	1994	111	1342
Brett Perriman, Det	1995	108	1488
Sterling Sharpe, GB	1992	108	1461
Jerry Rice, SF	1996	108	1254

Rushing

Yards Gained	Year	Car	Yds	Avg
Eric Dickerson, LA Rams	1984	379	2105	5.6
Barry Sanders, Det	1997	335	2053	6.1
Terrell Davis, Den	1998	392	2008	5.1
O.J. Simpson, Buf	1973	332	2003	6.0
Earl Campbell, Hou	1980	373	1934	5.2
Barry Sanders, Det	1994	331	1883	5.7
Jim Brown, Cle	1963	291	1863	6.4
Walter Payton, Chi	1977	339	1852	5.5
Jamal Anderson, Atl	1998	410	1846	4.5
Eric Dickerson, LA Rams	1986	404	1821	4.5
O.J. Simpson, Buf	1975	329	1817	5.5
Eric Dickerson, LA Rams	1983	390	1808	4.6

Scoring
Points

	Year	TD	PAT	FG	Pts
Paul Hornung, GB	1960	15	41	15	176
Gary Anderson, Min	1998	0	59	35	164
Mark Moseley, Wash	1983	0	62	33	161
Gino Cappelletti, Bos	1964	7	38	25	155
Emmitt Smith, Dal	1995	25	0	0	150
Chip Lohmiller, Wash	1991	0	56	31	149
Gino Cappelletti, Bos	1961	8	48	17	147
Paul Hornung, GB	1961	10	41	15	146
Jim Turner, Jets	1968	0	43	34	145
John Kasay, Car.	1996	0	34	37	145
John Riggins, Wash	1983	24	0	0	144
Kevin Butler, Chi	1985	0	51	31	144
Norm Johnson, Pit	1995	0	39	34	141
Tony Franklin, NE	1986	0	44	32	140
Steve Christie, Buf.	1998	0	41	33	140

Touchdowns

	Year	Rush	Rec	Ret	Total
Emmitt Smith, Dal	1995	25	0	0	25
John Riggins, Wash	1983	24	0	0	24
Terrell Davis, Den	1998	21	2	0	23
O.J. Simpson, Buf	1975	16	7	0	23
Jerry Rice, SF	1987	1	22	0	23
Gale Sayers, Chi	1966	14	6	2	22
Chuck Foreman, Min	1975	13	9	0	22
Emmitt Smith, Dal	1994	21	1	0	22
Jim Brown, Cle	1965	17	4	0	21
Joe Morris, NY Giants	1985	21	0	0	21
Terry Allen, Wash	1996	21	0	0	21
Lenny Moore, Bal	1964	16	3	1	20
Leroy Kelly, Cle	1968	16	4	0	20
Eric Dickerson, LA Rams	1983	18	2	0	20

Note: The NFL regular season schedule grew from 12 games (1947-60) to 14 (1961-77) to 16 (1978-present). The AFL regular season schedule was always 14 games (1960-69).

Touchdowns Passing

	Year	No
Dan Marino, Miami	1984	48
Dan Marino, Miami	1986	44
Brett Favre, Green Bay	1996	39
Brett Favre, Green Bay	1995	38
George Blanda, Houston	1961	36
Y.A. Tittle, NY Giants	1963	36
Steve Young, San Francisco	1998	36
Brett Favre, Green Bay	1997	35
Steve Young, San Francisco	1994	35
Randall Cunningham, Minnesota	1998	34
Y.A. Tittle, NY Giants	1962	33
Dan Fouts, San Diego	1981	33
Warren Moon, Houston	1990	33
Jim Kelly, Buffalo	1991	33
Brett Favre, Green Bay	1994	33
Warren Moon, Minnesota	1995	33
Vinny Testaverde, Baltimore	1996	33

Touchdowns Receiving

	Year	No
Jerry Rice, San Francisco	1987	22
Mark Clayton, Miami	1984	18
Sterling Sharpe, Green Bay	1994	18
Don Hutson, Green Bay	1942	17
Elroy (Crazylegs) Hirsch, LA Rams	1951	17
Bill Groman, Houston	1961	17
Jerry Rice, San Francisco	1989	17
Cris Carter, Minnesota	1995	17
Carl Pickens, Cincinnati	1995	17
Randy Moss, Minnesota	1998	17
Art Powell, Oakland	1963	16
Cloyce Box, Detroit	1952	15
Sonny Randle, St. Louis	1960	15
Jerry Rice, San Francisco	1986	15
Jerry Rice, San Francisco	1993	15
Andre Rison, Atlanta	1993	15
Jerry Rice, San Francisco	1995	15

All-Time NFL Leaders (Cont.)

Touchdowns Rushing

	Year	No
Emmitt Smith, Dallas	1995	25
John Riggins, Washington	1983	24
Joe Morris, NY Giants	1985	21
Emmitt Smith, Dallas	1994	21
Terry Allen, Washington	1996	21
Terrell Davis, Denver	1998	21
Jim Taylor, Green Bay	1962	19
Earl Campbell, Houston	1979	19
Chuck Muncie, San Diego	1981	19
Eric Dickerson, LA Rams	1983	18
George Rogers, Washington	1986	18
Emmitt Smith, Dallas	1992	18
Jim Brown, Cleveland	1958	17
Jim Brown, Cleveland	1965	17
Six tied with 16 each.		

Field Goals

	Year	Att	No
John Kasay, Carolina	1996	45	37
Cary Blanchard, Indianapolis	1996	40	36
Al Del Greco, Tennessee	1998	39	36
Ali Haji-Sheikh, NY Giants	1983	42	35
Jeff Jaeger, LA Raiders	1993	44	35
Gary Anderson, Minnesota	1998	35	35
Richie Cunningham, Dallas	1997	37	34
Nick Lowery, Kansas City	1990	37	34
Jim Turner, NY Jets	1968	46	34
Jason Hanson, Detroit	1993	43	34
John Carney, San Diego	1994	38	34
Fuad Reveiz, Minnesota	1994	39	34
Norm Johnson, Pittsburgh	1995	41	34
Gary Anderson, Pittsburgh	1985	42	33
Mark Moseley, Washington	1983	47	33
Chester Marcol, Green Bay	1972	48	33
Steve Christie, Buffalo	1998	41	33

Interceptions

	Year	No
Dick (Night Train) Lane, Detroit	1952	14
Dan Sandifer, Washington	1948	13
Spec Sanders, NY Yanks	1950	13
Lester Hayes, Oakland	1980	13

Punting

Qualifiers	Year	Avg
Sammy Baugh, Washington	1940	51.4
Yale Lary, Detroit	1963	48.9
Sammy Baugh, Washington	1941	48.7

Kickoff Returns

	Year	Avg
Travis Williams, Green Bay	1967	41.1
Gale Sayers, Chicago Bears	1967	37.7
Ollie Matson, Chicago Cards	1958	35.5

Punt Returns

	Year	Avg
Herb Rich, Baltimore	1950	23.0
Jack Christiansen, Detroit	1952	21.5
Dick Christy, NY Titans	1961	21.3
Bob Hayes, Dallas	1968	20.8

Sacks

	Year	No		Year	No
Mark Gastineau, NY Jets	1984	22	Chris Doleman, Minnesota	1989	21
Reggie White, Philadelphia	1987	21	Lawrence Taylor, NY Giants	1986	20½

Note: The NFL did not begin officially compiling sacks until 1982. Cincinnati's Coy Bacon is widely, although not officially, credited with 26 sacks during the 1976 season.

SINGLE GAME

Passing

Yards Gained	Date	Yds
Norm Van Brocklin, LA vs NY Yanks	9/28/51	554
Warren Moon, Hou vs KC	12/16/90	527
Boomer Esiason, Ariz vs Wash.	11/10/96	522
Dan Marino, Mia vs NYJ	10/23/88	521
Phil Simms, NYG vs Cin	10/13/85	513

Completions	Date	No
Drew Bledsoe, NE vs Min	11/13/94	45
Richard Todd, NYJ vs SF	9/21/80	42
Vinny Testaverde, NYJ vs Sea.	12/6/98	42
Warren Moon, Hou vs Dal	11/10/91	41
Ken Anderson, Cin vs SD	12/20/82	40
Phil Simms, NYG vs Cin	10/13/85	40

Receiving

Catches	Date	No
Tom Fears, LA vs GB	12/3/50	18
Clark Gaines, NYJ vs SF	9/21/80	17
Sonny Randle, St.L vs NYG	11/4/62	16
Keenan McCardell, Jax vs St.L.	10/20/96	16
Jerry Rice, SF vs LA Rams	11/20/94	16

Yards Gained	Date	Yds
Flipper Anderson, LA Rams vs NO	11/26/89	336
Stephone Paige, KC vs SD	12/22/85	309
Jim Benton, Cle vs Det	11/22/45	303
Cloyce Box, Det vs Bal	12/3/50	302
Jerry Rice, SF vs Det	9/25/95	289
John Taylor, SF vs LA Rams	12/11/89	286

Rushing

Yards Gained	Date	Yds
Walter Payton, Chi vs Min	11/20/77	275
O.J. Simpson, Buf vs Det	11/25/76	273
O.J. Simpson, Buf vs NE	9/16/73	250
Willie Ellison, LA Rams vs NO	12/5/71	247
Corey Dillon, Cin vs Ten.	12/4/97	246
Cookie Gilchrist, Buf vs NYJ	12/8/63	243

All-Purpose Yards

	Date	Yds
Glyn Milburn, Den vs Sea	12/10/95	404
Billy Cannon, Hou vs NY Titans	12/10/61	373
Tyrone Hughes, NO vs LA Rams	10/23/94	347
Lionel James, SD vs Raiders	11/10/85	345
Timmy Brown, Phi vs St.L.	12/16/62	341
Gale Sayers, Chi vs Min	12/18/66	339
Gale Sayers, Chi vs SF	12/12/65	336
Flipper Anderson, LA Rams vs NO	11/26/89	336

Scoring

Points

	Date	Pts
Ernie Nevers, Chi. Cards vs Chi. Bears	11/28/29	40
Dub Jones, Cle vs Chi. Bears	11/25/51	36
Gale Sayers, Chi vs SF	12/12/65	36
Paul Hornung, GB vs Bal	10/8/61	33
Bob Shaw, Chi. Cards vs Bal	10/2/50	30
Jim Brown, Cle vs Bal	11/1/59	30
Abner Haynes, Dal. Texans vs Oak	11/26/61	30
Billy Cannon, Hou vs NY Titans	12/10/61	30
Cookie Gilchrist, Buf vs NY Jets	12/8/63	30
Kellen Winslow, SD vs Oak	11/22/81	30
Jerry Rice, SF vs Atl	10/14/90	30
James Stewart, Jax vs Phi	10/12/97	30

Note: Nevers celebrated Thanksgiving, 1929, by scoring all of the Chicago Cardinals' points on six rushing TDs and four PATs. The Cards beat Red Grange and the Chicago Bears, 40-6.

Touchdowns Passing

	Date	No
Sid Luckman, Chi. Bears vs NYG	11/14/43	7
Adrian Burk, Phi vs Wash	10/17/54	7
George Blanda, Hou vs NY Titans	11/19/61	7
Y.A. Tittle, NYG vs Wash	10/28/62	7
Joe Kapp, Min vs Bal	9/28/69	7

Touchdowns Receiving

	Date	No
Bob Shaw, Chi. Cards vs Bal	10/2/50	5
Kellen Winslow, SD vs Oak	11/22/81	5
Jerry Rice, SF vs Atl	10/14/90	5

Touchdowns Rushing

	Date	No
Ernie Nevers, Chi. Cards vs Chi. Bears	11/28/29	6
Jim Brown, Cle vs Bal	11/1/59	5
Cookie Gilchrist, Buf vs NY Jets	12/8/63	5
James Stewart, Jax vs Phi	10/12/97	5

Field Goals

	Date	No
Jim Bakken, St.L vs Pit	9/24/67	7
Chris Boniol, Dal vs GB	11/18/96	7
Rich Karlis, Min vs LA Rams	11/5/89	7

14 players tied with 6 FGs.
Note: Bakken was 7-for-9, Boniol and Karlis 7-for-7.

Extra Point Kicks

	Date	No
Pat Harder, Cards vs NYG	10/17/48	9
Bob Waterfield, LA Rams vs Bal	10/22/50	9
Charlie Gogolak, Wash vs NYG	11/27/66	9

Interceptions

	No
By 17 players	4

Sacks

	Date	No
Derrick Thomas, KC vs Sea	11/11/90	7
Fred Dean, SF vs NO	11/13/83	6
Derrick Thomas, KC vs Oak	9/6/98	6
William Gay, Det vs TB	9/4/83	5½

Longest Plays

Passing (all for TDs)

	Date	Yds
Frank Filchock to Andy Farkas, Wash vs Pit	10/15/39	99
George Izo to Bobby Mitchell, Wash vs Cle	9/15/63	99
Karl Sweetan to Pat Studstill, Det vs Bal	10/16/66	99
Sonny Jurgensen to Gerry Allen, Wash vs Chi	9/15/68	99
Jim Plunkett to Cliff Branch, LA Raiders vs Wash	10/2/83	99
Ron Jaworski to Mike Quick, Phi vs Atl	11/10/85	99
Stan Humphries to Tony Martin, SD vs Sea	9/18/94	99
Brett Favre to Robert Brooks, GB vs Chi	9/11/95	99

Runs from Scrimmage (all for TDs)

	Date	Yds
Tony Dorsett, Dal vs Min	1/3/83	99
Andy Uram, GB vs Chi. Cards	10/8/39	97
Bob Gage, Pit vs Bears	12/4/49	97
Jim Spavital, Balt. Colts vs GB	11/5/50	96
Bob Hoernschemeyer, Det vs NY Yanks	11/23/50	96
Garrison Hearst, SF vs NYJ	9/6/98	96

Punts

	Date	Yds
Steve O'Neal, NYJ vs Den	9/21/69	98
Joe Lintzenich, Chi. Bears vs NYG	11/15/31	94
Shawn McCarthy, NE vs Buf	11/3/91	93

Field Goals

	Date	Yds
Tom Dempsey, NO vs Det	11/8/70	63
Jason Elam, Den vs Jax	10/25/98	63
Steve Cox, Cle vs Cin	10/21/84	60
Morten Andersen, NO vs Chi	10/27/91	60
Tony Franklin, Phi vs Dal	11/12/79	59
Pete Stoyanovich, Mia vs NYJ	11/12/89	59
Steve Christie, Buf vs Mia	9/26/93	59
Morten Andersen, Atl vs SF	12/24/95	59

Punt Returns (all for TDs)

	Date	Yds
Robert Bailey, Rams vs NO	10/23/94	103
Gil LeFebvre, Cin vs Bklyn	12/3/33	98
Charlie West, Min vs Wash	11/3/68	98
Dennis Morgan, Dal vs St.L	10/13/74	98
Terance Mathis, NYJ vs Dal	11/4/90	98
Greg Pruitt, LA Raiders vs Wash	10/2/83	97

Kickoff Returns (all for TDs)

	Date	Yds
Al Carmichael, GB vs Chi. Bears	10/7/56	106
Noland Smith, KC vs Den	12/17/67	106
Roy Green, St.L vs Dal	10/21/79	106

Interception Returns (all for TDs)

	Date	Yds
James Willis (14 yds) lateral to Troy Vincent (90 yds), Phi vs Dal	11/3/96	104
Vencie Glenn, SD vs Den	11/29/87	103
Louis Oliver, Mia vs Buf	10/4/92	103

Six players tied with 102-yd returns.

Chicago College All-Star Game

On Aug. 31, 1934, a year after sponsoring Major League Baseball's first All-Star Game, *Chicago Tribune* sports editor Arch Ward presented the first Chicago College All-Star Game at Soldier Field. A crowd of 79,432 turned out to see an all-star team of graduated college seniors battle the 1933 NFL champion Chicago Bears to a scoreless tie. The preseason game was played at Soldier Field and pitted the College All-Stars against the defending NFL champions (1933–1966) or Super Bowl champions (1967–75) every year except 1935 until it was cancelled in 1977. The NFL champs won the series, 31-9-1.

Year
1934 Chi. Bears 0, All-Stars 0
1935 Chi. Bears 5, All-Stars 0
1936 Detroit 7, All-Stars 0
1937 All-Stars 6, Green Bay 0
1938 All-Stars 28, Washington 16
1939 NY Giants 9, All-Stars 0

1940 Green Bay 45, All-Stars 28
1941 Chi. Bears 37, All-Stars 13
1942 Chi. Bears 21, All-Stars 0
1943 All-Stars 27, Washington 7
1944 Chi. Bears 24, All-Stars 21
1945 Green Bay 19, All-Stars 7
1946 All-Stars 16, LA Rams 0
1947 All-Stars 16, Chi. Bears 0
1948 Chi. Cards 28, All-Stars 0

Year
1949 Philadelphia 38, All-Stars 0

1950 All-Stars 17, Philadelphia 7
1951 Cleveland 33, All-Stars 0
1952 LA Rams 10, All-Stars 7
1953 Detroit 24, All-Stars 10
1954 Detroit 31, All-Stars 6
1955 All-Stars 30, Cleveland 27
1956 Cleveland 26, All-Stars 0
1957 NY Giants 22, All-Stars 12
1958 All-Stars 35, Detroit 19
1959 Baltimore 29, All-Stars 0

1960 Baltimore 32, All-Stars 7
1961 Philadelphia 28, All-Stars 14
1962 Green Bay 42, All-Stars 20
1963 All-Stars 20, Green Bay 17

Year
1964 Chi. Bears 28, All-Stars 17
1965 Cleveland 24, All-Stars 16
1966 Green Bay 38, All-Stars 0
1967 Green Bay 27, All-Stars 0
1968 Green Bay 34, All-Stars 17
1969 NY Jets 26, All-Stars 24

1970 Kansas City 24, All-Stars 3
1971 Baltimore 24, All-Stars 17
1972 Dallas 20, All-Stars 7
1973 Miami 14, All-Stars 3
1974 No Game (NFLPA Strike)
1975 Pittsburgh 21, All-Stars 14
1976 Pittsburgh 24, All-Stars 0*

*Downpour flooded field, game called with 1:22 left in 3rd quarter.

Number One Draft Choices

In an effort to blunt the dominance of the Chicago Bears and New York Giants in the 1930s and distribute talent more evenly throughout the league, the NFL established the college draft in 1936. The first player chosen in the first draft was Jay Berwanger, who was also college football's first Heisman Trophy winner. In all, 16 Heisman winners have also been the NFL's No. 1 draft choice. They are noted in **bold** type. The American Football League (formed in 1960) held its own draft for six years before agreeing to merge with the NFL and select players in a common draft starting in 1967.

Year	Team	Player
1936	Philadelphia	**Jay Berwanger**, HB, Chicago
1937	Philadelphia	Sam Francis, FB, Nebraska
1938	Cleveland Rams	Corbett Davis, FB, Indiana
1939	Chicago Cards	Ki Aldrich, C, TCU
1940	Chicago Cards	George Cafego, HB, Tennessee
1941	Chicago Bears	**Tom Harmon**, HB, Michigan
1942	Pittsburgh	Bill Dudley, HB, Virginia
1943	Detroit	**Frank Sinkwich**, HB, Georgia
1944	Boston Yanks	**Angelo Bertelli**, QB, N. Dame
1945	Chicago Cards	Charley Trippi, HB, Georgia
1946	Boston Yanks	Frank Dancewicz, QB, N. Dame
1947	Chicago Bears	Bob Fenimore, HB, Okla. A&M
1948	Washington	Harry Gilmer, QB, Alabama
1949	Philadelphia	Chuck Bednarik, C, Penn
1950	Detroit	**Leon Hart**, E, Notre Dame
1951	NY Giants	Kyle Rote, HB, SMU
1952	LA Rams	Bill Wade, QB, Vanderbilt
1953	San Francisco	Harry Babcock, E, Georgia
1954	Cleveland	Bobby Garrett, QB, Stanford
1955	Baltimore	George Shaw, QB, Oregon
1956	Pittsburgh	Gary Glick, DB, Colo. A&M
1957	Green Bay	**Paul Hornung**, QB, N. Dame
1958	Chicago Cards	King Hill, QB, Rice
1959	Green Bay	Randy Duncan, QB, Iowa
1960	NFL–LA Rams	**Billy Cannon**, HB, LSU
	AFL–No choice	
1961	NFL–Minnesota	Tommy Mason, HB, Tulane
	AFL–Buffalo	Ken Rice, G, Auburn
1962	NFL–Washington	**Ernie Davis**, HB, Syracuse
	AFL–Oakland	Roman Gabriel, QB, N.C. State
1963	NFL–LA Rams	**Terry Baker**, QB, Oregon St.
	AFL–Kan.City	Buck Buchanan, DT, Grambling
1964	NFL–San Fran	Dave Parks, E, Texas Tech
	AFL–Boston	Jack Concannon, QB, Boston Col.
1965	NFL–NY Giants	Tucker Frederickson, FB, Auburn
	AFL–Houston	Lawrence Elkins, E, Baylor

Year	Team	Player
1966	NFL–Atlanta	Tommy Nobis, LB, Texas
	AFL–Miami	Jim Grabowski, FB, Illinois
1967	Baltimore	Bubba Smith, DT, Michigan St.
1968	Minnesota	Ron Yary, T, USC
1969	Buffalo	**O.J. Simpson**, RB, USC
1970	Pittsburgh	Terry Bradshaw, QB, La.Tech
1971	New England	**Jim Plunkett**, QB, Stanford
1972	Buffalo	Walt Patulski, DE, Notre Dame
1973	Houston	John Matuszak, DE, Tampa
1974	Dallas	Ed (Too Tall) Jones, DE, Tenn. St.
1975	Atlanta	Steve Bartkowski, QB, Calif.
1976	Tampa Bay	Lee Roy Selmon, DE, Oklahoma
1977	Tampa Bay	Ricky Bell, RB, USC
1978	Houston	**Earl Campbell**, RB, Texas
1979	Buffalo	Tom Cousineau, LB, Ohio St.
1980	Detroit	**Billy Sims**, RB, Oklahoma
1981	New Orleans	**George Rogers**, RB, S. Carolina
1982	New England	Kenneth Sims, DT, Texas
1983	Baltimore	John Elway, QB, Stanford
1984	New England	Irving Fryar, WR, Nebraska
1985	Buffalo	Bruce Smith, DE, Va. Tech
1986	Tampa Bay	**Bo Jackson**, RB, Auburn
1987	Tampa Bay	**V. Testaverde**, QB, Miami-FL
1988	Atlanta	Aundray Bruce, LB, Auburn
1989	Dallas	Troy Aikman, QB, UCLA
1990	Indianapolis	Jeff George, QB, Illinois
1991	Dallas	Russell Maryland, DT, Miami-FL
1992	Indianapolis	Steve Emtman, DT, Washington
1993	New England	Drew Bledsoe, QB, Washington St.
1994	Cincinnati	Dan Wilkinson, DT, Ohio St.
1995	Cincinnati	Ki-Jana Carter, RB, Penn St.
1996	NY Jets	Keyshawn Johnson, WR, USC
1997	St. Louis	Orlando Pace, OT, Ohio St.
1998	Indianapolis	Peyton Manning, QB, Tennessee
1999	Cleveland	Tim Couch, QB, Kentucky

AP/Wide World Photos
Don Shula

Atlanta Falcons
Dan Reeves

New Orleans Saints
Mike Ditka

AP/Wide World Photos
Vince Lombardi

All-Time Winningest NFL Coaches

NFL career victories through the 1998 season. Career, regular season and playoff records are noted along with NFL, AFL and Super Bowl titles won. Coaches active during 1998 season in **bold** type.

		Yrs	Career				Regular Season				Playoffs			
			W	L	T	Pct	W	L	T	Pct	W	L	Pct.	League Titles
1	Don Shula	33	**347**	173	6	.665	328	156	6	.676	19	17	.528	2 Super Bowls and 1 NFL
2	George Halas	40	**324**	151	31	.671	318	148	31	.671	6	3	.667	5 NFL
3	Tom Landry	29	**270**	178	6	.601	250	162	6	.605	20	16	.556	2 Super Bowls
4	Curly Lambeau	33	**229**	134	22	.623	226	132	22	.624	3	2	.600	6 NFL
5	Chuck Noll	23	**209**	156	1	.572	193	148	1	.566	16	8	.667	4 Super Bowls
6	Chuck Knox	22	**193**	158	1	.550	186	147	1	.558	7	11	.389	—None—
7	**Dan Reeves**	18	**172**	125	1	.579	162	117	1	.580	10	8	.556	—None—
8	Paul Brown	21	**170**	108	6	.609	166	100	6	.621	4	8	.333	3 NFL
9	Bud Grant	18	**168**	108	5	.607	158	96	5	.620	10	12	.455	1 NFL
10	Marv Levy	17	**154**	120	0	.562	143	112	0	.561	11	8	.579	—None—
11	Steve Owen	23	**153**	108	17	.581	151	100	17	.595	2	8	.200	2 NFL
12	**M. Schottenheimer**	15	**150**	96	1	.609	145	85	1	.630	5	11	.313	—None—
13	**Bill Parcells**	13	**141**	98	1	.590	130	92	1	.585	11	6	.647	2 Super Bowls
14	Joe Gibbs	12	**140**	65	0	.683	124	60	0	.674	16	5	.762	3 Super Bowls
15	Hank Stram	17	**136**	100	10	.573	131	97	10	.571	5	3	.625	1 Super Bowl and 3 AFL
16	Weeb Ewbank	20	**134**	130	7	.507	130	129	7	.502	4	1	.800	1 Super Bowl, 2 NFL, and 1 AFL
17	**Mike Ditka**	13	**124**	88	0	.585	118	82	0	.590	6	6	.500	1 Super Bowl
18	Sid Gillman	18	**123**	104	7	.541	122	99	7	.550	1	5	.167	1 AFL
19	George Allen	12	**118**	54	5	.681	116	47	5	.705	2	7	.222	—None—
20	Don Coryell	14	**114**	89	1	.561	111	83	1	.572	3	6	.333	—None—
21	John Madden	10	**112**	39	7	.731	103	32	7	.750	9	7	.563	1 Super Bowl
22	George Seifert	8	**108**	35	0	.755	98	30	0	.766	10	5	.667	2 Super Bowls
23	Buddy Parker	15	**107**	76	9	.581	104	75	9	.577	3	1	.750	2 NFL
24	Vince Lombardi	10	**105**	35	6	.740	96	34	6	.728	9	1	.900	2 Super Bowls and 5 NFL
	Tom Flores	12	**105**	90	0	.538	97	87	0	.527	8	3	.727	2 Super Bowls

Notes: The NFL does not recognize records from the All-American Football Conference (1946-49). If it did, **Paul Brown** (52-4-3 in four AAFC seasons) would move up from 8th to 5th on the all-time list with the following career stats— 25 Yrs; 222 Wins; 112 Losses; 9 Ties; .660 Pct; 9-8 playoff record; and 4 AAFC titles.

The NFL also considers the Playoff Bowl or "Runner-up Bowl" (officially: the Bert Bell Benefit Bowl) as a post-season exhibition game. The Playoff Bowl was contested every year from 1960-69 in Miami between Eastern and Western Conference second place teams. While the games did not count, six of the coaches above went to the Playoff Bowl at least once and came away with the following records— Allen (2-0), Brown (0-1), Grant (0-1), Landry (1-2), Lombardi (1-1) and Shula (2-0).

Where They Coached

Allen—LA Rams (1966-70), Washington (1971-77); **Brown**—Cleveland (1950-62), Cincinnati (1968-75); **Coryell**—St. Louis (1973-77), San Diego (1978-86); **Ditka**— Chicago (1982-92), New Orleans (1997—); **Ewbank**— Baltimore (1954-62), NY Jets (1963-73); **Flores**—Oakland-LA Raiders (1979-87), Seattle (1992-94); **Gibbs**—Washington (1981-92); **Gillman**—LA Rams (1955-59), LA-San Diego Chargers (1960-69), Houston (1973-74).

Grant—Minnesota (1967-83,1985); **Halas**—Chicago Bears (1920-29,33-42,46-55,58-67); **Knox**— LA Rams (1973-77, 1992-94); Buffalo (1978-82), Seattle (1983-91); **Lambeau**— Green Bay (1921-49), Chicago Cards (1950-51), Washington (1952-53); **Landry**—Dallas (1960-88); **Levy**— Kansas City (1978-82), Buffalo (1986-97); **Lombardi**— Green Bay (1959-67), Washington (1969); **Madden**—Oakland (1969-78).

Noll—Pittsburgh (1969-91); **Owen**—NY Giants (1931-53); **Parcells**— NY Giants (1983-90), New England (1993-97), NY Jets (1997—); **Parker**—Chicago Cards (1949), Detroit (1951-56), Pittsburgh (1957-64); **Reeves**— Denver (1981-92), NY Giants (1993-96), Atlanta (1997—); **Schottenheimer**—Cleveland (1984-88), Kansas City (1989-98); **Seifert**—San Francisco (1989-96), Carolina (1999—); **Shula**—Baltimore (1963-69), Miami (1970-95); **Stram**—Dallas-Kansas City (1960-74), New Orleans (1976-77).

Top Winning Percentages

Minimum of 85 NFL victories, including playoffs.

		Yrs	W	L	T	Pct
1	George Seifert	8	108	35	0	.755
2	Vince Lombardi	10	105	35	6	.740
3	John Madden	10	112	39	7	.731
4	Joe Gibbs	12	140	65	0	.683
5	George Allen	12	118	54	5	.681
6	George Halas	40	324	151	31	.671
7	Don Shula	33	347	173	6	.665
8	Curly Lambeau	33	229	134	22	.623
9	Bill Walsh	10	102	63	1	.617
10	**M. Schottenheimer**	15	150	96	1	.609
11	Paul Brown	21	170	108	6	.609
12	Bud Grant	18	168	108	5	.607
13	Tom Landry	29	270	178	6	.601
14	**Bill Parcells**	14	141	98	1	.590
15	**Mike Ditka**	13	124	88	0	.585
16	Steve Owen	23	153	108	17	.581
17	Buddy Parker	15	107	76	9	.581
18	**Dan Reeves**	18	172	125	1	.579
19	Hank Stram	17	136	100	10	.573
20	Chuck Noll	23	209	156	1	.572
21	Marv Levy	17	154	120	0	.562
22	Don Coryell	14	114	89	1	.561
23	Jimmy Conzelman	15	89	68	17	.560
24	Chuck Knox	22	193	158	1	.550
25	Sid Gillman	18	123	104	7	.541

Note: If AAFC records are included, **Paul Brown** moves from 11th to 8th with a percentage of .660 (25 yrs, 222-112-9) and Buck Shaw would be 10th at .619 (8 yrs, 91-55-5).

Active Coaches' Victories

Through 1998 season, including playoffs.

		Yrs	W	L	T	Pct
1	Dan Reeves, Atlanta	17	**172**	125	1	.579
2	Bill Parcells, NY Jets	14	**141**	98	1	.590
3	Mike Ditka, New Orleans	13	**124**	88	0	.585
4	George Seifert, Carolina	8	**108**	35	0	.755
5	Jim Mora, Indianapolis	12	**96**	91	0	.513
6	Mike Holmgren, Seattle	7	**84**	42	0	.667
7	Jimmy Johnson, Miami	8	**79**	59	0	.572
8	Bill Cowher, Pittsburgh	7	**76**	47	0	.618
9	Dennis Green, Minnesota	7	**73**	47	0	.608
10	Dick Vermeil, St. Louis	9	**66**	74	0	.471
11	Bobby Ross, Detroit	7	**64**	55	0	.538
12	Mike Shanahan, Denver	7	**62**	30	0	.674
13	Bruce Coslet, Cincinnati	7	**43**	63	0	.406
14	Tom Coughlin, Jacksonville	4	**38**	32	0	.543
15	Norv Turner, Washington	5	**32**	47	1	.406
	Jeff Fisher, Tennessee	5	**32**	38	0	.457
17	Ray Rhodes, Green Bay	4	**30**	36	1	.455
18	Wade Phillips, Buffalo	4	**27**	27	0	.500
	Steve Mariucci, San Fran	2	**27**	9	0	.750
20	Pete Carroll, New England	3	**26**	25	0	.510
21	Tony Dungy, Tampa Bay	3	**25**	25	0	.500
22	Vince Tobin, Arizona	3	**21**	29	0	.420
23	Jim Fassel, NY Giants	2	**18**	14	1	.545
24	Chan Gailey, Dallas	1	**10**	7	0	.588
25	Jon Gruden, Oakland	1	**8**	8	0	.500
26	Brian Billick, Baltimore	0	**0**	0	0	.000
	Gunther Cunningham, KC	0	**0**	0	0	.000
	Dick Jauron, Chicago	0	**0**	0	0	.000
	Chris Palmer, Cleveland	0	**0**	0	0	.000
	Andy Reid, Philadelphia	0	**0**	0	0	.000
	Mike Riley, San Diego	0	**0**	0	0	.000

Annual Awards
Most Valuable Player

The NFL awarded the Joe F. Carr Trophy (Carr was NFL president from 1921-39) to the league MVP from 1938 to 1946. There hadn't been an official, league-sanctioned MVP award until 1997 when the NFL/Miller Lite Player of the Year was introduced. However, four principal MVP awards have been given out throughout the years and are noted below: UPI (1953-69), AP (since 1957), the Maxwell Club of Philadelphia's Bert Bell Trophy (since 1959) and the Pro Football Writers Assn. (since 1976). UPI switched to AFC and NFC Player of the Year awards in 1970 and then discontinued its awards in 1997.

Multiple winners (more than one season): Jim Brown (4); Randall Cunningham, Brett Favre, Johnny Unitas and Y.A. Tittle (3); Earl Campbell, Otto Graham, Don Hutson, Joe Montana, Walter Payton, Barry Sanders, Ken Stabler, Joe Theismann and Steve Young (2).

Year	Awards
1938 Mel Hein, NY Giants, C	Carr
1939 Parker Hall, Cleveland Rams, HB	Carr
1940 Ace Parker, Brooklyn, HB	Carr
1941 Don Hutson, Green Bay, E	Carr
1942 Don Hutson, Green Bay, E	Carr
1943 Sid Luckman, Chicago Bears, QB	Carr
1944 Frank Sinkwich, Detroit, HB	Carr
1945 Bob Waterfield, Cleveland Rams, QB	Carr
1946 Bill Dudley, Pittsburgh, HB	Carr
1947-52 No award	
1953 Otto Graham, Cleveland Browns, QB	UPI
1954 Joe Perry, San Francisco, FB	UPI
1955 Otto Graham, Cleveland, QB	UPI
1956 Frank Gifford, NY Giants, HB	UPI
1957 Y.A. Tittle, San Francisco, QB	UPI
& Jim Brown, Cleveland, FB	AP
1958 Jim Brown, Cleveland, FB	UPI
& Gino Marchetti, Baltimore, DE	AP
1959 Johnny Unitas, Baltimore, QB	UPI, Bell
& Charley Conerly, NY Giants, QB	AP
1960 Norm Van Brocklin, Phi., QB	UPI, AP (tie), Bell
& Joe Schmidt, Detroit, LB	AP (tie)
1961 Paul Hornung, Green Bay, HB	UPI, AP, Bell
1962 Y.A. Tittle, NY Giants, QB	UPI
Jim Taylor, Green Bay, FB	AP
& Andy Robustelli, NY Giants, DE	Bell

Year	Awards
1963 Jim Brown, Cleveland, FB	UPI, Bell
& Y.A. Tittle, NY Giants, QB	AP
1964 Johnny Unitas, Baltimore, QB	UPI, AP, Bell
1965 Jim Brown, Cleveland, FB	UPI, AP
& Pete Retzlaff, Philadelphia, TE	Bell
1966 Bart Starr, Green Bay, QB	UPI, AP
& Don Meredith, Dallas, QB	Bell
1967 Johnny Unitas, Baltimore, QB	UPI, AP, Bell
1968 Earl Morrall, Baltimore, QB	UPI, AP
& Leroy Kelly, Cleveland, RB	Bell
1969 Roman Gabriel, LA Rams, QB	UPI, AP, Bell
1970 John Brodie, San Francisco, QB	AP
& George Blanda, Oakland, QB-PK	Bell
1971 Alan Page, Minnesota, DT	AP
& Roger Staubach, Dallas, QB	Bell
1972 Larry Brown, Washington, RB	AP, Bell
1973 O.J. Simpson, Buffalo, RB	AP, Bell
1974 Ken Stabler, Oakland, QB	AP
& Merlin Olsen, LA Rams, DT	Bell
1975 Fran Tarkenton, Minnesota, QB	AP, Bell
1976 Bert Jones, Baltimore, QB	AP, PFWA
& Ken Stabler, Oakland, QB	Bell
1977 Walter Payton, Chicago, RB	AP, PFWA
& Bob Griese, Miami, QB	Bell
1978 Terry Bradshaw, Pittsburgh, QB	AP, Bell
& Earl Campbell, Houston, RB	PFWA

Year	Awards	Year	Awards
1979	Earl Campbell, Houston, RB ....AP, Bell, PFWA	1989	Joe Montana, San Francisco, QB ....AP, Bell, PFWA
1980	Brian Sipe, Cleveland, QB ....AP, PFWA	1990	Randall Cunningham, Phila., QB ....Bell, PFWA
	& Ron Jaworski, Philadelphia, QB..............Bell		& Joe Montana, San Francisco, QB..............AP
1981	Ken Anderson, Cincinnati, QB......AP, Bell, PFWA	1991	Thurman Thomas, Buffalo, RB............AP, PFWA
1982	Mark Moseley, Washington, PK.................AP		& Barry Sanders, Detroit, RB..................Bell
	Joe Theismann, Washington, QB...............Bell	1992	Steve Young, San Francisco, QB.....AP, Bell, PFWA
	& Dan Fouts, San Diego, QB................PFWA	1993	Emmitt Smith, Dallas, RB............AP, Bell, PFWA
1983	Joe Theismann, Washington, QB.......AP, PFWA	1994	Steve Young, San Francisco, QB.....AP, Bell, PFWA
	& John Riggins, Washington, RB..............Bell	1995	Brett Favre, Green Bay, QB..........AP, Bell, PFWA
1984	Dan Marino, Miami, QB............AP, Bell, PFWA	1996	Brett Favre, Green Bay, QB..........AP, Bell, PFWA
1985	Marcus Allen, LA Raiders, RB............AP, PFWA	1997	Barry Sanders, Detroit, RB....AP*, Bell, PFWA, NFL
	& Walter Payton, Chicago, RB................Bell		& Brett Favre, Green Bay, QB.................AP*
1986	Lawrence Taylor, NY Giants, LB.....AP, Bell, PFWA	1998	Terrell Davis, Denver, RB............AP, Bell, PFWA
1987	Jerry Rice, San Francisco, WR ....Bell, PFWA		& Randall Cunningham, Minnesota, QB........NFL
	& John Elway, Denver, QB....................AP		*In 1997 for the first time in history, two players tied for the
1988	Boomer Esiason, Cincinnati, QB.........AP, PFWA		AP MVP award.
	& Randall Cunningham, Phila, QB.............Bell		

Offensive Player of the Year

Selected by The Associated Press in balloting by a nationwide media panel. Given out since 1972. Rookie winners are in **bold** type.

Multiple winners: Earl Campbell (3); Terrell Davis, Jerry Rice and Barry Sanders (2).

Year		Pos	Year		Pos	Year		Pos
1972	Larry Brown, Was	RB	1981	Ken Anderson, Cin.	QB	1990	Warren Moon, Hou	QB
1973	O.J. Simpson, Buf	RB	1982	Dan Fouts, SD	QB	1991	Thurman Thomas, Buf	RB
1974	Ken Stabler, Oak	QB	1983	Joe Theismann, Was	QB	1992	Steve Young, SF	QB
1975	Fran Tarkenton, Min	QB	1984	Dan Marino, Mia	QB	1993	Jerry Rice, SF	WR
1976	Bert Jones, Bal	QB	1985	Marcus Allen, Raiders	RB	1994	Barry Sanders, Det	RB
1977	Walter Payton, Chi	RB	1986	Eric Dickerson, Rams	RB	1995	Brett Favre, GB	QB
1978	**Earl Campbell**, Hou	RB	1987	Jerry Rice, SF	WR	1996	Terrell Davis, Den	RB
1979	Earl Campbell, Hou	RB	1988	Roger Craig, SF	RB	1997	Barry Sanders, Det	RB
1980	Earl Campbell, Hou	RB	1989	Joe Montana, SF	QB	1998	Terrell Davis, Den	RB

Defensive Player of the Year

Selected by The Associated Press in balloting by a nationwide media panel. Given out since 1971. Rookie winners are in **bold** type.

Multiple winners: Lawrence Taylor (3); Joe Greene, Mike Singletary, Bruce Smith and Reggie White (2).

Year		Pos	Year		Pos	Year		Pos
1971	Alan Page, Min	DT	1981	**Lawrence Taylor**, NYG	LB	1991	Pat Swilling, NO	LB
1972	Joe Greene, Pit	DT	1982	Lawrence Taylor, NYG	LB	1992	Cortez Kennedy, Sea	DT
1973	Dick Anderson, Mia	S	1983	Doug Betters, Mia	DE	1993	Rod Woodson, Pit	CB
1974	Joe Greene, Pit	DT	1984	Kenny Easley, Sea	S	1994	Deion Sanders, SF	CB
1975	Mel Blount, Pit	CB	1985	Mike Singletary, Chi	LB	1995	Bryce Paup, Buf	LB
1976	Jack Lambert, Pit	LB	1986	Lawrence Taylor, NYG	LB	1996	Bruce Smith, Buf	DE
1977	Harvey Martin, Dal	DE	1987	Reggie White, Phi	DE	1997	Dana Stubblefield, SF	DT
1978	Randy Gradishar, Den	LB	1988	Mike Singletary, Chi	LB	1998	Reggie White, GB	DE
1979	Lee Roy Selmon, TB	DE	1989	Keith Millard, Min	DT			
1980	Lester Hayes, Oak	CB	1990	Bruce Smith, Buf	DE			

NFC Player of the Year

Given out by UPI from 1970-96. Offensive and defensive players honored since 1983. Rookie winners are in **bold** type.

Multiple winners: Eric Dickerson, Reggie White and Mike Singletary (3); Brett Favre, Charles Haley, Walter Payton, Lawrence Taylor and Steve Young (2).

Year		Pos	Year		Pos	Year		Pos
1970	John Brodie, SF	QB		Def—Lawrence Taylor, NYG	LB		Def—Charles Haley, SF	LB
1971	Alan Page, Min	DT	1984	Off—Eric Dickerson, Rams	RB	1991	Off—Mark Rypien, Was	QB
1972	Larry Brown, Was	RB		Def—Mike Singletary, Chi	LB		Def—Reggie White, Phi	DE
1973	John Hadl, Rams	QB	1985	Off—Walter Payton, Chi	RB	1992	Off—Steve Young, SF	QB
1974	Jim Hart, St.L	QB		Def—Mike Singletary, Chi	LB		Def—Chris Doleman, Min	DE
1975	Fran Tarkenton, Min	QB	1986	Off—Eric Dickerson, Rams	RB	1993	Off—Emmitt Smith, Dal	RB
1976	Chuck Foreman, Min	RB		Def—Lawrence Taylor, NYG	LB		Def—Eric Allen, Phi	CB
1977	Walter Payton, Chi	RB	1987	Off—Jerry Rice, SF	WR	1994	Off—Steve Young, SF	QB
1978	Archie Manning, NO	QB		Def—Reggie White, Phi	DE		Def—Charles Haley, Dal	DE
1979	Ottis Anderson, St.L	RB	1988	Off—Roger Craig, SF	RB	1995	Off—Brett Favre, GB	QB
1980	Ron Jaworski, Phi	QB		Def—Mike Singletary, Chi	LB		Def—Reggie White, GB	DE
1981	Tony Dorsett, Dal	RB	1989	Off—Joe Montana, SF	QB	1996	Off—Brett Favre, GB	QB
1982	Mark Moseley, Was	PK		Def—Keith Millard, Min	DT		Def—Kevin Greene, Car	LB
1983	Off—Eric Dickerson, Rams	RB	1990	Off—Randall Cunningham, Phi.	QB	1997	Award discontinued.	

Annual Awards (Cont.)
AFL-AFC Player of the Year

Presented by UPI to the top player in the AFL (1960-69) and AFC (1970-96). Offensive and defensive players have been honored since 1983. Rookie winners are in **bold** type.

Multiple winners: Bruce Smith (4); O.J. Simpson (3); Cornelius Bennett, George Blanda, John Elway, Dan Fouts, Daryle Lamonica, Dan Marino and Curt Warner (2).

Year		Pos	Year		Pos	Year		Pos
1960	**Abner Haynes**, Dal	HB	1978	**Earl Campbell**, Hou	RB	1989	Off–Christian Okoye, KC	RB
1961	George Blanda, Hou	QB	1979	Dan Fouts, SD	QB		Def–Michael Dean Perry, Cle	NT
1962	Cookie Gilchrist, Buf	FB	1980	Brian Sipe, Cle	QB	1990	Off–Warren Moon, Hou	QB
1963	Lance Alworth, SD	FL	1981	Ken Anderson, Cin	QB		Def–Bruce Smith, Buf	DE
1964	Gino Cappelletti, Bos	FL-PK	1982	Dan Fouts, SD	QB	1991	Off–Thurman Thomas, Buf	RB
1965	Paul Lowe, SD	HB	1983	Off–**Curt Warner**, Sea	RB		Def–Cornelius Bennett, Buf	LB
1966	Jim Nance, Bos	FB		Def–Rod Martin, Raiders	LB	1992	Off–Barry Foster, Pit	RB
1967	Daryle Lamonica, Raiders	QB	1984	Off–Dan Marino, Mia	QB		Def–Junior Seau, SD	LB
1968	Joe Namath, NYJ	QB		Def–Mark Gastineau, NYJ	DE	1993	Off–John Elway, Den	QB
1969	Daryle Lamonica, Raiders	QB	1985	Off–Marcus Allen, Raiders	RB		Def–Rod Woodson, Pit	CB
1970	George Blanda, Raiders	QB-PK		Def–Andre Tippett, NE	LB	1994	Off–Dan Marino, Mia	QB
1971	Otis Taylor, KC	WR	1986	Off–Curt Warner, Sea	RB		Def–Greg Lloyd, Pit	LB
1972	O.J. Simpson, Buf	RB		Def–Rulon Jones, Den	DE	1995	Off–Jim Harbaugh, Ind	QB
1973	O.J. Simpson, Buf	RB	1987	Off–John Elway, Den	QB		Def–Bryce Paup, Buf	LB
1974	Ken Stabler, Raiders	QB		Def–Bruce Smith, Buf	DE	1996	Off–Terrell Davis, Den	RB
1975	O.J. Simpson, Buf	RB	1988	Off–Boomer Esiason, Cin	QB		Def–Bruce Smith, Buf	DE
1976	Bert Jones, Bal	QB		Def–Bruce Smith, Buf	DE	1997	Award discontinued.	
1977	Craig Morton, Den	QB		& Cornelius Bennett, Buf	LB			

NFL-NFC Rookie of the Year

Presented by UPI to the top rookie in the NFL (1955-69) and NFC (1970-96). Players who were the overall first pick in the NFL draft are in **bold** type.

Year		Pos	Year		Pos	Year		Pos
1955	Alan Ameche, Bal	FB	1970	Bruce Taylor, SF	DB	1985	Jerry Rice, SF	WR
1956	Lenny Moore, Bal	HB	1971	John Brockington, GB	RB	1986	Reuben Mayes, NO	RB
1957	Jim Brown, Cle	FB	1972	Chester Marcol, GB	PK	1987	Robert Awalt, St.L	TE
1958	Jimmy Orr, Pit	FL	1973	Charle Young, Phi	TE	1988	Keith Jackson, Phi	TE
1959	Boyd Dowler, GB	FL	1974	John Hicks, NY	G	1989	Barry Sanders, Det	RB
1960	Gail Cogdill, Det	FL	1975	Mike Thomas, Wash	RB	1990	Mark Carrier, Chi	S
1961	Mike Ditka, Chi	TE	1976	Sammy White, Min	WR	1991	Lawrence Dawsey, TB	WR
1962	Ronnie Bull, Chi	FB	1977	Tony Dorsett, Dal	RB	1992	Robert Jones, Dal	LB
1963	Paul Flatley, Min	FL	1978	Bubba Baker, Det	DE	1993	Jerome Bettis, LA	RB
1964	Charley Taylor, Wash	HB	1979	Ottis Anderson, St.L	RB	1994	Bryant Young, SF	DT
1965	Gale Sayers, Chi	HB	1980	**Billy Sims**, Det	RB	1995	Rashaan Salaam, Chi	RB
1966	Johnny Roland, St.L	HB	1981	**George Rogers**, NO	RB	1996	Simeon Rice, Ari	DE
1967	Mel Farr, Det	RB	1982	Jim McMahon, Chi	QB	1997	Award discontinued.	
1968	Earl McCullough, Det	FL	1983	Eric Dickerson, LA	RB			
1969	Calvin Hill, Dal	RB	1984	Paul McFadden, Phi	PK			

AFL-AFC Rookie of the Year

Presented by UPI to the top rookie in the AFL (1960-69) and AFC (1970-96). Players who were the overall first pick in the AFL or NFL draft are in **bold** type.

Year		Pos	Year		Pos	Year		Pos
1960	Abner Haynes, Dal	HB	1973	Bobbie Clark, Cin	RB	1986	Leslie O'Neal, SD	DE
1961	Earl Faison, SD	DE	1974	Don Woods, SD	RB	1987	Shane Conlan, Buf	LB
1962	Curtis McClinton, Dal	FB	1975	Robert Brazile, Hou	LB	1988	John Stephens, NE	RB
1963	Billy Joe, Den	FB	1976	Mike Haynes, NE	DB	1989	Derrick Thomas, KC	LB
1964	Matt Snell, NY	FB	1977	A.J. Duhe, Mia	DE	1990	Richmond Webb, Mia	OT
1965	Joe Namath, NY	QB	1978	**Earl Campbell**, Hou	RB	1991	Mike Croel, Den	LB
1966	Bobby Burnett, Buf	HB	1979	Jerry Butler, Buf	WR	1992	Dale Carter, KC	CB
1967	George Webster, Hou	LB	1980	Joe Cribbs, Buf	RB	1993	Rick Mirer, Sea	QB
1968	Paul Robinson, Cin	RB	1981	Joe Delaney, KC	RB	1994	Marshall Faulk, Ind	RB
1969	Greg Cook, Cin	QB	1982	Marcus Allen, LA	RB	1995	Curtis Martin, NE	RB
1970	Dennis Shaw, Buf	QB	1983	Curt Warner, Sea	RB	1996	Terry Glenn, NE	WR
1971	**Jim Plunkett**, NE	QB	1984	Louis Lipps, Pit	WR	1997	Award discontinued.	
1972	Franco Harris, Pit	RB	1985	Kevin Mack, Cle	RB			

Offensive Rookie of the Year

Selected by The Associated Press in balloting by a nationwide media panel. Given out since 1967.

Year	Pos	Year	Pos	Year	Pos
1967 Mel Farr, Det	RB	1978 Earl Campbell, Hou	RB	1989 Barry Sanders, Det	RB
1968 Earl McCullouch, Det	OE	1979 Ottis Anderson, St.L	RB	1990 Emmitt Smith, Dal	RB
1969 Calvin Hill, Dal	RB	1980 Billy Sims, Det	RB	1991 Leonard Russell, NE	RB
1970 Dennis Shaw, Buf	QB	1981 George Rogers, NO	RB	1992 Carl Pickens, Cin	WR
1971 John Brockington, GB	RB	1982 Marcus Allen, Raiders	RB	1993 Jerome Bettis, Rams	RB
1972 Franco Harris, Pit	RB	1983 Eric Dickerson, Rams	RB	1994 Marshall Faulk, Ind	RB
1973 Chuck Foreman, Min	RB	1984 Louis Lipps, Pit	WR	1995 Curtis Martin, NE	RB
1974 Don Woods, SD	RB	1985 Eddie Brown, Cin	WR	1996 Eddie George, Hou	RB
1975 Mike Thomas, Was	RB	1986 Reuben Mayes, NO	RB	1997 Warrick Dunn, TB	RB
1976 Sammy White, Min	WR	1987 Troy Stradford, Mia	RB	1998 Randy Moss, Min	WR
1977 Tony Dorsett, Dal	RB	1988 John Stephens, NE	RB		

Defensive Rookie of the Year

Selected by The Associated Press in balloting by a nationwide media panel. Given out since 1967.

Year	Pos	Year	Pos	Year	Pos
1967 Lem Barney, Det	CB	1978 Al Baker, Det	DE	1988 Erik McMillan, NYJ	S
1968 Claude Humphrey, Atl	DE	1979 Jim Haslett, Buf	LB	1989 Derrick Thomas, KC	LB
1969 Joe Greene, Pit	DT	1980 Buddy Curry, Atl	LB	1990 Mark Carrier, Chi	S
1970 Bruce Taylor, SF	CB	& Al Richardson, Atl	LB	1991 Mike Croel, Den	LB
1971 Isiah Robertson, Rams	LB	1981 Lawrence Taylor, NYG	LB	1992 Dale Carter, KC	CB
1972 Willie Buchanon, GB	CB	1982 Chip Banks, Cle	LB	1993 Dana Stubblefield, SF	DT
1973 Wally Chambers, Chi	DT	1983 Vernon Maxwell, Bal	LB	1994 Tim Bowens, Mia	DT
1974 Jack Lambert, Pit	LB	1984 Bill Maas, KC	DT	1995 Hugh Douglas, NYJ	DE
1975 Robert Brazile, Hou	LB	1985 Duane Bickett, Ind	LB	1996 Simeon Rice, Ari	DE
1976 Mike Haynes, NE	CB	1986 Leslie O'Neal, SD	DE	1997 Peter Boulware, Bal	LB
1977 A.J. Duhe, Mia	DE	1987 Shane Conlan, Buf	LB	1998 Charles Woodson, Raiders	CB

Coach of the Year

Presented by UPI to the top coach in the AFL-NFL (1955-69) and AFC-NFC (1970-96). In 1997, the UPI awards were discontinued. Awards beginning in 1997 are the consensus selections from presenters such as AP, The Maxwell Football Club of Philadelphia, The Sporting News and the Pro Football Writers Association. Records indicate the team's change in record from the previous season.

Multiple winners: Dan Reeves (4); Paul Brown, Chuck Knox and Don Shula (3); George Allen, Leeman Bennett, Mike Ditka, George Halas, Tom Landry, Marv Levy, Bill Parcells, Jack Pardee, Sam Rutigliano, Lou Saban, Allie Sherman, Marty Schottenheimer and Bill Walsh (2).

Year	Improvement	Year	Improvement
1955 NFL–Joe Kuharich, Washington	3.9 to 8-4	AFC–Chuck Noll, Pittsburgh	6-8 to 11-3
1956 NFL–Buddy Parker, Detroit	3-9 to 9-3	1973 NFC–Chuck Knox, Los Angeles	6-7-1 to 12-2
1957 NFL–Paul Brown, Cleveland	5-7 to 9-2-1	AFC–John Ralston, Denver	5-9 to 7-5-2
1958 NFL–Weeb Ewbank, Baltimore	7-5 to 9-3	1974 NFC–Don Coryell, St. Louis	4-9-1 to 10-4
1959 NFL–Vince Lombardi, Green Bay	1-10-1 to 7-5	AFC–Sid Gillman, Houston	1-13 to 7-7
1960 NFL–Buck Shaw, Philadelphia	7-5 to 10-2	1975 NFC–Tom Landry, Dallas	8-6 to 10-4
AFL–Lou Rymkus, Houston	10-4	AFC–Ted Marchibroda, Baltimore	2-12 to 10-4
1961 NFL–Allie Sherman, New York	6-4-2 to 10-3-1	1976 NFC–Jack Pardee, Chicago	4-10 to 7-7
AFL–Wally Lemm, Houston	10-4 to 10-3-1	AFC–Chuck Fairbanks, New England	3-11 to 11-3
1962 NFL–Allie Sherman, New York	10-3-1 to 12-2	1977 NFC–Leeman Bennett, Atlanta	4-10 to 7-7
AFL–Jack Faulkner, Denver	3-11 to 7-7	AFC–Red Miller, Denver	9-5 to 12-2
1963 NFL–George Halas, Chicago	9-5 to 11-1-2	1978 NFC–Dick Vermeil, Philadelphia	5-9 to 9-7
AFL–Al Davis, Oakland	1-13 to 10-4	AFC–Walt Michaels, New York	3-11 to 8-8
1964 NFL–Don Shula, Baltimore	8-6 to 12-2	1979 NFC–Jack Pardee, Washington	8-8 to 10-6
AFL–Lou Saban, Buffalo	7-6-1 to 12-2	AFC–Sam Rutigliano, Cleveland	8-8 to 9-7
1965 NFL–George Halas, Chicago	5-9 to 9-5	1980 NFC–Leeman Bennett, Atlanta	6-10 to 12-4
AFL–Lou Saban, Buffalo	12-2 to 10-3-1	AFC–Sam Rutigliano, Cleveland	9-7 to 11-5
1966 NFL–Tom Landry, Dallas	7-7 to 10-3-1	1981 NFC–Bill Walsh, San Francisco	6-10 to 13-3
AFL–Mike Holovak, Boston	4-8-2 to 8-4-2	AFC–Forrest Gregg, Cincinnati	6-10 to 12-4
1967 NFL–George Allen, Los Angeles	8-6 to 11-1-2	1982 NFC–Joe Gibbs, Washington	8-8 to 8-1
AFL–John Rauch, Oakland	8-5-1 to 13-1	AFC–Tom Flores, Los Angeles	7-9 to 8-1
1968 NFL–Don Shula, Baltimore	11-1-2 to 13-1	1983 NFC–John Robinson, Los Angeles	2-7 to 9-7
AFL–Hank Stram, Kansas City	9-5 to 12-2	AFC–Chuck Knox, Seattle	4-5 to 9-7
1969 NFL–Bud Grant, Minnesota	8-6 to 12-2	1984 NFC–Bill Walsh, San Francisco	10-6 to 15-1
AFL–Paul Brown, Cincinnati	3-11 to 4-9-1	AFC–Chuck Knox, Seattle	9-7 to 12-4
1970 NFC–Alex Webster, New York	6-8 to 9-5	1985 NFC–Mike Ditka, Chicago	10-6 to 15-1
AFC–Paul Brown, Cincinnati	4-9-1 to 8-6	AFC–Raymond Berry, New England	9-7 to 11-5
1971 NFC–George Allen, Washington	6-8 to 9-4-1	1986 NFC–Bill Parcells, New York	10-6 to 14-2
AFC–Don Shula, Miami	10-4 to 10-3-1	AFC–Marty Schottenheimer, Cleveland	8-8 to 12-4
1972 NFC–Dan Devine, Green Bay	4-8-2 to 10-4	1987 NFC–Jim Mora, New Orleans	7-9 to 12-3

Annual Awards (Cont.)

Year		Improvement
	AFC–Ron Meyer, Indianapolis	3-13 to 9-6
1988	NFC–Mike Ditka, Chicago	11-4 to 12-4
	AFC–Marv Levy, Buffalo	7-8 to 12-4
1989	NFC–Lindy Infante, Green Bay	4-12 to 10-6
	AFC–Dan Reeves, Denver	8-8 to 11-5
1990	NFC–Jimmy Johnson, Dallas	1-15 to 7-9
	AFC–Art Shell, Los Angeles	8-8 to 12-4
1991	NFC–Wayne Fontes, Detroit	6-10 to 12-4
	AFC–Dan Reeves, Denver	5-11 to 12-4
1992	NFC–Dennis Green, Minnesota	8-8 to 11-5
	AFC–Bobby Ross, San Diego	4-12 to 11-5

Year		Improvement
1993	NFC–Dan Reeves, New York	6-10 to 11-5
	AFC–Marv Levy, Buffalo	11-5 to 12-4
1994	NFC–Dave Wannstedt, Chicago	7-9 to 9-7
	AFC–Bill Parcells, New England	5-11 to 10-6
1995	NFC–Ray Rhodes, Philadelphia	7-9 to 10-6
	AFC–Marty Schottenheimer, Kansas City	9-7 to 13-3
1996	NFC–Dom Capers, Carolina	7-9 to 12-4
	AFC–Tom Coughlin, Jacksonville	4-12 to 9-7
1997	NFL–Jim Fassel, NY Giants	6-10 to 10-5-1
1998	NFL–Dan Reeves, Atlanta	7-9 to 14-2

CANADIAN FOOTBALL

The Grey Cup

Earl Grey, the Governor-General of Canada (1904-11), donated a trophy in 1909 for the Rugby Football Championship of Canada. The trophy, which later became known as the Grey Cup, was originally open to competition for teams registered with the Canada Rugby Union. Since 1954, the Cup has gone to the champion of the Canadian Football League (CFL).

Overall multiple winners: Toronto Argonauts (14); Edmonton Eskimos (11); Winnipeg Blue Bombers (9); Hamilton Tiger-Cats and Ottawa Rough Riders (7); Calgary Stampeders and Hamilton Tigers (5); Montreal Alouettes and University of Toronto (4); B.C. Lions and Queen's University (3); Ottawa Senators, Sarnia Imperials, Saskatchewan Roughriders and Toronto Balmy Beach (2).

CFL multiple winners (since 1954): Edmonton (11); Winnipeg (7); Hamilton (6); Ottawa (5); Toronto (4); B.C. Lions, Calgary and Montreal (3); Saskatchewan (2).

Year	Cup Final
1909	Univ. of Toronto 26, Toronto Parkdale 6
1910	Univ. of Toronto 16, Hamilton Tigers 7
1911	Univ. of Toronto 14, Toronto Argonauts 4
1912	Hamilton Alerts 11, Toronto Argonauts 4
1913	Hamilton Tigers 44, Toronto Parkdale 2
1914	Toronto Argonauts 14, Univ. of Toronto 2
1915	Hamilton Tigers 13, Toronto Rowing 7
1916-19	Not held (WWI)
1920	Univ. of Toronto 16, Toronto Argonauts 3
1921	Toronto Argonauts 23, Edmonton Eskimos 0
1922	Queens Univ. 13, Edmonton Elks 1
1923	Queens Univ. 54, Regina Roughriders 0
1924	Queens Univ. 11, Toronto Balmy Beach 3
1925	Ottawa Senators 24, Winnipeg Tigers 1
1926	Ottawa Senators 10, Univ. of Toronto 7
1927	Toronto Balmy Beach 9, Hamilton Tigers 6
1928	Hamilton Tigers 30, Regina Roughriders 0
1929	Hamilton Tigers 14, Regina Roughriders 3
1930	Toronto Balmy Beach 11, Regina Roughriders 6
1931	Montreal AAA 22, Regina Roughriders 0
1932	Hamilton Tigers 25, Regina Roughriders 6
1933	Toronto Argonauts 4, Sarnia Imperials 3

Year	Cup Final
1934	Sarnia Imperials 20, Regina Roughriders 12
1935	Winnipeg 'Pegs 18, Hamilton Tigers 12
1936	Sarnia Imperials 26, Ottawa Rough Riders 20
1937	Toronto Argonauts 4, Winnipeg Blue Bombers 3
1938	Toronto Argonauts 30, Winnipeg Blue Bombers 7
1939	Winnipeg Blue Bombers 8, Ottawa Rough Riders 7
1940	Gm 1: Ottawa Rough Riders 8, Toronto B-Beach 2
	Gm 2: Ottawa Rough Riders 12, Toronto B-Beach 5
1941	Winnipeg Blue Bombers 18, Ottawa Rough Riders 16
1942	Toronto RACF 8, Winnipeg RACF 5
1943	Hamilton Wildcats 23, Winnipeg RACF 14
1944	Montreal HMCS 7, Hamilton Wildcats 6
1945	Toronto Argonauts 35, Winnipeg Blue Bombers 0
1946	Toronto Argonauts 28, Winnipeg Blue Bombers 6
1947	Toronto Argonauts 10, Winnipeg Blue Bombers 9
1948	Calgary Stampeders 12, Ottawa Rough Riders 7
1949	Montreal Alouettes 28, Calgary Stampeders 15
1950	Toronto Argonauts 13, Winnipeg Blue Bombers 0
1951	Ottawa Rough Riders 21, Saskatch. Roughriders 14
1952	Toronto Argonauts 21, Edmonton Eskimos 11
1953	Hamilton Tiger-Cats 12, Winnipeg Blue Bombers 6

Year	Winner	Head Coach	Score	Loser	Head Coach	Site
1954	Edmonton	Frank (Pop) Ivy	26-25	Montreal	Doug Walker	Toronto
1955	Edmonton	Frank (Pop) Ivy	34-19	Montreal	Doug Walker	Vancouver
1956	Edmonton	Frank (Pop) Ivy	50-27	Montreal	Doug Walker	Toronto
1957	Hamilton	Jim Trimble	32-7	Winnipeg	Bud Grant	Toronto
1958	Winnipeg	Bud Grant	35-28	Hamilton	Jim Trimble	Vancouver
1959	Winnipeg	Bud Grant	21-7	Hamilton	Jim Trimble	Toronto
1960	Ottawa	Frank Clair	16-6	Edmonton	Eagle Keys	Vancouver
1961	Winnipeg	Bud Grant	21-14(OT)	Hamilton	Jim Trimble	Toronto
1962	Winnipeg	Bud Grant	28-27*	Hamilton	Jim Trimble	Toronto
1963	Hamilton	Ralph Sazio	21-10	B.C. Lions	Dave Skrien	Vancouver
1964	B.C. Lions	Dave Skrien	34-24	Hamilton	Ralph Sazio	Toronto
1965	Hamilton	Ralph Sazio	22-16	Winnipeg	Bud Grant	Toronto
1966	Saskatchewan	Eagle Keys	29-14	Ottawa	Frank Clair	Vancouver
1967	Hamilton	Ralph Sazio	24-1	Saskatchewan	Eagle Keys	Ottawa
1968	Ottawa	Frank Clair	24-21	Calgary	Jerry Williams	Toronto
1969	Ottawa	Frank Clair	29-11	Saskatchewan	Eagle Keys	Montreal
1970	Montreal	Sam Etcheverry	23-10	Calgary	Jim Duncan	Toronto
1971	Calgary	Jim Duncan	14-11	Toronto	Leo Cahill	Vancouver
1972	Hamilton	Jerry Williams	13-10	Saskatchewan	Dave Skrien	Hamilton
1973	Ottawa	Jack Gotta	22-18	Edmonton	Ray Jauch	Toronto

Year	Winner	Head Coach	Score	Loser	Head Coach	Site
1974	Montreal	Marv Levy	20-7	Edmonton	Ray Jauch	Vancouver
1975	Edmonton	Ray Jauch	9-8	Montreal	Marv Levy	Calgary
1976	Ottawa	George Brancato	23-20	Saskatchewan	John Payne	Toronto
1977	Montreal	Marv Levy	41-6	Edmonton	Hugh Campbell	Montreal
1978	Edmonton	Hugh Campbell	20-13	Montreal	Joe Scannella	Toronto
1979	Edmonton	Hugh Campbell	17-9	Montreal	Joe Scannella	Montreal
1980	Edmonton	Hugh Campbell	48-10	Hamilton	John Payne	Toronto
1981	Edmonton	Hugh Campbell	26-23	Ottawa	George Brancato	Montreal
1982	Edmonton	Hugh Campbell	32-16	Toronto	Bob O'Billovich	Toronto
1983	Toronto	Bob O'Billovich	18-17	B.C. Lions	Don Matthews	Vancouver
1984	Winnipeg	Cal Murphy	47-17	Hamilton	Al Bruno	Edmonton
1985	B.C. Lions	Don Matthews	37-24	Hamilton	Al Bruno	Montreal
1986	Hamilton	Al Bruno	39-15	Edmonton	Jack Parker	Vancouver
1987	Edmonton	Joe Faragalli	38-36	Toronto	Bob O'Billovich	Vancouver
1988	Winnipeg	Mike Riley	22-21	B.C. Lions	Larry Donovan	Ottawa
1989	Saskatchewan	John Gregory	43-40	Hamilton	Al Bruno	Toronto
1990	Winnipeg	Mike Riley	50-11	Edmonton	Joe Faragalli	Vancouver
1991	Toronto	Adam Rita	36-21	Calgary	Wally Buono	Winnipeg
1992	Calgary	Wally Buono	24-10	Winnipeg	Urban Bowman	Toronto
1993	Edmonton	Ron Lancaster	33-23	Winnipeg	Cal Murphy	Calgary
1994	B.C. Lions	Dave Ritchie	26-23	Baltimore	Don Matthews	Vancouver
1995	Baltimore	Don Matthews	37-20	Calgary	Wally Buono	Regina
1996	Toronto	Don Matthews	43-37	Edmonton	Ron Lancaster	Hamilton
1997	Toronto	Don Matthews	47-23	Saskatchewan	Jim Daley	Edmonton
1998	Calgary	Wally Buono	26-24	Hamilton	Ron Lancaster	Winnipeg

*Halted by fog in 4th quarter, final 9:29 played the following day.

CFL Most Outstanding Player

Regular season Player of the Year as selected by The Football Reporters of Canada since 1953.

Multiple winners: Doug Flutie (6); Russ Jackson and Jackie Parker (3); Dieter Brock, Ron Lancaster and Mike Pringle (2).

Year		Year		Year	
1953	Billy Vessels, Edmonton, RB	1968	Bill Symons, Toronto, RB	1983	Warren Moon, Edmonton, QB
1954	Sam Etcheverry, Montreal, QB	1969	Russ Jackson, Ottawa, QB	1984	Willard Reaves, Winnipeg, RB
1955	Pat Abbruzzi, Montreal, RB	1970	Ron Lancaster, Saskatch., QB	1985	Merv Fernandez, B.C. Lions, WR
1956	Hal Patterson, Montreal, E-DB	1971	Don Jonas, Winnipeg, QB	1986	James Murphy, Winnipeg, WR
1957	Jackie Parker, Edmonton, RB	1972	Garney Henley, Hamilton, WR	1987	Tom Clements, Winnipeg, QB
1958	Jackie Parker, Edmonton, QB	1973	Geo. McGowan, Edmonton, WR	1988	David Williams, B.C. Lions, WR
1959	Johnny Bright, Edmonton, RB	1974	Tom Wilkinson, Edmonton, QB	1989	Tracy Ham, Edmonton, QB
1960	Jackie Parker, Edmonton, QB	1975	Willie Burden, Calgary, RB	1990	Mike Clemons, Toronto, RB
1961	Bernie Faloney, Hamilton, QB	1976	Ron Lancaster, Saskatch., QB	1991	Doug Flutie, B.C. Lions, QB
1962	George Dixon, Montreal, RB	1977	Jimmy Edwards, Hamilton, RB	1992	Doug Flutie, Calgary, QB
1963	Russ Jackson, Ottawa, QB	1978	Tony Gabriel, Ottawa, TE	1993	Doug Flutie, Calgary, QB
1964	Lovell Coleman, Calgary, RB	1979	David Green, Montreal, RB	1994	Doug Flutie, Calgary, QB
1965	George Reed, Saskatchewan, RB	1980	Dieter Brock, Winnipeg, QB	1995	Mike Pringle, Baltimore, RB
1966	Russ Jackson, Ottawa, QB	1981	Dieter Brock, Winnipeg, QB	1996	Doug Flutie, Toronto, QB
1967	Peter Liske, Calgary, QB	1982	Condredge Holloway, Tor., QB	1997	Doug Flutie, Toronto, QB
				1998	Mike Pringle, Montreal, RB

All-Time CFL Leaders

Through the 1998 season. Players active in 1998 are in **bold** type.

Passing Yards

		Yrs	Att	Cmp	Yards	Cmp Pct	Avg Gain	TD	Int	Rating
1	Ron Lancaster	19	6233	3384	50,535	54.3	14.9	333	396	72.4
2	Matt Dunigan	14	5476	3057	43,857	55.8	14.3	306	211	84.5
3	**Damon Allen**	14	5434	2949	41,730	54.3	14.2	231	190	78.9
4	Doug Flutie	8	4854	2975	41,355	61.3	13.9	270	155	93.9
5	Tom Clements	12	4657	2807	39,041	60.3	13.9	252	214	86.1
6	**Tracy Ham**	11	4731	2542	38,603	53.7	15.2	273	161	85.9
7	Kent Austin	10	4700	2709	36,030	57.6	13.3	198	191	79.2
8	Dieter Brock	11	4535	2602	34,830	57.4	13.4	210	158	82.8
9	Tom Burgess	10	4034	2118	30,308	52.5	14.3	190	191	73.1
10	Sam Etcheverry	7	2829	1630	25,582	57.6	15.7	183	163	85.3

Rushing Yards

		Yrs	Car	Yards	Avg	TD
1	George Reed	13	3243	16,116	5.0	134
2	Johnny Bright	13	1969	10,909	5.5	69
3	Normie Kwong	13	1745	9,022	5.2	78
4	**Mike Pringle**	7	1481	8,922	6.0	56
5	Leo Lewis	11	1351	8,861	6.5	48

Receiving Yards

		Yrs	Ct	Yards	Avg	TD
1	Ray Elgaard	14	830	13,198	16.0	78
2	**Allen Pitts**	9	792	12,397	15.7	101
3	**Don Narcisse**	12	872	11,766	13.5	74
4	Brian Kelly	9	575	11,169	19.4	97
5	Tom Scott	11	649	10,837	16.7	88

NFL EUROPE

The World League of American Football was formed in 1991 with hopes of expanding the popularity of the NFL to overseas markets. Funded by the NFL, the inaugural league in 1991 consisted of three European teams (London, Barcelona and Frankfurt), and seven North American teams (New York/New Jersey, Orlando, Montreal, Raleigh-Durham, Birmingham, Sacramento and San Antonio). The second season used the same format with Columbus, Ohio, replacing Raleigh-Durham.

In the fall of 1992, the NFL and WLAF Board of Directors voted to restructure the league to include more European teams. Play was subsequently suspended. In 1993, NFL clubs approved a six-team European-only league to resume play in 1995 with teams in Amsterdam, Barcelona, Frankfurt, London, Rhein and Scotland. In January 1998, the name of the league was changed to NFL Europe. Berlin was added for the 1999 season and London was disbanded.

The World Bowl

The first World Bowl was held in 1991 in front of 61,108 fans at London's Wembley Stadium. In 1991 and 1992, when the league consisted of three divisions, the top team from each division and one wild-card team advanced to the playoffs, with the winners of each game advancing to the World Bowl. There was no game played in 1993 or 1994. Since 1995, the top two regular season teams advance directly to the World Bowl.

Year	Winner	Head Coach	Score	Loser	Head Coach	Site
1991	London	Larry Kennan	21-0	Barcelona	Jack Bicknell	London
1992	Sacramento	Kay Stephenson	21-17	Orlando	Galen Hall	Montreal
1995	Frankfurt	Ernie Stautner	26-22	Amsterdam	Al Luginbill	Amsterdam
1996	Scotland	Jim Criner	32-27	Frankfurt	Ernie Stautner	Edinburgh, Scot.
1997	Barcelona	Jack Bicknell	38-24	Rhein	Galen Hall	Barcelona
1998	Rhein	Galen Hall	34-10	Frankfurt	Dick Curl	Frankfurt
1999	Frankfurt	Dick Curl	38-24	Barcelona	Jack Bicknell	Dusseldorf

World Bowl MVP

Year	Year	Year
1991 Dan Crossman, London, S	1996 Yo Murphy, Scotland, WR	1999 Andy McCullough, Frankfurt, WR
1992 Davis Archer, Sacramento, QB	1997 Jon Kitna, Barcelona, QB	
1995 Paul Justin, Frankfurt, QB	1998 Jim Arellanes, Rhein, QB	

Most Valuable Player

Regular season Offensive and Defensive Most Valuable Players as selected by league head coaches since 1991.

Year	Year	Year
1991 Off—Stan Gelbaugh, Lon., QB	1996 Off—Sean LaChapelle, Scot., WR	1999 Off—Lawrence Phillips, Bar., RB
Def—Anthony Parker, NY/NJ, CB	Def—Ty Parten, Scot., DL	Def—Mike Maslowski, Bar., LB
& Danny Lockett, Lon., LB	1997 Off—T.J. Rubley, Rhe., QB	
1992 Off—David Archer, Sac., QB	Def—Jason Simmons, Scot., DE	
Def—Adrian Jones, Bar., CB	1998 Off—Marcus Robinson, Rhe., WR	
1995 Off—Paul Justin, Frank., QB	Def—Josh Taves, Bar., DE	
Def—Malcolm Showell, Ams., DE		

ARENA FOOTBALL

The Arena Football League debuted in June of 1987 with four teams in Chicago, Denver, Pittsburgh and Washington D.C. Currently there are 16 teams in the league, divided into two conferences and four divisions.

ArenaBowl

Bowl	Year	Winner	Head Coach	Score	Loser	Head Coach	Site
I	1987	Denver	Tim Marcum	45-16	Pittsburgh	Joe Haering	Pittsburgh
II	1988	Detroit	Tim Marcum	24-13	Chicago	Perry Moss	Chicago
III	1989	Detroit	Tim Marcum	39-26	Pittsburgh	Joe Haering	Detroit
IV	1990	Detroit	Perry Moss	51-27	Dallas	Ernie Stautner	Detroit
V	1991	Tampa Bay	Fran Curci	48-42	Detroit	Tim Marcum	Detroit
VI	1992	Detroit	Tim Marcum	56-38	Orlando	Perry Moss	Orlando
VII	1993	Tampa Bay	Lary Kuharich	51-31	Detroit	Tim Marcum	Detroit
VIII	1994	Arizona	Danny White	36-31	Orlando	Perry Moss	Orlando
IX	1995	Tampa Bay	Tim Marcum	48-35	Orlando	Perry Moss	St. Petersburg
X	1996	Tampa Bay	Tim Marcum	42-38	Iowa	John Gregory	Des Moines
XI	1997	Arizona	Danny White	55-33	Iowa	John Gregory	Phoenix
XII	1998	Orlando	Jay Gruden	62-31	Tampa Bay	Tim Marcum	Tampa
XIII	1999	Albany	Mike Dailey	59-48	Orlando	Jay Gruden	Albany

ArenaBowl MVP

Year	Year	Year
1987 No award given.	1992 George LaFrance, Detroit, OS	1997 Donnie Davis, Arizona, QB
1988 Steve Griffin, Detroit, WR/DB	1993 Jay Gruden, Tampa Bay, QB	1998 Rick Hamilton, Orlando, FB/LB
1989 George LaFrance, Detroit, WR/DB	1994 Sherdrick Bonner, Arizona, QB	1999 Eddie Brown, Albany, OS
1990 Art Schlichter, Detroit, QB	1995 George LaFrance, Tampa Bay, OS	
1991 Jay Gruden, Tampa Bay, QB	1996 Stevie Thomas, Tampa Bay, WR/LB	

College Basketball

Oh man is UConn point guard **Khalid El-Amin** excited about the upset unfolding in his team's Final Four game with Duke.

Hot Dogs Roll

Jim Calhoun's UConn Huskies relish their big win against the heavily favored Duke Blue Devils.

by
Chris Fowler

It was the year of the Blue Devils. Right up until the season's final 40 minutes, when Duke's coronation became, instead, Connecticut's vindication.

The Huskies spent five quiet months in the shadow of Duke's dominance—their own amazing campaign obscured by the blizzard of Blue Devil hype. During the regular season they waltzed through the revitalized Big East, won at Stanford without top scorer Richard Hamilton and beat Big Ten champion and eventual Final Four participant Michigan State by 14 points. Had anybody noticed?

Against Duke, the Huskies were big underdogs, nearly 10 points. But this Championship Game was no shocker. It looked, to me, like the best team won. It would've been a great best-of-seven series anyway. Hamilton and Khalid El-Amin made big shots, Ricky Moore out-toughed his former

rival from the playgrounds of Georgia, Will Avery. UConn's role players responded to the challenge of Duke's depth.

But the Huskies' triumph had as much to do with attitude as athleticism. The Huskies feared no one. They could not be intimidated. They believed the name on the front of their jerseys carries as much weight as any. Heck, you've got to be tough-minded to survive a week of Jim Calhoun's practices.

For the UConn coach, the title delivered long overdue recognition, after so often being so close, only to feel snakebitten. Fair or not, coaches are now judged almost solely by their tournament record. So are teams. Lose a bunch in the regular season, then make an NCAA run, you become a "great tournament coach." Job offers or raises quickly follow. Kick butt for 30 games, then lose in March to some little school with a three-point phenom and you're an underachiever.

Chris Fowler is the host of ESPN's *College GameDay*.

Connecticut head coach **Jim Calhoun** is in the middle of it all during the postgame celebration following his team's victory over Duke in the 1999 National Championship Game.

So, where does that leave Duke? The Blue Devils gave us one of the great regular seasons in decades, including a 19-0 record in ACC games. They wore huge targets, survived rock-star fanfare everywhere they went and never lost sight of the ultimate goal. One loss in St. Pete doesn't make them underachievers or chokers. But it sure did short-circuit a new "Duke Dynasty" before it could even get started.

Suddenly, not even Coach K's program is immune to the Early-Exodus Syndrome that plagues college basketball these days. For the first time ever at Duke, two sophomores and a freshman chose to declare for the NBA draft. Elton Brand's decision was a no-brainer. As the consensus National Player of the Year his stock couldn't get much higher. His choice was quickly validated when the Chicago Bulls made him the first overall pick.

Brand's roomie, Avery, had a tougher call but, in the end, chose to test the draft waters. The big surprise was freshman Corey Maggette. His college "career" consisted of a few starts, a dozen or so highlight reel dunks and 17 minutes spent on the bench in the second half of the National Championship Game. A great talent, but still far from a great basketball player.

Still, it's hard to blame young guys like Maggette for taking the money, considering that pro potential weighs more than college production when it comes to NBA dollars. Even though he was taken 13th overall (one pick before Avery), personally, I would have taken another year on Duke's lovely campus, playing a featured role for Coach K in front of the Cameron Crazies and taken another crack at the title that was taken from them. ∎

AP/Wide World Photos

Things didn't go exactly according to plan for **Mike Krzyzewski** and his Duke Blue Devils in 1999. His team tied a single-season record with 37 wins but dropped the big one to UConn.

Dick Vitale's Highlights of the Year in College Basketball

10. The highly-touted and much-anticipated **Lamar Odom** finally makes his college debut and plays brilliantly for Jim Harrick and Rhode Island as he leads the Rams to the A-10 tournament title.

9. **Steve Alford and his Southwest Missouri State Bears** shock just about everyone during March Madness by advancing to the Sweet 16.

8. **Dr. Tom Davis** is a lame-duck coach at the University of Iowa but sparkles as he directs the Hawkeyes over Arkansas and into the Sweet 16 in his 13th and final season at Iowa.

7. **Elton Brand** earns consensus National Player of the Year honors after being benched by Coach K. at Duke earlier in the season for not being in tiptop shape.

6. The surprising **Gonzaga Bulldogs capture** the nation's attention during March Madness as they march their way into the Final Eight.

5. **Richard Hamilton**, the Connecticut Huskies' scoring sensation, climbs in stature by deciding to return to school instead of entering the NBA draft and then becomes the Most Outstanding Player of the NCAA tournament.

4. **Michigan State wins** the Big Ten championship and plays brilliantly under head coach Tom Izzo in gaining a Final Four berth.

3. **The Ohio State Buckeyes**, under Jim O'Brien, go from 1-15 a year ago in the Big Ten to earning a much-deserved spot in the Final Four.

2. **Duke goes unbeaten** in the ACC regular season, wins the ACC tournament and is sensational in finishing the year with an incredible 37-2 record despite falling just short of the program's ultimate goal of a third national championship.

1. Connecticut head coach **Jim Calhoun adds** to his already superb resume with a long-awaited national championship as the Huskies upend the Duke Blue Devils for the 1999 national title. ∎

THE **NUMBERS**

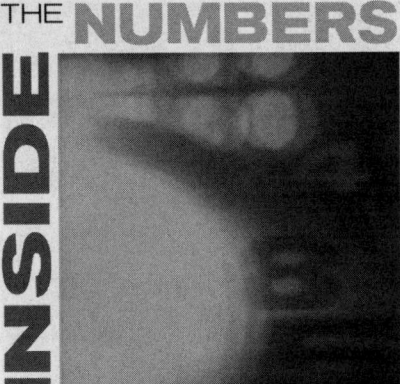

SCORNIN' THE BAYOU

While Duke lost three underclassmen to the draft this year, the school is not even close to the top of the list when it comes to losing early entry candidates to the pros. The problem with recruiting too well is that your best players often move on before using all four years of their eligibility. Below is a list of the schools with the least success at holding onto their star players since the first early entry candidates declared in 1976.

Underclassmen lost	School
9	LSU
8	Michigan
	North Carolina
6	Alabama
	Georgia
	Kentucky
5	Arkansas
	Houston
	Maryland
	Memphis St.
	Syracuse
	UNLV

The nine players that LSU has lost early are as follows: junior DeWayne Scales (1980), junior Jerry Reynolds (1985), sophomore John Williams (1986), Hernan Montenegro (1988, Montenegro had withdrawn from school in 1987), sophomore Chris Jackson (1990), junior Shaquille O'Neal (1992), junior Jamie Brandon (1994), junior Ronnie Henderson (1996) and sophomore Randy Livingston (1996).

DEVIL OF AN UPSET

Connecticut's upset of Duke in the NCAA men's championship game was big. But was it the biggest ever? Yes, at least according to the betting spreads. Here is a list of the biggest upsets in title game history.

Result	Year	Spread
UConn 77, Duke 74	1999	9½
Villanova 66, Georgetown 64	1985	9
Kansas 83, Oklahoma 79	1988	8
N.C. State 54, Houston 52	1983	8
Cincinnati 70, Ohio St. 65 OT	1961	8
Texas Western 72, Kentucky 65	1966	6

DRAFT FELT IN DURHAM

This year Duke became the first school in history to have four players drafted in the first round in a single NBA draft. They might have been more excited if three of the four weren't underclassmen. Here is a listing of schools with the most players taken in the first round at a single draft.

School	Year	Players	Drafted
Duke	1999	Elton Brand	1
		Trajan Langdon	11
		Corey Maggette	13
		William Avery	14
Kentucky	1996	Antoine Walker	6
		Tony Delk	16
		Walter McCarty	19
Arkansas	1992	Todd Day	8
		Oliver Miller	22
		Lee Mayberry	23
UNLV	1991	Larry Johnson	1
		Stacey Augmon	9
		Greg Anthony	12
Michigan	1990	Rumeal Robinson	10
		Loy Vaught	13
		Terry Mills	16
UCLA	1979	David Greenwood	2
		Roy Hamilton	10
		Brad Holland	14
Indiana	1976	Scott May	2
		Quinn Buckner	7
		Bob Wilkerson	11

AP/Wide World Photos

Longtime Iowa head coach **Dr. Tom Davis** made his exit from college basketball in 1999, but not before his team made some noise in the NCAA tournament.

FINALLY FOUR

Connecticut got its first Final Four bid in 21 tries this year. Until UConn broke through this year they had the most NCAA tournament appearances without making it to a Final Four. Here are the leaders in this dubious category.

NCAA appearances		First Final Four
21	UConn	1999
18	BYU	none
17	Missouri	none
16	Maryland	none
	Miami-OH	none
	Oregon St.	none
14	Alabama	none
	Notre Dame	1978
12	Utah St.	none
	Xavier	none
	Weber St.	none

Note: Notre Dame has had tournament appearances since 1978 but they are not counted here.

BAD TO GOOD

Ohio State completed an incredible single-season turnaround when it went from 8-22 in 1998 to the Final Four in 1999. The Buckeyes' 180-degree turn wasn't the most startling change of fortune in Final Four history however. Wisconsin went from 5-15 to a national championship in 1941. Here is a look at Final Four teams with the worst records in the previous season.

School	Final 4 (record)	Previous record
Wisconsin	1941 (20-3)	5-15
Ohio St.	1999 (27-9)	8-22
Kansas	1974 (23-7)	8-18
Georgetown	1943 (22-5)	9-11
DePaul	1943 (19-5)	10-12
Utah	1944 (21-4)	10-12
California	1946 (30-6)	7-8
Ohio St.	1944 (14-7)	8-9
Michigan	1992 (25-9)	14-15

COLLEGE BASKETBALL
S T A T I S T I C S

SEC
A

THE SEASON IN REVIEW
1998-1999
TOP 25 • NCAA'S • STANDINGS

THE 2000
INFORMATION PLEASE
SPORTS
ALMANAC

PAGE
285

Final Regular Season AP Men's Top 25 Poll

Taken **before** start of NCAA tournament.

The sportswriters & broadcasters poll: first place votes in parentheses; records through Monday, March 8, 1999; total points (based on 25 for 1st, 24 for 2nd, etc.); record in NCAA tourney and team lost to; head coach (career years and record including 1999 postseason), and preseason ranking. Teams in **bold** type went on to reach NCAA Final Four.

		Mar. 8 Record	Points	NCAA Recap	Head Coach	Preseason Rank
1	**Duke** (69)	32-1	1749	5-1 (Connecticut)	Mike Krzyzewski (24 yrs: 542-214)	1
2	**Michigan St.** (1)	29-4	1654	4-1 (Duke)	Tom Izzo (4 yrs: 88-41)	5
3	Connecticut	28-2	1635	6-0	Jim Calhoun (27 yrs: 554-258)	2
4	Auburn	27-3	1469	2-1 (Ohio St.)	Cliff Ellis (24 yrs: 444-271)	NR
5	Maryland	26-5	1434	2-1 (St. John's)	Gary Williams (21 yrs: 399-246)	6
6	Utah	27-4	1396	1-1 (Miami-OH)	Rick Majerus (15 yrs: 337-116)	10
7	Stanford	25-6	1316	1-1 (Gonzaga)	Mike Montgomery (21 yrs: 415-216)	3
8	Kentucky	25-8	1165	3-1 (Michigan St.)	Tubby Smith (8 yrs: 187-75)	4
9	St. John's	25-8	1122	3-1 (Ohio St.)	Mike Jarvis (14 yrs: 281-150)	33
10	Miami-FL	22-6	1089	1-1 (Purdue)	Leonard Hamilton (13 yrs: 177-199)	44
11	Cincinnati	22-6	1082	1-1 (Temple)	Bob Huggins (18 yrs: 414-155)	15
12	Arizona	22-6	1063	0-1 (Oklahoma)	Lute Olson (26 yrs: 587-212)	18
13	North Carolina	24-9	895	0-1 (Weber St.)	Bill Guthridge (1 yr: 34-4)	11
14	**Ohio St.**	23-8	832	4-1 (Connecticut)	Jim O'Brien (19 yrs: 270-248)	NR
15	UCLA	22-8	801	0-1 (Detroit)	Steve Lavin (3 yrs: 70-26)	12
16	College of Charleston	28-2	695	0-1 (Tulsa)	John Kresse (20 yrs: 493-121)	41
17	Arkansas	22-10	518	1-1 (Iowa)	Nolan Richardson (19 yrs: 456-166)	19
18	Wisconsin	22-9	464	0-1 (SW Missouri St.)	Dick Bennett (23 yrs: 430-242)	NR
19	Indiana	22-10	373	1-1 (St. John's)	Bobby Knight (34 yrs: 743-281)	22
20	Tennessee	20-8	356	1-1 (SW Missouri St.)	Jerry Green (16 yrs: 264-195)	9
21	Iowa	18-9	282	2-1 (Connecticut)	Tom Davis (28 yrs: 543-290)	NR
22	Kansas	22-9	268	1-1 (Kentucky)	Roy Williams (11 yrs: 305-72)	8
23	Florida	20-8	239	2-1 (Gonzaga)	Billy Donovan (5 yrs: 84-61)	46
24	NC-Charlotte	22-10	220	0-1 (Oklahoma)	Bob Lutz (10 yrs: 203-100)	NR
25	New Mexico	24-8	95	1-1 (Connecticut)	Dave Bliss (24 yrs: 465-271)	20t

Others receiving votes: 26. **Temple** (21-10) 71 pts; 27. **Oklahoma** (22-10) 56; 28. **Gonzaga** (25-6) 53; 29. **Syracuse** (21-11) 49; 30. **Texas** (19-12) 47; 31. **Minnesota** (17-10) 40; 32. **Missouri** (20-8) 37; 33. **Louisville** (19-10) 30; 34. **Rhode Island** (20-12) 27; 35. **Tulsa** (23-10) 26; 36. **Murray St.** (27-5) 17; 37. **Iowa St.** (14-15) and **Purdue** (19-12) 12; 39. **Detroit** (24-5) and **Kent** (23-6) 11; 41. **Miami-OH** (22-7) 10; 42. **Creighton** (21-8) 9; 43. **Villanova** (21-10) 7; 44. **George Washington** (20-8) 4; 45. **Weber St.** (24-7) 3; 46. **New Mexico St.** (21-9), **Pennsylvania** (21-5) and **Siena** (25-5) 2.

NCAA Men's Division I Tournament Seeds

	WEST		MIDWEST		SOUTH		EAST
1	Connecticut (28-2)	1	Michigan St. (29-4)	1	Auburn (27-3)	1	Duke (32-1)
2	Stanford (25-6)	2	Utah (27-4)	2	Maryland (26-5)	2	Miami-FL (22-6)
3	North Carolina (24-9)	3	Kentucky (25-8)	3	St. John's (25-8)	3	Cincinnati (26-5)
4	Arkansas (22-10)	4	Arizona (22-6)	4	Ohio St. (23-8)	4	Tennessee (20-8)
5	Iowa (18-9)	5	NC-Charlotte (22-10)	5	UCLA (22-8)	5	Wisconsin (22-9)
6	Florida (20-8)	6	Kansas (22-9)	6	Indiana (22-10)	6	Temple (21-10)
7	Minnesota (17-10)	7	Washington (17-11)	7	Louisville (19-10)	7	Texas (19-12)
8	Missouri (20-8)	8	Villanova (21-10)	8	Syracuse (21-11)	8	College of Charleston (28-2)
9	New Mexico (24-8)	9	Mississippi (19-12)	9	Oklahoma St. (22-10)	9	Tulsa (22-9)
10	Gonzaga (25-6)	10	Miami-OH (22-7)	10	Creighton (21-8)	10	Purdue (19-12)
11	Penn (21-5)	11	Evansville (23-9)	11	G. Washington (20-8)	11	Kent (23-6)
12	UAB (20-11)	12	Rhode Island (20-12)	12	Detroit (24-5)	12	SW Missouri St. (20-10)
13	Siena (25-5)	13	Oklahoma (20-10)	13	Murray St. (27-5)	13	Delaware (25-5)
14	Weber St. (24-7)	14	N. Mexico St. (23-9)	14	Samford (24-5)	14	George Mason (19-10)
15	Alcorn St. (23-6)	15	Arkansas St. (18-11)	15	Valparaiso (23-8)	15	Lafayette (22-7)
16	TX-San Antonio (18-10)	16	Mt. St. Mary's (15-14)	16	Winthrop (21-7)	16	Florida A&M (12-18)

1999 NCAA BASKETBALL MEN'S DIVISION I

EAST

FIRST ROUND March 11-12		SECOND ROUND March 13-14	REGIONALS March 19 & 21
1 Duke	99	Duke 97	
16 Florida A&M	58		Duke 78
8 Coll. of Charleston	53	Tulsa 56	
9 Tulsa	62		
5 Wisconsin	32	SW Mo. St. 81	SW Mo. St. 61
12 SW Mo. St.	43		
4 Tennessee	62	Tennessee 51	
13 Delaware	52		Duke 85
6 Temple	61	Temple 64	
11 Kent	54		Temple 77
3 Cincinnati	72	Cincinnati 54	
14 George Mason	48		
7 Texas	54	Purdue 73	Purdue 55
10 Purdue	58		Temple 64
2 Miami-FL	75	Miami-FL 63	
15 Lafayette	54		

Duke 68

MIDWEST

FIRST ROUND March 11-12		SECOND ROUND March 13-14	REGIONALS March 19 & 21
1 Michigan St.	76	Michigan St. 74	
16 Mt. St. Mary's	53		Michigan St. 54
8 Villanova	70	Mississippi 66	
9 Mississippi	72		
5 NC-Charlotte	81	NC-Char. 72	Oklahoma 46
12 Rhode Island	70		
4 Arizona	60	Oklahoma 85	
13 Oklahoma	61		Michigan St. 73
6 Kansas	95	Kansas 88	
11 Evansville	74		Kentucky 58
3 Kentucky	80	Kentucky 92	
14 New Mexico St.	58		
7 Washington	58	Miami-OH 66	Kentucky 66
10 Miami-OH	59		Miami-OH 43
2 Utah	80	Utah 58	
15 Arkansas St.	58		

Michigan St. 62

SOUTH

FIRST ROUND March 11-12		SECOND ROUND March 13-14	REGIONALS March 18 & 20
1 Auburn	80	Auburn 81	
16 Winthrop	41		Auburn 64
8 Syracuse	61	Oklahoma St. 74	
9 Oklahoma St.	69		
5 UCLA	53	Detroit 44	Ohio St. 72
12 Detroit	56		
4 Ohio St.	72	Ohio St. 75	
13 Murray St.	58		Ohio St. 77
6 Indiana	108	Indiana 61	
11 G. Washington	99		St. John's 74
3 St. John's	69	St. John's 86	
14 Samford	43		
7 Louisville	58	Creighton 63	Maryland 62
10 Creighton	62		St. John's 76
2 Maryland	82	Maryland 75	
15 Valparaiso	60		

Ohio St. 58

WEST

FIRST ROUND March 11-12		SECOND ROUND March 13-14	REGIONALS March 18 & 20
1 Connecticut	91	Connecticut 78	
16 Texas-SA	66		Connecticut 78
8 Missouri	59	New Mexico 56	
9 New Mexico	61		
5 Iowa	77	Iowa 82	Iowa 68
12 UAB	64		
4 Arkansas	94	Arkansas 72	
13 Siena	80		Connecticut 67
6 Florida	75	Florida 82 (OT)	
11 Penn	61		Florida 72
3 N. Carolina	74	Weber St. 74	
14 Weber St.	76		
7 Minnesota	63	Gonzaga 82	Gonzaga 73
10 Gonzaga	75		Gonzaga 62
2 Stanford	69	Stanford 74	
15 Alcorn St.	57		

Connecticut 64

NATIONAL CHAMPIONSHIP

Connecticut 77
Duke 74

FINAL FOUR

Tropicana Field
in St. Petersburg, Fla.
***
Semifinals: March 27
Finals: March 29

NCAA Men's Championship Game

61st NCAA Division I Championship Game. **Date:** Monday, March 29, at Tropicana Field. **Coaches:** Jim Calhoun of Connecticut and Mike Krzyzewski of Duke. **Favorite:** Duke by 9½.
Attendance: 41,340; **Officials:** Tim Higgins, Gerald Boudreaux, Scott Thornley; **TV Rating:** 17.2/27 share (CBS).

Connecticut 77

	Min	FG M-A	FT M-A	Pts	Reb O-T	A	PF
Kevin Freeman	32	3-6	0-0	6	5-8	0	1
Richard Hamilton	38	10-22	5-6	27	4-7	3	1
Jake Voskuhl	28	1-1	0-0	2	0-3	2	3
Ricky Moore	37	6-10	0-1	13	0-8	2	4
Khalid El-Amin	22	5-12	2-4	12	3-4	4	3
Souleymane Wane	8	2-2	0-0	4	0-0	0	4
Albert Mouring	17	3-4	0-1	6	0-3	0	1
Edmund Saunders	11	1-3	2-4	4	0-3	0	3
Rashamel Jones	6	1-1	1-2	3	0-2	0	0
Antric Klaiber	1	0-0	0-0	0	0-0	0	0
TOTALS	200	32-61	10-18	77	12-38	11	20

Three-point FG: 3-8 (Hamilton 2-4, Moore 1-1, El-Amin 0-2, Mouring 0-1); **Team Rebounds:** 3; **Blocked Shots:** 6 (Freeman 3, Voskuhl 2, Mouring); **Turnovers:** 16 (El-Amin 6, Freeman 3, Moore 3, Mouring 2, Jones, Saunders); **Steals:** 4 (Hamilton 2, Moore, Wane); **Percentages:** 2-Pt FG (.547), 3-Pt FG (.375), Total FG (.525), Free Throws (.556).

Duke 74

	Min	FG M-A	FT M-A	Pts	Reb O-T	A	PF
Chris Carrawell	31	3-7	3-4	9	0-4	2	4
Shane Battier	33	2-7	1-2	6	3-4	2	3
Elton Brand	38	5-8	5-8	15	2-13	0	3
William Avery	36	3-12	4-4	11	2-4	5	4
Trajan Langdon	38	7-15	6-7	25	0-1	1	2
Nate James	6	0-0	0-0	0	0-1	0	0
Corey Maggette	11	3-7	2-2	8	0-0	0	2
Chris Burgess	7	0-0	0-0	0	0-0	0	1
TOTALS	200	23-56	21-27	74	7-27	10	19

Three-point FG: 7-19 (Carrawell 0-2, Battier 1-3, Avery 1-3, Langdon 5-10, Maggette 0-1); **Team Rebounds:** 2; **Blocked Shots:** 4 (Carrawell 2, Brand 2); **Turnovers:** 19 (Carrawell 4, Brand 3, Langdon 2, Maggette 2, Avery); **Steals:** 6 (Langdon 3, Brand 2, Carrawell). **Percentages:** 2-Pt FG (.432), 3-Pt FG (.368), Total FG (.411), Free Throws (.778).

Connecticut (Big East)	37	40—	**77**
Duke (ACC)	39	35—	**74**

THE FINAL FOUR

Tropicana Field in St. Petersburg, Fla.
(Mar. 27-29).

Semifinal—Game One

West Regional champ Connecticut vs. South Regional champ Ohio State; Saturday, Mar. 27 (5:31 p.m. tipoff). **Coaches:** Jim Calhoun, Connecticut and Jim O'Brien, Ohio State. **Favorite:** Connecticut by 5½.

Ohio St. (Big Ten)	35	23—	**58**
Connecticut (Big East)	36	28—	**64**

High scorers— Richard Hamilton, UConn (24) and Michael Redd, Ohio St. (15); **Att**— 41,340; **TV rating**—9.2/21 share (CBS).

Semifinal—Game Two

East Regional champion Duke vs. Midwest Regional champ Michigan State; Saturday, Mar. 27 (8:12 p.m. tipoff). **Coaches:** Mike Krzyzewski, Duke and Tom Izzo, Michigan State. **Favorite:** Duke by 11½.

Duke (ACC)	32	36—	**68**
Michigan St. (Big Ten)	20	42—	**62**

High scorers— Elton Brand, Duke (18) and Peterson, Michigan St. (15); **Att**— 41,340; **TV rating**—10.9/20 share (CBS).

Most Outstanding Player

Richard Hamilton, Junior forward, Connecticut. SEMIFINAL—33 minutes, 24 points, 5 rebounds, 1 assist; FINAL—38 minutes, 27 points, 7 rebounds, 3 assists, 2 steals.

All-Tournament Team

Hamilton, guard Khalid El-Amin and guard Ricky Moore of Connecticut, guard Trajan Langdon and center Elton Brand of Duke.

Final ESPN/*USA Today* Coaches' Poll

Taken **after** NCAA Tournament.

Voted on by a panel of 26 Division I head coaches following the NCAA tournament: first place votes in parentheses with total points (based on 25 for 1st, 24 for 2nd, etc.). Schools on major probation are ineligible to be ranked.

		W-L	Pts	Before NCAAs W-L	Rank
1	Connecticut (26)	34-2	650	28-2	3
2	Duke	37-2	624	32-1	1
3	Michigan St.	33-5	596	29-4	2
4	Ohio St.	27-9	557	23-8	14
5	Kentucky	28-9	511	25-8	11
	St. John's	28-9	511	25-8	8
7	Auburn	29-4	477	27-3	4
8	Maryland	28-6	429	26-5	5
9	Stanford	26-7	400	25-6	7
10	Utah	28-5	344	27-4	6
11	Cincinnati	27-6	330	26-5	9
12	Miami-FL	23-7	296	22-6	12
	Gonzaga	28-7	296	25-6	NR
14	Temple	24-11	285	21-10	NR
15	Iowa	20-10	270	18-9	20
16	Arizona	22-7	257	22-6	10
17	Florida	22-9	178	20-8	25
18	North Carolina	24-10	172	24-9	13
19	Oklahoma	22-11	158	20-10	NR
20	Miami-OH	24-8	157	22-7	NR
21	UCLA	22-9	138	22-8	15
22	Purdue	21-13	136	19-12	NR
23	Kansas	23-10	133	22-9	22
24	SW Missouri St.	22-11	96	20-10	NR
25	Arkansas	23-11	81	22-10	19

Others receiving votes: 26. **Indiana** (23-11, 64 pts); 27. **Oklahoma St.** (23-11, 49); 28. **Wisconsin** (22-10, 43); 29. **NC-Charlotte** (23-11, 34); 30. **College of Charleston** (28-3, 29); 31. **New Mexico** (25-9, 28); 32. **Detroit** (25-6, 19); 33. **St. John's** (21-10, 9); 34. **Detroit** (23-6, 19); 35. **California** (22-11, 18); 36. **Creighton** (22-9, 15), **Syracuse** (20-12, 15) and **Texas** (19-13, 15); 39. **Tennessee** (21-9, 9); 40. **Louisville** (19-11, 6), **Murray St.** (26-6, 6) and **Weber St.** (22-8, 6); 43. **Minnesota** (17-11, 4) and **N. Mexico St.** (21-9, 4); 45. **Clemson** (19-5, 3); 46. **Missouri** (20-9, 1).

NCAA Finalists' Tournament and Season Statistics

At least 10 games played during the overall season.

Duke (37-2)

| | NCAA Tournament | | | | | | Overall Season | | | | |
| | | | —Per Game— | | | | | | —Per Game— | | |
	Gm	FG%	TPts	Pts	Reb	Ast	Gm	FG%	TPts	Pts	Reb	Ast
Elton Brand	6	.649	102	17.0	9.2	0.8	39	.620	691	17.7	9.8	1.1
Trajan Langdon	6	.537	91	18.2	4.0	1.4	36	.462	622	17.3	3.4	1.9
William Avery	6	.409	84	14.0	5.3	2.8	39	.483	580	14.9	3.5	5.0
Chris Carrawell	6	.426	62	10.3	4.5	3.2	39	.454	386	9.9	4.8	3.3
Corey Maggette	6	.514	51	8.5	3.7	1.5	39	.525	414	10.6	3.9	1.5
Shane Battier	6	.469	49	8.2	4.7	2.3	37	.545	338	9.1	4.9	1.5
Nate James	6	.500	22	3.7	1.5	1.5	39	.454	196	5.0	2.6	0.9
Taymon Domzalski	3	.583	18	6.0	3.7	0.0	30	.534	115	3.8	3.0	0.3
Chris Burgess	6	.667	17	2.8	2.7	0.5	39	.614	212	5.4	3.9	0.8
J.D. Simpson	4	.000	4	1.0	0.8	0.0	26	.125	10	0.4	0.3	0.2
D. Bryant	3	.000	1	0.3	0.3	0.3	13	.333	8	0.6	0.2	0.2
Justin Caldbeck	3	.000	0	0.0	0.0	0.0	20	.300	7	0.4	0.6	0.2
Ryan Caldbeck	3	.000	0	0.0	0.7	0.0	12	.333	2	0.2	0.5	0.0
DUKE	6	.504	501	83.5	37.7	14.7	39	.514	3581	91.8	42.2	16.2
OPPONENTS	6	.389	378	63.0	30.5	10.0	39	.391	2619	67.2	33.4	12.0

Three-pointers: NCAA TOURNAMENT— Langdon (17-32), Avery (15-29), Battier (9-19), James (4-6), Carrawell (3-8), Maggette (1-8), Simpson (0-1), R. Caldbeck (0-1), Team (49-104 for .471 pct.); OVERALL— Langdon (112-254), Avery (76-185), Battier (39-94), Maggette (29-84), Carrawell (19-55), James (15-52), Burgess (2-4), Bryant (1-3), Simpson (0-6), R. Caldbeck (0-2), Team (293-739 for .396 pct.).

Connecticut (34-2)

| | NCAA Tournament | | | | | | Overall Season | | | | |
| | | | —Per Game— | | | | | | —Per Game— | | |
	Gm	FG%	TPts	Pts	Reb	Ast	Gm	FG%	TPts	Pts	Reb	Ast
Richard Hamilton	6	.500	145	24.2	4.7	2.0	34	.443	732	21.5	4.8	2.7
Khalid El-Amin	6	.417	84	14.0	3.3	5.2	36	.412	497	13.8	2.8	3.9
Kevin Freeman	6	.522	59	9.8	8.3	0.2	36	.588	440	12.2	7.3	0.8
Ricky Moore	6	.421	48	8.0	5.3	3.2	36	.423	243	6.8	3.6	3.6
Edmund Saunders	6	.630	42	7.0	5.3	0.2	35	.562	211	6.0	4.7	0.7
Jake Voskuhl	6	.450	22	3.7	6.2	1.0	34	.512	186	5.5	6.4	1.1
Rashamel Jones	6	.462	17	2.8	2.0	0.5	32	.516	113	3.5	1.7	0.8
Albert Mouring	5	.500	17	3.4	1.4	0.8	32	.439	228	7.1	2.5	1.1
E. J. Harrison	5	.500	15	3.0	0.8	1.0	26	.455	49	1.9	0.8	0.8
Souleymane Wane	5	.429	6	1.2	1.4	0.6	30	.385	61	2.0	2.8	0.4
Antric Klaiber	2	—	0	0.0	0.0	0.0	23	.294	15	0.7	1.0	0.1
CONNECTICUT	6	.482	455	75.8	38.2	14.2	36	.467	2781	77.3	40.3	15.3
OPPONENTS	6	.369	384	64.0	30.5	10.7	36	.387	2207	61.3	33.1	11.9

Three-pointers: NCAA TOURNAMENT—Hamilton (7-23), El-Amin (5-21), Moore (4-12), Mouring (3-6), Harrison (2-3), Jones (0-1), Team (21-66 for .318 pct.); OVERALL— Hamilton (68-196), El-Amin (51-151), Mouring (32-85), Ricky Moore (18-51), Harrison (3-9), Jones (1-9), Saunders (1-1), Freeman (0-2), Klaiber (0-1), Tonella (0-1), Team (174-506 for .344 pct.).

Duke's Schedule

Reg. Season
(29-1)

W	Fairfield	98-66
W	at Davidson	94-61
W	S.Carolina St.	120-56
W	at Notre Dame	111-82
W	at Fresno State	93-82
L	at Cincinnati	75-77
W	at Michigan St.	73-67
W	N.C. State	89-69
W	Florida	116-86
W	Michigan	108-64
W	N.C. A&T	88-53
W	at Kentucky	71-60
W	NC-Greensboro	104-58
W	at Maryland	82-64
W	Georgia Tech	99-58
W	Virginia	115-69
W	at Wake Forest	82-72
W	Florida St.	98-73
W	at Clemson	82-60
W	at St. John's	92-88
W	North Carolina	89-77
W	at N.C. State	80-61

W	Maryland	95-77
W	at Georgia Tech	87-79
W	at Virginia	100-54
W	Wake Forest	102-71
W	at Florida St.	85-59
W	Clemson	92-65
W	at DePaul	96-64
W	at North Carolina	81-61

ACC Tourney
(3-0)

W	Virginia	104-67
W	N.C. State	83-68
W	North Carolina	96-73

NCAA Tourney
(5-1)

W	Florida A&M	99-58
W	Tulsa	97-56
W	SW Mo. St.	78-61
W	Temple	85-64
W	Michigan St.	68-62
L	Connecticut	74-77

Connecticut's Schedule

Reg. Season
(25-2)

W	Quinnipiac	102-60
W	Richmond	77-57
W	Hartford	95-58
W	Wagner	111-46
W	Washington	69-48
W	Michigan St.	82-68
W	at Massachusetts	59-54
W	at Pittsburgh	70-69
W	Fairfield	102-67
W	Villanova	100-76
W	Georgetown	87-64
W	at Boston College	91-78
W	at West Virginia	80-45
W	Notre Dame	101-70
W	Pittsburgh	81-58
W	at Miami	70-68
W	Seton Hall	62-47
W	at Georgetown	78-71
W	at St. John's	78-74
L	Syracuse	42-59
W	at Stanford	70-59

W	Boston College	66-50
W	at Seton Hall	53-48
W	Rutgers	77-64
L	Miami	71-73
W	at Providence	72-65
W	at Syracuse	70-58

Big East Tourney
(3-0)

W	Seton Hall	57-56
W	Syracuse	71-50
W	St. John's	82-63

NCAA Tourney
(6-0)

W	Texas-San Antonio	91-66
W	New Mexico	78-56
W	Iowa	78-68
W	Gonzaga	67-62
W	Ohio State	64-58
W	Duke	77-74

Final NCAA Men's Division I Standings

Conference records include regular season games only. Overall records include all postseason tournament games.

America East Conference

Team	Conference			Overall		
	W	L	Pct	W	L	Pct
*Delaware	15	3	.833	25	7	.781
Drexel	15	3	.833	20	9	.690
†Hofstra	14	4	.778	22	11	.667
Maine	13	5	.722	19	9	.679
Hartford	9	9	.500	11	16	.407
Vermont	7	11	.389	11	16	.407
Northeastern	6	12	.333	10	18	.357
Boston University	5	13	.278	9	18	.333
Towson	4	14	.222	6	22	.214
New Hampshire	2	16	.111	4	23	.148

Conf. Tourney Final: Delaware 86, Drexel 67.
***NCAA Tourney (0-1):** Delaware (0-1).
†**NIT (0-1):** Hofstra (0-1).

Atlantic Coast Conference

Team	Conference			Overall		
	W	L	Pct	W	L	Pct
*Duke	16	0	1.000	37	2	.949
*Maryland	13	3	.813	28	6	.824
*North Carolina	10	6	.625	24	9	.727
†Wake Forest	7	9	.438	17	14	.548
†N.C. State	6	10	.375	19	14	.576
†Georgia Tech	6	10	.375	15	16	.484
†Clemson	5	11	.313	20	15	.571
Florida St	5	11	.313	13	17	.433
Virginia	4	12	.250	14	16	.467

Conf. Tourney Final: Duke 96, North Carolina 73.
***NCAA Tourney (7-3):** Duke (5-1), Maryland (2-1), North Carolina (0-1).
†**NIT (6-4):** Wake Forest (1-1), N.C. State (1-1), Georgia Tech (0-1), Clemson (4-1, NIT runner-up).

Atlantic 10 Conference

East	Conference			Overall		
	W	L	Pct	W	L	Pct
*Temple	13	3	.813	24	11	.686
*Rhode Island	10	6	.625	20	13	.606
Massachusetts	9	7	.562	14	16	.467
St. Bonaventure	8	8	.500	14	15	.483
Fordham	5	11	.313	12	15	.444
St. Joseph's-PA	5	11	.313	12	18	.400

West	W	L	Pct	W	L	Pct
*Geo. Washington	13	3	.813	20	9	.690
†Xavier-OH	12	4	.750	25	11	.694
La Salle	8	8	.500	13	15	.464
Virginia Tech	7	9	.438	13	15	.464
Dayton	5	11	.313	11	17	.393
Duquesne	1	15	.063	5	23	.179

Note: There are 12 teams in the Atlantic 10.
Conf. Tourney Final: Rhode Island 62, Temple 59.
***NCAA Tourney (3-3):** Temple (3-1), Rhode Island (0-1), George Washington (0-1).
†**NIT (4-1):** Xavier-OH (4-1).

Big East Conference

Team	Conference			Overall		
	W	L	Pct	W	L	Pct
*Connecticut	16	2	.889	34	2	.944
*Miami-FL	15	3	.833	23	7	.767
*St. John's	14	4	.778	28	9	.757
*Villanova	10	8	.556	21	11	.656
*Syracuse	10	8	.556	21	12	.636
†Rutgers	9	9	.500	19	13	.594
†Providence	9	9	.500	16	14	.533
†Seton Hall	8	10	.444	15	15	.500
Notre Dame	8	10	.444	14	16	.467
†Georgetown	6	12	.333	15	16	.484
Pittsburgh	5	13	.278	14	16	.467
West Virginia	4	14	.222	10	19	.345
Boston College	3	15	.167	6	21	.222

Conf. Tourney Final: Connecticut 82, St. John's 63.
***NCAA Tourney (10-4):** Connecticut (6-0), Miami-FL (1-1), St. John's (3-1), Villanova (0-1), Syracuse (0-1).
†**NIT (1-4):** Rutgers (1-1), Providence (0-1), Seton Hall (0-1), Georgetown (0-1).

Big Sky Conference

Team	Conference			Overall		
	W	L	Pct	W	L	Pct
*Weber St	13	3	.813	25	8	.758
Northern Arizona	12	4	.750	21	8	.724
Portland St	9	7	.563	17	11	.607
Cal St.-Northridge	9	7	.563	17	12	.586
Montana St	9	7	.563	16	13	.552
Eastern Washington	7	9	.438	10	17	.370
Montana	6	10	.375	13	14	.481
Idaho St	4	12	.250	6	20	.231
Cal St.-Sacramento	3	13	.188	3	23	.115

Conf. Tourney Final: Weber St. 82, Northern Arizona 75.
***NCAA Tourney (1-1):** Weber St. (1-1).

Big South Conference

Team	Conference			Overall		
	W	L	Pct	W	L	Pct
*Winthrop	9	1	.900	21	8	.724
Radford	8	2	.800	20	8	.714
NC-Asheville	5	5	.500	11	18	.379
Charleston Southern	4	6	.400	12	16	.429
Coastal Carolina	4	6	.400	7	20	.259
Liberty	0	10	.000	11	17	.393
Elon	0	0	.000	11	16	.407
High Point	0	0	.000	4	22	.154

Conf. Tourney Final: Winthrop 86, Radford 74.
***NCAA Tourney (0-1):** Winthrop (0-1).
Note: Elon and High Point were provisional members of the Big South Conference in the 1998-99 season and were ineligible for the conference championship.

Final NCAA Men's Division I Standings (Cont.)

Big Ten Conference

Team	Conference			Overall		
	W	L	Pct	W	L	Pct
*Michigan St	15	1	.938	33	5	.868
*Ohio St	12	4	.750	27	9	.750
*Indiana	9	7	.563	21	11	.676
*Wisconsin	9	7	.563	22	10	.688
*Iowa	9	7	.563	20	10	.688
*Minnesota	8	8	.500	17	11	.607
*Purdue	7	9	.438	21	13	.618
†Northwestern	6	10	.400	15	14	.517
Michigan	5	11	.313	12	19	.387
Penn St	5	11	.313	13	14	.482
Illinois	3	13	.188	14	18	.336

Note: There are 11 teams in the Big 10.
Conf. Tourney Final: Michigan St. 67, Illinois 50.
*NCAA Tourney (13-7): Michigan St. (4-1), Ohio St. (4-1), Indiana (1-1), Wisconsin (0-1), Iowa (2-1), Minnesota (0-1), Purdue (2-1).
†NIT (0-1): Northwestern (0-1).

Big 12 Conference

Team	Conference			Overall		
	W	L	Pct	W	L	Pct
*Texas	13	3	.813	19	13	.594
*Missouri	11	5	.688	20	9	.690
*Kansas	11	5	.688	23	10	.697
*Oklahoma	11	5	.688	22	11	.688
*Oklahoma St.	10	6	.625	23	11	.676
†Nebraska	10	6	.625	20	13	.606
†Kansas St	7	9	.438	20	13	.606
†Colorado	7	9	.438	18	15	.545
Iowa St.	6	10	.375	15	15	.500
Texas A&M	5	11	.312	12	15	.444
Texas Tech	5	11	.312	13	17	.433
Baylor	0	16	.000	6	24	.200

Conf. Tourney Final: Kansas 53, Oklahoma St. 37.
*NCAA Tourney (4-5): Texas (0-1), Missouri (0-1), Kansas (1-1), Oklahoma (2-1), Oklahoma St. (1-1).
†NIT (2-3): Nebraska (1-1), Kansas St. (0-1), Colorado (1-1).

Big West Conference

Team	Conference			Overall		
	W	L	Pct	W	L	Pct
Boise St.	12	4	.750	21	8	.724
*New Mexico St.	12	4	.750	23	10	.697
Idaho	11	5	.688	16	11	.593
Utah St	8	8	.500	15	13	.536
Nevada	4	12	.250	8	18	.308
North Texas	4	12	.250	4	22	.154

Team	Conference			Overall		
	W	L	Pct	W	L	Pct
UC-Santa Barbara	12	4	.750	15	13	.536
Long Beach St	9	7	.563	13	15	.464
Pacific	9	7	.563	14	13	.519
Cal St.-Fullerton	7	9	.438	13	14	.481
Cal Poly-SLO	6	10	.375	11	16	.407
UC-Irvine	2	14	.125	6	20	.231

Conf. Tourney Final: New Mexico St. 79, Boise St. 69.
*NCAA Tourney (0-1): New Mexico St. (0-1).

Colonial Athletic Association

Team	Conference			Overall		
	W	L	Pct	W	L	Pct
*George Mason	13	3	.813	19	11	.633
†Old Dominion	11	5	.688	25	8	.758
Richmond	10	6	.625	15	12	.556
James Madison	9	7	.563	16	11	.593
NC-Wilmington	9	7	.563	11	17	.393
Va. Commonwealth	8	8	.500	15	16	.484
East Carolina	7	9	.438	13	14	.481
William & Mary	3	13	.188	8	19	.296
American	2	14	.125	7	21	.250

Conf. Tourney Final: George Mason 63, Old Dominion 58.
*NCAA Tourney (0-1): George Mason (0-1).
†NIT (1-1): Old Dominion (1-1).

Conference USA

American Division	Conference			Overall		
	W	L	Pct	W	L	Pct
*Cincinnati	12	4	.750	28	6	.824
*Louisville	11	5	.688	18	10	.643
*NC-Charlotte	10	6	.625	20	12	.625
†DePaul	10	6	.625	17	13	.567
St. Louis	8	8	.500	14	15	.483
Marquette	6	10	.375	14	14	.500

National Division	Conference			Overall		
	W	L	Pct	W	L	Pct
*Ala-Birmingham	10	6	.625	19	10	.655
So. Florida	6	10	.375	13	14	.481
So. Mississippi	6	10	.375	15	16	.484
Memphis	6	10	.375	14	15	.483
Tulane	6	10	.375	15	14	.517
Houston	5	11	.313	10	17	.370

Conf. Tourney Final: Tulane 58, Cincinnati 44.
*NCAA Tourney (2-4): Cincinnati (1-1), Louisville (0-1), NC-Charlotte (1-1), Alabama-Birmingham (0-1).
†NIT (1-1): DePaul (1-1).

Ivy League

Team	Conference			Overall		
	W	L	Pct	W	L	Pct
*Pennsylvania	13	1	.929	21	6	.778
Princeton	11	3	.786	20	7	.741
Dartmouth	10	4	.714	14	12	.538
Harvard	7	7	.500	13	13	.500
Cornell	6	8	.429	11	15	.423
Columbia	5	9	.357	10	16	.385
Brown	2	12	.143	4	22	.154
Yale	2	12	.143	4	22	.154

Conf. Tourney Final: Ivy League has no tournament.
*NCAA Tourney (0-1): Pennsylvania (0-1).

Metro Atlantic Conference

Team	Conference			Overall		
	W	L	Pct	W	L	Pct
*Siena	13	5	.722	25	6	.806
Niagara	13	5	.722	17	12	.586
Iona	12	6	.647	16	14	.533
Canisius	11	7	.611	15	12	.556
St. Peter's	10	8	.556	14	15	.483
Marist	8	10	.444	16	12	.571
Rider	7	11	.389	12	16	.429
Fairfield	7	11	.389	12	15	.444
Loyola-MD	6	12	.333	13	15	.464
Manhattan	3	15	.167	5	22	.185

Conf. Tourney Final: Siena 82, St. Peter's 67.
*NCAA Tourney (0-1): Siena (0-1).

Mid-American Conference

East	Conference W	L	Pct	Overall W	L	Pct
*Miami-OH	15	3	.833	24	8	.750
*Kent	13	5	.722	23	7	.767
Akron	12	6	.667	18	9	.667
Bowling Green	12	6	.667	18	10	.643
Ohio	12	6	.667	18	10	.643
Marshall	11	7	.611	16	11	.593
Buffalo	1	17	.056	5	24	.172

West	Conference W	L	Pct	Overall W	L	Pct
†Toledo	11	7	.611	19	9	.679
Ball St.	10	8	.556	16	11	.593
Central Mich	7	11	.389	10	16	.385
Western Mich	6	12	.333	11	15	.423
Eastern Mich	5	13	.278	5	20	.200
N. Illinois	2	16	.111	6	20	.231

Conf. Tourney Final: Kent 49, Miami-OH 43.
***NCAA Tourney (2-2):** Miami-OH (2-1), Kent (0-1).
†NIT (0-1): Toledo (0-1).

Mid-Continent Conference

Team	Conference W	L	Pct	Overall W	L	Pct
*Valparaiso	10	4	.714	23	9	.719
Oral Roberts	10	4	.714	17	11	.607
Western Illinois	9	5	.643	16	12	.571
Youngstown St.	9	5	.643	14	14	.500
Southern Utah	6	8	.429	13	17	.433
Indiana-Purdue	6	8	.429	11	16	.407
Missouri-KC	3	11	.214	8	22	.267
Chicago St.	3	11	.214	3	24	.100
Oakland	0	0	.000	12	15	.444

Conf. Tourney Final: Valparaiso 73, Oral Roberts 69.
***NCAA Tourney (0-1):** Valparaiso (0-1).
Note: Oakland was a provisional member of the Mid-Continent Conference in 1998-99 and was not eligible for the conference championship.

Mid-Eastern Athletic Conference

Team	Conference W	L	Pct	Overall W	L	Pct
South Carolina St.	14	4	.778	17	12	.586
Coppin St.	14	4	.778	15	14	.517
Morgan St.	12	6	.667	14	14	.500
Norfolk St.	11	7	.611	15	12	.556
Bethune-Cookman	10	9	.526	11	16	.407
N. Carolina A&T	9	9	.500	13	15	.464
Hampton	8	10	.444	8	19	.296
*Florida A&M	8	11	.421	12	18	.400
MD-Eastern Shore	7	11	.389	10	17	.370
Delaware St.	5	13	.278	8	19	.296
Howard	2	16	.111	2	25	.074

Conf. Tourney Final: Florida A&M 64, S.C. State 61.
***NCAA Tourney (0-1):** Florida A&M (0-1).

Midwestern Collegiate Conference

Team	Conference W	L	Pct	Overall W	L	Pct
*Detroit	12	2	.857	25	6	.806
†Butler	11	3	.786	22	10	.688
WI-Green Bay	9	5	.643	20	11	.645
Loyola-IL	7	7	.500	9	18	.333
Cleveland St.	6	8	.429	14	14	.500
WI-Milwaukee	5	9	.357	8	19	.296
Wright St	4	10	.286	9	18	.333
Illinois-Chicago	2	12	.143	7	20	.259

Conf. Tourney Final: Detroit 72, Butler 65.
***NCAA Tourney (1-1):** Detroit (1-1).
†NIT (2-1): Butler (2-1).

Missouri Valley Conference

Team	Conference W	L	Pct	Overall W	L	Pct
*Evansville	13	5	.722	23	10	.697
*Creighton	11	7	.611	22	9	.710
*SW Missouri St.	11	7	.611	22	11	.667
†Bradley	11	7	.611	17	12	.586
Indiana St.	10	8	.556	15	12	.556
Southern Illinois	10	8	.556	15	12	.556
Illinois St	7	11	.389	16	15	.516
Wichita St.	6	12	.333	13	17	.433
Northern Iowa	6	12	.333	9	18	.333
Drake	5	13	.278	10	17	.370

Conf. Tourney Final: Creighton 70, Evansille 61.
***NCAA Tourney (3-3):** Evansville (0-1), Creighton (1-1), SW Missouri St. (2-1).
†NIT (0-1): Bradley (0-1).

Northeast Conference

Team	Conference W	L	Pct	Overall W	L	Pct
MD-Baltimore County	17	3	.850	19	9	.679
St. Francis-NY	16	4	.800	20	8	.714
Robert Morris	12	8	.600	15	12	.556
Central Connecticut St.	11	9	.550	19	13	.594
LIU Brooklyn	10	10	.500	19	10	.370
*Mt. St. Mary's	10	10	.500	15	15	.500
Fairleigh Dickinson	9	11	.450	12	16	.429
Wagner	7	13	.350	9	18	.333
St. Francis-PA	7	13	.350	9	17	.346
Quinnipiac	6	14	.300	9	18	.333
Monmouth	5	15	.250	5	21	.192

Conf. Tourney Final: Mount St. Mary's 72, Central Connecticut St. 56.
***NCAA Tourney (0-1):** Mount St. Mary's (0-1).

Ohio Valley Conference

Team	Conference W	L	Pct	Overall W	L	Pct
*Murray St.	16	2	.889	27	6	.818
SE Missouri St	15	3	.833	20	9	.690
Morehead St	9	9	.500	13	15	.464
Tennessee St.	9	9	.500	12	15	.444
Austin Peay	9	9	.500	11	16	.407
Middle Tenn. St	9	9	.500	12	19	.387
Eastern Illinois	8	10	.444	13	16	.448
Tennessee Tech	8	10	.444	12	15	.444
Tennessee-Martin	5	13	.278	8	18	.308
Eastern Kentucky	2	16	.111	3	23	.115

Conf. Tourney Final: Murray St. 62, SE Missouri St. 61.
***NCAA Tourney (0-1):** Murray St. (0-1).

Pacific-10 Conference

Team	Conference W	L	Pct	Overall W	L	Pct
*Stanford	15	3	.833	26	7	.788
*Arizona	13	5	.722	22	7	.759
*UCLA	12	6	.667	22	9	.710
*Washington	10	8	.556	17	12	.586
†California	8	10	.444	22	11	.667
†Oregon	8	10	.444	19	13	.594
†USC	7	11	.389	15	13	.536
Oregon St	7	11	.389	13	14	.481
Arizona St	6	12	.333	14	16	.467
Washington St	4	14	.222	10	19	.345

Conf. Tourney Final: Pac-10 has no tournament.
***NCAA Tourney (1-4):** Stanford (1-1), Arizona (0-1), UCLA (0-1), Washington (0-1).
†NIT (8-2): California (5-0, NIT Champion), Oregon (3-1), USC (0-1).

Final NCAA Men's Division I Standings (Cont.)

Patriot League

Team	Conference			Overall		
	W	L	Pct	W	L	Pct
*Lafayette	10	2	.833	22	8	.733
Navy	9	3	.750	20	7	.741
Bucknell	9	3	.750	16	13	.552
Colgate	7	5	.583	14	14	.500
Army	4	8	.333	8	19	.296
Holy Cross	3	9	.250	7	20	.259
Lehigh	0	12	.000	6	22	.214

Conf. Tourney Final: Lafayette 67, Bucknell 63.
*NCAA Tourney (0-1): Lafayette (0-1).

Southeastern Conference

Eastern Div.	Conference			Overall		
	W	L	Pct	W	L	Pct
*Tennessee	12	4	.750	21	9	.700
*Kentucky	11	5	.688	28	9	.757
*Florida	10	6	.625	22	9	.710
†Georgia	6	10	.375	15	15	.500
Vanderbilt	5	11	.313	14	15	.483
South Carolina	3	13	.188	8	2	.276

Western Div.	Conference			Overall		
	W	L	Pct	W	L	Pct
*Auburn	14	2	.875	29	4	.879
*Arkansas	9	7	.563	23	11	.676
*Mississippi	8	8	.500	20	13	.606
†Mississippi St	8	8	.500	20	13	.606
†Alabama	6	10	.375	17	15	.531
LSU	4	12	.250	12	15	.444

Conf. Tourney Final: Kentucky 76, Arkansas 63.
*NCAA Tourney (10-6): Tennessee (1-1), Kentucky (3-1), Florida (2-1), Auburn (2-1), Arkansas (1-1), Mississippi (1-1).
†NIT (0-3): Georgia (0-1), Mississippi St. (0-1), Alabama (0-1).

Southern Conference

North Div.	Conference			Overall		
	W	L	Pct	W	L	Pct
Appalachian St	13	3	.813	21	8	.724
Davidson	11	5	.688	16	11	.593
East Tennessee St	9	7	.563	17	11	.607
Virginia Military	9	7	.563	12	15	.444
NC-Greensboro	5	11	.313	7	20	.259
W. Carolina	2	14	.125	8	21	.276

South Div.	Conference			Overall		
	W	L	Pct	W	L	Pct
*College of Charleston	16	0	1.000	28	3	.903
Tenn-Chattanooga	9	7	.563	16	12	.571
Wofford	8	8	.500	11	16	.407
Georgia Southern	6	10	.375	11	17	.393
Furman	5	11	.313	12	16	.428
The Citadel	3	13	.188	9	18	.333

Conf. Tourney Final: College of Charleston 77, Appalachian St. 67.
*NCAA Tourney (0-1): College of Charleston (0-1).

Southland Conference

Team	Conference			Overall		
	W	L	Pct	W	L	Pct
SW Texas St.	13	5	.722	19	9	.679
*Texas-San Antonio	12	6	.667	18	11	.620
Nicholls St	12	6	.667	14	15	.483
NE Louisiana	12	6	.667	13	14	.481
Lamar	11	7	.611	17	11	.607
McNeese St.	11	7	.611	13	15	.464
Northwestern St.	8	10	.444	11	15	.423
Texas-Arlington	8	10	.444	10	16	.385
Sam Houston St.	7	11	.389	10	16	.385
SE Louisiana	3	15	.167	6	20	.231
Stephen F. Austin	2	16	.111	4	22	.154

Conf. Tourney Final: Texas-San Antonio 71, Southwest Texas St. 63.
*NCAA Tourney (0-1): Texas-San Antonio (0-1).

Southwestern Athletic Conference

Team	Conference			Overall		
	W	L	Pct	W	L	Pct
*Alcorn St.	14	2	.875	23	7	.767
Southern	13	3	.813	21	7	.750
Jackson St	11	5	.688	16	12	.571
Miss. Valley St.	10	6	.625	14	13	.519
Alabama St	8	8	.500	11	16	.407
Texas Southern	6	10	.375	8	19	.296
Grambling	5	11	.313	6	21	.222
Prairie View A&M	4	12	.250	6	21	.222
Ark-Pine Bluff	1	15	.063	3	24	.111

Conf. Tourney Final: Alcorn St. 89, Southern 83.
*NCAA Tourney (0-1): Alcorn St. (0-1).

Sun Belt Conference

Team	Conference			Overall		
	W	L	Pct	W	L	Pct
Louisiana Tech	10	4	.714	19	9	.679
*Arkansas St	9	5	.643	18	12	.600
SW Louisiana	7	7	.500	13	16	.448
Florida International	7	7	.500	13	16	.448
Western Kentucky	7	7	.500	13	16	.448
South Alabama	6	8	.429	11	16	.407
New Orleans	5	9	.357	14	16	.467
Ark-Little Rock	5	9	.357	12	15	.444

Conf. Tourney Final: Arkansas St. 65, Western Kentucky 48.
*NCAA Tourney (0-1): Arkansas St. (0-1).

Trans America Athletic Conference

Team	Conference			Overall		
	W	L	Pct	W	L	Pct
*Samford	15	1	.938	24	6	.800
Central Florida	13	3	.813	19	10	.655
Georgia St.	11	5	.688	17	13	.567
Stetson	10	6	.625	14	13	.519
Centenary	9	7	.563	14	14	.500
Jacksonville	7	9	.438	12	15	.444
Troy St.	6	10	.375	9	18	.333
Campbell	6	10	.375	9	18	.333
Mercer	5	11	.313	8	18	.308
Florida Atlantic	3	13	.188	6	20	.231
Jacksonville St.	3	13	.188	8	18	.308

Conf. Tourney Final: Samford 89, Central Florida 61.
*NCAA Tourney (0-1): Samford (0-1).

West Coast Conference

Team	Conference			Overall		
	W	L	Pct	W	L	Pct
*Gonzaga	12	2	.857	28	7	.800
†Pepperdine	9	5	.643	19	13	.594
San Diego	9	5	.643	18	9	.667
Santa Clara	8	6	.571	14	15	.483
Loyola Marymount	6	8	.429	11	16	.407
St. Mary's-CA	5	9	.357	13	18	.419
San Francisco	4	10	.286	12	18	.400
Portland	3	11	.214	9	18	.333

Conf. Tourney Final: Gonzaga 91, Santa Clara 66.
*NCAA Tourney (3-1): Gonzaga (3-1).
†NIT (0-1): Pepperdine (0-1).

Best in Show

Conferences with at least two wins in the 1999 NCAA's; number of tournament teams in parentheses.

	W-L		W-L
Big Ten (7)	13-7	WAC (3)	3-3
Big East (5)	10-4	Atlantic 10 (3)	3-3
SEC (6)	10-6	Missouri Valley (3)	3-3
ACC (3)	7-3	Mid American (2)	2-2
Big 12 (5)	4-5	Conference USA (4)	2-4
West Coast (1)	3-1		

Western Athletic Conference

Pacific

	Conference			Overall		
Pacific	W	L	Pct	W	L	Pct
*Utah	14	0	1.00	28	5	.848
*New Mexico	9	5	.643	25	9	.735
†Fresno St.	9	5	.643	21	12	.636
UTEP	8	6	.571	16	12	.571
Brigham Young	6	8	.429	12	16	.429
San Jose St.	5	9	.357	12	16	.429
Hawaii	3	11	.214	6	20	.231
San Diego St.	2	12	.143	4	22	.154

Mountain

	Conference			Overall		
Mountain	W	L	Pct	W	L	Pct
†UNLV	9	5	.643	16	13	.552
*Tulsa	9	5	.643	23	10	.697
Rice	8	6	.571	18	10	.643
†TCU	7	7	.500	21	11	.656
SMU	7	7	.500	15	15	.500
†Colorado St.	7	7	.500	18	10	.643
†Wyoming	7	7	.500	18	10	.643
Air Force	2	12	.143	10	16	.385

Conf. Tourney Final: Utah 60, New Mexico 45.
*NCAA Tourney (3-3): Utah (1-1), New Mexico (1-1), Tulsa (1-1).
†NIT (5-5): Fresno St. (0-1), UNLV (0-1), TCU (2-1), Colorado St. (2-1), Wyoming (1-1).

Division I Independent

	W	L	Pct
Belmont	14	13	.519
Denver	10	17	.370
Texas-Pan American	5	22	.185

Annual Awards

Player of the Year

Elton Brand, Duke.....AP, NABC, *TSN*, USBWA, Naismith, Wooden

Wooden Award Voting

Presented since 1977 by the Los Angeles Athletic Club and named after the former Purdue All-America and UCLA coach John Wooden. Voting done by 1,038-member panel of national media; candidates must have a cumulative college grade point average of 2.0 (out of 4.0) and be making progress toward graduation.

		Cl	Pos	Pts
1	Elton Brand, Duke	So.	C	4312
2	Andre Miller, Utah	Sr.	G	3616
3	Wally Szczerbiak, Miami-OH	Sr.	F	3108
4	Mateen Cleaves, Michigan St.	Sr.	G	2964
5	Richard Hamilton, UConn	Jr.	G	2865
6	Jason Terry, Arizona	Sr.	G	2745
7	Trajan Langdon, Duke	Sr.	G	2069
8	Chris Porter, Auburn	Jr.	F	1437
9	Evan Eschmeyer, Northwestern	Sr.	C	1127
10	Scott Padgett, Kentucky	Sr.	F	1048

Div. II and III Annual Awards

Awarded by the National Association of Basketball Coaches.

Players of the Year
Div. II ....Antonio Garcia, Ky. Wesleyan
Div. III.........Merrill Breunson, WI-Platteville
Coaches of the Year
Div. II ....Ray Harper, Ky. Wesleyan
Div. III.........Bo Ryan, WI-Platteville
NAIA..........Kim Elders, Cornerstone (Mich.)
JuCo..........Ryan Cross, Barton County (Kan.)

Coaches of the Year

Cliff Ellis, Auburn..........................AP, USBWA
Mike Krzyzewski, Duke.................NABC, Naismith
Jim O'Brien, Ohio St...............................NABC
Note: Krzyzewski and O'Brien shared the NABC Coach of the Year Award.

Consensus All-America Team

The NCAA Division I players cited most frequently by the following All-America selectors: AP, U.S. Basketball Writers, National Assn. of Basketball Coaches and Wooden Award Committee. (*) indicates unanimous first team selection.

First Team

	Class	Hgt	Pos
Elton Brand, Duke*	So.	6-8	C
Richard Hamilton, UConn*	Jr.	6-6	F/G
Andre Miller, Utah*	Sr.	6-2	G
Mateen Cleaves, Michigan St.*	Sr.	6-2	G
Jason Terry, Arizona*	Sr.	6-2	G

Second Team

	Class	Hgt	Pos
Evan Eschmeyer, Northwestern	Sr.	6-11	C
Chris Porter, Auburn	Jr.	6-7	F
Wally Szczerbiak, Miami-OH	Sr.	6-7	F
Steve Francis, Maryland	Jr.	6-3	G
Trajan Langdon, Duke	Sr.	6-3	G

Third Team

	Class	Hgt	Pos
Scoonie Penn, Ohio St.	Jr.	5-10	G
Baron Davis, UCLA	So.	6-3	G
Ron Artest, St. John's	So.	6-6	G/F
Quincy Lewis, Minnesota	Sr.	6-7	F
Tim James, Miami-FL	Sr.	6-7	F

NCAA Men's Division I Leaders

Includes games through NCAA and NIT tourneys.

INDIVIDUAL

Scoring

	Cl	Gm	FG%	3FG/Att	FT%	Reb	Ast	Stl	Blk	Pts	Avg	Hi
Alvin Young, Niagara	Sr.	29	.473	65/160	.789	167	65	72	6	728	25.1	44
Ray Minlend, St. Francis-NY	Sr.	28	.465	31/121	.751	95	77	79	2	680	24.3	39
Wally Szczerbiak, Miami-OH	Sr.	32	.522	63/177	.831	272	93	39	32	775	24.2	43
Brian Merriweather, Tex.-Pan Am.	So.	27	.408	110/272	.914	72	34	56	5	641	23.7	38
Damian Woolfolk, Nofolk St.	Jr.	27	.487	46/131	.793	111	50	39	6	635	23.5	35
Quincy Lewis, Minnesota	Sr.	27	.457	53/133	.811	160	38	50	16	625	23.1	36
Jason Hartman, Portland St.	Sr.	28	.456	79/209	.812	156	51	20	7	639	22.8	35
Lee Nailon, TCU	Sr.	31	.508	4/15	.715	288	79	38	29	707	22.8	44
Maurice Evans, Wichita St.	So.	31	.461	69/164	.792	130	57	23	22	632	22.6	38
Harold Arceneaux, Weber St.	Jr.	32	.511	34/103	.758	193	57	55	50	713	22.3	39
Roberto Bergersen, Boise St.	Sr.	29	.480	71/179	.856	116	66	54	12	644	22.2	36
Robert Johnson, Rice	Sr.	28	.434	83/230	.727	120	59	25	7	617	22.0	32
Jamel Thomas, Providence	Sr.	30	.423	58/183	.754	217	63	39	11	661	22.0	38
Jason Terry, Arizona	Sr.	29	.443	76/191	.839	97	159	80	6	635	21.9	37
Damon Arnette, Fla. Atlantic	Sr.	24	.472	46/116	.698	197	43	76	7	525	21.9	32
Kevin Martin, NC-Asheville	Sr.	29	.485	28/79	.746	153	111	40	3	634	21.9	33
Jason Rowe, Loyola-MD	Jr.	28	.505	58/161	.787	136	161	95	2	612	21.9	32
Mike Pegues, Delaware	Jr.	31	.495	2/6	.782	224	85	32	16	675	21.8	38
Richard Hamilton, Connecticut	Jr.	34	.443	68/196	.833	163	91	40	9	732	21.5	39
Courtney Alexander, Fresno St.	Jr.	32	.469	50/158	.757	121	82	50	7	684	21.4	37

Rebounding

	Cl	Gm	No	Avg
Ian McGinnis, Dartmouth	So.	26	317	12.2
Todd MacCulloch, Washington	Sr.	29	345	11.9
Jeff Foster, SW Texas St.	Sr.	28	316	11.3
Chris Mihm, Texas	So.	32	351	11.0
K'Zell Wesson, La Salle	Sr.	28	301	10.8
Bud Eley, SE Mo. St.	Sr.	29	310	10.7
Quentin Richardson, DePaul	Fr.	31	327	10.5
Michael Ruffin, Tulsa	Sr.	33	342	10.4
Derek Hood, Arkansas	Sr.	34	349	10.3
Eric Dow, Denver	Sr.	27	276	10.2
Venson Hamilton, Nebraska	Sr.	33	335	10.2
Evan Eschmeyer, Northwestern	Sr.	29	292	10.1
Cal Bowdler, Old Dominion	Sr.	34	339	10.0
Kenny Thomas, New Mexico	Sr.	26	259	10.0
Darren Phillip, Fairfield	Jr.	27	268	9.9

Assists

	Cl	Gm	No	Avg
Doug Gottlieb, Oklahoma St.	Jr.	34	299	8.8
Chico Fletcher, Arkansas St.	Jr.	30	250	8.3
Ali Ton, Davidson	Sr.	25	190	7.6
Ed Cota, North Carolina	Jr.	32	238	7.4
Chris Herren, Fresno St.	Sr.	25	181	7.2
Mateen Cleaves, Michigan St.	Jr.	38	274	7.2
Prince Fowler, TCU	Sr.	32	226	7.1
Devan Clark, Southern U.	So.	28	194	6.9
Shawnta Rogers, G. Washington	Sr.	29	196	6.8
Tim Hill, Harvard	Sr.	26	172	6.6
Mark Dickel, UNLV	Jr.	29	190	6.6
Andy Bedard, Maine	Jr.	28	181	6.5
Tyris Livas, Bethune-Cookman	Jr.	27	174	6.4
Terrell Stokes, Maryland	Sr.	34	213	6.3
Lalo Rios, Texas-Pan Am	Sr.	27	169	6.3
Lamar Taylor, Va. Commonwealth	So.	31	194	6.3

Field Goal Percentage

Minimum 5 Field Goals made per game.

	Cl	Gm	FG	FGA	Pct
Todd MacCulloch, Washington	Sr.	29	210	317	66.2
Quincy Gause, Georgia St.	Sr.	23	144	221	65.2
Ryan Moss, Ark-Little Rock	Sr.	24	135	210	64.3
Elton Brand, Duke	So.	39	255	411	62.0
Damous Anderson, Florida St.	Jr.	23	115	190	60.5
Charles Gosa, N. Mexico St.	Sr.	33	199	329	60.5
David Tompkins, Yale	Sr.	26	165	275	60.0
Bud Eley, SE Mo. St.	Sr.	29	170	286	59.4
J.R. Van Hoose, Marshall	Fr.	27	149	251	59.4
Evan Eschmeyer, Northwestern	Sr.	29	180	308	58.4

Free Throw Percentage

Minimum 2.5 Free Throws made per game.

	Cl	Gm	FT	FTA	Pct
Lonnie Cooper, La. Tech	Sr.	25	70	76	92.1
Haywood Eaddy, Loyola Mary.	Sr.	21	79	88	89.8
Marcus Wilson, Evansville	Sr.	33	165	184	89.7
Jermel President, C. of Charleston	Sr.	31	94	105	89.5
Arthur Lee, Stanford	Sr.	33	140	158	88.6
Matt Sundblad, Lamar	Sr.	28	84	95	88.4
Rayford Young, Texas Tech	Jr.	25	100	114	87.7
Brandon Welsch, Robert Morris	Jr.	27	71	81	87.7
Brian Earl, Princeton	Sr.	30	77	88	87.5
Mike DeRocckis, Drexel	Sr.	29	77	88	87.5
Ronnie McCollum, Centenary	So.	28	125	143	87.4

Oklahoma St.
Doug Gottlieb
Assists

Dartmouth
Ian McGinnis
Rebounding

Washington
Todd MacCulloch
FG Percentage

Niagara
Alvin Young
Scoring

3-Pt Field Goal Percentage

Minimum 1.5 Three-Point FG made per game.

	Cl	Gm	FG	FGA	Pct
Rodney Thomas, IUPUI	Jr.	26	59	113	52.2
Ross Land, N. Arizona	Jr.	29	83	163	50.9
Brian Grawer, Missouri	So.	29	64	129	49.6
Ryan Borowicz, WI-Green Bay	Sr.	31	78	159	49.1
Alan Puckett, Citadel	Fr.	27	55	113	48.7
Kevin Worley, Canisius	Sr.	27	54	111	48.6
Scott Thomason, Pacific	Sr.	27	54	111	48.6
Tim Heskett, Oklahoma	So.	32	79	167	47.3
Nathan Jameson, NC-Greensboro	So.	27	56	119	47.1
Keith Greene, TX-Arlington	Jr.	26	65	139	46.8

3-Pt Field Goals Per Game

	Cl	Gm	No	Avg
Brian Merriweather, TX-Pan Am	So.	27	110	4.1
Shannon Taylor, E. Washington	Sr.	27	103	3.8
Alan Barksdale, Ark-Little Rock	Jr.	25	95	3.8
Josh Heard, Tenn. Tech	Jr.	27	98	3.6
Fred Warrick, Coppin St.	Sr.	29	98	3.4
Clay McKnight, Pacific	Jr.	27	90	3.3
Leslie Ballard, Radford	Sr.	28	92	3.3
Greg Buth, Dartmouth	So.	26	83	3.2
Jan-Michael Thomas, Washington	Jr.	28	89	3.2
Jamie Roberts, Tenn. St.	So.	25	78	3.1

Blocked Shots

	Cl	Gm	No	Avg
Tarvis Williams, Hampton	Jr.	27	135	5.0
Henry Jordan, Miss. Valley St.	So.	27	108	4.0
Etan Thomas, Syracuse	Jr.	33	131	4.0
Wojciech Myrda, NE Louisiana	Fr.	27	96	3.6
Calvin Booth, Penn St.	Sr.	27	95	3.5
Alvin Jones, Georgia Tech	So.	31	107	3.5
Frantz Pierre-Louis, Wagner	Sr.	27	84	3.1
Kris Hunter, Virginia	Jr.	29	88	3.0
John Bennett, Delaware	Sr.	31	93	3.0
Joel Przybilla, Minnesota	Fr.	28	84	3.0
Vincent Jones, Jackson St.	Jr.	28	84	3.0
Caswell Cyrus, St. Bonaventure	Jr.	28	84	3.0

Steals

	CL	Gm	No	Avg
Shawnta Rogers, G. Washington	Sr.	29	103	3.6
Tim Winn, St. Bonaventure	Jr.	23	81	3.5
Jason Rowe, Loyola-MD	Jr.	28	95	3.4
John Linehan, Providence	So.	30	98	3.3
Cookie Belcher, Nebraska	Jr.	32	102	3.2
Damon Arnette, Fla. Atlantic	Sr.	24	76	3.2
Pepe Sanchez, Temple	Jr.	33	101	3.1
Jason Hart, Syracuse	Jr.	33	101	3.1
Gene Nabors, Robert Morris	Jr.	27	82	3.0
Skip Victor, Navy	Sr.	27	80	3.0

Single Game Highs

Points

No		Opponent	Date
44	Lee Nailon, TCU	Gonzaga	Dec. 30
44	Alvin Young, Niagara	Siena	Feb. 8

Rebounds

No		Opponent	Date
24	Darren Phillip, Fairfield	Loyola-MD	Dec. 5

Assists

No		Opponent	Date
18	Doug Gottlieb, Oklahoma St.	Fla. Atlantic	Dec. 1

Blocks

No		Opponent	Date
12	Tarvis Williams, Hampton	N.C. A&T	Jan. 9

Steals

No		Opponent	Date
12	Richard Duncan, Mid. Tenn St.	Eastern Ky.	Feb. 20

NCAA Men's Division I Leaders (Cont.)
TEAM

Scoring Offense

	Gm	W-L	Pts	Avg
Duke	39	37-2	3581	91.8
TCU	32	21-11	2776	86.8
Siena	31	25-6	2686	86.6
Norfolk St.	27	15-12	2330	86.3
Cal Poly SLO	27	11-16	2293	84.9
Southern U.	28	21-7	2372	84.7
Maryland	34	28-6	2873	84.5
Arizona	29	22-7	2383	82.2
CS-Northridge	29	17-12	2378	82.0
Wyoming	28	18-10	2286	81.6
Auburn	33	29-4	2680	81.2
Niagara	29	17-12	2341	80.7
Maine	28	19-9	2257	80.6
Florida	31	22-9	2488	80.3
St. Francis-NY	28	20-8	2246	80.2

Scoring Defense

	Gm	W-L	Pts	Avg
Princeton	30	22-8	1581	52.7
Wisconsin	32	22-10	1766	55.2
Detroit	31	25-6	1713	55.3
Utah	33	28-5	1827	55.4
WI-Green Bay	31	20-11	1736	56.0
Northwestern	29	15-14	1655	57.1
Temple	35	24-11	2048	58.5
Col. of Charleston	31	28-3	1834	59.2
Michigan St.	38	33-5	2262	59.5
Butler	32	22-10	1921	60.0
Hofstra	32	22-10	1933	60.4
Miami-OH	32	24-8	1933	60.4
Pennsylvania	27	21-6	1640	60.7
Stanford	33	26-7	2006	60.8
Iowa St.	30	15-15	1825	60.8

Scoring Margin

	Off	Def	Mar.
Duke	91.8	67.2	24.7
Auburn	81.2	61.6	19.6
Maryland	84.5	66.4	18.1
Connecticut	77.3	61.3	15.9
Utah	71.3	55.4	15.9
Col. of Charleston	72.8	59.2	13.7
St. John's-NY	79.0	65.4	13.6
Gonzaga	78.4	65.1	13.2
Cincinnati	73.9	61.2	12.7
Kentucky	75.4	62.7	12.7
Stanford	73.5	60.8	12.7
Michigan St.	71.7	59.5	12.2
Murray St.	78.5	67.1	11.4
N. Arizona	77.2	66.7	10.4
Pennsylvania	71.1	60.7	10.4

Won-Lost Percentage

	W	L	Pct.
Duke	37	2	.949
Connecticut	34	2	.944
Col. of Charleston	28	3	.903
Auburn	29	4	.879
Michigan St.	33	5	.868
Utah	28	5	.848
Maryland	28	6	.824
Cincinnati	27	6	.818
Murray St.	27	6	.818
Delaware	25	6	.806
Detroit	25	6	.806
Siena	25	6	.806
Gonzaga	28	7	.800
Samford	24	6	.800
Stanford	26	7	.788

Field Goal Percentage

	FG	FGA	PCT.
N. Arizona	783	1497	52.3
Duke	1244	2422	51.4
Evansville	879	1739	50.5
Maryland	1044	2108	49.5
TCU	1006	2050	49.1
Samford	729	1487	49.0
Col. of Charleston	830	1702	48.8
Montana St.	821	1688	48.6
Oral Roberts	782	1625	48.1
Loyola-MD	790	1642	48.1
Weber St.	947	1978	47.9
Kentucky	1034	2163	47.8
Utah	863	1808	47.7
Utah St.	740	1551	47.7
Washington	749	1571	47.7

Field Goal Percentage Defense

	FG	FGA	PCT.
Kansas St.	729	1963	37.1
Detroit	590	1583	37.3
Northwestern	577	1548	37.3
SW Texas St.	597	1601	37.3
Old Dominion	797	2116	37.7
Navy	575	1519	37.9
Rice	606	1599	37.9
Stanford	719	1894	38.0
Kentucky	823	2162	38.1
Cincinnati	703	1841	38.2
Tulsa	693	1814	38.2
Tennessee	688	1797	38.3
Miami-FL	695	1810	38.4
Temple	698	1812	38.5
Connecticut	828	2141	38.7

Rebound Margin

	Off	Def	Mar
Navy	.43.6	33.7	10.0
Michigan St.	.36.3	27.1	9.2
Auburn	.44.0	34.8	9.2
North Carolina	.39.9	31.0	8.9
Duke	.42.2	33.4	8.8
Stanford	.40.7	32.1	8.6
Stetson	.38.5	29.9	8.6
Clemson	.38.7	30.5	8.2
Utah	.36.0	27.8	8.2
Arizona	.41.7	33.6	8.1
Kansas St.	.42.5	34.5	8.0
Alcorn St.	.45.5	37.6	7.9
Murray St.	.41.1	33.4	7.6
Lamar	.43.1	35.5	7.6
Fairleigh Dickinson	.38.3	30.9	7.4

Free Throw Percentage

	FT	FTA	Pct
Siena	.672	854	78.7
Evansville	.515	667	77.2
Western Mich.	.435	568	76.6
Miami-OH	.436	570	76.5
Robert Morris	.452	594	76.1
Detroit	.416	553	75.2
Michigan	.481	640	75.2
N. Arizona	.429	571	75.1
New Mexico	.531	707	75.1
Akron	.519	692	75.0
Brown	.335	447	74.9
Penn St.	.373	500	74.6
Maine	.437	590	74.1
Wisconsin	.413	558	74.0
Princeton	.335	453	74.0

3-point FG Percentage

	3PT	3PTA	Pct
Northern Arizona	.243	546	44.5
WI-Green Bay	.219	521	42.0
Evansville	.229	563	40.7
IUPUI	.165	407	40.5
Gonzaga	.291	730	39.9
Canisius	.153	385	39.7
Duke	.293	739	39.6
Pennsylvania	.208	529	39.3
Lamar	.190	485	39.2
Texas Tech	.178	455	39.1
Montana St.	.224	576	38.9
Northern Iowa	.167	430	38.8
TCU	.228	588	38.8
Oklahoma	.274	707	38.8
Morehead St.	.209	545	38.3

3-point FG Made Per Game

	Gm	No	Avg
Cal Poly SLO	.27	255	9.4
Florida	.31	289	9.3
Samford	.30	278	9.3
Air Force	.26	233	9.0
Portland St.	.28	250	8.9
E. Washington	.27	241	8.9
Arkansas	.34	296	8.7
St. Mary's-CA	.31	267	8.6
Creighton	.31	263	8.5
Troy St.	.27	229	8.5
N. Arizona	.29	243	8.4
Pacific	.27	226	8.4
Vanderbilt	.29	242	8.3
Gonzaga	.35	291	8.3
Oklahoma	.33	274	8.3

Underclassmen in NBA Draft

Sixteen Division I players (7 juniors, 8 sophomores and 1 freshman), 2 high school seniors, 4 players from overseas, 3 junior college players, 1 Division II junior and 1 Division II sophomore forfeited the remainder of their college eligibility and declared for the 1999 NBA Draft which took place at the MCI Center in Washington, D.C. on June 23.

Players are listed in alphabetical order; first round selections in **bold** type, high school players in *italics*.

	Cl	Drafted by	Overall Pick
Ron Artest, St. John's	So.	Chicago	16
William Avery, Duke	So.	Minnesota	14
Jonathan Bender, Picayune			
(Miss.)	HS	Toronto	5
Carl Boyd, California	Jr.	Not drafted	—
Elton Brand, Duke	So.	Chicago	1
Nikola Dacevic, Limoges, France	—	Not drafted	—
Baron Davis, UCLA	So.	Charlotte	3
Steve Francis, Maryland	Jr.	Vancouver	2
Dwayne Franklin, Shaw (Div. II)	So.	Not drafted	—
Dion Glover, Georgia Tech	So.	Atlanta	20
Richard Hamilton, UConn	Jr.	Washington	7
Rico Harris, CS-Northridge	Jr.	Not drafted	—
Hrvoje Henjak, Split, Croatia	—	Not drafted	—
Kendric Johnson, West Hills Coll.	Fr.	Not drafted	—
Jumaine Jones, Georgia	So.	Atlanta	27
Shawn Kenney, Cleveland St.	So.	Not drafted	—
A. Kirilenko, CSKA Moscow	—	Utah	24
Corey Maggette, Duke	Fr.	Seattle	13
Shawn Marion, UNLV	Jr.	Phoenix	9
Michael Maxwell, W. N. Mexico	Jr.	Not drafted	—
Greg Minor, CS-Northridge	Jr.	Not drafted	—
Lamar Odom, Rhode Island	So.	LA Clippers	4
Josko Poljak, Split, Croatia	—	Not drafted	—
Alek Redojevic, Barton CC	So.	Toronto	12
Gene Shipley, San Jose City Coll.	Fr.	Not drafted	—
Leon Smith, King HS (Illinois)	HS	San Antonio	29
Albert White, Missouri	Jr.	Not drafted	—

Note: Harold Arceneaux (Weber St.), Edwin Daniels (UNLV), Giorgos Diamantopolous (Greece), Antonis Fotsis (Greece), DeeAndre Hullett (College of the Sequoias), Guilherme Joanoni (Brazil), Lamont Long (New Mexico), Jamaal Magloire (Kentucky), Olumide Oyedeji (Nigeria), Igor Rakocevic (Yugoslavia), Tyron Triplett (Tallahassee CC) and Kostas Tsartsaris (Greece) declared for the draft and then withdrew their names before the June 23 deadline.

High School Players to enter NBA

Player	Pro career
Tony Kappen	1946-47
Connie Simmons	1946-56
Joe Graboski	1948-62
Reggie Harding	1963-68
Moses Malone	1974-95
Bill Willoughby	1975-84
Darryl Dawkins	1975-89
Kevin Garnett	1995—
Kobe Bryant	1996—
Jermaine O'Neal	1996—
Tracy McGrady	1997—
Al Harrington	1998—
Rashard Lewis	1998—
Korleone Young	1998—

Note: Kappen started out in the American Basketball League and Malone started out in the American Basketball Association. Because they enrolled in a college, Lloyd Daniels (Mount St. Antonio), Thomas Hamilton (Pittsburgh) and Shawn Kemp (Kentucky/Trinity Valley CC) were not included on this list.

Other 1999 Men's Tournaments

NIT Tournament

The 62nd annual National Invitation Tournament had a 32-team field. First three rounds played on home courts of higher seeded teams. Semifinal, Third Place and Championship games played March 23-25 at Madison Square Garden in New York City.

1st Round

at Rutgers 58	Hofstra 45
at Clemson 77	Georgia 57
at Old Dominion 75	Seton Hall 56
Butler 51	at Bradley 50
Xavier 86	at Toledo 84
at Wake Forest 73	Alabama 57
at N.C. State 82	Providence 76
at Princeton 54	Georgetown 47
at California 79	Fresno St. 71
at DePaul 69	Northwestern 64
at Colorado 65	Pepperdine 61
at Colorado St. 69	Mississippi St.56
at Oregon 67	Georgia Tech 64
at Wyoming 81	USC 77
at Nebraska 68	UNLV 53
TCU 72	at Kansas St. 71

2nd Round

at Butler 75	Old Dominion 62
at Xavier 87	Wake Forest 76
Princeton 61	at N.C. State 58
at TCU 101	Nebraska 89
at Oregon 93	Wyoming 72
at Colorado St. 86	Colorado 76
Clemson 78	at Rutgers 68
California 58	at DePaul 57

Quarterfinals

at Clemson 89	Butler 69
at Xavier 65	Princeton 58
at California 71	Colorado St. 62
Oregon 77	at TCU 68

Semifinals

Clemson 79	Xavier 76
California 85	Oregon 69

Third Place

Xavier 106 .... Oregon 75

Championship

California 61 .... Clemson 60

NCAA Division II

The eight regional winners of the 48-team field: NORTHEAST— St. Rose, N.Y. (26-5); EAST— Salem-Teikyo, W. Va. (28-3); SOUTH ATLANTIC— Lander, S.C. (25-6); SOUTH— Florida Southern (27-7); SOUTH CENTRAL— Truman State, Mo. (25-6); GREAT LAKES— Kentucky Wesleyan (32-2); NORTH CENTRAL— Metropolitan State, Colo. (26-5); WEST— CS-San Bernardino (23-7).

The Elite Eight was played March 17-20, at the Commonwealth Convention Center in Louisville, Ky. There was no Third Place game.

Quarterfinals

Metropolitan St. 89	Salem-Teikyo 84
Truman St. 106	St. Rose 101 3 OT
Florida Southern 84	CS-San Bernardino 69
Ky. Wesleyan 74	Lander 69

Semifinals

Metropolitan St. 69	Truman St. 65
Ky. Wesleyan 87	Florida Southern 67

Championship

Ky. Wesleyan 75 .... Metropolitan St. 60

NCAA Division III

Sixty-four teams played into the 32-team Division III field. The four sectional winners: ATLANTIC— William Paterson, N.J. (19-10); NORTHEAST— Connecticut College (27-0); SOUTH— Hampden-Sydney. (28-2); MIDWEST— Wisconsin-Platteville (28-2).

The Final Four was played March 19-20, at Salem Civic Center in Salem, Va.

Semifinals

WI-Platteville 75	William Paterson 51
Hampden-Sydney 74	Connecticut College 58

Third Place

Connecticut College 92 .... Wm. Paterson 83

Championship

WI-Platteville 76 .... Hampden-Sydney 75 (2 OT)

NAIA Division I

The quarterfinalists, in alphabetical order, after two rounds of the 32-team NAIA tournament: Azusa Pacific, Calif. (30-5); Biola, Calif. (29-7); Concordia, Calif. (83-67); Life, Ga. (35-10); Mobile, Ala. (32-5); Oklahoma Baptist (31-6); Union, Tenn. (35-2); Westmont, Calif. (28-5).

All tournament games played, March 16-22, at the Donald W. Reynolds Center in Tulsa, Okla. There was no Third Place game.

Quarterfinals: Mobile def. Biola, 71-59; Westmont def. Oklahoma Baptist, 67-54; Azusa Pacific def. Union, 85-77; Life def. Concordia, 83-67.

Semifinals: Mobile def. Westmont, 71-63; Life def. Azusa Pacific, 77-71.

Championship: Life def. Mobile, 63-60.

NAIA Division II

The semifinalists, in alphabetical order, after three rounds of the 32-team NAIA tournament: Berea College, Ky. (24-6); Bethel College, Ind. (33-5); Cornerstone College, Mich. (35-3); Mount Senario College, Wisc. (24-12).

All tournament games played, March 10-16, at Nampa, Idaho. There was no Third Place game.

Semifinals: Cornerstone def. Berea, 100-85; Bethel def. Mt. Senario, 90-72.

Championship: Cornerstone def. Bethel, 113-109.

Purdue Done It

by Mimi Griffin

Although it was generally predicted that, in 1999, Tennessee would easily defend their national title, this season was expected to be one of overall parity. Eleven of the preseason's top 15 teams had at least four starters returning. These teams were loaded with talent and experience. But it was chemistry that was the determining component to success during the 1998-99 season. This is the quality that sets teams apart when talent and experience are equally distributed.

Carolyn Peck's Purdue Boilermakers had great chemistry. This team almost always faced a disadvantage in height or quickness, yet they continually found a way to win. They were a patient team that operated effectively in the half court and always seized the opportunity to run when available. They were tenacious on defense, making up in intensity and effort what they lacked in other physical attributes.

This team was a "throwback," they didn't have the best collection of athletes on the floor but they had the best basketball players. Two seniors that comprised the best backcourt in the nation, Stephanie White-McCarty and Ukari Figgs, led them. These two players operated as coaches on the floor, calling plays and switching defenses to exploit their opponent's weaknesses.

White-McCarty has often been compared to Larry Bird, and rightfully so. She has an uncanny sense of timing and positioning and was one of the most efficient and fundamental players in all of college basketball this season. She contributed exactly what her team needed at all times whether it was points, rebounds, assists or even just encouragement.

It didn't take White-McCarty and Purdue long to establish themselves this season. In their first game of the year their victim was the No. 1 ranked Lady Vols of Tennessee. The Lady Vols had just come off an undefeated season, won a third straight national championship (their sixth in 12 years) and had everyone coming back from a team that was labeled the best of all time. Their fourth consecutive national championship would be a cakewalk, right? Wrong! Tennessee never attained the consistent excellence they displayed during the previous year. The pressure of expectation was stifling.

They found the regular season and all the resulting hype from the previous season to be a nuisance. They waited with great anticipation for the time of the year that really mattered, the month of March. Once the postseason began however, it was hard to just "flick the switch" to turn up the intensity and sharpen the consistency. Their trademark pressure defense lacked the ferocity of previous years and their inability to be effective in the half court, due to a lack of perimeter scorers, was exposed by Duke in the East Regional Final.

San Jose

Duke was another team that struggled with the pressure of expectation. The Blue Devils returned all five starters from the previous year yet lost three of their first four games because of injury problems. They used mental imagery to get them through the tough times and help them maintain their composure, confidence and chemistry. Their efforts and their focus on teamwork paid off as Duke won a berth in the Final Four for the first time in the program's history.

Another team with a noteworthy performance this season was Louisiana Tech. Although the team had incredible talent, they sometimes lacked leadership and direction. The real turning point came during the weekend of the Connecticut game in Ruston, La. It was the 25th anniversary of women's basketball at Tech and many of the alums attended the game and talked with the team about the "Tech Tradition."

Purdue's win over Tennessee early in the season reverberated throughout the women's basketball world. It served notice to dozens of teams that anything was possible. Forty-one different teams shared space in the Top 25 during the year, a record number. As we begin to see new and different teams at the Final Four in the coming years, the magnitude of Tennessee's accomplishment of three consecutive national championships will gain even greater clarity. It's a feat that won't soon be repeated. ∎

Mimi Griffin is ESPN's Women's college basketball analyst.

Final Regular Season AP Women's Top 25 Poll

Taken **before** start of NCAA tournament.

The sportswriters & broadcasters poll: first place votes in parentheses; records through Sunday, February 28, 1999; total points (based on 25 for 1st, 24 for 2nd, etc.); record in NCAA tourney and team lost to; head coach (career years and record including 1999 postseason), and preseason ranking. Teams in **bold** type went on to reach the NCAA Final Four.

		Feb. 28 Record	Points	NCAA Recap	Head Coach	Preseason Rank
1	**Purdue** (37)	27-1	1020	6-0	Carolyn Peck (2 yrs: 57-11)	5
2	Tennessee (2)	28-2	983	3-1 (Duke)	Pat Summitt (25 yrs: 695-146)	1
3	**Louisiana Tech** (1)	24-2	945	4-1 (Purdue)	Leon Barmore (17 yrs: 489-74)	2
4	Colorado St. (1)	29-1	899	2-1 (UCLA)	Tom Collen (2 yrs: 57-9)	NR
5	Old Dominion	23-3	846	2-1 (Duke)	Wendy Larry (15 yrs: 329-126)	15
6	Connecticut	25-4	819	2-1 (Iowa St.)	Geno Auriemma (14 yrs: 357-94)	3
7	Rutgers	26-4	759	3-1 (Purdue)	Vivian Stringer (27 yrs: 595-183)	12
8	Notre Dame	24-3	720	1-1 (LSU)	Muffet McGraw (17 yrs: 349-151)	17
9	Texas Tech	25-3	666	2-1 (Rutgers)	Marsha Sharp (17 yrs: 406-129)	14
10	**Duke**	24-6	623	5-1 (Purdue)	Gail Goestenkors (7 yrs: 148-68)	4
11	North Carolina	26-6	569	2-1 (Purdue)	Sylvia Hatchell (24 yrs: 541-213)	10
12	Virginia Tech	26-2	564	2-1 (Tennessee)	Bonnie Henrickson (2 yrs: 50-13)	NR
13	Clemson	23-5	545	2-1 (Georgia)	Jim Davis (13 yrs: 278-124)	NR
14	**Georgia**	23-6	490	4-1 (Duke)	Andy Landers (20 yrs: 486-148)	7
15	Oregon	23-4	438	1-1 (Iowa St.)	Jody Runge (6 yrs: 120-53)	NR
16	UCLA	21-7	424	3-1 (La. Tech)	Kathy Olivier (6 yrs: 97-74)	6
17	Santa Barbara	23-3	320	1-1 (SW Mo. St.)	Mark French (20 yrs: 334-225)	24
18	Penn St.	21-7	305	1-1 (La. Tech)	Rene Portland (23 yrs: 523-180)	NR
19	Virginia	20-8	257	0-1 (Penn St.)	Debbie Ryan (22 yrs: 501-174)	8
20	LSU	20-7	250	2-1 (La. Tech)	Sue Gunter (29 yrs: 588-266)	NR
21	Iowa St.	20-6	219	3-1 (Georgia)	Bill Fennelly (11 yrs: 250-91)	22t
22	Alabama	19-10	149	1-1 (UNC)	Rick Moody (10 yrs: 219-92)	9
23	Florida International	21-5	102	0-1 (Xavier)	Cindy Russo (22 yrs: 463-172)	NR
24	Tulane	23-5	68	0-1 (St. Joe's)	Lisa Stockton (8 yrs: 185-65)	NR
25	Kansas	21-8	67	1-1 (Purdue)	Marian Washington (26 yrs: 503-276)	11

Others receiving votes: 26. **Auburn** (19-8) 63 pts; 27. **SW Missouri St.** (23-5) 50; 28. **Cincinnati** (20-9) 26; 29. **Kentucky** (20-10) 24; 30. **Illinois** (18-10) 22; 31. **Toledo** (24-5) 21; 32. **Xavier** (23-7) 12; 33. **St. Mary's-CA** (26-6) 11; 34. **Arizona** (16-9) 10; 35. **Western Ky.** (20-6) 9; 36. **Boston College** (21-7) and **Marquette** (21-8) 8; 38. **St. Joseph's-PA** (21-7) 4; 39. **Kansas St.** (14-12) and **Stanford** (16-11) 3; 41. **New Mexico** (21-5) 2; 42. **Georgetown** (18-10) and **Utah** (21-5) 1.

NCAA Women's Division I Tournament Seeds

	WEST		MIDWEST		MIDEAST		EAST
1	La. Tech (26-2)	1	Purdue (28-1)	1	Connecticut (27-4)	1	Tennessee (28-2)
2	Colorado St. (31-2)	2	Clemson (24-5)	2	Texas Tech (28-3)	2	Old Dominion (26-3)
3	UCLA (23-7)	3	Rutgers (26-5)	3	Georgia (23-6)	3	Duke (24-6)
4	LSU (20-7)	4	North Carolina (26-7)	4	Iowa St. (22-7)	4	Va. Tech (26-2)
5	Notre Dame (25-4)	5	Alabama (19-10)	5	Oregon (24-5)	5	Auburn (19-8)
6	Kentucky (20-10)	6	Arizona (17-10)	6	Toledo (25-5)	6	Tulane (24-5)
7	SW Missouri St. (24-6)	7	Mississippi St. (17-10)	7	Illinois (18-11)	7	Stanford (18-11)
8	Penn St. (21-7)	8	Marquette (21-7)	8	Xavier (23-8)	8	Boston College (21-7)
9	Virginia (20-8)	9	Kansas (22-9)	9	Florida Int'l. (23-6)	9	Ohio St. (17-11)
10	UC-Santa Barbara (26-3)	10	N.C. State (16-11)	10	Louisville (21-10)	10	Maine (23-6)
11	Nebraska (21-11)	11	Florida (19-13)	11	SMU (19-10)	11	St. Joseph's (23-7)
12	St. Mary's-CA (26-6)	12	Grambling (25-4)	12	Cincinnati (22-8)	12	Texas (16-11)
13	Evansville (19-10)	13	Northeastern (22-7)	13	Santa Clara (22-6)	13	St. Peter's (25-5)
14	WI-Green Bay (19-9)	14	Dartmouth (19-8)	14	Liberty (21-7)	14	Holy Cross (21-7)
15	CS-Northridge (21-7)	15	S.F. Austin (17-11)	15	Fla. A&M (18-11)	15	Tennessee Tech (21-8)
16	Cent. Florida (20-9)	16	Oral Roberts (17-12)	16	St. Francis (18-11)	16	Appalachian St. (14-14)

1999 NCAA BASKETBALL WOMEN'S DIVISION I

MIDWEST

First Round March 12 & 13	Second Round March 14 & 15	Regionals March 20-22
1 Purdue 68		
16 Oral Roberts 48	Purdue 55	
8 Marquette 58		Purdue 82
9 Kansas 64	Kansas 41	
5 Alabama 80		
12 Grambling 68	Alabama 56	
4 N. Carolina 64		N. Carolina 59
13 Northeastern 55	N. Carolina 70	
6 Arizona 87		
11 Florida 84	Arizona 47	
14 Dartmouth 70		Rutgers 53
7 Mississippi St. 57	Rutgers 90	
10 NC State 76		
2 Texas Tech 80	NC State 78	
15 S.F. Austin 54	Texas Tech 85	Texas Tech 42

Purdue 75 / Rutgers 62 → Purdue 77

WEST

First Round March 12 & 13	Second Round March 14 & 15	Regionals March 20-22
1 Louisiana Tech 90		
16 Central Fla. 48	La. Tech 79	
8 Penn St. 82		La. Tech 73
9 Virginia 69	Penn St. 62	
5 Notre Dame 61		
12 St. Mary's 57	Notre Dame 64	
4 LSU 78		LSU 52
13 Evansville 69	LSU 74	
6 Kentucky 98		
11 Nebraska 92	Kentucky 63	
3 UCLA 76		UCLA 77
14 WI-Green Bay 69	UCLA 87	
7 SW Mo. St. 72		
10 UC-Santa Barb. 71	SW Mo. St. 70	
2 Colorado St. 71	Colorado St. 86	Colorado St. 68
15 CS-Northridge 59		

La. Tech 88 / UCLA 62 → La. Tech 63

EAST

First Round March 12 & 13	Second Round March 14 & 15	Regionals March 20-22
1 Tennessee 113		
16 Appalachian St. 54	Tennessee 89	
8 Boston Coll. 72		Tennessee 63
9 Ohio St. 59	Boston Coll. 62	
5 Auburn 69		
12 Texas 61	Auburn 61	
4 Virginia Tech 73		Virginia Tech 52
13 St. Peter's 48	Virginia Tech 76	
6 Tulane 72		
11 St. Joseph's 83	St. Joseph's 60	
3 Duke 79		Duke 76
14 Holy Cross 51	Duke 66	
7 Stanford 58		
10 Maine 60	Maine 62	
2 Old Dominion 74	Old Dominion 72	Old Dominion 63
15 Tennessee Tech 48		

Tennessee 63 / Duke 69 → Duke 81

MIDEAST

First Round March 12 & 13	Second Round March 14 & 15	Regionals March 20-22
1 Connecticut 97		
16 St. Francis 46	Connecticut 86	
8 Xavier 85		Connecticut 58
9 Florida Int'l 71	Xavier 84	
5 Oregon 65		
12 Cincinnati 56	Oregon 70	
4 Iowa St. 74		Iowa St. 64
13 Santa Clara 61	Iowa St. 85	
6 Toledo 76		
11 SMU 91	SMU 55	
3 Georgia 73		Georgia 67
14 Liberty 52	Georgia 68	
7 Illinois 69		
10 Louisville 67	Illinois 51	
2 Clemson 76	Clemson 63	Clemson 54
15 Florida A&M 45		

Iowa St. 71 / Georgia 89 → Georgia 69

NATIONAL CHAMPIONSHIP

Duke 45 / Purdue 62

FINAL FOUR

San Jose Arena
in San Jose, Calif.
***
Semifinals: March 26
Finals: March 28

NCAA Championship Game

Duke 45

	Min	FG M-A	FT M-A	Pts	Reb O-T	A	PF
Peppi Browne	31	2-13	1-2	5	5-9	0	2
Georgia Schweitzer	18	0-3	0-0	0	0-4	1	3
Michele Van Gorp	32	7-10	1-2	15	2-5	0	4
Nicole Erickson	37	3-9	0-0	9	0-3	2	2
Rochelle Parent	21	2-3	2-2	6	2-5	4	3
Lauren Rice	20	1-5	0-0	2	1-8	0	3
Payton Black	1	0-0	0-0	0	0-0	0	0
Krista Gingrich	5	0-5	0-0	0	0-0	1	1
TOTALS	200	18-55	4-6	45	10-36	12	23

Three-point FG: 5-21 (Howard 3-6, Erickson 2-6, Browne 0-1, Schweitzer 0-1, Van Gorp 0-1, Gingrich 0-2, Rice 0-4); **Team Rebounds:** 2; **Blocked Shots:** 2 (Van Gorp, Rice); **Turnovers:** 20 (Schweitzer 6, Howard 4, Browne 3, Rice 3, Erickson 2, Van Gorp 2); **Steals:** 2 (Rice, Van Gorp); **Percentages:** 2-Pt FG (.382); 3-Pt FG (.238); Total FG (.327); Free Throws (.667).

Purdue 62

	Min	FG M-A	FT M-A	Pts	Reb O-T	A	PF
S. White-McCarty	36	6-17	0-1	12	0-1	2	3
Michelle Duhart	37	2-3	1-2	5	2-5	2	3
Camille Cooper	36	5-9	3-6	13	2-7	0	3
Ukari Figgs	40	5-15	8-9	18	0-3	1	1
Katie Douglas	36	3-9	6-8	13	2-5	2	3
Candi Crawford	4	0-0	0-0	0	0-0	0	1
Tiffany Young	3	0-2	0-0	0	1-2	0	0
Kelly Komara	8	0-0	1-2	1	0-2	1	0
TOTALS	200	21-55	19-28	62	7-25	8	14

Three-point FG: 1-13 (Douglas 1-3, Figgs 0-5, White-McCarty 0-4, Young 0-1); **Team Rebounds:** 8; **Blocked Shots:** 3 (Duhart, Cooper, Douglas); **Turnovers:** 8 (Figgs 5, Douglas 2, White-McCarty); **Steals:** 7 (Figgs 3, Duhart 2, Douglas, White-McCarty); **Percentages:** 2-Pt FG (.476); 3-Pt FG (.077); Total FG (.382); Free Throws (.679).

Duke (ACC)	22	23—	45
Purdue (Big Ten)	17	45—	62

Technical Fouls: None. **Officials:** Bob Trammell, Melissa Barlow, Teresa Dahlem. **Attendance:** 17,773. **TV Rating:** 4.3 (ESPN).

Final ESPN/USA Today Coaches' Poll

Taken **after** NCAA tournament.

Voted on by panel of 33 women's coaches and media following the NCAA tournament: first place votes in parentheses with final overall records.

		Pts			Pts
1	Purdue (33)	825	14	Virginia Tech	398
2	Duke	783	15	North Carolina	369
3	La. Tech	751	16	LSU	345
4	Tennessee	724	17	Notre Dame	298
5	Georgia	704	18	Penn St.	269
6	Rutgers	625	19	Oregon	211
7	UCLA	555	20	SW Missouri St.	99
8	Connecticut	535		Virginia	99
9	Texas Tech	506	22	Kansas	98
10	Old Dominion	500	23	UC-Santa Barbara	86
11	Iowa St.	486	24	Xavier	76
12	Colorado St.	470	25	Alabama	72
13	Clemson	462			

WOMEN'S FINAL FOUR

at San Jose Arena in San Jose, Calif. (March 26-28).

Semifinals

Duke 81	Georgia 69
Purdue 77	La. Tech 63

Championship

Purdue 62	Duke 45

Final Records: Purdue (34-1), Duke (29-7), La. Tech (30-3), Georgia (27-7).

Most Outstanding Player: Ukari Figgs, Purdue senior guard. SEMIFINAL— 40 minutes, 24 points, 10 rebounds, 4 assists, 2 blocks; FINAL— 40 minutes, 18 points, 3 rebounds, 3 steals, 1 assist.

All-Tournament Team: Figgs, forward Stephanie White-McCarty and guard Katie Douglas of Purdue, center Michele Van Gorp and guard Nicole Erickson of Duke.

Annual Awards

Player of the Year

Chamique Holdsclaw, Tennessee....AP, Naismith, USBWA, WBCA

Stephanie White-McCarty, Purdue ....Wade

Coach of the Year

Carolyn Peck, Purdue ......AP, Naismith, WBCA, Wooden

Consensus All-America Team

The NCAA Division I players cited most frequently by the Associated Press, US Basketball Writers Assn., the Women's Basketball Coaches Assn. and the Women's Basketball News Service. Holdover from the 1997-98 All-America first team are in **bold** type; (*) indicates unanimous first team selection.

First Team

	Class	Hgt	Pos
Chamique Holdsclaw, Tenn.*	Jr.	6-2	F
Stephanie White-McCarty, Purdue*	Sr.	5-11	G/F
Tamika Catchings, Tenn.	So.	6-1	F
Dominique Canty, Alabama	Sr.	5-10	G/F
Becky Hammon, Colo. St.	Sr.	5-6	G

Second Team

	Class	Hgt	Pos
Semeka Randall, Tennessee	So.	5-10	G
Amanda Wilson, La. Tech	Sr.	6-0	F
Svetlana Abrosimova, Connecticut	So.	6-2	F
Angie Braziel, Texas Tech	Sr.	6-3	C
Tamika Whitmore, Memphis	Sr.	6-2	C

Other Women's Tournaments

WNIT (Mar. 23 at Fayetteville, Ark.): Final— Arkansas def. Wisconsin, 67-64.

NCAA Division II (Mar. 20 at Pine Bluff, Ark.): Final— North Dakota def. Arkansas Tech, 80-63.

NCAA Division III (Mar. 20 at Danbury, Conn.): Final— Washington (Mo.) def. College of St. Benedict (Minn.), 74-65.

NAIA Division I (Mar. 23 at Jackson, Tenn.): Final— Oklahoma City def. Simon Fraser (B.C.), 72-55.

NAIA Division II (Mar. 16 at Sioux City, Iowa): Final— Shawnee St. (Ohio) def. St. Francis (Ind.), 80-65.

NCAA Women's Division I Leaders

Includes games through NCAA and NIT tourneys.

INDIVIDUAL

Scoring

	Cl	Gm	Pts	Avg
Tamika Whitmore, Memphis	Sr.	32	843	26.3
Jackie Stiles, SW Missouri St.	So.	32	823	25.7
Kim Knuth, Toledo	Sr.	31	788	25.4
Kristina Behnfeldt, Marshall	Sr.	26	621	23.9
Jamie Cassidy, Maine	Jr.	31	738	23.8
Linda Froehlich, UNLV	Fr.	28	657	23.5
Becky Hammon, Colorado St.	Sr.	36	824	22.9
Diana Caramonico, Pennsylvania	So.	26	590	22.7
Chari Nordgaard, WI-Green Bay	Sr.	29	653	22.5
Jess Zinobile, St. Francis	Jr.	29	653	22.5
Karalyn Church, Vermont	Jr.	28	627	22.4
Amy O'Brien, Holy Cross	Sr.	29	643	22.2
Summer Erb, N.C. State	Jr.	29	624	21.5
Leah Aldrich, Eastern Ill.	Jr.	26	556	21.4
Lisa Baswell, Jacksonville	Jr.	29	618	21.3
Hilary Waltman, St. Bonaventure	Jr.	27	575	21.3
Chamique Holdsclaw, Tennessee	Sr.	34	724	21.3
Tesha Tinsley, Northeastern	Sr.	30	637	21.2
Jackie Raterman, Bowling Green	Sr.	27	561	20.8
Megan Gardiner, Mt. St. Mary's	Sr.	28	579	20.7

Assists

	Cl	Gm	No	Avg
Dalma Ivanyi, Fla. Int'l	Sr.	30	265	8.8
Nikki Kremer, Xavier-OH	Sr.	32	275	8.6
Lisa Witherspoon, Virginia Tech	Sr.	30	246	8.2
Amy Vachon, Maine	Jr.	29	234	8.1
Amy Sheiron, Sam Houston St.	Sr.	27	215	8.0
Helen Darling, Penn St.	Jr.	30	226	7.5
Brandi McCain, Florida	Fr.	33	246	7.5
Milena Flores, Stanford	Jr.	30	219	7.3
Tasha Pointer, Rutgers	So.	33	226	6.8
Kristen Pool, UNLV	Sr.	28	191	6.8
Erica Gomez, UCLA	Jr.	34	227	6.7
Megan Stafford, UC-Irvine	Jr.	24	156	6.5
Niele Ivey, Notre Dame	Jr.	28	181	6.5
Maureen DiJulia, Hartford	Sr.	26	168	6.5
Jenny Knight, Louisville	Jr.	32	204	6.4
Gina Graziani, Miami-FL	Jr.	24	153	6.4
Letitia Hall, Southern U.	Jr.	27	172	6.4
Angela Zampella, St. Joseph's-PA	Jr.	31	193	6.2
LaTonya Blanton, Pittsburgh	Sr.	27	161	6.0
Kathy Coyner, Massachusetts	So.	30	178	5.9

Rebounding

	Cl	Gm	No	Avg
Monica Logan, UMBC	Sr.	27	364	13.5
Diana Caramonico, Pennsylvania	So.	26	333	12.8
Malveata Johnson, North Carolina	So.	28	353	12.6
AuBree Hamilton, Miami-OH	Jr.	24	285	11.9
Carolyn Harvey, St. Francis-NY	Jr.	27	314	11.6
Kate Sanford, Charleston Southern	Jr.	28	323	11.5
Kiesha Brooks, Coppin St.	So.	26	298	11.5
Amy Herrig, Iowa	Sr.	27	306	11.3
Elise James, Robert Morris	Jr.	26	287	11.0
April Cromartie, Campbell	Fr.	28	306	10.9
Megan Gibbons, Colgate	Sr.	27	295	10.9
Jess Zinobile, St. Francis-PA	Jr.	29	314	10.8
Shea Lunsford, Western Ky.	Sr.	28	303	10.8
Felicia Tarver, Prairie View	Sr.	26	281	10.8
Mercy Aghedo, St. Peter's	Jr.	31	334	10.8

Blocked Shots

	Cl	Gm	No	Avg
Teresa Jenkins, Florida A&M	Sr.	29	127	4.4
Rhonda Smith, Long Beach St.	Jr.	29	118	4.1
Ruth Riley, Notre Dame	So.	31	101	3.3
Malveata Johnson, North Carolina	So.	28	88	3.1
DeMya Walker, Virginia	Sr.	29	83	2.9

Steals

	Cl	Gm	No	Avg
Denee Rivera, Hofstra	Jr.	27	119	4.4
Nicole Kubik, Nebraska	Jr.	33	136	4.1
Termika Mitchell, Grambling	Sr.	30	119	4.0
Sheryl Klick, Niagara	Jr.	28	109	3.9
Cher Dyson, Stetson	So.	27	103	3.8

TEAM

Scoring Offense

	Gm	W-L	Pts	Avg
Connecticut	34	29-5	3100	91.2
La. Tech	33	30-3	2888	87.5
Tennessee	34	31-3	2952	86.8
Grambling	30	25-5	2600	86.7
UCLA	34	26-8	2896	85.2
UC-Santa Barbara	30	26-4	2538	84.6
North Carolina	36	28-8	2950	81.9
Georgia	34	27-7	2786	81.9
Notre Dame	31	26-5	2512	81.0

Scoring Defense

	Gm	W-L	Pts	Avg
Utah	28	21-7	1543	55.1
Princeton	27	16-11	1498	55.5
Rutgers	35	29-6	1952	55.8
Loyola-MD	28	21-7	1603	57.3
Coastal Carolina	28	18-10	1620	57.9
St. Joseph's-PA	31	23-8	1797	58.0
Morgan St.	28	12-16	1632	58.3
Northeastern	30	22-8	1753	58.4
New Mexico	31	24-7	1812	58.5
Clemson	32	26-6	1871	58.5

Scoring Margin

	Off	Def	Mar
Connecticut	91.2	61.5	29.7
La. Tech	87.5	59.2	28.4
Tennessee	86.8	63.1	23.7
UC-Santa Barbara	84.6	66.2	18.4
Old Dominion	79.3	61.0	18.3
Grambling	86.7	68.9	17.7
Colorado St.	79.3	62.6	16.6
Purdue	76.5	60.0	16.5
Notre Dame	81.0	65.5	15.5

High-Point Games

Individual

No		Opponent	Date
52	Jackie Stiles, SW Mo. St.	Baylor	12/2
46	Lisa Baswell, Jacksonville St.	Ala. A&M	12/15
44	Paula Corder, SE Mo. St.	E. Kentucky	1/2
43	Malveata Johnson, NC A&T	Coppin St.	1/2
42	J. Fambrough, Miss. St.	Northwestern St.	12/19
42	Amy Herrig, Iowa	Northwestern	2/14

THE 2000 ESPN INFORMATION PLEASE SPORTS ALMANAC

COLLEGE BASKETBALL
STATISTICS
THROUGH THE YEARS
1901-1999
NCAA'S • ALL-TIME LEADERS

SEC B
PAGE 304

National Champions

The Helms Foundation of Los Angeles, under the direction of founder Bill Schroeder, selected national college basketball champions from 1942-82 and researched retroactive picks from 1901-41. The first NIT tournament and then the NCAA tournament have settled the national championship since 1938, but there are four years (1939, '40, '44 and '54) where the Helms selections differ. Please note that the column titled Outstanding Player is not a list of the official NCAA tournament Most Outstanding Players but rather a subjective list of each team's best player over the course of the season. For a list of official tournament Most Outstanding Players turn to page 307.

Multiple champions (1901-37): Chicago, Columbia and Wisconsin (3); Kansas, Minnesota, Notre Dame, Penn, Pittsburgh, Syracuse and Yale (2). **Multiple champions (since 1938):** UCLA (11); Kentucky (7); Indiana (5); North Carolina (3); Cincinnati, Duke, Kansas, Louisville, N.C. State, Oklahoma A&M (now Oklahoma St.) and San Francisco (2).

Year		Record	Head Coach	Outstanding Player
1901	Yale	10-4	No coach	G.M. Clark, F
1902	Minnesota	11-0	Louis Cooke	W.C. Deering, F
1903	Yale	15-1	W.H. Murphy	R.B. Hyatt, F
1904	Columbia	17-1	No coach	Harry Fisher, F
1905	Columbia	19-1	No coach	Harry Fisher, F
1906	Dartmouth	16-2	No coach	George Grebenstein, F
1907	Chicago	22-2	Joseph Raycroft	John Schommer, C
1908	Chicago	21-2	Joseph Raycroft	John Schommer, C
1909	Chicago	12-0	Joseph Raycroft	John Schommer, C
1910	Columbia	11-1	Harry Fisher	Ted Kiendl, F
1911	St. John's-NY	14-0	Claude Allen	John Keenan, F/C
1912	Wisconsin	15-0	Doc Meanwell	Otto Stangel, F
1913	Navy	9-0	Louis Wenzell	Laurence Wild, F
1914	Wisconsin	15-0	Doc Meanwell	Gene Van Gent, C
1915	Illinois	16-0	Ralph Jones	Ray Woods, G
1916	Wisconsin	20-1	Doc Meanwell	George Levis, F
1917	Washington St	25-1	Doc Bohler	Roy Bohler, G
1918	Syracuse	16-1	Edmund Dollard	Joe Schwarzer, G
1919	Minnesota	13-0	Louis Cooke	Arnold Oss, F
1920	Penn	22-1	Lon Jourdet	George Sweeney, F
1921	Penn	21-2	Edward McNichol	Danny McNichol, G
1922	Kansas	16-2	Phog Allen	Paul Endacott, G
1923	Kansas	17-1	Phog Allen	Paul Endacott, G
1924	North Carolina	25-0	Bo Shepard	Jack Cobb, F
1925	Princeton	21-2	Al Wittmer	Art Loeb, G
1926	Syracuse	19-1	Lew Andreas	Vic Hanson, F
1927	Notre Dame	19-1	George Keogan	John Nyikos, C
1928	Pittsburgh	21-0	Doc Carlson	Chuck Hyatt, F
1929	Montana St.	36-2	Schubert Dyche	John (Cat) Thompson, F
1930	Pittsburgh	23-2	Doc Carlson	Chuck Hyatt, F
1931	Northwestern	16-1	Dutch Lonborg	Joe Reiff, C
1932	Purdue	17-1	Piggy Lambert	John Wooden, G
1933	Kentucky	20-3	Adolph Rupp	Forest Sale, F
1934	Wyoming	26-3	Willard Witte	Les Witte, G
1935	NYU	19-1	Howard Cann	Sid Gross, F
1936	Notre Dame	22-2-1	George Keogan	John Moir, F
1937	Stanford	25-2	John Bunn	Hank Luisetti, F

Year		Record	Winner	Head Coach	Outstanding Player
1938	Temple	23-2	NIT	James Usilton	Meyer Bloom, G
1939	Oregon	29-5	NCAA	Howard Hobson	Slim Wintermute, C
	& LIU-Brooklyn (Helms)	24-0	NIT	Clair Bee	Irv Torgoff, F
1940	Indiana	20-3	NCAA	Branch McCracken	Marv Huffman, G
	& USC (Helms)	20-3	*	Sam Barry	Ralph Vaughn, F
1941	Wisconsin	20-3	NCAA	Bud Foster	Gene Englund, F
1942	Stanford	27-4	NCAA	Everett Dean	Jim Pollard, F
1943	Wyoming	31-2	NCAA	Everett Shelton	Kenny Sailors, G
1944	Utah	21-4	NCAA	Vadal Peterson	Arnie Ferrin, F
	& Army (Helms)	15-0	**	Ed Kelleher	Dale Hall, F

Year		Record	Winner	Head Coach	Outstanding Player
1945	Oklahoma A&M	27-4	NCAA	Hank Iba	Bob Kurland, C
1946	Oklahoma A&M	31-2	NCAA	Hank Iba	Bob Kurland, C
1947	Holy Cross	27-3	NCAA	Doggie Julian	George Kaftan, F
1948	Kentucky	36-3	NCAA	Adolph Rupp	Ralph Beard, G
1949	Kentucky	32-2	NCAA	Adolph Rupp	Alex Groza, C
1950	CCNY	24-5	NCAA & NIT	Nat Holman	Irwin Dambrot, G
1951	Kentucky	32-2	NCAA	Adolph Rupp	Bill Spivey, C
1952	Kansas	28-3	NCAA	Phog Allen	Clyde Lovellette, C
1953	Indiana	23-3	NCAA	Branch McCracken	Don Schlundt, C
1954	La Salle	26-4	NCAA	Ken Loeffler	Tom Gola, F
	& Kentucky (Helms)	25-0	***	Adolph Rupp	Cliff Hagan, C
1955	San Francisco	28-1	NCAA	Phil Woolpert	Bill Russell, C
1956	San Francisco	29-0	NCAA	Phil Woolpert	Bill Russell, C
1957	North Carolina	32-0	NCAA	Frank McGuire	Lennie Rosenbluth, F
1958	Kentucky	23-6	NCAA	Adolph Rupp	Vern Hatton, G
1959	California	25-4	NCAA	Pete Newell	Darrall Imhoff, C
1960	Ohio St.	25-3	NCAA	Fred Taylor	Jerry Lucas, C
1961	Cincinnati	27-3	NCAA	Ed Jucker	Bob Wiesenhahn, F
1962	Cincinnati	29-2	NCAA	Ed Jucker	Paul Hogue, C
1963	Loyola-IL	29-2	NCAA	George Ireland	Jerry Harkness, F
1964	UCLA	30-0	NCAA	John Wooden	Walt Hazzard, G
1965	UCLA	28-2	NCAA	John Wooden	Gail Goodrich, G
1966	Texas Western	28-1	NCAA	Don Haskins	Bobby Joe Hill, G
1967	UCLA	30-0	NCAA	John Wooden	Lew Alcindor, C
1968	UCLA	29-1	NCAA	John Wooden	Lew Alcindor, C
1969	UCLA	29-1	NCAA	John Wooden	Lew Alcindor, C
1970	UCLA	28-2	NCAA	John Wooden	Sidney Wicks, F
1971	UCLA	29-1	NCAA	John Wooden	Sidney Wicks, F
1972	UCLA	30-0	NCAA	John Wooden	Bill Walton, C
1973	UCLA	30-0	NCAA	John Wooden	Bill Walton, C
1974	N.C. State	30-1	NCAA	Norm Sloan	David Thompson, F
1975	UCLA	28-3	NCAA	John Wooden	Dave Meyers, F
1976	Indiana	32-0	NCAA	Bob Knight	Scott May, F
1977	Marquette	25-7	NCAA	Al McGuire	Butch Lee, G
1978	Kentucky	30-2	NCAA	Joe B. Hall	Jack Givens, F
1979	Michigan St	26-6	NCAA	Jud Heathcote	Magic Johnson, G
1980	Louisville	33-3	NCAA	Denny Crum	Darrell Griffith, G
1981	Indiana	26-9	NCAA	Bob Knight	Isiah Thomas, G
1982	North Carolina	32-2	NCAA	Dean Smith	James Worthy, F
1983	N.C. State	26-10	NCAA	Jim Valvano	Sidney Lowe, G
1984	Georgetown	34-3	NCAA	John Thompson	Patrick Ewing, C
1985	Villanova	25-10	NCAA	Rollie Massimino	Ed Pinckney, C
1986	Louisville	32-7	NCAA	Denny Crum	Pervis Ellison, C
1987	Indiana	30-4	NCAA	Bob Knight	Steve Alford, G
1988	Kansas	27-11	NCAA	Larry Brown	Danny Manning, C
1989	Michigan	30-7	NCAA	Steve Fisher	Glen Rice, F
1990	UNLV	35-5	NCAA	Jerry Tarkanian	Larry Johnson, F
1991	Duke	32-7	NCAA	Mike Krzyzewski	Christian Laettner, F/C
1992	Duke	34-2	NCAA	Mike Krzyzewski	Christian Laettner, C
1993	North Carolina	34-4	NCAA	Dean Smith	Eric Montross, C
1994	Arkansas	31-3	NCAA	Nolan Richardson	Corliss Williamson, F
1995	UCLA	31-2	NCAA	Jim Harrick	Ed O'Bannon, F
1996	Kentucky	34-2	NCAA	Rick Pitino	Tony Delk, G
1997	Arizona	25-9	NCAA	Lute Olson	Miles Simon, G
1998	Kentucky	35-4	NCAA	Tubby Smith	Jeff Sheppard, G
1999	Connecticut	34-2	NCAA	Jim Calhoun	Richard Hamilton, G

*USC was beaten by Kansas in the West Regional of the NCAA tournament.
**Army did not lift its policy against postseason play until accepting a bid to the 1961 NIT.
***Unbeaten Kentucky turned down a bid to the 1954 NCAA tournament after the NCAA declared seniors Cliff Hagan, Frank Ramsey and Lou Tsioropoulos ineligible for postseason play.

The Red Cross Benefit Games, 1943-45

For three seasons during World War II, the NCAA and NIT champions met in a benefit game at Madison Square Garden in New York to raise money for the Red Cross. The NCAA champs won all three games.

Year	Winner	Score	Loser
1943	Wyoming (NCAA)	52-47	St. John's (NIT)
1944	Utah (NCAA)	43-36	St. John's (NIT)
1945	Oklahoma A&M (NCAA)	52-44	DePaul (NIT)

NCAA Final Four

The NCAA basketball tournament began in 1939 under the sponsorship of the National Association of Basketball Coaches, but was taken over by the NCAA in 1940. From 1939-51, the winners of the Eastern and Western Regionals played for the national championship, while regional runners-up shared third place. The concept of a Final Four originated in 1952 when four teams qualified for the first national semifinals. Consolation games to determine overall third place were held between regional finalists from 1946-51 and then national semifinalists from 1952-81. Consolation games were discontinued in 1982.

Multiple champions: UCLA (11); Kentucky (7); Indiana (5); North Carolina (3); Cincinnati, Duke, Kansas, Louisville, N.C. State, Oklahoma A&M (now Oklahoma St.) and San Francisco (2).

Year	Champion	Runner-up	Score	Final Four	———Third Place———	
1939	Oregon	Ohio St.	46-33	@ Evanston, IL	Oklahoma	Villanova
1940	Indiana	Kansas	60-42	@ Kansas City	Duquesne	USC
1941	Wisconsin	Washington St.	39-34	@ Kansas City	Arkansas	Pittsburgh
1942	Stanford	Dartmouth	53-38	@ Kansas City	Colorado	Kentucky
1943	Wyoming	Georgetown	46-34	@ New York	DePaul	Texas
1944	Utah	Dartmouth	42-40 (OT)	@ New York	Iowa St.	Ohio St.
1945	Oklahoma A&M	NYU	49-45	@ New York	Arkansas	Ohio St.

Year	Champion	Runner-up	Score	Final Two	Third Place	Fourth Place
1946	Oklahoma A&M	North Carolina	43-40	@ New York	Ohio St.	California
1947	Holy Cross	Oklahoma	58-47	@ New York	Texas	CCNY
1948	Kentucky	Baylor	58-42	@ New York	Holy Cross	Kansas St.
1949	Kentucky	Oklahoma A&M	46-36	@ Seattle	Illinois	Oregon St.
1950	CCNY	Bradley	71-68	@ New York	N.C. State	Baylor
1951	Kentucky	Kansas St.	68-58	@ Minneapolis	Illinois	Oklahoma A&M

Year	Champion	Runner-up	Score	Third Place	Fourth Place	Final Four
1952	Kansas	St. John's	80-63	Illinois	Santa Clara	@ Seattle
1953	Indiana	Kansas	69-68	Washington	LSU	@ Kansas City
1954	La Salle	Bradley	92-76	Penn St.	USC	@ Kansas City
1955	San Francisco	La Salle	77-63	Colorado	Iowa	@ Kansas City
1956	San Francisco	Iowa	83-71	Temple	SMU	@ Evanston, IL
1957	North Carolina	Kansas	54-53 (3OT)	San Francisco	Michigan St.	@ Kansas City
1958	Kentucky	Seattle	84-72	Temple	Kansas St.	@ Louisville
1959	California	West Virginia	71-70	Cincinnati	Louisville	@ Louisville
1960	Ohio St.	California	75-55	Cincinnati	NYU	@ San Francisco
1961	Cincinnati	Ohio St.	70-65 (OT)	St. Joseph's-PA	Utah	@ Kansas City
1962	Cincinnati	Ohio St.	71-59	Wake Forest	UCLA	@ Louisville
1963	Loyola-IL	Cincinnati	60-58 (OT)	Duke	Oregon St.	@ Louisville
1964	UCLA	Duke	98-83	Michigan	Kansas St.	@ Kansas City
1965	UCLA	Michigan	91-80	Princeton	Wichita St.	@ Portland, OR
1966	Texas Western	Kentucky	72-65	Duke	Utah	@ College Park, MD
1967	UCLA	Dayton	79-64	Houston	North Carolina	@ Louisville
1968	UCLA	North Carolina	78-55	Ohio St.	Houston	@ Los Angeles
1969	UCLA	Purdue	92-72	Drake	North Carolina	@ Louisville
1970	UCLA	Jacksonville	80-69	New Mexico St.	St. Bonaventure	@ College Park, MD
1971	UCLA	Villanova	68-62	Western Ky.	Kansas	@ Houston
1972	UCLA	Florida St.	81-76	North Carolina	Louisville	@ Los Angeles
1973	UCLA	Memphis St.	87-66	Indiana	Providence	@ St. Louis
1974	N.C. State	Marquette	76-64	UCLA	Kansas	@ Greensboro, NC
1975	UCLA	Kentucky	92-85	Louisville	Syracuse	@ San Diego
1976	Indiana	Michigan	86-68	UCLA	Rutgers	@ Philadelphia
1977	Marquette	North Carolina	67-59	UNLV	NC-Charlotte	@ Atlanta
1978	Kentucky	Duke	94-88	Arkansas	Notre Dame	@ St. Louis
1979	Michigan St.	Indiana St.	75-64	DePaul	Penn	@ Salt Lake City
1980	Louisville	UCLA	59-54	Purdue	Iowa	@ Indianapolis
1981	Indiana	North Carolina	63-50	Virginia	LSU	@ Philadelphia

Year	Champion	Runner-up	Score	———Third Place———		Final Four
1982	North Carolina	Georgetown	63-62	Houston	Louisville	@ New Orleans
1983	N.C. State	Houston	54-52	Georgia	Louisville	@ Albuquerque
1984	Georgetown	Houston	84-75	Kentucky	Virginia	@ Seattle
1985	Villanova	Georgetown	66-64	Memphis St.	St. John's	@ Lexington
1986	Louisville	Duke	72-69	Kansas	LSU	@ Dallas
1987	Indiana	Syracuse	74-73	Providence	UNLV	@ New Orleans
1988	Kansas	Oklahoma	83-79	Arizona	Duke	@ Kansas City
1989	Michigan	Seton Hall	80-79 (OT)	Duke	Illinois	@ Seattle
1990	UNLV	Duke	103-73	Arkansas	Georgia Tech	@ Denver
1991	Duke	Kansas	72-65	North Carolina	UNLV	@ Indianapolis
1992	Duke	Michigan	71-51	Cincinnati	Indiana	@ Minneapolis
1993	North Carolina	Michigan	77-71	Kansas	Kentucky	@ New Orleans
1994	Arkansas	Duke	76-72	Arizona	Florida	@ Charlotte
1995	UCLA	Arkansas	89-78	North Carolina	Oklahoma St.	@ Seattle
1996	Kentucky	Syracuse	76-67	UMass	Mississippi St.	@ E. Rutherford, NJ
1997	Arizona	Kentucky	84-79 (OT)	Minnesota	North Carolina	@ Indianapolis
1998	Kentucky	Utah	78-69	Stanford	North Carolina	@ San Antonio
1999	Connecticut	Duke	77-74	Michigan St.	Ohio St.	@ St. Petersburg, FL

Note: Six teams have had their standing in the Final Four vacated for using ineligible players: 1961–St. Joseph's-PA (3rd place); 1971–Villanova (Runner-up) and Western Kentucky (3rd place); 1980–UCLA (Runner-up); 1985–Memphis St. (3rd place); 1996–UMass (3rd place).

Most Outstanding Player

A Most Outstanding Player has been selected every year of the NCAA tournament. Winners who did not play for the tournament champion are listed in **bold** type. The 1939 and 1951 winners are unofficial and not recognized by the NCAA. Statistics listed are for Final Four games only.

Multiple winners: Lew Alcindor (3); Alex Groza, Bob Kurland, Jerry Lucas and Bill Walton (2).

Year		Gm	FGM	Pct	3PTM	3PTA	FTM	Pct	Reb	Ast	Blk	Stl	PPG
1939	**Jimmy Hull**, Ohio St............	2	15	—	—	—	10	—	—	—	—	—	20.0
1940	Marv Huffman, Indiana	2	7	—	—	—	4	—	—	—	—	—	9.0
1941	John Kotz, Wisconsin	2	8	—	—	—	6	—	—	—	—	—	11.0
1942	Howie Dallmar, Stanford	2	8	—	—	—	4	.667	—	—	—	—	10.0
1943	Kenny Sailors, Wyoming	2	10	—	—	—	8	.727	—	—	—	—	14.0
1944	Arnie Ferrin, Utah	2	11	—	—	—	6	—	—	—	—	—	14.0
1945	Bob Kurland, Okla. A&M........	2	16	—	—	—	5	—	—	—	—	—	18.5
1946	Bob Kurland, Okla. A&M........	2	21	—	—	—	10	.667	—	—	—	—	26.0
1947	George Kaftan, Holy Cross	2	18	—	—	—	12	.706	—	—	—	—	24.0
1948	Alex Groza, Kentucky...........	2	16	—	—	—	5	—	—	—	—	—	18.5
1949	Alex Groza, Kentucky...........	2	19	—	—	—	14	—	—	—	—	—	26.0
1950	Irwin Dambrot, CCNY	2	12	.429	—	—	4	.500	—	—	—	—	14.0
1951	Bill Spivey, Kentucky	2	20	—	—	—	10	—	—	—	—	—	25.0
1952	Clyde Lovellette, Kansas	2	24	—	—	—	18	—	—	—	—	—	33.0
1953	**B.H. Born**, Kansas	2	17	—	—	—	17	—	—	—	—	—	25.5
1954	Tom Gola, La Salle	2	12	—	—	—	14	—	—	—	—	—	19.0
1955	Bill Russell, San Francisco	2	19	—	—	—	9	—	—	—	—	—	23.5
1956	**Hal Lear**, Temple..............	2	32	—	—	—	16	—	—	—	—	—	40.0
1957	**Wilt Chamberlain**, Kansas	2	18	.514	—	—	19	.704	—	25	—	—	32.5
1958	**Elgin Baylor**, Seattle	2	18	.340	—	—	12	.750	—	41	—	—	24.0
1959	**Jerry West**, West Virginia......	2	22	.667	—	—	22	.688	—	25	—	—	33.0
1960	Jerry Lucas, Ohio St............	2	16	.667	—	—	3	1.000	—	23	—	—	17.5
1961	**Jerry Lucas**, Ohio St...........	2	20	.714	—	—	16	.941	—	25	—	—	28.0
1962	Paul Hogue, Cincinnati	2	23	.639	—	—	12	.632	—	38	—	—	29.0
1963	**Art Heyman**, Duke	2	18	.409	—	—	15	.682	—	19	—	—	25.5
1964	Walt Hazzard, UCLA	2	11	.550	—	—	8	.667	10	—	—	—	15.0
1965	**Bill Bradley**, Princeton.........	2	34	.630	—	—	19	.950	24	—	—	—	43.5
1966	**Jerry Chambers**, Utah	2	25	.532	—	—	20	.833	35	—	—	—	35.0
1967	Lew Alcindor, UCLA	2	14	.609	—	—	11	.458	38	—	—	—	19.5
1968	Lew Alcindor, UCLA	2	22	.629	—	—	9	.900	34	—	—	—	26.5
1969	Lew Alcindor, UCLA	2	23	.676	—	—	16	.640	41	—	—	—	31.0
1970	Sidney Wicks, UCLA............	2	15	.714	—	—	9	.600	34	—	—	—	19.5
1971	**Howard Porter**, Villanova	2	20	.488	—	—	7	.778	24	—	—	—	23.5
1972	Bill Walton, UCLA	2	20	.690	—	—	17	.739	41	—	—	—	28.5
1973	Bill Walton, UCLA	2	28	.824	—	—	2	.400	30	—	—	—	29.0
1974	David Thompson, N.C. State.....	2	19	.514	—	—	11	.786	17	—	—	—	24.5
1975	Richard Washington, UCLA......	2	23	.548	—	—	8	.727	20	—	—	—	27.0
1976	Kent Benson, Indiana	2	17	.500	—	—	7	.636	18	—	—	—	20.5
1977	Butch Lee, Marquette...........	2	11	.344	—	—	8	1.000	6	2	1	1	15.0
1978	Jack Givens, Kentucky	2	28	.651	—	—	8	.667	17	4	1	3	32.0
1979	Magic Johnson, Michigan St.	2	17	.680	—	—	19	.864	17	3	0	2	26.5
1980	Darrell Griffith, Louisville	2	23	.622	—	—	11	.688	7	15	0	2	28.5
1981	Isiah Thomas, Indiana	2	14	.560	—	—	9	.818	4	9	3	4	18.5
1982	James Worthy, N. Carolina	2	20	.741	—	—	2	.286	8	9	0	4	21.0
1983	**Akeem Olajuwon**, Houston	2	16	.552	—	—	9	.643	40	3	5	2	20.5
1984	Patrick Ewing, Georgetown	2	8	.571	—	—	2	1.000	18	1	15	1	9.0
1985	Ed Pinckney, Villanova	2	8	.571	—	—	12	.750	15	6	3	0	14.0
1986	Pervis Ellison, Louisville........	2	15	.600	—	—	6	.750	24	2	3	1	18.0
1987	Keith Smart, Indiana	2	14	.636	0	1	7	.778	7	7	0	2	17.5
1988	Danny Manning, Kansas	2	25	.556	0	1	6	.667	17	4	8	9	28.0
1989	Glen Rice, Michigan............	2	24	.490	7	16	4	1.000	16	1	0	3	29.5
1990	Anderson Hunt, UNLV...........	2	19	.613	9	16	2	.500	4	9	1	1	24.5
1991	Christian Laettner, Duke	2	12	.545	1	1	21	.913	17	2	1	2	23.0
1992	Bobby Hurley, Duke	2	10	.417	7	12	8	.800	3	11	0	3	17.5
1993	Donald Williams, N. Carolina	2	15	.652	10	14	10	1.000	4	1	0	2	25.0
1994	Corliss Williamson, Arkansas	2	21	.500	0	0	10	.714	21	8	3	4	26.0
1995	Ed O'Bannon, UCLA............	2	16	.457	3	8	10	.769	25	3	1	7	22.5
1996	Tony Delk, Kentucky	2	15	.417	8	16	6	.546	9	2	3	2	22.0
1997	Miles Simon, Arizona...........	2	17	.459	3	10	17	.773	8	6	0	1	27.0
1998	Jeff Sheppard, Kentucky.........	2	16	.552	4	10	7	.778	10	7	0	4	21.5
1999	Richard Hamilton, Connecticut ...	2	20	.513	3	7	8	.727	12	4	1	2	25.5

Final Four All-Decade Teams

To celebrate the 50th anniversary of the NCAA tournament in 1989, five All-Decade teams were selected by a blue ribbon panel of coaches and administrators. An All-Time Final Four team was also chosen. Selections were actually made prior to the 1988 tournament.

Selection panel: Vic Bubas, Denny Crum, Wayne Duke, Dave Gavitt, Joe B. Hall, Jud Heathcote, Hank Iba, Pete Newell, Dean Smith, John Thompson and John Wooden.

All-1950s

	Years
Elgin Baylor, Seattle	1958
Wilt Chamberlain, Kansas	1957
Tom Gola, La Salle	1954
K.C. Jones, San Francisco	1955
Clyde Lovellette, Kansas	1952
Oscar Robertson, Cinn.	1959-60
Guy Rodgers, Temple	1958
Lennie Rosenbluth, N. Carolina	1957
Bill Russell, San Francisco	1955-56
Jerry West, West Virginia	1959

All-1970s

	Years
Kent Benson, Indiana	1976
Larry Bird, Indiana St	1979
Jack Givens, Kentucky	1978
Magic Johnson, Mich. St	1979
Marques Johnson, UCLA	1975-76
Scott May, Indiana	1976
David Thompson, N.C. State	1974
Bill Walton, UCLA	1972-74
Sidney Wicks, UCLA	1969-71
Keith Wilkes, UCLA	1972-74

All-Time Team

	Years
Lew Alcindor, UCLA	1967-69
Larry Bird, Indiana St.	1979
Wilt Chamberlain, Kansas	1957
Magic Johnson, Mich. St.	1979
Michael Jordan, N. Carolina	1982

All-1940s

	Years
Ralph Beard, Kentucky	1948-49
Howie Dallmar, Stanford	1942
Dwight Eddleman, Illinois	1949
Arnie Ferrin, Utah	1944
Alex Groza, Kentucky	1948-49
George Kaftan, Holy Cross	1947
Bob Kurland, Okla. A&M	1945-46
Jim Pollard, Stanford	1942
Kenny Sailors, Wyoming	1943
Gerry Tucker, Oklahoma	1947

All-1960s

	Years
Lew Alcindor, UCLA	1967-69
Bill Bradley, Princeton	1965
Gail Goodrich, UCLA	1964-65
John Havlicek, Ohio St.	1961-62
Elvin Hayes, Houston	1967
Walt Hazzard, UCLA	1964
Jerry Lucas, Ohio St	1960-61
Jeff Mullins, Duke	1964
Cazzie Russell, Michigan	1965
Charlie Scott, N. Carolina	1968-69

All-1980s

	Years
Steve Alford, Indiana	1987
Johnny Dawkins, Duke	1986
Patrick Ewing, Georgetown	1982-84
Darrell Griffith, Louisville	1980
Michael Jordan, N. Carolina	1982
Rodney McCray, Louisville	1980
Akeem Olajuwon, Houston	1983-84
Ed Pinckney, Villanova	1985
Isiah Thomas, Indiana	1981
James Worthy, N. Carolina	1982

Note: Lew Alcindor later changed his name to Kareem Abdul-Jabbar; Keith Wilkes later changed his first name to Jamaal; and Akeem Olajuwon later changed the spelling of his first name to Hakeem.

Seeds at the Final Four

Year	Seeds (Total)	Teams
1979	1,2,2,9 (14)	Indiana St., **Michigan St.**, DePaul, Pennsylvania
1980	2,5,6,8 (21)	**Louisville**, Iowa, Purdue, UCLA
1981	1,1,2,3 (7)	Virginia, LSU, N. Carolina, **Indiana**
1982	1,1,3,6 (11)	**N. Carolina**, Georgetown, Louisville, Houston
1983	1,1,4,6 (12)	Houston, Louisville, Georgia, **N.C. State**
1984	1,1,2,7 (11)	Kentucky, **Georgetown**, Houston, Virginia
1985	1,1,2,8 (12)	St. John's, Georgetown, Memphis, **Villanova**
1986	1,1,2,11 (15)	Duke, Kansas, **Louisville**, LSU
1987	1,1,2,6 (10)	UNLV, **Indiana**, Syracuse, Providence
1988	1,1,2,6 (10)	Arizona, Oklahoma, Duke, **Kansas**
1989	1,2,3,3 (9)	Illinois, Duke, Seton Hall, **Michigan**
1990	1,3,4,4 (12)	**UNLV**, Duke, Ga. Tech, Arkansas
1991	1,1,2,3 (7)	UNLV, N. Carolina, **Duke**, Kansas
1992	1,2,4,6 (13)	**Duke**, Indiana, Cincinnati, Michigan
1993	1,1,1,2 (5)	**N. Carolina**, Kentucky, Michigan, Kansas
1994	1,2,2,3 (8)	**Arkansas**, Arizona, Duke, Florida
1995	1,2,2,4 (9)	**UCLA**, Arkansas, N. Carolina, Okla. St.
1996	1,1,4,5 (11)	**Kentucky**, UMass, Syracuse, Miss. St.
1997	1,1,1,4 (7)	Kentucky, N. Carolina, Minnesota, **Arizona**
1998	1,2,3,3 (9)	N. Carolina, **Kentucky**, Stanford, Utah
1999	1,1,1,4 (7)	**Connecticut**, Duke, Michigan St., Ohio St.

All Time Seeds Records

All-time records of NCAA tournament seeds since tourney expanded to 64 teams in 1985. Records are through the 1999 NCAA Tournament. Note that 1st refers to championships. 2nd refers to runners-up and FF refers to Final Four appearances.

Seed	W	L	Pct.	1st	2nd	FF
1	254	75	.772	10	9	23
2	186	79	.702	5	5	11
3	124	82	.602	2	4	4
4	117	83	.585	1	1	8
5	93	85	.522	0	0	2
6	116	82	.586	2	1	3
7	67	84	.444	0	0	1
8	60	83	.420	1	1	0
9	51	84	.378	0	0	1
10	55	84	.396	0	0	0
11	35	80	.304	0	0	1
12	31	80	.279	0	0	0
13	15	60	.200	0	0	0
14	15	60	.200	0	0	0
15	3	60	.048	0	0	0
16	0	60	.000	0	0	0

Collegiate Commissioners Association Tournament

The Collegiate Commissioners Association staged an eight-team tournament for teams that didn't make the NCAA tournament in 1974 and '75.

Most Valuable Players: 1974–Kent Benson, Indiana; 1975–Bob Elliot, Arizona.

Year	Winner	Score	Loser	Site
1974	Indiana	85-60	USC	St. Louis
1975	Drake	83-76	Arizona	Louisville

NCAA Tournament Appearances

App	W-L	F4	Championships	App	W-L	F4	Championships
41 Kentucky	86-36	13	7 (1948-49,51,58,78,96,98)	19 Ohio St.	35-18	9	1 (1960)
35 UCLA	75-27	15	11 (1964-65,67-73,75,95)	18 Houston	26-23	5	None
33 N. Carolina	76-33	14	3 (1957,82,93)	18 BYU	11-21	0	None
28 Louisville	48-30	7	2 (1980,86)	18 West Virginia	13-18	1	None
28 Indiana	52-23	7	5 (1940,53,76,81,87)	18 Arizona	26-17	3	1 (1997)
28 Kansas	58-28	10	2 (1952,88)	18 Cincinnati	34-17	6	2 (1961-62)
25 Villanova	37-25	3	1 (1985)	18 Iowa	25-20	3	None
25 St. John's	26-27	2	None	18 Oklahoma	22-18	3	None
25 Syracuse	37-26	3	None	18 Purdue	22-18	2	None
24 Notre Dame	25-28	1	None	17 N.C. State	27-16	3	2 (1974,83)
24 Arkansas	39-24	6	1 (1994)	17 Texas	16-20	2	None
23 Duke	65-21	12	2 (1991-92)	17 Missouri	13-17	0	None
23 Temple	27-23	2	None	17 Pennsylvania	13-19	1	None
22 Kansas St.	27-26	4	None	16 Maryland	21-16	0	None
21 Georgetown	36-20	4	1 (1984)	16 Oklahoma St.	27-15	5	2 (1945-46)
21 Utah	31-24	4	1 (1944)	16 San Francisco	21-14	3	2 (1955-56)
21 Marquette	28-22	2	1 (1977)	16 Memphis	18-16	3	None
21 Connecticut	26-21	1	1 (1999)	16 Oregon St.	12-19	2	None
21 Princeton	13-25	1	None	16 Western Ky.	15-17	1	None
20 DePaul	20-23	2	None	16 Miami-OH	6-18	0	None
20 Michigan	41-19	6	1 (1989)	16 New Mexico St.	10-18	1	None
19 Illinois	23-20	4	None				

Note: Although all NCAA tournament appearances are included above, the NCAA has officially voided the records of Villanova (4-1) and Western Ky. (4-1) in 1971, UCLA (5-1) in 1980, Oregon St. (2-3) from 1980-82, Memphis (9-5) from 1982-86, DePaul (6-4) from 1986-89, N.C. State from 1987-88 and Kentucky (2-1) in 1988.

All-Time NCAA Division I Tournament Leaders

Through 1999; minimum of six games; **Last** column indicates final year played.

CAREER

Scoring

Points

		Yrs	Last	Gm	Pts
1	Christian Laettner, Duke	4	1992	23	407
2	Elvin Hayes, Houston	3	1968	13	358
3	Danny Manning, Kansas	4	1988	16	328
4	Oscar Robertson, Cincinnati	3	1960	10	324
5	Glen Rice, Michigan	4	1989	13	308
6	Lew Alcindor, UCLA	3	1969	12	304
7	Bill Bradley, Princeton	3	1965	9	303
8	Austin Carr, Notre Dame	3	1971	7	289
9	Juwan Howard, Michigan	3	1994	16	280
10	Calbert Cheaney, Indiana	3	1993	13	279

Average

		Yrs	Last	Pts	Avg
1	Austin Carr, Notre Dame	3	1971	289	41.3
2	Bill Bradley, Princeton	3	1965	303	33.7
3	Oscar Robertson, Cincinnati	3	1960	324	32.4
4	Jerry West, West Virginia	3	1960	275	30.6
5	Bob Pettit, LSU	3	1954	183	30.5
6	Dan Issel, Kentucky	3	1970	176	29.3
	Jim McDaniels, Western Ky	2	1971	176	29.3
8	Dwight Lamar, SW Louisiana	2	1973	175	29.2
9	Bo Kimble, Loyola-CA	3	1990	204	29.1
10	David Robinson, Navy	3	1987	200	28.6

Rebounds

Total

		Yrs	Last	Gm	No
1	Elvin Hayes, Houston	3	1968	13	222
2	Lew Alcindor, UCLA	3	1969	12	201
3	Jerry Lucas, Ohio St.	3	1962	12	197
4	Bill Walton, UCLA	3	1974	12	176
5	Christian Laettner, Duke	4	1992	23	169
6	Paul Hogue, Cincinnati	3	1962	12	160
7	Sam Lacey, New Mexico St.	3	1970	11	157
8	Derrick Coleman, Syracuse	4	1990	14	155
9	Akeem Olajuwon, Houston	3	1984	15	153
10	Patrick Ewing, Georgetown	4	1985	18	144

Average

		Yrs	Last	Reb	Avg
1	Johnny Green, Michigan St.	2	1959	118	19.7
2	Artis Gilmore, Jacksonville	2	1971	115	19.2
3	Paul Silas, Creighton	3	1964	111	18.5
4	Len Chappell, Wake Forest	2	1962	137	17.1
5	Elvin Hayes, Houston	3	1968	222	17.1
6	Lew Alcindor, UCLA	3	1969	201	16.8
7	Jerry Lucas, Ohio St.	3	1962	197	16.4
8	Bill Walton, UCLA	3	1974	176	14.7
9	Sam Lacey, New Mexico St.	3	1970	157	14.3
10	Bob Lanier, St. Bonaventure	3	1970	85	14.2

3-Pt Field Goals

Total

		Yrs	Last	Gm	No
1	Bobby Hurley, Duke	4	1993	20	42
2	Jeff Fryer, Loyola-CA	3	1990	7	38
3	Glen Rice, Michigan	4	1989	13	35
4	Anderson Hunt, UNLV	3	1991	15	34
5	Dennis Scott, Georgia Tech	3	1990	8	33

Assists

Total

		Yrs	Last	Gm	No
1	Bobby Hurley, Duke	4	1993	20	145
2	Sherman Douglas, Syracuse	4	1989	14	106
3	Greg Anthony, UNLV	3	1991	15	100
4	Mark Wade, UNLV	2	1987	8	93
	Rumeal Robinson, Michigan	3	1990	11	93

SINGLE TOURNAMENT

Scoring

Points

		Year	Gm	Pts
1	Glen Rice, Michigan	1989	6	184
2	Bill Bradley, Princeton	1965	5	177
3	Elvin Hayes, Houston	1968	5	167
4	Danny Manning, Kansas	1988	6	163
5	Hal Lear, Temple	1956	5	160
	Jerry West, West Virginia	1959	5	160

Average

		Year	Gm	Pts	Avg
1	Austin Carr, Notre Dame	1970	3	158	52.7
2	Austin Carr, Notre Dame	1971	3	125	41.7
3	Jerry Chambers, Utah	1966	4	143	35.8
	Bo Kimble, Loyola-CA	1990	4	143	35.8
5	Bill Bradley, Princeton	1965	5	177	35.4
6	Clyde Lovellette, Kansas	1952	4	141	35.3

Rebounds

Total	Year	Gm	No	Avg
1 Elvin Hayes, Houston	1968	5	97	19.4
2 Artis Gilmore, Jacksonville	1970	5	93	18.6
3 Elgin Baylor, Seattle	1958	5	91	18.2
4 Sam Lacey, New Mexico St.	1970	5	90	18.0
5 Clarence Glover, Western Ky.	1971	5	89	17.8

Assists

Total	Year	Gm	No	Avg
1 Mark Wade, UNLV	1987	5	61	12.2
2 Rumeal Robinson, Michigan	1989	6	56	9.3
3 Sherman Douglas, Syracuse	1987	6	49	8.2
4 Bobby Hurley, Duke	1992	6	47	7.8
5 Michael Jackson, Georgetown	1985	6	45	7.5

SINGLE GAME

Scoring

Points	Year	Pts
1 Austin Carr, Notre Dame vs Ohio Univ	1970	61
2 Bill Bradley, Princeton vs Wichita St.	1965	58
3 Oscar Robertson, Cincinnati vs Arkansas	1958	56
4 Austin Carr, Notre Dame vs Kentucky	1970	52
Austin Carr, Notre Dame vs TCU	1971	52
6 David Robinson, Navy vs Michigan	1987	50
7 Elvin Hayes, Houston vs Loyola-IL	1968	49
8 Hal Lear, Temple vs SMU	1956	48
9 Austin Carr, Notre Dame vs Houston	1971	47
10 Dave Corzine, DePaul vs Louisville	1978	46
11 Bob Houbregs, Washington vs Seattle	1953	45
Austin Carr, Notre Dame vs Iowa	1970	45
Bo Kimble, Loyola-CA vs New Mexico St.	1990	45
14 Seven players tied with 44 each.		

Rebounds

Total	Year	No
1 Fred Cohen, Temple vs UConn	1956	34
2 Nate Thurmond, Bowl. Green vs Miss. St.	1963	31
3 Jerry Lucas, Ohio St. vs Kentucky	1961	30
4 Toby Kimball, UConn vs St. Joseph's-PA	1965	29
5 Elvin Hayes, Houston vs Pacific	1966	28

Assists

Total	Year	No
1 Mark Wade, UNLV vs Indiana	1987	18
2 Sam Crawford, N. Mexico St. vs Nebraska	1993	16
3 Kenny Patterson, DePaul vs Syracuse	1985	15
4 Keith Smart, Indiana vs Auburn	1987	15
5 Five players tied with 14 each.		

SINGLE FINAL FOUR GAME

Letters in the **Year** column indicate the following: C for Consolation Game, F for Final and S for Semifinal.

Scoring

Points	Year	Pts
1 Bill Bradley, Princeton vs Wichita St	1965-C	58
2 Hal Lear, Temple vs SMU	1956-C	48
3 Bill Walton, UCLA vs Memphis St	1973-F	44
4 Bob Houbregs, Washington vs LSU	1953-C	42
Jack Egan, St. Joseph's-PA vs Utah	1961-C	42*
Gail Goodrich, UCLA vs Michigan	1965-C	42
7 Jack Givens, Kentucky vs Duke	1978-F	41
8 Oscar Robertson, Cincinnati vs L'ville	1959-C	39
Al Wood, N. Carolina vs Virginia	1981-S	39
10 Jerry West, West Va. vs Louisville	1959-S	38
Jerry Chambers, Utah vs Texas Western	1966-S	38
Freddie Banks, UNLV vs Indiana	1987-S	38

*Four overtimes.

Rebounds

Total	Year	No
1 Bill Russell, San Francisco vs Iowa	1956-F	27
2 Elvin Hayes, Houston vs UCLA	1967-S	24
3 Bill Russell, San Francisco vs SMU	1956-S	23
4 Four players tied with 22 each.		

Assists

Total	Year	No
1 Mark Wade, UNLV vs Indiana	1987-S	18
2 Rumeal Robinson, Michigan vs Illinois	1989-S	12
3 Michael Jackson, G'town vs St. John's	1985-S	11
4 Milt Wagner, Louisville vs LSU	1986-S	11
5 Rumeal Robinson, Mich. vs Seton Hall	1989-F	11*

*Overtime.

Teams in Both NCAA and NIT

Fourteen teams played in both the NCAA and NIT tournaments from 1940-52. Colorado (1940), Utah (1944), Kentucky (1949) and BYU (1951) won one of the titles, while CCNY won two in 1950, beating Bradley in both championship games.

Year	NIT	NCAA
1940 Colorado	**Won Final**	Lost 1st Rd
Duquesne	Lost Final	Lost 2nd Rd
1944 Utah	Lost 1st Rd	**Won Final**
1949 Kentucky	Lost 2nd Rd	**Won Final**
1950 CCNY	**Won Final**	**Won Final**
Bradley	Lost Final	Lost Final
1951 BYU	**Won Final**	Lost 2nd Rd
St. John's	Lost 3rd Rd	Lost 2nd Rd
N.C. State	Lost 2nd Rd	Lost 2nd Rd
Arizona	Lost 2nd Rd	Lost 1st Rd
1952 St. John's	Lost Final	Lost 2nd Rd
Dayton	Lost 1st Rd	Lost Final
Duquesne	Lost 2nd Rd	Lost 2nd Rd
Saint Louis	Lost 2nd Rd	Lost 2nd Rd

Most Popular Final Four Sites

The NCAA has staged its Men's Division I championship—the Final Two (1939-51) and Final Four (since 1952)—at 31 different arenas and indoor stadiums in 27 different cities. The following facilities have all hosted the event more than once. Note that the RCA Dome was scheduled to host the Final Four again in 2000.

No	Arena	Years
9	Municipal Auditorium (KC)	1940-42, 53-55, 57, 61, 64
7	Madison Sq. Garden (NYC)	1943-48, 50
6	Freedom Hall (Louisville)	1958-59, 62-63, 67, 69
3	Kingdome (Seattle)	1984, 89, 95
	Superdome (New Orleans)	1982, 87, 93
2	Cole Field House (College Park, Md.)	1966, 70
	Edmundson Pavilion (Seattle)	1949, 52
	LA Sports Arena	1968, 72
	RCA Dome (Indianapolis)	1991, 97
	St. Louis Arena	1973, 78
	Spectrum (Philadelphia)	1976, 81

NIT Championship

The National Invitation Tournament began under the sponsorship of the Metropolitan New York Basketball Writers Association in 1938. The NIT is now administered by the Metropolitan Intercollegiate Basketball Association. All championship games have been played at Madison Square Garden.

Multiple winners: St. John's (5); Bradley (4); BYU, Dayton, Kentucky, LIU-Brooklyn, Michigan, Minnesota, Providence, Temple, Virginia and Virginia Tech (2).

Year	Winner	Score	Loser	Year	Winner	Score	Loser
1938	Temple	60-36	Colorado	1969	Temple	89-76	Boston Coll.
1939	LIU-Brooklyn	44-32	Loyola-IL	1970	Marquette	65-53	St. John's
1940	Colorado	51-40	Duquesne	1971	North Carolina	84-66	Georgia Tech
1941	LIU-Brooklyn	56-42	Ohio Univ.	1972	Maryland	100-69	Niagara
1942	West Virginia	47-45	Western Ky.	1973	Virginia Tech	92-91 (OT)	Notre Dame
1943	St. John's	48-27	Toledo	1974	Purdue	97-81	Utah
1944	St. John's	47-39	DePaul	1975	Princeton	80-69	Providence
1945	DePaul	71-54	Bowling Green	1976	Kentucky	71-67	NC-Charlotte
1946	Kentucky	46-45	Rhode Island	1977	St. Bonaventure	94-91	Houston
1947	Utah	49-45	Kentucky	1978	Texas	101-93	N.C. State
1948	Saint Louis	65-52	NYU	1979	Indiana	53-52	Purdue
1949	San Francisco	48-47	Loyola-IL	1980	Virginia	58-55	Minnesota
1950	CCNY	69-61	Bradley	1981	Tulsa	86-84 (OT)	Syracuse
1951	BYU	62-43	Dayton	1982	Bradley	67-58	Purdue
1952	La Salle	75-64	Dayton	1983	Fresno St.	69-60	DePaul
1953	Seton Hall	58-46	St. John's	1984	Michigan	83-63	Notre Dame
1954	Holy Cross	71-62	Duquesne	1985	UCLA	65-62	Indiana
1955	Duquesne	70-58	Dayton	1986	Ohio St.	73-63	Wyoming
1956	Louisville	93-80	Dayton	1987	Southern Miss.	84-80	La Salle
1957	Bradley	84-83	Memphis St.	1988	Connecticut	72-67	Ohio St.
1958	Xavier-OH	78-74 (OT)	Dayton	1989	St. John's	73-65	Saint Louis
1959	St. John's	76-71 (OT)	Bradley	1990	Vanderbilt	74-72	Saint Louis
1960	Bradley	88-72	Providence	1991	Stanford	78-72	Oklahoma
1961	Providence	62-59	Saint Louis	1992	Virginia	81-76 (OT)	Notre Dame
1962	Dayton	73-67	St. John's	1993	Minnesota	62-61	Georgetown
1963	Providence	81-66	Canisius	1994	Villanova	80-73	Vanderbilt
1964	Bradley	86-54	New Mexico	1995	Virginia Tech	65-64 (OT)	Marquette
1965	St. John's	55-51	Villanova	1996	Nebraska	60-56	St. Joseph's
1966	BYU	97-84	NYU	1997	Michigan	82-72	Florida St.
1967	Southern Illinois	71-56	Marquette	1998	Minnesota	79-72	Penn St.
1968	Dayton	61-48	Kansas	1999	California	61-60	Clemson

Most Valuable Player

A Most Valuable Player has been selected every year of the NIT tournament. Winners who did not play for the tournament champion are listed in **bold** type.

Multiple winners: None. However, Tom Gola of La Salle is the only player to be named MVP in the NIT (1952) and Most Outstanding Player of the NCAA tournament (1954).

Year		Year		Year	
1938	Don Shields, Temple	1963	Ray Flynn, Providence	1987	Randolph Keys, So. Miss.
1939	**Bill Lloyd**, St. John's	1964	Lavern Tart, Bradley	1988	Phil Gamble, Connecticut
1940	Bob Doll, Colorado	1965	Ken McIntyre, St. John's	1989	Jayson Williams, St. John's
1941	**Frank Baumholtz**, Ohio U.	1966	**Bill Melchionni**, Villanova	1990	Scott Draud, Vanderbilt
1942	Rudy Baric, West Virginia	1967	Walt Frazier, So. Illinois	1991	Adam Keefe, Stanford
1943	Harry Boykoff, St. John's	1968	Don May, Dayton	1992	Bryant Stith, Virginia
1944	Bill Kotsores, St. John's	1969	**Terry Driscoll,** Boston College	1993	Voshon Lenard, Minnesota
1945	George Mikan, DePaul	1970	Dean Meminger, Marquette	1994	**Doremus Bennerman**, Siena
1946	**Ernie Calverley**, Rhode Island	1971	Bill Chamberlain, N. Carolina	1995	Shawn Smith, Va. Tech
1947	Vern Gardner, Utah	1972	Tom McMillen, Maryland	1996	Erick Strickland, Nebraska
1948	Ed Macauley, Saint Louis	1973	**John Shumate**, Notre Dame	1997	Robert Traylor, Michigan
1949	Don Lofgan, San Francisco	1974	**Mike Sojourner**, Utah	1998	Kevin Clark, Minnesota
1950	Ed Warner, CCNY	1975	**Ron Lee**, Oregon	1999	Sean Lampley, California
1951	Roland Minson, BYU	1976	**Cedric Maxwell**, NC-Charlotte		
1952	Tom Gola, La Salle	1977	Greg Sanders, St. Bonaventure		
	& Norm Grekin, La Salle	1978	Ron Baxter, Texas		
1953	Walter Dukes, Seton Hall		& Jim Krivacs, Texas		
1954	Togo Palazzi, Holy Cross	1979	Clarence Carter, Indiana		
1955	**Maurice Stokes**, St. Francis-PA		& Ray Tolbert, Indiana		
1956	Charlie Tyra, Louisville	1980	Ralph Sampson, Virginia		
1957	**Win Wilfong**, Memphis St.	1981	Greg Stewart, Tulsa		
1958	Hank Stein, Xavier-OH	1982	Mitchell Anderson, Bradley		
1959	Tony Jackson, St. John's	1983	Ron Anderson, Fresno St.		
1960	**Lenny Wilkens**, Providence	1984	Tim McCormick, Michigan		
1961	Vinny Ernst, Providence	1985	Reggie Miller, UCLA		
1962	Bill Chmielewski, Dayton	1986	Brad Sellers, Ohio St.		

All-Time NIT Team

As selected by a media panel (Mar. 15, 1997).

Walt Frazier, S. Illinois
George Mikan, DePaul
Tom Gola, La Salle
Maurice Stokes, St. Francis-PA
Ralph Beard, Kentucky

All-Time Winningest Division I Teams

Top 25 Winning Percentage

Division I schools with best winning percentages through 1997-98 season (including tournament games). Years in Division I only; minimum 20 years. NCAA tournament columns indicate years in tournament, record and number of championships.

		First Year	Yrs	Games	Won	Lost	Tied	Pct	NCAA Tourney Yrs	W-L	Titles
1	Kentucky	1903	96	2287	1748	538	1	.765	40	86-36	7
2	North Carolina	1911	89	2342	1733	609	0	.740	33	76-33	3
3	UNLV	1959	41	1166	846	320	0	.726	13	30-12	1
4	Kansas	1899	101	2411	1687	724	0	.700	28	58-28	2
5	UCLA	1920	80	2066	1444	622	0	.699	35	79-28	11
6	St. John's	1908	92	2297	1582	715	0	.689	25	26-27	0
7	Syracuse	1901	98	2201	1497	704	0	.680	25	37-26	0
8	Duke	1906	94	2340	1585	755	0	.677	23	65-21	2
9	Western Kentucky	1915	80	2064	1379	685	0	.668	16	15-17	0
10	Arkansas	1924	76	1997	1315	682	0	.658	24	39-24	1
11	Utah	1909	91	2139	1402	737	0	.655	21	31-24	1
12	Indiana	1901	99	2231	1453	778	0	.651	28	52-23	5
13	Louisville	1912	85	2083	1356	727	0	.651	27	48-30	2
14	Temple	1895	103	2343	1520	823	0	.649	23	27-23	0
15	DePaul	1924	76	1864	1205	659	0	.646	20	20-23	0
16	Notre Dame	1898	94	2233	1441	791	1	.646	24	25-28	0
17	Purdue	1897	101	2175	1404	771	0	.646	18	23-18	0
18	Weber St.	1963	37	1048	676	372	0	.645	12	6-13	0
19	Illinois	1906	94	2122	1358	764	0	.640	19	23-20	0
20	Penn	1897	99	2315	1475	838	2	.638	17	13-19	0
21	Villanova	1921	79	2021	1288	733	0	.637	25	37-25	1
22	New Orleans	1970	30	854	544	310	0	.637	4	1-4	0
23	Arizona	1906	94	2091	1331	754	0	.637	18	26-17	1
24	Illinois St.	1972	27	819	518	301	0	.632	5	3-5	0
25	Murray St.	1926	74	1894	1197	697	0	.632	10	1-10	0

Top 35 All-Time Victories

Division I schools with most victories through 1998-99 (including postseason tournaments). Minimum 20 years in Division I.

		Wins			Wins			Wins			Wins
1	Kentucky	1748	10	Indiana	1453	19	Illinois	1358		Arkansas	1315
2	North Carolina	1733	11	UCLA	1444	20	Louisville	1356	29	Montana St.	1298
3	Kansas	1687	12	Notre Dame	1441	21	Bradley	1355	30	Ohio St.	1291
4	Duke	1585	13	Princeton	1407	22	N.C. State	1345	31	Villanova	1288
5	St. John's	1582	14	Purdue	1404	23	Cincinnati	1338	32	Iowa	1285
6	Temple	1520	15	Washington	1402	24	Fordham	1331	33	Alabama	1283
7	Syracuse	1497		Utah	1402		Arizona	1331	34	USC	1274
8	Penn	1475	17	Western Ky.	1379	26	Washington St.	1320	35	St. Joseph's-PA	1271
9	Oregon St.	1467	18	West Virginia	1359	27	Texas	1315			

Top 28 Single-Season Victories

Division I schools with most victories in a season through 1998-99 (including postseason tournaments). NCAA champions in **bold** type.

		Year	Record		Year	Record		Year	Record
1	UNLV	1987	37-2	Kansas	1997	34-2	Bradley	1986	32-3
	Duke	1999	37-2	Kentucky	1947	34-3	Connecticut*	1996	32-3
	Duke	1986	37-3	**Georgetown**	1984	34-3	Duke	1998	32-4
4	**Kentucky**	1948	36-3	Arkansas	1991	34-4	Louisville	1983	32-4
5	Massachusetts*	1996	35-2	**N. Carolina**	1993	34-4	Kentucky	1986	32-4
	Georgetown	1985	35-3	N. Carolina	1998	34-4	N. Carolina	1987	32-4
	Arizona	1988	35-3	24	Indiana St.	1979	33-1	Temple	1987	32-4
	Kansas	1986	35-4	**Louisville**	1980	33-3	Bradley	1950	32-5
	Kansas	1998	35-4	Michigan St.	1999	33-5	Connecticut	1998	32-5
	Kentucky	1998	35-4	UNLV	1986	33-5	Marshall	1947	32-5
	Oklahoma	1988	35-4	28	**N. Carolina**	1957	32-0	Houston	1984	32-5
	UNLV	1990	35-5	**Indiana**	1976	32-0	Bradley	1951	32-6
	Kentucky	1997	35-5	**Kentucky**	1949	32-2	**Louisville**	1986	32-7
14	UNLV	1991	34-1	**Kentucky**	1951	32-2	**Duke**	1991	32-7
	Connecticut	1999	34-2	**N. Carolina**	1982	32-2	Arkansas	1995	32-7
	Duke	1992	34-2	Temple	1988	32-2			
	Kentucky	1996	34-2	Arkansas	1978	32-3			

*NCAA later stripped UMass of its four 1996 tournament victories after learning that center Marcus Camby accepted gifts from an agent. UConn was stripped of its two 1996 tournament victories because two players illegally accepted plane tickets.

Associated Press Final Polls

Taken before NCAA, NIT and Collegiate Commissioner's Association (1974-75) tournaments.

The Associated Press introduced its weekly college basketball poll of sportswriters (later, sportswriters and broadcasters) during the 1948-49 season.

Since the NCAA Division I tournament has determined the national champion since 1939, the final AP poll ranks the nation's best teams through the regular season and conference tournaments.

Except for four seasons (see AP Post-Tournament Final Polls), the final AP poll has been released prior to the NCAA and NIT tournaments and has gone from a Top 10 (1949 and 1963-67) to a Top 20 (1950-62 and 1968-89) to a Top 25 (since 1990). Tournament champions are in **bold** type.

1949

			Before Tourns	Head Coach	Final Record
1	**Kentucky**	29-1		Adolph Rupp	32-2
2	Oklahoma A&M	21-4		Hank Iba	23-5
3	Saint Louis	22-3		Eddie Hickey	22-4
4	Illinois	19-3		Harry Combes	21-4
5	Western Ky.	25-3		Ed Diddle	25-4
6	Minnesota	18-3		Ozzie Cowles	same
7	Bradley	25-6		Forddy Anderson	27-8
8	**San Francisco**	21-5		Pete Newell	25-5
9	Tulane	24-4		Cliff Wells	same
10	Bowling Green	21-6		Harold Anderson	24-7

NCAA Final Four (at Edmundson Pavilion, Seattle): **Third Place**–Illinois 57, Oregon St. 53. **Championship** –Kentucky 46, Oklahoma A&M 36.

NIT Final Four (at Madison Square Garden): **Semifinals**–San Francisco 49, Bowling Green 39; Loyola-IL 55, Bradley 50. **Third Place**–Bowling Green 82, Bradley 77. **Championship**–San Francisco 48, Loyola-IL 47.

1951

			Before Tourns	Head Coach	Final Record
1	**Kentucky**	28-2		Adolph Rupp	32-2
2	Oklahoma A&M	27-4		Hank Iba	29-6
3	Columbia	22-0		Lou Rossini	22-1
4	Kansas St.	22-3		Jack Gardner	25-4
5	Illinois	19-4		Harry Combes	22-5
6	Bradley	32-6		Forddy Anderson	same
7	Indiana	19-3		Branch McCracken	same
8	N.C. State	29-4		Everett Case	30-7
9	St. John's	22-3		Frank McGuire	26-5
10	Saint Louis	21-7		Eddie Hickey	22-8
11	**BYU**	22-8		Stan Watts	26-10
12	Arizona	24-4		Fred Enke	24-6
13	Dayton	24-4		Tom Blackburn	27-5
14	Toledo	23-8		Jerry Bush	same
15	Washington	22-5		Tippy Dye	24-6
16	Murray St.	21-6		Harlan Hodges	same
17	Cincinnati	18-3		John Wiethe	18-4
18	Siena	19-8		Dan Cunha	same
19	USC	21-6		Forrest Twogood	same
20	Villanova	25-6		Al Severance	25-7

NCAA Final Four (at Williams Arena, Minneapolis): **Third Place**–Illinois 61, Oklahoma St. 46. **Championship**–Kentucky 68, Kansas St. 58.

NIT Final Four (at Madison Sq. Garden): **Semifinals**–Dayton 69, St. John's 62 (OT); BYU 69, Seton Hall 59. **Third Place**–St. John's 70, Seton Hall 68 (2 OT). **Championship**–BYU 62, Dayton 43.

1950

			Before Tourns	Head Coach	Final Record
1	Bradley	28-3		Forddy Anderson	32-5
2	Ohio St.	21-3		Tippy Dye	22-4
3	Kentucky	25-4		Adolph Rupp	25-5
4	Holy Cross	27-2		Buster Sheary	27-4
5	N.C. State	25-5		Everett Case	27-6
6	Duquesne	22-5		Dudey Moore	23-6
7	UCLA	24-5		John Wooden	24-7
8	Western Ky.	24-5		Ed Diddle	25-6
9	St. John's	23-4		Frank McGuire	24-5
10	La Salle	20-3		Ken Loeffler	21-4
11	Villanova	25-4		Al Severance	same
12	San Francisco	19-6		Pete Newell	19-7
13	LIU-Brooklyn	20-4		Clair Bee	20-5
14	Kansas St.	17-7		Jack Gardner	same
15	Arizona	26-4		Fred Enke	26-5
16	Wisconsin	17-5		Bud Foster	same
17	San Jose St.	21-7		Walter McPherson	same
18	Washington St.	19-13		Jack Friel	same
19	Kansas	14-11		Phog Allen	same
20	Indiana	17-5		Branch McCracken	same

Note: Unranked **CCNY**, coached by Nat Holman, won both the NCAAs and NIT. The Beavers entered the postseason at 17-5 and had a final record of 24-5.

NCAA Final Four (at Madison Square Garden): **Third Place**–N. Carolina St. 53, Baylor 41. **Championship**–CCNY 71, Bradley 68.

NIT Final Four (at Madison Square Garden): **Semifinals**–Bradley 83, St. John's 72; CCNY 62, Duquesne 52. **Third Place**–St. John's 69, Duquesne 67 (OT). **Championship**–CCNY 69, Bradley 61.

1952

			Before Tourns	Head Coach	Final Record
1	Kentucky	28-2		Adolph Rupp	29-3
2	Illinois	19-3		Harry Combes	22-4
3	Kansas St.	19-5		Jack Gardner	same
4	Duquesne	21-1		Dudey Moore	23-4
5	Saint Louis	22-6		Eddie Hickey	23-8
6	Washington	25-6		Tippy Dye	same
7	Iowa	19-3		Bucky O'Connor	same
8	**Kansas**	24-3		Phog Allen	28-3
9	West Virginia	23-4		Red Brown	same
10	St. John's	22-3		Frank McGuire	25-5
11	Dayton	24-3		Tom Blackburn	28-5
12	Duke	24-6		Harold Bradley	same
13	Holy Cross	23-3		Buster Sheary	24-4
14	Seton Hall	25-2		Honey Russell	25-3
15	St. Bonaventure	19-5		Ed Melvin	21-6
16	Wyoming	27-6		Everett Shelton	28-7
17	Louisville	20-5		Peck Hickman	20-6
18	Seattle	29-7		Al Brightman	29-8
19	UCLA	19-10		John Wooden	19-12
20	SW Texas St.	30-1		Milton Jowers	same

Note: Unranked La Salle, coached by Ken Loeffler, won the NIT. The Explorers entered the postseason at 21-7 and had a final record of 25-7.

NCAA Final Four (at Edmundson Pavillion, Seattle): **Semifinals**–St. John's 61, Illinois 59; Kansas 74, Santa Clara 59. **Third Place**–Illinois 67, Santa Clara 64. **Championship**–Kansas 80, St. John's 63.

NIT Final Four (at Madison Sq. Garden): **Semifinals**–La Salle 59, Duquesne 46; Dayton 69, St. Bonaventure 62. **Third Place**–St. Bonaventure 48, Duquesne 34. **Championship**–La Salle 75, Dayton 64.

Associated Press Final Polls (Cont.)

1953

		Before Tourns	Head Coach	Final Record
1	**Indiana**	18-3	Branch McCracken	23-3
2	La Salle	25-2	Ken Loeffler	25-3
3	**Seton Hall**	28-2	Honey Russell	31-2
4	Washington	27-2	Tippy Dye	30-3
5	LSU	22-1	Harry Rabenhorst	24-3
6	Kansas	16-5	Phog Allen	19-6
7	Oklahoma A&M	22-6	Hank Iba	23-7
	Kansas St.	17-4	Jack Gardner	same
9	Western Ky.	25-5	Ed Diddle	25-6
10	Illinois	18-4	Harry Combes	same
11	Oklahoma City	18-4	Doyle Parrick	18-6
12	N.C. State	26-6	Everett Case	same
13	Notre Dame	17-4	John Jordan	19-5
14	Louisville	21-5	Peck Hickman	22-6
	Seattle	27-3	Al Brightman	29-4
16	Miami-OH	17-5	Bill Rohr	17-6
17	Eastern Ky.	16-8	Paul McBrayer	16-9
18	Duquesne	18-7	Dudey Moore	21-8
	Navy	16-4	Ben Carnevale	16-5
20	Holy Cross	18-5	Buster Sheary	20-6

NCAA Final Four (at Municipal Auditorium, Kansas City):
Semifinals—Indiana 80, LSU 67; Kansas 79, Washington
53. **Third Place**—Washington 88, LSU 69.
Championship—Indiana 69, Kansas 68.

NIT Final Four (at Madison Sq. Garden): **Semifinals**—
Seton Hall 74, Manhattan 56; St. John's 64, Duquesne 55.
Third Place—Duquesne 81, Manhattan 67.
Championship—Seton Hall 58, St. John's 46.

1954

		Before Tourns	Head Coach	Final Record
1	Kentucky	25-0	Adolph Rupp	same*
2	Indiana	19-3	Branch McCracken	20-4
3	Duquesne	24-2	Dudey Moore	26-3
4	Western Ky.	28-1	Ed Diddle	29-3
5	Oklahoma A&M	23-4	Hank Iba	24-5
6	Notre Dame	20-2	John Jordan	22-3
7	Kansas	16-5	Phog Allen	same
8	**Holy Cross**	23-2	Buster Sheary	26-2
9	LSU	21-3	Harry Rabenhorst	21-5
10	**La Salle**	21-4	Ken Loeffler	26-4
11	Iowa	17-5	Bucky O'Connor	same
12	Duke	22-6	Harold Bradley	same
13	Colorado A&M	22-5	Bill Strannigan	22-7
14	Illinois	17-5	Harry Combes	same
15	Wichita	27-3	Ralph Miller	27-4
16	Seattle	26-1	Al Brightman	26-2
17	N.C. State	26-6	Everett Case	28-7
18	Dayton	24-6	Tom Blackburn	25-7
	Minnesota	17-5	Ozzie Cowles	same
20	Oregon St.	19-10	Slats Gill	same
	UCLA	18-7	John Wooden	same
	USC	17-12	Forrest Twogood	19-14

*Kentucky turned down invitation to NCAA tournament after
NCAA declared seniors Cliff Hagan, Frank Ramsey and Lou
Tsioropoulos ineligible for postseason play.
NCAA Final Four (at Municipal Auditorium, Kansas City):
Semifinals—La Salle 69, Penn St. 54; Bradley 74, USC 72.
Third Place—Penn St. 70, USC 61. **Championship**—La
Salle 92, Bradley 76.
NIT Final Four (at Madison Square Garden):
Semifinals—Duquesne 66, Niagara 51; Holy Cross 75,
Western Ky. 69. **Third Place**—Niagara 71, Western Ky. 65.
Championship—Holy Cross 71, Duquesne 62.

1955

		Before Tourns	Head Coach	Final Record
1	**San Francisco**	23-1	Phil Woolpert	28-1
2	Kentucky	22-2	Adolph Rupp	23-3
3	La Salle	22-4	Ken Loeffler	26-5
4	N.C. State	28-4	Everett Case	same
5	Iowa	17-5	Bucky O'Connor	19-7
6	**Duquesne**	19-4	Dudey Moore	22-4
7	Utah	23-3	Jack Gardner	24-4
8	Marquette	22-2	Jack Nagle	24-3
9	Dayton	23-3	Tom Blackburn	25-4
10	Oregon St.	21-7	Slats Gill	22-8
11	Minnesota	15-7	Ozzie Cowles	same
12	Alabama	19-5	Johnny Dee	same
13	UCLA	21-5	John Wooden	same
14	G. Washington	24-6	Bill Reinhart	same
15	Colorado	16-5	Bebe Lee	19-6
16	Tulsa	20-6	Clarence Iba	21-7
17	Vanderbilt	16-6	Bob Polk	same
18	Illinois	17-5	Harry Combes	same
19	West Virginia	19-10	Fred Schaus	19-11
20	Saint Louis	19-7	Eddie Hickey	20-8

NCAA Final Four (at Municipal Auditorium, Kansas City):
Semifinals—La Salle 76, Iowa 73; San Francisco 62, Colo-
rado 50. **Third Place**—Colorado 75, Iowa 74.
Championship—San Francisco 77, La Salle 63.

NIT Final Four (at Madison Square Garden):
Semifinals—Dayton 79, St. Francis-PA 73 (OT); Duquesne
65, Cincinnati 51. **Third Place**—Cincinnati 96, St.
Francis-PA 91 (OT). **Championship**—Duquesne 70, Dayton
58.

1956

		Before Tourns	Head Coach	Final Record
1	**San Francisco**	25-0	Phil Woolpert	29-0
2	N.C. State	24-3	Everett Case	24-4
3	Dayton	23-3	Tom Blackburn	25-4
4	Iowa	17-5	Bucky O'Connor	20-6
5	Alabama	21-3	Johnny Dee	same
6	**Louisville**	23-3	Peck Hickman	26-3
7	SMU	22-2	Doc Hayes	25-4
8	UCLA	21-5	John Wooden	22-6
9	Kentucky	19-5	Adolph Rupp	20-6
10	Illinois	18-4	Harry Combes	same
11	Oklahoma City	18-6	Abe Lemons	20-7
12	Vanderbilt	19-4	Bob Polk	same
13	North Carolina	18-5	Frank McGuire	same
14	Holy Cross	22-4	Roy Leenig	22-5
15	Temple	23-3	Harry Litwack	27-4
16	Wake Forest	19-9	Murray Greason	same
17	Duke	19-7	Harold Bradley	same
18	Utah	21-5	Jack Gardner	22-6
19	Oklahoma A&M	18-8	Hank Iba	18-9
20	West Virginia	21-8	Fred Schaus	21-9

NCAA Final Four (at McGaw Hall, Evanston, IL):
Semifinals—Iowa 83, Temple 76; San Francisco 76, SMU
68. **Third Place**—Temple 90, SMU 81. **Championship**—
San Francisco 83, Iowa 71.

NIT Final Four (at Madison Square Garden):
Semifinals—Dayton 89, St. Francis-NY 58; Louisville 89, St.
Joseph's-PA 79. **Third Place**—St. Joseph's-PA 93, St.
Francis-NY 82. **Championship**—Louisville 93, Dayton 80.

1957

			Before Tourns	Head Coach	Final Record
1	N. Carolina	27-0		Frank McGuire	32-0
2	Kansas	21-2		Dick Harp	24-3
3	Kentucky	22-4		Adolph Rupp	23-5
4	SMU	21-3		Doc Hayes	22-4
5	Seattle	24-2		John Castellani	24-3
6	Louisville	21-5		Peck Hickman	same
7	West Va.	25-4		Fred Schaus	25-5
8	Vanderbilt	17-5		Bob Polk	same
9	Oklahoma City	...17-8		Abe Lemons	19-9
10	Saint Louis	19-7		Eddie Hickey	19-9
11	Michigan St.	14-8		Forddy Anderson	16-10
12	Memphis St.	21-5		Bob Vanatta	24-6
13	California	20-4		Pete Newell	21-5
14	UCLA	22-4		John Wooden	same
15	Mississippi St.	...17-8		Babe McCarthy	same
16	Idaho St.	24-2		John Grayson	25-4
17	Notre Dame	18-7		John Jordan	20-8
18	Wake Forest	19-9		Murray Greason	same
19	Canisius	20-5		Joe Curran	22-6
20	Oklahoma A&M	.17-9		Hank Iba	same

Note: Unranked **Bradley**, coached by Chuck Orsborn, won the NIT. The Braves entered the tourney at 19-7 and had a final record of 22-7.
NCAA Final Four (at Municipal Auditorium, Kansas City): **Semifinals**—North Carolina 74, Michigan St. 70 (3 OT); Kansas 80, San Francisco 56. **Third Place**—San Francisco 67, Michigan St. 60. **Championship**—North Carolina 54, Kansas 53 (3 OT).
NIT Final Four (at Madison Square Garden): **Semifinals**—Memphis St. 80, St. Bonaventure 78; Bradley 78, Temple 66. **Third Place**—Temple 67, St. Bonaventure 50. **Championship**—Bradley 84, Memphis St. 83.

1958

			Before Tourns	Head Coach	Final Record
1	West Virginia	26-1		Fred Schaus	26-2
2	Cincinnati	24-2		George Smith	25-3
3	Kansas St.	20-3		Tex Winter	22-5
4	San Francisco	24-1		Phil Woolpert	25-2
5	Temple	24-2		Harry Litwack	27-3
6	Maryland	20-6		Bud Millikan	22-7
7	Kansas	18-5		Dick Harp	same
8	Notre Dame	22-4		John Jordan	24-5
9	Kentucky	19-6		Adolph Rupp	23-6
10	Duke	18-7		Harold Bradley	same
11	Dayton	23-3		Tom Blackburn	25-4
12	Indiana	12-10		Branch McCracken	13-11
13	North Carolina	..19-7		Frank McGuire	same
14	Bradley	20-6		Chuck Orsborn	20-7
15	Mississippi St.	...20-6		Babe McCarthy	same
16	Auburn	16-6		Joel Eaves	same
17	Michigan St.	16-6		Forddy Anderson	same
18	Seattle	20-6		John Castellani	24-7
19	Oklahoma St.	19-7		Hank Iba	21-8
20	N.C. State	18-6		Everett Case	same

Note: Unranked **Xavier-OH**, coached by Jim McCafferty, won the NIT. The Musketeers entered the tourney at 15-11 and had a final record of 19-11.
NCAA Final Four (at Freedom Hall, Louisville): **Semifinals**—Kentucky 61, Temple 60; Seattle 73, Kansas St. 51. **Third Place**—Temple 67, Kansas St. 57. **Championship**—Kentucky 84, Seattle 72.
NIT Final Four (at Madison Square Garden): **Semifinals**—Dayton 80, St. John's 56; Xavier-OH 72, St. Bonaventure 53. **Third Place**—St. Bonaventure 84, St. John's 69. **Championship**—Xavier-OH 78, Dayton 74 (OT).

1959

			Before Tourns	Head Coach	Final Record
1	Kansas St.	24-1		Tex Winter	25-2
2	Kentucky	23-2		Adolph Rupp	24-3
3	Mississippi St.	...24-1		Babe McCarthy	same*
4	Bradley	23-3		Chuck Orsborn	25-4
5	Cincinnati	23-3		George Smith	26-4
6	N.C. State	22-4		Everett Case	same
7	Michigan St.	18-3		Forddy Anderson	19-4
8	Auburn	20-2		Joel Eaves	same
9	North Carolina	...20-4		Frank McGuire	20-5
10	West Virginia	25-4		Fred Schaus	29-5
11	California	21-4		Pete Newell	25-4
12	Saint Louis	20-5		John Benington	20-6
13	Seattle	23-6		Vince Cazzetta	same
14	St. Joseph's-PA	...22-3		Jack Ramsay	22-5
15	St. Mary's-CA	18-5		Jim Weaver	19-6
16	TCU	19-5		Buster Brannon	20-6
17	Oklahoma City	...20-6		Abe Lemons	20-7
18	Utah	21-5		Jack Gardner	21-7
19	St. Bonaventure	..20-2		Eddie Donovan	20-3
20	Marquette	22-4		Eddie Hickey	23-6

*Mississippi St. turned down invitation to NCAA tournament because it was an integrated event.
Note: Unranked **St. John's**, coached by Joe Lapchick, won the NIT. The Redmen entered the tourney at 16-6 and had a final record of 20-6.
NCAA Final Four (at Freedom Hall, Louisville): **Semifinals**—West Virginia 94, Louisville 79; California 64, Cincinnati 58. **Third Place**—Cincinnati 98, Louisville 85. **Championship**—California 71, West Virginia 70.
NIT Final Four (at Madison Square Garden): **Semifinals**—Bradley 59, NYU 79; St. John's 76, Providence 55. **Third Place**—NYU 71, Providence 57. **Championship**—St. John's 76, Bradley 71 (OT).

1960

			Before Tourns	Head Coach	Final Record
1	Cincinnati	25-1		George Smith	28-2
2	California	24-1		Pete Newell	28-2
3	Ohio St.	21-3		Fred Taylor	25-3
4	Bradley	24-2		Chuck Orsborn	27-2
5	West Virginia	24-4		Fred Schaus	26-5
6	Utah	24-2		Jack Gardner	26-3
7	Indiana	20-4		Branch McCracken	same
8	Utah St.	22-4		Cecil Baker	24-5
9	St. Bonaventure	..19-3		Eddie Donovan	21-5
10	Miami-FL	23-3		Bruce Hale	23-4
11	Auburn	19-3		Joel Eaves	same
12	NYU	19-4		Lou Rossini	22-5
13	Georgia Tech	21-5		Whack Hyder	22-6
14	Providence	21-4		Joe Mullaney	24-5
15	Saint Louis	19-7		John Benington	19-8
16	Holy Cross	20-5		Roy Leenig	20-6
17	Villanova	19-5		Al Severance	20-6
18	Duke	15-10		Vic Bubas	17-11
19	Wake Forest	21-7		Bones McKinney	same
20	St. John's	17-7		Joe Lapchick	17-8

NCAA Final Four (at the Cow Palace, San Fran.): **Semifinals**—Ohio St. 76, NYU 54; California 77, Cincinnati 69. **Third Place**—Cincinnati 95, NYU 71. **Championship**—Ohio St. 75, California 55.
NIT Final Four (at Madison Square Garden): **Semifinals**—Bradley 82, St. Bonaventure 71; Providence 68, Utah St. 62. **Third Place**—Utah St. 99, St. Bonaventure 93. **Championship**—Bradley 88, Providence 72.

Associated Press Final Polls (Cont.)

1961

			Before Tourns	Head Coach	Final Record
1	Ohio St.	24-0		Fred Taylor	27-1
2	**Cincinnati**	23-3		Ed Jucker	27-3
3	St. Bonaventure	..22-3		Eddie Donovan	24-4
4	Kansas St.	22-3		Tex Winter	23-4
5	North Carolina.	...19-4		Frank McGuire	same
6	Bradley	21-5		Chuck Orsborn	same
7	USC	20-6		Forrest Twogood	21-8
8	Iowa.	18-6		S. Scheuerman	same
9	West Virginia	..23-4		George King	same
10	Duke	22-6		Vic Bubas	same
11	Utah	21-6		Jack Gardner	23-8
12	Texas Tech.	14-9		Polk Robison	15-10
13	Niagara	16-4		Taps Gallagher	16-5
14	Memphis St.	20-2		Bob Vanatta	20-3
15	Wake Forest.	...17-10		Bones McKinney	19-11
16	St. John's	20-4		Joe Lapchick	20-5
17	St. Joseph's-PA	..22-4		Jack Ramsay	25-5
18	Drake	19-7		Maury John	same
19	Holy Cross	19-4		Roy Leenig	22-5
20	Kentucky	18-8		Adolph Rupp	19-9

Note: Unranked **Providence**, coached by Joe Mullaney, won the NIT. The Friars entered the tourney at 20-5 and had a final record of 24-5.

NCAA Final Four (at Municipal Auditorium, Kansas City): **Semifinals**—Ohio St. 95, St. John's-PA 69; Cincinnati 82, Utah 67. **Third Place**—St. Joseph's-PA 127, Utah 120 (4 OT). **Championship**—Cincinnati 70, Ohio St. 65 (OT).

NIT Final Four (at Madison Square Garden)—St. Louis 67, Dayton 60; Providence 90, Holy Cross 83 (OT). **Third Place**—Holy Cross 85, Dayton 67. **Championship**—Providence 62, St. Louis 59.

1962

			Before Tourns	Head Coach	Final Record
1	Ohio St.	23-1		Fred Taylor	26-2
2	**Cincinnati**	25-2		Ed Jucker	29-2
3	Kentucky	22-2		Adolph Rupp	23-3
4	Mississippi St.	19-6		Babe McCarthy	same
5	Bradley	21-6		Chuck Orsborn	21-7
6	Kansas St.	22-3		Tex Winter	same
7	Utah	23-3		Jack Gardner	same
8	Bowling Green	...21-3		Harold Anderson	same
9	Colorado.	18-6		Sox Walseth	19-7
10	Duke	20-5		Vic Bubas	same
11	Loyola-IL	21-3		George Ireland	23-4
12	St. John's	19-4		Joe Lapchick	21-5
13	Wake Forest	18-8		Bones McKinney	22-9
14	Oregon St.	22-4		Slats Gill	24-5
15	West Virginia	...24-5		George King	24-6
16	Arizona St.	23-3		Ned Wulk	23-4
17	Duquesne	20-5		Red Manning	22-7
18	Utah St.	21-5		Ladell Andersen	22-7
19	UCLA	16-9		John Wooden	18-11
20	Villanova.	19-6		Jack Kraft	21-7

Note: Unranked **Dayton**, coached by Tom Blackburn, won the NIT. The Flyers entered the tourney at 20-6 and had a final record of 24-6.

NCAA Final Four (at Freedom Hall, Louisville): **Semifinals**—Ohio St. 84, Wake Forest 68; Cincinnati 72, UCLA 70. **Third Place**—Wake Forest 82, UCLA 80. **Championship**—Cincinnati 71, Ohio St. 59.

NIT Final Four (at Madison Square Garden): **Semifinals**—Dayton 98, Loyola-IL 82; St. John's 76, Duquesne 65. **Third Place**—Loyola-IL 95, Duquesne 84. **Championship**—Dayton 73, St. John's 67.

1963

AP ranked only 10 teams from the 1962-63 season through 1967-68.

			Before Tourns	Head Coach	Final Record
1	Cincinnati	23-1		Ed Jucker	26-2
2	Duke	24-2		Vic Bubas	27-3
3	**Loyola-IL**	24-2		George Ireland	29-2
4	Arizona St.	24-2		Ned Wulk	26-3
5	Wichita	19-7		Ralph Miller	19-8
6	Mississippi St.	...21-5		Babe McCarthy	22-6
7	Ohio St.	20-4		Fred Taylor	same
8	Illinois	19-5		Harry Combes	20-6
9	NYU.	17-3		Lou Rossini	18-5
10	Colorado.	18-6		Sox Walseth	19-7

Note: Unranked **Providence**, coached by Joe Mullaney, won the NIT. The Friars entered the tourney at 21-4 and had a final record of 24-4.

NCAA Final Four (at Freedom Hall, Louisville): **Semifinals**—Loyola-IL 94, Duke 75; Cincinnati 80, Oregon St. 46. **Third Place**—Duke 85, Oregon St. 63. **Championship**—Loyola-IL 60, Cincinnati 58 (OT).

NIT Final Four (at Madison Square Garden): **Semifinals**—Providence 70, Marquette 64; Canisius 61, Villanova 46. **Third Place**—Marquette 66, Villanova 58. **Championship**—Providence 81, Canisius 66.

1964

AP ranked only 10 teams from the 1962-63 season through 1967-68.

			Before Tourns	Head Coach	Final Record
1	**UCLA**	26-0		John Wooden	30-0
2	Michigan.	20-4		Dave Strack	23-5
3	Duke	23-4		Vic Bubas	26-5
4	Kentucky	21-4		Adolph Rupp	21-6
5	Wichita St.	22-5		Ralph Miller	23-6
6	Oregon St.	25-3		Slats Gill	25-4
7	Villanova.	22-3		Jack Kraft	24-4
8	Loyola-IL.	20-5		George Ireland	22-6
9	DePaul.	21-3		Ray Meyer	21-4
10	Davidson.	22-4		Lefty Driesell	22-4

Note: Unranked **Bradley**, coached by Chuck Orsborn, won the NIT. The Braves entered the tourney at 20-6 and finished with a record of 23-6.

NCAA Final Four (at Municipal Auditorium, Kansas City): **Semifinals**—Duke 91, Michigan 80; UCLA 90, Kansas St. 84. **Third Place**—Michigan 100, Kansas St. 90. **Championship**—UCLA 98, Duke 83.

NIT Final Four (at Madison Square Garden): **Semifinals**—New Mexico 72, NYU 65; Bradley 67, Army 52. **Third Place**—Army 60, NYU 59. **Championship**—Bradley 86, New Mexico 54.

Undefeated National Champions

Seven NCAA seasons have ended with an undefeated national champion. UCLA has accomplished the feat four times.

Year		W-L
1956	San Francisco	.29-0
1957	North Carolina	.32-0
1964	UCLA	.30-0
1967	UCLA	.30-0
1972	UCLA	.30-0
1973	UCLA	.30-0
1976	Indiana	.32-0

1965

AP ranked only 10 teams from the 1962-63 season through 1965-68.

		Before Tourns	Head Coach	Final Record
1	Michigan	21-3	Dave Strack	24-4
2	UCLA	24-2	John Wooden	28-2
3	St. Joseph's-PA	25-1	Jack Ramsay	26-3
4	Providence	22-1	Joe Mullaney	24-2
5	Vanderbilt	23-3	Roy Skinner	24-4
6	Davidson	24-2	Lefty Driesell	same
7	Minnesota	19-5	John Kundla	same
8	Villanova	21-4	Jack Kraft	23-5
9	BYU	21-5	Stan Watts	21-7
10	Duke	20-5	Vic Bubas	same

Note: Unranked **St. John's**, coached by Joe Lapchick, won the NIT. The Redmen entered the tourney at 17-8 and finished with a record of 21-8.
NCAA Final Four (at Memorial Coliseum, Portland, OR): **Semifinals**—Michigan 93, Princeton 76; UCLA 108, Wichita St. 89. **Third Place**—Princeton 118, Wichita St. 82. **Championship**—UCLA 91, Michigan 80.
NIT Final Four (at Madison Square Garden): **Semifinals**—Villanova 91, NYU 69; St. John's 67, Army 60. **Third Place**—Army 75, NYU 74. **Championship**— St. John's 55, Villanova 51.

1966

AP ranked only 10 teams from the 1962-63 season through 1967-68.

		Before Tourns	Head Coach	Final Record
1	Kentucky	24-1	Adolph Rupp	27-2
2	Duke	23-3	Vic Bubas	26-4
3	**Texas Western**	23-1	Don Haskins	28-1
4	Kansas	22-3	Ted Owens	23-4
5	St. Joseph's-PA	22-4	Jack Ramsay	24-5
6	Loyola-IL	22-2	George Ireland	22-3
7	Cincinnati	21-5	Tay Baker	21-7
8	Vanderbilt	22-4	Roy Skinner	same
9	Michigan	17-7	Dave Strack	18-8
10	Western Ky.	23-2	Johnny Oldham	25-3

Note: Unranked **BYU**, coached by Stan Watts, won the NIT. The Cougars entered the tourney at 17-5 and had a final record of 20-5.
NCAA Final Four (at Cole Fieldhouse, College Park, MD): **Semifinals**—Kentucky 83, Duke 79; Texas Western 85, Utah 78. **Third Place**—Duke 79, Utah 77. **Championship**—Texas Western 72, Kentucky 65.
NIT Final Four (at Madison Square Garden): **Semifinals**—BYU 66, Army 60; NYU 69, Villanova 63. **Third Place**—Villanova 76, Army 65. **Championship**—BYU 97, NYU 84.

1967

AP ranked only 10 teams from the 1962-63 season through 1967-68.

		Before Tourns	Head Coach	Final Record
1	UCLA	26-0	John Wooden	30-0
2	Louisville	23-3	Peck Hickman	23-5
3	Kansas	22-3	Ted Owens	23-4
4	North Carolina	24-4	Dean Smith	26-6
5	Princeton	23-2	B. van Breda Kolff	25-3
6	Western Ky.	23-2	Johnny Oldham	23-3
7	Houston	23-3	Guy Lewis	27-4
8	Tennessee	21-5	Ray Mears	21-7
9	Boston College	19-2	Bob Cousy	21-3
10	Texas Western	20-5	Don Haskins	22-6

Note: Unranked **Southern Illinois**, coached by Jack Hartman, won the NIT. The Salukis entered the tourney at 20-2 and had a final record of 24-2.
NCAA Final Four (at Freedom Hall, Louisville): **Semifinals**—Dayton 76, N. Carolina 62; UCLA 73, Houston 58. **Third Place**—Houston 84, N. Carolina 62. **Championship**—UCLA 79, Dayton 64.
NIT Final Four (at Madison Square Garden): **Semifinals**—Marquette 83, Marshall 78; Southern Ill. 79, Rutgers 70. **Third Place**—Rutgers 93, Marshall 76. **Championship**—Southern Ill. 71, Marquette 56.

1968

AP ranked only 10 teams from the 1962-63 season through 1967-68.

		Before Tourns	Head Coach	Final Record
1	Houston	28-0	Guy Lewis	31-2
2	UCLA	25-1	John Wooden	29-1
3	St. Bonaventure	22-0	Larry Weise	23-2
4	North Carolina	25-3	Dean Smith	28-4
5	Kentucky	21-4	Adolph Rupp	22-5
6	New Mexico	23-3	Bob King	23-5
7	Columbia	21-4	Jack Rohan	23-5
8	Davidson	22-4	Lefty Driesell	24-5
9	Louisville	20-6	John Dromo	21-7
10	Duke	21-5	Vic Bubas	22-6

Note: Unranked **Dayton**, coached by Don Donoher, won the NIT. The Flyers entered the tourney at 17-9 and had a final record of 21-9.
NCAA Final Four (at the Sports Arena, Los Angeles): **Semifinals**—N. Carolina 80, Ohio St. 66; UCLA 101, Houston 69. **Third Place**—Ohio St. 89, Houston 85. **Championship**—UCLA 78, N. Carolina 55.
NIT Final Four (at Madison Square Garden): **Semifinals**—Dayton 76, Notre Dame 74 (OT); Kansas 58, St. Peter's 46. **Third Place**—Notre Dame 81, St.Peter's 78. **Championship**—Dayton 61, Kansas 48.

All-Time AP Top 20

The composite AP Top 20 from the 1948-49 season through 1998-99, based on the final regular season rankings of each year. The final AP poll has been taken before the NCAA and NIT tournaments each season since 1949 except in 1953 and '54 and again in 1974 and '75 when the final poll came out after the postseason. Team point totals are based on 20 points for all 1st place finishes, 19 for each 2nd, etc. Also listed are the number of times ranked No.1 by AP going into the tournaments, and times ranked in the pre-tournament Top 10 and Top 20.

		Pts	No.1	Top 10	Top 20			Pts	No.1	Top 10	Top 20
1	Kentucky	581	7	33	38	11	N.C. State	176	1	9	16
2	North Carolina	475	4	26	34	12	UNLV	173	2	8	13
3	UCLA	441	7	22	33	13	Marquette	166	0	11	15
4	Duke	337	3	19	28		Arizona	166	0	7	15
5	Kansas	293	1	16	23	15	Illinois	164	0	8	18
6	Indiana	292	4	16	23	16	Arkansas	162	0	9	14
7	Louisville	233	0	11	22	17	Ohio St.	156	2	9	11
8	Cincinnati	207	2	9	15	18	Syracuse	150	0	9	15
9	Notre Dame	195	0	13	17	19	Kansas St.	147	1	8	12
10	Michigan	191	2	10	14	20	DePaul	141	2	8	10

Associated Press Final Polls (Cont.)

1969

		Head Coach	Before Tourns	Final Record
1	**UCLA**	John Wooden	25-1	29-1
2	La Salle	Tom Gola	23-1	same*
3	Santa Clara	Dick Garibaldi	26-1	27-2
4	North Carolina	Dean Smith	25-3	27-5
5	Davidson	Lefty Driesell	24-2	26-3
6	Purdue	George King	20-4	23-5
7	Kentucky	Adolph Rupp	22-4	23-5
8	St. John's	Lou Carnesecca	22-4	23-6
9	Duquesne	Red Manning	19-4	21-5
10	Villanova	Jack Kraft	21-4	21-5
11	Drake	Maury John	23-4	26-5
12	New Mexico St.	Lou Henson	23-3	24-5
13	South Carolina	Frank McGuire	20-6	21-7
14	Marquette	Al McGuire	22-4	24-5
15	Louisville	John Dromo	20-5	21-6
16	Boston College	Bob Cousy	21-3	24-4
17	Notre Dame	Johnny Dee	20-6	20-7
18	Colorado	Sox Walseth	20-6	21-7
19	Kansas	Ted Owens	20-6	20-7
20	Illinois	Harvey Schmidt	19-5	same

*On probation

Note: Unranked **Temple**, coached by Harry Litwack, won the NIT. The Owls entered the tourney at 18-8 and finished with a record of 22-8.

NCAA Final Four (at Freedom Hall, Louisville): **Semifinals**—Purdue 92, N. Carolina 65; UCLA 85, Drake 82. **Third Place**—Drake 104, N. Carolina 84. **Championship**—UCLA 92, Purdue 72.

NIT Final Four (at Madison Square Garden): **Semifinals**—Temple 63, Tennessee 58; Boston College 73, Army 61. **Third Place**—Tennessee 64, Army 52. **Championship**—Temple 89, Boston College 76.

1970

		Head Coach	Before Tourns	Final Record
1	Kentucky	Adolph Rupp	25-1	26-2
2	**UCLA**	John Wooden	24-2	28-2
3	St. Bonaventure	Larry Weise	22-1	25-3
4	Jacksonville	Joe Williams	23-1	27-2
5	New Mexico St.	Lou Henson	23-2	27-3
6	South Carolina	Frank McGuire	25-3	25-3
7	Iowa	Ralph Miller	19-4	20-5
8	**Marquette**	Al McGuire	22-3	26-3
9	Notre Dame	Johnny Dee	20-6	21-8
10	N.C. State	Norm Sloan	22-6	23-7
11	Florida St.	Hugh Durham	23-3	23-3
12	Houston	Guy Lewis	24-3	25-5
13	Penn	Dick Harter	25-1	25-2
14	Drake	Maury John	21-6	22-7
15	Davidson	Terry Holland	22-4	22-5
16	Utah St.	Ladell Andersen	20-6	22-7
17	Niagara	Frank Layden	21-5	22-7
18	Western Ky.	John Oldham	22-2	22-3
19	Long Beach St.	Jerry Tarkanian	23-3	24-5
20	USC	Bob Boyd	18-8	18-8

NCAA Final Four (at Cole Fieldhouse, College Park, MD): **Semifinals**—Jacksonville 91, St. Bonaventure 83; UCLA 93, New Mexico St. 77. **Third Place**—N. Mexico St. 79, St. Bonaventure 73. **Championship**—UCLA 80, Jacksonville 69.

NIT Final Four (at Madison Square Garden): **Semifinals**—St. John's 96, Army 79; Marquette 101, LSU 79. **Third Place**—Army 75, LSU 68. **Championship**—Marquette 65, St. John's 53.

1971

		Head Coach	Before Tourns	Final Record
1	**UCLA**	John Wooden	25-1	29-1
2	Marquette	Al McGuire	26-0	28-1
3	Penn	Dick Harter	26-0	28-1
4	Kansas	Ted Owens	25-1	27-3
5	USC	Bob Boyd	24-2	24-2
6	South Carolina	Frank McGuire	23-4	23-6
7	Western Ky.	John Oldham	20-5	24-6
8	Kentucky	Adolph Rupp	22-4	22-6
9	Fordham	Digger Phelps	25-1	26-3
10	Ohio St.	Fred Taylor	19-5	20-6
11	Jacksonville	Tom Wasdin	22-3	22-4
12	Notre Dame	Johnny Dee	19-7	20-9
13	N. Carolina	Dean Smith	22-6	26-6
14	Houston	Guy Lewis	20-6	22-7
15	Duquesne	Red Manning	21-3	21-4
16	Long Beach St.	Jerry Tarkanian	21-4	23-5
17	Tennessee	Ray Mears	20-6	21-7
18	Villanova	Jack Kraft	19-5	23-6
19	Drake	Maury John	20-7	21-8
20	BYU	Stan Watts	18-9	18-11

NCAA Final Four (at the Astrodome, Houston): **Semifinals**—Villanova 92, Western Ky. 89 (2 OT); UCLA 68, Kansas 60. **Third Place**—Western Ky. 77, Kansas 75. **Championship**—UCLA 68, Villanova 62.

NIT Final Four (at Madison Square Garden): **Semifinals**—N. Carolina 73, Duke 76; St. Bonaventure 71 (2 OT). **Third Place**—St. Bonaventure 92, Duke 88 (OT). **Championship**—N. Carolina 84, Ga.Tech 66.

1972

		Head Coach	Before Tourns	Final Record
1	**UCLA**	John Wooden	26-0	30-0
2	North Carolina	Dean Smith	23-4	26-5
3	Penn	Chuck Daly	23-2	25-3
4	Louisville	Denny Crum	23-4	26-5
5	Long Beach St.	Jerry Tarkanian	23-3	25-4
6	South Carolina	Frank McGuire	22-4	24-5
7	Marquette	Al McGuire	24-2	25-4
8	SW Louisiana	Beryl Shipley	23-3	25-4
9	BYU	Stan Watts	21-4	21-5
10	Florida St.	Hugh Durham	23-5	27-6
11	Minnesota	Bill Musselman	17-6	18-7
12	Marshall	Carl Tacy	23-3	23-4
13	Memphis St.	Gene Bartow	21-6	21-7
14	**Maryland**	Lefty Driesell	23-5	27-5
15	Villanova	Jack Kraft	19-6	20-8
16	Oral Roberts	Ken Trickey	25-1	26-2
17	Indiana	Bob Knight	17-7	17-8
18	Kentucky	Adolph Rupp	20-6	21-7
19	Ohio St.	Fred Taylor	18-6	same
20	Virginia	Bill Gibson	21-6	21-7

NCAA Final Four (at the Sports Arena, Los Angeles): **Semifinals**—Florida St. 79, N. Carolina 75; UCLA 96, Louisville 77. **Third Place**—N. Carolina 105, Louisville 91. **Championship**—UCLA 81, Florida St. 76.

NIT Final Four (at Madison Square Garden): **Semifinals**—Maryland 91, Jacksonville 77; Niagara 69, St. John's 67. **Third Place**—Jacksonville 83, St. John's 80. **Championship**—Maryland 100, Niagara 69.

1973

	Before Tourns	Head Coach	Final Record
1	**UCLA** 26-0	John Wooden	30-0
2	N.C. State......27-0	Norm Sloan	same*
3	Long Beach St. ..24-2	Jerry Tarkanian	26-3
4	Providence 24-2	Dave Gavitt	27-4
5	Marquette 23-3	Al McGuire	25-4
6	Indiana 19-5	Bob Knight	22-6
7	SW Louisiana ...23-2	Beryl Shipley	24-5
8	Maryland 22-6	Lefty Driesell	23-7
9	Kansas St.......22-4	Jack Hartman	23-5
10	Minnesota......20-4	Bill Musselman	21-5
11	North Carolina...22-7	Dean Smith	25-8
12	Memphis St......21-5	Gene Bartow	24-6
13	Houston.........23-3	Guy Lewis	23-4
14	Syracuse 22-4	Roy Danforth	24-5
15	Missouri.........21-5	Norm Stewart	21-6
16	Arizona St......18-7	Ned Wulk	19-9
17	Kentucky 19-7	Joe B. Hall	20-8
18	Penn............20-5	Chuck Daly	21-7
19	Austin Peay......21-5	Lake Kelly	22-7
20	San Francisco ...22-4	Bob Gaillard	23-5

*N.C. State was ineligible for NCAA tournament for using improper methods to recruit David Thompson.

Note: Unranked **Virginia Tech**, coached by Don DeVoe, won the NIT. The Hokies entered the tourney at 18-5 and finished with a record of 22-5.

NCAA Final Four (at The Arena, St. Louis): **Semifinals**—Memphis St. 98, Providence 85; UCLA 70, Indiana 59. **Third Place**—Indiana 97, Providence 79. **Championship**—UCLA 87, Memphis St. 66.

NIT Final Four (at Madison Square Garden): **Semifinals**—Va. Tech 74, Alabama 73; Notre Dame 78, N. Carolina 71. **Third Place**—N. Carolina 88, Alabama 71. **Championship**—Va. Tech 92, Notre Dame 91 (OT).

1974

	Before Tourns	Head Coach	Final Record
1	**N.C. State** 26-1	Norm Sloan	30-1
2	UCLA..........23-3	John Wooden	26-4
3	Notre Dame 24-2	Digger Phelps	26-3
4	Maryland 23-5	Lefty Driesell	same
5	Providence 26-3	Dave Gavitt	28-4
6	Vanderbilt 23-3	Roy Skinner	23-5
7	Marquette 22-4	Al McGuire	26-5
8	North Carolina...22-5	Dean Smith	22-6
9	Long Beach St....24-2	Lute Olson	same
10	**Indiana**.......20-5	Bob Knight	23-5
11	Alabama........22-4	C.M. Newton	same
12	Michigan........21-4	Johnny Orr	22-5
13	Pittsburgh 23-3	Buzz Ridl	25-4
14	Kansas..........21-5	Ted Owens	23-7
15	USC............22-4	Bob Boyd	24-5
16	Louisville 21-6	Denny Crum	21-7
17	New Mexico....21-6	Norm Ellenberger	22-7
18	South Carolina...22-4	Frank McGuire	22-5
19	Creighton 22-6	Eddie Sutton	23-7
20	Dayton.........19-7	Don Donoher	20-9

NCAA Final Four (at Greensboro, NC, Coliseum): **Semifinals**—N.C. State 80, UCLA 77 (2 OT); Marquette 64, Kansas 51. **Third Place**—UCLA 78, Kansas 61. **Championship**—N.C. State 76, Marquette 64.

NIT Final Four (at Madison Square Garden): **Semifinals**—Purdue 78, Jacksonville 63; Utah 117, Boston Col. 93. **Third Place**—Boston Col. 87, Jacksonville 77. **Championship**—Purdue 87, Utah 81.

CCA Final Four (at The Arena, St. Louis): Semifinals—Indiana 73, Toledo 72; USC 74, Bradley 73. Championship—Indiana 85, USC 60.

1975

	Before Tourns	Head Coach	Final Record
1	Indiana 29-0	Bob Knight	31-1
2	**UCLA** 23-3	John Wooden	28-3
3	Louisville 24-2	Denny Crum	28-3
4	Maryland 22-4	Lefty Driesell	24-5
5	Kentucky 22-4	Joe B. Hall	26-5
6	North Carolina...21-7	Dean Smith	23-8
7	Arizona St.......23-3	Ned Wulk	25-4
8	N.C. State 22-6	Norm Sloan	22-6
9	Notre Dame 18-8	Digger Phelps	19-10
10	Marquette 23-3	Al McGuire	23-4
11	Alabama........22-4	C.M. Newton	22-5
12	Cincinnati 21-5	Gale Catlett	23-6
13	Oregon St.......18-10	Ralph Miller	19-12
14	**Drake** 16-10	Bob Ortegel	19-10
15	Penn............23-4	Chuck Daly	23-5
16	UNLV...........22-4	Jerry Tarkanian	24-5
17	Kansas St.......18-8	Jack Hartman	20-9
18	USC............18-7	Bob Boyd	18-8
19	Centenary.......25-4	Larry Little	same
20	Syracuse 20-7	Roy Danforth	23-9

NCAA Final Four (at San Diego Sports Arena): **Semifinals**—Kentucky 95, Syracuse 79; UCLA 75, Louisville 74 (OT). **Third Place**—Louisville 96, Syracuse 88 (OT). **Championship**—UCLA 92, Kentucky 85.

NIT Championship (at Madison Sq. Garden): Princeton 80, Providence 69. No Top 20 teams played in NIT.

CCA Championship (at Freedom Hall, Louisville): Drake 83, Arizona 76. No.14 Drake and No.18 USC were only Top 20 teams in CCA.

1976

	Before Tourns	Head Coach	Final Record
1	**Indiana**........27-0	Bob Knight	32-0
2	Marquette 25-1	Al McGuire	27-2
3	UNLV...........28-1	Jerry Tarkanian	29-2
4	Rutgers.........28-0	Tom Young	31-2
5	UCLA...........24-3	Gene Bartow	28-4
6	Alabama........22-4	C.M. Newton	23-5
7	Notre Dame 22-5	Digger Phelps	23-6
8	North Carolina...25-3	Dean Smith	25-4
9	Michigan........21-6	Johnny Orr	25-7
10	Western Mich. ...24-2	Eldon Miller	25-3
11	Maryland 22-6	Lefty Driesell	same
12	Cincinnati 25-5	Gale Catlett	25-6
13	Tennessee 21-5	Ray Mears	21-6
14	Missouri........24-4	Norm Stewart	26-5
15	Arizona 22-8	Fred Snowden	24-9
16	Texas Tech......24-5	Gerald Myers	25-6
17	DePaul.........19-8	Ray Meyer	20-9
18	Virginia.........18-11	Terry Holland	18-12
19	Centenary.......22-4	Larry Little	same
20	Pepperdine 21-5	Gary Colson	22-6

NCAA Final Four (at the Spectrum, Phila.); **Semifinals**—Michigan 86, Rutgers 70; Indiana 65, UCLA 51. **Third Place**—UCLA 106, Rutgers 92. **Championship**—Indiana 86, Michigan 68.

NIT Championship (at Madison Square Garden): Kentucky 71, NC-Charlotte 67. No Top 20 teams played in NIT.

Associated Press Final Polls (Cont.)

1977

		Head Coach	Before Tourns	Final Record
1	Michigan	Johnny Orr	24-3	26-4
2	UCLA	Gene Bartow	24-3	25-4
3	Kentucky	Joe B. Hall	24-3	26-4
4	UNLV	Jerry Tarkanian	25-2	29-3
5	North Carolina	Dean Smith	24-4	28-5
6	Syracuse	Jim Boeheim	25-3	26-4
7	**Marquette**	Al McGuire	20-7	25-7
8	San Francisco	Bob Gaillard	29-1	29-2
9	Wake Forest	Carl Tacy	20-7	22-8
10	Notre Dame	Digger Phelps	21-6	22-7
11	Alabama	C.M. Newton	23-4	25-6
12	Detroit	Dick Vitale	24-3	25-4
13	Minnesota	Jim Dutcher	24-3	same*
14	Utah	Jerry Pimm	22-6	23-7
15	Tennessee	Ray Mears	22-5	22-6
16	Kansas St.	Jack Hartman	23-6	24-7
17	NC-Charlotte	Lee Rose	25-3	28-5
18	Arkansas	Eddie Sutton	26-1	26-2
19	Louisville	Denny Crum	21-6	21-7
20	VMI	Charlie Schmaus	25-3	26-4

*On probation

NCAA Final Four (at the Omni, Atlanta): **Semifinals**—Marquette 51, NC-Charlotte, 49; N. Carolina 84, UNLV 83. **Third Place**—UNLV 106, NC-Charlotte 94. **Championship**—Marquette 67, N. Carolina 59.

NIT Championship (at Madison Square Garden): St. Bonaventure 94, Houston 91. No.11 Alabama was only Top 20 team in NIT.

1978

		Head Coach	Before Tourns	Final Record
1	**Kentucky**	Joe B. Hall	25-2	30-2
2	UCLA	Gary Cunningham	24-2	25-3
3	DePaul	Ray Meyer	25-2	27-3
4	Michigan St.	Jud Heathcote	23-4	25-5
5	Arkansas	Eddie Sutton	28-3	32-3
6	Notre Dame	Digger Phelps	20-6	23-8
7	Duke	Bill Foster	23-6	27-7
8	Marquette	Hank Raymonds	24-3	24-4
9	Louisville	Denny Crum	22-6	23-7
10	Kansas	Ted Owens	24-4	24-5
11	San Francisco	Bob Gaillard	22-5	23-6
12	New Mexico	Norm Ellenberger	24-3	24-4
13	Indiana	Bob Knight	20-7	21-8
14	Utah	Jerry Pimm	22-5	23-6
15	Florida St.	Hugh Durham	23-5	23-6
16	North Carolina	Dean Smith	23-7	23-8
17	**Texas**	Abe Lemons	22-5	26-5
18	Detroit	Dave Gaines	24-3	25-4
19	Miami-OH	Darrell Hedric	18-8	19-9
20	Penn	Bob Weinhauer	19-7	20-8

NCAA Final Four (at the Checkerdome, St. Louis): **Semifinals**—Kentucky 64, Arkansas 59; Duke 90, Notre Dame 86. **Third Place**—Arkansas 71, Notre Dame 69. **Championship**—Kentucky 94, Duke 88.

NIT Championship (at Madison Square Garden): Texas 101, N.C. State 93. No. 17 Texas and No. 18 Detroit were only Top 20 teams in NIT.

1979

		Head Coach	Before Tourns	Final Record
1	Indiana St.	Bill Hodges	29-0	33-1
2	UCLA	Gary Cunningham	23-4	25-5
3	**Michigan St.**	Jud Heathcote	21-6	26-6
4	Notre Dame	Digger Phelps	22-5	24-6
5	Arkansas	Eddie Sutton	23-4	25-5
6	DePaul	Ray Meyer	22-5	26-6
7	LSU	Dale Brown	22-5	23-6
8	Syracuse	Jim Boeheim	25-3	26-4
9	North Carolina	Dean Smith	23-5	23-6
10	Marquette	Hank Raymonds	21-6	22-7
11	Duke	Bill Foster	22-7	22-8
12	San Francisco	Dan Belluomini	21-6	22-7
13	Louisville	Denny Crum	23-7	24-8
14	Penn	Bob Weinhauer	21-5	25-7
15	Purdue	Lee Rose	23-7	27-8
16	Oklahoma	Dave Bliss	20-9	21-10
17	St. John's	Lou Carnesecca	18-10	21-11
18	Rutgers	Tom Young	21-8	22-9
19	Toledo	Bob Nichols	21-6	22-7
20	Iowa	Lute Olson	20-7	20-8

NCAA Final Four (at Special Events Center, Salt Lake City): **Semifinals**—Michigan St. 101, Penn 67; Indiana St. 76, DePaul 74; **Third Place**—DePaul 96, Penn 93. **Championship**—Michigan St. 75, Indiana St. 64.

NIT Championship (at Madison Square Garden): Indiana 53, Purdue 52. No. 15 Purdue was the only Top 20 team in NIT.

1980

		Head Coach	Before Tourns	Final Record
1	DePaul	Ray Meyer	26-1	26-2
2	**Louisville**	Denny Crum	28-3	33-3
3	LSU	Dale Brown	24-5	26-6
4	Kentucky	Joe B. Hall	28-5	29-6
5	Oregon St.	Ralph Miller	26-3	26-4
6	Syracuse	Jim Boeheim	25-3	26-4
7	Indiana	Bob Knight	20-7	21-8
8	Maryland	Lefty Driesell	23-6	24-7
9	Notre Dame	Digger Phelps	20-7	20-8
10	Ohio St.	Eldon Miller	24-5	21-8
11	Georgetown	John Thompson	24-5	26-6
12	BYU	Frank Arnold	24-4	24-5
13	St. John's	Lou Carnesecca	24-4	24-5
14	Duke	Bill Foster	22-8	24-9
15	North Carolina	Dean Smith	21-7	21-8
16	Missouri	Norm Stewart	23-5	25-6
17	Weber St.	Neil McCarthy	26-2	26-3
18	Arizona St.	Ned Wulk	21-6	22-7
19	Iona	Jim Valvano	28-4	29-5
20	Purdue	Lee Rose	19-9	23-10

NCAA Final Four (at Market Square Arena, Indianapolis): **Semifinals**—Louisville 80, Iowa 72; UCLA 67, Purdue 62; **Championship**—Louisville 59, UCLA 54.

NIT Championship (at Madison Square Garden): Virginia 58, Minnesota 55. No Top 20 teams played in NIT.

1981

		Before Tourns	Head Coach	Final Record
1	DePaul	27-1	Ray Meyer	27-2
2	Oregon St.	26-1	Ralph Miller	26-2
3	Arizona St.	24-3	Ned Wulk	24-4
4	LSU	28-3	Dale Brown	31-5
5	Virginia	25-3	Terry Holland	29-4
6	North Carolina	25-7	Dean Smith	29-8
7	Notre Dame	22-5	Digger Phelps	23-6
8	Kentucky	22-5	Joe B. Hall	22-6
9	**Indiana**	21-9	Bob Knight	26-9
10	UCLA	20-6	Larry Brown	20-7
11	Wake Forest	22-6	Carl Tacy	22-7
12	Louisville	21-8	Denny Crum	21-9
13	Iowa	21-6	Lute Olson	21-7
14	Utah	24-4	Jerry Pimm	25-5
15	Tennessee	20-7	Don DeVoe	21-8
16	BYU	22-6	Frank Arnold	25-7
17	Wyoming	23-5	Jim Brandenburg	24-6
18	Maryland	20-9	Lefty Driesell	21-10
19	Illinois	20-7	Lou Henson	21-8
20	Arkansas	22-7	Eddie Sutton	24-8

NCAA Final Four (at the Spectrum, Phila.): **Semifinals**–N. Carolina 78, Virginia 65; Indiana 67, LSU 49. **Third Place**–Virginia 78, LSU 74. **Championship**–Indiana 63, N. Carolina 50.
NIT Championship (at Madison Square Garden): Tulsa 86, Syracuse 84. No Top 20 teams played in NIT.

1982

		Before Tourns	Head Coach	Final Record
1	**N. Carolina**	27-2	Dean Smith	32-2
2	DePaul	26-1	Ray Meyer	26-2
3	Virginia	29-3	Terry Holland	30-4
4	Oregon St.	23-4	Ralph Miller	25-5
5	Missouri	26-3	Norm Stewart	27-4
6	Georgetown	26-6	John Thompson	30-7
7	Minnesota	22-5	Jim Dutcher	23-6
8	Idaho	26-2	Don Monson	27-3
9	Memphis St.	23-4	Dana Kirk	24-5
10	Tulsa	24-5	Nolan Richardson	24-6
11	Fresno St.	26-2	Boyd Grant	27-3
12	Arkansas	23-5	Eddie Sutton	23-6
13	Alabama	23-6	Wimp Sanderson	24-7
14	West Virginia	26-3	Gale Catlett	27-4
15	Kentucky	22-7	Joe B. Hall	22-8
16	Iowa	20-7	Lute Olson	21-8
17	Ala-Birmingham	23-5	Gene Bartow	25-6
18	Wake Forest	20-8	Carl Tacy	21-9
19	UCLA	21-6	Larry Farmer	21-6
20	Louisville	20-9	Denny Crum	23-10

NCAA Final Four (at the Superdome, New Orleans): **Semifinals**–N. Carolina 68, Houston 63; Georgetown 50, Louisville 46. **Championship**–N. Carolina 63, Georgetown 62.
NIT Championship (at Madison Square Garden): Bradley 67, Purdue 58. No Top 20 teams played in NIT.

1983

		Before Tourns	Head Coach	Final Record
1	Houston	27-2	Guy Lewis	31-3
2	Louisville	29-3	Denny Crum	32-4
3	St. John's	27-4	Lou Carnesecca	28-5
4	Virginia	27-4	Terry Holland	29-5
5	Indiana	23-5	Bob Knight	24-6
6	UNLV	28-2	Jerry Tarkanian	28-3
7	UCLA	23-5	Larry Farmer	23-6
8	North Carolina	26-7	Dean Smith	28-8
9	Arkansas	25-3	Eddie Sutton	26-4
10	Missouri	26-7	Norm Stewart	26-8
11	Boston College	24-6	Gary Williams	25-7
12	Kentucky	22-7	Joe B. Hall	23-8
13	Villanova	22-7	Rollie Massimino	24-8
14	Wichita St.	25-3	Gene Smithson	same*
15	Tenn.-Chatt.	26-3	Murray Arnold	26-4
16	**N.C. State**	20-10	Jim Valvano	26-10
17	Memphis St.	22-7	Dana Kirk	23-8
18	Georgia	21-9	Hugh Durham	24-10
19	Oklahoma St.	24-6	Paul Hansen	24-7
20	Georgetown	21-9	John Thompson	22-10

*On probation

NCAA Final Four (at The Pit, Albuquerque, NM): **Semifinals**–N.C. State 67, Georgia 60; Houston 94, Louisville 81. **Championship**–N.C. State 54, Houston 52.
NIT Championship (at Madison Square Garden): Fresno St. 69, DePaul 60. No Top 20 teams played in NIT.

1984

		Before Tourns	Head Coach	Final Record
1	North Carolina	27-2	Dean Smith	28-3
2	**Georgetown**	29-3	John Thompson	34-3
3	Kentucky	26-4	Joe B. Hall	29-5
4	DePaul	26-2	Ray Meyer	27-3
5	Houston	28-4	Guy Lewis	32-5
6	Illinois	24-4	Lou Henson	26-5
7	Oklahoma	29-4	Billy Tubbs	29-5
8	Arkansas	25-6	Eddie Sutton	25-7
9	UTEP	27-3	Don Haskins	27-4
10	Purdue	22-6	Gene Keady	22-7
11	Maryland	23-7	Lefty Driesell	24-8
12	Tulsa	27-3	Nolan Richardson	27-4
13	UNLV	27-5	Jerry Tarkanian	29-6
14	Duke	24-9	Mike Krzyzewski	24-10
15	Washington	22-6	Marv Harshman	24-7
16	Memphis St.	24-6	Dana Kirk	26-7
17	Oregon St.	22-6	Ralph Miller	22-7
18	Syracuse	22-8	Jim Boeheim	23-9
19	Wake Forest	21-8	Carl Tacy	23-9
20	Temple	25-4	John Chaney	26-5

NCAA Final Four (at the Kingdome, Seattle): **Semifinals**–Houston 49, Virginia 47 (OT); Georgetown 53, Kentucky 40. **Championship**–Georgetown 84, Houston 75.
NIT Championship (at Madison Square Garden): Michigan 83, Notre Dame 63. No Top 20 teams played in NIT.

Highest-Rated College Games on TV

The dozen highest-rated college basketball games seen on U.S. television have been NCAA tournament championship games, led by the 1979 Michigan State-Indiana State final that featured Magic Johnson and Larry Bird.

Listed below are the finalists (winning team first), date of game, TV network, and TV rating and audience share (according to Nielson Media Research).

		Date	Net	Rtg/Sh			Date	Net	Rtg/Sh
1	Michigan St.-Indiana St.	3/26/79	NBC	24.1/38	7	N. Carolina-Georgetown	3/29/82	CBS	21.6/31
2	Villanova-Georgetown	4/1/85	CBS	23.3/33	8	UCLA-Kentucky	3/31/75	NBC	21.3/33
3	Duke-Michigan	4/6/92	CBS	22.7/35	9	Michigan-Seton Hall	4/3/89	CBS	21.3/33
4	N.C. State-Houston	4/4/83	CBS	22.3/32	10	Louisville-Duke	3/31/86	CBS	20.7/31
5	N. Carolina-Michigan	4/5/93	CBS	22.2/34	11	Indiana-N. Carolina	3/30/81	NBC	20.7/29
6	Arkansas-Duke	4/4/94	CBS	21.6/33	12	UCLA-Memphis St.	3/26/73	NBC	20.5/32

Associated Press Final Polls (Cont.)

1985

		Before Tourns	Head Coach	Final Record
1	Georgetown	30-2	John Thompson	35-3
2	Michigan	25-3	Bill Frieder	26-4
3	St. John's	27-3	Lou Carnesecca	31-4
4	Oklahoma	28-5	Billy Tubbs	31-6
5	Memphis St.	27-3	Dana Kirk	31-4
6	Georgia Tech	24-7	Bobby Cremins	27-8
7	North Carolina	24-8	Dean Smith	27-9
8	Louisiana Tech	27-2	Andy Russo	29-3
9	UNLV	27-3	Jerry Tarkanian	28-4
10	Duke	22-7	Mike Krzyzewski	23-8
11	VCU	25-5	J.D. Barnett	26-6
12	Illinois	24-8	Lou Henson	26-9
13	Kansas	25-7	Larry Brown	26-8
14	Loyola-IL	25-5	Gene Sullivan	27-6
15	Syracuse	21-8	Jim Boeheim	22-9
16	N.C. State	20-9	Jim Valvano	23-10
17	Texas Tech	23-7	Gerald Myers	23-8
18	Tulsa	23-7	Nolan Richardson	23-8
19	Georgia	21-8	Hugh Durham	22-9
20	LSU	19-9	Dale Brown	19-10

Note: Unranked **Villanova**, coached by Rollie Massimino, won the NCAAs. The Wildcats entered the tourney at 19-10 and had a final record of 25-10.

NCAA Final Four (at Rupp Arena, Lexington, KY): **Semifinals**– Georgetown 77, St. John's 59; Villanova 52, Memphis St. 45. **Championship**–Villanova 66, Georgetown 64.

NIT Championship (at Madison Square Garden): UCLA 65, Indiana 62. No Top 20 teams played in NIT.

1986

		Before Tourns	Head Coach	Final Record
1	Duke	32-2	Mike Krzyzewski	37-3
2	Kansas	31-3	Larry Brown	35-4
3	Kentucky	29-3	Eddie Sutton	32-4
4	St. John's	30-4	Lou Carnesecca	31-5
5	Michigan	27-4	Bill Frieder	28-5
6	Georgia Tech	25-6	Bobby Cremins	27-7
7	**Louisville**	26-7	Denny Crum	32-7
8	North Carolina	26-5	Dean Smith	28-6
9	Syracuse	25-5	Jim Boeheim	26-6
10	Notre Dame	23-5	Digger Phelps	23-6
11	UNLV	31-4	Jerry Tarkanian	33-5
12	Memphis St.	27-5	Dana Kirk	28-6
13	Georgetown	23-7	John Thompson	24-8
14	Bradley	31-2	Dick Versace	32-3
15	Oklahoma	25-8	Billy Tubbs	26-9
16	Indiana	21-7	Bob Knight	21-8
17	Navy	27-4	Paul Evans	30-5
18	Michigan St.	21-7	Jud Heathcote	23-8
19	Illinois	21-9	Lou Henson	22-10
20	UTEP	27-5	Don Haskins	27-6

NCAA Final Four (at Reunion Arena, Dallas): **Semifinals**–Duke 71, Kansas 67; Louisville 88, LSU 77. **Championship**–Louisville 72, Duke 69.

NIT Championship (at Madison Square Garden): Ohio St. 73, Wyoming 63. No Top 20 teams played in NIT.

1987

		Before Tourns	Head Coach	Final Record
1	UNLV	33-1	Jerry Tarkanian	37-2
2	North Carolina	29-3	Dean Smith	32-4
3	**Indiana**	24-4	Bob Knight	30-4
4	Georgetown	26-4	John Thompson	29-5
5	DePaul	26-2	Joey Meyer	28-3
6	Iowa	27-4	Tom Davis	30-5
7	Purdue	24-4	Gene Keady	25-5
8	Temple	31-3	John Chaney	32-4
9	Alabama	26-4	Wimp Sanderson	28-5
10	Syracuse	26-6	Jim Boeheim	31-7
11	Illinois	23-7	Lou Henson	23-8
12	Pittsburgh	24-7	Paul Evans	25-8
13	Clemson	25-5	Cliff Ellis	25-6
14	Missouri	24-9	Norm Stewart	24-10
15	UCLA	24-6	Walt Hazzard	25-7
16	New Orleans	25-3	Benny Dees	26-4
17	Duke	22-8	Mike Krzyzewski	24-9
18	Notre Dame	22-7	Digger Phelps	24-8
19	TCU	23-6	Jim Killingsworth	24-7
20	Kansas	23-10	Larry Brown	25-11

NCAA Final Four (at the Superdome, New Orleans): **Semifinals**–Syracuse 77, Providence 63; Indiana 97, UNLV 93. **Championship**–Indiana 74, Syracuse 73.

NIT Championship (at Madison Square Garden): Southern Miss. 84, La Salle 80. No Top 20 teams played in NIT.

1988

		Before Tourns	Head Coach	Final Record
1	Temple	29-1	John Chaney	32-2
2	Arizona	31-2	Lute Olson	35-3
3	Purdue	27-3	Gene Keady	29-4
4	Oklahoma	30-3	Billy Tubbs	35-4
5	Duke	24-6	Mike Krzyzewski	28-7
6	Kentucky	25-5	Eddie Sutton	27-6
7	North Carolina	24-6	Dean Smith	27-7
8	Pittsburgh	23-6	Paul Evans	24-7
9	Syracuse	25-8	Jim Boeheim	26-9
10	Michigan	24-7	Bill Frieder	26-8
11	Bradley	26-4	Stan Albeck	26-5
12	UNLV	27-5	Jerry Tarkanian	28-6
13	Wyoming	26-5	Benny Dees	26-6
14	N.C. State	24-7	Jim Valvano	24-8
15	Loyola-CA	27-3	Paul Westhead	28-4
16	Illinois	22-9	Lou Henson	23-10
17	Iowa	22-9	Tom Davis	24-10
18	Xavier-OH	26-3	Pete Gillen	26-4
19	BYU	25-5	Ladell Andersen	26-6
20	Kansas St.	22-8	Lon Kruger	25-9

Note: Unranked **Kansas**, coached by Larry Brown, won the NCAAs. The Jayhawks entered the tourney at 21-11 and had a final record of 27-11.

NCAA Final Four (at Kemper Arena, Kansas City): **Semifinals**–Kansas 66, Duke 59; Oklahoma 86, Arizona 78. **Championship**–Kansas 83, Oklahoma 79.

NIT Championship (at Madison Square Garden): Connecticut 72, Ohio St. 67. No Top 20 teams played in NIT.

1989

		Before Tourns	Head Coach	Final Record
1	Arizona	27-3	Lute Olson	29-4
2	Georgetown	26-4	John Thompson	29-5
3	Illinois	27-4	Lou Henson	31-5
4	Oklahoma	28-5	Billy Tubbs	30-6
5	North Carolina	27-7	Dean Smith	29-8
6	Missouri	27-7	Norm Stewart & Rich Daly	29-8
7	Syracuse	27-7	Jim Boeheim	30-8
8	Indiana	25-7	Bob Knight	27-8
9	Duke	24-7	Mike Krzyzewski	28-8
10	**Michigan**	24-7	Bill Frieder & Steve Fisher	30-7
11	Seton Hall	26-6	P.J. Carlesimo	31-7
12	Louisville	22-8	Denny Crum	24-9
13	Stanford	26-6	Mike Montgomery	26-7
14	Iowa	22-9	Tom Davis	23-10
15	UNLV	26-7	Jerry Tarkanian	29-8
16	Florida St.	22-7	Pat Kennedy	22-8
17	West Virginia	25-4	Gale Catlett	26-5
18	Ball State	28-2	Rick Majerus	29-3
19	N.C. State	20-8	Jim Valvano	22-9
20	Alabama	23-7	Wimp Sanderson	23-8

NCAA Final Four (at The Kingdome, Seattle): **Semifinals**—Seton Hall 95, Duke 78; Michigan 83, Illinois 81. **Championship**—Michigan 80, Seton Hall 79 (OT).
NIT Championship (at Madison Square Garden): St. John's 73, St. Louis 65. No Top 20 teams played in NIT.

1990

		Before Tourns	Head Coach	Final Record
1	Oklahoma	26-4	Billy Tubbs	27-5
2	UNLV	29-5	Jerry Tarkanian	35-5
3	Connecticut	28-5	Jim Calhoun	31-6
4	Michigan St.	26-5	Jud Heathcote	28-6
5	Kansas	29-4	Roy Williams	30-5
6	Syracuse	24-6	Jim Boeheim	26-7
7	Arkansas	26-4	Nolan Richardson	30-5
8	Georgetown	23-6	John Thompson	24-7
9	Georgia Tech	24-6	Bobby Cremins	28-7
10	Purdue	21-7	Gene Keady	22-8
11	Missouri	26-5	Norm Stewart	26-6
12	La Salle	29-1	Speedy Morris	30-2
13	Michigan	22-7	Steve Fisher	23-8
14	Arizona	24-6	Lute Olson	25-7
15	Duke	24-8	Mike Krzyzewski	29-9
16	Louisville	26-7	Denny Crum	27-8
17	Clemson	24-8	Cliff Ellis	26-9
18	Illinois	21-7	Lou Henson	21-8
19	LSU	22-8	Dale Brown	23-9
20	Minnesota	20-8	Clem Haskins	23-9
21	Loyola-CA	23-5	Paul Westhead	26-6
22	Oregon St.	22-6	Jim Anderson	22-7
23	Alabama	24-8	Wimp Sanderson	26-9
24	New Mexico St.	26-4	Neil McCarthy	26-5
25	Xavier-OH	26-4	Pete Gillen	28-5

NCAA Final Four (at McNichols Sports Arena, Denver): **Semifinals**—Duke 97, Arkansas 83; UNLV 90, Georgia Tech 81. **Championship**—UNLV 103, Duke 73.
NIT Championship (at Madison Square Garden): Vanderbilt 74, St.Louis 72. No Top 25 teams played in NIT.

1991

		Before Tourns	Head Coach	Final Record
1	UNLV	30-0	Jerry Tarkanian	34-1
2	Arkansas	31-3	Nolan Richardson	34-4
3	Indiana	27-4	Bob Knight	29-5
4	North Carolina	25-5	Dean Smith	29-6
5	Ohio St.	25-3	Randy Ayers	27-4
6	**Duke**	26-7	Mike Krzyzewski	32-7
7	Syracuse	26-5	Jim Boeheim	26-6
8	Arizona	26-6	Lute Olson	28-7
9	Kentucky	22-6	Rick Pitino	same*
10	Utah	28-3	Rick Majerus	30-4
11	Nebraska	26-7	Danny Nee	26-8
12	Kansas	22-7	Roy Williams	27-8
13	Seton Hall	22-8	P.J. Carlesimo	25-9
14	Oklahoma St.	22-7	Eddie Sutton	24-8
15	New Mexico St.	23-5	Neil McCarthy	23-6
16	UCLA	23-8	Jim Harrick	23-9
17	E.Tennessee St.	28-4	Alan LaForce	28-5
18	Princeton	24-2	Pete Carril	24-3
19	Alabama	21-9	Wimp Sanderson	23-10
20	St. John's	20-8	Lou Carnesecca	23-9
21	Mississippi St.	20-8	Richard Williams	20-9
22	LSU	20-9	Dale Brown	20-10
23	Texas	22-8	Tom Penders	23-9
24	DePaul	20-8	Joey Meyer	20-9
25	Southern Miss.	21-7	M.K. Turk	21-8

*On probation

NCAA Final Four (at the Hoosier Dome, Indianapolis): **Semifinals**—Kansas 79, North Carolina 73; Duke 79, UNLV 77. **Championship**—Duke 72, Kansas 65.
NIT Championship (at Madison Square Garden): Stanford 78, Oklahoma 72. No Top 25 teams played in NIT.

1992

		Before Tourns	Head Coach	Final Record
1	**Duke**	28-2	Mike Krzyzewski	34-2
2	Kansas	26-4	Roy Williams	27-5
3	Ohio St.	23-5	Randy Ayers	26-6
4	UCLA	25-4	Jim Harrick	28-5
5	Indiana	23-6	Bob Knight	27-7
6	Kentucky	26-6	Rick Pitino	29-7
7	UNLV	26-2	Jerry Tarkanian	same*
8	USC	23-5	George Raveling	24-6
9	Arkansas	25-7	Nolan Richardson	26-8
10	Arizona	24-6	Lute Olson	24-7
11	Oklahoma St.	26-7	Eddie Sutton	28-8
12	Cincinnati	25-4	Bob Huggins	29-5
13	Alabama	25-8	Wimp Sanderson	26-9
14	Michigan St.	21-7	Jud Heathcote	22-8
15	Michigan	20-8	Steve Fisher	25-9
16	Missouri	20-8	Norm Stewart	21-9
17	Massachusetts	28-4	John Calipari	30-5
18	North Carolina	21-9	Dean Smith	23-10
19	Seton Hall	21-8	P.J. Carlesimo	23-9
20	Florida St.	20-9	Pat Kennedy	22-10
21	Syracuse	21-9	Jim Boeheim	22-10
22	Georgetown	21-9	John Thompson	22-10
23	Oklahoma	21-8	Billy Tubbs	21-9
24	DePaul	20-8	Joey Meyer	20-9
25	LSU	20-9	Dale Brown	21-10

*On probation

NCAA Final Four (at the Metrodome, Minneapolis): **Semifinals**—Michigan 76, Cincinnati 72; Duke 81, Indiana 78. **Championship**—Duke 71, Michigan 51.
NIT Championship (at Madison Square Garden): Virginia 81, Notre Dame 76 (OT). No Top 25 teams played in NIT.

Associated Press Final Polls (Cont.)

1993

		Before Tourns	Head Coach	Final Record
1	Indiana	28-3	Bob Knight	31-4
2	Kentucky	26-3	Rick Pitino	30-4
3	Michigan	26-4	Steve Fisher	31-5
4	N. Carolina	28-4	Dean Smith	34-4
5	Arizona	24-3	Lute Olson	24-4
6	Seton Hall	27-6	P.J. Carlesimo	28-7
7	Cincinnati	24-4	Bob Huggins	27-5
8	Vanderbilt	26-5	Eddie Fogler	28-6
9	Kansas	25-6	Roy Williams	29-7
10	Duke	23-7	Mike Krzyzewski	24-8
11	Florida St.	22-9	Pat Kennedy	25-10
12	Arkansas	20-8	Nolan Richardson	22-9
13	Iowa	22-8	Tom Davis	23-9
14	Massachusetts	23-6	John Calipari	24-7
15	Louisville	20-8	Denny Crum	22-9
16	Wake Forest	19-8	Dave Odom	21-9
17	New Orleans	26-3	Tim Floyd	26-4
18	Georgia Tech	19-10	Bobby Cremins	19-11
19	Utah	23-6	Rick Majerus	24-7
20	Western Ky.	24-5	Ralph Willard	26-6
21	New Mexico	24-6	Dave Bliss	24-7
22	Purdue	18-9	Gene Keady	18-10
23	Oklahoma St.	19-8	Eddie Sutton	20-9
24	New Mexico St.	25-7	Neil McCarthy	26-8
25	UNLV	21-7	Rollie Massimino	21-8

NCAA Final Four (at the Superdome, New Orleans): **Semifinals**–North Carolina 78, Kansas 68; Michigan 81, Kentucky 78 (OT). **Championship**–North Carolina 77, Michigan 71.

NIT Championship (at Madison Square Garden): Minnesota 62, Georgetown 61. No. 25 UNLV was the only Top 25 team that played in the NIT.

1994

		Before Tourns	Head Coach	Final Record
1	North Carolina	27-6	Dean Smith	28-7
2	Arkansas	25-3	Nolan Richardson	31-3
3	Purdue	26-4	Gene Keady	29-5
4	Connecticut	27-4	Jim Calhoun	29-5
5	Missouri	25-3	Norm Stewart	28-4
6	Duke	23-5	Mike Krzyzewski	28-6
7	Kentucky	26-6	Rick Pitino	27-7
8	Massachusetts	27-6	John Calipari	28-7
9	Arizona	25-5	Lute Olson	29-6
10	Louisville	26-5	Denny Crum	28-6
11	Michigan	21-7	Steve Fisher	24-8
12	Temple	22-7	John Chaney	23-8
13	Kansas	25-7	Roy Williams	27-8
14	Florida	25-7	Lon Kruger	29-8
15	Syracuse	21-6	Jim Boeheim	23-7
16	California	22-7	Todd Bozeman	22-8
17	UCLA	21-6	Jim Harrick	21-7
18	Indiana	19-8	Bob Knight	21-9
19	Oklahoma St.	23-9	Eddie Sutton	24-10
20	Texas	24-7	Tom Penders	26-8
21	Marquette	22-8	Kevin O'Neill	24-9
22	Nebraska	20-9	Danny Nee	20-10
23	Minnesota	20-11	Clem Haskins	21-12
24	Saint Louis	23-5	Charlie Spoonhour	23-6
25	Cincinnati	22-9	Bob Huggins	22-10

NCAA Final Four (at the Charlotte Coliseum): **Semifinals**– Arkansas 91, Arizona 82; Duke 70, Florida 65. **Championship**– Arkansas 76, Duke 72.

NIT Championship (at Madison Square Garden): Villanova 80, Vanderbilt 73. No top 25 teams played in NIT.

1995

		Before Tourns	Head Coach	Final Record
1	UCLA	25-2	Jim Harrick	31-2
2	Kentucky	25-4	Rick Pitino	28-5
3	Wake Forest	24-5	Dave Odom	26-6
4	North Carolina	24-5	Dean Smith	28-6
5	Kansas	23-5	Roy Williams	25-6
6	Arkansas	27-6	Nolan Richardson	32-7
7	Massachusetts	26-4	John Calipari	26-5
8	Connecticut	25-4	Jim Calhoun	28-5
9	Villanova	25-7	Steve Lappas	25-8
10	Maryland	24-7	Gary Williams	26-8
11	Michigan St.	22-5	Jud Heathcote	22-6
12	Purdue	24-6	Gene Keady	25-7
13	Virginia	22-8	Jeff Jones	25-9
14	Oklahoma St.	23-9	Eddie Sutton	27-10
15	Arizona	23-7	Lute Olson	23-8
16	Arizona St.	22-8	Bill Frieder	24-9
17	Oklahoma	23-8	Kelvin Sampson	23-9
18	Mississippi St.	20-7	Richard Williams	22-8
19	Utah	27-5	Rick Majerus	28-6
20	Alabama	22-9	David Hobbs	23-10
21	Western Ky.	26-3	Matt Kilcullen	27-4
22	Georgetown	19-9	John Thompson	21-10
23	Missouri	19-8	Norm Stewart	20-9
24	Iowa St.	22-10	Tim Floyd	23-11
25	Syracuse	19-9	Jim Boeheim	20-10

NCAA Final Four (at the Kingdome, Seattle): **Semifinals**– UCLA 74, Oklahoma St. 61; Arkansas 75, North Carolina 68. **Championship**– UCLA 89, Arkansas 78.

NIT Championship (at Madison Square Garden): Virginia Tech 65, Marquette 64 (OT). No top 25 teams played in NIT.

1996

		Before Tourns	Head Coach	Final Record
1	Massachusetts	31-1	John Calipari	35-2
2	Kentucky	28-2	Rick Pitino	34-2
3	Connecticut	30-2	Jim Calhoun	32-3
4	Georgetown	26-7	John Thompson	29-8
5	Kansas	26-4	Roy Williams	29-5
6	Purdue	25-5	Gene Keady	26-6
7	Cincinnati	25-4	Bob Huggins	28-5
8	Texas Tech	28-1	James Dickey	30-2
9	Wake Forest	23-5	Dave Odom	26-6
10	Villanova	25-6	Steve Lappas	26-7
11	Arizona	24-6	Lute Olson	26-7
12	Utah	25-6	Rick Majerus	27-7
13	Georgia Tech	22-11	Bobby Cremins	24-12
14	UCLA	23-7	Jim Harrick	23-8
15	Syracuse	24-8	Jim Boeheim	29-9
16	Memphis	22-7	Larry Finch	22-8
17	Iowa St.	23-8	Tim Floyd	24-9
18	Penn St.	21-6	Jerry Dunn	21-7
19	Mississippi St.	22-7	Richard Williams	26-8
20	Marquette	22-7	Mike Deane	23-8
21	Iowa	22-8	Tom Davis	23-9
22	Virginia Tech	22-5	Bill Foster	23-6
23	New Mexico	27-4	Dave Bliss	28-5
24	Louisville	20-11	Denny Crum	22-12
25	North Carolina	20-10	Dean Smith	21-11

NCAA Final Four (at the Meadowlands, E. Rutherford, N.J.): **Semifinals**– Kentucky 81, Massachusetts 74; Syracuse 77, Mississippi St. 69. **Championship**– Kentucky 76, Syracuse 67.

NIT Championship (at Madison Square Garden): Nebraska 60, St. Joseph's 56. No top 25 teams played in NIT.

1997

		Before Tourns	Head Coach	Final Record
1	Kansas	32-1	Roy Williams	34-2
2	Utah	26-3	Rick Majerus	29-4
3	Minnesota	27-3	Clem Haskins	31-4
4	North Carolina	24-6	Dean Smith	28-7
5	Kentucky	30-4	Rick Pitino	35-5
6	South Carolina	24-7	Eddie Fogler	24-8
7	UCLA	21-7	Steve Lavin	24-8
8	Duke	23-8	Mike Krzyzewski	24-9
9	Wake Forest	23-6	Dave Odom	24-7
10	Cincinnati	25-7	Bob Huggins	26-8
11	New Mexico	24-7	Dave Bliss	25-8
12	St. Joseph's	24-6	Phil Martelli	26-7
13	Xavier	22-5	Skip Prosser	23-6
14	Clemson	21-9	Rick Barnes	23-10
15	**Arizona**	19-9	Lute Olsen	25-9
16	Charleston	28-2	John Kresse	29-3
17	Georgia	24-8	Tubby Smith	24-9
18	Iowa St.	20-8	Tim Floyd	22-9
19	Illinois	21-9	Lon Kruger	22-10
20	Villanova	23-9	Steve Lappas	24-10
21	Stanford	20-7	Mike Montgomery	22-8
22	Maryland	21-10	Gary Williams	21-11
23	Boston College	21-8	Jim O'Brien	22-9
24	Colorado	21-9	Ricardo Patton	22-10
25	Louisville	23-8	Denny Crum	26-9

NCAA Final Four (at the RCA Dome, Indianapolis): **Semifinals**– Kentucky 78, Minnesota 69; Arizona 66, North Carolina 58. **Championship**– Arizona 84, Kentucky 79 (OT).

NIT Championship (at Madison Square Garden): Michigan 82, Florida St. 72. No top 25 teams played in NIT.

1998

		Before Tourns	Head Coach	Final Record
1	North Carolina	30-3	Bill Guthridge	34-4
2	Kansas	34-3	Roy Williams	35-4
3	Duke	29-3	Mike Krzyzewski	32-4
4	Arizona	27-4	Lute Olsen	30-5
5	**Kentucky**	29-4	Tubby Smith	35-4
6	Connecticut	29-4	Jim Calhoun	32-5
7	Utah	25-3	Rick Majerus	30-4
8	Princeton	26-1	Bill Carmody	27-2
9	Cincinnati	26-5	Bob Huggins	27-6
10	Stanford	26-4	Mike Montgomery	30-5
11	Purdue	26-7	Gene Keady	28-8
12	Michigan	24-8	Brian Ellerbe	25-9
13	Mississippi	22-6	Rob Evans	22-7
14	South Carolina	23-7	Eddie Fogler	23-8
15	TCU	27-5	Billy Tubbs	27-6
16	Michigan St.	20-7	Tom Izzo	22-8
17	Arkansas	23-8	Nolan Richardson	24-9
18	New Mexico	23-7	Dave Bliss	24-8
19	UCLA	22-8	Steve Lavin	24-9
20	Maryland	19-10	Gary Williams	21-11
21	Syracuse	24-8	Jim Boeheim	26-9
22	Illinois	22-9	Lon Kruger	23-10
23	Xavier	22-7	Skip Prosser	22-8
24	Temple	21-8	John Chaney	21-9
25	Murray St.	29-3	Mark Gottfried	29-4

NCAA Final Four (at the Alamodome, San Antonio): **Semifinals**– Kentucky 86, Stanford 85 (OT); Utah 65, North Carolina 59. **Championship**– Kentucky 78, Utah 69.

NIT Championship (at Madison Square Garden): Minnesota 79, Penn St. 72. No top 25 teams played in NIT.

AP Post-Tournament Final Polls

The final AP Top 20 poll has been released after the NCAA tournament and NIT four times– in 1953 and '54 and again in 1974 and '75. Those four polls are listed below; teams that were not included in the last regular season polls are in *CAPITAL* italic letters.

	1953	Final Record		1954	Final Record		1974	Final Record		1975	Final Record
1	Indiana	23-3	1	Kentucky	25-0	1	N.C. State	30-1	1	UCLA	28-3
2	Seton Hall	31-2	2	La Salle	26-4	2	UCLA	26-4	2	Kentucky	26-5
3	Kansas	19-6	3	Holy Cross	26-2	3	Marquette	26-5	3	Indiana	31-1
4	Washington	30-3	4	Indiana	20-4	4	Maryland	23-5	4	Louisville	28-3
5	LSU	24-3	5	Duquesne	26-3	5	Notre Dame	26-3	5	Maryland	24-5
6	La Salle	25-3	6	Notre Dame	22-3	6	Michigan	22-5	6	Syracuse	23-9
7	*ST. JOHN'S*	17-6	7	*BRADLEY*	19-13	7	Kansas	23-7	7	N.C. State	22-6
8	Okla. A&M	23-7	8	Western Ky.	29-3	8	Providence	28-4	8	Arizona St.	25-4
9	Duquesne	21-8	9	*PENN ST.*	18-6	9	Indiana	23-5	9	North Carolina	23-8
10	Notre Dame	19-5	10	Okla. A&M	24-5	10	Long Beach St.	24-2	10	Alabama	22-5
11	Illinois	18-4	11	USC	19-14	11	*PURDUE*	22-8	11	Marquette	23-4
12	Kansas St.	17-4	12	*GEO. WASH.*	23-3	12	North Carolina	22-6	12	*PRINCETON*	22-8
13	Holy Cross	20-6	13	Iowa	17-5	13	Vanderbilt	23-5	13	Cincinnati	23-6
14	Seattle	29-4	14	LSU	21-5	14	Alabama	22-4	14	Notre Dame	19-10
15	*WAKE FOREST*	22-7	15	Duke	22-6	15	*UTAH*	22-8	15	Kansas St.	20-9
16	*SANTA CLARA*	20-7	16	*NIAGARA*	24-6	16	Pittsburgh	25-4	16	Drake	19-10
17	Western Ky.	25-6	17	Seattle	26-2	17	USC	24-5	17	UNLV	24-5
18	N.C. State	26-6	18	Kansas	16-5	18	*ORAL ROBERTS*	23-6	18	Oregon St.	19-12
19	*DEPAUL*	19-9	19	Illinois	17-5	19	South Carolina	22-5	19	*MICHIGAN*	19-8
20	*SW MISSOURI*	24-4	20	*MARYLAND*	23-7	20	Dayton	20-9	20	Penn	23-5

Pre-Tournament Records

1953– St. John's (Al DeStefano, 14-5); Wake Forest (Murray Greason, 21-6); Santa Clara (Bob Feerick, 18-6); DePaul (Ray Meyer, 18-7); SW Missouri St. (Bob Vanatta, 19-4 before NAIA tourney). **1954**– Bradley (Forddy Anderson, 15-12); Penn St. (Elmer Gross, 14-5); George Washington (Bill Reinhart, 23-2); Niagara (Taps Gallagher, 22-5); Maryland (Bud Millikan, 23-7). **1974**– Purdue (Fred Schaus, 18-8); Utah (Bill Foster, 19-7); Oral Roberts (Ken Trickey, 21-5). **1975**– Princeton (Pete Carril, 18-8); Michigan (Johnny Orr, 19-7).

AP Final Polls (Cont.)
1999

	Before Tourns	Head Coach	Final Record
1 Duke	32-1	Mike Krzyzewski	37-2
2 Michigan St.	29-4	Tom Izzo	33-5
3 **Connecticut**	28-2	Jim Calhoun	34-2
4 Auburn	27-3	Cliff Ellis	29-4
5 Maryland	26-5	Gary Williams	28-6
6 Utah	27-4	Rick Majerus	28-5
7 Stanford	25-6	Mike Montgomery	26-7
8 Kentucky	25-8	Tubby Smith	28-9
9 St. John's	25-8	Mike Jarvis	28-9
10 Miami-FL	22-6	Leonard Hamilton	23-7
11 Cincinnati	26-5	Bob Huggins	27-6
12 Arizona	22-6	Lute Olson	22-7
13 North Carolina	24-9	Bill Guthridge	24-10
14 Ohio St.	23-8	Jim O'Brien	27-9
15 UCLA	22-8	Steve Lavin	22-9
16 College of Charleston	28-2	John Kresse	28-3
17 Arkansas	22-10	Nolan Richardson	23-11
18 Wisconsin	22-9	Dick Bennett	22-10
19 Indiana	22-10	Bobby Knight	23-11
20 Tennessee	20-8	Jerry Green	21-9
21 Iowa	18-9	Tom Davis	20-10
22 Kansas	22-9	Roy Williams	23-10
23 Florida	20-8	Billy Donovan	22-9
24 NC-Charlotte	22-10	Bob Lutz	23-11
25 New Mexico	24-8	Dave Bliss	25-9

NCAA Final Four (at the Tropicana Field, St. Petersburg): **Semifinals**– Duke 68, Michigan St. 62; Connecticut 64, Ohio St. 58. **Championship**– Connecticut 77, Duke 74.
NIT Championship (at Madison Square Garden): California 61, Clemson 60. No top 25 teams played in NIT.

Division I Winning Streaks
Full Season
(Including tournaments)

No		Seasons	Broken by	Score
88	UCLA	1971-74	Notre Dame	71-70
60	San Francisco	1955-57	Illinois	62-33
47	UCLA	1966-68	Houston	71-69
45	UNLV	1990-91	Duke	79-77
44	Texas	1913-17	Rice	24-18
43	Seton Hall	1939-41	LIU-Bklyn	49-26
43	LIU-Brooklyn	1935-37	Stanford	45-31
41	UCLA	1968-69	USC	46-44
39	Marquette	1970-71	Ohio St.	60-59
37	Cincinnati	1962-63	Wichita St.	65-64
37	North Carolina	1957-58	West Virginia	75-64
36	N.C. State	1974-75	Wake Forest	83-78
35	Arkansas	1927-29	Texas	26-25

Regular Season
(Not including tournaments)

No		Seasons	Broken by	Score
76	UCLA	1971-74	Notre Dame	71-70
57	Indiana	1975-77	Toledo	59-57
56	Marquette	1970-72	Detroit	70-49
54	Kentucky	1952-55	Georgia Tech	59-58
51	San Francisco	1955-57	Illinois	62-33
48	Penn	1970-72	Temple	57-52
47	Ohio St	1960-62	Wisconsin	86-67
44	Texas	1913-17	Rice	24-18
43	UCLA	1966-68	Houston	71-69
43	LIU-Brooklyn	1935-37	Stanford	45-31
42	Seton Hall	1939-41	LIU-Bklyn	49-26

Home Court

No		Seasons	Broken By	Score
129	Kentucky	1943-55	Georgia Tech	59-58
99	St. Bonaventure	1948-61	Detroit	77-70
98	UCLA	1970-76	Oregon	65-45
86	Cincinnati	1957-64	Kansas	51-47
81	Arizona	1945-51	Kansas St.	76-57
81	Marquette	1967-73	Notre Dame	71-69
80	Lamar	1978-84	Louisiana Tech	68-65
75	Long Beach St.	1968-74	San Francisco	94-84
72	UNLV	1974-78	New Mexico	102-98
71	Arizona	1987-92	UCLA	89-87

All-Time Highest Scoring Teams
SINGLE SEASON
Scoring Offense

Team	Season	Gm	Pts	Avg
Loyola-CA	1990	32	3918	122.4
Loyola-CA	1989	31	3486	112.5
UNLV	1976	31	3426	110.5
Loyola-CA	1988	32	3528	110.3
UNLV	1977	32	3426	107.1
Oral Roberts	1972	28	2943	105.1
Southern-BR	1991	28	2924	104.4
Loyola-CA	1991	31	3211	103.6
Oklahoma	1988	39	4012	102.9
Oklahoma	1989	36	3680	102.2

Scoring Defense
Before 1965

Team	Season	Gm	Pts	Avg
Oklahoma A&M	1948	31	1006	32.5
Oklahoma A&M	1949	28	985	35.2
Oklahoma A&M	1950	27	1059	39.2
Alabama	1948	27	1070	39.6
Creighton	1948	23	925	40.2

Since 1965

Team	Season	Gm	Pts	Avg
Fresno St.	1982	30	1412	47.1
Princeton	1992	28	1349	48.2
Princeton	1991	27	1320	48.9
N.C. State	1982	32	1570	49.1
Princeton	1982	26	1277	49.1

Scoring Margin

Team	Season	Off	Def	Mar
UCLA	1972	94.6	64.3	30.3
N.C. State	1948	75.3	47.2	28.1
Kentucky	1954	87.5	60.3	27.2
Kentucky	1952	82.3	55.4	26.9
UNLV	1991	97.7	71.0	26.7
UCLA	1968	93.4	67.2	26.2
UCLA	1967	89.6	63.7	25.9
Houston	1968	97.8	72.5	25.3
Duke	1999	91.8	67.2	24.7
Kentucky	1948	69.0	44.4	24.6

NCAA Champs With Most Losses

11	Kansas (27-11)	1988
10	Villanova (25-10)	1985
10	N.C. State (26-10)	1983
9	Arizona (25-9)	1997
9	Indiana (26-9)	1981

Annual NCAA Division I Leaders
Scoring

The NCAA did not begin keeping individual scoring records until the 1947-48 season. All averages include postseason games where applicable.

Multiple winners: Pete Maravich and Oscar Robertson (3); Darrell Floyd, Charles Jones, Harry Kelly, Frank Selvy and Freeman Williams (2).

Year		Gm	Pts	Avg	Year		Gm	Pts	Avg
1948	Murray Wier, Iowa	19	399	21.0	1974	Larry Fogle, Canisius	25	835	33.4
1949	Tony Lavelli, Yale	30	671	22.4	1975	Bob McCurdy, Richmond	26	855	32.9
1950	Paul Arizin, Villanova	29	735	25.3	1976	Marshall Rodgers, Texas-Pan Am	25	919	36.8
1951	Bill Mlkvy, Temple	25	731	29.2	1977	Freeman Williams, Portland St.	26	1010	38.8
1952	Clyde Lovellette, Kansas	28	795	28.4	1978	Freeman Williams, Portland St.	27	969	35.9
1953	Frank Selvy, Furman	25	738	29.5	1979	Lawrence Butler, Idaho St.	27	812	30.1
1954	Frank Selvy, Furman	29	1209	41.7	1980	Tony Murphy, Southern-BR	29	932	32.1
1955	Darrell Floyd, Furman	25	897	35.9	1981	Zam Fredrick, S. Carolina	27	781	28.9
1956	Darrell Floyd, Furman	28	946	33.8	1982	Harry Kelly, Texas Southern	29	862	29.7
1957	Grady Wallace, S. Carolina	29	906	31.2	1983	Harry Kelly, Texas Southern	29	835	28.8
1958	Oscar Robertson, Cincinnati	28	984	35.1	1984	Joe Jakubick, Akron	27	814	30.1
1959	Oscar Robertson, Cincinnati	30	978	32.6	1985	Xavier McDaniel, Wichita St	31	844	27.2
1960	Oscar Robertson, Cincinnati	30	1011	33.7	1986	Terrance Bailey, Wagner	29	854	29.4
1961	Frank Burgess, Gonzaga	26	842	32.4	1987	Kevin Houston, Army	29	953	32.9
1962	Billy McGill, Utah	26	1009	38.8	1988	Hersey Hawkins, Bradley	31	1125	36.3
1963	Nick Werkman, Seton Hall	22	650	29.5	1989	Hank Gathers, Loyola-CA	31	1015	32.7
1964	Howie Komives, Bowling Green	23	844	36.7	1990	Bo Kimble, Loyola-CA	32	1131	35.3
1965	Rick Barry, Miami-FL	26	973	37.4	1991	Kevin Bradshaw, US Int'l	28	1054	37.6
1966	Dave Schellhase, Purdue	24	781	32.5	1992	Brett Roberts, Morehead St	29	815	28.1
1967	Jimmy Walker, Providence	28	851	30.4	1993	Greg Guy, Texas-Pan Am	19	556	29.3
1968	Pete Maravich, LSU	26	1138	43.8	1994	Glenn Robinson, Purdue	34	1030	30.3
1969	Pete Maravich, LSU	26	1148	44.2	1995	Kurt Thomas, TCU	27	781	28.9
1970	Pete Maravich, LSU	31	1381	44.5	1996	Kevin Granger, Texas Southern	24	648	27.0
1971	Johnny Neumann, Ole Miss	23	923	40.1	1997	Charles Jones, LIU-Brooklyn	30	903	30.1
1972	Dwight Lamar, SW La.	29	1054	36.3	1998	Charles Jones, LIU-Brooklyn	30	869	29.0
1973	Bird Averitt, Pepperdine	25	848	33.9	1999	Alvin Young, Niagara	29	728	25.1

Note: Seventeen underclassmen have won the title. **Sophomores** (4)–Robertson (1958), Maravich (1968), Neumann (1971) and Fogle (1974); **Juniors** (13)–Selvy (1953), Floyd (1955), Robertson (1959), Werkman (1963), Maravich (1969), Lamar (1972), Williams (1977), Kelly (1982), Bailey (1986), Gathers (1989), Guy (1993), Robinson (1994) and Jones (1997).

Rebounds

The NCAA did not begin keeping individual rebounding records until the 1950-51 season. From 1956-62, the championship was decided on highest percentage of recoveries out of all rebounds made by both teams in all games. All averages include postseason games where applicable.

Multiple winners: Artis Gilmore, Jerry Lucas, Xavier McDaniel, Kermit Washington and Leroy Wright (2).

Year		Gm	No	Avg	Year		Gm	No	Avg
1951	Ernie Beck, Penn	27	556	20.6	1976	Sam Pellom, Buffalo	26	420	16.2
1952	Bill Hannon, Army	17	355	20.9	1977	Glenn Mosley, Seton Hall	29	473	16.3
1953	Ed Conlin, Fordham	26	612	23.5	1978	Ken Williams, N. Texas	28	411	14.7
1954	Art Quimby, Connecticut	26	588	22.6	1979	Monti Davis, Tennessee St.	26	421	16.2
1955	Charlie Slack, Marshall	21	538	25.6	1980	Larry Smith, Alcorn State	26	392	15.1
1956	Joe Holup, G. Washington	26	604	25.6	1981	Darryl Watson, Miss. Valley St.	27	379	14.0
1957	Elgin Baylor, Seattle	25	508	23.5	1982	LaSalle Thompson, Texas	27	365	13.5
1958	Alex Ellis, Niagara	25	536	26.2	1983	Xavier McDaniel, Wichita St.	28	403	14.4
1959	Leroy Wright, Pacific	26	652	23.8	1984	Akeem Olajuwon, Houston	37	500	13.5
1960	Leroy Wright, Pacific	17	380	23.4	1985	Xavier McDaniel, Wichita St.	31	460	14.8
1961	Jerry Lucas, Ohio St.	27	470	19.8	1986	David Robinson, Navy	35	455	13.0
1962	Jerry Lucas, Ohio St.	28	499	21.1	1987	Jerome Lane, Pittsburgh	33	444	13.5
1963	Paul Silas, Creighton	27	557	20.6	1988	Kenny Miller, Loyola-IL	29	395	13.6
1964	Bob Pelkington, Xavier-OH	26	567	21.8	1989	Hank Gathers, Loyola-CA	31	426	13.7
1965	Toby Kimball, Connecticut	23	483	21.0	1990	Anthony Bonner, St. Louis	33	456	13.8
1966	Jim Ware, Oklahoma City	29	607	20.9	1991	Shaquille O'Neal, LSU	28	411	14.7
1967	Dick Cunningham, Murray St.	22	479	21.8	1992	Popeye Jones, Murray St.	30	431	14.4
1968	Neal Walk, Florida	25	494	19.8	1993	Warren Kidd, Mid. Tenn. St.	26	386	14.8
1969	Spencer Haywood, Detroit	22	472	21.5	1994	Jerome Lambert, Baylor	24	355	14.8
1970	Artis Gilmore, Jacksonville	28	621	22.2	1995	Kurt Thomas, TCU	27	393	14.6
1971	Artis Gilmore, Jacksonville	26	603	23.2	1996	Marcus Mann, Miss. Valley St.	29	394	13.6
1972	Kermit Washington, American	23	455	19.8	1997	Tim Duncan, Wake Forest	31	457	14.7
1973	Kermit Washington, American	22	439	20.0	1998	Ryan Perryman, Dayton	33	412	12.5
1974	Marvin Barnes, Providence	32	597	18.7	1999	Ian McGinnis, Dartmouth	26	317	12.2
1975	John Irving, Hofstra	21	323	15.4					

Note: Only three players have ever led the NCAA in scoring and rebounding in the same season: Xavier McDaniel of Wichita St. (1985), Hank Gathers of Loyola-Marymount (1989) and Kurt Thomas of TCU (1995).

Assists

The NCAA did not begin keeping individual assist records until the 1983-84 season. All averages include postseason games where applicable.

Multiple winner: Avery Johnson (2).

Year		Gm	No	Avg
1984	Craig Lathen, IL-Chicago	29	274	9.45
1985	Rob Weingard, Hofstra	24	228	9.50
1986	Mark Jackson, St. John's	36	328	9.11
1987	Avery Johnson, Southern-BR	31	333	10.74
1988	Avery Johnson, Southern-BR	30	399	13.30
1989	Glenn Williams, Holy Cross	28	278	9.93
1990	Todd Lehmann, Drexel	28	260	9.29
1991	Chris Corchiani, N.C. State	31	299	9.65
1992	Van Usher, Tennessee Tech	29	254	8.76
1993	Sam Crawford, N. Mexico St	34	310	9.12
1994	Jason Kidd, California	30	272	9.06
1995	Nelson Haggerty, Baylor	28	284	10.14
1996	Raimonds Miglinieks, UC-Irvine	27	230	8.52
1997	Kenny Mitchell, Dartmouth	26	203	7.81
1998	Ahlon Lewis, Arizona St.	32	294	9.19
1999	Doug Gottlieb, Oklahoma St.	34	299	8.79

Blocked Shots

The NCAA did not begin keeping individual blocked shots records until the 1985-86 season. All averages include post-season games where applicable.

Multiple winner: Keith Closs and David Robinson (2).

Year		Gm	No	Avg
1986	David Robinson, Navy	35	207	5.91
1987	David Robinson, Navy	32	144	4.50
1988	Rodney Blake, St. Joe's-PA	29	116	4.00
1989	Alonzo Mourning, G'town	34	169	4.97
1990	Kenny Green, Rhode Island	26	124	4.77
1991	Shawn Bradley, BYU	34	177	5.21
1992	Shaquille O'Neal, LSU	30	157	5.23
1993	Theo Ratliff, Wyoming	28	124	4.43
1994	Grady Livingston, Howard	26	115	4.42
1995	Keith Closs, Cen. Conn. St.	26	139	5.35
1996	Keith Closs, Cen. Conn. St.	28	178	6.36
1997	Adonal Foyle, Colgate	28	180	6.43
1998	Jerome James, Florida A&M	27	125	4.63
1999	Tarvis Williams, Hampton	27	135	5.00

All-Time NCAA Division I Individual Leaders

Through 1998-99; includes regular season and tournament games; **Last** column indicates final year played.

CAREER

Scoring

	Points	Yrs	Last	Gm	Pts
1	Pete Maravich, LSU	3	1970	83	3667
2	Freeman Williams, Port. St.	4	1978	106	3249
3	Lionel Simmons, La Salle	4	1990	131	3217
4	Alphonzo Ford, Miss. Val. St.	4	1993	109	3165
5	Harry Kelly, Texas Southern	4	1983	110	3066
6	Hersey Hawkins, Bradley	4	1988	125	3008
7	Oscar Robertson, Cincinnati	3	1960	88	2973
8	Danny Manning, Kansas	4	1988	147	2951
9	Alfredrick Hughes, Loyola-IL	4	1985	120	2914
10	Elvin Hayes, Houston	3	1968	93	2884
11	Larry Bird, Indiana St.	3	1979	94	2850
12	Otis Birdsong, Houston	4	1977	116	2832
13	Kevin Bradshaw, US Int'l	4	1991	111	2804
14	Allan Houston, Tennessee	4	1993	128	2801
15	Hank Gathers, USC/Loyola-CA	4	1990	117	2723
16	Reggie Lewis, Northeastern	4	1987	122	2708
17	Daren Queenan, Xavier-OH	4	1988	118	2703
18	Byron Larkin, Xavier-OH	4	1988	121	2696
19	David Robinson, Navy	4	1987	127	2669
20	Wayman Tisdale, Oklahoma	3	1985	104	2661

	Average	Yrs	Last	Pts	Avg
1	Pete Maravich, LSU	3	1970	3667	44.2
2	Austin Carr, Notre Dame	3	1971	2560	34.6
3	Oscar Robertson, Cinn	3	1960	2973	33.8
4	Calvin Murphy, Niagara	3	1970	2548	33.1
5	Dwight Lamar, SW La	2	1973	1862	32.7
6	Frank Selvy, Furman	3	1954	2538	32.5
7	Rick Mount, Purdue	3	1970	2323	32.3
8	Darrell Floyd, Furman	3	1956	2281	32.1
9	Nick Werkman, Seton Hall	3	1964	2273	32.0
10	Willie Humes, Idaho St.	2	1971	1510	31.5
11	William Averitt, Pepperdine	2	1973	1541	31.4
12	Elgin Baylor, Idaho/Seattle	3	1958	2500	31.3
13	Elvin Hayes, Houston	3	1968	2884	31.0
14	Freeman Williams, Port. St.	4	1978	3249	30.7
15	Larry Bird, Indiana St.	3	1979	2850	30.3
16	Bill Bradley, Princeton	3	1965	2503	30.2
17	Rich Fuqua, Oral Roberts	2	1973	1617	29.9
18	Wilt Chamberlain, Kansas	2	1958	1433	29.9
19	Rick Barry, Miami-FL	3	1965	2298	29.8
20	Doug Collins, Illinois St.	3	1973	2240	29.1

	Field Goal Pct.	Yrs	Last	FG	FGA	Pct
1	Ricky Nedd, Appalach. St.	4	1994	412	597	.690
2	Stephen Scheffler, Purdue	4	1990	408	596	.685
3	Steve Johnson, Ore. St.	4	1981	828	1222	.678
4	Murray Brown, Fla. St.	4	1980	566	847	.668
5	Lee Campbell, SW Mo.St.	3	1990	411	618	.665
6	Warren Kidd, M.Tenn.St.	3	1993	496	747	.664
7	Todd MacCulloch, Wash.	4	1999	702	1058	.664
8	Joe Senser, West Chester	4	1979	476	719	.662
9	Kevin McGee, UC-Irvine	2	1982	552	841	.656
10	O. Phillips, Pepperdine	2	1983	404	618	.654

Note: minimum 400 FGs made.

	Free Throw Pct.	Yrs	Last	FT	FTA	Pct
1	Greg Starrick, Ky/So.Ill	4	1972	341	375	.909
2	Jack Moore, Nebraska	4	1982	446	495	.901
3	Steve Henson, Kansas St.	4	1990	361	401	.900
4	Steve Alford, Indiana	4	1987	535	596	.898
5	Bob Lloyd, Rutgers	3	1967	543	605	.898
6	Jim Barton, Dartmouth	4	1989	394	440	.895
7	Tommy Boyer, Arkansas	3	1963	315	353	.892
8	Rob Robbins, N. Mexico	4	1991	309	348	.888
9	Marcus Wilson, Evansville	4	1999	455	513	.887
10	Sean Miller, Pitt	4	1992	317	358	.885

Note: minimum 300 FTs made.

	3-Pt Field Goals	Yrs	Last	Gm	3FG
1	Curtis Staples, Virginia	4	1998	122	413
2	Keith Veney, Lamar/Marshall	4	1997	111	409
3	Doug Day, Radford	4	1993	117	401
4	Ronnie Schmitz, Missouri-KC	4	1993	112	378
5	Mark Alberts, Akron	4	1993	107	375

	3-Pt Field Goal Pct.	Yrs	Last	3FG	Att	Pct
1	Tony Bennett, Wisc-GB	4	1992	290	584	.497
2	Keith Jennings, E.Tenn.St.	4	1991	223	452	.493
3	Kirk Manns, Michigan St.	4	1990	212	446	.475
4	Tim Locum, Wisconsin	4	1991	227	481	.472
5	David Olson, Eastern Ill.	4	1992	262	562	.466

Note: minimum 200 3FGs made.

Rebounds

Total (before 1973)

		Yrs	Last	Gm	No
1	Tom Gola, La Salle	4	1955	118	2201
2	Joe Holup, G. Washington	4	1956	104	2030
3	Charlie Slack, Marshall	4	1956	88	1916
4	Ed Conlin, Fordham	4	1955	102	1884
5	Dickie Hemric, Wake Forest	4	1955	104	1802
6	Paul Silas, Creighton	3	1964	81	1751
7	Art Quimby, Connecticut	4	1955	80	1716
8	Jerry Harper, Alabama	4	1956	93	1688
9	Jeff Cohen, Wm. & Mary	4	1961	103	1679
10	Steve Hamilton, Morehead St.	4	1958	102	1675

Total (since 1973)

		Yrs	Last	Gm	No
1	Tim Duncan, Wake Forest	4	1997	128	1570
2	Derrick Coleman, Syracuse	4	1990	143	1537
3	Ralph Sampson, Virginia	4	1983	132	1511
4	Pete Padgett, Nevada-Reno	4	1976	104	1464
5	Lionel Simmons, La Salle	4	1990	131	1429
6	Anthony Bonner, St. Louis	4	1990	133	1424
7	Tyrone Hill, Xavier-OH	4	1990	126	1380
8	Popeye Jones, Murray St.	4	1992	123	1374
9	Michael Brooks, La Salle	4	1980	114	1372
10	Xavier McDaniel, Wichita St.	4	1985	117	1359

Average (before 1973)

		Yrs	Last	No	Avg
1	Artis Gilmore, Jacksonville	2	1971	1224	22.7
2	Charlie Slack, Marshall	4	1956	1916	21.8
3	Paul Silas, Creighton	3	1964	1751	21.6
4	Leroy Wright, Pacific	3	1960	1442	21.5
5	Art Quimby, Connecticut	4	1955	1716	21.5

Note: minimum 800 rebounds.

Average (since 1973)

		Yrs	Last	No	Avg
1	Glenn Mosley, Seton Hall	4	1977	1263	15.2
2	Bill Campion, Manhattan	3	1975	1070	14.2
3	Pete Padgett, Nevada-Reno	4	1976	1464	14.1
4	Bob Warner, Maine	4	1976	1304	13.6
5	Shaquille O'Neal, LSU	3	1992	1217	13.5

Note: minimum 650 rebounds.

Assists

Total

		Yrs	Last	Gm	No
1	Bobby Hurley, Duke	4	1993	140	1076
2	Chris Corchiani, N.C. State	4	1991	124	1038
3	Keith Jennings, E. Tenn. St.	4	1991	127	983
4	Sherman Douglas, Syracuse	4	1989	138	960
5	Tony Miller, Marquette	4	1995	123	956
6	Greg Anthony, Portland/UNLV	4	1991	138	950
7	Gary Payton, Oregon St.	4	1990	120	938
8	Orlando Smart, San Fran.	4	1994	116	902
9	Andre LaFleur, Northeastern	4	1987	128	894
10	Jim Les, Bradley	4	1986	118	884

Average

		Yrs	Last	No	Avg
1	A. Johnson, Cameron/Southern	3	1988	838	8.91
2	Sam Crawford, N. Mexico St.	2	1993	592	8.84
3	Mark Wade, Okla/UNLV	3	1987	693	8.77
4	Chris Corchiani, N.C. State	4	1991	1038	8.37
5	Taurence Chisholm, Delaware	4	1988	877	7.97
6	Van Usher, Tennessee Tech	3	1992	676	7.95
7	Anthony Manuel, Bradley	3	1989	855	7.92
8	Gary Payton, Oregon St.	4	1990	938	7.82
9	Orlando Smart, San Fran.	4	1994	902	7.78
10	Tony Miller, Marquette	4	1995	956	7.77

Note: minimum 550 assists.

Blocked Shots

Average

		Yrs	Last	No	Avg
1	Keith Closs, Cen. Conn. St.	2	1996	317	5.87
2	Adonal Foyle, Colgate	3	1997	492	5.66
3	David Robinson, Navy	2	1987	351	5.24
4	Shaquille O'Neal, LSU	3	1992	412	4.58
5	Jerome James, Fla. A&M	3	1998	363	4.48

Note: minimum 200 blocked shots.

Steals

Average

		Yrs	Last	No	Avg
1	Mookie Blaylock, Oklahoma	2	1989	281	3.80
2	Ronn McMahon, Eastern Wash.	3	1990	225	3.52
3	Jason Kidd, California	2	1994	204	3.46
4	Eric Murdock, Providence	4	1991	376	3.21
5	Van Usher, Tennessee Tech	3	1992	270	3.18

Note: minimum 200 steals.

2000 Points/1000 Rebounds

For a combined total of 4000 or more.

		Gm	Pts	Reb	Total
1	Tom Gola, La Salle	118	2462	2201	4663
2	Lionel Simmons, La Salle	131	3217	1429	4646
3	Elvin Hayes, Houston	93	2884	1602	4486
4	Dickie Hemric, W. Forest	104	2587	1802	4389
5	Oscar Robertson, Cinn.	88	2973	1338	4311
6	Joe Holup, G. Wash.	104	2226	2030	4256
7	Harry Kelly, TX-Southern	110	3066	1085	4151
8	Danny Manning, Kansas	147	2951	1187	4138
9	Larry Bird, Indiana St.	94	2850	1247	4097
10	Elgin Baylor, Col. Idaho/ Seattle	80	2500	1559	4059
11	Michael Brooks, La Salle	114	2628	1372	4000

Years Played– Baylor (1956-58); Bird (1977-79); Brooks (1977-80); Gola (1952-55); Hayes (1966-68); Hemric (1952-55); Holup (1953-56); Kelly (1980-83); Manning (1985-88); Robertson (1958-60); Simmons (1987-90).

SINGLE SEASON
Scoring

Points

		Year	Gm	Pts
1	Pete Maravich, LSU	1970	31	1381
2	Elvin Hayes, Houston	1968	33	1214
3	Frank Selvy, Furman	1954	29	1209
4	Pete Maravich, LSU	1969	26	1148
5	Pete Maravich, LSU	1968	26	1138
6	Bo Kimble, Loyola-CA	1990	32	1131
7	Hersey Hawkins, Bradley	1988	31	1125
8	Austin Carr, Notre Dame	1970	29	1106
9	Austin Carr, Notre Dame	1971	29	1101
10	Otis Birdsong, Houston	1977	36	1090

Average

		Year	Gm	Pts	Avg
1	Pete Maravich, LSU	1970	31	1381	44.5
2	Pete Maravich, LSU	1969	26	1148	44.2
3	Pete Maravich, LSU	1968	26	1138	43.8
4	Frank Selvy, Furman	1954	29	1209	41.7
5	Johnny Neumann, Ole Miss	1971	23	923	40.1
6	Freeman Williams, Port. St.	1977	26	1010	38.8
7	Billy McGill, Utah	1962	26	1009	38.8
8	Calvin Murphy, Niagara	1968	24	916	38.2
9	Austin Carr, Notre Dame	1970	29	1106	38.1
10	Austin Carr, Notre Dame	1971	29	1101	38.0

All-Time NCAA Division I Individual Leaders (Cont.)

Field Goal Pct.

		Year	FG	FGA	Pct
1	Steve Johnson, Oregon St.	1981	235	315	.746
2	Dwayne Davis, Florida	1989	179	248	.722
3	Keith Walker, Utica	1985	154	216	.713
4	Steve Johnson, Oregon St.	1980	211	297	.710
5	Oliver Miller, Arkansas	1991	254	361	.704

Free Throw Pct.

		Year	FT	FTA	Pct
1	Craig Collins, Penn St.	1985	94	98	.959
2	Rod Foster, UCLA	1982	95	100	.950
3	Carlos Gibson, Marshall	1978	84	89	.944
4	Danny Basile, Marist	1994	84	89	.944
5	Jim Barton, Dartmouth	1986	65	69	.942

3-Pt Field Goal Pct.

		Year	3FG	Att	Pct
1	Glenn Tropf, Holy Cross	1988	52	82	.634
2	Sean Wightman, W. Mich	1992	48	76	.632
3	Keith Jennings, E. Tenn. St.	1991	84	142	.592
4	Dave Calloway, Monmouth	1989	48	82	.585
5	Steve Kerr, Arizona	1988	114	199	.573

Assists

	Average	Year	Gm	No	Avg
1	Avery Johnson, Southern-BR	1988	30	399	13.3
2	Anthony Manuel, Bradley	1988	31	373	12.0
3	Avery Johnson, Southern-BR	1987	31	333	10.7
4	Mark Wade, UNLV	1987	38	406	10.7
5	Glenn Williams, Holy Cross	1989	28	278	9.9

Rebounds

	Average (before 1973)	Year	Gm	No	Avg
1	Charlie Slack, Marshall	1955	21	538	25.6
2	Leroy Wright, Pacific	1959	26	652	25.1
3	Art Quimby, Connecticut	1955	25	611	24.4
4	Charlie Slack, Marshall	1956	22	520	23.6
5	Ed Conlin, Fordham	1953	26	612	23.5

	Average (since 1973)	Year	Gm	No	Avg
1	Kermit Washington, American	1973	25	511	20.4
2	Marvin Barnes, Providence	1973	30	571	19.0
3	Marvin Barnes, Providence	1974	32	597	18.7
4	Pete Padgett, Nevada	1973	26	462	17.8
5	Jim Bradley, Northern Ill	1973	24	426	17.8

Blocked Shots

	Average	Year	Gm	No	Avg
1	Adonal Foyle, Colgate	1997	28	180	6.42
2	Keith Closs, Cen. Conn. St.	1996	28	178	6.36
3	David Robinson, Navy	1986	35	207	5.91
4	Keith Closs, Cen. Conn. St.	1995	26	139	5.35
5	Shaquille O'Neal, LSU	1992	30	157	5.23

Steals

	Average	Year	Gm	No	Avg
1	Darron Brittman, Chicago St.	1986	28	139	4.96
2	Aldwin Ware, Florida A&M	1988	29	142	4.90
3	Ronn McMahon, East Wash	1990	29	130	4.48
4	Pointer Williams, McNeese St.	1996	27	118	4.37
5	Jim Paguaga, St. Francis-NY	1986	28	120	4.29

SINGLE GAME

Scoring

Points vs Div. I Team

		Year	Pts
1	Kevin Bradshaw, US Int'l vs Loyola-CA	1991	72
2	Pete Maravich, LSU vs Alabama	1970	69
3	Calvin Murphy, Niagara vs Syracuse	1969	68
4	Jay Handlan, Wash. & Lee vs Furman	1951	66
	Pete Maravich, LSU vs Tulane	1969	66
	Anthony Roberts, Oral Rbts vs N.C. A&T	1977	66
7	Anthony Roberts, Oral Rbts vs Ore	1977	65
	Scott Haffner, Evansville vs Dayton	1989	65
9	Pete Maravich, LSU vs Kentucky	1970	64
10	Johnny Neumann, Ole Miss vs LSU	1971	63
	Hersey Hawkins, Bradley vs Detroit	1988	63

Points vs Non-Div. I Team

		Year	Pts
1	Frank Selvy, Furman vs Newberry	1954	100
2	Paul Arizin, Villanova vs Phi. NAMC	1949	85
3	Freeman Williams, Port. St. vs Rocky Mt	1978	81
4	Bill Mlkvy, Temple vs Wilkes	1951	73
5	Freeman Williams, Port. St. vs So. Ore	1977	71

Note: Bevo Francis of Division II Rio Grande (Ohio) scored an overall collegiate record 113 points against Hillsdale in 1954. He also scored 84 against Alliance and 82 against Bluffton that same season.

Assists

		Year	No
1	Tony Fairley, Baptist vs Armstrong St.	1987	22
	Avery Johnson, Southern-BR vs TX-South	1988	22
	Sherman Douglas, Syracuse vs Providence	1989	22
4	Mark Wade, UNLV vs Navy	1986	21
	Kelvin Scarborough, N. Mexico vs Hawaii	1987	21
	Anthony Manuel, Bradley vs UC-Irvine	1987	21
	Avery Johnson, Southern-BR vs Ala. St.	1988	21

3-Pt Field Goals

		Year	No
1	Keith Veney, Marshall vs Morehead St.	1996	15
2	Dave Jamerson, Ohio U. vs Charleston	1989	14
	Askia Jones, Kansas St. vs Fresno St.	1994	14
4	Gary Bosserd, Niagara vs Siena	1987	12
	Darrin Fitzgerald, Butler vs Detroit	1987	12
	Al Dillard, Arkansas vs Delaware St.	1993	12
	Mitch Taylor, South-BR vs La. Christian	1995	12
	David McMahan, Winthrop vs C. Carolina	1996	12

Rebounds

Total (before 1973)

		Year	No
1	Bill Chambers, Wm. & Mary vs Virginia	1953	51
2	Charlie Slack, Marshall vs M. Harvey	1954	43
3	Tom Heinsohn, Holy Cross vs BC	1955	42
4	Art Quimby, UConn vs BU	1955	40
5	Three players tied with 39 each.		

Total (since 1973)

		Year	No
1	David Vaughn, Oral Roberts vs Brandeis	1973	34
2	Robert Parish, Centenary vs So. Miss	1973	33
3	Durand Macklin, LSU vs Tulane	1976	32
	Jervaughn Scales, South-BR vs Grambling	1994	32
5	Jim Bradley, Northern Ill. vs WI-Milw	1973	31
	Calvin Natt, NE La. vs Ga. Southern	1976	31

Blocked Shots

		Year	No
1	David Robinson, Navy vs NC-Wilmington	1986	14
	Shawn Bradley, BYU vs Eastern Ky	1990	14
	Roy Rogers, Alabama vs Georgia	1996	14
4	Kevin Robinson, Vermont vs UNH	1992	13
	Jim McIlvaine, Marquette vs No. Ill	1993	13
	Keith Closs, C. Conn. St. vs St. Fran-PA	1994	13

Steals

		Year	No
1	Mookie Blaylock, Oklahoma vs Centenary	1987	13
	Mookie Blaylock, Oklahoma vs Loyola-CA	1988	13
3	Kenny Robertson, Cleve. St. vs Wagner	1988	12
	Terry Evans, Oklahoma vs Florida A&M	1993	12
5	Nine players tied with 11 each, including Darron Brittman of Chicago St., who did it twice.		

Annual Awards

UPI picked the first national Division I Player of the Year in 1955. Since then, the U.S. Basketball Writers Assn. (1959), the Commonwealth Athletic Club of Kentucky's Adolph Rupp Trophy (1961), the Atlanta Tip-Off Club (1969), the National Assn. of Basketball Coaches (1975), and the LA Athletic Club's John Wooden Award (1977) have joined in. UPI discontinued its award in 1997.

Since 1977, the first year all the following awards were given out, the same player has won all of them in the same season 12 times: Marques Johnson in 1977, Larry Bird in 1979, Ralph Sampson in both 1982 and '83, Michael Jordan in 1984, David Robinson in 1987, Lionel Simmons in 1990, Calbert Cheaney in 1993, Glenn Robinson in 1994, Tim Duncan in 1997, Antawn Jamison in 1998 and Elton Brand in 1999.

United Press International

Voted on by a panel of UPI college basketball writers and first presented in 1955.

Multiple winners: Oscar Robertson, Ralph Sampson and Bill Walton (3); Lew Alcindor and Jerry Lucas (2).

Year	Year	Year
1955 Tom Gola, La Salle	1970 Pete Maravich, LSU	1985 Chris Mullin, St. John's
1956 Bill Russell, San Francisco	1971 Austin Carr, Notre Dame	1986 Walter Berry, St. John's
1957 Chet Forte, Columbia	1972 Bill Walton, UCLA	1987 David Robinson, Navy
1958 Oscar Robertson, Cincinnati	1973 Bill Walton, UCLA	1988 Hersey Hawkins, Bradley
1959 Oscar Robertson, Cincinnati	1974 Bill Walton, UCLA	1989 Danny Ferry, Duke
1960 Oscar Robertson, Cincinnati	1975 David Thompson, N.C. State	1990 Lionel Simmons, La Salle
1961 Jerry Lucas, Ohio St.	1976 Scott May, Indiana	1991 Shaquille O'Neal, LSU
1962 Jerry Lucas, Ohio St.	1977 Marques Johnson, UCLA	1992 Jim Jackson, Ohio St.
1963 Art Heyman, Duke	1978 Butch Lee, Marquette	1993 Calbert Cheaney, Indiana
1964 Gary Bradds, Ohio St.	1979 Larry Bird, Indiana St.	1994 Glenn Robinson, Purdue
1965 Bill Bradley, Princeton	1980 Mark Aguirre, DePaul	1995 Joe Smith, Maryland
1966 Cazzie Russell, Michigan	1981 Ralph Sampson, Virginia	1996 Ray Allen, UConn
1967 Lew Alcindor, UCLA	1982 Ralph Sampson, Virginia	1997 award discontinued
1968 Elvin Hayes, Houston	1983 Ralph Sampson, Virginia	
1969 Lew Alcindor, UCLA	1984 Michael Jordan, N. Carolina	

U.S. Basketball Writers Association

Voted on by the USBWA and first presented in 1959.

Multiple winners: Ralph Sampson and Bill Walton (3); Lew Alcindor, Jerry Lucas and Oscar Robertson (2).

Year	Year	Year
1959 Oscar Robertson, Cincinnati	1973 Bill Walton, UCLA	1987 David Robinson, Navy
1960 Oscar Robertson, Cincinnati	1974 Bill Walton, UCLA	1988 Hersey Hawkins, Bradley
1961 Jerry Lucas, Ohio St.	1975 David Thompson, N.C. State	1989 Danny Ferry, Duke
1962 Jerry Lucas, Ohio St.	1976 Adrian Dantley, Notre Dame	1990 Lionel Simmons, La Salle
1963 Art Heyman, Duke	1977 Marques Johnson, UCLA	1991 Larry Johnson, UNLV
1964 Walt Hazzard, UCLA	1978 Phil Ford, North Carolina	1992 Christian Laettner, Duke
1965 Bill Bradley, Princeton	1979 Larry Bird, Indiana St.	1993 Calbert Cheaney, Indiana
1966 Cazzie Russell, Michigan	1980 Mark Aguirre, DePaul	1994 Glenn Robinson, Purdue
1967 Lew Alcindor, UCLA	1981 Ralph Sampson, Virginia	1995 Ed O'Bannon, UCLA
1968 Elvin Hayes, Houston	1982 Ralph Sampson, Virginia	1996 Marcus Camby, UMass
1969 Lew Alcindor, UCLA	1983 Ralph Sampson, Virginia	1997 Tim Duncan, Wake Forest
1970 Pete Maravich, LSU	1984 Michael Jordan, N. Carolina	1998 Antawn Jamison, N. Carolina
1971 Sidney Wicks, UCLA	1985 Chris Mullin, St. John's	1999 Elton Brand, Duke
1972 Bill Walton, UCLA	1986 Walter Berry, St. John's	

Rupp Trophy

Voted on by AP sportswriters and broadcasters and first presented in 1961 by the Commonwealth Athletic Club of Kentucky in the name of former University of Kentucky coach Adolph Rupp.

Multiple winners: Ralph Sampson (3); Lew Alcindor, Jerry Lucas, David Thompson and Bill Walton (2).

Year	Year	Year
1961 Jerry Lucas, Ohio St.	1975 David Thompson, N.C. State	1989 Sean Elliott, Arizona
1962 Jerry Lucas, Ohio St.	1976 Scott May, Indiana	1990 Lionel Simmons, La Salle
1963 Art Heyman, Duke	1977 Marques Johnson, UCLA	1991 Shaquille O'Neal, LSU
1964 Gary Bradds, Ohio St.	1978 Butch Lee, Marquette	1992 Christian Laettner, Duke
1965 Bill Bradley, Princeton	1979 Larry Bird, Indiana St.	1993 Calbert Cheaney, Indiana
1966 Cazzie Russell, Michigan	1980 Mark Aguirre, DePaul	1994 Glenn Robinson, Purdue
1967 Lew Alcindor, UCLA	1981 Ralph Sampson, Virginia	1995 Joe Smith, Maryland
1968 Elvin Hayes, Houston	1982 Ralph Sampson, Virginia	1996 Marcus Camby, UMass
1969 Lew Alcindor, UCLA	1983 Ralph Sampson, Virginia	1997 Tim Duncan, Wake Forest
1970 Pete Maravich, LSU	1984 Michael Jordan, N. Carolina	1998 Antawn Jamison, N. Carolina
1971 Austin Carr, Notre Dame	1985 Patrick Ewing, Georgetown	1999 Elton Brand, Duke
1972 Bill Walton, UCLA	1986 Walter Berry, St. John's	
1973 Bill Walton, UCLA	1987 David Robinson, Navy	
1974 David Thompson, N.C. State	1988 Hersey Hawkins, Bradley	

Naismith Award

Voted on by a panel of coaches, sportswriters and broadcasters and first presented in 1969 by the Atlanta Tip-Off Club in 1969 in the name of the inventor of basketball, Dr. James Naismith.

Multiple winners: Ralph Sampson and Bill Walton (3).

Year	Year	Year
1969 Lew Alcindor, UCLA	1980 Mark Aguirre, DePaul	1991 Larry Johnson, UNLV
1970 Pete Maravich, LSU	1981 Ralph Sampson, Virginia	1992 Christian Laettner, Duke
1971 Austin Carr, Notre Dame	1982 Ralph Sampson, Virginia	1993 Calbert Cheaney, Indiana
1972 Bill Walton, UCLA	1983 Ralph Sampson, Virginia	1994 Glenn Robinson, Purdue
1973 Bill Walton, UCLA	1984 Michael Jordan, N. Carolina	1995 Joe Smith, Maryland
1974 Bill Walton, UCLA	1985 Patrick Ewing, Georgetown	1996 Marcus Camby, UMass
1975 David Thompson, N.C. State	1986 Johnny Dawkins, Duke	1997 Tim Duncan, Wake Forest
1976 Scott May, Indiana	1987 David Robinson, Navy	1998 Antawn Jamison, N. Carolina
1977 Marques Johnson, UCLA	1988 Danny Manning, Kansas	1999 Elton Brand, Duke
1978 Butch Lee, Marquette	1989 Danny Ferry, Duke	
1979 Larry Bird, Indiana St.	1990 Lionel Simmons, La Salle	

National Association of Basketball Coaches

Voted on by the National Assn. of Basketball Coaches and presented by the Eastman Kodak Co. from 1975-94.

Multiple winner: Ralph Sampson (2).

Year	Year	Year
1975 David Thompson, N.C. State	1984 Michael Jordan, N. Carolina	1993 Calbert Cheaney, Indiana
1976 Scott May, Indiana	1985 Patrick Ewing, Georgetown	1994 Glenn Robinson, Purdue
1977 Marques Johnson, UCLA	1986 Walter Berry, St. John's	1995 Shawn Respert, Mich. St.
1978 Phil Ford, North Carolina	1987 David Robinson, Navy	1996 Marcus Camby, UMass
1979 Larry Bird, Indiana St.	1988 Danny Manning, Kansas	1997 Tim Duncan, Wake Forest
1980 Michael Brooks, La Salle	1989 Sean Elliott, Arizona	1998 Antawn Jamison, N. Carolina
1981 Danny Ainge, BYU	1990 Lionel Simmons, La Salle	1999 Elton Brand, Duke
1982 Ralph Sampson, Virginia	1991 Larry Johnson, UNLV	
1983 Ralph Sampson, Virginia	1992 Christian Laettner, Duke	

Wooden Award

Voted on by a panel of coaches, sportswriters and broadcasters and first presented in 1977 by the Los Angeles Athletic Club in the name of former Purdue All-America and UCLA coach John Wooden. Unlike the other five Player of the Year awards, candidates for the Wooden must have a minimum grade point average of 2.00 (out of 4.00).

Multiple winner: Ralph Sampson (2).

Year	Year	Year
1977 Marques Johnson, UCLA	1985 Chris Mullin, St. John's	1993 Calbert Cheaney, Indiana
1978 Phil Ford, North Carolina	1986 Walter Berry, St. John's	1994 Glenn Robinson, Purdue
1979 Larry Bird, Indiana St.	1987 David Robinson, Navy	1995 Ed O'Bannon, UCLA
1980 Darrell Griffith, Louisville	1988 Danny Manning, Kansas	1996 Marcus Camby, UMass
1981 Danny Ainge, BYU	1989 Sean Elliott, Arizona	1997 Tim Duncan, Wake Forest
1982 Ralph Sampson, Virginia	1990 Lionel Simmons, La Salle	1998 Antawn Jamison, N. Carolina
1983 Ralph Sampson, Virginia	1991 Larry Johnson, UNLV	1999 Elton Brand, Duke
1984 Michael Jordan, N. Carolina	1992 Christian Laettner, Duke	

Players of the Year and Top Draft Picks

Consensus College Players of the Year and first overall selections in NBA draft since the abolition of the NBA's territorial draft in 1966. Top draft picks who became Rookie of the Year are in **bold** type; (*) indicates top draft pick chosen as junior and (**) indicates top draft pick chosen as sophomore.

Year	Player of the Year	Top Draft Pick	Year	Player of the Year	Top Draft Pick
1966	Cazzie Russell, Mich.	Cazzie Russell, NY	1984	Michael Jordan, N. Caro.	Akeem Olajuwon, Hou.
1967	Lew Alcindor, UCLA	Jimmy Walker, Det.	1985	Patrick Ewing, G'town	
1968	Elvin Hayes, Houston	Elvin Hayes, SD		& Chris Mullin, St. John's	**Patrick Ewing**, NY
1969	Lew Alcindor, UCLA	**Lew Alcindor**, Mil.	1986	Walter Berry, St. John's	Brad Daugherty, Cle.
1970	Pete Maravich, LSU	Bob Lanier, Det.	1987	David Robinson, Navy	**David Robinson**, SA
1971	Sidney Wicks, UCLA	Austin Carr, Cle.	1988	Hersey Hawkins, Bradley	
1972	Bill Walton, UCLA	LaRue Martin, Por.		& Danny Manning, Kan.	Danny Manning, LAC
1973	Bill Walton, UCLA	Doug Collins, Phi.	1989	Sean Elliott, Arizona	
1974	Bill Walton, UCLA	Bill Walton, Por.		& Danny Ferry, Duke	Pervis Ellison, Sac.
1975	David Thompson, N.C. St.	David Thompson, Atl.	1990	Lionel Simmons, La Salle	**Derrick Coleman**, NJ
1976	Scott May, Indiana	John Lucas, Hou.	1991	Shaquille O'Neal, LSU	**Larry Johnson**, Cha.
1977	Marques Johnson, UCLA	Kent Benson, Ind.	1992	Christian Laettner, Duke	**Shaquille O'Neal**, Orl.*
1978	Butch Lee, Marquette		1993	Calbert Cheaney, Ind.	**Chris Webber**, Orl.**
	& Phil Ford, N. Caro.	Mychal Thompson, Por.	1994	Glenn Robinson, Purdue	Glenn Robinson, Mil.*
1979	Larry Bird, Indiana St.	Magic Johnson, LAL**	1995	Ed O'Bannon, UCLA	
1980	Mark Aguirre, DePaul	Joe Barry Carroll, G. St.		& Joe Smith, Maryland	Joe Smith, G. St.**
1981	Ralph Sampson, Va.		1996	Marcus Camby, UMass	**Allen Iverson**, Phi.**
	& Danny Ainge, BYU	Mark Aguirre, Dal.	1997	Tim Duncan, Wake Forest	**Tim Duncan**, SA
1982	Ralph Sampson, Va.	James Worthy, LAL*	1998	Antawn Jamison, N. Caro.	M. Olowokandi, LAC
1983	Ralph Sampson, Va.	**Ralph Sampson**, Hou.	1999	Elton Brand, Duke	Elton Brand, Chi.**

All-Time Winningest Division I Coaches

Minimum of 10 seasons as Division I head coach; regular season and tournament games included; coaches active during 1998-99 in **bold** type.

Top 30 Winning Percentage

		Yrs	W	L	Pct
1	Clair Bee	21	412	87	**.826**
2	Adolph Rupp	41	876	190	**.822**
3	**Roy Williams**	11	304	72	**.817**
4	**Jerry Tarkanian**	28	707	169	**.807**
5	John Wooden	29	664	162	**.804**
6	Dean Smith	36	879	254	**.776**
7	Harry Fisher	13	147	44	**.770**
8	Frank Keaney	27	387	117	**.768**
9	George Keogan	24	385	117	**.767**
10	Jack Ramsay	11	231	71	**.765**
11	Vic Bubas	10	213	67	**.761**
12	Chick Davies	21	314	106	**.748**
13	Ray Mears	21	399	135	**.747**
14	**Rick Majerus**	15	335	116	**.743**
15	Rick Pitino	15	352	124	**.739**
16	Al McGuire	20	405	143	**.739**
17	Everett Case	18	376	133	**.739**
18	Phog Allen	48	746	264	**.739**
19	**Jim Boeheim**	23	540	193	**.737**
20	**John Chaney**	27	605	218	**.735**
21	Walter Meanwell	22	280	101	**.735**
22	**Nolan Richardson**	19	456	166	**.733**
23	Bill Musselman	12	232	85	**.732**
24	**Lute Olson**	26	586	215	**.732**
25	**Bob Huggins**	18	415	154	**.729**
26	**Bob Knight**	34	743	281	**.726**
27	Lew Andreas	25	355	134	**.726**
28	Lou Carnesecca	24	526	200	**.725**
29	Fred Schaus	12	251	96	**.723**
30	Cam Henderson	35	630	243	**.722**

Top 30 Victories

		Yrs	W	L	Pct
1	Dean Smith	36	879	254	.776
2	Adolph Rupp	41	876	190	.822
3	**Jim Phelan**	45	800	443	.644
4	Hank Iba	41	767	338	.694
5	Ed Diddle	42	759	302	.715
6	Phog Allen	48	746	264	.739
7	**Bob Knight**	34	743	281	.726
8	**Norm Stewart**	38	731	375	.661
9	Ray Meyer	42	724	354	.672
10	**Don Haskins**	38	718	353	.670
11	**Lefty Driesell**	37	715	360	.665
12	**Jerry Tarkanian**	28	707	169	.807
13	**Lou Henson**	36	702	352	.666
14	John Wooden	29	664	162	.804
15	Ralph Miller	38	657	382	.632
16	Marv Harshman	40	654	449	.593
17	Gene Bartow	34	647	353	.647
18	**Denny Crum**	29	644	264	.709
19	Cam Henderson	35	630	243	.722
20	Norm Sloan	37	624	393	.614
21	**Eddie Sutton**	29	621	252	.711
22	**John Chaney**	27	605	218	.735
23	Slats Gill	36	599	392	.604
24	Abe Lemons	34	597	344	.634
25	**John Thompson**	27	596	239	.714
26	Guy Lewis	30	592	279	.680
27	**Lute Olson**	26	586	215	.732
28	Eldon Miller	36	568	419	.575
29	Gary Colson	34	563	385	.594
30	Tony Hinkle	41	557	393	.586

Note: Clarence (Bighouse) Gaines of Division II Winston-Salem St. (1947-93) retired after the 1992-93 season to finish his 47-year career ranked No. 3 on the all-time NCAA list of all coaches regardless of division. His record is 828-446 with a .650 winning percentage.

Where They Coached

Allen–Baker (1906-08), Kansas (1908-09), Haskell (1909), Central Mo. St. (1913-19), Kansas (1920-56); **Andreas**–Syracuse (1925-43; 45-50); **Bartow**–Central Mo. St. (1962-64), Valparaiso (1965-70), Memphis St. (1971-74), Illinois (1975), UCLA (1976-77), UAB (1979-96); **Bee**–Rider (1929-31), LIU-Brooklyn (1932-45, 46-51); **Boeheim**–Syracuse (1977–); **Bubas**–Duke (1960-69); **Carnesecca**–St. John's (1966-70, 74-92); **Case**–N.C. State (1947-64); **Chaney**–Cheyney St. (1973-82), Temple (1983–); **Colson**–Valdosta St. (1959-68), Pepperdine (1969-79), New Mexico (1981-88), Fresno St. (1991-95); **Crum**–Louisville (1972–); **Davies**–Duquesne (1925-43, 47-48); **Diddle**–Western Ky. (1923-64); **Driesell**–Davidson (1961-69), Maryland (1970-86), J. Madison (1989-97), Georgia St. (1997–); **Fisher**–Columbia (1907-16), Army (1922-23, 25).

Gill–Oregon St. (1929-64); **Harshman**–Pacific Lutheran (1946-58), Wash. St. (1959-71), Washington (1972-85); **Haskins**–UTEP (1962-99); **Henderson**–Muskingum (1920-22), Davis & Elkins (1923-35), Marshall (1936-55); **Henson**–Hardin-Simmons (1963-66), N. Mexico St. (1967-75), Illinois (1976-96), N. Mexico St. (1997–); **Hinkle**–Butler (1927-42, 46-70); **Huggins**–Walsh (1981-83), Akron (1985-89), Cincinnati (1990–); **Iba**–NW Missouri St. (1930-33), Colorado (1934), Oklahoma St. (1935-70); **Keaney**–Rhode Island (1921-48); **Keogan**–St. Louis (1916), Allegheny (1919), Valparaiso (1920-21), Notre Dame (1924-43); **Knight**–Army (1966-71), Indiana (1972–).

Lapchick–St. John's (1937-47, 57-65); **Lemons**–Okla. City (1956-73), Pan American (1974-76), Texas (1977-82), Okla. City (1984-90); **Lewis**– Houston (1957-86); **Majerus**–Marquette (1984-86), Ball St. (1988-89), Utah (1991–); **A. McGuire**–Belmont Abbey (1958-64), Marquette (1965-77); **Meanwell**–Wisconsin (1912-17, 21-34), Missouri (1918-20); **Mears**–Wittenberg (1957-62), Tennessee (1963-77); **Meyer**–DePaul (1943-84); **E. Miller**–Western Mich. (1970-75), Ohio St. (1976-85), Northern Iowa (1986–); **R. Miller**–Wichita St. (1952-64), Iowa (1965-70), Oregon St. (1971-89); **Musselman**–Ashland (1966-71), Minnesota (1972-75), S. Alabama (1996-97); **Olson**–Long Beach St. (1974), Iowa (1975-83), Arizona (1984–); **Phelan**–Mount St. Mary's (1955–); **Pitino**–Boston Univ. (1979-83), Providence (1986-87), Kentucky (1990-97).

Ramsay–St. Joseph's-PA (1956-66); **Richardson**–Tulsa (1981-85), Arkansas (1986–); **Rupp**–Kentucky (1931-72); **Schaus**–West Va. (1955-60), Purdue (1973-78); **Sloan**–Presbyterian (1952-55), Citadel (1957-60), Florida (1961-66), N.C. State (1967-80), Florida (1981-89); **Smith**–North Carolina (1962-97); **Stewart**–No. Iowa (1962-67), Missouri (1968-99); **Sutton**–Creighton (1970-74), Arkansas (1975-85), Kentucky (1986-89), Oklahoma St. (1991–); **Tarkanian**–Long Beach St. (1969-73), UNLV (1974-92), Fresno St. (1995–); **Thompson**–Georgetown (1973-99); **Wilkes**–Stetson (1958-93); **Williams**– Kansas (1989–); **Wooden**–Indiana St. (1947-48), UCLA (1949-75).

Most NCAA Tournaments

Through 1999; listed are number of appearances, overall tournament record, times reaching Final Four, and number of NCAA championships.

App		W-L	F4	Championships
27	Dean Smith	65-27	11	2 (1982, 93)
23	**Bob Knight**	42-20	5	3 (1976, 81, 87)
22	**Denny Crum**	42-22	6	2 (1980, 86)
20	Adolph Rupp	30-18	6	4 (1948-49, 51, 58)
20	**John Thompson**	34-19	3	1 (1984)
20	**Lute Olson**	31-20	4	1 (1997)
20	**Eddie Sutton**	29-20	2	None
19	**Lou Henson**	19-20	2	None
19	**Jim Boeheim**	29-19	2	None
18	Lou Carnesecca	17-20	1	None
16	John Wooden	47-10	12	10 (1964-65, 67-73, 75)
16	**Jerry Tarkanian**	37-16	4	1 (1990)
16	**Norm Stewart**	12-16	0	None
16	**Gene Keady**	15-16	0	None
15	**Mike Krzyzewski**	48-13	8	2 (1991-92)
15	Digger Phelps	17-17	1	None
15	**John Chaney**	19-15	0	None
14	**Don Haskins**	14-13	1	1 (1966)
14	Guy Lewis	26-18	5	None
13	**Jim Calhoun**	25-12	1	1 (1999)
13	Dale Brown	15-14	2	None
13	Ray Meyer	14-16	2	None

Active Coaches' Victories

Minimum five seasons in Division I.

		Yrs	W	L	Pct
1	Jim Phelan, Mt. St. Mary's	45	**800**	443	.644
2	Bob Knight, Indiana	34	**743**	281	.726
3	Norm Stewart, Missouri	38	**731**	375	.661
4	Lefty Driesell, Georgia St.	37	**715**	360	.665
5	Jerry Tarkanian, Fresno St.	28	**707**	169	.807
6	Lou Henson, N. Mexico St.	36	**702**	352	.666
7	Denny Crum, Louisville	29	**644**	264	.709
8	Eddie Sutton, Okla. St.	29	**621**	253	.711
9	John Chaney, Temple	27	**605**	218	.735
10	Lute Olson, Arizona	26	**586**	215	.732
11	Jim Calhoun, UConn.	27	**554**	258	.682
12	Hugh Durham, Jacksonville	31	**545**	344	.613
13	Mike Krzyzewski, Duke	24	**542**	214	.717
14	Jim Boeheim, Syracuse	23	**540**	193	.737
15	Billy Tubbs, TCU	25	**539**	258	.676
16	Gale Catlett, West Va.	27	**526**	279	.653
17	Tom Penders, Geo. Wash.	28	**498**	328	.603
18	Davey Whitney, Alcorn St.	28	**495**	302	.621
19	Calvin Luther, Tenn-Martin	38	**491**	462	.515
20	John Kresse, C. of Charleston	20	**490**	121	.802
21	Larry Hunter, Ohio	23	**469**	200	.701
22	Dave Bliss, N. Mexico	24	**464**	271	.631
23	Rollie Massimino, Cleveland St.	25	**458**	326	.584
24	Nolan Richardson, Arkansas	19	**456**	166	.733
25	Gene Keady, Purdue	21	**453**	200	.694

Annual Awards

UPI picked the first national Division I Coach of the Year in 1955. Since then, the U.S. Basketball Writers Assn. (1959), AP (1967), the National Assn. of Basketball Coaches (1969) and the Atlanta Tip-Off Club (1987) have joined in. Since 1987, the first year all five awards were given out, no coach has won all of them in the same season.

United Press International

Voted on by a panel of UPI college basketball writers and first presented in 1955.

Multiple winners: John Wooden (6); Bob Knight, Ray Meyer, Adolph Rupp, Norm Stewart, Fred Taylor and Phil Woolpert (2).

Year	Year	Year
1955 Phil Woolpert, San Francisco	1970 John Wooden, UCLA	1985 Lou Carnesecca, St. John's
1956 Phil Woolpert, San Francisco	1971 Al McGuire, Marquette	1986 Mike Krzyzewski, Duke
1957 Frank McGuire, North Carolina	1972 John Wooden, UCLA	1987 John Thompson, Georgetown
1958 Tex Winter, Kansas St.	1973 John Wooden, UCLA	1988 John Chaney, Temple
1959 Adolph Rupp, Kentucky	1974 Digger Phelps, Notre Dame	1989 Bob Knight, Indiana
1960 Pete Newell, California	1975 Bob Knight, Indiana	1990 Jim Calhoun, Connecticut
1961 Fred Taylor, Ohio St.	1976 Tom Young, Rutgers	1991 Rick Majerus, Utah
1962 Fred Taylor, Ohio St.	1977 Bob Gaillard, San Francisco	1992 Perry Clark, Tulane
1963 Ed Jucker, Cincinnati	1978 Eddie Sutton, Arkansas	1993 Eddie Fogler, Vanderbilt
1964 John Wooden, UCLA	1979 Bill Hodges, Indiana St.	1994 Norm Stewart, Missouri
1965 Dave Strack, Michigan	1980 Ray Meyer, DePaul	1995 Leonard Hamilton, Miami-FL
1966 Adolph Rupp, Kentucky	1981 Ralph Miller, Oregon St.	1996 Gene Keady, Purdue
1967 John Wooden, UCLA	1982 Norm Stewart, Missouri	1997 award discontinued
1968 Guy Lewis, Houston	1983 Jerry Tarkanian, UNLV	
1969 John Wooden, UCLA	1984 Ray Meyer, DePaul	

U.S. Basketball Writers Association

Voted on by the USBWA and first presented in 1959.

Multiple winners: John Wooden (5); Bob Knight (3); Lou Carnesecca, John Chaney, Ray Meyer and Fred Taylor (2).

Year	Year	Year
1959 Eddie Hickey, Marquette	1973 John Wooden, UCLA	1987 John Chaney, Temple
1960 Pete Newell, California	1974 Norm Sloan, N.C. State	1988 John Chaney, Temple
1961 Fred Taylor, Ohio St.	1975 Bob Knight, Indiana	1989 Bob Knight, Indiana
1962 Fred Taylor, Ohio St.	1976 Bob Knight, Indiana	1990 Roy Williams, Kansas
1963 Ed Jucker, Cincinnati	1977 Eddie Sutton, Arkansas	1991 Randy Ayers, Ohio St.
1964 John Wooden, UCLA	1978 Ray Meyer, DePaul	1992 Perry Clark, Tulane
1965 Butch van Breda Kolff, Princeton	1979 Dean Smith, North Carolina	1993 Eddie Fogler, Vanderbilt
1966 Adolph Rupp, Kentucky	1980 Ray Meyer, DePaul	1994 Charlie Spoonhour, St. Louis
1967 John Wooden, UCLA	1981 Ralph Miller, Oregon St.	1995 Kelvin Sampson, Oklahoma
1968 Guy Lewis, Houston	1982 John Thompson, Georgetown	1996 Gene Keady, Purdue
1969 Maury John, Drake	1983 Lou Carnesecca, St. John's	1997 Clem Haskins, Minnesota
1970 John Wooden, UCLA	1984 Gene Keady, Purdue	1998 Tom Izzo, Michigan St.
1971 Al McGuire, Marquette	1985 Lou Carnesecca, St. John's	1999 Cliff Ellis, Auburn
1972 John Wooden, UCLA	1986 Dick Versace, Bradley	

Associated Press

Voted on by AP sportswriters and broadcasters and first presented in 1967.
Multiple winners: John Wooden (5); Bob Knight (3); Guy Lewis, Ray Meyer, Ralph Miller and Eddie Sutton (2).

Year	Year	Year
1967 John Wooden, UCLA	1978 Eddie Sutton, Arkansas	1989 Bob Knight, Indiana
1968 Guy Lewis, Houston	1979 Bill Hodges, Indiana St.	1990 Jim Calhoun, Connecticut
1969 John Wooden, UCLA	1980 Ray Meyer, DePaul	1991 Randy Ayers, Ohio St.
1970 John Wooden, UCLA	1981 Ralph Miller, Oregon St.	1992 Roy Williams, Kansas
1971 Al McGuire, Marquette	1982 Ralph Miller, Oregon St.	1993 Eddie Fogler, Vanderbilt
1972 John Wooden, UCLA	1983 Guy Lewis, Houston	1994 Norm Stewart, Missouri
1973 John Wooden, UCLA	1984 Ray Meyer, DePaul	1995 Kelvin Sampson, Oklahoma
1974 Norm Sloan, N.C. State	1985 Bill Frieder, Michigan	1996 Gene Keady, Purdue
1975 Bob Knight, Indiana	1986 Eddie Sutton, Kentucky	1997 Clem Haskins, Minnesota
1976 Bob Knight, Indiana	1987 Tom Davis, Iowa	1998 Tom Izzo, Michigan St.
1977 Bob Gaillard, San Francisco	1988 John Chaney, Temple	1999 Cliff Ellis, Auburn

National Association of Basketball Coaches

Voted on by NABC membership and first presented in 1969.
Multiple winners: John Wooden (3); Mike Krzyzewski (2).

Year	Year	Year
1969 John Wooden, UCLA	1980 Lute Olson, Iowa	1991 Mike Krzyzewski, Duke
1970 John Wooden, UCLA	1981 Ralph Miller, Oregon St.	1992 George Raveling, USC
1971 Jack Kraft, Villanova	& Jack Hartman, Kansas St.	1993 Eddie Fogler, Vanderbilt
1972 John Wooden, UCLA	1982 Don Monson, Idaho	1994 Nolan Richardson, Arkansas
1973 Gene Bartow, Memphis St.	1983 Lou Carnesecca, St. John's	& Gene Keady, Purdue
1974 Al McGuire, Marquette	1984 Marv Harshman, Washington	1995 Jim Harrick, UCLA
1975 Bob Knight, Indiana	1985 John Thompson, Georgetown	1996 John Calipari, UMass
1976 Johnny Orr, Michigan	1986 Eddie Sutton, Kentucky	1997 Clem Haskins, Minnesota
1977 Dean Smith, North Carolina	1987 Rick Pitino, Providence	1998 Bill Guthridge, N. Carolina
1978 Bill Foster, Duke	1988 John Chaney, Temple	1999 Mike Krzyzewski, Duke
& Abe Lemons, Texas	1989 P.J. Carlesimo, Seton Hall	& Jim O'Brien, Ohio St.
1979 Ray Meyer, DePaul	1990 Jud Heathcote, Michigan St.	

Naismith Award

Voted on by a panel of coaches, sportswriters and broadcasters and first presented by the Atlanta Tip-Off Club in 1987 in the name of the inventor of basketball, Dr. James Naismith.
Multiple winner: Mike Krzyzewski (3).

Year	Year	Year
1987 Bob Knight, Indiana	1992 Mike Krzyzewski, Duke	1997 Roy Williams, Kansas
1988 Larry Brown, Kansas	1993 Dean Smith, North Carolina	1998 Bill Guthridge, N. Carolina
1989 Mike Krzyzewski, Duke	1994 Nolan Richardson, Arkansas	1999 Mike Krzyzewski, Duke
1990 Bobby Cremins, Georgia Tech	1995 Jim Harrick, UCLA	
1991 Randy Ayers, Ohio St.	1996 John Calipari, UMass	

Other Men's Champions

The NCAA has sanctioned national championship tournaments for Division II since 1957 and Division III since 1975. The NAIA sanctioned a single tournament from 1937-91, then split into two divisions in 1992.

NCAA Div. II Finals

Multiple winners: Kentucky Wesleyan (7); Evansville (5); CS-Bakersfield (3); North Alabama and Virginia Union (2).

Year	Winner	Score	Loser	Year	Winner	Score	Loser
1957	Wheaton, IL	89-65	Ky. Wesleyan	1965	Evansville	85-82*	Southern Illinois
1958	South Dakota	75-53	St. Michael's, VT	1966	Ky. Wesleyan	54-51	Southern Illinois
1959	Evansville, IN	83-67	SW Missouri St.	1967	Winston-Salem, NC	77-74	SW Missouri St.
1960	Evansville	90-69	Chapman, CA	1968	Ky. Wesleyan	63-52	Indiana St.
1961	Wittenberg, OH	42-38	SE Missouri St.	1969	Ky. Wesleyan	75-71	SW Missouri St.
1962	Mt. St. Mary's, MD	58-57*	CS-Sacramento	1970	Phila. Textile	76-65	Tennessee St.
1963	South Dakota St.	42-40	Wittenberg, OH	1971	Evansville	97-82	Old Dominion, VA
1964	Evansville	72-59	Akron, OH	1972	Roanoke, VA	84-72	Akron, OH

Player of the Year and NBA MVP

College Players of the Year who have gone on to win the NBA's Most Valuable Player award:

Bill Russell COLLEGE–San Francisco (1956); PROS–Boston Celtics (1958, 1961, 1962, 1963 and 1965).
Oscar Robertson COLLEGE–Cincinnati (1958, 1959 and 1960); PROS–Cincinnati Royals (1964).
Kareem Abdul-Jabbar COLLEGE–UCLA (1967 and 1969); PROS–Milwaukee Bucks (1971, 1972 and 1974) and LA Lakers (1976, 1977 and 1980).
Bill Walton COLLEGE–UCLA (1972, 1973 and 1974); PROS–Portland Trail Blazers (1978).
Larry Bird COLLEGE–Indiana St. (1979); PROS–Boston Celtics (1984, 1985 and 1986).
Michael Jordan COLLEGE–North Carolina (1984); PROS–Chicago Bulls (1988, 1991, 1992, 1996 and 1998).
David Robinson COLLEGE–Navy (1987); PROS–San Antonio Spurs (1995).

Year	Winner	Score	Loser	Year	Winner	Score	Loser
1973	Ky. Wesleyan	78-76*	Tennessee St.	1987	Ky. Wesleyan	92-74	Gannon, PA
1974	Morgan St., MD	67-52	SW Missouri St.	1988	Lowell, MA	75-72	AK-Anchorage
1975	Old Dominion	76-74	New Orleans	1989	N.C. Central	73-46	SE Missouri St.
1976	Puget Sound, WA	83-74	Tennessee-Chatt.	1990	Ky. Wesleyan	93-79	CS-Bakersfield
1977	Tennessee-Chatt.	71-62	Randolph-Macon	1991	North Alabama	79-72	Bridgeport, CT
1978	Cheyney, PA	47-40	WI-Green Bay	1992	Virginia Union	100-75	Bridgeport
1979	North Alabama	64-50	WI-Green Bay	1993	CS-Bakersfield	85-72	Troy St., AL
1980	Virginia Union	80-74	New York Tech	1994	CS-Bakersfield	92-86	Southern Ind.
1981	Florida Southern	73-68	Mt. St. Mary's, MD	1995	Southern Indiana	71-63	UC-Riverside
1982	Dist. of Columbia	73-63	Florida Southern	1996	Fort Hays St.	70-63	N. Kentucky
1983	Wright St., OH	92-73	Dist. of Columbia	1997	CS-Bakersfield	57-56	N. Kentucky
1984	Central Mo. St.	81-77	St. Augustine's, NC	1998	UC-Davis	83-77	Ky. Wesleyan
1985	Jacksonville St.	74-73	South Dakota St.	1999	Ky. Wesleyan	75-60	Metropolitan St.
1986	Sacred Heart, CT	93-87	SE Missouri St.	*Overtime			

NCAA Div. III Finals

Multiple winners: North Park (5); WI-Platteville (4); Potsdam St., Scranton and WI-Whitewater (2).

Year	Winner	Score	Loser	Year	Winner	Score	Loser
1975	LeMoyne-Owen, TN	57-54	Glassboro St., NJ	1989	WI-Whitewater	94-86	Trenton St., NJ
1976	Scranton, PA	60-57	Wittenberg, OH	1990	Rochester, NY	43-42	DePauw, IN
1977	Wittenberg, OH	79-66	Oneonta St., NY	1991	WI-Platteville	81-74	Franklin Marshall
1978	North Park, IL	69-57	Widener, PA	1992	Calvin, MI	62-49	Rochester, NY
1979	North Park, IL	66-62	Potsdam St., NY	1993	Ohio Northern	71-68	Augustana, IL
1980	North Park, IL	83-76	Upsala, NJ	1994	Lebanon Valley, PA	66-59*	NYU
1981	Potsdam St., NY	67-65*	Augustana, IL	1995	WI-Platteville	69-55	Manchester, IN
1982	Wabash, IN	83-62	Potsdam St., NY	1996	Rowan, NJ	100-93	Hope, MI
1983	Scranton, PA	64-63	Wittenberg, OH	1997	Illinois Wesleyan	89-86	Neb-Wesleyan
1984	WI-Whitewater	103-86	Clark, MA	1998	WI-Platteville	69-56	Hope, MI
1985	North Park, IL	72-71	Potsdam St., NY	1999	WI-Platteville	76-75**	Hampden-Sydney
1986	Potsdam St., NY	76-73	LeMoyne-Owen, TN	*Overtime			
1987	North Park, IL	106-100	Clark, MA	**Double overtime			
1988	Ohio Wesleyan	92-70	Scranton, PA				

NAIA Finals, 1937-91

Multiple winners: Grand Canyon, Hamline, Kentucky St. and Tennessee St. (3); Central Missouri, Central St., Fort Hays St. and SW Missouri St. (2).

Year	Winner	Score	Loser	Year	Winner	Score	Loser
1937	Central Missouri	35-24	Morningside, IA	1973	Guilford, NC	99-96	MD-Eastern Shore
1938	Central Missouri	45-30	Roanoke, VA	1974	West Georgia	97-79	Alcorn St., MS
1939	Southwestern, KS	32-31	San Diego St.	1975	Grand Canyon, AZ	65-54	M'western St., TX
1940	Tarkio, MO	52-31	San Diego St.	1976	Coppin St., MD	96-91	Henderson St., AR
1941	San Diego St.	36-32	Murray St., KY	1977	Texas Southern	71-44	Campbell, NC
1942	Hamline, MN	33-31	SE Oklahoma	1978	Grand Canyon	79-75	Kearney St., NE
1943	SE Missouri St.	34-32	NW Missouri St.	1979	Drury, MO	60-54	Henderson St., AR
1944	Not held			1980	Cameron, OK	84-77	Alabama St.
1945	Loyola-LA	49-36	Pepperdine, CA	1981	Beth. Nazarene, OK	86-85*	AL-Huntsville
1946	Southern Illinois	49-40	Indiana St.	1982	SC-Spartanburg	51-38	Biola, CA
1947	Marshall, WV	73-59	Mankato St., MN	1983	Charleston, SC	57-53	WV-Wesleyan
1948	Louisville, KY	82-70	Indiana St.	1984	Fort Hays St., KS	48-46*	WI-Stevens Pt.
1949	Hamline, MN	57-46	Regis, CO	1985	Fort Hays St.	82-80*	Wayland Bapt., TX
1950	Indiana St.	61-47	East Central, OK	1986	David Lipscomb, TN	67-54	AR-Monticello
1951	Hamline, MN	69-61	Millikin, IL	1987	Washburn, KS	59-77	West Virginia St.
1952	SW Missouri St.	73-64	Murray St., KY	1988	Grand Canyon	88-86*	Auburn-Montg, AL
1953	SW Missouri St.	79-71	Hamline, MN	1989	St.Mary's, TX	61-58	East Central, OK
1954	St.Benedict's, KS	62-56	Western Illinois	1990	Birm-Southern, AL	88-80	WI-Eau Claire
1955	East Texas St.	71-54	SE Oklahoma	1991	Oklahoma City	77-74	Central Arkansas
1956	McNeese St., LA	60-55	Texas Southern	*Overtime			
1957	Tennessee St.	92-73	SE Oklahoma				
1958	Tennessee St.	85-73	Western Illinois				
1959	Tennessee St.	97-87	Pacific-Luth., WA				
1960	SW Texas St.	66-44	Westminster, PA				
1961	Grambling, LA	95-75	Georgetown, KY	## NAIA Div. I Finals			
1962	Prairie View, TX	62-53	Westminster, PA				

NAIA split tournament into two divisions in 1992.

Multiple winner: Oklahoma City (3), Life (2).

Year	Winner	Score	Loser
1963	Pan American, TX	73-62	Western Carolina				
1964	Rockhurst, MO	66-56	Pan American, TX	1992	Oklahoma City	82-73*	Central Arkansas
1965	Central St., OH	85-51	Oklahoma Baptist	1993	Hawaii Pacific	88-83	Okla. Baptist
1966	Oklahoma Baptist	88-59	Georgia Southern	1994	Oklahoma City	99-81	Life, GA
1967	St.Benedict's, KS	71-65	Oklahoma Baptist	1995	Birm-Southern	92-76	Pfeiffer, NC
1968	Central St., OH	51-48	Fairmont St., WV	1996	Oklahoma City	86-80	Georgetown, KY
1969	Eastern N. Mex	99-76	MD-Eastern Shore	1997	Life	73-64	Okla. Baptist
1970	Kentucky St.	79-71	Central Wash.	1998	Georgetown, KY	83-69	So. Nazarene
1971	Kentucky St.	102-82	Eastern Michigan	1999	Life	63-60	Mobile, AL
1972	Kentucky St.	71-62	WI-Eau Claire	*Overtime			

NAIA Div. II Finals

NAIA split tournament into two divisions in 1992.

Multiple winner: Bethel, IN (3).

Year	Winner	Score	Loser	Year	Winner	Score	Loser
1992	Grace, IN	85-79*	Northwestern-IA	1997	Bethel	95-94	Siena Heights, MI
1993	Williamette, OR	63-56	Northern St., SD	1998	Bethel	89-87	Oregon Tech
1994	Eureka, IL	98-95*	Northern St.	1999	Cornerstone, MI	113-109	Bethel
1995	Bethel, IN	103-95*	NW Nazarene, ID	*Overtime			
1996	Albertson, ID	81-72*	Whitworth, WA				

WOMEN

NCAA Final Four

Replaced the Association of Intercollegiate Athletics for Women (AIAW) tournament in 1982 as the official playoff for the national championship.

Multiple winners: Tennessee (6); Louisiana Tech, Stanford and USC (2).

Year	Champion	Head Coach	Score	Runner-up	—Third Place—	
1982	Louisiana Tech	Sonya Hogg	76-62	Cheyney	Maryland	Tennessee
1983	USC	Linda Sharp	69-67	Louisiana Tech	Georgia	Old Dominion
1984	USC	Linda Sharp	72-61	Tennessee	Cheyney	Louisiana Tech
1985	Old Dominion	Marianne Stanley	70-65	Georgia	NE Louisiana	Western Ky.
1986	Texas	Jody Conradt	97-81	USC	Tennessee	Western Ky.
1987	Tennessee	Pat Summitt	67-44	Louisiana Tech	Long Beach St.	Texas
1988	Louisiana Tech	Leon Barmore	56-54	Auburn	Long Beach St.	Tennessee
1989	Tennessee	Pat Summitt	76-60	Auburn	Louisiana Tech	Maryland
1990	Stanford	Tara VanDerveer	88-81	Auburn	Louisiana Tech	Virginia
1991	Tennessee	Pat Summitt	70-67 (OT)	Virginia	Connecticut	Stanford
1992	Stanford	Tara VanDerveer	78-62	Western Kentucky	SW Missouri St.	Virginia
1993	Texas Tech	Marsha Sharp	84-82	Ohio St.	Iowa	Vanderbilt
1994	North Carolina	Sylvia Hatchell	60-59	Louisiana Tech	Alabama	Purdue
1995	Connecticut	Geno Auriemma	70-64	Tennessee	Georgia	Stanford
1996	Tennessee	Pat Summitt	83-65	Georgia	Connecticut	Stanford
1997	Tennessee	Pat Summitt	68-59	Old Dominion	Stanford	Notre Dame
1998	Tennessee	Pat Summitt	93-75	Louisiana Tech	Arkansas	N.C. State
1999	Purdue	Carolyn Peck	62-45	Duke	Louisiana Tech	Georgia

Final Four sites: 1982 (Norfolk, Va.), **1983** (Norfolk, Va.), **1984** (Los Angeles), **1985** (Austin), **1986** (Lexington), **1987** (Austin), **1988** (Tacoma), **1989** (Tacoma), **1990** (Knoxville), **1991** (New Orleans), **1992** (Los Angeles), **1993** (Atlanta), **1994** (Richmond), **1995** (Minneapolis), **1996** (Charlotte), **1997** (Cincinnati), **1998** (Kansas City), **1999** (San Jose).

Most Outstanding Player

A Most Outstanding Player has been selected every year of the NCAA tournament. Winner who did not play for the tournament champion is listed in **bold**, type.

Multiple winner: Chamique Holdsclaw and Cheryl Miller (2).

Year	Year	Year
1982 Janice Lawrence, La. Tech	1988 Erica Westbrooks, La. Tech	1994 Charlotte Smith, N. Carolina
1983 Cheryl Miller, USC	1989 Bridgette Gordon, Tennessee	1995 Rebecca Lobo, Connecticut
1984 Cheryl Miller, USC	1990 Jennifer Azzi, Stanford	1996 Michelle Marciniak, Tennessee
1985 Tracy Claxton, Old Dominion	1991 **Dawn Staley**, Virginia	1997 Chamique Holdsclaw, Tenn.
1986 Clarissa Davis, Texas	1992 Molly Goodenbour, Stanford	1998 Chamique Holdsclaw, Tenn.
1987 Tonya Edwards, Tennessee	1993 Sheryl Swoopes, Texas Tech	1999 Ukari Figgs, Purdue

All-Time NCAA Division I Tournament Leaders

Through 1998-99; minimum of six games; **Last** column indicates final year played.

CAREER

Scoring

	Total Points	Yrs	Last	Pts	Avg
1	**Chamique Holdsclaw**, Tenn.	4	1999	**479**	21.8
2	Bridgette Gordon, Tenn	4	1989	**388**	21.6
3	Cheryl Miller, USC	4	1986	**333**	20.8
4	Janice Lawrence, La. Tech	3	1984	**312**	22.3
5	Penny Toler, Long Beach St.	4	1989	**291**	22.4
6	Dawn Staley, Virginia	4	1992	**274**	18.3
7	Cindy Brown, Long Beach St	4	1987	**263**	21.9
	Venus Lacy, La. Tech	3	1990	**263**	18.8
9	Clarissa Davis, Texas	3	1989	**261**	21.8
10	Janet Harris, Georgia	4	1985	**254**	19.5

Rebounds

	Total Rebounds	Yrs	Last	No	Avg
1	**Chamique Holdsclaw**, Tenn.	4	1999	**188**	8.5
2	Cheryl Miller, USC	4	1986	**170**	10.6
3	Sheila Frost, Tennessee	4	1989	**162**	9.0
4	Val Whiting, Stanford	4	1993	**161**	10.1
5	Venus Lacy, La. Tech	3	1990	**148**	10.6
6	Bridgette Gordon, Tenn	4	1989	**142**	7.9
7	Kirsten Cummings, Long Beach St.	4	1985	**136**	10.5
8	Nora Lewis, La. Tech	3	1989	**130**	9.3
9	Pam McGee, USC	3	1984	**127**	9.8
10	Daedra Charles, Tenn	3	1991	**125**	9.6
	Paula McGee, USC	3	1984	**125**	9.6

SINGLE GAME

Scoring

		Year	Pts
1	Lorri Bauman, Drake vs Maryland	1982	50
2	Sheryl Swoopes, Texas Tech vs Ohio St	1993	47
3	Barbara Kennedy, Clemson vs Penn St	1982	43
4	LaTaunya Pollard, L. Beach St. vs Howard	1982	40
	Cindy Brown, L. Beach St. vs Ohio St.	1987	40
6	Kerry Bascom, UConn vs Toledo	1991	39
	Portia Hill, S.F. Austin St. vs Arkansas	1990	39
	Delmonica DeHorney, Ark. vs Stanford	1990	39
	Sheri Sam, Vanderbilt vs Harvard	1996	39
	Chamique Holdsclaw, Tenn. vs Boston Col.	1999	39

Rebounds

		Year	No
1	Cheryl Taylor, Tenn. Tech vs Georgia	1985	23
	Charlotte Smith, N. Car. vs La. Tech	1994	23
3	Daedra Charles, Tenn. vs SW Missouri	1991	22
4	Cherie Nelson, USC vs Western Ky	1987	21
5	Alison Lang, Oregon vs Missouri	1982	20
	Shelda Arceneaux, S.D. St. vs L. Beach St.	1984	20
	Tracy Claxton, ODU vs Georgia	1985	20
	Brigette Combs, West. Ky. vs West Va	1989	20
	Tandreia Green, West. Ky. vs West Va	1989	20
10	Seven tied with 19 each.		

Associated Press Final Top 10 Polls

The Associated Press weekly women's college basketball poll was begun by Mel Greenberg of *The Philadelphia Inquirer* during the 1976-77 season. Although the poll was started as a Top 20 in 1977 and was expanded to a Top 25 in 1990, only the Top 10 from each poll are listed below due to space constraints. The Association of Intercollegiate Athletics for Women (AIAW) Tournament determined the Division I national champion for 1972-81. The NCAA began its women's Division I tournament in 1982. The final AP Polls were taken before the NCAA tournament. Eventual national champions are in **bold** type.

1977
1 **Delta St.**
2 Immaculata
3 St. Joseph's-PA
4 CS-Fullerton
5 Tennessee
6 Tennessee Tech
7 Wayland Baptist
8 Montclair St.
9 S.F. Austin St.
10 N.C. State

1978
1 Tennessee
2 Wayland Baptist
3 N.C. State
4 Montclair St.
5 **UCLA**
6 Maryland
7 Queens-NY
8 Valdosta St.
9 Delta St.
10 LSU

1979
1 **Old Dominion**
2 Louisiana Tech
3 Tennessee
4 Texas
5 S.F. Austin St.
6 UCLA
7 Rutgers
8 Maryland
9 Cheyney
10 Wayland Baptist

1980
1 **Old Dominion**
2 Tennessee
3 Louisiana Tech
4 South Carolina
5 S.F. Austin St.
6 Maryland
7 Texas
8 Rutgers
9 Long Beach St.
10 N.C. State

1981
1 **Louisiana Tech**
2 Tennessee
3 Old Dominion
4 USC
5 Cheyney
6 Long Beach St.
7 UCLA
8 Maryland
9 Rutgers
10 Kansas

1982
1 **Louisiana Tech**
2 Cheyney
3 Maryland
4 Tennessee
5 Texas
6 USC
7 Old Dominion
8 Rutgers
9 Long Beach St.
10 Penn St.

1983
1 **USC**
2 Louisiana Tech
3 Texas
4 Old Dominion
5 Cheyney
6 Long Beach St.
7 Maryland
8 Penn St.
9 Georgia
10 Tennessee

1984
1 Texas
2 Louisiana Tech
3 Georgia
4 Old Dominion
5 **USC**
6 Long Beach St.
7 Kansas St.
8 LSU
9 Cheyney
10 Mississippi

1985
1 Texas
2 NE Louisiana
3 Long Beach St.
4 Louisiana Tech
5 **Old Dominion**
6 Mississippi
7 Ohio St.
8 Georgia
9 Penn St.
10 Auburn

1986
1 **Texas**
2 Georgia
3 USC
4 Louisiana Tech
5 Western Ky.
6 Virginia
7 Auburn
8 Long Beach St.
9 LSU
10 Rutgers

1987
1 Texas
2 Auburn
3 Louisiana Tech
4 Long Beach St.
5 Rutgers
6 Georgia
7 **Tennessee**
8 Mississippi
9 Iowa
10 Ohio St.

1988
1 Tennessee
2 Iowa
3 Auburn
4 Texas
5 **Louisiana Tech**
6 Ohio St.
7 Long Beach St.
8 Rutgers
9 Maryland
10 Virginia

1989
1 **Tennessee**
2 Auburn
3 Louisiana Tech
4 Stanford
5 Maryland
6 Texas
7 Long Beach St.
8 Iowa
9 Colorado
10 Georgia

1990
1 Louisiana Tech
2 **Stanford**
3 Washington
4 Tennessee
5 UNLV
6 S.F. Austin St.
7 Georgia
8 Texas
9 Auburn
10 Iowa

1991
1 Penn St.
2 Virginia
3 Georgia
4 **Tennessee**
5 Purdue
6 Auburn
7 N.C. State
8 LSU
9 Arkansas
10 Western Ky.

1992
1 Virginia
2 Tennessee
3 **Stanford**
4 S.F. Austin St.
5 Mississippi
6 Miami-FL
7 Iowa
8 Maryland
9 Penn St.
10 SW Missouri St.

1993
1 Vanderbilt
2 Tennessee
3 Ohio St.
4 Iowa
5 **Texas Tech**
6 Stanford
7 Auburn
8 Penn St.
9 Virginia
10 Colorado

1994
1 Tennessee
2 Penn St.
3 Connecticut
4 **North Carolina**
5 Colorado
6 Louisiana Tech
7 USC
8 Purdue
9 Texas Tech
10 Virginia

1995
1 **Connecticut**
2 Colorado
3 Tennessee
4 Stanford
5 Texas Tech
6 Vanderbilt
7 Penn St.
8 Louisiana Tech
9 Western Ky.
10 Virginia

1996
1 Louisiana Tech
2 Connecticut
3 Stanford
4 **Tennessee**
5 Georgia
6 Old Dominion
7 Iowa
8 Penn St.
9 Texas Tech
10 Alabama

1997
1 Connecticut
2 Old Dominion
3 Stanford
4 North Carolina
5 Louisiana Tech
6 Georgia
7 Florida
8 Alabama
9 LSU
10 **Tennessee**

1998
1 **Tennessee**
2 Old Dominion
3 Connecticut
4 Louisiana Tech
5 Stanford
6 Texas Tech
7 North Carolina
8 Duke
9 Arizona
10 N.C. State

1999
1 **Purdue**
2 Tennessee
3 Louisiana Tech
4 Colorado St.
5 Old Dominion
6 Connecticut
7 Rutgers
8 Notre Dame
9 Texas Tech
10 Duke

All-Time AP Top 10

The composite AP Top 10 from the 1976-77 season through 1998-99, based on the final regular season rankings of each year. Team points are based on 10 points for all 1st place finishes, 9 for each 2nd, etc. Also listed are the number of times ranked No. 1 by AP going into the tournaments, and times ranked in the pre-tournament Top 10.

		Pts	No. 1	Top 10
1	Tennessee	151	5	20
2	Louisiana Tech	140	4	18
3	Old Dominion	81	2	11
4	Texas	80	4	17
5	Stanford	58	0	8
6	Georgia	51	0	10
7	Connecticut	50	2	6
8	Long Beach St.	45	0	10
9	Auburn	42	0	8
10	USC	40	1	6

All-Time Winningest Division I Teams

Division I schools with best winning percentages and most victories through 1998-99 (including postseason tournaments). Although official NCAA women's basketball records didn't begin until the 1981-82 season, results from previous seasons are included below.

Top 10 Winning Percentage

		Yrs	W	L	Pct
1	Louisiana Tech	25	706	120	.855
2	Montana	21	493	131	.790
3	Texas	25	646	178	.785
4	Tennessee	54	788	203	.770
5	S. F. Austin St.	27	636	210	.752
6	Old Dominion	30	650	217	.750
7	Mount St. Mary's*	25	499	173	.743
8	Norfolk St.	24	495	188	.725
9	Virginia	26	548	206	.727
10	Auburn	28	564	219	.720

*Includes records prior to Division I.

Top 10 Victories

		Yrs	W	L	Pct
1	Tennessee	54	788	203	.770
2	Louisiana Tech	25	706	120	.855
3	Old Dominion	30	650	217	.750
4	James Madison	77	649	367	.641
5	Texas	25	646	177	.785
6	Long Beach St.	37	638	262	.709
7	S.F. Austin St.	27	636	210	.752
8	Tennessee Tech	29	627	259	.706
9	Richmond	79	602	404	.598
10	Ohio St.	34	575	258	.690

Annual NCAA Division I Leaders

All averages include postseason games

Scoring

Multiple winner: Cindy Blodgett and Andrea Congreaves (2).

Year		Gm	Pts	Avg
1982	Barbara Kennedy, Clemson	31	908	29.3
1983	LaTaunya Pollard, L. Beach St	31	907	29.3
1984	Deborah Temple, Delta St	28	873	31.2
1985	Anucha Browne, Northwestern	28	855	30.5
1986	Wanda Ford, Drake	30	919	30.6
1987	Tresa Spaulding, BYU	28	810	28.9
1988	LeChandra LeDay, Grambling	28	850	30.4
1989	Patricia Hoskins, Miss. Valley	27	908	33.6
1990	Kim Perrot, SW Louisiana	28	839	30.0

Year		Gm	Pts	Avg
1991	Jan Jensen, Drake	30	888	29.6
1992	Andrea Congreaves, Mercer	28	925	33.0
1993	Andrea Congreaves, Mercer	26	805	31.0
1994	Kristy Ryan, CS-Sacramento	26	727	28.0
1995	Koko Lahanas, CS-Fullerton	29	778	26.8
1996	Cindy Blodgett, Maine	32	889	27.8
1997	Cindy Blodgett, Maine	30	810	27.0
1998	Allison Feaster, Harvard	28	797	28.5
1999	Tamika Whitmore, Memphis	32	843	26.3

Rebounds

Multiple winner: Patricia Hoskins (2).

Year		Gm	No	Avg	Year		Gm	No	Avg
1982	Anne Donovan, Old Dominion	28	412	14.7	1992	Christy Greis, Evansville	28	383	13.7
1983	Deborah Mitchell, Miss. Col	28	447	16.0	1993	Ann Barry, Nevada	25	355	14.2
1984	Joy Kellog, Oklahoma City	23	373	16.2	1994	DeShawne Blocker, E. Tenn. St.	26	450	17.3
1985	Rosina Pearson, Beth-Cookman	26	480	18.5	1995	Tera Sheriff, Jackson St	29	401	13.8
1986	Wanda Ford, Drake	30	506	16.9	1996	Dana Wynne, Seton Hall	29	372	12.8
1987	Patricia Hoskins, Miss. Valley St.	28	476	17.0	1997	Etolia Mitchell, Georgia St.	25	330	13.2
1988	Katie Beck, East Tenn. St.	25	441	17.6	1998	Alisha Hill, Howard	30	397	13.2
1989	Patricia Hoskins, Miss. Valley St.	27	440	16.3	1999	Monica Logan, UMBC	27	364	13.5
1990	Pam Hudson, Northwestern St	29	438	15.1					
1991	Tarcha Hollis, Grambling	29	443	15.3					

Note: Wanda Ford (1986) and Patricia Hoskins (1989) each led the country in scoring and rebounds in the same year.

All-Time NCAA Division I Individual Leaders

Through 1998-99; includes regular season and tournament games; Official NCAA women's basketball records began with 1981-82 season. Players who competed earlier than that are not included below; **Last** column indicates final year played.

CAREER

Scoring

		Yrs	Last	Pts	Avg
1	Patricia Hoskins, Miss. Valley St.	4	1989	3122	28.4
2	Sandra Hodge, New Orleans	4	1984	2860	26.7
3	Lorri Bauman, Drake	4	1984	3115	26.0
4	Andrea Congreaves, Mercer	4	1993	2796	25.9
5	Cindy Blodgett, Maine	4	1998	3005	25.5
6	Valorie Whiteside, Aplach St.	4	1988	2944	25.4
7	Joyce Walker, LSU	4	1984	2906	24.8
8	Tarcha Hollis, Grambling	4	1991	2058	24.2
9	Korie Hlede, Duquesne	4	1998	2631	24.1
10	Karen Pelphrey, Marshall	4	1986	2746	24.1

Rebounds

		Yrs	Last	Reb	Avg
1	Wanda Ford, Drake	4	1986	1887	16.1
2	Patricia Hoskins, Miss. Valley St.	4	1989	1662	15.1
3	Tarcha Hollis, Grambling	4	1991	1185	13.9
4	Katie Beck, East Tenn. St.	4	1988	1404	13.4
5	Marilyn Stephens, Temple	4	1984	1519	13.0
6	Natalie Williams, UCLA	4	1994	1137	12.8
7	Cheryl Taylor, Tenn. Tech	4	1987	1532	12.8
8	DeShawne Blocker, E. Tenn. St.	4	1995	1361	12.7
9	Olivia Bradley, West Virginia	4	1985	1484	12.7
10	Judy Mosley, Hawaii	4	1990	1441	12.6

SINGLE SEASON
Scoring

	Average	Year	Gm	Pts	Avg
1	Patricia Hoskins, Miss.Valley St.	1989	27	908	33.6
2	Andrea Congreaves, Mercer	1992	28	925	33.0
3	Deborah Temple, Delta St.	1984	28	873	31.2
4	Andrea Congreaves, Mercer	1993	26	805	31.0
5	Wanda Ford, Drake	1986	30	919	30.6
6	Anucha Browne, Northwestern	1985	28	855	30.5
7	LeChandra LeDay, Grambling	1988	28	850	30.4
8	Kim Perrot, SW Louisiana	1990	28	841	30.0
9	Tina Hutchinson, San Diego St.	1984	30	898	29.9
10	Jan Jensen, Drake	1991	30	888	29.6

SINGLE GAME
Scoring

		Year	Pts
1	Cindy Brown, Long Beach St. vs San Jose St.	1987	60
2	Lorri Bauman, Drake vs SW Missouri St.	1984	58
	Kim Perrot, SW La. vs SE La	1990	58
4	Patricia Hoskins, Miss.Valley St. vs South-BR	1989	55
	Patricia Hoskins, Miss.Valley St. vs Ala. St.	1989	55
6	Wanda Ford, Drake vs SW Missouri St.	1986	54
	Anjinea Hopson, Grambling vs Jackson St.	1994	54
	Mary Lowry, Baylor vs Texas	1994	54
9	Chris Starr, Nevada vs CS-Sacramento	1983	53
	Felisha Edwards, NE La. vs Southern Miss.	1991	53
	Sheryl Swoopes, Texas Tech vs Texas	1993	53

Winningest Active Division I Coaches

Minimum of five seasons as Division I head coach; regular season and tournament games included.

Top 10 Winning Percentage

		Yrs	W	L	Pct
1	Leon Barmore, La. Tech	17	489	74	.869
2	Pat Summitt, Tennessee	25	695	146	.826
3	Geno Auriemma, Connecticut	14	357	94	.792
4	Robin Selvig, Montana	21	493	131	.790
5	Tara VanDerveer, Stanford	20	476	133	.782
6	Bill Sheahan, Mt. St. Mary's	18	393	111	.780
7	Andy Landers, Georgia	20	486	148	.767
8	Jody Conradt, Texas	30	725	222	.766
9	Vivian Stringer, Rutgers	27	595	183	.765
10	Joe Ciampi, Auburn	22	507	160	.760

Top 10 Victories

		Yrs	W	L	Pct
1	Jody Conradt, Texas	30	725	222	.766
2	Pat Summitt, Tennessee	25	695	146	.826
3	Vivian Stringer, Rutgers	27	595	183	.765
4	Sue Gunter, LSU	29	588	266	.689
5	Kay Yow, N.C. State	28	571	233	.710
6	Sylvia Hatchell, N. Carolina	24	541	213	.718
7	Theresa Grentz, Illinois	25	537	200	.729
8	Rene Portland, Penn St.	23	523	180	.744
9	Mike Granelli, St. Peter's	27	513	195	.725
10	Joe Ciampi, Auburn	22	507	160	.760

Annual Awards

The Broderick Award was first given out to the Women's Division I or Large School Player of the Year in 1977. Since then, the National Assn. for Girls and Women in Sports (1978), the Women's Basketball Coaches Assn. (1983), the Atlanta Tip-Off Club (1983) and the Associated Press (1995) have joined in.

Since 1983, the first year as many as four awards were given out, the same player has won all of them in the same season twice: Cheryl Miller of USC in 1985 and Rebecca Lobo of Connecticut in 1995.

Associated Press

Voted on by AP sportswriters and broadcasters and first presented in 1995.
Multiple winners: Chamique Holdsclaw (2).

Year	Year	Year
1995 Rebecca Lobo, Connecticut	1997 Kara Wolters, Connecticut	1999 Chamique Holdsclaw, Tennessee
1996 Jennifer Rizzotti, Connecticut	1998 Chamique Holdsclaw, Tennessee	

Broderick Award

Voted on by a national panel of women's collegiate athletic directors and first presented by the late Thomas Broderick, an athletic outfitter, in 1977. Honda has presented the award since 1987. Basketball Player of the Year is one of 10 nominated for Collegiate Woman Athlete of the Year; (*) indicates player also won Athlete of the Year.
Multiple winners: Chamique Holdsclaw, Nancy Lieberman, Cheryl Miller and Dawn Staley (2).

Year	Year	Year
1977 Lucy Harris, Delta St.*	1985 Cheryl Miller, USC	1993 Sheryl Swoopes, Texas Tech
1978 Ann Meyers, UCLA*	1986 Kamie Ethridge, Texas*	1994 Lisa Leslie, USC
1979 Nancy Lieberman, Old Dominion*	1987 Katrina McClain, Georgia	1995 Rebecca Lobo, Connecticut
1980 Nancy Lieberman, Old Dominion*	1988 Teresa Weatherspoon, La. Tech*	1996 Jennifer Rizzotti, Connecticut
1981 Lynette Woodard, Kansas	1989 Bridgette Gordon, Tennessee	1997 Chamique Holdsclaw, Tennessee
1982 Pam Kelly, La. Tech	1990 Jennifer Azzi, Stanford	1998 Chamique Holdsclaw, Tennessee*
1983 Anne Donovan, Old Dominion	1991 Dawn Staley, Virginia	
1984 Cheryl Miller, USC*	1992 Dawn Staley, Virginia	

Wade Trophy

Voted on by the National Assn. for Girls and Women in Sports (NAGWS) and awarded for academics and community service as well as player performance. First presented in 1978 in the name of former Delta St. coach Margaret Wade.
Multiple winner: Nancy Lieberman (2).

Year	Year	Year
1978 Carol Blazejowski, Montclair St.	1986 Kamie Ethridge, Texas	1994 Carol Ann Shudlick, Minnesota
1979 Nancy Lieberman, Old Dominion	1987 Shelly Pennefather, Villanova	1995 Rebecca Lobo, Connecticut
1980 Nancy Lieberman, Old Dominion	1988 Teresa Weatherspoon, La. Tech	1996 Jennifer Rizzotti, Connecticut
1981 Lynette Woodard, Kansas	1989 Clarissa Davis, Texas	1997 DeLisha Milton, Florida
1982 Pam Kelly, La. Tech	1990 Jennifer Azzi, Stanford	1998 Ticha Penicheiro, Old Dominion
1983 LaTaunya Pollard, L. Beach St.	1991 Daedra Charles, Tennessee	1999 Stephanie White-McCarty,
1984 Janice Lawrence, La. Tech	1992 Susan Robinson, Penn St.	Purdue
1985 Cheryl Miller, USC	1993 Karen Jennings, Nebraska	

Naismith Trophy

Voted on by a panel of coaches, sportwriters and broadcasters and first presented in 1983 by the Atlanta Tip-Off Club in the name of the inventor of basketball, Dr. James Naismith.
Multiple winners: Cheryl Miller (3); Clarissa Davis, Chamique Holdsclaw and Dawn Staley (2).

Year	Year	Year
1983 Anne Donovan, Old Dominion	1989 Clarissa Davis, Texas	1995 Rebecca Lobo, Connecticut
1984 Cheryl Miller, USC	1990 Jennifer Azzi, Stanford	1996 Saudia Roundtree, Georgia
1985 Cheryl Miller, USC	1991 Dawn Staley, Virgina	1997 Kate Starbird, Stanford
1986 Cheryl Miller, USC	1992 Dawn Staley, Virginia	1998 Chamique Holdsclaw, Tennessee
1987 Clarissa Davis, Texas	1993 Sheryl Swoopes, Texas Tech	1999 Chamique Holdsclaw, Tennessee
1988 Sue Wicks, Rutgers	1994 Lisa Leslie, USC	

Women's Basketball Coaches Association

Voted on by the WBCA and first presented by Champion athletic outfitters in 1983.
Multiple winners: Chamique Holdsclaw, Cheryl Miller and Dawn Staley (2).

Year	Year	Year
1983 Anne Donovan, Old Dominion	1989 Clarissa Davis, Texas	1995 Rebecca Lobo, Connecticut
1984 Janice Lawrence, La. Tech	1990 Venus Lacy, La. Tech	1996 Saudia Roundtree, Georgia
1985 Cheryl Miller, USC	1991 Dawn Staley, Virgina	1997 Kate Starbird, Stanford
1986 Cheryl Miller, USC	1992 Dawn Staley, Virginia	1998 Chamique Holdsclaw, Tennessee
1987 Katrina McClain, Georgia	1993 Sheryl Swoopes, Texas Tech	1999 Chamique Holdsclaw, Tennessee
1988 Michelle Edwards, Iowa	1994 Lisa Leslie, USC	

Coach of the Year Award

Voted on by the Women's Basketball Coaches Assn. and first presented by Converse athletic outfitters in 1983.
Multiple winners: Pat Summitt (3), Jody Conradt and Vivian Stringer (2).

Year	Year	Year
1983 Pat Summitt, Tennessee	1989 Tara VanDerveer, Stanford	1995 Pat Summitt, Tennessee
1984 Jody Conradt, Texas	1990 Kay Yow, N.C. State	1996 Leon Barmore, La. Tech
1985 Jim Foster, St. Joseph's-PA	1991 Rene Portland, Penn St.	1997 Geno Auriemma, Connecticut
1986 Jody Conradt, Texas	1992 Ferne Labati, Miami-FL	1998 Pat Summitt, Tennessee
1987 Theresa Grentz, Rutgers	1993 Vivian Stringer, Iowa	1999 Carolyn Peck, Purdue
1988 Vivian Stringer, Iowa	1994 Marsha Sharp, Texas Tech	

Other Women's Champions

The NCAA has sanctioned national championship tournaments for Division II and Division III since 1982. The NAIA sanctioned a single tournament from 1981-91, then split in to two divisions in 1992.

NCAA Div. II Finals

Multiple winners: North Dakota St. (5); Cal Poly Pomona, Delta St. and North Dakota (3).

Year	Winner	Score	Loser
1982	Cal Poly Pomona	93-74	Tuskegee, AL
1983	Virginia Union	73-60	Cal Poly Pomona
1984	Central Mo.St.	80-73	Virginia Union
1985	Cal Poly Pomona	80-69	Central Mo.St.
1986	Cal Poly Pomona	70-63	North Dakota St.
1987	New Haven, CT	77-75	Cal Poly Pomona
1988	Hampton, VA	65-48	West Texas St.
1989	Delta St., MS	88-58	Cal Poly Pomona
1990	Delta St., MS	77-43	Bentley, MA
1991	North Dakota St.	81-74	SE Missouri St.
1992	Delta St., MS	65-63	North Dakota St.
1993	North Dakota St.	95-63	Delta St.
1994	North Dakota St.	89-56	CS-San Bernadino
1995	North Dakota St.	98-85	Portland St.
1996	North Dakota St.	104-78	Shippensburg, PA
1997	North Dakota	94-78	S. Indiana
1998	North Dakota	92-76	Emporia St.
1999	North Dakota	80-63	Arkansas Tech

NCAA Div. III Finals

Multiple winners: Capital, Elizabethtown and Washington (2).

Year	Winner	Score	Loser
1982	Elizabethtown, PA	67-66	*NC-Greensboro
1983	North Central, IL	83-71	Elizabethtown, PA
1984	Rust College, MS	51-49	Elizabethtown, PA
1985	Scranton, PA	68-59	New Rochelle, NY
1986	Salem St., MA	89-85	Bishop, TX
1987	WI-Stevens Pt.	81-74	Concordia, MN
1988	Concordia, MN	65-57	St. John Fisher, NY
1989	Elizabethtown, PA	66-65	CS-Stanislaus
1990	Hope, MI	65-63	St. John Fisher
1991	St. Thomas, MN	73-55	Muskingum, OH
1992	Alma, MI	79-75	Moravian, PA
1993	Central Iowa	71-63	Capital, OH
1994	Capital, OH	82-63	Washington, MO
1995	Capital, OH	59-55	WI-Oshkosh
1996	WI-Oshkosh	66-50	Mt. Union, OH
1997	NYU	72-70	WI-Eau Claire
1998	Washington, MO	77-69	So. Maine
1999	Washington, MO	74-65	College of St. Benedict, MN

*Overtime

NAIA Finals

Multiple winners: One tournament–SW Oklahoma (4); Div. I tourney–Southern Nazarene (4), Arkansas Tech (2); Div. II tourney–Northern St. and Western Oregon (2).

Year	Winner	Score	Loser
1981	Kentucky St.	73-67	Texas Southern
1982	SW Oklahoma	80-45	Mo. Southern
1983	SW Oklahoma	80-68	AL-Huntsville
1984	NC-Asheville	72-70	*Portland, OR
1985	SW Oklahoma	55-54	Saginaw Val., MI
1986	Francis Marion, SC	75-65	Wayland Baptist, TX
1987	SW Oklahoma	60-58	North Georgia
1988	Oklahoma City	113-95	Claflin, SC
1989	So. Nazarene, OK	98-96	Claflin, SC
1990	SW Oklahoma	82-75	AR-Monticello
1991	Ft. Hays St., KS	57-53	SW Oklahoma
1992	I– Arkansas Tech	84-68	Wayland Baptist, TX
	II– Northern St., SD	73-56	Tarleton St., TX
1993	I– Arkansas Tech	76-75	Union, TN
	II– No. Montana	71-68	Northern St., SD
1994	I– So. Nazarene	97-74	David Lipscomb, TN
	II– Northern St., SD	48-45	Western Oregon
1995	I– So. Nazarene	78-77	SE Oklahoma
	II– Western Oregon	75-67	NW Nazarene, ID
1996	I– So. Nazarene	80-79	SE Oklahoma
	II– Western Oregon	80-77	Huron, SD
1997	I– So. Nazarene	78-73	Union, TN
	II– NW Nazarene	64-46	Black Hills St., SD
1998	I– Union, TN	73-70	So. Nazarene
	II– Walsh, OH	73-66	Mary Hardin-Baylor
1999	I– Oklahoma City	72-55	Simon Fraser, B.C.
	II– Shawnee St., OH	80-65	St. Francis, IN

*Overtime

AIAW Finals

The Association of Intercollegiate Athletics for Women Large College tournament determined the women's national champion for 10 years until supplanted by the NCAA.

In 1982, most Division I teams entered the first NCAA tournament rather than the last one staged by the AIAW.

Year	Winner	Score	Loser
1972	Immaculata, PA	52-48	West Chester, PA
1973	Immaculata, PA	59-52	Queens College, NY
1974	Immaculata, PA	68-53	Mississippi College
1975	Delta St., MS	90-81	Immaculata, PA
1976	Delta St., MS	69-64	Immaculata, PA
1977	Delta St., MS	68-55	LSU
1978	UCLA	90-74	Maryland
1979	Old Dominion	75-65	Louisiana Tech
1980	Old Dominion	68-53	Tennessee
1981	Louisiana Tech	79-59	Tennessee
1982	Rutgers	83-77	Texas

Pro Basketball

Spurs **David Robinson** and **Tim Duncan** played tall enough to keep the trophies out of the reach of the pesky Knicks in the NBA Finals.

Tall Win in Short Season

Seven-footers Tim Duncan and David Robinson lead the Spurs to an NBA title in a lockout-shortened season.

by
David Aldridge

When you think about it, the San Antonio Spurs were the perfect transition champion from the glitz and glamour of the Bulls. There is no glitz in San Antonio. It's a hardscrabble town of working men and women. So it's appropriate that its team was a blue-collar bunch, utterly lacking in flash but deep in fundamentals. A defensive dynamo that stuffed opponents' halfcourt game. A brutally effective offensive bunch that proved two seven-footers could play together. If they're Tim Duncan and David Robinson.

The Spurs were what economists call a "correction," an antidote for an overheating league. A league with too many players who forget that what made Magic, Bird and Jordan great was that they won, not how they looked winning.

San Antonio's best player was Duncan, a laconic 23-year-old who might take the trash out but won't talk it. And his first on-court strut will be news to us. Its foundation was Robinson, the 10-year vet whose biggest NBA crime to this point was being too nice. But Duncan deftly became the best player in the league and Robinson won his redemption. After a shaky start that threatened Coach Gregg Popovich's job, the Spurs went 46-7 the rest of the way.

Still, the Spurs' pulverizing run through the Timberwolves, Lakers, Blazers and Knicks to the title couldn't cover up the problems the NBA faced in 1999. The lockout nearly destroyed the league and severely damaged the game's relationship with its fans. Attendance was down and ratings went through the

---

David Aldridge is ESPN's NBA analyst.

AP/Wide World Photos

Tim Duncan proved that he, not **Shaquille O'Neal**, is the big man of the future–and for that matter the present–leading his Spurs to the first NBA title of the post-Jordan era.

floor—perhaps expected in the wake of Michael Jordan's retirement, but exacerbated by the ill feelings of fans who felt they were ignored by both sides during the labor dispute.

The league pointed to a new, promising batch of rookies. It embraced Allen Iverson's spectacular play in Philadelphia after keeping him at arm's length for two years. And it could rightly celebrate the nightly excellence of Jason Kidd in Phoenix, Kevin Garnett in Minnesota and Alonzo Mourning in Miami. Portland and Utah were standard-bearers for most of the season out west and Paul Silas helped resuscitate the Hornets after a brutal start and the resignation of coach Dave Cowens.

But the league is in desperate need of new rivalries, new standard-bearers. It needs to develop a worthy challenger to San Antonio in the west.

The Lakers, who finally courted Phil Jackson out of daily work in Bill Bradley's campaign, think they've got the answer. The NBA needs a new colossus to replace Chicago in the east. It needs Iverson to continue to mature both on and off the floor. It needs flash and dunks. But more importantly, it needs fundamentals—and about a dozen more players with the game and demeanor of Duncan to bring people's attention back between the lines. ■

David Aldridge's Top 10 Stories of the NBA Season

10. **The Thrilla in Vanilla Meets Vinsanity.** Two spectacular rookies—Sacramento's Jason Williams and Toronto's Vince Carter—help breathe life into two of the league's dumpier franchises. Williams will do anything

The NBA player lockout ended at 191 days when NBA Players' Association Executive Director **Billy Hunter**, left, and NBA Commissioner **David Stern** shook hands on a new collective bargaining agreement on Jan. 7, 1999 in New York.

from anywhere on the floor, and along with Chris Webber and Vlade Divac, reintroduces the Kings to the league. Carter's dunk packages are breathtaking, but his all-around game is the real revelation.

9. **Dennis in Denial.** Dennis Rodman comes back for an utterly bizarre run with the Lakers. After he finally signs, the Lakers promptly roll off 10 straight wins, but Rodman's erratic behavior provides no comfort for a team that has already fired Del Harris and will trade Eddie Jones and Elden Campbell for Glen Rice. After five weeks of missed practices and indifference, the Lakers cut him.

8. **Coach Cal's K.O.** The Nets implode after a promising 1997-98 season and John Calipari pays the price. Injuries and new ownership are too much for Calipari to overcome; the acquisition of Stephon Marbury from the Timberwolves comes too late to save his job.

7. **The Antonio McDyess Tilt-a-Whirl.** McDyess, who forced a trade from Denver to Phoenix a year ago, now goes back to Denver as a free agent after being lobbied hard during the lockout by Nuggets guard Nick Van Exel. A last-minute pilgrimage to Denver by Suns guards Jason Kidd and Rex Chapman almost changes McDyess's mind. The Suns don't stew for long; they promptly snatch Tom Gugliotta from Minnesota.

AP/Wide World Photos

Michael Jordan announces his retirement from the NBA on Jan. 13, 1999 at the United Center in Chicago while league commissioner David Stern wonders how a Jordan-less and post-lockout NBA will thrive.

6. **Slippen' Pippen?** Scottie Pippen takes off for Houston and $82 million, but the dominance expected from the uniting of Pippen with Hakeem Olajuwon and Charles Barkley never materializes. Pippen struggles with an offense that doesn't feature movement but does feature a lot of giving Olajuwon the ball on the left block.

5. **Smash and Grab.** It used to be the term for robbing passengers in their cars. Now it describes the way halfcourt defense is played in the NBA. Scores around the league plummet. The Sacramento Kings are the only team in the league to average more than 100 points a game in the regular season. Rules designed to help in-crease offensive flow are approved for the 1999-2000 season.

4. **The Rebirth of Latrell Sprewell.** How does a guy go from being everything that's wrong with pro sports to a celebrity admired by millions? By playing in New York, where everything's OK as long as you wear the home white. Sprewell wasn't a thug/criminal when he was in Golden State, and he isn't an angel now. It just reads that way in the New York tabloids.

3. **Knick Capades.** This soap opera never goes into hiatus. Ernie Grunfeld deals Charles Oakley to Toronto for Marcus Camby, then acquires Sprewell from Golden State for fan favorite John Starks. Grunfeld's disagreements with Coach Jeff Van Gundy about the roles of the new players and style the team should play explode into open feuding. Madison Square Garden President Dave Checketts fires Grunfeld with nine games left and pursues Phil Jackson, then lies about it. Bombarded with daily questions about the future, and playing without injured Patrick Ewing, the Knicks, naturally, go to the Finals with Sprewell and Camby leading the way.

2. **Where's my Key? Oh, I Forgot. I'm Locked Out.** David Stern and the owners, determined to put the brakes on spiraling player salaries, terminate the old collective bargaining agreement and lock the players out for seven months. The season is nearly cancelled. But when the smoke clears, the owners have what they want: limits on what star players can make, more

drug testing and a rookie scale that binds young star players to their teams for up to five years.

1. **MJ Decides to Call it Quits.** What other way could Michael Jordan go out? A sixth league championship in hand and his place in league history secure, Jordan retired—this time, for good; this time, on his own terms. His departure leaves the league scrambling to find itself and find something that non-fanatic fans will be compelled to watch. ■

THE **NUMBERS**

INSIDE

FOUL SHOOTERS

Three active players are the worst in NBA history from the free throw line. No, Shaquille O'Neal is not one of them. Here are the five biggest foul-ups at the foul line.

	FT Pct.
Chris Dudley (1987-99)	.462
Bo Outlaw (1993-99)	.508
Dale Davis (1991-99)	.510
Wilt Chamberlain (1959-73)	.511
Larry Smith (1980-93)	.531

Note: Shaquille O'Neal's career free throw percentage is .536

TOP PICK TO TITLE

It appears that San Antonio used their top draft choice in the 1997 NBA draft wisely when they took Tim Duncan. The former number one pick won an NBA championship with the Spurs in just his second year in the league. Here is a look at the fastest top picks to help his team win a title.

Player	Rookie Year	Title Year
Magic Johnson, LA Lakers	1980	1980
Tim Duncan, San Antonio	1998	1999
Lew Alcindor, Milwaukee	1970	1971
Bill Walton, Portland	1975	1977
James Worthy, LA Lakers	1983	1985

PARTY CRASHERS

The New York Knicks became the first 8-seed to make the NBA Finals with their fantastic post-season run. Below is a rundown on the lowest seeds to make it to the NBA Finals since the playoffs expanded to 16 teams in 1984.

Year	Seed	Team	Regular Season W-L
1999	8	New York	27-23
1995	6	Houston	47-35
1991	3	LA Lakers	58-24
1990	3	Portland	59-23

Note: Houston won the NBA championship in 1995.

DELAY OF GAME

The six-month long NBA lockout ended in January, narrowly preventing the cancellation of the season. Here is a look at the longest labor-related interruptions in the four major sports.

League	Days	Dates
MLB (strike)	232	8/12/94-3/31/95
NBA (lockout)	191	7/1/98-1/7/99
NHL (lockout)	103	10/1/94-1/13/95
NBA (lockout)	79	7/1-9/17/95
NFL (strike)	57	9/21-11/16/82
MLB (strike)	50	6/12-7/31/81

■

PRO BASKETBALL
S T A T I S T I C S

THE SEASON IN REVIEW
1998-1999
STANDINGS • PLAYOFFS

SEC **A**

PAGE **349**

THE 2000 ESPN INFORMATION PLEASE SPORTS ALMANAC

Final NBA Standings

Division champions (*) and playoff qualifiers (†) are noted. Number of seasons listed after each head coach refers to current tenure with club.

Western Conference

Midwest Division

	W	L	Pct	GB	Per Game For	Opp
*San Antonio	37	13	.740	—	92.8	84.7
†Utah	37	13	.740	—	93.3	86.8
†Houston	31	19	.620	6	94.2	91.9
†Minnesota	25	25	.500	12	92.9	92.6
Dallas	19	31	.380	18	91.6	94.0
Denver	14	36	.280	23	93.5	100.1
Vancouver	8	42	.160	29	88.9	97.5

Head Coaches: SA— Gregg Popovich (3rd season); **Utah—** Jerry Sloan (11th); **Hou—** Rudy Tomjanovich (8th); **Min—** Phil Saunders (4th); **Dal—** Don Nelson (2nd); **Den—** Mike D'Antoni (1st); **Van—** Brian Hill (2nd).
1997-98 Standings: 1. Utah (62-20); 2. San Antonio (56-26); 3. Minnesota (45-37); 4. Houston (41-41); 5. Dallas (20-62); 6. Vancouver (19-63); 7. Denver (11-71).

Pacific Division

	W	L	Pct	GB	Per Game For	Opp
*Portland	35	15	.700	—	94.8	88.5
†LA Lakers	31	19	.620	4	99.0	96.0
†Sacramento	27	23	.540	8	100.2	100.6
†Phoenix	27	23	.540	8	95.6	93.3
Seattle	25	25	.500	10	94.9	95.9
Golden St.	21	29	.420	14	88.3	90.8
LA Clippers	9	41	.180	26	90.4	99.2

Head Coaches: Port— Mike Dunleavy (2nd season); **LAL—** Del Harris (4th, 6-6) was fired and replaced with assistant Kurt Rambis Feb. 26, 1999 (1st, 25-13); **Sac—** Eddie Jordan (3rd); **Pho—** Danny Ainge (3rd); **Sea—** Paul Westphal (1st); **GS—** P.J. Carlesimo (2nd); **LAC—** Chris Ford (1st).
1997-98 Standings: 1. Seattle (61-21); 2. LA Lakers (61-21); 3. Phoenix (56-26); 4. Portland (46-36); 5. Sacramento (27-55); 6. Golden St. (19-63); 7. LA Clippers (17-65).

Eastern Conference

Atlantic Division

	W	L	Pct	GB	Per Game For	Opp
*Miami	33	17	.660	—	89.0	84.0
†Orlando	33	17	.660	—	89.5	86.9
†Philadelphia	28	22	.560	5	89.7	87.6
†New York	27	23	.540	6	86.4	85.4
Boston	19	31	.380	14	93.0	94.9
Washington	18	32	.360	15	91.2	93.4
New Jersey	16	34	.320	17	91.4	95.2

Head Coaches: Mia— Pat Riley (4th season); **Orl—** Chuck Daly (2nd); **Phi—** Larry Brown (2nd); **NY—** Jeff Van Gundy (4th); **Bos—** Rick Pitino (2nd); **Wash—** Bernie Bickerstaff (3rd); **NJ—** John Calipari (3rd, 3-17) fired and replaced with assistant Don Casey on an interim basis Mar. 15, 1999 (13-17).
1997-98 Standings: 1. Miami (55-27); 2. New Jersey (43-39); 3. New York (43-39); 4. Washington (42-40); 5. Orlando (41-41); 6. Boston (36-46); 7. Philadelphia (31-51).

Central Division

	W	L	Pct	GB	Per Game For	Opp
*Indiana	33	17	.660	—	94.7	90.9
†Atlanta	31	19	.620	2	86.3	83.4
†Detroit	29	21	.580	4	90.4	86.9
†Milwaukee	28	22	.560	5	91.7	90.0
Charlotte	26	24	.520	7	92.9	93.0
Toronto	23	27	.460	10	91.1	92.8
Cleveland	22	28	.440	11	86.4	88.2
Chicago	13	37	.260	20	81.9	91.4

Head Coaches: Ind— Larry Bird (2nd season); **Atl—** Lenny Wilkens (6th); **Det—** Alvin Gentry (2nd); **Mil—** George Karl (1st); **Char—** Dave Cowens (3rd, 4-11) fired and replaced with assistant Paul Silas Mar. 8, 1999 (1st, 22-13); **Tor—** Butch Carter (2nd); **Cle—** Mike Fratello (6th); **Chi—** Tim Floyd (1st).
1997-98 Standings: 1. Chicago (62-20); 2. Indiana (58-24); 3. Charlotte (51-31); 4. Atlanta (50-32); 5. Cleveland (47-35); 6. Detroit (37-45); 7. Milwaukee (36-46); 8. Toronto (16-66).

Overall Conference Standings

Sixteen teams—eight from each conference—qualify for the NBA Playoffs; (*) indicates division champions.

Western Conference

		W	L	Home	Away	Div	Conf
1	San Antonio*	37	13	21-4	16-9	17-4	33-11
2	Utah	37	13	22-3	15-10	15-3	33-11
3	Portland*	35	15	22-3	13-12	15-7	30-14
4	LA Lakers	31	19	18-7	13-12	14-8	28-16
5	Houston	31	19	19-6	12-13	12-9	28-16
6	Sacramento	27	23	16-9	11-14	11-9	23-21
7	Phoenix	27	23	15-10	12-13	9-10	26-18
8	Minnesota	25	25	18-7	7-18	11-9	22-22
	Seattle	25	25	17-8	8-17	11-10	23-21
	Golden St.	21	29	13-12	8-17	8-11	18-26
	Dallas	19	31	15-10	4-21	8-12	16-28
	Denver	14	36	12-23	2-23	5-16	12-32
	LA Clippers	9	41	6-19	3-22	3-16	8-36
	Vancouver	8	42	17-18	1-24	3-18	8-36

Eastern Conference

		W	L	Home	Away	Div	Conf
1	Miami*	33	17	18-7	15-10	12-8	30-15
2	Indiana*	33	17	18-7	15-10	15-7	30-14
3	Orlando	33	17	21-4	12-13	12-6	30-14
4	Atlanta	31	19	16-9	15-10	13-8	27-18
5	Detroit	29	21	17-8	12-13	13-8	25-19
6	Philadelphia	28	22	17-8	11-14	9-10	25-19
7	Milwaukee	28	22	17-8	11-14	13-11	25-20
8	New York	27	23	19-6	8-17	12-8	24-21
	Charlotte	26	24	16-9	10-15	12-10	23-21
	Toronto	23	27	14-11	9-16	9-14	19-26
	Cleveland	22	28	15-10	7-18	9-13	18-26
	Boston	19	31	10-15	9-16	10-9	16-28
	Washington	18	32	13-12	5-20	6-13	16-28
	New Jersey	16	34	12-13	4-21	6-13	14-30
	Chicago	13	37	8-17	5-20	4-19	11-33

Michael Jordan: The Stats

Michael Jordan, arguably the greatest player in basketball history, retired on Jan. 13, 1999 after 13 seasons and six world titles with the NBA's Chicago Bulls. Below is a rundown of his career statistics in college basketball, pro basketball and minor league baseball.

Position: Guard. **Height:** 6-6. **Weight:** 216 pounds. **Birthdate:** Feb. 17, 1963. **Birthplace:** Brooklyn, NY. **High School:** Laney HS (Wilmington, NC). **College:** North Carolina '85. **Drafted:** Taken third overall in the 1984 NBA Draft by the Chicago Bulls (behind two 7-foot centers: Houston's Akeem Olajuwon and Kentucky's Sam Bowie). **Jersey Number:** #23 (wore #45 for the 1994-95 season before switching back).

University of North Carolina

Year	Gm	FG	FGA	FG%	FT	FTA	FT%	Reb	Ast	Stl	Pts	PPG
1981-82	34	191	358	.534	78	108	.722	149	61	41	460	13.5
1982-83	36	282	527	.535	123	167	.737	197	56	78	721	20.0
1983-84	31	247	448	.551	113	145	.779	163	64	50	607	19.6
TOTALS	101	720	1333	.540	314	420	.748	509	181	169	1788	17.7

Note: Jordan declared himself eligible for the NBA draft following his junior season at UNC.

Chicago Bulls

Regular Season	Gm	FG	FGA	FG%	FT	FTA	FT%	RPG	APG	Stl	Blk	Pts	PPG
1984-85	82	837	1625	.515	630	746	.845	6.5	5.9	196	69	2313	28.2
1985-86	18	150	328	.457	105	125	.840	3.6	2.9	37	21	408	22.7
1986-87	82	1098	2279	.482	833	972	.857	5.2	4.6	236	125	3041	37.1†
1987-88	82	1069	1998	.535	723	860	.841	5.5	5.9	259†	131	2868	35.0†
1988-89	81	966	1795	.538	674	793	.850	8.0	8.0	234	65	2633	32.5†
1989-90	82	1034	1964	.526	593	699	.848	6.9	6.3	227†	54	2753	33.6†
1990-91*	82	990	1837	.539	571	671	.851	6.0	5.5	223	83	2580	31.5†
1991-92*	80	943	1818	.519	491	590	.832	6.4	6.1	182	75	2404	30.1†
1992-93*	78	992	2003	.495	476	569	.837	6.7	5.5	221†	61	2541	32.6†
1994-95	17	166	404	.411	109	136	.801	6.9	5.3	30	13	457	26.9
1995-96*	82	916	1850	.495	548	657	.834	6.6	4.3	180	42	2491	30.4†
1996-97*	82	920	1892	.486	480	576	.833	5.9	4.3	140	44	2431	29.6†
1997-98*	82	881	1893	.465	565	721	.784	5.8	3.5	141	45	2357	28.7†
TOTALS	930	10962	21686	.505	6798	8115	.838	6.3	5.4	2306	828	29277	31.5

Playoffs	Gm	FG	FGA	FG%	FT	FTA	FT%	RPG	APG	Stl	Blk	Pts	PPG
1984-85	4	34	78	.436	48	58	.828	5.8	8.5	11	4	117	29.3
1985-86	3	48	95	.505	34	39	.872	6.3	5.7	7	4	131	43.7
1986-87	3	35	84	.417	35	39	.897	7.0	6.0	6	7	107	35.7
1987-88	10	138	260	.531	86	99	.869	7.1	4.7	24	11	363	36.3
1988-89	17	199	390	.510	183	229	.799	7.0	7.6	42	13	591	34.8
1989-90	16	219	426	.514	133	159	.836	7.2	6.8	45	14	587	36.7
1990-91*	17	197	376	.524	125	148	.845	6.4	8.4	40	23	529	31.1
1991-92*	22	290	581	.499	162	189	.857	6.2	5.8	44	16	759	34.5
1992-93*	19	251	528	.475	136	169	.805	6.7	6.0	39	17	666	35.1
1994-95	10	120	248	.484	64	79	.810	6.5	4.5	23	14	315	31.5
1995-96*	18	187	407	.459	153	187	.818	4.9	4.1	33	6	552	30.7
1996-97*	19	227	498	.456	123	148	.831	7.9	4.8	30	17	590	31.1
1997-98*	21	243	526	.462	181	223	.812	5.1	3.5	32	12	680	32.4
TOTALS	179	2188	4497	.487	1463	1766	.828	6.4	5.7	376	158	5987	33.4

Note: Jordan left basketball before the 1993-94 season to attempt a career at professional baseball.
*won NBA championship.
†led league.

Minor League Baseball

Birmingham Barons AA (Chicago White Sox)

Position: Outfield. **Batted:** Right. **Threw:** Right. **How obtained:** Signed as a free agent by the White Sox on Feb. 7, 1994. **Retired from baseball:** Mar. 10, 1995. **Jersey Number:** #45.

Year	Avg	Gm	AB	R	H	TB	2B	3B	HR	RBI	BB	SO	SB	E
1994	.202	127	436	46	88	116	17	1	3	51	51	114	30	11

NBA Awards

Award	Year
Regular Season MVP	1988, 91, 92, 96, 98
Finals MVP	1991, 92, 93, 96, 97, 98
Rookie of the Year	1985
All-NBA First Team	1987, 88, 89, 90, 91, 92, 93, 96, 97, 98
Defensive Player of the Year	1998
All-NBA Defensive First Team	1988, 89, 90, 91, 92, 93, 97, 98
NBA All-Star	1985, 86, 87, 88, 89, 90, 91, 92, 93, 96, 97, 98
All-Star Game MVP	1988, 96, 98
Slam Dunk champion	1987, 88

Philadelphia 76ers
Allen Iverson
Scoring

Los Angeles Lakers
Shaquille O'Neal
Field Goal Pct.

Miami Heat
Alonzo Mourning
Blocked Shots

Phoenix Suns
Jason Kidd
Assists

NBA Regular Season Individual Leaders

Scoring

	Gm	Min	FG	FG%	3pt/Att	FT	FT%	Reb	Ast	Stl	Blk	Pts	Avg	Hi
Allen Iverson, Phi.	48	1990	435	.412	58/199	356	.751	236	223	110	7	1284	26.8	46
Shaquille O'Neal, LAL	49	1705	510	.576	0/1	269	.540	525	114	36	82	1289	26.3	38
Karl Malone, Utah	49	1832	393	.493	0/1	378	.788	463	201	62	28	1164	23.8	38
Shareef Abdur-Rahim, Van.	50	2021	386	.432	11/36	369	.841	374	172	69	55	1152	23.0	39
Keith Van Horn, NJ	42	1576	322	.428	16/53	256	.852	358	65	43	53	916	21.8	35
Tim Duncan, SA	50	1963	418	.495	1/7	247	.690	571	121	45	126	1084	21.7	39
Gary Payton, Sea	50	2008	401	.434	83/281	199	.721	244	436	109	12	1084	21.7	34
Stephon Marbury, Min-NJ	49	1895	378	.428	66/197	222	.799	142	437	59	8	1044	21.3	41
Antonio McDyess, Den	50	1937	415	.471	1/9	230	.680	537	82	73	115	1061	21.2	46
Grant Hill, Det	50	1852	384	.479	0/14	285	.752	355	300	80	27	1053	21.1	46
Kevin Garnett, Min	47	1780	414	.460	4/14	145	.704	489	202	78	83	977	20.8	30
Shawn Kemp, Cle	42	1475	277	.482	1/2	307	.789	388	101	48	45	862	20.5	32
Michael Finley, Dal	50	2051	389	.444	45/136	186	.823	194	218	66	15	1009	20.2	36
Alonzo Mourning, Mia	46	1753	324	.511	0/2	276	.652	507	74	34	180	924	20.1	34
Kobe Bryant, LAL	50	1896	362	.465	27/101	245	.839	264	190	72	50	996	19.9	38
Mitch Richmond, Was	50	1912	331	.412	70/221	251	.857	172	122	64	10	983	19.7	35
Hakeem Olajuwon, Hou	50	1784	373	.514	4/13	195	.717	478	88	82	123	945	18.9	32
Toni Kukoc, Chi	44	1654	315	.420	39/137	159	.747	310	235	49	11	828	18.8	32
Reggie Miller, Ind	50	1787	294	.438	106/275	226	.915	135	112	37	9	920	18.4	34
Glenn Robinson, Mil	47	1579	347	.459	31/79	140	.870	276	100	46	41	865	18.4	33
Vince Carter, Tor	50	1760	345	.450	19/66	204	.761	283	149	55	77	913	18.3	32
Tim Hardaway, Mia	48	1772	301	.400	112/311	121	.812	152	352	57	6	835	17.4	32
Ray Allen, Mil	50	1719	303	.450	74/208	176	.903	276	100	53	7	856	17.1	31
Tom Gugliotta, Pho	43	1563	277	.483	2/7	173	.794	381	121	59	21	729	17.0	33
Jason Kidd, Pho	50	2060	310	.444	45/123	181	.757	339	539	114	19	846	16.9	30

Rebounds

	Gm	Off	Def	Tot	Avg
Chris Webber, Sac	42	149	396	545	13.0
Charles Barkley, Hou	42	167	349	516	12.3
Dikembe Mutombo, Atl	50	192	418	610	12.2
Danny Fortson, Den	50	210	371	581	11.6
Tim Duncan, SA	50	159	412	571	11.4
Alonzo Mourning, Mia	46	166	341	507	11.0
Antonio McDyess, Den	50	168	369	537	10.7
Shaquille O'Neal, LAL	49	187	338	525	10.7
Kevin Garnett, Min	47	166	323	489	10.4
Vlade Divac, Cha	50	140	361	501	10.0
David Robinson, SA	49	148	344	492	10.0
Brian Grant, Por	48	173	297	470	9.8
Hakeem Olajuwon, Hou	50	106	372	478	9.6
Karl Malone, Utah	49	107	356	463	9.4
Tom Gugliotta, Pho	43	131	250	381	8.9

Assists

	Gm	Ast	Avg
Jason Kidd, Pho	50	539	10.8
Rod Strickland, Was	44	434	9.9
Stephon Marbury, Min	49	437	8.9
Gary Payton, Sea	50	436	8.7
Terrell Brandon, Min	36	309	8.6
Mark Jackson, Ind	49	386	7.9
Brevin Knight, Cle	39	302	7.7
John Stockton, Utah	50	374	7.5
Avery Johnson, SA	50	369	7.4
Nick Van Exel, LAL	50	368	7.4
Tim Hardaway, Mia	48	352	7.3
Darrell Armstrong, Orl	50	335	6.7
Mike Bibby, Van	50	325	6.5
David Wesley, Cha	50	322	6.4
Eric Snow, Phi	48	301	6.3

Field Goal Pct.

	Gm	FG	Att	Pct
Shaquille O'Neal, LAL	.49	510	885	.576
Otis Thorpe, Was	.49	240	440	.545
Hakeem Olajuwon, Hou	.50	373	725	.514
Alonzo Mourning, Mia	.46	324	634	.511
David Robinson, SA	.49	268	527	.509
Rasheed Wallace, Por	.49	242	476	.508
Bison Dele, Det	.49	216	431	.501
Tim Duncan, SA.	.50	418	845	.495
Danny Fortson, Den	.50	191	386	.495
Vitaly Potapenko, Bos.	.50	204	412	.495

Free Throw Pct.

	Gm	FT	Att	Pct
Reggie Miller, Ind	.50	226	247	.915
Chauncey Billups, Den	.45	157	172	.913
Darrell Armstrong, Orl	.50	161	178	.904
Ray Allen, Mil	.50	176	195	.903
Hersey Hawkins, Sea	.50	119	132	.902
Jeff Hornacek, Utah	.48	125	140	.893
Chris Mullin, Ind	.50	80	92	.870
Glenn Robinson, Mil.	.47	140	161	.870
Mario Elie, SA.	.47	103	119	.866
Eric Piatkowski, LAC	.49	88	102	.863

3-Point Field Goal Pct.

	Gm	3FG	Att	Pct
Dell Curry, Mil.	.42	69	145	.476
Chris Mullin, Ind	.50	73	157	.465
Hubert Davis, Dal	.50	65	144	.451
Walt Williams, Por	.48	63	144	.438
Michael Dickerson, Hou.	.50	71	164	.433
Jeff Hornacek, Phi	.48	34	81	.420
Clifford Robinson, Pho	.50	58	139	.417
George McCloud, Pho	.48	69	166	.416
Jud Buechler, Det	.50	61	148	.412

High-Point Games

	Opp	Date	FG-FT—Pts
Allen Iverson, Phi	SA	2/12	14-15—46
Antonio McDyess, Den	Van.	2/28	16-14—46
Grant Hill, Det	Was.	2/8	14-18—46
Allen Iverson, Phi	LAL	3/19	17-4—41
Stephon Marbury, Min	Mil	5/5	13-11—41
Stephon Marbury, Min	Hou	2/17	16-8—40

Six tied at 39 points each, including Iverson and McDyess who each did it twice.

Blocked Shots

	Gm	Blk	Avg
Alonzo Mourning, Mia	.46	180	3.91
Shawn Bradley, Dal	.49	159	3.24
Theo Ratliff, Phi	.50	149	2.98
Dikembe Mutombo, Atl	.50	147	2.94
Greg Ostertag, Uta.	.48	131	2.73
Patrick Ewing, NY	.38	100	2.63
Tim Duncan, SA.	.50	126	2.52
Hakeem Olajuwon, Hou	.50	123	2.46
David Robinson, SA	.49	119	2.43
Antonio McDyess, Den.	.50	115	2.30

Steals

	Gm	Stl	Avg
Kendall Gill, NJ	.50	134	2.68
Eddie Jones, Cha	.50	125	2.50
Allen Iverson, Phi.	.48	110	2.29
Jason Kidd, Pho.	.50	114	2.28
Doug Christie, Tor	.50	113	2.26
Anfernee Hardaway, Orl	.50	111	2.22
Gary Payton, Sea	.50	109	2.18
Darrell Armstrong, Orl	.50	108	2.16
Eric Snow, Phi	.48	100	2.08
Mookie Blaylock, Atl.	.48	99	2.06

Rookie Leaders

Scoring	Gm	FG	FT	Pts	Avg
Vince Carter, Tor	.50	345	204	913	18.3
Paul Pierce, Bos.	.48	284	139	791	16.5
Mike Bibby, Van	.50	260	127	662	13.2
Jason Williams, Sac	.50	231	79	641	12.8
Michael Dickerson, Hou.	.50	215	46	547	10.9

Field Goal Pct.	Gm	FG	Att	Pct
Robert Traylor, Mil	.49	108	201	.537
Michael Doleac, Orl.	.49	125	267	.468
Michael Dickerson, Hou.	.50	215	462	.465
Matt Harpring, Orl	.50	148	320	.463
Antawn Jamison, GS	.47	178	394	.452

Rebounds	Gm	Off	Def	Tot	Avg
Michael Olowokandi, LAC	.45	120	237	357	7.9
Antawn Jamison, GS	.47	131	170	301	6.4
Paul Pierce, Bos.	.48	117	192	309	6.4
Vince Carter, Tor	.50	94	189	283	5.7
Matt Harpring, Orl	.50	88	126	214	4.3

Assists	Gm	No	Avg
Mike Bibby, Van	.50	325	6.5
Jason Williams, Sac	.50	299	6.0
Vince Carter, Tor	.50	149	3.0
Cuttino Mobley, Hou	.49	121	2.5
Paul Pierce, Bos.	.48	115	2.4

Personal Fouls

Danny Fortson, Den	.212
Otis Thorpe, Was	.196
Charles Oakley, Tor	.182
Bison Dele, Det	.181
Theo Ratliff, Phi	.180

Disqualifications

Otis Thorpe, Was.	.9
Danny Fortson, Den	.9
Theo Ratliff, Phi.	.8
Rasheed Wallace, Por.	.6

Four tied with 5 each.

Turnovers

Shareef Abdur-Rahim, Van.	.186
Grant Hill, Det	.184
Allen Iverson, Phi.	.167
Stephon Marbury, Min	.164
Karl Malone, Utah.	.162

Triple Doubles

Jason Kidd, Pho	.7
Scottie Pippen, Hou	.2

Nine tied with 1 each.

Minutes Played

Jason Kidd, Pho	.2060
Michael Finley, Dal	.2051
Shareef Abdur-Rahim, Van	.2021
Scottie Pippen, Hou	.2011
Gary Payton, Sea	.2008

Technical Fouls

Gary Payton, Sea	.22
Rasheed Wallace, Por.	.12
Karl Malone, Utah	.11

Five tied with 9 each.

Team by Team Statistics

Players who competed for more than one team during the regular season are listed with their final club; (*) indicates rookies.

Atlanta Hawks

	Gm	FG%	Tpts	PPG	RPG	APG
Steve Smith	36	.402	672	18.7	4.2	3.3
Mookie Blaylock	48	.379	640	13.3	4.7	5.8
Alan Henderson	38	.442	474	12.5	6.6	0.7
Dikembe Mutombo	50	.512	541	10.8	12.2	1.1
LaPhonso Ellis	20	.421	204	10.2	5.5	0.9
Grant Long	50	.421	489	9.8	5.9	1.1
Tyrone Corbin	47	.391	352	7.5	3.1	0.9
Chris Crawford	42	.431	288	6.9	2.1	0.6
Anthony Johnson	49	.404	244	5.0	1.5	0.4
Ed Gray	30	.291	146	4.9	0.9	0.4
Roshown McLeod*	34	.380	162	4.8	15	0.4
Jeff Sheppard*	18	.385	40	2.2	1.2	0.9
Shammond Williams	2	.000	3	1.5	0.0	0.5
Mark West	49	.373	60	1.2	2.6	0.3

Triple Doubles: Blaylock (1). **3-pt FG leader:** Blaylock (77).
Steals leader: Blaylock (99). **Blocks leader:** Mutombo (147).
Signed: G Sheppard (Mar. 29).

Boston Celtics

	Gm	FG%	Tpts	PPG	RPG	APG
Antoine Walker	42	.412	784	18.7	8.5	3.1
Ron Mercer	41	.431	698	17.0	3.8	2.5
Paul Pierce*	48	.439	791	16.5	6.4	2.4
Kenny Anderson	34	.451	412	12.1	3.0	5.7
Vitaly Potapenko	50	.495	499	10.0	6.6	1.5
Dana Barros	50	.453	464	9.3	2.1	4.2
Tony Battie	50	.519	335	6.7	6.0	1.1
Walter McCarty	32	.362	181	5.7	3.6	1.3
Damon Jones*	24	.361	125	5.2	1.8	1.8
Greg Minor	44	.417	214	4.9	2.7	1.1
Popeye Jones	18	.392	54	3.0	2.9	0.8
Bruce Bowen	30	.280	70	2.3	1.7	0.9
Eric Riley	35	.519	78	2.2	2.8	0.4
Marlon Garnett	24	.294	51	2.1	0.9	0.8
Dwayne Schintzius	16	.250	11	0.7	1.2	0.5

Triple Doubles: none. **3-pt FG leader:** Pierce (84).
Steals leader: Pierce (82). **Blocks leader:** Battie (71).
Acquired: C/F Potapenko from the Cleveland Cavaliers for F/C Andrew DeClercq and a first-round pick (Mar. 11).

Charlotte Hornets

	Gm	FG%	Tpts	PPG	RPG	APG
Eddie Jones	50	.437	780	15.6	3.9	3.7
Bobby Phills	43	.433	613	14.3	4.0	3.5
David Wesley	50	.446	706	14.1	3.2	6.4
Derrick Coleman	37	.414	486	13.1	8.9	2.1
Elden Campbell	49	.477	616	12.6	8.1	1.4
Chucky Brown	48	.472	407	8.5	3.6	1.2
Brad Miller*	38	.565	238	6.3	3.1	0.6
Chuck Person	50	.388	303	6.1	2.6	1.2
Eldridge Recasner	44	.446	222	5.0	1.8	2.1
Ricky Davis*	46	.405	209	4.5	1.8	1.3
Charles Shackleford	32	.489	107	3.3	4.0	0.4
Travis Williams	8	.462	15	1.9	2.4	0.3
Corey Beck	24	.462	45	1.9	1.2	0.8
Willie Burton	3	.143	4	1.3	2.0	0.0
Joe Wolf	3	.000	0	0.0	0.3	0.0

Triple Doubles: none. **3-pt FG leader:** Phills (68).
Steals leader: Jones (125). **Blocks leader:** Campbell (73).
Signed: G Beck (Apr. 6).
Acquired: G Jones and C Campbell from the Los Angeles Lakers for F Glen Rice, G B.J. Armstrong and F J.R. Reid (Mar. 10).

Chicago Bulls

	Gm	FG%	Tpts	PPG	RPG	APG
Toni Kukoc	44	.420	828	18.8	7.0	5.3
Ron Harper	35	.377	392	11.2	5.1	3.3
Brent Barry	37	.396	412	11.1	3.9	3.1
Dickey Simpkins	50	.463	456	9.1	6.8	1.3
Mark Bryant	45	.483	407	9.0	5.2	1.1
Randy Brown	39	.414	342	8.8	3.4	3.8
Kornel David*	50	.449	308	6.2	3.5	0.8
Rusty LaRue	43	.359	203	4.7	1.3	1.5
Cory Carr*	42	.329	171	4.1	1.2	1.6
Andrew Lang	21	.323	80	3.8	1.3	0.3
Corey Benjamin*	31	.376	118	3.8	1.3	0.3
Bill Wennington	38	.348	143	3.8	2.1	0.5
Charles Jones*	29	.317	108	3.7	1.4	1.4
Keith Booth	39	.325	120	3.1	2.4	1.0
Mario Bennett	3	.333	7	2.3	1.7	0.0

Triple Doubles: none. **3-pt FG leader:** Kukoc (39).
Steals leader: Brown (68). **Blocks leader:** Harper (35).

Cleveland Cavaliers

	Gm	FG%	Tpts	PPG	RPG	APG
Shawn Kemp	42	.482	862	20.5	9.2	2.4
Zydrunas Ilgauskas	5	.509	76	15.2	8.8	0.8
Wesley Person	45	.453	503	11.2	3.2	1.8
Derek Anderson	38	.398	409	10.8	2.9	3.8
Brevin Knight	39	.425	373	9.6	3.4	7.7
Cedric Henderson	50	.417	454	9.1	3.9	2.3
Andrew DeClercq	47	.500	371	7.9	5.4	0.7
Danny Ferry	50	.476	349	7.0	2.0	1.1
Johnny Newman	50	.422	303	6.1	1.5	0.8
Mitchell Butler	31	.482	168	5.4	1.4	0.7
Bob Sura	50	.333	214	4.3	2.0	3.0
Earl Boykins*	22	.380	65	3.0	0.8	1.5
Corie Blount	34	.360	100	2.9	1.9	0.3
Ryan Stack*	18	.378	47	2.6	1.9	0.3
Antonio Lang	10	.667	13	1.3	1.6	0.1
Litterial Green	1	.000	0	0.0	0.0	0.0

Triple Doubles: none. **3-pt FG leader:** Person (75).
Steals leader: Knight (70). **Blocks leader:** Kemp (45).
Signed: G Butler (Mar. 19), F Blount (Mar. 13), G Boykins (Mar. 10).
Acquired: F/C DeClercq and a first round draft choice from the Boston Celtics for F/C Vitaly Potapenko.

Dallas Mavericks

	Gm	FG%	Tpts	PPG	RPG	APG
Michael Finley	50	.444	1009	20.2	5.3	4.4
Gary Trent	45	.477	719	16.0	7.8	1.7
Cedric Ceballos	13	.421	163	12.5	6.5	0.9
Hubert Davis	50	.438	457	9.1	1.7	1.8
Robert Pack	25	.431	222	8.9	1.4	3.2
Shawn Bradley	49	.480	420	8.6	8.0	0.8
Dirk Nowitzki*	47	.405	385	8.2	3.4	1.0
Steve Nash	40	.363	315	7.9	2.9	5.5
Erick Strickland	33	.403	249	7.5	2.5	1.9
Samaki Walker	39	.463	229	5.9	3.7	0.2
A.C Green	50	.422	246	4.9	4.6	0.5
Chris Antsey	41	.360	134	3.3	2.4	0.7
Bruno Sundov*	3	.286	4	1.3	0.0	0.3
John Williams	25	.333	29	1.3	3.3	0.6

Triple Doubles: none. **3-pt FG leader:** Davis (65).
Steals leader: Finley (66). **Blocks leader:** Bradley (159).
Signed: C Sundov (Mar. 29).

Denver Nuggets

	Gm	FG%	Tpts	PPG	RPG	APG
Antonio McDyess	50	.471	1061	21.2	10.7	1.6
Nick Van Exel	50	.398	826	16.5	2.3	7.4
Chauncey Billups	45	.386	624	13.9	2.1	3.8
Raef LaFrentz*	12	.457	166	13.8	7.6	0.7
Danny Fortson	50	.495	550	11.0	11.6	0.6
Eric Williams	38	.365	277	7.3	2.1	1.0
Cory Alexander	36	.373	261	7.3	2.1	3.3
Bryant Stith	46	.393	320	7.0	2.3	1.8
Johnny Taylor	36	.414	207	5.8	2.8	0.7
Eric Washington	38	.397	205	5.4	2.3	0.8
Tyson Wheeler*	1	1.000	4	4.0	0.0	2.0
Keon Clark*	28	.450	93	3.3	3.4	0.4
Carl Herrera	28	.395	65	2.3	2.2	0.1
Kelly McCarty*	2	.667	4	2.0	1.5	0.0
Loren Meyer	14	.250	16	1.1	1.1	0.1
Monty Williams	1	.000	1	1.0	0.0	0.0

Triple Doubles: none. **3-pt FG leader:** Billups (85).
Steals leader: McDyess (73). **Blocks leader:** McDyess (115).

Detroit Pistons

	Gm	FG%	Tpts	PPG	RPG	APG
Grant Hill	50	.479	1053	21.1	7.1	6.0
Jerry Stackhouse	42	.371	607	14.5	2.5	2.8
Lindsey Hunter	49	.435	582	11.9	3.4	3.9
Joe Dumars	38	.411	428	11.3	1.8	3.5
Bison Dele	49	.501	513	10.5	5.6	1.4
Christian Laettner	16	.358	121	7.6	3.4	1.5
Jerome Williams	50	.500	355	7.1	7.0	0.5
Jud Buechler	50	.417	274	5.5	2.7	1.1
Don Reid	47	.557	242	5.1	3.6	0.7
Korleone Young*	3	.500	13	4.3	1.3	0.3
Loy Vaught	37	.381	127	3.4	3.9	0.3
Charles O'Bannon	18	.429	56	3.1	1.9	0.7
Khalid Reeves	11	.381	25	2.3	0.6	1.0
Eric Montross	46	.525	95	2.1	3.0	0.3
Mikki Moore	2	1.000	4	2.0	0.5	0.0
Mark Macon	7	.200	9	1.3	0.7	0.6
Steve Henson	4	.500	4	1.0	0.0	0.8

Triple Doubles: Hill (1). **3-pt FG leader:** Dumars (158).
Steals leader: Hill (143). **Blocks leader:** Stackhouse (59).
Signed: G Reeves (Mar. 14).

Golden St. Warriors

	Gm	FG%	Tpts	PPG	RPG	APG
John Starks	50	.370	690	13.8	3.3	4.7
Donyell Marshall	48	.421	530	11.0	7.1	1.4
Chris Mills	47	.411	483	10.3	5.0	2.2
Antawn Jamison*	47	.452	449	9.6	6.4	0.7
Bimbo Coles	48	.442	455	9.5	2.4	4.6
Terry Cummings	50	.439	454	9.1	5.1	1.2
Erick Dampier	50	.389	442	8.8	7.6	1.1
Jason Caffey	35	.444	308	8.8	5.9	0.5
Tony Delk	36	.364	246	6.8	1.5	2.6
Mugsy Bogues	36	.494	183	5.1	2.0	3.7
Adonal Foyle	44	.430	129	2.9	4.4	0.4
Felton Spencer	26	.455	42	1.6	1.8	0.0
Duane Ferrell	8	.071	5	0.6	0.8	0.0

Triple Doubles: none. **3-pt FG leader:** Starks (78).
Steals leader: Starks (69). **Blocks leader:** Dampier (58).

Houston Rockets

	Gm	FG%	Tpts	PPG	RPG	APG
Hakeem Olajuwon	50	.514	945	18.9	9.6	1.8
Charles Barkley	42	.478	676	16.1	12.3	4.6
Scottie Pippen	50	.432	726	14.5	6.5	5.9
Michael Dickerson*	50	.465	547	10.9	1.7	1.9
Sam Mack	44	.435	472	10.7	2.2	1.3
Cuttino Mobley*	49	.425	487	9.9	2.3	2.5
Othella Harrington	41	.513	400	9.8	6.0	0.4
Brent Price	40	.483	292	7.3	2.0	2.8
Eddie Johnson	3	.462	12	4.0	0.7	0.3
Bryce Drew*	34	.364	118	3.5	0.9	1.5
Matt Bullard	41	.377	117	2.9	1.0	0.4
Antoine Carr	18	.404	47	2.6	1.7	0.5
Anthony Miller	29	.467	70	2.4	2.3	0.2
Stanley Roberts	6	.385	14	2.3	1.8	0.0
Matt Maloney	15	.179	21	1.4	0.7	1.4

Triple Doubles: Pippen (2). **3-pt FG leader:** Mack (87).
Steals leader: Pippen (98). **Blocks leader:** Olajuwon (123).
Signed: C Roberts (Feb. 5).

Indiana Pacers

	Gm	FG%	Tpts	PPG	RPG	APG
Reggie Miller	50	.438	920	18.4	2.7	2.2
Rik Smits	49	.490	728	14.9	5.6	1.1
Jalen Rose	49	.403	542	11.1	3.1	1.9
Chris Mullin	50	.477	507	10.1	3.2	1.6
Antonio Davis	49	.471	463	9.4	7.0	0.7
Dale Davis	50	.533	398	8.0	8.3	0.4
Mark Jackson	49	.419	373	7.6	3.8	7.9
Travis Best	49	.416	346	7.1	1.6	3.4
Sam Perkins	48	.400	238	5.0	2.9	0.5
Derrick McKey	13	.442	60	4.6	3.2	1.0
Austin Croshere	27	.427	92	3.4	1.7	0.4
Al Harrington*	21	.321	45	2.1	1.9	0.2
Fred Hoiberg	12	.286	19	1.6	0.9	0.3
Mark Pope	4	.143	2	0.5	1.0	0.0

Triple Doubles: Jackson (1). **3-pt FG leader:** Miller (106).
Steals leader: Rose (50). **Blocks leader:** D. Davis (57).

Los Angeles Clippers

	Gm	FG%	Tpts	PPG	RPG	APG
Maurice Taylor	46	.461	773	16.8	5.3	1.5
Lamond Murray	50	.391	612	12.2	3.9	1.2
Eric Piatkowski	49	.432	513	10.5	2.9	1.1
Tyrone Nesby*	50	.449	503	10.1	3.5	1.6
M. Olowokandi*	45	.431	401	8.9	7.9	0.6
Sherman Douglas	30	.438	247	8.2	1.9	4.1
Darrick Martin	37	.367	296	8.0	1.3	3.9
Rodney Rogers	47	.441	348	7.4	3.8	1.6
Troy Hudson	25	.400	169	6.8	2.2	3.7
Lorenzen Wright	48	.458	319	6.6	7.5	0.7
Brian Skinner*	21	.465	86	4.1	2.5	0.0
Charles Smith	23	.361	84	3.7	1.0	0.6
Pooh Richardson	11	.333	28	2.5	1.2	2.7
Keith Closs	15	.552	32	2.1	1.7	0.0
Stojko Vrankovic	2	.250	2	1.0	3.0	0.0

Triple Doubles: none. **3-pt FG leader:** Piatkowski (65).
Steals leader: Nesby (77). **Blocks leader:** Olowokandi (55).
Signed: G Douglas (Feb. 4), G Hudson (Apr. 2).

Individual Single Game Highs

Most Field Goals Made
19 ....Tim Duncan, SA vs. Van (4/1)

Most Field Goals Attempted
36 ....Allen Iverson, Phi. vs. LAL (3/19)

Most Assists
20 ....Stephon Marbury, NJ vs. Ind. (4/25)

Most Rebounds
25 ....Lorenzen Wright, LAC vs. Sac. (3/11)

Most 3-point Field Goals Made
9 ....Dee Brown, Tor. at Mil. (4/28)

Most 3-point Field Goals Attempted
18 ....Dee Brown, Tor. at Mil. (4/28)

Los Angeles Lakers

	Gm	FG%	Tpts	PPG	RPG	APG
Shaquille O'Neal	49	.576	1289	26.3	10.7	2.3
Kobe Bryant	50	.465	996	19.9	5.3	3.8
Glen Rice	27	.432	472	17.5	3.7	2.6
J.R. Reid	41	.477	369	9.0	5.2	1.2
Rick Fox	44	.448	394	9.0	2.0	2.0
Derek Harper	45	.412	309	6.9	1.5	4.2
Derek Fisher	50	.376	296	5.9	1.8	3.9
Tyronn Lue*	15	.431	75	5.0	0.4	1.7
Robert Horry	38	.459	188	4.9	4.0	1.5
Travis Knight	37	.515	156	4.2	3.5	0.8
Sam Jacobson*	2	.600	8	4.0	1.5	0.0
Sean Rooks	36	.405	98	2.7	2.0	0.3
Ruben Patterson*	24	.412	65	2.7	1.3	0.1
Dennis Rodman	23	.348	49	2.1	11.2	1.3

Triple Doubles: none. **3-pt FG leader:** Rice (53).
Steals leader: Bryant (72). **Blocks leader:** O'Neal (82).
Signed: F Rodman (Feb. 23).
Acquired: F Rice, G Armstrong, F Reid from the Charlotte Hornets for G Eddie Jones and C Elden Campbell. (Mar. 10).

Miami Heat

	Gm	FG%	Tpts	PPG	RPG	APG
Alonzo Mourning	46	.511	924	20.1	11.0	1.6
Tim Hardaway	48	.400	835	17.4	3.2	7.3
Jamal Mashburn	24	.451	356	14.8	6.1	3.1
P.J. Brown	50	.480	571	11.4	6.9	1.3
Terry Porter	50	.465	525	10.5	2.8	2.9
Terry Mills	1	.375	9	9.0	4.0	0.0
C. Weatherspoon	48	.534	397	8.1	5.0	0.7
Dan Majerle	48	.396	3337	7.0	4.3	3.1
Voshon Lenard	12	.392	82	6.8	1.3	0.8
Mark Strickland	32	.445	119	3.7	2.4	0.3
Blue Edwards	24	.444	77	3.2	1.4	1.3
Rex Walters	33	.368	101	3.1	1.5	1.8
Duane Causwell	19	.571	44	2.3	1.8	0.1
Mark Davis	4	.333	9	2.3	1.8	0.3
Keith Askins	33	.323	53	1.6	1.3	0.3
Marty Conlon	7	.231	8	1.1	0.7	0.2
Jamie Watson	3	.500	2	0.7	0.3	0.3

Triple Doubles: none. **3-pt FG leader:** Hardaway (112).
Steals leader: Hardaway (57). **Blocks leader:** Mourning (180).
Signed: G Edwards (Feb. 14).

Milwaukee Bucks

	Gm	FG%	Tpts	PPG	RPG	APG
Glenn Robinson	47	.459	865	18.4	5.9	2.1
Ray Allen	50	.450	856	17.1	4.2	3.6
Sam Cassell	8	.419	127	15.9	1.9	4.5
Dell Curry	42	.485	423	10.1	2.0	1.1
Armon Gilliam	34	19.6	281	8.3	3.7	0.6
Tim Thomas	50	.473	358	7.2	2.5	0.9
Haywoode Workman	29	.429	200	6.9	3.5	5.9
Vinny Del Negro	48	.422	281	5.9	2.1	3.6
Chris Gatling	48	.442	272	5.7	3.7	0.7
Robert Traylor*	49	.537	259	5.3	3.7	0.8
Ervin Johnson	50	.508	256	5.1	6.4	0.4
Michael Curry	50	.437	244	4.9	2.2	1.6
Scott Williams	7	.294	14	2.0	2.0	0.1
Adonis Jordan	4	.500	6	1.5	0.0	0.8
Paul Grant	6	.333	4	0.7	0.2	0.0

Triple Doubles: none. **3-pt FG leader:** Robinson (31).
Steals leader: Allen (53). **Blocks leader:** Johnson (57).
Signed: G Del Negro (Feb. 2), G Workman (Mar. 17)
Acquired: F Thomas and F Williams from the Philadelphia 76ers for F Tyrone Hill and G Jerald Honeycutt, G Cassell and F Gatling from the New Jersey Nets and F Paul Grant from the Minnesota Timberwolves via a three team deal which sent G Terrell Brandon from the Bucks to the Minnesota Timberwolves and F Brian Evans, a 1999 first round draft choice and an undisclosed draft choice from the Nets to the Timberwolves. The Timberwolves sent G Stephon Marbury, F Bill Curley and G Chris Carr to the New Jersey Nets. (Mar. 11).

Minnesota Timberwolves

	Gm	FG%	Tpts	PPG	RPG	APG
Kevin Garnett	47	.460	977	20.8	10.4	4.3
Terrell Brandon	36	.418	501	13.9	3.7	8.8
Joe Smith	43	.427	588	13.7	8.2	1.6
Sam Mitchell	50	.408	561	11.2	3.6	2.0
Anthony Peeler	28	.379	270	9.6	3.0	2.8
Malik Sealy	31	.411	251	8.1	3.0	1.2
Bobby Jackson	50	.405	353	7.1	2.7	3.3
Dennis Scott	36	.408	234	6.5	1.6	1.1
James Robinson	31	.362	183	5.9	2.0	1.8
Dean Garrett	49	.502	270	5.5	5.2	0.6
Tom Hammonds	49	.458	212	4.3	2.8	0.4
Radoslav Nesterovic*	2	.250	4	4.0	4.0	0.5
Andrae Patterson*	35	.443	114	3.3	1.9	0.4
Bill Curley	35	.403	78	2.2	1.5	0.4
Brian Evans	16	.295	34	2.1	1.2	0.9
Reggie Jordan	27	.278	51	1.9	2.2	1.5
Trevor Winter	1	—	0	0.0	3.0	0.0

Triple Doubles: none. **3-pt FG leader:** Scott (37).
Steals leader: Garnett (78). **Blocks leader:** Garnett (83).
Signed: G/F Scott (Mar. 17).
Acquired: G Brandon from the Milwaukee Bucks and F Brian Evans, a 1999 first round draft choice and an undisclosed draft choice from the New Jersey Nets in a three team deal which sent G Stephon Marbury, F Bill Curley and G Chris Carr from the Timberwolves to the New Jersey Nets and F Paul Grant to the Milwaukee Bucks. The Nets sent G Sam Cassell and F Chris Gatling to Milwaukee. (Mar. 11).

New Jersey Nets

	Gm	FG%	Tpts	PPG	RPG	APG
Keith Van Horn	42	.428	916	21.8	8.5	1.5
Stephon Marbury	49	.428	1044	21.3	2.9	8.9
Kerry Kittles	46	.370	592	12.9	4.2	2.5
Kendall Gill	50	.398	588	11.8	4.9	2.5
Jayson Williams	30	.445	242	8.1	12.0	1.1
Eric Murdock	15	.395	119	7.9	2.3	4.4
Scott Burrell	32	.361	212	6.6	3.7	1.4
Jamie Feick	28	.500	177	6.3	10.3	0.9
Mark Hendrickson	22	.443	120	5.5	3.1	0.6
Lucious Harris	36	.403	193	5.4	1.9	0.9
Chris Carr	39	.371	207	5.3	1.8	0.6
Elliot Perry	35	.379	98	2.8	1.0	1.3
Jim McIlvaine	22	.431	48	2.2	2.5	0.1
Rony Seikaly	9	.200	15	1.7	2.3	0.2
William Cunningham	16	.167	6	0.4	1.8	0.1
Gheorghe Muresan	1	.000	0	0.0	0.0	0.0

Triple Doubles: Gill (1). **3-pt FG leader:** Marbury (66).
Steals leader: Gill (134). **Blocks leader:** Williams (60).
Acquired: G Marbury, F Curley and G Carr from the Minnesota Timberwolves for F Brian Evans, a 1999 first round draft choice and an undisclosed draft choice in a three team deal which sent G Sam Cassell and G Chris Gatling from New Jersey to the Milwaukee Bucks. Minnesota sent F Paul Grant to the Milwaukee Bucks for G Terrell Brandon (Mar. 11).
Signed: G Burrell (Feb. 3), F Feick (Mar. 22), F Hendrickson (Mar. 25).

New York Knicks

	Gm	FG%	Tpts	PPG	RPG	APG
Patrick Ewing	38	.435	657	17.3	9.9	1.1
Latrell Sprewell	37	.415	606	16.4	4.2	2.5
Allan Houston	50	.418	813	16.3	2.0	2.7
Larry Johnson	49	.459	587	12.0	5.8	2.4
Kurt Thomas	50	.462	406	8.1	5.7	1.1
Charlie Ward	50	.404	378	7.6	3.4	5.4
Marcus Camby	46	.521	329	7.2	5.5	0.3
Chris Childs	48	.427	328	6.8	2.8	4.0
Chris Dudley	46	.440	115	2.5	4.2	0.2
Ben Davis	8	.412	17	2.1	1.4	0.4
Herb Williams	6	.500	10	1.7	1.0	0.0
Rick Brunson	17	.286	17	1.0	0.6	1.1
David Wingate	20	.438	14	0.7	0.4	0.3

Triple Doubles: none. **3-pt FG leader:** Houston (57).
Steals leader: Ward (103). **Blocks leader:** Ewing (100).

Orlando Magic

	Gm	FG%	Tpts	PPG	RPG	APG
Anfernee Hardaway	.50	.420	791	15.8	5.7	5.3
Nick Anderson	.47	.395	701	14.9	5.9	1.9
Darrell Armstrong	.50	.441	690	13.8	3.6	6.7
Isaac Austin	.49	.408	690	9.7	4.8	1.8
Horace Grant	.50	.434	443	8.9	7.0	1.8
Matt Harpring*	.50	.463	408	8.2	4.3	0.9
Bo Outlaw	.31	.545	203	6.5	5.4	1.8
Michael Doleac*	.49	.468	304	6.2	3.0	0.4
Derek Strong	.44	.422	223	5.1	3.7	0.4
Dominique Wilkins	.27	.379	134	5.0	2.6	0.6
B.J. Armstrong	.32	.455	105	3.3	3.7	1.4
Kevin Ollie	.7	.231	6	1.6	0.6	0.4
Danny Schayes	.19	.379	28	1.5	0.7	0.2
Gerald Wilkins	.3	.000	2	0.7	0.3	0.3
Miles Simon*	.5	.200	2	0.4	0.4	0.0
Jonathan Kerner*	.1	.000	0	0.0	0.0	0.0

Triple Doubles: none. **3-pt FG leader:** Anderson (96).
Steals leader: Hardaway 111). **Blocks leader:** Grant (60).
Signed: F Wilkins (Feb. 5) G Armstrong (Mar. 14).

Philadelphia 76ers

	Gm	FG%	Tpts	PPG	RPG	APG
Allen Iverson	.48	.412	1284	26.8	4.9	4.6
Matt Geiger	.50	.479	674	13.5	7.2	1.2
Theo Ratliff	.50	.470	560	11.2	8.1	0.6
Larry Hughes*	.50	.411	455	9.1	3.8	1.5
Eric Snow	.48	.428	413	8.6	3.4	6.3
Tyrone Hill	.38	.455	325	8.6	7.6	0.9
George Lynch	.43	.421	356	8.3	6.5	1.8
Aaron McKie	.50	.401	240	4.8	2.8	2.0
Doug Overton	.24	.429	92	3.8	0.9	1.0
Harvey Grant	.47	.369	146	3.1	2.3	0.5
Jerald Honeycutt	.16	.281	30	1.9	0.8	0.2
Nazr Mohammed*	.26	.357	42	1.6	1.4	0.1
Anthony Parker	.2	1.000	2	1.0	0.0	0.0
Rick Mahorn	.16	.278	13	0.8	1.4	0.1
Benoit Benjamin	.6	.286	4	0.7	1.3	0.2
Casey Shaw	.9	.125	2	0.2	0.3	0.0

Triple Doubles: none. **3-pt FG leader:** Iverson (58).
Steals leader: Iverson (110). **Blocks leader:** Ratliff (149).
Acquired: F Hill and G Honeycutt from the Milwaukee Bucks for F Tim Thomas and F Scott Williams. (Mar. 11).
Signed: F/C Mahorn (Feb. 24), G Overton (Mar. 27).

Phoenix Suns

	Gm	FG%	Tpts	PPG	RPG	APG
Tom Gugliotta	.43	.483	729	17.0	8.9	2.8
Jason Kidd	.50	.444	846	16.9	6.8	10.8
Cliff Robinson	.50	.475	819	16.4	4.5	2.6
Rex Chapman	.38	.359	459	12.1	2.7	2.9
Randy Livingston	.1	.625	12	12.0	2.0	3.0
Danny Manning	.50	.484	453	9.1	4.4	2.3
George McCloud	.48	.438	428	8.9	3.4	1.6
Luc Longley	.39	.483	339	8.7	5.7	1.2
Pat Garrity*	.39	.500	217	5.6	1.9	0.5
Chris Morris	.44	.430	184	4.2	2.8	0.5
Shawn Respert	.12	.361	37	3.1	1.1	0.7
Toby Bailey*	.27	.395	78	2.9	2.0	0.5
Gerald Brown*	.33	.371	80	2.4	0.7	0.9
Joe Kleine	.31	.405	68	2.2	2.2	0.4
Jimmy Oliver	.2	.333	3	1.5	0.0	0.0
Marko Milic	.11	.400	16	1.5	0.5	0,2

Triple Doubles: Kidd (7). **3-pt FG leader:** McCloud (69).
Steals leader: Kidd (114). **Blocks leader:** Robinson (59).
Signed: F Morris (Feb. 3).

Portland Trailblazers

	Gm	FG%	Tpts	PPG	RPG	APG
Isaiah Rider	.47	.412	651	13.9	4.2	2.2
Rasheed Wallace	.49	.508	628	12.8	4.9	1.2
Damon Stoudamire	.50	.396	631	12.6	3.3	6.2
Arvydas Sabonis	.50	.485	606	12.1	7.9	2.4
Brian Grant	.48	.479	550	11.5	9.8	1.4
Walt Williams	.48	.424	446	9.3	3.0	1.7
Jim Jackson	.49	.411	414	8.4	3.2	2.6
Greg Anthony	.50	.414	319	6.4	1.3	2.0
Bonzi Wells*	.7	.550	31	4.4	1.3	2.0
Stacey Augmon	.48	.448	208	4.3	2.6	1.2
Kelvin Cato	.43	.450	151	3.5	3.5	0.4
Jermaine O'Neal	.36	.434	90	2.5	2.7	0.4
Carlos Rogers	.2	1.000	5	2.5	0.5	0.5
Brian Shaw	.1	.000	0	0.0	1.0	1.0
Gary Grant	.2	.000	0	0.0	0.0	1.5

Triple Doubles: none. **3-pt FG leader:** Anthony (49).
Steals leader: Anthony (66). **Blocks leader:** Sabonis (63).
Signed: G Shaw (Apr. 6).

Sacramento Kings

	Gm	FG%	Tpts	PPG	RPG	APG
Chris Webber	.42	.486	839	20.0	13.0	4.1
Vlade Divac	.50	.470	714	14.3	10.0	4.3
Corliss Williamson	.50	.485	659	13.2	4.1	1.3
Jason Williams*	.50	.374	641	12.8	3.1	6.0
Vernon Maxwell	.46	.390	492	10.7	1.8	1.7
Tariq Abdul-Wahad	.49	.435	454	9.3	3.8	1.0
L. Funderburke	.47	.559	420	8.9	4.7	0.6
Predrag Stojakovic*	.48	.378	402	8.4	3.0	1.5
Scott Pollard	.16	.541	82	5.1	5.1	0.3
Jon Barry	.43	.428	213	5.0	2.2	2.6
Oliver Miller	.4	.455	10	2.5	2.0	0.0
Jerome James*	.16	.375	24	1.5	1.1	0.1
Michael Hawkins	.24	.350	36	1.5	1.0	1.1
Peter Aluma	.2	.500	2	1.0	1.0	0.0

Triple Doubles: Divac and Webber (1). **3-pt FG leader:** Williams (100).
Steals leader: Williams (95). **Blocks leader:** Webber (89).
Signed: C Pollard (Feb. 24).
Claimed: G Hawkins off waivers (Feb. 22).

More Individual Single Game Highs

Most Free Throws Made

18	Steve Smith, Atl vs. NJ (2/6)
	Grant Hill, Det vs. Was. (2/8)
	Karl Malone, Utah vs. GS (4/8)

Most Free Throws Attempted

22	Shaquille O'Neal, LAL vs. Utah (2/7)
	Grant Hill, Det. vs. Was. (2/8)
	Jason Kidd, Pho. vs. Van. (3/22)

Most Blocked Shots

9	Five tied

Most Steals

11	Kendall Gill, NJ vs. Min. (4/3)

Most Turnovers

10	Jason Kidd, Pho at LAC (4/6)

Most Minutes

56	Shareef Abdur-Rahim, Van vs Bos (2/17)*

*overtime

San Antonio Spurs

	Gm	FG%	Tpts	PPG	RPG	APG
Tim Duncan	50	.495	1084	21.7	11.4	2.4
David Robinson	49	.509	775	15.8	10.0	2.1
Sean Elliott	50	.410	561	11.2	4.3	2.3
Avery Johnson	50	.473	487	9.7	2.4	7.4
Mario Elie	47	.471	455	9.7	2.9	1.9
Jaren Jackson	47	.380	301	6.4	2.1	1.0
Malik Rose	47	.463	284	6.0	3.9	0.6
Antonio Daniels	47	.454	220	4.7	1.1	2.3
Steve Kerr	44	.391	192	4.4	1.0	1.1
Jerome Kersey	45	.340	145	3.2	2.9	0.9
Will Perdue	37	.633	90	2.4	3.7	0.5
Gerard King*	19	.429	23	1.2	0.7	0.2
Andrew Gaze	19	.320	21	1.1	0.3	0.3
Brandon Williams	3	.000	2	0.7	0.3	0.0

Triple Doubles: none. **3-pt FG leader:** Jackson (53).
Steals leader: Robinson (69). **Blocks leader:** Duncan (126).

Seattle Supersonics

	Gm	FG%	Tpts	PPG	RPG	APG
Gary Payton	50	.434	1084	21.7	4.9	8.7
Detlef Schrempf	50	.472	752	15.0	7.4	3.7
Vin Baker	34	.453	468	13.8	6.2	1.6
Don MacLean	17	.396	185	10.9	3.8	0.9
Hersey Hawkins	50	.419	516	10.3	4.0	2.5
Dale Ellis	48	.411	495	10.3	2.4	0.8
Billy Owens	21	.394	163	7.8	3.8	1.8
Olden Polynice	48	.472	368	7.7	8.9	0.9
John Crotty	27	.411	159	5.9	1.1	2.3
Vladimir Stephania*	23	.424	127	5.5	3.3	0.5
Jelani McCoy*	26	.737	133	5.1	3.0	0.2
Aaron Williams	40	.423	158	4.0	3.2	0.6
Moochie Norris	12	.325	38	3.2	1.7	2.0
James Cotton	10	.333	25	2.5	1.0	0.0
Rashard Lewis*	20	.365	47	2.4	1.3	0.2
Drew Barry*	17	.313	37	2.2	1.2	1.7

Triple Doubles: Payton (1). **3-pt FG leader:** Payton (83).
Steals leader: Payton (109). **Blocks leader:** Baker (34).

Toronto Raptors

	Gm	FG%	Tpts	PPG	RPG	APG
Vince Carter*	50	.450	913	18.3	5.7	3.0
Doug Christie	50	.388	760	15.2	4.1	3.7
Kevin Willis	42	.459	504	12.0	8.3	1.6
Dee Brown	49	.378	549	11.2	2.1	2.9
Tracy McGrady	49	.436	458	9.3	5.7	2.3
John Wallace	48	.432	411	8.6	3.6	1.0
Charles Oakley	48	.428	348	7.0	7.5	3.4
Alvin Williams	50	.401	248	5.0	1.6	2.6
John Thomas	39	.577	169	4.3	3.4	0.4
Reggie Slater	30	.383	115	3.8	2.3	0.2
Michael Stewart	42	.415	61	1.5	2.4	0.1
Sean Marks*	8	.625	11	1.4	0.1	0.0
Negele Knight	6	.375	8	1.3	1.0	1.3
Michael Williams	2	.200	2	1.0	0.5	0.0
Mark Baker	1	.000	0	0.0	0.0	0.0

Triple Doubles: none. **3-pt FG leader:** Brown (135).
Steals leader: Christie (113). **Blocks leader:** Carter (77).

Utah Jazz

	Gm	FG%	Tpts	PPG	RPG	APG
Karl Malone	49	.493	1164	23.8	9.4	4.1
Bryon Russell	50	.464	622	12.4	5.3	1.5
Jeff Hornacek	48	.477	587	12.2	3.3	4.0
John Stockton	50	.488	553	11.1	2.9	7.5
Shandon Anderson	50	.446	427	8.5	2.6	1.1
Howard Eisley	50	.446	368	7.4	1.9	3.7
Greg Ostertag	48	.476	273	5.7	7.3	0.5
Thurl Bailey	43	.446	181	4.2	2.2	0.6
Adam Keefe	44	.452	174	4.0	3.2	0.6
Todd Fuller	42	.452	142	3.4	2.4	0.1
Greg Foster	42	.377	118	2.8	2.0	0.6
Jacques Vaughn	19	.367	44	2.3	0.6	0.6
Anthony Avent	5	.308	9	1.8	2.4	0.2
Chris King	8	.286	4	0.5	1.4	0.1

Triple Doubles: Malone (1). **3-pt FG leader:** Russell (52).
Steals leader: Stockton (81). **Blocks leader:** Ostertag (131).
Acquired: C Fuller from the Golden State Warriors for a second-round draft choice in 2000. (Feb. 4).

Vancouver Grizzlies

	Gm	FG%	Tpts	PPG	RPG	APG
Shareef Abdur-Rahim	50	.432	1152	23.0	7.5	3.4
Mike Bibby*	50	.430	662	13.2	2.7	6.5
Tony Massenburg	43	.487	481	11.2	6.0	0.5
Bryant Reeves	25	.406	271	10.8	5.5	1.5
Felipe Lopez*	47	.446	437	9.3	3.5	1.3
Doug West	14	.477	81	5.8	1.8	1.4
Cherokee Parks	48	.429	266	5.5	5.1	0.8
Michael Smith	48	.535	230	4.8	7.3	1.0
DeJuan Wheat	46	.378	208	4.5	1.0	2.2
Pete Chilcutt	46	.366	166	3.6	2.5	0.7
Rodrick Rhodes	13	.250	43	3.3	1.3	0.8
J.R. Henderson*	30	.365	97	3.2	1.6	0.7
Terry Dehere	26	.365	83	3.2	0.9	1.0
Lee Mayberry	9	.368	20	2.2	0.3	2.6
Jason Sasser	6	.571	9	1.5	1.0	0.3
Makhtar Ndiaye*	4	.250	5	1.3	1.3	0.3

Triple Doubles: none. **3-pt FG leader:** Chilcutt (26).
Steals leader: Bibby (78). **Blocks leader:** Abdur-Rahim (55).
Acquired: G Rhodes from the Houston Rockets for G Sam Mack (Mar. 11).
Signed: G Dehere (Mar. 23).

Washington Wizards

	Gm	FG%	Tpts	PPG	RPG	APG
Mitch Richmond	50	.412	983	19.7	3.4	2.4
Juwan Howard	36	.474	682	18.9	8.1	3.0
Rod Strickland	44	.416	690	15.7	4.8	9.9
Otis Thorpe	49	.545	554	11.3	6.8	2.1
Calbert Cheaney	50	.414	385	7.7	2.8	1.5
Tracy Murray	36	.350	233	6.6	2.3	0.8
Ben Wallace	46	.578	277	6.0	8.3	0.4
Chris Whitney	39	.410	187	4.8	1.2	1.8
Randell Jackson*	27	.426	114	4.2	2.0	0.3
Tim Legler	30	.443	119	4.0	1.3	2.1
Jeff McInnis	35	.373	130	3.7	0.6	2.1
Terry Davis	37	.533	49	2.5	2.9	0.1
Jahidi White*	20	.531	49	2.5	2.9	0.1
John Coker	14	.419	31	2.2	1.6	0.0
Etdrick Bohannon	2	—	0	0.0	0.0	0.0

Triple Doubles: Strickland (1). **3-pt FG leader:** Whitney (32).
Steals leader: Strickland (76). **Blocks leader:** Wallace (90).

More Individual Single Game Highs

Most Offensive Rebounds

11	Danny Fortson, Den. at Hou. (3/9)
	Shaquille O'Neal, LAL at Cle. (3/18)
	Jerome Williams, Det. at Bos. (4/27)
	Erick Dampier, GS vs. Por. (2/14)*

Most Defensive Rebounds

19	Lorenzen Wright, LAC vs. Sac. (3/11)

*overtime

NBA Regular Season Team Leaders
Offense

WEST	—Per Game—			FGM-FGA	FG%	3PM-3PA	3Pt%	FTM-FTA	FT%	OFF-DEF	TRB	TO	BLKS
	Pts	Reb	Ast										
Sacramento	100.2	45.6	22.6	1918-4307	.445	290-943	.308	883-1293	.683	706-1573	2279	842	232
LA Lakers	99.0	42.0	21.9	1841-3935	.468	241-685	.352	1027-1503	.683	619-1482	2101	754	304
Phoenix	95.6	40.3	25.0	1797-4003	.449	261-702	.372	924-1215	.760	599-1418	2017	681	200
Seattle	94.9	42.0	21.7	1756-3976	.442	309-899	.344	922-1354	.681	676-1422	2098	765	201
Portland	94.8	44.3	21.5	1747-3956	.442	246-675	.364	1002-1349	.743	646-1570	2216	771	290
Houston	94.2	41.6	21.2	1755-3798	.462	336-914	.368	865-1187	.729	536-1540	2076	812	260
Denver	93.5	40.8	19.4	1681-3989	.421	302-922	.328	1010-1325	.762	648-1391	2039	739	274
Utah	93.3	41.3	24.1	1684-3620	.465	140-388	.361	1158-1510	.767	555-1508	2063	814	276
Minnesota	92.9	42.9	24.4	1838-4327	.425	122-410	.298	849-1143	.743	754-1392	2146	641	272
San Antonio	92.8	44.0	22.0	1740-3812	.456	172-521	.330	988-1415	.698	614-1584	2198	759	351
Dallas	91.6	42.5	18.4	1749-4033	.434	202-595	.339	881-1210	.728	645-1478	2123	692	292
LA Clippers	90.4	39.2	16.4	1711-4007	.427	214-668	.320	883-1225	.721	665-1293	1958	796	236
Vancouver	88.9	40.2	19.3	1643-3838	.428	148-453	.327	1009-1408	.717	650-1359	2009	848	199
Golden State	88.3	47.5	20.7	1730-4173	.415	162-565	.287	794-1175	.676	816-1559	2375	768	226

EAST	—Per Game—			FGM-FGA	FG%	3PM-3PA	3Pt%	FTM-FTA	FT%	ORB-DRB	TRB	TO	BLKS
	Pts	Reb	Ast										
Indiana	94.7	40.5	20.1	1731-3866	.448	294-799	.368	977-1228	.796	574-1452	2026	649	224
Boston	93.0	42.8	21.5	1816-4163	.436	273-758	.360	745-1077	.692	680-1458	2138	809	255
Charlotte	92.9	39.5	22.2	1671-3717	.450	268-735	.365	1034-1384	.747	480-1493	1973	796	247
Milwaukee	91.7	42.9	20.6	1753-3818	.459	231-619	.373	847-1155	.733	754-1392	2146	641	272
New Jersey	91.4	43.0	18.5	1691-4170	.406	225-679	.331	962-1251	.769	715-1437	2152	750	273
Washington	91.2	40.0	21.3	1768-3969	.445	179-580	.309	845-1198	.705	595-1403	1998	736	200
Toronto	91.1	43.2	20.7	1660-3940	.421	226-662	.341	1011-1330	.760	712-1447	2159	799	321
Detroit	90.4	40.4	20.2	1660-3716	.447	248-679	.365	950-1283	.740	606-1412	2018	790	208
Philadelphia	89.7	43.1	18.7	1656-3883	.426	98-371	.264	1073-1486	.722	729-1428	2157	822	271
Orlando	89.5	42.7	21.3	1687-3943	.428	223-675	.330	876-1252	.700	688-1445	2133	819	213
Miami	89.0	40.2	20.4	1616-3565	.453	289-804	.359	928-1262	.735	503-1509	2012	744	304
Cleveland	86.4	35.8	21.9	1562-3561	.439	182-534	.341	1016-1356	.749	472-1316	1788	785	205
New York	86.4	41.2	19.3	1610-3704	.435	208-589	.353	892-1218	.732	551-1510	2061	804	262
Atlanta	86.3	43.5	15.6	1539-3759	.409	197-644	.306	1040-1422	.731	675-1499	2174	745	260
Chicago	81.9	39.3	20.3	1539-3837	.401	177-612	.289	840-1185	.709	573-1394	1967	774	169

Defense

WEST	—Per Game—			FGM-FGA	FG%	3PM-3PA	3Pt%	FTM-FTA	FT%	OFF-DEF	TRB	TO	BLKS
	Pts	Reb	Ast										
San Antonio	84.7	42.1	18.8	1631-4061	.402	170-559	.304	805-1148	.701	696-1407	2103	730	243
Utah	86.8	38.6	18.1	1595-3863	.413	214-666	.321	936-1299	.721	636-1294	1930	744	264
Portland	88.5	40.1	19.2	1644-3938	.417	201-631	.318	916-1263	.725	616-1388	2004	785	244
Golden State	90.8	43.2	20.5	1617-3848	.420	193-575	.336	1114-1531	.728	656-1503	2159	735	305
Houston	91.9	41.1	20.7	1793-4136	.434	230-645	.357	779-1062	.734	664-1391	2055	653	245
Minnesota	92.6	43.1	22.3	1680-3823	.439	213-654	.326	1055-1470	.718	591-1563	2154	836	262
Phoenix	93.3	42.4	21.3	1772-3936	.450	272-755	.360	850-1224	.694	614-1506	2120	812	205
Dallas	94.0	43.6	21.5	1815-4037	.450	216-686	.315	855-1193	.717	660-1519	2179	699	244
Seattle	95.9	42.0	22.2	1838-4026	.457	264-765	.345	857-1187	.722	652-1446	2098	746	224
LA Lakers	96.0	40.6	21.2	1759-3992	.551	217-653	.332	1064-1501	.709	628-1403	2031	716	201
Vancouver	97.5	42.6	23.8	1813-3917	.463	229-653	.351	1021-1400	.729	673-1456	2129	779	327
LA Clippers	99.2	42.9	22.0	1830-3858	.474	222-627	.354	1078-1445	.746	640-1506	2146	782	289
Denver	100.1	42.4	23.5	1885-4017	.469	237-640	.370	997-1339	.745	620-1502	2122	701	291
Sacramento	100.6	47.0	23.3	2009-4498	.447	219-652	.336	793-1113	.712	750-1598	2348	790	221

EAST	—Per Game—			FGM-FGA	FG%	3PM-3PA	3Pt%	FTM-FTA	FT%	OFF-DEF	TRB	TO	BLKS
	Pts	Reb	Ast										
Atlanta	83.4	39.0	17.9	1598-3883	.412	190-634	.300	784-1076	.729	581-1369	1950	675	243
Miami	84.0	39.2	17.1	1565-3804	.411	211-606	.348	860-1167	.737	618-1342	1960	677	188
New York	85.4	40.8	18.5	1528-3790	.403	234-662	.353	979-1335	.733	616-1426	2042	677	188
Detroit	86.9	38.5	20.9	1585-3639	.436	236-682	.346	941-1317	.715	548-1378	1926	770	225
Orlando	86.9	40.4	20.8	1708-3856	.443	230-667	.345	697-986	.707	595-1424	2019	863	239
Philadelphia	87.6	40.4	20.0	1599-3784	.423	241-716	.337	941-1288	.731	619-1402	2021	896	263
Cleveland	88.2	39.9	20.1	1597-3664	.436	236-675	.350	978-1316	.743	592-1405	1997	821	282
Milwaukee	90.0	41.1	20.4	1600-3746	.427	272-814	.334	1029-1369	.752	658-1397	2055	830	194
Indiana	90.9	41.0	19.1	1706-3935	.434	206-634	.325	928-1227	.756	626-1426	2052	652	238
Chicago	91.4	42.4	22.0	1723-3786	.455	208-612	.340	914-1247	.733	551-1568	2119	782	285
Toronto	92.8	40.1	21.9	1694-3855	.439	255-686	.372	996-1368	.728	614-1393	2007	773	267
Charlotte	93.0	42.9	21.8	1739-4003	.438	212-637	.333	959-1306	.734	655-1491	2146	762	232
Washington	93.4	42.7	21.6	1705-3826	.446	218-619	.352	1044-1418	.736	617-1517	2134	794	212
Boston	94.9	43.7	20.4	1725-3896	.443	175-561	.312	1118-1506	.742	642-1544	2186	841	253
New Jersey	95.2	44.0	19.4	1796-3968	.453	223-654	.341	943-1298	.727	624-1577	2201	813	326

Series Summaries

WESTERN CONFERENCE

FIRST ROUND (Best of 5)

	W-L	Avg.	Leading Scorer
Minnesota	1-3	80.5	Garnett (21.8)
San Antonio	3-1	86.8	Johnson (19.5)

Date	Winner	Home Court
May 9	Spurs, 99-86	at San Antonio
May 11	Timberwolves, 80-71	at San Antonio
May 13	Spurs, 85-71	at Minnesota
May 15	Spurs, 92-85	at Minnesota

	W-L	Avg.	Leading Scorer
Phoenix	0-3	90.7	Robinson (15.7)
Portland	3-0	102.7	Rider (20.0)

Date	Winner	Home Court
May 8	Trailblazers, 95-80	at Portland
May 10	Trailblazers, 110-99	at Portland
May 12	Trailblazers, 103-93	at Phoenix

	W-L	Avg.	Leading Scorer
Sacramento	2-3	90.6	Divac (16.2)
Utah	3-2	95.4	Malone (23.8)

Date	Winner	Home Court
May 8	Jazz, 117-87	at Utah
May 10	Kings, 101-90	at Utah
May 12	Kings, 84-81 (OT)	at Sacramento
May 14	Jazz, 90-89	at Sacramento
May 16	Jazz, 99-92 (2OT)	at Utah

	W-L	Avg.	Leading Scorer
Houston	1-3	96.3	Barkley (23.5)
LA Lakers	3-1	97.8	O'Neal (29.5)

Date	Winner	Home Court
May 9	Lakers, 101-100	at Los Angeles
May 11	Lakers, 110-98	at Los Angeles
May 13	Rockets, 102-88	at Houston
May 15	Lakers, 92-85	at Houston

SEMIFINALS (Best of 7)

	W-L	Avg.	Leading Scorer
Utah	2-4	84.0	Malone (20.2)
Portland	4-2	84.7	Rider (19.3)

Date	Winner	Home Court
May 18	Jazz, 93-83	at Portland
May 20	Trailblazers, 84-81	at Portland
May 22	Trailblazers, 97-87	at Utah
May 23	Trailblazers, 81-75	at Utah
May 25	Jazz, 88-71	at Utah
May 27	Trailblazers, 92-80	at Portland

	W-L	Avg.	Leading Scorer
LA Lakers	0-4	88.8	O'Neal (23.8)
San Antonio	4-0	96.8	Duncan (29.0)

Date	Winner	Home Court
May 17	Spurs, 87-81	at San Antonio
May 19	Spurs, 79-76	at San Antonio
May 22	Spurs, 103-91	at Los Angeles
May 23	Spurs, 118-107	at Los Angeles

CHAMPIONSHIP (Best of 7)

	W-L	Avg.	Leading Scorer
Portland	0-4	76.0	Wallace (20.0)
San Antonio	4-0	86.3	Robinson (17.5)

Date	Winner	Home Court
May 29	Spurs, 80-76	at San Antonio
May 31	Spurs, 86-85	at San Antonio
June 4	Spurs, 85-63	at Portland
June 6	Spurs, 94-80	at Portland

EASTERN CONFERENCE

FIRST ROUND (Best of 5)

	W-L	Avg.	Leading Scorer
New York	3-2	83.0	Houston (15.2)
Miami	2-3	79.0	Mourning (21.6)

Date	Winner	Home Court
May 8	Knicks, 95-75	at Miami
May 10	Heat, 83-73	at Miami
May 12	Knicks, 97-73	at New York
May 14	Heat, 87-72	at New York
May 16	Knicks, 78-77	at Miami

	W-L	Avg.	Leading Scorer
Milwaukee	0-3	95.3	Allen (22.3)
Indiana	3-0	105.7	Miller (26.3)

Date	Winner	Home Court
May 9	Pacers, 110-88	at Indiana
May 11	Pacers, 108-107 (OT)	at Indiana
May 13	Pacers, 99-91	at Milwaukee

	W-L	Avg.	Leading Scorer
Philadelphia	3-1	92.5	Iverson (28.8)
Orlando	1-3	86.3	Hardaway (15.8)

Date	Winner	Home Court
May 9	76ers, 104-90	at Orlando
May 11	Magic, 79-68	at Orlando
May 13	76ers, 97-85	at Philadelphia
May 15	76ers, 101-91	at Philadelphia

	W-L	Avg.	Leading Scorer
Detroit	2-3	79.2	Hill (19.4)
Atlanta	3-2	82.2	Smith (18.2)

Date	Winner	Home Court
May 8	Hawks, 90-70	at Atlanta
May 10	Hawks, 89-69	at Atlanta
May 12	Pistons, 79-63	at Detroit
May 14	Pistons, 103-82	at Detroit
May 16	Hawks, 87-75	at Atlanta

SEMIFINALS (Best of 7)

	W-L	Avg.	Leading Scorer
New York	4-0	86.5	Houston (18.0)
Atlanta	0-4	76.5	Smith (16.3)

Date	Winner	Home Court
May 18	Knicks, 100-92	at Atlanta
May 20	Knicks, 77-70	at Atlanta
May 23	Knicks, 90-78	at New York
May 25	Knicks, 79-66	at New York

	W-L	Avg.	Leading Scorer
Philadelphia	0-4	86.0	Iverson (22.8)
Indiana	4-0	91.3	Miller (21.8)

Date	Winner	Home Court
May 17	Pacers, 94-90	at Indiana
May 19	Pacers, 85-82	at Indiana
May 21	Pacers, 97-86	at Philadelphia
May 23	Pacers, 89-86	at Philadelphia

CHAMPIONSHIP (Best of 7)

	W-L	Avg.	Leading Scorer
New York	4-2	90.0	Houston (19.0)
Indiana	2-4	89.2	Miller (16.2)

Date	Winner	Home Court
May 30	Knicks, 93-90	at Indiana
June 1	Pacers, 88-86	at Indiana
June 5	Knicks, 92-91	at New York
June 7	Pacers, 90-78	at New York
June 9	Knicks, 101-94	at Indiana
June 11	Knicks, 90-82	at New York

NBA FINALS (Best of 7)

	W-L	Avg.	Leading Scorer
New York	1-4	79.8	Sprewell (26.0)
San Antonio	4-1	84.8	Duncan (27.4)

Date	Winner	Home Court
June 16	Spurs, 89-77	at San Antonio
June 18	Spurs, 80-67	at San Antonio
June 21	Knicks, 89-81	at New York
June 23	Spurs, 96-89	at New York
June 25	Spurs, 78-77	at New York

Most Valuable Player
Tim Duncan, San Antonio, F
27.4 points, 14.0 rebounds, 2.2 blocks

Final Playoff Standings
(Ranked by victories)

	Gm	W	L	Pct	Per Game For	Per Game Opp
San Antonio	17	15	2	.882	88.4	81.2
New York	20	12	8	.600	85.0	83.0
Indiana	13	9	4	.692	93.6	90.0
Portland	13	7	6	.538	86.1	86.6
Utah	11	5	6	.455	89.1	87.3
LA Lakers	8	3	5	.375	94.0	96.8
Philadelphia	8	3	5	.375	89.2	88.7
Atlanta	9	3	6	.333	79.6	82.4
Detroit	5	2	3	.400	79.2	82.2
Sacramento	5	2	3	.400	90.6	95.4
Houston	4	1	3	.250	97.0	99.2
Minnesota	4	1	3	.250	80.5	86.7
Milwaukee	3	0	3	.000	95.3	105.6
Phoenix	3	0	3	.000	92.3	102.6

Off-Season Coaching Changes

Team	Old Coach	Why left?	New Coach	Old Job
LA Lakers	Kurt Rambis	Interim	Phil Jackson	Former Coach, Bulls
Orlando	Chuck Daly	Retired	Doc Rivers	TV analyst, Turner Sports
Cleveland	Mike Fratello	Fired	Randy Wittman	Asst. Coach, Timberwolves
Washington	Jim Brovelli	Interim	Gar Heard	Asst. Coach, Pistons
Denver	Mike D'Antoni	Fired	Dan Issel	GM & VP, Nuggets

NBA Playoff Leaders

Scoring

	Gm	FG	FT	Pts	Avg
Allen Iverson, Philadelphia	8	88	37	228	28.5
Shaquille O'Neal, LA Lakers	8	79	55	213	26.6
Charles Barkley, Houston	4	36	20	94	23.5
Tim Duncan, San Antonio	17	144	107	395	23.2
Ray Allen, Milwaukee	3	25	8	67	22.3
Kevin Garnett, Minnesota	4	35	17	87	21.8
Karl Malone, Utah	11	86	68	240	21.8
Alonzo Mourning, Miami	5	38	32	108	21.6
Nick Anderson, Orlando	4	29	14	83	20.8
Glenn Robinson, Milwaukee	3	21	16	62	20.7
Latrell Sprewell, New York	20	145	113	407	20.4
Reggie Miller, Indiana	13	79	77	263	20.2
Kobe Bryant, LA Lakers	8	61	28	158	19.8
Grant Hill, Detroit	5	42	13	97	19.4
Terrell Brandon, Minnesota	4	31	12	77	19.3
Anfernee Hardaway, Orlando	4	20	30	76	19.0
Allan Houston, New York	20	135	91	370	18.5
Scottie Pippen, Houston	4	23	21	73	18.3
Glen Rice, LA Lakers	7	45	28	128	18.3

High Point Games

	Date	FG-FT—Pts
Scottie Pippen, Hou vs LAL	5/13	12-10—37
Allen Iverson, Phi vs Orl	5/15	14-5—37
Shaquille O'Neal, LAL vs Hou	5/15	14-9—37
Tim Duncan, SA vs LAL	5/22	9-19—37

Rebounds

	Gm	Off	Def	Tot	Avg
Dikembe Mutombo, Atl	9	36	89	125	13.9
Charles Barkley, Hou	4	13	42	55	13.8
Kevin Garnett, Minn	4	16	32	48	12.0
Scottie Pippen, Hou	4	20	27	47	11.8
Shaquille O'Neal, LAL	8	44	49	93	11.6
Tim Duncan, SA	17	55	140	195	11.5

Assists

	Gm	No	Avg
Jason Kidd, Pho	3	31	10.3
Sam Cassell, Mil	3	26	8.7
Mark Jackson, Ind	13	112	8.6
John Stockton, Utah	11	92	8.4
Grant Hill, Det	5	37	7.4
Avery Johnson, SA	17	126	7.4
Eric Snow, Phi	8	57	7.1
Terrell Brandon, Min	4	28	7.0

NBA Finalists' Composite Box Scores

New York Knicks (12-8)

		Overall Playoffs		—Per Game—				Finals vs. San Antonio		—Per Game—		
	Gm	FG%	TPts	Pts	Reb	Ast	Gm	FG%	TPts	Pts	Reb	Ast
Latrell Sprewell	20	.419	407	20.4	4.8	2.2	5	.410	130	26.0	6.6	2.6
Allan Houston	20	.443	370	18.5	2.7	2.6	5	.427	108	21.6	3.2	2.6
Marcus Camby	20	.566	207	10.4	7.7	0.3	5	.500	48	9.6	7.8	0.2
Larry Johnson	20	.426	229	11.5	4.9	1.6	5	.286	38	7.6	4.8	1.4
Charlie Ward	20	.366	92	4.6	2.3	3.8	5	.462	29	5.8	3.2	3.6
Kurt Thomas	20	.355	106	5.3	5.5	0.4	5	.344	28	5.6	7.6	0.4
Chris Childs	20	.355	94	4.7	2.4	3.7	5	.227	12	2.4	1.2	2.2
Chris Dudley	18	.421	43	2.4	4.6	0.3	5	.250	6	1.2	3.8	0.2
Herb Williams	8	.200	2	0.3	0.4	0.0	2	.000	0	0.0	0.0	0.0
Rick Brunson	9	.400	6	0.7	0.1	0.2	1	–	0	0.0	0.0	0.0
Patrick Ewing	11	.430	144	13.1	8.7	0.5	–	–	–	–	–	–
KNICKS	20	.429	1700	85.0	39.3	15.0	5	.392	399	79.8	38.2	14.0
OPPONENTS	20	.406	1660	83.0	38.9	16.8	5	.445	424	84.8	40.6	20.2

Three-pointers: PLAYOFFS—Johnson (24-for-82), Ward (18-56), Childs (9-28), Houston (9-36), Sprewell (4-25), Team (64-228 for .281 pct.); FINALS—Ward (4-for-12), Sprewell (2-7), Houston (2-12), Johnson (2-18), Childs (1-5), Team (11-54 for .204 pct.).

San Antonio Spurs (15-2)

		Overall Playoffs		—Per Game—				Finals vs. New York		—Per Game—		
	Gm	FG%	TPts	Pts	Reb	Ast	Gm	FG%	TPts	Pts	Reb	Ast
Tim Duncan	17	.511	395	23.2	11.5	2.8	5	.537	137	27.4	14.0	2.4
David Robinson	17	.483	265	15.6	9.9	2.5	5	.424	83	16.6	11.8	2.4
Mario Elie	17	.384	135	7.9	3.5	2.9	5	.447	58	11.6	4.0	2.6
Avery Johnson	17	.487	215	12.6	2.5	7.4	5	.500	46	9.2	2.6	7.2
Sean Elliot	17	.444	203	11.9	3.4	2.6	5	.333	40	8.0	3.0	3.0
Jaren Jackson	17	.382	140	8.2	2.4	1.1	5	.324	33	6.6	3.0	3.0
Antonio Daniels	15	.429	27	1.8	0.7	1.1	4	.800	10	2.5	0.5	1.0
Steve Kerr	11	.267	24	2.2	0.8	0.7	5	.400	9	1.8	1.0	0.4
Malik Rose	17	.368	46	2.7	2.3	0.2	5	.200	6	1.2	2.4	0.4
Jerome Kersey	14	.349	36	2.6	2.1	0.3	2	1.000	2	1.0	0.0	0.0
Gerard King	8	.500	4	0.5	0.5	0.1	2	–	0	0.0	0.0	0.0
Will Perdue	12	.545	13	1.1	2.3	0.0	–	–	–	–	–	–
SPURS	17	.451	1503	88.4	40.2	21.3	5	.445	424	84.8	40.6	20.2
OPPONENTS	17	.399	1380	81.2	39.6	16.6	5	.392	399	79.8	38.2	14.0

Three-pointers: PLAYOFFS—Jackson (31-for-86), Elliot (22-55), Elie (8-30), Daniels (4-6), Kerr (3-13), Johnson (1-3), Kersey (1-4), Team (70-200 for .350 pct.); FINALS—Jackson (9-for-24), Elliot (5-18), Elie (4-13), Daniels (2-2), Kerr (1-2), Team (21-62 for .339 pct.).

Annual Awards

Most Valuable Player

The Maurice Podoloff Trophy; voting by 118-member panel of local and national pro basketball writers and broadcasters. Each ballot has five entries; points awarded on 10-7-5-3-1 basis.

	1st	2nd	3rd	4th	5th	Pts
Karl Malone, Utah	44	29	31	8	5	827
Alonzo Mourning, Mia	36	32	30	11	6	773
Tim Duncan, San Antonio	30	36	31	9	6	740
Allen Iverson, Phi.	5	11	10	40	22	319
Jason Kidd, Phoenix	2	4	6	21	18	159
Shaquille O'Neal, LA Lakers	1	2	3	11	17	89
Chris Webber, Sac.	0	2	2	5	12	51
Grant Hill, Detroit	0	1	3	3	8	39
Gary Payton, Seattle	0	1	1	4	11	35
Kevin Garnett, Minn.	0	0	0	2	3	9
Shawn Kemp. Cle.	0	0	0	2	1	7
David Robinson, San Antonio	0	0	1	0	1	6
Hakeem Olajuwon, Hou.	0	0	0	1	0	3
Arvydas Sabonis, Port	0	0	0	1	0	3
Darrell Armstrong, Orl.	0	0	0	0	2	2
Vince Carter, Tor.	0	0	0	0	1	1
Anfernee Hardaway, Orl.	0	0	0	0	1	1
Mark Jackson, Ind.	0	0	0	0	1	1
Glenn Robinson, Mil	0	0	0	0	1	1
Steve Smith, Atl.	0	0	0	0	1	1
Rasheed Wallace, Port	0	0	0	0	1	1

All-NBA Teams

Voting by a 118-member panel of local and national pro basketball writers and broadcasters. Each ballot has entries for three teams; points awarded on 5-3-1 basis. First Team repeaters from 1997-98 are in **bold** type.

Pos	First Team	1st	Pts
F	**Karl Malone**, Utah	113	580
F	**Tim Duncan**, San Antonio	112	576
C	Alonzo Mourning, Miami	95	542
G	Allen Iverson, Phi.	93	532
G	Jason Kidd, Pho.	86	516

Pos	Second Team	1st	Pts
F	Chris Webber, Sac.	3	278
F	Grant Hill, Detroit	4	263
C	Shaquille O'Neal, LA Lakers	23	382
G	Gary Payton, Seattle	51	440
G	Tim Hardaway, Miami	1	168

Pos	Third Team	1st	Pts
F	Kevin Garnett, Minn.	2	231
F	Antonio McDyess, Denver	0	80
C	Hakeem Olajuwon, Houston	0	67
G	Kobe Bryant, LA Lakers	1	75
G	John Stockton, Utah	1	75

All-Defensive Teams

Voting by NBA head coaches. Each ballot has entries for two teams; two points given for 1st team, one for 2nd. Coaches cannot vote for own players. First Team repeaters from 1997-98 are in **bold** type.

Pos	First Team	1st	Pts
F	Tim Duncan, San Antonio	16	38
F	**Karl Malone**, Utah	10	22
F	**Scottie Pippen**, Houston	9	22
C	Alonzo Mourning, Miami	19	46
G	**Gary Payton**, Seattle	22	47
G	Jason Kidd, Phoenix	24	10

Pos	Second Team	1st	Pts
F	P.J. Brown, Miami	4	15
F	Theo Ratliff, Philadelphia	4	14
C	Dikembe Mutombo, Atlanta	10	37
G	Mookie Blaylock, Atlanta	5	23
G	Eddie Jones, Charlotte	3	16

Coach of the Year

The Red Auerbach Trophy; voting by 118-member panel of local and national pro basketball writers and broadcasters. Each ballot has one entry.

	Votes	Improvement
Mike Dunleavy, Portland	48	46-36 to 35-15
Larry Brown, Philadelphia	23	31-51 to 28-22
Jerry Sloan, Utah	15	62-20 to 37-13
Chuck Daly, Orlando	13	41-41 to 33-17
Pat Riley, Miami	8	55-27 to 33-17
Gregg Popovich, San Antonio	4	56-26 to 37-13
Paul Silas, Charlotte	4	51-31 to 26-24
George Karl, Milwaukee	1	36-46 to 28-22
Butch Carter, Toronto	1	16-66 to 23-27
Lenny Wilkens, Atlanta	1	50-32 to 31-19

Rookie of the Year

The Eddie Gottlieb Trophy; voting by 118-member panel of local and national pro basketball writers and broadcasters. Each ballot has one entry.

	Pos	Votes
Vince Carter, Toronto	F	113
Jason Williams, Sacramento	G	3
Paul Pierce, Boston	F	2

All-Rookie Team

Voting by NBA's 29 head coaches, who cannot vote for players on their team. Each ballot has entries for two five-man teams, regardless of position; two points given for 1st team, one for 2nd. First team votes in parentheses.

First Team	College	Pts
Vince Carter, Toronto (28)	N. Carolina	56
Paul Pierce, Boston (28)	Kansas	56
Jason Williams, Sacramento (27)	Florida	55
Mike Bibby, Vancouver (19)	Arizona	19
Matt Harpring, Orlando (10)	Ga. Tech	10

Second Team	College	Pts
Michael Dickerson, Houston (9)	Arizona	33
Michael Doleac, Orlando (9)	Utah	30
Cuttino Mobley, Houston (3)	Rhode Island	26
Michael Olowokandi, LAC (4)	Pacific	22
Antawn Jamison, Golden St. (3)	N. Carolina	21

IBM Award

Created prior to the 1983-84 season to honor the player who contributes most to his team's overall success and utilizes a computer evaluation of key offensive and defensive statistics to determine an overall leader. The formula is as follows: (Player pts.-FGA+REB+AST+STL+BLK-PF-TO+(team wins x 10) x 250)/(team pts.-FGA+REB+AST+STL+BLK-PF-TO).

	Pos	Pts
Dikembe Mutombo, Atlanta	C	115.67
Shaquille O'Neal, LAL	C	102.86
Alonzo Mourning, Miami	C	100.63
Karl Malone, Utah	F	98.27
Jason Kidd, Phoenix	G	98.21
Tim Duncan, San Antonio	F	94.17
David Robinson, San Antonio	C	91.85
Kevin Garnett, Minnesota	F	87.25

Other Awards

Defensive Player of the Year— Alonzo Mourning, Miami; **Most Improved Player**—Darrell Armstrong, Orlando; **Sixth Man Award**— Darrell Armstrong, Orlando; **Kennedy PBWAA Citizenship Award**— Brian Grant, Portland; **NBA Sportsmanship Award**— Hersey Hawkins, Seattle; **The Sporting News Executive of the Year**— Geoff Petrie, Sacramento.

1999 College Draft

First and second round picks at the 53rd annual NBA College Draft held June 30, 1999 at the MCI Center in Washington, D.C. The order of the first 13 positions were determined by a Draft Lottery held May 22, in Secaucus, N.J. Positions 14 through 29 reflect regular season records in reverse order. Underclassmen selected are noted in CAPITAL letters.

First Round

Team		Pos
1 Chicago	ELTON BRAND, Duke	F
2 Vancouver	STEVE FRANCIS, Maryland	G
3 Charlotte	BARON DAVIS, UCLA	G
4 LA Clippers	LAMAR ODOM, Rhode Island	F
5 Toronto	JONATHAN BENDER, Picayune (Miss.) H.S.	F
6 Minnesota	Wally Szczerbiak, Miami-OH	F
7 Washington	RICHARD HAMILTON, Connecticut	G
8 **a**-Cleveland	Andre Miller, Utah	G
9 **b**-Phoenix	SHAWN MARION, UNLV	F
10 **c**-Atlanta	Jason Terry, Arizona	G
11 Cleveland	Trajan Langdon, Duke	G
12 Toronto	ALEX RADOJEVIC, Barton County CC	C
13 **d**-Seattle	COREY MAGGETTE, Duke	F
14 Minnesota	WILLIAM AVERY, Duke	G
15 New York	Frederic Weis, Limoges, France	C
16 **e**-Chicago	RON ARTEST, St. John's	G/F
17 **f**-Atlanta	Cal Bowdler, Old Dominion	F
18 **g**-Denver	James Possey, Xavier	G/F
19 **h**-Utah	Quincy Lewis, Minnesota	F
20 **i**-Atlanta	DION GLOVER, Georgia Tech	G
21 **j**-Golden State	Jeff Foster, SW Texas St.	F/C
22 Houston	Kenny Thomas, New Mexico	F
23 LA Lakers	Devean George, Augsburg (Minn.)	G/F
24 **k**-Utah	ANDREI KIRIKENKO, CSKA (Russia)	F
25 Miami	Tim James, Miami	F
26 **l**-Indiana	Vonteego Cummings, Pittsburgh	G
27 **m**-Atlanta	JUMAINE JONES, Georgia	F
28 Utah	Scott Padgett, Kentucky	F
29 **n**-San Antonio	LEON SMITH, M.L. King H.S. (Chicago)	F

Second Round

Team		Pos
30 **o**-LA Lakers	John Celestand, Villanova	G
31 LA Clippers	Rico Hill, Illinois State	F
32 Chicago	Michael Ruffin, Tulsa	F
33 Denver	Chris Herren, Fresno St.	G
34 New Jersey	Evan Eschmeyer, Northwestern	C
35 Washington	Calvin Booth, Penn St.	C
36 Dallas	Wang Zhi-Zhi, China	C
37 **p**-Vancouver	Obinna Ekezie, Maryland	F/C
38 **q**-Orlando	Laron Profit, Maryland	G/F
39 Cleveland	A.J. Bramlett, Arizona	C
40 **r**-Dallas	Gordan Giricek, Cibona-Zagreb (Croatia)	F
41 **s**-Denver	Francisco Elson, California	C
42 **t**-Minnesota	Louis Bullock, Michigan	G
43 Charlotte	Lee Nailon, Texas Christian	F
44 **u**-Houston	Tyrone Washington, Mississippi St.	F
45 Sacramento	Ryan Robertson, Kansas	G
46 New York	J.R. Koch, Iowa	F
47 Philadelphia	Todd MacCulloch, Washington	C
48 Milwaukee	Galen Young, UNC-Charlotte	G
49 **v**-Chicago	Lari Ketner, Massachusetts	C/F
50 Houston	Venson Hamilton, Nebraska	C
51 **w**-Vancouver	Antwain Smith, St. Paul's College	F
52 **x**-Atlanta	Roberto Bergersen, Boise St.	G
53 Miami	Rodney Buford, Creighton	G
54 **y**-Detroit	Melvin Levett, Cincinnati	G
55 **z**-Boston	Kris Clack, Texas	C
56 **1**-Golden State	Tim Young, Stanford	C
57 San Antonio	Emmanuel Ginobili, Reggio Calabria (Italy)	F
58 Utah	Edward Lucas, Virginia Tech	G/F

Acquired Picks

FIRST ROUND: **a**-from New Jersey; **b**-from Boston; **c**-from Golden State, Atlanta traded Mookie Blaylock and their first round pick for the Warriors first pick, Bimbo Coles and Duane Ferrell; **d**-Seattle traded the draft rights of Maggette and the contracts of Billy Owens, Dale Ellis and Don MacLean to Orlando for Horace Grant and two future second-round draft picks; **e**-from Phoenix; **f**-from Sacramento; **g**-from Milwaukee and Phoenix; **h**-from Philadelphia; **i**-from Detroit; **j**-from Atlanta, Golden State traded their first pick, Bimbo Coles and Duane Ferrell for the Hawks first pick and Mookie Blaylock; Golden State traded the rights to Jeff Foster to Indiana in exchange for the draft rights of Vonteego Cummings and a future first-round draft pick; **k**-from Orlando; **l**-traded to Golden State; **m**-from Portland via Detroit, traded to Philadelphia for a future first-round pick; **n**-traded to Dallas for Gordan Giricek and a future second-round pick. SECOND ROUND: **o**-from Vancouver; **p**-from Boston; **q**-from Golden State; **r**-from Toronto, traded to San Antonio; **s**-from Seattle; **t**-traded to Orlando for cash considerations; **u**-from Phoenix; **v**-from Detroit via Atlanta; **w**-from LA Lakers; **x**-traded to Portland for cash considerations; **y**-from Indiana; **z**-from Orlando via Denver; **1**-from Portland.

Tournament of the Americas

The Pre-Olympic Tournament of the Americas was held at the Roberto Clemente Coliseum in San Juan, Puerto Rico, July 14-25, 1999. The winners of the two semifinal games, the USA and Canada, will represent the Americas in the 2000 Olympic Games at Sydney.

First Round

(*) indicates team advanced to second round.

Group A	W	L
*United States	4	0
*Canada	3	1
*Argentina	2	2
*Uruguay	1	3
Cuba	0	4

Group B	W	L
*Puerto Rico	4	0
*Venezuela	3	1
*Brazil	2	2
*Dominican Republic	1	3
Panama	0	4

Second Round

The top four teams from each preliminary group advance to form one second round group of eight teams. Each team keeps its results against the other teams that advance. The fifth place teams Cuba and Panama were eliminated.

	W	L
United States	7	0
Puerto Rico	5	2
Argentina	5	2
Canada	5	2
Venezuela	3	4
Brazil	2	5
Dominican Republic	1	6
Uruguay	0	7

Semifinals

The top four finishing teams from the second round advanced to the semifinals on July 24. Teams finishing fifth to eighth place were eliminated.

United States 88 ..... Argentina 59
Canada 83 .... Puerto Rico 71

Bronze Medal

July 25.

Argentina 103 ..... Puerto Rico 101

Gold Medal

July 25.

United States 92 .... Canada 66

Continental Basketball Association
Final Standings

QW refers to quarters won. Teams get 3 points for a win, 1 point for each quarter won and ½ point for any quarters tied. Avg refers to average points per game played. (*) denotes playoff qualifiers.

American Conference

	W	L	QW	Pts	Home	Road
*Connecticut	37	19	124.5	235.5	25-3	12-16
*Grand Rapids	27	29	121.0	202.0	16-12	11-17
*Fort Wayne	28	28	103.5	187.5	21-7	7-21
Rockford	23	33	103.5	172.5	14-14	9-19

National Conference

	W	L	QW	Pts	Home	Road
*Sioux Falls	32	24	128.5	224.5	18-10	14-14
*Yakima	30	26	122.5	212.5	21-7	9-19
*Quad City	29	27	100.0	187.0	18-10	11-17
*Idaho	25	31	104.0	179.0	17-11	8-20
La Crosse	21	35	100.5	163.5	16-12	5-23

Playoffs

First two rounds are Best of 5

First Round

Connecticut def. Rockford, 3 games to 0
Sioux Falls def. Idaho, 3 games to 2
Yakima def. Quad City, 3 games to 2
Grand Rapids def. Fort Wayne, 3 games to 2

Second Round

Connecticut def. Grand Rapids, 3 games to 1
Sioux Falls def. Quad City, 3 games to 2

Finals (Best of 7)

Connecticut wins series, 4 games to 1

	W-L	Avg	Leading Scorer
Sioux Falls	1-4	108.8	Livingston (21.6)
Connecticut	4-1	111.0	Griffin (20.0)

Date	Winner	Home Court
Apr. 21	Connecticut, 109-104	at Connecticut
Apr. 23	Connecticut, 115-97	at Connecticut
Apr. 25	Connecticut, 115-105	at Sioux Falls
Apr. 26	Sioux Falls, 135-111	at Sioux Falls
Apr. 27	Connecticut, 105-103	at Sioux Falls

CBA Annual Awards

Most Valuable Player: Adrian Griffin, Conn.
Newcomer of the Year: Damon Jones, Idaho
Rookie of the Year: Bakari Hendrix, Quad City
Def. Player of the Year: James Martin, Conn.
Coach of the Year: Tyler Jones, Conn.
Finals MVP: Adrian Griffin, Conn.

CBA Regular Season Individual Leaders

Scoring

	Gm	Pts	Avg
Damon Jones, Idaho	35	758	21.7
Victor Page, Sioux Falls	39	749	19.2
Dennis Edwards, Rockford	48	916	19.1
Adrian Griffin, Connecticut	47	888	18.9
Jason Sasser, Sioux Falls	33	576	17.5

Rebounding

	Gm	Reb	Avg
Jerome Lane, Idaho	34	492	14.5
Nick Davis, Sioux Falls	54	510	9.4
James Martin, Connecticut	56	510	9.1
Rocky Walls, Yakima	50	440	8.8
Jason Sasser, Sioux Falls	33	271	8.2

Field Goal Pct.

	FGM	FGA	Pct
Mikki Moore, Fort Wayne	156	277	.563
Otis Hill, Connecticut	244	439	.556
Ira Newble, Idaho	148	267	.554
Darrin Hancock, Fort Wayne	234	424	.552
Courtney James, Fort Wayne	169	310	.545
Dennis Edwards, Rockford	382	707	.540
Demetrius Alexander, Idaho	206	390	.528

Assists

	Gm	Ast	Avg
Damon Bailey, Fort Wayne	44	297	6.8
Randy Livingston, Sioux Falls	40	259	6.5
Damon Jones, Idaho	35	222	6.3

Blocks

	Gm	Blk	Avg
Nick Davis, Sioux Falls	54	105	1.9
Mikki Moore, Fort Wayne	29	51	1.8
Matt Steigenga, Rockford	44	75	1.7
Elmore Spencer, Sioux Falls	30	49	1.6
Rahsaan Smith, Yakima	40	54	1.4
Maceo Baston, Quad City	42	52	1.2
Shawn Harvey, Yakima	54	60	1.1
Dennis Davis, La Crosse	29	32	1.1

Steals

	Gm	Stl	Avg
James Blackwell, La Crosse	47	120	2.6
Chris Garner, Fort Wayne	47	104	2.2
Adrian Griffin, Connecticut	47	104	2.2
Ronnie Fields, Rockford	56	112	2.0
Darrin Hancock, Fort Wayne	43	82	1.9
Randy Livingston, Sioux Falls	40	70	1.8

Women's National Basketball Association
Final WNBA Standings

Conference champions (*) and playoff qualifiers (†) are noted. GB refers to Games Behind leader. Number of seasons listed after each head coach refers to current tenure with club.

Eastern Conference

	W	L	Pct	GB	Home	Road
*New York	18	14	.563	—	12-4	6-10
†Charlotte	15	17	.469	3	8-8	7-9
†Detroit	15	17	.469	3	7-9	8-8
Orlando	15	17	.469	3	8-8	7-9
Washington	12	20	.375	6	6-10	6-10
Cleveland	7	25	.219	11	5-15	2-14

Head Coaches: NY–Richie Adubato (1st season); **Char**–Dan Hughes (10-9) named interim head coach on July 11, 1999 replacing Marynell Meadors (5-8); **Det**–Nancy Lieberman-Cline (2nd); **Orl**–Carolyn Peck (1st); **Wash**–Nancy Darsch (1st); **Cle**–Linda Hill-McDonald (3rd). **1998 Standings:** 1. Cleveland (20-10); 2. Charlotte (18-12); 3. New York (18-12); 4. Detroit (17-13); 5. Washington (3-27).

Western Conference

	W	L	Pct	GB	Home	Road
*Houston	26	6	.813	—	15-1	11-5
†Los Angeles	20	12	.625	6	13-3	7-9
†Sacramento	19	13	.594	7	11-5	8-8
Phoenix	15	17	.469	11	12-4	3-13
Minnesota	15	17	.469	11	8-8	7-9
Utah	15	17	.469	11	11-5	4-12

Head Coaches: Hou–Van Chancellor (3rd season); **LA**–Orlando Woolridge (2nd); **Sac**–Sonny Allen (1st); **Pho**–Cheryl Miller (2nd); **Minn**–Brian Agler (1st); **Utah**–Fred Williams (1st). **1998 Standings:** 1. Houston (27-3); 2. Phoenix (19-11); 3. Los Angeles (12-18); 4. Sacramento (8-22); 5. Utah (8-22).

WNBA Playoffs
First Round

Single game. Winners advance to semifinals to face conference champions.

	1	2	– F
Aug. 24 Charlotte	22	38	—60
at Detroit	26	28	—54
attendance: 6,917			

	1	2	– F
Aug. 24 Sacramento	32	26	—58
at Los Angeles	21	50	—71
attendance: 8,569			

Semifinals (Best of 3)

Date	Result
Aug. 27	at Charlotte 78, New York 67
Aug. 29	at New York 74, Charlotte 70
Aug. 30	at New York 69, Charlotte 54
	New York wins series, 2-1

Date	Result
Aug. 26	at Los Angeles 75, Houston 60
Aug. 29	at Houston 83, Los Angeles 55
Aug. 30	at Houston 72, Los Angeles 62
	Houston wins series, 2-1

Championship Series (Best of 3)
Houston wins series, 2 games to 1

	W-L	Avg	Leading Scorer
Houston	2-1	66.3	Cooper (21.7 ppg)
New York	1-2	58.3	Robinson (12.7 ppg)

Date	Winner
Sept. 2	Houston 73, at New York 60
Sept. 4	New York 68, at Houston 67
Sept. 5	at Houston 59, New York 47

Finals MVP: Cynthia Cooper, Houston, G (21.7 ppg, 4.3 rpg, 4.3 apg, 2.7 spg)

WNBA 1999 Attendance

Attendance figures below are for the regular season and teams are listed in alphabetical order.

Team	Home Games	Total Attendance	Average Attendance
Charlotte Sting	16	113,303	7,081
Cleveland Rockers	16	149,595	9,350
Detroit Shock	16	135,753	8,485
Houston Comets	16	190,503	11,906
Los Angeles Sparks	16	122,000	7,625
Minnesota Lynx	16	167,901	10,494
New York Liberty	16	224,748	14,047
Orlando Miracle	16	156,818	9,801
Phoenix Mercury	16	195,508	12,219
Sacramento Monarchs	16	138,009	8,626
Utah Starzz	16	120,706	7,544
Washington Mystics	16	244,889	15,306
WNBA totals	192	1,959,733	10,207

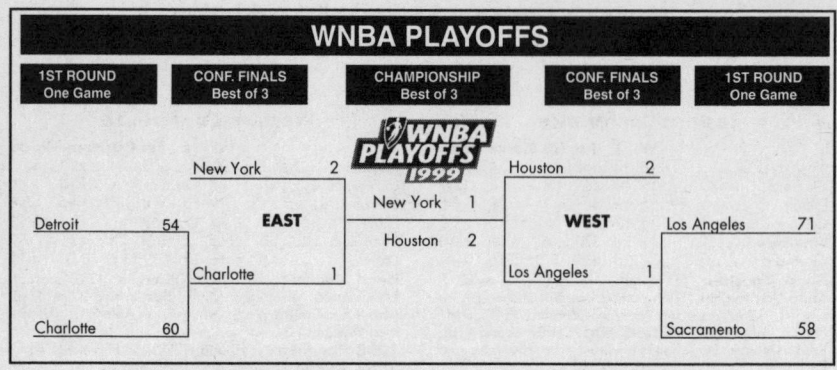

WNBA PLAYOFFS

| 1ST ROUND One Game | CONF. FINALS Best of 3 | CHAMPIONSHIP Best of 3 | CONF. FINALS Best of 3 | 1ST ROUND One Game |

WNBA PLAYOFFS 1999

New York 2

New York 1

Detroit 54   **EAST**

Houston 2

Charlotte 1

Charlotte 60

Houston 2

WEST

Los Angeles 1

Los Angeles 71

Sacramento 58

WNBA Regular Season Individual Leaders

Scoring

	Gm	Pts	Avg
Cynthia Cooper, Houston	31	686	22.1
Yolanda Griffith, Sacramento	29	545	18.8
Sheryl Swoopes, Houston	32	585	18.3
Natalie Williams, Utah	28	504	18.0
Nikki McCray, Washington	32	561	17.5
Chamique Holdsclaw, Washington	31	525	16.9
Brandy Reed, Minnesota	25	402	16.1
Lisa Leslie, Los Angeles	32	500	15.6
Jennifer Gillom, Phoenix	32	485	15.2
Adrienne Goodson, Utah	32	476	14.9

Field Goal Pct.

	Gm	FGM	FGA	Pct
Muriel Page, Washington	32	105	183	.574
Yolanda Griffith, Sacramento	29	200	370	.541
Alisa Burras, Cleveland	31	103	191	.539
Latasha Byears, Sacramento	32	130	242	.537
DeLisha Milton, Los Angeles	32	125	236	.530

Free Throw Pct.

	Gm	FTM	FTA	Pct
Eva Nemcova, Cleveland	31	62	63	.984
Dawn Staley, Charlotte	32	85	91	.934
Cynthia Cooper, Houston	31	204	229	.891
Korie Hlede, Utah	32	72	82	.878
Penny Toler, Los Angeles	30	39	45	.867

3-Point Field Goal Pct.

	Gm	FGM	FGA	Pct
Jennifer Azzi, Detroit	28	30	58	.517
Sandy Brondello, Detroit	32	37	76	.487
Taj McWilliams, Orlando	32	20	45	.444
Crystal Robinson, New York	32	76	174	.437
Gordana Grubin, Los Angeles	32	40	93	.430

Assists

	Gm	Ast	Avg
Ticha Penicheiro, Sacramento	32	226	7.1
Teresa Weatherspoon, New York	32	205	6.4
Dawn Staley, Charlotte	32	177	5.5
Cynthia Cooper, Houston	31	162	5.2
Debbie Black, Utah	32	161	5.0
Michele Timms, Phoenix	30	151	5.0

Rebounding

	Gm	Reb	Avg
Yolanda Griffith, Sacramento	29	329	11.3
Natalie Williams, Utah	28	257	9.2
Chamique Holdsclaw, Washington	31	246	7.9
Lisa Leslie, Los Angeles	32	248	7.8
Taj McWilliams, Orlando	32	239	7.5
Marlies Askamp, Phoenix	30	215	7.2
Sue Wicks, New York	32	223	7.0
Vicky Bullett, Charlotte	32	219	6.8
Muriel Page, Washington	32	213	6.7
Val Whiting, Detroit	31	207	6.7

Blocks

	Gm	Blk	Avg
Malgorzata Dydek, Utah	32	77	2.41
Maria Stepnova, Phoenix	32	62	1.94
Yolanda Griffith, Sacramento	29	54	1.86
Lisa Leslie, Los Angeles	32	49	1.53
Sheryl Swoopes, Houston	32	46	1.44

Steals

	Gm	Stl	Avg
Yolanda Griffith, Sacramento	29	73	2.52
Teresa Weatherspoon, New York	32	78	2.44
Debbie Black, Utah	32	77	2.41
Sheryl Swoopes, Houston	32	76	2.38
Nykesha Sales, Orlando	32	69	2.16

WNBA Annual Awards

Most Valuable Player:
Yolanda Griffith, Sacramento

Rookie of the Year:
Chamique Holdsclaw, Washington

Newcomer of the Year:
Yolanda Griffith, Sacramento

Def. Player of the Year:
Yolanda Griffith, Sacramento.

Coach of the Year:
Van Chancellor, Houston

THE 2000 ESPN INFORMATION PLEASE SPORTS ALMANAC

PRO BASKETBALL STATISTICS

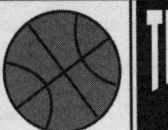

THROUGH THE YEARS
1947-1999
CHAMPIONS • NBA LEADERS

SEC B

PAGE 367

The NBA Finals

Although the National Basketball Association traces its first championship back to the 1946-47 season, the league was then called the Basketball Association of America (BAA). It did not become the NBA until after the 1948-49 season when the BAA and the National Basketball League (NBL) agreed to merge.

In the chart below, the Eastern finalists (representing the NBA Eastern Division from 1947-70, and the NBA Eastern Conference since 1971) are listed in CAPITAL letters. Also, each NBA champion's wins and losses are noted in parentheses after the series score.

Multiple winners: Boston (16); Minneapolis-LA Lakers (11); Chicago Bulls (6); Phi-SF-Golden St. Warriors and Syracuse Nationals-Phi. 76ers (3); Detroit, Houston and New York (2).

Year	Winner	Head Coach	Series	Loser	Head Coach
1947	PHILADELPHIA WARRIORS	Eddie Gottlieb	4-1 (WWWLW)	Chicago Stags	Harold Olsen
1948	Baltimore Bullets	Buddy Jeannette	4-2 (LWWWLW)	PHILA. WARRIORS	Eddie Gottlieb
1949	Minneapolis Lakers	John Kundla	4-2 (WWWLLW)	WASH. CAPITOLS	Red Auerbach
1950	Minneapolis Lakers	John Kundla	4-2 (WLWLWW)	SYRACUSE	Al Cervi
1951	Rochester	Les Harrison	4-3 (WWWLLLW)	NEW YORK	Joe Lapchick
1952	Minneapolis Lakers	John Kundla	4-3 (WLWLWLW)	NEW YORK	Joe Lapchick
1953	Minneapolis Lakers	John Kundla	4-1 (LWWWW)	NEW YORK	Joe Lapchick
1954	Minneapolis Lakers	John Kundla	4-3 (WLWLWLW)	SYRACUSE	Al Cervi
1955	SYRACUSE	Al Cervi	4-3 (WWLLLWW)	Ft. Wayne Pistons	Charley Eckman
1956	PHILADELPHIA WARRIORS	George Senesky	4-1 (LWWWW)	Ft. Wayne Pistons	Charley Eckman
1957	BOSTON	Red Auerbach	4-3 (LWLWWLW)	St. Louis Hawks	Alex Hannum
1958	St. Louis Hawks	Alex Hannum	4-2 (WLWLWW)	BOSTON	Red Auerbach
1959	BOSTON	Red Auerbach	4-0	Mpls. Lakers	John Kundla
1960	BOSTON	Red Auerbach	4-3 (WLWLWLW)	St. Louis Hawks	Ed Macauley
1961	BOSTON	Red Auerbach	4-1 (WWWLW)	St. Louis Hawks	Paul Seymour
1962	BOSTON	Red Auerbach	4-3 (WLLWLWW)	LA Lakers	Fred Schaus
1963	BOSTON	Red Auerbach	4-2 (WWLWLW)	LA Lakers	Fred Schaus
1964	BOSTON	Red Auerbach	4-1 (WWLWW)	SF Warriors	Alex Hannum
1965	BOSTON	Red Auerbach	4-1 (WWLWW)	LA Lakers	Fred Schaus
1966	BOSTON	Red Auerbach	4-3 (LWWWLLW)	LA Lakers	Fred Schaus
1967	PHILADELPHIA 76ERS	Alex Hannum	4-2 (WWLWLW)	SF Warriors	Bill Sharman
1968	BOSTON	Bill Russell	4-2 (WLWLWW)	LA Lakers	B.van Breda Kolff
1969	BOSTON	Bill Russell	4-3 (LLWWLWW)	LA Lakers	B.van Breda Kolff
1970	NEW YORK	Red Holzman	4-3 (WLWLWLW)	LA Lakers	Joe Mullaney
1971	Milwaukee	Larry Costello	4-0	BALT. BULLETS	Gene Shue
1972	LA Lakers	Bill Sharman	4-1 (LWWWW)	NEW YORK	Red Holzman
1973	NEW YORK	Red Holzman	4-1 (LWWWW)	LA Lakers	Bill Sharman
1974	BOSTON	Tommy Heinsohn	4-3 (WLWLWLW)	Milwaukee	Larry Costello
1975	Golden St. Warriors	Al Attles	4-0	WASH. BULLETS	K.C. Jones
1976	BOSTON	Tommy Heinsohn	4-2 (WWLLWW)	Phoenix	John MacLeod
1977	Portland	Jack Ramsay	4-2 (LLWWWW)	PHILA. 76ERS	Gene Shue
1978	WASHINGTON BULLETS	Dick Motta	4-3 (LWLWLWW)	Seattle	Lenny Wilkens
1979	Seattle	Lenny Wilkens	4-1 (LWWWW)	WASH. BULLETS	Dick Motta
1980	LA Lakers	Paul Westhead	4-2 (WLWLWW)	PHILA. 76ERS	Billy Cunningham
1981	BOSTON	Bill Fitch	4-2 (WLWLWW)	Houston	Del Harris
1982	LA Lakers	Pat Riley	4-2 (WLWLWL)	PHILA. 76ERS	Billy Cunningham
1983	PHILADELPHIA 76ERS	Billy Cunningham	4-0	LA Lakers	Pat Riley
1984	BOSTON	K.C. Jones	4-3 (LWLWWLW)	LA Lakers	Pat Riley
1985	LA Lakers	Pat Riley	4-2 (LWWWLW)	BOSTON	K.C. Jones
1986	BOSTON	K.C. Jones	4-2 (WWLWLW)	Houston	Bill Fitch
1987	LA Lakers	Pat Riley	4-2 (WWLLWW)	BOSTON	K.C. Jones
1988	LA Lakers	Pat Riley	4-3 (LWWLLWW)	DETROIT PISTONS	Chuck Daly
1989	DETROIT PISTONS	Chuck Daly	4-0	LA Lakers	Pat Riley
1990	DETROIT	Chuck Daly	4-1 (WLWWW)	Portland	Rick Adelman
1991	CHICAGO	Phil Jackson	4-1 (LWWWW)	LA Lakers	Mike Dunleavy
1992	CHICAGO	Phil Jackson	4-2 (WLWWLW)	Portland	Rick Adelman
1993	CHICAGO	Phil Jackson	4-2 (WWLWLW)	Phoenix	Paul Westphal

Year	Winner	Head Coach	Series	Loser	Head Coach
1994	Houston	Rudy Tomjanovich	4-3 (WLWLLWW)	NEW YORK	Pat Riley
1995	Houston	Rudy Tomjanovich	4-0	ORLANDO	Brian Hill
1996	CHICAGO	Phil Jackson	4-2 (WWWLLW)	Seattle	George Karl
1997	CHICAGO	Phil Jackson	4-2 (WWLLWW)	Utah	Jerry Sloan
1998	CHICAGO	Phil Jackson	4-2 (LWWWLW)	Utah	Jerry Sloan
1999	San Antonio	Gregg Popovich	4-1 (WWLWW)	NEW YORK	Jeff Van Gundy

Note: Four finalists were led by player-coaches: **1948**—Buddy Jeannette (guard) of Baltimore; **1950**—Al Cervi (guard) of Syracuse; **1968**—Bill Russell (center) of Boston; **1969**—Bill Russell (center) of Boston.

Most Valuable Player

Selected by an 11-member media panel. Winner who did not play for the NBA champion is in **bold** type.

Multiple winners: Michael Jordan (6); Magic Johnson (3); Kareem Abdul-Jabbar, Larry Bird, Hakeem Olajuwon and Willis Reed (2).

Year		Year		Year	
1969	**Jerry West**, LA Lakers, G	1980	Magic Johnson, LA Lakers, G/C	1991	Michael Jordan, Chicago, G
1970	Willis Reed, New York, C	1981	Cedric Maxwell, Boston, F	1992	Michael Jordan, Chicago, G
1971	Lew Alcindor, Milwaukee, C	1982	Magic Johnson, LA Lakers, G	1993	Michael Jordan, Chicago, G
1972	Wilt Chamberlain, LA Lakers, C	1983	Moses Malone, Philadelphia, C	1994	Hakeem Olajuwon, Houston, C
1973	Willis Reed, New York, C	1984	Larry Bird, Boston, F	1995	Hakeem Olajuwon, Houston, C
1974	John Havlicek, Boston, F	1985	K. Abdul-Jabbar, LA Lakers, C	1996	Michael Jordan, Chicago, G
1975	Rick Barry, Golden State, F	1986	Larry Bird, Boston, F	1997	Michael Jordan, Chicago, G
1976	Jo Jo White, Boston, G	1987	Magic Johnson, LA Lakers, G	1998	Michael Jordan, Chicago, G
1977	Bill Walton, Portland, C	1988	James Worthy, LA Lakers, F	1999	Tim Duncan, San Antonio, F/C
1978	Wes Unseld, Washington, C	1989	Joe Dumars, Detroit, G		
1979	Dennis Johnson, Seattle, G	1990	Isiah Thomas, Detroit, G		

Note: Lew Alcindor changed his name to Kareem Abdul-Jabbar after the 1970-71 season.

All-Time NBA Playoff Leaders

Through the 1999 playoffs.

CAREER

Years listed indicate number of playoff appearances. Players active in 1999 playoffs in **bold** type.

Points

		Yrs	Gm	Pts	Avg
1	Michael Jordan	13	179	5987	33.4
2	Kareem Abdul-Jabbar	18	237	5762	24.3
3	Jerry West	13	153	4457	29.1
4	**Karl Malone**	14	148	3931	26.6
5	Larry Bird	12	164	3897	23.8
6	John Havlicek	13	172	3776	22.0
7	**Hakeem Olajuwon**	14	140	3727	26.6
8	Magic Johnson	13	190	3701	19.5
9	Elgin Baylor	12	134	3623	27.0
10	Wilt Chamberlain	13	160	3607	22.5
11	**Scottie Pippen**	12	182	3290	18.1
12	Kevin McHale	13	169	3182	18.8
13	Dennis Johnson	13	180	3116	17.3
14	Julius Erving	11	141	3088	21.9
15	James Worthy	9	143	3022	21.1
16	Clyde Drexler	15	145	2963	20.4
17	Sam Jones	12	154	2909	18.9
18	**Charles Barkley**	13	123	2833	23.0
19	Robert Parish	16	184	2820	15.3
20	Bill Russell	13	165	2673	16.2

Scoring Average

Minimum of 25 games or 700 points.

		Yrs	Gm	Pts	Avg
1	Michael Jordan	13	179	5987	33.4
2	Jerry West	13	153	4457	29.1
3	Elgin Baylor	12	134	3623	27.0
4	George Gervin	9	59	1592	27.0
5	**Shaquille O'Neal**	6	66	1762	26.7
6	**Hakeem Olajuwon**	14	140	3727	26.6
7	**Karl Malone**	14	148	3931	26.6
8	Dominique Wilkins	9	55	1421	25.8
9	Bob Pettit	9	88	2240	25.5
10	Rick Barry	7	74	1833	24.8
11	Bernard King	5	28	687	24.5
12	Alex English	10	68	1661	24.4
13	Kareem Abdul-Jabbar	18	237	5762	24.3
14	Paul Arizin	8	49	1186	24.2
15	Larry Bird	12	164	3897	23.8
16	George Mikan	9	91	2141	23.5
17	**Charles Barkley**	13	123	2833	23.0
18	**Reggie Miller**	9	78	1793	23.0
19	Bob Love	6	47	1076	22.9
20	**Tim Duncan**	2	26	581	22.3

Field Goals

		Yrs	FG	Att	Pct
1	Kareem Abdul-Jabbar	18	2356	4422	.533
2	Michael Jordan	13	2188	4497	.487
3	Jerry West	13	1622	3460	.469
4	**Hakeem Olajuwon**	12	1469	2771	.530
5	Larry Bird	12	1458	3090	.472
6	John Havlicek	13	1451	3329	.436
7	**Karl Malone**	14	1429	3074	.465
8	Wilt Chamberlain	13	1425	2728	.522
9	Elgin Baylor	12	1388	3161	.439
10	Magic Johnson	13	1291	2552	.506

Free Throws

		Yrs	FT	Att	Pct
1	Michael Jordan	13	1463	1766	.828
2	Jerry West	13	1213	1507	.805
3	**Karl Malone**	14	1070	1455	.735
4	Kareem Abdul-Jabbar	18	1050	1419	.740
5	Magic Johnson	12	1040	1241	.838
6	Larry Bird	12	901	1012	.891
7	John Havlicek	13	874	1046	.836
8	Elgin Baylor	12	847	1101	.769
9	Kevin McHale	13	766	972	.788
10	Wilt Chamberlain	13	757	1627	.465

Assists

		Yrs	Gm	No	Avg
1	Magic Johnson	13	190	2346	12.3
2	**John Stockton**	15	158	1613	10.2
3	Larry Bird	12	164	1062	6.5
4	Michael Jordan	13	179	1022	5.7
5	Dennis Johnson	13	180	1006	5.6

Rebounds

		Yrs	Gm	No	Avg
1	Bill Russell	13	165	4104	24.9
2	Wilt Chamberlain	13	160	3913	24.5
3	Kareem Abdul-Jabbar	18	237	2481	10.5
4	Wes Unseld	12	119	1777	14.9
5	Robert Parish	16	184	1765	9.6

Appearances

	No		No
Kareem Abdul-Jabbar	18	Bob Cousy	13
Robert Parish	16	Hal Greer	13
Dolph Schayes	15	John Havlicek	13
John Stockton	15	Kevin McHale	13
Paul Silas	14	Dennis Johnson	13
Karl Malone	14	Magic Johnson	13
Hakeem Olajuwon	14	Michael Jordan	13
Charles Barkley	13	Bill Russell	13
Wilt Chamberlain	13	Chet Walker	13
Maurice Cheeks	13	Jerry West	13

Games Played

	No		No
K. Abdul-Jabbar	237	John Havlicek	170
Danny Ainge	193	Kevin McHale	169
Magic Johnson	190	Michael Cooper	168
Robert Parish	184	Bill Russell	165
Byron Scott	183	Larry Bird	164
Scottie Pippen	182	Paul Silas	163
Dennis Johnson	180	Wilt Chamberlain	160
Michael Jordan	179		

SINGLE GAME

Points

	Date	FG-FT-Pts
Michael Jordan, Chi at Bos*	4/20/86	22-19-63
Elgin Baylor, LA at Bos	4/14/62	22-17-61
Wilt Chamberlain, Phi vs Syr	3/22/62	22-12-56
Michael Jordan, Chi at Mia.	4/29/92	20-16-56
Charles Barkley, Pho vs G.St.	5/4/94	23-7-56
Rick Barry, SF vs Phi	4/18/67	22-11-55
Michael Jordan, Chi vs Cle	5/1/88	24-7-55
Michael Jordan, Chi at Cle	4/16/93	21-13-55
Michael Jordan, Chi vs. Wash	4/27/97	22-10-55

*Double overtime.

Field Goals

	Date	FG	Att
Wilt Chamberlain, Phi vs Syr	3/14/60	24	42
John Havlicek, Bos vs Atl	4/1/73	24	36
Michael Jordan, Chi vs Cle	5/1/88	24	45

Eight tied with 22 each.

Miscellaneous

3-Pt Field Goals

	Date	No
Rex Chapman, Pho at Sea	4/25/97	9
Dan Majerle, Pho vs Sea	6/1/93	8

Eight tied with 7 each.

Assists

	Date	No
Magic Johnson, LA vs Pho	5/15/84	24
John Stockton, Utah at LA Lakers	5/17/88	24
Magic Johnson, LA Lakers at Port	5/3/85	23
John Stockton, Utah vs Port	4/25/96	23
Doc Rivers, Atl vs Bos	5/16/88	22

Four tied with 21 each.

Rebounds

	Date	No
Wilt Chamberlain, Phi vs Bos	4/5/67	41
Bill Russell, Bos vs Phi	3/23/58	40
Bill Russell, Bos vs St.L	3/29/60	40
Bill Russell, Bos vs LA*	4/18/62	40

Three tied with 39 each.

*Overtime.

Appearances in NBA Finals

Standings of all NBA teams that have reached the NBA Finals since 1947.

App		Titles	Last Won
24	Minneapolis-LA Lakers	11	1988
19	Boston Celtics	16	1986
8	Syracuse Nats-Phila. 76ers	3	1983
8	New York Knicks	2	1973
6	Chicago Bulls	6	1998
6	Phila-SF-Golden St. Warriors	3	1975
5	Ft. Wayne-Detroit Pistons	2	1990
4	Houston Rockets	2	1995
4	St. Louis Hawks	1	1958
4	Baltimore-Washington Bullets	1	1978
3	Portland Trail Blazers	1	1977
3	Seattle SuperSonics	1	1979
2	Milwaukee Bucks	1	1971
2	Phoenix Suns	0	—
2	Utah Jazz	0	—
1	Baltimore Bullets	1	1948
1	San Antonio Spurs	1	1999
1	Chicago Stags	0	—
1	Orlando Magic	0	—
1	Rochester Royals	0	—
1	Washington Capitols	0	—

Change of address: The St. Louis Hawks now play in Atlanta and the Rochester Royals are now the Sacramento Kings.

Teams now defunct: Baltimore Bullets (1947-55), Chicago Stags (1946-50) and Washington Capitols (1946-51).

NBA FINALS

Points

Series		Year	Pts
4-Gm	Hakeem Olajuwon, Hou vs Orl	1995	131
5-Gm	Jerry West, LA vs Bos	1965	169
6-Gm	Michael Jordan, Chi vs Pho	1993	246
7-Gm	Elgin Baylor, LA vs Bos	1962	284

Field Goals

Series		Year	No
4-Gm	Hakeem Olajuwon, Hou vs Orl	1995	56
5-Gm	Michael Jordan, Chi vs LAL	1991	63
6-Gm	Michael Jordan, Chi vs Pho	1993	101
7-Gm	Elgin Baylor, LA vs Bos	1962	101

Assists

Series		Year	No
4-Gm	Bob Cousy, Bos vs Mpls	1959	51
5-Gm	Magic Johnson, LAL vs Chi	1991	62
6-Gm	Magic Johnson, LAL vs Bos	1985	84
7-Gm	Magic Johnson, LA vs Bos.	1984	95

Rebounds

Series		Year	No
4-Gm	Bill Russell, Bos vs Mpls	1959	118
5-Gm	Bill Russell, Bos vs St.L	1961	144
6-Gm	Wilt Chamberlain, Phi vs SF	1967	171
7-Gm	Bill Russell, Bos vs LA	1962	189

The National Basketball League

Formed in 1937 by three corporations– General Electric and the Firestone and Goodyear rubber companies of Akron, Ohio– which were interested in moving up from their midwestern industrial league origins and backing a fully professional league. The NBL started with 13 previously independent teams in 1937-38 and although GE, Firestone and Goodyear were gone by late 1942, ran 12 years before merging with the three-year-old Basketball Association of America in 1949 to form the NBA.

Multiple champions: Akron Firestone Non-Skids, Fort Wayne Zollner Pistons, Oshkosh All-Stars (2).

Year	Winner	Series	Loser	Year	Winner	Series	Loser
1938	Goodyear Wingfoots	2-1	Oshkosh All-Stars	1944	Ft. Wayne Pistons	3-0	Sheboygan Redskins
1939	Firestone Non-Skids	3-2	Oshkosh All-Stars	1945	Ft. Wayne Pistons	3-2	Sheboygan Redskins
1940	Firestone Non-Skids	3-2	Oshkosh All-Stars	1946	Rochester Royals	3-0	Sheboygan Redskins
1941	Oshkosh All-Stars	3-0	Sheboygan Redskins	1947	Chicago Gears	3-2	Rochester Royals
1942	Oshkosh All-Stars	2-1	Ft. Wayne Pistons	1948	Minneapolis Lakers	3-1	Rochester Royals
1943	Sheboygan Redskins	2-1	Ft. Wayne Pistons	1949	Anderson Packers	3-0	Oshkosh All-Stars

NBA All-Star Game

The NBA staged its first All-Star Game before 10,094 at Boston Garden on March 2, 1951. From that year on, the game has matched the best players in the East against the best in the West. Winning coaches are listed first. East leads series, 31-17.

Multiple MVP winners: Bob Pettit (4); Michael Jordan and Oscar Robertson (3); Bob Cousy, Julius Erving, Magic Johnson, Karl Malone and Isiah Thomas (2).

Year		Host	Coaches	Most Valuable Player
1951	East 111, West 94	Boston	Joe Lapchick, John Kundla	Ed Macauley, Boston
1952	East 108, West 91	Boston	Al Cervi, John Kundla	Paul Arizin, Philadelphia
1953	West 79, East 75	Ft. Wayne	John Kundla, Joe Lapchick	George Mikan, Minneapolis
1954	East 98, West 93 (OT)	New York	Joe Lapchick, John Kundla	Bob Cousy, Boston
1955	East 100, West 91	New York	Al Cervi, Charley Eckman	Bill Sharman, Boston
1956	West 108, East 94	Rochester	Charley Eckman, George Senesky	Bob Pettit, St. Louis
1957	East 109, West 97	Boston	Red Auerbach, Bobby Wanzer	Bob Cousy, Boston
1958	East 130, West 118	St. Louis	Red Auerbach, Alex Hannum	Bob Pettit, St. Louis
1959	West 124, East 108	Detroit	Ed Macauley, Red Auerbach	Bob Pettit, St. Louis & Elgin Baylor, Minneapolis
1960	East 125, West 115	Philadelphia	Red Auerbach, Ed Macauley	Wilt Chamberlain, Philadelphia
1961	West 153, East 131	Syracuse	Paul Seymour, Red Auerbach	Oscar Robertson, Cincinnati
1962	West 150, East 130	St. Louis	Fred Schaus, Red Auerbach	Bob Pettit, St. Louis
1963	East 115, West 108	Los Angeles	Red Auerbach, Fred Schaus	Bill Russell, Boston
1964	East 111, West 107	Boston	Red Auerbach, Fred Schaus	Oscar Robertson, Cincinnati
1965	East 124, West 123	St. Louis	Red Auerbach, Alex Hannum	Jerry Lucas, Cincinnati
1966	East 137, West 94	Cincinnati	Red Auerbach, Fred Schaus	Adrian Smith, Cincinnati
1967	West 135, East 120	San Francisco	Fred Schaus, Red Auerbach	Rick Barry, San Francisco
1968	East 144, West 124	New York	Alex Hannum, Bill Sharman	Hal Greer, Philadelphia
1969	East 123, West 112	Baltimore	Gene Shue, Richie Guerin	Oscar Robertson, Cincinnati
1970	East 142, West 135	Philadelphia	Red Holzman, Richie Guerin	Willis Reed, New York
1971	West 108, East 107	San Diego	Larry Costello, Red Holzman	Lenny Wilkens, Seattle
1972	West 112, East 110	Los Angeles	Bill Sharman, Tom Heinsohn	Jerry West, Los Angeles
1973	East 104, West 84	Chicago	Tom Heinsohn, Bill Sharman	Dave Cowens, Boston
1974	West 134, East 123	Seattle	Larry Costello, Tom Heinsohn	Bob Lanier, Detroit
1975	East 108, West 102	Phoenix	K.C. Jones, Al Attles	Walt Frazier, New York
1976	East 123, West 109	Philadelphia	Tom Heinsohn, Al Attles	Dave Bing, Washington
1977	West 125, East 124	Milwaukee	Larry Brown, Gene Shue	Julius Erving, Philadelphia
1978	East 133, West 125	Atlanta	Billy Cunningham, Jack Ramsay	Randy Smith, Buffalo
1979	West 134, East 129	Detroit	Lenny Wilkens, Dick Motta	David Thompson, Denver
1980	East 144, West 136 (OT)	Washington	Billy Cunningham, Lenny Wilkens	George Gervin, San Antonio
1981	East 123, West 120	Cleveland	Billy Cunningham, John MacLeod	Nate Archibald, Boston
1982	East 120, West 118	New Jersey	Bill Fitch, Pat Riley	Larry Bird, Boston
1983	East 132, West 123	Los Angeles	Billy Cunningham, Pat Riley	Julius Erving, Philadelphia
1984	East 154, West 145 (OT)	Denver	K.C. Jones, Frank Layden	Isiah Thomas, Detroit
1985	West 140, East 129	Indiana	Pat Riley, K.C. Jones	Ralph Sampson, Houston
1986	East 139, West 132	Dallas	K.C. Jones, Pat Riley	Isiah Thomas, Detroit
1987	West 154, East 149 (OT)	Seattle	Pat Riley, K.C. Jones	Tom Chambers, Seattle
1988	East 138, West 133	Chicago	Mike Fratello, Pat Riley	Michael Jordan, Chicago
1989	West 143, East 134	Houston	Pat Riley, Lenny Wilkens	Karl Malone, Utah
1990	East 130, West 113	Miami	Chuck Daly, Pat Riley	Magic Johnson, LA Lakers
1991	East 116, West 114	Charlotte	Chris Ford, Rick Adelman	Charles Barkley, Philadelphia
1992	West 153, East 113	Orlando	Don Nelson, Phil Jackson	Magic Johnson, LA Lakers
1993	West 135, East 132 (OT)	Salt Lake City	Paul Westphal, Pat Riley	Karl Malone, Utah & John Stockton, Utah
1994	East 127, West 118	Minneapolis	Lenny Wilkens, George Karl	Scottie Pippen, Chicago
1995	West 139, East 112	Phoenix	Paul Westphal, Brian Hill	Mitch Richmond, Sacramento
1996	East 129, West 118	San Antonio	Phil Jackson, George Karl	Michael Jordan, Chicago
1997	East 132, West 120	Cleveland	Doug Collins, Rudy Tomjanovich	Glen Rice, Charlotte
1998	East 135, West 114	New York	Larry Bird, George Karl	Michael Jordan, Chicago
1999	Not held–due to lockout			

NBA Franchise Origins

Here is what the current 29 teams in the National Basketball Association have to show for the years they have put in as members of the National Basketball League (NBL), Basketball Association of America (BAA), the NBA, and the American Basketball Association (ABA). League titles are noted by year won.

Western Conference

	First Season		League Titles	Franchise Stops
Dallas Mavericks	1980-81	(NBA)	None	• Dallas (1980–)
Denver Nuggets	1967-68	(ABA)	None	• Denver (1967–)
Golden St. Warriors	1946-47	(BAA)	1 BAA (1947) 2 NBA (1956,75)	• Philadelphia (1946-62) San Francisco (1962-71) Oakland (1971–)
Houston Rockets	1967-68	(NBA)	2 NBA (1994-95)	• San Diego (1967-71) Houston (1971–)
Los Angeles Clippers	1970-71	(NBA)	None	• Buffalo (1970-78) San Diego (1978-84) Los Angeles (1984–)
Los Angeles Lakers	1947-48	(NBL)	1 NBL (1947) 1 BAA (1949) 10 NBA (1950,52-54,72, 80,82,85,87-88)	• Minneapolis (1947-60) Los Angeles (1960-67) Inglewood, CA (1967-99) Los Angeles (1999–)
Minnesota Timberwolves	1989-90	(NBA)	None	• Minneapolis (1989–)
Phoenix Suns	1968-69	(NBA)	None	• Phoenix (1968–)
Portland Trail Blazers	1970-71	(NBA)	1 NBA (1977)	• Portland (1970–)
Sacramento Kings	1945-46	(NBL)	1 NBL (1946) 1 NBA (1951)	• Rochester, NY (1945-58) Cincinnati (1958-72) KC-Omaha (1972-75) Kansas City (1975-85) Sacramento (1985–)
San Antonio Spurs	1967-68	(ABA)	1 NBA (1999)	• Dallas (1967-73) San Antonio (1973–)
Seattle SuperSonics	1967-68	(NBA)	1 NBA (1979)	• Seattle (1967–)
Utah Jazz	1974-75	(NBA)	None	• New Orleans (1974-79) Salt Lake City (1979–)
Vancouver Grizzlies	1995-96	(NBA)	None	• Vancouver (1995–)

Eastern Conference

	First Season		League Titles	Franchise Stops
Atlanta Hawks	1946-47	(NBL)	1 NBA (1958)	• Tri-Cities (1946-51) Milwaukee (1951-55) St. Louis (1955-68) Atlanta (1968–)
Boston Celtics	1946-47	(BAA)	16 NBA (1957,59-66,68-69 74,76,81,84,86)	• Boston (1946–)
Charlotte Hornets	1988-89	(NBA)	None	• Charlotte (1988–)
Chicago Bulls	1966-67	(NBA)	6 NBA (1991-93,96-98)	• Chicago (1966–)
Cleveland Cavaliers	1970-71	(NBA)	None	• Cleveland (1970-74) Richfield, OH (1974-94) Cleveland (1994–)
Detroit Pistons	1941-42	(NBL)	2 NBL (1944-45) 2 NBA (1989-90)	• Ft. Wayne, IN (1941-57) Detroit (1957-78) Pontiac, MI (1978-88) Auburn Hills, MI (1988–)
Indiana Pacers	1967-68	(ABA)	3 ABA (1970,72-73)	• Indianapolis (1967–)
Miami Heat	1988-89	(NBA)	None	• Miami (1988–)
Milwaukee Bucks	1968-69	(NBA)	1 NBA (1971)	• Milwaukee (1968–)
New Jersey Nets	1967-68	(ABA)	2 ABA (1974,76)	• Teaneck, NJ (1967-68) Commack, NY (1968-69) W. Hempstead, NY (1969-71) Uniondale, NY (1971-77) Piscataway, NJ (1977-81) E. Rutherford, NJ (1981–)
New York Knicks	1946-47	(BAA)	2 NBA (1970,73)	• New York (1946–)
Orlando Magic	1989-90	(NBA)	None	• Orlando, FL (1989–)
Philadelphia 76ers	1949-50	(NBA)	3 NBA (1955,67,83)	• Syracuse, NY (1949-63) Philadelphia (1963–)
Toronto Raptors	1995-96	(NBA)	None	• Toronto (1995–)
Washington Wizards	1961-62	(NBA)	1 NBA (1978)	• Chicago (1961-63) Baltimore (1963-73) Landover, MD (1973–)

Note: The Tri-Cities Blackhawks represented Moline and Rock Island, Ill., and Davenport, Iowa.

The Growth of the NBA

Of the 11 franchises that comprised the Basketball Association of America (BAA) at the start of the 1946-47 season, only three remain—the Boston Celtics, New York Knickerbockers and Golden State Warriors (originally Philadelphia Warriors).

Just before the start of the 1948-49 season, four teams from the more established **National Basketball League** (NBL)—the Ft. Wayne Pistons (now Detroit), Indianapolis Jets, Minneapolis Lakers (now Los Angeles) and Rochester Royals (now Sacramento Kings)—joined the BAA.

A year later, the six remaining NBL franchises—Anderson (Ind.), Denver, Sheboygan (Wisc.), the Syracuse Nationals (now Philadelphia 76ers), Tri-Cities Blackhawks (now Atlanta Hawks) and Waterloo (Iowa)—joined along with the new Indianapolis Olympians and the BAA became the 17-team **National Basketball Association**.

The NBA was down to 10 teams by the 1950-51 season and slipped to eight by 1954-55 with Boston, New York, Philadelphia and Syracuse in the Eastern Division, and Ft. Wayne, Milwaukee (formerly Tri-Cities), Minneapolis and Rochester in the West.

By 1960, five of those surviving eight teams had moved to other cities but by the end of the decade the NBA was a 14-team league. It also had a rival, the **American Basketball Association**, which began play in 1967 with a red, white and blue ball, a three-point line and 11 teams. After a nine-year run, the ABA merged four clubs—the Denver Nuggets, Indiana Pacers, New York Nets and San Antonio Spurs—with the NBA following the 1975-76 season. The NBA adopted the three-point play in 1979-80.

Expansion/Merger Timetable

For teams currently in NBA.

1948—Added NBL's Ft. Wayne Pistons (now Detroit), Minneapolis Lakers (now Los Angeles) and Rochester Royals (now Sacramento Kings); **1949**—Syracuse Nationals (now Philadelphia 76ers) and Tri-Cities Blackhawks (now Atlanta Hawks).

1961—Chicago Packers (now Washington Wizards); **1966**—Chicago Bulls; **1967**—San Diego Rockets (now Houston) and Seattle SuperSonics; **1968**—Milwaukee Bucks and Phoenix Suns.

1970—Buffalo Braves (now Los Angeles Clippers), Cleveland Cavaliers and Portland Trail Blazers; **1974**—New Orleans Jazz (now Utah); **1976**—added ABA's Denver Nuggets, Indiana Pacers, New York Nets (now New Jersey) and San Antonio Spurs.

1980—Dallas Mavericks; **1988**—Charlotte Hornets and Miami Heat; **1989**—Minnesota Timberwolves and Orlando Magic.

1995—Toronto Raptors and Vancouver Grizzlies.

City and Nickname Changes

1951—Tri-Cities Blackhawks, who divided home games between Moline and Rock Island, Ill., and Davenport, Iowa, move to Milwaukee and become the Hawks; **1955**—Milwaukee Hawks move to St. Louis; **1957**—Ft. Wayne Pistons move to Detroit, while Rochester Royals move to Cincinnati.

1960—Minneapolis Lakers move to Los Angeles; **1962**—Chicago Packers renamed Zephyrs, while Philadelphia Warriors move to San Francisco; **1963**—Chicago Zephyrs move to Baltimore and become Bullets, while Syracuse Nationals move to Philadelphia and become 76ers; **1968**—St. Louis Hawks move to Atlanta.

1971—San Diego Rockets move to Houston, while San Francisco Warriors move to Oakland and become Golden State Warriors; **1972**—Cincinnati Royals move to Midwest, divide home games between Kansas City, Mo., and Omaha, Neb., and become Kings; **1973**—Baltimore Bullets move to Landover, Md., outside Washington and become Capital Bullets; **1974**—Capital Bullets renamed Washington Bullets; **1975**—KC-Omaha Kings settle in Kansas City; **1977**—New York Nets move from Uniondale, N.Y., to Piscataway, N.J. (later East Rutherford) and become New Jersey Nets; **1978**—Buffalo Braves move to San Diego and become Clippers; **1979**—New Orleans Jazz move to Salt Lake City and become Utah Jazz.

1984—San Diego Clippers move to Los Angeles; **1985**—Kansas City Kings move to Sacramento; **1997**—Washington Bullets become Washington Wizards.

Defunct NBA Teams

Teams that once played in the BAA and NBA, but no longer exist.
Anderson (Ind.)—Packers (1949-50); **Baltimore**—Bullets (1947-55); **Chicago**—Stags (1946-50); **Cleveland**—Rebels (1946-47); **Denver**—Nuggets (1949-50); **Detroit**—Falcons (1946-47); **Indianapolis**—Jets (1948-49) and Olympians (1949-53); **Pittsburgh**—Ironmen (1946-47); **Providence**—Steamrollers (1946-49); **St. Louis**—Bombers (1946-50); **Sheboygan (Wisc.)**—Redskins (1949-50); **Toronto**—Huskies (1946-47); **Washington**—Capitols (1946-51); **Waterloo (Iowa)**—Hawks (1949-50).

ABA Teams (1967-76)

Anaheim—Amigos (1967-68, moved to LA); **Baltimore**—Claws (1975, never played); **Carolina**—Cougars (1969-74, moved to St. Louis); **Dallas**—Chaparrals (1967-73, called Texas Chaparrals in 1970-71, moved to San Antonio); **Denver**—Rockets (1967-76, renamed Nuggets in 1974-76); **Miami**—Floridians (1968-72, called simply Floridians from 1970-72).

Houston—Mavericks (1967-69, moved to North Carolina); **Indiana**—Pacers (1967-76); **Kentucky**—Colonels (1967-76); **Los Angeles**—Stars (1968-70, moved to Utah); **Memphis**—Pros (1970-75, renamed Tams in 1972 and Sounds in 1974, moved to Baltimore); **Minnesota**—Muskies (1967-68, moved to Miami) and Pipers (1968-69, moved back to Pittsburgh); **New Jersey**—Americans (1967-68, moved to New York).

New Orleans—Buccaneers (1967-70, moved to Memphis); **New York**—Nets (1968-76); **Oakland**—Oaks (1967-69, moved to Washington); **Pittsburgh**—Pipers (1967-68, moved to Minnesota), Pipers 1969-72, renamed Condors in 1970); **St. Louis**—Spirits of St. Louis (1974-76); **San Antonio**—Spurs (1973-76); **San Diego**—Conquistadors (1972-75, renamed Sails in 1975); **Utah**—Stars (1970-75); **Virginia**—Squires (1970-76); **Washington**—Caps (1969-70, moved to Virginia).

Annual NBA Leaders
Scoring

Decided by total points from 1947-69, and per game average since 1970.

Multiple winners: Michael Jordan (10); Wilt Chamberlain (7); George Gervin (4); Neil Johnston, Bob McAdoo and George Mikan (3); Kareem Abdul-Jabbar, Paul Arizin, Adrian Dantley and Bob Pettit (2).

Year		Gm	Pts	Avg	Year		Gm	Pts	Avg
1947	Joe Fulks, Phi	60	1389	23.2	1974	Bob McAdoo, Buf	74	2261	30.6
1948	Max Zaslofsky, Chi	48	1007	21.0	1975	Bob McAdoo, Buf	82	2831	34.5
1949	George Mikan, Mpls	60	1698	28.3	1976	Bob McAdoo, Buf	78	2427	31.1
1950	George Mikan, Mpls	68	1865	27.4	1977	Pete Maravich, NO	73	2273	31.1
1951	George Mikan, Mpls	68	1932	28.4	1978	George Gervin, SA	82	2232	27.2
1952	Paul Arizin, Phi	66	1674	25.4	1979	George Gervin, SA	80	2365	29.6
1953	Neil Johnston, Phi	70	1564	22.3	1980	George Gervin, SA	78	2585	33.1
1954	Neil Johnston, Phi	72	1759	24.4	1981	Adrian Dantley, Utah.	80	2452	30.7
1955	Neil Johnston, Phi	72	1631	22.7	1982	George Gervin, SA	79	2551	32.3
1956	Bob Pettit, St.L	72	1849	25.7	1983	Alex English, Den	82	2326	28.4
1957	Paul Arizin, Phi	71	1817	25.6	1984	Adrian Dantley, Utah.	79	2418	30.6
1958	George Yardley, Det	72	2001	27.8	1985	Bernard King, NY	55	1809	32.9
1959	Bob Pettit, St.L	72	2105	29.2	1986	Dominique Wilkins, Atl	78	2366	30.3
1960	Wilt Chamberlain, Phi	72	2707	37.6	1987	Michael Jordan, Chi	82	3041	37.1
1961	Wilt Chamberlain, Phi	79	3033	38.4	1988	Michael Jordan, Chi	82	2868	35.0
1962	Wilt Chamberlain, Phi	80	4029	50.4	1989	Michael Jordan, Chi	81	2633	32.5
1963	Wilt Chamberlain, SF	80	3586	44.8	1990	Michael Jordan, Chi	82	2753	33.6
1964	Wilt Chamberlain, SF	80	2948	36.9	1991	Michael Jordan, Chi	82	2580	31.5
1965	Wilt Chamberlain, SF-Phi	73	2534	34.7	1992	Michael Jordan, Chi	80	2404	30.1
1966	Wilt Chamberlain, Phi	79	2649	33.5	1993	Michael Jordan, Chi	78	2541	32.6
1967	Rick Barry, SF	78	2775	35.6	1994	David Robinson, SA	80	2383	29.8
1968	Dave Bing, Det	79	2142	27.1	1995	Shaquille O'Neal, Orl	79	2315	29.3
1969	Elvin Hayes, SD	82	2327	28.4	1996	Michael Jordan, Chi	82	2491	30.4
1970	Jerry West, LA	74	2309	31.2	1997	Michael Jordan, Chi	82	2431	29.7
1971	Lew Alcindor, Mil	82	2596	31.7	1998	Michael Jordan, Chi	82	2357	28.7
1972	Kareem Abdul-Jabbar, Mil	81	2822	34.8	1999	Allen Iverson, Phi	48	1284	26.8
1973	Nate Archibald, KC-Omaha	80	2719	34.0					

Note: Lew Alcindor changed his name to Kareem Abdul-Jabbar after the 1970-71 season.

Rebounds

Decided by total rebounds from 1951-69 and per game average since 1970.

Multiple winners: Wilt Chamberlain (11); Dennis Rodman (7); Moses Malone (6); Bill Russell (4); Elvin Hayes and Hakeem Olajuwon (2).

Year		Gm	No	Avg	Year		Gm	No	Avg
1951	Dolph Schayes, Syr	66	1080	16.4	1976	Kareem Abdul-Jabbar, LA	82	1383	16.9
1952	Larry Foust, Ft. Wayne	66	880	13.3	1977	Bill Walton, Port.	65	934	14.4
	& Mel Hutchins, Mil	66	880	13.3	1978	Len Robinson, NO	82	1288	15.7
1953	George Mikan, Mpls	70	1007	14.4	1979	Moses Malone, Hou	82	1444	17.6
1954	Harry Gallatin, NY	72	1098	15.3	1980	Swen Nater, SD	81	1216	15.0
1955	Neil Johnston, Phi	72	1085	15.1	1981	Moses Malone, Hou	80	1180	14.8
1956	Bob Pettit, St.L	72	1164	16.2	1982	Moses Malone, Hou	81	1188	14.7
1957	Maurice Stokes, Roch	72	1256	17.4	1983	Moses Malone, Phi	78	1194	15.3
1958	Bill Russell, Bos	69	1564	22.7	1984	Moses Malone, Phi	71	950	13.4
1959	Bill Russell, Bos	70	1612	23.0	1985	Moses Malone, Phi	79	1031	13.1
1960	Wilt Chamberlain, Phi	72	1941	27.0	1986	Bill Laimbeer, Det	82	1075	13.1
1961	Wilt Chamberlain, Phi	79	2149	27.2	1987	Charles Barkley, Phi	68	994	14.6
1962	Wilt Chamberlain, Phi	80	2052	25.7	1988	Michael Cage, LA Clippers	72	938	13.0
1963	Wilt Chamberlain, SF	80	1946	24.3	1989	Hakeem Olajuwon, Hou	82	1105	13.5
1964	Bill Russell, Bos	78	1930	24.7	1990	Hakeem Olajuwon, Hou	82	1149	14.0
1965	Bill Russell, Bos	78	1878	24.1	1991	David Robinson, SA	82	1063	13.0
1966	Wilt Chamberlain, Phi	79	1943	24.6	1992	Dennis Rodman, Det	82	1530	18.7
1967	Wilt Chamberlain, Phi	81	1957	24.2	1993	Dennis Rodman, Det	62	1232	18.3
1968	Wilt Chamberlain, Phi	82	1952	23.8	1994	Dennis Rodman, SA	79	1132	17.3
1969	Wilt Chamberlain, LA	81	1712	21.1	1995	Dennis Rodman, SA	49	823	16.8
1970	Elvin Hayes, SD	82	1386	16.9	1996	Dennis Rodman, Chi	64	952	14.9
1971	Wilt Chamberlain, LA	82	1493	18.2	1997	Dennis Rodman, Chi	55	883	16.1
1972	Wilt Chamberlain, LA	82	1572	19.2	1998	Dennis Rodman, Chi	80	1201	15.0
1973	Wilt Chamberlain, LA	82	1526	18.6	1999	Chris Webber, Sac	42	545	13.0
1974	Elvin Hayes, Cap*	81	1463	18.1					
1975	Wes Unseld, Wash	73	1077	14.8					

*The Baltimore Bullets moved to Landover, MD in 1973-74 and became first the Capital Bullets, then the Washington Bullets in 1974-75.

Assists

Decided by total assists from 1952-69 and per game average since 1970.

Multiple winners: John Stockton (9); Bob Cousy (8); Oscar Robertson (6); Magic Johnson and Kevin Porter (4); Andy Phillip and Guy Rodgers (2).

Year		No	Year		No	Year		No
1947	Ernie Calverly, Prov	202	1965	Oscar Robertson, Cin	861	1983	Magic Johnson, LA	10.5
1948	Howie Dallmar, Phi	120	1966	Oscar Robertson, Cin	847	1984	Magic Johnson, LA	13.1
1949	Bob Davies, Roch	321	1967	Guy Rodgers, Chi	908	1985	Isiah Thomas, Det	13.9
			1968	Wilt Chamberlain, Phi	702	1986	Magic Johnson, Lakers	12.6
1950	Dick McGuire, NY	386	1969	Oscar Robertson, Cin	772	1987	Magic Johnson, Lakers	12.2
1951	Andy Phillip, Phi	414				1988	John Stockton, Utah	13.8
1952	Andy Phillip, Phi	539	1970	Lenny Wilkens, Sea	9.1	1989	John Stockton, Utah	13.6
1953	Bob Cousy, Bos	547	1971	Norm Van Lier, Chi	10.1			
1954	Bob Cousy, Bos	518	1972	Jerry West, LA	9.7	1990	John Stockton, Utah	14.5
1955	Bob Cousy, Bos	557	1973	Nate Archibald, KC-O	11.4	1991	John Stockton, Utah	14.2
1956	Bob Cousy, Bos	642	1974	Ernie DiGregorio, Buf	8.2	1992	John Stockton, Utah	13.7
1957	Bob Cousy, Bos	478	1975	Kevin Porter, Wash	8.0	1993	John Stockton, Utah	12.0
1958	Bob Cousy, Bos	463	1976	Slick Watts, Sea	8.1	1994	John Stockton, Utah	12.6
1959	Bob Cousy, Bos	557	1977	Don Buse, Ind	8.5	1995	John Stockton, Utah	12.3
			1978	Kevin Porter, Det-NJ	10.2	1996	John Stockton, Utah	11.2
1960	Bob Cousy, Bos	715	1979	Kevin Porter, Det	13.4	1997	Mark Jackson, Den-Ind	11.4
1961	Oscar Robertson, Cin	690				1998	Rod Strickland, Wash	10.5
1962	Oscar Robertson, Cin	899	1980	M.R. Richardson, NY	10.1	1999	Jason Kidd, Pho	10.8
1963	Guy Rodgers, SF	825	1981	Kevin Porter, Wash	9.1			
1964	Oscar Robertson, Cin	868	1982	Johnny Moore, SA	9.6			

Field Goal Percentage

Multiple winners: Wilt Chamberlain (9); Artis Gilmore (4); Neil Johnston and Shaquille O'Neal (3); Bob Feerick, Johnny Green, Alex Groza, Cedric Maxwell, Kevin McHale, Gheorghe Muresan, Kenny Sears and Buck Williams (2).

Year		Pct	Year		Pct	Year		Pct
1947	Bob Feerick, Wash	.401	1965	W. Chamberlain, SF-Phi	.510	1983	Artis Gilmore, SA	.626
1948	Bob Feerick, Wash	.340	1966	Wilt Chamberlain, Phi	.540	1984	Artis Gilmore, SA	.631
1949	Arnie Risen, Roch	.423	1967	Wilt Chamberlain, Phi	.683	1985	James Donaldson, LAC	.637
			1968	Wilt Chamberlain, Phi	.595	1986	Steve Johnson, SA	.632
1950	Alex Groza, Indpls	.478	1969	Wilt Chamberlain, LA	.583	1987	Kevin McHale, Bos	.604
1951	Alex Groza, Indpls	.470				1988	Kevin McHale, Bos	.604
1952	Paul Arizin, Phi	.448	1970	Johnny Green, Cin	.559	1989	Dennis Rodman, Det.	.595
1953	Neil Johnston, Phi	.452	1971	Johnny Green, Cin	.587			
1954	Ed Macauley, Bos	.486	1972	Wilt Chamberlain, LA	.649	1990	Mark West, Pho.	.625
1955	Larry Foust, Ft.W	.487	1973	Wilt Chamberlain, LA	.727	1991	Buck Williams, Port	.602
1956	Neil Johnston, Phi	.457	1974	Bob McAdoo, Buf	.547	1992	Buck Williams, Port	.604
1957	Neil Johnston, Phi	.447	1975	Don Nelson, Bos	.539	1993	Cedric Ceballos, Pho	.576
1958	Jack Twyman, Cin	.452	1976	Wes Unseld, Wash	.561	1994	Shaquille O'Neal, Orl	.599
1959	Kenny Sears, NY	.490	1977	K. Abdul-Jabbar, LA	.579	1995	Chris Gatling, G.St	.633
			1978	Bobby Jones, Den	.578	1996	Gheorghe Muresan, Wash.	.584
1960	Kenny Sears, NY	.477	1979	Cedric Maxwell, Bos	.584	1997	Gheorghe Muresan, Wash.	.604
1961	Wilt Chamberlain, Phi	.509				1998	Shaquille O'Neal, LAL	.584
1962	Walt Bellamy, Chi	.519	1980	Cedric Maxwell, Bos	.609	1999	Shaquille O'Neal, LAL	.576
1963	Wilt Chamberlain, SF	.528	1981	Artis Gilmore, Chi.	.670			
1964	Jerry Lucas, Cin	.527	1982	Artis Gilmore, Chi.	.652			

Free Throw Percentage

Multiple winners: Bill Sharman (7); Larry Bird (6); Rick Barry and Dolph Schayes (3); Mahmoud Abdul-Rauf, Larry Costello, Ernie DiGregorio, Bob Feerick, Kyle Macy, Reggie Miller, Calvin Murphy, Oscar Robertson and Larry Siegfried (2).

Year		Pct	Year		Pct	Year		Pct
1947	Fred Scolari, Wash	.811	1965	Larry Costello, Phi	.877	1983	Calvin Murphy, Hou	.920
1948	Bob Feerick, Wash	.788	1966	Larry Siegfried, Bos	.881	1984	Larry Bird, Bos	.888
1949	Bob Feerick, Wash	.859	1967	Adrian Smith, Cin	.903	1985	Kyle Macy, Pho	.907
			1968	Oscar Robertson, Cin	.873	1986	Larry Bird, Bos	.896
1950	Max Zaslofsky, Chi	.843	1969	Larry Siegfried, NY	.864	1987	Larry Bird, Bos	.910
1951	Joe Fulks, Phi	.855				1988	Jack Sikma, Mil	.922
1952	Bob Wanzer, Roch	.904	1970	Flynn Robinson, Mil	.898	1989	Magic Johnson, LAL	.911
1953	Bill Sharman, Bos	.850	1971	Chet Walker, Chi	.859			
1954	Bill Sharman, Bos	.844	1972	Jack Marin, Bal	.894	1990	Larry Bird, Bos	.930
1955	Bill Sharman, Bos	.897	1973	Rick Barry, G.St.	.902	1991	Reggie Miller, Ind	.918
1956	Bill Sharman, Bos	.867	1974	Ernie DiGregorio, Buf	.902	1992	Mark Price, Cle	.947
1957	Bill Sharman, Bos	.905	1975	Rick Barry, G.St.	.904	1993	Mark Price, Cle	.948
1958	Dolph Schayes, Syr	.904	1976	Rick Barry, G.St.	.923	1994	M. Abdul-Rauf, Den	.956
1959	Bill Sharman, Bos	.932	1977	Ernie DiGregorio, Buf	.945	1995	Spud Webb, Sac	.934
			1978	Rick Barry, G.St.	.924	1996	M. Abdul-Rauf, Den	.930
1960	Dolph Schayes, Syr	.892	1979	Rick Barry, Hou	.947	1997	Mark Price, G.St.	.906
1961	Bill Sharman, Bos	.921				1998	Chris Mullin, Ind.	.939
1962	Dolph Schayes, Syr	.896	1980	Rick Barry, Hou	.935	1999	Reggie Miller, Ind	.915
1963	Larry Costello, Syr	.881	1981	Calvin Murphy, Hou	.958			
1964	Oscar Robertson, Cin	.853	1982	Kyle Macy, Pho	.899			

Blocked Shots

Decided by per game average since 1973-74 season.

Multiple winners: Kareem Abdul-Jabbar and Mark Eaton (4); George Johnson, Dikembe Mutombo and Hakeem Olajuwon (3); Manute Bol (2).

Year		Gm	No	Avg
1974	Elmore Smith, LA	.81	393	4.85
1975	Kareem Abdul-Jabbar, Mil	.65	212	3.26
1976	Kareem Abdul-Jabbar, LA	.82	338	4.12
1977	Bill Walton, Port	.65	211	3.25
1978	George Johnson, NJ	.81	274	3.38
1979	Kareem Abdul-Jabbar, LA	.80	316	3.95
1980	Kareem Abdul-Jabbar, LA	.82	280	3.41
1981	George Johnson, SA	.82	278	3.39
1982	George Johnson, SA	.75	234	3.12
1983	Tree Rollins, Atl	.80	343	4.29
1984	Mark Eaton, Utah	.82	351	4.28
1985	Mark Eaton, Utah	.82	456	5.56
1986	Manute Bol, Wash	.80	397	4.96
1987	Mark Eaton, Utah	.79	321	4.06
1988	Mark Eaton, Utah	.82	304	3.71
1989	Manute Bol, G.St.	.80	345	4.31
1990	Akeem Olajuwon, Hou	.82	376	4.59
1991	Hakeem Olajuwon, Hou	.56	221	3.95
1992	David Robinson, SA	.68	305	4.49
1993	Hakeem Olajuwon, Hou	.82	342	4.17
1994	Dikembe Mutombo, Den	.82	336	4.10
1995	Dikembe Mutombo, Den	.82	321	3.91
1996	Dikembe Mutombo, Den	.74	332	4.49
1997	Shawn Bradley, Dal-NJ	.73	248	3.40
1998	Marcus Camby, Tor	.63	230	3.65
1999	Alonzo Mourning, Mia	.46	180	3.91

Note: Akeem Olajuwon changed the spelling of his first name to Hakeem during the 1990-91 season.

Steals

Decided by per game average since 1973-74 season.

Multiple winners: Michael Jordan, Micheal Ray Richardson and Alvin Robertson (3); Mookie Blaylock, Magic Johnson and John Stockton (2).

Year		Gm	No	Avg
1974	Larry Steele, Port	.81	217	2.68
1975	Rick Barry, G.St.	.80	228	2.85
1976	Slick Watts, Sea	.82	261	3.18
1977	Don Buse, Ind	.81	281	3.47
1978	Ron Lee, Pho	.82	225	2.74
1979	M.L. Carr, Det	.80	197	2.46
1980	Micheal Ray Richardson, NY	.82	265	3.23
1981	Magic Johnson, LA	.37	127	3.43
1982	Magic Johnson, LA	.78	208	2.67
1983	Micheal Ray Richardson, G. ST-NJ	.64	182	2.84
1984	Rickey Green, Utah	.81	215	2.65
1985	Micheal Ray Richardson, NJ	.82	243	2.96
1986	Alvin Robertson, SA	.82	301	3.67
1987	Alvin Robertson, SA	.81	260	3.21
1988	Michael Jordan, Chi	.82	259	3.16
1989	John Stockton, Utah	.82	263	3.21
1990	Michael Jordan, Chi	.82	227	2.77
1991	Alvin Robertson, SA	.81	246	3.04
1992	John Stockton, Utah	.82	244	2.98
1993	Michael Jordan, Chi	.78	221	2.83
1994	Nate McMillan, Sea	.73	216	2.96
1995	Scottie Pippen, Chi	.79	232	2.94
1996	Gary Payton, Sea	.81	231	2.85
1997	Mookie Blaylock, Atl.	.78	212	2.72
1998	Mookie Blaylock, Atl.	.70	183	2.61
1999	Kendall Gill, NJ	.50	134	2.68

All-Time NBA Regular Season Leaders

Through the 1999 regular season.

CAREER

Players active in 1999 in **bold** type.

Points

		Yrs	Gm	Pts	Avg
1	Kareem Abdul-Jabbar	20	1560	38,387	24.6
2	Wilt Chamberlain	14	1045	31,419	30.1
3	Michael Jordan	13	930	29,277	31.5
4	**Karl Malone**	14	1110	28,946	26.1
5	Moses Malone	19	1329	27,409	20.6
6	Elvin Hayes	16	1303	27,313	21.0
7	Oscar Robertson	14	1040	26,710	25.7
8	**Dominique Wilkins**	15	1074	26,668	24.8
9	John Havlicek	16	1270	26,395	20.8
10	Alex English	15	1193	25,613	21.5
11	**Hakeem Olajuwon**	15	1075	25,367	23.6
12	Jerry West	14	932	25,192	27.0
13	**Charles Barkley**	15	1053	23,468	22.3
14	Robert Parish	21	1611	23,334	14.5
15	Adrian Dantley	15	955	23,177	24.3
16	Elgin Baylor	14	846	23,149	27.4
17	**Patrick Ewing**	14	977	22,736	23.3
18	Clyde Drexler	15	1086	22,195	20.4
19	Larry Bird	13	897	21,791	24.3
20	Hal Greer	15	1122	21,586	19.2
21	Walt Bellamy	14	1043	20,941	20.1
22	Bob Pettit	11	792	20,880	26.4
23	George Gervin	10	791	20,708	26.2
24	**Tom Chambers**	16	1107	20,049	18.1
25	Bernard King	14	874	19,655	22.5
26	Walter Davis	15	1033	19,521	18.9
27	Bob Lanier	14	959	19,248	20.1
28	Dolph Schayes	16	1059	19,247	18.2
29	**Eddie Johnson**	17	1199	19,202	16.0
30	Gail Goodrich	14	1031	19,181	18.6

Scoring Average

Minimum of 400 games and 10,000 points.

		Yrs	Gm	Pts	Avg
1	Michael Jordan	13	930	29,277	31.5
2	Wilt Chamberlain	14	1045	31,419	30.1
3	Elgin Baylor	14	846	23,149	27.4
4	**Shaquille O'Neal**	7	455	12,343	27.1
5	Jerry West	14	932	25,192	27.0
6	Bob Pettit	11	792	20,880	26.4
7	George Gervin	10	791	20,708	26.2
8	**Karl Malone**	14	1110	28,946	26.1
9	Oscar Robertson	14	1040	26,710	25.7
10	**Dominique Wilkins**	15	1074	26,668	24.8
11	Kareem Abdul-Jabbar	20	1560	38,387	24.6
12	**David Robinson**	10	685	16,715	24.4
13	Larry Bird	13	897	21,791	24.3
14	Adrian Dantley	15	955	23,177	24.3
15	Pete Maravich	10	658	15,948	24.2
16	**Hakeem Olajuwon**	15	1075	25,367	23.6
17	**Patrick Ewing**	14	977	22,736	23.3
18	Rick Barry	10	794	18,395	23.2
19	**Mitch Richmond**	11	801	18,354	22.9
20	Paul Arizin	10	713	16,266	22.8
21	George Mikan	9	520	11,764	22.6
22	Bernard King	14	874	19,655	22.5
23	**Charles Barkley**	15	1053	23,468	22.3
24	David Thompson	8	509	11,264	22.1
25	Bob McAdoo	14	852	18,787	22.1
26	Julius Erving	11	836	18,364	22.0
27	Alex English	15	1193	25,613	21.5
28	Elvin Hayes	16	1303	27,313	21.0
29	Billy Cunningham	9	654	13,626	20.8
30	John Havlicek	16	1270	26,395	20.8

NBA-ABA Top 20

Points

All-Time combined regular season scoring leaders, including ABA service (1968-76). NBA players with ABA experience are listed in CAPITAL letters. Players active during 1996-97 are in **bold** type.

		Yrs	Pts	Avg
1	Kareem Abdul-Jabbar	20	38,387	24.6
2	Wilt Chamberlain	14	31,419	30.1
3	JULIUS ERVING	16	30,026	24.2
4	MOSES MALONE	21	29,580	20.3
5	Michael Jordan	13	29,277	31.5
6	**Karl Malone**	14	28,946	26.1
7	DAN ISSEL	15	27,482	22.6
8	Elvin Hayes	16	27,313	21.0
9	Oscar Robertson	14	26,710	25.7
10	**Dominique Wilkins**	15	26,668	24.8
11	GEORGE GERVIN	14	26,595	25.1
12	John Havlicek	16	26,395	20.8
13	Alex English	15	25,613	21.5
14	**Hakeem Olajuwon**	15	25,367	23.6
15	RICK BARRY	14	25,279	24.8
16	Jerry West	14	25,192	27.0
17	ARTIS GILMORE	17	24,941	18.8
18	Robert Parish	21	23,334	14.5
19	Adrian Dantley	15	23,177	24.3
20	Elgin Baylor	14	23,149	27.4

ABA Totals: BARRY (4 yrs, 226 gm, 6884 pts, 30.5 avg); ERVING (5 yrs, 407 gm, 11,662 pts, 28.7 avg); GERVIN (4 yrs, 269 gm, 5887 pts, 21.9 avg); GILMORE (5 yrs, 420 gm, 9362 pts, 22.3 avg); ISSEL (6 yrs, 500 gm, 12,823 pts, 25.6 avg); MALONE (2 yrs, 126 gm, 2171 pts, 17.2 avg).

Field Goals

		Yrs	FG	Att	Pct
1	Kareem Abdul-Jabbar	20	15,837	28,307	.559
2	Wilt Chamberlain	14	12,681	23,497	.540
3	Elvin Hayes	16	10,976	24,272	.452
4	Michael Jordan	13	10,958	21,686	.505
5	**Karl Malone**	14	10,683	20,301	.526
6	Alex English	15	10,659	21,036	.507
7	John Havlicek	16	10,513	23,930	.439
8	**Hakeem Olajuwon**	15	10,079	19,584	.515
9	**Dominique Wilkins**	15	9,963	21,589	.461
10	Robert Parish	21	9,614	17,914	.537

Note: If field goals made in the ABA are included, consider these NBA-ABA totals: Julius Erving (11,818), Dan Issel (10,431), George Gervin (10,368), Moses Malone (10,277) and Rick Barry (9,695).

Free Throws

		Yrs	FT	Att	Pct
1	Moses Malone	19	8531	11,090	.769
2	Oscar Robertson	14	7694	9,185	.838
3	**Karl Malone**	14	7511	10,288	.730
4	Jerry West	14	7160	8,801	.814
5	Dolph Schayes	16	6979	8,273	.844
6	Adrian Dantley	15	6832	8,351	.818
7	Michael Jordan	13	6798	8,115	.838
8	Kareem Abdul-Jabbar	20	6712	9,304	.721
9	**Charles Barkley**	13	6278	8,533	.736
10	Bob Pettit	11	6182	8,119	.761

Note: If free throws made in the ABA are included, consider these totals: Moses Malone (9,018), Dan Issel (6,591), Julius Erving (6,256) and Artis Gilmore (6,132).

Assists

		Yrs	Gm	No	Avg
1	**John Stockton**	15	1176	13,087	11.1
2	Magic Johnson	13	906	10,141	11.2
3	Oscar Robertson	14	1040	9,887	9.5
4	Isiah Thomas	13	979	9,061	9.3
5	**Mark Jackson**	12	926	7,924	8.6
6	Maurice Cheeks	15	1101	7,392	6.7
7	Lenny Wilkens	15	1077	7,211	6.7
8	Bob Cousy	14	924	6,955	7.5
9	Guy Rodgers	12	892	6,917	7.8
10	Kevin Johnson	11	729	6,687	9.2

Rebounds

		Yrs	Gm	No	Avg
1	Wilt Chamberlain	14	1045	23,924	22.9
2	Bill Russell	13	963	21,620	22.5
3	Kareem Abdul-Jabbar	20	1560	17,440	11.2
4	Elvin Hayes	16	1303	16,279	12.5
5	Moses Malone	19	1329	16,212	12.2
6	Robert Parish	21	1611	14,715	9.1
7	Nate Thurmond	14	964	14,464	15.0
8	Walt Bellamy	14	1043	14,241	13.7
9	Wes Unseld	13	984	13,769	14.0
10	Buck Williams	17	1307	13,017	10.0

Note: If rebounds accumulated in the ABA are included, consider the following totals: Moses Malone (17,834) and Artis Gilmore (16,330).

Steals

		Yrs	Gm	No
1	**John Stockton**	15	1176	2701
2	Maurice Cheeks	15	1101	2310
3	Michael Jordan	13	930	2306
4	Clyde Drexler	15	1086	2207
5	Alvin Robertson	10	779	2112

Note: Steals have only been an official stat since the 1973-74 season.

Blocked Shots

		Yrs	Gm	No
1	**Hakeem Olajuwon**	15	1075	3582
2	Kareem Abdul-Jabbar	20	1560	3189
3	Mark Eaton	11	875	3064
4	**Patrick Ewing**	14	977	2674
5	Tree Rollins	18	1156	2542

Note: Blocked shots have only been an official stat since the 1973-74 season. Also, note that if ABA records are included, consider the following block totals: Artis Gilmore (3,178).

Games Played

		Yrs	Career	Gm
1	Robert Parish	21	1976-97	1611
2	Kareem Abdul-Jabbar	20	1970-89	1560
3	Moses Malone	19	1976-95	1329
4	Buck Williams	17	1982-98	1307
5	Elvin Hayes	16	1969-84	1303

Note: If ABA records are included, consider the following game totals: Moses Malone (1,455) and Artis Gilmore (1,329).

Personal Fouls

		Yrs	Gm	Fouls	DQ
1	Kareem Abdul-Jabbar	20	1560	4657	48
2	Robert Parish	21	1611	4443	86
3	Buck Williams	17	1307	4267	58
4	Elvin Hayes	16	1303	4193	53
5	James Edwards	19	1168	4042	96

Note: If ABA records are included, consider the following personal foul totals: Artis Gilmore (4,529) and Caldwell Jones (4,436).

SINGLE SEASON

Scoring Average

		Season	Avg
1	Wilt Chamberlain, Phi	1961-62	50.4
2	Wilt Chamberlain, SF	1962-63	44.8
3	Wilt Chamberlain, Phi	1960-61	38.4
4	Elgin Baylor, LA	1961-62	38.3
5	Wilt Chamberlain, Phi	1959-60	37.6
6	Michael Jordan, Chi	1986-87	37.1
7	Wilt Chamberlain, SF	1963-64	36.9
8	Rick Barry, SF	1966-67	35.6
9	Michael Jordan, Chi	1987-88	35.0
10	Elgin Baylor, LA	1960-61	34.8
	Kareem Abdul-Jabbar, Mil	1971-72	34.8

Field Goal Pct.

		Season	Pct
1	Wilt Chamberlain, LA	1972-73	.727
2	Wilt Chamberlain, SF	1966-67	.683
3	Artis Gilmore, Chi	1980-81	.670
4	Artis Gilmore, Chi	1981-82	.652
5	Wilt Chamberlain, LA	1971-72	.649

Free Throw Pct.

		Season	Pct
1	Calvin Murphy, Hou	1980-81	.958
2	Mahmoud Abdul-Rauf, Den	1993-94	.956
3	Mark Price, Cle	1992-93	.948
4	Mark Price, Cle	1991-92	.947
	Rick Barry, Hou	1978-79	.947

3-Pt Field Goal Pct.

		Season	Pct
1	Steve Kerr, Chi	1994-95	.524
2	Jon Sundvold, Mia	1988-89	.522
3	Tim Legler, Wash	1995-96	.522
4	Steve Kerr, Chi	1995-96	.515
5	Detlef Schrempf, Sea	1994-95	.514

Assists

		Season	Avg
1	John Stockton, Utah	1989-90	14.5
2	John Stockton, Utah	1990-91	14.2
3	Isiah Thomas, Det	1984-85	13.9
4	John Stockton, Utah	1987-88	13.8
5	John Stockton, Utah	1991-92	13.7
6	John Stockton, Utah	1988-89	13.6
7	Kevin Porter, Det	1978-79	13.4
8	Magic Johnson, LA Lakers	1983-84	13.1
9	Magic Johnson, LA Lakers	1988-89	12.8
10	Magic Johnson, LA Lakers	1984-85	12.6
	John Stockton, Utah	1993-94	12.6

Rebounds

		Season	Avg
1	Wilt Chamberlain, Phi	1960-61	27.2
2	Wilt Chamberlain, Phi	1959-60	27.0
3	Wilt Chamberlain, Phi	1961-62	25.7
4	Bill Russell, Bos	1963-64	24.7
5	Wilt Chamberlain, Phi	1965-66	24.6

Blocked Shots

		Season	Avg
1	Mark Eaton, Utah	1984-85	5.56
2	Manute Bol, Wash	1985-86	4.96
3	Elmore Smith, LA	1973-74	4.85
4	Mark Eaton, Utah	1985-86	4.61
5	Hakeem Olajuwon, Hou	1989-90	4.59

Steals

		Season	Avg
1	Alvin Robertson, SA	1985-86	3.67
2	Don Buse, Ind	1976-77	3.47
3	Magic Johnson, LA Lakers	1980-81	3.43
4	Micheal Ray Richardson, NY	1979-80	3.23
5	Alvin Robertson, SA	1986-87	3.21

SINGLE GAME

Points

	Date	FG-FT	Pts
Wilt Chamberlain, Phi vs NY	3/2/62	36-28-	100
Wilt Chamberlain, Phi vs LA***	12/8/61	31-16-	78
Wilt Chamberlain, Phi vs Chi	1/13/62	29-15-	73
Wilt Chamberlain, SF at NY	11/16/62	29-15-	73
David Thompson, Den at Det	4/9/78	28-17-	73
Wilt Chamberlain, SF vs LA	11/3/62	29-14-	72
Elgin Baylor, LA at NY	11/15/60	28-15-	71
David Robinson, SA at LAC	4/24/94	26-18-	71
Wilt Chamberlain, SF at Syr	3/10/63	27-16-	70
Michael Jordan, Chi at Cle*	3/28/90	23-21-	69
Wilt Chamberlain, Phi at Chi	12/16/67	30- 8-	68
Pete Maravich, NO vs NYK	2/25/77	26-16-	68
Wilt Chamberlain, Phi vs NY	3/9/61	27-13-	67
Wilt Chamberlain, Phi at St. L	2/17/62	26-15-	67
Wilt Chamberlain, Phi vs NY	2/25/62	27-15-	67
Wilt Chamberlain, SF vs LA	1/11/63	28-11-	67
Wilt Chamberlain, LA vs Pho	2/9/69	29- 8-	66
Wilt Chamberlain, Phi at Cin	2/13/62	24-17-	65
Wilt Chamberlain, Phi at St. L	2/27/62	25-15-	65
Wilt Chamberlain, Phi vs LA	2/7/66	28- 9-	65
Elgin Baylor, Mpls vs Bos	11/8/59	25-14-	64
Rick Barry, G.St. vs Port	3/26/74	30- 4-	64
Michael Jordan, Chi vs Orl	1/16/93	27- 9-	64

*Overtime
***Triple overtime.
Note: Wilt Chamberlain's 100-point game vs New York was played at Hershey, Pa.

Field Goals

	Date	FG	Att
Wilt Chamberlain, Phi vs NY	3/2/62	36	63
Wilt Chamberlain, Phi vs LA***	12/8/61	31	62
Wilt Chamberlain, Phi at Chi	12/16/67	30	40
Rick Barry, G.St. vs Port	2/26/74	30	45

Wilt Chamberlain made 29 four times.
***Triple overtime.

Free Throws

	Date	FT	Att
Wilt Chamberlain, Phi vs NY	3/2/62	28	32
Adrian Dantley, Utah vs Hou	1/4/84	28	29
Adrian Dantley, Utah vs Den	11/25/83	27	31
Adrian Dantley, Utah vs Dal	10/31/80	26	29
Michael Jordan, Chi vs NJ	2/26/87	26	27

3-Pt Field Goals

	Date	No
Dennis Scott, Orl vs Atl	4/18/96	11
Brian Shaw, Mia at Mil	4/8/93	10
Joe Dumars, Det vs Min	11/8/94	10
George McCloud, Dal vs Pho	12/16/95	10*

Many tied with 9 each
* Overtime

Assists

	Date	No
Scott Skiles, Orl vs Den	12/30/90	30
Kevin Porter, NJ vs Hou	2/24/78	29
Bob Cousy, Bos vs Mpls	2/27/59	28
Guy Rodgers, SF vs St.L	3/14/63	28
John Stockton, Utah vs SA	1/15/91	28

Rebounds

	Date	No
Wilt Chamberlain, Phi vs Bos	11/24/60	55
Bill Russell, Bos vs Syr	2/5/60	51
Bill Russell, Bos vs Phi	11/16/57	49
Bill Russell, Bos vs Det	3/11/65	49
Wilt Chamberlain, Phi vs Syr	2/6/60	45
Wilt Chamberlain, Phi vs LA	1/21/61	45

Blocked Shots

	Date	No
Elmore Smith, LA vs Port	10/28/73	17
Manute Bol, Wash vs Atl	1/25/86	15
Manute Bol, Wash vs Ind	2/26/87	15
Shaquille O'Neal, Orl at NJ	11/20/93	15

Steals

	Date	No
Larry Kenon, San Antonio at KC	12/26/76	11
Kendall Gill, NJ vs Mia.	4/3/99	11

14 different players tied with 10 each, including Alvin Robertson, who had 10 steals in a game four times.

All-Time Winningest NBA Coaches

Top 25 NBA career victories through the 1999 season. Career, regular season and playoff records are noted along with NBA titles won. Coaches active during 1999 season in **bold** type.

			Career			Regular Season			Playoffs			
		Yrs	W	L	Pct	W	L	Pct	W	L	Pct	NBA Titles
1	**Lenny Wilkens**	26	**1223**	1012	.547	1151	927	.554	72	85	.459	1 (1979)
2	**Pat Riley**	17	**1096**	497	.688	947	404	.701	149	93	.616	4 (1982,85,87-88)
3	Red Auerbach	20	**1037**	548	.654	938	479	.662	99	69	.589	9 (1957, 59-66)
4	Bill Fitch	25	**999**	1157	.463	944	1106	.460	55	54	.505	1 (1981)
5	Dick Motta	25	**991**	1087	.477	935	1017	.479	56	70	.444	1 (1978)
6	**Don Nelson**	21	**937**	771	.549	886	710	.555	51	61	.455	None
7	Jack Ramsay	21	**908**	841	.519	864	783	.525	44	58	.431	1 (1977)
8	Cotton Fitzsimmons	21	**867**	824	.513	832	775	.518	35	49	.417	None
9	Gene Shue	22	**814**	908	.473	784	861	.477	30	47	.390	None
10	Red Holzman	18	**754**	652	.536	696	604	.535	58	48	.547	2 (1970, 73)
	John MacLeod	18	**754**	711	.515	707	657	.518	47	54	.465	None
12	**Jerry Sloan**	14	**746**	456	.621	676	392	.633	70	64	.522	None
13	**Larry Brown**	16	**727**	600	.548	683	553	.553	44	47	.484	None
14	**Chuck Daly**	14	**713**	488	.594	638	437	.593	75	51	.595	2 (1989-90)
15	Doug Moe	15	**661**	579	.533	628	529	.543	33	50	.398	None
16	Phil Jackson	9	**656**	234	.737	545	193	.738	111	41	.730	6 (1991-93,96-98)
17	K.C. Jones	10	**603**	309	.661	522	252	.674	81	57	.587	2 (1984,86)
18	Del Harris	14	**594**	507	.540	556	457	.549	38	50	.432	None
19	**Mike Fratello**	14	**592**	499	.543	572	465	.552	20	34	.370	None
20	Al Attles	14	**588**	548	.518	557	518	.518	31	30	.508	1 (1975)
21	**George Karl**	12	**576**	400	.590	531	348	.604	45	52	.464	None
22	Billy Cunningham	8	**520**	235	.689	454	196	.698	66	39	.629	1 (1983)
23	Alex Hannum	12	**518**	446	.536	471	412	.533	47	34	.580	2 (1958, 67)
24	John Kundla	11	**485**	338	.589	423	302	.583	62	36	.633	5 (1949-50, 52-54)
25	Kevin Loughery	17	**480**	683	.413	474	662	.417	6	21	.222	None

Note: The NBA does not recognize records from the National Basketball League (1937-49), the American Basketball League (1961-62) or the American Basketball Assn. (1968-76), so the following NBL, ABL and ABA overall coaching records are not included above: NBL–**John Kundla** (51-19 and a title in 1 year). ABA– **Larry Brown** (249-129 in 4 yrs), **Alex Hannum** (194-164 and one title in 4 yrs), **K.C. Jones** (30-58 in 1 yr); **Kevin Loughery** (189-95 and one title in 3 yrs).

Where They Coached

Attles—Golden St. (1970-80,80-83); **Auerbach**—Washington (1946-49), Tri-Cities (1949-50), Boston (1950-66); **Brown**—Denver (1976-79), New Jersey (1981-83), San Antonio (1988-92), LA Clippers (1992-93), Indiana (1993-97), Philadelphia (1997–); **Cunningham**—Philadelphia (1977-85); **Daly**—Cleveland (1981-82), Detroit (1983-92), New Jersey (1992-94), Orlando (1997-99); **Fitch**—Cleveland (1970-79), Boston (1979-83), Houston (1983-88), New Jersey (1989-92), LA Clippers (1994-98); **Fitzsimmons**—Phoenix (1970-72), Atlanta (1972-76), Buffalo (1977-78), Kansas City (1978-84), San Antonio (1984-86), Phoenix (1988-92, 95-96); **Fratello**—Atlanta (1980-90), Cleveland (1993-99).

Hannum—St. Louis (1957-58), Syracuse (1960-63), San Francisco (1963-66), Phila. 76ers (1966-68), Houston (1970-71); **Harris**—Houston (1979-83), Milwaukee (1987-92), LA Lakers (1994-99); **Holzman**—Milwaukee-St. Louis Hawks (1954-57), NY Knicks (1968-77,78-82); **Jackson**—Chicago (1989-98); **Jones**—Washington (1973-76), Boston (1983-88), Seattle (1990-92), Seattle (1990-92); **Karl**—Cleveland (1984-86); Golden St. (1986-88), Seattle (1991-98), Milwaukee (1999–); **Kundla**—Minneapolis (1948-57,58-59); **Loughery**—Philadelphia (1972-73), NY-NJ Nets (1976-81), Atlanta (1981-83), Chicago (1983-85), Washington (1985-88), Miami (1991-95); **MacLeod**—Phoenix (1973-87), Dallas (1987-89), NY Knicks (1990-91); **Moe**—San Antonio (1976-80), Denver (1981-90), Philadelphia (1992-93).

Motta—Chicago (1968-76), Washington (1976-80), Dallas (1980-87), Sacramento (1990-91), Dallas (1994-96), Denver (1997); **Nelson**—Milwaukee (1976-87), Golden St. (1988-95), New York (1995-96), Dallas (1997–); **Ramsay**—Philadelphia (1968-72), Buffalo (1972-76), Portland (1976-86), Indiana (1986-89); **Riley**—LA Lakers (1981-90), New York (1991-95), Miami (1995–); **Shue**—Baltimore (1967-73), Philadelphia (1973-77), San Diego Clippers (1978-80), Washington (1980-86), LA Clippers (1987-89); **Sloan**—Chicago (1979-82), Utah (1988–); **Wilkens**—Seattle (1969-72), Portland (1974-76), Seattle (1977-85), Cleveland (1986-93), Atlanta (1993–).

Top Winning Percentages

Minimum of 350 victories, including playoffs; coaches active during 1999 season in **bold** type.

		Yrs	W	L	Pct
1	Phil Jackson	9	656	234	**.737**
2	Billy Cunningham	8	520	235	**.689**
3	**Pat Riley**	17	1096	497	**.688**
4	K.C. Jones	10	603	309	**.661**
5	Red Auerbach	20	1037	548	**.654**
6	**Jerry Sloan**	14	746	456	**.621**
7	Tommy Heinsohn	9	474	296	**.616**
8	**Rudy Tomjanovich**	8	404	258	**.610**
9	**Chuck Daly**	14	713	488	**.594**
10	Larry Costello	10	467	323	**.591**
11	**George Karl**	12	576	400	**.590**
12	John Kundla	11	485	338	**.589**
13	Bill Sharman	7	368	267	**.580**
14	**Rick Adelman**	9	422	311	**.576**
15	Al Cervi	9	359	267	**.573**
16	Joe Lapchick	9	356	277	**.562**
17	**Don Nelson**	21	937	771	**.549**
18	**Larry Brown**	16	727	600	**.548**
19	**Lenny Wilkens**	26	1223	1012	**.547**
20	**Mike Fratello**	14	592	499	**.543**
21	Bill Russell	8	375	317	**.542**
22	**Del Harris**	14	594	507	**.540**
23	Alex Hannum	12	518	446	**.537**
24	Red Holzman	18	754	651	**.536**
25	Doug Moe	15	661	579	**.533**

Active Coaches' Victories

Through 1999 season, including playoffs.

		Yrs	W	L	Pct
1	Lenny Wilkens, Atlanta	26	1223	1012	.547
2	Pat Riley, Miami	17	1096	497	.688
3	Don Nelson, Dallas	21	937	771	.549
4	Jerry Sloan, Utah	14	746	456	.621
5	Larry Brown, Philadelphia	16	727	600	.548
6	Phil Jackson, LA Lakers	9	656	234	.737
7	George Karl, Milwaukee	12	576	400	.590
8	Rick Adelman, Sacramento	9	422	311	.576
9	Rudy Tomjanovich, Houston	8	404	258	.610
10	Chris Ford, LA Clippers	8	313	340	.479
11	Mike Dunleavy, Portland	8	310	374	.453
12	Paul Westphal, Seattle	5	241	132	.646
13	Brian Hill, Vancouver	6	236	227	.510
14	P.J. Carlesimo, Golden St.	5	180	210	.462
15	Jeff Van Gundy, New York	4	166	119	.582
16	Rick Pitino, Boston	4	151	158	.489
17	Phil Saunders, Minnesota	4	133	154	.463
18	Gregg Popovich, San Antonio	3	129	93	.581
19	Danny Ainge, Phoenix	3	126	92	.578
20	Larry Bird, Indiana	2	110	51	.683
21	Dan Issel, Denver	3	102	108	.486
22	Paul Silas, Charlotte	4	100	181	.356
23	Alvin Gentry, Detroit	3	62	66	.484
24	Don Casey, New Jersey	3	54	102	.346
25	Butch Carter, Toronto	2	28	55	.337
26	Tim Floyd, Chicago	1	13	37	.260
27	Gar Heard, Washington	1	9	44	.170
28	Randy Wittman, Cleveland	0	0	0	—
	Doc Rivers, Orlando	0	0	0	—

Annual Awards
Most Valuable Player

The Maurice Podoloff Trophy for regular season MVP. Named after the first commissioner (then president) of the NBA. Winners first selected by the NBA players (1956-80) then a national panel of pro basketball writers and broadcasters (since 1981). Winners' scoring averages are provided; (*) indicates led league.

Multiple winners: Kareem Abdul-Jabbar (6); Michael Jordan and Bill Russell (5); Wilt Chamberlain (4); Larry Bird, Magic Johnson and Moses Malone (3); Karl Malone and Bob Pettit (2).

Year		Avg	Year		Avg
1956	Bob Pettit, St. Louis, F	25.7*	1978	Bill Walton, Portland, C	18.9
1957	Bob Cousy, Boston, G	20.6	1979	Moses Malone, Houston, C	24.8
1958	Bill Russell, Boston, C	16.6			
1959	Bob Pettit, St. Louis, F	29.2*	1980	Kareem Abdul-Jabbar, LA, C	24.8
			1981	Julius Erving, Philadelphia, F	24.6
1960	Wilt Chamberlain, Philadelphia, C	37.6*	1982	Moses Malone, Houston, C	31.1
1961	Bill Russell, Boston, C	16.9	1983	Moses Malone, Philadelphia, C	24.5
1962	Bill Russell, Boston, C	18.9	1984	Larry Bird, Boston, F	24.2
1963	Bill Russell, Boston, C	16.8	1985	Larry Bird, Boston, F	28.7
1964	Oscar Robertson, Cincinnati, G	31.4	1986	Larry Bird, Boston, F	25.8
1965	Bill Russell, Boston, C	14.1	1987	Magic Johnson, LA Lakers, G	23.9
1966	Wilt Chamberlain, Philadelphia, C	33.5*	1988	Michael Jordan, Chicago, G	35.0*
1967	Wilt Chamberlain, Philadelphia, C	24.1	1989	Magic Johnson, LA Lakers, G	22.5
1968	Wilt Chamberlain, Philadelphia, C	24.3			
1969	Wes Unseld, Baltimore, C	13.8	1990	Magic Johnson, LA Lakers, G	22.3
			1991	Michael Jordan, Chicago, G	31.5*
1970	Willis Reed, New York, C	21.7	1992	Michael Jordan, Chicago, G	30.1*
1971	Lew Alcindor, Milwaukee, C	31.7*	1993	Charles Barkley, Phoenix, F	25.6
1972	Kareem Abdul-Jabbar, Milwaukee, C	34.8*	1994	Hakeem Olajuwon, Houston, C	27.3
1973	Dave Cowens, Boston, C	20.5	1995	David Robinson, San Antonio, C	27.6
1974	Kareem Abdul-Jabbar, Milwaukee, C	27.0	1996	Michael Jordan, Chicago, G	30.4*
1975	Bob McAdoo, Buffalo, F	34.5*	1997	Karl Malone, Utah, F	27.4
1976	Kareem Abdul-Jabbar, LA, C	27.7	1998	Michael Jordan, Chicago, G	28.7*
1977	Kareem Abdul-Jabbar, LA, C	26.2	1999	Karl Malone, Utah, F	23.8

Note: Lew Alcindor changed his name to Kareem Abdul-Jabbar after the 1970-71 season.

Rookie of the Year

The Eddie Gottlieb Trophy for outstanding rookie of the regular season. Named after the pro basketball pioneer and owner-coach of the first NBA champion Philadelphia Warriors. Winners selected by a national panel of pro basketball writers and broadcasters. Winners' scoring averages provided; (*) indicated led league; winners who were also named MVP are in **bold** type.

Year	Avg	Year	Avg
1953 Don Meineke, Ft. Wayne, F	10.8	1977 Adrian Dantley, Buffalo, F	20.3
1954 Ray Felix, Baltimore, C	17.6	1978 Walter Davis, Phoenix, G	24.2
1955 Bob Pettit, Milwaukee Hawks, F	20.4	1979 Phil Ford, Kansas City, G	15.9
1956 Maurice Stokes, Rochester, F/C	16.8		
1957 Tommy Heinsohn, Boston, F	16.2	1980 Larry Bird, Boston, F	21.3
1958 Woody Sauldsberry, Philadelphia, F/C	12.8	1981 Darrell Griffith, Utah, G	20.6
1959 Elgin Baylor, Minneapolis, F	24.9	1982 Buck Williams, New Jersey, F	15.5
		1983 Terry Cummings, San Diego, F	23.7
1960 **Wilt Chamberlain**, Philadelphia, C	37.6*	1984 Ralph Sampson, Houston, C	21.0
1961 Oscar Robertson, Cincinnati, G	30.5	1985 Michael Jordan, Chicago, G	28.2
1962 Walt Bellamy, Chicago Packers, C	31.6	1986 Patrick Ewing, New York, C	20.0
1963 Terry Dischinger, Chicago Zephyrs, F	25.5	1987 Chuck Person, Indiana, F	18.8
1964 Jerry Lucas, Cincinnati, F/C	17.7	1988 Mark Jackson, New York, G	13.6
1965 Willis Reed, New York, C	19.5	1989 Mitch Richmond, Golden St., G	22.0
1966 Rick Barry, San Francisco, F	25.7		
1967 Dave Bing, Detroit, G	20.0	1990 David Robinson, San Antonio, C	24.3
1968 Earl Monroe, Baltimore, G	24.3	1991 Derrick Coleman, New Jersey, F	18.4
1969 **Wes Unseld**, Baltimore, C	13.8	1992 Larry Johnson, Charlotte, F	19.2
		1993 Shaquille O'Neal, Orlando,C	23.4
1970 Lew Alcindor, Milwaukee Bucks, C	28.8	1994 Chris Webber, Golden St., F	17.5
1971 Dave Cowens, Boston, C	17.0	1995 Grant Hill, Detroit, F	19.9
& Geoff Petrie, Portland, G	24.8	& Jason Kidd, Dallas, G	11.7
1972 Sidney Wicks, Portland, F	24.5	1996 Damon Stoudamire, Toronto, G	19.0
1973 Bob McAdoo, Buffalo, C/F	18.0	1997 Allen Iverson, Philadelphia, G	23.5
1974 Ernie DiGregorio, Buffalo, G	15.2	1998 Tim Duncan, San Antonio, F/C	21.6
1975 Keith Wilkes, Golden St., F	14.2	1999 Vince Carter, Toronto, F	18.3
1976 Alvan Adams, Phoenix, C	19.0		

Note: The Chicago Packers changed their name to the Zephyrs after 1961-62 season. Also, Lew Alcindor changed his name to Kareem Abdul-Jabbar after the 1970-71 season.

Sixth Man Award

Awarded to the Best Player Off the Bench for the regular season. Winners selected by a national panel of pro basketball writers and broadcasters.

Multiple winners: Kevin McHale, Ricky Pierce and Detlef Schrempf (2).

Year	Year	Year
1983 Bobby Jones, Phi., F	1989 Eddie Johnson, Pho., F	1995 Anthony Mason, NY, F
1984 Kevin McHale, Bos., F	1990 Ricky Pierce, Mil., G/F	1996 Toni Kukoc, Chi., F
1985 Kevin McHale, Bos., F	1991 Detlef Schrempf, Ind., F	1997 John Starks, NY, G
1986 Bill Walton, Bos., F/C	1992 Detlef Schrempf, Ind., F	1998 Danny Manning, Pho., F
1987 Ricky Pierce, Mil., G/F	1993 Cliff Robinson, Port., F	1999 Darrell Armstrong, Orl., G
1988 Roy Tarpley, Dal., F	1994 Dell Curry, Char., G	

Number One Draft Choices

Overall first choices in the NBA draft since the abolition of the territorial draft in 1966. Players who became Rookie of the Year are in **bold** type. The draft lottery began in 1985.

Year	Overall 1st Pick	Year	Overall 1st Pick
1966 New York	Cazzie Russell, Michigan	1983 Houston	**Ralph Sampson**, Virginia
1967 Detroit	Jimmy Walker, Providence	1984 Houston	Akeem Olajuwon, Houston
1968 San Diego	Elvin Hayes, Houston	1985 New York	**Patrick Ewing**, Georgetown
1969 Milwaukee	**Lew Alcindor**, UCLA	1986 Cleveland	Brad Daugherty, N. Carolina
		1987 San Antonio	**David Robinson**, Navy
1970 Detroit	Bob Lanier, St. Bonaventure	1988 LA Clippers	Danny Manning, Kansas
1971 Cleveland	Austin Carr, Notre Dame	1989 Sacramento	Pervis Ellison, Louisville
1972 Portland	LaRue Martin, Loyola-Chicago		
1973 Philadelphia	Doug Collins, Illinois St.	1990 New Jersey	**Derrick Coleman**, Syracuse
1974 Portland	Bill Walton, UCLA	1991 Charlotte	**Larry Johnson**, UNLV
1975 Atlanta	David Thompson, N.C. State	1992 Orlando	**Shaquille O'Neal**, LSU
1976 Houston	John Lucas, Maryland	1993 Orlando	**Chris Webber**, Michigan
1977 Milwaukee	Kent Benson, Indiana	1994 Milwaukee	Glenn Robinson, Purdue
1978 Portland	Mychal Thompson, Minnesota	1995 Golden St.	Joe Smith, Maryland
1979 LA Lakers	Magic Johnson, Michigan St.	1996 Philadelphia	**Allen Iverson**, Georgetown
		1997 San Antonio	**Tim Duncan**, Wake Forest
1980 Golden St	Joe Barry Carroll, Purdue	1998 LA Clippers	Michael Olowokandi, Pacific
1981 Dallas	Mark Aguirre, DePaul	1999 Chicago	Elton Brand, Duke
1982 LA Lakers	James Worthy, N. Carolina		

Note: Lew Alcindor changed his name to Kareem Abdul-Jabbar after the 1970-71 season; Akeem Olajuwon changed his first name to Hakeem in 1991; in 1975 David Thompson signed with Denver of the ABA and did not play for Atlanta; David Robinson joined NBA for 1989-90 season after fulfilling military obligation.

Defensive Player of the Year

Awarded to the Best Defensive Player for the regular season. Winners selected by a national panel of pro basketball writers and broadcasters.

Multiple winners: Dikembe Mutombo (3); Mark Eaton, Sidney Moncrief, Hakeem Olajuwon and Dennis Rodman (2).

Year	Year	Year
1983 Sidney Moncrief, Mil., G	1989 Mark Eaton, Utah, C	1995 Dikembe Mutombo, Den., C
1984 Sidney Moncrief, Mil., G	1990 Dennis Rodman, Det., F	1996 Gary Payton, Sea., G
1985 Mark Eaton, Utah, C	1991 Dennis Rodman, Det., F	1997 Dikembe Mutombo, Atl., C
1986 Alvin Robertson, SA, G	1992 David Robinson, SA, C	1998 Dikembe Mutombo, Atl., C
1987 Michael Cooper, LAL, F	1993 Hakeem Olajuwon, Hou., C	1999 Alonzo Mourning, Mia., C
1988 Michael Jordan, Chi., G	1994 Hakeem Olajuwon, Hou., C	

Most Improved Player

Awarded to the Most Improved Player for the regular season. Winners selected by a national panel of pro basketball writers and broadcasters.

Year	Year	Year
1986 Alvin Robertson, SA, G	1991 Scott Skiles, Orl., G	1996 Gheorghe Muresan, Wash., C
1987 Dale Ellis, Sea., G	1992 Pervis Ellison, Wash., C	1997 Isaac Austin, Miami, C
1988 Kevin Duckworth, Port., C	1993 Mahmoud Abdul-Rauf, Den., G	1998 Alan Henderson, Atl., F
1989 Kevin Johnson, Pho., G	1994 Don MacLean, Wash., F	1999 Darrell Armstrong, Orl., G
1990 Rony Seikaly, Mia., C	1995 Dana Barros, Phi., G	

Coach of the Year

The Red Auerbach Trophy for outstanding coach of the year. Renamed in 1967 for the former Boston coach who led the Celtics to nine NBA titles. Winners selected by a national panel of pro basketball writers and broadcasters. Previous season and winning season records are provided; (*) indicates division title.

Multiple winners: Don Nelson and Pat Riley (3); Bill Fitch, Cotton Fitzsimmons and Gene Shue (2).

Year			Improvement	Year			Improvement
1963	Harry Gallatin, St. L	.29-51	to 48-32	1982	Gene Shue, Wash	.39-43	to 43-39
1964	Alex Hannum, SF	.31-49	to 48-32*	1983	Don Nelson, Mil.	.55-27*	to 51-31*
1965	Red Auerbach, Bos	.59-21*	to 61-18*	1984	Frank Layden, Utah	.30-52	to 45-37*
1966	Dolph Schayes, Phi	.40-40	to 55-25*	1985	Don Nelson, Mil.	.50-32*	to 59-23*
1967	Johnny Kerr, Chi.	.Expan.	to 33-48	1986	Mike Fratello, Atl	.34-48	to 50-32
1968	Richie Guerin, St. L	.39-42	to 56-26*	1987	Mike Schuler, Port	.40-42	to 49-33
1969	Gene Shue, Balt	.36-46	to 57-25*	1988	Doug Moe, Den	.37-45	to 54-28*
1970	Red Holzman, NY	.54-28	to 60-22*	1989	Cotton Fitzsimmons, Pho	.28-54	to 55-27
1971	Dick Motta, Chi	.39-43	to 51-31	1990	Pat Riley, LA Lakers	.57-25*	to 63-19*
1972	Bill Sharman, LA	.48-34*	to 69-13*	1991	Don Chaney, Hou	.41-41	to 52-30
1973	Tommy Heinsohn, Bos	.56-26*	to 68-14*	1992	Don Nelson, GS	.44-38	to 55-27
1974	Ray Scott, Det	.40-42	to 52-30	1993	Pat Riley, NY	.51-31	to 60-22
1975	Phil Johnson, KC-Omaha	.33-49	to 44-38	1994	Lenny Wilkens, Atl	.43-39	to 57-25*
1976	Bill Fitch, Cle	.40-42	to 49-33*	1995	Del Harris, LA Lakers	.33-49	to 48-34
1977	Tom Nissalke, Hou	.40-42	to 49-33*	1996	Phil Jackson, Chi.	.47-35	to 72-10*
1978	Hubie Brown, Atl	.31-51	to 41-41	1997	Pat Riley, Mia	.42-40	to 61-21
1979	Cotton Fitzsimmons, KC	.31-51	to 48-34*	1998	Larry Bird, Ind	.39-43	to 58-24
1980	Bill Fitch, Bos	.29-53	to 61-21*	1999	Mike Dunleavy, Port.	.46-36	to 35-15*
1981	Jack McKinney, Ind	.37-45	to 44-38				

World Championships

The World Basketball Championships for men and women have been played regularly at four-year intervals (give or take a year) since 1970. The men's tournament began in 1950 and the women's in 1953. The Federation Internationale de Basketball Amateur (FIBA), which governs the World and Olympic tournaments, was founded in 1932. FIBA first allowed professional players from the NBA to participate in 1994.

Men

Multiple wins: Yugoslavia (4); Soviet Union and USA (3); Brazil (2).

Year	
1950	**Argentina**, United States, Chile
1954	**United States**, Brazil, Philippines
1959	**Brazil**, United States, Chile
1963	**Brazil**, Yugoslavia, Soviet Union
1967	**Soviet Union**, Yugoslavia, Brazil
1970	**Yugoslavia**, Brazil, Soviet Union
1974	**Soviet Union**, Yugoslavia, United States
1978	**Yugoslavia**, Soviet Union, Brazil
1982	**Soviet Union**, United States, Yugoslavia
1986	**United States**, Soviet Union, Yugoslavia
1990	**Yugoslavia**, Soviet Union, United States
1994	**United States**, Russia, Croatia
1998	**Yugoslavia**, Russia, United States
2002	at Indianapolis (August)

Women

Multiple wins: Soviet Union and USA (6).

Year	
1953	**United States**, Chile, France
1957	**United States**, Soviet Union, Czechoslovakia
1959	**Soviet Union**, Bulgaria, Czechoslovakia
1964	**Soviet Union**, Czechoslovakia, Bulgaria
1967	**Soviet Union**, South Korea, Czechoslovakia
1971	**Soviet Union**, Czechoslovakia, Brazil
1975	**Soviet Union**, Japan, Czechoslovakia
1979	**United States**, South Korea, Canada
1983	**Soviet Union**, United States, China
1986	**United States**, Soviet Union, Canada
1990	**United States**, Yugoslavia, Cuba
1994	**Brazil**, China, United States
1998	**United States**, Russia, Australia
2002	at China (May)

NBA Photos

NBA's 50 Greatest Players

In October 1996, as part of its 50th anniversary celebration, the NBA named the 50 greatest players in league history. The voting was done by a league-approved panel of media, former players and coaches, current and former general managers and team executives. The players are listed alphabetically along with the dates of their professional careers and positions. Active players are in **bold** type.

Player	Pos	Player	Pos	Player	Pos
Kareem Abdul-Jabbar, 1969-89	C	George Gervin, 1972-86	G	Bob Pettit, 1954-65	F/C
Nate Archibald, 1970-84	G	Hal Greer, 1958-73	G	**Scottie Pippen**, 1987—	F
Paul Arizin, 1950-61	F/G	John Havlicek, 1962-78	F/G	Willis Reed, 1964-74	C
Charles Barkley, 1984—	F	Elvin Hayes, 1968-84	F/C	Oscar Robertson, 1960-74	G
Rick Barry, 1965-80	F	Magic Johnson, 1979-91, 96	G	**David Robinson**, 1989—	C
Elgin Baylor, 1958-72	F	Sam Jones, 1957-69	G	Bill Russell, 1956-69	C
Dave Bing, 1966-78	G	Michael Jordan, 1984-93, 95-98	G	Dolph Schayes, 1948-64	F/C
Larry Bird, 1979-92	F	Jerry Lucas, 1963-74	F/C	Bill Sharman, 1950-61	G
Wilt Chamberlain, 1959-73	C	**Karl Malone**, 1985—	F	**John Stockton**, 1984—	G
Bob Cousy, 1950-63, 69-70	G	Moses Malone, 1974-95	C	Isiah Thomas, 1981-94	G
Dave Cowens, 1970-80, 1982-83	C	Pete Maravich, 1970-80	G	Nate Thurmond, 1963-77	C/F
Billy Cunningham, 1965-76	G	Kevin McHale, 1980-93	F	Wes Unseld, 1968-81	C/F
Dave DeBusschere, 1962-74	F	George Mikan, 1946-54, 55-56	C	Bill Walton, 1974-88	C
Clyde Drexler, 1983-98	G	Earl Monroe, 1967-80	G	Jerry West, 1960-74	G
Julius Erving, 1971-87	F	**Hakeem Olajuwon**, 1984—	C	Lenny Wilkens, 1960-75	G
Patrick Ewing, 1985—	C	**Shaquille O'Neal**, 1992—	C	James Worthy, 1982-94	F
Walt Frazier, 1967-80	G	Robert Parish, 1976-97	C		

Note: Rick Barry, Billy Cunningham, Julius Erving, George Gervin and Moses Malone all played part of their pro careers in the ABA.

NBA's 10 Greatest Coaches

In December 1996, as part of its 50th anniversary celebration, the NBA named the 10 greatest coaches in league history. The voting was done by a league-approved panel of media. The coaches are listed alphabetically along with the dates of their professional coaching careers and overall records, including playoff games, and number of NBA titles won. Active coaches are in **bold** type.

Coach	W	L	Pct.	Titles	Coach	W	L	Pct.	Titles
Red Auerbach, 1946-66	1037	548	.654	9	**Don Nelson**, 1976-96, 97—	.937 771	549	.549	0
Chuck Daly, 1981-94, 97-99	.713	488	.594	2	Jack Ramsay, 1968-89	908	841	.519	1
Bill Fitch, 1970-98	.999	1157	.463	1	**Pat Riley**, 1981—	1096	497	.688	4
Red Holzman, 1953-82	.754	652	.536	2	**Lenny Wilkens**, 1969—	1223	1012	.547	1
Phil Jackson, 1989-98, 99—	.656	234	.737	6	TOTALS	8808	6538	.574	31
John Kundla, 1947-59	.485	338	.589	5					

American Basketball Association
ABA Finals

The American Basketball Assn. began play in 1967-68 as a 10-team rival of the 21-year-old NBA. The ABA, which introduced the three-point basket, a multi-colored ball and the All-Star Game Slam Dunk Contest, lasted nine seasons before folding following the 1975-76 season. Four ABA teams–Denver, Indiana, New York and San Antonio–survived to enter the NBA in 1976-77. The NBA also adopted the three-point basket (in 1979-80) and the All-Star Game Slam Dunk Contest. The older league, however, refused to take in the ABA ball.

Multiple winners: Indiana (3); New York (2).

Year	Winner	Head Coach	Series	Loser	Head Coach
1968	Pittsburgh Pipers	Vince Cazzetta	4-3 (WLLWLWW)	New Orleans Bucs	Babe McCarthy
1969	Oakland Oaks	Alex Hannum	4-1 (WLWWW)	Indiana Pacers	Bob Leonard
1970	Indiana Pacers	Bob Leonard	4-2 (WWLWLW)	Los Angeles Stars	Bill Sharman
1971	Utah Stars	Bill Sharman	4-3 (WWLLWLW)	Kentucky Colonels	Frank Ramsey
1972	Indiana Pacers	Bob Leonard	4-2 (WLWLWW)	New York Nets	Lou Carnesecca
1973	Indiana Pacers	Bob Leonard	4-3 (WLLWWLW)	Kentucky Colonels	Joe Mullaney
1974	New York Nets	Kevin Loughery	4-1 (WWWLW)	Utah Stars	Joe Mullaney
1975	Kentucky Colonels	Hubie Brown	4-1 (WWWLW)	Indiana Pacers	Bob Leonard
1976	New York Nets	Kevin Loughery	4-2 (WLWWLW)	Denver Nuggets	Larry Brown

Most Valuable Player

Winners' scoring averages provided; (*) indicates led league.

Multiple winners: Julius Erving (3); Mel Daniels (2).

Year		Avg
1968	Connie Hawkins, Pittsburgh, C	26.8*
1969	Mel Daniels, Indiana, C	24.0
1970	Spencer Haywood, Denver, C	30.0*
1971	Mel Daniels, Indiana, C	21.0
1972	Artis Gilmore, Kentucky, C	23.8
1973	Billy Cunningham, Carolina, F	24.1
1974	Julius Erving, New York, F	27.4*
1975	George McGinnis, Indiana, F	29.8*
	& Julius Erving, New York, F	27.9
1976	Julius Erving, New York, F	29.3*

Rookie of the Year

Winners' scoring averages provided; (*) indicates led league. Rookies who were also named Most Valuable Player are in **bold** type.

Year		Avg
1968	Mel Daniels, Minnesota, C	22.2
1969	Warren Armstrong, Oakland, G	21.5
1970	**Spencer Haywood**, Denver, C	30.0*
1971	Dan Issel, Kentucky, C	29.8*
	& Charlie Scott, Virginia, G	27.1
1972	**Artis Gilmore**, Kentucky, C	23.8
1973	Brian Taylor, New York, G	15.3
1974	Swen Nater, Virginia-SA, C	14.1
1975	Marvin Barnes, St. Louis, C	24.0
1976	David Thompson, Denver, F	26.0

Note: Warren Armstrong changed his name to Warren Jabali after the 1970-71 season.

Coach of the Year

Previous season and winning season records are provided; (*) indicates division title.

Multiple winner: Larry Brown (3).

Year		Improvement
1968	Vince Cazzetta, Pittsburgh	54-24*
1969	Alex Hannum, Oakland	22-56 to 60-18*
1970	Joe Belmont, Denver	44-34 to 51-33*
	& Bill Sharman, LA Stars	33-45 to 43-41
1971	Al Bianchi, Virginia	44-40 to 55-29*
1972	Tom Nissalke, Dallas	30-54 to 42-42
1973	Larry Brown, Carolina	35-49 to 57-27*
1974	Babe McCarthy, Kentucky	56-28 to 53-31
	& Joe Mullaney, Utah	55-29* to 51-33*
1975	Larry Brown, Denver	37-47 to 65-19*
1976	Larry Brown, Denver	65-19* to 60-24*

Scoring Leaders

Scoring championship decided by per game point average every season.

Multiple winner: Julius Erving (3).

Year		Gm	Avg	Pts
1968	Connie Hawkins, Pittsburgh	70	1875	26.8
1969	Rick Barry, Oakland	35	1190	34.0
1970	Spencer Haywood, Denver	84	2519	30.0
1971	Dan Issel, Kentucky	83	2480	29.8
1972	Charlie Scott, Virginia	73	2524	34.6
1973	Julius Erving, Virginia	71	2268	31.9
1974	Julius Erving, New York	84	2299	27.4
1975	George McGinnis, Indiana	79	2353	29.8
1976	Julius Erving, New York	84	2462	29.3

ABA All-Star Game

The ABA All-Star Game was an Eastern Division vs. Western Division contest from 1968-75. League membership had dropped to seven teams by 1976, the ABA's last season, so the team in first place at the break (Denver) played an All-Star team made up from the other six clubs.

Series: East won 5, West 3 and Denver 1.

Year	Result	Host	Coaches	Most Valuable Player
1968	East 126, West 120	Indiana	Jim Pollard, Babe McCarthy	Larry Brown, New Orleans
1969	West 133, East 127	Louisville	Alex Hannum, Gene Rhodes	John Beasley, Dallas
1970	West 128, East 98	Indiana	Babe McCarthy, Bob Leonard	Spencer Haywood, Denver
1971	East 126, West 122	Carolina	Al Bianchi, Bill Sharman	Mel Daniels, Indiana
1972	East 142, West 115	Louisville	Joe Mullaney, Ladell Andersen	Dan Issel, Kentucky
1973	West 123, East 111	Utah	Ladell Andersen, Larry Brown	Warren Jabali, Denver
1974	East 128, West 112	Virginia	Babe McCarthy, Joe Mullaney	Artis Gilmore, Kentucky
1975	East 151, West 124	San Antonio	Kevin Loughery, Larry Brown	Freddie Lewis, St. Louis
1976	Denver 144, ABA 138	Denver	Larry Brown, Kevin Loughery	David Thompson, Denver

Continental Basketball Association

Formed on April 23, 1946, the CBA is the oldest professional basketball league in the world. Originally named the Eastern Pennsylvania Basketball League, the league changed names several times before becoming known as the Eastern Basketball Association. In 1978, the EBA was redubbed the CBA.

Multiple champions: Allentown and Wilkes-Barre (8); Scranton, Tampa Bay and Williamsport (3); Albany, La Crosse, Pottsville, Rochester and Wilmington (2).

Year		Year		Year	
1947	Wilkes-Barre Barons	1966	Wilmington Blue Bombers	1985	Tampa Bay Thrillers
1948	Reading Keys	1967	Wilmington Blue Bombers	1986	Tampa Bay Thrillers
1949	Pottsville Packers	1968	Allentown Jets	1987	Rapid City Thrillers*
1950	Williamsport Billies	1969	Wilkes-Barre Barons	1988	Albany Patroons
1951	Sunbury Mercuries	1970	Allentown Jets	1989	Tulsa Fast Breakers
1952	Pottsville Packers	1971	Scranton Apollos	1990	La Crosse Catbirds
1953	Williamsport Billies	1972	Allentown Jets	1991	Wichita Falls Texans
1954	Williamsport Billies	1973	Wilkes-Barre Barons	1992	La Crosse Catbirds
1955	Wilkes-Barre Barons	1974	Hartford Capitols	1993	Omaha Racers
1956	Wilkes-Barre Barons	1975	Allentown Jets	1994	Quad City Thunder
1957	Scranton Miners	1976	Allentown Jets	1995	Yakima Sun Kings
1958	Wilkes-Barre Barons	1977	Scranton Apollos	1996	Sioux Falls Skyforce
1959	Wilkes-Barre Barons	1978	Wilkes-Barre Barons	1997	Oklahoma City Calvary
1960	Easton Madisons	1979	Rochester Zeniths	1998	Quad City Thunder
1961	Baltimore Bullets	1980	Anchorage Northern Knights	1999	Connecticut Pride
1962	Allentown Jets	1981	Rochester Zeniths		
1963	Allentown Jets	1982	Lancaster Lightning	*The Tampa Bay Thrillers moved to	
1964	Camden Bullets	1983	Detroit Spirits	Rapid City, S.D. at the end of the 1987	
1965	Allentown Jets	1984	Albany Patroons	regular season.	

WOMEN

American Basketball League
League Champions

The American Basketball League began play in 1996 as an eight-team league. Before the 1997-98 season the league added an expansion franchise in Long Beach, Calif. while the Richmond Rage was relocated to Philadelphia. In the spring of 1998, the league announced plans to dissolve an original franchise, the Atlanta Glory, and expand to Chicago and Nashville before the 1998-99 season, increasing the league's size to 10 teams. The ABL finals was a best of five series. Each ABL champion's wins and losses are noted in parentheses after the series score. The ABL folded before the 1999 season.

Multiple winner: Columbus (2).

Year	Champions	Head Coach	Series	Runners-up	Head Coach
1997	Columbus Quest	Brian Agler	3-2 (WLLWW)	Richmond Rage	Lisa Boyer
1998	Columbus Quest	Brian Agler	3-2 (LLWWW)	Long Beach StingRays	Maura McHugh
1999	league folded				

Most Valuable Player

Winner's scoring averages provided; (*) indicates led league.

Year		Avg
1997	Nikki McCray, Columbus	19.9
1998	Natalie Williams, Portland	21.9*

Coach of the Year

Previous season and winning season's record are provided; (*) indicates division title.

Year		Improvement
1997	Brian Agler, Columbus	31-9*
1998	Lin Dunn, Portland	14-26 to 27-17

Women's National Basketball Association
League Champions

The WNBA, owned and operated by the NBA, began play in 1997 as an eight-team summer league. The league added two teams prior to its second season (1998) and again expanded by two teams before its third season in 1999. Four more teams were added to begin play in the 2000 season, bringing the total number of teams to 16. The WNBA champion was determined by a single-game playoff between the winners of the semifinals in the league's 1997 inaugural season, before going to a best-of-three championship series in 1998.

Multiple winner: Houston (3).

Year	Champions	Head Coach	Score	Runners-up	Head Coach
1997	Houston Comets	Van Chancellor	65-51	New York Liberty	Nancy Darsch
1998	Houston Comets	Van Chancellor	2-1 (LWW)	Phoenix Mercury	Cheryl Miller
1999	Houston Comets	Van Chancellor	2-1 (WLW)	New York Liberty	Richie Adubato

Most Valuable Player

Winner's scoring averages provided; (*) indicates led league.

Multiple winner: Cynthia Cooper (2).

Year		Avg
1997	Cynthia Cooper, Houston	22.2*
1998	Cynthia Cooper, Houston	22.7*
1999	Yolanda Griffith, Sacramento	18.8

Coach of the Year

Previous season and winning season's record are provided; (*) indicates division title.

Multiple winner: Van Chancellor (3).

Year		Improvement
1997	Van Chancellor, Houston	18-10*
1998	Van Chancellor, Houston	18-10 to 27-3*
1999	Van Chancellor, Houston	27-3 to 26-6*

Hockey

During his 20-year career, the only thing that surpassed **Wayne Gretzky's** level of talent was the level of class he brought to the game.

AP/Wide World Photos

Starstruck in Big D

Brett Hull's disputed triple OT goal gives Dallas its first Stanley Cup title.

by
Steve Levy

The National Hockey League doesn't want or need your sympathy, but maybe it deserves some. Finally after four consecutive sweeps, we were treated to a terrific, competitive Stanley Cup Final as the Dallas Stars needed six "rock'em sock'em" games to polish off the Buffalo Sabres for the rights to Lord Stanley's cup. Unfortunately the series will be remembered for the controversial way in which it was won — on Brett Hull's goal in triple overtime with his skate apparently touching the crease.

Let's face it. The Sabres were probably not going to win the series, but the fact remains it was a tarnished goal. If the exact same goal was scored in a less meaningful game in November, it would be reviewed and disallowed. The league responded to the controversy a couple of days later with a new, reworked version of the crease rule. But the truth is, the change was really made a couple of

days before and simply announced after game six.

I had the unenviable task of breaking the bad news to Hull that the play was under review. As I was interviewing him on ESPN just as he had returned from the ice, my colleague Al Morganti whispered in my ear that the Sabres refused to open their locker room to the press. The team felt that Hull was in the crease and wanted an explanation. So, on the air, I relayed that to Hull and all the air in his body seemed to seep right out of him. I felt as if I had just ruined his long-awaited Stanley Cup celebration.

After the interview was finished, I watched him talking to his jubilant teammates in front of his locker stall, and he began pointing at me in an animated fashion, telling them that the Sabres thought he was in the crease. Five minutes later during an interview with "Hockey Night in Canada," Hull was first shown the replay of the goal.

"See, look I'm not in the crease!" he claimed. "My skate is out, out, out..." He then paused and said, "Oh

Steve Levy is a *SportsCenter* anchor and host of ESPN's *National Hockey Night.*

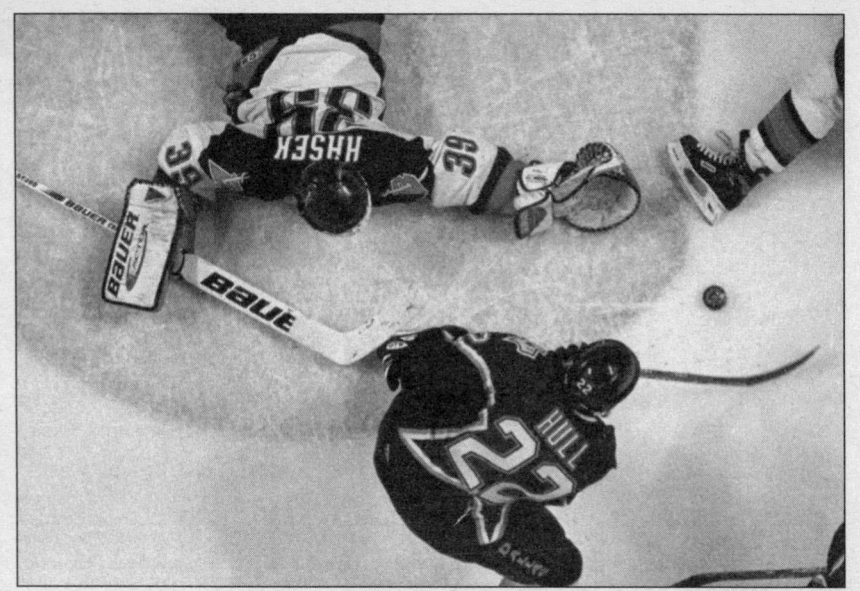

Dallas' **Brett Hull** clearly has his left skate in the crease before the puck goes in. Referees later claimed Hull had control of the puck when it was within the crease and kept control of it when it bounced out, which would make it a legal goal. The Sabres weren't buying it.

no. It's in." After a moment to regroup and think rationally, he added, "Well what are they going to do — make us put our skates on and get back out there?"

Personally, I'm happy for Brett Hull. I root for guys like him. The NHL, and for that matter the entire sports world, needs more people like him — players who are free-spirited and aren't afraid to speak their minds, rather than speak in the usual clichés. He also proved to the world this year that he wasn't just a goal scorer. The running joke in the Dallas locker room was that he along with Mike Modano and Jere Lehtinen were just a checking line — a really expensive checking line. Hull effectively played all three zones, and while his ice time and scoring stats suffered, he would be the first to say that it was his best

season ever. It's all about the ring. And now he has one.

The entire playoffs were simply a joy to watch. It seems rare these days when a team ponies up the money for a high-priced free agent and the move actually pays off. It did for Hull in Dallas and it did for Curtis Joseph and the Toronto Maple Leafs. It was great to have Toronto, one of the league's Original Six, in the conference finals, though it wasn't so great to see the Rangers, Blackhawks and the supposedly on-the-rise Los Angeles Kings miss the playoffs entirely.

The New Jersey Devils might as well have missed the playoffs. After finishing first overall in the Eastern Conference once again, they were ousted in round one by an under-manned and overall less-skilled group of Penguins led by the brilliant

AP/Wide World Photos

In one of the more spectacular goals of the year, a sprawling **Jaromir Jagr** backhands the puck towards the Philadelphia goal while being hauled down by defender Luke Richardson. Flyers goalie Ron Hextall made the initial save but Jagr batted the puck out of midair and into the net.

Jaromir Jagr. I gained a new respect for Jagr, adding to the abundance of respect I already had for him. He really rose to the occasion, not just playing through the pain of a groin injury, but dominating through it. He was a worthy Hart Trophy winner and now things appear to be getting even brighter in Pittsburgh. The Penguins were already one of the more entertaining teams in the league to watch, and now they've got themselves a magnificent owner (Mario Lemieux) who will not allow them to play poorly. He never did. ∎

Steve Levy's Top Ten Highlights of the 1998-99 Hockey Season.

10. **Four on Four Overtime.** Personally, I want to see the shootout, but at least this is an improvement and a sign that the league is moving in the right direction on the matter.

9. **The NHL Draft** is not usually a thriller, but the 1999 edition was very entertaining, complete with plenty of twists and turns in the first round and lots of trades involving the top ten selections.

8. **Dominik Hasek announces** that the upcoming season will be his last. The Sabres figure they'll be covered with top prospect Martin Biron, but no one covers up quite like the Dominator.

7. **Teemu Selanne scores** 47 goals and wins the first ever Rocket Richard Trophy. I love that the NHL added an award and named it properly and I also love that Selanne is its first recipient.

6. **Detroit proves** that you can't necessarily buy the Stanley Cup. Acquisitions at the trading deadline should have made it the best team in the league, but it didn't work

AP/Wide World Photos

Dallas center **Joe Nieuwendyk** stayed healthy for the entire postseason, led all scorers with 11 goals and took home the Conn Smythe Trophy for Most Valuable Player of the playoffs. Here he is with an even better trophy.

out that way. This is good news for teams like the Edmonton Oilers who are trying to do it the right way.

5. **The re-emergence of the Maple Leafs.** The NHL needs a strong presence from one of its Canadian teams and Montreal just wasn't helping out.

4. **Mario Lemieux saves** the Penguins for the second time — this time by buying them.

3. **The instant replay rule** goes away, at least when it concerns the crease. That call will now be made on the ice by the referee who will use nothing but good judgment and common sense.

2. **Conn Smythe Award winner Joe Nieuwendyk**, after missing almost all of the previous postseason with a serious knee injury, responds by scoring 11 goals in the playoffs, including seven game winners, on his way to a Stanley Cup win.

1. **Number 99.** No one will ever be allowed to put the number 99 on

an NHL sweater again. Wayne Gretzky's final skate around the ice as an NHL player is something I'll never forget. I was in the building that afternoon for his final game at the Garden. It's the only ticket stub I've ever kept. ■

1998-99 season. Aside from that whipper-snapper Pronger, the rest of the top five are all over 30.

	Age	Min/Gm
Chris Pronger, St.L	25	30.61
Brian Leetch, NYR	31	29.87
Ray Bourque, Bos.	39	29.51
Al MacInnis, St.L	36	29.12
Chris Chelios, Chi.-Det.	37	26.66

Note: Age given is as of Dec. 31, 1999.

RAY OF FIGHT

Buffalo's Rob Ray led the NHL in penalty minutes in 1998-99 with 261. Though no one will confuse him for a choir boy, Ray has actually mellowed since he set the AHL record for penalty minutes 10 years ago. Below are the all-time highest single-season totals for various pro and minor league teams.

League	PM		
IHL	648	Kevin Evans, Kalamazoo, 1986-87	
NHL	472	Dave Schultz, Philadelphia, 1974-75	
AHL	446	Rob Ray, Rochester, 1988-89	
CHL	411	Randy Holt, Dallas, 1974-75	
WHA	365	Curt Brackenbury, Min/Que, 1975-76	

WHO ARE YOU CALLING OLD?

Many of the league's top defensemen are starting to get, shall we say, a bit long in the tooth. But you certainly wouldn't know it from the amount of ice time they log. Listed are the NHL leaders in minutes per game for the

SMART SHOPPING

Los Angeles Kings left wing Luc Robitaille netted the 500th goal of his career on Jan. 7, 1999. Not bad for a ninth-round draft choice. In fact, in 1984 the Kings actually drafted Atlanta Braves pitcher Tom Glavine ahead of Robitaille (No. 69 overall). Below are the lowest draft choices used on future 500-goal scorers.

	Year	Round	Pick
Luc Robitaille, LA	1984	9	171
Brett Hull, Calg.	1984	6	117
Jari Kurri, Edm.	1980	4	69
Mark Messier, Edm.	1979	3	48

WAYNE'S WORLD

Wayne Gretzky's hockey domination didn't stop outside of North America. In the eight international competitions he played in, Gretzky was the leading scorer in six. He led Canada to three Canada Cups and in his first competition, the 1978 World Juniors, he led all scorers as a 16-year old, despite playing against players that were 18-20.

Year		Gm	G	A	Pts	Medal
1978	World Juniors	6	8	9	17	B
1981	Canada Cup	7	5	7	12	S
1982	World Champs.	10	6	8	14	B
1984	Canada Cup	8	5	7	12	G
1987	Canada Cup	9	3	18	21	G
1991	Canada Cup	7	4	8	12	G
1996	World Cup	8	3	4	7	S
1998	Olympics	6	0	4	4	—
	TOTAL	61	34	65	99	—

■

Final NHL Standings

Division champions (*) and playoff qualifiers (†) are noted. Number of seasons listed after each head coach refers to current tenure with club through 1998-99 season.

Western Conference
Central Division

	W	L	T	Pts	GF	GA	Dif
*Detroit	43	32	7	93	245	202	+43
†St. Louis	37	32	13	87	237	209	+28
Chicago	29	41	12	70	202	248	-46
Nashville	28	47	7	63	190	261	-71

Head Coaches: Det— Scotty Bowman (6th season); **St.L**— Joel Quenneville (3rd); **Chi**— fired Dirk Graham (1st, 16-35-8) on Feb. 22 and replaced him with Lorne Molleken (13-6-4); **Nash**— Barry Trotz (1st).

Northwest Division

	W	L	T	Pts	GF	GA	Dif
*Colorado	44	28	10	98	239	205	+34
†Edmonton	33	37	12	78	230	226	+4
Calgary	30	40	12	72	211	234	-23
Vancouver	23	47	12	58	192	258	-66

Head Coaches: Col— Bob Hartley (1st season); **Edm**— Ron Low (5th); **Cal**— Brian Sutter (2nd); **Van**— fired Mike Keenan (2nd; 15-24-6) on Jan. 24 and replaced him with Marc Crawford (8-23-6).

Pacific Division

	W	L	T	Pts	GF	GA	Dif
*Dallas	51	19	12	114	236	168	+68
†Phoenix	39	31	12	90	205	197	+8
†Anaheim	35	34	13	83	215	206	+9
†San Jose	31	33	18	80	196	191	+5
Los Angeles	32	45	5	69	189	222	-33

Head Coaches: Dal— Ken Hitchcock (4th season); **Pho**— Jim Schoenfeld (2nd); **Ana**— Craig Hartsburg (1st); **SJ**— Darryl Sutter (2nd); **LA**— Larry Robinson (4th).

Eastern Conference
Northeast Division

	W	L	T	Pts	GF	GA	Dif
*Ottawa	44	23	15	103	239	179	+60
†Toronto	45	30	7	97	268	231	+37
†Boston	39	30	13	91	214	181	+33
†Buffalo	37	28	17	91	207	175	+32
Montreal	32	39	11	75	184	209	-25

Head Coaches: Ott— Jacques Martin (4th season); **Tor**— Pat Quinn (1st); **Bos**— Pat Burns (2nd); **Buf**— Lindy Ruff (2nd); **Mon**— Alain Vigneault (2nd).

Atlantic Division

	W	L	T	Pts	GF	GA	Dif
*New Jersey	47	24	11	105	248	196	+52
†Philadelphia	37	26	19	93	231	196	+35
†Pittsburgh	38	30	14	90	242	225	+17
NY Rangers	33	38	11	77	217	227	-10
NY Islanders	24	48	10	58	194	244	-50

Head Coaches: NJ— Robbie Ftorek (1st season); **Phi**— Roger Neilson (2nd); **Pit**— Kevin Constantine (2nd); **NYR**— John Muckler (2nd); **NYI**— GM/coach Mike Milbury (2nd, 13-29-3) replaced himself as coach on Jan. 21 with Bill Stewart (11-19-7).

Southeast Division

	W	L	T	Pts	GF	GA	Dif
*Carolina	34	30	18	86	210	202	+8
Florida	30	34	18	78	210	228	-18
Washington	31	45	6	68	200	218	-18
Tampa Bay	19	54	9	47	179	292	-113

Head Coaches: Car— Paul Maurice (4th season); **Fla**— Terry Murray (1st); **Was**— Ron Wilson (2nd); **TB**— Jacques Demers (2nd).

Home & Away, Division, Conference Records

Sixteen teams— eight from each conference— qualify for the Stanley Cup Playoffs; (*) indicates division champions.

Western Conference

		Pts	Home	Away	Div	Conf
1	Dallas*	114	29-8-4	22-11-8	18-4-2	35-14-7
2	Colorado*	98	21-14-6	23-14-4	8-8-2	29-19-8
3	Detroit*	93	27-12-2	16-20-5	12-4-2	30-20-4
4	Phoenix	90	23-13-5	16-18-7	11-11-2	28-21-7
5	St. Louis	87	18-17-6	19-15-7	10-6-2	27-20-8
6	Anaheim	83	21-14-6	14-20-7	12-7-5	25-24-8
7	San Jose	80	17-15-9	14-18-9	7-14-3	21-26-9
8	Edmonton	78	17-19-5	16-18-7	12-4-2	25-24-6
	Calgary	72	15-20-6	15-20-6	6-10-2	21-25-8
	Chicago	70	20-17-4	9-24-8	7-10-1	18-29-7
	Los Angeles	69	18-20-3	14-25-2	6-18-0	21-32-4
	Nashville	63	15-22-4	13-25-3	4-13-1	21-30-4
	Vancouver	58	14-21-6	9-26-6	6-10-2	15-32-8

Eastern Conference

		Pts	Home	Away	Div	Conf
1	New Jersey*	105	19-14-8	28-10-3	15-4-1	35-15-8
2	Ottawa*	103	22-11-8	22-12-7	8-8-4	30-18-9
3	Carolina*	86	20-12-9	14-18-9	5-2-8	25-19-15
4	Toronto	97	23-13-5	22-17-2	8-11-1	25-26-5
5	Philadelphia	93	21-9-11	16-17-8	7-8-5	22-21-13
6	Boston	91	22-10-9	17-20-4	11-7-2	29-20-9
7	Buffalo	91	23-12-6	14-16-11	10-6-4	28-17-12
8	Pittsburgh	90	21-10-10	17-20-4	5-11-4	26-23-9
	Florida	78	17-17-7	13-17-11	6-4-5	20-25-11
	NY Rangers	77	17-19-5	16-19-6	8-8-4	21-27-9
	Montreal	75	21-15-5	11-24-6	7-12-1	21-28-7
	Washington	68	16-23-2	15-22-4	8-5-2	25-26-5
	NY Islanders	58	11-23-7	13-25-3	7-11-2	17-36-4
	Tampa Bay	47	12-25-4	7-29-5	2-10-3	12-35-8

1999 NHL All-Star Game

North America, 8-6

49th NHL All-Star Game. **Date:** Jan. 24 at the Ice Palace in Tampa; **Coaches:** Lindy Ruff, Buffalo (World) and Ken Hitchcock, Dallas (North America); **MVP:** Wayne Gretzky, NY Rangers center (North America) — one goal, two assists.

For the second consecutive year, the NHL voted to abandon its usual all-star game format of Eastern Conference vs. Western Conference in favor of a game pitting the North American all-stars vs. the rest of the world's all-stars.

Starters were chosen by fan vote while reserves were selected by the NHL's Hockey Operations Department, after consultation with NHL general managers. Head coaches whose teams had the best winning percentage in the Eastern Conference (World) and Western Conference (North America) on Dec. 29 were named all-star head coaches.

Defensemen Mattias Norstrom and Mattias Ohlund were added to the **World** team as injury replacements for Uwe Krupp and Kenny Jonsson. Teppo Numminen replaced Krupp in the starting lineup. Viktor Kozlov was injured and did not play.

Left wing Luc Robitaille and goalie Ron Tugnutt were added to the **North American** team as injury replacements for Steve Yzerman and Curtis Joseph, respectively. Eric Lindros replaced Yzerman in the starting lineup.

The World

	Starters	G	A	Pts	PM
C	Peter Forsberg, Colorado	0	1	1	0
W	Jaromir Jagr, Pittsburgh	0	1	1	0
W	Teemu Selanne, Anaheim	1	0	1	0
D	Nicklas Lidstrom, Detroit	0	0	0	0
D	Teppo Numminen, Phoenix	0	0	0	0
	Reserves				
W	Mats Sundin, Toronto	1	3	4	0
D	Mattias Ohlund, Vancouver	1	1	2	0
W	Pavol Demitra, St. Louis	1	0	1	0
C	Bobby Holik, New Jersey	0	1	1	0
G	Arturs Irbe, Carolina	0	1	1	0
W	Dmitri Kristich, Boston	0	1	1	0
W	Markus Naslund, Vancouver	1	0	1	0
W	Marco Sturm, San Jose	1	0	1	0
C	Alexei Yashin, Ottawa	0	1	1	0
D	Alexei Zhitnik, Buffalo	0	1	1	0
D	Sergei Zubov, Dallas	1	0	1	0
W	Peter Bondra, Washington	0	0	0	0
D	Roman Hamrlik, Edmonton	0	0	0	0
W	Sergei Krivokrasov, Nashville	0	0	0	0
D	Mattias Norstrom, Los Angeles	0	0	0	0
W	Martin Straka, Pittsburgh	0	0	0	0
	TOTALS	6	12	18	0

Goaltenders	Mins	Shots	Saves	GA
Dominik Hasek, Buf.	20:00	19	15	4
Arturs Irbe, Car. (L)	20:00	15	12	3
Nikolai Khabibulin, Pho.	19:13	15	14	1
TOTALS	59:13	49	41	8

North America

	Starters	G	A	Pts	PM
D	Ray Bourque, Boston	1	0	1	0
W	Paul Kariya, Anaheim	1	0	1	0
C	Eric Lindros, Philadelphia	0	0	0	0
D	Al MacInnis, St. Louis	0	0	0	2
W	Brendan Shanahan, Detroit	0	0	0	0
	Reserves				
C	Mike Modano, Dallas	1	3	4	0
C	Wayne Gretzky, NY Rangers	1	2	3	0
W	Tony Amonte, Chicago	0	2	2	0
W	Theo Fleury, Calgary	0	2	2	0
D	Chris Pronger, St. Louis	0	2	2	0
W	Mark Recchi, Montreal	1	1	2	0
W	Luc Robitaille, Los Angeles	1	0	1	0
D	Rob Blake, Los Angeles	1	0	1	0
W	Wendel Clark, Tampa Bay	0	1	1	0
C	Jeremy Roenick, Phoenix	0	1	1	0
D	Darryl Sydor, Dallas	1	0	1	0
D	John LeClair, Philadelphia	0	0	0	0
D	Larry Murphy, Detroit	0	0	0	0
C	Keith Primeau, Carolina	0	0	0	0
D	Scott Stevens, New Jersey	0	0	0	0
W	Keith Tkachuk, Phoenix	0	0	0	0
	TOTALS	8	15	23	2

Goaltenders	Mins	Shots	Saves	GA
Martin Brodeur, NJ	20:00	9	8	1
Ron Tugnutt, Ott. (W)	20:00	15	12	3
Ed Belfour, Dal.	20:00	12	10	2
TOTALS	60:00	36	30	6

Score by Periods

	1	2	3	Final
World	1	3	2	— 6
North America	4	3	1	— 8

Power plays: World — 0/1; North America — 0/0.
Officials: Paul Devorski (referee), Pierre Champoux and Brian Murphy (linesmen). **Attendance:** 19,758.

1999 NHL Skills Competition

World, 13-11

Puck Control Relay
Team: North America
Individual: Paul Kariya (North America)
Fastest Skater
Team: World (14.66 sec.)
Individual: Peter Bondra, World (14.64 sec.)
Hardest Shot
Team: North America (96.1 mph)
Individual: Al MacInnis, North America (98.5 mph)
Goalie Goals (goals/attempts)
Team: World (1/6, made by Dominik Hasek)

Rapid Fire Relay
Team: World (25 saves- Irbe, Hasek and Khabibulin)
Shooting Accuracy (targets/shots)
Team: North America (16/26)
Individual: Ray Bourque, Keith Tkachuk and Jeremy Roenick, North America (4/6)
Breakaway Relay (goals/shots)
Team: World wins, 9-5
Goaltender Competition
Individual: Arturs Irbe, World (14 saves)

THE GREAT ONE: FOR THE RECORD

NY Rangers center Wayne Gretzky, voted the greatest hockey player of all-time in a recent poll conducted by *The Hockey News*, retired after the 1998-99 season with four Stanley Cups, ten scoring titles and nine Hart Trophies (MVP). He finished his career with 894 goals, 1,963 assists and 2,857 points—all likely untouchable records.

Year by Year Statistics

Season	Age	Club	Gm	G	A	Pts	PM	Gm	G	A	Pts	PM	—Awards—
				—Regular Season —				—Playoffs —					
1978-79	18	Indianapolis.........8		3	3	6	0	—	—	—	—	—	
		Edmonton..........72		43	61	104	19	13	10*	10	20*	2	WHA Top Rookie
1979-80	19	Edmonton...........79		51	86*	137†	21	3	2	1	3	0	Hart, Byng
1980-81	20	Edmonton..........80		55	109*	164*	28	9	7	14	21	4	Hart, Ross
1981-82	21	Edmonton..........80		92*	120*	212*	26	5	5	7	12	8	Hart, Ross
1982-83	22	Edmonton..........80		71*	125*	196*	59	16	12	26*	38*	4	Hart, Ross
1983-84	23	Edmonton.........74		87*	118*	205*	39	19	13	22*	35*	12	Hart, Ross
1984-85	24	Edmonton..........80		73*	135*	208*	52	18	17	30*	47*	4	Hart, Ross & Smythe
1985-86	25	Edmonton..........80		52	163*	215*	46	10	8	11	19	2	Hart, Ross
1986-87	26	Edmonton.........79		62*	121*	183*	28	21	5	29*	34*	6	Hart, Ross
1987-88	27	Edmonton..........64		40	109*	149	24	19	12	31*	43*	16	Smythe
1988-89	28	Los Angeles......78		54	114†	168	26	11	5	17	22	0	Hart
1989-90	29	Los Angeles 73		40	102*	142*	42	7	3	7	10	0	Ross
1990-91	30	Los Angeles 78		41	122*	163*	16	12	4	11	15	2	Ross, Byng
1991-92	31	Los Angeles 74		31	90*	121	34	6	2	5	7	2	Byng
1992-93	32	Los Angeles 45		16	49	65	6	24	15*	25*	40*	4	—
1993-94	33	Los Angeles 81		38	92†	130*	20	—	—	—	—	—	Byng
1995	34	Los Angeles 48		11	37	48	6	—	—	—	—	—	—
1995-96	35	LA, St. Louis 80		23	79	102	34	13	2	14	16	0	—
1996-97	36	NY Rangers........82		25	72†	97	28	15	10	10	20	2	—
1997-98	37	NY Rangers........82		23	67†	90	28	—	—	—	—	—	—
1998-99	38	NY Rangers........70		9	53	62	14	—	—	—	—	—	Byng
		WHA totals 80		46	64	110	19	13	10	10	20	2	
		NHL totals.......1487		894	1963	2857	577	208	122	260	382	66	

*Led league
†Tied for league lead

NHL Records

Over his illustrious twenty-year career, Gretzky set or tied 61 NHL records — 40 regular season records, 15 playoff records, and six all-star game records.

Regular Season

Goals, career	894
Goals, incl. playoffs	1016
Goals, season	92
Goals, season, incl. playoffs	100
Goals, first 50 games of a season	61†
Goals, period	4*
Assists, career	1963
Assists, incl. playoffs	2223
Assists, season	163
Assists, season, incl. playoffs	174
Assists, game	7*#
Assists, road game	7*
Points, career	2857
Points, incl. playoffs	3239
Points, season	215
Points, season, incl. playoffs	255
Overtime assists, career	15
Goals by a center, career	894
Goals by a center, season	92
Assists by a center, career	1963
Assists by a center, season	163
Points by a center, career	2857
Points by a center, season	215
Assists by a rookie, game	7

Regular Season

Goals per game avg., season	1.18
Assists per game avg., season	2.04
Assists per game avg., career	1.32
Points per game avg., season	2.77
40-or-more goal seasons	12
Consecutive 40-or-more goal seasons	12
50-or-more goal seasons	9*
60-or-more goal seasons	5*
Consecutive 60-or-more goal seasons	4
100-or-more point seasons	15
Consecutive 100-or-more point seasons	13
Hat tricks, career	50
Hat tricks, season	10†
Consecutive games with assist	23
Consecutive games with point	51
Consecutive games with point from start of season	51

Playoffs

Goals, career	122
Assists, career	260
Assists, season	31

Playoffs

Assists, non-finals series	14*
Assists, final series	10
Assists, game	6*
Assists, period	3*@
Points, career	382
Points, season	47
Points, final series	13
Points, period	4*
Shorthanded goals, season	3*†
Shorthanded goals, game	2*
Game-winning goals, career	24
Hat tricks, career	10

All-Star Games

Goals, career	13
Goals, game	4*
Goals, period	4
Assists, career	12*
Points, career	25
Points, period	4*

*tied for the record
†did it twice
#did it three times
@did it five times

Pittsburgh Penguins	Mighty Ducks of Anaheim	Buffalo Sabres	Ottawa Senators
Jaromir Jagr	**Teemu Selanne**	**Rob Ray**	**Ron Tugnutt**
Scoring, Assists	Goals, PP Goals	Penalty Minutes	GAA

NHL Regular Season Individual Leaders

(*) indicates rookie eligible for Calder Trophy.

Scoring

	Pos	Gm	G	A	Pts	+/-	PM	PP	SH	GW	GT	Shots	Pct
Jaromir Jagr, Pittsburgh	R	81	44	83	127	17	66	10	1	7	2	343	12.8
Teemu Selanne, Anaheim	R	75	47	60	107	18	30	25	0	7	1	281	16.7
Paul Kariya, Anaheim	L	82	39	62	101	17	40	11	2	4	0	429	9.1
Peter Forsberg, Colorado	C	78	30	67	97	27	108	9	2	7	0	217	13.8
Joe Sakic, Colorado	C	73	41	55	96	23	29	12	5	6	1	255	16.1
Alexei Yashin, Ottawa	C	82	44	50	94	16	54	19	0	5	1	337	13.1
Eric Lindros, Philadelphia	C	71	40	53	93	35	120	10	1	2	3	242	16.5
Theo Fleury, Calg-Col	R	75	40	53	93	26	86	8	3	5	2	301	13.3
John LeClair, Philadelphia	L	76	43	47	90	36	30	16	0	7	3	246	17.5
Pavol Demitra, St. Louis	L	82	37	52	89	13	16	14	0	10	1	259	14.3
Martin Straka, Pittsburgh	C	80	35	48	83	12	26	5	4	4	1	177	19.8
Mats Sundin, Toronto	C	82	31	52	83	22	58	4	0	6	0	209	14.8
Mike Modano, Dallas	C	77	34	47	81	29	44	6	4	7	1	224	15.2
Jason Allison, Boston	C	82	23	53	76	5	68	5	1	3	0	158	14.6
Tony Amonte, Chicago	R	82	44	31	75	0	60	14	3	8	0	256	17.2
Luc Robitaille, Los Angeles	L	82	39	35	74	-1	54	11	0	7	0	292	13.4
Steve Yzerman, Detroit	C	80	29	45	74	8	42	13	2	4	0	231	12.6
Rod Brind'Amour, Philadelphia	C	82	24	50	74	3	47	10	0	3	2	191	12.6
Steve Thomas, Toronto	L	78	28	45	73	26	33	11	0	7	0	209	13.4
Petr Sykora, New Jersey	C	80	29	43	72	16	22	15	0	7	0	222	13.1

Goals

Selanne, Ana	47
Jagr, Pit	44
Amonte, Chi	44
Yashin, Ott	44
LeClair, Phi	43
Sakic, Col	41
Lindros, Phi	40
Fleury, Calg-Col	40
Satan, Buf	40
Kariya, Ana	39
Robitaille, LA	39
Graves, NYR	38

Plus/Minus

Karpovtsev, NYR-Tor	39
LeClair, Phi	36
Lindros, Phi	35
Arvedson, Ott	33
MacInnis, St.L	33
Lehtinen, Dal	29
Stevens, NJ	29
Modano, Dal	29
Shannon, Buf	28
Daneyko, NJ	27
Forsberg, Col	27

Assists

Jagr, Pit	83
Forsberg, Col	67
Kariya, Ana	62
Selanne, Ana	60
Sakic, Col	55
Gretzky, NYR	53
Lindros, Phi	53
Fleury, Calg-Col	53
Allison, Bos	53
Demitra, St.L	52
Sundin, Tor	52
Brind'Amour, Phi	50
Yashin, Ott	50

Penalty Minutes

Ray, Buf	261
Odgers, Col	259
Worrell*, Fla	258
Cote*, Nash	242
Oliwa, NJ	240
Lambert, Nash	218
Laus, Fla	218
Brashear, Van	209
Probert, Chi	206
Brown*, Mon-Chi	205
Domi, Tor	198

Defensemen Points

MacInnis, St.L	62
Lidstrom, Det	57
Bourque, Bos	57
Olausson, Ana	56
Leetch, NYR	55
Housley, Calg	54
Murphy, Det	52
Desjardins, Phi	51
Zubov, Dal	51
Mironov, Edm-Chi	49
Sydor, Dal	48

Power Play Goals

Selanne, Ana	25
Yashin, Ott	19
Aucoin, Van	18
LeClair, Phi	16
Hull, Dal	15
Sykora, NJ	15
Naslund, Van	15
Graves, NYR	14
Amonte, Chi	14
Demitra, St.L	14

Rookie Points

Hejduk, Col	48
Morrison, NJ	46
Drury, Col	44
Hrdina, Pit	42
Parrish, Fla	37
Muckalt, Van	36
Hossa, Ott	30
Korolyuk, SJ	30
LeCavalier, TB	28
Sharifijanov, NJ	27
Watt, NYI	25
Kvasha, Fla	25

Short-Handed Goals

Rolston, NJ	5
Pellerin, St.L	5
Sakic, Col	5
Dvorak, Fla	4
Arvedson, Ott	4
Modano, Dal	4
Straka, Pit	4

Goaltending
(Minimum 26 games)

	Gm	Min	GAA	GA	Shots	Sv%	EN	ShO	Record	G	A	Pts	PM
Ron Tugnutt, Ottawa	43	2508	**1.79**	75	1005	.925	2	3	22-10-8	0	0	0	0
Dominik Hasek, Buffalo	64	3817	**1.87**	119	1877	.937	2	9	30-18-14	0	0	0	14
Ed Belfour, Dallas	61	3536	**1.99**	117	1373	.915	0	5	35-15-9	0	0	0	26
Byron Dafoe, Boston	68	4001	**1.99**	133	1800	.926	3	10	32-23-11	0	2	2	25
Roman Turek, Dallas	26	1382	**2.08**	48	562	.915	1	1	16-3-3	0	0	0	0
Nikolai Khabibulin, Phoenix	63	3657	**2.13**	130	1681	.923	6	8	32-23-7	0	0	0	8
John Vanbiesbrouck, Philadelphia	62	3712	**2.18**	135	1380	.902	4	6	27-18-15	0	1	1	12
Steve Shields, San Jose	37	2162	**2.22**	80	1011	.921	1	4	15-11-8	0	1	1	6
Arturs Irbe, Carolina	62	3643	**2.22**	135	1753	.923	3	6	27-20-12	0	0	0	10
Mike Vernon, San Jose	49	2831	**2.27**	107	1200	.911	3	4	16-22-10	0	0	0	8
Patrick Roy, Colorado	61	3648	**2.29**	139	1673	.917	4	5	32-19-8	0	2	2	28
Martin Brodeur, New Jersey	70	4239	**2.29**	162	1728	.906	4	4	39-21-10	0	4	4	4
Jamie McLennan, St. Louis	33	1763	**2.38**	70	640	.891	3	3	13-14-4	0	0	0	0
Jamie Storr*, Los Angeles	28	1525	**2.40**	61	724	.916	3	4	12-12-2	0	1	1	6
Chris Osgood, Detroit	63	3691	**2.42**	149	1654	.910	4	3	34-25-4	0	3	3	8

Wins

Brodeur, NJ	39
Belfour, Dal	35
Joseph, Tor	35
Osgood, Det	34
Roy, Col	32
Khabibulin, Pho	32
Dafoe, Bos	32
Hebert, Ana	31
Hasek, Buf	30

Three tied with 27 each.

Shutouts

Dafoe, Bos	10
Hasek, Buf	9
Khabibulin, Pho	8
Vanbiesbrouck, Phi	6
Irbe, Car	6
Hebert, Ana	6
Snow, Van	6

Five tied with 5 each.

Save Pct.

Hasek, Buf	.937
Dafoe, Bos	.926
Tugnutt, Ott	.925
Irbe, Car	.923
Khabibulin, Pho	.923
Hebert, Ana	.922
Shields, SJ	.921
Roy, Col	.917
Storr*, LA	.916
Belfour, Dal	.915

Losses

Kolzig, Wash	31
Snow, Van	31
Richter, NYR	30
Thibault, Mon-Chi	30
Hebert, Ana	29
Salo, NYI-Edm	28
Hackett, Chi-Mon	26
Osgood, Det	25
Schwab, TB	25
Joseph, Tor	24

Team Goaltending

WESTERN	GAA	Mins	GA	Shots	Sv%	EN	SO	EASTERN	GAA	Mins	GA	Shots	Sv%	EN	SO
Dallas	**2.02**	4986	168	1965	.915	1	6	Buffalo	**2.09**	5020	175	2461	.929	4	10
San Jose	**2.28**	5016	191	2217	.914	4	8	Ottawa	**2.15**	4999	179	2068	.913	5	6
Phoenix	**2.37**	4985	197	2249	.912	7	9	Boston	**2.17**	5001	181	2226	.919	5	11
Detroit	**2.44**	4962	202	2215	.909	5	3	Philadelphia	**2.34**	5025	196	1877	.896	4	7
Colorado	**2.47**	4974	205	2280	.910	5	5	New Jersey	**2.36**	4986	196	2026	.903	4	5
Anaheim	**2.48**	4990	206	2596	.921	4	7	Carolina	**2.41**	5022	202	2399	.916	6	8
St. Louis	**2.51**	4989	209	1868	.888	5	6	Montreal	**2.51**	4988	209	2207	.905	3	7
Los Angeles	**2.69**	4960	222	2456	.910	10	8	Washington	**2.64**	4959	218	2143	.898	8	6
Edmonton	**2.71**	4997	226	2223	.898	5	3	Pittsburgh	**2.69**	5011	225	2129	.894	10	9
Calgary	**2.81**	4990	234	2415	.903	7	2	NY Rangers	**2.73**	4996	227	2476	.908	8	4
Chicago	**2.98**	4989	248	2404	.897	11	4	Florida	**2.73**	5017	228	2355	.903	4	5
Vancouver	**3.11**	4981	258	2412	.893	5	7	Toronto	**2.79**	4972	231	2359	.902	6	3
Nashville	**3.15**	4964	261	2709	.904	8	2	NY Islanders	**2.93**	4990	244	2331	.895	8	5
								Tampa Bay	**3.52**	4974	292	2633	.889	5	4

Power Play/Penalty Killing

Power play and penalty killing conversions. Power play: No— number of opportunities; GF— goals for; Pct— percentage. Penalty killing: No— number of times shorthanded; GA— goals against; Pct— percentage of penalties killed; SH— shorthanded goals for.

WESTERN	Power Play			Penalty Killing				EASTERN	Power Play			Penalty Killing			
	No	GF	Pct	No	GA	Pct	SH		No	GF	Pct	No	GA	Pct	SH
Anaheim	378	83	22.0	387	60	84.5	6	NY Rangers	348	71	20.4	336	48	85.7	7
St. Louis	301	61	20.3	387	47	87.9	7	New Jersey	304	60	19.7	325	47	85.5	7
Colorado	375	71	18.9	386	63	83.7	7	Pittsburgh	363	65	17.9	302	56	81.5	10
Dallas	393	74	18.8	319	43	86.5	6	Boston	368	65	17.7	305	33	89.2	3
Detroit	415	67	16.1	355	45	87.3	14	Washington	301	52	17.3	353	55	84.4	8
Vancouver	358	57	15.9	450	77	82.9	17	Philadelphia	386	65	16.8	333	53	84.1	4
Chicago	335	50	14.9	405	80	80.2	8	NY Islanders	341	54	15.8	363	60	83.5	8
Edmonton	438	63	14.4	374	67	82.1	8	Ottawa	397	59	14.9	317	44	86.1	6
Calgary	357	51	14.3	386	78	79.8	12	Montreal	344	50	14.5	344	44	87.2	8
San Jose	399	53	13.3	407	61	85.0	8	Toronto	367	53	14.4	325	64	80.3	7
Los Angeles	327	43	13.1	330	47	85.8	12	Tampa Bay	310	43	13.9	387	68	82.4	11
Nashville	324	40	12.3	357	75	79.0	7	Buffalo	363	49	13.5	399	55	86.2	6
Phoenix	342	41	12.0	348	45	87.1	8	Florida	380	51	13.4	370	67	81.9	10
								Carolina	382	42	11.0	346	51	85.3	5

Team by Team Statistics

High scorers and goaltenders with at least ten games played. Players who competed for more than one team during the regular season are listed with their final club; (*) indicates rookies eligible for Calder Trophy.

Mighty Ducks of Anaheim

Top Scorers	Gm	G	A	Pts	+/-	PM	PP
Teemu Selanne	.75	47	60	107	18	30	25
Paul Kariya	.82	39	62	101	17	40	11
Steve Rucchin	.69	23	39	62	11	22	5
Fredrik Olausson	.74	16	40	56	17	30	10
Marty McInnis	.81	19	35	54	-15	42	11
CALG	.6	1	1	2	-1	6	0
ANA	.75	18	34	52	-14	36	11
Tomas Sandstrom	.58	15	17	32	-5	42	7
Travis Green	.79	13	17	30	-7	81	3
Matt Cullen	.75	11	14	25	-12	47	5
Ruslan Salei	.74	2	14	16	1	65	1
Ted Drury	.75	5	6	11	2	83	0
Jim McKenzie	.73	5	4	9	-18	99	1
Jeff Nielsen	.80	5	4	9	-12	34	0
Johan Davidsson*	.64	3	5	8	-9	14	1
Antti Aalto*	.73	3	5	8	-12	24	2
Jason Marshall	.72	1	7	8	-5	142	0
Kevin Haller	.82	1	6	7	-1	122	0
Pascal Trepanier*	.45	2	4	6	0	48	0
Mike Crowley*	.20	2	3	5	-10	16	1
Pavel Trnka	.63	0	4	4	-6	60	0
Stu Grimson	.73	3	0	3	0	158	0
Jamie Pushor	.70	1	2	3	-20	112	0

Acquired: C McInnis from Chi. for undisclosed draft pick (Oct. 27).

Goalies (10 Gm)	Gm	Min	GAA	Record	SV%
Guy Hebert	.69	4083	2.42	31-29-9	.922
Dominic Roussel	.18	884	2.51	4-5-4	.923
ANAHEIM	.82	4990	2.48	35-34-13	.921

Shutouts: Hebert (6), Roussel (1). **Assists:** Hebert (1). **PM:** none.

Boston Bruins

Top Scorers	Gm	G	A	Pts	+/-	PM	PP
Jason Allison	.82	23	53	76	5	68	5
Dmitri Khristich	.79	29	42	71	11	48	13
Ray Bourque	.81	10	47	57	-7	34	8
Sergei Samsonov	.79	25	26	51	-6	18	6
Joe Thornton	.81	16	25	41	3	69	7
Anson Carter	.55	16	40	40	7	22	6
Steve Heinze	.73	22	18	40	7	30	9
Kyle McLaren	.52	6	18	24	1	48	3
Rob DiMaio	.71	7	14	21	-14	95	1
Darren Van Impe	.60	5	15	20	-5	66	4
P.J. Axelsson	.77	7	10	17	-14	18	0
Peter Ferraro	.46	6	8	14	10	44	1
Grant Ledyard	.47	4	8	12	-8	33	1
Don Sweeney	.81	2	10	12	14	64	0
Tim Taylor	.49	4	7	11	-10	55	0
Hal Gill	.80	3	7	10	-10	63	0
Shawn Bates*	.33	5	4	9	3	2	0
Chris Taylor	.37	3	5	8	-3	12	0
Cameron Mann*	.33	5	2	7	0	17	1
Ken Belanger	.54	2	5	7	-1	182	0
NYI	.9	1	1	2	1	30	0
BOS	.45	1	4	5	-2	152	0
Landon Wilson	.22	3	3	6	0	10	0
Mattias Timander	.22	0	6	6	4	10	0
Dave Ellett	.54	0	6	6	11	25	0

Acquired: LW Belanger from NYI for LW Ted Donato (Nov. 7).

Goalies (10 Gm)	Gm	Min	GAA	Record	SV%
Byron Dafoe	.68	4001	1.99	32-23-11	.926
Rob Tallas	.17	987	2.61	7-7-2	.898
BOSTON	.82	5001	2.17	39-30-13	.919

Shutouts: Dafoe (10), Tallas (1). **PM:** Dafoe (25).

Buffalo Sabres

Top Scorers	Gm	G	A	Pts	+/-	PM	PP
Miroslav Satan	.81	40	26	66	24	44	13
Michael Peca	.82	27	29	56	7	81	10
Michal Grosek	.76	20	30	50	21	102	4
Curtis Brown	.78	16	31	47	23	56	5
Dixon Ward	.78	20	24	44	10	44	2
Joe Juneau	.72	15	28	43	-4	22	2
WASH	.63	14	27	41	-3	20	2
BUF	.9	1	1	2	-1	2	0
Jason Woolley	.80	10	33	43	16	62	4
Stu Barnes	.81	20	16	36	-11	30	13
PIT	.64	20	12	32	-12	20	13
BUF	.17	0	4	4	1	10	0
Brian Holzinger	.81	17	17	34	2	45	5
Alexei Zhitnik	.81	7	26	33	-6	96	3
Vaclav Varada	.72	7	24	31	11	61	1
Geoff Sanderson	.75	12	18	30	8	22	1
Darryl Shannon	.71	3	12	15	28	52	1
Richard Smehlik	.72	3	11	14	-9	44	0
Wayne Primeau	.67	5	8	13	-6	38	0
Erik Rasmussen*	.42	3	7	10	6	37	0

Acquired: C Barnes from Pit. for RW Matthew Barnaby (Mar. 11); C Juneau and '99 third-round pick from Wash. for D Alexei Tezikov and future considerations (Mar. 23).

Goalies (10 Gm)	Gm	Min	GAA	Record	SV%
Dominik Hasek	.64	3817	1.87	30-18-14	.937
Dwayne Roloson	.18	911	2.77	6-8-2	.909
BUFFALO	.82	5020	2.09	37-28-17	.929

Shutouts: Hasek (9), Roloson (1). **Assists:** none. **PM:** Hasek (14), Roloson (4).

Calgary Flames

Top Scorers	Gm	G	A	Pts	+/-	PM	PP
Cory Stillman	.76	27	30	57	7	38	9
Phil Housley	.79	11	43	54	14	52	4
Valeri Bure	.80	26	27	53	0	22	7
Jarome Iginla	.82	28	23	51	1	58	7
Andrew Cassels	.70	12	25	37	-12	18	4
Derek Morris	.71	7	27	34	4	73	3
Rene Corbet	.73	13	18	31	1	68	3
COL	.53	8	14	22	3	58	2
CALG	.20	5	4	9	-2	10	1
Jeff Shantz	.76	13	17	30	14	44	1
CHI	.7	1	0	1	-1	4	0
CALG	.69	12	17	29	15	40	1
Jason Wiemer	.78	8	13	21	-12	177	1
Clarke Wilm*	.78	10	8	18	11	53	2
Andre Nazarov	.62	7	9	16	-4	73	0
TB	.26	2	0	2	-5	43	0
CALG	.36	5	9	14	1	30	0
Steve Smith	.69	1	14	15	3	80	0
Steve Dubinsky	.62	4	10	14	-7	14	0
CHI	.1	0	0	0	0	0	0
CALG	.61	4	10	14	-7	14	0

Acquired: C Shantz and C Dubinsky from Chi. for D Jamie Allison, C Marty McInnis and C Erik Andersson (Oct. 27); RW Nazarov from TB for C Michael Nylander (Jan. 19); LW Corbet, D Wade Belak and future considerations from Col. for RW Theo Fleury and LW Chris Dingman (Feb. 28).

Goalies (10 Gm)	Gm	Min	GAA	Record	SV%
Fred Brathwaite	.28	1663	2.45	11-9-7	.915
Tyler Moss*	.11	550	2.51	3-7-0	.922
Ken Wregget	.27	1590	2.53	10-12-4	.906
J.S. Giguere*	.15	860	3.21	6-7-1	.897
CALGARY	.82	4990	2.81	30-40-12	.903

Shutouts: Brathwaite and Wregget (1). **Assists:** Brathwaite, Moss, Wregget and Giguere (1). **PM:** Wregget (8), Giguere (4), Brathwaite (2).

Carolina Hurricanes

Top Scorers	Gm	G	A	Pts	+/-	PM	PP
Keith Primeau	.78	30	32	62	8	75	9
Sami Kapanen	.81	24	35	59	-1	10	5
Ray Sheppard	.74	25	33	58	4	16	5
Ron Francis	.82	21	31	52	-2	34	8
Gary Roberts	.77	14	28	42	2	178	1
Andrei Kovalenko	.74	19	21	40	-6	32	3
EDM	.43	13	14	27	-4	30	2
PHI	.13	0	1	1	-5	2	0
CAR	.18	6	6	12	3	0	1
Jeff O'Neill	.75	16	15	31	3	66	4
Martin Gelinas	.76	13	15	28	3	67	0
Robert Kron	.75	9	16	25	-13	10	3
Glen Wesley	.74	7	17	24	14	44	0
Paul Ranheim	.78	9	10	19	4	39	0
Kevin Dineen	.67	8	10	18	5	97	0
Bates Battaglia	.60	7	11	18	7	22	0
Kent Manderville	.81	5	11	16	9	38	0
Nolan Pratt	.61	1	14	15	15	95	0
Paul Coffey	.54	2	12	14	-7	28	1
CHI	.10	0	4	4	-6	0	0
CAR	.44	2	8	10	-1	28	1
Marek Malik	.52	2	9	11	-6	36	1

Acquired: D Coffey from Chi. for RW Nelson Emerson (Dec. 29); LW Kovalenko from Phi. for D Adam Burt (Mar. 6).

Goalies (10 Gm)	Gm	Min	GAA	Record	Sv%
Arturs Irbe	.62	3643	2.22	27-20-12	.923
Trevor Kidd	.25	1358	2.70	7-10-6	.905
CAROLINA	.82	5022	2.41	34-30-18	.916

Shutouts: Irbe (6), Kidd (2). **Assists:** none. **PM:** Irbe (10).

Chicago Blackhawks

Top Scorers	Gm	G	A	Pts	+/-	PM	PP
Tony Amonte	.82	44	31	75	0	60	14
Alexei Zhamnov	.76	20	41	61	-10	50	8
Doug Gilmour	.72	16	40	56	-16	56	7
Boris Mironov	.75	11	38	49	13	131	5
EDM	.63	11	29	40	6	104	5
CHI	.12	0	9	9	7	27	0
Eric Daze	.72	22	20	42	-13	22	8
Dean McAmmond	.77	10	20	30	8	38	1
EDM	.65	9	16	25	5	36	1
CHI	.12	1	4	5	3	2	0
Ed Olczyk	.61	10	15	25	-3	29	2
Dave Manson	.75	6	17	23	1	155	2
MON	.11	0	2	2	-3	48	0
CHI	.64	6	15	21	4	107	2
Bob Probert	.78	7	14	21	-11	206	0
Anders Eriksson	.72	2	18	20	11	34	0
DET	.61	2	10	12	5	34	0
CHI	.11	0	8	8	6	0	0
J.P. Dumont*	.25	9	6	15	7	10	0
Doug Zmolek	.62	0	14	14	1	102	0
Todd White*	.35	5	8	13	-1	20	2
Reid Simpson	.53	5	4	9	5	145	1

Acquired: G Thibault, D Manson and D Brad Brown from Mon. for G Jeff Hackett, D Eric Weinrich, D Alain Nasreddine and future considerations (Nov. 16); D Mironov, LW McAmmond and D Jonas Elofsson from Edm. for C Chad Kilger, LW Ethan Moreau, D Christian Laflamme and LW Daniel Cleary (Mar. 20); D Eriksson, '99 first-round pick and '01 first-round pick from Det. for D Chris Chelios (Mar. 23).

Goalies (10 Gm)	Gm	Min	GAA	Record	Sv%
Jocelyn Thibault	.62	3544	2.69	24-30-7	.906
MON	.10	529	2.61	3-4-2	.908
CHI	.52	3014	2.71	21-26-5	.905
Mark Fitzpatrick	.27	1403	2.74	6-8-6	.906
CHICAGO	.82	4989	2.98	29-41-12	.897

Shutouts: Thibault (5). **Assists:** Thibault and Fitzpatrick (1). **PM:** Fitzpatrick (8), Thibault (2).

Colorado Avalanche

Top Scorers	Gm	G	A	Pts	+/-	PM	PP
Peter Forsberg	.78	30	67	97	27	108	9
Joe Sakic	.73	41	55	96	23	29	12
Theo Fleury	.75	40	53	93	26	86	8
CALG	.60	30	39	69	18	68	7
COL	.15	10	14	24	8	18	1
Claude Lemieux	.82	27	24	51	0	102	11
Adam Deadmarsh	.66	22	27	49	-2	99	10
Milan Hejduk*	.82	14	34	48	8	26	4
Chris Drury*	.79	20	24	44	9	62	6
Valeri Kamensky	.65	14	30	44	1	28	2
Sandis Ozolinsh	.39	7	25	32	10	22	4
Adam Foote	.64	5	16	21	20	92	3
Sylvain Lefebvre	.76	2	18	20	18	48	0
Shean Donovan	.68	7	12	19	4	37	1
Aaron Miller	.76	5	13	18	3	42	1
Stephane Yelle	.72	8	7	15	-8	40	1
Alexei Gusarov	.54	3	10	13	12	24	1
Dale Hunter	.62	2	9	11	-7	119	0
WASH	.50	0	5	5	-7	102	0
COL	.12	2	4	6	0	17	0
Shjon Podein	.55	3	6	9	-5	24	0
PHI	.14	1	0	1	-2	0	0
COL	.41	2	6	8	-3	24	0

Acquired: LW Podein from Phi. for RW Keith Jones (Nov. 12); RW Fleury and LW Chris Dingman from Calg. for LW Rene Corbet, D Wade Belak and future considerations (Feb. 28); C Hunter and '00 third-round pick from Wash. for '99 second-round pick (Mar. 23).

Goalies (10 Gm)	Gm	Min	GAA	Record	SV%
Patrick Roy	.61	3648	2.29	32-19-8	.917
Craig Billington	.21	1086	2.87	11-8-1	.894
COLORADO	.82	4974	2.47	44-28-10	.910

Shutouts: Roy (5). **Assists:** Roy (2). **PM:** Roy (28), Billington (2).

Dallas Stars

Top Scorers	Gm	G	A	Pts	+/-	PM	PP
Mike Modano	.77	34	47	81	29	44	6
Brett Hull	.60	32	26	58	19	30	15
Joe Nieuwendyk	.67	28	27	55	11	34	8
Jere Lehtinen	.74	20	32	52	29	18	7
Sergei Zubov	.81	10	41	51	9	20	5
Darryl Sydor	.74	14	34	48	-1	50	9
Jamie Langenbrunner	.75	12	33	45	10	62	4
Pat Verbeek	.78	17	17	34	11	133	8
Grant Marshall	.82	13	18	31	1	85	2
Derian Hatcher	.80	9	21	30	21	102	3
Benoit Hogue	.74	12	17	29	-10	54	2
TB	.62	11	14	25	-12	50	2
DAL	.12	1	3	4	2	4	0
Mike Keane	.81	6	23	29	-2	62	1
Tony Hrkac	.69	13	14	27	2	26	2
Derek Plante	.51	6	14	20	4	16	1
BUF	.41	4	11	15	3	12	0
DAL	.10	2	3	5	1	4	1
Dave Reid	.73	6	11	17	0	16	1
Guy Carbonneau	.74	4	12	16	-3	31	0
Richard Matvichuk	.64	3	9	12	23	51	1
Shawn Chambers	.61	2	9	11	6	18	1
Craig Ludwig	.80	2	6	8	5	87	0

Acquired: LW Hogue and a conditional '01 pick from TB for D Sergei Gusev (Mar. 21); C Plante from Buf. for '99 second-round pick (Mar. 23).

Goalies (10 Gm)	Gm	Min	GAA	Record	SV%
Ed Belfour	.61	3536	1.99	35-15-9	.915
Roman Turek	.26	1382	2.08	16-3-3	.915
DALLAS	.82	4986	2.02	51-19-12	.915

Shutouts: Belfour (5), Turek (1). **Assists:** none. **PM:** Belfour (26).

Detroit Red Wings

Top Scorers

Top Scorers	Gm	G	A	Pts	+/-	PM	PP
Steve Yzerman	80	29	45	74	8	42	13
Sergei Fedorov	77	26	37	63	9	66	6
Igor Larionov	75	14	49	63	13	48	4
Brendan Shanahan	81	31	27	58	2	123	5
Vyacheslav Kozlov	79	29	29	58	10	45	6
Nicklas Lidstrom	81	14	43	57	14	14	6
Larry Murphy	80	10	42	52	21	42	5
Wendel Clark	77	32	16	48	-24	37	11
TB	65	28	14	42	-25	35	11
DET	12	4	2	6	1	2	0
Darren McCarty	69	14	26	40	10	108	6
Chris Chelios	75	9	27	36	1	93	3
CHI	65	8	26	34	-4	89	2
DET	10	1	1	2	5	4	1
Tomas Holmstrom	82	13	21	34	-11	69	5
Martin Lapointe	77	16	13	29	7	141	7
Doug Brown	80	9	19	28	5	42	3
Kris Draper	80	4	14	18	2	79	0
Kirk Maltby	53	8	6	14	-6	34	0
Mathieu Dandenault	75	4	10	14	17	59	0

Acquired: D Chelios from Chi. for D Anders Eriksson, '99 first-round pick and '01 first-round pick (Mar. 23); LW Clark and '99 sixth-round pick from TB for G Kevin Hodson and '99 second-round pick (Mar. 23); D Samuelsson from NYR for '99 second-round pick and '99 third-round pick (Mar. 23); G Ranford from TB for '99 conditional pick (Mar. 23).

Goalies (10 Gm)

Goalies (10 Gm)	Gm	Min	GAA	Record	Sv%
Norm Maracle	16	821	2.27	6-5-2	.918
Chris Osgood	63	3691	2.42	34-25-9	.910
Bill Ranford	36	1812	3.64	6-18-4	.885
TB	32	1568	3.90	3-18-3	.881
DET	4	244	1.97	3-0-1	.918
DETROIT	82	4962	2.44	43-32-7	.909

Shutouts: Osgood (3), Ranford (1). **Assists:** Osgood (3). **PM:** Osgood (8), Ranford (2).

Edmonton Oilers

Top Scorers

Top Scorers	Gm	G	A	Pts	+/-	PM	PP
Bill Guerin	80	30	34	64	7	133	13
Josef Beranek	66	19	30	49	6	23	7
Mike Grier	82	20	24	44	5	54	3
Pat Falloon	82	17	23	40	-4	20	8
Rem Murray	78	21	18	39	4	20	4
Doug Weight	43	6	31	37	-8	12	1
Todd Marchant	82	14	22	36	3	65	3
Alexander Selivanov	72	14	19	33	-8	42	2
TB	43	6	13	19	-8	18	1
EDM	29	8	6	14	0	24	1
Roman Hamrlik	75	8	24	32	9	70	3
Ryan Smyth	71	13	18	31	0	62	6
Janne Niinimaa	81	4	24	28	7	88	2
Chad Kilger	77	15	12	27	-4	34	2
CHI	64	14	11	25	-1	30	2
EDM	13	1	1	2	-3	4	0
Ethan Moreau	80	10	11	21	-3	92	0
CHI	66	9	6	15	-5	84	0
EDM	14	1	5	6	2	8	0
Tom Poti*	73	5	16	21	10	42	2

Acquired: C Alexandre Daigle from Phi. for LW Andrei Kovalenko and then RW Selivanov from TB for Daigle (Jan. 29); C Kilger, LW Moreau, D Christian Laflamme and LW Daniel Cleary from Chi. for D Boris Mironov, D Jonas Elofsson and LW Dean McAmmond (Mar. 20); G Salo from NYI for C Mats Lindgren and '99 eighth-round pick (Mar. 20).

Goalies (10 Gm)

Goalies (10 Gm)	Gm	Min	GAA	Record	Sv%
Tommy Salo	64	3717	2.57	25-28-9	.903
NYI	51	3018	2.62	17-26-7	.904
EDM	13	700	2.31	8-2-2	.903
Bob Essensa	39	2091	2.75	12-14-6	.901
EDMONTON	82	4997	2.71	33-37-12	.898

Shutouts: Salo (5). **Assists:** Essensa (1). **PM:** Salo (12).

Florida Panthers

Top Scorers

Top Scorers	Gm	G	A	Pts	+/-	PM	PP
Ray Whitney	81	26	38	64	-3	18	7
Rob Niedermayer	82	18	33	51	-13	50	6
Viktor Kozlov	65	16	35	51	13	24	5
Scott Mellanby	67	18	27	45	5	85	4
Radek Dvorak	82	19	24	43	7	29	0
Mark Parrish*	73	24	13	37	-6	25	5
Robert Svehla	80	8	29	37	-13	83	4
Bill Lindsay	75	12	15	27	-1	92	0
Oleg Kvasha*	68	12	13	25	5	45	4
Bret Hedican	67	5	18	23	5	51	0
VAN	42	2	11	13	7	34	0
FLA	25	3	7	10	-2	17	0
Johan Garpenlov	64	8	9	17	-9	42	0
Pavel Bure	11	13	3	16	3	4	5
Kirk Muller	82	4	11	15	-11	49	0
Jaroslav Spacek*	63	3	12	15	15	28	2
Terry Carkner	62	2	9	11	0	54	0
Paul Laus	75	1	9	10	-1	218	0
Peter Worrell*	62	4	5	9	0	258	0
Dan Boyle*	22	3	5	8	0	6	1
Dino Ciccarelli	14	6	1	7	-1	27	5
Gord Murphy	51	0	7	7	4	16	0
Alex Hicks	55	0	7	7	-5	62	0
SJ	4	0	1	1	-1	4	0
FLA	51	0	6	6	-4	58	0

Acquired: LW Hicks and '99 fifth-round pick from SJ for D Jeff Norton (Nov. 11); RW Bure, D Hedican, D Brad Ference and a conditional third-round pick from Van. for C Dave Gagner, D Ed Jovanovski, LW Mike Brown, G Kevin Weekes and a conditional first-round pick (Jan. 17).

Goalies (10 Gm)

Goalies (10 Gm)	Gm	Min	GAA	Record	Sv%
Sean Burke	59	3402	2.66	21-24-14	.907
Kirk McLean	30	1597	2.74	9-10-4	.900
FLORIDA	82	5017	2.73	30-34-18	.903

Shutouts: Burke (3), McLean (2). **Assists:** Burke (4). **PM:** Burke (27), McLean (2).

Los Angeles Kings

Top Scorers

Top Scorers	Gm	G	A	Pts	+/-	PM	PP
Luc Robitaille	82	39	35	74	-1	54	11
Donald Audette	49	18	18	36	7	51	6
Rob Blake	62	12	23	35	-7	128	5
Jozef Stumpel	64	13	21	34	-18	10	1
Glen Murray	61	16	15	31	-14	36	3
Ray Ferraro	65	13	18	31	0	59	4
Vladimir Tsyplakov	69	11	12	23	-7	32	0
Olli Jokinen*	66	9	12	21	-10	44	3
Craig Johnson	69	7	12	19	-12	32	2
Russ Courtnall	57	6	13	19	-9	19	0
Pavel Rosa*	29	4	12	16	0	6	0
Garry Galley	60	4	12	16	-9	30	3
Doug Bodger	65	3	11	14	1	34	0
Sean O'Donnell	80	1	13	14	1	186	0
Ian Laperriere	72	3	10	13	-5	138	0
Brandon Convery	15	2	7	9	4	12	0
VAN	12	2	7	9	5	8	0
LA	3	0	0	0	-1	4	0
Dave Babych*	41	2	6	8	-2	22	2
PHI	33	2	4	6	0	20	2
LA	8	0	2	2	-2	2	0
Philippe Boucher	45	2	6	8	-12	32	1
Mattias Norstrom	78	2	5	7	-10	36	0

Acquired: RW Audette from Buf. for '99 second-round pick (Dec. 18); D Babych from Phi. for D Steve Duchesne (Mar. 23). **Claimed:** C Convery off waivers from Van. (Nov. 19).

Goalies (10 Gm)

Goalies (10 Gm)	Gm	Min	GAA	Record	Sv%
Jamie Storr*	28	1525	2.40	12-12-2	.916
Stephane Fiset	42	2403	2.60	18-21-1	.915
Manny Legace	17	899	2.60	2-9-2	.911
LOS ANGELES	82	4960	2.69	32-45-5	.910

Shutouts: Storr (4), Fiset (3). **Assists:** Storr and Legace (1). **PM:** Storr (6), Fiset (2).

Montreal Canadiens

Top Scorers	Gm	G	A	Pts	+/-	PM	PP
Saku Koivu	.65	14	30	44	-7	38	4
Martin Rucinsky	.73	17	17	34	-25	50	5
Vladimir Malakhov	.62	13	21	34	-7	77	8
Shayne Corson	.63	12	20	32	-10	147	7
Benoit Brunet	.60	14	17	31	-1	31	4
Turner Stevenson	.69	10	17	27	6	88	0
Stephane Quintal	.82	8	19	27	-23	84	1
Brian Savage	.54	16	10	26	-14	20	5
Patrick Poulin	.81	8	17	25	6	21	0
Sergei Zholtok	.70	7	15	22	-12	6	2
Eric Weinrich	.80	7	15	22	-25	89	4
CHI	.14	1	3	4	-13	12	0
MON	.66	6	12	18	-12	77	4
Jonas Hoglund	.74	8	10	18	-5	16	1
Dainius Zubrus	.80	6	10	16	-8	29	0
PHI	.63	3	5	8	-5	25	0
MON	.17	3	5	8	-3	4	0
Jason Dawe	.59	6	8	14	0	22	1
NYI	.22	2	3	5	0	8	0
MON	.37	4	5	9	0	14	1
Patrice Brisebois	.54	3	9	12	-8	28	1
Igor Ulanov	.76	3	9	12	-3	109	0

Acquired: G Hackett, D Weinrich, D Alain Nasreddine and future considerations from Chi. for G Jocelyn Thibault, D Dave Manson and D Brad Brown (Nov. 16); RW Zubrus and a choice of picks from Phi. for RW Mark Recchi (Mar. 10). **Claimed:** RW Dawe off waivers from NYI (Dec. 15).

Goalies (10 Gm)	Gm	Min	GAA	Record	Sv%
Frederic Chabot	.11	430	2.23	1-3-0	.915
Jeff Hackett	.63	3616	2.49	26-26-10	.907
CHI	.10	524	3.78	2-6-1	.871
MON	.53	3091	2.27	24-20-9	.914
Jose Theodore*	.18	913	3.29	4-12-0	.877
MONTREAL	.82	4988	2.51	32-39-11	.905

Shutouts: Hackett (5), Theodore (1). **Assists:** Hackett (1). **PM:** Hackett (12), Chabot (2).

Nashville Predators

Top Scorers	Gm	G	A	Pts	+/-	PM	PP
Cliff Ronning	.79	20	40	60	-3	42	10
PHO	.7	2	5	7	3	2	2
NASH	.72	18	35	53	-6	40	8
Greg Johnson	.68	16	34	50	-8	24	2
Sergei Krivokrasov	.70	25	23	48	-5	42	10
Sebastien Bordeleau	.72	16	24	40	-14	26	1
Scott Walker	.71	15	25	40	0	103	0
Tom Fitzgerald	.80	13	19	32	-18	48	0
Patric Kjellberg	.71	11	20	31	-13	24	2
Andrew Brunette	.77	11	20	31	-10	26	7
Jamie Heward	.63	6	12	18	-24	44	4
Vitali Yachmenev	.55	7	10	17	-10	10	0
Drake Berehowsky	.74	2	15	17	-9	140	0
Denny Lambert	.76	5	11	16	-3	218	1
Joel Bouchard	.64	4	11	15	-10	60	0
John Slaney	.46	2	12	14	-12	14	0
Bob Boughner	.79	3	10	13	-6	137	0
Kimmo Timonen*	.50	4	8	12	-4	30	1
Jan Vopat	.55	5	6	11	0	28	0
Ville Peltonen	.14	5	5	10	1	2	1
Darren Turcotte	.40	4	5	9	-11	16	0
Rob Valicevic	.19	4	2	6	4	2	0
Mark Mowers*	.30	0	6	6	-4	4	0
Jeff Daniels	.9	1	3	4	-1	2	0

Acquired: C Ronning and D Richard Lintner from Pho. for future considerations (Oct. 31).

Goalies (10 Gm)	Gm	Min	GAA	Record	Sv%
Tomas Vokoun*	.37	1954	2.95	12-18-4	.908
Mike Dunham	.44	2472	3.08	16-23-3	.908
NASHVILLE	.82	4964	3.15	28-47-7	.904

Shutouts: Vokoun and Dunham (1). **Assists:** Vokoun (1). **PM:** Vokoun (6), Dunham (4).

New Jersey Devils

Top Scorers	Gm	G	A	Pts	+/-	PM	PP
Petr Sykora	.80	29	43	72	16	22	15
Bobby Holik	.78	27	37	64	16	119	5
Brian Rolston	.82	24	33	57	11	14	5
Jason Arnott	.74	27	27	54	10	79	8
Patrik Elias	.74	17	33	50	19	34	3
Brendan Morrison*	.76	13	33	46	-4	18	5
Scott Niedermayer	.72	11	35	46	16	26	1
Randy McKay	.70	17	20	37	10	143	3
Lyle Odelein	.70	5	26	31	6	114	1
Dave Andreychuk	.52	15	13	28	1	20	4
Jay Pandolfo	.70	14	13	27	3	10	1
Vadim Sharifijanov*	.53	11	16	27	11	28	1
Scott Stevens	.75	5	22	27	29	64	0
Denis Pederson	.76	11	12	23	-10	66	3
Sergei Nemchinov	.77	12	8	20	-13	28	2
NYI	.67	8	8	16	-17	22	1
NJ	.10	4	0	4	4	6	1
Sergei Brylin	.47	5	10	15	8	28	3
Krzysztof Oliwa	.64	5	7	12	4	240	0
Ken Daneyko	.82	2	9	11	27	63	0
Kevin Dean	.62	1	10	11	4	22	1
Bob Carpenter	.56	2	8	10	-3	36	0
Brad Bombardir	.56	1	7	8	-4	16	0
Sheldon Souray	.70	1	7	8	5	110	0

Acquired: C Nemchinov from NYI for '99 fourth-round pick (Mar. 22).

Goalies (10 Gm)	Gm	Min	GAA	Record	Sv%
Martin Brodeur	.70	4239	2.29	39-21-10	.906
Chris Terreri	.12	726	2.48	8-3-1	.898
NEW JERSEY	.82	4986	2.36	47-24-11	.903

Shutouts: Brodeur (4), Terreri (1). **Assists:** Brodeur (4), Terreri (1). **PM:** Brodeur (4).

New York Islanders

Top Scorers	Gm	G	A	Pts	+/-	PM	PP
Zigmund Palffy	.50	22	28	50	-6	34	5
Trevor Linden	.82	18	29	47	-14	32	8
Bryan Smolinski	.82	16	24	40	-7	49	7
Mariusz Czerkawski	.78	21	17	38	-10	14	4
Claude Lapointe	.82	14	23	37	-19	62	2
Mark Lawrence	.60	14	16	30	-8	38	4
Craig Janney	.56	5	22	27	-15	14	2
TB	.38	4	18	22	-13	10	2
NYI	.18	1	4	5	-2	4	0
Kenny Jonsson	.63	8	18	26	-18	34	6
Mats Lindgren	.60	10	15	25	6	24	3
EDM	.48	5	12	17	4	22	0
NYI	.12	5	3	8	2	2	3
Mike Watt*	.75	8	17	25	-2	12	0
Barry Richter	.72	6	18	24	-4	34	0
Eric Brewer*	.63	5	6	11	-14	32	2
Brad Isbister	.32	4	4	8	1	46	0
PHO	.32	4	4	8	1	46	0
NYI	.0	0	0	0	0	0	0
Zdeno Chara*	.59	2	6	8	-8	83	0
David Harlock	.70	2	6	8	-16	68	0
Gino Odjick	.23	4	3	7	-2	133	1
Kevin Miller	.33	1	5	6	-5	13	0
Rich Pilon	.52	0	4	4	-8	88	0

Acquired: G Potvin from Tor. for D Bryan Berard and exchange of '99 sixth-round picks (Jan. 9); C Janney from TB for '99 sixth-round pick (Jan. 18); LW Isbister and '99 third-round pick from Pho. for C Robert Reichel and '99 third and fourth-round picks; C Lindgren and '99 eighth-round pick from Edm. for G Tommy Salo (Mar. 20).

Goalies (10 Gm)	Gm	Min	GAA	Record	Sv%
Wade Flaherty	.20	1048	3.03	5-11-2	.892
Felix Potvin	.16	905	3.71	5-9-1	.885
TOR	.5	299	3.81	3-2-0	.866
NYI	.11	606	3.66	2-7-1	.893
NY ISLANDERS	.82	4990	2.93	24-48-10	.895

Shutouts: none. **Assists:** none. **PM:** Flaherty (4).

New York Rangers

Top Scorers

Top Scorers	Gm	G	A	Pts	+/-	PM	PP
Wayne Gretzky	.70	9	53	62	-23	14	3
John MacLean	.82	28	27	55	5	46	11
Brian Leetch	.82	13	42	55	-7	42	4
Adam Graves	.82	38	15	53	-12	47	14
Petr Nedved	.56	20	27	47	-6	50	9
Marc Savard	.70	9	36	45	-7	38	4
Kevin Stevens	.81	23	20	43	-10	64	8
Niklas Sundstrom	.81	13	30	43	-2	20	1
Mike Knuble	.82	15	20	35	-7	26	3
Mathieu Schneider	.75	10	24	34	-19	71	5
Todd Harvey	.37	11	17	28	-1	72	6
Manny Malhotra	.73	8	8	16	-2	13	1
Mike Maneluk	.45	6	9	15	5	20	1
PHI	.13	2	6	8	4	8	0
CHI	.28	4	3	7	2	8	1
NYR	.4	0	0	0	-1	4	0
Brent Fedyk	.67	4	6	10	-11	30	0
Jeff Beukeboom	.45	0	9	9	-2	60	0
Kevin Brown	.12	4	2	6	-2	0	2
EDM	.12	4	2	6	-2	0	2
NYR	.0	0	0	0	0	0	0
Scott Fraser	.28	2	4	6	-12	14	1
Chris Tamer	.63	1	5	6	-14	124	0
PIT	.11	0	0	0	-2	32	0
NYR	.52	1	5	6	-12	92	0

Acquired: D Schneider from Tor. for D Alexander Karpovtsev and '99 fourth-round pick (Oct. 14); C Nedved. C Sean Pronger and D Tamer from Pit. for RW Alexei Kovalev, C Harry York and future considerations (Nov. 25); RW Brown from Edm. for LW Vladimir Vorobiev (Mar. 23). **Claimed:** RW Maneluk off waivers from Chi. (Mar. 4).

Goalies (10 Gm)

Goalies (10 Gm)	Gm	Min	GAA	Record	Sv%
Mike Richter	.68	3878	2.63	27-30-8	.910
Dan Cloutier	.22	1097	2.68	6-8-3	.914
NY RANGERS	.82	4996	2.73	33-38-11	.908

Shutouts: Richter (4). **Assists:** none. **PM:** Cloutier (2).

Ottawa Senators

Top Scorers

Top Scorers	Gm	G	A	Pts	+/-	PM	PP
Alexei Yashin	.82	44	50	94	16	54	19
Shawn McEachern	.77	31	25	56	8	46	7
Andreas Dackell	.77	15	35	50	9	30	6
Magnus Arvedson	.80	21	26	47	33	50	0
Andreas Johansson	.69	21	16	37	1	34	7
Nelson Emerson	.65	13	24	37	8	51	3
CAR	.35	8	13	21	1	36	3
CHI	.27	4	10	14	8	13	0
OTT	.3	1	1	2	-1	2	0
Vaclav Prospal	.79	10	26	36	8	58	2
Jason York	.79	4	31	35	17	48	2
Daniel Alfredsson	.58	11	22	33	8	14	4
Radek Bonk	.81	16	16	32	15	48	0
Marian Hossa*	.60	15	15	30	18	37	1
Wade Redden	.72	8	21	29	7	54	3
Ted Donato	.82	11	16	27	-8	41	3
BOS	.14	1	3	4	0	4	0
NYI	.55	7	11	18	-10	27	2
OTT	.13	3	2	5	2	10	1
Igor Kravchuk	.79	4	21	25	14	32	3
Sami Salo*	.61	7	12	19	20	24	2
Shaun Van Allen	.79	6	11	17	3	30	0
Bruce Gardiner	.59	4	8	12	-6	43	0
Janne Laukkanen	.50	1	11	12	18	40	0
Patrick Traverse*	.46	1	9	10	12	22	0

Acquired: LW Donato from NYI for '99 fourth-round pick (Mar. 20); RW Emerson from Chi. for RW Chris Murray (Mar. 23).

Goalies (10 Gm)

Goalies (10 Gm)	Gm	Min	GAA	Record	Sv%
Ron Tugnutt	.43	2508	1.79	22-10-8	.925
Damian Rhodes	.45	2480	2.44	22-13-7	.905
OTTAWA	.82	4999	2.15	44-23-15	.913

Shutouts: Tugnutt and Rhodes (3). **Goals:** Rhodes (1). **Assists:** Rhodes (1). **PM:** Rhodes (4).

Philadelphia Flyers

Top Scorers

Top Scorers	Gm	G	A	Pts	+/-	PM	PP
Eric Lindros	.71	40	53	93	35	120	10
John LeClair	.76	43	47	90	36	30	16
Rod Brind'Amour	.82	24	50	74	3	47	10
Keith Jones	.78	20	33	53	23	98	3
COL	.12	2	2	4	-6	20	1
PHI	.66	18	31	49	29	78	2
Mark Recchi	.71	16	37	53	-7	34	3
MON	.61	12	35	47	-4	28	3
PHI	.10	4	2	6	-3	6	0
Eric Desjardins	.68	15	36	51	18	38	6
Dan McGillis	.78	8	37	45	16	61	6
Mikael Renberg	.66	15	23	38	5	18	6
TB	.20	4	8	12	-2	4	2
PHI	.46	11	15	26	7	14	4
Daymond Langkow	.78	14	19	33	-8	39	4
TB	.22	4	6	10	0	15	1
PHI	.56	10	13	23	-8	24	3
Steve Duchesne	.71	6	24	30	-6	24	3
LA	.60	4	19	23	-6	22	1
PHI	.11	2	5	7	0	2	1
Valeri Zelepukin	.74	16	9	25	0	48	0
Chris Therien	.74	3	15	18	16	48	0

Acquired: RW Jones from Col. for LW Shjon Podein (Nov. 12); RW Renberg and C Langkow from TB for C Chris Gratton and C Mike Sillinger (Dec. 12); RW Recchi from Mon. for RW Dainius Zubrus and a choice of picks (Mar. 10); D Duchesne from LA for D Dave Babych and '00 fifth-round pick (Mar. 23).

Goalies (10 Gm)

Goalies (10 Gm)	Gm	Min	GAA	Record	Sv%
John Vanbiesbrouck	.62	3712	2.18	27-18-15	.902
Ron Hextall	.23	1235	2.53	10-7-4	.888
PHILADELPHIA	.82	5025	2.34	37-26-19	.896

Shutouts: Vanbiesbrouck (6). **Assists:** Hextall (2), Vanbiesbrouck (1). **PM:** Vanbiesbrouck (12), Hextall (2).

Phoenix Coyotes

Top Scorers

Top Scorers	Gm	G	A	Pts	+/-	PM	PP
Jeremy Roenick	.78	24	48	72	7	130	4
Robert Reichel	.83	26	43	69	-13	54	8
NYI	.70	19	37	56	-15	50	5
PHO	.13	7	6	13	2	4	3
Keith Tkachuk	.68	36	32	68	22	151	11
Rick Tocchet	.81	26	30	56	5	147	6
Greg Adams	.75	19	24	43	-1	26	5
Teppo Numminen	.82	10	30	40	3	30	1
Dallas Drake	.53	9	22	31	17	65	0
Jyrki Lumme	.60	7	21	28	5	34	1
Oleg Tverdovsky	.82	7	18	25	11	32	2
Juha Ylonen	.59	6	17	23	18	20	2
Daniel Briere*	.64	8	14	22	-3	30	2
Shane Doan	.79	6	16	22	-5	54	0
Bob Corkum	.77	9	10	19	-9	17	0
Mike Stapleton	.76	9	9	18	-6	34	0
Keith Carney	.82	2	14	16	15	62	0
Deron Quint	.60	5	8	13	-10	20	1
J.J. Daigneault	.70	2	9	11	-12	70	1
NASH	.35	2	2	4	-4	38	1
PHO	.35	0	7	7	-8	32	0
Jim Cummins	.55	1	7	8	3	190	0

Acquired: D Daigneault from Nash. for future considerations (Jan. 13); G Shtalenkov from Edm. for '00 third-round pick (Mar. 11); C Reichel and '99 third and fourth-round picks from NYI for LW Brad Isbister and '99 third-round pick.

Goalies (10 Gm)

Goalies (10 Gm)	Gm	Min	GAA	Record	Sv%
Nikolai Khabibulin	.63	3657	2.13	32-23-7	.923
Mikhail Shtalenkov	.38	2063	2.62	13-19-4	.898
EDM	.34	1819	2.67	12-17-3	.898
PHO	.4	243	2.22	1-2-1	.913
Jim Waite	.16	898	2.74	6-5-4	.895
PHOENIX	.82	4995	2.30	39-31-12	.912

Shutouts: Khabibulin (8), Shtalenkov (3), Waite (1). **Assists:** none. **PM:** Khabibulin (8), Shtalenkov (2), Waite (2).

Pittsburgh Penguins

Top Scorers	Gm	G	A	Pts	+/-	PM	PP
Jaromir Jagr	81	44	83	127	17	66	10
Martin Straka	80	35	48	83	12	26	5
German Titov	72	11	45	56	18	34	3
Alexei Kovalev	77	23	30	53	2	49	6
NYR	14	3	4	7	-6	12	1
PIT	63	20	26	46	8	37	5
Robert Lang	72	21	23	44	-10	24	7
Kip Miller	77	19	23	42	1	22	1
Jan Hrdina*	82	13	29	42	-2	40	3
Kevin Hatcher	66	11	27	38	11	24	4
Rob Brown	58	13	11	24	-15	16	9
Brad Werenka	81	6	18	24	17	93	1
Jiri Slegr	63	3	20	23	13	86	1
Matthew Barnaby	62	6	16	22	-12	177	1
BUF	44	4	14	18	-2	143	0
PIT	18	2	2	4	-10	34	1
Aleksey Morozov	67	9	10	19	5	14	0
Dan Kesa	67	2	8	10	-9	27	0
Bobby Dollas	70	2	8	10	-3	60	0
Ian Moran	62	4	5	9	1	37	0
Maxim Galanov*	51	4	3	7	-8	14	2
Jeff Serowik	26	0	6	6	-4	16	0
Darius Kasparaitis	48	1	4	5	12	70	0

Acquired: RW Kovalev, C Harry York and future considerations from NYR for C Petr Nedved, C Sean Pronger and D Chris Tamer (Nov. 25); RW Barnaby from Buf. for C Stu Barnes (Mar. 11).

Goalies (10 Gm)	Gm	Min	GAA	Record	Sv%
J-S Aubin*	17	756	2.22	4-3-6	.908
Tom Barrasso	43	2306	2.55	19-16-3	.901
Peter Skudra*	37	1914	2.79	15-11-5	.892
PITTSBURGH	82	5011	2.69	38-30-14	.894

Shutouts: Barrasso (4), Skudra (3), Aubin (2). **Assists:** Barrasso (3). **PM:** Barrasso (20), Skudra (2).

St. Louis Blues

Top Scorers	Gm	G	A	Pts	+/-	PM	PP
Pavol Demitra	82	37	52	89	13	16	14
Pierre Turgeon	67	31	34	65	4	36	10
Al MacInnis	82	20	42	62	33	70	11
Scott Young	75	24	28	52	8	27	8
Chris Pronger	67	13	33	46	3	113	8
Scott Pellerin	80	20	21	41	1	42	0
Craig Conroy	69	14	25	39	14	38	0
Mike Eastwood	82	9	21	30	6	36	0
Terry Yake	60	9	18	27	-9	34	3
Pascal Rheaume	60	9	18	27	10	24	2
Jim Campbell	55	4	21	25	-8	41	1
Michel Picard	45	11	11	22	5	16	0
Blair Atcheynum	65	10	8	18	-8	18	2
NASH	53	8	6	14	-10	16	2
ST.L	12	2	2	4	2	2	0
Lubos Bartecko*	32	5	11	16	4	6	0
Michal Handzus*	66	4	12	16	-9	30	0
Ricard Persson	54	1	12	13	4	94	0
Geoff Courtnall	24	5	7	12	2	28	1
Marty Reasoner*	22	3	7	10	2	8	1
Kelly Chase	45	3	7	10	2	143	0
Jamal Mayers*	34	4	5	9	-3	40	0
Tony Twist	63	2	6	8	0	149	0
Jamie Rivers	76	2	5	7	-3	47	1

Acquired: RW Atcheynum from Nash. for '00 sixth-round pick (Mar. 23).

Goalies (10 Gm)	Gm	Min	GAA	Record	Sv%
Jamie McLennan	33	1763	2.38	13-14-4	.891
Grant Fuhr	39	2193	2.44	16-11-8	.892
Rich Parent*	10	519	2.54	4-3-1	.886
ST. LOUIS	82	4989	2.51	37-32-13	.888

Shutouts: McLennan (3), Fuhr (2), Parent (1). **Assists:** none. **PM:** Fuhr (12), Parent (2).

San Jose Sharks

Top Scorers	Gm	G	A	Pts	+/-	PM	PP
Jeff Friesen	78	22	35	57	3	42	10
Vincent Damphousse	77	19	30	49	-4	50	6
MON	65	12	24	36	-7	46	3
SJ	12	7	6	13	3	4	3
Joe Murphy	76	25	23	48	10	73	7
Patrick Marleau	81	21	24	45	10	24	4
Owen Nolan	78	19	26	45	16	129	6
Mike Ricci	82	13	26	39	1	68	2
Marco Sturm	78	16	22	38	7	52	3
Bill Houlder	76	9	23	32	8	40	7
Alex Korolyuk*	55	12	18	30	3	26	2
Stephane Matteau	68	8	15	23	2	73	0
Jeff Norton	72	4	18	22	2	44	2
FLA	3	0	0	0	0	2	0
SJ	69	4	18	22	2	42	2
Ronnie Stern	78	4	9	16	-3	158	1
Dave Lowry	61	6	9	15	-5	24	2
Mike Rathje	82	5	9	14	15	36	2
Murray Craven	43	4	10	14	-3	18	0
Marcus Ragnarsson	74	0	13	13	7	66	0
Tony Granato	35	6	6	12	4	54	0
Bob Rouse	70	0	11	11	0	44	0

Acquired: D Norton from Fla. for LW Alex Hicks and '99 fifth-round pick (Nov. 11); C Damphousse from Mon. for '99 fifth-round pick, '00 second-round pick and future considerations (Mar. 23).

Goalies (10 Gm)	Gm	Min	GAA	Record	Sv%
Steve Shields	37	2162	2.22	15-11-8	.921
Mike Vernon	49	2831	2.27	16-22-10	.911
SAN JOSE	82	5016	2.28	31-33-18	.914

Shutouts: Shields and Vernon (4). **Assists:** Shields (1). **PM:** Vernon (8), Shields (6).

Tampa Bay Lightning

Top Scorers	Gm	G	A	Pts	+/-	PM	PP
Darcy Tucker	82	21	22	43	-34	176	8
Chris Gratton	78	8	26	34	-28	143	1
PHI	26	1	7	8	-8	41	0
TB	52	7	19	26	-20	102	1
Stephane Richer	64	12	21	33	-10	22	3
Vincent Lecavalier*	82	13	15	28	-19	23	2
Petr Svoboda	59	5	18	23	1	81	1
PHI	25	4	2	6	5	28	1
TB	34	1	16	17	-4	53	0
Pavel Kubina*	68	9	12	21	-33	80	3
Colin Forbes	80	12	8	20	-5	61	0
PHI	66	9	7	16	0	51	0
TB	14	3	1	4	-5	10	0
Rob Zamuner	58	8	11	19	-15	24	1
Cory Cross	67	2	16	18	-25	92	0
Alexandre Daigle	63	9	8	17	-13	4	4
PHI	31	3	2	5	-1	2	1
TB	32	6	6	12	-12	2	3
Jassen Cullimore	78	5	12	17	-22	81	1
Michael Nylander	33	4	10	14	-9	8	1
CALG	22	2	3	5	1	2	1
TB	24	2	7	9	-10	6	0
Mike Sillinger	79	8	5	13	-29	36	0
PHI	25	0	3	3	-9	8	0
TB	54	8	2	10	-20	28	0

Acquired: C Gratton and C Sillinger from Phi. for RW Mikael Renberg and C Damond Langkow (Dec. 12); D Svoboda from Phi. for D Karl Dykhuis (Dec. 28); C Nylander from Calg. for RW Andrei Nazarov (Jan. 19); C Daigle from Edm. for RW Alexander Selivanov (Jan. 29); LW Forbes and a conditional pick from Phi. for RW Sandy McCarthy and LW Mikael Andersson (Mar. 20).

Goalies (10 Gm)	Gm	Min	GAA	Record	Sv%
Daren Puppa	13	691	2.87	5-6-1	.906
Corey Schwab	40	2146	3.52	8-25-3	.891
TAMPA BAY	82	4974	3.52	19-54-9	.889

Shutouts: Puppa (2). **Assists:** Schwab (4), Puppa (1). **PM:** Schwab (4).

Toronto Maple Leafs

Top Scorers

Top Scorers	Gm	G	A	Pts	+/-	PM	PP
Mats Sundin	82	31	52	83	22	58	4
Steve Thomas	78	28	45	73	26	33	11
Sergei Berezin	76	37	22	59	16	12	9
Derek King	81	24	28	52	15	20	8
Igor Korolev	66	13	34	47	11	46	1
Mike Johnson	79	20	24	44	13	35	5
Yanic Perreault	76	17	25	42	7	42	4
LA	64	10	17	27	-3	30	2
TOR	12	7	8	15	10	12	2
Steve Sullivan	63	20	20	40	12	28	4
Bryan Berard	69	9	25	34	1	48	4
NYI	31	4	11	15	-6	26	2
TOR	38	5	14	19	7	22	2
Fredrik Modin	67	16	15	31	14	35	1
Garry Valk	77	8	21	29	8	53	1
Sylvain Cote	79	5	24	29	22	28	0
Dimitri Yushkevich	78	6	22	28	25	88	2
Alexander Karpovtsev	58	3	25	28	39	52	1
NYR	2	1	0	1	1	0	0
TOR	56	2	25	27	38	52	1
Alyn McCauley	39	9	15	24	7	2	1
Tie Domi	72	8	14	22	5	198	0
Tomas Kaberle*	57	4	18	22	3	12	0
Todd Warriner	53	9	10	19	-6	28	1
Daniil Markov*	57	4	8	12	5	47	0

Acquired: D Karpovtsev and '99 fourth-round pick from NYR for D Mathieu Schneider (Oct. 14); D Berard and exchange of '99 sixth-round picks from NYI for G Felix Potvin (Jan. 9); C Perreault from LA for RW Jason Podollan (Mar. 23).

Goalies (10 Gm)	Gm	Min	GAA	Record	Sv%
Curtis Joseph	67	4001	2.56	35-24-7	.910
TORONTO	82	4972	2.79	45-30-7	.902

Shutouts: Joseph (3). **Assists:** Joseph (5). **PM:** Joseph (6).

Vancouver Canucks

Top Scorers

Top Scorers	Gm	G	A	Pts	+/-	PM	PP
Markus Naslund	80	36	30	66	-13	74	15
Mark Messier	59	13	35	48	-12	33	4
Alexander Mogilny	59	14	31	45	0	58	3
Bill Muckalt*	73	16	20	36	-9	98	4
Mattias Ohlund	74	9	26	35	-19	83	2
Adrian Aucoin	82	23	11	34	-14	77	18
Dave Gagner	69	6	22	28	-16	63	2
FLA	36	4	10	14	-7	39	2
VAN	33	2	12	14	-9	24	0
Ed Jovanovski	72	5	22	27	-9	126	1
FLA	41	3	13	16	-4	82	1
VAN	31	2	9	11	-5	44	0
Dave Scatchard	82	13	13	26	-12	140	0
Bryan McCabe	69	7	14	21	-11	120	1
Donald Brashear	82	8	10	18	-25	209	2
Brad May	66	6	11	17	-14	102	1
Todd Bertuzzi	32	8	8	16	-6	44	1
Harry York	56	7	9	16	-3	24	1
NYR	5	0	0	0	-1	4	0
PIT	2	0	0	0	0	0	0
VAN	49	7	9	16	-2	20	1

Acquired: C Gagner, D Jovanovski, LW Mike Brown, G Weekes and a conditional first-round pick for RW Pavel Bure, D Bret Hedican, D Brad Ference and a conditional third-round pick (Jan. 17). **Claimed:** C York off waivers from Pit. (Dec. 8).

Goalies (10 Gm)	Gm	Min	GAA	Record	Sv%
Garth Snow	65	3501	2.93	20-31-8	.900
Corey Hirsch	20	919	3.13	3-8-3	.890
Kevin Weekes*	11	532	3.83	0-8-1	.868
VANCOUVER	82	4981	3.11	23-47-12	.893

Shutouts: Snow (6), Hirsch (1). **Assists:** Snow (1). **PM:** Snow (34).

Washington Capitals

Top Scorers

Top Scorers	Gm	G	A	Pts	+/-	PM	PP
Peter Bondra	66	31	24	55	-1	56	6
Adam Oates	59	12	41	53	-1	22	3
Brian Bellows	76	17	19	36	-12	26	8
Andrei Nikolishin	73	8	27	35	0	28	0
Sergie Gonchar	53	21	10	31	1	57	13
James Black	75	16	14	30	5	14	1
Calle Johansson	67	8	21	29	10	22	2
Steve Konowalchuk	45	12	12	24	0	26	4
Jan Bulis	38	7	16	23	3	6	3
Ken Klee	78	7	13	20	-9	80	0
Richard Zednik	49	9	8	17	-6	50	1
Dmitri Mironov	46	2	14	16	-5	80	2
Jaroslav Svejkovsky	25	6	8	14	-2	12	4
Michal Pivonka	36	5	6	11	-6	12	2
Chris Simon	23	3	7	10	-4	48	0
Joe Reekie	73	0	10	10	12	68	0
Benoit Gratton*	16	4	3	7	-1	16	0
Brendan Witt	54	2	5	7	-6	87	0
Kelly Miller	62	2	5	7	-5	29	0
Mike Eagles	52	4	2	6	-5	50	0
Jeff Toms	21	1	5	6	0	2	0
Mark Tinordi	48	0	6	6	-6	108	0
Enrico Ciccone	59	3	1	4	-8	127	0
TB	16	1	1	2	-1	24	0
WASH	43	2	0	2	-7	103	0
Matt Herr*	30	2	2	4	-7	8	1
Trevor Halverson*	17	0	4	4	-5	28	0

Acquired: C Black from Chi. for future considerations (Oct. 15); D Ciccone from TB for future considerations (Dec. 28).

Goalies (10 Gm)	Gm	Min	GAA	Record	Sv%
Rick Tabaracci	23	1193	2.51	4-12-3	.906
Olaf Kolzig	64	3586	2.58	26-31-3	.900
WASHINGTON	82	4959	2.64	31-45-6	.898

Shutouts: Kolzig (4), Tabaracci (2). **Assists:** Kolzig (2). **PM:** Kolzig (19), Tabaracci (2).

NHL Expansion through 2000-2001

In the 1999-2000 season, the Atlanta Thrashers joined the Eastern Conference's Southeast Division.

In the 2000-2001 season, the Columbus Blue Jackets and Minnesota Wild will each join the Western Conference, with Columbus going to the Central Division and Minnesota to the Northwest.

WESTERN	EASTERN
Central	**Northeast**
Chicago	Boston
Columbus	Buffalo
Detroit	Montreal
Nashville	Ottawa
St. Louis	Toronto
Northwest	**Atlantic**
Calgary	New Jersey
Colorado	NY Islanders
Edmonton	NY Rangers
Minnesota	Philadelphia
Vancouver	Pittsburgh
Pacific	**Southeast**
Anaheim	Atlanta
Dallas	Carolina
Los Angeles	Florida
Phoenix	Tampa Bay
San Jose	Washington

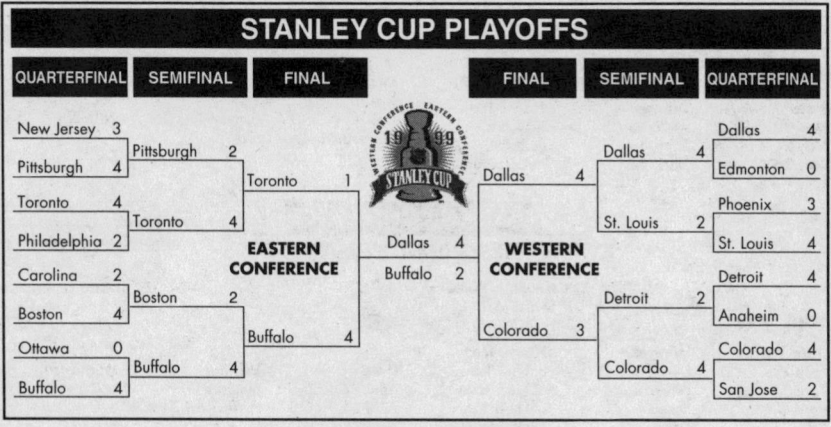

STANLEY CUP PLAYOFFS

| QUARTERFINAL | SEMIFINAL | FINAL | | FINAL | SEMIFINAL | QUARTERFINAL |

EASTERN CONFERENCE

New Jersey 3
Pittsburgh 4 — Pittsburgh 2
Toronto 4 — Toronto 1
Philadelphia 2 — Toronto 4
Carolina 2
Boston 4 — Boston 2 — Dallas 4
Ottawa 0 — Buffalo 4 — Buffalo 2
Buffalo 4 — Buffalo 4

WESTERN CONFERENCE

Dallas 4
St. Louis 2 — Dallas 4
Colorado 3 — Detroit 2 — Colorado 4

Dallas 4 — Edmonton 0
Phoenix 3 — St. Louis 4
Detroit 4 — Anaheim 0
Colorado 4 — San Jose 2

Stanley Cup Playoffs
Series Summaries

WESTERN CONFERENCE

FIRST ROUND (Best of 7)

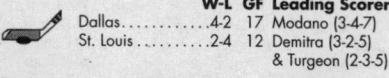

	W-L	GF	Leading Scorers
Dallas	4-0	11	Modano (1-3-4)
Edmonton	0-4	7	Moreau (0-3-3) & Smyth (3-0-3)

Date	Winner	Home Ice
April 21	Stars, 2-1	at Dallas
April 23	Stars, 3-2	at Dallas
April 25	Stars, 3-2	at Edmonton
April 27	Stars, 3-2 (3OT)	at Edmonton

	W-L	GF	Leading Scorers
Detroit	4-0	17	Yzerman (5-2-7)
Anaheim	0-4	6	Selanne (2-2-4) & Kariya (1-3-4)

Date	Winner	Home Ice
April 21	Red Wings, 5-3	at Detroit
April 23	Red Wings, 5-1	at Detroit
April 25	Red Wings, 4-2	at Anaheim
April 27	Red Wings, 3-0	at Anaheim

Shutout: Osgood, Detroit.

	W-L	GF	Leading Scorers
Colorado	4-2	19	Sakic (3-9-12)
San Jose	2-4	17	Norton (0-7-7)

Date	Winner	Home Ice*
April 24	Avalanche, 3-1	at San Jose
April 26	Avalanche, 2-1 (OT)	at San Jose
April 28	Sharks, 4-2	at Colorado
April 30	Sharks, 7-3	at Colorado
May 1	Avalanche, 6-2	at Colorado
May 3	Avalanche, 3-2 (OT)	at San Jose

* The first two games of the series were postponed due to the shootings in Littleton, CO. The series then followed a 2-3-1-1 format with the first two games played in San Jose.

	W-L	GF	Leading Scorers
St. Louis	4-3	19	MacInnis (3-6-9)
Phoenix	3-4	16	Drake (4-3-7)

Date	Winner	Home Ice
April 22	Blues, 3-1	at Phoenix
April 24	Coyotes, 4-3 (OT)	at Phoenix
April 25	Coyotes, 5-4	at St. Louis
April 27	Coyotes, 2-1	at St. Louis
April 30	Blues, 2-1	at Phoenix
May 2	Blues, 5-3	at St. Louis
May 4	Blues, 1-0 (OT)	at Phoenix

Shutout: Fuhr, St. Louis.

SEMIFINALS (Best of 7)

	W-L	GF	Leading Scorers
Dallas	4-2	17	Modano (3-4-7)
St. Louis	2-4	12	Demitra (3-2-5) & Turgeon (2-3-5)

Date	Winner	Home Ice
May 6	Stars, 3-0	at Dallas
May 8	Stars, 5-4 (OT)	at Dallas
May 10	Blues, 3-2 (OT)	at St. Louis
May 12	Blues, 3-2 (OT)	at St. Louis
May 15	Stars, 3-1	at Dallas
May 17	Stars, 2-1	at St. Louis

Shutout: Belfour, Dallas.

	W-L	GF	Leading Scorers
Colorado	4-2	21	Forsberg (4-5-9)
Detroit	2-4	14	Yzerman (4-2-6)

Date	Winner	Home Ice
May 7	Red Wings, 3-2	at Colorado
May 9	Red Wings, 4-0	at Colorado
May 11	Avalanche, 5-3	at Detroit
May 13	Avalanche, 6-2	at Detroit
May 16	Avalanche, 3-0	at Colorado
May 18	Avalanche, 5-2	at Detroit

Shutouts: Ranford, Detroit; Roy, Colorado.

CHAMPIONSHIP (Best of 7)

	W-L	GF	Leading Scorers
Dallas	4-3	23	Nieuwendyk (3-6-9)
Colorado	3-4	16	Forsberg (2-5-7)

Date	Winner	Home Ice
May 22	Avalanche, 2-1	at Dallas
May 24	Stars, 4-2	at Dallas
May 26	Stars, 3-0	at Colorado

Date	Winner	Home Ice
May 28	Avalanche, 3-2 (OT)	at Colorado
May 30	Avalanche, 7-5	at Dallas
June 1	Stars, 4-1	at Colorado
June 4	Stars, 4-1	at Dallas

Shutout: Belfour, Dallas.

EASTERN CONFERENCE

FIRST ROUND (Best of 7)

	W-L	GF	Leading Scorers
Pittsburgh	4-3	21	Straka (6-5-11)
New Jersey	3-4	18	Holik (0-7-7)

Date	Winner	Home Ice
April 22	Devils, 3-1	at New Jersey
April 24	Penguins, 4-1	at New Jersey
April 25	Penguins, 4-2	at Pittsburgh
April 27	Devils, 4-2	at Pittsburgh
April 30	Devils, 4-3	at New Jersey
May 2	Penguins, 3-2 (OT)	at Pittsburgh
May 4	Penguins, 4-2	at New Jersey

	W-L	GF	Leading Scorers
Boston	4-2	16	Bourque (1-5-6)
			& Allison (0-6-6)
Carolina	2-4	10	Sheppard (5-1-6)

Date	Winner	Home Ice
April 22	Bruins, 2-0	at Carolina
April 24	Hurricanes, 3-2 (OT)	at Carolina
April 26	Hurricanes, 3-2	at Boston
April 28	Bruins, 4-1	at Boston
April 30	Bruins, 4-3 (2OT)	at Carolina
May 2	Bruins, 2-0	at Boston

Shutouts: Dafoe, Boston (2).

	W-L	GF	Leading Scorers
Buffalo	4-0	12	Peca (1-5-6)
Ottawa	0-4	6	Emerson (1-3-4)

Date	Winner	Home Ice
April 21	Sabres, 2-1	at Ottawa
April 23	Sabres, 3-2 (2OT)	at Ottawa
April 25	Sabres, 3-0	at Buffalo
April 27	Sabres, 4-3	at Buffalo

Shutout: Hasek, Buffalo.

	W-L	GF	Leading Scorers
Toronto	4-2	9	Berard (0-5-5)
Philadelphia	2-4	11	Desjardins (2-2-4)
			& Brind'Amour (1-3-4)

Date	Winner	Home Ice
April 22	Flyers, 3-0	at Toronto
April 24	Maple Leafs, 2-1	at Toronto
April 26	Maple Leafs, 2-1	at Philadelphia
April 28	Flyers, 5-2	at Philadelphia
April 30	Maple Leafs, 2-1 (OT)	at Toronto
May 2	Maple Leafs, 1-0	at Philadelphia

Shutouts: Vanbiesbrouck, Philadelphia; Joseph, Toronto.

SEMIFINALS (Best of 7)

	W-L	GF	Leading Scorers
Toronto	4-2	18	Bohonos (3-4-7)
			& Sundin (3-4-7)
Pittsburgh	2-4	14	Jagr (3-4-7)

Date	Winner	Home Ice
May 7	Penguins, 2-0	at Toronto
May 9	Maple Leafs, 4-2	at Toronto
May 11	Penguins, 4-3	at Pittsburgh
May 13	Maple Leafs, 3-2 (OT)	at Pittsburgh
May 15	Maple Leafs, 4-1	at Toronto
May 17	Maple Leafs, 4-3	at Pittsburgh

Shutout: Barrasso, Pittsburgh.

	W-L	GF	Leading Scorers
Buffalo	4-2	17	Zhitnik (2-4-6)
Boston	2-4	14	Allison (2-3-5)

Date	Winner	Home Ice
May 8	Bruins, 4-2	at Boston
May 10	Sabres, 3-1	at Boston
May 12	Sabres, 3-2	at Buffalo
May 14	Sabres, 3-0	at Buffalo
May 14	Bruins, 5-3	at Boston
May 14	Sabres, 3-2	at Buffalo

Shutout: Hasek, Buffalo.

CHAMPIONSHIP (Best of 7)

	W-L	GF	Leading Scorers
Buffalo	4-1	21	Barnes (4-2-6)
Toronto	1-4	16	Sundin (4-3-7)

Date	Winner	Home Ice
May 23	Sabres, 5-4	at Toronto
May 25	Maple Leafs, 6-3	at Toronto
May 27	Sabres, 4-2	at Buffalo
May 29	Sabres, 5-2	at Buffalo
May 31	Sabres, 4-2	at Toronto

STANLEY CUP FINAL (Best of 7)

	W-L	GF	Leading Scorers
Dallas	4-2	13	Modano (0-7-7)
Buffalo	2-4	9	Three tied with 3 each.

	Winner	Home Ice
June 8	Sabres, 3-2 (OT)	at Dallas
June 10	Stars, 4-2	at Dallas
June 12	Stars, 2-1	at Buffalo
June 15	Sabres, 2-1	at Buffalo
June 17	Stars, 2-0	at Dallas
June 19	Stars, 2-1 (3OT)	at Buffalo

Shutout: Belfour, Dallas.

Conn Smythe Trophy (Playoff MVP)
Joe Nieuwendyk, Dallas, C
23 games, 11 goals, 10 assists, 21 points
Six game-winning goals

Stanley Cup Final Box Scores

Game 1
Tuesday, June 8, at Dallas

Buffalo ....0 0 2 1 — 3
Dallas ....1 0 1 0 — 2
1st Period: DAL— Hull 6 (Modano, Lehtinen) 10:17 (pp). **3rd Period:** BUF— Barnes 5 (Juneau, Smehlik) 8:33; BUF— Primeau 3 (Zhitnik, Smehlik) 13:37 (pp); DAL— Lehtinen 8 (Modano, Zubov) 19:11.
Overtime: BUF— Woolley 4 (Brown) 15:30.
Shots on Goal: Buffalo— 5-4-10-5–24; Dallas— 11-13-6-7–37. **Power plays:** Buffalo 1-4; Dallas 1-10. **Goalies:** Buffalo, Hasek (37 shots, 35 saves); Dallas, Belfour (24 shots, 21 saves). **Attendance:** 17,001.

Game 2
Thursday, June 10, at Dallas

Buffalo ....0 1 1 — 2
Dallas ....0 1 3 — 4
2nd Period: BUF— Peca 5 (Woolley, Satan) 7:22 (pp); DAL— Langenbrunner 10 (Matvichuk, Nieuwendyk) 18:26.
3rd Period: DAL— Ludwig 1 (Skrudland) 4:25; BUF— Zhitnik 4 (unassisted) 5:36 (pp); DAL— Hull 7 (Hrkac, Chambers) 17:10; DAL— Hatcher 1 (Zubov) 19:34 (en).
Shots on Goal: Buffalo— 7-10-4–21; Dallas— 5-7-19–31. **Power plays:** Buffalo 2-4; Dallas 0-6. **Goalies:** Buffalo, Hasek (30 shots, 27 saves); Dallas, Belfour (21 shots, 19 saves). **Attendance:** 17,001.

Game 3
Saturday, June 12, at Buffalo

Dallas ....0 1 1 — 2
Buffalo ....0 1 0 — 1
2nd Period: BUF— Barnes 6 (Smehlik, Holzinger) 7:51; DAL— Nieuwendyk 10 (Reid, Langenbrunner) 15:33.
3rd Period: DAL— Nieuwendyk 11 (Langenbrunner, Reid) 9:35.
Shots on Goal: Dallas— 8-13-8–29; Buffalo— 3-6-3–12. **Power plays:** Dallas 0-2; Buffalo 0-8. **Goalies:** Dallas, Belfour (12 shots, 11 saves); Buffalo, Hasek (29 shots, 27 saves). **Attendance:** 18,595.

Game 4
Tuesday, June 15, at Buffalo

Dallas ....1 0 0 — 1
Buffalo ....1 1 0 — 2
1st Period: BUF— Sanderson 4 (unassisted) 8:09; DAL— Lehtinen 9 (Modano, Hatcher) 10:14 (pp).
2nd Period: BUF— Ward 7 (unassisted) 7:37.
Shots on Goal: Dallas— 9-9-13–31; Buffalo— 7-9-2–18.
Power plays: Dallas 1-3; Buffalo 0-5. **Goalies:** Dallas, Belfour (18 shots, 16 saves); Buffalo, Hasek (31 shots, 30 saves). **Attendance:** 18,595.

Game 5
Thursday, June 17, at Dallas

Buffalo ....0 0 0 — 0
Dallas ....0 1 1 — 2
2nd Period: DAL— Sydor 3 (Modano, Zubov) 2:23 (pp).
3rd Period: DAL— Verbeek 3 (Matvichuk, Modano) 15:21.
Shots on Goal: Buffalo— 9-5-9–23; Dallas— 8-7-6–21.
Power plays: Buffalo 0-3; Dallas 1-3. **Goalies:** Buffalo, Hasek (21 shots, 19 saves); Dallas, Belfour (23 shots, 23 saves). **Attendance:** 17,001.

Game 6
Thursday, June 19, at Buffalo

Dallas ....1 0 0 0 0 1 — 2
Buffalo ....0 1 0 0 0 0 — 1
1st Period: DAL— Lehtinen 10 (Modano, Ludwig) 8:09.
2nd Period: BUF— Barnes 7 (Primeau, Zhitnik) 18:21.
3rd Overtime: DAL— Hull 8 (Lehtinen, Modano) 14:51.
Shots on Goal: Dallas— 5-11-10-4-13-7–50; Buffalo— 11-15-6-6-12-4–54. **Power plays:** Dallas 0-2; Buffalo 0-2. **Goalies:** Dallas, Belfour (54 shots, 53 saves); Buffalo, Hasek (50 shots, 48 saves). **Attendance:** 18,595.

Stanley Cup Leaders

Scoring

	Gm	G	A	Pts	+/-	PM	PP
Peter Forsberg, Col	19	8	16	24	7	31	1
Mike Modano, Dal	23	5	18	23	6	16	1
Joe Nieuwendyk, Dal	23	11	10	21	7	19	3
Joe Sakic, Col	19	6	13	19	-2	8	1
Theo Fleury, Col	18	5	12	17	-2	20	2
Jamie Langenbrunner, Dal	23	10	7	17	7	16	4
Mats Sundin, Tor	17	8	8	16	2	16	3

Four tied with 15 each.

Plus/Minus

McKee, Buf	+13
Zubov, Dal	+13
Warrener, Buf	+12
Markov, Tor	+9
Lehtinen, Dal	+8
Sydor, Dal	+8
Miller, Col	+8

Penalty Minutes

Zhitnik, Buf	52
Hunter, Col	38
Barnaby, Pit	35
Holzinger, Buf	33
Warrener, Buf	32
Ward, Buf	32
Forsberg, Col	31

Goals

Nieuwendyk, Dal	11
Langenbrunner, Dal	10
Lehtinen, Dal	10
Yzerman, Det	9
Sundin, Tor	8
Deadmarsh, Col	8
Forsberg, Col	8
Hull, Dal	8

Assists

Modano, Dal	18
Forsberg, Col	16
Sakic, Col	13
Fleury, Col	12
Zubov, Dal	12
Lemieux, Col	11
Woolley, Buf	11
Zhitnik, Buf	11

Goaltending
(Minimum 420 minutes)

	Gm	Min	W-L	ShO	GAA
Ed Belfour, Dal	23	1544	16-7	3	1.67
Dominik Hasek, Buf	19	1217	13-6	2	1.77
Byron Dafoe, Bos	12	768	6-6	2	2.03
Grant Fuhr, St.L	13	790	6-6	1	2.35
Nikolai Khabibulin, Pho	7	449	3-4	0	2.41
Curtis Joseph, Tor	17	1011	9-8	1	2.43
Patrick Roy, Col	19	1173	11-8	1	2.66

Power Play Goals

Yzerman, Det	4
Barnes, Buf	4
Zhitnik, Buf	4
Langenbrunner, Dal	4

Overtime Goals

Turgeon, St.L	2
Hejduk, Col	2
Nieuwendyk, Dal	2

Wins

Belfour, Dal	16-7
Hasek, Buf	13-6
Roy, Col	11-8
Joseph, Tor	9-8

Three tied with 6 each.

Save Pct.

Hasek, Buf	.939
Belfour, Dal	.930
Khabibulin, Pho	.924
Dafoe, Bos	.921
Roy, Col	.920

Finalists' Composite Box Scores
Dallas Stars (16-7)

Top Scorers	Pos	Overall Playoffs								Finals vs Buffalo							
		Gm	G	A	Pts	+/-	PM	PP	S	Gm	G	A	Pts	+/-	PM	PP	S
Mike Modano	C	23	5	18	23	6	16	1	83	6	0	7	7	4	8	0	19
Joe Nieuwendyk	C	23	11	10	21	7	19	3	72	6	2	1	3	3	9	0	19
Jamie Langenbrunner	C	23	10	7	17	7	16	4	46	6	1	2	3	2	4	0	6
Brett Hull	R	22	8	7	15	3	4	3	86	5	3	0	3	2	2	1	18
Jere Lehtinen	R	23	10	3	13	8	2	1	55	6	3	2	5	5	0	1	14
Sergei Zubov	D	23	1	12	13	13	4	0	46	6	0	3	3	2	2	0	20
Darryl Sydor	D	23	3	9	12	8	16	1	49	6	1	0	1	2	8	1	16
Dave Reid	L	23	2	8	10	4	14	0	30	6	0	2	2	2	2	0	9
Mike Keane	R	23	5	2	7	-1	6	0	41	6	0	1	1	-3	0	0	12
Pat Verbeek	R	18	3	4	7	4	14	0	33	6	1	0	1	0	4	0	13
Derian Hatcher	D	18	1	6	7	4	24	0	28	6	1	1	2	2	10	0	14
Guy Carbonneau	C	17	2	4	6	0	6	0	29	6	0	0	0	-3	0	0	9
Richard Matvichuk	D	22	1	5	6	4	20	0	26	6	0	2	2	3	6	0	10
Craig Ludwig	D	23	1	4	5	2	20	0	6	6	1	1	2	-1	10	0	3
Grant Marshall	R	14	0	3	3	1	20	0	23	6	0	0	0	0	0	0	0
Tony Hrkac	C	5	0	2	2	3	4	0	3	3	0	1	1	2	2	0	3
Benoit Hogue	C	14	0	2	2	-1	16	0	20	2	0	0	0	0	2	0	1
Shawn Chambers	D	17	0	2	2	-1	18	0	19	6	0	1	1	-1	2	0	9
Blake Sloan*	R	19	0	2	2	1	8	0	7	6	0	0	0	-1	0	0	2
Brian Skrudland	C	19	0	2	2	0	16	0	10	6	0	1	1	0	8	0	1
Derek Plante	C	6	1	0	1	0	4	0	8	0	0	0	0	0	0	0	0
Brad Lukowich*	D	8	0	1	1	3	4	0	6	0	0	0	0	0	0	0	0
Doug Lidster	D	4	0	0	0	0	2	0	1	0	0	0	0	0	0	0	0
Jon Sim*	C	4	0	0	0	-1	0	0	1	2	0	0	0	-1	0	0	1

Overtime goals— OVERALL (Nieuwendyk 2, Hull, Modano); FINALS (Hull). **Shorthanded goals—** OVERALL (Keane, Lehtinen, Modano); FINALS (none). **Power Play conversions—**OVERALL (13 for 107, 12.1%); FINALS (3 for 26, 11.5%).

Goaltending	Overall Playoffs							Finals vs Buffalo							
	Gm	Min	GAA	GA	SA	Sv%	W-L	Gm	Min	GAA	GA	SA	Sv%	W-L
Ed Belfour	23	1544	1.67	43	617	.930	16-7	6	429	1.26	9	152	.941	4-2
TOTAL	23	1547	1.71	44	618	.929	16-7	6	429	1.26	9	152	.941	4-2

Empty Net Goals— OVERALL (one), FINALS (none). **Shutouts—** OVERALL (Belfour 3), FINALS (Belfour). **Assists—** OVERALL (none), FINALS (none). **Penalty Minutes—** OVERALL (Belfour 4), FINALS (none).

Buffalo Sabres (14-7)

Top Scorers	Pos	Overall Playoffs								Finals vs Dallas							
		Gm	G	A	Pts	+/-	PM	PP	S	Gm	G	A	Pts	+/-	PM	PP	S
Jason Woolley	D	21	4	11	15	0	10	2	43	6	1	1	2	0	6	0	9
Alexei Zhitnik	D	21	4	11	15	-6	52	4	58	6	1	2	3	-4	18	1	16
Curtis Brown	C	21	7	6	13	3	10	3	34	6	0	1	1	-2	0	0	9
Michael Peca	C	21	5	8	13	1	18	2	37	6	1	0	1	-3	2	1	10
Dixon Ward	R	21	7	5	12	6	32	0	38	6	1	0	1	-2	8	0	5
Joe Juneau	C	20	3	8	11	-2	10	0	29	6	0	1	1	0	0	0	4
Stu Barnes	C	21	7	3	10	-1	6	4	30	6	1	2	3	-3	0	0	13
Geoff Sanderson	L	19	4	6	10	0	6	1	53	6	1	0	1	1	4	0	16
Vaclav Varada	R	21	5	4	9	2	14	1	38	6	0	0	0	-2	6	0	6
Miroslav Satan	L	12	3	5	8	3	2	1	25	6	0	1	1	-3	2	0	10
Brian Holzinger	C	21	3	5	8	1	33	1	32	6	0	1	1	1	9	0	9
Wayne Primeau	C	19	3	4	7	0	6	1	22	6	1	1	2	-1	4	1	7
Erik Rasmussen*	C	21	2	4	6	2	18	0	23	6	0	0	0	-2	2	0	5
Rhett Warrener	D	20	1	3	4	12	32	0	21	5	0	0	0	6	6	0	5
Michal Grosek	L	13	0	4	4	1	28	0	20	1	0	0	0	0	0	0	0
Richard Smehlik	D	21	0	3	3	-4	10	0	20	6	0	3	3	-4	2	0	4
Jay McKee	D	21	0	3	3	13	24	0	13	6	0	0	0	-1	2	0	4
Rob Ray	R	5	1	0	1	1	0	0	0	1	0	0	0	0	0	0	0
James Patrick	D	20	0	1	1	6	12	0	11	6	0	0	0	2	4	0	7
Darryl Shannon	D	2	0	0	0	-1	0	0	7	1	0	0	0	0	0	0	0
Randy Cunneyworth	L	3	0	0	0	1	0	0	2	3	0	0	0	-1	0	0	2
Dean Sylvester*	R	4	0	0	0	-1	2	0	2	0	0	0	0	0	0	0	0
Paul Kruse	L	10	0	0	0	0	4	0	1	1	0	0	0	-1	0	0	1

Overtime goals— OVERALL (Satan, Woolley); FINALS (Woolley). **Shorthanded goals—** OVERALL (Ward 2, Juneau, Peca); FINALS (none). **Power Play conversions—** OVERALL (19 for 95, 20.0%); FINALS (3 for 26, 11.5%).

Goaltending	Overall Playoffs							Finals vs Dallas							
	Gm	Min	GAA	GA	SA	Sv%	W-L	Gm	Min	GAA	GA	SA	Sv%	W-L
Dominik Hasek	19	1217	1.77	36	587	.939	13-6	6	427	1.69	12	198	.939	2-4
Dwayne Roloson	4	139	4.32	10	67	.851	1-1	0	0	0	–	0	–	0-0
TOTAL	21	1361	2.16	49	657	.925	14-7	6	430	1.81	13	199	.935	2-4

Empty Net Goals— OVERALL (three), FINALS (one). **Shutouts—** OVERALL (Hasek 2); FINALS (none). **Assists—** OVERALL (Hasek); FINALS (none). **Penalty Minutes—** OVERALL (Hasek 8), FINALS (Hasek 2).

Annual Awards

Except for the Vezina Trophy and Adams Award, voting is done by a 56-member panel of the Pro Hockey Writers Association, while full PHWA membership voted for Masterton Trophy. Vezina Trophy is voted on by NHL general managers and Adams Award by NHL broadcasters. Points are awarded on 10–7–5–3–1 basis except for the Vezina Trophy and the Adams Award which are awarded 5–3–1.

Hart Trophy
For Most Valuable Player

	Pos	1st	2nd	3rd	4th	5th	Pts
Jaromir Jagr, Pit	R	51	4	1	0	0—	543
Alexei Yashin, Ott	C	0	23	9	5	5—	226
Dominik Hasek, Buf	G	4	10	8	5	7—	172
Curtis Joseph, Tor	G	1	5	10	7	2—	118
Teemu Selanne, Ana	R	0	3	14	5	5—	111
Eric Lindros, Phi	C	0	4	5	6	6—	77

Calder Trophy
For Rookie of the Year

	Pos	1st	2nd	3rd	4th	5th	Pts
Chris Drury, Col	C	32	15	2	4	1—	448
Marian Hossa, Ott	L	12	9	11	8	7—	269
Milan Hejduk, Col	R	4	11	8	6	9—	184
Mark Parrish, Fla	L	5	5	11	6	10—	168
Brendan Morrison, NJ	C	1	5	15	12	7—	163

Norris Trophy
For Best Defenseman

	1st	2nd	3rd	4th	5th	Pts
Al MacInnis, St.L	54	0	1	1	0—	548
Nicklas Lidstrom, Det	0	21	9	13	3—	234
Ray Bourque, Bos	0	9	12	8	10—	157
Chris Pronger, St.L	1	5	9	3	8—	107
Eric Desjardins, Phi	0	6	4	6	11—	91

Vezina Trophy
For Outstanding Goaltender

	1st	2nd	3rd	Pts
Dominik Hasek, Buf	8	10	3—	73
Curtis Joseph, Tor	10	4	2—	64
Byron Dafoe, Bos	8	4	6—	58
Martin Brodeur, NJ	1	1	9—	17
Ron Tugnutt, Ott	0	4	1—	13

Lady Byng Trophy
For Sportsmanship and Gentlemanly Play

	Pos	1st	2nd	3rd	4th	5th	Pts
Wayne Gretzky, NYR	C	20	7	2	2	3—	268
Nicklas Lidstrom, Det	D	13	10	3	5	3—	233
Teemu Selanne, Ana	R	9	12	6	5	3—	222
Pavol Demitra, St.L	L	7	8	13	6	7—	216
Joe Sakic, Col	C	1	6	12	4	2—	126

Selke Trophy
For Best Defensive Forward

	Pos	1st	2nd	3rd	4th	5th	Pts
Jere Lehtinen, Dal	R	23	16	7	5	1—	393
Magnus Arvedson, Ott	L	19	9	7	6	5—	311
Michael Peca, Buf	C	11	12	16	3	3—	286
Steve Yzerman, Det	C	1	1	2	4	5—	44
Curtis Brown, Buf	C	1	1	3	2	0—	38
Craig Conroy, St.L	C	0	3	1	3	3—	38

Adams Award
For Coach of the Year

	1st	2nd	3rd	Pts
Jacques Martin, Ott	43	16	7—	270
Pat Quinn, Tor	18	24	14—	176
Ken Hitchcock, Dal	7	20	13—	108
Pat Burns, Bos	0	8	9—	33
Kevin Constantine, Pit	3	2	10—	31
Robbie Ftorek, NJ	2	2	8—	24

AP/Wide World Photos

Pittsburgh's **Jaromir Jagr** added his first Hart Trophy to his rapidly growing NHL resume.

Other Awards

Lester B. Pearson Award (NHL Players Assn. MVP)— Jaromir Jagr, Pittsburgh; **Jennings Trophy** (goaltenders with a minimum of 25 games played for team with fewest goals against)— Ed Belfour and Roman Turek, Dallas; **Maurice "Rocket" Richard Trophy** (regular season goal-scoring leader)— Teemu Selanne, Anaheim; **Art Ross Trophy** (regular season points leader)— Jaromir Jagr, Pittsburgh; **Masterton Trophy** (perseverance, sportsmanship, and dedication to hockey)— John Cullen, Tampa Bay; **King Clancy Trophy** (leadership and humanitarian contributions to community)— Rob Ray, Buffalo; **Lester Patrick Trophy** (outstanding service to hockey in the U.S.)— Boston Bruins President and GM Harry Sinden and the 1998 U.S. Olympic Women's Hockey Team.

All-NHL Team

Voting by Pro Hockey Writers' Association (PHWA). Holdover from 1997-98 All-NHL first team in **bold** type.

	First Team		Second Team
G	**Dominik Hasek**, Buf	G	Byron Dafoe, Bos
G	Al MacInnis, St.L	G	Ray Bourque, Bos
D	**Nicklas Lidstrom**, Det	D	Eric Desjardins, Phi
C	**Peter Forsberg**, Col	C	Alexei Yashin, Ott
R	**Jaromir Jagr**, Pit	R	Teemu Selanne, Ana
L	Paul Kariya, Ana	L	**John LeClair**, Phi

All-Rookie Team

Voting by PHWA. Vote totals not released.

Pos		Pos	
G	Jamie Storr, LA	F	Chris Drury, Col
D	Sami Salo, Ott	F	Milan Hejduk, Col
D	Tom Poti, Edm	F	Marian Hossa, Ott

1999 NHL Draft

First and second round selections at the 37th annual NHL Entry Draft held June 26, 1999, in Boston. The order of the first 12 positions (11 non-playoff teams plus expansion Atlanta) were determined by a draft lottery held May 16 in New York. Positions 13 through 28 reflect regular season records in reverse order. The top 28 picks are first round selections and the remaining 22 are from the second round.

Top 50 Picks

Team		Pos	Team		Pos
1 **a-**Atlanta	Patrik Stefan, Long Beach	C	26 Ottawa	Martin Havlat, Trinec	C
2 **b-**Vancouver	Daniel Sedin, MoDo	L	27 New Jersey	Ari Ahonen, Jyvaskyla	G
3 Vancouver	Henrik Sedin, MoDo	C	28 **j-**NY Islanders	Kristian Kudroc, Michalovce	D
4 **c-**NY Rangers	Pavel Brendl, Calgary	R	29 **k-**Washington	Michal Sivek, Kladno	C
5 NY Islanders	Tim Connolly, Erie	C	30 Atlanta	Luke Sellars, Ottawa	D
6 Nashville	Brian Finley, Barrie	G	31 **l-**Washington	Charlie Stephens, Guelph	C
7 Washington	Kris Beech, Calgary	C	32 **m-**Dallas	Michael Ryan, BC High	R
8 **d-**NY Islanders	Taylor Pyatt, Sudbury	L	33 Nashville	Jonas Andersson, AIK	R
9 **e-**NY Rangers	Jamie Lundmark, Moose Jaw	C	34 Washington	Ross Lupaschuk, Prince Albert	D
10 **f-**NY Islanders	Branislav Mezei, Belleville	D	35 **n-**Buffalo	Milan Bartovic, Trencin	R
11 **g-**Calgary	Oleg Saprykin, Seattle	L	36 Edmonton	Alexei Semenov, Sudbury	D
12 Florida	Denis Shvidki, Barrie	R	37 Washington*	Nolan Yonkman, Kelowna	C
13 Edmonton	Jani Rita, Jokerit	R	38 Calgary	Dan Cavanaugh, BU	C
14 San Jose	Jeff Jillson, Michigan	D	39 Montreal	Alexander Buturlin, CSKA	L
15 **h-**Phoenix	Scott Kelman, Seattle	C	40 **o-**Florida	Alexander Auld, North Bay	G
16 Carolina	David Tanabe, Wisconsin	D	41 Edmonton*	Tony Salmelainen, IFK Helsinki	L
17 St. Louis	Barret Jackman, Regina	D	42 New Jersey*	Mike Commodore, N. Dakota	D
18 Pittsburgh	Konstantin Koltsov, Cherepovets	L	43 Los Angeles*	Andrei Shefer, Cherepovets	L
19 Phoenix	Kiril Safranov, SKA	D	44 **p-**Anaheim	Jordan Leopold, Minnesota	D
20 Buffalo	Barrett Heisten, Maine	L	45 **q-**Colorado	Martin Grenier, Quebec	D
21 Boston	Nick Boynton, Ottawa	D	46 Chicago	Dmitri Levinski, Cherepovets	R
22 Philadelphia	Maxime Ouellet, Quebec	G	47 **r-**Tampa Bay	Sheldon Keefe, Barrie	R
23 **i-**Chicago	Steve McCarthy, Kootenay	D	48 **s-**Ottawa	Simon Lajeunesse, Moncton	G
24 Toronto	Luca Cereda, Ambri	C	49 Carolina	Brett Lysak, Regina	C
25 Colorado	Mikhail Kuleshov, Cherepovets	L	50 **t-**New Jersey	Brett Clouthier, Kingston	L

Acquired picks: a— from Vancouver via Tampa Bay; **b—** from Atlanta; **c—** from Chicago via Vancouver and Tampa Bay; **d—** from Los Angeles; **e—** from Calgary; **f—** from Montreal; **g—** from NY Rangers; **h—** from Anaheim; **i—** from Detroit; **j—** from Dallas; **k—** from Tampa Bay; **l—** from Colorado via Vancouver; **m—** from NY Islanders; **n—** from Los Angeles; **o—** from St. Louis; **p—** from NY Rangers via Ottawa; **q—** from Florida via Nashville; **r—** from Detroit via San Jose; **s—** from Anaheim; **t—** from St. Louis.
*compensatory pick

U.S. Division I College Hockey

Final regular season standings; overall records, including all postseason tournament games, in parentheses.

Central Collegiate Hockey Assn.

	W	L	T	Pts	GF	GA
*Michigan St. (29-6-7)	20	3	7	47	91	40
*Michigan (25-11-6)	17	8	5	39	98	72
*Ohio St. (21-16-4)	17	10	3	37	88	67
Notre Dame (19-14-5)	15	11	4	34	92	68
*N. Michigan (22-15-5)	14	11	5	33	94	83
Ferris St. (14-16-6)	13	12	5	31	76	69
Bowling Green (17-18-3)	13	14	3	29	102	105
Lake Superior St. (11-23-4)	10	17	3	23	79	93
Miami-OH (11-20-5)	9	17	4	22	78	104
W. Michigan (6-20-8)	5	17	8	18	69	119
Alaska-Fairbanks (11-22-1)	8	21	1	17	77	124

Conf. Tourney Final: Michigan 5, N. Michigan 1.
*NCAA Tourney (2-4): Michigan St. (1-1), Michigan (1-1), Ohio St. (0-1), N. Michigan (0-1).

Eastern Collegiate Athletic Conf.

	W	L	T	Pts	GF	GA
*Clarkson (25-11-1)	18	4	0	36	91	48
*St. Lawrence (23-13-3)	15	4	3	33	80	47
Rensselaer (23-12-2)	13	7	2	28	89	62
Princeton (20-12-2)	13	8	1	27	69	62
Colgate (19-12-4)	12	8	2	26	66	56
Yale (13-14-4)	11	7	4	26	65	56
Cornell (12-15-4)	9	10	3	21	67	63
Harvard (14-16-2)	8	12	2	18	64	67
Vermont (13-18-2)	7	13	2	16	53	67
Brown (9-16-6)	5	12	5	15	56	72
Dartmouth (10-17-2)	6	14	2	14	60	79
Union (3-26-3)	1	18	2	4	32	93

Conf. Tourney Final: Clarkson 3, St. Lawrence 2.
*NCAA Tourney (0-2): Clarkson (0-1), St. Lawrence (0-1).

Hockey East Association

	W	L	T	Pts	GF	GA
*New Hampshire (31-7-3)	18	3	3	39	100	49
*Maine (31-6-4)	17	5	2	36	94	64
*Boston College (27-12-4)	15	7	2	32	99	73
Providence (20-17-1)	12	11	1	25	90	81
Boston University (14-20-3)	8	13	3	19	72	86
UMass-Lowell (17-19-0)	9	15	0	18	65	85
UMass-Amherst (12-21-2)	8	14	2	18	56	86
Merrimack (11-24-1)	7	16	1	15	67	94
Northeastern (11-20-3)	6	16	2	14	74	101

Conf. Tourney Final: Boston College 5, New Hampshire 4 (OT).
*NCAA Tourney (8-2): Maine (4-0), New Hampshire (2-1), Boston College (2-1).

Western Collegiate Hockey Assn.

	W	L	T	Pts	GF	GA
*North Dakota (32-6-2)	24	2	2	50	142	76
*Colorado College (29-12-1)	20	8	0	40	103	68
*Denver (25-12-1)	15	11	2	32	101	95
Wisconsin (15-19-4)	13	13	3	29	76	81
Minnesota (15-19-9)	10	12	6	26	90	99
Alaska-Anchorage (13-18-5)	10	13	5	25	57	71
St. Cloud St. (16-18-5)	8	16	4	20	79	95
Michigan Tech (9-28-1)	9	19	0	18	67	99
Minnesota-Duluth (7-27-4)	4	20	4	12	71	102

Conf. Tourney Final: Denver 4, North Dakota 3.
*NCAA Tourney (1-3): Colorado College (1-1), North Dakota (0-1), Denver (0-1).

Metro Atlantic Athletic Conf.

	W	L	T	Pts	GF	GA
Quinnipiac (26-6-2) 22	4	2	46	131	63
Holy Cross (22-9-4) 19	6	3	41	107	63
Connecticut (20-10-4)........18	6	4	40	106	70
Canisius (16-15-5) 12	11	5	29	112	82
American Int'l (12-16-4).......11	13	4	26	92	93
Iona (13-18-2)..............12	15	1	25	116	115
Sacred Heart (7-23-1)........7	20	1	15	81	128
Fairfield (1-31-0)............1	27	0	2	55	186

Conf. Tourney Final: Holy Cross 4, Canisius 3.
*NCAA Tourney (0-0).

Independents

(Listed alphabetically)	Gm	W	L	T	Pts	GF	GA
Air Force 36	15	19	2	32	113	128
Army 26	8	16	2	18	74	89
Minn. St.-Mankato 39	19	15	5	43	149	124
Nebraska-Omaha............35	10	25	0	20	90	135
Niagara 32	17	12	3	37	103	85

*NCAA Tourney (0-0).

USA Today/American Hockey Magazine Coaches Poll

Taken April 5, 1999 after the NCAA Tournament. First place votes are in parentheses.

	League	W	L	T	Pts
1 Maine (10)..................HE	31	6	4	100
2 New Hampshire ....HE	31	7	3	89
3 Michigan St. ....CCHA	29	6	7	77
4 Boston College ....HE	27	12	4	73
5 North Dakota ....WCHA	32	6	2	61
6 Colorado College ....WCHA	29	12	1	49
7 Michigan ....CCHA	25	11	6	41
8 Denver ....WCHA	26	13	2	28
9 Clarkson ....ECAC	25	11	1	22
10 St. Lawrence ....ECAC	23	13	3	8

Also receiving votes: Ohio St. (2 pts).

Scoring Leaders

Including postseason games.

	Cl	Gm	G	A	Pts
Jason Krog, UNH ....Sr.	41	34	51	**85**
Jason Blake, North Dakota ...Sr.	38	28	41	**69**
Brian Swanson. Colorado Col. .Sr.	42	25	41	**66**
Steve Kariya, Maine..........Sr.	41	27	38	**65**
Mike Souza, UNH ....Jr.	41	23	42	**65**
Ryan Carter, Iona ....Fr.	33	33	30	**63**
Darren Haydar, UNH ....Fr.	41	31	30	**61**

Goaltending Leaders

Including postseason games; minimum 15 games.

	Cl	Record	Sv%	GAA
Joe Blackburn, Michigan St.... So.	21-5-7	.928	**1.55**
Ty Conklin, UNH ....So.	18-3-1	.922	**1.84**
Scott Simpson, Holy Cross .....Sr.	16-5-2	.915	**2.22**
Josh Blackburn, Michigan......Fr.	25-10-6	.905	**2.28**
Shep Harder, Colgate ....Jr.	15-7-1	.923	**2.28**
Greg Naumenko, Alaska-Anch.. Jr.	11-13-5	.920	**2.31**
Alfie Michaud, Maine ....Jr.	28-6-3	.910	**2.32**

Hobey Baker Award

For College Player of the Year. Presented by Koho and USA Hockey, Inc. Voting done by 18-member panel of national media, coaches, pro scouts and a member of USA Hockey. Vote totals not released.

	Cl	Pos
Winner: Jason Krog, UNH ....Sr.		F
Runner-up: Mike York, Michigan St. ....Sr.		F

NCAA Division I Tournament
Regional Seeds

Frozen Four teams in **bold**.

West
1 North Dakota (32-5-2)
2 **Michigan St.** (28-5-7)
3 Colorado Coll. (28-11-1)
4 **Boston College** (25-11-4)
5 N. Michigan (22-14-5)
6 St. Lawrence (23-12-3)

East
1 **New Hampshire** (29-6-3)
2 Clarkson (25-10-1)
3 **Maine** (27-6-4)
4 Denver (26-12-2)
5 Michigan (24-10-6)
6 Ohio St. (21-15-4)

West Regional

Held at the Dane County Coliseum in Madison, Wisc., March 27-28. Single elimination, two second round winners advance to Frozen Four.

First Round

Colorado College 5.....................St. Lawrence 2
Boston College 2...................Northern Michigan 1
(Byes: Michigan St. and North Dakota)

Second Round

Boston College 3 ....North Dakota 1
Michigan St. 4......................Colorado College 3

East Regional

Held at the Worcester (Mass.) Centrum, March 26-27. Single elimination, two second round winners advance to Final Four.

First Round

Maine 4 ....Ohio St. 2
Michigan 5 ....Denver 3
(Byes: New Hampshire and Clarkson)

Second Round

New Hampshire 2.........OT ....Michigan 1
Maine 7 ....Clarkson 2

THE FROZEN FOUR

Held at Arrowhead Pond in Anaheim, Calif., April 1 and April 3. Single elimination; no consolation game.

Semifinals

New Hampshire 5 .... Michigan St. 3
Maine 2 ....OT ....Boston College 1

Championship Game

Maine, 3-2 (OT)

Maine (HE)......................1	1	0	1	–	**3**
New Hampshire (HE) 0	1	1	0	–	**2**

1st Period: UM— Ben Guite (Jason Vitorino, Dan Kerluke), 15:47 (pp).
2nd Period: UM— Niko Dimitrakos (David Cullen, Peter Metcalf), 4:10; NH— Darren Haydar (Mike Souza, Ty Conklin), 15:58 (sh).
3rd Period: NH— Souza (Jason Krog, Haydar), 3:33.
Overtime: UM— Marcus Gustafsson (Cory Larose), 10:50.
Goalies: UM— Alfie Michaud (48 shots, 46 saves); NH— Ty Conklin (39 shots, 36 saves). **Attendance:** 14,447.
Final records: Maine (31-6-4); New Hampshire (31-7-3); Michigan St. (29-6-7); Boston College (27-12-4).
Outstanding Player: Alfie Michaud, Maine junior goalie; SEMIFINAL— 36 shots, 35 saves; FINAL— 48 shots, 46 saves.
All-Tournament Team: Michaud, forward Niko Dimitrakos and defenseman David Cullen of Maine; forwards Jason Krog and Mike Souza and defenseman Jayme Filipowicz of New Hampshire.

Division I All-America

First team Titan Division I All-Americans as chosen by the American Hockey Coaches Association. Holdover from 1997-98 All-America first teams is in **bold** type.

West Team

Pos		Yr	Hgt	Wgt
G	Joe Blackburn, Michigan St.	So.	5-11	180
D	Scott Swanson, Colorado Coll.	Sr.	6-2	205
D	Brad Williamson, North Dakota	Sr.	5-10	175
F	Jason Blake, North Dakota	Sr.	5-10	180
F	Brian Swanson, Colorado Coll.	Sr.	5-10	185
F	**Mike York**, Michigan St.	Sr.	5-10	185

East Team

Pos		Yr	Hgt	Wgt
G	Eric Heffler, St. Lawrence	Sr.	6-3	190
D	David Cullen, Maine	Sr.	6-1	211
D	Mike Motteau, Boston College	Jr.	6-0	192
F	Brian Gionta, Boston College	So.	5-7	160
F	Steve Kariya, Maine	Sr.	5-9	165
F	Jason Krog, UNH	Sr.	5-11	191

Other NCAA Tournaments

Division II

Two teams selected from limited national field. Championship decided in two games with mini-game (one 15-minute period), if necessary.

Final Two

March 12-13 in Essex Junction, Vt.
Championship: GAME ONE— St. Michael's (Vt.) 4, New Hampshire College 4; GAME TWO— St. Michael's 8, New Hampshire College 5.
Final records: St. Michael's (16-10-2), New Hampshire College (17-8-2).

Division III

Final Four

March 19-20 in Northfield, Vt.
Semifinals— Wisc-Superior 4, Norwich (Vt.) 2; Middlebury (Vt.) 9, R.I.T. 3. **Third Place**—Norwich 9, R.I.T. 2. **Championship**— Middlebury 5, Wisc-Superior 0.
Final records: Middlebury (21-5-1); Wisc-Superior (22-8-3); Norwich (27-2-2); R.I.T. (26-3-2).

Women's College Hockey

National Championship

Women's hockey is not an officially sanctioned NCAA sport, but a championship is sponsored by the American Women's College Hockey Alliance (AWCHA).

March 27 in Minneapolis, Minn.
Championship: Harvard 6, New Hampshire 5 (OT)
Consolation: Minnesota 3, Brown 2
Final records: Harvard (33-1-0), New Hampshire (23-7-5), Minnesota (29-4-3), Brown (20-7-4).

First-Team All-America

As determined by the AWCHA.

G Ali Brewer, Brown, Jr.
D Nicki Luongo, UNH, Sr.
D Angela Ruggerio, Harvard, Fr.
F Jennifer Botterill, Harvard, Fr.
F A.J. Mleczko*, Harvard, Sr.
F Tammy Shewchuk, Harvard, So.
*winner of the Patty Kazmaier Memorial Award as college hockey's top player.

MINOR LEAGUE HOCKEY

American Hockey League

Division champions (*) and playoff qualifiers (†) are noted. GF and GA refer to goals for and against. Losses in overtime are designated in parentheses and worth one point in the standings.

Eastern Conference
Atlantic Division

Team (Affiliate)	W	L	T	Pts	GF	GA
*Lowell (NYI)	33	34(2)	13	81	219	237
†St. John's (Tor.)	34	39(4)	7	79	246	270
†Fredericton (Mon.)	33	41(5)	6	77	246	246
†Saint John (Calg.)	31	41(1)	8	71	238	296
Portland (Wash.)	23	50(2)	7	55	214	273

New England Division

Team (Affiliate)	W	L	T	Pts	GF	GA
*Providence (Bos.)	56	20(4)	4	120	321	223
†Hartford (NYR)	38	37(6)	5	87	256	256
†Springfield (Pho. & LA)	35	36(1)	9	80	245	232
†Worcester (St.L & Ott.)	34	38(2)	8	78	237	260
New Haven (Car. & Fla.)	33	40(5)	7	78	240	250

Western Conference
Empire Division

Team (Affiliate)	W	L	T	Pts	GF	GA
*Rochester (Buf.)	52	22(1)	6	111	287	176
†Albany (NJ)	46	28(2)	6	100	275	230
†Hamilton (Edm.)	40	33(4)	7	91	229	206
†Adirondack (Det.)	21	51(3)	8	53	184	280
Syracuse (Van. & Pit.)	18	53(3)	9	48	220	327

Mid-Atlantic Division

Team (Affiliate)	W	L	T	Pts	GF	GA
*Philadelphia (Phi.)	47	24(2)	9	105	272	221
†Kentucky (SJ & Fla.)	44	29(3)	7	98	272	214
†Hershey (Col.)	37	33(1)	10	85	242	224
†Cincinnati (Ana.)	35	41(2)	4	76	227	249

Scoring Leaders

	Gm	G	A	Pts	PM
Dominic Pittis, Roch	76	38	66	104	108
Randy Robitaille, Pro	74	28	74	102	34
John Madden, Alb	75	38	60	98	44
Peter White, Phi	77	31	59	90	20
Jim Montgomery, Phi	78	29	58	87	89

Goaltending Leaders

	GP	GAA	Sv%	Record
Martin Biron, Roch	52	2.08	.930	36-13-3
Steve Passmore, Ham	54	2.24	.929	24-21-7
Jim Carey, Pro	30	2.34	.919	17-8-3

Calder Cup Finals

	W-L	GF	Leading Scorers
Providence	4-1	20	Mann (4-4-8)
Rochester	1-4	9	Cunneyworth (1-3-4)

Date	Winner	Home Ice
June 5	Providence, 4-2	at Providence
June 6	Providence, 6-0	at Providence
June 9	Providence, 3-2 (3OT)	at Rochester
June 11	Rochester, 4-2	at Rochester
June 13	Providence, 5-1	at Providence

International Hockey League

Division champions (*) and playoff qualifiers (†) are noted. GF and GA refer to goals for and against. SOL refers to shootout losses and are worth one point in the standings.

Eastern Conference
Northeast Division

Team (Affiliate)	W	L	SOL	Pts	GF	GA
*Detroit (Ott.)	50	21	11	111	259	195
†Orlando (Indep.)	45	33	4	94	264	253
†Cincinnati (Indep.)	44	32	6	94	269	270
Grand Rapids (Indep.)	34	40	8	76	256	281

Central Division

Team (Affiliate)	W	L	SOL	Pts	GF	GA
*Michigan (Dal.)	35	34	13	83	232	253
†Fort Wayne (Indep.)	34	33	15	83	251	279
†Indianapolis (Chi.)	32	37	13	77	242	278
Cleveland (TB)	28	47	7	63	248	310

Scoring Leaders

	Gm	G	A	Pts	PM
Brian Wiseman, Hou	77	21	87	108	106
Steve Maltais, Chi	82	56	44	100	164
Bill Bowler, Man	82	26	67	93	59
Todd Simon, Cin	81	26	62	88	72
Gilbert Dionne, Cin	76	35	52	87	123

Goaltending Leaders

	GP	GAA	Sv%	Record
Kevin Weekes, Det	33	2.07	.919	19-5-7
Manny Legace, Long	33	2.25	.912	22-8-1
Manny Fernandez, Hou	51	2.36	.916	34-6-10

Western Conference
Midwest Division

Team (Affiliate)	W	L	SOL	Pts	GF	GA
*Chicago (Indep.)	49	21	12	110	285	246
†Manitoba (Indep.)	47	21	14	108	269	236
†Kansas City (Indep.)	44	31	7	95	256	270
†Milwaukee (Nash.)	38	28	16	92	254	265

Southwest Division

Team (Affiliate)	W	L	SOL	Pts	GF	GA
*Houston (Indep.)	54	15	13	121	307	209
†Long Beach (LA)	48	28	6	102	260	237
Utah (Indep.)	39	34	9	87	244	254
Las Vegas (Pho.)	35	39	8	78	247	307

Turner Cup Finals

	W-L	GF	Leading Scorers
Houston	4-3	30	Stewart (6-4-10)
Orlando	3-4	23	Panteleyev (6-3-9)

Date	Winner	Home Ice
May 23	Houston, 6-3	at Houston
May 25	Orlando, 4-2	at Houston
May 27	Houston, 6-1	at Orlando
May 29	Houston, 5-4 (OT)	at Orlando
June 1	Orlando, 5-4 (OT)	at Orlando
June 3	Orlando, 3-2	at Houston
June 5	Houston, 5-3	at Houston

East Coast Hockey League

Division champions (*) and playoff qualifiers (†) are noted. GF and GA refer to goals for and against. SOL refers to shootout losses and are worth one point in the standings.

Northern Conference
Northeast Division

Team (Affiliate)	W	L	SOL	Pts	GF	GA
*Roanoke (NYI)	38	22	10	86	224	201
†Hampton Roads (Wash./Nash.)	38	24	8	84	215	213
†Richmond (SJ)	40	27	3	83	239	196
†Chesapeake (TB)	34	25	11	79	229	206
Johnstown (Calg.)	27	34	9	63	218	265

Northwest Division

Team (Affiliate)	W	L	SOL	Pts	GF	GA
*Columbus (Chi.)	39	24	7	85	257	242
†Peoria (St.L)	39	25	6	84	243	230
†Toledo (Det.)	39	26	5	83	256	246
†Dayton (Dal.)	34	27	9	77	239	241
Huntington (Ana.)	31	33	6	68	221	253
Wheeling (Pit.)	27	37	6	60	206	249

Scoring Leaders

	Gm	G	A	Pts	PM
John Spoltore, Lou	69	36	73	109	96
Jamie Ling, Day	70	39	56	95	32
Chris Valicevic, Lou	70	20	72	92	63
Jamey Hicks, Bir	65	16	75	91	60
Dany Bousquet, PD	62	36	54	90	63

Goaltending Leaders

	GP	GAA	Sv%	Record
Maxime Gingras, Rich	50	2.26	.924	30-13-10
Marc Magliarditi, Fla	47	2.27	.914	32-10-8
Bujar Amidovski, Lou	27	2.32	.923	17-5-3

Southern Conference
Southeast Division

Team (Affiliate)	W	L	SOL	Pts	GF	GA
*Pee Dee (Indep.)	51	15	4	106	289	191
†Florida (Car.)	45	20	5	95	253	190
†South Carolina (Buf.)	40	20	10	90	235	216
†Augusta (NJ & Van.)	38	27	5	81	235	233
†Jacksonville (Indep.)	35	33	2	72	235	255
Charlotte (NYR)	29	30	11	69	221	262
Miami (Fla.)	28	32	10	66	208	266
Greenville (Bos.)	26	33	11	63	208	241

Southwest Division

Team (Affiliate)	W	L	SOL	Pts	GF	GA
*Louisiana (Indep.)	46	18	6	98	297	205
†Mississippi (LA & Pho.)	41	22	7	89	251	215
†Birmingham (Indep.)	37	29	4	78	251	267
†New Orleans (Edm. & Mon.)	30	27	13	73	244	261
†Mobile (Indep.)	31	31	8	70	231	259
†Baton Rouge (Indep.)	30	30	10	70	222	228
Tallahassee (Indep.)	27	34	9	63	212	250
Pensacola (Indep.)	25	41	4	54	199	267

Kelly Cup Finals

	W-L	GF	Leading Scorers
Mississippi	4-3	21	Hurd (4-3-7)
Richmond	3-4	17	Kraft (2-4-6)

Date	Winner	Home Ice
May 15	Richmond, 2-0	at Mississippi
May 16	Mississippi, 5-3	at Mississippi
May 19	Richmond, 5-3	at Richmond
May 23	Richmond, 1-0	at Richmond
May 24	Mississippi, 2-0	at Mississippi
May 28	Mississippi, 7-3	at Richmond
May 30	Mississippi, 4-3 (2OT)	at Mississippi

World Hockey Championships

MEN

The World Hockey Championships, held in Oslo, Hamar and Lillehammer, Norway May 1-16, 1999. Top two teams (*) in each pool after preliminary round-robin advance to the qualifying round. Third place teams play in a consolation round. Top two teams from each pool of the qualifying round advance to the semifinals. The semifinals and finals are best-of-two series with a 10-minute overtime if necessary. If teams are still tied, a shootout decides the winner.

Final Round Robin Standings

POOL A	W-L-T	Pts	GF	GA
*Canada	3-0-0	6	12	6
*Slovakia	2-1-0	4	17	9
Norway	1-2-0	2	9	14
Italy	0-3-0	0	8	17

POOL B	W-L-T	Pts	GF	GA
*Sweden	3-0-0	6	14	5
*Switzerland	2-1-0	4	12	9
Latvia	1-2-0	2	14	14
France	0-3-0	0	6	18

POOL C	W-L-T	Pts	GF	GA
*Czech Republic	3-0-0	6	23	5
*United States	2-1-0	4	15	7
Austria	1-2-0	2	6	14
Japan	0-3-0	0	5	23

POOL D	W-L-T	Pts	GF	GA
*Finland	2-0-1	5	10	5
*Russia	1-0-2	4	9	6
Belarus	1-1-1	3	6	7
Ukraine	0-3-0	0	2	13

Qualifying Round

POOL E	W-L-T	Pts	GF	GA
*Finland	3-0-0	6	13	6
*Canada	2-1-0	4	14	7
United States	1-2-0	2	7	8
Switzerland	0-3-0	0	3	16

POOL F	W-L-T	Pts	GF	GA
*Czech Republic	2-1-0	4	11	8
*Sweden	2-1-0	4	6	4
Russia	1-1-1	3	9	7
Slovakia	0-2-1	1	5	12

Semifinals (best of two)

Finland 3 . . . . Sweden 1
Sweden 2 . . . . Finland 1†

Canada 2 . . . . Czech Republic 1
Czech Republic 4* . . . . Canada 3
†Finland advances with a goal in OT.
*Czech Republic wins shootout, 4-3.

Bronze Medal Game

Sweden 3 . . . . Canada 2

Championship (best of two)

Czech Republic 3 . . . . Finland 1
Finland 4 . . . . Czech Republic 1*
*Czech Republic wins championship with goal in OT.

Scoring Leaders

	Gm	G	A	Pts	PM
Saku Koivu, Finland	10	4	12	**16**	4
Teemu Selanne, Finland	11	3	8	**11**	2
Markus Naslund, Sweden	10	6	4	**10**	16
Zigmund Palffy, Slovakia	6	5	5	**10**	6
Jan Hlavac, Czech Republic	12	5	5	**10**	4
Martin Rucinsky, Czech Republic	12	4	6	**10**	16
Alexei Yashin, Russia	6	8	1	**9**	6
Daniel Alfredsson, Sweden	10	4	5	**9**	8

Goaltending Leaders

(At least 180 minutes)	Gm	Min	GAA
Parris Duffus, USA	5	258	**1.63**
Andrei Mezin, Belarus	6	360	**1.67**
Tommy Salo, Sweden	8	423	**1.84**
Ari Sulander, Finland	9	464	**1.94**
Ron Tugnutt, Canada	7	328	**2.01**

World All-Star Team
(Selected by media)

First team: G— Tommy Salo, Sweden; **D—** Pavel Kubina, Czech Republic; Jere Karalahti, Finland; **F—** Martin Rucinsky, Czech Republic; Saku Koivu, Finland; Teemu Selanne, Finland.

WOMEN

The fifth sanctioned Women's World Hockey Championship, held in Espoo, Finland March 8-14, 1999. Top five teams from the 1998 Winter Olympics qualified (USA, Canada, Finland, China and Sweden) along with the top three teams from a qualification tournament (Germany, Switzerland and Russia). Top two teams (*) in each group after preliminary round-robin advance to the medal round.

Final Round Robin Standings

POOL A	W-L-T	Pts	GF	GA
*United States	3-0-0	6	27	2
*Sweden	2-1-0	4	10	12
China	1-2-0	2	4	11
Russia	0-3-0	0	4	20

POOL B	W-L-T	Pts	GF	GA
*Canada	3-0-0	6	24	0
*Finland	2-1-0	4	16	1
Germany	1-2-0	2	5	26
Switzerland	0-3-0	0	4	22

Medal Round

Canada 4 . . . . Sweden 1
United States 3 . . . . Finland 1

Bronze Medal: Finland 8 . . . . Sweden 2
Gold Medal: Canada 3 . . . . United States 1

World All-Star Team
(Selected by media)

First team: G— Sami Jo Small, Canada; **D—** Sue Merz, USA; Kirsi Hanninen, Finland; **F—** Hayley Wickenheiser, Canada; Jayna Hefford, Canada; Jenny Schmidgall, USA.

THE 2000 ESPN INFORMATION PLEASE SPORTS ALMANAC

HOCKEY STATISTICS

THROUGH THE YEARS 1893-1999

STANLEY CUP • NHL LEADERS

SEC B

PAGE 413

The Stanley Cup

The Stanley Cup was originally donated to the Canadian Amateur Hockey Association by Sir Frederick Arthur Stanley, Lord Stanley of Preston and 16th Earl of Derby, who had become interested in the sport while Governor General of Canada from 1888 to 1893. Stanley wanted the trophy to be a challenge cup, contested for each year by the best amateur hockey teams in Canada.

In 1893, the Cup was presented without a challenge to the AHA champion Montreal Amateur Athletic Association team. Every year since, however, there has been a playoff. In 1914, Cup trustees limited the field challenging for the trophy to the champion of the eastern professional National Hockey Association (NHA, organized in 1910) and the western professional Pacific Coast Hockey Association (PCHA, organized in 1912).

The NHA disbanded in 1917 and the National Hockey League (NHL) was formed. From 1918 to 1926, the NHL and PCHA champions played for the Cup with the Western Canada Hockey League (WCHL) champion joining in a three-way challenge in 1923 and '24. The PCHA disbanded in 1924, while the WCHL became the Western Hockey League (WHL) for the 1925-26 season and folded the following year. The NHL playoffs have decided the winner of the Stanley Cup ever since.

Champions, 1893-1917

Multiple winners: Montreal Victorias and Montreal Wanderers (4); Montreal Amateur Athletic Association and Ottawa Silver Seven (3); Montreal Shamrocks, Ottawa Senators, Quebec Bulldogs and Winnipeg Victorias (2).

Year		Year		Year	
1893	Montreal AAA	1901	Winnipeg Victorias	1909	Ottawa Senators
1894	Montreal AAA	1902	Montreal AAA	1910	Montreal Wanderers
1895	Montreal Victorias	1903	Ottawa Silver Seven	1911	Ottawa Senators
1896 (Feb.)	Winnipeg Victorias	1904	Ottawa Silver Seven	1912	Quebec Bulldogs
(Dec.)	Montreal Victorias	1905	Ottawa Silver Seven	1913	Quebec Bulldogs
1897	Montreal Victorias	1906	Montreal Wanderers	1914	Toronto Blueshirts (NHA)
1898	Montreal Victorias	1907 (Jan.)	Kenora Thistles	1915	Vancouver Millionaires (PCHA)
1899	Montreal Shamrocks	(Mar.)	Montreal Wanderers	1916	Montreal Canadiens (NHA)
1900	Montreal Shamrocks	1908	Montreal Wanderers	1917	Seattle Metropolitans (PCHA)

Champions Since 1918

Multiple winners: Montreal Canadiens (23); Toronto Arenas-St. Pats-Maple Leafs (13); Detroit Red Wings (9); Boston Bruins and Edmonton Oilers (5); NY Islanders, NY Rangers and Ottawa Senators (4); Chicago Blackhawks (3); Philadelphia Flyers, Pittsburgh Penguins and Montreal Maroons (2).

Year	Winner	Head Coach	Series	Loser	Head Coach
1918	Toronto Arenas	Dick Carroll	3-2 (WLWLW)	Vancouver (PCHA)	Frank Patrick
1919	No Decision*				
1920	Ottawa	Pete Green	3-2 (WWLLW)	Seattle (PCHA)	Pete Muldoon
1921	Ottawa	Pete Green	3-2 (LWWLW)	Vancouver (PCHA)	Frank Patrick
1922	Toronto St. Pats	Eddie Powers	3-2 (LWWLW)	Vancouver (PCHA)	Frank Patrick
1923	Ottawa	Pete Green	3-1 (WLWW)	Vancouver (PCHA)	Frank Patrick
			2-0	Edmonton (WCHL)	K.C. McKenzie
1924	Montreal	Leo Dandurand	2-0	Vancouver (PCHA)	Frank Patrick
			2-0	Calgary (WCHL)	Eddie Oatman
1925	Victoria (WCHL)	Lester Patrick	3-1 (WWLW)	Montreal	Leo Dandurand
1926	Montreal Maroons	Eddie Gerard	3-1 (WWLW)	Victoria (WHL)	Lester Patrick
1927	Ottawa	Dave Gill	2-0 (TWTW)	Boston	Art Ross
1928	NY Rangers	Lester Patrick	3-2 (LWLWW)	Montreal Maroons	Eddie Gerard
1929	Boston	Cy Denneny	2-0	NY Rangers	Lester Patrick
1930	Montreal	Cecil Hart	2-0	Boston	Art Ross
1931	Montreal	Cecil Hart	3-2 (WLLWW)	Chicago	Art Duncan
1932	Toronto	Dick Irvin	3-0	NY Rangers	Lester Patrick
1933	NY Rangers	Lester Patrick	3-1 (WWLW)	Toronto	Dick Irvin
1934	Chicago	Tommy Gorman	3-1 (WWLW)	Detroit	Jack Adams
1935	Montreal Maroons	Tommy Gorman	3-0	Toronto	Dick Irvin
1936	Detroit	Jack Adams	3-1 (WWLW)	Toronto	Dick Irvin
1937	Detroit	Jack Adams	3-2 (LWLWW)	NY Rangers	Lester Patrick
1938	Chicago	Bill Stewart	3-1 (WLWW)	Toronto	Dick Irvin
1939	Boston	Art Ross	4-1 (WLWWW)	Toronto	Dick Irvin
1940	NY Rangers	Frank Boucher	4-2 (WWLLWW)	Toronto	Dick Irvin

Year	Winner	Head Coach	Series	Loser	Head Coach
1941	Boston	Cooney Weiland	4-0	Detroit	Jack Adams
1942	Toronto	Hap Day	4-3 (LLLWWWW)	Detroit	Jack Adams
1943	Detroit	Ebbie Goodfellow	4-0	Boston	Art Ross
1944	Montreal	Dick Irvin	4-0	Chicago	Paul Thompson
1945	Toronto	Hap Day	4-3 (WWWLLLW)	Detroit	Jack Adams
1946	Montreal	Dick Irvin	4-1 (WWWLW)	Boston	Dit Clapper
1947	Toronto	Hap Day	4-2 (LWWWLW)	Montreal	Dick Irvin
1948	Toronto	Hap Day	4-0	Detroit	Tommy Ivan
1949	Toronto	Hap Day	4-0	Detroit	Tommy Ivan
1950	Detroit	Tommy Ivan	4-3 (WLWLLWW)	NY Rangers	Lynn Patrick
1951	Toronto	Joe Primeau	4-1 (WLWW)	Montreal	Dick Irvin
1952	Detroit	Tommy Ivan	4-0	Montreal	Dick Irvin
1953	Montreal	Dick Irvin	4-1 (WLWWW)	Boston	Lynn Patrick
1954	Detroit	Tommy Ivan	4-3 (WLWWLLW)	Montreal	Dick Irvin
1955	Detroit	Jimmy Skinner	4-3 (WWLLWLW)	Montreal	Dick Irvin
1956	Montreal	Toe Blake	4-1 (WWLWW)	Detroit	Jimmy Skinner
1957	Montreal	Toe Blake	4-1 (WWLWW)	Boston	Milt Schmidt
1958	Montreal	Toe Blake	4-2 (WLWLWW)	Boston	Milt Schmidt
1959	Montreal	Toe Blake	4-1 (WWLWW)	Toronto	Punch Imlach
1960	Montreal	Toe Blake	4-0	Toronto	Punch Imlach
1961	Chicago	Rudy Pilous	4-2 (WLWLWW)	Detroit	Sid Abel
1962	Toronto	Punch Imlach	4-2 (WWLLWW)	Chicago	Rudy Pilous
1963	Toronto	Punch Imlach	4-1 (WWWLW)	Detroit	Sid Abel
1964	Toronto	Punch Imlach	4-3 (WLLWLWW)	Detroit	Sid Abel
1965	Montreal	Toe Blake	4-3 (WLWWLW)	Chicago	Billy Reay
1966	Montreal	Toe Blake	4-2 (LLWWWW)	Detroit	Sid Abel
1967	Toronto	Punch Imlach	4-2 (LWWLWW)	Montreal	Toe Blake
1968	Montreal	Toe Blake	4-0	St. Louis	Scotty Bowman
1969	Montreal	Claude Ruel	4-0	St. Louis	Scotty Bowman
1970	Boston	Harry Sinden	4-0	St. Louis	Scotty Bowman
1971	Montreal	Al MacNeil	4-3 (LLWWLWW)	Chicago	Billy Reay
1972	Boston	Tom Johnson	4-2 (WWWLWL)	NY Rangers	Emile Francis
1973	Montreal	Scotty Bowman	4-2 (WWLWLW)	Chicago	Billy Reay
1974	Philadelphia	Fred Shero	4-2 (LWWWLW)	Boston	Bep Guidolin
1975	Philadelphia	Fred Shero	4-2 (WWLLWW)	Buffalo	Floyd Smith
1976	Montreal	Scotty Bowman	4-0	Philadelphia	Fred Shero
1977	Montreal	Scotty Bowman	4-0	Boston	Don Cherry
1978	Montreal	Scotty Bowman	4-2 (WWLLWW)	Boston	Don Cherry
1979	Montreal	Scotty Bowman	4-1 (LWWWW)	NY Rangers	Fred Shero
1980	NY Islanders	Al Arbour	4-2 (WLWWLW)	Philadelphia	Pat Quinn
1981	NY Islanders	Al Arbour	4-1 (WWWLW)	Minnesota	Glen Sonmor
1982	NY Islanders	Al Arbour	4-0	Vancouver	Roger Neilson
1983	NY Islanders	Al Arbour	4-0	Edmonton	Glen Sather
1984	Edmonton	Glen Sather	4-1 (WLWWW)	NY Islanders	Al Arbour
1985	Edmonton	Glen Sather	4-1 (LWWWW)	Philadelphia	Mike Keenan
1986	Montreal	Jean Perron	4-1 (LWWWW)	Calgary	Bob Johnson
1987	Edmonton	Glen Sather	4-3 (WWLWLLW)	Philadelphia	Mike Keenan
1988	Edmonton	Glen Sather	4-0	Boston	Terry O'Reilly
1989	Calgary	Terry Crisp	4-2 (WLLLWW)	Montreal	Pat Burns
1990	Edmonton	John Muckler	4-1 (WWLWW)	Boston	Mike Milbury
1991	Pittsburgh	Bob Johnson	4-2 (LWLWWW)	Minnesota	Bob Gainey
1992	Pittsburgh	Scotty Bowman	4-0	Chicago	Mike Keenan
1993	Montreal	Jacques Demers	4-1 (LWWWW)	Los Angeles	Barry Melrose
1994	NY Rangers	Mike Keenan	4-3 (LWWWLLW)	Vancouver	Pat Quinn
1995	New Jersey	Jacques Lemaire	4-0	Detroit	Scotty Bowman
1996	Colorado	Marc Crawford	4-0	Florida	Doug MacLean
1997	Detroit	Scotty Bowman	4-0	Philadelphia	Terry Murray
1998	Detroit	Scotty Bowman	4-0	Washington	Ron Wilson
1999	Dallas	Ken Hitchcock	4-2 (LWWLWW)	Buffalo	Lindy Ruff

* The 1919 finals were cancelled after five games due to an influenza epidemic with Montreal and Seattle (PCHA) tied at 2-2-1.

M.J. O'Brien Trophy

Donated by Canadian mining magnate M.J. O'Brien, whose son Ambrose founded the National Hockey Association in 1910. Originally presented to the NHA champion until the league's demise in 1917, the trophy then passed to the NHL champion through 1927. It was awarded to the NHL's Canadian Division winner from 1927-38 and the Stanley Cup runner-up from 1939-50 before being retired in 1950.

NHA winners included the Montreal Wanderers (1910), original Ottawa Senators (1911 and '15), Quebec Bulldogs (1912 and '13), Toronto Blueshirts (1914) and Montreal Canadiens (1916 and '17).

Conn Smythe Trophy

The Most Valuable Player of the Stanley Cup Playoffs, as selected by the Pro Hockey Writers Association. Presented since 1965 by Maple Leaf Gardens Limited in the name of the former Toronto coach, GM and owner, Conn Smythe. Winners who did not play for the Cup champion are in **bold** type.

Multiple winners: Wayne Gretzky, Mario Lemieux, Bobby Orr, Bernie Parent and Patrick Roy (2).

Year	Year	Year
1965 Jean Beliveau, Mon., C	1977 Guy Lafleur, Mon., RW	1989 Al MacInnis, Calg., D
1966 **Roger Crozier**, Det., G	1978 Larry Robinson, Mon., D	1990 Bill Ranford, Edm., G
1967 Dave Keon, Tor., C	1979 Bob Gainey, Mon., LW	1991 Mario Lemieux, Pit., C
1968 **Glenn Hall**, St.L., G	1980 Bryan Trottier, NYI, C	1992 Mario Lemieux, Pit., C
1969 Serge Savard, Mon., D	1981 Butch Goring, NYI, C	1993 Patrick Roy, Mon., G
1970 Bobby Orr, Bos., D	1982 Mike Bossy, NYI, RW	1994 Brian Leetch, NYR, D
1971 Ken Dryden, Mon., G	1983 Billy Smith, NYI, G	1995 Claude Lemieux, NJ, RW
1972 Bobby Orr, Bos., D	1984 Mark Messier, Edm., LW	1996 Joe Sakic, Col., C
1973 Yvan Cournoyer, Mon., RW	1985 Wayne Gretzky, Edm., C	1997 Mike Vernon, Det., G
1974 Bernie Parent, Phi., G	1986 Patrick Roy, Mon., G	1998 Steve Yzerman, Det., C
1975 Bernie Parent, Phi., G	1987 **Ron Hextall**, Phi., G	1999 Joe Nieuwendyk, Dal., C
1976 **Reggie Leach**, Phi., RW	1988 Wayne Gretzky, Edm., C	

Note: Ken Dryden (1971) and Patrick Roy (1986) are the only players to win as rookies.

All-Time Stanley Cup Playoff Leaders
CAREER

Stanley Cup Playoff leaders through 1999. Years listed indicate number of playoff appearances. Players active in 1999 are in **bold** type; (DNP) indicates active player that did not participate in 1999 playoffs.

Scoring

Points

		Yrs	Gm	G	A	Pts
1	**Wayne Gretzky** (DNP)	16	208	122	260	382
2	**Mark Messier** (DNP)	17	236	109	186	295
3	Jari Kurri	14	200	106	127	233
4	Glenn Anderson	15	225	93	121	214
5	**Paul Coffey**	16	194	59	137	196
6	Bryan Trottier	17	221	71	113	184
7	Jean Beliveau	17	162	79	97	176
8	Denis Savard	16	169	66	109	175
9	**Doug Gilmour** (DNP)	14	152	54	117	171
10	Denis Potvin	14	185	56	108	164
11	**Ray Bourque**	19	180	36	125	161
12	Mike Bossy	10	129	85	75	160
	Gordie Howe	20	157	68	92	160
	Bobby Smith	13	184	64	96	160
15	Mario Lemieux	7	89	70	85	155
16	Stan Mikita	18	155	59	91	150
17	Brian Propp	13	160	64	84	148
	Steve Yzerman	14	145	61	87	148
19	**Claude Lemieux**	14	198	76	71	147
20	**Larry Murphy**	18	200	35	111	146
21	Larry Robinson	20	227	28	116	144
22	Jacques Lemaire	11	145	61	78	139
23	**Adam Oates** (DNP)	11	126	38	100	138
	Al MacInnis	15	142	36	102	138
25	Phil Esposito	15	130	61	76	137

Goals

		Yrs	Gm	G
1	**Wayne Gretzky** (DNP)	16	208	122
2	**Mark Messier** (DNP)	17	236	109
3	Jari Kurri	15	200	106
4	Glenn Anderson	15	225	93
5	Mike Bossy	10	129	85
6	Maurice Richard	15	133	82
7	Jean Beliveau	17	162	79
8	**Brett Hull**	14	130	77
9	**Claude Lemieux**	14	198	76
10	**Dino Ciccarelli** (DNP)	14	141	73
11	**Esa Tikkanen** (DNP)	13	186	72
12	Bryan Trottier	17	221	71
13	Mario Lemieux	7	89	70
14	Gordie Howe	20	157	68
15	Denis Savard	16	169	66

Assists

		Yrs	Gm	A
1	**Wayne Gretzky** (DNP)	16	208	260
2	**Mark Messier** (DNP)	17	236	186
3	**Paul Coffey**	16	194	137
4	Jari Kurri	15	200	127
5	**Ray Bourque**	19	180	125
6	Glenn Anderson	15	225	121
7	**Doug Gilmour**	14	152	117
8	Larry Robinson	20	227	116
9	Bryan Trottier	17	221	113
10	**Larry Murphy**	18	200	111
11	Denis Savard	16	169	109
12	Denis Potvin	14	185	108
13	**Al MacInnis**	15	142	102
14	**Adam Oates** (DNP)	11	126	100
15	Jean Beliveau	17	162	97

Goaltending

Wins

		Gm	W-L	Pct	GAA
1	**Patrick Roy**	179	110-67	.621	2.41
2	**Grant Fuhr**	150	92-50	.648	2.92
3	Billy Smith	132	88-36	.710	2.73
4	Ken Dryden	112	80-32	.714	2.40
5	**Mike Vernon**	134	77-52	.597	2.67
6	Jacques Plante	112	71-37	.657	2.17
7	Andy Moog	132	68-57	.544	3.04
8	**Ed Belfour**	108	61-42	.592	2.19
9	**Tom Barrasso**	113	59-50	.541	3.04
10	Turk Broda	102	58-42	.580	1.98
11	Terry Sawchuk	106	54-48	.529	2.54
12	Glenn Hall	115	49-65	.430	2.79
13	Gerry Cheevers	88	47-35	.573	2.69
	Ron Hextall (DNP)	93	47-43	.522	3.04
15	Tony Esposito	99	45-53	.459	3.07

Shutouts

		Gm	GAA	No
1	Clint Benedict	48	1.80	15
	Jacques Plante	112	2.17	15
3	Turk Broda	102	1.98	13
4	Terry Sawchuk	106	2.54	12
	Patrick Roy	179	2.41	12

Goals Against Average
Minimum of 50 games played

		Gm	Min	GA	GAA
1	George Hainsworth	52	3486	112	1.93
2	**Martin Brodeur**	61	3875	126	1.95
3	Turk Broda	101	6389	211	1.98
4	**Dominik Hasek**	56	3383	116	2.06
5	**Chris Osgood**	53	3077	111	2.16
6	Jacques Plante	112	6652	240	2.16
7	**Ed Belfour**	108	6525	238	2.19
8	Ken Dryden	112	6846	274	2.40
9	**Patrick Roy**	179	11055	444	2.41
10	Bernie Parent	71	4302	174	2.43

Note: Clint Benedict had an average of 1.80 but played in only 48 games.

Games Played

		Yrs	Gm
1	**Patrick Roy**, Mon-Col	13	179
2	**Grant Fuhr**, Edm-Buf-St.L	14	150
3	**Mike Vernon**, Calg-Det-SJ	13	134
4	Billy Smith, NY Islanders	13	132
	Andy Moog, Edm-Bos-Dal-Mon	16	132

Appearances in Cup Finals
Standings of all teams that have reached the Stanley Cup championship round, since 1918.

App		Cups	Last Won
32	Montreal Canadiens	23*	1993
21	Toronto Maple Leafs	13†	1967
21	Detroit Red Wings	9	1998
17	Boston Bruins	5	1972
10	New York Rangers	4	1994
10	Chicago Blackhawks	3	1961
7	Philadelphia Flyers	2	1975
6	Edmonton Oilers	5	1990
5	New York Islanders	4	1983
5	Vancouver Millionaires (PCHA)	0	—
4	(original) Ottawa Senators	4	1927
3	Montreal Maroons	2	1935
3	Minnesota/Dallas (North) Stars	1	1999
3	St. Louis Blues	0	—
2	Pittsburgh Penguins	2	1992
2	Calgary Flames	1	1989
2	Victoria Cougars (WCHL-WHL)	1	1925
2	Buffalo Sabres	0	—
2	Seattle Metropolitans (PCHA)	0	—
2	Vancouver Canucks	0	—
1	Colorado Avalanche	1	1996
1	New Jersey Devils	1	1995
1	Calgary Tigers (WCHL)	0	—
1	Edmonton Eskimos (WCHL)	0	—
1	Florida Panthers	0	—
1	Los Angeles Kings	0	—
1	Washington Capitals	0	—

*Les Canadiens also won the Cup in 1916 for a total of 24. Also, their final with Seattle in 1919 was cancelled due to an influenza epidemic that claimed the life of the Habs' Joe Hall.

†Toronto has won the Cup under three nicknames—Arenas (1918), St. Pats (1922) and Maple Leafs (1932,42,45,47-49,51,62-64,67).

Teams now defunct (7): Calgary Tigers, Edmonton Eskimos, Montreal Maroons, (original) Ottawa Senators, Seattle, Vancouver Millionaires and Victoria. Edmonton (1923) and Calgary (1924) represented the WCHL and later the WHL, while Vancouver (1918,1921-24) and Seattle (1919-20) played out of the PCHA.

Miscellaneous
Championships

		Yrs	Cups
1	Henri Richard, Montreal	18	11
2	Yvan Cournoyer, Montreal	15	10
	Jean Beliveau, Montreal	17	10
4	Claude Provost, Montreal	14	9
5	Jacques Lemaire, Montreal	11	8
	Maurice Richard, Montreal	15	8
	Red Kelly, Detroit-Toronto	19	8

Years in Playoffs

		Yrs	Gm
1	Gordie Howe, Detroit-Hartford	20	157
	Larry Robinson, Montreal-Los Angeles	20	227
3	Red Kelly, Detroit-Toronto	19	164
	Ray Bourque, Boston	19	180
5	Kevin Lowe, Edm-NYR-Edm	18	214
	Larry Murphy, LA-Wash-Min-Pit-Tor-Det	18	200
	Dale Hunter, Que-Wash-Col	18	186
	Henri Richard, Montreal	18	180
	Stan Mikita, Chicago	18	155

Games Played

		Yrs	Gm
1	**Mark Messier**, Edm-NYR-Van (DNP)	17	236
2	Larry Robinson, Montreal-Los Angeles	20	227
3	Glenn Anderson, Edm-Tor-NYR-St.L	15	225
4	Bryan Trottier, NY Isles-Pittsburgh	17	221
5	Kevin Lowe, Edm-NYR-Edm	18	214

Penalty Minutes

		Yrs	Gm	Min
1	**Dale Hunter**, Que-Wash-Col	18	186	729
2	Chris Nilan, Mon-NYR-Bos-Mon	12	111	541
3	**Claude Lemieux**, Mon-NJ-Col	14	198	489
4	Willi Plett, Atl-Calg-Min-Bos	10	83	466
5	Dave Williams, Tor-Van-LA	12	83	455

SINGLE SEASON
Scoring
Points

		Year	Gm	G	A	Pts
1	Wayne Gretzky, Edm	1985	18	17	30	47
2	Mario Lemieux, Pit	1991	23	16	28	44
3	Wayne Gretzky, Edm	1988	19	12	31	43
4	Wayne Gretzky, LA	1993	24	15	25	40
5	Wayne Gretzky, Edm	1983	16	12	26	38
6	Paul Coffey, Edm	1985	18	12	25	37
7	Mike Bossy, NYI	1981	18	17	18	35
	Wayne Gretzky, Edm	1984	19	13	22	35
	Doug Gilmour, Tor	1993	21	10	25	35
10	Mario Lemieux, Pit	1992	15	16	18	34
	Mark Messier, Edm	1988	19	11	23	34
	Mark Recchi, Pit	1991	24	10	24	34
	Wayne Gretzky, Edm	1987	21	5	29	34
	Brian Leetch, NYR	1994	23	11	23	34
	Joe Sakic, Col	1996	22	18	16	34

Goals

		Year	Gm	No
1	Reggie Leach, Philadelphia	1976	16	19
	Jari Kurri, Edmonton	1985	18	19
3	Joe Sakic, Colorado	1996	22	18
4	Newsy Lalonde, Montreal	1919	10	17
	Mike Bossy, NY Islanders	1981	18	17
	Wayne Gretzky, Edmonton	1985	18	17
	Steve Payne, Minnesota	1981	19	17
	Mike Bossy, NY Islanders	1982	19	17
	Mike Bossy, NY Islanders	1983	19	17
	Kevin Stevens, Pittsburgh	1991	24	17

Assists

		Year	Gm	No
1	Wayne Gretzky, Edmonton	1988	19	31
2	Wayne Gretzky, Edmonton	1985	18	30
3	Wayne Gretzky, Edmonton	1987	21	29
4	Mario Lemieux, Pittsburgh	1991	23	28
5	Wayne Gretzky, Edmonton	1983	16	26
6	Paul Coffey, Edmonton	1985	18	25
	Doug Gilmour, Toronto	1993	21	25
	Wayne Gretzky, Los Angeles	1993	24	25
9	Al MacInnis, Calgary	1989	22	24
	Mark Recchi, Pittsburgh	1991	24	24

Goaltending
Wins

		Year	Gm	Min	W-L
1	Grant Fuhr, Edm	1988	19	1136	16-2
	Mike Vernon, Det	1997	20	1229	16-4
	Patrick Roy, Mon	1993	20	1293	16-4
	Martin Brodeur, NJ	1995	20	1222	16-4
	Mike Vernon, Calg	1989	22	1381	16-5
	Tom Barrasso, Pit	1992	21	1233	16-5
	Chris Osgood, Det	1998	22	1361	16-6
	Bill Ranford, Edm	1990	22	1401	16-6
	Patrick Roy, Col	1996	22	1454	16-6
	Mike Richter, NYR	1994	23	1417	16-7
	Ed Belfour, Dal	1999	23	1544	16-7

Shutouts

		Year	Gm	No
1	Clint Benedict, Mon. Maroons	1926	8	4
	Terry Sawchuk, Detroit	1952	8	4
	Clint Benedict, Mon. Maroons	1928	9	4
	Dave Kerr, NY Rangers	1937	9	4
	Frank McCool, Toronto	1945	13	4
	Ken Dryden, Montreal	1977	14	4
	Bernie Parent, Philadelphia	1975	17	4
	Olaf Kolzig, Washington	1998	21	4
	Mike Richter, NY Rangers	1994	23	4
	Kirk McLean, Vancouver	1994	24	4

Goals Against Average
(Minimum of eight games played.)

		Year	Gm	Min	GA	GAA
1	Terry Sawchuk, Det	1952	8	480	5	0.63
2	Clint Benedict, Mon-M	1928	9	555	8	0.89
3	Turk Broda, Tor	1951	9	509	9	1.06
4	Dave Kerr, NYR	1937	9	553	10	1.11
5	Jacques Plante, Mon	1960	8	489	11	1.35
6	Rogie Vachon, Mon	1969	8	507	12	1.42
7	Jacques Plante, St.L	1969	10	589	14	1.43
8	Frankie Brimsek, Bos	1939	12	863	18	1.50
9	Chuck Gardiner, Chi	1934	8	602	12	1.50
10	Ken Dryden, Mon	1977	14	849	22	1.55

Note: Average determined by games played through 1942-43 season and by minutes played since then.

SINGLE SERIES
Scoring
Points

	Year	Rd	G-A—Pts
Rick Middleton, Bos vs Buf	1983	DF	5-14—19
Wayne Gretzky, Edm vs Chi	1985	CF	4-14—18
Mario Lemieux, Pit vs Wash	1992	DSF	7-10—17
Barry Pedersen, Bos vs Buf	1983	DF	7-9—16
Doug Gilmour, Tor vs SJ	1994	CSF	3-13—16
Jari Kurri, Edm vs Chi	1985	CF	12-3—15
Tim Kerr, Phi vs Pit	1989	DF	10-5—15
Mario Lemieux, Pit vs Bos	1991	CF	6-9—15
Wayne Gretzky, Edm vs LA	1987	DSF	2-13—15

Goals

	Year	Rd	No
Jari Kurri, Edm vs Chi	1985	CF	12
Newsy Lalonde, Mon vs Ott	1919	SF*	11
Tim Kerr, Phi vs Pit	1989	DF	10

Five tied with nine each.
*NHL final prior to Stanley Cup series with Seattle.

Assists

	Year	Rd	No
Rick Middleton, Bos vs Buf	1983	DF	14
Wayne Gretzky, Edm vs Chi	1985	CF	14
Wayne Gretzky, Edm vs LA	1987	DSF	13
Doug Gilmour, Tor vs SJ	1994	CSF	13

Four tied with 11 each.

SINGLE GAME
Scoring
Points

	Date	G	A	Pts
Patrik Sundstrom, NJ vs Wash	4/22/88	3	5	8
Mario Lemieux, Pit vs Phi	4/25/89	5	3	8
Wayne Gretzky, Edm at Calg	4/17/83	4	3	7
Wayne Gretzky, Edm at Win	4/25/85	3	4	7
Wayne Gretzky, Edm vs LA	4/9/87	1	6	7

Goals

	Date	No
Newsy Lalonde, Mon vs Ott	3/1/19	5
Maurice Richard, Mon vs Tor	3/23/44	5
Darryl Sittler, Tor vs Phi	4/22/76	5
Reggie Leach, Phi vs Bos	5/6/76	5
Mario Lemieux, Pit vs Phi	4/25/89	5

Assists

	Date	No
Mikko Leinonen, NYR vs Phi	4/8/82	6
Wayne Gretzky, Edm vs LA	4/9/87	6

Ten tied with five each.

Ten Longest Playoff Overtime Games

The 10 longest overtime games in Stanley Cup history. Note the following Series initials: SF (semifinals), CQF (conference quarterfinal), DSF (division semifinal), QF (quarterfinal) and Final (Cup final). Series winners are in **bold** type; (*) indicates deciding game of series.

		OTs	Elapsed Time	Goal Scorer	Date	Series	Location
1	**Detroit** 1, Montreal Maroons 0	6	176:30	Mud Bruneteau	3/24/36	SF, Gm 1	Montreal
2	**Toronto** 1, Boston 0	6	164:46	Ken Doraty	4/3/33	SF, Gm 5	Toronto
3	**Pittsburgh** 3 Washington 2	4	139:15	Petr Nedved	4/24/96	CQF, Gm 4	Washington
4	Toronto 3, **Detroit** 2	4	130:18	Jack McLean	3/23/43	SF, Gm 2	Detroit
5	**Montreal** 2, NY Rangers 1	4	128:52	Gus Rivers	3/28/30	SF, Gm 1	Montreal
6	**NY Islanders** 3, Washington 2	4	128:47	Pat LaFontaine	4/18/87	DSF, Gm 7*	Washington
7	Buffalo 1, **New Jersey** 0	4	125:43	Dave Hannan	4/27/94	QF, Gm 6	Buffalo
8	**Montreal** 3, Detroit 2	4	121:09	Maurice Richard	3/27/51	SF, Gm 1	Detroit
9	**NY Americans** 3, NY Rangers 2	4	120:40	Lorne Carr	3/27/38	QF, Gm 3*	New York
10	**NY Rangers** 4, Montreal 3	3	119:32	Fred Cook	3/26/32	SF, Gm 2	Montreal

NHL All-Star Game

Three benefit NHL All-Star games were staged in the 1930s for forward Ace Bailey and the families of Howie Morenz and Babe Siebert. Bailey, of Toronto, suffered a fractured skull on a career-ending check by Boston's Eddie Shore. Morenz, the Montreal Canadiens' legend, died of a heart attack at 35 after a severely broken leg ended his career. Siebert, who played with both Montreal teams, drowned at age 35.

The All-Star Game was revived at the start of the 1947-48 season as an annual exhibition match between the defending Stanley Cup champion and All-Stars from the league's other five teams. The format has changed several times since then. The game was moved to midseason in 1966-67 and became an East vs. West contest in 1968-69. The Eastern (East, 1968-1974; Wales, 1975-93) Conference leads the series 18-7-1. In 1998, as a preview for the upcoming Winter Olympics, the East-West format was abandoned for one pitting North American all-stars against all-stars from the rest of the world. The format was kept in 1999.

Benefit Games

Date	Occasion		Host	Coaches
2/14/34	Ace Bailey Benefit	Toronto 7, All-Stars 3	Toronto	Dick Irvin, Lester Patrick
11/3/37	Howie Morenz Memorial	All-Stars 6, Montreals* 5	Montreal	Jack Adams, Ceil Hart
10/29/39	Babe Seibert Memorial	All-Stars 5, Canadiens 3	Montreal	Art Ross, Pit Lepine

*Combined squad of Montreal Canadiens and Montreal Maroons.

All-Star Games

Multiple MVP winners: Wayne Gretzky and Mario Lemieux (3); Bobby Hull and Frank Mahovlich (2).

Year		Host	Coaches	Most Valuable Player
1947	All-Stars 4, Toronto 3	Toronto	Dick Irvin, Hap Day	No award
1948	All-Stars 3, Toronto 1	Chicago	Tommy Ivan, Hap Day	No award
1949	All-Stars 3, Toronto 1	Toronto	Tommy Ivan, Hap Day	No award
1950	Detroit 7, All-Stars 1	Detroit	Tommy Ivan, Lynn Patrick	No award
1951	1st Team 2, 2nd Team 2	Toronto	Joe Primeau, Hap Day	No award
1952	1st Team 1, 2nd Team 1	Detroit	Tommy Ivan, Dick Irvin	No award
1953	All-Stars 3, Montreal 1	Montreal	Lynn Patrick, Dick Irvin	No award
1954	All-Stars 2, Detroit 2	Detroit	King Clancy, Jim Skinner	No award
1955	Detroit 3, All-Stars 1	Detroit	Jim Skinner, Dick Irvin	No award
1956	All-Stars 1, Montreal 1	Montreal	Jim Skinner, Toe Blake	No award
1957	All-Stars 5, Montreal 3	Montreal	Milt Schmidt, Toe Blake	No award
1958	Montreal 6, All-Stars 3	Montreal	Toe Blake, Milt Schmidt	No award
1959	Montreal 6, All-Stars 1	Montreal	Toe Blake, Punch Imlach	No award
1960	All-Stars 2, Montreal 1	Montreal	Punch Imlach, Toe Blake	No award
1961	All-Stars 3, Chicago 1	Chicago	Sid Abel, Rudy Pilous	No award
1962	Toronto 4, All-Stars 1	Toronto	Punch Imlach, Rudy Pilous	Eddie Shack, Tor., RW
1963	All-Stars 3, Toronto 3	Toronto	Sid Abel, Punch Imlach	Frank Mahovlich, Tor., LW
1964	All-Stars 3, Toronto 2	Toronto	Sid Abel, Punch Imlach	Jean Beliveau, Mon., C
1965	All-Stars 5, Montreal 2	Montreal	Billy Reay, Toe Blake	Gordie Howe, Det., RW
1966	No game (see below)			
1967	Montreal 3, All-Stars 0	Montreal	Toe Blake, Sid Abel	Henri Richard, Mon., C
1968	Toronto 4, All-Stars 3	Toronto	Punch Imlach, Toe Blake	Bruce Gamble, Tor., G
1969	West 3, East 3	Montreal	Scotty Bowman, Toe Blake	Frank Mahovlich, Det., LW
1970	East 4, West 1	St. Louis	Claude Ruel, Scotty Bowman	Bobby Hull, Chi., LW
1971	West 2, East 1	Boston	Scotty Bowman, Harry Sinden	Bobby Hull, Chi., LW
1972	East 3, West 2	Minnesota	Al MacNeil, Billy Reay	Bobby Orr, Bos., D
1973	East 5, West 4	NY Rangers	Tom Johnson, Billy Reay	Greg Polis, Pit., LW
1974	West 6, East 4	Chicago	Billy Reay, Scotty Bowman	Garry Unger, St.L., C
1975	Wales 7, Campbell 1	Montreal	Bep Guidolin, Fred Shero	Syl Apps Jr., Pit., C
1976	Wales 7, Campbell 5	Philadelphia	Floyd Smith, Fred Shero	Peter Mahovlich, Mon., C
1977	Wales 4, Campbell 3	Vancouver	Scotty Bowman, Fred Shero	Rick Martin, Buf., LW
1978	Wales 3, Campbell 2 (OT)	Buffalo	Scotty Bowman, Fred Shero	Billy Smith, NYI, G
1979	No game (see below)			
1980	Wales 6, Campbell 3	Detroit	Scotty Bowman, Al Arbour	Reggie Leach, Phi., RW
1981	Campbell 4, Wales 1	Los Angeles	Pat Quinn, Scotty Bowman	Mike Liut, St.L., G
1982	Wales 4, Campbell 2	Washington	Al Arbour, Glen Sonmor	Mike Bossy, NYI, RW
1983	Campbell 9, Wales 3	NY Islanders	Roger Neilson, Al Arbour	Wayne Gretzky, Edm., C
1984	Wales 7, Campbell 6	New Jersey	Al Arbour, Glen Sather	Don Maloney, NYR, LW
1985	Wales 6, Campbell 4	Calgary	Al Arbour, Glen Sather	Mario Lemieux, Pit., C
1986	Wales 4, Campbell 3 (OT)	Hartford	Mike Keenan, Glen Sather	Grant Fuhr, Edm., G
1987	No game (see below)			
1988	Wales 6, Campbell 5 (OT)	St. Louis	Mike Keenan, Glen Sather	Mario Lemieux, Pit., C
1989	Campbell 9, Wales 5	Edmonton	Glen Sather, Terry O'Reilly	Wayne Gretzky, LA, C
1990	Wales 12, Campbell 7	Pittsburgh	Pat Burns, Terry Crisp	Mario Lemieux, Pit., C
1991	Campbell 11, Wales 5	Chicago	John Muckler, Mike Milbury	Vincent Damphousse, Tor., LW
1992	Campbell 10, Wales 6	Philadelphia	Bob Gainey, Scotty Bowman	Brett Hull, St.L., RW
1993	Wales 16, Campbell 6	Montreal	Scotty Bowman, Mike Keenan	Mike Gartner, NYR, RW
1994	East 9, West 8	NY Rangers	Jacques Demers, Barry Melrose	Mike Richter, NYR, G
1995	No game (see below)			
1996	East 5, West 4	Boston	Doug MacLean, Scotty Bowman	Ray Bourque, Bos., D
1997	East 11, West 7	San Jose	Doug MacLean, Ken Hitchcock	Mark Recchi, Mon., RW
1998	North America 8, World 7	Vancouver	Jacques Lemaire, Ken Hitchcock	Teemu Selanne, World, RW
1999	North America 8, World 6	Tampa	Ken Hitchcock, Lindy Ruff	Wayne Gretzky, N. Amer., C

No All-Star Game: in 1966 (moved from start of season to mid-season); in 1979 (replaced by Challenge Cup series with USSR); in 1987 (replaced by Rendez-Vous '87 series with USSR); and in 1995 (cancelled when NHL lockout shortened season to 48 games).

NHL Franchise Origins

Here is what the current 28 teams in the National Hockey League have to show for the years they have put in as members of the NHL, the early National Hockey Association (NHA) and the more recent World Hockey Association (WHA). League titles and Stanley Cup championships are noted by year won. The Stanley Cup has automatically gone to the NHL champion since the 1926-27 season. Following the 1992-93 season, the NHL renamed the Clarence Campbell Conference the Western Conference, while the Prince of Wales Conference became the Eastern Conference.

Western Conference

	First Season	League Titles	Franchise Stops
Anaheim, Mighty Ducks of	1993-94 (NHL)	None	•Anaheim, CA (1993—)
Calgary Flames	1972-73 (NHL)	1 Cup (1989)	•Atlanta (1972-80) Calgary (1980—)
Chicago Blackhawks	1926-27 (NHL)	3 Cups (1934,38,61)	•Chicago (1926—)
Colorado Avalanche	1972-73 (WHA)	1 WHA (1977) 1 Cup (1996)	•Quebec City (1972-95) Denver (1995—)
Dallas Stars	1967-68 (NHL)	1 Cup (1999)	•Bloomington, MN (1967-93) Dallas (1993—)
Detroit Red Wings	1926-27 (NHL)	9 Cups (1936- 37,43,50,52,54-55,97,98)	•Detroit (1926—)
Edmonton Oilers	1973-74 (WHA)	5 Cups (1984-85,87-88,90)	•Edmonton (1972—)
Los Angeles Kings	1967-68 (NHL)	None	•Inglewood, CA (1967-99) Los Angeles (1999—)
Nashville Predators	1998-99 (NHL)	None	•Nashville, TN (1998—)
Phoenix Coyotes	1972-73 (WHA)	3 WHA (1976, 78-79)	•Winnipeg (1972-96) Phoenix (1996—)
St. Louis Blues	1967-68 (NHL)	None	•St. Louis (1967—)
San Jose Sharks	1991-92 (NHL)	None	•San Francisco (1991-93) San Jose (1993—)
Vancouver Canucks	1970-71 (NHL)	None	•Vancouver (1970—)

Eastern Conference

	First Season	League Titles	Franchise Stops
Atlanta Thrashers	1999-00 (NHL)	None	•Atlanta (1999—)
Boston Bruins	1924-25 (NHL)	5 Cups (1929,39,41,70,72)	•Boston (1924—)
Buffalo Sabres	1970-71 (NHL)	None	•Buffalo (1970—)
Carolina Hurricanes	1972-73 (WHA)	1 WHA (1973)	•Boston (1972-74) W. Springfield, MA (1974-75) Hartford, CT (1975-78) Springfield, MA (1978-80) Hartford (1980-97) Greensboro (1997-99) Raleigh (1999—)
Florida Panthers	1993-94 (NHL)	None	•Miami (1993-98) Sunrise, FL (1998—)
Montreal Canadiens	1909-10 (NHA)	2 NHA (1916-17) 2 NHL (1924-25) 24 Cups (1916,24,30- 31,44,46,53,56-60,65- 66,68-69,71,73,76- 79,86,93)	•Montreal (1909—)
New Jersey Devils	1974-75 (NHL)	1 Cup (1995)	•Kansas City (1974-76) Denver (1976-82) E. Rutherford, NJ (1982—)
New York Islanders	1972-73 (NHL)	4 Cups (1980-83)	•Uniondale, NY (1972—)
New York Rangers	1926-27 (NHL)	4 Cups (1928,33,40,94)	•New York (1926—)
Ottawa Senators	1992-93 (NHL)	None	•Ottawa (1992-1996) Kanata, Ont. (1996—)
Philadelphia Flyers	1967-68 (NHL)	2 Cups (1974-75)	•Philadelphia (1967—)
Pittsburgh Penguins	1967-68 (NHL)	2 Cups (1991-92)	•Pittsburgh (1967—)
Tampa Bay Lightning	1992-93 (NHL)	None	•Tampa, FL (1992-93) St. Petersburg, FL (1993-96) Tampa, FL (1996—)
Toronto Maple Leafs	1916-17 (NHA)	2 NHL (1918,22) 13 Cups (1918,22,32,42,45,47- 49,51,62-64,67)	•Toronto (1916—)
Washington Capitals	1974-75 (NHL)	None	•Landover, MD (1974-97) Washington, D.C. (1997—)

Note: The Hartford Civic Center roof collapsed after a snowstorm in January 1978, forcing the Whalers to move their home games to Springfield, Mass., for two years.

The Growth of the NHL

Of the four franchises that comprised the National Hockey League (NHL) at the start of the 1917-18 season, only two remain—the Montreal Canadiens and the Toronto Maple Leafs (originally the Toronto Arenas). From 1919-26, eight new teams joined the league, but only four—the Boston Bruins, Chicago Blackhawks (originally Black Hawks), Detroit Red Wings (originally Cougars) and New York Rangers—survived.

It was 41 years before the NHL expanded again, doubling in size for the 1967-68 season with new teams in Los Angeles, Minnesota, Oakland, Philadelphia, Pittsburgh and St. Louis. The league had 16 clubs by the start of the 1972-73 season, but it also had a rival in the **World Hockey Association,** which debuted that year with 12 teams.

The NHL added two more teams in 1974 and merged the struggling Cleveland Barons (originally the Oakland Seals) and Minnesota North Stars in 1978, before absorbing four WHA clubs—the Edmonton Oilers, Hartford Whalers, Quebec Nordiques and Winnipeg Jets—in time for the 1979-80 season. Seven expansion teams have joined the league so far in the 1990s, giving the NHL its current 28-team roster. Two more will be added in 2000 to make it an even 30.

Expansion/Merger Timetable

For teams currently in NHL.

1919—Quebec Bulldogs finally take the ice after sitting out NHL's first two seasons; **1924**—Boston Bruins and Montreal Maroons; **1925**—New York Americans and Pittsburgh Pirates; **1926**—Chicago Black Hawks (now Blackhawks), Detroit Cougars (now Red Wings) and New York Rangers; **1932**—Ottawa Senators return after sitting out 1931-32 season.

1967—California Seals (later Cleveland Barons), Los Angeles Kings, Minnesota North Stars, Philadelphia Flyers, Pittsburgh Penguins and St. Louis Blues.

1970—Buffalo Sabres and Vancouver Canucks; **1972**—Atlanta Flames (now Calgary) and New York Islanders; **1974**—Kansas City Scouts (now New Jersey Devils) and Washington Capitals; **1978**—Cleveland Barons merge with Minnesota North Stars (now Dallas Stars) and team remains in Minnesota; **1979**—added WHA's Edmonton Oilers, Hartford Whalers, Quebec Nordiques (now Colorado Avalanche) and Winnipeg Jets (now Phoenix Coyotes).

1991—San Jose Sharks; **1992**—Ottawa Senators and Tampa Bay Lightning; **1993**—Mighty Ducks of Anaheim and Florida Panthers; **1998**—Nashville Predators; **1999**—Atlanta Thrashers.

Looking forward: 2000—Columbus Blue Jackets and Minnesota Wild.

City and Nickname Changes

1919—Toronto Arenas renamed St. Pats; **1920**—Quebec moves to Hamilton and becomes Tigers (will fold in 1925); **1926**—Toronto St. Pats renamed Maple Leafs; **1929**—Detroit Cougars renamed Falcons.

1930—Pittsburgh Pirates move to Philadelphia and become Quakers (will fold in 1931); **1932**—Detroit Falcons renamed Red Wings; **1934**—Ottawa Senators move to St. Louis and become Eagles (will fold in 1935); **1941**—New York Americans renamed Brooklyn Americans (will fold in 1942).

1967—California Seals renamed Oakland Seals three months into first season; **1970**—Oakland Seals renamed California Golden Seals; **1975**—California Golden Seals renamed Seals; **1976**—California Seals move to Cleveland and become Barons, while Kansas City Scouts move to Denver and become Colorado Rockies; **1978**—Cleveland Barons merge with Minnesota North Stars and become Minnesota North Stars.

1980—Atlanta Flames move to Calgary; **1982**—Colorado Rockies move to East Rutherford, N.J., and become New Jersey Devils; **1986**—Chicago Black Hawks renamed Blackhawks; **1993**—Minnesota North Stars move to Dallas and become Stars. **1995**—Quebec Nordiques move to Denver and become Colorado Avalanche; **1996**—Winnipeg Jets move to Phoenix and become Coyotes; **1997**—Hartford Whalers move to Greensboro and become Carolina Hurricanes; **1999**—Carolina Hurricanes move to Raleigh.

Defunct NHL Teams

Teams that once played in the NHL, but no longer exist.

Brooklyn—Americans (1941-42, formerly NY Americans from 1925-41); **Cleveland**—Barons (1976-78, originally California-Oakland Seals from 1967-76); **Hamilton (Ont.)**—Tigers (1920-25, originally Quebec Bulldogs from 1919-20); **Montreal**—Maroons (1924-38) and Wanderers (1917-18); **New York**—Americans (1925-41, later Brooklyn Americans for 1941-42); **Oakland**—Seals (1967-76, also known as California Seals and Golden Seals and later Cleveland Barons from 1976-78); **Ottawa**—Senators (1917-31 and 1932-34, later St. Louis Eagles for 1934-35); **Philadelphia**—Quakers (1930-31, originally Pittsburgh Pirates from 1925-30); **Pittsburgh**—Pirates (1925-30, later Philadelphia Quakers for 1930-31); **Quebec**—Bulldogs (1919-20, later Hamilton Tigers from 1920-25); **St. Louis**—Eagles (1934-35), originally Ottawa Senators (1917-31 and 1932-34).

WHA Teams (1972-79)

Baltimore—Blades (1975); **Birmingham**—Bulls (1976-78); **Calgary**—Cowboys (1975-77); **Chicago**—Cougars (1972-75); **Cincinnati**—Stingers (1975-79); **Cleveland**—Crusaders (1972-76, moved to Minnesota); **Denver**—Spurs (1975-76, moved to Ottawa); **Edmonton**—Oilers (1972-79, originally called Alberta Oilers in 1972-73); **Houston**—Aeros (1972-78); **Indianapolis**—Racers (1974-78).

Los Angeles—Sharks (1972-74, moved to Michigan); **Michigan**—Stags (1974-75, moved to Baltimore); **Minnesota**—Fighting Saints (1972-76) and New Fighting Saints (1976-77); **New England**—Whalers (1972-79, played in Boston from 1972-74, West Springfield, MA from 1974-75, Hartford from 1975-78 and Springfield, MA in 1979); **New Jersey**—Knights (1973-74, moved to San Diego); **New York**—Raiders (1972-73, renamed Golden Blades in 1973, moved to New Jersey).

Ottawa—Nationals (1972-73, moved to Toronto) and Civics (1976); **Philadelphia**—Blazers (1972-73, moved to Vancouver); **Phoenix**—Roadrunners (1974-77); **Quebec**—Nordiques (1972-79); **San Diego**—Mariners (1974-77); **Toronto**—Toros (1973-76, moved to Birmingham, AL); **Vancouver**—Blazers (1973-75, moved to Calgary); **Winnipeg**—Jets (1972-79).

Annual NHL Leaders

Art Ross Trophy (Scoring)

Given to the player who leads the league in points scored and named after the former Boston Bruins general manager-coach. First presented in 1948, names of prior leading scorers have been added retroactively. A tie for the scoring championship is broken three ways: 1. total goals; 2. fewest games played; 3. first goal scored.

Multiple Winners: Wayne Gretzky (10); Gordie Howe and Mario Lemieux (6); Phil Esposito (5); Stan Mikita (4); Jaromir Jagr and Guy Lafleur (3); Max Bentley, Charlie Conacher, Bill Cook, Babe Dye, Bernie Geoffrion, Bobby Hull, Elmer Lach, Newsy Lalonde, Joe Malone, Dickie Moore, Howie Morenz, Bobby Orr and Sweeney Schriner (2).

Year		Gm	G	A	Pts	Year		Gm	G	A	Pts
1918	Joe Malone, Mon	20	44	0	44	1960	Bobby Hull, Chi	70	39	42	81
1919	Newsy Lalonde, Mon	17	23	9	32	1961	Bernie Geoffrion, Mon	64	50	45	95
1920	Joe Malone, Que	24	39	6	45	1962	Bobby Hull, Chi	70	50	34	84
1921	Newsy Lalonde, Mon	24	33	8	41	1963	Gordie Howe, Det	70	38	48	86
1922	Punch Broadbent, Ott	24	32	14	46	1964	Stan Mikita, Chi	70	39	50	89
1923	Babe Dye, Tor	22	26	11	37	1965	Stan Mikita, Chi	70	28	59	87
1924	Cy Denneny, Ott	21	22	1	23	1966	Bobby Hull, Chi	65	54	43	97
1925	Babe Dye, Tor	29	38	6	44	1967	Stan Mikita, Chi	70	35	62	97
1926	Nels Stewart, Maroons	36	34	8	42	1968	Stan Mikita, Chi	72	40	47	87
1927	Bill Cook, NYR	44	33	4	37	1969	Phil Esposito, Bos	74	49	77	126
1928	Howie Morenz, Mon	43	33	18	51	1970	Bobby Orr, Bos	76	33	87	120
1929	Ace Bailey, Tor	44	22	10	32	1971	Phil Esposito, Bos	78	76	76	152
1930	Cooney Weiland, Bos	44	43	30	73	1972	Phil Esposito, Bos	76	66	67	133
1931	Howie Morenz, Mon	39	28	23	51	1973	Phil Esposito, Bos	78	55	75	130
1932	Busher Jackson, Tor	48	28	25	53	1974	Phil Esposito, Bos	78	68	77	145
1933	Bill Cook, NYR	48	28	22	50	1975	Bobby Orr, Bos	80	46	89	135
1934	Charlie Conacher, Tor	42	32	20	52	1976	Guy Lafleur, Mon	80	56	69	125
1935	Charlie Conacher, Tor	47	36	21	57	1977	Guy Lafleur, Mon	80	56	80	136
1936	Sweeney Schriner, NYA	48	19	26	45	1978	Guy Lafleur, Mon	79	60	72	132
1937	Sweeney Schriner, NYA	48	21	25	46	1979	Bryan Trottier, NYI	76	47	87	134
1938	Gordie Drillon, Tor	48	26	26	52	1980	Marcel Dionne, LA	80	53	84	137
1939	Toe Blake, Mon	48	24	23	47	1981	Wayne Gretzky, Edm	80	55	109	164
1940	Milt Schmidt, Bos	48	22	30	52	1982	Wayne Gretzky, Edm	80	92	120	212
1941	Bill Cowley, Bos	46	17	45	62	1983	Wayne Gretzky, Edm	80	71	125	196
1942	Bryan Hextall, NYR	48	24	32	56	1984	Wayne Gretzky, Edm	74	87	118	205
1943	Doug Bentley, Chi	50	33	40	73	1985	Wayne Gretzky, Edm	80	73	135	208
1944	Herbie Cain, Bos	48	36	46	82	1986	Wayne Gretzky, Edm	80	52	163	215
1945	Elmer Lach, Mon	50	26	54	80	1987	Wayne Gretzky, Edm	79	62	121	183
1946	Max Bentley, Chi	47	31	30	61	1988	Mario Lemieux, Pit	77	70	98	168
1947	Max Bentley, Chi	60	29	43	72	1989	Mario Lemieux, Pit	76	85	114	199
1948	Elmer Lach, Mon	60	30	31	61	1990	Wayne Gretzky, LA	73	40	102	142
1949	Roy Conacher, Chi	60	26	42	68	1991	Wayne Gretzky, LA	78	41	122	163
1950	Ted Lindsay, Det	69	23	55	78	1992	Mario Lemieux, Pit	64	44	87	131
1951	Gordie Howe, Det	70	43	43	86	1993	Mario Lemieux, Pit	60	69	91	160
1952	Gordie Howe, Det	70	47	39	86	1994	Wayne Gretzky, LA	81	38	92	130
1953	Gordie Howe, Det	70	49	46	95	1995	Jaromir Jagr, Pit	48	32	38	70
1954	Gordie Howe, Det	70	33	48	81	1996	Mario Lemieux, Pit	70	69	92	161
1955	Bernie Geoffrion, Mon	70	38	37	75	1997	Mario Lemieux, Pit	76	50	72	122
1956	Jean Beliveau, Mon	70	47	41	88	1998	Jaromir Jagr, Pit	77	35	67	102
1957	Gordie Howe, Det	70	44	45	89	1999	Jaromir Jagr, Pit	81	44	83	127
1958	Dickie Moore, Mon	70	36	48	84						
1959	Dickie Moore, Mon	70	41	55	96						

Note: The three times players have tied for total points in one season the player with more goals has won the trophy. In 1961-62, Hull outscored Andy Bathgate of NY Rangers, 50 goals to 28. In 1979-80, Dionne outscored Wayne Gretzky of Edmonton, 53-51. In 1995, Jagr outscored Eric Lindros of Philadelphia, 32-29.

NHL 500-Goal Scorers

Of the 27 500-goal scorers listed below, five (Ciccarelli, Bobby Hull, Kurri, Lemieux and Messier) went on to score over 600, three (Dionne, Esposito and Gartner) scored over 700, and two (Gretzky and Howe) have scored over 800. Players active in 1999 are in **bold** type.

	Date	Game #		Date	Game #
Maurice Richard, Mon vs Chi	10/19/57	863	Bryan Trottier, NYI vs Calg	2/13/90	1104
Gordie Howe, Det at NYR	3/14/62	1045	Mike Gartner, NYR vs Wash	10/14/91	936
Bobby Hull, Chi vs NYR	2/21/70	861	Michel Goulet, Chi vs Calg	2/16/92	951
Jean Beliveau, Mon vs Min	2/11/71	1101	Jari Kurri, LA vs Bos	10/17/92	833
Frank Mahovlich, Mon vs Van	3/21/73	1105	**Dino Ciccarelli,** Det at LA	1/8/94	946
Phil Esposito, Bos vs Det	12/22/74	803	Mario Lemieux, Pit at NYI	10/26/95	605
John Bucyk, Bos vs St.L	10/30/75	1370	**Mark Messier,** NYR vs Calg	11/6/95	1141
Stan Mikita, Chi vs Van	2/27/77	1221	**Steve Yzerman,** Det vs Col	1/17/96	906
Marcel Dionne, LA at Wash	12/14/82	887	Dale Hawerchuk, St.L at Tor	1/31/96	1103
Guy Lafleur, Mon at NJ	12/20/83	918	**Brett Hull,** St.L vs LA	12/22/96	693
Mike Bossy, NYI vs Bos	1/2/86	647	Joe Mullen, Pit at Col	3/14/97	1052
Gilbert Perreault, Buf vs NJ	3/9/86	1159	**Dave Andreychuk,** NJ vs Wash	3/15/97	1070
Wayne Gretzky, Edm vs Van	11/22/86	575	**Luc Robitaille,** LA vs Buf	1/7/99	928
Lanny McDonald, Calg vs NYI	3/21/89	1107			

Goals

Multiple Winners: Bobby Hull (7); Phil Esposito (6); Charlie Conacher, Wayne Gretzky, Gordie Howe and Maurice Richard (5); Bill Cooke, Babe Dye, Brett Hull, Mario Lemieux and Teemu Selanne (3); Jean Beliveau, Doug Bentley, Peter Bondra, Mike Bossy, Bernie Geoffrion, Bryan Hextall, Joe Malone and Nels Stewart (2).

Year		No	Year		No	Year		No
1918	Joe Malone, Mon	44	1945	Maurice Richard, Mon	50	1974	Phil Esposito, Bos	68
1919	Odie Cleghorn, Mon	23	1946	Gaye Stewart, Tor	37	1975	Phil Esposito, Bos	61
	& Newsy Lalonde, Mon	23	1947	Maurice Richard, Mon	45	1976	Reggie Leach, Phi	61
1920	Joe Malone, Que	39	1948	Ted Lindsay, Det	33	1977	Steve Shutt, Mon	60
1921	Babe Dye, Ham-Tor	35	1949	Sid Abel, Det	28	1978	Guy Lafleur, Mon	60
1922	Punch Broadbent, Ott	32	1950	Maurice Richard, Mon	43	1979	Mike Bossy, NYI	69
1923	Babe Dye, Tor	26	1951	Gordie Howe, Det	43	1980	Danny Gare, Buf	56
1924	Cy Denneny, Ott	22	1952	Gordie Howe, Det	47		Charlie Simmer, LA	56
1925	Babe Dye, Tor	38	1953	Gordie Howe, Det	49		& Blaine Stoughton, Hart	56
1926	Nels Stewart, Maroons	34	1954	Maurice Richard, Mon	37	1981	Mike Bossy, NYI	68
1927	Bill Cook, NYR	33	1955	Bernie Geoffrion, Mon	38	1982	Wayne Gretzky, Edm	92
1928	Howie Morenz, Mon	33		& Maurice Richard, Mon	38	1983	Wayne Gretzky, Edm	71
1929	Ace Bailey, Tor	22	1956	Jean Beliveau, Mon	47	1984	Wayne Gretzky, Edm	87
1930	Cooney Weiland, Bos	43	1957	Gordie Howe, Det	44	1985	Wayne Gretzky, Edm	73
1931	Charlie Conacher, Tor	31	1958	Dickie Moore, Mon	36	1986	Jari Kurri, Edm	68
1932	Charlie Conacher, Tor	34	1959	Jean Beliveau, Mon	45	1987	Wayne Gretzky, Edm	62
	& Bill Cook, NYR	34	1960	Bronco Horvath, Bos	39	1988	Mario Lemieux, Pit	70
1933	Bill Cook, NYR	28		& Bobby Hull, Chi	39	1989	Mario Lemieux, Pit	85
1934	Charlie Conacher, Tor	32	1961	Bernie Geoffrion, Mon	50	1990	Brett Hull, St.L	72
1935	Charlie Conacher, Tor	36	1962	Bobby Hull, Chi	50	1991	Brett Hull, St.L	86
1936	Charlie Conacher, Tor	23	1963	Gordie Howe, Det	38	1992	Brett Hull, St.L	70
	& Bill Thoms, Tor	23	1964	Bobby Hull, Chi	43	1993	Alexander Mogilny, Buf	76
1937	Larry Aurie, Det	23	1965	Norm Ullman, Tor	42		& Teemu Selanne, Win	76
	& Nels Stewart, Bos-NYA	23	1966	Bobby Hull, Chi	54	1994	Pavel Bure, Van	60
1938	Gordie Drillon, Tor	26	1967	Bobby Hull, Chi	52	1995	Peter Bondra, Wash	34
1939	Roy Conacher, Bos	26	1968	Bobby Hull, Chi	44	1996	Mario Lemieux, Pit	69
1940	Bryan Hextall, NYR	24	1969	Bobby Hull, Chi	58	1997	Keith Tkachuk, Pho	52
1941	Bryan Hextall, NYR	26	1970	Phil Esposito, Bos	43	1998	Teemu Selanne, Ana	52
1942	Lynn Patrick, NYR	32	1971	Phil Esposito, Bos	76		& Peter Bondra, Wash	52
1943	Doug Bentley, Chi	33	1972	Phil Esposito, Bos	66	1999	Teemu Selanne, Ana	47
1944	Doug Bentley, Chi	38	1973	Phil Esposito, Bos	55			

Assists

Multiple Winners: Wayne Gretzky (16); Bobby Orr (5); Frank Boucher, Bill Cowley, Phil Esposito, Gordie Howe, Elmer Lach, Mario Lemieux, Stan Mikita and Joe Primeau (3); Syl Apps, Andy Bathgate, Jean Beliveau, Doug Bentley, Art Chapman, Bobby Clarke, Ron Francis, Jaromir Jagr, Ted Lindsay, Bert Olmstead, Henri Richard and Bryan Trottier (2).

Year		No	Year		No	Year		No
1918	No official records kept.		1946	Elmer Lach, Mon	34	1974	Bobby Orr, Bos	90
1919	Newsy Lalonde, Mon	9	1947	Billy Taylor, Det	46	1975	Bobby Clarke, Phi	89
1920	Corbett Denneny, Tor	12	1948	Doug Bentley, Chi	37		& Bobby Orr, Bos	89
1921	Louis Berlinquette, Mon	9	1949	Doug Bentley, Chi	43	1976	Bobby Clarke, Phi	89
	Harry Cameron, Tor	9	1950	Ted Lindsay, Det	55	1977	Guy Lafleur, Mon	80
	& Joe Matte, Ham	9	1951	Gordie Howe, Det	43	1978	Bryan Trottier, NYI	77
1922	Punch Broadbent, Ott	14		& Teeder Kennedy, Tor	43	1979	Bryan Trottier, NYI	87
	& Leo Reise, Ham	14	1952	Elmer Lach, Mon	50	1980	Wayne Gretzky, Edm	86
1923	Ed Bouchard, Ham	12	1953	Gordie Howe, Det	46	1981	Wayne Gretzky, Edm	109
1924	King Clancy, Ott	8	1954	Gordie Howe, Det	48	1982	Wayne Gretzky, Edm	120
1925	Cy Denneny, Ott	15	1955	Bert Olmstead, Mon	48	1983	Wayne Gretzky, Edm	125
1926	Frank Nighbor, Ott	13	1956	Bert Olmstead, Mon	56	1984	Wayne Gretzky, Edm	118
1927	Dick Irvin, Chi	18	1957	Ted Lindsay, Det	55	1985	Wayne Gretzky, Edm	135
1928	Howie Morenz, Mon	18	1958	Henri Richard, Mon	52	1986	Wayne Gretzky, Edm	163
1929	Frank Boucher, NYR	16	1959	Dickie Moore, Mon	55	1987	Wayne Gretzky, Edm	121
1930	Frank Boucher, NYR	36	1960	Don McKenney, Bos	49	1988	Wayne Gretzky, Edm	109
1931	Joe Primeau, Tor	32	1961	Jean Beliveau, Mon	58	1989	Wayne Gretzky, LA	114
1932	Joe Primeau, Tor	37	1962	Andy Bathgate, NYR	56		& Mario Lemieux, Pit	114
1933	Frank Boucher, NYR	28	1963	Henri Richard, Mon	50	1990	Wayne Gretzky, LA	102
1934	Joe Primeau, Tor	32	1964	Andy Bathgate, NYR-Tor	58	1991	Wayne Gretzky, LA	122
1935	Art Chapman, NYA	34	1965	Stan Mikita, Chi	59	1992	Wayne Gretzky, LA	90
1936	Art Chapman, NYA	28	1966	Jean Beliveau, Mon	48	1993	Adam Oates, Bos	97
1937	Syl Apps, Tor	29		Stan Mikita, Chi	48	1994	Wayne Gretzky, LA	92
1938	Syl Apps, Tor	29		& Bobby Rousseau, Mon	48	1995	Ron Francis, Pit	48
1939	Bill Cowley, Bos	34	1967	Stan Mikita, Chi	62	1996	Ron Francis, Pit	92
1940	Milt Schmidt, Bos	30	1968	Phil Esposito, Bos	49		& Mario Lemieux, Pit	92
1941	Bill Cowley, Bos	45	1969	Phil Esposito, Bos	77	1997	Mario Lemieux, Pit	72
1942	Phil Watson, NYR	37	1970	Bobby Orr, Bos	87		& Wayne Gretzky, NYR	72
1943	Bill Cowley, Bos	45	1971	Bobby Orr, Bos	102	1998	Jaromir Jagr, Pit	67
1944	Clint Smith, Chi	49	1972	Bobby Orr, Bos	80		& Wayne Gretzky, NYR	67
1945	Elmer Lach, Mon	54	1973	Phil Esposito, Bos	75	1999	Jaromir Jagr, Pit	83

Goals Against Average

Average determined by games played through 1942-43 season and by minutes played since then. Minimum of 15 games from 1917-18 season through 1925-26; minimum of 25 games since 1926-27 season. Not to be confused with the Vezina Trophy. Goaltenders who posted the season's lowest goals against average, but did not win the Vezina are in **bold** type.

Multiple Winners: Jacques Plante (9); Clint Benedict and Bill Durnan (6); Johnny Bower, Ken Dryden and Tiny Thompson (4); Patrick Roy and Georges Vezina (3); Ed Belfour, Frankie Brimsek, Turk Broda, George Hainsworth, Dominik Hasek, Harry Lumley, Bernie Parent, Pete Peeters and Terry Sawchuk (2).

Year		GAA	Year		GAA	Year		GAA
1918	Georges Vezina, Mon	3.82	1946	Bill Durnan, Mon	2.60	1974	Bernie Parent, Phi	1.89
1919	Clint Benedict, Ott	2.94	1947	Bill Durnan, Mon	2.30	1975	Bernie Parent, Phi	2.03
1920	Clint Benedict, Ott	2.67	1948	Turk Broda, Tor	2.38	1976	Ken Dryden, Mon	2.03
1921	Clint Benedict, Ott	3.13	1949	Bill Durnan, Mon	2.10	1977	Bunny Larocque, Mon	2.09
1922	Clint Benedict, Ott	3.50	1950	Bill Durnan, Mon	2.20	1978	Ken Dryden, Mon	2.05
1923	Clint Benedict, Ott	2.25	1951	Al Rollins, Tor	1.77	1979	Ken Dryden, Mon	2.30
1924	Georges Vezina, Mon	2.00	1952	Terry Sawchuk, Det	1.90	1980	Bob Sauve, Buf	2.36
1925	Georges Vezina, Mon	1.87	1953	Terry Sawchuk, Det	1.90	1981	Richard Sevigny, Mon	2.40
1926	Alex Connell, Ott	1.17	1954	Harry Lumley, Tor	1.86	1982	**Denis Herron,** Mon	2.64
1927	**Clint Benedict,** Mon-M	1.51	1955	**Harry Lumley,** Tor	1.94	1983	Pete Peeters, Bos	2.36
1928	Geo. Hainsworth, Mon	1.09	1956	Jacques Plante, Mon	1.86	1984	**Pat Riggin,** Wash	2.66
1929	Geo. Hainsworth, Mon	0.98	1957	Jacques Plante, Mon	2.02	1985	**Tom Barrasso,** Buf	2.66
1930	Tiny Thompson, Bos	2.23	1958	Jacques Plante, Mon	2.11	1986	**Bob Froese,** Phi	2.55
1931	Roy Worters, NYA	1.68	1959	Jacques Plante, Mon	2.16	1987	**Brian Hayward,** Mon	2.81
1932	Chuck Gardiner, Chi	1.92	1960	Jacques Plante, Mon	2.54	1988	**Pete Peeters,** Wash	2.78
1933	Tiny Thompson, Bos	1.83	1961	Johnny Bower, Tor	2.50	1989	Patrick Roy, Mon	2.47
1934	**Wilf Cude,** Det-Mon	1.57	1962	Jacques Plante, Mon	2.37	1990	**Mike Liut,** Hart-Wash	2.53
1935	Lorne Chabot, Chi	1.83	1963	**Jacques Plante,** Mon	2.49	1991	Ed Belfour, Chi	2.47
1936	Tiny Thompson, Bos	1.71	1964	**Johnny Bower,** Tor	2.11	1992	Patrick Roy, Mon	2.36
1937	Norm Smith, Det	2.13	1965	Johnny Bower, Tor	2.38	1993	**Felix Potvin,** Tor	2.50
1938	Tiny Thompson, Bos	1.85	1966	**Johnny Bower,** Tor	2.25	1994	Dominik Hasek, Buf	1.95
1939	Frankie Brimsek, Bos	1.58	1967	Glenn Hall, Chi	2.38	1995	Dominik Hasek, Buf	2.11
1940	Dave Kerr, NYR	1.60	1968	Gump Worsley, Mon	1.98	1996	**Ron Hextall,** Phi	2.17
1941	Turk Broda, Tor	2.06	1969	**Jacques Plante,** St.L	1.96	1997	**Martin Brodeur,** NJ	1.88
1942	Frankie Brimsek, Bos	2.45	1970	**Ernie Wakely,** St.L	2.11	1998	**Ed Belfour,** Dal	1.88
1943	Jim Mowers, Det	2.47	1971	**Jacques Plante,** Tor	1.88	1999	**Ron Tugnutt,** Ott	1.79
1944	Bill Durnan, Mon	2.18	1972	Tony Esposito, Chi	1.77			
1945	Bill Durnan, Mon	2.42	1973	Ken Dryden, Mon	2.26			

Penalty Minutes

Multiple Winners: Red Horner (8); Gus Mortson and Dave Schultz (4); Bert Corbeau, Lou Fontinato and Tiger Williams (3); Billy Boucher, Carl Brewer, Red Dutton, Pat Egan, Bill Ezinicki, Joe Hall, Tim Hunter, Keith Magnuson, Chris Nilan, Jimmy Orlando and Rob Ray (2).

Year		Min	Year		Min	Year		Min
1918	Joe Hall, Mon	60	1946	Jack Stewart, Det	73	1974	Dave Schultz, Phi	348
1919	Joe Hall, Mon	85	1947	Gus Mortson, Tor	133	1975	Dave Schultz, Phi	472
1920	Cully Wilson, Tor	79	1948	Bill Barilko, Tor	147	1976	Steve Durbano, Pit-KC	370
1921	Bert Corbeau, Mon	86	1949	Bill Ezinicki, Tor	145	1977	Tiger Williams, Tor	338
1922	Sprague Cleghorn, Mon	63	1950	Bill Ezinicki, Tor	144	1978	Dave Schultz, LA-Pit	405
1923	Billy Boucher, Mon	52	1951	Gus Mortson, Tor	142	1979	Tiger Williams, Tor	298
1924	Bert Corbeau, Tor	55	1952	Gus Kyle, Bos	127	1980	Jimmy Mann, Win	287
1925	Billy Boucher, Mon	92	1953	Maurice Richard, Mon	112	1981	Tiger Williams, Van	343
1926	Bert Corbeau, Tor	121	1954	Gus Mortson, Chi	132	1982	Paul Baxter, Pit	409
1927	Nels Stewart, Mon-M	133	1955	Fern Flaman, Bos	150	1983	Randy Holt, Wash	275
1928	Eddie Shore, Bos	165	1956	Lou Fontinato, NYR	202	1984	Chris Nilan, Mon	338
1929	Red Dutton, Mon-M	139	1957	Gus Mortson, Chi	147	1985	Chris Nilan, Mon	358
1930	Joe Lamb, Ott	119	1958	Lou Fontinato, NYR	152	1986	Joey Kocur, Det	377
1931	Harvey Rockburn, Det	118	1959	Ted Lindsay, Chi	184	1987	Tim Hunter, Calg	361
1932	Red Dutton, NYA	107	1960	Carl Brewer, Tor	150	1988	Bob Probert, Det	398
1933	Red Horner, Tor	144	1961	Pierre Pilote, Chi	165	1989	Tim Hunter, Calg	375
1934	Red Horner, Tor	146	1962	Lou Fontinato, Mon	167	1990	Basil McRae, Min	351
1935	Red Horner, Tor	125	1963	Howie Young, Det	273	1991	Rob Ray, Buf	350
1936	Red Horner, Tor	167	1964	Vic Hadfield, NYR	151	1992	Mike Peluso, Chi	408
1937	Red Horner, Tor	124	1965	Carl Brewer, Tor	177	1993	Marty McSorley, LA	399
1938	Red Horner, Tor	82	1966	Reg Fleming, Bos-NYR	166	1994	Tie Domi, Win	347
1939	Red Horner, Tor	85	1967	John Ferguson, Mon	177	1995	Enrico Ciccone, TB	225
1940	Red Horner, Tor	87	1968	Barclay Plager, St.L	153	1996	Matthew Barnaby, Buf	335
1941	Jimmy Orlando, Det	99	1969	Forbes Kennedy, Phi-Tor	219	1997	Gino Odjick, Van	371
1942	Pat Egan, NYA	124	1970	Keith Magnuson, Chi	213	1998	Donald Brashear, Van	372
1943	Jimmy Orlando, Det	99	1971	Keith Magnuson, Chi	291	1999	Rob Ray, Buf	261
1944	Mike McMahon, Mon	98	1972	Bryan Watson, Pit	212			
1945	Pat Egan, Bos	86	1973	Dave Schultz, Phi	259			

All-Time NHL Regular Season Leaders

Through 1999 regular season.

CAREER

Players active during 1999 season in **bold** type.

Points

		Yrs	Gm	G	A	Pts
1	**Wayne Gretzky**	20	1487	894	1963	2857
2	Gordie Howe	26	1767	801	1049	1850
3	Marcel Dionne	18	1348	731	1040	1771
4	**Mark Messier**	20	1413	610	1050	1660
5	Phil Esposito	18	1282	717	873	1590
6	Mario Lemieux	12	745	613	881	1494
7	**Paul Coffey**	19	1322	385	1102	1487
8	**Ron Francis**	18	1329	449	1037	1486
9	**Steve Yzerman**	16	1178	592	891	1483
10	**Ray Bourque**	20	1453	385	1083	1468
11	Stan Mikita	22	1394	541	926	1467
12	Bryan Trottier	18	1279	524	901	1425
13	Dale Hawerchuk	16	1188	518	891	1409
14	Jari Kurri	17	1251	601	797	1398
15	John Bucyk	23	1540	556	813	1369
16	Guy Lafleur	17	1126	560	793	1353
17	Denis Savard	17	1196	473	865	1338
18	Mike Gartner	19	1432	708	627	1335
19	Gilbert Perreault	17	1191	512	814	1326
20	Alex Delvecchio	24	1549	456	825	1281
21	Jean Ratelle	21	1281	491	776	1267
22	Peter Stastny	15	977	450	789	1239
23	**Doug Gilmour**	16	1197	397	835	1232
24	Norm Ullman	20	1410	490	739	1229
25	Jean Beliveau	20	1125	507	712	1219
26	Bobby Clarke	15	1144	358	852	1210
27	**Bernie Nicholls**	18	1127	475	734	1209
28	**Dino Ciccarelli**	19	1232	608	592	1200
29	Bobby Hull	16	1063	610	560	1170
30	**Larry Murphy**	19	1477	275	880	1155

Goals

		Yrs	Gm	No
1	**Wayne Gretzky**	20	1487	894
2	Gordie Howe	26	1767	801
3	Marcel Dionne	18	1348	731
4	Phil Esposito	18	1282	717
5	Mike Gartner	19	1432	708
6	Mario Lemieux	12	745	613
7	Bobby Hull	16	1063	610
	Mark Messier	20	1413	610
9	**Dino Ciccarelli**	19	1232	608
10	Jari Kurri	17	1251	601
11	**Steve Yzerman**	16	1178	592
12	**Brett Hull**	14	861	586
13	Mike Bossy	10	752	573
14	Guy Lafleur	17	1126	560
15	John Bucyk	23	1540	556
16	Michel Goulet	15	1089	548
17	Maurice Richard	18	978	544
18	Stan Mikita	22	1394	541
19	Frank Mahovlich	18	1181	533
20	**Dave Andreychuk**	17	1210	532
21	Bryan Trottier	18	1279	524
22	Dale Hawerchuk	16	1188	518
23	**Luc Robitaille**	13	971	517
24	Gilbert Perreault	17	1191	512
25	Jean Beliveau	20	1125	507
26	Joe Mullen	17	1062	502
27	Lanny McDonald	16	1111	500
28	Glenn Anderson	16	1128	498
29	Jean Ratelle	21	1281	491
30	Norm Ullman	20	1410	490

Assists

		Yrs	Gm	No
1	**Wayne Gretzky**	20	1487	1963
2	**Paul Coffey**	19	1322	1102
3	**Ray Bourque**	20	1453	1083
4	**Mark Messier**	20	1413	1050
5	Gordie Howe	26	1767	1049
6	Marcel Dionne	18	1348	1040
7	**Ron Francis**	18	1329	1037
8	Stan Mikita	22	1394	926
9	Bryan Trottier	18	1279	901
10	**Steve Yzerman**	16	1178	891
	Dale Hawerchuk	16	1188	891
12	Mario Lemieux	12	745	881
13	**Larry Murphy**	19	1477	880
14	Phil Esposito	18	1281	873
15	Denis Savard	17	1196	865
16	Bobby Clarke	15	1144	852
17	**Adam Oates**	14	967	838
18	**Doug Gilmour**	16	1197	835
19	Alex Delvecchio	24	1549	825
20	Gilbert Perreault	17	1191	814

Penalty Minutes

		Yrs	Gm	Min
1	Tiger Williams	14	962	3966
2	**Dale Hunter**	19	1407	3565
3	**Marty McSorley**	16	934	3319
4	Tim Hunter	16	815	3146
5	Chris Nilan	13	688	3043
6	**Bob Probert**	13	726	2907
7	**Rick Tocchet**	15	990	2773
8	**Pat Verbeek**	17	1225	2665
9	**Craig Berube**	13	796	2651
10	**Dave Manson**	13	919	2604
11	Willi Plett	12	834	2572
12	**Rob Ray**	10	645	2529
13	**Joey Kocur**	15	820	2519
14	**Scott Stevens**	17	1275	2504
15	**Tie Domi**	10	558	2458

NHL-WHA Top 15

All-time regular season scoring leaders, including games played in World Hockey Association (1972-79). NHL players with WHA experience are listed in CAPITAL letters. Players active during 1999 are in **bold** type.

Points

		Yrs	G	A	Pts
1	**WAYNE GRETZKY**	21	940	2027	2967
2	GORDIE HOWE	32	975	1383	2358
3	BOBBY HULL	23	913	895	1808
4	Marcel Dionne	18	731	1040	1771
5	**MARK MESSIER**	21	611	1060	1671
6	Phil Esposito	18	717	873	1590
7	Mario Lemieux	12	613	881	1494
8	**Paul Coffey**	19	385	1102	1487
9	**Ron Francis**	18	449	1037	1486
10	**Steve Yzerman**	16	592	891	1483
11	**Ray Bourque**	20	385	1083	1468
12	Stan Mikita	22	541	926	1467
13	Bryan Trottier	18	524	901	1425
14	Dale Hawerchuk	16	512	891	1409
15	Jari Kurri	17	601	797	1398

WHA Totals: GRETZKY (1 yr, 80 gm, 46-64—110); HOWE (6 yrs, 419 gm, 174-334—508); HULL (7 yrs, 411 gm, 303-335—638); MESSIER (1 yr, 52 gm, 1-10—11).

Years Played

		Yrs	Career	Gm
1	Gordie Howe	26	1946-71, 79-80	1767
2	Alex Delvecchio	24	1950-74	1549
	Tim Horton	24	1949-50, 51-74	1446
4	John Bucyk	23	1955-78	1540
5	Stan Mikita	22	1958-80	1394
	Doug Mohns	22	1953-75	1390
	Dean Prentice	22	1952-74	1378
8	Harry Howell	21	1952-73	1411
	Ron Stewart	21	1952-73	1353
	Jean Ratelle	21	1960-81	1281
	Allan Stanley	21	1948-69	1244
	Eric Nesterenko	21	1951-72	1219
	Marcel Pronovost	21	1950-70	1206
	George Armstrong	21	1949-50, 51-71	1187
	Terry Harper	21	1949-70	971
	Gump Worsley	21	1952-53, 54-74	862

Note: Combined NHL-WHA years played: Howe (32); Howell (24); Bobby Hull (23); Norm Ullman, Nesterenko, Frank Mahovlich and Dave Keon (22).

Games Played

		Yrs	Career	Gm
1	Gordie Howe	26	1946-71, 79-80	1767
2	Alex Delvecchio	24	1950-74	1549
3	John Bucyk	23	1955-78	1540
4	**Wayne Gretzky**	20	1979-99	1487
5	**Larry Murphy**	19	1980—	1477
6	**Ray Bourque**	20	1979—	1453
7	Tim Horton	24	1949-50, 51-74	1446
8	Mike Gartner	19	1979-98	1432
9	**Mark Messier**	20	1979—	1413
10	Harry Howell	21	1952-73	1411
11	Norm Ullman	20	1955-75	1410
12	**Dale Hunter**	19	1980-99	1407
13	Stan Mikita	22	1958-80	1394
14	Doug Mohns	22	1953-75	1390
15	Larry Robinson	20	1972-92	1384

Note: Combined NHL-WHA games played: Howe (2,186), Dave Keon (1,597), Howell (1,581), Gretzky (1,567), Ullman (1,554), Gartner (1,510), Bobby Hull (1,474), Messier (1,465) and Frank Mahovlich (1,418).

Goaltending

Wins

		Yrs	Gm	W	L	T	Pct
1	Terry Sawchuk	21	971	**447**	330	172	.562
2	Jacques Plante	18	837	**434**	247	146	.614
3	Tony Esposito	16	886	**423**	306	152	.566
4	**Patrick Roy**	14	778	**412**	243	95	.613
5	Glenn Hall	18	906	**407**	326	163	.545
6	**Grant Fuhr**	18	845	**398**	282	112	.573
7	Andy Moog	18	713	**372**	209	88	.622
8	Rogie Vachon	16	795	**355**	291	127	.541
9	**Mike Vernon**	16	673	**347**	223	83	.595
10	**Tom Barrasso**	16	708	**345**	248	79	.572
11	Gump Worsley	21	861	**335**	352	150	.490
12	**J. Vanbiesbrouck**	17	779	**333**	303	105	.520
13	Harry Lumley	16	804	**330**	329	143	.501
14	Billy Smith	18	680	**305**	233	105	.556
15	Turk Broda	12	629	**302**	224	101	.562
16	**Ron Hextall**	13	608	**296**	214	69	.571
17	Mike Liut	13	663	**294**	271	74	.518
18	Ed Giacomin	13	610	**289**	208	97	.568
19	Dan Bouchard	14	655	**286**	232	113	.543
20	Tiny Thompson	12	553	**284**	194	75	.581

Losses

		Yrs	Gm	W	L	T	Pct
1	Gump Worsley	21	861	335	**352**	150	.490
2	Gilles Meloche	18	788	270	**351**	131	.446
3	Terry Sawchuk	21	971	447	**330**	172	.562
4	Harry Lumley	16	804	330	**329**	143	.501
5	Glenn Hall	18	906	407	**326**	163	.545

Goals Against Average
Minimum of 300 games played.

Before 1950

		Gm	Min	GA	GAA
1	George Hainsworth	465	29,415	937	1.91
2	Alex Connell	416	26,030	837	2.01
3	Chuck Gardiner	316	19,687	664	2.02
4	Lorne Chabot	412	25,309	861	2.04
5	Tiny Thompson	552	34,174	1183	2.08

Since 1950

		Gm	Min	GA	GAA
1	**Martin Brodeur**	375	21,627	789	2.19
2	Ken Dryden	397	23,352	870	2.24
3	**Dominik Hasek**	414	23,902	901	2.26
4	Jacques Plante	837	49,533	1965	2.38
5	**Ed Belfour**	550	31,553	1319	2.51

Shutouts

		Yrs	Games	No
1	Terry Sawchuk	21	971	103
2	George Hainsworth	11	465	94
3	Glenn Hall	18	906	84
4	Jacques Plante	18	837	82
5	Alex Connell	12	417	81
	Tiny Thompson	12	553	81
7	Tony Esposito	16	886	76
8	Lorne Chabot	11	411	73
9	Harry Lumley	16	804	71
10	Roy Worters	12	484	66
11	Turk Broda	14	629	62
12	John Roach	14	491	58
13	Clint Benedict	13	362	57
14	Bernie Parent	13	608	54
	Ed Giacomin	13	610	54

NHL-WHA Top 15

All-Time regular season wins leaders, including games played in World Hockey Association (1972-79). NHL goaltenders with WHA experience are listed in CAPITAL letters. Players active during 1999 are in **bold** type.

Wins

		Yrs	W	L	T	Pct
1	JACQUES PLANTE	19	449	261	147	.610
2	Terry Sawchuk	21	447	330	172	.562
3	Tony Esposito	16	423	306	152	.566
4	**Patrick Roy**	14	412	243	95	.613
5	Glenn Hall	18	407	326	163	.545
6	**Grant Fuhr**	18	398	282	112	.573
7	Andy Moog	18	372	209	88	.622
8	Rogie Vachon	16	355	291	127	.541
9	**Mike Vernon**	16	347	223	83	.595
10	**Tom Barrasso**	16	345	248	79	.572
11	Gump Worsley	21	335	352	150	.490
12	**J. Vanbiesbrouck**	17	333	303	105	.520
13	Harry Lumley	16	330	329	143	.501
14	GERRY CHEEVERS	17	329	180	83	.626
15	MIKE LIUT	15	325	310	78	.511

WHA Totals: PLANTE (1 yr, 31 gm, 15-14-1); CHEEVERS (4 yrs, 191 gm, 99-78-9); LIUT (2 yrs, 81 gm, 31-39-4).

All-Time NHL Regular Season Leaders (Cont.)
SINGLE SEASON

Scoring
Points

		Season	G	A	Pts
1	Wayne Gretzky, Edm	1985-86	52	163	215
2	Wayne Gretzky, Edm	1981-82	92	120	212
3	Wayne Gretzky, Edm	1984-85	73	135	208
4	Wayne Gretzky, Edm	1983-84	87	118	205
5	Mario Lemieux, Pit	1988-89	85	114	199
6	Wayne Gretzky, Edm	1982-83	71	125	196
7	Wayne Gretzky, Edm	1986-87	62	121	183
8	Mario Lemieux, Pit	1987-88	70	98	168
9	Wayne Gretzky, LA	1988-89	54	114	168
10	Wayne Gretzky, Edm	1980-81	55	109	164
11	Wayne Gretzky, LA	1990-91	41	122	163
12	Mario Lemieux, Pit	1995-96	69	92	161
13	Mario Lemieux, Pit	1992-93	69	91	160
14	Steve Yzerman, Det	1988-89	65	90	155
15	Phil Esposito, Bos	1970-71	76	76	152
16	Bernie Nicholls, LA	1988-89	70	80	150
17	Jaromir Jagr, Pit	1995-96	62	87	149
	Wayne Gretzky, Edm	1987-88	40	109	149
19	Pat LaFontaine, Buf	1992-93	53	95	148
20	Mike Bossy, NYI	1981-82	64	83	147

WHA 150 points or more: 154—Marc Tardif, Que. (1977-78).

Goals

		Season	Gm	No
1	Wayne Gretzky, Edm	1981-82	80	92
2	Wayne Gretzky, Edm	1983-84	74	87
3	Brett Hull, St.L	1990-91	78	86
4	Mario Lemieux, Pit	1988-89	76	85
5	Alexander Mogilny, Buf	1992-93	77	76
	Phil Esposito, Bos	1970-71	78	76
	Teemu Selanne, Win	1992-93	84	76
8	Wayne Gretzky, Edm	1984-85	80	73
9	Brett Hull, St.L	1989-90	80	72
10	Jari Kurri, Edm	1984-85	73	71
	Wayne Gretzky, Edm	1982-83	80	71
12	Brett Hull, St.L	1991-92	73	70
	Mario Lemieux, Pit	1987-88	77	70
	Bernie Nicholls, LA	1988-89	79	70
15	Mario Lemieux, Pit	1992-93	60	69
	Mario Lemieux, Pit	1995-96	70	69
	Mike Bossy, NYI	1978-79	80	69
18	Phil Esposito, Bos	1973-74	78	68
	Jari Kurri, Edm	1985-86	78	68
	Mike Bossy, NYI	1980-81	79	68

WHA 70 goals or more: 77—Bobby Hull, Win. (1974-75); 75—Real Cloutier, Que. (1978-79); 71—Marc Tardif, Que. (1975-76); 70—Anders Hedberg, Win. (1976-77).

Assists

		Season	Gm	No
1	Wayne Gretzky, Edm	1985-86	80	163
2	Wayne Gretzky, Edm	1984-85	80	135
3	Wayne Gretzky, Edm	1982-83	80	125
4	Wayne Gretzky, LA	1990-91	78	122
5	Wayne Gretzky, Edm	1986-87	79	121
6	Wayne Gretzky, Edm	1981-82	80	120
7	Wayne Gretzky, Edm	1983-84	74	118
8	Mario Lemieux, Pit	1988-89	76	114
	Wayne Gretzky, LA	1988-89	78	114
10	Wayne Gretzky, Edm	1987-88	64	109
	Wayne Gretzky, Edm	1980-81	80	109
12	Wayne Gretzky, LA	1989-90	73	102
	Bobby Orr, Bos	1970-71	78	102
14	Mario Lemieux, Pit	1987-88	77	98
15	Adam Oates, Bos	1992-93	84	97

WHA 95 assists or more: 106—Andre Lacroix, S.Diego (1974-75).

Goaltending
Wins

		Season	Record
1	Bernie Parent, Phi	1973-74	47-13-12
2	Bernie Parent, Phi	1974-75	44-14- 9
	Terry Sawchuk, Det	1950-51	44-13-13
	Terry Sawchuk, Det	1951-52	44-14-12
5	Martin Brodeur, NJ	1997-98	43-17- 8
	Tom Barrasso, Pit	1992-93	43-14- 5
	Ed Belfour, Chi	1990-91	43-19- 7
8	Jacques Plante, Mon	1955-56	42-12-10
	Jacques Plante, Mon	1961-62	42-14-14
	Ken Dryden, Mon	1975-76	42-10- 8
	Mike Richter, NYR	1993-94	42-12- 6

Most WHA wins in one season: 44—Richard Brodeur, Que. (1975-76).

Losses

		Season	Record
1	Gary Smith, Cal	1970-71	19-48- 4
2	Al Rollins, Chi	1953-54	12-47- 7
3	Peter Sidorkiewicz, Ott	1992-93	8-46- 3
4	Harry Lumley, Chi	1951-52	17-44- 9
5	Harry Lumley, Chi	1950-51	12-41-10
	Craig Billington, Ott	1993-94	11-41- 4

Most WHA losses in one season: 36—Don McLeod, Van. (1974-75) and Andy Brown, Ind. (1974-75).

Shutouts

		Season	Gm	No
1	George Hainsworth, Mon	1928-29	44	22
2	Alex Connell, Ottawa	1925-26	36	15
	Alex Connell, Ottawa	1927-28	44	15
	Hal Winkler, Bos	1927-28	44	15
	Tony Esposito, Chi	1969-70	63	15

Most WHA shutouts in one season: 5—Gerry Cheevers, Cle. (1972-73) and Joe Daly, Win. (1975-76).

Goals Against Average
Before 1950

		Season	Gm	GAA
1	George Hainsworth, Mon	1928-29	44	0.98
2	George Hainsworth, Mon	1927-28	44	1.09
3	Alex Connell, Ottawa	1925-26	36	1.17
4	Tiny Thompson, Bos	1928-29	44	1.18
5	Roy Worters, NY Americans	1928-29	38	1.21

Since 1950

		Season	Gm	GAA
1	Tony Esposito, Chi	1971-72	48	1.77
2	Al Rollins, Tor	1950-51	40	1.77
3	**Ron Tugnutt**, Ott	1998-99	43	1.79
4	Harry Lumley, Tor	1953-54	69	1.86
5	Jacques Plante, Mon	1955-56	64	1.86

Penalty Minutes

		Season	PM
1	Dave Schultz, Phi	1974-75	472
2	Paul Baxter, Pit	1981-82	409
3	Mike Peluso, Chi	1991-92	408
4	Dave Schultz, LA-Pit	1977-78	405
5	Marty McSorley, LA	1992-93	399
6	Bob Probert, Det	1987-88	398
7	Basil McRae, Min	1987-88	382
8	Joey Kocur, Det	1985-86	377
9	Tim Hunter, Calg	1988-89	375
10	Donald Brashear, Van	1997-98	372

WHA 355 minutes or more: 365—Curt Brackenbury, Min-Que. (1975-76).

SINGLE GAME
Scoring

Points

	Date	G-A—Pts
Darryl Sittler, Tor vs Bos	2/7/76	6-4—10
Maurice Richard, Mon vs Det	12/28/44	5-3—8
Bert Olmstead, Mon vs Chi	1/9/54	4-4—8
Tom Bladon, Phi vs Cle	12/11/77	4-4—8
Bryan Trottier, NYI vs NYR	12/23/78	5-3—8
Peter Stastny, Que at Wash	2/22/81	4-4—8
Anton Stastny, Que at Wash	2/22/81	3-5—8
Wayne Gretzky, Edm vs NJ	11/19/83	3-5—8
Wayne Gretzky, Edm vs Min	1/4/84	4-4—8
Paul Coffey, Edm vs Det	3/14/86	2-6—8
Mario Lemieux, Pit vs St.L	10/15/88	2-6—8
Bernie Nicholls, LA vs Tor	12/1/88	2-6—8
Mario Lemieux, Pit vs NJ	12/31/88	5-3—8

Goals

	Date	No
Joe Malone, Que vs Tor	1/31/20	7
Newsy Lalonde, Mon vs Tor	1/10/20	6
Joe Malone, Que vs Ott	3/10/20	6
Corb Denneny, Tor vs Ham	1/26/21	6
Cy Denneny, Ott vs Ham	3/7/21	6
Syd Howe, Det vs NYR	2/3/44	6
Red Berenson, St.L at Phi	11/7/68	6
Darryl Sittler, Tor vs Bos	2/7/76	6

Assists

	Date	No
Billy Taylor, Det at Chi	3/16/47	7
Wayne Gretzky, Edm vs Wash	2/15/80	7
Wayne Gretzky, Edm at Chi	12/11/85	7
Wayne Gretzky, Edm vs Que	2/14/86	7
24 players tied with 6 each.		

Penalty Minutes

	Date	Min
Randy Holt, LA at Phi	3/11/79	67
Frank Bathe, Phi vs LA	3/11/79	55
Russ Anderson, Pit vs Edm	1/19/80	51

Penalties

	Date	No
Chris Nilan, Bos vs Har	3/31/91	10*
Eight tied with 9 each.		

* Nilan accumulated six minors, two majors, one 10-minute misconduct and one game misconduct.

The NHL Top 50

To celebrate its fiftieth anniversary, *The Hockey News* presented its list of the "Top 50 NHL Players of All-Time" on January 9, 1998. The list was determined by a panel of 50 hockey experts representing past and present NHL players, coaches, executives and journalists. Voting was conducted before the 1997 Stanley Cup playoffs. Players active during the 1998-99 season are in **bold** type.

No.	Player	Pos
1	**Wayne Gretzky**, 1979-1999	C
2	Bobby Orr, 1966-1979	D
3	Gordie Howe, 1946-71, 79-80	RW
4	Mario Lemieux, 1984-1997	C
5	Maurice Richard, 1942-1960	RW
6	Doug Harvey, 1947-69	D
7	Jean Beliveau, 1950-71	C
8	Bobby Hull, 1957-72, 79-80	LW
9	Terry Sawchuk, 1949-70	G
10	Eddie Shore, 1926-40	D
11	Guy Lafleur, 1971-85, 88-91	RW
12	**Mark Messier**, 1979—	C
13	Jacques Plante, 1952-65, 67-73	G
14	**Ray Bourque**, 1979—	D
15	Howie Morenz, 1923-37	C
16	Glenn Hall, 1952-71	G
17	Stan Mikita, 1958-80	C
18	Phil Esposito, 1963-81	C
19	Denis Potvin, 1973-88	D
20	Mike Bossy, 1977-87	RW
21	Ted Lindsay, 1944-60, 64-65	LW
22	Red Kelly, 1947-67	D
23	Bobby Clarke, 1969-84	C
24	Larry Robinson, 1972-92	D
25	Ken Dryden, 1970-79	G
26	Frank Mahovlich, 1956-74	LW
27	Milt Schmidt, 1936-42, 45-55	C
28	**Paul Coffey**, 1980—	D
29	Henri Richard, 1955-75	C
30	Bryan Trottier, 1975-92, 93-94	C
31	Dickie Moore, 1951-65, 67-68	LW
32	Newsy Lalonde, 1917-21, 25-27	C
33	Syl Apps, 1936-48	C
34	Bill Durnan, 1943-50	G
35	**Patrick Roy**, 1984—	G
36	Charlie Conacher, 1929-41	RW
37	**Jaromir Jagr**, 1990—	RW
38	Marcel Dionne, 1971-89	C
39	Joe Malone, 1917-24	C
40	**Chris Chelios**, 1983—	D
41	Dit Clapper, 1927-47	D
42	Bernie Geoffrion, 1950-64, 66-68	RW
43	Tim Horton, 1949-50, 51-74	D
44	Bill Cook, 1926-37	RW
45	Johnny Bucyk, 1955-78	LW
46	George Hainsworth, 1926-37	G
47	Gilbert Perreault, 1970-87	C
48	Max Bentley, 1940-43, 45-54	C
49	Brad Park, 1968-85	D
50	Jari Kurri, 1980-1998	RW

All-Time Winningest NHL Coaches

Top 20 NHL career victories through the 1999 season. Career, regular season and playoff records are noted along with NHL titles won. Coaches active during 1999 season in **bold** type.

		Career				Regular Season				Playoffs				
	Yrs	W	L	T	Pct	W	L	T	Pct	W	L	T	Pct	Stanley Cups
1 **Scotty Bowman**	27	**1300**	630	285	.651	1100	515	285	.654	200	115	0	.635	8 (1973, 76-79, 92, 97-98)
2 Al Arbour	22	**904**	663	248	.566	781	577	248	.564	123	86	0	.589	4 (1980-83)
3 Dick Irvin	26	**790**	609	228	.556	690	521	226	.559	100	88	2	.532	4 (1932,44,46,53)
4 Billy Reay	16	**599**	445	175	.563	542	385	175	.571	57	60	0	.487	None
5 **Mike Keenan**	14	**597**	441	117	.568	506	372	117	.567	91	69	0	.569	1 (1994)
6 Toe Blake	13	**582**	292	159	.640	500	255	159	.634	82	37	0	.689	8 (1956-60,65-66,68)
7 Glen Sather	11	**553**	305	110	.628	464	268	110	.616	89	37	0	.706	4 (1984-85,87-88)
8 Bryan Murray	13	**518**	412	123	.550	484	368	123	.559	34	44	0	.436	None
9 Jack Adams	21	**475**	449	163	.512	423	397	162	.513	52	52	1	.500	3 (1936-37, 43)
10 **Pat Quinn**	13	**464**	373	109	.548	402	315	109	.553	62	58	0	.517	None
Jacques Demers	14	**464**	510	130	.479	409	467	130	.471	55	43	0	.561	1 (1993)
12 **Roger Neilson**	14	**454**	403	147	.525	414	355	147	.532	40	48	0	.455	None
13 Fred Shero	10	**451**	272	119	.606	390	225	119	.612	61	47	0	.565	2 (1974-75)
14 **Pat Burns**	10	**446**	330	109	.566	385	271	109	.575	61	59	0	.508	None
15 Punch Imlach	15	**439**	384	148	.528	395	336	148	.534	44	48	0	.478	4 (1962-64,67)
16 Emile Francis	13	**433**	326	112	.561	393	273	112	.577	40	53	0	.430	None
17 Sid Abel	16	**414**	470	155	.473	382	426	155	.477	32	44	0	.421	None
18 Bob Berry	11	**395**	377	121	.510	384	355	121	.517	11	22	0	.333	None
19 Art Ross	18	**393**	310	95	.552	361	277	90	.558	32	33	5	.493	1 (1939)
20 Michel Bergeron	10	**369**	387	104	.490	338	350	104	.492	31	37	0	.456	None

Note: The NHL does not recognize records from the World Hockey Association (1972-79), so the following WHA overall coaching records are not included above: **Demers** (155-164-44 in 4 yrs); **Sather** (103-97-1 in 3 yrs).

Where They Coached

Abel—Chicago (1952-54), Detroit (1957-68,69-70), St. Louis (1971-72), Kansas City (1975-76); **Adams**—Toronto (1922-23), Detroit (1927-47); **Arbour**—St. Louis (1970-73), NY Islanders (1973-86,88-94); **Bergeron**—Quebec (1980-87), NY Rangers (1987-89), Quebec (1989-90); **Berry**—Los Angeles (1978-81), Montreal (1981-84), Pittsburgh (1984-87), St. Louis (1992-94); **Blake**—Montreal (1955-68); **Bowman**—St. Louis (1967-71), Montreal (1971-79), Buffalo (1979-87), Pittsburgh (1991-93), Detroit (1993—); **Burns**—Montreal (1988-92), Toronto (1992-96), Boston (1997—).

Demers—Quebec (1979-80), St. Louis (1983-86), Detroit (1986-90), Montreal (1992-95), Tampa Bay (1997-99); **Francis**—NY Rangers (1965-75), St. Louis (1976-77,81-83); **Imlach**—Toronto (1958-69), Buffalo (1970-72), Toronto (1979-81); **Irvin**—Chicago (1930-31,55-56), Toronto (1931-40), Montreal (1940-55); **Keenan**—Philadelphia (1984-88), Chicago (1988-92), NY Rangers (1993-94), St. Louis (1994-96), Vancouver (1997-99); **Murray**—Washington (1982-90), Detroit (1990-93), Florida (1997-98).

Neilson—Toronto (1977-79), Buffalo (1979-81), Vancouver (1982-83), Los Angeles (1984), NY Rangers (1989-93), Florida (1993-95), Philadelphia (1998—); **Quinn**—Philadelphia (1978-82), Los Angeles (1984-87), Vancouver (1990-94, 96), Toronto (1998—); **Reay**—Toronto (1957-59), Chicago (1963-77); **Ross**—Montreal Wanderers (1917-18), Hamilton (1922-23), Boston (1924-28,29-34,36-39,41-45); **Sather**—Edmonton (1979-89, 93-94); **Shero**—Philadelphia (1971-78), NY Rangers (1978-81).

Top Winning Percentages

Minimum of 275 victories, including playoffs.

	Yrs	W	L	T	Pct.
1 Scotty Bowman	27	1300	630	285	**.651**
2 Toe Blake	13	582	292	159	**.640**
3 Glen Sather	11	553	305	110	**.628**
4 Fred Shero	10	451	272	119	**.606**
5 Don Cherry	6	281	177	77	**.597**
6 Tommy Ivan	9	324	205	111	**.593**
7 Jacques Lemaire	7	296	193	69	**.592**
8 Mike Keenan	14	597	441	117	**.568**
9 Al Arbour	22	904	663	248	**.566**
10 Pat Burns	10	446	330	109	**.566**
11 Billy Reay	16	599	445	175	**.563**
12 Emile Francis	13	433	326	112	**.561**
13 Terry Murray	9	357	271	76	**.561**
14 Hap Day	10	308	237	81	**.557**
15 Dick Irvin	26	790	609	228	**.556**
16 Lester Patrick	13	312	242	115	**.552**
17 Art Ross	18	393	310	95	**.552**
18 Bryan Murray	13	518	412	123	**.550**
19 Pat Quinn	13	464	373	109	**.548**
20 Bob Johnson	6	275	223	58	**.547**
21 Punch Imlach	15	439	384	148	**.528**
22 Brian Sutter	9	356	314	93	**.528**
23 Roger Neilson	14	454	403	147	**.525**
24 Terry Crisp	9	310	286	78	**.518**
25 Jack Adams	21	475	449	163	**.512**

Active Coaches' Victories

Through 1999 season, including playoffs.

	Yrs	W	L	T	Pct.
1 Scotty Bowman, Det.	27	**1300**	630	285	.651
2 Pat Quinn, Tor.	13	**464**	373	109	.548
3 Roger Neilson, Phi	14	**454**	403	147	.525
4 Pat Burns, Bos.	10	**446**	330	109	.566
5 Terry Murray, Fla	9	**357**	271	76	.561
6 Brian Sutter, Calg.	9	**356**	314	93	.528
7 John Muckler, NYR	9	**283**	281	73	.502
8 Ron Wilson, Wash.	6	**207**	236	49	.471
9 Marc Crawford, Van.	5	**204**	132	47	.594
10 Jacques Martin, Ott.	6	**200**	210	72	.490
11 Ken Hitchcock, Dal.	4	**192**	108	36	.625
12 Darryl Sutter, SJ	5	**190**	174	54	.519
13 Kevin Constantine, Pit	5	**152**	157	56	.493
14 Craig Hartsburg, Ana	4	**147**	148	53	.499
15 Paul Maurice, Car.	4	**130**	147	45	.474
16 Robbie Ftorek, NJ	3	**120**	95	22	.553
17 Joel Quenneville, St.L.	3	**114**	91	28	.549
18 Lindy Ruff, Buf	2	**97**	69	34	.570
19 Alain Vigneault, Mon.	2	**73**	77	24	.489
20 Bob Hartley, Col.	1	**55**	36	10	.594
21 Butch Goring, NYI	2	**42**	41	13	.505
22 Barry Trotz, Nash.	1	**28**	47	7	.384
23 Lorne Molleken, Chi.	1	**13**	6	4	.652
24 Bobby Francis, Pho	0	**0**	0	0	.000
Curt Fraser, Atl.	0	**0**	0	0	.000
Kevin Lowe, Edm.	0	**0**	0	0	.000
Steve Ludzik, TB	0	**0**	0	0	.000
Andy Murray, LA	0	**0**	0	0	.000

Annual Awards
Hart Memorial Trophy

Awarded to the player "adjudged to be the most valuable to his team" and named after Cecil Hart, the former manager-coach of the Montreal Canadiens. Winners selected by Pro Hockey Writers Assn. (PHWA). Winners' scoring statistics or goaltender W-L records and goals against average are provided; (*) indicates led or tied for league lead.

Multiple Winners: Wayne Gretzky (9); Gordie Howe (6); Eddie Shore (4); Bobby Clarke, Mario Lemieux, Howie Morenz and Bobby Orr (3); Jean Beliveau, Bill Cowley, Phil Esposito, Dominik Hasek, Bobby Hull, Guy Lafleur, Mark Messier, Stan Mikita and Nels Stewart (2).

Year		G	A	Pts	Year		G	A	Pts
1924	Frank Nighbor, Ottawa, C	10	3	13	1962	Jacques Plante, Mon., G	42-14-14;		2.37*
1925	Billy Burch, Hamilton, C	20	4	24	1963	Gordie Howe, Det., RW	38	48	86*
1926	Nels Stewart, Maroons, C	34	8	42*	1964	Jean Beliveau, Mon., C	28	50	78
1927	Herb Gardiner, Mon., D	6	6	12	1965	Bobby Hull, Chi., LW	39	32	71
1928	Howie Morenz, Mon., C	33	18	51	1966	Bobby Hull, Chi., LW	54	43	97*
1929	Roy Worters, NYA, G	16-13-9,		1.21	1967	Stan Mikita, Chi., C	35	62	97*
1930	Nels Stewart, Maroons, C	39	16	55	1968	Stan Mikita, Chi., C	40	47	87*
1931	Howie Morenz, Mon., C	28	23	51*	1969	Phil Esposito, Bos., C	49	77	126*
1932	Howie Morenz, Mon., C	24	25	49	1970	Bobby Orr, Bos., D	33	87	120*
1933	Eddie Shore, Bos., D	8	27	35	1971	Bobby Orr, Bos., D	37	102	139
1934	Aurel Joliat, Mon., LW	22	15	37	1972	Bobby Orr, Bos., D	37	80	117
1935	Eddie Shore, Bos., D	7	26	33	1973	Bobby Clarke, Phi., C	37	67	104
1936	Eddie Shore, Bos., D	3	16	19	1974	Phil Esposito, Bos., C	68	77	145*
1937	Babe Siebert, Mon., D	8	20	28	1975	Bobby Clarke, Phi., C	27	89	116
1938	Eddie Shore, Bos., D	3	14	17	1976	Bobby Clarke, Phi., C	30	89	119
1939	Toe Blake, Mon., LW	24	23	47*	1977	Guy Lafleur, Mon., RW	56	80	136*
1940	Ebbie Goodfellow, Det., D	11	17	28	1978	Guy Lafleur, Mon., RW	60	72	132*
1941	Bill Cowley, Bos., C	17	45	62*	1979	Bryan Trottier, NYI., C	47	87	134*
1942	Tommy Anderson, NYA, D	12	29	41	1980	Wayne Gretzky, Edm., C	51	86	137*
1943	Bill Cowley, Bos., C	27	45	72	1981	Wayne Gretzky, Edm., C	55	109	164*
1944	Babe Pratt, Tor., D	17	40	57	1982	Wayne Gretzky, Edm., C	92	120	212*
1945	Elmer Lach, Mon., C	26	54	80*	1983	Wayne Gretzky, Edm., C	71	125	196*
1946	Max Bentley, Chi., C	31	30	61*	1984	Wayne Gretzky, Edm., C	87	118	205*
1947	Maurice Richard, Mon., RW	45	26	71	1985	Wayne Gretzky, Edm., C	73	135	208*
1948	Buddy O'Connor, NYR, C	24	36	60	1986	Wayne Gretzky, Edm., C	52	163	215*
1949	Sid Abel, Det., C	28	26	54	1987	Wayne Gretzky, Edm., C	62	121	183*
1950	Chuck Rayner, NYR, G	28-30-11;		2.62	1988	Mario Lemieux, Pit., C	70	98	168*
1951	Milt Schmidt, Bos., C	22	39	61	1989	Wayne Gretzky, LA, C	54	114	168
1952	Gordie Howe, Det., RW	47	39	86*	1990	Mark Messier, Edm., C	45	84	129
1953	Gordie Howe, Det., RW	49	46	95*	1991	Brett Hull, St. L., RW	86	45	131
1954	Al Rollins, Chi., G	12-47-7;		3.23	1992	Mark Messier, NYR, C	35	72	107
1955	Ted Kennedy, Tor., C	10	42	52	1993	Mario Lemieux, Pit., C	69	91	160*
1956	Jean Beliveau, Mon., C	47	41	88	1994	Sergei Fedorov, Det., C	56	64	120
1957	Gordie Howe, Det., RW	44	45	89*	1995	Eric Lindros, Phi., C	29	41	70*
1958	Gordie Howe, Det., RW	33	44	77	1996	Mario Lemieux, Pit., C	69	92	161*
1959	Andy Bathgate, NYR, RW	40	48	88	1997	Dominik Hasek, Buf., G	37-20-10;		2.27
1960	Gordie Howe, Det., RW	28	45	73	1998	Dominik Hasek, Buf., G	33-23-13,		2.09
1961	Bernie Geoffrion, Mon., RW	50	45	95*	1999	Jaromir Jagr, Pit., RW	44	83	127*

Calder Memorial Trophy

Awarded to the most outstanding rookie of the year and named after Frank Calder, the late NHL president (1917-43). Since the 1990-91 season, all eligible candidates must not have attained their 26th birthday by Sept. 15 of their rookie year. Winners selected by PHWA. Winners' scoring statistics or goaltender W-L record & goals against average are provided.

Year		G	A	Pts	Year		G	A	Pts
1933	Carl Voss, NYR-Det., C	8	15	23	1952	Bernie Geoffrion, Mon., RW	30	24	54
1934	Russ Blinco, Maroons, C	14	9	23	1953	Gump Worsley, NYR, G	13-29-8;		3.06
1935	Sweeney Schriner, NYA, LW	18	22	40	1954	Camille Henry, NYR, LW	24	15	39
1936	Mike Karakas, Chi., G	21-19-8;		1.92	1955	Ed Litzenberger, Mon-Chi., RW	23	28	51
1937	Syl Apps, Tor., C	16	29	45	1956	Glenn Hall, Det., G	30-24-16;		2.11
1938	Cully Dahlstrom, Chi., C	10	9	19	1957	Larry Regan, Bos., RW	14	19	33
1939	Frankie Brimsek, Bos., G	33-9-1;		1.58	1958	Frank Mahovlich, Tor., LW	20	16	36
1940	Kilby MacDonald, NYR, LW	15	13	28	1959	Ralph Backstrom, Mon., C	18	22	40
1941	John Quilty, Mon., C	18	16	34	1960	Billy Hay, Chi., C	18	37	55
1942	Knobby Warwick, NYR, RW	16	17	33	1961	Dave Keon, Tor., C	20	25	45
1943	Gaye Stewart, Tor., LW	24	23	47	1962	Bobby Rousseau, Mon., RW	21	24	45
1944	Gus Bodnar, Tor., C	22	40	62	1963	Kent Douglas, Tor., D	7	15	22
1945	Frank McCool, Tor., G	24-22-4;		3.22	1964	Jacques Laperriere, Mon., D	2	28	30
1946	Edgar Laprade, NYR, C	15	19	34	1965	Roger Crozier, Det., G	40-23-7;		2.42
1947	Howie Meeker, Tor., RW	27	18	45	1966	Brit Selby, Tor., LW	14	13	27
1948	Jim McFadden, Det., C	24	24	48	1967	Bobby Orr, Bos., D	13	28	41
1949	Penny Lund, NYR, RW	14	16	30	1968	Derek Sanderson, Bos., C	24	25	49
1950	Jack Gelineau, Bos., G	22-30-15;		3.28	1969	Danny Grant, Min., LW	34	31	65
1951	Terry Sawchuk, Det., G	44-13-13;		1.99	1970	Tony Esposito, Chi., G	38-17-8;		2.17

Annual Awards (Cont.)

Year		G	A	Pts	Year		G	A	Pts
1971	Gilbert Perreault, Buf., C	38	34	72	1986	Gary Suter, Calg., D	18	50	68
1972	Ken Dryden, Mon., G	39-8-15;		2.24	1987	Luc Robitaille, LA, LW	45	39	84
1973	Steve Vickers, NYR, LW	30	23	53	1988	Joe Nieuwendyk, Calg., C	51	41	92
1974	Denis Potvin, NYI, D	17	37	54	1989	Brian Leetch, NYR, D	23	48	71
1975	Eric Vail, Atl., LW	39	21	60	1990	Sergei Makarov, Calg., RW	24	62	86
1976	Bryan Trottier, NYI, C	32	63	95	1991	Ed Belfour, Chi., G	43-19-7;		2.47
1977	Willi Plett, Atl., RW	33	23	56	1992	Pavel Bure, Van., RW	34	26	60
1978	Mike Bossy, NYI, RW	53	38	91	1993	Teemu Selanne, Win., RW	76	56	132
1979	Bobby Smith, Min., C	30	44	74	1994	Martin Brodeur, NJ, G	27-11-8;		2.40
1980	Ray Bourque, Bos., D	17	48	65	1995	Peter Forsberg, Que., C	15	35	50
1981	Peter Stastny, Que., C	39	70	109	1996	Daniel Alfredsson, Ott., RW	26	35	61
1982	Dale Hawerchuk, Win., C	45	58	103	1997	Bryan Berard, NYI, D	8	40	48
1983	Steve Larmer, Chi., RW	43	47	90	1998	Sergei Samsonov, Bos., LW	22	25	47
1984	Tom Barrasso, Buf., G	26-12-3;		2.84	1999	Chris Drury, Col., C	20	24	44
1985	Mario Lemieux, Pit., C	43	57	100					

Vezina Trophy

From 1927-80, given to the principal goaltender(s) on the team allowing the fewest goals during the regular season. Trophy named after 1920's goalie Georges Vezina of the Montreal Canadiens, who died of tuberculosis in 1926. Since the 1980-81 season, the trophy has been awarded to the most outstanding goaltender of the year as selected by the league's general managers.

Multiple Winners: Jacques Plante (7, one of them shared); Bill Durnan (6); Ken Dryden (5, three shared); Dominik Hasek (5); Bunny Larocque (4, all shared); Terry Sawchuk (4, one shared); Tiny Thompson (4); Tony Esposito (3, one shared); George Hainsworth (3); Glenn Hall (3, two shared); Patrick Roy (3); Ed Belfour (2); Johnny Bower (2, one shared); Frankie Brimsek (2); Turk Broda (2); Chuck Gardiner (2); Charlie Hodge (2, one shared); Bernie Parent (2, one shared); Gump Worsley (2, both shared).

Year		Record	GAA	Year		Record	GAA
1927	George Hainsworth, Mon	28-14-2	1.52	1968	Gump Worsley, Mon	19-9-8	1.98
1928	George Hainsworth, Mon	26-11-7	1.09		& Rogie Vachon, Mon	23-13-2	2.48
1929	George Hainsworth, Mon	22-7-15	0.98	1969	Jacques Plante, St.L	18-12-6	1.96
1930	Tiny Thompson, Bos	38-5-1	2.23		& Glenn Hall, St.L	19-12-8	2.17
1931	Roy Worters, NYA	18-16-10	1.68	1970	Tony Esposito, Chi	38-17-8	2.17
1932	Chuck Gardiner, Chi	18-19-11	1.92	1971	Ed Giacomin, NYR	27-10-7	2.16
1933	Tiny Thompson, Bos	25-15-8	1.83		& Gilles Villemure, NYR	22-8-4	2.30
1934	Chuck Gardiner, Chi	20-17-11	1.73	1972	Tony Esposito, Chi	31-10-6	1.77
1935	Lorne Chabot, Chi	26-17-5	1.83		& Gary Smith, Chi	14-5-6	2.42
1936	Tiny Thompson, Bos	22-20-6	1.71	1973	Ken Dryden, Mon	33-7-13	2.26
1937	Norm Smith, Det	25-14-9	2.13	1974	(Tie) Bernie Parent, Phi	47-13-12	1.89
1938	Tiny Thompson, Bos	30-11-7	1.85		Tony Esposito, Chi	34-14-21	2.04
1939	Frankie Brimsek, Bos	33-9-1	1.58	1975	Bernie Parent, Phi	44-14-10	2.03
1940	Dave Kerr, NYR	27-11-10	1.60	1976	Ken Dryden, Mon	42-10-8	2.03
1941	Turk Broda, Tor	28-14-6	2.06	1977	Ken Dryden, Mon	41-6-8	2.14
1942	Frankie Brimsek, Bos	24-17-6	2.45		& Bunny Larocque, Mon	19-2-4	2.09
1943	John Mowers, Det	25-14-11	2.47	1978	Ken Dryden, Mon	37-7-7	2.05
1944	Bill Durnan, Mon	38-5-7	2.18		& Bunny Larocque, Mon	22-3-4	2.67
1945	Bill Durnan, Mon	38-8-4	2.42	1979	Ken Dryden, Mon	30-10-7	2.30
1946	Bill Durnan, Mon	24-11-5	2.60		& Bunny Larocque, Mon	22-7-4	2.84
1947	Bill Durnan, Mon	34-16-10	2.30	1980	Bob Sauve, Buf	20-8-4	2.36
1948	Turk Broda, Tor	32-15-13	2.38		& Don Edwards, Buf	27-9-12	2.57
1949	Bill Durnan, Mon	28-23-9	2.10	1981	Richard Sevigny, Mon	20-4-3	2.40
1950	Bill Durnan, Mon	26-21-17	2.20		Denis Herron, Mon	6-9-6	3.50
1951	Al Rollins, Tor	27-5-8	1.77		& Bunny Larocque, Mon	16-9-3	3.03
1952	Terry Sawchuk, Det	44-14-12	1.90	1982	Billy Smith, NYI	32-9-4	2.97
1953	Terry Sawchuk, Det	32-15-16	1.90	1983	Pete Peeters, Bos	40-11-9	2.36
1954	Harry Lumley, Tor	32-24-13	1.86	1984	Tom Barrasso, Buf	26-12-3	2.84
1955	Terry Sawchuk, Det	40-17-11	1.96	1985	Pelle Lindbergh, Phi	40-17-7	3.02
1956	Jacques Plante, Mon	42-12-10	1.86	1986	John Vanbiesbrouck, NYR	31-21-5	3.32
1957	Jacques Plante, Mon	31-18-12	2.02	1987	Ron Hextall, Phi	37-21-6	3.00
1958	Jacques Plante, Mon	34-14-8	2.11	1988	Grant Fuhr, Edm	40-24-9	3.43
1959	Jacques Plante, Mon	38-16-13	2.16	1989	Patrick Roy, Mon	33-5-6	2.47
1960	Jacques Plante, Mon	40-17-12	2.54	1990	Patrick Roy, Mon	31-16-5	2.53
1961	Johnny Bower, Tor	33-15-10	2.50	1991	Ed Belfour, Chi	43-19-7	2.47
1962	Jacques Plante, Mon	42-14-14	2.37	1992	Patrick Roy, Mon	36-22-8	2.36
1963	Glenn Hall, Chi	30-20-16	2.55	1993	Ed Belfour, Chi	41-18-11	2.59
1964	Charlie Hodge, Mon	33-18-11	2.26	1994	Dominik Hasek, Buf	30-20-6	1.95
1965	Johnny Bower, Tor	13-13-8	2.38	1995	Dominik Hasek, Buf	19-14-7	2.11
	& Terry Sawchuk, Tor	17-13-6	2.56	1996	Jim Carey, Wash	35-24-9	2.26
1966	Gump Worsley, Mon	29-14-6	2.36	1997	Dominik Hasek, Buf	37-20-10	2.27
	& Charlie Hodge, Mon	12-7-2	2.58	1998	Dominik Hasek, Buf	33-23-13	2.09
1967	Glenn Hall, Chi	19-5-5	2.38	1999	Dominik Hasek, Buf	30-18-14	1.87
	& Denis Dejordy, Chi	22-12-7	2.46				

Lady Byng Memorial Trophy

Awarded to the player "adjudged to have exhibited the best type of sportsmanship and gentlemanly conduct combined with a high standard of playing ability" and named after Lady Evelyn Byng, the wife of former Canadian Governor General (1921-26) Baron Byng of Vimy. Winners selected by PHWA.

Multiple winners: Frank Boucher (7); Wayne Gretzky (5); Red Kelly (4); Bobby Bauer, Mike Bossy and Alex Delvecchio (3); Johnny Bucyk, Marcel Dionne, Ron Francis, Paul Kariya, Dave Keon, Stan Mikita, Joey Mullen, Frank Nighbor, Jean Ratelle, Clint Smith and Sid Smith (2).

Year	Year	Year
1925 Frank Nighbor, Ott., C	1950 Edgar Laprade, NYR, C	1975 Marcel Dionne, Det., C
1926 Frank Nighbor, Ott., C	1951 Red Kelly, Det., D	1976 Jean Ratelle, NY-Bos., C
1927 Billy Burch, NYA, C	1952 Sid Smith, Tor., LW	1977 Marcel Dionne, LA, C
1928 Frank Boucher, NYR, C	1953 Red Kelly, Det., D	1978 Butch Goring, LA, C
1929 Frank Boucher, NYR, C	1954 Red Kelly, Det., D	1979 Bob MacMillan, Atl., RW
1930 Frank Boucher, NYR, C	1955 Sid Smith, Tor., LW	1980 Wayne Gretzky, Edm., C
1931 Frank Boucher, NYR, C	1956 Earl Reibel, Det., C	1981 Rick Kehoe, Pit., RW
1932 Joe Primeau, Tor., C	1957 Andy Hebenton, NYR, RW	1982 Rick Middleton, Bos., RW
1933 Frank Boucher, NYR, C	1958 Camille Henry, NYR, LW	1983 Mike Bossy, NYI, RW
1934 Frank Boucher, NYR, C	1959 Alex Delvecchio, Det., LW	1984 Mike Bossy, NYI, RW
1935 Frank Boucher, NYR, C	1960 Don McKenney, Bos., C	1985 Jari Kurri, Edm., RW
1936 Doc Romnes, Chi., F	1961 Red Kelly, Tor., D	1986 Mike Bossy, NYI, RW
1937 Marty Barry, Det., C	1962 Dave Keon, Tor., C	1987 Joey Mullen, Calg., RW
1938 Gordie Drillon, Tor., RW	1963 Dave Keon, Tor., C	1988 Mats Naslund, Mon., LW
1939 Clint Smith, NYR, C	1964 Ken Wharram, Chi., RW	1989 Joey Mullen, Calg., RW
1940 Bobby Bauer, Bos., RW	1965 Bobby Hull, Chi., LW	1990 Brett Hull, St.L., RW
1941 Bobby Bauer, Bos., RW	1966 Alex Delvecchio, Det., LW	1991 Wayne Gretzky, LA, C
1942 Syl Apps, Tor., C	1967 Stan Mikita, Chi., C	1992 Wayne Gretzky, LA, C
1943 Max Bentley, Chi., C	1968 Stan Mikita, Chi., C	1993 Pierre Turgeon, NYI, C
1944 Clint Smith, Chi., C	1969 Alex Delvecchio, Det., LW	1994 Wayne Gretzky, LA, C
1945 Bill Mosienko, Chi., RW	1970 Phil Goyette, St.L., C	1995 Ron Francis, Pit., C
1946 Toe Blake, Mon., LW	1971 Johnny Bucyk, Bos., LW	1996 Paul Kariya, Ana., LW
1947 Bobby Bauer, Bos., RW	1972 Jean Ratelle, NYR, C	1997 Paul Kariya, Ana., LW
1948 Buddy O'Connor, NYR, C	1973 Gilbert Perreault, Buf., C	1998 Ron Francis, Pit., C
1949 Bill Quackenbush, Det., D	1974 Johnny Bucyk, Bos., LW	1999 Wayne Gretzky, NYR, C

Note: Bill Quackenbush and Red Kelly are the only defensemen to win the Lady Byng.

James Norris Memorial Trophy

Awarded to the most outstanding defenseman of the year and named after James Norris, the late Detroit Red Wings owner-president. Winners selected by PHWA.

Multiple winners: Bobby Orr (8); Doug Harvey (7); Ray Bourque (5); Chris Chelios, Paul Coffey, Pierre Pilote and Denis Potvin (3); Rod Langway, Brian Leetch and Larry Robinson (2).

Year	Year	Year
1954 Red Kelly, Detroit	1970 Bobby Orr, Boston	1986 Paul Coffey, Edmonton
1955 Doug Harvey, Montreal	1971 Bobby Orr, Boston	1987 Ray Bourque, Boston
1956 Doug Harvey, Montreal	1972 Bobby Orr, Boston	1988 Ray Bourque, Boston
1957 Doug Harvey, Montreal	1973 Bobby Orr, Boston	1989 Chris Chelios, Montreal
1958 Doug Harvey, Montreal	1974 Bobby Orr, Boston	1990 Ray Bourque, Boston
1959 Tom Johnson, Montreal	1975 Bobby Orr, Boston	1991 Ray Bourque, Boston
1960 Doug Harvey, Montreal	1976 Denis Potvin, NY Islanders	1992 Brian Leetch, NY Rangers
1961 Doug Harvey, Montreal	1977 Larry Robinson, Montreal	1993 Chris Chelios, Chicago
1962 Doug Harvey, NY Rangers	1978 Denis Potvin, NY Islanders	1994 Ray Bourque, Boston
1963 Pierre Pilote, Chicago	1979 Denis Potvin, NY Islanders	1995 Paul Coffey, Detroit
1964 Pierre Pilote, Chicago	1980 Larry Robinson, Montreal	1996 Chris Chelios, Chicago
1965 Pierre Pilote, Chicago	1981 Randy Carlyle, Pittsburgh	1997 Brian Leetch, NY Rangers
1966 Jacques Laperriere, Montreal	1982 Doug Wilson, Chicago	1998 Rob Blake, Los Angeles
1967 Harry Howell, NY Rangers	1983 Rod Langway, Washington	1999 Al MacInnis, St. Louis
1968 Bobby Orr, Boston	1984 Rod Langway, Washington	
1969 Bobby Orr, Boston	1985 Paul Coffey, Edmonton	

Frank Selke Trophy

Awarded to the outstanding defensive forward of the year and named after the late Montreal Canadiens general manager. Winners selected by the PHWA.

Multiple winners: Bob Gainey (4); Guy Carbonneau (3); Sergei Fedorov and Jere Lehtinen (2).

Year	Year	Year
1978 Bob Gainey, Mon., LW	1986 Troy Murray, Chi., C	1994 Sergei Fedorov, Det., C
1979 Bob Gainey, Mon., LW	1987 Dave Poulin, Phi., C	1995 Ron Francis, Pit., C
1980 Bob Gainey, Mon., LW	1988 Guy Carbonneau, Mon., C	1996 Sergei Fedorov, Det., C
1981 Bob Gainey, Mon., LW	1989 Guy Carbonneau, Mon., C	1997 Michael Peca, Buf., C
1982 Steve Kasper, Bos., C	1990 Rick Meagher, St.L., C	1998 Jere Lehtinen, Dal., RW
1983 Bobby Clarke, Phi., C	1991 Dirk Graham, Chi., RW	1999 Jere Lehtinen, Dal., RW
1984 Doug Jarvis, Wash., C	1992 Guy Carbonneau, Mon., C	
1985 Craig Ramsay, Buf., LW	1993 Doug Gilmour, Tor., C	

Annual Awards (Cont.)
Jack Adams Award

Awarded to the coach "adjudged to have contributed the most to his team's success" and named after the late Detroit Red Wings coach and general manager. Winners selected by NHL Broadcasters' Assn.; (*) indicates division champion.

Multiple winners: Pat Burns (3); Scotty Bowman, Jacques Demers and Pat Quinn (2).

Year		Improvement		Year		Improvement	
1974	Fred Shero, Phi	37-30-11	to 50-16-12*	1987	Jacques Demers, Det	17-57-6	to 34-36-10
1975	Bob Pulford, LA	41-14-23	to 37-35-8	1988	Jacques Demers, Det	34-36-10	to 41-28-11*
1976	Don Cherry, Bos	40-26-14	to 48-15-17*	1989	Pat Burns, Mon	45-22-13	to 53-18-9*
1977	Scotty Bowman, Mon	58-11-11*	to 60-8-12*	1990	Bob Murdoch, Win	26-42-12	to 37-32-11
1978	Bobby Kromm, Det	6-55-9	to 32-34-14	1991	Brian Sutter, St.L	37-34-9	to 47-22-11
1979	Al Arbour, NYI	48-17-15*	to 51-15-14*	1992	Pat Quinn, Van	28-43-9	to 42-26-12*
1980	Pat Quinn, Phi	40-25-15	to 48-12-20*	1993	Pat Burns, Tor	30-43-7	to 44-29-11
1981	Red Berenson, St.L	34-34-12	to 45-18-17*	1994	Jacques Lemaire, NJ	40-37-7	to 47-25-12
1982	Tom Watt, Win	9-57-14	to 33-33-14	1995	Marc Crawford, Que	34-42-8	to 30-13-5*
1983	Orval Tessier, Chi	30-38-12	to 47-23-10	1996	Scotty Bowman, Det	33-11-4*	to 62-13-7*
1984	Bryan Murray, Wash	39-25-16	to 48-27-5	1997	Ted Nolan, Buf	33-42-7	to 40-30-12*
1985	Mike Keenan, Phi	44-26-10	to 53-20-7*	1998	Pat Burns, Bos	26-47-9	to 39-30-13
1986	Glen Sather, Edm	49-20-11*	to 56-17-7*	1999	Jacques Martin, Ott	34-33-15	to 44-23-15*

Lester B. Pearson Award

Awarded to the season's most outstanding player and named after the former diplomat, Nobel Peace Prize winner and Canadian prime minister. Winners selected by the NHL Players Assn.

Multiple winners: Wayne Gretzky (5); Mario Lemieux (4); Guy Lafleur (3); Marcel Dionne, Phil Esposito, Dominik Hasek and Mark Messier (2).

Year	Year	Year
1971 Phil Esposito, Bos., C	1981 Mike Liut, St.L., G	1991 Brett Hull, St.L., RW
1972 Jean Ratelle, NYR, C	1982 Wayne Gretzky, Edm., C	1992 Mark Messier, NYR, C
1973 Bobby Clarke, Phi., C	1983 Wayne Gretzky, Edm., C	1993 Mario Lemieux, Pit., C
1974 Phil Esposito, Bos., C	1984 Wayne Gretzky, Edm., C	1994 Sergei Fedorov, Det., C
1975 Bobby Orr, Bos., D	1985 Wayne Gretzky, Edm., C	1995 Eric Lindros, Phi., C
1976 Guy Lafleur, Mon., RW	1986 Mario Lemieux, Pit., C	1996 Mario Lemieux, Pit., C
1977 Guy Lafleur, Mon., RW	1987 Wayne Gretzky, Edm., C	1997 Dominik Hasek, Buf., G
1978 Guy Lafleur, Mon., RW	1988 Mario Lemieux, Pit., C	1998 Dominik Hasek, Buf., G
1979 Marcel Dionne, LA, C	1989 Steve Yzerman, Det., C	1999 Jaromir Jagr, Pit., RW
1980 Marcel Dionne, LA, C	1990 Mark Messier, Edm., C	

Bill Masterton Trophy

Awarded to the player who "best exemplifies the qualities of perseverance, sportsmanship and dedication to hockey" and named after the 29-year-old rookie center of the Minnesota North Stars who died of a head injury sustained in a 1968 NHL game. Presented by the PHWA.

Year	Year	Year
1968 Claude Provost, Mon., RW	1979 Serge Savard, Mon., D	1990 Gord Kluzak, Bos., D
1969 Ted Hampson, Oak., C	1980 Al MacAdam, Min., RW	1991 Dave Taylor, LA, RW
1970 Pit Martin, Chi., C	1981 Blake Dunlop, St.L., C	1992 Mark Fitzpatrick, NYI, G
1971 Jean Ratelle, NYR, C	1982 Chico Resch, Colo., G	1993 Mario Lemieux, Pit., C
1972 Bobby Clarke, Phi., C	1983 Lanny McDonald, Calg., RW	1994 Cam Neely, Bos., RW
1973 Lowell MacDonald, Pit., RW	1984 Brad Park, Det., D	1995 Pat LaFontaine, Buf., C
1974 Henri Richard, Mon., C	1985 Anders Hedberg, NYR, RW	1996 Gary Roberts, Calg., LW
1975 Don Luce, Buf., C	1986 Charlie Simmer, Bos., LW	1997 Tony Granato, SJ, LW
1976 Rod Gilbert, NYR, RW	1987 Doug Jarvis, Hart., C	1998 Jamie McLennan, St.L, G
1977 Ed Westfall, NYI, RW	1988 Bob Bourne, LA, C	1999 John Cullen, TB, C
1978 Butch Goring, LA, C	1989 Tim Kerr, Phi., C	

Number One Draft Choices

Overall first choices in the NHL draft since the league staged its first universal amateur draft in 1969. Players are listed with team that selected them; those who became Rookie of the Year are in **bold** type.

Year	Year	Year
1969 Rejean Houle, Mon., LW	1980 Doug Wickenheiser, Mon., C	1991 Eric Lindros, Que., C
1970 **Gilbert Perreault,** Buf., C	1981 **Dale Hawerchuk,** Win., C	1992 Roman Hamrlik, TB, D
1971 Guy Lafleur, Mon., RW	1982 Gord Kluzak, Bos., D	1993 Alexandre Daigle, Ott., C
1972 Billy Harris, NYI, RW	1983 Brian Lawton, Min., C	1994 Ed Jovanovski, Fla., D
1973 **Denis Potvin,** NYI, D	1984 **Mario Lemieux,** Pit., C	1995 **Bryan Berard,** Ott., D
1974 Greg Joly, Wash., D	1985 Wendel Clark, Tor., LW/D	1996 Chris Phillips, Ott., D
1975 Mel Bridgman, Phi., C	1986 Joe Murphy, Det., C	1997 Joe Thornton, Bos., C
1976 Rick Green, Wash., D	1987 Pierre Turgeon, Buf., C	1998 Vincent Lecavalier, TB, C
1977 Dale McCourt, Det., C	1988 Mike Modano, Min., C	1999 Patrik Stefan, Atl., C
1978 **Bobby Smith,** Min., C	1989 Mats Sundin, Que., RW	
1979 Rob Ramage, Colo., D	1990 Owen Nolan, Que., RW	

World Hockey Association
WHA Finals

The World Hockey Association began play in 1972-73 as a 12-team rival of the 56-year-old NHL. The WHA played for the AVCO World Trophy in its seven playoff finals (Avco Financial Services underwrote the playoffs).

Multiple winners: Winnipeg (3); Houston (2).

Year	Winner	Head Coach	Series	Loser	Head Coach
1973	New England Whalers	Jack Kelley	4-1 (WWLWW)	Winnipeg Jets	Bobby Hull
1974	Houston Aeros	Bill Dineen	4-0	Chicago Cougars	Pat Stapleton
1975	Houston Aeros	Bill Dineen	4-0	Quebec Nordiques	Jean-Guy Gendron
1976	Winnipeg Jets	Bobby Kromm	4-0	Houston Aeros	Bill Dineen
1977	Quebec Nordiques	Marc Boileau	4-3 (LWLWWLW)	Winnipeg Jets	Bobby Kromm
1978	Winnipeg Jets	Larry Hillman	4-0	NE Whalers	Harry Neale
1979	Winnipeg Jets	Larry Hillman	4-2 (WWLWLW)	Edmonton Oilers	Glen Sather

Playoff MVPs—1973—No award; **1974**—No award; **1975**—Ron Grahame, Houston, G; **1976**—Ulf Nilsson, Winnipeg, C; **1977**—Serg Bernier, Quebec, C; **1978**—Bobby Guindon, Winnipeg, C; **1979**—Rich Preston, Winnipeg, RW.

Most Valuable Player
(Gordie Howe Trophy, 1976-79)

Year		G	A	Pts
1973	Bobby Hull, Win., LW	51	52	103
1974	Gordie Howe, Hou., RW	31	69	100
1975	Bobby Hull, Win., LW	77	65	142
1976	Marc Tardif, Que., LW	71	77	148
1977	Robbie Ftorek, Pho., C	46	71	117
1978	Marc Tardif, Que., LW	65	89	154
1979	Dave Dryden, Edm., G	41-17-2; 2.89		

Scoring Leaders

Year		Gm	G	A	Pts
1973	Andre Lacroix, Phi.	78	50	74	124
1974	Mike Walton, Min.	78	57	60	117
1975	Andre Lacroix, S. Diego.	78	41	106	147
1976	Marc Tardif, Que	81	71	77	148
1977	Real Cloutier, Que.	76	66	75	141
1978	Marc Tardif, Que.	78	65	89	154
1979	Real Cloutier, Que.	77	75	54	129

Note: In 1979, 18 year-old Rookie of the Year Wayne Gretzky finished third in scoring (46-64—110).

Rookie of the Year

Year		G	A	Pts
1973	Terry Caffery, N. Eng., C	39	61	100
1974	Mark Howe, Hou., LW	38	41	79
1975	Anders Hedberg, Win., RW	53	47	100
1976	Mark Napier, Tor., RW	43	50	93
1977	George Lyle, N. Eng., LW	39	33	72
1978	Kent Nilsson, Win., C	42	65	107
1979	Wayne Gretzky, Ind.-Edm., C	46	64	110

Best Goaltender

Year		Record	GAA
1973	Gerry Cheevers, Cleveland	32-20-0	2.84
1974	Don McLeod, Houston	33-13-3	2.56
1975	Ron Grahame, Houston	33-10-0	3.03
1976	Michel Dion, Indianapolis	14-15-1	2.74
1977	Ron Grahame, Houston	27-10-2	2.74
1978	Al Smith, New England	30-20-3	3.22
1979	Dave Dryden, Edmonton	41-17-2	2.89

Best Defenseman

Year	
1973	J.C. Tremblay, Quebec
1974	Pat Stapleton, Chicago
1975	J.C. Tremblay, Quebec
1976	Paul Shmyr, Cleveland
1977	Ron Plumb, Cincinnati
1978	Lars-Erik Sjoberg, Winnipeg
1979	Rick Ley, New England

Coach of the Year

Year		Improvement	
1973	Jack Kelley, N. Eng		46-30-2*
1974	Billy Harris, Tor	35-39-4	to 41-33-4
1975	Sandy Hucul, Pho	Expan.	to 39-31-8
1976	Bobby Kromm, Win	38-35-5	to 52-27-2*
1977	Bill Dineen, Hou	53-27-0*	to 50-24-6*
1978	Bill Dineen, Hou	50-24-6*	to 42-34-4
1979	John Brophy, Birm	36-41-3	to 32-42-6

*Won Division.

WHA All-Star Game

The WHA All-Star Game was an Eastern Division vs Western Division contest from 1973-75. In 1976, the league's five Canadian-based teams played the nine teams in the US. Over the final three seasons—East played West in 1977; AVCO Cup champion Quebec played a WHA All-Star team in 1978; and in 1979, a full WHA All-Star team played a three-game series with Moscow Dynamo of the Soviet Union.

Year	Result	Host	Coaches	Most Valuable Player
1973	East 6, West 2	Quebec	Jack Kelley, Bobby Hull	Wayne Carleton, Ottawa
1974	East 8, West 4	St. Paul, MN	Jack Kelley, Bobby Hull	Mike Walton, Minnesota
1975	West 6, East 4	Edmonton	Bill Dineen, Ron Ryan	Rejean Houle, Quebec
1976	Canada 6, USA 1	Cleveland	Jean-Guy Gendron, Bill Dineen	Can—Real Cloutier, Que. USA—Paul Shmyr, Cleve.
1977	East 4, West 2	Hartford	Jacques Demers, Bobby Kromm	East—L. Levasseur, Min. West—W. Lindstrom, Win.
1978	Quebec 5, WHA 4	Quebec	Marc Boileau, Bill Dineen	Quebec—Marc Tardif WHA—Mark Howe, NE
1979	WHA def. Moscow Dynamo 3 games to none (4-2, 4-2, 4-3)	Edmonton	Larry Hillman, P. Iburtovich	No awards

World Championship
Men

The World Hockey Championship tournament has been played regularly since 1930. The International Ice Hockey Federation (IIHF), which governs both the World and Winter Olympic tournaments, considers the Olympic champions from 1920-68 to also be the World champions. However the IIHF has not recognized an Olympic champion as World champion since 1968. The IIHF has sanctioned separate World Championships in Olympic years three times—in 1972, 1976 and again in 1992. The world championship is officially vacant for the three Olympic years from 1980-88.

Multiple winners: Soviet Union/Russia (23); Canada (21); Sweden (7); Czechoslovakia (6) Czech Republic and USA (2).

Year		Year		Year		Year	
1920	Canada	1950	Canada	1967	Soviet Union	1984	Not held
1924	Canada	1951	Canada	1968	Soviet Union	1985	Czechoslovakia
1928	Canada	1952	Canada	1969	Soviet Union	1986	Soviet Union
1930	Canada	1953	Sweden	1970	Soviet Union	1987	Sweden
1931	Canada	1954	Soviet Union	1971	Soviet Union	1988	Not held
1932	Canada	1955	Canada	1972	Czechoslovakia	1989	Soviet Union
1933	United States	1956	Soviet Union	1973	Soviet Union	1990	Soviet Union
1934	Canada	1957	Sweden	1974	Soviet Union	1991	Sweden
1935	Canada	1958	Soviet Union	1975	Soviet Union	1992	Sweden
1936	Great Britain	1959	Canada	1976	Czechoslovakia	1993	Russia
1937	Canada	1960	United States	1977	Czechoslovakia	1994	Canada
1938	Canada	1961	Canada	1978	Czechoslovakia	1995	Finland
1939	Canada	1962	Sweden	1979	Soviet Union	1996	Czech Republic
1940-46	Not held	1963	Soviet Union	1980	Not held	1997	Canada
1947	Czechoslovakia	1964	Soviet Union	1981	Soviet Union	1998	Sweden
1948	Czechoslovakia	1965	Soviet Union	1982	Soviet Union	1999	Czech Republic
1949	Czechoslovakia	1966	Soviet Union	1983	Soviet Union		

Women

The women's World Hockey Championship tournament is governed by the International Ice Hockey Federation (IIHF).

Multiple winners: Canada (5).

Year		Year		Year		Year	
1990	Canada	1994	Canada	1997	Canada	1999	Canada
1992	Canada						

Canada vs. USSR Summits

The first competition between the Soviet National Team and the NHL took place Sept. 2-28, 1972. A team of NHL All-Stars emerged as the winner of the heralded 8-game series, but just barely—winning with a record of 4-3-1 after trailing 1-3-1.

Two years later a WHA All-Star team played the Soviet Nationals and could win only one game and tie three others in eight contests. Two other Canada vs USSR series took place during NHL All-Star breaks: the three-game Challenge Cup at New York in 1979, and the two-game Rendez-Vous '87 in Quebec City in 1987.

The NHL All-Stars played the USSR in a three-game Challenge Cup series in 1979.

1972 Team Canada vs. USSR
NHL All-Stars vs Soviet National Team.

Date	City	Result	Goaltenders
9/2	Montreal	USSR, 7-3	Tretiak/Dryden
9/4	Toronto	Canada, 4-1	Esposito/Tretiak
9/6	Winnipeg	Tie, 4-4	Tretiak/Esposito
9/8	Vancouver	USSR, 5-3	Tretiak/Dryden
9/22	Moscow	USSR, 5-4	Tretiak/Esposito
9/24	Moscow	Canada, 3-2	Dryden/Tretiak
9/26	Moscow	Canada, 4-3	Esposito/Tretiak
9/28	Moscow	Canada, 6-5	Dryden/Tretiak

Standings

	W	L	T	Pts	GF	GA
Team Canada (NHL)	4	3	1	9	32	32
Soviet Union	3	4	1	7	32	32

Leading Scorers

1. Phil Esposito, Canada, (7-6—13); **2.** Aleksandr Yakushev, USSR (7-4—11); **3.** Paul Henderson, Canada (7-2—9); **4.** Boris Shadrin, USSR (3-5—8); **5.** Valeri Kharlamov, USSR (3-4—7) and Vladimir Petrov, USSR (3-4—7); **7.** Bobby Clarke, Canada (2-4—6) and Yuri Liapkin, USSR (1-5—6).

1974 Team Canada vs. USSR
WHA All-Stars vs Soviet National Team.

Date	City	Result	Goaltenders
9/17	Quebec City	Tie, 3-3	Tretiak/Cheevers
9/19	Toronto	Canada, 4-1	Cheevers/Tretiak
9/21	Winnipeg	USSR, 8-5	Tretiak/McLeod
9/23	Vancouver	Tie, 5-5	Tretiak/Cheevers
10/1	Moscow	USSR, 3-2	Tretiak/Cheevers
10/3	Moscow	USSR, 5-2	Tretiak/Cheevers
10/5	Moscow	Tie, 4-4	Cheevers/Tretiak
10/6	Moscow	USSR, 3-2	Sidelinkov/Cheevers

Standings

	W	L	T	Pts	GF	GA
Soviet Union	4	1	3	11	32	27
Team Canada (WHA)	1	4	3	5	27	32

Leading Scorers

1. Bobby Hull, Canada (7-2—9); **2.** Aleksandr Yakushev, USSR (6-2—8), Ralph Backstrom, Canada (4-4—8) and Valeri Kharlamov, USSR (2-6—8); **5.** Gordie Howe, Canada (3-4—7), Andre Lacroix, Canada (1-6—7) and Vladimir Petrov, USSR (1-6—7).

1979 Challenge Cup Series
NHL All-Stars vs Soviet National Team

Date	City	Result	Goaltenders
2/8	New York	NHL, 4-2	K. Dryden/Tretiak
2/10	New York	USSR, 5-4	Tretiak/K. Dryden
2/11	New York	USSR, 6-0	Myshkin/Cheevers

Rendez-Vous '87
NHL All-Stars vs Soviet National Team

Date	City	Result	Goaltenders
2/11	Quebec	NHL, 4-3	Fuhr/Belosheykhin
2/13	Quebec	USSR, 5-3	Belosheykhin/Fuhr

The Canada Cup

After organizing the historic 8-game Team Canada-Soviet Union series of 1972, NHL Players Association executive director Alan Eagleson and the NHL created the Canada Cup in 1976. For the first time, the best players from the world's six major hockey powers—Canada, Czechoslovakia, Finland, Russia, Sweden and the USA—competed together in one tournament.

1976
Round Robin Standings

	W	L	T	Pts	GF	GA
Canada	4	1	0	8	22	6
Czechoslovakia	3	1	1	7	19	9
Soviet Union	2	2	1	5	23	14
Sweden	2	2	1	5	16	18
United States	1	3	1	3	14	21
Finland	1	4	0	2	16	42

Finals (Best of 3)

Date	City	Score
9/13	Toronto	Canada 6, Czechoslovakia 0
9/15	Montreal	Canada 5, Czechoslovakia 4 (OT)

Note: Darryl Sittler scored the winning goal for Canada at 11:33 in overtime to clinch the Cup, 2 games to none.

Leading Scorers

1. Victor Hluktov, USSR (5-4—9), Bobby Orr, Canada (2-7—9) and Denis Potvin, Canada (1-8—9); **4.** Bobby Hull, Canada (5-3—8) and Milan Novy, Czechoslovakia (5-3—8).

Team MVPs

Canada—Rogie Vachon   Sweden—Borje Salming
Czech.—Milan Novy   USA—Robbie Ftorek
USSR—Alexandr Maltsev   Finland—Matti Hagman
Tournament MVP—Bobby Orr, Canada

1981
Round Robin Standings

	W	L	T	Pts	GF	GA
Canada	4	0	1	9	32	13
Soviet Union	3	1	1	7	20	13
Czechoslovakia	2	1	2	6	21	13
United States	2	2	1	5	17	19
Sweden	1	4	0	2	13	20
Finland	0	4	1	1	6	31

Semifinals

Date	City	Score
9/11	Ottawa	USSR 4, Czechoslovakia 1
9/11	Montreal	Canada 4, United States 1

Finals

Date	City	Score
9/13	Montreal	USSR 8, Canada 1

Leading Scorers

1. Wayne Gretzky, Canada (5-7—12); **2.** Mike Bossy, Canada (8-3—11), Bryan Trottier, Canada (3-8—11), Guy Lafleur, Canada (2-9—11), Alexei Kasatonov, USSR (1-10—11).

All-Star Team

Goal—Vladislav Tretiak, USSR; **Defense**—Arnold Kadlec, Czech. and Alexei Kasatonov, USSR; **Forwards**—Mike Bossy, Canada, Gil Perreault, Canada, and Sergei Shepelev, USSR. **Tournament MVP**—Tretiak.

1984
Round Robin Standings

	W	L	T	Pts	GF	GA
Soviet Union	5	0	0	10	22	7
United States	3	1	1	7	21	13
Sweden	3	2	0	6	15	16
Canada	2	2	1	5	23	18
West Germany	0	4	1	1	13	29
Czechoslovakia	0	4	1	1	10	21

Semifinals

Date	City	Score
9/12	Edmonton	Sweden 9, United States 2
9/15	Montreal	Canada 3, USSR 2 (OT)

Note: Mike Bossy scored the winning goal for Canada at 12:29 in overtime.

Finals (Best of 3)

Date	City	Score
9/16	Calgary	Canada 5, Sweden 2
9/18	Edmonton	Canada 6, Sweden 5

Leading Scorers

1. Wayne Gretzky, Canada (5-7—12); **2.** Michel Goulet, Canada (5-6—11), Kent Nilsson, Sweden (3-8—11), Paul Coffey, Canada (3-8—11); **5.** Hakan Loob, Sweden (6-4—10).

All-Star Team

Goal—Vladimir Myshkin, USSR; **Defense**—Paul Coffey, Canada and Rod Langway, USA; **Forwards**—Wayne Gretzky, Canada, John Tonelli, Canada, and Sergei Makarov, USSR. **Tournament MVP**—Tonelli.

1987
Round Robin Standings

	W	L	T	Pts	GF	GA
Canada	3	0	2	8	19	13
Soviet Union	3	1	1	7	22	13
Sweden	3	2	0	6	17	14
Czechoslovakia	2	2	1	5	12	15
United States	2	3	0	4	13	14
Finland	0	5	0	0	9	23

Semifinals

Date	City	Score
9/8	Hamilton	USSR 4, Sweden 2
9/9	Montreal	Canada 5, Czechoslovakia 3

Finals (Best of 3)

Date	City	Score
9/11	Montreal	USSR 6, Canada 5 (OT)
9/13	Hamilton	Canada 6, USSR 5 (2 OT)
9/15	Hamilton	Canada 6, USSR 5

Note: In Game 1, Alexander Semak of USSR scored at 5:33 in overtime. In Game 2, Mario Lemieux of Canada scored at 10:01 in the second overtime period. Lemieux also won Game 3 on a goal with 1:26 left in regulation time.

Leading Scorers

1. Wayne Gretzky, Canada (3-18—18); **2.** Mario Lemieux, Canada (11-7—18); **3.** Sergei Makarov, USSR (7-8—15); **4.** Vladimir Krutov, USSR (7-7—14); **5.** Viacheslav Bykov, USSR (2-7—9); **6.** Ray Bourque, Canada (2-6—8).

All-Star Team

Goal—Grant Fuhr, Canada; **Defense**—Ray Bourque, Canada and Viacheslav Fetisov, USSR; **Forwards**—Wayne Gretzky, Canada, Mario Lemieux, Canada, and Vladimir Krutov, USSR. **Tournament MVP**—Gretzky.

1991

Round Robin Standings

	W	L	T	Pts	GF	GA
Canada	3	0	2	8	21	11
United States	4	1	0	8	19	15
Finland	2	2	1	5	10	13
Sweden	2	3	0	4	13	17
Soviet Union	1	3	1	3	14	14
Czechoslovakia	1	4	0	2	11	18

Semifinals

Date	City	Score
9/11	Hamilton	United States 7, Finland 3
9/12	Toronto	Canada 4, Sweden 0

Finals (Best of 3)

Date	City	Score
9/14	Montreal	Canada 4, United States 1
9/16	Hamilton	Canada 4, United States 2

Leading Scorers

1. Wayne Gretzky, Canada (4-8—12); **2.** Steve Larmer, Canada (6-5—11); **3.** Brett Hull, USA (2-7—9); **4.** Mike Modano, USA (2-7—9); **5.** Mark Messier, Canada (2-6—8).

All-Star Team

Goal—Bill Ranford, Canada; **Defense**—Al MacInnis, Canada and Chris Chelios, USA; **Forwards**—Wayne Gretzky, Canada, Jeremy Roenick, USA and Mats Sundin, Sweden. **Tournament MVP**—Bill Ranford.

The World Cup

Formed jointly by the NHL and the NHL Players Association in cooperation with the International Ice Hockey Federation. The inaugural World Cup held games in nine different cities throughout North America and Europe, the most ever by a single international hockey tournament.

1996

Round Robin Standings

European Pool	W	L	T	Pts	GF	GA
Sweden	3	0	0	6	14	3
Finland	2	1	0	4	17	11
Germany	1	2	0	2	11	15
Czech Republic	0	3	0	0	4	17

North American Pool	W	L	T	Pts	GF	GA
United States	3	0	0	6	19	8
Canada	2	1	0	4	11	10
Russia	1	2	0	2	12	14
Slovakia	0	3	0	0	10	18

Semifinals

Date	City	Score
9/7	Philadelphia	Canada 3, Sweden 2 (OT)
9/8	Ottawa	United States 5, Russia 2

Finals (Best of 3)

Date	City	Score
9/10	Philadelphia	Canada 4, United States 3 (OT)
9/12	Montreal	United States 5, Canada 2
9/14	Montreal	United States 5, Canada 2

Leading Scorers

1. Brett Hull, USA (7-4—11); **2.** John LeClair, USA (6-4—10); **3.** Mats Sundin, Sweden (4-3—7); Wayne Gretzky, Canada (3-4—7); Doug Weight, USA (3-4—7); Paul Coffey, Canada (0-7—7); Brian Leetch, USA (0-7—7).

All-Tournament Team

Goal—Mike Richter, USA; **Defense**—Calle Johansson, Sweden and Chris Chelios, USA; **Forwards**—Brett Hull, USA; John LeClair, USA and Mats Sundin, Sweden. **Tournament MVP**—Mike Richter, USA.

U.S. DIVISION I COLLEGE HOCKEY

NCAA Final Four

The NCAA Division I hockey tournament began in 1948 and was played at the Broadmoor Ice Palace in Colorado Springs from 1948-57. Since 1958, the tournament has moved around the country, stopping for consecutive years only at Boston Garden from 1972-74. Consolation games to determine third place were played from 1949-89 and discontinued in 1990.

Multiple Winners: Michigan (9); North Dakota (6); Denver and Wisconsin (5); Boston University (4); Lake Superior St., Michigan Tech and Minnesota (3); Colorado College, Cornell, Maine, Michigan St. and RPI (2).

Year	Champion	Head Coach	Score	Runner-up	Third Place	
1948	Michigan	Vic Heyliger	8-4	Dartmouth	Colorado College and Boston College	

Year	Champion	Head Coach	Score	Runner-up	Third Place	Score	Fourth Place
1949	Boston College	Snooks Kelley	4-3	Dartmouth	Michigan	10-4	Colorado Col.
1950	Colorado College	Cheddy Thompson	13-4	Boston Univ.	Michigan	10-6	Boston College
1951	Michigan	Vic Heyliger	7-1	Brown	Boston Univ.	7-4	Colorado College
1952	Michigan	Vic Heyliger	4-1	Colorado Col.	Yale	4-1	St. Lawrence
1953	Michigan	Vic Heyliger	7-3	Minnesota	RPI	6-3	Boston Univ.
1954	RPI	Ned Harkness	5-4*	Minnesota	Michigan	7-2	Boston College
1955	Michigan	Vic Heyliger	5-3	Colorado Col.	Harvard	6-3	St. Lawrence
1956	Michigan	Vic Heyliger	7-5	Michigan Tech	St. Lawrence	6-2	Boston College
1957	Colorado College	Tom Bedecki	13-6	Michigan	Clarkson	2-1†	Harvard
1958	Denver	Murray Armstrong	6-2	North Dakota	Clarkson	5-1	Harvard
1959	North Dakota	Bob May	4-3*	Michigan St.	Boston College	7-6†	St. Lawrence
1960	Denver	Murray Armstrong	5-3	Michigan Tech	Boston Univ.	7-6	St. Lawrence
1961	Denver	Murray Armstrong	12-2	St. Lawrence	Minnesota	4-3	RPI
1962	Michigan Tech	John MacInnes	7-1	Clarkson	Michigan	5-1	St. Lawrence
1963	North Dakota	Barry Thorndycraft	6-5	Denver	Clarkson	5-3	Boston College
1964	Michigan	Allen Renfrew	6-3	Denver	RPI	2-1	Providence
1965	Michigan Tech	John MacInnes	8-2	Boston College	North Dakota	9-5	Brown
1966	Michigan St.	Amo Bessone	6-1	Clarkson	Denver	4-3	Boston Univ.
1967	Cornell	Ned Harkness	4-1	Boston Univ.	Michigan St.	6-1	North Dakota
1968	Denver	Murray Armstrong	4-0	North Dakota	Cornell	6-1	Boston College
1969	Denver	Murray Armstrong	4-3	Cornell	Harvard	6-5†	Michigan Tech
1970	Cornell	Ned Harkness	6-4	Clarkson	Wisconsin	6-5	Michigan Tech
1971	Boston Univ.	Jack Kelley	4-2	Minnesota	Denver	1-0	Harvard

Year	Champion	Head Coach	Score	Runner-up	Third Place	Score	Fourth Place
1972	Boston Univ.	Jack Kelley	4-0	Cornell	Wisconsin	5-2	Denver
1973	Wisconsin	Bob Johnson	4-2	Denver	Boston College	3-1	Cornell
1974	Minnesota	Herb Brooks	4-2	Michigan Tech	Boston Univ.	7-5	Harvard
1975	Michigan Tech	John MacInnes	6-1	Minnesota	Boston Univ.	10-5	Harvard
1976	Minnesota	Herb Brooks	6-4	Michigan Tech	Brown	8-7	Boston Univ.
1977	Wisconsin	Bob Johnson	6-5*	Michigan	Boston Univ.	6-5	N. Hampshire
1978	Boston Univ.	Jack Parker	5-3	Boston College	Bowl. Green	4-3	Wisconsin
1979	Minnesota	Herb Brooks	4-3	North Dakota	Dartmouth	7-3	N. Hampshire
1980	North Dakota	Gino Gasparini	5-2	N. Michigan	Dartmouth	8-4	Cornell
1981	Wisconsin	Bob Johnson	6-3	Minnesota	Mich. Tech	5-2	N. Michigan
1982	North Dakota	Gino Gasparini	5-2	Wisconsin	Northeastern	10-4	N. Hampshire
1983	Wisconsin	Jeff Sauer	6-2	Harvard	Providence	4-3	Minnesota
1984	Bowling Green	Jerry York	5-4*	Minn-Duluth	North Dakota	6-5†	Michigan St.
1985	RPI	Mike Addesa	2-1	Providence	Minn-Duluth	7-6†	Boston College
1986	Michigan St.	Ron Mason	6-5	Harvard	Minnesota	6-4	Denver
1987	North Dakota	Gino Gasparini	5-3	Michigan St.	Minnesota	6-3	Harvard
1988	Lake Superior St.	Frank Anzalone	4-3*	St. Lawrence	Maine	5-2	Minnesota
1989	Harvard	Billy Cleary	4-3*	Minnesota	Michigan St.	7-4	Maine

Year	Champion	Head Coach	Score	Runner-up	Third Place
1990	Wisconsin	Jeff Sauer	7-3	Colgate	Boston College and Boston Univ.
1991	Northern Michigan	Rick Comley	8-7*	Boston Univ.	Maine and Clarkson
1992	Lake Superior St.	Jeff Jackson	5-3	Wisconsin	Michigan and Michigan St.
1993	Maine	Shawn Walsh	5-4	Lake Superior St.	Boston Univ. and Michigan
1994	Lake Superior St.	Jeff Jackson	9-1	Boston Univ.	Harvard and Minnesota
1995	Boston Univ.	Jack Parker	6-2	Maine	Michigan and Minnesota
1996	Michigan	Red Berenson	3-2*	Colorado Col.	Vermont and Boston Univ.
1997	North Dakota	Dean Blais	6-4	Boston Univ.	Colorado College and Michigan
1998	Michigan	Red Berenson	3-2*	Boston College	New Hampshire and Ohio St.
1999	Maine	Shawn Walsh	3-2*	New Hampshire	Boston College and Michigan St.

*Championship game overtime goals:1954—1:54; 1959—4:22; 1977—0: 23; 1984—7:11 in 4th OT; 1988—4:46; 1989—4:16; 1991—1:57 in 3rd OT; 1996—3:35; 1998—17:51; 1999—10:50.

†Consolation game overtimes ended in 1st OT except in 1957, '59, and '69, which all ended in 2nd OT.

Note: Runners-up Denver (1973) and Wisconsin (1992) had participation voided by the NCAA for using ineligible players.

Most Outstanding Player

The Most Outstanding Players of each NCAA Div. I tournament since 1948. Winners of the award who did not play for the tournament champion are in **bold** type. In 1960, three players, none on the winning team, shared the award.

Multiple Winners: Lou Angotti and Marc Behrend (2).

Year
1948 **Joe Riley,** Dartmouth, F
1949 **Dick Desmond,** Dart., G
1950 **Ralph Bevins,** Boston U., G
1951 **Ed Whiston,** Brown, G
1952 **Ken Kinsley,** Colo. Col., G
1953 John Matchetts, Mich., F
1954 Abbie Moore, RPI, F
1955 **Phil Hilton,** Colo. Col., D
1956 Lorne Howes, Mich., G
1957 Bob McCusker, Colo. Col., F
1958 Murray Massier, Denver, F
1959 Reg Morelli, N. Dakota, F
1960 **Lou Angotti,** Mich. Tech, F;
     Bob Marquis, Boston U., F;
     & **Barry Urbanski,** BU, G
1961 Bill Masterton, Denver, F
1962 Lou Angotti, Mich. Tech, F
1963 Al McLean, N. Dakota, F

Year
1964 Bob Gray, Michigan, G
1965 Gary Milroy, Mich. Tech, F
1966 Gaye Cooley, Mich. St., G
1967 Walt Stanowski, Cornell, D
1968 Gerry Powers, Denver, G
1969 Keith Magnuson, Denver, D
1970 Dan Lodboa, Cornell, D
1971 Dan Brady, Boston U., G
1972 Tim Regan, Boston, U., G
1973 Dean Talafous, Wisc., F
1974 Brad Shelstad, Minn., G
1975 Jim Warden, Mich. Tech, G
1976 Tom Vanelli, Minn., F
1977 Julian Baretta, Wisc., G
1978 Jack O'Callahan, Boston U., D
1979 Steve Janaszak, Minn., G
1980 Doug Smail, N. Dakota, F
1981 Marc Behrend, Wisc., G

Year
1982 Phil Sykes, N. Dakota, F
1983 Marc Behrend, Wisc., G
1984 Gary Kruzich, Bowl. Green, G
1985 **Chris Terreri,** Prov., G
1986 Mike Donnelly, Mich. St., F
1987 Tony Hrkac, N. Dakota, F
1988 Bruce Hoffort, Lk. Superior, G
1989 Ted Donato, Harvard, F
1990 Chris Tancill, Wisconsin, F
1991 Scott Beattie, No. Mich., F
1992 Paul Constantin, Lk. Superior, F
1993 Jim Montgomery, Maine, F
1994 Sean Tallaire, Lk. Superior, F
1995 Chris O'Sullivan, Boston U., F
1996 Brendan Morrison, Michigan, F
1997 Matt Henderson, N. Dakota, F
1998 Marty Turco, Michigan, G
1999 Alfie Michaud, Maine, G

Hobey Baker Award

College hockey's Player of the Year award; voted on by a national panel of sportswriters, broadcasters, college coaches and pro scouts. First presented in 1981 by the Decathlon Athletic Club of Bloomington, Minn., in the name of the Princeton collegiate hockey and football star who was killed in a plane crash.

Year
1981 Neal Broten, Minnesota, F
1982 George McPhee, Bowl. Green, F
1983 Mark Fusco, Harvard, D
1984 Tom Kurvers, Minn-Duluth, D
1985 Bill Watson, Minn-Duluth, F
1986 Scott Fusco, Harvard, F
1987 Tony Hrkac, North Dakota, F

Year
1988 Robb Stauber, Minnesota, G
1989 Lane MacDonald, Harvard, F
1990 Kip Miller, Michigan St., F
1991 Dave Emma, Boston College, F
1992 Scott Pellerin, Maine, F
1993 Paul Kariya, Maine, F
1994 Chris Marinucci, Minn-Duluth, F

Year
1995 Brian Holzinger, Bowl. Green, F
1996 Brian Bonin, Minnesota, F
1997 Brendan Morrison, Michigan, F
1998 Chris Drury, Boston U., F
1999 Jason Krog, UNH, F

Coach of the Year

The Penrose Memorial Trophy, voted on by the American Hockey Coaches Association and first presented in 1951 in the name of Colorado gold and copper magnate Spencer T. Penrose. Penrose built the Broadmoor hotel and athletic complex in Colorado Springs that originally hosted the NCAA hockey championship from 1948-57.

Multiple winners: Len Ceglarski and Charlie Holt (3); Rick Comley, Eddie Jeremiah, Snooks Kelly, John MacInnes, Jack Parker, Jack Riley and Cooney Weiland (2).

Year
1951 Eddie Jeremiah, Dartmouth
1952 Cheddy Thompson, Colo. Col.
1953 John Mariucci, Minnesota
1954 Vic Heyliger, Michigan
1955 Cooney Weiland, Harvard
1956 Bill Harrison, Clarkson
1957 Jack Riley, Army
1958 Harry Cleverly, BU
1959 Snooks Kelly, BC

1960 Jack Riley, Army
1961 Murray Armstrong, Denver
1962 Jack Kelley, Colby
1963 Tony Frasca, Colorado Col.
1964 Tom Eccleston, Providence
1965 Jim Fullerton, Brown
1966 Amo Bessone, Michigan St.
    & Len Ceglarski, Clarkson
1967 Eddie Jeremiah, Dartmouth

Year
1968 Ned Harkness, Cornell
1969 Charlie Holt, New Hampshire

1970 John MacInnes, Michigan Tech
1971 Cooney Weiland, Harvard
1972 Snooks Kelly, BC
1973 Len Ceglarski, BC
1974 Charlie Holt, New Hampshire
1975 Jack Parker, BU
1976 John MacInnes, Michigan Tech
1977 Jerry York, Clarkson
1978 Jack Parker, BU
1979 Charlie Holt, New Hampshire

1980 Rick Comley, No. Michigan
1981 Bill O'Flarety, Clarkson
1982 Fern Flaman, Northeastern
1983 Bill Cleary, Harvard
1984 Mike Sertich, Minn-Duluth
1985 Len Ceglarski, BC

Year
1986 Ralph Backstrom, Denver
1987 Gino Gasparini, N. Dakota
1988 Frank Anzalone, Lk. Superior
1989 Joe March, St. Lawrence

1990 Terry Slater, Colgate
1991 Rick Comley, No. Michigan
1992 Ron Mason, Michigan St.
1993 George Gwozdecky, Miami-OH
1994 Don Lucia, Colorado Col.
1995 Shawn Walsh, Maine
1996 Bruce Crowder, UMass-Lowell
1997 Dean Blais, N. Dakota
1998 Tim Taylor, Yale
1999 Dick Umile, UNH
Note: 1960 winner Jack Riley won the award for coaching the USA to its first hockey gold medal in the Winter Olympics at Squaw Valley.

All-Time Tournament Appearances

	App	Record		App	Record
Boston Univ.	24	32-28-0	RPI	8	8-8-1
Michigan	22	35-15-0	Providence	7	9-12-0
Minnesota	22	28-24-0	N. Michigan	7	8-8-0
Boston College	20	17-29-0	Dartmouth	5	4-5-0
Michigan St.	19	23-22-1	Minn.-Duluth	4	5-6-0
Wisconsin	17	29-15-1	Brown	4	2-5-0
Clarkson	17	12-20-0	Northeastern	3	3-3-1
North Dakota	16	25-13-0	UMass-Lowell	3	2-3-1
Harvard	16	14-24-1	Ala-Anchorage	3	2-5-0
Denver	14	19-12-0	Vermont	3	1-4-0
Colorado Coll.	14	12-15-0	W. Michigan	3	0-4-0
St. Lawrence	13	5-22-0	Ohio St.	2	2-2-0
Cornell	11	10-12-0	Yale	2	1-2-0
Lake Superior St.	10	20-11-1	Miami-OH.	2	0-2-0
Michigan Tech	10	13-9-0	Colgate	1	3-1-0
New Hampshire	10	7-14-0	Merrimack	1	2-2-0
Bowling Green	9	8-12-1	Princeton	1	0-1-0
Maine	8	18-10-0	St. Cloud St.	1	0-2-0

Note: The NCAA voided tournament participation of Denver in 1973 and Wisconsin in 1992 for using ineligible players.

NCAA All-Time Team

To celebrate the 50th anniversary of the NCAA tournament in 1997, the NCAA announced its 50th Anniversary Team and introduced it during the 1997 championship game in Milwaukee. The team was chosen by current Division I coaches, coaches of teams that have participated in the NCAA tournament, and members of the Division I Hockey Committee. Players named to the team had to have played in at least one NCAA tournament game. Tournament years are listed below.

Forwards

Tony Amonte, Boston Univ., 1981, '83
Lou Angotti, Michigan Tech, 1960, '62
Red Berenson, Michigan, 1962
Bill Cleary, Harvard, 1955
Tony Hrkac, North Dakota, 1987
Paul Kariya, Maine, 1993
Bill Masterton, Denver, 1960, '61
John Matchetts, Michigan, 1951, '53
John Mayasich, Minnesota, 1953, '54
Jim Montgomery, Maine, 1990, '91, '92, '93
Tom Rendall, Michigan, 1955, '56, '57
Phil Sykes, North Dakota, 1979, '80, '82

Defensemen

Chris Chelios, Wisconsin, 1982, '83
Bruce Driver, Wisconsin, 1981, '82, '83
George Konik, Denver, 1960, '61
Dan Lodboa, Cornell, 1970
Keith Magnuson, Denver, 1968, '69
Jack O'Callahan, Boston Univ., 1976, '77, '78

Goaltenders

Marc Behrend, Wisconsin, 1981, '83
Ken Dryden, Cornell, 1967, '68, '69
Chris Terreri, Providence, 1983, '85

College Sports

John Thompson, who helped shape the lives of many over his 27-year coaching tenure at Georgetown, retired during the 1999 season.

Storrs is Rip City

Richard Hamilton decides to stay one more year at UConn and is rewarded with an NCAA championship.

by
Steve Cyphers

You heard about his decision in the spring to stay at Connecticut and not jump to the pros. He actually liked college life and thought his team had a chance to win it all. But privately you thought, "Why would he leave? He's not ready anyway."

Then you saw the news in the summer that he broke his right foot and you thought what you always think when an athlete is injured. "Too bad. Tough break."

Throughout the season you noticed his numbers in the box scores and the wins his Huskies posted. You went out of your way to watch the Connecticut-Stanford matchup on television in February. You wanted to see for yourself just how good these Huskies were — and how good he was. But alas, a thigh bruise kept him out, but his team won anyway.

On "Selection Sunday," you saw Connecticut sent out west. You knew you'd be there too.

And then you saw him. Richard "Rip" Hamilton, in person, at practice the day before the Sweet 16 game with Iowa. He was even skinnier than you thought — with legs as big as your forearm. You wondered how this frail-looking, 6-6 body belonged to the scorer that Notre Dame coach John MacLeod referred to as "a weapon."

The answer came when you saw his game. Smooth, fluid, slashing his way to the basket before stopping, pulling up and shooting from the wing. He made it look so easy. No wasted energy. Not a single unnecessary move. All this against a bruising Iowa attack that simply couldn't faze him. A game-high 24 points left the Hawkeyes frustrated and the Huskies moving on.

Against gutsy Gonzaga in the Elite Eight, he led the Huskies again with 21 points despite being asked to focus

---

Steve Cyphers is a reporter for ESPN's *Sports-Center* and *College GameDay*.

UConn's lanky shooting guard **Richard Hamilton** averaged 24.1 points-per-game in the NCAA tournament and was voted Most Outstanding Player of the Final Four.

on defense. Though he joked that defense wasn't his forte, he held the Bulldogs' sharpshooting Richie Frahm to seven points, just 2 of 11 from the floor. He was named the region's MVP and for the first time in its 21 trips to the NCAA Tournament, Connecticut was headed to the Final Four, balanced squarely on the frail frame of "Rip" Hamilton.

It was then that you learned of his inspiration. His grandfather, Edmund, had died of lung cancer before the season began. You heard him say that his own foot surgery was a blessing because it gave him so much time to be with his "grandpa," to just sit and talk sometimes for hours at a time. He told you that the Final Four trip to St. Petersburg meant more to Edmund Hamilton than to anyone else.

You couldn't help yourself. You pulled for Edmund's grandson as you packed for St. Pete too.

At Tropicana Field it was business as usual. He led the team with 24 points in the semifinal and by now you had seen enough games to know that the clinching bucket was vintage "Rip." With under two minutes to play, you saw him shake an Ohio State defender on the wing and bury one with the shot clock winding down to give the Huskies an insurmountable six-point lead.

The championship game pitted favored Duke, "the team for the ages," and UConn, "the team of destiny." The game actually exceeded the hype!

And it was his game. An uncharacteristic first half was followed by the most important 20 minutes of his

Iowa State's **Cael Sanderson**, right, puts the hurt on Minnesota's Brandon Eggum in the 184-pound final of the NCAA Division I wrestling championship. Sanderson was the first freshman in history to be named the tournament's Most Outstanding Wrestler.

career. With 16 second-half points on 5 of 9 shooting, he led all scorers with 27 points and UConn delivered the 77-74 upset.

He was named Most Outstanding Player of the Final Four, and in the locker room you heard the unassuming star credit his teammates and coaches for his success.

While the Huskies danced and celebrated their first national championship, you heard passionate Connecticut fans chanting, "One more year! One more year!"

But you knew he would leave. You had seen enough. You had seen him average over 24 points-per-game in tournament play. You saw him with the nets around his neck. And this time, you thought, "If he should leave, he's ready." ■

Steve Cyphers' Top Ten Highlights of the 1999 College Sports Season

10. Hats off to the **Iowa wrestling** team. Again! As underdogs this time, the Hawkeyes capture their 19th national championship. Iowa State freshman Cael Sanderson is named Most Outstanding Wrestler of the tournament, the first freshman to win the award.

9. **Kansas State** has one of its best football seasons in school history, winning 11 in a row before losing the last two. But why did it seem like the Wildcats never had a chance to enjoy it?

8. **The NCAA is not in Kansas anymore.** The governing body of college athletics pack up and move to

AP/Wide World Photos

Athletic directors, from left, **Rodger Jehlicka** of Adams State (Div. II), **Michael Dinning** of Simon Fraser (NAIA), **Ted Leland** of Stanford (Div. I), and **Gary Guerin** of Williams College (Div. III) stand with their school's Directors' Cups, given for athletic excellence.

its posh new digs in Indianapolis. However, over 70 percent of its employees decide there's no place like home and don't make the move.

7. **Bizarre coaching exits.** Iowa hoops coach Tom Davis, after being told *before* the season began that he would be out, rallies the Hawkeyes to the Sweet 16 — and he never grumbled.

6. **Bizarre coaching exits — part two.** After his wife seeks a restraining order against him, Weber State basketball coach Ron Abegglen is forced to resign, but not until after the season. All he does is lead his team to a 25-8 record, and a win over North Carolina in the first round of the tournament.

5. **Brian Shay**, the barely 5-8 feature back from Division II Emporia State in Kansas, breaks all-division career records for rushing yards, touchdowns and all-purpose yards.

4. **Suzanne Yoculan does it!** One of the more intense and interesting coaches in any sport at any level leads her Georgia Bulldogs to a second consecutive gymnastics championship, becoming just the second school to successfully defend the title.

3. **The Washington women** enter the NCAA championship regatta as overwhelming favorites, having won the previous two rowing championships, but Brown upsets them for their first title. Washington settles for third in the fastest-growing collegiate sport.

2. **Duke's women's basketball team** enjoys every second of their run to the NCAA title game. Like the men, they don't come away with a win. But unlike the men, they don't need a victory to ensure their place in history.

1. **Ricky Williams.** Sure, he can run the football. Just ask Tony Dorsett. But Williams can also engage anyone in interesting conversation on almost any topic. The relationship he established with Doak Walker before the former SMU great died is a story we should someday tell our children.

■

THE NUMBERS

INSIDE

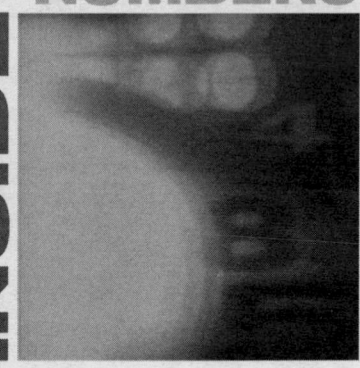

THAT WOULD BE PERFECTION

In 1998-99, eight NCAA teams rolled through their seasons without a loss. They are listed below, in alphabetical order.

School	Sport	Record
Amherst	Wom. Tennis - Div. III	20-0
BYU-Hawaii	Wom. Tennis - Div. II	31-0
Long Beach St.	Wom. Volleyball - Div. I	36-0
Maryland	Wom. Lacrosse - Nat.	21-0
Middlebury	Wom. Lacrosse - Div. III	17-0
Mount Union	Football - Div. III	14-0
NW Missouri St.	Football - Div. II	15-0
Wash. (MO)	Wom. Basketball - Div. III	30-0

CALIFORNIA GOLD RUSH

Listed are the Division I men's and women's programs with the most all-time NCAA championships. Three of the top five men's, and two of the top five women's programs are from California, led by USC with 70 overall men's titles. Of course, 26 outdoor track championships doesn't hurt.

School	Men Titles
USC	70
UCLA	63
Stanford	51
Oklahoma St.	42
Arkansas	34

School	Women Titles
Stanford	25
Texas	20
LSU	19
North Carolina	19
UCLA	16

ON THE RISE

According to NCAA figures, women's basketball total attendance has increased every year since 1982, the first year women's basketball championships were offered and the first year such statistics were compiled. In 1999, attendance broke the eight million mark for the first time in history, led by Tennessee with 231,915 spectators in its 14 home games (an average of 16,565). Below is a list of overall attendance figures over the last 10 years.

Year	Attendance
1999	8,010,227
1998	7,387,335
1997	6,734,141
1996	5,233,954
1995	4,961,946
1994	4,557,066
1993	4,193,243
1992	3,827,711
1991	3,407,247
1990	3,183,871

■

NCAA Division I Basketball Schools
1999-2000 Season
Conferences and coaches as of Sept. 10, 1999.

Joining Big South in 1999-2000: HIGH POINT from Division II.
Joining Big South in 1999-2000: ELON from Division II.
Joining Sun Belt in 1999-2000: DENVER from Independent.
Joining Northeast in 1999-2000: SACRED HEART from Division II.
Joining Division I as an Independent in 1999-2000: ALBANY and STONY BROOK from Division II.
Joining Mountain West in 1999-2000: AIR FORCE, BRIGHAM YOUNG, COLORADO ST., NEW MEXICO, SAN DIEGO ST., UNLV, UTAH and WYOMING from WAC.
Joining WAC in 2000: NEVADA from Big West.

	Nickname	Conference	Head Coach	Location	Colors
Air Force	Falcons	Mountain West	Reggie Minton	Colo. Springs, CO	Blue/Silver
Akron	Zips	Mid-American	Dan Hipsher	Akron, OH	Blue/Gold
Alabama	Crimson Tide	SEC-West	Mark Gottfried	Tuscaloosa, AL	Crimson/White
Alabama A&M	Bulldogs	SWAC	Vann Pettaway	Huntsville, AL	Maroon/White
Ala.-Birmingham	Blazers	USA	Murray Bartow	Birmingham, AL	Green/Gold
Alabama St.	Hornets	SWAC	Rob Spivery	Montgomery, AL	Black/Gold
Albany	Great Danes	Independent	Scott Hicks	Albany, NY	Purple/Gold
Alcorn St.	Braves	SWAC	Davey Whitney	Lorman, MS	Purple/Gold
American	Eagles	Colonial	Art Perry	Washington, DC	Red/Blue
Appalachian St.	Mountaineers	Southern	Buzz Peterson	Boone,NC	Black/Gold
Arizona	Wildcats	Pac-10	Lute Olson	Tucson, AZ	Cardinal/Navy
Arizona St.	Sun Devils	Pac-10	Rob Evans	Tempe, AZ	Maroon/Gold
Arkansas	Razorbacks	SEC-West	Nolan Richardson	Fayetteville, AR	Cardinal/White
Ark.-Little Rock	Trojans	Sun Belt	Sidney Moncrief	Little Rock, AR	Maroon/White
Ark.-Pine Bluff	Golden Lions	SWAC	Harold Blevins	Pine Bluff, AR	Black/Gold
Arkansas St.	Indians	Sun Belt	Dickey Nutt	State Univ., AR	Scarlet/Black
Army	Cadets, Black Knights	Patriot	Pat Harris	West Point, NY	Black/Gold/Gray
Auburn	Tigers	SEC-West	Cliff Ellis	Auburn, AL	Orange/Blue
Austin Peay St.	Governors	Ohio Valley	Dave Loos	Clarksville, TN	Red/White
Ball St.	Cardinals	Mid-American	Ray McCallum	Muncie, IN	Cardinal/White
Baylor	Bears	Big 12	Dave Bliss	Waco, TX	Green/Gold
Belmont	Bruins	Independent	Rick Byrd	Nashville, TN	Navy Blue/Red
Bethune-Cookman	Wildcats	Mid-Eastern	Horace Broadnax	Daytona Beach, FL	Maroon/Gold
Boise St.	Broncos	Big West	Rod Jensen	Boise, ID	Orange/Blue
Boston College	Eagles	Big East	Al Skinner	Chestnut Hill, MA	Maroon/Gold
Boston University	Terriers	America East	Dennis Wolff	Boston, MA	Scarlet/White
Bowling Green	Falcons	Mid-American	Dan Dakich	Bowling Green, OH	Orange/Brown
Bradley	Braves	Mo. Valley	Jim Molinari	Peoria, IL	Red/White
Brigham Young	Cougars	Mountain West	Steve Cleveland	Provo, UT	Royal Blue/White
Brown	Bears	Ivy	Glen Miller	Providence, RI	Brown/Cardinal/White
Bucknell	Bison	Patriot	Pat Flannery	Lewisburg, PA	Orange/Blue
Buffalo	Bulls	Mid-American	Tim Cohane	Buffalo, NY	Royal Blue/White
Butler	Bulldogs	Midwestern	Barry Collier	Indianapolis, IN	Blue/White
California	Golden Bears	Pac-10	Ben Braun	Berkeley, CA	Blue/Gold
Cal Poly SLO	Mustangs	Big West	Jeff Schneider	San Luis Obispo, CA	Green/Gold
CS-Fullerton	Titans	Big West	Bob Hawking	Fullerton, CA	Blue/Orange/White
CS-Northridge	Matadors	Big Sky	Bobby Braswell	Northridge, CA	Red/White/Black
CS-Sacramento	Hornets	Big Sky	Tom Abatemarco	Sacramento, CA	Green/Gold
Campbell	Fighting Camels	Trans Am	Billy Lee	Buies Creek, NC	Orange/Black
Canisius	Golden Griffins	Metro Atlantic	Mike MacDonald	Buffalo, NY	Blue/Gold
Centenary	Gentlemen	Independent	Kevin Johnson	Shreveport, LA	Maroon/White
Central Conn. St.	Blue Devils	Northeast	Howie Dickenman	New Britain, CT	Blue/White
Central Florida	Golden Knights	Trans Am	Kirk Speraw	Orlando, FL	Black/Gold
Central Michigan	Chippewas	Mid-American	Jay Smith	Mt. Pleasant, MI	Maroon/Gold
Charleston So.	Buccaneers	Big South	Tom Conrad	Charleston, SC	Blue/Gold

NCAA Division I Basketball Schools (Cont.)

	Nickname	Conference	Head Coach	Location	Colors
Chicago St.	Cougars	Mid-Continent	Bo Ellis	Chicago, IL	Green/White
Cincinnati	Bearcats	USA	Bob Huggins	Cincinnati, OH	Red/Black
The Citadel	Bulldogs	Southern	Pat Dennis	Charleston, SC	Blue/White
Clemson	Tigers	ACC	Larry Shyatt	Clemson, SC	Purple/Orange
Cleveland St.	Vikings	Midwestern	Rollie Massimino	Cleveland, OH	Forest Green/White
Coastal Carolina	Chanticleers	Big South	Pete Strickland	Conway, SC	Green/Bronze/Black
Colgate	Red Raiders	Patriot	Emmett Davis	Hamilton, NY	Maroon/Gray/White
College of Charleston	Cougars	Southern	John Kresse	Charleston, SC	Maroon/White
Colorado	Buffaloes	Big 12	Ricardo Patton	Boulder, CO	Silver/Gold/Black
Colorado St.	Rams	Mountain West	Ritchie McKay	Ft. Collins, CO	Green/Gold
Columbia	Lions	Ivy	Armond Hill	New York, NY	Lt. Blue/White
Connecticut	Huskies	Big East	Jim Calhoun	Storrs, CT	Blue/White
Coppin St.	Eagles	Mid-Eastern	Ron Mitchell	Baltimore, MD	Royal Blue/Gold
Cornell	Big Red	Ivy	Scott Thompson	Ithaca, NY	Carnelian/White
Creighton	Bluejays	Mo. Valley	Dana Altman	Omaha, NE	Blue/White
Dartmouth	Big Green	Ivy	Dave Faucher	Hanover, NH	Green/White
Davidson	Wildcats	Southern	Bob McKillop	Davidson, NC	Red/Black
Dayton	Flyers	Atlantic 10	Oliver Purnell	Dayton, OH	Red/Blue
Delaware	Fightin' Blue Hens	America East	Mike Brey	Newark, DE	Blue/Gold
Delaware St.	Hornets	Mid-Eastern	Tony Sheals	Dover, DE	Red/Columbia Blue
Denver	Pioneers	Sun Belt	Marty Fletcher	Denver, CO	Crimson/Gold
DePaul	Blue Demons	USA	Pat Kennedy	Chicago, IL	Scarlet/Blue
Detroit Mercy	Titans	Midwestern	Perry Watson	Detroit, MI	Red/White/Blue
Drake	Bulldogs	Mo. Valley	Kurt Kanaskie	Des Moines, IA	Blue/White
Drexel	Dragons	America East	Steve Seymour	Philadelphia, PA	Navy Blue/Gold
Duke	Blue Devils	ACC	Mike Krzyzewski	Durham, NC	Royal Blue/White
Duquesne	Dukes	Atlantic 10	Darelle Porter	Pittsburgh, PA	Red/Blue
East Carolina	Pirates	Colonial	Bill Herrion	Greenville, NC	Purple/Gold
East Tenn. St.	Buccaneers	Southern	Ed DeChellis	Johnson City, TN	Blue/Gold
Eastern Illinois	Panthers	Ohio Valley	Rick Samuels	Charleston, IL	Blue/Gray
Eastern Kentucky	Colonels	Ohio Valley	Scott Perry	Richmond, KY	Maroon/White
Eastern Michigan	Eagles	Mid-American	Milton Barnes	Ypsilanti, MI	Green/White
Eastern Washington	Eagles	Big Sky	Steve Aggers	Cheney, WA	Red/White
Elon	Fightin Christians	Big South	Mark Simons	Elon, NC	Maroon/Gold
Evansville	Aces	Mo. Valley	Jim Crews	Evansville, IN	Purple/White
Fairfield	Stags	Metro Atlantic	Tim O'Toole	Fairfield, CT	Cardinal Red
Fairleigh Dickinson	Knights	Northeast	Tom Green	Teaneck, NJ	Blue/Black
Florida	Gators	SEC-East	Billy Donovan	Gainesville, FL	Orange/Blue
Florida A&M	Rattlers	Mid-Eastern	Mickey Clayton	Tallahassee, FL	Orange/Green
Florida Atlantic	Owls	Trans Am	Sidney Green	Boca Raton, FL	Blue/Red
Florida Int'l	Golden Panthers	Sun Belt	Shakey Rodriguez	Miami, FL	Blue/Gold
Florida St.	Seminoles	ACC	Steve Robinson	Tallahassee, FL	Garnet/Gold
Fordham	Rams	Atlantic 10	Bob Hill	Bronx, NY	Maroon/White
Fresno St.	Bulldogs	WAC	Jerry Tarkanian	Fresno, CA	Cardinal/Blue
Furman	Paladins	Southern	Larry Davis	Greenville, SC	Purple/White
George Mason	Patriots	Colonial	Jim Larranaga	Fairfax, VA	Green/Gold
George Washington	Colonials	Atlantic 10	Tom Penders	Washington, DC	Buff/Blue
Georgetown	Hoyas	Big East	Craig Esherick	Washington, DC	Blue/Gray
Georgia	Bulldogs, 'Dawgs	SEC-East	Jim Harrick	Athens, GA	Red/Black
Georgia Southern	Eagles	Southern	Jeff Price	Statesboro, GA	Blue/White
Georgia St.	Panthers	Trans Am	Lefty Driesell	Atlanta, GA	Roy. Blue/White
Georgia Tech	Yellow Jackets	ACC	Bobby Cremins	Atlanta, GA	Old Gold/White
Gonzaga	Bulldogs, Zags	West Coast	Mark Few	Spokane, WA	Blue/White/Red
Grambling St.	Tigers	SWAC	Larry Wright	Grambling, LA	Black/Gold
Hampton	Pirates	Mid-Eastern	Steve Merfeld	Hampton, VA	Royal Blue/White
Hartford	Hawks	America East	Paul Brazeau	W. Hartford, CT	Scarlet/White
Harvard	Crimson	Ivy	Frank Sullivan	Cambridge, MA	Crimson/Black/White
Hawaii	Rainbows	WAC	Riley Wallace	Honolulu, HI	Green/White
High Point	Panthers	Big South	Jerry Steele	High Point, NC	Purple/White
Hofstra	Flying Dutchmen	America East	Jay Wright	Hempstead, NY	Blue/White/Gold
Holy Cross	Crusaders	Patriot	Ralph Willard	Worcester, MA	Royal Purple
Houston	Cougars	USA	Clyde Drexler	Houston, TX	Scarlet/White
Howard	Bison	Mid-Eastern	Kirk Saulny	Washington, DC	Blue/White/Red
Idaho	Vandals	Big West	David Farrar	Moscow, ID	Silver/Gold
Idaho St.	Bengals	Big Sky	Doug Oliver	Pocatello, ID	Orange/Black
Illinois	Fighting Illini	Big Ten	Lon Kruger	Champaign, IL	Orange/Blue
Illinois-Chicago	Flames	Midwestern	Jim Collins	Chicago, IL	Navy Blue/Red

	Nickname	Conference	Head Coach	Location	Colors
Illinois St.	Redbirds	Mo. Valley	Tom Richardson	Normal, IL	Red/White
Indiana	Hoosiers	Big Ten	Bob Knight	Bloomington, IN	Cream/Crimson
IU/PU-Indianapolis	Jaguars	Mid-Continent	Ron Hunter	Indianapolis, IN	Red/Gold
Indiana St.	Sycamores	Mo. Valley	Royce Waltman	Terre Haute, IN	Blue/White
Iona	Gaels	Metro Atlantic	Jeff Ruland	New Rochelle, NY	Maroon/Gold
Iowa	Hawkeyes	Big Ten	Steve Alford	Iowa City, IA	Old Gold/Black
Iowa St.	Cyclones	Big 12	Larry Eustachy	Ames, IA	Cardinal/Gold
Jackson St.	Tigers	SWAC	Andy Stoglin	Jackson, MS	Blue/White
Jacksonville	Dolphins	Trans Am	Hugh Durham	Jacksonville, FL	Green/White
Jacksonville St.	Gamecocks	Trans Am	Mark Turgeon	Jacksonville, AL	Red/White
James Madison	Dukes	Colonial	Sherman Dillard	Harrisonburg, VA	Purple/Gold
Kansas	Jayhawks	Big 12	Roy Williams	Lawrence, KS	Crimson/Blue
Kansas St.	Wildcats	Big 12	Tom Asbury	Manhattan, KS	Purple/White
Kent St.	Golden Flashes	Mid-American	Gary Waters	Kent, OH	Navy Blue/Gold
Kentucky	Wildcats	SEC-East	Tubby Smith	Lexington, KY	Blue/White
La Salle	Explorers	Atlantic 10	Speedy Morris	Philadelphia, PA	Blue/Gold
Lafayette	Leopards	Patriot	Fran O'Hanlon	Easton, PA	Maroon/White
Lamar	Cardinals	Southland	Mike Deane	Beaumont, TX	Red/White
Lehigh	Mountain Hawks, Engineers	Patriot	Sal Mentesana	Bethlehem, PA	Brown/White
Liberty	Flames	Big South	Mel Hankinson	Lynchburg, VA	Red/White/Blue
Long Beach St.	49ers	Big West	Wayne Morgan	Long Beach, CA	Black/Gold
LIU-Brooklyn	Blackbirds	Northeast	Ray Martin	Brooklyn, NY	Blue/White
LSU	Fighting Tigers	SEC-West	John Brady	Baton Rouge, LA	Purple/Gold
Louisiana Tech	Bulldogs	Sun Belt	Keith Richard	Ruston, LA	Red/Blue
Louisville	Cardinals	USA	Denny Crum	Louisville, KY	Red/Black/White
Loyola Marymount	Lions	West Coast	Charles Bradley	Los Angeles, CA	Crimson/Blue
Loyola-IL	Ramblers	Midwestern	Larry Farmer	Chicago, IL	Maroon/Gold
Loyola-MD	Greyhounds	Metro Atlantic	Dino Gaudio	Baltimore, MD	Green/Gray
Maine	Black Bears	America East	John Giannini	Orono, ME	Blue/White
Manhattan	Jaspers	Metro Atlantic	Bobby Gonzalez	Riverdale, NY	Kelly Green/White
Marist	Red Foxes	Metro Atlantic	Dave Magarity	Poughkeepsie, NY	Red/White
Marquette	Golden Eagles	USA	Tom Crean	Milwaukee, WI	Blue/Gold
Marshall	Thundering Herd	Mid-American	Greg White	Huntington, WV	Green/White
Maryland	Terrapins, Terps	ACC	Gary Williams	College Park, MD	Red/Wt./Black/Gold
MD-Balt. County	Retrievers	Northeast	Tom Sullivan	Baltimore, MD	Black/Gold/Red
MD-Eastern Shore	Hawks	Mid-Eastern	Lonnie Williams	Princess Anne, MD	Maroon/Gray
Massachusetts	Minutemen	Atlantic 10	James Bruiser Flint	Amherst, MA	Maroon/White
McNeese St.	Cowboys	Southland	Ron Everhart	Lake Charles, LA	Blue/Gold
Memphis	Tigers	USA	Tic Price	Memphis, TN	Blue/Gray
Mercer	Bears	Trans Am	Mark Slonaker	Macon, GA	Orange/Black
Miami-FL	Hurricanes	Big East	Leonard Hamilton	Coral Gables, FL	Orange/Green/White
Miami-OH	RedHawks	Mid-American	Charlie Coles	Oxford, OH	Red/White
Michigan	Wolverines	Big Ten	Brian Ellerbe	Ann Arbor, MI	Maize/Blue
Michigan St.	Spartans	Big Ten	Tom Izzo	East Lansing, MI	Green/White
Middle Tenn. St.	Blue Raiders	Ohio Valley	Randy Wiel	Murfreesboro, TN	Blue/White
Minnesota	Golden Gophers	Big Ten	Dan Monson	Minneapolis, MN	Maroon/Gold
Mississippi	Ole Miss, Rebels	SEC-West	Rod Barnes	Oxford, MS	Red/Blue
Mississippi St.	Bulldogs	SEC-West	Rick Stansbury	Starkville, MS	Maroon/White
Miss. Valley St.	Delta Devils	SWAC	Lafayette Stribling	Itta Bena, MS	Green/White
Missouri	Tigers	Big 12	Quin Snyder	Columbia, MO	Old Gold/Black
Missouri-KC	Kangaroos	Mid-Continent	Bob Sundvold	Kansas City, MO	Blue/Gold
Monmouth	Hawks	Northeast	Dave Calloway	W. Long Branch, NJ	Royal Blue/White
Montana	Grizzlies	Big Sky	Don Holst	Missoula, MT	Copper/Silver/Gold
Montana St.	Bobcats	Big Sky	Mick Durham	Bozeman, MT	Blue/Gold
Morehead St.	Eagles	Ohio Valley	Kyle Macy	Morehead, KY	Blue/Gold
Morgan St.	Bears	Mid-Eastern	Chris Fuller	Baltimore, MD	Blue/Orange
Mt. St. Mary's	Mountaineers	Northeast	Jim Phelan	Emmitsburg, MD	Blue/White
Murray St.	Racers	Ohio Valley	Tevester Anderson	Murray, KY	Blue/Gold
Navy	Midshipmen	Patriot	Don DeVoe	Annapolis, MD	Navy Blue/Gold
Nebraska	Cornhuskers	Big 12	Danny Nee	Lincoln, NE	Scarlet/Cream
Nevada	Wolf Pack	Big West	Trent Johnson	Reno, NV	Silver/Blue
New Hampshire	Wildcats	America East	Phil Rowe	Durham, NH	Blue/White
New Mexico	Lobos	Mountain West	Fran Fraschilla	Albuquerque, NM	Cherry/Silver
New Mexico St.	Aggies	Big West	Lou Henson	Las Cruces, NM	Crimson/White
New Orleans	Privateers	Sun Belt	Joey Stiebing	New Orleans, LA	Royal Blue/Silver
Niagara	Purple Eagles	Metro Atlantic	Joe Mihalich	Lewiston, NY	Purple/White/Gold
Nicholls St.	Colonels	Southland	Rickey Broussard	Thibodaux, LA	Red/Gray
Norfolk State	Spartans	Mid-Eastern	Mel Coleman	Norfolk, VA	Green/Gold
North Carolina	Tar Heels	ACC	Bill Guthridge	Chapel Hill, NC	Carolina Blue/White

NCAA Division I Basketball Schools (Cont.)

	Nickname	Conference	Head Coach	Location	Colors
North Carolina A&T	Aggies	Mid-Eastern	Curtis Hunter	Greensboro, NC	Blue/Gold
North Carolina St.	Wolfpack	ACC	Herb Sendek	Raleigh, NC	Red/White
NC-Asheville	Bulldogs	Big South	Eddie Biedenbach	Asheville, NC	Royal Blue/White
NC-Charlotte	49ers	USA	Bobby Lutz	Charlotte, NC	Green/White
NC-Greensboro	Spartans	Southern	Fran McCaffrey	Greensboro, NC	Gold/White/Navy
NC-Wilmington	Seahawks	Colonial	Jerry Wainwright	Wilmington, NC	Green/Gold/Navy
North Texas	Mean Green	Big West	Vic Trilli	Denton, TX	Green/White
NE Louisiana	Indians	Southland	Mike Vining	Monroe, LA	Maroon/Gold
Northeastern	Huskies	America East	Rudy Keeling	Boston, MA	Red/Black
Northern Arizona	Lumberjacks	Big Sky	Mike Adras	Flagstaff, AZ	Blue/Gold
Northern Illinois	Huskies	Mid-American	Brian Hammel	De Kalb, IL	Cardinal/Black
Northern Iowa	Panthers	Mo. Valley	Sam Weaver	Cedar Falls, IA	Purple/Old Gold
Northwestern	Wildcats	Big Ten	Kevin O'Neill	Evanston, IL	Purple/White
Northwestern St.	Demons	Southland	Mike McConathy	Natchitoches, LA	Purple/Orange/Wt.
Notre Dame	Fighting Irish	Big East	Matt Doherty	Notre Dame, IN	Gold/Blue
Oakland-MI	Pioneers	Mid-Continent	Greg Kampe	Rochester, MI	Black/Gold
Ohio	Bobcats	Mid-American	Larry Hunter	Athens, OH	Hunter Green/White
Ohio St.	Buckeyes	Big Ten	Jim O'Brien	Columbus, OH	Scarlet/Gray
Oklahoma	Sooners	Big 12	Kelvin Sampson	Norman, OK	Crimson/Cream
Oklahoma St.	Cowboys	Big 12	Eddie Sutton	Stillwater, OK	Orange/Black
Old Dominion	Monarchs	Colonial	Jeff Capel	Norfolk, VA	Slate Blue/Silver
Oral Roberts	Golden Eagles	Mid-Continent	Scott Sutton	Tulsa, OK	Navy Blue/White
Oregon	Ducks	Pac-10	Ernie Kent	Eugene, OR	Green/Yellow
Oregon St.	Beavers	Pac-10	Eddie Payne	Corvallis, OR	Orange/Black
Pacific	Tigers	Big West	Bob Thomason	Stockton, CA	Orange/Black
Pennsylvania	Quakers	Ivy	Fran Dunphy	Philadelphia, PA	Red/Blue
Penn St.	Nittany Lions	Big Ten	Jerry Dunn	University Park, PA	Blue/White
Pepperdine	Waves	West Coast	Jan Van Breda Kolff	Malibu, CA	Blue/Orange
Pittsburgh	Panthers	Big East	Ben Howland	Pittsburgh, PA	Gold/Blue
Portland	Pilots	West Coast	Rob Chavez	Portland, OR	Purple/White
Portland St.	Vikings	Big Sky	Joel Sobotka	Portland, OR	Green/White
Prairie View A&M	Panthers	SWAC	Elwood Plummer	Prairie View, TX	Purple/Gold
Princeton	Tigers	Ivy	Bill Carmody	Princeton, NJ	Orange/Black
Providence	Friars	Big East	Tim Welsh	Providence, RI	Black/White
Purdue	Boilermakers	Big Ten	Gene Keady	W. Lafayette, IN	Old Gold/Black
Quinnipiac	Braves	Northeast	Joe DeSantis	Hamden, CT	Blue/Gold
Radford	Highlanders	Big South	Ron Bradley	Radford, VA	Blue/Red/Green/Wt.
Rhode Island	Rams	Atlantic 10	Jerry DeGregorio	Kingston, RI	Lt. Blue/White/Navy
Rice	Owls	WAC	Willis Wilson	Houston, TX	Blue/Gray
Richmond	Spiders	Colonial	John Beilein	Richmond, VA	Red/Blue
Rider	Broncs	Metro Atlantic	Don Harnum	Lawrenceville, NJ	Cranberry/White
Robert Morris	Colonials	Northeast	Jim Boone	Moon Township, PA	Blue/White
Rutgers	Scarlet Knights	Big East	Kevin Bannon	New Brunswick, NJ	Scarlet
Sacred Heart	Pioneers	Northeast	Dave Bike	Fairfield, CT	Scarlet/White
St. Bonaventure	Bonnies	Atlantic 10	Jim Baron	St. Bonaventure, NY	Brown/White
St. Francis-NY	Terriers	Northeast	Ron Ganulin	Brooklyn, NY	Red/Blue
St. Francis-PA	Red Flash	Northeast	Bobby Jones	Loretto, PA	Red/White
St. John's	Red Storm	Big East	Mike Jarvis	Jamaica, NY	Red/White
St. Joseph's-PA	Hawks	Atlantic 10	Phil Martelli	Philadelphia, PA	Crimson/Gray
Saint Louis	Billikens	USA	Lorenzo Romar	St. Louis, MO	Blue/White
St. Mary's-CA	Gaels	West Coast	Dave Bollwinkel	Moraga, CA	Red/Blue
St. Peter's	Peacocks	Metro Atlantic	Rodger Blind	Jersey City, NJ	Blue/White
Sam Houston St.	Bearkats	Southland	Bob Marlin	Huntsville, TX	Orange/White
Samford	Bulldogs	Trans Am	Jimmy Tillette	Birmingham, AL	Red/Blue
San Diego	Toreros	West Coast	Brad Holland	San Diego, CA	Lt. Blue/Navy
San Diego St.	Aztecs	Mountain West	Steve Fisher	San Diego, CA	Scarlet/Black
San Francisco	Dons	West Coast	Phil Mathews	San Francisco, CA	Green/Gold
San Jose St.	Spartans	WAC	Steve Barnes	San Jose, CA	Gold/White/Blue
Santa Clara	Broncos	West Coast	Dick Davey	Santa Clara, CA	Bronco Red/White
Seton Hall	Pirates	Big East	Tommy Amaker	South Orange, NJ	Blue/White
Siena	Saints	Metro Atlantic	Paul Hewitt	Loudonville, NY	Green/Gold
South Alabama	Jaguars	Sun Belt	Bob Weltlich	Mobile, AL	Red/White/Blue
South Carolina	Gamecocks	SEC-East	Eddie Fogler	Columbia, SC	Garnet/Black
South Carolina St.	Bulldogs	Mid-Eastern	Cy Alexander	Orangeburg, SC	Garnet/Blue
South Florida	Bulls	USA	Seth Greenberg	Tampa, FL	Green/Gold
SE Missouri St.	Indians	Ohio Valley	Gary Garner	Cape Girardeau, MO	Red/Black
SE Louisiana	Lions	Southland	Billy Kennedy	Hammond, LA	Green/Gold
Southern Illinois	Salukis	Mo. Valley	Bruce Weber	Carbondale, IL	Maroon/White

	Nickname	Conference	Head Coach	Location	Colors
SMU	Mustangs	WAC	Mike Dement	Dallas, TX	Red/Blue
Southern Miss	Golden Eagles	USA	James Green	Hattiesburg, MS	Black/Gold
Southern Utah	Thunderbirds	Mid-Continent	Bill Evans	Cedar City, UT	Scarlet/White
Southern-BR	Jaguars	SWAC	Tommy Green	Baton Rouge, LA	Blue/Gold
SW Missouri St.	Bears	Mo. Valley	Barry Hinson	Springfield, MO	Maroon/White
SW Texas St.	Bobcats	Southland	Mike Miller	San Marcos, TX	Maroon/Gold
SW Louisiana	Ragin' Cajuns	Sun Belt	Jessie Evans	Lafayette, LA	Vermilion/White
Stanford	Cardinal	Pac-10	Mike Montgomery	Stanford, CA	Cardinal/White
S.F. Austin St.	Lumberjacks	Southland	Derek Allister	Nacogdoches, TX	Purple/White
Stetson	Hatters	Trans Am	Murray Arnold	DeLand, FL	Green/White
Stony Brook	Seawolves	Independent	Nick Macarchuk	Stony Brook, NY	Scarlet/Gray
Syracuse	Orangemen	Big East	Jim Boeheim	Syracuse, NY	Orange
Temple	Owls	Atlantic 10	John Chaney	Philadelphia, PA	Cherry/White
Tennessee	Volunteers	SEC-East	Jerry Green	Knoxville, TN	Orange/White
Tenn-Chattanooga	Mocs	Southern	Henry Dickerson	Chattanooga, TN	Navy Blue/Old Gold
Tenn-Martin	Skyhawks	Ohio Valley	Bret Campbell	Martin, TN	Orange/Wt./Royal Blue
Tennessee St.	Tigers	Ohio Valley	Frankie Allen	Nashville, TN	Blue/White
Tennessee Tech	Golden Eagles	Ohio Valley	Jeff Lebo	Cookeville, TN	Purple/Gold
Texas	Longhorns	Big 12	Rick Barnes	Austin, TX	Burnt Orange/White
Texas A&M	Aggies	Big 12	Melvin Watkins	College Station, TX	Maroon/White
TCU	Horned Frogs	WAC	Billy Tubbs	Ft. Worth, TX	Purple/White
Texas Southern	Tigers	SWAC	Robert Moreland	Houston, TX	Maroon/Gray
Texas Tech	Red Raiders	Big 12	James Dickey	Lubbock, TX	Scarlet/Black
TX-Arlington	Mavericks	Southland	Eddie McCarter	Arlington, TX	Royal Blue/White
TX-Pan American	Broncs	Independent	TBA	Edinburg, TX	Green/White
TX-San Antonio	Roadrunners	Southland	Tim Carter	San Antonio, TX	Orange/Navy/White
Toledo	Rockets	Mid-American	Stan Joplin	Toledo, OH	Blue/Gold
Towson	Tigers	America East	Mike Jaskulski	Towson, MD	Gold/White/Black
Troy St.	Trojans	Trans Am	Don Maestri	Troy, AL	Cardinal/Silver/Black
Tulane	Green Wave	USA	Perry Clark	New Orleans, LA	Olive Green/Sky Blue
Tulsa	Golden Hurricane	WAC	Bill Self	Tulsa, OK	Blue/Red/Gold
UC-Irvine	Anteaters	Big West	Pat Douglass	Irvine, CA	Blue/Gold
UCLA	Bruins	Pac-10	Steve Lavin	Los Angeles, CA	Blue/Gold
UC-Santa Barbara	Gauchos	Big West	Bob Williams	Santa Barbara, CA	Blue/Gold
UNLV	Runnin' Rebels	Mountain West	Billy Bayno	Las Vegas, NV	Scarlet/Gray
USC	Trojans	Pac-10	Henry Bibby	Los Angeles, CA	Cardinal/Gold
Utah	Utes	Mountain West	Rick Majerus	Salt Lake City, UT	Crimson/White
Utah St.	Aggies	Big West	Stew Morrill	Logan, UT	Navy Blue/White
UTEP	Miners	WAC	Jason Rabedeaux	El Paso, TX	Orange/Blue/Wt.
Valparaiso	Crusaders	Mid-Continent	Homer Drew	Valparaiso, IN	Brown/Gold
Vanderbilt	Commodores	SEC-East	Kevin Stallings	Nashville, TN	Black/Gold
Vermont	Catamounts	America East	Tom Brennan	Burlington, VT	Green/Gold
Villanova	Wildcats	Big East	Steve Lappas	Villanova, PA	Blue/White
Virginia	Cavaliers	ACC	Pete Gillen	Charlottesville, VA	Orange/Blue
VCU	Rams	Colonial	Mack McCarthy	Richmond, VA	Black/Gold
VMI	Keydets	Southern	Bart Bellairs	Lexington, VA	Red/White/Yellow
Virginia Tech	Hokies, Gobblers	Atlantic 10	Ricky Stokes	Blacksburg, VA	Orange/Maroon
Wagner	Seahawks	Northeast	Dereck Whittenburg	Staten Island, NY	Green/White
Wake Forest	Demon Deacons	ACC	Dave Odom	Winston-Salem, NC	Old Gold/Black
Washington	Huskies	Pac-10	Bob Bender	Seattle, WA	Purple/Gold
Washington St.	Cougars	Pac-10	Paul Graham	Pullman, WA	Crimson/Gray
Weber St.	Wildcats	Big Sky	Joe Cravens	Ogden, UT	Purple/White
West Virginia	Mountaineers	Big East	Gale Catlett	Morgantown, WV	Old Gold/Blue
Western Carolina	Catamounts	Southern	Phil Hopkins	Cullowhee, NC	Purple/Gold
Western Illinois	Leathernecks	Mid-Continent	Jim Kerwin	Macomb, IL	Purple/Gold
Western Kentucky	Hilltoppers	Sun Belt	Dennis Felton	Bowling Green, KY	Red/White
Western Michigan	Broncos	Mid-American	Bob Donewald	Kalamazoo, MI	Brown/Gold
Wichita St.	Shockers	Mo. Valley	Randy Smithson	Wichita, KS	Yellow/Black
William & Mary	Tribe	Colonial	Charlie Woollum	Williamsburg, VA	Green/Gold/Silver
Winthrop	Eagles	Big South	Gregg Marshall	Rock Hill, SC	Garnet/Gold
Wisconsin	Badgers	Big Ten	Dick Bennett	Madison, WI	Cardinal/White
WI-Green Bay	Phoenix	Midwestern	Mike Heideman	Green Bay, WI	Green/White/Red
WI-Milwaukee	Panthers	Midwestern	Bo Ryan	Milwaukee, WI	Black/Gold
Wofford	Terriers	Southern	Richard Johnson	Spartanburg, SC	Old Gold/Black
Wright St.	Raiders	Midwestern	Ed Schilling	Dayton, OH	Green/Gold
Wyoming	Cowboys	Mountain West	Steve McClain	Laramie, WY	Brown/Yellow
Xavier	Musketeers	Atlantic 10	Skip Prosser	Cincinnati, OH	Blue/White
Yale	Bulldogs, Elis	Ivy	James Jones	New Haven, CT	Yale Blue/White
Youngstown St.	Penguins	Mid-Continent	John Robic	Youngstown, OH	Red/White

NCAA Division I-A Football Schools
1999 Season
Conferences and coaches as of Sept. 10, 1999.

Joining Mid-American in 1999: BUFFALO from Div. I-AA Independent.
Joining Conference USA in 1999: ALABAMA-BIRMINGHAM from Independent.
Joining Big West in 1999: ARKANSAS STATE from Independent.
Joining I-A as an Independent in 1999: MIDDLE TENNESSEE ST. from Div. I-AA Ohio Valley.
Joining Mountain West in 1999: AIR FORCE, BRIGHAM YOUNG, COLORADO ST., NEW MEXICO, SAN DIEGO ST., UNLV, UTAH and WYOMING from WAC.
Joining WAC in 2000: NEVADA from Big West.

	Nickname	Conference	Head Coach	Location	Colors
Air Force	Falcons	Mountain West	Fisher DeBerry	Colo. Springs, CO	Blue/Silver
Akron	Zips	Mid-American	Lee Owens	Akron, OH	Blue/Gold
Alabama	Crimson Tide	SEC-West	Mike DuBose	Tuscaloosa, AL	Crimson/White
Ala.-Birmingham	Blazers	USA	Watson Brown	Birmingham, AL	Green/Gold
Arizona	Wildcats	Pac-10	Dick Tomey	Tucson, AZ	Cardinal/Navy
Arizona St.	Sun Devils	Pac-10	Bruce Snyder	Tempe, AZ	Maroon/Gold
Arkansas	Razorbacks	SEC-West	Houston Nutt	Fayetteville, AR	Cardinal/White
Arkansas St.	Indians	Big West	Joe Hollis	State Univ., AR	Scarlet/Black
Army	Cadets, Black Knights	USA	Bob Sutton	West Point, NY	Black/Gold/Gray
Auburn	Tigers	SEC-West	Tommy Tuberville	Auburn, AL	Orange/Blue
Ball St.	Cardinals	Mid-American	Bill Lynch	Muncie, IN	Cardinal/White
Baylor	Bears	Big 12	Kevin Steele	Waco, TX	Green/Gold
Boise St.	Broncos	Big West	Dirk Koetter	Boise, ID	Orange/Blue
Boston College	Eagles	Big East	Tom O'Brien	Chestnut Hill, MA	Maroon/Gold
Bowling Green	Falcons	Mid-American	Gary Blackney	Bowling Green, OH	Orange/Brown
Buffalo	Bulls	Mid-American	Craig Cirbus	Buffalo, NY	Royal Blue/White
Brigham Young	Cougars	Mountain West	LaVell Edwards	Provo, UT	Royal Blue/White
California	Golden Bears	Pac-10	Tom Holmoe	Berkeley, CA	Blue/Gold
Central Florida	Golden Knights	Independent	Mike Kruczek	Orlando, FL	Black/Gold
Central Michigan	Chippewas	Mid-American	Dick Flynn	Mt. Pleasant, MI	Maroon/Gold
Cincinnati	Bearcats	USA	Rick Minter	Cincinnati, OH	Red/Black
Clemson	Tigers	ACC	Tommy Bowden	Clemson, SC	Purple/Orange
Colorado	Buffaloes	Big 12	Gary Barnett	Boulder, CO	Silver/Gold/Black
Colorado St.	Rams	Mountain West	Sonny Lubick	Ft. Collins, CO	Green/Gold
Duke	Blue Devils	ACC	Carl Franks	Durham, NC	Royal Blue/White
East Carolina	Pirates	USA	Steve Logan	Greenville, NC	Purple/Gold
Eastern Michigan	Eagles	Mid-American	Rick Rasnick	Ypsilanti, MI	Green/White
Florida	Gators	SEC-East	Steve Spurrier	Gainesville, FL	Orange/Blue
Florida St.	Seminoles	ACC	Bobby Bowden	Tallahassee, FL	Garnet/Gold
Fresno St.	Bulldogs	WAC	Pat Hill	Fresno, CA	Cardinal/Blue
Georgia	Bulldogs	SEC-East	Jim Donnan	Athens, GA	Red/Black
Georgia Tech	Yellow Jackets	ACC	George O'Leary	Atlanta, GA	Old Gold/White
Hawaii	Rainbow Warriors	WAC	June Jones	Honolulu, HI	Green/White
Houston	Cougars	USA	Kim Helton	Houston, TX	Scarlet/White
Idaho	Vandals	Big West	Chris Tormey	Moscow, ID	Silver/Gold
Illinois	Fighting Illini	Big Ten	Ron Turner	Champaign, IL	Orange/Blue
Indiana	Hoosiers	Big Ten	Cam Cameron	Bloomington, IN	Cream/Crimson
Iowa	Hawkeyes	Big Ten	Kirk Ferentz	Iowa City, IA	Old Gold/Black
Iowa St.	Cyclones	Big 12	Dan McCarney	Ames, IA	Cardinal/Gold
Kansas	Jayhawks	Big 12	Terry Allen	Lawrence, KS	Crimson/Blue
Kansas St.	Wildcats	Big 12	Bill Snyder	Manhattan, KS	Purple/White
Kent St.	Golden Flashes	Mid-American	Dean Pees	Kent, OH	Navy Blue/Gold
Kentucky	Wildcats	SEC-East	Hal Mumme	Lexington, KY	Blue/White
LSU	Fighting Tigers	SEC-West	Gerry DiNardo	Baton Rouge, LA	Purple/Gold
Louisiana Tech	Bulldogs	Independent	Jack Bicknell III	Ruston, LA	Red/Blue
Louisville	Cardinals	USA	John L. Smith	Louisville, KY	Red/Black/White
Marshall	Thundering Herd	Mid-American	Bob Pruett	Huntington, WV	Green/White
Maryland	Terrapins, Terps	ACC	Ron Vanderlinden	College Park, MD	Red/White/Black/Gold
Memphis	Tigers	USA	Rip Scherer	Memphis, TN	Blue/Gray
Miami-FL	Hurricanes	Big East	Butch Davis	Coral Gables, FL	Orange/Green/White
Miami-OH	RedHawks	Mid-American	Terry Hoeppner	Oxford, OH	Red/White
Michigan	Wolverines	Big Ten	Lloyd Carr	Ann Arbor, MI	Maize/Blue
Michigan St.	Spartans	Big Ten	Nick Saban	E. Lansing, MI	Green/White
Middle Tenn. St.	Blue Raiders	Independent	Andy McCollum	Murfreesboro, TN	Blue/White
Minnesota	Golden Gophers	Big Ten	Glen Mason	Minneapolis, MN	Maroon/Gold
Mississippi	Ole Miss, Rebels	SEC-West	David Cutcliffe	Oxford, MS	Cardinal/Navy Blue
Mississippi St.	Bulldogs	SEC-West	Jackie Sherrill	Starkville, MS	Maroon/White
Missouri	Tigers	Big 12	Larry Smith	Columbia, MO	Old Gold/Black

	Nickname	Conference	Head Coach	Location	Colors
Navy	Midshipmen	Independent	Charlie Weatherbie	Annapolis, MD	Navy Blue/Gold
Nebraska	Cornhuskers	Big 12	Frank Solich	Lincoln, NE	Scarlet/Cream
Nevada	Wolf Pack	Big West	Jeff Tisdel	Reno, NV	Silver/Blue
New Mexico	Lobos	Mountain West	Rocky Long	Albuquerque, NM	Cherry/Silver
New Mexico St.	Aggies	Big West	Tony Samuel	Las Cruces, NM	Crimson/White
North Carolina	Tar Heels	ACC	Carl Torbush	Chapel Hill, NC	Carolina Blue/White
North Carolina St.	Wolfpack	ACC	Mike O'Cain	Raleigh, NC	Red/White
North Texas	Mean Green	Big West	Darrell Dickey	Denton, TX	Green/White
NE Louisiana	Indians	Independent	Bobby Keasler	Monroe, LA	Maroon/Gold
Northern Illinois	Huskies	Mid-American	Joe Novak	De Kalb, IL	Cardinal/Black
Northwestern	Wildcats	Big Ten	Randy Walker	Evanston, IL	Purple/White
Notre Dame	Fighting Irish	Independent	Bob Davie	Notre Dame, IN	Gold/Blue
Ohio University	Bobcats	Mid-American	Jim Grobe	Athens, OH	Ohio Green/White
Ohio St.	Buckeyes	Big Ten	John Cooper	Columbus, OH	Scarlet/Gray
Oklahoma	Sooners	Big 12	Bob Stoops	Norman, OK	Crimson/Cream
Oklahoma St.	Cowboys	Big 12	Bob Simmons	Stillwater, OK	Orange/Black
Oregon	Ducks	Pac-10	Mike Bellotti	Eugene, OR	Green/Yellow
Oregon St.	Beavers	Pac-10	Dennis Erickson	Corvallis, OR	Orange/Black
Penn St.	Nittany Lions	Big Ten	Joe Paterno	University Park, PA	Blue/White
Pittsburgh	Panthers	Big East	Walt Harris	Pittsburgh, PA	Blue/Gold
Purdue	Boilermakers	Big Ten	Joe Tiller	W. Lafayette, IN	Old Gold/Black
Rice	Owls	WAC	Ken Hatfield	Houston, TX	Blue/Gray
Rutgers	Scarlet Knights	Big East	Terry Shea	New Brunswick, NJ	Scarlet
San Diego St.	Aztecs	Mountain West	Ted Tollner	San Diego, CA	Scarlet/Black
San Jose St.	Spartans	WAC	Dave Baldwin	San Jose, CA	Gold/White/Blue
South Carolina	Gamecocks	SEC-East	Lou Holtz	Columbia, SC	Garnet/Black
SMU	Mustangs	WAC	Mike Cavan	Dallas, TX	Red/Blue
Southern Miss.	Golden Eagles	USA	Jeff Bower	Hattiesburg, MS	Black/Gold
SW Louisiana	Ragin' Cajuns	Independent	Jerry Baldwin	Lafayette, LA	Vermilion/White
Stanford	Cardinal	Pac-10	Tyrone Willingham	Stanford, CA	Cardinal/White
Syracuse	Orangemen	Big East	Paul Pasqualoni	Syracuse, NY	Orange
Temple	Owls	Big East	Bobby Wallace	Philadelphia, PA	Cherry/White
Tennessee	Volunteers	SEC-East	Phillip Fulmer	Knoxville, TN	Orange/White
Texas	Longhorns	Big 12	Mack Brown	Austin, TX	Burnt Orange/White
Texas A&M	Aggies	Big 12	R.C. Slocum	College Station, TX	Maroon/White
TCU	Horned Frogs	WAC	Dennis Franchione	Ft. Worth, TX	Purple/White
Texas Tech	Red Raiders	Big 12	Spike Dykes	Lubbock, TX	Scarlet/Black
Toledo	Rockets	Mid-American	Gary Pinkel	Toledo, OH	Blue/Gold
Tulane	Green Wave	USA	Chris Scelfo	New Orleans, LA	Olive Green/Sky Blue
Tulsa	Golden Hurricane	WAC	Dave Rader	Tulsa, OK	Blue/Gold
UCLA	Bruins	Pac-10	Bob Toledo	Los Angeles, CA	Blue/Gold
UNLV	Rebels	Mountain West	John Robinson	Las Vegas, NV	Scarlet/Gray
USC	Trojans	Pac-10	Paul Hackett	Los Angeles, CA	Cardinal/Gold
Utah	Utes	Mountain West	Ron McBride	Salt Lake City, UT	Crimson/White
Utah St.	Aggies	Big West	Dave Arslanian	Logan, UT	Navy Blue/White
UTEP	Miners	WAC	Charlie Bailey	El Paso, TX	Orange/Blue/Wt.
Vanderbilt	Commodores	SEC-East	Woody Widenhofer	Nashville, TN	Black/Gold
Virginia	Cavaliers	ACC	George Welsh	Charlottesville, VA	Orange/Blue
Virginia Tech	Hokies, Gobblers	Big East	Frank Beamer	Blacksburg, VA	Orange/Maroon
Wake Forest	Demon Deacons	ACC	Jim Caldwell	Winston-Salem, NC	Old Gold/Black
Washington	Huskies	Pac-10	Rick Neuheisel	Seattle, WA	Purple/Gold
Washington St.	Cougars	Pac-10	Mike Price	Pullman, WA	Crimson/Gray
West Virginia	Mountaineers	Big East	Don Nehlen	Morgantown, WV	Old Gold/Blue
Western Michigan	Broncos	Mid-American	Gary Darnell	Kalamazoo, MI	Brown/Gold
Wisconsin	Badgers	Big Ten	Barry Alvarez	Madison, WI	Cardinal/White
Wyoming	Cowboys	Mountain West	Dana Dimel	Laramie, WY	Brown/Yellow

Most Popular Sports

In 1998-99, 983 NCAA schools had men's basketball programs, making it by far the most popular sport. Below are the top five most-offered college men's and women's sports. Note that football is in eighth place for men, sponsored by 607 NCAA institutions. Source: NCAA.

MEN'S	I	II	III	Total
Basketball	312	291	380	983
Baseball	277	232	338	847
Cross-Country	295	225	309	829
Tennis	273	180	314	767
Soccer	191	169	358	718

WOMEN'S	I	II	III	Total
Basketball	306	289	409	1004
Volleyball	299	272	392	963
Cross-Country	308	251	332	891
Tennis	301	219	357	877
Softball	232	244	356	832

NCAA Division I-AA Football Schools
1999 Season
Coaches as of Sept. 10, 1999.

Joining Metro Atlantic in 1999: LA SALLE from Independent.
Joining Northeast in 1999: STONY BROOK from Division II.
Joining Northeast in 1999: ALBANY from Division II.
Joining Ohio Valley in 1999: WESTERN KENTUCKY from Independent.
Joining Division I-AA in 2001: FLORIDA ATLANTIC (new program).

	Nickname	Conference	Head Coach	Location	Colors
Alabama A&M	Bulldogs	SWAC	Ron Cooper	Huntsville, AL	Maroon/White
Alabama St.	Hornets	SWAC	Ron Dickerson	Montgomery, AL	Black/Gold
Albany	Great Danes	Northeast	Bob Ford	Albany, NY	Purple/Gold
Alcorn St.	Braves	SWAC	Johnny Thomas	Lorman, MS	Purple/Gold
Appalachian St.	Mountaineers	Southern	Jerry Moore	Boone, NC	Black/Gold
Ark.-Pine Bluff	Golden Lions	SWAC	Lee Hardman	Pine Bluff, AR	Black/Gold
Austin Peay St.	Governors	Independent	Bill Schmitz	Clarksville, TN	Red/White
Bethune-Cookman	Wildcats	Mid-Eastern	Alvin Wyatt	Daytona Beach, FL	Maroon/Gold
Brown	Bears	Ivy	Phil Estes	Providence, RI	Brown/Red/White
Bucknell	Bison	Patriot	Tom Gadd	Lewisburg, PA	Orange/Blue
Butler	Bulldogs	Pioneer	Ken LaRose	Indianapolis, IN	Blue/White
Cal Poly SLO	Mustangs	Independent	Larry Welsh	San Luis Obispo, CA	Green/Gold
CS-Northridge	Matadors	Big Sky	Jeff Kearin	Northridge, CA	Red/White/Black
CS-Sacramento	Hornets	Big Sky	John Volek	Sacramento, CA	Green/Gold
Canisius	Golden Griffins	Metro Atlantic	Chuck Williams	Buffalo, NY	Blue/Gold
Central Conn. St.	Blue Devils	Northeast	Sal Cintorino	New Britain, CT	Blue/White
Charleston So.	Buccaneers	Independent	David Dowd	Charleston, SC	Blue/Gold
The Citadel	Bulldogs	Southern	Don Powers	Charleston, SC	Blue/White
Colgate	Red Raiders	Patriot	Dick Biddle	Hamilton, NY	Maroon/White/Gray
Columbia	Lions	Ivy	Ray Tellier	New York, NY	Lt. Blue/White
Connecticut	Huskies	Atlantic 10	Randy Edsall	Storrs, CT	Blue/White
Cornell	Big Red	Ivy	Pete Mangurian	Ithaca, NY	Carnelian/White
Dartmouth	Big Green	Ivy	John Lyons	Hanover, NH	Green/White
Davidson	Wildcats	Independent	Tim Landis	Davidson, NC	Red/Black
Dayton	Flyers	Pioneer	Mike Kelly	Dayton, OH	Red/Blue
Delaware	Blue Hens	Atlantic 10	Tubby Raymond	Newark, DE	Blue/Gold
Delaware St.	Hornets	Mid-Eastern	John McKenzie	Dover, DE	Red/Blue
Drake	Bulldogs	Pioneer	Rob Ash	Des Moines, IA	Blue/White
Duquesne	Dukes	Metro Atlantic	Greg Gattuso	Pittsburgh, PA	Red/Blue
East Tenn. St.	Buccaneers	Southern	Paul Hamilton	Johnson City, TN	Blue/Gold
Eastern Illinois	Panthers	Ohio Valley	Bob Spoo	Charleston, IL	Blue/Gray
Eastern Kentucky	Colonels	Ohio Valley	Roy Kidd	Richmond, KY	Maroon/White
Eastern Wash.	Eagles	Big Sky	Mike Kramer	Cheney, WA	Red/White
Elon	Fightin Christians	Independent	Al Seagraves	Elon, NC	Maroon/Gold
Fairfield	Stags	Metro Atlantic	Kevin Kiesel	Fairfield, CT	Cardinal Red
Florida A&M	Rattlers	Mid-Eastern	Billy Joe	Tallahassee, FL	Orange/Green
Fordham	Rams	Patriot	Dave Clawson	Bronx, NY	Maroon/White
Furman	Paladins	Southern	Bobby Johnson	Greenville, SC	Purple/White
Georgetown	Hoyas	Metro Atlantic	Bob Benson	Washington, DC	Blue/Gray
Georgia Southern	Eagles	Southern	Paul Johnson	Statesboro, GA	Blue/White
Grambling St.	Tigers	SWAC	Doug Williams	Grambling, LA	Black/Gold
Hampton	Pirates	Mid-Eastern	Joe Taylor	Hampton, VA	Royal Blue/White
Harvard	Crimson	Ivy	Tim Murphy	Cambridge, MA	Crimson/Black/White
Hofstra	Flying Dutchmen	Independent	Joe Gardi	Hempstead, NY	Gray/White/Gold
Holy Cross	Crusaders	Patriot	Dan Allen	Worcester, MA	Royal Purple
Howard	Bison	Mid-Eastern	Steve Wilson	Washington, DC	Blue/Wt./Red
Idaho St.	Bengals	Big Sky	Larry Lewis	Pocatello, ID	Orange/Black
Illinois St.	Redbirds	Gateway	Todd Berry	Normal, IL	Red/White
Indiana St.	Sycamores	Gateway	Tim McGuire	Terre Haute, IN	Royal Blue/White
Iona	Gaels	Metro Atlantic	Fred Mariani	New Rochelle, NY	Maroon/Gold
Jackson St.	Tigers	SWAC	Robert Hughes	Jackson, MS	Blue/White
Jacksonville	Dolphins	Independent	Steve Gilbert	Jacksonville, FL	Green/White
Jacksonville St.	Gamecocks	Southland	Mike Williams	Jacksonville, AL	Red/White
James Madison	Dukes	Atlantic 10	Mickey Matthews	Harrisonburg, VA	Purple/Gold
Lafayette	Leopards	Patriot	Bill Russo	Easton, PA	Maroon/White
La Salle	Explorers	Metro Atlantic	Bill Manlove	Philadelphia, PA	Blue/Gold
Lehigh	Engineers	Patriot	Kevin Higgins	Bethlehem, PA	Brown/White
Liberty	Flames	Independent	Sam Rutigliano	Lynchburg, VA	Red/White/Blue
Maine	Black Bears	Atlantic 10	Jack Cosgrove	Orono, ME	Blue/White
Marist	Red Foxes	Metro Atlantic	Jim Parady	Poughkeepsie, NY	Red/White

	Nickname	Conference	Head Coach	Location	Colors
Massachusetts	Minutemen	Atlantic 10	Mark Whipple	Amherst, MA	Maroon/White
McNeese St.	Cowboys	Southland	Kirby Bruchhaus	Lake Charles, LA	Blue/Gold
Miss. Valley St.	Delta Devils	SWAC	LaTraia Jones	Itta Bena, MS	Green/White
Monmouth	Hawks	Northeast	Kevin Callahan	W. Long Branch, NJ	Royal Blue/White
Montana	Grizzlies	Big Sky	Mick Dennehy	Missoula, MT	Maroon/Gray
Montana St.	Bobcats	Big Sky	Cliff Hysell	Bozeman, MT	Blue/Gold
Morehead St.	Eagles	Independent	Matt Ballard	Morehead, KY	Blue/Gold
Morgan St.	Bears	Mid-Eastern	Stanley Mitchell	Baltimore, MD	Blue/Orange
Murray St.	Racers	Ohio Valley	Denver Johnson	Murray, KY	Blue/Gold
New Hampshire	Wildcats	Atlantic 10	Sean McDonnell	Durham, NH	Blue/White
Nicholls St.	Colonels	Southland	Daryl Daye	Thibodaux, LA	Red/Gray
Norfolk State	Spartans	Mid-Eastern	Maurice Forte	Norfolk, VA	Green/Gold
North Carolina A&T	Aggies	Mid-Eastern	Bill Hayes	Greensboro, NC	Blue/Gold
Northeastern	Huskies	Atlantic 10	Barry Gallup	Boston, MA	Red/Black
Northern Arizona	Lumberjacks	Big Sky	Jerome Souers	Flagstaff, AZ	Blue/Gold
Northern Iowa	Panthers	Gateway	Mike Dunbar	Cedar Falls, IA	Purple/Old Gold
Northwestern St.	Demons	Southland	Sam Goodwin	Natchitoches, LA	Purple/White
Pennsylvania	Quakers	Ivy	Al Bagnoli	Philadelphia, PA	Red/Blue
Portland St.	Vikings	Big Sky	Tim Walsh	Portland, OR	Green/Gray
Prairie View A&M	Panthers	SWAC	Gregory Johnson	Prairie View, TX	Purple/Gold
Princeton	Tigers	Ivy	Steve Tosches	Princeton, NJ	Orange/Black
Rhode Island	Rams	Atlantic 10	Floyd Keith	Kingston, RI	Light Blue/Navy/Wt.
Richmond	Spiders	Atlantic 10	Jim Reid	Richmond, VA	Red/Blue
Robert Morris	Colonials	Northeast	Joe Walton	Moon Township, PA	Blue/White
Sacred Heart	Pioneers	Northeast	Tom Radulski	Fairfield, CT	Scarlet/White
St. Francis-PA	Red Flash	Northeast	David Jaumotte	Loretto, PA	Red/White
St. John's-NY	Red Storm	Independent	Bob Ricca	Jamaica, NY	Red/White
St. Mary's-CA	Gaels	Independent	Mike Rasmussen	Moraga, CA	Red/Blue
St. Peter's	Peacocks	Metro Atlantic	Rob Stern	Jersey City, NJ	Blue/White
Sam Houston St.	Bearkats	Southland	Ron Randleman	Huntsville, TX	Orange/White
Samford	Bulldogs	Independent	Pete Hurt	Birmingham, AL	Crimson/Blue
San Diego	Toreros	Pioneer	Kevin McGarry	San Diego, CA	Lt. Blue/Navy
Siena	Saints	Metro Atlantic	Chris Phelps	Loudonville, NY	Green/Gold
South Carolina St.	Bulldogs	Mid-Eastern	Willie Jeffries	Orangeburg, SC	Garnet/Blue
South Florida	Bulls	Indepedent	Jim Leavitt	Tampa, FL	Green/Gold
SE Missouri St.	Indians	Ohio Valley	John Mumford	Cape Girardeau, MO	Red/Black
Southern-BR	Jaguars	SWAC	Pete Richardson	Baton Rouge, LA	Blue/Gold
Southern Illinois	Salukis	Gateway	Jan Quarless	Cardondale, IL	Maroon/White
Southern Utah	Thunderbirds	Independent	C. Ray Gregory	Cedar City, UT	Scarlet/White
SW Missouri St.	Bears	Gateway	Randy Ball	Springfield, MO	Maroon/White
SW Texas St.	Bobcats	Southland	Bob DeBesse	San Marcos, TX	Maroon/Gold
S.F. Austin St.	Lumberjacks	Southland	Mike Santiago	Nacogdoches, TX	Purple/White
Stony Brook	Seawolves	Northeast	Ron Cooper	Stony Brook, NY	Scarlet/Gray
Tenn-Chattanooga	Mocs	Southern	Buddy Green	Chattanooga, TN	Navy Blue/Old Gold
Tenn-Martin	Skyhawks	Ohio Valley	Jim Marshall	Martin, TN	Orange/White/Blue
Tennessee St.	Tigers	Ohio Valley	L.C. Cole	Nashville, TN	Blue/White
Tennessee Tech	Golden Eagles	Ohio Valley	Mike Hennigan	Cookeville, TN	Purple/Gold
Texas Southern	Tigers	SWAC	Bill Thomas	Houston, TX	Maroon/Gray
Towson	Tigers	Patriot	Gordy Combs	Towson, MD	Gold/White
Troy St.	Trojans	Southland	Larry Blakeney	Troy, AL	Cardinal/Gray/Black
Valparaiso	Crusaders	Pioneer	Tom Horne	Valparaiso, IN	Brown/Gold
Villanova	Wildcats	Atlantic 10	Andy Talley	Villanova, PA	Blue/White
VMI	Keydets	Southern	Cal McCombs	Lexington, VA	Red/White/Yellow
Wagner	Seahawks	Northeast	Walt Hameline	Staten Island, NY	Green/White
Weber St.	Wildcats	Big Sky	Jerry Graybeal	Ogden, UT	Royal Purple/White
Western Carolina	Catamounts	Southern	Bill Bleil	Cullowhee, NC	Purple/Gold
Western Illinois	Leathernecks	Gateway	Don Patterson	Macomb, IL	Purple/Gold
Western Kentucky	Hilltoppers	Ohio Valley	Jack Harbaugh	Bowling Green, KY	Red/White
William & Mary	Tribe	Atlantic 10	Jimmye Laycock	Williamsburg, VA	Green/Gold/Silver
Wofford	Terriers	Southern	Mike Ayers	Spartanburg, SC	Old Gold/Black
Yale	Bulldogs, Elis	Ivy	Jack Siedlecki	New Haven, CT	Yale Blue/White
Youngstown St.	Penguins	Gateway	Jim Tressel	Youngstown, OH	Red/White

Native American Nicknames Down to 9

At the start of the 1998-99 academic year the number of Native American nickname variations stood at 9 in Division I basketball and football: INDIANS (3)– Arkansas St., Northeast Louisiana and Southeast Missouri St.; BRAVES (2)– Alcorn St. and Bradley; CHIPPEWAS– Central Michigan; FIGHTING ILLINI– Illinois; SEMINOLES– Florida St.; TRIBE– William & Mary.

UALR

Sidney Moncrief
Arkansas-Little Rock

Iowa

Steve Alford
SW Missouri St. to Iowa

Georgia

Jim Harrick
Rhode Island to Georgia

Clemson

Tommy Bowden
Tulane to Clemson

Coaching Changes

New head coaches were named at 52 Division 1 basketball schools while 20 Division 1-A and 19 Division 1-AA football schools changed head coaches after the 1998-99 season. Coaching changes listed below are as of September 10, 1999.

Division I Basketball

	Old Coach	Record	Why Left?	New Coach	Old Job
Ark.-Little Rock	Wimp Sanderson	12-15	resigned	Sidney Moncrief	First coaching position
Baylor	Harry Miller	6-24	resigned	Dave Bliss	Coach, New Mexico
Brown	Frank Dobbs	4-22	resigned	Glen Miller	Coach, Connecticut Coll.
Centenary	Billy Kennedy	14-14	to SE Louisiana*	Kevin Johnson	Asst., Centenary
Delaware St.	James Dubose	8-19	to Coppin St.**	Tony Sheals	Asst., Towson
Drexel	Bill Herrion	20-9	to East Carolina*	Steve Seymour	Asst., Drexel
East Carolina	Joe Dooley	13-14	resigned	Bill Herrion	Coach, Drexel
Florida Atlantic	Kevin Billerman	6-20	fired	Sidney Green	Coach, North Florida
Fordham	Nick Macarchuk	12-15	to Stony Brook*	Bob Hill	Fmr. Coach, NBA Spurs
Georgetown	John Thompson	7-6#	retired	Craig Esherick	Asst., Georgetown
Georgia	Ron Jirsa	15-15	fired	Jim Harrick	Coach, Rhode Island
Georgia Southern	Gregg Polinsky	11-17	fired	Jeff Price	Coach, Lynn-FL
Gonzaga	Dan Monson	28-7	to Minnesota*	Mark Few	Asst., Gonzaga
Grambling St.	Lacey Reynolds	6-21	fired	Larry Glenn Wright	Fmr. asst., Grambling
Holy Cross	Bill Raynor	7-20	fired	Ralph Willard	Coach, Pittsburgh
Illinois St.	Kevin Stallings	16-15	to Vanderbilt*	Tom Richardson	Asst., Illinois State
Iowa	Tom Davis	20-10	retired	Steve Alford	Coach, SW Missouri St.
Lamar	Grey Giovanine	17-11	resigned	Mike Deane	Coach, Marquette
Manhattan	John Leonard	5-22	fired	Bobby Gonzalez	Asst., Virginia
Marquette	Mike Deane	14-15	fired	Tom Crean	Asst., Michigan St.
Minnesota	Clem Haskins	17-11	resigned	Dan Monson	Coach, Gonzaga
Missouri	Norm Stewart	20-9	retired	Quin Snyder	Asst., Duke
Nevada	Pat Foster	8-18	resigned	Trent Johnson	Asst., Stanford
New Hampshire	Jeff Jackson	4-23	to Vanderbilt**	Phil Rowe	Coach, Keene St.
New Mexico	Dave Bliss	25-9	to Baylor*	Fran Fraschilla	Fmr. coach, St. John's
North Carolina A&T	Roy Thomas	13-15	resigned	Curtis Hunter†	Asst., North Carolina A&T
NC-Greensboro	Randy Peele	7-20	resigned	Fran McCaffrey	Asst., Notre Dame
Northern Arizona	Ben Howland	21-8	to Pittsburgh*	Mike Adras	Asst., N. Arizona
Northwestern St.	J.D. Barnett	11-15	resigned	Mike McConathy	Coach, Bossier Parish C.C.
Notre Dame	John MacLeod	14-16	resigned	Matt Doherty	Asst., Kansas
Oral Roberts	Barry Hinson	17-11	to SW Missouri St.*	Scott Sutton	Asst., Oral Roberts
Pepperdine	Lorenzo Romar	19-13	to Saint Louis*	Jan Van Breda Kolff	Coach, Vanderbilt
Pittsburgh	Ralph Willard	14-16	to Holy Cross*	Ben Howland	Coach, N. Arizona
Rhode Island	Jim Harrick	20-13	to Georgia*	Jerry DeGregorio	Asst., Rhode Island
St Francis-PA	Tom McConnell	9-17	resigned	Bobby Jones	Asst., Minnesota
Saint Louis	Charlie Spoonhour	15-16	retired	Lorenzo Romar	Coach, Pepperdine
San Diego St.	Fred Trenkle	4-22	resigned	Steve Fisher	Asst., NBA Kings
San Jose St.	Phil Johnson	12-16	to NBA Chicago**	Steve Barnes	Asst., San Jose St.
SE Louisiana	John Lyles	6-20	resigned	Billy Kennedy	Coach, Centenary
SW Missouri St.	Steve Alford	22-11	to Iowa*	Barry Hinson	Coach, Oral Roberts
Stony Brook	Bernard Tomlin	11-16	re-assigned	Nick Macarchuk	Coach, Fordham
Tenn.-Martin	Cal Luther	8-18	retired	Bret Campbell	Asst., Austin Peay
Texas-Pan Am	Delray Brooks	5-22	fired	TBA	—
UTEP	Don Haskins	16-12	retired	Jason Rabedeaux	Asst., Oklahoma
Vanderbilt	Jan Van Breda Kolff	14-15	to Pepperdine*	Kevin Stallings	Coach, Illinois State

	Old Coach	Record	Why Left?	New Coach	Old Job
Virginia Tech	Bob Hussey	13-15	fired	Ricky Stokes	Asst., Texas
Wagner	Tim Capstraw	9-18	fired	Dereck Whittenburg	Asst., Georgia Tech
Washington St.	Kevin Eastman	10-19	resigned	Paul Graham	Asst., Oklahoma St.
Weber St.	Ron Abegglen	25-8	resigned	Joe Cravens	Asst., Weber St.
WI-Milwaukee	Ric Cobb	8-19	re-assigned	Bo Ryan	Coach, WI-Platteville
Yale	Dick Kuchen	4-22	fired	James Jones	Asst., Ohio
Youngstown St.	Dan Peters	14-14	to Cincinnati**	John Robic	Asst., Massachusetts

* as head coach
** as assistant coach
# Thompson retired on Jan. 8 with a 7-6 record. The team finished the year 15-16.
† on an interim basis

Division I-A Football

	Old Coach	Record	Why Left?	New Coach	Old Job
Auburn	Terry Bowden	1-5	resigned#	Tommy Tuberville	Coach, Ole Miss
Baylor	Dave Roberts	2-9	fired	Kevin Steele	Asst., NFL Carolina
Clemson	Tommy West	3-8	fired	Tommy Bowden	Coach, Tulane
Colorado	Rick Neuheisel	8-4	to Washington*	Gary Barnett	Coach, Northwestern
Duke	Fred Goldsmith	4-7	fired	Carl Franks	Asst., Florida
Hawaii	Fred vonAppen	0-12	fired	June Jones	Coach, NFL San Diego
Iowa	Hayden Fry	3-8	retired	Kirk Ferentz	Asst., NFL Baltimore
Louisiana Tech	Gary Crowton	6-6	to NFL Chicago%	Jack Bicknell III	Asst., Louisiana Tech
Miami-OH	Randy Walker	10-1	to Northwestern*	Terry Hoeppner	Asst., Miami-OH
Mid. Tenn. St.	Boots Donnelly	5-5	resigned	Andy McCollum	Asst., Baylor
Mississippi	Tommy Tuberville	7-5@	to Auburn*	David Cutcliffe	Asst., Tennessee
NE Louisiana	Ed Zaunbrecher	5-6	fired	Bobby Keasler	Coach, McNeese St.
Northwestern	Gary Barnett	3-9	to Colorado*	Randy Walker	Coach, Miami-OH
Oklahoma	John Blake	5-6	fired	Bob Stoops	Def. coord., Florida
Oregon State	Mike Riley	5-6	to NFL San Diego*	Dennis Erickson	Coach, NFL Seattle
South Carolina	Brad Scott	1-10	fired	Lou Holtz	Fmr. Coach, Notre Dame
SW Louisiana	Nelson Stokley	2-9	retired	Jerry Baldwin	Asst., LSU
Tulane	Tommy Bowden	12-0	to Clemson*	Chris Scelfo	Asst., Georgia
UNLV	Jeff Horton	0-11	fired	John Robinson	Fmr. Coach, USC
Washington	Jim Lambright	6-6	fired	Rick Neuheisel	Coach, Colorado

* as head coach
% as offensive coordinator
# Bowden resigned on Oct. 23, 1998 and was replaced by defensive coordinator Bill Oliver (2-3) for the remainder of the season.
@ Tuberville left on Nov. 28 when the team was 6-5. Cutcliffe coached the team to a win in the Independence Bowl.

Division I-AA Football

	Old Coach	Record	Why Left?	New Coach	Old Job
CS-Northridge	Ron Ponciano	7-4	fired	Jeff Kearin†	Asst., CS-Northridge
Connecticut	Skip Holtz	10-3	to South Carolina%	Randy Edsall	Def. coord., Georgia Tech
Fordham	Ken O'Keefe	4-7	to Iowa%	Dave Clawson	Off. coord., Villanova
Idaho St.	Tom Walsh	3-8	fired	Larry Lewis	Asst., Washington St.
Jackson St.	James Carson	7-4	reassigned	Robert Hughes†	Asst., Jackson St.
James Madison	Alex Wood	3-8	to NFL Minnesota**	Mickey Matthews	Def. coord., Baylor
McNeese St.	Bobby Keasler	9-3	to Northeast Louisiana*	Kirby Bruchhaus	Def. coord., McNeese
Mississippi Valley	Larry Dorsey	1-10	fired	LaTraia Jones	Def. coord., Arkansas-Pine Bluff
Morgan St.	Stump Mitchell	1-10	to NFL Seattle**	Stanley Mitchell†	Asst., Morgan St.
New Hampshire	Bill Bowes	4-7	retired	Sean McDonnell	Off. coord., UNH
Nicholls St.	Darren Barbier	4-7	to Tulane**	Daryl Daye	Def. coord., Liberty
Norfolk St.	Darnell Moore	2-9	fired	Maurice Forte	Fmr. asst., NFL Detroit
St. Francis-PA	Kevin Doherty	0-10	to Connecticut**	David Jaumotte	Asst., Ashland-OH
St. Peter's	Mark Collins	0-10	fired	Rob Stern	Coach, Hudson Cath. HS (NJ)
Siena	Ed Zaloom	4-6	to WPI*	Chris Phelps	Off. coord., Hobart
SW Missouri St.	Del Miller	5-6	resigned	Randy Ball	Coach, Western Illinois
S.F. Austin St.	John Pearce	3-8	to UCLA**	Mike Santiago	Off. coord., McNeese St.
VMI	Ted Cain	1-10	fired@	Cal McCombs	Def. coord., Air Force
Western Illinois	Randy Ball	11-3	to SW Missouri St.*	Don Patterson	Off. coord., Iowa

* as head coach
** as an assistant coach
% as offensive coordinator
† on an interim basis
@ Cain was fired on Nov. 9 when the team was 1-9. Athletic Director Donny White coached the final game of the season.

1998-99 Directors' Cup

Officially, it is the Sears Directors' Cup and sponsored by the National Association of Collegiate Directors of Athletics. Introduced in 1993-94 to honor the nation's best overall NCAA Division I athletic department (combining men's and women's sports), winners in NCAA Division II and III and NAIA were named for the first time following the 1995-96 season.

Standings computed by NACDA with points awarded for each Div. I school's finish in 20 sports (top 10 scoring sports for both men and women). Div. II schools are awarded points in 14 sports (top 7 scoring sports for both men and women). Div III schools are awarded points in 18 sports (top 9 scoring sports for both men and women). NAIA schools are awarded points in 12 sports (top 6 scoring sports for both men and women). National champions in each sport earn 100 points, while 2nd through 64th-place finishers earn decreasing points depending on the size of the tournament field. Division I-A football points based on final *USA Today*/ESPN Coaches' Top 25 poll. Listed below are team conferences (for Div. I only), combined Final Four finishes (1st through 4th place) for men's and women's programs, overall points in **bold** type, and the previous year's ranking (for Div. I only).

Multiple Winners: Stanford (5); Simon Fraser, BC and Williams, MA (3); UC-Davis (2)

Division I

		Conf	1-2-3-4	Pts	97-98 Rank			Conf	1-2-3-4	Pts	97-98 Rank
1	Stanford	Pac-10	1-7-3-0	**970**	1		Nebraska	Big 12	0-0-2-0	**420**	9
2	Georgia	SEC	4-1-1-1	**720**	7	15	Ohio St.	Big Ten	0-2-1-0	**410**	23
3	Penn St.	Big Ten	1-1-2-2	**600**	15	16	LSU	SEC	0-1-1-0	**390**	10
4	Florida	SEC	1-1-1-1	**580**	2	17	Arkansas	SEC	3-0-0-0	**370**	14
5	UCLA	Pac-10	1-2-0-0	**570**	4		N. Carolina	ACC	0-1-0-0	**370**	2
6	Michigan	Big Ten	1-1-0-1	**520**	5		Tennessee	SEC	1-0-0-0	**370**	19
7	Duke	ACC	1-2-2-0	**510**	NR	20	Auburn	SEC	1-0-0-1	**340**	25
8	Virginia	ACC	1-2-1-0	**490**	13	21	Minnesota	Big Ten	0-1-0-0	**330**	17
9	Arizona	Pac-10	0-0-0-3	**470**	6		Washington	Pac-10	0-1-1-1	**330**	8
	USC	Pac-10	1-0-1-0	**470**	10	23	California	Pac-10	0-0-2-1	**320**	19
11	Texas	Big 12	2-0-1-0	**440**	15	24	Maryland	ACC	1-0-1-0	**310**	19
12	Arizona St.	Pac-10	0-1-0-1	**420**	12	25	Notre Dame	Big East	0-1-0-0	**300**	NR
	BYU	WAC	1-1-0-0	**420**	18		Wisconsin	Big Ten	0-0-0-0	**300**	NR

Division II

		1-2-3-4	Pts			1-2-3-4	Pts
1	Adams St., CO	2-0-2-0	**340**		Lynn, FL	1-0-0-1	**220**
2	Abilene Christian	4-0-0-0	**330**	17	West Florida	0-1-1-0	**210**
	UC-Davis	0-0-0-1	**330**	18	Hawaii Pacific	1-0-0-0	**200**
4	Florida Southern	1-1-1-0	**320**	19	Edinboro, PA	0-0-0-1	**190**
	North Dakota St.	0-1-0-1	**320**	20	Nebraska-Kearney	0-1-0-0	**180**
6	North Dakota	1-1-0-1	**310**	21	Barry, FL	0-1-0-0	**170**
7	Western St., CO	0-2-0-0	**280**	22	Adelphi, NY	1-0-0-0	**160**
8	South Dakota	0-0-2-0	**260**		Armstrong Atlantic, GA	0-1-0-1	**160**
	Truman St., MO	0-0-2-0	**260**		CS-Chico	1-0-0-0	**160**
10	Ashland, OH	0-0-1-0	**250**		Carson-Newman, TN	0-1-0-0	**160**
11	Shippensburg, PA	0-0-1-0	**240**		Central Oklahoma	0-0-1-0	**160**
12	CS-Bakersfield	0-1-0-0	**230**		Metropolitan St., CO	0-1-0-0	**160**
	Drury, MO	2-0-0-0	**230**		NW Missouri St.	1-0-0-0	**160**
14	Bloomsburg, PA	1-0-0-0	**220**		Seattle Pacific	0-0-1-0	**160**
	Kennesaw St., GA	0-1-1-0	**220**		St. Augustine's, NC	0-4-0-0	**160**

Division III

		1-2-3-4	Pts			1-2-3-4	Pts
1	Williams, MA	1-1-3-0	**640**	16	St. Thomas, MN	0-0-0-0	**240**
2	Middlebury, VT	3-1-0-0	**560**	17	Ithaca, NY	0-0-1-0	**230**
3	College of New Jersey	0-2-2-0	**470**		Ohio Wesleyan	1-0-0-0	**230**
4	Amherst, MA	1-1-0-0	**430**		Wisconsin-Stevens Pt.	0-0-0-1	**230**
	Rowan, NJ	0-1-2-1	**430**	20	Mt. Union, OH	1-0-0-2	**220**
6	UC-San Diego	0-1-3-1	**360**		Pacific Lutheran, WA	0-1-1-0	**220**
7	Calvin, MI	1-1-0-1	**350**	22	Emory, GA	0-0-0-0	**210**
8	Cortland St., NY	0-0-0-0	**310**		Kenyon, OH	2-0-0-0	**210**
9	Trinity, TX	0-0-2-1	**300**		North Central, IL	1-0-0-0	**210**
10	Wisconsin-Eau Claire	0-0-1-2	**280**	25	Gustavus Adolphus, MN	0-0-0-0	**200**
	Wisconsin-La Crosse	0-1-1-1	**280**		Hobart/William Smith, NY	0-1-1-0	**200**
	Wisconsin-Oshkosh	0-1-1-0	**280**		Johns Hopkins, MD	0-0-1-0	**200**
13	Methodist, NC	2-0-0-0	**260**		Lincoln, PA	3-0-0-1	**200**
	Washington, MO	1-0-0-0	**260**		Wartburg, IA	1-0-0-0	**200**
15	Denison, OH	0-2-1-0	**250**				

NAIA

	1-2-3-4	Pts			1-2-3-4	Pts
1	Simon Fraser, BC............3-4-2-0	790	14	Lewis-Clark St., ID..............1-0-1-0	250
2	Azusa Pacific, CA............2-0-2-3	500		Nebraska Wesleyan..........0-0-1-0	250
3	Life, GA...................3-1-0-1	490		Puget Sound, WA.............1-1-0-0	250
4	Lindewood, MO...............0-3-1-0	440	17	Berry, GA 0-0-0-1	240
	Oklahoma City.............2-1-1-0	440	18	Malone, OH.................0-1-0-1	220
6	Mobile, AL 0-1-1-0	320		Olivet Nazarene, IL...........0-1-0-0	220
7	Findlay, OH 0-1-0-0	310	20	Spring Hill, AL 0-0-2-0	210
	Southern Nazarene, OK........1-0-1-0	310	21	Lindsey Wilson, KY 1-0-0-0	200
	Westmont, CA 0-0-1-0	310		Oklahoma Baptist..............0-0-0-0	200
10	Mary, ND...................0-1-0-1	290		Oklahoma Christian.............0-0-0-1	200
11	McKendree, IL 2-0-0-0	270		Pt. Loma Nazarene, CA 0-0-0-0	200
12	Auburn-Montgomery, AL........1-1-0-0	260		Texas Lutheran 0-1-0-0	200
	Cumberland, KY 0-0-1-1	260			

NCAA Division I Schools on Probation

As of Sept. 1, 1999, there were 19 Division I member institutions serving NCAA probations.

School	Sport	Yrs	Penalty To End	School	Sport	Yrs	Penalty To End
LSU...............	M Basketball	1	9/26/99	Texas Southern	M/W Track and XC	5	8/11/01
Michigan St........	Football	4	12/1/99		Football	5	8/11/01
Kansas St..........	W Basketball	3	5/31/00		Baseball	5	8/11/01
	& Football	2	5/31/00		M Tennis	5	8/11/01
Cal-Berkeley	M Basketball	3	6/1/00		& M Golf	5	8/11/01
Maine	M Ice Hockey	4	6/3/00	Purdue	M Basketball	2	4/9/01
	Baseball	4	6/3/00	Texas Tech.........	M & W Basketball	4	4/24/02
	Football	4	6/3/00		Football	4	4/24/02
	M/W Track and XC	4	6/3/00		Baseball	4	4/24/02
	W Soccer	4	6/3/00		Golf	4	4/24/02
	Field Hockey	4	6/3/00		M Track	4	4/24/02
	M Basketball	4	6/3/00		W Soccer	4	4/24/02
	& M Golf	4	6/3/00		W Volleyball	4	4/24/02
Texas-Pan American.	M Basketball	8	7/25/00		& M Tennis	4	4/24/02
Cincinnati	M Basketball	2	8/7/00	Texas-El Paso.......	M & W Basketball	5	5/1/02
Weber St.	M Basketball	4	8/7/00		Football	5	5/1/02
Wisconsin	No Specific Sport	2	11/13/00		& W Rifle	5	5/1/02
SE Missouri St.	M Basketball	3	1/31/01	Gonzaga..........	M Basketball	4	6/5/02
UCLA	Softball	3	4/30/01	CS-Fullerton........	M Basketball	4	11/14/02
	& M Basketball	3	4/30/01	Bucknell	M Wrestling	4	2/7/03
Louisville	M Basketball	5	8/9/01				
	& W Volleyball	5	8/9/01				

Remaining postseason and TV sanctions
1999-2000 postseason ban: Bucknell wrestling.
1999-2000 television ban: None.

NCAA Graduation Rates

The following table compares graduation rates of NCAA Division I student athletes with the entire student body in those schools. Years given denote the year in which students entered college. Rates are based on students who enrolled as freshmen, received an athletics scholarship and graduated in six years or less. All figures are percentages.
Source: NCAA Graduation-Rate Report, 1999.

	1987	1988	1989	1990	1991	1992
All Student Athletes	57	58	58	58	57	58
Entire Student Body	56	57	57	56	56	56
Male Student Athletes	53	53	53	53	51	52
Male Student Body	54	55	55	54	53	54
Female Student Athletes	67	69	67	68	67	68
Female Student Body	58	58	59	58	58	59
Div. I-A Football Players	55	56	56	52	50	51
Male Basketball Players	46	42	44	45	41	41
Female Basketball Players	62	65	65	67	66	62

1998-99 NCAA Team Champions

Ten schools won two or more national championships during the 1998-99 academic year, led by Division I Georgia and Division II Abilene Christian with four each.

Multiple winners: Four— ABILENE CHRISTIAN (Div. II men's indoor track, women's indoor track, men's outdoor track and women's outdoor track); GEORGIA (Div. I men's golf, men's tennis, women's swimming and National Division of women's gymnastics). **Three**— ARKANSAS (Div. I men's cross country, men's indoor track and men's outdoor track); LINCOLN, PA (Div. III men's indoor track, men's outdoor track and women's outdoor track); MIDDLEBURY, VT (Div. III men's ice hockey, women's field hockey and women's lacrosse). **Two**— ADAMS ST., CO (Div. II men's cross country and women's cross country); DRURY, MO (Div. II men's swimming & diving and women's swimming & diving); KENYON, OH (Div. III men's swimming & diving and women's swimming & diving); METHODIST, NC (Div. III men's golf and Div. II/III women's golf); TEXAS (Div. I women's indoor track and women's outdoor track).

Overall titles in parentheses; (*) indicates defending champions.

FALL
Cross Country
Men

Div.	Winner		Runner-Up	Score
I	Arkansas	(9)	Stanford*	97-114
II	Adams St., CO	(4)	Western St., CO	68-74
III	North Central, IL*	(11)	Calvin, MI	106-122

Women

Div.	Winner		Runner-Up	Score
I	Villanova	(7)	Brigham Young*	106-110
II	Adams St., CO*	(7)	Western St., CO	56-79
III	Calvin, MI	(1)	College of NJ	124-170

Field Hockey

Div.	Winner		Runner-Up	Score
I	Old Dominion	(8)	Princeton	3-2
II	Bloomsburg, PA*	(5)	Lock Haven, PA	4-3 (OT)
III	Middlebury, VT	(1)	William Smith*	3-2 (OT)

Football

Div.	Winner		Runner-Up	Score
I-A	Tennessee	(2)	Florida St.	AP poll
I-AA	Massachusetts	(1)	Georgia Southern	55-43
II	NW Missouri St.	(1)	Carson-Newman, TN	24-6
III	Mt. Union, OH*	(4)	Rowan, NJ	44-24

Note: There is no official Div. I-A playoff.

Soccer
Men

Div.	Winner		Runner-Up	Score
I	Indiana	(4)	Stanford	3-1
II	Southern Conn. St.	(5)	S. Car.-Spartanburg	1-0
III	Ohio Wesleyan	(1)	Greensboro, NC	2-1 (OT)

Women

Div.	Winner		Runner-Up	Score
I	Florida	(1)	North Carolina*	1-0
II	Lynn, FL	(1)	Sonoma St., CA	3-1
III	Macalester, MN	(1)	College of NJ	1-0 (4OT)

Volleyball
Women

Div.	Winner		Runner-Up	Score
I	Long Beach St.	(3)	Penn St.	5 games
II	Hawaii Pacific	(1)	North Dakota St.	4 games
III	Central, IA	(1)	UC-San Diego*	5 games

Water Polo
Men

Div.	Winner		Runner-Up	Score
National	USC	(1)	Stanford	9-8 (2OT)

WINTER
Basketball
Men

Div.	Winner		Runner-Up	Score
I	Connecticut	(1)	Duke	77-74
II	Kentucky Wesleyan	(7)	Metropolitan St., CO	75-60
III	Wisc.-Platteville	(4)	Hampden-Sydney, VA	76-75 (2OT)

Women

Div.	Winner		Runner-Up	Score
I	Purdue	(1)	Duke	62-45
II	North Dakota*	(3)	Arkansas Tech	80-63
III	Washington, MO*	(2)	St. Benedict, ME	74-65

Fencing

Div.	Winner		Runner-Up	Score
Combined	Penn St.*	(7)	Notre Dame	171-139

Gymnastics

Div.	Winner		Runner-Up	Margin
Men	Michigan	(3)	Ohio St.	by 1.700
Women	Georgia*	(5)	Michigan	by .300

Ice Hockey

Div.	Winner		Runner-Up	Score
I	Maine	(2)	New Hampshire	3-2 (OT)
II	St. Michael's, VT	(1)	New Hampshire Coll.	4-4, 8-5†
III	Middlebury, VT*	(5)	Wisc-Superior	5-0

†Div. II championship is decided by a two-game series.

Real Gender Equity

Schools whose men's and women's teams won NCAA championships in the same sport, or its equivalent during the 1998-99 season.

School	Div.	Sports	School	Div.	Sports
Abilene Christian	II	Men's Indoor Track	Kenyon, OH	III	Men's Swimming
		Women's Indoor Track			Women's Swimming
		Men's Outdoor Track	Lincoln, PA	III	Men's Outdoor Track
		Women's Outdoor Track			Women's Outdoor Track
Adams St., CO	II	Men's Cross Country	Methodist, SC	III	Men's Golf
		Women's Cross Country		II/III	Women's Golf
Drury, MO	II	Men's Swimming			
		Women's Swimming			

Rifle

Div.	Winner		Runner-Up	Score
Combined	AK-Fairbanks	(2)	Navy	6276-6168

Skiing

Div.	Winner		Runner-Up	Score
Combined	Colorado*	(15)	Denver	650-636

Swimming & Diving
Men

Div.	Winner		Runner-Up	Score
I	Auburn	(2)	Stanford*	467½-414½
II	Drury, MO	(1)	CS-Bakersfield*	829-557
III	Kenyon, OH	(20)	Denison, OH	670-383½

Women

Div.	Winner		Runner-Up	Score
I	Georgia	(1)	Stanford*	504½-441
II	Drury, MO*	(3)	North Dakota	613-603½
III	Kenyon, OH*	(16)	Denison, OH	664½-503

Indoor Track
Men

Div.	Winner		Runner-Up	Score
I	Arkansas*	(15)	Stanford	65-42½
II	Abilene Christian*	(7)	St. Augustine's	85-50
III	Lincoln, PA*	(5)	Wisc.-Oshkosh	60-37

Women

Div.	Winner		Runner-Up	Score
I	Texas*	(5)	LSU	61-57
II	Abilene Christian*	(11)	St. Augustine's	119-44
III	Wheaton, MA*	(1)	Wisc.-La Crosse	43-38

Wrestling

Div.	Winner		Runner-Up	Score
I	Iowa*	(19)	Minnesota	100½-98½
II	Pitt.-Johnstown	(2)	Neb.-Omaha	110-105½
III	Wartburg, IA	(2)	Augsburg, MN*	117½-116

SPRING
Baseball

Div.	Winner		Runner-Up	Score
I	Miami-FL	(3)	Florida St.	6-5
II	CS-Chico	(2)	Kennesaw St., GA	11-5
III	NC Wesleyan	(2)	St. Thomas, MN	1-0

Golf
Men

Div.	Winner		Runner-Up	Score
I	Georgia	(1)	Oklahoma St.	1180-1183
II	Florida Southern*	(10)	SC-Aiken	1125-1157
III	Methodist, NC*	(9)	UC-San Diego	1190-1217

Women

Div.	Winner		Runner-Up	Score
I	Duke	(1)	Arizona St.* & Georgia (tie)	895-903†
II and III	Methodist, NC*	(3)	Fla. Southern	1282-1285

†rain-shortened

Lacrosse
Men

Div.	Winner		Runner-Up	Score
I	Virginia	(2)	Syracuse	12-10
II	Adelphi, NY*	(6)	C.W. Post	11-8
III	Salisbury St., MD	(3)	Middlebury, VT	13-6

Women

Div.	Winner		Runner-Up	Score
National	Maryland*	(7)	Virginia	16-6
III	Middlebury, VT	(2)	Amherst, MA	10-9

Rowing
Women

Div.	Winner		Runner-Up	Score
National	Brown	(1)	Virginia	56-56†

†Both teams finished with the same amount of points, but Brown was awarded the title thanks to a higher finish in the Varsity Eight.

Note: The 1997 National Collegiate Women's Rowing Championships were the first to be sponsored by the NCAA. National championships had been held without NCAA sponsorship since 1979.

Softball

Div.	Winner		Runner-Up	Score
I	UCLA	(8)	Washington	3-2
II	Humboldt St., CA	(1)	Nebraska-Kearney	7-2
III	Simpson, IA	(2)	Chapman, CA	6-0

Tennis

Note that both Div. II tournaments were team-only.

Men

Div.	Winner		Runner-Up	Score
I	Georgia	(3)	UCLA	4-3
II	Lander, SC*	(7)	Barry, FL	5-1
III	Williams, MA	(1)	Kalamazoo, MI	4-1

Women

Div.	Winner		Runner-Up	Score
I	Stanford	(10)	Florida*	5-2
II	BYU-Hawaii	(1)	Armstrong Atlantic	5-1
III	Amherst, MA	(1)	Williams, MA	5-2

Outdoor Track
Men

Div.	Winner		Runner-Up	Score
I	Arkansas*	(9)	Stanford	59-52
II	Abilene Christian	(10)	St. Augustine's*	93-73
III	Lincoln, PA	(5)	Pacific Lutheran	62-47

Women

Div.	Winner		Runner-Up	Score
I	Texas*	(3)	UCLA	62-60
II	Abilene Christian*	(9)	St. Augustine's	145½-98
III	Lincoln, PA	(2)	Wheaton, MA	54-48

Volleyball
Men

Div.	Winner		Runner-Up	Score
National	BYU	(1)	Long Beach St.	3 games

Colorado
Adam Goucher
Cross-country

AK-Fairbanks
Kelly Mansfield
Rifle

Iowa St.
Cael Sanderson
Wrestling

Arizona
Ryk Neethling
Swimming

1998-99 Division I Individual Champions
Repeat champions in **bold** type.

FALL
Cross-country

Men (10,000 meters)	**Time**
1 Adam Goucher, Colorado	29:26.90
2 Abdi Abdirahman, Arizona	29:49.90
3 Julius Mwangi, Butler	30:00.00

Women (5,000 meters)	**Time**
1 Katie McGregor, Michigan	16:47.21
2 Amy Skieresz, Arizona	16:53.52
3 Amy Yoder, Arkansas	17:03.05

WINTER
Fencing
Men

Event		Score
Foil	Felix Reichling, Stanford	15-11
Epee	Alex Roytblat, St. John's	15-11
Sabre	Keeth Smart, St. John's	15-4

Women

Event		Score
Foil	Monique DeBruin, Stanford	15-7
Epee	Felicia Zimmerman, Stanford	8-7

Gymnastics
Men

Event		Points
All-Around	Jason Hardabura, Nebraska	58.050
Floor Exercise	Jason Hardabura, Nebraska	9.8000
Pommel Horse	Brandon Stefaniak, Penn St.	9.7750
Rings	Cortney Bramwell, BYU	9.9250
Vault	Guard Young, BYU	9.8125
High Bar	**Todd Bishop**, Oklahoma	9.9000
Parallel Bars	Justin Toman, Michigan	9.8375

Women

Event		Points
All-Around	Theresa Kulikowski, Utah	39.675
Vault	Heidi Moneymaker, UCLA	9.8625
Uneven Bars	Angie Leonard, Utah	9.9500
Balance Beam (tie)	Kiralee Hayashi, UCLA	9.9000
	Theresa Kulikowski, Utah	9.9000
	& Andreé Pickens, Alabama	9.9000
Floor Exercise	Marny Oestreng, Bowling Green	9.9250

Rifle
Combined
Smallbore

	Points
1 Kelly Mansfield, AK-Fairbanks	1185
2 Jonah Lindberg, AK-Fairbanks	1172
3 Mary Elsass, Kentucky	1170
Joacim Trybom, AK-Fairbanks	1170

Air Rifle

	Points
1 Kelly Mansfield, AK-Fairbanks	396
2 Emily Caruso, Norwich	395
3 Grant Mecozzi, AK-Fairbanks	394

Skiing
Men

Event		Time
Slalom	Jayme Smithers, Denver	1:33.32
Giant Slalom	**David Viele**, Dartmouth	2:11.63
10-k Freestyle	Rune Kollerud, Utah	27:19.6
20-k Classic	Ove Erik Tronvoll, Colorado	56:17.0

Women

Event		Time
Slalom	Linda Wikstrom, Colorado	1:45.08
Giant Slalom	Aimee-Noel Hartley, Colorado	2:22.91
5-k Freestyle	Ekaterina Ivanova, Vermont	15:17.9
15-k Classic	Britta Wienand, Denver	51:11.6

Wrestling

Wgt	Champion	Runner-Up
125	Stephen Abas, Fresno St.	Jeremy Hunter, Penn St.
133	**Eric Guerrero**, Okla. St.	Cody Sanderson, Iowa St.
141	Doug Schwab, Iowa	Michael Lightner, Okla.
149	T.J. Williams, Iowa	Tony Davis, N. Iowa
157	Casey Cunningham, C. Mich.	Clint Musser, Penn St.
165	Kirk White, Boise St.	Rodney Jones, Okla.
174	Glenn Pritzlaff, Penn St.	Otto Olson, Mich.
184	Cael Sanderson, Iowa St.	Brandon Eggum, Minn.
197	**Tim Hartung**, Minn.	Lee Fullhart, Iowa
Hvy	**Stephen Neal**, CS-Bakers.	Brock Lesnar, Minn.

Georgia	Washington St.	Texas	Arizona St.
Kristy Kowal	**Bernard Lagat**	**Suziann Reid**	**Grace Park**
Swimming	Track & Field	Track & Field	Golf

Swimming & Diving
(*) indicates meet record

Men

Event (yards)	Time
50 free..............Aaron Ciarla, Auburn	19.36
100 free.......Bart Kizierowski, California	42.70
200 free.........**Ryk Neethling**, Arizona	1:33.59
500 free.........**Ryk Neethling**, Arizona	4:13.80
1650 free.........**Ryk Neethling**, Arizona	14:35.57
100 back.......Michael Gilliam, Tennessee	47.12
200 back..........**Tate Blahnik**, Stanford	1:41.42
100 breast...Brendon Dedekind, Florida St.	53.16
200 breast.........Dave Denniston, Auburn	1:55.51
100 butterfly.........Dod Wales, Stanford	45.89
200 butterfly.....Shamek Pietucha, Virginia	1:43.50
200 IM.............Lionel Moreau, Auburn	1:45.24
400 IM............Tim Siciliano, Michigan	3:43.54
200 free relay.....................Auburn	1:16.63†
400 free relay.....................Auburn	2:50.90*
800 free relay.....................**Texas**	6:23.03
200 medley relay..................**Auburn**	1:26.12
400 medley relay..................Auburn	3:09.17

Diving	Points
1-meter.........**Rio Ramirez**, Miami-FL	643.10
3-meter................Troy Dumais, Texas	688.70
Platform..........**Rio Ramirez**, Miami-FL	901.60

†set meet record in prelims with 1:16.50.

Women

Event (yards)	Time
50 free..........**Catherine Fox**, Stanford	22.13
100 free......**Martina Moravcova**, SMU	48.05
200 free......**Martina Moravcova**, SMU	1:43.84
500 free..............Lindsay Benko, USC	4:40.22
1650 free..........Julie Varozza, Georgia	15:59.66
100 back......Marylyn Chiang, California	52.36*
200 back........Keegan Walkley, Georgia	1:53.63
100 breast.......**Kristy Kowal**, Georgia	59.25
200 breast.......**Kristy Kowal**, Georgia	2:07.66*
100 butterfly.....**Misty Hyman**, Stanford	51.77
200 butterfly............Limin Liu, Nevada	1:53.36*
200 IM......**Martina Moravcova**, SMU	1:55.64
400 IM.......Madeleine Crippen, Villanova	4:06.76
200 free relay......................SMU	1:28.94
400 free relay...................**Arizona**	3:16.49
800 free relay...................Stanford	7:06.22
200 medley relay..............**Stanford**	1:37.77*
400 medley relay..............**Stanford**	3:33.75

Diving	Points
1-meter...........Jenny Lingamfelter, SMU	444.40
3-meter.................Jenny Keim, Miami	576.90
Platform.............Laura Wilkinson, Texas	664.75

Indoor Track
(*) indicates meet record

Men

Event	Time
60 meters.........Leonard Scott, Tennessee	6.58
200 meters.............Coby Miller, Auburn	20.68
400 meters...........Ato Modibo, Clemson	46.11
800 meters.......Derrick Peterson, Missouri	1:45.88
Mile.........Bernard Lagat, Washington St.	3:55.65
3000 meters..Bernard Lagat, Washington St.	7:54.92
5000 meters.......**Brad Hauser**, Stanford	13:52.79
60-m hurdles...Terrence Trammell, S. Carolina	7.52
4x400-m relay.....................Clemson	3:07.80
Distance medley relay...............UCLA	9:33.17

Event	Hgt/Dist
High Jump.............Mark Boswell, Texas	7-7
Pole Vault..............Jacob Davis, Texas	19-2¼*
Long Jump..Maurice Wignall, George Mason	26-1½
Triple Jump.......Melvin Lister, Arkansas	55-0¾
Shot Put........**Brad Snyder**, S. Carolina	64-11½
35-lb Throw.....**Libor Charfreitag**, SMU	72-3½

Women

Event	Time
60 meters........Debbie Ferguson, Georgia	7.24
200 meters.........Peta-Gaye Dowdie, LSU	22.83*
400 meters.........**Suziann Reid**, Texas	51.68
800 meters..........**Hazel Clark**, Florida	2:01.77*
Mile...........Kate Vermeulen, W. Virginia	4:39.07
3000 meters.....Carrie Tollefson, Villanova	9:15.05
5000 meters.......Leigh Daniel, Texas Tech	16:01.11
60-m hurdles.............Joyce Bates, LSU	8.02*
4x400-m relay......................Texas	3:31.55*
Distance medley relay.........Georgetown	11:10.16

Event	Hgt/Dist
High Jump.............**Erin Aldrich**, Texas	6-3½
Pole Vault.....**Melissa Price**, Fresno St.	13-11¼
Long Jump........**Trecia Smith**, Pittsburgh	21-5¼
Triple Jump..Nicole Gamble, North Carolina	46-1¼
Shot Put..........Marika Tuliniemi, SMU	54-11¼
20-lb Throw..........Toyinda Smith, Purdue	68-9

Spring
Golf
Men

		Total
1	Luke Donald, Northwestern........73-68-72-71—284	
2	Ryuji Imada, Georgia............72-76-72-67—287	
	Troy Kelly, Washington..........75-71-70-71—287	

Women

		Total
1	Grace Park, Arizona St.	69-73-70—212
2	Candy Hannemann, Duke	71-72-70—213
3	Shauna Estes, Georgia	77-70-69—216

Note: The women's tournament was shortened to three rounds due to rain.

Tennis

Men

Singles— Jeff Morrison (Florida) def. James Blake (Harvard), 7-6 (2), 2-6, 6-4.

Doubles— Ryan Wolters & K.J. Hippensteel (Stanford) def. Nenad Toroman & Gareth Williams (Tulsa), 6-3, 6-2.

Women

Singles— Zuzana Lesenarova (San Diego) def. Marissa Irvin (Stanford), 4-6, 6-3, 7-6 (3).

Doubles— Amanda Augustus & **Amy Jensen** (California) def. Vanessa Castellano & Marissa Catlin (Georgia), 4-6, 7-5, 6-1.

Outdoor Track

(*) indicates meet record

Men

Event		Time
100 meters	**Leonard Myles-Mills**, BYU	9.98
200 meters	John Capel, Florida	19.87*
400 meters	Clement Chukwu, Eastern Mich.	44.79
800 meters	Derrick Peterson, Missouri	1:46.97
1500 meters	Clyde Colenso, SMU	3:47.54
5000 meters	Bernard Lagat, Washington St.	14:01.09
10,000 meters	Nathan Nutter, Stanford	29:11.96
110-m hurdles	Terrence Trammell, S. Carolina	13.45
400-m hurdles	Bayano Kamani, Baylor	48.68
3000-m steeple	**Matt Kerr**, Arkansas	8:44.29
4x100-m relay	South Carolina	38.92
4x400-m relay	UCLA	3:02.12

Event		Hgt/Dist
High Jump	Mark Boswell, Texas	7-7¾
Pole Vault	Jacob Davis, Texas	18-2¾
Long Jump	Melvin Lister, Arkansas	26-10
Triple Jump	LeVar Anderson, Stanford	56-2
Shot Put	Janus Robberts, SMU	65-11½
Discus	Gábor Máté, Auburn	202-1
Javelin	Matti Närhi, UTEP	261-7
Hammer	Andras Haklits, NE Louisiana	243-1
Decathlon	Tom Pappas, Tennessee	8184 pts

Women

Event		Time
100 meters	Angela Williams, USC	11.04
200 meters	LaTasha Williams, Ball St.	22.29
400 meters	**Suziann Reid**, Texas	51.08
800 meters	Claudine Williams, LSU	2:03.38
1500 meters	Mary Jayne Harrelson, App. St.	4:21.06
3000 meters	Carrie Tollefson, Villanova	9:26.51
5000 meters	Carrie Tollefson, Villanova	16:09.51
10,000 meters	Leigh Daniel, Texas Tech	34:01.63
100-m hurdles	Yolanda McCray, Miami-FL	12.85
400-m hurdles	Joanna Hayes, UCLA	55.16
4x100-m relay	**Texas**	42.95
4x400-m relay	**Texas**	3:27.08*

Event		Hgt/Dist
High Jump	Kajsa Bergqvist, SMU	6-2¾
Pole Vault	Paula Serrano, Cal Poly SLO	13-5¼*
Long Jump	Trecia Smith, Pittsburgh	21-8¼
Triple Jump	Stacey Bowers, Baylor	45-10
Shot Put	Seilala Sua, UCLA	57-9
Discus	**Seilala Sua**, UCLA	210-10*
Javelin	Vigdis Gudjonsdóttir, Georgia	182-3
Hammer	Florence Ezeh, SMU	207-2
Heptathlon	Tracye Lawyer, Stanford	5855 pts

Championship Most Outstanding Players
Men

Baseball	Marshall McDougall, Florida St.
Basketball	Richard Hamilton, Connecticut
Cross-country	Adam Goucher, Colorado*
Golf	Luke Donald, Northwestern*
Gymnastics	Jason Hardabura, Nebraska*
Ice Hockey	Alfie Michaud, Maine
Lacrosse	Conor Gill, Virginia
Soccer: Offense	Aleksey Korol, Indiana
Soccer: Defense	Nick Garcia, Indiana
Swimming & Diving	Ryk Neethling, Arizona
Tennis	Jeff Morrison, Florida*
Track: Indoor	Bernard Lagat, Washington St.*
Track: Outdoor	John Capel, Florida,* Janus Robberts, SMU,* & Terrence Trammell, S. Carolina*
Volleyball	Ossie Antonetti, BYU
Water Polo: Offense	Marko Pintaric, USC
Water Polo: Defense	Ivan Babic, USC & Chris Aguilera, Stanford
Wrestling	Cael Sanderson, Iowa St.

Women

Basketball	Ukari Figgs, Purdue
Cross-country	Katie McGregor, Michigan*
Golf	Grace Park, Arizona St.*
Gymnastics	Theresa Kulikowski, Utah*
Lacrosse	Jen Adams, Maryland
Soccer: Offense	Danielle Fotopolous, Florida
Soccer: Defense	Meredith Flaherty, Florida
Softball	Julie Adams, UCLA
Swimming & Diving	Kristy Kowal, Georgia
Tennis	Zuzana Lesenarova, San Diego*
Track: Indoor	Suziann Reid, Texas*
Track: Outdoor	Carrie Tollefson, Villanova* & Seilala Sua, UCLA*
Volleyball	Misty May, Long Beach St. & Lauren Cacciamani, Penn St.

(*) indicates won individual or all-around NCAA championship; There were no official Outstanding Players in field hockey or the men's and women's combined sports of fencing, riflery and skiing. Outstanding players in indoor and outdoor track are the individuals earning the most points in the NCAA Championships.

1998-99 NAIA Team Champions
Total NAIA titles in parentheses.

FALL

Cross Country: MEN'S–Life, GA (1); WOMEN'S–Simon Fraser, BC (5). **Football:** MEN'S– Azusa Pacific, CA (1). **Soccer:** MEN'S– Lindsey Wilson, KY (3); WOMEN'S–Azusa Pacific, CA (1). **Volleyball:** WOMEN'S– Columbia, MO (1).

WINTER

Basketball: MEN'S– Division I: Life, GA (2) and Division II: Cornerstone, MI (1); WOMEN'S– Division I: Oklahoma City (2) and Division II: Shawnee St., OH (1). **Swimming & Diving:** MEN'S– Simon Fraser, BC (3); WOMEN'S– Puget Sound, WA (5). **Indoor Track:** MEN'S– California Baptist (1); WOMEN'S– McKendree, IL (1). **Wrestling:** MEN'S– Montana St.-Northern (4).

SPRING

Baseball: MEN'S– Lewis-Clark, ID (10); **Golf:** MEN'S– Texas Wesleyan (6); WOMEN'S– Southern Nazarene, OK (1); **Softball:** WOMEN'S– Oklahoma City (2); **Tennis:** MEN'S– Oklahoma City (2); WOMEN'S– (tie) Auburn-Montgomery, AL (2) & Brenau (1); **Outdoor Track:** MEN'S– Life, GA (3); WOMEN'S– McKendree, IL (1).

Annual NCAA Division I Team Champions

Men's and women's NCAA Division I team champions from Cross-country to Wrestling. Rowing is included, although the NCAA does not sanction championships on the men's side. Also see team champions for baseball, basketball, football, golf, ice hockey, soccer and tennis in the appropriate chapters throughout the almanac. See pages 460-462 for list of 1998-99 individual champions.

CROSS-COUNTRY

Men

Arkansas cruised past two-time defending champion Stanford to capture its all-time leading ninth cross-country team title. Dehydration forced Arkansas' Michael Power to the sidelines but the team's depth managed to carry the Razorbacks to victory with 97 points. Stanford was runner-up with 114 points. Sean Kaley (fifth place, 30:12.1) was the first Razorback to finish the 10,000 meter course. Colorado's Adam Goucher won the individual crown, setting a course record with a time of 29:26.9. (*Lawrence, Kan.; Nov. 23, 1998.*)

Multiple winners: Arkansas (9); Michigan St. (8); UTEP (7); Oregon and Villanova (4); Drake, Indiana, Penn St. and Wisconsin (3); Iowa St., San Jose St., Stanford and Western Michigan (2).

Year		Year		Year		Year		Year	
1938	Indiana	1950	Penn St.	1963	San Jose St.	1976	UTEP	1989	Iowa St.
1939	Michigan St.	1951	Syracuse	1964	Western Mich.	1977	Oregon	1990	Arkansas
1940	Indiana	1952	Michigan St.	1965	Western Mich.	1978	UTEP	1991	Arkansas
1941	Rhode Island	1953	Kansas	1966	Villanova	1979	UTEP	1992	Arkansas
1942	Indiana	1954	Oklahoma St.	1967	Villanova	1980	UTEP	1993	Arkansas
	& Penn St.	1955	Michigan St.	1968	Villanova	1981	UTEP	1994	Iowa St.
1943	Not held	1956	Michigan St.	1969	UTEP	1982	Wisconsin	1995	Arkansas
1944	Drake	1957	Notre Dame	1970	Villanova	1983	Vacated	1996	Stanford
1945	Drake	1958	Michigan St.	1971	Oregon	1984	Arkansas	1997	Stanford
1946	Drake	1959	Michigan St.	1972	Tennessee	1985	Wisconsin	1998	Arkansas
1947	Penn St.	1960	Houston	1973	Oregon	1986	Arkansas		
1948	Michigan St.	1961	Oregon St.	1974	Oregon	1987	Arkansas		
1949	Michigan St.	1962	San Jose St.	1975	UTEP	1988	Wisconsin		

Women

Villanova grabbed four of the top 18 spots to win its seventh women's cross-country championship and reclaim its once-familiar spot at the top. Defending champ Brigham Young took the second spot with 110 points, four behind Villanova's 106 and one ahead of Stanford's 111. Michigan's Katie McGregor became the first Wolverine to win the individual championship, covering the 5,000-meter course in 16:47.21. (*Lawrence, Kan.; Nov. 23, 1998.*)

Multiple winners: Villanova (7); Oregon, Virginia and Wisconsin (2).

Year		Year		Year		Year		Year	
1981	Virginia	1985	Wisconsin	1989	Villanova	1993	Villanova	1997	Brigham Young
1982	Virginia	1986	Texas	1990	Villanova	1994	Villanova	1998	Villanova
1983	Oregon	1987	Oregon	1991	Villanova	1995	Providence		
1984	Wisconsin	1988	Kentucky	1992	Villanova	1996	Stanford		

FENCING

Men & Women

Penn State continued to dominate the college fencing world, becoming the first team in the history of the sport to win five consecutive team titles. The Nittany Lions amassed 171 points to finish ahead of perennial runner-up Notre Dame (139) and Stanford (136). Felicia Zimmermann of Stanford became the first woman ever to win an individual title in two different weapons. Last year she was the women's foil champion, while this year she captured the epee title. No Penn State competitor won an individual title, but two took seconds. (*Waltham, Mass.; Mar. 18-21, 1999.*)

Multiple winners: Penn St. (7); Columbia/Barnard (2). **Note:** Prior to 1990, men and women held separate championships. Men's multiple winners included: NYU (12); Columbia (11); Wayne St. (7); Navy, Notre Dame and Penn (3); Illinois (2). Women's multiple winners included: Wayne St. (3); Yale (2).

Year		Year		Year		Year		Year	
1990	Penn St.	1993	Columbia/	1994	Notre Dame	1996	Penn St.	1998	Penn St.
1991	Penn St.		Barnard	1995	Penn St.	1997	Penn St.	1999	Penn St.
1992	Columbia/								
	Barnard								

FIELD HOCKEY

Women

Old Dominion thwarted a second-half Princeton rally to win the Division I field hockey title with a 3-2 victory. It was the first title for the Lady Monarchs since 1992 and their eighth overall as they ran their season record to 23-2. Marina DiGiacomo netted two goals for Old Dominion and goaltender Jaime Hill made seven saves en route to the victory. Princeton's Alison Morris put the Tigers in striking distance with a goal with 10:41 remaining to close the gap to 3-2, but the ODU defense shut them down the rest of the way to secure the championship. (*Philadelphia, Penn.; Nov. 22, 1998.*)

Multiple winners: Old Dominion (8); North Carolina (4); Connecticut and Maryland (2).

Year		Year		Year		Year		Year	
1981	Connecticut	1985	Connecticut	1989	North Carolina	1993	Maryland	1997	North Carolina
1982	Old Dominion	1986	Iowa	1990	Old Dominion	1994	J. Madison	1998	Old Dominion
1983	Old Dominion	1987	Maryland	1991	Old Dominion	1995	North Carolina		
1984	Old Dominion	1988	Old Dominion	1992	Old Dominion	1996	North Carolina		

Annual NCAA Division I Team Champions (Cont.)

GYMNASTICS

Men

After suffering through a winless season just three years ago, Michigan came full circle, winning its first gymnastics national title since 1970. They recorded 232.55 points to beat out runner-up and Big Ten rival Ohio State. Host Nebraska's Jason Hardabura won the all-around title with 58.05 points, edging Michigan's Justin Toman (57.9). Toman won the parallel bar competition, placed third in the high bar and fifth in the pommel horse to pace the Wolverines. *(Lincoln, Neb.; Apr. 22-24, 1999.)*

Multiple winners: Illinois and Penn St. (9); Nebraska (8); California and So. Illinois (4); Iowa St., Michigan, Oklahoma and Stanford (3); Florida St., Ohio St. and UCLA (2).

Year	Year	Year	Year	Year
1938 Chicago	1955 Illinois	1967 So.Illinois	& Oklahoma	1990 Nebraska
1939 Illinois	1956 Illinois	1968 California	1978 Oklahoma	1991 Oklahoma
1940 Illinois	1957 Penn St.	1969 Iowa	1979 Nebraska	1992 Stanford
1941 Illinois	1958 Michigan St.	& Michigan (T)	1980 Nebraska	1993 Stanford
1942 Illinois	& Illinois	1970 Michigan &	1981 Nebraska	1994 Nebraska
1943-47 Not held	1959 Penn St.	Michigan (T)	1982 Nebraska	1995 Stanford
1948 Penn St.	1960 Penn St.	1971 Iowa St.	1983 Nebraska	1996 Ohio St.
1949 Temple	1961 Penn St.	1972 So. Illinois	1984 UCLA	1997 California
1950 Illinois	1962 USC	1973 Iowa St.	1985 Ohio St.	1998 California
1951 Florida St.	1963 Michigan	1974 Iowa St.	1986 Arizona St.	1999 Michigan
1952 Florida St.	1964 So. Illinois	1975 California	1987 UCLA	(T) indicates won
1953 Penn St.	1965 Penn St.	1976 Penn St.	1988 Nebraska	trampoline competi-
1954 Penn St.	1966 So.Illinois	1977 Indiana St.	1989 Illinois	tion (1969-70).

Women

Georgia defended its team title at the Division I women's gymnastics championships, becoming only the second school ever to repeat as champions. Georgia finished with an immaculate 32-0 record for the year and is 67-0 over the past two years. The Bulldogs narrowly outscored runner-up Michigan, 196.850-196.550 while Alabama placed third. Utah's Theresa Kulikowski won the all-around individual championship, edging Georgia's Karin Lichey. Aside from placing second in the individual competition, Lichey paced her squad with three first-place finishes in the team finals. *(Salt Lake City, Utah; Apr. 22-24, 1999.)*

Multiple winners: Utah (9); Georgia (5); Alabama (3).

Year	Year	Year	Year	Year
1982 Utah	1986 Utah	1990 Utah	1994 Utah	1998 Georgia
1983 Utah	1987 Georgia	1991 Alabama	1995 Utah	1999 Georgia
1984 Utah	1988 Alabama	1992 Utah	1996 Alabama	
1985 Utah	1989 Georgia	1993 Georgia	1997 UCLA	

LACROSSE

Men

Virginia had been to the championship game four times since its victory in 1972 and came out on the short end in overtime each game. Not this year. The Cavaliers defeated Syracuse 12-10 for their second NCAA Division I men's lacrosse championship. Virginia pulled out to an 8-3 halftime lead and was up 10-4 in the fourth quarter when Syracuse made a charge, scoring five consecutive goals to cut the lead to 10-9. Cavalier freshman Conor Gill, the games Most Outstanding Player, then put the game on ice, scoring the insurance goal and assisting on another. *(College Park, Md.; May 29-31, 1999.)*

Multiple winners: Johns Hopkins (7); Syracuse (6); Princeton (5); North Carolina (4); Cornell (3); Maryland and Virginia (2).

Year	Year	Year	Year	Year
1971 Cornell	1977 Cornell	1983 Syracuse	1989 Syracuse	1995 Syracuse
1972 Virginia	1978 Johns Hopkins	1984 Johns Hopkins	1990 Syracuse	1996 Princeton
1973 Maryland	1979 Johns Hopkins	1985 Johns Hopkins	1991 North Carolina	1997 Princeton
1974 Johns Hopkins	1980 Johns Hopkins	1986 North Carolina	1992 Princeton	1998 Princeton
1975 Maryland	1981 North Carolina	1987 Johns Hopkins	1993 Syracuse	1999 Virginia
1976 Cornell	1982 North Carolina	1988 Syracuse	1994 Princeton	

Women

Maryland continued its unstoppable run through the women's college lacrosse world with a 16-6 victory over Virginia in the NCAA championship game. The win capped a perfect 21-0 season for the Terrapins and marked the team's record fifth consecutive title. Tournament MVP Jen Adams chipped in four goals to pace the offense, Kristin Sommar pumped in three and Quinn Carney scored two and assisted on five others. Goaltender Alex Kehoe stopped 18 Virginia shots en route to the win. *(Baltimore, Md.; May 14-16, 1999.)*

Multiple winners: Maryland (7); Penn St., Temple and Virginia (2).

Year	Year	Year	Year	Year
1982 Massachusetts	1986 Maryland	1990 Harvard	1994 Princeton	1998 Maryland
1983 Delaware	1987 Penn St.	1991 Virginia	1995 Maryland	1999 Maryland
1984 Temple	1988 Temple	1992 Maryland	1996 Maryland	
1985 New Hampshire	1989 Penn St.	1993 Virginia	1997 Maryland	

RIFLE
Men & Women

Alaska-Fairbanks dethroned four-time defending champion West Virginia to capture its second college rifle team championship. The Nanooks registered an NCAA record 6,276 points to finish ahead of the U.S. Naval Academy and West Virginia, respectively. Shooters Melissa Mulloy, Kelly Mansfield and Dan Jordan carried the Nanooks to the team high score in both the air rifle and smallbore competitions. Individually, Mansfield won both the air rifle and smallbore titles as well. (*Northfield, Vt.; Mar. 10-13, 1999.*)

Multiple winners: West Virginia (13); Tennessee Tech (3); Alaska-Fairbanks and Murray St. (2).

Year		Year		Year		Year		Year	
1980	Tenn. Tech	1984	West Virginia	1988	West Virginia	1992	West Virginia	1996	West Virginia
1981	Tenn. Tech	1985	Murray St.	1989	West Virginia	1993	West Virginia	1997	West Virginia
1982	Tenn. Tech	1986	West Virginia	1990	West Virginia	1994	AK-Fairbanks	1998	West Virginia
1983	West Virginia	1987	Murray St.	1991	West Virginia	1995	West Virginia	1999	AK-Fairbanks

ROWING
NCAA Championships
Women

Brown emerged victorious in the championship's final event, the I Varsity Eights, to win the NCAA Women's Rowing Championship, the school's first NCAA title of any kind. Virginia held a three point lead over Brown going into the race but the Bears (6:46.89) wouldn't be denied, pulling away in the final 500 meters to beat the Cavaliers (6:50.9) by four seconds. The two teams actually tied in overall points with 56, but the win in the I Varsity Eights was the tiebreaker that gave them the team title. Two-time defending champion Washington finished third with 42 points. (*Rancho Cordova, Calif.; May 28-30, 1999*).

Multiple winners: Washington (2).

Year	Overall winner	Varsity Eights	Year	Overall winner	Varsity Eights
1997	Washington	Washington	1999	Brown	Brown
1998	Washington	Washington			

Intercollegiate Rowing Association Regatta
VARSITY EIGHTS
Men

The 97th IRA championships regatta went to California, who tore through the 2,000-meter course in record fashion for their 11th overall win and first since 1976. Princeton, back in fifth place with 1,000 meters remaining, surged to second place and challenged California for the lead until the Golden Bears finally pulled away to win by a length (5:23.6 to 5:26.3). (*Cooper River, Camden, N.J.; May 30, 1999.*)

The IRA was formed in 1895 by several Northeastern colleges after Harvard and Yale quit the Rowing Association (established in 1871) to stage an annual race of their own. Since then the IRA Regatta has been contested over courses of varing lengths in Poughkeepsie, N.Y., Marietta, Ohio, Syracuse, N.Y. and Camden, N.J.

Distances: 4 miles (1895-97,1899-1916,1925-41); 3 miles (1898,1921-24,1947-49,1952-63,1965-67); 2 miles (1920,1950-51); 2000 meters (1964, since 1968).

Multiple winners: Cornell (24); Navy (13); California and Washington (11); Penn (9); Brown and Wisconsin (7); Syracuse (6); Columbia (4); Princeton (3); Northeastern (2).

Year		Year		Year		Year		Year	
1895	Columbia	1915	Cornell	1937	Washington	1961	California	1981	Cornell
1896	Cornell	1916	Syracuse	1938	Navy	1962	Cornell	1982	Cornell
1897	Cornell	1917-19	Not held	1939	California	1963	Cornell	1983	Brown
1898	Penn					1964	California	1984	Navy
1899	Penn	1920	Syracuse	1940	Washington	1965	Navy	1985	Princeton
		1921	Navy	1941	Washington	1966	Wisconsin	1986	Brown
1900	Penn	1922	Navy	1942-46	Not held	1967	Penn	1987	Brown
1901	Cornell	1923	Washington	1947	Navy	1968	Penn	1988	Northeastern
1902	Cornell	1924	Washington	1948	Washington	1969	Penn	1989	Penn
1903	Cornell	1925	Navy	1949	California				
1904	Syracuse	1926	Washington			1970	Washington	1990	Wisconsin
1905	Cornell	1927	Columbia	1950	Washington	1971	Cornell	1991	Northeastern
1906	Cornell	1928	California	1951	Wisconsin	1972	Penn	1992	Dartmouth,
1907	Cornell	1929	Columbia	1952	Navy	1973	Wisconsin		Navy & Penn†
1908	Syracuse			1953	Navy	1974	Wisconsin	1993	Brown
1909	Cornell	1930	Cornell	1954	Navy*	1975	Wisconsin	1994	Brown
		1931	Navy	1955	Cornell	1976	California	1995	Brown
1910	Cornell	1932	California	1956	Cornell	1977	Cornell	1996	Princeton
1911	Cornell	1933	Not held	1957	Cornell	1978	Syracuse	1997	Washington
1912	Cornell	1934	California	1958	Cornell	1979	Brown	1998	Princeton
1913	Syracuse	1935	California	1959	Wisconsin			1999	California
1914	Columbia	1936	Washington			1980	Navy		
				1960	California				

*In 1954, Navy was disqualified because of an ineligible coxwain; no trophies were given.
†First dead heat in history of IRA Regatta.

Annual NCAA Division I Team Champions (Cont.)

The Harvard-Yale Regatta

Harvard had won 13 of the past 14 meetings but Yale proved to be the better crew this time as they defeated Harvard in the 134th running of the Harvard/Yale Regatta. Yale completed the four-mile course on the Thames River in New London, Conn. in 20:45.94, just ahead of the Crimson, who recorded a time of 20:51.98. Amidst heavy winds and choppy water, the Elis came from behind to pull ahead of Harvard after the three-mile mark. The Harvard/Yale Regatta is the nation's oldest intercollegiate sporting event. Harvard holds an 81-53 series edge.

National Rowing Championship
VARSITY EIGHTS
Men

National championship raced annually from 1982-96 in Bantam, Ohio over a 2,000-meter course on Lake Harsha. Winner received the Herschede Cup. Regatta discontinued in 1997.

Multiple winners: Harvard (6); Brown (3); Wisconsin (2).

Year	Champion	Time	Runner-up	Time	Year	Champion	Time	Runner-up	Time
1982	Yale	5:50.8	Cornell	5:54.15	1990	Wisconsin	5:52.5	Harvard	5:56.84
1983	Harvard	5:59.6	Washington	6:00.0	1991	Penn	5:58.21	Northeastern	5:58.48
1984	Washington	5:51.1	Yale	5:55.6	1992	Harvard	5:33.97	Dartmouth	5:34.28
1985	Harvard	5:44.4	Princeton	5:44.87	1993	Brown	5:54.15	Penn	5:56.98
1986	Wisconsin	5:57.8	Brown	5:59.9	1994	Brown	5:24.52	Harvard	5:25.83
1987	Harvard	5:35.17	Brown	5:35.63	1995	Brown	5:23.40	Princeton	5:25.83
1988	Harvard	5:35.98	Northeastern	5:37.07	1996	Princeton	5:57.47	Penn	6:03.28
1989	Harvard	5:36.6	Washington	5:38.93	1997	discontinued			

Women

National championship held over various distances at 10 different venues from 1979-96. Distances— 1000 meters (1979-81); 1500 meters (1982-83); 1000 meters (1984); 1750 meters (1985); 2000 meters (1986-88, since 1991); 1852 meters (1989-90). Winner received the Ferguson Bowl. Regatta discontinued in 1997.

Multiple winners: Washington (7); Princeton (4); Boston University (2).

Year	Champion	Time	Runner-up	Time	Year	Champion	Time	Runner-up	Time
1979	Yale	3:06	California	3:08.6	1988	Washington	6:41.0	Yale	6:42.37
1980	California	3:05.4	Oregon St.	3:05.8	1989	Cornell	5:34.9	Wisconsin	5:37.5
1981	Washington	3:20.6	Yale	3:22.9	1990	Boston Univ.	7:03.2	Cornell	7:06.21
1982	Washington	4:56.4	Wisconsin	4:59.83	1991	Boston Univ.	6:28.79	Cornell	6:32.79
1983	Washington	4:57.5	Dartmouth	5:03.02	1992	Princeton	6:40.75	Washington	6:43.86
1984	Washington	3:29.48	Radcliffe	3:31.08	1993	Princeton	6:11.38	Yale	6:14.46
1985	Washington	5:28.4	Wisconsin	5:32.0	1994	Princeton	6:11.98	Washington	6:12.69
1986	Wisconsin	6:53.28	Radcliffe	6:53.34	1995	Brown	6:45.7	Princeton	6:49.3
1987	Washington	6:33.8	Yale	6:37.4	1996	discontinued			
					1997				

SKIING

Men & Women

Colorado successfully defended its title by winning its second consecutive and 15th overall NCAA skiing championship. The Buffaloes accumulated 650 points to outscore second-place Denver (636) and third-place Vermont (600). Colorado senior Ove Erik Tronvoll won the men's 20-kilometer classic race by an amazing 96 seconds, Linda Wikstrom won the women's slalom and Aimee-Noel Hartley took the women's giant slalom to pace the Buffaloes. It was Colorado's fourth team title in the last nine seasons. (Bethel, Me.; Mar. 10-13, 1999.)

Multiple winners: Colorado (15); Denver (14); Utah (9); Vermont (5); Dartmouth and Wyoming (2).

Year		Year		Year		Year		Year	
1954	Denver	1964	Denver	1974	Colorado	1983	Utah	1993	Utah
1955	Denver	1965	Denver	1975	Colorado	1984	Utah	1994	Vermont
1956	Denver	1966	Denver	1976	Colorado	1985	Wyoming	1995	Colorado
1957	Denver	1967	Denver		& Dartmouth	1986	Utah	1996	Utah
1958	Dartmouth	1968	Wyoming	1977	Colorado	1987	Utah	1997	Utah
1959	Colorado	1969	Denver	1978	Colorado	1988	Utah	1998	Colorado
1960	Colorado	1970	Denver	1979	Colorado	1989	Vermont	1999	Colorado
1961	Denver	1971	Denver	1980	Vermont	1990	Vermont		
1962	Denver	1972	Colorado	1981	Utah	1991	Colorado		
1963	Denver	1973	Colorado	1982	Colorado	1992	Vermont		

SOFTBALL

Women

UCLA pitcher Courtney Dale recorded the win and blasted a second-inning home run to lead the Bruins to a 3-2 victory over Washington in the Division I Women's Softball Championship. It was the Bruins' eighth softball title and first since 1992. The Bruins jumped out to an early first-inning lead on a two-run single by tournament MVP Julie Adams, who was playing with a hurt shoulder. Washington threatened in the seventh, pulling to within one, but their rally fell short. Dale finished the season at 33-1 while Washington's Jennifer Spediacci took the loss to fall to 24-9. (*Oklahoma City, Okla.; May 27-31, 1999.*)

Multiple winners: UCLA (8); Arizona (5); Texas A&M (2).

Year		Year		Year		Year		Year	
1982	UCLA	1986	CS-Fullerton	1990	UCLA	1994	Arizona	1998	Fresno St.
1983	Texas A&M	1987	Texas A&M	1991	Colorado	1995	UCLA*	1999	UCLA
1984	UCLA	1988	UCLA	1992	UCLA	1996	Arizona		
1985	UCLA	1989	UCLA	1993	Arizona	1997	Arizona		

*Title was later vacated due to action by the NCAA Committee on Infractions.

SWIMMING & DIVING

Men

Auburn won a total of seven events (four relays and three individual) to cruise to its second NCAA Division I swimming title in the last three years. The Tigers amassed 467½ points overall to easily outdistance defending champ Stanford (414½) and in impressive fashion. Auburn broke the NCAA and U.S. open records in both the 200 and 400 freestyle relays. They won the 200 and 400 medley relays and also got wins from Dave Denniston in the 200 breaststroke, Aaron Ciarla in the 50 freestyle and Lionel Moreau in the 200 individual medley.

For the third consecutive year, Arizona's Ryk Neethling won the 1,650 freestyle and he also defended his title in the 200 and 500 freestyles. He now has six NCAA titles on his resume in his first three years at Arizona. Miami junior Rio Ramirez won the 1-meter diving championship for the third consecutive year and added a title in the platform diving competition. (*Indianapolis, Ind.; Mar. 25-27, 1999.*)

Multiple winners: Michigan and Ohio St. (11); USC (9); Stanford (8); Indiana and Texas (6); Yale (4); Auburn, California and Florida (2).

1937 Michigan	1950 Ohio St.	1963 USC	1976 USC	1989 Texas
1938 Michigan	1951 Yale	1964 USC	1977 USC	1990 Texas
1939 Michigan	1952 Ohio St.	1965 USC	1978 Tennessee	1991 Texas
1940 Michigan	1953 Yale	1966 USC	1979 California	1992 Stanford
1941 Michigan	1954 Ohio St.	1967 Stanford	1980 California	1993 Stanford
1942 Yale	1955 Ohio St.	1968 Indiana	1981 Texas	1994 Stanford
1943 Ohio St.	1956 Ohio St.	1969 Indiana	1982 UCLA	1995 Michigan
1944 Yale	1957 Michigan	1970 Indiana	1983 Florida	1996 Texas
1945 Ohio St.	1958 Michigan	1971 Indiana	1984 Florida	1997 Auburn
1946 Ohio St.	1959 Michigan	1972 Indiana	1985 Stanford	1998 Stanford
1947 Ohio St.	1960 USC	1973 Indiana	1986 Stanford	1999 Auburn
1948 Michigan	1961 Michigan	1974 USC	1987 Stanford	
1949 Ohio St.	1962 Ohio St.	1975 USC	1988 Texas	

Women

Georgia junior Kristy Kowal won the 100 and 200-yard breaststrokes to lead her team to its first ever NCAA Division I swimming title. The Bulldogs scored 504½ points, ahead of last year's champion Stanford (441) and SMU (370½). Julie Varozza and Keegan Walkley gave Georgia its other victories, taking the 1,650-yard freestyle and 200-yard backstroke, respectively.

SMU's Martina Moravcova ended her illustrious college career as she began it, in dominating fashion. She captured three individual titles (100 and 200-yard freestyles and the 200-yard individual medley) which ran her all-time NCAA Championships total to ten. She was also a part of SMU's winning 200-yard freestyle relay team. Stanford's Catherine Fox repeated as 50-yard freestyle champ and teammate Misty Hyman successfully defended her 100-yard butterfly title. (*Athens, Ga.; Mar. 18-20, 1999.*)

Multiple winners: Stanford (8); Texas (7).

Year		Year		Year		Year		Year	
1982	Florida	1986	Texas	1990	Texas	1994	Stanford	1998	Stanford
1983	Stanford	1987	Texas	1991	Texas	1995	Stanford	1999	Georgia
1984	Texas	1988	Texas	1992	Stanford	1996	Stanford		
1985	Texas	1989	Stanford	1993	Stanford	1997	USC		

Annual NCAA Division I Team Champions (Cont.)

INDOOR TRACK

Men

Unsurprisingly, Arkansas emerged victorious once again at the NCAA Division I Indoor Track and Field Championships. It was the Razorbacks' 15th win over the last 16 years. They scored 65 points to beat Stanford (42½) and third-place Clemson (28). Melvin Lister kept up a long tradition of Arkansas championship triple jumpers, recording his team's only individual title with a jump of 55-0¾. Kenyan long-distance star Bernard Lagat of Washington State pulled off a double victory with a win in the mile (3:55.65) and the 3000-meters (7:54.92). Arkansas really took charge of the meet after the mile run, in which Seneca Lassiter and Ryan Travis finished third and sixth, respectively. Sean Kaley was another top scorer for Arkansas with a third place finish in both the 3000 and the 5000-meters. (*Indianapolis, Ind.; March 5-6, 1999.*)

Multiple winners: Arkansas (15); UTEP (7); Kansas and Villanova (3); USC (2).

Year		Year		Year		Year		Year	
1965	Missouri	1972	USC	1979	Villanova	1986	Arkansas	1993	Arkansas
1966	Kansas	1973	Manhattan	1980	UTEP	1987	Arkansas	1994	Arkansas
1967	USC	1974	UTEP	1981	UTEP	1988	Arkansas	1995	Arkansas
1968	Villanova	1975	UTEP	1982	UTEP	1989	Arkansas	1996	George Mason
1969	Kansas	1976	UTEP	1983	SMU	1990	Arkansas	1997	Arkansas
1970	Kansas	1977	Washington St.	1984	Arkansas	1991	Arkansas	1998	Arkansas
1971	Villanova	1978	UTEP	1985	Arkansas	1992	Arkansas	1999	Arkansas

Women

Texas won its fifth Division I women's track title and its second in a row with a tightly-fought victory over rival LSU. Both teams were knotted at 51 points apiece going into the 4x400-meter relay but Texas emerged victorious with a meet record 3:31.55. LSU finished third in the event. The Longhorns took the championship with 61 points, ahead of LSU (57) and SMU (25).

Star sprinter Suziann Reid led Texas with a win in the 400-meters, a third-place showing in the 200, and a 51.5 second anchor leg in the winning 4x400. Sophomore Erin Aldrich also gave the Longhorns ten points by defending her title in the high jump (6-3½). Joyce Bates (60-meter hurdles) and Peta Gaye-Dowdie each recorded individual wins for runners-up LSU. Villanova's Carrie Tollefson, the 1997 cross-country champion, capped a triumphant comeback from a tumor in her heel to win the 3000-meters in 9:15.05. (*Indianapolis, Ind.; March 5-6, 1999.*)

Multiple winners: LSU (8); Texas (5); Nebraska (2).

Year		Year		Year		Year		Year	
1983	Nebraska	1987	LSU	1991	LSU	1995	LSU	1999	Texas
1984	Nebraska	1988	Texas	1992	Florida	1996	LSU		
1985	Florida St.	1989	LSU	1993	LSU	1997	LSU		
1986	Texas	1990	Texas	1994	LSU	1998	Texas		

OUTDOOR TRACK

Men

Stanford held a 22-point lead heading into the final day but Arkansas roared back behind the running of senior Matt Kerr to win its eighth consecutive Division I Outdoor Track and Field Championship and ninth overall. Kerr defended his title in the 3000-meter steeplechase, winning in 8:44.29 to give the Razorbacks a much-needed ten points. Two-time defending 1500-meter champ Seneca Lassiter placed second this year (behind SMU's Clyde Colenso) and Kenny Evans took third in the high jump to pace Arkansas (59 points).

Stanford finished in second place, as they did last year, with 52 points and SMU followed closely with 49. Florida's John Capel tied a meet record by running a 19.87 in the 200-meters. He also took second place in the 100-meter race behind BYU's Leonard Myles-Mills who repeated as champion. (*Boise, Id.; June 2-5, 1999.*)

Multiple winners: USC (26); Arkansas (9); UCLA (8); UTEP (6); Illinois and Oregon (5); Kansas, LSU and Stanford (3); SMU and Tennessee (2).

Year		Year		Year		Year		Year	
1921	Illinois	1938	USC	1954	USC	1970	BYU, Kansas	1986	SMU
1922	California	1939	USC	1955	USC		& Oregon	1987	UCLA
1923	Michigan	1940	USC	1956	UCLA	1971	UCLA	1988	UCLA
1924	Not held	1941	USC	1957	Villanova	1972	UCLA	1989	LSU
1925	Stanford*	1942	USC	1958	USC	1973	UCLA		
1926	USC*	1943	USC	1959	Kansas	1974	Tennessee	1990	LSU
1927	Illinois*	1944	Illinois			1975	UTEP	1991	Tennessee
1928	Stanford	1945	Navy	1960	Kansas	1976	USC	1992	Arkansas
1929	Ohio St.	1946	Illinois	1961	USC	1977	Arizona St.	1993	Arkansas
1930	USC	1947	Illinois	1962	Oregon	1978	UCLA & UTEP	1994	Arkansas
1931	USC	1948	Minnesota	1963	USC	1979	UTEP	1995	Arkansas
1932	Indiana	1949	USC	1964	Oregon			1996	Arkansas
1933	LSU			1965	Oregon & USC	1980	UTEP	1997	Arkansas
1934	Stanford	1950	USC	1966	UCLA	1981	UTEP	1998	Arkansas
1935	USC	1951	USC	1967	USC	1982	UTEP	1999	Arkansas
1936	USC	1952	USC	1968	USC	1983	SMU		
1937	USC	1953	USC	1969	San Jose St.	1984	Oregon		
						1985	Arkansas		

(*) indicates unofficial championship.

AP/Wide World Photos

An ecstatic Long Beach State squad shows us all who's No. 1 in women's volleyball after its 3-2 championship finals victory over Penn State. The win completed a perfect 36-0 season.

Women

Texas won the meet's final race, the 1600-meter relay, in record fashion to boost them ahead of UCLA for their second consecutive Division I Women's Track and Field Championship. The Longhorns won with 62 points, just two ahead of UCLA (60) and four ahead of USC (58). Star Suziann Reid ran the anchor leg for a Texas squad that broke the 1600-meter relay collegiate record (3:27.08). As usual, Reid also won the individual 400-meter race for the third time in her career, becoming the first woman in history to do so.

UCLA's Seilala Sua won her third consecutive discus title and also added a victory in the shot put, becoming the first to record the double since 1990. USC freshman Angela Williams upset defending champ Debbie Ferguson of Georgia in the 100-m. Miami's Yolanda McCray captured a victory in the 100-m hurdles with a time of 12.85. (*Boise, Id.; June 2-5, 1999.*)

Multiple winners: LSU (11); Texas (3); UCLA (2).

Year	Year	Year	Year	Year
1982 UCLA	1986 Texas	1990 LSU	1994 LSU	1998 Texas
1983 UCLA	1987 LSU	1991 LSU	1995 LSU	1999 Texas
1984 Florida St.	1988 LSU	1992 LSU	1996 LSU	
1985 Oregon	1989 LSU	1993 LSU	1997 LSU	

VOLLEYBALL

Men

Brigham Young upended Long Beach State in three games, 15-9, 15-7, 15-10 to win its first NCAA volleyball title in its first championship appearance. The win makes the Cougars only the second championship team from outside of California (Penn St. was the other in 1994). They fought back from a 7-0 deficit in the third game before finally putting the 49ers away. Tournament Most Outstanding Player Ossie Antonetti led all players with 22 kills and also recorded a team-high 13 digs. Fellow all-tournament team selection Ryan Millar contributed 15 kills and Hector Lebron was solid as the team's playmaker, dishing out 59 assists. David McKenzie led Long Beach State with 19 kills and 15 digs. (*Los Angeles, Calif.; May 8, 1999.*)

Multiple winners: UCLA (17); Pepperdine and USC (4).

Year	Year	Year	Year	Year
1970 UCLA	1976 UCLA	1982 UCLA	1988 USC	1994 Penn St.
1971 UCLA	1977 USC	1983 UCLA	1989 UCLA	1995 UCLA
1972 UCLA	1978 Pepperdine	1984 UCLA	1990 USC	1996 UCLA
1973 San Diego St.	1979 UCLA	1985 Pepperdine	1991 Long Beach St.	1997 Stanford
1974 UCLA	1980 USC	1986 Pepperdine	1992 Pepperdine	1998 UCLA
1975 UCLA	1981 UCLA	1987 UCLA	1993 UCLA	1999 Brigham Young

Annual NCAA Division I Team Champions (Cont.)
Women

Long Beach State capped off a perfect 36-0 season with a tightly-contested championship win over Penn State to garner its third women's volleyball championship. Long Beach started strong, cruising to 15-3, 15-10 wins in the first two games, only to see Penn State claw even by taking the next two, 15-13, 16-14. The Nittany Lions took an early 7-2 lead in the deciding game but were outplayed the rest of the way by the 49ers, who ultimately went on to win 15-12.

Final Four co-MVP Misty May led the 49ers with nine kills, 11 digs, four blocks and 70 assists. Penn State ended its phenomenal season at 35-1 but settled for second place for the second consecutive year. The match was played in front of a record crowd of 13,194 at the University of Wisconsin. (*Madison, Wisc.; Dec. 19, 1998.*)

Multiple winners: Stanford (4); Hawaii, Long Beach St. and UCLA (3); Pacific (2).

Year	Year	Year	Year	Year
1981 USC	1985 Pacific	1989 Long Beach St.	1993 Long Beach St.	1997 Stanford
1982 Hawaii	1986 Pacific	1990 UCLA	1994 Stanford	1998 Long Beach St.
1983 Hawaii	1987 Hawaii	1991 UCLA	1995 Nebraska	
1984 UCLA	1988 Texas	1992 Stanford	1996 Stanford	

WATER POLO
Men

Senior driver Marco Pintaric scored a two-pointer in the second overtime to give USC a 9-8 win over Stanford and its first NCAA water polo championship. The Trojans trailed the Cardinal 8-7 when Pintaric unleashed his blast with 1:38 to give USC the lead for keeps. The Trojans had lost the past two championship games (to UCLA in 1996 and Pepperdine in 1997) but would not be denied this time. Pintaric was named most outstanding offensive player for the tournament, while Stanford's goalkeeper Chris Aguilera shared the defensive honor with USC's Ivan Babic. (*Newport Beach, Calif.; Dec. 6, 1998.*)

Multiple winners: California (11); Stanford (8); UCLA (5); UC-Irvine (3).

Year	Year	Year	Year	Year
1969 UCLA	1975 California	1981 Stanford	1987 California	1993 Stanford
1970 UC-Irvine	1976 Stanford	1982 UC-Irvine	1988 California	1994 Stanford
1971 UCLA	1977 California	1983 California	1989 UC-Irvine	1995 UCLA
1972 UCLA	1978 Stanford	1984 California	1990 California	1996 UCLA
1973 California	1979 UC-S. Barbara	1985 Stanford	1991 California	1997 Pepperdine
1974 California	1980 Stanford	1986 Stanford	1992 California	1998 USC

WRESTLING
Men

Wrestling juggernaut Iowa made it five titles in a row, eight of the last nine, and 19 of the last 25 by winning the 1999 NCAA Division I Wrestling Championship. The Hawkeyes finished with 100½ points, just two ahead of runner-up Minnesota who had previously broken Iowa's 25-year reign as Big Ten champion.

Iowa was led by Doug Schwab in the 141-pound class and T.J. Williams at 149. Each registered individual wins. Williams' win capped off a perfect 40-0 season. Iowa State's stellar freshman Cael Sanderson at the 184-pound class took home the tournament's Most Outstanding Wrestler award. He also finished the season undefeated (38-0). Cal State-Bakersfield heavyweight Stephen Neal took down Minnesota's Brock Lesnar, which allowed Iowa to claim the title. (*State College, Pa.; Mar. 18-20, 1999.*)

Multiple winners: Oklahoma St. (30); Iowa (19); Iowa St. (8); Oklahoma (7).

Year	Year	Year	Year	Year
1928 Okla. A&M*	1941 Okla. A&M	1957 Oklahoma	1971 Okla. St.	1985 Iowa
1929 Okla. A&M	1942 Okla. A&M	1958 Okla. St.	1972 Iowa St.	1986 Iowa
1930 Okla. A&M	1943-45 Not held	1959 Okla. St.	1973 Iowa St.	1987 Iowa St.
1931 Okla. A&M*	1946 Okla. A&M	1960 Oklahoma	1974 Oklahoma	1988 Arizona St.
1932 Indiana*	1947 Cornell Col.	1961 Okla. St.	1975 Iowa	1989 Okla. St.
1933 Okla. A&M*	1948 Okla. A&M	1962 Okla. St.	1976 Iowa	1990 Okla. St.
& Iowa St.*	1949 Okla. A&M	1963 Oklahoma	1977 Iowa St.	1991 Iowa
1934 Okla. A&M	1950 Northern Iowa	1964 Okla. St.	1978 Iowa	1992 Iowa
1935 Okla. A&M	1951 Oklahoma	1965 Iowa St.	1979 Iowa	1993 Iowa
1936 Oklahoma	1952 Oklahoma	1966 Okla. St.	1980 Iowa	1994 Okla. St.
1937 Okla. A&M	1953 Penn St.	1967 Michigan St.	1981 Iowa	1995 Iowa
1938 Okla. A&M	1954 Okla. A&M	1968 Okla. St.	1982 Iowa	1996 Iowa
1939 Okla. A&M	1955 Okla. A&M	1969 Iowa St.	1983 Iowa	1997 Iowa
1940 Okla. A&M	1956 Okla. A&M	1970 Iowa St.	1984 Iowa	1998 Iowa
				1999 Iowa

(*) indicates unofficial champions. Note: Oklahoma A&M became Oklahoma St. in 1958.

Halls of Fame & Awards

Finally, a bust former Giant linebacker Lawrence Taylor can enjoy.
Taylor was league MVP in 1986,
but has faced legal troubles since
his retirement.

AP/Wide World Photos

BASEBALL

National Baseball Hall of Fame & Museum

Established in 1935 by Major League Baseball to celebrate the game's 100th anniversary. **Address:** P.O. Box 590, Cooperstown, NY 13326. **Telephone:** (607) 547-7200.

Eligibility: Nominated players must have played at least part of 10 seasons in the major leagues and be retired for at least five but no more than 20 years. Voting done by Baseball Writers' Association of America. Certain nominated players not elected by the writers can become eligible via the Veterans' Committee 23 years after retirement. The Hall of Fame board of directors voted unanimously on Feb. 4, 1991, to exclude players on baseball's ineligible list from consideration. Pete Rose is the only living ex-player on that list.

Class of 1999 (7): BBWAA vote—pitcher **Nolan Ryan**, New York Mets (1966-71), California (1972-79), Houston (1980-88), Texas (1989-93); third baseman **George Brett**, Kansas City (1973-93); shortstop **Robin Yount**, Milwaukee (1974-93). VETERAN'S COMMITTEE vote—first baseman **Orlando Cepeda**, San Francisco (1958-66), St. Louis (1966-68), Atlanta (1969-72), Oakland (1972), Boston (1973), Kansas City (1974); umpire **Nestor Chylak**, (1954-78); manager **Frank Selee**, Boston-NL (1890-1901), Chicago-NL (1902-05), Negro Leagues pitcher **Joe Williams**, several clubs (1910-32).

1999 Top 10 vote-getters (473 BBWAA ballots cast, 355 needed to elect): 1. **Nolan Ryan** (491); 2. **George Brett** (488); 3. **Robin Yount** (385); 4. **Carlton Fisk** (330); 5. **Tony Perez** (302); 6. **Gary Carter** (168); 7. **Steve Garvey** (150); 8. **Jim Rice** (146), 9. **Bruce Sutter** (121), 10. **Jim Kaat** (100).

Elected first year on ballot (34): Hank Aaron, Ernie Banks, Johnny Bench, George Brett, Lou Brock, Rod Carew, Steve Carlton, Ty Cobb, Bob Feller, Bob Gibson, Reggie Jackson, Walter Johnson, Al Kaline, Sandy Koufax, Mickey Mantle, Christy Mathewson, Willie Mays, Willie McCovey, Joe Morgan, Stan Musial, Jim Palmer, Brooks Robinson, Frank Robinson, Jackie Robinson, Babe Ruth, Nolan Ryan, Mike Schmidt, Tom Seaver, Warren Spahn, Willie Stargell, Honus Wagner, Ted Williams, Carl Yastrzemski and Robin Yount.

Members are listed with years of induction; (+) indicates deceased members.

Catchers

Bench, Johnny 1989	+ Cochrane, Mickey..........1947	+ Hartnett, Gabby 1955
Berra, Yogi 1972	+ Dickey, Bill 1954	+ Lombardi, Ernie 1986
+ Bresnahan, Roger 1945	+ Ewing, Buck 1939	+ Schalk, Ray 1955
+ Campanella, Roy 1969	+ Ferrell, Rick 1984	

1st Basemen

+ Anson, Cap 1939	+ Connor, Roger 1976	McCovey, Willie 1986
+ Beckley, Jake 1971	+ Foxx, Jimmie...............1951	+ Mize, Johnny 1981
+ Bottomley, Jim.............1974	Gehrig, Lou 1939	+ Sisler, George 1939
+ Brouthers, Dan 1945	+ Greenberg, Hank 1956	+ Terry, Bill 1954
Cepeda, Orlando 1999	+ Kelly, George 1973	
+ Chance, Frank............1946	Killebrew, Harmon 1984	

2nd Basemen

Carew, Rod 1991	+ Frisch, Frankie 1947	+ Lazzeri, Tony 1991
+ Collins, Eddie..............1939	+ Gehringer, Charlie 1949	Morgan, Joe...............1990
Doerr, Bobby 1986	+ Herman, Billy 1975	+ Robinson, Jackie 1962
+ Evers, Johnny 1946	+ Hornsby, Rogers 1942	Schoendienst, Red..........1989
+ Fox, Nellie 1997	+ Lajoie, Nap 1937	

Shortstops

Aparicio, Luis..............1984	+ Jackson, Travis 1982	+ Vaughan, Arky 1985
+ Appling, Luke.............1964	+ Jennings, Hugh 1945	+ Wagner, Honus 1936
+ Bancroft, Dave............1971	+ Maranville, Rabbit..........1954	+ Wallace, Bobby 1953
Banks, Ernie 1977	+ Reese, Pee Wee 1984	+ Ward, Monte 1964
Boudreau, Lou 1970	Rizzuto, Phil 1994	Yount, Robin...............1999
+ Cronin, Joe................1956	+ Sewell, Joe 1977	
Davis, George 1998	+ Tinker, Joe 1946	

3rd Basemen

+ Baker, Frank...............1955	Kell, George................1983	Robinson, Brooks...........1983
Brett, George 1999	+ Lindstrom, Fred 1976	Schmidt, Mike 1995
+ Collins, Jimmy 1945	Mathews, Eddie............1978	+ Traynor, Pie 1948

Left Fielders

Brock, Lou..................1985	Kiner, Ralph 1975	+ Wheat, Zack 1959
+ Burkett, Jesse 1946	+ Manush, Heinie 1964	Williams, Billy 1987
+ Clarke, Fred 1945	+ Medwick, Joe 1968	Williams, Ted 1966
+ Delahanty, Ed.............1945	Musial, Stan................1969	Yastrzemski, Carl..........1989
+ Goslin, Goose 1968	+ O'Rourke, Jim.............1945	
+ Hafey, Chick 1971	+ Simmons, Al 1953	
+ Kelley, Joe................1971	Stargell, Willie 1988	

Center Fielders

+ Ashburn, Richie 1995	Doby, Larry 1998	Snider, Duke 1980
+ Averill, Earl. 1975	+ Duffy, Hugh 1945	+ Speaker, Tris 1937
+ Carey, Max 1961	+ Hamilton, Billy 1961	+ Waner, Lloyd 1967
+ Cobb, Ty 1936	+ Mantle, Mickey 1974	+ Wilson, Hack. 1979
+ Combs, Earle 1970	Mays, Willie 1979	
+ DiMaggio, Joe 1955	+ Roush, Edd 1962	

Right Fielders

Aaron, Hank 1982	Jackson, Reggie 1993	+ Rice, Sam 1963
+ Clemente, Roberto. 1973	Kaline, Al 1980	Robinson, Frank. 1982
+ Crawford, Sam 1957	+ Keeler, Willie 1939	+ Ruth, Babe 1936
+ Cuyler, Kiki 1968	+ Kelly, King 1945	Slaughter, Enos 1985
+ Flick, Elmer 1963	+ Klein, Chuck 1980	+ Thompson, Sam 1974
+ Heilmann, Harry 1952	+ McCarthy, Tommy 1946	+ Waner, Paul 1952
+ Hooper, Harry 1971	+ Ott, Mel 1951	+ Youngs, Ross 1972

Pitchers

+ Alexander, Grover 1938	+ Chesbro, Jack 1946	+ Faber, Red 1964
+ Bender, Chief. 1953	+ Clarkson, John 1963	Feller, Bob 1962
+ Brown, Mordecai 1949	+ Coveleski, Stan 1969	Fingers, Rollie 1992
Bunning, Jim. 1996	+ Dean, Dizzy 1953	Ford, Whitey 1974
Carlton, Steve 1994	+ Drysdale, Don 1984	+ Galvin, Pud 1965

Major League Baseball's All-Time Team—Then and Now

The Baseball Writers' Association of America originally selected an all-time team as part of major league baseball's 100th anniversary, announcing the outcome of its vote on July 21, 1969. Vote totals were not released. Recently, another vote was released when a panel of 36 BWAA members picked an all-time team for the Classic Sports Network just before the 1997 All-Star Game. This time vote totals were given, the single outfield category was divided into three (left, center and right) and two recently popularized positions—the designated hitter and relief pitcher—were added. In the most recent vote two points were awarded for first-place votes and one point for second place. Point totals follow the names with the number of first-place votes in parentheses. All-time team members are listed in **bold** type

1969 Vote

C	**Mickey Cochrane**, Bill Dickey, Roy Campanella	OF	**Babe Ruth**, **Ty Cobb**, **Joe DiMaggio**, Ted
1B	**Lou Gehrig**, George Sisler, Stan Musial		Williams, Tris Speaker, Willie Mays
2B	**Rogers Hornsby**, Charlie Gehringer, Eddie	RHP	**Walter Johnson**, Christy Mathewson, Cy Young
	Collins	LHP	**Lefty Grove**, Sandy Koufax, Carl Hubbell
SS	**Honus Wagner**, Joe Cronin, Ernie Banks	Mgr.	**John McGraw**, Casey Stengel, Joe McCarthy
3B	**Pie Traynor**, Brooks Robinson, Jackie Robinson		

1969 Vote All-Time Outstanding Player: **Ruth**, Cobb, Wagner, DiMaggio

1997 Vote

C   **Johnny Bench** (24) 52; Yogi Berra (4) 22; Roy Campanella (4) 17; Mickey Cochrane (1) 5; Bill Dickey (1) 4; Gabby Hartnett (1) 3; Carlton Fisk 2.

1B   **Lou Gehrig** (31) 66½; Jimmie Foxx (3) 19; George Sisler (2) 8; Willie McCovey 6; Hank Greenberg 2½; Stan Musial, Eddie Murray, Mark McGwire and Frank Thomas 1.

2B   **Rogers Hornsby** (17) 44; Joe Morgan (6) 23; Jackie Robinson (6) 15; Charley Gehringer (4) and Napolean Lajoie (3) 11; Eddie Collins (1) 3; Rod Carew 2; Ryne Sandberg 1.

SS   **Honus Wagner** (23) 55; Cal Ripken Jr. (6) 24; Ozzie Smith (5) 16; Ernie Banks (1) 8; Lou Boudreau and Luke Appling 1.

3B   **Mike Schmidt** (21) 50; Brooks Robinson (13) 37; Eddie Mathews 5; George Brett (1) 8; Pie Traynor 6; Pete Rose (1) 2; Frank Baker, Al Rosen and Wade Boggs 1.

LF   **Ted Williams** (32) 68; Stan Musial (4) 36; Pete Rose, Ralph Kiner, Rickey Henderson and Barry Bonds 1.

CF   **Willie Mays** (25) 57; Ty Cobb (7) 22; Joe DiMaggio (3) 17; Mickey Mantle (1) 10; Tris Speaker 2.

RF   **Babe Ruth** (31) 67; Hank Aaron (5) 36; Frank Robinson 2; Al Kaline, Roberto Clemente and Tony Gwynn 1.

DH   **Paul Molitor** (22) 48; Harold Baines (3) 12; Don Baylor (1) 10; Edgar Martinez (2) 9; Ty Cobb (2) 6; Hal McRae (1) 5; Mickey Mantle (1) and Dave Parker (1) 3; Joe DiMaggio (1) 2; Lee May, Frank Robinson and Tony Oliva 1.

RHP   **Walter Johnson** (9) 30, Cy Young (12) 25; Christy Mathewson (5) 18; Bob Feller (4) 10; Bob Gibson (2) 9; Nolan Ryan (2) 7; Tom Seaver (1) 3; Greg Maddux (1), Grover Cleveland Alexander and Juan Marichal 2.

LHP   **Sandy Koufax** (11) 32; Warren Spahn (11) 28; Lefty Grove (8) 25; Steve Carlton (4) 12; Carl Hubbell 6; Whitey Ford (1) 3; Eddie Plank (1) 2.

RP   **Dennis Eckersley** (16) 40; Rollie Fingers (9) 29; Lee Smith (4) 13; Hoyt Wilhelm (3) 10; Rich Gossage (3) 9; Bruce Sutter (1) 6, Dan Quisenberry 1.

Mgr.   **Casey Stengel** (6) 22; Joe McCarthy (6) 18; Connie Mack (7) 17; John McGraw (6) 14; Sparky Anderson (3) 11; Leo Durocher (2) 6; Dick Williams (1) 4; Billy Martin (1) 3; Al Lopez (1), Ned Hanlon (1), Whitey Herzog (1), Earl Weaver and Bobby Cox 2; Tony La Russa 1.

Baseball (Cont.)

Gibson, Bob...............1981	+ Lyons, Ted...............1955	Roberts, Robin...............1976
+ Gomez, Lefty..............1972	Marichal, Juan.............1983	+ Ruffing, Red................1967
+ Grimes, Burleigh...........1964	+ Marquard, Rube............1971	+ Rusie, Amos................1977
+ Grove, Lefty................1947	+ Mathewson, Christy........1936	Ryan, Nolan.................1999
+ Haines, Jess...............1970	+ McGinnity, Joe............1946	Seaver, Tom.................1992
+ Hoyt, Waite................1969	Niekro, Phil.................1997	Spahn, Warren..............1973
+ Hubbell, Carl..............1947	+ Newhouser, Hal............1992	Sutton, Don.................1998
+ Hunter, Catfish.............1987	+ Nichols, Kid...............1949	+ Vance, Dazzy...............1955
Jenkins, Ferguson...........1991	Palmer, Jim.................1990	+ Waddell, Rube..............1946
+ Johnson, Walter............1936	+ Pennock, Herb.............1948	+ Walsh, Ed..................1946
+ Joss, Addie................1978	Perry, Gaylord..............1991	+ Welch, Mickey..............1973
+ Keefe, Tim.................1964	+ Plank, Eddie...............1946	Wilhelm, Hoyt...............1985
Koufax, Sandy...............1972	+ Radbourne, Old Hoss.......1939	+ Willis, Vic.................1995
Lemon, Bob.................1976	+ Rixey, Eppa...............1963	+ Wynn, Early................1972
		+ Young, Cy..................1937

Managers

+ Alston, Walter.............1983	Lasorda, Tommy.............1997	+ McKechnie, Bill.............1962
+ Durocher, Leo..............1994	Lopez, Al...................1977	+ Robinson, Wilbert..........1945
+ Hanlon, Ned...............1996	+ Mack, Connie..............1937	+ Selee, Frank...............1999
+ Harris, Bucky..............1975	+ McCarthy, Joe.............1957	+ Stengel, Casey.............1966
+ Huggins, Miller............1964	+ McGraw, John.............1937	Weaver, Earl................1996

Umpires

+ Barlick, Al.................1989	+ Connolly, Tom.............1953	+ Klem, Bill..................1953
+ Chylak, Nestor.............1999	+ Evans, Billy...............1973	+ McGowan, Bill..............1992
+ Conlan, Jocko.............1974	+ Hubbard, Cal..............1976	

From Negro Leagues

+ Bell, Cool Papa (OF).......1974	+ Foster, Willie (P)..........1996	+ Paige, Satchel (P)..........1971
+ Charleston, Oscar (1B-OF)..1976	+ Gibson, Josh (C)...........1972	+ Rogan, Wilber (P)..........1998
+ Dandridge, Ray (3B).......1987	Irvin, Monte (OF)............1973	+ Wells, Willie (SS)..........1997
+ Day, Leon (P-OF-2B)......1995	+ Johnson, Judy (3B)........1975	+ Williams, Joe (P)..........1999
+ Dihigo, Martin (P-OF).....1977	+ Leonard, Buck (1B)........1972	
+ Foster, Rube (P-Mgr)......1981	+ Lloyd, Pop (SS)............1977	

Pioneers and Executives

+ Barrow, Ed.................1953	+ Giles, Warren..............1979	+ Rickey, Branch.............1967
+ Bulkeley, Morgan...........1937	+ Griffith, Clark.............1946	+ Spalding, Al................1939
+ Cartwright, Alexander.....1938	+ Harridge, Will.............1972	+ Veeck, Bill.................1991
+ Chadwick, Henry...........1938	+ Hulbert, William..........1995	+ Weiss, George.............1971
+ Chandler, Happy...........1982	+ Johnson, Ban..............1937	+ Wright, George............1937
+ Comiskey, Charles.........1939	+ Landis, Kenesaw..........1944	+ Wright, Harry.............1953
+ Cummings, Candy..........1939	+ MacPhail, Larry...........1978	+ Yawkey, Tom..............1980
+ Frick, Ford................1970	MacPhail, Lee..............1998	

Ford Frick Award

First presented in 1978 by the Hall of Fame for meritorious contributions by baseball broadcasters. Named in honor of the late newspaper reporter, broadcaster, National League president and commissioner, the Frick Award does not constitute induction into the Hall of Fame.

Year		Year		Year	
1978	Mel Allen & Red Barber	1985	Buck Canel	1992	Milo Hamilton
1979	Bob Elson	1986	Bob Prince	1993	Chuck Thompson
1980	Russ Hodges	1987	Jack Buck	1994	Bob Murphy
1981	Ernie Harwell	1988	Lindsey Nelson	1995	Bob Wolff
1982	Vin Scully	1989	Harry Caray	1996	Herb Carneal
1983	Jack Brickhouse	1990	Byrum Saam	1997	Jimmy Dudley
1984	Curt Gowdy	1991	Joe Garagiola	1998	Jaime Jarrin
				1999	Arch McDonald

J.G. Taylor Spink Award

First presented in 1962 by the Baseball Writers' Association of America for meritorious contributions by members of the BBWAA. Named in honor of the late publisher of *The Sporting News*, the Spink Award does not constitute induction into the Hall of Fame. Winners are honored in the year following their selection.

Year		Year		Year	
1962	J.G. Taylor Spink	1968	H.G. Salsinger	1973	Warren Brown, John Drebinger
1963	Ring Lardner	1969	Sid Mercer		& John F. Kieran
1964	Hugh Fullerton	1970	Heywood C. Broun	1974	John Carmichael
1965	Charley Dryden	1971	Frank Graham		& James Isaminger
1966	Grantland Rice	1972	Dan Daniel, Fred Lieb	1975	Tom Meany & Shirley Povich
1967	Damon Runyon		& J. Roy Stockton	1976	Harold Kaese & Red Smith

Year		Year		Year	
1977	Gordon Cobbledick & Edgar Munzel	1985	Earl Lawson	1993	John Wendell Smith
1978	Tim Murnane & Dick Young	1986	Jack Lang	1994	No award
1979	Bob Broeg & Tommy Holmes	1987	Jim Murray	1995	Joseph Durso
1980	Joe Reichler & Milt Richman	1988	Bob Hunter & Ray Kelly	1996	Charley Feeney
1981	Bob Addie & Allen Lewis	1989	Jerome Holtzman	1997	Sam Lacy
1982	Si Burick	1990	Phil Collier	1998	Bob Stevens
1983	Ken Smith	1991	Ritter Collett		
1984	Joe McGuff	1992	Leonard Koppett & Buzz Saidt		

BASKETBALL

Naismith Memorial Basketball Hall of Fame

Established in 1949 by the National Association of Basketball Coaches in memory of the sport's inventor, Dr. James Naismith. Original Hall opened in 1968 and current Hall in 1985. **Address:** 1150 West Columbus Avenue, Springfield, MA 01105. **Telephone:** (413) 781-6500.

Eligibility: Nominated players and referees must be retired for five years, coaches must have coached 25 years or be retired for five, and contributors must have already completed their noteworthy service to the game. Voting done by 24-member honors committee made up of media representatives, Hall of Fame members and trustees. Any nominee not elected after five years becomes eligible for consideration by the Veterans' Committee after a five-year wait.

Class of 1999 (5): PLAYERS—forward **Kevin McHale**, NBA (Boston 1980-92). COACHES—**John Thompson**, college (Georgetown, 1972-99); **Billie Moore**, women's college (Cal. State-Fullerton, 1969-76, UCLA, 1977-93). CONTRIBUTORS—executive **Wayne Embry**, Milwaukee (1968-1984), Indiana (1985), Cleveland (1986-99), **Fred Zollner**, owner, Pistons (1941-74), helped bring about use of the 24-second shot clock, six-foul rule and widening of free throw lane.

1999 finalists (nominated but not elected): PLAYERS—Bob McAdoo, Maurice Cheeks, Dennis Johnson, Gus Johnson, Ubiratan Pereira Maciel, Sidney Moncrief, Drazen Petrovic, Chet Walker and Jo Jo White. COACHES—Jim Phelan, Tex Winter and Morgan Wootten.

Note: John Wooden and **Lenny Wilkens**, who was rehonored by the Hall in 1998, are the only members to be inducted as both a player and a coach.

Members are listed with years of induction; (+) indicates deceased members.

Men

Abdul-Jabbar, Kareem	1995	Gola, Tom	1975	Mikan, George	1959
Archibald, Nate	1991	Goodrich, Gail	1996	Mikkelsen, Vern	1995
Arizin, Paul	1977	Greer, Hal	1981	Monroe, Earl	1990
+ Barlow, Thomas (Babe)	1980	+ Gruenig, Robert	1963	Murphy, Calvin	1993
Barry, Rick	1987	Hagan, Cliff	1977	+ Murphy, Charles (Stretch)	1960
Baylor, Elgin	1976	+ Hanson, Victor	1960	+ Page, Harlan (Pat)	1962
+ Beckman, John	1972	Havlicek, John	1983	Pettit, Bob	1970
Bellamy, Walt	1993	Hawkins, Connie	1992	Phillip, Andy	1961
Belov, Sergei	1992	Hayes, Elvin	1990	+ Pollard, Jim	1977
Bing, Dave	1990	Haynes, Marques	1998	Ramsey, Frank	1981
Bird, Larry	1998	Heinsohn, Tom	1986	Reed, Willis	1981
+ Borgmann, Benny	1961	+ Holman, Nat	1964	Risen, Arnie	1998
Bradley, Bill	1982	Houbregs, Bob	1987	Robertson, Oscar	1979
+ Brennan, Joe	1974	Howell, Bailey	1997	+ Roosma, John	1961
Cervi, Al	1984	Hyatt, Chuck	1959	Russell, Bill	1974
Chamberlain, Wilt	1978	Issel, Dan	1993	+ Russell, John (Honey)	1964
+ Cooper, Charles (Tarzan)	1976	+ Jeannette, Buddy	1994	Schayes, Dolph	1972
+ Cosic, Kresimir	1996	+ Johnson, Bill (Skinny)	1976	+ Schmidt, Ernest J	1973
Cousy, Bob	1970	+ Johnston, Neil	1990	+ Schommer, John	1959
Cowens, Dave	1991	Jones, K. C	1989	+ Sedran, Barney	1962
Cunningham, Billy	1986	Jones, Sam	1983	Sharman, Bill	1975
+ Davies, Bob	1969	+ Krause, Edward (Moose)	1975	+ Steinmetz, Christian	1961
+ DeBernardi, Forrest	1961	Kurland, Bob	1961	Thompson, David	1996
DeBusschere, Dave	1982	Lanier, Bob	1992	+ Thompson, John (Cat)	1962
+ Dehnert, Dutch	1968	+ Lapchick, Joe	1966	Thurmond, Nate	1984
+ Endacott, Paul	1971	Lovellette, Clyde	1988	Twyman, Jack	1982
English, Alex	1997	Lucas, Jerry	1979	Unseld, Wes	1988
Erving, Julius (Dr. J)	1993	Luisetti, Hank	1959	+ Vandivier, Robert (Fuzzy)	1974
Foster, Bud	1964	Macauley, Ed	1960	+ Wachter, Ed	1961
Frazier, Walt	1987	+ Maravich, Pete	1987	Walton, Bill	1993
+ Friedman, Marty	1971	Martin, Slater	1981	Wanzer, Bobby	1987
Fulks, Joe	1977	+ McCracken, Branch	1960	West, Jerry	1979
Gale, Laddie	1976	+ McCracken, Jack	1962	Wilkens, Lenny	1989
Gallatin, Harry	1991	+ McDermott, Bobby	1988	Wooden, John	1960
Gates, William (Pop)	1989	McGuire, Dick	1993	Yardley, George	1996
Gervin, George	1996	McHale, Kevin	1999		

Basketball (Cont.)

Women

Blazejowski, Carol 1994	Harris, Lucy 1992	Semenova, Juliana 1993
Crawford, Joan 1997	Lieberman-Cline, Nancy.....1996	White, Nera...............1992
Curry, Denise 1997	Meyers, Ann..............1993	
Donovan, Anne 1995	Miller, Cheryl.............1995	

Teams

Buffalo Germans 1961	New York Renaissance......1963	Original Celtics 1959
First Team 1959		

Referees

+ Enright, Jim...............1978	+ Leith, Lloyd 1982	+ Shirley, J. Dallas 1979
+ Hepbron, George 1960	+ Mihalik, Red..............1986	+ Strom, Earl 1995
+ Hoyt, George 1961	Nucatola, John............1977	Tobey, Dave 1961
+ Kennedy, Pat 1959	+ Quigley, Ernest (Quig) 1961	+ Walsh, David.............1961

Coaches

+ Allen, Forrest (Phog) 1959	+ Gill, Amory (Slats).........1967	+ McGuire, Frank 1976
+ Anderson, Harold (Andy)....1984	Gomelsky, Aleksandr 1995	+ Meanwell, Walter (Doc).....1959
Auerbach, Red.............1968	Hannum, Alex 1998	Meyer, Ray 1978
+ Barry, Sam 1978	Harshman, Marv 1984	Miller, Ralph..............1988
+ Blood, Ernest (Prof) 1960	Haskins, Don 1997	Moore, Billie..............1999
+ Cann, Howard.............1967	+ Hickey, Eddie.............1978	Nikolic, Aleksandar 1998
+ Carlson, Henry (Doc) 1959	+ Hobson, Howard (Hobby) ...1965	Ramsay, Jack 1992
Carnesecca, Lou 1992	+ Holzman, Red 1986	Rubini, Cesare 1994
Carnevale, Ben 1969	+ Iba, Hank 1968	+ Rupp, Adolph 1968
Carril, Pete 1997	+ Julian, Alvin (Doggie) 1967	+ Sachs, Leonard 1961
+ Case, Everett 1981	+ Keaney, Frank 1960	+ Shelton, Everett 1979
Conradt, Judy.............1998	+ Keogan, George 1961	Smith, Dean 1982
Crum, Denny 1994	Knight, Bob 1991	Taylor, Fred...............1985
Daly, Chuck 1994	Kundla, John 1995	Thompson, John 1999
+ Dean, Everett 1966	+ Lambert, Ward (Piggy) 1960	+ Wade, Margaret...........1984
Diaz-Miguel, Antonio 1997	Litwack, Harry 1975	Watts, Stan...............1985
+ Diddle, Ed 1971	+ Loeffler, Ken 1964	Wilkens, Lenny............1998
+ Drake, Bruce 1972	+ Lonborg, Dutch 1972	Wooden, John 1972
Gaines, Clarence (Bighouse).1981	+ McCutchan, Arad 1980	+ Woolpert, Phil 1992
Gardner, Jack 1983	McGuire, Al...............1992	

Contributors

+ Abbott, Senda Berenson.....1984	+ Irish, Ned 1964	+ Ripley, Elmer...............1972
+ Bee, Clair 1967	+ Jones, R. William 1964	+ St. John, Lynn W 1962
+ Brown, Walter A 1965	+ Kennedy, Walter 1980	+ Saperstein, Abe............1970
+ Bunn, John 1964	+ Liston, Emil (Liz) 1974	+ Schabinger, Arthur 1961
+ Douglas, Bob 1971	McLendon, John............1978	+ Stagg, Amos Alonzo.........1959
+ Duer, Al..................1981	+ Mokray, Bill 1965	Stankovic, Boris 1991
Embry, Wayne 1999	+ Morgan, Ralph.............1959	+ Steitz, Ed.................1983
Fagen, Clifford B 1983	+ Morgenweck, Frank (Pop) ...1962	+ Taylor, Chuck 1968
+ Fisher, Harry 1973	+ Naismith, James............1959	+ Teague, Bertha............1984
+ Fleisher, Larry.............1991	Newell, Pete..............1978	+ Tower, Oswald.............1959
+ Gottlieb, Eddie.............1971	+ O'Brien, John J. (Jack)......1961	+ Trester, Arthur (A.L.) 1961
+ Gulick, Luther..............1959	+ O'Brien, Larry 1991	+ Wells, Cliff 1971
+ Harrison, Les 1979	+ Olsen, Harold G 1959	+ Wilke, Lou 1982
+ Hepp, Ferenc 1980	+ Podoloff, Maurice 1973	+ Zollner, Fred..............1999
+ Hickox, Ed 1959	+ Porter, Henry (H.V.)........1960	
+ Hinkle, Tony 1965	+ Reid, William A............1963	

Curt Gowdy Award

First presented in 1990 by the Hall of Fame Board of Trustees for meritorious contributions by the media. Named in honor of the former NBC sportscaster, the Gowdy Award does not constitute induction into the Hall of Fame.

Year	Year	Year
1990 Curt Gowdy & Dick Herbert	1994 Leonard Koppett	1997 Marv Albert & Bob Ryan
1991 Dave Dorr & Marty Glickman	& Cawood Ledford	1998 Dick Vitale, Larry Donald &
1992 Sam Goldaper & Chick Hearn	1995 Dick Enberg & Bob Hammel	Dick Weiss
1993 Leonard Lewin & Johnny Most	1996 Billy Packer & Bob Hentzen	

BOWLING

National Bowling Hall of Fame & Museum

The National Bowling Hall is one museum with separate wings for honorees of the American Bowling Congress (ABC), Professional Bowlers' Association (PBA) and Women's International Bowling Congress (WIBC). The museum does not include the new Ladies Pro Bowlers Tour Hall of Fame, which is located in Las Vegas. **Address:** 111 Stadium Plaza, St. Louis, MO 63102. **Telephone:** (314) 231-6340.

Professional Bowlers Association

Established in 1975. **Eligibility:** Nominees must be PBA members and at least 35 years old. Voting done by 50-member panel that includes writers who have covered bowling for at least 12 years.

Class of 1999 (1): MERITORIOUS SERVICE—**Keijiro Nakano**.

Members are listed with years of induction; (+) indicates deceased members.

Performance

+ Allen, Bill 1983	Ferraro, Dave.............1997	Salvino, Carmen 1975
Anthony, Earl 1986	Godman, Jim 1987	Semiz, Teata...............1998
Aulby, Mike 1996	Hardwick, Billy 1977	Smith, Harry...............1975
Berardi, Joe 1990	Holman, Marshall 1990	Soutar, Dave 1979
Bluth, Ray 1975	Hudson, Tommy...........1989	Stefanich, Jim..............1980
Buckley, Roy...............1992	Husted, Dave 1996	Voss, Brian 1994
Burton, Nelson Jr 1979	Johnson, Don 1977	Webb, Wayne 1993
Carter, Don 1975	Laub, Larry 1985	Weber, Dick 1975
Colwell, Paul 1991	Monacelli, Amleto 1997	Weber, Pete 1998
Cook, Steve 1993	Ozio, David 1995	+ Welu, Billy 1975
Davis, Dave 1978	Pappas, George 1986	Williams, Walter Ray Jr......1995
Dickinson, Gary............1988	Petraglia, John 1982	Zahn, Wayne...............1981
Durbin, Mike 1984	Ritger, Dick 1978	
+ Fazio, Buzz 1976	Roth, Mark 1987	

Veterans

Allison, Glenn 1984	+ Joseph, Joe 1985	McGrath, Mike 1988
Asher, Barry 1988	Limongello, Mike 1994	Schlegel, Ernie.............1997
Foremsky, Skee 1992	Marzich, Andy..............1990	+ St. John, Jim 1989
Guenther, Johnny...........1986	McCune, Don...............1991	Strampe, Bob 1987

Meritorious Service

+ Antenora, Joe...............1993	+ Frantz, Lou 1978	Pezzano, Chuck............1975
Archibald, John 1989	Golden, Harry 1983	Reichert, Jack 1992
Clemens, Chuck............1994	Hoffman, Ted Jr 1985	+ Richards, Joe 1976
+ Elias, Eddie 1976	Jowdy, John 1988	Schenkel, Chris 1976
Esposito, Frank.............1975	Kelley, Joe..................1989	Stitzlein, Lorraine...........1980
Evans, Dick 1986	Lichstein, Larry 1996	Thompson, Al 1991
Firestone, Raymond........1987	+ Nagy, Steve 1977	Zeller, Roger...............1995
Fisher, E.A. (Bud)..........1984	Nakano, Keijiro............1999	

American Bowling Congress

Established in 1941 and open to professional and amateur bowlers. **Eligibility:** Nominated bowlers must have competed in at least 20 years of ABC tournaments. Voting done by 170-member panel made up of ABC officials, Hall of Fame members and media representatives.

Class of 1999 (4): MERITORIOUS SERVICE— **Darold Dobs**. PIONEER— **John Wilcox**. PERFORMANCE— **Paul Colwell** and **Don Scudder**.

Members are listed with years of induction; (+) indicates deceased members.

Performance

Allison, Glenn 1979	Burton, Nelson Jr..........1981	Ellis, Don...................1981
Anthony, Earl 1986	+ Burton, Nelson Sr 1964	+ Falcaro, Joe 1968
Asher, Barry...............1998	+ Campi, Lou.................1968	+ Faragalli, Lindy 1968
+ Asplund, Harold 1978	+ Carlson, Adolph 1941	+ Fazio, Buzz 1963
Baer, Gordy 1987	Carter, Don 1970	Fehr, Steve 1993
Beach, Bill 1991	+ Caruana, Frank 1977	+ Gersonde, Russ 1968
+ Benkovic, Frank............1958	+ Cassio, Marty 1972	+ Gibson, Therm.............1965
Berlin, Mike 1994	+ Castellano, Graz...........1976	Godman, Jim 1987
+ Billick, George............1982	+ Clause, Frank 1980	Goike, Robert...............1996
+ Blouin, Jimmy.............1953	Cohn, Alfred 1985	Golembiewski, Billy.........1979
Bluth, Ray 1973	Colwell, Paul 1999	Griffo, Greg.................1995
+ Bodis, Joe 1941	+ Crimmins, Johnny 1962	Guenther, Johnny............1988
+ Bomar, Buddy 1966	Davis, Dave 1990	Hardwick, Billy 1985
+ Brandt, Allie 1960	+ Daw, Charlie 1941	Hart, Bob 1994
+ Brosius, Eddie 1976	+ Day, Ned 1952	Hennessey, Tom 1976
+ Bujack, Fred 1967	Dickinson, Gary............1992	Hoover, Dick 1974
Bunetta, Bill 1968	+ Easter, Sarge 1963	Horn, Bud..................1992

Bowling (Cont.)

Howard, George...........1986
Jackson, Eddie............1988
Johnson, Don 1982
Johnson, Earl 1987
+ Joseph, Joe 1969
+ Jouglard, Lee 1979
+ Kartheiser, Frank 1967
+ Kawolics, Ed 1968
+ Kissoff, Joe 1976
+ Klares, John 1982
+ Knox, Billy 1954
+ Koster, John 1941
+ Krems, Eddie 1973
  Kristof, Joe 1968
+ Krumske, Paul 1968
+ Lange, Herb 1941
+ Lauman, Hank 1976
  Lillard, Bill 1972
  Lindemann, Tony 1979
+ Lindsey, Mort 1941
+ Lippe, Harry.............1989
  Lubanski, Ed 1971
  Lucci, Vince Sr 1978
+ Marino, Hank............1941
+ Martino, John.............1969
  Marzich, Andy............1993

+ Allen, Lafayette Jr.........1994
+ Briell, Frank 1996
+ Carow, Rev. Charles......1995
+ Celestine, Sydney 1993
+ Curtis, Thomas...........1993
  de Freitas, Eric..........1994
  Hall, William Sr. 1994

+ Allen, Harold 1966
  Archibald, John 1996
+ Baker, Frank 1975
+ Baumgarten, Elmer 1963
+ Bellisimo, Lou 1986
+ Bensinger, Bob 1969
+ Chase, LeRoy 1972
+ Coker, John 1980
+ Collier, Chuck 1963
+ Cruchon, Steve 1983
+ Ditzen, Walt 1973
  Dobs, Darold 1999
+ Doehrman, Bill 1968
  Elias, Eddie 1985
  Esposito, Frank...........1997

McGrath, Mike 1993
+ McMahon, Junie 1967
+ Meisel, Draold...........1998
+ Mercurio, Skang 1967
+ Meyers, Norm 1984
+ Nagy, Steve 1963
  Norris, Joe 1954
  O'Donnell, Chuck 1968
  Pappas, George 1989
+ Patterson, Pat 1974
  Ritger, Dick 1984
+ Rogoznica, Andy..........1993
  Salvino, Carmen 1979
  Schissler, Les............1991
  Schlegel, Ernie 1997
  Schroeder, Jim 1990
+ Schwoegler, Connie 1968
  Scudder, Don 1999
  Semiz, Teata.............1991
+ Sielaff, Lou 1968
+ Sinke, Joe 1977
+ Sixty, Billy 1961
  Smith, Harry.............1978
+ Smith, Jimmy 1941
  Soutar, Dave 1985
+ Sparando, Tony 1968

+ Spinella, Barney 1968
+ Steers, Harry 1941
  Stefanich, Jim............1983
+ Stein, Otto Jr 1971
  Stoudt, Bud 1991
  Strampe, Bob............1977
+ Thoma, Sykes............1971
  Toft, Rod 1991
  Tountas, Pete 1989
+ Totsky, Mike 1996
  Tucker, Bill.............1988
  Tuttle, Tommy 1995
+ Varipapa, Andy...........1957
+ Ward, Walter.............1959
  Weber, Dick 1970
+ Welu, Billy 1975
+ Wilman, Joe 1951
+ Wolf, Phil 1961
  Wonders, Rich 1990
+ Young, George 1959
  Zahn, Wayne 1980
  Zikes, Les 1983
+ Zunker, Gil 1941

Pioneers

Hirashima, Hirohito........1995
+ Karpf, Samuel 1993
+ Moore, Henry 1996
+ Pasdeloup, Frank..........1993
+ Rhodman, Bill............1997
+ Satow, Masao 1994
+ Schutte, Louis 1993

Shimada, Fuzzy...........1997
  Stein, Louis 1997
+ Thompson, William V.......1993
+ Timm, Dr. Henry..........1993
  Wilcox, John 1999

Meritorious Service

Evans, Dick.............1992
  Franklin, Bill 1992
+ Hagerty, Jack 1963
+ Hattstrom, H.A. (Doc) 1980
+ Hermann, Cornelius 1968
+ Howley, Pete 1941
+ Kennedy, Bob............1981
+ Langtry, Abe.............1963
+ Levine, Sam 1971
+ Luby, David.............1969
  Luby, Mort Jr.............1988
+ Luby, Mort Sr.............1974
  Matzelle, Al 1995
+ McCullough, Howard.......1971
+ Patterson, Morehead.......1985

+ Petersen, Louie 1963
  Pezzano, Chuck...........1982
  Picchietti, Remo 1993
  Pluckhahn, Bruce 1989
+ Raymer, Milt.............1972
+ Reed, Elmer 1978
  Reichert, Jack 1998
  Rudo, Milt...............1984
  Schenkel, Chris 1988
+ Sweeney, Dennis 1974
  Tessman, Roger 1994
+ Thum, Joe 1980
  Weinstein, Sam 1970
+ Whitney, Eli 1975
  Wolf, Fred 1976

Women's International Bowling Congress

Established in 1953. **Eligibility:** Performance nominees must have won at least one WIBC Championship Tournament title, a WIBC Queens tournament title or an international competition title and have bowled in at least 15 national WIBC Championship Tournaments (unless injury or illness cut career short).

Class of 1999 (3): PERFORMANCE—**Jeanne Naccarato** and **Lucy Givinco-Sandelin**; MERITORIOUS SERVICE—**Pearl Keller**.

Members are listed with years of induction; (+) indicates deceased members.

Performance

Abel, Joy.................1984
Adamek, Donna 1996
Ann, Patty 1995
Bolt, Mae 1978
Bouvia, Gloria 1987
Boxberger, Loa..........1984
Buckner, Pam 1990
+ Burling, Catherine 1958
+ Burns, Nina 1977

Cantaline, Anita 1979
Carter, LaVerne 1977
Carter, Paula 1994
Coburn, Cindy C. 1998
Coburn, Doris 1976
Costello, Pat 1986
Costello, Patty 1989
Dryer, Pat 1978
Duval, Helen 1970

Fellmeth, Catherine 1970
Fothergill, Dotty 1980
+ Fritz, Deane 1966
  Garms, Shirley...........1971
  Gianulias, Nikki 1997
  Givinco-Sandelin, Lucy 1999
  Gloor, Olga 1976
  Gonzalez, Ashie 1998
  Graham, Linda...........1992

Graham, Mary Lou 1989	+ Matthews, Merle 1974	+ Rump, Anita 1962
+ Greenwald, Goldie 1953	+ McCutcheon, Floretta 1956	+ Ruschmeyer, Addie 1961
Grinfelds, Vesma 1991	Merrick, Marge 1980	+ Ryan, Esther 1963
+ Harman, Janet 1985	+ Mikiel, Val 1979	+ Sablatnik, Ethel 1979
+ Hartrick, Stella 1972	Miller, Carol 1997	+ Schulte, Myrtle 1965
+ Hatch, Grayce 1953	+ Miller, Dorothy 1954	+ Shablis, Helen 1977
Havlish, Jean 1987	Mivelaz, Betty 1991	Sill, Aleta 1996
+ Hoffman, Martha 1979	Mohacsi, Mary 1994	+ Simon, Violet (Billy) 1960
Holm, Joan 1974	Morris, Betty...............1983	+ Small, Tess 1971
+ Humphreys, Birdie..........1979	Naccarato, Jeanne 1999	+ Smith, Grace 1968
Ignizio, Mildred 1975	Nichols, Lorrie 1989	Soutar, Judy 1976
Jacobson, D.D 1981	Norman, Edie Jo 1993	+ Stockdale, Louise..........1953
+ Jaeger, Emma..............1953	Norton, Virginia 1988	Toepfer, Elvira 1976
Kelly, Annese 1985	Notaro, Phyllis 1979	+ Twyford, Sally 1964
+ Knechtges, Doris 1983	Ortner, Bev.................1972	+ Warmbier, Marie...........1953
Kuczynski, Betty............1981	+ Powers, Connie 1973	Wilkinson, Dorothy 1990
Ladewig, Marion 1964	Rickard, Robbie 1994	+ Winandy, Cecelia 1975
Martin, Sylvia Wene 1966	+ Robinson, Leona 1969	Zimmerman, Donna 1982
Martorella, Millie...........1975	Romeo, Robin.............1995	

Meritorious Service

Baetz, Helen...............1977	Herold, Mitzi 1998	+ Phaler, Emma 1965
+ Baker, Helen...............1989	+ Higley, Margaret...........1969	+ Porter, Cora 1986
+ Banker, Gladys 1994	+ Hochstadter, Bee 1967	+ Quin, Zoe.................1979
+ Bayley, Clover 1992	+ Kay, Nora.................1964	+ Rishling, Gertrude 1972
+ Berger, Winifred 1976	Keller, Pearl 1999	Simone, Anne 1991
+ Bohlen, Philena 1955	+ Kelly, Ellen 1979	Sloan, Catherine 1985
Borschuk, Lo 1988	Kelone, Theresa 1978	+ Speck, Berdie.............1966
+ Botkin, Freda 1986	+ Knepprath, Jeannette 1963	Spitalnick, Mildred 1994
+ Chapman, Emily 1957	+ Lasher, Iolia 1967	+ Spring, Alma 1979
+ Crowe, Alberta 1982	Marrs, Mabel..............1979	+ Switzer, Pearl 1973
+ Dornblaser, Gertrude 1979	+ McBride, Bertha 1968	Todd, Trudy...............1993
Duffy, Agnes...............1987	+ Menne, Catherine 1979	+ Veatch, Georgia 1974
Finke, Gertrude 1990	Mitchell, Flora 1996	+ White, Mildred 1975
+ Fisk, Rae 1983	+ Mraz, Jo 1959	+ Wood, Ann................1970
+ Haas, Dorothy 1977	O'Connor, Billie............1992	

Ladies Pro Bowlers Hall of Fame

Established in 1995 by the Ladies Pro Bowlers Tour. The LPBT has since been renamed the Professional Women Bowlers Association. **Address:** Sam's Town Hotel, Gambling Hall and Bowling Center, 5111 Boulder Highway, Las Vegas, NV 89122. **Telephone:** (815) 332-5756.

Eligibility: Nominees in performance category must have at least five titles from organizations including All-Star, World Invitational, LPBT, WPBA, PWBA, TPA and LPBA. Voting done by 10-member committee of bowling writers appointed by LPBT president John Falzone.

Class of 1999: had yet to be released as of press time.

Members are listed with year of induction; (+) indicates deceased member.

Performance

Adamek, Donna 1995	Gianulias, Nikki 1996	Morris, Betty...............1995
Colburn-Carroll, Cindy 1997	Grinfelds, Vesma...........1997	Nichols, Lorrie 1996
Costello, Pat...............1997	Johnson, Tish 1998	Romeo, Robin..............1996
Costello, Patty 1995	Ladewig, Marion...........1995	Sill, Aleta 1998
Fothergill, Dotty 1995	Martorella, Millie...........1995	Wagner, Lisa 1996

Pioneers

Able, Joy..................1998	Coburn, Doris 1996	Ortner, Bev................1998
Boxberger, Loa.............1997	Duval, Helen 1995	Soutar, Judy 1997
Carter, LaVerne 1995	Garms, Shirley.............1995	Zimmerman, Donna 1996

Builders

Buhler, Janet...............1996	Robinson, Jeanette..........1996	+ Veatch, Georgia 1995
Keller, Pearl 1997	Sommer Jr., John 1997	

BOXING

International Boxing Hall of Fame

Established in 1989 and opened in 1990. **Address:** 1 Hall of Fame Drive, Canastota, NY 13032. **Telephone:** (315) 697-7095.

Eligibility: All nominees must be retired for five years. Voting done by 142-member panel made up of Boxing Writers' Association members and world-wide boxing historians.

Class of 1999 (17): MODERN ERA—**Jimmy Bivins** (light heavyweight), **Khaosai Galaxy** (junior bantamweight), **Lew Jenkins** (lightweight), **Eusebio Pedroza** (featherweight), **Vicente Saldivar** (featherweight). OLD TIMERS—**Johnny Coulon** (bantamweight), **Sam McVey** (heavyweight), **Freddie Steele** (middleweight), **Lew Tendler** (lightweight). PIONEER—**Bill Richmond** (heavyweight). NON-PARTICIPANTS— **Irving Rudd** (press agent), **Jimmy Johnston** (manager/promoter), **Tom O'Rourke** (manager), **Mickey Duff** (boxer/manager/promoter), **Murray Goodman** (press agent), **Bob Arum** (promoter), **Giuseppe Ballarati** (historian).

Members are listed with year of induction; (+) indicates deceased member.

Modern Era

Ali, Muhammad 1990	Gomez, Wilfredo 1995	Ortiz, Carlos 1991
+ Angott, Sammy 1998	+ Graham, Billy..............1992	+ Ortiz, Manuel 1996
Arguello, Alexis 1992	+ Graziano, Rocky 1991	Patterson, Floyd 1991
+ Armstrong, Henry 1990	Griffith, Emile..............1990	Pedroza, Eusebio 1999
Basilio, Carmen 1990	Hagler, Marvelous Marvin ..1993	Pep, Willie 1990
Benitez, Wilfredo 1996	Harada, Masahiko (Fighting) .1995	+ Perez, Pascual 1995
Benvenuti, Nino...........1992	Jack, Beau 1991	Pryor, Aaron 1996
+ Berg, Jackie (Kid) 1994	+ Jenkins, Lew 1999	+ Robinson, Sugar Ray........1990
Bivins, Jimmy 1999	Jofre, Eder 1992	+ Rodriguez, Luis 1997
+ Brown, Joe 1996	Johnson, Harold...........1993	Saddler, Sandy 1990
+ Burley, Charley 1992	LaMotta, Jake 1990	+ Saldivar, Vicente 1999
Canto, Miguel 1998	Leonard, Sugar Ray 1997	+ Sanchez, Salvador 1991
+ Cerdan, Marcel 1991	+ Liston, Sonny 1991	Schmeling, Max.............1992
Cervantes, Antonio 1998	+ Louis, Joe 1990	Spinks, Michael 1994
+ Charles, Ezzard 1990	+ Marciano, Rocky 1990	+ Tiger, Dick 1991
+ Conn, Billy 1990	Maxim, Joey................1994	Torres, Jose................1997
+ Elorde, Gabriel (Flash) 1993	+ Montgomery, Bob 1995	+ Walcott, Jersey Joe 1990
Foster, Bob 1990	+ Monzon, Carlos 1990	+ Williams, Ike 1990
Frazier, Joe...............1990	+ Moore, Archie 1990	+ Wright, Chalky 1997
Fullmer, Gene..............1991	Muhammad, Matthew Saad .1998	+ Zale, Tony 1991
Galaxy, Khaosai 1999	Napoles, Jose 1990	Zarate, Carlos 1994
Gavilan, Kid...............1990	Norton, Ken 1992	+ Zivic, Fritzie 1993
Giardello, Joey 1993	Olivares, Ruben 1991	

Old-Timers

Ambers, Lou 1992	+ Genaro, Frankie 1998	+ McFarland, Packey 1992
+ Attell, Abe...............1990	+ Gibbons, Mike 1992	+ McGovern, Terry 1990
+ Baer, Max 1995	+ Gibbons, Tommy 1993	McLarnin, Jimmy 1991
+ Britton, Jack 1990	+ Greb, Harry 1990	+ McVey, Sam 1999
+ Brown, Panama Al 1992	+ Griffo, Young 1991	+ Miller, Freddie 1997
+ Burns, Tommy 1996	+ Herman, Pete 1997	+ Nelson, Battling 1992
+ Canzoneri, Tony 1990	+ Jackson, Peter.............1990	+ O'Brien, Philadelphia Jack ...1994
+ Carpentier, Georges 1991	+ Jeanette, Joe 1997	+ Rosenbloom, Maxie 1993
+ Chocolate, Kid.............1991	+ Jeffries, James J 1990	+ Ross, Barney 1990
+ Choynski, Joe.............1998	+ Johnson, Jack 1990	+ Ryan, Tommy 1991
+ Corbett, James J...........1990	+ Ketchel, Stanley 1990	+ Sharkey, Jack 1994
+ Coulon, Johnny 1999	+ Kilbane, Johnny 1995	+ Steele, Freddie 1999
+ Darcy, Les 1993	+ LaBarba, Fidel 1996	+ Stribling, Young 1996
+ Delaney, Jack.............1996	+ Langford, Sam 1990	+ Tendler, Lew 1999
+ Dempsey, Jack 1990	+ Lavigne, George (Kid) 1998	+ Tunney, Gene 1990
+ Dempsey, Jack (Nonpareil) ..1992	+ Leonard, Benny 1990	+ Villa, Pancho 1994
+ Dillon, Jack...............1995	+ Lewis, John Henry 1994	+ Walcott, Joe (Barbados) 1991
+ Dixon, George.............1990	+ Lewis, Ted (Kid) 1992	+ Walker, Mickey 1990
+ Driscoll, Jim 1990	+ Loughran, Tommy 1991	+ Welsh, Freddie 1997
+ Dundee, Johnny 1991	+ Lynch, Benny 1998	+ Wilde, Jimmy 1990
+ Fitzsimmons, Bob..........1990	+ Mandell, Sammy 1998	+ Williams, Kid 1996
+ Flowers, Theodore (Tiger)....1993	+ McAuliffe, Jack 1995	+ Wills, Harry 1992
+ Gans, Joe 1990	+ McCoy, Charles (Kid) 1991	

Pioneers

+ Belcher, Jem 1992	+ Donovan, Prof. Mike 1998	+ King, Tom 1992
+ Brain, Ben.................1994	+ Duffy, Paddy...............1994	+ Langham, Nat 1992
+ Broughton, Jack 1990	+ Figg, James 1992	+ Mace, Jem 1990
+ Burke, James (Deaf).........1992	+ Jackson, Gentleman John 1992	+ Mendoza, Daniel 1990
+ Cribb, Tom 1991	+ Johnson, Tom 1995	+ Molineaux, Tom............1997

+ Morrissey, John 1996
+ Pearce, Henry 1993
+ Richmond, Bill 1999

+ Sam, Dutch 1997
+ Sayers, Tom 1990
  Spring, Tom 1992

+ Sullivan, John L 1990
+ Thompson, William 1991
+ Ward, Jem 1995

Non-Participants

+ Andrews, Thomas S 1992
+ Arcel, Ray. 1991
  Arum, Bob 1999
+ Ballarati, Giuseppe 1999
+ Blackburn, Jack 1992
+ Brady, William A. 1998
  Brenner, Teddy 1993
+ Chambers, John Graham 1990
  Clancy, Gil 1993
+ Coffroth, James W. 1991
+ D'Amato, Cus. 1995
+ Donovan, Arthur 1993
  Duff, Mickey 1999
  Dundee, Angelo. 1992
+ Dundee, Chris 1994
+ Dunphy, Don 1993

  Duva, Lou 1998
+ Egan, Pierce 1991
+ Fleischer, Nat. 1990
+ Fox, Richard K. 1997
  Futch, Eddie 1994
+ Goldman, Charley 1992
+ Goldstein, Ruby 1994
  Goodman, Murray 1999
+ Humphreys, Joe 1997
+ Jacobs, Jimmy 1993
+ Jacobs, Mike 1990
+ Johnston, Jimmy 1999
+ Kearns, Jack (Doc) 1990
  King, Don 1997
+ Liebling, A.J. 1992
+ Lonsdale, Lord 1990

+ Markson, Harry 1992
  Mercante, Arthur 1995
+ Muldoon, William 1996
  Odd, Gilbert 1995
+ O'Rourke, Tom 1999
+ Parker, Dan 1996
+ Parnassus, George 1991
+ Queensberry, Marquis of 1990
+ Rickard, Tex 1990
  Rudd, Irving 1999
+ Siler, George 1995
+ Solomons, Jack 1995
  Steward, Emanuel 1996
+ Taub, Sam. 1994
+ Taylor, Herman 1998
+ Walker, James J. (Jimmy) 1992

Old *Ring* Hall Members Not in Int'l. Boxing Hall

Nat Fleischer, the late founder and editor-in-chief of *The Ring*, established his magazine's Boxing Hall of Fame in 1954, but it was abandoned after the 1987 inductions. One hundred and twelve members of the old *Ring* Hall have been elected to the International Hall since 1989. The 43 boxers and one sportswriter who have yet to be elected to the International Hall are listed below with their year of induction into the *Ring* Hall.

Modern Group

+ Apostoli, Fred. 1978
+ Braddock, James J. 1964
+ Escobar, Sixto 1975

+ Garcia, Ceferino 1977
+ Lesnevich, Gus. 1973
+ Petrolle, Billy. 1962

+ Shirai, Yoshio. 1977

Old-Timers

+ Berlenbach, Paul 1971
+ Britt, Jimmy 1976
+ Chaney, George (K.O.) 1974
+ Corbett, Young II 1965
+ Fields, Jackie 1977
+ Houck, Leo 1969
+ Jeffra, Harry 1982

+ Kid, The Dixie 1975
+ Klaus, Frank 1974
+ Levinsky, Battling 1966
+ Maher, Peter. 1978
+ Mitchell, Charley 1957
+ Papke, Billy. 1972
+ Ritchie, Willie 1962

+ Root, Jack 1961
+ Sharkey, Tom 1959
+ Smith, Jeff 1969
+ Taylor, Bud 1986
+ Willard, Jess. 1977
+ Wolgast, Ad. 1958

Pioneers

+ Aaron, Barney (Young) 1967
+ Chambers, Arthur 1954
+ Chandler, Tom 1972
+ Clark, Nobby 1971
+ Collyer, Sam 1964
+ Donnelly, Dan 1960
+ Goss, Joe 1969

+ Gully, John 1959
+ Heenan, John C. 1954
+ Hyer, Jacob 1968
+ Hyer, Tom 1954
+ Jackling, Thomas 1985
+ Kilrain, Jack 1965
+ Price, Ned. 1962

+ Ryan, Paddy. 1973

Non-Participant
+ Daniel, Dan (sportswriter). 1977

FOOTBALL

College Football Hall of Fame

Established in 1955 by the National Football Foundation. **Address:** 111 South St. Joseph St., South Bend, IN 46601. **Telephone:** (219) 235-9999.

Eligibility: Nominated players must be out of college 10 years and a first team All-America pick by a major selector during their careers; coaches must be retired three years. Voting done by 12-member panel of athletic directors, conference and bowl officials and media representatives. 1996 was the first year representatives from NCAA Div. I-AA, II, and III, and the NAIA are eligible for induction.

Class of 1999 (23): LARGE COLLEGE—DE **Ross Browner**, Notre Dame (1973, 75-77); E **Chuck Dicus**, Arkansas (1968-70); RB **Chris Gilbert**, Texas (1966-68); OG **John Hannah**, Alabama (1970-72); TB **Billy Kilmer**, UCLA (1958-60); LB **Steve Kiner**, Tennessee (1967-69); QB **Chuck Long**, Iowa (1981-85); DB **Frank Loria**, Virginia Tech (1965-67); MG **Joe Palumbo**, Virginia (1949-51); RB **Greg Pruitt**, Oklahoma (1970-72); RB **Herschel Walker**, Georgia (1980-82); DL **Ed White**, Cal-Berkeley (1965–68). COACHES—**Jerry Claiborne**, Virginia Tech (1961-70), Maryland (1972-81), Kentucky (1982-89); **Don Coryell**, Whitter (1957-59), San Diego (1961-72); **Jim Young**, Arizona (1973-76), Purdue (1977-81), Army (1983-90). SMALL COLLEGE—QB **George Bork**, Northern Illinois (1960-63); DB **Teel Bruner**, Centre, KY (1982-85); DB **George Floyd**, Eastern Kentucky (1978-81); HB **Willie Galimore**, Florida A&M (1953-56); LB **Jim LeClair**, North Dakota (1970-71), DT **Randy Trautman**, Boise St. (1961-64). COACHES—**Billy Nicks**, Morris Brown (1930-42), Praire View A&M (1945-47, 52-65); **James Sochor**, Cal-Davis (1970-89).

Note: Bobby Dodd and **Amos Alonzo Stagg** are the only members to be honored as both players and coaches.

Football (Cont.)

Players are listed with final year they played in college and coaches are listed with year of induction; (+) indicates deceased members.

Players

+ Abell, Earl-Colgate 1915
  Agase, Alex-Purdue/Ill 1946
+ Agganis, Harry-Boston U 1952
  Albert, Frank-Stanford 1941
+ Aldrich, Ki-TCU 1938
+ Aldrich, Malcolm-Yale 1921
+ Alexander, Joe-Syracuse 1920
  Alworth, Lance-Arkansas 1961
+ Ameche, Alan-Wisconsin 1954
+ Ames, Knowlton-Princeton . .1889
  Amling, Warren-Ohio St. 1946
  Anderson, Dick-Colorado 1967
  Anderson, Donny-Tex.Tech . .1966
+ Anderson, Hunk-N.Dame 1921
  Atkins, Doug-Tennessee 1952
  Babich, Bob-Miami-OH 1968
+ Bacon, Everett-Wesleyan 1912
+ Bagnell, Reds-Penn 1950
+ Baker, Hobey-Princeton 1913
+ Baker, John-USC 1931
+ Baker, Moon-N'western 1926
  Baker, Terry-Oregon St 1962
+ Ballin, Harold-Princeton 1914
+ Banker, Bill-Tulane 1929
  Banonis, Vince-Detroit 1941
+ Barnes, Stan-California 1921
+ Barrett, Charles-Cornell. 1915
+ Baston, Bert-Minnesota 1916
+ Battles, Cliff-WV Wesleyan . .1931
  Baugh, Sammy-TCU 1936
  Baughan, Maxie-Ga.Tech. 1959
+ Bausch, James-Kansas. 1930
  Beagle, Ron-Navy 1955
  Beban, Gary-UCLA 1967
  Bechtol, Hub-Texas 1946
  Beck, Ray-Ga. Tech 1951
+ Beckett, John-Oregon 1916
  Bednarik, Chuck-Penn 1948
  Behm, Forrest-Nebraska 1940
  Bell, Bobby-Minnesota 1962
  Bellino, Joe-Navy. 1960
  Below, Marty-Wisconsin 1923
+ Benbrook, Al-Michigan 1910
+ Berry, Charlie-Lafayette. 1924
+ Bertelli, Angelo-N.Dame. 1943
  Berwanger, Jay-Chicago 1935
+ Bettencourt, L.-St.Mary's 1927
  Biletnikoff, Fred-Fla.St. 1964
  Blanchard, Doc-Army 1946
+ Blozis, Al-Georgetown 1942
  Bock, Ed-Iowa St 1938
  Bomar, Lynn-Vanderbilt 1924
+ Bomeisler, Bo-Yale 1913
+ Booth, Albie-Yale 1931
+ Borries, Fred-Navy 1934
+ Bosley, Bruce-West Va. 1955
  Bosseler, Don-Miami,FL. 1956
  Bottari, Vic-California 1938
+ Boynton, Ben-Williams 1920
+ Brewer, Charles-Harvard 1895
+ Bright, Johnny-Drake 1951
  Brodie, John-Stanford 1956
+ Brooke, George-Penn 1895
  Brosky, Al-Illinois 1952
  Brown, Bob-Nebraska 1963
  Brown, Geo-Navy/S.Diego St.1947
+ Brown, Gordon-Yale 1900
  Brown, Jim-Syracuse 1956

+ Brown, John, Jr.-Navy 1913
+ Brown, Johnny Mack-Ala 1925
+ Brown, Tay-USC. 1932
  Browner, Ross-Notre Dame . .1977
  Buddie, Brad-USC 1979
+ Bunker, Paul-Army 1902
  Burford, Chris-Stanford 1959
  Burton, Ron-N'western 1959
  Butkus, Dick-Illinois 1964
+ Butler, Robert-Wisconsin 1912
+ Cafego, George-Tenn 1939
+ Cagle, Red-SWLa/Army. 1929
+ Cain, John-Alabama 1932
  Cameron, Ed-Wash.& Lee . . .1924
+ Campbell, David-Harvard 1901
  Campbell, Earl-Texas. 1977
+ Cannon, Jack-N.Dame 1929
  Cappelletti, John-Penn St 1973
+ Carideo, Frank-N.Dame. 1930
+ Carney, Charles-Illinois 1921
  Caroline, J.C.-Illinois. 1954
  Carpenter, Bill-Army 1959
+ Carpenter, Hunter-Va.Tech . . .1905
  Carroll, Chas.-Washington. . . .1928
  Casanova, Tommy-LSU 1971
+ Casey, Edward-Harvard 1919
  Cassady, Howard-Ohio St 1955
+ Chamberlin, Guy-Neb. 1915
  Chapman, Sam-California 1938
+ Chappuis, Bob-Michigan 1947
+ Christman, Paul-Missouri 1940
+ Clark, Dutch-Colo. Col. 1929
  Cleary, Paul-USC 1947
+ Clevenger, Zora-Indiana 1903
  Cloud, Jack-Wm. & Mary 1948
+ Cochran, Gary-Princeton 1897
+ Cody, Josh-Vanderbilt 1919
  Coleman, Don-Mich.St 1951
+ Conerly, Charlie-Miss 1947
  Connor, George-HC/ND 1947
+ Corbin, William-Yale. 1888
  Corbus, William-Stanford. 1933
+ Cowan, Hector-Princeton 1889
+ Coy, Edward (Ted)-Yale 1909
+ Crawford, Fred-Duke. 1933
  Crow, John David-Tex.A&M. .1957
+ Crowley, Jim-Notre Dame. . . .1924
  Csonka, Larry-Syracuse 1967
  Cutter, Slade-Navy 1934
+ Czarobski, Ziggie-N.Dame . .1947
  Dale, Carroll-Va.Tech 1959
+ Dalrymple, Gerald-Tulane 1931
+ Dalton, John-Navy. 1911
+ Daly, Chas.-Harvard/Army . . .1902
  Daniell, Averell-Pitt. 1936
+ Daniell, James-Ohio St 1941
  Davies, Tom-Pittsburgh 1921
+ Davis, Ernie-Syracuse 1961
  Davis, Glenn-Army 1946
  Davis, Robert-Ga. Tech 1947
  Dawkins, Pete-Army 1958
  DeLong, Steve-Tennessee 1964
+ DeRogatis, Al-Duke 1948
+ DesJardien, Paul-Chicago. . . .1914
+ Devine, Aubrey-Iowa 1921
+ DeWitt, John-Princeton 1903
  Dial, Buddy-Rice 1958
  Dicus, Chuck-Arkansas 1970

  Ditka, Mike-Pittsburgh 1960
  Dobbs, Glenn-Tulsa 1942
+ Dodd, Bobby-Tennessee 1930
  Donan, Holland-Princeton. . . .1950
+ Donchess, Joseph-Pitt. 1929
  Dorsett, Tony-Pitt. 1976
+ Dougherty, Nathan-Tenn 1909
  Drahos, Nick-Cornell. 1940
+ Driscoll, Paddy-N'western . . .1917
+ Drury, Morley-USC 1927
  Dudley, Bill-Virginia 1941
  Duncan, Randy-Iowa. 1958
  Easley, Kenny-UCLA 1980
+ Eckersall, Walter-Chicago . . .1906
+ Edwards, Turk-Wash.St 1931
+ Edwards, Wm.-Princeton 1899
+ Eichenlaub, Ray-N.Dame 1914
  Eisenhauer, Steve-Navy 1953
  Elkins, Larry-Baylor 1964
  Elliott, Bump-Mich/Purdue . .1947
  Elliott, Pete-Michigan 1948
  Elmendorf, Dave-Tex. A&M . .1970
+ Evans, Ray-Kansas 1947
+ Exendine, Albert-Carlisle 1907
  Falaschi, Nello-S.Clara 1936
  Fears, Tom-S.Clara/UCLA 1947
+ Feathers, Beattie-Tenn 1933
  Fenimore, Bob-Okla.St 1946
+ Fenton, Doc-LSU 1909
  Ferguson, Bob-Ohio St. 1961
  Ferraro, John-USC 1944
  Fesler, Wes-Ohio St. 1930
+ Fincher, Bill-Ga.Tech 1920
  Fischer, Bill-Notre Dame 1948
+ Fish, Hamilton-Harvard 1909
+ Fisher, Robert-Harvard 1911
+ Flowers, Allen-Ga.Tech 1920
  Flowers, Charlie-Ole Miss. . . .1959
+ Fortmann, Danny-Colgate 1935
  Fralic, Bill-Pittsburgh 1984
  Francis, Sam-Nebraska 1936
  Franco, Ed-Fordham 1937
+ Frank, Clint-Yale. 1937
  Franz, Rodney-California 1949
  Frederickson, Tucker-Auburn .1964
+ Friedman, Benny-Michigan . . .1926
  Gabriel, Roman-N.C. State . .1961
  Gain, Bob-Kentucky 1950
+ Galiffa, Arnold-Army 1949
+ Gallarneau, Hugh-Stanford . .1940
+ Garbisch, Edgar-W.& J./Army.1924
  Garrett, Mike-USC. 1965
+ Gelbert, Charles-Penn. 1896
+ Geyer, Forest-Oklahoma 1915
  Gibbs, Jake-Miss 1960
  Giel, Paul-Minnesota 1953
  Gifford, Frank-USC 1951
  Gilbert, Chris-Texas. 1968
+ Gilbert, Walter-Auburn 1936
  Gilmer, Harry-Alabama 1947
+ Gipp, George-N.Dame 1920
+ Gladchuk, Chet-Boston Col . .1940
  Glass, Bill-Baylor 1956
  Glover, Rich-Nebraska 1972
  Goldberg, Marshall-Pitt. 1938
  Goodreault, Gene-BC 1940
+ Gordon, Walter-Calif 1918
+ Governali, Paul-Columbia 1942

Grabowski, Jim-Illinois 1965
Gradishar, Randy-Ohio St. . . .1973
Graham, Otto-N'western 1943
+ Grange, Red-Illinois. 1925
+ Grayson, Bobby-Stanford. . . .1935
Green, Hugh-Pitt 1980
+ Green, Jack-Tulane/Army. 1945
Greene, Joe-N.Texas St 1968
Griese, Bob-Purdue 1966
Griffin, Archie-Ohio St 1975
Groom, Jerry-Notre Dame 1950
+ Gulick, Merle-Toledo/Hobart.1929
+ Guyon, Joe-Ga.Tech 1918
Hadl, John-Kansas. 1961
+ Hale, Edwin-Miss.College . . .1921
Hall, Parker-Miss 1938
Ham, Jack-Penn St 1970
+ Hamilton, Bob-Stanford. 1935
+ Hamilton, Tom-Navy 1926
Hannah, John-Alabama 1972
+ Hanson, Vic-Syracuse 1926
+ Harder, Pat-Wisconsin 1942
+ Hardwick, Tack-Harvard. 1914
+ Hare, T.Truxton-Penn 1900
+ Harley, Chick-Ohio St 1919
+ Harmon, Tom-Michigan 1940
+ Harpster, Howard-Carnegie. .1928
+ Hart, Edward-Princeton. 1911
Hart, Leon-Notre Dame 1949
Hartman, Bill-Georgia. 1937
+ Hazel, Homer-Rutgers. 1924
+ Hazeltine, Matt-Calif 1954
+ Healey, Ed.-Dartmouth 1916
+ Heffelfinger, Pudge-Yale 1891
+ Hein, Mel-Washington St 1930
+ Heinrich, Don-Washington. . . .1952
Hendricks, Ted-Miami,FL. 1968
+ Henry, Pete-Wash&Jeff 1919
+ Herschberger, C.-Chicago 1898
+ Herwig, Robert-Calif. 1937
+ Heston, Willie-Michigan. 1904
+ Hickman, Herman-Tenn. 1931
+ Hickok, William-Yale. 1894
Hill, Dan-Duke 1938
+ Hillebrand, Art-Princeton 1899
+ Hinkey, Frank-Yale. 1894
Hinkle, Carl-Vanderbilt 1937
Hinkle, Clarke-Bucknell 1931
Hirsch, Elroy-Wisc./Mich 1943
+ Hitchcock, James-Auburn 1932
Hoffmann, Frank-N.Dame 1931
+ Hogan, James J.-Yale 1904
+ Holland, Brud-Cornell 1938
+ Holleder, Don-Army 1955
+ Hollenback, Bill-Penn. 1908
Holovak, Mike-Boston Col 1942
Holub, E.J.-Texas Tech. 1960
Hornung, Paul-N.Dame 1956
+ Horrell, Edwin-California 1924
+ Horvath, Les-Ohio St 1944
+ Howe, Arthur-Yale 1911
+ Howell, Dixie-Alabama. 1934
+ Hubbard, Cal-Centenary 1926
+ Hubbard, John-Amherst 1906
+ Hubert, Pooley-Ala. 1925
Huff, Sam-West Virginia 1955
Humble, Weldon-Rice 1946
Hunley, Ricky-Arizona. 1983
+ Hunt, Joe-Texas A&M 1927
Huntington, Ellery-Colgate . .1914
+ Hutson, Don-Alabama. 1934
+ Ingram, Jonas-Navy 1906
+ Isbell, Cecil-Purdue 1937

+ Jablonsky, J.-Army/Wash 1933
Jackson, Bo-Auburn 1985
+ Janowicz, Vic-Ohio St. 1951
+ Jenkins, Darold-Missouri 1941
+ Jensen, Jackie-California 1948
+ Joesting, Herbert-Minn 1927
Johnson, Bob-Tennessee 1967
+ Johnson, Jimmie-Carlisle/
Northwestern 1903
Johnson, Ron-Michigan. 1968
+ Jones, Calvin-Iowa. 1955
+ Jones, Gomer-Ohio St 1935
Jordan, Lee Roy-Alabama. 1962
+ Juhan, Frank-U.of South 1910
Justice, Charlie-N.Car. 1949
+ Kaer, Mort-USC 1926
Karras, Alex-Iowa. 1957
Kavanaugh, Ken-LSU. 1939
+ Kaw, Edgar-Cornell 1922
Kazmaier, Dick-Princeton 1951
+ Keck, James-Princeton. 1921
Kelley, Larry-Yale 1936
+ Kelly, Wild Bill-Montana 1926
Kenna, Doug-Army 1944
+ Kerr, George-Boston Col 1941
Ketcham, Henry-Yale. 1913
Keyes, Leroy-Purdue 1968
+ Killinger, Glenn-Penn St 1921
Kilmer, Billy-UCLA 1960
Kiner, Steve-Tennessee 1969
+ Kilpatrick, John-Yale 1910
Kimbrough, John-Tex A&M. . . .1940
+ Kinard, Frank-Mississippi 1937
+ King, Phillip-Princeton 1893
+ Kinnick, Nile-Iowa. 1939
+ Kipke, Harry-Michigan 1923
+ Kitzmiller, John-Oregon. 1930
+ Koch, Barton-Baylor 1931
+ Koppisch, Walt-Columbia 1924
Kramer, Ron-Michigan 1956
Kroll, Alex-Rutgers. 1961
+ Krueger, Charlie-Tex. A&M . . .1957
Kutner, Malcolm-Texas 1941
Kwalick, Ted-Penn St 1968
+ Lach, Steve-Duke 1941
+ Lane, Myles-Dartmouth 1927
Lattner, Johnny-N.Dame 1953
Lauricella, Hank-Tenn 1952
+ Lautenschlaeger, Les-Tulane . .1925
+ Layden, Elmer-N.Dame. 1924
+ Layne, Bobby-Texas. 1947
+ Lea, Langdon-Princeton. 1895
LeBaron, Eddie-Pacific 1949
+ Leech, James-VMI 1920
+ Lester, Darrell-TCU 1935
Lilly, Bob-TCU 1960
Little, Floyd-Syracuse 1966
+ Lio, Augie-Georgetown. 1940
+ Locke, Gordon-Iowa 1922
Long, Chuck-Iowa 1985
Long, Mel-Toledo 1971
+ Loria, Frank-Virginia Tech 1967
+ Lourie, Don-Princeton 1921
Lucas, Richie-Penn St 1959
+ Luckman, Sid-Columbia 1938
Lujack, Johnny-N.Dame. 1947
+ Lund, Pug-Minnesota 1934
Lynch, Jim-Notre Dame 1966
+ Macomber, Bart-Illinois. 1915
MacLeod, Robert-Dart. 1938
Maegle, Dick-Rice 1954
+ Mahan, Eddie-Harvard. 1915
Majors, John-Tennessee 1956

+ Mallory, William-Yale 1923
Mancha, Vaughn-Ala 1947
+ Mann, Gerald-SMU. 1927
Manning, Archie-Miss. 1970
Manske, Edgar-N'western 1933
Marinaro, Ed-Cornell 1971
+ Markov, Vic-Washington 1937
+ Marshall, Bobby-Minn 1906
Martin, Jim-Notre Dame 1949
Matson, Ollie-San Fran. 1952
Matthews, Ray-TCU. 1927
+ Maulbetsch, John-Mich 1914
+ Mauthe, Pete-Penn St. 1912
+ Maxwell, Robert-Chicago/
Swarthmore 1906
McAfee, George-Duke 1939
McAfee, Ken-Notre Dame 1977
+ McClung, Thomas-Yale 1891
McColl, Bill-Stanford 1951
+ McCormick, Jim-Princeton 1907
McDonald, Tommy-Okla 1956
+ McDowall, Jack-N.C.State. 1927
McElhenny, Hugh-Wash 1951
+ McEver, Gene-Tennessee 1931
+ McEwan, John-Army 1916
McFadden, Banks-Clemson . . .1939
McFadin, Bud-Texas 1950
McGee, Mike-Duke 1959
+ McGinley, Edward-Penn 1924
+ McGovern, John-Minn 1910
McGraw, Thurman-Colo.St. . . .1949
+ McKeever, Mike-USC 1960
+ McLaren, George-Pitt 1918
McMahon, Jim-BYU 1981
+ McMillan, Dan-USC/Calif 1922
+ McMillin, Bo-Centre 1921
+ McWhorter, Bob-Georgia 1913
+ Mercer, LeRoy-Penn. 1912
Meredith, Don-SMU 1959
Merritt, Frank-Army 1943
+ Metzger, Bert-N.Dame 1930
+ Meylan, Wayne-Nebraska. 1967
Michaels, Lou-Kentucky. 1957
Michels, John-Tennessee 1952
Mickal, Abe-LSU 1935
Miller, Creighton-N.Dame 1943
+ Miller, Don-Notre Dame 1924
+ Miller, Eugene-Penn St 1913
+ Miller, Fred-Notre Dame 1928
Miller, Rip-Notre Dame 1924
Millner, Wayne-N.Dame 1935
+ Milstead, C.A.-Wabash/Yale. . .1923
+ Minds, John-Penn. 1897
Minisi, Skip-Penn/Navy 1947
Modzelewski, Dick-Md. 1952
+ Moffat, Alex-Princeton. 1883
+ Molinski, Ed-Tenn. 1940
Montgomery, Cliff-Columbia .1933
Moomaw, Donn-UCLA 1952
+ Morley, William-Columbia 1902
Morris, George-Ga.Tech. 1952
Morris, Larry-Ga.Tech 1954
+ Morton, Bill-Dartmouth 1931
Morton, Craig-California 1964
+ Moscrip, Monk-Stanford. 1935
+ Muller, Brick-California. 1922
+ Nagurski, Bronko-Minn. 1929
+ Nevers, Ernie-Stanford 1925
+ Newell, Marshall-Harvard 1893
Newman, Harry-Michigan 1932
+ Newsome, Ozzie-Alabama 1977
Nielson, Gifford-BYU 1977
Nobis, Tommy-Texas 1965

Football (Cont.)

Nomellini, Leo-Minnesota....1949
+ Oberlander, Andrew-Dart ..1925
+ O'Brien, Davey-TCU 1938
+ O'Dea, Pat-Wisconsin......1899
Odell, Bob-Penn............1943
+ O'Hearn, Jack-Cornell 1915
Olds, Robin-Army 1942
+ Oliphant, Elmer-Army/Pur ..1917
Olsen, Merlin-Utah St 1961
Onkotz, Dennis-Penn St......1969
+ Oosterbaan, Bennie-Mich ...1927
O'Rourke, Charles-BC.......1940
+ Orsi, John-Colgate..........1931
+ Osgood, Win-Cornell/Penn..1892
Osmanski, Bill-Holy Cross ...1938
+ Owen, George-Harvard.....1922
Owens, Jim-Oklahoma 1949
Owens, Steve-Oklahoma 1969
Page, Alan-Notre Dame 1966
Palumbo, Joe-Virginia 1951
Pardee, Jack-Texas A&M 1956
Parilli, Babe-Kentucky 1951
Parker, Ace-Duke 1936
Parker, Jackie-Miss.St 1953
Parker, Jim-Ohio St 1956
+ Pazzetti, Vince-Lehigh 1912
+ Peabody, Chub-Harvard....1941
+ Peck, Robert-Pittsburgh 1916
Pellegrini, Bob-Maryland 1955
+ Pennock, Stan-Harvard......1914
Pfann, George-Cornell 1923
+ Phillips, H.D.-Sewanee 1904
Phillips, Loyd-Arkansas 1966
Pihos, Pete-Indiana 1946
Pingel, John-Michigan St 1938
+ Pinckert, Erny-USC..........1931
Plunkett, Jim-Stanford.......1970
+ Poe, Arthur-Princeton.......1899
+ Pollard, Fritz-Brown.........1916
Poole, B.-Miss/NC/Army....1947
Powell, Marvin-USC 1976
Pregulman, Merv-Michigan ..1943
+ Price, Eddie-Tulane 1949
Pruitt, Greg-Oklahoma 1972
+ Pund, Peter-Georgia Tech ...1928
Ramsey, G.-Wm&Mary 1942
Redman, Rick-Wash 1964
+ Reeds, Claude-Oklahoma ...1913
Reid, Mike-Penn St..........1969
Reid, Steve-Northwestern ...1936
+ Reid, William-Harvard 1899
Reifsnyder, Bob-Navy 1958
Renfro, Mel-Oregon 1963
+ Rentner, Pug-N'western......1932
+ Reynolds, Bob-Stanford......1935
+ Reynolds, Bobby-Nebraska ..1952
Rhome, Jerry-SMU/Tulsa ...1964
Richter, Les-California 1951
Richter, Pat-Wisconsin 1962
+ Riley, Jack-Northwestern 1931
Rimington, Dave-Nebraska ..1982
+ Rinehart, Chas.-Lafayette ...1897
Ritcher, Jim-NC St...........1979
Roberts, J. D.-Oklahoma 1953
+ Robeson, Paul-Rutgers 1918
Robinson, Dave-Penn St......1962
Robinson, Jerry-UCLA 1978
+ Rodgers, Ira-West Va.......1919
+ Rogers, Ed-Carlisle/Minn ...1903
Rogers, George-S. Carolina ..1980
Roland, Johnny-Missouri 1965

Romig, Joe-Colorado........1961
+ Rosenberg, Aaron-USC......1933
Rote, Kyle-SMU 1950
+ Routt, Joe-Texas A&M 1937
+ Salmon, Red-Notre Dame ...1903
Sarkisian, Alex..............1948
+ Sauer, George-Nebraska 1933
Savitsky, George-Penn 1947
Saxton, Jimmy-Texas 1961
Sayers, Gale-Kansas 1964
Scarbath, Jack-Maryland 1952
+ Scarlett, Hunter-Penn 1908
Schloredt, Bob-Wash 1960
+ Schoonover, Wear-Ark.......1929
+ Schreiner, Dave-Wisconsin ..1942
+ Schultz, Germany-Mich 1908
+ Schwab, Dutch-Lafayette....1922
+ Schwartz, Marchy-N.Dame ..1931
+ Schwegler, Paul-Wash 1931
Scott, Clyde-Navy/Arkansas .1948
Scott, Richard-Navy 1947
Scott, Tom-Virginia.........1953
+ Seibels, Henry-Sewanee 1899
Sellers, Ron-Florida St 1968
Selmon, Lee Roy-Okla.......1975
+ Shakespeare, Bill-N.Dame ...1935
Shell, Donnie-S.Carolina St...1998
+ Shelton, Murray-Cornell 1915
+ Shevlin, Tom-Yale 1905
+ Shively, Bernie-Illinois 1926
+ Simons, Monk-Tulane 1934
Simpson, O.J.-USC 1968
Sims, Billy-Oklahoma 1979
Singletary, Mike-Baylor......1980
Sington, Fred-Alabama 1930
+ Sinkwich, Frank-Georgia 1942
+ Sitko, Emil-Notre Dame......1949
+ Skladany, Joe-Pittsburgh 1933
+ Slater, Duke-Iowa...........1921
+ Smith, Bruce-Minnesota 1941
Smith, Bubba-Michigan St ...1966
+ Smith, Clipper-N.Dame......1927
+ Smith, Ernie-USC 1932
Smith, Harry-USC 1939
Smith, Jim Ray-Baylor 1954
Smith, Riley-Alabama 1935
+ Smith, Vernon-Georgia 1931
+ Snow, Neil-Michigan 1901
Sparlis, Al-UCLA 1945
+ Spears, Clarence-Dart.......1915
Spears, W.D.-Vanderbilt.....1927
+ Sprackling, Wm.-Brown 1911
+ Sprague, Bud-Army/Texas ..1928
Spurrier, Steve-Florida.......1966
Stafford, Harrison-Texas 1932
+ Stagg, Amos Alonzo-Yale ...1889
Stanfill, Bill-Georgia 1968
+ Starcevich, Max-Wash 1936
Staubach, Roger-Navy 1964
+ Steffen, Walter-Chicago 1908
Steffy, Joe-Tenn/Army 1947
+ Stein, Herbert-Pitt 1921
Steuber, Bob-Missouri 1943
+ Stevens, Mal-Yale...........1923
Stillwagon, Jim-Ohio St......1970
+ Stinchcomb, Pete-Ohio St. ..1920
+ Stevenson, Vincent-Penn 1905
Strom, Brock-Air Force 1959
+ Strong, Ken-NYU............1928
+ Strupper, Ev-Ga.Tech.......1917
+ Stuhldreher, Harry-N.Dame ..1924

+ Sturhan, Herb-Yale..........1926
+ Stydahar, Joe-West Va 1935
+ Suffridge, Bob-Tennessee 1940
+ Suhey, Steve-Penn St 1947
Sullivan, Pat-Auburn 1971
+ Sundstrom, Frank-Cornell ...1923
Swann, Lynn-USC 1973
+ Swanson, Clarence-Neb......1921
+ Swiacki, Bill-Columbia/HC ..1947
Swink, Jim-TCU 1956
Taliaferro, Geo.-Indiana 1948
Tarkenton, Fran-Georgia.....1960
+ Tavener, John-Indiana 1944
+ Taylor, Chuck-Stanford 1942
Thomas, Aurelius-Ohio St....1957
+ Thompson, Joe-Pittsburgh ...1907
+ Thorne, Samuel-Yale 1895
+ Thorpe, Jim-Carlisle 1912
+ Ticknor, Ben-Harvard 1930
+ Tigert, John-Vanderbilt......1904
Tinsley, Gaynell-LSU 1936
Tipton, Eric-Duke 1938
+ Tonnemaker, Clayton-Minn...1949
+ Torrey, Bob-Pennsylvania ...1905
+ Travis, Brick-Missouri.......1920
Trippi, Charley-Georgia 1946
+ Tryon, Edward-Colgate 1925
+ Tubbs, Jerry-Oklahoma 1956
Turner, Bulldog-H.Simmons ..1939
Twilley, Howard-Tulsa 1965
+ Utay, Joe-Texas A&M 1907
+ Van Brocklin, Norm-Ore.....1948
+ Van Sickel, Dale-Florida 1929
+ Van Surdam, H.-Wesleyan ...1905
+ Very, Dexter-Penn St 1912
Vessels, Billy-Oklahoma 1952
+ Vick, Ernie-Michigan........1921
+ Wagner, Hube-Pittsburgh....1913
+ Walker, Doak-SMU 1949
Walker, Herschel-Georgia ...1982
+ Wallace, Bill-Rice...........1935
+ Walsh, Adam-N.Dame 1924
+ Warburton, Cotton, USC 1934
Ward, Bob-Maryland 1951
+ Warner, William-Cornell 1904
+ Washington, Kenny-UCLA ...1939
Weatherall, Jim-Okla........1951
Webster, George-Mich. St ...1966
Wedemeyer, H.-St. Mary's...1947
Weekes, Harold-Columbia ..1902
Weiner, Art-N. Carolina.....1949
+ Weir, Ed-Nebraska 1925
+ Welch, Gus-Carlisle.........1914
+ Weller, John-Princeton 1935
+ Wendell, Percy-Harvard 1912
+ West, Belford-Colgate.......1919
+ Westfall, Bob-Michigan 1941
+ Weyand, Babe-Army........1915
+ Wharton, Buck-Penn 1896
+ Wheeler, Arthur-Princeton ..1894
White, Byron-Colorado 1938
White, Charles-USC 1979
White, Danny-Ariz. St.......1973
White, Ed-Cal.Berkeley......1968
White, Randy-Maryland 1974
Whitmire, Don-Navy/Ala....1944
+ Wickhorst, Frank-Navy 1926
Widseth, Ed-Minnesota 1936
+ Wildung, Dick-Minnesota ...1942
Williams, Bob-N. Dame 1950
Williams, Froggie-Rice.......1949

Willis, Bill-Ohio St 1944
+ Wilson, Bobby-SMU 1935
+ Wilson, George-Wash 1925
+ Wilson, Harry-Army/Penn St.1926
Wilson, Marc-BYU 1979
Wilson, Mike-Lafayette 1928
Wistert, Albert-Michigan 1942
Wistert, Alvin-Michigan 1949

+ Wistert, Whitey-Michigan . . .1933
+ Wojciechowicz, Alex-Fordham. .1937
+ Wood, Barry-Harvard 1931
+ Wyant, Andy-Chicago 1894
+ Wyatt, Bowden-Tenn 1938
+ Wyckoff, Clint-Cornell. 1895
+ Yarr, Tommy-N.Dame 1931
Yary, Ron-USC 1967

+ Yoder, Lloyd-Carnegie. 1926
+ Young, Claude-Illinois 1946
+ Young, Harry-Wash.& Lee . . .1916
+ Young, Waddy-Okla 1938
Youngblood, Jack-Florida 1970
Zarnas, Gustave-Ohio St. 1937

Coaches

+ Aillet, Joe 1989
+ Alexander, Bill 1951
+ Anderson, Ed 1971
+ Armstrong, Ike 1957
+ Bachman, Charlie 1978
+ Banks, Earl 1992
+ Baujan, Harry 1990
+ Bell, Matty 1955
+ Bezdek, Hugo 1954
+ Bible, Dana X. 1951
+ Bierman, Bernie 1955
Blackman, Bob. 1987
+ Blaik, Earl (Red) 1965
Broyles, Frank 1983
+ Bryant, Paul (Bear) 1986
+ Butts, Wally 1997
+ Caldwell, Charlie 1961
+ Camp, Walter 1951
Casanova, Len 1977
+ Cavanaugh, Frank. 1954
Claiborne, Jerry 1999
+ Colman, Dick 1990
Coryell, Don. 1999
+ Crisler, Fritz 1954
+ Daugherty, Duffy 1984
+ Devaney, Bob. 1981
Devine, Dan 1985
+ Dobie, Gil. 1951
+ Dodd, Bobby 1993
+ Donohue, Michael. 1951
Dooley, Vince. 1994
+ Dorais, Gus 1954
+ Edwards, Bill 1986
+ Engle, Rip 1973
Faurot, Don 1961
+ Gaither, Jake 1973
Gillman, Sid. 1989
+ Godfrey, Ernest 1972
Graves, Ray 1990
+ Gustafson, Andy 1985
+ Hall, Edward 1951
+ Harding, Jack. 1980
+ Harlow, Richard. 1954

+ Harman, Harvey 1981
+ Harper, Jesse 1971
+ Haughton, Percy 1951
+ Hayes, Woody. 1983
+ Heisman, John W 1954
+ Higgins, Robert 1954
+ Hollingberry, Babe 1979
+ Howard, Frank. 1989
+ Ingram, Bill. 1973
James, Don. 1997
+ Jennings, Morley 1973
+ Jones, Biff. 1954
+ Jones, Howard. 1951
+ Jones, Tad. 1958
+ Jordan, Lloyd 1978
+ Jordan, Ralph (Shug). 1982
+ Kerr, Andy 1951
Kush, Frank. 1995
+ Leahy, Frank. 1970
+ Little, George 1955
+ Little, Lou 1960
+ Madigan, Slip 1974
Maurer, Dave 1991
McClendon, Charley. 1986
+ McCracken, Herb 1973
+ McGugin, Dan. 1951
McKay, John. 1988
+ McKeen, Allyn 1991
+ McLaughry, Tuss 1962
+ Merritt, John 1994
+ Meyer, Dutch 1956
+ Mollenkopf, Jack 1988
+ Moore, Bernie 1954
+ Moore, Scrappy 1980
+ Morrison, Ray 1954
+ Munger, George 1976
+ Munn, Clarence (Biggie) 1959
+ Murray, Bill. 1974
+ Murray, Frank 1983
+ Mylin, Ed (Hooks) 1974
+ Neale, Earle (Greasy). 1967
+ Neely, Jess 1971
+ Nelson, David 1987

+ Neyland, Robert 1956
+ Norton, Homer 1971
+ O'Neill, Frank (Buck) 1951
+ Owen, Bennie 1951
Parseghian, Ara. 1980
+ Perry, Doyt 1988
+ Phelan, Jimmy 1973
+ Prothro, Tommy 1991
Ralston, John 1992
+ Robinson, E.N. 1955
+ Rockne, Knute 1951
+ Romney, Dick 1954
+ Roper, Bill 1951
Royal,Darrell 1983
+ Sanders, Henry (Red) 1996
+ Sanford, George 1971
Schembechler, Bo 1993
+ Schmidt, Francis 1971
+ Schwartzwalder, Ben 1982
+ Shaughnessy, Clark. 1968
+ Shaw, Buck 1972
+ Smith, Andy 1951
+ Snavely, Carl 1965
+ Stagg, Amos Alonzo 1951
+ Sutherland, Jock. 1951
+ Tatum, Jim. 1984
+ Thomas, Frank 1951
+ Vann, Thad. 1987
Vaught, Johnny. 1979
+ Wade, Wallace 1955
+ Waldorf, Lynn (Pappy) 1966
+ Warner, Glenn (Pop). 1951
+ Wieman, E.E. (Tad). 1956
+ Wilce, John 1954
+ Wilkinson, Bud 1969
+ Williams, Henry. 1951
+ Woodruff, George. 1963
+ Woodson, Warren 1989
+ Wyatt, Bowden 1997
Young, Jim 1999
+ Yost, Fielding (Hurry Up) 1951
+ Zuppke, Bob. 1951

Small College
Players

Bentrim, Jeff-N.Dakota St. . . .1986
Bork, George-N. Illinois 1963
Brasdshaw, Terry-La. Tech. . .1969
Bruner, Teel-Centre KY. 1985
+ Buchanan, Buck-Grambling. . .1962
Cichy, Joe-N.Dakota St. 1970
Deery, Tom-Widener, PA. 1981
+ Delaney, Joe-N'western St. . . .1980
Dement, Kenneth-SE Mo. St. .1954
Den Herder, Vern-Central IA. .1970
Dryer, Fred-San Diego St. 1968

Dudek, Joe-Plymouth St. 1985
Floyd, George-E. Kentucky . . .1981
Galimore, Willie-Fla. A&M 1956
Grinnell, William-Tufts. 1934
Hawkins, Frank-Nevada. 1980
Holt, Pierce-Angelo St. 1987
Johnson, Billy-Widener, PA . . .1973
Johnson, Gary-Grambling St. . .1974
LeClair, Jim-North Dakota. . . .1971
Lomax, Neil-Portland St. 1980
McGriff, Tyrone-Jackson St. . .1974

Montgomery, Wilbert-Ab. Christ. . .1976
O'Brien, Ken-UC–Davis 1982
Payton, Walter-Jackson St. . . .1974
Pugh, Larry-Westminster 1964
Reasons, Gary-N'western St. . .1983
Ritchie, Richard-Texas A&I . . .1976
Shell, Donnie-S.C. State 1973
Taylor, Bruce-Boston U. 1969
Thomsen, Lynn-Augustana . . .1986
Trautman, Randy-Boise St. . . .1964
Youngblood, Jim-Tenn. Tech . .1972

Coaches

+ Burry, Harold 1996
Butterfield, Jim 1997
+ Hoernemann, Paul. 1997
Keade, Bob 1998

Klausing, Chuck. 1998
Nicks, Billy 1999
Rutschman, Ad. 1998
Sherman, Edgar. 1996

Sochor, James 1999
+ Steinke, Gilbert 1996
+ Tressel, Lee 1996

Pro Football Hall of Fame

Established in 1963 by National Football League to commemorate the sport's professional origins. **Address:** 2121 George Halas Drive NW, Canton, OH 44708. **Telephone:** (330) 456-8207.

Eligibility: Nominated players must be retired five years, coaches must be retired, and contributors can still be active. Voting done by 36-member panel made up of media representatives from all 30 NFL cities, one PFWA representative and five selectors-at-large.

Class of 1999 (5): PLAYERS—RB **Eric Dickerson**, LA Rams (1983-87), Indianapolis (1987-91), LA Raiders (1992), Atlanta (1993); G **Tom Mack**, LA Rams (1966-78); TE **Ozzie Newsome**, Cleveland (1978-90); G **Billy Shaw**, Buffalo (1961-69); LB **Lawrence Taylor**, NY Giants (1981-93).

Quarterbacks

Baugh, Sammy 1963	Graham, Otto 1965	Starr, Bart 1977
Blanda, George (also PK) . . .1981	Griese, Bob 1990	Staubach, Roger 1985
Bradshaw, Terry 1989	+ Herber, Arnie 1966	Tarkenton, Fran 1986
+ Clark, Dutch 1963	Jurgensen, Sonny 1983	Tittle, Y.A. 1971
+ Conzelman, Jimmy 1964	+ Layne, Bobby 1967	Unitas, Johnny 1979
Dawson, Len. 1987	+ Luckman, Sid 1965	+ Van Brocklin, Norm. 1971
+ Driscoll, Paddy 1965	Namath, Joe 1985	+ Waterfield, Bob 1965
Fouts, Dan 1993	Parker, Clarence (Ace) 1972	

Running Backs

+ Battles, Cliff 1968	+ Hinkle, Clarke 1964	+ Nevers, Ernie 1963
Brown, Jim 1971	Hornung, Paul 1986	Payton, Walter 1993
Campbell, Earl. 1991	Johnson, John Henry 1987	Perry, Joe 1969
Canadeo, Tony 1974	Kelly, Leroy 1994	Riggins, John 1992
Csonka, Larry. 1987	+ Leemans, Tuffy 1978	Sayers, Gale 1977
Dickerson, Eric. 1999	Matson, Ollie 1972	Simpson, O.J. 1985
Dorsett, Tony. 1994	McAfee, George 1966	+ Strong, Ken 1967
Dudley, Bill 1966	McElhenny, Hugh 1970	Taylor, Jim. 1976
Gifford, Frank 1977	+ McNally, Johnny (Blood) 1963	+ Thorpe, Jim. 1963
+ Grange, Red 1963	Moore, Lenny 1975	Trippi, Charley. 1968
+ Guyon, Joe 1966	+ Motley, Marion 1968	Van Buren, Steve 1965
Harris, Franco 1990	+ Nagurski, Bronko 1963	+ Walker, Doak. 1986

Ends & Wide Receivers

	Hirsch, Elroy (Crazylegs) 1968	
Alworth, Lance. 1978	+ Hutson, Don 1963	+ Millner, Wayne 1968
+ Badgro, Red 1981	Joiner, Charlie 1996	Mitchell, Bobby 1983
Berry, Raymond 1973	Largent, Steve 1995	Newsome, Ozzie 1999
Biletnikoff, Fred 1988	Lavelli, Dante 1975	Pihos, Pete 1970
+ Chamberlin, Guy 1965	Mackey, John 1992	Smith, Jackie 1994
Ditka, Mike. 1988	Maynard, Don 1987	Taylor, Charley 1984
Fears, Tom 1970	McDonald, Tommy 1998	Warfield, Paul 1983
+ Hewitt, Bill 1971		Winslow, Kellen 1995

Linemen (pre-World War II)

+ Edwards, Turk (T) 1969	+ Hubbard, Cal (T) 1963	Musso, George (T-G). 1982
+ Fortmann, Dan (G) 1985	+ Kiesling, Walt (G) 1966	+ Stydahar, Joe (T) 1967
+ Healey, Ed (T). 1964	+ Kinard, Bruiser (T) 1971	+ Trafton, George (C). 1964
+ Hein, Mel (C) 1963	+ Lyman, Link (T) 1964	+ Turner, Bulldog (C). 1966
+ Henry, Pete (T) 1963	+ Michalske, Mike (G) 1964	+ Wojciechowicz, Alex (C) 1968

Offensive Linemen

Bednarik, Chuck (C-LB) 1967	Langer, Jim (C) 1987	Ringo, Jim (C). 1981
Brown, Roosevelt (T) 1975	Little, Larry (G) 1993	St. Clair, Bob (T) 1990
Dierdorf, Dan (T) 1996	Mack, Tom (G) 1999	Shaw, Billy (G). 1999
Gatski, Frank (C) 1985	McCormack, Mike (T) 1984	Shell, Art (T) 1989
Gregg, Forrest (T-G) 1977	Mix, Ron (T-G) 1979	Stephenson, Dwight (C) 1998
Groza, Lou (T-PK) 1974	Munoz, Anthony (T) 1998	Upshaw, Gene (G) 1987
Hannah, John (G) 1991	Otto, Jim (C). 1980	Webster, Mike (C) 1997
Jones, Stan (T-G-DT). 1991	Parker, Jim (G) 1973	

Defensive Linemen

Atkins, Doug. 1982	Jones, Deacon 1980	Robustelli, Andy. 1971
+ Buchanan, Buck 1990	+ Jordan, Henry 1995	Selmon, Lee Roy 1995
Creekmur, Lou 1996	Lilly, Bob 1980	Stautner, Ernie 1969
Davis, Willie. 1981	Marchetti, Gino 1972	Weinmeister, Arnie 1984
Donovan, Art 1968	Nomellini, Leo 1969	White, Randy. 1994
+ Ford, Len. 1976	Olsen, Merlin 1982	Willis, Bill 1977
Greene, Joe 1987	Page, Alan 1988	

Linebackers

Bell, Bobby 1983	Hendricks, Ted 1990	Schmidt, Joe. 1973
Butkus, Dick 1979	Huff, Sam 1982	Singletary, Mike. 1998
Connor, George (DT-OT) 1975	Lambert, Jack 1990	Taylor, Lawrence 1999
+ George, Bill 1974	Lanier, Willie 1986	
Ham, Jack. 1988	+ Nitschke, Ray 1978	

NFL's 75th Anniversary All-Time Team

Selected by a 15-member panel of former players, NFL and Pro Football Hall of Fame officials and media representatives and released Sept. 1, 1994.

Offense

Wide Receivers (4): Lance Alworth, Raymond Berry, Don Hutson and Jerry Rice

Tight Ends (2): Mike Ditka and Kellen Winslow

Tackles (3): Roosevelt Brown, Forrest Gregg and Anthony Munoz

Guards (3): John Hannah, Jim Parker and Gene Upshaw

Centers (2): Mel Hein and Mike Webster

Quarterbacks (4): Sammy Baugh, Otto Graham, Joe Montana and Johnny Unitas

Running Backs (6): Jim Brown, Marion Motley, Bronko Nagurski, Walter Payton, O.J. Simpson and Steve Van Buren

Defense

Ends (3): Deacon Jones, Gino Marchetti and Reggie White

Tackles (3): Joe Greene, Bob Lilly and Merlin Olsen

Linebackers (7): Dick Butkus, Jack Ham, Ted Hendricks, Jack Lambert, Willie Lanier, Ray Nitschke and Lawrence Taylor

Cornerbacks (4): Mel Blount, Mike Haynes, Dick (Night Train) Lane and Rod Woodson

Safties (3): Ken Houston, Ronnie Lott and Larry Wilson

Specialists

Placekicker: Jan Stenerud
Punter: Ray Guy

Kick Returner: Gale Sayers
Punt Returner: Billy (White Shoes) Johnson

Defensive Backs

Adderley, Herb 1980	Haynes, Mike............1997	Lary, Yale 1979
Barney, Lem 1992	Houston, Ken 1986	Renfro, Mel...............1996
Blount, Mel...............1989	Johnson, Jimmy 1994	+ Tunnell, Emlen 1967
Brown, Willie 1984	Krause, Paul...............1998	Wilson, Larry 1978
+ Christiansen, Jack 1970	Lane, Dick (Night Train) 1974	Wood, Willie 1989

Placekicker

Stenerud, Jan 1991

Coaches

+ Brown, Paul 1967	Grant, Bud 1994	+ Neale, Earle (Greasy).......1969
+ Ewbank, Weeb 1978	+ Halas, George............1963	Noll, Chuck 1993
+ Flaherty, Ray 1976	+ Lambeau, Curly 1963	+ Owen, Steve 1966
Gibbs, Joe 1996	Landry, Tom 1990	Shula, Don 1997
Gillman, Sid 1983	+ Lombardi, Vince...........1971	Walsh, Bill 1993

Contributors

+ Bell, Bert 1963	+ Halas, George............1963	+ Ray, Hugh (Shorty) 1966
+ Bidwill, Charles 1967	Hunt, Lamar 1972	+ Reeves, Dan 1967
+ Carr, Joe 1963	+ Mara, Tim................1963	+ Rooney, Art...............1964
Davis, Al..................1992	Mara, Wellington 1997	+ Rozelle, Pete...............1985
+ Finks, Jim 1995	+ Marshall, George 1963	Schramm, Tex.............1991

Dick McCann Award

First presented in 1969 by the Pro Football Writers of America for long and distinguished reporting on pro football. Named in honor of the first director of the Hall, the McCann Award does not constitute induction into the Hall of Fame.

Year	Year	Year	Year
1969 George Strickler	1977 Art Daley	1985 Cooper Rollow	1993 Ira Miller
1970 Arthur Daley	1978 Murray Olderman	1986 Bill Wallace	1994 Don Pierson
1971 Joe King	1979 Pat Livingston	1987 Jerry Magee	1995 Ray Didinger
1972 Lewis Atchison	1980 Chuck Heaton	1988 Gordon Forbes	1996 Paul Zimmerman
1973 Dave Brady	1981 Norm Miller	1989 Vito Stellino	1997 Bob Roesler
1974 Bob Oates	1982 Cameron Snyder	1990 Will McDonough	1998 Dave Anderson
1975 John Steadman	1983 Hugh Brown	1991 Dick Connor	1999 Art Spander
1976 Jack Hand	1984 Larry Felser	1992 Frank Luska	

Pete Rozelle Award

First presented in 1989 by the Hall of Fame for exceptional longtime contributions to radio and TV in pro football. Named in honor of the former NFL commissioner, who was also a publicist and GM for the LA Rams, the Rozelle Award does not constitute induction into the Hall of Fame.

Year	Year	Year	Year
1989 Bill McPhail	1992 Chris Schenkel	1995 Frank Gifford	1998 Val Pinchbeck Jr.
1990 Lindsey Nelson	1993 Curt Gowdy	1996 Jack Buck	1999 Dick Enberg
1991 Ed Sabol	1994 Pat Summerall	1997 Charlie Jones	

Canadian Football Hall of Fame

Established in 1963. Current Hall opened in 1972. **Address:** 58 Jackson Street West, Hamilton, Ontario, L8P 1L4. **Telephone:** (905) 528-7566.

Eligibility: Nominated players must be retired three years, but coaches and builders can still be active. Voting done by 15-member panel of Canadian pro and amateur football officials.

Class of 1999 (3): PLAYERS—DB **Dickie Harris**, Montreal (1972-80); QB **Condredge Halloway**, Ottawa (1975-80), Toronto (1981-86), B.C. (1987). BUILDER—**Donald Barker**.

Members are listed with year of induction; (+) indicates deceased members.

Players

Ah You, Junior	1997	
Atchison, Ron	1978	
+ Bailey, Byron	1975	
Baker, Bill	1994	
Barrow, John	1976	
+ Batstone, Harry	1963	
+ Beach, Ormond	1963	
Benecick, Al	1996	
Box, Ab.	1965	
+ Breen, Joe	1963	
+ Bright, Johnny	1970	
Brown, Tom	1984	
Brock, Dieter	1995	
Campbell, Jerry (Soupy)	1996	
Casey, Tom	1964	
Charlton, Ken	1992	
Clarke, Bill	1996	
Clements, Tom	1994	
Coffey, Tommy Joe.	1977	
+ Conacher, Lionel	1963	
Copeland, Royal	1988	
Corrigall, Jim	1990	
+ Cox, Ernest	1963	
+ Craig, Ross	1964	
+ Cronin, Carl	1967	
Cutler, Dave	1998	
+ Cutler, Wes.	1968	
Dalla Riva, Peter	1993	
DiPietro, Rocky	1997	
+ Dixon, George	1974	
+ Eliowitz, Abe	1969	
+ Emerson, Eddie	1963	
Etcheverry, Sam	1969	
Evanshen, Terry	1984	
+ Faloney, Bernie	1974	
+ Fear, A.H. (Cap)	1967	
Fennell, Dave	1990	
+ Ferraro, John	1966	
Fieldgate, Norm	1979	
Fleming, Willie.	1982	
Gabriel, Tony	1985	
Gaines, Gene	1994	
+ Gall, Hugh	1963	
Golab, Tony	1964	

Grant, Tom	1995	
Gray, Herbert	1983	
+ Griffing, Dean	1965	
Halloway, Condredge	1999	
+ Hanson, Fritz	1963	
Harris, Dickie	1999	
Harris, Wayne	1976	
Harrison, Herm	1993	
Helton, John	1986	
Henley, Garney	1979	
Hinton, Tom	1991	
+ Huffman, Dick	1987	
+ Isbister, Bob Sr.	1965	
Jackson, Russ	1973	
+ Jacobs, Jack	1963	
+ James, Eddie (Dynamite)	1963	
James, Gerry	1981	
+ Kabat, Greg	1966	
Kapp, Joe	1984	
Keeling, Jerry	1989	
Kelly, Brian	1991	
Kelly, Ellison	1992	
Kepley, Dan	1996	
Krol, Joe	1963	
Kwong, Normie	1969	
Lancaster, Ron	1982	
+ Lawson, Smirle.	1963	
+ Leadlay, Frank (Pep)	1963	
+ Lear, Les	1974	
Lewis, Leo	1973	
Lunsford, Earl	1983	
Luster, Marv	1990	
Luzzi, Don	1986	
+ McCance, Ches	1976	
+ McGill, Frank	1965	
McQuarters, Ed	1988	
Miles, Rollie	1980	
+ Molson, Percy	1963	
Morris, Frank	1983	
+ Morris, Ted	1964	
Mosca, Angelo	1987	
+ Nelson, Roger	1986	
Neumann, Peter.	1979	
O'Quinn, John (Red)	1981	

Pajaczkowski, Tony	1988	
Parker, Jackie	1971	
Patterson, Hal.	1971	
Poplawski, Joe	1998	
Perry, Gordon	1970	
+ Perry, Norm	1963	
Ploen, Ken	1975	
+ Quilty, S.P. (Silver)	1966	
+ Rebholz, Russ	1963	
Reed, George	1979	
+ Reeve, Ted	1963	
Rigney, Frank	1985	
Robinson, Larry	1998	
+ Rodden, Mike	1964	
+ Rowe, Paul	1964	
Ruby, Martin.	1974	
+ Russel, Jeff	1963	
Scott, Tom	1998	
+ Scott, Vince	1982	
Shatto, Dick	1975	
+ Simpson, Ben	1963	
Simpson, Bob	1976	
+ Sprague, David	1963	
Stevenson, Art	1969	
Stewart, Ron	1977	
+ Stirling, Hugh (Bummer)	1966	
Sutherin, Don	1992	
Symons, Bill	1997	
Thelen, Dave	1989	
+ Timmis, Brian	1963	
Tinsley, Bud	1982	
+ Tommy, Andy	1989	
+ Trawick, Herb	1975	
+ Tubman, Joe	1968	
Tucker, Whit.	1993	
Urness, Ted	1989	
Vaughan, Kaye	1978	
Wagner, Virgil	1980	
+ Welch, Hawley (Huck)	1964	
Wilkinson, Tom	1987	
Wilson, Al	1997	
Wylie, Harvey	1980	
Young, Jim	1991	
+ Zock, Bill.	1985	

Builders

+ Back, Leonard	1971	
+ Bailey, Harold	1965	
+ Ballard, Harold	1987	
Barker, Donald.	1999	
+ Berger, Sam	1993	
+ Brook, Tom	1975	
+ Brown, D. Wes	1963	
+ Chipman, Arthur	1969	
Clair, Frank.	1981	
+ Cooper, Ralph	1992	
Coulter, Bruce	1997	
+ Crighton, Hec	1986	
+ Currie, Andrew	1974	
Custis, Bernard	1998	
+ Davies, Dr. Andrew	1969	
+ DeGruchy, John	1963	
Dojack, Paul.	1978	

+ Duggan, Eck.	1981	
+ DuMoulin, Seppi	1963	
+ Foulds, Willliam	1963	
Fulton, Greg	1995	
Gaudaur, J.G. (Jake).	1984	
Gibson, Frank	1996	
Grant, Bud	1983	
+ Grey, Lord Earl	1963	
+ Griffith, Dr. Harry	1963	
+ Halter, Sydney	1966	
+ Hannibal, Frank	1963	
+ Hayman, Lew	1975	
+ Hughes, W.P. (Billy)	1974	
Keys, Eagle	1990	
Kimball, Norman	1991	
+ Kramer, R.A. (Bob)	1987	
+ Lieberman, M.I. (Moe)	1973	

+ McBrien, Harry	1978	
+ McCaffrey, Jimmy	1967	
+ McCann, Dave	1966	
McNaughton, Don	1994	
+ McPherson, Don	1983	
+ Metras, Johnny	1980	
+ Montgomery, Ken	1970	
+ Newton, Jack	1964	
+ Preston, Ken	1990	
+ Ritchie, Alvin	1963	
+ Ryan, Joe B.	1968	
Sazio, Ralph.	1988	
+ Shaughnessy, Frank (Shag)	1963	
+ Shouldice, W.T. (Hap).	1977	
+ Simpson, Jimmie	1986	
+ Slocomb, Karl	1989	
+ Spring, Harry	1976	

Stukus, Annis 1974	+ Tindall, Frank............1985	+ Warwick, Bert 1964
+ Taylor, N.J. (Piffles) 1963	+ Warner, Clair............1965	+ Wilson, Seymour..........1984

GOLF

World Golf Hall of Fame

A new World Golf Hall of Fame opened its doors in 1998 at the World Golf Village outside of Jacksonville, Fla. The 71 members of the former Hall of Fame (established in 1974 but inactive since 1993) in Pinehurst, N.C. and LPGA Hall of Fame were "grandfathered" into the new Hall. **Address:** 21 World Golf Place, St. Augustine, FL 32092. **Telephone:** (904) 940-4000.

Eligibility: Professionals have three avenues into the WGHF. A PGA Tour player qualifies for the ballot if he has at least 10 victories in approved tournaments, or at least two victories among The Players Championship, Masters, U.S. Open, British Open and PGA Championship, is at least 40 years old and has been a member of the Tour for 10 years. A senior PGA Tour player qualifies if he has been a Senior Tour member for five years and has 20 wins between the PGA Tour and Senior Tour or five wins among the PGA majors, the Players Championship and the senior majors (U.S. Senior Open, Tradition, PGA Seniors' Championship and Senior Players Championship).

Any player qualifying for the LPGA Hall automatically qualifies for the WGHF. Until 1999, nominees must have had played 10 years on the LPGA tour and won 30 official events, including two major championships; 35 official events and one major; or 40 official events and no majors. The eligibility requirements were loosened somewhat in 1999. The new guidelines are based on a system which awards two points for winning a major and one point for winning other tournaments, the Vare trophy (for lowest scoring average) and the player of the year award. Players must win at least one major, Vare trophy, or player of the year award and accumulate a total of 27 points to be inducted. For players not eligible for either the PGA Tour or the LPGA Hall of Fame, a body of over 300 international golf writers and historians will vote each year.

Members are listed with year of induction; (+) indicates deceased members.

Class of 1999 (4): MEN—**Seve Ballesteros** and **Lloyd Mangrum**; WOMEN—**Beth Daniel** and **Amy Alcott**.
Note: Seve Ballesteros had already been voted in but was not inducted until 1999.

Men

+ Anderson, Willie 1975	+ Guldahl, Ralph.............1981	Nicklaus, Jack 1974
+ Armour, Tommy 1976	+ Hagen, Walter.............1974	+ Ouimet, Francis 1974
+ Ball, John, Jr.............1977	+ Hilton, Harold 1978	Palmer, Arnold.............1974
Ballesteros, Seve 1999	+ Hogan, Ben 1974	Player, Gary...............1974
+ Barnes, Jim 1989	Irwin, Hale 1992	Runyan, Paul 1990
+ Boros, Julius 1982	+ Jones, Bobby 1974	+ Sarazen, Gene 1974
+ Braid, James..............1976	+ Little, Lawson 1980	+ Smith, Horton 1990
Casper, Billy...............1978	Littler, Gene 1990	Snead, Sam 1974
Cooper, Lighthorse Harry....1992	+ Locke, Bobby 1977	+ Taylor, John H 1975
+ Cotton, Thomas 1980	+ Mangrum, Lloyd...........1999	Thomson, Peter.............1988
+ Demaret, Jimmy 1983	+ Middlecoff, Cary...........1986	+ Travers, Jerry 1976
De Vicenzo, Roberto........1989	Miller, Johnny 1998	+ Travis, Walter 1979
+ Evans, Chick 1975	+ Morris, Tom Jr. 1975	Trevino, Lee 1981
Faldo, Nick 1998	+ Morris, Tom Sr 1976	+ Vardon, Harry 1974
Floyd, Ray 1989	Nelson, Byron 1974	Watson, Tom 1988

Women

Alcott, Amy................1999	Jameson, Betty 1951	+ Vare, Glenna Collett 1975
Berg, Patty 1974	King, Betsy 1995	+ Wethered, Joyce 1975
Bradley, Pat 1991	Lopez, Nancy 1989	Whitworth, Kathy 1982
Carner, JoAnne 1985	Mann, Carol................1977	Wright, Mickey 1976
Daniel, Beth 1999	Rawls, Betsy 1987	+ Zaharias, Babe Didrikson ...1974
Haynie, Sandra 1977	Sheehan, Patty.............1993	
+ Howe, Dorothy C.H 1978	Suggs, Louise 1979	

Contributors

Campbell, William 1990	+ Harlow, Robert.............1988	+ Ross, Donald 1977
+ Corcoran, Fred 1975	Hope, Bob 1983	+ Shore, Dinah 1994
+ Crosby, Bing...............1978	Jones, Robert Trent 1987	+ Tufts, Richard 1992
+ Dey, Joe 1975	+ Roberts, Clifford...........1978	
+ Graffis, Herb 1977	Rodriguez, Chi Chi 1992	

Old PGA Hall Members Not in PGA/World Hall

The original PGA Hall of Fame was established in 1940 by the PGA of America, but abandoned after the 1982 inductions in favor of the PGA/World Hall of Fame. Twenty-nine members of the old PGA Hall have been elected to the PGA/World Hall since then. Players yet to make the cut are listed below with year of induction into old PGA Hall.

+ Brady, Mike 1960	Ford, Doug.................1975	+ Picard, Henry.............1961
+ Burke, Billy 1966	+ Ghezzi, Vic 1965	+ Revolta, Johnny 1963
Burke, Jack Jr 1975	+ Harbert, Chick............1968	+ Shute, Denny 1957
+ Cruickshank, Bobby 1967	Harper, Chandler 1969	+ Smith, Alex................1940
+ Diegel, Leo................1955	+ Harrison, Dutch 1962	+ Smith, Macdonald 1954
+ Dudley, Ed 1964	+ Hutchison, Jock Sr.........1959	+ Wood, Craig 1956
+ Dutra, Olin 1962	+ McDermott, John 1940	
+ Farroll, Johnny 1961	+ McLeod, Fred.............1960	

HOCKEY

Hockey Hall of Fame

Established in 1945 by the National Hockey League and opened in 1961. **Address:** BCE Place, 30 Yonge Street, Toronto, Ontario, M5E 1X8. **Telephone:** (416) 360-7735.

Eligibility: Nominated players and referees must be retired three years. However that waiting period has now been waived ten times. Players that have had the waiting period waived are indicated with an asterisk. Voting done by 15-member panel made up of pro and amateur hockey personalities and media representatives. A 15-member Veterans Committee selects older players.

Class of 1999 (3): PLAYER— forward **Wayne Gretzky**, Edmonton (1979-88), Los Angeles (1989-96), St. Louis (1996), New York Rangers (1996-99). BUILDER— **Ian "Scotty" Morrison**. REFEREE— **Andy van Hellemond**.

Members are listed with year of induction; (+) indicates deceased members.

Forwards

Abel, Sid...................1969	Gainey, Bob...............1992	+ Oliver, Harry 1967
+ Adams, Jack..............1959	+ Gardner, Jimmy 1962	Olmstead, Bert...........1985
+ Apps, Syl 1961	Geoffrion, Bernie..........1972	+ Patrick, Lynn 1980
Armstrong, George........1975	+ Gerard, Eddie 1945	Perreault, Gilbert...........1990
+ Bailey, Ace...............1975	Gilbert, Rod 1982	+ Phillips, Tom 1945
+ Bain, Dan 1945	+ Gilmour, Billy 1962	+ Primeau, Joe...............1963
+ Baker, Hobey.............1945	Goulet, Michel............1998	Pulford, Bob 1991
Barber, Bill 1990	Gretzky, Wayne* 1999	+ Rankin, Frank 1961
+ Barry, Marty 1965	+ Griffis, Si.................1950	Ratelle, Jean 1985
Bathgate, Andy 1978	+ Hay, George 1958	Richard, Henri 1979
+ Bauer, Bobby 1996	+ Hextall, Bryan 1969	Richard, Maurice (Rocket)* ..1961
Beliveau, Jean* 1972	+ Hooper, Tom..............1962	+ Richardson, George 1950
+ Bentley, Doug 1964	Howe, Gordie*............1972	+ Roberts, Gordie 1971
+ Bentley, Max 1966	+ Howe, Syd 1965	+ Russel, Blair 1965
+ Blake, Toe................1966	Hull, Bobby 1983	+ Russell, Ernie 1965
Bossy, Mike 1991	+ Hyland, Harry 1962	+ Ruttan, Jack 1962
+ Boucher, Frank 1958	+ Irvin, Dick 1958	+ Scanlan, Fred..............1965
+ Bowie, Dubbie............1945	+ Jackson, Busher 1971	Schmidt, Milt 1961
+ Broadbent, Punch 1962	+ Joliat, Aurel 1947	+ Schriner, Sweeney..........1962
Bucyk, John (Chief) 1981	+ Keats, Duke 1958	+ Seibert, Oliver 1961
+ Burch, Billy 1974	Kennedy, Ted (Teeder)......1966	Shutt, Steve...............1993
Clarke, Bobby 1987	Keon, Dave 1986	+ Siebert, Babe 1964
+ Colville, Neil 1967	Lach, Elmer...............1966	Sittler, Darryl 1989
+ Conacher, Charlie..........1961	Lafleur, Guy 1988	+ Smith, Alf 1962
Conacher, Roy.............1998	+ Lalonde, Newsy............1950	Smith, Clint 1991
+ Cook, Bill 1952	Laprade, Edgar 1993	+ Smith, Hooley..............1972
+ Cook, Bun.................1995	Lemaire, Jacques 1984	+ Smith, Tommy..............1973
Cournoyer, Yvan 1982	Lemieux, Mario* 1997	+ Stanley, Barney 1962
+ Cowley, Bill 1968	+ Lewis, Herbie 1989	Stastny, Peter 1998
+ Crawford, Rusty 1962	Lindsay, Ted* 1966	+ Stewart, Nels 1962
+ Darragh, Jack.............1962	+ MacKay, Mickey 1952	+ Stuart, Bruce..............1961
+ Davidson, Scotty 1950	Mahovlich, Frank...........1981	+ Taylor, Fred (Cyclone).......1947
+ Day, Hap 1961	+ Malone, Joe...............1950	+ Trihey, Harry 1950
Delvecchio, Alex 1977	+ Marshall, Jack 1965	Trottier, Bryan.............1997
+ Denneny, Cy...............1959	+ Maxwell, Fred 1962	Ullman, Norm 1982
Dionne, Marcel 1992	McDonald, Lanny 1992	+ Walker, Jack...............1960
+ Drillon, Gordie............1975	+ McGee, Frank 1945	+ Walsh, Marty..............1962
+ Drinkwater, Graham 1950	+ McGimsie, Billy 1962	Watson, Harry 1994
Dumart, Woody 1992	Mikita, Stan 1983	+ Watson, Harry (Moose) 1962
+ Dunderdale, Tommy 1974	Moore, Dickie 1974	+ Weiland, Cooney 1971
+ Dye, Babe.................1970	+ Morenz, Howie 1945	+ Westwick, Harry (Rat).......1962
Esposito, Phil 1984	+ Mosienko, Bill 1965	+ Whitcroft, Fred.............1962
+ Farrell, Arthur.............1965	+ Nighbor, Frank 1947	
+ Foyston, Frank 1958	+ Noble, Reg................1962	
+ Frederickson, Frank.........1958	+ O'Connor, Buddy 1988	

Goaltenders

+ Benedict, Clint 1965	+ Hainsworth, George 1961	Rayner, Chuck 1973
Bower, Johnny 1976	Hall, Glenn................1975	+ Sawchuk, Terry* 1971
+ Brimsek, Frankie 1966	+ Hern, Riley 1962	Smith, Billy 1993
+ Broda, Turk 1967	+ Holmes, Hap 1972	+ Thompson, Tiny 1959
Cheevers, Gerry 1985	+ Hutton, J.B. (Bouse) 1962	Tretiak, Vladislav...........1989
+ Connell, Alex 1958	+ Lehman, Hughie 1958	+ Vezina, Georges 1945
Dryden, Ken 1983	+ LeSueur, Percy 1961	Worsley, Gump 1980
+ Durnan, Bill................1964	+ Lumley, Harry..............1980	+ Worters, Roy 1969
Esposito, Tony 1988	+ Moran, Paddy 1958	
+ Gardiner, Chuck 1945	Parent, Bernie..............1984	
Giacomin, Eddie 1987	+ Plante, Jacques 1978	

Defensemen

Boivin, Leo 1986
+ Boon, Dickie. 1952
Bouchard, Butch 1966
+ Boucher, George 1960
+ Cameron, Harry 1962
+ Clancy, King. 1958
+ Clapper, Dit* 1947
+ Cleghorn, Sprague 1958
+ Conacher, Lionel 1994
Coulter, Art. 1974
+ Dutton, Red. 1958
Flaman, Fernie 1990
Gadsby, Bill 1970
+ Gardiner, Herb 1958
+ Goheen, F.X. (Moose) 1952
+ Goodfellow, Ebbie 1963
+ Grant, Mike 1950
+ Green, Wilf (Shorty) 1962

+ Hall, Joe 1961
+ Harvey, Doug. 1973
Horner, Red 1965
+ Horton, Tim. 1977
Howell, Harry 1979
+ Johnson, Ching 1958
+ Johnson, Ernie 1952
Johnson, Tom 1970
Kelly, Red* 1969
Laperriere, Jacques 1987
Lapointe, Guy 1993
+ Laviolette, Jack 1962
+ Mantha, Sylvio. 1960
+ McNamara, George. 1958
Orr, Bobby* 1979
Park, Brad. 1988
+ Patrick, Lester 1947
Pilote, Pierre 1975

+ Pitre, Didier 1962
Potvin, Denis. 1991
+ Pratt, Babe 1966
Pronovost, Marcel 1978
+ Pulford, Harvey 1945
Quackenbush, Bill 1976
Reardon, Kenny. 1966
Robinson, Larry 1995
+ Ross, Art 1945
Salming, Borje 1996
Savard, Serge 1986
Seibert, Earl 1963
+ Shore, Eddie 1947
+ Simpson, Joe 1962
Stanley, Allan 1981
+ Stewart, Jack 1964
+ Stuart, Hod. 1945
+ Wilson, Gordon (Phat) 1962

Referees & Linesmen

Armstrong, Neil. 1991
Ashley, John 1981
Chadwick, Bill 1964
D'Amico, John 1993
+ Elliott, Chaucer 1961

+ Hayes, George 1988
+ Hewitson, Bobby 1963
+ Ion, Mickey. 1961
Pavelich, Matt 1987
+ Rodden, Mike 1962

+ Smeaton, J. Cooper 1961
Storey, Red 1967
Udvari, Frank. 1973
van Hellemond, Andy. 1999

Builders

+ Adams, Charles. 1960
+ Adams, Weston W. Sr 1972
+ Ahearn, Frank 1962
+ Ahearne, J.F. (Bunny) 1977
+ Allan, Sir Montagu 1945
Allen, Keith 1992
Arbour, Al. 1996
+ Ballard, Harold 1977
+ Bauer, Fr. David. 1989
+ Bickell, J.P. 1978
Bowman, Scotty 1991
+ Brown, George 1961
+ Brown, Walter 1962
+ Buckland, Frank 1975
Butterfield, Jack 1980
+ Calder, Frank 1945
+ Campbell, Angus 1964
+ Campbell, Clarence 1966
+ Cattarinich, Joseph 1977
+ Dandurand, Leo 1963
Dilio, Frank. 1964
+ Dudley, George 1958
+ Dunn, James. 1968
Francis, Emile. 1982
+ Gibson, Jack 1976
+ Gorman, Tommy 1963
+ Griffiths, Frank A. 1993
+ Hanley, Bill 1986
+ Hay, Charles 1984

+ Hendy, Jim 1968
+ Hewitt, Foster 1965
+ Hewitt, W.A. 1945
+ Hume, Fred. 1962
+ Imlach, Punch 1984
+ Ivan, Tommy 1964
+ Jennings, Bill. 1975
+ Johnson, Bob 1992
+ Juckes, Gordon 1979
+ Kilpatrick, John 1960
+ Knox, Seymour III 1993
+ Leader, Al 1969
LeBel, Bob. 1970
+ Lockhart, Tom 1965
+ Loicq, Paul 1961
+ Mariucci, John 1985
Mathers, Frank. 1992
+ McLaughlin, Frederic 1963
+ Milford, Jake 1984
Molson, Hartland 1973
Morrison, Ian (Scotty) 1999
+ Murray, Athol (Pere) 1998
+ Nelson, Francis 1945
+ Norris, Bruce 1969
+ Norris, James D. 1962
+ Norris, James Sr 1958
+ Northey, William. 1945
+ O'Brien, J.A. 1962
O'Neill, Brian 1994

Page, Fred 1993
+ Patrick, Frank 1958
+ Pickard, Allan 1958
+ Pilous, Rudy 1985
Poile, Bud 1990
Pollock, Sam. 1978
+ Raymond, Donat 1958
+ Robertson, John Ross. 1945
+ Robinson, Claude 1945
+ Ross, Philip 1976
Sather, Glen 1997
Sebetzki, Gunther 1995
+ Selke, Frank 1960
Sinden, Harry 1983
+ Smith, Frank 1962
+ Smythe, Conn. 1958
Snider, Ed. 1988
+ Stanley, Lord of Preston 1945
+ Sutherland, James 1945
+ Tarasov, Anatoli 1974
Torrey, Bill 1995
+ Turner, Lloyd 1958
+ Tutt, William Thayer 1978
Voss, Carl. 1974
+ Waghorne, Fred 1961
+ Wirtz, Arthur 1971
Wirtz, Bill 1976
Ziegler, John. 1987

Note: Alan Eagleson was inducted into the Hockey Hall of Fame in 1989 but resigned in 1998 after being found guilty of fraud.

Elmer Ferguson Award

First presented in 1984 by the Professional Hockey Writers' Association for meritorious contributions by members of the PHWA. Named in honor of the late Montreal newspaper reporter, the Ferguson Award does not constitute induction into the Hall of Fame and is not necessarily an annual presentation.

1984 Jacques Beauchamp, Jim Burchard, Red Burnett, Dink Carroll, Jim Coleman, Ted Damata, Marcel Desjardins, Jack Dulmage, Milt Dunnell, Elmer Ferguson, Tom Fitzgerald, Trent Frayne, Al Laney, Joe Nichols, Basil O'Meara, Jim Vipond & Lewis Walter
1985 Charlie Barton, Red Fisher, George Gross, Zotique L'Esperance, Charles Mayer & Andy O'Brien
1986 Dick Johnston, Leo Monahan & Tim Moriarty
1987 Bill Brennan, Rex MacLeod, Ben Olan & Fran Rosa
1988 Jim Proudfoot & Scott Young
1989 Claude Larochelle & Frank Orr

1990 Bertrand Raymond
1991 Hugh Delano
1992 No award
1993 Al Strachan
1994 No award
1995 Jake Gatecliff
1996 No award
1997 Ken McKenzie
1998 Yvon Pedneault
1999 Russ Conway

Hockey (Cont.)
Foster Hewitt Award

First presented in 1984 by the NHL Broadcasters' Association for meritorious contributions by members of the NHLBA. Named in honor of Canada's legendary "Voice of Hockey," the Hewitt Award does not constitute induction into the Hall of Fame and is not necessarily an annual presentation.

1985 Budd Lynch & Doug Smith	1990 Jiggs McDonald	1995 Brian McFarlane
1986 Wes McKnight & Lloyd Pettit	1991 Bruce Martyn	1996 Bob Cole
1987 Bob Wilson	1992 Jim Robson	1997 Gene Hart
1988 Dick Irvin	1993 Al Shaver	1998 Howie Meeker
1989 Dan Kelly	1994 Ted Darling	1999 Richard Garneau

U.S. Hockey Hall of Fame

Established in 1968 by the Eveleth (Minn.) Civic Association Project H Committee and opened in 1973. **Address:** 801 Hat Trick Ave., P.O. Box 657, Eveleth, MN 55734. **Telephone:** (218) 744-5167.

Eligibility: Nominated players and referees must be American-born and retired five years; coaches must be American-born and must have coached predominantly American teams. Voting done by 12-member panel made up of Hall of Fame members and U.S. hockey officials.

Class of 1998 (4): PLAYERS—**Joe Mullen**, **Bruce Mather** and **Mike Curran**. COACH—**Lou Nanne**.

Members are listed with year of induction; (+) indicates deceased members.

Players

+ Abel, Clarence (Taffy) 1973	Ftorek, Robbie 1991	Moe, Bill 1974
+ Baker, Hobey 1973	+ Garrison, John 1974	Morrow, Ken 1995
Bartholome, Earl 1977	Garrity, Jack 1986	+ Moseley, Fred. 1975
+ Bessone, Peter 1978	+ Goheen, Frank (Moose) 1973	Mullen, Joe. 1998
Blake, Bob 1985	Grant, Wally 1994	+ Murray, Hugh (Muzz) Sr. 1987
Boucha, Henry. 1995	+ Harding, Austie 1975	+ Nelson, Hub. 1978
+ Brimsek, Frankie 1973	Iglehart, Stewart 1975	+ Nyrop, William D. 1997
Cavanaugh, Joe 1994	Ikola, Willard. 1990	Olson, Eddie 1977
+ Chaisson, Ray 1974	Johnson, Virgil 1974	+ Owen, George 1973
Chase, John 1973	+ Karakas, Mike 1973	+ Palmer, Winthrop 1973
Christian, Bill 1984	Kirrane, Jack 1987	Paradise, Bob 1989
Christian, Roger. 1989	+ Lane, Myles 1973	Purpur, Clifford (Fido) 1974
Cleary, Bill 1976	Langevin, Dave 1993	Riley, Bill. 1977
Cleary, Bob 1981	Larson, Reed. 1996	+ Romnes, Elwin (Doc) 1973
+ Conroy, Tony 1975	+ Linder, Joe. 1975	Rondeau, Dick 1985
Curran, Mike 1998	+ LoPresti, Sam 1973	Sheehey, Timothy. 1997
Dahlstrom, Carl (Cully) 1973	+ Mariucci, John 1973	+ Williams, Tom 1981
+ DesJardins, Vic. 1974	Matchefts, John 1991	+ Winters, Frank (Coddy) 1973
+ Desmond, Richard 1988	Mather, Bruce. 1998	+ Yackel, Ken. 1986
+ Dill, Bob 1979	Mayasich, John 1976	
Everett, Doug 1974	McCartan, Jack 1983	

Coaches

+ Almquist, Oscar. 1983	Heyliger, Vic. 1974	Pleban, Connie 1990
Bessone, Amo 1992	Holt Jr., Charles E.. 1997	Riley, Jack 1979
Brooks, Herb 1990	Ikola, Willard. 1990	+ Ross, Larry 1988
Ceglarski, Len 1992	+ Jeremiah, Eddie 1973	+ Thompson, Cliff 1973
+ Fullerton, James 1992	+ Johnson, Bob 1991	+ Stewart, Bill 1982
Gambucci, Sergio 1996	Kelley, Jack. 1993	+ Winsor, Ralph 1973
+ Gordon, Malcolm 1973	+ Kelly, John (Snooks). 1974	
Harkness, Ned. 1994	Nanne, Lou. 1998	

Referee

Chadwick, Bill 1974

Contributor

Schulz, Charles M. 1993

Administrators

+ Brown, George 1973	+ Jennings, Bill. 1981	Trumble, Hal. 1970
+ Brown, Walter 1973	+ Kahler, Nick 1980	+ Tutt, Thayer. 1973
Bush, Walter. 1980	+ Lockhart, Tom 1973	Wirtz, Bill 1967
+ Clark, Don 1978	Marvin, Cal 1982	+ Wright, Lyle 1973
Claypool, Jim. 1995	Patrick, Craig. 1996	
+ Gibson, J.L. (Doc) 1973	Ridder, Bob 1976	

Members of Both Hockey and U.S. Hockey Halls of Fame

Players	**Coach**	**Builders**	
Hobey Baker	Bob Johnson	George Brown	Tom Lockhart
Frankie Brimsek		Walter Brown	Thayer Tutt
Frank (Moose) Goheen	**Referee**	Doc Gibson	Bill Wirtz
John Mariucci	Bill Chadwick	Bill Jennings	

HORSE RACING

National Horse Racing Hall of Fame

Established in 1950 by the Saratoga Springs Racing Association and opened in 1955. **Address:** National Museum of Racing and Hall of Fame, 191 Union Ave., Saratoga Springs, NY 12866. **Telephone:** (518) 584-0400.

Eligibility: Nominated horses must be retired five years; jockeys must be active at least 15 years; trainers must be active at least 25 years. Voting done by 100-member panel of horse racing media.

Class of 1999 (5): JOCKEY—**Russell Baze**. TRAINER—**D. Wayne Lukas**. HORSES—**Exceller**, **Miesque** and **Gun Bow**.

Members are listed with year of induction; (+) indicates deceased members.

Jockeys

+ Adams, Frank (Dooley)*....1970	+ Garner, Andrew (Mack)....1969	+ Patrick, Gil 1970
+ Adams, John 1965	+ Garrison, Snapper 1955	Pincay, Laffit Jr. 1975
+ Aitcheson, Joe Jr.*.........1978	+ Gomez, Avelino............1982	+ Purdy, Sam 1970
+ Arcaro, Eddie 1958	+ Griffin, Henry..............1956	+ Reiff, John.................1956
Atkinson, Ted 1957	+ Guerin, Eric 1972	+ Robertson, Alfred..........1971
Baeza, Braulio.............1976	Hartack, Bill 1959	Rotz, John L................1983
Bailey, Jerry 1995	Hawley, Sandy 1992	+ Sande, Earl................1955
+ Barbee, George............1996	+ Johnson, Albert 1971	+ Schilling, Carroll 1970
+ Bassett, Carroll*...........1972	+ Knapp, Willie..............1969	Shoemaker, Bill 1958
Baze, Russell 1999	+ Kummer, Clarence..........1972	+ Simms, Willie..............1977
+ Blum, Walter 1987	+ Kurtsinger, Charley 1967	+ Sloan, Todhunter 1955
+ Bostwick, George H.* 1968	+ Loftus, Johnny 1959	+ Smithwick, A. Patrick* 1973
+ Boulmetis, Sam 1973	Longden, Johnny 1958	Stevens, Gary 1997
+ Brooks, Steve 1963	Maher, Danny 1955	+ Stout, James 1968
Brumfield, Don 1996	+ McAtee, Linus..............1956	+ Taral, Fred 1955
+ Burns, Tommy 1983	McCarron, Chris 1989	+ Tuckman, Bayard Jr.*.......1973
+ Butwell, Jimmy 1984	+ McCreary, Conn 1975	Turcotte, Ron...............1979
+ Byers, J.D. (Dolly) 1967	+ McKinney, Rigan 1968	+ Turner, Nash..............1955
Cauthen, Steve.............1994	+ McLaughlin, James 1955	Ussery, Robert 1980
+ Coltiletti, Frank............1970	+ Miller, Walter...............1955	Vasquez, Jacinto 1998
Cordero, Angel Jr...........1988	+ Murphy, Isaac 1955	Velasquez, Jorge 1990
+ Crawford, Robert (Specs)*...1973	+ Neves, Ralph 1960	+ Woolfe, George 1955
Day, Pat 1991	+ Notter, Joe 1963	+ Workman, Raymond.......1956
Delahoussaye, Eddie 1993	+ O'Connor, Winnie 1956	Ycaza, Manuel 1977
+ Ensor, Lavelle (Buddy).......1962	+ Odom, George 1955	
+ Fator, Laverne 1955	+ O'Neill, Frank 1956	*Steeplechase jockey
Fishback, Jerry*............1992	+ Parke, Ivan 1978	

Trainers

+ Barrera, Laz...............1979	+ Jacobs, Hirsch 1958	+ Parke, Burley 1986
+ Bedwell, H. Guy 1971	Jerkens, H. Allen 1975	+ Penna, Angel Sr............1988
+ Brown, Edward D...........1984	Johnson, Philip.............1997	+ Pincus, Jacob 1988
Burch, Elliot 1980	+ Johnson, William R. 1986	+ Rogers, John...............1955
+ Burch, Preston M. 1963	+ Jolley, LeRoy 1987	+ Rowe, James Sr............1955
Burch, W.P.................1955	+ Jones, Ben A...............1958	Schulhofer, Scotty 1992
+ Burlew, Fred 1973	Jones, H.A. (Jimmy).........1959	Sheppard, Jonathan 1990
+ Childs, Frank E.............1968	+ Joyner, Andrew 1955	+ Smith, Robert A............1976
+ Clark, Henry 1982	Kelly, Tom 1993	+ Smithwick, Mike 1976
+ Cocks, W. Burling..........1985	Laurin, Lucien 1977	+ Stephens, Woody 1976
Conway, James P...........1996	+ Lewis, J. Howard 1969	Tenny, Mesh 1991
Croll, Jimmy 1994	Lukas, D. Wayne 1999	+ Thompson, H.J. 1969
+ Duke, William 1956	+ Luro, Horatio 1980	+ Trotsek, Harry 1984
+ Feustel, Louis 1964	+ Madden, John 1983	Van Berg, Jack..............1985
+ Fitzsimmons, J. (Sunny Jim) ..1958	+ Maloney, Jim 1989	+ Van Berg, Marion 1970
Frankel, Bobby.............1995	Martin, Frank (Pancho) 1981	+ Veitch, Sylvester............1977
+ Gaver, John M. 1966	McAnally, Ron 1990	+ Walden, Robert 1970
+ Healey, Thomas............1955	+ McDaniel, Henry............1956	Walsh, Michael 1997
+ Hildreth, Samuel 1955	+ Miller, MacKenzie 1987	+ Ward, Sherrill 1978
+ Hirsch, Max 1959	+ Molter, William, Jr. 1960	Whiteley, Frank Jr............1978
+ Hirsch, W.J. (Buddy) 1982	Mott, Bill 1998	+ Whittingham, Charlie 1974
+ Hitchcock, Thomas Sr. 1973	+ Mulholland, Winbert........1967	+ Williamson, Ansel 1998
+ Hughes, Hollie 1973	+ Neloy, Eddie 1983	Winfrey, W.C. (Bill).........1971
+ Hyland, John 1956	Nerud, John 1972	

Horses

Year foaled in parentheses.

+ Ack Ack (1966)............1986	+ Alsab (1939) 1976	+ Armed (1941) 1963
Affectionately (1960) 1989	+ Alydar (1975) 1989	+ Artful (1902) 1956
Affirmed (1975).............1980	Alysheba (1984)............1993	+ Arts and Letters (1966)......1994
All-Along (1979) 1990	+ American Eclipse (1814) 1970	+ Assault (1943)..............1964

Horse Racing (Cont.)

+ Battleship (1927)...........1969
+ Bayakoa (1984) 1998
+ Bed O'Roses (1947)........1976
+ Beldame (1901) 1956
+ Ben Brush (1893) 1955
+ Bewitch (1945) 1977
+ Bimelech (1937)............1990
+ Black Gold (1919)..........1989
+ Black Helen (1932)..........1991
+ Blue Larkspur (1926)........1957
+ Bold 'n Determined (1977) ..1997
+ Bold Ruler (1954) 1973
+ Bon Nouvel (1960) 1976
+ Boston (1833) 1955
+ Broomstick (1901)..........1956
+ Buckpasser (1963) 1970
+ Busher (1942) 1964
+ Bushranger (1930) 1967
+ Cafe Prince (1970) 1985
+ Carry Back (1958) 1975
+ Cavalcade (1931)...........1993
+ Challedon (1936) 1977
+ Chris Evert (1971)..........1988
+ Cicada (1959)..............1967
+ Citation (1945) 1959
+ Coaltown (1945)............1983
+ Colin (1905) 1956
+ Commando (1898)..........1956
+ Count Fleet (1940) 1961
+ Crusader (1923) 1995
+ Dahlia (1971) 1981
+ Damascus (1964) 1974
+ Dark Mirage (1965) 1974
+ Davona Dale (1976)........1985
+ Desert Vixen (1970) 1979
+ Devil Diver (1939)..........1980
+ Discovery (1931) 1969
+ Domino (1891) 1955
+ Dr. Fager (1964) 1971
  Easy Goer (1986) 1997
+ Eight 30 (1936).............1994
+ Elkridge (1938) 1966
+ Emperor of Norfolk (1885) ..1988
+ Equipoise (1928)...........1957
  Exceller (1973) 1999
+ Exterminator (1915) 1957
+ Fairmount (1921) 1985

+ Fair Play (1905) 1956
+ Firenze (1885)..............1981
  Flatterer (1979) 1994
  Foolish Pleasure (1972) 1995
+ Forego (1971)..............1979
+ Fort Marcy (1964) 1998
+ Gallant Bloom (1966).......1977
+ Gallant Fox (1927).........1957
+ Gallant Man (1954) 1987
+ Gallorette (1942) 1962
+ Gamely (1964) 1980
  Genuine Risk (1977)........1986
+ Good and Plenty (1900) 1956
+ Go For Wand (1987)........1996
+ Granville (1933)............1997
+ Grey Lag (1918)............1957
+ Gun Bow (1960)............1999
+ Hamburg (1895)...........1986
+ Hanover (1884).............1955
+ Henry of Navarre (1891) 1985
+ Hill Prince (1947)...........1991
+ Hindoo (1878)..............1955
+ Imp (1894).................1965
+ Jay Trump (1957)...........1971
  John Henry (1975) 1990
+ Johnstown (1936)...........1992
+ Jolly Roger (1922)...........1965
+ Kingston (1884)............1955
+ Kelso (1957) 1967
+ Kentucky (1861) 1983
  Lady's Secret (1982).........1992
  La Prevoyante (1970).........1995
+ L'Escargot (1963) 1977
+ Lexington (1850)...........1955
+ Longfellow (1867)..........1971
+ Luke Blackburn (1877)......1956
+ Majestic Prince (1966).......1988
+ Man o' War (1917).........1957
  Miesque (1984)..............1999
+ Miss Woodford (1880).......1967
+ Myrtlewood (1933)..........1979
+ Nashua (1952)..............1965
+ Native Dancer (1950) 1963
+ Native Diver (1959).........1978
+ Northern Dancer (1961) 1976
+ Neji (1950) 1966
+ Oedipus (1941)............1978

+ Old Rosebud (1911).......1968
+ Omaha (1932).............1965
+ Pan Zareta (1910) 1972
+ Parole (1873) 1984
  Personal Ensign (1984) 1993
+ Peter Pan (1904)...........1956
  Princess Rooney (1980) 1991
+ Real Delight (1949)..........1987
+ Regret (1912) 1957
+ Reigh Count (1925) 1978
  Riva Ridge (1969)...........1998
+ Roamer (1911) 1981
+ Roseben (1901)............1956
+ Round Table (1954) 1972
+ Ruffian (1972) 1976
+ Ruthless (1864) 1975
+ Salvator (1886).............1955
+ Sarazen (1921).............1957
+ Seabiscuit (1933) 1958
+ Searching (1952) 1978
  Seattle Slew (1974) 1981
+ Secretariat (1970)..........1974
+ Shuvee (1966)..............1975
+ Silver Spoon (1956) 1978
+ Sir Archy (1805) 1955
+ Sir Barton (1916)...........1957
  Slew o'Gold (1980) 1992
+ Sun Beau (1925)............1996
  Sunday Silence (1986).......1996
+ Stymie (1941) 1975
+ Susan's Girl (1969)..........1976
+ Swaps (1952) 1966
+ Sword Dancer (1956)........1977
+ Sysonby (1902).............1956
+ Ta Wee (1966) 1994
+ Tim Tam (1955) 1985
+ Tom Fool (1949) 1960
+ Top Flight (1929)...........1966
+ Tosmah (1961)..............1984
+ Twenty Grand (1928)........1957
+ Twilight Tear (1941) 1963
+ War Admiral (1934).........1958
+ Whirlaway (1938) 1959
+ Whisk Broom II (1907)......1979
  Zaccio (1976) 1990
+ Zev (1920)..................1983

Harness Racing Living Hall of Fame

Established by the U.S. Harness Writers Association (USHWA) in 1958. **Address:** Trotting Horse Museum, 240 Main Street, P.O. Box 590, Goshen, NY 10924; **Telephone:** (914) 294-6330.

　　Eligibility: Open to all harness racing drivers, trainers and executives. Voting done by USHWA membership. There are 73 members of the Living Hall of Fame, but only the 37 drivers and trainer-drivers are listed below.

Class of 1999 (2): HORSES— **Abercrombie** and **Peace Corps**.

Members are listed with years of induction; (+) indicates deceased members.

Trainer-Drivers

　Abbatiello, Carmine 1986
　Abbatiello, Tony............1995
　Ackerman, Doug 1995
+ Avery, Earle 1975
+ Baldwin, Ralph.............1972
　Beissinger, Howard..........1975
　Bostwick, Dunbar...........1989
+ Cameron, Del...............1975
　Campbell, John 1991
+ Chapman, John 1980
　Cruise, Jimmy..............1987
　Dancer, Stanley 1970
+ Ervin, Frank 1969

　Farrington, Bob 1980
　Filion, Herve................1976
+ Garnsey, Glen 1983
　Galbraith, Clint 1990
　Gilmour, Buddy 1990
　Harner, Levi 1986
+ Haughton, Billy 1969
+ Hodgins, Clint 1973
　Insko, Del 1981
　Kopas, Jack 1996
　Lachance, Michel 1996
　Miller, Del 1969
+ O'Brien, Joe 1971

　O'Donnell, Bill 1991
　Patterson, John Sr 1994
+ Pownall, Harry.............1971
　Remmem, Ray 1998
　Riegle, Gene 1992
+ Russell, Sanders 1971
+ Shively, Bion...............1968
　Sholty, George.............1985
　Simpson, John Sr 1972
+ Smart, Curly 1970
　Sylvester, Charles 1998
　Waples, Keith 1987
　Waples, Ron................1994

Exemplars of Racing

+ Hanes, John W 1982   + Mellon, Paul 1989   Widener, George D 1971
+ Jeffords, Walter M.........1973

MEDIA

National Sportscasters and Sportswriters Hall of Fame

Established in 1959 by the National Sportscasters and Sportswriters Association. **Mailing Address:** P.O. Box 559, Salisbury, NC 28144. A permanent museum is tentatively scheduled to open in early 2000. **Telephone:** (704) 633-4275.

Eligibility: Nominees must be active for at least 25 years. Voting done by NSSA membership and other media representatives.

Class of 1999 (2): **Jon Miller** and **John Stedman**.

Members are listed with year of induction; (+) indicates deceased members.

Sportscasters

+ Allen, Mel.................1972	Glickman, Marty 1992	+ McNamee, Graham 1964
+ Barber, Walter (Red) 1973	Gowdy, Curt 1981	Michaels, Al...............1998
+ Brickhouse, Jack 1983	Harwell, Ernie 1989	Miller, Jon.................1999
Buck, Jack.................1990	Hearn, Chick 1997	+ Nelson, Lindsey 1979
+ Caray, Harry 1989	+ Hodges, Russ 1975	+ Prince, Bob..............1986
+ Cosell, Howard 1993	+ Hoyt, Waite 1987	Schenkel, Chris 1981
+ Dean, Dizzy.............1976	+ Husing, Ted 1963	+ Scott, Ray 1982
+ Dunphy, Don 1986	Jackson, Keith 1995	Scully, Vin...............1991
+ Elson, Bob 1995	+ McCarthy, Clem..........1970	+ Stern, Bill 1974
Enberg, Dick 1996	McKay, Jim................1987	Summerall, Pat............1994

Sportswriters

Anderson, Dave...........1990	+ Gould, Alan 1990	Pope, Edwin..............1994
Bisher, Furman 1989	+ Graham, Frank Sr...........1995	+ Povich, Shirley 1984
Broeg, Bob................1997	+ Grimsley, Will 1987	+ Rice, Grantland 1962
Burick, Si.................1985	Heinz, W.C................1987	+ Runyon, Damon 1964
+ Cannon, Jimmy 1986	Jenkins, Dan 1996	Russell, Fred 1988
+ Carmichael, John P.........1994	+ Kieran, John 1971	Sherrod, Blackie 1991
+ Connor, Dick 1992	+ Lardner, Ring 1967	+ Smith, Walter (Red) 1977
+ Considine, Bob 1980	+ Murphy, Jack 1988	+ Spink, J.G. Taylor 1969
+ Daley, Arthur 1976	+ Murray, Jim 1978	Stedman, John 1999
Deford, Frank............1998	Olderman, Murray 1993	+ Ward, Arch 1973
Durslag, Mel..............1995	+ Parker, Dan 1975	+ Woodward, Stanley 1974

American Sportscasters Hall of Fame

Established in 1984 by the American Sportscasters Association. **Mailing Address:** 5 Beekman Street, Suite 814, New York, NY 10038. **Permanent Address:** MCI Center, 601 F St. NW, Washington, D.C. 20001. **Telephone:** (212) 227-8080.

Eligibility: nominations made by selection committee of previous winners, voting by ASA membership.

Class of 1999 (1): **Ray Scott.**

Members are listed with year of induction; (+) indicates deceased members.

+ Allen, Mel.................1985	Gowdy, Curt 1985	+ Nelson, Lindsey 1986
+ Barber, Walter (Red) 1984	Harwell, Ernie 1991	Schenkel, Chris 1997
+ Brickhouse, Jack 1985	Hearn, Chick 1995	+ Scott, Ray 1999
Buck, Jack.................1990	+ Husing, Ted 1984	Scully, Vin................1992
+ Caray, Harry 1989	Jackson, Keith 1994	+ Stern, Bill 1984
+ Cosell, Howard 1993	+ McCarthy, Clem...........1987	Whitaker, Jack............1998
+ Dunphy, Don 1984	McKay, Jim................1987	
Glickman, Marty 1993	+ McNamee, Graham 1984	

MOTORSPORTS

Motorsports Hall of Fame of America

Established in 1989. **Mailing Address:** P.O. Box 194, Novi, MI 48376. **Telephone:** (248) 349-7223.

Eligibility: Nominees must be retired at least three years or engaged in their area of motor sports for at least 20 years. Areas include: open wheel, stock car, dragster, sports car, motorcycle, off road, power boat, air racing, land speed records, historic and at-large.

Class of 1999 (10): DRIVERS—**Jimmy Bryan** (open wheel), **Tim Slock** (stock car), **Frank Kurtis** (at-large), **Bart Markle** (motorcycle), **C.J. Hart** (dragster), **George Follmer** (historic), **Bill Seebold** (power boat) and **Frank Lockhart** (historic). PILOTS—**Lyle Shelton.** CONTRIBUTORS—**Harry Miller.**

Members are listed with year of induction; (+) indicates deceased members.

Drivers

Allison, Bobby 1992	Bettenhausen, Tony 1997	+ Campbell, Sir Malcolm......1994
Andretti, Mario 1990	Brabham, Jack 1998	Cantrell, Bill 1992
Arfons, Art 1991	Breedlove, Craig 1993	+ Chenoweth, Dean 1991
+ Baker, Cannonball 1989	Bryan, Jimmy 1999	Chrisman, Art...............1997

Motorsports (Cont.)

+ Clark, Jim 1990
+ Cook, Betty................1996
  Cunningham, Briggs........1997
  Davis, Jim 1997
  DeCoster, Roger...........1994
+ DePalma, Ralph 1992
+ DePaolo, Peter 1995
+ Donahue, Mark 1990
  Follmer, George...........1999
  Foyt, A.J 1989
  Garlits, Don 1989
  Glidden, Bob 1994
  Gurney, Dan...............1991
  Hanauer, Chip 1995
  Hart, C.J...................1999
  Hill, Phil 1989
+ Holbert, Al 1993
+ Horn, Ted 1993
  Jarrett, Ned 1997

  Jenkins, Bill (Grumpy) 1996
  Johnson, Junior............1991
  Jones, Parnelli 1992
  Kalitta, Connie.............1992
  Kurtis, Frank...............1999
  Leonard, Joe...............1991
  Lockhart, Frank 1999
+ McLaren, Bruce 1995
  Mann, Dick................1993
  Markle, Bart...............1999
+ Mays, Rex................1995
  Mears, Rick 1998
+ Meyer, Louis..............1993
  Muldowney, Shirley.........1990
+ Muncy, Bill 1989
+ Musson, Ron...............1993
  Nordskog, Bob 1997
+ Oldfield, Barney 1989
  Parks, Wally...............1993

  Pearson, David 1993
+ Petrali, Joe 1992
  Petty, Lee.................1996
  Petty, Richard 1989
  Prudhomme, Don..........1991
+ Revson, Peter 1996
+ Roberts, Fireball...........1995
  Roberts, Kenny............1990
  Rutherford, Johnny.........1996
  Seebold, Bill...............1999
+ Shaw, Wilbur...............1991
  Slock, Tim.................1999
  Smith, Malcolm 1996
+ Thompson, Mickey 1990
  Unser, Al..................1991
  Unser, Bobby 1994
+ Vukovich, Bill Sr...........1992
  Ward, Rodger 1995
+ Wood, Gar................1990
  Yarborough, Cale 1994

Pilots

+ Cochran, Jacqueline 1993
+ Curtiss, Glenn 1990
+ Doolittle, Jimmy 1989

+ Earhart, Amelia 1992
+ Falck, Bill 1994
  Greenmayer, Darryl 1997

  Shelton, Lyle 1999
+ Turner, Roscoe 1991

Contributors

+ Agajanian, J.C............1992
  Bignotti, George 1993
+ Black, Keith 1995
  Chapman, Colin 1997
+ Chevrolet, Louis 1995
  Duesenberg, Fred 1997

  Economacki, Chris 1994
+ Ford, Henry 1996
+ France, Bill Sr. 1990
  Hall, Jim 1994
+ Hulman, Tony 1991
  Little, Bernie 1994

  Miller, Harry..............1999
  Penske, Roger 1995
+ Rickenbacker, Eddie 1994
+ Rose, Mauri 1996
  Shelby, Carroll............1992
  Watson, A.J................1996

International Motorsports Hall of Fame

Established in 1990 by the International Motorsports Hall of Fame Commission. **Mailing Address:** P.O. Box 1018, Talladega, AL 35160. **Telephone:** (256) 362-5002.

Eligibility: Nominees must be retired from their specialty in motorsports for five years. Voting done by 150-member panel made up of the world-wide auto racing media.

Class of 1999 (5): DRIVERS—**Gordon Johncock**, **Alain Prost**, **Wendell Scott**, and **Louise Smith**. CONTRIBUTERS—**Harry Hyde**.

Members are listed with year of induction; (+) indicates deceased members.

Drivers

  Allison, Bobby 1993
+ Allison, Davey 1998
+ Ascari, Alberto............1992
  Baker, Buck...............1990
+ Bettenhausen, Tony 1991
  Brabham, Jack............1990
+ Campbell, Sir Malcolm.....1990
+ Caracciola, Rudolph.......1998
+ Clark, Jim 1990
+ DePalma, Ralph 1991
+ Donahue, Mark 1990
+ Evans, Richie 1996
+ Fangio, Juan Manuel 1990
+ Flock, Tim 1991
+ Gregg, Peter 1992
  Gurney, Dan...............1990
+ Haley, Donald 1996
+ Hill, Graham 1990
  Hill, Phil 1991

+ Holbert, Al 1993
+ Isaac, Bobby 1996
  Jarrett, Ned 1991
  Johncock, Gordon..........1999
  Johnson, Junior............1990
  Jones, Parnelli 1990
  Lauda, Niki................1993
  Lorenzen, Fred............1991
+ Lund, Tiny 1994
+ Mays, Rex................1993
+ McLaren, Bruce 1991
+ Meyer, Louis..............1992
  Moss, Stirling 1990
+ Nuvolari, Tazio 1998
+ Oldfield, Barney 1990
  Parsons, Benny 1994
  Pearson, David 1993
  Petty, Lee.................1990
  Prost, Alain 1999

+ Roberts, Fireball...........1990
  Roberts, Kenny............1992
  Rose, Mauri 1994
  Rutherford, Johnny.........1996
  Scott, Wendell 1999
+ Shaw, Wilbur...............1991
  Smith, Louise 1999
  Stewart, Jackie.............1990
  Surtees, John 1996
  Thomas, Herb..............1994
+ Turner, Curtis 1992
  Unser, Al Sr................1998
  Unser, Bobby 1990
+ Vukovich, Bill 1991
  Ward Rodger..............1992
+ Weatherly, Joe 1994
  Yarborough, Cale 1993

Contributors

  Bignotti, George 1993
+ Chapman, Colin 1994
+ Chevrolet, Louis 1992
+ Ferrari, Enzo 1994
+ Ford, Henry 1993
+ France, Bill Sr............1990
  Granatelli, Andy 1992

+ Hulman, Tony.............1990
  Hyde, Harry...............1999
  Marcum, John 1994
+ Matthews, Banjo 1998
  Moody, Ralph 1994
  Parks, Wally 1992
  Penske, Roger 1998

+ Porsche, Ferdinand 1996
+ Rickenbacker, Eddie 1992
  Shelby, Carroll............1991
+ Thompson, Mickey 1990
  Yunick, Smokey 1990

OLYMPICS

U.S. Olympic Hall of Fame

Established in 1983 by the United States Olympic Committee. **Mailing Address:** U.S. Olympic Committee, 1750 East Boulder Street, Colorado Springs, CO 80909. Plans for a permanent museum site have been suspended due to lack of funding. **Telephone:** (719) 578-4529.

Eligibility: Nominated athletes must be five years removed from active competition. Voting done by National Sportscasters and Sportswriters Association, Hall of Fame members and the USOC board members of directors.

Voting for membership in the Hall was suspended in 1993.

Members are listed with year of induction; (+) indicates deceased members.

Teams

1956 Basketball Dick Boushka, Carl Cain, Chuck Darling, Bill Evans, Gib Ford, Burdy Haldorson, Bill Hougland, Bob Jeangerard, K.C. Jones, Bill Russell, Ron Tomsic, +Jim Walsh and coach +Gerald Tucker.

1960 Basketball Jay Arnette, Walt Bellamy, Bob Boozer, Terry Dischinger, Burdy Haldorson, Darrall Imhoff, Allen Kelley, +Lester Lane, Jerry Lucas, Oscar Robertson, Adrian Smith, Jerry West and coach Pete Newell.

1964 Basketball Jim Barnes, Bill Bradley, Larry Brown, Joe Caldwell, Mel Counts, Richard Davies, Walt Hazzard, Luke Jackson, John McCaffrey, Jeff Mullins, Jerry Shipp, George Wilson and coach +Hank Iba.

1960 Ice Hockey Billy Christian, Roger Christian, Billy Cleary, Bob Cleary, Gene Grazia, Paul Johnson, Jack Kirrane, John Mayasich, Jack McCartan, Bob McKay, Dick Meredith, Weldon Olson, Ed Owen, Rod Paavola, Larry Palmer, Dick Rodenheiser, +Tom Williams and coach Jack Riley.

1980 Ice Hockey Bill Baker, Neal Broten, Dave Christian, Steve Christoff, Jim Craig, Mike Eruzione, John Harrington, Steve Janaszak, Mark Johnson, Ken Morrow, Rob McClanahan, Jack O'Callahan, Mark Pavelich, Mike Ramsey, Buzz Schneider, Dave Silk, Eric Strobel, Bob Suter, Phil Verchota, Mark Wells and coach Herb Brooks.

Alpine Skiing

Mahre, Phil 1992

Bobsled

+ Eagan, Eddie (see Boxing) . . . 1983

Boxing

Clay, Cassius* 1983
+ Eagan, Eddie (see Bobsled) . . 1983
Foreman, George 1990
Frazier, Joe 1989
Leonard, Sugar Ray 1985
Patterson, Floyd 1987
*Clay changed name to Muhammad Ali in 1964.

Cycling

Carpenter-Phinney, Connie . . . 1992

Diving

King, Miki 1992
Lee, Sammy 1990
Louganis, Greg 1985
McCormick, Pat 1985

Figure Skating

Albright, Tenley 1988
Button, Dick 1983
Fleming, Peggy 1983
Hamill, Dorothy 1991
Hamilton, Scott 1990

Gymnastics

Conner, Bart 1991
Retton, Mary Lou 1985
Vidmar, Peter 1991

Rowing

+ Kelly, Jack Sr. 1990

Speed Skating

Heiden, Eric 1983

Swimming

Babashoff, Shirley 1987
Caulkins, Tracy 1990
+ Daniels, Charles 1988
de Varona, Donna 1987
+ Kahanamoku, Duke 1984
+ Madison, Helene 1992
Meyer, Debbie 1986
Naber, John 1984
Schollander, Don 1983
Spitz, Mark 1983
+ Weissmuller, Johnny 1983

Track & Field

Beamon, Bob 1983
Boston, Ralph 1985
+ Calhoun, Lee 1991
Campbell, Milt 1992
Davenport, Willie 1991
Davis, Glenn 1986
+ Didrikson, Babe 1983
Dillard, Harrison 1983
Evans, Lee 1989
+ Ewry, Ray 1983
Fosbury, Dick 1992
Jenner, Bruce 1986
Johnson, Rafer 1983
+ Kraenzlein, Alvin 1985
Lewis, Carl 1985
Mathias, Bob 1983

Mills, Billy 1984
Morrow, Bobby 1989
Moses, Edwin 1985
O'Brien, Parry 1984
Oerter, Al 1983
+ Owens, Jesse 1983
+ Paddock, Charley 1991
Richards, Bob 1983
+ Rudolph, Wilma 1983
+ Sheppard, Mel 1989
Shorter, Frank 1984
+ Thorpe, Jim 1983
Toomey, Bill 1984
Tyus, Wyomia 1985
Whitfield, Mal 1988
+ Wykoff, Frank 1984

Weight Lifting

+ Davis, John 1989
Kono, Tommy 1990

Wrestling

Gable, Dan 1985

Contributors

Arledge, Roone 1989
+ Brundage, Avery 1983
+ Bushnell, Asa 1990
Hull, Col. Don 1992
+ Iba, Hank 1985
+ Kane, Robert 1986
+ Kelly, Jack Jr. 1992
McKay, Jim 1988
Miller, Don 1984
Simon, William 1991
Walker, LeRoy 1987

The Olympic Order

Established in 1974 by the International Olympic Committee (IOC) to honor athletes, officials and media members who have made remarkable contributions to the Olympic movement. The IOC's Council of the Olympic Order is presided over by the IOC president and active IOC members are not eligible for consideration. Through 1998, only three American officials have received the Order's highest commendation—the gold medal:

Avery Brundage, president of USOC (1928-53) and IOC (1952-72), was given the award posthumously in 1975.

Peter Ueberroth, president of Los Angeles Olympic Organizing Committee, was given the award in 1984.

Billy Payne, president of the Atlanta Committee for the Olympic Games, was given the award in 1996.

SOCCER

International Soccer Hall of Champions

Established in 1998 by FIFA, soccer's international governing body. Located at Disneyland Paris.

Eligibility: Nominated players and coaches must be retired at least five years. Nominations made by a committee composed of FIFA members, the Hall of Champions management and three ad hoc members then submit a list to a panel of 32 soccer journalists from around the world who also have the chance to add nominees of their own as well as voting for a specific number of candidates in each category.

Class of 1999 (12): PLAYERS—**Just Fontaine, Garrincha, Bobby Moore, Gerd Müller** and **Dino Zoff**. MANAGERS—**Bill Shankly**. REFEREES—**Jack Taylor**. CLUB TEAMS—**Ajax Amsterdam**. NATIONAL TEAMS—**Germany**. PIONEERS—**Joao Havelange**. MEDIA—**Jacques Ferran**. FOR THE GOOD OF THE GAME—**Fernand Sastre**.

Players

Beckenbauer, Franz (W. Ger)..1998	Fontaine, Just (FRA).........1999	Pele (BRA)..................1998
Charlton, Sir Bobby (ENG)....1998	+ Garrincha (BRA) 1999	Plantini, Michel (FRA) 1998
Cruyff, Johan (NED) 1998	Matthews, Sir Stanley (ENG).1998	Puskas, Ferenc (HUN/SPA) ..1998
Distefano, Alfredo (ARG/SPA).1998	+ Moore, Bobby (ENG) 1999	+ Yashin, Lev (RUS)...........1998
Eusebio (POR) 1998	Müller, Gerd (W. Ger) 1999	Zoff, Dino (ITA)..............1999

Managers

+ Busby, Sir Matt (SCO).......1998	Michels, Rinus (NED) 1998	+ Shankly, Bill (SCO) 1999

Referees

Taylor, Jack (ENG)..........1999	Vautrot, Michel (FRA) 1998

Pioneers

Havelange, Joao (BRA)......1999	+ Rimet, Jules (FRA)...........1998

Club Teams

Ajax Amsterdam (NED) 1999	Real Madrid (SPA).........1998

National Teams

Brazil....................1998	Germany..................1999

Media

Ferran, Jacques (FRA).......1999	Goddett, Jacques (FRA) 1998

For the Good of the Game

+ Dassler, Horst (GER) 1998	+ Sastre, Fernard (FRA) 1999

National Soccer Hall of Fame

Established in 1950 by the Philadelphia Oldtimers Association. First exhibit unveiled in Oneonta, NY in 1982. Moved into new Hall of Fame building in the summer of 1999. **Address:** 18 Stadium Circle, Oneonta, NY 13820. **Telephone:** (607) 432-3351.

Eligibility: Nominated players must have represented the U.S. in international competition and be retired five years; other categories include Meritorious Service and Special Commendation.

Nominations made by state organizations and a veterans' committee. Voting done by nine-member committee made up of Hall of Famers, U.S. Soccer officials and members of the national media.

Class of 1999: None. Will resume inductions in 2000.

Members are listed with home state and year of induction; (+) indicates deceased members.

Members

Abronzino, Umberto (CA) ...1971	+ Booth, Joseph (CT)..........1952	+ Chesney, Stan (NY).........1966
Aimi, Milton (TX) 1991	Borghi, Frank (MO)..........1976	Chyzowych, Walter (PA) 1997
+ Alonso, Julie (NY) 1972	Boulos, Frenchy (NY) 1980	+ Coll, John (NY) 1986
+ Andersen, William (NY).....1956	+ Boxer, Matt (CA) 1961	+ Collins, George M. (MA)....1951
+ Ardizzone, John (CA) 1971	Bradley, Gordon (Eng) 1996	Collins, Peter (NY)...........1998
Armstrong, James (NY).....1952	+ Briggs, Lawrence E. (MA)...1978	+ Colombo, Charlie (MO)......1976
+ Auld, Andrew (RI) 1986	+ Brittan, Harold (PA) 1951	+ Commander, Colin (OH) 1967
Bahr, Walter (PA)...........1976	+ Brock, John (MA)...........1950	+ Cordery, Ted (CA) 1975
Barr, George (NY)..........1983	+ Brown, Andrew M. (OH) 1950	+ Craddock, Robert (PA) 1959
+ Barriskill, Joe (NY)..........1953	+ Brown, David (NJ) 1951	+ Craggs, Edmund (WA)......1969
+ Beardsworth, Fred (MA)....1965	Brown, George (NJ) 1995	Craggs, George (WA) 1981
Beckenbauer, Franz (Ger)..1998	Brown, James (NY)..........1986	+ Cummings, Wilfred R. (IL) ...1953
Berling, Clay (CA).........1995	+ Cahill, Thomas W (NY) 1950	+ Delach, Joseph (PA).........1973
Bernabei, Ray (PA).........1978	+ Carenza, Joe (MO)..........1982	DeLuca, Enzo (NY) 1979
Best, John O. (CA)..........1982	+ Caraffi, Ralph (OH)..........1959	+ Dick, Walter (CA) 1989
+ Bookie, Michael (PA)........1986	Chacurian, Chico (CT) 1992	Diorio, Nick (PA)...........1974

+ Donaghy, Edward J. (NY) ...1951
+ Donelli, Buff (PA) 1954
+ Donnelly, George (NY).....1989
+ Douglas, Jimmy (NJ) 1954
+ Dresmich, John W. (PA) 1968
+ Duff, Duncan (CA) 1972
+ Dugan, Thomas (NJ) 1951
+ Dunn, James (MO) 1974
   Edwards, Gene (WI).........1985
   Ely, Alexander (PA) 1997
+ Epperleim, Rudy (NJ) 1951
+ Fairfield, Harry (PA) 1951
   Feibusch, Ernst (CA) 1984
+ Ferguson, John (PA)..........1950
+ Fernley, John A. (MA) 1951
+ Ferro, Charles (NY)...........1958
+ Fishwick, George E. (IL) 1974
+ Flamhaft, Jack (NY)...........1964
+ Fleming, Harry G. (PA)......1967
+ Florie, Thomas (NJ) 1986
+ Foulds, Pal (MA) 1953
+ Foulds, Sam (MA) 1969
+ Fowler, Dan (NY)............1970
+ Fowler, Peg (NY) 1979
   Fricker, Werner (PA) 1992
+ Fryer, William J. (NJ) 1951
+ Gaetjens, Joe (NY) 1976
+ Gallagher, James (NY) 1986
+ Garcia, Pete (MO) 1964
+ Gentle, James (PA)...........1986
   Getzinger, Rudy (IL).........1991
+ Giesler, Walter (MO) 1962
   Glover, Teddy (NY) 1965
+ Gonsalves, Billy (MA).........1950
   Gormley, Bob (PA)...........1989
+ Gould, David L. (PA) 1953
+ Govier, Sheldon (IL)..........1950
   Greer, Don (CA) 1985
   Gryzik, Joe (IL) 1973
+ Guelker, Bob (MO) 1980
   Guennel, Joe (CO) 1980
   Harker, Al (PA).............1979
+ Healy, George (MI) 1951
   Heilpern, Herb (NY) 1988
   Heinrichs, April (CO) 1998
+ Hemmings, William (IL)......1961
+ Hudson, Maurice (CA) 1966
   Hunt, Lamar (TX) 1982
   Hynes, John (NY)............1977
+ Iglehart, Alfredda (MD) 1951
+ Japp, John (PA) 1953
+ Jeffrey, William (PA) 1951
   Jewell, Frank (FA)............1996
+ Johnson, Jack (IL) 1952
   Kabanica, Mike (WI) 1987
   Kehoe, Bob (MO) 1990

   Kelly, Frank (NJ)............1994
+ Kempton, George (WA) 1950
   Keough, Harry (MO).......1976
+ Klein, Paul (NJ) 1953
   Kleinaitis, Al (IN) 1995
+ Koszma, Oscar (CA).........1964
   Kracher, Frank (IL) 1983
   Kraft, Granny (MD) 1984
+ Kraus, Harry (NY) 1963
   Kropfelder, Nicholas........1996
+ Kunter, Rudy (NY) 1963
+ Lamm, Kurt (NY) 1979
   Lang, Millard (MD) 1950
   Larson, Bert (CT) 1988
   Leonard, Abbot (Eng) 1996
+ Lewis, H. Edgar (PA) 1950
   Lombardo, Joe (NY) 1984
   Long, Denny (MO)...........1993
+ MacEwan, John J. (MI) 1953
+ Maca, Joe (NY) 1976
+ Magnozzi, Enzo (NY)........1978
+ Maher, Jack (IL) 1970
+ Manning, Dr. Randolf (NY) ..1950
+ Marre, John (MO) 1953
   McBride, Pat (MO) 1994
+ McClay, Allan (MA) 1971
+ McGhee, Bart (NY) 1986
+ McGrath, Frank (MA) 1978
+ McGuire, Jimmy (NY) 1951
+ McGuire, John (NY) 1951
+ McIlveney, Eddie (PA) 1976
   McLaughlin, Bennie (PA).....1977
+ McSkimming, Dent (MO) 1951
   Merovich, Pete (PA)..........1971
+ Mieth, Werner (NJ) 1974
+ Millar, Robert (NY) 1950
   Miller, Al (OH)..............1995
+ Miller, Milton (NY)...........1971
+ Mills, Jimmy (PA) 1954
   Monson, Lloyd (NY) 1994
   Moore, James F. (MO) 1971
   Moore, Johnny (CA) 1997
+ Moorehouse, George (NY) ..1986
+ Morrison, Robert (PA) 1951
+ Morrissette, Bill (MA) 1967
   Nanoski, Jukey (NY).........1993
+ Netto, Fred (IL)..............1958
   Newman, Ron (CA).........1992
+ Niotis, D.J. (IL) 1963
+ O'Brien, Shamus (NY) 1990
   Olaff, Gene (NJ) 1971
+ Oliver, Arnie (MA)...........1968
   Oliver, Len (PA) 1996
+ Palmer, William (PA) 1952
   Pariani, Gino (MO)..........1976
+ Patenaude, Bert (MA) 1971

+ Pearson, Eddie (GA) 1990
+ Peel, Peter (IL)..............1951
   Pelé (Brazil) 1993
   Peters, Wally (NJ) 1967
   Phillipson, Don (CO)........1987
+ Piscopo, Giorgio (NY) 1978
+ Pomeroy, Edgar (CA) 1955
+ Ramsden, Arnold (TX) 1957
+ Ratican, Harry (MO).........1950
   Reese, Doc (MD) 1957
+ Renzulli, Pete (NY)...........1951
   Ringsdorf, Gene (MD).......1979
   Roe, James (MO)............1997
   Roth, Werner (NY)...........1989
+ Rottenberg, Jack (NJ) 1971
   Roy, Willy (IL)..............1989
+ Ryan, Hun (PA)..............1958
+ Sager, Tom (PA)............1968
   Saunders, Harry (NY)........1981
   Schaller, Willy (IL) 1995
   Schellscheidt, Mannie (NJ)...1990
   Schillinger, Emil (PA) 1960
+ Schroeder, Elmer (PA) 1951
+ Scwarcz, Erno (NY) 1951
+ Shields, Fred (PA) 1968
+ Single, Erwin (NY)...........1981
+ Slone, Philip (NY) 1986
+ Smith, Alfred (PA) 1951
   Smith, Patrick (OH) 1998
+ Souza, Ed (MA)..............1976
   Souza, Clarkie (MA)..........1976
+ Spalding, Dick (PA) 1951
+ Stark, Archie (NJ) 1950
+ Steelink, Nicolaas (CA) 1971
+ Steur, August (NY)...........1969
+ Stewart, Douglas (PA) 1950
+ Stone, Robert T. (CO) 1971
+ Swords, Thomas (MA) 1976
+ Tintle, Joseph (NJ) 1952
+ Tracey, Ralph (MO)..........1986
+ Triner, Joseph (IL) 1951
+ Vaughan, Frank (MO) 1986
+ Walder, Jimmy (PA)..........1971
+ Wallace, Frank (MO) 1976
+ Washauer, Adolph (CA).....1977
+ Webb, Tom (WA)............1987
+ Weir, Alex (NY)..............1975
+ Weston, Victor (WA) 1956
+ Wilson, Peter (NJ) 1950
+ Wood, Alex (MI) 1986
+ Woods, John W. (IL) 1952
   Woosnam, Phil (GA)........1997
   Yeagley, Jerry (IN)..........1989
+ Young, John (CA)...........1958
+ Zampini, Dan (PA)..........1963
   Zerhusen, Al (CA)...........1978

International Swimming Hall of Fame

Established in 1965 by the U.S. College Coaches' Swim Forum. **Address:** One Hall of Fame Drive, Ft. Lauderdale, FL 33316. **Telephone:** (954) 462-6536.

Categories for induction are: swimming, diving, water polo, synchronized swimming, coaching, pioneers and contributors. Of the 481 members, 266 are from the United States. Contributors are not included in the following list. Only U.S. men, women and coaches listed below.

Members are listed with year of induction; (+) indicates deceased members.

U.S. Men

+ Anderson, Miller 1967
   Barrowman, Mike 1997
   Biondi, Matt 1997
+ Boggs, Phil 1985
   Brack, Walter...............1997

   Breen, George..............1975
+ Browning, Skippy 1975
   Bruner, Mike................1988
   Burton, Mike................1977
+ Cann, Tedford 1967

   Carey, Rick.................1993
   Clark, Earl 1972
   Clark, Steve 1966
   Cleveland, Dick.............1991
   Clotworthy, Robert..........1980

+ Crabbe, Buster............1965
+ Daniels, Charlie...........1965
  Degener, Dick 1971
  DeMont, Rick 1990
  Dempsey, Frank...........1996
+ Desjardins, Pete..........1966
  Edgar, David 1996
+ Faricy, John 1990
+ Farrell, Jeff 1968
+ Fick, Peter..............1978
+ Flanagan, Ralph 1978
  Ford, Alan 1966
  Furniss, Bruce...........1987
  Gaines, Rowdy 1995
  Garton, Tim 1997
  Glancy, Harrison.........1990
+ Goodwin, Budd 1971
  Graef, Jed..............1988
  Haines, George 1977
  Hall, Gary 1981
+ Harlan, Bruce...........1973
+ Hebner, Harry 1968
  Hencken, John 1988
  Hickcox, Charles.........1976
  Higgins, John 1971
  Holiday, Harry 1991
  Irwin, Juno Stover 1980
  Jastremski, Chet.........1977
+ Kahanamoku, Duke 1965
+ Kealoha, Warren.........1968
  Kiefer, Adolph 1965
  Kinsella, John 1986
+ Kojac, George...........1968

  Konno, Ford.............1972
+ Kruger, Stubby...........1986
+ Kuehn, Louis 1988
+ Langer, Ludy............1988
  Larson, Lance 1980
  Lee, Dr. Sammy 1968
  Lemmons, Kelley 1999
+ LeMoyne, Harry 1988
  Louganis, Greg 1993
  Lundquist, Steve 1990
  Mann, Thompson.........1984
  McCormick, Pat..........1965
+ McDermott, Turk.........1969
+ McGillivray, Perry 1981
  McKenzie, Don 1989
  McKinney, Frank 1975
  McLane, Jimmy 1970
+ Medica, Jack 1966
  Montgomery, Jim 1986
  Mullikan, Bill 1984
  Naber, John 1982
  Nakama, Keo 1975
+ O'Connor, Wally.........1966
  Oyakawa, Yoshi 1979
+ Patnik, Al 1969
  Phillips, William Berge 1997
+ Riley, Mickey 1977
+ Ris, Wally 1966
  Robie, Carl.............1976
  Roper, Gail.............1997
  Ross, Clarence 1988
+ Ross, Norman 1967
  Roth, Dick 1987

+ Ruddy, Joe 1986
  Russell, Doug 1985
  Saari, Roy..............1976
+ Schaeffer, E. Carroll 1968
  Scholes, Clarke 1980
  Schollander, Don 1965
  Shaw, Tim..............1989
+ Sheldon, George.........1989
+ Skelton, Robert..........1988
  Smith, Bill 1966
+ Smith, Dutch 1979
+ Smith, Jimmy 1992
  Smith, R. Jackson 1983
  Spitz, Mark.............1977
  Stack, Allen 1979
  Stickles, Ted 1995
  Stock, Tom 1989
+ Swendsen, Clyde.........1991
  Tobian, Gary 1978
  Troy, Mike..............1971
  Vande Weghe, Albert.......1990
  Vassallo, Jesse 1997
+ Verdeur, Joe 1966
  Vogel, Matt.............1996
+ Vollmer, Hal 1990
  Wayne, Marshall.........1981
  Webster, Bob............1970
+ Weissmuller, Johnny 1965
+ White, Al 1965
  Wrightson, Bernie 1984
  Yorzyk, Bill 1971

U.S. Women

  Anderson, Terry 1986
  Atwood, Sue 1992
  Babashoff, Shirley........1982
  Babb-Sprigue, Kristen 1999
  Ball, Catie..............1976
+ Bauer, Sybil 1967
  Bean, Dawn Pawson........1996
  Belote, Melissa...........1983
  Bleibtrey, Ethelda........1967
+ Boyle, Charlotte..........1988
  Burke, Lynne............1978
  Bush, Lesley 1986
  Callen, Gloria 1984
  Caretto, Patty 1987
  Carr, Cathy 1988
  Caulkins, Tracy 1990
+ Chadwick, Florence 1970
  Chandler, Jennifer 1987
  Cohen, Tiffany 1996
+ Coleman, Georgia 1966
  Cone, Carin 1984
  Costie, Candy 1995
  Crlenkovich, Helen 1981
  Curtis, Ann 1966
  Daniel, Ellie 1997
  de Varona, Donna.........1969
  Dean, Penny 1996
+ Dorfner, Olga...........1970
  Draves, Vickie 1969
  Duenkel, Ginny 1985
  Ederle, Gertrude 1965
  Ellis, Kathy 1991
  Ferguson, Cathy 1978
  Finneran, Sharon..........1985

+ Galligan, Claire............1970
+ Garatti-Seville, Eleanor......1992
  Gestring, Marjorie.........1976
  Gossick, Sue 1988
+ Guest, Irene 1990
  Hall, Kaye 1979
  Henne, Jan 1979
  Holm, Eleanor 1966
  Hunt-Newman, Virginia 1993
  Johnson, Gail 1983
  Josephson, Karen 1997
  Josephson, Sarah 1997
  Kane, Marion............1981
+ Kaufman, Beth 1967
  Kight, Lenore 1981
  King, Micki.............1978
  Kolb, Claudia 1975
+ Lackie, Ethel 1969
  Linehan, Kim 1997
  Lord-Landon, Alice........1993
+ Madison, Helene 1966
  Mann, Shelly 1966
  McCormick, Kelly 1999
  McGrath, Margo 1989
  McKim, Josephine 1991
  Meagher, Mary T..........1993
+ Meany, Helen 1971
  Merlino, Maxine 1999
  Meyer, Debbie 1977
  Mitchell, Michele 1995
  Moe, Karen 1992
  Morris, Pam 1965
  Neilson, Sandra 1986
  Neyer, Megan 1997

+ Norelius, Martha..........1967
  Olsen, Zoe-Ann 1989
  O'Rourke, Heidi 1980
+ Osipowich, Albina 1986
  Pedersen, Susan 1995
  Pinkston, Betty Becker.....1967
  Pope, Paula Jean Meyers....1979
  Potter, Cynthia 1987
+ Poynton, Dorothy 1968
+ Rawls, Katherine 1965
  Redmond, Carol 1989
  Riggin, Aileen 1967
  Ross, Anne 1984
  Rothammer, Keena 1991
  Ruiz-Conforto, Tracie.......1993
  Ruuska, Sylvia 1976
  Schuler, Carolyn 1989
  Seller, Peg..............1988
+ Smith, Caroline 1988
  Steinseifer, Carrie 1999
  Stouder, Sharon 1972
+ Toner, Vee..............1995
+ Vilen, Kay..............1978
  Von Saltza, Chris.........1966
  Oho Wahle 1996
+ Wainwright, Helen 1972
+ Watson, Lillian (Pokey) 1984
  Wehselau, Mariechen.......1989
  Welshons, Kim 1988
  Wichman, Sharon 1991
  Williams, Esther..........1966
+ Woodbridge, Margaret 1989

U.S. Coaches

+ Armbruster, Dave 1966
+ Bachrach, Bill 1966
  Billingsley, Hobie 1983
+ Brandsten, Ernst 1966
+ Brauninger, Stan 1972
  Bussard, Ray 1999
+ Cady, Fred 1969
+ Center, George (Dad) 1991
  Chavoor, Sherman 1977
+ Cody, Jack 1970
  Counsilman, Dr. James 1976
+ Curtis, Katherine 1979
  Daland, Peter 1977
+ Daughters, Ray 1971

+ Draves, Lyle 1989
+ Gambril, Don 1983
  Haines, George 1977
  Handley, L. de B. 1967
  Hannula, Dick 1987
  Kimball, Dick 1985
+ Kiphuth, Bob 1965
  Mann, Matt II 1965
+ McCormick, Glen 1995
  Moriarty, Phil 1980
  Mowerson, Robert 1986
  Muir, Bob 1989
+ Neuschaufer, Al 1967
  Nitzkowski, Monte 1991

  O'Brien, Ron 1988
+ Papenguth, Richard 1986
+ Peppe, Mike 1966
+ Pinkston, Clarence 1966
+ Robinson, Tom 1965
  Sakamoto, Soichi 1966
+ Sava, Charlie 1970
+ Schlueter, Walt 1978
  Schubert, Mark 1997
  Smith, Dick 1979
  Stager, Gus 1982
  Thornton, Nort 1995
  Tinkham, Stan 1989

TENNIS

International Tennis Hall of Fame

Originally the National Tennis Hall of Fame. Established in 1953 by James Van Alen and sanctioned by the U.S. Tennis Association in 1954. Renamed the International Tennis Hall of Fame in 1976. **Address:** 194 Bellevue Ave., Newport, RI 02840. **Telephone:** (401) 849-3990.

Eligibility: Nominated players must be five years removed from being a "significant factor" in competitive tennis. Voting done by members of the international tennis media.

Class of 1999 (2): PLAYERS— **John McEnroe** and **Ken McGregor**.

Members are listed with year of induction; (+) indicates deceased members.

Men

+ Adee, George 1964
+ Alexander, Fred 1961
+ Allison, Wilmer 1963
+ Alonso, Manuel 1977
+ Ashe, Arthur 1985
+ Behr, Karl 1969
  Borg, Bjorn 1987
+ Borotra, Jean 1976
  Bromwich, John 1984
+ Brookes, Norman 1977
+ Brugnon, Jacques 1976
  Budge, Don 1964
+ Campbell, Oliver 1955
+ Chace, Malcolm 1961
+ Clark, Clarence 1983
+ Clark, Joseph 1955
+ Clothier, William 1956
+ Cochet, Henri 1976
  Connors, Jimmy 1998
  Cooper, Ashley 1991
+ Crawford, Jack 1979
  David, Herman 1998
+ Doeg, John 1962
+ Doherty, Lawrence 1980
+ Doherty, Reginald 1980
  Drobny, Jaroslav 1983
+ Dwight, James 1955
  Emerson, Roy 1982
+ Etchebaster, Pierre 1978
  Falkenburg, Bob 1974
  Fraser, Neale 1984
+ Garland, Chuck 1969
+ Gonzales, Pancho 1968
+ Grant, Bryan (Bitsy) 1972
+ Griffin, Clarence 1970
+ Hackett, Harold 1961

  Hewitt, Bob 1992
+ Hoad, Lew 1980
+ Hovey, Fred 1974
+ Hunt, Joe 1966
+ Hunter, Frank 1961
+ Johnston, Bill 1958
+ Jones, Perry 1970
  Kodes, Jan 1990
  Kramer, Jack 1968
+ Lacoste, Rene 1976
+ Larned, William 1956
  Larsen, Art 1969
  Laver, Rod 1981
+ Lott, George 1964
  Mako, Gene 1973
  McEnroe, John 1999
  McGregor, Ken 1999
+ McKinley, Chuck 1986
+ McLoughlin, Maurice 1957
  McMillan, Frew 1992
+ McNeill, Don 1965
  Mulloy, Gardnar 1972
+ Murray, Lindley 1958
+ Myrick, Julian 1963
  Nastase, Ilie 1991
  Newcombe, John 1986
+ Nielsen, Arthur 1971
  Olmedo, Alex 1987
+ Osuna, Rafael 1979
  Parker, Frank 1966
+ Patterson, Gerald 1989
+ Patty, Budge 1977
+ Perry, Fred 1975
+ Pettitt, Tom 1982
  Pietrangeli, Nicola 1986
+ Quist, Adrian 1984

  Ralston, Dennis 1987
+ Renshaw, Ernest 1983
+ Renshaw, William 1983
+ Richards, Vincent 1961
+ Riggs, Bobby 1967
  Roche, Tony 1986
  Rosewall, Ken 1980
  Santana, Manuel 1984
  Savitt, Dick 1976
  Schroeder, Ted 1966
+ Sears, Richard 1955
  Sedgman, Frank 1979
  Segura, Pancho 1984
  Seixas, Vic 1971
+ Shields, Frank 1964
+ Slocum, Henry 1955
  Smith, Stan 1987
  Stolle, Fred 1985
+ Talbert, Bill 1967
+ Tilden, Bill 1959
  Trabert, Tony 1970
  Van Ryn, John 1963
  Vilas, Guillermo 1991
+ Vines, Ellsworth 1962
+ von Cramm, Gottfried 1977
+ Ward, Holcombe 1956
+ Washburn, Watson 1965
+ Whitman, Malcolm 1955
+ Wilding, Anthony 1978
+ Williams, Richard 2nd 1957
  Wood, Sidney 1964
+ Wrenn, Robert 1955
+ Wright, Beals 1956

Women

+ Atkinson, Juliette 1974
  Austin, Bunny 1997
  Austin, Tracy 1992
+ Barger-Wallach, Maud 1958
  Betz Addie, Pauline 1965
+ Bjurstedt Mallory, Molla 1958

  Bowrey, Lesley Turner 1997
  Brough Clapp, Louise 1967
+ Browne, Mary 1957
  Bueno, Maria 1978
+ Cahill, Mabel 1976
  Casals, Rosie 1996

+ Connolly Brinker, Maureen . .1968
+ Dod, Charlotte (Lottie) 1983
+ Douglass Chambers, Dorothy . .1981
  Evert, Chris 1995
  Fry Irvin, Shirley 1970
  Gibson, Althea 1971

Tennis (Cont.)

Goolagong Cawley, Evonne . .	1988
+ Hansell, Ellen	1965
Hard, Darlene	1973
Hart, Doris	1969
Haydon Jones, Ann	1985
Heldman, Gladys	1979
+ Hotchkiss Wightman, Hazel . . .	1957
+ Jacobs, Helen Hull	1962
King, Billie Jean	1987
+ Lenglen, Suzanne	1978
Mandlikova, Hana	1994
+ Marble, Alice	1964
+ McKane Godfree, Kitty	1978
+ Moore, Elisabeth	1971
Mortimer Barrett, Angela	1993
+ Nuthall Shoemaker, Betty	1977
Osborne duPont, Margaret	1967
+ Palfrey Danzig, Sarah	1963
+ Roosevelt, Ellen	1975
+ Round Little, Dorothy	1986
+ Ryan, Elizabeth	1972
+ Sears, Eleanora	1968
Smith Court, Margaret	1979
+ Sutton Bundy, May	1956
+ Townsend Toulmin, Bertha	1974
Wade, Virginia	1989
+ Wagner, Marie	1969
+ Wills Moody Roark, Helen	1959

Contributors

+ Baker, Lawrence Sr	1975
Chatrier, Philippe	1992
Collins, Bud	1994
Cullman, Joseph F. 3rd	1990
+ Danzig, Allison	1968
+ Davis, Dwight	1956
+ Gray, David	1985
+ Gustaf, V (King of Sweden) . .	1980
+ Hester, W.E. (Slew)	1981
+ Hopman, Harry	1978
Hunt, Lamar	1993
+ Laney, Al	1979
Martin, Alastair	1973
Martin, William M	1982
Maskell, Dan	1996
+ Outerbridge, Mary	1981
+ Pell, Theodore	1966
+ Tingay, Lance	1982
+ Tinling, Ted	1986
+ Van Alen, James	1965
+ Wingfield, Walter Clopton . . .	1997

TRACK & FIELD

National Track & Field Hall of Fame

Established in 1974 by the The Athletics Congress (now USA Track & Field). Originally located in Charleston, WV, the Hall moved to Indianapolis in 1983 and reopened at the Hoosier Dome (now RCA Dome) in 1986. **Address:** One RCA Dome, Indianapolis, IN 46225. **Telephone:** (317) 261-0500.

Eligibility: Nominated athletes must be retired three years and coaches must have coached at least 20 years if retired or 35 years if still coaching. Voting done by 800-member panel made up of Hall of Fame and USA Track & Field officials, Hall of Fame members, current U.S. champions and members of the Track & Field Writers of America.

Class of 1998 (4): MEN—**Greg Foster**, **Jay Silvester** and **Dwight Stones**; WOMEN—**Francie Larrieu Smith**. Members are listed with year of induction; (+) indicates deceased members.

Men

+ Albritton, Dave	1980
Ashenfelter, Horace	1975
+ Bausch, James	1979
Beamon, Bob	1977
Beatty, Jim	1990
Bell, Greg	1988
+ Boeckmann, Dee	1976
Boston, Ralph	1974
Bragg, Don	1996
+ Calhoun, Lee	1974
Campbell, Milt	1989
Carr, Henry	1997
+ Clark, Ellery	1991
Connolly, Harold	1984
Courtney, Tom	1978
+ Cunningham, Glenn	1974
+ Curtis, William	1979
Davenport, Willie	1982
Davis, Glenn	1974
Davis, Harold	1974
Dillard, Harrison	1974
Dumas, Charley	1990
Evans, Lee	1983
+ Ewell, Barney	1986
+ Ewry, Ray	1974
+ Flanagan, John	1975
Fosbury, Dick	1981
Foster, Greg	1998
+ Gordien, Fortune	1979
Greene, Charlie	1992
+ Hahn, Archie	1983
+ Hardin, Glenn	1978
Hayes, Bob	1976
Held, Bud	1987
Hines, Jim	1979
+ Houser, Bud	1979
+ Hubbard, DeHart	1979
Jenkins, Charlie	1992
Jenner, Bruce	1980
+ Johnson, Cornelius	1994
Johnson, Rafer	1974
Jones, Hayes	1976
Kelley, John	1980
Kiviat, Abel	1985
+ Kraenzlein, Alvin	1974
Laird, Ron	1986
+ Lash, Don	1995
Laskau, Henry	1997
Liquori, Marty	1995
Long, Dr. Dallas	1996
Mathias, Bob	1974
Matson, Randy	1984
McCluskey, Joe	1996
+ Meadows, Earle	1996
+ Meredith, Ted	1982
+ Metcalfe, Ralph	1975
+ Milburn, Rod	1993
Mills, Billy	1976
Moore, Tom	1988
Morrow, Bobby	1975
+ Mortensen, Jess	1992
Moses, Edwin	1994
+ Myers, Lawrence	1974
Nehemiah, Renaldo	1997
O'Brien, Parry	1974
Oerter, Al	1974
+ Osborn, Harold	1974
+ Owens, Jesse	1974
+ Paddock, Charley	1976
Patton, Mel	1985
+ Peacock, Eulace	1987
+ Prefontaine, Steve	1976
+ Ray, Joie	1976
+ Rice, Greg	1977
Richards, Bob	1975
+ Rose, Ralph	1976
Ryun, Jim	1980
+ Scholz, Jackson	1977
Schul, Bob	1991
Seagren, Bob	1986
+ Sheppard, Mel	1976
+ Sheridan, Martin	1988
Shorter, Frank	1989
Silvester, Jay	1998
Sime, Dave	1981
+ Simpson, Robert	1974
Smith, Tommie	1978
+ Stanfield, Andy	1977
Steers, Les	1974
Stones, Dwight	1998
+ Tewksbury, Dr. Walter	1996
Thomas, John	1985
+ Thomson, Earl	1977
+ Thorpe, Jim	1975
+ Tolan, Eddie	1982
Toomey, Bill	1975
+ Towns, Forrest (Spec)	1976
Warmerdam, Cornelius	1974
Whitfield, Mal	1974
Wilkins, Mac	1993
+ Williams, Archie	1992
Wohlhuter, Rick	1990
+ Woodruff, John	1978
Wottle, Dave	1982
+ Wykoff, Frank	1977
Young, George	1981

Women

Ashford, Evelyn 1997	Heritage, Doris Brown 1990	+ Schmidt, Kate..............1994
Brisco, Valerie 1995	+ Jackson, Nell 1989	+ Shiley Newhouse, Jean 1993
Coachman, Alice..........1975	Larrieu Smith, Francie.......1998	+ Stephens, Helen............1975
+ Copeland, Lillian 1994	Manning, Madeline 1984	Tyus, Wyomia 1980
+ Didrikson, Babe.............1974	McDaniel, Mildred 1983	+ Walsh, Stella 1975
Faggs, Mae 1976	McGuire, Edith 1979	Watson, Martha 1987
Ferrell, Barbara 1988	Ritter, Louise 1995	White, Willye..............1981
+ Griffith Joyner, Florence 1995	+ Robinson, Betty 1977	
+ Hall Adams, Evelyne........1988	+ Rudolph, Wilma............1974	

Coaches

+ Abbott, Cleve..............1996	+ Hamilton, Brutus............1974	+ Murphy, Michael 1974
+ Baskin, Weems 1982	+ Haydon, Ted...............1975	Rosen, Mel 1995
+ Beard, Percy.............1981	+ Hayes, Billy 1976	+ Snyder, Larry 1978
Bell, Sam................1992	+ Haylett, Ward 1979	Temple, Ed 1989
+ Botts, Tom 1983	+ Higgins, Ralph 1982	+ Templeton, Dink 1976
Bowerman, Bill.............1981	+ Hillman, Harry 1976	Walker, LeRoy 1983
Bush, Jim.................1987	+ Hurt, Edward 1975	+ Wilt, Fred 1981
+ Cromwell, Dean............1974	+ Hutsell, Wilbur 1977	+ Winter, Bud 1985
+ Doherty, Ken 1976	+ Jones, Thomas 1977	Wolfe, Vern 1996
+ Easton, Bill 1975	Jordan, Payton 1982	Wright, Stan..............1993
+ Elliott, Jumbo 1981	+ Littlefield, Clyde 1981	+ Yancy, Joseph.............1984
+ Giegengack, Bob 1978	+ Moakley, Jack 1988	

Contributors

+ Abramson, Jesse 1981	+ Ferris, Dan 1974	Nelson, Cordner 1988
Andersen, Roxanne.........1991	+ Griffith, John...............1979	+ Sullivan, James.............1977
+ Bakjian, Andy 1986	+ Lebow, Fred 1994	
+ Brundage, Avery 1974	+ Nelson, Bert 1991	

VOLLEYBALL

Volleyball Hall of Fame

Established in 1985. **Address:** P.O. Box 1895, 444 Dwight St., Holyoke, MA 01041 **Telephone:** (413) 536-0926.

Eligibility: Nominees must have contributed at least seven years of outstanding service to volleyball within his/her respective category. Nominees in the player or official category must be retired for five years. A nominee may appear on the ballot a maximum of seven times at which point he/she can be nominated in the Veterans category an unlimited number of times. Voting is done by a panel of no more than 30 individuals from the greater volleyball community.

Class of 1999 (2): VETERAN—**James Wortham**; LEADER—**Wilber H. Peck**.

Members are listed with year of induction; (+) indicates deceased members.

Men

Bright, Mike 1993	+ Haine, Thomas.............1991	Stanley, Jon 1992
Buck, Craig 1998	O'Hara, Michael...........1989	Timmons, Steve 1998
Dvorak, Dusty..............1998	Rundle, Larry 1994	Velasco, Pedro "Pete" 1997
Engen, Rolf................1991	Selznick, Eugene 1988	Von Hagen, Ron 1992

Women

Bright, Patti................1996	Green, Debbie.............1995	Ward, Jane................1988
Dowdell, Patty.............1994	+ Hyman, Flo................1988	Weishoff, Paula 1998
Gregory, Kathy 1989	Peppler, Mary Jo 1990	

Coaches

Banachowski, Andy 1997	Dunphy, Marv 1994	Shondell, Donald...........1996
Beal, Douglas..............1989	Matsudaira, Yasutaka.......1998	+ Wilson, Harry 1988
Coleman, Dr. James 1992	Scates, Al 1993	
DeGroot, Col. Edward 1990	Selinger, Arie 1995	

Veteran

+ Wortham, James 1999	

Leaders

Baird, Bill 1998	+ Gibson, Leonard 1988	Monaco, Jr., Albert 1997
+ Fisher, Dr. George J.........1991	+ Koch, John 1994	+ Morgan, Dr. William G......1985
+ Friermood, Dr. Harold T......1986	+ Lindsey, Robert L...........1995	Peck, Wilber H..............1999

Officials

Davies, Glen 1989	Ignacio, Catalino............1991	Miller, C.L. (Bobb) 1995
+ Fish, Alton.................1990	Kennedy, Merton H. 1992	

WOMEN

International Women's Sports Hall of Fame

Established in 1980 by the Women's Sports Foundation. **Address:** Women's Sports Foundation, Eisenhower Park, East Meadow, NY 11554. **Telephone:** (516) 542-4700.

Eligibility: Nominees' achievements and commitment to the development of women's sports must be internationally recognized. Athletes are elected in two categories—Pioneer (before 1960) and Contemporary (since 1960). Members are divided below by sport for the sake of easy reference; (*) indicates member inducted in Pioneer category. Coaching nominees must have coached at least 10 years.

Class of 1998 (4): CONTEMPORARY—**Florence Griffith Joyner** (track and field). PIONEER—**Margaret Osbourne du Pont** (tennis) and **Shirley Strickland de la Hunty** (track and field). COACH—**Tara Van Derveer** (basketball).

Members are listed with year of induction; (+) indicates deceased members.

Alpine Skiing
Cranz, Christl* 1991
Golden Brosnihan, Diana....1997
Lawrence, Andrea Mead*...1983
Moser-Pröll, Annemarie 1982

Auto Racing
Guthrie, Janet................1980

Aviation
+ Coleman, Bessie* 1992
+ Earhart, Amelia* 1980
+ Marvingt, Marie* 1987

Badminton
Hashman, Judy Devlin* 1995

Baseball
Stone, Toni* 1993

Basketball
Meyers, Ann................1985
Miller, Cheryl...............1991

Bowling
Ladewig, Marion*..........1984

Cycling
Carpenter Phinney, Connie ..1990

Diving
King, Micki.................1983
McCormick, Pat*...........1984
Riggin, Aileen* 1988

Equestrian
Hartel, Lis 1994

Fencing
Schacherer-Elek, Ilona* 1989

Figure Skating
Albright, Tenley* 1983
+ Blanchard, Theresa Weld* ..1989
Fleming, Peggy 1981
Heiss Jenkins, Carol* 1992
+ Henie, Sonja* 1982
Protopopov, Ludmila 1992
Rodnina, Irena 1988
Scott-King, Barbara Ann* ...1997

Golf
Berg, Patty* 1980
Carner, JoAnne 1987
Hicks, Betty* 1995
Mann, Carol................1982
Rawls, Betsy*...............1986
Suggs, Louise*..............1987
+ Vare, Glenna Collett* 1981
Whitworth, Kathy 1984
Wright, Mickey 1981

Golf/Track & Field
+ Zaharias, Babe Didrikson* ..1980

Gymnastics
Caslavska, Vera 1991
Comaneci, Nadia 1990
Korbut, Olga 1982
Latynina, Larysa*..........1985
Retton, Mary Lou 1993
Tourischeva, Lyudmila 1987

Shooting
Murdock, Margaret.........1988

Softball
Joyce, Joan 1989

Speed Skating
+ Klein Outland, Kit* 1993
Young, Sheila..............1981

Swimming
Caulkins, Tracy 1986
+ Chadwick, Florence* 1996
Curtis Cuneo, Ann* 1985
de Varona, Donna..........1983
Ederle, Gertrude* 1980
Fraser, Dawn 1985
Holm, Eleanor* 1980
Meagher, Mary T. 1993
Meyer-Reyes, Debbie 1987

Tennis
+ Connolly, Maureen* 1987
+ Dod, Charlotte (Lottie)*.....1986
Evert, Chris.................1981
Gibson, Althea* 1980
Goolagong Cawley, Evonne .1989

+ Hotchkiss Wightman, Hazel* .1986
King, Billie Jean............1980
+ Lenglen, Suzanne* 1984
Navratilova, Martina 1984
Osbourne du Pont, Margaret*.1998
+ Sears, Eleanora* 1984
Smith Court, Margaret 1986

Track & Field
Ashford, Evelyn 1997
Blankers-Koen, Fanny* 1982
Cheng, Chi................1994
Coachman Davis, Alice* 1991
Faggs Star, Aeriwentha Mae* .1996
+ Griffith Joyner, Florence 1998
Manning Mims, Madeline ...1987
+ Rudolph, Wilma............1980
+ Stephens, Helen* 1983
Strickland de la Hunty, Shirley* .1998
Szewinska, Irena 1992
Tyus, Wyomia 1981
Waitz, Grete 1995
White, Willye..............1988

Volleyball
+ Hyman, Flo................1986

Water Skiing
McGuire, Willa Worthington*...1990

Orienteering
Kringstad, Annichen 1995

Coaches
Applebee, Constance 1991
Backus, Sharron............1993
Conradt, Judy...............1995
Emery, Gail 1997
Grossfeld, Muriel 1991
Holum, Diana..............1996
Jacket, Barbara 1995
+ Jackson, Nell 1990
Kanakogi, Rusty............1994
Summitt, Pat Head..........1990
Van Derveer, Tara 1998
+ Wade, Margaret 1992

Women's Global Challenge

The Women's Sports Foundation announced the creation of the "Women's Global Challenge" to feature the best amateur and professional female athletes and to be held every two years beginning in 2001. After originally planning for a 1999 debut, the Women's Sports Foundation decided that a 2001 start was more prudent. The inaugural event will be held in Washington D.C. and will consist of eight sports — basketball, beach volleyball, diving, figure skating, gymnastics, soccer, swimming and track & field. The top ten athletes in each individual sport and the top four to eight teams in each team sport will be invited to compete. The inaugural "Challenge" will be broadcast by CBS, Lifetime Television and Trans World International and will be syndicated to an estimated 100 countries.

RETIRED NUMBERS

Major League Baseball

The New York Yankees have retired the most uniform numbers (14) in the major leagues; followed the Brooklyn/Los Angeles Dodgers (10), the St. Louis Cardinals (9), the Chicago White Sox and the Pittsburgh Pirates (8) and the New York/San Francisco Giants (7). **Jackie Robinson** had his #42 retired by Major League Baseball in 1997. Players who were already wearing the number were allowed to continue to do so. Los Angeles had already retired Robinson's number so he's only listed with the Dodgers below. **Nolan Ryan** has had his number retired by three teams—#34 by Texas and Houston and #30 by California. Four players and a manager have had their numbers retired by two teams: **Hank Aaron**—#44 by the Boston/Milwaukee/Atlanta Braves and the Milwaukee Brewers; **Rod Carew**—#29 by Minnesota and California; **Rollie Fingers**—#34 by Milwaukee and Oakland; **Frank Robinson**—#20 by Cincinnati and Baltimore; **Casey Stengel**—#37 by the New York Yankees and New York Mets.

Numbers retired in 1999 (2): MILWAUKEE—#4 worn by shortstop **Paul Molitor** (1978-92 with Brewers); SAN FRANCISCO—#30 worn by first baseman **Orlando Cepeda** (1958-66 with Giants).

American League

Three AL teams—the Seattle Mariners, Tampa Bay Devil Rays and the Toronto Blue Jays—have not retired any numbers. The Blue Jays have a "level of excellence" which includes Dave Steib (#11) and George Bell (#37). Both numbers have been used in recent years, however.

Anaheim Angels
11 Jim Fregosi
26 Gene Autry
29 Rod Carew
30 Nolan Ryan
50 Jimmie Reese

Baltimore Orioles
4 Earl Weaver
5 Brooks Robinson
20 Frank Robinson
22 Jim Palmer
33 Eddie Murray

Boston Red Sox
1 Bobby Doerr
4 Joe Cronin
8 Carl Yastrzemski
9 Ted Williams

Chicago White Sox
2 Nellie Fox
3 Harold Baines
4 Luke Appling
9 Minnie Minoso
11 Luis Aparicio
16 Ted Lyons
19 Billy Pierce
72 Carlton Fisk

Cleveland Indians
3 Earl Averill
5 Lou Boudreau
14 Larry Doby
18 Mel Harder
19 Bob Feller
21 Bob Lemon

Detroit Tigers
2 Charlie Gehringer
5 Hank Greenberg
6 Al Kaline
16 Hal Newhouser

Kansas City Royals
5 George Brett
10 Dick Howser
20 Frank White

Minnesota Twins
3 Harmon Killebrew
6 Tony Oliva
14 Kent Hrbek
29 Rod Carew
34 Kirby Puckett

New York Yankees
1 Billy Martin
3 Babe Ruth
4 Lou Gehrig
5 Joe DiMaggio
7 Mickey Mantle
8 Yogi Berra & Bill Dickey
9 Roger Maris
10 Phil Rizzuto
15 Thurman Munson
16 Whitey Ford
23 Don Mattingly
32 Elston Howard
37 Casey Stengel
44 Reggie Jackson

Oakland Athletics
27 Catfish Hunter
34 Rollie Fingers

Texas Rangers
34 Nolan Ryan

National League

Two NL teams—the Arizona Diamondbacks and Colorado Rockies—have not retired any numbers. San Francisco has honored former NY Giants Christy Mathewson and John McGraw even though they played before numbers were worn.

Atlanta Braves
3 Dale Murphy
21 Warren Spahn
35 Phil Niekro
41 Eddie Mathews
44 Hank Aaron

Chicago Cubs
14 Ernie Banks
26 Billy Williams

Cincinnati Reds
1 Fred Hutchinson
5 Johnny Bench
8 Joe Morgan
18 Ted Kluszewski
20 Frank Robinson

Florida Marlins
5 Carl Barger

Houston Astros
25 Jose Cruz
32 Jim Umbricht
33 Mike Scott
34 Nolan Ryan
40 Don Wilson

Los Angeles Dodgers
1 Pee Wee Reese
2 Tommy Lasorda
4 Duke Snider
19 Jim Gilliam
20 Don Sutton
24 Walter Alston
32 Sandy Koufax
39 Roy Campanella
42 Jackie Robinson
53 Don Drysdale

Milwaukee Brewers
4 Paul Molitor
19 Robin Yount
34 Rollie Fingers
44 Hank Aaron

Montreal Expos
8 Gary Carter
10 Rusty Staub
& Andre Dawson

New York Mets
14 Gil Hodges
37 Casey Stengel
41 Tom Seaver

Philadelphia Phillies
1 Richie Ashburn
20 Mike Schmidt
32 Steve Carlton
36 Robin Roberts

Pittsburgh Pirates
1 Billy Meyer
4 Ralph Kiner
8 Willie Stargell
9 Bill Mazeroski
20 Pie Traynor
21 Roberto Clemente
33 Honus Wagner
40 Danny Murtaugh

St. Louis Cardinals
1 Ozzie Smith
2 Red Schoendienst
6 Stan Musial
9 Enos Slaughter
14 Ken Boyer
17 Dizzy Dean
20 Lou Brock
45 Bob Gibson
85 August (Gussie) Busch

San Diego Padres
6 Steve Garvey
35 Randy Jones

San Francisco Giants
3 Bill Terry
4 Mel Ott
11 Carl Hubbell
24 Willie Mays
27 Juan Marichal
30 Orlando Cepeda
44 Willie McCovey

Retired Numbers (Cont.)
National Basketball Association

Boston has retired the most numbers (20) in the NBA, followed by Portland (8); the Los Angeles Lakers, Milwaukee, New York Knicks and the KC/Sacramento Kings have (7); Detroit, New Jersey, the Rochester/Cincinnati Royals and the Syracuse Nats/Philadelphia 76ers have (6); Cleveland and Phoenix have (5). Six players have had their numbers retired by two teams: **Kareem Abdul-Jabbar**—#33 by LA Lakers and Milwaukee; **Wilt Chamberlain**—#13 by the Los Angeles Lakers and Philadelphia; **Julius Erving**—#6 by Philadelphia and #32 by New Jersey; **Bob Lanier**—#16 by Detroit and Milwaukee; **Oscar Robertson**—#1 by Milwaukee and #14 by Sacramento; **Nate Thurmond**—#42 by Cleveland and Golden State.

Numbers retired in 1999 (2): NEW JERSEY—#52 worn by forward **Buck Williams** (1981-89 with Nets); SEATTLE—#10 for guard **Nate McMillan** (1988-97 with Supersonics). The Phoenix Suns honored forward Tom Chambers in 1999 and inducted him into their new Ring of Honor but have announced that they no longer retire numbers.

Eastern Conference

Three Eastern teams—the Miami Heat, Orlando Magic, and Toronto Raptors—have not retired any numbers.

Boston Celtics
1 Walter A. Brown
2 Red Auerbach
3 Dennis Johnson
6 Bill Russell
10 Jo Jo White
14 Bob Cousy
15 Tom Heinsohn
16 Tom (Satch) Sanders
17 John Havlicek
18 Dave Cowens
19 Don Nelson
21 Bill Sharman
22 Ed Macauley
23 Frank Ramsey
24 Sam Jones
25 K.C. Jones
32 Kevin McHale
33 Larry Bird
35 Reggie Lewis
00 Robert Parish
Loscy Jim Loscutoff
Radio mic Johnny Most

Atlanta Hawks
9 Bob Pettit
23 Lou Hudson

Charlotte Hornets
6 Fans ("Sixth Man")

Chicago Bulls
4 Jerry Sloan
10 Bob Love
23 Michael Jordan

Cleveland Cavaliers
7 Bingo Smith
22 Larry Nance
34 Austin Carr
42 Nate Thurmond
43 Brad Daugherty

Detroit Pistons
2 Chuck Daly
11 Isiah Thomas
15 Vinnie Johnson
16 Bob Lanier
21 Dave Bing
40 Bill Laimbeer

Indiana Pacers
30 George McGinnis
34 Mel Daniels
35 Roger Brown

Milwaukee Bucks
1 Oscar Robertson
2 Junior Bridgeman
4 Sidney Moncrief
14 Jon McGlocklin
16 Bob Lanier
32 Brian Winters
33 Kareem Abdul-Jabbar

New York Knicks
10 Walt Frazier
12 Dick Barnett
15 Dick McGuire
   & Earl Monroe
19 Willis Reed
22 Dave DeBusschere
24 Bill Bradley
613 Red Holzman

New Jersey Nets
3 Drazen Petrovic
4 Wendell Ladner
23 John Williamson
25 Bill Melchionni
32 Julius Erving
52 Buck Williams

Philadelphia 76ers
6 Julius Erving
10 Maurice Cheeks
13 Wilt Chamberlain
15 Hal Greer
24 Bobby Jones
32 Billy Cunningham
P.A. mic Dave Zinkoff

Washington Wizards
11 Elvin Hayes
25 Gus Johnson
41 Wes Unseld

Western Conference

Three Western teams—the Los Angeles Clippers, Minnesota Timberwolves and Vancouver Grizzlies—have not retired any numbers.

Dallas Mavericks
15 Brad Davis

Denver Nuggets
2 Alex English
33 David Thompson
40 Byron Beck
44 Dan Issel

Golden St. Warriors
14 Tom Meschery
16 Al Attles
24 Rick Barry
42 Nate Thurmond

Houston Rockets
23 Calvin Murphy
24 Moses Malone
45 Rudy Tomjanovich

Los Angeles Lakers
13 Wilt Chamberlain
22 Elgin Baylor
25 Gail Goodrich
32 Magic Johnson
33 Kareem Abdul-Jabbar
42 James Worthy
44 Jerry West

Phoenix Suns
5 Dick Van Arsdale
6 Walter Davis
33 Alvan Adams
42 Connie Hawkins
44 Paul Westphal

Portland Trail Blazers
1 Larry Weinberg
13 Dave Twardzik
15 Larry Steele
20 Maurice Lucas
32 Bill Walton
36 Lloyd Neal
45 Geoff Petrie
77 Jack Ramsay

Sacramento Kings
1 Nate Archibald
6 Fans ("Sixth Man")
11 Bob Davies
12 Maurice Stokes
14 Oscar Robertson
27 Jack Twyman
44 Sam Lacey

San Antonio Spurs
13 James Silas
44 George Gervin
00 Johnny Moore

Seattle SuperSonics
10 Nate McMillan
19 Lenny Wilkens
32 Fred Brown
43 Jack Sikma
Radio Mic Bob Blackburn

Utah Jazz
1 Frank Layden
7 Pete Maravich
35 Darrell Griffith
53 Mark Eaton

National Football League

The Chicago Bears have retired the most uniform numbers (13) in the NFL; followed by the New York Giants (10); the Dallas Texans/Kansas City Chiefs and San Francisco (8); the Baltimore-Indianapolis Colts and the Boston-New England Patriots (7); Detroit and Philadelphia (6); Cleveland (5). No player has ever had his number retired by more than one NFL team.

Numbers retired in 1999 (2): DENVER—#7 worn by quarterback **John Elway** (1983-98 with Broncos); ST. LOUIS—#29 worn by running back **Eric Dickerson** (1983-87 with Rams).

AFC

Five AFC teams—the Baltimore Ravens, Buffalo Bills, Oakland Raiders, Pittsburgh Steelers and Jacksonville Jaguars—have not retired any numbers.

Cincinnati Bengals
54 Bob Johnson

Cleveland Browns
14 Otto Graham
32 Jim Brown
45 Ernie Davis
46 Don Fleming
76 Lou Groza

Denver Broncos
7 John Elway
18 Frank Tripucka
44 Floyd Little

Indianapolis Colts
19 Johnny Unitas
22 Buddy Young
24 Lenny Moore
70 Art Donovan
77 Jim Parker
82 Raymond Berry
89 Gino Marchetti

Kansas City Chiefs
3 Jan Stenerud
16 Len Dawson
28 Abner Haynes
33 Stone Johnson
36 Mack Lee Hill
63 Willie Lanier
78 Bobby Bell
86 Buck Buchanan

Miami Dolphins
12 Bob Griese

New England Patriots
14 Steve Grogan
20 Gino Cappelletti
40 Mike Haynes
57 Steve Nelson
73 John Hannah
79 Jim Hunt
89 Bob Dee

New York Jets
12 Joe Namath
13 Don Maynard

San Diego Chargers
14 Dan Fouts

Seattle Seahawks
12 Fans ("12th Man")
80 Steve Largent

Tennessee Titans
34 Earl Campbell
43 Jim Norton
63 Mike Munchak
65 Elvin Bethea

NFC

Atlanta, Dallas and the Carolina Panthers are the only NFC teams that haven't officially retired any numbers. The Falcons haven't issued uniforms #10 (Steve Bartowski), #23 (Bobby Butler), #31 (William Andrews), #57 (Jeff Van Note and Clay Matthews), #60 (Tommy Nobis) and #78 (Mike Kenn) since those players retired. The Cowboys have a "Ring of Honor" at Texas Stadium that includes nine players and one coach—Tony Dorsett, Chuck Howley, Lee Roy Jordan, Tom Landry, Bob Lilly, Don Meredith, Don Perkins, Mel Renfro, Roger Staubach and Randy White.

Arizona Cardinals
8 Larry Wilson
77 Stan Mauldin
88 J.V. Cain
99 Marshall Goldberg

Chicago Bears
3 Bronko Nagurski
5 George McAfee
7 George Halas
28 Willie Galimore
34 Walter Payton
40 Gale Sayers
41 Brian Piccolo
42 Sid Luckman
51 Dick Butkus
56 Bill Hewitt
61 Bill George
66 Bulldog Turner
77 Red Grange

Detroit Lions
7 Dutch Clark
22 Bobby Layne
37 Doak Walker
56 Joe Schmidt
85 Chuck Hughes
88 Charlie Sanders

Green Bay Packers
3 Tony Canadeo
14 Don Hutson
15 Bart Starr
66 Ray Nitschke

Minnesota Vikings
10 Fran Tarkenton
88 Alan Page

New Orleans Saints
31 Jim Taylor
81 Doug Atkins

New York Giants
1 Ray Flaherty
4 Tuffy Leemans
7 Mel Hein
11 Phil Simms
14 Y.A. Tittle
32 Al Blozis
40 Joe Morrison
42 Charlie Conerly
50 Ken Strong
56 Lawrence Taylor

Philadelphia Eagles
15 Steve Van Buren
40 Tom Brookshier
44 Pete Retzlaff
60 Chuck Bednarik
70 Al Wistert
99 Jerome Brown

St. Louis Rams
7 Bob Waterfield
29 Eric Dickerson
74 Merlin Olsen
78 Jackie Slater

San Francisco 49ers
12 John Brodie
16 Joe Montana
34 Joe Perry
37 Jimmy Johnson
39 Hugh McElhenny
70 Charlie Krueger
73 Leo Nomellini
87 Dwight Clark

Tampa Bay Bucs
63 Lee Roy Selmon

Wash. Redskins
33 Sammy Baugh

AP/Wide World Photos

The National Hockey League honored retiring legend **Wayne Gretzky** by announcing that his #99 will not be worn in the NHL ever again.

National Hockey League

The Boston Bruins and Montreal Canadiens have retired the most uniform numbers (7) in the NHL; followed by Detroit (6); Chicago and N.Y. Islanders (5); Buffalo, St. Louis and Philadelphia (4). Following his retirement in 1999, the NHL announced that the league will retire Wayne Gretzky's #99. Two players have had their numbers retired by two teams: Gordie Howe—#9 by Detroit and Hartford; and Bobby Hull—#9 by Chicago and Winnipeg.

Numbers retired in 1999 (1): NHL—# 99 **Wayne Gretzky** (1979-88 with Edmonton, 1988-96 with Los Angeles, 1996 with St. Louis and 1996-99 with NY Rangers).

Eastern Conference

Five Eastern teams—the Atlanta Thrashers, Carolina Hurricanes, New Jersey Devils, Tampa Bay Lightning and Florida Panthers—have not retired any numbers. The Hartford Whalers had retired three numbers: #2 Rick Ley, #9 Gordie Howe and #19 John McKenzie.

Boston Bruins
2 Eddie Shore
3 Lionel Hitchman
4 Bobby Orr
5 Dit Clapper
7 Phil Esposito
9 John Bucyk
15 Milt Schmidt

Buffalo Sabres
2 Tim Horton
7 Rick Martin
11 Gilbert Perreault
14 Rene Robert

Montreal Canadiens
1 Jacques Plante
2 Doug Harvey
4 Jean Beliveau
9 Howie Morenz
9 Maurice Richard
10 Guy Lafleur
16 Henri Richard

New York Islanders
5 Denis Potvin
9 Clark Gilles
22 Mike Bossy
23 Bob Nystrom
31 Billy Smith

New York Rangers
1 Eddie Giacomin
7 Rod Gilbert

Ottawa Senators
8 Frank Finnigan

Philadelphia Flyers
1 Bernie Parent
4 Barry Ashbee
7 Bill Barber
16 Bobby Clarke

Pittsburgh Penguins
21 Michel Briere
66 Mario Lemieux

Toronto Maple Leafs
5 Bill Barilko
6 Ace Bailey

Washington Capitals
5 Rod Langway
7 Yvon Labre

Western Conference

Four Western teams—the Colorado Avalanche, San Jose Sharks, Mighty Ducks of Anaheim and Nashville Predators—have not retired any numbers. Note, the Quebec Nordiques retired the numbers of J.C. Tremblay (3), Marc Tardiff (8) and Michel Goulet (16) but these numbers have been worn since the team moved to Colorado.

Calgary Flames
9 Lanny McDonald

Chicago Blackhawks
1 Glenn Hall
9 Bobby Hull
18 Denis Savard
21 Stan Mikita
35 Tony Esposito

Dallas Stars
7 Neal Broten

8 Bill Goldsworthy
19 Bill Masterton

Detroit Red Wings
1 Terry Sawchuk
6 Larry Aurie
7 Ted Lindsay
9 Gordie Howe
10 Alex Delvecchio
12 Sid Abel

Edmonton Oilers
3 Al Hamilton

Los Angeles Kings
16 Marcel Dionne
18 Dave Taylor
30 Rogie Vachon

Phoenix Coyotes
9 Bobby Hull
25 Thomas Steen

St. Louis Blues
3 Bob Gassoff
8 Barclay Plager
11 Brian Sutter
24 Bernie Federko

Vancouver Canucks
12 Stan Smyl

AWARDS

Associated Press Athletes of the Year
Selected annually by AP newspaper sports editors since 1931.

Male

Mark McGwire's home run race with Sammy Sosa re-energized baseball and riveted sports fans across the country in 1998. When it was all over McGwire, the St. Louis first baseman, had an amazing 70 home runs, far surpassing the mark of 61 held by Roger Maris for 37 years.

The Top 10 vote-getters (first place votes in parentheses): 1. **Mark McGwire**, baseball (101), 332 pts; 2. **Sammy Sosa**, baseball (16), 177 pts; 3. **Terrell Davis**, football (10), 63 pts; 4. **Michael Jordan**, basketball (4), 54 pts; 5. **John Elway**, football (3), 50 pts; 6. **Jeff Gordon**, auto racing (1), 42 pts; 7. **Ricky Williams**, college football (1), 37 pts; 8. **Dominik Hasek**, hockey (4), 36 pts; 9. **Mark O'Meara**, golf (1), 23 pts; 10. **Oscar De La Hoya**, boxing (2), 11 pts.

Multiple winners: Michael Jordan (3); Don Budge, Sandy Koufax, Carl Lewis, Joe Montana and Byron Nelson (2).

Year		Year		Year	
1931	**Pepper Martin**, baseball	1952	**Bob Mathias**, track	1975	**Fred Lynn**, baseball
1932	**Gene Sarazen**, golf	1953	**Ben Hogan**, golf	1976	**Bruce Jenner**, track
1933	**Carl Hubbell**, baseball	1954	**Willie Mays**, baseball	1977	**Steve Cauthen**, horse racing
1934	**Dizzy Dean**, baseball	1955	**Hopalong Cassady**, col. football	1978	**Ron Guidry**, baseball
1935	**Joe Louis**, boxing			1979	**Willie Stargell**, baseball
1936	**Jesse Owens**, track	1956	**Mickey Mantle**, baseball	1980	**U.S. Olympic hockey team**
1937	**Don Budge**, tennis	1957	**Ted Williams**, baseball	1981	**John McEnroe**, tennis
1938	**Don Budge**, tennis	1958	**Herb Elliott**, track	1982	**Wayne Gretzky**, hockey
1939	**Nile Kinnick**, college football	1959	**Ingemar Johansson**, boxing	1983	**Carl Lewis**, track
1940	**Tom Harmon**, college football	1960	**Rafer Johnson**, track	1984	**Carl Lewis**, track
1941	**Joe DiMaggio**, baseball	1961	**Roger Maris**, baseball	1985	**Dwight Gooden**, baseball
1942	**Frank Sinkwich**, college football	1962	**Maury Wills**, baseball	1986	**Larry Bird**, pro basketball
1943	**Gunder Haegg**, track	1963	**Sandy Koufax**, baseball	1987	**Ben Johnson**, track
1944	**Byron Nelson**, golf	1964	**Don Schollander**, swimming	1988	**Orel Hershiser**, baseball
1945	**Byron Nelson**, golf	1965	**Sandy Koufax**, baseball	1989	**Joe Montana**, pro football
1946	**Glenn Davis**, college football	1966	**Frank Robinson**, baseball	1990	**Joe Montana**, pro football
1947	**Johnny Lujack**, college football	1967	**Carl Yastrzemski**, baseball	1991	**Michael Jordan**, pro basketball
1948	**Lou Boudreau**, baseball	1968	**Denny McLain**, baseball	1992	**Michael Jordan**, pro basketball
1949	**Leon Hart**, college football	1969	**Tom Seaver**, baseball	1993	**Michael Jordan**, pro basketball
1950	**Jim Konstanty**, baseball	1970	**George Blanda**, pro football	1994	**George Foreman**, boxing
1951	**Dick Kazmaier**, college football	1971	**Lee Trevino**, golf	1995	**Cal Ripken Jr.**, baseball
		1972	**Mark Spitz**, swimming	1996	**Michael Johnson**, track
		1973	**O.J. Simpson**, pro football	1997	**Tiger Woods**, golf
		1974	**Muhammad Ali**, boxing	1998	**Mark McGwire**, baseball

Female

Se Ri Pak, the LPGA rookie from South Korea, won two majors in 1998 including the most memorable U.S. Women's Open in history, winning the tournament on the 20th playoff hole over Jenny Chuasiriporn. Pak, 20, became the youngest person to win the U.S. Open and the youngest person to win two majors in one year.

The Top 10 vote-getters (first place votes in parentheses): 1. **Se Ri Pak**, golf (19), 156 points; 2. **Chamique Holdsclaw**, basketball (27), 142 pts; 3. **Tara Lipinski**, figure skating (21), 105 pts; 4. **Marion Jones**, track and field (24), 101 pts; 5. **Lindsay Davenport**, tennis (15), 85 pts; 6. **Cynthia Cooper**, basketball (10), 55 pts; 7. **Martina Hingis**, tennis (8), 49 pts; 8. **Picabo Street**, skiing (5), 45 pts; 9. **Michelle Kwan**, figure skating (7), 37 pts; 10. **Ila Borders**, baseball (5), 27 pts.

Multiple winners: Babe Didrikson Zaharias (6); Chris Evert (4); Patty Berg and Maureen Connolly (3); Tracy Austin, Althea Gibson, Billie Jean King, Nancy Lopez, Alice Marble, Martina Navratilova, Wilma Rudolph, Monica Seles, Kathy Whitworth and Mickey Wright (2).

Year		Year		Year	
1931	**Helene Madison**, swimming	1950	**Babe Didrikson Zaharias**, golf	1969	**Debbie Meyer**, swimming
1932	**Babe Didrikson**, track	1951	**Maureen Connolly**, tennis	1970	**Chi Cheng**, track
1933	**Helen Jacobs**, tennis	1952	**Maureen Connolly**, tennis	1971	**Evonne Goolagong**, tennis
1934	**Virginia Van Wie**, golf	1953	**Maureen Connolly**, tennis	1972	**Olga Korbut**, gymnastics
1935	**Helen Wills Moody**, tennis	1954	**Babe Didrikson Zaharias**, golf	1973	**Billie Jean King**, tennis
1936	**Helen Stephens**, track	1955	**Patty Berg**, golf	1974	**Chris Evert**, tennis
1937	**Katherine Rawls**, swimming	1956	**Pat McCormick**, diving	1975	**Chris Evert**, tennis
1938	**Patty Berg**, golf	1957	**Althea Gibson**, tennis	1976	**Nadia Comaneci**, gymnastics
1939	**Alice Marble**, tennis	1958	**Althea Gibson**, tennis	1977	**Chris Evert**, tennis
1940	**Alice Marble**, tennis	1959	**Maria Bueno**, tennis	1978	**Nancy Lopez**, golf
1941	**Betty Hicks Newell**, golf	1960	**Wilma Rudolph**, track	1979	**Tracy Austin**, tennis
1942	**Gloria Callen**, swimming	1961	**Wilma Rudolph**, track	1980	**Chris Evert Lloyd**, tennis
1943	**Patty Berg**, golf	1962	**Dawn Fraser**, swimming	1981	**Tracy Austin**, tennis
1944	**Ann Curtis**, swimming	1963	**Mickey Wright**, golf	1982	**Mary Decker Tabb**, track
1945	**Babe Didrikson Zaharias**, golf	1964	**Mickey Wright**, golf	1983	**Martina Navratilova**, tennis
1946	**Babe Didrikson Zaharias**, golf	1965	**Kathy Whitworth**, golf	1984	**Mary Lou Retton**, gymnastics
1947	**Babe Didrikson Zaharias**, golf	1966	**Kathy Whitworth**, golf	1985	**Nancy Lopez**, golf
1948	**Fanny Blankers-Koen**, track	1967	**Billie Jean King**, tennis	1986	**Martina Navratilova**, tennis
1949	**Marlene Bauer**, golf	1968	**Peggy Fleming**, skating	1987	**Jackie Joyner-Kersee**, track

Awards (Cont.)

Year		Year		Year	
1988	**Florence Griffith Joyner**, track	1992	**Monica Seles**, tennis	1996	**Amy Van Dyken**, swimming
1989	**Steffi Graf**, tennis	1993	**Sheryl Swoopes**, basketball	1997	**Martina Hingis**, tennis
1990	**Beth Daniel**, golf	1994	**Bonnie Blair**, speed skating	1998	**Se Ri Pak**, golf
1991	**Monica Seles**, tennis	1995	**Rebecca Lobo**, col. basketball		

UPI International Athletes of the Year

Selected annually by United Press International's European newspaper sports editors from 1974-95.

Male

Multiple winners: Sebastian Coe, Alberto Juantorena and Carl Lewis (2).

Year		Year		Year	
1974	**Muhammad Ali**, boxing	1982	**Daley Thompson**, track	1990	**Stefan Edberg**, tennis
1975	**Joao Oliveira**, track	1983	**Carl Lewis**, track	1991	**Sergei Bubka**, track
1976	**Alberto Juantorena**, track	1984	**Carl Lewis**, track	1992	**Kevin Young**, track
1977	**Alberto Juantorena**, track	1985	**Steve Cram**, track	1993	**Miguel Indurain**, cycling
1978	**Henry Rono**, track	1986	**Diego Maradona**, soccer	1994	**Johan Olav Koss**, speed
1979	**Sebastian Coe**, track	1987	**Ben Johnson**, track		skating
1980	**Eric Heiden**, speed skating	1988	**Matt Biondi**, swimming	1995	**Jonathan Edwards**, track
1981	**Sebastian Coe**, track	1989	**Boris Becker**, tennis	1996	discontinued

Female

Multiple winners: Nadia Comaneci, Steffi Graf, Marita Koch and Monica Seles (2).

Year		Year		Year	
1974	**Irena Szewinska**, track	1982	**Marita Koch**, track	1990	**Merlene Ottey**, track
1975	**Nadia Comaneci**, gymnastics	1983	**Jarmila Kratochvilova**, track	1991	**Monica Seles**, tennis
1976	**Nadia Comaneci**, gymnastics	1984	**Martina Navratilova**, tennis	1992	**Monica Seles**, tennis
1977	**Rosie Ackermann**, track	1985	**Mary Decker Slaney**, track	1993	**Wang Junxia**, track
1978	**Tracy Caulkins**, swimming	1986	**Heike Drechsler**, track	1994	**Le Jingyi**, swimming
1979	**Marita Koch**, track	1987	**Steffi Graf**, tennis	1995	**Gwen Torrence**, track
1980	**Hanni Wenzel**, alpine skiing	1988	**Florence Griffith Joyner**, track	1996	discontinued
1981	**Chris Evert Lloyd**, tennis	1989	**Steffi Graf**, tennis		

Jesse Owens International Trophy

Presented annually by the International Amateur Athletic Association since 1981 and selected by a worldwide panel of electors. The Jesse Owens International Trophy is named after the late American Olympic champion, who won four gold medals at the 1936 Summer Games in Berlin.

Year		Year		Year	
1981	**Eric Heiden**, speed skating	1988	**Ben Johnson**, track	1995	**Johan Olva Koss**, speed
1982	**Sebastian Coe**, track	1990	**Roger Kingdom**, track		skating
1983	**Mary Decker**, track	1991	**Greg LeMond**, cycling	1996	**Michael Johnson**, track
1984	**Edwin Moses**, track	1992	**Mike Powell**, track	1997	**Michael Johnson**, track
1985	**Carl Lewis**, track	1993	**Vitaly Scherbo**, gymnastics	1998	**Haile Gebrselassie**, track
1986	**Said Aouita**, track	1994	**Wang Junxia**, track	1999	**Marion Jones**, track
1987	**Greg Louganis**, diving				

James E. Sullivan Memorial Award

Presented annually by the Amateur Athletic Union since 1930. The Sullivan Award is named after the former AAU president and given to the athlete who, "by his or her performance, example and influence as an amateur, has done the most during the year to advance the cause of sportsmanship." An athlete cannot win the award more than once.

The 1998 winner was college basketball player **Chamique Holdsclaw**. Holdsclaw swept the player of the year awards and led the Tennessee Lady Vols to a perfect 39-0 record and their third straight national championship in 1998. Holdsclaw became the second University of Tennessee athlete to win the award in as many years. The other ten finalists are listed alphabetically: **Elton Brand**, basketball; **Pat Burrell**, baseball; **Jenny Chuasiriporn**, golf; **Tim Couch**, football; **Sammie Henson**, wrestling; **Matt Kuchar**, golf; **Kristin Maloney**, gymnastics; **Mark Ruiz**, diving; **Angelo Taylor**, track; **Ricky Williams**, football. Vote totals were not released.

Year		Year		Year	
1930	**Bobby Jones**, golf	1943	**Gilbert Dodds**, track	1956	**Pat McCormick**, diving
1931	**Barney Berlinger**, track	1944	**Ann Curtis**, swimming	1957	**Bobby Morrow**, track
1932	**Jim Bausch**, track	1945	**Doc Blanchard**, football	1958	**Glenn Davis**, track
1933	**Glenn Cunningham**, track	1946	**Arnold Tucker**, football	1959	**Parry O'Brien**, track
1934	**Bill Bonthron**, track	1947	**John B. Kelly, Jr.**, rowing	1960	**Rafer Johnson**, track
1935	**Lawson Little**, golf	1948	**Bob Mathias**, track	1961	**Wilma Rudolph**, track
1936	**Glenn Morris**, track	1949	**Dick Button**, skating	1963	**John Pennel**, track
1937	**Don Budge**, tennis	1950	**Fred Wilt**, track	1964	**Don Schollander**, swimming
1938	**Don Lash**, track	1951	**Bob Richards**, track	1965	**Bill Bradley**, basketball
1939	**Joe Burk**, rowing	1952	**Horace Ashenfelter**, track	1966	**Jim Ryun**, track
1940	**Greg Rice**, track	1953	**Sammy Lee**, diving	1967	**Randy Matson**, track
1941	**Leslie MacMitchell**, track	1954	**Mal Whitfield**, track	1968	**Debbie Meyer**, swimming
1942	**Cornelius Warmerdam**, track	1955	**Harrison Dillard**, track	1969	**Bill Toomey**, track

Year		Year		Year	
1970	**John Kinsella**, swimming	1981	**Carl Lewis**, track	1992	**Bonnie Blair**, speed skating
1971	**Mark Spitz**, swimming	1982	**Mary Decker**, track	1993	**Charlie Ward**, football
1972	**Frank Shorter**, track	1983	**Edwin Moses**, track	1994	**Dan Jansen**, speed skating
1973	**Bill Walton**, basketball	1984	**Greg Louganis**, diving	1995	**Bruce Baumgartner**, wrestling
1974	**Rich Wohlhuter**, track	1985	**Joan B. Samuelson**, track	1996	**Michael Johnson**, track
1975	**Tim Shaw**, swimming	1986	**Jackie Joyner-Kersee**, track	1997	**Peyton Manning**, football
1976	**Bruce Jenner**, track	1987	**Jim Abbott**, baseball	1998	**Chamique Holdsclaw**,
1977	**John Naber**, swimming	1988	**Florence Griffith Joyner**, track		basketball
1978	**Tracy Caulkins**, swimming	1989	**Janet Evans**, swimming		
1979	**Kurt Thomas**, gymnastics	1990	**John Smith**, wrestling		
1980	**Eric Heiden**, speed skating	1991	**Mike Powell**, track		

USOC Sportsman & Sportswoman of the Year

To the outstanding overall male and female athletes from within the U.S. Olympic Committee member organizations. Winners are chosen from nominees of the national governing bodies for Olympic and Pan American Games and affiliated organizations. Voting is done by members of the national media, USOC board of directors and Athletes' Advisory Council.

Sportsman

Multiple winners: Eric Heiden and Michael Johnson (3); Matt Biondi and Greg Louganis (2).

Year		Year		Year	
1974	**Jim Bolding**, track	1983	**Rick McKinney**, archery	1992	**Pablo Morales**, swimming
1975	**Clint Jackson**, boxing	1984	**Edwin Moses**, track	1993	**Michael Johnson**, track
1976	**John Naber**, swimming	1985	**Willie Banks**, track	1994	**Dan Jansen**, speed skating
1977	**Eric Heiden**, speed skating	1986	**Matt Biondi**, swimming	1995	**Michael Johnson**, track
1978	**Bruce Davidson**, equestrian	1987	**Greg Louganis**, diving	1996	**Michael Johnson**, track
1979	**Eric Heiden**, speed skating	1988	**Matt Biondi**, swimming	1997	**Pete Sampras**, tennis
1980	**Eric Heiden**, speed skating	1989	**Roger Kingdom**, track	1998	**Jonny Moseley**, skiing
1981	**Scott Hamilton**, fig. skating	1990	**John Smith**, wrestling		
1982	**Greg Louganis**, diving	1991	**Carl Lewis**, track		

Sportswoman

Multiple winners: Bonnie Blair, Tracy Caulkins, Jackie Joyner-Kersee, Picabo Street and Sheila Young Ochowicz (2).

Year		Year		Year	
1974	**Shirley Babashoff**, swimming	1982	**Melanie Smith**, equestrian	1991	**Kim Zmeskal**, gymnastics
1975	**Kathy Heddy**, swimming	1983	**Tamara McKinney**, skiing	1992	**Bonnie Blair**, speed skating
1976	**Sheila Young**, speedskating	1984	**Tracy Caulkins**, swimming	1993	**Gail Devers**, track
1977	**Linda Fratianne**, fig. skating	1985	**Mary Decker Slaney**, track	1994	**Bonnie Blair**, speed skating
1978	**Tracy Caulkins**, swimming	1986	**Jackie Joyner-Kersee**, track	1995	**Picabo Street**, skiing
1979	**Sippy Woodhead**, swimming	1987	**Jackie Joyner-Kersee**, track	1996	**Amy Van Dyken**, swimming
1980	**Beth Heiden**, speed skating	1988	**Florence Griffith Joyner**, track	1997	**Tara Lipinski**, figure skating
1981	**Sheila Ochowicz**, speed	1989	**Janet Evans**, swimming	1998	**Picabo Street**, skiing
	skating & cycling	1990	**Lynn Jennings**, track		

Honda Broderick Cup

To the outstanding collegiate woman athlete of the year in NCAA competition. Winner is chosen from nominees in each of the NCAA's 10 competitive sports. Final voting is done by member athletic directors. Award is named after founder and sportswear manufacturer Thomas Broderick.

Multiple winner: Tracy Caulkins (2).

Year		Year		
1977	**Lucy Harris**, Delta St ....basketball	1988	**Teresa Weatherspoon**, La. Tech ....basketball
1978	**Ann Meyers**, UCLA ....basketball	1989	**Vicki Huber**, Villanova ....track
1979	**Nancy Lieberman**, Old Dominion ......basketball	1990	**Suzy Favor**, Wisconsin ....track
1980	**Julie Shea**, N.C. State ....track & field	1991	**Dawn Staley**, Virginia ....basketball
1981	**Jill Sterkel**, Texas ....swimming	1992	**Missy Marlowe**, Utah ....gymnastics
1982	**Tracy Caulkins**, Florida................swimming	1993	**Lisa Fernandez**, UCLA....................softball
1983	**Deitre Collins**, Hawaii ....volleyball	1994	**Mia Hamm**, North Carolina ....soccer
1984	**Tracy Caulkins**, Florida................swimming	1995	**Rebecca Lobo**, UConn..................basketball
	& **Cheryl Miller**, USC.................basketball	1996	**Jennifer Rizzotti**, UConn ....basketball
1985	**Jackie Joyner**, UCLA.................track & field	1997	**Cindy Daws**, Notre Dame ....soccer
1986	**Kamie Ethridge**, Texas ....basketball	1998	**Chamique Holdsclaw**, Tennessee ......basketball
1987	**Mary T. Meagher**, California...........swimming	1999	**Misty May**, Long Beach St..............volleyball

Flo Hyman Award

Presented annually since 1987 by the Women's Sports Foundation for "exemplifying dignity, spirit and commitment to excellence" and named in honor of the late captain of the 1984 U.S. Women's Volleyball team. Voting by WSF members.

Year		Year		Year	
1987	**Martina Navratilova**, tennis	1991	**Diana Golden**, skiing	1995	**Mary Lou Retton**, gymnastics
1988	**Jackie Joyner-Kersee**, track	1992	**Nancy Lopez**, golf	1996	**Donna de Varona**, swimming
1989	**Evelyn Ashford**, track	1993	**Lynette Woodard**, basketball	1997	**Billie Jean King**, tennis
1990	**Chris Evert**, tennis	1994	**Patty Sheehan**, golf	1998	**Nadia Comaneci**, gymnastics

Awards (Cont.)
ESPY Awards

The ESPY Awards, which represent the convergence of the sports and entertainment communities, were created by ESPN in 1993 and are given for Excellence in Sports Performance in more than 30 categories. ESPYs are awarded in by a panel of sports executives, journalists and retired athletes whose decisions are based on the performances of the nominees during the year preceding the awards ceremony. Note that not all categories are listed below.

Breakthrough Athlete of the Year

1993 Gary Sheffield, San Diego Padres
1994 Mike Piazza, Los Angeles Dodgers
1995 Jeff Bagwell, Houston Astros
1996 Hideo Nomo, Los Angeles Dodgers
1997 Tiger Woods, golf
1998 Nomar Garciaparra, Boston Red Sox
1999 Randy Moss, Minnesota Vikings

Coach/Manager of the Year

1993 Jimmy Johnson, Dallas Cowboys
1994 Jimmy Johnson, Dallas Cowboys
1995 George Siefert, San Francisco 49ers
1996 Gary Barnett, Northwestern
1997 Joe Torre, New York Yankees
1998 Jim Leyland, Florida Marlins
1999 Joe Torre, New York Yankees

Comeback Athlete of the Year

1993 Dave Winfield, Toronto Blue Jays
1994 Mario Lemieux, Pittsburgh Penguins
1995 Dan Marino, Miami Dolphins
1996 Michael Jordan, Chicago Bulls
1997 Evander Holyfield, boxer
1998 Roger Clemens, Toronto Blue Jays
1999 Eric Davis, Baltimore Orioles

Outstanding Female Athlete of the Year

1993 Monica Seles, tennis
1994 Julie Krone, jockey
1995 Bonnie Blair, speed skater
1996 Rebecca Lobo, basketball
1997 Amy Van Dyken, swimming
1998 Mia Hamm, soccer
1999 Chamique Holdsclaw, college basketball

Outstanding Male Athlete of the Year

1993 Michael Jordan, Chicago Bulls
1994 Barry Bonds, San Francisco Giants
1995 Steve Young, San Francisco 49ers
1996 Cal Ripken, Baltimore Orioles
1997 Michael Johnson, Olympic sprinter
1998 Tiger Woods, golf
1999 Mark McGwire, St. Louis Cardinals

Outstanding Performance Under Pressure

1993 Christian Laettner, Duke
1994 Joe Carter, Toronto Blue Jays
1995 Mark Messier, New York Rangers
1996 Martin Broduer, New Jersey Devils
1997 Kerri Strug, Olympic gymnast
1998 Terrell Davis, Denver Broncos
1999 Mark O'Meara, golf

Outstanding Team

1993 Dallas Cowboys
1994 Toronto Blue Jays
1995 New York Rangers
1996 UConn women's hoops
1997 New York Yankees

1998 Denver Broncos
1999 New York Yankees

Outstanding Baseball Performer of the Year

1993 Dennis Eckersley, Oakland A's
1994 Barry Bonds, San Francisco Giants
1995 Jeff Bagwell, Houston Astros
1996 Greg Maddux, Atlanta Braves
1997 Ken Caminiti, San Diego Padres
1998 Larry Walker, Colorado Rockies
1999 Mark McGwire, St. Louis Cardinals

Outstanding Pro Football Performer of the Year

1993 Emmitt Smith, Dallas Cowboys
1994 Emmitt Smith, Dallas Cowboys
1995 Barry Sanders, Detroit Lions
1996 Brett Favre, Green Bay Packers
1997 Brett Favre, Green Bay Packers
1998 Barry Sanders, Detroit Lions
1999 Terrell Davis, Denver Broncos

Outstanding Pro Basketball Performer of the Year

1993 Michael Jordan, Chicago Bulls
1994 Charles Barkley, Phoenix Suns
1995 Hakeem Olajuwon, Houston Rockets
1996 Hakeem Olajuwon, Houston Rockets
1997 Michael Jordan, Chicago Bulls
1998 Michael Jordan, Chicago Bulls
1999 Michael Jordan, Chicago Bulls

Outstanding Pro Hockey Performer of the Year

1993 Mario Lemieux, Pittsburgh Penguins
1994 Mario Lemieux, Pittsburgh Penguins
1995 Mark Messier, New York Rangers
1996 Eric Lindros, Philadelphia Flyers
1997 Joe Sakic, Colorado Avalanche
1998 Mario Lemieux, Pittsburgh Penguins
1999 Dominik Hasek, Buffalo Sabres

Outstanding College Football Performer of the Year

1993 Garrison Hearst, Georgia
1994 Charlie Ward, Florida State
1995 Rashaan Salaam, Colorado
1996 Eddie George, Ohio State
1997 Danny Wuerffel, Florida
1998 Peyton Manning, Tennessee
1999 Ricky Williams, Texas

Outstanding College Basketball Performer of the Year

1993 Christian Laettner, Duke
1994 Bobby Hurley, Duke
1995 Grant Hill, Duke
1996 Ed O'Bannon, UCLA
1997 Tim Duncan, Wake Forest
1998 Keith Van Horn, Utah
1999 Antawn Jamison, North Carolina

Outstanding Women's College Hoops Performer of the Year

1993 Dawn Staley, Virginia
1994 Sheryl Swoopes, Texas Tech
1995 Charlotte Smith, North Carolina
1996 Rebecca Lobo, Connecticut
1997 Saudia Roundtree, Georgia
1998 Chamique Holdsclaw, Tennessee
1999 Chamique Holdsclaw, Tennessee

Outstanding Men's Tennis Performer of the Year

1993 Jim Courier
1994 Pete Sampras
1995 Pete Sampras
1996 Pete Sampras
1997 Pete Sampras
1998 Pete Sampras
1999 Pete Sampras

Outstanding Women's Tennis Performer of the Year

1993 Monica Seles
1994 Steffi Graf
1995 Aranxta Sanchez-Vicario
1996 Steffi Graf
1997 Steffi Graf
1998 Martina Hingis
1999 Lindsay Davenport

Outstanding Men's Golf Performer of the Year

1993 Fred Couples
1994 Nick Price
1995 Nick Price
1996 Corey Pavin
1997 Tom Lehman
1998 Tiger Woods
1999 Mark O'Meara

Outstanding Women's Golf Performer of the Year

1993 Dottie Monroe
1994 Betsy King
1995 Laura Davies
1996 Annika Sorenstam
1997 Karrie Webb
1998 Annika Sorenstam
1999 Annika Sorenstam

Outstanding Jockey of the Year

1994 Mike Smith
1995 Chris McCarron
1996 Jerry Bailey
1997 Jerry Bailey
1998 Gary Stevens
1999 Kent Desormeaux

Outstanding Bowling Performer of the Year

1995 Norm Duke
1996 Mike Aulby
1997 Bob Learn Jr.
1998 Walter Ray Williams Jr.
1999 Walter Ray Williams Jr.

Outstanding Auto Racing Performer of the Year

1993 Nigel Mansell
1994 Nigel Mansell
1995 Al Unser Jr.
1996 Jeff Gordon
1997 Jimmy Vasser
1998 Jeff Gordon
1999 Jeff Gordon

Outstanding Men's Track Performer of the Year

1993 Kevin Young
1994 Michael Johnson
1995 Dennis Mitchell
1996 Michael Johnson
1997 Michael Johnson
1998 Wilson Kipketer
1999 Maurice Greene

Outstanding Women's Track Performer of the Year

1993 Evelyn Ashford
1994 Gail Devers
1995 Gwen Torrence
1996 Kim Batten
1997 Marie-Jose Perec
1998 Marion Jones
1999 Marion Jones

Outstanding Boxing Performer of the Year

1993 Riddick Bowe
1994 Evander Holyfield
1995 George Foreman
1996 Roy Jones Jr.
1997 Evander Holyfield
1998 Evander Holyfield
1999 Oscar De La Hoya

Game of the Year

1996 AFC championship between Colts and Steelers
1997 Ohio State edges Arizona State in the Rose Bowl
1998 Super Bowl XXXII, Broncos over Packers
1999 not awarded

Presidential Medal of Freedom

Since President John F. Kennedy established the Medal of Freedom as America's highest civilian honor in 1963, only nine sports figures have won the award. Note that (*) indicates the presentation was made posthumously.

Year		President	Year		President
1963	**Bob Kiphuth**, swimming	Kennedy	1986	**Earl (Red) Blaik**, football	Reagan
1976	**Jesse Owens**, track & field	Ford	1991	**Ted Williams**, baseball	Bush
1977	**Joe DiMaggio**, baseball	Ford	1992	**Richard Petty**, auto racing	Bush
1983	**Paul (Bear) Bryant***, football	Reagan	1993	**Arthur Ashe***, tennis	Clinton
1984	**Jackie Robinson***, baseball	Reagan			

Awards (Cont.)
Arthur Ashe Award for Courage

Presented since 1993 on the annual ESPN "ESPYs" telecast. Given to a member of the sports community who has exemplified the same courage, spirit and determination to help others despite personal hardship that characterized Arthur Ashe, the late tennis champion and humanitarian. Voting done by select 26-member committee of media and sports personalities.

Year		Year		Year	
1993	**Jim Valvano**, basketball	1996	**Loretta Clairborne**, special	1998	**Dean Smith**, college basketball
1994	**Steve Palermo**, baseball		olympics	1999	**Billie Jean King**, tennis
1995	**Howard Cosell**, TV & radio	1997	**Muhammad Ali**, boxing		

The Hickok Belt

Officially known as the S. Rae Hickok Professional Athlete of the Year Award and presented by the Kickik Manufacturing Co. of Arlington, Texas, from 1950-76. The trophy was a large belt of gold, diamonds and other jewels, reportedly worth $30,000 in 1976, the last year it was handed out. Voting was done by 270 newspaper sports editors from around the country.

Multiple winner: Sandy Koufax (2).

Year		Year		Year	
1950	**Phil Rizzuto**, baseball	1960	**Arnold Palmer**, golf	1970	**Brooks Robinson**, baseball
1951	**Allie Reynolds**, baseball	1961	**Roger Maris**, baseball	1971	**Lee Trevino**, golf
1952	**Rocky Marciano**, boxing	1962	**Maury Wills**, baseball	1972	**Steve Carlton**, baseball
1953	**Ben Hogan**, golf	1963	**Sandy Koufax**, baseball	1973	**O.J. Simpson**, football
1954	**Willie Mays**, baseball	1964	**Jim Brown**, football	1974	**Muhammad Ali**, boxing
1955	**Otto Graham**, football	1965	**Sandy Koufax**, baseball	1975	**Pete Rose**, baseball
1956	**Mickey Mantle**, baseball	1966	**Frank Robinson**, baseball	1976	**Ken Stabler**, football
1957	**Carmen Basilio**, boxing	1967	**Carl Yastrzemski**, baseball	1977	Discontinued
1958	**Bob Turley**, baseball	1968	**Joe Namath**, football		
1959	**Ingemar Johansson**, boxing	1969	**Tom Seaver**, baseball		

ABC's "Wide World of Sports" Athlete of the Year

Selected annually by the producers of ABC Sports since 1962.

Multiple winner: Greg LeMond (2).

Year		Year		Year	
1962	**Jim Beatty**, track	1974	**Muhammad Ali**, boxing	1987	**Dennis Conner**, yachting
1963	**Valery Brumel**, track	1975	**Jack Nicklaus**, golf	1988	**Greg Louganis**, diving
1964	**Don Schollander**, swimming	1976	**Nadia Comaneci**, gymnastics	1989	**Greg LeMond**, cycling
1965	**Jim Clark**, auto racing	1977	**Steve Cauthen**, horse racing	1990	**Greg LeMond**, cycling
1966	**Jim Ryun**, track	1978	**Ron Guidry**, baseball	1991	**Carl Lewis**, track
1967	**Peggy Fleming**, figure skating	1979	**Willie Stargell**, baseball		& **Kim Zmeskal**, gymnastics
1968	**Bill Toomey**, track	1980	**U.S. Olympic hockey team**	1992	**Bonnie Blair**, speed skating
1969	**Mario Andretti**, auto racing	1981	**Sugar Ray Leonard**, boxing	1993	**Evander Holyfield**, boxing
1970	**Willis Reed**, basketball	1982	**Wayne Gretzky**, hockey	1994	**Al Unser Jr.**, auto racing
1971	**Lee Trevino**, golf	1983	**Australia II**, yachting	1995	**Miguel Induráin**, cycling
1972	**Olga Korbut**, gymnastics	1984	**Edwin Moses**, track	1996	**Michael Johnson**, track
1973	**O.J. Simpson**, football	1985	**Pete Rose**, baseball	1997	**Tiger Woods**, golf
	& **Jackie Stewart**, auto racing	1986	**Debi Thomas**, figure skating	1998	**Mark McGwire**, baseball

The Sporting News Sportsman of the Year

Selected annually by the editors of The Sporting News since 1968. 'Man of the Year' changed to 'Sportsman' of the Year in 1993.

Multiple Winner: Mark McGwire (2).

Year		Year		Year	
1968	**Denny McLain**, baseball	1980	**George Brett**, baseball	1992	**Mike Krzyzewski**, col. bask.
1969	**Tom Seaver**, baseball	1981	**Wayne Gretzky**, hockey	1993	**Cito Gaston**
1970	**John Wooden**, basketball	1982	**Whitey Herzog**, baseball		& **Pat Gillick**, baseball
1971	**Lee Trevino**, golf	1983	**Bowie Kuhn**, baseball	1994	**Emmitt Smith**, pro football
1972	**Charles O. Finley**, baseball	1984	**Peter Ueberroth**, LA Olympics	1995	**Cal Ripken Jr.**, baseball
1973	**O.J. Simpson**, pro football	1985	**Pete Rose**, baseball	1996	**Joe Torre**, baseball
1974	**Lou Brock**, baseball	1986	**Larry Bird**, pro basketball	1997	**Mark McGwire**, baseball
1975	**Archie Griffin**, football	1987	No award	1998	**Mark McGwire**
1976	**Larry O'Brien**, basketball	1988	**Jackie Joyner-Kersee**, track		& **Sammy Sosa**, baseball
1977	**Steve Cauthen**, horse racing	1989	**Joe Montana**, football		
1978	**Ron Guidry**, baseball	1990	**Nolan Ryan**, baseball		
1979	**Willie Stargell**, baseball	1991	**Michael Jordan**, basketball		

Time Man of the Year

Since Charles Lindbergh was named Time magazine's first Man of the Year for 1927, two individuals with significant sports credentials have won the honor.

Year	
1984	**Peter Ueberroth**, president of the Los Angeles Olympic Organizing Committee.
1991	**Ted Turner**, owner-president of Turner Broadcasting System, founder of CNN cable news network, owner of the Atlanta Braves (NL) and Atlanta Hawks (NBA), and former winning America's Cup skipper.

TROPHY CASE

From the first organized track meet at Olympia in 776 B.C., to the Atlanta Summer Olympics over 2,700 years later, championships have been officially recognized with prizes that are symbolically rich and eagerly pursued. Here are 15 of the most coveted trophies in America.

(Illustrations by Lynn Mercer Michaud)

America's Cup

First presented by England's Royal Yacht Squadron to the winner of an invitational race around the Isle of Wight on Aug. 22, 1851. . . originally called the Hundred Guinea Cup. . . renamed after the U.S. boat America, winner of the first race. . . made of sterling silver and designed by London jewelers R. & G. Garrard. . . measures 2 feet, 3 inches high and weighs 16 lbs. . . originally cost 100 guineas ($500), now valued at $250,000 . . . bell-shaped base added in 1958. . . challenged for every three to four years. . . trophy held by yacht club sponsoring winning boat...Cup was badly damaged when a Maori protester repeatedly smashed it with a sledgehammer on March 14, 1997. It was sent back to the original maker and fully restored.

Vince Lombardi Trophy

First presented at the AFL-NFL World Championship Game (now Super Bowl) on Jan. 15, 1967. . . originally called the World Championship Game Trophy . . . renamed in 1971 in honor of former Green Bay Packers GM-coach and two-time Super Bowl winner Vince Lombardi, who died in 1970 as coach of Washington . . . made of sterling silver and designed by Tiffany & Co. of New York . . . measures 21 inches high and weighs 7 lbs (football depicted is regulation size). . . valued at $12,500. . . competed for annually-. . . winning team keeps trophy.

Olympic Gold Medal

First presented by International Olympic Committee in 1908 (until then winners received silver medals). . . second and third place finishers also got medals of silver and bronze for first time in 1908. . . each medal must be at least 2.4 inches in diameter and 0.12 inches thick. . . the gold medal is actually made of silver, but must be gilded with at least 6 grams (0.21 ounces) of pure gold. . . the medals for the 1996 Atlanta Games were designed by Malcolm Grear Designers and produced by Reed & Barton of Taunton, Mass...604 gold, 604 silver and 630 bronze medals were made. . . competed for every two years as Winter and Summer Games alternate. . . winners keep medals.

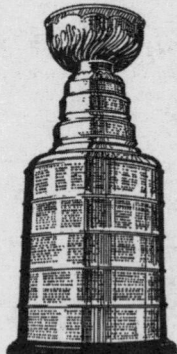

Stanley Cup

Donated by Lord Stanley of Preston, the Governor General of Canada and first presented in 1893. . . original cup was made of sterling silver by an unknown London silversmith and measured 7 inches high with an 11½-inch diameter. . . in order to accommodate all the rosters of winning teams, the cup now measures 35½ inches high with a base 54 inches around and weighs 32 lbs. . . in order to add new names each year, bands on the trophy are often retired and displayed at the Hall of Fame. . . originally bought for 10 guineas ($48.67), it is now insured for $75,000. . . actual cup retired to Hall of Fame and replaced in 1970. . . presented to NHL playoff champion since 1918. . . trophy loaned to winning team for one year.

World Cup

First presented by the Federation Internationale de Football Association (FIFA). . . originally called the World Cup Trophy. . . renamed the Jules Rimet Cup (after the then FIFA president) in 1946, but retired by Brazil after that country's third title in 1970. . . new World Cup trophy created in 1974. . . designed by Italian sculptor Silvio Gazzaniga and made of solid 18 carat gold with two malachite rings inlaid at the base. . . measures 14.2 inches high and weighs 11 lbs. . . insured for $200,000 (U.S.). . . competed for every four years. . . winning team gets gold-plated replica.

Commissioner's Trophy

First presented by the Commissioner of baseball to the winner of the 1967 World Series. . . also known as the World Championship Trophy. . . made of brass and gold plate with an ebony base and a baseball in the center made of pewter with a silver finish. . . designed by Balfour & Co. of Attleboro, Mass. . . 30 pennants represent 14 AL and 16 NL teams . . . measures 30 inches high and 36 inches around at the base and weighs 30 lbs. . . valued at $15,000. . . competed for annually. . . winning team keeps trophy.

Larry O'Brien Trophy

First presented in 1978 to winner of NBA Finals. . . originally called the Walter A. Brown Trophy after the league pioneer and Boston Celtics owner (an earlier NBA championship bowl was also named after Brown). . . renamed in 1984 in honor of outgoing commissioner O'Brien, who served from 1975-84 . . . made of sterling silver with 24 carat gold overlay and designed by Tiffany & Co. of New York. . . measures 2 feet high and weighs 14½ lbs (basketball depicted is regulation size). . . valued at $13,500. . . competed for annually. . . winning team keeps trophy.

Heisman Trophy

First presented in 1935 to the best college football player east of the Mississippi by the Downtown Athletic Club of New York. . . players across the entire country eligible since 1936. . . originally called the DAC Trophy. . . renamed in 1936 following the death of DAC athletic director and former college coach John W. Heisman. . . made of bronze and designed by New York sculptor Frank Eliscu, it measures 13½ in. high, 6½ in. wide and 14 in. long at the base and weighs 25 lbs. . . valued at $2,000 . . . voting done by national media and former Heisman winners. . . trophy sponsor American Suzuki announced plans for limited fan voting starting in 1999. . . awarded annually. . . winner keeps trophy.

James E. Sullivan Memorial Award

First presented by the Amateur Athletic Union (AAU) in 1930 as a gold medal and given to the nation's outstanding amateur athlete. . . trophy given since 1933. . . named after the amateur sports movement pioneer, who was a founder and past president of AAU and the director of the 1904 Olympic Games in St. Louis. . . made of bronze with a marble base, it measures 17½ in. high and 11 in. wide at the base and weighs 13½ lbs. . . valued at $2,500. . . voting done by AAU and USOC officials, former winners and selected media. . . awarded annually. . . winner keeps trophy.

Ryder Cup

Donated in 1927 by English seed merchant Samuel Ryder, who offered the gold cup for a biennial match between teams of golfing pros from Great Britain and the United States. . . the format changed in 1977 to include the best players on the European PGA Tour . . . made of 14 carat gold on a wood base and designed by Mappin and Webb of London. . . the golfer depicted on the top of the trophy is Ryder's friend and teaching pro Abe Mitchell. . . . the cup measures 16 in. high and weighs 4 lbs. . . insured for $50,000 . . . competed for every two years at alternating European and U.S. sites . . . the cup is held by the PGA headquarters of the winning side.

Davis Cup

Donated by American college student and U.S. doubles champion Dwight F. Davis in 1900 and presented by the International Tennis Federation (ITF) to the winner of the annual 16-team men's competition. . . officially called the International Lawn Tennis Challenge Trophy. . . made of sterling silver and designed by Shreve, Crump and Low of Boston, the cup has a matching tray (added in 1921) and a very heavy two-tiered base containing rosters of past winning teams. . . it stands 34½ in. high and 108 in. around at the base and weighs 400 lbs. . . insured for $150,000. . . competed for annually. . . trophy loaned to winning country for one year.

Borg-Warner Trophy

First presented by the Borg-Warner Automotive Co. of Chicago in 1936 to the winner of the Indianapolis 500. . . replaced the Wheeler-Schebler Trophy which went to the 400-mile leader from 1911-32. . . made of sterling silver with bas-relief sculptured heads of each winning driver and a gold bas-relief head of Tony Hulman, the owner of the Indy Speedway from 1945-77 . . . designed by Robert J. Hill and made by Gorham, Inc. of Rhode Island . . . measures 51½ in. high and weighs over 80 lbs. . . new base added in 1988 and the entire trophy restored in 1991. . . competed for annually. . . insured for $1 million. . . trophy stays at Speedway Hall of Fame. . . winner gets a 14-in. high replica valued at $30,000.

NCAA Championship Trophy

First presented in 1952 by the NCAA to all 1st, 2nd and 3rd place teams in sports with sanctioned tournaments. . . 1st place teams receive gold-plated awards, 2nd place award is silver-plated and 3rd is bronze. . . replaced silver cup given to championship teams from 1939-1951. . . made of walnut, the trophy stands 24¾ in. high, 14⅛ in. wide and 4½ in. deep at the base and weighs 15 lbs . . . designed by Medallic Art Co. of Danbury, Conn. and made by House of Usher of Kansas City since 1990. . . valued at $500. . . competed for annually. . . winning teams keep trophies.

World Championship Belt

First presented in 1921 by the World Boxing Association, one of the three organizations (the World Boxing Council and International Boxing Federation are the others) generally accepted as sanctioning legitimate world championship fights. . . belt weighs 8 lbs. and is made of hand tanned leather. . . the outsized buckle measures 10½ in. high and 8 in. wide, is made of pewter with 24 carat gold plate and contains crystal and semi-precious stones . . . side panels of polished brass are for engraving title bout results . . . currently made by Phil Valentino Originals of Jersey City, N.J.. . . champions keep belts even if they lose their title.

World Championship Ring

Rings decorated with gems and engraving date back to ancient Egypt where the wealthy wore heavy gold and silver rings to indicate social status. . . championship rings in sports serve much the same purpose, indicating the wearer is a champion. . . As an example, the Dallas Cowboys' ring for winning Superbowl XXX on Jan. 28, 1996 was designed by Diamond Cutters International of Houston. . . each ring is made of 14–carat yellow gold, weighs 48–51 penny weights and features five trimmed marquis diamonds interlocking in the shape of the Cowboys' star logo as well as five more marquis diamonds (for the team's five Super Bowl wins) on a bed of 51 smaller diamonds. . . rings were appraised at over $30,000 each.

Who's Who

Pete Rose, baseball's disgraced all-time hit leader, was banned from the game for life in 1989 but voted to baseball's All-Century Team a decade later.

Sports Personalities

Eight hundred fifty-six entries dating back to the turn of the century. Entries updated through September 21, 1999.

Hank Aaron (b. Feb. 5, 1934): Baseball OF; led NL in HRs and RBI 4 times each and batting twice with Milwaukee and Atlanta Braves; MVP in 1957; played in 24 All-Star Games, all-time leader in HRs (755) and RBI (2,297), 3rd in hits (3,771); executive with Braves and TBS, Inc.

Kareem Abdul-Jabbar (b. Lew Alcindor, Apr. 16, 1947): Basketball C; led UCLA to 3 NCAA titles (1967-69); Final 4 MOP 3 times; Player of Year twice; led Milwaukee (1) and LA Lakers (5) to 6 NBA titles; playoff MVP twice (1971,85), regular season MVP 6 times (1971-72,74,76-77,80); retired in 1989 after 20 seasons as all-time leader in over 20 categories.

Andre Agassi (b. Apr. 29, 1970): Tennis; 42 career tournament wins including the career grand slam; Wimbledon (1992), U.S. Open (1994,99), Australian Open (1996), French Open (1999); helped U.S. win 2 Davis Cup finals (1990,92); regained the world No. 1 ranking in 1999 for the first time since 1996.

Troy Aikman (b. Nov. 21, 1966): Football QB; consensus All-America at UCLA (1988); 1st overall pick in 1989 NFL Draft (by Dallas); led Cowboys to 3 Super Bowl titles (1992,93,95 seasons); MVP in Super Bowl XXVII.

Marv Albert (b. June 12, 1941): Radio-TV; Former NBC announcer and radio broadcaster for the New York Knicks, Rangers and Giants who pled guilty to a misdemeanor assault charge amid embarrassing allegations of his sex life. Rehired to MSG and Turner networks in 1998 and NBC in '99.

Tenley Albright (b. July 18, 1935): Figure skater; 2-time world champion (1953,55); won Olympic silver (1952) and gold (1956) medals; became a surgeon.

Amy Alcott (b. Feb. 22, 1956): Golfer; 29 career wins, including five majors; inducted into World Golf Hall of Fame in 1999.

Grover Cleveland (Pete) Alexander (b. Feb. 26, 1887, d. Nov. 4, 1950): Baseball RHP; won 20 or more games 9 times; 373 career wins and 90 shutouts.

Muhammad Ali (b. Cassius Clay, Jan. 17, 1942): Boxer; 1960 Olympic light heavyweight champion; 3-time world heavyweight champ (1964-67, 1974-78,1978-79); defeated Sonny Liston (1964), George Foreman (1974) and Leon Spinks (1978) for title; fought Joe Frazier in 3 memorable bouts (1971-75), winning twice; adopted Black Muslim faith in 1964 and changed name; stripped of title in 1967 after conviction for refusing induction into U.S. Army; verdict reversed by Supreme Court in 1971; career record of 56-5 with 37 KOs and 19 successful title defenses; lit the flaming cauldron to signal the beginning of the 1996 Summer Olympics in Atlanta

Forrest (Phog) Allen (b. Nov. 18, 1885, d. Sept. 16, 1974): Basketball; college coach 48 years; directed Kansas to NCAA title (1952); 6th on all-time Div. I list with 746 career wins.

Bobby Allison (b. Dec. 3, 1937): Auto racer; 3-time winner of Daytona 500 (1978,82,88); NASCAR national champ in 1983; father of Davey.

Davey Allison (b. Feb. 25, 1961, d. July 13, 1993): Auto racer; stock car Rookie of Year (1987); winner of 19 NASCAR races, including 1992 Daytona 500; killed at age 32 in helicopter accident at Talladega Superspeedway; son of Bobby.

Roberto Alomar (b. Feb. 5, 1968): Baseball; six-time Gold Glove second baseman; eight-time All-Star; MVP of 1992 ALCS; became known well beyond baseball for spitting in the face of umpire John Hirschbeck during final weekend of 1996 season; named MVP of 1998 All-Star Game.

Walter Alston (b. Dec. 1, 1911, d. Oct. 1, 1984): Baseball; managed Brooklyn-LA Dodgers 23 years, won 7 pennants and 4 World Series (1955,59,63,65); retired after 1976 season with 2,063 wins (2,040 regular season and 23 postseason).

Sparky Anderson (b. Feb. 22, 1934): Baseball; only manager to win World Series in each league — Cincinnati in NL (1975-76) and Detroit in AL (1984); 3rd-ranked skipper on all-time career list with 2,228 wins (2,194 regular season and 34 postseason).

Willie Anderson (b. May 1878, d. Oct. 25, 1910): Scottish golfer; became a US citizen and won 4 U.S. Opens, including 3 straight (1901,03-05).

Mario Andretti (b. Feb. 28, 1940): Auto racer; 4-time USAC-CART national champion (1965-66,69,84); only driver to win Daytona 500 (1967), Indy 500 (1969) and Formula One world title (1978); Indy 500 Rookie of Year (1965); retired after 1994 racing season ranked 1st in poles (67) and starts (407) and 2nd in wins (52) on all-time CART list; father of Michael and Jeff, uncle of John.

Michael Andretti (b. Oct. 5, 1962): Auto racer; 1991 CART national champion with single-season record 8 wins; Indy 500 Rookie of Year (1984); left IndyCar circuit for ill-fated Formula One try in 1993; returned to IndyCar in '94; son of Mario.

Earl Anthony (b. Apr. 27, 1938): Bowler; 6-time PBA Bowler of Year; 41 career titles; first to earn $100,000 in 1 season (1975); first to earn $1 million in career. Came out of retirement in '96.

Luis Aparicio (b. Apr. 29, 1934): Baseball SS; retired as all-time leader in most games, assists and double plays by shortstop; led AL in stolen bases 9 times (1956-64); 506 career steals.

Al Arbour (b. Nov. 1, 1932): Hockey; coached NY Islanders to 4 straight Stanley Cup titles (1980-83); retired after 1993-94 season 2nd on all-time career list with 904 wins (781 regular season and 123 postseason); elected to Hockey Hall of Fame in 1996.

Eddie Arcaro (b. Feb. 19, 1916, d. Nov. 14, 1997): Jockey; 2-time Triple Crown winner (Whirlaway in 1941, Citation in '48); from 1938-55, he won Kentucky Derby 5 times, Preakness and Belmont 6 times each.

Roone Arledge (b. July 8, 1931): Sports TV innovator of live events, anthology shows, Olympic coverage and "Monday Night Football"; ran ABC Sports from 1968-86; ran ABC News from 1977-98.

Henry Armstrong (b. Dec. 12, 1912, d. Oct. 22, 1988): Boxer; held feather-, light- and welterweight titles simultaneously in 1938; pro record 152-21-8 with 100 KOs.

Lance Armstrong (b. Sept. 18, 1971): Cyclist; returned from treatment for testicular cancer to become improbable winner of 1999 Tour de France, becoming only the second American winner in the race's history.

Arthur Ashe (b. July 10, 1943, d. Feb. 6, 1993): Tennis; first black man to win U.S. Championship (1968) and Wimbledon (1975); 1st U.S. player to earn $100,000 in 1 year (1970); won Davis Cup as player (1968-70) and captain (1981-82); wrote black sports history, Hard Road to Glory; announced in 1992 that he was infected with AIDS virus from a blood transfusion during 1983 heart surgery; in 1997, the new home for the U.S. Open was named Arthur Ashe Stadium.

Evelyn Ashford (b. Apr. 15, 1957): Track & Field; winner of 4 Olympic gold medals — 100m in 1984, and 4x100m in 1984, '88 and '92; also won silver medal in 100m in '88; member of 5 U.S. Olympic teams (1976-92); Inducted into Track and Field and Women's Sports Halls of Fame in 1998.

Red Auerbach (b. Sept. 20, 1917): Basketball; 3rd winningest coach (regular season and playoffs) in NBA history; won 1,037 times in 20 years; as coach-GM, led Boston to 9 NBA titles, including 8 in a row (1959-66); also coached defunct Washington Capitols (1946-49); NBA Coach of the Year award named after him; retired as Celtics coach in 1966 and as GM in '84; club president from 1970 to 1997.

Tracy Austin (b. Dec. 12, 1962): Tennis; youngest player to win U.S. Open (age 16 in 1979); won 2nd U.S. Open in '81; named AP Female Athlete of Year twice before she was 20; recurring neck and back injuries shortened career after 1983; youngest player ever inducted into Tennis Hall of Fame (age 29 in 1992).

Donovan Bailey (b. Dec. 16, 1967): Track; Jamaican-born Canadian sprinter who set world record in the 100m (9.84) in gold medal-winning performance at 1996 Olympics which stood until '99; set indoor record in 50m (5.56) in 1996; member of Canadian 4x100 relay that won gold in 1996 Olympics.

Oksana Baiul (b. Feb. 26, 1977): Ukrainian figure skater; 1993 world champion at age 15; edged Nancy Kerrigan by a 5-4 judges' vote for 1994 Olympic gold medal.

Hobey Baker (b. Jan. 15, 1892, d. Dec. 21, 1918): Football and hockey star at Princeton (1911-14); member of college football and pro hockey Halls of Fame; college hockey Player of Year award named after him; killed in plane crash.

Seve Ballesteros (b. Apr. 9, 1957): Spanish golfer; has won British Open 3 times (1979,84,88) and Masters twice (1980,83); 3-time European Golfer of Year (1986,88,91); has led Europe to 5 Ryder Cup titles (1985,87,89,95,97); 72 world-wide victories.

Ernie Banks (b. Jan. 31, 1931): Baseball SS-1B; led NL in home runs and RBI twice each; 2-time MVP (1958-59) with Chicago Cubs; 512 career HRs.

Roger Bannister (b. Mar. 23, 1929): British runner; first to run mile in less than 4 minutes (3:59.4 on May 6, 1954).

Walter (Red) Barber (b. Feb. 17, 1908, d. Oct. 22, 1992): Radio-TV; renowned baseball play-by-play broadcaster for Cincinnati, Brooklyn and N.Y. Yankees from 1934-66; won Peabody Award for radio commentary in 1991.

Charles Barkley (b. Feb. 20, 1963): Basketball F; 5-time All-NBA 1st team with Philadelphia and Phoenix; traded to Suns for 3 players (June 17, 1992); U.S. Olympic Dream Team member in '92; NBA regular season MVP in 1993. Traded to Houston Rockets in 1996.

Leon Barmore (b. June 3, 1944): college basketball coach; respected coach of Louisiana Tech Lady Techsters; career win pct. of .869 (489-74, 17 yrs) entering 1999-2000 season is best all-time.

Rick Barry (b. Mar. 28, 1944): Basketball F; only player to lead both NBA and ABA in scoring; 5-time All-NBA 1st team; Finals MVP with Golden St. in 1975.

Sammy Baugh (b. Mar. 17, 1914): Football QB-DB-P; led Washington to NFL titles in 1937 (his rookie year) and '42; led league in passing 6 times, punting 4 times and interceptions once.

Elgin Baylor (b. Sept. 16, 1934): Basketball F; MOP of Final 4 in 1958; led Minneapolis-LA Lakers to 8 NBA Finals; 10-time All-NBA 1st team (1959-65,67-69); LA Clippers' vice president of basketball operations.

Bob Beamon (b. Aug. 29, 1946): Track & Field; won 1968 Olympic gold medal in long jump with world record (29-ft, 2½in.) that shattered old mark by nearly 2 feet; record finally broken by 2 inches in 1991 by Mike Powell.

Franz Beckenbauer (b. Sept. 11, 1945): Soccer; captain of West German World Cup champions in 1974 then coached West Germany to World Cup title in 1990; invented sweeper position; played in U.S. for NY Cosmos (1977-80,83); Member of International Soccer Hall of Champions.

Boris Becker (b. Nov. 22, 1967): German tennis player; 3-time Wimbledon champ (1985-86,89); youngest male (17) to win Wimbledon; led country to 1st Davis Cup win in 1988; has also won U.S. (1989) and Australian (1991,96) Opens.

Chuck Bednarik (b. May 1, 1925): Football C-LB; 2-time All-America at Penn and 7-time All-Pro with NFL Eagles as both center (1950) and linebacker (1951-56); missed only 3 games in 14 seasons; led Eagles to 1960 NFL title as a 35-year-old two-way player.

Clair Bee (b. Mar. 2, 1896, d. May 20, 1983): Basketball coach who led LIU to 2 undefeated seasons (1936,39) and 2 NIT titles (1939,41); his teams won 95 percent of their games between 1931-51, including 43 in a row from 1935-37; coached NBA Baltimore Bullets from 1952-54, but was only 34-116; contributions to game include 1-3-1 zone defense, 3-second rule and NBA 24-second clock.

Jean Beliveau (b. Aug. 31, 1931): Hockey C; led Montreal to 10 Stanley Cups in 17 playoffs; playoff MVP (1965); 2-time regular season MVP (1956,64).

Bert Bell (b. Feb. 25, 1895, d. Oct. 11, 1959): Football; team owner and 2nd NFL commissioner (1946-59); proposed college draft in 1935 and instituted TV blackout rule.

James (Cool Papa) Bell (b. May 17, 1903, d. Mar. 8, 1991): Baseball; member of the Negro Leagues; widely considered the fastest player ever to play baseball; tremendous hitter and base runner; also coached for the Kansas City Monarchs, teaching such players as Jackie Robinson; member of the National Baseball Hall of Fame.

Albert Belle (b. August 25, 1966): Baseball OF; tremendous hitter and stupendous troublemaker; five-time All-Star; three-time AL RBI leader; was fined $50,000 for a profanity-laced tirade aimed at NBC's Hannah Storm during 1995 World Series; in 1996, was suspended for a brutal hit on Brewers' Fernando Vina; suspended 10 games in 1994 for using a corked bat.

Deane Beman (b. Apr. 22, 1938): Golf; 1st commissioner of PGA Tour (1974-94); introduced "stadium golf"; as player, won U.S. Amateur twice and British Amateur once.

Johnny Bench (b. Dec. 7, 1947): Baseball C; led NL in HRs twice and RBI 3 times; 2-time regular season MVP (1970,72) with Cincinnati, World Series MVP in 1976; 389 career HRs.

Patty Berg (b. Feb. 13, 1918): Golfer; 57 career pro wins, including 15 majors; 3-time AP Female Athlete of Year (1938,43,55).

Chris Berman (b. May 10, 1955): Radio-TV; 5-time Sportscaster of Year known for his nicknames and jovial studio anchoring on ESPN; play-by-play man only year Brown University football team won Ivy League (1976); began doing weekly highlights on "Monday Night Football" in 1996.

Yogi Berra (b. May 12, 1925): Baseball C; played on 10 World Series winners with NY Yankees; holds WS records for games played (75), at bats (259) and hits (71); 3-time AL MVP (1951,54-55); managed both Yankees (1964) and NY Mets (1973) to pennants.

Jay Berwanger (b. Mar. 19, 1914): Football HB; Univ. of Chicago star; won 1st Heisman Trophy in 1935.

Gary Bettman (b. June 2, 1952): Hockey; former NBA executive, who was named first commissioner of NHL on Dec. 11, 1992; took office on Feb. 1, 1993.

Matt Biondi (b. Oct. 8, 1965): Swimmer; won 7 medals in 1988 Olympics, including 5 gold (2 individual, 3 relay); has won a total of 11 medals (8 gold, 2 silver and a bronze) in 3 Olympics (1984,88,92).

Larry Bird (b. Dec. 7, 1956): Basketball F; college Player of Year (1979) at Indiana St.; 1980 NBA Rookie of Year; 9-time All-NBA 1st team; 3-time regular season MVP (1984-86); led Boston to 3 NBA titles (1981,84, 86); 2-time Finals MVP (1984,86); U.S. Olympic Dream Team member in '92; in 1997, named coach of Indiana Pacers and won Coach of the Year honors in first season; inducted into Hall of Fame in 1998.

The Black Sox: Eight Chicago White Sox players who were banned from baseball for life in 1921 for allegedly throwing the 1919 World Series— RHP Eddie Cicotte (1884-1969), OF Happy Felsch (1891-1964), 1B Chick Gandil (1887-1970), OF Shoeless Joe Jackson (1889-1951), INF Fred McMullin (1891-1952), SS Swede Risberg (1894-1975), 3B-SS Buck Weaver (1890-1956), and LHP Lefty Williams (1893-1959).

Earl (Red) Blaik (b. Feb. 15, 1897, d. May 6, 1989): Football; coached Army to consecutive national titles in 1944-45; 166 career wins and 3 Heisman winners (Blanchard, Davis, Dawkins).

Bonnie Blair (b. Mar. 18, 1964): Speedskater; only American woman to win 5 Olympic gold medals in Winter Games; won 500-meters in 1988, then 500m and 1,000m in both 1992 and '94; added 1,000m bronze in 1988; Sullivan Award winner (1992); retired on 31st birthday as reigning world sprint champ.

Hector (Toe) Blake (b. Aug. 21, 1912, d. May 17, 1995): Hockey LW; led Montreal to 2 Stanley Cups as a player and 8 more as coach; regular season MVP in 1939.

Felix (Doc) Blanchard (b. Dec. 11, 1924): Football FB; 3-time All-America; led Army to national titles in 1944-45; Glenn Davis' running mate; won Heisman Trophy and Sullivan Award in 1945.

George Blanda (b. Sept. 17, 1927): Football QB-PK; pro football's all-time leading scorer (2,002 points); led Houston to 2 AFL titles (1960-61); played 26 pro seasons; retired at 48.

Fanny Blankers-Koen (b. Apr. 26, 1918): Dutch sprinter; 30-year-old mother of two, who won 4 gold medals (100m, 200m, 800m hurdles and 4x100m relay) at 1948 Olympics.

Drew Bledsoe (b. Feb. 14, 1972): Football QB; 1st overall pick in 1993 NFL draft (by New England); holds NFL season record for most passes attempted (691) and game records for most passes completed (45) and attempted (70).

Wade Boggs (b. June 15, 1958): Baseball 3B; 5 AL batting titles (1983,85-88) with Boston Red Sox; 11-time All-Star; two Gold Gloves; has since played with NY Yankees and Tampa Bay; got 3000th career hit with a home run Aug. 7, 1999 against Cleveland.

Barry Bonds (b. July 24, 1964): Baseball OF; 3-time NL MVP, twice with Pittsburgh (1990,92) and once with San Francisco (1993); NL's HR and RBI leader in 1993; one of only three players with 40 homers and 40 stolen bases in same season (1996); son of Bobby.

Bjorn Borg (b. June 6, 1956): Swedish tennis player; 2-time Player of Year (1979-80); won 6 French Opens and 5 straight Wimbledons (1976-80); led Sweden to 1st Davis Cup win in 1975; retired in 1983 at age 26; attempted unsuccessful comeback in 1991.

Mike Bossy (b. Jan. 22, 1957): Hockey RW; led NY Isles to 4 Stanley Cups; playoff MVP in 1982; 50 goals or more 9 straight years; 573 career goals.

Ralph Boston (b. May 9, 1939): Track & Field; medaled in 3 consecutive Olympic long jumps— gold (1960), silver (1964), bronze (1968).

Ray Bourque (b. Dec. 28, 1960): Hockey D; 12-time All-NHL 1st team, has won Norris Trophy 5 times (1987-88,1990-91,94) with Boston; '96 All-Star Game MVP.

Bobby Bowden (b. Nov. 8, 1929): Football; coached Florida St. to a national title in 1993; over 290 career wins, including a 16-5-1 bowl record in 33 years as coach at Samford, West Va. and FSU; father of Terry.

Terry Bowden (b. Feb. 24, 1956): Football; led Auburn to 11-0 record in his first season as Division I-A head coach in 1993; NCAA probation earned under previous staff prevented bowl appearance; resigned under fire during 1998 season; son of Bobby.

Scotty Bowman (b. Sept. 18, 1933): Hockey coach; all-time winningest NHL coach in both regular season and playoffs over 26 seasons; coached a record-tying eight Stanley Cup winners with Montreal (1973,76-79), Pittsburgh (1992) and Detroit (1997,98).

Jack Brabham (b. Apr. 2, 1926): Australian auto racer; 3-time Formula One champion (1959-60,66); 14 career wins; member of the Hall of Fame.

Bill Bradley (b. July 28, 1943): Basketball F; 2-time All-America at Princeton; Player of the Year and Final 4 MOP in 1965; captain of gold medal-winning 1964 U.S. Olympic team; Sullivan Award winner (1965); led NY Knicks to 2 NBA titles (1970,73); U.S. Senator (D, N.J.) 1979-95; running for President in 2000.

Pat Bradley (b. Mar. 24, 1951): Golfer; 2-time LPGA Player of Year (1986,91); has won all four majors on LPGA tour, including 3 du Maurier Classics; inducted into the LPGA Hall of Fame on Jan. 18, 1992; entered 2000 among all-time LPGA money leaders and tournament winners (31).

Terry Bradshaw (b. Sept. 2, 1948): Football QB; led Pittsburgh to 4 Super Bowl titles (1975-76,79-80); 2-time Super Bowl MVP (1979-80) and regular season MVP in 1978; Fox TV studio analyst.

George Brett (b. May 15, 1953): Baseball 3B-1B; AL batting champion in 3 different decades (1976,80,90); MVP in 1980; led KC to World Series title in 1985; retired after 1993 season with 3,154 hits and .305 career average; inducted into Hall of Fame in '99.

Valerie Brisco-Hooks (b. July 6, 1960): Track & Field; won three gold medals at the 1984 Olympics (200 meters, 400 meters and 4x100 relay); first athlete to ever win the 200 and 400 in the same Olympics.

Lou Brock (b. June 18, 1939): Baseball OF; former all-time stolen base leader (938); led NL in steals 8 times; led St. Louis to 2 World Series titles (1964,67); had 3,023 career hits.

Herb Brooks (b. Aug. 5, 1937): Hockey; former U.S. Olympic player (1964,68) who coached 1980 team to gold medal; coached Minnesota to 3 NCAA titles (1974,76,78); also coached NY Rangers, Minnesota and New Jersey in NHL.

Jim Brown (b. Feb. 17, 1936): Football FB; All-America at Syracuse (1956) and NFL Rookie of Year (1957); led NFL in rushing 8 times; 8-time All-Pro (1957-61,63-65); 3-time MVP (1958,63,65) with Cleveland; ran for 12,312 yards and scored 126 touchdowns in just 9 seasons.

Larry Brown (b. Sept. 14, 1940): Basketball; played in ACC, AAU, 1964 Olympics and ABA; 3-time assist leader (1968-70) and 3-time Coach of Year (1973,75-76) in ABA; coached ABA's Carolina and Denver and NBA's Denver, N. J., San Antonio, LA Clippers, Indiana and Phila.; also coached UCLA to NCAA Final (1980) and Kansas to NCAA title (1988).

Mordecai (Three-Finger) Brown (b. Oct. 18, 1876, d. Feb. 14, 1948): Baseball; nickname derived from loss of three fingers in a childhood accident; injury gave him a particularly nasty curve ball; won the decisive game of the 1907 World Series as a Chicago Cub; in 1908, first pitcher to record 4 consecutive shutouts and finished at 29-9; career record of 239-130 with lifetime ERA of 2.06; member of Hall of Fame.

Paul Brown (b. Sept. 7, 1908, d. Aug. 5, 1991): Football innovator; coached Ohio St. to national title in 1942; in pros, directed Cleveland Browns to 4 straight AAFC titles (1946-49) and 3 NFL titles (1950,54-55); formed Cincinnati Bengals as head coach and part-owner in 1968 (reached playoffs in '70).

Valery Brumel (b. Apr. 14, 1942): Soviet high jumper; dominated event from 1961-64; broke world record 5 times; won silver medal in 1960 Olympics and gold in 1964; highest jump was 7-5.

Avery Brundage (b. Sept. 28, 1887, d. May 5, 1975): Amateur sports czar for over 40 years as president of AAU (1928-35), U.S. Olympic Committee (1929-53) and Int'l Olympic Committee (1952-72).

Kobe Bryant (b. Aug. 23, 1978): Basketball; guard/forward for the Los Angeles Lakers; graduated from Lower Merion HS in Pennsylvania and made the jump directly to the NBA; youngest player (18 yrs., 2 mos., 11 days) ever to appear in an NBA game; became the youngest all-star in NBA history in 1998 and scored a team-high 18 points.

Paul (Bear) Bryant (b. Sept. 11, 1913, d. Jan. 26, 1983): Football; coached at 4 colleges over 38 years; directed Alabama to 5 national titles (1961,64-65,78-79); 323-85-17 record; 15 bowl wins, including 8 Sugar Bowls.

Sergey Bubka (b. Dec. 4, 1963): Ukrainian pole vaulter; 1st man to clear 20 feet both indoors and out (1991); holder of indoor (20-2) and outdoor (20-1¾) world records as of Sept. 21, 1999; 6-time world champion (1983,87,91,93,95,97); won Olympic gold medal in 1988, but failed to clear any height in 1992 Games.

Buck Buchanan (b. Sept. 10, 1940, d. July 16, 1992): Football; played both ways in college at Grambling; first player chosen in the first AFL draft by the Dallas Texans who later became the KC Chiefs; missed one game in a 13-year pro career; played in six AFL All-Star games and two Pro Bowls at def. tackle; defensive star of the Chiefs team that won Super Bowl IV; later coached for the New Orleans Saints and Cleveland Browns; member of Pro Football Hall of Fame.

Don Budge (b. June 13, 1915): Tennis; in 1938 became 1st player to win the Grand Slam— the French, Wimbledon, U.S. and Australian titles in 1 year; led U.S. to 2 Davis Cups (1937-38); turned pro in late '38.

Maria Bueno (b. Oct. 11, 1939): Brazilian tennis player; won 4 U.S. Championships (1959,63-64,66) and 3 Wimbledons (1959-60,64).

Leroy Burrell (b. Feb. 21, 1967): Track & Field; set former world record of 9.85 in 100 meters, July 6, 1994; previously held record (9.90) in 1991; member of 4 world record-breaking 4x100m relay teams.

Susan Butcher (b. Dec. 26, 1956): Sled Dog racer; 4-time winner of Iditarod Trail race (1986-88,90).

Dick Butkus (b. Dec. 9, 1942): Football LB; 2-time All-America at Illinois (1963-64); All-Pro 7 of 9 NFL seasons with Chicago Bears.

Dick Button (b. July 18, 1929): Figure skater; 5-time world champion (1948-52); 2-time Olympic champ (1948,52); Sullivan Award winner (1949); won Emmy Award as Best Analyst for 1980-81 TV season.

Walter Byers (b. Mar. 13, 1922): College athletics; 1st exec. director of NCAA, serving from 1951-88.

Frank Calder (b. Nov. 17, 1877, d. Feb. 4, 1943): Hockey; 1st NHL president (1917-43); guided league through its formative years; NHL's Rookie of the Year award named after him.

Walter Camp (b. Apr. 7, 1859, d. Mar. 14, 1925): Football coach and innovator; established scrimmage line, center snap, downs, 11 players per side; elected 1st All-America team (1889).

Roy Campanella (b. Nov. 19, 1921, d. June 26, 1993): Baseball C; 3-time NL MVP (1951,53,55); led Brooklyn to 5 pennants and 1st World Series title (1955); career cut short when 1958 car accident left him paralyzed.

Clarence Campbell (b. July 9, 1905, d. June 24, 1984): Hockey; 3rd NHL president (1946-77), league tripled in size from 6 to 18 teams during his tenure.

Earl Campbell (b. Mar. 29, 1955): Football RB; won Heisman Trophy in 1977; led NFL in rushing 3 times; 3-time All-Pro; 2-time MVP (1978-79) at Houston.

John Campbell (b. Apr. 8, 1955): Harness racing; 5-time winner of Hambletonian (1987,88,90,95,98); 3-time Driver of Year; first driver to go over $100 million in career winnings.

Jimmy Cannon (b. 1910, d. Dec. 5, 1973): Tough, opinionated New York sportswriter and essayist who viewed sports as an extension of show business; protégé of Damon Runyon; covered World War II for Stars & Stripes.

Jose Canseco (b. July 2, 1964): Baseball OF/DH; AL Rookie of the Year in 1986 and Most Valuable Player in 1988 with the Oakland A's; in 1988 he became the first player in history with 40 HRs and 40 steals in a season; led AL in HRs in 1988 and tied for lead in 1991.

Jennifer Capriati (b. Mar. 29, 1976): Tennis; youngest Grand Slam semifinalist ever (age 14 in 1990 French Open); also youngest to win a match at Wimbledon (1990); upset Steffi Graf to win gold medal at 1992 Olympics; left tour from 1994 to '96 due to personal problems including an arrest for marijuana possession.

Harry Caray (b. Mar. 1, 1917, d. Feb. 18, 1998): Radio-TV; baseball play-by-play broadcaster for St. Louis Cardinals, Oakland, Chicago White Sox and Cubs 1945-98; father of sportscaster Skip and grandfather of sportscaster Chip.

Rod Carew (b. Oct. 1, 1945): Baseball 2B-1B; led AL in batting 7 times (1969,72-75,77-78) with Minnesota; MVP in 1977; had 3,053 career hits.

Steve Carlton (b. Dec. 22, 1944): Baseball LHP; won 20 or more games 6 times; 4-time Cy Young winner (1972,77,80,82) with Philadelphia; 329-244 career record.

JoAnne Carner (b. Apr. 4, 1939): Golfer; 5-time U.S. Amateur champion; 2-time U.S. Open champ; 3-time LPGA Player of Year (1974,81-82); 7th in career wins (42).

Don Carter (b. July 29, 1926): Bowler; 6-time Bowler of Year (1953-54,57-58,60-61); voted Greatest of All-Time in 1970.

Alexander Cartwright (b. Apr. 17, 1820, d. July 12, 1892): Baseball; engineer and draftsman who spread gospel of baseball from New York City to California gold fields; widely regarded as the father of modern game; his guidelines included setting 3 strikes for an out and 3 outs for each half inning.

Billy Casper (b. June 4, 1931): Golfer; 2-time PGA Player of Year (1966,70); has won U.S. Open (1959,66), Masters (1970), U.S. Senior Open (1983); compiled 51 PGA Tour wins and 9 on Senior Tour.

Tracy Caulkins (b. Jan. 11, 1963): Swimmer; won 3 gold medals (2 individual) at 1984 Olympics; set 5 world records and won 48 U.S. national titles from 1978-84; Sullivan Award winner (1978); 2-time Honda Broderick Cup winner (1982,84).

Steve Cauthen (b. May 1, 1960): Jockey; became youngest jockey (18) to win the Triple Crown with Affirmed in 1978; won a record $6.1 million in 1977, winning the Eclipse Award as the nation's top rider and the award for AP male athlete of the year.

Evonne Goolagong Cawley (b. July 31, 1951): Australian tennis player; won Australian Open 4 times, Wimbledon twice (1971,80), French once (1971).

Florence Chadwick (b. Nov. 9, 1917, d. Mar. 15, 1995): Dominant distance swimmer of 1950s; set English Channel records from France to England (1950) and England to France (1951 and '55).

Wilt Chamberlain (b. Aug. 21, 1936): Basketball C; consensus All-America in 1957 and '58 at Kansas; Final Four MOP in 1957; led NBA in scoring 7 times and rebounding 11 times; 7-time All-NBA first team; 4-time MVP (1960,66-68) in Philadelphia; scored 100 points vs. NY Knicks in Hershey, Pa., Mar. 2, 1962; led 76ers (1967) and LA Lakers (1972) to NBA titles; Finals MVP in 1972.

A.B. (Happy) Chandler (b. July 14, 1898, d. June 15, 1991): Baseball; former Kentucky governor and U.S. Senator who succeeded Judge Landis as commissioner in 1945; backed Branch Rickey's move in 1947 to make Jackie Robinson 1st black player in major leagues; deemed too pro-player and ousted by owners in 1951.

Julio Cesar Chavez (b. July 12, 1962): Mexican boxer; world jr. welterweight champ (1989-94); also held titles as jr. lightweight (1984-87) and lightweight (1987-89); fought Pernell Whitaker to controversial draw for welterweight title on Sept. 10, 1993; career record of 101-2-2 record with 84 KOs; 90-bout unbeaten streak ended Jan. 29, 1994 when Frankie Randall won title on split decision; Chavez won title back four months later.

Linford Christie (b. Apr. 2, 1960): British sprinter; won 100-meter gold medals at both 1992 Olympics (9.96) and '93 World Championships (9.87).

Jim Clark (b. Mar. 14, 1936, d. Apr. 7, 1968): Scottish auto racer; 2-time Formula One world champion (1963,65); won Indy 500 in 1965; killed in car crash.

Bobby Clarke (b. Aug. 13, 1949): Hockey C; led Philadelphia Flyers to consecutive Stanley Cups in 1974-75; 3-time regular season MVP (1973,75-76); currently Flyers general manager.

Ron Clarke (b. Feb. 21, 1937): Australian runner; from 1963-70 set 17 world records in races from 2 miles to 20,000m; never won Olympic gold medal.

Roger Clemens (b. Aug. 4, 1962): Baseball RHP; twice fanned MLB record 20 batters in 9-inning game (April 29, 1986 and Sept. 18, 1996); 5 Cy Young Awards with Boston (1986-87,91) and Toronto (1997,98); AL MVP in 1986.

Roberto Clemente (b. Aug. 18, 1934, d. Dec. 31, 1972): Baseball OF; hit over .300 13 times with Pittsburgh; led NL in batting 4 times; World Series MVP in 1971; regular season MVP in 1966; had 3,000 career hits; killed in plane crash.

Alice Coachman (b. Nov. 9, 1923): Track & Field; became the first black woman to win an Olympic gold medal with her win in the high jump in 1948 (London); broke the high school and college high jump records despite not wearing any shoes; member of the National Track & Field Hall of Fame.

Ty Cobb (b. Dec. 18, 1886, d. July 17, 1961): Baseball OF; all-time highest career batting average (.367); hit over .400 3 times; led AL in batting 12 times and stolen bases 6 times with Detroit; MVP in 1911; had 4,191 career hits and 892 steals.

Mickey Cochrane (b. Apr. 6, 1903, d. June 28, 1962): Baseball C; led Philadelphia A's (1929-30) and Detroit (1935) to 3 World Series titles; 2-time AL MVP (1928,34).

Sebastian Coe (b. Sept. 29, 1956): British runner; won gold medal in 1500m and silver medal in 800m at both 1980 and '84 Olympics; long-time world record holder in 800m and 1000m; elected to Parliament as Conservative in 1992.

Paul Coffey (b. June 1, 1961): Hockey D; holds NHL record for assists and points by a defenseman; member of four Stanley Cup championship teams at Edmonton (1984-85,87) and Pittsburgh (1991).

Rocky Colavito (b. August 10, 1933): Baseball OF; six-time all-star who hit 374 HRs over his 14-year career; led the league in HRs in 1959 with 42 and RBI in 1965 with 108; hit four consecutive HRs in one game.

Eddie Collins (b. May 2, 1887, d. Mar. 25, 1951): Baseball 2B; led Phila. A's (1910-11) and Chicago White Sox (1917) to 3 World Series titles; AL MVP in 1914; had 3,311 career hits and 743 stolen bases.

Nadia Comaneci (b. Nov. 12, 1961): Romanian gymnast; 1st to record perfect 10 in Olympics; won 3 individual golds at 1976 Olympics and 2 more in '80.

Lionel Conacher (b. May 24, 1901, d. May 26, 1954): Canada's greatest all-around athlete; NHL hockey (2 Stanley Cups), CFL football (1 Grey Cup), minor league baseball, soccer, lacrosse, track, amateur boxing champion; member of Parliament (1949-54).

Gene Conley (b. Nov. 10, 1930): Baseball and Basketball; played for World Series and NBA champions with Milwaukee Braves (1957) and Boston Celtics (1959-61); winning pitcher in 1954 All-Star Game; 91-96 record in 11 seasons.

Dennis Conner (b. Sept. 16, 1942): Sailing; 3-time America's Cup-winning skipper aboard *Freedom* (1980), *Stars & Stripes* (1987) and the *Stars & Stripes* catamaran (1988); only American skipper to lose Cup, first in 1983 when *Australia II* beat *Liberty* and again in '95 when New Zealand's *Black Magic* swept Conner and his *Stars & Stripes* crew aboard the borrowed *Young America*.

Maureen Connolly (b. Sept. 17, 1934, d. June 21, 1969): Tennis; in 1953 1st woman to win Grand Slam (at age 18); riding accident ended her career in '54; won both Wimbledon and U.S. titles 3 times (1951-53); 3-time AP Female Athlete of Year (1951-53).

Jimmy Connors (b. Sept. 2, 1952): Tennis; No.1 player in world 5 times (1974-78); won 5 U.S. Opens, 2 Wimbledons and 1 Australian; rose from No. 936 at the close of 1990 to U.S. Open semifinals in 1991 at age 39; NCAA singles champ (1971); all-time leader in pro singles titles (109) and matches won at U.S. Open (98) and Wimbledon (84); inducted into Hall of Fame in 1998.

Jack Kent Cooke (b. Oct. 25, 1912, d. April 6, 1997): Football; sole owner of NFL Washington Redskins from 1985-97; teams have won 2 Super Bowls (1988,92); also owned NBA Lakers and NHL Kings in LA; built LA Forum for $12 million in 1967.

Cynthia Cooper (b. April 14, 1963): Women's basketball G; won two NCAA basketball titles at USC (1983-84); 2-time WNBA MVP with Houston Comets.

Angel Cordero Jr. (b. Nov. 8, 1942): Jockey; retired third on all-time list with 7,057 wins in 38,646 starts; won Kentucky Derby 3 times (1974,76,85), Preakness twice and Belmont once; 2-time Eclipse Award winner (1982-83).

Howard Cosell (b. Mar. 25, 1920, d. Apr. 23, 1995): Radio-TV; former ABC commentator on *Monday Night Football* and *Wide World of Sports*, who energized TV sports journalism with abrasive "tell it like it is" style.

Bob Costas (b. Mar. 22, 1952): Radio-TV; NBC anchor for NBA, NFL and Summer Olympics as well as baseball play-by-play man; 8-time Emmy winner and 6-time Sportscaster of Year.

James (Doc) Counsilman (b. Dec. 28, 1920): Swimming; coached Indiana men's swim team to 6 NCAA championships (1968-73); coached the 1964 and '76 U.S. men's Olympic teams that won a combined 21 of 24 gold medals; in 1979 became oldest person (59) to swim English Channel; retired in 1990 with dual meet record of 287-36-1.

Fred Couples (b. Oct. 3, 1959): Golfer; 2-time PGA Tour Player of the Year (1991,92); 14 Tour victories, including 1992 Masters.

Jim Courier (b. Aug. 17, 1970): Tennis; No. 1 player in world in 1992, has won 2 Australian Opens (1992-93) and 2 French (1991-92); played on 1992 Davis Cup winner; Nick Bollettieri Academy classmate of Andre Agassi.

Margaret Smith Court (b. July 16, 1942): Australian tennis player; won Grand Slam in both singles (1970) and mixed doubles (1963 with Ken Fletcher); record 24 Grand Slam singles titles—11 Australian, 5 U.S., 5 French and 3 Wimbledon.

Bob Cousy (b. Aug. 9, 1928): Basketball G; led NBA in assists 8 times; 10-time All-NBA 1st team; 1957 MVP; led Boston to 6 NBA titles (1957,59-63).

Buster Crabbe (b. Feb. 7, 1910, d. Apr. 23, 1983): Swimmer; 2-time Olympic freestyle medalist with bronze in 1928 (1500m) and gold in '32 (400m); became movie star and King of Serials as Flash Gordon and Buck Rogers.

Ben Crenshaw (b. Jan. 11, 1952): Golfer; co-NCAA champion with Tom Kite in 1972; battled Graves' disease in mid-1980s; 19 career Tour victories; won Masters for second time on April 9, 1995 and dedicated it to 90-year-old mentor Harvey Penick, who had died on April 2; captain of 1999 Ryder Cup team.

Joe Cronin (b. Oct. 12, 1906, d. Sept. 7, 1984): Baseball SS; hit over .300 and drove in over 100 runs 8 times each; player-manager in Washington and Boston (1933-47); AL president (1959-73).

Larry Csonka (b. Dec. 25, 1946): Football RB; powerful runner and blocker who gained 8,081 yards in 11 seasons in the AFL and NFL; won two consecutive Super Bowls with the Miami Dolphins (1973-74); member of the College and Pro Football Halls of Fame.

Ann Curtis (b. Mar. 6, 1926): Swimming; won 2 gold medals and 1 silver in 1948 Olympics; set 4 world and 18 U.S. records during career; 1st woman and swimmer to win Sullivan Award (1944).

Bjorn Dählie (b. June 19, 1967): Norwegian cross-country skier; winner of a record eight gold and 12 overall Winter Olympic medals from 1992-98.

Chuck Daly (b. July 20, 1930): Basketball; coached Detroit to two NBA titles (1989-90) before leaving in 1992 to coach New Jersey; coached NBA "Dream Team" to gold medal in 1992 Olympics; retired in 1994 but returned in 1997 to coach Orlando Magic for two seasons.

John Daly (b. Apr. 28, 1966): Golfer; surprise winner of 1991 PGA Championship as unknown 25-year-old; battled through personal troubles in 1994 to return in '95 and win 2nd major at British Open, beating Italy's Costantino Rocca in 4-hole playoff.

Stanley Dancer (b. July 25, 1927): Harness racing; winner of 4 Hambletonians; trainer-driver of Triple Crown winners in trotting (Nevele Pride in 1968 and Super Bowl in '72) and pacing (Most Happy Fella in 1970).

Beth Daniel (b. Oct. 14, 1956): Golfer; 32 career wins, including 1 major; inducted into World Golf Hall of Fame in 1999.

Tamas Darnyi (b. June 3, 1967): Hungarian swimmer; 2-time double gold medal winner in 200m and 400m individual medley at 1988 and '92 Olympics; set world records in both at '91 worlds; 1st swimmer to break 2 minutes in 200m IM (1:59:36).

Lindsay Davenport (b. June 8, 1976): Tennis player; first American female to be ranked No. 1 in the world (1998) since Chris Evert in 1985; won U.S. Open (1998) and Wimbledon (1999); Olympic gold medalist at Atlanta.

Al Davis (b. July 4, 1929): Football; GM-coach of Oakland 1963-66; helped force AFL-NFL merger as AFL commissioner in 1966; returned to Oakland as managing general partner and directed club to 3 Super Bowl wins (1977,81,84); defied fellow NFL owners and moved Raiders to LA in 1982; turned down owners' 1995 offer to build him a new stadium in LA and moved back to Oakland instead.

Dwight Davis (b. July 5, 1879, d. Nov. 28, 1945): Tennis; donor of Davis Cup; played for winning U.S. team in 1st two Cup finals (1900,02); won U.S. and Wimbledon doubles titles in 1901; Secretary of War (1925-29) under President Coolidge.

Ernie Davis (b. Dec. 14, 1939, d. May 18, 1963): Football; star running back at Syracuse University; first black to win the Heisman Trophy, in 1961; drafted by the Washington Redskins and traded to Cleveland but died the following year of leukemia before playing a pro game.

Glenn Davis (b. Dec. 26, 1924): Football HB; 3-time All-America; led Army to national titles in 1944-45; Doc Blanchard's running mate; won Heisman Trophy in 1946.

Terrell Davis (b. Oct. 28, 1972): Football RB; 1998 NFL MVP, rushing for an league-leading 2,008 yards (3rd all-time); played for two Super Bowl winners in Denver (XXXII and XXXIII), earning MVP honors in the former with Super Bowl-record 3 rushing TDs.

Pat Day (b. Oct. 13, 1953): Jockey; 4-time Eclipse award winner; ranked 3rd all-time in career wins; inducted into Hall of Fame in 1991.

Dizzy Dean (b. Jan. 16 1911, d. July 17, 1974): Baseball RHP; led NL in strikeouts and complete games 4 times; last NL pitcher to win 30 games (30-7 in 1934); MVP in 1934 with St. Louis; 150-83 record.

Dave DeBusschere (b. Oct. 16, 1940): Basketball F; youngest coach in NBA history (24 in 1964); player-coach of Detroit Pistons (1964-67); played in 8 All-Star games; won 2 NBA titles as player with NY Knicks; ABA commissioner (1975-76); also pitched 2 seasons for Chicago White Sox (1962-63) with 3-4 record.

Pierre de Coubertin (b. Jan. 1, 1863, d. Sept. 2, 1937): French educator; father of the Modern Olympic Games; IOC president from 1896-1925.

Anita DeFrantz (b. Oct. 4, 1952): Olympics; attorney who is one of 2 American delegates to the International Olympic Committee (James Easton is the other); first woman to represent U.S. on IOC; member of USOC Executive Committee; member of bronze medal U.S. women's eight-oared shell at Montreal in 1976.

Oscar De La Hoya (b. Feb. 4, 1973): Boxing; won the IBF lightweight title with a TKO of Rafael Ruelas in 1995; won WBC Super Lightweight title over Julio Cesar Chavez in 1996 and the WBC Welterweight title over Pernell Whitaker in 1997; won Olympic gold medal in 1992 as a lightweight; lost WBC Welterweight belt to Felix Trinidad in a majority decision on Sept. 18, 1999.

Jack Dempsey (b. June 24, 1895, d. May 31, 1983): Boxer; world heavyweight champion from 1919-26; lost title to Gene Tunney, then lost "Long Count" rematch in 1927 when he floored Tunney in 7th round but failed to retreat to neutral corner; pro record 64-6-9 with 49 KOs.

Donna de Varona (b. Apr. 26, 1947): Swimming; won gold medals in 400 IM and 400 freestyle relay at 1964 Olympics; set 18 world records during career; co-founder of Women's Sports Foundation.

Gail Devers (b. Nov. 19, 1966): Track & Field; fastest-ever woman sprinter-hurdler; overcame thyroid disorder (Graves' disease) that sidelined her in 1989-90 and nearly resulted in having both feet amputated; won Olympic gold medal in 100 meters in 1992 and '96; world champion in 100 meters (1993) and 100-meter hurdles (1993,95).

Klaus Dibiasi (b. Oct. 6, 1947): Italian diver; won 3 consecutive Olympic gold medals in platform event (1968,72,76).

Eric Dickerson (b. Sept. 2, 1960): Football RB; led NFL in rushing 4 times (1983-84,86,88); ran for single-season record 2,105 yards in 1984; All-Pro 5 times; traded from LA Rams to Indianapolis (Oct. 31, 1987) in 3-team, 10-player deal (including draft picks); 3rd on all-time career rushing list with 13,259 yards in 11 seasons; entered Pro Football Hall of Fame in '99.

Joe DiMaggio (b. Nov. 25, 1914, d. Mar. 8, 1999): Baseball OF; hit safely in 56 straight games (1941); led AL in batting, HRs and RBI twice each; 3-time MVP (1939,41,47); hit .325 with 361 HRs over 13 seasons; led NY Yankees to 10 World Series titles.

Marcel Dionne (b. Aug. 3, 1951): Hockey C; third on NHL's all-time points list (1,771) and goals list (731); tied Wayne Gretzky for the league lead in points (137) in 1980; scored 50 goals in a season 6 times; won the Lady Byng Award for gentlemanly play in 1975 with Detroit and in 1977 with the L.A. Kings; member of the Hockey Hall of Fame.

Mike Ditka (b. Oct. 18, 1939): Football; All-America at Pitt (1960); NFL Rookie of Year (1961); 5-time Pro Bowl tight end for Chicago Bears; also played for Philadelphia and Dallas in 12-year career; returned to Chicago as head coach in 1982; won Super Bowl XX; compiled 112-68-0 record in 11 seasons with Bears; left Bears in 1992; named head coach of New Orleans Saints in 1997.

Larry Doby (b. Dec. 13, 1924): Baseball OF; first black player in the AL; joined the Cleveland Indians in July 1947, three months after Jackie Robinson entered the Majors with the NL's Brooklyn Dodgers; an all-star centerfielder from 1949-55; managed the Chicago White Sox in 1978, becoming the second black major league manager; inducted into the Hall of Fame in 1998.

Charlotte (Lottie) Dod (b. Sept. 24, 1871, d. June 27, 1960): British athlete; was 5-time Wimbledon singles champion (1887-88,91-93); youngest player ever to win Wimbledon (15 in 1887); archery silver medalist at 1908 Olympics; member of national field hockey team in 1899; British Amateur golf champ in 1904.

Tony Dorsett (b. Apr. 7, 1954): Football RB; won Heisman Trophy leading Pitt to national title in 1976; 2nd all-time in NCAA Div. I-A rushing with 6,082 yards; led Dallas to Super Bowl title as NFC Rookie of Year (1977); NFC Player of Year (1981); ranks 4th on all-time NFL list with 12,739 yards gained in 12 years.

James (Buster) Douglas (b. Apr. 7, 1960): Boxing; 42-1 shot who knocked out undefeated Mike Tyson in 10th round on Feb. 10, 1990 to win heavyweight title in Tokyo; 8 1/2 months later, lost only title defense to Evander Holyfield by KO in 3rd round.

The Dream Team Head coach Chuck Daly's "Best Ever" 12-man NBA All-Star squad that headlined the 1992 Summer Olympics in Barcelona and easily won the basketball gold medal; co-captained by Larry Bird and Magic Johnson, with veterans Charles Barkley, Clyde Drexler, Patrick Ewing, Michael Jordan, Karl Malone, Chris Mullin, Scottie Pippen, David Robinson, John Stockton and Duke's Christian Laettner.

Heike Drechsler (b. Dec. 16, 1964): German long jumper and sprinter; East German before reunification in 1991; set world long jump record (24-2 1/4) in 1988; won long jump gold medals at 1992 Olympics and 1983 and '93 World Championships; won silver medal in long jump and bronze medals in both 100- and 200-meter sprints at 1988 Olympics.

Ken Dryden (b. Aug. 8, 1947): Hockey G; led Montreal to 6 Stanley Cup titles; playoff MVP as rookie in 1971; won or shared 5 Vezina trophies; 2.24 career GAA; currently President of Toronto Maple Leafs.

Don Drysdale (b. July 23, 1936, d. July 3, 1993): Baseball RHP; led NL in strikeouts 3 times and games started 4 straight years; pitched record 6 shutouts in a row in 1968; won Cy Young (1962); had 209-166 record and hit 29 HRs in 14 years.

Charley Dumas (b. Feb. 12, 1937): U.S. high jumper; first man to clear 7 feet (7-0 1/2) on June 29, 1956; won gold medal at 1956 Olympics.

Tim Duncan (b. Apr. 25, 1976): Basketball; consensus College Player of the Year as a senior at Wake Forest; #1 overall pick by the San Antonio Spurs (1997); 1998 NBA Rookie of the Year; became only the ninth rookie in NBA history to be named to the All-NBA first team (1998), 1999 NBA Finals MVP as he led Spurs to NBA title.

Margaret Osborne du Pont (b. Mar. 4, 1918): Tennis; won 5 French, 7 Wimbledon and an unprecedented 25 U.S. national titles in singles, doubles and mixed doubles from 1941-62.

Roberto Duran (b. June 16, 1951): Panamanian boxer; one of only 4 fighters to hold 4 different world titles— lightweight (1972-79), welterweight (1980), junior middleweight (1983) and middleweight (1989-90); lost famous "No Mas" welterweight title bout when he quit in 8th round against Sugar Ray Leonard (1980); pro record of 102-14 (69 KOs).

Leo Durocher (b. July 27, 1905, d. Oct. 7, 1991): Baseball; managed in NL 24 years; won 2,015 games, including postseason; 3 pennants with Brooklyn (1941) and NY Giants (1951,54); won World Series in 1954.

Eddie Eagan (b. Apr. 26, 1898, d. June 14, 1967): Only athlete to win gold medals in both Summer and Winter Olympics (Boxing–1920, Bobsled–1932).

Alan Eagleson (b. Apr. 24, 1933): Hockey; Toronto lawyer, agent and 1st executive director of NHL Players Assn. (1967-90); midwifed Team Canada vs. Soviet series (1972) and Canada Cup; charged with racketeering and defrauding NHLPA in indictment handed down by U.S. grand jury in 1994; was sentenced to 18 months in jail in Jan. 1998 after pleading guilty but only served 6 months; resigned from Hall of Fame in 1998.

Dale Earnhardt (b. Apr. 29, 1952): Auto racer; 7-time NASCAR national champion (1980,86-87,90-91,93-94); Rookie of Year in 1979; all-time NASCAR money leader with over $34 million won and 6th on career wins list with 73; finally won Daytona 500 in 1998 on 20th attempt.

Dick Ebersol (b. July 28, 1947): Radio-TV; protégé of ABC Sports czar Roone Arledge; key NBC exec in launching of *Saturday Night Live* in 1975; became president of NBC Sports in 1989; won U.S. TV rights to both 2000 Summer and 2002 Winter Olympics with combined bid of $1.27 billion in August 1995.

Dennis Eckersley (b. Oct. 3, 1954): Baseball P; began his career as a starter in 1975 with the Cleveland Indians; pitched a no-hitter against California in 1977; won 20 games in 1978 with Boston; moved to the bullpen after 12 seasons as a starter and became one of the best closers of all time with Oakland; won the AL Cy Young Award and MVP (1992).

Stefan Edberg (b. Jan. 19, 1966): Swedish tennis player; 2-time No.1 player (1990-91); 2-time winner of Australian Open (1985,87), Wimbledon (1988,90) and U.S. Open (1991-92).

Gertrude Ederle (b. Oct. 23, 1906): Swimmer; 1st woman to swim English Channel, breaking men's record by 2 hours in 1926; won 3 medals in 1924 Olympics.

Lee Elder (b. July 14, 1934): Golf; in 1975, he became the first black golfer to play in the Masters Tournament; also played in the 1977 Masters; member of the 1979 U.S. Ryder Cup team; played in South Africa's first integrated tournament in 1972.

Todd Eldredge (b. Aug. 28, 1971): Figure Skater; five-time U.S. champion (1990,91,95,97,98); 1996 World Champion; has won U.S. titles at all three levels (novice, junior and senior); most decorated American figure skater without an Olympic medal.

Bill Elliott (b. Oct. 8, 1955): Auto racer; 2-time winner of Daytona 500 (1985,87); NASCAR national champ in 1988; 40 NASCAR wins as of Sept. 1999.

Herb Elliott (b. Feb. 25, 1938): Australian runner; undefeated from 1958-60; ran 17 sub-4:00 miles; 3 world records; won gold medal in 1500 meters at 1960 Olympics; retired at age 22.

John Elway (b. June 28, 1960): Football QB; All-American at Stanford; first overall pick in the famous quarterback draft of 1983; known for his last-minute, game-winning scoring drives; led Broncos to three Super Bowl losses before back-to-back wins in Super Bowl XXXII and XXXIII; 1987 NFL MVP; four-time Pro Bowl selection; first QB to receive a pass in the Super Bowl (1987); one of only two QBs in league history (Marino) to throw for over 3,000 yards in 12 seasons; retired after '98 season.

Roy Emerson (b. Nov. 3, 1936): Australian tennis player; won 12 majors in singles— 6 Australian, 2 French, 2 Wimbledon and 2 U.S. from 1961-67.

Kornelia Ender (b. Oct. 25, 1958): East German swimmer; 1st woman to win 4 gold medals at one Olympics (1976), all in world-record time.

Julius Erving (b. Feb. 22, 1950): Basketball F; in ABA (1971-76)— 3-time MVP, 2-time playoff MVP, led NY Nets to 2 titles (1974,76); in NBA (1976-87)— 5-time All-NBA 1st team, MVP in 1981, led Philadelphia 76ers to title in 1983.

Phil Esposito (b. Feb. 20, 1942): Hockey C; 1st NHL player to score 100 points in a season (126 in 1969); 6-time All-NHL 1st team with Boston (1969-74); 2-time MVP (1969,74); 5-time scoring champ; star of 1972 Canada-Soviet series; former president-GM of Tampa Bay Lightning.

Janet Evans (b. Aug. 28, 1971): Swimmer; won 3 individual gold medals (400m & 800m freestyle, 400m IM) at 1988 Olympics; 1989 Sullivan Award winner; won 1 gold (800m) and 1 silver (400m) at 1992 Olympics; world record-holder in 400m, 800m and 1500m freestyles as of Sept. 1999.

Lee Evans (b. Feb. 25, 1947): Track & Field; dominant quarter-miler in world from 1966-72; world record in 400m set at 1968 Olympics stood 20 years.

Chris Evert (b. Dec. 21, 1954): Tennis; No.1 player in world 5 times (1975-77,80-81); won at least 1 Grand Slam singles title every year from 1974-86; 18 majors in all— 7 French, 6 U.S., 3 Wimbledon and 2 Australian; retired after 1989 season.

Weeb Ewbank (b. May 6, 1907, d. Nov. 18, 1998): Football; only coach to win NFL and AFL titles; led Baltimore to 2 NFL titles (1958-59) and NY Jets to Super Bowl III win.

Patrick Ewing (b. Aug. 5, 1962): Basketball C; 3-time All-America; led Georgetown to 3 NCAA Finals and 1984 title; Final 4 MOP in '84; NBA Rookie of Year with New York in '86; All-NBA in 1990; on U.S. Olympic gold medal-winning teams in 1984 and '92; named one of the NBA's 50 greatest players of all-time.

Ray Ewry (b. Oct. 14, 1873, d. Sept. 29, 1937): Track & Field; won 10 gold medals (although 2 are not recognized by IOC) over 4 consecutive Olympics (1900,04,06,08); all events he won (Standing HJ, LJ and TJ) were discontinued in 1912.

Nick Faldo (b. July 18, 1957): British golfer; 3-time winner of British Open (1987,90,92) and Masters (1989, 90, 96); 3-time European Golfer of Year (1989-90,92); PGA Player of Year in 1990.

Juan Manuel Fangio (b. June 24, 1911, d. July 17, 1995): Argentine auto racer; 5-time Formula One world champion (1951,54-57); 24 career wins, retired in 1958.

Brett Favre (b. Oct. 10, 1969): Football QB; Selected in the second round (33rd overall) by the Atlanta Falcons in the 1991 NFL draft; traded to Green Bay Packers in 1992; league MVP in 1995, '96 and '97; five-time Pro Bowl QB; 100th TD pass came in his 62nd game, third-fastest in league history; 39 TD passes in 1996 season broke his own NFC record of 38 set in 1995; led Packers to Super Bowl victory in 1997.

Sergei Fedorov (b. Dec. 13, 1969): Hockey C; first Russian to win NHL Hart Trophy as 1993-94 regular season MVP; 3-time All-Star with Detroit.

Bob Feller (b. Nov. 3, 1918): Baseball RHP; led AL in strikeouts 7 times and wins 6 times with Cleveland; threw 3 no-hitters and 12 one-hitters; 266-162 record.

Tom Ferguson (b. Dec. 20, 1950): Rodeo; 6-time All-Around champion (1974-79); 1st cowboy to win $100,000 in one season (1978); 1st to win $1 million in career (1986).

Herve Filion (b. Feb. 1, 1940): Harness racing; 10-time Driver of Year; all-time leader in races won with 14,783 in 35 years.

Rollie Fingers (b. Aug. 25, 1946): Baseball RHP; relief ace with 341 career saves; won AL MVP and Cy Young awards in 1981 with Milwaukee; World Series MVP in 1974 with Oakland.

Charles O. Finley (b. Feb. 22, 1918, d. Feb, 19, 1997): Baseball owner; moved KC A's to Oakland in 1968; won 3 straight World Series from 1972-74; also owned teams in NHL and ABA.

Bobby Fischer (b. Mar. 9, 1943): Chess; at 15, became youngest international grandmaster in chess history; only American to hold world championship (1972-75); was stripped of title in 1975 after refusing to defend against Anatoly Karpov and became recluse; re-emerged to defeat old foe and former world champion Boris Spassky in 1992.

Carlton Fisk (b. Dec. 26, 1947): Baseball C; holds all-time major league record for games caught (2,229); also all-time HR leader for catchers (376); AL Rookie of Year (1972) and 10-time All-Star; hit epic, 12th-inning Game 6 homer for Boston Red Sox in 1975 World Series.

Emerson Fittipaldi (b. Dec. 12, 1946): Brazilian auto racer; 2-time Formula One world champion (1972,74); 2-time winner of Indy 500 (1989,93); won overall IndyCar title in 1989.

James (Sunny Jim) Fitzsimmons (b. July 23, 1874, d. Mar. 11, 1966): Horse racing; trained horses that won over 2,275 races, including 2 Triple Crown winners— Gallant Fox in 1930 and Omaha in '35.

Jim Fixx (b. Apr. 23, 1932, d. July 20, 1984): Running; author who popularized the sport of running; his 1977 bestseller *The Complete Book of Running*, is credited with helping start America's fitness revolution; died of a heart attack while running.

Larry Fleisher (b. Sept. 26, 1930, d. May 4, 1989): Basketball; led NBA players union from 1961-89; increased average yearly salary from $9,400 in 1967 to $600,000 without a strike.

Peggy Fleming (b. July 27, 1948): Figure skating; 3-time world champion (1966-68); won Olympic gold medal in 1968.

Curt Flood (b. Jan. 18, 1938, d. Jan. 20, 1997): Baseball OF; played 15 years (1956-69,71) mainly with St. Louis; hit over .300 6 times with 7 Gold Gloves; refused trade to Phillies in 1969; lost challenge to baseball's reserve clause in Supreme Court in 1972 (see Peter Seitz).

Ray Floyd (b. Sept. 14, 1942): Golfer; has 22 PGA victories in 4 decades; joined Senior PGA Tour in 1992; has won Masters (1976), U.S. Open (1986), PGA twice (1969,82) and PGA Seniors Championship (1995); only player to ever win on PGA and Senior tours in same year (1992); member of 8 Ryder Cup teams and captain in 1989.

Doug Flutie (b. Oct. 23, 1962): Football QB; won Heisman Trophy at Boston College (1984); has played in USFL, NFL and CFL; 6-time CFL MVP with B.C. Lions (1991), Calgary (1992-94) and Toronto (1996-97); led Calgary to Grey Cup title in '92 and Toronto in 1996-97; returned to NFL with Buffalo in 1998.

Whitey Ford (b. Oct. 21, 1928): Baseball LHP; all-time leader in World Series wins (10); led AL in wins 3 times; won Cy Young and World Series MVP in 1961 with NY Yankees; 236-106 record

George Foreman (b. Jan. 10, 1949): Boxer; Olympic heavyweight champ (1968); world heavyweight champ (1973-74 and 94-95); lost title to Muhammad Ali (KO-8th) in '74; recaptured it on Nov. 5, 1994 at age 45 with a 10-round KO of WBA/IBF champ Michael Moorer, becoming the oldest man to win heavyweight crown; named AP Male Athlete of Year 20 years after losing title to Ali; stripped of WBA title on Mar. 4, 1995 after declining to fight No. 1 contender; successfully defended title at age 46 against 26-year-old Axel Schultz of Germany in controversial majority decision on Apr. 22; gave up IBF title in June after refusing rematch with Schultz.

Dick Fosbury (b. Mar. 6, 1947): Track & Field; revolutionized high jump with back-first "Fosbury Flop"; won gold medal at 1968 Olympics.

The Four Horsemen Senior backfield that led Notre Dame to national collegiate football championship in 1924; put together as sophomores by Irish coach Knute Rockne; immortalized by sportswriter Grantland Rice, whose report of the Oct. 19, 1924, Notre Dame-Army game began: "Outlined against a blue, gray October sky the Four Horsemen rode again . . .": HB Jim Crowley (b. Sept. 10, 1902, d. Jan. 15, 1986), FB Elmer Layden (b. May 4, 1903, d. June 30, 1973), HB Don Miller (b. May 30, 1902, d. July 28, 1979) and QB Harry Stuhldreher (b. Oct. 14, 1901, d. Jan. 26, 1965).

The Four Musketeers French quartet that dominated men's tennis in 1920s and '30s, winning 8 straight French singles titles (1925-32), 6 Wimbledons in a row (1924-29) and 6 consecutive Davis Cups (1927-32)— Jean Borotra (b. Aug. 13, 1898, d. July 17, 1994), Jacques Brugnon (b. May 11, 1895, d. Mar. 20, 1978), Henri Cochet (b. Dec. 14, 1901, d. Apr. 1, 1987), Rene Lacoste (b. July 2, 1905, d. Oct. 13, 1996).

Nellie Fox (b. Dec. 25, 1927, d. Dec. 1, 1975): Baseball 2B; batted .306 in 1959 to win the AL MVP award with the pennant-winning Chicago White Sox; led the league in fielding percentage six times, hits four times and triples once; ended his 19-year career with 2,663 hits, 1,279 runs and .288 average.

Jimmie Foxx (b. Oct. 22, 1907, d. July 21, 1967): Baseball 1B; led AL in HRs 4 times and batting twice; won Triple Crown in 1933; 3-time MVP (1932-33,38) with Philadelphia and Boston; hit 30 HRs or more 12 years in a row; 534 career HRs.

A.J. Foyt (b. Jan. 16, 1935): Auto racer; 7-time USAC-CART national champion (1960-61,63-64,67,75,79); 4-time Indy 500 winner (1961,64,67,77); only driver in history to win Indy 500, Daytona 500 (1972) and 24 Hours of LeMans (1967 with Dan Gurney); retired in 1993 as all-time CART wins leader with 67.

Bill France Sr. (b. Sept. 26, 1909, d. June 7, 1992): Stock car pioneer and promoter; founded NASCAR in 1948; guided race circuit through formative years; built both Daytona (Fla.) Int'l Speedway and Talladega (Ala.) Superspeedway.

Dawn Fraser (b. Sept. 4, 1937): Australian swimmer; won gold medals in 100m freestyle at 3 consecutive Olympics (1956,60,64).

Joe Frazier (b. Jan. 12, 1944): Boxer; 1964 Olympic heavyweight champion; world heavyweight champ (1970-73); fought Muhammad Ali 3 times and won once; pro record 32-4-1 with 27 KOs.

Walt Frazier (b. March 29, 1945): Basketball G; won the NBA championship two times (1970 and 73) with the New York Knicks; 35 points and 19 assists in the 1970 championship game vs. the Lakers; averaged 18.9 PPG and 6.1 APG over his career; four-time all-NBA and a member of the Hall of Fame; nicknamed "Clyde the Glide."

Ford Frick (b. Dec. 19, 1894, d. Apr. 8, 1978): Baseball; sportswriter and radio announcer who served as NL president (1934-51) and commissioner (1951-65); convinced record-keepers to list Roger Maris' and Babe Ruth's season records separately; major leagues moved to West Coast and expanded from 16 to 20 teams during his tenure.

Frankie Frisch (b. Sept. 9, 1898, d. Mar. 12, 1973): Baseball 2B; played on 8 NL pennant winners in 19 years with NY and St. Louis; hit .300 or better 11 years in a row (1921-31); MVP in 1931; player-manager from 1933-37.

Dan Gable (b. Oct. 25, 1948): Wrestling; career wrestling record of 118-1 at Iowa St., where he was a 2-time NCAA champ (1968,69) and tourney MVP in 1969 (137 lbs); won gold medal (149 lbs) at 1972 Olympics; coached U.S. freestyle team in 1988; coached Iowa to 9 straight NCAA titles (1978-86) and 15 overall in 21 years.

Eddie Gaedel (b. June 8, 1925, d. June 18, 1961): Baseball PH; St. Louis Browns' midget whose career lasted one at bat (he walked) on Aug 19, 1951.

Clarence (Big House) Gaines (b. May 21, 1924): Basketball; retired as coach of Div. II Winston-Salem after 1992-93 season with 828-447 record in 47 years; ranks 3rd on all-time NCAA list behind Dean Smith (879) and Adolph Rupp (876).

Alonzo (Jake) Gaither (b. Apr. 11, 1903, d. Feb. 18, 1994): Football; head coach at Florida A&M for 25 years; led Rattlers to 6 national black college titles; retired after 1969 season with record of 203-36-4 and a winning percentage of .844; coined phrase, "I like my boys agile, mobile and hostile."

Lou Gehrig (b. June 19, 1903, d. June 2, 1941): Baseball 1B; played in 2,130 consecutive games from 1925-39 a major league record until Cal Ripken Jr. surpassed it in 1995; led AL in RBI 5 times and HRs 3 times; drove in 100 runs or more 13 years in a row; 2-time MVP (1927,36); hit .340 with 493 HRs over 17 seasons; led NY Yankees to 6 World Series titles; died at age 37 of Amyotrophic Lateral Sclerosis (ALS), a rare and incurable disease of the nervous system now better known as Lou Gehrig's disease.

Bernie Geoffrion (b. Feb. 14, 1931): Hockey RW; credited with popularizing the slap shot, earning his nickname "Boom Boom"; scored 30 goals in 1952 to win the NHL's Calder Trophy (Rookie of the Year Award); won the MVP award (Hart) in 1955; became the second player in history to score 50 goals in one season; led the league in points in 1955 and 61; won 6 Stanley Cups with Montreal; member of the Hockey Hall of Fame.

George Gervin (b. April 27, 1952): Basketball G/F; joined the ABA in 1972 and came to the NBA with San Antonio in 1976; a five-time NBA all-star; led the league in scoring four times; elected to the Basketball Hall of Fame in 1996.

A. Bartlett Giamatti (b. Apr. 14, 1938, d. Sept. 1, 1989): Scholar and 7th commissioner of baseball; banned Pete Rose for life for betting on Major League games and associating with known gamblers; also served as president of Yale (1978-86) and National League (1986-89).

Joe Gibbs (b. Nov. 25, 1940): Football; coached Washington to 140 victories and 3 Super Bowl titles in 12 seasons before retiring in 1993; owner of NASCAR racing team that won 1993 Daytona 500.

Althea Gibson (b. Aug. 25, 1927): Tennis; won both Wimbledon and U.S. championships in 1957 and '58; 1st black to play in either tourney and 1st to win each title.

Bob Gibson (b. Nov. 9, 1935): Baseball RHP; won 20 or more games 5 times; won 2 NL Cy Youngs (1968,70); MVP in 1968; led St. Louis to 2 World Series titles (1964,67); 251-174 record.

Josh Gibson (b. Dec. 21, 1911, d. Jan. 20, 1947): Baseball C; the "Babe Ruth of the Negro Leagues"; Satchel Paige's battery mate with Pittsburgh Crawfords. The Negro Leagues did not keep accurate records but Gibson hit 84 home runs in one season and his Baseball Hall of Fame plaque says he hit "almost 800" home runs in his seventeen-year career.

Kirk Gibson (b. May 28, 1957): Baseball OF; All-America flanker at Mich. St. in 1978; chose baseball career and was AL playoff MVP with Detroit in 1984 and NL regular season MVP with Los Angeles in 1988.

Frank Gifford (b. Aug. 16, 1930): Football HB; 4-time All-Pro (1955-57,59); NFL MVP in 1956; led NY Giants to 3 NFL title games; TV sportscaster since 1958, beginning career while still a player; scandal struck the married Gifford after he was videotaped in a compromising position with a former stewardess in 1997.

Sid Gillman (b. Oct. 26, 1911): Football innovator; only coach in both College and Pro Football Halls of Fame; led college teams at Miami-OH and Cincinnati to combined 81-19-2 record from 1944-54; coached LA Rams (1955-59) in NFL, then led LA-San Diego Chargers to 5 Western titles and 1 league championship in first six years of AFL.

George Gipp (b. Feb. 18, 1895, d. Dec. 14, 1920): Football FB; died of throat infection 2 weeks before he made All-America; rushed for 2,341 yards, scored 156 points and averaged 38 yards a punt in 4 years (1917-20).

Marc Girardelli (b. July 18, 1963): Luxembourg Alpine skier; Austrian native who refused to join Austrian Ski Federation because he wanted to be coached by his father; won unprecedented 5th overall World Cup title in 1993; winless at Olympics, although he won 2 silver medals in 1992.

Tom Glavine (b. Mar. 26, 1966): Baseball LHP; Atlanta Braves' pitcher led the majors in wins from 1991-95 with 91; 2-time NL Cy Young winner (1991,98); six-time All-Star and was the NL starter twice; World Series MVP (1995).

Tom Gola (b. Jan. 13, 1933): Basketball F; 4-time All-America and 1955 Player of Year at La Salle; MOP in 1952 NIT and '54 NCAA Final 4, leading Pioneers to both titles; won NBA title as rookie with Philadelphia Warriors in 1956; 4-time NBA All-Star.

Lefty Gomez (b. Nov. 26, 1908, d. Feb. 17, 1989): Baseball LHP; 4-time 20-game winner with NY Yankees; holds World Series record for most wins (6) without a defeat; pitched on 5 world championship clubs in 1930s.

Pancho Gonzales (b. May 9, 1928, d. July 3, 1995): Tennis; won consecutive U.S. Championships in 1947-48 before turning pro at 21; dominated pro tour from 1950-61; in 1969 at age 41, played longest Wimbledon match ever (5:12), beating Charlie Pasarell 22-24,1-6,16-14,6-3,11-9.

Bob Goodenow (b. Oct. 29, 1952): Hockey; succeeded Alan Eagleson as executive director of NHL Players Assn. in 1990; led players out on 10-day strike (Apr. 1-10) in 1992 and during 103-day owners' lockout in 1994-95.

Gail Goodrich (b. April 23, 1943): Basketball G; starred at UCLA and won two national championships in 1964 and 1965 under legendary coach John Wooden's tutelage; won the NBA championship with the L.A. Lakers in 1972 and led the team in scoring (25.9 ppg); averaged 18.6 ppg over his 14-year career.

Jeff Gordon (b. Aug. 4, 1971): Auto racer; NASCAR Rookie of Year (1993); 3-time Winston Cup champion (1995,97,98); won inaugural Brickyard 400 in 1994; in 1997, at 25 became youngest winner of the Daytona 500; in 1998 he tied Richard Petty for the modern-era record for wins in a single season with 13.

Dr. Harold Gores (b. Sept. 20, 1909, d. May 28, 1993): Educator and first president of Education Facilities Laboratories in New York; in 1964 hired Monsanto Co. to produce a synthetic turf that kids could play on in city schoolyards; resulting ChemGrass proved too expensive for playground use, but it was just what the Houston Astros were looking for in 1966 to cover the floor of the Astrodome, where grass refused to grow. Thus, AstroTurf was born.

Goose Gossage (b. July 5, 1951): Baseball RHP; Nine-time All Star (1975-78, 80-82, 84-85); intimidating relief pitcher; Fireman of the Year in 1975 with White Sox and 1978 with Yankees; led AL in saves with 26 (1975), 27 (1978); 1,002 career appearances; 310 saves.

Shane Gould (b. Nov. 23, 1956): Australian swimmer; set world records in 5 different freestyle events between July 1971 and Jan. 1972; won 3 gold medals, a silver and bronze in 1972 Olympics then retired at age 16.

Alf Goullet (b. Apr. 5, 1891, d. Mar. 11, 1995): Cycling; Australian who gained fame and fortune early in century as premier performer on U.S. 6-day bike race circuit; won 8 annual races at Madison Square Garden with 6 different partners from 1913-23.

Curt Gowdy (b. July 31, 1919): Radio-TV; former radio voice of NY Yankees and then Boston Red Sox from 1949-66; TV play-by-play man for AFL, NFL and major league baseball; has broadcast World Series, All-Star Games, Rose Bowls, Super Bowls, Olympics and NCAA Final Fours for all 3 networks; hosted "The American Sportsman."

Steffi Graf (b. June 14, 1969): German tennis player; won Grand Slam and Olympic gold medal in 1988 at age 19; won three of four majors in 1993, '95 and '96; won 22 Grand Slam singles titles— 7 at Wimbledon, 6 French, 5 U.S. and 4 Australian Opens, retired in 1999 as 3rd all-time with 107 career singles titles and as all-time tour leader in career earnings with over $21 million in prize money.

Otto Graham (b. Dec. 6, 1921): Football QB and basketball All-America at Northwestern; in pro ball, led Cleveland Browns to 7 league titles in 10 years, winning 4 AAFC championships (1946-49) and 3 NFL (1950,54-55); 5-time All-Pro; 2-time NFL MVP (1953,55).

Red Grange (b. June 13, 1903, d. Jan. 28, 1991): Football HB; 3-time All-America at Illinois who brought 1st huge crowds to pro football when he signed with Chicago Bears in 1925; formed 1st AFL with manager-promoter C.C. Pyle in 1926, but league folded and he returned to Bears.

Bud Grant (b. May 20, 1927): Football and Basketball; only coach to win 100 games in both CFL and NFL and only member of both CFL and U.S. Pro Football Halls of Fame; led Winnipeg to 4 Grey Cup titles (1958-59,61-62) in 6 appearances, but his Minnesota Vikings lost all 4 Super Bowl attempts in 1970s; all-time rank of 6th in CFL wins (122) and 9th in NFL wins (168); also All-Big Ten at Minnesota in the late 1940s; a 3-time CFL All-Star offensive end; also member of 1950 NBA champion Minneapolis Lakers.

Rocky Graziano (b. June 7, 1922, d. May 22, 1990): Boxer; world middleweight champion (1946-47); fought Tony Zale for title 3 times in 21 months, losing twice; pro record 67-10-6 with 52 KOs; movie "Somebody Up There Likes Me" based on his life.

Hank Greenberg (b. Jan. 1, 1911, d. Sept. 4, 1986): Baseball 1B; led AL in HRs and RBI 4 times each; 2-time MVP (1935,40) with Detroit; 331 career HRs, including 58 in 1938.

Joe Greene (b. Sept. 24, 1946): Football DT; 5-time All-Pro (1972-74,77,79); led Pittsburgh to 4 Super Bowl titles in 1970s; nicknamed "Mean Joe."

Bud Greenspan (b. Sept. 18, 1926): Filmmaker specializing in the Olympic Games; has won Emmy awards for 22-part "The Olympiad" (1976-77) and historical vignettes for ABC-TV's coverage of 1980 Winter Games; won 1994 Emmy award for edited special on Lillehammer Winter Olympics.

Wayne Gretzky (b. Jan. 26, 1961): Hockey C; 10-time NHL scoring champion; 9-time regular season MVP (1979-87,89) and 9-time All-NHL first team; has scored 200 points or more in a season 4 times; led Edmonton to 4 Stanley Cups (1984-85,87-88); 2-time playoff MVP (1985,88); traded to LA Kings (Aug. 9, 1988); broke Gordie Howe's all-time NHL goal scoring record of 801 on Mar. 23, 1994; all-time NHL leader in points (2857), goals (894) and assists (1963); also all-time Stanley Cup leader in points, goals and assists; spent the end of the 1996 season with the St. Louis Blues and then signed a free agent contract with the New York Rangers; retired in 1999 at age 38 with 61 NHL scoring records in 20 seasons. See page 393.

Bob Griese (b. Feb. 3, 1945): Football QB; 2-time All-Pro (1971,77); led Miami to undefeated season (17-0) in 1972 and consecutive Super Bowl titles (1973-74).

Ken Griffey Jr. (b. Nov. 21, 1969): Baseball OF; overall 1st pick of 1987 draft by Seattle; 9-time Gold Glove winner; 10-time All-Star; 1997 AL MVP; among the youngest ever to reach certain statistical plateaus, like 200 homers, 300 homers and 1,000 hits; MVP of 1992 All-Star game at age 23; hit home runs in 8 consecutive games in 1993; son of Ken Sr. and in 1990 they became the first father-son combination to appear in the same major league lineup.

Archie Griffin (b. Aug. 21, 1954): Football RB; only college player to win two Heisman Trophies (1974-75); rushed for 5,177 yards in career at Ohio St.

Emile Griffith (b. Feb. 3, 1938): Boxer; world welterweight champion (1961,62-63,63-65); world middleweight champ (1966-67,67-68); pro record 85-24-2 with 23 KOs.

Dick Groat (b. Nov. 4, 1930): Basketball and Baseball SS; 2-time basketball All-America at Duke and college Player of Year in 1951; won NL MVP award as shortstop with Pittsburgh in 1960; won World Series with Pirates (1960) and St. Louis (1964).

Lefty Grove (b. Mar. 6, 1900, d. May 23, 1975): Baseball LHP; won 20 or more games 8 times; led AL in ERA 9 times and strikeouts 7 times; 31-4 record and MVP in 1931 with Philadelphia; 300-141 record.

Lou Groza (b. Jan. 25, 1924): Football T-PK; 6-time All-Pro; played in 13 championship games for Cleveland from 1946-67; kicked winning field goal in 1950 NFL title game; 1,608 career points (1,349 in NFL).

Janet Guthrie (b. Mar. 7, 1938): Auto racer; in 1977, became 1st woman to race in Indianapolis 500; placed 9th at Indy in 1978.

Tony Gwynn (b. May 9, 1960): Baseball OF; 8-time NL batting champion (1984,87-89,94-97) with San Diego, 15-time All-Star; got 3,000th career hit Aug. 6, 1999 at Montreal; played basketball at San Diego St. leaving as school's all-time assist leader; drafted in 10th round of 1981 NBA draft by San Diego Clippers.

Harvey Haddix (b. Sept. 18, 1925, d. Jan. 9, 1994): Baseball LHP; pitched 12 perfect innings for Pittsburgh, but lost to Milwaukee in the 13th, 1-0 (May 26, 1959); won Game 7 of 1960 World Series.

Walter Hagen (b. Dec. 21, 1892, d. Oct. 5, 1969): Pro golf pioneer; won 2 U.S. Opens (1914,19), 4 British Opens (1922,24,28-29), 5 PGA Championships (1921,24-27) and 5 Western Opens; retired with 40 PGA wins; 6-time U.S. Ryder Cup captain.

Marvin Hagler (b. May 23, 1954): Boxer; world middleweight champion 1980-87; enjoyed his nickname "Marvelous Marvin" so much he had his name legally changed; pro record of 62-3-2 with 52 KOs.

Mika Hakkinen (b. Sept. 28, 1968): Finnish auto racer; won 1998 Formula One championship with eight wins, 13 career F1 wins as of Sept. 21, 1999.

George Halas (b. Feb. 2, 1895, d. Oct. 31, 1983): Football pioneer; MVP in 1919 Rose Bowl; player-coach-owner of Chicago Bears from 1920-83; signed Red Grange in 1925; coached Bears for 40 seasons and won 8 NFL titles (1921,33,40-41,43,46,63); 2nd on all-time career list with 324 wins; elected to NFL Hall of Fame in 1963.

Dorothy Hamill (b. July 26, 1956): Figure skater; won Olympic gold medal and world championship in 1976; Ice Capades headliner from 1977-84; bought the financially-strapped Ice Capades in 1993 and sold it several years later.

Scott Hamilton (b. Aug. 28, 1958): Figure skater; 4-time world champion (1981-84); won gold medal at 1984 Olympics.

Mia Hamm (b. Mar. 17, 1972): Soccer F; became all-time leading scorer in international soccer with her 108th goal on May 22, 1999; Member of the 1991 and 1999 U.S. World Cup championship teams, third-place 1995 World Cup team and 1996 Olympic gold medal team; named U.S. Soccer's Female Athlete of the Year for five consecutive years (1994-98); MVP of both U.S. Women's Cup '97 and U.S. Women's Cup '95; made the U.S. National Team at 15; a three-time collegiate All-American; led the Univ. of North Carolina to four national championships (1989,90,92,93).

Tonya Harding (b. Nov. 12, 1970): Figure skater; 1991 U.S. women's champion; involved in bizarre plot hatched by ex-husband Jeff Gillooly to injure rival Nancy Kerrigan on Jan. 6, 1994 and keep her off Olympic team; won '94 U.S. women's title in Kerrigan's absence; denied any role in assault and sued USOC when her berth on Olympic team was threatened; finished 8th at Lillehammer (Kerrigan recovered and won silver medal); pled guilty on Mar. 16 to conspiracy to hinder investigation; stripped of 1994 title by U.S. Figure Skating Assn.

Tom Harmon (b. Sept. 28, 1919, d. Mar. 17, 1990): Football HB; 2-time All-America at Michigan; won Heisman Trophy in 1940; played in AFL NY Americans in 1941 and NFL LA Rams (1946-47); World War II fighter pilot who won Silver Star and Purple Heart; became radio-TV commentator.

Franco Harris (b. Mar. 7, 1950): Football RB; ran for over 1,000 yards a season 8 times; rushed for 12,120 yards in 13 years; led Pittsburgh to 4 Super Bowl titles.

Leon Hart (b. Nov. 2, 1928): Football E; only player to win 3 national championships in college and 3 more in the NFL; won his titles at Notre Dame (1946-47,49) and with Detroit Lions (1952-53,57); 3-time All-America and last lineman to win Heisman Trophy (1949); All-Pro on both offense and defense in 1951.

Bill Hartack (b. Dec. 9, 1932): Jockey; won Kentucky Derby 5 times (1957,60,62,64,69), Preakness 3 times (1956,64,69), but the Belmont only once (1960).

Doug Harvey (b. Dec. 19, 1924, d. Dec. 26, 1989): Hockey D; 10-time All-NHL 1st team; won Norris Trophy 7 times (1955-58,60-62); led Montreal to 6 Stanley Cups.

Dominik Hasek (b. Jan. 29, 1965): Czech hockey G; 2-time NHL MVP (1997,98) with Buffalo; 5-time Vezina Trophy winner (1994,95,97,98,99); led Czech Republic to Olympic gold medal in 1998 at Nagano; announced plans to retire following 1999-2000 season.

Billy Haughton (b. Nov. 2, 1923, d. July 15, 1986): Harness racing; 4-time winner of Hambletonian; trainer-driver of one Pacing Triple Crown winner (1968); 4,910 career wins.

João Havelange (b. May 8, 1916): Soccer; Brazilian-born president of Federation Internationale de Football Assoc. (FIFA) 1974-98; also member of International Olympic Committee.

John Havlicek (b. Apr. 8, 1940): Basketball F; played in 3 NCAA Finals at Ohio St. (1960-62); led Boston to 8 NBA titles (1963-66,68-69,74,76); Finals MVP in 1974; 4-time All-NBA 1st team.

Bob Hayes (b. Dec. 20, 1942): Track & Field and Football; won gold medal in 100m at 1964 Olympics; all-pro SE for Dallas in 1966; convicted of drug trafficking in 1979 and served 18 months of a 5-year sentence.

Elvin Hayes (b. Nov. 17, 1945): Basketball C; Known as "the Big E"; Overall number one pick of the 1968 NBA draft; three-time All-NBA first team (1975,77,79); 1978 Finals MVP; 12-time NBA all-star (1969-80); named to NBA's 50 Greatest Players; 6th leading scorer in NBA history with 27,313 points; member of NBA Hall of Fame.

Woody Hayes (b. Feb. 14, 1913, d. Mar. 12, 1987): Football; coached Ohio St. to 3 national titles (1954,57,68) and 4 Rose Bowl victories; 238 career wins in 28 seasons at Denison, Miami-OH and OSU.

Thomas Hearns (b. Oct. 18, 1958): Boxer; has held world titles as welterweight, junior middleweight, middleweight and light heavyweight; pro record of 59-4-1 and 46 KOs.

Eric Heiden (b. June 14, 1958): Speedskater; 3-time overall world champion (1977-79); won all 5 men's gold medals at 1980 Olympics, setting records in each; Sullivan Award winner (1980).

Mel Hein (b. Aug. 22, 1909, d. Jan. 31, 1992): Football C; NFL All-Pro 8 straight years (1933-40); MVP in 1938 with Giants; didn't miss a game in 15 years.

John W. Heisman (b. Oct. 23, 1869, d. Oct. 3, 1936): Football; coached at 9 colleges from 1892-1927; won 185 games; Director of Athletics at Downtown Athletic Club in NYC (1928-36); DAC named Heisman Trophy after him.

Carol Heiss (b. Jan. 20, 1940): Figure skater; 5-time world champion (1956-60); won Olympic silver medal in 1956 and gold in '60; married 1956 men's gold medalist Hayes Jenkins.

Rickey Henderson (b. Dec. 25, 1958): Baseball OF; AL playoff MVP (1989) and AL regular season MVP (1990); set single-season base stealing record of 130 in 1982; has led AL in steals a record 12 times; broke Lou Brock's all-time record of 938 on May 1, 1991; all-time leader in steals and HRs as leadoff batter.

Sonja Henie (b. Apr. 8, 1912, d. Oct. 12, 1969): Norwegian figure skater; 10-time world champion (1927-36); won 3 consecutive Olympic gold medals (1928,32,36); became movie star.

Foster Hewitt (b. Nov. 21, 1902, d. Apr. 21, 1985): Radio-TV; Canada's premier hockey play-by-play broadcaster from 1923-81; coined phrase, "He shoots, he scores! "

Damon Hill (b. Sept. 17, 1960): British auto racer; 1996 Formula One champion; 22 F1 wins for second place among active drivers as of Sept. 21, 1999.

Graham Hill (b. Feb. 15, 1929, d. Nov. 29, 1975): British auto racer; 2-time Formula One world champion (1962,68); won Indy 500 in 1966; killed in plane crash; father of fellow driver Damon.

Phil Hill (b. Apr. 20, 1927): Auto racer; first U.S. driver to win Formula One championship (1961); 3 career wins (1958-64).

Martina Hingis (b. Sept. 30, 1980): Tennis player; in March 1997 at 16 years, 6 months, she became the youngest No. 1 ranked player since the ranking system began in 1975; has won Wimbledon (1997), U.S. Open (1997) and 3 Australian Opens (1997,98,99); first woman to surpass the $3 million mark in earnings for one season (1997).

Max Hirsch (b. July 30, 1880, d. Apr. 3, 1969): Horse racing; trained 1,933 winners from 1908-68; won Triple Crown with Assault in 1946.

Tommy Hitchcock (b. Feb. 11, 1900, d. Apr. 19, 1944): Polo; world class player at 20; achieved 10-goal rating 18 times from 1922-40.

Lew Hoad (b. Nov. 23, 1934, d. July 3, 1994): Australian tennis player; 2-time Wimbledon winner (1956-57); won Australian, French and Wimbledon titles in 1956, but missed capturing Grand Slam at Forest Hills when beaten by Ken Rosewall in 4-set final.

Gil Hodges (b. Apr. 4, 1924, d. Apr. 2, 1972): Baseball 1B-Manager; tied Major League record with four home runs in one game on Aug 31, 1950; won three Gold Gloves (1957-59); drove in 100 runs in seven consecutive seasons (1949-55); hit 370 home runs and 1,274 RBIs lifetime; won 660 games as a manager (Senators and Mets).

Ben Hogan (b. Aug. 13, 1912, d. July 25, 1997): Golfer; 4-time PGA Player of Year; one of only four players to win all four Grand Slam titles (others are Nicklaus, Player and Sarazen); won 4 U.S. Opens, 2 Masters, 2 PGAs and 1 British Open between 1946-53; only player to win three of the four current majors in one year when he won Masters, U.S. Open and British Open in 1953; nearly killed in Feb. 2, 1949 car accident, but came back to win U.S. Open in '50; third on all-time list with 63 career wins.

Chamique Holdsclaw (b. Aug. 9, 1977): Basketball F; 2-time national player of the year, leading Tennessee to 3 straight national championships (1996,97,98); 1998 Sullivan Award winner; 1999 WNBA No. 1 draft choice and Rookie of the Year.

Eleanor Holm (b. Dec. 6, 1913): Swimmer; won gold medal in 100m backstroke at 1932 Olympics; thrown off '36 U.S. team for drinking champagne in public and shooting craps on boat to Germany.

Nat Holman (b. Oct. 18, 1896, d. Feb. 12, 1995): Basketball pioneer; played with Original Celtics (1920-28); coached CCNY to both NCAA and NIT titles in 1950 (a year later, several of his players were caught up in a point-shaving scandal); 423 career wins.

Larry Holmes (b. Nov. 3, 1949): Boxer; heavyweight champion (WBC or IBF) from 1978-85; successfully defended title 20 times before losing to Michael Spinks; returned from first retirement in 1988 and was KO'd in 4th by champ Mike Tyson; launched second comeback in 1991; fought and lost title bids against Evander Holyfield in '92 and Oliver McCall in '95; pro record of 67-6 and 43 KOs.

Lou Holtz (b. Jan. 6, 1937): Football; coached Notre Dame to national title in 1988; 2-time Coach of Year (1977,88) retired after 1996 season with 216-95-7 record in 27 seasons with 5 schools; also coached NFL NY Jets for 13 games (3-10) in 1976; returned to coaching with Univ. of South Carolina in 1999.

Evander Holyfield (b. Oct. 19, 1962): Boxer; KO'd Buster Douglas in 3rd round to become world hvywt. champion in 1990; 2 of first 4 title defenses included wins over 42-year-old ex-champs George Foreman and Larry Holmes; lost title to Riddick Bowe by unanimous dec. in 1992; beat Bowe by majority dec. to reclaim title in 1993; lost title again to Michael Moorer by majority dec. in 1994; after retiring in '94 due to an apparent heart defect, he returned to the ring in 1995 with a clean bill of health; defeated Mike Tyson in 1996 to win WBA belt; in 1997 rematch, Tyson was DQ'd for twice biting Holyfield's ear; escaped with controversial draw in 1999 unification bout with Lennox Lewis.

Red Holzman (b. Aug. 10, 1920, d. Nov. 13, 1998): Basketball; played for NBL and NBA champions at Rochester (1946,51); coached NY Knicks to 2 NBA titles (1970,73); Coach of Year (1970); ranks 10th on all-time NBA list with 754 wins.

Rogers Hornsby (b. Apr. 27, 1896, d. Jan. 5, 1963): Baseball 2B; hit .400 three times, including .424 in 1924; led NL in batting 7 times; 2-time MVP (1925,29); career average of .358 over 23 years is all-time highest in NL.

Paul Hornung (b. Dec. 23, 1935): Football HB-PK; only Heisman Trophy winner to play for losing team (2-8 Notre Dame in 1956); 3-time NFL scoring leader (1959-61) at Green Bay; 176 points in 1960, an all-time record; MVP in 1961; suspended by NFL for 1963 season for betting on his own team.

Gordie Howe (b. Mar. 31, 1928): Hockey RW; played 32 seasons in NHL and WHA from 1946-80; led NHL in scoring 6 times; All-NHL 1st team 12 times; MVP 6 times in NHL (1952-53,57-58,60,63) with Detroit and once in WHA (1974) with Houston; ranks 2nd on all-time NHL list in goals (801) and points (1,850) to Wayne Gretzky.

Cal Hubbard (b. Oct. 31, 1900, d. Oct. 19, 1977): Member of college football, pro football and baseball halls of fame; 9 years in NFL; 4-time All-Pro at end and tackle; AL umpire (1936-51).

William DeHart Hubbard (b. Nov. 25, 1903, d. June 23, 1976): Track & Field; won the long jump at the 1924 Olympics, becoming the first black athlete to win an Olympic gold medal in an individual event; set the long jump world record in 1925 (25-10¾) and tied the 100-yard dash record (9.6) in 1926.

Carl Hubbell (b. June 22, 1903, d. Nov. 21, 1988): Baseball LHP; led NL in wins and ERA 3 times each; 2-time MVP (1933,36) with NY Giants; fanned Ruth, Gehrig, Foxx, Simmons and Cronin in succession in 1934 All-Star Game; 253-154 career record.

Sam Huff (b. Oct. 4, 1934): Football LB; glamorized NFL's middle linebacker position with NY Giants from 1956-63; subject of "The Violent World of Sam Huff" TV special in 1961; helped club win 6 division titles and a world championship (1956).

Miller Huggins (b. Mar. 27, 1879, d. Sept. 25, 1929): Baseball; managed NY Yankees from 1918 until his death late in '29 season; led Yanks to 6 pennants and 3 World Series titles from 1921-28.

H. Wayne Huizenga (b. Dec. 29, 1937): Owner; formerly vice chairman of Viacom Inc. and chairman/CEO of Blockbuster Entertainment; owner of NFL Miami Dolphins, NHL Florida Panthers and Pro Player Stadium and former majority owner of MLB's Florida Marlins; criticized for dismantling 1997 World Champion Marlins in off-season to cut payroll.

Bobby Hull (b. Jan. 3, 1939): Hockey LW; led NHL in scoring 3 times; 2-time MVP (1965-66) with Chicago; All-NHL first team 10 times; jumped to WHA in 1972, 2-time MVP there (1973,75) with Winnipeg; scored 913 goals in both leagues; father of Brett.

Brett Hull (b. Aug. 9, 1964): Hockey RW; NHL MVP in 1991 with St. Louis; holds single season RW scoring record with 86 goals; he and father Bobby have both won Hart (MVP), Lady Byng (sportsmanship) and All-Star Game MVP trophies.

Jim (Catfish) Hunter (b. Apr. 8, 1946, d. Sept. 9, 1999): Baseball RHP; won 20 games or more 5 times (1971-75); played on 5 World Series winners with Oakland and NY Yankees; threw perfect game in 1968; won AL Cy Young Award in 1974; 224-166 career record.

Ibrahim Hussein (b. June 3, 1958): Kenyan distance runner; 3-time winner of Boston Marathon (1988,91-92) and 1st African runner to win in Boston; won New York Marathon in 1987.

Flo Hyman (b. July 31, 1954, d. Jan. 24, 1986): Volleyball; 3-time All-America spiker at Houston and captain of 1984 U.S. Women's Olympic team; died of heart attack caused by Marfan Syndrome during a match in Japan in 1986.

Hank Iba (b. Aug. 6, 1904, d. Jan. 15, 1993): Basketball; coached Oklahoma A&M to 2 straight NCAA titles (1945-46); 767 career wins in 41 years; coached U.S. Olympic team to 2 gold medals (1964,68), but lost to Soviets in controversial '72 final.

Mike Ilitch (b. July 20, 1929): Baseball and Hockey owner; owns Little Caesar's, the international pizza chain; bought Detroit Red Wings for $8 million in 1982 and Detroit Tigers for $85 million in 1992.

Punch Imlach (b. Mar. 15, 1918, d. Dec. 1, 1987): Hockey; directed Toronto to 4 Stanley Cups (1962-64,67) in 11 seasons as GM-coach.

Miguel Induráin (b. July 16, 1964): Spanish cyclist; won a record 5th straight Tour de France in 1995, joining legends Jacques Anquetil and Bernard Hinault of France and Eddy Merckx of Belgium as the only 5-time winners; won gold in time trial at '96 Olympics; retired in 1997.

Hale Irwin (b. June 3, 1945): Golfer; oldest player ever to win U.S. Open (45 in 1990); NCAA champion in 1967; 20 PGA victories, including 3 U.S. Opens (1974,79,90); 5-time Ryder Cup team member; joined senior PGA tour in 1995 and had already won 25 titles through Aug. 1999.

Bo Jackson (b. Nov. 30, 1962): Baseball OF and Football RB; won Heisman Trophy in 1985 and MVP of baseball All-Star Game in 1989; starter for both baseball's KC Royals and NFL's LA Raiders in 1988 and '89; severely injured left hip Jan. 13, 1991, in NFL playoffs; waived by Royals but signed by Chicago White Sox in 1991; missed entire 1992 season recovering from hip surgery; played for White Sox in 1993 and California in '94 before retiring.

Joe Jackson (b. July 16, 1889, d. Dec. 5, 1951): Baseball OF; hit .300 or better 11 times; nicknamed "Shoeless Joe"; career average of .356 (see Black Sox).

Phil Jackson (b. Sept. 17, 1945): Basketball; NBA champion as reserve forward with New York in 1973 (injured when Knicks won in '70); coached Chicago to six NBA titles in eight years (1991-93, 96-98); coach of the year in 1996 and 97; all-time leader in winning percentage for NBA coaches with 500 or more wins; returned to coach the LA Lakers in 1999.

Reggie Jackson (b. May 18, 1946): Baseball OF; led AL in HRs 4 times; MVP in 1973; played on 5 World Series winners with Oakland, NY Yankees; 1977 Series MVP with 5 HRs; 563 career HRs; all-time strikeout leader (2,597); member of the Hall of Fame.

Dr. Robert Jackson (b. Aug. 6, 1932): Surgeon; revolutionized sports medicine by popularizing the use of arthroscopic surgery to treat injuries; learned technique from Japanese physician that allowed athletes to return quickly from potentially career-ending injuries.

Helen Jacobs (b. Aug. 6, 1908): Tennis; 4-time winner of U.S. Championship (1932-35); Wimbledon winner in 1936; lost 4 Wimbledon finals to arch-rival Helen Wills Moody.

Jaromir Jagr (b. Feb. 15, 1972): Czech Hockey RW; fifth overall pick by Pittsburgh (1990); NHL All-Rookie team (1991); NHL MVP (1999); Won Art Ross Trophy (1995,98,99); NHL All-Star First Team (1995,96,97,98,99); NHL single season record for most points by a right winger (149); NHL single season record for most assists by a right winger (87).

Dan Jansen (b. June 17, 1965): Speedskater; 1993 world record-holder in 500m; fell in 500m and 1,000m in 1988 Olympics at Calgary after learning of death of sister Jane; placed 4th in 500m and didn't attempt 1,000m 4 years later in Albertville; fell in 500m at '94 Games in Lillehammer, but finally won an Olympic medal with world record (1:12.43) effort in 1,000m, then took victory lap with baby daughter Jane in his arms; won 1994 Sullivan Award.

James J. Jeffries (b. Apr. 15, 1875, d. Mar. 3, 1953): Boxer; world heavyweight champion (1899-1905); retired undefeated but came back to fight Jack Johnson in 1910 and lost (KO, 15th).

David Jenkins (b. June 29, 1936): Figure skater; brother of Hayes; 3-time world champion (1957-59); won gold medal at 1960 Olympics.

Hayes Jenkins (b. Mar. 23, 1933): Figure skater; 4-time world champion (1953-56); won gold medal at 1956 Olympics; married 1960 women's gold medalist Carol Heiss.

Bruce Jenner (b. Oct. 28, 1949): Track & Field; won gold medal in 1976 Olympic decathlon.

Jackie Jensen (b. Mar. 9, 1927, d. July 14, 1982): Football RB and Baseball OF; All-America at California in 1948; American League MVP with Boston Red Sox in 1958.

Ben Johnson (b. Dec. 30, 1961): Canadian sprinter; set 100m world record (9.83) at 1987 World Championships; won 100m at 1988 Olympics, but flunked drug test and forfeited gold medal; 1987 world record revoked in '89 for admitted steroid use; returned drug-free in 1991, but performed poorly; banned for life by IAAF in 1993 for testing positive after a meet in Montreal.

Bob Johnson (b. Mar. 4, 1931, d. Nov. 26, 1991): Hockey; coached Pittsburgh Penguins to 1st Stanley Cup title in 1991; led Wisconsin to 3 NCAA titles (1973,77,81) in 15 years; also coached 1976 U.S. Olympic team and NHL Calgary (1982-87).

Earvin (Magic) Johnson (b. Aug. 14, 1959): Basketball G; led Michigan St. to NCAA title in 1979 and was Final 4 MOP; All-NBA 1st team 9 times; 3-time MVP (1987,89-90); led LA Lakers to 5 NBA titles; 3-time Finals MVP (1980, 82, 87); 2nd all-time in NBA assists with 10,141; retired on Nov. 7, 1991 after announcing he was HIV-positive; returned to score 25 points in 1992 NBA All-Star Game; U.S. Olympic Dream Team member in '92; announced NBA comeback then retired again before start of 1992-93 season; named head coach of Lakers on Mar. 23, 1994, but finished season at 5-11 and quit; later became minority owner of team; came back a final time and played 32 games during 1995-96 season before retiring for good.

Jack Johnson (b. Mar. 31, 1878, d. June 10, 1946): Boxer; controversial heavyweight champion (1908-15) and 1st black to hold title; defeated Tommy Burns for crown at age 30; fled to Europe in 1913 after Mann Act conviction; lost title to Jess Willard in Havana, but claimed to have taken a dive; pro record 78-8-12 with 45 KOs.

Jimmy Johnson (b. July 16, 1943): Football; All-SWC defensive lineman on Arkansas' 1964 national championship team; coached Miami-FL to national title in 1987; college record of 81-34-3 in 10 years; hired by old friend and new Dallas owner Jerry Jones to succeed Tom Landry in 1989; went 1-15 in '89, then led Cowboys to consecutive Super Bowl victories in 1992 and '93 seasons; quit in 1994 after issues with Jones; became TV analyst; replaced Don Shula as Miami Dolphins head coach in 1996.

Judy Johnson (b. Oct. 26, 1899, d. June 13, 1989): Baseball IF; one of the great stars of the Negro Leagues; a great fielding third baseman who regularly batted over .300; when baseball integrated Johnson's playing days were over but he coached and scouted for the Philadelphia Athletics, Boston Braves and Philadelphia Phillies; member of Hall of Fame.

Junior Johnson (b. 1930): Auto Racing; won the second Daytona 500 in 1960; also won 13 NASCAR races in 1965, including the Rebel 300 at Darlington; retired from racing to become a highly successful car owner; his first driver was Bobby Allison.

Michael Johnson (b. Sep 13, 1967): Track & Field; Shattered world record in 200m (19.32) and set Olympic record in 400m (43.49) to become first man to win the gold in both races in the same Olympic Games at Atlanta in 1996; two-time world champion in 200 (1991,95) and four-time world champ in 400 (1993,95,97,99); set world record in 400m (43.18) at '99 world championships in Seville.

Rafer Johnson (b. Aug. 18, 1935): Track & Field; won silver medal in 1956 Olympic decathlon and gold medal in 1960.

Randy Johnson (b. Sept. 10, 1963): Baseball LHP; 6'10" flamethrower; threw no-hitter June 2, 1990 for Seattle; struck out over 300 batters 3 times (1993,98,99); led majors in Ks in 1993,94,98,99; AL Cy Young Award (1995); traded to Houston in 1998 and signed a free agent contract with Arizona in 1999.

Walter Johnson (b. Nov. 6, 1887, d. Dec. 10, 1946): Baseball RHP; won 20 games or more 10 straight years; led AL in ERA 5 times, wins 6 times and strikeouts 12 times; twice MVP (1913, 24) with Washington; all-time leader in shutouts (110) and 2nd in wins (417); nicknamed "Big Train."

Ben A. Jones (b. Dec. 31, 1882, d. June 13, 1961): Horse racing; Calumet Farm trainer (1939-47); saddled 6 Kentucky Derby champions, including 2 Triple Crown winners—Whirlaway in 1941 and Citation in '48.

Bobby Jones (b. Mar. 17, 1902, d. Dec. 18, 1971): Won U.S. and British Opens plus U.S. and British Amateurs in 1930 to become golf's only Grand Slam winner ever; from 1922-30, won 4 U.S. Opens, 5 U.S. Amateurs, 3 British Opens, and played in 6 Walker Cups; founded Masters tournament in 1934.

Deacon Jones (b. Dec. 9, 1938): Football DE; 5-time All-Pro (1965-69) with LA Rams; unofficially 2nd all-time in NFL sacks with 173½ in 14 years.

Jerry Jones (b. Oct. 13, 1942): Football; owner-GM of Dallas Cowboys; maverick who bought declining team (3-13) and Texas Stadium for $140 million in 1989; hired old pal Jimmy Johnson to replace legendary Tom Landry as coach; their partnership led Cowboys to 2 Super Bowl titles (1993-94); when feud developed in 1994, he fired Johnson and hired Barry Switzer, who won Super Bowl in 1996.

Marion Jones (b. Oct. 12, 1975): Track & Field; American sprinter who aims to be first to win 5 track golds (100, 200, LJ, 4x100, 4x400) in an Olympics in Sydney 2000; 2-time world champion in 100m (1997,99); former college basketball star at North Carolina; voted Women's Athlete of the Year by Track & Field News in 1997 and 1998; winner of the 1999 Jesse Owens Award.

Roy Jones Jr. (b. Jan. 16, 1969): Boxing; robbed of gold medal at 1988 Summer Olympics due to an error in scoring; still voted Outstanding Boxer of the Games; won IBF middleweight crown by beating Bernard Hopkins in 1993; moved up to super middleweight and won IBF title from James Toney in 1994; moved up to light heavyweight division winning WBC (in 1997), WBA (1998) and IBF titles (1999).

Michael Jordan (b. Feb. 17, 1963): Basketball G; College Player of Year with North Carolina in 1984; NBA Rookie of the Year (1985); led NBA in scoring 7 years in a row (1987-93) and also 1996-98; 10-time All-NBA 1st team; 5-time regular season MVP (1988,91-92,96,98) and 6-time MVP of NBA Finals (1991-93,96-98); 3-time AP Male Athlete of Year; led U.S. Olympic team to gold medals in 1984 and '92; stunned sports world when he retired at age 30 on Oct. 6, 1993; signed as OF with Chi. White Sox and spent summer of '94 in AA with Birmingham; struggled with .204 average; made one of the most anticipated comebacks in sports history when he returned to the Bulls lineup on Mar. 19, 1995 but Bulls were eliminated by Orlando in second round of playoffs later that season; led Bulls to NBA titles for the next three years for 6 titles in all (1991-93,96-98); retired in 1999 (see p. 350).

Florence Griffith Joyner (b. Dec. 21, 1959, d. Sept. 21, 1998): Track & Field; set world records in 100 and 200 meters in 1988; won 3 gold medals at '88 Olympics (100m, 200m, 4x100m relay); Sullivan Award winner (1988); retired in 1989; named as co-chairperson of President's Council on Physical Fitness and Sports in 1993; sister-in-law of Jackie Joyner-Kersee; died of suffocation during an epileptic seizure in 1998.

Jackie Joyner-Kersee (b. Mar. 3, 1962): Track & Field; 2-time world champion in both long jump (1987,91) and heptathlon (1987,93); won heptathlon gold medals at 1988 and '92 Olympics and LJ gold at '88 Games; also won Olympic silver (1984) in heptathlon and bronze (1992,96) in LJ; Sullivan Award winner (1986); only woman to receive The Sporting News Man of Year award.

Sonny Jurgensen (b. Aug. 23, 1934): Football QB; played 18 seasons with Philadelphia and Washington; led NFL in passing twice (1967,69); All-Pro in 1961; 255 career TD passes.

Duke Kahanamoku (b. Aug. 24, 1890, d. Jan. 22, 1968): Swimmer; won 3 gold medals and 2 silver over 3 Olympics (1912,20,24); also surfing pioneer.

Al Kaline (b. Dec. 19, 1934): Baseball; youngest player (at age 20) to win batting title (led AL with .340 in 1955); had 3,007 hits, 399 HRs in 22 years with Detroit.

Anatoly Karpov (b. May 23, 1951): Chess; Soviet world champion from 1975-85; regained International Chess Federation (FIDE) version of championship in 1993 when countryman Garry Kasparov was stripped of title after forming new Professional Chess Association; held FIDE title until 1999.

Garry Kasparov (b. Apr. 13, 1963): Chess; Azerbaijani who became youngest player (22 years, 210 days) ever to win world championship as Soviet in 1985; defeated countryman Anatoly Karpov for title; split with International Chess Federation (FIDE) to form Professional Chess Association (PCA) in 1993; stripped of FIDE title in '93 but successfully defended PCA title against Briton Nigel Short; beat IBM supercomputer "Deep Blue" 4 games to 2 in 1996 much-publicized match in New York; lost rematch to computer in 1997.

Ewing Kauffman (b. Sept. 21, 1916, d. Aug. 1, 1993): Baseball; pharmaceutical billionaire and long-time owner of Kansas City Royals; Royals Stadium renamed for Kauffman on July 2, 1993, one month before his death.

Mike Keenan (b. Oct. 21, 1949): Hockey; coach who finally led NY Rangers to Stanley Cup title in 1994 after 53 unsuccessful years; quit a month later in pay dispute and signed with St. Louis as coach-GM; since moved on to Vancouver; left coaching in 1999 tied for fifth all-time with 597 wins (including playoffs).

Kipchoge (Kip) Keino (b. Jan. 17, 1940): Kenyan runner; policeman who beat USA's Jim Ryun to win 1,500m gold medal at 1968 Olympics; won again in steeplechase at 1972 Summer Games; his success spawned long line of international distance champions from Kenya.

Johnny Kelley (b. Sept. 6, 1907): Distance runner; ran in his 61st and final Boston Marathon at age 84 in 1992, finishing in 5:58:36; won Boston twice (1935,45) and was 2nd 7 times.

Jim Kelly (b. Feb. 14, 1960): Football QB; led Buffalo to four consecutive Super Bowl appearances, and is only QB to lose four times; named to AFC Pro Bowl team 5 times.

Walter Kennedy (b. June 8, 1912, d. June 26, 1977): Basketball; 2nd NBA commissioner (1963-75); league doubled in size to 18 teams during his term of office.

Nancy Kerrigan (b. Oct. 13, 1969): Figure skating; 1993 U.S. women's champion and Olympic medalist in 1992 (bronze) and '94 (silver); victim of Jan. 6, 1994 assault at U.S. nationals in Detroit when Shane Stant clubbed her in right knee with metal baton after a practice session; conspiracy hatched by Jeff Gillooly, ex-husband of rival Tonya Harding; although unable to compete in nationals, she quickly recovered and was granted berth on Olympic team; finished 2nd in Lillehammer to Oksana Baiul of Ukraine by a 5-4 judges' vote.

Billy Kidd (b. Apr. 13, 1943): Skiing; the first great Amercian male Alpine skier; first American male to win an Olympic medal when he won a silver in the slalom and a bronze in the Alpine combined in 1964; competed respectably with the great Jean-Claude Killy; won the world Alpine combined event in 1970, which was the first world championship for an American male.

Harmon Killebrew (b. June 29, 1936): Baseball 3B-1B; led AL in HRs 6 times and RBI 3 times; MVP in 1969 with Minnesota; 573 career homers ranks him fifth all-time.

Jean-Claude Killy (b. Aug. 30, 1943): French alpine skier; 2-time World Cup champion (1967-68); won 3 gold medals at 1968 Olympics in Grenoble; co-president of 1992 Winter Games in Albertville.

Ralph Kiner (b. Oct. 27, 1922): Baseball OF; led NL in home runs 7 straight years (1946-52) with Pittsburgh; 369 career HRs and 1,015 RBI in 10 seasons; long-time NY Mets announcer.

Betsy King (b. Aug. 13, 1955): Golfer; 2-time LPGA Player of Year (1984,89); 3-time winner of Dinah Shore (1987,90,97) and 2-time winner of U.S. Open (1989,90); 31 overall Tour wins; member of LPGA Hall of Fame; Tour's all-time leading money winner with $6.3 million in earnings as of Sept. 1999.

Billie Jean King (b. Nov. 22, 1943): Tennis; women's rights pioneer; Wimbledon singles champ 6 times; U.S. champ 4 times; first woman athlete to earn $100,000 in one year (1971); beat 55-year-old Bobby Riggs 6-4,6-3,6-3, in "Battle of the Sexes" to win $100,000 at Astrodome in 1973.

Don King (b. Aug. 20, 1931): Boxing promoter; first major black promoter who controlled heavyweight title from 1978-90 while Larry Holmes and Mike Tyson were champions; first big promotion was Muhammad Ali's fight against George Foreman in 1974; former numbers operator who served 4 years for manslaughter (1967-70); acquitted of tax evasion and fraud in 1985; regained control of heavyweight title in 1994 with wins by Oliver McCall (WBC) and Bruce Seldon (WBA); also promoted Evander Holyfield, Roberto Duran and Julio Cesar Chavez among others; also famous for his gravity-defying hairstyle and his catchphrase "Only in America!"

Karch Kiraly (b. Nov. 3, 1960): Volleyball; USA's preeminent volleyball player; led UCLA to three NCAA championships (1979,81,82); played on US national teams that won Olympic gold medals in 1984 and '88, world championships in '82 and '86; won the inaugural gold medal for Olympic beach volleyball with Kent Steffes in 1996.

Tom Kite (b. Dec. 9, 1949): Golfer; entered 1999 as 3rd on all-time PGA Tour money list with over $10 million; finally won 1st major with victory in 1992 U.S. Open at Pebble Beach; co-NCAA champion with Ben Crenshaw (1972); PGA Rookie of Year (1973); PGA Player of Year (1989); captain of losing 1997 US Ryder Cup team; 17 career PGA wins.

Gene Klein (b. Jan. 29, 1921, d. Mar. 12, 1990): Horseman; won 3 Eclipse awards as top owner (1985-87); his filly Winning Colors won 1988 Kentucky Derby; also owned San Diego Chargers football team (1966-84).

Bob Knight (b. Oct. 25, 1940): Basketball; has coached Indiana to 3 NCAA titles (1976,81,87); 3-time Coach of Year (1975-76,89); coached 1984 U.S. Olympic team to gold medal; 6th on all-time NCAA list with 743 wins in 34 years.

Phil Knight (b. Feb. 24, 1938): Founder and chairman of Nike, Inc., the multi-billion dollar shoe and fitness company founded in 1972 and based in Beaverton, Ore.; stable of endorsees includes Michael Jordan, Tiger Woods and Brazilian soccer phenom Ronaldo; named "The Most Powerful Man in Sports" by The Sporting News in 1992.

Bill Koch (b. June 7, 1955): Cross-country skiing; first highly accomplished American male in his sport; first American male to win a cross-country Olympic medal when he took home a silver in the 30-kilometer race in 1976; in 1982, he was the first American male to win the Nordic World Cup.

Olga Korbut (b. May 16, 1955): Soviet gymnast; 3 gold medals at 1972 Olympics; first to perform back somersault on balance beam.

Johann Olav Koss (b. Oct. 29, 1968): Norwegian speedskater; won three gold medals at 1994 Olympics in Lillehammer with world records in the 1,500m, 5,000m and 10,000m; also won 1,500m gold and 10,000m silver in 1992 Games; retired shortly after '94 Olympics.

Sandy Koufax (b. Dec. 30, 1935): Baseball LHP; led NL in strikeouts 4 times and ERA 5 straight years; won 3 Cy Young Awards (1963,65,66) with LA Dodgers; MVP in 1963; 2-time World Series MVP (1963, 65); threw perfect game against Chicago Cubs (1-0, Sept. 9, 1965) and had 3 other no-hitters in career.

Alvin Kraenzlein (b. Dec. 12, 1876, d. Jan. 6, 1928): Track & Field; won 4 individual gold medals in 1900 Olympics (60m, long jump and the 110m and 200m hurdles).

Ingrid Kristiansen (b. Mar. 21, 1956): Norwegian runner; 2-time Boston Marathon winner (1986,89); won New York City Marathon in 1989; former world record holder in the marathon.

Julie Krone (b. July 24, 1963): Jockey; only woman to ride winning horse in a Triple Crown race when she captured Belmont Stakes aboard Colonial Affair in 1993; retired in 1999 as all-time winningest female jockey with over 3,000 wins.

Mike Krzyzewski (b. Feb. 13, 1947): Basketball; has coached Duke to 8 Final Four appearances; won consecutive NCAA titles in 1991 and '92; missed most of 1994-95 season with a back injury and stress-related exhaustion; 24-year record of 547-214.

Bowie Kuhn (b. Oct. 28, 1926): Baseball Commissioner; Elected commissioner on Feb. 4, 1969 and served until Sept. 30, 1984; kept Willie Mays and Mickey Mantle out of baseball for their employment with casinos; handed down one-year suspensions of several players for drug involvement; nixed Charlie Finley's sale of three players for $3.5 million; baseball enjoyed unprecedented attendance and television contracts during his reign.

Alan Kulwicki (b. Dec. 14, 1954, d. Apr. 1, 1993): Auto racer; 1992 NASCAR national champion; 1st college grad and Northerner to win title; NASCAR Rookie of Year in 1986; famous for driving car backwards on victory lap; killed at age 38 in plane crash near Bristol, Tenn.

Michelle Kwan (b. July 7, 1980): Figure Skater; 1998 Olympic silver medalist at Nagano; U.S. Champion (1996,98,99) and World Champ (1996,98); was U.S. alternate to the Olympics in 1994 as a 13-year-old.

Marion Ladewig (b. Oct. 30, 1914): Bowler; named Woman Bowler of the Year 9 times (1950-54,57-59,63).

Guy Lafleur (b. Sept. 20, 1951): Hockey RW; led NHL in scoring 3 times (1976-78); 2-time MVP (1977-78), played for 5 Stanley Cup winners in Montreal; playoff MVP in 1977; returned to NHL as player in 1988 after election to Hall of Fame; retired again in 1991 with 560 goals and 1,353 points.

Napoleon (Nap) Lajoie (b. Sept. 5, 1874, d. Feb. 7, 1959): Baseball 2B; led AL in batting 3 times (1901,03-04); batted .422 in 1901; hit .339 for career with 3,251 hits.

Jack Lambert (b. July 8, 1952): Football LB; 6-time All-Pro (1975-76,79-82); led Pittsburgh to 4 Super Bowl titles.

Kenesaw Mountain Landis (b. Nov. 20, 1866, d. Nov. 25, 1944): U.S. District Court judge who became first baseball commissioner (1920-44); banned eight Chicago Black Sox from baseball for life.

Tom Landry (b. Sept. 11, 1924): Football; All-Pro DB for NY Giants (1954); coached Dallas for 29 years (1960-88); won 2 Super Bowls (1972,78); 3rd on NFL all-time list with 270 wins.

Steve Largent (b. Sept. 28, 1954): Football WR; retired in 1989 after 14 years in Seattle with then NFL records in passes caught (819) and TD passes caught (100); elected to U.S. House of Representatives (R, Okla.) in 1994 and Pro Football Hall of Fame in '95.

Don Larsen (b. Aug. 7, 1929): Baseball RHP; NY Yankees hurler who pitched the only perfect game in World Series history— a 2-0 victory over Brooklyn in Game 5 of the 1956 Series (Oct. 8); Series MVP that year; had career record of 81-91 in 14 seasons with 6 clubs.

Tommy Lasorda (b. Sept. 22, 1927): Baseball; managed LA Dodgers to 2 World Series titles (1981,88) in 4 appearances; retired as manager during 1996 season with 1,599 regular-season wins in 21 years; named interim GM of Dodgers in 1998; member of Baseball Hall of Fame.

Larissa Latynina (b. Dec. 27, 1934): Soviet gymnast; won total of 18 medals, (9 gold) in 3 Olympics (1956,60,64).

Nikki Lauda (b. Feb. 22, 1949): Austrian auto racer; 3-time world Formula One champion (1975,77,84); 25 career wins from 1971-85.

Rod Laver (b. Aug. 9, 1938): Australian tennis player; only player to win Grand Slam twice (1962,69); Wimbledon champion 4 times; 1st to earn $1 million in prize money.

Bobby Layne (b. Dec. 19, 1926, d. Dec. 1, 1986): Football QB; college star at Texas; master of 2-minute offense; led Detroit to 4 divisional titles and 3 NFL championships in 1950s.

Frank Leahy (b. Aug. 27, 1908, d. June 21, 1973): Football; coached Notre Dame to four national titles (1943,46-47,49); career record of 107-13-9 for a winning pct. of .864.

Jacques Lemaire (b. Sept. 7, 1945): Hockey C; member of 8 Stanley Cup champions in Montreal; scored 366 goals in 12 seasons; coached Canadiens from 1983-85; directed New Jersey Devils to surprising 4-game sweep of Detroit to win 1995 Stanley Cup.

Mario Lemieux (b. Oct. 5, 1965): Hockey C; 6-time NHL scoring leader (1988-89,92-93,96,97); Rookie of Year (1985); 3-time regular season MVP (1988,93,96); 3-time All-Star Game MVP; led Pittsburgh to consecutive Stanley Cup titles (1991 and '92); won 1993 scoring title despite missing 24 games to undergo radiation treatments for Hodgkin's disease; missed 62 games during 1993-94 season and entire 94-95 season due to back injuries and fatigue; returned in 1995-96 to lead NHL in scoring and win the MVP trophy; retired after 1996-97 season and inducted into the Hall of Fame; headed group of investors that bought bankrupt Penguins in 1999.

Greg LeMond (b. June 26, 1961): Cyclist; 3-time Tour de France winner (1986,89-90); only non-European to win the event until Lance Armstrong in 1999; retired in Dec. 1994 after being diagnosed with a rare muscular disease known as mitochondrial myopathy.

Ivan Lendl (b. Mar. 7, 1960): Czech tennis player; No. 1 player in world 4 times (1985-87,89); has won both French and U.S. Opens 3 times and Australian twice; owns 94 career tournament wins.

Suzanne Lenglen (b. May 24, 1899, d. July 4, 1938): French tennis player; dominated women's tennis from 1919-26; won both Wimbledon and French singles titles 6 times.

Sugar Ray Leonard (b. May 17, 1956): Boxer; light welterweight Olympic champ (1976); won world welterweight title 1979 and four more titles; retired after losing to Terry Norris on Feb. 9, 1991, with record of 36-2-1 and 25 KOs; misguided comeback in 1997 resulted in resounding defeat by Hector Camacho.

Walter (Buck) Leonard (b. Sept. 8, 1907, d. Nov. 27, 1997): Baseball 1B; won Negro League championship nine years in a row behind the Homestead Grays; hit .391 in 1948 to lead the league; usually batted cleanup behind Josh Gibson; retired at the age of 48; member of the National Baseball Hall of Fame.

Marv Levy (b. Aug. 3, 1928): Football; coached Buffalo to four consecutive Super Bowls, but is one of two coaches who are 0-4 (Bud Grant is the other); won 50 games and two CFL Grey Cups with Montreal (1974,77).

Bill Lewis (b. Nov. 30, 1868, d. Jan. 1, 1949): Football; college star at Amherst College and then Harvard; first black player to be selected as an All-American (1892-93); also the first black admitted to the American Bar Association (1911); was U.S. Assistant Attorney General.

Carl Lewis (b. July 1, 1961): Track & Field; won 9 Olympic gold medals; 4 in 1984 (100m, 200m, 4x100m, LJ), 2 in '88 (100m, LJ), 2 in '92 (4x100m, LJ) and 1 in '96 (LJ); has record 8 World Championship titles and 9 medals in all; Sullivan Award winner (1981); two-time AP Male Athlete of the Year (1983-84).

Lennox Lewis (b. Sept. 2, 1965): British boxer; won 1988 Olympic super heavyweight gold medal for Canada; WBC heavyweight champion whose apparent win over IBF champ Evander Holyfield on Mar. 13, 1999 was controversially ruled a draw; pro record of 34-1-1 (27 KOs) as of Sept. 21, 1999.

Nancy Lieberman-Cline (b. July 1, 1958): Basketball; 3-time All-America and 2-time Player of Year (1979-80); led Old Dominion to consecutive AIAW titles in 1979 and '80; played in defunct WPBL and WABA and became 1st woman to play in men's pro league (USBL) in 1986; played in the inaugural season of the WNBA for the Phoenix Mercury and named coach/GM of Detroit Shock in '98.

Eric Lindros (b. Feb. 28, 1973): Hockey C; No. 1 pick in 1991 NHL draft by the Nordiques; sat out 1991-92 season rather than play in Quebec; traded to Philadelphia in 1992 for 6 players, 2 No. 1 picks and $15 million; elected Flyers captain at age 22; won Hart Trophy as league MVP in 1995.

Tara Lipinski (b. June 10, 1982): Figure Skater; won the 1998 women's figure skating gold medal at the Olympics in Nagano, becoming the youngest in history (15 yrs., 7 mos.) to do so; she and Michelle Kwan gave the U.S. its first 1-2 finish in that event since 1956; 1997 U.S. and World champion; turned pro in April 1998.

Sonny Liston (b. May 8, 1932, d. Dec. 30, 1970): Boxer; heavyweight champion (1962-64), who knocked out Floyd Patterson twice in the first round, then lost title to Muhammad Ali (then Cassius Clay) in 1964; pro record of 50-4 with 39 KOs.

Rebecca Lobo (b. Oct. 6, 1973): Basketball F; women's college basketball Player of the Year in 1995; led Connecticut to undefeated season (35-0) and national title; member of 1996 U.S. Olympic team; helped lead NY Liberty to WNBA's first championship game in 1997 but lost to Houston Comets.

Vince Lombardi (b. June 11, 1913, d. Sept. 3, 1970): Football; coached Green Bay to 5 NFL titles; won first 2 Super Bowls (1967-68); died as NFL's all-time winningest coach with percentage of .740 (105-35-6); Super Bowl trophy named in his honor.

Johnny Longden (b. Feb. 14, 1907): Jockey; first to win 6,000 races; rode Count Fleet to Triple Crown in 1943.

Nancy Lopez (b. Jan. 6, 1957): Golfer; 4-time LPGA Player of the Year (1978-79,85,88); Rookie of Year (1977); 3-time winner of LPGA Championship; reached Hall of Fame by age 30 with 35 victories; 48 career wins.

Donna Lopiano (b. Sept. 11, 1946): Former basketball and softball star who was women's athletic director at Texas for 18 years before leaving to become executive director of Women's Sports Foundation in 1992.

Greg Louganis (b. Jan. 29, 1960): U.S. diver; won platform and springboard gold medals at both 1984 and '88 Olympics; revealed on Feb. 22, 1995 that he has AIDS.

Joe Louis (b. May 13, 1914, d. Apr. 12, 1981): Boxer; world heavyweight champion from June 22, 1937 to Mar. 1, 1949; his reign of 11 years, 8 months longest in division history; successfully defended title 25 times; retired in 1949, but returned to lose title shot against successor Ezzard Charles in 1950 and then to Rocky Marciano in '51; pro record of 63-3 with 49 KOs.

Sid Luckman (b. Nov. 21, 1916, d. July 5, 1998): Football QB; 6-time All-Pro; led Chicago Bears to 4 NFL titles (1940-41,43,46); MVP in 1943.

Hank Luisetti (b. June 16, 1916): Basketball F; 3-time All-America at Stanford (1935-38); revolutionized game with one-handed shot.

Johnny Lujack (b. Jan. 4, 1925): Football QB; led Notre Dame to three national titles (1943,46-47); won Heisman Trophy in 1947.

Darrell Wayne Lukas (b. Sept. 2, 1935): Horse racing; 4-time Eclipse-winning trainer who saddled Horses of Year Lady's Secret in 1988 and Criminal Type in 1990; first trainer to earn over $100 million in purses; led nation in earnings 11 times from 1983-94; Grindstone's Kentucky Derby win in 1996 gave him six Triple Crown wins in a row; has won Preakness 5 times, Kentucky Derby 4 times and Belmont 3 times.

Gen. Douglas MacArthur (b. Jan. 26, 1880, d. Apr. 5, 1964): Controversial U.S. general of World War II and Korea; president of U.S. Olympic Committee (1927-28); college football devotee, National Football Foundation MacArthur Bowl named after him.

Connie Mack (b. Dec. 22, 1862, d. Feb. 8, 1956): Baseball owner; managed Philadelphia A's until he was 87 (1901-50); all-time major league wins leader with 3,755, including World Series; won 9 AL pennants and 5 World Series (1910-11,13,29-30); also finished last 17 times.

Andy MacPhail (b. Apr. 5, 1953): Baseball; Chicago Cubs president, who was GM of 2 World Series champions in Minnesota (1987,91); won first title at age 34; son of Lee, grandson of Larry.

Larry MacPhail (b. Feb. 3, 1890, d. Oct. 1, 1975): Baseball executive and innovator; introduced major leagues to night games at Cincinnati (May 24, 1935); won pennant in Brooklyn (1941) and World Series with NY Yankees (1947); father of Lee.

Lee MacPhail (b. Oct. 25, 1917): Baseball; AL president (1974-83); president of owners' Player Relations Committee (1984-85); also GM of Baltimore (1959-65) and NY Yankees (1967-74); son of Larry and father of Andy.

John Madden (b. Apr. 10, 1936): Football and Radio-TV; won 112 games and a Super Bowl (1976 season) as coach of Oakland Raiders; has won 11 Emmy Awards since 1982 as NFL analyst with CBS and Fox; signed 4-year, $32 million deal with Fox in 1994— a richer contract than any NFL player at the time.

Greg Maddux (b. Apr. 14, 1966): Baseball RHP; won unprecedented 4 straight NL Cy Young Awards with Cubs (1992) and Atlanta (1993-95); has led NL in ERA four times (1993-95,98); won 9th straight gold glove in 1998.

Phil Mahre (b. May 10, 1957): Alpine skier; 3-time World Cup overall champ (1981-83); finished 1-2 with twin brother Steve in 1984 Olympic slalom.

Karl Malone (b. July 24, 1963): Basketball F; 11-time All-NBA 1st team (1989-99) with Utah; member of the 1992 and '96 Olympic Dream Teams; 2-time NBA MVP (1997,99); named one of the NBA's 50 greatest players.

Moses Malone (b. Mar. 23, 1955): Basketball C; signed with Utah of ABA at age 19; led NBA in rebounding 6 times; 4-time All-NBA 1st team; 3-time NBA MVP (1979,82-83); Finals MVP with Philadelphia in 1983; played in 21st pro season in 1994-95.

Nigel Mansell (b. Aug. 8, 1953): British auto racer; won 1992 Formula One driving championship with record 9 victories and 14 poles; quit Grand Prix circuit to race Indy cars in 1993; 1st rookie to win IndyCar title; 3rd driver to win IndyCar and F1 titles; returned to F1 after 1994 IndyCar season and won '94 Australian Grand Prix; left F1 again on May 23, 1995 with 31 wins and 32 poles in 15 years.

Mickey Mantle (b. Oct. 20, 1931, d. Aug. 13, 1995): Baseball OF; led AL in home runs 4 times; won Triple Crown in 1956; hit 52 HRs in 1956 and 54 in '61; 3-time MVP (1956-57,62); hit 536 career HRs; played in 12 World Series with NY Yankees and won 7 times; all-time Series leader in HRs (18), RBI (40), runs (42) and strikeouts (54).

Diego Maradona (b. Oct. 30, 1960): Soccer F; captain and MVP of 1986 World Cup champion Argentina; also led national team to 1990 World Cup final; consensus Player of Decade in 1980s; led Napoli to 2 Italian League titles (1987,90) and UEFA Cup (1989); tested positive for cocaine and suspended 15 months by FIFA in 1991; returned to World Cup as Argentine captain in 1994, but was kicked out of tournament after two games when doping test found 5 banned substances in his urine.

Pete Maravich (b. June 27, 1947, d. Jan. 5, 1988): Basketball; NCAA scoring leader 3 times at LSU (1968-70); averaged NCAA-record 44.2 points a game over career; Player of Year in 1970; NBA scoring champ in '77 with New Orleans.

Alice Marble (b. Sept. 28, 1913, d. Dec. 13, 1990): Tennis; 4-time U.S. champion (1936,38-40); won Wimbledon in 1939; swept U.S. singles, doubles and mixed doubles from 1938-40.

Rocky Marciano (b. Sept. 1, 1923, d. Aug. 31, 1969): Boxer; heavyweight champion (1952-56); retired undefeated; pro record of 49-0 with 43 KOs; killed in plane crash in Iowa.

Juan Marichal (b. Oct. 20, 1938): Baseball RHP; won 21 or more games 6 times for S.F. Giants from 1963-69; ended 16-year career at 243-142.

Dan Marino (b. Sept. 15, 1961): Football QB; 4-time leading passer in AFC (1983-84,86,89); set NFL single-season records for TD passes (48) and passing yards (5,084) with Miami in 1984; all-time leader in career TD passes, passing yards, attempts and completions.

Roger Maris (b. Sept. 10, 1934, d. Dec. 14, 1985): Baseball OF; broke Babe Ruth's season HR record with 61 in 1961; 2-time AL MVP (1960-61) with NY Yankees; 275 HRs in 12 years.

Billy Martin (b. May 16, 1928, d. Dec. 25, 1989): Baseball; 5-time manager of NY Yankees; won 2 pennants and 1 World Series (1977); also managed Minnesota, Detroit, Texas and Oakland; played on 5 Yankee world champions in 1950s.

Pedro Martinez (b. Oct. 25, 1971): Baseball RHP; one of baseball's premier pitchers; won 1997 NL Cy Young award with Montreal; traded to Boston Red Sox on Nov. 18, 1997 for pitchers Carl Pavano and Tony Armas; won AL pitching Triple Crown with Boston in 1999.

Eddie Mathews (b. Oct. 13, 1931): Baseball 3B; led NL in HRs twice (1953,59); hit 30 or more home runs 9 straight years; 512 career HRs.

Christy Mathewson (b. Aug. 12, 1880, d. Oct. 7, 1925): Baseball RHP; won 22 or more games 12 straight years (1903-14); 373 career wins; pitched 3 shutouts in 1905 World Series.

Bob Mathias (b. Nov. 17, 1930): Track & Field; youngest winner of decathlon with gold medal in 1948 Olympics at age 17; first to repeat as decathlon champ in 1952; Sullivan Award winner (1948); 4-term member of U.S. Congress (R, Calif.) from 1967-74.

Ollie Matson (b. May 1, 1930): Football HB; All-America at San Francisco (1951); bronze medal winner in 400m at 1952 Olympics; 4-time All-Pro for NFL Chicago Cardinals (1954-57); traded to LA Rams for 9 players in 1959; accounted for 12,884 all-purpose yards and scored 73 TDs in 14 seasons.

Don Mattingly (b. Apr. 20, 1961): Baseball 1B; American League MVP (1985); won AL batting title in 1984 (.343) and led AL with 207 hits and 44 doubles; led majors with 145 RBI in 1985; led AL with 238 hits (Yankee record), 53 doubles and a .573 slugging percentage in 1986; won 9 Gold Glove Awards (1985-89, 91-94); back injury shortened career.

Willie Mays (b. May 6, 1931): Baseball OF; nicknamed the "Say Hey Kid"; led NL in HRs and stolen bases 4 times each; 2-time MVP (1954,65) with NY-SF Giants; Hall of Famer who played in 24 All-Star Games; 660 HRs and 3,283 hits in career.

Bill Mazeroski (b. Sept. 5, 1936): Baseball 2B; career .260 hitter who won the 1960 World Series for Pittsburgh with a lead-off HR in the bottom of the 9th inning of Game 7; the pitcher was Ralph Terry of the NY Yankees, the count was 1-0 and the score was tied 9-9; also a sure-fielder, Maz won 8 Gold Gloves in 17 seasons.

Bob McAdoo (b. Sept. 25, 1951): Basketball F/C; 1972 *Sporting News* First Team All-American; NBA Rookie of the Year (1973); NBA MVP (1975); All-NBA First Team (1975); Led NBA in scoring three consecutive years (1974-76); 5-time All-Star (1974-78); two championships with LA Lakers (1982,85).

Joe McCarthy (b. Apr. 21, 1887, d. Jan. 13, 1978): Baseball; first manager to win pennants in both leagues (Chicago Cubs in 1929 and NY Yankees in 1932); greatest success came with Yankees when he won seven pennants and six World Series championships from 1936 to 1943; first manager to win four World Series in a row (1936-39); finished his career with the Boston Red Sox (1948-'50); lifetime record of 2125-1333; member of Baseball Hall of Fame.

Pat McCormick (b. May 12, 1930): U.S. diver; won women's platform and springboard gold medals in both 1952 and '56 Olympics.

Willie McCovey (b. Jan. 10, 1938): Baseball 1B; led NL in HRs 3 times and RBI twice; MVP in 1969 with SF; 521 career HRs; indicted for tax evasion in July 1995, pled guilty.

John McEnroe (b. Feb. 16, 1959): Tennis; No.1 player in the world 4 times (1981-84); 4-time U.S. Open champ (1979-81,84); 3-time Wimbledon champ (1981,83-84); played on 5 Davis Cup winners (1978,79,81,82,92); won NCAA singles title (1978); finished career with 77 singles championships, 77 more in men's doubles (including 9 Grand Slam titles), and U.S. Davis Cup records for years played (13) and singles matches won (41).

John McGraw (b. Apr. 7, 1873, d. Feb. 25, 1934): Baseball; managed NY Giants to 9 NL pennants between 1905-24; won 3 World Series (1905,21-22); 2nd on all-time career list with 2,810 wins in 33 seasons (2,784 regular season and 26 World Series).

Frank McGuire (b. Nov. 8, 1916, d. Oct. 11, 1994): Basketball; winner of 731 games as high school, college and pro coach; only coach to win 100 games at 3 colleges — St. John's (103), North Carolina (164) and South Carolina (283); won 550 games in 30 college seasons; 1957 UNC team went 32-0 and beat Kansas 54-53 in triple OT to win NCAA title; coached NBA Philadelphia Warriors to 49-31 record in 1961-62 season, but refused to move with team to San Francisco.

Mark McGwire (b. Oct. 1, 1963): Baseball 1B; *Sporting News* college player of the year (1984); Member of 1984 U.S. Olympic baseball team; won AL Rookie of the Year and hit rookie-record 49 HRs in 1987; broke Roger Maris' season home run record (61) in 1998 with St. Louis finishing with 70; only player with at least 50 HRs in 4 straight seasons.

Jim McKay (b. Sept. 24, 1921): Radio-TV; host and commentator of ABC's Olympic coverage and "Wide World of Sports" show since 1961; 12-time Emmy winner; also given Peabody Award in 1988 and Life Achievement Emmy in 1990; became part owner of Baltimore Orioles in 1993.

John McKay (b. July 5, 1923): Football; coached USC to 3 national titles (1962,67,72); won Rose Bowl 5 times; reached NFL playoffs 3 times with Tampa Bay.

Tamara McKinney (b. Oct. 16, 1962): Skiing; first American woman to win overall Alpine World Cup championship (1983); won World Cup slalom (1984) and giant slalom titles twice (1981,83).

Denny McLain (b. Mar. 29, 1944): Baseball RHP; last pitcher to win 30 games (1968); 2-time Cy Young winner (1968-69) with Detroit; convicted of racketeering, extortion and drug possession in 1985, served 29 months of 25-year jail term, sentence overturned when court ruled he had not received a fair trial; he has faced subsequent legal troubles.

Rick Mears (b. Dec. 3, 1951): Auto racer; 3-time CART national champ (1979,81-82); 4-time winner of Indy 500 (1979,84,88,91) and only driver to win 6 Indy 500 poles; Indy 500 Rookie of Year (1978); retired after 1992 season with 29 CART wins and 40 poles.

Mark Messier (b. Jan. 18, 1961): Hockey C; 2-time NHL MVP with Edmonton (1990) and NY Rangers (1992); captain of 1994 Rangers team that won 1st Stanley Cup since 1940; ranks 2nd in all-time playoff points and assists; signed free agent contract with Vancouver Canucks in 1997.

Anne Meyers (b. Mar. 26, 1955): Basketball G; In 1974, became first high school student to play for U.S. national team; 4-time All-American at UCLA (1976-79); member of 1976 U.S. Olympic team; Broderick Award and Cup winner (1978); Signed $50,000 no cut contract with NBA's Indiana Pacers (1980); married Dodger great Don Drysdale.

George Mikan (b. June 18, 1924): Basketball C; 3-time All-America (1944-46); led DePaul to NIT title (1945); led Minneapolis Lakers to 5 NBA titles in 6 years (1949-54); first commissioner of ABA (1967-69).

Stan Mikita (b. May 20, 1940): Hockey C; led NHL in scoring 4 times; won both MVP and Lady Byng awards in 1967 and '68 with Chicago.

Cheryl Miller (b. Jan. 3, 1964): Basketball; 3-time College Player of Year (1984-86); led USC to NCAA title and U.S. to Olympic gold medal in 1984; coached USC to 44-14 record in 2 seasons before quitting to join Turner Sports as NBA reporter; coach/GM of WNBA's Phoenix Mercury; sister of NBA star Reggie Miller.

Del Miller (b. July 5, 1913): Harness racing; driver, trainer, owner, breeder, seller and track owner; drove to 2,441 wins from 1939-90.

Marvin Miller (b. Apr. 14, 1917): Baseball labor leader; executive director of Players' Assn. from 1966-82; increased average salary from $19,000 to over $240,000; led 13-day strike in 1972 and 50-day walkout in '81.

Tommy Moe (b. Feb. 17, 1970): Alpine skier; won Downhill gold and Super-G silver at 1994 Winter Olympics; 1st U.S. man to win 2 Olympic alpine medals in one year.

Joe Montana (b. June 11, 1956): Football QB; led Notre Dame to national title in 1977; led San Francisco to 4 Super Bowl titles in 1980s; only 3-time Super Bowl MVP; 2-time NFL MVP (1989-90); led NFL in passing 5 times; traded to Kansas City in 1993; ranks 2nd in all-time passing efficiency (92.3), 6th in TD passes (273) and yards passing (40,551).

Helen Wills Moody (b. Oct. 6, 1905, d. Jan. 1, 1998): Tennis; won 8 Wimbledon singles titles, 7 U.S. and 4 French from 1923-38.

Warren Moon (b. Nov. 18, 1956): Football QB; MVP of 1978 Rose Bowl with Washington; MVP of CFL with Edmonton in 1983; led Eskimos to 5 consecutive Grey Cup titles (1978-82) and was playoff MVP twice (1980,82); entered NFL in 1984 and has played for four different teams; picked for 9 Pro Bowls including a QB-record 8 staight (1988-95).

Archie Moore (b. Dec. 13, 1913, d. Dec. 9, 1998): Boxer; world light-heavyweight champion (1952-60); pro record 199-26-8 with a record 145 KOs.

Michael Moorer (b. Nov. 12, 1967): Boxer; became first left-hander to win heavyweight title when he scored majority decision over Evander Holyfield on Apr. 22, 1994; lost title to George Foreman on 10th round KO Nov. 5, 1994; won IBF belt in 1996, defended it twice before losing it to Holyfield on Nov. 8, 1997; pro record of 39-2 with 31 KOs.

Noureddine Morceli (b. Feb. 28, 1970): Algerian runner; 3-time world champion at 1,500 meters (1991,93,95); former holder of world records in several middle distance events.

Howie Morenz (b. June 21, 1902, d. Mar. 8, 1937): Hockey C; 3-time NHL MVP (1928,31,32); led Montreal Canadiens to 3 Stanley Cups; voted Outstanding Player of the Half-Century in 1950.

Joe Morgan (b. Sept. 19, 1943): Baseball 2B; led NL in walks 4 times; regular-season MVP both years he led Cincinnati to World Series titles (1975-76); 4th behind Babe Ruth, Ted Williams and Rickey Henderson in career walks with 1,865.

Bobby Morrow (b. Oct. 15, 1935): Track & Field; won 3 gold medals at 1956 Olympics (100m, 200m and 4x400m relay).

Willie Mosconi (b. June 27, 1913, d. Sept. 12, 1993): Pocket Billiards; 14-time world champion from 1941-57.

Annemarie Moser-Pröll (b. Mar. 27, 1953): Austrian alpine skier; won World Cup overall title 6 times (1971-75,79); all-time women's World Cup leader in career wins with 61; won Downhill in 1980 Olympics.

Edwin Moses (b. Aug. 31, 1955): Track & Field; won 400m hurdles at 1976 and '84 Olympics, bronze medal in '88; also winner of 122 consecutive races from 1977-87.

Marion Motley (b. June 5, 1920, d. June 27, 1999): Football FB; all-time leading AAFC rusher; rushed for over 4,700 yards and 31 TDs for Cleveland Browns (1946-53).

Rupert Murdoch (b. Mar. 11, 1931): Australian media magnate and Los Angeles Dodgers owner; Bought the Dodgers and Dodger Stadium on Mar. 19, 1998 for a reported $350 million.

Calvin Murphy (b. May 9, 1948): Basketball G; NBA All-Rookie team (1971); holds NBA single season free throw percentage (.958); third all-time career free throw pct. (.892); elected to Basketball Hall of Fame in 1992; though only 5'9'' and 165 pounds, he is regarded as one of the best guards ever.

Dale Murphy (b. Mar. 12, 1956): Baseball OF; led NL in RBI 3 times and HRs twice; 2-time MVP (1982-83) with Atlanta; also played with Philadelphia and Colorado; retired in 1993 with 398 HRs.

Jack Murphy (b. Feb. 5, 1923, d. Sept. 24, 1980): Sports editor and columnist of *The San Diego Union* from 1951-80; instrumental in bringing AFL Chargers south from LA in 1961, landing Padres as NL expansion team in '69; and lobbying for 54,000-seat San Diego stadium that would later bear his name.

Eddie Murray (b. Feb. 24, 1956): Baseball 1B-DH; AL Rookie of Year in 1977; became 20th player in history, but only 2nd switch hitter (after Pete Rose) to get 3,000 hits; one of only 3 men (Aaron and Mays) with 500 HRs and 3,000 hits.

Jim Murray (b. Dec. 29, 1919, d. Aug. 16, 1998): Sports columnist for *LA Times* 1961-98; 14-time Sportswriter of the Year; won Pulitzer Prize for commentary in 1990.

Ty Murray (b. Oct. 11, 1969): Rodeo cowboy; 6-time All-Around world champion (1989-94); Rookie of Year in 1988; youngest (age 20) to win All-Around title; set single season earnings mark with $297,896 in 1993; career shortened by injury.

Stan Musial (b. Nov. 21, 1920): Baseball OF-1B; led NL in batting 7 times; 3-time MVP (1943,46,48) with St. Louis; played in 24 All-Star Games; had 3,630 career hits and .331 average.

John Naber (b. Jan. 20, 1956): Swimmer; won 4 gold medals and a silver in 1976 Olympics.

Bronko Nagurski (b. Nov. 3, 1908, d. Jan. 7, 1990): Football FB-T; All-America at Minnesota (1929); All-Pro with Chicago Bears (1932-34); charter member of college and pro Halls of Fame.

James Naismith (b. Nov. 6, 1861, d. Nov. 28, 1939): Canadian physical education instructor who invented basketball in 1891 at the YMCA Training School (now Springfield College) in Springfield, Mass.

Joe Namath (b. May 31, 1943): Football QB; signed for unheard-of $400,000 as rookie with AFL's NY Jets in 1965; 2-time All-AFL (1968-69) and All-NFL (1972); led Jets to Super Bowl upset as MVP in '69.

Ilie Nastase (b. July 19, 1946): Romanian tennis player; No.1 in the world twice (1972-73); won U.S. (1972) and French (1973) Opens; has since entered Romanian politics.

Martina Navratilova (b. Oct. 18, 1956): Tennis player; No.1 player in the world 7 times (1978-79,82-86); won her record 9th Wimbledon singles title in 1990; also won 4 U.S. Opens, 3 Australian and 2 French; in all, won 18 Grand Slam singles titles and 37 Grand Slam doubles titles; retired as all-time leader among men and women in singles titles (167) and money won ($20.3 million) over 21 years.

Cosmas Ndeti (b. Nov. 24, 1971): Kenyan distance runner; winner of three consecutive Boston Marathons (1993-95), set course record of 2:07:15 in 1994.

Earle (Greasy) Neale (b. Nov. 5, 1891, d. Nov. 2, 1973): Baseball and Football; hit .357 for Cincinnati in 1919 World Series; also played with pre-NFL Canton Bulldogs; later coached Philadelphia Eagles to 2 NFL titles (1948-49).

Primo Nebiolo (b. July 14, 1923): Italian president of International Amateur Athletic Federation (IAAF) since 1981; also an at-large member of International Olympic Committee; regarded as dictatorial, but credited with elevating track & field to world class financial status.

Byron Nelson (b. Feb. 4, 1912): Golfer; 2-time winner of both Masters (1937,42) and PGA (1940,45); also U.S. Open champion in 1939; won 19 tournaments in 1945, including 11 in a row; also set all-time PGA stroke average with 68.33 strokes per round over 120 rounds in '45.

Lindsey Nelson (b. May 25, 1919, d. June 10, 1995): Radio-TV; all-purpose play-by-play broadcaster for CBS, NBC and others; 4-time Sportscaster of the Year (1959-62); voice of Cotton Bowl for 25 years and NY Mets from 1962-78; given Life Achievement Emmy Award in 1991.

Ernie Nevers (b. July 11, 1903, d. May 3, 1976): Football FB; earned 11 letters in four sports at Stanford; played pro football, baseball and basketball; scored 40 points for Chicago Cardinals in one NFL game (1929).

Paula Newby-Fraser (b. June 2, 1962): Zimbabwean triathlete; 8-time winner of Ironman Triathlon in Hawaii; established women's record of 8:55:28 in 1992.

John Newcombe (b. May 23, 1944): Australian tennis player; No.1 player in world 3 times (1967,70-71); won Wimbledon 3 times and U.S. and Australian championships twice each.

Pete Newell (b. Aug. 31, 1915): Basketball; coached at Univ. of San Francisco, Michigan St. and the Univ. of California; first coach to win NIT (San Francisco-1949), NCAA (California-1959) and Olympic gold medal (1960); later served as the general manager of the San Diego Rockets and LA Lakers in the NBA; member of Basketball Hall of Fame.

Bob Neyland (b. Feb. 17, 1892, d. Mar. 28, 1962): Football; 3-time coach at Tennessee; had 173-31-12 record in 21 years; won national title in 1951; Vols' stadium named for him; also Army general who won Distinguished Service Cross as supply officer in World War II.

Jack Nicklaus (b. Jan. 21, 1940): Golfer; all-time leader in major tournament wins with 20— including 6 Masters, 5 PGAs, 4 U.S. Opens and 3 British Opens; oldest player to win Masters (46 in 1986); PGA Player of Year 5 times (1967,72-73,75-76); named Golfer of the Century by PGA in 1988; 6-time Ryder Cup player and 2-time captain (1983,87); won NCAA title (1961) and 2 U.S. Amateurs (1959,61); 70 PGA Tour wins (2nd to Sam Snead's 81); third win in Tradition in 1995 gave him 7 majors in 6 years on Senior PGA Tour; nicknamed "the Golden Bear."

Chuck Noll (b. Jan. 5, 1932): Football; coached Pittsburgh to 4 Super Bowl titles (1975-76,79-80); retired after 1991 season ranked 5th on all-time list with 209 wins (including playoffs) in 23 years.

Greg Norman (b. Feb. 10, 1955): Australian golfer; PGA Tour's all-time money winner ($11.9 million), passing Tom Kite on Aug. 27, 1995; 73 tournament wins worldwide; 2-time British Open winner (1986,93); lost Masters by a stroke in both 1986 (to Jack Nicklaus) and '87 (to Larry Mize in sudden death).

James D. Norris (b. Nov. 6, 1906, d. Feb. 25, 1966): Boxing promoter and NHL owner; president of International Boxing Club from 1949 until U.S. Supreme Court ordered its break-up (for anti-trust violations) in 1958; only NHL owner to win Stanley Cups in two cities; Detroit (1936-37,43) and Chicago (1961).

Paavo Nurmi (b. June 13, 1897, d. Oct. 2, 1973): Finnish runner; won 9 gold medals (6 individual) in 1920, '24 and '28 Olympics; from 1921-31 broke 23 world outdoor records in events ranging from 1,500 to 20,000 meters.

Dan O'Brien (b. July 18, 1966): Track & Field; Olympic decathlon gold medalist (1996); set former world record in decathlon (8,891 pts) in 1992, after shockingly failing to qualify for event at U.S. Olympic Trials; three-time gold medalist at World Championships (1991,93,95).

Larry O'Brien (b. July 7, 1917, d. Sept. 27, 1990): Basketball; former U.S. Postmaster General and 3rd NBA commissioner (1975-84); league absorbed 4 ABA teams and created salary cap during his term in office.

Al Oerter (b. Sept. 19, 1936): Track & Field; his 4 discus golds in consecutive Olympics from 1956-68 is an unmatched Olympic record.

Sadaharu Oh (b. May 20, 1940): Baseball 1B; led Japan League in HRs 15 times; 9-time MVP for Tokyo Giants; hit 868 HRs in 22 years.

Hakeem Olajuwon (b. Jan. 21, 1963): Basketball C; Nigerian native who was consensus All-America in 1984 and Final Four MOP in 1983 for Houston; overall 1st pick by Houston Rockets in 1984 NBA draft; led Rockets to back-to-back NBA titles (1994-95); regular season MVP ('94) and Finals MVP (1994-95); 6-time All-NBA 1st team (1987-89,93-95). Member of Dream Team III.

Jose Maria Olazabal (b. Feb. 5, 1966): Spanish golfer; has 24 worldwide victories including 2 Masters (1994,99); played on 6 European Ryder Cup teams.

Barney Oldfield (b. Jan. 29, 1878, d. Oct. 4, 1946): Auto racing pioneer; drove cars built by Henry Ford; first man to drive car a mile per minute (1903).

Walter O'Malley (b. Oct. 9, 1903, d. Aug. 9, 1979): Baseball owner; moved Brooklyn Dodgers to Los Angeles after 1957 season; won 4 World Series (1955,59,63,65).

Shaquille O'Neal (b. Mar. 6, 1972): Basketball C; 2-time All-America at LSU (1991-92); overall 1st pick (as a junior) by Orlando in 1992 NBA draft; Rookie of Year in 1993; led NBA in scoring in 1995; member of Dream Teams II and III. Signed with LA Lakers in 1996.

Bobby Orr (b. Mar. 20, 1948): Hockey D; 8-time Norris Trophy winner as best defenseman; led NHL in scoring twice and assists 5 times; All-NHL 1st team 8 times; regular season MVP 3 times (1970-72); playoff MVP twice (1970,72) with Boston.

Tom Osborne (b. Feb. 23, 1937): Football; Nebraska head coach from 1973-97; career record of 255-49-3; his win pct. of .835 is fifth all-time; finally won national championship in 1994; followed it with 2nd national title in '95 and shared national title with Michigan in '97.

Mel Ott (b. Mar. 2, 1909, d. Nov. 21, 1958): Baseball OF; joined NY Giants at age 16; led NL in HRs 6 times; had 511 HRs and 1,860 RBI in 22 years.

Kristin Otto (b. Feb. 7, 1966): East German swimmer; 1st woman to win 6 gold medals (4 individual) at one Olympics (1988).

Francis Ouimet (b. May 8, 1893, d. Sept. 3, 1967): Golfer; won 1913 U.S. Open as 20-year-old amateur playing on Brookline, Mass. course where he used to caddie; won U.S. Amateur twice; 8-time Walker Cup player.

Steve Owen (b. Apr. 21, 1898, d. May 17, 1964): Football; All-Pro guard (1927); coached NY Giants for 23 years (1931-53); won 153 career games and 2 NFL titles (1934,38).

Jesse Owens (b. Sept. 12, 1913, d. Mar. 31, 1980): Track & Field; broke 5 world records in one afternoon at Big Ten Championships (May 25, 1935); a year later, he upstaged Hitler by winning 4 golds (100m, 200m, 4x100m relay and long jump) at 1936 Olympics in Berlin.

Alan Page (b. Aug. 7, 1945): Football DE; All-America at Notre Dame in 1966 and member of two national championship teams; 6-time NFL All-Pro and 1971 Player of Year with Minnesota Vikings; later a lawyer who was elected to Minnesota Supreme Court in 1992.

Satchel Paige (b. July 7, 1906, d. June 6, 1982): Baseball RHP; pitched 55 career no-hitters over 20 seasons in Negro Leagues, entered major leagues with Cleveland in 1948 at age 42; had 28-31 record in 5 years; returned to AL at age 59 to start 1 game for Kansas City in 1965 (went 3 innings, gave up a hit and got a strikeout).

Se Ri Pak (b. Sept. 28, 1977): Golfer; won two Majors as a rookie in 1998; won the LPGA Championship and then the U.S. Open on the second hole of sudden death with amateur Jenny Chuasiriporn after an additional 18 holes failed to break the tie; finished second on the 1998 money list.

Arnold Palmer (b. Sept. 10, 1929): Golfer; winner of 4 Masters, 2 British Opens and a U.S. Open; 2-time PGA Player of Year (1960,62); 1st player to earn over $1 million in career (1968); annual PGA Tour money leader award named after him; 60 wins on PGA Tour and 10 more on Senior Tour.

Jim Palmer (b. Oct. 15, 1945): Baseball RHP; 3-time Cy Young Award winner (1973,75-76); won 20 or more games 8 times with Baltimore; 1991 comeback attempt at age 45 scrubbed in spring training.

Bill Parcells (b. Aug. 22, 1941): Football; coached NY Giants to 2 Super Bowl titles (1987,91); retired after 1990 season then returned in '93 as coach of New England; led Patriots to Super Bowl loss in 1997; left Patriots in 1997 and signed to coach the New York Jets.

Jack Pardee (b. Apr. 19, 1936): Football; All-America linebacker at Texas A&M; 2-time All-Pro with LA Rams (1963) and Washington (1971); 2-time NFL Coach of Year (1976,79) and winner of 87 games in 11 seasons; only man hired as head coach in NFL, WFL, USFL and CFL; also coached at Univ. of Houston.

Bernie Parent (b. Apr. 3, 1945): Hockey G; led Philadelphia Flyers to 2 Stanley Cups as playoff MVP (1974,75); 2-time Vezina Trophy winner; posted 55 career shutouts and 2.55 GAA in 13 seasons.

Joe Paterno (b. Dec. 21, 1926): Football; has coached Penn St. to 2 national titles (1982,86) and 18-9-1 bowl record in 31 years; also had three unbeaten teams that didn't finish No. 1; 4-time Coach of Year (1968,78,82,86); entered 1999 season 4th on all-time list with 307 wins.

Craig Patrick (b. May 20, 1946): Hockey; GM of 2-time Cup champion Pittsburgh Penguins (1991-92); also captain of 1969 NCAA champion at Denver; assistant coach-GM of 1980 gold medal-winning U.S. Olympic team; scored 72 goals in 8 NHL seasons and won 69 games in 3 years as coach; grandson of Lester.

Lester Patrick (b. Dec. 30, 1883, d. June 1, 1960): Hockey; pro hockey pioneer as player, coach and general manager for 43 years; led NY Rangers to Stanley Cups as coach (1928,33) and GM (1940); grandfather of Craig.

Floyd Patterson (b. Jan. 4, 1935): Boxer; Olympic middleweight champ in 1952; world heavyweight champion (1956-59,60-62); 1st to regain heavyweight crown; fought Ingemar Johansson 3 times in 22 months from 1959-61 and won last two; pro record 55-8-1 with 40 KOs.

Walter Payton (b. July 25, 1954): Football RB; NFL's all-time leading rusher with 16,726 yards; scored 125 career TDs; All-Pro 7 times with Chicago; MVP in 1977; led Bears to Super Bowl title in Jan. 1986.

Calvin Peete (b. July 18, 1943): Golf; began playing golf at the age of 23; earned over $2 million in career earnings; selected to the U.S. Ryder Cup teams in 1983 and 1985.

Pelé (b. Oct. 23, 1940): Brazilian soccer F; given name— Edson Arantes do Nascimento; led Brazil to 3 World Cup titles (1958,62,70); came to U.S. in 1975 to play for NY Cosmos in NASL; scored 1,281 goals in 22 years; currently Brazil's minister of sport.

Roger Penske (b. Feb. 20, 1937): Auto racing; national sports car driving champion (1964); established racing team in 1961; co-founder of Championship Auto Racing Teams (CART); Penske Racing entered 1999 with a record 99 CART victories, including 10 Indianapolis 500s and 9 CART points titles; shocked racing world by failing to qualify car for 1995 Indy 500.

Willie Pep (b. Sept. 19, 1922): Boxer; 2-time world featherweight champion (1942-48,49-50); pro record 230-11-1 with 65 KOs.

Marie-Jose Perec (b. 1968): Track & Field; French sprinter who became 2nd woman to win the 200m and 400m events in the same Olympics (1996); her time in the 400 (48.25) set an Olympic record; Valerie Brisco-Hooks did it in the boycotted 1984 games; also won the 400M in 1992 Games.

Fred Perry (b. May 18, 1909, d. Feb. 2, 1995): British tennis player; 3-time Wimbledon champ (1934-36); first player to win all four Grand Slam singles titles, though not in same year; last native to win All-England men's title.

Gaylord Perry (b. Sept. 15, 1938): Baseball RHP; only pitcher to win a Cy Young Award in both leagues; retired in 1983 with 314-265 record and 3,534 strikeouts over 22 years and 8 teams; brother Jim won 215 games for family total of 529.

Bob Pettit (b. Dec. 12, 1932): Basketball F; All-NBA 1st team 10 times (1955-64); 2-time MVP (1956,59) with St. Louis Hawks; first player to score 20,000 points.

Richard Petty (b. July 2, 1937): Auto racer; 7-time winner of Daytona 500; 7-time NASCAR national champ (1964,67,71-72,74-75,79); first stock car driver to win $1 million in career; all-time NASCAR leader in races won (200), poles (127) and wins in a single season (27 in 1967); retired after 1992 season; son of Lee (54 career wins) and father of Kyle (7 career wins).

Laffit Pincay Jr. (b. Dec. 29, 1946): Jockey; 5-time Eclipse Award winner (1971,73-74,79,85); winner of 3 Belmonts and 1 Kentucky Derby (aboard Swale in 1984); entered 1999 with 8,601 career wins, trailing only Bill Shoemaker's 8,833.

Scottie Pippen (b. Sept. 25, 1965): Basketball F; started on six NBA champions with Chicago (1991-93, 96-98); 3-time all-NBA first team (1994-96). Voted one of NBA's 50 Greatest Players.

Uta Pippig (b. Sept. 7, 1965): German marathoner; won three-straight Boston Marathons (1994,95,96); she set a new course record in '94.

Nelson Piquet (b. Aug. 17, 1952): Brazilian auto racer; 3-time Formula One world champion (1981,83, 87); left circuit in 1991 with 23 career wins.

Rick Pitino (b. Sept. 18, 1952): Basketball; won 1996 NCAA title in his 7th year at Kentucky; previously coached the New York Knicks in the NBA (96-85 overall), Providence College (42-23) and Boston University (46-24); in 1997, became coach and president of Boston Celtics.

Jacques Plante (b. Jan. 17, 1929, d. Feb. 27, 1986): Hockey G; led Montreal to 6 Stanley Cups (1953,56-60); won 7 Vezina Trophies; MVP in 1962; first goalie to regularly wear a mask; posted 82 shutouts with 2.38 GAA.

Gary Player (b. Nov. 1, 1936): South African golfer; 3-time winner of Masters and British Open; only player in 20th century to win British Open in three different decades (1959,68,74); one of only four players to win all four Grand Slam titles (others are Hogan, Nicklaus and Sarazen); has also won 2 PGAs, a U.S. Open and 2 U.S. Senior Opens; owner of 21 wins on PGA Tour and 17 more on Senior Tour.

Jim Plunkett (b. Dec. 5, 1947): Football QB; Heisman Trophy winner (Stanford) in 1970; AFL Rookie of the Year in 1971; led Oakland-LA Raiders to Super Bowl wins in 1981 and '84; MVP in '81.

Maurice Podoloff (b. Aug. 18, 1890, d. Nov. 24, 1985): Basketball; engineered merger of Basketball Assn. of America and National Basketball League into NBA in 1949; NBA commissioner (1949-63); league MVP trophy named after him.

Fritz Pollard (b. Jan. 27, 1894, d. May 11, 1986): Football; 1st black All-America RB (1916 at Brown); 1st black to play in Rose Bowl; 7-year NFL pro (1920-26); 1st black NFL coach, at Milwaukee and Hammond, Ind.

Sam Pollock (b. Dec. 15, 1925): Hockey GM; managed NHL Montreal Canadiens to 9 Stanley Cups in 14 years (1965-78).

Denis Potvin (b. Oct. 29, 1953): Hockey D; won Norris Trophy 3 times (1976,78-79); 5-time All-NHL 1st-team; led NY Islanders to 4 Stanley Cups.

Mike Powell (b. Nov. 10, 1963): Track & Field; broke Bob Beamon's 23-year-old long jump world record by 2 inches with leap of 29-ft., 4½-in. at the 1991 World Championships; Sullivan Award winner (1991); won long jump silver medals in 1988 and '92 Olympics; repeated as world champ in 1993.

Steve Prefontaine (b. Jan. 25, 1951, d. June 1, 1975): Track & Field; All-America distance runner at Oregon; first athlete to win same event at NCAA championships 4 straight years (5,000 meters from 1970-73); finished 4th in 5,000 at 1972 Munich Olympics; first athlete to endorse Nike running shoes; killed in a one-car accident.

Nick Price (b. Jan. 28, 1957): Zimbabwean golfer; PGA Player of Year in 1993 and '94; became 1st since Nick Faldo in 1990 to win 2 Grand Slam titles in same year when he took British Open and PGA Championship in 1994; also won PGA in '92.

Alain Prost (b. Feb. 24, 1955): French auto racer; 4-time Formula One world champion (1985-86,89,93); sat out 1992 then returned to win title in 1993; retired after '93 season as all-time F1 wins leader with 51.

Kirby Puckett (b. Mar. 14, 1961): Baseball OF; led Minnesota Twins to World Series titles in 1987 and '91; retired in 1996 due to an eye ailment with a batting title (1989), 2,304 hits and a .318 career average in 12 seasons.

C.C. Pyle (b. 1882, d. Feb. 3, 1939): Promoter; known as "Cash and Carry"; hyped Red Grange's pro football debut by arranging 1925 barnstorming tour with Chicago Bears; had Grange bolt NFL for new AFL in 1926 (AFL folded in '27); also staged 2 Transcontinental Races (1928-29), known as "Bunion Derbies."

Bobby Rahal (b. Jan. 10, 1953): Auto racer; 3-time PPG Cup champ (1986,87,92); 24 career Indy-Car wins, including 1986 Indy 500.

Jack Ramsay (b. Feb. 21, 1925): Basketball; coach who won 239 college games with St. Joseph's-PA in 11 seasons and 906 NBA games (including playoffs) with 4 teams over 21 years; placed 3rd in 1961 Final Four; led Portland to NBA title in 1977.

Bill Rassmussen (b. Oct. 15, 1932): Radio-TV; unemployed radio broadcaster who founded ESPN, the nation's first 24-hour all-sports cable-TV network, in 1978; bought out by Getty Oil in 1981.

Willis Reed (b. June 25, 1942): Basketball C; led NY Knicks to NBA titles in 1970 and '73, Finals MVP both years; regular season MVP 1970. Voted one of NBA's 50 Greatest Players.

Pee Wee Reese (b. July 23, 1919, d. Aug. 14, 1999): Baseball SS; member of Brooklyn/Los Angeles Dodgers from 1940-58; led NL in runs scored (132) in 1949 and stolen bases (30) in 1952; hit over .300 in a season once (.309 in 1954); led the NL in putouts four times; real name was Harold H. Reese.

Mary Lou Retton (b. Jan. 24, 1968): Gymnast; won gold medal in women's All-Around at the 1984 Olympics; also won 2 silvers and 2 bronzes.

Butch Reynolds (b. June 8, 1964): Track & Field; held world record in 400 meters from 1988 to 1999 when it was finally broken by Michael Johnson; banned for 2½ years for allegedly failing drug test in 1990; sued IAAF and won $27.4 million judgment in 1992, but award was voided in '94; won silver medal in 400 meters and gold as member of U.S. 4x400-meter relay team at both 1993 and '95 World Championships.

Grantland Rice (b. Nov. 1, 1880, d. July 13, 1954): First celebrated American sportswriter; chronicled the Golden Age of Sport in 1920s; immortalized Notre Dame's "Four Horsemen."

Jerry Rice (b. Oct. 13, 1962): Football WR; 2-time Div. I-AA All-America at Mississippi Valley St. (1983-84); 10-time All-Pro; regular season MVP in 1987 and Super Bowl MVP in 1989 with San Francisco; NFL all-time leader in touchdowns and receptions.

Henri Richard (b. Feb. 29, 1936): Hockey C; leap year baby who played on more Stanley Cup championship teams (11) than anybody else; at 5-foot-7, known as the "Pocket Rocket"; brother of Maurice.

Maurice Richard (b. Aug. 4, 1921): Hockey RW; the "Rocket"; 8-time NHL 1st team All-Star; MVP in 1947; 1st to score 50 goals in one season (1944-45); 544 career goals; played on 8 Stanley Cup winners in Montreal.

Bob Richards (b. Feb. 2, 1926): Track & Field; pole vaulter, ordained minister and original *Wheaties* pitchman, who won gold medals at 1952 and '56 Olympics; remains only 2-time Olympic pole vault champ.

Tex Rickard (b. Jan. 2, 1870, d. Jan. 6, 1929): Promoter who handled boxing's first $1 million gate (Dempsey vs. Carpentier in 1921); built Madison Square Garden in 1925; founded NY Rangers as Garden tenant in 1926 and named NHL team after himself (Tex's Rangers); also built Boston Garden in 1928.

Eddie Rickenbacker (b. Oct. 8, 1890, d. July 23, 1973): Mechanic and auto racer; became America's top flying ace (22 kills) in World War I; owned Indianapolis Speedway (1927-45) and ran Eastern Air Lines (1938-59).

Branch Rickey (b. Dec. 20, 1881, d. Dec. 9, 1965): Baseball innovator; revolutionized game with creation of modern farm system while general manager of St. Louis Cardinals (1917-42); integrated major leagues in 1947 as president-GM of Brooklyn Dodgers when he brought up Jackie Robinson (whom he had signed on Oct. 23, 1945); later GM of Pittsburgh Pirates.

Leni Riefenstahl (b. Aug. 22, 1902): German filmmaker of 1930s; directed classic sports documentary "Olympia" on 1936 Berlin Summer Olympics; infamous, however, for also making 1934 Hitler propaganda film "Triumph of the Will."

Roy Riegels (b. Apr. 4, 1908, d. Mar. 26, 1993): Football; California center who picked up fumble in 2nd quarter of 1929 Rose Bowl and raced 70 yards in the wrong direction to set up a 2-point safety in 8-7 loss to Georgia Tech.

Bobby Riggs (b. Feb. 25, 1918, d. Oct. 25, 1995): Tennis; won Wimbledon once (1939) and U.S. title twice (1939,41); legendary hustler who made his biggest score in 1973 as 55-year-old male chauvinist challenging the best women players; beat No. 1 Margaret Smith Court 6-2,6-1, but was thrashed by No. 2 Billie Jean King, 6-4,6-3,6-3 in nationally televised "Battle of the Sexes" on Sept. 20, before 30,492 at the Astrodome.

Pat Riley (b. Mar. 20, 1945): Basketball; coached LA Lakers to 4 of their 5 NBA titles in 1980s (1982,85,87-88); coached New York from 1991-95; 2-time Coach of Year (1990,93) and all-time NBA leader in playoff wins (137); quit Knicks after 1994-95 season with year left on contract; signed with Miami Heat on Sept. 2 as coach, team president and part-owner after Knicks agreed to drop tampering charges in exchange for $1 million and a conditional first round draft pick.

Cal Ripken Jr. (b. Aug. 24, 1960): Baseball SS; broke Lou Gehrig's major league Iron Man record of 2,130 consecutive games played on Sept. 6, 1995; record streak began on May 30, 1982 and ended Sept. 19, 1998 after 2,632 games; 2-time AL MVP (1983,91) for Baltimore; AL Rookie of Year (1982); AL starter in All-Star Game since 1984; holds record for career home runs by a shortstop with 400 and counting.

Phil Rizzuto (b. Sept. 25, 1918): Baseball SS; nicknamed "the Scooter"; AL MVP with the Yankees in 1950; 5-time All-Star; retired in 1956 and became Yankees radio and television announcer; elected to the Hall of Fame in 1994.

Joe Robbie (b. July 7, 1916, d. Jan. 7, 1990): Football; original owner of Miami Dolphins (1966-90); won 2 Super Bowls (1973-74); built $115-million Joe Robbie Stadium (now named Pro Player Stadium) with private funds in 1987.

Oscar Robertson (b. Nov. 24, 1938): Basketball G; 3-time College Player of Year (1958-60) at Cincinnati; led 1960 U.S. Olympic team to gold medal; NBA Rookie of Year (1961); 9-time All-NBA 1st team; MVP in 1964 with Cincinnati Royals; NBA champion in 1971 with Milwaukee Bucks; 3rd in career assists with 9,887.

Paul Robeson (b. Apr. 8, 1898, d. Jan. 23, 1976): Black 4-sport star and 2-time football All-America (1917-18) at Rutgers; 3-year NFL pro; also scholar, lawyer, singer, actor and political activist; long-tainted by Communist sympathies, he was finally inducted into College Football Hall of Fame in 1995.

Brooks Robinson (b. May 18, 1937): Baseball 3B; led AL in fielding 12 times from 1960-72 with Baltimore; AL MVP in 1964; World Series MVP in 1970; 16 Gold Gloves; entered Hall of Fame in 1983.

David Robinson (b. Aug. 6, 1965): Basketball C; College Player of Year at Navy in 1987 NBA draft; overall 1st pick by San Antonio in 1987 NBA draft; served in military from 1987-89; NBA Rookie of Year in 1990 and MVP in '95; 2-time All-NBA 1st team (1991,92); led NBA in scoring in 1994; member of 1988, '92 and '96 U.S. Olympic teams.

Eddie Robinson (b. Feb. 13, 1919): Football; head coach at Div. I-AA Grambling from 1941-97; winningest coach in college history (408-165-15); led Tigers to 8 national black college titles.

Frank Robinson (b. Aug. 31, 1935): Baseball OF; won MVP in NL (1961) and AL (1966); Triple Crown winner and World Series MVP in 1966 with Baltimore; 1st black manager in major leagues with Cleveland in 1975; also managed in SF and Baltimore.

Jackie Robinson (b. Jan. 31, 1919, d. Oct. 24, 1972): Baseball 1B-2B-3B; 4-sport athlete at UCLA (baseball, basketball, football and track); hit .387 with K.C. Monarchs of Negro Leagues in 1945; signed by Brooklyn Dodgers on Oct. 23, 1945 and broke major league baseball's color line in 1947; Rookie of Year in 1947 and NL's MVP in '49; hit .311 over 10 seasons. His #42 was retired by MLB in 1997.

Sugar Ray Robinson (b. May 3, 1921, d. Apr. 12, 1989): Boxer; world welterweight champion (1946-51); 5-time middleweight champ; retired at age 45 after 25 years in the ring; pro record 174-19-6 with 109 KOs.

Knute Rockne (b. Mar. 4, 1888, d. Mar. 31, 1931): Football; coached Notre Dame to 3 consensus national titles (1924,29,30); highest winning percentage in college history (.881) with record of 105-12-5 over 13 seasons; killed in plane crash.

Bill Rodgers (b. Dec. 23, 1947): Distance runner; won Boston and New York City marathons 4 times each from 1975-80.

Dennis Rodman (b. May 13, 1961): Basketball F; ferocious rebounder and tenacious defender; also known for dyeing his hair various colors and for getting suspended regularly; in 1997, he was suspended for 11 games for kicking a courtside cameraman; led the NBA in rebounding 7 years in a row, 1992-98; member of 5 NBA champion teams, Detroit (1989,90) and Chicago(1996-98); 2-time All Star (1990,92), 2-time defensive player of the year (1990-91) and 6-time member of the NBA All-Defensive team (1989-93,96).

Irina Rodnina (b. Sept. 12, 1949): Soviet figure skater; won 10 world championships and 3 Olympic gold medals in pairs competition from 1971-80.

Alex Rodriguez (b. July 27, 1975): Baseball SS; one of baseball's best all-around players; led AL in his first full season in the majors (1996) with .358 batting average and 141 runs, also hit 36 home runs and had 123 RBIs; in 1998 became just third player ever to hit 40 HRs and get 40 steals in one season.

Ronaldo (b. Sept. 22, 1976): Soccer; Brazilian forward who has been compared to the great Pele; signed with a first division club in Brazil, Cruzeiro Belo Horizonte, before he was 18 and scored 58 goals in 60 games; named to the Brazilian National Team when he was 17; named FIFA Player of the Year in 1996 and '97; European Player of the Year in '97; named 1998 World Cup MVP.

Art Rooney (b. Jan. 27, 1901, d. Aug. 25, 1988): Race track legend and pro football pioneer; bought Pittsburgh Steelers franchise in 1933 for $2,500; finally won NFL title with 1st of 4 Super Bowls in 1974 season.

Theodore Roosevelt (b. Oct. 27, 1858, d. Jan. 6, 1919): 26th President of the U.S.; physical fitness buff who boxed as undergraduate at Harvard; credited with presidential assist in forming of Intercollegiate Athletic Assn. (now NCAA) in 1905-06.

Mauri Rose (b. May 26, 1906, d. Jan. 1, 1981): Auto racer; 3-time winner of Indy 500 (1941,47-48).

Murray Rose (b. Jan. 6, 1939): Australian swimmer; won 3 gold medals at 1956 Olympics; added a gold, silver and bronze in 1960.

Pete Rose (b. Apr. 14, 1941): Baseball OF-IF; all-time hits leader with 4,256; led NL in batting 3 times; regular-season MVP in 1973; World Series MVP 1975; had 44-game hitting streak in '78; managed Cincinnati (1984-89); banned for life in 1989 for conduct detrimental to baseball; convicted of tax evasion in 1990 and sentenced to 5 months in prison; released Jan. 7, 1991.

Ken Rosewall (b. Nov. 2, 1934): Tennis; won French and Australian singles titles at age 18; U.S. champ twice, but never won Wimbledon.

Mark Roth (b. Apr. 10, 1951): Bowler; 4-time PBA Player of Year (1977-79,84); entered 1999 with 34 tournament wins; victory in Apr. 15, 1995 Foresters Open was first in 7 years; U.S. Open champ in 1984.

Alan Rothenberg (b. Apr. 10, 1939): Soccer; president of U.S. Soccer 1990-98; surprised European skeptics by directing hugely successful 1994 World Cup tournament; successfully got oft-delayed outdoor Major League Soccer off ground in 1996.

Patrick Roy (b. Oct. 5, 1965): Hockey G; led Montreal to 2 Stanley Cup titles; playoff MVP as rookie in 1986 and again in '93; has won Vezina Trophy 3 times (1989-90,92); won 3rd Stanley Cup with Colorado ('96).

Pete Rozelle (b. Mar. 1, 1926, d. December 6, 1996): Football; NFL Commissioner from 1960-89; presided over growth of league from 12 to 28 teams, merger with AFL, creation of Super Bowl and advent of huge TV rights fees.

Wilma Rudolph (b. June 23, 1940, d. Nov. 12, 1994): Track & Field; won 3 gold medals (100m, 200m and 4x100m relay) at 1960 Olympics; also won relay silver in '56 Games; 2-time AP Athlete of Year (1960-61) and Sullivan Award winner in 1961.

Damon Runyon (b. Oct. 4, 1884, d. Dec. 10, 1946): Kansas native who gained fame as New York journalist, sports columnist and short-story writer; best known for 1932 story collection, "Guys and Dolls."

Adolph Rupp (b. Sept. 2, 1901, d. Dec. 10, 1977): Basketball; 2nd in all-time college coaching wins with 876; led Kentucky to 4 NCAA championships (1948-49,51,58) and 1 NIT title (1946).

Bill Russell (b. Feb. 12, 1934): Basketball C; won titles in college, Olympics and pros; 5-time NBA MVP; led Boston to 11 titles from 1957-69; also became first black NBA head coach in 1966.

Babe Ruth (b. Feb. 6, 1895, d. Aug. 16, 1948): Baseball LHP-OF; two-time 20-game winner with Boston Red Sox (1916-17); had a 94-46 record with a 2.28 ERA, while he was 3-0 in the World Series with an ERA of 0.87; sold to New York Yankees for $100,000 in 1920; AL MVP in 1923; led AL in slugging average 13 times, HRs 12 times, RBI 6 times and batting once (.378 in 1924); hit 60 HRs in 1927 and at least 54 3 other times; ended career with Boston Braves in 1935 with 714 HRs, 2,211 RBI and a batting average of .342; remains all-time leader in walks (2,056) and slugging average (.690); member of the Hall of Fame's inaugural class of 1936.

Johnny Rutherford (b. Mar. 12, 1938): Auto racer; 3-time winner of Indy 500 (1974,76,80); CART national champion in 1980.

Nolan Ryan (b. Jan. 31, 1947): Baseball RHP; recorded 7 no-hitters against Kansas City and Detroit (1973), Minnesota (1974), Baltimore (1975), LA Dodgers (1981), Oakland A's (1990) and Toronto (1991 at age 44); 2-time 20-game winner (1973-74); 2-time NL leader in ERA (1981,87); led AL in strikeouts 9 times and NL twice in 27 years; retired after 1993 season with 324 wins, 292 losses and all-time records for strikeouts (5,714) and walks (2,795); never won Cy Young Award; inducted into Hall of Fame in 1999.

Samuel Ryder (b. Mar. 24, 1858, d. Jan. 2, 1936): Golf; English seed merchant who donated the Ryder Cup in 1927 for competition between pro golfers from Great Britain and the U.S.; made his fortune by coming up with idea of selling seeds in small packages.

Toni Sailer (b. Nov. 17, 1935): Austrian skier; 1st to win 3 alpine gold medals in Winter Olympics — taking downhill, slalom and giant slalom events in 1956.

Alberto Salazar (b. Aug. 7, 1958): Track and Field; set one world and six U.S. records during his career; broke 12-year-old record at New York Marathon in 1981 and broke Boston Marathon record in 1982; won three straight NY Marathons (1980-82); qualified for the 1980 and 1984 U.S. Olympic teams

Juan Antonio Samaranch (b. July 17, 1920): president of International Olympic Committee since 1980; the native of Barcelona was reelected in 1996 after IOC's move in '95 to bump membership age limit to 80.

Pete Sampras (b. Aug. 12, 1971): Tennis; No.1 player in world 1993-98; overtaken only briefly several times; youngest ever U.S. Open men's champion (19 years, 28 days) in 1990; has won 12 majors: 2 Australian Opens (1994,97), 6 Wimbledons (1993,94,95, 97,98,99) and 4 U.S. Opens (1990,93,95,96).

Joan Benoit Samuelson (b. May 16, 1957): Distance runner; has won Boston Marathon twice (1979,83); won first women's Olympic marathon in 1984 Games at Los Angeles; Sullivan Award recipient in 1985.

Arantxa Sanchez Vicario (b. Dec. 18, 1971): Spanish tennis player; 27 tour victories including 3 French Opens (1989,94,98) and 1 U.S. Open (1994); finalist in three of four Grand Slam finals in '95; teamed with Conchita Martinez to win 5 Federation Cups from 1991-98.

Earl Sande (b. Nov. 13, 1898, d. Aug. 19, 1968): Jockey; rode Gallant Fox to Triple Crown in 1930; won 5 Belmonts and 3 Kentucky Derbies.

Barry Sanders (b. July 16, 1968): Football RB; won 1988 Heisman Trophy as junior at Oklahoma St.; all-time NCAA single season leader in rushing (2,628 yards), scoring (234 points) and TDs (39); 4-time NFL rushing leader with Detroit Lions (1990,94,96,97); NFC Rookie of Year (1988); 2-time NFL Player of Year (1991,97); NFC MVP (1994); rushed for 2,053 yards in 1997, second-best season total ever; No. 2 all-time rusher with 15,269 yards; abruptly retired just prior to 1999 season.

Deion Sanders (b. Aug. 9, 1967): Baseball OF and Football DB-KR-WR; 2-time All-America at Florida St. in football (1987-88); 7-time NFL All-Pro CB with Atlanta, San Francisco and Dallas (1991-94,96-98); led majors in triples (14) with Atlanta in 1992 and hit .533 in World Series the same year; played on 2 Super Bowl winners (SF in XXIX, and Dallas in XXX); first 2-way starter in NFL since Chuck Bednarik in 1962; only athlete to play in both World Series and Super Bowl.

Abe Saperstein (b. July 4, 1901, d. Mar. 15, 1966): Basketball; founded all-black, Harlem Globetrotters barnstorming team in 1927; coached sharpshooting comedians to 1940 world pro title in Chicago and established troupe as game's foremost goodwill ambassadors; also served as 1st commissioner of American Basketball League (1961-62).

Gene Sarazen (b. Feb. 27, 1902, d. May 13, 1999): Golfer; one of only four players to win all four Grand Slam titles (others are Hogan, Nicklaus and Player); won Masters, British Open, 2 U.S. Opens and 3 PGA titles between 1922-35; invented sand wedge in 1930.

Glen Sather (b. Sept. 2, 1943): Hockey; GM-coach of 4 Stanley Cup winners in Edmonton (1984-85,87-88) and GM-only for another in 1990; ranks 7th on all-time NHL list with 553 wins (including playoffs); entered Hockey Hall of Fame in 1997.

Terry Sawchuk (b. Dec. 28, 1929, d. May 31, 1970): Hockey G; recorded 103 shutouts in 21 NHL seasons; 4-time Vezina Trophy winner; played on 4 Stanley Cup winners at Detroit and Toronto; posted career 2.52 GAA.

Gale Sayers (b. May 30, 1943): Football HB; 2-time All-America at Kansas; NFL Rookie of Year (1965) and 5-time All-Pro with Chicago; scored then-record 22 TDs in rookie year.

Chris Schenkel (b. Aug. 21, 1923): Radio-TV; 4-time Sportscaster of Year; easy-going baritone who covered basketball, bowling, football, golf and the Olympics for ABC and CBS; host of ABC's Pro Bowlers Tour for 33 years; received lifetime achievement Emmy Award in 1993.

Vitaly Scherbo (b. Jan. 13, 1972): Russian gymnast; winner of unprecedented 6 gold medals in gymnastics, including men's All-Around, for Unified Team in 1992 Olympics; won 3 bronze in '96 Games.

Mike Schmidt (b. Sept. 27, 1949): Baseball 3B; led NL in HRs 8 times; 3-time MVP (1980,81,86) with Philadelphia; 548 career HRs and 10 Gold Gloves; inducted into Hall of Fame in 1995.

Don Schollander (b. Apr. 30, 1946): Swimming; won 4 gold medals at 1964 Olympics, plus one gold and one silver in 1968; won Sullivan Award in 1964.

Dick Schultz (b. Sept. 5, 1929): Reform-minded executive director of NCAA from 1988-93; announced resignation on May 11, 1993 in wake of special investigator's report citing Univ. of Virginia with improper student-athlete loan program during Schultz's tenure as athletic director (1981-87); named executive director of the USOC on June 23, 1995.

Michael Schumacher (b. Jan. 3, 1969): German auto racer; Formula One's active win leader (and 3rd all-time) with 36 career victories as of Sept. 21 1999; world champion in 1994 and '95.

Bob Seagren (b. Oct. 17, 1946): Track & Field; won gold medal in pole vault at 1968 Olympics; broke world outdoor record 5 times.

Tom Seaver (b. Nov. 17, 1944): Baseball RHP; won 3 Cy Young Awards (1969,73,75); had 311 wins, 3,640 strikeouts and 2.86 ERA over 20 years.

George Seifert (b. Jan. 22, 1940): Football; coached San Francisco to a record 17 wins in his 1st season as head coach in 1989; 2-time Super Bowl-winning coach with 49ers (1989,94); left team in 1997 as all-time NFL leader in win pct. (.755); returned to NFL in 1999 with Carolina.

Peter Seitz (b. May 17, 1905, d. Oct. 17, 1983): Baseball arbitrator; ruled on Dec. 23, 1975 that players who perform for one season without a signed contract can become free agents; decision ushered in big money era for players.

Monica Seles (b. Dec. 2, 1973): Tennis; No. 1 in the world in 1991 and '92 after winning Australian, French and U.S. Opens both years; won 4 Australian, 3 French and 2 US Opens; winner of 30 singles titles in just 5 years before she was stabbed in the back by Steffi Graf fan Gunter Parche on Apr. 30, 1993 during match in Hamburg, Germany; spent remainder of 1993, all of '94 and most of '95 recovering; returned to WTA Tour with win at the Canadian Open in 1995; comeback complete with 1996 Australian Open win.

Bud Selig (b. July 30, 1934): Baseball; Milwaukee car dealer who bought AL Seattle Pilots for $10.8 million in 1970 and moved team to Midwest; as de facto comissioner, he presided over 232-day players' strike that resulted in cancellation of World Series for first time since 1904 and delayed opening of 1995 season until Apr. 25; officially named baseball's ninth commissioner on July 2, 1998.

Frank Selke (b. May 7, 1893, d. July 3, 1985): Hockey; GM of 6 Stanley Cup champions in Montreal (1953,56-60); the annual NHL trophy for best defensive forward bears his name.

Ayrton Senna (b. Mar. 21, 1960, d. May 1, 1994): Brazilian auto racer; 3-time Formula One champion (1988,90-91); died as all-time F1 leader in poles (65) and 2nd in wins (41); killed in crash at Imola, Italy during '94 San Marino Grand Prix.

Wilbur Shaw (b. Oct. 13, 1902, d. Oct. 30, 1954): Auto racer; 3-time winner and 3-time runner-up of Indy 500 from 1933-1940.

Patty Sheehan (b. Oct. 27, 1956): Golfer; LPGA Player of Year in 1983; clinched entry into LPGA Hall of Fame with her 30th career win in 1993; 3 LPGA titles (1983-84,93) and 2 U.S. Opens (1992,94).

Bill Shoemaker (b. Aug. 19, 1931): Jockey; all-time career wins leader with 8,833; 3-time Eclipse Award winner as jockey (1981) and special award recipient (1976,81); won Belmont 5 times, Kentucky Derby 4 times and Preakness twice; oldest jockey to win Kentucky Derby (age 54, aboard Ferdinand in 1986); retired in 1990 to become trainer; paralyzed in 1991 auto accident but continued to train horses.

Eddie Shore (b. Nov. 25, 1902, d. Mar. 16, 1985): Hockey D; only NHL defenseman to win Hart Trophy as MVP 4 times (1933,35-36,38); led Boston Bruins to Stanley Cup titles in 1929 and '39; had 105 goals and 1,047 penalty minutes in 14 seasons.

Frank Shorter (b. Oct. 31, 1947): Track & Field; won gold medal in marathon at 1972 Olympics, 1st American to win in 64 years.

Don Shula (b. Jan. 4, 1930): Football; retired after 1995 season with an NFL-record 347 career wins (including playoffs) and a winning percentage of .670; took six teams to Super Bowl and won twice with Miami (VII, VIII); 4-time Coach of Year, twice with Baltimore (1964,68) and twice with Miami (1970-71); coached 1972 Dolphins to 17-0 record, the only undefeated team in NFL history.

Charlie Sifford (b. June 2, 1922): Golf; won the Hartford Open in 1967 with a final-round 64, becoming the first black player to win a PGA event; won the PGA Seniors Championship in 1975; amassed over $1 million in career earnings; published his autobiography "Just Let Me Play" in 1992.

Al Simmons (b. May 22, 1902, d. May 26, 1956): Baseball OF; led AL in batting twice (1930-31) with Philadelphia A's and knocked in 100 runs or more 11 straight years (1924-34).

O.J. Simpson (b. July 9, 1947): Football RB; won Heisman Trophy in 1968 at USC; ran for 2,003 yards in NFL in 1973; All-Pro 5 times; MVP in 1973; rushed for 11,236 career yards; TV analyst and actor after career ended; arrested June 17, 1994 as suspect in double murder of ex-wife Nicole Brown Simpson and her friend Ronald Goldman; acquitted on Oct. 3, 1995 by a Los Angeles jury in criminal trial but forced to make financial reparations after losing civil suit.

George Sisler (b. Mar. 24, 1893, d. Mar. 26, 1973): Baseball 1B; hit over .400 twice (1920,22); 257 hits in 1920 still a major league record.

Mary Decker Slaney (b. Aug. 4, 1958): U.S. middle distance runner; has held 7 separate American track & field records from the 800 to 10,000 meters; won both 1,500 and 3,000 meters at 1983 World Championships in Helsinki, but no Olympic medals.

Raisa Smetanina (b. Feb. 29, 1952): Russian Nordic skier; all-time Winter Olympics medalist with 10 cross-country medals (4 gold, 5 silver and a bronze) in 5 appearances (1976,80,84,88,92).

Billy Smith (b. Dec. 12, 1950): Hockey G; led NY Islanders to 4 consecutive Stanley Cups (1980-83); won Vezina Trophy in 1982; Stanley Cup MVP in 1983.

Dean Smith (b. Feb. 28, 1931): Basketball; No. 1 on all-time NCAA coaches victory list (879); led North Carolina to 25 NCAA tournaments in 34 years, reaching Final Four 10 times and winning championship twice (1982,93); coached U.S. Olympic team to gold medal in 1976.

Emmitt Smith (b. May 15, 1969): Football RB; consensus All-America (1989) at Florida; 4-time NFL rushing leader (1991-93,95); 4-time All-Pro (1992-95); regular season and Super Bowl MVP in 1993; played on three Super Bowl champions (1993,94,96).

John Smith (b. Aug. 9, 1965): Wrestler; 2-time NCAA champion for Oklahoma St. at 134 lbs (1987-88) and Most Outstanding Wrestler of '88 championships; 3-time world champion; gold medal winner at 1988 and '92 Olympics at 137 lbs; won Sullivan Award (1990); coached Oklahoma St. to 1994 NCAA title and brother Pat was Most Outstanding Wrestler.

Lee Smith (b. Dec. 4, 1957): Baseball RHP; 3-time NL saves leader (1983,91-92); retired as all-time saves leader with 478 and an ERA of 3.03; 10 seasons with 30 or more saves and 3 times saved over 40.

Michelle Smith deBruin (b. Apr. 7, 1969): Irish swimmer; won three gold medals at the 1996 Olympics; accused of using performance-enhancing drugs but passed all tests until she was suspended for 4 years by FINA in 1998 for tampering with a urine sample.

Ozzie Smith (b. Dec. 26, 1954): Baseball SS; won 13 straight Gold Gloves (1980-92); played in 12 straight All-Star Games (1981-92); MVP of 1985 NL playoffs; holds all-time assist record for SS with 8,375.

Walter (Red) Smith (b. Sept. 25, 1905, d. Jan. 15, 1982): Sportswriter for newspapers in Philadelphia and New York from 1936-82; won Pulitzer Prize for commentary in 1976.

Conn Smythe (b. Feb. 1, 1895, d. Nov. 18, 1980): Hockey pioneer; built Maple Leaf Gardens in 1931; managed Toronto to 7 Stanley Cups before retiring in 1961.

Sam Snead (b. May 27, 1912): Golfer; won both Masters and PGA 3 times and British Open once; runner-up in U.S. Open 4 times; PGA Player of Year in 1949; oldest player (52 years, 10 months) to win PGA event with Greater Greensboro Open title in 1965; all-time PGA Tour career victory leader with 81.

Duke Snider (b. Sept. 26, 1926): Baseball OF; hit 40 or more home runs five straight seasons (1953-57); played in six World Series with the Dodgers and batted .286 with 11 home runs; nicknamed "Duke of Flatbush"; in 18 seasons hit 407 home runs, scored 1,259 runs and had 1,333 RBI.

Annika Sorenstam (b. Oct. 9, 1970): Swedish golfer; won the 1995 U.S. Women's Open as her first LPGA victory; won the event again in 1996; College Player of the Year and NCAA champion in 1991.

Sammy Sosa (b. Nov. 12, 1968): Baseball OF; slugging Chicago Cub who surpassed Roger Maris' season home run record (61), just after Mark McGwire did, in 1998 and finished the year with 66; NL MVP (1998).

Javier Sotomayor (b. Oct. 13, 1967): Cuban high jumper; first man to clear 8 feet (8-0) on July 29, 1989; won gold medal at 1992 Olympics with jump of only 7-ft, 8-in.; broke world record with leap of 8-0½ in 1993.

Warren Spahn (b. Apr. 23, 1921): Baseball LHP; led NL in wins 8 times; won 20 or more games 13 times; Cy Young winner in 1957; most career wins (363) by a left-hander.

Tris Speaker (b. Apr. 4, 1888, d. Dec. 8, 1958): Baseball OF; all-time leader in outfield assists (449) and doubles (792); had .344 career BA and 3,515 hits.

J.G. Taylor Spink (b. Nov. 6, 1888, d. Dec. 7, 1962): Publisher of *The Sporting News* from 1914-62; Baseball Writers' Assn. annual meritorious service award named after him.

Leon Spinks (b. July 11, 1953): Boxing; won heavyweight crown in split decision over Muhammad Ali in Feb.1978; Ali regained title seven months later; won gold medal in light heavyweight division at 1976 Olympics; brother Michael won the heavyweight title in 1983; were the only brothers to hold world titles; known more for frequent traffic violations and lavish lifestyle than bouts late in career; filed for bankruptcy in 1986.

Mark Spitz (b. Feb. 10, 1950): Swimmer; set 23 world and 35 U.S. records; won all-time record 7 gold medals (4 individual, 3 relay) in 1972 Olympics; also won 4 medals (2 gold, a silver and a bronze) in 1968 Games for a total of 11; comeback attempt at age 41 foundered in 1991.

Latrell Sprewell (b. Sept. 8, 1970): Basketball G; became an NBA All-Star in just his second pro season out of Alabama; led Golden State in scoring four years in a row; made headlines in 1997 after being suspended by the NBA for attacking Warriors head coach P.J. Carlesimo during a practice.

Amos Alonzo Stagg (b. Aug. 16, 1862, d. Mar. 17, 1965): Football innovator; coached at U. of Chicago for 41 seasons and College of the Pacific for 14 more; 314-199-35 record; elected to both college football and basketball Halls of Fame.

Willie Stargell (b. Mar. 6, 1940): Baseball OF-1B; led NL in home runs twice (1971,73); 475 career HRs; NL co-MVP and World Series MVP in 1979.

Bart Starr (b. Jan. 9, 1934): Football QB; led Green Bay to 5 NFL titles and 2 Super Bowl wins from 1961-67; regular season MVP in 1966; MVP of Super Bowls I and II.

Roger Staubach (b. Feb. 5, 1942): Football QB; Heisman Trophy winner as Navy junior in 1963; led Dallas to 2 Super Bowl titles (1972,78) and was Super Bowl MVP in 1972; 5-time leading passer in NFC (1971,73,77-79).

George Steinbrenner (b. July 4, 1930): Baseball; principal owner of NY Yankees since 1973; teams have won 6 pennants and 4 World Series (1977-78,96,98); has changed managers 21 times and GMs 11 times in 25 years; ordered by baseball commish Fay Vincent in 1990 to surrender control of club for dealings with small-time gambler; reinstated in 1993.

Casey Stengel (b. July 30, 1890, d. Sept. 29, 1975): Baseball; player for 14 years and manager for 25; outfielder and lifetime .284 hitter with 5 clubs (1912-25); guided NY Yankees to 10 AL pennants and 7 World Series titles from 1949-60; 1st NY Mets skipper from 1962-65.

Ingemar Stenmark (b. Mar. 18, 1956): Swedish alpine skier; 3-time World Cup overall champ (1976-78); posted 86 World Cup wins in 16 years; won 2 gold medals at 1980 Olympics.

Helen Stephens (b. Feb. 3, 1918, d. Jan. 17, 1994): Track & Field; set 3 world records in 100-yard dash and 4 more in 100 meters in 1935-36; won gold medals in 100 meters and 4x100-meter relay in 1936 Olympics; retired in 1937.

Woody Stephens (b. Sept. 1, 1913, d. Aug. 22, 1998): Horse racing; trainer who saddled an unprecedented 5 straight winners in Belmont Stakes (1982-86); also had two Kentucky Derby winners (1974,84); trained 1982 Horse of Year Conquistador Cielo; won Eclipse award as nation's top trainer in 1983.

David Stern (b. Sept. 22, 1942): Basketball; marketing expert and NBA commissioner since 1984; took office the year Michael Jordan turned pro; has presided over stunning artistic and financial success of NBA both nationally and internationally; league has grown from 23 teams to 29 during his watch and opened offices worldwide; oversaw launch of WNBA in 1997.

Teófilo Stevenson (b. Mar. 29, 1952): Cuban boxer; won 3 consecutive gold medals as Olympic heavyweight (1972,76,80); did not turn pro.

Jackie Stewart (b. June 11, 1939): Auto racer; won 27 Formula One races and 3 world driving titles from 1965-73.

John Stockton (b. Mar 26, 1962): Basketball G; all-time NBA leader in every major assist category, including most in a season (1,164), highest average in a season (14.4 per game) and most overall (13,087); also holds the NBA record for career steals (2,701); All-NBA team in '94 and '95; member of 1992 and '96 US Olympic basketball Dream Teams; 8-time All-Star.

Dwight Stones (b. Dec. 6, 1953): Track & Field; set three world records in the high jump, the last in 1976 (7-7¼); won bronze medal at 1972 Summer Games and silver in 1976; won NCAA indoor and outdoor titles in 1976; competed until 1979 when he was suspended for taking money for a television appearance; attempted comeback in 1983 but failed to make 1984 Olympic squad.

Curtis Strange (b. Jan. 30, 1955): Golfer; won consecutive U.S. Open titles (1988-89); 3-time leading money winner on PGA Tour (1985,87-88); first PGA player to win $1 million in one year (1988).

Picabo Street (b. Apr. 3, 1971): Skiing; 2-time Olympic medalist, gold (Super G in 1998) and silver (downhill in 1994); her 1995 World Cup downhill series title first-ever by U.S. woman, she repeated the feat in 1996.

Kerri Strug (b. Nov. 19, 1977): Gymnastics; delivered the most dramatic moment of the 1996 Summer Olympics when she completed a vault (9.712) after spraining her ankle; the second vault assured the first all-around gold medal for a US Women's gymnastics team; a poor performance by the Russian team on the beam had clinched the gold medal for the US but Strug was unaware when she made the second vault, the injury prevented her from participating in any individual events.

Louise Suggs (b. Sept. 7, 1923): Golfer; won 11 majors and 50 LPGA events overall from 1949-62.

James E. Sullivan (b. Nov. 18, 1862, d. Sept. 16, 1914): Track & Field; pioneer who founded Amateur Athletic Union (AAU) in 1888; director of St. Louis Olympic Games in 1904; AAU's Sullivan Award for performance and sportsmanship named after him.

John L. Sullivan (b. Oct. 15, 1858, d. Feb. 2, 1918): Boxer; world heavyweight champion (1882-92); last of bare-knuckle champions.

Pat Summitt (b. June 14, 1952): Basketball; women's basketball coach at Tennessee (1974—); 2nd all-time in career victories to Jody Conradt of Texas; coached 1984 US women's basketball team to its first Olympic gold medal; has coached Lady Vols to 6 national championships (1987,89,91,96,97,98).

Don Sutton (b. April 2, 1945): Baseball RHP; won 324 games and tossed 58 shutouts in his 23-year career; recorded NL record five career 1-hitters; played with Dodgers, Astros, Brewers, Athletics, Angels and was a 4-time All-Star; elected to Hall of Fame in 1998.

Lynn Swann (b. Mar. 7, 1952): Football WR; played nine seasons with Pittsburgh (1974-82); appeared in four Super Bowls and had 16 catches for 364 yards and three TDs; named MVP of Super Bowl X for 4-161, 1 TD performance.

Barry Switzer (b. Oct. 5, 1937): Football; coached Oklahoma to 3 national titles (1974-75,85); 4th on all-time winning pct list at .837 (157-29-4); resigned in 1989 after OU was slapped with 3-year NCAA probation and 5 players were brought up on criminal charges; hired as Dallas Cowboys head coach in 1994 and led team to victory in Super Bowl XXX in 1996, resigning before '98 season.

Paul Tagliabue (b. Nov. 24, 1940): Football; NFL attorney who was elected league's 4th commissioner in 1989; ushered in salary cap in 1994; league expanded by 2 teams in 1995 for 1st time since '76; brought $300 million suit against Dallas owner Jerry Jones on Sept. 18, 1995 for Jones' rogue sponsorship deals with Pepsi and Nike.

Anatoli Tarasov (b. 1918, d. June 23, 1995): Hockey; coached Soviet Union to 9 straight world championships and 3 Olympic gold medals (1964,68,72).

Jerry Tarkanian (b. Aug. 30, 1930): Basketball; 4th all-time winningest college coach with .807 win pct.; has amassed over 700 wins in 28 years at Long Beach St., UNLV and Fresno St.; led UNLV to 4 Final Fours and 1 national title (1990); fought 16-year battle with NCAA over purity of UNLV program; quit as coach after going 26-2 in 1991-92; fired after 20 games (9-11) as coach of NBA San Antonio Spurs in 1992; unretired in 1995 to coach his alma mater, Fresno St.

Fran Tarkenton (b. Feb. 3, 1940): Football QB; 2-time NFL All-Pro (1973,75); Player of Year (1975); threw for 47,003 yards and 342 TDs (both former NFL records) in 18 seasons with Vikings and Giants.

Chuck Taylor (b. June 24, 1901, d. June 23, 1969): Converse traveling salesman whose name came to grace the classic, high-top canvas basketball sneakers known as "Chucks"; over 500 million pairs have been sold since 1917; he also ran clinics worldwide and edited Converse Basketball Yearbook (1922-68).

Lawrence Taylor (b. Feb. 4, 1959): Football LB; All-America at North Carolina (1980); only defensive player in NFL history to be consensus Player of Year (1986); led NY Giants to Super Bowl titles in 1986 and '90 seasons; played in a record 10 Pro Bowls (1981-90); retired after 1993 season with 132½ sacks and has had several drug-related arrests since; inducted into Hall of Fame in 1999.

Gustavo Thoeni (b. Feb. 28, 1951): Italian alpine skier; 4-time World Cup overall champion (1971-73,75); won giant slalom at 1972 Olympics.

Frank Thomas (b. May 27, 1968): Baseball 1B; All-America at Auburn in 1989; 2-time AL MVP with Chicago (1993,94); has hit 40 home runs 3 times (1993,95,96); nicknamed "the Big Hurt."

Isiah Thomas (b. Apr. 30, 1961): Basketball; led Indiana to NCAA title as sophomore and Final 4 MOP in 1981; consensus All-America guard in '81; led Detroit to 2 NBA titles in 1989 and '90; NBA Finals MVP in 1990; 3-time All-NBA 1st team (1984-86); retired in 1994 at age 33 after tearing right Achilles tendon; purchased struggling CBA in 1999.

Thurman Thomas (b. May 16, 1966): Football RB; 3-time AFC rushing leader (1990-91,93); 2-time All-Pro (1990-91); NFL Player of Year (1991); led Buffalo to 4 straight Super Bowls (1991-94).

Daley Thompson (b. July 30, 1958): British Track & Field; won consecutive gold medals in decathlon at 1980 and '84 Olympics.

John Thompson (b. Sept. 2, 1941): Basketball; coached centers Patrick Ewing, Alonzo Mourning and Dikembe Mutombo at Georgetown; reached NCAA tourney final 3 out of 4 years with Ewing, winning title in 1984; also led Hoyas to 6 Big East tourney titles; coached 1988 U.S. Olympic team to bronze medal; retired abruptly during 1999 season with 27-year mark of 596-239.

Bobby Thomson (b. Oct. 25, 1923): Baseball OF; career .270 hitter who won the 1951 NL pennant for the NY Giants with a 1-out, 3-run HR in the bottom of the 9th inning of Game 3 of a best-of-3 playoff with Brooklyn; the pitcher was Ralph Branca, the count was 0-1 and the Dodgers were ahead 4-2; the Giants had trailed Brooklyn by 13½ games on Aug. 11.

Jim Thorpe (b. May 28, 1888, d. May 28, 1953): 2-time All-America in football; won both pentathlon and decathlon at 1912 Olympics; stripped of medals a month later for playing semi-pro baseball prior to Games; medals restored in 1982; played major league baseball (1913-19) and pro football (1920-26,28); chosen "Athlete of the Half Century" by AP in 1950.

Bill Tilden (b. Feb. 10, 1893, d. June 5, 1953): Tennis; won 7 U.S. and 3 Wimbledon titles in 1920s; led U.S. to 7 straight Davis Cup victories (1920-26).

Tinker to Evers to Chance Chicago Cubs double play combination from 1903-10; immortalized in poem by New York sportswriter Franklin P. Adams— SS Joe Tinker (1880-1948), 2B Johnny Evers (1883-1947) and 1B Frank Chance (1877-1924); all 3 managed the Cubs and made the Hall of Fame.

Y.A. Tittle (b. Oct. 24, 1926): Football QB; played 17 years in AAFC and NFL; All-Pro 4 times; league MVP with San Francisco (1957) and NY Giants (1962); passed for 28,339 career yards.

Alberto Tomba (b. Dec. 19, 1966): Italian alpine skier; all-time Olympic alpine medalist with 5 (3 gold, 2 silver); became 1st alpine skier to win gold medals in 2 consecutive Winter Games when he won the slalom and giant slalom in 1988 then repeated in the GS in '92; also won silvers in slalom in 1992 and '94.

Vladislav Tretiak (b. Apr. 25, 1952): Hockey G; led USSR to Olympic gold medals in 1972 and '76; starred for Soviets against Team Canada in 1972, and again in 2 Canada Cups (1976,81).

Lee Trevino (b. Dec. 1, 1939): Golfer; 2-time winner of 3 majors—U.S. Open (1968,71), British Open (1971-72) and PGA (1974,84); Player of Year once on PGA Tour (1971) and 3 times with Seniors (1990,92,94); 27 PGA Tour and 28 Senior Tour wins.

Felix Trinidad (b. Jan. 10, 1973): Puerto Rican boxer; undefeated WBC/IBF welterweight champion; won WBC belt with a majority decision over the slightly-favored Oscar De La Hoya in their highly-anticipated meeting on Sept. 18, 1999.

Bryan Trottier (b. July 17, 1956): Hockey C; led NY Islanders to 4 straight Stanley Cups (1980-83); Rookie of Year (1976); scoring champion (134 points) and regular season MVP in 1979; playoff MVP (1980); added 5th and 6th Cups with Pittsburgh in 1991 and '92; entered Hockey Hall of Fame in 1997.

Gene Tunney (b. May 25, 1897, d. Nov. 7, 1978): Boxer; world heavyweight champion from 1926-28; beat 31-year-old champ Jack Dempsey in unanimous 10 round decision in 1926; beat him again in famous "long count" rematch in '27; quit while still champion in 1928 with 65-1-1 record and 47 KOs.

Ted Turner (b. Nov. 19, 1938): Sportsman and TV mogul; skippered *Courageous* to America's Cup win in 1977; owner of Atlanta Braves, Hawks and expansion NHL Thrashers; owner of CNN, TNT and WTBS; founder of Goodwill Games; 1991 *Time* Man of Year.

Mike Tyson (b. June 30, 1966): Boxer; youngest (age 19) to win heavyweight title (WBC in 1986); undisputed champ from 1987 until upset loss to 42-1 shot Buster Douglas on Feb. 10, 1990, in Tokyo; found guilty on Feb. 10, 1992, of raping 18-year-old Miss Black America contestant Desiree Washington in Indianapolis on July 19, 1991; sentenced to 6-year prison term; released May 9, 1995 after serving 3 years; reclaimed WBC and WBA belts with wins over Frank Bruno and Bruce Seldon in 1996; lost WBA title to Evander Holyfield in 1996; brought his career to a halt when he bit Holyfield twice in the ear during their WBA championship fight in 1997; returned to jail in 1999 for assaulting two motorists during a 1998 traffic dispute; see career fight record in Boxing chapter.

Wyomia Tyus (b. Aug. 29, 1945): Track & Field; 1st woman to win consecutive Olympic gold medals in 100m (1964-68).

Peter Ueberroth (b. Sept. 2, 1937): Organizer of 1984 Summer Olympics in LA; 1984 *Time* Man of Year; baseball commissioner from 1984-89; headed Rebuild Los Angeles for one year after 1992 riots.

Johnny Unitas (b. May 7, 1933): Football QB; led Baltimore Colts to 2 NFL titles (1958-59) and a Super Bowl win (1971); All-Pro 5 times; 3-time MVP (1959,64,67); passed for 40,239 career yards and 290 TDs.

Al Unser Jr. (b. Apr. 19, 1962): Auto racer; 2-time CART-IndyCar national champion (1990,94); captured Indy 500 for 2nd time in 3 years in '94, giving Unser family 9 overall titles at the Brickyard; 31 CART wins in 17 years; son of Al and nephew of Bobby.

Al Unser Sr. (b. May 29, 1939): Auto racer; 3-time USAC-CART national champion (1970,83,85); 4-time winner of Indy 500 (1970-71,78,87); retired in 1994 ranked 3rd on all-time CART list with 39 wins; younger brother of Bobby and father of Al Jr.

Bobby Unser (b. Feb. 20, 1934): Auto racer; 2-time USAC-CART national champion (1968,74); 3-time winner of Indy 500 (1968,75,81); retired after 1981 season; ranks 5th on all-time IndyCar list with 35 wins.

Gene Upshaw (b. Aug. 15, 1945): Football G; 2-time All-AFL and 3-time All-NFL selection with Oakland; helped lead Raiders to 2 Super Bowl titles in 1976 and '80 seasons; executive director of NFL Players Assn. since 1987; agreed to application of salary cap in 1994.

Jim Valvano (b. Mar. 10, 1946, d. Apr. 28, 1993): Basketball; coach at N.C. State whose team upset Houston to win national title in 1983; in 19 seasons as a coach appeared in 8 NCAA tournaments; career record 346-212; AD at N.C. State (1986-89) when a recruiting and admissions scandal forced him out of the job; worked as a broadcaster for ESPN and ABC; died after a year-long battle with cancer; The V Foundation for cancer research is named for him.

Norm Van Brocklin (b. Mar. 15, 1926, d. May 2, 1983): Football QB-P; led NFL in passing 3 times and punting twice; led LA Rams (1951) and Philadelphia (1960) to NFL titles; MVP in 1960.

Amy Van Dyken (b. Feb. 17, 1973): Swimming; first American woman to win four gold medals in one Olympics (1996); won the individual 50M freestyle, 100M butterfly, and was on the US team for the 4x100 freestyle and 4x50 medley.

Johnny Vander Meer (b. Nov. 2, 1914, d. Oct. 6, 1997): Baseball LHP; only major leaguer to pitch consecutive no-hitters (June 11 & 15, 1938).

Harold S. Vanderbilt (b. July 6, 1884, d. July 4, 1970): Sportsman; successfully defended America's Cup 3 times (1930, 34,37); also invented contract bridge in 1926.

Glenna Collett Vare (b. June 20, 1903, d. Feb. 10, 1989): Golfer; won record 6 U.S. Women's Amateur titles from 1922-35; "the female Bobby Jones."

Andy Varipapa (b. Mar. 31, 1891, d. Aug. 25, 1984): Bowler; trick-shot artist; won consecutive All-Star match game titles (1947-48) at age 55 and 56.

Mo Vaughn (b. Dec. 15, 1967): Baseball 1B; 1995 AL MVP with Boston; 3-time All-Star; signed a 6-year, $80 million deal with Anaheim in 1999.

Bill Veeck (b. Feb. 9, 1914, d. Jan. 2, 1986): Maverick baseball executive; owned AL teams in Cleveland, St. Louis and Chicago from 1946-80; introduced ballpark giveaways, exploding scoreboards, Wrigley Field's ivy-covered walls and midget Eddie Gaedel; won World Series with Indians (1948) and pennant with White Sox (1959).

Jacques Villeneuve (b. Apr. 9, 1971): Canadian auto racer; Indianapolis 500 runner-up and IndyCar Rookie of Year in 1994; won 500 and IndyCar driving championship in 1995; jumped to Formula One racing in 1996 and won the F1 title in 1997.

Fay Vincent (b. May 29, 1938): Baseball; became 8th commissioner after death of A. Bartlett Giamatti in 1989; presided over World Series earthquake, owners' lockout and banishment of NY Yankees owner George Steinbrenner in his first year on the job; contentious relationship with owners resulted in his resignation on Sept. 7, 1992, four days after 18-9 "no confidence" vote.

Lasse Viren (b. July 22, 1949): Finnish runner; won gold medals at 5,000 and 10,00 meters in 1972 Munich Olympics; repeated 5,000/10,000 double in 1976 Games and added a 5th place in the marathon.

Dick Vitale (b. June 9, 1939): Broadcaster; Radio and television commentator for ESPN and ABC Sports known for his enthusiastic, almost spastic style; had successful college and pro basketball coaching career with the University of Detroit (1973-77) and the Detroit Pistons (1978-79); he's been nominated for a Cable ACE award eight times and won once in 1995.

Lanny Wadkins (b. Dec. 5, 1949): Golfer; member of 8 Ryder Cup teams and captain of 1995 team; 21 PGA Tour wins.

Honus Wagner (b. Feb. 24, 1874, d. Dec. 6, 1955): Baseball SS; hit .300 for 17 consecutive seasons (1897-1913) with Louisville and Pittsburgh; led NL in batting 8 times; ended career with 3,430 career hits, a .329 average and 722 stolen bases.

Lisa Wagner (b. May 19, 1961): Bowler; 3-time LPBT Player of Year (1983,88,93); 1980's Bowler of Decade; first woman to earn $100,000 in a season; winner of a record 32 pro titles as of Sept. 1999.

Grete Waitz (b. Oct. 1, 1953): Norwegian runner; 9-time winner of New York City Marathon from 1978-88; won silver medal at 1984 Olympics.

Jersey Joe Walcott (b. Jan. 31, 1914, d. Feb. 27, 1994): Boxer; oldest heavyweight (37) to ever win the championship; lost four championship bouts before knocking out Ezzard Charles in the seventh round in 1951; lost the title the following year, losing to Rocky Marciano; won 50 bouts, 30 by knockout, lost 17 and fought one draw as a professional; later became sheriff of Camden County, NJ.

Doak Walker (b. Jan. 1, 1927, d. Sept. 27, 1998): Football HB; won Heisman Trophy as SMU junior in 1948; led Detroit to 2 NFL titles (1952-53); All-Pro 4 times in 6 years.

Herschel Walker (b. Mar. 3, 1962): Football RB; led Georgia to national title as freshman in 1980; won Heisman in 1982 then jumped to upstart USFL in '83; signed by Dallas Cowboys after USFL folded; led NFL in rushing in 1988; traded to Minnesota in 1989 for 5 players and 6 draft picks; later played for Philadelphia and NY Giants and again with Dallas.

Rusty Wallace (b. Aug. 14, 1956): Auto racing; NASCAR Winston Cup champion in 1989 and runner-up in 1980, 1988 and 1993; recorded 18 victories and $3,616,226 from 1993-94; has earned $1 million in earnings 9 different seasons.

Bill Walsh (b. Nov. 30, 1931): Football; Hall of Fame coach and GM of 3 Super Bowl winners with San Francisco (1982,85,89); retired after 1989 Super Bowl; returned to college coaching in 1992 for his second stint at Stanford; retired after 1994 season; returned as 49er GM in 1999.

Bill Walton (b. Nov. 5, 1952): Basketball C; 3-time College Player of Year (1972-74); led UCLA to 2 national titles (1972-73); led Portland to NBA title as MVP in 1977; regular season MVP in 1978.

Darrell Waltrip (b. Feb. 5, 1947): Auto racing; 3-time NASCAR Winston Cup champion (1981,82,85); active leader with 84 career Winston Cup wins and 59 poles.

Arch Ward (b. Dec. 27, 1896, d. July 9, 1955): Promoter and sports editor of *Chicago Tribune* from 1930-55; founder of baseball All-Star Game (1933), Chicago College All-Star Football Game (1934) and the All-America Football Conference (1946-49).

Charlie Ward (b. Oct. 12, 1970): Football QB and Basketball G; first Heisman winner to play for national champs (Florida St. in 1993) since Tony Dorsett in 1976, won Sullivan Award (1993); not taken in NFL Draft; 1st round pick of NY Knicks in 1994 NBA draft.

Glenn (Pop) Warner (b. Apr. 5, 1871, d. Sept. 7, 1954): Football innovator; coached at 7 colleges over 49 years; 319 career wins 2nd only to Bear Bryant's 323 in Div. I-A; produced 47 All-Americas, including Jim Thorpe and Ernie Nevers.

Tom Watson (b. Sept. 4, 1949): Golfer; 6-time PGA Player of the Year (1977-80,82,84); has won 5 British Opens, 2 Masters and a U.S. Open; 4-time Ryder Cup member; 34 PGA tour wins.

Earl Weaver (b. Aug. 14, 1930): Baseball; managed the Baltimore Orioles to 6 Eastern Division titles, four AL pennants and a World Series victory in 1970; was ejected 91 times and suspended four times for outbursts against umpires; record of 1,480-1,060 from 1968-82 and 1985-86.

Dick Weber (b. Dec. 23, 1929): Bowler; 3-time PBA Bowler of the Year (1961,63,65); won 30 PBA titles in 4 decades.

Johnny Weissmuller (b. June 2, 1904, d. Jan. 20 1984): Swimmer; won 3 gold medals at 1924 Olympics and 2 more at 1928 Games; became Hollywood's most famous Tarzan.

Jerry West (b. May 28, 1938): Basketball G; 2-time All-America and NCAA Final 4 MOP (1959) at West Virginia; led 1960 U.S. Olympic team to gold medal; 10-time All-NBA 1st-team; NBA finals MVP (1969); led LA Lakers to NBA title once as player (1972) and 5 times as GM in 1980s; his silhouette serves as the NBA's logo.

Pernell Whitaker (b. Jan. 2, 1964): Boxer; won Olympic gold medal as lightweight in 1984; has won 4 world championships as lightweight, jr. welterweight, welterweight and jr. middleweight; outfought but failed to beat Julio Cesar Chavez when Sept. 10, 1993 welterweight title defense ended in controversial draw; pro record of 41-3-1 (17 KOs).

Bill White (b. Jan. 28, 1934): Baseball; NL president and highest ranking black executive in sports from 1989-94; as 1st baseman, won 7 Gold Gloves and hit .286 with 202 HRs in 13 seasons.

Byron (Whizzer) White (b. June 8, 1917): Football; All-America HB at Colorado (1937); signed with Pittsburgh in 1938 for the then largest contract in pro history ($15,800); took Rhodes Scholarship in 1939; returned to NFL in 1940 to lead league in rushing and retired in 1941; named to U.S. Supreme Court by President Kennedy in 1962 and stepped down in 1993.

Reggie White (b. Dec. 19, 1961): Football DE; consensus All-America in 1983 at Tennessee; 7-time All-NFL (1986-92) with Philadelphia; signed as free agent with Green Bay in 1993 for $17 million over 4 years; played key role in Packers 1997 Super Bowl victory; made headlines in 1998 after making controversial public comments about gays and minorities; retired in 1999 as all-time NFL leader in sacks (192½).

Kathy Whitworth (b. Sept. 27, 1939): Golf; 7-time LPGA Player of the Year (1966-69,71-73); won 6 majors; 88 tour wins, most on LPGA or PGA tour.

Hazel Hotchkiss Wightman (b. Dec. 20, 1886, d. Dec. 5, 1974): Tennis; won 16 U.S. national titles; 4-time U.S. Women's champion (1909-11,19); donor of Wightman Cup.

Hoyt Wilhelm (b. July 26, 1923): Baseball RHP; Knuckleballer who is 3rd all-time in games pitched (1,070) and 1st in games finished (651) and games won in relief (123); career ERA of 2.52 and 227 saves; 1st reliever inducted into Hall of Fame (1985).

Lenny Wilkens (b. Oct. 28, 1937): Basketball; NBA's all-time winningest coach (1223-1012 including playoffs); MVP of 1960 NIT as Providence guard; played 15 years in NBA, including 4 as player-coach; coached Seattle to NBA title in 1979; Coach of Year in 1994 with Atlanta; one of only two men (John Wooden) to be honored by the Hall of Fame as player and coach.

Dominique Wilkins (b. Jan. 12, 1960): Basketball F; last player to lead NBA in scoring (1986) before Michael Jordan's reign; All-NBA 1st team in 1986; elder statesman of Dream Team II.

Bud Wilkinson (b. Apr. 23, 1916, d. Feb. 9, 1994): Football; played on 1936 national championship team at Minnesota; coached Oklahoma to 3 national titles (1950,55,56); won 4 Orange and 2 Sugar Bowls; teams had winning streaks of 47 (1953-57) and 31 (1948-50); retired after 1963 season with 145-29-4 record in 17 years; also coached St. Louis of NFL to 9-20 record in 1978-79.

Ricky Williams (b. May 21, 1977): Football RB; became all-time NCAA Div. IA leader in rushing yards (6,279) and touchdowns (75) at Texas; 1998 Heisman Trophy winner; Mike Ditka and New Orleans Saints made history by trading their entire draft to take him fifth overall in 1999 NFL draft.

Serena Williams (b. Sept. 26, 1981): Tennis; beat Martina Hingis for 1999 U.S. Open championship becoming the first black woman to win a Grand Slam title since Althea Gibson in 1958; won doubles title at the 1999 U.S. and French Opens with sister Venus.

Ted Williams (b. Aug. 30, 1918): Baseball OF; led AL in batting 6 times, and HRs and RBI 4 times each; won Triple Crown twice (1942,47); 2-time MVP (1946,49); last player to bat .400 when he hit .406 in 1941; Marine Corps combat pilot who missed three full seasons during World War II (1943-45) and most of two others (1952-53) during Korean War; hit .344 lifetime with 521 HRs in 19 years with Boston Red Sox.

Venus Williams (b. June 17, 1980): Tennis; reached the finals of the 1997 U.S. Open and the semis in 1998 and 1999; won doubles title at the 1999 U.S. and French Opens with sister Serena; recorded fastest serve in WTA history with 127 mph blast.

Walter Ray Williams Jr. (b. Oct. 6, 1959): Bowling and Horseshoes; 5-time PBA Bowler of Year (1986,93,96,97,98); won 6 World Horseshoe Pitching titles.

Hack Wilson (b. Apr. 26, 1900, d. Nov. 23, 1948): Baseball; as a Chicago Cub, he produced one of baseball's most outstanding seasons in 1930 with 56 homeruns, .356 batting average, 105 walks and, most amazingly, a major league record 191 RBIs that still stands; finished with 1,461 hits, 244 homers, 1,062 RBIs; member of Baseball Hall of Fame.

Dave Winfield (b. Oct. 3, 1951): Baseball OF-DH; selected in 4 major sports league drafts in 1973— NFL, NBA, ABA, and MLB; chose baseball and has played in 12 All-Star Games over 22-year career; at age 41, helped lead Toronto to World Series title in 1992; 3,110 hits and 465 HRs.

Katarina Witt (b. Dec. 3, 1965): East German figure skater; 4-time world champion (1984-85,87-88); won consecutive Olympic gold medals (1984,88).

John Wooden (b. Oct. 14, 1910): Basketball; College Player of Year at Purdue in 1932; coached UCLA to 10 national titles (1964-65,67-73,75); one of only two men (Lenny Wilkens) to be honored by the Hall of Fame as player and coach.

Tiger Woods (b. Dec. 30, 1975): Golfer; youngest (18) and first minority to win U.S. Amateur in 1994, won it again in '95 and '96; turned pro in Sept. of '96 and won the fifth event he entered, the Las Vegas Invitational; in first full year on the tour, he won 6 of 25 events and broke the single season money record; won 1997 Masters by a record 18 under par and 13 stroke margin of victory, the latter being a record for all majors; won second major at 1999 PGA Championship.

Mickey Wright (b. Feb. 14, 1935): Golfer; won 3 of 4 majors (LPGA, U.S. Open, Titleholders) in 1961; 4-time winner of both U.S. Open and LPGA titles; 82 career wins including 13 majors.

Early Wynn (b. Jan. 6, 1920, d. Mar. 4, 1999): Baseball RHP; won 20 games 5 times; Cy Young winner in 1959; 300-244 record in 23 years.

Kristi Yamaguchi (b. July 12, 1971): Figure Skating; finished second in the 1991 American nationals but won the world title that year; dominated the sport in 1992 by winning the national, world and Olympic titles and then turned professional.

Cale Yarborough (b. Mar. 27, 1940): Auto racer; 3-time NASCAR national champion (1976-78); 4-time winner of Daytona 500 (1968,77,83-84); ranks 5th on NASCAR all-time list with 83 wins.

Carl Yastrzemski (b. Aug. 22, 1939): Baseball OF; led AL in batting 3 times; won Triple Crown and MVP in 1967; had 3,419 hits and 452 HRs in 23 years with Boston; member of Hall of Fame.

Cy Young (b. Mar. 29, 1867, d. Nov. 4, 1955): Baseball RHP; all-time leader in wins (511), losses (313), complete games (751) and innings pitched (7,356); had career 2.63 ERA in 22 years (1890-1911); 30-game winner 5 times and 20-game winner 11 other times; threw 3 no-hitters and perfect game (1904); AL and NL pitching awards named after him.

Sheila Young (b. Oct. 14, 1950): Speed skater and cyclist; 1st U.S. athlete to win 3 medals at Winter Olympics (1976); won speed skating overall and sprint cycling world titles in 1976.

Steve Young (b. Oct. 11, 1961): Football QB; All-America at BYU (1983); NFL Player of Year (1992) with SF 49ers; only QB to lead NFL in passer rating 4 straight years (1991-94); rating of 112.8 in 1994 was highest ever; threw record 6 TD passes in MVP performance in Super Bowl XXIX; holds NFL career records for highest passer rating (97.6) and completion percentage (64.5), entering 1999.

Robin Yount (b. Sept. 16, 1955): Baseball SS-OF; AL MVP at 2 positions— as SS in 1982 and OF in '89; retired after 1993 season with 3,142 hits, 251 HRs and a major-league-record 123 sacrifice flies after 20 seasons with Milwaukee Brewers; inducted into Hall of Fame in 1999.

Steve Yzerman (b. May 9, 1965): Hockey C; Captained the Detroit Red Wings to back-to-back Stanley Cup sweeps in '96-97 and '97-98; took home the Conn Smythe Trophy as the playoff MVP in 1998.

Mario Zagalo (b. Aug. 9, 1931): Soccer; Brazilian forward who is one of only two men (Franz Beckenbauer is the other) to serve as both captain (1962) and coach (1970,94) of World Cup champion.

Babe Didrikson Zaharias (b. June 26, 1911, d. Sept. 27, 1956): All-around athlete who was chosen AP Female Athlete of Year 6 times from 1932-54; won 2 gold medals (javelin and 80-meter hurdles) and a silver (high jump) at 1932 Olympics; took up golf in 1935 and went on to win 55 pro and amateur events; won 10 majors, including 3 U.S. Opens (1948,50,54); helped found LPGA in 1949; chosen female "Athlete of the Half Century" by AP in 1950.

Frank Zamboni (b. Jan. 16, 1901, d. July 27, 1988): Mechanic, ice salesman and skating rink owner in Paramount, Calif.; invented 1st ice-resurfacing machine in 1949; over 4,000 sold in more than 33 countries since.

Emil Zatopek (b. Sept. 19, 1922): Czech distance runner; winner of 1948 Olympic gold medal at 10,000 meters; 4 years later, won unprecedented Olympic triple crown (5,000 meters, 10,000 meters and marathon) at 1952 Games in Helsinki.

John Ziegler (b. Feb. 9, 1934): Hockey; NHL president from 1977-92; negotiated settlement with rival WHA in 1979 that led to inviting four WHA teams (Edmonton, Hartford, Quebec and Winnipeg) to join NHL; stepped down June 12, 1992, 2 months after settling 10-day players' strike.

Pirmin Zurbriggen (b. Feb. 4, 1963): Swiss alpine skier; 4-time World Cup overall champ (1984,87-88,90) and 3-time runner-up; 40 World Cup wins in 10 years; won gold and bronze medals at 1988 Olympics.

Ballparks & Arenas

The final price for Seattle's SAFECO Field was well over the $500 million mark, making it the most expensive baseball stadium ever built.

AP/Wide World Photos

Patriot Games

New England Patriots owner Bob Kraft got an offer he couldn't refuse from the state of Connecticut. Somehow he refused it anyway.

by
Karl Ravech

I remember the phone call as if it were yesterday. I remember it so well because I had made it. The morning after the owner of the New England Patriots, Bob Kraft, had announced along with the Governor of Connecticut, John Rowland, that the two had agreed to build a new state of the art facility to house the NFL franchise in downtown Hartford, I placed a call to Kraft's son Jonathan.

He was in all the news clips standing proudly next to his father, and considering the age similarities between myself and him, I figured we'd be able to connect. We did connect, though unfortunately, it wasn't too long after that I learned the connection was as weak as a broken promise.

My history with the New England Patriots goes back some 25 years and as my family goes, their relationship with the team dates back even further.

As long as I can remember enjoying sports, and that basically means as long as I can remember, my father had a pair of season tickets. Despite the team's ineptitudes, going to the games was an event. The same way many fathers talk about taking their little boys to baseball games, I shared the experience with my dad at football games. And you know, as the years go by, those times become more special.

To me, the Patriots were not just a football team, they were a large part of my childhood and as a father of a 4-year-old boy myself, the thought of having Sam and I share the same bond that my father and I did took on added significance.

The deal the State of Connecticut put on the table to entice the team to move 90 miles from Foxboro was financially unbalanced. In essence the governor had pledged to provide the Kraft family with a $374 million dollar facility. The cost to the Kraft family was as much as it costs to breathe,

Karl Ravech has been an ESPN anchor and reporter since 1993.

AP/Wide World Photos

Connecticut governor **John Rowland**, left, is shown here presenting Patriots owner **Bob Kraft** with a Connecticut license plate. Rowland thought he had swung a deal to bring the team to Hartford until a loophole allowed Kraft to back out and keep the team in Massachusetts.

and yet they choked as if someone were forcing a fistful of knuckles down their throats instead of a fistful of dollars.

Why did the deal unravel? Perhaps it was the pressure of the NFL to keep a team in the Boston television market. Perhaps Kraft felt an obligation to the city and state in which he grew up. Clearly the decision was not a financial one, as the deal Massachusetts offered him was comical in relation to what Connecticut was offering.

In the end there was Rowland, standing in the middle of a burning building with a pipette full of water trying to put it out. "Failure is not an option," he uttered with regards to having the deal fall apart. But it did fall apart and in the opinion of most in the state of Connecticut, that was a good thing. I saw it as devastating.

The investment I had made in the dream was sincere. I remember lying in bed with my son explaining the rules of the game to him. He had just about figured out what a touchdown was when I had to explain the game of life to him. Business decisions, deceit, lies, broken dreams, broken promises.

My life and my relationship with Sam will be just fine without the Patriots. In fact, I guess in a way I owe Bob Kraft and his son a heartfelt thank you. All of the energies we would have committed to rooting for a faceless football team can now be focused on each other. ■

Karl Ravech's Top Ten List of Ballparks and Arenas in the News

10. **Staples Center**. The new top-of-the-line home of the Clippers,

Tiger Stadium, which opened five days after the Titanic sunk in 1912, was closed down after the 1999 season as the Tigers move to the new Comerica Park in downtown Detroit for the 2000 season.

Lakers and Kings opens with a Bruce Springsteen concert and will become the first building to house three major league teams simultaneously. Good luck to the NBA and NHL schedule makers.

9. **Golf Courses**. I know this is supposed to be about ballparks and stadiums but there is more construction of new golf courses than any other sports venues. In fact, many are called stadium courses. The game's popularity is rising and like many new sports facilities, the new courses are shrines.

8. **Los Angeles Football**. Does the NFL need L.A.? Larry King says no. If they had a team it would limit the number of televised games they get each week. The biggest obstacle in returning the NFL to Los Angeles? A stadium.

They don't have one. Several individuals have offered huge sums of money to build one. For now the league goes on and so does life in Los Angeles. Did somebody say "punt?"

7. **Candlestick Park**. It was in the middle of the summer but it was the equivalent of a November in New England. The fact is Pacific Bell Park has a Fenway Park flavor to it. Players can hit homers into the bay. Fans will be able to see the skyline and the bridge. In the end, the Stick will be remembered for the quake and the cold.

6. **Cleveland Browns Stadium**. For three years some of the best football fans in America went without their beloved Browns. A return to the NFL was met with great anticipation and a brand new facility.

552

AP/Wide World Photos

Tragedy struck **Miller Park** in Milwaukee on July 14 when a 480-foot crane fell while lifting a section of the park's retractable roof. Three workers were killed and the park's opening was moved from April 2000 to March 2001.

Jacobs Field raised the bar in Cleveland. The Indians success raised expectations. The Browns will struggle for a while but when dogs get treated like kings, life is good.

5. **Miller Park**. A tragic accident which claimed the lives of three construction workers left a black cloud over the damaged ballpark, the organization and the city. Bud Selig's daughter now runs the team and under her guidance the future is very positive. The stadium won't open on time but Brewers fans should keep an open mind and in time it will all work out.

4. **Conseco Fieldhouse**. Two years ago the Indiana Pacers hired Larry Bird to coach the team. Continu-

ing their throwback theme, they've built a fieldhouse for the future. Unlike the fieldhouses which dot the Hoosier state, this one is state of the art. It looks like it was built in the 1940's but has all the amenities and luxuries of the next millennium.

3. **SAFECO Field**. Seattle has opened its beautiful new ballpark. The problem is neither of the team's stars, Ken Griffey Jr. or Alex Rodriguez, seem to want to share the future with it. Kevin Costner and Co. wanted us to believe "if you build it, they will come." In this case, they've built it and it may force them to leave.

2. **Fenway Park**. Bostonians, who are among the most provincial in the country, are waging a battle

553

reminiscent of the Tea Party to save the old ballpark that was built in 1912. The fact that a group has listed the park as one of the 10 most endangered historic resources will not be enough to save it. The memories live forever, as will the Green Monster. Within five years a new park should rise along with a familiar green wall in left field.

1. **Tiger Stadium**. The ballyard which was at baseball's most famous address, the corner of Michigan and Trumbull streets, will be vacated following the 1999 season. For over a century Tiger fans came, cried and carried the banner for what made the game great. The $285 million Comerica Park brings all the amenities. Will it bring victories? ■

THE **NUMBERS**

INSIDE

TIGER STADIUM TRIBUTE

Major League Baseball lost one of the good ones in 1999 as Tiger Stadium closed its doors, in favor of the brand new Comerica Park in downtown Detroit. The following list merely scratches the surface of memorable occurrences from the corner of Michigan and Trumbull.

First game — April 20, 1912 (Detroit 6, Cleveland 5)

First hit — April 20, 1912 (Nap Lajoie, Cleveland)

First run — April 20, 1912 (Shoeless Joe Jackson, Cleveland)

First HR — May 5, 1912 (Del Pratt, St. Louis, thanks to a flukey bounce that found its way through the centerfield scoreboard.)

First HR hit entirely out of the rebuilt Tiger Stadium — May 4, 1939 (Ted Williams, Boston)

WHAT A RELIEF

Lost in all the talk about luxury boxes and naming rights is the effect the ballparks and arenas of the next millennium will have on the average fan. Well, we should be able to rest more comfortably in the future with more restrooms than ever before. Here are the planned increases in restrooms for six of next year's new stadiums.

	Old	New	%Change
Staples Center (L.A.)	4	55	+1,275
AmericanAirlines Arena (Miami)	10	50	+400
Raleigh Ent. & Sports Arena (Carolina)	8	38	+375
Pepsi Center (Denver)	11	41	+273
Conseco Fieldhouse (Ind.)	12	22	+120
Philips Arena (Atlanta)	12	30	+150

OPEN AND SHUT CASE

As a public service to fans in Milwaukee, Houston and New York who are waiting for their teams to begin playing in ballparks with retractable roofs, here's a look at how the three major league teams with the option of putting the top down have fared in those games. (Through Sept. 19, 1999)

Team	Open	Win %	Closed	Win %
Toronto	211-211	.500	220-148	.598
Arizona	31-29	.517	50-45	.526
Seattle	20-13	.606	1-5	.166

Note: Toronto's totals include postseason games. Also, Toronto is 31-26 in games categorized by the team as "other." These are games in which the roof was closed during the game or only partially closed. ■

BALLPARKS & ARENAS
COMING ATTRACTIONS

1999

BASEBALL

Seattle (AL): Grand opening of SAFECO Field (SAFECO Corp. is the title sponsor) occurred on July 15, 1999. A crowd of 44,607 watched the Mariners lose 3-2 to the San Diego Padres. Located on the site of the old Kingdome parking lot; seating capacity of 47,115 for baseball only; retractable-roof, grass field; includes 69 luxury suites; estimated cost: $498 million.

NBA BASKETBALL

Atlanta (East) Philips Arena (Royal Philips Electronics NV is the title sponsor), home of the NBA Hawks and NHL-expansion Thrashers, was scheduled to open on Sept. 18, 1999 for a preseason Thrashers game. The arena has a capacity of 20,000 for basketball and 18,750 for hockey including 96 luxury suites; located on the old site of the Omni which was demolished on July 27, 1997. The Hawks home opener on the $213 million facility was scheduled for Nov. 4, 1999 against the Milwaukee Bucks.

Denver (West): Grand opening of the Pepsi Center (Pepsi-Cola is the title sponsor) was scheduled for Oct. 1, 1999 for a concert by Canadian songstress Celine Dion; seats 19,300 for NBA Nuggets and 18,129 for NHL Avalanche; includes 95 luxury suites; estimated cost: $160 million. Nuggets home opener was scheduled for Nov. 2, 1999 against the Phoenix Suns.

Indiana (East): Grand opening of 18,500-seat Conseco Fieldhouse (Conseco Inc. is the title sponsor) was scheduled for Nov. 6, 1999 for a game between the Pacers and the Boston Celtics. The retro-styled building is located in downtown Indianapolis between Pennsylvania and Delaware streets. Estimated cost: $175 million. The arena has 69 luxury suites and serves as home to the Pacers and IHL's Indianapolis Ice.

Los Angeles (West): Grand opening of the Staples Center (Staples Inc. is the title sponsor), which will house the NBA Clippers and Lakers and NHL Kings, was scheduled for a Bruce Springsteen concert on Oct. 17. It will be the first facility to host three major professional teams simultaneously. The complex, which is near the downtown L.A. Convention Center, will seat 20,000 for basketball, 18,500 for hockey and include 160 prime-level suites. Estimated cost: $240 million. Clippers home opener was scheduled for Nov. 2, 1999 against Seattle. Lakers home opener scheduled for Nov. 3, 1999 against Vancouver.

Miami (East): Grand opening of AmericanAirlines Arena (American Airlines is the title sponsor) was scheduled for a concert by Gloria Estefan on Dec. 31, 1999; arena is located on the FEC tract next to Bayside on the Miami waterfront. Arena seats approximately 19,600 for NBA Heat and has 156 luxury suites. Estimated cost: $228 million. Heat home opener was scheduled for Jan. 2, 2000 against the Orlando Magic.

Toronto (East): Grand opening of the Air Canada Centre (Air Canada is the title sponsor) took place on Feb. 20, 1999 with a 3-2 victory by the NHL Maple Leafs over the Canadiens. The new home to the NBA Raptors and NHL Maple Leafs is located on site of Old Canada Post Building at corner of Bay Street and Lake Shore Road; arena seats 19,800 for basketball and 18,800 for hockey; includes 65 suites on the 200 level; estimated cost: $172 million (US). Raptors' home opener was Feb. 21, 1999 with a 102-87 win over the Vancouver Grizzlies.

NFL FOOTBALL

Cleveland (AFC): Grand opening of Cleveland Browns Stadium was a preseason NFL game against the Vikings on Aug. 21, 1999. The Browns lost to the Vikings 24-17 in front of 71,398 fans. The 72,000-seat open-air stadium is located on the old site of Cleveland Stadium and includes 148 luxury suites. Estimated cost: $280 million. The field is natural turf and is heated to keep the field from freezing.

Tennessee (AFC): Grand opening of Adelphia Coliseum (Adelphia Communications is the title sponsor) for the redubbed NFL Tennessee Titans was a preseason NFL game against the Falcons on Aug. 27, 1999. The Titans beat Atlanta 17-3 in front 65,729 fans. The natural grass, open-air stadium seats 67,000 and has 144 luxury suites; located in the East Bank area of downtown Nashville. The coliseum is also home to Tennessee State football; Estimated cost: $290 million.

NHL HOCKEY

Atlanta (expansion team): Philips Arena (Royal Philips Electronics NV is the title sponsor), home of the NHL-expansion Thrashers and NBA Hawks was scheduled to open on Sept. 18, 1999 for a preseason Thrashers game. The arena has a capacity of 18,750 for hockey and 20,000 for basketball including 96 luxury suites; located on the old site of the Omni which was demolished on July 27, 1997.

Carolina (East): The Raleigh Entertainment and Sports Arena (title sponsor pending) was set to open for the start of the 1999-2000 NHL season. The building, located next to Carter Finley Stadium and the North Carolina State Fairgrounds, has a capacity of 19,000 for basketball and 20,000 for hockey and include 75 luxury suites; estimated cost: $152 million. The arena will also be home to N.C. State basketball. Hurricanes home opener was set for Oct. 29, 1999 against the New Jersey Devils.

Colorado (West): Grand opening of the Pepsi Center (Pepsi-Cola is the title sponsor) was scheduled for Oct. 1, 1999 for a concert by Canadian songstress Celine Dion; seats 18,129 for NHL Avalanche and 19,300 for NBA Nuggets; includes 95 luxury suites; estimated cost: $160 million. Avalanche's home opener was scheduled for Oct. 13, 1999 against the Boston Bruins.

Los Angeles (West): Grand opening of the Staples Center (Staples Inc. is the title sponsor), which will house the NHL Kings and NBA Clippers and Lakers was scheduled for a Bruce Springsteen concert on Oct. 17, 1999. The complex, which is near the downtown L.A. Convention Center, will have 18,500 seats for hockey and 20,000 seats for basketball, 160 prime-level suites and 2,500 club seats. The Staples Center will be the first facility to host three major professional teams during the same season. Estimated cost: $240 million. Kings home opener was scheduled for Oct. 20, 1999 against the Boston Bruins.

Toronto (East): Grand opening of the Air Canada Centre (Air Canada is the title sponsor) took place on Feb. 20, 1999 with a 3-2 victory by the Maple Leafs over the Canadiens. The new home to the NHL Maple Leafs and NBA Raptors is located on site of Old Canada Post Building at corner of Bay Street and Lake Shore Road; seats 18,800 for hockey and 19,800 for basketball; includes 65 suites; estimated cost: $172 million (US). Leafs home opener was scheduled for Oct. 4, 1999 against the Boston Bruins.

2000

BASEBALL

Detroit (AL): Ground was broken for Comerica Park (Comerica Bank is the title sponsor) on Oct. 29, 1997. Located near a new stadium for the Detroit Lions in downtown Detroit's Foxtown Theater district about one mile from existing Tiger Stadium; baseball-only park will seat approximately 40,000 and have 80 luxury suites; estimated cost: $290 million. Grand opening slated for opening day 2000.

Houston (NL): Groundbreaking for the Enron Field (Enron Oil & Gas Co. is the title sponsor) on the east side of downtown Houston occurred on October 30, 1997. The natural grass ballpark will feature a retractable roof which can open and close in 12 minutes; will seat 42,000 and have over 60 luxury suites; left field will be connected to Union train station, which will also house the Astros administrative offices, retail stores and a cafe. Estimated cost: $260 million. Grand opening slated for opening day 2000.

San Francisco (NL): Construction of Pacific Bell Park (Pacific Bell is the title sponsor) is well underway; to be located right on the waterfront at China Basin; the open-air baseball-only park will seat 40,800, including 5,300 club seats and 67 luxury suites; estimated cost: $306 million. Giants' home opener scheduled for April 2000.

NFL FOOTBALL

Cincinnati (AFC): Groundbreaking for Paul Brown Stadium took place on April 25, 1998. The project will cost approximately $400 million. The open-air, grass-field stadium will have a futuristic design and seat 64,000 for football, including 7,600 club seats and 104 luxury suites; Bengals' home opener scheduled for August 2000.

NHL HOCKEY

Columbus (expansion): Groundbreaking for Nationwide Arena (Nationwide Insurance is the title sponsor) took place on May 26, 1998. The privately-funded arena for the NHL expansion Columbus Blue Jackets will seat 18,500 for hockey and cost an estimated $150 million. The building will have 76 luxury suites and is scheduled to open in August 2000.

Minnesota (expansion): Groundbreaking for New Saint Paul Arena (title sponsor pending) took place on June 23, 1998. The multi-purpose arena will seat 18,600 for the NHL expansion Minnesota Wild, including 74 luxury suites, and feature a transparent glass exterior. The building, located in downtown St. Paul in front of the old St. Paul Civic Center, will cost an estimated $130 million and is scheduled to open in September 2000.

2001

BASEBALL

Milwaukee (AL): Groundbreaking for Miller Park (Miller Brewing Co. is the title sponsor) on a site adjacent to the existing County Stadium took place Nov. 9, 1996. The retractable-roof stadium will have natural grass, an asymmetrical outfield and seat approximately 43,000 including 70 luxury suites; Brewers' home opener originally scheduled for April 2000 but that has been delayed to April 2001 in wake of an accident that killed three ironworkers when a 567-foot, 2,100-ton crane collapsed on July 14, 1999 during construction on the new park; estimated cost: $250 million plus an estimated $50-75 million to repair accident damage.

Pittsburgh (NL): Groundbreaking for PNC Park (PNC Bank is the title sponsor) took place April 7, 1999. To be located on a site on the Allegheny River between Three Rivers Stadium and the Roberto Clemente Bridge (formerly Sixth Street Bridge). The baseball-only park would seat 38,127, have 69 luxury suites and cost an estimated $228 million; Stadium would be part of city's larger construction project, including enlarged convention center and new ballpark for NFL's Steelers; earliest Pirates' home opener would be April 2001.

NFL FOOTBALL

Pittsburgh (AFC): Groundbreaking for new open-air, grass-field stadium took place June 18, 1999. Stadium will seat 65,000 and contain 120 luxury suites. To be located 300 yards west of Three Rivers Stadium as part of city's larger construction project, including enlarged convention center and PNC Park for MLB's Pirates. Estimated cost for new football stadium: $233 million. Earliest opening would be September 2001.

2002

BASEBALL

New York (NL): New ballpark is in planning stages. To be located adjacent to Shea Stadium in Queens. The retractable-roof stadium would seat 45,000, including 78 luxury suites and 5,000 club seats. The stadium will have a grass field on a platform that can be rolled out into the parking lot to receive enough sunshine and moisture. With the field out, the stadium could seat 60,000 for hockey, basketball or other events. Estimated cost: $500 million. Earliest opening would be April 2002.

San Diego (NL): New ballpark is in planning stages. To be located on a one-square-block downtown lot and be part of a larger redevelopment project that would include a new hotel, office space and retail space. The as-yet-unnamed baseball-only park would seat approximately 42,000. Earliest Padres' home opener would be April 2002.

Philadelphia (NL): New ballpark is in planning stages. Several key factors for the baseball only, grass-field park, including location, need to be finalized. Ballpark would seat 45,000 and be part of a retail complex. Estimated cost of entire project: $315 million. Earliest Phillies home opener would be April 2002.

NFL FOOTBALL

Seattle (AFC): Construction for the as-yet-unnamed stadium is set to begin in April 2000. Stadium and exhibition center are to be located on old site of Kingdome; would seat 67,000 (expanded capacity: 72,000) and include 82 luxury suites and 7,000 club seats; open-air, grass-field stadium and exhibition center would cost an estimated $400 million. The Seahawks would compete at Husky Stadium for two years during construction. Earliest Seahawks home opener would be August 2002.

Philadelphia (NFC): New stadium for the Eagles is in the planning stages. Several key factors including financing and location need to be finalized. Estimated cost: $300 million. Earliest Eagles home opener could be August 2002 but will most likely be later.

2003

BASEBALL

Cincinnati (NL): New ballpark is in planning stages. Many details, including the site, are still to be determined. Estimated cost of project: $235 million. Earliest opening would be spring 2003. Stay tuned.

Boston (AL): New Fenway Park is in the planning stages. The open-air, grass field park would be located adjacent to the existing Fenway Park and emulate many of the Fenway's features including the Green Monster and Pesky's Pole; part of the project includes preserving portions of the old ballpark as a public park; would seat 44,130 and the earliest Red Sox home opener would be April 2003.

NFL FOOTBALL

New England (AFC): New, as-yet-unnamed, stadium to be located next to existing Foxboro Stadium is in the planning stages. The new stadium would have 68,000 seats and include 80 luxury suites and over 7,000 club seats; Estimated cost: $285 million. Earliest Patriots home opener would be August 2003.

Home, Sweet Home

The home fields, home courts and home ice of the AL, NL, NBA, NFL, CFL, NHL, WNBA, NCAA Division I-A college football and Division I basketball. Also included are Formula One, IndyCar, Indy Racing League and NASCAR auto racing tracks.

Attendance figures for the 1998 NFL regular season and the 1998-99 NBA and NHL regular seasons are provided. See Baseball chapter for 1999 AL and NL attendance figures.

MAJOR LEAGUE BASEBALL

American League

	Built	Capacity	LF	LCF	CF	RCF	RF	Field
Anaheim Angels . . . .**Edison International Field of Anaheim**	1966	**45,050**	365	380	400	370	365	Grass
Baltimore Orioles. . . . .**Oriole Park at Camden Yards**	1992	**48,262**	333	364	410	373	318	Grass
Boston Red Sox. . . . .**Fenway Park**	1912	**33,871**	310	379	390*	380	302	Grass
Chicago White Sox . . . .**Comiskey Park**	1991	**44,321**	347	375	400	375	347	Grass
Cleveland Indians . . . .**Jacobs Field**	1994	**43,368**	325	370	405	375	325	Grass
Detroit Tigers . . . .**Comerica Park**	2000	**40,000**	345	398	420	380	330	Grass
Kansas City Royals . . . .**Kauffman Stadium**	1973	**40,529**	330	375	400	375	330	Grass
Minnesota Twins. . . . .**Hubert H. Humphrey Metrodome**	1982	**48,678**	343	385	408	367	327	Turf
New York Yankees . . . .**Yankee Stadium**	1923	**57,746**	318	399	408	385	314	Grass
Oakland Athletics . . . . .**Network Associates Coliseum**	1966	**43,662**	330	367	400	367	330	Grass
Seattle Mariners . . . .**SAFECO Field**	1999	**45,611**	331	390	405	386	326	Grass
Tampa Bay Devil Rays . . . .**Tropicana Field**	1990	**44,027**	370	415	404	370	322	Turf
Texas Rangers. . . . .**The Ballpark in Arlington**	1994	**52,000**	332	390	400	407	381	Grass
Toronto Blue Jays . . . .**SkyDome**	1989	**50,516**	328	375	400	375	328	Turf

*The staight-away centerfield fence at Fenway Park is 390 feet from home plate but the deepest part of centerfield, a.k.a. "the Triangle," is 420 feet away. The left-field fence, known as "the Green Monster," is 37 feet tall topped with a 23-foot screen.

National League

	Built	Capacity	LF	LCF	CF	RCF	RF	Field
Arizona Diamondbacks. . . . .**Bank One Ballpark**	1998	**49,075**	330	376	407	376	334	Grass
Atlanta Braves . . . .**Turner Field**	1996	**50,062**	335	380	401	385	330	Grass
Chicago Cubs . . . .**Wrigley Field**	1914	**38,957**	355	368	400	368	353	Grass
Cincinnati Reds . . . .**Cinergy Field**	1970	**52,953**	330	375	404	375	330	Turf
Colorado Rockies . . . .**Coors Field**	1995	**50,381**	347	390	415	375	350	Grass
Florida Marlins . . . .**Pro Player Stadium**	1987	**42,531**	330	385	434	385	345	Grass
Houston Astros. . . . .**Enron Field**	2000	**42,000**	315	TBD	436	TBD	326	Grass
Los Angeles Dodgers . . . .**Dodger Stadium**	1962	**56,000**	330	385	395	385	330	Grass
Milwaukee Brewers . . . .**County Stadium**	1953	**53,192**	315	392	402	392	315	Grass
Montreal Expos. . . . .**Olympic Stadium**	1976	**46,500**	325	375	404	375	325	Turf
New York Mets . . . .**Shea Stadium**	1964	**55,775**	338	371	410	371	338	Grass
Philadelphia Phillies . . . .**Veterans Stadium**	1971	**62,411**	330	378	408	378	330	Turf
Pittsburgh Pirates . . . .**Three Rivers Stadium**	1970	**47,972**	335	375	400	375	335	Turf
St. Louis Cardinals. . . . .**Busch Stadium**	1966	**49,625**	330	372	402	372	330	Grass
San Diego Padres . . . .**Qualcomm Stadium**	1967	**53,166**	327	370	405	370	327	Grass
San Francisco Giants . . . .**Pacific Bell Park**	2000	**40,800**	335	TBD	404	420	307	Grass

Rank by Capacity

AL		NL	
New York.	.57,746	Philadelphia	.62,411
Texas	.52,000	Los Angeles	.56,000
Toronto.	.50,516	New York.	.55,775
Minnesota	.48,678	San Diego	.53,166
Baltimore	.48,262	Cincinnati	.52,953
Seattle	.45,611	Colorado	.50,381
Anaheim	.45,050	Atlanta	.50,062
Chicago.	.44,321	St. Louis	.49,625
Tampa Bay	.44,027	Arizona	.49,075
Oakland	.43,662	Pittsburgh	.47,972
Cleveland	.43,368	Montreal	.46,500
Kansas City	.40,529	Milwaukee	.43,000
Detroit	.40,000	Florida	.42,531
Boston	.33,871	Houston	.42,000
		San Francisco	.40,800
		Chicago.	.38,957

Rank by Age

AL		NL	
Boston	.1912	Chicago.	.1914
New York	.1923	Milwaukee	.1953
Anaheim	.1966	Los Angeles.	.1962
Oakland	.1966	New York	.1964
Kansas City	.1973	St. Louis	.1966
Minnesota	.1982	San Diego	.1967
Toronto	.1989	Cincinnati	.1970
Tampa Bay	.1990	Pittsburgh.	.1970
Chicago.	.1991	Philadelphia	.1971
Baltimore	.1992	Montreal	.1976
Cleveland	.1994	Florida.	.1987
Texas	.1994	Atlanta	.1993
Seattle	.1999	Colorado	.1995
Detroit	.2000	Arizona	.1998
		Houston	.2000
		San Francisco	.2000

Note: New York's Yankee Stadium (AL) was rebuilt in 1976.

Major League Baseball (Cont.)
Home Fields

Listed below are the principal home fields used through the years by current American and National League teams. The NL became a major league in 1876, the AL in 1901.

The capacity figures in the right-hand column indicate the largest seating capacity of the ballpark while the club played there. Capacity figures before 1915 (and the introduction of concrete grandstands) are sketchy at best and have been left blank.

American League

Anaheim Angels

1961	Wrigley Field (Los Angeles)	20,457
1962-65	Dodger Stadium	56,000
1966–	Edison International Field of Anaheim	45,050
	(1966 capacity-43,250)	

Baltimore Orioles

1901	Lloyd Street Grounds (Milwaukee)	–
1902-53	Sportsman's Park II (St. Louis)	30,500
1954-91	Memorial Stadium (Baltimore)	53,371
1992–	Oriole Park at Camden Yards	48,262

Boston Red Sox

1901-11	Huntington Ave. Grounds	–
1912–	Fenway Park	33,871
	(1934 capacity-27,000)	

Chicago White Sox

1901-10	Southside Park	–
1910-90	Comiskey Park I	43,931
1991–	Comiskey Park II	44,321

Cleveland Indians

1901-09	League Park I	–
1910-46	League Park II	21,414
1932-93	Cleveland Stadium	74,483
1994–	Jacobs Field	43,368

Detroit Tigers

1901-11	Bennett Park	–
1912-99	Tiger Stadium	46,945
2000–	Comerica Park	40,000
	(1912 capacity-23,000)	

Kansas City Royals

1969-72	Municipal Stadium	35,020
1973–	Kauffman Stadium	40,529
	(1973 capacity-40,762)	

Minnesota Twins

1901-02	American League Park (Washington, DC)	–
1903-60	Griffith Stadium	27,410
1960-81	Metropolitan Stadium (Bloomington, MN)	45,919
1982–	HHH Metrodome (Minneapolis)	48,678
	(1982 capacity-54,000)	

New York Yankees

1901-02	Oriole Park (Baltimore)	–
1903-12	Hilltop Park (New York)	–
1913-22	Polo Grounds II	38,000
1923-73	Yankee Stadium I	67,224
1974-75	Shea Stadium	55,101
1976–	Yankee Stadium II	57,746
	(1976 capacity-57,145)	

Oakland Athletics

1901-08	Columbia Park (Philadelphia)	–
1909-54	Shibe Park	33,608
1955-67	Municipal Stadium (Kansas City)	35,020
1968–	Network Associates Coliseum	43,662
	(1968 capacity-48,621)	

Seattle Mariners

1977-99	The Kingdome	59,166
1999–	SAFECO Field	45,611

Tampa Bay Devil Rays

1990–	Tropicana Field	44,027

Texas Rangers

1961	Griffith Stadium (Washington, DC)	27,410
1962-71	RFK Stadium	45,016
1972-93	Arlington Stadium (Texas)	43,521
1994-	The Ballpark in Arlington	52,000

Toronto Blue Jays

1977-89	Exhibition Stadium	43,737
1989–	SkyDome	50,516
	(1989 capacity-49,500)	

Ballpark Name Changes: ANAHEIM—**Edison International Field of Anaheim** originally Anaheim Stadium (1966-98); CHICAGO—**Comiskey Park I** originally White Sox Park (1910-12), then Comiskey Park in 1913, then White Sox Park again in 1962, then Comiskey Park again in 1976; CLEVELAND—**League Park** renamed Dunn Field in 1920, then League Park again in 1928; **Cleveland Stadium** originally Municipal Stadium (1932-74); DETROIT—**Tiger Stadium** originally Navin Field (1912-37), then Briggs Stadium (1938-60); KANSAS CITY—**Kauffman Stadium** originally Royals Stadium (1973-93); LOS ANGELES—**Dodger Stadium** referred to as Chavez Revine by AL while Angels played there (1962-65); OAKLAND—**Network Associates Coliseum** originally Oakland Alameda Coliseum (1968-98); PHILADELPHIA—**Shibe Park** renamed Connie Mack Stadium in 1953; ST. LOUIS—**Sportsman's Park** renamed Busch Stadium in 1953; WASHINGTON—**Griffith Stadium** originally National Park (1892-1920), **RFK Stadium** originally D.C. Stadium (1961-68).

National League

Arizona Diamondbacks

1998–	Bank One Ballpark	45,075

Atlanta Braves

1876-94	South End Grounds I (Boston)	–
1894-1914	South End Grounds II	–
1915-52	Braves Field	40,000
1953-65	County Stadium (Milwaukee)	43,394
1966-96	Atlanta-Fulton County Stadium	52,769
	(1966 capacity-50,000)	
1997–	Turner Field	50,062

Chicago Cubs

1876-77	State Street Grounds	–
1878-84	Lakefront Park	–
1885-91	West Side Park	–
1891-93	Brotherhood Park	–
1893-1915	West Side Grounds	–
1916–	Wrigley Field	38,957
	(1916 capacity-16,000)	

Cincinnati Reds

1876-79	Avenue Grounds	–
1880	Bank Street Grounds	–
1890-1901	Redland Field I	–
1902-11	Palace of the Fans	–
1912-70	Crosley Field	29,603
1970–	Cinergy Field	52,953
	(1970 capacity-52,000)	

Colorado Rockies

1993-94	Mile High Stadium (Denver)	76,100
1995–	Coors Field	50,381

Florida Marlins

1993–	Pro Player Stadium (Miami)	42,531

Houston Astros

1962-64	Colt Stadium	32,601
1965-99	The Astrodome	54,370
	(1965 capacity-45,011)	
2000–	Enron Field	42,000

Los Angeles Dodgers

1890	Washington Park I (Brooklyn)	–
1891-97	Eastern Park	–
1898-1912	Washington Park II	–
1913-56	Ebbets Field	31,497
1957	Ebbets Field	31,497
	& Roosevelt Stadium (Jersey City)	24,167
1958-61	Memorial Coliseum (Los Angeles)	93,600
1962–	Dodger Stadium	56,000

Milwaukee Brewers

1969	Sick's Stadium (Seattle)	59,166
1970-99	County Stadium (Milwaukee)	53,192
	(1970 capacity-46,620)	
2000	Miller Park	43,000

Montreal Expos

1969-76	Jarry Park	28,000
1977–	Olympic Stadium	46,500
	(1977 capacity-58,500)	

New York Mets

1962-63	Polo Grounds	55,987
1964–	Shea Stadium	55,775
	(1964 capacity-55,101)	

Philadelphia Phillies

1883-86	Recreation Park	–
1887-94	Huntingdon Ave. Grounds	–
1895-1938	Baker Bowl	18,800
1938-70	Shibe Park	33,608
1971–	Veterans Stadium	62,411
	(1971 capacity-56,371)	

Pittsburgh Pirates

1887-90	Recreation Park	–
1891-1909	Exposition Park	–
1909-70	Forbes Field	35,000
1970–	Three Rivers Stadium	47,972
	(1970 capacity-50,235)	

St. Louis Cardinals

1876-77	Sportsman's Park I	–
1885-86	Vandeventer Lot	–
1892-1920	Robison Field	18,000
1920-66	Sportsman's Park II	30,500
1966–	Busch Stadium	49,625
	(1966 capacity-50,126)	

San Diego Padres

1969–	Qualcomm Stadium	53,166
	(1969 capacity-47,634)	

San Francisco Giants

1876	Union Grounds (Brooklyn)	–
1883-88	Polo Grounds I (New York)	–
1889-90	Manhattan Field	–
1891-1957	Polo Grounds II	55,987
1958-59	Seals Stadium (San Francisco)	22,900
1960-99	3Com Park	63,000
	(1960 capacity-42,553)	
2000–	Pacific Bell Park	40,800

Ballpark Name Changes: ATLANTA—**Atlanta-Fulton County Stadium** originally Atlanta Stadium (1966-74), **Turner Field** originally Centennial Olympic Stadium (1996); CHICAGO—**Wrigley Field** originally Weeghman Park (1914-17), then Cubs Park (1918-25); CINCINNATI—**Redland Field** originally League Park (1890-93), **Crosley Field** originally Redland Field II (1912-33) and **Cinergy Field** originally Riverfront Stadium (1970-96); FLORIDA—**Pro Player Stadium** originally Joe Robbie Stadium (1987-96); HOUSTON—**Astrodome** originally Harris County Domed Stadium before it opened in 1965; PHILADELPHIA—**Shibe Park** renamed Connie Mack Stadium in 1953; ST. LOUIS—**Robison Field** originally Vandeventer Lot, then League Park, then Cardinal Park all before becoming Robison Field in 1901, **Sportsman's Park** renamed Busch Stadium in 1953, and **Busch Stadium** originally Busch Memorial Stadium (1966-82); SAN DIEGO—**Qualcomm Stadium** originally San Diego Stadium (1967-81) and San Diego/Jack Murphy Stadium (1982-96); SAN FRANCISCO—**3Com Park** originally Candlestick Park (1960-95).

NATIONAL BASKETBALL ASSOCIATION

Western Conference

		Location	Built	Capacity
Dallas Mavericks	**Reunion Arena**	Dallas, Texas	1980	**18,042**
Denver Nuggets	**Pepsi Center**	Denver, Colo.	1999	**19,300**
Golden State Warriors	**The Arena in Oakland**	Oakland, Calif.	1997	**19,596**
Houston Rockets	**Compaq Center**	Houston, Texas	1975	**16,285**
Los Angeles Clippers	**Staples Center**	Los Angeles, Calif.	1999	**20,000**
Los Angeles Lakers	**Staples Center**	Los Angeles, Calif.	1999	**20,000**
Minnesota Timberwolves	**Target Center**	Minneapolis, Minn.	1990	**19,006**
Phoenix Suns	**America West Arena**	Phoenix, Ariz.	1992	**19,023**
Portland Trail Blazers	**Rose Garden**	Portland, Ore.	1995	**19,980**
Sacramento Kings	**ARCO Arena**	Sacramento, Calif.	1988	**17,317**
San Antonio Spurs	**Alamodome**	San Antonio, Texas	1993	**20,557**
Seattle SuperSonics	**KeyArena at Seattle Center**	Seattle, Wash.	1962	**17,100**
Utah Jazz	**Delta Center**	Salt Lake City, Utah	1991	**19,911**
Vancouver Grizzlies	**General Motors Place**	Vancouver, B.C.	1995	**19,193**

Notes: Seattle's Key Arena was originally the Seattle Coliseum before being rebuilt in 1995; San Antonio's Alamodome seating is expandable to hold 34,215 while Portland's Rose Garden was "downsized" from a capacity of 21,538 to 19,980 prior to the 1998-99 season

National Basketball Association (Cont.)
Eastern Conference

		Location	Built	Capacity
Atlanta Hawks	**Philips Arena**	Atlanta, Ga.	1999	**20,000**
Boston Celtics	**FleetCenter**	Boston, Mass.	1995	**18,624**
Charlotte Hornets	**Charlotte Coliseum**	Charlotte, N.C.	1988	**23,799**
Chicago Bulls	**United Center**	Chicago, Ill.	1994	**21,711**
Cleveland Cavaliers	**Gund Arena**	Cleveland, Ohio	1994	**20,562**
Detroit Pistons	**The Palace of Auburn Hills**	Auburn Hills, Mich.	1988	**21,960**
Indiana Pacers	**Conseco Fieldhouse**	Indianapolis, Ind.	1999	**18,500**
Miami Heat	**Miami Arena**	Miami, Fla.	1988	**15,200**
	& AmericanAirlines Arena	Miami, Fla.	1999	**19,600**
Milwaukee Bucks	**Bradley Center**	Milwaukee, Wisc.	1988	**18,717**
New Jersey Nets	**Continental Airlines Arena**	E. Rutherford, N.J.	1981	**20,049**
New York Knicks	**Madison Square Garden**	New York, N.Y.	1968	**19,763**
Orlando Magic	**Orlando Arena**	Orlando, Fla.	1989	**17,248**
Philadelphia 76ers	**First Union Center**	Philadelphia, Pa.	1996	**20,444**
Toronto Raptors	**Air Canada Centre**	Toronto, Ont.	1999	**19,800**
Washington Wizards	**MCI Center**	Washington, D.C.	1997	**20,500**

Rank by Capacity

West		East	
San Antonio	20,557	Charlotte	23,799
LA Clippers	20,000	Detroit	21,960
LA Lakers	20,000	Chicago	21,711
Portland	19,980	Cleveland	20,562
Utah	19,911	Washington	20,500
Golden St.	19,596	Philadelphia	20,444
Denver	19,300	New Jersey	20,049
Vancouver	19,193	Atlanta	20,000
Phoenix	19,023	Toronto	19,800
Minnesota	19,006	New York	19,763
Dallas	18,042	Miami	19,600
Sacramento	17,317	Milwaukee	18,717
Seattle	17,100	Boston	18,624
Houston	16,285	Indiana	18,500
		Orlando	17,248

Note: Alamodome seating is expandable to 32,500.

Rank by Age

West		East	
Seattle	1962	New York	1968
Houston	1975	New Jersey	1981
Dallas	1980	Charlotte	1988
Sacramento	1988	Detroit	1988
Minnesota	1990	Milwaukee	1988
Utah	1991	Orlando	1989
Phoenix	1992	Chicago	1994
San Antonio	1993	Cleveland	1994
Portland	1995	Boston	1995
Vancouver	1995	Philadelphia	1996
Golden St.	1997	Washington	1997
Denver	1999	Toronto	1999
LA Clippers	1999	Atlanta	1999
LA Lakers	1999	Indiana	1999
		Miami	1999

Note: The Seattle Coliseum was rebuilt and renamed KeyArena in 1995.

1999 NBA Attendance

Official overall attendance in the NBA for the 1999 season was 12,134,906 for an average per game crowd of 16,738 over 50 games. Teams in each conference are ranked by attendance over 25 home games based on total tickets distributed; sellouts are listed in S/O column. Numbers in parentheses indicate rank in 1997-98.

Western Conference

	Attendance	S/O	Average
1 San Antonio (3)	527,357	9	21,094
2 Utah (2)	493,120	18	19,725
3 Portland (1)	486,556	14	19,462
4 Phoenix (4)	472,283	17	18,891
5 LA Lakers (7)	430,007	22	17,200
6 Minnesota (5)	427,974	4	17,119
7 Seattle (6)	426,800	25	17,072
8 Sacramento (10)	418,751	14	16,750
9 Vancouver (9)	417,966	7	16,719
10 Houston (8)	407,125	25	16,285
11 Dallas (11)	362,837	4	14,513
12 Golden St. (12)	335,837	1	13,433
13 Denver (13)	296,965	3	11,879
14 LA Clippers (14)	256,568	1	10,263
TOTAL	12,124906	164	16,738

Note: LA Clippers played 19 games at LA Sports Arena (0 sellouts and 8,448 avg.) and 6 at The Arrowhead Pond in Anaheim (1 sellout and 10,518 avg.)

Eastern Conference

	Attendance	S/O	Average
1 Chicago (1)	560,012	25	22,400
2 Charlotte (2)	480,807	0	19,232
3 New York (3)	494,075	25	19,763
4 Washington (4)	402,481	2	16,099
5 Detroit (5)	444,585	3	17,783
6 Boston (6)	440,602	6	17,624
7 New Jersey (7)	415,353	3	16,614
8 Atlanta (8)	331,831	3	13,273
9 Orlando (9)	411,091	10	16,444
10 Cleveland (10)	352,992	1	14,210
11 Toronto (11)	439,190	4	17,568
12 Philadelphia (12)	436,444	5	17,458
13 Indiana (13)	404,536	15	16,181
14 Milwaukee (14)	381,948	1	15,278
15 Miami (15)	378,813	21	15,153
TOTAL	12,134,906	124	16,738

Note: Washington played 5 games at USAir Arena (4 sellouts and 18,661 avg.) and 36 at their new MCI Center (19 sellouts, 19,665 avg.).

Home Courts

Listed below are the principal home courts used through the years by current NBA teams. The largest capacity of each arena is noted in the right-hand column. ABA arenas (1972-76) are included for Denver, Indiana, New Jersey and San Antonio.

Western Conference

Dallas Mavericks

1980–	Reunion Arena	18,042

Denver Nuggets

1967-75	Auditorium Arena	6,841
1975-99	McNichols Sports Arena	17,171
	(1975 capacity-16,700)	
1999–	Pepsi Center	19,300

Golden State Warriors

1946-52	Philadelphia Arena	7,777
1952-62	Convention Hall (Philadelphia)	9,200
	&Philadelphia Arena	7,777
1962-64	Cow Palace (San Francisco)	13,862
1964-66	Civic Auditorium	7,500
	& (USF Memorial Gym)	6,000
1966-67	Cow Palace, Civic Auditorium	
	& Oakland Coliseum Arena	15,000
1967-71	Cow Palace	14,500
1971-96	Oakland Coliseum Arena	15,025
	(1971 capacity-12,905)	
1996-97	San Jose Arena	18,500
1997–	The Arena in Oakland	19,596

Houston Rockets

1967-71	San Diego Sports Arena	14,000
1971-72	Hofheinz Pavilion (Houston)	10,218
1972-73	Hofheinz Pavilion	10,218
	&HemisFair Arena (San Antonio)	10,446
1973-75	Hofheinz Pavilion	10,218
1975–	Compaq Center	16,285
	(1975 capacity-15,600)	

Los Angeles Clippers

1970-78	Memorial Auditorium (Buffalo)	17,300
1978-84	San Diego Sports Arena	12,167
1985-94	Los Angeles Sports Arena	16,005
1994-99	Los Angeles Sports Arena	16,021
	&Arrowhead Pond	18,211
1999–	Staples Center	20,000

Los Angeles Lakers

1948-60	Minneapolis Auditorium	10,000
1960-67	Los Angeles Sports Arena	14,781
1967-99	Great Western Forum (Inglewood, CA)	17,505
	(1967 capacity-17,086)	
1999–	Staples Center	20,000

Minnesota Timberwolves

1989-90	Hubert H. Humphrey Metrodome	23,000
1990–	Target Center	19,006

Phoenix Suns

1968-92	Arizona Veterans' Memorial Coliseum	14,487
1992–	America West Arena	19,023

Portland Trail Blazers

1970-95	Memorial Coliseum	12,888
1995–	Rose Garden	19,980
	(1995 capacity-21,538)	

Sacramento Kings

1948-55	Edgarton Park Arena (Rochester, NY)	5,000
1955-58	Rochester War Memorial	10,000
1958-72	Cincinnati Gardens	11,438
1972-74	Municipal Auditorium (Kansas City)	9,929
	&Omaha (NE) Civic Auditorium	9,136
1974-78	Kemper Arena (Kansas City)	16,785
	&Omaha Civic Auditorium	9,136
1978-85	Kemper Arena	16,785
1985-88	ARCO Arena I	10,333
1988–	ARCO Arena II	17,317
	(1988 capacity-16,517)	

San Antonio Spurs

1967-70	Memorial Auditorium (Dallas)	8,088
	&Moody Coliseum (Dallas)	8,500
1970-71	Moody Coliseum	8,500
	Tarrant Convention Center (Ft. Worth)	13,500
	&Municipal Coliseum (Lubbock)	10,400
1971-73	Moody Coliseum	9,500
	&Memorial Auditorium	8,088
1973-93	HemisFair Arena (San Antonio)	16,057
1993–	The Alamodome	20,557

Seattle SuperSonics

1967-78	Seattle Center Coliseum	14,098
1978-85	Kingdome	40,192
1985-94	Seattle Center Coliseum	14,252
1994-95	Tacoma Dome	19,000
1995–	Key Arena at Seattle Center	17,100

Utah Jazz

1974-75	Municipal Auditorium	7,853
	& Louisiana Superdome	47,284
1975-79	Superdome	47,284
1979-83	Salt Palace (Salt Lake City)	12,519
1983-84	Salt Palace	12,519
	&Thomas & Mack Center (Las Vegas)	18,500
1985-91	Salt Palace	12,616
1991–	Delta Center	19,911

Vancouver Grizzlies

1995–	General Motors Place	19,193

Eastern Conference

Atlanta Hawks

1949-51	Wharton Field House (Moline, IL)	6,000
1951-55	Milwaukee Arena	11,000
1955-68	Kiel Auditorium (St. Louis)	10,000
1968-72	Alexander Mem. Coliseum (Atlanta)	7,166
1972-96	The Omni	16,378
1997-99	Georgia Dome	21,570
	&Alexander Mem. Coliseum	9,300
1999–	Philips Arena	20,000

Boston Celtics

1946-95	Boston Garden	14,890
1995–	FleetCenter	18,624

Note: From 1975-95 the Celtics played some regular season games at the Hartford Civic Center (15,418).

Charlotte Hornets

1988–	Charlotte Coliseum	23,799
	(1988 capacity-23,500)	

Chicago Bulls

1966-67	Chicago Amphitheater	11,002
1967-94	Chicago Stadium	18,676
1994–	United Center	21,711

Cleveland Cavaliers

1970-74	Cleveland Arena	11,000
1974-94	The Coliseum (Richfield, OH)	20,273
1994–	Gund Arena	20,562

National Basketball Association (Cont.)

Detroit Pistons

1948-52	North Side H.S. Gym (Ft. Wayne, IN)	.3,800
1952-57	Memorial Coliseum (Ft. Wayne)	9,306
1957-61	Olympia Stadium (Detroit)	14,000
1961-78	Cobo Arena	11,147
1978-88	Silverdome (Pontiac, MI)	22,366
1988–	The Palace of Auburn Hills	21,960

Indiana Pacers

1967-74	State Fairgrounds (Indianapolis)	9,479
1974-99	Market Square Arena	16,530
	(1974 capacity-17,287)	
1999–	Conseco Fieldhouse	18,500

Miami Heat

1988-99	Miami Arena	15,200
2000–	AmericanAirlines Arena	19,600

Milwaukee Bucks

1968-88	Milwaukee Arena (The Mecca)	11,052
1988–	Bradley Center	18,717

New Jersey Nets

1967-68	Teaneck (NJ) Armory	3,500
1968-69	Long Island Arena (Commack, NY)	6,500
1969-71	Island Garden (W. Hempstead, NY)	5,200
1971-77	Nassau Coliseum (Uniondale, NY)	15,500
1977-81	Rutgers Ath. Center (Piscataway, NJ)	9,050
1981–	Continental Airlines Arena (E. Ruth., NJ)	20,049

New York Knicks

1946-68	Madison Sq. Garden III (50th St.)	18,496
1968–	Madison Sq. Garden IV (33rd St.)	19,763
	(1968 capacity-19,694)	

Orlando Magic

1989–	Orlando Arena	17,248

Philadelphia 76ers

1949-51	State Fair Coliseum (Syracuse, NY)	7,500
1951-63	Onondaga County (NY) War Memorial	8,000
1963-67	Convention Hall (Philadelphia)	12,000
	&Philadelphia Arena	7,777
1967-96	CoreStates Spectrum	18,136
1996–	First Union Center	20,444

Toronto Raptors

1995-99	SkyDome	20,125
1999–	Air Canada Centre	19,800

Washington Wizards

1961-62	Chicago Amphitheater	11,000
1962-63	Chicago Coliseum	7,100
1963-73	Baltimore Civic Center	12,289
1973-97	USAir Arena (Landover, MD)	18,756
1997–	MCI Center	20,500

Note: From 1988-96 the Wizards (then Bullets) played four regular season games at Baltimore Arena (12,756).

Building Name Changes: HOUSTON– **Compaq Center** originally The Summit (1975-97); NEW JERSEY– **Continental Airlines Arena** originally Byrne Meadowlands Arena (1981-96); PHILADELPHIA– **First Union Center** originally the CoreStates Center (1996-98) and **CoreStates Spectrum** originally The Spectrum (1967-94); WASHINGTON– **USAir Arena** originally Capital Centre (1973-93).

NATIONAL FOOTBALL LEAGUE

American Football Conference

		Location	Built	Capacity	Field
Baltimore Ravens	**PSInet Stadium**	Baltimore, Md.	1998	68,400	Grass
Buffalo Bills	**Ralph Wilson Stadium**	Orchard Park, N.Y.	1973	75,339	Turf
Cincinnati Bengals	**Paul Brown Stadium**	Cincinnati, Ohio	2000	64,000	Grass
Cleveland Browns	**Cleveland Browns Stadium**	Cleveland, Ohio	1999	72,000	Grass
Denver Broncos	**Mile High Stadium**	Denver, Colo.	1948	76,098	Grass
Indianapolis Colts	**RCA Dome**	Indianapolis, Ind.	1984	60,597	Turf
Jacksonville Jaguars	**ALLTEL Stadium**	Jacksonville, Fla.	1995	73,000	Grass
Kansas City Chiefs	**Arrowhead Stadium**	Kansas City, Mo.	1972	79,409	Grass
Miami Dolphins	**Pro Player Stadium**	Miami, Fla.	1987	74,192	Grass
New England Patriots	**Foxboro Stadium**	Foxboro, Mass.	1971	60,292	Grass
New York Jets	**Giants Stadium**	E. Rutherford, N.J.	1976	79,466	Grass
Oakland Raiders	**Network Associates Coliseum**	Oakland, Calif.	1966	63,026	Grass
Pittsburgh Steelers	**Three Rivers Stadium**	Pittsburgh, Pa.	1970	59,600	Turf
San Diego Chargers	**Qualcomm Stadium**	San Diego, Calif.	1967	71,000	Grass
Seattle Seahawks	**Kingdome**	Seattle, Wash.	1976	66,400	Turf
Tennessee Titans	**Adelphia Stadium**	Nashville, Tenn.	1999	67,000	Grass

National Football Conference

		Location	Built	Capacity	Field
Arizona Cardinals	**Sun Devil Stadium**	Tempe, Ariz.	1958	73,273	Grass
Atlanta Falcons	**Georgia Dome**	Atlanta, Ga.	1992	71,228	Turf
Carolina Panthers	**Ericsson Stadium**	Charlotte, N.C.	1996	73,250	Grass
Chicago Bears	**Soldier Field**	Chicago, Ill.	1924	66,944	Grass
Dallas Cowboys	**Texas Stadium**	Irving, Texas	1971	65,675	Turf
Detroit Lions	**Pontiac Silverdome**	Pontiac, Mich.	1975	80,335	Turf
Green Bay Packers	**Lambeau Field**	Green Bay, Wisc.	1957	60,790	Grass
Minnesota Vikings	**Hubert H. Humphrey Metrodome**	Minneapolis, Minn.	1982	64,121	Turf
New Orleans Saints	**Louisiana Superdome**	New Orleans, La.	1975	70,200	Turf
New York Giants	**Giants Stadium**	E. Rutherford, N.J.	1976	79,466	Grass
Philadelphia Eagles	**Veterans Stadium**	Philadelphia, Pa.	1971	65,352	Turf
St. Louis Rams	**Trans World Dome**	St. Louis, Mo.	1995	66,000	Turf
San Francisco 49ers	**3Com Park**	San Francisco, Calif.	1960	70,140	Grass
Tampa Bay Buccaneers	**Raymond James Stadium**	Tampa, Fla.	1998	65,000	Grass
Washington Redskins	**Jack Kent Cooke Stadium**	Raljon, MD	1997	80,166	Grass

Rank by Capacity

AFC		NFC	
NY Jets	79,466	Detroit	80,335
Kansas City	79,409	Washington	80,166
Denver	76,098	NY Giants	79,466
Buffalo	75,399	Arizona'	73,273
Miami	74,192	Carolina	73,250
Jacksonville	73,000	Atlanta	71,228
Cleveland	72,000	New Orleans	70,200
San Diego	71,000	San Francisco	70,140
Baltimore	68,400	Chicago	66,944
Tennessee	67,000	St. Louis	66,000
Seattle	66,400	Dallas	65,675
Cincinnati	64,000	Philadelphia	65,352
Oakland	63,026	Tampa Bay	65,000
Indianapolis	60,597	Minnesota	64,121
New England	60,292	Green Bay	60,790
Pittsburgh	59,600		

Rank by Age

AFC		NFC	
Denver	1948	Chicago	1924
Oakland	1966	Green Bay	1957
San Diego	1967	Arizona	1958
Cincinnati	1970	San Francisco	1960
Pittsburgh	1970	Dallas	1971
New England	1971	Philadelphia	1971
Kansas City	1972	New Orleans	1975
Buffalo	1973	Detroit	1975
NY Jets	1976	NY Giants	1976
Seattle	1976	Minnesota	1982
Indianapolis	1984	Atlanta	1992
Miami	1987	St. Louis	1995
Jacksonville	1995	Carolina	1996
Baltimore	1998	Washington	1997
Cleveland	1999	Tampa Bay	1998
Tennessee	1999		

1998 NFL Attendance

Official overall paid attendance in the NFL for the 1998 season was 14,977,356 for an average per game crowd of 62,406 over 240 games. Teams in each conference are ranked by attendance over eight home games. Rank column indicates rank in entire league. Numbers in parentheses indicate conference rank in 1997.

AFC

		Attendance	Rank	Average
1	Denver (2)	597,462	1	74,683
2	N.Y. Jets (5)	589,768	2	73,721
3	Kansas City (1)	589,038	3	73,630
4	Miami (3)	581,784	4	72,723
5	Jacksonville (4)	561,472	7	70,184
6	Buffalo (6)	560,570	8	70,071
7	Baltimore (8)	549,531	10	68,691
8	Seattle (11)	500,210	16	62,526
9	San Diego (9)	476,718	19	59,590
10	New England (7)	475,828	20	59,479
11	Pittsburgh (10)	464,619	21	58,077
12	Cincinnati (13)	444,335	23	55,542
13	Indianapolis (12)	440,930	24	55,116
14	Oakland (14)	386,548	29	48,319
15	Tennessee (15)	299,555	30	37,444
	TOTAL	7,518,368	—	62,653

NFC

		Attendance	Rank	Average
1	NY Giants (2)	576,708	5	72,089
2	Detroit (3)	571,416	6	71,427
3	Washington (1)	552,099	9	69,012
4	San Francisco (9)	537,385	11	67,173
5	Philadelphia (5)	527,990	12	65,999
6	Tampa Bay (4)	518,047	13	64,766
7	Minnesota (10)	510,741	14	63,843
8	Dallas (8)	510,438	15	63,805
9	Carolina (6)	489,622	17	61,203
10	Green Bay (11)	479,292	18	59,912
11	Atlanta (15)	457,477	22	57,185
12	New Orleans (12)	436,473	25	54,559
13	St. Louis (7)	431,143	26	53,893
14	Arizona (14)	430,552	27	53,819
15	Chicago (13)	429,607	28	53,701
	TOTAL	7,458,990	—	62,159

Home Fields

Listed below are the principal home fields used through the years by current NFL teams. The largest capacity of each stadium is noted in the right-hand column. All-America Football Conference stadiums (1946-49) are included for Cleveland and San Francisco.

AFC

Baltimore Ravens

1996-97	Memorial Stadium	65,000
1998–	PSInet Stadium	68,400

Buffalo Bills

1960-72	War Memorial Stadium	45,748
1973–	Ralph Wilson Stadium (Orchard Park, NY)	75,339
	(1973 capacity-80,020)	

Cincinnati Bengals

1968-69	Nippert Stadium (Univ. of Cincinnati)	26,500
1970-99	Cinergy Field	60,389
	(1970 capacity-56,200)	
2000–	Paul Brown Stadium	64,000

Cleveland Browns

1946-95	Cleveland Stadium	78,512
	(1946 capacity-85,703)	
1999–	Cleveland Browns Stadium	72,000

Denver Broncos

1960–	Mile High Stadium	76,098
	(1960 capacity-34,000)	

Indianapolis Colts

1953-83	Memorial Stadium (Baltimore)	60,020
1984–	RCA Dome (Indianapolis)	60,597
	(1984 capacity-60,127)	

Jacksonville Jaguars

1995–	ALLTEL Stadium	73,000

Kansas City Chiefs

1960-62	Cotton Bowl (Dallas)	72,000
1963-71	Municipal Stadium (Kansas City)	47,000
1972–	Arrowhead Stadium	79,409
	(1972 capacity-78,097)	

Miami Dolphins

1966-86	Orange Bowl	75,206
1987–	Pro Player Stadium	74,192
	(1987 capacity-75,500)	

New England Patriots

1960-62	Nickerson Field (Boston Univ.)	17,369
1963-68	Fenway Park	33,379
1969	Alumni Stadium (Boston College)	26,000
1970	Harvard Stadium	37,300
1971–	Foxboro Stadium	60,292
	(1971 capacity-61,114)	

National Football League (Cont.)

New York Jets

1960-63	Polo Grounds	55,987
1964-83	Shea Stadium	60,372
1984–	Giants Stadium (E. Rutherford, NJ)	79,466

Oakland Raiders

1960	Kesar Stadium (San Francisco)	59,636
1961	Candlestick Park	42,500
1962-65	Frank Youell Field (Oakland)	20,000
1966-81	Oakland-Alameda County Coliseum	54,587
1982-94	Memorial Coliseum (Los Angeles)	67,800
1995–	Network Associates Coliseum	63,026

Pittsburgh Steelers

1933-57	Forbes Field	35,000
1958-63	Forbes Field	35,000
	&Pitt Stadium	54,500
1964-69	Pitt Stadium	54,500
1970–	Three Rivers Stadium	59,600
	(1970 capacity-49,000)	

San Diego Chargers

1960	Memorial Coliseum (Los Angeles)	92,604
1961-66	Balboa Stadium (San Diego)	34,000
1967–	Qualcomm Stadium	71,000
	(1967 capacity-54,000)	

Seattle Seahawks

1976-94	Kingdome	66,000
1994	Kingdome	66,400
	&Husky Stadium	72,500
1995–	Kingdome	66,400

Tennessee Titans

1960-64	Jeppesen Stadium (Houston)	23,500
1965-67	Rice Stadium (Rice Univ.)	70,000
1968-96	Astrodome	59,969
1997	Liberty Bowl (Memphis)	62,380
1998	Vanderbilt Stadium (Nashville)	41,600
1999–	Adelphia Stadium (Nashville)	67,000

Ballpark Name Changes: BALTIMORE—**Cleveland Stadium** originally Municipal Stadium (1932-74), **PSInet Stadium** originally Ravens' Stadium (1998-99); BUFFALO—**Ralph Wilson Stadium** originally Rich Stadium (1973-99); CINCINNATI—**Cinergy Field** originally Riverfront Stadium (1970-96); DENVER—**Mile High Stadium** originally Bears Stadium (1948-66); INDIANAPOLIS—**RCA Dome** originally Hoosier Dome (1984-94); JACKSONVILLE—**ALLTEL Stadium** originally Jacksonville Municipal Stadium (1995-97); MIAMI—**Pro Player Stadium** originally Joe Robbie Stadium (1987-96); NEW ENGLAND—**Foxboro Stadium** originally Schaefer Stadium (1971-82), then Sullivan Stadium (1983-89); OAKLAND—**Network Associates Coliseum** originally Oakland Alameda Coliseum (1995-99); SAN DIEGO—**Qualcomm Stadium** originally San Diego Stadium (1967-81) then San Diego/Jack Murphy Stadium (1981-96).

NFC

Arizona Cardinals

1920-21	Normal Field (Chicago)	7,500
1922-25	Comiskey Park	28,000
1926-28	Normal Field	7,500
1929-59	Comiskey Park	52,000
1960-65	Busch Stadium (St. Louis)	34,000
1966-87	Busch Memorial Stadium	54,392
1988–	Sun Devil Stadium (Tempe, AZ)	73,273

Atlanta Falcons

1966-91	Atlanta-Fulton County Stadium	59,643
1992–	Georgia Dome	71,228

Carolina Panthers

1995	Memorial Stadium (Clemson, SC)	81,473
1996–	Ericsson Stadium	73,250

Chicago Bears

1920	Staley Field (Decatur, IL)	–
1921-70	Wrigley Field (Chicago)	37,741
1971–	Soldier Field	66,944
	(1971 capacity-55,049)	

Dallas Cowboys

1960-70	Cotton Bowl	72,132
1971–	Texas Stadium (Irving, TX)	65,675
	(1971 capacity-65,101)	

Detroit Lions

1930-33	Spartan Stadium (Portsmouth, OH)	8,200
1934-37	Univ. of Detroit Stadium	25,000
1938-74	Tiger Stadium	54,468
1975–	Pontiac Silverdome	80,335
	(1975 capacity-80,638)	

Green Bay Packers

1921-22	Hagemeister Brewery Park	–
1923-24	Bellevue Park	–
1925-56	City Stadium I	24,800
1957–	Lambeau Field	60,790
	(1957 capacity-32,150)	

Note: The Packers played games in Milwaukee from 1933-94: at Borchert Field, State Fair Park and Marquette Stadium (1933-52), and County Stadium (1953-94).

Minnesota Vikings

1961-81	Metropolitan Stadium (Bloomington)	48,446
1982–	HHH Metrodome (Minneapolis)	64,121
	(1982 capacity-62,220)	

New Orleans Saints

1967-74	Tulane Stadium	80,997
1975–	Louisiana Superdome	70,200
	(1975 capacity-74,472)	

New York Giants

1925-55	Polo Grounds II	55,200
1956-73	Yankee Stadium I	63,800
1973-74	Yale Bowl (New Haven, CT)	70,896
1975	Shea Stadium	60,372
1976–	Giants Stadium (E. Rutherford, NJ)	79,466
	(1976 capacity-76,800)	

Philadelphia Eagles

1933-35	Baker Bowl	18,800
1936-39	Municipal Stadium	73,702
1940	Shibe Park	33,608
1941	Municipal Stadium	73,702
1942	Shibe Park	33,608
1943	Forbes Field (Pittsburgh)	34,528
1944-57	Shibe Park	33,608
1958-70	Franklin Field (Univ. of Penn.)	60,546
1971–	Veterans Stadium	65,352
	(1971 capacity-65,000)	

St. Louis Rams

1937-42	Municipal Stadium (Cleveland)	85,703
1945	Suspended operations for one year.	
1944-45	Municipal Stadium	85,703
1946-79	Memorial Coliseum (Los Angeles)	92,604
1980-94	Anaheim Stadium	69,008
1995–	Trans World Dome	66,000

San Francisco 49ers

1946-70	Kezar Stadium	59,636
1971–	3Com Park	70,140
	(1971 capacity-61,246)	

Tampa Bay Buccaneers

1976-97	Houlihan's Stadium	74,300
1998–	Raymond James Stadium	65,000

Washington Redskins

1932	Braves Field (Boston)	40,000
1933-36	Fenway Park	27,000
1937-60	Griffith Stadium (Washington, DC)	35,000
1961-97	RFK Stadium	56,454
1997–	Jack Kent Cooke Stadium (Raljon, MD)	..80,166

Ballpark Name Changes: ATLANTA—**Atlanta-Fulton County Stadium** originally Atlanta Stadium (1966-74); CHICAGO— **Wrigley Field** originally Cubs Park (1916-25), also, **Comiskey Park** originally White Sox Park (1910-12); DETROIT—**Tiger Stadium** originally Navin Field (1912-37), then Briggs Stadium (1938-60), also, **Pontiac Silverdome** originally Pontiac Metropolitan Stadium (1975); GREEN BAY—**Lambeau Field** originally City Stadium II (1957-64); PHILADELPHIA—**Shibe Park** renamed Connie Mack Stadium in 1953; ST. LOUIS—**Busch Memorial Stadium** renamed Busch Stadium in 1983; SAN FRANCISCO—**3Com Park** originally Candlestick Park (1960-94); TAMPA BAY—**Raymond James Stadium** originally Tampa Stadium (1976-96), then **Houlihan's Stadium** (1996-98); WASHINGTON—**RFK Stadium** originally D.C. Stadium (1961-68).

NATIONAL HOCKEY LEAGUE

Western Conference

	Location	Built	Capacity
Anaheim, Mighty Ducks of ....**Arrowhead Pond**	Anaheim, Calif.	1993	**17,174**
Calgary Flames ....**Canadian Airlines Saddledome**	Calgary, Alb.	1983	**17,139**
Chicago Blackhawks.....................................**United Center**	Chicago, Ill.	1994	**20,500**
Colorado Avalanche ....**Pepsi Center**	Denver, Colo.	1999	**18,129**
Dallas Stars..**Reunion Arena**	Dallas, Texas	1980	**17,001**
Detroit Red Wings.............................**Joe Louis Arena**	Detroit, Mich.	1979	**19,983**
Edmonton Oilers ....**Skyreach Centre**	Edmonton, Alb.	1974	**17,100**
Los Angeles Kings.............................**Staples Center**	Los Angeles, Calif.	1999	**18,500**
Nashville Predators ....**Gaylord Entertainment Center**	Nashville, Tenn.	1994	**17,298**
Phoenix Coyotes ....**America West**	Phoenix, Ariz.	1992	**16,210**
St. Louis Blues...**Kiel Center**	St. Louis, Mo.	1994	**19,260**
San Jose Sharks....................................**San Jose Arena**	San Jose, Calif.	1993	**17,483**
Vancouver Canucks.........................**General Motors Place**	Vancouver, B.C.	1995	**18,422**

Eastern Conference

	Location	Built	Capacity
Atlanta Thrashers ....**Philips Arena**	Atlanta, Ga.	1999	**18,750**
Boston Bruins...**FleetCenter**	Boston, Mass.	1995	**17,565**
Buffalo Sabres................................**Marine Midland Arena**	Buffalo, N.Y.	1996	**18,500**
Carolina Hurricanes ....**Entertainment and Sports Arena**	Raleigh, N.C.	1999	**19,000**
Florida Panthers ....**National Car Rental Center**	Sunrise, Fla.	1998	**19,250**
Montreal Canadiens ....**Molson Centre**	Montreal, Que.	1996	**21,273**
New Jersey Devils ....**Continental Airlines Arena**	E. Rutherford, N.J.	1981	**19,040**
New York Islanders ....**Nassau Veterans' Mem. Coliseum**	Uniondale, N.Y.	1972	**16,297**
New York Rangers.........................**Madison Square Garden**	New York, N.Y.	1968	**18,200**
Ottawa Senators.......................................**Corel Centre**	Kanata, Ont.	1996	**18,500**
Philadelphia Flyers ....**First Union Center**	Philadelphia, Pa.	1996	**19,519**
Pittsburgh Penguins..**Civic Arena**	Pittsburgh, Pa.	1961	**16,958**
Tampa Bay Lightning...**Ice Palace**	Tampa Bay, Fla.	1996	**19,758**
Toronto Maple Leafs ....**Air Canada Centre**	Toronto, Ont.	1999	**18,800**
Washington Capitals ....**MCI Center**	Washington, D.C.	1997	**20,000**

Rank by Capacity

Western		Eastern	
Chicago..........20,500		Montreal 21,273	
Detroit 19,983		Washington.......20,000	
St. Louis 19,260		Tampa Bay 19,758	
Los Angeles.......18,500		Philadelphia 19,519	
Vancouver 18,422		Florida 19,250	
Colorado..........18,129		New Jersey 19,040	
San Jose..........17,483		Carolina..........19,000	
Nashville 17,298		Toronto...........18,800	
Anaheim 17,174		Atlanta 18,750	
Calgary 17,139		Buffalo...........18,500	
Edmonton.........17,100		Ottawa...........18,500	
Dallas.............17,001		NY Rangers.......18,200	
Phoenix 16,210		Boston 17,565	
		Pittsburgh.........16,958	
		NY Islanders......16,297	

Rank by Age

Western		Eastern	
Edmonton 1974		Pittsburgh...........1961	
Detroit 1979		NY Rangers.........1968	
Dallas...............1980		NY Islanders........1972	
Calgary 1983		New Jersey 1981	
Phoenix 1992		Boston 1995	
Anaheim 1993		Montreal 1996	
San Jose 1993		Ottawa 1996	
Chicago.............1994		Buffalo 1996	
St. Louis 1994		Philadelphia 1996	
Nashville............1994		Tampa Bay 1996	
Vancouver 1995		Washington.........1997	
Colorado............1999		Florida 1998	
Los Angeles.........1999		Toronto.............1999	
		Carolina 1999	
		Atlanta 1999	

National Hockey League (Cont.)
1998-99 NHL Attendance

Official overall paid attendance for the 1998-99 season according to the NHL accounting office was 17,896,042 (paid tickets) for an average per game crowd of 16,166 over 1107 games. Teams in each conference are ranked by attendance over 41 home games. There were no neutral site games. Number of sellouts are listed in S/O column. Numbers in parentheses indicate rank in 1997-98.

Western Conference

		Attendance	S/O	Average
1	Detroit (1)	819,303	41	19,983
2	St. Louis (7)	749,334	17	18,276
3	Chicago (2)	710,503	4	17,329
4	San Jose (3)	701,494	19	17,110
5	Dallas (8)	693,225	38	16,908
6	Edmonton (9)	666,641	19	16,260
7	Nashville (N/A)	664,282	17	16,202
8	Colorado (10)	658,501	41	16,061
9	Calgary (6)	648,050	10	16,201
10	Anaheim (5)	647,973	9	15,804
11	Vancouver (4)	647,913	7	15,803
12	Phoenix (12)	637,467	17	15,548
13	Los Angeles (13)	524,599	5	12,795
	TOTAL	8,769,285	244	16,453

Eastern Conference

		Attendance	S/O	Average
1	Montreal (1)	850,371	16	20,741
2	Philadelphia (2)	804,105	37	19,612
3	Florida (11)	758,542	13	18,501
4	NY Rangers (3)	746,200	41	18,200
5	Washington (8)	708,531	20	17,281
6	Ottawa (5)	705,990	16	17,219
7	Toronto (6)	687,372	36	16,765
8	New Jersey (4)	683,480	6	16,670
9	Boston (9)	668,020	17	16,293
10	Buffalo (7)	641,034	10	15,635
11	Pittsburgh (10)	607,822	5	14,825
12	Tampa Bay (12)	471,518	1	11,500
13	NY Islanders (13)	458,076	3	11,173
14	Carolina (14)	335,696	4	8,188
	TOTAL	9,126,757	225	15,900

Home Ice

Listed below are the principal home buildings used through the years by current NHL teams. The largest capacity of each arena is noted in the right hand column. World Hockey Association arenas (1972-76) are included for Edmonton, Hartford (now Carolina), Quebec (now Colorado) and Winnipeg (now Phoenix).

Western Conference

Anaheim, Mighty Ducks of

1993–	Arrowhead Pond	17,174

Calgary Flames

1972-80	The Omni (Atlanta)	15,278
1980-83	Calgary Corral	7,424
1983–	Canadian Airlines Saddledome	17,139
	(1983 capacity-16,674)	

Chicago Blackhawks

1926-29	Chicago Coliseum	5,000
1929-94	Chicago Stadium	17,317
1994–	United Center	20,500

Colorado Avalanche

1972-95	Le Colisee de Quebec	15,399
1995-99	McNichols Arena (Denver)	16,061
1999–	Pepsi Center	18,129

Dallas Stars

1967-93	Met Center (Bloomington, MN)	15,174
1993–	Reunion Arena (Dallas)	17,001

Detroit Red Wings

1926-27	Border Cities Arena (Windsor, Ont.)	3,200
1927-79	Olympia Stadium (Detroit)	16,700
1979–	Joe Louis Arena	19,983

Edmonton Oilers

1972-74	Edmonton Gardens	7,200
1974–	Skyreach Centre	17,100
	(1974 capacity-15,513)	

Los Angeles Kings

1967-99	Great Western Forum (Inglewood)	16,005
	(1967 capacity-15,651)	
1999–	Staples Center	18,500

Note: The Kings played 17 games at Long Beach Sports Arena and LA Sports Arena at the start of the 1967-68 season.

Nashville Predators

1998–	Nashville Arena	17,298

Phoenix Coyotes

1972– 96	Winnipeg Arena	15,393
	(1972 capacity-10,177)	
1996–	America West (Phoenix)	16,210

St. Louis Blues

1967-94	St. Louis Arena	17,188
1994–	Kiel Center	19,260

San Jose Sharks

1991-93	Cow Palace (Daly City, CA)	11,100
1993–	San Jose Arena	17,483

Vancouver Canucks

1970-95	Pacific Coliseum	16,150
1995–	General Motors Place	18,422

Building Name Changes: CALGARY—**Canadian Airlines Saddledome** originally Olympic Saddledome (1983-1995); DALLAS—**Met Center** in Minneapolis originally Metropolitan Sports Center (1967-82); EDMONTON—**Skyreach Centre** formerly named Edmonton Coliseum (1995-99) which was originally Northlands Coliseum (1974-94); LOS ANGELES—**Great Western Forum** originally The Forum (1967-88); ST. LOUIS—**St. Louis Arena** renamed The Checkerdome in 1977, then St. Louis Arena again in 1982.

Eastern Conference

Atlanta Thrashers

1999–	Philips Arena	18,750

Boston Bruins

1924-28	Boston Arena	6,200
1928-95	Boston Garden	14,448
1995–	FleetCenter	17,565

Buffalo Sabres

| 1970-96 | Memorial Auditorium (The Aud) . . . . . . .16,284 (1970 capacity-10,429) |
| 1996- | Marine Midland Arena . . . . .18,500 |

Carolina Hurricanes

1972-73	Boston Garden 14,442
1973-74	Boston Garden (regular season). . . . . . . .14,442 West Springfield (MA) Big E (playoffs) . . .5,513
1974-75	West Springfield Big E . . . . .5,513 & Hartford (CT) Civic Center 10,507
1975-77	Hartford Civic Center. 10,507
1977-78	Hartford Civic Center. . . . . .10,507 & Springfield (MA) Civic Center. 7,725
1978-79	Springfield Civic Center. 7,725
1979-80	Springfield Civic Center. . . . . .7,725 & Hartford Civic Center II 14,250
1980-97	Hartford Civic Center II 15,635
1997-99	Greensboro Coliseum 21,500
1999-	Entertainment and Sports Arena. 19,000

Note: The Hartford Civic Center roof caved in January 1978, forcing the Whalers to move their home games to Springfield, MA for two years.

Florida Panthers

| 1993-98 | Miami Arena . . . . .14,703 |
| 1998- | National Car Rental Center . . . . .19,250 |

Montreal Canadiens

1910-20	Jubilee Arena. 3,200
1913-18	Montreal Arena (Westmount) 6,000
1918-26	Mount Royal Arena. 6,750
1926-68	Montreal Forum I 15,500
1968-96	Montreal Forum II 17,959
1996-	Molson Centre .21,273

New Jersey Devils

1974-76	Kemper Arena (Kansas City). 16,300
1976-82	McNichols Arena (Denver) 15,900
1982-	Continental Airlines Arena 19,040 (1982 capacity-19,023)

New York Islanders

| 1972- | Nassau Veterans' Mem. Coliseum . . . . . .16,297 (1972 capacity-14,500) |

New York Rangers

| 1925-68 | Madison Square Garden III . . . . .15,925 |
| 1968- | Madison Square Garden IV . . . . .18,200 (1968 capacity-17,250) |

Ottawa Senators

| 1992-95 | Ottawa Civic Center . . . . .10,755 |
| 1996- | Corel Centre (Kanata) . . . . .18,500 |

Philadelphia Flyers

| 1967-96 | CoreStates Spectrum . . . . .17,380 (1967 capacity-14,558) |
| 1996- | First Union Center. . . . . .19,519 |

Pittsburgh Penguins

| 1967- | Civic Arena . . . . .16,958 (1967 capacity-12,508) |

Tampa Bay Lightning

1992-93	Expo Hall (Tampa) 10,500
1993-96	ThunderDome (St. Petersburg). 26,000
1996-	Ice Palace 19,758

Toronto Maple Leafs

1917-31	Mutual Street Arena 8,000
1931-99	Maple Leaf Gardens 15,746 (1931 capacity-13,542)
1999-	Air Canada Centre 18,800

Washington Capitals

| 1974-97 | USAir Arena (Landover, MD) . . . . .18,130 |
| 1997- | MCI Center . . . . .20,000 |

Building Name Changes: NEW JERSEY—**Continental Airlines Arena** originally Meadowlands Arena (1982-96); PHILADELPHIA—**First Union Center** originally the CoreStates Center (1996-98) and **CoreStates Spectrum** originally The Spectrum (1967-94); WASHINGTON—**USAir Arena** originally Capital Centre (1974-93).

AUTO RACING

Formula One, NASCAR Winston Cup, CART and Indy Racing League (IRL) racing circuits. Qualifying records accurate as of Aug. 1, 1998. Capacity figures for NASCAR, CART and IRL tracks are approximate and pertain to grandstand seating only. Standing room and hillside terrain seating featured at most road courses are not included.

CART

	Location	Miles	Qual.mph record	Set by	Seats
Belle Isle Park	Detroit, Mich.	2.346**	114.773	Juan Montoya (1999)	18,000
Burke Lakefront Airport.	Cleveland, Ohio	2.106**	134.385	Jimmy Vasser (1998)	36,000
California Speedway	Fontana, Calif.	2.029	240.942	Mauricio Gugelmin (1997)	69,000
Chicago Motor Speedway	Cicero, Ill.	1.029	162.559	Max Papis (1999)	40,000
Exhibition Place	Toronto, Ont.	1.721**	110.565	Gil de Ferran (1999)	60,000
Gateway International Raceway	Madison, Ill.	1.27	187.963	Raul Boesel (1997)	35,000
Homestead Motorsports Complex.	Homestead, Fla.	1.502	217.541	Greg Moore (1998)	50,000
Houston Grand Prix	Houston, Tex.	1.527**	92.377	Greg Moore (1998)	60,000
Laguna Seca Raceway.	Monterey, Calif.	2.24*	118.666	Bryan Herta (1997)	8,000
Long Beach	Long Beach, Calif.	1.824**	111.226	Bryan Herta (1998)	45,000
Michigan Speedway	Brooklyn, Mich.	2.0	234.665	Jimmy Vasser (1996)	112,000
Mid-Ohio Sports Car Course	Lexington, Ohio	2.258*	124.394	Dario Franchitti (1999)	6,000
The Milwaukee Mile	West Allis, Wisc.	1.032	185.500	Patrick Carpentier (1998)	36,800
Nazareth Speedway	Nazareth, Pa.	.946	184.896	Patrick Carpentier (1998)	35,000
Pacific Place	Vancouver, B.C.	1.781**	105.730	Juan Montoya (1999)	65,000
Portland International Raceway	Portland, Ore.	1.969*	121.808	Juan Montoya (1999)	27,000
Piquet International Raceway.	Rio de Janeiro, Brazil	1.864	174.002	Christian Fittipaldi (1999)	80,000
Road America.	Elkhart Lake, Wisc.	4.048*	145.745	Michael Andretti (1998)	10,000
Surfers Paradise	Gold Coast, Australia	2.804	109.028	Dario Franchitti (1998)	55,000
Twin Ring Motegi.	Motegi, Japan	1.549	219.000	Gil de Ferran (1999)	50,000

*Road courses (not ovals). **Temporary street circuits.

Auto Racing (Cont.)
Indy Racing League

Founded by Indianapolis Motor Speedway president Tony George, the Indy Racing League competes with CART and fielded 10 races, anchored by the Indianapolis 500, in 1999.

	Location	Miles	Qual.mph Record	Set by	Seats
Atlanta Motor Speedway	Hampton, Ga.	1.54	224.145	Billy Boat (1998)	124,000
Lowe's Motor Speedway	Harrisburg, N.C.	1.5	220.498	Tony Stewart (1998)	132,000
Dover Downs Int'l. Speedway	Dover, Del.	1.0	185.204	Tony Stewart (1998)	122,000
Indianapolis Motor Speedway	Indianapolis, Ind.	2.5	237.498	Arie Luyendyk (1996)	265,000
Las Vegas Motor Speedway	Las Vegas, Nev.	1.5	226.491	Arie Luyendyk (1996)	102,000
Phoenix International Raceway	Phoenix, Ariz.	1.0	183.599	Arie Luyendyk (1996)	72,500
Pikes Peak Int'l. Raceway	Fountain, Colo.	1.0	178.571	Billy Boat (1998)	42,787
Texas Motor Speedway	Fort Worth, Tex.	1.5	225.979	Billy Boat (1998)	154,861
Walt Disney World Speedway	Orlando, Fla.	1.1	181.388	Buddy Lazier (1996)	55,000

NASCAR

	Location	Miles	Qual.mph Record	Set By	Seats
Atlanta Motor Speedway	Hampton, Ga.	1.54	197.478	Geoff Bodine (1997)	78,000
Bristol Motor Speedway	Bristol, Tenn.	0.533	125.142	Rusty Wallace (1999)	135,000
California Speedway	Fontana, Calif.	2.0	183.753	Greg Sacks (1997)	86,450
Lowe's Motor Speedway	Concord, N.C.	1.5	185.759	Ward Burton (1994)	157,000
Darlington International Raceway	Darlington, N.C.	1.37	173.797	Ward Burton (1996)	60,000
Daytona International Speedway	Daytona Beach, Fla.	2.5	210.364	Bill Elliott (1987)	160,000
Dover Downs International Speedway	Dover, Del.	1.0	159.320	Bobby Labonte (1999)	55,000
Indianapolis Motor Speedway	Indianapolis, Ind.	2.5	179.612	Jeff Gordon (1999)	265,000
Las Vegas Motor Speedway	Las Vegas, Nev.	1.5	170.643	Bobby Labonte (1999)	107,000
Martinsville Speedway	Martinsville, Va.	0.526	95.275	Tony Stewart (1999)	77,500
Homestead-Miami Speedway	Homestead, Fla.	1.5	—	TBD	72,000
Michigan Speedway	Brooklyn, Mich.	2.0	188.843	Ward Burton (1999)	70,000
New Hampshire Int'l Speedway	Loudon, N.H.	1.058	131.171	Jeff Gordon (1999)	83,000
North Carolina Speedway	Rockingham, N.C.	1.017	157.885	Mark Martin (1997)	60,122
Phoenix International Raceway	Phoenix, Ariz.	1.0	131.579	Bobby Hamilton (1996)	78,500
Pocono Raceway	Long Pond, Pa.	2.5	170.506	Sterling Marlin (1999)	77,000
Richmond International Raceway	Richmond, Va.	0.75	126.499	Jeff Gordon (1999)	95,920
Sears Point International Raceway	Sonoma, Calif.	2.52*	98.711	Jeff Gordon (1998)	42,500
Talladega Superspeedway	Talladega, Ala.	2.66	212.809	Bill Elliott (1987)	108,000
Texas Motor Speedway	Ft. Worth, Tex.	1.5	190.154	Kenny Irwin (1999)	154,861
Watkins Glen	Watkins Glen, N.Y.	2.45*	121.234	Rusty Wallace (1999)	35,000

*Road courses (not ovals).
Notes: Richmond sells reserved seats only (no infield) for Winston Cup races.

Formula One
Race track capacity figures unavailable.

Grand Prix		Miles	Qual.mph Record	Set by
Argentine	**Oscar A. Galvez** (Buenos Aires)	2.646	112.722	Jacques Villeneuve (1997)
Austrian	**A1-Ring** (Zeltwig, Austria)	2.684	134.657	Jacques Villeneuve (1997)
Australian	**Albert Park** (Melbourne)	3.295	132.731	Jacques Villeneuve (1997)
Belgian	**Spa-Francorchamps**	4.333	143.394	Mika Hakkinen (1998)
Brazilian	**Interlagos** (Sao Paulo)	2.667	127.799	Nigel Mansell (1992)
British	**Silverstone** (Towcester)	3.194	148.043	Nigel Mansell (1992)
Canadian	**Circuit Gilles Villeneuve** (Montreal)	2.747	127.181	David Coulthard (1998)
Luxembourg	**Nürburgring** (Nürburg, Germany)	2.822	131.219	Teo Fabi (1985)
French	**Magny Cours** (Nevers)	2.641	128.709	Nigel Mansell (1992)
German	**Hockenheimring** (Hockenheim)	4.240	156.722	Nigel Mansell (1991)
Hungarian	**Hungaroring** (Budapest)	2.468	117.602	Riccardo Patrese (1992)
Italian	**Autodromo Nazionale di Monza** (Milan)	3.585	159.951	Ayrton Senna (1991)
Japanese	**Suzuka** (Nagoya)	3.644	138.515	Gerhard Berger (1991)
Malaysian	**Sepang**	3.444	—	first race was Oct. 1999
Monaco	**Monte Carlo**	2.092	96.286	Heinz-Harald Frentzen (1997)
San Marino	**Ferrari Circuit** (Imola, Italy)	3.063	138.265	Ayrton Senna (1994)
Spanish	**Catalunya** (Barcelona)	2.937	138.205	Jacques Villeneuve (1997)

SOCCER

World's Premier Soccer Stadiums

(Listed by city)

Stadium	Location	Seats	Stadium	Location	Seats
Olimpiako	Athens, Greece	74,160	Olympiastadion	Munich, Germany	74,000
Eden Park	Auckland, New Zealand	48,000	San Paolo	Naples, Italy	72,810
Nou Camp	Barcelona, Spain	115,000	Parc des Princes	Paris, France	49,700
Olympiastadion	Berlin, Germany	76,234	Rose Bowl	Pasadena, Calif.	102,083
Népstadion	Budapest, Hungary	72,000	Spartakiadni Stadion.	Prague, Czech Republic	250,000
Monumental	Buenos Aires, Argentina	77,000	Rungnado	Pyongyang, N. Korea	150,000
D.A. Nasser	Cairo, Egypt	100,000	Maracana	Rio de Janeiro, Brazil	165,000
Westfalenstadion	Dortmund, Germany	42,800	King Fahd II	Riyadh, Saudi Arabia	75,000
Lansdowne Road	Dublin, Ireland	51,000	Olimpico	Rome, Italy	86,517
Hampden Park	Glasgow, Scotland	50,000	Stade de France	Saint-Denis, France	80,000
Ellis Park	Johannesburg, S. Africa	62,000	Nacional	Santiago, Chile	75,000
Republikansky	Kiev, Ukraine	100,000	Morumbi	Sao Paulo, Brazil	120,000
Estadio da Luz	Lisbon, Portugal	130,000	Olympic Stadium	Seoul, S. Korea	100,000
Wembley	London, England	80,000	Olympic Stadium	Sydney, Australia	120,000
Santiago Bernabeu	Madrid, Spain	110,000	Olympic Stadium	Tokyo, Japan	62,000
Azteca	Mexico City, Mexico	114,000	Delle Alpi	Turin, Italy	71,012
Guiseppe Meazza	Milan, Italy	83,107	Prater	Vienna, Austria	62,958
Centenario	Montevideo, Uruguay	76,609	Dziesieiolecia	Warsaw, Poland	100,000
Luzhniki Stadion	Moscow, Russia	100,000			

Major League Soccer

The 12-team MLS is the only U.S. Division I professional outdoor league sanctioned by FIFA and U.S. Soccer. Note that all capacity figures are approximate given the adjustments of football stadium seating to soccer.

Western Conference

	Stadium	Built	Seats	Field
Chicago Fire	Soldier Field	1924	24,955	Grass
Colorado Rapids	Mile High	1948	17,500	Grass
Dallas Burn	Cotton Bowl	1935	22,528	Grass
Kansas City Wizards	Arrowhead	1972	20,571	Grass
L.A. Galaxy	Rose Bowl	1922	30,000	Grass
San Jose Clash	Spartan	1933	26,000	Grass

Eastern Conference

	Stadium	Built	Seats	Field
Columbus Crew	Columbus Crew Stadium	1999	22,500	Grass
D.C. United	RFK	1961	26,169	Grass
Metro Stars (N.Y./N.J.)	Giants	1976	25,576	Both
Miami Fusion	Lockhart	1959	20,450	Grass
N.E. Revolution	Foxboro	1971	24,871	Grass
Tampa Bay Mutiny	Raymond James	1998	17,482	Grass

MISCELLANEOUS

Minor League Baseball

AAA Ballparks
International League

East		Built	Seats	Field
Buffalo (Indians)	Dunn Tire Park	1988	20,900	Grass
Ottawa (Expos)	JetForm Park	1993	10,332	Grass
Pawtucket (Red Sox)	McCoy Stadium	1942	10,031	Grass
Rochester (Orioles)	Frontier Field	1997	10,868	Grass
Scranton/Wilkes-Barre (Phillies)	Lackawanna County Stadium	1989	10,982	Turf
Syracuse (Blue Jays)	P&C Stadium	1997	11,604	Turf
West		**Built**	**Seats**	**Field**
Columbus (Yankees)	Cooper Stadium	1932	15,000	Grass
Indianapolis (Reds)	Victory Field	1996	15,500	Grass
Louisville (Brewers)	Slugger Field	2000	13,000	Grass
Toledo (Tigers)	Ned Skeldon Stadium	1965	10,197	Grass
South		**Built**	**Seats**	**Turf**
Charlotte (White Sox)	Knights Stadium	1990	10,000	Grass
Durham (Devil Rays)	Durham Bulls Athletic Park	1994	10,000	Grass
Norfolk (Mets)	Harbor Park	1993	12,067	Grass
Richmond (Braves)	The Diamond	1985	12,134	Grass

Pacific Coast League

East Division		Built	Seats	Field
Oklahoma (Rangers)	Southwestern Bell Bricktown Ballpark	1998	12,000	Grass
Memphis (Cardinals)	Tim McCarver Stadium	1963	8,800	Grass
Nashville (Pirates)	Herschel Greer Stadium	1978	10,700	Grass
New Orleans (Astros)	Zephyr Field	1997	10,000	Grass

Miscellaneous (Cont.)

North Division		Built	Seats	Field
Calgary (Marlins)	**Burns Stadium**	1966	8,000	Grass
Edmonton (Angels)	**TELUS Field**	1995	9,200	Grass
Tacoma (Mariners)	**Cheney Stadium**	1960	9,600	Grass
Vancouver (Athletics)	**Nat Bailey Stadium**	1951	6,500	Grass
Central Division		**Built**	**Seats**	**Field**
Albuquerque (Dodgers)	**Albuquerque Sports Stadium**	1969	5,500	Grass
Colorado Springs (Rockies)	**Sky Sox Stadium**	1988	9,000	Grass
Iowa (Cubs)	**Sec Taylor Stadium**	1992	11,000	Grass
Omaha (Royals)	**Rosenblatt Stadium**	1948	24,000	Turf
South Division		**Built**	**Seats**	**Field**
Las Vegas (Padres)	**Cashman Field**	1983	9,334	Grass
Fresno (Giants)	**Beiden Field**	1987	6,575	Grass
Salt Lake (Twins)	**Franklin Covey Field**	1993	15,500	Grass
Tucson (Diamondbacks)	**Tucson Electric Park**	1998	11,000	Grass

Note: The Vancouver Canadians will relocate to Sacramento starting in the 2000 season.

Japanese Baseball League
Central League

		Location	Built	Seats	Field
Chunichi Dragons	**Nagoya Dome**	Nagoya	1997	40,500	Turf
Hanshin Tigers	**Koshien Stadium**	Nisinomiya	1924	55,000	Grass
Hiroshima Carp	**Hiroshima Municipal Stadium**	Hiroshima	1957	32,000	Grass
Yakult Swallows	**Meiji Jingu Stadium**	Tokyo	1926	48,785	Grass
Yokohama BayStars	**Yokohama Stadium**	Yokohama	1978	30,000	Turf
Yomiuri Giants	**Tokyo Dome**	Tokyo	1988	48,000	Turf

Pacific League

		Location	Built	Seats	Field
Chiba Lotte Marines	**Chiba Marine Stadium**	Chiba	1991	30,000	Turf
Fukuoka Daiei Hawks	**Fukuoka Dome**	Fukuoka	1993	48,000	Turf
Kintetsu Buffaloes	**Osaka Dome**	Osaka	1997	55,000	Turf
Nippon Ham Fighters	**Tokyo Dome**	Tokyo	1988	48,000	Turf
Orix Blue Wave	**Green Stadium Kobe**	Kobe	1988	35,000	Grass
Seibu Lions	**Seibu Stadium**	Tokorozawa	1979	37,000	Turf

Canadian Football League
East Division

		Location	Built	Seats	Field
Hamilton Tiger-Cats	**Ivor Wynne Stadium**	Hamilton, Ont.	1932	28,830	Turf
Montreal Alouettes	**Molson Stadium (McGill)**	Montreal, Que.	1976	18,027	Turf
Toronto Argonauts	**SkyDome**	Toronto, Ont.	1989	31,600	Turf
Winnipeg Blue Bombers	**Winnipeg Stadium**	Winnipeg, Man.	1953	29,544	Turf

West Division

		Location	Built	Seats	Field
British Columbia Lions	**B.C. Place**	Vancouver, B.C.	1983	40,800	Turf
Calgary Stampeders	**McMahon Stadium**	Calgary, Alb.	1960	37,317	Turf
Edmonton Eskimos	**Commonwealth Stadium**	Edmonton, Alb.	1978	60,081	Grass
Saskatchewan Roughriders	**Taylor Field**	Regina, Sask.	1948	27,732	Turf

NFL Europe

		Location	Seats
Amsterdam Admirals	**Amsterdam Arena**	Amsterdam, Netherlands	51,328
Barcelona Dragons	**Estadi Olimpic de Monthuic**	Barcelona, Spain	54,000
Berlin Thunder	**Jahn Sportspark**	Berlin, Germany	20,000
Frankfurt Galaxy	**WaldStadion**	Frankfurt, Germany	54,000
Rhein Fire	**Rheinstadion**	Dusseldorf, Germany	57,000
Scottish Claymores	**Murrayfield Stadium**	Edinburgh, Scotland	67,000
	& Hampden Park	Glasgow, Scotland	52,000

Arena Football League
American Conference

Western Division		Location	Built	Seats
Arizona Rattlers	**America West Arena**	Phoenix, Ariz.	1992	16,923
Los Angeles Avengers	**Staples Center**	Los Angeles, Calif.	1999	18,000
Portland Forest Dragons	**Rose Garden**	Portland, Ore.	1995	18,800
San Jose SaberCats	**San Jose Arena**	San Jose, Calif.	1990	16,929
Central Division				
Iowa Barnstormers	**Veterans Auditorium**	Des Moines, Iowa	1955	11,250
Grand Rapids Rampage	**Van Andel Arena**	Grand Rapids, Mich.	1996	10,618
Houston Terror	**Compaq Center**	Houston, Texas	1975	15,050
Milwaukee Mustangs	**Bradley Center**	Milwaukee, Wisc.	1988	17,819

National Conference

Southern Division		Location	Built	Seats
Florida Bobcats	**National Car Rental Center**	Sunrise, Fla.	1998	17,900
Nashville Kats	**Nashville Arena**	Nashville, Tenn.	1996	16,121
New England Sea Wolves	**Hartford Civic Center**	Hartford, Conn.	1975	18,900
Orlando Predators	**Orlando Arena**	Orlando, Fla.	1989	16,613
Eastern Division		**Location**	**Built**	**Seats**
Albany Firebirds	**Pepsi Arena**	Albany, N.Y.	1990	13,652
Buffalo Destroyers	**Marine Midland Arena**	Buffalo, N.Y.	1996	18,127
New Jersey Red Dogs	**Continental Airlines Arena**	E. Rutherford, N.J.	1981	17,500
Tampa Bay Storm	**Ice Palace**	Tampa Bay, Fla.	1996	20,282

Women's Professional Basketball
Women's National Basketball Association

The WNBA teams play in the same arenas as the NBA teams in their respective cities. However, the capacities of the venues are "down-sized" for some games. The new, smaller capacity for WNBA games is listed below where applicable.

Eastern		Location	Built	Seats
Charlotte Sting	**Charlotte Coliseum**	Charlotte, N.C.	1988	12,884
Cleveland Rockers	**Gund Arena**	Cleveland, Ohio	1994	11,751
Detroit Shock	**The Palace of Auburn Hills**	Auburn Hills, Mich.	1988	22,076
Indiana (expansion)	**Conseco Fieldhouse**	Indianapolis, Ind.	1999	18,500
Miami (expansion)	**AmericanAirlines Arena**	Miami, Fla.	1999	19,600
New York Liberty	**Madison Square Garden**	New York, N.Y.	1968	19,763
Orlando Miracle	**Orlando Arena**	Orlando, Fla.	1989	17,240
Washington Mystics	**MCI Center**	Washington, D.C.	1997	20,500
Western		**Location**	**Built**	**Seats**
Houston Comets	**Compaq Center**	Houston, Tex.	1975	16,285
Los Angeles Sparks	**Great Western Forum**	Inglewood, Calif.	1967	17,505
Minnesota Lynx	**Target Center**	Minneapolis, Minn.	1990	13,000
Phoenix Mercury	**America West Arena**	Phoenix, Ariz.	1992	17,623
Portland (expansion)	**Rose Garden**	Portland, Ore.	1995	19,980
Sacramento Monarchs	**ARCO Arena**	Sacramento, Calif.	1988	17,317
Seattle (expansion)	**KeyArena at Seattle Center**	Seattle, Wash.	1962	17,100
Utah Starzz	**Delta Center**	Salt Lake City, Utah	1991	19,911

Horse Racing
Triple Crown race tracks

Race	Racetrack	Seats	Infield
Kentucky Derby	Churchill Downs	48,500	100,000
Preakness	Pimlico Race Course	40,000	60,000
Belmont Stakes	Belmont Park	32,941	50,000

Record crowds: Kentucky Derby– 163,628 (1974); Preakness– 101,000 (1999); Belmont–85,818 (1999).

Tennis
Grand Slam center courts

Event	Main Stadium	Seats
Australian Open	Melbourne Park	15,000
French Open	Stade Roland Garros	16,500
Wimbledon	Centre Court	13,850
U.S. Open	Arthur Ashe Stadium	22,500

COLLEGE BASKETBALL

The 50 Largest Arenas

The 50 largest arenas in Division I for the 1999-2000 NCAA regular season. Note that (*) indicates part-time home court.

		Seats	Home Team			Seats	Home Team
1	Carrier Dome	33,000	Syracuse	26	Pittsburgh Civic Arena	16,725	Pittsburgh*
2	Thompson-Boling Arena	24,535	Tennessee	27	Assembly Hall	16,450	Illinois
3	Rupp Arena	23,000	Kentucky	28	Allen Field House	16,300	Kansas
4	Marriott Center	22,700	BYU	29	Hartford Civic Center	16,294	UConn*
5	Dean Smith Center	21,572	N. Carolina	30	Erwin Center	16,175	Texas
6	First Union Center	21,000	Villanova*	31	LA Sports Arena	15,509	USC
7	MCI Center	20,600	Georgetown*	32	Carver-Hawkeye Arena	15,500	Iowa
8	The Pyramid	20,142	Memphis		Pepsi Arena	15,500	Siena*
9	Continental Airlines Arena	20,029	Seton Hall*	34	Bryce Jordan Center	15,261	Penn St.
10	Ent. and Sports Arena	20,000	N.C. State	35	Miami Arena	15,200	Miami
	Kiel Center	20,000	Saint Louis	36	Breslin Events Center	15,138	Michigan St.
12	The Rose Garden	19,980	Portland St.	37	Coleman Coliseum	15,043	Alabama
13	Marine Midland Arena	19,500	Canisius* & Niagara*	38	Arena-Auditorium	15,028	Wyoming
14	Bud Walton Arena	19,200	Arkansas	39	Huntsman Center	15,000	Utah
15	Bradley Center	19,150	Marquette		United Spirit Arena	15,000	Texas Tech
16	Freedom Hall	18,865	Louisville	41	Cole Fieldhouse	14,500	Maryland
17	Thomas & Mack Center	18,500	UNLV	42	McKale Center	14,489	Arizona
18	Madison Square Garden	18,470	St. John's*	43	Joel Memorial Coliseum	14,407	Wake Forest
19	University Arena (The Pit)	18,018	New Mexico	44	Williams Arena	14,321	Minnesota
20	Alltel Arena	18,000	Arkansas-Little Rock	45	Devaney Sports Center	14,200	Nebraska
	New Orleans Arena	18,000	Tulane	46	University Activity Center	14,198	Arizona St.
22	Rosemont Horizon	17,500	DePaul*	47	Maravich Assembly Ctr.	14,164	LSU
	Value City Arena	17,500	Ohio St.	48	Mackey Arena	14,123	Purdue
24	Assembly Hall	17,357	Indiana	49	Hilton Coliseum	14,020	Iowa St.
25	Kohl Center	17,142	Wisconsin	50	WVU Coliseum	14,000	West Va.

Division I Conference Home Courts

NCAA Division I conferences for the 1999-2000 season. Teams with home games in more than one arena are noted.

America East

	Home Floor	Seats
Boston University	Case Gym	1,800
Delaware	Bob Carpenter Center	5,000
Drexel	Phys. Education Center	2,300
Hartford	Chase Family Arena	4,475
Hofstra	Physical Fitness Center	2,500
	& Hofstra Arena	5,112
Maine	Alfond Arena	5,712
New Hampshire	Whittemore Center	7,200
Northeastern	Cabot Center	2,500
Towson	Towson Center	5,000
Vermont	Patrick Gym	3,228

Atlantic Coast

	Home Floor	Seats
Clemson	Littlejohn Coliseum	11,020
Duke	Cameron Indoor Stadium	9,314
Florida St.	Leon County Civic Center	12,500
Georgia Tech	Alexander Mem. Stadium	10,000
Maryland	Cole Field House	14,500
North Carolina	Dean Smith Center	21,572
N.C. State	Entertainment and Sports Arena	20,000
Virginia	University Hall	8,457
Wake Forest	Joel Mem. Coliseum	14,407

Atlantic 10

	Home Floor	Seats
Dayton	U. of Dayton Arena	13,511
Duquesne	Palumbo Center	6,200
Fordham	Rose Hill Gym	3,470
G. Washington	Smith Center	5,000
La Salle	Hayman Center	4,000
Massachusetts	Mullins Center	9,493
Rhode Island	Keaney Gymnasium	3,385
	& Providence Civic Center	12,681
St. Bonaventure	Reilly Center	6,000
St. Joseph's-PA	Alumni Mem. Fieldhouse	3,200
Temple	Apollo Center	10,224
Virginia Tech	Cassell Coliseum	10,052
Xavier-OH	Cincinnati Gardens	10,100

Big East

	Home Floor	Seats
Boston College	Conte Forum	8,606
Connecticut	Gampel Pavilion	10,027
	& Hartford Civic Center	16,294
Georgetown	MCI Center	20,600
Miami-FL	Miami Arena	15,200
Notre Dame	Joyce Center	11,418
Pittsburgh	Fitzgerald Field House	6,798
	& Pittsburgh Civic Arena	16,725
Providence	Providence Civic Center	12,993
Rutgers	Brown Athletic Center	9,000
St. John's	Alumni Hall	6,008
	& Madison Square Garden	18,470
Seton Hall	Continental Airlines Arena	20,029
Syracuse	Carrier Dome	33,000
Villanova	The Pavilion	6,500
	First Union Center	21,000
West Virginia	WVU Coliseum	14,000

Big Sky

	Home Floor	Seats
CS-Northridge	The Matadome	1,600
CS-Sacramento	Memorial Auditorium	2,603
Eastern Wash.	Reese Court	6,000
Idaho St.	Holt Arena	8,000
Montana	Adams Center	7,500
Montana St.	Worthington Arena	7,250
Northern Arizona	Walkup Skydome	7,000
Portland St.	Rose Garden	19,980
	& Memorial Coliseum	12,000
Weber St.	Dee Events Center	12,000

Big South

	Home Floor	Seats
Charleston So	CSU Fieldhouse	1,500
Coastal Carolina	Kimbel Gymnasium	1,480
Elon	Koury Center	2,000
High Point	Millis Center	1,800
Liberty	Vines Center	9,000
NC-Asheville	Justice Center	1,570
	& Asheville Civic Center	6,000
Radford	Dedmon Center	5,000
Winthrop	Winthrop Coliseum	6,100

Big Ten

	Home Floor	Seats
Illinois	Assembly Hall	16,450
Indiana	Assembly Hall	17,357
Iowa	Carver-Hawkeye Arena	15,500
Michigan	Crisler Arena	13,562
Michigan St.	Breslin Events Center	15,138
Minnesota	Williams Arena	14,321
Northwestern	Welsh-Ryan Arena	8,117
Ohio St.	Value City Arena	17,500
Penn St.	Bryce Jordan Center	15,261
Purdue	Mackey Arena	14,123
Wisconsin	Kohl Center	17,142

Note: There are 11 schools in the Big Ten.

Big 12

North	Home Floor	Seats
Colorado	Coors Events Conference Ctr.	11,198
Iowa St.	Hilton Coliseum	14,020
Kansas	Allen Fieldhouse	16,300
Kansas St.	Bramlage Coliseum	13,500
Missouri	Hearnes Center	13,300
Nebraska	Devaney Sports Center	14,200

South	Home Floor	Seats
Baylor	Ferrell Center	10,284
Oklahoma	Lloyd Noble Center	11,100
Oklahoma St.	Gallagher-Iba Arena	6,381
Texas	Erwin Center	16,175
Texas A&M	Reed Arena	12,700
Texas Tech	United Spirit Arena	15,000

Big West

	Home Floor	Seats
Boise St.	BSU Pavilion	12,380
Cal Poly-SLO	Mott Gym	3,500
CS-Fullerton	Titan Gym	3,500
Idaho	Kibbie Dome	10,000
Long Beach St.	The Pyramid	5,000
Nevada	Lawlor Events Center	11,200
New Mexico St.	Pan American Center	13,071
North Texas	The Super Pit	10,000
Pacific	Spanos Center	6,150
UC-Irvine	Bren Events Center	5,000
UC-Santa Barbara	The Thunderdome	6,000
Utah St.	The Smith Spectrum	10,270

Note: Nevada will join the WAC in July 2000.

Colonial

	Home Floor	Seats
American	Bender Arena	5,000
East Carolina	Minges Coliseum	7,500
George Mason	Patriot Center	10,000
James Madison	JMU Convocation Center	7,156
NC-Wilmington	Trask Coliseum	6,100
Old Dominion	Norfolk Scope	10,253
Richmond	Robins Center	9,171
VCU	Siegel Center	7,500
Wm. & Mary	William & Mary Hall	8,600

Conference USA

	Home Floor	Seats
UAB	Bartow Arena	8,500
Cincinnati	Shoemaker Center	13,176
DePaul	Rosemont Horizon	17,500
Houston	Hofheinz Pavilion	8,479
Louisville	Freedom Hall	18,865
Marquette	Bradley Center	19,150
Memphis	The Pyramid	20,142
UNC Charlotte	Halton Arena	9,105
Saint Louis	Kiel Center	20,000
South Florida	Sun Dome	10,411
Southern Miss	Green Coliseum	8,095
Tulane	New Orleans Arena	18,000

Ivy League

	Home Floor	Seats
Brown	Pizzitola Sports Center	2,800
Columbia	Levien Gymnasium	3,408
Cornell	Newman Arena	4,750
Dartmouth	Leede Arena	2,200
Harvard	Briggs Athletic Center	2,195
Penn	The Palestra	8,700
Princeton	Jadwin Gymnasium	6,854
Yale	Lee Amphitheater	3,100

Metro Atlantic

	Home Floor	Seats
Canisius	Marine Midland Arena	19,500
	& Koessler Athletic Center	1,800
Fairfield	Alumni Hall	2,479
Iona	Mulcahy Center	3,200
Loyola-MD	Reitz Arena	3,000
Manhattan	Draddy Gymnasium	3,000
Marist	McCann Center	3,944
Niagara	Marine Midland Arena	19,500
	& Gallagher Center	3,200
Rider	Alumni Gymnasium	1,650
St. Peter's	Yanitelli Center	3,200
Siena	Pepsi Arena	15,500

Mid American

	Home Floor	Seats
Akron	JAR Arena	5,942
Ball St.	University Arena	11,500
Bowling Green	Anderson Arena	5,200
Buffalo	Alumni Arena	8,500
Central Mich.	Rose Arena	5,200
Eastern Mich.	Convocation Center	4,800
Kent	MAC Center	6,327
Marshall	Henderson Center	9,043
Miami-OH	Millett Hall	9,200
Northern Illinois	Chick Evans Field House	6,044
Ohio Univ.	The Convo	13,000
Toledo	Savage Hall	9,000
Western Mich.	University Arena	5,800

Mid-Continent

	Home Floor	Seats
Chicago St.	Dickens Athletic Center	2,500
IU-PUI	IU-PUI Gym	2,000
Missouri-K.C.	Municipal Auditorium	9,287
Oakland	Oakland Arena	3,000
Oral Roberts	Mabee Center	10,575
Southern Utah	Centrum	5,300
Valparaiso	Athletics-Recreation Center	4,500
Western Ill.	Western Hall	5,139
Youngstown St.	Beeghly Center	8,000

College Basketball (Cont.)

Mid-Eastern Athletic

	Home Floor	Seats
Bethune-Cookman	Moore Gym	3,000
Coppin St.	Coppin Center	3,000
Delaware St.	Memorial Hall	3,000
Florida A&M	Gaither Gym	3,350
Hampton	Hampton Convocation Center	7,200
Howard	Burr Gym	3,000
MD-East.Shore	Tawes Gym	1,200
Morgan St.	Hill Fieldhouse	5,000
Norfolk St.	Echols Hall	7,600
N. Carolina A&T	Corbett Sports Center	7,500
S. Carolina St.	SHM Center	3,200

Midwestern

	Home Floor	Seats
Butler	Hinkle Fieldhouse	11,043
Cleveland St.	CSU Convocation Center	13,610
Detroit Mercy	Calihan Hall	8,837
IL-Chicago	UIC Pavilion	8,000
Loyola-IL	Gentile Center	5,200
WI-Green Bay	Brown County Arena	5,600
WI-Milwaukee	Klotsche Center	5,000
Wright St.	Nutter Center	10,632

Missouri Valley

	Home Floor	Seats
Bradley	Carver Arena	10,825
Creighton	Omaha Civic Auditorium	9,493
Drake	Knapp Center	7,002
Evansville	Roberts Stadium	12,300
Illinois St.	Redbird Arena	10,200
Indiana St.	Hulman Center	10,200
Northern Iowa	UNI-Dome	10,000
Southern Ill.	SIU Arena	10,014
SW Missouri St.	Hammons Student Center	8,846
Wichita St.	Levitt Arena	10,423

Mountain West

	Home Floor	Seats
Air Force	Clune Arena	6,003
BYU	Marriott Center	22,700
Colorado St.	Moby Arena	8,754
San Diego St.	Aztec Bowl Arena	12,000
UNLV	Thomas & Mack Center	18,500
New Mexico	University Arena (The Pit)	18,018
Utah	Huntsman Center	15,000
Wyoming	Arena-Auditorium	15,028

Northeast

	Home Floor	Seats
Central Conn. St.	Detrick Gym	4,500
Farleigh Dickinson	Rothman Center	5,000
LIU-Brooklyn	Schwartz Athletic Center	1,200
MD-Balt. County	Retriever Activity Center	4,024
Monmouth	Boylan Gym	2,500
Mt. St. Mary's	Knott Arena	3,196
Quinnipiac	Burt Kahn Court	1,500
Robert Morris	Sewall Center	3,056
Sacred Heart	Pitt Center	5,000
St. Francis-NY	Phys. Ed. Center	1,400
St. Francis-PA	DeGol Arena	3,500
Wagner	Spiro Sports Center	2,100

Ohio Valley

	Home Floor	Seats
Austin Peay	Dunn Center	9,000
Eastern Illinois	Lantz Gym	5,300
Eastern Ky.	McBrayer Arena	6,500
Middle Tenn. St.	Murphy Center	11,520
Morehead St.	Johnson Arena	6,500
Murray St.	Regional Special Events Ctr.	8,600
SE Missouri St.	Show Me Center	7,000
Tennessee-Martin	Skyhawk Arena	6,700
Tennessee St.	Gentry Complex	10,500
Tennessee Tech	Eblen Center	10,152

Pacific-10

	Home Floor	Seats
Arizona	McKale Center	14,489
Arizona St.	Wells Fargo Arena	14,198
California	Haas Pavillion	12,100
Oregon	McArthur Court	9,087
Oregon St.	Gill Coliseum	10,400
Stanford	Maples Pavilion	7,500
UCLA	Pauley Pavilion	12,819
USC	LA Sports Arena	15,509
Washington	Hec Edmundson Pavilion	7,800
Washington. St.	Friel Court	12,058

Patriot League

	Home Floor	Seats
Army	Christl Arena	5,043
Bucknell	Davis Gym	2,380
Colgate	Cotterell Court	3,000
Holy Cross	Hart Recreation Center	3,600
Lafayette	Kirby Field House	3,500
Lehigh	Stabler Arena	5,600
Navy	Alumni Hall	5,710

Southeastern

Eastern	Home Floor	Seats
Florida	O'Connell Center	12,000
Georgia	Stegeman Coliseum	10,523
Kentucky	Rupp Arena	23,000
South Carolina	McGuire Arena	12,401
Tennessee	Thompson-Boling Arena	24,535
Vanderbilt	Memorial Gymnasium	14,100

Western	Home Floor	Seats
Alabama	Coleman Coliseum	15,043
Arkansas	Bud Walton Arena	19,200
Auburn	Eaves-Memorial Coliseum	10,108
LSU	Maravich Assembly Center	14,164
Mississippi	Tad Smith Coliseum	8,135
Mississippi St.	Humphrey Coliseum	10,500

Southern

	Home Floor	Seats
Appalachian St.	Varsity Gymnasium	8,000
The Citadel	McAlister Field House	6,200
Coll. of Charleston	Kresse Arena	3,500
Davidson	Belk Arena	5,700
E. Tenn. St.	Memorial Center	12,000
Furman	Timmons Arena	5,000
Ga. Southern	Hanner Fieldhouse	5,500
NC-Greensboro	Fleming Gymnasium	2,320
Tenn-Chatt.	UTC Arena	11,218
VMI	Cameron Hall	5,029
W. Carolina	Ramsey Center	7,286
Wofford	Johnson Arena	3,500

Southland

	Home Floor	Seats
Lamar	Montagne Center	10,800
McNeese St.	Burton Coliseum	8,000
Nicholls St.	Stopher Gym	3,800
NE Louisiana	Ewing Coliseum	8,000
Northwestern St.	Prather Coliseum	3,900
Sam Houston St.	Johnson Coliseum	6,172
SE Louisiana	University Center	7,500
SW Texas St.	Strahan Coliseum	7,200
S.F. Austin St.	W.R. Johnson Coliseum	7,200
TX-Arlington	Texas Hall	4,200
TX-San Antonio	Convocation Center	5,100

Southwestern

	Home Floor	Seats
Alabama A&M	T.M. Elmore Gym	8,000
Alabama St.	Joe Reed Acadome	7,000
Alcorn St.	Whitney Complex	7,000
Arkansas-Pine Bluff	Johnson Complex	4,500
Grambling St.	Memorial Gym	4,500
Jackson St.	Williams Center	8,000
Miss.Valley St.	Harrison Athletic Complex	6,000
Prairie View A&M	The Baby Dome	6,600
Southern-BR	Clark Activity Center	7,500
TX Southern	Health & P.E. Building	8,100

Sun Belt

	Home Floor	Seats
Ark-Little Rock	Alltel Arena	18,000
Arkansas St	Convocation Center	10,563
Denver	Magness Arena	7,200
Florida International	Golden Panther Arena	5,000
Louisiana Tech	Thomas Assembly Center	8,000
New Orleans	Lakefront Arena	10,000
South Alabama	Mitchell Center	10,000
SW Louisiana	The Cajundome	12,800
Western Ky.	E.A. Diddle Arena	11,300

Trans America

	Home Floor	Seats
Campbell	Carter Gym	1,050
Central Fla.	UCF Arena	5,100
Fla. Atlantic	FAU Gym	5,000
Georgia St.	GSU Sports Arena	5,500
Jacksonville	Memorial Coliseum	9,150
Jacksonville St.	Mathews Coliseum	5,500
Mercer	Macon Coliseum	2,500
Samford	Seibert Hall	4,000
Stetson	Edmunds Center	5,000
Troy St.	Sartain Hall	3,000

West Coast

	Home Floor	Seats
Gonzaga	Martin Centre	4,000
Loyola Marymount	Gersten Pavilion	4,156
Pepperdine	Firestone Fieldhouse	3,104
Portland	Chiles Center	5,000
St. Mary's-CA	McKeon Pavilion	3,500
San Diego	USD Sports Center	2,500
San Francisco	War Memorial Gym	5,300
Santa Clara	Toso Pavilion	5,000

Western Athletic

	Home Floor	Seats
Fresno St.	Selland Arena	10,132
Hawaii	Stan Sherif Center	10,225
Rice	Autry Court	5,000
San Jose St.	The Events Center	5,000
SMU	Moody Coliseum	8,998
TCU	Daniel-Meyer Coliseum	7,166
Tulsa	Reynolds Center	8,310
UTEP	Haskins Center	12,222

Note: Nevada will join the WAC in July 2000.

Independents

	Home Floor	Seats
Albany	Rec. and Convocation Center	5,000
Belmont	Striplin Gym	2,500
Centenary	Gold Dome	3,000
Stonybrook	Pritchard Gym	5,226
Texas-Pan Am	Health/PE Fieldhouse	3,500

Future NCAA Final Four Sites

Men

Year	Arena	Seats	Location
2000	RCA Dome	47,100	Indianapolis
2001	Metrodome	50,000	Minneapolis
2002	Georgia Dome	40,000	Atlanta
2003	Louisiana Superdome	53,500	New Orleans
2004	Alamodome	20,557*	San Antonio
2005	Trans World Dome	66,000	St. Louis
2006	RCA Dome	47,100	Indianapolis
2007	Georgia Dome	40,000	Atlanta

*This is the listed capacity for Spurs games at the Alamodome. It is likely that the seating will be reconfigured to fit more spectators for the Final Four.

Women

Year	Arena	Seats	Location
2000	First Union Center	20,444	Philadelphia
2001	Kiel Center	20,000	St. Louis
2002	Alamodome	26,000	San Antonio
2003	Georgia Dome	40,000	Atlanta
2004	New Orleans Sports Arena	17,832	New Orleans

COLLEGE FOOTBALL

The 40 Largest I-A Stadiums

The 40 largest stadiums in NCAA Division I-A college football heading into the 1999 season. Note that (*) indicates stadium not on campus.

		Location	Seats	Home Team	Conference	Built	Field
1	Michigan Stadium	Ann Arbor, Mich.	107,501	Michigan	Big Ten	1927	Grass
2	Ohio Stadium	Columbus, Ohio	103,801	Ohio St.	Big Ten	1922	Grass
3	Neyland Stadium	Knoxville, Tenn.	102,854	Tennessee	SEC-East	1921	Grass
4	Rose Bowl*	Pasadena, Calif.	98,636	UCLA	Pac-10	1922	Grass
5	Beaver Stadium	University Park, Pa.	93,967	Penn St.	Big Ten	1960	Grass
6	LA Memorial Coliseum*	Los Angeles, Calif.	92,000	USC	Pac-10	1923	Grass
7	Sanford Stadium	Athens, Ga.	86,117	Georgia	SEC-East	1929	Grass
8	Stanford Stadium	Stanford, Calif.	85,500	Stanford	Pac-10	1921	Grass
9	Jordan-Hare Stadium	Auburn, Ala.	85,214	Auburn	SEC-West	1939	Grass
10	Bryant-Denny Stadium	Tuscaloosa, Ala.	83,818	Alabama	SEC-West	1929	Grass
11	Kyle Field	College Station, Tex.	80,210	Texas A&M	Big 12-South	1925	Grass
12	Legion Field*	Birmingham, Ala.	83,091	Alabama/UAB	SEC/Indy	1927	Grass
13	Florida Field	Gainesville, Fla.	83,000	Florida	SEC-East	1929	Grass
14	Memorial Stadium	Clemson, S.C.	81,474	Clemson	ACC	1942	Grass
15	Williams-Brice Stadium	Columbia, S.C.	80,250	South Carolina	SEC-East	1934	Grass
16	Royal-Memorial Stadium	Austin, Tex.	80,082	Texas	Big 12-South	1924	Grass
17	Notre Dame Stadium	Notre Dame, Ind.	80,012	Notre Dame	Independent	1930	Grass
18	Doak Campbell Stadium	Tallahasse, Fla.	80,000	Florida St.	ACC	1950	Grass
	Tiger Stadium	Baton Rouge, La.	80,000	LSU	SEC-West	1924	Grass
20	Camp Randall Stadium	Madison, Wisc.	76,129	Wisconsin	Big Ten	1917	Turf
21	Memorial Stadium	Berkeley, Calif.	75,028	California	Pac-10	1923	Grass
22	Oklahoma Memorial Field	Norman, Okla.	75,004	Oklahoma	Big 12-South	1924	Grass
23	Memorial Stadium	Lincoln, Neb.	74,506	Nebraska	Big 12-North	1923	Turf
24	Sun Devil Stadium	Tempe, Ariz.	73,379	Arizona St.	Pac-10	1959	Grass
25	Husky Stadium	Seattle, Wash.	72,500	Washington	Pac-10	1920	Turf
26	Orange Bowl*	Miami, Fla.	72,314	Miami-FL	Big East	1935	Grass
27	Spartan Stadium	East Lansing, Mich.	72,027	Michigan St.	Big Ten	1957	Turf
28	Qualcomm Stadium*	San Diego, Calif.	71,400	San Diego St.	Mountain West	1967	Grass
29	Memorial Stadium	Champaign, Ill.	70,904	Illinois	Big Ten	1923	Turf
30	Kinnick Stadium	Iowa City, Iowa	70,397	Iowa	Big Ten	1929	Grass
31	Citrus Bowl*	Orlando, Fla.	70,188	Central Florida	Independent	1936	Grass
32	Rice Stadium	Houston, Tex.	70,000	Rice	WAC	1950	Turf
33	Superdome*	New Orleans, La.	69,767	Tulane	USA	1975	Turf
34	Cotton Bowl*	Dallas, Tex.	68,252	SMU	WAC	1932	Grass
35	Commonwealth	Lexington, Ky.	68,000	Kentucky	SEC	1973	Grass
36	Ross-Ade Stadium	W. Lafayette, Ind.	67,861	Purdue	Big Ten	1924	Grass
37	Veterans Stadium*	Philadelphia, Pa.	66,592	Temple	Big East	1971	Turf
38	Cougar Stadium	Provo, Utah	65,000	BYU	Mountain West	1964	Grass
39	HHH Metrodome*	Minneapolis, Minn.	63,699	Minnesota	Big Ten	1982	Turf
40	Mountaineer Field	Morgantown, W. Va.	63,500	West Virginia	Big East	1980	Turf

1999 Conference Home Fields

NCAA Division I-A conference by conference listing includes member teams heading into the 1999 season. Note that (*) indicates stadium is not on campus.

Atlantic Coast

	Stadium	Built	Seats	Field
Clemson	Memorial	1942	81,474	Grass
Duke	Wallace Wade	1929	33,941	Grass
Florida St.	Doak Campbell	1950	80,000	Grass
Ga. Tech	Bobby Dodd	1913	46,000	Grass
Maryland	Byrd	1950	48,055	Grass
N. Carolina	Kenan Memorial	1927	60,000	Grass
N.C. State	Carter-Finley	1966	51,500	Grass
Virginia	Scott	1931	44,000	Grass
Wake Forest	Groves	1968	31,500	Grass

Big East

	Stadium	Built	Seats	Field
Boston Col.	Alumni	1957	44,500	Turf
Miami-FL	Orange Bowl*	1935	72,314	Grass
Pittsburgh	Pitt	1925	56,150	Turf
Rutgers	Rutgers	1994	41,500	Grass
Syracuse	Carrier Dome	1980	49,550	Turf
Temple	Veterans*	1971	66,592	Turf
Va. Tech	Lane	1965	50,000	Grass
West Va.	Mountaineer Fld.	1980	63,500	Turf

University of Michigan

Michigan Stadium added more than 5,000 seats in 1998. The Wolverines can once again lay claim to playing their home games at the nation's largest college football venue.

Big Ten

	Stadium	Built	Seats	Field
Illinois	Memorial	1923	70,904	Turf
Indiana	Memorial	1960	52,354	Grass
Iowa	Kinnick	1929	70,397	Grass
Michigan	Michigan	1927	107,501	Grass
Michigan St.	Spartan	1957	72,027	Turf
Minnesota	Metrodome*	1982	63,699	Turf
Northwestern	Ryan Field	1926	49,256	Grass
Ohio St.	Ohio	1922	103,801	Grass
Penn St.	Beaver	1960	93,967	Grass
Purdue	Ross-Ade	1924	67,861	Grass
Wisconsin	Camp Randall	1917	76,129	Turf

Big 12

NORTH	Stadium	Built	Seats	Field
Colorado	Folsom Field	1924	51,808	Turf
Iowa St.	Trice Field	1975	43,000	Grass
Kansas	Memorial	1921	50,250	Turf
Kansas St.	Wagner Field	1968	50,000	Turf
Missouri	Faurot Field	1926	62,000	Grass
Nebraska	Memorial	1923	74,506	Turf

SOUTH	Stadium	Built	Seats	Field
Baylor	Floyd Casey	1950	50,000	Grass
Oklahoma	Memorial	1924	75,004	Grass
Oklahoma St.	Lewis Field	1920	50,614	Turf
Texas	Royal-Mem.	1924	80,082	Grass
Texas A&M	Kyle Field	1925	80,210	Grass
Texas Tech	Jones	1947	50,500	Turf

Note: The annual Oklahoma-Texas game has been played at the Cotton Bowl (capacity 68,252) in Dallas since 1937.

Big West

	Stadium	Built	Seats	Field
Arkansas St.	Indian	1974	33,410	Grass
Boise St.	Bronco	1970	30,000	Turf
Idaho	Martin Stadium	1972	37,500	Turf
Nevada	Mackay	1967	31,545	Grass
New Mexico St.	Aggie Memorial	1978	30,343	Grass
North Texas	Fouts Field	1952	30,500	Turf
Utah St.	Romney	1968	30,257	Grass

Conference USA

	Stadium	Built	Seats	Field
UAB	Legion	1927	83,091	Grass
Army	Michie	1924	39,929	Turf
Houston	Robertson	1942	31,000	Grass
Cincinnati	Nippert	1924	35,000	Turf
E. Carolina	Dowdy-Ficklen	1963	42,700	Grass
Louisville	Papa John's Cardinal	1998	42,000	Turf
Memphis	Liberty Bowl*	1965	62,380	Grass
Southern Miss	Roberts	1976	33,000	Grass
Tulane	Superdome*	1975	69,767	Turf

I-A Independents

	Stadium	Built	Seats	Field
C. Florida	Citrus Bowl	1936	70,188	Grass
Louisiana Tech	Joe Aillet	1968	30,600	Grass
Middle Tennessee St.	Johnny Red Floyd	1933	30,880	Turf
Navy	Navy-Marine Corps Memorial	1959	30,000	Grass
NE Louisiana	Malone	1978	30,427	Grass
Notre Dame	Notre Dame	1930	80,012	Grass
SW Louisiana	Cajun Field	1971	31,000	Grass

College Football (Cont.)

Mid-American

	Stadium	Built	Seats	Field
Akron	Rubber Bowl*	1940	35,202	Turf
Ball St.	Ball State	1967	21,581	Grass
Buffalo	UB	1993	31,000	Grass
Bowling Green	Doyt Perry	1966	30,599	Grass
Central Mich.	Kelly/Shorts	1972	30,199	Turf
Eastern Mich.	Rynearson	1969	30,200	Turf
Kent	Dix	1969	30,520	Turf
Marshall	Marshall	1991	30,000	Turf
Miami-OH	Fred Yager	1983	30,012	Grass
Northern Ill.	Huskie	1965	31,000	Turf
Ohio Univ.	Peden	1929	20,000	Grass
Toledo	Glass Bowl	1937	26,248	Turf
Western Mich.	Waldo	1939	30,200	Grass

Mountain West

	Stadium	Built	Seats	Field
Air Force	Falcon	1962	52,480	Grass
BYU	Cougar	1964	65,000	Grass
Colorado St.	Hughes	1968	30,000	Grass
New Mexico	University	1960	31,218	Grass
San Diego St.	Qualcomm*	1967	71,400	Grass
UNLV	Sam Boyd*	1971	40,000	Grass
Utah	Rice-Eccles	1927†	45,634	Grass
Wyoming	War Memorial	1950	33,500	Grass

Note: The new Mountain West Conference was created in 1999 when the eight teams above broke off from the WAC.
†Utah's Rice-Eccles Stadium was rebuilt in 1998.

Pacific-10

	Stadium	Built	Seats	Field
Arizona	Arizona	1928	56,500	Grass
Arizona St.	Sun Devil	1959	73,379	Grass
California	Memorial	1923	75,028	Grass
Oregon	Autzen	1967	41,698	Turf
Oregon St.	Reser's	1953	35,362	Turf
Stanford	Stanford	1921	85,500	Grass
UCLA	Rose Bowl*	1922	98,636	Grass
USC	LA Coliseum*	1923	92,000	Grass
Washington	Husky	1920	72,500	Turf
Washington St.	Martin	1972	37,600	Grass

Southeastern

EAST	Stadium	Built	Seats	Field
Florida	Florida Field	1929	83,000	Grass
Georgia	Sanford	1929	86,117	Grass
Kentucky	Commonwealth	1973	68,000	Grass
S. Carolina	Williams-Brice	1934	80,250	Grass
Tennessee	Neyland	1921	102,854	Grass
Vanderbilt	Vanderbilt	1981	41,600	Grass

WEST	Stadium	Built	Seats	Field
Alabama	Bryant-Denny	1929	83,818	Grass
	& Legion	1927	83,091	Grass
Arkansas	Razorback	1938	50,019	Grass
	& War Memorial*	1948	53,727	Grass
Auburn	Jordan-Hare	1939	85,214	Grass
LSU	Tiger	1924	80,000	Grass
Mississippi	Vaught-Hem'way	1941	50,577	Grass
Miss. St.	Scott Field	1915	40,656	Grass

Note: EAST–Vanderbilt Stadium was rebuilt in 1981.

SEC Championship Game

The first two SEC Championship Games were played at Legion Field in Birmingham, Ala., in 1992 and 1993. The game was moved to Atlanta's 71,228-seat Georgia Dome in 1994.

Western Athletic

	Stadium	Built	Seats	Field
Fresno St.	Bulldog	1980	41,031	Grass
Hawaii	Aloha*	1975	50,000	Turf
Rice	Rice	1950	70,000	Turf
San Jose St.	Spartan	1933	30,578	Grass
SMU	Cotton Bowl*	1932	68,252	Grass
TCU	Amon Carter	1929	44,800	Grass
Tulsa	Skelly	1930	40,385	Turf
UTEP	Sun Bowl*	1963	52,000	Turf

Note: Eight teams from the WAC (Air Force, BYU, Colorado St., San Diego St., UNLV, New Mexico, Utah and Wyoming) broke off and formed the new Mountain West Conference in 1999. The WAC membership will change again in July 2000 with the addition of Nevada.

Bowl Games

Listed alphabetically and updated as of Sept. 1, 1999. The Bowl Championship Series calls for the national championship game (No. 1 vs. No. 2) to rotate between the Fiesta Bowl (1999), Sugar Bowl (2000), Orange Bowl (2001) and Rose Bowl (2002). See The Bowl Championship Series.

	Stadium	Built	Seats	Field
Alamo	Alamodome	1993	65,000	Turf
Aloha	Aloha	1975	50,000	Turf
Cotton	Cotton	1930	68,252	Grass
Fiesta	Sun Devil	1959	73,471	Grass
Fla. Citrus	Fla. Citrus Bowl	1936	65,000	Grass
Gator	Alltel	1995	72,223	Grass
Holiday	Qualcomm	1967	71,400	Grass
Humanitarian	Bronco	1970	30,000	Turf
Independence	Independence	1936	50,459	Grass
Insight.com	Arizona	1928	57,803	Grass
Las Vegas	Sam Boyd	1971	40,000	Turf
Liberty	Liberty Bowl	1965	62,800	Grass

	Stadium	Built	Seats	Field
Micron/PC	Pro Player	1987	74,916	Grass
Mobile Alabama	Ladd Peeble	1948	41,000	Grass
Motor City	Pontiac Silverdome	1975	80,335	Turf
Music City	Adelphia	1999	67,000	Grass
Oahu	Aloha	1975	50,000	Turf
Orange	Pro Player	1987	75,192	Grass
Outback	Houlihan's	1967	65,000	Grass
Peach	Georgia Dome	1992	71,228	Turf
Rose	Rose Bowl	1922	102,083	Grass
Sugar	Superdome	1975	76,000	Turf
Sun	Sun Bowl	1963	57,127	Turf

Playing Sites

Alamo— San Antonio; **Aloha**— Honolulu; **Cotton**— Dallas; **Fiesta**— Tempe; **Florida Citrus**— Orlando; **Gator**— Jacksonville; **Holiday**— San Diego; **Humanitarian**— Boise; **Independence**— Shreveport; **Insight.com**—Tucson; **Las Vegas**— Las Vegas; **Liberty**— Memphis; **Micron/PC**—Miami; **Mobile Alabama**—Mobile; **Motor City**— Pontiac; **Music City**— Nashville; **Oahu**— Honolulu; **Orange**— Miami; **Outback**— Tampa; **Peach**— Atlanta; **Rose**— Pasadena; **Sugar**— New Orleans; **Sun**— El Paso.

Business

With the hopes of the Penguins remaining in Pittsburgh in serious jeopardy, former star **Mario Lemieux** swooped in and rescued them from bankruptcy.

AP/Wide World Photos

Owning Up to It

These days major sports franchise owners seem to be bigger celebrities than the players that work for them.

by
Bob Stevens

Trade you an Art Modell for an Al Lerner? Sure, if you throw in a Mike Ilitch. Okay, but only if you'll throw in a Tom Hicks.

Remember the days when you and your buddies argued the virtues of Mays, Mantle and Snider? Or the 90's Cowboys versus the 80's 49ers versus the 70's Steelers? Well, except for baseball's young shortstops and football's quarterbacks, the players and the teams are no longer the stars. It's the owners who define their teams, and their entire cities, for better (Dallas' Hicks and Jerry Jones) or worse (Cincinnati's Marge Schott, who's finally gone, and Mike Brown, with whom the Queen City is stuck).

Unfortunately, fans are stuck with their owners, except in the rare cases of Cleveland with the aforementioned Modell, who in 1999 began the search for help in squandering his Baltimore windfall, and Cincy with Schott, who

finally had her stake in the Reds taken over by the minority owners. Don't you think fans in Chicago would love to trade owners with Pittsburgh? They have the young, creative Kevin McClatchy, who is breathing new life into the Pirates, the esteemed yet still competitive Rooneys of the Steelers, and Mario Lemieux who's willing to forego lawsuits to save the Penguins.

Or maybe Chicago would trade with Cleveland, which boasts a wealthy but quiet "hire good management and leave them alone" triumvirate in the Indians' Dick Jacobs, Browns' Al Lerner and Cavs' Gordon Gund (who probably would have won as many titles with Michael Jordan as Jerry Reinsdorf).

Unfortunately many of the "good" owners see the corporate invasion of team ownership and are bailing out. Jacobs is trying to sell the Indians, the late Leon Hess' Jets will likely go corporate in 2000. In place of the O'Malleys and the Autrys, you have

Bob Stevens is an anchor for ESPN's *Sports-Center*.

Once content to just watch from their luxury box, or not even come to the games at all, team owners like the Cowboys' **Jerry Jones** have been taking a much more active approach to running their teams. Some may even call it meddlesome.

Fox and Disney. And can you say either the Dodgers or Angels are better for it? Kansas City used to have the most stable, and arguably one of the most successful, football-baseball combos anywhere with Lamar Hunt and Ewing Kauffman, men with keen interest, deep pockets, and no desire to upstage their teams. Kauffman's death signaled the collapse of the Royals, and baseball still hasn't found a worthy ownership group to take control.

Fans in Detroit and Phoenix get the best and worst of both worlds. In Motown, Ilitch has actively spent on his Red Wings and is footing the bill for the Tigers' new ballpark to give them a chance to be competitive. But the Ford family continues to wallow in NFL mediocrity and won't even commit to joining Ilitch in the revitalization of downtown Detroit. Arizona is celebrating a baseball division title in its second season under the perpetual motion machine, Jerry Colangelo, who also keeps the Suns perennially competitive. Cardinals owner Bill Bidwill followed a rare playoff run by playing hardball with a half-dozen important veterans.

The ownership game has changed so much in the last decade that George Steinbrenner has actually become one of the good guys. His ego-maniacal rule of the Yankees was once considered the bane of professional sports, but ever since he turned over the day-to-day operation to real baseball people, he's now considered a voice of reason and sanity.

The best owners of all, though, still have to be the men and women who back the Green Bay Packers, pro sports' only community-owned team.

AP/Wide World Photos

Former Detroit Pistons star **Isiah Thomas** had originally planned to buy a CBA expansion team for Detroit. Instead, he bought the entire league for approximately $10 million and plans to reorganize it.

They have money, they hire good people and leave them alone, and the only time you hear them rising up in unison is to cheer another Green Bay touchdown. Few fans would trade that opportunity for anything. ∎

Bob Stevens' Top Ten 1999 Sports Business Highlights

10. **Sign of the times?** A group of Ottawa Senators season ticket holders threaten to sue over the holdout of star scorer Alexei Yashin, claiming the product they bought includes Yashin.

9. **Americans retake the "Beach."** The Pebble Beach Golf Links are finally back in the hands of Americans, bought for $820 million by a group led by Peter Ueberroth, Arnold Palmer and Clint Eastwood.

8. **De La Hoya vs. Trinidad.** Say what you will about the decision, the best decision was having this fight in the first place. The two middleweights got rich. De La Hoya earned over $21 million and Trinidad $10.5 million. The pay-per-view audience is the largest ever for a non-heavyweight fight, with HBO reporting 1.25 million buys.

7. **Mario buys the Penguins.** Mario Lemieux turns $32 million in money owed him by the bankrupt Pittsburgh Penguins into a $25 million controlling ownership stake in the "new" Penguins. The 34-year-old becomes the first former player to own a major sports franchise.

AP/Wide World Photos

Good sections still available! Only 100 fans were in attendance at the start of the Marlins-Expos game on Sept. 21 in Florida. Marlins owner **John Henry**, left, invited each of the fans down to the batters box seats to be his guest.

6. **Isiah buys a league.** Not a new children's sports book, Isiah Thomas actually buys the entire Continental Basketball Association (the NBA's quasi-minor league) for $10 million.

5. **Olympic bribery scandal.** The Olympic movement takes a huge hit image-wise, but the biggest business loss is John Hancock, who backs out of its sponsorship of the 2002 games in Salt Lake City.

4. **Baseball ownership changes.** Marge Schott is gone in Cincinnati, selling to her minority partners, but other owners won't approve proposals for new owners of the Royals and A's. The Twins and Expos are also gasping for green. A September game in Flor-ida between the Marlins and Expos draws a counted crowd of about 100. It was so small players could hear cell-phones ringing in the stadium.

3. **Baseball economics, part two.** Four old stadiums close, to be replaced by new cash machines that owners promise will make their teams competitive again. Goodbye Tiger Stadium, 3Com (Candlestick), Kingdome and Astrodome. Hello Comerica, Pacific Bell, SAFECO and Enron Fields.

2. **Ryder Cup fiasco.** Just in time for the PGA Championship, members of the American Ryder Cup team express their displeasure at being paid only expenses to play for their country. They receive the support of almost no one, inside

the game or out. The PGA of America makes over $20 million in profit from the matches, but funds many of its outreach programs with the money.

1. **NFL franchise follies.** At 34, Daniel Snyder buys the Washington Redskins and their stadium (for which he'll sell the name) for $800 million. The NFL is still looking for a deal to put a 32nd team in Los Angeles, or is it a 32nd owner for one team? Connecticut offers a free new stadium to the Patriots, who use the leverage to get a deal from Massachusetts and the NFL to fund a new stadium in Foxboro. ∎

THE **NUMBERS**

INSIDE

RICKY MIGHT LOSE HIS NUMBERS

Rookie running back Ricky Williams signed a very risky, incentive-laden contract to play with the New Orleans Saints for the next seven years (with a possibility of an eighth). The deal could earn Williams $68.4 million but could also be as low as $11.1 million. Listed are his base salary figures over the seven years and just some of his possible incentives.

Year	Base Salary
1999	$175,000
2000	250,000
2001	325,000
2002	350,000
2003	375,000
2004	400,000
2005	400,000
Goal	**Bonus**
Involved in 35 percent of off. plays	$50,000
Average 4.5 yards-per-carry	50,000
12 rushing touchdowns	50,000
12 receiving touchdowns	50,000
76 points scored	50,000
1,601 yards of total offense	50,000
Keep weight below 240 pounds	100,000
Goal - rushing yards	**Bonus**
1,600 yards	$1 million
1,800 yards	1.5 million
2,000 yards	2 million
2,100 yards	2.1 million
2,106 yards*	3 million

*This would establish a new NFL single-season record.

JOCKS ON FILM

Can you guess the top-grossing sports movie of all-time? It's probably not what you think. According to USA Today and official box office totals, The Waterboy, starring Adam Sandler, ranks atop the list, having pulled in a whopping $161.5 million. And you probably thought it was Youngblood, huh? Below are the top-grossing sports movies, the amount they've made and their overall standing with regard to non-sports related films. By the way, Titanic is on top with over $600 million.

Movie (overall rank)	Gross (in millions)
1. The Waterboy (59)	$161.5
2. Jerry Maguire (66)	153.6
3. Rocky IV (104)	127.9
4. Rocky III (114)	122.8
5. Rocky (129)	117.2
6. The Karate Kid, Part II (133)	115.1
7. A League of Their Own (153)	107.5

Note: Figures are as of Sept. 20, 1999. ∎

BUSINESS 585

1998-99 Top Rated TV Sports Events

Final 1998-99 network television ratings for nationally-telecast sports events, according to Nielsen Media Research. Covers period from Oct. 1, 1998 through Aug. 29, 1999. Events are listed with ratings points and audience share; each ratings point represents 994,000 households and shares indicate percentage of TV sets in use.

Multiple entries: SPORTS—NFL Football (57); Major League Baseball (6); NBA Basketball (5); NCAA Football bowl games (3); NCAA Basketball (2). NETWORKS—FOX (30); ABC (20); CBS (19); NBC (6).

		Date	Net	Rtg/Sh
1	**Super Bowl XXXIII** (Broncos vs Falcons)	1/31/99	FOX	40.2/61
2	**AFC Championship Game** (Jets at Broncos)	1/17/99	CBS	26.6/48
3	**NFC Championship Game** (Falcons at Vikings)	1/17/99	FOX	25.7/54
4	**NFC Playoff Game** (Packers at 49ers)	1/3/99	FOX	23.6/40
5	**NFC Playoff Game** (Cardinals at Vikings)	1/10/99	FOX	21.4/39
6	**NFC Playoff Game** (Cardinals at Cowboys)	1/2/99	ABC	21.2/40
7	**AFC Playoff Game** (Jaguars at Jets)	1/10/99	CBS	20.1/45
8	**AFC Playoff Game** (Dolphins at Broncos)	1/9/99	CBS	18.4/37
9	**AFC Playoff Game** (Patriots at Jaguars)	1/3/99	CBS	18.3/38
10	**NFC Playoff Game** (49ers at Falcons)	1/9/99	FOX	18.2/42
11	**AFC Playoff Game** (Bills at Dolphins)	1/2/99	ABC	18.1/40
12	**Fiesta Bowl** (Florida St. vs Tennessee)	1/4/99	ABC	17.2/26
	NCAA Men's Basketball Championship Game (Duke vs UConn)	3/29/99	CBS	17.2/27
14	**NFL Monday Night Football** (Vikings at Packers)	10/5/98	ABC	16.8/27
15	**NFL Regular Season Late Game** (Various teams)	11/1/98	FOX	16.7/32
16	**MLB World Series - Game 4** (Yankees at Padres)	10/21/98	FOX	16.6/27
17	**NFL Thanksgiving Day Late Game** (Vikings at Cowboys)	11/26/98	FOX	16.5/43
	NFL Regular Season Late Game (Various teams)	12/6/98	CBS	16.5/33
19	**NFL Monday Night Football** (Broncos at Dolphins)	12/21/98	ABC	16.3/27
20	**NFL Regular Season Late Game** (Various teams)	11/22/98	CBS	16.2/32
21	**NFL Monday Night Football** (Packers at Steelers)	11/9/98	ABC	15.6/25
	NFL Thanksgiving Day Early Game (Steelers at Lions)	11/26/98	CBS	15.6/42
23	**MLB World Series - Game 3** (Yankees at Padres)	10/20/98	FOX	15.4/25
	NFL Monday Night Football (Packers at Buccaneers)	12/7/98	ABC	15.4/25
25	**NFL Monday Night Football** (Dolphins at Patriots)	11/23/98	ABC	15.1/24
26	**NFL Regular Season Late Game** (Various teams)	12/13/98	FOX	14.7/30
	NFC Playoff Game (Cardinals at Vikings)	1/10/99	FOX	14.7/24
28	**Monday Night Football** (Jets at Patriots)	10/19/98	ABC	14.6/23
29	**Monday Night Football** (Steelers at Chiefs)	10/26/98	ABC	14.5/23
	NFL Regular Season Early Game (Various teams)	11/8/98	FOX	14.5/34
	NFL Regular Season Late Game (Various teams)	12/20/98	FOX	14.5/30
32	**NFL Regular Season Late Game** (Various Teams)	12/27/98	CBS	14.4/30

AP/Wide World Photos

John Elway led the Denver Broncos to their second consecutive Super Bowl title on Jan. 31 in what was by far the most-watched television program of the year.

		Date	Net	Rtg/Sh
33	**Monday Night Football** (Giants at 49ers)	11/30/98	ABC	14.0/22
34	**NFL Regular Season Late Game** (Various teams)	11/15/98	FOX	13.9/28
	Monday Night Football (Broncos at Chiefs)	11/16/98	ABC	13.9/22
36	**NFL Regular Season Late Game** (Various teams)	10/19/98	FOX	13.8/29
37	**NFL Regular Season Late Game** (Various teams)	11/8/98	CBS	13.7/26
38	**NFL Regular Season Early Game** (Various teams)	12/13/98	CBS	13.4/32
39	**Rose Bowl** (UCLA vs Wisconsin)	1/1/99	ABC	13.3/25
40	**NFL Regular Season Late Game** (Various teams)	10/25/98	CBS	13.2/26
	Monday Night Football (Cowboys at Eagles)	11/2/98	ABC	13.2/20
42	**NFL Regular Season Late Game** (Various teams)	11/29/98	FOX	13.0/25
43	**MLB ALCS - Game 6** (Indians at Yankees)	10/13/98	NBC	12.9/22
44	**NFL Regular Season Early Game** (Various teams)	11/22/98	FOX	12.7/30
45	**MLB World Series - Game 2** (Padres at Yankees)	10/18/98	FOX	12.6/20

	Date	Net	Rtg/Sh
46 **MLB World Series - Game 1**			
(Padres at Yankees)......10/17/98	FOX	12.4/23
47 **NBA Finals - Game 3**			
(Spurs at Knicks) 6/21/99	NBC	12.1/21
48 **NFL Regular Season Early Post Game**			
(Various teams)...........11/8/98	FOX	12.0/27
NBA Finals - Game 4			
(Spurs at Knicks) 6/23/99	NBC	12.0/22
MLB 1999 All-Star Game			
(Boston, MA) 7/13/99	FOX	12.0/22
51 **Monday Night Football**			
(Lions at 49ers) 12/14/98	ABC	11.9/19
52 **NFL Regular Season Late Game**			
(Various teams)...........10/4/98	FOX	11.8/24
53 **Monday Night Football**			
(Dolphins at Jaguars).....10/12/98	ABC	11.7/19
54 **Monday Night Football**			
(Steelers at Jaguars) 12/28/98	ABC	11.5/19
Sugar Bowl			
(Ohio St. vs Texas A&M)....1/1/99	ABC	11.5/20
NBA Finals - Game 1			
(Knicks at Spurs) 6/16/99	NBC	11.5/21
57 **Women's World Cup Final**			
(USA vs China)..........7/10/99	ABC	11.4/31
58 **NFL Regular Season Late Post Game**			
(Various teams) 12/20/98	FOX	11.3/21
59 **NFL Regular Season Early Game**			
(Various teams)..........12/27/98	FOX	11.1/27
60 **NFL Regular Season Late Game**			
(Various teams) 10/11/98	CBS	11.0/24

	Date	Net	Rtg/Sh
NBA Finals - Game 5			
(Spurs at Knicks) 6/25/99	NBC	11.0/22
62 **NFL Regular Season Early Game**			
(Various teams)...........11/1/98	CBS	10.9/26
NFL Regular Season Early Game			
(Various teams) 11/15/98	CBS	10.9/27
NCAA Men's Basketball National Semifinal			
(Duke vs Michigan St.) 3/27/99	CBS	10.9/20
65 **NFL Regular Season Early Game**			
(Various teams)...........12/6/98	FOX	10.8/26
66 **NFL Regular Season Early Game**			
(Various teams) 10/25/98	FOX	10.5/26
NFL Regular Season Late Game			
(Various teams) 11/29/98	CBS	10.5/20
68 **NFL Regular Season Late Post Game**			
(Various teams) 12/13/98	FOX	10.4/19
NFL Regular Season Early Game			
(Various teams) 12/20/98	CBS	10.4/25
70 **NFL Regular Season Early Game**			
(Various teams) 12/26/98	FOX	10.3/29
71 **NBA Eastern Conference Finals - Game 6**			
(Pacers at Knicks).........6/11/99	NBC	10.2/21
72 **Masters Golf - Final Round**			
(Augusta, GA) 4/11/99	CBS	10.1/22
NFL Hall of Fame Game			
(Browns at Cowboys) 8/9/99	ABC	10.1/18
74 **NFL Regular Season Early Post Game**			
(Various teams) 11/2/98	FOX	10.0/22
NFL Regular Season Early Post Game			
(Various teams) 12/27/98	FOX	10.0/23

AP/Wide World Photos

These four die-hard Packers fans decided to brave the cold and watch Super Bowl XXXII in the parking lot of Green Bay's Lambeau Field. They came away cold and disappointed as the Packers lost to Denver, but they did help make the game the 28th highest-rated program of all-time.

All-Time Top-Rated TV Programs

NFL Football dominates television's All-Time Top-Rated 50 Programs with 21 Super Bowls and the 1981 NFC Championship Game making the list. Rankings based on surveys taken from January 1961 through August 22, 1999; include only sponsored programs seen on individual networks; and programs under 30 minutes scheduled duration are excluded. Programs are listed with ratings points, audience share and number of households watching, according to Nielsen Media Research.

Multiple entries: The Super Bowl (21); "Roots" (7); "The Beverly Hillbillies" and "The Thorn Birds" (3); "The Bob Hope Christmas Show," "The Ed Sullivan Show," "Gone With The Wind" and 1994 Winter Olympics (2).

	Program	Episode/Game	Net	Date	Rating	Share	Households
1	M*A*S*H (series)	Final episode	CBS	2/28/83	**60.2**	77	50,150,000
2	Dallas (series)	"Who Shot J.R.?"	CBS	11/21/80	**53.3**	76	41,470,000
3	Roots (mini-series)	Part 8	ABC	1/30/77	**51.1**	71	36,380,000
4	Super Bowl XVI	49ers 26, Bengals 21	CBS	1/24/82	**49.1**	73	40,020,000
5	Super Bowl XVII	Redskins 27, Dolphins 17	NBC	1/30/83	**48.6**	69	40,480,000
6	XVII Winter Olympics	Women's Figure Skating	CBS	2/23/94	**48.5**	64	45,690,000
7	Super Bowl XX	Bears 46, Patriots 10	NBC	1/26/86	**48.3**	70	41,490,000
8	Gone With the Wind (movie)	Part 1	NBC	11/7/76	**47.7**	65	33,960,000
9	Gone With the Wind (movie)	Part 2	NBC	11/8/76	**47.4**	64	33,750,000
10	Super Bowl XII	Cowboys 27, Broncos 10	CBS	1/15/78	**47.2**	67	34,410,000
11	Super Bowl XIII	Steelers 35, Cowboys 31	NBC	1/21/79	**47.1**	74	35,090,000
12	Bob Hope Special	Christmas Show	NBC	1/15/70	**46.6**	64	27,260,000
13	Super Bowl XVIII	Raiders 38, Redskins 9	CBS	1/22/84	**46.4**	71	38,800,000
	Super Bowl XIX	49ers 38, Dolphins 16	ABC	1/20/85	**46.4**	63	39,390,000
15	Super Bowl XIV	Steelers 31, Rams 19	CBS	1/20/80	**46.3**	67	35,330,000
16	Super Bowl XXX	Cowboys 27, Steelers 17	NBC	1/28/96	**46.0**	68	44,114,400
	ABC Theater (special)	"The Day After"	ABC	11/20/83	**46.0**	62	38,550,000
18	Roots (mini-series)	Part 6	ABC	1/28/77	**45.9**	66	32,680,000
	The Fugitive (series)	Final episode	ABC	8/29/67	**45.9**	72	25,700,000
20	Super Bowl XXI	Giants 39, Broncos 20	CBS	1/25/87	**45.8**	66	40,030,000
21	Roots (mini-series)	Part 5	ABC	1/27/77	**45.7**	71	32,540,000
22	Super Bowl XXVIII	Cowboys 30, Bills 13	NBC	1/29/94	**45.5**	66	42,860,000
	Cheers	Final episode	NBC	5/20/93	**45.5**	64	42,360,500
24	The Ed Sullivan Show	Beatles' 1st appearance	CBS	2/9/64	**45.3**	60	23,240,000
25	Super Bowl XXVII	Cowboys 52, Bills 17	NBC	1/31/93	**45.1**	66	41,988,100
26	Bob Hope Special	Christmas Show	NBC	1/14/71	**45.0**	61	27,050,000
27	Roots (mini-series)	Part 3	ABC	1/25/77	**44.8**	68	31,900,000
28	Super Bowl XXXII	Denver 31, Green Bay 24	NBC	1/25/98	**44.5**	67	43,630,000
29	Super Bowl XI	Raiders 32, Vikings 14	NBC	1/9/77	**44.4**	73	31,610,000
	Super Bowl XV	Raiders 27, Eagles 10	NBC	1/25/81	**44.4**	63	34,540,000
31	Super Bowl VI	Cowboys 24, Dolphins 3	CBS	1/16/72	**44.2**	74	27,450,000
32	XVII Winter Olympics	Women's Figure Skating	CBS	2/25/94	**44.1**	64	41,540,000
	Roots (mini-series)	Part 2	ABC	1/24/77	**44.1**	62	31,400,000
34	The Beverly Hillbillies	Regular episode	CBS	1/8/64	**44.0**	65	22,570,000
35	Roots (mini-series)	Part 4	ABC	1/26/77	**43.8**	66	31,190,000
	The Ed Sullivan Show	Beatles' 2nd appearance	CBS	2/16/64	**43.8**	60	22,445,000
37	Super Bowl XXIII	49ers 20, Bengals 16	NBC	1/22/89	**43.5**	68	39,320,000
38	The Academy Awards	John Wayne wins Oscar	ABC	4/7/70	**43.4**	78	25,390,000
39	Super Bowl XXXI	Packers 35, Patriots 21	FOX	1/26/97	**43.3**	65	42,000,000
40	The Thorn Birds (mini-series)	Part 3	ABC	3/29/83	**43.2**	62	35,990,000
41	The Thorn Birds (mini-series)	Part 4	ABC	3/30/83	**43.1**	62	35,900,000
42	NFC Championship Game	49ers 28, Cowboys 27	CBS	1/10/82	**42.9**	62	34,940,000
43	The Beverly Hillbillies	Regular episode	CBS	1/15/64	**42.8**	62	21,960,000
44	Super Bowl VII	Dolphins 14, Redskins 7	NBC	1/14/73	**42.7**	72	27,670,000
45	The Thorn Birds (mini-series)	Part 2	ABC	3/28/83	**42.5**	59	35,400,000
46	Super Bowl IX	Steelers 16, Vikings 6	NBC	1/12/75	**42.4**	72	29,040,000
	The Beverly Hillbillies	Regular episode	CBS	2/26/64	**42.4**	60	21,750,000
48	Super Bowl X	Steelers 21, Cowboys 17	CBS	1/18/76	**42.3**	78	29,440,000
	ABC Sunday Night Movie	"Airport"	ABC	11/11/73	**42.3**	63	28,000,000
	ABC Sunday Night Movie	"Love Story"	ABC	10/1/72	**42.3**	62	27,410,000
	Cinderella	Musical special	CBS	2/22/65	**42.3**	59	22,250,000
	Roots (mini-series)	Part 7	ABC	1/29/77	**42.3**	65	30,120,000

Note: Between October 1, 1998 and August 22, 1999, the highest-rated program was Super Bowl XXXIII on January 31. With a 40.2 rating, it tied 1983's "The Winds of War – Part 2" for 83rd on the all-time list.

All-Time Top-Rated Cable TV Sports Events

All-time cable television for sports events, according to ESPN, Turner Sports research and *The Sports Business Daily*. Covers period from Sept. 1, 1980 through Sept. 1, 1999.

NFL Telecasts

		Date	Net	Rtg
1	Chicago at Minnesota	12/6/87	ESPN	17.6
2	Detroit at Miami	12/25/94	ESPN	15.1
3	Chicago at Minnesota	12/3/89	ESPN	14.7
4	Cleveland at San Fran	11/29/87	ESPN	14.2
5	Pittsburgh at Houston	12/30/90	ESPN	13.8

Non-NFL Telecasts

		Date	Net	Rtg
1	MLB: Chicago (NL)-St. Louis	9/7/98	ESPN	9.5
2	NBA: Detroit-Boston	6/1/88	TBS	8.8
3	NBA: Chicago-Detroit	5/31/89	TBS	8.2
4	NBA: Detroit-Boston	5/26/88	TBS	8.1
	MLB: Giants-Chicago (NL)	9/28/98	ESPN	8.1

Teams Bought in 1999

Twelve major league clubs acquired new majority owners or significant minority owners from Nov. 1, 1998 through Sept. 23, 1999.

Major League Baseball

Cincinnati Reds: The long-standing yet controversial reign of Marge Schott as the owner of the Reds is now over. On September 15, 1999, the league approved the $67 million sale of Schott's controlling interest of the club to Great American Insurance Co. owner Carl Lindner, already one of the team's limited partners. Schott, who had owned 6 of the 15 shares in the team's partnership, agreed to sell 5½ to Lindner and limited partners George Strike and William Reik.

Major League Baseball had been taking steps to oust Schott since 1993, when she was suspended for making racially insensitive comments. In 1996 after more inflammatory remarks, the league suspended her again and took away her day-to-day control of the club.

Florida Marlins: South Florida native John Henry purchased the Marlins from H. Wayne Huizenga on January 13, 1999 for $150 million. After spending $52.5 million for players in 1997 that resulted in a World Series title, Huizenga became increasingly disappointed with the situation in Florida when the state refused to publicly finance a new ballpark. He pared the payroll down to $19.1 million to make the team more financially attractive, albeit much less successful. Henry has been a limited partner of the New York Yankees and is chairman of John W. Henry & Co., an alternative investment firm.

NFL Football

Washington Redskins: Communications mogul Daniel Snyder purchased the Redskins and Jack Kent Cooke Stadium on May 25, 1999 for $800 million, by far the highest price paid for a franchise in U.S. sports history. It beats out the $550 million paid for the Cleveland Browns just last year. At 34, Snyder becomes the youngest current NFL owner. To help finance the package, he brought in Fred Drasner and Mort Zuckerman, co-owners of New York's *Daily News*. The $800 million also included a hefty $300 million down payment.

NBA Basketball

Charlotte Hornets: Owner George Shinn came to an agreement on July 29, 1999 to sell up to 50 percent of the team to Ray Wooldridge, the president and CEO of Space Master Building Systems in Atlanta. No financial terms were disclosed, but the deal was estimated to be worth between $75 and $80 million. Shinn had previously been in discussions with Michael Jordan, but talks ultimately broke when Shinn refused Jordan's demands for more authority in business decisions.

Denver Nuggets: Colorado businessman Donald Sturm purchased the Nuggets, along with the NHL's Colorado Avalanche and the Pepsi Center Arena from Ascent Entertainment Group for $461 million on July 27, 1999. Sturm was the highest bidder for the three assets at an auction that also included a $450 million bid from Saudi princess Thara Al Saud and a $438 million bid from a group that included John Elway.

Bill Laurie and his wife Nancy, the Wal-Mart heiress, had originally purchased the assets in March for $400 million but the bidding process was re-opened when shareholders of Ascent filed two lawsuits, claiming the price should have been higher.

Sacramento Kings: On July 1, 1999 the Maloof family, led by Joe and Gavin Maloof, officially gained controlling interest of the Kings, the WNBA's Sacramento Monarchs and ARCO Arena. Terms of the deal were not disclosed. The Maloofs had previously purchased a minority interest in the Kings from owner Jim Thomas in January 1998 with an option for controlling interest in the future. The family had previously owned the NBA's Houston Rockets from 1979-82.

Vancouver Grizzlies: Wal-Mart heirs Bill and Nancy Laurie agreed to a deal on September 23, 1999 to purchase the Grizzlies from John McCaw and Orca Bay Sports and Entertainment for approximately $200 million. Official financial terms were not disclosed. Speculation was high that the team would eventually be moved to St. Louis, as the Lauries also purchased the St. Louis Blues and the Kiel Center (see below).

NHL Hockey

Colorado Avalanche: See NBA's Denver Nuggets.

Pittsburgh Penguins: On September 3, 1999, Mario Lemieux was granted final approval to take control of the financially-strapped Penguins. The Hall of Famer became the first retired player to become the owner of the major sports team on which he played. The Penguins, estimated to have a market value of approximately $85 million, had declared bankruptcy during the season and the future of the team in Pittsburgh was in serious jeopardy. Lemieux and his group of investors had raised $52 million by Sept. 3 and was hoping for more. Lemieux converted $25 million in cash and deferred salary into equity, giving him the largest stake in the ownership group. Civic Arena will be under control of its current owners, SMG, until 2004 when Lemieux will gain control.

St. Louis Blues: After unsuccessfully bidding for the package that included the Denver Nuggets and Colorado Avalanche, Wal-Mart heirs Bill and Nancy Laurie purchased the Blues and the Kiel Center for a bargain price of $100 million on Sept. 6, 1999. The Blues alone had been estimated at $100 million and the Kiel Center cost $135 million to build five years ago. The couple did agree to assume the Kiel Center's $96 million debt. Nancy Laurie is the daughter of the late Bud Walton, who co-founded the Wal-Mart chain.

Tampa Bay Lightning: Palace Sports & Entertainment, led by Detroit Pistons owner William Davidson, agreed to purchase the Lightning and the Ice Palace from Art Williams on March 3, 1999. The cost of the deal was estimated at $110 million, less than the $117 million Williams paid just 38 weeks prior. Williams had become increasingly frustrated with the team's losing ways and low attendance, which led to his quick surrender of ownership. Davidson, who had inquired about the purchase of the team twice in the past, also owns the IHL's Detroit Vipers.

Washington Capitals: On June 22, 1999 the NHL's Board of Governors approved the sale of the Capitals from original owner Abe Pollin to a group comprised of America Online executive Ted Leonsis, local businessman Jon Ledecky and team president Dick Patrick. The trio also purchased a minority stake in the NBA's Washington Wizards and the MCI Center. They are said to have invested approximately $200 million overall, about $85 million for the Capitals. The sale marks the end of Pollin's 26-year tenure as Capitals' owner.

Top 10 Salaries In Each Sport

The top 10 highest paid athletes over the 1998-99 season for the NBA, Major League Baseball and NHL and the 1998 season for the NFL. Figures are in millions of dollars.

Source: *Street & Smith's SportsBusiness Journal* and *USA Today.*

NFL

		Position	Team	Salary
1	Deion Sanders	Cornerback	Dallas	$7.579
2	Dan Marino	Quarterback	Miami	7.577
3	Drew Bledsoe	Quarterback	N. England	7.098
4	Hugh Douglas	Def. Lineman	Philadelphia	5.701
5	Brett Favre	Quarterback	Green Bay	5.624
6	Troy Aikman	Quarterback	Dallas	5.561
7	Eric Swann	Def. Lineman	Arizona	5.000
8	John Randle	Def. Lineman	Minnesota	4.540
9	Herman Moore	Wide Receiver	Detroit	4.370
10	Bobby Taylor	Cornerback	Philadelphia	4.304

MLB

		Position	Team	Salary
1	Albert Belle	Left Field	Baltimore	$11.950
2	Pedro Martinez	Pitcher	Boston	11.000
3	Kevin Brown	Pitcher	Los Angeles	10.700
4	Greg Maddux	Pitcher	Atlanta	10.600
5	Gary Sheffield	Left Field	Los Angeles	9.920
6	Bernie Williams	Center Field	NY Yankees	9.860
7	Barry Bonds	Left Field	San Francisco	9.380
8	Randy Johnson	Pitcher	Arizona	9.350
9	Sammy Sosa	Right Field	Chicago-NL	9.000
	Raul Mondesi	Right Field	Los Angeles	9.000

NBA

		Position	Team	Salary
1	Kevin Garnett	Forward	Minnesota	$21.000
2	Shaquille O'Neal	Center	Los Angeles	17.140
3	Patrick Ewing	Center	New York	17.000
4	Juwan Howard	Forward	Washington	15.070
5	Alonzo Mourning	Center	Miami	15.000
6	Shawn Kemp	Forward	Cleveland	14.210
7	Gary Payton	Guard	Seattle	12.570
8	Hakeem Olajuwon	Center	Houston	12.500
9	David Robinson	Center	San Antonio	11.000
	Jayson Williams	Center	New Jersey	11.000

NHL

		Position	Team	Salary
1	Sergei Fedorov	Center	Detroit	$14.000
2	Paul Kariya	Left Wing	Anaheim	8.500
	Eric Lindros	Center	Philadelphia	8.500
4	Dominik Hasek	Goalie	Buffalo	8.000
5	Pavel Bure	Right Wing	Florida	6.400
6	Mats Sundin	Center	Toronto	6.350
7	Peter Forsberg	Center	Colorado	6.000
	Doug Gilmour	Center	Chicago	6.000
	Wayne Gretzky	Center	NY Rangers	6.000
	Mark Messier	Center	Vancouver	6.000

Highest and Lowest Ticket Prices

The most expensive and least expensive average ticket prices for NFL, NBA, Major League Baseball and NHL franchises over the 1998-99 season.

Source: Team Marketing Report

NFL

Highest		Venue	Avg. Price
1	Washington	Jack Kent Cooke	$74.28
2	Tampa Bay	Raymond James Stad.	64.65
3	Jacksonville	ALLTEL Stadium	57.79
4	Tennessee	Vanderbilt Stadium	55.63
5	Carolina	Ericsson Stadium	55.45

Lowest		Venue	Avg. Price
1	St. Louis	Trans World Dome	$33.99
2	Detroit	Pontiac Silverdome	35.65
3	Seattle	Kingdome	35.68
4	Philadelphia	Veterans Stadium	37.59
5	Cincinnati	Cinergy Field	37.77

MLB

Highest		Venue	Avg. Price
1	Boston	Fenway Park	$24.05
2	NY Yankees	Yankee Stadium	23.33
3	Texas	Ballpark in Arlington	19.93
4	NY Mets	Shea Stadium	19.89
5	Baltimore	Camden Yards	19.82

Lowest		Venue	Avg. Price
1	Minnesota	HHH Metrodome	$8.46
2	Montreal	Olympic Stadium	9.38
3	Cincinnati	Cinergy Field	9.71
4	Oakland	Network Assoc. Col.	10.10
5	Pittsburgh	Three Rivers Stadium	10.71

NBA

Highest		Venue	Avg. Price
1	NY Knicks	Madison Sq. Garden	$79.34
2	Seattle	KeyArena	63.47
3	Washington	MCI Center	61.40
4	Philadelphia	First Union Center	60.23
5	Houston	Compaq Center	58.18

Lowest		Venue	Avg. Price
1	Toronto	SkyDome	$26.17
2	Charlotte	Charlotte Coliseum	28.12
3	Milwaukee	Bradley Center	29.06
4	Denver	McNichols Arena	30.53
5	LA Clippers	LA Sports Arena	31.75
		& Arrowhead Pond	

NHL

Highest		Venue	Avg. Price
1	NY Rangers	Madison Sq. Garden	$58.83
2	Philadelphia	First Union Center	53.25
3	Washington	MCI Center	52.71
4	Colorado	McNichols Arena	49.28
5	Detroit	Joe Louis Arena	48.36

Lowest		Venue	Avg. Price
1	Calgary	Canadian Airlines Saddledome	$26.04
2	Edmonton	Edmonton Coliseum	29.82
3	Ottawa	Corel Centre	32.60
4	Vancouver	General Motors Place	36.09
5	Tampa Bay	Ice Palace	36.80

The 1998 *Forbes* Top 40

The 40 highest-paid athletes of 1998 (including salary, winnings, endorsements, etc.), according to *Forbes* magazine. The list below is in conjunction with the "*Forbes* Power 100", which is a ranking of the 100 most powerful celebrities for 1998. Nationality, birth date, and each athlete's rank on the 1997 list are also given. Age refers to athlete's age as of Dec. 31, 1998.

Dollar amounts given are in millions.

		Sport	Salary/ Winnings	Other Income	Total	Nat	Birthdate	Age	1997 Rank
1	Michael Jordan	Basketball	$29.0	$40.0	**$69.0**	USA	Feb. 17, 1963	35	1
2	Michael Schumacher	Auto Racing	25.0	13.0	**38.0**	GBR	Jan. 3, 1969	29	4
3	Sergei Fedorov	Hockey	29.0	0.8	**29.8**	RUS	Dec. 13, 1969	29	NR
4	Tiger Woods	Golf	1.8	25.0	**26.8**	USA	Dec. 30, 1975	23	6
5	Dale Earnhardt	Auto Racing	4.6	19.5	**24.1**	USA	Apr. 29, 1952	46	8
6	Grant Hill	Basketball	4.6	17.0	**21.6**	USA	Oct. 5, 1972	26	10
7	Oscar De La Hoya	Boxing	17.0	1.5	**18.5**	USA	Feb. 4, 1973	25	3
8	Patrick Ewing	Basketball	17.5	0.8	**18.3**	USA	Aug. 5, 1962	36	NR
9	Arnold Palmer	Golf	0.1	18.0	**18.1**	USA	Sept. 10, 1929	69	12
10	Gary Sheffield	Baseball	17.0	0.2	**17.2**	USA	Nov. 18, 1968	30	NR
11	Andre Agassi	Tennis	1.8	14.0	**15.8**	USA	Apr. 29, 1970	28	16
12	Dennis Rodman	Basketball	9.0	6.3	**15.3**	USA	May 13, 1961	37	27
13	Wayne Gretzky	Hockey	6.6	8.0	**14.6**	CAN	Jan. 26, 1961	37	28
14	Jeff Gordon	Auto Racing	6.2	8.3	**14.5**	USA	Aug. 4, 1971	27	32
15	Cal Ripken Jr.	Baseball	6.4	7.7	**14.1**	USA	Aug. 24, 1960	38	17
16	Greg Norman	Golf	0.3	13.3	**13.6**	AUS	Feb. 10, 1955	43	11
17	Brett Favre	Football	7.3	5.8	**13.1**	USA	Oct. 10, 1969	29	40
18	David Robinson	Basketball	10.9	2.0	**12.9**	USA	Aug. 6, 1965	33	18
19	Gary Payton	Basketball	9.0	3.7	**12.7**	USA	July 23, 1968	30	24
20	Ken Griffey Jr.	Baseball	7.8	4.9	**12.7**	USA	Nov. 21, 1969	29	19
21	Alonzo Mourning	Basketball	10.4	1.7	**12.1**	USA	Feb. 8, 1970	28	20
22	Shawn Kemp	Basketball	8.6	3.5	**12.1**	USA	Nov. 26, 1969	29	NR
23	Mike Piazza	Baseball	8.0	4.0	**12.0**	USA	Sept. 4, 1968	30	29
24	Roy Jones Jr.	Boxing	12.0	0.0	**12.0**	USA	Jan. 16, 1969	29	NR
25	Mo Vaughn	Baseball	11.7	0.2	**11.9**	USA	Dec. 15, 1967	31	NR
26	Pete Sampras	Tennis	3.9	7.8	**11.7**	USA	Aug. 12, 1971	27	15
27	Peyton Manning	Football	10.1	1.5	**11.6**	USA	Mar. 24, 1976	22	NR
28	Deion Sanders	Football	5.3	6.2	**11.5**	USA	Aug. 9, 1967	31	NR
29	Lennox Lewis	Boxing	11.0	0.4	**11.4**	GBR	Sept. 2, 1965	33	35
30	Hakeem Olajuwon	Basketball	9.8	1.2	**11.0**	NGR	Jan. 21, 1963	35	26
31	Jack Nicklaus	Golf	0.3	10.5	**10.8**	USA	Jan. 20, 1940	58	38
32	Pedro Martinez	Baseball	10.0	0.7	**10.7**	DOM	Oct. 25, 1971	27	NR
33	Horace Grant	Basketball	10.3	0.3	**10.6**	USA	July 4, 1965	33	13
34	Albert Belle	Baseball	10.0	0.3	**10.3**	USA	Aug. 25, 1966	32	31
35	Michael Chang	Tennis	1.2	9.0	**10.2**	USA	Feb. 22, 1972	26	21
36	Martina Hingis	Tennis	3.4	6.7	**10.1**	SWI	Sept. 30, 1980	18	NR
37	Sammy Sosa	Baseball	9.0	1.0	**10.0**	DOM	Nov. 12, 1968	30	37
38	Ronaldo	Soccer	5.0	5.0	**10.0**	BRA	Sept. 22, 1976	22	NR
39	Mark McGwire	Baseball	8.6	1.4	**10.0**	USA	Oct. 1, 1963	35	NR
40	Shaquille O'Neal	Basketball	0.0*	9.8	**9.8**	USA	Mar. 6, 1972	26	7

*O'Neal's contract called for a lump payment at the beginning of the season, which was in Oct. 1997.

Most Valuable Teams

The top 25 most valuable franchises in North American sports according to *Forbes* magazine. Estimates are based on 1997 revenues and expenses for MLB and NFL teams and 1998 figures for NBA and NHL teams.

Dollar amounts given are in millions.

		League	Profit	Current Value			League	Profit	Current Value
1	Dallas Cowboys	NFL	$41.3	**$413**	15	Cincinnati Bengals	NFL	1.7	**311**
2	Washington Redskins	NFL	31.7	**403**	16	Colorado Rockies	MLB	38.3	**303**
3	Carolina Panthers	NFL	0.7	**365**	17	Chicago Bulls	NBA	8.6	**303**
4	New York Yankees	MLB	21.4	**362**	18	Pittsburgh Steelers	NFL	-1.6	**300**
5	Tampa Bay Buccaneers	NFL	2.6	**346**	19	Atlanta Braves	MLB	18.2	**299**
6	Miami Dolphins	NFL	31.6	**304**	20	New York Knicks	NBA	18.3	**296**
7	Baltimore Ravens	NFL	-1.0	**329**	21	Jacksonville Jaguars	NFL	-14.1	**294**
8	Seattle Seahawks	NFL	-10.9	**324**	22	New York Giants	NFL	0.4	**288**
9	Baltimore Orioles	MLB	18.7	**323**	23	Los Angeles Lakers	NBA	24.8	**268**
10	Cleveland Indians	MLB	15.4	**322**	24	New York Jets	NFL	2.1	**259**
11	Tennessee Oilers	NFL	-0.4	**322**	25	Kansas City Chiefs	NFL	3.7	**257**
12	St. Louis Rams	NFL	17.1	**322**					
13	Denver Broncos	NFL	2.5	**320**					
14	Detroit Lions	NFL	-20.9	**312**					

Note: There are no NHL teams in the the top 25. The most valuable NHL franchise is the NY Rangers in 51st with a value of $195 million.

The Peabody Award

Presented annually since 1940 for outstanding achievement in radio and television broadcasting. Named after Georgia banker and philanthropist George Foster Peabody, the awards are administered by the Henry W. Grady College of Journalism and Mass Communication at the University of Georgia.

Television

Year

1960 **CBS** for coverage of 1960 Winter and Summer Olympic Games
1966 ABC's **"Wide World of Sports"** (for Outstanding Achievement in Promotion of International Understanding).
1968 **ABC Sports** coverage of both the 1968 Winter and Summer Olympic Games.
1972 **ABC Sports** coverage of the 1972 Summer Olympics in Munich.
1973 **Joe Garagiola** of NBC Sports (for "The Baseball World of Joe Garagiola").
1976 **ABC Sports** coverage of both the 1976 Winter and Summer Olympic Games.
1984 **Roone Arledge**, president of ABC News & Sports (for significant contributions to news and sports programming).
1986 **WFAA-TV**, Dallas for its investigation of the Southern Methodist University football program.
1988 **Jim McKay** of ABC Sports (for pioneering efforts and career accomplishments in the world of TV sports).
1991 **CBS Sports** coverage of the 1991 Masters golf tournament
   & **HBO Sports** and Black Canyon Productions for the baseball special "When It Was A Game."
1995 **Kartemquin Educational Films** and **KTCA-TV** in St. Paul, MN, presented on PBS for "Hoop Dreams"
   & **Turner Original Productions** for the baseball special "Hank Aaron: Chasing the Dream."
1996 **HBO Sports** for its documentary "The Journey of the African-American Athlete
   & **Bud Greenspan**, a personal award for excellence in chronicling the Olympic Games.
1997 **HBO Pictures** and **The Thomas Carter Company** for the original movie "Don King: Only in America."
1998 **KTVX-TV**, Salt Lake City for its investigation into the policies and practices of the IOC during the Olympic bribery
   scandal & **HBO Sports** for its ongoing series of sports documentaries.

Radio

Year

1974 **WSB** radio in Atlanta for "Henry Aaron: A Man with a Mission."
1991 **Red Barber** of National Public Radio (for his six decades as a broadcaster and his 10 years as a commentator on
   NPR's "Morning Edition").

National Emmy Awards
Sports Programming

Presented by the Academy of Television Arts and Sciences since 1948. Eligibility period covered the calendar year from 1948-57 and since 1988.

   Multiple major award winners: ABC "Wide World of Sports" (19), NFL Films Football coverage (10); ABC Olympics coverage (9); ABC "Monday Night Football" (8); CBS NFL Football coverage, ESPN "Outside the Lines" series (6); CBS NCAA Basketball coverage and CBS "NFL Today" (5); ESPN "SportsCenter" and NBC Olympics coverage (4); ABC "The American Sportsman," ABC Indianapolis 500 coverage, ESPN "GameDay" and HBO "Real Sports with Bryant Gumbel" (3); ABC Kentucky Derby coverage, ABC "Sportsbeat," Bud Greenspan Olympic specials, CBS Olympics coverage, CBS Golf coverage, ESPN "Speedworld," Fox "NFL Sunday", MTV Sports series and NBC World Series coverage (2).

1949

Coverage—"Wrestling" (KTLA, Los Angeles)

1950

Program—"Rams Football" (KNBH-TV, Los Angeles)

1954

Program—"Gillette Cavalcade of Sports" (NBC)

1965-66

Programs—"Wide World of Sports" (ABC), "Shell's Wonderful World of Golf" (NBC) and "CBS Golf Classic" (CBS)

1966-67

Program—"Wide World of Sports" (ABC)

1967-68

Program—"Wide World of Sports" (ABC)

1968-69

Program—"1968 Summer Olympics" (ABC)

1969-70

Programs—"NFL Football" (CBS) and "Wide World of Sports" (ABC)

1970-71

Program—"Wide World of Sports" (ABC)

1971-72

Program—"Wide World of Sports" (ABC)

1972-73

News Special—"Coverage of Munich Olympic Tragedy" (ABC)
Sports Programs—"1972 Summer Olympics" (ABC) and "Wide World of Sports" (ABC)

1973-74

Program—"Wide World of Sports" (ABC)

1974-75

Non-Edited Program—"Jimmy Connors vs. Rod Laver Tennis Challenge" (CBS)
Edited Program—"Wide World of Sports" (ABC)

1975-76

Live Special—"1975 World Series: Cincinnati vs. Boston" (NBC)
Live Series—"NFL Monday Night Football" (ABC)
Edited Specials—"1976 Winter Olympics" (ABC) and "Triumph and Tragedy: The Olympic Experience" (ABC)
Edited Series—"Wide World of Sports" (ABC)

1976-77

Live Special—"1976 Summer Olympics" (ABC)
Live Series—"The NFL Today/NFL Football" (CBS)
Edited Special—"1976 Summer Olympics Preview" (ABC)
Edited Series—"The Olympiad" (PBS)

National Emmy Awards (Cont.)

1977-78
Live Special—"Muhammad Ali vs. Leon Spinks Heavyweight Championship Fight" (CBS)
Live Series—"The NFL Today/NFL Football" (CBS)
Edited Special—"The Impossible Dream: Ballooning Across the Atlantic" (CBS)
Edited Series—"The Way It Was" (PBS)

1978-79
Live Special—"Super Bowl XIII: Pittsburgh vs Dallas" (NBC)
Live Series—"NFL Monday Night Football" (ABC)
Edited Special—"Spirit of '78: The Flight of Double Eagle II" (ABC)
Edited Series—"The American Sportsman" (ABC)

1979-80
Live Special—"1980 Winter Olympics" (ABC)
Live Series—"NCAA College Football" (ABC)
Edited Special—"Gossamer Albatross: Flight of Imagination" (CBS)
Edited Series—"NFL Game of the Week" (NFL Films)

1980-81
Live Special—"1981 Kentucky Derby" (ABC)
Live Series—"PGA Golf Tour" (CBS)
Edited Special—"Wide World of Sports 20th Anniversary Show" (ABC)
Edited Series—"The American Sportsman" (ABC)

1981-82
Live Special—"1982 NCAA Basketball Final: North Carolina vs Georgetown" (CBS)
Live Series—"NFL Football" (CBS)
Edited Special—"1982 Indianapolis 500" (ABC)
Edited Seris—"Wide World of Sports" (ABC)

1982-83
Live Special—"1982 World Series: St. Louis vs Milwaukee" (NBC)
Live Series—"NFL Football" (CBS)
Edited Special—"Wimbledon '83" (NBC)
Edited Series—"Wide World of Sports" (ABC)
Journalism—"ABC Sportsbeat" (ABC)

1983-84
No awards given—

1984-85
Live Special—"1984 Summer Olympics" (ABC)
Live Series—No award given
Edited Special—"Road to the Super Bowl '85" (NFL Films)
Edited Series—"The American Sportsman" (ABC)
Journalism—"ABC Sportsbeat" (ABC), "CBS Sports Sunday" (CBS), Dick Schaap features (ABC) and 1984 Summer Olympic features (ABC)

1985-86
No awards given—

1986-87
Live Special—"1987 Daytona 500" (CBS)
Live Series—"NFL Football" (CBS)
Edited Special—"Wide World of Sports 25th Anniversary Special" (ABC)
Edited Series—"Wide World of Sports" (ABC)

1987-88
Live Special—"1987 Kentucky Derby" (ABC)
Live Series—"NFL Monday Night Football" (ABC)
Edited Special—"Paris-Roubaix Bike Race" (CBS)
Edited Series—"Wide World of Sports" (ABC)

1988
Live Special—"1988 Summer Olympics" (NBC)
Live Series—"1988 NCAA Basketball" (CBS)
Edited Special—"Road to the Super Bowl '88" (NFL Films)
Edited Series—"Wide World of Sports" (ABC)
Studio Show—"NFL GameDay" (ESPN)
Journalism—1988 Summer Olympic reporting (NBC)

1989
Live Special—"1989 Indianapolis 500" (ABC)
Live Series—"NFL Monday Night Football" (ABC)
Edited Special—"Trans-Antarctica! The International Expedition" (ABC)
Edited Series—"This is the NFL" (NFL Films)
Studio Show—"NFL Today" (CBS)
Journalism—1989 World Series Game 3 earthquake coverage (ABC)

1990
Live Special—"1990 Indianapolis 500" (ABC)
Live Series—"1990 NCAA Basketball Tournament" (CBS)
Edited Special—"Road to Super Bowl XXIV" (NFL Films)
Edited Series—"Wide World of Sports" (ABC)
Studio Show—"SportsCenter" (ESPN)
Journalism—"Outside the Lines: The Autograph Game" (ESPN)

1991
Live Special—"1991 NBA Finals: Chicago vs LA Lakers" (NBC)
Live Series—"1991 NCAA Basketball Tournament" (CBS)
Edited Special—"Wide World of Sports 30th Anniversary Special" (ABC)
Edited Series—"This is the NFL" (NFL Films)
Studio Show—"NFL GameDay" (ESPN) and "NFL Live" (NBC)
Journalism—"Outside the Lines: Steroids–Whatever It Takes" (ESPN)

1992
Live Special—"1992 Breeders' Cup" (NBC)
Live Series—"1992 NCAA Basketball Tournament" (CBS)
Edited Special—"1992 Summer Olympics" (NBC)
Edited Series—"MTV Sports" (MTV)
Studio Show—"The NFL Today" (CBS)
Journalism—"Outside the Lines: Portraits in Black and White" (ESPN)

1993
Live Special—"1993 World Series" (CBS)
Live Series—"Monday Night Football" (ABC)
Edited Special—"Road to the Super Bowl" (NFL Films)
Edited Series—"This is the NFL" (NFL Films)
Studio Show—"The NFL Today" (CBS)
Journalism (TIE)—"Outside the Lines: Mitch Ivey Feature" (ESPN) and "SportsCenter: University of Houston Football" (ESPN).
Feature—"Arthur Ashe: His Life, His Legacy" (NBC).

1994
Live Special —"NHL Stanley Cup Finals" (ESPN)
Live Series —"Monday Night Football" (ABC)
Edited Special —"Lillehammer '94: 16 Days of Glory" (Disney/Cappy Productions)
Edited Series —"MTV Sports" (MTV)
Studio Show —"NFL GameDay" (ESPN)
Journalism —"1994 Winter Olympic Games: Mossad feature" (CBS)
Feature (TIE) —"Heroes of Telemark" on Winter Olympic Games (CBS); and "SportsCenter: Vanderbilt running back Brad Gaines" (ESPN).

"Baseball" Wins Prime Time Emmy

Ken Burns's miniseries "Baseball" won the 1994 Emmy Award for Outstanding Informational Series. The nine-part documentary aired from Sept. 18-28, 1994 and ran more than 18 hours, drawing the largest audience in PBS history.

1995

Live Special —"Cal Ripken 2131" (ESPN)
Live Series —"ESPN Speedworld" (ESPN)
Edited Special (quick turn-around) —"Outside the Lines: Playball– Opening Day in America" (ESPN)
Edited Special (long turn-around) —"Lillehammer, an Olympic Diary" (CBS)
Edited Series —"NFL Films Presents" (NFL Films)
Studio Show (TIE) —"NFL GameDay" (ESPN) and "Fox NFL Sunday"(Fox)
Journalism —"Real Sports with Bryant Gumbel: Broken Promises" (HBO)
Feature (TIE) —"SportsCenter: Jerry Quarry" (ESPN) and "Real Sports with Bryant Gumbel: Coach" (HBO).

1996

Live Special —"1996 World Series" (Fox)
Live Series —"ESPN Speedworld" (ESPN)
Edited Special —"Football America" (TNT/NFL Films)
Edited Series —"NFL Films Presents" (NFL Films)
Live Event Turnaround —"The Centennial Olympic Games" (NBC)
Studio Show —"SportsCenter" (ESPN)
Journalism —"Outside the Lines: AIDS in Sports" (ESPN)
Feature —"Real Sports with Bryant Gumbel: 1966 Texas Western NCAA Champs" (HBO).

1997

Live Special —"The NBA Finals" (NBC)
Live Series —"NFL Monday Night Football" (ABC)
Edited Special —"Ironman Triathlon World Championship" (NBC/World Triathlon Corporation)
Edited Series —"NFL Films Presents" (NFL Films)
Live Event Turnaround —"Outside The Lines: Inside The Kentucky Derby" (ESPN)
Studio Show —"Fox NFL Sunday" (FOX)
Journalism —"Real Sports With Bryant Gumbel: Pros and Cons" (HBO)
Feature —"NFL Films Presents: Eddie George" (NFL Films).

1998

Live Special —"McGwire's 62nd Home Run Game" (FOX)
Live Series —"NBC Golf Tour" (NBC)
Edited Special —"A Cinderella Season: The Lady Vols Fight Back" (HBO)
Edited Series —"Real Sports With Bryant Gumbel" (HBO)
Live Event Turnaround —"Wimbledon '98" (NBC)
Studio Show —"Fox NFL Sunday" (FOX)
Journalism (TIE)—"Real Sports With Bryant Gumbel: Winning At All Costs" (HBO) and "Real Sports With Bryant Gumbel: Diamond Bucks" (HBO)
Feature —"NFL Films Presents: Steve Mariucci" (ESPN2 and NFL Films).

Sportscasters of the Year
National Emmy Awards

An Emmy Award for Sportscasters was first introduced in 1968 and given for Outstanding Host/Commentator for the 1967-68 TV season. Two awards, one for Outstanding Host or Play-by-Play and the other for Outstanding Analyst, were first presented in 1981 for the 1980-81 season. Three awards, for Outstanding Studio Host, Play-by-Play and Analyst, have been given since the 1993 season

Multiple winners: John Madden (11); Bob Costas and Jim McKay (9); Dick Enberg (4); Keith Jackson and Al Michaels (3); Cris Collinsworth (2). Note that Jim McKay has won a total of 12 Emmy awards: eight for Host/Commentator, one for Host/Play-by-Play, two for Sports Writing, and one for News Commentary.

Season	Host/Commentator	Season	Host/Play-by-Play	Season	Analyst
1967-68	Jim McKay, ABC	1980-81	Dick Enberg, NBC	1980-81	Dick Button, ABC
1968-69	No award	1981-82	Jim McKay, ABC	1981-82	John Madden, CBS
1969-70	No award	1982-83	Dick Enberg, NBC	1982-83	John Madden, CBS
1970-71	Jim McKay, ABC	1983-84	No award	1983-84	No award
	& Don Meredith, ABC	1984-85	George Michael, NBC	1984-85	No award
1971-72	No award	1985-86	No award	1985-86	No award
1972-73	Jim McKay, ABC	1986-87	Al Michaels, ABC	1986-87	John Madden, CBS
1973-74	Jim McKay, ABC	1987-88	Bob Costas, NBC	1987-88	John Madden, CBS
1974-75	Jim McKay, ABC	1988	Bob Costas, NBC	1988	John Madden, CBS
1975-76	Jim McKay, ABC	1989	Al Michaels, ABC	1989	John Madden, CBS
1976-77	Frank Gifford, ABC	1990	Dick Enberg, NBC	1990	John Madden, CBS
1977-78	Jack Whitaker, CBS	1991	Bob Costas, NBC	1991	John Madden, CBS
1978-79	Jim McKay, ABC	1992	Bob Costas, NBC	1992	John Madden, CBS
1979-80	Jim McKay, ABC				

Year	Studio Host	Year	Play-by-Play	Year	Analyst
1993	Bob Costas, NBC	1993	Dick Enberg, NBC	1993	Billy Packer, CBS
1994	Bob Costas, NBC	1994	Keith Jackson, ABC	1994	John Madden, Fox
1995	Bob Costas, NBC	1995	Al Michaels, ABC	1995	John Madden, Fox
1996	Bob Costas, NBC	1996	Keith Jackson, ABC	1996	Howie Long, Fox
1997	Dan Patrick, ESPN	1997	Bob Costas, NBC	1997	Cris Collinsworth, HBO/NBC
1998	James Brown, FOX	1998	Keith Jackson, ABC	1998	Cris Collinsworth, HBO/FOX

Life Achievement Emmy Award

For outstanding work as an exemplary television sportscaster over many years.

Year		Year		Year		Year	
1989	Jim McKay	1992	Chris Schenkel	1995	Vin Scully	1998	Keith Jackson
1990	Lindsey Nelson	1993	Pat Summerall	1996	Frank Gifford		
1991	Curt Gowdy	1994	Howard Cosell	1997	Jim Simpson		

National Sportscasters and Sportswriters Assn. Award

Sportscaster of the Year presented annually since 1959 by the National Sportscasters and Sportswriters Association, based in Salisbury, N.C. Voting is done by NSSA members and selected national media.

Multiple winners: Bob Costas (7); Chris Berman and Keith Jackson (5); Lindsey Nelson and Chris Schenkel (4); Dick Enberg, Al Michaels and Vin Scully (3); Curt Gowdy and Ray Scott (2).

Year		Year		Year		Year	
1959	Lindsey Nelson	1970	Chris Schenkel	1980	Dick Enberg	1990	Chris Berman
1960	Lindsey Nelson	1971	Ray Scott		& Al Michaels	1991	Bob Costas
1961	Lindsey Nelson	1972	Keith Jackson	1981	Dick Enberg	1992	Bob Costas
1962	Lindsey Nelson	1973	Keith Jackson	1982	Vin Scully	1993	Chris Berman
1963	Chris Schenkel	1974	Keith Jackson	1983	Al Michaels	1994	Chris Berman
1964	Chris Schenkel	1975	Keith Jackson	1984	John Madden	1995	Bob Costas
1965	Vin Scully	1976	Keith Jackson	1985	Bob Costas	1996	Chris Berman
1966	Curt Gowdy	1977	Pat Summerall	1986	Al Michaels	1997	Bob Costas
1967	Chris Schenkel	1978	Vin Scully	1987	Bob Costas	1998	Jim Nance
1968	Ray Scott	1979	Dick Enberg	1988	Bob Costas		
1969	Curt Gowdy			1989	Chris Berman		

American Sportscasters Association Award

Sportscaster of the Year presented annually from 1984-94, with the exception of 1988, by the New York-based American Sportscasters Association. Two awards were presented beginning in 1995 to honor top play-by-play personality and studio host. Two more were added in 1998 to honor the top color analyst and sideline reporter. Voting is done by ASA members and officials.

Multiple winners: Dick Enberg (5); Bob Costas (4); Chris Berman (3).

Sportscaster of the Year

Year		Year		Year		Year	
1984	Dick Enberg	1987	Dick Enberg	1990	Dick Enberg	1993	Bob Costas
1985	Vin Scully	1988	No award	1991	Bob Costas	1994	Pat Summerall
1986	Dick Enberg	1989	Bob Costas	1992	Bob Costas		

Play-by-Play		**Studio Host**		**Color Analyst**		**Sideline Reporter**	
Year		Year		Year		Year	
1995	Al Michaels	1995	Chris Berman	1998	Joe Morgan	1998	Jim Gray
1996	Marv Albert	1996	Chris Berman		& John Madden (tie)		
1997	Dick Enberg	1997	Chris Berman				
1998	Jon Miller	1998	Jim Nance				

The Pulitzer Prize

The Pulitzer Prizes for journalism, letters and music have been presented annually since 1917 in the name of Joseph Pulitzer (1847-1911), the publisher of the *New York World*. Prizes are awarded by the president of Columbia University on the recommendation of a board of review. Fifteen Pulitzers have been awarded for newspaper sports reporting, sports commentary and sports photography.

News Coverage

1935 **Bill Taylor,** *NY Herald Tribune,* for his reporting on the 1934 America's Cup yacht races.

Special Citation

1952 **Max Kase,** *NY Journal-American,* for his reporting on the 1951 college basketball point-shaving scandal.

Meritorious Public Service

1954 **Newsday** (Garden City, N.Y.) for its expose of New York State's race track scandals and labor racketeering.

General Reporting

1956 **Arthur Daley,** *NY Times,* for his 1955 columns.

Investigative Reporting

1981 **Clark Hallas** & **Robert Lowe,** *(Tucson) Arizona Daily Star,* for their 1980 investigation of the University of Arizona athletic department.

1986 **Jeffrey Marx** & **Michael York,** Lexington (Ky.) *Herald-Leader,* for their 1985 investigation of the basketball program at the University of Kentucky and other major colleges.

Specialized Reporting

1985 **Randall Savage** & **Jackie Crosby,** Macon (Ga.) *Telegraph and News,* for their 1984 investigation of athletics and academics at the University of Georgia and Georgia Tech.

Feature Writing

1996 **Lisa Pollak**, *Baltimore Sun,* for her story about baseball umpire John Hirschbeck dealing with the death of one son and the illness of another from the same disease.

Commentary

1976 **Red Smith**, *NY Times,* for his 1975 columns.
1981 **Dave Anderson,** *NY Times,* for his 1980 columns.
1990 **Jim Murray**, *LA Times,* for his 1989 columns.

Photography

1949 **Nat Fein**, *NY Herald Tribune,* for his photo, "Babe Ruth Bows Out."

1952 **John Robinson** & **Don Ultang,** *Des Moines* (Iowa) *Register and Tribune,* for their sequence of six pictures of the 1951 Drake-Oklahoma A&M football game, in which Drake's Johnny Bright had his jaw broken.

1985 **The Photography Staff** of the *Orange County* (Calif.) *Register,* for their coverage of the 1984 Summer Olympics in Los Angeles.

1993 **William Snyder** & **Ken Geiger,** *The Dallas Morning News,* for their coverage of the 1992 Summer Olympics in Barcelona, Spain.

Sportswriter of the Year
NSSA Award

Presented annually since 1959 by the National Sportscasters and Sportswriters Association, based in Salisbury, N.C. Voting is done by NSSA members and selected national media.

Multiple winners: Jim Murray (14); Frank Deford (6); Rick Reilly and Red Smith (5); Will Grimsley (4); Peter Gammons (3).

Year	Year	Year
1959 Red Smith, *NY Herald-Tribune*	1973 Jim Murray, *LA Times*	1987 Frank Deford, *Sports Ill.*
1960 Red Smith, *NY Herald-Tribune*	1974 Jim Murray, *LA Times*	1988 Frank Deford, *Sports Ill.*
1961 Red Smith, *NY Herald-Tribune*	1975 Jim Murray, *LA Times*	1989 Peter Gammons, *Sports Ill.*
1962 Red Smith, *NY Herald-Tribune*	1976 Jim Murray, *LA Times*	1990 Peter Gammons, *Boston Globe*
1963 Arthur Daley, *NY Times*	1977 Jim Murray, *LA Times*	1991 Rick Reilly, *Sports Ill.*
1964 Jim Murray, *LA Times*	1978 Will Grimsley, *AP*	1992 Rick Reilly, *Sports Ill.*
1965 Red Smith, *NY Herald-Tribune*	1979 Jim Murray, *LA Times*	1993 Peter Gammons, *Boston Globe*
1966 Jim Murray, *LA Times*	1980 Will Grimsley, *AP*	1994 Rick Reilly, *Sports Ill.*
1967 Jim Murray, *LA Times*	1981 Will Grimsley, *AP*	1995 Rick Reilly, *Sports Ill.*
1968 Jim Murray, *LA Times*	1982 Frank Deford, *Sports Ill.*	1996 Rick Reilly, *Sports Ill.*
1969 Jim Murray, *LA Times*	1983 Will Grimsley, *AP*	1997 Dave Kindred, *The Sporting News*
1970 Jim Murray, *LA Times*	1984 Frank Deford, *Sports Ill.*	1998 Mitch Albom, *Detroit Free Press*
1971 Jim Murray, *LA Times*	1985 Frank Deford, *Sports Ill.*	
1972 Jim Murray, *LA Times*	1986 Frank Deford, *Sports Ill.*	

Best Newspaper Sports Sections of 1998

Winners of the Annual Associated Press Sports Editors contest for best daily and Sunday sports sections. Awards are divided into different categories, based on circulation figures. Selections are made by a committee of APSE members.

Circulation Over 175,000

Top 10 Daily		Top 10 Sunday	
Atlanta Journal and Constitution	Los Angeles Times	Atlanta Journal and Constitution	Los Angeles Times
Boston Globe	New York Daily News	Chicago Sun Times	New York Daily News
Chicago Tribune	New York Times	Chicago Tribune	New York Times
Dallas Morning News	San Diego Union-Tribune	Dallas Morning News	Rocky Mountain News
Detroit Free Press	Washington Post	Fort Worth Star-Telegram	St. Petersburg Times

Circulation 50,000-175,000

Top 10 Daily		Top 10 Sunday	
Akron Beacon Journal	Raleigh News and Observer	Akron Beacon Journal	Quad-City Times
Ann Arbor News	The Hackensack Record	Arkansas Democrat-Gazette	(Davenport, Iowa)
Deseret News	San Francisco Examiner	Columbia (S.C.) State	Raleigh News and Observer
(Salt Lake City)	Spokesman-Review	Connecticut Post	The Record (Hackensack, N.J.)
Lexington (Ky.) Herald-	(Spokane, Wash.)	(Bridgeport)	The News Tribune
Leader	The News Tribune	Lexington (Ky.) Herald-	(Tacoma, Wash.)
Newport News (Va.) Daily Press	(Tacoma, Wash.)	Leader	Vancouver (B.C.) Province

Best Sportswriting of 1998

Winners of the Annual Associated Press Sports Editors Contest for best sportswriting in 1998. Eventual winners were chosen from five finalists in each writing division. Selections are made by a committee of APSE members. Note the investigative writing division included all circulation categories.

Circulation over 175,000

Column:	Mitch Albom, *Detroit Free Press*	**Game Story:**	Rick Bozich, *Louisville Courier-Journal*
Enterprise:	Scott Fowler, *Charlotte Observer*	**News story:**	Steve Fainaru, *Boston Globe*
Feature:	Michael McLeod, *Orlando Sentinel*		

Circulation 50,000-175,000

Column:	Gwen Knapp, *San Francisco Examiner*	**Game Story:**	Beth Bragg, *Anchorage Daily News*
Enterprise:	Dave Fairbank and David Teel, *Newport-News (Va.) Daily Press*	**News story:**	Cedric Harmon, *Spartanburg (S.C.) Herald-Journal*
Feature:	Chuck Culpepper, *Lexington (Ky.) Herald-Leader*		

All Categories

Investigative:	Mike Fish, David Milliron and Mike Tierney, *Atlanta Journal and Constitution*

Directory of Organizations

Listing of the major sports organizations, teams and media addresses and officials as Sept. 23, 1999.

AUTO RACING

CART
(Championship Auto Racing Teams, Inc.)
755 W. Big Beaver Rd., Suite 800, Troy, MI 48084
(248) 362-8800
President-CEO ....Andrew Craig
Director of Publicity ....Mike Zizzo

IRL
(Indy Racing League)
4565 West 16th St., Indianapolis, IN 46222
(317) 484-6526
Founder ....Tony George
Dir. of Racing Ops. ....Brian Barnhart
Director of Public Relations ....Mai Lindstrom

FIA— Formula One
(Federation Internationale de L'Automobile)
2 Chemin de Blandonnet, 1215 Geneva 15, Switzerland
TEL: 011-41-2254-4400
President ....Max Mosley
Secretary General ....Pierre de Coninck
Director of Public Relations ...Francesco Longanesi-Cattani

NASCAR
(National Assn. for Stock Car Auto Racing)
P.O. Box 2875, Daytona Beach, FL 32120
(904) 253-0611
President ....William C. France
Director of Communications-Worldwide ......John Griffin

NHRA
(National Hot Rod Association)
2035 Financial Way, Glendora, CA 91741
(626) 914-4761
President ....Dallas Gardner
Executive V.P./General Manager ....Tom Compton
Director of Communications ....Matt Blaty

MAJOR LEAGUE BASEBALL

Office of the Commissioner
245 Park Ave., 31st Floor, New York, NY 10160
(212) 931-7800
Commissioner ....Bud Selig
President-COO ....Paul Beeston
General Counsel ....Thomas Ostertag
Executive Dir. of Public Relatons ....Richard Levin

Player Relations Committee
350 Park Ave.
New York, NY 10022
(212) 339-7400
Chief Labor Negotiator ....Randy Levine
Associate Counsels ....John Westhoff
                                        & Louis Melendez

Major League Baseball Players Association
12 East 49th St., 24th Floor
New York, NY 10017
(212) 826-0808
Exec. Director & General Counsel ....Donald Fehr
Associate General Counsel ....Gene Orza

AL

American League Office
245 Park Ave., 28th Floor, New York, NY 10167
(212) 931-7600

Anaheim Angels
P. O. Box 2000, Anaheim, CA 92803
(714) 940-2000
Chairman ....Michael Eisner
Owner ....Walt Disney Co.
President & CEO ....Tony Tavares
V.P. & General Manager ....Bill Bavasi
V.P. of Communications ....Tim Mead

Baltimore Orioles
333 West Camden St., Baltimore, MD 21201
(410) 685-9800
CEO ....Peter Angelos
Vice Chairman, Business & Finance ....Joseph Foss
General Manager ....Frank Wren
Director of Public Relations ....John Maroon

Boston Red Sox
Fenway Park, 4 Yawkey Way, Boston, MA 02215
(617) 267-9440
General Partner ....Jean R. Yawkey Trust
CEO ....John Harrington
Exec. V.P./General Manager ....Dan Duquette
Director of Communications ....Kevin Shea

Chicago White Sox
Comiskey Park, 333 W. 35th St., Chicago, IL 60616
(312) 674-1000
Chairman ....Jerry Reinsdorf
Vice Chairman ....Eddie Einhorn
Senior V.P./General Manager ....Ron Schueler
Director of Public Relations ....Scott Reifert

Cleveland Indians
Jacobs Field, 2401 Ontario St., Cleveland, OH 44115
(216) 420-4200
Owner-Chairman-CEO ....Richard Jacobs
Exec. V.P./General Manager ....John Hart
V.P., Public Relations ....Bob DiBiasio

Detroit Tigers
Tiger Stadium, 2121 Trumbull Ave., Detroit, MI 48216
(313) 962-4000
Owner-Chairman ....Mike Ilitch
Owner-Secretary-Treasurer ....Marian Ilitch
President/CEO ....John McHale Jr.
V.P./General Manager ....Randy Smith
Director of Public Relations ....Tyler Barnes

Kansas City Royals
P.O. Box 419969, Kansas City, MO 64141
(816) 921-8000
Owner ....Greater K.C. Community Foundation
Chairman-CEO ....David Glass
V.P./General Manager ....Herk Robinson
Director of Media Relations ....Steve Fink

Minnesota Twins
Hubert H. Humphrey Metrodome
34 Kirby Puckett Place, Minneapolis, MN 55415
(612) 375-1366
Owner ....Carl Pohlad
President ....Jerry Bell
V.P./General Manager ....Terry Ryan
Manager of Media Relations ....Sean Harlin

New York Yankees
Yankee Stadium, Bronx, NY 10451
(718) 293-4300
Principal Owner ....George Steinbrenner
General Partners ....Hal Steinbrenner & Stephen Swindal
V.P./General Manager ....Brian Cashman
Dir. of Media Relations/Publicity ....Rick Cerrone

Oakland Athletics
7677 Oakport, Oakland, CA 94621
(510) 638-4900
Co-Owners . . . . .Steve Schott and Ken Hofmann
President . . . . .Mike Crowley
General Manager . . . . .Billy Beane
Baseball Information Manager . . . . .Mike Selleck

Seattle Mariners
P.O. Box 4100, Seattle, WA 98104
(206) 346-4000
Chairman-CEO . . . . John Ellis
President-COO . . . . .Chuck Armstrong
V.P., Baseball Operations . . . . .TBA
Director of Baseball Information . . . . .Tim Hevly

Tampa Bay Devil Rays
Tropicana Field, One Tropicana Dr.
St. Petersburg, FL 33705
(727) 825-3137
Managing General Partner/CEO . . . . . . .Vincent J. Naimoli
Senior V.P., Baseball Ops./GM . . . . .Chuck Lamar
VP Public Relations . . . . .Rick Vaughn

Texas Rangers
1000 Ballpark Way, Arlington, TX 76011
(817) 273-5222
Owner . . . . .Thomas Hicks
President . . . . .Jim Lites
V.P., General Manager .Doug Melvin
V.P., Public Relations . . . . .John Blake

Toronto Blue Jays
SkyDome, One Blue Jays Way, Suite 3200
Toronto, Ontario M5V 1J1
(416) 341-1000
Owner . . . . .Labatt Brewing Co.
Senior Chairman . . . . .Sam Pollock
President/General Manager . . . . .Gord Ash
Vice President of Media . . . . .Howie Starkman

NL

National League Office
245 Park Ave., 28th Floor, New York, NY 10167
(212) 931-7700

Arizona Diamondbacks
P.O. Box 2095, Phoenix, AZ 85001
(602) 462-6500
Chairman/CEO . . . . .Jerry Colangelo
President . . . . .Richard H. Dozer
V.P./General Manager . . . . .Joe Garagiola Jr.
Direcor of Public Relations . . . . .Mike Swanson

Atlanta Braves
P.O. Box 4064, Atlanta, GA 30302
(404) 522-7630
Owner . . . . .Ted Turner
President . . . . .Stan Kasten
Exec. V.P./General Manager . . . . .John Schuerholz
Director of Public Relations . . . . .Jim Schultz

Chicago Cubs
1060 West Addison St., Chicago, IL 60613
(773) 404-2827
Owner . . . . .The Tribune Company
President-CEO . . . . .Andy MacPhail
V.P./General Manager . . . . .Ed Lynch
Director of Media Relations . . . . .Sharon Pannozzo

Cincinnati Reds
100 Cinergy Field, Cincinnati, OH 45202
(513) 421-4510
Majority Owner . . . . .Carl Lindner
General Manager . . . . .Jim Bowden
Director of Media Relations . . . . .Rob Butcher

Colorado Rockies
Coors Field, 2001 Blake St., Denver, CO 80205
(303) 292-0200
Chairman-President-CEO . . . . .Jerry McMorris
Executive V.P./General Manager . . . . .Dan O'Dowd
V.P. of Business Ops. .Keli McGregor
Director of Public Relations . . . . .Jay Alves

Florida Marlins
2267 N.W. 199th St., Miami, FL 33056
(305) 626-7400
Owner . . . . .John W. Henry
Exec. V.P./General Manager . . . . .Dave Dombrowski
Director of Media Relations . . . . .Ron Colangelo

Houston Astros
The Astrodome, P.O. Box 288, Houston, TX 77001
(713) 799-9500
Chairman-CEO . . . . .Drayton McLane Jr.
President . . . . .Tal Smith
General Manager .Gerry Hunsicker
Director of Media Relations . . . . .Rob Matwick

Los Angeles Dodgers
1000 Elysian Park Ave., Los Angeles, CA 90012
(323) 224-1500
Owner . . . . .Fox Group
President . . . . .Bob Graziano
General Manager . . . . .Kevin Malone
Director of Media Relations/Pub. . . . . .Brent Shyer

Milwaukee Brewers
County Stadium, P.O. Box 3099, Milwaukee, WI 53201
(414) 933-4114
President-CEO . . . . .Wendy Selig-Prieb
Asst. to President . . . . .Sal Bando
General Manager . . . . .Dean Taylor
Director of Media Relations . . . . .Jon Greenberg

Montreal Expos
P.O. Box 500, Station M, Montreal, Quebec H1V 3P2
(514) 253-3434
General Partner-President . . . . .Claude Brochu
V.P./General Manager . . . . .Jim Beattie
V.P., Baseball Operations . . . . .Bill Stoneman
Director of Media Relations . . . . .Peter Loyello

New York Mets
123-01 Roosevelt Ave., Flushing, NY 11368
(718) 507-6387
Chairman . . . . .Nelson Doubleday
President-CEO . . . . .Fred Wilpon
General Manager . . . . .Steve Phillips
Director of Media Relations . . . . Jay Horwitz

Philadelphia Phillies
P.O. Box 7575, Philadelphia, PA 19101
(215) 463-6000
Managing Gen. Partner/Pres./CEO . . .David Montgomery
General Partner/Chairman . . . . .Bill Giles
General Manager . . . . .Ed Wade
V.P. of Public Relations . . . . .Larry Shenk

Pittsburgh Pirates
P.O. Box 7000, Pittsburgh, PA 15212
(412) 323-5000
CEO/Managing General Partner . . . . .Kevin McClatchy
COO . . . . .Richard Freeman
Senior V.P. & General Manager . . . . .Cam Bonifay
Director of Media Relations . . . . .Jim Trdinich

St. Louis Cardinals
250 Stadium Plaza, St. Louis, MO 63102
(314) 421-3060
Owner . . . . .Frederick O. Hanser
President . . . . .Mark Lamping
V.P./General Manager . . . . .Walt Jocketty
Director of Public Relations . . . . .Brian Bartow

San Diego Padres
P.O. Box 122000, San Diego, CA 92112
(619) 881-6500
Chairman ....John Moores
President-CEO ....Larry Lucchino
V.P., Baseball Operations & G.M ....Kevin Towers
Director of Media Relations ....Glenn Geffner

San Francisco Giants
3Com Park at Candlestick Point, San Francisco, CA 94124
(415) 468-3700
President ....Peter Magowan
Executive V.P./COO ....Laurence Baer
Senior V.P./General Manager ....Brian Sabean
V.P. of Communications ....Bob Rose

PRO BASKETBALL

NBA

League Office
Olympic Tower, 645 Fifth Ave., New York, NY 10022
(212) 407-8000
Commissioner ....David Stern
Senior V.P. of Basketball Ops. ....Rod Thorn
Deputy Commissioner ....Russell Granik
V.P., Public Relations ....Brian McIntyre
V.P., Media Relations ....Chris Rienza

NBA Players Association
1700 Broadway, Suite 1400, New York, NY 10019
(212) 655-0880
Exec. Director ....William Hunter
General Counsel ....Robert Lanza
President ....Patrick Ewing

Atlanta Hawks
One CNN Center, South Tower, Suite 405
Atlanta, GA 30303
(404) 827-3800
Owner ....Ted Turner
President ....Stan Kasten
General Manager ....Pete Babcock
V.P. of Communications ....Arthur Triche

Boston Celtics
151 Merrimac St., 4th Floor, Boston, MA 02114
(617) 523-6050
Chairman ....Paul Gaston
President & Head Coach ....Rick Pitino
General Manager ....Chris Wallace
V.P. of Media Relations ....Jeff Twiss

Charlotte Hornets
100 Hive Drive, Charlotte, NC 28217
(704) 357-0252
Owners ....George Shinn and Ray Wooldridge
Executive V.P., Basketball Operations ....Bob Bass
V.P. of Public Relations ....Harold Kaufman

Chicago Bulls
United Center, 1901 West Madison St., Chicago, IL 60612
(312) 455-4000
Chairman ....Jerry Reinsdorf
V.P., Basketball Operations ....Jerry Krause
Director of Media Services ....Tim Hallam

Cleveland Cavaliers
One Centre Court, Cleveland, OH 44115
(216) 420-2000
Owner-Chairman ....Gordon Gund
Owner-Vice Chairman ....George Gund III
President & COO ....Wayne Embry
Senior V.P./General Manager ....Jim Paxson
Director of Media Relations ....Bob Zink

Dallas Mavericks
Reunion Arena, 777 Sports St., Dallas, TX 75207
(214) 748-1808
Owners ..Ross Perot Jr., David McDavid & Frank Zaccanelli
General Manager ....Don Nelson
VP Communications ....Greg Anderson

Denver Nuggets
1635 Clay St., Denver, CO 80204
(303) 405-1100
Owner ....Donald Sturm
General Manager & Head Coach ....Dan Issel
Director of Media Services ....Tommy Sheppard

Detroit Pistons
The Palace of Auburn Hills
Two Championship Dr., Auburn Hills, MI 48326
(248) 377-0100
Managing Partner ....William Davidson
President ....Tom Wilson
General Manager ....Rick Sund
V.P. of Public Relations ....Matt Dobek

Golden State Warriors
1011 Broadway, Oakland, CA 94607
(510) 986-2200
Owner-CEO ....Chris Cohan
General Manager ....Garry St. Jean
Director of Public Relations ....Raymond Ridder

Houston Rockets
2 Greenway Plaza, Suite 400, Houston, TX 77046
(713) 627-3865
Owner ....Leslie L. Alexander
COO ....George Postolos
Sr. Exec. V.P. of Basketball Affairs ....Robert Barr
Manager of Team Communications ....Tim Frank

Indiana Pacers
125 S. Pennsylvania St., Indianapolis, IN 46204
(317) 263-2100
Owners ....Melvin Simon & Herb Simon
President ....Donnie Walsh
General Manager ....David Kahn
Executive V.P./Head Coach ....Larry Bird
Director of Media Relations ....David Benner

Los Angeles Clippers
Staples Center
1111 S. Figueroa St., Suite 1000, Los Angeles, CA 90015
(213) 745-0400
Owner-Chairman ....Donald T. Sterling
Executive V.P. ....Andy Roeser
V.P., Basketball Operations ....Elgin Baylor
Director of Communications ....Jill Wiggins

Los Angeles Lakers
Great Western Forum
3900 W. Manchester Blvd., Inglewood, CA 90305
(310) 419-3100
Owner ....Jerry Buss
Exec. V.P., Basketball Operations ....Jerry West
General Manager ....Mitch Kupchak
Director of Public Relations ....John Black

Miami Heat
Suntrust International Bldg, 1 SE 3rd Ave., Suite 2300, Miami, FL 33131
(305) 577-4328
Managing General Partner ....Micky Arison
President & Head Coach ....Pat Riley
General Manager ....Randy Pfund
Director of Media Relations ....Tim Donovan

Milwaukee Bucks
Bradley Center, 1001 N. Fourth St., Milwaukee, WI 53203
(414) 227-0500
President ....Sen. Herb Kohl (D., Wisc.)
General Manager ....Ernie Grunfeld
Director of Publicity ....TBA

Minnesota Timberwolves
Target Center
600 First Ave. North, Minneapolis, MN 55403
(612) 673-1600
Owner ....Glen Taylor
President ....Rob Moor
V.P., Basketball Operations ....Kevin McHale
General Manager & Head Coach ....Flip Saunders
Dir. of Public Relations/Communications ....Kent Wipf

New Jersey Nets
390 Murray Hill Pkwy., East Rutherford, NJ 07073
(201) 935-8888
Co-Chairman/CEO ....Finn Wentworth
Co-Chair/Owner ....Lewis Katz
General Manager ....John Nash
Director of Public Relations ....John Mertz

New York Knickerbockers
Madison Square Garden
2 Penn Plaza, 14th Floor, New York, NY 10121
(212) 465-6000
Owner ....Cablevision Systems Inc.
President (MSG) ....Dave Checketts
General Manager ....Scott Layden
V.P. of Communications ....Chris Weiller

Orlando Magic
2 Magic Place
870 Matland Summit Blvd., Orlando, FL 32810
(407) 916-2400
Owner ....Rich DeVos
President ....Bob Vander Weide
V.P., Basketball Ops. & GM ....John Gabriel
Sr. Dir. of Publicity/Media Relations ....Scott Bowman

Philadelphia 76ers
First Union Center
3601 S. Broad St., Philadelphia, PA 19148
(215) 339-7600
Owner-President ....Pat Croce
General Manager ....Billy King
Player Personnel Director ....Tony DiLeo
Director of Communications ....Karen Frascona

Phoenix Suns
P.O. Box 1369, Phoenix, AZ 85001
(602) 379-7900
President-CEO ....Jerry Colangelo
Executive V.P./General Manager ....Bryan Colangelo
Sr. V.P. of Player Personnel ....Dick Van Arsdale
V.P. of Basketball Communications ....Julie Fie

Portland Trail Blazers
One Center Court, Suite 200, Portland, OR 97227
(503) 234-9291
Owner-Chairman ....Paul Allen
President & General Manager ....Bob Whitsitt
Assistant General Manager ....Mark Wakenstein
Director of Communications ....John Christensen

Sacramento Kings
One Sports Parkway, Sacramento, CA 95834
(916) 928-0000
Controlling Partners ....Joe Maloof and Gavin Maloof
President ....John Thomas
V.P., Basketball Operations ....Geoff Petrie
Director of Media Relations ....Troy Hanson

San Antonio Spurs
Alamodome
100 Montana St., San Antonio, TX 78203
(210) 554-7700
Chairman ....Peter Holt
GM & Head Coach ....Gregg Popovich
Director of Player Personnel ....Sam Schuler
Director of Media Services ....Tom James

Seattle SuperSonics
190 Queen Anne Ave. N., Suite 200
Seattle, WA 98109
(206) 281-5800
Owner-Chairman ....Barry Ackerley
President & General Manager ....Wally Walker
Executive V.P. of Basketball Ops. ....Billy McKinney
Director of Media Relations ....Cheri Hanson

Toronto Raptors
40 Bay St., Suite 400
Toronto, Ontario 5MJ 2X2
(416) 815-5600
President ....Richard Peddie
V.P./General Manager ....Glen Grunwald
V.P of Comms./Community Dev. ....John Lashway

Utah Jazz
Delta Center, 301 West South Temple
Salt Lake City, UT 84101
(801) 325-2500
Owner ....Larry Miller
President ....Frank Layden
General Manager ....R. Tim Howells
V.P. of Basketball Operations ....Kevin O'Connor
Director of Media Relations ....Kim Turner

Vancouver Grizzlies
General Motors Place, 800 Griffiths Way
Vancouver, B.C. V6B 6G1
(604) 899-7650
Owners ....Bill and Nancy Laurie
President/G.M. ....Stu Jackson
Director, Media Relations ....Steve Frost

Washington Wizards
MCI Center, 601 F Street NW
Washington, D.C., 20004
(202) 661-5000
Chairman ....Abe Pollin
President ....Susan O'Malley
Executive V.P./General Manager ....Wes Unseld
Director of Public Relations ....Maureen Lewis

Other Men's Pro Leagues

Continental Basketball Association
400 North 5th St., Suite 1425, Phoenix, AZ 85004
(602) 254-6677
Commissioner ....Gary Hunter
Dir. of Media Relations ....Deron Filip
   Member teams (9): Connecticut Pride, Ft. Wayne (IN) Fury, Grand Rapids Hoops, Idaho Stampede, LaCrosse Bobcats, Quad City (IL) Thunder, Rockford (IL) Lightning, Sioux Falls (SD) Skyforce, and Yakima (WA) Sun Kings.

United States Basketball League
46 Quirk Road, Milford, CT 06460
(203) 877-9508
Commissioner ....Daniel T. Meisenheimer III
Dir. of Public Relations ....Sean Fisher
   Member teams (13): Atlanta Trojans, Atlantic City Seagulls, Brooklyn Kings, Connecticut Skyhawks, Gulf Coast Sundogs, Kansas Cagerz, Long Island Surf, New Jersey Shorecats, New Hampshire Thunder Loons, Pennsylvania Valleydawgs, Raleigh Cougars, Tampa Bay Windjammers, Washington D.C. Congressionals.

WNBA
Women's National Basketball Association
645 5th Ave., New York, NY 10022
(212) 688-9622
President ....Val Ackerman
Manager, Communications ....Gail Fuller
Director of Media Relations ....Mark Pray

Charlotte Sting
3308 Oaklace Blvd., Ste. B
Charlotte, NC 28208
(704) 357-0252
Executive V.P. ....Sam Russo
Head Coach ....Dan Hughes
Director of Media Relations ....John Maxwell

Cleveland Rockers
Gund Arena, One Center Court
Cleveland, OH 44115
(216) 420-2000
President/COO ....Wayne Embry
Head Coach ....TBA
Director of Media Relations ....Lori Montgomery

Detroit Shock
The Palace at Auburn Hills
Two Championship Dr.
Auburn Hills, MI 48326
(248) 377-0100
GM/Head Coach ....Nancy Lieberman-Cline
Dir. of Public Relations ....Dennis Sampier

Houston Comets
Two Greenway Plaza, Suite 400
Houston, TX 77046-3865
(713) 627-9622
Owner/President ....Leslie L. Alexander
GM/Head Coach ....Van Chancellor
Director of Media Relations ....Megan Bonifas

Los Angeles Sparks
Great Western Forum
3900 W. Manchester Blvd.
Inglewood, CA 90306
(310) 330-2434
Interim General Manager ....Johnny Best
Head Coach ....Orlando Woolridge
Director of Media Relations ....Stacey Terrien

Minnesota Lynx
Target Center
600 First Ave. N.
Minneapolis, MN 55403
(612) 673-1600
COO ....Roger Griffth
GM/Head Coach ....Brain Agler
Manager of Media Relations ....Caryn Fine

New York Liberty
Two Penn Plaza
New York, NY 10121
(212) 564-9622
General Manager ....Carol Blazejowski
Head Coach ....Richie Adubato
Director of Public Relations ....Maureen Coyle

Orlando Miracle
2 Magic Place
8701 Matland Summit Blvd.
Orlando, FL, 32810
(407) 916-2400
President ....Bob Vander Weide
GM/Head Coach ....Carolyn Peck
Sr. Director of Public/Media Relations ......Scott Bowman
Dir. of Media Relations ....Joel Glass

Phoenix Mercury
America West Arena
201 E. Jefferson St.
Phoenix, AZ 85004
(602) 514-8333
Chairman/CEO ....Jerry Colangelo
GM/Head Coach ....Cheryl Miller
Director of Communications ....Nedia Kia

Sacramento Monarchs
ARCO Arena, One Sports Pkwy.
Sacramento, CA 95834
(916) 928-0000
General Manager ....Jerry Reynolds
Head Coach ....Sonny Allen
Director of Communications/Ops. ....Andrea Lepore

Utah Starzz
Delta Center, 301 West South Temple
Salt Lake City, UT 84101
(801) 325-2500
General Manager ....R. Tim Howells
Head Coach ....Fred Williams
Director of Public/Comm. Relations ....Tami Scott

Washington Mystics
MCI Center, 601 F St. NW
Washington D.C. 20004
(202) 661-5000
Executive V.P./General Manager ....Wes Unseld
Head Coach ....Nancy Darsch
Director of Public Relations ....Julie Demeo

BOWLING

ABC
(American Bowling Congress)
5301 South 76th St., Greendale, WI 53129
(414) 421-6400
Executive Director ....Roger Dalken
Director of PR/Marketing ....Michael Deering

BPAA
(Bowling Proprietors' Assn. of America)
P.O. Box 5802, Arlington, TX 76005
(817) 649-5105
CEO ....Don A. Harris
President ....Rex Haney
Director of Public Relations ....Cary Richmond

PWBA
(Professional Women's Bowling Association)
7171 Cherryvale Blvd., Rockford, IL 61112
(815) 332-5756
President ....John Falzone
Media Director ....John Takacs

PBA
(Professional Bowlers Association)
1720 Merriman Road, P.O. Box 5118
Akron, OH 44334
(330) 836-5568
Commissioner ....Mark Gerberich
Public Relations Director ....Dave Schroeder

WIBC
(Women's International Bowling Congress, Inc.)
5301 South 76th St., Greendale, WI 53129
(414) 421-9000
President ....Joyce Deitch
Public Relations Manager ....Mark Whitney

BOXING

IBF
(International Boxing Federation)
134 Evergreen Place, 9th Floor
East Orange, NJ 07018
(973) 414-0300
President ....Robert W. Lee
Executive Secretary ....Marian Muhammad
Ratings Chairman ....Daryl Peoples

WBA
(World Boxing Association)
P.O. Box 377, Maracay 2110–A
Venezuela
TEL: 011-58-44-63-1584
President ....Gilberto Mendoza
General Counsel/U.S. Spokesman ....Jimmy Binns
1735 Market St., 39th Floor, Phila., PA 19103
(215) 557-8000
Ratings Chairman ....Bolivar Icaza
P.O. Box 1833, Panama 1, Rep. de Panama
TEL: 011-507-63-5167

WBC
(World Boxing Council)
Genova 33-503, Col. Juarez,
MEXICO, 06600, D.F., Mexico
TEL: 011-525-208-2440
President ....Jose Sulaiman
Ratings Chairman ....Frank Quill
Press Information/U.S. Spokesman ....John Brister
411 Ballentine St., Bay St. Louis, MS 39520
(228) 467-3304

WBO
(World Boxing Organization)
1st Federal Bldg., 1056 Ave Munoz Revera, Suite 714
San Juan, P.R. 00927
(787) 765-4444
President ....Francisco Paco Valcarcel
Past Pres./Attorney ....Louis Batista Salas
Ratings Chairman ....Louis Perez
Public Relations Dir. ....Mario Rivera-Martino

Don King Productions, Inc.
501 Fairway Dr.
Deerfield Beach, FL 33441
(954) 418-5800
President ....Don King
V.P. of Boxing Ops. ....Bob Goodman
Director of Public Relations ....Greg Fritz

Top Rank
3980 Howard Hughes Pkwy. Ste. 580
Las Vegas, NV 89109
(702) 732-2717
Chairman ....Bob Arum
Director of Marketing ....Michael Malitz

COLLEGE SPORTS

CCA
(Collegiate Commissioners Association)
2201 Stemmons Freeway, Dallas, TX 75207
(214) 742-1212
President ....John Steinbrecher (Mid-Continent)
Exec. V.P. ....Michael Slive (Conf. USA)
Secretary-Treasurer ....Britton Banowsky (Big 12)

NAIA
(National Assn. of Intercollegiate Athletics)
6120 South Yale, Suite 1450, Tulsa, OK 74136
(918) 494-8828
President-CEO ....Steve Baker
Public Relations Director ....Darin David

NCAA
(National Collegiate Athletic Association)
P.O. Box 6222, Indianapolis, IN 46206
(317) 957-6222
Chief Operating Officer ....Daniel Boggan Jr.
President ....Cedric Dempsey
Group Exec. Dir. for Enforcement ....David Berst
Director of Public Relations ....Wallace I. Renfro

WSF
(Women's Sports Foundation)
Eisenhower Park, East Meadow, NY 11554
(516) 542-4700
Executive Director ....Donna Lopiano
President ....Nancy Lieberman-Cline
Director of Public Relations ....Coni Diggs

Major NCAA Conferences
See pages 445-453 for basketball coaches, football coaches, nicknames and colors of all Division I basketball schools and Division I-A and I-AA football schools.

ATLANTIC COAST CONFERENCE
P.O. Drawer ACC
Greensboro, NC 27417-6724
(336) 854-8787   Founded: 1953
Commissioner ....John Swofford
Asst. Commis. of Media Relations ....Brian Morrison
1999-00 members: BASKETBALL & FOOTBALL (9)—
Clemson, Duke, Florida St., Georgia Tech, Maryland, North Carolina, North Carolina St., Virginia and Wake Forest.

Clemson University
Clemson, SC 29633   Founded: 1889
SID: (864) 656-2114   Enrollment: 16,435
President ....Deno Curris
Athletic Director ....Bobby Robinson
Sports Information Director ....Tim Baurret

Duke University
Durham, NC 27708   Founded: 1838
SID: (919) 684-2633   Enrollment: 6,072
President ....Nannerl Keohane
Athletic Director ....Joe Alleva
Sports Information Director ....Mike Cragg

Florida State University
Tallahassee, FL 32316   Founded: 1857
SID: (850) 644-1403   Enrollment: 30,519
President ....Talbot (Sandy) D'Alemberte
Athletic Director ....Dave Hart Jr.
Sports Information Director ....Rob Wilson

Georgia Tech
Atlanta, GA 30332   Founded: 1885
SID: (404) 894-5445   Enrollment: 10,304
President ....Wayne Clough
Athletic Director ....Dave Braine
Sports Information Director ....Mike Finn

University of Maryland
College Park, MD 20741   Founded: 1807
SID: (301) 314-7064   Enrollment: 33,600
President ....Dr. Clayton D. Mote Jr.
Athletic Director ....Deborah Yow
Sports Information Director ....Dave Haglund

University of North Carolina
Chapel Hill, NC 27514   Founded: 1789
SID: (919) 962-2123   Enrollment: 24,255
Chancellor ....Michael K. Hooker
Athletic Director ....Dick Baddour
Sports Information Director ....Steve Kirschner

North Carolina State University
Raleigh, NC 27695   Founded: 1887
SID: (919) 515-2102   Enrollment: 27,196
Chancellor ....Mary Anne E. Fox
Athletic Director ....Les Robinson
Sports Information Director ....Annabelle Vaughan

University of Virginia
Charlottesville, VA 22903   Founded: 1819
SID: (804) 982-5500   Enrollment: 18,279
President ....John T. Casteen III
Athletic Director ....Terry Holland
Sports Information Director ....Rich Murray

Wake Forest University
Winston-Salem, NC 27109   Founded: 1834
SID: (336) 758-5640   Enrollment: 3,836
President ....Thomas K. Hearn Jr.
Athletic Director ....Ron Wellman
Sports Information Director ....John Justus

       ❧   ❧   ❧

BIG EAST CONFERENCE
56 Exchange Terrace
Providence, RI 02903
(401) 272-9108   Founded: 1979
Commissioner ....Mike Tranghese
Assoc. Commissioner/P.R ....John Paquette
   1999-00 members: BASKETBALL (13)— Boston College, Connecticut, Georgetown, Miami-FL, Notre Dame, Pittsburgh, Providence, Rutgers, St. John's, Seton Hall, Syracuse, Villanova and West Virginia; FOOTBALL (8)— Boston College, Miami-FL, Pittsburgh, Rutgers, Syracuse, Temple, Virginia Tech and West Virginia.

Boston College
Chestnut Hill, MA 02467   Founded: 1863
SID: (617) 552-3004   Enrollment: 8,958
President ....Rev. William P. Leahy, S.J.
Athletic Director ....Gene DeFillippo
Sports Information Director ....Chris Cameron

University of Connecticut
Storrs, CT 06269   Founded: 1881
SID: (860) 486-3531   Enrollment: 21,901
President ....Philip Austin
Athletic Director ....Lew Perkins
Sports Information Director ....Tim Tolokan

Georgetown University
Washington, DC 20057   Founded: 1789
SID: (202) 687-2492   Enrollment: 6,338
President ....Rev. Leo J. O'Donovan, S.J.
Athletic Director ....Joseph C. Lang
Sports Information Director ....Bill Shapland

University of Miami
Coral Gables, FL 33146   Founded: 1926
SID: (305) 284-3244   Enrollment: 13,842
President ....Edward T. Foote II
Athletic Director ....Paul Dee
Sports Information Director ....Bob Burda

University of Notre Dame
Notre Dame, IN 46556   Founded: 1842
SID: (219) 631-7516   Enrollment: 7,838
President ....Rev. Edward (Monk) Malloy
Athletic Director ....Michael Wadsworth
Sports Information Director ....John Heisler

University of Pittsburgh
Pittsburgh, PA 15213   Founded: 1787
SID: (412) 648-8240   Enrollment: 32,293
Chancellor ....Mark A. Nordenberg
Athletic Director ....Steve Pederson
Sports Information Director ................E.J. Borghetti

Providence College
Providence, RI 02918   Founded: 1917
SID: (401) 865-2272   Enrollment: 3,700
President ....Philip A. Smith, OP
Athletic Director ....John Marinatto
Sports Information Director ....Tim Connor

Rutgers University
New Brunswick, NJ 08903   Founded: 1766
SID: (732) 445-4200   Enrollment: 34,500
President ....Francis L. Lawrence
Athletic Director ....Robert E. Mulcahy III
Sports Information Director ....John Wooding

St. John's University
Jamaica, NY 11439   Founded: 1870
SID: (718) 990-6367   Enrollment: 17,200
President ....Rev. Donald J. Harrington, CM
Athletic Director ....Edward J. Manetta Jr.
Sports Information Director ....Dominic Scianna

Seton Hall University
South Orange, NJ 07079   Founded: 1856
SID: (973) 761-9493   Enrollment: 9,527
Chancellor ....Rev. Thomas R. Peterson, OP
Athletic Director ....Jeff Fogelson
Sports Information Director ....Marie Wozniak

Syracuse University
Syracuse, NY 13244   Founded: 1870
SID: (315) 443-2608   Enrollment: 10,400
Chancellor ....Kenneth Shaw
Athletic Director ....Jake Crouthamel
Sports Information Director ....Sue Edson

Temple University
Philadelphia, PA 19122   Founded: 1884
SID: (215) 204-7445   Enrollment: 30,000
President ....Peter J. Liacouras
Athletic Director ....David O'Brien
Sports Information Director ....Brian Kirschner

Villanova University
Villanova, PA 19085   Founded: 1842
SID: (610) 519-4120   Enrollment: 6.039
President ....Rev. Edmund J. Dobbin, OSA
Athletic Director ....Tim Hofferth
Sports Information Director .....:.........Dean Kenefick

Virginia Tech
Blacksburg, VA 24061   Founded: 1872
SID: (540) 231-6796   Enrollment: 24,812
President ....Paul Torgersen
Athletic Director ....Jim Weaver
Sports Information Director ....Dave Smith

West Virginia University
Morgantown, WV 26507   Founded: 1867
SID: (304) 293-2821   Enrollment: 22,000
President ....David Hardesty
Athletic Director ....Ed Pastilong
Sports Information Director ....Shelly Poe

       ❧   ❧   ❧

BIG 12 CONFERENCE
2201 Stemmons Fwy., 28th Floor
Dallas, TX 75207
(214) 742-1212   Founded: 1996
Commissioner ....Kevin Weiberg
Media Relations Director ....Bo Carter
   1999-00 members: BASKETBALL & FOOTBALL (12)— Baylor, Colorado, Iowa St., Kansas, Kansas St., Missouri, Nebraska, Oklahoma, Oklahoma St., Texas, Texas A&M and Texas Tech.

Baylor University
Waco, TX 76711   Founded: 1845
SID: (254) 710-2743   Enrollment: 11,124
President ....Robert B. Sloan
Athletic Director ....Tom Stanton
Sports Information Director ....Brian McCallum

University of Colorado
Boulder, CO 80309   Founded: 1876
SID: (303) 492-5626   Enrollment: 24,622
President ....Dr. John Buechner
Athletic Director ....Dick Tharp
Sports Information Director ....Dave Plati

Iowa State University
Ames, IA 50011
SID: (515) 294-3372
President ....Martin Jischke
Athletic Director ....Eugene Smith
Sports Information Director ....Tom Kroeschell

Founded: 1858
Enrollment: 25,585

University of Kansas
Lawrence, KS 66045
SID: (785) 864-3417
Chancellor ....Robert Hemenway
Athletic Director ....Bob Frederick
Sports Information Director ....Dean Buchan

Founded: 1866
Enrollment: 25,108

Kansas State University
Manhattan, KS 66502
SID: (785) 532-6735
President ....Jon Wefald
Athletic Director ....Max Urick
Sports Information Director ....Kent Brown

Founded: 1863
Enrollment: 20,885

University of Missouri
Columbia, MO 65205
SID: (573) 882-3241
Chancellor ....Richard Wallace
Athletic Director ....Michael Alden
Sports Information Director ....Bob Brendel

Founded: 1839
Enrollment: 22,723

University of Nebraska
Lincoln, NE 68588
SID: (402) 472-2263
Chancellor ....Dr. James Moeser
Athletic Director ....Bill Byrne
Sports Information Director ....Chris Anderson

Founded: 1869
Enrollment: 25,000

University of Oklahoma
Norman, OK 73019
SID: (405) 325-8231
President ....David Boren
Athletic Director ....Joe Castiglione
Sports Information Director ....Mike Prusinski

Founded: 1890
Enrollment: 25,400

Oklahoma State University
Stillwater, OK 74078
SID: (405) 707-7830
President ....James Halligan
Athletic Director ....Terry Don Phillips
Sports Information Director ....Steve Buzzard

Founded: 1890
Enrollment: 20,466

University of Texas
Austin, TX 78713
SID: (512) 471-7437
President ....Dr. Larry Faulkner
Athletic Director ....De Loss Dodds
Sports Information Director ....John Biancoa

Founded: 1883
Enrollment: 48,8869

Texas A&M University
College Station, TX 77843
SID: (409) 845-5725
President ....Ray Bowen
Athletic Director ....Wally Groff
Sports Information Director ....Alan Cannon

Founded: 1876
Enrollment: 43,406

Texas Tech University
Lubbock, TX 79409
SID: (806) 742-2770
Chancellor ....John Montford
Athletic Director ....Gerald Myers
Sports Information Director ....TBA

Founded: 1923
Enrollment: 25,000

ๆ   ๆ   ๆ

BIG TEN CONFERENCE
1500 West Higgins Road, Park Ridge, IL 60068-6300
(847) 696-1010
Commissioner ....Jim Delany
Assistant Commssioner of Media Relations ......Sue Ryan

Founded: 1895

1999-00 members: BASKETBALL & FOOTBALL (11)—
Illinois, Indiana, Iowa, Michigan, Michigan St., Minnesota,
Northwestern, Ohio St., Penn St., Purdue and Wisconsin.

University of Illinois
Champaign, IL 61820
SID: (217) 333-1390
President ....James J. Stukel
Athletic Director ....Ron Guenther
Dir. of Communications ....Barbara Butler

Founded: 1867
Enrollment: 36,000

Indiana University
Bloomington, IN 47408
SID: (812) 855-9399
President ....Myles Brand
Athletic Director ....Clarence Doninger
Sports Information Director ....Kit Klingelhoffer

Founded: 1820
Enrollment: 35,551

University of Iowa
Iowa City, IA 52242
SID: (319) 335-9411
President ....Mary Sue Coleman
Athletic Director ....Bob Bowlsby
Sports Information Director ....Phil Haddy

Founded: 1847
Enrollment: 28,705

University of Michigan
Ann Arbor, MI 48109
SID: (734) 763-1381
President ....Lee Bollinger
Athletic Director ....Tom Goss
Sports Information Director ....Bruce Madej

Founded: 1817
Enrollment: 37,197

Michigan State University
East Lansing, MI 48824
SID: (517) 355-2271
President ....Peter McPherson
Interim Athletic Director ....Clarence Underwood
Sports Information Director ....John Lewandowski

Founded: 1855
Enrollment: 42,603

University of Minnesota
Minneapolis, MN 55455
SID: (612) 625-4090
President ....Mark Yudof
Athletic Director ....Dr. Mark Dienhart
Sports Information Director ....Marc Ryan

Founded: 1851
Enrollment: 38,000

Northwestern University
Evanston, IL 60208
SID: (847) 491-7503
President ....Henry S. Bienen
Athletic Director ....Rick Taylor
Sports Information Director ....Brad Hurlbut

Founded: 1851
Enrollment: 7,400

Ohio State University
Columbus, OH 43210
SID: (614) 292-6861
President ....William E. Kirwan
Athletic Director ....Andy Geiger
Sports Information Director ....Gerry Emig

Founded: 1870
Enrollment: 48,300

Penn State University
University Park, PA 16802
SID: (814) 865-1757
President ....Graham Spanier
Athletic Director ....Tim Curley
Sports Information Director ....Jeff Nelson

Founded: 1855
Enrollment: 41,050

Purdue University
West Lafayette, IN 47907
SID: (765) 494-3202
President ....Steven C. Beering
Athletic Director ....Morgan Burke
Sports Information Director ....Tom Schott

Founded: 1869
Enrollment: 36,878

University of Wisconsin
Madison, WI 53711
Founded: 1848
SID: (608) 262-1811
Enrollment: 40,109
Chancellor ....David Ward
Athletic Director ....Pat Richter
Sports Information Director ....Steve Malchow

           ੈ   ੈ   ੈ

BIG WEST CONFERENCE
Two Corporate Park, Suite 206
Irvine, CA 92606
(949) 261-2525
Founded: 1969
Commissioner ....Dennis Farrell
Director of Information ....Michael Daniels
  1999-00 members: BASKETBALL (12)— Boise St.,
CS-Fullerton, Cal Poly-SLO, Idaho, Long Beach St., Nevada,
New Mexico St., North Texas, Pacific, UC-Irvine, UC-Santa
Barbara, Utah St.; FOOTBALL (7)— Arkansas St., Boise St.,
Idaho, Nevada, New Mexico St., North Texas, Utah St.

Arkansas State University
State University, AR 72467
Founded: 1909
SID: (870) 972-2541
Enrollment: 10,050
President ....Les Wyatt
Athletic Director ....Barry Dowd
Sports Information Director ....Gina Bowman

Boise State
Boise, ID 83725
Founded: 1932
SID: (208) 385-1515
Enrollment: 15,832
President ....Charles P. Ruch
Athletic Director ....Gene Bleymaier
Sports Information Director ....Max Corbet

Cal State-Fullerton
Fullerton, CA 92834
Founded: 1957
SID: (714) 278-3970
Enrollment: 25,000
President ....Milton A. Gordon
Athletic Director ....John Easterbrook
Sports Information Director ....Mel Franks

Cal Poly SLO
San Luis Obispo, CA 93407
Founded: 1901
SID: (805) 756-6531
Enrollment: 17,000
President ....Dr. Warren J. Baker
Athletic Director ....John McCutcheon
Sports Information Director ....Jason Sullivan

University of Idaho
Moscow, ID 83844
Founded: 1889
SID: (208) 885-0211
Enrollment: 11,437
President ....Bob Hoover
Athletic Director ....Mike Bohn
Sports Information Director ....Becky Paull

Long Beach State
Long Beach, CA 90840
Founded: 1949
SID: (562) 985-8569
Enrollment: 28,000
President ....Robert Maxson
Athletic Director ....Bill Shumard
Sports Information Director ....Steve Janisch

University of Nevada
Reno, NV 89557
Founded: 1874
SID: (775) 784-6900
Enrollment: 12,500
President ....Joe Crowley
Athletic Director ....Chris Ault
Sports Information Director ....Paul Stuart

New Mexico State University
Las Cruces, NM 88003
Founded: 1888
SID: (505) 646-3929
Enrollment: 15,409
President ....Dr. William Conroy
Athletic Director ....TBA
Sports Information Director ....Heath Nielsen

University of North Texas
Denton, TX 76203
Founded: 1890
SID: (940) 565-2476
Enrollment: 25,000
Chancellor ....Dr. Alfred F. Hurley
Athletic Director ....Craig Helwig
Sports Information Director ....Sean Johnson

University of the Pacific
Stockton, CA 95211
Founded: 1851
SID: (209) 946-2479
Enrollment: 6,000
President ....Donald DeRosa
Athletic Director ....TBA
Sports Information Director ....Mike Millerick

University of California, Irvine
Irvine, CA 92697
Founded: 1962
SID: (949) 824-5814
Enrollment: 17,776
Chancellor ....Ralph Cicerone
Athletic Director ....Dan Guerrero
Sports Information Director ....Bob Olson

University of California, Santa Barbara
Santa Barbara, CA 93106
Founded: 1944
SID: (805) 893-3428
Enrollment: 18,400
Chancellor ....Henry Yang
Athletic Director ....Gary Cunningham
Sports Information Director ....Bill Mahoney

Utah State University
Logan, UT 84322
Founded: 1888
SID: (435) 797-1361
Enrollment: 20,808
President ....George Emert
Athletic Director ....Bruce Van de Velde
Sports Information Director ....Mike Strauss

           ੈ   ੈ   ੈ

CONFERENCE USA
35 East Wacker Drive, Suite 650, Chicago, IL 60601
(312) 553-0483
Founded: 1995
Commissioner ....Mike Slive
Asst. Commissioner ....Brian Teter
  1999-00 members: BASKETBALL (12)— UAB, Cincin-
nati, DePaul, Houston, Louisville, Marquette, Memphis,
UNC-Charlotte, Saint Louis, South Florida, Southern Miss
and Tulane; FOOTBALL (9)— UAB, Army, Cincinnati, East
Carolina, Houston, Louisville, Memphis, Southern Miss and
Tulane.

University of Alabama at Birmingham
Birmingham, AL 35294
Founded: 1969
SID: (205) 934-0722
Enrollment: 16,016
President ....Dr. W. Ann Reynolds
Athletic Director ....Gene Bartow
Sports Information Director ....Grant Shingleton

Army— U.S. Military Academy
West Point, NY 10996
Founded: 1802
SID: (914) 938-3303
Enrollment: 4,000
Superintendent ....Lt. Gen. Daniel W. Christman
Athletic Director ....Rick Greenspan
Sports Information Director ....Bob Beretta

University of Cincinnati
Cincinnati, OH 45221
Founded: 1819
SID: (513) 556-5191
Enrollment: 35,000
President ....Dr. Joseph A. Steger
Athletic Director ....Bob Goin
Sports Information Director ....Tom Hathaway

DePaul University
Chicago, IL 60614
Founded: 1898
SID: (773) 325-7525
Enrollment: 17,133
President ....Rev. John P. Minogue
Athletic Director ....Bill Bradshaw
Sports Information Director ....John Lanctot

East Carolina University

Greenville, NC 27858 — Founded: 1907
SID: (252) 328-4522 — Enrollment: 18,000
Chancellor ....Richard Eakin
Athletic Director ....Mike Hamrick
Sports Information Director ....Norm Reilly

University of Houston

Houston, TX 77204 — Founded: 1927
SID: (713) 743-9404 — Enrollment: 30,757
President ....Arthur K. Smith
Athletic Director ....Chet Gladchuk
Sports Information Director ....Chris Buckhalter

University of Louisville

Louisville, KY 40292 — Founded: 1798
SID: (502) 852-6581 — Enrollment: 22,000
President ....Dr. John W. Shumaker
Athletic Director ....Tom Jurich
Sports Information Director ....Kenny Klein

Marquette University

Milwaukee, WI 53233 — Founded: 1881
SID: (414) 288-7447 — Enrollment: 10,600
President ....Rev. Robert A. Wild S.J.
Athletic Director ....Bill Cords
Sports Information Director ....Kathleen Hohl

University of Memphis

Memphis, TN 38152 — Founded: 1912
SID: (901) 678-2337 — Enrollment: 20,100
President ....V. Lane Rawlins
Athletic Director ..........................R.C. Johnson
Sports Information Director ....Bob Winn

University of North Carolina at Charlotte

Charlotte, NC 28223 — Founded: 1946
SID: (704) 547-4937 — Enrollment: 16,370
Chancellor ....J. H. Woodward
Athletic Director ....Judy Rose
Sports Information Director ....Tom Whitestone

Saint Louis University

St. Louis, MO 63103 — Founded: 1818
SID: (314) 977-2524 — Enrollment: 11,000
President ....Rev. Lawrence Biondi, S.J.
Athletic Director ....Doug Woolard
Sport Information Director ....Doug McIlhagga

University of South Florida

Tampa, FL 33620 — Founded: 1956
SID: (813) 974-4086 — Enrollment: 37,000
President ....Betty Castor
Athletic Director ....Paul Griffin
Sports Information Director ....John Gerdes

University of Southern Mississippi

Hattiesburg, MS 39406 — Founded: 1910
SID: (601) 266-4503 — Enrollment: 14,000
President ....Dr. Horace W. Fleming Jr.
Athletic Director ....Rich Gianniani
Sports Information Director ....Regiel Napier

Tulane University

New Orleans, LA 70118 — Founded: 1834
SID: (504) 865-5506 — Enrollment: 11,300
President ....Dr. Scott S. Cowen
Athletic Director ....TBA
Sports Information Director ....Scott Stricklin

≫ઢ   ≫ઢ   ≫ઢ

MID-AMERICAN CONFERENCE

24 Public Square, 15th Floor, Cleveland, OH 44113
(216) 566-4622 — Founded: 1946
Commissioner ....Rick Chryst
Director of Communications ....Gary Richter

1999-00 members: BASKETBALL & FOOTBALL (13)—
Akron, Ball St., Bowling Green, Buffalo, Central Michigan,
Eastern Michigan, Kent, Marshall, Miami-OH, Northern
Illinois, Ohio University, Toledo and Western Michigan.

University of Akron

Akron, OH 44325 — Founded: 1870
SID: (330) 972-7468 — Enrollment: 23,508
President ....Louis Proenza
Athletic Director ....Dennis Helsel
Sports Information Director ....Jeff Brewer

Ball State University

Muncie, IN 47306 — Founded: 1918
SID: (765) 285-8242 — Enrollment: 18,528
President ....John Worthen
Athletic Director ....Andrea Seger
Sports Information Director ....Joe Hernandez

Bowling Green State University

Bowling Green, OH 43403 — Founded: 1910
SID: (419) 372-7075 — Enrollment: 16,900
President ....Sidney Ribeau
Athletic Director ....Paul Krebs
Sports Information Director ....Steve Barr

University of Buffalo

Buffalo, NY 14260 — Founded: 1846
SID: (716) 645-6311 — Enrollment: 23,000
President ....William P. Greiner
Athletic Director ....Nelson Townsend
Sports Information Director ....Paul Vecchio

Central Michigan University

Mt. Pleasant, MI 48859 — Founded: 1892
SID: (517) 774-3277 — Enrollment: 25,595
President ....Leonard Plachta
Athletic Director ....Herb Deromedi
Sports Information Director ....Fred Stabley Jr.

Eastern Michigan University

Ypsilanti, MI 48197 — Founded: 1849
SID: (734) 487-0317 — Enrollment: 24,000
President ....William Shelton
Athletic Director ....Dr. David Dials
Sports Information Director ....Jim Streeter

Kent State University

Kent, OH 44242 — Founded: 1910
SID: (330) 672-2110 — Enrollment: 29,862
President ....Carol Cartwright
Athletic Director ....Laing Kennedy
Sports Information Director ....Will Roleson

Marshall University

Huntington, WV 25715 — Founded: 1837
SID: (304) 696-4660 — Enrollment: 16,000
President ....TBA
Athletic Director ....Lance West
Sports Information Director ....Clark Haptonstall

Miami University

Oxford, OH 45056 — Founded: 1809
SID: (513) 529-4327 — Enrollment: 16,000
President ....James C. Garland
Athletic Director ....Joel Maturi
Sports Information Director ....Mike Wolf

Northen Illinois University

DeKalb, IL 60115 — Founded: 1895
SID: (815) 753-1706 — Enrollment: 22,473
President ....John LaTourette
Athletic Director ....Cary Groth
Sports Information Director ....Michael Korcek

Ohio University
Athens, OH 45701
Founded: 1804
SID: (740) 593-1298
Enrollment: 27,605
President ....Robert Glidden
Athletic Director ....Tom Boeh
Sports Information Director ....Heather Czeczok

University of Toledo
Toledo, OH 43606
Founded: 1872
SID: (419) 530-3790
Enrollment: 20,307
President ....Dr. Vik Kapoor
Athletic Director ....Pete Liske
Sports Information Director ....Paul Helgren

Western Michigan University
Kalamazoo, MI 49008
Founded: 1903
SID: (616) 387-4138
Enrollment: 25,669
President ....Dr. Elson Floyd
Athletic Director ....Kathy Beauregard
Sports Information Director ....Dan Jankowski

ঽ৯   ঽ৯   ঽ৯

MOUNTAIN WEST CONFERENCE
P.O. Box 35670
Colorado Springs, CO 80935
(719) 533-9500
Founded: 1999
Commissioner ....Craig Thompson
Media Relations Director ....Amy Turner
1999-00 members: BASKETBALL & FOOTBALL (8)—
Air Force, BYU, Colorado State, UNLV, New Mexico, San
Diego St., Utah, Wyoming.

U.S. Air Force Academy
US Academy, CO 80840
Founded: 1959
SID: (719) 333-2313
Enrollment: 4,100
Superintendent ....Lt. Gen. Tad Oelstrom
Athletic Director ....Col. Randall W. Spetman
Sports Information Director ....Dave Kellogg

Brigham Young University
Provo, UT 84602
Founded: 1875
SID: (801) 378-4911
Enrollment: 28,300
President ....Merril J. Bateman
Athletic Director ....Val Hale
Sports Information Director ....Jeff Reynolds

Colorado State University
Fort Collins, CO 80523
Founded: 1870
SID: (970) 491-5067
Enrollment: 22,344
President ....Dr. Albert Yates
Athletic Director ....Tim Wieser
Sports Information Director ....Gary Ozzello

University of New Mexico
Albuquerque, NM 87131
Founded: 1889
SID: (505) 925-5520
Enrollment: 23,744
President ....Dr. William Gordon
Athletic Director ....Rudy Davalos
Sports Information Director ....Greg Remington

San Diego State University
San Diego, CA 92182
Founded: 1897
SID: (619) 594-5547
Enrollment: 29,000
President ....Dr. Stephen L. Weber
Athletic Director ....Rick Bay
Sports Information Director ....John Rosenthal

UNLV— University of Nevada, Las Vegas
Las Vegas, NV 89154
Founded: 1957
SID: (702) 895-3207
Enrollment: 21,200
President ....Dr. Carol Harter
Athletic Director ....Charles Cavognaro
Sports Information Director ....Jim Gemma

University of Utah
Salt Lake City, UT 84112
Founded: 1850
SID: (801) 581-3510
Enrollment: 25,213
President ....Dr. Bernard Machen
Athletic Director ....Dr. Chris Hill
Sports Information Director ....Liz Abel

University of Wyoming
Laramie, WY 82071
Founded: 1886
SID: (307) 766-2256
Enrollment: 10,600
President ....Philip Dubois
Athletic Director ....Lee Moon
Sports Information Director ....Kevin McKinney

ঽ৯   ঽ৯   ঽ৯

PACIFIC-10 CONFERENCE
800 South Broadway, Suite 400, Walnut Creek, CA 94596
(925) 932-4411
Founded: 1915
Commissioner ....Thomas Hansen
Asst. Commissioner, Public Relations ....Jim Muldoon
1999-00 members: BASKETBALL & FOOTBALL (10)—
Arizona, Arizona St., California, Oregon, Oregon St.,
Stanford, UCLA, USC, Washington and Washington St.

University of Arizona
Tucson, AZ 85721
Founded: 1885
SID: (520) 621-4163
Enrollment: 35,000
President ....Peter Likins
Athletic Director ....Jim Livengood
Sports Information Director ....Tom Duddleston

Arizona State University
Tempe, AZ 85287
Founded: 1885
SID: (602) 965-6592
Enrollment: 44,255
President ....Lattie F. Coor
Athletic Director ....Kevin White
Sports Information Director ....Mark Brand

University of California
Berkeley, CA 94720
Founded: 1868
SID: (510) 642-5363
Enrollment: 31,000
Chancellor ....Robert Berdahl
Athletic Director ....John Kasser
Sports Information Director ....Kevin Reneau

University of Oregon
Eugene, OR 97401
Founded: 1876
SID: (541) 346-5488
Enrollment: 17,300
President ....David Frohnmeyer
Athletic Director ....Bill Moos
Sports Information Director ....Dave Williford

Oregon State University
Corvallis, OR 97331
Founded: 1868
SID: (541) 737-3720
Enrollment: 15,000
President ....Paul G. Risser
Athletic Director ....Mitch Barnhart
Sports Information Director ....Hal Cowan

Stanford University
Stanford, CA 94305
Founded: 1891
SID: (650) 723-4418
Enrollment: 13,075
President ....Gerhard Casper
Athletic Director ....Ted Leland
Sports Information Director ....Gary Migdol

UCLA— Univ. of California, Los Angeles
Los Angeles, CA 90024
Founded: 1919
SID: (310) 206-6831
Enrollment: 34,000
Chancellor ....Albert Carnesale
Athletic Director ....Pete Dalis
Sports Information Director ....Marc Dellins

USC— Univ. of Southern California
Los Angeles, CA 90089
Founded: 1880
SID: (213) 740-8480
Enrollment: 28,100
President ....Steven Sample
Athletic Director ....Mike Garrett
Sports Information Director ....Tim Tessalone

University of Washington
Seattle, WA 98195 — Founded: 1861
SID: (206) 543-2230 — Enrollment: 26,000
President ....Richard McCormick
Athletic Director ....Barbara Hedges
Sports Information Director ....Jim Daves

Washington State University
Pullman, WA 99164 — Founded: 1890
SID: (509) 335-2684 — Enrollment: 20,000
President ....Samuel Smith
Athletic Director ....Rick Dickson
Sports Information Director ....Rod Commons

ॡ   ॡ   ॡ

SOUTHEASTERN CONFERENCE
2201 Civic Center Blvd.
Birmingham, AL 35203
(205) 458-3000 — Founded: 1933
Commissioner ....Roy Kramer
Asst. Commis. of Media Relations ....Charles Bloom
1999-00 members: BASKETBALL & FOOTBALL (12)—
Alabama, Arkansas, Auburn, Florida, Georgia, Kentucky,
LSU, Mississippi St., Ole Miss, South Carolina, Tennessee
and Vanderbilt.

University of Alabama
Tuscaloosa, AL 35487 — Founded: 1831
SID: (205) 348-6084 — Enrollment: 19,000
President ....Dr. Andrew Sorensen
Interim Athletic Director ....Finus Gaston
Sports Information Director ....Larry White

University of Arkansas
Fayetteville, AR 72701 — Founded: 1871
SID: (501) 575-2751 — Enrollment: 14,577
Chancellor ....John White
Athletic Director ....Frank Broyles
Women's Athletic Director ....Bev Lewis
Sports Information Director ....Rick Schaeffer

Auburn University
Auburn, AL 36831 — Founded: 1856
SID: (334) 844-9800 — Enrollment: 21,505
President ....William V. Muse
Athletic Director ....David Housel
Sports Information Director ....Kent Partridge

University of Florida
Gainesville, FL 32604 — Founded: 1853
SID: (352) 375-4683 ext. 6100 — Enrollment: 42,000
President ....John Lombardi
Athletic Director ....Jeremy Foley
Sports Information Director ....John Humenik

University of Georgia
Athens, GA 30603 — Founded: 1785
SID: (706) 542-1621 — Enrollment: 30,009
President ....Michael F. Adams
Athletic Director ....Vince Dooley
Sports Information Director ....Claude Felton

University of Kentucky
Lexington, KY 40506 — Founded: 1865
SID: (606) 257-3838 — Enrollment: 24,200
President ....Charles T. Wethington Jr.
Athletic Director .........................C.M. Newton
Sports Information Director ....Rena Vicini

LSU— Louisiana State University
Baton Rouge, LA 70894 — Founded: 1860
SID: (225) 388-8226 — Enrollment: 28,077
Chancellor ....Mark Emmert
Athletic Director ....Joe Dean
Sports Information Director ....Herb Vincent

Mississippi State University
Starkville, MS 39762 — Founded: 1878
SID: (601) 325-2703 — Enrollment: 15,714
President ....Dr. Malcolm Portera
Athletic Director ....Larry Templeton
Sports Information Director ....Mike Nemeth

Ole Miss— University of Mississippi
U. of M., MS 38677 — Founded: 1848
SID: (601) 232-7522 — Enrollment: 13,168
Chancellor ....Dr. Robert C. Khayat
Athletic Director ....John Shafer
Sports Information Director ....Langston Rogers

University of South Carolina
Columbia, SC 29208 — Founded: 1801
SID: (803) 777-5204 — Enrollment: 23,489
President ....John Palms
Athletic Director ....Mike McGee
Sports Information Director ....Kerry Tharp

University of Tennessee
Knoxville, TN 37996 — Founded: 1794
SID: (423) 974-1212 — Enrollment: 25,612
President ....J. Wade Gilley
Athletic Director ....Doug Dickey
Women's Athletic Director ....Joan Cronan
Sports Information Director ....Bud Ford

Vanderbilt University
Nashville, TN 37212 — Founded: 1873
SID: (615) 322-4121 — Enrollment: 5,927
Chancellor ....Joe B. Wyatt
Athletic Director ....Todd Turner
Sports Information Director ....Rod Williamson

ॡ   ॡ   ॡ

WESTERN ATHLETIC CONFERENCE
9250 East Costilla Ave., Suite 300
Englewood, CO 80112
(303) 799-9221 — Founded: 1962
Commissioner ....Karl Benson
Directors of Communications .....Dave Chaffin & Lisa Vad
1999-00 members: BASKETBALL & FOOTBALL (8)—
Fresno St., Hawaii, Rice, San Jose St., SMU, TCU, Tulsa,
and UTEP.

Fresno State University
Fresno, CA 93740 — Founded: 1911
SID: (559) 278-2509 — Enrollment: 18,113
President ....Dr. John D. Welty
Athletic Director ....Dr. Al Bohl
Sports Information Director ....Rose Pietrzak

University of Hawaii
Honolulu, HI 96822 — Founded: 1907
SID: (808) 956-7523 — Enrollment: 17,353
President ....Dr. Kenneth Mortimer
Athletic Director ....Hugh Yoshida
Sports Information Director ....Lois Manin

Rice University
Houston, TX 77005 — Founded: 1912
SID: (713) 737-5775 — Enrollment: 2,600
President ....Dr. Malcolm Gillis
Athletic Director ....Bobby May
Sports Information Director ....Bill Cousins

San Jose State University
San Jose, CA 95192 — Founded: 1857
SID: (408) 924-1217 — Enrollment: 30,578
President ....Dr. Robert L. Caret
Athletic Director ....Chuck Bell
Sports Information Director ....Lawrence Fan

SMU— Southern Methodist University
Dallas, TX 75275   Founded: 1911
SID: (214) 768-2883   Enrollment: 10,038
President ....Dr. R. Gerald Turner
Athletic Director ....Jim Copeland
Sports Information Director ....Jon Jackson

TCU— Texas Christian University
Fort Worth, TX 76129   Founded: 1873
SID: (817) 257-7969   Enrollment: 7,240
Chancellor ....Dr. Michael Ferrari
Athletic Director ....Eric Hyman
Sports Information Director ....Rick Covington

University of Tulsa
Tulsa, OK 74104   Founded: 1894
SID: (918) 631-2395   Enrollment: 4,300
President ....Dr. Bob Lawless
Athletic Director ....Judy MacLeod
Sports Information Director ....Don Tomkalski

UTEP— University of Texas at El Paso
El Paso, TX 79902   Founded: 1914
SID: (915) 747-6653   Enrollment: 15,393
President ....Dr. Diana Natalicio
Athletic Director ....Bob Stull
Sports Information Director ....Jeff Darby

🐚   🐚   🐚

MAJOR INDEPENDENTS
Division I-A football independents in 1999.

University of Central Florida
Orlando, FL 32816   Founded: 1963
SID: (407) 823-2729   Enrollment: 32,000
President ....Dr. John C. Hitt
Athletic Director ....Steve Sloan
Sports Information Director ....John Marini

Louisiana Tech University
Ruston, LA 71272   Founded: 1894
SID: (318) 257-3144   Enrollment: 9,664
President ....Dan Reneau
Athletic Director ....Jim Oakes
Sports Information Director ....TBA

Middle Tennessee State University
Murfreesboro, TN 37132   Founded: 1911
SID: (615) 898-2425   Enrollment: 18,432
President ....Dr. James Walker
Athletic Director ....Lee Fowler
Media Relations Director ....Mark Owens

Navy— U.S. Naval Academy
Annapolis, MD 21402   Founded: 1845
SID: (410) 268-6226   Enrollment: 4,000
Superintendent ....Adm. John Ryan
Athletic Director ....Jack Lengyel
Sports Information Director ....Scott Strasemeier

Northeast Louisiana University
Monroe, LA 71209   Founded: 1931
SID: (318) 342-5460   Enrollment: 10,427
President ....Lawson Swearingen, Jr.
Athletic Director ....TBA
Sports Information Director ....Cory Rogers

University of Notre Dame
Notre Dame, IN 46556   Founded: 1842
SID: (219) 631-7516   Enrollment: 7,838
President ....Rev. Edward (Monk) Malloy
Athletic Director ....Michael Wadsworth
Sports Information Director ....John Heisler

University of Southwestern Louisiana
Lafayette, LA 70506   Founded: 1898
SID: (318) 482-6331   Enrollment: 17,000
President ....Ray Authement
Athletic Director ....Nelson Schexnayder
Sports Information Director ....Dan McDonald

🐚   🐚   🐚

OTHER MAJOR DIVISION I CONFERENCES
Conferences that play either Division I basketball or Division I-AA football, or both.

America East
10 High St., Suite 860, Boston, MA 02110
(617) 695-6369   Founded: 1979
Commissioner ....Chris Monasch
Director of Communications ....Matt Bourque
   1999-00 members: BASKETBALL (10)— Boston University, Delaware, Drexel, Hartford, Hofstra, Maine, New Hampshire, Northeastern, Towson and Vermont.

Atlantic 10 Conference
2 Penn Center Plaza
Philadelphia, PA 19102   Founded: 1976
(215) 751-0500   A-10 Football founded: 1997
Executive Director ....Carolyn Femovich
Director of Information ....Sue Hoffman
   1999-00 members: BASKETBALL (12)— Dayton, Duquesne, Fordham, George Washington, La Salle, Massachusetts, Rhode Island, St. Bonaventure, St. Joseph's-PA, Temple, Virginia Tech and Xavier-OH. FOOTBALL (11)— Connecticut, Delaware, James Madison, Maine, Massachusetts, New Hampshire, Northeastern, Rhode Island, Richmond, Villanova and William & Mary.

Big Sky Conference
P.O. Box 1459, Ogden, UT 84401
(801) 392-1978, ext. 2   Founded: 1963
Commissioner ....Douglas Fullerton
Asst. Commissioner, Media Relations ....Eric Capper
   1999-00 members: BASKETBALL & FOOTBALL (9)— Cal St. Northridge, Cal. St. Sacramento, Eastern Washington, Idaho St., Montana, Montana St., Northern Arizona, Portland St. and Weber St.

Big South Conference
6428 Bannington Dr., Ste A
Charlotte, NC 28226
(704) 341-7990   Founded: 1983
Commissioner ....Kyle Kallander
Director of Media Relations ....Drew Dickerson
   1999-00 members: BASKETBALL (8)— Charleston Southern, Coastal Carolina, Elon, High Point, Liberty, NC-Asheville, Radford and Winthrop.

Colonial Athletic Association
8625 Patterson Ave., Richmond, VA 23229
(804) 754-1616   Founded: 1985
Commissioner ....Thomas E. Yeager
Sports Information Director ....Steve Vehorn
   1999-00 members: BASKETBALL (9)— American, East Carolina, George Mason, James Madison, NC-Wilmington, Old Dominion, Richmond, Virginia Commonwealth and William & Mary.

Division I Hockey Conferences
The five Division I hockey conferences are the Eastern Collegiate Athletic Conference (ECAC) in Centerville, Mass., (508) 771-5060; the Central Collegiate Hockey Assn. (CCHA) in Ann Arbor, Mich. (248) 888-0600; Hockey East in Lawrence, Mass., (978) 687-8535; the Metro Atlantic Athletic Assn. in Edison, N.J. (732) 225-0202 and the Western Collegiate Hockey Assn. in Madison, Wisc. (608) 829-0100.

Gateway Football Conference
1000 Union Station, Suite 105
St. Louis, MO 63103
(314) 421-2268   Founded: 1985
Commissioner ....Patty Viverito
Asst. Commissioner ....Mike Kern
   1999 members: FOOTBALL (7)— Illinois St., Indiana St., Northern Iowa, Southern Illinois, SW Missouri St., Western Illinois and Youngstown St..

Ivy League
330 Alexander Street
Princeton, NJ 08544
(609) 258-6426   Founded: 1954
Executive Director ....Jeffrey Orleans
Director of Information ....Chuck Yrigoyen
   1999-00 members: BASKETBALL & FOOTBALL (8)— Brown, Columbia, Cornell, Dartmouth, Harvard, Pennsylvania, Princeton and Yale.

Metro Atlantic Athletic Conference
1090 Amboy Avenue
Edison, NJ 08837
(732) 225-0202   Founded: 1980
Commissioner ....Richard Ensor
Director of Media Relations ....Catherine Hughes
   1999-00 members: BASKETBALL (10)— Canisius, Fairfield, Iona, Loyola-MD, Manhattan, Marist, Niagara, Rider, St. Peter's and Siena. FOOTBALL (9)— Canisius, Duquesne, Fairfield, Georgetown, Iona, La Salle, Marist, St. Peter's and Siena.

Mid-Continent Conference
340 West Butterfield Rd., Ste 3D
Elmhurst, IL 60126
(630) 516-0661   Founded: 1982
Commissioner ....Jon Steinbrecher
Director of Media Relations ....Nancy Smith
   1999-00 members: BASKETBALL (9)— Chicago St., Indiana U-Purdue U Indianapolis, Missouri/K.C., Oakland, Oral Roberts, Southern Utah, Valparaiso, Western Illinois, Youngstown St.

Mid-Eastern Athletic Conference
102 North Elm St. SE Building, Suite 401
Greensboro, NC 27401
(336) 275-9961   Founded: 1970
Commissioner ....Charles S. Harris
Asst. Commissioner, Media Relations ...Bradford Evans, Jr.
   1999-00 members: BASKETBALL (11)— Bethune-Cookman, Coppin St., Delaware St., Florida A&M, Hampton, Howard, MD-Eastern Shore, Morgan St., Norfolk St., North Carolina A&T and South Carolina St.; FOOTBALL (9)— all but Coppin St. and MD-Eastern Shore.

Midwestern Collegiate Conference
201 South Capitol Ave., Suite 500
Indianapolis, IN 46225
(317) 237-5622   Founded: 1979
Commissioner ....John LeCrone
Director of Communications ....Josh Lehman
   1999-00 members: BASKETBALL (8)— Butler, Cleveland St., Detroit Mercy, Illinois-Chicago, Loyola-IL, Wisconsin-Green Bay, Wisconsin-Milwaukee and Wright St.

Missouri Valley Conference
1000 St. Louis Union Station, Suite 105
St. Louis, MO 63103
(314) 421-0339   Founded: 1907
Commissioner ....Doug Elgin
Asst. Commissioner ....Jack Watkins
   1999-00 members: BASKETBALL (10)— Bradley, Creighton, Drake, Evansville, Illinois St., Indiana St., Northern Iowa, Southern Illinois, SW Missouri St., and Wichita St.

Northeast Conference
220 Old New Brunswick Rd.
Piscataway, NJ 08854
(732) 562-0877   Founded: 1981
Commissioner ....John Iamarino
Asst. Commissioner, Public Relations ....Ron Ratner
   1999-00 members: BASKETBALL (12)— Cent. Conn. St., Fairleigh Dickinson, LIU-Brooklyn, Maryland-Baltimore County, Monmouth, Mount St. Mary's, Quinnipiac, Robert Morris, Sacred Heart, St. Francis-NY, St. Francis-PA and Wagner. FOOTBALL (8)—Albany, Cent. Conn. St., Monouth, Robert Morris, Sacred Heart, St. Francis (PA), Stony Brook and Wagner.

Ohio Valley Conference
278 Franklin Road, Suite 103
Brentwood, TN 37027
(615) 371-1698   Founded: 1948
Commissioner ....Dan Beebe
Asst. Commis., Info. and Champs. ....Rob Washburn
   1999-00 members: BASKETBALL (10)— Austin Peay St., Eastern Illinois, Eastern Kentucky, Middle Tennessee St., Morehead St., Murray St., SE Missouri St., Tennessee-Martin, Tennessee St. and Tennessee Tech; FOOTBALL (8)— Eastern Illinois, Eastern Kentucky, Murray St., SE Missouri St., Tennessee-Martin, Tennessee St., Tennessee Tech and Western Kentucky

Patriot League
3897 Adler Place, Building C, Suite 310
Bethlehem, PA 18017
(610) 691-2414   Founded: 1984
Executive Director ....Carolyn Femovich
Director of Information ....Sue Hofmann
   1999-00 members: BASKETBALL (7)— Army, Bucknell, Colgate, Holy Cross, Lafayette, Lehigh and Navy; FOOTBALL (7)— Bucknell, Colgate, Fordham, Holy Cross, Lafayette, Lehigh and Towson.

Pioneer Football League
1000 St. Louis Union Station, Suite 105
St. Louis, MO 63103
(314) 421-2268   Founded: 1993
Commissioner ....Patty Viverito
Media Relations ....Cindy Kern
   1999 members: FOOTBALL (5): Butler, Dayton, Drake, San Diego and Valparaiso.

Southern Conference
1 West Pack Square, Suite 1508
Asheville, NC 28801
(828) 255-7872   Founded: 1921
Commissioner ....Alfred B. White
Asst. Commissioner, Public Affairs ....TBA
   1999-00 members: BASKETBALL (12)— Appalachian St., The Citadel, College of Charleston, Davidson, East Tennessee St., Furman, Georgia Southern, UNC-Greensboro, Tennessee-Chattanooga, VMI, Western Carolina and Wofford; FOOTBALL (9)—all except College of Charleston, Davidson and UNC-Greensboro.

Southland Conference
8150 North Central Expressway, Suite 930
Dallas, TX 75206
(214) 750-7522   Founded: 1963
Commissioner ....Greg Sankey
Director of Media Relations ....Bruce Ludlow
   1999-00 members: BASKETBALL (11)— Lamar, McNeese St., Nicholls St., NE Louisiana, Northwestern St., Sam Houston St., SE Louisiana, Southwest Texas St., Stephen F. Austin St., Texas-Arlington and Texas-San Antonio; FOOTBALL (8)— Jacksonville St., McNeese St., Nicholls St., Northwestern St., Sam Houston St., Southwest Texas St., Stephen F. Austin St. and Troy St.

Southwestern Athletic Conference
1500 Sugar Bowl Drive, Superdome
New Orleans, LA 70112
(504) 523-7574 Founded: 1920
Commissioner . . . . .Rudy Washington
Director of Publicity . . . . .Lonza Hardy Jr.
   1999-00 members: BASKETBALL & FOOTBALL (10)—
Alabama A&M, Alabama St., Alcorn St., Arkansas-Pine
Bluff, Grambling St., Jackson St., Mississippi Valley St.,
Prairie View A&M, Southern-Baton Rouge and Texas South-
ern.

Sun Belt Conference
One Galleria Boulevard, Suite 2115
Metairie, LA 70001
(504) 834-6600 Founded: 1976
Commissioner . . . . .Wright Waters
Director of Media Services . . . . .Dayna Wells
   1999-00 members: BASKETBALL (9)— Arkansas-Little
Rock, Arkansas St., Denver, Florida International, Louisiana
Tech, New Orleans, South Alabama, SW Louisiana and
Western Kentucky.

Trans America Athletic Conference
3370 Vineville Ave., Suite 108-B,
Macon, GA 31204
(912) 474-3394 Founded: 1978
Commissioner . . . . .Bill Bibb
Director of Information . . . . .Tom Snyder
   1999-00 members: BASKETBALL (10)— Campbell,
Central Florida, Florida Atlantic, Georgia St., Jacksonville,
Jacksonville St., Mercer, Samford, Stetson and Troy St.

West Coast Conference
1200 Bayhill Dr.
San Bruno, CA 94066
(650) 873-8622 Founded: 1952
Commissioner . . . . .Michael Gilleran
Director of Information . . . . .Don Ott
   1999-00 members: BASKETBALL (8)— Gonzaga,
Loyola Marymount, Pepperdine, Portland, St. Mary's, San
Diego, San Francisco and Santa Clara.

PRO FOOTBALL

National Football League

League Office
280 Park Ave.
New York, NY 10017
(212) 450-2000
Commissioner . . . . .Paul Tagliabue
President . . . . .Neil Austrian
Exec. V.P. & League Counsel . . . . .Jeff Pash
AFC Info. Coordinator . . . . .Dan Masonson
NFC Info. Coordinator . . . . .Chris McCloskey

NFL Management Council
280 Park Ave.
New York, NY 10017
(212) 450-2000
Chairman . . . . .Harold Henderson
V.P. & General Counsel . . . . .Dennis Curran

NFL Players Association
2021 L Street NW, Suite 600
Washington, DC 20036
(202) 463-2200
Executive Director . . . . .Gene Upshaw
Asst. Exec. Director . . . . .Doug Allen
General Counsel . . . . .Richard Berthelsen
Director of Public Relations . . . . .Frank Woschitz

AFC

Baltimore Ravens
11001 Owings Mills Blvd.
Owings Mills, MD 21117
(410) 654-6200
Owner/CEO . . . . .Arthur B. Modell
President/COO . . . . .David Modell
Secretary/General Counsel . . . . .Jim Bailey
V.P., Communications .Kevin Byrne

Buffalo Bills
One Bills Drive, Orchard Park, NY 14127
(716) 648-1800
Owner-President . . . . .Ralph C. Wilson Jr.
Exec. V.P./General Manager . . . . .John Butler
V.P. of Communications . . . . .Scott Berchtold

Cincinnati Bengals
One Bengals Drive, Cincinnati, OH 45204
(513) 621-3550
Chairman . . . . .Austin E. Knowlton
President . . . . .Mike Brown
Public Relations Director . . . . .Jack Brennan

Cleveland Browns
76 Lou Groza Blvd., Berea, OH 44017
(440) 891-5000
Owner/Chairman . . . . .Al Lerner
President/CEO . . . . .Carmen Policy
V.P., Director of Football Ops. . . . . .Dwight Clark
V.P., Director of Communications . . . . .Alex Martins

Denver Broncos
13655 Broncos Parkway, Englewood, CO 80112
(303) 649-9000
Owner-President-CEO . . . . .Pat Bowlen
General Manager . . . . .Neal Dahlen
Director of Media Relations . . . . .Jim Saccomano

Indianapolis Colts
7001 W 56th St., Indianapolis, IN 46254
(317) 297-2658
Owner-CEO . . . . .Jim Irsay
President . . . . .Bill Polian
Dir. of Football Operations . . . . .Dom Anile
V.P. of Public Relations . . . . .Craig Kelley

Jacksonville Jaguars
One ALLTEL Stadium Place
Jacksonville, FL 32202
(904) 633-6000
Chairman-CEO-President . . . . .Wayne Weaver
Sr. V.P., Football Operations . . . . .Michael Huyghue
Exec. Director of Communications . . . . .Dan Edwards

Kansas City Chiefs
One Arrowhead Drive, Kansas City, MO 64129
(816) 920-9300
Owner-Founder . . . . .Lamar Hunt
Chairman . . . . .Jack Steadman
President-CEO-General Manager . . . . .Carl Peterson
Director of Public Relations . . . . .Bob Moore

Miami Dolphins
7500 SW 30th St., Davie, FL 33314
(954) 452-7000
Owner-Chairman . . . . .H. Wayne Huizenga
President & COO . . . . .Eddie Jones
GM & Head Coach . . . . .Jimmy Johnson
V.P., Media Relations . . . . .Harvey Greene

New England Patriots
Foxboro Stadium, 60 Washington St., Foxboro, MA 02035
(508) 543-8200
Owner-President-CEO & General Manager . . . . . .Bob Kraft
Dir. of Player Personnel . . . . .Bobby Grier
Director of Media Relations . . . . .Stacey James

New York Jets
1000 Fulton Ave.
Hempstead, NY 11550
(516) 560-8100
Owner-Chairman . . . . .Leon Hess Estate
President . . . . .Steve Gutman
Chief Football Ops. Officer & Head Coach . . . .Bill Parcells
Director of Public Relations . . . . .Frank Ramos

Oakland Raiders
1220 Harbor Bay Parkway
Alameda, CA 94502
(510) 864-5000
Managing General Partner . . . . .Al Davis
Executive Assistant . . . . .Al LoCasale
Director of Public Relations . . . . .Mike Taylor

Pittsburgh Steelers
300 Stadium Circle
Pittsburgh, PA 15212
(412) 323-0300
Owner-President . . . . .Dan Rooney
V.P.s . . . . John McGinley, Art Rooney Jr. & Art Rooney II
Communications Coordinator . . . . .Ron Wahl

San Diego Chargers
4020 Murphy Canyon Rd.
San Diego, CA 92123
(619) 874-4500
Owner-Chairman . . . . .Alex Spanos
President-Vice Chairman . . . . .Dean Spanos
General Manager . . . . .Bobby Beathard
Director of Public Relations . . . . .Bill Johnston

Seattle Seahawks
11220 NE 53rd Street, Kirkland, WA 98033
(425) 827-9777
Owner . . . . .Paul Allen
President . . . . .Bob Whitsitt
V.P./GM/Head Coach . . . . .Mike Holmgren
Public Relations Director . . . . .Dave Pearson

Tennessee Titans
460 Great Circle Road, Nashville, TN 37228
(615) 565-4000
Owner-President .K.S. (Bud) Adams Jr.
Exec. V.P./General Manager . . . . .Floyd Reese
Director of Media Services . . . . .Tony Wyllie

NFC

Arizona Cardinals
P.O. Box 888, Phoenix, AZ 85001
(602) 379-0101
Owner-President . . . . .Bill Bidwill
Vice President . . . . .Bill Bidwill, Jr.
General Manager . . . . .Bob Ferguson
Public Relations Director . . . . .Paul Jensen

Atlanta Falcons
One Falcon Place
Suwanee, GA 30024
(770) 945-1111
Owner-President . . . . .Taylor Smith
Exec. V.P. Football Ops./Head Coach . . . . .Dan Reeves
V.P., Football Ops. . . . . .Ron Hill
Director of Public Relations . . . . .Aaron Salkin

Carolina Panthers
800 South Mint St.
Charlotte, NC 28202-1502
(704) 358-7000
Founder-Owner . . . . .Jerry Richardson
President . . . . .Mark Richardson
Dir. of Player Personnel . . . . .Jack Bushofsky
Director of Communications . . . . .Charlie Dayton

Chicago Bears
1000 Football Drive, Lake Forest, IL 60045
(847) 295-6600
Owner-Chairman Emeritus . . . . .Edward McCaskey
Chairman of the Board . . . . .Michael McCaskey
President-CEO . . . . .Ted Phillips
Director of Public Relations . . . . .Bryan Harlan

Dallas Cowboys
Cowboys Center
One Cowboys Parkway, Irving, TX 75063
(972) 556-9900
Owner-President-GM . . . . .Jerry Jones
V.P./Dir. of Player Personnel . . . . .Stephen Jones
Public Relations Director . . . . .Rich Dalrymple

Detroit Lions
Pontiac Silverdome
1200 Featherstone Rd., Pontiac, MI 48342
(248) 335-4131
Owner-President . . . . .William Clay Ford
Executive V.P. & COO .Chuck Schmidt
V.P. of Player Personnel . . . . .Ron Hughes
Director of Media Relations . . . . .Mike Murray

Green Bay Packers
1265 Lombardi Ave., P.O. Box 10628
Green Bay, WI 54307
(920) 496-5700
President-CEO . . . . .Bob Harlan
Exec. V.P./ General Manager . . . . .Ron Wolf
Exec. Dir. of Public Relations . . . . .Lee Remmel

Minnesota Vikings
9520 Viking Drive, Eden Prairie, MN 55344
(612) 828-6500
Owner . . . . .Red McCombs
President . . . . .Gary Woods
Exec. V.P./General Manager . . . . .Tim Connolly
Director of Public Relations . . . . .Bob Hagan

New Orleans Saints
5800 Airline Drive, Metairie, LA 70003
(504) 733-0255
Owner . . . . .Tom Benson
President & General Manager . . . . .Bill Kuharich
V.P. of Football Ops./Asst. GM . . . . .Charles Bailey
Director of Media/Public Relations . . . . .Greg Bensel

New York Giants
Giants Stadium
East Rutherford, NJ 07073
(201) 935-8111
President/co-CEO . . . . .Wellington Mara
Chairman/co-CEO . . . . .Preston Robert Tisch
V.P. & General Manager . . . . .Ernie Accorsi
V.P. of Communications . . . . .Pat Hanlon

Philadelphia Eagles
Veterans Stadium
3501 S. Broad St.
Philadelphia, PA 19148
(215) 463-2500
Owner . . . . .Jeff Lurie
Executive V.P. & CEO . . . . .Joe Banner
Director of Football Operations . . . . .Tom Modrak
Director of Public Relations . . . . .Ron Howard

St. Louis Rams
One Rams Way, St. Louis, MO 63045
(314) 982-7267
Owner-Chairman . . . . .Georgia Frontiere
Owner-Vice Chairman . . . . .Stan Kroenke
President . . . . .John Shaw
Pres., Football Ops./Head Coach . . . . .Dick Vermeil
Director of Public Relations . . . . .Rick Smith

San Francisco 49ers
4949 Centennial Blvd.
Santa Clara, CA 95054
(408) 562-4949
Owners . .Edward J. DeBartolo Corp., Edward DeBartolo Jr.
and Denise DeBartolo-York
V.P./General Manager . . . . .Bill Walsh
Director of Public Relations . . . . .Kirk Reynolds

Tampa Bay Buccaneers
One Buccaneer Place, Tampa, FL 33607
(813) 870-2700
Owner-President . . . . .Malcolm Glazer
General Manager . . . . .Rich McKay
Director of Communications . . . . .Reggie Roberts

Washington Redskins
Redskin Park
P.O. Box 17247, Washington D.C. 20041
(703) 478-8900
Owner . . . . .Daniel M. Snyder
General Manager . . . . .Charley Casserly
Director of Public Relations . . . . .Mike McCall

Canadian Football League

League Office
CFL Building, 110 Eglinton Avenue West, 5th Floor
Toronto, Ontario M4R 1A3
(416) 322-9650
Chairman/Acting Commissioner . . . . .John Tory
President/COO . . . . Jeff Giles
V.P., Football Operations . . . . .Ed Chalupka
Director of Communications . . . . .Jim Neish

CFL Players Association
467 Speers Rd., Unit 5
Oakville, Ontario L6K 3S4
(905) 844-7852
President . . . . .Dan Ferrone
Legal Counsel . . . . .Ed Molstad

British Columbia Lions
10605 135th St.
Surrey, B.C. V3T 4C8
(604) 930-5466
Owner . . . . .David Braylay
President & CEO . . . . .Glen Ringdal
Dir. of Media/Public Relations . . . . .Eric Stansfield

Calgary Stampeders
McMahon Stadium
1817 Crowchild Trail, NW
Calgary, Alberta T2M 4R6
(403) 289-0205
Owner . . . . .Sig Gutsche
President . . . . .Stan Schwartz
General Manager & Head Coach . . . . .Wally Buono
V.P., Marketing & Communications . . . . .Ron Rooke

Edmonton Eskimos
9023 111th Ave.
Edmonton, Alberta T5B 0C3
(780) 448-1525
Owner . . . . .Community-owned
President . . . . .Hugh Campbell
General Manager . . . . .Tom Higgins

Hamilton Tiger-Cats
75 Balsam Ave. N
Hamilton, Ontario L8L 8C1
(905) 547-2418
Chairman/Owner . . . . .David M. Macdonald
Vice Chairman/Owner . . . . .George Grant
GM/Dir. of Business Ops. . . . . .Neil Lumsden
Communications Director . . . . .Norm Miller

Montreal Alouettes
1255 University St., Suite 120
Montreal, Quebec H3B 3A9
(514) 252-4600
Owner . . . . .Robert Wetenhall
President & CEO . . . . .Larry Smith
Dir. of Football Ops/GM . . . . .Jim Popp
Dir. of Communications . . . . .Louis-Philippe Doraif

Saskatchewan Roughriders
2940 — 10th Avenue, P.O. Box 1277
Regina, Saskatchewan S4P 3B8
(306) 569-2323
Owner . . . . .Community-owned
President . . . . .Bob Ellard
CEO & General Manager . . . . .Alan Ford
Media Coordinator . . . . .Tony Playter

Toronto Argonauts
1 Blue Jays Way, Toronto, Ontario M5V 1J3
(416) 341-5151
Owners . . . . .Labatt Brewing Co.
President . . . . .Bob Nicholson
General Manager . . . . .Eric Tillman
Director of Public Relations . . . . .Greg Mandziuk

Winnipeg Blue Bombers
1465 Maroons Road, Winnipeg, Manitoba R3G 0L6
(204) 784-2583
Owner . . . . .Community-owned
President . . . . .Robert Miles
General Manager . . . . .Ken Bishop
Dir., Media/Public Relations . . . . .J.D. Boyd

NFL Europe

President . . . . .Oliver Luck
Director of Public Relations . . . . .David Tossell
Public Relations Assistant . . . . .Michael Signora

League Offices

Frankfurt
Westerbach Str. 47
Frankfurt, Geramny 60489
011-49-69-978-2790

London
26A Albemarle St.
London, England W1X 3FA
011-44-171-355-1955

New York
280 Park Avenue, New York, NY 10017
(212) 450-2000
   Member teams (6): Amsterdam Admirals, Barcelona
Dragons, Berlin Thunder, Frankfurt Galaxy, Rhein Fire (Dusseldorf), Scottish Claymores (Edinburgh).

Arena Football League
75 E Wacker, Suite 400
Chicago, IL 60601
(312) 332-5510
Commissioner . . . . .C. David Baker
Deputy Commissioner . . . . .Ronald J. Kurpiers II
V.P., Football Operations . . . . .Jerry Trice
V.P., Media Services . . . . .David Cooper
   Member teams (16): American Conference— Arizona
Rattlers, Grand Rapids Rampage, Houston Thunderbears,
Iowa Barnstormers, Los Angeles Avengers, Milwaukee Mus-
tangs, Portland (OR) Forest Dragons and San Jose Sabre-
cats. National Conference— Albany (NY) Firebirds, Buffalo
Destroyers, Florida Bobcats, Nashville Kats, New Jersey
Red Dogs, New England Sea Wolves, Orlando Predators
and Tampa Bay Storm.

GOLF

LPGA Tour
(Ladies' Professional Golf Association)
100 International Golf Drive
Daytona Beach, FL 32124
(904) 274-6200
Commissioner . . . . .Ty Votaw
Deputy Commissioner . . . . .Jim Webb
Director of Communications . . . . .Leslie King

PGA of America
100 Avenue of the Champions
Palm Beach Gardens, FL 33410
(561) 624-8400
President . . . . .Will Mann
CEO . . . . .Jim Awtrey
Director of Communications . . . . .Terry McSweeney

PGA European Tour
Wentworth Drive, Virginia Water
Surrey, England GU25 4LX
TEL: 011-44-1344-842881
Executive Director . . . . .Ken Schofield
Director of Communications . . . . .Mitchell Platts

PGA Tour
112 PGA Tour Blvd.
Ponte Vedra, FL 32082
(904) 285-3700
Commissioner . . . . .Tim Finchem
Director of Information . . . . .Dave Lancer

Royal & Ancient Golf Club of St. Andrews
St. Andrews, Fife
Scotland KY16 9JD
TEL: 011-44-1334-472112
Secretary . . . . .Peter Dawson
Press Officer . . . . .Stewart McDougall

USGA
(United States Golf Association)
P.O. Box 708, Liberty Corner Road
Far Hills, NJ 07931
(908) 234-2300
President . . . . .Buzz Taylor
Executive Director . . . . .David Fay
Sr. Director of Communications . . . . .Marty Parkes

PRO HOCKEY

NHL

National Hockey League

Commissioner . . . . .Gary Bettman
Pres., NHL Enterprises . . . . .Richie Woodworth
Senior V.P., Dir. of Hockey Ops. . . . . .Colin Campbell
V.P., Media Relations . . . . .Frank Brown

League Offices

Montreal
1800 McGill College Ave., Suite 2600
Montreal, Quebec H3A 3J6
(514) 288-9220

New York
1251 Sixth Ave., 47th Floor, New York, NY 10020
(212) 789-2000

Toronto
1 International Blvd.
Rexdale, Ontario M9W 6L9
(416) 981-2777

NHL Players' Association
777 Bay St., Suite 2400, P.O. Box 121
Toronto, Ontario M5G 2C8
(416) 408-4040
Executive Director . . . . .Bob Goodenow
Associate Counsel . . . . .Ian Pulver,
Jeff Citron, Chris DiFrancesco and Rick Olczyk
Media Relations Mgr. . . . . .Devin Smith

Anaheim, Mighty Ducks of
Arrowhead Pond of Anaheim
Anaheim, CA 92806
(714) 940-2900
Owner . . . . .Walt Disney Co.
Anaheim Sports, Inc. Pres. . . . . .Tony Tavares
President/General Manager . . . . .Pierre Gauthier
Dir., Communications and Team Services . . . . . .Rob Scichili

Atlanta Thrashers
1 CNN Center
Box 105583, Atlanta, GA 30348
(404) 584-7825
Owner . . . . .Turner Sports
President/Governor . . . . .Dr. Harvey W Schiller
Executive V.P. . . . . .Dave Maggard
V.P./General Manager . . . . .Don Waddell
Public Relations Director .Tom Hughes

Boston Bruins
1 FleetCenter, Suite 250, Boston, MA 02114
(617) 624-1900
Owner . . . . .Jeremy Jacobs
President & General Manager . . . . .Harry Sinden
Director of Media Relations . . . . .Heidi Holland

Buffalo Sabres
Marine Midland Arena, One Seymour H. Knox III Plaza,
Buffalo, NY 14203-3096
(716) 855-4100
CEO . . . . .Timothy Rigas
General Manager . . . . .Darcy Regier
V.P. of Communications . . . . .Michael Gilbert

Calgary Flames
Canadian Airlines Saddledome, P.O. Box 1540 Station M
Calgary, Alberta T2P 3B9
(403) 777-2177
Owners . . . . . . .Harley Hotchkiss, Grant A. Bartlett, Murray
Edwards, Ronald V. Joyce, Alvin G. Libin, Allan P. Markin,
J.R. McCaig, Byron and Daryl Seamen
President & CEO . . . . .Ron Bremner
Executive V.P./General Manager . . . . .Al Coates
Director of Communications . . . . .Peter Hanlon

Carolina Hurricanes
The Raleigh Entertainment Sports Arena
1400 Edward Mill Rd., Raleigh, NC 27607
(919) 467-7825
Owner-CEO . . . . .Peter Karmanos Jr.
General Partner . . . . .Thomas Thewes
President & General Manager . . . . .Jim Rutherford
Dir., Media Relations/Team Services . . . . .Chris Brown

Chicago Blackhawks
United Center, 1901 West Madison St.
Chicago, IL 60612
(312) 455-7000
Owner-President . . . . .William Wirtz
General Manager . . . . .Bob Murray
Executive Director of P.R. . . . . .Jim DeMaria

Colorado Avalanche
1635 Clay St., Denver, CO 80204
(303) 405-1100
Owner . . . . .Donald Sturm
President/GM/Alt. Governor . . . . .Pierre Lacroix
Dir., Media Relations/Team Services . . . . . .Jean Martineau

Dallas Stars
211 Cowboys Parkway, Irving, TX 75063
(972) 868-2890
Owner . . . . .Thomas O. Hicks
President . . . . Jim Lites
General Manager . . . . .Bob Gainey
Director of Public Relations . . . . .Larry Kelly

Detroit Red Wings
Joe Louis Arena, 600 Civic Center Drive
Detroit, MI 48226
(313) 396-7544
Owner/President . . . . .Mike Ilitch
Owner/Secretary-Treasurer . . . . .Marian Ilitch
General Manager . . . . .Ken Holland
Director of Media Relations . . . . .John Hahn

Edmonton Oilers
11230 110th St., Edmonton, Alberta, T5G 3H7
(614) 414-4000
Owners . . . . .Edmonton Investors Group, Ltd.
President & General Manager . . . . .Glen Sather
Exec. V.P. & Assistant GM . . . . .Bruce MacGregor
Director of Public Relations . . . . .Bill Tuele

Florida Panthers
National Car Rental Center
1 Panther Parkway, Sunrise, FL 33323
(954) 835-7000
Owner . . . . .H. Wayne Huizenga
President . . . . .Bill Torrey
General Manager . . . . .Bryan Murray
Dir. of Public & Media Relations . . . . .Mike Hanson

Los Angeles Kings
Staples Center
1111 S. Figueroa, Los Angeles, CA 90017
(310) 419-3160
Majority Owners . . . . .Philip Anschutz and Ed Roski
President . . . . .Tim Leiweke
General Manager . . . . .Dave Taylor
Director of Media Relations . . . . .Mike Altieri

Montreal Canadiens
Molson Centre, 1260 Gauchetière St. West
Montreal, Quebec H3B 5E8
(514) 932-2582
Owner . . . . .Molson Companies, Ltd.
President . . . . .Pierre Boivin
General Manager . . . . .Rejean Houle
Director of Communications . . . . .Don Beauchamp

Nashville Predators
501 Broadway, Nashville, TN 57203
(615) 770-2300
Chairman and Maj. Owner . . . . .Craig Leipold
President . . . . .Jack Diller
General Manager . . . . .David Poile
Mgr., Team Services/Media Relations . . . . .Frank Buonomo

New Jersey Devils
Continental Airlines Arena, P.O. Box 504
East Rutherford, NJ 07073
(201) 935-6050
Chairman . . . . .John McMullen
President & GM . . . . .Lou Lamoriello
Director of Public Relations . . . . .Kevin Dessart

New York Islanders
Nassau Veterans' Memorial Coliseum, Uniondale, NY 11553
(516) 794-4100
Owner .Stephen Gluckstern, Howard P. Milstein and Edward
Milstein
General Manager . . . . .Mike Milbury
Director of Media Relations . . . . .Chris Botta

New York Rangers
2 Penn Plaza, 14th Floor
New York, NY 10121
(212) 465-6486
Owner . . . . .Cablevision Systems Inc.
President (MSG) . . . . .Dave Checketts
President & General Manager . . . . .Neil Smith
Director of Public Relations . . . . .John Rosasco

Ottawa Senators
1000 Palladium Dr.
Kanata, Ontario, K2V 1A4
(613) 599-0250
Chairman & Gov. . . . . .Rod Bryden
President & CEO . . . . .Roy Mlakar
General Manager .Marshall Johnston
Director of Media Relations . . . . .Morgan Quarry

Philadelphia Flyers
3601 S. Broad St., Philadelphia, PA 19148
(215) 465-4500
Chairman . . . . .Ed Snider
President & General Manager . . . . .Bob Clarke
Director of Media Relations . . . . .Zack Hill

Phoenix Coyotes
Cellular One Ice Den, 9375 E. Bell Rd.
Scottsdale, AZ 85260
(602) 473-5600
Owner . . . . .Richard Burke
President . . . . .Shawn Hunter
General Manager . . . . .Bobby Smith
Director of Media Relations . . . . .Richard Nairn

Pittsburgh Penguins
Civic Arena, Pittsburgh, PA 15219
(412) 642-1800
Owner/Chairman . . . . .Mario Lemieux
President & General Manager . . . . .Craig Patrick
V.P., Communications . . . . .Thomas McMillan

St. Louis Blues
Kiel Center, 1401 Clark Ave.
St. Louis, MO 63103
(314) 622-2500
Owners . . . . .Bill and Nancy Laurie
General Manager . . . . .Larry Pleau
Director of Public Relations . . . . .Jeff Trammel

San Jose Sharks
525 West Santa Clara St., San Jose, CA 95113
(408) 287-7070
Owner-Chairman . . . . .George Gund III
Co-Owner . . . . .Gordon Gund
President-CEO . . . . .Greg Jamison
Exec. V.P.& GM . . . . .Dean Lombardi
Director of Media Relations . . . . .Ken Arnold

Tampa Bay Lightning
401 Channelside Drive, Tampa, FL 33602
(813) 301-6500
Owner . . . . .Palace Sports & Ent.
CEO & Governor . . . . .Tom Wilson
President . . . . .Ron Campbell
V.P./General Manager . . . . .Rick Dudley
Director of Public Relations . . . . .Jay Preble

Toronto Maple Leafs
Air Canada Center
40 Bay Street, Toronto, Ontario M5J 2X2
(416) 815-5500
Chairman-CEO . . . . .Steve Stavro
President . . . . .Ken Dryden
Coach/G.M. . . . . .Pat Quinn
Manager of Media Relations . . . . .Pat Park

Vancouver Canucks
General Motors Place, 800 Griffiths Way
Vancouver, B.C. V6B 6G1
(604) 899-4600
Owners ....Bill and Nancy Laurie
CEO ....Stephen Bellringer
President & General Manager ....Brian Burke
Manager of Media Relations ....Chris Brumwell

Washington Capitals
MCI Center, 601 F St. NW
Washington, D.C. 20004
(202) 628-3200
Owners ....Ted Leonsis, Jon Ledecky, Dick Patrick
President ....Dick Patrick
V.P./General Manager ....George McPhee
V.P. of Communications ....Matt Williams

AHL

American Hockey League
One Monarch Place, Springfield, MA 01144
(413) 781-2030
President ....David Andrews
Director of Hockey Ops. ....Jim Mill
Manager, Media Relations ....Jamie Leaver

IHL

International Hockey League
1395 E. Twelve Mile Rd., Madison Heights, MI 48701
(248) 546-3230
President/CEO ....Doug Moss
VP, Communications ....Jim Anderson

IIHF

International Ice Hockey Federation
Parkring 11
CH-8002 Zurich, Switzerland
TEL: 011-411-289-8600
President ....Rene Fasel
General Secretary ....Jan-Ake Edvinsson
PR/Marketing Mgr. ....Kimmo Leinonen

HORSE RACING

Breeders' Cup Limited
230 Lexington Green Circle, Suite 310
Lexington, KY 40503
(606) 223-5444
President ...........................D.G. Van Clief, Jr.
Communications Manager ....TBA

National Museum of Racing and Hall of Fame
191 Union Ave., Saratoga Springs, NY 12866
(518) 584-0400
Executive Director ....Peter Hammell
Assistant Director ....Catherine Maguire
Communications Officer ....Richard Hamilton

The Jockeys' Guild
P.O. Box 250, Lexington, KY 40588-0250
(606) 259-3211
President ....Gary Stevens
National Manager ....John Giovanni
Communications ....John Ball

NTRA
(National Thoroughbred Racing Association)
2343 Alexandria Drive, Ste. 210, Lexington, KY 40504
(606) 223-0658
CEO-Commissioner ....Tim Smith
Executive Dir. ....Nick Nicholson
VP. of Communications ....Chip Tuttle

TRA
(Thoroughbred Racing Associations of N. America, Inc.)
420 Fair Hill Drive, Suite 1, Elkton, MD 21921
(410) 392-9200
President ....Stella Thayer
Executive V.P ....Chris Scherf

NTRA Communications
(National Thoroughbred Racing Association Communications)
444 Madison Ave., Suite 503
New York, NY 10022
(212) 907-9280
V.P. of Communications ....Chip Tuttle
Director of Media Relations ....Eric Wing

USTA
(United States Trotting Association)
750 Michigan Ave., Columbus, OH 43215
(614) 224-2291
President ....Corwin Nixon
Executive V.P. ....Fred Noe
Director of Public Relations ....John Pawlak

MEDIA

PERIODICALS

ESPN, The Magazine
19 E 34th St., 7th Floor, New York, NY 10016
(212) 515-1000
Editor in Chief ....John Papanek
Executive Editors ....Gary Hoenig, Steve Wulf
V.P., Publisher ....Michael Rooney
Public Relations Manager ....Kim Shapiro

Sports Illustrated
Time & Life Bldg., Rockefeller Center, New York, NY 10020
(212) 522-1212
President/CEO ....Don Logan
Managing Editor ....William Colson
Executive Editors .....B. Peter Carry, Rob Fleder and David Bauer

The Sporting News
10176 Corporate Square Dr., Suite 200
St. Louis, MO 63132
(314) 997-7111
Senior V.P./Editorial Director ....John D. Rawlings
President ....James H. Nuckols

The Sports Business Daily
120 West Morehead St., Ste. 220
Charlotte, NC 28202
(704) 973-1500
President ....Sal Schiliro
Editor ....Abe Madkour
Media Relations Mgr. ....Bill Magrath

USA Today
1000 Wilson Blvd., Arlington, VA 22229
(703) 276-3400
Owner ....Gannett Co.
President-Publisher ....Tom Curley
Managing Editor/Sports ....Monte Lorell

WIRE SERVICES

Associated Press
50 Rockefeller Plaza, New York, NY 10020
(212) 621-1630
Sports Editor ....Terry Taylor
Deputy Sports Editor ....Brian Friedman

United Press International
1510 H Street, Washington, DC 20005
(202) 898-8000
Sports Editor ....Ron Colbert

The Sports Network
95 James Way, Suite 107 & 109
Southampton, PA 18966
(215) 942-7890
President ....Mickey Charles
Director of Operations ....Phil Sokol
Managing Editor ....Jim Gillis

Sportsticker
600 Plaza Two, Harborside Financial Ctr., Jersey City, NJ 07311
(201) 309-1200
V.P./General Manager ....Rick Alessandri
Exec. Director, News ....Jim Morganthaler

TV NETWORKS

ABC Sports
47 West 66th St., 13th Floor
New York, NY 10023
(212) 456-4867
President ....Howard Katz
Senior V.P., Production ....John Filippelli
Director of Media Relations ....Mark Mandel

CBC Sports
P.O. Box 500, Station A 5H 100
Toronto, Ontario M5W 1E6
(416) 205-6523
Head of Sports ....Alan Clark
Sr. Executive Producer ....Joel Darling
Publicist ....Susan Procter

CBS Sports
51 West 52nd St., 25th Floor
New York, NY 10019
(212) 975-5230
President ....Sean McManus
Executive Producer ....Terry Ewert
Sr. V.P., Programming/Bus. Affairs ....Tony Petitti
V.P., Communications ....Leslie Ann Wade

ESPN
ESPN Plaza, Bristol, CT 06010
(860) 585-2000
President-CEO ....Steve Bornstein
Sr. V.P., Programming ....John Wildhack
Sr. V.P. & Executive Editor ....John Walsh
Asst. Managing Editor/News Dir. ....Vince Doria
Director of Communications ....Mike Soltys

ESPN Classic
ESPN Plaza, Bristol, CT 06010
(860) 585–2000
Executive Producer ....Vince Doria
Communications Coordinator ....Amy Swanson

FOX Sports
10201 W. Pico Blvd., Los Angeles, CA 90035
(310) 369-1000
President ....David Hill
Exec. Producer ....Ed Goren
V.P., Media Relations (NYC) ....Vince Wladika

The Golf Channel
7580 Commerce Center Drive, Orlando, FL 32819
(407) 345-4653
President-CEO ....Joe Gibbs
V.P., Production ....Tony Tortorici
Director of Public Relations ....Debra Sweeney

HBO Sports
1100 Ave. of the Americas, New York, NY 10036
(212) 512-1987
President-CEO ....Seth Abraham
V.P., Executive Producer ....Ross Greenburg
Sr. V.P., Programming ....Lou DiBella
Director of Publicity ....Ray Stallone

MTV Sports
1633 Broadway, 32nd Floor, New York, NY 10019
(212) 654-6177
Executive Prorducer ....Patrick Byrns
Supervising Producer ....Greg Johnston
Publicity Contact ....Greg Baldwin

NBC Sports
30 Rockefeller Plaza, New York, NY 10112
(212) 664-2160
Chairman ....Dick Ebersol
President ....Ken Schanzer
Executive Producer ....Tommy Roy
Director of Public Relations ....Ed Markey

Rainbow Sports
111 Stewart Ave.
Bethpage, NY 11714
(516) 396-3000
President ....Greg Moyer
Vice President.of Marketing ....Dan Ronayne

TSN-The Sports Network
2225 Shepherd Ave. East, Suite 100
Willowdale, Ontario, M2J-5C2
(416) 494-1212
Chairman & CEO ....Gordon Craig
President ....Rick Brace
Communications Manager ....David Rosenbloom

Turner Sports
One CNN Center
13th Floor, Atlanta, GA 30303
(404) 827-1735
President ....Dr. Harvey Schiller
Sr. V.P., Programming ....Kevin O'Malley
V.P., Production ....Mike Pearl
V.P.,Public Relations ....Greg Hughes

Univision (Spanish)
9405 NW 41st St., Miami, FL 33178
(305) 477-3412
V.P. of Ops./Sports ....Tony Oquendo
Publicity Coordinator ....Rosalyn Sariol

USA Network
1230 Ave. of the Americas, New York, NY 10020
(212) 408-9100
Sr. V.P., Production in Sports ....Gordon Beck
V.P., Sports Programming ....Kevin Landy
Sports Publicity ....David Schwarz

OLYMPICS

IOC
(International Olympic Committee)
Chateau de Vidy
CH-1007 Lausanne, Switzerland
TEL: 011-41-21-621-6111
President ....Juan Antonio Samaranch
Director General ....Francois Carrard
Secretary General ....Francoise Zweifel
Dir. of International Cooperation ....Fekrou Kidane
Director of Communications/New Media ..Franklin Servan-Schreiber

2000 SUMMER GAMES

Sydney Olympic Organizing Committee
GPO Box 2000, Sydney, Australia NSW 2001
TEL: 011-61-29-297-2000
  Time difference: 14 hours ahead of New York (EDT)
CEO . . . . .Sandy Hollway
M.P., President . . . . .Hon. Michael Knight
General Manager, Media . . . . .Milton Cockburn
  (Games of XXVIIth Olympiad, Sept. 15-Oct. 1)

2002 WINTER GAMES

Salt Lake Olympic Organizing Committee
257 East, 200 South, Suite 600, Salt Lake City, UT 84111
(801) 212-2002
Chairman . . . . .Robert H. Garff
President & CEO . . . . .W. Mitt Romney
CFO/COO . . . . .Frasier Bullock
Senior V.P., Communications . . . . .Shelly Thomas
  (XIXth Olympic Winter Games, Feb. 8-24)

2004 SUMMER GAMES

Athens Olympic Organizing Committee
Zappio, Megaro, Athens, Greece
TEL: 011-30-1-12004
  Time difference: 7 hours ahead of New York (EDT)
Chairman . . . . .Stratis Stratigis
Managing Director . . . . .Kostas Bakouris
  (XXVIIIth Olympic Summer Games, Aug. 13-29)

COA
(Canadian Olympic Association)
2380 Avenue Pierre Dupuy, Montreal, Quebec H3C-3R4
(514) 861-3371
CEO . . . . .Carol Anne Letheren
President . . . . .Bill Warren
IOC members . . . . . .Carol Anne Letheren & Richard Pound
Media Relations . . . . .Lisa Beatty (Tor.) . . . . .Dina Bell (Ott.)

USOC
(United States Olympic Committee)
One Olympic Plaza, Colorado Springs, CO 80909
(719) 632-5551
President . . . . .Bill Hybl
Director . . . . .Dick Schultz
IOC members .Anita DeFrantz, James Easton & George Killian
Director of Public/Media Relations . . . . .Mike Moran

2006 WINTER GAMES

Turin Olympic Organizing Committee
Via Nizza 262/58–10126, Turin, Italy
TEL: 39-011-63-10-511
Exec. President . . . . .Giorgetto Giugiaro
Director General . . . . .Evelina Christillin

U.S. OLYMPICS TRAINING CENTERS

Colorado Springs Training Center
One Olympic Plaza, Colorado Springs, CO 80909
(719) 578-4500
Sr. Dir. of Sport Services . . . . Benita Fitzgerald-Mosley
Sports Services . . . . John Smyth

Lake Placid Training Center
421 Old Military Road, Lake Placid, NY 12946
(518) 523-2600
Director . . . . .Jack Favro
Operations Manager . . . . .Tracy Lamb

San Diego Training Center
2800 Olympic Parkway, Chula Vista, CA 91915
(619) 656-1500
Director . . . . .Patrice Milkovich

U.S. OLYMPIC ORGANIZATIONS

National Archery Association
One Olympic Plaza, Colorado Springs, CO 80909
(719) 578-4576
President . . . . .Jane Johnson
Executive Director . . . . .George Greenway
Media Contact . . . . .Bill Kellick

U.S. Badminton Association
One Olympic Plaza, Colorado Springs, CO 80909
(719) 578-4808
President . . . . .Steve Kearney
Executive Director . . . . .Steve Cloppas

USA Baseball
3400 E Camino Camtestre, Tucson, AZ 85716
(520) 327-9700
Executive Director & CEO . . . . .Daniel F. O'Brien
Dir. of Media Relations .Jim Street

USA Basketball
5465 Mark Dabling Blvd., Colorado Springs, CO 80918
(719) 590-4800
President . . . . .Russell Granik
Executive Director . . . . .Warren S. Brown
Director of Public Relations . . . . .Craig Miller

U.S. Biathlon Association
29 Ethan Allen Ave.
Colchester, VT 05446
(802) 654-7833
President . . . . .Lyle Nelson
Exec. Director . . . . .Stephen Sands
Director of Summer Biathlon . . . . Jerry Kokesh
Public Relations Contact . . . . .Mary Grace

U.S. Bobsled and Skeleton Federation
421 Old Military Road
Lake Placid, NY 12946
(518) 523-1842
President . . . . .Jim Morris
Executive Director . . . . .Matt Roy
Media/P.R. Director . . . . .TBA

USA Boxing
One Olympic Plaza, Colorado Springs, CO 80909
(719) 578-4506
President . . . . .Gary Tony
Executive Director . . . . .Paul Montville
Dir. of Media/Public Relations . . . . .Shilpa Bakre

U.S. Canoe and Kayak Team
421 Old Military Rd., P.O. Box 789
Lake Placid, NY 12946
(518) 523-1855
Chairman . . . . .Howard Turner
Executive Director . . . . .Terry Kent
Public Relations Director . . . . .Lisa Fish

USA Curling
1100 Center Point Drive, Box 866
Stevens Point, WI 54481
(715) 344-1199
President . . . . .Leland Rich
Executive Director . . . . .David Garber
Media Contact . . . . .Rick Patzke

USA Cycling
One Olympic Plaza
Colorado Springs, CO 80909
(719) 578-4581
President . . . . .Mike Plant
Executive Director & CEO . . . . .Lisa Voight
COO . . . . .Phil Milburn
Director of Communications . . . . .Rich Wanninger

United States Diving, Inc.
Pan American Plaza, Suite 430,
201 South Capitol Avenue, Indianapolis, IN 46225
(317) 237-5252
President ....William Walker
Executive Director ....Todd Smith
Director of Communications ....Seth Pederson

U.S. Equestrian Team
Pottersville Road, Gladstone, NJ 07934
(908) 234-1251
President ....Finn M. W. Capersen
Executive Director ....Bob Standish
Director of Public Relations ....Marty Bauman
                                (508) 698-6810

U.S. Fencing Association
One Olympic Plaza, Colorado Springs, CO 80909
(719) 578-4511
President ....Donald Alperstein
Executive Director ....Michael Massik
Media Relations Coord. ....Coleen Walker Mar

U.S. Field Hockey Assocation
One Olympic Plaza, Colorado Springs, CO 80909
(719) 578-4567
President ....Jenepher Shillingford
Executive Director ....Jane Betts
Director of Media/Public Relations ......Howard Thomas

U.S. Figure Skating Association
20 First Street, Colorado Springs, CO 80906
(719) 635-5200
President ....James W. Disbrow
Executive Director ....John Le Fevre
Director of Events ....Heather Linhart

USA Gymnastics (Artistic & Rythmic)
Pan American Plaza, Suite 300
201 South Capitol Avenue, Indianapolis, IN 46225
(317) 237-5050
President-Exec. Director ....Robert V. Colarossi
Director of Public Relations ....Courtney Caress

USA Hockey, Inc.
1775 Bob Johnson Dr., Colorado Springs, CO 80906
(719) 576-8724
President ....Walter Bush Jr.
Executive Director ....Doug Palazzari
Dir. of Public Relations & Media ....Darryl Seibel

United States Judo, Inc.
One Olympic Plaza, Suite 202
Colorado Springs, CO 80909
(719) 578-4730
President ....Yosh Uchida
Public Relations Director ....Clay Morgan

U.S. Luge Association
P.O. Box 651, Lake Placid, NY 12946
(518) 523-2071
President ....Doug Bateman
Executive Director ....Ron Rossi
Public Relations Manager ....Sandy Caligiore
Communications Manager ....Dmitry Feld

USA Pentathlon
7330 San Pedro, Box 10, San Antonio, TX 78216
(210) 528-2999
President ....Dr. Risto Hurme
Executive Director ....Rob Stull

U.S. Rowing
Pan American Plaza, Suite 400
201 South Capitol Avenue, Indianapolis, IN 46225
(317) 237-5656
President ....Dave Vogel
Executive Director ....Frank Coyle
Media Contact ....Maureen Merhoff

U.S. Sailing Association
P.O. Box 1260, 15 Maritime Drive, Portsmouth, RI 02871
(401) 683-0800
President ....James P. Muldoon
Executive Director ....Terry D. Harper
Media Liaison ....Barby MacGowan
                                (401) 849-0220

U.S. Shooting Team
One Olympic Plaza
Colorado Springs, CO 80909
(719) 578-4670
Executive Director ....Robert Jursnick
Public Relations Director ....Betsy Abbey

U.S. Ski & Snowboard Assoc.
P.O. Box 100, 1500 Kearns Blvd.
Park City, UT 84060
(435) 649-9090
Chairman ....Jim McCarthy
CEO/President ....Bill Marolt
V.P. of Public Relations ....Tom Kelly
Public Information Manager ....TBA

U.S. Soccer Federation
U.S. Soccer House
1801-1811 South Prairie Ave.
Chicago, IL 60616
(312) 808-1300
President ....Dr. S. Robert Contiguglia
Exec. Director/Sec. General ....Hank Steinbrecher
Director of Communications ....Jim Moorhouse

Amateur Softball Association
2801 N.E. 50th Street
Oklahoma City, OK 73111
(405) 424-5266
President ....G. Pat Adkinson
Executive Director ....Ron Radigonda
Director of Communications ....Brian McCall

U.S. Speedskating
P.O. Box 450639, Westlake, OH 44145
(440) 899-0128
President ....Bill Cushman
Executive Director ....Katie Marquard
Public Relations Director ....TBA

U.S.A. Swimming
One Olympic Plaza, Colorado Springs, CO 80909
(719) 578-4578
President ....Dale Neuberger
Executive Director ....Chuck Weilgus
Director of Communications ....Charlie Snyder

U.S. Synchronized Swimming, Inc.
Pan American Plaza, Suite 901
201 South Capitol Avenue
Indianapolis, IN 46225
(317) 237-5700
President ....Laurette Longmire
Executive Director ....Debbie Hesse
Media Relations Director ....Brian Eaton

USA Table Tennis
One Olympic Plaza
Colorado Springs, CO 80909
(719) 578-4583
President ....Sherri Pittman
Interim Executive Director ....Linda Gleeson
Communications Director ....TBA

USA Team Handball
1903 Towers Ferry Rd., Ste. 230, Atlanta, GA 30339
(770) 956-7660
President ....Dennis Berkholtz
Executive Director ....Mike Cavanaugh
Director of Programs ....Danette Leininger

U.S. Tennis Association
70 West Red Oak Lane, White Plains, NY 10604
(914) 696-7000
President ....Julia A. Levering
Executive Director ....Richard D. Fermin
Dir. of Communications ....TBA

USA Track and Field
P.O. Box 120, Indianapolis, IN 46206
(317) 261-0500
President ....Patricia Rico
CEO ....Craig Masback
Director of Communications ....Jennifer Tilden

USA Triathlon
3595 East Fountain Blvd., Ste. F-1, Colorado Springs, CO 80910
(719) 597-9090
President ....Mike Highfield
Executive Director ....Steven M. Locke
Communications Director ....Mike McCarley

USA Volleyball
715 S. Circle Dr., 2nd Floor
Colorado Springs, CO 80910
(719) 228-6800
President ....Rebecca Howard
Director of Communications ....Lorene Graves

United States Water Polo
1685 W. Uintah St., Colorado Springs, CO 80904
(719) 634-0699
President ....Bret B. Bernard
Executive Director ....Bruce Wigo
Dir. of Media/Public Relations ....Kyle Utsumi

USA Weightlifting
One Olympic Plaza, Colorado Springs, CO 80909
(719) 578-4508
President ....Brian Derwin
Exec. Dir./Comm. Dir. ....James J. Fox

USA Wrestling
6155 Lehman Drive, Colorado Springs, CO 80918
(719) 598-8181
President ....Bruce Baumgartner
Executive Director ....Jim Scherr
Dir. of Communications ....Gary Abbott

PAN AMERICAN SPORT ORGANIZATIONS

USA Bowling
5301 South 76th St., Greendale, WI 53129
(414) 421-9008
President ....Kevin Dornberger
Executive Director ....Gerald Koenig

USA National Karate-Do Federation, Inc.
P.O. Box 77083, 8351 15th Ave. NW, Seattle, WA 98177-7083
(206) 440-8386
President ....Julius Thiry
Executive Director ....Brian Lynch
Public/Media Information ....Howard High

United States Raquetball Association
1685 West Uintah, Colorado Springs, CO 80904
(719) 635-5396
President ....Otto Dietrich
Executive Director ....Luke Saint Onge
Assoc. Exec. Dir/Communications ....Linda Mojer

USA Roller Skating
P.O. Box 6579, Lincoln, NE 68506
(402) 483-7551
President ....Sue Dooley
Executive Director ....George Pickard
Information Director ....Bill Wolf

U.S. Squash Racquets Association
P.O. Box 1216 (23 Cynwyd Rd.)
Bala Cynwyd, PA 19004
(610) 667-4006
President ....Eben Hardie
Executive Director ....Craig W. Brand

U.S. Taekwondo Union
One Olympic Plaza, Colorado Springs, CO 80909
(719) 578-4632
President ....Dr. Sang Chul Lee
Executive Director ....R. Jay Warwick

USA Water Ski Association
799 Overlook Drive, S.E., Winter Haven, FL 33884
(941) 324-4341
President ....Andrea Plough
Executive Director ....Steve McDermett
Director of Communications ....Greg Nixon

AFFILIATED ORGANIZATIONS

U.S. Orienteering Federation
P.O. Box 1444, Forest Park, GA 30298
(404) 363-2110
President ....Charles Ferguson
Executive Director ....Robin Shannonhouse
Media Contact ....Jon Nash

USA Rugby
3595 East Fountain Blvd., Ste. M2
Colorado Springs, CO 80910
(719) 637-1022
President ....Anne Barry
Executive V.P. ....Neal Brendel
Communications Director ....Jen Pope

U.S. Sports Acrobatics Federation
P.O. Box 41356, Sacramento, CA 95841-0356
(916) 488-9499
President ....Tonya Case-Patterson

Underwater Society of America
P.O. Box 628, Daly City, CA 94080
(650) 583-0614
President/Exec. Director ....Carol Rose

SOCCER

FIFA

(Federation Internationale de Football Assn.)
P.O. Box 85, 8030 Zurich, Switzerland
TEL: 011-41-1-384-9595
President ....Joseph Blatter
General Secretary ....Michael Zen-Russinen
Director of Communications ....Keith Cooper

MLS

Major League Soccer
110 E. 42nd Street, 10th Floor
New York, NY 10017
(212) 450-1200
Founder ....Alan I. Rothenberg
Commissioner ....Don Garber
V.P. of Communications ....Dan Courtemanche
Director of Information ....Trey Fitz-Gerald

Chicago Fire
311 W Superior St., #444
Chicago, IL 60610
(312) 705-7200
Investor/Operator ....Philip F. Anschutz
General Manager ....Peter Wilt
Director of Communications ....Adam Low

Colorado Rapids
555 17th Street, Suite 3350, Denver, CO 80202
(303) 299-1570
Investor/Operator ....Philip F. Anschutz
General Manager ....Dan Counce
Media Relations ....Ben Grossman

Columbus Crew
Columbus Crew Stadium
2121 Velma Ave., Columbus, OH 43211
(614) 447-2739
Investor/Operator ....Lamar Hunt and Family
President/GM ....Jamey Rootes
Director of Media Relations ....Jeff Wuerth

Dallas Burn
2602 McKinney, Suite 200, Dallas, TX 75204
(214) 979-0303
Investor/Operator ....League-owned
President/GM ....Billy Hicks
Director of Media Relations ....Chris Ward

Kansas City Wizards
706 Broadway St., Suite 706
Kansas City, MO 64105
(816) 472-4625
Investor/Operator ....Lamar Hunt and Family
General Manager ....Doug Newman
Director of Media Relations ....Rob Thomson

Los Angeles Galaxy
1010 Rose Bowl Dr., Pasadena, CA 91103
(626) 432-1540
Investor/Operator ....Philip F. Anschutz
President ....Tim Leiweke
General Manager ....Sergio del Prado
Director of Media Relations ....Luis Garcia

Miami Fusion
2200 Commercial Blvd., Ste. 104
Ft. Lauderdale, FL 33309
(954) 717-2200
Investor/Operator ....Kenneth Horowitz
V.P./General Manager ....Doug Hamilton
Director of Public Relations ....Gabe Gabor

New England Revolution
Foxboro Stadium, 60 Washington St.
Foxboro, MA 02035
(508) 543-5001
Investor/Operator ....Robert Kraft and Family
General Manager ....Brian O'Donovan
Director of Media Relations ....Derek Aframe

New York/New Jersey MetroStars
One Harmon Plaza, 3rd Floor
Seacaucus, NJ 07094
(201) 583-7000
Investor/Operator ....John Kluge and Stuart Subotnick
V.P./General Manager ....Charlie Stillitano
Media Relations ....Richard Schneider

San Jose Clash
3550 Stevens Creek Blvd., Suite 200
San Jose, CA 95117
(408) 241-9922
Investor/Operator ....Kraft Family Sports Group
General Manager ....Lynne Meterssparel
Director of Media Relations ....Rick La Plante

Tampa Bay Mutiny
Raymond-James Stadium
4042 N. Himes, Tampa, FL 33607
(813) 386-2000
Investor/Operator ....League-owned
President/GM ....Nick Sakiewicz
Director of Media Relations ....Tracey Judd

Washington D.C. United
13832 Redskin Drive, Herndon, VA 20171
(703) 478-6600
Owner ....Washington Soccer, L.P.
President/GM ....Kevin Payne
Director of Communications ....Rick Lawes

Other Soccer

CONCACAF
(Confederation of North, Central American &
Caribbean Association Football)
725 Fifth Ave., 17th Floor
New York, NY 10022
(212) 308-0044
President ....Jack Austin Warner
General Secretary ....Chuck Blazer
Senior Consultant ....Clive Toye
Press Officer ....Carlos Giron

U.S. Soccer
(United States Soccer Federation)
Soccer House, 1801-1811 South Prairie Ave.
Chicago, IL 60616
(312) 808-1300
President ....Dr. S. Robert Contiguglia
Exec. Director/Sec. General ....Hank Steinbrecher
Director of Communications ....Jim Moorhouse

NPSL
(National Professional Soccer League)
115 Dewalt Avenue NW, 5th Fl.
Canton, OH 44702
(330) 455-4625
Commissioner ....Steve M. Paxos
Director of Operations ....Paul Luchowski
Director of Media Relations ....Chuck Murr
   Member teams (13): Baltimore Spirit, Buffalo Blizzard,
Cleveland Crunch, Detroit Rockers, Edmonton Drillers,
Florida Thundercats, Harrisburg Heat, Kansas City Attack,
Milwaukee Wave, Montreal Impact, Philadelphia Kixx, St.
Louis Ambush and Wichita Wings.

USL
(United Soccer Leagues)
14497 N. Dale Mabry Hwy., Ste. 201
Tampa, FL 33618
(813) 963-3909
Commissioner ....Francisco Marcos
Administrative Manager ....Beverly Wright
Director of Public Relations ....Scott Creighton

SWIMMING

FINA
(Federation Internationale de Natation Amateur)
9 ave de Beaumont
1012 Lausanne, Switzerland
TEL: 011-4121-312-6602
President ....Mustapha Larfaoui
Honrary Secretary ....Gunnar Werner

TENNIS

ATP Tour
(Association of Tennis Professionals)
201 ATP Tour Blvd.
Ponte Vedra Beach, FL 32082
(904) 285-8000
Chief Executive Officer ....Mark Miles
V.P., Communications and Media Relations .Graeme Agars
Dir. of Media Services/Ops. ....Joe Lynch

**ITF
(International Tennis Federation)**
Palliser Rd., Barons Court
London, England W14 9EN
TEL: 011-44-181-878-6464
President ....Ricci Bitti
Executive V.P. ....Juan Margets
Head of Communications ....Alun James

World TeamTennis
445 North Wells, Suite 404, Chicago, IL 60610
(312) 245-5300
Chief Executive Officer ....Billie Jean King
Executive Director ....Ilana Kloss
Communications Director ....Tracey Maltby

**USTA
(United States Tennis Association)**
70 West Red Oak Lane, White Plains, NY 10604
(914) 696-7000
President ....Juila A. Levering
Executive Director ....Richard D. Fermin
Dir. of Communications ....TBA

**WTA Tour
(Women's Tennis Association)**
1266 East Main St. 4th Floor, Stamford, CT 06902
(203) 978-1740
CEO ....Bartlett H. McGuire
COO ....Elizabeth Garger
V.P. of Communications/Development ....Joe Favorito

TRACK & FIELD

**IAAF
(International Ameteur Athletics Federation)**
17 Rue Princesse Florestine
BP 359, MC-98007, Monaco Cedex
TEL: 377-93-10-8888
President ....Primo Nebiolo
Senior V.P. ....Lamaine Diack
General Secretariat ....Sandrine Steva
Director of Information ....Sandrine Steva

USA Track & Field
P.O. Box 120, Indianapolis, IN 46206
(317) 261-0500
President ....Patricia Rico
CEO ....Craig Masbak
Director of Communications ....Jennifer Tilden

YACHTING

1999-2000 America's Cup

**New Zealand Defense Committee
(Royal New Zealand Yacht Squadron)**
P.O. Box 1927, Auckland, New Zealand
TEL: 011-64-9-357-6712
  Time difference: 16 hours ahead of New York (EDT)
Exec. Director & Contact ....Alan Sefton
  (Next America's Cup defense scheduled to begin in Oct.
1999 and run through Feb. 2000, off the coast of Auck-
land.)

MISCELLANEOUS

**AAU
(Amateur Athletic Union)**
c/o Walt Disney World Resorts, P.O. Box 10000
Lake Buena Vista, FL 32830-1000
(407) 934-7200
President ....Bobby Dodd
Media/Public Relations Director ....Melissa Wilson

All-American Soap Box Derby
P.O. Box 7225, Akron, OH 44306
(330) 733-8723
President ....Robert McLaughlin
Chairman of the Board ....Roy Hartzi
Executive Director ....Anthony DeLuca
Public Relations Director ....Bob Troyer

American Powerboating Association
P.O. Box 377, Eastpointe, MI 48021
(810) 773-9700
President ....Mike Jones
Executive Director ....Gloria Urbin

Association of Surfing Professionals
P.O. Box 1095, Coolangatta
Queensland, Australia 4225
61-07-5599-1550
President/CEO ....Wayne Bartholomew
Tour Director ....Peter Whittaker
Tour Supervisor ....Al Hunt

**BASS, Inc.
(Bass Anglers Sportsmen Society)**
5845 Carmichael Road
Mongomery, AL 36117
(334) 272-9530
CEO ....Helen Sevier
Publicity Director ....MarJean Corkran

Iditarod Trail Committee
P.O. Box 870800, Wasilla, AK 99687
(907) 376-5155
Executive Director ....Stan Hooley
Race Director ....Joanne Potts

International Game Fish Association
300 Gulf Steam Way
Dania Baech, FL 33004
(954) 927-2628
Chairman ....George Matthews
President ....Mike Leach
Editor ....Ray Crawford

Little League Baseball Incorporated
P.O. Box 3485, Williamsport, PA 17701
(570) 326-1921
CEO-President ....Steven Keener
Director of Communications ....Dennis Sullivan
Dir., Publications/Media Relations ....Lance Van Auken

**National Association for Girls and Women
in Sport**
1900 Association Drive
Reston, VA 20191
(703) 476-3452
Executive Director ....Dr. Diana Everett
President ....Dr. Jane Rintala

National Lacrosse League
237 Main St., Ste 1500
Buffalo, NY 14203
(716) 855-1NLL
Commissioner ....John Livsey Jr.
V.P. of Public Relations ....Bruce Wawrzyniak
  Member teams (8): Albany, Baltimore, Buffalo, Long
Island (N.Y.), Philadelphia, Rochester (N.Y.), Syracuse
(N.Y.) and Toronto.

National Rifle Assocation
11250 Waples Mill Road
Fairfax, VA 22030
(703) 267-1000
Executive VP ....Wayne LaPierre
Public Affairs Director ....Bill Powers

National Sports Foundation
P.O. Box 888886
Atlanta, GA 30356
(770) 698-8600
Executive Director ....Ed Harris

NORBA
(National Off-Road Bicycle Association)
One Olympic Plaza
Colorado Springs, CO 80909
(719) 578-4717
Managing Directors ....Leslie Klein and Eric Moore
Communications Coordinator ....Patrice Quintero

Professional Billiards Tour, Inc.
4412 Commercial Way
Spring Hill, FL 34606
(352) 596-7808
CEO ....Don Mackey

Professional Rodeo Cowboys Association
101 Pro Rodeo Drive
Colorado Springs, CO 80919
(719) 593-8840
Commissioner ....Steve Hatchell
Director of Communications ....Steve Fleming

Roller Hockey International
650 S. Cherry Creek Dr., Ste. 1025
Denver, CO 80246
(303) 399-0800
Commissioner ....Ralph Backstrom
CEO ....Bernie Mullin
Media Relations ....Mark Ehrhart

Special Olympics
1325 G St. NW Suite 500
Washington, DC 20005
(202) 628-3630
Founder ....Eunice Kennedy Shriver
COB ....Sargent Shriver
COO ....Kim Elliott
Sr. Media Relations Manager ....Mike Janes

U.S. Polo Association
4059 Iron Works Pkwy., Ste. 1
Lexington, KY 40511
(606) 255-0593
Executive Director ....George Alexander Jr.

U.S. Pro Beach Volleyball
P.O. Box 57
Huntington Beach, CA 92648
(714) 536-4900
President ....Gary Pope

U.S. Windsurfing
P.O. Box 978, Hood River, OR 97031
(541) 386-8708
President ....Dick Tillman
Executive Director ....Holly Macpherson

Wheelchair Sports USA
3595 East Fountain Blvd., Suite L-1
Colorado Springs, CO 80910
(719) 574-1150
Chairman ....Paul DePace
Executive Director ....Patricia Shepherd

Commissioners and Presidents
Chief Executives of Established Major Sports Organizations since 1876

Major League Baseball

Commissioner	Tenure
Kenesaw Mountain Landis*	.1920-44
Albert (Happy) Chandler	...1945-51
Ford Frick	.1951-65
William Eckert	.1965-68
Bowie Kuhn	.1969-84
Peter Ueberroth	.1984-89
A. Bartlett Giamatti*	1989
Fay Vincent	.1989-92
Bud Selig†	.1998—

*Died in office.
†Served as interim commissioner from 1992-98.

National League

President	Tenure
Morgan G. Bulkeley	.1876
William A. Hulbert*	.1877-82
A.G. Mills	.1883-84
Nicholas Young	.1885-1902
Henry Pulliam*	.1903-09
Thomas J. Lynch	.1910-13
John K. Tener	.1914-18
John A. Heydler	.1918-34
Ford Frick	.1935-51
Warren Giles	.1951-69
Charles (Chub) Feeney	...1970-86
A. Bartlett Giamatti	.1987-89
Bill White	.1989-94
Leonard Coleman	.1994-99

*Died in office.
Note: League president jobs were eliminated after the 1999 season.

American League

President	Tenure
Bancroft (Ban) Johnson	.1901-27
Ernest Barnard*	1927-31
William Harridge	.1931-59
Joe Cronin	.1959-73
Lee McPhail	.1974-83
Bobby Brown	.1984-94
Gene Budig	.1994-99

*Died in office.
Note: League president jobs were eliminated after the 1999 season.

NBA

Commissioner	Tenure
Maurice Podoloff	1949-63
Walter Kennedy	.1963-75
Larry O'Brien	.1975-84
David Stern	.1984—

NFL

President	Tenure
Jim Thorpe	.1920
Joe Carr	.1921-39
Carl Storck	.1939-41

Commissioner	
Elmer Layden	.1941-46
Bert Bell*	.1946-59
Austin Gunsel	.1959-60
Pete Rozelle	.1960-89
Paul Tagliabue	.1989—

*Died in office.

NHL

President	Tenure
Frank Calder*	.1917-43
Red Dutton	.1943-46
Clarence Campbell	.1946-77
John Ziegler	.1977-92
Gil Stein	.1992-93

Commissioner	
Gary Bettman	.1993—

*Died in office.

NCAA

Executive Director	Tenure
Walter Byers	.1951-88
Dick Schultz	.1988-93
Cedric Dempsey	.1993—

IOC

President	Tenure
Demetrius Vikelas, Greece	.1894-96
Baron Pierre de Coubertin, France	.1896-1925
Count Henri de Baillet-Latour, Belgium	.1925-42
Vacant	.1942-46
J. Sigfried Edstrom, Sweden	.1946-52
Avery Brundage, USA	.1952-72
Lord Michael Killanin, Ireland	.1972-80
Juan Antonio Samaranch, Spain	.1980—

Olympics

U.S. Olympians Tommie Smith, center, and John Carlos raised their fists and the ire of many Olympic officials in a controversial racial protest during the 1968 Summer Games in Mexico City.

AP/Wide World Photos

THE 2000 ESPN INFORMATION PLEASE SPORTS ALMANAC

OLYMPICS STATISTICS

SEC A

THROUGH THE YEARS 1896-1996

SUMMER OLYMPICS

PAGE 624

Modern Olympic Games

The original Olympic Games were celebrated as a religious festival from 776 B.C. until 393 A.D., when Roman emperor Theodosius I banned all pagan festivals (the Olympics celebrated the Greek god Zeus). On June 23, 1894, French educator Baron Pierre de Coubertin, speaking at the Sorbonne in Paris to a gathering of international sports leaders, proposed that the ancient games be revived on an international scale. The idea was enthusiastically received and the Modern Olympics were born. The first Olympics were held two years later in Athens, where 245 athletes from 14 nations competed in the ancient Panathenaic stadium to large and ardent crowds. Americans captured nine out of 12 track and field events, but Greece won the most medals with 47.

The Summer Olympics

Year	No	Location	Dates	Nations	Most medals	USA Medals	
1896	I	Athens, GRE	Apr. 6-15	14	Greece (10-19-18—47)	11- 6- 2 — 19	(2nd)
1900	II	Paris, FRA	May 20-Oct. 28	26	France (26-37-32—95)	18-14-15 — 47	(2nd)
1904	III	St. Louis, USA.	July 1-Nov. 23	13	USA (78-84-82—244)	78-84-82—244	(1st)
1906-a	—	Athens, GRE	Apr. 22-May 2	20	France (15-9-16—40)	12- 6- 6 — 24	(3rd)
1908	IV	London, GBR	Apr. 27-Oct. 31	22	Britain (54-46-38—138)	23-12-12 — 47	(2nd)
1912	V	Stockholm, SWE	May 5-July 22	28	Sweden (23-24-17—64)	25-18-20 — 63	(2nd)
1916	VI	Berlin, GER	Cancelled (WWI)				
1920	VII	Antwerp, BEL	Apr. 20-Sept. 12	29	USA (41-27-27—95)	41-27-27 — 95	(1st)
1924	VIII	Paris, FRA	May 4-July 27	44	USA (45-27-27—99)	45-27-27 — 99	(1st)
1928	IX	Amsterdam, NED	May 17-Aug. 12	46	USA (22-18-16—56)	22-18-16 — 56	(1st)
1932	X	Los Angeles, USA.	July 30-Aug. 14	37	USA (41-32-30—103)	41-32-30 — 103	(1st)
1936	XI	Berlin, GER	Aug. 1-16	49	Germany (33-26-30—89)	24-20-12 — 56	(2nd)
1940-b	XII	Tokyo, JPN	Cancelled (WWII)				
1944	XIII	London, GBR	Cancelled (WWII)				
1948	XIV	London, GBR	July 29-Aug. 14	59	USA (38-19-19—84)	38-27-19 — 84	(1st)
1952-cd	XV	Helsinki, FIN	July 19-Aug. 3	69	USA (40-19-17—76)	40-19-17— 76	(1st)
1956-e	XVI	Melbourne, AUS	Nov. 22-Dec .8	72	USSR (37-29-32—98)	32-25-17— 74	(2nd)
1960	XVII	Rome, ITA	Aug. 25-Sept. 11	83	USSR (43-29-31—103)	34-21-16— 71	(2nd)
1964	XVIII	Tokyo, JPN	Oct. 10-24	93	USSR (30-31-35—96)	36-26-28— 90	(2nd)
1968-f	XIX	Mexico City, MEX	Oct. 12-27	112	USA (45-28-34—107)	45-28-34—107	(1st)
1972	XX	Munich, W. GER	Aug. 26-Sept. 10	121	USSR (50-27-22—99)	33-31-30— 94	(2nd)
1976-g	XXI	Montreal, CAN	July 17-Aug. 1	92	USSR (49-41-35—125)	34-35-25— 94	(3rd)
1980-h	XXII	Moscow, USSR	July 19-Aug. 3	80	USSR (80-69-46—195)	Boycotted Games	
1984-i	XXIII	Los Angeles, USA.	July 28-Aug. 12	140	USA (83-61-30—174)	83-61-30—174	(1st)
1988	XXIV	Seoul, S. KOR	Sept. 17-Oct. 2	159	USSR (55-31-46—132)	36-31-27— 94	(3rd)
1992-j	XXV	Barcelona, SPA	July 25-Aug. 9	169	UT (45-38-29—112)	37-34-37—108	(2nd)
1996	XXVI	Atlanta, USA	July 20-Aug. 4	197	USA (44-32-25—101)	44-32-25—101	(1st)
2000	XXVII	Sydney, AUS	Sept. 15-Oct. 1				
2004	XXVIII	Athens, GRE	Aug. 13-29				

a—The 1906 Intercalated Games in Athens are considered unofficial by the IOC because they did not take place in the four-year cycle established in 1896. However, most record books include these interim games with the others.

b—The 1940 Summer Games are originally scheduled for Tokyo, but Japan resigns as host after the outbreak of the Sino-Japanese War in 1937. Helsinki is the next choice, but the IOC cancels the Games after Soviet troops invade Finland in 1939.

c—Germany and Japan are allowed to rejoin the Olympic community for the first Summer Games since 1936. Though a divided country, the Germans send a joint East-West team until 1964.

d—The Soviet Union (USSR) participates in its first Olympics, Winter or Summer, since the Russian revolution in 1917 and takes home the second most medals (22-30-19—71).

e—Due to Australian quarantine laws, the equestrian events for the 1956 Games are held in Stockholm, June 10-17.

f—East Germany and West Germany send separate teams for the first time and will continue to do so through 1988.

g—The 1976 Games are boycotted by 32 nations, most of them from black Africa, because the IOC will not ban New Zealand. Earlier that year, a rugby team from New Zealand had toured racially-segregated South Africa.

h—The 1980 Games are boycotted by 64 nations, led by the USA, to protest the Soviet invasion of Afghanistan on Dec. 27, 1979.

i—The 1984 Games are boycotted by 14 Eastern Bloc nations, led by the USSR, to protest America's overcommercialization of the Games, inadequate security and an anti-Soviet attitude by the U.S. government. Most believe, however, the communist walkout is simply revenge for 1980.

j—Germany sends a single team after East and West German reunification in 1990 and the USSR competes as the Unified Team after the breakup of the Soviet Union in 1991.

1896

Athens

The ruins of ancient Olympia were excavated by the German archaeologist Ernst Curtius from 1875-81.

Among the remains uncovered was the ancient stadium where the original Olympic Games were celebrated from 776 B.C. to 393 A.D., when Roman emperor Theodosius I banned all pagan festivals.

Athletics played an important role in the religious festivals of the ancient Greeks, who believed competitive sports pleased the spirits of the dead. The festivals honoring gods like Zeus were undertaken by many Greek tribes and cities and usually held every four years.

During the first 13 Olympiads (an Olympiad is an interval of four years between celebrations of the Olympic Games), the only contested event was a foot race of 200 yards. Longer races were gradually introduced and by 708 B.C., field events like the discus, javelin throw and the long jump were part of the program. Wrestling and boxing followed and in 640 B.C., four-horse chariot races became a fixture at the Games.

During the so-called Golden Age of Greece, which most historians maintain lasted from 477 to 431 B.C., Olympia was considered holy ground. Victorious athletes gave public thanks to the gods and were revered as heroes. Three-time winners had statues erected in their likeness and received various gifts and honors, including exemption from taxation.

Eventually, however, winning and the rewards that went with victory corrupted the original purpose of the Ancient Games. Idealistic amateurs gave way to skilled foreign athletes who were granted the citizenship needed to compete and were paid handsomely by rich Greek gamblers.

There is evidence to suggest that the Games continued until the temples of Olympia were physically demolished in 426 A.D. by a Roman army sent by Theodosius II. Over the next 15 centuries, earthquakes and floods buried the site, until its discovery in 1875.

On June 23, 1894, French educator Baron Pierre de Coubertin, speaking at the Sorbonne in Paris to a gathering of international sports leaders from nine nations— including the United States and Russia— proposed that the ancient Games be revived on an international scale. The idea was enthusiastically received and the Modern Olympics, as we know them, were born.

The first Olympiad was celebrated two years later in Athens, where an estimated 245 athletes (all men) from 14 nations competed in the ancient Panathenaic stadium before large and ardent crowds.

Americans won nine of the 12 track and field events, but Greece won the most medals with 47.

The highlight was the victory by native peasant Spiridon Louis in the first marathon race, which was run over the same course covered by the Greek hero Pheidippides after the battle of Marathon in 490 B.C.

Top 10 Standings

National medal standings are not recognized by the IOC. The unofficial point totals are based on 3 points for a gold medal, 2 for a silver and 1 for a bronze.

		Gold	Silver	Bronze	Total	Pts
1	Greece	10	19	18	47	86
2	USA	11	6	2	19	47
3	Germany	7	5	3	15	34
4	France	5	4	2	11	25
5	Great Britain	3	3	1	7	16
6	Denmark	1	2	4	7	11
	Hungary	2	1	3	6	11
8	Austria	2	0	3	5	9
9	Switzerland	1	2	0	3	7
10	Australia	2	0	0	2	6

Leading Medal Winners

Number of individual medals won on the left; gold, silver and bronze breakdown to the right.

No		Sport	G-S-B
6	Hermann Weingärtner, GER	Gymnastics	3-2-1
4	Karl Schuman, GER	Gymnastics & Wrestling	4-0-0
4	Alfred Flatow, GER	Gymnastics	3-1-0
4	Bob Garrett, USA	Track/Field	2-1-1
4	Viggo Jensen, DEN	Shooting & Weightlifting	1-2-1
3	Paul Masson, FRA	Cycling	3-0-0
3	Teddy Flack, AUS	Track/Field & Tennis	2-0-1
3	Jules Zutter, SWI	Gymnastics	1-2-0
3	James Connolly, USA	Track/Field	1-1-1
3	Leon Flameng, FRA	Cycling	1-1-1
3	Adolf Schmal, AUT	Cycling	1-0-2
3	Efstathios Choraphas, GRE	Swimming	0-1-2
3	Holger Nielsen, DEN	Shooting	0-1-2

Track & Field

Event		Time
100m	Tom Burke, USA	12.0
400m	Tom Burke, USA	54.2
800m	Teddy Flack, AUS	2:11.0
1500m	Teddy Flack, AUS	4:33.2
Marathon	Spiridon Louis, GRE	2:58:50
110m H	Tom Curtis, USA	17.6

Event		Mark
High Jump	Ellery Clark, USA	5-11¼
Pole Vault	William Hoyt, USA	10-10
Long Jump	Ellery Clark, USA	20-10
Triple Jump	James Connolly, USA	44-11¾
Shot Put	Bob Garrett, USA	36-9¾
Discus	Bob Garrett, USA	95-7½

Swimming

Event		Time
100m Free	Alfréd Hajós, HUN	1:22.2
500m Free	Paul Neumann, AUT	8:12.6
1200m Free	Alfréd Hajós, HUN	18:22.2

Other		Time
Sailors' 100m Free	Ioannis Malokinis, GRE	2:20.4

Team Sports

None

Also Contested

Cycling, Fencing, Gymnastics, Shooting, Tennis, Weightlifting and Greco-Roman Wrestling.

1900

Paris

The success of the revived Olympics moved Greece to declare itself the rightful host of all future Games, but de Coubertin and the International Olympic Committee were determined to move the athletic feast around. In France, however, the Games were overshadowed by the brand new Eiffel Tower and all but ignored by the organizers of the 1900 Paris Exposition.

Despite their sideshow status, the Games attracted 1,225 athletes from 26 nations and enjoyed more publicity, if not bigger crowds, than in Athens.

University of Pennsylvania roommates Alvin Kraenzlein, Irving Baxter and John Tewksbury and Purdue grad Ray Ewry dominated the 23 track and field events, winning 11 and taking five seconds and a third. Kraenzlein remains the only track and fielder to win four individual titles in one year. Women were invited to compete for the first time and Britain's Charlotte Cooper won the singles and mixed doubles in tennis.

No gold medals were given out in Paris. Winners received silver medals with bronze for second place.

Top 10 Standings

National team medal standings are not recognized by the IOC. The unofficial point totals are based on 3 points for a gold medal, 2 for a silver and 1 for a bronze.

		Gold	Silver	Bronze	Total	Pts
1	France	26	37	32	95	184
2	USA	18	14	15	47	97
3	Great Britain	16	6	8	30	68
4	Belgium	6	5	5	16	33
5	Switzerland	6	1	1	8	21
6	Germany	3	2	2	7	15
7	Denmark	1	3	2	6	11
	Hungary	1	3	2	6	11
9	Australia	2	0	4	6	10
	Holland	1	2	3	6	10

Leading Medal Winners

Number of individual medals won on the left; gold, silver and bronze breakdown to the right.

MEN

No		Sport	G-S-B
5	Irving Baxter, USA	Track/Field	2-3-0
5	John W. Tewksbury, USA	Track/Field	2-2-1
4	Alvin Kraenzlein, USA	Track/Field	4-0-0
4	Konrad Stäheli, SWI	Shooting	3-0-1
4	Achille Paroche, FRA	Shooting	1-2-1
4	Stan Rowley, AUS	Track/Field	1-0-3
4	Ole Östmo, NOR	Shooting	0-2-2
3	Ray Ewry, USA	Track/Field	3-0-0
3	Charles Bennett, AUS	Track/Field	2-1-0
3	Emil Kellenberger, SWI	Shooting	2-1-0
3	Laurie Doherty, GBR	Tennis	2-0-1
3	Reggie Doherty, GBR	Tennis	2-0-1
3	E. Michelet, FRA	Yachting	1-0-2
3	F. Michelet, FRA	Yachting	1-0-2
3	Anders Nielsen, DEN	Shooting	0-3-0
3	Zoltán Halmay, HUN	Swimming	0-2-1
3	Léon Moreaux, FRA	Shooting	0-2-1

WOMEN

No		Sport	G-S-B
2	Charlotte Cooper, GBR	Tennis	2-0-0
2	Marion Jones, USA	Tennis	0-0-2

Track & Field

Event		Time	
60m	Alvin Kraenzlein, USA	7.0	WR
100m	Frank Jarvis, USA	11.0	OR
200m	John W. Tewksbury, USA	22.2	
400m	Maxey Long, USA	49.4	OR
800m	Alfred Tysoe, GBR	2:01.2	
1500m	Charles Bennett, GBR	4:06.2	WR
Marathon	Michel Théato, FRA	2:59:45	
110m H	Alvin Kraenzlein, USA	15.4	OR
200m H	Alvin Kraenzlein, USA	25.4	
400m H	John W. Tewksbury, USA	57.6	
3000m Steeple	George Orton, CAN	7:34.4	
4000m Steeple	John Rimmer, GBR	12:58.4	
5000m Team	GBR (Charles Bennett, John Rimmer, Sidney Robinson, Alfred Tysoe, Stanley Rowley)	26 pts	

Event		Mark	
High Jump	Irving Baxter, USA	6- 2¾	OR
Pole Vault	Irving Baxter, USA	10-10	
Long Jump	Alvin Kraenzlein, USA	23- 6¾	OR
Triple Jump	Meyer Prinstein, USA	47- 5¾	OR
Shot Put	Richard Sheldon, USA	46- 3	OR
Discus	Rudolf Bauer, HUN	118- 3	OR
Hammer	John Flanagan, USA	163- 1	

Standing		Mark	
High Jump	Ray Ewry, USA	5- 5	WR
Long Jump	Ray Ewry, USA	10- 6¼	
Triple Jump	Ray Ewry, USA	34- 8½	

Swimming

Event		Time
220yd Free	Frederick Lane, AUS	2:25.2
1000m Free	John Jarvis, GBR	13:40.2
4000m Free	John Jarvis, GBR	58:24.0
200m Back	Ernst Hoppenberg, GER	2:47.0
200m Team	GER (Ernst Hoppenberg, Max Hainle, Max Schone, Julius Frey, Herbert von Petersdorff)	32 pts

Team Sports

Sport	Champion
Cricket	Great Britain
Polo	Great Britain/USA
Rugby	France
Soccer	Great Britain
Tug-of-War	Sweden/Norway
Water Polo	Great Britain

Note: In Polo, Foxhunters Hurlingham defeated Club Rugby in a contest of teams made up of British and American players. A combined 6-man team of Swedes and Norwegians won the Tug- of-War.

Also Contested

Archery, Croquet, Cycling, Equestrian, Fencing, Golf, Gymnastics, Rowing, Shooting, Tennis and Yachting.

1904

St. Louis

Originally scheduled for Chicago, the Games were moved to St. Louis and held in conjunction with the centennial celebration of the Louisiana Purchase.

The program included more sports than in Paris, but with only 13 nations sending athletes, the first Olympics to be staged in the United States had a decidedly All-American flavor—over 500 of the 687 competitors were Americans. Little wonder the home team won 80 percent of the medals.

The rout was nearly total in track and field where the U.S.–led by triple-winners Ray Ewry, Archie Hahn, Jim Lightbody and Harry Hillman–took 23 of 25 gold medals and swept 20 events.

The marathon, which was run over dusty roads in brutally hot weather, was the most bizarre event of the Games. Thomas Hicks of the U.S. won, but only after his handlers fed him painkillers during the race. And an impostor nearly stole the victory when Fred Lorz, who dropped out after nine miles, was seen trotting back to the finish line to retrieve his clothes. Amused that officials thought he had won the race, Lorz played along until he was found out shortly after the medal ceremony. Banned for life by the AAU, Lorz was reinstated a year later and won the 1905 Boston Marathon.

Top 10 Standings

National medal standings are not recognized by the IOC. The unofficial point totals are based on 3 points for a gold medal, 2 for a silver and 1 for a bronze.

		Gold	Silver	Bronze	Total	Pts
1	USA	78	84	82	244	484
2	Germany	4	4	4	12	24
3	Canada	4	1	1	6	15
4	Hungary	2	1	1	4	9
	Cuba	3	0	0	3	9
6	Austria	1	1	1	3	6
	Britain/Ireland	1	1	1	3	6
8	Greece	1	0	1	2	4
	Switzerland	1	0	1	2	4
10	Cuba/USA	1	0	0	1	3

Leading Medal Winners

Number of individual medals won on the left; gold, silver and bronze breakdown to the right.

MEN

No		Sport	G-S-B
6	Anton Heida, USA	Gymnastics	5-1-0
6	George Eyser, USA	Gymnastics	3-2-1
6	Burton Downing, USA	Cycling	2-3-1
5	Marcus Hurley, USA	Cycling	4-0-1
5	Charles Daniels, USA	Swimming	3-1-1
5	Albertson Van Zo Post, USA	Fencing	2-1-2
5	William Merz, USA	Gymnastics	0-1-4
4	Jim Lightbody, USA	Track/Field	3-1-0
4	Francis Gailey, USA	Swimming	0-3-1
4	Teddy Billington, USA	Cycling	0-1-3
4	Frank Kungler, USA	Weightlifting, Wrestling & Tug of War	0-1-3
3	Ray Ewry, USA	Track/Field	3-0-0
3	Ramón Fonst, CUB	Fencing	3-0-0
3	Archie Hahn, USA	Track/Field	3-0-0
3	Harry Hillman, USA	Track/Field	3-0-0
3	Julius Lenhart, AUT	Gymnastics	2-1-0
3	George Bryant, USA	Archery	2-0-1
3	Emil Rausch, GER	Swimming	2-0-1
3	Robert Williams, USA	Archery	1-2-0
3	Ralph Rose, USA	Track/Field	1-1-1
3	William Thompson, USA	Archery	1-0-2
3	Charles Tatham, USA	Fencing	0-2-1
3	William Hogenson, USA	Track/Field	0-1-2
3	Emil Voigt, USA	Gymnastics	0-1-2

WOMEN

No		Sport	G-S-B
2	Lida Howell, USA	Archery	2-0-0
2	Emma Cooke, USA	Archery	0-2-0
2	Jessie Pollack, USA	Archery	0-0-2

Track & Field

Event		Time	
60m	Archie Hahn, USA	7.0	=WR
100m	Archie Hahn, USA	11.0	
200m	Archie Hahn, USA	21.6	OR
400m	Harry Hillman, USA	49.2	OR
800m	Jim Lightbody, USA	1:56.0	OR
1500m	Jim Lightbody, USA	4:05.4	WR
Marathon	Thomas Hicks, USA	3:28:53	
110m H	Frederick Schule, USA	16.0	
200m H	Harry Hillman, USA	24.6	OR
400m H	Harry Hillman, USA	53.0	
3000m Steeple	Jim Lightbody, USA	7:39.6	
4-mile Team	New York AC (Arthur Newton, George Underwood, Paul Pilgrim, Howard Valentine, David Munson)	27 pts	

Event		Mark	
High Jump	Sam Jones, USA	5-11	
Pole Vault	Charles Dvorak, USA	11- 5¾	
Long Jump	Meyer Prinstein, USA	24- 1	OR
Triple Jump	Meyer Prinstein, USA	47- 1	
Shot Put	Ralph Rose, USA	48- 7	WR
56-lb Throw	Étienne Desmarteau, CAN	34- 4	
Discus	Martin Sheridan, USA	128-10½	OR
Hammer	John Flanagan, USA	168- 1	OR
Triathlon	Max Emmerich, USA	35.7 pts	
Decathlon	Tom Kiely, IRL	6036 pts	

Note: Sheridan won Discus throw-off after tying with Rose for 1st.

Standing		Mark	
High Jump	Ray Ewry, USA	5- 3	
Long Jump	Ray Ewry, USA	11- 4⅞	WR
Triple Jump	Ray Ewry, USA	34- 7¼	

Swimming

Event		Time
50yd Free	Zoltán Halmay, HUN	28.0
100yd Free	Zoltán Halmay, HUN	1:02.8
220yd Free	Charles Daniels, USA	2:44.2
440yd Free	Charles Daniels, USA	6:16.2
880yd Free	Emil Rausch, GER	13:11.4
Mile Free	Emil Rausch, GER	27:18.2
100yd Back	Walter Brack, GER	1:16.8
400yd Brst	Georg Zacharias, GER	7:23.6
4x50yd Free	USA (Joe Ruddy, Leo Goodwin, Louis Handle, Charles Daniels)	2:04.6

Note: Halmay won 50-Free in swim-off with Scott Leary of USA.

Diving		Points
Platform	George Sheldon, USA	12.66

Plunge		Mark
for Distance	William Dickey, USA	62-6

Team Sports

Sport	Champion
Lacrosse	Canada (Shamrock-Winnipeg)
Soccer	Canada (Galt Football Club)
Tug-of-War	USA (Milwaukee AC)
Water Polo	USA (New York AC)

Also Contested

Archery, Boxing, Cycling, Fencing, Golf, Gymnastics, Roque (Croquet), Rowing, Tennis, Weightlifting and Freestyle Wrestling.

1906

Athens

After disappointing receptions in Paris and St. Louis, the Olympic movement returned to Athens for the Intercalated Games of 1906.

The mutual desire of Greece and Baron de Coubertin to recapture the spirit of the 1896 Games led to an understanding that the Greeks would host an interim games every four years between Olympics.

Nearly 900 athletes from 20 countries came to Athens, including, for the first time, an official American team picked by the USOC.

As usual, the U.S. dominated track and field, taking 11 of 21 events, including double wins by Martin Sheridan (shot put and freestyle discus), Ray Ewry (standing high and long jumps) and Paul Pilgrim (400 and 800 meters). The previously unknown Pilgrim had been an 11th-hour addition to the team.

Verner Järvinen, the first Finn to compete in the Olympics, won the Greek-style discus throw and placed second in the freestyle discus. He returned home a national hero and inspired Finland to become a future Olympic power.

The Intercalated Games were cancelled due to political unrest in 1910 and never reappeared. Medals won are considered unofficial by the IOC.

Top 10 Standings

National medal standings are not recognized by the IOC. The unofficial point totals are based on 3 points for a gold medal, 2 for a silver and 1 for a bronze.

		Gold	Silver	Bronze	Total	Pts
1	France	15	9	16	40	79
2	Greece	8	13	12	33	62
3	USA	12	6	6	24	54
4	Great Britain	8	11	5	24	51
5	Italy	7	6	3	16	36
6	Switzerland	5	6	4	15	31
7	Germany	4	6	5	15	29
8	Sweden	2	5	7	14	23
9	Hungary	2	5	3	10	19
10	Austria	3	3	2	8	17
	Norway	4	2	1	7	17

Leading Medal Winners

Number of individual medals won on the left; gold, silver and bronze breakdown to the right.

MEN

No		Sport	G-S-B
6	Louis Richardet, SWI	Shooting	4-2-0
5	Martin Sheridan, USA	Track/Field	2-3-0
5	Konrad Stäheli, SWI	Shooting	2-2-1
5	Léon Moreaux, FRA	Shooting	2-1-2
5	Jean Reich, SWI	Shooting	1-1-3
4	Gudbrand Skatteboe, NOR	Shooting	3-1-0
4	Gustav Casmir, GER	Fencing	2-2-0
4	Eric Lemming, SWE	Track/Field & Tug of War	1-0-3
3	Francesco Verri, ITA	Cycling	3-0-0
3	Enrico Bruna, ITA	Rowing	3-0-0
3	Georgio Cesana, ITA	Rowing	3-0-0
3	Max Decugis, FRA.	Tennis	3-0-0
3	Emilio Fontanella, ITA	Rowing	3-0-0
3	Georges Dillon-Cavanaugh, FRA	Fencing	2-1-0
3	Henry Taylor, GBR	Swimming	1-1-1
3	Fernand Vast, FRA	Cycling	1-0-2
3	Raoul de Boigne, FRA	Shooting	0-1-2
3	John Jarvis, GBR	Swimming	0-1-2

WOMEN

No		Sport	G-S-B
2	Sophia Marinou, GRE	Tennis	0-2-0

Track & Field

Event		Time
100m	Archie Hahn, USA	11.2
400m	Paul Pilgrim, USA	53.2
800m	Paul Pilgrim, USA	2:01.5
1500m	Jim Lightbody, USA	4:12.0
5 Miles	Henry Hawtrey, GBR	26:11.8
Marathon	Billy Sherring, CAN	2:51:23.6
110m H	Robert Leavitt, USA	16.2
500m Walk	George Bonhag, USA	7:12.6
3000m Walk	György Sztantics, HUN	15:13.2

Event		Mark
High Jump	Con Leahy, GBR/IRL	5-10
Pole Vault	Fernand Gonder, FRA	11-5¾
Long Jump	Meyer Prinstein, USA	23-7½
Triple Jump	Peter O'Connor, GBR/IRL	46-2¼
Shot Put	Martin Sheridan, USA	40-5¼
Stone Throw	Nicolaos Georgantas, GRE	65-4½
Discus	Martin Sheridan, USA	136-0
Greek Discus	Verner Järvinen, FIN	115-4½
Freestyle		
Javelin	Eric Lemming, SWE	176-10　**WR**
Pentathlon	Hjalmar Mellander, SWE	24 pts

Notes: Weight in Stone Throw was 14.08 lbs; spinning not allowed in Greek-style Discus.

Standing		Mark
High Jump	Ray Ewry, USA	5- 1¼
Long Jump	Ray Ewry, USA	10-10

Swimming

Event		Time
100m Free	Charles Daniels, USA	1:13.4
400m Free	Otto Scheff, AUT	6:23.8
Mile Free	Henry Taylor, GBR	28:28.0
4x250m Free	HUN (József Ónody, Henrik Hajós, Geza Kiss, Zoltán Halmay)	16:52.4

Diving		Points
Platform	Gottlob Walz, GER	156.0

Team Sports

Sport	Champion
Soccer	Denmark
Tug-of-War	Germany

Also Contested

Canoeing, Cycling, Fencing, Gymnastics, Rowing, Shooting, Tennis, Weightlifting and Greco-Roman Wrestling.

1908

London

The fourth Olympic Games were certainly the wettest and probably the most contentious in history.

Held at a new 68,000-seat stadium in the Shepherds Bush section of London, the 1908 Games were played out under continually rainy skies and suffered from endless arguments between British officials and many of the other countries involved–especially the United States.

"The Battle of Shepherds Bush" began almost immediately, when the U.S. delegation noticed that there was no American flag among the national flags decorating the stadium for the opening ceremonies. U.S. flag bearer and discus champion Martin Sheridan responded by refusing to dip the Stars and Stripes when he passed King Edward VII's box in the parade of athletes. "This flag dips to no earthly king," Sheridan said. And it hasn't since.

The Americans, at least, got to march with their flag. Finland, then ruled by Russia, could not. Informed they would have to use a Russian flag, the furious Finns elected to march with no flag at all.

Once again the marathon proved to be the Games' most memorable event. Laid out over a 26-mile, 365-yard course that stretched from Windsor Castle to the royal box at Shepherds Bush, the race ended in controversy when leader Dorando Pietri of Italy staggered into the packed stadium, took a wrong turn, collapsed, was helped up by

doctors, wobbled and fell three more times before being half-carried across the finish line by race officials. Caught up in the drama of Pietri's agony, the cheering crowd hardly noticed that he was declared the winner just as second place runner, Johnny Hayes of the U.S., entered the stadium.

Pietri was later disqualified in favor of Hayes, but only after British and U.S. officials argued for an hour and fights had broken out in the stands.

Top 10 Standings

National medal standings are not recognized by the IOC. The unofficial point totals are based on 3 points for a gold medal, 2 for a silver and 1 for a bronze.

		Gold	Silver	Bronze	Total	Pts
1	Great Britain	54	46	38	138	292
2	USA	23	12	12	47	105
3	Sweden	8	6	11	25	47
4	France	5	5	9	19	34
5	Canada	3	3	10	16	25
6	Germany	3	5	5	13	24
7	Hungary	3	4	2	9	19
8	Norway	2	3	3	8	15
	Belgium	1	5	2	8	15
10	Italy	2	2	0	4	10

Leading Medal Winners

Number of individual medals won on the left; gold, silver and bronze breakdown to the right.

MEN

No		Sport	G-S-B
3	Mel Sheppard, USA	Track/Field	3-0-0
3	Henry Taylor, GBR	Swimming	3-0-0
3	Benjamin Jones, GBR	Cycling	2-1-0
3	Martin Sheridan, USA	Track/Field	2-0-1
3	Oscar Swahn, SWE	Shooting	2-0-1
3	Josiah Ritchie, GBR	Tennis	1-1-1
3	Ted Ranken, GBR	Shooting	0-3-0

WOMEN

No		Sport	G-S-B
2	Madge Syers, GBR	Figure Skating	1-0-1

Note: Figure Skating was part of the Summer Olympics in 1908 and '20.

Track & Field

Event		Time	
100m	Reggie Walker, S. Afr.	10.8	=OR
200m	Bobby Kerr, CAN	22.6	
400m	Wyndham Halswelle, GBR	50.0	
800m	Mel Sheppard, USA	1:52.8	WR
1500m	Mel Sheppard, USA	4:03.4	OR
5 Miles	Emil Voigt, GBR	25:11.2	
Marathon	Johnny Hayes, USA	2:55:18.4	OR
110m H	Forrest Smithson, USA	15.0	WR
400m H	Charley Bacon, USA	55.0	WR
3200m Steeple	Arthur Russell, GBR	10:47.8	
3500m Walk	George Larner, GBR	14:55.0	
10-mi Walk	George Larner, GBR	1:15:57.4	
Medley Relay	USA (William Hamilton, Nathaniel Cartmell, John Taylor, Mel Sheppard)	3:29.4	
3-mile Relay	GBR (Joseph Deakin, Archie Robertson, Wilfred Coales)	6 pts	

Note: Medley Relay made up of two 200m runs, a 400m and an 800m.

Event		Mark	
High Jump	Harry Porter, USA	6-3	OR
Pole Vault	Edward Cooke, USA	12-2	OR
Long Jump	Frank Irons, USA	24-6½	OR
Triple Jump	Timothy Ahearne, GBR/IRL	48-11½	OR
Shot Put	Ralph Rose, USA	46-7½	
Discus	Martin Sheridan, USA	134-2	OR
Greek Discus	Martin Sheridan, USA	128-4	OR
Hammer	John Flanagan, USA	170-4	OR
Javelin	Eric Lemming, SWE	179-10	WR
Freestyle Javelin	Eric Lemming, SWE	178-7½	

Note: Spinning not allowed in Greek-style Discus.

Standing		Mark
High Jump	Ray Ewry, USA	5-2
Long Jump	Ray Ewry, USA	10-11¼

Swimming
MEN

Event		Time	
100m Free	Charles Daniels, USA	1:05.6	WR
400m Free	Henry Taylor, GBR	5:36.8	
1500m Free	Henry Taylor, GBR	22:48.4	WR
100m Back	Arno Bieberstein, GER	1:24.6	WR
200m Brst	Frederick Holman, GBR	3:09.2	WR
4x200m Free	GBR (John Derbyshire, Paul Radmilovic, William Foster, Henry Taylor)	10:55.6	WR

Diving		Points
Platform	Hjalmar Johansson, SWE	83.75
Spring	Albert Zürner, GER	85.5

Team Sports

Sport	Champion
Field Hockey	Great Britain (England)
Lacrosse	Canada
Polo	Great Britain (Roehampton)
Rugby	Australia
Soccer	Great Britain
Tug-of-War	Great Britain (City Police)
Water Polo	Great Britain

Also Contested

Archery, Boxing, Cycling, Fencing, Figure Skating, Gymnastics, Jeu de Paume (court tennis), Racquets, Rowing, Shooting, Tennis, Freestyle Wrestling, Greco-Roman Wrestling and Yachting.

1912

Stockholm

The belligerence of 1908 was replaced with benevolence four years later, as Sweden provided a well-organized and pleasant haven for the troubled Games.

And then there were Jim Thorpe and Hannes Kolehmainen.

Thorpe, a 24-year-old American Indian who was a two-time consensus All-America football player at Carlisle (Pa.) Institute, won the two most demanding events in track and field—the pentathlon and decathlon. And he did it with ease. "You sir," said the Swedes' King Gustav V at the medal ceremony, "are the greatest athlete in the world." To which Thorpe is said to have replied, "Thanks, King."

Kolehmainen, a 22-year-old Finnish vegetarian, ran away with three distance events being run for the first time—the 5,000 and 10,000-meter races and the 12,000-meter cross-country run. He also picked up a silver medal in the 12,000-meter team race.

Ralph Craig of the U.S. was the only other winner of two individual track gold medals, taking both the 100 and 200-meter runs. The 100 final had seven false starts, one with Craig sprinting the entire distance before being called back.

Although Thorpe returned to the U.S. a hero, a year later it was learned that he had played semipro baseball for $25 a week in 1909 and 1910. The IOC, with the full support of the American Olympic Committee, stripped him of his medals and erased his records.

The medals and records were restored in 1982—29 years after Thorpe's death.

Top 10 Standings

National medal standings are not recognized by the IOC. The unofficial point totals are based on 3 points for a gold medal, 2 for a silver and 1 for a bronze.

		Gold	Silver	Bronze	Total	Pts
1	Sweden	23	24	17	64	134
2	USA	25	18	20	63	131
3	Great Britain	10	15	16	41	76
4	Finland	9	8	9	26	52
5	Germany	5	13	7	25	48
6	France	7	4	3	14	32
7	Denmark	1	6	5	12	20
8	Norway	3	2	5	10	18
9	Canada	3	2	3	8	16
	Hungary	3	2	3	8	16
	South Africa	4	2	0	6	16

Leading Medal Winners

Number of individual medals won on the left; gold, silver and bronze breakdown to the right.

MEN

No		Sport	G-S-B
6	Louis Richardet, SWI	Shooting	4-2-0
5	Wilhelm Carlberg, SWE	Shooting	3-2-0
4	Hannes Kolehmainen, FIN	Track/Field	3-1-0
4	Eric Carlberg, SWE	Shooting	2-2-0
4	Johan von Holst, SWE	Shooting	2-1-1
4	Carl Osburn, USA	Shooting	1-2-1
3	Alfred Lane, USA	Shooting	3-0-0
3	Åke Lundeberg, SWE	Shooting	2-1-0
3	Frederick Hird, USA	Shooting	2-0-1
3	Jean Cariou, FRA	Equestrian	1-1-1
3	Charles Dixon, GBR	Tennis	1-1-1
3	Harold Hardwick, AUS	Swimming	1-0-2
3	Jack Hatfield, GBR	Swimming	0-2-1
3	Charles Stewart, GBR	Shooting	0-0-3

WOMEN

No		Sport	G-S-B
2	Edith Hannam, GBR	Tennis	2-0-0
2	Jennie Fletcher, GBR	Swimming	1-0-1
2	Sigrid Fick, SWE	Tennis	0-1-1

Track & Field

Event		Time	
100m	Ralph Craig, USA	10.8	=OR
200m	Ralph Craig, USA	21.7	
400m	Charlie Reidpath, USA	48.2	OR
800m	Ted Meredith, USA	1:51.9	WR
1500m	Arnold Jackson, GBR	3:56.8	OR
5000m	Hannes Kolehmainen, FIN	14:36.6	WR
10,000m	Hannes Kolehmainen, FIN	31:20.8	
X-country (12,000m)	Hannes Kolehmainen, FIN	45:11.6	
Marathon	Kenneth McArthur, S. Afr.	2:36:54.8	
110m H	Frederick Kelly, USA	15.1	
10k Walk	George Goulding, CAN	46:28.4	
4x100m	GBR (David Jacobs, Harold Macintosh, Victor d'Arcy, William Applegarth)	42.4	OR
4x400m	USA (Mel Sheppard, Edward Lindberg, Ted Meredith, Charlie Reidpath)	3:16.6	WR
3000m Team	USA (Tel Berna, Norman Taber, George Bonhag)	9 pts	
X-country (12,000m)	SWE (Hjalmar Andersson, John Eke, Josef Ternström)	10 pts	

Event		Mark	
High Jump	Alma Richards, USA	6-4	OR
Pole Vault	Harry Babcock, USA	12-11½	OR
Long Jump	Albert Gutterson, USA	24-11¼	OR
Triple Jump	Gustaf Lindblom, SWE	48-5¼	
Shot Put	Babe McDonald, USA	50-4	OR
Discus	Armas Taipale, FIN	148-3	OR
Hammer	Matt McGrath, USA	179-7	OR
Javelin	Eric Lemming, SWE	198-11	WR
Pentathlon	Jim Thorpe, USA	7 pts	
Decathlon	Jim Thorpe, USA	8412 pts	WR

Event		Mark
High Jump	Platt Adams, USA	5-4¼
Long Jump	Constantin Tsiklitiras, GRE	11-0¾

Both Hands		Mark
Shot Put	Ralph Rose, USA	90-10½
Discus	Armas Taipale, FIN	271-10
Javelin	Juho Saaristo, FIN	359-0

Swimming

MEN

Event		Time	
100m Free	Duke Kahanamoku, USA	1:03.4	
400m Free	George Hodgson, CAN	5:24.4	
1500m Free	George Hodgson, CAN	22:00.0	WR
100m Back	Harry Hebner, USA	1:21.2	
200m Brst	Walter Bathe, GER	3:01.8	OR
400m Brst	Walter Bathe, GER	6:29.6	OR
4x200m Free	AUS (Cecil Healy, Malcolm Champion, Leslie Boardman, Harold Hardwick)	10:11.6	WR

Diving		Points
Spring	Paul Günther, GER	79.23
Platform	Erik Adlerz, SWE	73.94
Plain High	Erik Adlerz, SWE	40.0

WOMEN

Event		Time	
100m Free	Fanny Durack, AUS	1:22.2	
4x100m Free	GBR (Bella Moore, Jennie Fletcher, Annie Speirs, Irene Steer)	5:52.8	WR

Diving		Points
Platform	Greta Johansson, SWE	39.9

Team Sports

Sports	Champion
Soccer	Great Britain
Tug-of-War	Sweden
Water Polo	Great Britain

Also Contested

Cycling, Equestrian, Fencing, Gymnastics, Modern Pentathlon, Rowing, Shooting, Tennis, Greco-Roman Wrestling and Yachting.

- VIIᵉ OLYMPIADE - ANVERS (BELGIQUE) 1920 AOUT-SEPTEMBRE 1920

1920

Antwerp

The Olympic quadrennial, scheduled for Berlin in 1916, was interrupted by World War I–the so-called "War to End All Wars," which had involved 28 countries and killed nearly 10 million troops in four years.

The four-year cycle of Olympiads–Berlin would have been the sixth–is still counted, however, even though the Games were not played.

Less than two years after the armistice, the Olympics resumed in Belgium, a symbolic and austere choice considering it had been occupied for four years by enemy forces. Still, 29 countries (one more than participated in the war) sent a record 2,600 athletes to the Games. Germany and Austria, the defeated enemies of Belgium and the Allies, were not invited.

The United States turned in the best overall team performance, winning 41 gold medals, but the talk of the Games was 23-year-old distance runner Paavo Nurmi of Finland. Nurmi won the 10,000-meter run and 8,000-meter cross-country, took a third gold in the team cross-country and silver in the 5,000-meter run. In all, Finland won nine track and field gold medals to break the U.S. dominance in the sport.

Elsewhere, Albert Hill of Britain made his Olympic debut at age 36 and won both the 800 and 1,500-meter runs. World record holder Charley Paddock of the U.S. won the 100 meters, but was upset in the 200 by teammate Allen Woodring, who was a last-minute addition to the team. And in swimming, the U.S. won 11 of 15 events, led by triple gold medalists Norman Ross and Ethelda Bleibtrey, defending men's 100-meter freestyle champion Duke Kahanamoku and 14-year-old springboard diving champion Aileen Riggin.

The Antwerp Games were also noteworthy for the introduction of the Olympic oath–uttered for the first time by Belgium fencer Victor Bion–and the Olympic flag, with its five multicolored, intersecting rings.

Top 10 Standings

National medal standings are not recognized by the IOC. The unofficial point totals are based on 3 points for a gold medal, 2 for a silver and 1 for a bronze.

		Gold	Silver	Bronze	Total	Pts
1	USA	41	27	27	95	204
2	Sweden	19	20	25	64	122
3	Great Britain	14	15	13	42	85
4	France	9	19	13	41	78
5	Finland	15	10	9	34	74
	Belgium	13	11	11	35	72
7	Norway	13	9	9	31	66
8	Italy	13	5	5	23	54
9	Denmark	3	9	1	13	28
10	Holland	4	2	5	11	21

Leading Medal Winners

Number of individual medals won on the left; gold, silver and bronze breakdown to the right.

MEN

No		Sport	G-S-B
7	Willis Lee, USA	Shooting	5-1-1
7	Lloyd Spooner, USA	Shooting	4-1-2
6	Hubert van Innis, BEL	Archery	4-2-0
6	Carl Osburn, USA	Shooting	4-1-1
5	Nedo Nadi, ITA	Fencing	5-0-0
5	Otto Olsen, NOR	Shooting	3-2-0
5	Larry Nuesslein, USA	Shooting	2-1-2
5	Julien Brulé, FRA	Archery	1-3-1
4	Dennis Fenton, USA	Shooting	3-0-1
4	Aldo Nadi, ITA	Fencing	3-1-0
4	Paavo Nurmi, FIN	Track/Field	3-1-0
4	Harold Natvig, NOR	Shooting	2-1-1
4	Östen Östensen, NOR	Shooting	0-2-2
4	Erik Backman, SWE	Track/Field	0-1-3
4	Fritz Kuchen, SWI	Shooting	0-0-4
3	Norman Ross, USA	Swimming	3-0-0
3	Albert Hill, GBR	Track/Field	2-1-0
3	Morris Kirksey, USA	Track/Field & Rugby	2-1-0
3	Charley Paddock, USA	Track/Field	2-1-0
3	Bevil Rudd, S. Afr.	Track/Field	1-0-2
3	Ettore Caffaratti, ITA	Equestrian	0-1-2

Fourteen shooters tied with 3 each.

WOMEN

No		Sport	G-S-B
3	Ethelda Bleibtrey, USA	Swimming	3-0-0
3	Suzanne Lenglen, FRA	Tennis	2-0-1
3	Kitty McKane, GBR	Tennis	1-1-1
3	Frances Schroth, USA	Swimming	1-0-2
2	Irene Guest, USA	Swimming	1-1-0
2	Margaret Woodbridge, USA	Swimming	1-1-0
2	Dorothy Holman, GBR	Tennis	0-2-0

Track & Field

Event		Time	
100m	Charley Paddock, USA	10.8	
200m	Allen Woodring, USA	22.0	
400m	Bevil Rudd, S. Afr.	49.6	
800m	Albert Hill, GBR	1:53.4	
1500m	Albert Hill, GBR	4:01.8	
5000m	Joseph Guillemot, FRA	14:55.6	
10,000m	Paavo Nurmi, FIN	31:45.8	
X-country (8000m)	Paavo Nurmi, FIN	27:15.0	
Marathon	Hannes Kolehmainen, FIN.	2:32:35.8	WB
110m H	Earl Thomson, CAN	14.8	WR
400m H	Frank Loomis, USA	54.0	WR
3000m Steeple	Percy Hodge, GBR	10:00.4	OR
3k Walk	Ugo Frigerio, ITA	13:14.2	OR
10k Walk	Ugo Frigerio, ITA	48:06.2	
4x100m	USA (Charley Paddock, Jackson Scholz, Loren Murchison, Morris Kirksey)	42.2	WR
4x400m	GBR (Cecil Griffiths, Robert Lindsay, John Ainsworth-Davis, Guy Butler)	3:22.2	
3000m Team	USA (Horace Brown, Arlie Schardt, Ivan Dresser)	10 pts	
X-country (8000m)	FIN (Paavo Nurmi, Heikki Liimatainen, Teodor Koskenniemi)	10 pts	

Event		Mark	
High Jump	Richmond Landon, USA	6-4	=OR
Pole Vault	Frank Foss, USA	13-5	WR
Long Jump	William Petersson, SWE	23-5½	
Triple Jump	Vilho Tuulos, FIN	47-7	
Shot Put	Ville Pörhölä, FIN	48-7¼	
56-lb Throw	Babe McDonald, USA	36-11½	OR
Discus	Elmer Niklander, FIN	146-7	
Hammer	Pat Ryan, USA	173-5	
Javelin	Jonni Myyrä, FIN	215-10	OR
Pentathlon	Eero Lehtonen, FIN	14 pts	
Decathlon	Helge Lövland, NOR	6803 pts	

Swimming

MEN

Event		Time	
100m Free	Duke Kahanamoku, USA	1:01.4	
400m Free	Norman Ross, USA	5:26.8	
1500m Free	Norman Ross, USA	22:23.2	
100m Back	Warren Kealoha, USA	1:15.2	
200m Brst	Håkan Malmroth, SWE	3:04.4	
400m Brst	Håkan Malmroth, SWE	6:31.8	
4x200m Free	USA (Perry McGillivray, Pua Kealoha, Norman Ross, Duke Kahanamoku)	10:04.4	WR

Diving		Points
Plain High	Arvid Wallman, SWE	183.5
Platform	Clarence Pinkston, USA	100.67
Spring	Louis Kuehn, USA	675.4

WOMEN

Event		Time	
100m Free	Ethelda Bleibtrey, USA	1:13.6	WR
300m Free	Ethelda Bleibtrey, USA	4:34.0	WR
4x100m Free	USA (Margaret Woodbridge, Frances Schroth, Irene Guest, Ethelda Bleibtrey)	5:11.6	WR

Diving		Points
Platform	Stefani Fryland-Clausen, DEN	34.6
Spring	Aileen Riggin, USA	539.9

Team Sports

Sport	Champion
Field Hockey	Great Britain
Ice Hockey	Canada
Polo	Great Britain
Soccer	Belgium
Rugby	United States
Tug-of-War	Great Britain
Water Polo	Great Britain/Ireland

Also Contested

Archery, Boxing, Cycling, Equestrian, Fencing, Figure Skating, Gymnastics, Modern Pentathlon, Rowing, Shooting, Tennis, Weightlifting, Freestyle Wrestling, Greco-Roman Wrestling and Yachting.

PARIS 1924
JEUX OLYMPIQUES

1924

Paris

Paavo Nurmi may have been the talk of Antwerp in 1920, but he was the sensation of Paris four years later.

It wasn't just that the "Flying Finn" won five gold medals, it was the way he did it. Running with a stopwatch on his wrist, Peerless Paavo captured the 1,500 and 5,000-meter finals within an hour of each other and set Olympic records in both. Two days later, he blew away the field in the 10,000-meter cross-country run where the heat and an unusually difficult course combined to knock out 23 of 38 starters (Finland also won the team gold in the event). And finally, the next day he led the Finns to victory in the 3,000-meter team race. His performance overshadowed the four gold medals of teammate Ville Ritola.

The gold medals won by British runners Harold Abrahams in the 100 meters and Eric Liddell in the 400 were chronicled in the 1981 Academy Award-winning film "Chariots of Fire." The movie, however, was not based on fact. Liddell, a devout Christian, knew months in advance that the preliminary for the 100 (his best event) was on a Sunday, so he had plenty of time to change plans and train for the 400. Also, he and Abrahams never competed against each other in real life.

Speaking of the movies, Johnny Weissmuller of the U.S. won three swimming gold medals in the 100 and 400-meter freestyles and the 4x200 freestyle relay. He would later become Hollywood's most famous Tarzan.

Top 10 Standings

National medal standings are not recognized by the IOC. The unofficial point totals are based on 3 points for a gold medal, 2 for a silver and 1 for a bronze.

		Gold	Silver	Bronze	Total	Pts
1	USA	45	27	27	99	216
2	France	13	15	10	38	79
3	Finland	14	13	10	37	78
4	Great Britain	9	13	12	34	65
5	Sweden	4	13	12	29	50
6	Switzerland	7	8	10	25	47
7	Italy	8	3	5	16	35
8	Belgium	3	7	3	13	26
9	Norway	5	2	3	10	22
10	Holland	4	1	5	10	19

Leading Medal Winners

Number of individual medals won on the left; gold, silver and bronze breakdown to the right.

MEN

No		Sport	G-S-B
6	Ville Ritola, FIN	Track/Field	4-2-0
5	Paavo Nurmi, FIN	Track/Field	5-0-0
5	Roger Ducret, FRA	Fencing	3-2-0
4	Johnny Weissmuller, USA	Swimming & Water Polo	3-0-1
3	Ole Lilloe-Olsen, NOR	Shooting	2-1-0
3	Vincent Richards, USA	Tennis	2-1-0
3	Albert Séquin, FRA	Gymnastics	1-2-0
3	Boy Charlton, AUS	Swimming	1-1-1
3	August Güttinger, SWI	Gymnastics	1-0-2
3	Robert Prazák, CZE	Gymnastics	0-3-0
3	Arne Borg, SWE	Swimming	0-2-1
3	Jean Gutweniger, SWI	Gymnastics	0-2-1
3	Henri Hoevenaers, BEL	Cycling	0-2-1

WOMEN

No		Sport	G-S-B
3	Gertrude Ederle, USA	Swimming	1-0-2
2	Ethel Lackie, USA	Swimming	2-0-0
2	Hazel Wightman, USA	Tennis	2-0-0
2	Helen Wills, USA	Tennis	2-0-0
2	Betty Becker, USA	Diving	1-1-0
2	Mariechen Wehselau, USA	Swimming	1-1-0
2	Kitty McKane, GBR	Tennis	0-1-1
2	Aileen Riggin, USA	Swimming & Diving	0-1-1

Track & Field

Event		Time	
100m	Harold Abrahams, GBR	10.6	=OR
200m	Jackson Scholz, USA	21.6	
400m	Eric Liddell, GBR	47.6	OR
800m	Douglas Lowe, GBR	1:52.4	
1500m	Paavo Nurmi, FIN	3:53.6	OR
5000m	Paavo Nurmi, FIN	14:31.2	OR
10,000m	Ville Ritola, FIN	30:23.2	WR
X-country (10,000m)	Paavo Nurmi, FIN	32:54.8	
Marathon	Albin Stenroos, FIN	2:41:22.6	
110m H	Daniel Kinsey, USA	15.0	
400m H	Morgan Taylor, USA	52.6	
3000m Steeple	Ville Ritola, FIN	9:33.6	OR
10k Walk	Ugo Frigerio, ITA	47:49.0	
4x100m	USA (Francis Hussey, Louis Clarke, Loren Murchison, Alfred Leconey)	41.0	=WR
4x400M	USA (C.S. Cochrane, Alan Helffrich, J.O. MacDonald, William Stevenson)	3:16.0	WR
3000m Team	FIN (Paavo Nurmi, Ville Ritola, Elias Katz)	8 pts	
X-country (10,000m)	FIN (Paavo Nurmi, Ville Ritola, Hekki Liimatainen)	11 pts	

Event		Mark	
High Jump	Harold Osborn, USA	6-6	OR
Pole Vault	Lee Barnes, USA	12-11½	
Long Jump	De Hart Hubbard, USA	24-5	
Triple Jump	Nick Winter, AUS	50-11¼	WR
Shot Put	Bud Houser, USA	49-2¼	
Discus	Bud Houser, USA	151-4	OR
Hammer	Fred Tootell, USA	174-10	
Javelin	Jonni Myyrä, FIN	206-7	
Pentathlon	Eero Lehtonen, FIN	14 pts	
Decathlon	Harold Osborn, USA	7711 pts	WR

Swimming

MEN

Event		Time	
100m Free	Johnny Weissmuller, USA	59.0	OR
400m Free	Johnny Weissmuller, USA	5:04.2	OR
1500m Free	Boy Charlton, AUS	20:06.6	WR
100m Back	Warren Kealoha, USA	1:13.2	OR
200m Brst	Robert Skelton, USA	2:56.6	

Event		Time	
4x200m Free	USA (Wallace O'Connor, Harry Glancy, Ralph Breyer, Johnny Weissmuller)	.........9:53.4	**WR**

Diving		Points	
Plain High	Richmond Eve, AUS	..........160.0	
Platform	Albert White, USA	.........97.46	
Spring	Albert White, USA	...........696.4	

WOMEN

Event		Time	
100m Free	Ethel Lackie, USA	...........1:12.4	
400m Free	Martha Norelius, USA	.......6:02.2	**OR**
100m Back	Sybil Bauer, USA	.............1:23.2	**OR**
200m Brst	Lucy Morton, GBR	..........3:33.2	**OR**
4x100m Free	USA (Gertrude Ederle, Euphrasia Donnelly, Ethel Lackie, Mariechen Wehselau)	........4:58.8	**WR**

Diving		Points	
Platform	Caroline Smith, USA	..........33.2	
Spring	Elizabeth Becker, USA	.......474.5	

Team Sports

Sport	Champion
Polo	....Argentina
Rugby	....................................United States
Soccer	....Uruguay
Water Polo	....France

Also Contested

Boxing, Cycling, Equestrian, Fencing, Gymnastics, Modern Pentathlon, Rowing, Shooting, Tennis, Weightlifting, Freestyle Wrestling, Greco-Roman Wrestling and Yachting.

1928

Amsterdam

"We are here to represent the greatest country on earth. We did not come here to lose gracefully. We came here to win–and win decisively."

So ordered American Olympic Committee president Gen. Douglas Mac-Arthur before the start of the 1928 Games. His athletes would deliver, easily winning the unofficial national standings for the third Olympiad in a row.

The U.S. men won eight gold medals in track and field, but were victorious in only one individual running race (Ray Barbuti in the 400 meters). In the sprints, Canada's Percy Williams became the first non-American to win both the 100 and 200. Finland claimed four running titles, including Paavo Nurmi's victory in the 10,000 meters–his ninth overall gold medal in three Olympic Games. Teammate and arch-rival Ville Ritola placed second in the 10,000 and outran Nurmi in the 5,000.

These Games marked Germany's return to the Olympic fold after serving a 10-year probation for its "aggressiveness" in World War I. It was also the first Olympics that women were allowed to partici-

pate in track and field (despite objections from Pope Pius IX). And in swimming, the U.S. got double gold performances from Martha Norelius, Albina Osipowich and Johnny Weissmuller, as well as diver Pete Desjardins.

Top 10 Standings

National medal standings are not recognized by the IOC. The unofficial point totals are based on 3 points for a gold medal, 2 for a silver and 1 for a bronze.

		Gold	Silver	Bronze	Total	Pts
1	USA	22	18	16	56	118
2	Germany	10	7	14	31	58
3	Finland	8	8	9	25	49
4	Sweden	7	6	12	25	45
5	France	6	10	5	21	43
6	Holland	6	9	4	19	40
7	Italy	7	5	7	19	38
8	Great Britain	3	10	7	20	36
9	Switzerland	7	4	4	15	33
10	Canada	4	4	7	15	27

Leading Medal Winners

Number of individual medals won on the left; gold, silver and bronze breakdown to the right.

MEN

No		Sport	G-S-B
4	Georges Miez, SWI	Gymnastics	3-1-0
4	Hermann Hänggi, SWI	Gymnastics	2-1-1
3	Lucien Gaudin, FRA	Fencing	2-1-0
3	Eugen Mack, SWI	Gymnastics	2-0-1
3	Paavo Nurmi, FIN	Track/Field	1-2-0
3	Ladislav Vácha, CZE	Gymnastics	1-2-0
3	Leon Stukelj, YUG	Gymnastics	1-0-2
3	Emanuel Löffler, CZE	Gymnastics	0-2-1

WOMEN

No		Sport	G-S-B
3	Joyce Cooper, GBR	Swimming	0-1-2
2	Martha Norelius, USA	Swimming	2-0-0
2	Albina Osipowich, USA	Swimming	2-0-0
2	Maria Braun, NED	Swimming	1-1-0
2	Eleanor Garatti, USA	Swimming	1-1-0
2	Betty Robinson, USA	Track/Field	1-1-0
2	Fanny Rosenfeld, CAN	Track/Field	1-1-0
2	Ethel Smith, CAN	Track/Field	1-0-1
2	Ellen King, GBR	Swimming	0-2-0
2	Georgia Coleman, USA	Diving	0-1-1

Track & Field
MEN

Event		Time	
100m	Percy Williams, CAN	............10.8	
200m	Percy Williams, CAN	............21.8	
400m	Ray Barbuti, USA	...............47.8	
800m	Douglas Lowe, GBR	............1:51.8	**OR**
1500m	Harri Larva, FIN	...............3:53.2	**OR**
5000m	Ville Ritola, FIN	..............14:38.0	
10,000m	Paavo Nurmi, FIN	.........30:18.8	**OR**
Marathon	Mohamed El Ouafi, FRA	...2:32:57.0	
110m H	Syd Atkinson, S. Afr.	...........14.8	
400m H	David Burghley, GBR	...........53.4	**OR**
3000m Steeple	Toivo Loukola, FIN	...........9:21.8	**WR**
4x100m	USA (Frank Wykoff, Jimmy Quinn, Charley Borah, Hank Russell)	....41.0	**WR**
4x400m	USA (George Baird, Bud Spencer, Fred Alderman, Ray Barbuti)	.................3:14.2	**WR**

Event		Mark
High Jump	Bob King, USA	.6-4½
Pole Vault	Sabin Carr, USA	.13-9¼ **OR**
Long Jump	Ed Hamm, USA	.25- 4½ **OR**
Triple Jump	Mikio Oda, JPN	.49-11
Shot Put	Johnny Kuck, USA	.52-0¾ **WR**
Discus	Bud Houser, USA	.155- 3 **OR**
Hammer	Pat O'Callaghan, IRL	.168- 7
Javelin	Erik Lundkvist, SWE	.218- 6 **OR**
Decathlon	Paavo Yrjölä, FIN	.8053 pts **WR**

WOMEN

Event		Time
100m	Betty Robinson, USA	.12.2 **=WR**
800m	Lina Radke, GER	.2:16.8 **WR**
4x100m	CAN (Fanny Rosenfeld, Ethel Smith, Florence Bell, Myrtle Cook)	. 48.4 **WR**

Event		Mark
High Jump	Ethel Catherwood, CAN	.5- 2½
Discus	Halina Konopacka, POL	.129-11¾ **WR**

Swimming
MEN

Event		Time
100m Free	Johnny Weissmuller, USA	.58.6 **OR**
400m Free	Alberto Zorilla, ARG	.5:01.6 **OR**
1500m Free	Arne Borg, SWE	.19:51.8 **OR**
100m Back	George Kojac, USA	.1:08.2 **WR**
200m Brst	Yoshiyuki Tsuruta, JPN	.2:48.8 **OR**

Event		Time
4x200m Free	USA (Austin Clapp, Walter Laufer, Gorge Kojac, Johnny Weissmuller)	.9:36.2 **WR**

Diving		Points
Platform	Pete Desjardins, USA	.98.74
Spring	Pete Desjardins, USA	.185.04

WOMEN

Event		Time
100m Free	Albina Osipowich, USA	.1:11.0 **OR**
400m Free	Martha Norelius, USA	.5:42.8 **WR**
100m Back	Maria Braun, NED	.1:22.0
200m Brst	Hilde Schrader, GER	.3:12.6
4x100m Free	USA (Adelaide Lambert, Eleanor Garatti, Albina Osipowich, Martha Norelius)	. 4:47.6 **WR**

Diving		Points
Platform	Elizabeth Becker Pinkston, USA	.31.6
Spring	Helen Meany, USA	.78.62

Team Sports

Sport	Champion
Field Hockey	India
Soccer	Uruguay
Water Polo	Germany

Also Contested

Boxing, Cycling, Equestrian, Fencing, Gymnastics, Modern Pentathlon, Rowing, Weightlifting, Freestyle Wrestling, Greco-Roman Wrestling and Yachting.

1932

Los Angeles

Despite a world-wide economic depression and predictions that the 1932 Summer Olympics were doomed to failure, 37 countries sent over 1,300 athletes to southern California and the Games were a huge success.

Energized by perfect weather and the buoyant atmosphere of the first Olympic Village, the competition was fierce. Sixteen world and Olympic records fell in men's track and field alone.

In women's track, 21-year-old Babe Didrikson, who had set world records in the 80-meter hurdles, javelin and high jump at the AAU Olympic Trials three weeks before, came to L.A. and announced, "I am out to beat everybody in sight." She almost did too–winning the hurdles and javelin, but taking second in the high jump (despite tying teammate Jean Shiley for first) when her jumping style was ruled illegal.

Didrikson's heroics, along with American Eddie Tolan's double in the 100 and 200 meters and Italian Luigi Beccali's upset victory in the 1,500, were among the Games' highlights, but they didn't quite make up for the absence of Finland's famed distance runner Paavo Nurmi.

Just before the Games, the IOC said that Nurmi would not be allowed to participate in his fourth Olympics because he had received excessive expense money on a trip to Germany in 1929. The ruling came as no surprise in the track world where it was said, "Nurmi has the lowest heartbeat and the highest asking price of any athlete in the world."

The Japanese men and American women dominated in swimming, each winning five of six events. Helene Madison of the U.S. won two races and anchored the winning relay team.

Top 10 Standings

National medal standings are not recognized by the IOC. The unofficial point totals are based on 3 points for a gold medal, 2 for a silver and 1 for a bronze.

		Gold	Silver	Bronze	Total	Pts
1	USA	41	32	30	103	217
2	Italy	12	12	12	36	72
3	Sweden	9	5	9	23	46
4	France	10	5	4	19	44
5	Finland	5	8	12	25	43
6	Germany	3	12	5	20	38
7	Japan	7	7	4	18	39
8	Great Britain	4	7	5	16	31
	Hungary	6	4	5	15	31
10	Canada	2	5	8	15	24

Leading Medal Winners

Number of individual medals won on the left; gold, silver and bronze breakdown to the right.

MEN

No		Sport	G-S-B
4	István Pelle, HUN	Gymnastics	2-2-0
4	Giulio Gaudini, ITA	Fencing	0-3-1
4	Heikki Savolainen, FIN	Gymnastics	0-1-3
3	Romeo Neri, ITA	Gymnastics	3-0-0
3	Alex Wilson, CAN	Track/Field	0-1-2
3	Philip Edwards, CAN	Track/Field	0-0-3

WOMEN

No		Sport	G-S-B
3	Helene Madison, USA	Swimming	3-0-0
3	Babe Didrikson, USA	Track/Field	2-1-0
2	Georgia Coleman, USA	Diving	1-1-0
2	Eleanor Garatti, USA	Swimming	1-0-1
2	Willy den Ouden, HOL	Swimming	0-2-0
2	Valerie Davies, GBR	Swimming	0-0-2

Track & Field
MEN

Event		Time	
100m	Eddie Tolan, USA	10.3	OR
200m	Eddie Tolan, USA	21.2	OR
400m	Bill Carr, USA	46.2	WR
800m	Tommy Hampson, GBR	1:49.7	WR
1500m	Luigi Beccali, ITA	3:51.2	OR
5000m	Lauri Lehtinen, FIN	14:30.0	OR
10,000m	Janusz Kusocinski, POL	30:11.4	OR
Marathon	Juan Carlos Zabala, ARG	2:31:36.0	OR
110m H	George Saling, USA	14.6	
400m H	Bob Tisdall, IRL	51.7	
3000m Steeple	Volmari Iso-Hollo, FIN	10:33.4	
50k Walk	Thomas Green, GBR	4:50:10	
4x100m	USA (Bob Kiesel, Emmett Toppino, Hector Dyer, Frank Wykoff)	40.0	WR
4x400m	USA (Ivan Fuqua, Edgar Ablowich, Karl Warner, Bill Carr)	3:08.2	WR

Note: Due to a lap count error, the 3000-meter steeplechase actually went 3460 meters, or one lap too many.

Event		Mark	
High Jump	Duncan McNaughton, CAN	6- 5½	
Pole Vault	Bill Miller, USA	14- 1¾	OR
Long Jump	Edward Gordon, USA	25- 0¾	
Triple Jump	Chuhei Nambu, JPN	51- 7	WR
Shot Put	Leo Sexton, USA	52- 6	OR
Discus	John Anderson, USA	162- 4	OR
Hammer	Pat O'Callaghan, IRL	176-11	
Javelin	Matti Järvinen, FIN	238- 6	OR
Decathlon	Jim Bausch, USA	8462 pts	WR

WOMEN

Event		Time	
100m	Stella Walsh, POL*	11.9	=WR
80m H	Babe Didrikson, USA	11.7	WR
4x100m	USA (Mary Carew, Evelyn Furtsch, Annette Rogers, Wilhelmina Von Bremen)	46.9	WR

*An autopsy performed after Walsh's death in 1980 revealed that she was a man.

Event		Mark	
High Jump	Jean Shiley, USA	5- 5¼	WR
Discus	Lillian Copeland, USA	133- 2	OR
Javelin	Babe Didrikson, USA	143- 4	OR

Swimming
MEN

Event		Time	
100m Free	Yasuji Miyazaki, JPN	58.2	
400m Free	Buster Crabbe, USA	4:48.4	OR
1500m Free	Kusuo Kitamura, JPN	19:12.4	OR
100m Back	Masaji Kiyokawa, JPN	1:08.6	
200m Brst	Yoshiyuki Tsuruta, JPN	2:45.4	
4x200m Free	JPN (Yasuji Miyazaki, Masonori Yusa, Takashi Yokoyama, Hisakichi Toyoda)	8:58.4	WR

Diving		Points
Platform	Harold Smith, USA	124.80
Spring	Michael Galitzen, USA	161.38

WOMEN

Event		Time	
100m Free	Helene Madison, USA	1:06.8	OR
400m Free	Helene Madison, USA	5:28.5	WR
100m Back	Eleanor Holm, USA	1:19.4	
200m Brst	Clare Dennis, AUS	3:06.3	OR
4x100m Free	USA (Josephine McKim, Helen Johns, Eleanor Saville-Garatti, Helene Madison)	4:38.0	WR

Diving		Points
Platform	Dorothy Poynton, USA	40.26
Spring	Georgia Coleman, USA	87.52

Team Sports

Sport	Champion
Field Hockey	India
Water Polo	Hungary

Also Contested

Boxing, Cycling, Equestrian, Fencing, Gymnastics, Modern Pentathlon, Rowing, Shooting, Weightlifting, Freestyle Wrestling, Greco-Roman Wrestling and Yachting.

1936

Berlin

At the Big Ten Track and Field Championships of 1935, Ohio State's Jesse Owens equaled or set world records in four events: the 100 and 220-yard dashes, 200-yard low hurdles and the long jump. He was also credited with world marks in the 200-meter run and 200-meter hurdles. That's six world records in one afternoon, and he did it all in 45 minutes!

The following year, he swept the 100 and 200 meters and long jump at the Olympic Trials and headed for Germany favored to win all three.

In Berlin, dictator Adolf Hitler and his Nazi followers felt sure that the Olympics would be the ideal venue to demonstrate Germany's oft-stated racial superiority. He directed that $25 million be spent on the finest facilities, the cleanest streets and the temporary withdrawal of all outward signs of the state-run anti-Jewish campaign. By the time over 4,000 athletes from 49 countries arrived for the Games, the stage was set.

Then Owens, a black sharecropper's son from Alabama, stole the show—winning his three individual events and adding a fourth gold medal in the 4x100-meter relay. The fact that four other American blacks also won did little to please Herr Hitler, but the applause from the German crowds, especially for Owens, was thunderous. As it was for New Zealander Jack Lovelock's thrilling win over Glenn Cunningham and defending champ Luigi Beccali in the 1,500 meters.

Germany won only five combined gold medals in men's and women's track and field, but saved face for the "master race" in the overall medal count with an 89-56 margin over the United States.

The top female performers in Berlin were 17-year-old Dutch swimmer Rie Mastenbroek, who won three gold medals, and 18-year-old American runner Helen Stephens, who captured the 100 meters and anchored the winning 4x100-meter relay team.

Basketball also made its debut as a medal sport and was played outdoors. The U.S. men easily won the first gold medal championship game with a 19-8 victory over Canada in the rain.

Top 10 Standings

National medal standings are not recognized by the IOC. The unofficial point totals are based on 3 points for a gold medal, 2 for a silver and 1 for a bronze.

		Gold	Silver	Bronze	Total	Pts
1	Germany	33	26	30	89	181
2	USA	24	20	12	56	124
3	Italy	8	9	5	22	47
4	Finland	7	6	6	19	39
	France	7	6	6	19	39
6	Sweden	6	5	9	20	37
	Hungary	10	1	5	16	37
8	Japan	6	4	8	18	34
9	Holland	6	4	7	17	33
10	Great Britain	4	7	3	14	29

Leading Medal Winners

Number of individual medals won on the left; gold, silver and bronze breakdown to the right.

MEN

No		Sport	G-S-B
6	Konrad Frey, GER	Gymnastics	3-1-2
5	Alfred Schwarzmann, GER	Gymnastics	3-0-2
5	Eugen Mack, SWI	Gymnastics	0-4-1
4	Jesse Owens, USA	Track/Field	4-0-0
3	Robert Charpentier, FRA	Cycling	3-0-0
3	Guy Lapébie, FRA	Cycling	2-1-0
3	Jack Medica, USA	Swimming	1-2-0
3	Matthias Volz, GER	Gymnastics	1-0-2

WOMEN

No		Sport	G-S-B
4	Rie Mastenbroek, NED	Swimming	3-1-0
2	Helen Stephens, USA	Track/Field	2-0-0
2	Dorothy Poynton Hill, USA	Diving	1-0-1
2	Gisela Arendt, GER	Swimming	0-1-1

Track & Field

MEN

Event		Time	
100m	Jesse Owens, USA	10.3	
200m	Jesse Owens, USA	20.7	OR
400m	Archie Williams, USA	46.5	
800m	John Woodruff, USA	1:52.9	
1500m	Jack Lovelock, NZE	3:47.8	WR
5000m	Gunnar Höckert, FIN	14:22.2	OR
10,000m	Ilmari Salminen, FIN	30:15.4	
Marathon	Sohn Kee-chung, JPN	2:29:19.2	OR
110m H	Forrest Towns, USA	14.2	
400m H	Glenn Hardin, USA	52.4	
3000m Steeple	Volmari Iso-Hollo, FIN	9:03.8	WR
50k walk	Harold Whitlock, GBR	4:30:41.4	OR

Note: Marathon winner Sohn was a Korean, but was forced to run for Japan, which occupied his country.

Event		Time	
4x100m	USA (Jesse Owens, Ralph Metcalfe, Foy Draper, Frank Wykoff)	39.8	WR
4x400m	GBR (Frederick Wolff, Godfrey Rampling, William Roberts, A.G. Brown)	3:09.0	

Event		Mark	
High Jump	Cornelius Johnson, USA	6-8	OR
Pole Vault	Earle Meadows, USA	14-3¼	OR
Long Jump	Jesse Owens, USA	26-5½	OR
Triple Jump	Naoto Tajima, JPN	52-6	WR
Shot Put	Hans Woellke, GER	53-1¾	OR
Discus	Ken Carpenter, USA	165-7	OR
Hammer	Karl Hein, GER	185-4	OR
Javelin	Gerhard Stöck, GER	235-8	
Decathlon	Glenn Morris, USA	7900 pts	WR

WOMEN

Event		Time	
100m	Helen Stephens, USA	11.5^w	
80m H	Trebisonda Valla, ITA	11.7	
4x100m	USA (Harriet Bland, Annette Rogers, Betty Robinson, Helen Stephens)	46.9	

^{w} indicates wind-aided.

Event		Mark	
High Jump	Ibolya Csák, HUN	5-3	
Discus	Gisela Mauermayer, GER	156-3	OR
Javelin	Tilly Fleischer, GER	148-3	OR

Swimming

MEN

Event		Time	
100m Free	Ferenc Csík, HUN	57.6	
400m Free	Jack Medica, USA	4:44.5	OR
1500m Free	Noboru Terada, JPN	19:13.7	
100m Back	Adolf Kiefer, USA	1:05.9	OR
200m Brst	Tetsuo Hamuro, JPN	2:41.5	OR
4x200m Free	JPN (Masanori Yusa, Shigeo Sugiura, Masaharu Taguchi, Shigeo Arai)	8:51.5	WR

Diving		Points
Platform	Marshall Wayne, USA	113.58
Spring	Richard Degener, USA	163.57

WOMEN

Event		Time	
100m Free	Rie Mastenbroek, NED	1:05.9	OR
400m Free	Rie Mastenbroek, NED	5:26.4	OR
100m Back	Nida Senff, NED	1:18.9	
200m Brst	Hideko Maehata, JPN	3:03.6	
4x100m Free	NED (Johanna Selbach, Catherina Wagner, Willemijntje den Ouden, Rie Mastenbroek)	4:36.0	OR

Diving		Points
Platform	Dorothy Poynton Hill, USA	33.93
Spring	Marjorie Gestring, USA	89.27

Team Sports

Sport	Champion
Basketball	United States
Field Hockey	India
Handball	Germany
Polo	Argentina
Soccer	Italy
Water Polo	Hungary

Note: In Water Polo, both Hungary and Germany finished with records of 8-0-1. The Hungarians were awarded the gold medal on total goals (57-56).

Also Contested

Boxing, Canoeing, Cycling, Equestrian, Fencing, Gymnastics, Modern Pentathlon, Rowing, Shooting, Weightlifting, Freestyle Wrestling, Greco-Roman Wrestling and Yachting.

OLYMPIC GAMES

29 JULY 1948 14 AUGUST
L O N D O N

1948

London

The Summer Olympics were scheduled for Tokyo in 1940, but by mid-1938, Japan was at war with China and withdrew as host. The IOC immediately transferred the Games to Helsinki and the Finns eagerly began preparations only to be invaded by the Soviet Union in 1939.

By then, of course, Germany had marched into Poland and World War II was on. The Japanese attacked Pearl Harbor two years later, and the bombs didn't stop falling until 1945. Against this backdrop of global conflict, the Olympic Games were cancelled again in 1940 and '44. Many of the participants in the 1936 Games died in the war.

Eager to come back after two dormant Olympiads, the IOC offered the 1948 Games to London. Much of the British capital had been reduced to rubble in the blitz, but the offer was accepted and the Games went on–successfully, without frills, and without invitations extended to Germany and Japan. The Soviet Union was invited, but chose not to show.

The United States reclaimed its place at the top of the overall medal standings, but the primary individual stars were a 30-year-old Dutch mother of two and a 17-year-old kid from California.

Fanny Blankers-Koen duplicated Jesse Owens' track and field grand slam of 12 years before by winning the 100-meter and 200-meter runs, the 80-meter hurdles, and anchoring the women's 4x100-meter relay.

And Bob Mathias, just two months after graduating from Tulare High School, won the gold medal in the decathlon, an event he had taken up for the first time earlier in the year.

Top 10 Standings

National medal standings are not recognized by the IOC. The unofficial point totals are based on 3 points for a gold medal, 2 for a silver and 1 for a bronze.

		Gold	Silver	Bronze	Total	Pts
1	USA	38	27	19	84	187
2	Sweden	16	11	17	44	87
3	Italy	8	12	9	29	57
4	France	10	6	13	29	55
5	Hungary	10	5	12	27	52
6	Great Britain	3	14	6	23	43
	Finland	8	7	5	20	43
8	Switzerland	5	10	5	20	40
9	Denmark	5	7	8	20	37
10	Holland	5	2	9	16	28
	Turkey	6	4	2	12	28

Leading Medal Winners

Number of individual medals won on the left; gold, silver and bronze breakdown to the right.

MEN

No		Sport	G-S-B
5	Veikko Huhtanen, FIN	Gymnastics	3-1-1
4	Paavo Aaltonen, FIN	Gymnastics	3-0-1
3	Jimmy McLane, USA	Swimming	2-1-0
3	Humberto Mariles, MEX	Equestrian	2-0-1
3	Mal Whitfield, USA	Track/Field	2-0-1
3	Barney Ewell, USA	Track/Field	1-2-0
3	Michael Reusch, SWI	Gymnastics	1-2-0
3	Josef Stalder, SWI	Gymnastics	1-1-1
3	Ferenc Pataki, HUN	Gymnastics	1-0-2
3	Walter Lehmann, SWI	Gymnastics	0-3-0
3	Edoardo Mangiarotti, ITA	Fencing	0-2-1
3	János Mogyorósi, HUN	Gymnastics	0-1-2

WOMEN

No		Sport	G-S-B
4	Fanny Blankers-Koen, NED	Track/Field	4-0-0
3	Ann Curtis, USA	Swimming	2-1-0
3	Micheline Ostermeyer, FRA	Track/Field	2-0-1
3	Karen-Margrete Harup, DEN	Swimming	1-2-0
3	Shirley Strickland, AUS	Track/Field	0-1-2

Track & Field
MEN

Event		Time	
100m	Harrison Dillard, USA	10.3	=OR
200m	Mel Patton, USA	21.1	
400m	Arthur Wint, JAM	46.2	
800m	Mal Whitfield, USA	1:49.2	OR
1500m	Henri Eriksson, SWE	3:49.8	
5000m	Gaston Reiff, BEL	14:17.6	OR
10,000m	Emil Zátopek, CZE	29:59.6	OR
Marathon	Delfo Cabrera, ARG	2:34:51.6	
110m H	Bill Porter, USA	13.9	OR
400m H	Roy Cochran, USA	51.1	OR
3000m Steeple	Thore Sjöstrand, SWE	9:04.6	
10k Walk	John Mikaelsson, SWE	45:13.2	
50k Walk	John Ljunggren, SWE	4:41:52	
4x100m	USA (Barney Ewell, Lorenzo Wright, Harrison Dillard, Mel Patton)	40.6	
4x400m	USA (Art Harnden, Cliff Bourland, Roy Cochran, Mal Whitfield)	3:10.4	

Event		Mark	
High Jump	John Winter, AUS	6-6	
Pole Vault	Guinn Smith, USA	14-1¼	
Long Jump	Willie Steele, USA	25-8	
Triple Jump	Arne Åhman, SWE	50-6¼	
Shot Put	Wilbur Thompson, USA	56-2	OR
Discus	Adolfo Consolini, ITA	173-2	OR
Hammer	Imre Németh, HUN	183-11	
Javelin	Tapio Rautavaara, FIN	228-10	
Decathlon	Bob Mathias, USA	7139 pts	

WOMEN

Event		Time	
100m	Fanny Blankers-Koen, NED	11.9	
200m	Fanny Blankers-Koen, NED	24.4	
80m H	Fanny Blankers-Koen, NED	11.2	OR
4x100m	NED (Xenia Stad-de Jong, Jeanette Witziers-Timmer, Gerda van der Kade-Koudijs, Fanny Blankers-Koen)	47.5	

Event		Mark
High Jump	Alice Coachman, USA...........5-6	OR
Long Jump	Olga Gyarmati, HUN 18-8¼	
Shot Put	Micheline Ostermeyer, FRA....45-1½	
Discus	Micheline Ostermeyer, FRA 137-6	
Javelin	Herma Bauma, AUT..........149-6	

Note: Coachman and Dorothy Odam of Britain tied for 1st place, but Coachman was awarded gold medal for making height on first try.

Swimming
MEN

Event		Time	
100m Free	Wally Ris, USA 57.3	OR
400m Free	Bill Smith, USA.............4:41.0	OR
1500m Free	Jimmy McLane, USA........19:18.5	
100m Back	Allen Stack, USA............1:06.4	
200m Brst	Joe Verdeur, USA............2:39.3	OR
4x200m Free	USA (Wally Ris, Jimmy McLane, Wally Wolf, Bill Smith) 8:46.0	WR

Diving		Points
Platform	Sammy Lee, USA..........130.05
Spring	Bruce Harlan, USA 163.64

WOMEN

Event		Time	
100m Free	Greta Andersen, DEN 1:06.3	
400m Free	Ann Curtis, USA 5:17.8	OR
100m Back	Karen M. Harup, DEN 1:14.4	OR
200m Brst	Nel van Vliet, NED 2:57.2	
4x100m Free	USA (Marie Corridon, Thelma Kalama, Brenda Helser, Ann Curtis) 4:29.2	OR

Diving		Points
Platform	Vicki Draves, USA 68.87
Spring	Vicki Draves, USA 108.74

Team Sports

Sport	Champion
Basketball...............................United States
Field Hockey ....India
Soccer ....Sweden
Water Polo...................................Italy

Also Contested

Boxing, Canoeing, Cycling, Equestrian, Fencing, Gymnastics, Modern Pentathlon, Rowing, Shooting, Weightlifting, Freestyle Wrestling, Greco-Roman Wrestling and Yachting.

1952

Helsinki

The Soviet Union returned to the Olympic fold in 1952 after a 40-year absence, a period of time that included a revolution and two world wars. Ironically, the Soviets chose to make their comeback in Finland, a country they had invaded twice during World War II.

This time it was the United States that was surprised by the Soviets, and the USA had to scramble on the last day of competition to hold off the USSR's assault on first place in the overall standings. It was the beginning of an all-consuming 36-year Cold War rivalry.

Despite the Soviets' impressive debut, it was a Communist from another Iron Curtain country who turned in the most memorable individual performance of the Games. Emil Zátopek of Czechoslovakia, the 10,000-meter champion in London, not only repeated at 10,000 meters, but also won at 5,000 and in the marathon—an event he had never run before. He also set Olympic records in each race and topped it off by watching his wife Dana Zátopková win the women's javelin.

Zátopek's unique triple was wildly applauded by the distance-minded Finns, but their greatest outburst came in the opening ceremonies when legendary countryman Paavo Nurmi, now 56, ran into the stadium with the Olympic torch and handed it off to another native legend Hannes Kolehmainen, now 62, who lit the flame to start the Games.

Also, Harrison Dillard of the U.S. won the 110-meter hurdles. In 1948, Dillard, the world's best hurdler, failed to qualify for the hurdles and won the 100-meter dash instead.

Top 10 Standings

National medal standings are not recognized by the IOC. The unofficial point totals are based on 3 points for a gold medal, 2 for a silver and 1 for a bronze.

		Gold	Silver	Bronze	Total	Pts
1	USA...............40		19	17	76	175
2	USSR.............21		30	18	69	141
3	Hungary...........16		10	16	42	84
4	Sweden............12		13	10	35	72
5	Italy..............8		9	4	21	46
6	Finland 6		3	13	22	37
7	France 6		6	6	18	36
8	Germany............0		7	17	24	31
9	Czechoslovakia 7		3	3	13	30
10	Australia 6		2	3	11	25

Leading Medal Winners

Number of individual medals won on the left; gold, silver and bronze breakdown to the right.

MEN

No		Sport	G-S-B
6	Viktor Chukarin, USSR...........Gymnastics	4-2-0
4	Edoardo Mangiarotti, ITA ....Fencing	2-2-0
4	Grant Shaginyan, USSR ....Gymnastics	2-2-0
4	Josef Stalder, SWI ....Gymnastics	0-2-2
3	Emil Zátopek, CZE ....Track/Field	3-0-0
3	Ford Konno, USA................Swimming	2-1-0
3	Herb McKenley, JAM............Track/Field	1-2-0
3	Hans Eugster, SWI ....Gymnastics	1-1-1

WOMEN

No		Sport	G-S-B
7	Maria Gorokhovskaya, USSR ....Gymnastics	2-5-0
6	Margit Korondi, HUN ....Gymnastics	1-1-4
4	Nina Bocharova, USSR...........Gymnastics	2-2-0
4	Ágnes Keleti, HUN ....Gymnastics	1-1-2
3	Yekaterina Kalinchuk, USSR ......Gymnastics	2-1-0
3	Éva Novák, HUN................Swimming	1-2-0
3	Galina Minaicheva, USSR ....Gymnastics	1-1-1
3	Aleksandra Chudina, USSR ......Track/Field	0-2-1

Track & Field
MEN

Event		Time	
100m	Lindy Remigino, USA	.10.4	
200m	Andy Stanfield, USA	.20.7	
400m	George Rhoden, JAM	.45.9	OR
800m	Mal Whitfield, USA	1:49.2	=OR
1500m	Josy Barthel, LUX	3:45.1	OR
5000m	Emil Zátopek, CZE	14:06.6	OR
10,000m	Emil Zátopek, CZE	.29:17.0	OR
Marathon	Emil Zátopek, CZE	2:23:03.2	OR
110m H	Harrison Dillard, USA	.13.7	OR
400m H	Charley Moore, USA	.50.8	OR
3000m Steeple	Horace Ashenfelter, USA	8:45.4	WR
10k Walk	John Mikaelsson, SWE	.45:02.8	OR
50k Walk	Giuseppe Dordoni, ITA	4:28:07.8	OR
4x100m	USA (Dean Smith, Harrison Dillard, Lindy Remigino, Andy Stanfield)	.40.1	
4x400m	JAM (Arthur Wint, Leslie Laing, Herb McKenley, George Rhoden)	3:03.9	WR

Event		Mark	
High Jump	Walt Davis, USA	6- 8½	OR
Pole Vault	Bob Richards, USA	.14-11	OR
Long Jump	Jerome Biffle, USA	.24-10	
Triple Jump	Adhemar da Silva, BRA	.53- 2¾	WR
Shot Put	Parry O'Brien, USA	.57- 1½	OR
Discus	Sim Iness, USA	.180- 6	OR
Hammer	József Csermák, HUN	.197-11	WR
Javelin	Cy Young, USA	.242- 1	OR
Decathlon	Bob Mathias, USA	.7887 pts	WR

WOMEN

Event		Time	
100m	Marjorie Jackson, AUS	.11.5	WR
200m	Marjorie Jackson, AUS	.23.7	
80m H	Shirley Strickland, AUS	.10.9	WR
4x100m	USA (Mae Faggs, Barbara Jones, Janet Moreau, Catherine Hardy)	.45.9	WR

Event		Mark	
High Jump	Esther Brand, S.Afr.	.5- 5¾	
Long Jump	Yvette Williams, NZE	.20- 5¾	OR
Shot Put	Galina Zybina, USSR	.50- 1¾	WR
Discus	Nina Romaschkova, USSR	.168- 8	OR
Javelin	Dana Zátopková, CZE	.165- 7	

Swimming
MEN

Event		Time	
100m Free	Clarke Scholes, USA	.57.4	
400m Free	Jean Boiteux, FRA	4:30.7	OR
1500m Free	Ford Konno, USA	18:30.3	OR
100m Back	Yoshi Oyakawa, USA	1:05.4	OR
200m Brst	John Davies, AUS	2:34.4	OR
4x200m Free	USA (Wayne Moore, Bill Woolsey, Ford Konno, Jimmy McLane)	8:31.1	OR

Diving		Points
Platform	Sammy Lee, USA	.156.28
Spring	Skippy Browning, USA	.205.29

WOMEN

Event		Time	
100m Free	Katalin Szöke, HUN	1:06.8	
400m Free	Valéria Gyenge, HUN	5:12.1	OR
100m Back	Joan Harrison, S. Afr.	1:14.3	
200m Brst	Éva Szekely, HUN	2:51.7	OR
4x100m Free	HUN (Ilona Novák, Judit Temes, Eva Novák, Katalin Szöke)	4:24.4	WR

Diving		Points
Platform	Pat McCormick, USA	.79.37
Spring	Pat McCormick, USA	.147.30

Team Sports

Sport	Champion
Basketball	United States
Field Hockey	India
Soccer	Hungary
Water Polo	Hungary

Also Contested

Boxing, Canoeing, Cycling, Equestrian, Fencing, Gymnastics, Modern Pentathlon, Rowing, Shooting, Weightlifting, Freestyle Wrestling, Greco-Roman Wrestling and Yachting.

1956

Melbourne

Armed conflicts in Egypt and Hungary threatened to disrupt the 1956 Games, which were scheduled to begin on Nov. 22 (during the summer Down Under).

In July, Egypt seized the Suez Canal from British and French control. In October, Britain and France invaded Egypt in an attempt to retake the canal. Then in November, Soviet tanks rolled into Hungary to crush an anti-Communist revolt.

The only direct bearing these events had in Melbourne came when the Soviet water polo team met the Hungarians in the semifinals. Hungary won 4-0, but the match turned ugly after a Hungarian player was pulled bleeding from the pool with a deep gash over his eye from a Soviet head butt. A brawl quickly ensued involving both players and spectators and the police had to step in to prevent a riot.

Otherwise, the Soviets outmedaled the U.S. for the first time, cleaning up in gymnastics and winning their first track and field titles when Vladimir Kuts ran off with the 5,000 and 10,000 meters.

The American men won 15 track and field titles, including three golds for sprinter Bobby Morrow and Al Oerter's first victory in the discus.

Harold Connolly of the U.S. won the hammer throw and the heart of the women's discus champion, Olga Fikotová of Czechoslovakia. Their romance captured the imagination of the world and three months after the Games they were married.

Emil Zátopek, the Czech hero of Helsinki, returned to defend his marathon title but came in sixth. Winner Alain Mimoun of France had finished second to Zátopek three times in previous Olympic races.

Top 10 Standings

National medal standings are not recognized by the IOC. The unofficial point totals are based on 3 points for a gold medal, 2 for a silver and 1 for a bronze.

		Gold	Silver	Bronze	Total	Pts
1	USSR	37	29	32	98	201
2	USA	32	25	17	74	163
3	Australia	13	8	14	35	69
4	Hungary	9	10	7	26	54
5	Germany	6	13	7	26	51
6	Italy	8	8	9	25	49
7	Great Britain	6	7	11	24	43
8	Sweden	8	5	6	19	40
9	Japan	4	10	5	19	37
10	Romania	5	3	5	13	26
	France	4	4	6	14	26

Leading Medal Winners

Number of individual medals won on the left; gold, silver and bronze breakdown to the right.

MEN

No		Sport	G-S-B
5	Viktor Chukarin, USSR	Gymnastics	3-1-1
5	Takashi Ono, JPN	Gymnastics	1-3-1
4	Valentin Muratov, USSR	Gymnastics	3-1-0
4	Yuriy Titov, USSR	Gymnastics	1-1-2
4	Masao Takemoto, JPN	Gymnastics	0-1-3
3	Bobby Morrow, USA	Track/Field	3-0-0
3	Murray Rose, AUS	Swimming	3-0-0
3	Edoardo Mangiarotti, ITA	Fencing	2-0-1
3	Thane Baker, USA	Track/Field	1-1-1
3	Masami Kubota, JPN	Gymnastics	0-2-1
3	George Breen, USA	Swimming	0-1-2

WOMEN

No		Sport	G-S-B
6	Agnes Keleti, HUN	Gymnastics	4-2-0
6	Larissa Latynina, USSR	Gymnastics	4-1-1
4	Tamara Manina, USSR	Gymnastics	1-2-1
3	Sofiya Muratova, USSR	Gymnastics	1-0-3
3	Betty Cuthbert, AUS	Track/Field	3-0-0
3	Lorraine Crapp, AUS	Swimming	2-1-0
3	Dawn Fraser, AUS	Swimming	2-1-0
3	Olga Tass, HUN	Gymnastics	1-1-1

Track & Field

MEN

Event		Time	
100m	Bobby Morrow, USA	10.5	
200m	Bobby Morrow, USA	20.6	OR
400m	Charley Jenkins, USA	46.7	
800m	Tom Courtney, USA	1:47.7	OR
1500m	Ron Delany, IRL	3:41.2	OR
5000m	Vladimir Kuts, USSR	13:39.6	OR
10,000m	Vladimir Kuts, USSR	28:45.6	OR
Marathon	Alain Mimoun, FRA	2:25:00.0	
110m H	Lee Calhoun, USA	13.5	OR
400m H	Glenn Davis, USA	50.1	=OR
3000m Steeple	Chris Brasher, GBR	8:41.2	OR
20k Walk	Leonid Spirin, USSR	1:31:27.4	
50k Walk	Norman Read, NZE	4:30:42.8	
4x100m	USA (Ira Murchison, Leamon King, Thane Baker, Bobby Morrow)	39.5	WR
4x400m	USA (Lou Jones, Jesse Mashburn, Charlie Jenkins, Tom Courtney)	3:04.8	

Event		Mark	
High Jump	Charley Dumas, USA	6-11½	OR
Pole Vault	Bob Richards, USA	14-11½	OR
Long Jump	Greg Bell, USA	25-8¼	OR
Triple Jump	Adhemar da Silva, BRA	53-7¾	OR
Shot Put	Parry O'Brien, USA	60-11¼	OR
Discus	Al Oerter, USA	184-11	OR
Hammer	Harold Connolly, USA	207-3	OR
Javelin	Egil Danielson, NOR	281-2	WR
Decathlon	Milt Campbell, USA	7937 pts	OR

WOMEN

Event		Time	
100m	Betty Cuthbert, AUS	11.5	
200m	Betty Cuthbert, AUS	23.4	=OR
80m H	Shirley Strickland, AUS	10.7	OR
4x100m	AUS (Shirley Strickland, Norma Croker, Fleur Mellor, Betty Cuthbert)	44.5	WR

Event		Mark	
High Jump	Mildred McDaniel, USA	5-9¼	WR
Long Jump	Elzbieta Krzesinska, POL	20-10	=OR
Shot Put	Tamara Tyshkevich, USSR	54-5	OR
Discus	Olga Fikotová, CZE	176-1	OR
Javelin	Inese Jaunzeme, USSR	176-8	

Swimming

MEN

Event		Time	
100m Free	Jon Henricks, AUS	55.4	OR
400m Free	Murray Rose, AUS	4:27.3	OR
1500m Free	Murray Rose, AUS	17:58.9	
100m Back	David Theile, AUS	1:02.2	OR
200m Brst	Masaru Furukawa, JPN	2:34.7	OR
200m Fly	Bill Yorzyk, USA	2:19.3	OR
4x200m Free	AUS (Kevin O'Halloran, John Devitt, Murray Rose, Jon Henricks)	8:23.6	WR

Diving		Points	
Platform	Joaquin Capilla, MEX	152.44	
Spring	Bob Clotworthy, USA	159.56	

WOMEN

Event		Time	
100m Free	Dawn Fraser, AUS	1:02.0	WR
400m Free	Lorraine Crapp, AUS	4:54.6	OR
100m Back	Judy Grinham, GBR	1:12.9	OR
200m Brst	Ursula Happe, GER	2:53.1	OR
100m Fly	Shelly Mann, USA	1:11.0	OR
4x100m Free	AUS (Dawn Fraser, Faith Leech, Sandra Morgan, Lorraine Crapp)	4:17.1	WR

Diving		Points	
Platform	Pat McCormick, USA	84.85	
Spring	Pat McCormick, USA	142.36	

Team Sports

Sport	Champion
Basketball	United States
Field Hockey	India
Soccer	Soviet Union
Water Polo	Hungary

Also Contested

Boxing, Canoeing, Cycling, Equestrian, Fencing, Gymnastics, Modern Pentathlon, Rowing, Shooting, Weightlifting, Freestyle Wrestling, Greco-Roman Wrestling and Yachting.

Note: Equestrian events were held in Stockholm, Sweden, June 10-17, due to Australian quarantine laws.

JEUX DE LA XVII OLYMPIADE
ROMA 25.VIII-11.IX

1960

Rome

Free of political entanglements, save the ruling that Nationalist China had to compete as Formosa, the 1960 Games attracted a record 5,348 athletes from 83 countries. More importantly, it was the first Summer Games covered by U.S. television. CBS bought the rights for $394,000.

Rome was a coming-out party for 18-year-old Louisville boxer Cassius Clay. The brash but engaging Clay, who would later change his name to Muhammad Ali and hold the world heavyweight title three times, won the Olympic light heavyweight crown, pummeling Polish opponent Zbigniew Pietryskowsky in the final. Clay was so proud of his gold medal that he didn't take it off for two days.

Sprinter Wilma Rudolph and swimmer Chris von Saltza each won three gold medals for the U.S. Rudolph, who was one of her father's 22 children and who couldn't walk without braces until she was nine, struck gold at 100 and 200 meters and anchored the winning 400-meter relay team. Von Saltza won the 400-meter freestyle, placed second in the 100-free and anchored the winning 4x100-free and medley relays.

The U.S. men won nine track and field titles, including repeat gold medals for Lee Calhoun, Glenn Davis and Al Oerter. Rafer Johnson and C.K. Yang of Formosa, college teammates at UCLA, finished 1-2 in the decathlon.

Among the other stars in Rome were barefoot Ethiopian marathoner Abebe Bikila, Australia's Herb Elliott in the 1,500 meters, Soviet gymnasts Boris Shakhlin and Larissa Latynina.

Finally, the greatest amateur basketball team ever assembled represented the U.S. and won easily. The 12-man roster included Oscar Robertson, Jerry West, Jerry Lucas, Walt Bellamy and Terry Dischinger—four of whom would become NBA Rookies of the Year from 1961-64.

Top 10 Standings

National medal standings are not recognized by the IOC. The unofficial point totals are based on 3 points for a gold medal, 2 for a silver and 1 for a bronze.

	Gold	Silver	Bronze	Total	Pts
1 USSR	43	29	31	103	218
2 USA	34	21	16	71	160
3 Germany	12	19	11	42	85
4 Italy	13	10	13	36	72
5 Australia	8	8	6	22	46
6 Hungary	6	8	7	21	41
7 Poland	4	6	11	21	35
8 Japan	4	7	7	18	33
9 Great Britain	2	6	12	20	30
10 Turkey	7	2	0	9	25

Leading Medal Winners

Number of individual medals won on the left; gold, silver and bronze breakdown to the right.

MEN

No		Sport	G-S-B
7	Boris Shakhlin, USSR	Gymnastics	4-2-1
6	Takashi Ono, JPN	Gymnastics	3-1-2
3	Murray Rose, AUS	Swimming	1-1-1
3	John Konraads, AUS	Swimming	1-0-2
3	Yuri Titov, USSR	Gymnastics	0-2-1

WOMEN

No		Sport	G-S-B
6	Larissa Latynina, USSR	Gymnastics	3-2-1
4	Chris von Saltza, USA	Swimming	3-1-0
4	Polina Astakhova, USSR	Gymnastics	2-1-1
4	Sofia Muratova, USSR	Gymnastics	1-2-1
3	Wilma Rudolph, USA	Track/Field	3-0-0
3	Dawn Fraser, AUS	Swimming	1-2-0
3	Tamara Lyukhina, USSR	Gymnastics	1-0-2

Track & Field

MEN

Event		Time	
100m	Armin Hary, GER	10.2	OR
200m	Livio Berruti, ITA	20.5	=WR
400m	Otis Davis, USA	44.9	WR
800m	Peter Snell, NZE	1:46.3	OR
1500m	Herb Elliott, AUS	3:35.6	WR
5000m	Murray Halberg, NZE	13:43.4	
10,000m	Pyotr Bolotnikov, USSR	28:32.2	OR
Marathon	Abebe Bikila, ETH	2:15:16.2	WB
110m H	Lee Calhoun, USA	13.8	
400m H	Glenn Davis, USA	49.3	=OR
3000m Steeple	Zdzislaw Krzyszkowiak, POL	8:34.2	OR
20k Walk	Vladimir Golubnichiy, USSR	1:34:07.2	
50k Walk	Don Thompson, GBR	4:25:30.0	OR
4x100m	GER (Bernd Cullmann, Armin Hary, Walter Mahlendorf, Martin Lauer)	39.5	=WR
4x400m	USA (Jack Yerman, Earl Young, Glenn Davis, Otis Davis)	3:02.2	WR

Event		Mark	
High Jump	Robert Shavlakadze, USSR	7- 1	OR
Pole Vault	Don Bragg, USA	15- 5	OR
Long Jump	Ralph Boston, USA	26-7¾	OR
Triple Jump	Józef Schmidt, POL	55- 2	OR
Shot Put	Bill Nieder, USA	64- 6¾	OR
Discus	Al Oerter, USA	194-2	OR
Hammer	Vasily Rudenkov, USSR	220- 2	OR
Javelin	Viktor Tsibulenko, USSR	277- 8	OR
Decathlon	Rafer Johnson, USA	8392 pts	OR

WOMEN

Event		Time	
100m	Wilma Rudolph, USA	11.0ʷ	
200m	Wilma Rudolph, USA	24.0	
800m	Lyudmila Shevtsova, USSR	2:04.3	=WR
80m H	Irina Press, USSR	10.8	
4x100m	USA (Martha Hudson, Lucinda Williams, Barbara Jones, Wilma Rudolph)	44.5	

ʷ indicates wind-aided.

Event		Mark	
High Jump	Iolanda Balas, ROM	6- 0¾	OR
Long Jump	Vyera Krepkina, USSR	20-10¾	OR
Shot Put	Tamara Press, USSR	56-10	OR
Discus	Nina R. Ponomaryeva, USSR	180- 9	OR
Javelin	Elvira Ozolina, USSR	183- 8	OR

Boxing

Weight Class	Champion
Flyweight (112 lbs)	Gyula Török, HUN
Bantamweight (119)	Oleg Grigoryev, USSR
Featherweight (125)	Francesco Musso, ITA
Lightweight (132)	Kazimierz Pazdzior, POL
Lt. Welterweight (139)	Bohumil Nemecek, CZE
Welterweight (148)	Nino Benvenuti, ITA
Lt. Middleweight (156)	Skeeter McClure, USA
Middleweight (165)	Eddie Crook, USA
Lt. Heavyweight (178)	Cassius Clay, USA
Heavyweight (178+)	Franco De Piccoli, ITA

Gymnastics

MEN

Individual		Points
All-Around	Boris Shakhlin, USSR	115.95
Floor	Nobuyuki Aihara, JPN	19.45
Horiz.Bar	Takashi Ono, JPN	19.60
Paral.Bars	Boris Shakhlin, USSR	19.40
Rings	Albert Azaryan, USSR	19.725
Side Horse	Boris Shakhlin, USSR	
	Eugen Ekman, FIN	19.375
Vault	Boris Shakhlin, USSR	
	Takashi Ono, JPN	19.35

Team		Points
All-Around	JPN (Ono, Tsurumi, Aihara, Endo, Takemoto, Mitsukuri)	575.20

WOMEN

Individual		Points
All-Around	Larissa Latynina, USSR	77.031
Bal.Beam	Eva Bosáková, CZE	19.283
Floor	Larissa Latynina, USSR	19.583
Uneven Bars	Polina Astakhova, USSR	19.616
Vault	Margarita Nikolayeva, USSR	19.316

Team		Points
All-Around	USSR (Latynina, Muratova, Astakhova, Nikolayeva, Ivanova, Lyukhina)	382.320

Swimming

MEN

Event		Time	
100m Free	John Devitt, AUS	55.2	OR
400m Free	Murray Rose, AUS	4:18.3	OR
1500m Free	John Konrads, AUS	17:19.6	OR
100m Back	David Theile, AUS	1:09.9	OR
200m Brst	Bill Mulliken, USA	2:37.4	
200m Fly	Mike Troy, USA	2:12.8	WR
4x200m Free	USA (George Harrison, Dick Blick, Mike Troy, Jeff Farrell)	8:10.2	WR
4x100m Mdly	USA (Frank McKinney, Paul Hait, Lance Larson, Jeff Farrell)	4:05.4	WR

Diving		Points
Platform	Bob Webster, USA	165.56
Spring	Gary Tobian, USA	170.00

WOMEN

Event		Time	
100m Free	Dawn Fraser, AUS	1:01.2	OR
400m Free	Chris von Saltza, USA	4:50.6	OR
100m Back	Lynn Burke, USA	1:09.3	OR
200m Brst	Anita Lonsbrough, GBR	2:49.5	WR
100m Fly	Carolyn Schuler, USA	1:09.5	OR
4x100m Free	USA (Joan Spillane, Shirley Stobs, Carolyn Wood, Chris von Saltza)	4:08.9	WR
4x100m Mdly	USA (Lynn Burke, Patty Kempner, Carolyn Schuler, Chris von Saltza)	4:41.1	WR

Diving

		Points
Platform	Ingrid Krämer, GER	91.28
Spring	Ingrid Krämer, GER	155.81

Team Sports

Men	Champion
Basketball	United States
Field Hockey	Pakistan
Soccer	Yugoslavia
Water Polo	Italy

Also Contested

Canoeing, Cycling, Equestrian, Fencing, Modern Pentathlon, Rowing, Shooting, Weightlifting, Freestyle Wrestling, Greco-Roman Wrestling and Yachting.

1964

Tokyo

Twenty-six years after Japan's wartime government forced the Japanese Olympic Committee to resign as hosts of the 1940 Summer Games, Tokyo welcomed the world to the first Asian Olympics. The new Japan spared no expense–a staggering $3 billion was spent to rebuild the city– and was rewarded with a record-breaking fortnight.

Twelve world and six Olympic records fell in swimming alone, with Americans accounting for 13. Eighteen-year-old Don Schollander led the way, winning two individual and two relay gold medals to become the first swimmer to win four events in one Games. Sharon Stouder collected three golds and a silver for the U.S. women, but the most remarkable performance of all belonged to Australian Dawn Fraser, who won the 100-meter freestyle for the third straight Olympics.

In track and field, Al Oerter of the U.S. won the discus for the third straight time. His record toss was one of 25 world and Olympic marks broken. Another fell when Billy Mills of the U.S. electrified the Games by coming from behind for an upset win in the 10,000 meters. New Zealander Peter Snell, the defending 800-meter champion, won both the 800 and 1,500 (last done in 1920).

Sprinter Bob Hayes of the U.S. equaled the world record of 10 seconds flat in the 100 meters, but stunned the crowd with a sub-nine second, come-from-behind anchor leg to lead the U.S. to set a world record in the 4x100 meters.

Abebe Bikila of Ethiopia became the first runner to win consecutive marathons. The remarkable Betty Cuthbert of Australia, who won three sprint gold medals in Melbourne, came back eight years later at age 26 to win the 400. And Soviet gymnast Larissa Latynina won six medals for the second straight Olympics in a row.

Top 10 Standings

National medal standings are not recognized by the IOC. The unofficial point totals are based on 3 points for a gold medal, 2 for a silver and 1 for a bronze.

	Gold	Silver	Bronze	Total	Pts
1 USA	36	26	28	90	188
2 USSR	30	31	35	96	187
3 Germany	10	22	18	50	92
4 Japan	16	5	8	29	66
5 Italy	10	10	7	27	57
6 Hungary	10	7	5	22	49
7 Poland	7	6	10	23	43
8 Great Britain	4	12	2	18	38
9 Australia	6	2	10	18	32
10 Czechoslovakia	5	6	3	14	30

Leading Medal Winners

Number of individual medals won on the left; gold, silver and bronze breakdown to the right.

MEN

No		Sport	G-S-B
4	Don Schollander, USA	Swimming	4-0-0
4	Yukio Endo, JPN	Gymnastics	3-1-0
4	Shuji Tsurumi, JPN	Gymnastics	1-3-0
4	Boris Shakhlin, USSR	Gymnastics	1-2-1
4	Viktor Lisitsky, USSR	Gymnastics	0-4-0
4	Hans-Joachim Klein, GER	Swimming	0-3-1
3	Steve Clark, USA	Swimming	3-0-0
3	Franco Menichelli, ITA	Gymnastics	1-1-1
3	Frank Wiegard, GER	Swimming	0-3-0

WOMEN

No		Sport	G-S-B
6	Larissa Latynina, USSR	Gymnastics	2-2-2
4	Vera Cáslavská, CZE	Gymnastics	3-1-0
4	Polina Astakhova, USSR	Gymnastics	2-1-1
4	Sharon Stouder, USA	Swimming	3-1-0
4	Kathy Ellis, USA	Swimming	2-0-2
3	Irena Kirszenstein, POL	Track/Field	1-2-0
3	Ada Kok, NED	Swimming	1-2-0
3	Edith Maguire, USA	Track/Field	1-2-0
3	Mary Rand, GBR	Track/Field	1-1-1

Track & Field

MEN

Event		Time	
100m	Bob Hayes, USA	10.0	=WR
200m	Henry Carr, USA	20.3	OR
400m	Mike Larrabee, USA	45.1	
800m	Peter Snell, NZE	1:45.1	OR
1500m	Peter Snell, NZE	3:38.1	
5000m	Bob Schul, USA	13:48.8	
10,000m	Billy Mills, USA	28:24.4	OR
Marathon	Abebe Bikila, ETH	2:12:11.2	WB
110m H	Hayes Jones, USA	13.6	
400m H	Rex Cawley, USA	49.6	
3000m Steeple	Gaston Roelants, BEL	8:30.8	OR
20k Walk	Ken Matthews, GBR	1:29:34.0	OR
50k Walk	Abdon Pamich, ITA	4:11:12.4	OR
4x100m	USA (Paul Drayton, Gerald Ashworth, Richard Stebbins, Bob Hayes)	39.0	WR
4x400m	USA (Ollan Cassell, Mike Larrabee, Ulis Williams, Henry Carr)	3:00.7	WR

WB indicates world best.

Event		Mark	
High Jump	Valery Brumel, USSR	7- 1¾	OR
Pole Vault	Fred Hansen, USA	16- 8¾	OR
Long Jump	Lynn Davies, GBR	26- 5¾	
Triple Jump	Józef Schmidt, POL	55- 3½	OR
Shot Put	Dallas Long, USA	66- 8½	OR
Discus	Al Oerter, USA	200- 1	OR
Hammer	Romuald Klim, USSR	228-10	OR
Javelin	Pauli Nevala, FIN	271- 2	
Decathlon	Willi Holdorf, GER	7887 pts	

WOMEN

Event		Time	
100m	Wyomia Tyus, USA	11.4	
200m	Edith McGuire, USA	23.0	OR
400m	Betty Cuthbert, AUS	52.0	OR
800m	Ann Packer, GBR	2:01.1	OR
80m H	Karin Balzer, GER	10.5[w]	
4x100m	POL (Teresa Ciepla, Irena Kirszenstein, Halina Górecka, Ewa Klobukowska)	43.6	

[w] indicates wind-aided.

Event		Mark	
High Jump	Iolanda Balas, ROM	6- 2¾	OR
Long Jump	Mary Rand GBR	22- 2¼	WR
Shot Put	Tamara Press, USSR	59- 6¼	OR
Discus	Tamara Press, USSR	187-10	OR
Javelin	Mihaela Penes, ROM	198- 7	
Pentathlon	Irina Press, USSR	5246 pts	WR

Boxing

Weight Class	Champion
Flyweight (112 lbs)	Fernando Atzori, ITA
Bantamweight (119)	Takao Sakurai, JPN
Featherweight (125)	Stanislav Stepashkin, USSR
Lightweight (132)	Józef Grudzien, POL
Lt. Welterweight (139)	Jerzy Kulej, POL
Welterweight (148)	Marian Kasprzyk, POL
Lt. Middleweight (156)	Boris Lagutin, USSR
Middleweight (165)	Valery Popenchenko, USSR
Lt. Heavyweight (178)	Cosimo Pinto, ITA
Heavyweight (178+)	Joe Frazier, USA

Gymnastics

MEN

Individual		Points
All-Around	Yukio Endo, JPN	115.95
Floor	Franco Menichelli, ITA	19.45
Horiz.Bar	Boris Shakhlin, USSR	19.625
Paral.Bars	Yukio Endo, JPN	19.675
Rings	Takuji Haytta, JPN	19.475
Side Horse	Miroslav Cerar, YUG	19.525
Vault	Haruhiro Yamashita, JPN	19.60

Team		Points
All-Around	JPN (Endo, Tsurumi, Yamashita, Hayata, Mitsukuri, Ono)	577.95

WOMEN

Individual		Points
All-Around	Vera Cáslavská, CZE	77.564
Bal.Beam	Vera Cáslavská, CZE	19.449
Floor	Larissa Latynina, USSR	19.599
Uneven Bars	Polina Astakhova, USSR	19.332
Vault	Vera Cáslavská, CZE	19.483

Team		Points
All-Around	USSR (Latynina, Astakhova, Volchetskaya, Zamotailova, Manina, Gromova)	280.890

Swimming

MEN

Event		Time	
100m Free	Don Schollander, USA	.53.4	OR
400m Free	Don Schollander, USA	4:12.2	WR
1500m Free	Robert Windle, AUS	17:01.7	OR
200m Back	Jed Graef, USA	2:10.3	WR
200m Brst	Ian O'Brien, AUS	2:27.8	WR
200m Fly	Kevin Berry, AUS	2:06.6	WR
400m I.M.	Dick Roth, USA	4:45.4	WR
4x100m Free	USA (Steve Clark, Mike Austin, Gary Ilman, Don Schollander)	3:32.3	WR
4x200m Free	USA (Steve Clark, Roy Saari, Gary Ilman, Don Schollander)	7:52.1	WR
4x100m Mdly	USA (Thompson Mann, Bill Craig, Fred Schmidt, Steve Clark)	3:58.4	WR

Diving		Points
Platform	Bob Webster, USA	148.58
Spring	Ken Sitzberger, USA	159.90

WOMEN

Event		Time	
100m Free	Dawn Fraser, AUS	.59.5	OR
400m Free	Ginny Duenkel, USA	4:43.3	OR
100m Back	Cathy Ferguson, USA	1:07.7	OR
200m Brst	G. Prozumenshikova, USSR	2:46.4	OR
100m Fly	Sharon Stouder, USA	1:04.7	WR

Event		Time	
400m Mdly	Donna de Varona, USA	5:18.7	OR
4x100m Free	USA (Sharon Stouder, Donna de Varona, Pokey Watson, Kathy Ellis)	4:03.8	WR
4x100m Mdly	USA (Cathy Ferguson, Cynthia Goyette, Sharon Stouder, Kathy Ellis)	4:33.9	WR

Diving		Points
Platform	Lesley Bush, USA	99.80
Spring	Ingrid Engel-Krämer, GER	145.00

Team Sports

Men	Champion
Basketball	United States
Field Hockey	India
Soccer	Hungary
Volleyball	Soviet Union
Water Polo	Hungary

Women	Champion
Volleyball	Japan

Also Contested

Canoeing, Cycling, Equestrian, Fencing, Judo, Modern Pentathlon, Rowing, Shooting, Weightlifting, Freestyle Wrestling, Greco-Roman Wrestling and Yachting.

1968

Mexico City

The Games of the Nineteenth Olympiad were the highest and most controversial ever held.

Staged at 7,349 feet above sea level where the thin air was a major concern to many competing countries, the Mexico City Olympics were another chapter in a year buffeted by the Vietnam War, the assassinations of Martin Luther King and Robert Kennedy, the Democratic Convention in Chicago, and the Soviet invasion of Czechoslovakia.

Ten days before the Olympics were scheduled to open on Oct. 12, over 30 Mexico City university students were killed by army troops when a campus protest turned into a riot. Still, the Games began on time and were free of discord until black Americans Tommie Smith and John Carlos, who finished 1-3 in the 200-meter run, bowed their heads and gave the Black Power salute during the national anthem as a protest against racism in the U.S.

They were immediately thrown off the team by the USOC.

The thin air helped shatter records in every men's and women's race up to 1,500 meters and may have played a role in U.S. long jumper Bob Beamon's incredible gold medal leap of 29 feet, 2½ inches –beating the existing world mark by nearly two feet.

Other outstanding American performances included Al Oerter's record fourth consecutive discus title, Debbie Meyer's three individual swimming gold medals, the innovative Dick Fosbury winning the high jump with his backwards "flop" and Wyomia Tyus becoming the first woman to win back-to-back golds in the 100 meters.

Top 10 Standings

National medal standings are not recognized by the IOC. The unofficial point totals are based on 3 points for a gold medal, 2 for a silver and 1 for a bronze.

		Gold	Silver	Bronze	Total	Pts
1	USA	45	28	34	107	225
2	USSR	29	32	30	91	181
3	Hungary	10	10	12	32	62
4	Japan	11	7	7	25	54
5	E. Germany	9	9	7	25	52
6	W. Germany	5	10	10	25	45
7	Australia	5	7	5	17	34
8	France	7	3	5	15	32
9	Poland	5	2	11	18	30
10	Czechoslovakia	7	2	4	13	29
	Romania	4	6	5	15	29

Leading Medal Winners

Number of individual medals won on the left; gold, silver and bronze breakdown to the right.

MEN

No		Sport	G-S-B
7	Mikhail Voronin, USSR	Gymnastics	2-4-1
6	Akinori Nakayama, JPN	Gymnastics	4-1-1
4	Charles Hickcox, USA	Swimming	3-1-0
4	Sawao Kato, JPN	Gymnastics	3-0-1
4	Mark Spitz, USA	Swimming	2-1-1
4	Mike Wenden, AUS	Swimming	2-1-1
3	Roland Matthes, E. Ger.	Swimming	2-1-0
3	Ken Walsh, USA	Swimming	2-1-0
3	Pierre Trentin, FRA	Cycling	2-0-1
3	Vladimir Kosinski, USSR	Swimming	0-2-1
3	Leonid Ilyichev, USSR	Swimming	0-1-2

WOMEN

No		Sport	G-S-B
6	Vera Cáslavská, CZE	Gymnastics	4-2-0
4	Sue Pedersen, USA	Swimming	2-2-0
4	Natalya Kuchinskaya, USSR	Gymnastics	2-0-2
4	Jan Henne, USA	Swimming	2-1-1
4	Zinaida Voronina, USSR	Gymnastics	1-1-2
3	Debbie Meyer, USA	Swimming	3-0-0
3	Kaye Hall, USA	Swimming	2-0-1
3	Larissa Petrik, USSR	Gymnastics	2-0-1
3	Ellie Daniel, USA	Swimming	1-1-1
3	Linda Gustavson, USA	Swimming	1-1-1
3	Elaine Tanner, CAN	Swimming	0-2-1

Track & Field
MEN

Event		Time	
100m	Jim Hines, USA	9.95	WR
200m	Tommie Smith, USA	19.83	WR
400m	Lee Evans, USA	43.86	WR
800m	Ralph Doubell, AUS	1:44.3	=WR
1500m	Kip Keino, KEN	3:34.9	OR
5000m	Mohamed Gammoudi, TUN	14:05.0	
10,000m	Naftali Temu, KEN	29:27.4	
Marathon	Mamo Wolde, ETH	2:20:26.4	
110m H	Willie Davenport, USA	13.3	OR
400m H	David Hemery, GBR	48.12	WR
3000m Steeple	Amos Biwott, KEN	8:51.0	
20k Walk	Vladimir Golubnichiy, USSR	1:33:58.4	
50k Walk	Christoph Höhne, E. Ger	4:20:13.6	
4x100m	USA (Charlie Greene, Mel Pender, Ronnie Ray Smith, Jim Hines)	38.2	WR
4x400m	USA (Vince Matthews, Ron Freeman, Larry James, Lee Evans)	2:56.16	WR

Event		Mark	
High Jump	Dick Fosbury, USA	7- 4¼	OR
Pole Vault	Bob Seagren, USA	17- 8½	OR
Long Jump	Bob Beamon, USA	29- 2½	WR
Triple Jump	Viktor Saneyev, USSR	57- 0¾	WR
Shot Put	Randy Matson, USA	67- 4¾	OR
Discus	Al Oerter, USA	212- 6	OR
Hammer	Gyula Zsivóyzky, HUN	240- 8	OR
Javelin	Janis Lusis, USSR	295- 7	OR
Decathlon	Bill Toomey, USA	8193 pts	OR

WOMEN

Event		Time	
100m	Wyomia Tyus, USA	11.0	WR
200m	Irena K. Szewinska, POL	22.5	WR
400m	Colette Besson, FRA	52.0	=OR
800m	Madeline Manning, USA	2:00.9	OR
80m H	Maureen Caird, AUS	10.3	OR
4x100m	USA (Barbara Ferrell, Margaret Bailes, Mildrette Netter, Wyomia Tyus)	42.8	WR

Event		Mark	
High Jump	Miloslava Rezková, CZE	5-11½	
Long Jum	Viorica Viscopoleanu, ROM	22- 4½	WR
Shot Put	Margitta Gummel, E. Ger	64- 4	WR
Discus	Lia Manoliu, ROM	191- 2	OR
Javelin	Angéla Németh, HUN	198- 0	
Pentathlon	Ingrid Becker, GER	5098 pts	

Boxing

Weight Class	Champion
Lt. Flyweight (106 lbs)	Francisco Rodriguez, VEN
Flyweight (112)	Ricardo Delgado, MEX
Bantamweight (119)	Valery Sokolov, USSR
Featherweight (125)	Antonio Roldan, MEX
Lightweight (132)	Ron Harris, USA
Lt. Welterweight (139)	Jerzy Kulej, POL
Welterweight (148)	Manfred Wolke, E. Ger
Lt. Middleweight (156)	Boris Lagutin, USSR
Middleweight (165)	Chris Finnegan, GBR
Lt. Heavyweight (178)	Dan Poznjak, USSR
Heavyweight (178+)	George Foreman, USA

Gymnastics
MEN

Individual		Points
All-Around	Sawao Kato, JPN	115.9
Floor	Sawao Kato, JPN	19.475
Horiz.Bar	Akinori Nakayama, JPN	
	Mikhail Voronin, USSR	19.55
Paral.Bars	Akinori Nakayama, JPN	19.475
Rings	Akinori Nakayama, JPN	19.45
Side Horse	Miroslav Cerar, YUG	19.325
Vault	Mikhail Voronin, USSR	19.00

Team		Points
All-Around	JPN (Kato, Nakayama, Kenmotsu, Kato, Endo, Tsukahara)	575.90

WOMEN

Individual		Points
All-Around	Vera Cáslavská, CZE	78.25
Bal.Beam	Natayla Kuchinskaya, USSR	19.65
Floor	Vera Cáslavská, CZE	
	Larissa Petrik, USSR	19.675
Uneven Bars	Vera Cáslavská, CZE	19.65
Vault	Vera Cáslavská, CZE	19.775

Team		Points
All-Around	USSR (Voronina, Kuchinskaya, Petrik, Karasseva, Touricheva, Burda)	382.85

Swimming
MEN

Event		Time	
100m Free	Mike Wenden, AUS	52.2	WR
200m Free	Mike Wenden, AUS	1:55.2	OR
400m Free	Mike Burton, USA	4:09.0	OR
1500m Free	Mike Burton, USA	16:38.9	OR
100m Back	Roland Matthes, E. Ger	58.7	OR
200m Back	Roland Matthes, E. Ger	2:09.6	OR
100m Brst	Don McKenzie, USA	1:07.7	OR
200m Brst	Felipe Muñoz, MEX	2:28.7	
100m Fly	Doug Russell, USA	55.9	OR
200m Fly	Carl Robie, USA	2:08.7	
200m I.M.	Charles Hickcox, USA	2:12.0	OR
400m I.M.	Charles Hickcox, USA	4:48.4	
4x100m Free	USA (Zack Zorn, Steve Rerych, Mark Spitz, Ken Walsh)	3:31.7	WR
4x200m Free	USA (John Nelson, Steve Rerych, Mark Spitz, Don Schollander)	7:52.33	
4x100m Mdly	USA (Charles Hickcox, Don McKenzie, Doug Russell, Ken Walsh)	3:54.9	WR

Diving		Points
Platform	Klaus Dibiasi, ITA	164.18
Spring	Bernie Wrightson, USA	170.15

WOMEN

Event		Time	
100m Free	Jan Henne, USA	1:00.0	
200m Free	Debbie Meyer, USA	2:10.5	OR
400m Free	Debbie Meyer, USA	4:31.8	OR
800m Free	Debbie Meyer, USA	9:24.0	OR
100m Back	Kaye Hall, USA	1:06.2	WR
200m Back	Pokey Watson, USA	2:24.8	OR
100m Brst	Djurdjica Bjedov, YUG	1:15.8	OR
200m Brst	Sharon Wichman, USA	2:44.4	OR

Event		Time	
100m Fly	Lyn McClements, AUS	1:05.5	
200m Fly	Ada Kok, NED	2:24.7	**OR**
200m I.M.	Claudia Kolb, USA	2:24.7	**OR**
400m I.M.	Claudia Kolb, USA	5:08.5	**OR**
4x100m Free	USA (Jane Barkman, Linda Gustavson, Sue Pedersen, Jan Henne)	4:02.5	**OR**
4x100m Mdly	USA (Kaye Hall, Catie Ball, Ellie Daniel, Sue Pedersen)	4:28.3	**OR**

Diving		Points
Platform	Milena Duchková, CZE	109.59
Spring	Sue Gossick, USA	150.77

Team Sports

Men	Champion
Basketball	United States
Field Hockey	Pakistan
Soccer	Hungary
Volleyball	Soviet Union
Water Polo	Yugoslavia

Women	Champion
Volleyball	Soviet Union

Also Contested

Canoeing, Cycling, Equestrian, Fencing, Modern Pentathlon, Rowing, Shooting, Weightlifting, Freestyle Wrestling, Greco-Roman Wrestling and Yachting.

1972

Munich

On Sept. 5, with six days left in the Games, eight Arab commandos slipped into the Olympic Village, killed two Israeli team members and seized nine others as hostages. Early the next morning, all nine were killed in a shootout between the terrorists and West German police at a military airport.

The tragedy stunned the world and stopped the XXth Olympiad in its tracks. But after suspending competition for 24 hours and holding a memorial service attended by 80,000 at the main stadium, 84-year-old outgoing IOC president Avery Brundage and his committee ordered "the Games must go on."

They went on without 22-year-old swimmer Mark Spitz, who had set an Olympic gold medal record by winning four individual and three relay events, all in world record times. Spitz, an American Jew, was an inviting target for further terrorism and agreed with West German officials when they advised him to leave the country.

The pall that fell over Munich quieted an otherwise boisterous Games in which American swimmer Rick DeMont was stripped of a gold medal for taking asthma medication and track medalists Vince Matthews and Wayne Collett of the U.S. were banned for life for fooling around on the victory stand during the American national anthem.

The United States also lost an Olympic basketball game for the first time ever (they were 62-0) when the Soviets were given three chances to convert a last-second inbound pass and finally won, 51-50. The U.S. refused the silver medal.

Munich was also where 17-year-old Soviet gymnast Olga Korbut and 16-year-old swimmer Shane Gould of Australia won three gold medals each and Britain's 33-year-old Mary Peters won the pentathlon.

Top 10 Standings

National medal standings are not recognized by the IOC. The unofficial point totals are based on 3 points for a gold medal, 2 for a silver and 1 for a bronze.

		Gold	Silver	Bronze	Total	Pts
1	USSR	50	27	22	99	226
2	USA	33	31	30	94	191
3	E. Germany	20	23	23	66	129
4	W. Germany	13	11	16	40	77
5	Japan	13	8	8	29	63
6	Hungary	6	13	16	35	60
7	Bulgaria	6	10	5	21	43
8	Australia	8	7	2	17	40
	Poland	7	5	9	21	40
10	Italy	5	3	10	18	31
	Great Britain	4	5	9	18	31

Leading Medal Winners

Number of individual medals won on the left; gold, silver and bronze breakdown to the right.

MEN

No		Sport	G-S-B
7	Mark Spitz, USA	Swimming	7-0-0
5	Sawao Kato, JPN	Gymnastics	3-2-0
4	Jerry Heidenreich, USA	Swimming	2-1-1
4	Roland Matthes, E. Ger.	Swimming	2-1-1
4	Akinori Nakayama, JPN	Gymnastics	2-1-1
4	Shigeru Kasamatsu, JPN	Gymnastics	1-1-2
4	Eizo Kenmotsu, JPN	Gymnastics	1-1-2
3	Valery Borsov, USSR	Track/Field	2-1-0
3	Mitsuo Tsukahara, JPN	Gymnastics	2-0-1
3	Steve Genter, USA	Swimming	1-2-0
3	Viktor Klimenko, USSR	Gymnastics	1-2-0
3	Mike Stamm, USA	Swimming	1-2-0
3	Vladimir Bure, USSR	Swimming	0-1-2

WOMEN

No		Sport	G-S-B
5	Shane Gould, AUS	Swimming	3-1-1
5	Karin Janz, E. Ger	Gymnastics	2-2-1
4	Olga Korbut, USSR	Gymnastics	3-1-0
4	Lyudmila Tourischeva, USSR	Gymnastics	2-1-1
4	Tamara Lazakovitch, USSR	Gymnastics	1-1-2

Track & Field

MEN

Event		Time	
100m	Valery Borzov, USSR	10.14	
200m	Valery Borzov, USSR	20.00	
400m	Vince Matthews, USA	44.66	
800m	Dave Wottle, USA	1:45.9	
1500m	Pekka Vasala, FIN	3:36.3	
5000m	Lasse Viren, FIN	13:26.4	**OR**
10,000m	Lasse Viren, FIN	27:38.4	**WR**
Marathon	Frank Shorter, USA	2:12:19.8	
110m H	Rod Milburn, USA	13.24	**=WR**
400m H	John Akii-Bua, UGA	47.82	**WR**
3000m Steeple	Kip Keino, KEN	8:23.6	**OR**
20k Walk	Peter Frenkel, E. Ger	1:26:42.4	**OR**

Event		Time	
50k Walk	Bernd Kannenberg, W. Ger.	3:56:11.6	OR
4x100m	USA (Larry Black, Robert Taylor, Gerald Tinker, Eddie Hart)	38.19	=WR
4x400m	KEN (Charles Asati, Hezaklah Nyamau, Robert Ouko, Julius Sang)	2:59.8	

Event		Mark	
High Jump	Yuri Tarmak, USSR	7- 3¾	
Pole Vault	Wolfgang Nordwig, E. Ger	18- 0½	OR
Long Jump	Randy Williams, USA	27- 0½	
Triple Jump	Viktor Saneyev, USSR	56-11¼	
Shot Put	Wladyslaw Komar, POL	69- 6	OR
Discus	Ludvik Danek, CZE	211- 3	
Hammer	Anatoly Bondarchuk, USSR	247- 8	OR
Javelin	Klaus Wolfermann, W. Ger	296-10	OR
Decathlon	Nikolai Avilov, USSR	8454 pts	WR

WOMEN

Event		Time	
100m	Renate Stecher, E. Ger	11.07	
200m	Renate Stecher, E. Ger	22.40	=WR
400m	Monika Zehrt, E. Ger	51.08	OR
800m	Hildegard Falck, W. Ger	1:58.55	OR
1500m	Lyudmila Bragina, USSR	4:01.4	WR
100m H	Annelie Ehrhardt, E. Ger	12.59	WR
4x100m	W. Ger. (Christiane Krause, Ingrid Mickler, Annegret Richter, Heidemarie Rosendahl)	42.81	=WR
4x400m	E. Ger. (Dagmar Kasling, Rita Kühne, Helga Seidler, Monika Zehrt)	3:23.0	WR

Event		Mark	
High Jump	Ulrike Meyfarth, W. Ger	6- 3½	=WR
Long Jump	Heidemarie Rosendahl, W. Ger	22- 3	
Shot Put	Nadezhda Chizhova, USSR	69- 0	WR
Discus	Faina Melnik, USSR	218- 7	OR
Javelin	Ruth Fuchs, E. Ger	209- 7	OR
Pentathlon	Mary Peters, GBR	4801 pts	WR

Boxing

Weight Class	Champion
Lt. Flyweight (106 lbs)	György Gedó, HUN
Flyweight (112)	Georgi Kostadinov, BUL
Bantamweight (119)	Orlando Martinez, CUB
Featherweight (125)	Boris Kousnetsov, USSR
Lightweight (132)	Jan Szczepanski, POL
Lt. Welterweight (139)	Ray Seales, USA
Welterweight (148)	Emilio Correa, CUB
Lt. Middleweight (156)	Dieter Kottysch, W. Ger
Middleweight (165)	Vyacheslav Lemechev, USSR
Lt. Heavyweight (178)	Mate Parlov, YUG
Heavyweight (178+)	Teófilo Stevenson, CUB

Gymnastics
MEN

Individual		Points
All-Around	Sawao Kato, JPN	114.650
Floor	Nikolai Andrianov, USSR	19.175
Horiz.Bar	Mitsuo Tsukahara, JPN	19.725
Paral.Bars	Sawao Kato, JPN	19.475
Rings	Akinori Nakayama, JPN	19.35
Side Horse	Viktor Klimenko, USSR	19.125
Vault	Klaus Köste, E. Ger	18.85

Team		Points
All-Around	JPN (Kato, Kenmotsu, Kasamatsu, Nakayama, Tsukahara, Okamura)	571.25

WOMEN

Individual		Points
All-Around	Lyudmila Tourischeva, USSR	77.025
Bal.Beam	Olga Korbut, USSR	19.40
Floor	Olga Korbut, USSR	19.575
Uneven Bars	Karin Janz, E. Ger	19.675

Individual		Points
Vault	Karin Janz, E. Ger	19.525

Team		Points
All-Around	USSR (Tourischeva, Korbut, Lazakovitch, Burda, Saadi, Koshel)	380.50

Swimming
MEN

Event		Time	
100m Free	Mark Spitz, USA	51.22	WR
200m Free	Mark Spitz, USA	1:52.78	WR
400m Free	Brad Cooper, USA	4:00.27	OR
1500m Free	Mike Burton, USA	15:52.58	WR
100m Back	Roland Matthes, E. Ger	56.58	OR
200m Back	Roland Matthes, E. Ger	2:02.82	=WR
100m Brst	Nobutaka Taguchi, JPN	1:04.94	WR
200m Brst	John Hencken, USA	2:21.55	WR
100m Fly	Mark Spitz, USA	54.27	WR
200m Fly	Mark Spitz, USA	2:00.70	WR
200m I.M.	Gunnar Larsson, SWE	2:07.17	WR
400m I.M.	Gunnar Larsson, SWE	4:31.98	OR
4x100m Free	USA (Dave Edgar, John Murphy, Jerry Heidenreich, Mark Spitz)	3:26.42	WR
4x200m Free	USA (John Kinsella, Fred Tyler, Steve Genter, Mark Spitz)	7:35.78	WR
4x100m Mdly	USA (Mike Stamm, Tom Bruce, Mark Spitz, Jerry Heidenreich)	3:48.16	WR

Diving		Points
Platform	Klaus Dibiasi, ITA	504.12
Spring	Vladimir Vasin, USSR	594.09

WOMEN

Event		Time	
100m Free	Sandra Neilson, USA	58.59	OR
200m Free	Shane Gould, AUS	2:03.56	WR
400m Free	Shane Gould, AUS	4:19.44	WR
800m Free	Keena Rothhammer, USA	8:53.68	WR
100m Back	Melissa Belote, USA	1:05.78	OR
200m Back	Melissa Belote, USA	2:19.19	WR
100m Brst	Cathy Carr, USA	1:13.58	WR
200m Brst	Beverly Whitfield, AUS	2:41.71	OR
100m Fly	Mayumi Aoki, JPN	1:03.34	WR
200m Fly	Karen Moe, USA	2:15.57	WR
200m I.M.	Shane Gould, AUS	2:23.07	WR
400m I.M.	Gail Neall, AUS	5:02.97	WR
4x100m Free	USA (Sandra Neilson, Jennifer Kemp, Jane Barkman, Shirley Babashoff)	3:55.19	WR
4x100m Mdly	USA (Melissa Belote, Cathy Carr, Deena Deardurff, Sandra Neilson)	4:20.75	WR

Diving		Points
Platform	Ulrika Knape, SWE	390.00
Spring	Micki King, USA	450.03

Team Sports

Men	Champion
Basketball	Soviet Union
Field Hockey	West Germany
Handball	Yugoslavia
Soccer	Poland
Volleyball	Japan
Water Polo	Soviet Union

Women	Champion
Volleyball	Soviet Union

Also Contested

Archery, Canoeing, Cycling, Equestrian, Fencing, Judo, Modern Pentathlon, Rowing, Shooting, Weightlifting, Freestyle Wrestling, Greco-Roman Wrestling and Yachting.

1976

CANADA
1976

Montreal

In 1970, when Montreal was named to host the Summer Olympics '76, organizers estimated it would cost $310 million to stage the Games. However, due to political corruption, mismanagement, labor disputes, inflation and a $100 million outlay for security to prevent another Munich, the final bill came to more than $1.5 billion.

Then, right before the Games were scheduled to open in July, 32 nations, most of them from black Africa, walked out when the IOC refused to ban New Zealand because its national rugby team was touring racially segregated South Africa. Taiwan also withdrew when Communist China pressured trading partner Canada to deny the Taiwanese the right to compete as the Republic of China.

When the Games finally got started they were quickly stolen by 14-year-old Romanian gymnast Nadia Comaneci, who scored seven perfect 10s on her way to three gold medals.

East Germany's Kornelia Ender did Comaneci one better, winning four times as the GDR captured 11 of 13 events in women's swimming. John Naber (4 gold) and the U.S. men did the East German women one better when they won 12 of 13 gold medals in swimming.

In track and field, Cuba's Alberto Juantorena won the 400 and 800-meter runs, and Finland's Lasse Viren took the 5,000 and 10,000. Viren missed a third gold when he placed fifth in the marathon.

Four Americans who became household names during the Games were decathlon winner Bruce Jenner and three future world boxing champions—Ray Leonard and the Spinks brothers, Michael and Leon.

Top 10 Standings

National medal standings are not recognized by the IOC. The unofficial point totals are based on 3 points for a gold medal, 2 for a silver and 1 for a bronze.

	Gold	Silver	Bronze	Total	Pts
1 USSR	49	41	35	125	264
2 USA	34	35	25	94	197
3 E. Germany	40	25	25	90	195
4 W. Germany	10	12	17	39	71
5 Japan	9	6	10	25	49
6 Poland	7	6	13	26	46
7 Romania	4	9	14	27	44
8 Bulgaria	6	9	7	22	43
9 Cuba	6	4	3	13	29
10 Hungary	4	5	13	22	35

Leading Medal Winners

Number of individual medals won on the left; gold, silver and bronze breakdown to the right.

MEN

No		Sport	G-S-B
7	Nikolai Andrianov, USSR	Gymnastics	4-2-1
5	John Naber, USA	Swimming	4-1-0
5	Mitsuo Tsukahara, JPN	Gymnastics	2-1-2
4	Jim Montgomery, USA	Swimming	3-0-1
3	John Hencken, USA	Swimming	2-1-0
3	Sawao Kato, JPN	Gymnastics	2-1-0
3	Eizo Kenmotsu, JPN	Gymnastics	1-2-0
3	Rüdiger Helm, E. Ger	Canoeing	1-0-2

WOMEN

No		Sport	G-S-B
5	Kornelia Ender, E. Ger	Swimming	4-1-0
5	Nadia Comaneci, ROM	Gymnastics	3-1-1
5	Shirley Babashoff, USA	Swimming	1-4-0
4	Nelli Kim, USSR	Gymnastics	3-1-0
4	Andrea Pollack, E. Ger	Swimming	2-2-0
4	Lyudmila Tourischeva, USSR	Gymnastics	1-2-1
3	Ulrike Richter, E. Ger	Swimming	3-0-0
3	Annagret Richter, W. Ger	Track/Field	1-2-0
3	Renate Stecher, E. Ger	Track/Field	1-1-1
3	Teodora Ungureanu, ROM	Gymnastics	0-2-1

Track & Field
MEN

Event		Time	
100m	Hasely Crawford, TRI	10.06	
200m	Donald Quarrie, JAM	20.23	
400m	Alberto Juantorena, CUB	44.26	
800m	Alberto Juantorena, CUB	1:43.50	WR
1500m	John Walker, NZE	3:39.17	
5000m	Lasse Viren, FIN	13:24.76	
10,000m	Lasse Viren, FIN	27:40.38	
Marathon	Waldemar Cierpinski, E. Ger	2:09:55	OR
110m H	Guy Drut, FRA	13.30	
400m H	Edwin Moses, USA	47.64	WR
3000m Steeple	Anders Gärdeud, SWE	8:08.2	WR
20k Walk	Daniel Bautista, MEX	1:24:40.6	OR
4x100m	USA (Harvey Glance, Johnny Jones, Millard Hampton, Steve Riddick)	38.33	
4x400m	USA (Herman Frazier, Benjamin Brown, Fred Newhouse, Maxie Parks)	2:58.65	

Event		Mark	
High Jump	Jacek Wszola, POL	7- 4½	OR
Pole Vault	Tadeusz Slusarski, POL	18- 0½	=OR
Long Jump	Arnie Robinson, USA	27- 4¾	
Triple Jump	Viktor Saneyev, USSR	56- 8¾	
Shot Put	Udo Beyer, E. Ger	69- 0¾	
Discus	Mac Wilkins, USA	221- 5	
Hammer	Yuri Sedykh, USSR	254- 4	OR
Javelin	Miklos Nèmeth, HUN	310- 4	WR
Decathlon	Bruce Jenner, USA	8617 pts	WR

WOMEN

Event		Time	
100m	Annegret Richter, W. Ger	11.08	
200m	Bärbel Eckert, E. Ger	22.37	OR
400m	Irena K. Szewinska, POL	49.29	WR
800m	Tatyana Kazankina, USSR	1:54.94	WR
1500m	Tatyana Kazankina, USSR	4:05.48	
100m H	Johanna Schaller, E. Ger	12.77	

Event		Time
4x100m	E. Ger. (Marlies Oelsner, Renate Stecher, Carla Bodendorf, Barbel Eckert)	42.55 **OR**
4x400m	E. Ger. (Doris Maletzki, Brigitte Rohde, Ellen Streidt, Christina Brehmer)	3:19.23 **WR**

Event		Mark
High Jump	Rosemarie Ackermann, E. Ger	6- 4 **OR**
Long Jump	Angela Voigt, E. Ger	22- 0¾
Shot Put	Ivanka Hristova, BUL	69- 5¼ **OR**
Discus	Evelin Schlaak, E. Ger	226- 4 **OR**
Javelin	Ruth Fuchs, E. Ger	216- 4 **OR**
Pentathlon	Siegrun Siegl, E. Ger	4745 pts

Boxing

Weight Class	Champion
Lt. Flyweight (106 lbs)	Jorge Hernandez, CUB
Flyweight (112)	Leo Randolph, USA
Bantamweight (119)	Gu Yong-Ju, N. Kor
Featherweight (125)	Angel Herrera, CUB
Lightweight (132)	Howard Davis, USA
Lt. Welterweight (139)	Ray Leonard, USA
Welterweight (148)	Jochen Bachfeld, E. Ger
Lt. Middleweight (156)	Jerzy Rybicki, POL
Middleweight (165)	Michael Spinks, USA
Lt. Heavyweight (178)	Leon Spinks, USA
Heavyweight (178+)	Teófilo Stevenson, CUB

Gymnastics
MEN

Individual		Points
All-Around	Nikolai Andrianov, USSR	116.65
Floor	Nikolai Andrianov, USSR	19.45
Horiz.Bar	Mitsuo Tsukahara, JPN	19.675
Paral.Bars	Sawao Kato, JPN	19.675
Rings	Nikolai Andrianov, USSR	19.65
Side Horse	Zoltan Magyar, HUN	19.70
Vault	Nikolai Andrianov, USSR	19.45

Team		Points
All-Around	JPN (Kato, Tsukahara, Kajiyama, Kenmotsu, Igarashi, Fujimoto)	576.85

WOMEN

Individual		Points
All-Around	Nadia Comaneci, ROM	79.275
Bal.Beam	Nadia Comaneci, ROM	19.95
Floor	Nelli Kim, USSR	19.85
Uneven Bars	Nadia Comaneci, ROM	20.00
Vault	Nelli Kim, USSR	19.80

Team		Points
All-Around	USSR (Kim, Tourischeva, Korbut, Saadi, Filatova, Grozdova)	466.00

Swimming
MEN

Event		Time
100m Free	Jim Montgomery, USA	49.99 **WR**
200m Free	Bruce Furniss, USA	1:50.29 **WR**
400m Free	Brian Goodell, USA	3:51.93 **WR**
1500m Free	Brian Goodell, USA	15:02.40 **WR**
100m Back	John Naber, USA	55.49 **WR**
200m Back	John Naber, USA	1:59.19 **WR**
100m Brst	John Hencken, USA	1:03.11 **WR**
200m Brst	David Wilkie, GBR	2:15.11 **WR**
100m Fly	Matt Vogel, USA	54.35
200m Fly	Mike Bruner, USA	1:59.23 **WR**
400m I.M.	Rod Strachan, USA	4:23.68 **WR**
4x200m Free	USA (Mike Bruner, Bruce Furniss, John Naber, Jim Montgomery)	7:23.22 **WR**

Event		Time
4x100m Mdly	USA (John Naber, John Hencken, Matt Vogel, Jim Montgomery)	3:42.22 **WR**

Diving		Points
Platform	Klaus Dibiasi, ITA	600.51
Spring	Phil Boggs, USA	619.05

WOMEN

Event		Time
100m Free	Kornelia Ender, E. Ger	55.65 **WR**
200m Free	Kornelia Ender, E. Ger	1:59.26 **WR**
400m Free	Petra Thümer, E. Ger	4:09.89 **WR**
800m Free	Petra Thümer, E. Ger	8:37.14 **WR**
100m Back	Ulrike Richter, E. Ger	1:01.83 **OR**
200m Back	Ulrike Richter, E. Ger	2:13.43 **OR**
100m Brst	Hannelore Anke, E. Ger	1:11.16
200m Brst	Marina Koshevaia, USSR	2:33.35 **WR**
100m Fly	Kornelia Ender, E. Ger	1:00.13 **WR**
200m Fly	Andrea Pollack, E. Ger	2:11.41 **OR**
400m I.M.	Ulrike Tauber, E. Ger	4:42.77 **WR**
4x100m Free	USA (Kim Peyton, Wendy Boglioli, Jill Sterkel, Shirley Babashoff)	3:44.82 **WR**
4x100m Mdly	E. Ger. (Ulrike Richter, Hannelore Anke, Andrea Pollack, Kornelia Ender)	4:07.95 **WR**

Diving		Points
Platform	Elena Vaytsekhovskaya, USSR	406.59
Spring	Jennifer Chandler, USA	506.19

Team Sports

Men	Champion
Basketball	United States
Field Hockey	New Zealand
Handball	Soviet Union
Soccer	East Germany
Volleyball	Poland
Water Polo	Hungary

Women	Champion
Basketball	Soviet Union
Handball	Soviet Union
Volleyball	Japan

Also Contested

Archery, Canoeing, Cycling, Equestrian, Fencing, Judo, Modern Pentathlon, Rowing, Shooting, Weightlifting, Freestyle Wrestling, Greco-Roman Wrestling and Yachting.

1980

Moscow

Four years after 32 nations walked out of the Montreal Games, twice that many chose to stay away from Moscow—many in support of an American-led boycott to protest the December 1979, Soviet invasion of Afghanistan.

Unable to persuade the IOC to cancel or move the Summer Games, U.S. President Jimmy Carter pressured the USOC to officially withdraw in April. Many western governments, like West Germany and Japan, followed suit and withheld their athletes. But others, like Britain and France, while supporting the boycott, allowed their Olympic committees to participate if they wished.

The first Games to be held in a Communist country opened in July with 80 nations competing and were dominated by the USSR and East Germany. They were also plagued by charges of rigged judging and poor sportsmanship by Moscow fans who, without the Americans around, booed the Poles and East Germans unmercifully.

While Soviet gymnast Aleksandr Dityatin became the first athlete to win eight medals in one year, the belle of Montreal, Nadia Comaneci of Romania, returned to win two more gold medals and Cuban heavyweight Teofilo Stevenson became the first boxer to win three golds in the same weight division.

In track and field, Miruts Yifter of Ethiopia won at 5,000 and 10,000 meters, but the most thrilling moment of the Games came in the last lap of the 1,500 meters where Sebastian Coe of Great Britain outran countryman Steve Ovett and Jurgen Straub of East Germany for the gold.

Top 10 Standings

National medal standings are not recognized by the IOC. The unofficial point totals are based on 3 points for a gold medal, 2 for a silver and 1 for a bronze.

		Gold	Silver	Bronze	Total	Pts
1	USSR	80	69	46	195	424
2	E. Germany	47	37	42	126	257
3	Bulgaria	8	16	17	41	73
4	Hungary	7	10	15	32	56
5	Poland	3	14	15	32	52
6	Cuba	8	7	5	20	43
	Romania	6	6	13	25	43
8	Great Britain	5	7	9	21	38
9	Italy	8	3	4	15	34
10	France	6	5	3	14	31

Leading Medal Winners

Number of individual medals won on the left; gold, silver and bronze breakdown to the right.

MEN

No		Sport	G-S-B
8	Aleksandr Dityatin, USSR	Gymnastics	3-4-1
5	Nikolai Andrianov, USSR	Gymnastics	2-2-1
4	Roland Brückner, E. Ger	Gymnastics	1-1-2
3	Vladimir Parfenovich, USSR	Canoeing	3-0-0
3	Vladimir Salnikov, USSR	Swimming	3-0-0
3	Sergei Kopliakov, USSR	Swimming	2-1-0
3	Aleksandr Tkachyov, USSR	Gymnastics	2-1-0
3	Andrei Krylov, USSR	Swimming	1-2-0
3	Arsen Miskarov, USSR	Swimming	0-2-1

WOMEN

No		Sport	G-S-B
5	Ines Diers, E. Ger	Swimming	2-2-1
4	Caren Metschuck, E. Ger	Swimming	3-1-0
4	Nadia Comaneci, ROM	Gymnastics	2-2-0
4	Natalya Shaposhnikova, USSR	Gymnastics	2-0-2
4	Maxi Gnauck, E. Ger	Gymnastics	1-1-2
3	Barbara Krause, E. Ger	Swimming	3-0-0
3	Rica Reinisch, E. Ger	Swimming	3-0-0
3	Yelena Davydova, USSR	Gymnastics	2-1-0
3	Steffi Kraker, E. Ger	Gymnastics	0-1-2
3	Melita Ruhn, ROM	Gymnastics	0-1-2

Track & Field
MEN

Event		Time
100m	Allan Wells, GBR	10.25
200m	Pietro Mennea, ITA	20.19
400m	Viktor Markin, USSR	44.60
800m	Steve Ovett, GBR	1:45.4
1500m	Sebastian Coe, GBR	3:38.4
5000m	Miruts Yifter, ETH	13:21.0
10,000m	Miruts Yifter, ETH	27:42.7
Marathon	Waldemar Cierpinski, E. Ger	.2:11:03
110m H	Thomas Munkelt, E. Ger	13.39
400m H	Volker Beck, E. Ger	48.70
3000m Steeple	Bronislaw Malinowski, POL	8:09.7
20k Walk	Maurizio Damilano, ITA	1:23:35.5 OR
50k Walk	Hartwig Gauder, E. Ger	3:49:24.0 OR
4x100m	USSR (Vladimir Muravyov, Nikolai Sidorov, Aleksandr Aksinin, Andrei Prokofiev)	38.26
4x400m	USSR (Remigius Valiulis, Mikhail Linge, Nikolai Chernetsky, Viktor Markin)	3:01.1

Event		Mark
High Jump	Gerd Wessig, E. Ger	7- 8¾ WR
Pole Vault	Wladyslaw Kozakiewicz, POL	18-11½ WR
Long Jump	Lutz Dombrowski, E. Ger	28- 0¼
Triple Jump	Jaak Uudmäe, USSR	56-11¼
Shot Put	Vladimir Kiselyov, USSR	70- 0½ OR
Discus	Viktor Rashchupkin, USSR	218- 8
Hammer	Yuri Sedykh, USSR	268- 4 WR
Javelin	Dainis Kula, USSR	299- 2
Decathlon	Daley Thompson, GBR	8495 pts

WOMEN

Event		Time
100m	Lyudmila Kondratyeva, USSR	11.06
200m	Bärbel E. Wöckel, E. Ger	22.03 OR
400m	Marita Koch, E. Ger	48.88 OR
800m	Nadezhda Olizarenko, USSR	.1:53.42 WR
1500m	Tatyana Kazankina, USSR	3:56.6 OR
100m H	Vera Komisova, USSR	12.56 OR
4x100m	E. Ger. (Romy Müller, Bärbel E. Wöckel, Ingrid Auerswald, Marlies O. Göhr)	41.60 WR
4x400m	USSR (Tatyana Prorochenko, Tatyana Goistchik, Nina Zyuskova, Irina Nazarova)	3:20.2

Event		Mark
High Jump	Sara Simeoni, ITA	6- 5½ OR
Long Jump	Tatiana Kolpakova, USSR	23- 2 OR
Shot Put	Ilona Slupianke, E. Ger	73- 6¼
Discus	Evelin S. Jahl, E. Ger	229- 6 OR
Javelin	Maria Colon, CUB	224- 5 OR
Pentathlon	Nadezhda Tkachenko, USSR	.5083 pts WR

Boxing

Weight Class	Champion
Lt. Flyweight (106 lbs)	Shamil Sabyrov, USSR
Flyweight (112)	Peter Lessov, BUL
Bantamweight (119)	Juan Hernandez, CUB
Featherweight (125)	Rudi Fink, E. Ger
Lightweight (132)	Angel Herrera, CUB
Lt. Welterweight (139)	Patrizio Oliva, ITA
Welterweight (148)	Andres Aldama, CUB
Lt. Middleweight (156)	Armando Martinez, CUB
Middleweight (165)	Jose Gomez, CUB
Lt. Heavyweight (178)	Slobodan Kacar, YUG
Heavyweight (178+)	Teofilo Stevenson, CUB

Gymnastics
MEN

Individual		Points
All-Around	Aleksandr Dityatin, USSR	118.65
Floor	Roland Brückner, E. Ger	19.75
Horiz.Bar	Stoyan Deltchev, BUL	19.825
Paral.Bars	Aleksandr Tkachyov, USSR	19.775
Rings	Aleksandr Dityatin, USSR	19.875
Side Horse	Zoltán Magyar, HUN	19.925
Vault	Nikolai Andrianov, USSR	19.825

Team		Points
All-Around	USSR (Dityatin, Andrianov, Azaryan, Tkachyov, Makuts, Markelov)	598.60

WOMEN

Individual		Points
All-Around	Yelena Davydova, USSR	79.15
Bal.Beam	Nadia Comaneci, ROM	19.80
Floor	Nadia Comaneci, ROM & Nelli Kim, USSR	19.875
Uneven Bars	Maxi Gnauk, E. Ger	19.875
Vault	Natalya Shaposhnikova, USSR	19.725

Team		Points
All-Around	USSR (Shaposhnikova, Davydova, Kim, Filatova, Zakharova, Naimuschina)	394.90

Swimming
MEN

Event		Time	
100m Free	Jörg Woithe, E. Ger	50.40	
200m Free	Sergei Kopliakov, USSR	1:49.91	OR
400m Free	Vladimir Salnikov, USSR	3:51.31	OR
1500m Free	Vladimir Salnikov, USSR	14:58.27	WR
100m Back	Bengt Baron, SWE	56.33	
200m Back	Sándor Wladár, HUN	2:01.93	
100m Brst	Duncan Goodhew, GBR	1:03.44	
200m Brst	Robertas Zhulpa, USSR	2:15.85	
100m Fly	Pär Arvidsson, SWE	54.92	
200m Fly	Sergei Fesenko, USSR	1:59.76	
400m I.M.	Aleksandr Sidorenko, USSR	4:22.89	OR
4x200m Free	USSR (Sergei Kopliakov, Vladimir, Salnikov, Ivar Stukolkin, Andrei Krylov)	7:23.50	
4x100m Mdly	AUS (Mark Kerry, Peter Evans, Mark Tonelli, Neil Brooks)	3:45.70	

Diving		Points
Platform	Falk Hoffmann, E. Ger	835.650
Spring	Aleksandr Portnov, USSR	905.025

WOMEN

Event		Time	
100m Free	Barbara Krause, E. Ger	54.79	WR
200m Free	Barbara Krause, E. Ger	1:58.33	OR
400m Free	Ines Diers, E. Ger	4:08.76	OR
800m Free	Michelle Ford, AUS	8:28.90	OR
100m Back	Rica Reinisch, E. Ger	1:00.86	WR
200m Back	Rica Reinisch, E. Ger	2:11.77	WR
100m Brst	Ute Geweniger, E. Ger	1:10.22	
200m Brst	Lina Kaciusytė, USSR	2:29.54	OR
100m Fly	Caren Metschuck, E. Ger	1:00.42	
200m Fly	Ines Geissler, E. Ger	2:10.44	OR
400m I.M.	Petra Schneider, E. Ger	4:36.29	WR
4x100m Free	E. Ger. (Barbara Krause, Caren Metschuck, Ines Diers, Sarina Hülsenbeck)	3:42.71	WR
4x100m Mdly	E. Ger. (Rica Reinisch, Ute Geweniger, Andrea Pollack, Caren Metschuck)	4:06.67	WR

Diving		Points
Platform	Martina Jäschke, E. Ger	596.25
Spring	Irina Kalinina, USSR	725.91

Team Sports

Men	Champion
Basketball	Yugoslavia
Field Hockey	India
Handball	East Germany
Soccer	Czechoslovakia
Volleyball	Soviet Union
Water Polo	Soviet Union

Women	Champion
Basketball	Soviet Union
Field Hockey	Zimbabwe
Handball	Soviet Union
Volleyball	Soviet Union

Also Contested

Archery, Canoeing, Cycling, Equestrian, Fencing, Judo, Modern Pentathlon, Rowing, Shooting, Weightlifting, Freestyle Wrestling, Greco-Roman Wrestling and Yachting.

1984

Los Angeles

For the third consecutive Olympiad, a boycott prevented all member nations from attending the Summer Games. This time, the Soviet Union and 13 Communist allies stayed home in an obvious payback for the West's snub of Moscow in 1980. Romania was the only Warsaw Pact country to come to L.A.

While a record 140 nations did show up, the level of competition was hardly what it might have been had the Soviets and East Germans made the trip. As a result, the United States won a record 83 gold medals in the most lopsided Summer Games since St. Louis 80 years before.

The American gold rush was led by 23-year-old Carl Lewis, who duplicated Jesse Owens' 1936 track and field grand slam by winning the 100 and 200 meters and the long jump, and anchoring the 4x100 meter relay. Teammate Valerie Brisco-Hooks won three times, taking the 200, 400 and 4x100 relay.

Sebastian Coe of Britain became the first repeat winner of the 1,500 meters since Jim Lightbody of the U.S. in 1906. Other repeaters were Briton Daley Thompson in the decathlon and U.S. hurdler Edwin Moses, who won in 1976 but was not allowed to defend his title in '80.

Romanian gymnast Ecaterina Szabó matched Lewis' four gold medals and added a silver, but the darling of the Games was little (4-foot-8¾), 16-year-old Mary Lou Retton, who won the women's All-Around with a pair of 10s in her last two events.

The L.A. Olympics were the first privately financed Games ever and made an unheard of profit of $215 million. *Time* magazine was so impressed it named organizing president Peter Ueberroth its Man of the Year.

Top 10 Standings

National medal standings are not recognized by the IOC. The unofficial point totals are based on 3 points for a gold medal, 2 for a silver and 1 for a bronze.

		Gold	Silver	Bronze	Total	Pts
1	USA	83	61	30	174	401
2	W. Germany	17	19	23	59	112
3	Romania	20	16	17	53	109
4	Canada	10	18	16	44	82
5	China	15	8	9	32	70
6	Italy	14	6	12	32	66
7	Japan	10	8	14	32	60
8	Great Britain	5	11	21	37	58
9	France	5	7	16	28	45
10	Australia	4	8	12	24	40

Leading Medal Winners

Number of individual medals won on the left; gold, silver and bronze breakdown to the right.

MEN

No		Sport	G-S-B
6	Li Ning, CHN	Gymnastics	3-2-1
5	Koji Gushiken, JPN	Gymnastics	2-1-2
4	Carl Lewis, USA	Track/Field	4-0-0
4	Mike Heath, USA	Swimming	3-1-0
4	Michael Gross, W. Ger	Swimming	2-2-0
4	Mitch Gaylord, USA	Gymnastics	1-1-2
3	Rick Carey, USA	Swimming	3-0-0
3	Ian Ferguson, NZE	Canoeing	3-0-0
3	Rowdy Gaines, USA	Swimming	3-0-0
3	Peter Vidmar, USA	Gymnastics	2-1-0
3	Victor Davis, CAN	Swimming	1-2-0
3	Pablo Morales, USA	Swimming	1-2-0
3	Lou Yun, CHN	Gymnastics	1-2-0
3	Shinji Morisue, JPN	Gymnastics	1-1-1
3	Lars-Erik Moberg, SWE	Canoeing	0-3-0
3	Mark Stockwell, AUS	Swimming	0-2-1

WOMEN

No		Sport	G-S-B
5	Ecaterina Szabó, ROM	Gymnastics	4-1-0
5	Mary Lou Retton, USA	Gymnastics	1-2-2
4	Nancy Hogshead, USA	Swimming	3-1-0
3	Valerie Brisco-Hooks, USA	Track/Field	3-0-0
3	Tracy Caulkins, USA	Swimming	3-0-0
3	Mary T. Meagher, USA	Swimming	3-0-0
3	Agneta Andersson, SWE	Canoeing	2-1-0
3	Chandra Cheeseborough, USA	Track/Field	2-1-0
3	Simona Pauca, ROM	Gymnastics	2-0-1
3	Julie McNamara, USA	Gymnastics	1-2-0
3	Anne Ottenbrite, CAN	Swimming	1-1-1
3	Karin Seick, W. Ger	Swimming	0-1-2
3	Annemarie Verstappen, NED	Swimming	0-1-2

Track & Field
MEN

Event		Time	
100m	Carl Lewis, USA	9.99	
200m	Carl Lewis, USA	19.80	OR
400m	Alonzo Babers, USA	44.27	
800m	Joaquim Cruz, BRA	1:43.00	OR
1500m	Sebastian Coe, GBR	3:32.53	OR
5000m	Said Aouita, MOR	13:05.59	OR
10,000m	Alberto Cova, ITA	27:47.54	
Marathon	Carlos Lopes, POR	2:09:21	OR
110m H	Roger Kingdom, USA	13.20	OR
400m H	Edwin Moses, USA	47.75	
3000m Steeple	Julius Korir, KEN	8:11.80	
20k Walk	Ernesto Canto, MEX	1:23:13.0	OR
50k Walk	Raúl González, MEX	3:47:26.0	OR
4x100m	USA (Sam Graddy, Ron Brown, Calvin Smith, Carl Lewis)	37.83	WR

Event		Time	
4x400m	USA (Sunder Nix, Ray Armstead, Alonzo Babers, Antonio McKay)	2:57.91	

Event		Mark	
High Jump	Dietmar Mögenburg, W. Ger	7-8½	
Pole Vault	Pierre Quinon, FRA	18-10¼	
Long Jump	Carl Lewis, USA	28-0¼	
Triple Jump	Al Joyner, USA	56-7½	
Shot Put	Alessandro Andrei, ITA	69-9	
Discus	Rolf Danneberg, W. Ger	218-6	
Hammer	Juha Tiainen, FIN	256-2	
Javelin	Arto Härkönen, FIN	284-8	
Decathlon	Daley Thompson, GBR	8798 pts	=WR

WOMEN

Event		Time	
100m	Evelyn Ashford, USA	10.97	OR
200m	Valerie Brisco-Hooks, USA	21.81	OR
400m	Valerie Brisco-Hooks, USA	48.83	OR
800m	Doina Melinte, ROM	1:57.60	
1500m	Gabriella Dorio, ITA	4:03.25	
3000m	Maricica Puica, ROM	8:35.96	OR
Marathon	Joan Benoit, USA	2:24.52	
100m H	Benita Fitzergald-Brown, USA	12.84	
400m H	Nawal El Moutawakel, MOR	54.61	OR
4x100m	USA (Alice Brown, Jeanette Bolden, Chandra Cheeseborough, Evelyn Ashford)	41.65	
4x400m	USA (Lillie Leatherwood, Sherri Howard, Valerie Brisco-Hooks, Chandra Cheeseborough)	3:18.29	OR

Event		Mark	
High Jump	Ulrike Meyfarth, W. Ger	6-7½	OR
Long Jump	Anisoara Stanciu, ROM	22-10	
Shot Put	Claudia Losch, W. Ger	67-2¼	
Discus	Ria Stalman, NED	214-5	
Javelin	Tessa Sanderson, GBR	228-2	OR
Heptathlon	Glynis Nunn, AUS	6390 pts	OR

Boxing

Weight Class	Champion
Lt. Flyweight (106 lbs)	Paul Gonzales, USA
Flyweight (112)	Steve McCrory, USA
Bantamweight (119)	Maurizio Stecca, ITA
Featherweight (125)	Meldrick Taylor, USA
Lightweight (132)	Pernell Whitaker, USA
Lt. Welterweight (139)	Jerry Page, USA
Welterweight (148)	Mark Breland, USA
Lt. Middleweight (156)	Frank Tate, USA
Middleweight (165)	Shin Joon-Sup, S. Kor
Lt. Heavyweight (178)	Anton Josipovic, YUG
Heavyweight (200)	Henry Tillman, USA
Super Heavyweight (200+)	Tyrell Biggs, USA

Gymnastics
MEN

Individual		Points
All-Around	Koji Gushiken, JPN	118.7
Floor	Li Ning, CHN	19.925
Horiz.Bar	Shinji Morisue, JPN	20.00
Paral.Bars	Bart Conner, USA	19.95
Rings	Koji Gushiken, JPN	
	Li Ning, CHN	19.85
Side Horse	Li Ning, CHN	
	Peter Vidmar, USA	19.95
Vault	Lou Yun, CHN	19.95

Team		Points
All-Around	USA (Peter Vidmar, Bart Conner, Mitch Gaylord, Tim Daggett, James Hartung, Scott Johnson)	591.40

WOMEN

Individual		Points
All-Around	Mary Lou Retton, USA	79.175
Bal.Beam	Simona Pauca, ROM	
	Ecaterina Szabó, ROM	19.80
Floor	Ecaterina Szabó, ROM	19.975
Uneven Bars	Julie McNamara, USA	
	Ma Yanhong, CHN	19.95
Vault	Ecaterina Szabó, ROM	19.875

Team		Points
All-Around	ROM (Szabó, Cutina, Pauca, Grigoras, Stanulet, Agache)	392.02

Rhythmic		Points
All-Around	Lori Fung, CAN	57.950

Swimming

MEN

Event		Time	
100m Free	Rowdy Gaines, USA	49.80	OR
200m Free	Michael Gross, W. Ger	1:47.44	WR
400m Free	George DiCarlo, USA	3:51.23	OR
1500m Free	Mike O'Brien, USA	15:05.20	
100m Back	Rick Carey, USA	55.79	
200m Back	Rick Carey, USA	2:00.23	
100m Brst	Steve Lundquist, USA	1:01.65	WR
200m Brst	Victor Davis, CAN	2:13.34	WR
100m Fly	Michael Gross, W. Ger	53.08	WR
200m Fly	Jon Sieben, AUS	1:57.04	WR
200m I.M.	Alex Baumann, CAN	2:01.42	WR
400m I.M.	Alex Baumann, CAN	4:17.41	WR
4x100m Free	USA (Chris Cavanaugh, Mike Heath, Matt Biondi, Rowdy Gaines)	3:19.03	WR
4x200m Free	USA (Mike Heath, David Larson, Jeff Float, Bruce Hayes)	7:15.69	WR
4x100m Mdly	USA (Rick Carey, Steve Lundquist, Pablo Morales, Rowdy Gaines)	3:39.30	WR

Diving		Points
Platform	Greg Louganis, USA	710.91
Spring	Greg Louganis, USA	754.41

WOMEN

Event		Time	
100m Free	Nancy Hogshead, USA	55.92	
200m Free	Mary Wayte, USA	1:59.23	
400m Free	Tiffany Cohen, USA	4:07.10	OR
800m Free	Tiffany Cohen, USA	8:24.95	OR
100m Back	Theresa Andrews, USA	1:02.55	
200m Back	Jolanda de Rover, NED	2:12.38	
100m Brst	Petra van Staveren, NED	1:09.88	OR
200m Brst	Anne Ottenbrite, CAN	2:30.38	
100m Fly	Mary T. Meagher, USA	59.26	
200m Fly	Mary T. Meagher, USA	2:06.90	OR
200m I.M.	Tracy Caulkins, USA	2:12.64	OR
400m I.M.	Tracy Caulkins, USA	4:39.24	
4x100m Free	USA (Jenna Johnson, Carrie Steinseifer, Dara Torres, Nancy Hogshead)	3:43.43	
4x100m Mdly	USA (Theresa Andrews, Tracy Caulkins, Mary T. Meagher, Nancy Hogshead)	4:08.34	

Diving		Points
Platform	Zhou Jihong, CHN	435.51
Spring	Sylvie Bernier, CAN	530.70

Team Sports

Men	Champion
Basketball	United States
Field Hockey	Pakistan
Handball	Yugoslavia
Soccer	France
Volleyball	United States
Water Polo	Yugoslavia

Women	Champion
Basketball	United States
Field Hockey	Holland
Handball	Yugoslavia
Volleyball	China

Also Contested

Archery, Canoeing, Cycling, Equestrian, Fencing, Judo, Modern Pentathlon, Rowing, Shooting, Synchronized Swimming, Weightlifting, Freestyle Wrestling, Greco-Roman Wrestling and Yachting.

1988

Seoul

SÉOUL 1988

For the first time since Munich in 1972, there was no organized boycott of the Summer Olympics. Cuba and Ethiopia stayed away in support of North Korea (the IOC turned down the North Koreans' demand to co-host the Games, so they refused to participate), but that was about it.

More countries (159) sent more athletes (9,465) to South Korea than to any previous Olympics. There were also more security personnel (100,000) than ever before given Seoul's proximity (30 miles) to the North and the possibility of student demonstrations for reunification.

Ten days into the Games, Canadian Ben Johnson beat defending champion Carl Lewis in the 100-meter dash with a world record time of 9.79. Two days later, however, Johnson was stripped of his gold medal and sent packing by the IOC when his post-race drug test indicated steroid use.

Lewis, who finished second in the 100, was named the winner. He also repeated in the long jump, but was second in the 200 and did not run the 4x100-relay. Teammate Florence Griffith Joyner claimed four medals—gold in the 100, 200 and 4x100-meter relay, and silver in the 4x400 relay. Her sister-in-law, Jackie Joyner-Kersee, won the long jump and heptathlon.

The most gold medals were won by swimmers—Kristin Otto of East Germany (6) and American Matt Biondi (5). Otherwise, Steffi Graf added an Olympic gold medal to her Grand Slam sweep in tennis, Greg Louganis won both men's diving events for the second straight time, and the U.S. men's basketball team had to settle for third place after losing to the gold medal-winning Soviets, 82-76, in the semifinals.

Top 10 Standings

National medal standings are not recognized by the IOC. The unofficial point totals are based on 3 points for a gold medal, 2 for a silver and 1 for a bronze.

	Gold	Silver	Bronze	Total	Pts
1 USSR	55	31	46	132	273
2 E. Germany	37	35	30	102	211
3 USA	36	31	27	94	197
4 W. Germany	11	14	15	40	76
5 Bulgaria	10	12	13	35	67
South Korea	12	10	11	33	67
7 Hungary	11	6	6	23	51
8 China	5	11	12	28	49
Romania	7	11	6	24	49
10 Great Britain	5	10	9	24	44

Leading Medal Winners

Number of individual medals won on the left; gold, silver and bronze breakdown to the right.

MEN

No		Sport	G-S-B
7	Matt Biondi, USA	Swimming	5-1-1
5	Vladimir Artemov, USSR	Gymnastics	4-1-0
4	Dmitri Bilozerchev, USSR	Gymnastics	3-0-1
4	Valeri Lyukin, USSR	Gymnastics	2-2-0
3	Chris Jacobs, USA	Swimming	2-1-0
3	Carl Lewis, USA	Track/Field	2-1-0
3	Holger Behrendt, E. Ger	Gymnastics	1-1-1
3	Uwe Dassler, E. Ger	Swimming	1-1-1
3	Paul McDonald, NZE	Canoeing	1-1-1
3	Igor Polianski, USSR	Swimming	1-0-2
3	Gennadi Prigoda, USSR	Swimming	0-1-2
3	Sven Tippelt, E. Ger	Gymnastics	0-1-2

WOMEN

No		Sport	G-S-B
6	Kristin Otto, E. Ger	Swimming	6-0-0
6	Daniela Silivas, ROM	Gymnastics	3-2-1
4	Florence Griffith Joyner, USA	Track/Field	3-1-0
4	Svetlana Boguinskaya, USSR	Gymnastics	2-1-1
4	Elena Shushunova, USSR	Gymnastics	2-1-1
3	Janet Evans, USA	Swimming	3-0-0
3	Silke Hörner, E. Ger	Swimming	2-0-1
3	Daniela Hunger, E. Ger	Swimming	2-0-1
3	Katrin Meissner, E. Ger	Swimming	2-0-1
3	Birgit Schmidt, E. Ger	Canoeing	2-1-0
3	Birte Weigang, E. Ger	Swimming	1-2-0
3	Vania Guecheva, BUL	Canoeing	1-1-1
3	Gabriela Potorac, ROM	Gymnastics	0-2-1
3	Heike Drechsler, E. Ger	Track/Field	0-1-2

Track & Field

MEN

Event		Time	
100m	Carl Lewis, USA	9.92	OR
200m	Joe DeLoach, USA	19.75	OR
400m	Steve Lewis, USA	43.87	
800m	Paul Ereng, KEN	1:43.45	
1500m	Peter Rono, KEN	3:35.96	
5000m	John Ngugi, KEN	13:11.70	
10,000m	Brahim Boutaib, MOR	27:21.46	OR
Marathon	Gelindo Bordin, ITA	2:10:32	
110m H	Roger Kingdom, USA	12.98	OR
400m H	Andre Phillips, USA	47.19	OR
3000m			
Steeple	Julius Kariuki, KEN	8:05.51	OR
20k Walk	Jozef Pribilinec, CZE	1:19:57	OR
50k Walk	Viacheslav Ivanenko, USSR	3:38:29	OR
4x100m	USSR (Victor Bryzgine, Vladimir Krylov, Vladimir Mouraviev, Vitaly Savine)	38.19	

Event		Time	
4x400m	USA (Danny Everett, Steve Lewis, Kevin Robinzine, Butch Reynolds)	2:56.16	=WR

Event		Mark	
High Jump	Guennadi Avdeenko, USSR	7- 9¾	OR
Pole Vault	Sergey Bubka, USSR	19- 4¼	OR
Long Jump	Carl Lewis, USA	28- 7¼	
Triple Jump	Hristo Markov, BUL	57- 9¼	OR
Shot Put	Ulf Timmermann, E. Ger	73- 8¾	OR
Discus	Jürgen Schult, E. Ger	225- 9	OR
Hammer	Sergey Litvinov, USSR	278- 2	OR
Javelin	Tapio Korjus, FIN	276- 6	
Decathlon	Christian Schenk, E. Ger	8488 pts	

WOMEN

Event		Time	
100m	Florence Griffith Joyner, USA	10.54	OR
200m	Florence Griffith Joyner, USA	21.34	WR
400m	Olga Bryzgina, USSR	48.65	OR
800m	Sigrun Wodars, E. Ger	1:56.10	
1500m	Paula Ivan, ROM	3:53.96	OR
3000m	Tatiana Samolenko, USSR	8:26.53	OR
10,000m	Olga Bondarenko, USSR	31:05.21	OR
Marathon	Rosa Mota, POR	2:25:40	
100m H	Yordanka Donkova, BUL	12.38	OR
400m H	Debra Flintoff-King, AUS	53.17	OR
4x100m	USA (Alice Brown, Sheila Echols, Florence Griffith Joyner, Evelyn Ashford)	41.98	
4x400m	USSR (Tatyana Ledovskaia, Olga Nazarova, Maria Piniguina, Olga Bryzgina)	3:15.18	WR

Event		Mark	
High Jump	Louise Ritter, USA	6- 8	OR
Long Jump	Jackie Joyner-Kersee, USA	24- 3¼	OR
Shot Put	Natalya Lisovskaya, USSR	72-11¼	
Discus	Martina Hellmann, E. Ger	237- 2½	OR
Javelin	Petra Felke, E. Ger	245- 0	OR
Heptathlon	Jackie Joyner-Kersee, USA	7291 pts	WR

Boxing

Weight Class	Champion
Lt. Flyweight (106 lbs)	Ivailo Hristov, BUL
Flyweight (112)	Kim Kwang-Sun, S. Kor
Bantamweight (119)	Kennedy McKinney, USA
Featherweight (125)	Giovanni Parisi, ITA
Lightweight (132)	Andreas Zuelow, E. Ger
Lt. Welterweight (139)	Vyacheslav Yanovsky, USSR
Welterweight (148)	Robert Wangila, KEN
Lt. Middleweight (156)	Park Si-Hun, S. Kor
Middleweight (165)	Henry Maske, E. Ger
Lt. Heavyweight (178)	Andrew Maynard, USA
Heavyweight (200)	Ray Mercer, USA
Super Heavyweight (200+)	Lennox Lewis, CAN

Gymnastics

MEN

Individual		Points
All-Around	Vladimir Artemov, USSR	119.125
Floor	Sergey Kharkov, USSR	19.925
Horiz.Bar	Vladimir Artemov, USSR	
	Valeri Lyukin, USSR	19.900
Paral.Bars	Vladimir Artemov, USSR	19.925
Rings	Dmitri Bilozerchev, USSR	
	Holger Behrendt, E. Ger	19.925
Side Horse	Dmitri Bilozerchev, USSR, Lyubomir Geraskov, BUL, Zsolt Borkai, HUN	19.950
Vault	Lou Yun, CHN	19.875

Team		Points
All-Around	USSR (Artemov, Bilozerchev, Kharkov, Lyukin, Gogoladze, Nouvikov)	593.350

WOMEN

Individual		Points
All-Around	Yelena Shushunova, USSR	79.662
Bal.Beam	Daniela Silivas, ROM	19.924
Floor	Daniela Silivas, ROM	19.937
Uneven Bars	Daniela Silivas, ROM	20.000
Vault	Svetlana Boguinskaya, USSR	19.905

Team		Points
All-Around	USSR (Shushunova, Boguinskaya, Baitova, Chevtchenko, Strajeva, Lachtchenova)	395.475

Rhythmic		Points
All-Around	Marina Lobatch, USSR	60.0

Swimming
MEN

Event		Time	
50m Free	Matt Biondi, USA	22.14	WR
100m Free	Matt Biondi, USA	48.63	OR
200m Free	Duncan Armstrong, AUS	1:47.25	WR
400m Free	Uwe Dassler, E. Ger.	3:46.95	WR
1500m Free	Vladimir Salnikov, USSR	15:00.04	
100m Back	Daichi Suzuki, JPN	55.05	
200m Back	Igor Polianski, USSR	1:59.37	
100m Brst	Adrian Moorhouse, GBR	1:02.04	
200m Brst	József Szabó, HUN	2:13.52	
100m Fly	Anthony Nesty, SUR	53.00	OR
200m Fly	Michael Gross, W. Ger	1:56.94	OR
200m I.M.	Tamás Darnyi, HUN	2:00.17	WR
400m I.M.	Tamás Darnyi, HUN	4:14.75	WR
4x100mFree	USA (Chris Jacobs, Troy Dalbey, Tom Jager, Matt Biondi)	3:16.53	WR
4x200m Free	USA (Troy Dalbey, Matt Cetlinski, Doug Gjertsen, Matt Biondi)	7:12.51	WR

Event		Time	
4x100m Med	USA (David Berkoff, Rich Schroeder, Matt Biondi, Chris Jacobs)	3:36.93	WR

Diving		Points
Platform	Greg Louganis, USA	638.61
Spring	Greg Louganis, USA	730.80

WOMEN

Event		Time	
50m Free	Kristin Otto, E. Ger.	25.49	OR
100m Free	Kristin Otto, E. Ger.	54.93	
200m Free	Heike Freidrich, E. Ger	1:57.65	OR
400m Free	Janet Evans, USA	4:03.85	WR
800m Free	Janet Evans, USA	8:20.20	
100m Back	Kristin Otto, E. Ger.	1:00.89	
200m Back	Krisztina Egerszegi, HUN	2:09.29	OR
100m Brst	Tania Dangalakova, BUL	1:07.95	OR
200m Brst	Silke Hörner, E. Ger.	2:26.71	WR
100m Fly	Kristin Otto, E. Ger.	59.00	OR
200m Fly	Kathleen Nord, E. Ger.	2:09.51	
200m I.M.	Daniela Hunger, E. Ger	2:12.59	OR
400m I.M.	Janet Evans, USA	4:37.76	
4x100m Free	E. Ger. (Kristin Otto, Katrin Meissner, Daniela Hunger, Manuela Stellmach)	3:40.63	OR
4x100m Med	E. Ger. (Kristin Otto, Silke Horner, Birte Weigang, Katrin Meissner)	4:03.74	OR

Diving		Points
Platform	Xu Yanmei, CHN	445.20
Spring	Gao Min, CHN	580.23

Tennis
MEN

Singles: Miloslav Mecir, CZE, def. Tim Mayotte, USA, 3-6, 6-2, 6-4, 6-2

Doubles: Ken Flach & Robert Seguso, USA, def. Emilio Sanchez & Sergio Casal, SPA, 6-3, 6-4, 6-7, 6-7, 9-7

WOMEN

Singles: Steffi Graf, W. Ger, def. Gabriela Sabatini, ARG, 6-3,6-3

Doubles: Pam Shriver and Zina Garrison, USA, def. Jana Novotna and Helena Sukova, CZE, 4-6,6-2,10-8

Team Sports

Men	Champion
Basketball	Soviet Union
Field Hockey	Great Britain
Handball	Soviet Union
Soccer	Soviet Union
Volleyball	United States
Water Polo	Yugoslavia

Women	Champion
Basketball	United States
Field Hockey	Australia
Handball	South Korea
Volleyball	Soviet Union

Also Contested

Archery, Canoeing, Cycling, Equestrian, Fencing, Judo, Modern Pentathlon, Shooting, Synchronized Swimming, Table Tennis, Weightlifting, Freestyle Wrestling, Greco-Roman Wrestling and Yachting.

1992

Barcelona

The year IOC president Juan Antonio Samaranch brought the Olympics to his native Spain marked the first renewal of the Summer Games since the fall of communism in Eastern Europe and the reunification of Germany in 1990.

A record 10,563 athletes from 172 nations gathered without a single country boycotting the Games. Both Cuba and North Korea returned after 12 years and South Africa was welcomed back after 32, following the national government's denunciation of apartheid racial policies.

While Germany competed under one flag for the first time since 1964, 12 nations from the former Soviet Union joined forces one last time as the Unified Team.

This was also the year the IOC threw open the gates to professional athletes after 96 years of high-minded opposition. Basketball was the chief beneficiary as America's popular "Dream Team" of NBA All-Stars easily won the gold.

Carl Lewis earned his seventh and eighth career gold medals with a third consecutive Olympic win in the long jump, and an anchor-leg performance on the American 4x100-meter relay team that helped establish a world record. Gail Devers of the U.S., whose feet had nearly been amputated by doctors in 1990 as a result of radiation treatment for Graves' disease, won the women's 100 meters.

Other track and field athletes stumbled, however. After Olympic favorite and world champion Dan O'Brien failed to even make the U.S. team, Dave Johnson, the new favorite, settled for the bronze. Ukrainian pole vaulter Sergey Bubka, who had dominated the sport for the past decade, was the heavy favorite, but he failed to clear any height.

China's Fu Mingxia, 13, won the women's platform diving gold, becoming the second-youngest person to win an individual gold medal. In gymnastics, Vitaly Scherbo of Belarus, competing for the Unified Team, won six golds. Cuba made its Olympic return rewarding, capturing seven boxing golds as well as the gold in baseball.

Top 10 Standings

National medal standings are not recognized by the IOC. The unofficial point totals are based on 3 points for a gold medal, 2 for a silver and 1 for a bronze.

		Gold	Silver	Bronze	Total	Pts
1	Unified Team	45	38	29	112	240
2	United States	37	34	37	108	216
3	Germany	33	21	28	82	169
4	China	16	22	16	54	108
5	Cuba	14	6	11	31	65
6	Hungary	11	12	7	30	64
7	South Korea	12	5	12	29	58
8	Spain	13	7	2	22	55
9	France	8	5	16	29	50
	Australia	7	9	11	27	50

Leading Medal Winners

Number of individual medals won on the left; gold, silver and bronze breakdown to the right.

MEN

No		Sport	G-S-B
6	Vitaly Scherbo, UT	Gymnastics	6-0-0
5	Grigory Misiutin, UT	Gymnastics	1-4-0
4	Aleksandr Popov, UT	Gymnastics	2-2-0
3	Yevgeny Sadovyi, UT	Swimming	3-0-0
3	Matt Biondi, USA	Swimming	2-1-0
3	Jon Olsen, USA	Swimming	2-0-1
3	Mel Stewart, USA	Swimming	2-0-1
3	Vladimir Pychnenko, UT	Swimming	1-2-0
3	Li Xiaoshuang, CHN	Gymnastics	1-1-1
3	Li Jing, CHN	Gymnastics	0-3-0
3	Anders Holmertz, SWE	Swimming	0-2-1
3	Andreas Wecker, GER	Gymnastics	0-1-2

WOMEN

No		Sports	G-S-B
5	Shannon Miller, USA	Gymnastics	0-2-3
4	Tatiana Gutsu, UT	Gymnastics	2-1-1
4	Lavinia Milosovici, ROM	Gymnastics	2-1-1
4	Summer Sanders, USA	Swimming	2-1-1
4	Franziska van Almsick, GER	Swimming	0-2-2
3	Krisztina Egerszegi, HUN	Swimming	3-0-0
3	Nicole Haislett, USA	Swimming	3-0-0
3	Crissy Ahmann-Leighton, USA	Swimming	2-1-0
3	Jenny Thompson, USA	Swimming	2-1-0
3	Gwen Torrence, USA	Track/Field	2-1-0
3	Tatyana Lysenko, UT	Gymnastics	2-0-1
3	Lin Li, CHN	Swimming	1-2-0
3	Dagmar Hase, GER	Swimming	1-2-0
3	Zhuang Yong, CHN	Swimming	1-2-0
3	Rita Koban, HUN	Kayaking	1-1-1
3	Anita Hall, USA	Swimming	1-1-1
3	Daniela Hunger, GER	Swimming	0-1-2

Track & Field
MEN

Event		Time	
100m	Linford Christie, GBR	9.96	
200m	Mike Marsh, USA	20.01	
400m	Quincy Watts, USA	43.50	OR
800m	William Tanui, KEN	1:43.66	
1500m	Fermin Cacho, SPA	3:40.12	
5000m	Dieter Baumann, GER	13:12.52	
10,000m	Khalid Skah, MOR	27:46.70	
Marathon	Hwang Young-Cho, S. Kor	2:13.23	
110m H	Mark McKoy, CAN	13.12	
400m H	Kevin Young, USA	46.78	WR
3000m Steeple	Matthew Birir, KEN	8:08.84	
20k Walk	Daniel Plaza Montero, SPA	1:21:45	
50k Walk	Andrei Perlov, UT	3:50:13	
4x100m	USA (Mike Marsh, Leroy Burrell, Dennis Mitchell, Carl Lewis)	37.40	WR
4x400m	USA (Andrew Valmon, Quincy Watts, Michael Johnson, Steve Lewis)	2:55.74	WR

Event		Mark	
High Jump	Javier Sotomayor, CUB	7-8	
Pole Vault	Maksim Tarasov, UT	19-0¼	
Long Jump	Carl Lewis, USA	28-5½	
Triple Jump	Mike Conley, USA	59-7½"	
Shot Put	Michael Stulce, USA	71-2½	
Discus	Romas Ubartas, LIT	213-8	
Hammer	Andrei Abduvaliyev, UT	270-9	
Javelin	Jan Zelezny, CZE	294-2	OR
Decathlon	Robert Zmelik, CZE	8611 pts	

ʷ indicates wind-aided.

WOMEN

Event		Time
100m	Gail Devers, USA	10.82
200m	Gwen Torrence, USA	21.81
400m	Marie-Jose Perec, FRA	48.83
800m	Ellen van Langen, NED	1:55.54
1500m	Hassiba Boulmerka, ALG	3:55.30
3000m	Elena Romanova, UT	8:46.04
10,000m	Derartu Tulu, ETH	31:06.02
Marathon	Valentina Yegorova, UT	2:32:41
100m H	Paraskevi Patoulidou, GRE	12.64
400m H	Sally Gunnell, GBR	53.23
10K Walk	Chen Yueling, CHN	44.32
4x100m	USA (Evelyn Ashford, Esther Jones, Carlette Guidry-White, Gwen Torrence)	42.11
4x400m	UT (Yelena Ruzina, Lyudmila Dzhigalova, Olga Nazarova, Olga Bryzgina)	3:20.20

Event		Mark
High Jump	Heike Henkel, GER	6-7½
Long Jump	Heike Drechsler, GER	23-5¼
Shot Put	Svetlana Krivaleva, UT	69-1¼
Discus	Maritza Marten, CUB	229-10
Javelin	Silke Renk, GER	224-2
Heptathlon	Jackie Joyner-Kersee, USA	7044 pts

Boxing

Weight Class	Champion
Lt. Flyweight (106 lbs)	Rogelio Marcelo, CUB
Flyweight (112)	Su Choi-Chol, N. Kor
Bantamweight (119)	Joel Casamayor, CUB
Featherweight (125)	Andreas Tews, GER
Lightweight (132)	Oscar De La Hoya, USA
Lt. Welterweight (139)	Hector Vinent, CUB
Welterweight (147)	Michael Carruth, IRE
Lt. Middleweight (156)	Juan Lemus, CUB

Weight Class	Champion
Middleweight (165)	Ariel Hernandez, CUB
Lt. Heavyweight (178)	Torsten May, GER
Heavyweight (201)	Felix Savon, CUB
Super Heavyweight (200+)	Roberto Balado, CUB

Gymnastics
MEN

Individual		Points
All-Around	Vitaly Scherbo, UT	59.025
Floor	Li Xiaosahuang, CHN	9.925
Horiz.Bar	Trent Dimas, USA	9.875
Paral.Bars	Vitaly Scherbo, UT	9.900
Rings	Vitaly Scherbo, UT	9.937
Side Horse	Vitaly Scherbo, UT	
	Pae Gil-Su, N. Kor	9.925
Vault	Vitaly Scherbo, UT	9.856
Team		**Points**
All Around	UT (Scherbo, Belenki, Misiutin, Korobchinski, Voropayev, Sharipov)	585.450

WOMEN

Individual		Points
All-Around	Tatiana Gutsu, UT	39.737
Bal.Beam	Tatiana Lyssenko, UT	9.975
Floor	Lavinia Milosovici, ROM	10.000
Uneven Bars	Lu Li, CHN	10.000
Vault	Henrietta Onodi, HUN	
	& Lavinia Milosovici, ROM	9.925
Team		**Points**
All Around	UT (Boginskaya, Lyssenko, Galiyeva, Goutsou, Grudneva, Chusovitina)	395.666
Rythmic		**Points**
All Around	Aleksandra Timoshenko, UT	59.037

Swimming
MEN

Event		Time	
50m Free	Aleksandr Popov, UT	21.91	OR
100m Free	Aleksandr Popov, UT	49.02	
200m Free	Yevgeny Sadovyi, UT	1:46.70	OR
400m Free	Yevgeny Sadovyi, UT	3:45.00	WR
1500m Free	Kieren Perkins, AUS	14:43.48	WR
100m Back	Mark Tewksbury, CAN	53.98	OR
200m Back	Martin Lopez-Zubero, SPA	1:58.47	OR
100m Brst	Nelson Diebel, USA	1:01.50	OR
200m Brst	Mike Barrowman, USA	2:10.16	WR
100m Fly	Pablo Morales, USA	53.32	
200m Fly	Mel Stewart, USA	1:56.26	OR
200m I.M.	Tamas Darnyi, HUN	2:00.76	
400m I.M.	Tamas Darnyi, HUN	4:14.23	OR
4x100m Free	USA (Joe Hudepohl, Matt Biondi, Tom Jager, Jon Olsen)	3:16.74	
4x200m Free	UT (Dmitri Lepikov, Vladimir Pyshnenko, Veniamin Tayanovich, Yevgeny Sadovyi)	7:11.95	WR
Diving		**Points**	
Platform	Sun Shuwei, CHN	677.31	
Spring	Mark Lenzi, USA	676.53	

WOMEN

Event		Time	
50m Free	Yang Wenyi, CHN	24.79	WR
100m Free	Zhuang Yong, CHN	54.64	OR
200m Free	Nicole Haislett, USA	1:57.90	
400m Free	Dagmar Hase, GER	4:07.18	
800m Free	Janet Evans, USA	8:25.52	
100m Back	Krisztina Egerszegi, HUN	1:00.68	OR
200m Back	Krisztina Egerszegi, HUN	2:07.06	OR
100m Brst	Yelena Rudkovskaya, UT	1:08.00	
200m Brst	Kyoko Iwasaki, JPN	2:26.65	OR
100m Fly	Qian Hong, CHN	58.62	OR
200m Fly	Summer Sanders, USA	2:08.67	

Event		Time	
200m I.M.	Lin Li, CHN	2:11.65	WR
400m I.M.	Krisztina Egerszegi, HUN	4:36.54	
4x100m Free	USA (Nicole Haislett, Dara Torres, Angel Martino, Jenny Thompson)	3:39.46	WR
4x100m Med	USA (Lea Loveless, Anita Nall, Crissy Ahmann-Leighton, Jenny Thompson)	4:02.54	WR
Diving		**Points**	
Platform	Fu Mingxia, CHN	461.43	
Spring	Gao Min, CHN	572.40	

Tennis
MEN

Singles: Marc Rosset, SWI, def. Jordi Arrese, SPA, 7-6, 6-4, 3-6, 4-6, 8-6.

Doubles: Boris Becker and Michael Stich, GER, def. Wayne Ferreira and Piet Norval, RSA, 7-6, 4-6, 7-6, 6-3.

WOMEN

Singles: Jennifer Capriati, USA, def. Steffi Graf, GER, 3-6, 6-3, 6-4.

Doubles: Gigi Fernandez and Mary Joe Fernandez, USA, def. Conchita Martinez and Arantxa Sanchez Vicario, SPA, 7-5, 2-6, 6-2.

Team Sports

Men	Champion
Baseball	Cuba
Basketball	United States
Field Hockey	Germany
Handball	Unified Team
Soccer	Spain
Volleyball	Brazil
Water Polo	Italy
Women	**Champion**
Basketball	Unified Team
Field Hockey	Spain
Handball	South Korea
Volleyball	Cuba

Also Contested

Archery, Badminton, Canoeing, Cycling, Equestrian, Fencing, Judo, Modern Pentathlon, Shooting, Table Tennis, Weightlifting, Freestyle Wrestling, Greco-Roman Wrestling and Yachting.

1996

Atlanta

The Atlanta Games were certainly the largest (a record 197 nations competed), most logistically complicated Olympics to date and perhaps the most hyped and overcommercialized as well. Despite all the troubles that organizers faced, from computer scoring snafus and transportation problems to a horrific terrorist attack, these Olympics had some of the best stories ever.

The Games began so joyously with Muhammad Ali, the world's best-known sports figure now stricken by illness, igniting the Olympic cauldron.

Sadly, just eight days later horror was the prevailing mood after a terrorist's bomb ripped apart a peaceful Friday evening in Centennial Olympic Park. In the explosion, one women was killed, 111 were injured and the entire world was reminded of the terror and tragedy of Munich in 1972.

As they did in '72, the Games would go on. In track and field, Michael Johnson delivered on his much-anticipated, yet still startling, double in the 200 and 400 meters. One thing that many didn't foresee is that he would be matched by France's Marie-Jose Perec, who converted her own 200-400 double, albeit with much less attention. Carl Lewis pulled out one last bit of magic to win the long jump for the ninth gold medal of his amazing Olympic career. Donovan Bailey set a world record in the 100 and led Canada to a win over a faltering U.S. team in the 4x100 relay.

The U.S. women's gymnastics squad took the team gold after Kerri Strug hobbled up and completed her final gutsy vault in the Games' most compelling moment. Swimmer Amy Van Dyken became the first American woman to win four golds in a single Games. Ireland's Michelle Smith won three golds (and a bronze) of her own, but her victories were somewhat tainted by controversy surrounding unproven charges of drug use.

The USA faired well in team sports also. The men's basketball "Dream Team" was back and, predictably, stomped the competition on its way back to the winners' podium. Also the U.S. women won gold at the Olympic debut of two sports–softball and soccer.

Top 10 Standings

National medal standings are not recognized by the IOC. The unofficial point totals are based on 3 points for a gold medal, 2 for a silver and 1 for a bronze.

		Gold	Silver	Bronze	Total	Pts
1	United States	44	32	25	101	221
2	Russia	26	21	16	63	136
3	Germany	20	18	27	65	123
4	China	16	22	12	50	104
5	France	15	7	15	37	74
6	Italy	13	10	12	35	71
7	Australia	9	9	23	41	68
8	South Korea	7	15	5	27	56
9	Cuba	9	8	8	25	51
10	Ukraine	9	2	12	23	43

Leading Medal Winners

Number of individual medals won on the left; gold, silver and bronze breakdown to the right.

MEN

No		Sport	G-S-B
6	Alexei Nemov, RUS	Gymnastics	2-1-3
4	Gary Hall Jr., USA	Swimming	2-2-0
4	Aleksandr Popov, RUS	Swimming	2-2-0
3	Josh Davis, USA	Swimming	3-0-0
3	Denis Pankratov, RUS	Swimming	2-1-0
3	Daniel Kowalski, AUS	Swimming	0-1-2
3	Vitaly Scherbo, BEL	Gymnastics	0-0-3

WOMEN

No		Sport	G-S-B
4	Amy Van Dyken, USA	Swimming	4-0-0
4	Michelle Smith, IRL	Swimming	3-0-1
4	Angel Martino, USA	Swimming	2-0-2
4	Simona Amanar, ROM	Gymnastics	1-1-2
4	Dagmar Hase, GER	Swimming	0-3-1
4	Gina Gogean, ROM	Gymnastics	0-1-3
3	Jenny Thompson, USA	Swimming	3-0-0
3	Lilia Podkopayeva, UKR	Gymnastics	2-1-0
3	Amanda Beard, USA	Swimming	1-2-0
3	Le Jingyi, CHN	Swimming	1-2-0
3	Wendy Hedgepeth, USA	Swimming	1-2-0
3	Susan O'Neill, AUS	Swimming	1-1-1
3	Merlene Ottey, JAM	Track & Field	0-2-1
3	Franziska van Almsick, GER	Swimming	0-2-1
3	Sandra Volker, GER	Swimming	0-1-2

Track & Field

MEN

Event		Time	
100m	Donovan Bailey, CAN	9.84	WR
200m	Michael Johnson, USA	19.32	WR
400m	Michael Johnson, USA	43.49	OR
800m	Vebjoern Rodal, NOR	1:42.58	OR
1500m	Noureddine Morceli, ALG	3:35.78	
5000m	Venuste Niyongabo, BUR	13:07.96	
10,000m	Haile Gebrselassie, ETH	27:07.34	OR
Marathon	Josia Thugwane, RSA	2:12:36	
110m H	Allen Johnson, USA	12.95	OR
400m H	Derrick Adkins, USA	47.54	
3000m Steeple	Joseph Keter, KEN	8:07.12	
20k Walk	Jefferson Perez, ECU	1:20:07	
50k Walk	Robert Korzeniowski, POL	3:43:30	
4x100m	Canada (Donavan Bailey, Robert Esmie, Glenroy Gilbert, Bruny Surin, Carlton Chambers)	37.69	
4x400m	USA (Anthuan Maybank, Derek Mills, LaMont Smith, Alvin Harrison, Jason Rouser)	2:55.99	

Event		Mark	
High Jump	Charles Austin, USA	7-10	OR
Pole Vault	Jean Galfione, FRA	19-5¼	OR
Long Jump	Carl Lewis, USA	27-10 ¾	
Triple Jump	Kenny Harrison, USA	59-4¼	OR
Shot Put	Randy Barnes, USA	70-11¼	
Discus	Lars Riedel, GER	227-8	
Hammer	Balazs Kiss, HUN	266-6	
Javelin	Jan Zelezny, CZE	289-3	
Decathlon	Dan O'Brien, USA	8824 pts	

WOMEN

Event		Time	
100m	Gail Devers, USA	10.94	
200m	Marie-Jose Perec, FRA	22.12	
400m	Marie-Jose Perec, FRA	48.25	OR
800m	Svetlana Masterkova, RUS	1:57.73	
1500m	Svetlana Masterkova, RUS	4:00.83	
5000m	Wang Junxia, CHN	14:59.88	
10,000m	Fernanda Ribeiro, POR	31:01.63	OR
Marathon	Fatuma Roba, ETH	2:26:05	
100m H	Ludmila Engquist, SWE	12.58	
400m H	Deon Hemmings, JAM	52.82	OR
10K Walk	Yelena Ninikolayeva, RUS	41:49	
4x100m	USA (Chryste Gaines, Gail Devers, Inger Miller, Gwen Torrence)	41.95	
4x400m	USA (Rochelle Stevens, Maicel Malone, Kim Graham, Jearl Miles, Linetta Wilson)	3:20.91	

Event		Mark
High Jump	Stefka Kostadinova, BUL	6-8¾
Long Jump	Chioma Ajunwa, NGR	23-4½
Triple Jump	Inessa Kravets, UKR	50-3½
Shot Put	Astrid Kumbernuss, GER	67-5½
Discus	Ilke Wyludda, GER	228-6
Javelin	Heli Rantanen, FIN	222-11
Heptathlon	Ghada Shouaa, SYR	6780 pts

Boxing

Weight Class	Champion
Lt. Flyweight (106 lbs)	Daniel Petrov Bojilov, BUL
Flyweight (112)	Maikro Romero, CUB
Bantamweight (119)	Istvan Kovacs, HUN
Featherweight (125)	Somluck Kamsing, THA
Lightweight (132)	Hocine Soltani, ALG
Lt. Welterweight (139)	Hector Vinent, CUB
Welterweight (147)	Oleg Saitov, RUS
Lt. Middleweight (156)	David Reid, USA
Middleweight (165)	Ariel Hernandez, CUB
Lt. Heavyweight (178)	Vasilii Jirov, KAZ
Heavyweight (201)	Felix Savon, CUB
Super Heavyweight (200+)	Vladimir Klichko, UKR

Gymnastics

MEN

Individual		Points
All-Around	Li Xiaosahuang, CHN	58.423
Floor	Ioannis Melissanidis, GRE	9.850
Horiz.Bar	Andreas Wecker, GER	9.850
Paral.Bars	Rustam Sharipov, UKR	9.837
Rings	Yuri Chechi, ITA	9.887
Side Horse	Li Donghua, SWI	9.875
Vault	Alexei Nemov, RUS	9.787

Team		Points
All-Around	Russia	576.778

WOMEN

Individual		Points
All-Around	Lilia Podkopayeva, UKR	39.255
Bal.Beam	Shannon Miller, USA	9.862
Floor	Lilia Podkopayeva, UKR	9.887
Uneven Bars	Svetlana Chorkina, RUS	9.850
Vault	Simona Amanar, ROM	9.775

Team		Points
All-Around	USA (Borden, Chow, Dawes, Miller, Moceanu, Phelps and Strug)	389.225

Rythmic		Points
All-Around	Ekaterina Serebryanskaya, UKR	39.683
Team	Spain	38.933

Swimming

MEN

Event		Time
50m Free	Aleksandr Popov, RUS	22.13
100m Free	Aleksandr Popov, UT	48.74
200m Free	Danyon Loader, NZE	1:47.63
400m Free	Danyon Loader, NZE	3:47.97
1500m Free	Kieren Perkins, AUS	14:56.40
100m Back	Jeff Rouse, USA	54.10
200m Back	Brad Bridgewater, USA	1:58.54
100m Brst	Fred Deburghgraeve, BEL	1:00.60
200m Brst	Norbert, Rozsa, HUN	2:12.57
100m Fly	Denis Pankratov, RUS	52.27
200m Fly	Denis Pankratov, RUS	1:56.51
200m I.M.	Attila Czene, HUN	1:59.51
400m I.M.	Tom Dolan, USA	4:14.90
4x100m Free	USA (Jon Olsen, Josh Davis, Bradley Schumacher, Gary Hall Jr.)	3:15.41
4x200m Free	USA (Josh Davis, Joe Hudepohl, Ryan Berube, Bradley Schumacher)	7:14.84
4x100m Med.	USA (Jeff Rouse, Mark Henderson, Gary Hall Jr., Jeremy Linn)	3:34.84

Diving		Points
Platform	Dmitri Saoutine, RUS	692.34
Spring	Xiong Ni, CHN	701.46

WOMEN

Event		Time
50m Free	Amy Van Dyken, USA	24.87
100m Free	Le Jingyi, CHN	54.50
200m Free	Claudia Poll, CRC	1:58.16
400m Free	Michelle Smith, IRL	4:07.25
800m Free	Brooke Bennett, USA	8:27.89
100m Back	Beth Botsford, USA	1:01.19
200m Back	Krisztina Egerszegi, HUN	2:07.83
100m Brst	Penny Heyns, RSA	1:07.73
200m Brst	Penny Heyns, RSA	2:25.41
100m Fly	Amy Van Dyken, USA	59.13
200m Fly	Susan O'Neill, AUS	2:07.76
200m I.M.	Michelle Smith, IRL	2:13.93
400m I.M.	Michelle Smith, IRL	4:39.18
4x100m Free	USA (Angel Martino, Amy Van Dyken, Catherine Fox, Jenny Thompson)	3:39.29
4x200m Free	USA (Jenny Thompson, Sheila Taorima, Trina Jackson, Christina Teuscher)	7:59.87
4x100m Med	USA (Angel Martino, Amy Van Dyken, Amanda Beard, Beth Botsford)	4:02.88

Diving		Points
Platform	Fu Mingxia, CHN	521.58
Spring	Fu Mingxia, CHN	547.68

Tennis

MEN

Singles: Andre Agassi, USA, def. Sergi Bruguera, SPA, 6-2, 6-3, 6-1.

Doubles: Todd Woodbridge and Mark Woodforde, AUS, def. Neil Broad and Tim Henman, GBR, 6-4, 6-4, 6-2.

WOMEN

Singles: Lindsay Davenport, USA, def. Arantxa Sanchez Vicario, SPA, 7-6 (8-6), 6-2.

Doubles: Gigi Fernandez and Mary Joe Fernandez, USA, def. Jana Novotna and Helena Sukova, CZE, 7-6 (8-6), 6-4.

Team Sports

Men	Champion
Baseball	Cuba
Basketball	United States
Field Hockey	Netherlands
Handball	Croatia
Soccer	Nigeria
Volleyball	Netherlands
Water Polo	Spain

Women	Champion
Basketball	United States
Field Hockey	Australia
Handball	Denmark
Soccer	United States
Softball	United States
Volleyball	Cuba

Also Contested

Archery, Badminton, Beach Volleyball, Canoeing, Cycling, Equestrian, Fencing, Judo, Modern Pentathlon, Mountain Biking, Shooting, Table Tennis, Weightlifting, Freestyle Wrestling, Greco-Roman Wrestling and Yachting.

New Events for 2000

Taekwondo and Triathlon will make their Summer Olympic debuts in Sydney. The triathlon will consist of 1.5-kilometer swim, 40-kilometer cycle and 10-kilometer run, while taekwondo will be contested in four separate weights classes for men and women. Also, women's water polo, canoe slalom and the gymnastic discipline of trampoline will appear for the first time.

Event-by-Event

Gold medal winners from 1896-1996 in the following events: Baseball, Basketball, Boxing, Diving, Field Hockey, Gymnastics, Soccer, Swimming, Tennis, and Track & Field.

BASEBALL

Multiple gold medals: Cuba (2).

Year		Year	
1992	**Cuba**, Taiwan, Japan	1996	**Cuba**, Japan, United States

BASKETBALL

MEN

Multiple gold medals: USA (11), USSR (2).

Year		Year	
1936	**United States**, Canada, Mexico	1972	**Soviet Union**, United States, Cuba
1948	**United States**, France, Brazil	1976	**United States**, Yugoslavia, Soviet Union
1952	**United States**, Soviet Union, Uruguay	1980	**Yugoslavia**, Italy, Soviet Union
1956	**United States**, Soviet Union, Uruguay	1984	**United States**, Spain, Yugoslavia
1960	**United States**, Soviet Union, Brazil	1988	**Soviet Union**, Yugoslavia, United States
1964	**United States**, Soviet Union, Brazil	1992	**United States**, Croatia, Lithuania
1968	**United States**, Yugoslavia, Soviet Union	1996	**United States**, Yugoslavia, Lithuania

U.S. Medal-Winning Men's Basketball Teams

1936 (gold medal): Sam Balter, Ralph Bishop, Joe Fortenberry, Tex Gibbons, Francis Johnson, Carl Knowles, Frank Lubin, Art Mollner, Don Piper, Jack Ragland, Carl Shy, Willard Schmidt, Duane Swanson and William Wheatley. Coach–Jim Needles; Assistant–Gene Johnson. Final: USA over Canada, 19-8.

1948 (gold medal): Cliff Barker, Don Barksdale, Ralph Beard, Louis Beck, Vince Boryla, Gordon Carpenter, Alex Groza, Wallace Jones, Bob Kurland, Ray Lumpp, R.C. Pitts, Jesse Renick, Robert (Jackie) Robinson and Ken Rollins. Coach–Omar Browning; Assistant–Adolph Rupp. Final: USA over France, 65-21.

1952 (gold medal): Ron Bontemps, Mark Freiberger, Wayne Glasgow, Charlie Hoag, Bill Hougland, John Keller, Dean Kelley, Bob Kenney, Bob Kurland, Bill Lienhard, Clyde Lovellette, Frank McCabe, Dan Pippin and Howie Williams. Coach–Warren Womble; Assistant–Forrest (Phog) Allen. Final: USA over USSR, 36-25.

1956 (gold medal): Dick Boushka, Carl Cain, Chuck Darling, Bill Evans, Gib Ford, Burdy Haldorson, Bill Hougland, Bob Jeangerard, K.C. Jones, Bill Russell, Ron Tomsic and Jim Walsh. Coach–Gerald Tucker; Assistant–Bruce Drake. Final: USA over USSR, 89-55.

1960 (gold medal): Jay Arnette, Walt Bellamy, Bob Boozer, Terry Dischinger, Jerry Lucas, Oscar Robertson, Adrian Smith, Burdy Haldorson, Darrall Imhoff, Allen Kelley, Lester Lane and Jerry West. Coach–Pete Newell; Assistant–Warren Womble. Final round: USA defeated USSR (81-57), Italy (112-81) and Brazil (90-63) in round robin.

1964 (gold medal): Jim (Bad News) Barnes, Bill Bradley, Larry Brown, Joe Caldwell, Mel Counts, Dick Davies, Walt Hazzard, Lucious Jackson, Pete McCaffrey, Jeff Mullins, Jerry Shipp and George Wilson. Coach–Hank Iba; Assistant–Henry Vaughn. Final: USA over USSR, 73-59.

1968 (gold medal): Mike Barrett, John Clawson, Don Dee, Cal Fowler, Spencer Haywood, Bill Hosket, Jim King, Glynn Saulters, Charlie Scott, Mike Silliman, Ken Spain, and JoJo White. Coach–Hank Iba; Assistant–Henry Vaughn. Final: USA over Yugoslavia, 65-50.

1972 (silver medal refused): Mike Bantom, Jim Brewer, Tom Burleson, Doug Collins, Kenny Davis, Jim Forbes, Tom Henderson, Bobby Jones, Dwight Jones, Kevin Joyce, Tom McMillen and Ed Ratleff. Coach–Hank Iba; Assistants– John Bach and Don Haskins. Final: USSR over USA, 51-50.

1976 (gold medal): Tate Armstrong, Quinn Buckner, Kenny Carr, Adrian Dantley, Walter Davis, Phil Ford, Ernie Grunfeld, Phil Hubbard, Mitch Kupchak, Tommy LaGarde, Scott May and Steve Sheppard. Coach–Dean Smith; Assistants–Bill Guthridge and John Thompson. Final: USA over Yugoslavia, 95-74.

1980 (no medal): USA boycotted Moscow Games. Final: Yugoslavia over Italy, 86-77.

1984 (gold medal): Steve Alford, Patrick Ewing, Vern Fleming, Michael Jordan, Joe Kleine, Jon Koncak, Chris Mullin, Sam Perkins, Alvin Robertson, Wayman Tisdale, Jeff Turner and Leon Wood. Coach–Bobby Knight; Assistants– Don Donoher and George Raveling. Final: USA over Spain, 96-65.

1988 (bronze medal): Stacey Augmon, Willie Anderson, Bimbo Coles, Jeff Grayer, Hersey Hawkins, Dan Majerle, Danny Manning, Mitch Richmond, J.R. Reid, David Robinson, Charles D. Smith and Charles E. Smith. Coach–John Thompson; Assistants–George Raveling and Mary Fenlon. Final: USSR over Yugoslavia, 76-63.

1992 (gold medal): Charles Barkley, Larry Bird, Clyde Drexler, Patrick Ewing, Magic Johnson, Michael Jordan, Christian Laettner, Karl Malone, Chris Mullin, Scottie Pippen, David Robinson and John Stockton. Coach–Chuck Daly; Assistants–Lenny Wilkens, Mike Krzyzewski and P.J. Carlesimo. Final: USA over Croatia, 117-85.

1996 (gold medal): Charles Barkley, Anfernee Hardaway, Grant Hill, Karl Malone, Reggie Miller, Hakeem Olajuwon, Shaquille O'Neal, Gary Payton, Scottie Pippen, David Robinson and John Stockton. Coach–Lenny Wilkens; Assistants–Bobby Cremins, Clem Haskins and Jerry Sloan. Final: USA over Yugoslavia, 95-69.

WOMEN

Multiple gold medals: USA and USSR/UT (3).

Year		Year	
1976	**Soviet Union**, United States, Bulgaria	1988	**United States**, Yugoslavia, Soviet Union
1980	**Soviet Union**, Bulgaria, Yugoslavia	1992	**Unified Team**, China, United States
1984	**United States**, South Korea, China	1996	**United States**, Brazil, Australia

U.S. Gold Medal-Winning Women's Basketball Teams

1984: Cathy Boswell, Denise Curry, Anne Donovan, Teresa Edwards, Lea Henry, Janice Lawrence, Pamela McGee, Carol Menken-Schaudt, Cheryl Miller, Kim Mulkey, Cindy Noble and Lynette Woodard. Coach–Pat Summitt; Assistant–Kay Yow. Final: USA over South Korea, 85-55.

1988: Cindy Brown, Vicky Bullett, Cynthia Cooper, Anne Donovan, Teresa Edwards, Kamie Ethridge, Jennifer Gillom, Bridgette Gordon, Andrea Lloyd, Katrina McClain, Suzie McConnell and Teresa Weatherspoon. Coach–Kay Yow; Assistants–Sylvia Hatchell and Susan Yow. Final: USA over Yugoslavia, 77-70.

Basketball (Cont.)

1996: Jennifer Azzi, Ruthie Bolton, Teresa Edwards, Venus Lacy, Lisa Leslie, Rebecca Lobo, Katrina McClain, Nikki McCray, Carla McGee, Dawn Staley, Katy Steding and Sheryl Swoopes. Coach—Tara VanDerveer; Assistants—Ceal Barry, Nancy Darsch and Marian Washington. Final: USA over Brazil, 111-87.

BOXING

Multiple gold medals: László Papp and Teófilo Stevenson (3); Ariel Hernandez, Angel Herrera, Oliver Kirk, Jerzy Kulej, Boris Lagutin, Harry Mallin, Felix Savon and Hector Vinent (2). All fighters won titles in consecutive Olympics, except Kirk, who won both the bantamweight and featherweight titles in 1904 (he only had to fight once in each division).

Light Flyweight (106 lbs)

Year		Final Match	Year		Final Match
1968	Francisco Rodriguez, VEN	Decision, 3-2	1984	Paul Gonzales, USA	Default
1972	György Gedó, HUN	Decision, 5-0	1988	Ivailo Hristov, BUL	Decision, 5-0
1976	Jorge Hernandez, CUB	Decision, 4-1	1992	Rogelio Marcelo, CUB	Decision, 24-10
1980	Shamil Sabyrov, USSR	Decision, 3-2	1996	Daniel Petrov Bojilov, BUL	Decision, 19-6

Flyweight (112 lbs)

Year		Final Match	Year		Final Match
1904	George Finnegan, USA	Stopped, 1st	1964	Fernando Atzori, ITA	Decision, 4-1
1920	Frank Di Gennara, USA	Decision	1968	Ricardo Delgado, MEX	Decision, 5-0
1924	Fidel LaBarba, USA	Decision	1972	Georgi Kostadinov, BUL	Decision, 5-0
1928	Antal Kocsis, HUN	Decision	1976	Leo Randolph, USA	Decision, 3-2
1932	István Énekes, HUN	Decision	1980	Peter Lessov, BUL	Stopped, 2nd
1936	Willi Kaiser, GER	Decision	1984	Steve McCrory, USA	Decision, 4-1
1948	Pascual Perez, ARG	Decision	1988	Kim Kwang-Sun, S. Kor	Decision, 4-1
1952	Nate Brooks, USA	Decision, 3-0	1992	Su Choi-Chol, N. Kor	Decision, 12-2
1956	Terence Spinks, GBR	Decision	1996	Maikro Romero, CUB	Decision, 12-11
1960	Gyula Török, HUN	Decision, 3-2			

Bantamweight (119 lbs)

Year		Final Match	Year		Final Match
1904	Oliver Kirk, USA	Stopped, 3rd	1960	Oleg Grigoryev, USSR	Decision
1908	Henry Thomas, GBR	Decision	1964	Takao Sakurai, JPN	Stopped, 2nd
1920	Clarence Walker, RSA	Decision	1968	Valery Sokolov, USSR	Stopped, 2nd
1924	William Smith, RSA	Decision	1972	Orlando Martinez, CUB	Decision, 5-0
1928	Vittorio Tamagnini, ITA	Decision	1976	Gu Yong-Ju, N. Kor	Decision, 5-0
1932	Horace Gwynne, CAN	Decision	1980	Juan Hernandez, CUB	Decision, 5-0
1936	Ulderico Sergo, ITA	Decision	1984	Maurizio Stecca, ITA	Decision, 4-1
1948	Tibor Csik, HUN	Decision	1988	Kennedy McKinney, USA	Decision, 5-0
1952	Pentti Hämäläinen, FIN	Decision, 2-1	1992	Joel Casamayor, CUB	Decision, 14-8
1956	Wolfgang Behrendt, GER	Decision	1996	Istvan Kovacs, HUN	Decision, 14-7

Featherweight (125 lbs)

Year		Final Match	Year		Final Match
1904	Oliver Kirk, USA	Decision	1960	Francesco Musso, ITA	Decision, 4-1
1908	Richard Gunn, GBR	Decision	1964	Stanislav Stepashkin, USSR	Decision, 3-2
1920	Paul Fritsch, FRA	Decision	1968	Antonio Roldan, MEX	Won on Disq.
1924	John Fields, USA	Decision	1972	Boris Kousnetsov, USSR	Decision, 3-2
1928	Lambertus van Klaveren, NED	Decision	1976	Angel Herrera, CUB	KO, 2nd
1932	Carmelo Robledo, ARG	Decision	1980	Rudi Fink, E. Ger	Decision, 4-1
1936	Oscar Casanovas, ARG	Decision	1984	Meldrick Taylor, USA	Decision, 5-0
1948	Ernesto Formenti, ITA	Decision	1988	Giovanni Parisi, ITA	Stopped, 1st
1952	Jan Zachara, CZE	Decision, 2-1	1992	Andreas Tews, GER	Decision, 16-7
1956	Vladimir Safronov, USSR	Decision	1996	Somluck Kamsing, THA	Decision, 8-5

Lightweight (132 lbs)

Year		Final Match	Year		Final Match
1904	Harry Spanger, USA	Decision	1960	Kazimierz Pazdzior, POL	Decision, 4-1
1908	Frederick Grace, GBR	Decision	1964	Józef Grudzien, POL	Decision
1920	Samuel Mosberg, USA	Decision	1968	Ronnie Harris, USA	Decision, 5-0
1924	Hans Nielsen, DEN	Decision	1972	Jan Szczepanski, POL	Decision, 5-0
1928	Carlo Orlandi, ITA	Decision	1976	Howard Davis, USA	Decision, 5-0
1932	Lawrence Stevens, RSA	Decision	1980	Angel Herrera, CUB	Stopped, 3rd
1936	Imre Harangi, HUN	Decision	1984	Pernell Whitaker, USA	Foe quit, 2nd
1948	Gerald Dreyer, RSA	Decision	1988	Andreas Zuelow, E. Ger	Decision, 5-0
1952	Aureliano Bolognesi, ITA	Decision, 2-1	1992	Oscar De La Hoya, USA	Decision, 7-2
1956	Richard McTaggart, GBR	Decision	1996	Hocine Soltani, ALG	Tiebreak, 3-3

Light Welterweight (139 lbs)

Year		Final Match	Year		Final Match
1952	Charles Adkins, USA	Decision, 2-1	1960	Bohumil Nemecek, CZE	Decision, 5-0
1956	Vladimir Yengibaryan, USSR	Decision	1964	Jerzy Kulej, POL	Decision, 5-0

Year	Final Match	Year	Final Match
1968 Jerzy Kulej, POL	Decision, 3-2	1984 Jerry Page, USA	Decision, 5-0
1972 Ray Seales, USA	Decision, 3-2	1988 Vyacheslav Yanovsky, USSR	Decision, 5-0
1976 Ray Leonard, USA	Decision, 5-0	1992 Hector Vinent, CUB	Decision, 11-1
1980 Patrizio Oliva, ITA	Decision, 4-1	1996 Hector Vinent, CUB	Decision, 20-13

Welterweight (147 lbs)

Year	Final Match	Year	Final Match
1904 Albert Young, USA	Decision	1964 Marian Kasprzyk, POL	Decision, 4-1
1920 Bert Schneider, CAN	Decision	1968 Manfred Wolke, E. Ger	Decision, 4-1
1924 Jean Delarge, BEL	Decision	1972 Emilio Correa, CUB	Decision, 5-0
1928 Edward Morgan, NZE	Decision	1976 Jochen Bachfeld, E. Ger	Decision, 3-2
1932 Edward Flynn, USA	Decision	1980 Andrés Aldama, CUB	Decision, 4-1
1936 Sten Suvio, FIN	Decision	1984 Mark Breland, USA	Decision, 5-0
1948 Julius Torma, CZE	Decision	1988 Robert Wangila, KEN	KO, 2nd
1952 Zygmunt Chychla, POL	Decision, 3-0	1992 Michael Carruth, IRL	Decision, 13-10
1956 Nicolae Linca, ROM	Decision, 3-2	1996 Oleg Saitov, RUS	Decision, 14-9
1960 Nino Benvenuti, ITA	Decision, 4-1		

Light Middleweight (156 lbs)

Year	Final Match	Year	Final Match
1952 László Papp, HUN	Decision, 3-0	1976 Jerzy Rybicki, POL	Decision, 5-0
1956 László Papp, HUN	Decision	1980 Armando Martinez, CUB	Decision, 4-1
1960 Skeeter McClure, USA	Decision, 4-1	1984 Frank Tate, USA	Decision, 5-0
1964 Boris Lagutin, USSR	Decision, 4-1	1988 Park Si-Hun, S. Kor	Decision, 3-2
1968 Boris Lagutin, USSR	Decision, 5-0	1992 Juan Lemus, CUB	Decision, 6-1
1972 Dieter Kottysch, W. Ger	Decision, 3-2	1996 David Reid, USA	KO, 3rd

Middleweight (165 lbs)

Year	Final Match	Year	Final Match
1904 Charles Mayer, USA	Stopped, 3rd	1960 Eddie Crook, USA	Decision, 3-2
1908 John Douglas, GBR	Decision	1964 Valery Popenchenko, USSR	Stopped, 1st
1920 Harry Mallin, GBR	Decision	1968 Christopher Finnegan, GBR	Decision, 3-2
1924 Harry Mallin, GBR	Decision	1972 Vyacheslav Lemechev, USSR	KO, 1st
1928 Piero Toscani, ITA	Decision	1976 Michael Spinks, USA	Stopped, 3rd
1932 Carmen Barth, USA	Decision	1980 José Gomez, CUB	Decision, 4-1
1936 Jean Despeaux, FRA	Decision	1984 Shin Joon-Sup, S. Kor	Decision, 3-2
1948 László Papp, HUN	Decision	1988 Henry Maske, E. Ger	Decision, 5-0
1952 Floyd Patterson, USA	KO, 1st	1992 Ariel Hernandez, CUB	Decision, 12-7
1956 Gennady Schatkov, USSR	KO, 1st	1996 Ariel Hernandez, CUB	Decision, 11-3

Light Heavyweight (178 lbs)

Year	Final Match	Year	Final Match
1920 Eddie Eagan, USA	Decision	1964 Cosimo Pinto, ITA	Decision, 3-2
1924 Harry Mitchell, GBR	Decision	1968 Dan Poznjak, USSR	Default
1928 Victor Avendaño, ARG	Decision	1972 Mate Parlov, YUG	Stopped, 2nd
1932 David Carstens, RSA	Decision	1976 Leon Spinks, USA	Stopped, 3rd
1936 Roger Michelot, FRA	Decision	1980 Slobodan Kacar, YUG	Decision, 4-1
1948 George Hunter, RSA	Decision	1984 Anton Josipovic, YUG	Default
1952 Norvel Lee, USA	Decision, 3-0	1988 Andrew Maynard, USA	Decision, 5-0
1956 Jim Boyd, USA	Decision	1992 Torsten May, GER	Decision, 8-3
1960 Cassius Clay, USA	Decision, 5-0	1996 Vasilii Jirov, KAZ	Decision, 17-4

Note: Cassius Clay changed his name to Muhammad Ali after winning the world heavyweight championship in 1964.

Heavyweight (201 lbs)

Year	Final Match	Year	Final Match
1984 Henry Tillman, USA	Decision, 5-0	1992 Felix Savon, CUB	Decision, 14-1
1988 Ray Mercer, USA	KO, 1st	1996 Felix Savon, CUB	Decision, 20-2

Super Heavyweight (Unlimited)

Year	Final Match	Year	Final Match
1904 Samuel Berger, USA	Decision	1960 Franco De Piccoli, ITA	KO, 1st
1908 Albert Oldham, GBR	KO, 1st	1964 Joe Frazier, USA	Decision, 3-2
1920 Ronald Rawson, GBR	Decision	1968 George Foreman, USA	Stopped, 2nd
1924 Otto von Porat, NOR	Decision	1972 Teófilo Stevenson, CUB	Default
1928 Arturo Rodriguez Jurado, ARG	Stopped, 1st	1976 Teófilo Stevenson, CUB	KO, 3rd
1932 Santiago Lovell, ARG	Decision	1980 Teófilo Stevenson, CUB	Decision, 4-1
1936 Herbert Runge, GER	Decision	1984 Tyrell Biggs, USA	Decision, 4-1
1948 Rafael Iglesias, ARG	KO, 2nd	1988 Lennox Lewis, CAN	Stopped, 2nd
1952 Ed Sanders, USA	Won on Disq.*	1992 Roberto Balado, CUB	Decision, 13-2
1956 Pete Rademacher, USA	Stopped, 1st	1996 Vladimir Klichko, UKR	Decision, 7-3

*Sanders' opponent, Ingemar Johansson, was disqualified in 2nd round for not trying.

Note: Called heavyweight through 1980.

DIVING

MEN

Multiple gold medals: Greg Louganis (4); Klaus Dibiasi (3); Pete Desjardins, Sammy Lee, Bob Webster and Albert White (2).

Springboard

Year		Points	Year		Points
1908	Albert Zürner, GER	85.5	1960	Gary Tobian, USA	170.00
1912	Paul Günther, GER	79.23	1964	Ken Sitzberger, USA	159.90
1920	Louis Kuehn, USA	675.4	1968	Bernie Wrightson, USA	170.15
1924	Albert White, USA	696.4	1972	Vladimir Vasin, USSR	594.09
1928	Pete Desjardins, USA	185.04	1976	Phil Boggs, USA	619.05
1932	Michael Galitzen, USA	161.38	1980	Aleksandr Portnov, USSR	905.03
1936	Richard Degener, USA	163.57	1984	Greg Louganis, USA	754.41
1948	Bruce Harlan, USA	163.64	1988	Greg Louganis, USA	730.80
1952	David Browning, USA	205.29	1992	Mark Lenzi, USA	676.53
1956	Bob Clotworthy, USA	159.56	1996	Ni Xiong, CHN	701.46

Platform

Year		Points	Year		Points
1904	George Sheldon, USA	12.66	1956	Joaquin Capilla, MEX	152.44
1906	Gottlob Walz, GER	156.0	1960	Bob Webster, USA	165.56
1908	Hjalmar Johansson, SWE	83.75	1964	Bob Webster, USA	148.58
1912	Erik Adlerz, SWE	73.94	1968	Klaus Dibiasi, ITA	164.18
1920	Clarence Pinkston, USA	100.67	1972	Klaus Dibiasi, ITA	504.12
1924	Albert White, USA	97.46	1976	Klaus Dibiasi, ITA	600.51
1928	Pete Desjardins, USA	98.74	1980	Falk Hoffmann, E. Ger	835.65
1932	Harold Smith, USA	124.80	1984	Greg Louganis, USA	710.91
1936	Marshall Wayne, USA	113.58	1988	Greg Louganis, USA	638.61
1948	Sammy Lee, USA	130.05	1992	Sun Shuwei, CHN	677.31
1952	Sammy Lee, USA	156.28	1996	Dmitri Saoutine, RUS	692.34

WOMEN

Multiple gold medals: Pat McCormick (4); Ingrid Engel-Krämer and Fu Mingxia (3); Vicki Draves, Dorothy Poynton Hill and Gao Min (2).

Springboard

Year		Points	Year		Points
1920	Aileen Riggin, USA	539.9	1964	Ingrid Engel-Kräamer, GER	145.00
1924	Elizabeth Becker, USA	474.5	1968	Sue Gossick, USA	150.77
1928	Helen Meany, USA	78.62	1972	Micki King, USA	450.03
1932	Georgia Coleman, USA	87.52	1976	Jennifer Chandler, USA	506.19
1936	Marjorie Gestring, USA	89.27	1980	Irina Kalinina, USSR	725.91
1948	Vicki Draves, USA	108.74	1984	Sylvie Bernier, CAN	530.70
1952	Pat McCormick, USA	147.30	1988	Gao Min, CHN	580.23
1956	Pat McCormick, USA	142.36	1992	Gao Min, CHN	572.40
1960	Ingrid Krämer, GER	155.81	1996	Fu Mingxia, CHN	547.68

Platform

Year		Points	Year		Points
1912	Greta Johansson, SWE	39.9	1964	Lesley Bush, USA	99.80
1920	Stefani Fryland-Clausen, DEN	34.6	1968	Milena Duchková, CZE	109.59
1924	Caroline Smith, USA	33.2	1972	Ulrika Knape, SWE	390.00
1928	Elizabeth Becker Pinkston, USA	31.6	1976	Elena Vaytsekhovskaya, USSR	406.59
1932	Dorothy Poynton, USA	40.26	1980	Martina Jäschke, E. Ger	596.25
1936	Dorothy Poynton Hill, USA	33.93	1984	Zhou Jihong, CHN	435.51
1948	Vicki Draves, USA	68.87	1988	Xu Yanmei, CHN	445.20
1952	Pat McCormick, USA	79.37	1992	Fu Mingxia, CHN	461.43
1956	Pat McCormick, USA	84.85	1996	Fu Mingxia, CHN	521.58
1960	Ingrid Krämer, GER	91.28			

FIELD HOCKEY

MEN

Multiple gold medals: India (8); Great Britain and Pakistan (3); West Germany/Germany (2).

Year		Year	
1908	**Great Britain**, Ireland, Scotland	1964	**India**, Pakistan, Australia
1920	**Great Britain**, Denmark, Belgium	1968	**Pakistan**, Australia, India
1928	**India**, Netherlands, Germany	1972	**West Germany**, Pakistan, India
1932	**India**, Japan, United States	1976	**New Zealand**, Australia, Pakistan
1936	**India**, Germany, Netherlands	1980	**India**, Spain, Soviet Union
1948	**India**, Great Britain, Netherlands	1984	**Pakistan**, West Germany, Great Britain
1952	**India**, Netherlands, Great Britain	1988	**Great Britain**, West Germany, Netherlands
1956	**India**, Pakistan, Germany	1992	**Germany**, Australia, Pakistan
1960	**Pakistan**, India, Spain	1996	**Netherlands**, Spain, Australia

WOMEN

Multiple gold medals: Australia (2).

Year		Year	
1980	**Zimbabwe**, Czechoslovakia, Soviet Union	1992	**Spain**, Germany, Great Britain
1984	**Netherlands**, West Germany, United States	1996	**Australia**, South Korea, Netherlands
1988	**Australia**, South Korea, Netherlands		

GYMNASTICS

MEN

At least 4 gold medals (including team events): Sawao Kato (8); Nikolai Andrianov, Viktor Chukarin and Boris Shakhlin (7); Akinori Nakayama and Vitaly Scherbo (6); Yukio Endo, Anton Heida, Mitsuo Tsukahara and Takashi Ono (5); Vladimir Artemov, Georges Miez and Valentin Muratov (4).

All-Around

Year		Points	Year		Points
1900	Gustave Sandras, FRA	302	1956	Viktor Chukarin, USSR	114.25
1904	Julius Lenhart, AUT	69.80	1960	Boris Shakhlin, USSR	115.95
1906	Pierre Payssé, FRA	97.0	1964	Yukio Endo, JPN	115.95
1908	Alberto Braglia, ITA	317.0	1968	Sawao Kato, JPN	115.9
1912	Alberto Braglia, ITA	135.0	1972	Sawao Kato, JPN	114.650
1920	Giorgio Zampori, ITA	88.35	1976	Nikolai Andrianov, USSR	116.65
1924	Leon Stukelj, YUG	110.340	1980	Aleksandr Dityatin, USSR	118.65
1928	Georges Miez, SWI	247.500	1984	Koji Gushiken, JPN	118.7
1932	Romeo Neri, ITA	140.625	1988	Vladimir Artemov, USSR	119.125
1936	Alfred Schwarzmann, GER	113.100	1992	Vitaly Scherbo, UT	59.025
1948	Veikko Huhtanen, FIN	229.7	1996	Li Xiaoshuang, CHN	58.423
1952	Viktor Chukarin, USSR	115.7			

Horizontal Bar

Year		Points	Year		Points
1896	Hermann Weingärtner, GER	–	1964	Boris Shakhlin, USSR	19.625
1904	(TIE) Anton Heida, USA	40	1968	(TIE) Akinori Nakayama, JPN	19.55
	& Edward Hennig, USA	40		& Mikhail Voronin, USSR	19.55
1924	Leon Stukelj, YUG	19.73	1972	Mitsuo Tsukahara, JPN	19.725
1928	Georges Miez, SWI	19.17	1976	Mitsuo Tsukahara, JPN	19.675
1932	Dallas Bixler, USA	18.33	1980	Stoyan Deltchev, BUL	19.825
1936	Aleksanteri Saarvala, FIN	19.367	1984	Shinji Morisue, JPN	20.00
1948	Josef Stalder, SWI	19.85	1988	(TIE) Vladimir Artemov, USSR	19.900
1952	Jack Günthard, SWI	19.55		& Valeri Lyukin, USSR	19.900
1956	Takashi Ono, JPN	19.60	1992	Trent Dimas, USA	9.875
1960	Takashi Ono, JPN	19.60	1996	Andreas Wecker, GER	9.850

Parallel Bars

Year		Points	Year		Points
1896	Alfred Flatow, GER	–	1964	Yukio Endo, JPN	19.675
1904	George Eyser, USA	44	1968	Akinori Nakayama, JPN	19.475
1924	August Güttinger, SWI	21.63	1972	Sawao Kato, JPN	19.475
1928	Ladislav Vácha, CZE	18.83	1976	Sawao Kato, JPN	19.675
1932	Romeo Neri, ITA	18.97	1980	Aleksandr Tkachyov, USSR	19.775
1936	Konrad Frey, GER	19.067	1984	Bart Conner, USA	19.95
1948	Michael Reusch, SWI	19.75	1988	Vladimir Artemov, USSR	19.925
1952	Hans Eugster, SWI	19.65	1992	Vitaly Scherbo, UT	9.900
1956	Viktor Chukarin, USSR	19.20	1996	Rustam Sharipov, UKR	9.837
1960	Boris Shakhlin, USSR	19.40			

Vault

Year		Points	Year		Points
1896	Karl Schumann, GER	–	1960	(TIE) Takashi Ono, JPN	19.35
1904	(TIE) George Eyser, USA	36		& Boris Shakhlin, USSR	19.35
	& Anton Heida, USA	36	1964	Haruhiro Yamashita, JPN	19.60
1924	Frank Kriz, USA	9.98	1968	Mikhail Voronin, USSR	19.00
1928	Eugen Mack, SWI	9.58	1972	Klaus Köste, E. Ger	18.85
1932	Savino Guglielmetti, ITA	18.03	1976	Nikolai Andrianov, USSR	19.45
1936	Alfred Schwarzmann, GER	19.20	1980	Nikolai Andrianov, USSR	19.825
1948	Paavo Aaltonen, FIN	19.55	1984	Lou Yun, CHN	19.95
1952	Viktor Chukarin, USSR	19.20	1988	Lou Yun, CHN	19.875
1956	(TIE) Helmut Bantz, GER	18.85	1992	Vitaly Scherbo, UT	9.856
	& Valentin Muratov, USSR	18.85	1996	Alexei Nemov, RUS	9.787

Gymnastics (Cont.)
Pommel Horse

Year		Points
1896	Louis Zutter, SWI	–
1904	Anton Heida, USA	.42
1924	Josef Wilhelm, SWI	21.23
1928	Hermann Hänggi, SWI	19.75
1932	Istvän Pelle, HUN	19.07
1936	Konrad Frey, GER	19.333
1948	(TIE) Paavo Aaltonen, FIN	19.35
	Veikko Huhtanen, FIN	19.35
	& Heikki Savolainen, FIN	19.35
1952	Viktor Chukarin, USSR	19.50
1956	Boris Shakhlin, USSR	19.25
1960	(TIE) Eugen Ekman, FIN	19.375
	& Boris Shakhlin, USSR	19.375
1964	Miroslav Cerar, YUG	19.525
1968	Miroslav Cerar, YUG	19.325
1972	Viktor Klimenko, SOV	19.125
1976	Zoltán Magyar, HUN	19.70
1980	Zoltán Magyar, HUN	19.925
1984	(TIE) Li Ning, CHN	19.95
	& Peter Vidmar, USA	19.95
1988	(TIE) Dmitri Bilozerchev, USSR,	19.95
	Zsolt Borkai, HUN	19.95
	& Lyubomir Geraskov, BUL	19.95
1992	(TIE) Pae Gil-Su, N. Kor	9.925
	& Vitaly Scherbo, UT	9.925
1996	Li Donghua, SWI	9.875

Rings

Year		Points
1896	Ioannis Mitropoulos, GRE	–
1904	Hermann Glass, USA	.45
1924	Francesco Martino, ITA	21.553
1928	Leon Stukelj, YUG	19.25
1932	George Gulack, USA	18.97
1936	Alois Hudec, CZE	19.433
1948	Karl Frei, SWI	19.80
1952	Grant Shaginyan, USSR	19.75
1956	Albert Azaryan, USSR	19.35
1960	Albert Azaryan, USSR	19.725
1964	Takuji Haytta, JPN	19.475
1968	Akinori Nakayama, JPN	19.45
1972	Akinori Nakayama, JPN	19.35
1976	Nikolai Andrianov, USSR	19.65
1980	Aleksandr Dityatin, USSR	19.875
1984	(TIE) Koji Gushiken, JPN	19.85
	& Li Ning, CHN	19.85
1988	(TIE) Holger Behrendt, E. Ger	19.925
	& Dmitri Bilozerchev, USSR	19.925
1992	Vitaly Scherbo, UT	9.937
1996	Yuri Chechi, ITA	9.887

Floor Exercise

Year		Points
1932	Istvan Pelle, HUN	9.60
1936	Georges Miez, SWI	18.666
1948	Ferenc Pataki, HUN	19.35
1952	William Thoresson, SWE	19.25
1956	Valentin Muratov, USSR	19.20
1960	Nobuyuki Aihara, JPN	19.45
1964	Franco Menichelli, ITA	19.45
1968	Sawao Kato, JPN	19.475
1972	Nikolai Andrianov, USSR	19.175
1976	Nikolai Andrianov, USSR	19.45
1980	Roland Brückner, E. Ger	19.75
1984	Li Ning, CHN	19.925
1988	Sergei Kharkov, USSR	19.925
1992	Li Xiaosahuang, CHN	9.925
1996	Ioannis Melissanidis, GRE	9.850

Team Combined Exercises

Year		Points
1904	United States	374.43
1906	Norway	19.00
1908	Sweden	438
1912	Italy	265.75
1920	Italy	359.855
1924	Italy	839.058
1928	Switzerland	1718.625
1932	Italy	541.850
1936	Germany	657.430
1948	Finland	1358.30
1952	Soviet Union	574.40
1956	Soviet Union	568.25
1960	Japan	575.20
1964	Japan	577.95
1968	Japan	575.90
1972	Japan	571.25
1976	Japan	576.85
1980	Soviet Union	598.60
1984	United States	591.40
1988	Soviet Union	593.35
1992	Unified Team	585.45
1996	Russia	576.778

WOMEN

At least 4 gold medals (including team events): Larissa Latynina (9); Vera Cáslavská (7); Polina Astakhova, Nadia Comaneci, Agnes Keleti and Nelli Kim (5); Olga Korbut, Ecaterina Szabó and Lyudmila Tourischeva (4).

All-Around

Year		Points
1952	Maria Gorokhovskaya, USSR	76.78
1956	Larissa Latynina, USSR	74.933
1960	Larissa Latynina, USSR	77.031
1964	Vera Cáslavská, CZE	77.564
1968	Vera Cáslavská, CZE	78.25
1972	Lyudmila Tourischeva, USSR	77.025
1976	Nadia Comaneci, ROM	79.275
1980	Yelena Davydova, USSR	79.15
1984	Mary Lou Retton, USA	79.175
1988	Yelena Shushunova, USSR	79.662
1992	Tatiana Gutsu, UT	39.737
1996	Lilia Podkopayeva, UKR	39.255

Vault

Year		Points	Year		Points
1952	Yekaterina Kalinchuk, USSR	19.20	1980	Natalia Shaposhnikova, USSR	19.725
1956	Larissa Latynina, USSR	18.833	1984	Ecaterina Szabó, ROM	19.875
1960	Margarita Nikolayeva, USSR	19.316	1988	Svetlana Boginskaya, USSR	19.905
1964	Vera Cáslavská, CZE	19.483	1992	(TIE) Henrietta Onodi, HUN	9.925
1968	Vera Cáslavská, CZE	19.775		& Lavinia Milosovici, ROM	9.925
1972	Karin Janz, E. Ger	19.525	1996	Simona Amanar, ROM	9.775
1976	Nelli Kim, USSR	19.80			

Uneven Bars

Year		Points	Year		Points
1952	Margit Korondi, HUN	19.40	1980	Maxi Gnauck, E. Ger	19.875
1956	Agnes Keleti, HUN	18.966	1984	(TIE) Julianne McNamara, USA	19.95
1960	Polina Astakhova, USSR	19.616		& Ma Yanhong, CHN	19.95
1964	Polina Astakhova, USSR	19.332	1988	Daniela Silivas, ROM	20.00
1968	Vera Cáslavská, CZE	19.65	1992	Lu Li, CHN	10.00
1972	Karin Janz, E. Ger	19.675	1996	Svetlana Chorkina, RUS	9.850
1976	Nadia Comaneci, ROM	20.00			

Balance Beam

Year		Points	Year		Points
1952	Nina Bocharova, USSR	19.22	1980	Nadia Comaneci, ROM	19.80
1956	Agnes Keleti, HUN	18.80	1984	(TIE) Simona Pauca, ROM	19.80
1960	Eva Bosakova, CZE	19.283		& Ecaterina Szabó, ROM	19.80
1964	Vera Cáslavská, CZE	19.449	1988	Daniela Silivas, ROM	19.924
1968	Natalya Kuchinskaya, USSR	19.65	1992	Tatiana Lyssenko, UT	9.975
1972	Olga Korbut, USSR	19.40	1996	Shannon Miller, USA	9.862
1976	Nadia Comaneci, ROM	19.95			

Floor Exercise

Year		Points	Year		Points
1952	Agnes Keleti, HUN	19.36	1976	Nelli Kim, USSR	19.85
1956	(TIE) Agnes Keleti, HUN	18.733	1980	(TIE) Nadia Comaneci, ROM	19.875
	& Larissa Latynina, USSR	18.733		& Nelli Kim, USSR	19.875
1960	Larissa Latynina, USSR	19.583	1984	Ecaterina Szabó, ROM	19.975
1964	Larissa Latynina, USSR	19.599	1988	Daniela Silivas, ROM	19.937
1968	(TIE) Vera Cáslavská, CZE	19.675	1992	Lavinia Milosovici, ROM	10.000
	& Larissa Petrik, USSR	19.675	1996	Lilia Podkopayeva, UKR	9.887
1972	Olga Korbut, USSR	19.575			

Team Combined Exercises

Year		Points	Year		Points
1928	Netherlands	316.75	1972	Soviet Union	380.50
1936	Germany	506.50	1976	Soviet Union	466.00
1948	Czechoslovakia	445.45	1980	Soviet Union	394.90
1952	Soviet Union	527.03	1984	Romania	392.02
1956	Soviet Union	444.800	1988	Soviet Union	395.475
1960	Soviet Union	382.320	1992	Unified Team	395.666
1964	Soviet Union	280.890	1996	United States	389.225
1968	Soviet Union	382.85			

SOCCER

MEN

Multiple gold medals: Great Britain and Hungary (3); Uruguay and USSR (2).

Year		Year	
1900	**Great Britain**, France, Belgium	1956	**Soviet Union**, Yugoslavia, Bulgaria
1904	**Canada**, USA I, USA II	1960	**Yugoslavia**, Denmark, Hungary
1906	**Denmark**, Smyrna (Int'l entry), Greece	1964	**Hungary**, Czechoslovakia, Germany
1908	**Great Britain**, Denmark, Netherlands	1968	**Hungary**, Bulgaria, Japan
1912	**Great Britain**, Denmark, Netherlands	1972	**Poland**, Hungary, East Germany & Soviet Union
1920	**Belgium**, Spain, Netherlands	1976	**East Germany**, Poland, Soviet Union
1924	**Uruguay**, Switzerland, Sweden	1980	**Czechoslovakia**, East Germany, Soviet Union
1928	**Uruguay**, Argentina, Italy	1984	**France**, Brazil, Yugoslavia
1936	**Italy**, Austria, Norway	1988	**Soviet Union**, Brazil, West Germany
1948	**Sweden**, Yugoslavia, Denmark	1992	**Spain**, Poland, Ghana
1952	**Hungary**, Yugoslavia, Sweden	1996	**Nigeria**, Argentina, Brazil

WOMEN

Year	
1996	**United States**, China, Norway

SWIMMING

World and Olympic records below that appear to be broken or equaled by winning times in subsequent years, but are not so indicated, were all broken in preliminary heats leading up to the finals. Some events were not held at every Olympics.

MEN

At least 4 gold medals (including relays): Mark Spitz (9); Matt Biondi (8); Charles Daniels, Tom Jager, Don Schollander, and Johnny Weissmuller (5); Tamás Darnyi, Roland Matthes, John Naber, Aleksandr Popov, Murray Rose, Vladimir Salnikov and Henry Taylor (4).

50-meter Freestyle

Year		Time		Year		Time	
1904	Zoltán Halmay, HUN (50 yds)	.28.0		1992	Aleksandr Popov, UT	21.91	**OR**
1906-84	Not held			1996	Aleksandr Popov, RUS	22.13	
1988	Matt Biondi, USA	.22.14	**WR**				

100-meter Freestyle

Year		Time		Year		Time	
1896	Alfréd Hajós, HUN	1:22.2	**OR**	1956	Jon Henricks, AUS	.55.4	**OR**
1904	Zoltán Halmay, HUN (100 yds)	1:02.8		1960	John Devitt, AUS	.55.2	**OR**
1906	Charles Daniels, USA	1:13.4		1964	Don Schollander, USA	.53.4	**OR**
1908	Charles Daniels, USA	1:05.6	**WR**	1968	Michael Wenden, AUS	.52.2	**WR**
1912	Duke Kahanamoku, USA	1:03.4		1972	Mark Spitz, USA	.51.22	**WR**
1920	Duke Kahanamoku, USA	1:00.4	**WR**	1976	Jim Montgomery, USA	.49.99	**WR**
1924	Johnny Weissmuller, USA	.59.0	**OR**	1980	Jorg Woithe, E. Ger.	.50.40	
1928	Johnny Weissmuller, USA	.58.6	**OR**	1984	Rowdy Gaines, USA	.49.80	**OR**
1932	Yasuji Miyazaki, JPN	.58.2		1988	Matt Biondi, USA	.48.63	**OR**
1936	Ferenc Csik, HUN.	.57.6		1992	Aleksandr Popov, UT	.49.02	
1948	Wally Ris, USA	.57.3	**OR**	1996	Aleksandr Popov, RUS	.48.74	
1952	Clarke Scholes, USA	.57.4					

200-meter Freestyle

Year		Time		Year		Time	
1900	Frederick Lane, AUS (220 yds)	2:25.2	**OR**	1980	Sergei Kopliakov, USSR.	1:49.81	**OR**
1904	Charles Daniels, USA (220 yds)	2:44.2		1984	Michael Gross, W. Ger.	1:47.44	**WR**
1968	Michael Wenden, AUS	1:55.2	**OR**	1988	Duncan Armstrong, AUS	1:47.25	**WR**
1972	Mark Spitz, USA.	1:52.78	**WR**	1992	Yevgeny Sadovyi, UT	1:46.70	**OR**
1976	Bruce Furniss, USA.	1:50.29	**WR**	1996	Danyon Loader, NZE	1:47.63	

400-meter Freestyle

Year		Time		Year		Time	
1896	Paul Neumann, AUT (550m)	8:12.6		1956	Murray Rose, AUS	4:27.3	**OR**
1904	Charles Daniels, USA (440 yds)	6:16.2		1960	Murray Rose, AUS	4:18.3	**OR**
1906	Otto Scheff, AUT.	6:23.8		1964	Don Schollander, USA	4:12.2	**WR**
1908	Henry Taylor, GBR	5:36.8		1968	Mike Burton, USA.	4:09.0	**OR**
1912	George Hodgson, CAN.	5:24.4		1972	Bradford Cooper, AUS*	4:00.27	**OR**
1920	Norman Ross, USA	5:26.8		1976	Brian Goodell, USA.	3:51.93	**WR**
1924	Johnny Weissmuller, USA.	5:04.2	**OR**	1980	Vladimir Salnikov, USSR	3:51.31	**OR**
1928	Alberto Zorilla, ARG.	5:01.6	**OR**	1984	George DiCarlo, USA	3:51.23	**OR**
1932	Buster Crabbe, USA	4:48.4	**OR**	1988	Uwe Dassler, E. Ger.	3:46.95	**WR**
1936	Jack Medica, USA	4:44.5	**OR**	1992	Yevgeny Sadovyi, UT	3:45.00	**WR**
1948	Bill Smith, USA	4:41.0	**OR**	1996	Danyon Loader, NZE	3:47.97	
1952	Jean Boiteux, FRA	4:30.7	**OR**				

*Cooper finished second to Rick DeMont of the U.S., who was disqualified when he flunked the post-race drug test (his asthma medication was on the IOC's banned list).

1500-meter Freestyle

Year		Time		Year		Time	
1896	Alfréd Hajós, HUN (1200m)	18:22.2	**OR**	1952	Ford Konno, USA	18:30.3	**OR**
1900	John Arthur Jarvis, GBR (1000m)	13:40.2		1956	Murray Rose, AUS	17:58.9	
1904	Emil Rausch, GER (1 mile)	27:18.2		1960	Jon Konrads, AUS	17:19.6	**OR**
1906	Henry Taylor, GBR (1 mile)	28:28.0		1964	Robert Windle, AUS	17:01.7	**OR**
1908	Henry Taylor, GBR	22:48.4	**WR**	1968	Mike Burton, USA	16:38.9	**OR**
1912	George Hodgson, CAN	22:00.0	**WR**	1972	Mike Burton, USA	15:52.58	**WR**
1920	Norman Ross, USA	22:23.2		1976	Brian Goodell, USA.	15:02.40	**WR**
1924	Andrew (Boy) Charlton, AUS	20:06.6	**WR**	1980	Vladimir Salnikov, USSR	14:58.27	**WR**
1928	Arne Borge, SWE.	19:51.8	**OR**	1984	Mike O'Brien, USA	15:05.20	
1932	Kusuo Kitamura, JPN	19:12.4	**OR**	1988	Vladimir Salnikov, USSR	15:00.40	
1936	Noboru Terada, JPN	19:13.7		1992	Kieren Perkins, AUS.	14:43.48	**WR**
1948	James McLane, USA.	19:18.5		1996	Kieren Perkins, AUS.	14:56.40	

100-meter Backstroke

Year		Time		Year		Time	
1904	Walter Brack, GER (100 yds)	1:16.8		1956	David Theile, AUS.	1:02.2	OR
1908	Arno Bieberstein, GER	1:24.6	WR	1960	David Theile, AUS.	1:01.9	OR
1912	Harry Hebner, USA	1:21.2		1968	Roland Matthes, E. Ger	.58.7	OR
1920	Warren Kealoha, USA	1:15.2		1972	Roland Matthes, E. Ger	.56.58	OR
1924	Warren Kealoha, USA	1:13.2	OR	1976	John Naber, USA	.55.49	WR
1928	George Kojac, USA	1:08.2	WR	1980	Bengt Baron, SWE	.56.33	
1932	Masaji Kiyokawa, JPN	1:08.6		1984	Rick Carey, USA.	.55.79	
1936	Adolf Kiefer, USA	1:05.9	OR	1988	Daichi Suzuki, JPN.	.55.05	
1948	Allen Stack, USA.	1:06.4		1992	Mark Tewksbury, CAN	.53.98	OR
1952	Yoshinobu Oyakawa, USA	1:05.4	OR	1996	Jeff Rouse, USA	.54.10	

200-meter Backstroke

Year		Time		Year		Time	
1900	Ernst Hoppenberg, GER	2:47.0		1980	Sándor Wládár, HUN	2:01.93	
1964	Jed Graef, USA.	2:10.3	WR	1984	Rick Carey, USA.	2:00.23	
1968	Roland Matthes, E. Ger	2:09.6	OR	1988	Igor Poliansky, USSR	1:59.37	
1972	Roland Matthes, E. Ger	2:02.82	=WR	1992	Martin Lopez-Zubero, SPA.	1:58.47	OR
1976	John Naber, USA	1:59.19	WR	1996	Brad Bridgewater, USA	1:58.54	

100-meter Breaststroke

Year		Time		Year		Time	
1968	Don McKenzie, USA	1:07.7	OR	1984	Steve Lundquist, USA	1:01.65	WR
1972	Nobutaka Taguchi, JPN	1:04.94	WR	1988	Adrian Moorhouse, GBR	1:02.04	
1976	John Hencken, USA	1:03.11	WR	1992	Nelson Diebel, USA	1:01.50	OR
1980	Duncan Goodhew, GBR	1:03.44		1996	Fred deBurghgraeve, BEL	1:00.60	

200-meter Breaststroke

Year		Time		Year		Time	
1908	Frederick Holman, GBR	3:09.2	WR	1960	Bill Mulliken, USA	2:37.4	
1912	Walter Bathe, GER	3:01.8	OR	1964	Ian O'Brien, AUS	2:27.8	WR
1920	Hakan Malmroth, SWE	3:04.4		1968	Felipe Muñoz, MEX	2:28.7	
1924	Robert Skelton, USA	2:56.6		1972	John Hencken, USA	2:21.55	WR
1928	Yoshiyuki Tsuruta, JPN	2:48.8	OR	1976	David Wilkie, GBR	2:15.11	WR
1932	Yoshiyuki Tsuruta, JPN	2:45.4		1980	Robertas Zhulpa, USSR	2:15.85	
1936	Tetsuo Hamuro, JPN	2:41.5	OR	1984	Victor Davis, CAN	2:13.34	WR
1948	Joseph Verdeur, USA	2:39.3	OR	1988	József Szabó, HUN	2:13.52	
1952	John Davies, AUS	2:34.4	OR	1992	Mike Barrowman, USA	2:10.16	WR
1956	Masaru Furukawa, JPN	2:34.7*	OR	1996	Norbert Rozsa, HUN	2:12.57	

*In 1956, the butterfly stroke and breaststroke were separated into two different events.

100-meter Butterfly

Year		Time		Year		Time	
1968	Doug Russell, USA	.55.9	OR	1984	Michael Gross, W. Ger.	.53.08	WR
1972	Mark Spitz, USA	.54.27	WR	1988	Anthony Nesty, SUR	.53.0	OR
1976	Matt Vogel, USA.	.54:35		1992	Pablo Morales, USA	.53.32	
1980	Pär Arvidsson, SWE	.54.92		1996	Dennis Pankratov, RUS	.52.27	

200-meter Butterfly

Year		Time		Year		Time	
1956	Bill Yorzyk, USA	2:19.3	OR	1980	Sergei Fesenko, USSR	1:59.76	
1960	Mike Troy, USA	2:12.8	WR	1984	Jon Sieben, AUS.	1:57.04	WR
1964	Kevin Berry, AUS	2:06.6	WR	1988	Michael Gross, W. Ger.	1:56.94	OR
1968	Carl Robie, USA	2:08.7		1992	Melvin Stewart, USA	1:56.26	WR
1972	Mark Spitz, USA.	2:00.70	WR	1996	Dennis Pankratov, RUS.	1:56.51	
1976	Mike Bruner, USA	1:59.23	WR				

200-meter Individual Medley

Year		Time		Year		Time	
1968	Charles Hickcox, USA	2:12.0	OR	1988	Tamás Darnyi, HUN.	2:00.17	WR
1972	Gunnar Larsson, SWE	2:07.17	WR	1992	Tamás Darnyi, HUN.	2:00.76	
1984	Alex Baumann, CAN	2:01.42	WR	1996	Attila Czene, HUN.	1:59.91	

400-meter Individual Medley

Year		Time		Year		Time	
1964	Richard Roth, USA	4:45.4	WR	1984	Alex Baumann, CAN.	4:17.41	WR
1968	Charles Hickcox, USA	4:48.4		1988	Tamás Darnyi, HUN.	4:14.75	WR
1972	Gunnar Larsson, SWE	4:31.98	OR	1992	Tamás Darnyi, HUN.	4:14.23	OR
1976	Rod Strachan, USA	4:23.68	WR	1996	Tom Dolan, USA.	4:14.90	
1980	Aleksandr Sidorenko, USSR	4:22.89	OR				

Swimming (Cont.)

4x100-meter Freestyle Relay

Year		Time		Year		Time	
1964	United States	3:32.2	WR	1984	United States	3:19.03	WR
1968	United States	3:31.7	WR	1988	United States	3:16.53	WR
1972	United States	3:26.42	WR	1992	United States	3:16.74	
1976-80 Not held				1996	United States	3:15.41	

4x200-meter Freestyle Relay

Year		Time		Year		Time	
1906	Hungary (x250m)	16:52.4		1960	United States	8:10.2	WR
1908	Great Britain	10:55.6	WR	1964	United States	7:52.1	WR
1912	Australia/New Zealand	10:11.6	WR	1968	United States	7:52.33	
1920	United States	10:04.4	WR	1972	United States	7:35.78	WR
1924	United States	9:53.4	WR	1976	United States	7:23.22	WR
1928	United States	9:36.2	WR	1980	Soviet Union	7:23.50	
1932	Japan	8:58.4	WR	1984	United States	7:15.69	WR
1936	Japan	8:51.5	WR	1988	United States	7:12.51	WR
1948	United States	8:46.0	WR	1992	Unified Team	7:11.95	WR
1952	United States	8:31.1	OR	1996	United States	7:14.84	
1956	Australia	8:23.6	WR				

4x100-meter Medley Relay

Year		Time		Year		Time	
1960	United States	4:05.4	WR	1980	Australia	3:45.70	
1964	United States	3:58.4	WR	1984	United States	3:39.30	WR
1968	United States	3:54.9	WR	1988	United States	3:36.93	WR
1972	United States	3:48.16	WR	1992	United States	3:36.93	=WR
1976	United States	3:42.22	WR	1996	United States	3:34.84	

WOMEN

At least 4 gold medals (including relays): Kristin Otto (6); Krisztina Egerszegi and Jenny Thompson (5), Kornelia Ender, Janet Evans, Dawn Fraser and Amy Van Dyken (4).

50-meter Freestyle

Year		Time		Year		Time	
1988	Kristin Otto, E. Ger	25.49	OR	1996	Amy Van Dyken, USA	24.87	
1992	Yang Wenyi, CHN	24.79	WR				

100-meter Freestyle

Year		Time		Year		Time	
1912	Fanny Durack, AUS	1:22.2		1964	Dawn Fraser, AUS	59.5	OR
1920	Ethelda Bleibtrey, USA	1:13.6	WR	1968	Jan Henne, USA	1:00.0	
1924	Ethel Lackie, USA	1:12.4		1972	Sandra Neilson, USA	58.59	OR
1928	Albina Osipowich, USA	1:11.0	OR	1976	Kornelia Ender, E. Ger	55.65	WR
1932	Helene Madison, USA	1:06.8	OR	1980	Barbara Krause, E. Ger	54.79	WR
1936	Rie Mastenbroek, NED	1:05.9	OR	1984	(TIE) Nancy Hogshead, USA	55.92	
1948	Greta Andersen, DEN	1:06.3			Carrie Steinseifer, USA	55.92	
1952	Katalin Szöke, HUN	1:06.8		1988	Kristin Otto, E. Ger	54.93	
1956	Dawn Fraser, AUS	1:02.0	WR	1992	Zhuang Yong, CHN	54.65	OR
1960	Dawn Fraser, AUS	1:01.2	OR	1996	Le Jingyi, CHN	54.50	

200-meter Freestyle

Year		Time		Year		Time	
1968	Debbie Meyer, USA	2:10.5	OR	1984	Mary Wayte, USA	1:59.23	
1972	Shane Gould, AUS	2:03.56	WR	1988	Heike Friedrich, E. Ger	1:57.65	OR
1976	Kornelia Ender, E. Ger	1:59.26	WR	1992	Nicole Haislett, USA	1:57.90	
1980	Barbara Krause, E. Ger	1:58.33	OR	1996	Claudia Poll, CRC	1:58.16	

400-meter Freestyle

Year		Time		Year		Time	
1920	Ethelda Bleibtrey, USA (300m)	4:34.0	WR	1964	Ginny Duenkel, USA	4:43.3	OR
1924	Martha Norelius, USA	6:02.2	OR	1968	Debbie Meyer, USA	4:31.8	OR
1928	Martha Norelius, USA	5:42.8	WR	1972	Shane Gould, AUS	4:19.44	WR
1932	Helene Madison, USA	5:28.5	WR	1976	Petra Thümer, E. Ger	4:09.89	WR
1936	Rie Mastenbroek, NED	5:26.4	OR	1980	Ines Diers, E. Ger	4:08.76	OR
1948	Ann Curtis, USA	5:17.8	OR	1984	Tiffany Cohen, USA	4:07.10	OR
1952	Valéria Gyenge, HUN	5:12.1	OR	1988	Janet Evans, USA	4:03.85	WR
1956	Lorraine Crapp, AUS	4:54.6	OR	1992	Dagmar Hase, GER	4:07.18	
1960	Chris von Saltza, USA	4:50.6	OR	1996	Michelle Smith, IRL	4:07.25	

800-meter Freestyle

Year		Time		Year		Time	
1968	Debbie Meyer, USA	9:24.0	OR	1984	Tiffany Cohen, USA	8:24.95	OR
1972	Keena Rothhammer, USA	8:53.68	WR	1988	Janet Evans, USA	8:20.20	OR
1976	Petra Thümer, E. Ger	8:37.14	WR	1992	Janet Evans, USA	8:25.52	
1980	Michelle Ford, AUS	8:28.90	OR	1996	Brooke Bennett, USA	8:27.89	

100-meter Backstroke

Year		Time		Year		Time	
1924	Sybil Bauer, USA	1:23.2	OR	1968	Kaye Hall, USA	1:06.2	WR
1928	Maria Braun, NED	1:22.0		1972	Melissa Belote, USA	1:05.78	OR
1932	Eleanor Holm, USA	1:19.4		1976	Ulrike Richter, E. Ger	1:01.83	OR
1936	Dina Senff, NED	1:18.9		1980	Rica Reinisch, E. Ger	1:00.86	WR
1948	Karen-Margrete Harup, DEN	1:14.4	OR	1984	Theresa Andrews, USA	1:02.55	
1952	Joan Harrison, S. Afr.	1:14.3		1988	Kristin Otto, E. Ger.	1:00.89	
1956	Judy Grinham, GBR	1:12.9	OR	1992	Krisztina Egerszegi, HUN	1:00.68	OR
1960	Lynn Burke, USA	1:09.3	OR	1996	Beth Botsford, USA	1:01.19	
1964	Cathy Ferguson, USA	1:07.7	WR				

200-meter Backstroke

Year		Time		Year		Time	
1968	Pokey Watson, USA	2:24.8	OR	1984	Jolanda de Rover, NED	2:12.38	
1972	Melissa Belote, USA	2:19.19	WR	1988	Krisztina Egerszegi, HUN	2:09.29	OR
1976	Ulrike Richter, E. Ger	2:13.43	OR	1992	Krisztina Egerszegi, HUN	2:07.06	OR
1980	Rica Reinisch, E. Ger	2:11.77	WR	1996	Krisztina Egerszegi, HUN	2:07.83	

100-meter Breaststroke

Year		Time		Year		Time	
1968	Djurdjica Bjedov, YUG	1:15.8	OR	1984	Petra van Staveren, NED	1:09.88	OR
1972	Cathy Carr, USA	1:13.58	WR	1988	Tania Dangalakova, BUL	1:07.95	OR
1976	Hannelore Anke, E. Ger	1:11.16		1992	Yelena Rudkovskaya, UT	1:08.00	
1980	Ute Geweniger, E. Ger	1:10.22		1996	Penny Heyns, S. Afr.	1:07.73	

200-meter Breaststroke

Year		Time		Year		Time	
1924	Lucy Morton, GBR	3:33.2	OR	1968	Sharon Wichman, USA	2:44.4	OR
1928	Hilde Schrader, GER	3:12.6		1972	Beverley Whitfield, AUS	2:41.71	OR
1932	Clare Dennis, AUS	3:06.3	OR	1976	Marina Koshevaya, USSR	2:33.35	WR
1936	Hideko Maehata, JPN	3:03.6		1980	Lina Kaciusyte, USSR	2:29.54	OR
1948	Petronella van Vliet, NED	2:57.2		1984	Anne Ottenbrite, CAN	2:30.38	
1952	Éva Székely, HUN	2:51.7	OR	1988	Silke Hörner, E. Ger	2:26.71	OR
1956	Ursula Happe, GER	2:53.1	OR	1992	Kyoko Iwasaki, JPN	2:26.65	OR
1960	Anita Lonsbrough, GBR	2:49.5	WR	1996	Penny Heyns, S. Afr.	2:25.41	
1964	Galina Prozumenshikova, USSR	2:46.4	OR				

100-meter Butterfly

Year		Time		Year		Time	
1956	Shelly Mann, USA	1:11.0	OR	1980	Caren Metschuck, E. Ger	1:00.42	
1960	Carolyn Schuler, USA	1:09.5	OR	1984	Mary T. Meagher, USA	59.26	
1964	Sharon Stouder, USA	1:04.7	WR	1988	Kristin Otto, E. Ger	59.00	OR
1968	Lynn McClements, AUS	1:05.5		1992	Qian Hong, CHN	58.62	OR
1972	Mayumi Aoki, JPN	1:03.34	WR	1996	Amy Van Dyken, USA	59.13	
1976	Kornelia Ender, E. Ger	1:00.13	=WR				

200-meter Butterfly

Year		Time		Year		Time	
1968	Ada Kok, NED	2:24.7	OR	1984	Mary T. Meagher, USA	2:06.90	OR
1972	Karen Moe, USA	2:15.57	WR	1988	Kathleen Nord, E. Ger	2:09.51	
1976	Andrea Pollack, E. Ger	2:11.41	OR	1992	Summer Sanders, USA	2:08.67	
1980	Ines Geissler, E. Ger	2:10.44	OR	1996	Susan O'Neill, AUS	2:07.76	

200-meter Individual Medley

Year		Time		Year		Time	
1968	Claudia Kolb, USA	2:24.7	OR	1988	Daniela Hunger, E. Ger	2:12.59	OR
1972	Shane Gould, AUS	2:23.07	WR	1992	Lin Li, CHN	2:11.65	WR
1984	Tracy Caulkins, USA	2:12.64	OR	1996	Michelle Smith, IRL	2:13.93	

400-meter Individual Medley

Year		Time		Year		Time	
1964	Donna de Varona, USA	5:18.7	OR	1984	Tracy Caulkins, USA	4:39.24	
1968	Claudia Kolb, USA	5:08.5	OR	1988	Janet Evans, USA	4:37.76	
1972	Gail Neall, AUS	5:02.97	WR	1992	Krisztina Egerszegi, HUN	4:36.54	
1976	Ulrike Tauber, E. Ger	4:42.77	WR	1996	Michelle Smith, IRL	4:39.18	
1980	Petra Schneider, E. Ger	4:36.29	WR				

Swimming (Cont.)

4x100-meter Freestyle Relay

Year		Time		Year		Time	
1912	Great Britain	5:52.8	WR	1964	United States	4:03.8	WR
1920	United States	5:11.6	WR	1968	United States	4:02.5	OR
1924	United States	4:58.8	WR	1972	United States	3:55.19	WR
1928	United States	4:47.6	WR	1976	United States	3:44.82	WR
1932	United States	4:38.0	WR	1980	East Germany	3:42.71	WR
1936	Netherlands	4:36.0	OR	1984	United States	3:43.43	
1948	United States	4:29.2	OR	1988	East Germany	3:40.63	OR
1952	Hungary	4:24.4	WR	1992	United States	3:39.46	WR
1956	Australia	4:17.1	WR	1996	United States	3:39.29	
1960	United States	4:08.9	WR				

4x200-meter Freestyle Relay

Year		Time
1996	United States	7:59.87

4x100-meter Medley Relay

Year		Time		Year		Time	
1960	United States	4:41.1	WR	1980	East Germany	4:06.67	WR
1964	United States	4:33.9	WR	1984	United States	4:08.34	
1968	United States	4:28.3	OR	1988	East Germany	4:03.74	OR
1972	United States	4:20.75	WR	1992	United States	4:02.54	WR
1976	East Germany	4:07.95	WR	1996	United States	4:02.88	

TENNIS

MEN

Multiple gold medals (including men's doubles): John Boland, Max Decugis, Laurie Doherty, Reggie Doherty, Arthur Gore, Andre Grobert, Vincent Richards, Charles Winslow and Beals Wright (2).

Singles

Year			Year		
1896	John Boland	Great Britain/Ireland	1920	Louis Raymond	South Africa
1900	Laurie Doherty,	Great Britain	1924	Vincent Richards	United States
1904	Beals Wright	United States	1928-84	Not held	
1906	Max Decugis	France	1988	Miloslav Mecir	Czechoslovakia
1908	Josiah Ritchie	Great Britain	1992	Marc Rosset	Switzerland
	(Indoor) Arthur Gore	Great Britain	1996	Andre Agassi	United States
1912	Charles Winslow	South Africa			
	(Indoor) André Gobert	France			

Doubles

Year		Year	
1896	John Boland, IRL & Fritz Traun, GER	1920	Noel Turnbull & Max Woosnam, GBR
1900	Laurie and Reggie Doherty, GBR	1924	Vincent Richards & Frank Hunter, USA
1904	Edgar Leonard & Beals Wright, USA	1928-84	Not held
1906	Max Decugis & Maurice Germot, FRA	1988	Ken Flach & Robert Seguso, USA
1908	George Hillyard & Reggie Doherty, GBR	1992	Boris Becker & Michael Stich, GER
	(Indoor) Arthur Gore & Herbert Barrett, GBR	1996	Todd Woodbridge & Mark Woodforde, AUS
1912	Charles Winslow & Harold Kitson, S. Afr.		
	(Indoor) Andre Gobert & Maurice Germot, FRA		

WOMEN

Multiple gold medals (including women's doubles): Helen Wills, Gigi Fernandez and Mary Joe Fernandez (2).

Singles

Year			Year		
1900	Charlotte Cooper	Great Britain	1920	Suzanne Lenglen	France
1906	Esmee Simiriotou	Greece	1924	Helen Wills	United States
1908	Dorothea Chambers	Great Britain	1928-84	Not held	
	(Indoor) Gwen Eastlake-Smith	Great Britain	1988	Steffi Graf	West Germany
1912	Marguerite Broquedis	France	1992	Jennifer Capriati	United States
	(Indoor) Edith Hannam	Great Britain	1996	Lindsay Davenport	United States

Doubles

Year		Year	
1920	Winifred McNair & Kitty McKane, GBR	1988	Pam Shriver & Zina Garrison, USA
1924	Hazel Wightman & Helen Wills, USA	1992	Gigi Fernandez & Mary Joe Fernandez, USA
1928-84	Not held	1996	Gigi Fernandez & Mary Joe Fernandez, USA

TRACK & FIELD

World and Olympic records below that appear to be broken or equaled by winning times, heights and distances in subsequent years, but are not so indicated, were all broken in preliminary races and field events leading up to the finals.

MEN

At least 4 gold medals (including relays and discontinued events): Ray Ewry (10); Carl Lewis and Paavo Nurmi (9); Ville Ritola and Martin Sheridan (5); Harrison Dillard, Archie Hahn, Hannes Kolehmainen, Alvin Kraenzlein, Eric Lemming, Jim Lightbody, Al Oerter, Jesse Owens, Meyer Prinstein, Mel Sheppard, Lasse Viren and Emil Zátopek (4). Note that all of Ewry's gold medals came before 1912, in the Standing High Jump, Standing Long Jump and Standing Triple Jump.

100 meters

Year		Time		Year		Time	
1896	Tom Burke, USA	12.0		1952	Lindy Remigino, USA	10.4	
1900	Frank Jarvis, USA	11.0		1956	Bobby Morrow, USA	10.5	
1904	Archie Hahn, USA	11.0		1960	Armin Hary, GER	10.2	OR
1906	Archie Hahn, USA	11.2		1964	Bob Hayes, USA	10.0	=WR
1908	Reggie Walker, S. Afr.	10.8	=OR	1968	Jim Hines, USA	9.95	WR
1912	Ralph Craig, USA	10.8		1972	Valery Borzov, USSR	10.14	
1920	Charley Paddock, USA	10.8		1976	Hasely Crawford, TRI	10.06	
1924	Harold Abrahams, GBR	10.6	=OR	1980	Allan Wells, GBR	10.25	
1928	Percy Williams, CAN	10.8		1984	Carl Lewis, USA	9.99	
1932	Eddie Tolan, USA	10.3	OR	1988	Carl Lewis, USA*	9.92	WR
1936	Jesse Owens, USA	10.3ʷ		1992	Linford Christie, GBR	9.96	
1948	Harrison Dillard, USA	10.3	=OR	1996	Donovan Bailey, CAN	9.84	WR

ʷindicates wind-aided.

*Lewis finished second to Ben Johnson of Canada, who set a world record of 9.79 seconds. Two days later, Johnson was stripped of his gold medal and his record when he tested positive for steroid use in a post-race drug test.

200 meters

Year		Time		Year		Time	
1900	John Walter Tewksbury, USA	22.2		1956	Bobby Morrow, USA	20.6	OR
1904	Archie Hahn, USA	21.6	OR	1960	Livio Berruti, ITA	20.5	=WR
1908	Bobby Kerr, CAN	22.6		1964	Henry Carr, USA	20.3	WR
1912	Ralph Craig, USA	21.7		1968	Tommie Smith, USA	19.83	WR
1920	Allen Woodring, USA	22.0		1972	Valery Borzov, USSR	20.00	
1924	Jackson Scholz, USA	21.6		1976	Donald Quarrie, JAM	20.23	
1928	Percy Williams, CAN	21.8		1980	Pietro Mennea, ITA	20.19	
1932	Eddie Tolan, USA	21.2	OR	1984	Carl Lewis, USA	19.80	OR
1936	Jesse Owens, USA	20.7	OR	1988	Joe DeLoach, USA	19.75	OR
1948	Mel Patton, USA	21.1		1992	Mike Marsh, USA	20.01	
1952	Andy Stanfield, USA	20.7		1996	Michael Johnson, USA	19.32	WR

400 meters

Year		Time		Year		Time	
1896	Tom Burke, USA	54.2		1952	George Rhoden, JAM	45.9	OR
1900	Maxey Long, USA	49.4	OR	1956	Charley Jenkins, USA	46.7	
1904	Harry Hillman, USA	49.2	OR	1960	Otis Davis, USA	44.9	WR
1906	Paul Pilgrim, USA	53.2		1964	Mike Larrabee, USA	45.1	
1908	Wyndham Halswelle, GBR	50.0		1968	Lee Evans, USA	43.86	WR
1912	Charlie Reidpath, USA	48.2	OR	1972	Vince Matthews, USA	44.66	
1920	Bevil Rudd, S. Afr.	49.6		1976	Alberto Juantorena, CUB	44.26	
1924	Eric Liddell, GBR	47.6	OR	1980	Viktor Markin, USSR	44.60	
1928	Ray Barbuti, USA	47.8		1984	Alonzo Babers, USA	44.27	
1932	Bill Carr, USA	46.2	WR	1988	Steve Lewis, USA	43.87	
1936	Archie Williams, USA	46.5		1992	Quincy Watts, USA	43.50	OR
1948	Arthur Wint, JAM	46.2		1996	Michael Johnson, USA	43.49	OR

800 meters

Year		Time		Year		Time	
1896	Teddy Flack, AUS	2:11.0		1952	Mal Whitfield, USA	1:49.2	=OR
1900	Alfred Tysoe, GBR	2:01.2		1956	Tom Courtney, USA	1:47.7	OR
1904	Jim Lightbody, USA	1:56.0	OR	1960	Peter Snell, NZE	1:46.3	OR
1906	Paul Pilgrim, USA	2:01.5		1964	Peter Snell, NZE	1:45.1	OR
1908	Mel Sheppard, USA	1:52.8	WR	1968	Ralph Doubell, AUS	1:44.3	=WR
1912	Ted Meredith, USA	1:51.9	WR	1972	Dave Wottle, USA	1:45.9	
1920	Albert Hill, GBR	1:53.4		1976	Alberto Juantorena, CUB	1:43.50	WR
1924	Douglas Lowe, GBR	1:52.4		1980	Steve Ovett, GBR	1:45.4	
1928	Douglas Lowe, GBR	1:51.8	OR	1984	Joaquim Cruz, BRA	1:43.00	OR
1932	Tommy Hampson, GBR	1:49.7	WR	1988	Paul Ereng, KEN	1:43.45	
1936	John Woodruff, USA	1:52.9		1992	William Tanui, KEN	1:43.66	
1948	Mal Whitfield, USA	1:49.2	OR	1996	Vebjoern Rodal, NOR	1:42.58	OR

1500 meters

Year		Time		Year		Time	
1896	Teddy Flack, AUS	4:33.2		1900	Charles Bennett, GBR	4:06.2	WR

Track & Field (Cont.)

Year		Time		Year		Time	
1904	Jim Lightbody, USA	4:05.4	WR	1956	Ron Delany, IRL	3:41.2	OR
1906	Jim Lightbody, USA	4:12.0		1960	Herb Elliott, AUS	3:35.6	WR
1908	Mel Sheppard, USA	4:03.4	OR	1964	Peter Snell, NZE	3:38.1	
1912	Arnold Jackson, GBR	3:56.8	OR	1968	Kip Keino, KEN	3:34.9	OR
1920	Albert Hill, GBR	4:01.8		1972	Pekka Vasala, FIN	3:36.3	
1924	Paavo Nurmi, FIN	3:53.6	OR	1976	John Walker, NZE	3:39.17	
1928	Harry Larva, FIN	3:53.2	OR	1980	Sebastian Coe, GBR	3:38.4	
1932	Luigi Beccali, ITA	3:51.2	OR	1984	Sebastian Coe, GBR	3:32.53	OR
1936	John Lovelock, NZE	3:47.8	WR	1988	Peter Rono, KEN	3:35.96	
1948	Henry Eriksson, SWE	3:49.8		1992	Fermin Cacho, SPA	3:40.12	
1952	Josy Barthel, LUX	3:45.1	OR	1996	Noureddine Morceli, ALG	3:35.78	

5000 meters

Year		Time		Year		Time	
1912	Hannes Kolehmainen, FIN	14:36.6	WR	1964	Bob Schul, USA	13:48.8	
1920	Joseph Guillemot, FRA	14:55.6		1968	Mohamed Gammoudi, TUN	14:05.0	
1924	Paavo Nurmi, FIN	14:31.2	OR	1972	Lasse Viren, FIN	13:26.4	OR
1928	Ville Ritola, FIN	14:38.0		1976	Lasse Viren, FIN	13:24.76	
1932	Lauri Lehtinen, FIN	14:30.0	OR	1980	Miruts Yifter, ETH	13:21.0	
1936	Gunnar Höckert, FIN	14:22.2	OR	1984	Said Aouita, MOR	13:05.59	OR
1948	Gaston Reiff, BEL	14:17.6	OR	1988	John Ngugi, KEN	13:11.70	
1952	Emil Zátopek, CZE	14:06.6	OR	1992	Dieter Baumann, GER	13:12.52	
1956	Vladimir Kuts, USSR	13:39.6	OR	1996	Venuste Niyongabo, BUR	13:07.96	
1960	Murray Halberg, NZE	13:43.4					

10,000 meters

Year		Time		Year		Time	
1912	Hannes Kolehmainen, FIN	31:20.8		1964	Billy Mills, USA	28:24.4	OR
1920	Paavo Nurmi, FIN	31:45.8		1968	Naftali Temu, KEN	29:27.4	
1924	Ville Ritola, FIN	30:23.2	WR	1972	Lasse Viren, FIN	27:38.4	WR
1928	Paavo Nurmi, FIN	30:18.8	OR	1976	Lasse Viren, FIN	27:40.38	
1932	Janusz Kusocinski, POL	30:11.4	OR	1980	Miruts Yifter, ETH	27:42.7	
1936	Ilmari Salminen, FIN	30:15.4		1984	Alberto Cova, ITA	27:47.54	
1948	Emil Zátopek, CZE	29:59.6	OR	1988	Brahim Boutaib, MOR	27:21.46	OR
1952	Emil Zátopek, CZE	29:17.0	OR	1992	Khalid Skah, MOR	27:46.70	
1956	Vladimir Kuts, USSR	28:45.6	OR	1996	Haile Gebrselassie, ETH	27:07.34	OR
1960	Pyotr Bolotnikov, USSR	28:32.2	OR				

Marathon

Year		Time		Year		Time	
1896	Spiridon Louis, GRE	2:58:50		1952	Emil Zátopek, CZE	2:23:03.2	OR
1900	Michel Théato, FRA	2:59:45		1956	Alain Mimoun, FRA	2:25:00.0	
1904	Thomas Hicks, USA	3:28:53		1960	Abebe Bikila, ETH	2:15:16.2	WB
1906	Billy Sherring, CAN	2:51:23.6		1964	Abebe Bikila, ETH	2:12:11.2	WB
1908	Johnny Hayes, USA*	2:55:18.4	OR	1968	Mamo Wolde, ETH	2:20:26.4	
1912	Kenneth McArthur, S. Afr.	2:36:54.8		1972	Frank Shorter, USA	2:12:19.8	
1920	Hannes Kolehmainen, FIN	2:32:35.8	WB	1976	Waldemar Cierpinski, E. Ger	2:09:55.0	OR
1924	Albin Stenroos, FIN	2:41:22.6		1980	Waldemar Cierpinski, E. Ger	2:11:03.0	
1928	Boughèra El Ouafi, FRA	2:32:57.0		1984	Carlos Lopes, POR	2:09:21.0	OR
1932	Juan Carlos Zabala, ARG	2:31:36.0	OR	1988	Gelindo Bordin, ITA	2:10:32	
1936	Sohn Kee-Chung, JPN†	2:29:19.2	OR	1992	Hwang Young-Cho, S. Kor	2:13:23	
1948	Delfo Cabrera, ARG	2:34:51.6		1996	Josia Thugwane, S. Afr.	2:12:36	

*Dorando Pietri of Italy placed first, but was disqualified for being helped across the finish line.
†Sohn was a Korean, but he was forced to compete under the name Kitei Son by Japan, which occupied Korea at the time.
Note: Marathon distances–40,000 meters (1896,1904); 40,260 meters (1900); 41,860 meters (1906); 42,195 meters (1908 and since 1924); 40,200 meters (1912); 42,750 meters (1920). Current distance of 42,195 meters measures 26 miles, 385 yards.

110-meter Hurdles

Year		Time		Year		Time	
1896	Tom Curtis, USA	17.6		1952	Harrison Dillard, USA	13.7	OR
1900	Alvin Kraenzlein, USA	15.4	OR	1956	Lee Calhoun, USA	13.5	OR
1904	Frederick Schule, USA	16.0		1960	Lee Calhoun, USA	13.8	
1906	Robert Leavitt, USA	16.2		1964	Hayes Jones, USA	13.6	
1908	Forrest Smithson, USA	15.0	WR	1968	Willie Davenport, USA	13.3	OR
1912	Frederick Kelly, USA	15.1		1972	Rod Milburn, USA	13.24	=WR
1920	Earl Thomson, CAN	14.8	WR	1976	Guy Drut, FRA	13.30	
1924	Daniel Kinsey, USA	15.0		1980	Thomas Munkelt, E. Ger	13.39	
1928	Syd Atkinson, S. Afr.	14.8		1984	Roger Kingdom, USA	13.20	OR
1932	George Saling, USA	14.6		1988	Roger Kingdom, USA	12.98	OR
1936	Forrest (Spec) Towns, USA	14.2		1992	Mark McKoy, CAN	13.12	
1948	William Porter, USA	13.9	OR	1996	Allen Johnson, USA	12.95	OR

400-meter Hurdles

Year		Time		Year		Time	
1900	John Walter Tewksbury, USA	57.6		1960	Glenn Davis, USA	49.3	OR
1904	Harry Hillman, USA	53.0		1964	Rex Cawley, USA	49.6	
1908	Charley Bacon, USA	55.0	WR	1968	David Hemery, GBR	48.12	WR
1920	Frank Loomis, USA	54.0	WR	1972	John Akii-Bua, UGA	47.82	WR
1924	Morgan Taylor, USA	52.6		1976	Edwin Moses, USA	47.64	WR
1928	David Burghley, GBR	53.4	OR	1980	Volker Beck, E. Ger	48.70	
1932	Bob Tisdall, IRL	51.7		1984	Edwin Moses, USA	47.75	
1936	Glenn Hardin, USA	52.4		1988	Andre Phillips, USA	47.19	OR
1948	Roy Cochran, USA	51.1	OR	1992	Kevin Young, USA	46.78	WR
1952	Charley Moore, USA	50.8	OR	1996	Derrick Adkins, USA	47.54	
1956	Glenn Davis, USA	50.1	=OR				

3000-meter Steeplechase

Year		Time		Year		Time	
1900	George Orton, CAN	7:34.4		1960	Zdzislaw Krzyszkowiak, POL	8:34.2	OR
1904	Jim Lightbody, USA	7:39.6		1964	Gaston Roelants, BEL	8:30.8	OR
1908	Arthur Russell, GBR	10:47.8		1968	Amos Biwott, KEN	8:51.0	
1920	Percy Hodge, GBR	10:00.4	OR	1972	Kip Keino, KEN	8:23.6	OR
1924	Ville Ritola, FIN	9:33.6	OR	1976	Anders Gärderud, SWE	8:08.2	WR
1928	Toivo Loukola, FIN	9:21.8	WR	1980	Bronislaw Malinowski, POL	8:09.7	
1932	Volmari Iso-Hollo, FIN	10:33.4*		1984	Julius Korir, KEN	8:11.80	
1936	Volmari Iso-Hollo, FIN	9:03.8	WR	1988	Julius Kariuki, KEN	8:05.51	OR
1948	Thore Sjöstrand, SWE	9:04.6		1992	Matthew Birir, KEN	8:08.84	
1952	Horace Ashenfelter, USA	8:45.4	WR	1996	Joseph Keter, KEN	8:07.12	
1956	Chris Brasher, GBR	8:41.2	OR				

*Iso-Hollo ran one extra lap due to lap counter's mistake.
Note: Other steeplechase distances– 2500 meters (1900); 2590 meters (1904); 3200 meters (1908) and 3460 meters (1932).

4x100-meter Relay

Year		Time		Year		Time	
1912	Great Britain	42.4		1964	United States	39.0	WR
1920	United States	42.2	WR	1968	United States	38.23	WR
1924	United States	41.0	=WR	1972	United States	38.19	WR
1928	United States	41.0	=WR	1976	United States	38.33	
1932	United States	40.0		1980	Soviet Union	38.26	
1936	United States	39.8		1984	United States	37.83	WR
1948	United States	40.6		1988	Soviet Union	38.19	
1952	United States	40.1		1992	United States	37.40	WR
1956	United States	39.5	WR	1996	Canada	37.69	
1960	Germany	39.5	=WR				

4x400-meter Relay

Year		Time		Year		Time	
1908	United States	3:29.4		1960	United States	3:02.2	WR
1912	United States	3:16.6	WR	1964	United States	3:00.7	WR
1920	Great Britain	3:22.2		1968	United States	2:56.16	WR
1924	United States	3:16.0	WR	1972	Kenya	2:59.8	
1928	United States	3:14.2	WR	1976	United States	2:58.65	
1932	United States	3:08.2	WR	1980	Soviet Union	3:01.1	
1936	Great Britain	3:09.0		1984	United States	2:57.91	
1948	United States	3:10.4		1988	United States	2:56.16	=WR
1952	Jamaica	3:03.9	WR	1992	United States	2:55.74	WR
1956	United States	3:04.8		1996	United States	2:55.99	

20-kilometer Walk

Year		Time		Year		Time	
1956	Leonid Spirin, USSR	1:31:27.4		1980	Maurizio Damilano, ITA	1:23:35.5	OR
1960	Vladimir Golubnichiy, USSR	1:34:07.2		1984	Ernesto Canto, MEX	1:23:13	OR
1964	Ken Matthews, GBR	1:29:34.0	OR	1988	Jozef Pribilinec, CZE	1:19:57	OR
1968	Vladimir Golubnichiy, USSR	1:33:58.4		1992	Daniel Plaza Montero, SPA	1:21:45	
1972	Peter Frenkel, E. Ger	1:26:42.4	OR	1996	Jefferson Perez, ECU	1:20:07	
1976	Daniel Bautista, MEX	1:24:40.6	OR				

50-kilometer Walk

Year		Time		Year		Time	
1932	Thomas Green, GBR	4:50:10		1972	Bernd Kannenberg, W. Ger	3:56:11.6	OR
1936	Harold Whitlock, GBR	4:30:41.4	OR	1976	Not held		
1948	John Ljunggren, SWE	4:41:52		1980	Hartwig Gauder, E. Ger	3:49:24.0	OR
1952	Giuseppe Dordoni, ITA	4:28:07.8	OR	1984	Raul Gonzalez, MEX	3:47:26	OR
1956	Norman Read, NZE	4:30:42.8		1988	Vyacheslav Ivanenko, USSR	3:38:29	OR
1960	Don Thompson, GBR	4:25:30.0	OR	1992	Andrei Perlov, UT	3:50:13	
1964	Abdon Pamich, ITA	4:11:12.4	OR	1996	Robert Korzeniowski, POL	3:43:30	
1968	Christoph Höhne, E. Ger	4:20:13.6					

Track & Field (Cont.)

High Jump

Year		Height		Year		Height	
1896	Ellery Clark, USA	5-11¼		1952	Walt Davis, USA	6- 8½	OR
1900	Irving Baxter, USA	6- 2¾	OR	1956	Charley Dumas, USA	6-11½	OR
1904	Sam Jones, USA	5-11		1960	Robert Shavlakadze, USSR	7- 1	OR
1906	Cornelius Leahy, GBR/IRL	5-10		1964	Valery Brumel, USSR	7- 1¾	OR
1908	Harry Porter, USA	6- 3	OR	1968	Dick Fosbury, USA	7- 4¼	OR
1912	Alma Richards, USA	6- 4	OR	1972	Yuri Tarmak, USSR	7- 3¾	
1920	Richmond Landon, USA	6- 4	=OR	1976	Jacek Wszola, POL	7- 4½	OR
1924	Harold Osborn, USA	6- 6	OR	1980	Gerd Wessig, E. Ger	7- 8¾	WR
1928	Bob King, USA	6- 4½		1984	Dietmar Mögenburg, W. Ger	7- 8½	
1932	Duncan McNaughton, CAN	6- 5½		1988	Gennady Avdeyenko, USSR	7- 9¾	OR
1936	Cornelius Johnson, USA	6- 8	OR	1992	Javier Sotomayor, CUB	7- 8	
1948	John Winter, AUS	6- 6		1996	Charles Austin, USA	7-10	

Pole Vault

Year		Height		Year		Height	
1896	William Hoyt, USA	10-10		1952	Bob Richards, USA	14-11	OR
1900	Irving Baxter, USA	10-10		1956	Bob Richards, USA	14-11½	OR
1904	Charles Dvorak, USA	11- 5¾		1960	Don Bragg, USA	15- 5	OR
1906	Fernand Gonder, FRA	11- 5¾		1964	Fred Hansen, USA	16- 8¾	OR
1908	(TIE) Edward Cooke, USA	12- 2		1968	Bob Seagren, USA	17- 8½	OR
	Alfred Gilbert, USA	12- 2	OR	1972	Wolfgang Nordwig, E. Ger	18- 0½	OR
1912	Harry Babcock, USA	12-11½	OR	1976	Tadeusz Slusarski, POL	18- 0½	=OR
1920	Frank Foss, USA	13- 5	WR	1980	Wladyslaw Kozakiewicz, POL	18-11½	WR
1924	Lee Barnes, USA	12-11½		1984	Pierre Quinon, FRA	18-10¼	
1928	Sabin Carr, USA	13- 9¼	OR	1988	Sergey Bubka, USSR	19- 4¼	OR
1932	Bill Miller, USA	14- 1¾	OR	1992	Maksim Tarasov, UT	19- 0¼	
1936	Earle Meadows, USA	14- 3¼	OR	1996	Jean Galfione, FRA	19-5¼	OR
1948	Guinn Smith, USA	14- 1¼					

Long Jump

Year		Distance		Year		Distance	
1896	Ellery Clark, USA	20-10		1952	Jerome Biffle, USA	24-10	
1900	Alvin Kraenzlein, USA	23- 6¾	OR	1956	Greg Bell, USA	25- 8¼	
1904	Meyer Prinstein, USA	24- 1	OR	1960	Ralph Boston, USA	26- 7¾	OR
1906	Meyer Prinstein, USA	23- 7½		1964	Lynn Davies, GBR	26- 5¾	
1908	Frank Irons, USA	24- 6½	OR	1968	Bob Beamon, USA	29- 2½	WR
1912	Albert Gutterson, USA	24-11¼	OR	1972	Randy Williams, USA	27- 0½	
1920	William Petersson, SWE	23- 5½		1976	Arnie Robinson, USA	27- 4¾	
1924	De Hart Hubbard, USA	24- 5		1980	Lutz Dombrowski, E. Ger	28- 0¼	
1928	Ed Hamm, USA	25- 4½	OR	1984	Carl Lewis, USA	28- 0¼	
1932	Ed Gordon, USA	25- 0¾		1988	Carl Lewis, USA	28- 7¼	
1936	Jesse Owens, USA	26- 5½	OR	1992	Carl Lewis, USA	28- 5½	
1948	Willie Steele, USA	25- 8		1996	Carl Lewis, USA	27-10¾	

Triple Jump

Year		Distance		Year		Distance	
1896	James Connolly, USA	44-11¾		1956	Adhemar da Silva, BRA	53- 7¾	OR
1900	Meyer Prinstein, USA	47- 5¾	OR	1960	Józef Schmidt, POL	55- 2	
1904	Meyer Prinstein, USA	47- 1		1964	Józef Schmidt, POL	55- 3½	OR
1906	Peter O'Connor, GBR/IRL	46- 2¼		1968	Viktor Saneyev, USSR	57- 0¾	WR
1908	Timothy Ahearne, GBR/IRL	48-11¼	OR	1972	Viktor Saneyev, USSR	56-11¼	
1912	Gustaf Lindblom, SWE	48- 5¼		1976	Viktor Saneyev, USSR	56- 8¾	
1920	Vilho Tuulos, FIN	47- 7		1980	Jaak Uudmäe, USSR	56-11¼	
1924	Nick Winter, AUS	50-11¼	WR	1984	Al Joyner, USA	56- 7½	
1928	Mikio Oda, JPN	49-11		1988	Khristo Markov, BUL	57- 9¼	OR
1932	Chuhei Nambu, JPN	51- 7	WR	1992	Mike Conley, USA	59-7½ ʷ	OR
1936	Naoto Tajima, JPN	52- 6	WR	1996	Kenny Harrison, USA	59-4¼	OR
1948	Arne Ahman, SWE	50- 6¼			ʷindicates wind-aided.		
1952	Adhemar da Silva, BRA	53- 2¾	WR				

Shot Put

Year		Distance		Year		Distance	
1896	Bob Garrett, USA	36- 9¾		1928	John Kuck, USA	52- 0¾	WR
1900	Richard Sheldon, USA	46- 3¼	OR	1932	Leo Sexton, USA	52- 6	OR
1904	Ralph Rose, USA	48- 7	WR	1936	Hans Woellke, GER	53- 1¾	OR
1906	Martin Sheridan, USA	40- 5¼		1948	Wilbur Thompson, USA	56- 2	OR
1908	Ralph Rose, USA	46- 7½		1952	Parry O'Brien, USA	57- 1½	OR
1912	Patrick McDonald, USA	50- 4	OR	1956	Parry O'Brien, USA	60-11¼	OR
1920	Ville Pörhölä, FIN	48- 7¼		1960	Bill Nieder, USA	64- 6¾	OR
1924	Bud Houser, USA	49- 2¼		1964	Dallas Long, USA	66- 8½	OR

Year		Distance		Year		Distance	
1968	Randy Matson, USA	67-4¾		1984	Alessandro Andrei, ITA	69-9	
1972	Wladyslaw Komar, POL	69-6	OR	1988	Ulf Timmermann, E. Ger	73-8¾	OR
1976	Udo Beyer, E. Ger	69-0¾		1992	Mike Stulce, USA	71-2½	
1980	Vladimir Kiselyov, USSR	70-0½	OR	1996	Randy Barnes, USA	70-11¼	

Discus Throw

Year		Distance		Year		Distance	
1896	Bob Garrett, USA	95-7½		1952	Sim Iness, USA	180-6	OR
1900	Rudolf Bauer, HUN	118-3		1956	Al Oerter, USA	184-11	OR
1904	Martin Sheridan, USA	128-10½	OR	1960	Al Oerter, USA	194-2	OR
1906	Martin Sheridan, USA	136-0		1964	Al Oerter, USA	200-1	OR
1908	Martin Sheridan, USA	134-2	OR	1968	Al Oerter, USA	212-6	OR
1912	Armas Taipale, FIN	148-3		1972	Ludvik Danek, CZE	211-3	
1920	Elmer Niklander, FIN	146-7		1976	Mac Wilkins, USA	221-5	
1924	Bud Houser, USA	151-4	OR	1980	Viktor Rashchupkin, USSR	218-8	
1928	Bud Houser, USA	155-3		1984	Rolf Danneberg, W. Ger	218-6	
1932	John Anderson, USA	162-4	OR	1988	Jürgen Schult, E. Ger	225-9	OR
1936	Ken Carpenter, USA	165-7	OR	1992	Romas Ubartas, LIT	213-8	
1948	Adolfo Consolini, ITA	173-2		1996	Lars Riedel, GER	227-8	

Hammer Throw

Year		Distance		Year		Distance	
1900	John Flanagan, USA	163-1		1956	Harold Connolly, USA	207-3	OR
1904	John Flanagan, USA	168-1	OR	1960	Vasily Rudenkov, USSR	220-2	OR
1908	John Flanagan, USA	170-4	OR	1964	Romuald Klim, USSR	228-10	OR
1912	Matt McGrath, USA	179-7	OR	1968	Gyula Zsivótzky, HUN	240-8	OR
1920	Pat Ryan, USA	173-5		1972	Anatoly Bondarchuk, USSR	247-8	OR
1924	Fred Tootell, USA	174-10		1976	Yuri Sedykh, USSR	254-4	OR
1928	Pat O'Callaghan, IRL	168-7		1980	Yuri Sedykh, USSR	268-4	WR
1932	Pat O'Callaghan, IRL	176-11		1984	Juha Tiainen, FIN	256-2	
1936	Karl Hein, GER	185-4	OR	1988	Sergey Litvinov, USSR	278-2	OR
1948	Imre Németh, HUN	183-11		1992	Andrei Abduvaliyev, UT	270-9	
1952	József Csérmák, HUN	197-11	WR	1996	Balazs Kiss, HUN	266-6	

Javelin Throw

Year		Distance		Year		Distance	
1908	Eric Lemming, SWE	179-10	WR	1960	Viktor Tsibulenko, USSR	277-8	
1912	Eric Lemming, SWE	198-11	WR	1964	Pauli Nevala, FIN	271-2	
1920	Jonni Myyrä, FIN	215-10		1968	Jänis Lüsis, USSR	295-7	OR
1924	Jonni Myyrä, FIN	206-7		1972	Klaus Wolfermann, W. Ger	296-10	OR
1928	Erik Lundkvist, SWE	218-6	OR	1976	Miklos Németh, HUN	310-4	WR
1932	Matti Järvinen, FIN	238-6		1980	Dainis Kula, USSR	299-2	
1936	Gerhard Stöck, GER	235-8		1984	Arto Härkönen, FIN	284-8	
1948	Kai Tapio Rautavaara, FIN	228-10		1988	Tapio Korjus, FIN	276-6	
1952	Cy Young, USA	242-1	OR	1992	Jan Zelezny, CZE	294-2*	
1956	Egil Danielson, NOR	281-2	WR	1996	Jan Zelezny, CZE	289-3	

*In 1986 the balance point of the javelin was modified and new records have been kept since.

Decathlon

Year		Points		Year		Points	
1904	Thomas Kiely, IRL	6036		1960	Rafer Johnson, USA	8392	OR
1906-08 Not held				1964	Willi Holdorf, GER	7887	
1912	Jim Thrope, USA	8412	WR	1968	Bill Toomey, USA	8193	OR
1920	Helge Lövland, NOR	6803		1972	Nikolai Avilov, USSR	8454	WR
1924	Harold Osborn, USA	7711	WR	1976	Bruce Jenner, USA	8617	WR
1928	Paavo Yrjölä, FIN	8053	WR	1980	Daley Thompson, GBR	8495	
1932	Jim Bausch, USA	8462	WR	1984	Daley Thompson, GBR	8798	=WR
1936	Glenn Morris, USA	7900	WR	1988	Christian Schenk, E. Ger	8488	
1948	Bob Mathias, USA	7139		1992	Robert Zmelik, CZE	8611	
1952	Bob Mathias, USA	7887	WR	1996	Dan O'Brien, USA	8824	
1956	Milt Campbell, USA	7937	OR				

WOMEN

At least 4 gold medals (including relays): Evelyn Ashford, Fanny Blankers-Koen, Betty Cuthbert and Bärbel Eckert Wöckel (4).

100 meters

Year		Time		Year		Time	
1928	Betty Robinson, USA	12.2	=WR	1948	Fanny Blankers-Koen, HOL	11.9	
1932	Stella Walsh, POL*	11.9	=WR	1952	Marjorie Jackson, AUS	11.5	=WR
1936	Helen Stephens, USA	11.5ʷ		1956	Betty Cuthbert, AUS	11.5	

Track & Field (Cont.)

Year		Time	
1960	Wilma Rudolph, USA	11.0 ᵂ	
1964	Wyomia Tyus, USA	11.4	
1968	Wyomia Tyus, USA	11.08	**WR**
1972	Renate Stecher, E. Ger	11.07	
1976	Annegret Richter, W. Ger	11.08	

Year		Time	
1980	Lyudmila Kondratyeva, USSR	11.06	
1984	Evelyn Ashford, USA	10.97	**OR**
1988	Florence Griffith Joyner, USA	10.54ᵂ	
1992	Gail Devers, USA	10.82	**OR**
1996	Gail Devers, USA	10.94	

*An autopsy performed after Walsh's death in 1980 revealed that she was a man.
ᵂindicates wind-aided.

200 meters

Year		Time	
1948	Fanny Blankers-Koen, NED	24.4	
1952	Marjorie Jackson, AUS	23.7	**OR**
1956	Betty Cuthbert, AUS	23.4	**=OR**
1960	Wilma Rudolph, USA	24.0	
1964	Edith McGuire, USA	23.0	**OR**
1968	Irena Szewinska, POL	22.5	**WR**
1972	Renate Stecher, E. Ger	22.40	**=WR**

Year		Time	
1976	Bärbel Eckert, E. Ger	22.37	**OR**
1980	Bärbel Eckert Wockel, E. Ger	22.03	**OR**
1984	Valerie Brisco-Hooks, USA	21.81	**OR**
1988	Florence Griffith Joyner, USA	21.34	**WR**
1992	Gwen Torrence, USA	21.81	
1996	Marie-Jose Perec, FRA	22.12	

400 meters

Year		Time	
1964	Betty Cuthbert, AUS	52.0	
1968	Colette Besson, FRA	52.03	**=OR**
1972	Monika Zehrt, E. Ger	51.08	**OR**
1976	Irena Szewinska, POL	49.29	**WR**
1980	Marita Koch, E. Ger	48.88	**OR**

Year		Time	
1984	Valerie Brisco-Hooks, USA	48.83	**OR**
1988	Olga Bryzgina, USSR	48.65	**OR**
1992	Marie-Jose Perec, FRA	48.83	
1996	Marie-Jose Perec, FRA	48.25	**OR**

800 meters

Year		Time	
1928	Lina Radke, GER	2:16.8	**WR**
1932-56	Not held		
1960	Lyudmila Shevtsova, USSR	2:04.3	**=WR**
1964	Ann Packer, GBR	2:01.1	**OR**
1968	Madeline Manning, USA	2:00.9	**OR**
1972	Hildegard Falck, W. Ger	1:58.55	**OR**

Year		Time	
1976	Tatyana Kazankina, USSR	1:54.94	**WR**
1980	Nadezhda Olizarenko, USSR	1:53.42	**WR**
1984	Doina Melinte, ROM	1:57.60	
1988	Sigrun Wodars, E. Ger	1:56.10	
1992	Ellen van Langen, NED	1:55.54	
1996	Svetlana Masterkova, RUS	1:57.73	

1500 meters

Year		Time	
1972	Lyudmila Bragina, USSR	4:01.4	**WR**
1976	Tatyana Kazankina, USSR	4:05.48	
1980	Tatyana Kazankina, USSR	3:56.6	**OR**
1984	Gabriella Dorio, ITA	4:03.25	

Year		Time	
1988	Paula Ivan, ROM	3:53.96	**OR**
1992	Hassiba Boulmerka, ALG	3:55.30	
1996	Svetlana Masterkova, RUS	4:00.83	

5000 meters

Year		Time	
1984	Maricica Puica, ROM	8:35.96	
1988	Tatyana Samolenko, USSR	8:26.53	**OR**
1992	Elena Romanova, UT	8:46.04	

Year		Time
1996	Wang Junxia, CHN	14:59.88

Note: Event held over 3000 meters from 1984-92.

10,000 meters

Year		Time	
1988	Olga Bondarenko, USSR	31:05.21	**OR**
1992	Derartu Tulu, ETH	31:06.02	

Year		Time	
1996	Fernanda Ribeiro, POR	31:01.63	**OR**

Marathon

Year		Time
1984	Joan Benoit, USA	2:24:52
1988	Rosa Mota, POR	2:25:40

Year		Time
1992	Valentina Yegorova, UT	2:32:41
1996	Fatuma Roba, ETH	2:26:05

100-meter Hurdles

Year		Time	
1932	Babe Didrikson, USA	11.7	**WR**
1936	Trebisonda Valla, ITA	11.7	
1948	Fanny Blankers-Koen, NED	11.2	**OR**
1952	Shirley Strickland, AUS	10.9	**WR**
1956	Shirley Strickland, AUS	10.7	**OR**
1960	Irina Press, USSR	10.8	
1964	Karin Balzer, GER	10.5ᵂ	
1968	Maureen Caird, AUS	10.3	**OR**
1972	Annelie Ehrhardt, E. Ger	12.59	**WR**

Year		Time	
1976	Johanna Schaller, E. Ger	12.77	
1980	Vera Komisova, USSR	12.56	**OR**
1984	Benita Fitzgerald-Brown, USA	12.84	
1988	Yordanka Donkova, BUL	12.38	**OR**
1992	Paraskevi Patoulidou, GRE	12.64	
1996	Ludmila Enquist, SWE	12.58	

ᵂindicates wind-aided.
Note: Event held over 80 meters from 1932-68.

400-meter Hurdles

Year		Time	
1984	Nawal El Moutawakel, MOR	54.61	**OR**
1988	Debra Flintoff-King, AUS	53.17	**OR**

Year		Time	
1992	Sally Gunnell, GBR	53.23	
1996	Deon Hemmings, JAM	52.82	**OR**

4x100-meter Relay

Year		Time		Year		Time	
1928	Canada	48.4	WR	1968	United States	42.87	WR
1932	United States	46.9	WR	1972	West Germany	42.81	WR
1936	United States	46.9		1976	East Germany	42.55	OR
1948	Holland	47.5		1980	East Germany	41.60	WR
1952	United States	45.9	WR	1984	United States	41.65	
1956	Australia	44.5	WR	1988	United States	41.98	
1960	United States	44.5		1992	United States	42.11	
1964	Poland	43.6		1996	United States	41.95	

4x400-meter Relay

Year		Time		Year		Time	
1972	East Germany	3:23.0	WR	1988	Soviet Union	3:15.18	WR
1976	East Germany	3:19.23	WR	1992	Unified Team	3:20.20	
1980	Soviet Union	3:20.2		1996	United States	3:20.91	
1984	United States	3:18.29	OR				

10-kilometer Walk

Year		Time	Year		Time
1992	Chen Yueling, CHN	44:32	1996	Yelena Ninikolayeva, RUS	41:49

High Jump

Year		Height		Year		Height	
1928	Ethel Catherwood, CAN	5- 2½		1968	Miloslava Rezkova, CZE	5-11½	
1932	Jean Shiley, USA	5- 5¼	WR	1972	Ulrike Meyfarth, W. Ger	6- 3½	=WR
1936	Ibolya Csák, HUN	5- 3		1976	Rosemarie Ackermann, E. Ger	6- 4	OR
1948	Alice Coachman, USA	5- 6	OR	1980	Sara Simeoni, ITA	6- 5½	OR
1952	Esther Brand, RSA	5- 5¾		1984	Ulrike Meyfarth, W. Ger	6- 7½	OR
1956	Mildred McDaniel, USA	5- 9¼	WR	1988	Louise Ritter, USA	6- 8	OR
1960	Iolanda Balas, ROM	6- 0¾	OR	1992	Heike Henkel, GER	6- 7½	
1964	Iolanda Balas, ROM	6- 2¾	OR	1996	Stefka Kostadinova, BUL	6-8¾	

Long Jump

Year		Distance		Year		Distance	
1948	Olga Gyarmati, HUN	18- 8¼		1976	Angela Voigt, E. Ger	22- 0¾	
1952	Yvette Williams, NZE	20- 5¾		1980	Tatyana Kolpakova, USSR	23- 2	OR
1956	Elzbieta Krzesinska, POL	20-10	=WR	1984	Anisoara Cusmir-Stanciu, ROM	22-10	
1960	Vyera Krepkina, USSR	20-10¾	OR	1988	Jackie Joyner-Kersee, USA	24- 3¼	OR
1964	Mary Rand, GBR	22- 2¼	WR	1992	Heike Drechsler, GER	23- 5¼	
1968	Viorica Viscopoleanu, ROM	22- 4½	WR	1996	Chioma Ajunwa, NGR	23-4½	
1972	Heidemarie Rosendahl, W. Ger	22- 3					

Triple Jump

Year		Distance
1996	Inessa Kravets, UKR	50-3½

Shot Put

Year		Distance		Year		Distance	
1948	Micheline Ostermeyer, FRA	45- 1½		1976	Ivanka Hristova, BUL	69- 5¼	OR
1952	Galina Zybina, USSR	50- 1¾	WR	1980	Ilona Slupianek, E. Ger	73- 6¼	OR
1956	Tamara Tyshkevich, USSR	54- 5	OR	1984	Claudia Losch, W. Ger	67- 2¼	
1960	Tamara Press, USSR	56-10	OR	1988	Natalia Lisovskaya, USSR	72-11¾	
1964	Tamara Press, USSR	59- 6¼	OR	1992	Svetlana Krivaleva, UT	69- 1¼	
1968	Margitta Gummel, E. Ger	64- 4	WR	1996	Astrid Kumbernuss, GER	67-5½	
1972	Nadezhda Chizhova, USSR	69- 0	WR				

Discus Throw

Year		Distance		Year		Distance	
1928	Halina Konopacka, POL	129-11¾	WR	1968	Lia Manoliu, ROM	191- 2	OR
1932	Lillian Copeland, USA	133- 2	OR	1972	Faina Melnik, USSR	218- 7	OR
1936	Gisela Mauermayer, GER	156- 3	OR	1976	Evelin Schlaak, E. Ger	226- 4	OR
1948	Micheline Ostermeyer, FRA	137- 6		1980	Evelin Schlaak Jahl, E. Ger	229- 6	OR
1952	Nina Romaschkova, USSR	168- 8	OR	1984	Ria Stalman, NED	214- 5	
1956	Olga Fikotová, CZE	176- 1	OR	1988	Martina Hellmann, E. Ger	237- 2½	OR
1960	Nina Ponomaryeva, USSR	180- 9	OR	1992	Maritza Marten, CUB	229-10	
1964	Tamara Press, USSR	187-10	OR	1996	Ilke Wyludda, GER	228-6	

Javelin Throw

Year		Distance		Year		Distance	
1932	Babe Didrikson, USA	143- 4		1948	Herma Bauma, AUT	149- 6	OR
1936	Tilly Fleischer, GER	148- 3	OR	1952	Dana Zátopková, CZE	165- 7	OR

Track & Field (Cont.)

Year		Distance		Year		Distance	
1956	Ineze Jaunzeme, USSR	176-8	**OR**	1980	Maria Colon Rueñes, CUB	224-5	**OR**
1960	Elvira Ozolina, USSR	183-8	**OR**	1984	Tessa Sanderson, GBR	228-2	**OR**
1964	Mihaela Penes, ROM	198-7	**OR**	1988	Petra Felke, E. Ger	245-0	**OR**
1968	Angéla Németh, HUN	198-0		1992	Silke Renk, GER	224-2	
1972	Ruth Fuchs, E. Ger	209-7	**OR**	1996	Heli Rantanen, FIN	222-11	
1976	Ruth Fuchs, E. Ger	216-4	**OR**				

Heptathlon

Year		Points		Year		Points	
1964	Irina Press, USSR	5246	**WR**	1984	Glynis Nunn, AUS	6390	**OR**
1968	Ingrid Becker, W. Ger	5098		1988	Jackie Joyner-Kersee, USA	7291	**WR**
1972	Mary Peters, GBR	4801	**WR**	1992	Jackie Joyner-Kersee, USA	7044	
1976	Siegrun Siegl, E. Ger	4745		1996	Ghada Shouaa, SYR	6780	
1980	Nadezhda Tkachenko, USSR	5083	**WR**				

Note: Seven-event Heptathlon replaced five-event Pentathlon in 1984.

All-Time Leading Medal Winners – Single Games

Athletes who have won the most medals in a single Summer Olympics. Totals include individual, relay and team medals. U.S. athletes are in **bold** type.

MEN

No		Sport	G-S-B
8	Aleksandr Dityatin, USSR (1980)	Gym	3-4-1
7	**Mark Spitz**, USA (1976)	Swim	7-0-0
7	**Willis Lee**, USA (1920)	Shoot	5-1-1
7	**Matt Biondi**, USA (1988)	Swim	5-1-1
7	Boris Shakhlin, USSR (1960)	Gym	4-2-1
7	**Lloyd Spooner**, USA (1920)	Shoot	4-1-2
7	Mikhail Voronin, USSR (1968)	Gym	2-4-1
7	Nikolai Andrianov, USSR (1976)	Gym	2-4-1
6	Vitaly Scherbo, UT (1992)	Gym	6-0-0
6	Li Ning (1984)	Gym	3-2-1
6	Akinori Nakayama, JPN (1968)	Gym	4-1-1
6	Takashi Ono, JPN (1960)	Gym	3-1-2
6	Viktor Chukarin, USSR (1956)	Gym	4-2-0
6	Konrad Frey, GER (1936)	Gym	3-1-2
6	Ville Ritola, FIN (1924)	Track	4-2-0
6	Hubert Van Innis, BEL (1920)	Arch	4-2-0
6	**Carl Osburn**, USA (1920)	Shoot	4-1-1
6	Louis Richardet, SWI (1906)	Shoot	3-3-0
6	**Anton Heida**, USA (1904)	Gym	5-1-0
6	**George Eyser**, USA (1904)	Gym	3-2-1
6	**Burton Downing**, USA (1904)	Cycle	2-3-1
6	Alexei Nemov, RUS (1996)	Gym	2-1-3

WOMEN

No		Sport	G-S-B
7	Maria Gorokhovskaya, USSR (1952)	Gym	2-5-0
6	Kristin Otto, E. Ger (1988)	Swim	6-0-0
6	Agnes Keleti, HUN (1956)	Gym	4-2-0
6	Vera Cáslavská, CZE (1968)	Gym	4-2-0
6	Larisa Latynina, USSR (1956)	Gym	4-1-1
6	Larisa Latynina, USSR (1960)	Gym	3-2-1
6	Daniela Silivas, ROM (1988)	Gym	3-2-1
6	Larisa Latynina, USSR (1964)	Gym	2-2-2
6	Margit Korondi, HUN, (1956)	Gym	1-1-4
6	Kornelia Ender, E. Ger (1976)	Swim	4-1-0
5	Ecaterina Szabó, ROM (1984)	Gym	4-1-0
5	Shane Gould, AUS (1972)	Swim	3-1-1
5	Nadia Comaneci, ROM (1976)	Gym	3-1-1
5	Karin Janz, E. Ger (1972)	Gym	2-2-1
5	Ines Diers, E. Ger (1980)	Swim	2-2-1
5	**Shirley Babashoff**, USA (1976)	Swim	1-4-0
5	**Mary Lou Retton**, USA (1984)	Gym	1-2-2
5	**Shannon Miller**, USA (1992)	Gym	0-2-3

All-Time Leading Medal Winners – Career

MEN

No		Sport	G-S-B
15	Nikolai Andrianov, USSR	Gymnastics	7-5-3
13	Boris Shakhlin, USSR	Gymnastics	7-4-2
13	Edoardo Mangiarotti, ITA	Fencing	6-5-2
13	Takashi Ono, JPN	Gymnastics	5-4-4
12	Paavo Nurmi, FIN	Track/Field	9-3-0
12	Sawao Kato, JPN	Gymnastics	8-3-1
11	**Mark Spitz**, USA	Swimming	9-1-1
11*	**Matt Biondi**, USA	Swimming	8-2-1
11	Viktor Chukarin, USSR	Gymnastics	7-3-1
11	**Carl Osburn**, USA	Shooting	5-4-2
10	**Ray Ewry**, USA	Track/Field	10-0-0
10	**Carl Lewis**, USA	Track/Field	9-1-0
10	Aladár Gerevich, HUN	Fencing	7-1-2
10	Akinori Nakayama, JPN	Gymnastics	6-2-2
10	Aleksandr Dityatin, USSR	Gymnastics	3-6-1
9	Vitaly Scherbo, BLR	Gymnastics	6-0-3
9	**Martin Sheridan**, USA	Track/Field	5-3-1
9	Zoltán Halmay, HUN	Swimming	3-5-1
9	Giulio Gaudini, ITA	Fencing	3-4-2
9	Mikhail Voronin, USSR	Gymnastics	2-6-1
9	Heikki Savolainen, FIN	Gymnastics	2-1-6
9	Yuri Titov, USSR	Gymnastics	1-5-3

*Includes gold medal as preliminary member of 1st-place relay team.

Note: Medals won by Ewry (2-0-0), Sheridan (2-3-0) and Halmay (1-1-0) at the 1906 Intercalated games are not officially recognized by the IOC.

Games Participated In

Andrianov (1972,76,80); **Biondi** (1984,88,92); **Chukarin** (1952,56); **Dityatin** (1976,80); **Ewry** (1900,04,06,08); **Gerevich** (1932,36,48,52,56,60); **Gaudini** (1928,32,36); **Halmay** (1900,04,06,08); **Kato** (1968,72,76); **Lewis** (1984,88,92,96); **Mangiarotti** (1936,48,52,56,60); **Nakayama** (1968,72); **Nurmi** (1920,24,28); **Ono** (1952,56,60,64); **Osburn** (1912,20, 24); **Savolainen** (1928,32,36,48,52); **Scherbo** (1992,96); **Shakhlin** (1956,60,64); **Sheridan** (1904,06,08); **Spitz** (1968,72); **Titov** (1956,60,64); **Voronin** (1968,72).

WOMEN

No		Sport	G-S-B
18	Larissa Latynina, USSR	Gymnastics	9-5-4
11	Vera Cáslavská, CZE	Gymnastics	7-4-0
10	Agnes Keleti, HUN	Gymnastics	5-3-2
10	Polina Astaknova, USSR	Gymnastics	5-2-3
9	Nadia Comaneci, ROM	Gymnastics	5-3-1
9	Lyudmila Tourischeva, USSR	Gymnastics	4-3-2
8	Kornelia Ender, E. Ger	Swimming	4-4-0
8	Dawn Fraser, AUS	Swimming	4-4-0
8	**Shirley Babashoff**, USA	Swimming	2-6-0
8	Sofia Muratova, USSR	Gymnastics	2-2-4
7	Krisztina Egerszegi, HUN	Swimming	5-1-1
7	Irena Kirszenstein Szewinska, POL	Track/Field	3-2-2
7	Shirley Strickland, AUS	Track/Field	3-1-3
7	Maria Gorokhovskaya, USSR	Gymnastics	2-5-0
7	Ildikó Ságiné-Ujlaki-Rejtö, HUN	Fencing	2-3-2
7	**Shannon Miller**, USA	Gymnastics	2-2-3
7	Merlene Ottey, JAM	Track/Field	0-2-5

Games Participated In

Astaknova (1956,60,64); **Babashoff** (1972,76); **Cáslavská** (1960,64,68); **Comaneci** (1976,80); **Egerszegi** (1988,92,96) **Ender** (1972,76); **Fraser** (1956,60,64); **Gorokhovskaya** (1952); **Keleti** (1952,56); **Latynina** (1956,60,64); **Miller** (1992,96); **Muratova** (1956,60); **Ottey** (1980,84,88,92,96) **Sdáginé-Ujlaki-Rejtä** (1960,64,68,72,76); **Strickland** (1948,52,56); **Szewinska** (1964,68,72,76,80); **Tourischeva** (1968, 72,76).

Most Individual Medals
Not including team competition.

		Sport	G-S-B
Men:	12-Nikolai Andrianov, USSR	Gym	6-3-3
Women:	14-Larissa Latynina, USSR	Gym	7-4-3

Most Gold Medals
MEN

No		Sport	G-S-B
10*	Ray Ewry, USA	Track/Field	10-0-0
9	Paavo Nurmi, FIN	Track/Field	9-3-0
9	**Mark Spitz**, USA	Swimming	9-1-1
9	**Carl Lewis**, USA	Track/Field	9-1-0
8	Sawao Kato, JPN	Gymnastics	8-3-1
8†	**Matt Biondi**, USA	Swimming	8-2-1
7	Nikolai Andrianov, USSR	Gymnastics	7-5-3
7	Boris Shakhlin, USSR	Gymnastics	7-4-2
7	Viktor Chukarin, USSR	Gymnastics	7-3-1
7	Aladar Gerevich, HUN	Fencing	7-1-2

*Medals won by Ewry (2-0-0) at the 1906 Intercalated games are not officially recognized by the IOC.
†Includes gold medal as preliminary member of 1st-place relay team.

WOMEN

No		Sport	G-S-B
9	Larissa Latynina, USSR	Gymnastics	9-5-4
7	Vera Cáslavská, CZE	Gymnastics	7-4-0
6	Kristin Otto, E. Ger	Swimming	6-0-0
5	Agnes Keleti, HUN	Gymnastics	5-3-2
5	Nadia Comaneci, ROM	Gymnastics	5-3-1
5	Polina Astaknova, USSR	Gymnastics	5-2-3
5	Krisztina Egerszegi, HUN	Swimming	5-1-1
5	**Jenny Thompson**, USA	Swimming	5-1-0
4	Kornelia Ender, E. Ger	Swimming	4-4-0
4	Dawn Fraser, AUS	Swimming	4-4-0
4	Lyudmila Tourischeva, USSR	Gymnastics	4-3-2
4	**Evelyn Ashford**, USA	Track/Field	4-1-0
4	**Janet Evans**, USA	Swimming	4-1-0
4	Fanny Blankers-Koen, NED	Track/Field	4-0-0
4	Betty Cuthbert, AUS	Track/Field	4-0-0
4	**Pat McCormick**, USA	Diving	4-0-0
4	**Amy Van Dyken**, USA	Swimming	4-0-0
4	Bärbel Eckert Wäckel, E. Ger	Track/Field	4-0-0

Most Silver Medals
MEN

No		Sport	G-S-B
6	Alexandr Dityatin, USSR	Gymnastics	3-6-1
6	Mikhail Voronin, USSR	Gymnastics	2-6-1
5	Nikolai Andrianov, USSR	Gymnastics	7-5-3
5	Edoardo Mangiarotti, ITA	Fencing	6-5-2
5	Zoltán Halmay, HUN	Swimming	3-5-1
5	Gustavo Marzi, ITA	Fencing	2-5-0
5	Yuri Titov, USSR	Gymnastics	1-5-3
5	Viktor Lisitsky, USSR	Gymnastics	0-5-0

WOMEN

No		Sport	G-S-B
6	**Shirley Babashoff**, USA	Swimming	2-6-0
5	Larissa Latynina, USSR	Gymnastics	9-5-4
5	Maria Gorokhovskaya, USSR	Gymnastics	2-5-0
4	Vera Cáslavská, CZE	Gymnastics	7-4-0
4	Kornelia Ender, E. Ger	Swimming	4-4-0
4	Dawn Fraser, AUS	Swimming	4-4-0
4	Erica Zuchold, E. Ger	Gymnastics	0-4-1

Most Bronze Medals
MEN

No		Sport	G-S-B
6	Heikki Savolainen, FIN	Gymnastics	2-1-6
5	Daniel Revenu, FRA	Fencing	1-0-5
5	Philip Edwards, CAN	Track/Field	0-0-5
5	Adrianus Jong, NED	Fencing	0-0-5

WOMEN

No		Sport	G-S-B
5	Merlene Ottey, JAM	Track/Field	0-2-5
4	Larissa Latynina, USSR	Gymnastics	9-5-4
4	Sofia Muratova, USSR	Gymnastics	2-2-4

All-Time Leading USA Medal Winners
Most Overall Medals
MEN

No		Sport	G-S-B	No		Sport	G-S-B
11	Mark Spitz	Swimming	9-1-1	6	Anton Heida	Gymnastics	5-1-0
11*	Matt Biondi	Swimming	8-2-1	6	Don Schollander	Swimming	5-1-0
11	Carl Osburn	Shooting	5-4-2	6	Johnny Weissmuller	Swim/Water Polo	5-0-1
10†	Ray Ewry	Track/Field	10-0-0	6	Alfred Lane	Shooting	5-0-1
10	Carl Lewis	Track/Field	9-1-0	6	Jim Lightbody	Track/Field	4-2-0
9†	Martin Sheridan	Track/Field	5-3-1	6	George Eyser	Gymnastics	3-2-1
8	Charles Daniels	Swimming	5-1-2	6	Michael Plumb	Equestrian	2-4-0
7‡	Tom Jager	Swimming	5-1-1	6	Burton Downing	Cycling	2-3-1
7	Willis Lee	Shooting	5-1-1	6	Bob Garrett	Track/Field	2-2-2
7	Lloyd Spooner	Shooting	4-1-2				

*Includes gold medal as prelim. member of 1st-place relay team.
†Medals won by Ewry (2-0-0) and Sheridan (2-3-0) at the 1906 Intercalated games are not officially recognized by the IOC.
‡Includes 3 gold medals as prelim. member of 1st-place relay teams.

Games Participated In

Biondi (1984,88,92); **Daniels** (1904,06,08); **Downing** (1904); **Ewry** (1900,04,06,08); **Eyser** (1904); **Garrett** (1896,1900); **Heida** (1904); **Jager** (1984,88,92); **Lane** (1912,20); **Lee** (1920); **Lewis** (1984,88,92,96); **Lightbody** (1904,06); **Osburn** (1912,20,24); **Plumb** (1960, 64,68,72,76,84); **Schollander** (1964, 68); **Sheridan** (1904,06,08); **Spitz** (1968,72); **Spooner** (1920); **Weissmuller** (1924,28).

WOMEN

No		Sport	G-S-B
8	Shirley Babashoff	Swimming	2-6-0
7	Shannon Miller	Gymnastics	2-2-3
6	Jenny Thompson	Swimming	5-1-0
6	Jackie Joyner-Kersee	Track/Field	3-1-2
5	Evelyn Ashford	Track/Field	4-1-0
5	Janet Evans	Swimming	4-1-0
5	*Mary T. Meagher	Swimming	3-1-1
5	Florence Griffith Joyner	Track/Field	3-2-0
5	Mary Lou Retton	Gymnastics	1-2-2
4	Pat McCormick	Diving	4-0-0
4	Amy Van Dyken	Swimming	4-0-0
4	Valerie Brisco-Hooks	Track/Field	3-1-0
4	Nancy Hogshead	Swimming	3-1-0
4	Sharon Stouder	Swimming	3-1-0

No		Sport	G-S-B
4	Wyomia Tyus	Track/Field	3-1-0
4	Wilma Rudolph	Track/Field	3-0-1
4	Chris von Saltza	Swimming	3-1-0
4	Sue Pederson	Swimming	2-2-0
4	Jan Henne	Swimming	2-1-1
4	Dorothy Poynton Hill	Diving	2-1-1
4	*Summer Sanders	Swimming	2-1-1
4	*Dara Torres	Swimming	2-1-1
4	Kathy Ellis	Swimming	2-0-2
4	Georgia Coleman	Diving	1-2-1

*Includes silver medal as prelim. member of 2nd-place relay team.

Games Participated In

Ashford (1976,84,88,92); **Babashoff** (1972,76); **Brisco-Hooks** (1984,88); **Coleman** (1928,32); **Ellis** (1964); **Evans** (1988,92); **Griffith Joyner** (1984,88); **Henne** (1968); **Hogshead** (1984); **Joyner-Kersee** (1984,88,92,96); **McCormick** (1952,56); **Meagher** (1984,88); **Miller** (1992, 96); **Pederson** (1968); **Poynton Hill** (1928,32,36); **Retton** (1984); **Rudolph** (1956,60); **Sanders** (1992); **Stouder** (1964); **Thompson** (1988,92,96); **Torres** (1984,88,92); **Tyus** (1964,68); **Van Dyken** (1996); **von Saltza** (1960).

Most Gold Medals

MEN

No		Sport	G-S-B
10	*Raymond Ewry	Track/Field	10-0-0
9	Mark Spitz	Swimming	9-1-1
9	Carl Lewis	Track/Field	9-1-0
8	‡Matt Biondi	Swimming	8-2-1
5	Carl Osburn	Shooting	5-4-2
5	*Martin Sheridan	Track/Field	5-3-1
5	Charles Daniels	Swimming	5-1-2
5	‡Tom Jager	Swimming	5-1-1
5	Willis Lee	Shooting	5-1-1
5	Anton Heida	Gymnastics	5-1-0
5	Don Schollander	Swimming	5-1-0
5	Johnny Weissmuller	Swim/Water Polo	5-0-1
5	Alfred Lane	Shooting	5-0-1
5	Morris Fisher	Shooting	5-0-0
4	Jim Lightbody	Track/Field	4-2-0
4	Lloyd Spooner	Shooting	4-1-2
4	Greg Louganis	Diving	4-1-0
4	John Naber	Swimming	4-1-0
4	Meyer Prinstein	Track/Field	4-1-0
4	Mel Sheppard	Track/Field	4-1-0
4	Marcus Hurley	Cycling	4-0-1
4	Harrison Dillard	Track/Field	4-0-0
4	Archie Hahn	Track/Field	4-0-0
4	Alvin Kraenzlein	Track/Field	4-0-0
4	Al Oerter	Track/Field	4-0-0
4	Jesse Owens	Track/Field	4-0-0

*Medals won by Ewry (2-0-0) and Sheridan (2-3-0) at the 1906 Intercalated games are not officially recognized by the IOC.

†Includes gold medal as prelim. member of 1st-place relay team.

‡ Includes 3 gold medals as prelim. member of 1st-place relay teams.

WOMEN

No		Sport	G-S-B
5	Jenny Thompson	Swimming	5-1-0
4	Evelyn Ashford	Track/Field	4-1-0
4	Janet Evans	Swimming	4-1-0

No		Sport	G-S-B
4	Pat McCormick	Diving	4-0-0
4	Amy Van Dyken	Swimming	4-0-0
3	Florence Griffith Joyner	Track/Field	3-2-0
3	Jackie Joyner-Kersee	Track/Field	3-1-2
3	*Mary T. Meagher	Swimming	3-1-1
3	Valerie Brisco-Hooks	Track/Field	3-1-0
3	Nancy Hogshead	Swimming	3-1-0
3	Sharon Stouder	Swimming	3-1-0
3	Wyomia Tyus	Track/Field	3-1-0
3	Chris von Saltza	Swimming	3-1-0
3	Wilma Rudolph	Track/Field	3-0-1
3	Melissa Belote	Swimming	3-0-0
3	Ethelda Bleibtrey	Swimming	3-0-0
3	Tracy Caulkins	Swimming	3-0-0
3	*Nicole Haislett	Swimming	3-0-0
3	Helen Madison	Swimming	3-0-0
3	Debbie Meyer	Swimming	3-0-0
3	Sandra Neilson	Swimming	3-0-0
3	Martha Norelius	Swimming	3-0-0
3	*Carrie Steinseifer	Swimming	3-0-0

*Includes gold medal as prelim. member of 1st-place relay team.

Most Silver Medals
MEN

No		Sport	G-S-B
4	Carl Osburn	Shooting	5-4-2
4	Michael Plumb	Equestrian	2-4-0
3	Martin Sheridan	Track/Field	5-3-1
3	Burton Downing	Cycling	2-3-1
3	Irving Baxter	Track/Field	2-3-0
3	Earl Thomson	Equestrian	2-3-0

WOMEN

No		Sport	G-S-B
6	Shirley Babashoff	Swimming	2-6-0

All-Time Medal Standings, 1896-1996

All-time Summer Games medal standings, according to *The Golden Book of the Olympic Games*. Medal counts include the 1906 Intercalated Games, which are not recognized by the IOC.

#	Country	G	S	B	Total
1	**United States**	832	634	553	2019
2	USSR (1952-88)	395	319	296	1010
3	Great Britain	169	223	218	610
4	France	175	179	206	560
5	Sweden	132	151	174	457
6	Italy	166	135	144	445
	East Germany (1968-88)	159	150	136	445
8	Hungary	142	129	155	426
9	Germany (1896-64,92–)	124	121	134	379
10	West Germany (1968-88)	77	104	120	301
11	Finland	99	80	113	292
	Australia	86	85	121	292
13	Japan	92	89	97	278
14	Romania	63	77	99	239
15	Poland	50	67	110	227
16	Canada	48	78	90	216
17	Netherlands	49	58	81	188
18	Bulgaria	43	76	63	182
19	Switzerland	46	69	59	174
20	China	52	63	49	164
21	Denmark	38	60	57	155
22	Czechoslovakia (1924-92)	49	49	44	142
23	Belgium	37	49	49	135
24	South Korea	38	42	46	126
25	Norway	45	41	38	124
26	Greece	28	42	43	113
27	Unified Team (1992)	45	38	29	112
28	Cuba	44	33	31	108
29	Yugoslavia (1924-88, 96)	27	31	32	90
30	Austria	18	31	34	83
31	New Zealand	29	12	29	70
32	Russia (1896-1912, 96–)	26	24	18	68
33	Spain	22	25	17	64
34	Turkey	30	16	13	59
35	South Africa	19	18	21	58
36	Brazil	12	13	29	54
37	Argentina	13	21	16	50
38	Kenya	14	17	16	47
39	Mexico	9	13	19	41
40	Iran	5	13	18	36
41	Jamaica	5	16	9	30
42	North Korea	8	6	12	26
43	Estonia	7	6	10	23
44	Great Britain/Ireland	6	11	3	20
45	Ireland	8	5	6	19
46	Ethiopia	8	1	7	16
	Egypt	6	5	5	16
48	India	8	3	4	15
	Portugal	3	4	8	15
50	Nigeria	2	5	7	14
	Mongolia	0	5	9	14
52	Czech Republic	4	3	4	11
	Morocco	4	2	5	11
54	Indonesia	3	4	3	10
	Pakistan	3	3	4	10
56	Uruguay	2	1	6	9
	Trinidad & Tobago	1	2	6	9
	Philippines	0	2	7	9
59	Venezuela	1	2	5	8
	Chile	0	6	2	8
61	Algeria	3	0	4	7
	Latvia	0	5	2	7
63	Uganda	1	3	2	6
	Tunisia	1	2	3	6
	Thailand	1	1	4	6
	Colombia	0	2	4	6
	Bohemia	0	1	5	6
	Puerto Rico	0	1	5	6
69	Croatia	1	2	2	5
	Chinese Taipei	0	3	2	5
71	Peru	1	3	0	4
	Bahamas	1	1	2	4
	Lithuania	1	0	3	4
	Namibia	0	4	0	4
	Lebanon	0	2	2	4
	Slovenia	0	2	2	4
	Ghana	0	1	3	4
78	Luxembourg	2	1	0	3
	Slovakia	1	1	1	3
	Israel	0	1	2	3
	Malaysia	0	1	2	3
82	Armenia	1	1	0	2
	Costa Rica	1	1	0	2
	Syria	1	1	0	2
	Japan/Korea	1	0	1	2
	Surinam	1	0	1	2
	Tanzania	0	2	0	2
	Cameroon	0	1	1	2
	Great Britain/USA	0	1	1	2
	Haiti	0	1	1	2
	Iceland	0	1	1	2
	Moldova	0	1	1	2
	Russia/Estonia	0	1	1	2
	United Arab Republic	0	1	1	2
	Uzbekistan	0	1	1	2
	Zambia	0	1	1	2
	The Antilles	0	0	2	2
	Georgia	0	0	2	2
	Panama	0	0	2	2
100	Australia/New Zealand	1	0	0	1
	Burkina Faso	1	0	0	1
	Cuba/USA	1	0	0	1
	Denmark/Sweden	1	0	0	1
	Ecuador	1	0	0	1
	Gr. Britain/Ireland/Germany	1	0	0	1
	Gr. Britain/Ireland/USA	1	0	0	1
	Hong Kong	1	0	0	1
	Ireland/USA	1	0	0	1
	Zimbabwe	1	0	0	1
	Azerbaijan	0	1	0	1
	Belgium/Greece	0	1	0	1
	Ceylon	0	1	0	1
	France/USA	0	1	0	1
	France/Gr. Britain/Ireland	0	1	0	1
	Ivory Coast	0	1	0	1
	Netherlands Antilles	0	1	0	1
	Senegal	0	1	0	1
	Singapore	0	1	0	1
	Smyrna	0	1	0	1
	Tonga	0	1	0	1
	Virgin Islands	0	1	0	1
	Australia/Great Britain	0	0	1	1
	Bermuda	0	0	1	1
	Bohemia/Great Britain	0	0	1	1
	Djibouti	0	0	1	1
	Dominican Republic	0	0	1	1
	France/Great Britain	0	0	1	1
	Guyana	0	0	1	1
	Iraq	0	0	1	1
	Mexico/Spain	0	0	1	1
	Mozambique	0	0	1	1
	Niger	0	0	1	1
	Qatar	0	0	1	1
	Scotland	0	0	1	1
	Thessalonika	0	0	1	1
	Wales	0	0	1	1

Combined totals:	G	S	B	Total
USSR/UT/Russia	466	381	343	1190
Germany/E. Ger/W. Ger	360	375	390	1125

THE 2000 ESPN INFORMATION PLEASE SPORTS ALMANAC

OLYMPICS STATISTICS

SEC B

THROUGH THE YEARS
1924-1998
WINTER OLYMPICS

PAGE 684

The Winter Olympics

The move toward a winter version of the Olympics began in 1908 when figure skating made an appearance at the Summer Games in London. Ten-time world champion Ulrich Salchow of Sweden, who originated the backwards, one revolution jump that bears his name, and Madge Syers of Britain were the first singles champions. Germans Anna Hubler and Heinrich Berger won the pairs competition.

Organizers of the 1916 Summer Games in Berlin planned to introduce a "Skiing Olympia," featuring nordic events in the Black Forest, but the Games were cancelled after the outbreak of World War I in 1914.

The Games resumed in 1920 at Antwerp, Belgium, where figure skating returned and ice hockey was added as a medal event. Sweden's Gillis Grafstrom and Magda Julin took individual honors, while Ludovika and Walter Jakobsson were the top pair. In hockey, Canada won the gold medal with the United States second and Czechoslovakia third.

Despite the objections of Modern Olympics' founder Baron Pierre de Coubertin and the resistance of the Scandinavian countries, which had staged their own Nordic championships every four or five years from 1901-26 in Sweden, the International Olympic Committee sanctioned an "International Winter Sports Week" at Chamonix, France, in 1924. The 11-day event, which included nordic skiing, speed skating, figure skating, ice hockey and bobsledding, was a huge success and was retroactively called the first Olympic Winter Games.

Seventy years after those first cold weather Games, the 17th edition of the Winter Olympics took place in Lillehammer, Norway, in 1994. The event ended the four-year Olympic cycle of staging both Winter and Summer Games in the same year and began a new schedule that calls for the two Games to alternate every two years.

Year	No	Location	Dates	Nations	Most medals	USA Medals
1924	I	Chamonix, FRA	Jan. 25-Feb. 4	16	Norway (4-7-6–17)	1-2-1– 4 (3rd)
1928	II	St. Moritz, SWI	Feb. 11-19	25	Norway (6-4-5–15)	2-2-2– 6 (2nd)
1932	III	Lake Placid, USA	Feb. 4-15	17	USA (6-4-2–12)	6-4-2–12 (1st)
1936	IV	Garmisch-Partenkirchen, GER	Feb. 6-16	28	Norway (7-5-3–15)	1-0-3– 4 (T-5th)
1940-a	–	Sapporo, JPN	Cancelled (WWII)			
1944	–	Cortina d'Ampezzo, ITA	Cancelled (WWII)			
1948	V	St. Moritz, SWI	Jan. 30-Feb. 8	28	Norway (4-3-3–10), Sweden (4-3-3–10) & Switzerland (3-4-3–10)	3-4-2– 9 (4th)
1952-b	VI	Oslo, NOR	Feb. 14-25	30	Norway (7-3-6–16)	4-6-1–11 (2nd)
1956-c	VII	Cortina d'Ampezzo, ITA	Jan. 26-Feb. 5	32	USSR (7-3-6–16)	2-3-2– 7 (T-4th)
1960	VIII	Squaw Valley, USA	Feb. 18-28	30	USSR (7-5-9–21)	3-4-3–10 (2nd)
1964	IX	Innsbruck, AUT	Jan. 29-Feb. 9	36	USSR (11-8-6–25)	1-2-3– 6 (7th)
1968-d	X	Grenoble, FRA	Feb. 6-18	37	Norway (6-6-2–14)	1-5-1– 7 (T-7th)
1972	XI	Sapporo, JPN	Feb. 3-13	35	USSR (8-5-3–16)	3-2-3– 8 (6th)
1976-e	XII	Innsbruck, AUT	Feb. 4-15	37	USSR (13-6-8–27)	3-3-4–10 (T-3rd)
1980	XIII	Lake Placid, USA	Feb. 14-23	37	E. Germany (9-7-7–23)	6-4-2–12 (3rd)
1984	XIV	Sarajevo, YUG	Feb. 7-19	49	USSR (6-10-9–25)	4-4-0– 8 (T-5th)
1988	XV	Calgary, CAN	Feb. 13-28	57	USSR (11-9-9–29)	2-1-3– 6 (T-8th)
1992-f	XVI	Albertville, FRA	Feb. 8-23	63	Germany (10-10-6–26)	5-4-2–11 (6th)
1994-g	XVII	Lillehammer, NOR	Feb. 12-27	67	Norway (10-11-5–26)	6-5-2–13 (T-5th)
1998	XVIII	Nagano, JPN	Feb. 7-22	72	Germany (12-9-8–29)	6-3-4–13 (5th)
2002	XIX	Salt Lake City, USA	Feb. 8-24			
2006	XX	Turin, ITA	TBA			

a–The 1940 Winter Games are originally scheduled for Sapporo, but Japan resigns as host in 1937 when the Sino-Japanese war breaks out. St. Moritz is the next choice, but the Swiss feel that ski instructors should not be considered professionals and the IOC withdraws its offer. Finally, Garmisch-Partenkirchen is asked to serve again as host, but the Germans invade Poland in 1939 and the Games are eventually cancelled.

b–Germany and Japan are allowed to rejoin the Olympic community for the first time since World War II. Though a divided country, the Germans send a joint East-West team through 1964.

c–The Soviet Union (USSR) participates in its first Winter Olympics and takes home the most medals, including the gold medal in ice hockey.

d–East Germany and West Germany officially send separate teams for the first time and will continue to do so through 1988.

e–The IOC grants the 1976 Winter Games to Denver in May 1970, but in 1972 Colorado voters reject a $5 million bond issue to finance the undertaking. Denver immediately withdraws as host and the IOC selects Innsbruck, the site of the 1964 Games, to take over.

f–Germany sends a single team after East and West German reunification in 1990 and the USSR competes as the Unified Team after the breakup of the Soviet Union in 1991.

g–The IOC moves the Winter Games' four-year cycle ahead two years in order to separate them from the Summer Games and alternate Olympics every two years.

Event-by-Event

Gold medal winners from 1924-98 in the following events: Alpine Skiing, Biathlon, Bobsled, Cross-country Skiing, Curling, Figure Skating, Ice Hockey, Luge, Nordic Combined, Ski Jumping, Snowboarding and Speed Skating.

ALPINE SKIING

MEN

Multiple gold medals: Jean-Claude Killy, Toni Sailer and Alberto Tomba (3); Hermann Maier, Henri Oreiller, Ingemar Stenmark and Markus Wasmeier (2).

Downhill

Year		Time	Year		Time
1948	Henri Oreiller, FRA	2:55.0	1976	Franz Klammer AUT	1:45.73
1952	Zeno Colò, ITA	2:30.8	1980	Leonhard Stock, AUS	1:45.50
1956	Toni Sailer, AUT	2:52.2	1984	Bill Johnson, USA	1:45.59
1960	Jean Vuarnet, FRA	2:06.0	1988	Pirmin Zurbriggen, SWI	1:59.63
1964	Egon Zimmermann, AUT	2:18.16	1992	Patrick Ortlieb, AUT	1:50.37
1968	Jean-Claude Killy, FRA	1:59.85	1994	Tommy Moe, USA	1:45.75
1972	Bernhard Russi, SWI	1:51.43	1998	Jean-Luc Cretier, FRA	1:50.11

Slalom

Year		Time	Year		Time
1948	Edi Reinalter, SWI	2:10.3	1976	Piero Gros, ITA	2:03.29
1952	Othmar Schneider, AUT	2:00.0	1980	Ingemar Stenmark, SWE	1:44.26
1956	Toni Sailer, AUT	3:14.7	1984	Phil Mahre, USA	1:39.41
1960	Ernst Hinterseer, AUT	2:08.9	1988	Alberto Tomba, ITA	1:39.47
1964	Pepi Stiegler, AUT	2:11.13	1992	Finn Christian Jagge, NOR	1:44.39
1968	Jean-Claude Killy, FRA	1:39.73	1994	Thomas Stangassinger, AUT	2:02.02
1972	Francisco Ochoa, SPA	1:49.27	1998	Hans-Petter Buraas, NOR	1:49.31

Giant Slalom

Year		Time	Year		Time
1952	Stein Eriksen, NOR	2:25.0	1980	Ingemar Stenmark, SWE	2:40.74
1956	Toni Sailer, AUS	3:00.1	1984	Max Julen, SWI	2:41.18
1960	Roger Staub, SWI	1:48.3	1988	Alberto Tomba, ITA	2:06.37
1964	Francois Bonlieu, FRA	1:46.71	1992	Alberto Tomba, ITA	2:06.98
1968	Jean-Claude Killy, FRA	3:29.28	1994	Markus Wasmeier, GER	2:52.46
1972	Gustav Thöni, ITA	3:09.62	1998	Hermann Maier, AUT	2:38.51
1976	Heini Hemmi, SWI	3:26.97			

Super Giant Slalom

Year		Time	Year		Time
1988	Frank Piccard, FRA	1:39.66	1994	Markus Wasmeier, GER	1:32.53
1992	Kjetil Andre Aamodt, NOR	1:13.04	1998	Hermann Maier, AUT	1:34.82

Alpine Combined

Year		Points	Year		Points
1936	Franz Pfnür, GER	99.25	1992	Josef Polig, ITA	14.58
1948	Henri Oreiller, FRA	3.27	Year		Time
1952-84 Not held			1994	Lasse Kjus, NOR	3:17.53
1988	Hubert Strolz, AUT	36.55	1998	Mario Reiter, AUT	3:08.06

WOMEN

Multiple gold medals: Deborah Compagnoni, Vreni Schneider and Katja Seizinger (3); Marielle Goitschel, Trude Jochum-Beiser, Petra Kronberger, Andrea Mead Lawrence, Rosi Mittermaier, Marie-Theres Nadig, Hanni Wenzel and Pernilla Wiberg (2).

Downhill

Year		Time	Year		Time
1948	Hedy Schlunegger, SWI	2:28.3	1976	Rosi Mittermaier, W. Ger	1:46.16
1952	Trude Jochum-Beiser, AUT	1:47.1	1980	Annemarie Moser-Pröll, AUT	1:37.52
1956	Madeleine Berthod, SWI	1:40.7	1984	Michela Figini, SWI	1:13.36
1960	Heidi Biebl, GER	1:37.6	1988	Marina Kiehl, W. Ger	1:25.86
1964	Christl Haas, AUT	1:55.39	1992	Kerrin Lee-Gartner, CAN	1:52.55
1968	Olga Pall, AUT	1:40.87	1994	Katja Seizinger, GER	1:35.93
1972	Marie-Theres Nadig, SWI	1:36.68	1998	Katja Seizinger, GER	1:28.89

Slalom

Year		Time	Year		Time
1948	Gretchen Fraser, USA	1:57.2	1976	Rosi Mittermaier, W. Ger	1:30.54
1952	Andrea Mead Lawrence, USA	2:10.6	1980	Hanni Wenzel, LIE	1:25.09
1956	Renée Colliard, SWI	1:52.3	1984	Paoletta Magoni, ITA	1:36.47
1960	Anne Heggtveit, CAN	1:49.6	1988	Vreni Schneider, SWI	1:36.69
1964	Christine Goitschel, FRA	1:29.86	1992	Petra Kronberger, AUT	1:32.68
1968	Marielle Goitschel, FRA	1:25.86	1994	Vreni Schneider, SWI	1:56.01
1972	Barbara Cochran, USA	1:31.24	1998	Hilde Gerg, GER	1:32.40

Giant Slalom

Year		Time	Year		Time
1952	Andrea Mead Lawrence, USA	2:06.8	1980	Hanni Wenzel, LIE	2:41.66
1956	Ossi Reichert, GER	1:56.5	1984	Debbie Armstrong, USA	2:20.98
1960	Yvonne Rügg, SWI	1:39.9	1988	Vreni Schneider, SWI	2:06.49
1964	Marielle Goitschel, FRA	1:52.24	1992	Pernilla Wiberg, SWE	2:12.74
1968	Nancy Greene, CAN	1:51.97	1994	Deborah Compagnoni, ITA	2:30.97
1972	Marie-Theres Nadig, SWI	1:29.90	1998	Deborah Compagnoni, ITA	2:50.59
1976	Kathy Kreiner, CAN	1:29.13			

Super Giant Slalom

Year		Time	Year		Time
1988	Sigrid Wolf, AUT	1:19.03	1994	Diann Roffe-Steinrotter, USA	1:22.15
1992	Deborah Compagnoni, ITA	1:21.22	1998	Picabo Street, USA	1:18.02

Alpine Combined

Year		Points	Year		Points
1936	Christl Cranz, GER	97.06	1992	Petra Kronberger, AUT	2.55
1948	Trude Beiser, AUT	6.58	**Year**		**Time**
1952-84	Not held		1994	Pernilla Wiberg, SWE	3:05.16
1988	Anita Wachter, AUT	29.25	1998	Katja Seizinger, GER	2:40.74

BIATHLON

MEN

Multiple gold medals (including relays): Aleksandr Tikhonov (4); Mark Kirchner and Ricco Gross (3); Anatoly Alyabyev, Ivan Biakov, Sergei Chepikov, Sven Fischer, Frank Luck, Viktor Mamatov, Frank-Peter Roetsch, Magnar Solberg and Dmitri Vasilyev (2).

10 kilometers

Year		Time	Year		Time
1980	Frank Ullrich, E. Ger	32:10.69	1992	Mark Kirchner, GER	26:02.3
1984	Erik Kvalfoss, NOR	30:53.8	1994	Sergei Chepikov, RUS	28:07.0
1988	Frank-Peter Roetsch, E. Ger	25:08.1	1998	Ole Einar Bjoerndalen, NOR	27:16.2

20 kilometers

Year		Time	Year		Time
1960	Klas Lestander, SWE	1:33:21.6	1984	Peter Angerer, W. Ger	1:11:52.7
1964	Vladimir Melanin, USSR	1:20:26.8	1988	Frank-Peter Roetsch, E. Ger	56:33.3
1968	Magnar Solberg, NOR	1:13:45.9	1992	Yevgeny Redkine, UT	57:34.4
1972	Magnar Solberg, NOR	1:15:55.50	1994	Sergei Tarasov, RUS	57:25.3
1976	Nikolai Kruglov, USSR	1:14:12.26	1998	Halvard Hanevold, NOR	56:16.4
1980	Anatoly Alyabyev, USSR	1:08:16.31			

4x7.5-kilometer Relay

Year		Time	Year		Time	Year		Time
1968	Soviet Union	2:13:02.4	1980	Soviet Union	1:34:03.27	1992	Germany	1:24:43.5
1972	Soviet Union	1:51:44.92	1984	Soviet Union	1:38:51.7	1994	Germany	1:30:22.1
1976	Soviet Union	1:57:55.64	1988	Soviet Union	1:22:30.0	1998	Germany	1:21.36.2

WOMEN

Multiple gold medals (including relays): Myriam Bedard and Anfisa Reztsova (2). Note that Reztsova won a third gold medal in 1988 in the Cross-country 4x5-kilometer Relay.

7.5 kilometers

Year		Time	Year		Time
1992	Anfisa Reztsova, UT	24:29.2	1998	Galina Koukleva, RUS	23:08.0
1994	Myriam Bedard, CAN	26:08.8			

15 kilometers

Year		Time	Year		Time
1992	Antje Misersky, GER	51:47.2	1998	Ekaterina Dafovska, BUL	54:52.0
1994	Myriam Bedard, CAN	52:06.6			

4x7.5-kilometer Relay

Year		Time	Year		Time	Year		Time
1992	France	1:15:55.6	1994	Russia	1:47:19.5	1998	Germany	1:40:13.6

Note: Event featured three skiers per team in 1992.

BOBSLED

Only drivers are listed in parentheses.

Multiple gold medals: DRIVERS—Meinhard Nehmer (3); Billy Fiske, Wolfgang Hoppe, Eugenio Monti, Andreas Ostler and Gustav Weder (2). CREW—Bernard Germeshausen (3); Donat Acklin, Luciano De Paolis, Cliff Gray, Lorenz Nieberl and Dietmar Schauerhammer (2).

Two-Man

Year		Time	Year		Time
1932	United States (Hubert Stevens)	8:14.74	1972	West Germany (Wolfgang Zimmerer)	4:57.07
1936	United States (Ivan Brown)	5:29.29	1976	East Germany (Meinhard Nehmer)	3:44.42
1948	Switzerland (Felix Endrich)	5:29.2	1980	Switzerland (Erich Schärer)	4:09.36
1952	Germany (Andreas Ostler)	5:24.54	1984	East Germany (Wolfgang Hoppe)	3:25.56
1956	Italy (Lamberto Dalla Costa)	5:30.14	1988	Soviet Union (Janis Kipurs)	3:54.19
1960	Not held		1992	Switzerland I (Gustav Weder)	4:03.26
1964	Great Britain (Anthony Nash)	4:21.90	1994	Switzerland I (Gustav Weder)	3:30.81
1968	Italy (Eugenio Monti)	4:41.54	1998	Italy I (Guenther Huber)	3:37.24

Four-Man

Year		Time	Year		Time
1924	Switzerland (Eduard Scherrer)	5:45.54	1968	Italy (Eugenio Monti)	2:17.39
1928	United States (Billy Fiske)	3:20.5	1972	Switzerland (Jean Wicki)	4:43.07
1932	United States (Billy Fiske)	7:53.68	1976	East Germany (Meinhard Nehmer)	3:40.43
1936	Switzerland (Pierre Musy)	5:19.85	1980	East Germany (Meinhard Nehmer)	3:59.92
1948	United States (Francis Tyler)	5:20.1	1984	East Germany (Wolfgang Hoppe)	3:20.22
1952	Germany (Andreas Ostler)	5:07.84	1988	Switzerland (Ekkehard Fasser)	3:47.51
1956	Switzerland (Franz Kapus)	5:10.44	1992	Austria I (Ingo Appelt)	3:53.90
1960	Not held		1994	Germany II (Harald Czudaj)	3:27.78
1964	Canada (Vic Emery)	4:14.46	1998	Germany II (Christoph Langen)	2:39.41

Note: Five-man sleds were used in 1928.

CROSS-COUNTRY SKIING

There have been two significant changes in men's and women's cross-country racing since the end of the 1984 Winter Games in Sarajevo. First, the classical and freestyle (i.e., skating) techniques were designated for specific events beginning in 1988, and the Pursuit race was introduced in 1992.

MEN

Multiple gold medals (including relays): Bjorn Dählie (8); Sixten Jernberg, Gunde Svan, Thomas Wassberg and Nikolai Zimyatov (4); Veikko Hakulinen, Eero Mäntyranta and Vegard Ulvang (3); Hallgeir Brenden, Harald Grönningen, Thorlief Haug, Jan Ottoson, Päl Tyldum and Vyacheslav Vedenine (2).

Multiple gold medals (including Nordic Combined): Johan Gröttumsbråten and Thorlief Haug (3).

10-kilometer Classical

Year		Time	Year		Time
1924-88	Not held		1994	Bjorn Dählie, NOR	24:20.1
1992	Vegard Ulvang, NOR	27:36.0	1998	Bjorn Dählie, NOR	27:24.5

15-kilometer Combined Pursuit

A 15-km Freestyle race in which the starting order is determined by order of finish in the 10-km Classical race. Time given is combined time of both events.

Year		Time	Year		Time
1924-88	Not held		1994	Bjorn Dählie, NOR	1:00.08.8
1992	Bjorn Dählie, NOR	1:05:37.9	1998	Thomas Alsgaard, NOR	1:07:01.7

15-kilometer Classical (Discont.)

Discontinued in 1992 and replaced by the freestyle 15-km Combined Pursuit. Event was held over 18 kilometers from 1924-52.

Year		Time	Year		Time
1924	Thorleif Haug, NOR	1:14:31.0	1964	Eero Mäntyranta, FIN	50:54.1
1928	Johan Gröttumsbråten, NOR	1:37:01.0	1968	Harald Grönningen, NOR	47:54.2
1932	Sven Utterström, SWE	1:23:07.0	1972	Sven-Ake Lundback, SWE	45:28.24
1936	Erik-August Larsson, SWE	1:14:38.0	1976	Nikolai Bazhukov, USSR	43:58.47
1948	Martin Lundström, SWE	1:13:50.0	1980	Thomas Wassberg, SWE	41:57.63
1952	Hallgeir Brenden, NOR	1:01:34.0	1984	Gunde Svan, SWE	41:25.6
1956	Hallgeir Brenden, NOR	49:39.0	1988	Mikhail Devyatyarov, USSR	41:18.9
1960	Hakon Brusveen NOR	51:55.5			

Youngest and Oldest Gold Medalists in an Individual Event

Youngest: MEN— Toni Nieminen, Finland, Large Hill Ski Jumping, 1992 (16 years, 261 days); WOMEN—Tara Lipinski, United States, Figure Skating, 1998 (15 years, 256 days).

Oldest: MEN— Magnar Solberg, NOR, 20-km Biathlon, 1972 (35 years, 4 days); WOMEN— Christina Baas-Kaiser, Holland, 3,000m Speed Skating, 1972 (33 years, 268 days).

30-kilometer Freestyle (Discont.)
Discontinued in 1998 and replaced by the 30-kilometer Classical.

Year	Time	Year	Time
1924-52 Not held		1976 Sergei Saveliev, USSR	1:30:29.38
1956 Veikko Hakulinen, FIN	1:44:06.0	1980 Nikolai Zimyatov, USSR	1:27:02.80
1960 Sixten Jernberg, SWE	1:51:03.9	1984 Nikolai Zimyatov, USSR	1:28:56.3
1964 Eero Mäntyranta, FIN	1:30:50.7	1988 Alexi Prokurorov, USSR	1:24:26.3
1968 Franco Nones, ITA	1:35:39.2	1992 Vegard Ulvang, NOR	1:22:27.8
1972 Vyacheslav Vedenine, USSR	1:36:31.15	1994 Thomas Alsgaard, NOR	1:12:26.4

30-kilometer Classical

Year	Time
1998 Mila Myllylae, FIN	1:33:55.8

50-kilometer Classical (Discont.)
Discontinued in 1998 and replaced by the 50-kilometer Freestyle.

Year	Time	Year	Time
1924 Thorleif Haug, NOR	3:44:32.0	1968 Ole Ellefsaeter, NOR	2:28:45.8
1928 Per Erik Hedlund, SWE	4:52:03.0	1972 Pål Tyldum, NOR	2:43:14.75
1932 Veli Saarinen, FIN	4:28:00.0	1976 Ivar Formo, NOR	2:37:30.05
1936 Elis Wiklund, SWE	3:30:11.0	1980 Nikolai Zimyatov, USSR	2:27:24.60
1948 Nils Karlsson, SWE	3:47:48.0	1984 Thomas Wassberg, SWE	2:15:55.8
1952 Veikko Hakulinen, FIN	3:33:33.0	1988 Gunde Svan, SWE	2:04:30.9
1956 Sixten Jernberg, SWE	2:50:27.0	1992 Bjorn Dählie, NOR	2:03:41.5
1960 Kalevi Hämäläinen, FIN	2:59:06.3	1994 Vladimir Smirnov, KAZ	2:07:20.3
1964 Sixten Jernberg, SWE	2:43:52.6		

50-kilometer Freestyle

Year	Time
1998 Bjorn Dählie, NOR	2:05:08.2

4x10-kilometer Mixed Relay
Two Classical and two Freestyle legs.

Year	Time	Year	Time	Year	Time
1936 Finland	2:41:33.0	1964 Sweden	2:18:34.6	1984 Sweden	1:55:06.3
1948 Sweden	2:32:08.0	1968 Norway	2:08:33.5	1988 Sweden	1:43:58.6
1952 Finland	2:20:16.0	1972 Soviet Union	2:04:47.94	1992 Norway	1:39:26.0
1956 Soviet Union	2:15:30.0	1976 Finland	2:07:59.72	1994 Italy	1:41:15.0
1960 Finland	2:18:45.6	1980 Soviet Union	1:57:03.46	1998 Norway	1:40:55.7

WOMEN

Multiple gold medals (including relays): Lyubov Egorova (6); Galina Kulakova and Raisa Smetanina (4); Claudia Boyarskikh and Marja-Liisa Hämäläinen (3); Manuela Di Centa, Toini Gustafson, Larisa Lazutina, Barbara Petzold and Elena Valbe (2).

Multiple gold medals (including relays and Biathlon): Anfisa Reztsova (2).

5-kilometer Classical

Year	Time	Year	Time
1964 Claudia Boyarskikh, USSR	17:50.5	1984 Marja-Liisa Hämäläinen, FIN	17:04.0
1968 Toini Gustafson, SWE	16:45.2	1988 Marjo Matikainen, FIN	15:04.0
1972 Galina Kulakova, USSR	17:00.50	1992 Marjut Lukkarinen, FIN	14:13.8
1976 Helena Takalo, FIN	15:48.69	1994 Lyubov Egorova, RUS	14:08.8
1980 Raisa Smetanina, USSR	15:06.92	1998 Larissa Lazutina, RUS	17:37.9

10-kilometer Combined Pursuit
A 10-km Freestyle race in which the starting order is determined by order of finish in the 5-km Classical race. Time given is combined time of both events.

Year	Time	Year	Time
1952-88 Not held		1994 Lyubov Egorova, RUS	41:38.1
1992 Lyubov Egorova, UT	40:07.7	1998 Larissa Lazutina, RUS	17:37.9

10-kilometer Classical (Discont.)
Discontinued in 1992 and replaced by the freestyle 10-km Combined Pursuit.

Year	Time	Year	Time
1952 Lydia Wideman, FIN	41:40.0	1972 Galina Kulakova, USSR	34:17.82
1956 Lyubov Kosyreva, USSR	38:11.0	1976 Raisa Smetanina, USSR	30:13.41
1960 Maria Gusakova, USSR	39:46.6	1980 Barbara Petzold, E. Ger.	30:31.54
1964 Claudia Boyarskikh, USSR	40:24.3	1984 Marja-Liisa Hämäläinen, FIN	31:44.2
1968 Toini Gustafson, SWE	36:46.5	1988 Vida Venciene, USSR	30:08.3

15-kilometer Freestyle (Discont.)
Discontinued in 1998 and replaced by the 15-kilometer Classical.

Year	Time	Year	Time
1992 Lyubov Egorova, UT	42:20.8	1994 Manuela Di Centa, ITA	39:44.5

15-kilometer Classical

Year	Time
1998 Olga Danilova, RUS	46:55.4

20-kilometer Classical (Discont.)
Discontinued in 1992 and replaced by the 30-kilometer Freestyle.

Year	Time	Year	Time
1984 Marja-Liisa Hämäläinen, FIN	1:01:45.0	1988 Tamara Tikhonova, USSR	55:53.6

30-kilometer Freestyle

Year	Time	Year	Time
1992 Stefania Belmondo, ITA	1:22:30.1	1998 Julija Tchepalova, RUS	1:22:01.5
1994 Manuela Di Centa, ITA	1:25:41.6		

4x5-kilometer Relay
Two Classical and two Freestyle legs since 1992. Event featured three skiers per team from 1956-72.

Year	Time	Year	Time	Year	Time
1956 Finland	1:09:01.0	1972 Soviet Union	48:46.15	1988 Soviet Union	59:51.1
1960 Sweden	1:04:21.4	1976 Soviet Union	1:07:49.75	1992 Unified Team	59:34.8
1964 Soviet Union	59:20.2	1980 East Germany	1:02:11.10	1994 Russia	57:12.5
1968 Norway	57:30.0	1984 Norway	1:06:49.7	1998 Russia	55:13.5

CURLING

MEN

Year	
1998	**Switzerland**, Canada, Norway

WOMEN

Year	
1998	**Canada**, Denmark, Sweden

FIGURE SKATING

MEN
Multiple gold medals: Gillis Grafström (3); Dick Button and Karl Schäfer (2).

Year		Year		Year	
1908 Ulrich Salchow	SWE	1948 Dick Button	USA	1976 John Curry	GBR
1912 Not held		1952 Dick Button	USA	1980 Robin Cousins	GBR
1920 Gillis Grafström	SWE	1956 Hayes Alan Jenkins	USA	1984 Scott Hamilton	USA
1924 Gillis Grafström	SWE	1960 David Jenkins	USA	1988 Brian Boitano	USA
1928 Gillis Grafström	SWE	1964 Manfred Schnelldorfer	GER	1992 Victor Petrenko	UT
1932 Karl Schäfer	AUT	1968 Wolfgang Schwarz	AUT	1994 Alexei Urmanov	RUS
1936 Karl Schäfer	AUT	1972 Ondrej Nepela	CZE	1998 Ilia Kulik	RUS

WOMEN
Multiple gold medals: Sonja Henie (3); Katarina Witt (2).

Year		Year		Year	
1908 Madge Syers	GBR	1948 Barbara Ann Scott	CAN	1976 Dorothy Hamill	USA
1912 Not held		1952 Jeanette Altwegg	GBR	1980 Anett Pötzsch	E. Ger
1920 Magda Julin-Mauroy	SWE	1956 Tenley Albright	USA	1984 Katarina Witt	E. Ger
1924 Herma Planck-Szabö	AUT	1960 Carol Heiss	USA	1988 Katarina Witt	E. Ger
1928 Sonja Henie	NOR	1964 Sjoukje Dijkstra	NED	1992 Kristi Yamaguchi	USA
1932 Sonja Henie	NOR	1968 Peggy Fleming	USA	1994 Oksana Baiul	UKR
1936 Sonja Henie	NOR	1972 Beatrix Schuba	AUT	1998 Tara Lipinski	USA

PAIRS

Multiple gold medals: MEN–Pierre Brunet, Artur Dmitriev, Sergei Grinkov, Oleg Protopopov and Aleksandr Zaitsev (2). WOMEN–Irina Rodnina (3); Ludmila Belousova, Ekaterina Gordeeva and Andree Joly Brunet (2).

Year		Year	
1908	Anna Hübler & Heinrich Burger...........Germany	1964	Ludmila Belousova & Oleg Protopopov........USSR
1912	Not held	1968	Ludmila Belousova & Oleg Protopopov........USSR
1920	Ludovika & Walter Jakobsson..............Finland	1972	Irina Rodnina & Aleksei Ulanov..............USSR
1924	Helene Engelmann & Alfred Berger........Austria	1976	Irina Rodnina & Aleksandr Zaitsev..........USSR
1928	Andrée Joly & Pierre Brunet...............France	1980	Irina Rodnina & Aleksandr Zaitsev..........USSR
1932	Andrée & Pierre Brunet...................France	1984	Elena Valova & Oleg Vasiliev...............USSR
1936	Maxi Herber & Ernst Baier................Germany	1988	Ekaterina Gordeeva & Sergei Grinkov.......USSR
1948	Micheline Lannoy & Pierre Baugniet.......Belgium	1992	Natalya Mishkutienok & Arthur Dmitriev......UT
1952	Ria & Paul Falk.......................Germany	1994	Ekaterina Gordeeva & Sergei Grinkov........RUS
1956	Elisabeth Schwartz & Kurt Oppelt..........Austria	1998	Oksana Kazakova & Artur Dmitriev...........RUS
1960	Barbara Wagner & Robert Paul...........Canada		

Ice Dancing

Multiple gold medals: Yevgeny Platov (2).

Year		Year	
1976	Lyudmila Pakhomova & Aleksandr Gorshkov...USSR	1992	Marina Klimova & Sergei Ponomarenko..........UT
1980	Natalia Linichuk & Gennady Karponosov.....USSR	1994	Oksana Gritschuk & Yevgeny Platov.........RUS
1984	Jayne Torvill & Christopher Dean......Great Britain	1998	Pasha Grishuk & Yevgeny Platov.............RUS
1988	Natalia Bestemianova & Andrei Bukin........USSR		

FREESTYLE SKIING

MEN
Aerials

Year		Points
1994	Andreas Schoebaechler, SWI..............234.67
1998	Eric Bergoust, USA.........................255.6

Moguls

Year		Points
1994	Jean-Luc Brassard, CAN...................27.24
1998	Jonny Moseley, USA......................26.93

WOMEN
Aerials

Year		Points
1994	Lina Cherjazova, UZB.....................166.84
1998	Nikki Stone, USA.........................193.00

Moguls

Year		Points
1994	Stine Lise Hattestad, NOR.................25.97
1998	Tae Satoya, JPN.........................25.06

ICE HOCKEY

MEN

Multiple gold medals: Soviet Union/Unified Team (8); Canada (6); United States (2).

Year		Year	
1920	**Canada**, United States Czechoslovakia	1976	**Soviet Union**, Czechoslovakia, West Germany
1924	**Canada**, United States, Great Britain	1980	**United States**, Soviet Union, Sweden
1928	**Canada**, Sweden, Switzerland	1984	**Soviet Union**, Czechoslovakia, Sweden
1932	**Canada**, United States, Germany	1988	**Soviet Union**, Finland, Sweden
1936	**Great Britain**, Canada, United States	1992	**Unified Team**, Canada, Czechoslovakia
1948	**Canada**, Czechoslovakia, Switzerland	1994	**Sweden**, Canada, Finland
1952	**Canada**, United States, Sweden	1998	**Czech Republic**, Russia, Finland
1956	**Soviet Union**, United States, Canada		
1960	**United States**, Canada, Soviet Union		
1964	**Soviet Union**, Sweden, Czechoslovakia		**WOMEN**
1968	**Soviet Union**, Czechoslovakia, Canada	Year	
1972	**Soviet Union**, United States, Czechoslovakia	1998	**United States**, Canada, Finland

U.S. Gold Medal Hockey Teams

1960
Forwards: Billy Christian, Roger Christian, Billy Cleary, Gene Grazia, Paul Johnson, Bob McVey, Dick Meredith, Weldy Olson, Dick Rodenheiser and Tom Williams. **Defensemen:** Bob Cleary, Jack Kirrane (captain), John Mayasich, Bob Owen and Rod Paavola. **Goaltenders:** Jack McCartan and Larry Palmer. **Coach:** Jack Riley.

1980
Forwards: Neal Broten, Steve Christoff, Mike Eruzione (captain), John Harrington, Mark Johnson, Rob McClanahan, Mark Pavelich, Buzz Schneider, Dave Silk, Eric Strobel, Phil Verchota and Mark Wells. **Defensemen:** Bill Baker, Dave Christian, Ken Morrow, Jack O'Callahan, Mike Ramsey and Bob Suter. **Goaltenders:** Jim Craig and Steve Janaszak. **Coach:** Herb Brooks.

1998
Forwards: Laurie Baker, Alana Blahoski, Lisa Brown-Miller, Karen Bye, Tricia Dunn, Cammi Granato, Katie King, Shelley Looney, A.J. Mleczko, Jenny Schmidgall, Gretchen Ulion, Sandra Whyte. **Defensemen:** Chris Bailey, Colleen Coyne, Sue Mertz, Tara Mounsey, Vicki Movessian, Angela Ruggiero. **Goaltenders:** Sarah DeCosta and Sarah Tueting. **Coach:** Ben Smith.

LUGE

MEN

Multiple gold medals: (including doubles): Georg Hackl (3); Norbert Hahn, Paul Hildgartner, Thomas Kohler and Hans Rinn (2).

Singles

Year	Time	Year	Time
1964 Thomas Köhler, GER	3:26.77	1984 Paul Hildgartner, ITA	3:04.258
1968 Manfred Schmid, AUT	2:52.48	1988 Jens Müller, E. Ger	3:05.548
1972 Wolfgang Scheidel, E. Ger	3:27.58	1992 Georg Hackl, GER	3:02.363
1976 Dettlef Günther, E. Ger	3:27.688	1994 Georg Hackl, GER	3:21.571
1980 Bernhard Glass, E. Ger	2:54.796	1998 Georg Hackl, GER	3:18.436

Doubles

Year	Time	Year	Time
1964 Austria	1:41.62	1984 West Germany	1:23.620
1968 East Germany	1:35.85	1988 East Germany	1:31.940
1972 (TIE) East Germany	1:28.35	1992 Germany	1:32.053
& Italy	1:28.35	1994 Italy	1:36.720
1976 East Germany	1:25.604	1998 Germany	1:41.105
1980 East Germany	1:19.331		

WOMEN

Multiple gold medals: Steffi Martin Walter (2).

Singles

Year	Time	Year	Time
1964 Ortrun Enderlein, GER	3:24.67	1984 Steffi Martin, E. Ger	2:46.570
1968 Erica Lechner, ITA	2:28.66	1988 Steffi Martin Walter, E. Ger	3:03.973
1972 Anna-Maria Müller, E. Ger	2:59.18	1992 Doris Neuner, AUT	3:06.696
1976 Margit Schumann, E. Ger	2:50.621	1994 Gerda Weissensteiner, ITA	3:15.517
1980 Vera Zozulya, USSR	2:36.537	1998 Silke Kraushaar, GER	3:23.779

NORDIC COMBINED

Multiple gold medals: Ulrich Wehling (3); Johan Gröttumsbråten (2).

Individual

Year	Points	Year	Points
1924 Thorleif Haug, NOR	18.906	1972 Ulrich Wehling, E. Ger	413.340
1928 Johan Gröttumsbråten, NOR	17.833	1976 Ulrich Wehling, E. Ger	423.39
1932 Johan Gröttumsbråten, NOR	446.00	1980 Ulrich Wehling, E. Ger	432.200
1936 Oddbjörn Hagen, NOR	430.3	1984 Tom Sandberg, NOR	422.595
1948 Heikki Hasu, FIN	448.80	1988 Hippolyt Kempf, SWI	432.230
1952 Simon Slattvik, NOR	451.621	1992 Fabrice Guy, FRA	426.470
1956 Sverre Stenersen, NOR	455.000	1994 Fred Borre Lundberg, NOR	457.970
1960 Georg Thoma, GER	457.952		**Time**
1964 Tormod Knutsen, NOR	469.28	1998 Bjarte Engen Vik, NOR	41:21.1
1968 Franz Keller, W. Ger	449.04		

Team

Year	Points	Year	Points
1924-84 Not held		1994 Japan	1368.860
1988 West Germany	792.08		**Time**
1992 Japan	1247.180	1998 Norway	54:11.5

SKI JUMPING

Multiple gold medals (including team jumping): Matti Nykänen (4); Jens Weissflog (3); Birger Ruud and Toni Nieminen (2).

Normal Hill–90 Meters

Year	Points	Year	Points
1924-60 Not held		1984 Jens Weissflog, E. Ger	215.2
1964 Veikko Kankkonen, FIN	229.9	1988 Matti Nykänen, FIN	229.1
1968 Jiri Raska, CZE	216.5	1992 Ernst Vettori, AUT	222.8
1972 Yukio Kasaya, JPN	244.2	1994 Espen Bredesen, NOR	282.0
1976 Hans-Georg Aschenbach, E. Ger	252.0	1998 Jani Soininen, FIN	234.5
1980 Anton Innauer, AUT	266.3	**Note:** Jump held at 70 meters from 1964-92.	

Large Hill–120 Meters

Year		Points	Year		Points
1924	Jacob Tullin Thams, NOR	18.960	1968	Vladimir Beloussov, USSR	231.3
1928	Alf Andersen, NOR	19.208	1972	Wojciech Fortuna, POL	219.9
1932	Birger Ruud, NOR	228.1	1976	Karl Schäabl, AUT	234.8
1936	Birger Ruud, NOR	232.0	1980	Jouko Törmänen, FIN	271.0
1948	Petter Hugsted, NOR	228.1	1984	Matti Nykänen, FIN	231.2
1952	Arnfinn Bergmann, NOR	226.0	1988	Matti Nykänen, FIN	224.0
1956	Antti Hyvärinen, FIN	227.0	1992	Toni Nieminen, FIN.	239.5
1960	Helmut Recknagel, GER	227.2	1994	Jens Weissflog, GER	274.5
1964	Toralf Engan, NOR.	230.7	1998	Kazuyoshi Funaki, JPN.	272.3

Note: Jump held at various lengths from 1924-56; at 80 meters from 1960-64; and at 90 meters from 1968-88.

Team Large Hill

Year		Points	Year		Points
1924-84	Not held		1994	Germany	970.1
1988	Finland	634.4	1998	Japan	933.0
1992	Finland	644.4			

SNOWBOARDING

MEN
Halfpipe

Year		Points
1998	Gian Simmen, SWI	85.2

WOMEN
Halfpipe

Year		Points
1998	Nicola Thost, GER.	74.6

Giant Slalom

Year		Points
1998	Ross Rebagliati, CAN.	2:03.96

Giant Slalom

Year		Points
1998	Karine Ruby, FRA	2:17.34

SPEED SKATING

MEN

Multiple gold medals: Eric Heiden and Clas Thunberg (5); Ivar Ballangrud, Yevgeny Grishin and Johann Olav Koss (4); Hjalmar Andersen, Tomas Gustafson, Irving Jaffee and Ard Schenk (3); Gaétan Boucher, Knut Johannesen, Erhard Keller, Uwe-Jens Mey, Gianni Romme and Jack Shea (2). Note that Thunberg's total includes the All-Around, which was contested for the only time in 1924.

500 meters

Year		Time		Year		Time	
1924	Charles Jewtraw, USA	44.0		1968	Erhard Keller, W. Ger.	40.3	
1928	(TIE) Bernt Evensen, NOR	43.4	**OR**	1972	Erhard Keller, W. Ger.	39.44	**OR**
	& Clas Thunberg, FIN.	43.4	**OR**	1976	Yevgeny Kulikov, USSR.	39.17	**OR**
1932	Jack Shea, USA	43.4	**=OR**	1980	Eric Heiden, USA	38.03	**OR**
1936	Ivar Ballangrud, NOR.	43.4	**=OR**	1984	Sergei Fokichev, USSR	38.19	
1948	Finn Helgesen, NOR.	43.1	**OR**	1988	Uwe-Jens Mey, E. Ger.	36.45	**WR**
1952	Ken Henry, USA	43.2		1992	Uwe-Jens Mey, GER.	37.14	
1956	Yevgeny Grishin, USSR.	40.2	**=WR**	1994	Aleksandr Golubev, RUS	36.33	**OR**
1960	Yevgeny Grishin, USSR.	40.2	**=WR**	1998	Hiroyashu Shimizu, JPN.	71.35	**OR**
1964	Terry McDermott, USA	40.1	**OR**				

1000 meters

Year		Time		Year		Time	
1924-72	Not held			1988	Nikolai Gulyaev, USSR	1:13.03	**OR**
1976	Peter Mueller, USA	1:19.32		1992	Olaf Zinke, GER	1:14.85	
1980	Eric Heiden, USA	1:15.18	**OR**	1994	Dan Jansen, USA	1:12.43	**WR**
1984	Gaétan Boucher, CAN	1:15.80		1998	Ids Postma, NED.	1:10.64	**OR**

1500 meters

Year		Time		Year		Time	
1924	Clas Thunberg, FIN.	2:20.8		1964	Ants Antson, USSR	2:10.3	
1928	Clas Thunberg, FIN.	2:21.1		1968	Kees Verkerk, NED.	2:03.4	**OR**
1932	Jack Shea, USA	2:57.5		1972	Ard Schenk, NED.	2:02.96	**OR**
1936	Charles Mathisen, NOR	2:19.2	**OR**	1976	Jan Egil Storholt, NOR.	1:59.38	**OR**
1948	Sverre Farstad, NOR.	2:17.6	**OR**	1980	Eric Heiden, USA	1:55.44	**OR**
1952	Hjalmar Andersen, NOR	2:20.4		1984	Gaétan Boucher, CAN	1:58.36	
1956	(TIE)Yevgeny Grishin, USSR	2:08.6	**WR**	1988	Andre Hoffman, E. Ger.	1:52.06	**WR**
	& Yuri Mikhailov, USSR.	2:08.6	**WR**	1992	Johann Olav Koss, NOR.	1:54.81	
1960	(TIE) Roald Aas, NOR.	2:10.4		1994	Johann Olav Koss, NOR.	1:51.29	**WR**
	& Yevgeny Grishin, USSR.	2:10.4		1998	Aadne Sondral, NOR	1:47.87	**WR**

5000 meters

Year		Time		Year		Time	
1924	Clas Thunberg, FIN	8:39.0		1968	Fred Anton Maier, NOR	7:22.4	WR
1928	Ivar Ballangrud, NOR	8:50.5		1972	Ard Schenk, NED	7:23.61	
1932	Irving Jaffee, USA	9:40.8		1976	Sten Stensen, NOR	7:24.48	
1936	Ivar Ballangrud, NOR	8:19.6	OR	1980	Eric Heiden, USA	7:02.29	OR
1948	Reidar Liaklev, NOR	8:29.4		1984	Tomas Gustafson, SWE	7:12.28	
1952	Hjalmar Andersen, NOR	8:10.6	OR	1988	Tomas Gustafson, SWE	6:44.63	WR
1956	Boris Shilkov, USSR	7:48.7	OR	1992	Geir Karlstad, NOR	6:59.97	
1960	Viktor Kosichkin, USSR	7:51.3		1994	Johann Olav Koss, NOR	6:34.96	WR
1964	Knut Johannesen, NOR	7:38.4	OR	1998	Gianni Romme, NED	6:22.20	WR

10,000 meters

Year		Time		Year		Time	
1924	Julius Skutnabb, FIN	18:04.8		1968	Johnny Höglin, SWE	15:23.6	OR
1928	Irving Jaffee, USA*	18:36.5		1972	Ard Schenk, NED	15:01.35	OR
1932	Irving Jaffee, USA	19:13.6		1976	Piet Kleine, NED	14:50.59	OR
1936	Ivar Ballangrud, NOR	17:24.3	OR	1980	Eric Heiden, USA	14:28.13	WR
1948	Ake Seyffarth, SWE	17:26.3		1984	Igor Malkov, USSR	14:39.90	
1952	Hjalmar Andersen, NOR	16:45.8	OR	1988	Tomas Gustafson, SWE	13:48.20	WR
1956	Sigvard Ericsson, SWE	16:35.9	OR	1992	Bart Veldkamp, NED	14:12.12	
1960	Knut Johannesen, NOR	15:46.6	WR	1994	Johann Olav Koss, NOR	13:30.55	WR
1964	Jonny Nilsson, SWE	15:50.1		1998	Gianni Romme, NED	13:15.33	WR

*Unofficial, according to the IOC. Jaffee recorded the fastest time, but the event was called off in progress due to thawing ice.

WOMEN

Multiple gold medals: Lydia Skoblikova (6); Bonnie Blair (5); Karin Enke, Gunda Niemann-Stirnemann and Yvonne van Gennip (3); Tatiana Averina, Claudia Pechstein and Christa Rothenburger (2).

500 meters

Year		Time		Year		Time	
1960	Helga Haase, GER	45.9		1984	Christa Rothenburger, E. Ger	41.02	OR
1964	Lydia Skoblikova, USSR	45.0	OR	1988	Bonnie Blair, USA	39.10	WR
1968	Lyudmila Titova, USSR	46.1		1992	Bonnie Blair, USA	40.33	
1972	Anne Henning, USA	43.33	OR	1994	Bonnie Blair, USA	39.25	
1976	Sheila Young, USA	42.76	OR	1998	Catriona Lemay-Doan, CAN	76.60	OR
1980	Karin Enke, E. Ger	41.78	OR				

1000 meters

Year		Time		Year		Time	
1960	Klara Guseva, USSR	1:34.1		1984	Karin Enke, E. Ger	1:21.61	OR
1964	Lydia Skoblikova, USSR	1:33.2	OR	1988	Christa Rothenburger, E. Ger	1:17.65	WR
1968	Carolina Geijssen, NED	1:32.6	OR	1992	Bonnie Blair, USA	1:21.90	
1972	Monika Pflug, W. Ger	1:31.40	OR	1994	Bonnie Blair, USA	1:18.74	
1976	Tatiana Averina, USSR	1:28.43	OR	1998	Marianne Timmer, NED	1:16.51	OR
1980	Natalia Petruseva, USSR	1:24.10	OR				

1500 meters

Year		Time		Year		Time	
1960	Lydia Skoblikova, USSR	2:25.2	WR	1984	Karin Enke, E. Ger	2:03.42	WR
1964	Lydia Skoblikova, USSR	2:22.6	OR	1988	Yvonne van Gennip, NED	2:00.68	OR
1968	Kaija Mustonen, FIN	2:22.4	OR	1992	Jacqueline Börner, GER	2:05.87	
1972	Dianne Holum, USA	2:20.85	OR	1994	Emese Hunyady, AUT	2:02.19	
1976	Galina Stepanskaya, USSR	2:16.58	OR	1998	Marianne Timmer, NED	1:57.58	WR
1980	Annie Borckink, NED	2:10.95	OR				

3000 meters

Year		Time		Year		Time	
1960	Lydia Skoblikova, USSR	5:14.3		1984	Andrea Schöne, E. Ger	4:24.79	OR
1964	Lydia Skoblikova, USSR	5:14.9		1988	Yvonne van Gennip, NED	4:11.94	WR
1968	Johanna Schut, NED	4:56.2	OR	1992	Gunda Niemann, GER	4:19.90	
1972	Christina Baas-Kaiser, NED	4:52.14	OR	1994	Svetlana Bazhanova, RUS	4:17.43	
1976	Tatiana Averina, USSR	4:45.19	OR	1998	Gunda Niemann-Stirnemann, GER	4:07.29	OR
1980	Bjorg Eva Jensen, NOR	4:32.13	OR				

5000 meters

Year		Time		Year		Time	
1960-84 Not held				1994	Claudia Pechstein, GER	7:14.37	
1988	Yvonne van Gennip, NED	7:14.13	WR	1998	Claudia Pechstein, GER	6:59.61	WR
1992	Gunda Niemann, GER	7:31.57					

AP/Wide World Photos

Norway's **Bjorn Dählie** collapses after crossing the finish line first in the 50km freestyle cross country event at Nagano in 1998. Perhaps it was all the gold around his neck. Norway has won more Winter Olympic medals than any other nation. Having guys like Dählie, who has won more medals than any other Winter Olympic athlete, doesn't hurt.

All-Time Leading Medal Winners

MEN

No		Sport	G-S-B
12	Bjorn Dählie, NOR	Cross-country	8-4-0
9	Sixten Jernberg, SWE	Cross-country	4-3-2
7	Clas Thunberg, FIN	Speed Skating	5-1-1
7	Ivar Ballangrud, NOR	Speed Skating	4-2-1
7	Veikko Hakulinen, FIN	Cross-country	3-3-1
7	Eero Mäntyranta, FIN	Cross-country	3-2-2
7	Bogdan Musiol, E. Ger/GER	Bobsled	1-5-1
6	Gunde Svan, SWE	Cross-country	4-1-1
6	Vegard Ulvang, NOR	Cross-country	3-2-1
6	Johan Gröttumsbråten, NOR	Nordic	3-1-2
6	Wolfgang Hoppe, E. Ger/GER	Bobsled	2-3-1
6	Eugenio Monti, ITA	Bobsled	2-2-2
6	Vladimir Smirnov, USSR/UT/KAZ	X-country	1-4-1
6	Mika Myllylae, FIN	Cross-country	1-1-4
6	Roald Larsen, NOR	Speed Skating	0-2-4
5	**Eric Heiden, USA**	Speed Skating	5-0-0
5	Yevgeny Grishin, USSR	Speed Skating	4-1-0
5	Johann Olav Koss, NOR	Speed Skating	4-1-0
5	Matti Nykänen, FIN	Ski Jumping	4-1-0
5	Aleksandr Tikhonov, USSR	Biathlon	4-1-0
5	Nikolai Zimyatov, USSR	Cross-country	4-1-0
5	Alberto Tomba, ITA	Alpine	3-2-0
5	Harald Grönningen, NOR	Cross-country	2-3-0
5	Pål Tyldum, NOR	Cross-country	2-3-0
5	Knut Johannesen, NOR	Speed Skating	2-2-1
5	Kjetil André Aamodt, NOR	Alpine	1-2-2
5	Peter Angerer, W. Ger/GER	Biathlon	1-2-2
5	Juha Mieto, FIN	Cross-country	1-2-2
5	Fritz Feierabend, SWI	Bobsled	0-3-2
5	Rintje Ritsma, NED	Speed Skating	0-2-3

WOMEN

No		Sport	G-S-B
10	Raisa Smetanina, USSR/UT	Cross-country	4-5-1
9	Lyubov Egorova, UT/RUS	Cross-country	6-3-0
8	Galina Kulakova, USSR	Cross-country	4-2-2
8	Karin (Enke) Kania, E. Ger	Speed Skating	3-4-1
8	Gunda Neimann-Stirnemann, GER	Speed Skating	3-4-1
7	Larisa Lazutina, UT/RUS	Cross-country	5-1-1
7	Marja-Liisa (Hämäläinen) Kirvesniemi, FIN	Cross-country	3-0-4
7	Elena Valbe, UT/RUS	Cross-country	3-0-4
7	Andrea (Mitscherlich, Schöne) Ehrig, E. Ger	Speed Skating	1-5-1
7	Stefania Belmondo, ITA	Cross-country	1-2-4
6	Lydia Skoblikova, USSR	Speed Skating	6-0-0
6	**Bonnie Blair, USA**	Speed Skating	5-0-1
6	Manuela Di Centa, ITA	Cross-country	2-2-2
6	Lee-Kyung Chun, KOR	ST Sp. Skating	4-0-1
5	Anfisa Reztsova, USSR/UT	CC/Biathlon	3-1-1
5	Vreni Schneider, SWI	Alpine	3-1-1
5	Katja Seizinger, GER	Alpine	3-0-2
5	Claudia Pechstein, GER	Speed Skating	2-1-2
5	Helena Takalo, FIN	Cross-country	1-3-1
5	Ursula Disl, GER	Biathlon	1-2-2
5	Alevtina Kolchina, USSR	Cross-country	1-1-3

Athletes with Winter and Summer Medals

Only three athletes have won medals in both the Winter and Summer Olympics:
Eddie Eagan, USA– Light Heavyweight Boxing gold (1920) and Four-man Bobsled gold (1932).
Jacob Tullin Thams, Norway– Ski Jumping gold (1924) and 8-meter Yachting silver (1936).
Christa Luding-Rothenburger, East Germany– Speed Skating gold at 500 meters (1984) and 1,000m (1988), silver at 500m (1988) and bronze at 500m (1992) and Match Sprint Cycling silver (1988). Luding-Rothenburger is the only athlete to ever win medals in both Winter and Summer Games in the same year.

Games Medaled In

MEN– **Aamodt** (1992,94); **Angerer** (1980,84,88); **Ballangrud** (1928,32,36); **Dählie** (1992,94,98); **Feierabend** (1936,48,52); **Grishin** (1956,60,64); **Gröttumsbråten** (1924,28,32); **Grönningen** (1960,64,68); **Hakulinen** (1952,56,60); **Heiden** (1980); **Hoppe** (1984,88,92,94); **Jernberg** (1956,60,64); **Johannesen** (1956,60,64); **Koss** (1992,94). **Larsen** (1924,28); **Mäntyranta** (1960,64,68); **Mieto** (1976,80,84); **Monti** (1956,60,64,68); **Musiol** (1980,84,88,92); **Myllylae** (1994,98); **Nykänen** (1984,88); **Ritsma** (1994,98); **Smirnov** (1988,92,94,98); **Svan** (1984,88); **Thunberg** (1924,28); **Tikhonov** (1968,72,76,80); **Tomba** (1988,92,94); **Tyldum** (1968,72,76); **Ulvang** (1988,92,94); **Zimyatov** (1980,84).

WOMEN– **Belmondo** (1992,94,98); **Blair** (1988,92,94); **Chun** (1994,98); **Di Centa** (1992,94); **Disl** (1994,98); **Egorova** (1992,94); **Ehrig** (1976,80,84,88); **Kania** (1980,84,88); **Kirvesniemi** (1984,88,94); **Kolchina** (1956,64,68); **Kulakova** (1968,72,76,80); **Lazutina** (1992,94,98); **Niemann-Stirnemann** (1992,94,98); **Pechstein** (1992,94,98); **Reztsova** (1988,92,94); **Schneider** (1988,92,94); **Seizinger** (1992,94,98); **Skoblikova** (1960,64); **Smetanina** (1976,80,84,88,92); **Takalo** (1972,76,80); **Valbe** (1992,94,98).

Most Gold Medals

MEN

No		Sport	G-S-B
8	Bjorn Dählie, NOR	Cross-country	8-4-0
5	Clas Thunberg, FIN	Speed Skating	5-1-1
5	**Eric Heiden, USA**	Speed Skating	5-0-0
4	Sixten Jernberg, SWE	Cross-country	4-3-2
4	Ivar Ballangrud, NOR	Speed Skating	4-2-1
4	Gunde Svan, SWE	Cross-country	4-1-1
4	Yevgeny Grishin, USSR	Speed Skating	4-1-0
4	Johann Olav Koss, NOR	Speed Skating	4-1-0
4	Matti Nykänen, FIN	Ski Jumping	4-1-0
4	Aleksandr Tikhonov, USSR	Biathlon	4-1-0
4	Nikolai Zimyatov, USSR	Cross-country	4-1-0
4	Thomas Wassberg, SWE	Cross-country	4-0-0
3	Veikko Hakulinen, FIN	Cross-country	3-3-1
3	Eero Mäntyranta, FIN	Cross-country	3-2-2
3	Vegard Ulvang, NOR	Cross-country	3-2-1
3	Alberto Tomba, ITA	Alpine	3-2-0
3	Johan Gröttumsbråten, NOR	Nordic	3-1-2
3	Bernhard Germeshausen, E. Ger	Bobsled	3-1-0
3	Gillis Grafström, SWE	Figure Skating	3-1-0
3	Tomas Gustafson, SWE	Speed Skating	3-1-0
3	Vladislav Tretiak, USSR	Ice Hockey	3-1-0
3	Jens Weissflog, E. Ger/GER	Ski Jumping	3-1-0
3	Meinhard Nehmer, E. Ger	Bobsled	3-0-1
3	Hjalmar Andersen, NOR	Speed Skating	3-0-0
3	Vitaly Davydov, USSR	Ice Hockey	3-0-0
3	Anatoly Firsov, USSR	Ice Hockey	3-0-0
3	Thorleif Haug, NOR	Cross-country	3-0-0
3	**Irving Jaffee, USA**	Speed Skating	3-0-0
3	Andrei Khomoutov, USSR/UT	Ice Hockey	3-0-0

No		Sport	G-S-B
3	Jean-Claude Killy, FRA	Alpine	3-0-0
3	Viktor Kuzkin, USSR	Ice Hockey	3-0-0
3	Aleksandr Ragulin, USSR	Ice Hockey	3-0-0
3	Toni Sailer, AUT	Alpine	3-0-0
3	Ard Schenk, NED	Speed Skating	3-0-0
3	Ulrich Wehling, E. Ger	Ski Jumping	3-0-0

WOMEN

No		Sport	G-S-B
6	Lyubov Egorova, UT/RUS	Cross-country	6-3-0
6	Lydia Skoblikova, USSR	Speed Skating	6-0-0
5	Larissa Lazutina, UT/RUS	Cross-country	5-1-1
5	**Bonnie Blair, USA**	Speed Skating	5-0-1
4	Raisa Smetanina, USSR/UT	Cross-country	4-5-1
4	Galina Kulakova, USSR	Cross-country	4-2-2
4	Lee-Kyung Chun, KOR	ST Sp. Skating	4-0-1
3	Karin (Enke) Kania, E. Ger	Speed Skating	3-4-1
3	Gunda Neimann-Stirnemann, GER	Speed Skating	3-4-1
3	Anfisa Reztsova, USSR/UT	CC/Biathlon	3-1-1
3	Vreni Schneider, SWI	Alpine	3-1-1
3	Marja-Liisa (Hämäläinen) Kirvesniemi, FIN	Cross-country	3-0-4
3	Elena Valbe, UT/RUS	Cross-country	3-0-4
3	Katja Seizinger, GER	Alpine	3-0-2
3	Claudia Boyarskikh, USSR	Cross-country	3-0-0
3	Sonja Henie, NOR	Figure Skating	3-0-0
3	Irina Rodnina, USSR	Figure Skating	3-0-0
3	Yvonne van Gennip, NED	Speed Skating	3-0-0

All-Time Leading USA Medalists
MEN

No		Sport	G-S-B
5	Eric Heiden	Speed Skating	5-0-0
3*	Irving Jaffee	Speed Skating	3-0-0
3	Pat Martin	Bobsled	1-2-0
3	John Heaton	Bobsled/Cresta	0-2-1
2	Dick Button	Figure Skating	2-0-0
2†	Eddie Eagan	Boxing/Bobsled	2-0-0

No		Sport	G-S-B
2	Billy Fiske	Bobsled	2-0-0
2	Cliff Gray	Bobsled	2-0-0
2	Jack Shea	Speed Skating	2-0-0
2	Billy Cleary	Ice Hockey	1-1-0
2	Jennison Heaton	Bobsled/Cresta	1-1-0
2	John Mayasich	Ice Hockey	1-1-0

No		Sport	G-S-B	No		Sport	G-S-B
2	Terry McDermott	Speed Skating	1-1-0	2	Stan Benham	Bobsled	0-2-0
2	Dick Meredith	Ice Hockey	1-1-0	2	Herb Drury	Ice Hockey	0-2-0
2	Tommy Moe	Alpine	1-1-0	2	Eric Flaim	Sp. Skate/ST Sp. Skate	0-2-0
2	Weldy Olson	Ice Hockey	1-1-0	2	Frank Synott	Ice Hockey	0-2-0
2	Dick Rodenheiser	Ice Hockey	1-1-0	2	John Garrison	Ice Hockey	0-1-1
2	David Jenkins	Figure Skating	1-1-0				

*Jaffee is generally given credit for a third gold medal in the 10,000-meter Speed Skating race of 1928. He had the fastest time before the race was cancelled due to thawing ice. The IOC considers the race unofficial.

†Eagan won the Light Heavyweight boxing title at the 1920 Summer Games in Antwerp and the four-man Bobsled at the 1932 Winter Games in Lake Placid. He is the only athlete ever to win gold medals in both the Winter and Summer Olympics.

WOMEN

No		Sport	G-S-B	No		Sport	G-S-B
6	Bonnie Blair	Speed Skating	5-0-1	2	Carol Heiss	Figure Skating	1-1-0
4	Cathy Turner	ST Sp. Skating	2-1-1	2	Picabo Street	Alpine	1-1-0
4	Dianne Holum	Speed Skating	1-2-1	2	Diann Roffe-Steinrotter	Alpine	1-1-0
3	Sheila Young	Speed Skating	1-1-1	2	Anne Henning	Speed Skating	1-0-1
3	Leah Poulos Mueller	Speed Skating	0-3-0	2	Penny Pitou	Alpine	0-2-0
3	Beatrix Loughran	Figure Skating	0-2-1	2	Nancy Kerrigan	Figure Skating	0-1-1
3	Amy Peterson	ST Sp. Skating	0-2-1	2	Jean Saubert	Alpine	0-1-1
2	Andrea Mead Lawrence	Alpine	2-0-0	2	Chris Witty	Sp. Skating	0-1-1
2	Tenley Albright	Figure Skating	1-1-0	2	Nikki Ziegelmeyer	ST Sp. Skating	0-1-1
2	Gretchen Fraser	Alpine	1-1-0				

Notes: The Cresta run is undertaken on a heavy sled ridden head first in the prone position and has only been held at St. Moritz in 1928 and '48. Also, the term ST Sp. Skating refers to Short Track (or pack) Speed Skating.

All-Time Medal Standings, 1924-98

All-time Winter Games medal standings, according to *The Golden Book of the Olympic Games*. Medal counts include figure skating medals (1908 and '20) and hockey medals (1920) awarded at the Summer Games. National medal standings for the Winter and Summer Games are not recognized by the IOC.

		G	S	B	Total			G	S	B	Total
1	Norway	83	87	69	239	22	Liechtenstein	2	2	5	9
2	Soviet Union (1956-88)	78	57	59	194	23	Hungary	0	2	4	6
3	**United States**	59	59	41	159	24	Kazakhstan (1994–)	1	2	2	5
4	Austria	39	53	53	145		Belgium	1	1	3	5
5	Finland	38	49	48	135	26	Poland	1	1	2	4
6	East Germany (1968-88)	43	39	36	118		Yugoslavia (1924-88)	0	3	1	4
7	Sweden	39	28	35	102		Belarus (1994–)	0	2	2	4
8	Switzerland	29	31	32	92	29	Czech Republic (1998–)	1	1	1	3
9	Germany (1928-36, 52-64, 92–)	35	30	25	90		Ukraine (1994–)	1	1	1	3
							Slovenia (1992–)	0	0	3	3
10	Canada	25	25	29	79	32	Bulgaria	1	0	1	2
11	Italy	27	27	23	77		Spain	1	0	1	2
12	Netherlands	19	23	19	61		Luxembourg	0	2	0	2
	France	18	17	26	61		North Korea	0	1	1	2
14	West Germany (1968-88)	18	20	19	57		Australia	0	0	2	2
15	Russia (1994–)	21	14	7	42	37	Uzbekistan (1994–)	1	0	0	1
16	Japan	8	9	12	29		Denmark	0	1	0	1
17	Czechoslovakia (1924-92)	2	8	16	26		New Zealand	0	1	0	1
18	Great Britain	7	4	13	24		Romania	0	0	1	1
19	Unified Team (1992)	9	6	8	23						
20	South Korea	9	3	4	16	**Combined totals**		**G**	**S**	**B**	**Total**
21	China	0	10	4	14	Germany/E. Ger/W. Ger		96	89	80	265
						USSR/UT/Russia		108	77	74	259

Notes: Athletes from the USSR participated in the Winter Games from 1956-88, returned as the Unified Team in 1992 after the breakup of the Soviet Union (in 1991) and then competed for the independent republics of Belarus, Kazakhstan, Russia, Ukraine, Uzbekistan and three others in 1994. Yugoslavia divided into Croatia and Bosnia-Herzegovina in 1991, while Czechoslovakia split into Slovakia and the Czech Republic the same year.

Germany was barred from the Olympics in 1924 and 1948 as an aggressor nation in both World Wars I and II. Divided into East and West Germany after WWII, both countries competed under one flag from 1952-64, then as separate teams from 1968-88. Germany was reunified in 1990.

International Sports

American sprinter **Michael Johnson** celebrates his world-record setting performance in the 400-meters at the World Track and Field Championships in Seville, Spain.

AP/Wide World Photos

The Strong Don't Just Survive

In the case of 1999 Tour de France winner Lance Armstrong, they win.

by
Jack Edwards

The man who should be dead will live forever in cycling history. Lance Armstrong had won the one-day World Championship in 1993 and individual stages at the Tour de France in '93 and '95, but hadn't demonstrated the ability to answer every challenge over the Tour's grueling three weeks — the ultimate test in the sport.

When he dismounted and left the '96 Tour, he felt sick. He wouldn't find out just how sick until October 1996, when he found out he had testicular cancer. An immediate diagnostic blood test revealed that the cancer had spread. A healthy patient's test number would be zero. Armstrong's count was 59,000. What were his chances of survival?

Jack Edwards has been with ESPN since 1991 as a *SportsCenter* anchor and now as a play-by-play announcer. He currently rides about 100 miles per week.

"Almost none," Dr. James Reeves, an Austin, Texas physician, explained. "We told Lance initially he had a 20 to 50 percent chance, mainly to give him hope."

The cancer was relentless. "I mean it was everywhere," said Armstrong. "I had 10 or 12 marble-to-golf-ball-sized tumors in the lung. Two on the brain. In the gut."

There is no mercy in cycling. Armstrong said, "Going out for five or six hours is a grind. Climbing for 15 miles straight is a grind. And cancer is a grind. The treatment is a grind. You lay in a bed. You can't think, you can't walk, you can't eat, you can't talk much. It's a grind and I think that's why, psychologically, I was so well prepared for that. I was so ready to dig in and go, 'All right. This is really going to suck. But I'm going to get through it.'"

AP/Wide World Photos

Lance Armstrong rides past the Arc de Triomphe during the final stage of his emotional Tour de France victory. The win capped an amazing comeback from cancer and made him just the second American in history to win the event.

Fifteen months after the initial diagnosis, his lung x-ray was clear. This case was, in Reeves' words, "miraculous. Nothing even close."

Two years and nine months after having one of his testicles removed and beginning chemotherapy, Lance Armstrong launched down the start ramp of the 1999 Tour de France prologue, the four-and-a-quarter mile sprint which sets the initial standing. He beat Switzerland's Alex Zuelle by seven seconds, and became the first American to wear the overall leader's yellow jersey since Greg LeMond in 1990.

LeMond had been the only American to win the Tour, but he did it with European-stocked teams. Armstrong was riding for the U.S. Postal Service team, made up of Americans Frankie Andreu, George Hincapie, Tyler Hamilton, Kevin Livingston, Christian Vande Velde, Jonathan Vaughters, and Frenchman Pascale Derame. They made sure Armstrong could conserve his energy for the crux of the 20-stage Tour, particularly stages eight and nine.

Stage eight is a 35-mile individual time trial, regarded as a "race of truth" because riders can't draft behind teammates. Stage nine is a brutal 130-mile trek into the Alps.

Armstrong, who often trains alone, beat Zuelle by 58 seconds in the time trial. The next day, with four miles to go in the climb into the Alps, Armstrong made his move. Zuelle asked his lungs to answer. They could not. No mercy. Grinding, relentless, confronting his inner voice and the blazing pain, Armstrong pounded out a 31-second win, expanding his overall lead to an insurmountable six minutes, three seconds.

AP/Wide World Photos

Sprinter **Marion Jones** lies on the track in pain after suffering back spasms during the 200-meter semifinal at the World Championships. She did win the 100-meter gold medal but was hoping for much more.

The Posties protected him until the penultimate stage a week and a half later. Armstrong won that time trial too. And on the Tour's last day, he wore the yellow into Paris for the largely-ceremonial ride 'round the Champs Elysees that celebrates not only the champions of the Tour de France, but also its survivors. ∎

Jack Edwards' Top Ten Newsmakers of the Year in International Sports

10. In the wake of a world-wide scandal, the **International Olympic Committee** invites further scrutiny by saying it has changed its bribe-demanding ways in the site bidding process. We'll see.

9. **Canadian Peter Reid** wins the Hawaii Ironman Triathlon in eight hours, 24 minutes, 20 seconds, with a time differential 1.5 percent better than second-place finisher Luc Van Lierde. Reid's wife, Lori Bowden, takes second in the women's race.

8. **Natascha Badmann** is the one woman better than Bowden, but not by much as the top three finishers are separated by a 0.7 percent time differential.

7. **Norway's Lasse Kjus and Kjetil Andre Aamodt** finish 1-2 in the men's overall World Cup Alpine Skiing standings. The win is Kjus' second overall World Cup championship (1996).

6. **The Austrian skiing dynasty** isn't dead though. Led by Olympic hero Hermann Maier, the Austrian men take eight of the top 11 overall World Cup Alpine spots (3-4-5-6-7-9-10-11).

5. Oh yeah, the **Austrian women** can ski too. Alexandra Meissnitzer wins the World Cup, with the three other Austrians in the top 8. The top American you ask? 36th, Kristina Koznick.

AP/Wide World Photos

A total of 12 world records were set at the 1999 Pan Pacific Championships in Sydney, four by South African **Penny Heyns**, who acknowledges the crowd here after setting a new standard in the 200-meter breaststroke.

FAST FORWARD

On June 16, Maurice Greene returned the 100-meter world record to the United States and proved to the world what he already knew — that he's the fastest man in the world. He not only broke the record, he shattered it by five one-hundredths of a second, the largest improvement since records were first compiled in 1912. The table below shows the progression of the world mark.

4. **Marion Jones** aims for four gold medals at the World Track and Field Championships in Seville, Spain and wins one (100-meters) before blowing out her back.

3. **Michael Johnson** breaks Butch Reynolds' 11-year-old 400-meter world record, blazing to a 43.18 at the World Championships.

2. In a record-breaking bonanza at the Pan Pacific Championships in Sydney, **Jenny Thompson swims** a 57.88 to break Mary T. Meagher's 18-year-old 100-meter butterfly world record.

1. **Lance Armstrong survives** cancer and wins the Tour de France. ∎

Time		Date
10.6	Donald Lippincott, USA	7/6/12
10.4	Charles Paddock, USA	4/23/21
10.3	Percy Williams, CAN	8/9/30
10.2	Jesse Owens, USA	6/20/36
10.1	Willie Williams, USA	8/3/56
10.0	Armin Hary, W. GER	6/21/60
9.99	Jim Hines, USA	6/20/68
9.95	Jim Hines, USA	10/14/68
9.93	Calvin Smith, USA	7/3/83
9.92	Carl Lewis, USA	9/24/88
9.90	Leroy Burrell, USA	6/14/91
9.86	Carl Lewis, USA	8/25/91
9.85	Leroy Burrell, USA	7/6/94
9.84	Donovan Bailey, CAN	7/27/96
9.79	Maurice Greene, USA	6/16/99

Note: Before 1968, times were registered in 10ths of a second.

AP/Wide World Photos

Apparently healed from his spectacular 1998 Olympic crash, Austria's **Hermann Maier** won the World Cup Super G title in 1999 and took two golds at the World Alpine Championships at Vail.

NEW AND IMPROVED

It's miraculous enough that Lance Armstrong returned to the cycling circuit at all after his bout with cancer, but what's truly amazing is that he returned even better than he was before the disease struck. He had always been considered a solid "single day" racer but finally put it all together in 1999 over the grueling, three-week test. Below are his overall finishes and stage wins from his four Tour de Frances before cancer and the one after.

Year	Overall Finish	Stage Wins
1993	withdrew	1 (Verdun)
1994	withdrew	0
1995	36th	1 (Limoges)
1996	withdrew	0
1999	1st	3 (Metz) (Sestrieres) (Futuroscope)

SPLITSVILLE

Most of us just can't fathom how fast elite marathoners really are. Take a look at the 5-kilometer split times (a distance the average runner is a little more familiar with) recorded by 1999 Boston Marathon winner Joseph Chebet. How's that for consistency? And note that he actually gets faster as the race goes on. Of the six marathons Chebet has run in his career, this one was his slowest.

Split	Time	Total Time Elapsed
5K	15:46	15:46
10K	15:41	31:27
15K	15:22	46:49
20K	15:17	1:02:06
25K	15:22	1:17:28
30K	15:27	1:32:55
35K	15:05	1:48:00
40K	15:03	2:03:03
Finish	—	2:09:52

Note: 5 kilometers = 3.1 miles ∎

INT'L SPORTS
STATISTICS

THE SEASON IN REVIEW
1998-1999
CHAMPIONS • RECORDS

SEC A

PAGE 703

THE 2000 ESPN INFORMATION PLEASE SPORTS ALMANAC

TRACK & FIELD

1999 IAAF World Championships

The 7th IAAF World Championships in athletics were held in Seville, Spain, Aug. 20-29, 1999. Note that (WR) indicates world record while (=WR) indicates the record was tied.

Final Medal Standings – Top Ten

		G	S	B	Total			G	S	B	Total
1	United States	11	3	3	17		Kenya	1	4	1	6
2	Russia	6	3	4	13		Jamaica	0	1	5	6
3	Germany	4	4	4	12	8	Morocco	2	2	1	5
4	Great Britain	1	4	2	7		Ethiopia	2	0	3	5
5	Greece	2	2	2	6	10	Six countries tied with 4 medals each.				

MEN

Event		Time
100 meters	Maurice Greene, USA	9.80
200 meters	Maurice Greene, USA	19.90
400 meters	Michael Johnson, USA	43.18 **WR**
800 meters	Wilson Kipketer, DEN	1:43.30
1500 meters	Hicham El Guerrouj, MOR	3:27.65
5000 meters	Salah Hissou, MOR	12:58.13
10,000 meters	Haile Gebrselassie, ETH	27:57.27
Marathon	Abel Anton, SPA	2:13:36
4x100m relay	USA (Drummond, Montgomery, Lewis, Greene)	37.59
4x400m relay	USA (Davis, Pettigrew, Taylor, Johnson)	2:56.45
110m hurdles	Colin Jackson, GBR	13.04
400m hurdles	Fabrizio Mori, ITA	47.72
3000m steeple	Christopher Koskei, KEN	8:11.76
20k walk	Ilya Markov, RUS	1:23:34
50k walk	German Skurygin, RUS	3:44:23

Event		Hgt/Dist
High Jump	Vyacheslav Voronin, RUS	7-9¼
Pole Vault	Maksim Tarasov, RUS	19-9
Long Jump	Ivan Pedroso, CUB	28-1
Triple Jump	Charles Michael Friedek, GER	57-8½
Shot Put	C.J. Hunter, USA	71-6
Discus	Anthony Washington, USA	226-7
Hammer	Karsten Kobs, GER	263-3
Javelin	Aki Parviainen, FIN	293-8
Decathlon	Tomas Dvorak, CZE	8744 pts

WOMEN

Event		Time
100 meters	Marion Jones, USA	10.70
200 meters	Inger Miller, USA	21.77
400 meters	Cathy Freeman, AUS	49.67
800 meters	Ludmila Formanova, CZE	1:56.68
1500 meters	Svetlana Masterkova, RUS	3:59.53
5000 meters	Gabriela Szabo, ROM	14:41.82
10,000 meters	Gete Wami, ETH	30:24.56
Marathon	Jong Song-Ok, N. Kor.	2:26:59
4x100m relay	Bahamas (Fynes, Sturrup, Davis-Thompson, Ferguson)	41.92
4x400m relay	Russia (Chebykina, Goncharenko, Kotlyarova, Nazarova)	3:21.98
100m hurdles	Gail Devers, USA	12.37
400m hurdles	Daima Pernia, CUB	52.89
20k walk	Hongyu Liu, CHN	1:30:50

Event		Hgt/Dist
High Jump	Inga Babakova, UKR	6-6¼
Pole Vault	Stacy Dragila, USA	15-1 **=WR**
Long Jump	Niurka Montalvo, SPA	23-2
Triple Jump	Paraskevi Tsiamita, GRE	48-10
Shot Put	Astrid Kumbernuss, GER	65-1½
Discus	Franka Dietzsch, GER	223-6
Hammer	Mihaela Melinte, ROM	246-8¾
Javelin	Mirela Manjani-Tzelili, GRE	220-1
Heptathlon	Eunice Barber, FRA	6861 pts

XIII Pan American Games

The 13th Pan American Games were held in Winnipeg, Canada from July 23-Aug. 8, 1999. More than 5,000 athletes from 42 countries in North, South and Central America and the Caribbean participated in 41 sports, making it the third-largest multi-sport event ever held in North America (behind the 1984 and 1996 Summer Olympics). The games have been held every four years since 1951.

Final Medal Standings – Top Ten

		G	S	B	Total			G	S	B	Total
1	United States	106	110	79	295	6	Mexico	11	16	30	57
2	Canada	64	52	80	196	7	Colombia	6	18	18	42
3	Cuba	70	40	47	157	8	Venezuela	7	16	17	40
4	Brazil	25	32	44	101	9	Jamaica	3	4	6	13
5	Argentina	25	19	28	72		Puerto Rico	1	3	9	13

1999 IAAF World Indoor Championships

The 7th IAAF World Indoor Championships in athletics were held in Maebashi, Japan, March 5-7, 1999. Note that (WR) indicates world record.

Final Medal Standings – Top Ten

		G	S	B	Total			G	S	B	Total
1	United States	3	8	9	20	6	Romania	3	1	0	4
2	Russia	3	3	1	7		Czech Republic	1	1	2	4
	Germany	3	0	4	7	8	Ethiopia	2	0	1	3
4	Great Britain	3	0	2	5		Bulgaria	1	1	1	3
	Poland	1	2	2	5	10	Six countries tied with 2 medals each.				

MEN

Event		Time
60 meters	Maurice Greene, USA	6.42
200 meters	Frank Fredericks, NAM	20.10
400 meters	Jamie Baulch, GBR	45.73
800 meters	Rohan Botha, S. Afr.	1:45.47
1500 meters	Haile Gebrselassie, ETH	3:33.77
3000 meters	Haile Gebrselassie, ETH	7:53.57
60-m hurdles	Colin Jackson, GBR	7.38
4x400-m relay	USA (Morris, Johnson, Minor, Campbell)	3:02.83 **WR**

Event		Hgt/Dist
High Jump	Javier Sotomayor, CUB	7-8¾
Pole Vault	Jean Galfione, FRA	19-8¼
Long Jump	Iván Pedroso, CUB	28-3½
Triple Jump	Charles Michael Friedek, GER	56-4½
Shot Put	Aleksandr Bagach, UKR	70-3
Heptathlon	Sebastian Chmara, POL	6386 pts

WOMEN

Event		Time
60 meters	Ekaterini Thanou, GRE	6.96
200 meters	Ionela Tirlea, ROM	22.39
400 meters	Grit Breuer, GER	50.80
800 meters	Ludmila Formanová, CZE	1:56.90
1500 meters	Gabriela Szabo, ROM	4:03.23
3000 meters	Gabriela Szabo, ROM	8:36.42
60-m hurdles	Olga Shishigina, KAZ	7.86
4x400-m relay	Russia (Chebykina, Goncharenko, Kotlyarova, Nazarova)	3:24.25 **WR**

Event		Hgt/Dist
High Jump	Khristina Kalcheva, BUL	6-6¼
Pole Vault	Nastja Ryshich, GER	14-9
Long Jump	Tatyana Kotova, RUS	22-6¼
Triple Jump	Ashia Hansen, GBR	49-3½
Shot Put	Svetlana Krivelyova, RUS	62-7¼
Pentathlon	DeDee Nathan, USA	4753 pts

World, Olympic and American Records

As of Sept. 7, 1999

World outdoor records officially recognized by the International Amateur Athletics Federation (IAAF).

MEN
Running

Event		Time		Date Set	Location
100 meters:	**World**	9.79	**Maurice Greene**, USA	June 16, 1999	Athens
	Olympic	9.84	Donovan Bailey, Canada	July 27, 1996	Atlanta
	American	9.79	Greene (same as World)	—	—
200 meters:	**World**	19.32	**Michael Johnson**, USA	Aug. 1, 1996	Atlanta
	Olympic	19.32	Johnson (same as World)	—	—
	American	19.32	Johnson (same as World)	—	—
400 meters:	**World**	43.18	**Michael Johnson**, USA	Aug. 26, 1999	Seville
	Olympic	43.49	Michael Johnson, USA	July 29, 1996	Atlanta
	American	43.18	Johnson (same as World)	—	—
800 meters:	**World**	1:41.11	**Wilson Kipketer**, Denmark	Aug. 24, 1997	Cologne
	Olympic	1:42.58	Vebjoern Rodal, Norway	July 31, 1996	Atlanta
	American	1:42.60	Johnny Gray	Aug. 28, 1985	Koblenz, W. Ger.
1000 meters:	**World**	2:12.18	**Sebastian Coe**, Great Britain	July 11, 1981	Oslo
	Olympic		Not an event		
	American	2:13.9	Rick Wohlhuter	July 30, 1974	Oslo
1500 meters:	**World**	3:26.00	**Hicham El Guerrouj**, Morocco	July 14, 1998	Rome
	Olympic	3:32.53	Sebastian Coe, Great Britain	Aug. 11, 1984	Los Angeles
	American	3:29.77	Sydney Maree	Aug. 25, 1985	Cologne
Mile:	**World**	3:43.13	**Hicham El Guerrouj**, Morocco	July 7, 1999	Rome
	Olympic		Not an event		
	American	3:47.69	Steve Scott	July 7, 1982	Oslo
2000 meters:	**World**	4:44.79	**Hicham El Guerrouj**, Morocco	Sept. 7, 1999	Berlin
	Olympic		Not an event		
	American	4:52.44	Jim Spivey	Sept. 15, 1987	Lausanne, SWI
3000 meters:	**World**	7:20.67	**Daniel Komen**, Kenya	Sept. 1, 1996	Riete, ITA
	Olympic		Not an event		
	American	7:30.84	Bob Kennedy	Aug. 8, 1998	Monte Carlo
5000 meters:	**World**	12:39.36	**Haile Gebrselassie**, Ethiopia	June 13, 1998	Helsinki
	Olympic	13:05.59	Said Aouita, Morocco	Aug. 11, 1984	Los Angeles
	American	12:58.21	Bob Kennedy	Aug. 14, 1996	Zurich
10,000 meters:	**World**	26:22.75	**Haile Gebrselassie**, Ethiopia	June 1, 1998	Hengelo, NED
	Olympic	27:07.34	Haile Gebrselassie, Ethiopia	July 29, 1996	Atlanta
	American	27:20.56	Mark Nenow	Sept. 5, 1986	Brussels

Event		Time		Date Set	Location
20,000 meters:	**World**	....56:55.6	**Arturo Barrios**, Mexico	Mar. 30, 1991	La Fleche, FRA
	Olympic		Not an event	—	—
	American	...58:15.0	Bill Rodgers	Aug. 9, 1977	Boston
Marathon:	**World**	....2:06:05	**Ronaldo da Costa**, Brazil	Sept. 20, 1998	Berlin
	Olympic	...2:09:21	Carlos Lopes, Portugal	Aug. 12, 1984	Los Angeles
	American	...2:09:35	Jerry Lawson	Oct. 19, 1997	Chicago
		..........2:08:52*	Alberto Salazar	Apr. 19, 1982	Boston

Note: The Mile run is 1,609.344 meters and the Marathon is 42,194.988 meters (26 miles, 385 yards).
*Former American record no longer officially recognized.

Relays

Event		Time		Date Set	Location
4 x 100m:	**World**	.......37.40	**USA** (Marsh, Burrell, Mitchell, C. Lewis)	Aug. 8, 1992	Barcelona
		...........37.40	**USA** (Drummond, Cason, Mitchell, Burrell)	Aug. 21, 1993	Stuttgart
	Olympic	.......37.40	USA (same as World)	—	—
	American	.....37.40	USA (same as World)	—	—
4 x 200m:	**World**	......1:18.68	**USA** (Marsh, Burrell, Heard, C. Lewis)	Apr. 17, 1994	Walnut, Calif.
	Olympic	....	Not an event	—	—
	American	...1:18.68	USA (same as World)	—	—
4 x 400m:	**World**	......2:54.20	**USA** (Young, Pettigrew, Washington, Johnson)	July 22, 1998	Uniondale, N.Y.
	Olympic	.....2:55.74	USA (Valmon, Watts, Johnson, S. Lewis)	Aug. 8, 1992	Barcelona
	American	...2:54.20	USA (same as World)	—	—
4 x 800m:	**World**	.....7:03.89	**Great Britain** (Elliott, Cook, Cram, Coe)	Aug. 30, 1982	London
	Olympic	....	Not an event	—	—
	American	.....7:06.5	Santa Monica TC (J. Robinson, Mack, E. Jones, Gray)	Apr. 26, 1986	Walnut, Calif.
4 x 1500m:	**World**	......14:38.8	**West Germany** (Wessinghage, Hudak, Lederer, Fleschen)	Aug. 17, 1977	Cologne
	Olympic	....	Not an event	—	—
	American	...14:46.3	USA (Aldredge, Clifford, Harbour, Duits)	June 24, 1979	Bourges, FRA

Hurdles

Event		Time		Date Set	Location
110 meters:	**World**	........12.91	**Colin Jackson**, Great Britain	Aug. 20, 1993	Stuttgart
	Olympic	.......12.95	Allen Johnson, USA	July 29, 1996	Atlanta
	American	......12.92	Roger Kingdom	Aug. 16, 1989	Zurich
		.............12.92	Allen Johnson	June 23, 1996	Atlanta
400 meters:	**World**	........46.78	**Kevin Young**, USA	Aug. 6, 1992	Barcelona
	Olympic	......46.78	Young (same as World)	—	—
	American	.....46.78	Young (same as World)	—	—

Note: The 10 hurdles at 110 meters are 3 feet, 6 inches high and those at 400 meters are 3 feet.

Walking

Event		Time		Date Set	Location
20 km:	**World**	......1:17:26	**Bernardo Segura**, Mexico	May 7, 1994	Fana, NOR
	Olympic	.....1:19:57	Jozef Pribilinec, Czechoslovakia	Sept. 23, 1988	Seoul
	American	...1:24:27	Allen James	May 7, 1994	Fana, NOR
50 km:	**World**	.....3:37:41	**Andrey Perlov**, Russia	Aug. 5, 1989	Leningrad
	Olympic	.....3:38:29	Vyacheslav Ivanenko, USSR	Sept. 30, 1988	Seoul
	American	...3:50:55	Curt Clausen	Aug. 25, 1999	Seville

Steeplechase

Event		Time		Date Set	Location
3000 meters:	**World**	.....7:55.72	**Bernard Barmasai**, Kenya	Aug. 24, 1997	Cologne
	Olympic	....8:05.51	Julius Kariuki, Kenya	Sept. 30, 1988	Seoul
	American	....8:09.17	Henry Marsh	Aug. 28, 1985	Koblenz

Note: A steeplechase course consists of 28 hurdles (3 feet high) and seven water jumps (12 feet long).

Field Events

Event		Mark		Date Set	Location
High Jump:	**World**	.......8-0½	**Javier Sotomayor**, Cuba	July 27, 1993	Salamanca, SPA
	Olympic	7-10	Charles Austin, USA	July 28, 1996	Atlanta
	American	....7-10½	Charles Austin	Aug. 7, 1991	Zurich
Pole Vault:	**World**	.....20-1¾	**Sergey Bubka**, Ukraine	July 31, 1994	Sestriere, ITA
	Olympic	.....19-5¼	Jean Galfione, France	Aug. 2, 1996	Atlanta
		...........19-5¼	Igor Trandenkov, Russia	Aug. 2, 1996	Atlanta
		...........19-5¼	Andrei Tiwontschik, Germany	Aug. 2, 1996	Atlanta
	American	...19-8½	Jeff Hartwig	July 21, 1998	Uniondale, N.Y.

Event		Mark		Date Set	Location
Long Jump:	World	29-4¾*	**Ivan Pedroso**, Cuba	July 29, 1995	Sestriere, ITA
		29-4½	**Mike Powell**, USA	Aug. 30, 1991	Tokyo
	Olympic	29-2½	Bob Beamon, USA	Oct. 18, 1968	Mexico City
	American	29-4½	Powell (same as World)	–	
Triple Jump:	World	60-0¼	**Jonathan Edwards**, GBR	Aug. 7, 1995	Göteborg, SWE
	Olympic	59-4¼	Kenny Harrison, USA	July 27, 1996	Atlanta
	American	59-4¼	Kenny Harrison (same as Olympic)	—	
Shot Put:	World	75-10¼	**Randy Barnes**, USA	May 20, 1990	Los Angeles
	Olympic	73-8¾	Ulf Timmermann, East Germany	Sept. 23, 1988	Seoul
	American	75-10¼	Barnes (same as World)	—	
Discus:	World	243-0	**Jurgen Schult**, East Germany	June 6, 1986	Neubrandenburg
	Olympic	227-8	Lare Reidel, Germany	July 31, 1996	Atlanta
	American	237-4	Ben Plucknett	July 7, 1981	Stockholm
Javelin:	World	323-1	**Jan Zelezny**, Czech Republic	May 25, 1996	Jena, GER
	Olympic	294-2	Jan Zelezny, Czechoslovakia	Aug. 8, 1992	Barcelona
	American	285-10	Tom Pukstys	May 25, 1997	Jena, GER
Hammer:	World	284-7	**Yuriy Sedykh**, USSR	Aug. 30, 1986	Stuttgart
	Olympic	278-2	Sergey Litvinov, USSR	Sept. 26, 1988	Seoul
	American	270-9	Lance Deal	Sept. 7, 1996	Milan

Note: The international weights for men— **Shot** (16 lbs); **Discus** (4 lbs/6.55 oz); **Javelin** (minimum 1 lb/124¼ oz.); **Hammer** (16 lbs).
*Apparent world record disallowed because of interference with wind gauge at altitude.

Decathlon

Event		Points		Date Set	Location
Ten Events:	World	8994	**Tomas Dvorak**, Czech.	July 3-4, 1999	Prague
	Olympic	8847	Daley Thompson, Great Britain	Aug. 8-9, 1984	Los Angeles
	American	8891	Dan O'Brien	Sept. 4-5, 1992	Talence, FRA

Note: Dvorak's WR times and distances, in order over two days— **100m** (10.54); **LJ** (25-11); **Shot** (55-0); **HJ** (6-8¼); **400m** (48.08); **110m H** (13.73); **Discus** (158-6); **PV** (16-0¾); **Jav** (237-3); **1500m** (4:37.20).

WOMEN
Running

Event		Time		Date Set	Location
100 meters:	World	10.49	**Florence Griffith Joyner**, USA	July 16, 1988	Indianapolis
	Olympic	10.62	Florence Griffith Joyner, USA	Sept. 24, 1988	Seoul
	American	10.49	Griffith Joyner (same as World)	—	
200 meters:	World	21.34	**Florence Griffith Joyner**, USA	Sept. 29, 1988	Seoul
	Olympic	21.34	Griffith Joyner (same as World)	—	
	American	21.34	Griffith Joyner (same as World)	—	
400 meters:	World	47.60	**Marita Koch**, East Germany	Oct. 6, 1985	Canberra, AUS
	Olympic	48.65	Olga Bryzgina, USSR	Sept. 26, 1988	Seoul
	American	48.83	Valerie Brisco	Aug. 6, 1984	Los Angeles
800 meters:	World	1:53.28	**Jarmila Kratochvilova**, Czech.	July 26, 1983	Munich
	Olympic	1:53.42	Nadezhda Olizarenko, USSR	July 27, 1980	Moscow
	American	1:56.43	Jearl Miles-Clark	Aug. 12, 1998	Zurich
1000 meters:	World	2:28.98	**Svetlana Masterkova**, Russia	Aug. 23, 1996	Brussels
	Olympic		Not an event		
	American	2:31.80	Regina Jacobs	July 3, 1999	Brunswick, Me.
1500 meters:	World	3:50.46	**Qu Yunxia**, China	Sept. 11, 1993	Beijing
	Olympic	3:53.96	Paula Ivan, Romania	Oct. 1, 1988	Seoul
	American	3:57.12	Mary Slaney	July 26, 1983	Stockholm
Mile:	World	4:12.56	**Svetlana Masterkova**, Russia	Aug. 14, 1996	Zurich
	Olympic		Not an event	—	—
	American	4:16.71	Mary Slaney	Aug. 21, 1985	Zurich
2000 meters:	World	5:25.36	**Sonia O'Sullivan**, Ireland	July 8, 1994	Edinburgh
	Olympic		Not an event	—	—
	American	5:32.7	Mary Slaney	Aug. 3, 1984	Eugene
3000 meters:	World	8:06.11	**Wang Junxia**, China	Sept. 13, 1993	Beijing
	Olympic	8:26.53	Tatyana Samolenko, USSR	Sept. 25, 1988	Seoul
	American	8:25.83	Mary Slaney	Sept. 7, 1985	Rome
5000 meters:	World	14:28.09	**Jiang Bo**, China	Oct. 23, 1997	Shanghai
	Olympic		Not an event	—	—
	American	14:52.49	Regina Jacobs	July 4, 1998	Brunswick, Me.
10,000 meters:	World	29:31.78	**Wang Junxia**, China	Sept. 8, 1993	Beijing
	Olympic	31:05.21	Olga Bondarenko, USSR	Sept. 30, 1988	Seoul
	American	31:19.89	Lynn Jennings	Aug. 7, 1992	Barcelona
Marathon:	World	2:20:47	**Tegla Loroupe**, Kenya	Apr. 19, 1998	Rotterdam
	Olympic	2:24:52	Joan Benoit, USA	Aug. 5, 1984	Los Angeles
	American	2:21:21	Joan Benoit Samuelson	Oct. 20, 1985	Chicago

Note: The Mile run is 1,609.344 meters and the Marathon is 42,194.988 meters (26 miles, 385 yards).

Relays

Event		Time		Date Set	Location
4 x 100m:	**World**	.......41.37	**East Germany** (Gladisch, Rieger, Auerswald, Gohr)	Oct. 6, 1985	Canberra, AUS
	Olympic	.......41.60	East Germany (Muller, Wockel, Auerswald, Gohr)	Aug. 1, 1980	Moscow
	American	......41.47	USA (Gaines, Jones, Miller, Devers)	Aug. 9, 1997	Athens
4 x 200m:	**World**	......1:28.15	**East Germany** (Gohr, Muller, Wockel, Koch)	Aug. 9, 1980	Jena, E. Ger.
	Olympic	....	Not an event	—	—
	American	....1:29.64	Nike International (Roberts, Miller, Green, Jones)	Apr. 25, 1998	Philadelphia
4 x 400m:	**World**	......3:15.17	**USSR** (Ledovskaya, Nazarova, Pinigina, Bryzgina)	Oct. 1, 1988	Seoul
	Olympic	.....3:15.17	USSR (same as World)	—	—
	American	....3:15.51	USA (Howard, Dixon, Brisco, Griffith Joyner)	Oct. 1, 1988	Seoul
4 x 800m:	**World**	......7:50.17	**USSR** (Olizarenko, Gurina, Borisova, Podyalovskaya)	Aug. 5, 1984	Moscow
	Olympic	....	Not an event	—	—
	American	....8:17.09	Athletics West (Addison, Arbogast, Decker Slaney, Mullen)	Apr. 24, 1983	Walnut, Calif.

Hurdles

Event		Time		Date Set	Location
100 meters:	**World**	.......12.21	**Yordanka Donkova**, Bulgaria	Aug. 20, 1988	Stara Zagora, BUL
	Olympic	.......12.38	Yordanka Donkova, Bulgaria	Sept. 30, 1988	Seoul
	American	.......12.37	Gail Devers	Aug. 28, 1999	Seville
400 meters:	**World**	.......52.61	**Kim Batten**, USA	Aug. 11, 1995	Göteborg, SWE
	Olympic	.......53.17	Debra Flintoff-King, Australia	Sept. 28, 1988	Seoul
	American	.......52.61	Batten (same as World)	—	—

Note: The 10 hurdles at 110 meters are 3 feet, 6 inches high and those at 400 meters are 3 feet.

Walking

Event		Time		Date Set	Location
5 km:	**World**	.....20:13.26	**Kerry Saxby-Junna**, Australia	Feb. 25, 1996	Hobart, AUS
	Olympic	....	Not an event	—	—
	American	..21:28.17	Teresa Vaill	Apr. 24, 1993	Philadelphia
10 km:	**World**	....41:56.23	**Nadezhda Ryashkina**, Russia	July 24, 1990	Seattle
	Olympic	...41.49*	Yelena Nikolayeva, Russia	July 29, 1996	Atlanta
	American	..44:41.87	Michelle Rohl	July 26, 1994	St. Petersburg

*road

Field Events

Event		Mark		Date Set	Location
High Jump:	**World**	......6-10¼	**Stefka Kostadinova**, Bulgaria	Aug. 30, 1987	Rome
	Olympic	6-8	Louise Ritter, USA	Sept. 30, 1988	Seoul
	American	6-8	Louise Ritter	July 8, 1988	Austin, Tex.
		6-8	Ritter (same as Olympic)	—	—
Pole Vault:	**World**	15-1	**Emma George**, Australia	Feb. 20, 1999	Sydney
		15-1	**Stacy Dragila**, USA	Aug. 21, 1999	Seville
	Olympic	....	Not an event	—	—
	American	15-1	Dragila (same as World)	—	—
Long Jump:	**World**	......24-8¼	**Galina Chistyakova**, USSR	June 11, 1988	Leningrad
	Olympic	...24-3¼	Jackie Joyner-Kersee, USA	Sept. 29, 1988	Seoul
	American	24-7	Jackie Joyner-Kersee	May 22, 1994	New York
Triple Jump:	**World**	.....50-10¼	**Inessa Kravets**, Ukraine	Aug. 8, 1995	Göteborg, SWE
	Olympic	....50-3½	Inessa Kravets, Ukraine	July 31, 1996	Atlanta
	American	..47-3½	Sheila Hudson	July 8, 1996	Stockholm
Shot Put:	**World**	74-3	**Natalya Lisovskaya**, USSR	June 7, 1987	Moscow
	Olympic	...73-6¼	Ilona Slupianek, E. Germany	July 24, 1980	Moscow
	American	..66-2½	Ramona Pagel	June 25, 1988	San Diego
Discus:	**World**	252-0	**Gabriele Reinsch**, E. Germany	July 9, 1988	Neubrandenburg
	Olympic	...237-2½	Martina Hellmann, E. Germany	Sept. 29, 1988	Seoul
	American	.216-10	Carol Cady	May 31, 1986	San Jose
Javelin:	**World**	....262-5*	**Petra Felke**, E. Germany	Sept. 9, 1988	Potsdam, E. Ger
	Olympic	...245-0*	Petra Felke, E. Germany	Sept. 26, 1988	Seoul
	American	.227-5*	Kate Schmidt	Sept. 10, 1977	Furth, W. Ger.
Hammer:	**World**	249-2	**Mihaela Melinte**, Romania	May 13, 1999	Clermont-Ferrand
	Olympic	....	Not an event	—	—
	American	...230-2	Dawn Ellerbe	Mar. 15, 1999	Laramie, Wyo.

*The IAAF changed the official design and weight for the women's javelin beginning April 1, 1999. The records shown are with the old-style javelins and will be removed from the record book on Jan. 1, 2000.

Note: The international weights for women— **Shot** (8 lbs/13 oz); **Discus** (2 lbs/3.27 oz); **Javelin** (minimum 1 lb/5.16 oz); **Hammer** (16 lbs).

Heptathlon

	Points		Date Set	Location
Seven Events:	**World** 7291*	**Jackie Joyner-Kersee**, USA	Sept. 23-24, 1988	Seoul
	Olympic 7291*	Joyner-Kersee (same as World)	—	—
	American 7291*	Joyner-Kersee (same as World)	—	—

*Due to the April 1, 1999 change in the design of the women's javelin, Joyner-Kersee's records will be replaced by new records, effective Jan. 1, 2000.
Note: Joyner-Kersee's WR times and distances, in order over two days— **100m H** (12.69); **HJ** (61¼); **Shot** (51-10); **200m** (22.56); **LJ** (2310¼); **Jav** (149-10); **800m** (2:08.51).

World and American Indoor Records
As of Sept. 1, 1999

World indoor records officially recognized by the International Amateur Athletics Federation (IAAF); (p) indicates record is pending ratification by the IAAF; (a) indicates record was set at an altitude over 1000 meters.

MEN
Running

Event	Time		Date Set	Location
50 meters:	**World** 5.56a	**Donovan Bailey**, Canada	Feb. 9, 1996	Reno, Nev.
	..............5.56p	**Maurice Greene**, USA	Feb. 13, 1999	Los Angeles
	American......5.56p	Greene (same as World)	Feb. 13, 1999	Los Angeles
60 meters:	**World** 6.39	**Maurice Greene**, USA	Feb. 3, 1998	Madrid
	American......6.39	Greene (same as World)	—	—
200 meters:	**World** 19.92	**Frankie Fredericks**, Namibia	Feb. 18, 1996	Lievin, FRA
	American 20.32	Rohsaan Griffin	Feb. 27, 1999	Atlanta
		& Kevin Little	Mar. 5, 1999	Maebashi, JPN
400 meters:	**World** 44.63	**Michael Johnson**, USA	Mar. 4, 1995	Atlanta
	American 44.63	Johnson (same as World)	—	—
800 meters:	**World** 1:42.67	**Wilson Kipketer**, Denmark	Mar. 9, 1997	Paris
	American 1:45.00	Johnny Gray	Mar. 8, 1992	Sindelfingen, GER
1000 meters:	**World** 2:15.26	**Noureddine Morceli**, Algeria	Feb. 22, 1992	Birmingham, ENG
	American 2:18.19	Ocky Clark	Feb. 12, 1989	Stuttgart
1500 meters:	**World** 3:31.18	**Hicham El Guerrouj**, Morocco	Feb. 2, 1997	Stuttgart
	American 3:38.12	Jeff Atkinson	Mar. 5, 1989	Budapest
Mile:	**World** 3:48.45	**Hicham El Guerrouj**, Morocco	Feb. 12, 1997	Ghent, BEL
	American 3:51.8	Steve Scott	Feb. 20, 1981	San Diego
3000 meters:	World......7:24.90	**Daniel Komen**, Kenya	Feb. 6, 1998	Budapest
	American 7:39.94	Steve Scott	Feb. 10, 1989	E. Rutherford, N.J.
5000 meters:	**World** ...12:50.38	**Haile Gebrselassie**, Ethiopia	Feb. 14, 1999	Birmingham, ENG
	American .13:20.55	Doug Padilla	Feb. 12, 1982	New York

Note: The Mile run is 1,609.344 meters.

Hurdles

Event	Time		Date Set	Location
50 meters:	**World** 6.25	**Mark McKoy**, Canada	Mar. 5, 1986	Kobe, JPN
	American 6.35	Greg Foster	Jan. 27, 1985	Rosemont, Ill.
	..............6.35	Greg Foster	Jan. 31, 1987	Ottawa
60 meters:	**World** 7.30	**Colin Jackson**, Britain	Mar. 6, 1994	Sindelfingen, GER
	American 7.36	Greg Foster	Jan. 16, 1987	Los Angeles

Note: The hurdles for both distances are 3 feet, 6 inches high. There are four hurdles in the 50 meters and five in the 60.

Relays

Event	Time		Date Set	Location
4 x 200 meters:	**World** 1:22.11	**Great Britain**	Mar. 3, 1991	Glasgow
	American 1:22.71	National Team	Mar. 3, 1991	Glasgow
4 x 400 meters:	**World** 3:02.83	**United States**	Mar. 7, 1999	Maebashi, JPN
	American 3:02.83	National Team (same as World)	Mar. 7, 1999	Maebashi, JPN

Field Events

Events	Time		Date Set	Location
High Jump:	**World** 7-11½	**Javier Sotomayor**, Cuba	Mar. 4, 1989	Budapest
	American 7-10½	Hollis Conway	Mar. 10, 1991	Seville
Pole Vault:	**World** 20-2	**Sergey Bubka**, Ukraine	Feb. 21, 1993	Donyetsk, UKR
	American 19-6¼	Jeff Hartwig	Mar. 6, 1999	Maebashi, JPN
Long Jump:	**World** 28-10¼	**Carl Lewis**, USA	Jan. 27, 1984	New York
	American 28-10¼	Lewis (same as World)	—	—
Triple Jump:	**World** 58-6	**Aliecer Urrutia**, Cuba	Mar. 1, 1997	Sindelfingen, GER
	American 58-3¼	Mike Conley	Feb. 27, 1987	New York
Shot Put:	**World** 74-4¼	**Randy Barnes**, USA	Jan. 20, 1989	Los Angeles
	American 74-4¼	Barnes (same as World)	—	—

Note: The international shot put weight for men is 16 lbs.

Heptathlon

		Points		Date Set	Location
Seven Events:	World	6476	**Dan O'Brien**, USA	Mar. 13-14, 1993	Toronto
	American	6476	O'Brien (same as World)	—	—

Note: O'Brien's WR times and distances, in order over two days— **60m** (6.67); **LJ** (25-8¾); **SP** (52-6¾); **HJ** (6-11¾); **60m H** (7.85); **PV** (17-0¾); **1000m** (2:57.96).

WOMEN
Running

Event		Time		Date Set	Location
50 meters:	World	5.96	**Irina Privalova**, Russia	Feb. 9, 1995	Madrid
	American	6.02p	Gail Devers	Feb. 21, 1999	Lievin, FRA
60 meters:	World	6.92	**Irina Privalova**, Russia	Feb. 11, 1993	Madrid
		6.92	**Irina Privalova**, Russia	Feb. 9, 1995	Madrid
	American	6.95	Gail Devers	Mar. 12, 1993	Toronto
		6.95	Marion Jones	Mar. 7, 1998	Maebashi, JPN
200 meters:	World	21.87	**Merlene Ottey**, Jamaica	Feb. 13, 1993	Lievin, FRA
	American	22.33	Gwen Torrence	Mar. 2, 1996	Atlanta
400 meters:	World	49.59	**Jarmila Kratochvilova**, Czech.	Mar. 7, 1982	Milan
	American	50.64	Diane Dixon	Mar. 10, 1991	Seville
800 meters:	World	1:56.36	**Maria Mutola**, Mozambique	Feb. 22, 1998	Lievin, FRA
	American	1:58.9	Mary Slaney	Feb. 22, 1980	San Diego
		1:58.92p	Suzy Hamilton	Feb. 7, 1999	Boston
1000 meters:	World	2:30.94	**Maria Mutola**, Mozambique	Feb. 25, 1999	Stockholm
	American	2:37.6	Mary Slaney	Jan. 21, 1989	Portland
1500 meters:	World	4:00.27	**Doina Melinte**, Romania	Feb. 9, 1990	E. Rutherford, N.J.
	American	4:00.8	Mary Slaney	Feb. 8, 1980	New York
Mile:	World	4:17.14	**Doina Melinte**, Romania	Feb. 9, 1990	E. Rutherford, N.J.
	American	4:20.5	Mary Slaney	Feb. 19, 1982	San Diego
3000 meters:	World	8:33.82	**Elly van Hulst**, Holland	Mar. 4, 1989	Budapest
	American	8:39.14	Regina Jacobs	Mar. 7, 1999	Maebashi, JPN
5000 meters:	World	14:47.35	**Gabriela Szabo**, Romania	Feb. 13, 1999	Dortmund, GER
	American	15:22.64	Lynn Jennings	Jan. 7, 1990	Hanover, N.H.

Note: The Mile run is 1,609.344 meters.

Hurdles

Event		Time		Date Set	Location
50 meters:	World	6.58	**Cornelia Oschkenat**, E. Ger.	Feb. 20, 1988	East Berlin
	American	6.67a	Jackie Joyner-Kersee	Feb. 10, 1995	Reno, Nev.
60 meters:	World	7.69	**Lyudmila Narozhilenko**, USSR	Feb. 4, 1990	Chelyabinsk, USSR
	American	7.81	Jackie Joyner-Kersee	Feb. 5, 1989	Fairfax, Va.

Note: The hurdles for both distances are 2 feet, 9 inches high. There are four hurdles in the 50 meters and five in the 60.

Walking

Event		Time		Date Set	Location
3000 meters:	World	11:40.33	**Claudia Iovan**, Romania	Jan. 30, 1999	Bucharest
	American	12:20.79	Debbi Lawrence	Mar. 12, 1993	Toronto

Relays

Event		Time		Date Set	Location
4 x 200 meters:	World	1:32.55	**West Germany**	Feb. 20, 1988	Dortmund, W. Ger.
		1:32.55	Germany	Feb. 21, 1999	Karlsruhe, GER
	American	1:33.24	National Team	Feb. 12, 1994	Glasgow
4 x 400 meters:	World	3:24.25	**Russia**	Mar. 7, 1999	Maebashi, JPN
	American	3:27.59	National Team	Mar. 7, 1999	Maebashi, JPN
4 x 800 meters:	World	8:18.71	**Russia**	Feb. 4, 1994	Moscow
	American	8:25.5p	Villanova	Feb. 7, 1987	Gainesville, Fla.

Field Events

Event		Mark		Date Set	Location
High Jump:	World	6-9½	**Heike Henkel**, Germany	Feb. 9, 1992	Karlsruhe, GER
	American	6-7	Tisha Waller	Feb. 28, 1998	Atlanta
Pole Vault:	World	14-11¼	**Nicole Humbert**, Germany	Feb. 25, 1999	Stochkolm
	American	14-9	Melissa Mueller	Feb. 7, 1999	Boston
Long Jump:	World	24-2¼	**Heike Drechsler**, E. Germany	Feb. 13, 1988	Vienna
	American	23-4¾	Jackie Joyner-Kersee	Mar. 5, 1992	Atlanta
Triple Jump:	World	49-9	**Ashia Hansen**, Great Britain	Feb. 28, 1998	Valencia, SPA
	American	46-8¼	Sheila Hudson	Mar. 4, 1995	Atlanta
Shot Put:	World	73-10	**Helena Fibingerova**, Czech.	Feb. 19, 1977	Jablonec, CZE
	American	65-0¾	Ramona Pagel	Feb. 20, 1987	Inglewood, Calif.

Note: The international shotput weight for women is 8 lbs. and 13 oz.

Pentathlon

		Points		Date Set	Location
Five Events:	World	4991	**Irina Byelova**, Russia	Feb. 14-15, 1992	Berlin
	American	4753	DeDee Nathan	Mar. 4-5, 1999	Maebashi, JPN

Note: Byelova's WR times and distances, in order over two days— **60m H** (8.22); **HJ** (6-4); **SP** (43-5¾); **LJ** (21-1¾); **800m** (2:10.26).

SWIMMING

Pan Pacific Championships

at Sydney, Australia, Aug. 22-29. Note that (WR) indicates world record.

Final Medal Standings

		G	S	B	Total			G	S	B	Total
1	United States	13	10	12	35	5	South Africa	3	1	4	8
2	Australia	13	13	6	32	6	Costa Rica	0	0	1	1
3	Canada	2	4	5	11	7	Nigeria, China Taipae, and Algeria did not medal.				
4	Japan	2	3	4	9						

MEN

Event		Time	
50m free	Brendon Dedekind, S. Afr.	22.06	
100m free	Michael Klim, AUS	48.98	
200m free	Ian Thorpe, AUS	1:46.00	WR
400m free	Ian Thorpe, AUS	3:41.83	WR
1500m free	Grant Hackett, AUS	14:45.60	
100m back	Lenny Krayzelburg, USA	53.60	WR
200m back	Lenny Krayzelburg, USA	1:55.87	WR
100m breast	Simon Cowley, AUS	1:02.06	
200m breast	Simon Cowley, AUS	2:12.98	
100m fly	Michael Klim, AUS	52.49	
200m fly	Tom Malchow, USA	1:55.41	
200m I.M.	Tom Wilkens, USA	2:01.01	
400m I.M.	Matthew Dunn, AUS	4:16.54	
5k open water	Klete Keller, USA	55:42	
25k open water	Mark Saliba, AUS	4:57:44	

Men's Relays

Event		Time	
400m free	Australia (Klim, English, Fydler, Thorpe)	3:16.08	
800m free	Australia (Thorpe, Kirby, Hackett, Klim)	7:08.79	WR
400m med	USA (Krayzelburg, Grote, Wales, Walker)	3:36.37	

WOMEN

Event		Time	
50m free	Jenny Thompson, USA	25.51	
100m free	Jenny Thompson, USA	54.89	
200m free	Susan O'Neill, AUS	1:58.17	
400m free	Brooke Bennett, USA	4:08.39	
800m free	Brooke Bennett, USA	8:25.06	
100m back	Mai Nakamura, JPN & Dyanna Calub, AUS	1:01.51	
200m back	Tomoka Hagiwara, JPN	2:11.36	
100m breast	Penny Heyns, S. Afr.	1:07.08*	WR
200m breast	Penny Heyns, S. Afr.	2:23.64	WR
100m fly	Jenny Thompson, USA	57.88	WR
200m fly	Susan O'Neill, AUS	2:06.60	
200m I.M.	Joanne Malar, CAN	2:13.63	
400m I.M.	Joanne Malar, CAN	4:40.23	
5k open water	Erica Rose, USA	58:11	
25k open water	Briley Bergen, USA	5:16:05	

*Heyns set a new world record in her qualifying heat on Aug. 23 with a time of 1:06.52.

Women's Relays

Event		Time
400m free	USA (Kolbisen, Fox, Benko, Thompson)	3:41.86
800m free	USA (Benko, Stonebraker, Thompson, Teuscher)	7:57.61
400m med	USA (Bedford, Quann, Thompson, Kolbisen)	4:03.09

World, Olympic and American Records

As of Sept. 1, 1999

World long course records officially recognized by the Federation Internationale de Natation Amateur (FINA). Note that (p) indicates preliminary heat; (r) relay lead-off split; and (s) indicates split time.

MEN
Freestyle

Distance		Time		Date Set	Location
50 meters:	World	21.81	Tom Jager, USA	Mar. 24, 1990	Nashville
	Olympic	21.91	Aleksandr Popov, Unified Team	July 30, 1992	Barcelona
	American	21.81	Jager (same as World)	—	
100 meters:	World	48.21	Aleksandr Popov, Russia	June 18, 1994	Monte Carlo
	Olympic	48.63	Matt Biondi, USA	Sept. 22, 1988	Seoul
	American	48.42	Matt Biondi	Aug. 10, 1988	Austin, Tex.
200 meters:	World	1:46.00	Ian Thorpe, Australia	Aug. 24, 1999	Sydney
	Olympic	1:46.70	Yevgeny Sadovyi, Unified Team	July 26, 1992	Barcelona
	American	1:47.72	Matt Biondi	Aug. 8, 1988	Austin, Tex.
400 meters:	World	3:41.83	Ian Thorpe, Australia	Aug. 22, 1999	Sydney
	Olympic	3:45.00	Yevgeny Sadovyi, Unified Team	July 29, 1992	Barcelona
	American	3:48.06	Matt Cetlinski	Aug. 11, 1988	Austin, Tex.
800 meters:	World	7:46.00s	Kieren Perkins, Australia	Aug. 24, 1994	Victoria, CAN
	Olympic		Not an event	—	
	American	7:52.45	Sean Killion	July 27, 1987	Clovis, Calif.
1500 meters:	World	14:41.66	Kieren Perkins, Australia	Aug. 24, 1994	Victoria, CAN
	Olympic	14:43.48	Kieren Perkins, Australia	July 31, 1992	Barcelona
	American	15:01.51	George DiCarlo	June 30, 1984	Indianapolis

Backstroke

Distance	Time		Date Set	Location
50 meters:	**World** 24.99	**Lenny Krayzelburg**, USA	Aug. 28, 1999	Sydney
	Olympic	Not an event	—	—
	American 24.99	Krayzelburg (same as World)	—	—
100 meters:	**World** 53.60	**Lenny Krayzelburg**, USA	Aug. 24, 1999	Sydney
	Olympic 53.86r	Jeff Rouse, USA	July 31, 1992	Barcelona
	American 53.60	Krayzelburg (same as World)	—	—
200 meters:	**World** 1:55.87	**Lenny Krayzelburg**, USA	Aug. 27, 1999	Sydney
	Olympic 1:58.47	Martin Zubero, Spain	July 28, 1992	Barcelona
	American ...1:55.87	Krayzelburg (same as World)	—	—

Breaststroke

Distance	Time		Date Set	Location
50 meters:	**World** 27.61	**Alexander Dzhaburiya**, UKR	April 27, 1996	Kharkov, UKR
	Olympic	Not an event	—	—
	American 28.64	Jeremy Linn, USA	July 20, 1996	Atlanta
100 meters:	**World** 1:00.60p	**Fred deBurghgraeve**, Belgium	July 20, 1996	Atlanta
	Olympic ...1:00.60	deBurghgraeve, BEL (same as World)	—	—
	American ...1:00.77	Jeremy Linn, USA	July 20, 1996	Atlanta
200 meters:	**World** 2:10.16	**Mike Barrowman**, USA	July 29, 1992	Barcelona
	Olympic ...2:10.16	Barrowman (same as World)	—	—
	American ...2:10.16	Barrowman (same as World)	—	—

Butterfly

Distance	Time		Date Set	Location
50 meters:	**World** 23.68	**Denis Pankratov**, Russia	Aug. 10, 1996	Mulhouse, AUS
	Olympic	Not an event	—	—
	American 23.89	Neil Walker	Aug. 12, 1997	Fukuoka, JPN
100 meters:	**World** 52.15	**Michael Klim**, Australia	Oct. 9, 1997	Brisbane, AUS
	Olympic 52.27	Denis Pankratov, Russia	July 24, 1996	Atlanta
	American 52.76	Neil Walker	Aug. 12, 1997	Fukuoka, JPN
200 meters:	**World** 1:55.22	**Denis Pankratov**, Russia	June 14, 1995	Canet, FRA
	Olympic 1:56.26	Melvin Stewart, USA	July 30, 1992	Barcelona
	American 1:55.41	Tom Malchow	Aug. 25, 1999	Sydney

Individual Medley

Distance	Time		Date Set	Location
200 meters:	**World** 1:58.16	**Jani Sievinen**, Finland	Sept. 11, 1994	Rome
	Olympic 1:59.91	Atilla Czene, Hungary	July 25, 1996	Atlanta
	American 2:00.11	David Wharton	Aug. 20, 1989	Tokyo
400 meters:	**World** 4:12.30	**Tom Dolan**, USA	Sept. 6, 1994	Rome
	Olympic 4:14.23	Tamas Darnyi, Hungary	July 27, 1992	Barcelona
	American 4:12.30	Dolan (same as World)	—	—

Relays

Distance	Time		Date Set	Location
4x100m medley:	**World** 3:34.84	**USA** (Rouse, Linn, Henderson, Hall Jr.)	July 26, 1996	Atlanta
	Olympic 3:34.84	USA (same as World)	—	—
	American 3:34.84	USA (same as World)	—	—
4x100m free:	**World** 3:15.11	**USA** (Fox, Hudepohl, Olsen, Hall)	Aug. 12, 1995	Atlanta
	Olympic 3:15.41	USA (Olsen, Davis, Schumacher, Hall Jr.)	July 23, 1996	Atlanta
	American 3:15.11	USA (same as World)	—	—
4x200m free:	**World** 7:08.79	**Australia** (Thorpe, Kirby, Hackett, Klim)	Aug. 25, 1999	Sydney
	Olympic 7:11.95	Unified Team (Lepikov, Pychnenko, Taianovitch, Sadovyi)	July 27, 1992	Barcelona
	American 7:12.51	USA (Dalbey, Cetlinski, Gjertsen, Biondi)	Sept. 21, 1988	Seoul

WOMEN
Freestyle

Distance	Time		Date Set	Location
50 meters:	**World** 24.51	**Le Jingyi**, China	Sept. 11, 1994	Rome
	Olympic 24.79	Yang Wenyi, China	July 31, 1992	Barcelona
	American 24.87	Amy Van Dyken	July 26, 1996	Atlanta
100 meters:	**World** 54.01	**Le Jingyi**, China	Sept. 5, 1994	Rome
	Olympic 54.50	Le Jingyi, China	July 20, 1996	Atlanta
	American 54.48p	Jenny Thompson	Mar. 1, 1992	Indianapolis
200 meters:	**World** 1:56.78	**Franziska Van Almsick**, Ger.	Sept. 6, 1994	Rome
	Olympic 1:57.65	Heike Friedrich, E. Germany	Sept. 21, 1988	Seoul
	American ...1:57.90	Nicole Haislett	July 27, 1992	Barcelona
400 meters:	**World** 4:03.85	**Janet Evans**, USA	Sept. 22, 1988	Seoul
	Olympic 4:03.85	Evans (same as World)	—	—
	American ...4:03.85	Evans (same as World)	—	—

Distance	Time		Date Set	Location
800 meters:	**World**.....8:16.22	**Janet Evans**, USA	Aug. 20, 1989	Tokyo
	Olympic....8:20.20	Janet Evans, USA	Sept. 24, 1988	Seoul
	American..8:16.22	Evans (same as World)	—	—
1500 meters:	**World** ...15:52.10	**Janet Evans**, USA	Mar. 26, 1988	Orlando
	Olympic..........	Not an event	—	—
	American .15:52.10	Evans (same as World)	—	—

Backstroke

Distance	Time		Date Set	Location
50 meters:	**World** 28.78	**Sandra Volker**, Germany	June 12, 1999	Monte Carlo
	Olympic..........	Not an event	—	—
	American 29.01	Natalie Coughlin	Aug. 6, 1998	Concord, Calif.
100 meters:	**World** 1:00.16r	**He Cihong**, China	Sept. 10, 1994	Rome
	Olympic...1:00.68	Krisztina Egerszegi, Hungary	July 28, 1992	Barcelona
	American..1:00.77p	Lea Maurer	Jan. 14, 1998	Perth, AUS
200 meters:	**World**.....2:06.62	**Krisztina Egerszegi**, Hungary	Aug. 25, 1991	Athens
	Olympic...2:07.06	Krisztina Egerszegi, Hungary	July 31, 1992	Barcelona
	American...2:08.60	Betsy Mitchell	June 27, 1986	Orlando

Breaststroke

Distance	Time		Date Set	Location
50 meters:	**World**.......30.83	**Penny Heyns**, South Africa	Aug. 28, 1999	Sydney
	Olympic............	Not an event	—	—
	American 31.98	Megan Quann	June 20, 1999	Federal Way, Wash.
100 meters:	**World**.....1:06.52	**Penny Heyns**, South Africa	Aug. 23, 1999	Sydney
	Olympic.....1:07.02	Penny Heyns, South Africa	July 21, 1996	Atlanta
	American...1:08.09	Amanda Beard	July 21, 1996	Atlanta
200 meters:	**World**.....2:23.64	**Penny Heyns**, South Africa	Aug. 27, 1999	Sydney
	Olympic.....2:25.41	Penny Heyns, South Africa	July 23, 1996	Atlanta
	American...2:25.35	Anita Nall	Mar. 2, 1992	Indianapolis

Butterfly

Distance	Time		Date Set	Location
50 meters:	**World**.......26.39	**Anna-Karin Kammerling**, Swe.	July 1, 1999	Halmsted, SWE
	Olympic............	Not an event	—	—
	American 26.55	Amy Van Dyken	May 17, 1996	Phoenix
100 meters:	**World**.......57.88	**Jenny Thompson**, USA	Aug. 23, 1999	Sydney
	Olympic.....58.62	Qian Hong, China	July 29, 1992	Barcelona
	American....57.88	Thompson (same as World)	—	—
200 meters:	**World**.....2:05.96	**Mary T. Meagher**, USA	Aug. 13, 1981	Brown Deer, Wisc.
	Olympic...2:06.90	Mary T. Meagher, USA	Aug. 4, 1984	Los Angeles
	American...2:05.96	Meagher (same as World)	—	—

Individual Medley

Distance	Time		Date Set	Location
200 meters:	**World**.....2:09.72	**Wu Yanyan**, China	Oct. 17, 1997	Shanghai
	Olympic.....2:11.65	Lin Li	July 30, 1992	Barcelona
	American....2:11.91	Summer Sanders	July 28, 1992	Barcelona
400 meters:	**World**.....4:34.79	**Yan Chen**, China	Oct. 13, 1997	Shanghai
	Olympic.....4:36.29	Petra Schneider, E. Germany	July 26, 1980	Moscow
	American....4:37.58	Summer Sanders	July 30, 1992	Barcelona

Relays

Distance	Time		Date Set	Location
4x100m free:	**World** 3:37.91	**China** (Jingyi, S.Ying, L. Ying, Lu)	Sept. 7, 1994	Rome
	Olympic 3:39.29	USA (Martino, Van Dyken, Fox, Thompson)	July 22, 1996	Atlanta
	American 3:39.29	USA (same as Olympic)	—	—
4x200m free:	**World** 7:55.47	**E. Germany** (Stellmach, Strauss, Mohring, Friedrich)	Aug. 18, 1987	Strasbourg, FRA
	Olympic......... 7:59.87	USA (Jackson, Teuscher, Taormina, Thompson)	July 25, 1996	Atlanta
	American 7:57.61	USA (Benko, Stonebraker, Thompson, Teuscher)	Aug. 26, 1999	Sydney
4x100m medley:	**World** 4:01.67	**China** (Cihong, Guohong, Limin, Jingyi)	Sept. 10, 1994	Rome
	Olympic 4:02.54	USA (Loveless, Nall, Ahmann-Leighton, Thompson)	July 30, 1992	Barcelona
	American 4:01.93	USA (Maurer, Kowal, Thompson, Van Dyken)	Jan. 16, 1998	Perth, AUS

WINTER SPORTS

Alpine Skiing
1999 World Championships
at Vail, Colorado (Feb. 1-14)

MEN

Slalom . . . . .Kalle Palander, Finland
Giant Slalom .Lasse Kjus, Norway
Super G . . . . .Lasse Kjus, Norway
& Hermann Maier, Austria (tie)
Downhill . . . . .Hermann Maier, Austria
Combined . . . . .Kjetil Andre Aamodt, Norway

WOMEN

Slalom . . . . .Zali Stegall, Austria
Giant Slalom . . . . .Alexandra Meissnitzer, Austria
Super G . . . . .Alexandra Meissnitzer, Austria
Downhill . . . . .Renate Goetschl, Austria
Combined . . . . .Pernilla Wiberg, Sweden

1999 World Cup Champions

MEN

Overall . . . . .Lasse Kjus, Norway
Downhill . . . . .Lasse Kjus, Norway
Slalom. . . . . .Thomas Stangassinger, Austria
Giant Slalom . . . . .Michael Von Gruenigen, Switzerland
Super G. . . . . .Hermann Maier, Austria
Nation's Cup . . . . .Austria

WOMEN

Overall . . . . .Alexandra Meissnitzer, Austria
Downhill . . . . .Renate Goetschl, Austria
Slalom . . . . .Sabine Egger, Austria
Giant Slalom . . . . .Alexandra Meissnitzer, Austria
Super G . . . . .Alexandra Meissnitzer, Austria
Nation's Cup . . . . .Austria

Freestyle Skiing
1999 World Championships
at Meiringen-Hasliberg, Switzerland (March 6-14)

MEN

Acroski. . . . . .Ian Edmondson, United States
Moguls . . . . .Janne Lahtela, Finland
Aerials . . . . .Eric Bergoust, United States
Dual Moguls . . . . .Johann Gregoire, France

WOMEN

Acroski. . . . . .Natalia Razumovskaya, Russia
Moguls . . . . .Ann Battelle, United States
Aerials . . . . .Jacqui Cooper, Australia
Dual Moguls. . . . . .Sandra Schmitt, Germany

World Cup Champions

MEN

Overall . . . . .Nicolas Fontaine, Canada
Aerials. . . . . .Nicolas Fontaine, Canada
Moguls . . . . .Janne Lahtela, Finland
Dual Moguls . . . . .Thony Hemery, France
Acroski . . . . .Steven Roxberg, United States
Nation's Cup . . . . .Canada

WOMEN

Overall . . . . .Jacqui Cooper, Australia
Aerials . . . . .Jacqui Cooper, Australia
Moguls. .Ann Battelle, United States
Dual Moguls. . . . . .Michelle Roark, United States
Acroski . . . . .Elena Batalova, Russia
Nation's Cup . . . . .United States

Nordic Skiing
1999 World Championships
at Ramsau, Austria (Feb. 18-28)

MEN

10-k Classic . . . . .Mika Myllylae, Finland
50-k Classic . . . . .Mika Myllylae, Finland
15-k Pursuit . . . . .Thomas Alsgaard, Norway
30-k Freestyle . . . . .Mika Myllylae, Finland
4x10-k Relay . . . . .Austria

WOMEN

5-k Classic . . . . .Bente Martinsen, Norway
30-k Classic . . . . .Larissa Lazutina, Russia
10-k Pursuit .Stefania Belmondo, Italy
15-k Freestyle . . . . .Stefania Belmondo, Italy
4x5-k Relay . . . . .Russia

Nordic Combined
90-meter jump/15-k cross country ski

Individual. . . . . .Bjarte Engen Vik, Norway
Team . . . . .Finland

Ski Jumping

Large Hill (120 meters) . . . . .Martin Schmitt, Germany
Normal Hill (90 meters). . . . . .Kazuyoshi Funaki, Japan
Team (120 meters). . . . . .Germany

World Cup Champions

MEN

1   Bjorn Dählie, Norway
2   Michal Botvinov, Austria
3   Mika Myllylae, Finland
4   Matthias Fredriksson, Sweden
5   Per Elofsson, Sweden
Nation's Cup: Norway

WOMEN

1   Bente Martinsen, Norway
2   Stefania Belmondo, Italy
3   Nina Gavriljuk, Russia
4   Kristina Smigun, Estonia
5   Larissa Lazutina, Russia
Nation's Cup: Russia

Nordic Combined
World Cup Champions

1 Bjarte Engen Vik, Norway
2 Hannu Manninen, Finland
3 Ladislav Rygl, Czech Republic
4 Felix Gottwald, Austria
5 Samppa Lajunen, Finland

Ski Jumping
World Cup Champions

1 Martin Schmitt, Germany
2 Janne Ahonen, Finland
3 Noriaki Kasai, Japan
4 Kazuyoshi Funaki, Japan
5 Hideharu Miyahira, Japan
Nation's Cup: Japan

Snowboarding
1999 World Championships
at Berchtesgaden, Germany (Jan. 11-17)

MEN

Halfpipe	Ricky Bower, United States
Slalom	Nicolas Huet, France
Giant Slalom	Markus Ebner, Germany
Cross	Henrik Jansson, Sweden
Parallel GS	Richard Richardsson, Sweden

WOMEN

Halfpipe	Kim Stacey, United States
Slalom	Marion Posch, Italy
Giant Slalom	Margherita Parini, Italy
Parallel GS	Isabelle Blanc, France
Cross	Julie Pomagalski, France

World Cup Champions

MEN

Overall	Mathieu Bozzetto, France
Halfpipe	Ross Powers, United States
Slalom	Mathieu Bozzetto, France
Giant Slalom	Stefan Kaltschuetz, Austria
Cross	Sylvian Duclos, France
Nation's Cup	France

WOMEN

Overall	Manuela Riegler, Austria
Halfpipe	Tricia Byrnes, United States
Slalom	Marion Posch, Italy
Giant Slalom	Margherita Parini, Italy
Cross	Ursula Fingerlos, Austria
Nation's Cup	France

Figure Skating
World Championships
at Helsinki, Finland (March 21-28)

Men's — 1. Alexei Yagudin, Russia; 2. Evgeny Plushenko, Russia; 3. Michael Weiss, USA

Women's — 1. Maria Butyrskaya, Russia; 2. Michelle Kwan, USA; 3. Julia Soldatova, Russia

Pairs — 1. Elena Berezhnaya & Anton Sikharulidze, Russia; 2. Xue Shen & Hongbo Zhao, China; 3. Dorota Zagorska & Mariusz Siudek, Poland

Ice Dance — 1. Anjelika Krylova & Oleg Ovsyannikov, Russia; 2. Marina Anissina & Gwendal Peizerat, France; 3. Shae-Lynn Bourne & Victor Kraatz, Canada

U.S. Championships
at Salt Lake City, Utah (Feb. 7-14)

Men's	Michael Weiss
Women's	Michelle Kwan
Pairs	Danielle Hartsell & Steve Hartsell
Ice Dance	Naomi Lang & Peter Tchernyshev

European Championships
at Prague, Czech Republic (Jan. 24-31)

Men's	Alexei Yagudin, Russia
Women's	Maria Butyrskaya, Russia
Pairs	Maria Petrova & Alexei Tikhonov, Russia
Ice Dance	Anjelika Krylova & Oleg Ovsyannikov, Russia

Speed Skating
World Cup Champions
MEN

500 meters	Jeremy Wotherspoon, Canada
1000 meters	Jeremy Wotherspoon, Canada
1500 meters	Adne Sondral, Norway
5000 meters	Bart Veldkamp, Belgium

WOMEN

500 meters	Catriona LeMay-Doan, Canada
1000 meters	Monique Garbrecht, Germany
1500 meters	Gunda Niemann-Stirnemann, Germany
3000/5000 meters	Gunda Niemann-Stirnemann, Germany

1999 World Championships
at Hamar, Norway (Feb. 6-7)

MEN

500 meters	Christain Breuer, Germany & Hiroyuki Noake, Japan (tie)
1500 meters	Adne Sondral, Norway
5000 meters	Vadim Sayutin, Russia
10,000 meters	Bart Veldkamp, Belgium
All-Around	Rintje Ritsma, Netherlands

WOMEN

500 meters	Annamarie Thomas, Netherlands
1500 meters	Annamarie Thomas, Netherlands
3000 meters	Gunda Niemann-Stirnemann, Germany
5000 meters	Gunda Niemann-Stirnemann, Germany
All-Around	Gunda Niemann-Stirnemann, Germany

SUMMER SPORTS

Cross-country
IAAF World Championships
The 27th IAAF World Cross Country Championships held at Belfast, Ireland (Mar. 21-22)

MEN		WOMEN	
12 km	1. Paul Tergat, Kenya 38:28	8 km	1. Gete Wami, Ethiopia 28:00
(7.46 mi)	2. Patrick Ivuti, Kenya 38:32	(4.97 mi)	2. Merima Denboba, Ethiopia 28:12
	3. Paulo Guerra, Portugal 38:46		3. Paula Radcliffe, Great Britain 28:12
	Best USA— Alan Culpepper, 21st, 41:10		*Best USA—* Deena Drossin, 10th, 28:53

Cycling
Tour de France
The 86th Tour de France (July 3-25) ran 20 stages plus a prologue, covering 2,287 miles starting in Puy-du-Fou, passing through the Alps and the Pyrenees and finishing on the Avenue des Champs-Elysees in Paris.

Against formidable odds, American Lance Armstrong, 27, rode to his first Tour de France victory in a time of 91 hours, 32 minutes and 16 seconds. His time was seven minutes, 37 seconds ahead of runner-up Alex Zuelle of Switzerland. Spain's Fernando Escartin took third, completing the course 10 minutes, 26 seconds behind Armstrong.

Less than three years before Armstrong rode down the Champs-Elysees for the victory, he was diagnosed with testicular cancer. The cancer then spread to his lungs and his brain and doctors gave him only a 50 percent chance of survival. He underwent two operations and extensive chemotherapy and began his comeback in early 1998. He is only the second American to win cycling's premier event.

		Team	Behind			Team	Behind
1	Lance Armstrong, USA	U.S. Postal	—	6	Abraham Olano, SPA	Once	16:47
2	Alex Zuelle, SWI	Banesto	7:37	7	Daniele Nardello, ITA	Mapei	17:02
3	Fernando Escartin, SPA	Kelme	10:26	8	Richard Virenque, FRA	Polti	17:28
4	Laurent Dufaux, SWI	Saeco	14:43	9	Wladimir Belli, ITA	Festina	17:37
5	Angel Casero, SPA	Vitalicio Seguros	15:11	10	Andrea Peron, ITA	Once	23:10

Other Worldwide Champions
1999 Major UCI (Union Cycliste Internationale) Road Results
MEN

Tour Down Under (AUS)	Stuart O'Grady, AUS	Ghent-Wevelgem (BEL)	Tom Steels, BEL
Mediterranean Tour (FRA)	Davide Rebellin, ITA	Fleche Wallone (BEL)	Michele Bartoli, ITA
Ruta del Sol (SPA)	Javier Pascual Rodriguez, SPA	Tour de Romandie (SWI)	Laurent Jalabert, FRA
Tour of Valencia (SPA)	Alexandre Vinokourov, KAZ	Giro d'Italia (ITA)	Ivan Gotti, ITA
Het Volk (BEL)	Frank Vandenbroucke, BEL	Dauphine Libere (FRA)	Alexandre Vinokourov, KAZ
Paris-Nice (FRA)	Michael Boogerd, NET	Tour of Switzerland (SWI)	Francesco Casagrande, ITA
Criterium International (FRA)	Jens Voigt, GER	Tour of Netherlands (NED)	Sergei Gontchar, UKR
Tour of the Basque Country (SPA)	Laurent Jalabert, FRA		

WOMEN

Canberra World Cup (AUS)	Anna Wilson, AUS	Wilmington Classic (USA)	Nicole Reinhart, USA
La Fleche Wallone (BEL)	Hanka Kufernagel, GER	H-P International (USA)	Jeannie Longo, FRA
Tour de L'Aude (FRA)	Lyne Bessette, CAN	Giro d'Italia Femminile (ITA)	Joanna Somarriba, SPA

Rowing
World Rowing Championships
at St. Catharines, Canada (Aug. 22-29)

MEN	WOMEN
Eights	United States, 6:01.58	Eights	Romania, 6:47.66
Coxed Pairs	United States, 6:48.56	Coxless Pairs	Canada, 7:00.85
Coxed Fours	United States, 6:38.31	Coxless Fours	Belarus, 6:26.25
Coxless Pairs	Australia, 6:19.00	Single Sculls	Ekaterina Karsten, BEL, 7:11.68
Coxless Fours	Great Britain, 5:48.57	Double Sculls	Germany, 6:41.98
Single Sculls	Rob Waddell, NZ, 6:36.68	Quad Sculls	Germany, 7:06.53
Double Sculls	Slovenia, 6:04.37		
Quad Sculls	Germany, 6:24.37		

Marathons
Boston Marathon

The 103rd edition of the Boston Marathon was held Monday, April 19, 1999 and run, as always, from Hopkinton through Ashland, Framingham, Natick, Wellesley, Newton and Brookline to Boston, Mass. Kenya's Joseph Chebet, race runner-up the previous two years, took the lead after the 22-mile mark and held on to record his first Boston win with a time of two hours, nine minutes and 52 seconds.

Ethiopia's Fatuma Roba ran the fourth fastest women's time (2:23:25) in Boston Marathon history to win her third consecutive race. Her time was four seconds off last year's pace. She joined Germany's Uta Pippig as the only women to win three consecutive Boston Marathons.

The highly-anticipated women's wheelchair race didn't disappoint as rivals Louise Sauvage and Jean Driscoll battled to the wire for the third consecutive year. And like the past two years, Sauvage (1:42:23) emerged victorious. Switzerland's Franz Nietlispach (1:21:36) took the men's wheelchair division for the fourth time in the last five years. Winners in the men's and women's divisions earned $80,000. **Distance:** 26.2 miles.

MEN

	Time
1 Joseph Chebet, KEN	2:09:52
2 Silvio Guerra, ECU	2:10:19
3 Frank Pooe, S. Afr	2:11:37
4 Abner Chipu, S. Afr	2:12:46
5 John Kagwe, KEN	2:13:58

Best USA: 13th — Joe LeMay, Connecticut, 2:16:11

WHEELCHAIR

	Time
1 Franz Nietlispach, SWI	1:21:36
2 Saul Mendoza, MEX	1:25:18
3 Scot A. Hollonbeck, USA	1:27:58

WOMEN

	Time
1 Fatuma Roba, ETH	2:23:25
2 Franziska Rochat-Moser, SWI	2:25:51
3 Yuko Arimori, JPN	2:26:39
4 Colleen De Reuck, S. Afr	2:27:54
5 Martha Tenorio, ECU	2:27:58

Best USA: 12th — Lynn Jennings, New Hampshire, 2:38:37

WHEELCHAIR

	Time
1 Louise Sauvage, AUS	1:42:23
2 Jean L. Driscoll, USA	1:42:23
3 Edith Hunkeler, SWI	1:43:48

Other 1999 Winners

Tokyo
Feb. 14	Men	Gert Thys, S. Afr	2:06:33
	(No women's division)		

Los Angeles
Mar. 14	Men	Simon Bor, KEN	2:09:25
	Women	Irina Bogacheva, KYR	2:30:32

London
Apr. 18	Men	Abdelkader El Mouaziz, MOR	2:07:57
	Women	Joyce Chepchumba, KEN	2:23:22

Rotterdam
Apr. 18	Men	Japhet Kosgei, KEN	2:07:09
	Women	Tegla Loroupe, KEN	2:22:48

Late 1998

New York City
Nov. 1	Men	John Kagwe, KEN	2:08:45
	Women	Franca Fiacconi, ITA	2:25:17

Fukuoka
Dec. 6	Men	Jackson Kabiga, KEN	2:08:42
	(No women's division)		

1999 Cricket World Cup

The Cricket World Cup is sponsored by the International Cricket Council (ICC) and has been held every four years since 1975. The seventh official World Cup was held at various locations in England, Scotland, Ireland and the Netherlands from May 7–June 20, 1999.

The top three teams (*) in each group after the preliminary round-robin series advance to the Super Six Round. The top four teams from the Super Six then advance to the semifinal round. NR denotes any contest that ends with "no result," commonly due to rain. Net RR refers to a team's "net run rate." Two points are awarded for a win, one for a tie and one for a NR.

Final Standings

GROUP A	W	L	NR	Pts	Net RR
*South Africa	4	1	0	8	0.86
*India	3	2	0	6	1.28
*Zimbabwe	3	2	0	6	0.02
England	3	2	0	6	-0.33
Sri Lanka	2	3	0	4	-0.81
Kenya	0	5	0	0	-1.20

Note: Zimbabwe advances over England due to a higher net run rate.

GROUP B	W	L	NR	Pts	Net RR
*Pakistan	4	1	0	8	0.51
*Australia	3	2	0	6	0.73
*New Zealand	3	2	0	6	0.58
West Indies	3	2	0	6	0.50
Bangladesh	2	3	0	4	-0.52
Scotland	0	5	0	0	-1.93

Note: New Zealand advances over West Indies due to a higher net run rate.

Super Six	W	L	NR	Pts	Net RR
Pakistan	3	2	0	6	0.65
Australia	3	2	0	6	0.36
South Africa	3	2	0	6	0.17
New Zealand	2	2	1	5	-0.52
Zimbabwe	2	2	1	5	-0.79
India	1	4	0	0	-0.15

Note: New Zealand advances over Zimbabwe due to a higher net run rate.

Semifinals

Pakistan defeats New Zealand by 9 wickets.
Australia and South Africa tied.†
†Australia advances due to a higher finish in the Super Six Round.

Finals

Australia defeats Pakistan by 8 wickets.

THE 2000 ESPN INFORMATION PLEASE SPORTS ALMANAC

INT'L SPORTS STATISTICS

SEC B

THROUGH THE YEARS
1896-1999
WINNERS • RECORDS

PAGE 717

TRACK & FIELD

IAAF World Championships

While the Summer Olympics have served as the unofficial world outdoor championships for track and field throughout the century, a separate World Championship meet was started in 1983 by the International Amateur Athletic Federation (IAAF). The meet was held every four years from 1983-91, but began an every-other-year cycle in 1993. World Championship sites include Helsinki (1983), Rome (1987), Tokyo (1991), Stuttgart (1993), Göteborg, Sweden (1995), Athens (1997) and Seville, Spain (1999). Note that (WR) indicates world record and (CR) indicates championship meet record.

MEN

Multiple gold medals (including relays): Michael Johnson (9); Carl Lewis (8); Sergey Bubka (6); Haile Gebrselassie, Maurice Greene, Lars Riedel and Calvin Smith (4); Donovan Bailey, Greg Foster, Werner Gunthor, Wilson Kipketer, Moses Kiptanui, Noureddine Morceli, Dan O'Brien, Ivan Pedroso, Antonio Pettigrew and Butch Reynolds (3); Andrey Abduvaliyev, Abel Anton, Leroy Burrell, Andre Cason, Maurizio Damilano, Jon Drummond, Tomas Dvorak, Hicham El Guerrouj, John Godina, Colin Jackson, Allen Johnson, Ismael Kirui, Billy Konchellah, Sergey Litvinov, Dennis Mitchell, Edwin Moses, Mike Powell, Javier Sotmayor and Jan Zelezny (2).

100 Meters

Year		Time	
1983	Carl Lewis, USA	10.07	
1987	Carl Lewis, USA	9.93	
1991	Carl Lewis, USA	9.86	WR
1993	Linford Christie, GBR	9.87	
1995	Donovan Bailey, CAN	9.97	
1997	Maurice Greene, USA	9.86	
1999	Maurice Greene, USA	9.80	CR

Note: Ben Johnson was the original winner in 1987, but was stripped of his title and world record time (9.83) following his 1989 admission of drug taking.

200 Meters

Year		Time	
1983	Calvin Smith, USA	20.14	
1987	Calvin Smith, USA	20.16	
1991	Michael Johnson, USA	20.01	
1993	Frank Fredericks, NAM	19.85	
1995	Michael Johnson, USA	19.79	CR
1997	Ato Boldon, USA	20.04	
1999	Maurice Greene, USA	19.90	

400 Meters

Year		Time	
1983	Bert Cameron, JAM	45.05	
1987	Thomas Schonlebe, E. Ger	44.33	
1991	Antonio Pettigrew, USA	44.57	
1993	Michael Johnson, USA	43.65	
1995	Michael Johnson, USA	43.39	
1997	Michael Johnson, USA	44.12	
1999	Michael Johnson, USA	43.18	WR

800 Meters

Year		Time	
1983	Willi Wülbeck, W. Ger	1:43.65	
1987	Billy Konchellah, KEN	1:43.06	CR
1991	Billy Konchellah, KEN	1:43.99	
1993	Paul Ruto, KEN	1:44.71	
1995	Wilson Kipketer, DEN	1:45.08	
1997	Wilson Kipketer, DEN	1:43.38	
1999	Wilson Kipketer, DEN	1:43.30	

1500 Meters

Year		Time	
1983	Steve Cram, GBR	3:41.59	
1987	Abdi Bile, SOM	3:36.80	
1991	Noureddine Morceli, ALG	3:32.84	
1993	Noureddine Morceli, ALG	3:34.24	
1995	Noureddine Morceli, ALG	3:33.73	
1997	Hicham El Guerrouj, MOR	3:35.83	
1999	Hicham El Guerrouj, MOR	3:27.65	CR

5000 Meters

Year		Time	
1983	Eammon Coghlan, IRL	13:28.53	
1987	Said Aouita, MOR	13:26.44	
1991	Yobes Ondieki, KEN	13:14.45	
1993	Ismael Kirui, KEN	13:02.75	
1995	Ismael Kirui, KEN	13:16.77	
1997	Daniel Komen, KEN	13:07.38	
1999	Salah Hissou, MOR	12:58.13	CR

10,000 Meters

Year		Time	
1983	Alberto Cova, ITA	28:01.04	
1987	Paul Kipkoech, KEN	27:38.63	
1991	Moses Tanui, KEN	27:38.74	
1993	Haile Gebrselassie, ETH	27:46.02	
1995	Haile Gebrselassie, ETH	27:12.95	CR
1997	Haile Gebrselassie, ETH	27:24.58	
1999	Haile Gebrselassie, ETH	27:57.27	

Marathon

Year		Time	
1983	Rob de Castella, AUS	2:10:03	CR
1987	Douglas Wakiihuri, KEN	2:11:48	
1991	Hiromi Taniguchi, JPN	2:14:57	
1993	Mark Plaatjes, USA	2:13:57	
1995	Martin Fíz, SPA	2:11:41	
1997	Abel Anton, SPA	2:13:16	
1999	Abel Anton, SPA	2:13:36	

110-Meter Hurdles

Year		Time	
1983	Greg Foster, USA	13.42	
1987	Greg Foster, USA	13.21	
1991	Greg Foster, USA	13.06	
1993	Colin Jackson, GBR	12.91	WR
1995	Allen Johnson, USA	13.00	
1997	Allen Johnson, USA	12.93	
1999	Colin Jackson, GBR	13.04	

Track & Field (Cont.)

400-Meter Hurdles

Year		Time	
1983	Edwin Moses, USA	47.50	
1987	Edwin Moses, USA	47.46	
1991	Samuel Matete, ZAM	47.64	
1993	Kevin Young, USA	47.18	CR
1995	Derrick Adkins, USA	47.98	
1997	Stephane Diagana, FRA	47.70	
1999	Fabrizio Mori, ITA	47.72	

3000-Meter Steeplechase

Year		Time	
1983	Patriz Ilg, W. Ger	8:15.06	
1987	Francesco Panetta, ITA	8:08.57	
1991	Moses Kiptanui, KEN	8:12.59	
1993	Moses Kiptanui, KEN	8:06.36	
1995	Moses Kiptanui, KEN	8:04.16	CR
1997	Wilson B. Kipketer, KEN	8:05.84	
1999	Christopher Koskei, KEN	8:11.76	

4 x 100-Meter Relay

Year		Time	
1983	United States	37.86	WR
1987	United States	37.90	
1991	United States	37.50	WR
1993	United States	37.48	CR
1995	Canada	38.31	
1997	Canada	37.86	
1999	United States	37.59	

4 x 400-Meter Relay

Year		Time	
1983	Soviet Union	3:00.79	
1987	United States	2:57.29	
1991	Great Britain	2:57.53	
1993	United States	2:54.29	WR
1995	United States	2:57.32	
1997	United States	2:56.47	
1999	United States	2:56.45	

20-Kilometer Walk

Year		Time	
1983	Ernesto Canto, MEX	1:20.49	
1987	Maurizio Damilano, ITA	1:20.45	
1991	Maurizio Damilano, ITA	1:19.37	CR
1993	Valentin Massana, SPA	1:22.31	
1995	Michele Didoni, ITA	1:19.59	
1997	Daniel Garcia, MEX	1:21:43	
1999	Ilya Markov, RUS	1:23:34	

50-Kilometer Walk

Year		Time	
1983	Ronald Weigel, E. Ger	3:43:08	
1987	Hartwig Gauder, E. Ger	3:40:53	CR
1991	Aleksandr Potashov, USSR	3:53:09	
1993	Jesus Angel Garcia, SPA	3:41:41	
1995	Valentin Kononen, FIN	3:43.42	
1997	Robert Korzeniowski, POL	3:44:46	
1999	German Skurygin, RUS	3:44:23	

High Jump

Year		Height	
1983	Gennedy Avdeyenko, USSR	7-7¼	
1987	Patrik Sjoberg, SWE	7-9¾	
1991	Charles Austin, USA	7-9¾	
1993	Javier Sotomayor, CUB	7-10½	CR
1995	Troy Kemp, BAH	7-9¼	
1997	Javier Sotomayor, CUB	7-9¼	
1999	Vyacheslav Voronin, RUS	7-9¼	

Pole Vault

Year		Height	
1983	Sergey Bubka, USSR	18-8¼	
1987	Sergey Bubka, USSR	19-2¼	
1991	Sergey Bubka, USSR	19-6¼	CR
1993	Sergey Bubka, UKR	19-8¼	
1995	Sergey Bubka, UKR	19-5	
1997	Sergey Bubka, UKR	19-8½	CR
1999	Maksim Tarasov, RUS	19-9	CR

Long Jump

Year		Distance	
1983	Carl Lewis, USA	28-0¾	
1987	Carl Lewis, USA	28-0¼	WR
1991	Mike Powell, USA	29-4½	WR
1993	Mike Powell, USA	28-2¼	
1995	Ivan Pedroso, CUB	28-6½	
1997	Ivan Pedroso, CUB	27-7½	
1999	Ivan Pedroso, CUB	28-1	

Triple Jump

Year		Distance	
1983	Zdzislaw Hoffmann, POL	57-2	
1987	Khristo Markov, BUL	58-9	
1991	Kenny Harrison, USA	58-4	
1993	Mike Conley, USA	58-7¼	
1995	Jonathan Edwards, GBR	60-0¼	WR
1997	Yoelvis Quesada, CUB	58-6¾	
1999	Charles Michael Friedek, GER	57-8½	

Shot Put

Year		Distance	
1983	Edward Sarul, POL	70-2¼	
1987	Werner Günthör, SWI	72-11¼	CR
1991	Werner Günthör, SWI	71-1¼	
1993	Werner Günthör, SWI	72-1	
1995	John Godina, USA	70-5¼	
1997	John Godina, USA	70-4¼	
1999	C.J. Hunter, USA	71-6	

Discus

Year		Distance	
1983	Imrich Bugar, CZE	222-2	
1987	Jurgen Schult, E. Ger	225-6	
1991	Lars Riedel, GER	217-2	
1993	Lars Riedel, GER	222-2	
1995	Lars Riedel, GER	225-7	CR
1997	Lars Riedel, GER	224-10	
1999	Anthony Washington, USA	226-7	CR

Hammer Throw

Year		Distance	
1983	Sergey Litvinov, USSR	271-3	
1987	Sergey Litvinov, USSR	272-6	CR
1991	Yuri Sedykh, USSR	268-0	
1993	Andrey Abduvaliyev, TAJ	267-10	
1995	Andrey Abduvaliyev, TAJ	267-7	
1997	Heinz Weis, GER	268-4	
1999	Karsten Kobs, GER	263-3	

Javelin

Year		Distance	
1983	Detlef Michel, E. Ger	293-7	
1987	Seppo Raty, FIN	274-1	
1991	Kimmo Kinnunen, FIN	297-11	CR
1993	Jan Zelezny, CZE	282-1	
1995	Jan Zelezny, CZE	293-11	
1997	Marius Corbett, S. Afr.	290-0	
1999	Aki Parviainen, FIN	293-8	

Decathlon

Year		Points	
1983	Daley Thompson, GBR	8714	
1987	Torsten Voss, E. Ger	8680	
1991	Dan O'Brien, USA	8812	CR

Year		Points	
1993	Dan O'Brien, USA	8817	CR
1995	Dan O'Brien, USA	8695	
1997	Tomas Dvorak, CZE	8837	CR
1999	Tomas Dvorak, CZE	8744	

WOMEN

Multiple gold medals (including relays): Gail Devers (5); Jackie Joyner-Kersee (4); Tatyana Samolenko Dorovskikh, Silke Gladisch, Marion Jones, Marita Koch, Astrid Kumbernuss, Jearl Miles, Merlene Ottey and Gwen Torrence (3); Hassiba Boulmerka, Sabine Braun, Olga Bryzgina, Mary Decker, Heike Daute Drechsler, Cathy Freeman, Chryste Gaines, Trine Hattestad, Martina Optiz Hellmann, Stefka Kostadinova, Katrin Krabbe, Jarmila Kratochvilova, Inger Miller, Marie-José Pérec, Ana Quirot, Gabriela Szabo and Huang Zhihong (2).

100 Meters

Year		Time	
1983	Marlies Gohr, E. Ger	10.97	
1987	Silke Gladisch, E. Ger	10.90	
1991	Katrin Krabbe, GER	10.99	
1993	Gail Devers, USA	10.81	CR
1995	Gwen Torrence, USA	10.85	
1997	Marion Jones, USA	10.83	
1999	Marion Jones, USA	10.70	CR

200 Meters

Year		Time	
1983	Marita Koch, E. Ger	22.13	
1987	Silke Gladisch, E. Ger	21.74	CR
1991	Katrin Krabbe, GER	22.09	
1993	Merlene Ottey, JAM	21.98	
1995	Merlene Ottey, JAM	22.12	
1997	Zhanna Pintusevich, UKR	22.32	
1999	Inger Miller, USA	21.77	

400 Meters

Year		Time	
1983	Jarmila Kratochvilova, CZE	47.99	WR
1987	Olga Bryzgina, USSR	49.38	
1991	Marie-José Pérec, FRA	49.13	
1993	Jearl Miles, USA	49.82	
1995	Marie-José Pérec, FRA	49.28	
1997	Cathy Freeman, AUS	49.77	
1999	Cathy Freeman, AUS	49.67	

800 Meters

Year		Time	
1983	Jarmila Kratochvilova, CZE	1:54.68	CR
1987	Sigrun Wodars, E. Ger	1:55.26	
1991	Lilia Nurutdinova, USSR	1:57.50	
1993	Maria Mutola, MOZ	1:55.43	
1995	Ana Quirot, CUB	1:56.11	
1997	Ana Quirot, CUB	1:57.14	
1999	Ludmila Formanova, CZE	1:56.68	

1500 Meters

Year		Time	
1983	Mary Decker, USA	4:00.90	
1987	Tatiana Samolenko, USSR	3:58.56	CR
1991	Hassiba Boulmerka, ALG	4:02.21	
1993	Liu Dong, CHN	4:00.50	
1995	Hassiba Boulmerka, ALG	4:02.42	
1997	Carla Sacramento, POR	4:04.24	
1999	Svetlana Masterkova, RUS	3:59.53	

5000 Meters

Held as 3000-meter race from 1983-93

Year		Time	
1983	Mary Decker, USA	8:34.62	
1987	Tatyana Samolenko, USSR	8:38.73	
1991	T. Samolenko Dorovskikh, USSR	8:35.82	
1993	Qu Yunxia, CHN	8:28.71	CR
1995	Sonia O'Sullivan, IRL	14:46.47	CR
1997	Gabriela Szabo, ROM	14:57.68	
1999	Gabriela Szabo, ROM	14:41.82	CR

10,000 Meters

Year		Time	
1983	Not held		
1987	Ingrid Kristiansen, NOR	31:05.85	
1991	Liz McColgan, GBR	31:14.31	
1993	Wang Junxia, CHN	30:49.30	CR
1995	Fernanda Ribeiro, POR	31:04.99	
1997	Sally Barsosio, KEN	31:32.92	
1999	Gete Wami, ETH	30:24.56	CR

Marathon

Year		Time	
1983	Grete Waitz, NOR	2:28:09	
1987	Rose Mota, POR	2:25:17	CR
1991	Wanda Panfil, POL	2:29:53	
1993	Junko Asari, JPN	2:30:03	
1995	Manuela Machado, POR	2:25:39	
1997	Hiromi Suzuki, JPN	2:29:48	
1999	Jong Song-Ok, N. Kor	2:26:59	

100-Meter Hurdles

Year		Time	
1983	Bettine Jahn, E. Ger	12.35ʷ	
1987	Ginka Zagorcheva, BUL	12.34	CR
1991	Lyudmila Narozhilenko, USSR	12.59	
1993	Gail Devers, USA	12.46	
1995	Gail Devers, USA	12.68	
1997	Ludmila Engquist, SWE	12.50	
1999	Gail Devers, USA	12.37	

ʷ indicates wind-aided.

400-Meter Hurdles

Year		Time	
1983	Yekaterina Fesenko, USSR	54.14	
1987	Sabine Busch, E. Ger	53.62	
1991	Tatiana Ledovskaya, USSR	53.11	
1993	Sally Gunnell, GBR	52.74	WR
1995	Kim Batten, USA	52.61	WR
1997	Nezha Bidouane, MOR	52.97	
1999	Daima Pernia, CUB	52.89	

4 x 100-Meter Relay

Year		Time	
1983	East Germany	41.76	
1987	United States	41.58	
1991	Jamaica	41.94	
1993	Russia	41.49	CR
1995	United States	42.12	
1997	United States	41.47	CR
1999	Bahamas	41.92	

4 x 400-Meter Relay

Year		Time	
1983	East Germany	3:19.73	
1987	East Germany	3:18.63	
1991	Soviet Union	3:18.43	
1993	United States	3:16.71	CR
1995	United States	3:22.39	
1997	Germany	3:20.92	
1999	Russia	3:21.98	

Track & Field (Cont.)

20-Kilometer Walk

Held as 10-Kilometer race from 1987-97

Year		Time	
1983	Not held		
1987	Irina Strakhova, USSR	44:12	
1991	Alina Ivanova, USSR	42:57	
1993	Sari Essayah, FIN	42:59	
1995	Irina Stankina, RUS	42:13	CR
1997	Anna Sidoti, ITA	42:55	
1999	Hongyu Liu, CHN	1:30:50	CR

High Jump

Year		Height	
1983	Tamara Bykova, USSR	6-7	
1987	Stefka Kostadinova, BUL	6-10¼	WR
1991	Heike Henkel, GER	6-8¾	
1993	Ioamnet Quintero, CUB	6-6¼	
1995	Stefka Kostadinova, BUL	6-7	
1997	Hanne Haugland, NOR	6-6¼	
1999	Inga Babakova, UKR	6-6¼	

Pole Vault

Year		Height	
1999	Stacy Dragila, USA	15-1	=WR

Long Jump

Year		Distance	
1983	Heike Daute, E. Ger	23-10¼w	
1987	Jackie Joyner-Kersee, USA	24-1¾	CR
1991	Jackie Joyner-Kersee, USA	24-0¼	
1993	Heike Drechsler, GER	23-4	
1995	Fiona May, ITA	22-10¾w	
1997	Lyudmila Galkina, RUS	23-1¾	
1999	Niurka Montalvo, SPA	23-2	

w indicates wind-aided.

Triple Jump

Year		Distance	
1993	Ana Biryukova, RUS	46-6¼	WR
1995	Inessa Kravets, UKR	50-10¾	WR
1997	Sarka Kasparkova, CZE	49-10½	
1999	Paraskevi Tsiamita, GRE	48-10	

Shot Put

Year		Distance	
1983	Helena Fibingerova, CZE	69-0	
1987	Natalia Lisovskaya, USSR	69-8	CR
1991	Huang Zhihong, CHN	68-4	
1993	Huang Zhihong, CHN	67-6	
1995	Astrid Kumbernuss, GER	69-7½	
1997	Astrid Kumbernuss, GER	67-11½	
1999	Astrid Kumbernuss, GER	65-1½	

Discus

Year		Distance	
1983	Martina Opitz, E. Ger	226-2	
1987	Martina Opitz Hellmann, E. Ger	235-0	CR
1991	Tsvetanka Khristova, BUL	233-0	
1993	Olga Burova, RUS	221-1	
1995	Ellina Zvereva, BLR	225-2	
1997	Beatrice Faumuina, NZL	219-3	
1999	Franka Dietzsch, GER	223-6	

Hammer Throw

Year		Distance	
1999	Mihaela Melinte, ROM	246-8¾	CR

Javelin

Year		Distance	
1983	Tiina Lillak, FIN	232-4	
1987	Fatima Whitbread, GBR	251-5	CR
1991	Xu Demei, CHN	225-8	
1993	Trine Hattestad, NOR	227-0	
1995	Natalya Shikolenko, BLR	221-8	
1997	Trine Hattestad, NOR	225-8	
1999	Mirela Manjani-Tzelili, GRE	220-1	

Heptathlon

Year		Points	
1983	Ramona Neubert, E. Ger	6770	
1987	Jackie Joyner-Kersee, USA	7128	CR
1991	Sabine Braun, GER	6672	
1993	Jackie Joyner-Kersee, USA	6837	
1995	Ghada Shouaa, SYR	6651	
1997	Sabine Braun, GER	6739	
1999	Eunice Barber, FRA	6861	

Marathons

Boston

America's oldest regularly contested foot race, the Boston Marathon is held on Patriots' Day every April. It has been run at four different distances: 24 miles, 1232 yards (1897-1923); 26 miles, 209 yards (1924-26); 26 miles, 385 yards (1927-52, since 1957); 25 miles, 958 yards (1953-56).

MEN

Multiple winners: Clarence DeMar (7); Gerard Cote and Bill Rodgers (4); Ibrahim Hussein, Cosmas Ndeti and Leslie Pawson (3); Tarzan Brown, Jim Caffrey, John A. Kelley, John Miles, Eino Oksanen, Toshihiko Seko, Geoff Smith, Moses Tanui and Aurele Vandendriessche (2).

Year		Time
1897	John McDermott, New York	2:55:10
1898	Ronald McDonald, Massachusetts	2:42:00
1899	Lawrence Brignolia, Massachusetts	2:54:38
1900	Jim Caffrey, Canada	2:39:44
1901	Jim Caffrey, Canada	2:29:23
1902	Sam Mellor, New York	2:43:12
1903	J.C. Lorden, Massachusetts	2:41:29
1904	Mike Spring, New York	2:38:04
1905	Fred Lorz, New York	2:38:25
1906	Tim Ford, Massachusetts	2:45:45
1907	Tom Longboat, Canada	2:24:24
1908	Tom Morrissey, New York	2:25:43
1909	Henri Renaud, New Hampshire	2:53:36
1910	Fred Cameron, Nova Scotia	2:28:52
1911	Clarence DeMar, Massachusetts	2:21:39

Year		Time
1912	Mike Ryan, Illinois	2:21:18
1913	Fritz Carlson, Minnesota	2:25:14
1914	James Duffy, Canada	2:25:01
1915	Edouard Fabre, Canada	2:31:41
1916	Arthur Roth, Massachusetts	2:27:16
1917	Bill Kennedy, New York	2:28:37
1918	World War relay race	
1919	Carl Linder, Massachusetts	2:29:13
1920	Peter Trivoulidas, New York	2:29:31
1921	Frank Zuna, New Jersey	2:18:57
1922	Clarence DeMar, Massachusetts	2:18:10
1923	Clarence DeMar, Massachusetts	2:23:37
1924	Clarence DeMar, Massachusetts	2:29:40
1925	Charles Mellor, Illinois	2:33:00
1926	John Miles, Nova Scotia	2:25:40

Year	Time
1927 Clarence DeMar, Massachusetts	2:40:22
1928 Clarence DeMar, Massachusetts	2:37:07
1929 John Miles, Nova Scotia	2:33:08
1930 Clarence DeMar, Massachusetts	2:34:48
1931 James Henigan, Massachusetts	2:46:45
1932 Paul deBruyn, Germany	2:33:36
1933 Leslie Pawson, Rhode Island	2:31:01
1934 Dave Komonen, Canada	2:32:53
1935 John A. Kelley, Massachusetts	2:32:07
1936 Ellison (Tarzan) Brown, Rhode Island	2:33:40
1937 Walter Young, Canada	2:33:20
1938 Leslie Pawson, Rhode Island	2:35:34
1939 Ellison (Tarzan) Brown, Rhode Island	2:28:51
1940 Gerard Cote, Canada	2:28:28
1941 Leslie Pawson, Rhode Island	2:30:38
1942 Joe Smith, Massachusetts	2:26:51
1943 Gerard Cote, Canada	2:28:25
1944 Gerard Cote, Canada	2:31:50
1945 John A. Kelley, Massachusetts	2:30:40
1946 Stylianos Kyriakides, Greece	2:29:27
1947 Yun Bok Suh, Korea	2:25:39
1948 Gerard Cote, Canada	2:31:02
1949 Karle Leandersson, Sweden	2:31:50
1950 Kee Yonh Ham, Korea	2:32:39
1951 Shigeki Tanaka, Japan	2:27:45
1952 Doroteo Flores, Guatemala	2:31:53
1953 Keizo Yamada, Japan	2:18:51
1954 Veiko Karvonen, Finland	2:20:39
1955 Hideo Hamamura, Japan	2:18:22
1956 Antti Viskari, Finland	2:14:14
1957 John J. Kelley, Connecticut	2:20:05
1958 Franjo Mihalic, Yugoslavia	2:25:54
1959 Eino Oksanen, Finland	2:22:42
1960 Paavo Kotila, Finland	2:20:54
1961 Eino Oksanen, Finland	2:23:39
1962 Eino Oksanen, Finland	2:23:48
1963 Aurele Vandendriessche, Belgium	2:18:58
1964 Aurele Vandendriessche, Belgium	2:19:59

Year	Time
1965 Morio Shigematsu, Japan	2:16:33
1966 Kenji Kimihara, Japan	2:17:11
1967 David McKenzie, New Zealand	2:15:45
1968 Amby Burfoot, Connecticut	2:22:17
1969 Yoshiaki Unetani, Japan	2:13:49
1970 Ron Hill, England	2:10:30
1971 Alvaro Mejia, Colombia	2:18:45
1972 Olavi Suomalainen, Finland	2:15:39
1973 Jon Anderson, Oregon	2:16:03
1974 Neil Cusack, Ireland	2:13:39
1975 Bill Rodgers, Massachusetts	2:09:55
1976 Jack Fultz, Pennsylvania	2:20:19
1977 Jerome Drayton, Canada	2:14:46
1978 Bill Rodgers, Massachusetts	2:10:13
1979 Bill Rodgers, Massachusetts	2:09:27
1980 Bill Rodgers, Massachusetts	2:12:11
1981 Toshihiko Seko, Japan	2:09:26
1982 Alberto Salazar, Oregon	2:08:52
1983 Greg Meyer, New Jersey	2:09:00
1984 Geoff Smith, England	2:10:34
1985 Geoff Smith, England	2:14:05
1986 Rob de Castella, Australia	2:07:51
1987 Toshihiko Seko, Japan	2:11:50
1988 Ibrahim Hussein, Kenya	2:08:43
1989 Abebe Mekonnen, Ethiopia	2:09:06
1990 Gelindo Bordin, Italy	2:08:19
1991 Ibrahim Hussein, Kenya	2:11:06
1992 Ibrahim Hussein, Kenya	2:08:14
1993 Cosmas Ndeti, Kenya	2:09:33
1994 Cosmas Ndeti, Kenya	2:07:15*
1995 Cosmas Ndeti, Kenya	2:09:22
1996 Moses Tanui, Kenya	2:09:16
1997 Lameck Aguta, Kenya	2:10:34
1998 Moses Tanui, Kenya	2:07:34
1999 Joseph Chebet, Kenya	2:09:52

*Course record.

WOMEN

Multiple winners: Rosa Mota, Uta Pippig and Fatuma Roba (3); Joan Benoit, Miki Gorman, Ingrid Kristiansen and Olga Markova (2).

Year	Time
1972 Nina Kuscsik, New York	3:08:58
1973 Jacqueline Hansen, California	3:05:59
1974 Miki Gorman, California	2:47:11
1975 Liane Winter, West Germany	2:42:24
1976 Kim Merritt, Wisconsin	2:47:10
1977 Miki Gorman, California	2:48:33
1978 Gayle Barron, Georgia	2:44:52
1979 Joan Benoit, Maine	2:35:15
1980 Jacqueline Gareau, Canada	2:34:28
1981 Allison Roe, New Zealand	2:26:46
1982 Charlotte Teske, West Germany	2:29:33
1983 Joan Benoit, Maine	2:22:43
1984 Lorraine Moller, New Zealand	2:29:28
1985 Lisa Larsen Weidenbach, Mass	2:34:06
1986 Ingrid Kristiansen, Norway	2:24:55

Year	Time
1987 Rosa Mota, Portugal	2:25:21
1988 Rosa Mota, Portugal	2:24:30
1989 Ingrid Kristiansen, Norway	2:24:33
1990 Rosa Mota, Portugal	2:25:23
1991 Wanda Panfil, Poland	2:24:18
1992 Olga Markova, CIS	2:23:43
1993 Olga Markova, Russia	2:25:27
1994 Uta Pippig, Germany	2:21:45*
1995 Uta Pippig, Germany	2:25:11
1996 Uta Pippig, Germany	2:27:12
1997 Fatuma Roba, Ethiopia	2:26:23
1998 Fatuma Roba, Ethiopia	2:23:21
1999 Fatuma Roba, Ethiopia	2:23:25

*Course record.

New York City

Started in 1970, the New York City Marathon is run in the fall, usually on the first Sunday in November. The route winds through all of the city's five boroughs and finishes in Central Park.

MEN

Multiple winners: Bill Rodgers (4); Alberto Salazar (3); Tom Fleming, John Kagwe, Orlando Pizzolato and German Silva (2).

Year	Time	Year	Time	Year	Time
1970 Gary Muhrcke, USA	2:31:38	1971 Norman Higgins, USA	2:22:54	1972 Sheldon Karlin, USA	2:27:52

Track & Field (Cont.)

Year	Time	Year	Time	Year	Time
1973 Tom Fleming, USA	2:21:54	1982 Alberto Salazar, USA	2:09:29	1991 Salvador Garcia, MEX	2:09:28
1974 Norbert Sander, USA	2:26:30	1983 Rod Dixon, NZ	2:08:59	1992 Willie Mtolo, S. Afr.	2:09:29
1975 Tom Fleming, USA	2:19:27	1984 Orlando Pizzolato, ITA.	2:14:53	1993 Andres Espinosa, MEX.	2:10:04
1976 Bill Rodgers, USA	2:10:09	1985 Orlando Pizzolato, ITA.	2:11:34	1994 German Silva, MEX	2:11:21
1977 Bill Rodgers, USA	2:11:28	1986 Gianni Poli, ITA	2:11:06	1995 German Silva, MEX	2:11:00
1978 Bill Rodgers, USA	2:12:12	1987 Ibrahim Hussein, KEN	2:11:01	1996 Giacomo Leone, ITA	2:09:54
1979 Bill Rodgers, USA	2:11:42	1988 Steve Jones, WAL	2:08:20	1997 John Kagwe, KEN	2:08:12
1980 Alberto Salazar, USA	2:09:41	1989 Juma Ikangaa, TAN	2:08:01*	1998 John Kagwe, KEN	2:08:45
1981 Alberto Salazar, USA	2:08:13	1990 Douglas Wakihuri, KEN	2:12:39	*Course record.	

WOMEN

Multiple winners: Grete Waitz (9); Miki Gorman, Nina Kuscsik and Tegla Loroupe (2).

Year	Time	Year	Time	Year	Time
1970 No Finisher		1980 Grete Waitz, NOR	2:25:41	1990 Wanda Panfil, POL	2:30:45
1971 Beth Bonner, USA	2:55:22	1981 Allison Roe, NZ	2:25:29	1991 Liz McColgan, SCO	2:27:23
1972 Nina Kuscsik, USA	3:08:41	1982 Grete Waitz, NOR	2:27:14	1992 Lisa Ondieki, AUS	2:24:40*
1973 Nina Kuscsik, USA	2:57:07	1983 Grete Waitz, NOR	2:27:00	1993 Uta Pippig, GER	2:26:24
1974 Katherine Switzer, USA	3:07:29	1984 Grete Waitz, NOR	2:29:30	1994 Tegla Loroupe, KEN	2:27:37
1975 Kim Merritt, USA	2:46:14	1985 Grete Waitz, NOR	2:28:34	1995 Tegla Loroupe, KEN	2:28:06
1976 Miki Gorman, USA	2:39:11	1986 Grete Waitz, NOR	2:28:06	1996 Anuta Catuna, ROM	2:28:18
1977 Miki Gorman, USA	2:43:10	1987 Priscilla Welch, GBR	2:30:17	1997 F. Rochat-Moser, SWI	2:28:43
1978 Grete Waitz, NOR	2:32:30	1988 Grete Waitz, NOR	2:28:07	1998 Franca Fiacconi, ITA	2:25:17
1979 Grete Waitz, NOR	2:27:33	1989 Ingrid Kristiansen, NOR	2:25:30	*Course record.	

Annual Awards
Track & Field News Athletes of the Year

Voted on by an international panel of track and field experts and presented since 1959 for men and 1974 for women.

MEN

Multiple winners: Carl Lewis (3); Sergey Bubka, Sebastian Coe, Haile Gebrselassie, Michael Johnson, Alberto Juantorena, Noureddine Morceli, Jim Ryun and Peter Snell (2).

Year	Event	Year	Event
1959 Martin Lauer, W. Germany	110H/Decathlon	1979 Sebastian Coe, Great Britain	800/1500
1960 Rafer Johnson, USA	Decathlon	1980 Edwin Moses, USA	400 Hurdles
1961 Ralph Boston, USA	Long Jump/110 Hurdles	1981 Sebastian Coe, Great Britain	800/1500
1962 Peter Snell, New Zealand	800/1500	1982 Carl Lewis, USA	100/200/Long Jump
1963 C.K. Yang, Taiwan	Decathlon/Pole Vault	1983 Carl Lewis, USA	100/200/Long Jump
1964 Peter Snell, New Zealand	800/1500	1984 Carl Lewis, USA	100/200/Long Jump
1965 Ron Clarke, Australia	5000/10,000	1985 Said Aouita, Morocco	1500/5000
1966 Jim Ryun, USA	800/1500	1986 Yuri Sedykh, USSR	Hammer Throw
1967 Jim Ryun, USA	1500	1987 Ben Johnson, Canada	100
1968 Bob Beamon, USA	Long Jump	1988 Sergey Bubka, USSR	Pole Vault
1969 Bill Toomey, USA	Decathlon	1989 Roger Kingdom, USA	110 Hurdles
1970 Randy Matson, USA	Shot Put	1990 Michael Johnson, USA	200/400
1971 Rod Milburn, USA	110 Hurdles	1991 Sergey Bubka, USSR	Pole Vault
1972 Lasse Viren, Finland	5000/10,000	1992 Kevin Young, USA	400 Hurdles
1973 Ben Jipcho, Kenya	1500/5000/Steeplechase	1993 Noureddine Morceli, Algeria	Mile/1500/3000
1974 Rick Wohlhuter, USA	800/1500	1994 Noureddine Morceli, Algeria	Mile/1500/3000
1975 John Walker, New Zealand	800/1500	1995 Haile Gebrselassie, Ethopia	5000/10,000
1976 Alberto Juantorena, Cuba	400/800	1996 Michael Johnson, USA	200/400
1977 Alberto Juantorena, Cuba	400/800	1997 Wilson Kipketer, Denmark	800
1978 Henry Rono, Kenya	5000/10,000/Steeplechase	1998 Haile Gebrselassie, Ethopia	3000/5000/10,000

WOMEN

Multiple winners: Marita Koch (4); Jackie Joyner-Kersee (3); Evelyn Ashford and Marion Jones (2).

Year	Event	Year	Event
1974 Irena Szewinska, Poland	100/200/400	1987 Jackie Joyner-Kersee, USA	100H/Heptathlon/LJ
1975 Faina Melnik, USSR	Shot Put/Discus	1988 Florence Griffith Joyner, USA	100/200
1976 Tatiana Kazankina, USSR	800/1500	1989 Ana Quirot, Cuba	400/800
1977 Rosemarie Ackermann, E. Germany	High Jump	1990 Merlene Ottey, Jamaica	100/200
1978 Marita Koch, E. Germany	100/200/400	1991 Heike Henkel, Germany	High Jump
1979 Marita Koch, E. Germany	100/200/400	1992 Heike Drechsler, Germany	Long Jump
1980 Ilona Briesenick, E. Germany	Shot Put	1993 Wang Junxia, China	1500/3000/10,000
1981 Evelyn Ashford, USA	100/200	1994 Jackie Joyner-Kersee, USA	100H/Heptathlon/LJ
1982 Marita Koch, E. Germany	100/200/400	1995 Sonia O'Sullivan, Ireland	1500/3000/5000
1983 Jarmila Kratochvilova, Czech	200/400/800	1996 Svetlana Masterkova, Russia	800/1500
1984 Evelyn Ashford, USA	100	1997 Marion Jones, USA	100/200
1985 Marita Koch, E. Germany	100/200/400	1998 Marion Jones, USA	100/200/LJ
1986 Jackie Joyner-Kersee, USA	Heptathlon/Long Jump		

SWIMMING & DIVING

FINA World Championships

While the Summer Olympics have served as the unofficial world championships for swimming and diving throughout the century, a separate World Championship meet was started in 1973 by the International Amateur Swimming Federation (FINA). The meet was held three times between 1973-78, then every four years since then. Sites have been Belgrade (1973); Cali, COL (1975); West Berlin (1978); Guayaquil, ECU (1982); Madrid (1986); Perth (1991 & 98) and Rome (1994).

MEN

Most gold medals (including relays): Jim Montgomery (7); Matt Biondi (6); Rowdy Gaines (5); Joe Bottom, Tamas Darnyi, Michael Gross, Tom Jager, Michael Klim, David McCagg, Vladimir Salnikov and Tim Shaw (4); Billy Forrester, Andras Hargitay, Roland Matthes, John Murphy, Aleksandr Popov, Jeff Rouse, Norbert Rozsa and David Wilkie (3).

50-Meter Freestyle

Year		Time	
1973-82 Not held			
1986	Tom Jager, USA	.22.49	
1991	Tom Jager, USA	.22.16	CR
1994	Aleksandr Popov, RUS	.22.17	
1998	Bill Pilczuk, USA	.22.29	

100-Meter Freestyle

Year		Time	
1973	Jim Montgomery, USA	.51.70	
1975	Tim Shaw, USA	.51.25	
1978	David McCagg, USA	.50.24	
1982	Jorg Woithe, E. Ger	.50.18	
1986	Matt Biondi, USA	.48.94	
1991	Matt Biondi, USA	.49.18	
1994	Aleksandr Popov, RUS	.49.12	
1998	Aleksandr Popov, RUS	.48.93	CR

200-Meter Freestyle

Year		Time	
1973	Jim Montgomery, USA	1:53.02	
1975	Tim Shaw, USA	1:52.04	
1978	Billy Forrester, USA	1:51.02	
1982	Michael Gross, W. Ger	1:49.84	
1986	Michael Gross, W. Ger	1:47.92	
1991	Giorgio Lamberti, ITA	1:47.27	
1994	Antti Kasvio, FIN	1:47.32	CR
1998	Michael Klim, AUS	1:47.41	

400-Meter Freestyle

Year		Time	
1973	Rick DeMont, USA	3:58.18	
1975	Tim Shaw, USA	3:54.88	
1978	Vladimir Salnikov, USSR	3:51.94	
1982	Vladimir Salnikov, USSR	3:51.30	
1986	Rainer Henkel, W. Ger	3:50.05	
1991	Jorg Hoffman, GER	3:48.04	
1994	Kieren Perkins, AUS	3:43.80	WR
1998	Ian Thorpe, AUS	3:46.29	

1500-Meter Freestyle

Year		Time	
1973	Stephen Holland, AUS	15:31.85	
1975	Tim Shaw, USA	15:28.92	
1978	Vladimir Salnikov, USSR	15:03.99	
1982	Vladimir Salnikov, USSR	15:01.77	
1986	Rainer Henkel, W. Ger	15:05.31	
1991	Jorg Hoffman, GER	14:50.36	WR
1994	Kieren Perkins, AUS	14:50.52	
1998	Grant Hackett, AUS	14:51.70	

100-Meter Backstroke

Year		Time	
1973	Roland Matthes, E. Ger	.57.47	
1975	Roland Matthes, E. Ger	.58.15	
1978	Bob Jackson, USA	.56.36	
1982	Dirk Richter, E. Ger	.55.95	
1986	Igor Polianski, USSR	.55.58	
1991	Jeff Rouse, USA	.55.23	
1994	Martin Lopez-Zubero, SPA	.55.17	CR
1998	Lenny Krayzelburg, USA	.55.00	

200-Meter Backstroke

Year		Time	
1973	Roland Matthes, E. Ger	2:01.87	
1975	Zoltan Varraszto, HUN	2:05.05	
1978	Jesse Vassallo, USA	2:02.16	
1982	Rick Carey, USA	2:00.82	
1986	Igor Polianski, USSR	1:58.78	CR
1991	Martin Zubero, SPA	1:59.52	
1994	Vladimir Selkov, RUS	1:57.42	
1998	Lenny Krayzelburg, USA	1:58.84	

100-Meter Breaststroke

Year		Time	
1973	John Hencken, USA	1:04.02	
1975	David Wilkie, GBR	1:04.26	
1978	Walter Kusch, W. Ger	1:03.56	
1982	Steve Lundquist, USA	1:02.75	
1986	Victor Davis, CAN	1:02.71	
1991	Norbert Rozsa, HUN	1:01.45	WR
1994	Norbert Rozsa, HUN	1:01.24	
1998	Frederik deBurghgraeve, BEL	1:01.34	

200-Meter Breaststroke

Year		Time	
1973	David Wilkie, GBR	2:19.28	
1975	David Wilkie, GBR	2:18.23	
1978	Nick Nevid, USA	2:18.37	
1982	Victor Davis, CAN	2:14.77	WR
1986	Jozsef Szabo, HUN	2:14.27	
1991	Mike Barrowman, USA	2:11.23	WR
1994	Norbert Rozsa, HUN	2:12.81	
1998	Kurt Grote, USA	2:13.40	

100-Meter Butterfly

Year		Time	
1973	Bruce Robertson, CAN	.55.69	
1975	Greg Jagenburg, USA	.55.63	
1978	Joe Bottom, USA	.54.30	
1982	Matt Gribble, USA	.53.88	
1986	Pablo Morales, USA	.53.54	
1991	Anthony Nesty, SUR	.53.29	
1994	Rafal Szukala, POL	.53.51	
1998	Michael Klim, AUS	.52.25	CR

200-Meter Butterfly

Year		Time	
1973	Robin Backhaus, USA	2:03.32	
1975	Billy Forrester, USA	2:01.95	
1978	Mike Bruner, USA	1:59.38	
1982	Michael Gross, W. Ger	1:58.85	
1986	Michael Gross, W. Ger	1:56.53	
1991	Melvin Stewart, USA	1:55.69	WR
1994	Denis Pankratov, RUS	1:56.54	
1998	Denys Sylantyev, UKR	1:56.61	

200-Meter Individual Medley

Year		Time	
1973	Gunnar Larsson, SWE	2:08.36	
1975	Andras Hargitay, HUN	2:07.72	
1978	Graham Smith, CAN	2:03.65	WR
1982	Alexander Sidorenko, USSR	2:03.30	
1986	Tamás Darnyi, HUN	2:01.57	
1991	Tamás Darnyi, HUN	1:59.36	WR
1994	Janis Sievinen, FIN	1:58.16	WR
1998	Marcel Wouda, NET	2:01.18	

Swimming & Diving (Cont.)

400-Meter Individual Medley

Year		Time
1973	Andras Hargitay, HUN	4:31.11
1975	Andras Hargitay, HUN	4:32.57
1978	Jesse Vassallo, USA	4:20.05 **WR**
1982	Ricardo Prado, BRA	4:19.78 **WR**
1986	Tamás Darnyi, HUN	4:18.98
1991	Tamás Darnyi, HUN	4:12.36 **WR**
1994	Tom Dolan, USA	4:12.30 **WR**
1998	Tom Dolan, USA	4:14.95

4 x 100-Meter Freestyle Relay

Year		Time
1973	United States	3:27.18
1975	United States	3:24.85
1978	United States	3:19.74
1982	United States	3:19.26 **WR**
1986	United States	3:19.98
1991	United States	3:17.15
1994	United States	3:16.90
1998	United States	3:16.69 **CR**

4 x 200-Meter Freestyle Relay

Year		Time
1973	United States	7:33.22 **WR**
1975	West Germany	7:39.44
1978	United States	7:20.82
1982	United States	7:21.09
1986	East Germany	7:15.91
1991	Germany	7:13.50 **CR**
1994	Sweden	7:17.34
1998	Australia	7:12.48

4 x 100-Meter Medley Relay

Year		Time
1973	United States	3:49.49
1975	United States	3:49.00
1978	United States	3:44.63
1982	United States	3:40.84 **WR**
1986	United States	3:41.25
1991	United States	3:39.66
1994	United States	3:37.74 **CR**
1998	Australia	3:37.98

WOMEN

Most gold medals (including relays): Kornelia Ender (8); Kristin Otto (7); Tracy Caulkins, Heike Friedrich, Le Jingyi, Rosemarie Kother, Ulrike Richter and Jenny Thompson (4); Hannalore Anke, Lu Bin, He Cihong, Janet Evans, Nicole Haislett, Lui Limin, Birgit Meineke, Joan Pennington, Manuela Stellmach, Amy Van Dyken, Renate Vogel and Cynthia Woodhead (3).

50-Meter Freestyle

Year		Time
1973-82 Not held		
1986	Tamara Costache, ROM	25.28 **WR**
1991	Zhuang Yong, CHN	25.47
1994	Le Jingyi, CHN	24.51 **WR**
1998	Amy Van Dyken, USA	25.15

100-Meter Freestyle

Year		Time
1973	Kornelia Ender, E. Ger	57.54
1975	Kornelia Ender, E. Ger	56.50
1978	Barbara Krause, E. Ger	55.68
1982	Birgit Meineke, E. Ger	55.79
1986	Kristin Otto, E. Ger	55.05
1991	Nicole Haislett, USA	55.17
1994	Le Jingyi, CHN	54.01 **WR**
1998	Jenny Thompson, USA	54.95

200-Meter Freestyle

Year		Time
1973	Keena Rothhammer, USA	2:04.99
1975	Shirley Babashoff, USA	2:02.50
1978	Cynthia Woodhead, USA	1:58.53 **WR**
1982	Annemarie Verstappen, HOL	1:59.53
1986	Heike Friedrich, E. Ger	1:58.26
1991	Hayley Lewis, AUS	2:00.48
1994	Franziska Van Almsick, GER	1:56.78 **WR**
1998	Claudia Poll, CST	1:58.90

400-Meter Freestyle

Year		Time
1973	Heather Greenwood, USA	4:20.28
1975	Shirley Babashoff, USA	4:22.70
1978	Tracey Wickham, AUS	4:06.28 **WR**
1982	Carmela Schmidt. E. Ger	4:08.98
1986	Heike Friedrich, E. Ger	4:07.45
1991	Janet Evans, USA	4:08.63
1994	Yang Aihua, CHN	4:09.64
1998	Yan Chen, CHN	4:06.72

800-Meter Freestyle

Year		Time
1973	Novella Calligaris, ITA	8:52.97
1975	Jenny Turrall, AUS	8:44.75
1978	Tracey Wickham, AUS	8:25.94
1982	Kim Linehan, USA	8:27.48
1986	Astrid Strauss, E. Ger	8:28.24
1991	Janet Evans, USA	8:24.05 **CR**
1994	Janet Evans, USA	8:29.85
1998	Brooke Bennett, USA	8:28.71

100-Meter Backstroke

Year		Time
1973	Ulrike Richter, E. Ger	1:05.42
1975	Ulrike Richter, E. Ger	1:03.30
1978	Linda Jezek, USA	1:02.55
1982	Kristin Otto, E. Ger	1:01.30
1986	Betsy Mitchell, USA	1:01.74
1991	Krisztina Egerszegi, HUN	1:01.78
1994	He Cihong, CHN	1:00.57 **WR**
1998	Lea Maurer, USA	1:01.16

200-Meter Backstroke

Year		Time
1973	Melissa Belote, USA	2:20.52
1975	Birgit Treiber, E. Ger	2:15.46 **WR**
1978	Linda Jezek, USA	2:11.93 **WR**
1982	Cornelia Sirch, E. Ger	2:09.91 **WR**
1986	Cornelia Sirch, E. Ger	2:11.37
1991	Krisztina Egerszegi, HUN	2:09.15
1994	He Cihong, CHN	2:07.40 **CR**
1998	Roxanna Maracineanu, FRA	2:11.26

100-Meter Breaststroke

Year		Time
1973	Renate Vogel, E. Ger	1:13.74
1975	Hannalore Anke, E. Ger	1:12.72
1978	Julia Bogdanova, USSR	1:10.31 **WR**
1982	Ute Geweniger, E. Ger	1:09.14
1986	Sylvia Gerasch, E. Ger	1:08.11 **WR**
1991	Linley Frame, AUS	1:08.81
1994	Samantha Riley, AUS	1:07.69 **WR**
1998	Kristy Kowal, USA	1:08.42

200-Meter Breaststroke

Year		Time
1973	Renate Vogel, E. Ger	2:40.01
1975	Hannalore Anke, E. Ger	2:37.25
1978	Lina Kachushite, USSR	2:31.42 **WR**
1982	Svetlana Varganova, USSR	2:28.82
1986	Silke Hoerner, E. Ger	2:27.40 **WR**

Year		Time	
1991	Elena Volkova, USSR	2:29.53	
1994	Samantha Riley, AUS	2:26.87	
1998	Agnes Kovacs, HUN	2:25.45	**CR**

100-Meter Butterfly

Year		Time	
1973	Kornelia Ender, E. Ger	1:02.53	
1975	Kornelia Ender, E. Ger	1:01.24	**WR**
1978	Joan Pennington, USA	1:00.20	
1982	Mary T. Meagher, USA	59.41	
1986	Kornelai Gressler, E. Ger	59.51	
1991	Qian Hong, CHN	59.68	
1994	Liu Limin, CHN	58.98	
1998	Jenny Thompson, USA	58.46	**CR**

200-Meter Butterfly

Year		Time	
1973	Rosemarie Kother, E. Ger	2:13.76	
1975	Rosemarie Kother, E. Ger	2:15.92	
1978	Tracy Caulkins, USA	2:09.78	**WR**
1982	Ines Geissler, E. Ger	2:08.66	
1986	Mary T. Meagher, USA	2:08.41	
1991	Summer Sanders, USA	2:09.24	
1994	Liu Limin, CHN	2:07.25	**CR**
1998	Susie O'Neill, AUS	2:07.93	

200-Meter Individual Medley

Year		Time	
1973	Andre Huebner, E. Ger	2:20.51	
1975	Kathy Heddy, USA	2:19.80	
1978	Tracy Caulkins, USA	2:19.80	**WR**
1982	Petra Schneider, E. Ger	2:11.79	**CR**
1986	Kristin Otto, E. Ger	2:15.56	
1991	Lin Li, CHN	2:13.40	
1994	Lu Bin, CHN	2:12.34	
1998	Yanyan Wu, CHN	2:10.88	**CR**

400-Meter Individual Medley

Year		Time	
1973	Gudrun Wegner, E. Ger	4:57.71	
1975	Ulrike Tauber, E. Ger	4:52.76	
1978	Tracy Caulkins, USA	4:40.83	**WR**
1982	Petra Schneider, E. Ger	4:36.10	**WR**
1986	Kathleen Nord, E. Ger	4:43.75	
1991	Lin Li, CHN	4:41.45	
1994	Dai Guohong, CHN	4:39.14	
1998	Yan Chen, CHN	4:36.66	

4 x 100-Meter Freestyle Relay

Year		Time	
1973	East Germany	3:52.45	
1975	East Germany	3:49.37	
1978	United States	3:43.43	**WR**
1982	East Germany	3:43.97	
1986	East Germany	3:40.57	
1991	United States	3:43.26	
1994	China	3:37.91	**WR**
1998	United States	3:42.11	

4 x 200-Meter Freestyle Relay

Year		Time	
1973-82 Not held			
1986	East Germany	7:59.33	**WR**
1991	Germany	8:02.56	
1994	China	7:57.96	**CR**
1998	Germany	8:01.46	

4 x 100-Meter Medley Relay

Year		Time	
1973	East Germany	4:16.84	
1975	East Germany	4:14.74	
1978	United States	4:08.21	
1982	East Germany	4:05.8	**WR**
1986	East Germany	4:04.82	
1991	United States	4:06.51	
1994	China	4:01.67	**CR**
1998	United States	4:01.93	

Diving

Multiple Gold Medals: MEN– Greg Louganis (5); Phil Boggs and Dmitry Sautin (3); Klaus Dibiasi and Yu Zhuocheng (2). WOMEN– Irina Kalinina and Gao Min (3); Fu Mingxia (2).

MEN
1-Meter Springboard

Year		Pts
1991	Edwin Jongejans, HOL	588.51
1994	Evan Stewart, ZIM	382.14
1998	Yu Zhuocheng, CHN	417.54

3-Meter Springboard

Year		Pts
1973	Phil Boggs, USA	618.57
1975	Phil Boggs, USA	597.12
1978	Phil Boggs, USA	913.95
1982	Greg Louganis, USA	752.67
1986	Greg Louganis, USA	750.06
1991	Kent Ferguson, USA	650.25
1994	Yu Zhuocheng, CHN	655.44
1998	Dmitry Sautin, RUS	746.79

Platform

Year		Pts
1973	Klaus Dibiasi, ITA	559.53
1975	Klaus Dibiasi, ITA	547.98
1978	Greg Louganis, USA	844.11
1982	Greg Louganis, USA	634.26
1986	Greg Louganis, USA	668.58
1991	Sun Shuwei, CHN	626.79
1994	Dmitry Sautin, RUS	634.71
1998	Dmitry Sautin, RUS	750.99

WOMEN
1-Meter Springboard

Year		Pts
1991	Gao Min, CHN	478.26
1994	Chen Lixia, CHN	279.30
1998	Irina Lashko, RUS	296.07

3-Meter Springboard

Year		Pts
1973	Christa Koehler, E. Ger	442.17
1975	Irina Kalinina, USSR	489.81
1978	Irina Kalinina, USSR	691.43
1982	Megan Neyer, USA	501.03
1986	Gao Min, CHN	582.90
1991	Gao Min, CHN	539.01
1994	Tan Shuping, CHN	548.49
1998	Yulia Pakhalina, RUS	544.52

Platform

Year		Pts
1973	Ulrike Knape, SWE	406.77
1975	Janet Ely, USA	403.89
1978	Irina Kalinina, USSR	412.71
1982	Wendy Wyland, USA	438.79
1986	Chen Lin, CHN	449.67
1991	Fu Mingxia, CHN	426.51
1994	Fu Mingxia, CHN	434.04
1998	Olena Zhupyna	550.41

ALPINE SKIING

World Cup Overall Champions

World Cup Overall Champions (downhill and slalom events combined) since the tour was organized in 1967.

MEN

Multiple winners: Marc Girardelli (5), Gustavo Thoeni and Pirmin Zurbriggen (4); Phil Mahre and Ingemar Stenmark (3); Jean-Claude Killy, Lasse Kjus and Karl Schranz (2).

Year		Year		Year	
1967	Jean-Claude Killy, France	1978	Ingemar Stenmark, Sweden	1989	Marc Girardelli, Luxembourg
1968	Jean Claude Killy, France	1979	Peter Luescher, Switzerland	1990	Pirmin Zurbriggen, Switzerland
1969	Karl Schranz, Austria	1980	Andreas Wenzel, Liechtenstein	1991	Marc Girardelli, Luxembourg
1970	Karl Schranz, Austria	1981	Phil Mahre, USA	1992	Paul Accola, Switzerland
1971	Gustavo Thoeni, Italy	1982	Phil Mahre, USA	1993	Marc Girardelli, Luxembourg
1972	Gustavo Thoeni, Italy	1983	Phil Mahre, USA	1994	Kjetil Andre Aamodt, Norway
1973	Gustavo Thoeni, Italy	1984	Pirmin Zurbriggen, Switzerland	1995	Alberto Tomba, Italy
1974	Piero Gros, Italy	1985	Marc Girardelli, Luxembourg	1996	Lasse Kjus, Norway
1975	Gustavo Thoeni, Italy	1986	Marc Girardelli, Luxembourg	1997	Luc Alphand, France
1976	Ingemar Stenmark, Sweden	1987	Pirmin Zurbriggen, Switzerland	1998	Hermann Maier, Austria
1977	Ingemar Stenmark, Sweden	1988	Pirmin Zurbriggen, Switzerland	1999	Lasse Kjus, Norway

WOMEN

Multiple winners: Annemarie Moser-Proell (6); Petra Kronberger and Vreni Schneider (3); Michela Figini, Nancy Greene, Erika Hess, Katja Seizinger, Maria Walliser and Hanni Wenzel (2).

Year		Year		Year	
1967	Nancy Greene, Canada	1978	Hanni Wenzel, Liechtenstein	1989	Vreni Schneider, Switzerland
1968	Nancy Greene, Canada	1979	Annemarie Moser-Pröll, Austria	1990	Petra Kronberger, Austria
1969	Gertrud Gabi, Austria	1980	Hanni Wenzel, Liechtenstein	1991	Petra Kronberger, Austria
1970	Michele Jacot, France	1981	Marie-Theres Nadig,Switzerland	1992	Petra Kronberger, Austria
1971	Annemarie Pröll, Austria	1982	Erika Hess, Switzerland	1993	Anita Wachter, Austria
1972	Annemarie Pröll, Austria	1983	Tamara McKinney, USA	1994	Vreni Schneider, Switzerland
1973	Annemarie Pröll, Austria	1984	Erika Hess, Switzerland	1995	Vreni Schneider, Switzerland
1974	Annemarie Pröll, Austria	1985	Michela Figini, Switzerland	1996	Katja Seizinger, Germany
1975	Annemarie Moser-Pröll, Austria	1986	Maria Walliser, Switzerland	1997	Pernilla Wiberg, Sweden
1976	Rosi Mittermaier, W. Germany	1987	Maria Walliser, Switzerland	1998	Katja Seizinger, Germany
1977	Lise-Marie Morerod, Switzerland	1988	Michela Figini, Switzerland	1999	Alexandra Meissnitzer, Austria

TOUR DE FRANCE

The world's premier cycling event, the Tour de France is staged throughout the country (sometimes passing through neighboring countries) over four weeks. The 1946 Tour, however, the first after World War II, was only a five-day race.

Multiple winners: Jacques Anquetil, Bernard Hinault, Miguel Induráin and Eddy Merckx (5); Louison Bobet, Greg LeMond and Phillippe Thys (3); Gino Bartali Ottavio Bottecchia, Fausto Coppi, Laurent Fignon, Nicholas Frantz, Firmin Lambot, André Leducq, Sylvere Maes, Antonin Magne, Lucien Petit-Breton and Bernard Thevenet (2).

Year		Year		Year	
1903	Maurice Garin, France	1932	André Leducq, France	1963	Jacques Anquetil, France
1904	Henri Cornet, France	1933	Georges Speicher, France	1964	Jacques Anquetil, France
1905	Louis Trousselier, France	1934	Antonin Magne, France	1965	Felice Gimondi, Italy
1906	René Pottier, France	1935	Romain Maes, Belgium	1966	Lucien Aimar, France
1907	Lucien Petit-Breton, France	1936	Sylvere Maes, Belgium	1967	Roger Pingeon, France
1908	Lucien Petit-Breton, France	1937	Roger Lapebie, France	1968	Jan Janssen, Holland
1909	Francois Faber, Luxembourg	1938	Gino Bartali, Italy	1969	Eddy Merckx, Belgium
1910	Octave Lapize, France	1939	Sylvere Maes, Belgium	1970	Eddy Merckx, Belgium
1911	Gustave Garrigou, France	1940-45	Not held	1971	Eddy Merckx, Belgium
1912	Odile Defraye, Belgium	1946	Jean Lazarides, France	1972	Eddy Merckx, Belgium
1913	Philippe Thys, Belgium	1947	Jean Robic, France	1973	Luis Ocana, Spain
1914	Philippe Thys, Belgium	1948	Gino Bartali, Italy	1974	Eddy Merckx, Belgium
1915-18	Not held	1949	Fausto Coppi, Italy	1975	Bernard Thevenet, France
1919	Firmin Lambot, Belgium	1950	Ferdinand Kubler, Switzerland	1976	Lucien van Impe, Belgium
1920	Philippe Thys, Belgium	1951	Hugo Koblet, Switzerland	1977	Bernard Thevenet, France
1921	Léon Scieur, Belgium	1952	Fausto Coppi, Italy	1978	Bernard Hinault, France
1922	Firmin Lambot, Belgium	1953	Louison Bobet, France	1979	Bernard Hinault, France
1923	Henri Pelissier, France	1954	Louison Bobet, France	1980	Joop Zoetemelk, Holland
1924	Ottavio Bottecchia, Italy	1955	Louison Bobet, France	1981	Bernard Hinault, France
1925	Ottavio Bottecchia, Italy	1956	Roger Walkowiak, France	1982	Bernard Hinault, France
1926	Lucien Buysse, Belgium	1957	Jacques Anquetil, France	1983	Laurent Fignon, France
1927	Nicholas Frantz, Luxembourg	1958	Charly Gaul, Luxembourg	1984	Laurent Fignon, France
1928	Nicholas Frantz, Luxembourg	1959	Federico Bahamontes, Spain	1985	Bernard Hinault, France
1929	Maurice Dewaele, Belgium	1960	Gastone Nencini, Italy	1986	Greg LeMond, USA
1930	André Leducq, France	1961	Jacques Anquetil, France	1987	Stephen Roche, Ireland
1931	Antonin Magne, France	1962	Jacques Anquetil, France	1988	Pedro Delgado, Spain

Year		Year		Year	
1989	Greg LeMond, USA	1993	Miguel Induráin, Spain	1997	Jan Ullrich, Germany
1990	Greg LeMond, USA	1994	Miguel Induráin, Spain	1998	Marco Pantani, Italy
1991	Miguel Induráin, Spain	1995	Miguel Induráin, Spain	1999	Lance Armstrong, USA
1992	Miguel Induráin, Spain	1996	Bjarne Riis, Denmark		

FIGURE SKATING

World Champions

Skaters who won World and Olympic championships in the same year are listed in **bold** type.

MEN

Multiple winners: Ulrich Salchow (10); Karl Schafer (7); Dick Button (5); Willy Bockl, Kurt Browning, Scott Hamilton and Hayes Jenkins (4); Emmerich Danzer, Gillis Grafstrom, Gustav Hugel, David Jenkins, Fritz Kachler, Ondrej Nepela and Elvis Stojko (3); Brian Boitano, Gilbert Fuchs, Jan Hoffmann, Felix Kaspar, Vladimir Kovalev, Tim Wood and Alexei Yagudin (2).

Year		Year		Year	
1896	Gilbert Fuchs, Germany	1933	Karl Schafer, Austria	1969	Tim Wood, USA
1897	Gustav Hugel, Austria	1934	Karl Schafer, Austria	1970	Tim Wood, USA
1898	Henning Grenander, Sweden	1935	Karl Schafer, Austria	1971	Ondrej Nepela, Czechoslovakia
1899	Gustav Hugel, Austria	1936	**Karl Schafer**, Austria	1972	**Ondrej Nepela**, Czechoslovakia
1900	Gustav Hugel, Austria	1937	Felix Kaspar, Austria	1973	Ondrej Nepela, Czechoslovakia
1901	Ulrich Salchow, Sweden	1938	Felix Kaspar, Austria	1974	Jan Hoffmann, E. Germany
1902	Ulrich Salchow, Sweden	1939	Graham Sharp, Britain	1975	Sergie Volkov, USSR
1903	Ulrich Salchow, Sweden	1940-46	Not held	1976	**John Curry**, Britain
1904	Ulrich Salchow, Sweden	1947	Hans Gerschwiler, Switzerland	1977	Vladimir Kovalev, USSR
1905	Ulrich Salchow, Sweden	1948	**Dick Button**, USA	1978	Charles Tickner, USA
1906	Gilbert Fuchs, Germany	1949	Dick Button, USA	1979	Vladimir Kovalev, USSR
1907	Ulrich Salchow, Sweden	1950	Dick Button, USA	1980	Jan Hoffmann, E. Germany
1908	**Ulrich Salchow**, Sweden	1951	Dick Button, USA	1981	Scott Hamilton, USA
1909	Ulrich Salchow, Sweden	1952	**Dick Button**, USA	1982	Scott Hamilton, USA
1910	Ulrich Salchow, Sweden	1953	Hayes Jenkins, USA	1983	Scott Hamilton, USA
1911	Ulrich Salchow, Sweden	1954	Hayes Jenkins, USA	1984	**Scott Hamilton**, USA
1912	Fritz Kachler, Austria	1955	Hayes Jenkins, USA	1985	Alexander Fadeev, USSR
1913	Fritz Kachler, Austria	1956	**Hayes Jenkins**, USA	1986	Brian Boitano, USA
1914	Gosta Sandhal, Sweden	1957	David Jenkins, USA	1987	Brian Orser, Canada
1915-21	Not held	1958	David Jenkins, USA	1988	**Brian Boitano**, USA
1922	Gillis Grafstrom, Sweden	1959	David Jenkins, USA	1989	Kurt Browning, Canada
1923	Fritz Kachler, Austria	1960	Alan Giletti, France	1990	Kurt Browning, Canada
1924	**Gillis Grafstrom,** Sweden	1961	Not held	1991	Kurt Browning, Canada
1925	Willy Bockl, Austria	1962	Donald Jackson, Canada	1992	**Viktor Petrenko**, CIS
1926	Willy Bockl, Austria	1963	Donald McPherson, Canada	1993	Kurt Browning, Canada
1927	Willy Bockl, Austria	1964	**Manfred Schnelldorfer**, W. Ger	1994	Elvis Stojko, Canada
1928	Willy Bockl, Austria			1995	Elvis Stojko, Canada
1929	Gillis Grafstrom, Sweden	1965	Alain Calmat, France	1996	Todd Eldredge, USA
1930	Karl Schafer, Austria	1966	Emmerich Danzer, Austria	1997	Elvis Stojko, Canada
1931	Karl Schafer, Austria	1967	Emmerich Danzer, Austria	1998	Alexei Yagudin, Russia
1932	**Karl Schafer**, Austria	1968	Emmerich Danzer, Austria	1999	Alexei Yagudin, Russia

WOMEN

Multiple winners: Sonja Henie (10); Carol Heiss and Herma Planck Szabo (5); Lily Kronberger and Katarina Witt (4); Sjoukje Dijkstra, Peggy Fleming, Meray Horvath (3); Tenley Albright, Linda Fratianne, Michelle Kwan, Anett Poetzsch, Beatrix Schuba, Barbara Ann Scott, Gabriele Seyfert, Megan Taylor, Alena Vrzanova and Kristi Yamaguchi (2).

Year		Year		Year	
1906	Madge Syers, Britain	1929	Sonja Henie, Norway	1952	Jacqueline Du Bief, France
1907	Madge Syers, Britian	1930	Sonja Henie, Norway	1953	Tenley Albright, USA
1908	Lily Kronberger, Hungary	1931	Sonja Henie, Norway	1954	Gundi Busch, W. Germany
1909	Lily Kronberger, Hungary	1932	**Sonja Henie**, Norway	1955	Tenley Albright, USA
1910	Lily Kronberger, Hungary	1933	Sonja Henie, Norway	1956	Carol Heiss, USA
1911	Lily Kronberger, Hungary	1934	Sonja Henie, Norway	1957	Carol Heiss, USA
1912	Meray Horvath, Hungary	1935	Sonja Henie, Norway	1958	Carol Heiss, USA
1913	Meray Horvath, Hungary	1936	**Sonja Henie**, Norway	1959	Carol Heiss, USA
1914	Meray Horvath, Hungary	1937	Cecilia Colledge, Britain	1960	**Carol Heiss**, USA
1915-21	Not held	1938	Megan Taylor, Britain	1961	Not held
1922	Herma Planck-Szabo, Austria	1939	Megan Taylor, Britain	1962	Sjoukje Dijkstra, Holland
1923	Herma Planck-Szabo, Austria	1940-46	Not held	1963	Sjoukje Dijkstra, Holland
1924	**Herma Planck-Szabo**, Austria	1947	Barbara Ann Scott, Canada	1964	**Sjoukje Dijkstra**, Holland
1925	Herma Planck-Szabo, Austria	1948	**Barbara Ann Scott**, Canada	1965	Petra Burka, Canada
1926	Herma Planck-Szabo, Austria	1949	Alena Vrzanova, Czechoslovakia	1966	Peggy Fleming, USA
1927	Sonja Henie, Norway	1950	Alena Vrzanova, Czechoslovakia	1967	Peggy Fleming, USA
1928	**Sonja Henie**, Norway	1951	Jeannette Altwegg, Britain	1968	**Peggy Fleming**, USA
				1969	Gabriele Seyfert, E. Germany

Year		Year		Year	
1970	Gabriele Seyfert, E. Germany	1980	**Anett Poetzsch**, E. Germany	1990	Jill Trenary, USA
1971	Beatrix Schuba, Austria	1981	Denise Biellmann, Switzerland	1991	Kristi Yamaguchi, USA
1972	**Beatrix Schuba**, Austria	1982	Elaine Zayak, USA	1992	**Kristi Yamaguchi**, USA
1973	Karen Magnussen, Canada	1983	Rosalyn Sumners, USA	1993	Oksana Baiul, Ukraine
1974	Christine Errath, E. Germany	1984	**Katarina Witt**, E. Germany	1994	Yuka Sato, Japan
1975	Dianne DeLeeuw, Holland	1985	Katarina Witt, E. Germany	1995	Lu Chen, China
1976	**Dorothy Hamill**, USA	1986	Debi Thomas, USA	1996	Michelle Kwan, USA
1977	Linda Fratianne, USA	1987	Katarina Witt, E. Germany	1997	Tara Lipinski, USA
1978	Anett Poetzsch, E. Germany	1988	**Katarina Witt**, E. Germany	1998	Michelle Kwan, USA
1979	Linda Fratianne, USA	1989	Midori Ito, Japan	1999	Maria Butyrskaya, Russia

U.S. Champions

Skaters who won U.S., World and Olympic championships in same year are in **bold** type.

MEN

Multiple winners: Dick Button and Roger Turner (7); Sherwin Badger, Todd Eldredge and Robin Lee (5); Brian Boitano, Scott Hamilton, David Jenkins, Hayes Jenkins and Charles Tickner (4); Gordon McKellen, Nathaniel Niles and Tim Wood (3); Scott Allen, Christopher Bowman, Scott Davis, Eugene Turner and Gary Visconti (2).

Year		Year		Year		Year	
1914	Norman Scott	1937	Robin Lee	1959	David Jenkins	1980	Charles Tickner
1915-17	Not held	1938	Robin Lee	1960	David Jenkins	1981	Scott Hamilton
1918	Nathaniel Niles	1939	Robin Lee	1961	Bradley Lord	1982	Scott Hamilton
1919	Not held	1940	Eugene Turner	1962	Monty Hoyt	1983	Scott Hamilton
1920	Sherwin Badger	1941	Eugene Turner	1963	Thomas Litz	1984	**Scott Hamilton**
1921	Sherwin Badger	1942	Robert Specht	1964	Scott Allen	1985	Brian Boitano
1922	Sherwin Badger	1943	Arthur Vaughn	1965	Gary Visconti	1986	Brian Boitano
1923	Sherwin Badger	1944-45	Not held	1966	Scott Allen	1987	Brian Boitano
1924	Sherwin Badger	1946	Dick Button	1967	Gary Visconti	1988	**Brian Boitano**
1925	Nathaniel Niles	1947	Dick Button	1968	Tim Wood	1989	Christopher Bowman
1926	Chris Christenson	1948	**Dick Button**	1969	Tim Wood	1990	Todd Eldredge
1927	Nathaniel Niles	1949	Dick Button	1970	Tim Wood	1991	Todd Eldredge
1928	Roger Turner	1950	Dick Button	1971	John (Misha) Petkevich	1992	Christopher Bowman
1929	Roger Turner	1951	Dick Button	1972	Ken Shelley	1993	Scott Davis
1930	Roger Turner	1952	**Dick Button**	1973	Gordon McKellen	1994	Scott Davis
1931	Roger Turner	1953	Hayes Jenkins	1974	Gordon McKellen	1995	Todd Eldredge
1932	Roger Turner	1954	Hayes Jenkins	1975	Gordon McKellen	1996	Rudy Galindo
1933	Roger Turner	1955	Hayes Jenkins	1976	Terry Kubicka	1997	Todd Eldredge
1934	Roger Turner	1956	**Hayes Jenkins**	1977	Charles Tickner	1998	Todd Eldredge
1935	Robin Lee	1957	David Jenkins	1978	Charles Tickner	1999	Michael Weiss
1936	Robin Lee	1958	David Jenkins	1979	Charles Tickner		

WOMEN

Multiple winners: Maribel Vinson (9); Theresa Weld Blanchard and Gretchen Merrill (6); Tenley Albright, Peggy Fleming, and Janet Lynn (5); Linda Fratianne and Carol Heiss (4); Dorothy Hamill, Michelle Kwan, Beatrix Loughran, Rosalyn Summers, Joan Tozzer and Jill Trenary (3); Yvonne Sherman and Debi Thomas (2).

Year		Year		Year		Year	
1914	Theresa Weld	1937	Maribel Vinson	1958	Carol Heiss	1979	Linda Fratianne
1915-17	Not held	1938	Joan Tozzer	1959	Carol Heiss	1980	Linda Fratianne
1918	Rosemary Beresford	1939	Joan Tozzer	1960	**Carol Heiss**	1981	Elaine Zayak
1919	Not held	1940	Joan Tozzer	1961	Laurence Owen	1982	Rosalyn Sumners
1920	Theresa Weld	1941	Jane Vaughn	1962	Barbara Pursley	1983	Rosalyn Sumners
1921	Theresa Blanchard	1942	Jane Sullivan	1963	Lorraine Hanlon	1984	Rosalyn Sumners
1922	Theresa Blanchard	1943	Gretchen Merrill	1964	Peggy Fleming	1985	Tiffany Chin
1923	Theresa Blanchard	1944	Gretchen Merrill	1965	Peggy Fleming	1986	Debi Thomas
1924	Theresa Blanchard	1945	Gretchen Merrill	1966	Peggy Fleming	1987	Jill Trenary
1925	Beatrix Loughran	1946	Gretchen Merrill	1967	Peggy Fleming	1988	Debi Thomas
1926	Beatrix Loughran	1947	Gretchen Merrill	1968	**Peggy Fleming**	1989	Jill Trenary
1927	Beatrix Loughran	1948	Gretchen Merrill	1969	Janet Lynn	1990	Jill Trenary
1928	Maribel Vinson	1949	Yvonne Sherman	1970	Janet Lynn	1991	Tonya Harding
1929	Maribel Vinson	1950	Yvonne Sherman	1971	Janet Lynn	1992	**Kristi Yamaguchi**
1930	Maribel Vinson	1951	Sonya Klopfer	1972	Janet Lynn	1993	Nancy Kerrigan
1931	Maribel Vinson	1952	Tenley Albright	1973	Janet Lynn	1994	vacated*
1932	Maribel Vinson	1953	Tenley Albright	1974	Dorothy Hamill	1995	Nicole Bobek
1933	Maribel Vinson	1954	Tenley Albright	1975	Dorothy Hamill	1996	Michelle Kwan
1934	Suzanne Davis	1955	Tenley Albright	1976	**Dorothy Hamill**	1997	Tara Lipinski
1935	Maribel Vinson	1956	Tenley Albright	1977	Linda Fratianne	1998	Michelle Kwan
1936	Maribel Vinson	1957	Carol Heiss	1978	Linda Fratianne	1999	Michelle Kwan

* Tonya Harding was stripped of the 1994 women's title and banned from membership in the U.S. Figure Skating Assn. for life on June 30, 1994 for violating the USFSA Code of Ethics after she pleaded guilty to a charge of conspiracy to hinder the prosecution related to the Jan. 6, 1994 attack on Nancy Kerrigan.

Soccer

U.S. co-captain **Julie Foudy** presents **President Clinton** with a jersey at a ceremony for the Women's World Cup winners at the White House.

Bra-vo!

Brandi Chastain and her U.S. Women's National teammates brought women's soccer to new heights with their thrilling shootout victory in the Women's World Cup.

by
Jack Edwards

The Women's World Cup was about strength, built and embodied. After being virtually ignored by NBC while winning a gold medal in Atlanta, this team had grown together, tactically and emotionally, to enrich a weak American soccer heritage. It even spent time in the weight room. At last, it had the world on its turf and the nation on its feet.

In the three weeks of the Cup, the U.S. drew an average of 68,748 fans per game. The crowd of 90,185 at the Rose Bowl finale, July 10, was the biggest ever to see a women's sports event, anywhere.

The U.S. dominated Denmark, winning the opener, 3-0. A giveaway goal against Nigeria two minutes into game two signaled the first of several defensive lapses. Of course, the best

Jack Edwards calls the play-by-play for MLS games among his ESPN assignments. He played Division I college soccer.

defense is a good offense — and the U.S. had firepower: three goals in four minutes in the 7-1 comeback over Nigeria, a 3-0 exercise against North Korea, a 13-1 cumulative scoring margin in round robin play. Now for the single-elimination games.

Five minutes into the quarterfinal match against Germany, Brandi Chastain mistakenly passed the ball toward the U.S. goal instead of wide of it, where keeper Briana Scurry was calling for the ball. Chastain put it in her own net. In the second half, she would bang one into the right goal, pulling the U.S. into a 2-2 tie. Then Shannon MacMillan, who had just subbed in, smoked a low line drive corner kick to Joy Fawcett, who hammered the header home to make it 3-2. On to the semi's.

Strength can be measured in what one gives up for others as well as what one appears to achieve alone. Against Brazil, the U.S. scored early

AP/Wide World Photos

Brandi Chastain strips to her sports bra after scoring the overtime penalty shot that won the Women's World Cup Final match against China in a 5-4 shootout.

and late. Cindy Parlow, five minutes in . . . and Michelle Akers 10 minutes from the end of the 2-0 decision. Mia Hamm was responsible for Akers' penalty kick goal, getting tripped inside the 18-yard box . . . but she didn't get a shot on goal, and hadn't scored in three straight matches. Few of her media critics understand the tactics of soccer. Hamm's job was to create chances. As the premiere target in the World Cup, she sometimes accomplished that by taking her defenders on a hike, thus creating space for teammates to attack. Hamm's fellow front-runner, Tiffeny Milbrett, took just five shots on goal during World Cup '99. She scored on three of them.

The U.S. played as one against China in the final. Teammates filled in behind one another to ensure against a short lapse, which the Chinese could make fatal. Joy Fawcett, 31 years old and a mother of two, unyielding in the middle of the defense; Chastain, with a daring slide tackle to steal the ball cleanly at the top of the box; Kristine Lilly, heading the ball off the line in overtime on the biggest play of the Cup; Akers, hurling her body around until she collapsed.

After 90 minutes of regulation, 30 more of overtime, and still no goals, it came down to the penalty kick shootout. Five players per side. Scurry guessed right, dove off the line and saved one. Chastain buried the clincher, stripped to her bra, and together they walked into legend.

Not that they'll inspire imitation. A week later, a Major League Soccer publicist was asked why the men on his team didn't pull off shirts in goal celebrations. He said, "Probably because they aren't as ripped." ∎

Jack Edwards' Ten Biggest Stories of the Year in Soccer

10. **Major League Soccer** considers having the game clocks count up instead of down for the 2000 season, reverting to the international standard of timekeeping in which only the referee on the field knows exactly how much time is left in the game (see item #2).

9. **MLS fires Commissioner Doug Logan** in mid-season and hires Don Garber as his replacement. Logan had served as the MLS top executive since the league's inception. Garber, formerly the Senior Vice President of the National Football League's International division, is a marketing whiz but a soccer neophyte.

8. **The U.S. Men's National Team** reaches the semifinal of the Confederations Cup in Mexico City but loses, 1-0, in sudden death overtime to eventual champion and archrival Mexico.

7. **Bruce Arena succeeds** Steve Sampson as the U.S. National Team head coach and announces that the team's nucleus will be comprised of the best Americans from the MLS. Arena, who won two MLS Cups as head coach of the D.C. United before taking his new assignment, compiles a 7-3-3 record in his first 10 months in charge.

AP/Wide World Photos

China goalkeeper **Gao Hong** dives but misses the final and winning overtime penalty shootout goal in the Women's World Cup Final at the Rose Bowl on July 10. U.S. goalkeeper Briana Scurry made a save on China's Liu Ying earlier to give the U.S. a one-goal advantage. The U.S. beat China 5-4 on penalty kicks after a 0-0 tie in regulation.

AP/Wide World Photos

English Premier League champ **Manchester United** celebrates its 2-1 miracle win over Bayern Munich of the German Bundesliga in the European Cup Final at Barcelona. Man U. was moments from a 1-0 defeat until scoring two goals in stoppage time for the thrilling come-from-behind win.

6. **The U.S. Men's National Team**, under new coach Bruce Arena, beats the highly-regarded German team twice in one year, shutting them out both times.

5. **The expansion Chicago Fire** win "U.S. Double": MLS Cup and the U.S. Open Cup.

4. **AC Milan**, under first-year head coach Alberto Zaccheroni, finishes their season with a rush to win Italy's Series A Championship following two lackluster seasons in which they finished in tenth and eleventh place.

3. **Manchester United wins** the rare "Triple": the English Premier League Championship, the FA Cup and the European Champions' Cup.

2. **Manchester United comes** from 0-1 down in stoppage time to shock Bayern Munich, 2-1, for European Champions' Cup. Bayern Munich grabs the early lead on a free kick and hits the woodwork twice in the final minutes before the Red Devils' Teddy Sheringham ties it up in the 91st minute, silencing the celebrating German fans. Late substitute Ole Gunnar Solskjaer then caps the miraculous comeback when he buries the game-winner seconds before the final whistle.

1. **U.S. Women's national team** wins the 1999 Women's World Cup in thrilling fashion on their home turf. ■

THE NUMBERS

INSIDE

CHUTES AND LADDERS

FIFA, the international governing body of soccer, publishes a monthly ranking of the world's men's national teams. Brazil has been ranked first every month since 1994. Although they haven't moved in the past year many other teams move around on the list. Here is a look at the biggest gainers and biggest losers, among teams ranked in the top 50, since the end of 1998.

Biggest Gainers	Sept. 99	Dec. 98	Change
Uruguay	41	76	**35**
Peru	45	72	**27**
Portugal	13	36	**23**
Turkey	34	57	**23**
Rep. of Ireland	34	56	**22**
Russia	19	40	**21**
Ukraine	26	47	**21**
Biggest Losers			
South Korea	40	17	**-23**
Iran	50	27	**-23**
Yugoslavia	17	6	**-11**
Egypt	38	28	**-10**
Jamaica	43	33	**-10**
Tunisia	30	21	**-9**

TRIPLE PLAY

In 1999, Manchester United became just the fourth club in history to win the European Cup, their domestic league and domestic cup titles in the same year. Below is a list of the teams that have pulled off the rare triple play.

	League	Year
Celtic Glasgow	Scottish	1967
Ajax Amsterdam	Dutch	1972
PSV Eindhoven	Dutch	1988
Manchester United	English Premier	1999

CROWDED HOUSES

The U.S. women played for packed stadiums during their championship run in the 1999 World Cup. In fact, all six of their games are included in the list of the 10 biggest crowds in women's soccer history.

Attendance	Teams	Site	Tourney	Date
90,185	USA-China	Rose Bowl	World Cup	July 10, 1999
78,972	USA-Denmark	Giants Stadium	World Cup	June 19, 1999
76,489	USA-China	Athens, Ga.	Olympics	Aug. 1, 1996
73,123	USA-Brazil	Palo Alto, Calif.	World Cup	July 4, 1999
65,080	USA-Nigeria	Soldier Field	World Cup	June 24, 1999
65,000	USA-China	Guangzhou, China	World Cup	Nov. 30, 1991
64,196	USA-Norway	Athens, Ga.	Olympics	July 28, 1996
54,642	USA-Germany	Landover, Md.	World Cup	July 1, 1999
50,484	USA-N. Korea	Foxboro, Mass.	World Cup	June 27, 1999
46,724	China-Sweden	Miami, Fla.	Olympics	July 21, 1996

Note: The largest crowd to watch a soccer game in U.S. history (men or women) is the audience of 101,799 for the France-Brazil match at the Rose Bowl during the 1984 Summer Olympics. The largest crowd ever to watch an American team play in the U.S. is 93,869 for the USA-Romania match in the 1994 World Cup at the Rose Bowl. The Women's World Cup final attendance of 90,185 ranks 13th overall. ∎

THE 2000
ESPN
INFORMATION PLEASE
SPORTS ALMANAC

S O C C E R
S T A T I S T I C S
THE SEASON IN REVIEW
1998-1999
WORLD • EUROPE • AMERICA

SEC A
PAGE 735

1999 Women's World Cup Tournament

The 3rd Women's World Cup hosted by the United States from June 19-July 10, 1999.

First Round

Round robin; each team played the other three teams in its group once. Note that three points were awarded for a win and one point for a tie. (*) indicates team advanced to second round.

Group A	Gm	W	L	T	Pts	GF	GA
*USA	3	3	0	0	9	13	1
*Nigeria	3	2	1	0	6	5	8
Korea DPR	3	1	2	0	3	4	6
Denmark	3	0	3	0	0	1	8

Results

6/19	New York (78,972)	USA 3, Denmark 0
6/20	Los Angeles (12,102)	Nigeria 2, Korea DPR 1
6/24	Chicago (65,080)	USA 7, Nigeria 1
6/24	Portland (20,169)	Korea DPR 3, Denmark 1
6/27	Boston (50,484)	USA 3, Korea DPR 0
6/27	Washington DC (22,109)	Nigeria 2, Denmark 0

Group B	Gm	W	L	T	Pts	GF	GA
*Brazil	3	2	0	1	7	12	4
*Germany	3	1	0	2	5	10	4
Italy	3	1	1	1	4	3	3
Mexico	3	0	3	0	0	1	15

Results

6/19	New York (78,972)	Brazil 7, Mexico 1
6/20	Los Angeles (15,102)	Germany 1, Italy 1
6/24	Chicago (65,080)	Brazil 2, Italy 0
6/24	Portland (20,169)	Germany 6, Mexico 0
6/27	Washington DC (22,109)	Germany 3, Brazil 3
6/27	Boston (50,484)	Italy 2, Mexico 0

Group C	Gm	W	L	T	Pts	GF	GA
*Norway	3	3	0	0	9	13	2
*Russia	3	2	1	0	6	10	3
Canada	3	0	2	1	1	3	12
Japan	3	0	2	1	1	1	10

Results

6/19	San Jose (23,298)	Japan 1, Canada 1
6/20	Boston (14,873)	Norway 2, Russia 1
6/23	Washington DC (16,448)	Norway 7, Canada 1
6/23	Portland (17,668)	Russia 5, Japan 0
6/26	Chicago (34,256)	Norway 4, Japan 0
6/26	New York (29,401)	Russia 4, Canada 1

Group D	Gm	W	L	T	Pts	GF	GA
*China	3	3	0	0	9	12	2
*Sweden	3	2	1	0	6	6	3
Australia	3	0	2	1	1	3	7
Ghana	3	0	2	1	1	1	10

Results

6/19	San Jose (23,298)	China 2, Sweden 1
6/20	Boston (14,873)	Australia 1, Ghana 1
6/23	Portland (17,668)	China 7, Ghana 0
6/23	Washington DC (16,448)	Sweden 3, Australia 1
6/26	New York (29,401)	China 3, Australia 1
6/26	Chicago (34,256)	Sweden 2, Ghana 0

Quarterfinals

Single elimination with two 15 minute sudden-death "golden goal" overtime periods. If still tied, games are decided by shootout.

6/30	San Jose (21,411)	Norway 3, Sweden 1
6/30	San Jose (21,411)	China 2, Russia 0
7/1	Washington DC (54,642)	USA 3, Germany 2
7/1	Washington DC (54,642)	Brazil 4, Nigeria 3*

*Brazil won in sudden-death "golden goal" overtime.

Semifinals

| 7/4 | Palo Alto (73,123) | USA 2, Brazil 0 |
| 7/4 | Boston (28,986) | China 5, Norway 0 |

Third Place

| 7/10 | Los Angeles (90,185) | Brazil 0, Norway 0* |

*Brazil won 5-4 on penalty kicks.

Final

| 7/10 | Los Angeles (90,185) | USA 0, China 0* |

*The United States won 5-4 on penalty kicks.

World Cup All-Star Team

Voting done by FIFA Technical Study Group and announced on July 7 before the July 10 championship game.

GK	Gao Hong, China
GK	Briana Scurry, United States
D	Wang Liping, China
D	Wen Lirong, China
D	Doris Fitschen, Germany
D	Carla Overbeck, United States
D	Brandi Chastain, United States
M	Sissi, Brazil
M	Zhao Lihong, China
M	Liu Ailing, China
M	Bettina Wiegmann, Germany
M	Michelle Akers, United States
F	Jin Yan, China
F	Sun Wen, China
F	Ann Kristin Aarones, Norway
F	Mia Hamm, United States

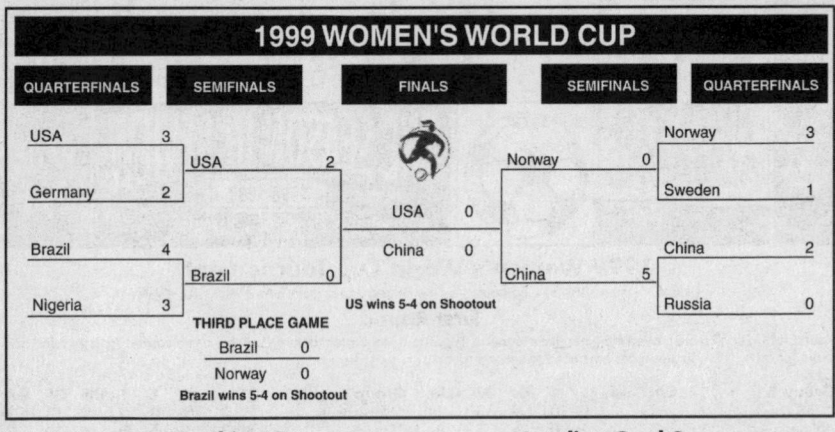

1999 WOMEN'S WORLD CUP

| QUARTERFINALS | SEMIFINALS | FINALS | SEMIFINALS | QUARTERFINALS |

| USA | 3 |
| Germany | 2 |

USA 2

Brazil 4
Nigeria 3

Brazil 0

USA 0
China 0

US wins 5-4 on Shootout

Norway 0
China 5

Norway 3
Sweden 1

China 2
Russia 0

THIRD PLACE GAME
Brazil 0
Norway 0
Brazil wins 5-4 on Shootout

USA 0, China 0

World Cup final played July 10, 1999 at the Rose Bowl in Los Angeles. **Attendance:** 90,185; **Referee:** Nicole Mouidi-Petignat (Switzerland); **Assistants:** Chislaine Peron-Labre (France), Ana Isabel Perez Assante (Peru); **Coaches:** Tony DiCicco (USA) and Yuanan Ma (China).

	1	2—	F
United States	0	0—	0
China	0	0—	0

Shootout

	Shooter	Result
1	Xie Huilin, China	Goal
	Carla Overbeck, USA	Goal
2	Qiu Haiyan, China	Goal
	Joy Fawcett, USA	Goal
3	Liu Ying, China	Saved
	Kristine Lilly, USA	Goal
4	Zhang Ouying, China	Goal
	Mia Hamm, USA	Goal
5	Sun Wen, China	Goal
	Brandi Chastain, USA	Goal

United States	China
1 Briana Scurry (GK)	18 Gao Hong (GK)
4 Carla Overbeck	2 Wang Liping
6 Brandi Chastain	3 Fan Yunje
9 Mia Hamm	6 Zhao Lihong
10 Michelle Akers	15 Qiu Haiyan (115th)
7 Sara Whalen (71st)	8 Jin Yan
11 Julie Foudy	5 Xie Huilin (119th)
12 Cindy Parlow	9 Sun Wen
8 Shannon MacMillan (57th)	10 Liu Ailing
13 Kristine Lilly	11 Pu Wei
14 Joy Fawcett	7 Zhang Ouying (59th)
16 Tiffeny Milbrett	12 Wen Lirong
15 Tisha Venturini (115th)	13 Liu Ying
20 Kate Sobrero	14 Bai Jie

Yellow Cards	Yellow Cards
10 Michelle Akers (74th)	7 Zhang Ouying (70th)
	10 Liu Ailing (80th)

USA	Match Stats	China
6	Corners	4
4	Offsides	1
11	Shots	12
5	SOG	3
5	Yellow Cards	2
0	Red Cards	0
13	Fouls	24

Leading Goal Scorers

		Goals
1	Sissi, Brazil	7
	Sun Wen, China	7
3	Ann Kristin Aarones, Norway	4
4	Inka Grings, Germany	3
	Jin Yan, China	3
	Liu Ailing, China	3
	Tiffeny Milbrett, USA	3
	Nkiru Okosieme, Nigeria	3
	Marianne Pettersen, Norway	3
	Pretinha, Brazil	3
	Hege Riise, Norway	3
	Bettina Wiegmann, Germany	3
13	Seventeen players tied	2

Assist Leaders

		Assists
1	Irina Grigorieva, Russia	4
2	Sissi, Brazil	3
	Sun Wen, China	3
	Olga Letuchova, Russia	3
	Julie Foudy, USA	3
	Unni Lehn, Norway	3
	Shannon MacMillan, USA	3
	Maren Meinhert, Germany	3
9	Twelve players tied	2

Leading Goalkeepers

		GA	GAA
1	Gao Hong, China	2	0.32
2	Briana Scurry, USA	3	0.47
3	Giorgia Brenzan, Italy	3	1.00
	Tracey Wheeler, Australia	1	1.00
5	Svetlana Petko, Russia	5	1.25
6	Bente Nordby, Norway	8	1.33
7	Maravilha, Brazil	9	1.46
8	Ulrika Karlsson, Sweden	6	1.50
9	Silke Rottenberg, Germay	7	1.75
10	Yong Sun Kye, N. Korea	6	2.00

FIFA Top 50 World Rankings

FIFA announced a new monthly world ranking system on Aug. 13, 1993 designed to "provide a constant international comparison of national team performances." The rankings are based on a mathematical formula that weighs strength of schedule, importance of matches and goals scored for and against. Games considered include World Cup qualifying and final rounds, Continental championship qualifying and final rounds, and friendly matches.

The formula was altered slightly in January 1999. Now the rankings annually take into account a team's seven best matches of the last eight years. Thereby favoring some teams that have been consistent over a long period of time but that may have stumbled just recently. At the end of the year, FIFA designates a Team of the Year. Teams of the Year so far have been Germany (1993) and Brazil (1994-98).

1998

		Points	1997 Rank				Points	1997 Rank				Points	1997 Rank
1	Brazil	73.44	1	18	Sweden		56.27	18	35	Belgium		51.31	41
2	France	68.86	6	19	Denmark		55.10	8	36	Portugal		50.56	30
3	Germany	66.87	2	20	Japan		55.01	14	37	China		49.77	55
4	Croatia	66.75	19	21	Tunisia		54.88	23	38	Scotland		49.58	37
5	Argentina	66.22	17	22	Austria		54.76	25	39	Australia		49.51	35
6	Yugoslavia	64.70	20	23	USA		54.74	26	40	Russia		49.12	12
7	Italy	63.82	9	24	Kuwait		54.69	44	41	Cameroon		48.73	53
8	Czech Republic	63.80	3	25	Paraguay		54.57	29	42	United Arab			
9	England	63.13	4	26	South Africa		53.64	31		Emirates		48.59	50
10	Mexico	61.93	5	27	Iran		53.61	46	43	Israel		48.08	61
11	Netherlands	61.67	22	28	Egypt		53.56	32	44	Ivory Coast		48.07	52
12	Romania	60.01	7	29	Zambia		53.31	21	45	Thailand		47.90	54
13	Morocco	59.58	15	30	Saudi Arabia		53.25	33	46	Hungary		47.47	77
14	Norway	58.99	13	31	Poland		52.34	48	47	Ukraine		46.39	49
15	Spain	58.63	11	32	Slovakia		52.04	34	48	Ghana		46.27	57
16	Chile	57.81	16	33	Jamaica		51.94	39	49	Bulgaria		45.33	36
17	South Korea	57.17	27	34	Colombia		51.64	10	50	Angola		44.61	58

1999 (as of Sept. 15)

		Points	1998 Rank				Points	1998 Rank				Points	1998 Rank
1	Brazil	838	1	18	Paraguay		647	25	35	Turkey		577	57
2	Czech Republic	772	8	19	Russia		642	40	36	Bulgaria		570	49
3	France	766	2	20	USA		621	23	37	Greece		568	53
4	Spain	757	15	21	Morocco		620	13	38	Egypt		565	28
5	Germany	735	3		Slovakia		620	32		Saudi Arabia		565	30
6	Croatia	727	4	23	Colombia		619	34	40	South Korea		559	17
7	Argentina	717	5	24	Chile		618	16	41	Uruguay		557	76
8	Italy	714	7		Israel		618	43	42	Trinidad and Tobago	554	51
9	Norway	712	14	26	Austria		615	22	43	Hungary		547	46
10	Mexico	709	10		Ukraine		615	47		Jamaica		547	33
	Romania	709	12	28	Scotland		606	38	45	Peru		546	72
12	England	683	9	29	Poland		595	31	46	Lithuania		543	54
13	Portugal	671	36	30	Tunisia		593	21		Ghana		543	48
14	Netherlands	668	11	31	South Africa		591	26	48	Ivory Coast		541	44
15	Sweden	667	18	32	Belgium		589	35	49	Iceland		536	64
16	Denmark	661	19	33	Zambia		582	29	50	Iran		534	27
17	Yugoslavia	656	6	34	Rep. of Ireland		576	56					

FIFA Confederations Cup

Contested by the continental champions of Africa, Asia, Europe, North America, Oceania and South America. Note that Germany replaced France as the European representative due to scheduling conflicts with the French national team after the tournament was rescheduled twice. Played in Mexico July 24-Aug. 4, 1999.

First Round

Round Robin; each team plays the other teams in its group once. Note that three points are awarded for a win and one for a tie. (*) indicates team advanced to semifinals.

Group A	W	L	T	GA	GA	Pts
*Mexico	2	0	1	8	3	7
*Saudi Arabia	1	1	1	6	6	4
Bolivia	0	1	2	2	2	2
Egypt	0	1	2	5	9	2

Group B	W	L	T	GF	GA	Pts
*Brazil	3	0	0	7	0	9
*USA	2	1	0	4	2	6
Germany	'1	2	0	2	6	3
New Zealand	0	3	0	1	6	0

Semifinals

8/1 Mexico City (65,000) .... Mexico 1, USA 0*
8/1 Guadalajara (48,000) .Brazil 8, Saudi Arabia 2
*Mexico won in sudden death "golden goal" overtime.

Third Place

8/3 Guadalajara (35,000)....USA 2, Saudi Arabia 0

Final

8/4 Mexico City (115,000) .... Mexico 4, Brazil 3

World Youth Championship

Championship for the Under-20 national teams contested for the 10th time since its inception in 1977. Held Apr. 3-24, 1999 in Nigeria.

First Round

Round Robin; each team plays the other teams in its group once. Note that three points are awarded for a win and one for a tie. (*) indicates team advanced to quarterfinals.

Group A	W	L	T	GF	GA	Pts
*Paraguay	2	1	0	5	6	6
*Nigeria	1	1	1	4	3	4
Costa Rica	1	1	1	4	5	4
Germany	1	2	0	5	4	3

RESULTS: **Apr. 3**—Nigeria 1, Costa Rica 1; **Apr. 4**—Germany 4, Paraguay 0; **Apr. 7**—Nigeria 2, Germany 0; Paraguay 3, Costa Rica 1; **Apr. 10**—Paraguay 2, Nigeria 1; Costa Rica 2, Germany 1.

Group B	W	L	T	GF	GA	Pts
*Ghana	2	0	1	5	1	7
*Croatia	1	0	2	6	2	5
Argentina	1	1	1	1	1	4
Kazakhstan	0	3	0	1	9	0

RESULTS: **Apr. 4**— Ghana 1, Croatia 1; Argentina 1, Kazakhstan 0; **Apr. 7**—Ghana 1, Argentina 0; Croatia 5, Kazakhstan 1; **Apr. 10**— Ghana 3, Kazakhstan 0; Croatia 0, Argentina 0.

Group C	W	L	T	GF	GA	Pts
*Mexico	2	0	1	5	2	7
*Ireland	2	1	0	6	1	6
Australia	1	2	0	4	8	3
Saudi Arabia	0	2	1	2	6	1

RESULTS: **Apr. 4**—Australia 3, Saudi Arabia 1; Mexico 1, Ireland 0; **Apr. 7**—Mexico 3, Australia 1; Ireland 2, Saudi Arabia 0; **Apr. 10**—Ireland 4, Australia 0; Mexico 1, Saudi Arabia 1.

Group D	W	L	T	GF	GA	Pts
*Mali	2	1	0	6	6	6
*Portugal	1	1	1	4	3	4
Uruguay	1	1	1	2	2	4
Korea Republic	1	2	0	5	6	3

RESULTS: **Apr. 5**—Mali 2, Uruguay 1; Portugal 3, Korea 1; **Apr. 8**— Uruguay 1, Korea 0; Mali 2, Portugal 1; **Apr. 11**—Uruguay 0, Portugal 0; Korea 4, Mali 2.

Group E	W	L	T	GF	GA	Pts
*Japan	2	1	0	6	3	6
*USA	2	1	0	5	4	6
Cameroon	2	1	0	4	4	6
England	0	3	0	0	4	0

RESULTS: **Apr. 5**—Cameroon 2, Japan 1; USA 1, England 0; **Apr. 8**— Cameroon 1, England 0; Japan 3, USA 1; **Apr. 11**—USA 3, Cameroon 1; Japan 2, England 0.

Group F	W	L	T	GF	GA	Pts
*Spain	2	0	1	5	1	7
*Brazil	2	1	0	8	3	6
Zambia	1	1	1	4	8	4
Honduras	0	3	0	4	10	0

RESULTS: **Apr. 5**— Zambia 4, Honduras 3; Spain 2, Brazil 0; **Apr. 8**— Zambia 0, Spain 0; Brazil 3, Honduras 0; **Apr. 11**— Brazil 5, Zambia 1; Spain 3, Honduras 1.

Round of 16

4/14	Kano (20,000)	Nigeria 1, Ireland 1*
4/14	Kaduna (1,000)	Ghana 2, Costa Rica 0
4/14	Lagos (1,500)	Paraguay 2, Uruguay 2*
4/14	Calabar (12,000)	Brazil 4, Croatia 0
4/15	Bauchi (8,000)	Japan 1, Portugal 1*
4/15	Port Harcourt (15,600)	Spain 3, USA 2
4/15	Ibadan (16,000)	Mexico 4, Argentina 1
4/15	Enugu (NA)	Mali 5, Cameroon 4†

*Games decided on penalty kicks. Nigeria beat Ireland 5-3, Uruguay beat Paraguay 10-9 and Japan beat Portugal 5-4.

Quarterfinals

4/18	Lagos (10,000)	Uruguay 2, Brazil 1
4/18	Enugu (22,000)	Mali 3, Nigeria 1
4/18	Ibadan (15,000)	Japan 2, Mexico 0
4/18	Kaduna (19,000)	Spain 1, Ghana 1*

*Game decided on penalty kicks. Spain beat Ghana 8-7.

Semifinals

4/21	Kaduna (16,000)	Spain 3, Mali 1
4/21	Lagos (8,000)	Japan 2, Uruguay 1

Third Place

4/24	Lagos (38,000)	Mali 1, Uruguay 0

Final

4/24	Lagos (38,000)	Spain 4, Japan 0

Pan Am Games

US Men's and Women's results during the Pan Am Games held in Winnipeg, Manitoba July 23-Aug. 7, 1999. A team comprised of players from the Men's Under-17, Under-20 and Under-23 teams and the Women's Under-18 team represented the United States. Other nations fielded their full Olympic teams.

Men

Record: 3-2-1. US Men won the bronze medal.

Date	Result	Scorers
July 23	Cuba	W, 1-0	Vagenas
July 25	Honduras	L, 1-2	Vagenas
July 29	Jamaica	W, 2-1	Victorine, Twellman
July 31	Uruguay	T, 0-0	—
Aug. 4	Mexico	L, 0-4	—
Aug. 6	Canada*	W, 2-1	Bocanegra, Donovan

*Bronze medal game.

Women

Record: 5-0-1. US Women won the gold medal.

Date	Result	Scorers
		Wallis, Sellers, Patrick,
July 23	Costa Rica	W, 6-0	Molinaro (2), Reddick
July 25	Mexico	T, 1-1	Wallis
July 29	Trinidad		Kraus, Wallis (3), Lewis,
	& Tobago	W, 9-1	Patrick (3), Molinaro
July 31	Canada	W, 3-0	Lindsey, Reddick, Patrick
Aug. 4	Costa Rica	W, 2-0	Wallis, Patrick
Aug. 6	Mexico*	W, 1-0	Reddick

*Gold medal game.

U.S. Men's National Team
1999 Schedule and Results
Through Sept. 8, 1999.

Date		Result	USA Goals	Site	Crowd
Jan. 24	Bolivia	T, 0-0	—	Santa Cruz, Bolivia	39,000
Feb. 6	Germany	W, 3-0	Kirovski, Sanneh, Reyna	Jacksonville, Fla.	17,259
Feb. 21	Chile	W, 2-1	Olsen, Lewis	Ft. Lauderdale, Fla.	14,898
Mar. 11	Guatemala	W, 3-1	Moore, McBride, Hejduk	Los Angeles, Calif.	34,154
Mar. 13	Mexico	L, 1-2	Hejduk	San Diego, Calif.	50,324
June 13	Argentina	W, 1-0	Moore	Washington, D.C.	40,119
July 13	Derby County (Eng.)*	W, 2-1	Lewis, Olsen	Denver, Colo.	20,376
July 24	New Zealand	W, 2-1	McBride, Kirovski	Guadalajara, Mex.	60,000
July 28	Brazil	L, 0-1	—	Guadalajara, Mex.	54,000
July 30	Germany	W, 2-0	Olsen, Moore	Guadalajara, Mex.	53,000
Aug. 1	Mexico	L, 0-1 (OT)	—	Mexico City, Mex.	80,000
Aug. 3	Saudi Arabia	W, 2-0	Bravo, McBride	Guadalajara, Mex.	35,000
Sept. 8	Jamaica	T, 2-2	Kreis, Albright	Kingston, Jamaica	20,000

*Exhibition match. Caps are not given and stats do not count.
Overall record: 7-3-2. **Team scoring:** Goals for– 18; Goals against– 9.

1999 U.S. Men's National Team Statistics
Individual records for season through Sept. 8, 1999. Note that the column labeled "Career C/G" refers to career caps and goals.

Forwards	GP	GS	Mins	G	A	Pts	Career C/G
Chris Albright	1	1	13	1	0	2	1/1
Paul Bravo	2	2	136	1	1	3	4/1
Roy Lassiter	4	1	84	0	0	0	29/4
Brian McBride	11	10	856	3	2	8	35/9
Joe-Max Moore	7	3	316	3	0	6	78/20
Ante Razov	3	1	150	0	1	1	4/0
Ernie Stewart	5	4	374	0	1	1	56/6

Defenders	GP	GS	Mins	G	A	Pts	Career C/G
Jeff Agoos	9	9	616	0	1	1	96/3
Marcelo Balboa	2	2	180	0	0	0	127/13
Gregg Berhalter	4	3	282	0	0	0	8/0
C.J. Brown	7	6	566	0	0	0	8/0
Leo Cullen	2	0	94	0	0	0	2/0
Steve Cherundolo	1	1	90	0	0	0	1/0
Thomas Dooley	1	1	90	0	0	0	81/7
Robin Fraser	7	6	630	0	1	1	22/0
Carlos Llamosa	4	4	338	0	0	0	5/0
Chad McCarty	1	0	23	0	0	0	1/0
Matt McKeon	2	2	147	0	0	0	2/0
Eddie Pope	3	2	198	0	0	0	29/3
David Regis	1	1	90	0	0	0	6/0
Greg Vanney	1	1	90	0	0	0	5/0

Midfielders	GP	GS	Mins	G	A	Pts	Career C/G
Chris Armas	6	5	480	0	0	0	7/0
Imad Baba	1	0	15	0	0	0	1/0
Chad Deering	1	1	66	0	0	0	12/1

Midfielders	GP	GS	Mins	G	A	Pts	Career C/G
Henry Gutierrez	1	1	77	0	0	0	1/0
John Harkes	3	3	243	0	0	0	89/6
Frankie Hejduk	8	5	510	2	0	2	22/4
Cobi Jones	8	7	642	0	0	0	119/8
Jovan Kirovski	10	9	900	2	1	5	35/6
Jason Kreis	1	1	45	1	0	2	8/1
Eddie Lewis	12	10	860	1	4	6	14/1
Clint Mathis	2	0	35	0	0	0	3/0
Ben Olsen	7	5	438	2	1	5	8/2
Claudio Reyna	3	3	270	1	0	2	65/7
Tony Sanneh	2	2	180	1	0	2	5/1
Billy Walsh	1	0	1	0	0	0	1/0
Richie Williams	7	6	564	0	0	0	7/0
Josh Wolff	1	0	44	0	0	0	1/0

Goalkeepers	GP	GS	Mins	Record	SO	Career Caps
Brad Friedel	2	2	180	2-0-0	2	59
Kevin Hartman	1	0	45	0-0-1	0	1
Kasey Keller	4	4	366	2-2-0	1	38
Tony Meola	3	3	197	1-0-1	2	90
Tom Presthus	1	0	45	1-0-0	0	1
Zach Thornton	4	2	253	1-1-0	0	6

Yellow cards: Agoos, Armas, Fraser, Harkes, Hejduk, McKeon (2), Berhalter, Bravo, Brown, Lewis, Llamosa, McBride, Moore, Olsen, Sanneh and Williams. **Red cards:** McKeon, Moore and Razov.
Head coach: Bruce Arena; **Assistant coaches:** Bob Bradley and Ivo Wortmann; **Goal coach:** Milutin Soskic; **General manager:** Pam Perkins.

U.S. Women's National Team
1999 Schedule and Results
Through Sept. 26, 1999. World Cup matches are in **bold** type.

Date		Result	USA Goals	Site	Crowd
Jan. 27	Portugal	W, 7-0	Chastain, Lilly (3), Akers, Hamm, MacMillan	Orlando, Fla.	—
Jan. 30	Portugal	W, 6-0	Lilly (2), Akers, Fotopoulos, Hamm, MacMillan	Ft. Lauderdale, Fla.	5,152
Feb. 14	FIFA World Stars	L, 1-2	Foudy	San Jose, Calif.	15,387
Feb. 24	Finland	W, 3-1	Grubb, Baggett, B. Keller	Orlando, Fla.	
Feb. 27	Finland	W, 2-0	Fawcett, Hamm	Tampa, Fla.	2,641
Mar. 14	Sweden	T, 1-1	Milbrett	Silves, Portugal	400
Mar. 16	Finland	W, 4-0	Milbrett (2), Parlow, Chastain	Quarteira, Portugal	200

Date		Result	USA Goals	Site	Crowd
Mar. 18	Norway	W, 2-1	Foudy, Lilly	Albufeire, Portugal	300
Mar. 20	China	L, 1-2	Milbrett	Loule, Portugal	800
Mar. 28	Mexico	W, 3-0	Foudy, Lilly (2)	Los Angeles, Calif.	27,034
Apr. 22	China	W, 2-1	Akers, Venturini	Hershey, Pa.	16,257
Apr. 25	China	L, 1-2	Foudy	E. Rutherford, N.J.	23,765
Apr. 29	Japan	W, 9-0	Akers, Lilly, Parlow, Milbrett (4), Wagner, Venturini	Charlotte, N.C.	10,119
May 2	Japan	W, 7-0	MacMillan (2), Hamm, Fotopoulos (2), Whalen, Venturini	Atlanta, Ga.	14,652
May 13	Holland	W, 5-0	Milbrett, Parlow, Lilly, Hamm, MacMillan	Milwaukee, Wisc.	6,767
May 16	Holland	W, 3-0	Chastain (2), Hamm	Chicago, Ill.	25,201
May 22	Brazil	W, 3-0	Hamm, Lilly, Milbrett	Orlando, Fla.	10,452
June 3	Australia	W, 4-0	Fotopoulos, Parlow, Lilly, Milbrett	Portland, Ore.	
June 6	Canada	W, 4-2	Hamm, Milbrett, Lilly, Parlow	Portland, Ore.	23,325
June 19	**Denmark**	W, 3-0	Hamm, Foudy, Lilly	E. Rutherford, N.J.	79,972
June 24	**Nigeria**	W, 7-1	Own goal, Hamm, Milbrett (2), Lilly, Akers, Parlow	Chicago, Ill.	65,080
June 27	**North Korea**	W, 3-0	MacMillan, Venturini (2)	Foxboro, Mass.	50,484
July 1	**Germany**	W, 3-2	Milbrett, Chastain, Fawcett	Landover, Md.	54,642
July 4	**Brazil**	W, 2-0	Parlow, Akers	Palo Alto, Calif.	73,123
July 10	**China**	W, 0-0 (5-4 PK)	—	Pasadena, Calif.	90,125
Sept. 4	Ireland	W, 5-0	Milbrett (2), Parlow, Fawcett, Lilly	Foxboro, Mass.	30,564
Sept. 26	Brazil	W, 6-0	Milbrett (2), MacMillan (2), Parlow, Fotopoulos	Denver, Colo.	25,099

Overall record: 23-2-1.
Team Scoring: Goals for– 95; Goals against– 13.
Note: the matches on Jan. 27, Feb. 24 and June 3 were closed door matches.

1999 U.S. Women's National Team Statistics

Individual records through Sept. 26, 1999. Note that the column labeled "Career C/G" refers to career caps and goals.

Forwards	GP	GS	Mins	G	A	Pts	Career C/G
Heather Aldama	1	0	13	0	0	0	2/0
Susan Bush	1	1	90	0	0	0	3/0
Mandy Clemens	1	1	90	0	0	0	1/0
Meredith Florence	1	0	45	0	0	0	1/0
D. Fotopolous	15	1	427	5	3	13	24/9
Mia Hamm	23	23	1859	10	13	33	180/111
S. MacMillan	23	7	1033	8	12	28	86/22
Tiffeny Milbrett	24	23	1870	19	11	49	126/66
Cindy Parlow	22	20	1510	8	10	26	64/25

Defenders	GP	GS	Mins	G	A	Pts	Career C/G
Samantha Baggett	1	1	90	1	0	2	2/0
Brandi Chastain	24	21	1722	5	4	14	103/21
Lorrie Fair	17	3	736	0	1	1	52/1
Joy Fawcett	24	23	2010	3	3	9	150/20
Michelle French	1	1	90	0	1	1	3/0
Jen Grubb	1	1	68	1	0	2	12/2
Heather Mitts	1	0	27	0	0	0	1/0
Carla Overbeck	24	24	1884	0	1	1	152/7
Christie Pearce	15	5	636	0	2	1	52/2
Danielle Slaton	1	1	63	0	0	0	1/0
Kate Sobrero	21	20	1755	0	0	0	33/0
Sara Whalen	15	5	777	1	2	4	39/2

Midfielders	GP	GS	Mins	G	A	Pts	Career C/G
Michelle Akers	20	18	1336	6	1	13	146/104
Aleisha Cramer	1	0	24	0	0	0	1/0
Julie Foudy	25	23	1844	5	5	15	163/32
Beth Keller	1	0	22	1	0	2	1/0
Kristine Lilly	25	24	2127	16	7	39	188/77
Tiffany Roberts	9	4	439	0	0	0	76/6
Laurie Schwoy	1	1	45	0	0	0	4/0
Jen Streiffer	1	1	90	0	1	1	1/0
Tisha Venturini	15	3	503	5	3	13	126/43
Aly Wagner	5	2	274	1	0	2	6/1

Goalkeepers	GP	GS	Mins	Record	SO	Career Caps
Briana Scurry	19	19	1695	17-2-0	11	97
Saskia Webber	6	5	495	4-0-1	3	27
Tracy Ducar	2	2	135	2-0-0	2	23
Siri Mullinix	1	0	45	0-0-0	0	1

Yellow Cards: Akers (4), Chastain (2), Fawcett, Fotopoulos, Foudy, Overbeck (2), Parlow and Pearce. **Red Cards:** none.

Head coach: Tony DiCiccio; **Assistant coaches:** Lauren Gregg and April Heinrichs; **Co-Captains:** Julie Foudy and Carla Overbeck.

Club Team Competition
1998 Toyota Cup

Also known as the Intercontinental Cup; a year-end match for the World Club Championship between the European Cup and Copa Libertadores winners. Played Dec. 1, 1998, before 51,000 at Tokyo's National Stadium.

Final

Real Madrid (Spain) 2 . . . . .Vasco da Gama (Brazil) 1
Scoring: Real Madrid—own goal (25th), Raul Gonzales (81st); Vasco da Gama— Juninho (43rd).

SOUTH AMERICA

1999 Liberatadores Cup

Contested by the league champions of South America's football union. Two-leg Semifinals and two-leg Final; home teams listed first. Winner Palmeiras of Brazil plays European Cup champion Manchester United of England in the 1999 World Club Championship in Tokyo in December.

Final Four: Cerro Porteño (Paraguay), Deportivo Cali (Colombia), Palmeiras (Brazil) and River Plate (Argentina).

Semifinals

Cerro Porteño vs. Deportivo Cali

Deportivo Cali 4 . . . . .Cerro Porteño 0
Cerro Porteño 3 . . . . .Deportivo Cali 2
Deportivo Cali wins 6-3 on aggregate

River Plate vs. Palmeiras

River Plate 1 . . . . .Palmeiras 0
Palmeiras 3 . . . . .River Plate 0
Palmeiras wins 3-1 on aggregate

Final

Deportivo Cali 1 . . . . .Palmeiras 0
Palmeiras 2 . . . . .Deportivo Cali 1
Aggregate tied 2-2, Palmeiras wins 4-3 on penalty kicks

EUROPE

There are three European club competitions sanctioned by the Union of European Football Associations (UEFA). The **European Cup** (officially, the Champions' Cup) is a knockout contest between national league champions of UEFA member countries; the **Cup Winners' Cup** is between winners of domestic cup competitions (note that a double winner– league and cup titles– would play for the European Cup and be replaced in the Cup Winners' Cup by the team it defeated in the domestic cup final); and the **UEFA Cup** is between the so-called "best of the rest," usually the national league runners-up. Note that home teams are listed first.

1998-99 European Cup

Champions League: Six-game double round robin in four 4-team groups (Sept. 16-Dec. 9, 1998); top two teams in each group advance to quarterfinal round. Winner Manchester United of England plays Libertadores Cup champion Palmeiras of Brazil in the 1999 World Club Championship this December in Tokyo.

Round Robin Standings

Group A	W	L	T	GF	GA	Pts
*Olympiakos (GRE)	3	1	2	8	6	11
Croatia Zagreb (CRO)	2	2	2	5	7	8
Porto (POR)	2	3	1	11	9	7
Ajax Amsterdam (NED)	2	3	1	4	6	7

Group B	W	L	T	GF	GA	Pts
*Juventus (ITA)	1	0	5	7	5	8
Galatasaray (TUR)	2	2	2	8	8	8
Rosenborg (NOR)	2	2	2	7	8	8
Athletico Bilbao (SPA)	1	2	3	5	6	6

Group C	W	L	T	GF	GA	Pts
*Inter Milan (ITA)	4	1	1	9	5	13
*Real Madrid (SPA)	4	2	0	17	8	12
Spartak Moscow (RUS)	2	2	2	7	6	8
Sturm Graz (AUT)	0	5	1	2	16	1

Group D	W	L	T	GF	GA	Pts
*Bayern Munich (GER)	3	1	2	9	6	11
*Manchester Utd. (ENG)	2	0	4	20	11	10
Barcelona (SPA)	2	2	2	11	9	8
Broendby (DEN)	1	5	0	4	18	3

Group E	W	L	T	GF	GA	Pts
*Dynamo Kiev (UKR)	3	1	2	11	7	11
Lens (FRA)	2	2	2	5	6	8
Arsenal (ENG)	2	2	2	8	8	8
Panathinaikos (GRE)	2	4	0	6	9	6

Group F	W	L	T	GF	GA	Pts
*FC Kaiserslautern (GER)	4	1	1	12	6	13
Benfica (POR)	2	2	2	8	9	8
PSV (NED)	2	3	1	10	11	7
HJK (Finland)	1	3	2	8	12	5

EUROPE (Cont.)
Quarterfinals
Two legs, total goals; home team listed first.

FC Kaiserlautern vs. Bayern Munich

Mar. 3 –Bayern Munich 2 . . . . .FC Kaiserslautern 0
Mar. 17 –FC Kaiserlautern 0 . . . . .Bayern Munich 4
Bayern Munich wins 6-0 on aggregate

Juventus vs. Olympiakos

Mar. 3 –Juventus 2 . . . . .Olympiakos 1
Mar. 17 –Olympiakos 1 . . . . .Juventus 1
Juventus wins 3-2 on aggregate

Internazionale FC vs. Manchester United

Mar. 3 –Manchester United 2 . . . . . .Internazionale FC 0
Mar. 17 –Internazionale FC 1 . . . . . .Manchester United 1
Manchester United wins 3-1 on aggregate

Real Madrid vs. Dynamo Kiev

Mar. 3 –Real Madrid 1 . . . . .Dynamo Kiev 1
Mar. 17 –Dynamo Kiev 2 . . . . .Real Madrid 0
Dynamo Kiev wins 3-1 on aggregate

Semifinals
Two legs, total goals; home team listed first.

Juventus vs. Manchester United

Apr. 7 –Manchester United 1 . . . . .Juventus 1
Apr. 21 –Juventus 2 . . . . .Manchester United 3
Manchester United wins 4-3 on aggregate

Bayern Munich vs. Dynamo Kiev

Apr. 7 –Dynamo Kiev 3 . . . . .Bayern Munich 3
Apr. 21 –Bayern Munich 1 . . . . .Dynamo Kiev 0
Bayern Munich wins 4-3 on aggregate

Final
May 26 at Barcelona. Attendance: 90,000

Manchester United 2 . . . . .Bayern Munich 1
Scoring: Manchester United—Teddy Sheringham (91st) and Ole Gunnar Solskjaer (92nd); Bayern Munich—Mario Basler (5th).

1999 Cup Winners' Cup
Two-leg Semifinals one-game Final; home team listed first.
Final Four: Chelsea (England), Lokomotiv Moscow (Russia), Mallorca (Spain) and Lazio of Rome (Italy).

Semifinals

Chelsea vs. Mallorca

Apr. 8 –Chelsea 1 . . . . .RCD Mallorca 1
Apr. 22 –Mallorca 1 .Chelsea 0
Mallorca wins 2-1 on aggregate

Lazio vs. Lokomotiv Moscow

Apr. 8 –Lokomotiv Moscow 1 . . . . .Lazio 1
Apr. 22 –Lazio 0 . . . . .Lokomotiv Moscow 0
Aggregate 1-1, Lazio advances on away goals

Final
May 19 at Birmingham, England. Attendance: 33,021

Lazio 2 . . . . Mallorca 1
Scoring: Lazio—Christian Vieri (7th), Pavel Nedved (81st); Mallorca—Dani (11th).

1999 UEFA Cup
Two-leg Semifinals, one-game Final; home team listed first.
Final Four: Atletico de Madrid (Spain), Bologna (Italy), Marseille (France) and Parma (Italy).

Semifinals

Atletico de Madrid vs. Parma

Apr. 6 –Atletico Madrid 1 . . . . .Parma 3
Apr. 20 –Parma 2 . . . . .Atletico Madrid 1
Parma wins 5-2 on aggregate

Marseille vs. Bologna

Apr. 6 –Marseille 0 . . . . .Bologna 0
Apr. 20 –Bologna 1 . . . . .Marseille 1
Aggregate 1-1, Marseille advances on away goals

Final
May 12 at Moscow. Attendance: 61,000

Parma 3 . . . . .Marseille 0
Scoring: Parma—Hernan Crespo (26th), Paolo Vanoli (36th), Enrico Chiesa (55th).

Major League Soccer
1999 Final Regular Season Standings

Conference champions (*) and playoff qualifiers (†) are noted. SOW refers to shootout wins. Teams receive three points for a win and one point for a shootout win. SOW are included in W (win) column. The GF and GA columns refer to Goals For and Goals Against in regulation play. Number of seasons listed after each head coach refers to current tenure with club through the 1999 season.

Eastern Conference

Team	W	L	Pts	GF	GA	SOW
* D.C. United	23	9	57	65	43	6
† Columbus Crew	19	13	45	48	39	6
† Tampa Bay Mutiny	14	18	32	51	50	5
† Miami Fusion	13	19	29	42	59	5
N. E. Revolution	12	20	26	38	53	5
NY/NJ MetroStars	7	25	15	32	64	3

Head Coaches: DC— Thomas Rongen (1st season); **Clb—** Tom Fitzgerald (4th); **TB—** replaced John Kowalski (2nd, 3-12) with Tim Hankinson on June 9; **Mia—** Ivo Wortmann (2nd); **NE—** replaced Walter Zenga (1st, 10-20) with interim Steve Nicol on Sept. 30; **NY/NJ—** Bora Multinovic (2nd).

Western Conference

Team	W	L	Pts	GF	GA	SOW
* Los Angeles Galaxy	20	12	54	49	29	3
† Dallas Burn	19	13	51	54	35	3
† Chicago Fire	18	14	48	51	36	3
† Colorado Rapids	20	12	48	38	39	6
San Jose Clash	19	13	37	48	49	10
Kansas City Wizards	8	24	20	33	53	2

Head Coaches: LA— Sigi Schmid (1st season); **Dal—** David Dir (4th); **Chi—** Bob Bradley (2nd); **Colo—** Glenn Myernick (3rd); **SJ—** replaced Brian Quinn (3rd, 15-12) with interim Jorge Espinoza on Sept. 16 until Lothar Osiander was available; **KC—** Bob Gansler (1st).

Leading Scorers

Points

	Gm	G	A	Pts
Jason Kreis, Dal	32	18	15	51
Roy Lassiter, DC	30	18	11	47
Ronald Cerritos, SJ	31	15	9	39
Stern John, Clb	28	18	2	38
Joe-Max Moore, NE	29	15	8	38
Ante Razov, Chi	30	14	7	35
Jaime Moreno, DC	25	10	13	33
Raul Diaz Arce, TB	31	13	7	33
Musa Shannon, TB	27	12	5	29
Jeff Cunningham, Clb	28	12	5	29

Goals

	Gm	No
Stern John, Clb	28	18
Roy Lassiter, DC	30	18
Jason Kreis, Dal	32	18
Joe-Max Moore, NE	29	15
Ronald Cerritos, SJ	31	15
Ante Razov, Chi	30	14
Raul Diaz Arce, TB	31	13
Musa Shannon, TB	27	12
Jeff Cunningham, Clb	28	12

Five players tied with 10 goals each.

Assists

	Gm	No
Steve Ralston, TB	32	18
Marco Etcheverry, DC	22	17
Mauricio Cienfuegos, LA	30	17
Carlos Valderrama, TB	31	15
Jason Kreis, Dal	32	15
Eddie Lewis, SJ	29	14
Henry Gutierrez, Mia	30	14
Jaime Moreno, DC	25	13
Robert Warzycha, Clb	28	12

Three players tied with 11 each.

Shots

	Gm	No
Jason Kreis, Dal	32	114
Stern John, Clb	28	104
Preki, KC	30	97
Mauricio Ramos, TB	30	95
Ante Razov, Chi	30	90

Shots on Goal

	Gm	No
Jason Kreis, Dal	32	57
Ante Razov, Chi	30	49
Joe-Max Moore, NE	29	47
Roy Lassiter, DC	30	47
Stern John, Clb	28	45
Ronald Cerritos, SJ	31	45

Game-Winning Goals

	Gm	GWG
Ante Razov, Chi	30	7
Jorge Dely Valdes, Col	32	7
Jason Kreis, Dal	32	6
Jaime Moreno, DC	25	5
Joe-Max Moore, NE	29	5

Shootout Goals

	Gm	No
Ronald Cerritos, SJ	31	9
Joey DiGiamarino, Col	26	6
Jaime Moreno, DC	25	5
Jamie Clark, SJ	26	5
Stern John, Clb	28	5
Eddie Lewis, SJ	29	5
Welton, Mia	29	5
Steve Ralston, TB	32	5

MLS Attendance

Number in parentheses indicates last year's rank.

	Gm	Total	Avg
Columbus (8)	16	283,129	17,696
Los Angeles (1)	16	282,113	17,632
Wash. D.C. (5)	16	278,711	17,419
New England (2)	16	267,752	16,735
Chicago (3)	16	256,261	16,016
San Jose (7)	16	239,350	14,959
N.Y./N.J.(4)	16	235,301	14,706
Colorado (6)	16	224,459	14,029
Tampa Bay (10)	16	209,700	13,106
Dallas (9)	16	195,381	12,211
Miami (11)	16	139,021	8,689
Kansas City (12)	16	130,924	8,183
TOTAL	192	2,742,102	14,282

Fouls Committed

	Gm	No
Matt McKeon, Col	.28	80
Geoff Aunger, DC	.25	75
Ben Olsen, DC	.28	65
Wade Barrett, SJ	.31	60
Richie Williams, DC	.23	56
Jeff Baicher, NE	.30	56

Fouls Suffered

	Gm	No
Cobi Jones, LA	.28	80
Preki, KC	.30	77
Jaime Moreno, DC	.25	74
Roman Kosecki, Chi	.25	66
Joe-Max Moore, NE	.29	66
Jeff Baicher, NE	.30	66

Offsides

	Gm	Offs
Roy Lassiter, DC	.30	43
Stern John, Clb	.28	37
Raul Diaz Arce, TB	.31	37
Ronald Cerritos, SJ	.31	35
Cobi Jones, LA	.28	32
Ante Razov, Chi	.30	32

Corner Kicks

	Gm	CKs
Marco Etcheverry, DC	.22	122
Steve Ralston, TB	.32	121
Henry Gutierrez, Mia	.30	119
Greg Vanney, LA	.31	109
Robert Warzycha, Clb	.28	105

MLS All-Star Game

West, 6-4

Date: Saturday, July 17, 1999 at Qualcomm Stadium in San Diego; **Attendance:** 23,227; **Coaches:** Thomas Rongen, D.C. (East) and Glenn Myernick, Col. (East); **MVP:** Preki, Kansas City midfielder (West) — two goals, one assist.

	1	2	Final
East	1	3	— 4
West	4	2	— 6

Scoring

1st Half: EAST— Roy Lassiter (Brian McBride) 1; WEST— Preki (Roman Kosecki) 13; WEST— Kosecki (Peter Nowak, Alexi Lalas) 32; WEST— Cobi Jones (Preki, Lubos Kubik) 36; WEST— Preki (Kosecki).

2nd Half: EAST— Joe-Max Moore (penalty) 62; EAST— Carlos Valderrama (Jaime Moreno) 73; EAST— Stern John (unassisted) 83; WEST— Mauricio Wright (Ronald Cerritos) 84; WEST— Cerritos (Mauricio Cienfuegos) 89.

Goaltenders

Saves: EAST— Tom Presthus 2. Walter Zenga 1; WEST— Matt Jordan 4, Zach Thornton 3.

Minutes Played

	Mins
Peter Vermes, Col	2880
Steve Ralston, TB	2872
Kevin Hartman, LA	2870
Jason Kreis, Dal	2815
Wade Barrett, SJ	2790
Brandon Pollard, Dal	2790
Greg Vanney, LA	2790

Leading Goaltenders

Goals Against Avg.

	Gm	Min	Shts	Svs	GAA	W-L
Kevin Hartman, LA	.32	2870	150	118	0.91	20-12
M. Hahnemann, Col	.13	1170	85	68	1.08	10-3
Matt Jordon, Dal	.29	2584	172	133	1.08	17-11
Zach Thornton, Chi	.30	2633	137	99	1.09	17-12
Mark Dougherty, Clb	.31	2745	152	106	1.15	18-12
Ian Feuer, Col	.19	1696	99	70	1.22	10-9
Scott Garlick, TB	.28	2471	193	152	1.31	14-13
Joe Cannon, SJ	.24	2160	129	95	1.33	14-10
Tom Presthus, DC	.26	2227	129	88	1.37	16-8
Chris Snitko, KC	.16	1395	95	66	1.68	4-10

Saves

	Gm	No
Scott Garlick, TB	.28	152
Matt Jordan, Dal	.29	133
Kevin Hartman, LA	.32	118
Mark Dougherty, Clb	.31	106
Zach Thornton, Chi	.30	99

Shutouts

	Gm	No
Matt Jordan, Dal	.29	11
Kevin Hartman, LA	.32	11
Ian Feuer, Col	.19	8
Zach Thornton, Chi	.30	7
Mark Dougherty, Clb	.31	6

Save Percentage

	Svs	SOG	SV Pct
Marcus Hahnemann, Col	.68	85	.800
Scott Garlick, TB	.152	193	.788
Kevin Hartman, LA	.118	150	.787
Matt Jordan, Dal	.133	172	.773
Joe Cannon, SJ	.95	129	.736

1999 U.S. Open Cup

Dating back to 1914, the U.S. Open Cup is the oldest soccer competition in the United States and is among the oldest in the world. The U.S. Open Cup is a single-elimination tournament open to all amateur and professional teams in the United States. Thirty-two teams competed for the 86-year-old Dewar Cup trophy in the 1999 U.S. Open Cup.

Quarterfinals

Aug. 11, 1999 at the Cotton Bowl and the Rose Bowl
Rochester Raging Rhinos (A-League) def. Dallas Burn (MLS), 2-1 OT
Columbus Crew (MLS) def. Los Angeles Galaxy (MLS), 3-1
Aug. 13 at Raymond James Stadium
Colorado Rapids (MLS) def. Tampa Bay Mutiny (MLS), 1-0
Aug. 18 at Blackbaud Stadium
Charleston Battery (A-League) def. Staten Island Vipers (A-League), 1-0

Semifinals

Sept. 1, 1999 at Hampton Roads, Va.
Colorado Rapids def. Charleston Battery, 3-0
Rochester Raging Rhinos def. Columbus Crew, 3-2

Final

Sept. 14, 1999 at Columbus, Ohio
Rochester Raging Rhinos def. Colorado Rapids, 2-0

Team-by-Team Statistics

At least two games played. Players who played with more than one club during the season are listed with final team.

Eastern Conference

Columbus Crew

	Pos	Gm	Min	G	A	Pts
Stern John . . . . .F		28	2293	18	2	38
Jeff Cunningham . . . . .F		28	1556	12	5	29
Brian McBride. . . . . .F		25	2209	5	10	20
Robert Warzycha . . . . . .M		28	2077	3	12	18
Brian Maisonneuve . . . . .M		29	2495	2	8	12
Ansil Elcock . . . . .D		28	1908	3	3	9
Mike Lapper . . . . .D		31	2700	1	4	6
Brian West . . . . .F		22	1074	1	4	6
Jason Farrell . . . . .M		28	1725	1	3	5
Andy Williams . . . . .F		21	1227	0	3	3
Michael Clark . . . . .D		30	2558	0	3	3
Matt Kmosko . . . . .M/D		14	785	0	3	3
Todd Yeagley . . . . .M		29	2356	1	1	3
John DeBrito . . . . .F		8	656	1	1	3
Thomas Dooley . . . . . .M/D		25	1697	0	1	1
Rob Smith . . . . .M		8	331	0	1	1
Billy Thompson . . . . .M		16	791	0	1	1
Matt Chulis. . . . . .D		4	260	0	0	0
Ubusuku Abukusumo. . . . .D		3	102	0	0	0

Goalkeepers	Gm	Min	W-L	Shts	Svs	GAA
Mark Dougherty 31		2745	18-12	152	106	1.15
Matt Napoleon 2		135	1-1	9	5	2.67

D.C. United

	Pos	Gm	Min	G	A	Pts
Roy Lassiter . . . . .F		30	2626	18	11	47
Jaime Moreno . . . . .F		25	2114	10	13	33
Marco Etcheverry . . . . . . .M		22	1890	4	17	25
A.J. Wood . . . . .F		24	1385	8	6	22
Ben Olsen . . . . .M		28	2296	5	11	21
Carey Talley . . . . .D		29	1603	4	4	12
Geoff Aunger . . . . .D		25	2128	3	5	11
Richie Williams . . . . .M		23	1996	2	6	10
John Maessner . . . . .M		24	1605	3	3	9
DC		11	743	3	2	8
MIA		13	862	0	1	1
Diego Sonora . . . . .M/D		27	2201	1	5	7
Jeff Agoos. . . . . .D		30	2610	2	2	6
Carlos Llamosa . . . . .D		17	1423	1	1	3
Clint Peay . . . . .D		5	241	1	1	3
Antonio Otero . . . . .M		12	719	0	2	2
Eddie Pope. . . . . .D		19	1647	1	0	2
Jason Moore . . . . .M		16	999	0	2	2
Chris Albright . . . . .F		8	347	0	1	1
David Hayes		5	44	0	0	0
Judah Cooks . . . . .M		6	148	0	0	0
Mike Slivinski . . . . .M		4	57	0	0	0

Goalkeepers	Gm	Min	W-L	Shts	Svs	GAA
Mark Simpson 9		653	6-1	48	37	1.24
Tom Presthus. 26		2227	16-8	129	88	1.37

New York/New Jersey MetroStars

	Pos	Gm	Min	G	A	Pts
Eduardo Hurtado . . . . . . .F		28	2377	7	3	17
Mark Chung . . . . .M		26	1995	3	7	13
Petter Villegas . . . . .M		30	1409	3	6	12
Henry Zambrano . . . . .F		14	1186	3	3	9
Brian Kelly . . . . .M		28	1843	2	4	8
Billy Walsh . . . . .M		30	2675	4	0	8
Sasa Curcic. . . . . .F		9	492	2	2	6
Nansha Kalonji . . . . .D		19	930	1	2	4
Mark Semioli . . . . .D		24	2106	2	0	4
Miles Joseph . . . . .F		20	1186	0	3	3
Mike Petke . . . . .D		25	2022	1	1	3
Lawrence Lozzano . . . . . M		19	1164	1	1	3
NY/NJ.		6	189	0	0	0
LA		13	975	1	1	3
Tab Ramos . . . . .M		5	347	0	3	3
Mike Sorber . . . . .M		24	1976	0	2	2
Ramiro Corrales . . . . .D		31	2659	0	2	2
Mike Duhaney . . . . .D		19	1037	1	0	2
John Wolyniec . . . . .F		4	69	1	0	2
Mohammad Khakpour . . .D		14	1260	0	1	1
Kevin Knight. . . . . .D		11	732	0	0	0
Eric Kvello . . . . .M		2	44	0	0	0

Goalkeepers	Gm	Min	W-L	Shts	Svs	GAA
Tim Howard 9		742	1-7	55	37	1.58
Mike Ammann. 24		2138	6-17	155	91	2.15

New England Revolution

	Pos	Gm	Min	G	A	Pts
Joe-Max Moore . . . . .F		29	2610	15	8	38
Giovanni Savarese . . . . . .F		27	2062	10	2	22
Ivan McKinley . . . . .D		29	2430	4	4	12
Johnny Torres . . . . .F		27	1248	3	3	9
John Harkes. . . . . .M		22	1880	0	8	8
Ted Chronopoulos . . . . . . .D		31	2710	1	5	7
Mike Burns		28	2505	1	4	6
Jeff Baicher . . . . .M		30	2397	4	9	17
SJ		20	1602	3	9	15
NE		10	795	1	0	2
Kris Kelderman . . . . .D		18	995	0	2	2
Carlos Parra . . . . .M		21	1095	1	1	3
MIA		9	622	0	1	1
NE		12	473	1	0	2
Jamar Beasley . . . . .F		18	502	0	1	1
Brian Dunseth . . . . .D		29	2370	0	1	1
Mario Gori . . . . .D		29	2294	0	1	1
MIA		12	945	0	0	0
NE		17	1349	0	1	1
Leonel Alvarez . . . . .M		29	2452	0	7	7
DAL		21	1794	0	6	6
NE		8	658	0	1	1
Paul Keegan . . . . .F		10	365	0	1	1
Walter Zenga . . . . .GK		25	2125	0	1	1
Paulo Dos Santos . . . . . . .M		16	652	0	0	0
Dan Calichman . . . . .D		25	2009	0	0	0
Richard Goulooze . . . . . . .D		11	805	0	0	0
Imad Baba . . . . .M		2	108	0	0	0
Chaka Daley . . . . .D		2	67	0	0	0
Manny Motajo. . . . . .D		2	56	0	0	0

Goalkeepers	Gm	Min	W-L	Shts	Svs	GAA
Jeff Causey. 16		755	7-7	49	32	0.95
Walter Zenga 25		2071	5-13	140	87	1.96

Miami Fusion

at least 5 games	Pos	Gm	Min	G	A	Pts
Henry Gutierrez	M	30	2415	6	14	26
Diego Serna	F	21	1862	10	2	22
Welton	F	29	2374	8	7	23
LA		9	638	0	1	1
MIA		20	1736	8	6	22
Tyrone Marshall	F	28	2223	4	5	13
Jay Heaps	M/D	29	2511	3	1	7
Edwin Gorter	M	21	1607	4	1	9
NE		6	359	1	0	2
MIA		15	1248	3	1	7
Nelson Vargas	M	22	1171	0	6	6
Eric Wynalda	F	6	487	2	1	5
Saul Martinez	F	15	491	2	0	4
Roberto Gaucho	F	5	295	1	2	4
Pablo Mastroeni	M	23	2025	0	3	3
Maurizio Rocha	M	11	555	0	3	3
Jim Rooney	M	13	847	0	2	2
NY/NJ		1	62	0	0	0
MIA		12	785	0	2	2
Brian Kamler	M	28	2063	1	4	6
DC		16	1302	1	2	4
MIA		12	761	0	2	2
Tim Sahaydak	D	9	276	0	2	2
Jeff Bilyk	M	11	901	0	1	1
Mickey Trotman	F	7	491	1	2	4
DAL		4	230	1	1	3
MIA		3	261	0	1	1
Arley Palacios	D	17	1370	1	0	2
NY/NJ		7	622	1	0	2
MIA		10	748	0	0	0
Jeremy Aldrich	D	18	1365	0	0	0
Tony Kuhn	F	16	484	0	0	0
NE		6	214	0	0	0
MIA		10	270	0	0	0
Wade Webber	D	7	540	0	0	0
Leo Cullen	D	30	2619	0	0	0

Goalkeepers	Gm	Min	W-L	Shts	Svs	GAA
Jeff Cassar	15	1304	5-10	83	45	1.73
Garth Lagerwey	16	1306	7-7	107	77	1.86

Tampa Bay Mutiny

	Pos	Gm	Min	G	A	Pts
Raul Diaz Arce	F	31	2586	13	7	33
SJ		18	1416	4	2	10
TB		13	1170	9	5	23
Musa Shannon	M/F	27	1829	12	5	29
Steve Ralston	M	32	2872	5	18	28
Carlos Valderrama	M	31	2762	4	15	23
MIA		4	360	1	2	4
TB		27	2402	3	13	19
Mauricio Ramos	M	30	2254	3	9	15
Manuel Lagos	M	19	872	4	5	13
CHI		10	737	4	5	13
TB		9	135	0	0	0
Jefferson Gottardi	F	11	762	4	1	9
Ritchie Kotschau	M	15	1072	3	2	8
CHI		4	214	0	0	0
TB		11	858	3	2	8
Dominic Kinnear	M	28	2151	0	7	7
Chad McCarty	D	30	2640	2	1	5
Steve Trittschuh	D	12	970	2	1	5
Eric Quill	F	15	431	1	1	3
Pete Marino	M	15	289	1	0	2
Harut Karapetyan	F	2	32	1	1	1
Scott Garlick	GK	28	2471	0	1	1
Chris Houser	D	9	529	0	1	1
Josh Keller	M	21	1787	0	0	0
R.T. Moore	D	17	1117	0	0	0
Joseph Addo	D	8	675	0	0	0
Jan Eriksson	D	6	525	0	0	0
Alan Prampin	F	4	117	0	0	0
Daniel Hernandez	M	14	901	0	0	0
LA		12	853	0	0	0
TB		2	48	0	0	0

Goalkeepers	Gm	Min	W-L	Shts	Svs	GAA
Scott Garlick	28	2471	14-13	193	152	1.31
Andy Kirk	6	409	0-5	32	18	3.08

Western Conference

Chicago Fire

	Pos	Gm	Min	G	A	Pts
Ante Razov	F	30	2068	14	7	35
Josh Wolff	F	28	1775	10	2	22
Peter Nowak	M	28	2480	6	8	20
Lubos Kubik	D	27	2387	5	8	18
Jerzy Podbrozny	M/F	29	2357	4	8	16
Roman Kosecki	F	25	1825	3	10	16
Diego Gutierrez	M	28	2164	3	5	11
Chris Armas	M	22	1935	1	5	7
Dema Kovalenko	F	11	291	3	0	6
Jesse Marsch	M	29	2364	1	2	4
Tom Soehn	D	23	1359	1	1	3
C.J. Brown	D	26	2238	0	2	2
Paul Dougherty	F	19	1079	0	5	5
TB		10	610	0	3	3
CHI		9	469	0	2	2
Frank Klopas	M/F	13	476	0	1	1
Sam George	M	27	2156	0	1	1
TB		17	1391	0	0	0
CHI		10	765	0	1	1
Andrew Lewis	D	9	363	0	1	1
John Ball	M	9	480	0	0	0
Francis Okaroh	D	26	2269	0	0	0

Goalkeepers	Gm	Min	W-L	Shts	Svs	GAA
Zach Thornton	30	2633	17-12	137	99	1.09
Greg Sutton	3	247	1-2	19	14	1.46

Colorado Rapids

	Pos	Gm	Min	G	A	Pts
Jorge Dely Valdes	F	32	2415	10	6	26
Wolde Harris	F	29	2096	8	8	24
Paul Bravo	M	25	1966	7	5	19
Ross Paule	M	26	2231	3	9	15
Anders Limpar	M	18	1358	2	6	10
Joey DiGiamarino	M	26	1913	3	2	8
Marcelo Balboa	D	27	2430	1	2	4
Kevin Anderson	M	17	920	1	2	4
Marcus Hahnemann	GK	13	1170	0	3	3
Matt McKeon	D	28	2415	0	2	2
Darren Sawatzky	M/F	14	494	1	0	2
Jason Bent	M	18	1497	0	2	2
Peter Vermes	D	32	2880	0	2	2
David Vaudreuil	M/D	31	2774	0	1	1
Marquis White	F	22	441	0	1	1
Tim Martin	D	19	1295	0	1	1
Tahj Jakins	D	19	803	0	0	0
Chris Martinez	D	16	798	0	0	0
Guillermo Jara	M/F	2	6	0	0	0

Goalkeepers	Gm	Min	W-L	Shts	Svs	GAA
Marcus Hahnemann	13	1170	10-3	85	68	1.08
Ian Feuer	19	1696	10-9	99	70	1.22

Dallas Burn

	Pos	Gm	Min	G	A	Pts
Jason Kreis	M	32	2815	18	15	51
Chad Deering	M	25	1936	4	7	15
Oscar Pareja	M	27	1954	4	6	14
Dante Washington	F	21	989	4	4	12
Ted Eck	M/F	31	2290	4	3	11
Ariel Graziani	F	11	935	4	1	9
NE		3	243	0	0	0
DAL		8	692	4	1	9
Jorge Rodriguez	M/D	30	2538	3	3	9
John Jairo Trellez	F	17	792	3	2	8
Mark Santel	M/D	26	1779	1	6	8
Richard Farrer	M/D	30	2608	2	1	5
Bobby Rhine	F	16	488	2	1	5
Paul Broome	M	13	627	1	2	4
Brian Haynes	M	18	532	1	2	4
Temoc Suarez	M	17	944	1	1	3
Sergi Daniv	M	13	1015	0	2	2
Brandon Pollard	D	31	2790	0	2	2
Matt Jordan	GK	29	2584	0	1	1
Kirk Wilson	M	5	222	0	0	0
Eric Dade	D	24	1630	0	0	0

Goalkeepers	Gm	Min	W-L	Shts	Svs	GAA
Matt Jordan	29	2584	17-11	172	133	1.08
Mark Dodd	6	296	2-2	23	18	1.22

Kansas City Wizards

	Pos	Gm	Min	G	A	Pts
Preki	M	30	2572	7	11	25
Chris Klein	M	30	2198	6	5	17
Chris Henderson	M	30	2625	3	6	12
Alex Bunbury	F	19	1579	4	4	12
Chris Brown	F	28	1679	4	3	11
Mo Johnston	F	29	2537	3	4	10
Alexi Lalas	D	30	2700	4	1	9
Brian Johnson	M	26	1674		5	5
Scott Vermillion	D	24	1630	0	3	3
Vitalis Takawira	F	18	651	0	2	2
Francisco Gomez	M	7	339	1	0	2
Jake Dancy	D	14	964	0	1	1
Brandon Prideaux	D	15	937	0	1	1
Uche Okafor	D	26	2269	0	1	1
Sean Bowers	D	25	1827	0	0	0
Vicente Figueroa	M	22	1312	0	0	0
Nino Da Silva	M	8	331	0	0	0
Paul Wright	F	6	148	0	0	0
Refik Sabanadzovic	M	6	436	0	0	0
Scott Uderitz	D	2	143	0	0	0
Tony Soto	D	4	176	0	0	0

Goalkeepers	Gm	Min	W-L	Shts	Svs	GAA
Tony Meola	9	765	1-8	48	36	1.18
Chris Snitko	16	1395	4-10	95	66	1.68

Los Angeles Galaxy

	Pos	Gm	Min	G	A	Pts
Cobi Jones	M	28	2488	8	8	24
Mauricio Cienfuegos	M	30	2621	3	17	23
Clint Mathis	M	27	1890	7	6	20
Carlos Hermosillo	F	16	1280	8	3	19
Roy Myers	M/F	26	1970	4	7	15
NY/NJ		7	552	0	1	1
LA		19	1418	4	6	14
Ezra Hendrickson	D	26	1708	4	3	11
Greg Vanney	M	31	2790	1	7	9
Danny Pena	D	27	2276	2	5	9
Simon Elliott	M/F	23	1691	2	5	9
Zak Ibsen	D	23	822	3	1	7
Steve Jolley	M	25	1940	2	1	5
Seth George	F	9	201	2	0	4
Paul Caligiuri	D	27	2275	1	1	3
Joe Franchino	M	25	1316	0	3	3
Marvin Quijano	F	7	167	0	1	1
Robin Fraser	D	24	2096	0	1	1
Jorge Salcedo	M	19	1178	0	1	1
TB		16	1108	0	1	1
LA		3	70	0	0	0

Goalkeepers	Gm	Min	W-L	Shts	Svs	GAA
Kevin Hartman	32	2870	20-12	150	118	0.91
Matt Reis	1	10	0-0	1	1	0.00

San Jose Clash

	Pos	Gm	Min	G	A	Pts
Ronald Cerritos	F	31	2721	15	9	39
Eddie Lewis	M	29	2546	4	14	22
Dario Brose	M	27	1288	4	2	10
Wade Barrett	M	31	2790	1	8	10
Alejandro Sequeria	F	25	1789	5	3	13
TB		11	833	2	1	5
SJ		14	956	3	2	8
Mauricio Wright	D	27	2430	3	2	8
Braeden Cloutier	M	26	1576	1	4	6
John Doyle	D	27	2150	1	4	6
Richard Mulrooney	M	32	2338	1	3	5
Mauricio Solis	M	12	1002	2	0	4
Jamie Clark	M	26	1894	2	0	4
Scott Bower	M	17	649	0	3	3
Jim Conrad	D	17	1163	1	1	3
Jair	M	21	1323	2	2	6
NE		18	1263	1	1	3
SJ		3	60	1	1	3
Ryan Tinsley	M	13	706	1	0	2
CHI		3	67	0	0	0
SJ		10	639	1	0	2
Joey Martinez	D	15	995	0	1	1
Joe Cannon	GK	24	2160	0	1	1
Adam Frye	D	3	117	0	1	1
Tim Weaver	D	1	90	0	0	0
Carlos Farias	M	2	72	0	0	0
Leighton O'Brien	M	4	62	0	0	0

Goalkeepers	Gm	Min	W-L	Shts	Svs	GAA
Joe Cannon	24	2160	14-10	129	95	1.33
David Kramer	8	720	5-3	55	35	2.13

1999 A-League Final Standings (Outdoor)

The A-League serves as a type of minor league system for Major League Soccer. The division II outdoor league is part of the United Systems of Independent Soccer Leagues (USISL) and is recognized by U.S. Soccer. MLS and the USISL have an agreement where MLS teams can assign players to the A-League and call-up A-League players when desired. Also, the U.S. Pro-40 Select team is made-up of players from the MLS's Project 40 program. Project 40 is a joint venture between MLS and U.S. Soccer aimed at developing young American players, giving them the chance to train with MLS clubs and play games at various professional levels. The U.S. Pro-40 team played all their games on the road.

Eastern Conference

Northeast Division	W	L	Pts	GF	GA
* Rochester Raging Rhinos	22	6	92	47	20
† Staten Island Vipers	19	9	82	52	31
† Long Island Rough Riders	18	10	74	57	44
† Pittsburgh Riverhounds	16	12	72	63	43
† Lehigh Valley Steam	15	13	63	42	44
Boston Bulldogs	12	16	61	49	36
Toronto Lynx	12	16	51	31	37
Connecticut Wolves	7	21	34	32	68

Atlantic Division	W	L	Pts	GF	GA
* Hershey Wildcats	17	11	75	54	33
† Richmond Kickers	17	11	69	51	44
† Charleston Battery	15	13	68	50	34
Atlanta Silverbacks	15	13	62	43	39
Jacksonville Cyclones	16	15	59	51	61
Hampton Roads Mariners	15	13	57	45	41
Raleigh Capital Express	11	17	47	32	50
Maryland Mania	3	25	13	16	85

Western Conference

Central Division	W	L	Pts	GF	GA
* Minnesota Thunder	22	6	88	57	17
† U.S. Pro-40	17	11	66	44	46
† New Orleans Storm	14	14	66	56	61
Indiana Blast	13	15	55	43	51
Milwaukee Rampage	13	15	54	44	49
Tennessee Rhythm	11	17	49	44	52
Cincinnati Riverhawks	7	21	34	45	71

Pacific Division	W	L	Pts	GF	GA
* San Diego Flash	20	8	90	65	30
† Vancouver 86ers	19	9	84	77	31
† Seattle Sounders	19	9	81	56	36
† Orange County Zodiac	17	11	73	59	49
† El Paso Patriots	12	16	55	49	59
San Francisco Bay Seals	9	19	40	37	54
Sacramento Geckos	0	28	1	16	91

Note: Three points are awarded for a victory in regulation or overtime. One point is awarded for a shootout win. Shootouts occur if a game is tied after a 15-minute sudden-death overtime.

Playoffs
Round of 16 (Single elimination)

Sept. 10	Rochester 2, Lehigh Valley 1	at Rochester
Sept. 10	San Diego 3, El Paso 1	at San Diego
Sept. 10	U.S. Pro-40 3, Vancouver 1	at Vancouver
Sept. 11	Staten Island 3, Richmond 2 OT	at Staten Island
Sept. 11	Hershey 3, Charleston 2	at Hershey
Sept. 11	Pittsburgh 4, Long Island 3	at Long Island
Sept. 11	Minnesota 4, New Orleans 0	at Minnesota
Sept. 11	Seattle 6, Orange County 3	at Seattle

Quarterfinals (Best of 3)

Eastern Conference
Hershey vs. Staten Island

Sept. 16	Hershey 2, Staten Island 0	at Hershey
Sept. 18	Hershey 2, Staten Island 0	at Staten Island
	Hershey wins series, 2-0	

Rochester vs. Pittsburgh

Sept. 18	Rochester 6, Pittsburgh 2	at Rochester
Sept. 25	Pittsburgh 1, Rochester 0	at Pittsburgh
Sept. 28	Rochester 2, Pittsburgh 0	at Rochester
	Rochester wins series, 3-1	

Western Conference
Minnesota vs. US Pro-40

Sept. 18	Minnesota 1, US Pro-40 0 OT	at Minnesota
Sept. 20	Minnesota 2, US Pro-40 0	at Minnesota
	Minnesota wins series, 2-0	

San Diego vs. Seattle

Sept. 18	San Diego 6, Seattle 0	at San Diego
Sept. 25	San Diego 1, Seattle 0	at Seattle
	San Diego wins series, 2-0	

Semifinals (Best of 3)

Eastern Conference
Rochester vs. Hershey

Oct. 3	Hershey 2, Rochester 1	at Hershey
Oct. 9	Rochester 1, Hershey 0	at Rochester
Oct. 11	Rochester 3, Hershey 1	at Rochester
	Rochester wins series, 2-1	

Western Conference
Minnesota vs. San Diego

Oct. 2	Minnesota 4, San Diego 1	at Minnesota
Oct. 7	Minnesota 2, San Diego 1	at San Diego
	Minnesota wins series, 2-0	

Final
Oct. 16, 1999 at Blaine, Minn. Attendance: 9,987

	1	2—	F
Minnesota	1	1—	2
Rochester	0	1—	1

Colleges

MEN

1998 Final *Soccer America* Top 20

Final 1998 regular season poll including games through Nov. 15. Conducted by the national weekly *Soccer America* and released in the Nov. 30 issue. Listing includes records through conference playoffs as well as NCAA tournament record and team lost to. Teams in **bold** type went on to reach NCAA Final Four. All tournament games decided by penalty kicks are considered ties.

		Nov.16 Record	NCAA Recap
1	Clemson	20-1-0	(2-1) Indiana
2	**Indiana**	18-2-0	(5-0)
3	Duke	18-3-0	(0-1) Jacksonville
4	Washington	16-3-0	(0-1) UNC-Greensboro
5	UCLA	16-3-0	(1-1) Creighton
6	South Carolina	15-4-0	(1-1) Virginia
7	Virginia	14-3-3	(2-1) Stanford
8	St. John's	14-4-3	(2-1) Santa Clara
9	**Stanford**	14-4-2	(4-1) Indiana
10	Cal State Fullerton	14-4-2	(0-1) San Diego
11	Creighton	14-3-2	(2-1) Maryland
12	Connecticut	17-3-0	(0-1) Penn St.
13	Akron	17-2-1	(0-1) Butler
14	Brown	12-2-2	(0-1) St. John's
15	Saint Louis	14-4-1	(0-1) Creighton
16	SMU	15-4-1	(0-1) Santa Clara
17	UNC Greensboro	18-3-2	(0-1) Santa Clara
18	**Maryland**	13-7-0	(3-1) Stanford
19	Georgetown	15-6-0	did not play
20	Butler	18-4-1	(1-1) Indiana

Note: The fourth Final Four team was **Santa Clara** which finished the regular season 12-4-2 and unranked.

NCAA Division I Tournament
First Round (Nov. 20-22)

at Clemson 5 ....Lafayette 0
William & Mary 2........2 OT ....at South Florida 1
at Butler 1 ....2 OT ....Cincinnati 0
at Indiana 3 ....2 OT ....Akron 2
at St. John's 1 ....2 OT ....Brown 0
Penn St. 1 ....at Connecticut 0
at Santa Clara 1 ....SMU 0
UNC-Greensboro 2 ....at Washington 1
Jacksonville 3...................................at Duke 2
at Maryland 2 ....Richmond 1
Creighton 4 ....2 OT ....at St. Louis 1
at UCLA 2...................................Fresno St. 1
San Diego 2 ....at Cal St.-Fullerton 1
at Stanford 3 ....3 OT ....San Jose St. 2
at S. Carolina 2...................VA. Commonwealth 1
at Virginia 3................................Rider 0

Second Round (Nov. 28-29)

at Clemson 1 ....William & Mary 0
at Indiana 2 ....2 OT...................Butler 1
at St. John's 1 ....Penn St. 0
at Santa Clara 4 ....UNC-Greensboro 0
at Maryland 3 ....Jacksonville 0
Creighton 2 ....at UCLA 0
at Stanford 3 ....2 OT...........San Diego 2
at Virginia 1 ....S. Carolina 0

Quarterfinals (Dec. 5-6)

Indiana 2.................................at Clemson 0
Santa Clara 2 ....at St. John's 1
at Maryland 3 ....Creighton 0
Stanford 3 ....at Virgina 0

FINAL FOUR
at Richmond, Va. (Dec. 11 & 13)
Semifinals

Indiana 4 ....Santa Clara 0
Stanford 1 ....Maryland 0

Championship

Indiana 3 ....Stanford 1
Scoring: IU— Dema Kovalenko (Yuri Lavrinenko), 6:54; IU— Lavrinenko (Kovalenko, Aleksey Korol), 19:09; SU— Simon Elliott (unassisted), 21:50; IU— Korol (Matt Fundenberger), 44:12.
Attendance: 15,202
Final records: Indiana (23-2), Stanford (18-5-2).

WOMEN

1998 Final *Soccer America* Top 20

Final 1998 regular season poll including games through Nov. 8. Conducted by the national weekly *Soccer America* and released in the Nov.30 issue. Listing includes records through conference playoffs as well as NCAA tournament record and team lost to. Teams in **bold** type went on to reach NCAA Final Four. All tournament games decided by penalty kicks are considered ties.

		Nov. 9 Record	NCAA Recap
1	North Carolina	21-0-0	(4-1) Florida
2	Santa Clara	19-0-1	(3-1) Florida
3	Florida	21-1-0	(5-0)
4	Notre Dame	19-2-1	(2-1) Portland
5	Portland	16-2-2	(3-1) North Carolina
6	Connecticut	19-1-2	(2-1) Santa Clara
7	Dartmouth	14-1-2	(2-1) North Carolina
8	Hartford	16-4-0	(1-1) Connecticut
9	Penn State	19-3-1	(2-1) Florida
10	San Diego State	18-2-1	(1-1) Portland
11	Clemson	15-6-0	(1-1) Penn St.
12	Virginia	13-6-2	(0-1) Georgia
13	BYU	18-4-0	(1-1) Santa Clara
14	Michigan	13-6-1	(0-1) Notre Dame
15	Nebraska	16-3-1	(1-1) Notre Dame
16	William & Mary	16-2-2	(1-1) North Carolina
17	Vanderbilt	16-5-0	(0-1) Clemson
18	UCLA	17-3-1	(0-1) BYU
19	Wake Forest	13-6-1	(0-1) Georgia
20	Baylor	15-4-1	(0-1) Northwestern

NCAA Division I Tournament
First Round (Nov. 11)

at UNC Charlotte 2.........................S. Carolina 0
at Maryland 4 ....Fairfield 3
at Georgia 5 ....Wake Forest 2
at Wisconsin 2......................Central Fla. 0
at Minnesota 6...............................Kentucky 1
at USC 2 ....Washington 1
at Texas A&M 3 ....Alabama 1
at Michigan 4 ....Xavier 2
at Pacific 2 ....California 1
at BYU 6..................................Stanford 1
at Harvard 4.......................Cen. Conn. St. 1
Syracuse 4 ....at Colgate 1
at Indiana 3 ....Wright St. 1
at Vanderbilt 5 ....UNC Greensboro 1
Northwestern 2.........................at Evansville 1
at James Madison 4 ....Radford 0

Second Round (Nov. 14-15)

at North Carolina 6 . . . . .UNC Charlotte 0
at William & Mary 2 . . . . .Maryland 0
Georgia 2 . . . . .at Virginia 2
(Georgia advances on PK's)
at Dartmouth . . . . .Wisconsin 0
at Portland 3 . . . . .Minnesota 0
at San Diego St. 1 . . . . . . .3 OT . . . . .USC 0
at Nebraska 7 . . . . .Texas A&M 0
at Notre Dame 3 . . . . .Michigan 0
at Santa Clara 5 . . . . .Pacific 0
BYU 2 . . . . .at UCLA 0
at Hartford 3 . . . . .Harvard 0
at Connecticut 2 . . . . .Syracuse 1
at Penn St. 2 . . . . .Indiana 1
at Clemson 2 . . . . .Vanderbilt 1
Northwestern 5 . . . . .at Baylor 4
at Florida 5 . . . . .James Madison 1

Third Round (Nov. 20-22)

at North Carolina 3 . . . . .William & Mary 0
at Dartmouth 2 . . . . .Georgia 1
at Portland . . . . .San Diego 2
at Notre Dame 2 . . . . .Nebraska 1
at Santa Clara 3 . . . . .BYU 0
at Connecticut 2 . . . . .Hartford 1
at Penn St. . . . . .Clemson 0
at Florida 1 . . . . .Northwestern 0

Quarterfinals (Nov. 27-29)

at North Carolina 3 .Dartmouth 0
Portland 2 . . . . .at Notre Dame 1
at Santa Clara 1 . . . . .Connecticut 0
at Florida 3 . . . . .Penn St. 1

FINAL FOUR
at Greensboro, N.C. (Dec. 4 and 6)
Semifinals

North Carolina 1 . . . . .Portland 0
Florida 1 . . . . .Santa Clara 0

Championship

Florida 1 . . . . .North Carolina 0
Scoring: F— Danielle Fotopoulos (unassisted) 5:23.
Attendance: 10,583
Final records: North Carolina (25-1), Connecticut (26-1).

1998 Annual Awards
Men's Players of the Year

Hermann Trophy . . . . .Wojtek Krakowiak, Clemson, MF
MAC Award . . . . .Jay Heaps, Duke, MF
Soccer America . . . . .Wojtek Krakowiak, Clemson, MF

Women's Player of the Year

Hermann Trophy . . . . .Cindy Parlow, North Carolina, F
MAC Award . . . . .Cindy Parlow, North Carolina, F
Soccer America . . . . .Danielle Fotopoulos, Florida, F

NSCAA Coaches of the Year

Division I: Women's . . . . .Becky Burleigh, Florida
Men's . . . . .Jerry Yeagley, Indiana

Division I All-America Teams
MEN

The combined 1998 first team All-America selections of the National Soccer Coaches Association of America (NSCAA) and the 11 *Soccer America* MVPs. Holdovers from the combined 1997 All-America team are in **bold** type.

GOALKEEPER— Adin Brown, William & Mary, Jr.
DEFENDERS— Carlos Bocanegra, UCLA, So.; Matt Chulis, Virginia, Sr.; Jamie Clark, Stanford, Sr.; Nick Garcia, Indiana, So.; Kevin Kalish, St. Louis, Sr.; Lee Morrison, Stanford, Fr.
MIDFIELDERS— **Lazo Alavanja**, Indiana, Sr.; Keith Beach, Maryland, Sr.; Jay Heaps, Duke, Sr.; Wojtek Krakowiak, Clemson, Jr.; Richard Mulrooney, Creighton, Sr.; Maurizio Rocha, Connecticut, Sr.;
FORWARDS— Chris Albright, Virginia, So.; **Seth George**, UCLA, Sr.; Aleksey Korol, Indiana, Jr.; **Dema Kovalenko**, Indiana, Jr.

WOMEN
The combined 1998 first team All-America selections of the National Soccer Coaches Association of America (NSCAA) and the 11 *Soccer America* MVPs. Holdovers from the combined 1997 All-America team are in **bold** type.
GOALKEEPER— Kristin Luckenbill, Dartmouth, So.
DEFENDERS— Suzanne Eastman, Dartmouth, Sr.; Lorrie Fair, North Carolina, Jr.; Michelle French, Portland, Sr.
MIDFIELDERS— **Erin Baxter**, Florida, Sr.; Kelly Convey, Penn St., Jr.; Asta Helgadottir, Vanderbilt, So.; **Anne Makinen**, Notre Dame, So.; Tiffany Roberts, North Carolina, Sr.; Nikki Serlenga, Santa Clara, Jr.
FORWARDS— **Mandy Clemens**, Santa Clara, Jr.; Kim Engesser, Nebraska, Sr.; Danielle Fotopoulos, Florida, Sr.; Mary Frances Monroe, Connecticut, Fr.; **Cindy Parlow**, North Carolina, Sr.

Small College Final Fours
MEN
NCAA Division II
at South Carolina-Spartanburg (Dec. 3-5)
Semifinals: Southern Conn. St. def. Seattle Pacific, 3-0; South Carolina-Spartanburg def. Mercyhurst (Penn.), 2-0.
Championship: Southern Conn. St. def. South Carolina-Spartanburg, 1-0. Final records: Southern Conn. St. (20-2-1), South Carolina-Spartanburg (23-1).

NCAA Division III
at Ohio Wesleyan (Nov. 28-29)
Semifinals: Greensboro (N.C.) def. Rowan (N.J.), 1-0; Ohio Wesleyan def. Williams (Mass.), 1-0.
Championship: Ohio Wesleyan def. Greensboro, 2-1 (OT). Final records: Ohio Wesleyan (18-6), Greensboro (17-4).

NAIA
at Birmingham, Ala. (Nov. 27-28)
Semifinals: Lindsey Wilson def. William Carey (Miss.), 4-0; Illinois-Springfield def. Seattle (Wash.), 1-0.
Championship: Lindsey Wilson def. Illinois-Springfield 2-1; Final records: Lindsey Wilson (24-0), Illinois-Springfield (20-6-1).

WOMEN
NCAA Division II
at Lynn University, Boca Raton, Fla. (Dec. 4-6)
Semifinals: Sonoma St. (Calif.) def. Ashland (Ohio), 5-2; Lynn University (Calif.) def. Franklin Pierce (NH), 4-0.
Championship: Lynn def. Sonoma St., 3-1. Final records: Lynn (19-1), Sonoma St. (22-2-1).

NCAA Division III
at Ithaca, N.Y. (Nov. 21-22)
Semifinals: College of New Jersey def. Ithaca (N.Y.), 2-0; Macalester def. Willamette, 1-0.
Championship: Macalester def. College of New Jersey, 1-0. Final records: Macalester (21-1-1), College of New Jersey (19-3-1).

NAIA
at Mobile, Ala. (Nov. 27-28)
Semifinals: Azusa Pacific (Calif.) def. Mobile (Ala.), 1-1 (Azusa Pacific advances on PK's); Simon Fraser (B.C.) def. Lindenwood (Mo.), 3-2.
Championship: Azusa Pacific def. Simon Fraser, 2-1; Final records: Azusa Pacific (24-0-1), Simon Fraser (15-4-2).

SOCCER STATISTICS

THE 2000 ESPN INFORMATION PLEASE SPORTS ALMANAC

THROUGH THE YEARS
1900-1999
WORLD • US • COLLEGE

SEC B

PAGE 751

The World Cup

The Federation Internationale de Football Association (FIFA) began the World Cup championship tournament in 1930 with a 13-team field in Uruguay. Sixty-four years later, 138 countries competed in qualifying rounds to fill 24 berths in the 1994 World Cup finals. FIFA increased the World Cup '98 tournament field from 24 to 32 teams, including automatic berths for defending champion Brazil and host France. The other 30 slots were allotted by region: Europe (14), Africa (5), South America (4), CONCACAF (3), Asia (3), and the one remaining position to the winner of a playoff between the fourth place team in Asia and the champion of Oceania.

The United States hosted the World Cup for the first time in '94 and American crowds shattered tournament attendance records (see Year-by-Year Comparisons). Tournaments have now been played three times in North America (Mexico 2 and U.S.), four times in South America (Argentina, Chile, Brazil and Uruguay) and nine times in Europe (France 2, Italy 2, England, Spain, Sweden, Switzerland and West Germany).

Brazil retired the first World Cup (called the Jules Rimet Trophy after FIFA's first president) in 1970 after winning it for the third time. The new trophy, first presented in 1974, is known as simply the World Cup.

Multiple winners: Brazil (4); Italy and West Germany (3); Argentina and Uruguay (2).

Year	Champion	Manager	Score	Runner-up	Host Country	Third Place
1930	Uruguay	Alberto Suppici	4-2	Argentina	Uruguay	No game
1934	Italy	Vittório Pozzo	2-1*	Czechoslovakia	Italy	Germany 3, Austria 2
1938	Italy	Vittório Pozzo	4-2	Hungary	France	Brazil 4, Sweden 2
1942-46 Not held						
1950	Uruguay	Juan Lopez	2-1	Brazil	Brazil	No game
1954	West Germany	Sepp Herberger	3-2	Hungary	Switzerland	Austria 3, Uruguay 1
1958	Brazil	Vicente Feola	5-2	Sweden	Sweden	France 6, W. Ger. 3
1962	Brazil	Aimoré Moreira	3-1	Czechoslovakia	Chile	Chile 1, Yugoslavia 0
1966	England	Alf Ramsey	4-2*	W. Germany	England	Portugal 2, USSR 1
1970	Brazil	Mario Zagalo	4-1	Italy	Mexico	W. Ger. 1, Uruguay 0
1974	West Germany	Helmut Schoen	2-1	Holland	W. Germany	Poland 1, Brazil 0
1978	Argentina	Cesar Menotti	3-1*	Holland	Argentina	Brazil 2, Italy 1
1982	Italy	Enzo Bearzot	3-1	W. Germany	Spain	Poland 3, France 2
1986	Argentina	Carlos Bilardo	3-2	W. Germany	Mexico	France 4, Belgium 2*
1990	West Germany	Franz Beckenbauer	1-0	Argentina	Italy	Italy 2, England 1
1994	Brazil	Carlos Parreira	0-0†	Italy	USA	Sweden 4, Bulgaria 0
1998	France	Aimé Jacquet	3-0	Brazil	France	Croatia 2, Holland 1
2002	at Japan/South Korea					

*Winning goals scored in overtime (no sudden death); †Brazil defeated Italy in shootout (3-2) after scoreless overtime period (30 minutes).

All-Time World Cup Leaders

Career Goals

World Cup scoring leaders through 1998. Years listed are years played in World Cup.

	No
Gerd Müller, West Germany (1970, 74)	14
Just Fontaine, France (1958)	13
Pelé, Brazil (1958, 62, 66, 70)	12
Sandor Kocsis, Hungary (1954)	11
Juergen Klinsmann, Germany (1990, 94, 98)	11
Helmut Rahn, West Germany (1954, 58)	10
Teofilo Cubillas, Peru (1970, 78)	10
Gregorz Lato, Poland (1974, 78, 82)	10
Gary Lineker, England (1986, 90)	10

Most Valuable Player

Officially, the Golden Ball Award, the Most Valuable Player of the World Cup tournament has been selected since 1982 by a panel of international soccer journalists.

Year		Year	
1982	Paolo Rossi, Italy	1994	Romario, Brazil
1986	Diego Maradona, Arg.	1998	Ronaldo, Brazil
1990	Toto Schillaci, Italy		

Single Tournament Goals

World Cup tournament scoring leaders through 1998.

Year		Gm	No
1930	Guillermo Stabile, Argentina	4	8
1934	Angelo Schiavio, Italy	3	4
	Oldrich Nejedly, Czechoslovakia	4	4
	& Edmund Conen, Germany	4	4
1938	Leônidas, Brazil	3	8
1950	Ademir, Brazil	6	7
1954	Sandor Kocsis, Hungary	5	11
1958	Just Fontaine, France	6	13
1962	Drazen Jerkovic, Yugoslavia	6	5
1966	Eusébio, Portugal	6	9
1970	Gerd Müller, West Germany	6	10
1974	Grzegorz Lato, Poland	7	7
1978	Mario Kempes, Argentina	7	6
1982	Paolo Rossi, Italy	7	6
1986	Gary Lineker, England	5	6
1990	Toto Schillaci, Italy	7	6
1994	Oleg Salenko, Russia	3	6
	Hristo Stoichkov, Bulgaria	7	6
1998	Davor Suker, Croatia	7	6

All-Time World Cup Ranking Table

Since the first World Cup in 1930, Brazil is the only country to play in all 16 final tournaments. The FIFA all-time table below ranks all nations that have ever qualified for a World Cup final tournament by points earned through 1998. Victories, which earned two points from 1930-90, were awarded three points starting in 1994. Note that Germany's appearances include 10 made by West Germany from 1954-90. Participants in the 1998 World Cup final are in **bold** type.

		App	Gm	W	L	T	Pts	GF	GA
1	**Brazil**	16	80	53	13	14	**120**	173	78
2	**Germany**	14	78	45	16	17	**107**	162	103
3	**Italy**	14	66	38	12	16	**92**	105	62
4	**Argentina**	12	57	29	18	10	**68**	100	69
5	**England**	10	45	20	12	13	**53**	62	42
6	**France**	10	41	21	14	6	**48**	86	58
7	**Spain**	10	40	16	14	10	**42**	61	48
8	**Yugoslavia**	9	37	16	13	8	**40**	60	46
	Uruguay	9	37	15	14	8	**38**	61	52
	Russia	8	34	16	12	6	**38**	60	40
11	Sweden	9	38	14	15	9	**37**	66	60
	Netherlands	7	31	14	9	9	**37**	56	36
13	Hungary	9	32	15	14	3	**33**	87	57
14	Poland	5	25	13	7	5	**31**	39	29
15	Austria	7	29	12	13	4	**28**	43	47
16	Czech Republic	8	30	11	14	5	**27**	44	45
17	**Mexico**	11	37	8	19	10	**26**	39	75
18	**Belgium**	10	32	9	16	7	**25**	40	56
19	**Romania**	7	21	8	8	5	**21**	30	32
20	**Chile**	7	25	7	12	6	**20**	31	40
21	**Scotland**	8	23	4	12	7	**15**	25	41
	Switzerland	7	22	6	13	3	**15**	33	51
23	**Bulgaria**	7	26	3	15	8	**14**	22	53
	Paraguay	5	15	4	6	5	**14**	19	27
25	**Cameroon**	4	14	3	5	6	**12**	13	26
	Portugal	2	9	6	3	0	**12**	19	12
27	Peru	4	15	4	8	3	**11**	19	31
	No. Ireland	3	13	3	5	5	**11**	13	23
	Denmark	2	9	5	3	1	**11**	19	13
30	**Croatia**	1	7	5	2	0	**10**	11	5
31	**USA**	6	17	4	12	1	**9**	18	38
32	**Morocco**	4	13	2	7	4	**8**	12	18
	Colombia	4	13	3	8	2	**8**	14	23

		App	Gm	W	L	T	Pts	GF	GA
	Nigeria	2	8	4	4	0	**8**	13	13
35	Ireland	2	9	1	3	5	**7**	4	7
	Norway	2	8	2	3	3	**7**	7	8
37	East Germany	1	6	2	2	2	**6**	5	5
38	**Saudi Arabia**	2	7	2	4	1	**5**	7	13
	Algeria	2	6	2	3	1	**5**	6	10
	Wales	1	5	1	1	3	**5**	4	4
41	**South Korea**	5	14	0	10	4	**4**	11	43
	Tunisia	2	6	1	3	2	**4**	4	6
	Costa Rica	1	4	2	2	0	**4**	4	6
44	**Iran**	2	6	1	4	1	**3**	4	12
	North Korea	1	4	1	2	1	**3**	5	9
	Cuba	1	3	1	1	1	**3**	5	12
	Jamaica	1	3	1	2	0	**3**	3	9
48	Egypt	2	4	0	2	2	**2**	3	6
	Honduras	1	3	0	1	2	**2**	2	3
	Israel	1	3	0	1	2	**2**	1	3
	Turkey	1	3	1	2	0	**2**	10	11
	South Africa	1	3	0	1	2	**2**	3	6
53	Bolivia	3	6	0	5	1	**1**	1	20
	Australia	1	3	0	2	1	**1**	0	5
	Kuwait	1	3	0	2	1	**1**	2	6
56	El Salvador	2	6	0	6	0	**0**	1	22
	Canada	1	3	0	3	0	**0**	0	5
	East Indies	1	1	0	1	0	**0**	0	6
	Greece	1	3	0	3	0	**0**	0	10
	Haiti	1	3	0	3	0	**0**	2	14
	Iraq	1	3	0	3	0	**0**	1	4
	Japan	1	3	0	3	0	**0**	1	4
	New Zealand	1	3	0	3	0	**0**	2	12
	UAE	1	3	0	3	0	**0**	2	11
	Zaire	1	3	0	3	0	**0**	0	14

The United States in the World Cup

While the United States has fielded a national team every year of the World Cup, only five of those teams have been able to make it past the preliminary competition and qualify for the final World Cup tournament. The 1994 national team automatically qualified because the U.S. served as host of the event for the first time. The U.S. played in three of the first four World Cups (1930, '34 and '50) and each of the last three (1990, '94 and '98). The Americans have a record of 4-12-1 in 17 World Cup matches, with two victories in 1930, a 1-0 upset of England in 1950, and a 2-1 shocker over Colombia in 1994.

1930

1st Round Matches

United States 3 .... Belgium 0
United States 3 .... Paraguay 0

Semifinals

Argentina 6 .... United States 1
U.S. Scoring—Bert Patenaude (3), Bart McGhee (2), James Brown and Thomas Florie.

1934

1st Round Match

Italy 7 .... United States 1
U.S. Scoring—Buff Donelli (who later became a noted college and NFL football coach).

1950

1st Round Matches

Spain 3 .... United States 1
United States 1 .... England 0
Chile 5 .... United States 2
U.S. Scoring—Joe Gaetjens, Joe Maca, John Souza and Frank Wallace.

1990

1st Round Matches

Czechoslovakia 5 .... United States 1
Italy 1 .... United States 0
Austria 2 .... United States 1
U.S. Scoring—Paul Caligiuri and Bruce Murray.

1994

1st Round Matches

United States 1 .... Switzerland 1
United States 2 .... Colombia 1
Romania 1 .... United States 0

Round of 16

Brazil 1 .... United States 0
Overall U.S. Scoring— Eric Wynalda, Ernie Stewart and own goal (Colombia defender Andres Escobar).

1998

1st Round Matches

Germany 2 .... United States 1
Iran 2 .... United States 1
Yugoslavia 1 .... United States 0
U.S. Scoring— Brian McBride.

World Cup Finals

Brazil and West Germany (now Germany) have played in the most Cup finals with six. Note that a four-team round robin determined the 1950 championship—the deciding game turned out to be the last one of the tournament between Uruguay and Brazil.

1930
Uruguay 4, Argentina 2
(at Montevideo, Uruguay)

	1	2-T
July 30 Uruguay (4-0)	1	3-4
Argentina (4-1)	2	0-2

Goals: Uruguay–Pablo Dorado (12th minute), Pedro Cea (54th), Santos Iriarte (68th), Castro (89th); Argentina–Carlos Peucelle (20th), Guillermo Stabile (37th).
Uruguay–Ballesteros, Nasazzi, Mascheroni, Andrade, Fernandez, Gestido, Dorado, Scarone, Castro, Cea, Iriarte.
Argentina–Botasso, Della Torre, Paternoster, J. Evaristo, Monti, Suarez, Peucelle, Varallo, Stabile, Ferreira, M. Evaristo.
Attendance: 90,000. **Referee:** Langenus (Belgium).

1934
Italy 2, Czechoslovakia 1 (OT)
(at Rome)

	1	2	OT-T
June 10 Italy (4-0-1)	0	1	1-2
Czechoslovakia (3-1)	0	1	0-1

Goals: Italy–Raimondo Orsi (80th minute), Angelo Schiavio (95th); Czechoslovakia–Puc (70th).
Italy–Combi, Monzeglio, Allemandi, Ferraris IV, Monti, Bertolini, Guaita, Meazza, Schiavio, Ferrari, Orsi.
Czechoslovakia–Planicka, Zenisek, Ctyroky, Kostalek, Cambal, Krcil, Junek, Svoboda, Sobotka, Nejedly, Puc.
Attendance: 55,000. **Referee:** Eklind (Sweden).

1938
Italy 4, Hungary 2
(at Paris)

	1	2-T
June 19 Italy (4-0)	3	1-4
Hungary (3-1)	1	1-2

Goals: Italy–Gino Colaussi (5th minute), Silvio Piola (16th), Colussi (35th), Piola (82nd); Hungary–Titkos (7th), Georges Sarosi (70th).
Italy–Olivieri, Foni, Rava, Serantoni, Andreolo, Locatelli, Biavati, Meazza, Piola, Ferrari, Colaussi.
Hungary–Szabo, Polgar, Biro, Szalay, Szucs, Lazar, Sas, Vincze, G. Sarosi, Szengeller, Titkos.
Attendance: 65,000. **Referee:** Capdeville (France).

1950
Uruguay 2, Brazil 1
(at Rio de Janeiro)

	1	2-T
July 16 Uruguay (3-0-1)	0	2-2
Brazil (4-1-1)	0	1-1

Goals: Uruguay–Juan Schiaffino (66th minute), Chico Ghiggia (79th); Brazil–Friaca (47th).
Uruguay–Maspoli, M. Gonzales, Tejera, Gambetta, Varela, Andrade, Ghiggia, Perez, Miguez, Schiaffino, Moran.
Brazil–Barbosa, Augusto, Juvenal, Bauer, Danilo, Bigode, Friaça, Zizinho, Ademir, Jair, Chico.
Attendance: 199,854. **Referee:** Reader (England).

1954
West Germany 3, Hungary 2
(at Berne, Switzerland)

	1	2-T
July 4 West Germany (4-1)	2	1-3
Hungary (4-1)	2	0-2

Goals: West Germany–Max Morlock (10th minute), Helmut Rahn (18th), Rahn (84th); Hungary–Ferenc Puskas (4th), Zoltan Czibor (9th).
West Germany–Turek, Posipal, Liebrich, Kohlmeyer, Eckel, Mai, Rahn, Morlock, O. Walter, F. Walter, Schaefer.
Hungary–Grosics, Buzansky, Lorant, Lantos, Bozsik, Zakarias, Czibor, Kocsis, Hidegkuti, Puskas, J. Toth.
Attendance: 60,000. **Referee:** Ling (England).

1958
Brazil 5, Sweden 2
(at Stockholm)

	1	2-T
June 29 Brazil (5-0-1)	2	3-5
Sweden (4-1-1)	1	1-2

Goals: Brazil–Vava (9th minute), Vava (32nd), Pelé (55th), Mario Zagalo (68th), Pelé (90th); Sweden–Nils Liedholm (3rd), Agne Simonsson (80th).
Brazil–Gilmar, D. Santos, N. Santos, Zito, Bellini, Orlando, Garrincha, Didi, Vava, Pelé, Zagalo.
Sweden–Svensson, Bergmark, Axbom, Boerjesson, Gustavsson, Parling, Hamrin, Gren, Simonsson, Liedholm, Skoglund.
Attendance: 49,737. **Referee:** Guigue (France).

1962
Brazil 3, Czechoslovakia 1
(at Santiago, Chile)

	1	2-T
June 17 Brazil (5-0-1)	1	2-3
Czechoslovakia (3-2-1)	1	0-1

Goals: Brazil–Amarildo (17th minute), Zito (68th), Vava (77th); Czechoslovakia–Josef Masopust (15th).
Brazil–Gilmar, D. Santos, N. Santos, Zito, Mauro, Zozimo, Garrincha, Didi, Vava, Amarildo, Zagalo.
Czechoslovakia–Schroiff, Tichy, Novak, Pluskal, Popluhar, Masopust, Pospichal, Scherer, Kvasniak, Kadraba, Jelinek.
Attendance: 68,679. **Referee:** Latishev (USSR).

1966
England 4, West Germany 2 (OT)
(at London)

	1	2	OT-T
July 30 England (5-0-1)	1	1	2-4
West Germany (4-1-1)	1	1	0-2

Goals: England–Geoff Hurst (18th minute), Martin Peters (78th), Hurst (101st), Hurst (120th); West Germany–Helmut Haller (12th), Wolfgang Weber (90th).
England–Banks, Cohen, Wilson, Stiles, J. Charlton, Moore, Ball, Hurst, B. Charlton, Hunt, Peters.
West Germany–Tilkowski, Hottges, Schnellinger, Beckenbauer, Schulz, Weber, Haller, Seeler, Held, Overath, Emmerich.
Attendance: 93,802. **Referee:** Dienst (Switzerland).

1970

Brazil 4, Italy 1
(at Mexico City)

	1	2–T
June 21 Brazil (6-0)	1	3–4
Italy (3-1-2)	1	0–1

Goals: Brazil–Pelé (18th minute), Gerson (65th), Jairzinho (70th), Carlos Alberto (86th); Italy–Roberto Boninsegna (37th).
Brazil–Felix, C. Alberto, Everaldo, Clodoaldo, Brito, Piazza, Jairzinho, Gerson, Tostão, Pelé, Rivelino.
Italy–Albertosi, Burgnich, Facchetti, Bertini (Juliano, 73rd), Rosato, Cera, Domenghini, Mazzola, Boninsegna (Rivera, 84th), De Sisti, Riva.
Attendance: 107,412. **Referee:** Glockner (E. Germany).

1974

West Germany 2, Holland 1
(at Munich)

	1	2–T
July 7 West Germany (6-1)	2	0–2
Holland (5-1-1)	1	0–1

Goals: West Germany–Paul Breitner (25th minute, penalty kick), Gerd Müller (43rd); Holland–Johan Neeskens (1st, penalty kick).
West Germany–Maier, Beckenbauer, Vogts, Breitner, Schwarzenbeck, Overath, Bonhof, Hoeness, Grabowski, Muller, Holzenbein.
Holland–Jongbloed, Suurbier, Rijsbergen (De Jong, 58th), Krol, Haan, Jansen, Van Hanegem, Neeskens, Rep, Cruyff, Rensenbrink (R. Van de Kerkhof, 46th).
Attendance: 77,833. **Referee:** Taylor (England).

1978

Argentina 3, Holland 1 (OT)
(at Buenos Aires)

	1	2	OT–T
June 25 Argentina (5-1-1)	1	0	2–3
Holland (3-2-2)	0	1	0–1

Goals: Argentina–Mario Kempes (37th minute), Kempes (104th), Daniel Bertoni (114th); Holland–Dirk Nanninga (81st).
Argentina–Fillol, Olguin, L. Galvan, Passarella, Tarantini, Ardiles (Larrosa, 65th), Gallego, Kempes, Luque, Bertoni, Ortiz (Houseman, 77th).
Holland–Jongbloed, Jansen (Suurbier, 72nd), Brandts, Krol, Poortvliet, Haan, Neeskens, W. Van de Kerkhof, R. Van de Kerkhof, Rep (Nanninga, 58th), Rensenbrink.
Attendance: 77,260. **Referee:** Gonella (Italy).

1982

Italy 3, West Germany 1
(at Madrid)

	1	2–T
July 11 Italy (4-0-3)	0	3–3
West Germany (4-2-1)	0	1–1

Goals: Italy–Paolo Rossi (57th minute), Marco Tardelli (68th), Alessandro Altobelli (81st); West Germany–Paul Breitner (83rd).
Italy–Zoff, Scirea, Gentile, Cabrini, Collovati, Bergomi, Tardelli, Oriali, Conti, Rossi, Graziani (Altobelli, 8th, and Causio, 89th).
West Germany–Schumacher, Stielike, Kaltz, Briegel, K.H. Forster, B. Forster, Breitner, Dremmler (Hrubesch, 61st), Littbarski, Fischer, Rummenigge (Muller, 69th).
Attendance: 90,080. **Referee:** Coelho (Brazil).

1986

Argentina 3, West Germany 2
(at Mexico City)

	1	2–T
June 29 Argentina (6-0-1)	1	2–3
West Germany (4-2-1)	0	2–2

Goals: Argentina–Jose Brown (22nd minute), Jorge Valdano (55th), Jorge Burruchaga (83rd); West Germany–Karl-Heinz Rummenigge (73rd), Rudi Voller (81st).
Argentina–Pumpido, Cuciuffo, Olarticoechea, Ruggeri, Brown, Batista, Burruchaga (Trobbiani, 89th), Giusti, Enrique, Maradona, Valdano.
West Germany–Schumacher, Jakobs, B. Forster, Berthold, Briegel, Eder, Brehme, Matthaus, Rummenigge, Magath (Hoeness, 61st), Allofs (Voller, 46th).
Attendance: 114,590. **Referee:** Filho (Brazil).

1990

West Germany 1, Argentina 0
(at Rome)

	1	2–T
July 8 West Germany (6-0-1)	0	1–1
Argentina (4-2-1)	0	0–0

Goals: West Germany–Andreas Brehme (85th minute, penalty kick).
West Germany–Illgner, Berthold (Reuter, 73rd), Kohler, Augenthaler, Buchwald, Brehme, Haessler, Matthaus, Littbarski, Klinsmann, Voller.
Argentina: Goycoechea, Ruggeri (Monzon, 46th), Simon, Serrizuela, Lorenzo, Basualdo, Troglio, Burruchaga (Calderon, 53rd), Sensini, Dezotti, Maradona.
Attendance: 73,603. **Referee:** Codesal (Mexico).

1994

Brazil 0, Italy 0 (Shootout)
(at Pasadena, Calif.)

	1	2	OT–T
July 17 Brazil (6-0-1)	0	0	0–0*
Italy (4-2-1)	0	0	0–0

*Brazil wins shootout, 3-2.
Shootout (five shots each, alternating): ITA–Baresi (miss, 0-0); BRA–Santos (blocked, 0-0); ITA– Albertini (goal, 1-0); BRA–Romario (goal, 1-1); ITA–Evani (goal, 2-1); BRA–Branco (goal, 2-2); ITA–Massaro (blocked, 2-2); BRA–Dunga (goal, 2-3); ITA–R. Baggio (miss, 2-3).
Brazil– Taffarel, Jorginho (Cafu, 21st minute), Branco, Aldair, Santos, Mazinho, Silva, Dunga, Zinho (Viola, 106th), Bebeto, Romario.
Italy– Pagliuca, Mussi (Apolloni, 35th minute), Baresi, Benarrivo, Maldini, Albertini, D. Baggio (Evani, 95th), Berti, Donadoni, R. Baggio, Massaro.
Attendance: 94,194. **Referee:** Puhl (Hungary).

1998

France 3, Brazil 0
(at Paris)

	1	2– T
July 12 Brazil (6-1)	0	0–0
France (7-0)	2	1–3

Goals: France– Zinedine Zidane (27th and 46th minutes), Petit (92).
Brazil– Taffarel, Cafu, Aldair, Baiano, Carlos, Sampaio (Edmundo, 74th minute), Dunga, Rivaldo, Leonardo (Denilson, 46th minute), Bebeto, Ronaldo.
France– Barthez, Lizarazu, Desailly, Thuram, Leboeuf, Djorkaeff (Viera, 75th minute), Deschamps, Zidane, Petit, Karembeu (Boghossian, 57th minute), Guivarc'h, Dugarry.
Attendance: 75,000. **Referee:** Belqola (Morocco).

Year-by-Year Comparisons

How the 16 World Cup tournaments have compared in nations qualifying, matches played, players participating, goals scored, average goals per game, overall attendance and attendance per game.

Year	Host	Continent	Nations	Matches	Players	Scored	Goals Per Game	Overall	Per Game
1930	Uruguay	So. America	13	18	189	70	3.8	589,300	32,739
1934	Italy	Europe	16	17	208	70	4.1	361,000	21,235
1938	France	Europe	15	18	210	84	4.7	376,000	20,889
1942-46	Not held								
1950	Brazil	So. America	13	22	192	88	4.0	1,044,763	47,489
1954	Switzerland	Europe	16	26	233	140	5.3	872,000	33,538
1958	Sweden	Europe	16	35	241	126	3.6	819,402	23,411
1962	Chile	So. America	16	32	252	89	2.8	892,812	27,900
1966	England	Europe	16	32	254	89	2.8	1,464,944	45,780
1970	Mexico	No. America	16	32	270	95	3.0	1,690,890	52,840
1974	West Germany	Europe	16	38	264	97	2.6	1,809,953	47,630
1978	Argentina	So. America	16	38	277	102	2.7	1,685,602	44,358
1982	Spain	Europe	24	52	396	146	2.8	2,108,723	40,552
1986	Mexico	No. America	24	52	414	132	2.5	2,393,031	46,020
1990	Italy	Europe	24	52	413	115	2.2	2,516,354	48,391
1994	United States	No. America	24	52	437	140	2.7	3,587,088	68,982
1998	France	Europe	32	64	704	171	2.7	2,775,400	43,366

World Team of the 20th Century

The team, comprised of the century's best players, was voted on by a panel that included 250 international soccer journalists and released on June 10, 1998 in conjunction with the opening of the 1998 World Cup. The panel first selected the European and South American Teams of the Century and then chose the World Team from those two lists.

World Team

Pos		Pos	
GK	Lev Yashin, Soviet Union	MF	Alfredo Di Stefano, Argentina
D	Carlos Alberto, Brazil	MF	Michel Platini, France
D	Franz Beckenbauer, West Germany	F	Pele, Brazil
D	Bobby Moore, England	F	Garrincha, Brazil
D	Nilton Santos, Brazil	F	Diego Maradona, Argentina
MF	Johan Cryuff, Netherlands		

European Team

Pos	
GK	Lev Yashin, Soviet Union
D	Paolo Maldini, Italy
D	Franz Beckenbauer, West Germany
D	Bobby Moore, England
D	Franco Baresi, Italy
MF	Johan Cryuff, Netherlands
MF	Eusebio, Portugal
MF	Michel Platini, France
F	Ferenc Puskas, Hungary
F	Bobby Charlton, England
F	Marco Van Basten, Netherlands

South American Team

Pos	
GK	Ubaldo Fillol, Argentina
D	Carlos Alberto, Brazil
D	Elias Figueroa, Chile
D	Daniel Passarella, Argentina
D	Nilton Santos, Brazil
MF	Didi, Brazil
MF	Alfredo Di Stefano, Argentina
MF	Rivelino, Brazil
F	Pele, Brazil
F	Garrincha, Brazil
F	Diego Maradona, Argentina

World Cup Shootouts

Introduced in 1982; winning sides in **bold** type.

Year	Round		Final	SO	Year	Round		Final	SO
1982	Semi	**W. Germany** vs. France	3-3	(5-4)		Semi	**W. Germany** vs. England	1-1	(4-3)
1986	Quarter	**Belgium** vs. Spain	1-1	(5-4)					
	Quarter	**France** vs. Brazil	1-1	(4-3)	1994	Second	**Bulgaria** vs. Mexico	1-1	(3-1)
	Quarter	**W. Germany** vs. Mexico	0-0	(4-1)		Quarter	**Sweden** vs. Romania	2-2	(5-4)
1990	Second	**Ireland** vs. Romania	0-0	(5-4)		Final	**Brazil** vs. Italy	0-0	(3-2)
	Quarter	**Argentina** vs. Yugoslavia	0-0	(3-2)	1998	Second	**Argentina** vs. England	2-2	(4-3)
	Semi	**Argentina** vs. Italy	1-1	(4-3)		Quarter	**France** vs. Italy	0-0	(4-3)

OTHER WORLDWIDE COMPETITION

The Olympic Games

Held every four years since 1896, except during World War I (1916) and World War II (1940-44). Soccer was not a medal sport in 1896 at Athens or in 1932 at Los Angeles. By agreement between FIFA and the IOC, Olympic soccer competition is currently limited to players 23-years old and under.

Multiple winners: England and Hungary (3); Soviet Union and Uruguay (2).

MEN

Year		Year	
1900	**England**, France, Belgium	1956	**Soviet Union**, Yugoslavia, Bulgaria
1904	**Canada**, USA I, USA II	1960	**Yugoslavia**, Denmark, Hungary
1906	**Denmark**, Smyrna (Int'l entry), Greece	1964	**Hungary**, Czechoslovakia, East Germany
1908	**England**, Denmark, Holland	1968	**Hungary**, Bulgaria, Japan
1912	**England**, Denmark, Holland	1972	**Poland**, Hungary, East Germany
1920	**Belgium**, Spain, Holland	1976	**East Germany**, Poland, Soviet Union
1924	**Uruguay**, Switzerland, Sweden	1980	**Czechoslovakia**, East Germany, Soviet Union
1928	**Uruguay**, Argentina, Italy	1984	**France**, Brazil, Yugoslavia
1936	**Italy**, Austria, Norway	1988	**Soviet Union**, Brazil, West Germany
1948	**Sweden**, Yugoslavia, Denmark	1992	**Spain**, Poland, Ghana
1952	**Hungary**, Yugoslavia, Sweden	1996	**Nigeria**, Argentina, Brazil

WOMEN

Year	
1996	**USA**, China, Norway

The Under-20 World Cup

Held every two years since 1977. Officially, the World Youth Championship for the FIFA/Coca-Cola Cup.

Multiple winners: Argentina and Brazil (3); Portugal (2).

Year		Year	
1977	Soviet Union	1991	Portugal
1979	Argentina	1993	Brazil
1981	West Germany	1995	Argentina
1983	Brazil	1997	Argentina
1985	Brazil	1999	Spain
1987	Yugoslavia	2001	(at Argentina)
1989	Portugal		

The Under-17 World Cup

Held every two years since 1985. Officially, the U-17 World Tournament for the FIFA/JVC Cup.

Multiple winners: Ghana and Nigeria (2).

Year		Year	
1985	Nigeria	1995	Ghana
1987	Soviet Union	1997	Brazil
1989	Saudi Arabia	1999	(at New Zealand)
1991	Ghana	2001	(at Trinidad &
1993	Nigeria		Tobago)

Indoor World Championship

First held in 1989. FIFA's only Five-a-Side tournament.

Multiple winners: Brazil (3).

Year		Year	
1989	Brazil	1996	Brazil
1992	Brazil	2000	(at Guatemala)

Women's World Cup

First held in 1991. Officially, the FIFA Women's World Championship.

Multiple winners: United States (2).

Year		Year	
1991	United States	1999	United States
1995	Norway		

Confederations Cup

First held in 1992. Contested by the Continental champions of Africa, Asia, Europe, North America and South America and originally called the Intercontinental Championship for the King Fahd Cup until it was redubbed the FIFA/Confederations Cup for the King Fahd Trophy in 1997.

Year		Year	
1992	Argentina	1997	Brazil
1995	Denmark	1999	Mexico

CONTINENTAL COMPETITION

European Championship

Held every four years since 1960. Officially, the European Football Championship. Winners receive the Henri Delaunay trophy, named for the Frenchman who first proposed the idea of a European Soccer Championship in 1927. The first one would not be played until five years after his death in 1955.

Multiple winner: West Germany (2).

Year		Year		Year		Year	
1960	Soviet Union	1972	West Germany	1984	France	1996	Germany
1964	Spain	1976	Czechoslovakia	1988	Holland	2000	(at Belgium/
1968	Italy	1980	West Germany	1992	Denmark		Netherlands)

Copa America

Held irregularly since 1916. Unofficially, the Championship of South America.

Multiple winners: Argentina and Uruguay (14); Brazil (6); Paraguay and Peru (2).

Year		Year		Year		Year		Year	
1916	Uruguay	1925	Argentina	1942	Uruguay	1957	Argentina	1987	Uruguay
1917	Uruguay	1926	Uruguay	1945	Argentina	1958	Argentina	1989	Brazil
1919	Brazil	1927	Argentina	1946	Argentina	1959	Uruguay	1991	Argentina
1920	Uruguay	1929	Argentina	1947	Argentina	1963	Bolivia	1993	Argentina
1921	Argentina	1935	Uruguay	1949	Brazil	1967	Uruguay	1995	Uruguay
1922	Brazil	1937	Argentina	1953	Paraguay	1975	Peru	1997	Brazil
1923	Uruguay	1939	Peru	1955	Argentina	1979	Paraguay	1999	Brazil
1924	Uruguay	1941	Argentina	1956	Uruguay	1983	Uruguay	2001	(at Colombia)

African Nations Cup

Contested since 1957 and held every two years since 1968.

Multiple winners: Egypt and Ghana (4); Congo/Zaire (3); Cameroon and Nigeria (2).

Year		Year		Year		Year		Year	
1957	Egypt	1968	Zaire	1978	Ghana	1988	Cameroon	1998	Egypt
1959	Egypt	1970	Sudan	1980	Nigeria	1990	Algeria	2000	(at Ghana/
1962	Ethiopia	1972	Congo	1982	Ghana	1992	Ivory Coast		Nigeria)
1963	Ghana	1974	Zaire	1984	Cameroon	1994	Nigeria		
1965	Ghana	1976	Morocco	1986	Egypt	1996	South Africa		

CONCACAF Gold Cup

The Confederation of North, Central American and Caribbean Football Championship. Contested irregularly from 1963-81 and revived as CONCACAF Gold Cup in 1991.

Multiple winners: Mexico (6); Costa Rica (2).

Year		Year		Year		Year	
1963	Costa Rica	1969	Costa Rica	1977	Mexico	1993	Mexico
1965	Mexico	1971	Mexico	1981	Honduras	1996	Mexico
1967	Guatemala	1973	Haiti	1991	United States	1998	Mexico

CLUB COMPETITION

Toyota Cup

Also known as the World Club Championship. Contested annually in December between the winners of the European Cup and South America's Copa Libertadores. Four European Cup winners refused to participate in the championship match in the 1970s and were replaced each time by the European Cup runner-up: Panathinaikos (Greece) for Ajax Amsterdam (Holland) in 1971; Juventus (Italy) for Ajax in 1973; Atlético Madrid (Spain) for Bayern Munich (West Germany) in 1974; and Malmo (Sweden) for Nottingham Forest (England) in 1979. Another European Cup winner, Marseille of France, was prohibited by the Union of European Football Associations (UEFA) from playing for the 1993 Toyota Cup because of its involvement in the match-rigging scandal.

Best-of-three game format from 1960-68, then a two-game/total goals format from 1969-79. Toyota became Cup sponsor in 1980, changed the format to a one-game championship and moved it to Toyko.

Multiple winners: AC Milan, Nacional and Penarol (3); Ajax Amsterdam, Independiente, Inter Milan, Juventus, Real Madrid, Santos and Sao Paulo (2).

Year		Year		Year	
1960	Real Madrid (Spain)	1973	Independiente (Argentina)	1986	River Plate (Argentina)
1961	Peñarol (Uruguay)	1974	Atlético Madrid (Spain)	1987	FC Porto (Portugal)
1962	Santos (Brazil)	1975	Not held	1988	Nacional (Uruguay)
1963	Santos (Brazil)	1976	Bayern MunichW. Germany)	1989	AC Milan (Italy)
1964	Inter Milan (Italy)	1977	Boca Juniors (Argentina)	1990	AC Milan (Italy)
1965	Inter Milan (Italy)	1978	Not held	1991	Red Star (Yugoslavia)
1966	Penarol (Uruguay)	1979	Olimpia (Paraguay)	1992	Sao Paulo (Brazil)
1967	Racing Club (Argentina)	1980	Nacional (Uruguay)	1993	Sao Paulo (Brazil)
1968	Estudiantes (Argentina)	1981	Flamengo (Brazil)	1994	Velez Sarsfield (Argentina)
1969	AC Milan (Italy)	1982	Peñarol (Uruguay)	1995	Ajax Amsterdam (Holland)
1970	Feyenoord (Holland)	1983	Gremio (Brazil)	1996	Juventus (Italy)
1971	Nacional (Uruguay)	1984	Independiente (Argentina)	1997	Borussia Dortmund (Germany)
1972	Ajax Amsterdam (Holland)	1985	Juventus (Italy)	1998	Real Madrid (Spain)

European Cup

Contested annually since the 1955-56 season by the league champions of the member countries of the Union of European Football Associations (UEFA).

Multiple winners: Real Madrid (7); AC Milan (5); Ajax Amsterdam and Liverpool (4); Bayern Munich (3); Benfica, Inter-Milan, Juventus and Nottingham Forest (2).

Year		Year		Year	
1956	Real Madrid (Spain)	1959	Real Madrid (Spain)	1961	Benfica (Portugal)
1957	Real Madrid (Spain)	1960	Real Madrid (Spain)	1962	Benfica (Portugal)
1958	Real Madrid (Spain)			1963	AC Milan (Italy)

Year	Year	Year
1964 Inter Milan (Italy)	1976 Bayern Munich (W. Germany)	1988 PSV Eindhoven (Holland)
1965 Inter Milan (Italy)	1977 Liverpool (England)	1989 AC Milan (Italy)
1966 Real Madrid (Spain)	1978 Liverpool (England)	
1967 Glasgow Celtic (Scotland)	1979 Nottingham Forest (England)	1990 AC Milan (Italy)
1968 Manchester United (England)		1991 Red Star Belgrade (Yugo.)
1969 AC Milan (Italy)	1980 Nottingham Forest (England)	1992 Barcelona (Spain)
	1981 Liverpool (England)	1993 Marseille (France)*
1970 Feyenoord (Holland)	1982 Aston Villa (England)	1994 AC Milan (Italy)
1971 Ajax Amsterdam (Holland)	1983 SV Hamburg (W. Germany)	1995 Ajax Amsterdam (Holland)
1972 Ajax Amsterdam (Holland)	1984 Liverpool (England)	1996 Juventus (Italy)
1973 Ajax Amsterdam (Holland)	1985 Juventus (Italy)	1997 Borussia Dortmund (Germany)
1974 Bayern Munich (W. Germany)	1986 Steaua Bucharest (Romania)	1998 Real Madrid (Spain)
1975 Bayern Munich (W. Germany)	1987 FC Porto (Portugal)	1999 Manchester United (England)

*title vacated

European Cup Winner's Cup

Contested annually since the 1960-61 season by the cup winners of the member countries of the Union of European Football Associations (UEFA).

Multiple winners: Barcelona (4); AC Milan, RSC Anderlecht, Chelsea and Dinamo Kiev (2).

Year	Year	Year
1961 Fiorentina (Italy)	1974 FC Magdeburg (E. Germany)	1987 Ajax Amsterdam (Holland)
1962 Atletico Madrid (Spain)	1975 Dinamo Kiev (USSR)	1988 Mechelen (Belgium)
1963 Tottenham Hotspur (England)	1976 RSC Anderlecht (Belgium)	1989 Barcelona (Spain)
1964 Sporting Lisbon (Portugal)	1977 SV Hamburg (W. Germany)	
1965 West Ham United (England)	1978 RSC Anderlecht (Belgium)	1990 Sampdoria (Italy)
1966 Borussia Dortmund (W.Germany)	1979 Barcelona (Spain)	1991 Manchester United (England)
1967 Bayern Munich (W. Germany)		1992 Werder Bremen (Germany)
1968 AC Milan (Italy)	1980 Valencia (Spain)	1993 Parma (Italy)
1969 Slovan Bratislava (Czech.)	1981 Dinamo Tbilisi (USSR)	1994 Arsenal (England)
	1982 Barcelona (Spain)	1995 Real Zaragoza (Spain)
1970 Manchester City (England)	1983 Aberdeen (Scotland)	1996 Paris St. Germain (France)
1971 Chelsea (England)	1984 Juventus (Italy)	1997 Barcelona (Spain)
1972 Glasgow Rangers (Scotland)	1985 Everton (England)	1998 Chelsea (England)
1973 AC Milan (Italy)	1986 Dinamo Kiev (USSR)	1999 Lazio (Italy)

UEFA Cup

Contested annually since the 1957-58 season by teams other than league champions and cup winners of the Union of European Football Associations (UEFA). Teams selected by UEFA based on each country's previous performance in the tournament. Teams from England were banned from UEFA Cup play from 1985-90 for the criminal behavior of their supporters.

Multiple winners: Barcelona, Inter Milan and Juventus (3); Borussia Mönchengladbach, IFK Göteborg, Leeds United, Liverpool, Parma, Real Madrid, Tottenham Hotspur and Valencia (2).

Year	Year	Year
1958 Barcelona (Spain)	1973 Liverpool (England)	1986 Real Madrid (Spain)
1959 Not held	1974 Feyenoord (Holland)	1987 IFK Göteborg (Sweden)
	1975 Borussia Mönchengladbach (W.	1988 Bayer Leverkusen (W. Germany)
1960 Barcelona (Spain)	Germany)	1989 Napoli (Italy)
1961 AS Roma (Italy)	1976 Liverpool (England)	
1962 Valencia (Spain)	1977 Juventus (Italy)	1990 Juventus (Italy)
1963 Valencia (Spain)	1978 PSV Eindhoven (Holland)	1991 Inter Milan (Italy)
1964 Real Zaragoza (Spain)	1979 Borussia Mönchengladbach (W.	1992 Ajax Amsterdam (Holland)
1965 Ferencvaros (Hungary)	Germany)	1993 Juventus (Italy)
1966 Barcelona (Spain)		1994 Inter Milan (Italy)
1967 Dinamo Zagreb (Yugoslavia)	1980 Eintracht Frankfurt (W. Germany)	1995 Parma (Italy)
1968 Leeds United (England)	1981 Ipswich Town (England)	1996 Bayern Munich (Germany)
1969 Newcastle United (England)	1982 IFK Göteborg (Sweden)	1997 Schalke 04 (Germany)
1970 Arsenal (England)	1983 RSC Anderlecht (Belgium)	1998 Inter Milan (Italy)
1971 Leeds United (England)	1984 Tottenham Hotspur (England)	1999 Parma (Italy)
1972 Tottenham Hotspur (England)	1985 Real Madrid (Spain)	

Copa Libertadores

Contested annually since the 1955-56 season by the league champions of South America's football union.

Multiple winners: Independiente (7); Peñarol (5); Estudiantes and Nacional-Uruguay (3); Boca Juniors, Cruzeiro, Gremio, Olimpia, River Plate, Santos and São Paulo (2).

Year	Year	Year
1960 Peñarol (Uruguay)	1967 Racing Club (Argentina)	1974 Independiente (Argentina)
1961 Peñarol (Uruguay)	1968 Estudiantes de la Plata (Argentina)	1975 Independiente (Argentina)
1962 Santos (Brazil)	1969 Estudiantes de la Plata (Argentina)	1976 Cruzeiro (Brazil)
1963 Santos (Brazil)		1977 Boca Juniors (Argentina)
1964 Independiente (Argentina)	1970 Estudiantes de la Plata (Argentina)	1978 Boca Juniors (Argentina)
1965 Independiente (Argentina)	1971 Nacional (Uruguay)	1979 Olimpia (Paraguay)
1966 Peñarol (Uruguay)	1972 Independiente (Argentina)	
	1973 Independiente (Argentina)	1980 Nacional (Uruguay)

Year		Year		Year	
1981	Flamengo (Brazil)	1988	Nacional (Uruguay)	1995	Gremio (Brazil)
1982	Peñarol (Uruguay)	1989	Nacional Medellin (Colombia)	1996	River Plate (Argentina)
1983	Gremio (Brazil)	1990	Olimpia (Paraguay)	1997	Cruzeiro (Brazil)
1984	Independiente (Argentina)	1991	Colo Colo (Chile)	1998	Vasco da Gama (Brazil)
1985	Argentinos Jrs. (Argentina)	1992	São Paulo (Brazil)	1999	Palmeiras (Brazil)
1986	River Plate (Argentina)	1993	São Paulo (Brazil)		
1987	Peñarol (Uruguay)	1994	Velez Sarsfield (Argentina)		

Annual Awards
World Player of the Year

Presented by FIFA, the European Sports Magazine Association (ESM) and Adidas, the sports equipment manufacturer, since 1991. Winners are selected by national team coaches from around the world.

Year		Nat'l Team	Year		Nat'l Team
1991	Lothar Matthäus, Inter Milan	Germany	1995	George Weah, AC Milan	Liberia
1992	Marco Van Basten, AC Milan	Holland	1996	Ronaldo, Barcelona	Brazil
1993	Roberto Baggio, Juventus	Italy	1997	Ronaldo, Inter Milan	Brazil
1994	Romario, Barcelona	Brazil	1998	Zinedine Zidane, Juventus	France

European Player of the Year

Officially, the "Ballon d'Or" and presented by *France Football* magazine since 1956. Candidates are limited to European players in European leagues and winners are selected by a panel of 49 European soccer journalists.

Multiple winners: Johan Cruyff, Michel Platini and Marco Van Basten (3); Franz Beckenbauer, Alfredo di Stéfano, Kevin Keegan and Karl-Heinz Rummenigge (2).

Year		Nat'l Team	Year		Nat'l Team
1956	Stanley Matthews, Blackpool	England	1978	Kevin Keegan, SV Hamburg	England
1957	Alfredo di Stéfano, Real Madrid	Arg./Spain	1979	Kevin Keegan, SV Hamburg	England
1958	Raymond Kopa, Real Madrid	France	1980	K.H. Rummenigge, Bayern Munich	W. Ger.
1959	Alfredo di Stéfano, Real Madrid	Arg./Spain	1981	K.H. Rummenigge, Bayern Munich	W. Ger.
1960	Luis Suarez, Barcelona	Spain	1982	Paolo Rossi, Juventus	Italy
1961	Enrique Sivori, Juventus	Arg./Italy	1983	Michel Platini, Juventus	France
1962	Josef Masopust, Dukla Prague	Czech.	1984	Michel Platini, Juventus	France
1963	Lev Yashin, Dinamo Moscow	Soviet Union	1985	Michel Platini, Juventus	France
1964	Denis Law, Manchester United	Scotland	1986	Igor Belanov, Dinamo Kiev	Soviet Union
1965	Eusébio, Benfica	Portugal	1987	Ruud Gullit, AC Milan	Holland
1966	Bobby Charlton, Manchester United	England	1988	Marco Van Basten, AC Milan	Holland
1967	Florian Albert, Ferencvaros	Hungary	1989	Marco Van Basten, AC Milan	Holland
1968	George Best, Manchester United	No. Ireland	1990	Lothar Matthäus, Inter Milan	W. Ger.
1969	Gianni Rivera, AC Milan	Italy	1991	Jean-Pierre Papin, Marseille	France
1970	Gerd Müller, Bayern Munich	W. Ger.	1992	Marco Van Basten, AC Milan	Holland
1971	Johan Cruyff, Ajax Amsterdam	Holland	1993	Roberto Baggio, Juventus	Italy
1972	Franz Beckenbauer, Bayern Munich	W. Ger.	1994	Hristo Stoitchkov, Barcelona	Bulgaria
1973	Johan Cruyff, Barcelona	Holland	1995	George Weah, AC Milan	Liberia
1974	Johan Cruyff, Barcelona	Holland	1996	Matthias Sammer, Bor. Dortmund	Germany
1975	Oleg Blokhin, Dinamo Kiev	Soviet Union	1997	Ronaldo, Inter Milan	Brazil
1976	Franz Beckenbauer, Bayern Munich	W. Ger.	1998	Zinedine Zidane, Juventus	France
1977	Allan Simonsen, B. Mönchengladbach	Denmark			

South American Player of the Year

Presented by El Pais of Uruguay since 1971. Candidates are limited to South American players in South American leagues and winners are selected by a panel of 80 Latin American sports editors.

Multiple winners: Elias Figueroa and Zico (3); Enzo Francescoli, Diego Maradona and Carlos Valderrama (2).

Year		Nat'l Team	Year		Nat'l Team
1971	Tostao, Cruzeiro	Brazil	1986	Antonio Alzamendi, River Plate	Uruguay
1972	Teofilo Cubillas, Alianza Lima	Peru	1987	Carlos Valderrama, Deportivo Cali	Colombia
1973	Pelé, Santos	Brazil	1988	Ruben Paz, Racing Buenos Aires	Uruguay
1974	Elias Figueroa, Internacional	Chile	1989	Bebeto, Vasco da Gama	Brazil
1975	Elias Figueroa, Internacional	Chile	1990	Raul Amarilla, Olimpia	Paraguay
1976	Elias Figueroa, Internacional	Chile	1991	Oscar Ruggeri, Velez Sarsfield	Argentina
1977	Zico, Flamengo	Brazil	1992	Rai, Sao Paulo	Brazil
1978	Mario Kempes, Valencia	Argentina	1993	Carlos Valderrama, Atl. Junior	Colombia
1979	Diego Maradona, Argentinos Juniors	Argentina	1994	Cafu, Sao Paulo	Brazil
1980	Diego Maradona, Boca Juniors	Argentina	1995	Enzo Francescoli, River Plate	Uruguay
1981	Zico, Flamengo	Brazil	1996	Jose Luis Chilavert, Velez Sarsfield	Paraguay
1982	Zico, Flamengo	Brazil	1997	Marcelo Salas, River Plate	Chile
1983	Socrates, Corinthians	Brazil	1998	Martin Palermo, Boca Juniors	Argentina
1984	Enzo Francescoli, River Plate	Uruguay			
1985	Julio Cesar Romero, Fluminense	Paraguay			

African Player of the Year

Officially, the African "Ballon d'Or" and presented by *France Football* magazine since 1970. All African players are eligible for the award and winners are selected by a panel of 52 African soccer journalists.

Multiple winners: George Weah (4); Abedi Pelé (3); Roger Milla and Thomas N'Kono (2).

Year	Year	Year
1970 Salif Keita, Mali	1980 Jean Manga Onguene, Cameroon	1989 George Weah, Liberia
1971 Ibrahim Sunday, Ghana	1981 Lakhdar Belloumi, Algeria	1990 Roger Milla, Cameroon
1972 Cherif Souleymane, Guinea	1982 Thomas N'Kono, Cameroon	1991 Abedi Pelé, Ghana
1973 Tshimimu Bwanga, Zaire	1983 Mahmoud Al-Khatib, Egypt	1992 Abedi Pelé, Ghana
1974 Paul Moukila, Congo	1984 Theophile Abega, Cameroon	1993 Abedi Pelé, Ghana
1975 Ahmed Faras, Morocco	1985 Mohamed Timoumi, Morocco	1994 George Weah, Liberia
1976 Roger Milla, Cameroon	1986 Badou Zaki, Morocco	1995 George Weah, Liberia
1977 Dhiab Tarak, Tunisia	1987 Rabah Madjer, Algeria	1996 George Weah, Liberia
1978 Abdul Razak, Ghana	1988 Kalusha Bwalya, Zambia	1997 Victor Ikpeba, Nigeria
1979 Thomas N'Kono, Cameroon		1998 Mustapha Hadji, Morocco

U.S. Player of the Year

Presented by Honda and the Spanish-speaking radio show "Futbol de Primera" since 1991. Candidates are limited to American players who have played with the U.S. National Team and winners are selected by a panel of U.S. soccer journalists.

Multiple winner: Eric Wynalda (2).

Year	Year	Year	Year
1991 Hugo Perez	1993 Thomas Dooley	1995 Alexi Lalas	1997 Eddie Pope
1992 Eric Wynalda	1994 Marcelo Balboa	1996 Eric Wynalda	1998 Cobi Jones

U.S. PRO LEAGUES

OUTDOOR

Major League Soccer

Sanctioned by U.S. Soccer and FIFA, the international soccer federation. MLS was founded on the heels of the successful 1994 World Cup tournament hosted by the United States and it remains the only FIFA-sanctioned division I outdoor league in the United States. The MLS title game is known as the MLS Cup.

Multiple Winner: D.C. United (2).

MLS Cup

Year	Winner	Head Coach	Score	Loser	Head Coach	Site
1996	D.C. United	Bruce Arena	3-2	Los Angeles Galaxy	Lothar Osiander	Foxboro, Mass.
1997	D.C. United	Bruce Arena	2-1	Colorado Rapids	Glen Myernick	Washington, D.C.
1998	Chicago Fire	Bob Bradley	2-0	D.C. United	Bruce Arena	Pasadena, Calif.

MLS Cup '96
D.C. United, 3-2 (OT)

Oct. 20 at Foxboro Stadium, Foxboro, Mass.
Attendance: 34,643

	1	2	OT	
Los Angeles Galaxy	1	1	0	—2
D.C. United	0	2	1	—3

First Half: LA—Eduardo Hurtado (Mauricio Cienfuegos), 5th minute.
Second Half: LA—Chris Armas (unassisted), 56th; DC—Tony Sanneh (Marco Etcheverry), 73rd; DC—Shawn Medved (unassisted), 82nd.
Overtime: DC—Eddie Pope (Etcheverry), 94th.
MVP: Marco Etcheverry, D.C. United, Midfielder

MLS Cup '97
D.C. United, 2-1

Oct. 26 at RFK Stadium, Washington, D.C.
Attendance: 57,431

	1	2	
Colorado Rapids	0	1	—1
D.C. United	1	1	—2

First Half: DC—Jaime Moreno (Tony Sanneh, David Vaudreuil), 37th minute.
Second Half: DC—Sanneh (John Harkes, Richie Williams), 68th; COL—Adrian Paz (David Patino, Matt Kmosko), 75th.
MVP: Jaime Moreno, D.C. United, Forward

MLS Cup '98
Chicago Fire, 2-0

Oct. 25 at the Rose Bowl, Pasadena, Calif.
Attendance: 51,350

	1	2	
D.C. United	0	0	—0
Chicago	2	0	—2

First Half: CHI—Jerzy Podbrozny (Peter Nowak, Ante Razov), 29th minute; CHI—Diego Gutierrez (Nowak), 45th.
MVP: Nowak, Chicago, Midfielder

Regular Season

Most Valuable Player

1996	Carlos Valderrama, Tampa Bay
1997	Preki, Kansas City
1998	Marco Etcheverry, D.C.

Leading Scorer	G	A	Pts
1996 Roy Lassiter, Tampa Bay	27	4	58
1997 Preki, Kansas City	12	17	41
1998 Stern John, Columbus	26	5	57

National Professional Soccer League (1967)

Not sanctioned by FIFA, the international soccer federation. The NPSL recruited individual players to fill the rosters of its 10 teams. The league lasted only one season.

	Playoff Final			**Regular Season**			
Year	Winner	Scores	Loser	Leading Scorer	G	A	Pts
1967	Oakland Clippers	0-1, 4-1	Baltimore Bays	Yanko Daucik, Toronto	20	8	48

United Soccer Association (1967)

Sanctioned by FIFA. Originally called the North American Soccer League, it became the USA to avoid being confused with the National Professional Soccer League (see above). Instead of recruiting individual players, the USA imported 12 entire teams from Europe to represent its 12 franchises. It, too, only lasted a season. The league champion Los Angeles Wolves were actually Wolverhampton of England and the runner-up Washington Whips were Aberdeen of Scotland.

	Playoff Final			**Regular Season**			
Year	Winner	Score	Loser	Leading Scorer	G	A	Pts
1967	Los Angeles Wolves	6-5 (OT)	Washington Whips	Roberto Boninsegna, Chicago	10	1	21

North American Soccer League (1968-84)

The NPSL and USA merged to form the NASL in 1968 and the new league lasted through 1984. The NASL championship was known as the Soccer Bowl from 1975-84. One game decided the NASL title every year but five. There were no playoffs in 1969; a two-game/aggregate goals format was used in 1968 and '70; and a best-of-three games format was used in 1971 and '84; (*) indicates overtime and (†) indicates game decided by shootout.

Multiple winners: NY Cosmos (5); Chicago (2).

	Playoff Final			**Regular Season**			
Year	Winner	Score(s)	Loser	Leading Scorer	G	A	Pts
1968	Atlanta Chiefs	0-0,3-0	San Diego Toros	John Kowalik, Chicago	30	9	69
1969	Kansas City Spurs	No game	Atlanta Chiefs	Kaiser Motaung, Atlanta	16	4	36
1970	Rochester Lancers	3-0,1-3	Washington Darts	Kirk Apostolidis, Dallas	16	3	35
1971	Dallas Tornado	1-2*,4-1,2-0	Atlanta Chiefs	Carlos Metidieri, Rochester	19	8	46
1972	New York Cosmos	2-1	St. Louis Stars	Randy Horton, New York	9	4	22
1973	Philadelphia Atoms	2-0	Dallas Tornado	Kyle Rote Jr., Dallas	10	10	30
1974	Los Angeles Aztecs	3-3†	Miami Toros	Paul Child, San Jose	15	6	36
1975	Tampa Bay Rowdies	2-0	Portland Timbers	Steve David, Miami	23	6	52
1976	Toronto Metros	3-0	Minnesota Kicks	Giorgio Chinaglia, New York............	19	11	49
1977	New York Cosmos	2-1	Seattle Sounders	Steve David, Los Angeles...............	26	6	58
1978	New York Cosmos	3-1	Tampa Bay Rowdies	Giorgio Chinaglia, New York............	34	11	79
1979	Vancouver Whitecaps	2-1	Tampa Bay Rowdies	Oscar Fabbiani, Tampa Bay.............	25	8	58
1980	New York Cosmos	3-0	Ft. Laud. Strikers	Giorgio Chinaglia, New York............	32	13	77
1981	Chicago Sting	0-0†	New York Cosmos	Giorgio Chinaglia, New York............	29	16	74
1982	New York Cosmos	1-0	Seattle Sounders	Giorgio Chinaglia, New York............	20	15	55
1983	Tulsa Roughnecks	2-0	Toronto Blizzard	Roberto Cabanas, New York	25	16	66
1984	Chicago Sting	2-1,3-2	Toronto Blizzard	Steve Zungul, Golden Bay...............	20	10	50

Note: In 1969, Kansas City won the NASL regular season championship with 110 points to 109 for Atlanta. There were no playoffs.

Regular Season MVP

Regular season Most Valuable Player as designated by the NASL.

Multiple winner: Carlos Metidieri (2).

Year	Year	Year
1967 Rueben Navarro, Phila (NPSL)	1973 Warren Archibald, Miami	1979 Johan Cruyff, Los Angeles
1968 John Kowalik, Chicago	1974 Peter Silvester, Baltimore	1980 Roger Davies, Seattle
1969 Cirilio Fernandez, KC	1975 Steve David, Miami	1981 Giorgio Chinaglia, New York
1970 Carlos Metidieri, Rochester	1976 Pelé, New York	1982 Peter Ward, Seattle
1971 Carlos Metidieri, Rochester	1977 Franz Beckenbauer, New York	1983 Roberto Cabanas, New York
1972 Randy Horton, New York	1978 Mike Flanagan, New England	1984 Steve Zungul, Golden Bay

A-League (American Professional Soccer League)

The American Professional Soccer League was formed in 1990 with the merger of the Western Soccer League and the New American Soccer League. The APSL was officially sanctioned as an outdoor pro league in 1992 and changed its name to the A-League in 1995.

Multiple winner: Colorado and Seattle (2).

Year	Year	Year
1990 Maryland Bays	1994 Montreal Impact	1998 Rochester Rhinos
1991 SF Bay Blackhawks	1995 Seattle Sounders	
1992 Colorado Foxes	1996 Seattle Sounders	
1993 Colorado Foxes	1997 Milwaukee Rampage	

INDOOR
Major Soccer League (1978-92)

Originally the Major Indoor Soccer League from 1978-79 season through 1989-90. The MISL championship was decided by one game in 1980 and 1981; a best-of-three games series in 1979, best-of-five games in 1982 and 1983; and best-of-seven games since 1984. The MSL folded after the 1991-92 season.

Multiple winners: San Diego (8); New York (4).

	Playoff Final			Regular Season			
Year	Winner	Series	Loser	Leading Scorer	G	A	Pts
1979	New York Arrows	2-0 (WW)	Philadelphia	Fred Grgurev, Philadelphia	46	28	74
1980	New York Arrows	7-4 (1 game)	Houston	Steve Zungul, New York	90	46	136
1981	New York Arrows	6-5 (1 game)	St. Louis	Steve Zungul, New York	108	44	152
1982	New York Arrows	3-2 (LWWLW)	St. Louis	Steve Zungul, New York	103	60	163
1983	San Diego Sockers	3-2 (WWLLW)	Baltimore	Steve Zungul, NY/Golden Bay	75	47	122
1984	Baltimore Blast	4-1 (LWWWW)	St. Louis	Stan Stamenkovic, Baltimore	34	63	97
1985	San Diego Sockers	4-1 (WWLWW)	Baltimore	Steve Zungul, San Diego	68	68	136
1986	San Diego Sockers	4-3 (WLLLWWW)	Minnesota	Steve Zungul, Tacoma	55	60	115
1987	Dallas Sidekicks	4-3 (LLWWLWW)	Tacoma	Tatu, Dallas	73	38	111
1988	San Diego Sockers	4-0	Cleveland	Eric Rasmussen, Wichita	55	57	112
1989	San Diego Sockers	4-3 (LWWWLLW)	Baltimore	Preki, Tacoma	51	53	104
1990	San Diego Sockers	4-2 (LWWWLW)	Baltimore	Tatu, Dallas	64	49	113
1991	San Diego Sockers	4-2 (WLWLWW)	Cleveland	Tatu, Dallas	78	66	144
1992	San Diego Sockers	4-2 (WWWLLW)	Dallas	Zoran Karic, Cleveland	39	63	102

Playoff MVPs

MSL playoff Most Valuable Players, selected by a panel of soccer media covering the playoffs.

Multiple winners: Zungul (4); Quinn (2).

Regular Season MVPs

MSL regular season Most Valuable Players, selected by a panel of soccer media from every city in the league.

Multiple winner: Zungul (6); Nogueira and Tatu (2).

Year		Year	
1979	Shep Messing, NY	1986	Brian Quinn, SD
1980	Steve Zungul, NY	1987	Tatu, Dallas
1981	Steve Zungul, NY	1988	Hugo Perez, SD
1982	Steve Zungul, NY	1989	Victor Nogueira, SD
1983	Juli Veee, SD	1990	Brian Quinn, SD
1984	Scott Manning, Bal.	1991	Ben Collins, SD
1985	Steve Zungul, SD	1992	Thompson Usiyan, SD

Year		Year	
1979	Steve Zungul, NY	1986	Steve Zungul, SD/Tac.
1980	Steve Zungul, NY	1987	Tatu, Dallas
1981	Steve Zungul, NY	1988	Erik Rasmussen, Wich.
1982	Steve Zungul, NY	1989	Preki, Tacoma
	& Stan Terlecki, Pit.	1990	Tatu, Dallas
1983	Alan Mayer, SD	1991	Victor Nogueira, SD
1984	Stan Stamenkovic, Bal.	1992	Victor Nogueira, SD
1985	Steve Zungul, SD		

NASL Indoor Champions (1980-84)

The North American Soccer League started an indoor league in the fall of 1979. The indoor NASL, which featured many of the same teams and players who played in the outdoor NASL, crowned champions from 1980-82 before suspending play. It was revived for the 1983-84 indoor season but folded for good in 1984. The NASL held indoor tournaments in 1975 (San Jose Earthquakes won) and 1976 (Tampa Bay Rowdies won) before the indoor league was started.

Multiple winners: San Diego (2).

Year		Year		Year		Year	
1980	Tampa Bay Rowdies	1982	San Diego Sockers	1983	Play suspended	1984	San Diego Sockers
1981	Edmonton Drillers						

National Professional Soccer League

The winter indoor NPSL began as the American Indoor Soccer Association in 1984-85, then changed its name in 1989-90.

Multiple winner: Canton (5); Cleveland (3); Kansas City (2).

Year		Year		Year		Year	
1985	Canton (OH) Invaders	1989	Canton Invaders	1993	Kansas City Attack	1997	Kansas City Attack
1986	Canton Invaders	1990	Canton Invaders	1994	Cleveland Crunch	1998	Milwaukee Wave
1987	Louisville Thunder	1991	Chicago Power	1995	St. Louis Ambush	1999	Cleveland Crunch
1988	Canton Invaders	1992	Detroit Rockers	1996	Cleveland Crunch		

Continental Indoor Soccer League (1993-97)

The summer indoor CISL played its first season in 1993 and folded following the 1997 season.

Multiple winners: Monterrey (2).

Year		Year		Year		Year	
1993	Dallas Sidekicks	1995	Monterrey La Raza	1996	Monterrey La Raza	1997	Seattle Seadogs
1994	Las Vegas Dustdevils						

U.S. COLLEGES

NCAA Men's Division I Champions

NCAA Division I champions since the first title was contested in 1959. The championship has been shared three times—in 1967, 1968 and 1989. There was a playoff for third place from 1974-81.

Multiple winners: Saint Louis (10); San Francisco and Virginia (5); Indiana (4); UCLA (3); Clemson, Howard and Michigan St. (2).

Year	Winner	Head Coach	Score	Runner-up	Host/Site	Semifinalists
1959	Saint Louis	Bob Guelker	5-2	Bridgeport	UConn	West Chester, CCNY
1960	Saint Louis	Bob Guelker	3-2	Maryland	Brooklyn	West Chester, UConn
1961	West Chester	Mel Lorback	2-0	Saint Louis	Saint Louis	Bridgeport, Rutgers
1962	Saint Louis	Bob Guelker	4-3	Maryland	Saint Louis	Mich. St., Springfield
1963	Saint Louis	Bob Guelker	3-0	Navy	Rutgers	Army, Maryland
1964	Navy	F.H. Warner	1-0	Michigan St.	Brown	Army, Saint Louis
1965	Saint Louis	Bob Guelker	1-0	Michigan St.	Saint Louis	Army, Navy
1966	San Francisco	Steve Negoesco	5-2	LIU-Brooklyn	California	Army, Mich. St.
1967-a	Michigan St. & Saint Louis	Gene Kenney Harry Keough	0-0	–	Saint Louis	LIU-Bklyn, Navy
1968-b	Michigan St. & Maryland	Gene Kenney Doyle Royal	2-2 (2 OT)	–	Ga. Tech	Brown, San Jose St.
1969	Saint Louis	Harry Keough	4-0	San Francisco	San Jose St.	Harvard, Maryland
1970	Saint Louis	Harry Keough	1-0	UCLA	SIU-Ed'sville	Hartwick, Howard
1971-c	Howard	Lincoln Phillips	3-2	Saint Louis	Miami	Harvard, San Fran.
1972	Saint Louis	Harry Keough	4-2	UCLA	Miami	Cornell, Howard
1973	Saint Louis	Harry Keough	2-1 (OT)	UCLA	Miami	Brown, Clemson

Year	Winner	Head Coach	Score	Runner-up	Host/Site	Third Place
1974	Howard	Lincoln Phillips	2-1 (4OT)	Saint Louis	Saint Louis	Hartwick 3, UCLA 1
1975	San Francisco	Steve Negoesco	4-0	SIU-Ed'sville	SIU-Ed'sville	Brown 2, Howard 0
1976	San Francisco	Steve Negoesco	1-0	Indiana	Penn	Hartwick 4, Clemson 3
1977	Hartwick	Jim Lennox	2-1	San Francisco	California	SIU-Ed'sville 3, Brown 2
1978-d	San Francisco	Steve Negoesco	4-3 (OT)	Indiana	Tampa	Clemson 6, Phi. Textile 2
1979	SIU-Ed'sville	Bob Guelker	3-2	Clemson	Tampa	Penn St. 2, Columbia 1
1980	San Francisco	Steve Negoesco	4-3 (OT)	Indiana	Tampa	Ala. A&M 2, Hartwick 0
1981	Connecticut	Joe Morrone	2-1 (OT)	Alabama A&M	Stanford	East. Ill. 4, Phi. Textile 2

Year	Winner	Head Coach	Score	Runner-up	Host/Site	Semifinalists
1982	Indiana	Jerry Yeagley	2-1 (8 OT)	Duke	Ft. Lauderdale	UConn, SIU-Ed'sville
1983	Indiana	Jerry Yeagley	1-0 (2 OT)	Columbia	Ft. Lauderdale	UConn, Virginia
1984	Clemson	I.M. Ibrahim	2-1	Indiana	Seattle	Hartwick, UCLA
1985	UCLA	Sigi Schmid	1-0 (8 OT)	American	Seattle	Evansville, Hartwick
1986	Duke	John Rennie	1-0	Akron	Tacoma	Fresno St., Harvard
1987	Clemson	I.M. Ibrahim	2-0	San Diego St.	Clemson	Harvard, N. Carolina
1988	Indiana	Jerry Yeagley	1-0	Howard	Indiana	Portland, S. Carolina
1989-e	Santa Clara & Virginia	Steve Sampson Bruce Arena	1-1 (2 OT)	–	Rutgers	Indiana, Rutgers
1990-f	UCLA	Sigi Schmid	0-0 (PKs)	Rutgers	South Fla.	Evansville, N.C. State
1991-g	Virginia	Bruce Arena	0-0 (PKs)	Santa Clara	Tampa	Indiana, Saint Louis
1992	Virginia	Bruce Arena	2-0	San Diego	Davidson	Davidson, Duke
1993	Virginia	Bruce Arena	2-0	South Carolina	Davidson	CS-Fullerton, Princeton
1994	Virginia	Bruce Arena	1-0	Indiana	Davidson	Rutgers, UCLA
1995	Wisconsin	Jim Launder	2-0	Duke	Richmond	Portland, Virginia
1996	St. John's	Dave Masur	4-1	Fla. International	Richmond	Creighton, NC-Charlotte
1997	UCLA	Sigi Schmid	2-0	Virginia	Richmond	Indiana, Saint Louis
1998	Indiana	Jerry Yeagley	3-1	Stanford	Richmond	Maryland, Santa Clara

a–game declared a draw due to inclement weather after regulation time; **b**–game declared a draw after two overtimes; **c**–Howard vacated title for using ineligible player; **d**–San Francisco vacated title for using ineligible player; **e**–game declared a draw due to inclement weather after two overtimes. **f**–UCLA wins on penalty kicks (4-3) after four overtimes; **g**–Virginia wins on penalty kicks (3-1) after four overtimes.

Women's NCAA Division I Champions

NCAA Division I women's champions since the first tournament was contested in 1982.

Multiple winner: North Carolina (14).

Year	Winner	Score	Runner-up	Year	Winner	Score	Runner-up
1982	North Carolina	2-0	Central Florida	1991	North Carolina	3-1	Wisconsin
1983	North Carolina	4-0	George Mason	1992	North Carolina	9-1	Duke
1984	North Carolina	2-0	Connecticut	1993	North Carolina	6-0	George Mason
1985	George Mason	2-0	North Carolina	1994	North Carolina	5-0	Notre Dame
1986	North Carolina	2-0	Colorado College	1995	Notre Dame	1-0 (3OT)	Portland
1987	North Carolina	1-0	Massachusetts	1996	North Carolina	1-0 (2OT)	Notre Dame
1988	North Carolina	4-1	N.C. State	1997	North Carolina	2-0	Connecticut
1989	North Carolina	2-0	Colorado College	1998	Florida	1-0	North Carolina
1990	North Carolina	6-0	Connecticut				

Annual Awards
MEN
Hermann Trophy

College Player of the Year. Voted on by Division I college coaches and selected sportswriters and first presented in 1967 in the name of Robert Hermann, one of the founders of the North American Soccer League. **Multiple winners:** Mike Fisher, Mike Seerey, Ken Snow and Al Trost (2).

Year	Year	Year
1967 Dov Markus, LIU	1978 Angelo DiBernardo, Indiana	1989 Tony Meola, Virginia
1968 Manuel Hernandez, San Jose St.	1979 Jim Stamatis, Penn St.	1990 Ken Snow, Indiana
1969 Al Trost, Saint Louis	1980 Joe Morrone, Jr. UConn	1991 Alexi Lalas, Rutgers
1970 Al Trost, Saint Louis	1981 Armando Betancourt, Indiana	1992 Brad Friedel, UCLA
1971 Mike Seerey, Saint Louis	1982 Joe Ulrich, Duke	1993 Claudio Reyna, Virginia
1972 Mike Seerey, Saint Louis	1983 Mike Jeffries, Duke	1994 Brian Maisonneuve, Indiana
1973 Dan Counce, Saint Louis	1984 Amr Aly, Columbia	1995 Mike Fisher, Virginia
1974 Farrukh Quraishi, Oneonta St.	1985 Tom Kain, Duke	1996 Mike Fisher, Virginia
1975 Steve Ralbovsky, Brown	1986 John Kerr, Duke	1997 Johnny Torres, Creighton
1976 Glenn Myernick, Hartwick	1987 Bruce Murray, Clemson	1998 Wojtek Krakowiak, Clemson
1977 Billy Gazonas, Hartwick	1988 Ken Snow, Indiana	

Missouri Athletic Club Award

College Player of the Year. Voted on by men's team coaches around the country from Division I to junior college level and first presented in 1986 by the Missouri Athletic Club of St. Louis. **Multiple winner:** Claudio Reyna and Ken Snow (2).

Year	Year	Year
1986 John Kerr, Duke	1991 Alexi Lalas, Rutgers	1996 Mike Fisher, Virginia
1987 John Harkes, Virginia	1992 Claudio Reyna, Virginia	1997 Johnny Torres, Creighton
1988 Ken Snow, Indiana	1993 Claudio Reyna, Virginia	1998 Jay Heaps, Duke
1989 Tony Meola, Virginia	1994 Todd Yeagley, Indiana	
1990 Ken Snow, Indiana	1995 Matt McKeon, St. Louis	

Coach of the Year

Men's Coach of the Year. Voted on by the National Soccer Coaches Association of America. **Multiple winner:** J. Yeagley (4).

Year	Year	Year
1973 Robert Guelker, SIU-Edwardsville	1982 John Rennie, Duke	1991 Mitch Murray, Santa Clara
1974 Jack MacKenzie, Quincy College	1983 Dieter Ficken, Columbia	1992 Charles Slagle, Davidson
1975 Paul Reinhardt, Vermont	1984 James Lennox, Hartwick	1993 Bob Bradley, Princeton
1976 Jerry Yeagley, Indiana	1985 Peter Mehlert, American	1994 Jerry Yeagley, Indiana
1977 Klass Deboer, Cleveland St.	1986 Steve Parker, Akron	1995 Jim Launder, Wisconsin
1978 Cliff McCrath, Seattle Pacific	1987 Anson Dorrance, N. Carolina	1996 Dave Masur, St. John's
1979 Walter Bahr, Penn St.	1988 Keith Tucker, Howard	1997 Sigi Schmid, UCLA
1980 Jerry Yeagley, Indiana	1989 Steve Sampson, Santa Clara	1998 Jerry Yeagley, Indiana
1981 Schellas Hyndman, E. Illinois	1990 Bob Reasso, Rutgers	

WOMEN
Hermann Trophy

Women's College Player of the year. Voted on by Division I college coaches and selected sportswriters and first presented in 1988 in the name of Robert Hermann, one of the founders of the North American Soccer League. **Multiple winners:** Mia Hamm and Cindy Parlow (2).

Year	Year	Year
1988 Michelle Akers, Central Fla.	1992 Mia Hamm, N. Carolina	1996 Cindy Daws, Notre Dame
1989 Shannon Higgins, N. Carolina	1993 Mia Hamm, N. Carolina	1997 Cindy Parlow, N. Carolina
1990 April Kater, Massachusetts	1994 Tisha Venturini, N. Carolina	1998 Cindy Parlow, N. Carolina
1991 Kristine Lilly, N. Carolina	1995 Shannon McMillan, Portland	

Missouri Athletic Club Award

Women's College Player of the Year. Voted on by women's team coaches around the country from Division I to junior college level and first presented in 1991 by the Missouri Athletic Club of St. Louis. **Multiple winner:** Mia Hamm and Cindy Parlow (2).

Year	Year	Year
1991 Kristine Lilly, N. Carolina	1994 Tisha Venturini, N. Carolina	1997 Cindy Parlow, N. Carolina
1992 Mia Hamm, N. Carolina	1995 Shannon McMillan, Portland	1998 Cindy Parlow, N. Carolina
1993 Mia Hamm, N. Carolina	1996 Cindy Daws, Notre Dame	

Coach of the Year

Women's Coach of the Year. Voted on by the National Soccer Coaches Association of America. **Multiple winners:** Kalenkeni M. Banda, Anson Dorrance and Chris Petrucelli (2).

Year	Year	Year
1982 Anson Dorrance, N. Carolina	1988 Larry Gross, N.C. State	1994 Chris Petrucelli, Norte Dame
1983 David Lombardo, Keene St.	1989 Austin Daniels, Hartford	1995 Chris Petrucelli, Norte Dame
1984 Phillip Picince, Brown	1990 Lauren Gregg, Virginia	1996 John Walker, Nebraska
1985 Kalenkeni M. Banda, UMass	1991 Greg Ryan, Wisc-Madison	1997 Len Tsantiris, UConn
1986 Anson Dorrance, N. Carolina	1992 Bell Hempen, Duke	1998 Becky Burleigh, Florida
1987 Kalenkeni M. Banda, UMass	1993 Jac Cicala, George Mason	

Bowling

The PBA took its act outdoors in 1999 with this tournament held in May at Bryant Park in New York City. Over 1,000 spectators were in attendance.

AP/Wide World Photos

Eddie's Legacy

*PBA founder Eddie Elias died in late 1998
but his influence on the sport remains intact.*

by

Mike Durbin

Late 1998 brought a spirit of sadness to professional bowling when a giant was cut down in its midst. Eddie Elias was that giant. The founder of the Professional Bowlers Association in 1959 and an innovative sports marketing genius, Elias is widely credited with officiating the marriage between professional sports and corporate sponsors. A consummate communicator and faithful friend, he is missed by those of us whose lives he touched. His creativity will never be forgotten.

Perhaps it is that spirit of innovation and creativity that is being summoned today, as professional bowling seeks to market itself to a generation of MTV viewers, while still retaining its Studio One faithful. Two televised championship rounds were held outside this year. The PBA Tour competed in New York City's Bryant Park, and the Senior Tour bowled in a Florida town square, both on specially constructed lanes with fans surrounding them on all sides.

Gone are the days of politely staid spectators clapping quietly, much to the dismay of some senior viewers. Not only that, but younger players have been pictured atop "Super Trucks" in a Texas promotion, while Senior Tour players are competing to win a house in a Florida retirement community.

More 1999 television memories include a buff Kim Adler of the Professional Women's Bowling Association revealing that she trains by trail riding and rock climbing in Nevada, and a silver-haired Dick Weber giving a maturing David Letterman bowling lessons on a Manhattan street corner. It's Eisenhower vs. Clinton. Is Elias watching this generational clash with approval? Undoubtedly.

The tournament promoters are not the only imaginative ones. The top players in each association are as well. Parker Bohn III is an innovator on the men's tour. He was the first to start his own fan club (dubbed "The Bohn

---

Mike Durbin is an analyst for ESPN's bowling coverage and a bowler on the Sr. PBA Tour.

The Eagle has landed. **Dale Eagle** dominated the Senior Tour in 1999, registering four victories and pulling in over $75,000 in the first 11 tournaments of the year.

Zone") and inadvertently was responsible for the tour's adoption of an instant replay rule, when a late and controversial foul line violation was called by the tournament official at the Columbia 300 Open. Bohn, from Jackson, N.J., was given a zero on a spare attempt due to the violation but still went on to win the tournament, one of four 1999 wins as of this writing. With earnings (including incentives) over $195,000, he has already surpassed his 1998 winnings, and leads the average list with a 227.20 over 16 tournaments. Several years ago, Bohn, now 36, expressed his goal of being named Player of the Year at least once in the 1990s. Though Jason Couch and Chris Barnes are outside contenders, Bohn's wish may come true.

On the Senior Tour another creative personality emerged in 1999. Dale Eagle, the 1996 Senior Tour Rookie of the Year, has won a record-tying four tournaments and has dominated the Senior Tour in every category. A crowd pleaser with his popular "Eagle" call (complete with flapping arms), Eagle demonstrated why staying in shape, a 90's concept, is vital for Senior Tour players as well.

After winning just three tournaments in a lengthy yet sporadic career on the PBA Tour, the 53-year-old Eagle has used daily workouts with weights and an amazing ability to focus during competitions to re-create himself as a Senior Tour standout. With over $75,000 in earnings and an average of 226.57 over the first 11 tournaments of the season, Eagle has all but wrapped up Senior Player of the Year honors.

The aforementioned Adler has dominated recent PWBA tournaments.

PBA Tour

It's Bohn. Parker Bohn. The 36-year-old gave his fan club, "The Bohn Zone" something to cheer about in 1999 with three wins through the PBA spring schedule.

By winning back-to-back tournaments in early August and finishing second in the following event, Adler, like Eagle, has also showed why keeping fit is a major asset in bowling. The Las Vegas native was named AMF Bowler of the Month in August and is a front-runner for the PWBA Player of the Year award along with Leanne Barrette and Wendy Macpherson.

The 1999 leaders on the three professional bowling tours have used a spirit of ingenuity and resolve to rise to a level of achievement they had previously not reached. Eddie Elias would be proud.

∎

Mike Durbin's Top Ten Stories from the Year in Bowling

10. **PBA adopts instant replay.** In the final round of the Columbia 300 Open in February, officials go to the video to determine if Parker Bohn III had fouled on a spare attempt. It is determined that he did and he is given a zero.

9. **Tom Baker is elected** to the PBA Hall of Fame. The tour veteran from Buffalo has earned over $1 million in prize money and is finally enshrined in the Hall.

8. **Brian Goebel wins** the PBA Tournament of Champions and the $60,000 first place prize with a 10-pin win over Steve Hoskins.

7. **Steve Jaros shoots** the 13th televised 300 game in history during the championship round of the Chattanooga Open, but due to "technical difficulties," many don't see it.

Twelve-year veteran **Carol Gianotti-Block**, a native of Perth, Australia, became the first international bowler to win the PWBA Player of the Year award at the close of 1998.

6. **PBA pulls the network plug.** After 41 years of commercial network television exposure, the PBA is casting its lot with ESPN.

5. **Carol Gianotti-Block** is named PWBA Player of the Year in 1998 after winning two tournaments and over $150,000 in prize money, the second-highest single-season total in PWBA history. Jody Ellis takes home Rookie of the Year honors.

4. **Walter Ray Williams Jr.** smashes the $200,000 mark once again and is the 1998 PBA Player of the Year. Pete Couture wins the prize on the senior circuit while Chris

Barnes grabs the trophy for PBA Rookie of the Year.

3. **Senior Tournament of Champions.** The Villages retirement community in Florida hosts the Senior Tour's first outdoor final round and offers a brand new, completely furnished home as a bonus to the winner.

2. **PBA takes over** Bryant Park in New York City for its first-ever outdoor event — "The New York City PBA Experience."

1. **PBA founder** Eddie Elias passes away at the age of 69. ■

THE NUMBERS

BAKER THE RECORD-BREAKER

PBA Senior Tour player Dick Baker didn't win the 1999 Boise Senior Open title on July 1, but his performance won't soon be forgotten. Baker rewrote three Senior Tour scoring records en route to a heartbreaking loss to Barry Gurney in the final.

	Baker	Difference (total pins)
9-game total	2,371	+74
18-game total	4,598	+182
42-game total	10,457	+61

THE 2000 ESPN INFORMATION PLEASE SPORTS ALMANAC

B O W L I N G S T A T I S T I C S SEC A

THE SEASON IN REVIEW
1998-1999
PBA • SENIORS • PWBA

PAGE 771

Tournament Results

Winners of stepladder finals in all PBA, Seniors and PWBA tournaments from Oct. 28, 1998, through Sept. 15, 1999; major tournaments in **bold** type.

PBA

Late 1998 Fall Tour

Final	Event	Winner	Earnings	Score	Runner-up
Oct. 28	Bay City Classic	Walter Ray Williams Jr.	$18,000	234-156	Tommy Delutz Jr.
Nov. 4	National Finance Challenge	Walter Ray Williams Jr.	20,000	237-231	Amleto Monacelli
Nov. 11	Brunswick Circuit Pro Bowling Classic	Norm Duke	19,000	245-195	Ryan Shafer
Nov. 21	**The Brunswick World TOC**	Bryan Goebel	60,000	245-235	Steve Hoskins
Dec. 10	Philip Morris Showdown	Walter Ray Williams Jr.	30,000	745-626†	Carol Gianotti-Block
Dec. 13	Philip Morris Mixed Doubles Champ.	Steve Hoskins/ Kim Canady	20,000 (each)	16,240- 15,871†	Parker Bohn III/ Cheryl Daniels

†Scoring in the Philip Morris Showdown and Mixed Doubles events is based on total pins.

1999 Winter/Spring Tour

Final	Event	Winner	Earnings	Score	Runner-up
Jan. 15	National/Senior Doubles	Jason Hurd/ Johnny Petraglia	$17,000 (each)	235-214	Paul Fleming/ Dale Eagle
Jan. 23	Albuquerque Open	Brian Himmler	17,000	228-161	Chris Barnes
Jan. 30	Don Carter PBA Classic	Mike Miller	17,000	232-223	Dave Wodka
Feb. 7	Columbia 300 Open	Parker Bohn III	22,000	225-211	Pete Weber
Feb. 13	Chattanooga Open	Steve Jaros	27,000*	226-224	Parker Bohn III
Feb. 20	Flagship Open	Chris Barnes	17,000	214-197	Rudy Kasimakis
Feb. 27	**PBA National Championship**	Tim Criss	28,000	238-161	Dave Arnold
Apr. 17	Empire State Open	Parker Bohn III	17,000	209-181	Rick Steelsmith
Apr. 24	Johnny Petraglia Open	Doug Kent	26,000	217-190	Rudy Kasimakis
May 1	NYC PBA Experience	Eric Forkel	17,000	243-231	Mark Mosayebi
May 8	**ABC Masters**	Brian Boghosian	40,000	247-231	Parker Bohn III
May 15	**Bayer/Brunswick TPC**	Steve Hoskins	40,000	246-183	Parker Bohn III
May 29	PBA Oregon Open	Chris Barnes	17,000	278-207	Norm Duke
June 5	Showboat Invitational	Parker Bohn III	24,000	241-220	Amleto Monacelli
June 12	Tucson Open	Walter Ray Williams Jr.	17,000	268-233	David Ozio
June 20	National Bowling Stadium Open	Ricky Ward	24,000	240-193	Mike Miller
June 26	ACDelco Classic	Tommy Delutz Jr.	31,000	223-186	Tony Reyes
Aug. 1	**BPAA U.S. Open**	Bob Learn Jr.	35,000	231-215	Jason Couch

*Jaros' earnings include a $10,000 bonus for rolling a 300 in a televised second-round victory over Ricky Ward. It was the 13th televised 300 game in PBA history.
Note: The American Bowling Congress Masters tournament is not a PBA Tour event.

SENIOR PBA

1999 Winter Tour

Final	Event	Winner	Earnings	Score	Runner-up
Jan. 9	ABC Senior Masters	Darrell Storkson	$20,000	225-204	Dale Eagle
Jan. 15	National/Senior Doubles	Jason Hurd/ Johnny Petraglia	17,000 (each)	235-214	Paul Fleming/ Dale Eagle
Jan. 21	Cal Bowl Senior Open	Dale Eagle	7,500	242-177	John Hricsina

1999 Spring/Summer Tour

Final	Event	Winner	Earnings	Score	Runner-up
Mar. 12	Senior World Open	Dale Eagle	$18,000	238-234	Mike Durbin
Apr. 15	Greater Hartford Senior Classic	Roger Workman	8,000	235-208	Gene Stus
June 10	Spokane Senior Open	Dale Eagle	9,000	280-169	Mike Pullin
June 18	Seattle Senior Open	Al Sanford	8,500	218-214	Dale Eagle
June 24	Northwest Senior Classic	Steve Neff	8,500	264-258	Pete Couture
July 1	Boise Senior Open	Barry Gurney	8,000	238-211	Dick Baker
July 8	Northern Calif. Senior Classic	Dale Eagle	7,500	258-248	Gary Mage
July 17	Showboat Senior Open	Vince Range	15,000	244-220	Dick Baker

PWBA
Late 1998 Fall Tour

Final	Event	Winner	Earnings	Score	Runner-up
Nov. 21	**Sam's Town Invitational**..........	Julie Gardner	$35,000	268-226	Dede Davidson
Dec. 10	Philip Morris Showdown	Walter Ray Williams Jr.	30,000	745-626†	Carol Gianotti-Block
Dec. 13	Philip Morris Mixed Doubles Champ. ..	Kim Canady/	20,000	16,240-	Cheryl Daniels/
		Steve Hoskins	(each)	15,871†	Parker Bohn III

†Scoring in the Philip Morris Showdown and Mixed Doubles is based on total pins.

1999 Winter/Spring Tour

Final	Event	Winner	Earnings	Score	Runner-up
Feb. 11	Greater Atlanta Open	Leanne Barrette	$11,500	256-233	Kim Adler
Feb. 18	Choo-Choo Classic	Lisa Bishop	11,500	215-204	Wendy Macpherson
Feb. 25	Greater Jacksonville Classic	Carolyn Dorin-Ballard	11,500	238-203	Michelle Feldman
Mar. 4	Greater Orlando Classic	Liz Johnson	11,500	269-180	Leanne Barrette
May 5	Track KO Punch Doubles	Lynda Norry/	11,000	287-236	Kelly Kulik/
		Kim Canady	(each)		Marianne DiRupo
May 12	Omaha Open	Lisa Wagner	11,500	257-199	Kim Canady
May 21	**WIBC Queens**....................	Leanne Barrette	20,000	256-174	Dede Davidson
May 27	St. Clair Classic...................	Wendy Macpherson	11,500	258-180	Leanne Barrette

Note: The Women's International Bowling Congress Queens tournament is not an official PWBA Tour event.

1999 Summer/Fall Tour

Final	Event	Winner	Earnings	Score	Runner-up
Aug. 1	**BPAA U.S. Open**.................	Kim Adler	$35,000	213-195	Lynda Barnes
Aug. 5	Lady Ebonite Classic................	Kim Adler	14,400	235-170	Leanne Barrette
Aug. 12	Storm Challenge	Lisa Wagner	14,400	223-166	Kim Adler
Aug. 19	Clabber Girl Open	Jennifer Swanson	11,500	209-201	Wendy Macpherson
Aug. 26	Hammer Players Championship	Lisa Bishop	16,000	210-156	Tish Johnson

1999 Fall Tour Schedules
PBA

Events: Japan Cup – Tokyo (Sept. 16-19); ACDelco Classic – Virginia Beach, VA (Oct. 2-6); Wichita Open – Wichita, KS (Oct. 8-12); Canandaigua Open – Canandaigua, NY (Oct. 16-20); Greater Detroit Open – Taylor, MI (Oct. 23-27); Bay City Classic – Bay City, MI (Oct. 30-Nov. 3); Indianapolis Open – Indianapolis, IN (Nov. 6-10); **Brunswick World Tournament of Champions** – Overland Park, KS (Nov. 15-19).

SENIOR PBA

Events: Naples Senior Open – Naples, FL (Sept. 25-29); Villages Senior Tournament of Champions – Lady Lake, FL (Oct. 3-7); Senior National Championship – Jackson, MI (Oct. 16-22).

PWBA

Events: Visionary Bowling Products Classic – Lancaster, OH (Sept. 26-30); **AMF Gold Cup** – Mechanicsville, VA (Oct. 2-7); Three Rivers Open – Pittsburg, PA (Oct. 9-14); Brunswick World Open – Lake Zurich, IL (Oct. 16-21); **Sam's Town Invitational** – Las Vegas, NV (Oct. 30-Nov. 6).

1999 Pan-American Games
(Aug. 2-7 in Winnipeg, Manitoba, CAN)

Since bowling has yet to achieve full-medal Olympic status, every four years since 1983 the Pan-American Games has served as the largest international multi-event competition for bowlers. Twelve nations competed in this year's team competition which was based on total pins. Two players from each nation entered the Masters competition, where total pinfalls plus bonus pins decided the medalists.

Masters Men	Total Pins	Men's Team	Total Pins
David Romero, Colombia	3,544	United States.....................	14,798
Michael J. Mullin, United States	3,529	Canada.........................	14,354
Marc H. Doi, Canada	3,518	Mexico.........................	14,157

Masters Women	Total Pins	Women's Team	Total Pins
J.L. Piesczynski, United States	3,328	United States.....................	13,816
Alicia Marcano, Venuzuela.....................	3,327	Colombia........................	13,516
Jennifer Willis, Canada.....................	3,282	Mexico.........................	13,514

Tour Leaders

Official standings for 1998 and unofficial standings for 1999. Note that (TB) indicates Tournaments Bowled; (CR) Championship Rounds as Stepladder Finalist; and (1st) Titles Won.

Final 1998

PBA

Top 10 Money Winners

		TB	CR	1st	Earnings
1	Walter Ray Williams Jr.	26	10	5	$238,225
2	Parker Bohn III	23	6	4	191,780
3	Steve Hoskins	26	6	2	154,105
4	Tim Criss	26	5	1	133,796
5	Norm Duke	24	5	3	106,095
6	Jason Couch	24	2	1	95,030
7	Pete Weber	21	4	1	93,143
8	Amleto Monacelli	21	6	0	86,782
9	Mike Aulby	21	4	1	86,340
10	Steve Jaros	26	2	0	77,270

Top 10 Averages

		TB	Games	Avg
1	Walter Ray Williams Jr.	26	973	226.13
2	Parker Bohn III	23	671	222.56
3	Norm Duke	24	755	222.37
4	Tim Criss	26	868	221.85
5	Amleto Monacelli	21	732	221.32
6	Ryan Shafer	25	851	220.24
	Pete Weber	21	717	220.24
8	Brian Himmler	25	710	219.93
9	Doug Kent	26	891	219.81
10	Steve Hoskins	26	813	219.79

SENIOR PBA

Top 5 Money Winners

		TB	CR	1st	Earnings
1	Pete Couture	12	9	4	$117,300
2	Gary Dickinson	12	6	1	60,950
3	Gene Stus	12	5	2	42,020
4	Mike Durbin	11	7	0	41,610
5	Ron Garr	10	1	0	40,215

Top 5 Averages

		TB	Games	Avg
1	Pete Couture	12	487	226.36
2	Johnny Petraglia	6	212	225.21
3	Gary Dickinson	12	534	225.09
4	Mike Durbin	11	439	224.00
5	Gene Stus	12	458	223.50

PWBA

Top 10 Money Winners

		TB	CR	1st	Earnings
1	Carol Gianotti-Block	23	9	2	$150,350
2	Aleta Sill	23	4	2	122,505
3	Dede Davidson	19	7	1	121,600
4	Carolyn Dorin-Ballard	23	7	2	118,478
5	Kim Adler	23	7	2	101,260
6	Marianne DiRupo	22	6	2	97,955
7	Dana Miller-Mackie	22	4	2	90,863
8	Kim Canady	23	2	1	81,820
9	Anne Marie Duggan	23	5	1	77,220
10	Wendy Macpherson	23	5	1	75,625

Note: Earnings include WIBC Queens.

Top 5 Averages

		TB	Games	Avg
1	Dede Davidson	19	660	217.25
2	Carol Gianotti-Block	23	948	215.81
3	Carolyn Dorin-Ballard	23	912	214.89
4	Marianne DiRupo	22	806	214.17
5	Kim Adler	23	841	213.53

1999 (through Sept. 15)

PBA

Top 10 Money Winners

		TB	CR	1st	Earnings
1	Parker Bohn III	16	7	3	$135,095
2	Chris Barnes	18	5	2	86,665
3	Bob Learn Jr.	18	3	1	72,895
4	Jason Couch	16	6	0	69,740
5	Steve Hoskins	15	2	1	67,660
6	Ricky Ward	13	5	1	67,400
7	Mike Miller	16	2	1	60,775
8	Tim Criss	18	2	1	54,750
9	Tommy Delutz Jr.	18	2	1	54,125
10	Walter Ray Williams Jr.	15	2	1	54,025

Top 10 Averages

		TB	Games	Avg
1	Parker Bohn III	16	533	227.20
2	Ryan Shafer	17	633	225.24
3	Walter Ray Williams Jr.	15	524	225.07
4	Chris Barnes	18	673	224.67
5	Jason Couch	16	633	224.06
6	Norm Duke	16	584	223.55
7	Amleto Monacelli	14	488	223.44
8	Bob Learn Jr.	18	689	223.38
9	Ricky Ward	13	421	223.11
10	Danny Wiseman	18	677	222.80

SENIOR PBA

Top 5 Money Winners

		TB	CR	1st	Earnings
1	Dale Eagle	11	8	4	$75,115
2	Roger Workman	9	3	1	25,380
3	Mike Durbin	11	4	0	24,360
4	Darrell Storkson	8	1	1	24,040
5	Al Sanford	11	2	1	23,965

Top 5 Averages

		TB	Games	Avg
1	Dale Eagle	11	470	226.57
2	Pete Couture	11	419	226.20
3	Dave Soutar	11	450	224.14
4	Ron Winger	11	446	223.12
5	Roger Workman	9	352	222.88

PWBA

Top 10 Money Winners

		TB	CR	1st	Earnings
1	Kim Adler	13	3	2	$76,990
2	Leanne Barrette	13	4	2	69,610
3	Wendy Macpherson	13	1	1	55,325
4	Carolyn Dorin-Ballard	13	1	1	44,760
5	Lisa Bishop	13	2	2	43,140
6	Lynda Barnes	13	1	0	41,510
7	Kim Canady	13	2	1	39,255
8	Lisa Wagner	13	2	2	38,400
9	Jennifer Swanson	12	1	1	34,955
10	Michelle Feldman	13	0	0	32,550

Note: Earnings include WIBC Queens.

Top 5 Averages

		TB	Games	Avg
1	Wendy Macpherson	13	531	217.91
2	Carolyn Dorin-Ballard	13	475	217.15
3	Kim Adler	13	462	216.30
4	Leanne Barrette	13	478	215.84
5	Kim Canady	13	449	215.36

THE 2000 ESPN INFORMATION PLEASE SPORTS ALMANAC — BOWLING STATISTICS — SEC B — THROUGH THE YEARS 1942-1999 CHAMPIONS • AWARDS — PAGE 774

Major Championships
MEN
BPAA U.S. Open

Started in 1941 by the Bowling Proprietors' Association of America, 18 years before the founding of the Professional Bowlers Association. Originally the BPAA All-Star Tournament, it became the U.S. Open in 1971. There were two BPAA All-Star tournaments in 1955, in January and December.

Multiple winners: Don Carter and Dick Weber (4); Dave Husted (3); Del Ballard, Jr., Marshall Holman, Junie McMahon, Connie Schwoegler, Andy Varipapa and Pete Weber (2)

Year		Year		Year		Year	
1942	John Crimmons	1957	Don Carter	1972	Don Johnson	1987	Del Ballard Jr.
1943	Connie Schwoegler	1958	Don Carter	1973	Mike McGrath	1988	Pete Weber
1944	Ned Day	1959	Billy Welu	1974	Larry Laub	1989	Mike Aulby
1945	Buddy Bomar			1975	Steve Neff		
1946	Joe Wilman	1960	Harry Smith	1976	Paul Moser	1990	Ron Palombi Jr.
1947	Andy Varipapa	1961	Bill Tucker	1977	Johnny Petraglia	1991	Pete Weber
1948	Andy Varipapa	1962	Dick Weber	1978	Nelson Burton Jr.	1992	Robert Lawrence
1949	Connie Schwoegler	1963	Dick Weber	1979	Joe Berardi	1993	Del Ballard Jr.
		1964	Bob Strampe			1994	Justin Hromek
1950	Junie McMahon	1965	Dick Weber	1980	Steve Martin	1995	Dave Husted
1951	Dick Hoover	1966	Dick Weber	1981	Marshall Holman	1996	Dave Husted
1952	Junie McMahon	1967	Les Schissler	1982	Dave Husted	1997	Not held
1953	Don Carter	1968	Jim Stefanich	1983	Gary Dickinson	1998	Walter Ray Williams Jr.
1954	Don Carter	1969	Billy Hardwick	1984	Mark Roth	1999	Bob Learn Jr.
1955	Steve Nagy			1985	Marshall Holman		
1956	Bill Lillard	1970	Bobby Cooper	1986	Steve Cook		
		1971	Mike Limongello				

PBA National Championship

The Professional Bowlers Association was formed in 1958 and its first national championship tournament was held in Memphis in 1960. The tournament has been held in Toledo, Ohio, since 1981.

Multiple winners: Earl Anthony (6); Mike Aulby, Dave Davis, Mike McGrath, Pete Weber and Wayne Zahn (2).

Year		Year		Year		Year	
1960	Don Carter	1970	Mike McGrath	1980	Johnny Petraglia	1990	Jim Pencak
1961	Dave Soutar	1971	Mike Limongello	1981	Earl Anthony	1991	Mike Miller
1962	Carmen Salvino	1972	Johnny Guenther	1982	Earl Anthony	1992	Eric Forkel
1963	Billy Hardwick	1973	Earl Anthony	1983	Earl Anthony	1993	Ron Palombi Jr.
1964	Bob Strampe	1974	Earl Anthony	1984	Bob Chamberlain	1994	David Traber
1965	Dave Davis	1975	Earl Anthony	1985	Mike Aulby	1995	Scott Alexander
1966	Wayne Zahn	1976	Paul Colwell	1986	Tom Crites	1996	Butch Soper
1967	Dave Davis	1977	Tommy Hudson	1987	Randy Pedersen	1997	Rick Steelsmith
1968	Wayne Zahn	1978	Warren Nelson	1988	Brian Voss	1998	Pete Weber
1969	Mike McGrath	1979	Mike Aulby	1989	Pete Weber	1999	Tim Criss

Brunswick World Tournament of Champions

Originally the Firestone Tournament of Champions (1965-93), the tournament has also been sponsored by General Tire (1994) and Brunswick Corp. (since 1995). Held annually in Akron, Ohio from 1965-94, the T of C was moved to suburban Chicago in 1995.

Multiple winners: Mike Durbin (3); Earl Anthony, Jim Godman, Marshall Holman and Mark Williams (2).

Year		Year		Year		Year	
1965	Billy Hardwick	1974	Earl Anthony	1983	Joe Berardi	1992	Marc McDowell
1966	Wayne Zahn	1975	Dave Davis	1984	Mike Durbin	1993	George Branham III
1967	Jim Stefanich	1976	Marshall Holman	1985	Mark Williams	1994	Norm Duke
1968	Dave Davis	1977	Mike Berlin	1986	Marshall Holman	1995	Mike Aulby
1969	Jim Godman	1978	Earl Anthony	1987	Pete Weber	1996	Dave D'Entremont
1970	Don Johnson	1979	George Pappas	1988	Mark Williams	1997	John Gant
1971	Johnny Petraglia	1980	Wayne Webb	1989	Del Ballard Jr.	1998	Bryan Goebel
1972	Mike Durbin	1981	Steve Cook	1990	Dave Ferraro		
1973	Jim Godman	1982	Mike Durbin	1991	David Ozio		

ABC Masters Tournament

Sponsored by the American Bowling Congress. The Masters is not a PBA event, but is considered one of the four major tournaments on the men's tour and is open to qualified pros and amateurs.

Multiple winners: Mike Aulby (3); Earl Anthony, Billy Golembiewski, Dick Hoover and Billy Welu (2).

Year		Year		Year		Year	
1951	Lee Jouglard	1964	Billy Welu	1977	Earl Anthony	1990	Chris Warren
1952	Willard Taylor	1965	Billy Welu	1978	Frank Ellenburg	1991	Doug Kent
1953	Rudy Habetler	1966	Bob Strampe	1979	Doug Myers	1992	Ken Johnson
1954	Red Elkins	1967	Lou Scalia	1980	Neil Burton	1993	Norm Duke
1955	Buzz Fazio	1968	Pete Tountas	1981	Randy Lightfoot	1994	Steve Fehr
1956	Dick Hoover	1969	Jim Chestney	1982	Joe Berardi	1995	Mike Aulby
1957	Dick Hoover	1970	Don Glover	1983	Mike Lastowski	1996	Ernie Schlegel
1958	Tom Hennessey	1971	Jim Godman	1984	Earl Anthony	1997	Jason Queen
1959	Ray Bluth	1972	Bill Beach	1985	Steve Wunderlich	1998	Mike Aulby
1960	Billy Golembiewski	1973	Dave Soutar	1986	Mark Fahy	1999	Brian Boghosian
1961	Don Carter	1974	Paul Colwell	1987	Rick Steelsmith		
1962	Billy Golembiewski	1975	Eddie Ressler	1988	Del Ballard Jr.		
1963	Harry Smith	1976	Nelson Burton Jr.	1989	Mike Aulby		

WOMEN

BPAA U.S. Open

Started by the Bowling Proprietors' Association of America in 1949, 11 years before the founding of the Professional Women's Bowling Association. Originally the BPAA Women's All-Star Tournament, it became the U.S. Open in 1971. There were two BPAA All-Star tournaments in 1955, in January and December. Note that (a) indicates amateur.

Multiple winners: Marion Ladewig (8); Donna Adamek, Paula Sperber Carter, Pat Costello, Dotty Fothergill, Dana Miller-Mackie, Aleta Sill and Sylvia Wene (2).

Year		Year		Year		Year	
1949	Marion Ladewig	1961	Phyllis Notaro	1975	Paula Sperber Carter	1988	Lisa Wagner
1950	Marion Ladewig	1962	Shirley Garms	1976	Patty Costello	1989	Robin Romeo
1951	Marion Ladewig	1963	Marion Ladewig	1977	Betty Morris	1990	Dana Miller-Mackie
1952	Marion Ladewig	1964	LaVerne Carter	1978	Donna Adamek	1991	Anne Marie Duggan
1953	Not held	1965	Ann Slattery	1979	Diana Silva	1992	Tish Johnson
1954	Marion Ladewig	1966	Joy Abel	1980	Pat Costello	1993	Dede Davidson
1955	Sylvia Wene	1967	Gloria Simon	1981	Donna Adamek	1994	Aleta Sill
1955	Anita Cantaline	1968	Dotty Fothergill	1982	Shinobu Saitoh	1995	Cheryl Daniels
1956	Marion Ladewig	1969	Dotty Fothergill	1983	Dana Miller	1996	Liz Johnson
1957	Not held	1970	Mary Baker	1984	Karen Ellingsworth	1997	Not held
1958	Merle Matthews	1971	a-Paula Sperber	1985	Pat Mercatanti	1998	Aleta Sill
1959	Marion Ladewig	1972	a-Lorrie Koch	1986	Wendy Macpherson	1999	Kim Adler
1960	Sylvia Wene	1973	Millie Martorella	1987	Carol Norman		
		1974	Pat Costello				

WIBC Queens

Sponsored by the Women's International Bowling Congress, the Queens is a double elimination, match play tournament. It is not a PWBA event, but is open to qualified pros and amateurs. Note that (a) indicates amateur.

Multiple winners: Millie Martorella (3); Donna Adamek, Dotty Fothergill, Aleta Sill and Katsuko Sugimoto (2).

Year		Year		Year		Year	
1961	Janet Harman	1971	Millie Martorella	1981	Katsuko Sugimoto	1991	Dede Davidson
1962	Dorothy Wilkinson	1972	Dotty Fothergill	1982	Katsuko Sugimoto	1992	Cindy Coburn-Carroll
1963	Irene Monterosso	1973	Dotty Fothergill	1983	Aleta Sill	1993	Jan Schmidt
1964	D.D. Jacobson	1974	Judy Soutar	1984	Kazue Inahashi	1994	Anne Marie Duggan
1965	Betty Kuczynski	1975	Cindy Powell	1985	Aleta Sill	1995	Sandra Postma
1966	Judy Lee	1976	Pam Rutherford	1986	Cora Fiebig	1996	Lisa Wagner
1967	Millie Martorella	1977	Dana Stewart	1987	Cathy Almeida	1997	Sandra Jo Odom
1968	Phyllis Massey	1978	Loa Boxberger	1988	Wendy Macpherson	1998	Lynda Norry
1969	Ann Feigel	1979	Donna Adamek	1989	Carol Gianotti	1999	Leanne Barrette
1970	Millie Martorella	1980	Donna Adamek	1990	a-Patty Ann		

Sam's Town Invitational

Originally held in Milwaukee as the Pabst Tournament of Champions, but discontinued after one year (1981). The event was revived in 1984, moved to Las Vegas and renamed the Sam's Town Tournament of Champions. Since then it has been known as the LPBT Tournament of Champions (1985), the Sam's Town National Pro/Am (1986-88) and the Sam's Town Invitational (since 1989).

Multiple winners: Tish Johnson (3); Aleta Sill (2).

Year		Year		Year		Year	
1981	Cindy Coburn	1987	Debbie Bennett	1993	Robin Romeo	1998	Julie Gardner
1982-83	Not held	1988	Donna Adamek	1994	Tish Johnson		
1984	Aleta Sill	1989	Tish Johnson	1995	Michelle Mullen		
1985	Patty Costello	1991	Lorrie Nichols	1996	Carol Gianotti-Block		
1986	Aleta Sill	1992	Tish Johnson	1997	Kim Adler		

Major Championships (Cont.)

WPBA National Championship (1960-1980)

The Women's Professional Bowling Association National Championship tournament was discontinued when the WPBA broke up in 1981. The WPBA changed its name from the Professional Women Bowlers Association (PWBA) in 1978.

Multiple winners: Patty Costello (3); Dotty Fothergill (2).

Year		Year		Year		Year		Year	
1960	Marion Ladewig	1965	Helen Duval	1970	Bobbe North	1975	Pam Buckner	1980	Donna Adamek
1961	Shirley Garms	1966	Judy Lee	1971	Patty Costello	1976	Patty Costello		
1962	Stephanie Balogh	1967	Betty Mivelaz	1972	Patty Costello	1977	Vesma Grinfelds		
1963	Janet Harman	1968	Dotty Fothergill	1973	Betty Morris	1978	Toni Gillard		
1964	Betty Kuczynski	1969	Dotty Fothergill	1974	Pat Costello	1979	Cindy Coburn		

Annual Leaders
Average
PBA Tour

The George Young Memorial Award, named after the late ABC Hall of Fame bowler. Based on at least 16 national PBA tournaments from 1959-78, and at least 400 games of tour competition since 1979.

Multiple winners: Mark Roth (6); Earl Anthony (5); Walter Ray Williams Jr. (4); Marshall Holman (3); Norm Duke, Billy Hardwick, Don Johnson and Wayne Zahn (2).

Year		Avg	Year		Avg	Year		Avg
1962	Don Carter	212.84	1975	Earl Anthony	219.06	1988	Mark Roth	218.04
1963	Bill Hardwick	210.35	1976	Mark Roth	215.97	1989	Pete Weber	215.43
1964	Ray Bluth	210.51	1977	Mark Roth	218.17	1990	Amleto Monacelli	218.16
1965	Dick Weber	211.90	1978	Mark Roth	219.83	1991	Norm Duke	218.21
1966	Wayne Zahn	208.63	1979	Mark Roth	221.66	1992	Dave Ferraro	219.70
1967	Wayne Zahn	212.14	1980	Earl Anthony	218.54	1993	Walter Ray Williams Jr.	222.98
1968	Jim Stefanich	211.90	1981	Mark Roth	216.70	1994	Norm Duke	222.83
1969	Billy Hardwick	212.96	1982	Marshall Holman	216.15	1995	Mike Aulby	225.49
1970	Nelson Burton Jr.	214.91	1983	Earl Anthony	216.65	1996	Walter Ray Williams Jr.	225.37
1971	Don Johnson	213.98	1984	Marshall Holman	213.91	1997	Walter Ray Williams Jr.	222.00
1972	Don Johnson	215.29	1985	Mark Baker	213.72	1998	Walter Ray Williams Jr.	226.13
1973	Earl Anthony	215.80	1986	John Gant	214.38			
1974	Earl Anthony	219.34	1987	Marshall Holman	216.80			

PWBA Tour

The Professional Women's Bowling Association (PWBA) went by the name Ladies Professional Bowling Tour (LPBT) from 1981-1997 and the Women's Professional Bowling Association prior to that. This table is based on at least 282 games of tour competition.

Multiple winners: Leanne Barrette, Nikki Gianulias and Lisa Rathgeber Wagner (3); Anne Marie Duggan, Wendy Macpherson and Aleta Sill (2).

Year		Avg	Year		Avg	Year		Avg
1981	Nikki Gianulias	213.71	1987	Wendy Macpherson	211.11	1993	Tish Johnson	215.39
1982	Nikki Gianulias	210.63	1988	Lisa Wagner	213.02	1994	Anne Marie Duggan	213.47
1983	Lisa Rathgeber	208.50	1989	Lisa Wagner	211.87	1995	Anne Marie Duggan	215.79
1984	Aleta Sill	210.68	1990	Leanne Barrette	211.53	1996	Tammy Turner	215.23
1985	Aleta Sill	211.10	1991	Leanne Barrette	211.48	1997	Wendy Macpherson	214.68
1986	Nikki Gianulias	213.89	1992	Leanne Barrette	211.36	1998	Dede Davidson	217.25

Money Won
PBA Tour

Multiple winners: Earl Anthony (6); Walter Ray Williams Jr. (5); Mark Roth and Dick Weber (4); Mike Aulby (3); Don Carter (2).

Year		Earnings	Year		Earnings	Year		Earnings
1959	Dick Weber	$7,672	1972	Don Johnson	$56,648	1986	Walter Ray Williams Jr.	$145,550
1960	Don Carter	22,525	1973	Don McCune	69,000	1987	Pete Weber	179,516
1961	Dick Weber	26,280	1974	Earl Anthony	99,585	1988	Brian Voss	225,485
1962	Don Carter	49,972	1975	Earl Anthony	107,585	1989	Mike Aulby	298,237
1963	Dick Weber	46,333	1976	Earl Anthony	110,833	1990	Amleto Monacelli	204,775
1964	Bob Strampe	33,592	1977	Mark Roth	105,583	1991	David Ozio	225,585
1965	Dick Weber	47,675	1978	Mark Roth	134,500	1992	Marc McDowell	176,215
1966	Wayne Zahn	54,720	1979	Mark Roth	124,517	1993	Walter Ray Williams Jr.	296,370
1967	Dave Davis	54,165	1980	Wayne Webb	116,700	1994	Norm Duke	273,752
1968	Jim Stefanich	67,375	1981	Earl Anthony	164,735	1995	Mike Aulby	219,792
1969	Billy Hardwick	64,160	1982	Earl Anthony	134,760	1996	Walter Ray Williams Jr.	244,630
1970	Mike McGrath	52,049	1983	Earl Anthony	135,605	1997	Walter Ray Williams Jr.	240,544
1971	Johnny Petraglia	85,065	1984	Mark Roth	158,712	1998	Walter Ray Williams Jr.	238,225
			1985	Mike Aulby	201,200			

WPBA and PWBA Tours

WPBA leaders through 1980; PWBA leaders since 1981.

Multiple winners: Aleta Sill (6); Donna Adamek (4); Patty Costello, Tish Johnson and Betty Morris (3); Dotty Fothergill and Wendy Macpherson.

Year	Earnings	Year	Earnings	Year	Earnings
1965 Betty Kuczynski	$ 3,792	1977 Betty Morris	$23,802	1989 Robin Romeo	$113,750
1966 Joy Abel	5,795	1978 Donna Adamek	31,000		
1967 Shirley Garms	4,920	1979 Donna Adamek	26,280	1990 Tish Johnson	94,420
1968 Dotty Fothergill	16,170			1991 Leanne Barrette	87,618
1969 Dotty Fothergill	9,220	1980 Donna Adamek	31,907	1992 Tish Johnson	96,872
		1981 Donna Adamek	41,270	1993 Aleta Sill	57,995
1970 Patty Costello	9,317	1982 Nikki Gianulias	45,875	1994 Aleta Sill	126,325
1971 Vesma Grinfelds	4,925	1983 Aleta Sill	42,525	1995 Tish Johnson	123,440
1972 Patty Costello	11,350	1984 Aleta Sill	81,452	1996 Wendy Macpherson	107,230
1973 Judy Cook	11,200	1985 Aleta Sill	52,655	1997 Wendy Macpherson	165,425
1974 Betty Morris	30,037	1986 Aleta Sill	36,962	1998 Carol Gianotti-Block	150,350
1975 Judy Soutar	20,395	1987 Betty Morris	63,735		
1976 Patty Costello	39,585	1988 Lisa Wagner	105,500		

All-Time Leaders

All-time leading money winners on the PBA and PWBA tours, through 1998. PBA figures date back to 1959, while PWBA figures include Women's Pro Bowlers Association (WPBA) earnings through 1980. National tour titles are also listed.

Money Won

PBA Top 20

		Titles	Earnings
1	Walter Ray Williams Jr.	29	$2,314,228
2	Pete Weber	24	2,111,158
3	Mike Aulby	26	1,941,415
4	Brian Voss	20	1,695,000
5	Marshall Holman	22	1,693,895
6	Amleto Monacelli	18	1,684,663
7	Parker Bohn III	17	1,587,549
8	Dave Husted	13	1,518,288
9	Mark Roth	34	1,514,050
10	Earl Anthony	41	1,441,061
11	Norm Duke	16	1,380,376
12	Wayne Webb	20	1,315,058
13	David Ozio	11	1,261,699
14	Gary Dickinson	8	1,236,661
15	Del Ballard Jr.	12	1,108,207
16	Mark Williams	7	1,094,727
17	Tom Baker	9	1,094,045
18	Dave Ferraro	9	1,044,176
19	Johnny Petraglia	14	952,220
20	Ernie Schlegel	6	944,497

WPBA-PWBA Top 12

		Titles	Earnings
1	Aleta Sill	30	$990,442
2	Tish Johnson	22	878,923
3	Lisa Wagner	30	775,076
4	Wendy Macpherson	14	754,405
5	Anne Marie Duggan	15	745,976
6	Carol Gianotti-Block	14	735,139
7	Leanne Barrette	19	699,058
8	Robin Mossontte	16	646,249
9	Cheryl Daniels	10	621,386
10	Nikki Gianulias	19	599,138
11	Dana Miller-Mackie	15	541,337
12	Dede Davidson	5	535,692

Senior PBA Top 5

		Titles	Earnings
1	John Handegard	14	$395,205
2	Gary Dickinson	10	349,593
3	Gene Stus	10	336,225
4	Teata Semiz	8	319,445
5	John Hricsina	7	310,218

Annual Awards

MEN

BWAA Bowler of the Year

Winners selected by Bowling Writers Association of America.

Multiple winners: Earl Anthony and Don Carter (6); Walter Ray Williams Jr. (5); Mark Roth (4); Mike Aulby and Dick Weber (3); Buddy Bomar, Ned Day, Billy Hardwick, Don Johnson, and Steve Nagy (2).

Year	Year	Year	Year
1942 Johnny Crimmins	1957 Don Carter	1972 Don Johnson	1987 Marshall Holman
1943 Ned Day	1958 Don Carter	1973 Don McCune	1988 Brian Voss
1944 Ned Day	1959 Ed Lubanski	1974 Earl Anthony	1989 Mike Aulby
1945 Buddy Bomar	1960 Don Carter	1975 Earl Anthony	
1946 Joe Wilman	1961 Dick Weber	1976 Earl Anthony	1990 Amleto Monacelli
1947 Buddy Bomar	1962 Don Carter	1977 Mark Roth	1991 David Ozio
1948 Andy Varipapa	1963 Dick Weber	1978 Mark Roth	1992 Marc McDowell
1949 Connie Schwoegler	1964 Billy Hardwick	1979 Mark Roth	1993 Walter Ray Williams Jr.
	1965 Dick Weber		1994 Norm Duke
1950 Junie McMahon	1966 Wayne Zahn	1980 Wayne Webb	1995 Mike Aulby
1951 Lee Jouglard	1967 Dave Davis	1981 Earl Anthony	1996 Walter Ray Williams Jr.
1952 Steve Nagy	1968 Jim Stefanich	1982 Earl Anthony	1997 Walter Ray Williams Jr.
1953 Don Carter	1969 Billy Hardwick	1983 Earl Anthony	1998 Walter Ray Williams Jr.
1954 Don Carter		1984 Mark Roth	
1955 Steve Nagy	1970 Nelson Burton Jr.	1985 Mike Aulby	
1956 Bill Lillard	1971 Don Johnson	1986 Walter Ray Williams Jr.	

Annual Awards (Cont.)
PBA Player of the Year

Winners selected by members of Professional Bowlers Association. The PBA Player of the Year has differed from the BWAA Bowler of the Year four times—in 1963, '64, '89 and '92.

Multiple winners: Earl Anthony (6); Walter Ray Williams Jr. (5); Mark Roth (4); Mike Aulby, Billy Hardwick, Don Johnson and Amleto Monacelli (2).

Year		Year		Year		Year	
1963	Billy Hardwick	1972	Don Johnson	1981	Earl Anthony	1990	Amleto Monacelli
1964	Bob Strampe	1973	Don McCune	1982	Earl Anthony	1991	David Ozio
1965	Dick Weber	1974	Earl Anthony	1983	Earl Anthony	1992	Dave Ferraro
1966	Wayne Zahn	1975	Earl Anthony	1984	Mark Roth	1993	Walter Ray Williams Jr.
1967	Dave Davis	1976	Earl Anthony	1985	Mike Aulby	1994	Norm Duke
1968	Jim Stefanich	1977	Mark Roth	1986	Walter Ray Williams Jr.	1995	Mike Aulby
1969	Billy Hardwick	1978	Mark Roth	1987	Marshall Holman	1996	Walter Ray Williams Jr.
1970	Nelson Burton Jr.	1979	Mark Roth	1988	Brian Voss	1997	Walter Ray Williams Jr.
1971	Don Johnson	1980	Wayne Webb	1989	Amleto Monacelli	1998	Walter Ray Williams Jr.

PBA Rookie of the Year

Winners selected by members of Professional Bowlers Association.

Year		Year		Year		Year	
1964	Jerry McCoy	1973	Steve Neff	1982	Mike Steinbach	1991	Ricky Ward
1965	Jim Godman	1974	Cliff McNealy	1983	Toby Contreras	1992	Jason Couch
1966	Bobby Cooper	1975	Guy Rowbury	1984	John Gant	1993	Mark Scroggins
1967	Mike Durbin	1976	Mike Berlin	1985	Tom Crites	1994	Tony Ament
1968	Bob McGregor	1977	Steve Martin	1986	Marc McDowell	1995	Billy Myers Jr.
1969	Larry Lichstein	1978	Joseph Groskind	1987	Ryan Shafer	1996	C.K. Moore
1970	Denny Krick	1979	Mike Aulby	1988	Rick Steelsmith	1997	Anthony Lombardo
1971	Tye Critchlow	1980	Pete Weber	1989	Steve Hoskins	1998	Chris Barnes
1972	Tommy Hudson	1981	Mark Fahy	1990	Brad Kiszewski		

WOMEN
BWAA Bowler of the Year

Winners selected by Bowling Writers Association of America.

Multiple winners: Marion Ladewig (9); Donna Adamek and Lisa Rathgeber Wagner (4); Tish Johnson and Betty Morris (3); Patty Costello, Dotty Forthergill, Shirley Garms, Wendy Macpherson, Val Mikiel, Aleta Sill, Judy Soutar and Sylvia Wene (2).

Year		Year		Year		Year	
1948	Val Mikiel	1961	Shirley Garms	1974	Betty Morris	1987	Betty Morris
1949	Val Mikiel	1962	Shirley Garms	1975	Judy Soutar	1988	Lisa Wagner
1950	Marion Ladewig	1963	Marion Ladewig	1976	Patty Costello	1989	Robin Romeo
1951	Marion Ladewig	1964	LaVerne Carter	1977	Betty Morris	1990	Tish Johnson
1952	Marion Ladewig	1965	Betty Kuczynski	1978	Donna Adamek	1991	Leanne Barrette
1953	Marion Ladewig	1966	Joy Abel	1979	Donna Adamek	1992	Tish Johnson
1954	Marion Ladewig	1967	Millie Martorella	1980	Donna Adamek	1993	Lisa Wagner
1955	Sylvia Wene	1968	Dotty Fothergill	1981	Donna Adamek	1994	Anne Marie Duggan
1956	Anita Cantaline	1969	Dotty Fothergill	1982	Nikki Gianulias	1995	Tish Johnson
1957	Marion Ladewig	1970	Mary Baker	1983	Lisa Rathgeber	1996	Wendy Macpherson
1958	Marion Ladewig	1971	Paula Sperber	1984	Aleta Sill	1997	Wendy Macpherson
1959	Marion Ladewig	1972	Patty Costello	1985	Aleta Sill	1998	Carol Gianotti-Block
1960	Sylvia Wene	1973	Judy Soutar	1986	Lisa Wagner		

PWBA Player of the Year

Winners selected by members of Professional Women's Bowling Association. The PWBA Player of the Year has differed from the BWAA Bowler of the Year three times—in 1985, '86 and '90.

Multiple winners: Lisa Rathgeber Wagner (3); Leanne Barrette, Tish Johnson and Wendy Macpherson (2).

Year		Year		Year		Year	
1983	Lisa Rathgeber	1988	Lisa Wagner	1993	Lisa Wagner	1998	Carol Gianotti-Block
1984	Aleta Sill	1989	Robin Romeo	1994	Anne Marie Duggan	**Note:** This award was
1985	Patty Costello	1990	Leanne Barrette	1995	Tish Johnson	known as the LPBT Player of
1986	Jeanne Maiden	1991	Leanne Barrette	1996	Wendy Macpherson	the Year Award from 1983–
1987	Betty Morris	1992	Tish Johnson	1997	Wendy Macpherson	97.

WPBA and PWBA Rookie of the Year

Winners selected by members of Women's Professional Bowlers Association (1978-80) and the Professional Women's Bowling Association (since 1981).

Year		Year		Year		Year	
1978	Toni Gillard	1984	Paula Vidad	1990	Debbie McMullen	1996	Liz Johnson
1979	Nikki Gianulias	1985	Dede Davidson	1991	Kim Kahrman	1997	Lisa Bishop
1980	Lisa Rathgeber	1986	Wendy Macpherson	1992	Marianne DiRupo	1998	Jody Ellis
1981	Cindy Mason	1987	Paula Drake	1993	Kathy Zielke		
1982	Carol Norman	1988	Mary Martha Cerniglia	1994	Tammy Turner		
1983	Anne Marie Pike	1989	Kim Terrell	1995	Krissy Stewart		

Horse Racing

Jockey **Chris Antley** jumps off Charismatic at the finish of the Belmont Stakes, after realizing his horse had pulled up lame.

AP/Wide World Photos

Tough Break

Lukas' Charismatic grabs the first two legs of the Triple Crown, then breaks a leg in the Belmont.

by
Hank Goldberg

Horse racing in 1999 simply belonged to D. Wayne Lukas. After a six-race hiatus from the winner's circle at the classics, Lukas trained Charismatic, a horse he had run twice for a claiming tag, to victories in the Kentucky Derby and the Preakness. This accomplishment gave him his 11th and 12th Triple Crown successes and put a stamp on the 64-year-old conditioner's election to the Horse Racing Hall of Fame.

Charismatic was ridden by Chris Antley, himself a comeback story after battling weight and substance abuse problems, and was less than a mild surprise at 31-1 in Kentucky and 8-1 at the Preakness.

In Kentucky, 19 horses went to the post on the first Saturday in May in what was a roughly-contested race, as 17 of them had trouble calls. Antley kept Charismatic free of difficulty and barely outlasted a closing Menifee

Hank Goldberg is an analyst for ESPN's horse racing coverage.

while another Lukas horse, Cat Thief, ran third.

The Preakness was an even more convincing effort for Charismatic as he prevailed by three lengths over Menifee, despite being five wide at the turn.

So for the third consecutive year, we had a chance for a Triple Crown winner at Belmont. Out of the gate, Charismatic hooked Bob Baffert's brilliant filly, Silverbulletday, in an early speed duel. Charismatic then took off and ran gallantly through the stretch as a pair of longshots, Lemon Drop Kid (29-1) and Vision and Verse (55-1) finally passed him. As he tried to battle back, he broke down crossing the finish line in third position. Antley courageously dismounted and put himself in harm's way to save his horse from further possible injury. Word came later that Charismatic had fractured two bones in his left front leg. He ultimately underwent successful surgery and was retired.

AP/Wide World Photos

Jockey **Chris Antley**, aboard Charismatic, signals his win as he crosses the finish line at the 125th running of the Kentucky Derby. The two teamed up to win the Preakness as well, but their Triple Crown bid was thwarted at the Belmont by Lemon Drop Kid.

Lemon Drop Kid was Flint Schulhofer's second Belmont winner, having scored in 1993 with Colonial Affair.

Baffert found himself without a Triple Crown winner for the first time since 1996, ending a two-year run that brought him four victories. He still appeared to be deep with his usual talent, which included General Challenge, Prime Timber, Exploit, and his pair of tremendous fillies, Excellent Meeting and the aforementioned Silverbulletday, who won the Kentucky Oaks and the Black-Eyed Susan Stakes among her eight wins in nine tries. It was still a fabulous year for Baffert. He won the Pimlico Special with Real Quiet, dominated the summer meet at Del Mar, won the Woodward with River Keen and now has the top 2-year-old filly in Chilukki.

It was quite a competitive year for 3-year-old colts. Just to prove that the Belmont was no fluke, Lemon Drop Kid and Vision and Verse ran 1-2 in the Travers at Saratoga. Cat Thief beat out General Challenge at the Swaps at Hollywood, but was then upended by Menifee at Monmouth's Haskell Invitational. Not to be outdone, General Challenge came back to win at the Pacific Classic. And of course there was Charismatic, who lived up to his name and just narrowly missed accomplishing what no horse had since 1978. ■

And at the wire it's...**Lemon Drop Kid** by a head over Vision and Verse and Charismatic! After a slow start that put him in eighth place after the first mile, jockey Jose Santos turned on the juice to capture the 1999 Belmont Stakes on June 5, the third leg of the Triple Crown.

Hank Goldberg's Top Stories of the Year in Horse Racing

10. **The 1999 Breeders' Cup**, run at Gulfstream Park in Florida, debuts another event — a mile and three-eighths turf race for fillies and mares.

9. **Shopping sprees** — Churchill Downs and Frank Stronach each drop some serious money over the year to acquire race tracks in California and Florida. Churchill purchases Hollywood Park for $140 million and Calder Race Course in Florida for $86 million. Stronach buys Santa Anita for $126 million and spends $95 million for Gulfstream.

8. **Shopping Sprees II** — Sheikh Mohammed al Maktoum buys thoroughbred racing powerhouse Worldly Manner from John and Betty Mabee's Golden Eagle Farm for $5 million. He then spends millions more duplicating Churchill Downs' conditions in his native Dubai to prepare the horse for the Kentucky Derby. He finishes in seventh.

7. **Horse racing loses** its share of legends during the year. Prominent owner and breeder Paul Mellon passes away at 91. Maryland-based trainer Dick Dutrow dies at 61, and Charlie Whittingham, who became the oldest trainer to win the Kentucky Derby with Ferdinand in 1986, succumbs to leukemia at the age of 86.

It was a busy year for trainer extraordinaire **D. Wayne Lukas**. It usually is. Lukas, here with Charismatic, was inducted into the National Horse Racing Hall of Fame and narrowly missed out on capturing the first Triple Crown since 1978.

6. **Northern California based jockey Russell Baze** joins D. Wayne Lukas and champion thoroughbreds Exceller, Miesque and Gun Bow as inductees into the Hall of Fame in Saratoga Springs.

5. **Churchill Downs hosts** the Breeders' Cup in November 1998. Answer Lively and Silverbulletday win the Juvenile Colt and Juvenile Filly, respectively, while Reraise wins the Sprint. Da Hoss, who missed all of 1997 with a variety of ailments, is a repeat winner in the Mile from Woodbine in 1996. Escena (Distaff), Buck's Boy (Turf) and Awesome Again (Classic) round out the victors.

4. **Skip Away**, despite running sixth in the Breeders' Cup Classic, has a sensational year in 1998 to win Horse of the Year honors for Carolyn and Sonny Hine.

3. **Behrens**, the 5-year-old horse trained by H. James Bond, is the outstanding older handicap horse of the year. He wins four stakes races in a row at one point, before Victory Gallop finally beats him by a nose at the Whitney.

2. **Lukas' Charismatic wins** the Kentucky Derby and the Preakness, so for the third consecutive year, a horse has a chance to be the first since Affirmed in 1978 to win the Triple Crown. He is passed down the stretch by Lemon Drop Kid and winds up third, but gives all horse racing fans a real thrill.

1. 1998 Eclipse Award Winners

Two-Year-Old Colt:
Answer Lively

Two-Year-Old Filly:
Silverbulletday

Three-Year-Old Colt:
Real Quiet

Three-Year-Old Filly:
Banshee Breeze

Older Male:
Skip Away

Older Filly or Mare:
Escena

Male Turf Horse:
Buck's Boy

Female Turf Horse:
Fiji

Sprinter:
Reraise

Steeplechase Horse:
Flat Top

Horse of the Year:
Skip Away ∎

THE **NUMBERS**

INSIDE

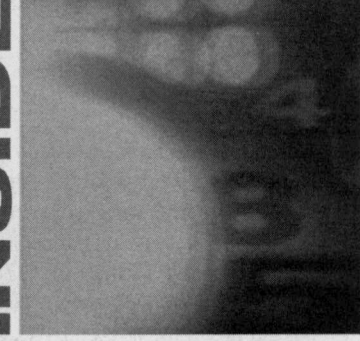

THE TRAINER KEEPS A ROLLIN'

There is no doubt that thoroughbred trainer D. Wayne Lukas was the centerpiece of the National Museum of Racing's Hall of Fame Class of 1999 which was inducted on Aug. 9. The 64-year-old Wisconsin native has led the nation in earnings 14 of the last 16 years and has amassed over $200 million in his 25-year career. Here are his other impressive numbers (as of Aug. 1, 1999):

Career Earnings	$201,228,839*
Season Earnings (1998)	$17,842,358*
Season Stakes victories (1987)	92*
Starts	20,341
Wins	3,805
Kentucky Derby victories	4
Preakness Stakes victories	5
Belmont Stakes victories	3
Breeders' Cup victories	13*
Eclipse Awards (Outstanding Trainer)	4*

*shares or holds all-time record.

CHEAP THRILLS

If not for the movie "The Blair Witch Project," the best investment of the year would have been the $62,500 Bob and Beverly Lewis spent for a red chestnut colt named Charismatic. The 3-year-old went on to win the first two legs of the Triple Crown and earn more than $2 million in 1999 before breaking his leg in a third place finish at the Belmont Stakes. His victory in the $1 million Kentucky Derby was the third-highest payoff in the race's 125-year history. Not a bad opening weekend.

Year	Horse	Payoff ($1)
1913	Donerail	$184.90
1940	Gallahadion	$72.40
1999	Charismatic	$64.60 ∎

HORSE RACING
STATISTICS

THE SEASON IN REVIEW
1998-1999
THOROUGHBRED • HARNESS

SEC A

PAGE 785

Thoroughbred Racing
Major Stakes Races

Winners of major stakes races from Nov. 7, 1998 through Sept. 19, 1999; (T) indicates turf race course; (F) indicates furlongs.

LATE 1998

Date	Race	Track	Miles	Winner	Jockey	Purse
Nov. 7	Breeders Cup - Juv. Fillies	Churchill Downs	1 1/16	Silverbulletday	Gary Stevens	$1,000,000
Nov. 7	Breeders Cup - Sprint	Churchill Downs	6F	Reraise	Corey Nakatani	1,000,000
Nov. 7	Breeders Cup - Distaff	Churchill Downs	1 1/8	Escena	Gary Stevens	2,000,000
Nov. 7	Breeders Cup - Mile	Churchill Downs	1	Da Hoss	John Velazquez	1,000,000
Nov. 7	Breeders Cup - Juvenile	Churchill Downs	1 1/16	Answer Lively	Jerry Bailey	1,000,000
Nov. 7	Breeders Cup - Turf	Churchill Downs	1 1/2 (T)	Buck's Boy	Shane Sellers	2,000,000
Nov. 7	Breeders Cup - Classic	Churchill Downs	1 1/4	Awesome Again	Pat Day	4,000,000
Nov. 29	Japan Cup	Tokyo Racecourse	2400 M	El Condor Pasa	Masayoshi Ebina	2,600,000
Nov. 29	Matriarch Stakes	Hollywood	1 1/4 (T)	Squeak	Alex O. Solis	700,000
Nov. 29	Hollywood Derby	Hollywood	1 1/8 (T)	Vergennes	John Velazquez	500,000
Dec. 12	Hollywood Turf Cup	Hollywood	1 1/2 (T)	Lazy Lode	Corey Naktani	500,000
Dec. 12	Hollywood Futurity	Hollywood	1 1/16	Tactical Cat	Laffit Pincay Jr.	403,000

1999 (through Sept. 19)

Date	Race	Track	Miles	Winner	Jockey	Purse
Jan. 3	Spectacular Bid B.C. Stakes*	Gulfstream	6 F	Texas Glitter	John R. Velazquez	$75,000
Jan. 9	San Miguel Stakes*	Santa Anita	6 F	Cape Canaveral	David Flores	100,000
Jan. 16	Holy Bull Stakes*	Gulfstream	1 1/16	Grits'n Hard Toast	Robbie G. Davis	100,000
Jan. 16	Golden Gate Derby	Golden Gate	1 1/16	Epic Honor	Lonnie Meche	150,000
Jan. 30	Donn Handicap	Gulfstream	1 1/8	Puerto Madero	Kent Desormeaux	500,000
Jan. 31	Hutcheson Stakes*	Gulfstream	7 F	Bet Me Best	Jerry Bailey	150,000
Jan. 31	Santa Catalina Stakes*	Santa Anita	1 1/16	General Challenge	Gary Stevens	106,500
Feb. 6	Charles H. Strub Stakes	Santa Anita	1 1/8	Event of the Year	Corey Nakatani	500,000
Feb. 6	San Vicente Stakes*	Santa Anita	7 F	Exploit	Chris McCarron	150,000
Feb. 20	Fountain of Youth Stakes*	Gulfstream	1 1/16	Vicar	Shane Sellars	200,000
Feb. 27	Southwest Stakes*	Oaklawn	1	Jim'smrtee	Travis Hightower	75,000
Feb. 27	Gulfstream Park Handicap	Gulfstream	1 1/4	Behrens	Jorge Chavez	350,000
Feb. 28	Rampart Handicap	Gulfstream	1 1/16	Banshee Breeze	Jerry Bailey	200,000
Feb. 28	San Rafael Stakes*	Santa Anita	1	Desert Hero	Corey Nakatani	200,000
Mar. 6	El Camino Real Derby*	Bay Meadows	1 1/16	Cliquot	David Flores	200,000
Mar. 6	*Santa Anita Handicap*	Santa Anita	1 1/4	Free House	Chris McCarron	1,000,000
Mar. 7	Santa Margarita Handicap	Santa Anita	1 1/8	Manistique	Gary Stevens	300,000
Mar. 13	Swale Stakes*	Gulfstream	7 F	Yes It's True	Jerry Bailey	100,000
Mar. 13	Florida Derby*	Gulfstream	1 1/8	Vicar	Shane Sellars	750,000
Mar. 13	San Felipe Stakes*	Santa Anita	1 1/16	Prime Timber	David Flores	250,000
Mar. 14	Louisiana Derby*	Fairgrounds	1 1/16	Kimberlite Pipe	Robby Albarado	600,000
Mar. 14	Santa Anita Oaks	Santa Anita	1 1/16	Excellent Meeting	Kent Desormeaux	250,000
Mar. 20	Rebel Stakes*	Oaklawn	1 1/16	Etbauer	Mike Smith	125,000
Mar. 21	Gotham Stakes*	Aqueduct	1	Badge	Shaun Bridgmonhan	150,000
Mar. 22	Tampa Bay Derby*	Tampa Bay	1 1/16	Pineaff	Jose Santos	150,000
Mar. 27	Gallery Furniture.com Stakes†*	Turfway	1 1/8	Stephen Got Even	Shane Sellers	750,000
Mar. 28	Dubai Classic	Nad al-Sheba	1 1/4	Almutawakel	Richard Hills	5,000,000
Apr. 3	Santa Anita Derby*	Santa Anita	1 1/8	General Challenge	Gary Stevens	750,000
Apr. 3	Flamingo Stakes	Hialeah	1 1/8	First American	Jose Velez Jr.	250,000
Apr. 3	Ashland Stakes	Keeneland	1 1/16	Silverbulletday	Jerry Bailey	500,000
Apr. 3	*Oaklawn Handicap*	Oaklawn	1 1/8	Behrens	Jorge Chavez	750,000
Apr. 7	Lafayette Stakes*	Keeneland	7 F	Yes It's True	Jerry Bailey	100,000
Apr. 9	Apple Blossom Handicap	Oaklawn	1 1/16	Banshee Breeze	Jerry Bailey	500,000
Apr. 10	Blue Grass Stakes*	Keeneland	1 1/8	Menifee	Pat Day	750,000
Apr. 10	Arkansas Derby*	Oaklawn	1 1/8	Valhol	Billy Patin	500,000

Date	Race	Track	Miles	Winner	Jockey	Purse
Apr. 10	Wood Memorial*	Aqueduct	1⅛	Adonis	Jorge Chavez	$600,000
Apr. 10	Bay Shore Stakes*	Aqueduct	7 F	Perfect Score	Edgar Prado	100,000
Apr. 17	Federico Tesio Stakes*	Pimlico	1⅛	Talk's Cheap	Michael J. Luzzi	200,000
Apr. 18	San Juan Capistrano Handicap	Santa Anita	1¾ (T)	Single Empire	Kent Desormeaux	400,000
Apr. 18	Lexington Stakes*	Keeneland	1¹⁄₁₆	Charismatic	Jerry Bailey	325,000
Apr. 18	Lone Star Derby*	Lone Star	1¹⁄₁₆	T.B. Track Star	Eddie Martin Jr.	300,000
Apr. 24	Derby Trial*	Churchill Downs	1	Patience Game	Corey Nakatani	100,000
Apr. 30	Kentucky Oaks	Churchill Downs	1⅛	Silverbulletday	Gary Stevens	500,000
May 1	**Kentucky Derby***	Churchill Downs	1¼	Charismatic	Chris Antley	1,000,000
May 1	Withers Stakes*	Aqueduct	1	Successful Appeal	Jose Espinoza	150,000
May 8	Pimlico Special	Pimlico	1³⁄₁₆	Real Quiet	Gary Stevens	500,000
May 8	Illinois Derby*	Sportsman's Park	1⅛	Vision and Verse	H. Castillo Jr.	500,000
May 14	Black-Eyed Susan Stakes	Pimlico	1⅛	Silverbulletday	Gary Stevens	200,000
May 15	**Preakness Stakes***	Pimlico	1³⁄₁₆	Charismatic	Chris Antley	1,000,000
May 23	Peter Pan Stakes*	Belmont	1⅛	Best of Luck	Jean-Luc Samyn	150,000
May 29	California Derby	Golden Gate	1⅛ (T)	Red Sky's	Russell Baze	125,000
May 29	Metropolitan Mile	Belmont	1	Sir Bear	John Velazquez	500,000
May 29	Massachusetts Handicap	Suffolk Downs	1⅛	Behrens	Jorge Chavez	600,000
May 29	The Californian	Hollywood Park	1⅛	Old Trieste	Chris McCarron	300,000
May 31	Charles Whittgham Handicap	Hollywood Park	1¼ (T)	River Bay	Alex Solis	400,000
June 4	Acorn Stakes	Belmont	1	Three Ring	Jerry Bailey	200,000
June 5	**Belmont Stakes***	Belmont	1½	Lemon Drop Kid	Jose Santos	1,000,000
June 5	Riva Ridge Stakes*	Belmont	7 F	Yes It's True	Jerry Bailey	150,000
June 5	Vodafone English Derby	Epsom Downs	1½ (T)	Oath	Kieren Fallon	795,500
June 12	Stephen Foster Handicap	Churchill Downs	1⅛	Victory Gallop	Jerry Bailey	750,000
June 13	Leonard Richards Stakes*	Delaware	1¹⁄₁₆	Stellar Brush	Michael McCarthy	200,000
June 13	Shoemaker BC Mile	Hollywood	1 (T)	Silic	Corey Nakatani	350,000
June 19	Jersey Shore BC*	Monmouth	7 F	Yes It's True	Jerry Bailey	100,000
June 26	Affirmed Handicap*	Hollywood Park	1¹⁄₁₆	General Challenge	David Flores	125,000
June 26	Vanity Handicap	Hollywood Park	1⅛	Manistique	Chris McCarron	400,000
June 26	Mother Goose Stakes	Belmont	1⅛	Dreams Gallore	Robby Albarado	250,000
June 27	Irish Derby	Curragh	1½ (T)	Montjeu	Cash Asmussen	1,208,210
June 27	Queen's Plate	Woodbine	1¼	Woodcarver	Mickey Walls	500,000
June 27	Hollywood Gold Cup	Hollywood Park	1¼	Real Quiet	Jerry Bailey	1,000,000
July 3	Beverly Hills Handicap	Hollywood Park	1¼ (T)	Virginie	Laffit Pincay Jr.	250,000
July 4	Philip H. Iselin Handicap	Monmouth	1¹⁄₁₆	Frisk Me Now	E. King Jr.	350,000
July 5	Suburban Handicap	Belmont	1¼	Behrens	Jorge Chavez	400,000
July 11	Dwyer Stakes*	Belmont	1¹⁄₁₆	Forestry	Jerry Bailey	150,000
July 17	Hollywood Oaks	Hollywood Park	1⅛	Smooth Player	Eddie Delahoussaye	150,000
July 17	Frank J. DeFrancis Memorial	Laurel Park	6 F	Yes It's True	Jerry Bailey	300,000
July 18	Swaps Stakes	Hollywood Park	1⅛	Cat Thief	Pat Day	500,000
July 24	Ohio Derby*	Thistledown	1⅛	Stellar Brush	Michael McCarthy	300,000
July 24	Coaching Club Am. Oaks	Belmont	1¼	On a Soapbox	Jerry Bailey	350,000
July 24	K. George VI and Q. Elizabeth Diamond Stakes	Ascot	1½ (T)	Daylami	Frankie Dettori	600,000
Aug. 1	Eddie Read Handicap	Del Mar	1⅛ (T)	Joe Who	Chris Antley	400,000
Aug. 1	Whitney Handicap	Saratoga	1⅛	Victory Gallop	Jerry Bailey	963,498
Aug. 6	Amsterdam Stakes*	Saratoga	1⅛-	Successful Appeal	Edgar Prado	75,000
Aug. 7	Go for Wand Handicap	Saratoga	1⅛	Banshee Breeze	Jerry Bailey	250,000
Aug. 8	Haskell Invitational*	Monmouth	1⅛	Menifee	Pat Day	1,000,000
Aug. 8	Jim Dandy Stakes*	Saratoga	1⅛	Ecton Park	Alex Solis	300,000
Aug. 21	Alabama Stakes	Saratoga	1¼	Silverbulletday	Jerry Bailey	400,000
Aug. 27	Personal Ensign Handicap	Saratoga	1¼	Beautiful Pleasure	Jorge Chavez	400,000
Aug. 28	King's Bishop Stakes*	Saratoga	7 F	Forestry	Chris Antley	200,000
Aug. 28	Travers Stakes*	Saratoga	1¼	Lemon Drop Kid	Jose Santos	1,000,000
Aug. 29	Pacific Classic	Del Mar	1¼	General Challenge	David Flores	1,000,000
Aug. 29	Saratoga BC Handicap	Saratoga	1¼	Running Stag	Shane Sellers	300,000
Sept. 5	Remington Park Derby	Remington	1¹⁄₁₆	Temperence Time	Timothy Doocy	300,000
Sept. 11	Man o' War Stakes	Belmont	1⅜ (T)	Val's Prince	Jorge Chavez	500,000
Sept. 18	The Woodward Stakes	Belmont	1⅛	River Keen	Chris Antley	500,000
Sept. 18	Ruffian Handicap	Belmont	1¹⁄₁₆	Catinca	Jerry Bailey	250,000
Sept. 19	Atto Mile	Woodbine	1	Quiet Resolve	Robert Landry	1,050,000

* VISA 3-Year-Old Championship Series race (see tables on p. 788).
Races in *italics* are part of the NTRA Champions on Fox series which premiered in 1999.
† formerly known as Jim Beam Stakes.

The 1999 Triple Crown

Thoroughbred racing's Triple Crown for 3-year-olds consists of the Kentucky Derby, Preakness Stakes and Belmont Stakes run over six weeks on May 1, May 15 and June 5, respectively.

125th KENTUCKY DERBY

Grade I for three-year olds; 8th race at Churchill Downs in Louisville. **Date**— May 1, 1999; **Distance**— 1¼ miles; **Stakes Purse**— $1,000,000 ($700,000 to winner; $170,000 for 2nd; $85,000 for 3rd; $45,000 for 4th); **Track**— Clear; **Off**— 5:29 p.m. EDT; **Favorite**— Excellent Meeting (9-2 odds) & General Challenge (9-2).

Winner— Charismatic; **Field**— 19 horses; **Time**— 2:03⅕; **Start**— Good for all; **Won**— Driving; **Sire**— Summer Squall; **Dam**— Bali Babe; **Record** (going into race)— 14 starts, 3 wins, 2 seconds, 3 thirds; **Last start**— 1st in Lexington Stakes (Apr. 18); **Breeder**— William Farish & Parrish Hill Farm.

Order of Finish	Jockey	PP	1/4	1/2	3/4	Mile	Stretch	Finish	To $1
Charismatic	Chris Antley	16	7-hd	7-½	7-1½	3-1½	2-hd	1-nk	31.30
Menifee	Pat Day	18	14-1	17-1½	15-1½	14-½	6-hd	2-¾	7.00
Cat Thief	Mike Smith	10	2-1½	2-1½	2-1½	1-hd	1½	3-1¼	7.40
Prime Timber	David Flores	13	10-hd	11-½	11-hd	5½	4-hd	4-no	6.30
Excellent Meeting	Kent Desormeaux	5	18-½	18-1½	16-½	13-hd	9-hd	5-½	4.80
Kimberlite Pipe	Robby Albarado	12	8-hd	8-½	9-hd	7-hd	5-½	6-1¼	11.60
Worldly Manner	Jerry Bailey	11	3-hd	3-½	3-½	2-1½	3-3½	7-½	14.50
K One King	Alex Solis	9	19	19	18-1	16-½	13-1	8-1	11.60
Lemon Drop Kid	Jose Santos	19	13-½	16-hd	17-1½	15-1½	15-hd	9-nk	11.60
Answer Lively	Craig Perret	7	6-1½	5-hd	4-hd	6-1½	7-1½	10-½	37.00
General Challenge	Gary Stevens	14	12-1½	12-½	12-hd	10-hd	10-1	11-¾	4.80
Ecton Park	Robbie Davis	3	16-hd	15-hd	13-½	18-5	16-1	12-½	11.60
Desert Hero	Corey Nakatani	6	5-hd	6-½	6-hd	9-1½	11-hd	13-1¼	19.70
Stephen Got Even	Chris McCarron	4	4-hd	4-½	8-hd	12-hd	14-½	14-1½	5.10
Valhol	Willie Martinez	8	1-½	1-½	1-hd	4-½	12-1½	15-2	11.60
First American	Eddie Delahoussaye	15	15-hd	13-1	5-½	8-hd	8-hd	16-2	34.90
Adonis	Jorge Chavez	1	17-1½	14-hd	19	17-1½	18-6	17-4¾	18.70
Vicar	Shane Sellers	17	11-hd	9-hd	14½	11-hd	17-1½	18-3¼	8.20
Three Ring	John Velazquez	2	9-½	10-hd	10-½	19	19	19	25.60

Times— 23⅖; 47⅘; 1:12⅖; 1:37⅖; 2:03⅕.

$2 Mutual Prices— #11 Charismatic ($64.60, $27.80, $14.40); #13 Menifee ($8.40, $5.80); #8 Cat Thief ($5.80).

Exacta— (11-13) for $727.80; **Trifecta**— (11-13-8) for $5,866.20; **Superfecta**— (11-13-8-9) for $24,015.50; **Pick Six**— (9-3-3-10-1-11) (5-correct) $12,956.90; **Scratched**— Aljabr; **Overweights**— none; **Attendance**— 151,051; **TV Rating**— 7.1/21 (ABC).

Trainers & Owners (by finish): **1**— D. Wayne Lukas & Robert/Beverly Lewis; **2**— Elliott Walden & Arthur B. Hancock III/ James Stone; **3**— D. Wayne Lukas & Overbrook Farm; **4**— Bob Baffert & Marie/Aaron Jones; **5**— Bob Baffert & Golden Eagle Farm; **6**— Dallas Stewart & John Gunther/Prairie Star Racing; **7**— Saeed bin Suroor & Godolphin Racing Inc.; **8**— Akiko Gothard & Madeleine/Allen Paulson; **9**— Scotty Schulhofer & Jeanne G. Vance; **10**— Bobby Barnett & John A. Franks; **11**— Bob Baffert & Golden Eagle Farm; **12**— Elliott Walden & Mark Stanley; **13**— Richard Mandella & The Thoroughbred Corp.; **14**— Nick Zito & Stephen Hilbert; **15**— Dallas Keen & James Jackson; **16**— Eduardo Caramori & T N T Stud; **17**— Nick Zito & Paraneck Stable; **18**— Carl Nafzger & James Tafel; **19**— Edward Plesa Jr. & Barry Schwartz.

124th PREAKNESS STAKES

Grade I for three-year olds; 10th race at Pimlico in Baltimore. **Date**— May 15, 1999; **Distance**— 1 3/16 miles; **Stakes Purse**— $1,000,000 ($650,000 to winner; $200,000 for 2nd; $100,000 for 3rd; $50,000 for 4th); **Track**— Fast and Clear; **Off**— 5:28 p.m. EDT; **Favorite**— Menifee (5-2).

Winner— Charismatic; **Field**— 13 horses; **Time**— 1:55⅕; **Start**— Good for all; **Won**— Driving; **Sire**— Summer Squall; **Dam**— Bali Babe; **Record** (going into race)— 15 starts, 4 wins, 2 seconds, 3 thirds; **Last start**— Won the Kentucky Derby (May 1); **Breeder**— William Farish & Parrish Hill Farm.

Order of Finish	Jockey	PP	1/4	1/2	3/4	Stretch	Finish	To $1
Charismatic	Chris Antley	6	10-1½	10-hd	8-1½	1-3	1-1½	8.40
Menifee	Pat Day	5	8-hd	8-hd	7-½	3-1	2-hd	2.00
Badge	Mike Luzzi	4	12-1½	11-1	9-½	5-1½	3-2½	58.00
Stephen Got Even	Gary Stevens	11	9-hd	9-½	10-1	7-1	4-3	11.00
Patience Game	Corey Nakatani	8	13	12-1	11-1½	8-7	5-½	15.60
Adonis	Jorge Chavez	9	7-1½	7-1	5-hd	6-hd	6-3¼	19.80
Cat Thief	Mike Smith	3	2-hd	1-hd	2-½	2-hd	7-¾	5.20
Kimberlite Pipe	Shane Sellers	2	3-2½	2-½	1-hd	4-hd	8-8¼	17.40
Valhol	Edgar Prado	12	4-1	5-hd	6-½	10-6	9-1	61.70
Vicar	Robbie Albarado	13	1-hd	3-4	3-2	9-3½	10-5¾	24.00

Times— 22⅖; 45⅕; 1:10⅕; 1:35⅕; 1:55⅕.

$2 Mutual Prices— #6 Charismatic ($18.80, $7.60, $5.80); #5 Menifee ($3.60, $3.20); #4 Badge ($18.80).

Exacta— (6-5) for $47.60; **Trifecta**— (6-5-4) for $2,049.80; **Pick Six**— none; **Scratched**— Silverbulletday; **Overweights**— none; **Attendance**— 100,311; **TV Rating**— 3.8/11 (ABC).

Trainers & Owners (by finish): **1**— D. Wayne Lukas & Robert/Beverly Lewis; **2**— Elliott Walden & Arthur B. Hancock III/ James Stone; **3**— Joe Aquilino & Southbelle Stable; **4**— Nick Zito & Stephen Hilbert; **5**— Alex Hassinger Jr. & The Thoroughbred Corp.; **6**— Nick Zito & Paraneck Stable; **7**— D. Wayne Lukas & Overbrook Farm; **8**— Dallas Stewart & John Gunther/ Prairie Star Racing; **9**— Dallas Keen & James Jackson; **10**— Carl Nafzger & James Tafel; **11**— Randy Morse & Phyllis Lamberth Raines/Mike Langford; **12**— Saeed bin Suroor & Godolphin Racing Inc. **13**— Bob Baffert & Golden Eagle Farm.

131st BELMONT STAKES

Grade I for three-year olds; 9th race at Belmont Park in Elmont, N.Y. **Date**— June 5, 1999; **Distance**— 1½ miles; **Stakes Purse**— $1,000,000 ($600,000 to winner; $200,000 for 2nd; $110,000 for 3rd; $60,000 for 4th; $30,000 for 5th); **Track**— Fast and Clear; **Off**— 5:29 p.m. EDT; **Favorite**— Charismatic (2-1).

Winner— Lemon Drop Kid; **Field**— 12 horses; **Time**— 2:27⅘; **Start**— Good for all; **Won**— Driving; **Sire**— Kingmambo (Mr. Prospector); **Dam**— Charming Lassie (Seattle Slew); **Record** (going into race): 10 starts, 3 wins, 2 seconds, 2 thirds; **Last Start**— 3rd in Peter Pan Stakes (May 23); **Breeder**— William Farish and William Kilroy.

Order of Finish	Jockey	PP	1/4	1/2	Mile	1 1/4-M	Stretch	Finish	To $1
Lemon Drop Kid	Jose Santos	6	8-3½	8-2	8-2½	4-hd	1½	1-hd	29.75
Vision and Verse	Heberto Castillo	2	3-hd	4-hd	4-2½	5-2½	3-1½	2-1½	54.75
Charismatic	Chris Antley	4	2-1	2½	2½	1-hd	2-hd	3-4¾	1.60
Best of Luck	Jean-Luc Samyn	12	11-5	11-9	10½	6½	6-2	4½	13.00
Stephen Got Even	Shane Sellers	11	5-1½	3½	3½	2-hd	4-11½	5-3½	9.30
Patience Game	Kent Desormeaux	7	6½	7-1	9-hd	8-1½	7-5	6-no	12.50
Silverbulletday	Jerry Bailey	3	1-hd	1-hd	1½	3-1	5-11½	7-7½	5.10
Menifee	Pat Day	10	4-hd	5-1	5-hd	9-4½	8-6	8-3¼	2.60
Pineaff	Sidney LeJuene	5	12	12	12	12	10½	9-8	60.00
Prime Directive	Mike Smith	9	7½	6½	6-hd	11-4	11-1	10-nk	76.00
Teletable	John Velazquez	1	9-1	9-2½	11-20	10-hd	9-2	11-2¾	75.75
Adonis	Jorge Chavez	8	10-6	10-4½	7½	7½	12	12	46.25

Times— 23⅗; 47⅗; 1:12; 1:36⅖; 2:01⅘; 2:27⅘.

$2 Mutual Prices— #6 Lemon Drop Kid ($61.50, $26.00, $10.60); #2 Vision and Verse ($44.40, $17.00); #4 Charismatic ($3.60).

Exacta— (6-2) for $1,537.00; **Trifecta**— (6-2-4) for $5,343.00; **Pick Three**— (4-3-6) for $2,450.00; **Scratched**— None; **Overweights**— None; **Attendance**— 85,818; **TV Rating**— 6.9/20 share (ABC).

Trainers & Owners (by finish): **1**— Flint S. Schulhofer & Jeanne G. Vance; **2**—Bill Mott & Bruce Lunsford; **3**— D. Wayne Lukas & Robert B. Lewis/Beverly J. Lewis; **4**— H. Allen Jerkens & Bohemia Stable; **5**— Nick Zito & Stephen C. Hilbert **6**— Alex L. Hassinger Jr. & Ahmed Bin Salman; **7**— Bob Baffert & Michael E. Pegram; **8**— Elliott Walden & Arthur B. Hancock III/James H. Stone; **9**— Kenneth G. McPeek & Joyce Monroe/Roy K. Monroe; **10**— Patrick B. Byrne & Noreen Carpenito; **11**— Alfredo Callejas & Robert Perez; **12**— Nick Zito & Paraneck Stable.

NTRA National Thoroughbred Poll

The NTRA Thoroughbred Poll conducted by National Thoroughbred Racing Association, covering races through Sept. 19, 1999. Rankings are based on the votes of sports and thoroughbred media representatives on a 10-9-8-7-6-5-4-3-2-1 basis. First place votes are in parentheses.

		Pts	Age	Sex	'99 Record Sts-1-2-3	Owner	Trainer
1	Behrens (14)	184	5	Horse	7—4-3-0	Rudlein Stable & W. Clifton Jr.	H. James Bond
2	Silverbulletday (5)	170	3	Filly	9—8-0-0	Michael E. Pegram	Bob Baffert
3	Lemon Drop Kid	156	3	Colt	7-3-1-1	Jeanne G. Vance	Scotty Schulhofer
4	Banshee Breeze	116	4	Filly	5—4-1-0	J. Tafel & Jayeff Stables	Carl Nafzger
5	General Challenge	93	3	Gelding	8—5-0-0	Golden Eagle Farm	Bob Baffert
6	Chilukki	83	2	Filly	5—5-0-0	Stonerside Stable	Bob Baffert
7	Charismatic	65	3	Colt	10—4-2-1	Robert & Beverly Lewis	D. Wayne Lukas
8	Menifee	36	3	Colt	8—3-3-1	A. Hancock III & J. Stone	Elliott Walden
9	Victory Gallop	32	4	Colt	4—3-0-1	Prestonwood Farms	Elliott Walden
10	More Than Ready	30	2	Colt	6—5-0-1	James T. Scatuorchio	Todd Pletcher

Others receiving votes: 11. River Keen (29 points); **12.** Forestry and Yagli (16); **14.** Real Quiet (12); **15.** Almutawakel (11); **16.** Tuzla (9); **17.** Beautiful Pleasure and Bevo (6); **19.** Running Stag and Yes It's True (5); **21.** Buck's Boy, Crafty Friend and Malek (4); **24.** Val's Prince and Vision and Verse (2); **26.** Affirmed Success, Forest Camp, Free House, Hawksley Hill (1).

Final VISA 3-year-old Series Standings

The VISA Championship Series consists of 45 stakes races to determine the VISA 3-Year-Old Champion. Points are awarded to the first, second and third-place finishers as follows: Triple Crown races are scored 20-10-7; Grade I races are scored 10-7-5; Grade II races 7-5-3; and Grade III and ungraded 5-3-1. Top horses and jockeys are listed below.

Horses

	Pts		Pts		Pts		Pts
1 Charismatic	57	6 Vicar	25	11 Prime Timber	19	16 Texas Glitter	13
2 Menifee	48	Yes It's True	25	12 Ecton Park	18	17 Badge	12
3 Cat Thief	46	8 Vision and Verse	24	13 Best of Luck	17	Certain	12
4 Lemon Drop Kid	38	9 Forestry	22	14 Desert Hero	15	Exploit	12
5 General Challenge	29	10 Successful Appeal	21	Stellar Brush	15		

Jockeys

	Pts		Pts		Pts		Pts
1 Pat Day	82	6 David Flores	40	11 Jorge Chavez	18	Edgar Prado	16
2 Jerry Bailey	61	Mike Smith	40	12 Herberto Castillo Jr.	17	17 Kent Desormeaux	15
3 Chris Antley	58	8 Gary Stevens	28	Jean-Luc Samyn	17	18 Mike Luzzi	12
4 Shane Sellers	53	9 Corey Nakatani	25	John Velazquez	17	Michael McCarthy	12
5 Jose Santos	43	10 Alex Solis	23	15 Chris McCarron	16		

1998-99 Money Leaders

Official Top 10 standings for 1998 and unofficial Top 10 standings for 1999, through Sept. 19, 1999.

Final 1998

HORSES	Age	Sts	1-2-3	Earnings
Silver Charm	4	9	6-2-0	$4,696,506
Awesome Again	4	6	6-0-0	3,845,990
Skip Away	5	9	7-0-1	2,740,000
Escena	5	9	5-3-0	2,032,425
Victory Gallop	3	8	3-4-0	1,981,720
Buck's Boy	5	10	6-2-1	1,874,020
Real Quiet	3	6	2-3-0	1,788,800
Coronado's Quest	3	11	5-2-0	1,739,950
Banshee Breeze	3	10	6-2-2	1,425,980
Silverbulletday	2	7	6-0-0	1,114,110

JOCKEYS	Mts	1st	Earnings
Gary Stevens	869	178	$19,358,840
Pat Day	1237	276	17,380,569
Jerry Bailey	1039	262	17,188,628
Kent Desormeaux	1053	198	14,592,355
Corey Nakatani	974	211	13,437,003
Shane Sellers	1286	252	12,887,304
Chris McCarron	728	156	10,815,559
John Velazquez	1360	231	10,714,006
Alex O. Solis	1057	166	10,587,417
Edgar Prado	1969	470	9,921,241

TRAINERS	Sts	1st	Earnings
Bob Baffert	538	139	$15,000,870
Bill Mott	581	136	10,012,899
D. Wayne Lukas	599	103	7,248,847
Neil Drysdale	277	73	6,574,484
Jerry Hollendorfer	922	241	6,385,111
Richard Mandella	324	62	5,483,995
Patrick Byrne	91	35	5,253,707
Elliott Walden	441	75	5,082,727
Todd Pletcher	545	109	5,045,923
Claude McGaughey III	294	62	5,001,211

1999 (through Sept. 19)

HORSES	Age	Sts	1-2-3	Earnings
Charismatic	3	10	4-2-1	$2,007,404
Silverbulletday	3	9	8-0-0	1,607,640
Menifee	3	8	3-3-1	1,595,400
Behrens	5	7	4-3-0	1,535,000
General Challenge	3	8	5-1-0	1,498,100
Victory Gallop	4	4	3-0-1	1,399,295
Lemon Drop Kid	3	7	3-3-1	1,319,400
Malek	6	6	1-3-1	1,293,570
Real Quiet	4	5	2-2-1	1,101,880
Free House	5	3	2-1-0	880,000

JOCKEYS	Mts	1st	Earnings
Jerry Bailey	79	201	$13,484,325
Pat Day	987	190	11,302,783
Jorge Chavez	1225	239	10,430,421
Shane Sellers	1034	205	10,267,243
Alex Solis	869	149	9,261,493
David Flores	911	161	9,083,883
John Velazquez	1090	202	8,286,273
Robby Albarado	1089	202	8,106,290
Edgar Prado	1364	318	7,379,567
Chris McCarron	536	104	7,165,029

TRAINERS	Sts	1st	Earnings
Bob Baffert	480	121	$12,577,762
D. Wayne Lukas	506	93	7,080,224
Elliott Walden	321	80	6,118,376
Richard Mandella	270	43	5,473,341
Bill Mott	364	78	4,521,651
Jerry Hollendorfer	688	155	3,874,916
Todd Plecher	478	75	3,702,105
John Kimmel	281	58	3,552,399
Bobby Barnett	389	56	3,441,863
Robert Frankel	218	37	3,436,942

Harness Racing

1998-99 Major Stakes Races

Winners of major stakes races from Nov. 7, 1998 through Sept. 23, 1999; all paces and trots cover one mile; (BC) indicates year-end Breeders' Crown series.

LATE 1998

Date	Race	Raceway	Winner	Time	Driver	Purse
Oct. 30	Three Diamonds Pace	Garden St.	Future Millbank	1:53⅗	Mike Lachance	$493,700
Oct. 30	Valley Victory	Garden St.	Starchip Enterprise	1:56	Jim Dougherty	343,400
Nov. 28	Governor's Cup	Garden St.	Island Fantasy	1:52	Mike Lachance	600,000
Dec. 4	Windy City Pace	Maywood	Take Down The Flag	1:53⅗	Paul MacDonell	270,000

1999 (through Sept. 23)

Date	Race	Raceway	Winner	Time	Driver	Purse
May 1	Berry's Creek	Meadowlands	Ideal Towne	1:52	Mike Lachance	$300,000
June 5	New Jersey Classic	Meadowlands	Art's Conquest	1:50	Mike Lachance	500,000
June 26	North America Cup	Woodbine	The Panderosa	1:49.4	John Campbell	1,000,000
July 9	Del Miller Memorial	Meadowlands	Lovelytobehold	1:54⅗	Jim Doherty	340,000
July 16	Budweiser Beacon Course	Meadowlands	CR Renegade	1:53⅘	Rod Allen	400,000
July 17	Meadowlands Pace	Meadowlands	The Panderosa	1:49⅗	John Campbell	1,000,000
July 31	BC Open Pace	Meadowlands	Red Bow Tie	1:50	Luc Oullette	300,000
July 31	BC Open Trot	Meadowlands	Supergrit	1:53⅕	Ron Pierce	500,000
July 31	BC Mare Pace	Meadowlands	Shore by Five	1:50⅘	Daniel Dube	250,000
Aug. 5	Sweetheart Pace	Meadowlands	Panything Goes	1:54⅗	George Brennan	517,600
Aug. 5	Peter Haughton Memorial	Meadowlands	Smok'n Lantern	1:58⅗	Berndt Lindstedt	458,000
Aug. 5	Merrie Annabelle Final	Meadowlands	Dream of Joy	1:58⅘	Jim Meittinis	412,400
Aug. 6	Woodrow Wilson Pace	Meadowlands	Richess Hanover	1:53	Mike Lachance	660,250
Aug. 7	**Hambletonian**	Meadowlands	Self Possessed	1:51⅗	Mike Lachance	1,000,000
Aug. 7	Hambletonian Oaks	Meadowlands	Oolong	1:54⅘	John Campbell	500,000
Aug. 7	Nat Ray	Meadowlands	Magician	1:52⅘	David Miller	400,000
Aug. 14	Adios Final	Ladbroke	Washington VC	1:52⅗	Dave Palone	500,000
Aug. 21	Maple Leaf Trot	Woodbine	Goodtimes	1:53⅖	Dave Wall	250,000
Aug. 21	Hoosier Cup	Hoosier Park	Art's Conquest	1:51⅖	Eric Ledford	400,000
Aug. 22	Confederation Cup XXIII	Flamboro	Teeth Of The Dog	1:55	John Stark Jr.	421,000

Date	Race	Raceway	Winner	Time	Driver	Purse
Aug. 28	Yonkers Trot	Yonkers	C R Renegade	1:58	Rod Allen	$350,000
Sept. 4	Metro Pace	Woodbine	The Firepan	1:51²/₅	John Campbell	600,000
Sept. 4	Cane Pace	Freehold	Blissfull Hall	1:51⁴/₅	Ron Pierce	350,000
Sept. 4	World Trotting Derby	Du Quoin	Enjoy Lavek	1:53¹/₅	Johnny Takter	525,000
Sept. 23	**Little Brown Jug**	Delaware	Blissfull Hall	1:55³/₅	Ron Pierce	550,000

1998-99 Money Leaders

Official Top 10 standings for 1998 and unofficial Top 10 standings for 1999 through Sept. 26, 1999.

Final 1998

HORSES	Age	Sts	1-2-3	Earnings
Muscles Yankee 3tc	12	9-1-1	$1,258,611
Shady Character 3pc	20	10-3-2	1,070,569
Artiscape 3pc	18	13-2-2	973,960
Day In A Life 3pc	27	7-8-5	948,917
Galleria 3pf	15	7-6-2	925,132
Red Bow Tie 4pg	30	17-4-2	839,137
Island Fantasy 2pc	17	10-2-2	799,919
Dragon Again 3pc	21	5-4-6	793,803
Ambro Romance 3pf	18	13-2-1	784,595
Grinfromeartoear 2pc	9	6-1-0	735,175

DRIVERS	Mts	1st	Earnings
John Campbell 1626	342	$10,768,771
Mike Lachance 2057	302	9,926,239
Luc Ouellette 2633	592	9,758,137
George Brennan. 2747	457	7,567,146
Ron Pierce 2481	329	5,927,575
Tony Morgan 3125	676	5,777,414
Jack Moiseyev 2636	415	5,647,414
Cat Manzi. 2919	399	5,438,686
Steve Condren 1715	245	4,590,460
Walter Case Jr. 2993	1079	4,472,338

1999 (through Sept. 26)

HORSES	Age	Sts	1-2-3	Earnings
The Panderosa 3pc	9	5-1-0	$1,075,066
Self Possessed 3tc	10	6-2-0	833,700
Red Bow Tie. 5pg	16	9-2-1	818,250
Art's Conquest 3pc	16	5-6-3	734,504
Supergrit 6tg	8	4-1-2	705,570
B.J.'s Whirlwind 5ph	28	5-10-5	672,680
Blissfull Hall 3pc	14	10-2-1	657,229
CR Renegade 3tc	17	8-3-2	594,529
Richess Hanover 2pc	11	8-2-1	504,437
Enjoy Lavec 3tc	11	5-0-3	499,934

DRIVERS	Mts	1st	Earnings
Luc Ouellette 2273	429	$8,438,134
John Campbell 1356	241	7,885,846
Mike Lachance 1766	229	7,390,368
David Miller 1966	252	5,366,730
Chris Christoforou 2424	474	4,605,232
Ron Pierce 2042	238	4,596,614
Jack Moiseyev 1709	253	4,160,663
George Brennan. 1558	240	3,859,325
Randall Waples 1763	333	3,660,951
Steve Condren 1161	178	3,203,606

Hambletonian Society/Breeders Crown Standardbred Poll

Final Poll conducted by Harness Racing Communications as of Sept. 20, 1999 and based on the votes of 35 harness racing media representatives. First place votes are in parentheses. (p-pacer, t-trotter, h-horse, f-filly, m-mare, c-colt, g-gelding)

		Pts	Age/Gait/Sex	'99 Sts—1-2-3	Earnings
1	Self Possessed (19).	310	3tc	10—6-2-0	$ 833,700
2	Red Bow Tie (9)	271	5pg	16—9-2-1	818,250
3	Moni Maker (5)	253	6tm	13—7-3-2	927,017*
4	Blissfull Hall	187	3pc	11—8-2-0	529,395
5	The Panderosa	185	3pc	8—5-1-0	1,075,066
6	Galleria	178	4pm	13—5-2-5	353,210
7	Big Tom (1).	87	4ph	19—16-1-0	313,500
8	Richess Hanover	82	2pc	10—8-1-1	492,859
9	Enjoy Lavec	54	3tc	11—5-0-3	499,934
10	BJ's Whirlwind.	40	5ph	28—5-10-5	672,680

Others receiving votes: 11. Dragon Again (38 points); **12.** Supergrit (34); **13.** Ohyouprettything (29); **14.** Incredible Tillie (17); **15.** CR Renegade (14); **16.** Bit O Candy (13); **17.** Goodtimes (9); **18.** Extreme Velocity (8); **19.** Jet Laag and Color Me Best (6); **21.** Oolong and Eternal Camnation (4); **23.** The Firepan and Smok'n Lantern (3); **25.** Teeth Of The Dog, Ramilette Hanover, Lovelytobehold and Island Fantasy (1).
*includes foreign earnings

Steeplechase Racing
1998-99 Major Stakes Races

Winners of major steeplechase races from Nov. 22, 1998 through Aug. 26, 1999.

LATE 1998

Date	Race	Location	Miles	Winner	Jockey	Purse
Nov. 22	Colonial Cup	Camden, S.C.	2 ¾	Flat Top	Colvin Ryan	$100,000

1999 (through Aug. 26)

Date	Race	Location	Miles	Winner	Jockey	Purse
Apr. 10	Atlanta Cup	Kingston, Ga.	2	Daulton River	Craig Thornton	$100,000
Apr. 17	Grand National	Butler, Md.	3	Welter Weight	Mike Elmore	30,000
Apr. 24	Maryland Hunt Cup	Glyndon, Md.	4	Welter Weight	Mike Elmore	50,000
May 1	Virginia Gold Cup	The Plains, Va.	4	Saluter	Jack Fisher	50,000
May 8	Iroquois	Nashville, Tenn.	3	Rowdy Irishman	Vincent Marzullo	100,000
Aug. 26	N.Y. Turf Writers Cup	Saratoga, N.Y.	2 ⅜	Campanile	Blythe Miller	112,100

THE 2000 — ESPΠ INFORMATION PLEASE SPORTS ALMANAC

HORSE RACING
STATISTICS
THROUGH THE YEARS
1867-1999
THOROUGHBRED • HARNESS

SEC B

PAGE 791

Thoroughbred Racing
The Triple Crown

The term "Triple Crown" was coined by sportswriter Charles Hatton while covering the 1930 victories of Gallant Fox in the Kentucky Derby, Preakness Stakes and Belmont Stakes. Before then, only Sir Barton (1919) had won all three races in the same year. Since then, nine horses have won the Triple Crown. Two trainers, James (Sunny Jim) Fitzsimmons and Ben A. Jones, have saddled two Triple Crown champions, while Eddie Arcaro is the only jockey to ride two champions.

Year		Jockey	Trainer	Owner	Sire/Dam
1919	**Sir Barton**	Johnny Loftus	H. Guy Bedwell	J.K.L. Ross	Star Shoot/Lady Sterling
1930	**Gallant Fox**	Earl Sande	J.E. Fitzsimmons	Belair Stud	Sir Gallahad III/Marguerite
1935	**Omaha**	Willie Saunders	J.E. Fitzsimmons	Belair Stud	Gallant Fox/Flambino
1937	**War Admiral**	Charley Kurtsinger	George Conway	Samuel Riddle	Man o' War/Brushup
1941	**Whirlaway**	Eddie Arcaro	Ben A. Jones	Calumet Farm	Blenheim II/Dustwhirl
1943	**Count Fleet**	Johnny Longden	Don Cameron	Mrs. J.D. Hertz	Reigh Count/Quickly
1946	**Assault**	Warren Mehrtens	Max Hirsch	King Ranch	Bold Venture/Igual
1948	**Citation**	Eddie Arcaro	Ben A. Jones	Calumet Farm	Bull Lea/Hydroplane II
1973	**Secretariat**	Ron Turcotte	Lucien Laurin	Meadow Stable	Bold Ruler/Somethingroyal
1977	**Seattle Slew**	Jean Cruguet	Billy Turner	Karen Taylor	Bold Reasoning/My Charmer
1978	**Affirmed**	Steve Cauthen	Laz Barrera	Harbor View Farm	Exclusive Native/Won't Tell You

Note: Gallant Fox (1930) is the only Triple Crown winner to sire another Triple Crown winner, Omaha (1935). Wm. Woodward Sr., owner of Belair Stud, was breeder-owner of both horses and both were trained by Sunny Jim Fitzsimmons.

Triple Crown Near Misses

Forty-four horses have won two legs of the Triple Crown. Of those, fifteen won the Kentucky Derby (KD) and Preakness Stakes (PS) only to be beaten in the Belmont Stakes (BS). Two others, Burgoo King (1932) and Bold Venture (1936), won the Derby and Preakness, but were forced out of the Belmont with the same injury–a bowed tendon–that effectively ended their racing careers. In 1978, Alydar finished second to Affirmed in all three races, the only time that has happened. Note that the Preakness preceded the Kentucky Derby in 1922, '23 and '31; (*) indicates won on disqualification.

Year		KD	PS	BS	Year		KD	PS	BS
1877	**Cloverbrook**	DNS	won	won	1963	**Chateaugay**	won	2nd	won
1878	**Duke of Magenta**	DNS	won	won	1964	**Northern Dancer**	won	won	3rd
					1966	**Kauai King**	won	won	4th
1880	**Grenada**	DNS	won	won	1967	**Damascus**	3rd	won	won
1881	**Saunterer**	DNS	won	won	1968	**Forward Pass**	won*	won	2nd
					1969	**Majestic Prince**	won	won	2nd
1895	**Belmar**	DNS	won	won					
					1971	**Canonero II**	won	won	4th
1920	**Man o' War**	DNS	won	won	1972	**Riva Ridge**	won	4th	won
1922	**Pillory**	DNS	won	won	1974	**Little Current**	5th	won	won
1923	**Zev**	won	12th	won	1976	**Bold Forbes**	won	3rd	won
1931	**Twenty Grand**	won	2nd	won	1979	**Spectacular Bid**	won	won	3rd
1932	**Burgoo King**	won	won	DNS					
1936	**Bold Venture**	won	won	DNS	1981	**Pleasant Colony**	won	won	3rd
1939	**Johnstown**	won	5th	won	1984	**Swale**	won	7th	won
1940	**Bimelech**	2nd	won	won	1987	**Alysheba**	won	won	4th
1942	**Shut Out**	won	5th	won	1988	**Risen Star**	3rd	won	won
1944	**Pensive**	won	won	2nd	1989	**Sunday Silence**	won	won	2nd
1949	**Capot**	2nd	won	won					
1950	**Middleground**	won	2nd	won	1991	**Hansel**	10th	won	won
1953	**Native Dancer**	2nd	won	won	1994	**Tabasco Cat**	6th	won	won
1955	**Nashua**	2nd	won	won	1995	**Thunder Gulch**	won	3rd	won
1956	**Needles**	won	2nd	won	1997	**Silver Charm**	won	won	2nd
1958	**Tim Tam**	won	won	2nd	1998	**Real Quiet**	won	won	2nd
					1999	**Charismatic**	won	won	3rd
1961	**Carry Back**	won	won	7th					

The Triple Crown Challenge (1987-93)

Seeking to make the Triple Crown more than just a media event and to insure that owners would not be attracted to more lucrative races, officials at Churchill Downs, the Maryland Jockey Club and the New York Racing Association created Triple Crown Productions in 1985 and announced that a $1 million bonus would be given to the horse that performs best in the Kentucky Derby, Preakness Stakes and Belmont Stakes. Furthermore, a bonus of $5 million would be presented to any horse winning all three races.

Revised in 1991, the rules stated that the winning horse must: 1. finish all three races; 2. earn points by finishing first, second, third or fourth in at least one of the three races; and 3. earn the highest number of points based on the following system–10 points to win, five to place, three to show and one to finish fourth. In the event of a tie, the $1 million is distributed equally among the top point-getters. From 1987-90, the system was five points to win, three to place and one to show. The Triple Crown Challenge was discontinued in 1994.

Year		KD	PS	BS	Pts
1987	1 **Bet Twice**	2nd	2nd	1st —	11
	2 Alysheba	1st	1st	4th —	10
	3 Cryptoclearance	4th	3rd	2nd —	4
1988	1 **Risen Star**	3rd	1st	1st —	11
	2 Winning Colors	1st	3rd	6th —	6
	3 Brian's Time	6th	2nd	3rd —	4
1989	1 **Sunday Silence**	1st	1st	2nd —	13
	2 Easy Goer	2nd	2nd	1st —	11
	3 Hawkster	5th	5th	5th —	0
1990	1 **Unbridled**	1st	2nd	4th —	8
	2 Summer Squall	2nd	1st	DNR —	8
	3 Go and Go	DNR	DNR	1st —	5
	(Unbridled was only horse to run all three races.)				

Year		KD	PS	BS	Pts
1991	1 **Hansel**	10th	1st	1st —	20
	2 Strike the Gold	1st	6th	2nd —	15
	3 Mane Minister	3rd	3rd	3rd —	9
1992	1 **Pine Bluff**	5th	1st	3rd —	13
	2 Casual Lies	2nd	3rd	5th —	8
	(No other horses ran all three races.)				
1993	1 **Sea Hero**	1st	5th	7th —	10
	2 Wild Gale	3rd	8th	3rd —	6
	(No other horses ran all three races.)				

Kentucky Derby

For three-year-olds. Held the first Saturday in May at Churchill Downs in Louisville, Ky. Inaugurated in 1875. Originally run at 1½ miles (1875-95), shortened to present 1¼ miles in 1896.

Trainers with most wins: Ben Jones (6); D. Wayne Lukas and Dick Thompson (4); Sunny Jim Fitzsimmons and Max Hirsch (3).

Jockeys with most wins: Eddie Arcaro and Bill Hartack (5); Bill Shoemaker (4); Angel Cordero Jr., Issac Murphy, Earl Sande and Gary Stevens (3).

Winning fillies: Regret (1915), Genuine Risk (1980) and Winning Colors (1988).

Year	Time	Jockey	Trainer	2nd place	3rd place
1875 **Aristides**	2:37¾	Oliver Lewis	Ansel Anderson	Volcano	Verdigris
1876 **Vagrant**	2:38¼	Bobby Swim	James Williams	Creedmore	Harry Hill
1877 **Baden-Baden**	2:38	Billy Walker	Ed Brown	Leonard	King William
1878 **Day Star**	2:37¼	Jimmy Carter	Lee Paul	Himyar	Leveler
1879 **Lord Murphy**	2:37	Charlie Shauer	George Rice	Falsetto	Strathmore
1880 **Fonso**	2:37½	George Lewis	Tice Hutsell	Kimball	Bancroft
1881 **Hindoo**	2:40	Jim McLaughlin	James Rowe Sr.	Lelex	Alfambra
1882 **Apollo**	2:40¼	Babe Hurd	Green Morris	Runnymede	Bengal
1883 **Leonatus**	2:43	Billy Donohue	John McGinty	Drake Carter	Lord Raglan
1884 **Buchanan**	2:40¼	Isaac Murphy	William Bird	Loftin	Audrain
1885 **Joe Cotton**	2:37¼	Babe Henderson	Alex Perry	Bersan	Ten Booker
1886 **Ben Ali**	2:36½	Paul Duffy	Jim Murphy	Blue Wing	Free Knight
1887 **Montrose**	2:39¼	Isaac Lewis	John McGinty	Jim Gore	Jacobin
1888 **MacBeth II**	2:38¼	George Covington	John Campbell	Gallifet	White
1889 **Spokane**	2:34½	Thomas Kiley	John Rodegap	Proctor Knott	Once Again
1890 **Riley**	2:45	Isaac Murphy	Edward Corrigan	Bill Letcher	Robespierre
1891 **Kingman**	2:52¼	Isaac Murphy	Dud Allen	Balgowan	High Tariff
1892 **Azra**	2:41½	Lonnie Clayton	John Morris	Huron	Phil Dwyer
1893 **Lookout**	2:39¼	Eddie Kunze	Wm. McDaniel	Plutus	Boundless
1894 **Chant**	2:41	Frank Goodale	Eugene Leigh	Pearl Song	Sigurd
1895 **Halma**	2:37½	Soup Perkins	Byron McClelland	Basso	Laureate
1896 **Ben Brush**	2:07¾	Willie Simms	Hardy Campbell	Ben Eder	Semper Ego
1897 **Typhoon II**	2:12½	Buttons Garner	J.C. Cahn	Ornament	Dr. Catlett
1898 **Plaudit**	2:09	Willie Simms	John E. Madden	Lieber Karl	Isabey
1899 **Manuel**	2:12	Fred Taral	Robert Walden	Corsini	Mazo
1900 **Lieut. Gibson**	2:06¼	Jimmy Boland	Charles Hughes	Florizar	Thrive
1901 **His Eminence**	2:07¾	Jimmy Winkfield	F.B. Van Meter	Sannazarro	Driscoll
1902 **Alan-a-Dale**	2:08¾	Jimmy Winkfield	T.C. McDowell	Inventor	The Rival
1903 **Judge Himes**	2:09	Hal Booker	J.P. Mayberry	Early	Bourbon
1904 **Elwood**	2:08½	Shorty Prior	C.E. Durnell	Ed Tierney	Brancas
1905 **Agile**	2:10¾	Jack Martin	Robert Tucker	Ram's Horn	Layson
1906 **Sir Huon**	2:08⅘	Roscoe Troxler	Pete Coyne	Lady Navarre	James Reddick
1907 **Pink Star**	2:12⅗	Andy Minder	W.H. Fizer	Zal	Ovelando
1908 **Stone Street**	2:15⅕	Arthur Pickens	J.W. Hall	Sir Cleges	Dunvegan
1909 **Wintergreen**	2:08⅕	Vincent Powers	Charles Mack	Miami	Dr. Barkley

Year	Time	Jockey	Trainer	2nd place	3rd place
1910 **Donau**	2:06⅖	Fred Herbert	George Ham	Joe Morris	Fighting Bob
1911 **Meridian**	2:05	George Archibald	Albert Ewing	Governor Gray	Colston
1912 **Worth**	2:09⅖	C.H. Shilling	Frank Taylor	Duval	Flamma
1913 **Donerail**	2:04⅘	Roscoe Goose	Thomas Hayes	Ten Point	Gowell
1914 **Old Rosebud**	2:03⅖	John McCabe	F.D. Weir	Hodge	Bronzewing
1915 **Regret**	2:05⅖	Joe Notter	James Rowe Sr.	Pebbles	Sharpshooter
1916 **George Smith**	2:04	Johnny Loftus	Hollie Hughes	Star Hawk	Franklin
1917 **Omar Khayyam**	2:04⅗	Charles Borel	C.T. Patterson	Ticket	Midway
1918 **Exterminator**	2:10⅘	William Knapp	Henry McDaniel	Escoba	Viva America
1919 **SIR BARTON**	2:09⅘	Johnny Loftus	H. Guy Bedwell	Billy Kelly	Under Fire
1920 **Paul Jones**	2:09	Ted Rice	Billy Garth	Upset	On Watch
1921 **Behave Yourself**	2:04⅕	Charles Thompson	Dick Thompson	Black Servant	Prudery
1922 **Morvich**	2:04⅗	Albert Johnson	Fred Burlew	Bet Mosie	John Finn
1923 **Zev**	2:05⅖	Earl Sande	David Leary	Martingale	Vigil
1924 **Black Gold**	2:05⅕	John Mooney	Hanly Webb	Chilhowee	Beau Butler
1925 **Flying Ebony**	2:07⅗	Earl Sande	William Duke	Captain Hal	Son of John
1926 **Bubbling Over**	2:03⅘	Albert Johnson	Dick Thompson	Bagenbaggage	Rock Man
1927 **Whiskery**	2:06	Linus McAtee	Fred Hopkins	Osmand	Jock
1928 **Reigh Count**	2:10⅖	Chick Lang	Bert Michell	Misstep	Toro
1929 **Clyde Van Dusen**	2:10⅘	Linus McAtee	Clyde Van Dusen	Naishapur	Panchio
1930 **GALLANT FOX**	2:07⅗	Earl Sande	Jim Fitzsimmons	Gallant Knight	Ned O.
1931 **Twenty Grand**	2:01⅘	Charley Kurtsinger	James Rowe Jr.	Sweep All	Mate
1932 **Burgoo King**	2:05⅕	Eugene James	Dick Thompson	Economic	Stepenfetchit
1933 **Brokers Tip**	2:06⅘	Don Meade	Dick Thompson	Head Play	Charley O.
1934 **Cavalcade**	2:04	Mack Garner	Bob Smith	Discovery	Agrarian
1935 **OMAHA**	2:05	Willie Saunders	Jim Fitzsimmons	Roman Soldier	Whiskolo
1936 **Bold Venture**	2:03⅗	Ira Hanford	Max Hirsch	Brevity	Indian Broom
1937 **WAR ADMIRAL**	2:03⅕	Charley Kurtsinger	George Conway	Pompoon	Reaping Reward
1938 **Lawrin**	2:04⅘	Eddie Arcaro	Ben Jones	Dauber	Can't Wait
1939 **Johnstown**	2:03⅖	James Stout	Jim Fitzsimmons	Challedon	Heather Broom
1940 **Gallahadion**	2:05	Carroll Bierman	Roy Waldron	Bimelech	Dit
1941 **WHIRLAWAY**	2:01⅖	Eddie Arcaro	Ben Jones	Staretor	Market Wise
1942 **Shut Out**	2:04⅖	Wayne Wright	John Gaver	Alsab	Valdina Orphan
1943 **COUNT FLEET**	2:04	Johnny Longden	Don Cameron	Blue Swords	Slide Rule
1944 **Pensive**	2:04⅕	Conn McCreary	Ben Jones	Broadcloth	Stir Up
1945 **Hoop Jr**	2:07	Eddie Arcaro	Ivan Parke	Pot O'Luck	Darby Dieppe
1946 **ASSAULT**	2:06⅗	Warren Mehrtens	Max Hirsch	Spy Song	Hampden
1947 **Jet Pilot**	2:06⅘	Eric Guerin	Tom Smith	Phalanx	Faultless
1948 **CITATION**	2:05⅖	Eddie Arcaro	Ben Jones	Coaltown	My Request
1949 **Ponder**	2:04⅕	Steve Brooks	Ben Jones	Capot	Palestinian
1950 **Middleground**	2:01⅗	William Boland	Max Hirsch	Hill Prince	Mr. Trouble
1951 **Count Turf**	2:02⅗	Conn McCreary	Sol Rutchick	Royal Mustang	Ruhe
1952 **Hill Gail**	2:01⅗	Eddie Arcaro	Ben Jones	Sub Fleet	Blue Man
1953 **Dark Star**	2:02	Hank Moreno	Eddie Hayward	Native Dancer	Invigorator
1954 **Determine**	2:03	Raymond York	Willie Molter	Hasty Road	Hasseyampa
1955 **Swaps**	2:01⅘	Bill Shoemaker	Mesh Tenney	Nashua	Summer Tan
1956 **Needles**	2:03⅖	David Erb	Hugh Fontaine	Fabius	Come On Red
1957 **Iron Liege**	2:02⅕	Bill Hartack	Jimmy Jones	Gallant Man	Round Table
1958 **Tim Tam**	2:05	Ismael Valenzuela	Jimmy Jones	Lincoln Road	Noureddin
1959 **Tomy Lee**	2:02⅕	Bill Shoemaker	Frank Childs	Sword Dancer	First Landing
1960 **Venetian Way**	2:02⅖	Bill Hartack	Victor Sovinski	Bally Ache	Victoria Park
1961 **Carry Back**	2:04	John Sellers	Jack Price	Crozier	Bass Clef
1962 **Decidedly**	2:00⅖	Bill Hartack	Horatio Luro	Roman Line	Ridan
1963 **Chateaugay**	2:01⅘	Braulio Baeza	James Conway	Never Bend	Candy Spots
1964 **Northern Dancer**	2:00	Bill Hartack	Horatio Luro	Hill Rise	The Scoundrel
1965 **Lucky Debonair**	2:01⅕	Bill Shoemaker	Frank Catrone	Dapper Dan	Tom Rolfe
1966 **Kauai King**	2:02	Don Brumfield	Henry Forrest	Advocator	Blue Skyer
1967 **Proud Clarion**	2:00⅗	Bobby Ussery	Loyd Gentry	Barbs Delight	Damascus
1968 **Forward Pass***	—	Ismael Valenzuela	Henry Forrest	Francie's Hat	T.V. Commercial
1969 **Majestic Prince**	2:01⅘	Bill Hartack	Johnny Longden	Arts and Letters	Dike
1970 **Dust Commander**	2:03⅖	Mike Manganello	Don Combs	My Dad George	High Echelon
1971 **Canonero II**	2:03⅕	Gustavo Avila	Juan Arias	Jim French	Bold Reason
1972 **Riva Ridge**	2:01⅘	Ron Turcotte	Lucien Laurin	No Le Hace	Hold Your Peace
1973 **SECRETARIAT**	1:59⅖	Ron Turcotte	Lucien Laurin	Sham	Our Native
1974 **Cannonade**	2:04	Angel Cordero Jr.	Woody Stephens	Hudson County	Agitate
1975 **Foolish Pleasure**	2:02	Jacinto Vasquez	LeRoy Jolley	Avatar	Diabolo
1976 **Bold Forbes**	2:01⅗	Angel Cordero Jr.	Laz Barrera	Honest Pleasure	Elocutionist
1977 **SEATTLE SLEW**	2:02⅕	Jean Cruguet	Billy Turner	Run Dusty Run	Sanhedrin

Kentucky Derby (Cont.)

Year	Time	Jockey	Trainer	2nd place	3rd place
1978 **AFFIRMED**	2:01⅕	Steve Cauthen	Laz Barrera	Alydar	Believe It
1979 **Spectacular Bid**	2:02⅖	Ron Franklin	Bud Delp	General Assembly	Golden Act
1980 **Genuine Risk**	2:02	Jacinto Vasquez	LeRoy Jolley	Rumbo	Jaklin Klugman
1981 **Pleasant Colony**	2:02	Jorge Velasquez	John Campo	Woodchopper	Partez
1982 **Gato Del Sol**	2:02⅖	E. Delahoussaye	Eddie Gregson	Laser Light	Reinvested
1983 **Sunny's Halo**	2:02⅕	E. Delahoussaye	David Cross Jr.	Desert Wine	Caveat
1984 **Swale**	2:02⅖	Laffit Pincay Jr.	Woody Stephens	Coax Me Chad	At The Threshold
1985 **Spend A Buck**	2:00⅕	Angel Cordero Jr.	Cam Gambolati	Stephan's Odyssey	Chief's Crown
1986 **Ferdinand**	2:02⅘	Bill Shoemaker	Chas. Whittingham	Bold Arrangement	Broad Brush
1987 **Alysheba**	2:03⅖	Chris McCarron	Jack Van Berg	Bet Twice	Avies Copy
1988 **Winning Colors**	2:02⅕	Gary Stevens	D. Wayne Lukas	Forty Niner	Risen Star
1989 **Sunday Silence**	2:05	Pat Valenzuela	Chas. Whittingham	Easy Goer	Awe Inspiring
1990 **Unbridled**	2:02	Craig Perret	Carl Nafzger	Summer Squall	Pleasant Tap
1991 **Strike the Gold**	2:03	Chris Antley	Nick Zito	Best Pal	Mane Minister
1992 **Lil E. Tee**	2:03	Pat Day	Lynn Whiting	Casual Lies	Dance Floor
1993 **Sea Hero**	2:02⅖	Jerry Bailey	Mack Miller	Prairie Bayou	Wild Gale
1994 **Go For Gin**	2:03⅗	Chris McCarron	Nick Zito	Strodes Creek	Blumin Affair
1995 **Thunder Gulch**	2:01⅕	Gary Stevens	D. Wayne Lukas	Tejano Run	Timber Country
1996 **Grindstone**	2:01	Jerry Bailey	D. Wayne Lukas	Cavonnier	Prince of Thieves
1997 **Silver Charm**	2:02⅖	Gary Stevens	Bob Baffert	Captain Bodgit	Free House
1998 **Real Quiet**	2:02⅕	Kent Desormeaux	Bob Baffert	Victory Gallop	Indian Charlie
1999 **Charismatic**	2:03⅕	Chris Antley	D. Wayne Lukas	Menifee	Cat Thief

*Dancer's Image finished first (in 2:02½), but was disqualified after traces of prohibited medication were found in his system.

Preakness Stakes

For three-year-olds. Held two weeks after the Kentucky Derby at Pimlico Race Course in Baltimore. Inaugurated 1873. Originally run at 1½ miles (1873-88), then at 1¼ miles (1889), 1½ miles (1890), 1¹⁄₁₆ miles (1894-1900), 1 mile & 70 yards (1901-07), 1¹⁄₁₆ miles (1908), 1 mile (1909-1910), 1⅛ miles (1911-24), and the present 1³⁄₁₆ miles since 1925.

Trainers with most wins: Robert W. Walden (7); T.J. Healey and D. Wayne Lukas (5); Sunny Jim Fitzsimmons and Jimmy Jones (4); and J. Whalen (3).

Jockeys with most wins: Eddie Arcaro (6); Pat Day (5); G. Barbee, Bill Hartack and Lloyd Hughes (3).

Winning fillies: Flocarline (1903), Whimsical (1906), Rhine Maiden (1915) and Nellie Morse (1924).

Year	Time	Jockey	Trainer	2nd place	3rd place
1873 **Survivor**	2:43	G. Barbee	A.D. Pryor	John Boulger	Artist
1874 **Culpepper**	2:56½	W. Donohue	H. Gaffney	King Amadeus	Scratch
1875 **Tom Ochiltree**	2:43½	L. Hughes	R.W. Walden	Viator	Bay Final
1876 **Shirley**	2:44¾	G. Barbee	W. Brown	Rappahannock	Compliment
1877 **Cloverbrook**	2:45½	C. Holloway	J. Walden	Bombast	Lucifer
1878 **Duke of Magenta**	2:41¾	C. Holloway	R.W. Walden	Bayard	Albert
1879 **Harold**	2:40½	L. Hughes	R.W. Walden	Jericho	Rochester
1880 **Grenada**	2:40½	L. Hughes	R.W. Walden	Oden	Emily F.
1881 **Saunterer**	2:40½	T. Costello	R.W. Walden	Compensation	Baltic
1882 **Vanguard**	2:44½	T. Costello	R.W. Walden	Heck	Col. Watson
1883 **Jacobus**	2:42½	G. Barbee	R. Dwyer	Parnell	(2-horse race)
1884 **Knight of Ellerslie**	2:39½	S. Fisher	T.B. Doswell	Welcher	(2-horse race)
1885 **Tecumseh**	2:49	Jim McLaughlin	C. Littlefield	Wickham	John C.
1886 **The Bard**	2:45	S. Fisher	J. Huggins	Eurus	Elkwood
1887 **Dunboyne**	2:39½	W. Donohue	W. Jennings	Mahoney	Raymond
1888 **Refund**	2:49	F. Littlefield	R.W. Walden	Bertha B.*	Glendale
1889 **Buddhist**	2:17½	W. Anderson	J. Rogers	Japhet	(2-horse race)
1890 **Montague**	2:36¾	W. Martin	E. Feakes	Philosophy	Barrister
1891-93 Not held					
1894 **Assignee**	1:49¼	F. Taral	W. Lakeland	Potentate	Ed Kearney
1895 **Belmar**	1:50½	F. Taral	E. Feakes	April Fool	Sue Kittie
1896 **Margrave**	1:51	H. Griffin	Byron McClelland	Hamilton II	Intermission
1897 **Paul Kauvar**	1:51¼	T. Thorpe	T.P. Hayes	Elkins	On Deck
1898 **Sly Fox**	1:49¾	W. Simms	H. Campbell	The Huguenot	Nuto
1899 **Half Time**	1:47	R. Clawson	F. McCabe	Filigrane	Lackland
1900 **Hindus**	1:48⅖	H. Spencer	J.H. Morris	Sarmatian	Ten Candles
1901 **The Parader**	1:47⅕	F. Landry	T.J. Healey	Sadie S.	Dr. Barlow
1902 **Old England**	1:45⅘	L. Jackson	G.B. Morris	Maj. Daingerfield	Namtor
1903 **Flocarline**	1:44⅘	W. Gannon	H.C. Riddle	Mackey Dwyer	Rightful
1904 **Bryn Mawr**	1:44⅕	E. Hildebrand	W.F. Presgrave	Wotan	Dolly Spanker
1905 **Cairngorm**	1:45⅘	W. Davis	A.J. Joyner	Kiamesha	Coy Maid
1906 **Whimsical**	1:45	Walter Miller	T.J. Gaynor	Content	Larabie
1907 **Don Enrique**	1:45⅖	G. Mountain	J. Whalen	Ethon	Zambesi
1908 **Royal Tourist**	1:46⅖	Eddie Dugan	A.J. Joyner	Live Wire	Robert Cooper

Year	Time	Jockey	Trainer	2nd place	3rd place
1909 **Effendi**	1:39⅘	Willie Doyle	F.C. Frisbie	Fashion Plate	Hill Top
1910 **Layminster**	1:40⅗	R. Estep	J.S. Healy	Dalhousie	Sager
1911 **Watervale**	1:51	Eddie Dugan	J. Whalen	Zeus	The Nigger
1912 **Colonel Holloway**	1:56⅗	C. Turner	D. Woodford	Bwana Tumbo	Tipsand
1913 **Buskin**	1:53⅖	James Butwell	J. Whalen	Kleburne	Barnegat
1914 **Holiday**	1:53⅘	A. Schuttinger	J.S. Healy	Brave Cunarder	Defendum
1915 **Rhine Maiden**	1:58	Douglas Hoffman	F. Devers	Half Rock	Runes
1916 **Damrosch**	1:54⅘	Linus McAtee	A.G. Weston	Greenwood	Achievement
1917 **Kalitan**	1:54⅖	E. Haynes	Bill Hurley	Al M. Dick	Kentucky Boy
1918 **War Cloud**	1:53⅗	Johnny Loftus	W.B. Jennings	Sunny Slope	Lanius
1918 **Jack Hare Jr**	1:53⅖	Charles Peak	F.D. Weir	The Porter	Kate Bright
1919 **SIR BARTON**	1:53	Johnny Loftus	H. Guy Bedwell	Eternal	Sweep On
1920 **Man o' War**	1:51⅗	Clarence Kummer	L. Feustel	Upset	Wildair
1921 **Broomspun**	1:54⅕	F. Coltiletti	James Rowe Sr.	Polly Ann	Jeg
1922 **Pillory**	1:51⅗	L. Morris	Thomas Healey	Hea	June Grass
1923 **Vigil**	1:53⅗	B. Marinelli	Thomas Healey	General Thatcher	Rialto
1924 **Nellie Morse**	1:57⅕	John Merimee	A.B. Gordon	Transmute	Mad Play
1925 **Coventry**	1:59	Clarence Kummer	William Duke	Backbone	Almadel
1926 **Display**	1:59⅘	John Maiben	Thomas Healey	Blondin	Mars
1927 **Bostonian**	2:01⅗	Whitey Abel	Fred Hopkins	Sir Harry	Whiskery
1928 **Victorian**	2:00⅕	Sonny Workman	James Rowe Jr.	Toro	Solace
1929 **Dr. Freeland**	2:01⅗	Louis Schaefer	Thomas Healey	Minotaur	African
1930 **GALLANT FOX**	2:00⅗	Earl Sande	Jim Fitzsimmons	Crack Brigade	Snowflake
1931 **Mate**	1:59	George Ellis	J.W. Healy	Twenty Grand	Ladder
1932 **Burgoo King**	1:59⅘	Eugene James	Dick Thompson	Tick On	Boatswain
1933 **Head Play**	2:02	Charley Kurtsinger	Thomas Hayes	Ladysman	Utopian
1934 **High Quest**	1:58⅕	Robert Jones	Bob Smith	Cavalcade	Discovery
1935 **OMAHA**	1:58⅖	Willie Saunders	Jim Fitzsimmons	Firethorn	Psychic Bid
1936 **Bold Venture**	1:59	George Woolf	Max Hirsch	Granville	Jean Bart
1937 **WAR ADMIRAL**	1:58⅖	Charley Kurtsinger	George Conway	Pompoon	Flying Scot
1938 **Dauber**	1:59⅘	Maurice Peters	Dick Handlen	Cravat	Menow
1939 **Challedon**	1:59⅘	George Seabo	Louis Schaefer	Gilded Knight	Volitant
1940 **Bimelech**	1:58⅗	F.A. Smith	Bill Hurley	Mioland	Gallahadion
1941 **WHIRLAWAY**	1:58⅘	Eddie Arcaro	Ben Jones	King Cole	Our Boots
1942 **Alsab**	1:57	Basil James	Sarge Swenke	Requested & Sun Again (dead heat)	
1943 **COUNT FLEET**	1:57⅖	Johnny Longden	Don Cameron	Blue Swords	Vincentive
1944 **Pensive**	1:59⅕	Conn McCreary	Ben Jones	Platter	Stir Up
1945 **Polynesian**	1:58⅘	W.D. Wright	Morris Dixon	Hoop Jr.	Darby Dieppe
1946 **ASSAULT**	2:01⅖	Warren Mehrtens	Max Hirsch	Lord Boswell	Hampden
1947 **Faultless**	1:59	Doug Dodson	Jimmy Jones	On Trust	Phalanx
1948 **CITATION**	2:02⅖	Eddie Arcaro	Jimmy Jones	Vulcan's Forge	Bovard
1949 **Capot**	1:56	Ted Atkinson	J.M. Gaver	Palestinian	Noble Impulse
1950 **Hill Prince**	1:59⅕	Eddie Arcaro	Casey Hayes	Middleground	Dooly
1951 **Bold**	1:56⅖	Eddie Arcaro	Preston Burch	Counterpoint	Alerted
1952 **Blue Man**	1:57⅖	Conn McCreary	Woody Stephens	Jampol	One Count
1953 **Native Dancer**	1:57⅘	Eric Guerin	Bill Winfrey	Jamie K.	Royal Bay Gem
1954 **Hasty Road**	1:57⅖	Johnny Adams	Harry Trotsek	Correlation	Hasseyampa
1955 **Nashua**	1:54⅗	Eddie Arcaro	Jim Fitzsimmons	Saratoga	Traffic Judge
1956 **Fabius**	1:58⅖	Bill Hartack	Jimmy Jones	Needles	No Regrets
1957 **Bold Ruler**	1:56⅕	Eddie Arcaro	Jim Fitzsimmons	Iron Liege	Inside Tract
1958 **Tim Tam**	1:57⅕	Ismael Valenzuela	Jimmy Jones	Lincoln Road	Gone Fishin'
1959 **Royal Orbit**	1:57	William Harmatz	R. Cornell	Sword Dancer	Dunce
1960 **Bally Ache**	1:57⅗	Bobby Ussery	Jimmy Pitt	Victoria Park	Celtic Ash
1961 **Carry Back**	1:57⅗	Johnny Sellers	Jack Price	Globemaster	Crozier
1962 **Greek Money**	1:56⅕	John Rotz	V.W. Raines	Ridan	Roman Line
1963 **Candy Spots**	1:56⅕	Bill Shoemaker	Mesh Tenney	Chateaugay	Never Bend
1964 **Northern Dancer**	1:56⅘	Bill Hartack	Horatio Luro	The Scoundrel	Hill Rise
1965 **Tom Rolfe**	1:56⅕	Ron Turcotte	Frank Whiteley	Dapper Dan	Hail To All
1966 **Kauai King**	1:55⅖	Don Brumfield	Henry Forrest	Stupendous	Amberoid
1967 **Damascus**	1:55⅕	Bill Shoemaker	Frank Whiteley	In Reality	Proud Clarion
1968 **Forward Pass**	1:56⅘	Ismael Valenzuela	Henry Forrest	Out Of the Way	Nodouble
1969 **Majestic Prince**	1:55⅗	Bill Hartack	Johnny Longden	Arts and Letters	Jay Ray
1970 **Personality**	1:56⅕	Eddie Belmonte	John Jacobs	My Dad George	Silent Screen
1971 **Canonero II**	1:54	Gustavo Avila	Juan Arias	Eastern Fleet	Jim French
1972 **Bee Bee Bee**	1:55⅗	Eldon Nelson	Red Carroll	No Le Hace	Key To The Mint
1973 **SECRETARIAT**	1:54⅖	Ron Turcotte	Lucien Laurin	Sham	Our Native
1974 **Little Current**	1:54⅗	Miguel Rivera	Lou Rondinello	Neapolitan Way	Cannonade
1975 **Master Derby**	1:56⅖	Darrel McHargue	Smiley Adams	Foolish Pleasure	Diabolo

Preakness Stakes (Cont.)

Year	Time	Jockey	Trainer	2nd place	3rd place
1976 **Elocutionist**	1:55	John Lively	Paul Adwell	Play The Red	Bold Forbes
1977 **SEATTLE SLEW**	1:54⅖	Jean Cruguet	Billy Turner	Iron Constitution	Run Dusty Run
1978 **AFFIRMED**	1:54⅖	Steve Cauthen	Laz Barrera	Alydar	Believe It
1979 **Spectacular Bid**	1:54⅕	Ron Franklin	Bud Delp	Golden Act	Screen King
1980 **Codex**	1:54⅕	Angel Cordero Jr.	D. Wayne Lukas	Genuine Risk	Colonel Moran
1981 **Pleasant Colony**	1:54⅗	Jorge Velasquez	John Campo	Bold Ego	Paristo
1982 **Aloma's Ruler**	1:55⅖	Jack Kaenel	John Lenzini Jr.	Linkage	Cut Away
1983 **Deputed Testamony**	1:55⅖	Donald Miller Jr.	Bill Boniface	Desert Wine	High Honors
1984 **Gate Dancer**	1:53⅗	Angel Cordero Jr.	Jack Van Berg	Play On	Fight Over
1985 **Tank's Prospect**	1:53⅖	Pat Day	D. Wayne Lukas	Chief's Crown	Eternal Prince
1986 **Snow Chief**	1:54⅘	Alex Solis	Melvin Stute	Ferdinand	Broad Brush
1987 **Alysheba**	1:55⅘	Chris McCarron	Jack Van Berg	Bet Twice	Cryptoclearance
1988 **Risen Star**	1:56⅕	E. Delahoussaye	Louie Roussel III	Brian's Time	Winning Colors
1989 **Sunday Silence**	1:53⅘	Pat Valenzuela	Chas. Whittingham	Easy Goer	Rock Point
1990 **Summer Squall**	1:53⅗	Pat Day	Neil Howard	Unbridled	Mister Frisky
1991 **Hansel**	1:54	Jerry Bailey	Frank Brothers	Corporate Report	Mane Minister
1992 **Pine Bluff**	1:55⅗	Chris McCarron	Tom Bohannan	Alydeed	Casual Lies
1993 **Prairie Bayou**	1:56⅗	Mike Smith	Tom Bohannan	Cherokee Run	El Bakan
1994 **Tabasco Cat**	1:56⅖	Pat Day	D. Wayne Lukas	Go For Gin	Concern
1995 **Timber Country**	1:54⅖	Pat Day	D. Wayne Lukas	Oliver's Twist	Thunder Gulch
1996 **Louis Quatorze**	1:53⅖	Pat Day	Nick Zito	Skip Away	Editor's Note
1997 **Silver Charm**	1:54⅖	Gary Stevens	Bob Baffert	Free House	Captain Bodgit
1998 **Real Quiet**	1:54⅘	Kent Desormeaux	Bob Baffert	Victory Gallop	Classic Cat
1999 **Charismatic**	1:55⅕	Chris Antley	D. Wayne Lukas	Menifee	Badge

* Later named Judge Murray.

Belmont Stakes

For three-year-olds. Held three weeks after Preakness Stakes at Belmont Park in Elmont, N.Y. Inaugurated in 1867 at Jerome Park, moved to Morris Park in 1890 and then to Belmont Park in 1905.

Originally run at 1 mile and 5 furlongs (1867-89), then 1¼ miles (1890-1905), 1⅜ miles (1906-25), and the present 1½ miles since 1926.

Trainers with most wins: James Rowe Sr. (8); Sam Hildreth (7); Sunny Jim Fitzsimmons (6); Woody Stephens (5); Max Hirsch and Robert W. Walden (4); Elliott Burch, Lucien Laurin, D. Wayne Lukas, F. McCabe and D. McDaniel (3).

Jockeys with most wins: Eddie Arcaro and Jim McLaughlin (6); Earl Sande and Bill Shoemaker (5); Braulio Baeza, Laffit Pincay Jr. and James Stout (3).

Winning fillies: Ruthless (1867) and Tanya (1905).

Year	Time	Jockey	Trainer	2nd place	3rd place
1867 **Ruthless**	3:05	J. Gilpatrick	A.J. Minor	DeCourcey	Rivoli
1868 **General Duke**	3:02	Bobby Swim	A. Thompson	Northumberland	Fanny Ludlow
1869 **Fenian**	3:04¼	C. Miller	J. Pincus	Glenelg	Invercauld
1870 **Kingfisher**	2:59½	W. Dick	R. Colston	Foster	Midday
1871 **Harry Bassett**	2:56	W. Miller	D. McDaniel	Stockwood	By the Sea
1872 **Joe Daniels**	2:58¼	James Roe	D. McDaniel	Meteor	Shylock
1873 **Springbok**	3:01¾	James Roe	D. McDaniel	Count d'Orsay	Strachino
1874 **Saxon**	2:39½	G. Barbee	W. Prior	Grinstead	Aaron Pennington
1875 **Calvin**	2:42¼	Bobby Swim	A. Williams	Aristides	Milner
1876 **Algerine**	2:40½	Billy Donohue	Major Doswell	Fiddlesticks	Barricade
1877 **Cloverbrook**	2:46	C. Holloway	J. Walden	Loiterer	Baden-Baden
1878 **Duke of Magenta**	2:43½	L. Hughes	R.W. Walden	Bramble	Sparta
1879 **Spendthrift**	2:42¾	George Evans	T. Puryear	Monitor	Jericho
1880 **Grenada**	2:47	L. Hughes	R.W. Walden	Ferncliffe	Turenne
1881 **Saunterer**	2:47	T. Costello	R.W. Walden	Eole	Baltic
1882 **Forester**	2:43	Jim McLaughlin	L. Stuart	Babcock	Wyoming
1883 **George Kinney**	2:42½	Jim McLaughlin	James Rowe Sr.	Trombone	Renegade
1884 **Panique**	2:42	Jim McLaughlin	James Rowe Sr.	Knight of Ellerslie	Himalaya
1885 **Tyrant**	2:43	Paul Duffy	W. Claypool	St. Augustine	Tecumseh
1886 **Inspector B**	2:41	Jim McLaughlin	F. McCabe	The Bard	Linden
1887 **Hanover**	2:43½	Jim McLaughlin	F. McCabe	Oneko	(2-horse race)
1888 **Sir Dixon**	2:40¼	Jim McLaughlin	F. McCabe	Prince Royal	(2-horse race)
1889 **Eric**	2:47¼	W. Hayward	J. Huggins	Diablo	Zephyrus
1890 **Burlington**	2:07¾	Pike Barnes	A. Cooper	Devotee	Padishah
1891 **Foxford**	2:08¾	Ed Garrison	M. Donavan	Montana	Laurestan
1892 **Patron**	2:12	W. Hayward	L. Stuart	Shellbark	(2-horse race)
1893 **Commanche**	1:53¼	Willie Simms	G. Hannon	Dr. Rice	Rainbow
1894 **Henry of Navarre**	1:56½	Willie Simms	B. McClelland	Prig	Assignee
1895 **Belmar**	2:11½	Fred Taral	E. Feakes	Counter Tenor	Nanki Poo

Year		Time	Jockey	Trainer	2nd place	3rd place
1896	**Hastings**	2:24½	H. Griffin	J.J. Hyland	Handspring	Hamilton II
1897	**Scottish Chieftain**	2:23¼	J. Scherrer	M. Byrnes	On Deck	Octagon
1898	**Bowling Brook**	2:32	F. Littlefield	R.W. Walden	Previous	Hamburg
1899	**Jean Beraud**	2:23	R. Clawson	Sam Hildreth	Half Time	Glengar
1900	**Ildrim**	2:21¼	Nash Turner	H.E. Leigh	Petruchio	Missionary
1901	**Commando**	2:21	H. Spencer	James Rowe Sr.	The Parader	All Green
1902	**Masterman**	2:22⅗	John Bullman	J.J. Hyland	Renald	King Hanover
1903	**Africander**	2:21¾	John Bullman	R. Miller	Whorler	Red Knight
1904	**Delhi**	2:06⅗	George Odom	James Rowe Sr.	Graziallo	Rapid Water
1905	**Tanya**	2:08	E. Hildebrand	J.W. Rogers	Blandy	Hot Shot
1906	**Burgomaster**	2:20	Lucien Lyne	J.W. Rogers	The Quail	Accountant
1907	**Peter Pan**	N/A	G. Mountain	James Rowe Sr.	Superman	Frank Gill
1908	**Colin**	N/A	Joe Notter	James Rowe Sr.	Fair Play	King James
1909	**Joe Madden**	2:21⅗	E. Dugan	Sam Hildreth	Wise Mason	Donald MacDonald
1910	**Sweep**	2:22	James Butwell	James Rowe Sr.	Duke of Ormonde	(2-horse race)
1911-12	Not held					
1913	**Prince Eugene**	2:18	Roscoe Troxler	James Rowe Sr.	Rock View	Flying Fairy
1914	**Luke McLuke**	2:20	Merritt Buxton	J.F. Schorr	Gainer	Charlestonian
1915	**The Finn**	2:18⅖	George Byrne	E.W. Heffner	Half Rock	Pebbles
1916	**Friar Rock**	2:22	E. Haynes	Sam Hildreth	Spur	Churchill
1917	**Hourless**	2:17⅘	James Butwell	Sam Hildreth	Skeptic	Wonderful
1918	**Johren**	2:20⅖	Frank Robinson	A. Simons	War Cloud	Cum Sah
1919	**SIR BARTON**	2:17⅖	John Loftus	H. Guy Bedwell	Sweep On	Natural Bridge
1920	**Man o' War**	2:14⅕	Clarence Kummer	L. Feustel	Donnacona	(2-horse race)
1921	**Grey Lag**	2:16⅘	Earl Sande	Sam Hildreth	Sporting Blood	Leonardo II
1922	**Pillory**	2:18⅘	C.H. Miller	T.J. Healey	Snob II	Hea
1923	**Zev**	2:19	Earl Sande	Sam Hildreth	Chickvale	Rialto
1924	**Mad Play**	2:18⅘	Earl Sande	Sam Hildreth	Mr. Mutt	Modest
1925	**American Flag**	2:16⅘	Albert Johnson	G.R. Tompkins	Dangerous	Swope
1926	**Crusader**	2:32⅕	Albert Johnson	George Conway	Espino	Haste
1927	**Chance Shot**	2:32⅖	Earl Sande	Pete Coyne	Bois de Rose	Flambino
1928	**Vito**	2:33⅕	Clarence Kummer	Max Hirsch	Genie	Diavolo
1929	**Blue Larkspur**	2:32⅘	Mack Garner	C. Hastings	African	Jack High
1930	**GALLANT FOX**	2:31⅗	Earl Sande	Jim Fitzsimmons	Whichone	Questionnaire
1931	**Twenty Grand**	2:29⅗	Charley Kurtsinger	James Rowe Jr.	Sun Meadow	Jamestown
1932	**Faireno**	2:32⅘	Tom Malley	Jim Fitzsimmons	Osculator	Flag Pole
1933	**Hurryoff**	2:32⅗	Mack Garner	H. McDaniel	Nimbus	Union
1934	**Peace Chance**	2:29⅕	W.D. Wright	Pete Coyne	High Quest	Good Goods
1935	**OMAHA**	2:30⅗	Willie Saunders	Jim Fitzsimmons	Firethorn	Rosemont
1936	**Granville**	2:30	James Stout	Jim Fitzsimmons	Mr. Bones	Hollyrood
1937	**WAR ADMIRAL**	2:28⅗	Charley Kurtsinger	George Conway	Sceneshifter	Vamoose
1938	**Pasteurized**	2:29⅖	James Stout	George Odom	Dauber	Cravat
1939	**Johnstown**	2:29⅗	James Stout	Jim Fitzsimmons	Belay	Gilded Knight
1940	**Bimelech**	2:29⅗	Fred Smith	Bill Hurley	Your Chance	Andy K.
1941	**WHIRLAWAY**	2:31	Eddie Arcaro	Ben Jones	Robert Morris	Yankee Chance
1942	**Shut Out**	2:29⅕	Eddie Arcaro	John Gaver	Alsab	Lochinvar
1943	**COUNT FLEET**	2:28⅕	Johnny Longden	Don Cameron	Fairy Manhurst	Deseronto
1944	**Bounding Home**	2:32⅕	G.L. Smith	Matt Brady	Pensive	Bull Dandy
1945	**Pavot**	2:30⅕	Eddie Arcaro	Oscar White	Wildlife	Jeep
1946	**ASSAULT**	2:30⅘	Warren Mehrtens	Max Hirsch	Natchez	Cable
1947	**Phalanx**	2:29⅖	R. Donoso	Syl Veitch	Tide Rips	Tailspin
1948	**CITATION**	2:28⅕	Eddie Arcaro	Jimmy Jones	Better Self	Escadru
1949	**Capot**	2:30⅕	Ted Atkinson	John Gaver	Ponder	Palestinian
1950	**Middleground**	2:28⅗	William Boland	Max Hirsch	Lights Up	Mr. Trouble
1951	**Counterpoint**	2:29	David Gorman	Syl Veitch	Battlefield	Battle Morn
1952	**One Count**	2:30⅕	Eddie Arcaro	Oscar White	Blue Man	Armageddon
1953	**Native Dancer**	2:28⅗	Eric Guerin	Bill Winfrey	Jamie K.	Royal Bay Gem
1954	**High Gun**	2:30⅘	Eric Guerin	Max Hirsch	Fisherman	Limelight
1955	**Nashua**	2:29	Eddie Arcaro	Jim Fitzsimmons	Blazing Count	Portersville
1956	**Needles**	2:29⅘	David Erb	Hugh Fontaine	Career Boy	Fabius
1957	**Gallant Man**	2:26⅗	Bill Shoemaker	John Nerud	Inside Tract	Bold Ruler
1958	**Cavan**	2:30⅕	Pete Anderson	Tom Barry	Tim Tam	Flamingo
1959	**Sword Dancer**	2:28⅖	Bill Shoemaker	Elliott Burch	Bagdad	Royal Orbit
1960	**Celtic Ash**	2:29⅕	Bill Hartack	Tom Barry	Venetian Way	Disperse
1961	**Sherluck**	2:29⅕	Braulio Baeza	Harold Young	Globemaster	Guadalcanal
1962	**Jaipur**	2:28⅘	Bill Shoemaker	B. Mulholland	Admiral's Voyage	Crimson Satan
1963	**Chateaugay**	2:30⅕	Braulio Baeza	James Conway	Candy Spots	Choker
1964	**Quadrangle**	2:28⅖	Manuel Ycaza	Elliott Burch	Roman Brother	Northern Dancer

Belmont Stakes (Cont.)

Year	Time	Jockey	Trainer	2nd place	3rd place
1965 **Hail to All**	2:28⅖	John Sellers	Eddie Yowell	Tom Rolfe	First Family
1966 **Amberoid**	2:29⅗	William Boland	Lucien Laurin	Buffle	Advocator
1967 **Damascus**	2:28⅘	Bill Shoemaker	F.Y. Whiteley Jr.	Cool Reception	Gentleman James
1968 **Stage Door Johnny**	2:27⅕	Gus Gustines	John Gaver	Forward Pass	Call Me Prince
1969 **Arts and Letters**	2:28⅘	Braulio Baeza	Elliott Burch	Majestic Prince	Dike
1970 **High Echelon**	2:34	John Rotz	John Jacobs	Needles N Pens	Naskra
1971 **Pass Catcher**	2:30⅖	Walter Blum	Eddie Yowell	Jim French	Bold Reason
1972 **Riva Ridge**	2:28	Ron Turcotte	Lucien Laurin	Ruritania	Cloudy Dawn
1973 **SECRETARIAT**	2:24	Ron Turcotte	Lucien Laurin	Twice A Prince	My Gallant
1974 **Little Current**	2:29⅕	Miguel Rivera	Lou Rondinello	Jolly Johu	Cannonade
1975 **Avatar**	2:28⅕	Bill Shoemaker	Tommy Doyle	Foolish Pleasure	Master Derby
1976 **Bold Forbes**	2:29	Angel Cordero Jr.	Laz Barrera	McKenzie Bridge	Great Contractor
1977 **SEATTLE SLEW**	2:29⅗	Jean Cruguet	Billy Turner	Run Dusty Run	Sanhedrin
1978 **AFFIRMED**	2:26⅘	Steve Cauthen	Laz Barrera	Alydar	Darby Creek Road
1979 **Coastal**	2:28⅗	Ruben Hernandez	David Whiteley	Golden Act	Spectacular Bid
1980 **Temperence Hill**	2:29⅘	Eddie Maple	Joseph Cantey	Genuine Risk	Rockhill Native
1981 **Summing**	2:29	George Martens	Luis Barerra	Highland Blade	Pleasant Colony
1982 **Conquistador Cielo**	2:28⅕	Laffit Pincay Jr.	Woody Stephens	Gato Del Sol	Illuminate
1983 **Caveat**	2:27⅘	Laffit Pincay Jr.	Woody Stephens	Slew o' Gold	Barberstown
1984 **Swale**	2:27⅕	Laffit Pincay Jr.	Woody Stephens	Pine Circle	Morning Bob
1985 **Creme Fraiche**	2:27	Eddie Maple	Woody Stephens	Stephan's Odyssey	Chief's Crown
1986 **Danzig Connection**	2:29⅘	Chris McCarron	Woody Stephens	Johns Treasure	Ferdinand
1987 **Bet Twice**	2:28⅕	Craig Perret	Jimmy Croll	Cryptoclearance	Gulch
1988 **Risen Star**	2:26⅖	E. Delahoussaye	Louie Roussel III	Kingpost	Brian's Time
1989 **Easy Goer**	2:26	Pat Day	Shug McGaughey	Sunday Silence	Le Voyageur
1990 **Go And Go**	2:27⅕	Michael Kinane	Dermot Weld	Thirty Six Red	Baron de Vaux
1991 **Hansel**	2:28	Jerry Bailey	Frank Brothers	Strike the Gold	Mane Minister
1992 **A.P. Indy**	2:26	E. Delahoussaye	Neil Drysdale	My Memoirs	Pine Bluff
1993 **Colonial Affair**	2:29⅘	Julie Krone	Scotty Schulhofer	Kissin Kris	Wild Gale
1994 **Tabasco Cat**	2:26⅘	Pat Day	D. Wayne Lukas	Go For Gin	Strodes Creek
1995 **Thunder Gulch**	2:32	Gary Stevens	D. Wayne Lukas	Star Standard	Citadeed
1996 **Editor's Note**	2:28⅘	Rene Douglas	D. Wayne Lukas	Skip Away	My Flag
1997 **Touch Gold**	2:28⅘	Chris McCarron	David Hofmans	Silver Charm	Free House
1998 **Victory Gallop**	2:29	Gary Stevens	Elliott Walden	Real Quiet	Thomas Jo
1999 **Lemon Drop Kid**	2:27⅘	Jose Santos	Scotty Schulhofer	Vision and Verse	Charismatic

Breeders' Cup Championship

Inaugurated on Nov. 10, 1984, the Breeders' Cup Championship consists of seven races on one track on one day late in the year to determine thoroughbred racing's principle champions.

The Breeders' Cup has been held at the following tracks (in alphabetical order): Aqueduct Racetrack (N.Y.) in 1985; Belmont Park (N.Y.) in 1990 and '95; Churchill Downs (Ky.) in 1988, '91, '94 and '98; Gulfstream Park (Fla.) in 1989 and '92; Hollywood Park (Calif.) in 1984, '87 and '97; Santa Anita Park (Calif.) in 1986 and '93 and Woodbine (Toronto) in 1996.

Trainers with most wins: D. Wayne Lukas (13); Shug McGaughey (7); Neil Drysdale and Bill Mott (5); Ron McAnally (4); Francois Boutin and Patrick Byrne (3).

Jockeys with most wins: Pat Day (10); Mike Smith (8); Jerry Bailey, Eddie Delahoussaye Chris McCarron and Laffit Pincay Jr. (7); Jose Santos, Gary Stevens and Pat Valenzuela (6); Angel Cordero, Corey Nakatani and Craig Perret (4); Randy Romero (3).

Juvenile

Distances: one mile (1984-85, 87); 1$\frac{1}{16}$ miles (1986 and since 1988).

Year	Time	Jockey	Trainer	2nd place	3rd place
1984 **Chief's Crown**	1:36⅕	Don MacBeth	Roger Laurin	Tank's Prospect	Spend A Buck
1985 **Tasso**	1:36⅕	Laffit Pincay Jr.	Neil Drysdale	Storm Cat	Scat Dancer
1986 **Capote**	1:43⅘	Laffit Pincay Jr.	D. Wayne Lukas	Qualify	Alysheba
1987 **Success Express**	1:35⅕	Jose Santos	D. Wayne Lukas	Regal Classic	Tejano
1988 **Is It True**	1:46⅗	Laffit Pincay Jr.	D. Wayne Lukas	Easy Goer	Tagel
1989 **Rhythm**	1:43⅗	Craig Perret	Shug McGaughey	Grand Canyon	Slavic
1990 **Fly So Free**	1:43⅖	Jose Santos	Scotty Schulhofer	Take Me Out	Lost Mountain
1991 **Arazi**	1:44⅗	Pat Valenzuela	Francois Boutin	Bertrando	Snappy Landing
1992 **Gilded Time**	1:43⅖	Chris McCarron	Darrell Vienna	It'sali'lknownfact	River Special
1993 **Brocco**	1:42⅘	Gary Stevens	Randy Winick	Blumin Affair	Tabasco Cat
1994 **Timber Country**	1:44⅖	Pat Day	D. Wayne Lukas	Eltish	Tejano Run
1995 **Unbridled's Song**	1:41⅗	Mike Smith	James Ryerson	Hennessy	Editor's Note
1996 **Boston Harbor**	1:43⅖	Jerry Bailey	D. Wayne Lukas	Acceptable	Ordway
1997 **Favorite Trick**	1:41⅖	Pat Day	Patrick Byrne	Dawson's Legacy	Nationalore
1998 **Answer Lively**	1:44	Jerry Bailey	Bobby Barnett	Aly's Alley	Cat Thief

Juvenile Fillies

Distances: one mile (1984-85, 87); 1 1/16 miles (1986 and since 1988).

Year	Time	Jockey	Trainer	2nd place	3rd place
1984 **Outstandingly***	1:37⅘	Walter Guerra	Pancho Martin	Dusty Heart	Fine Spirit
1985 **Twilight Ridge**	1:35⅘	Jorge Velasquez	D. Wayne Lukas	Family Style	Steal A Kiss
1986 **Brave Raj**	1:43⅕	Pat Valenzuela	Melvin Stute	Tappiano	Saros Brig
1987 **Epitome**	1:36⅖	Pat Day	Phil Hauswald	Jeanne Jones	Dream Team
1988 **Open Mind**	1:46⅗	Angel Cordero Jr.	D. Wayne Lukas	Darby Shuffle	Lea Lucinda
1989 **Go for Wand**	1:44⅕	Randy Romero	Wm. Badgett, Jr.	Sweet Roberta	Stella Madrid
1990 **Meadow Star**	1:44	Jose Santos	LeRoy Jolley	Private Treasure	Dance Smartly
1991 **Pleasant Stage**	1:46⅖	Eddie Delahoussaye	Chris Speckert	La Spia	Cadillac Women
1992 **Liza**	1:42⅘	Pat Valenzuela	Alex Hassingfer	Educated Risk	Boots 'n Jackie
1993 **Phone Chatter**	1:43	Laffit Pincay Jr.	Richard Mandella	Sardula	Heavenly Prize
1994 **Flanders**	1:45⅕	Pat Day	D. Wayne Lukas	Serena's Song	Stormy Blues
1995 **My Flag**	1:42⅖	Jerry Bailey	Shug McGaughey	Cara Rafaela	Golden Attraction
1996 **Storm Song**	1:43⅗	Craig Perret	Nick Zito	Love That Jazz	Critical Factor
1997 **Countess Diana**	1:42⅕	Shane Sellers	Patrick Byrne	Career Collection	Primaly
1998 **Silverbulletday**	1:43⅗	Gary Stevens	Bob Baffert	Excellent Meeting	Three Ring

*In 1984, winner Fran's Valentine was disqualified for interference in the stretch and placed 10th.

Sprint

Distance: six furlongs (since 1984).

Year	Time	Jockey	Trainer	2nd place	3rd place
1984 **Eillo**	1:10⅕	Craig Perret	Budd Lepman	Commemorate	Fighting Fit
1985 **Precisionist**	1:08⅖	Chris McCarron	L.R. Fenstermaker	Smile	Mt. Livermore
1986 **Smile**	1:08⅖	Jacinto Vasquez	Scotty Schulhofer	Pine Tree Lane	Bedside Promise
1987 **Very Subtle**	1:08⅘	Pat Valenzuela	Melvin Stute	Groovy	Exclusive Enough
1988 **Gulch**	1:10⅖	Angel Cordero Jr.	D. Wayne Lukas	Play The King	Afleet
1989 **Dancing Spree**	1:09	Angel Cordero Jr.	Shug McGaughey	Safely Kept	Dispersal
1990 **Safely Kept**	1:09⅗	Craig Perret	Alan Goldberg	Dayjur	Black Tie Affair
1991 **Sheikh Albadou**	1:09⅕	Pat Eddery	Alexander Scott	Pleasant Tap	Robyn Dancer
1992 **Thirty Slews**	1:08⅕	Eddie Delahoussaye	Bob Baffert	Meafara	Rubiano
1993 **Cardmania**	1:08⅗	Eddie Delahoussaye	Derek Meredith	Meafara	Gilded Time
1994 **Cherokee Run**	1:09⅖	Mike Smith	Frank Alexander	Soviet Problem	Cardmania
1995 **Desert Stormer**	1:09	Kent Desormeaux	Frank Lyons	Mr. Greeley	Lit de Justice
1996 **Lit de Justice**	1:08⅗	Corey Nakatani	Jenine Sahadi	Paying Dues	Honour and Glory
1997 **Elmhurst**	1:08⅕	Corey Nakatani	Jenine Sahadi	Hesabull	Bet On Sunshine
1998 **Reraise**	1:09	Corey Nakatani	Craig Dollase	Grand Slam	Kona Gold

Mile

Year	Time	Jockey	Trainer	2nd place	3rd place
1984 **Royal Heroine**	1:32⅗	Fernando Toro	John Gosden	Star Choice	Cozzene
1985 **Cozzene**	1:35	Walter Guerra	Jan Nerud	Al Mamoon*	Shadeed
1986 **Last Tycoon**	1:35⅕	Yves St.-Martin	Robert Collet	Palace Music	Fred Astaire
1987 **Miesque**	1:32⅘	Freddie Head	Francois Boutin	Show Dancer	Sonic Lady
1988 **Miesque**	1:38⅗	Freddie Head	Francois Boutin	Steinlen	Simply Majestic
1989 **Steinlen**	1:37⅕	Jose Santos	D. Wayne Lukas	Sabona	Most Welcome
1990 **Royal Academy**	1:35⅕	Lester Piggott	M.V. O'Brien	Itsallgreektome	Priolo
1991 **Opening Verse**	1:37⅖	Pat Valenzuela	Dick Lundy	Val des Bois	Star of Cozzene
1992 **Lure**	1:32⅘	Mike Smith	Shug McGaughey	Paradise Creek	Brief Truce
1993 **Lure**	1:33⅖	Mike Smith	Shug McGaughey	Ski Paradise	Fourstars Allstar
1994 **Barathea**	1:34⅖	Frankie Dettori	Luca Cumani	Johann Quatz	Unfinished Symph
1995 **Ridgewood Pearl**	1:43⅗	John Murtagh	John Oxx	Fastness	Sayyedati
1996 **Da Hoss**	1:35⅘	Gary Stevens	Michael Dickinson	Spinning World	Same Old Wish
1997 **Spinning World**	1:32⅗	Cash Asmussen	Jonathan Pease	Geri	Decorated Hero
1998 **Da Hoss**	1:35⅕	John Velazquez	Michael Dickinson	Hawksley Hill	Labeeb

*In 1985, 2nd place finisher Palace Music was disqualified for interference and placed 9th.

Distaff

Distances: 1¼ miles (1984-87); 1⅛ miles (since 1988).

Year	Time	Jockey	Trainer	2nd place	3rd place
1984 **Princess Rooney**	2:02⅖	Eddie Delahoussaye	Neil Drysdale	Life's Magic	Adored
1985 **Life's Magic**	2:02	Angel Cordero Jr.	D. Wayne Lukas	Lady's Secret	DontstopThemusic
1986 **Lady's Secret**	2:01⅕	Pat Day	D. Wayne Lukas	Fran's Valentine	Outstandingly
1987 **Sacahuista**	2:02⅘	Randy Romero	D. Wayne Lukas	Clabber Girl	Oueee Bebe
1988 **Personal Ensign**	1:52	Randy Romero	Shug McGaughey	Winning Colors	Goodbye Halo
1989 **Bayakoa**	1:47⅖	Laffit Pincay Jr.	Ron McAnally	Gorgeous	Open Mind
1990 **Bayakoa**	1:49⅕	Laffit Pincay Jr.	Ron McAnally	Colonial Waters	Valay Maid
1991 **Dance Smartly**	1:50⅘	Pat Day	Jim Day	Versailles Treaty	Brought to Mind
1992 **Paseana**	1:48	Chris McCarron	Ron McAnally	Versailles Treaty	Magical Maiden
1993 **Hollywood Wildcat**	1:48⅕	Eddie Delahoussaye	Neil Drysdale	Paseana	Re Toss
1994 **One Dreamer**	1:50⅗	Gary Stevens	Thomas Proctor	Heavenly Prize	Miss Dominique

Breeders' Cup Championship (Cont.)

Year	Time	Jockey	Trainer	2nd place	3rd place
1995 **Inside Information**	1:46	Mike Smith	Shug McGaughey	Heavenly Prize	Lakeway
1996 **Jewel Princess**	1:48⅕	Corey Nakatani	Wallace Dollase	Serena's Song	Different
1997 **Ajina**	1:47⅕	Mike Smith	Bill Mott	Sharp Cat	Escena
1998 **Escena**	1:49⅘	Gary Stevens	Bill Mott	Banshee Breeze	Keeper Hill

Turf

Distance: 1½ miles (since 1984).

Year	Time	Jockey	Trainer	2nd place	3rd place
1984 **Lashkari**	2:25⅕	Yves St.-Martin	de Royer-Dupre	All Along	Raami
1985 **Pebbles**	2:27	Pat Eddery	Clive Brittain	StrawberryRoad II	Mourjane
1986 **Manila**	2:25⅖	Jose Santos	Leroy Jolley	Theatrical	Estrapade
1987 **Theatrical**	2:24⅖	Pat Day	Bill Mott	Trempolino	Village Star II
1988 **Gt. Communicator**	2:35⅕	Ray Sibille	Thad Ackel	Sunshine Forever	Indian Skimmer
1989 **Prized**	2:28	Eddie Delahoussaye	Neil Drysdale	Sierra Roberta	Star Lift
1990 **In The Wings**	2:29⅗	Gary Stevens	Andre Fabre	With Approval	El Senor
1991 **Miss Alleged**	2:30⅘	Eric Legrix	Pascal Bary	Itsallgreektome	Quest for Fame
1992 **Fraise**	2:24	Pat Valenzuela	Bill Mott	Sky Classic	Quest for Fame
1993 **Kotashaan**	2:25	Kent Desormeaux	Richard Mandella	Bien Bien	Luazur
1994 **Tikkanen**	2:26⅖	Mike Smith	Jonathan Pease	Hatoof	Paradise Creek
1995 **Northern Spur**	2:42	Chris McCarron	Ron McAnally	Freedom Cry	Carnegie
1996 **Pilsudski**	2:30⅕	Walter Swinburn	Michael Stoute	Singspiel	Swain
1997 **Chief Bearhart**	2:24	Jose Santos	Mark Frostad	Borgia	Flag Down
1998 **Buck's Boy**	2:28⅗	Shane Sellers	Noel Hickey	Yagli	Dushyantor

Classic

Distance: 1¼ miles (since 1984).

Year	Time	Jockey	Trainer	2nd place	3rd place
1984 **Wild Again**	2:03⅖	Pat Day	Vincent Timphony	Slew o' Gold	Gate Dancer*
1985 **Proud Truth**	2:00⅘	Jorge Velasquez	John Veitch	Gate Dancer	Turkoman
1986 **Skywalker**	2:00⅖	Laffit Pincay Jr.	M. Whittingham	Turkoman	Precisionist
1987 **Ferdinand**	2:01⅖	Bill Shoemaker	C. Whittingham	Alysheba	Judge Angelucci
1988 **Alysheba**	2:04⅘	Chris McCarron	Jack Van Berg	Seeking the Gold	Waquoit
1989 **Sunday Silence**	2:00⅕	Chris McCarron	C. Whittingham	Easy Goer	Blushing John
1990 **Unbridled**	2:02⅕	Pat Day	Carl Nafzger	Ibn Bey	Thirty Six Red
1991 **Black Tie Affair**	2:02⅘	Jerry Bailey	Ernie Poulos	Twilight Agenda	Unbridled
1992 **A.P. Indy**	2:00⅕	Eddie Delahoussaye	Neil Drysdale	Pleasant Tap	Jolypha
1993 **Arcangues**	2:00⅘	Jerry Bailey	Andre Fabre	Bertrando	Kissin Kris
1994 **Concern**	2:02⅖	Jerry Bailey	Richard Small	Tabasco Cat	Dramatic Gold
1995 **Cigar**	1:59⅖	Jerry Bailey	Bill Mott	L'Carriere	Unaccounted For
1996 **Alphabet Soup**	2:01	Chris McCarron	David Hofmans	Louis Quatorze	Cigar
1997 **Skip Away**	1:59⅕	Mike Smith	Hubert Hine	Deputy Commander	Dowty
1998 **Awesome Again**	2:02	Pat Day	Patrick Byrne	Silver Charm	Swain

*In 1984, 2nd place finisher Gate Dancer was disqualified for interference and placed 3rd.

Breeders' Cup Leaders

The all-time money-winning horses and race winning jockeys in the history of the Breeders' Cup through 1998.

Top 10 Horses

		Sts	1-2-3	Earnings
1	Awesome Again	1	1-0-0	$2,662,400
2	Skip Away	2	1-0-0	2,288,000
3	Alysheba	3	1-1-1	2,133,000
4	Alphabet Soup	1	1-0-0	2,080,000
5	Cigar	2	1-0-1	2,040,000
6	Unbridled	2	1-0-1	1,710,000
7	Black Tie Affair (IRE)	3	1-0-1	1,668,000
8	A.P. Indy	1	1-0-0	1,560,000
	Arcangues	1	1-0-0	1,560,000
	Concern	1	1-0-0	1,560,000

Top 10 Jockeys

		Sts	1-2-3	Earnings
1	Pat Day	82	10-13-9	$17,233,000
2	Chris McCarron	84	7-11-7	12,740,000
3	Gary Stevens	70	6-13-8	10,934,680
4	Jerry Bailey	51	7-5-5	10,387,000
5	Mike Smith	36	8-3-3	7,860,200
6	Eddie Delahoussaye	64	7-3-6	7,719,000
7	Laffit Pincay Jr.	61	7-4-9	6,811,000
8	Angel Cordero Jr.	48	4-7-7	6,020,000
9	Jose Santos	44	6-1-4	5,587,000
10	Corey Nakatani	29	4-5-5	5,112,600

Top 10 Trainers

		Sts	1-2-3	Earnings
1	D. Wayne Lukas	120	13-18-12	$12,996,000
2	Bill Mott	27	5-5-4	7,870,000
3	Shug McGaughey	42	7-8-1	6,601,400
4	Andre Fabre	26	2-4-5	5,384,000
5	Neil Drysdale	19	5-3-1	4,983,600
6	Charlie Whittingham	24	2-2-3	$4,298,000
7	Patrick Byrne	6	3-0-0	3,718,000
8	Jack Van Berg	14	1-3-3	3,600,000
9	Ron McAnally	24	4-2-2	3,276,000
10	Robert Frankel	30	0-4-5	2,943,000

Annual Money Leaders
Horses

Annual money-leading horses since 1910, according to *The American Racing Manual*.

Multiple leaders: Round Table, Buckpasser, Alysheba and Cigar (2).

Year		Age	Sts	1st	Earnings	Year		Age	Sts	1st	Earnings
1910	Novelty	2	16	11	$ 72,630	1955	Nashua	3	12	10	$752,550
1911	Worth	2	13	10	16,645	1956	Needles	3	8	4	440,850
1912	Star Charter	4	17	6	14,655	1957	Round Table	3	22	15	600,383
1913	Old Rosebud	2	14	12	19,057	1958	Round Table	4	20	14	662,780
1914	Roamer	3	16	12	29,105	1959	Sword Dancer	3	13	8	537,004
1915	Borrow	7	9	4	20,195						
1916	Campfire	2	9	6	49,735	1960	Bally Ache	3	15	10	445,045
1917	Sun Briar	2	9	5	59,505	1961	Carry Back	3	16	9	565,349
1918	Eternal	2	8	6	56,173	1962	Never Bend	2	10	7	402,969
1919	Sir Barton	3	13	8	88,250	1963	Candy Spots	3	12	7	604,481
						1964	Gun Bow	4	16	8	580,100
1920	Man o' War	3	11	11	166,140	1965	Buckpasser	2	11	9	568,096
1921	Morvich	2	11	11	115,234	1966	Buckpasser	3	14	13	669,078
1922	Pillory	3	7	4	95,654	1967	Damascus	3	16	12	817,941
1923	Zev	3	14	12	272,008	1968	Forward Pass	3	13	7	546,674
1924	Sarzen	3	12	8	95,640	1969	Arts and Letters	3	14	8	555,604
1925	Pompey	2	10	7	121,630						
1926	Crusader	3	15	9	166,033	1970	Personality	3	18	8	444,049
1927	Anita Peabody	2	7	6	111,905	1971	Riva Ridge	2	9	7	503,263
1928	High Strung	2	6	5	153,590	1972	Droll Role	4	19	7	471,633
1929	Blue Larkspur	3	6	4	153,450	1973	Secretariat	3	12	9	860,404
						1974	Chris Evert	3	8	5	551,063
1930	Gallant Fox	3	10	9	308,275	1975	Foolish Pleasure	3	11	5	716,278
1931	Gallant Flight	2	7	7	219,000	1976	Forego	6	8	6	401,701
1932	Gusto	3	16	4	145,940	1977	Seattle Slew	3	7	6	641,370
1933	Singing Wood	2	9	3	88,050	1978	Affirmed	3	11	8	901,541
1934	Cavalcade	3	7	6	111,235	1979	Spectacular Bid	3	12	10	1,279,334
1935	Omaha	3	9	6	142,255						
1936	Granville	3	11	7	110,295	1980	Temperence Hill	3	17	8	1,130,452
1937	Seabiscuit	4	15	11	168,580	1981	John Henry	6	10	8	1,798,030
1938	Stagehand	3	15	8	189,710	1982	Perrault (GB)	5	8	4	1,197,400
1939	Challedon	3	15	9	184,535	1983	All Along (FRA)	4	7	4	2,138,963
						1984	Slew o' Gold	4	6	5	2,627,944
1940	Bimelech	3	7	4	110,005	1985	Spend A Buck	3	7	5	3,552,704
1941	Whirlaway	3	20	13	272,386	1986	Snow Chief	3	9	6	1,875,200
1942	Shut Out	3	12	8	238,872	1987	Alysheba	3	10	3	2,511,156
1943	Count Fleet	3	6	6	174,055	1988	Alysheba	4	9	7	3,808,600
1944	Pavot	2	8	8	179,040	1989	Sunday Silence	3	9	7	4,578,454
1945	Busher	3	13	10	273,735						
1946	Assault	3	15	8	424,195	1990	Unbridled	3	11	4	3,718,149
1947	Armed	6	17	11	376,325	1991	Dance Smartly	3	8	8	2,876,821
1948	Citation	3	20	19	709,470	1992	A.P. Indy	3	7	5	2,622,560
1949	Ponder	3	21	9	321,825	1993	Kotashaan (FRA)	5	10	6	2,619,014
						1994	Paradise Creek	5	11	8	2,610,187
1950	Noor	5	12	7	346,940	1995	Cigar	5	10	10	4,819,800
1951	Counterpoint	3	15	7	250,525	1996	Cigar	6	8	5	4,910,000
1952	Crafty Admiral	4	16	9	277,225	1997	Skip Away	4	11	4	4,089,000
1953	Native Dancer	3	10	9	513,425	1998	Silver Charm	4	9	6	4,696,506
1954	Determine	3	15	10	328,700						

Jockeys

Annual money-leading jockeys since 1910, according to *The American Racing Manual*.

Multiple leaders: Bill Shoemaker (10); Laffit Pincay Jr. (7); Eddie Arcaro (6); Braulio Baeza (5); Chris McCarron and Jose Santos (4); Jerry Bailey, Angel Cordero Jr. and Earl Sande (3); Ted Atkinson, Laverne Fator, Mack Garner, Bill Hartack, Charles Kurtsinger, Johnny Longden, Mike Smith, Gary Stevens, Sonny Workman and Wayne Wright (2).

Year		Mts	Wins	Earnings	Year		Mts	Wins	Earnings
1910	Carroll Shilling	506	172	$176,030	1920	Clarence Kummer	353	87	$292,376
1911	Ted Koerner	813	162	88,308	1921	Earl Sande	340	112	263,043
1912	Jimmy Butwell	684	144	79,843	1922	Albert Johnson	297	43	345,054
1913	Merritt Buxton	887	146	82,552	1923	Earl Sande	430	122	569,394
1914	J. McCahey	824	155	121,845	1924	Ivan Parke	844	205	290,395
1915	Mack Garner	775	151	96,628	1925	Laverne Fator	315	81	305,775
1916	John McTaggart	832	150	155,055	1926	Laverne Fator	511	143	361,435
1917	Frank Robinson	731	147	148,057	1927	Earl Sande	179	49	277,877
1918	Lucien Luke	756	178	201,864	1928	Linus McAtee	235	55	301,295
1919	John Loftus	177	65	252,707	1929	Mack Garner	274	57	314,975

Year		Mts	Wins	Earnings
1930	Sonny Workman	571	152	$420,438
1931	Charley Kurtsinger	519	93	392,095
1932	Sonny Workman	378	87	385,070
1933	Robert Jones	471	63	226,285
1934	Wayne Wright	919	174	287,185
1935	Silvio Coucci	749	141	319,760
1936	Wayne Wright	670	100	264,000
1937	Charley Kurtsinger	765	120	384,202
1938	Nick Wall	658	97	385,161
1939	Basil James	904	191	353,333
1940	Eddie Arcaro	783	132	343,661
1941	Don Meade	1164	210	398,627
1942	Eddie Arcaro	687	123	481,949
1943	Johnny Longden	871	173	573,276
1944	Ted Atkinson	1539	287	899,101
1945	Johnny Longden	778	180	981,977
1946	Ted Atkinson	1377	233	1,036,825
1947	Douglas Dodson	646	141	1,429,949
1948	Eddie Arcaro	726	188	1,686,230
1949	Steve Brooks	906	209	1,316,817
1950	Eddie Arcaro	888	195	1,410,160
1951	Bill Shoemaker	1161	257	1,329,890
1952	Eddie Arcaro	807	188	1,859,591
1953	Bill Shoemaker	1683	485	1,784,187
1954	Bill Shoemaker	1251	380	1,876,760
1955	Eddie Arcaro	820	158	1,864,796
1956	Bill Hartack	1387	347	2,343,955
1957	Bill Hartack	1238	341	3,060,501
1958	Bill Shoemaker	1133	300	2,961,693
1959	Bill Shoemaker	1285	347	2,843,133
1960	Bill Shoemaker	1227	274	2,123,961
1961	Bill Shoemaker	1256	304	2,690,819
1962	Bill Shoemaker	1126	311	2,916,844
1963	Bill Shoemaker	1203	271	2,526,925
1964	Bill Shoemaker	1056	246	2,649,553

Year		Mts	Wins	Earnings
1965	Braulio Baeza	1245	270	$2,582,702
1966	Braulio Baeza	1341	298	2,951,022
1967	Braulio Baeza	1064	256	3,088,888
1968	Braulio Baeza	1089	201	2,835,108
1969	Jorge Velasquez	1442	258	2,542,315
1970	Laffit Pincay Jr.	1328	269	2,626,526
1971	Laffit Pincay Jr.	1627	380	3,784,377
1972	Laffit Pincay Jr.	1388	289	3,225,827
1973	Laffit Pincay Jr.	1444	350	4,093,492
1974	Laffit Pincay Jr.	1278	341	4,251,060
1975	Braulio Baeza	1190	196	3,674,398
1976	Angel Cordero Jr.	1534	274	4,709,500
1977	Steve Cauthen	2075	487	6,151,750
1978	Darrel McHargue	1762	375	6,188,353
1979	Laffit Pincay Jr.	1708	420	8,183,535
1980	Chris McCarron	1964	405	7,666,100
1981	Chris McCarron	1494	326	8,397,604
1982	Angel Cordero Jr.	1838	397	9,702,520
1983	Angel Cordero Jr.	1792	362	10,116,807
1984	Chris McCarron	1565	356	12,038,213
1985	Laffit Pincay Jr.	1409	289	13,415,049
1986	Jose Santos	1636	329	11,329,297
1987	Jose Santos	1639	305	12,407,355
1988	Jose Santos	1867	370	14,877,298
1989	Jose Santos	1459	285	13,847,003
1990	Gary Stevens	1504	283	13,881,198
1991	Chris McCarron	1440	265	14,456,073
1992	Kent Desormeaux	1568	361	14,193,006
1993	Mike Smith	1510	343	14,024,815
1994	Mike Smith	1484	317	15,979,820
1995	Jerry Bailey	1367	287	16,311,876
1996	Jerry Bailey	1187	298	19,465,376
1997	Jerry Bailey	1136	269	18,206,013
1998	Gary Stevens	869	178	19,358,840

Trainers

Annual money-leading trainers since 1908, according to *The American Racing Manual*.

Multiple Leaders: D. Wayne Lukas (14); Sam Hildreth (9); Charlie Whittingham (7); Sunny Jim Fitzsimmons and Jimmy Jones (5); Laz Barrera, Ben Jones and Willie Molter (4); Hirsch Jacobs, Eddie Neloy and James Rowe Sr. (3); H. Guy Bedwell, Jack Gaver, John Schorr, Humming Bob Smith, Silent Tom Smith and Mesh Tenney (2).

Year		Wins	Earnings
1908	James Rowe Sr.	50	$284,335
1909	Sam Hildreth	73	123,942
1910	Sam Hildreth	84	148,010
1911	Sam Hildreth	67	49,418
1912	John Schorr	63	58,110
1913	James Rowe Sr.	18	45,936
1914	R.C. Benson	45	59,315
1915	James Rowe Sr.	19	75,596
1916	Sam Hildreth	39	70,950
1917	Sam Hildreth	23	61,698
1918	H. Guy Bedwell	53	80,296
1919	H. Guy Bedwell	63	208,728
1920	Louis Feustel	22	186,087
1921	Sam Hildreth	85	262,768
1922	Sam Hildreth	74	247,014
1923	Sam Hildreth	75	392,124
1924	Sam Hildreth	77	255,608
1925	G.R. Tompkins	30	199,245
1926	Scott Harlan	21	205,681
1927	W.H. Bringloe	63	216,563
1928	John Schorr	65	258,425
1929	James Rowe Jr.	25	314,881
1930	Sunny Jim Fitzsimmons	47	397,355
1931	Big Jim Healy	33	297,300
1932	Sunny Jim Fitzsimmons	68	266,650

Year		Wins	Earnings
1933	Humming Bob Smith	53	$135,720
1934	Humming Bob Smith	43	249,938
1935	Bud Stotler	87	303,005
1936	Sunny Jim Fitzsimmons	42	193,415
1937	Robert McGarvey	46	209,925
1938	Earl Sande	15	226,495
1939	Sunny Jim Fitzsimmons	45	266,205
1940	Silent Tom Smith	14	269,200
1941	Ben Jones	70	475,318
1942	Jack Gaver	48	406,547
1943	Ben Jones	73	267,915
1944	Ben Jones	60	601,660
1945	Silent Tom Smith	52	510,655
1946	Hirsch Jacobs	99	560,077
1947	Jimmy Jones	85	1,334,805
1948	Jimmy Jones	81	1,118,670
1949	Jimmy Jones	76	978,587
1950	Preston Burch	96	637,754
1951	Jack Gaver	42	616,392
1952	Ben Jones	29	662,137
1953	Harry Trotsek	54	1,028,873
1954	Willie Molter	136	1,107,860
1955	Sunny Jim Fitzsimmons	66	1,270,055
1956	Willie Molter	142	1,227,402
1957	Jimmy Jones	70	1,150,910
1958	Willie Molter	69	$1,116,544

Year		Wins	Earnings
1959	Willie Molter	.71	847,290
1960	Hirsch Jacobs	.97	748,349
1961	Jimmy Jones	.62	759,856
1962	Mesh Tenney	.58	1,099,474

Year		Sts	Wins	Earnings
1963	Mesh Tenney	192	40	$860,703
1964	Bill Winfrey	287	61	1,350,534
1965	Hirsch Jacobs	610	91	1,331,628
1966	Eddie Neloy	282	93	2,456,250
1967	Eddie Neloy	262	72	1,776,089
1968	Eddie Neloy	212	52	1,233,101
1969	Elliott Burch	156	26	1,067,936
1970	Charlie Whittingham	551	82	1,302,354
1971	Charlie Whittingham	393	77	1,737,115
1972	Charlie Whittingham	429	79	1,734,020
1973	Charlie Whittingham	423	85	1,865,385
1974	Pancho Martin	846	166	2,408,419
1975	Charlie Whittingham	487	3	2,437,244
1976	Jack Van Berg	2362	496	2,976,196
1977	Laz Barrera	781	127	2,715,848

Year		Sts	Wins	Earnings
1978	Laz Barrera	592	100	$3,307,164
1979	Laz Barrera	492	98	3,608,517
1980	Laz Barrera	559	99	2,969,151
1981	Charlie Whittingham	376	74	3,993,302
1982	Charlie Whittingham	410	63	4,587,457
1983	D. Wayne Lukas	595	78	4,267,261
1984	D. Wayne Lukas	805	131	5,835,921
1985	D. Wayne Lukas	1140	218	11,155,188
1986	D. Wayne Lukas	1510	259	12,345,180
1987	D. Wayne Lukas	1735	343	17,502,110
1988	D. Wayne Lukas	1500	318	17,842,358
1989	D. Wayne Lukas	1398	305	16,103,998
1990	D. Wayne Lukas	1396	267	14,508,871
1991	D. Wayne Lukas	1497	289	15,942,223
1992	D. Wayne Lukas	1349	230	9,806,436
1993	Bobby Frankel	345	79	8,933,252
1994	D. Wayne Lukas	693	147	9,247,457
1995	D. Wayne Lukas	837	194	12,834,483
1996	D. Wayne Lukas	1006	192	15,966,344
1997	D. Wayne Lukas	824	169	9,993,569
1998	Bob Baffert	538	139	15,000,870

All-Time Leaders

The all-time money-winning horses and race-winning jockeys of North America through 1998, according to *Thoroughbred Racing Communications, Inc.* Records include all available information on races in foreign countries.

Top 35 Horses — Money Won

Note that horses who raced in 1998 are in **bold** type.

		Sts	1st	2nd	3rd	Earnings
1	Cigar	33	19	4	5	$9,999,815
2	**Skip Away**	38	18	10	6	9,616,360
3	Alysheba	26	11	8	2	6,679,242
4	John Henry	83	39	15	9	6,597,947
5	**Silver Charm**	19	11	7	2	6,513,006
6	Singspiel	20	9	8	0	5,950,217
7	Best Pal	47	18	11	4	5,668,245
8	Taiki Blizzard	22	6	8	2	5,544,484
9	Sunday Silence	14	9	5	0	4,968,554
10	Easy Goer	20	14	5	1	4,873,770
11	Unbridled	24	8	6	6	4,489,875
12	Pilsudski	22	10	6	2	4,389,167
13	**Awesome Again**	12	9	0	2	4,374,590
14	Spend A Buck	15	10	3	2	4,220,689
15	Creme Fraiche	64	17	12	13	4,024,727
16	Devil His Due	41	11	12	3	3,920,405
17	Sandpit	40	14	11	6	3,802,971
18	Ferdinand	29	8	9	6	3,777,978
19	Slew o' Gold	21	12	5	1	3,533,534
20	Precisionist	46	20	10	4	3,485,398
21	Lando	23	10	2	1	3,484,413
22	Strike the Gold	31	6	8	5	3,457,026
23	Paradise Creek	25	14	7	1	3,386,925
24	Snow Chief	24	13	3	5	3,383,210
25	Cryptoclearance	44	12	10	7	3,376,327
26	Black Tie Affair	45	18	9	6	3,370,694
27	Bet Twice	26	10	6	4	3,308,599
28	Steinlen	45	20	10	7	3,300,100
29	Serena's Song (f)	38	18	11	3	3,283,388
30	Awad	70	14	10	11	3,270,131
31	Dance Smartly (f)	17	12	2	3	3,263,836
32	Sky Classic	29	15	6	1	3,240,398
33	Gentlemen	24	9	6	2	3,185,610
34	Paseana (f)	36	19	10	2	3,173,203
35	Siphon	24	12	6	2	3,098,619

Top 35 Jockeys — Races Won

Note that jockeys active in 1998 are in **bold** type.

		Yrs	Wins	Earnings
1	Bill Shoemaker	42	8833	$123,375,524
2	**Laffit Pincay Jr.**	33	8601	198,144,777
3	**Pat Day**	26	7363	206,062,411
4	**David Gall**	42	7259	24,181,749
5	Angel Cordero Jr.	35	7057	164,561,227
6	Jorge Velasquez	33	6794	125,534,962
7	**Chris McCarron**	25	6714	224,666,852
8	**Sandy Hawley**	31	6449	88,677,062
9	**Russell Baze**	25	6436	90,172,056
10	Larry Snyder	35	6388	47,207,289
11	Carl Gambardella	39	6349	29,389,041
12	Earlie Fires	34	6035	74,324,384
13	John Longden	41	6032	24,665,800
14	**E. Delahoussaye**	31	5988	169,793,214
15	Jacinto Vasquez	37	5232	80,780,712
16	**Ron Ardoin**	26	4834	50,926,698
17	Eddie Arcaro	31	4779	30,039,543
18	Don Brumfield	37	4573	43,567,861
19	Steve Brooks	34	4451	18,239,817
20	**Gary Stevens**	20	4446	180,922,371
21	**Jerry Bailey**	25	4434	168,451,086
22	Rodolfo Baez	24	4423	26,682,715
23	Walter Blum	22	4382	26,497,189
24	**Eddie Maple**	34	4369	104,526,553
25	**Randy Romero**	25	4277	74,645,195
26	Bill Hartack	22	4272	26,666,758
27	**Rick Wilson**	26	4245	57,810,814
28	**Craig Perret**	32	4214	100,532,196
29	**Jeffrey Lloyd**	22	4090	31,547,420
30	Avelino Gomez	34	4081	11,777,297
31	Hugo Dittfach	33	4000	13,506,052
32	Phil Grove	30	3990	16,507,393
33	Ted Atkinson	22	3795	17,449,360
34	David Whited	36	3784	25,067,466
35	Ralph Neves	21	3772	13,786,239

Horse of the Year (1936-70)

In 1971, the *Daily Racing Form*, the Thoroughbred Racing Associations, and the National Turf Writers Assn. joined forces to create the Eclipse Awards. Before then, however, the *Racing Form* (1936-70) and the TRA (1950-70) issued separate selections for Horse of the Year. Their picks differed only four times from 1950-70 and are so noted. Horses listed in CAPITAL letters are Triple Crown winners; (f) indicates female.

Multiple winners: Kelso (5); Challedon, Native Dancer and Whirlaway (2).

Year	Year	Year	Year
1936 Granville	1946 ASSAULT	1955 Nashua	1964 Kelso
1937 WAR ADMIRAL	1947 Armed	1956 Swaps	1965 Roman Brother (DRF)
1938 Seabiscuit	1948 CITATION	1957 Bold Ruler (DRF)	Moccasin (TRA)
1939 Challedon	1949 Capot	Dedicate (TRA)	1966 Buckpasser
1940 Challedon	1950 Hill Prince	1958 Round Table	1967 Damascus
1941 WHIRLAWAY	1951 Counterpoint	1959 Sword Dancer	1968 Dr. Fager
1942 Whirlaway	1952 One Count (DRF)	1960 Kelso	1969 Arts and Letters
1943 COUNT FLEET	Native Dancer (TRA)	1961 Kelso	1970 Fort Marcy (DRF)
1944 Twilight Tear (f)	1953 Tom Fool	1962 Kelso	Personality (TRA)
1945 Busher (f)	1954 Native Dancer	1963 Kelso	

Eclipse Awards (since 1971)

The Eclipse Awards, honoring the Horse of the Year and other champions of the sport, are sponsored by the National Thoroughbred Racing Association (NTRA), *Daily Racing Form* and the National Turf Writers Assn. In 1998, the NTRA replaced the Thoroughbred Racing Associations of North America as co-sponsor.

The awards are named after the 18th century racehorse and sire, Eclipse, who began racing at age five and was unbeaten in 18 starts (eight wins were walkovers). As a stallion, Eclipse sired winners of 344 races, including three Epsom Derby champions.

Horses listed in CAPITAL letters won the Triple Crown that year. Age of horse in parentheses where necessary.

Multiple winners: (horses): Forego (8); John Henry (7); Affirmed and Secretariat (5); Cigar, Flatterer, Lonesome Glory, Seattle Slew, Skip Away and Spectacular Bid (4); Ack Ack, Susan's Girl and Zaccio (3); All Along, Alysheba, Bayakoa, Black Tie Affair, Cafe Prince, Conquistador Cielo, Desert Vixen, Favorite Trick, Ferdinand, Flawlessly, Go for Wand, Holy Bull, Housebuster, Kotashaan, Lady's Secret, Life's Magic, Miesque, Morley Street, Open Mind, Paseana, Riva Ridge, Slew o' Gold and Spend A Buck (2).

Multiple winners: (people): Laffit Pincay Jr. (5); Laz Barrera, Pat Day, John Franks and D. Wayne Lukas (4); Jerry Bailey, Steve Cauthen, Harbor View Farm, Fred W. Hooper, Nelson Bunker Hunt, Mr. & Mrs. Gene Klein, Dan Lasater, John & Betty Mabee, Ogden Phipps, Bill Shoemaker, Edward Taylor and Charlie Whittingham (3); Braulio Baeza, Bob Baffert, C.T. Chenery, Claiborne Farm, Angel Cordero Jr., Kent Desormeaux, John W. Galbreath, Chris McCarron, Paul Mellon, Bill Mott, Allen Paulson and Mike Smith (2).

Horse of the Year

Year	Year	Year	Year
1971 Ack Ack (5)	1978 AFFIRMED (3)	1985 Spend A Buck (3)	1992 A.P. Indy (3)
1972 SECRETARIAT (2)	1979 Affirmed (4)	1986 Lady's Secret (4)	1993 Kotashaan (5)
1973 SECRETARIAT (3)	1980 Spectacular Bid (4)	1987 Ferdinand (4)	1994 Holy Bull (3)
1974 Forego (4)	1981 John Henry (6)	1988 Alysheba (4)	1995 Cigar (5)
1975 Forego (5)	1982 Conquistador Cielo (3)	1989 Sunday Silence (3)	1996 Cigar (6)
1976 Forego (6)	1983 All Along (4)	1990 Criminal Type (5)	1997 Favorite Trick (2)
1977 SEATTLE SLEW (3)	1984 John Henry (9)	1991 Black Tie Affair (5)	1998 Skip Away (5)

Older Male

Year	Year	Year	Year
1971 Ack Ack (5)	1978 Seattle Slew (4)	1985 Vanlandingham (4)	1992 Pleasant Tap (5)
1972 Autobiography (4)	1979 Affirmed (4)	1986 Turkoman (4)	1993 Bertrando (4)
1973 Riva Ridge (4)	1980 Spectacular Bid (4)	1987 Ferdinand (4)	1994 The Wicked North (4)
1974 Forego (4)	1981 John Henry (6)	1988 Alysheba (4)	1995 Cigar (5)
1975 Forego (5)	1982 Lemhi Gold (4)	1989 Blushing John (4)	1996 Cigar (6)
1976 Forego (6)	1983 Bates Motel (4)	1990 Criminal Type (5)	1997 Skip Away (4)
1977 Forego (7)	1984 Slew o' Gold (4)	1991 Black Tie Affair (5)	1998 Skip Away (5)

Older Filly or Mare

Year	Year	Year	Year
1971 Shuvee (5)	1978 Late Bloomer (4)	1985 Life's Magic (4)	1992 Paseana (5)
1972 Typecast (6)	1979 Waya (4)	1986 Lady's Secret (4)	1993 Paseana (6)
1973 Susan's Girl (4)	1980 Glorious Song (4)	1987 North Sider (5)	1994 Sky Beauty (4)
1974 Desert Vixen (4)	1981 Relaxing (5)	1988 Personal Ensign (4)	1995 Inside Information (4)
1975 Susan's Girl (6)	1982 Track Robbery (6)	1989 Bayakoa (5)	1996 Jewel Princess (4)
1976 Proud Delta (4)	1983 Amb. of Luck (4)	1990 Bayakoa (6)	1997 Hidden Lake (4)
1977 Cascapedia (4)	1984 Princess Rooney (4)	1991 Queena (5)	1998 Escena (5)

3-Year-Old Colt or Gelding

Year		Year		Year		Year	
1971	Canonero II	1978	AFFIRMED	1985	Spend A Buck	1992	A.P. Indy
1972	Key to the Mint	1979	Spectacular Bid	1986	Snow Chief	1993	Prairie Bayou
1973	SECRETARIAT	1980	Temperence Hill	1987	Alysheba	1994	Holy Bull
1974	Little Current	1981	Pleasant Colony	1988	Risen Star	1995	Thunder Gulch
1975	Wajima	1982	Conquistador Cielo	1989	Sunday Silence	1996	Skip Away
1976	Bold Forbes	1983	Slew o' Gold	1990	Unbridled	1997	Silver Charm
1977	SEATTLE SLEW	1984	Swale	1991	Hansel	1998	Real Quiet

3-Year-Old Filly

Year		Year		Year		Year	
1971	Turkish Trousers	1978	Tempest Queen	1985	Mom's Command	1992	Saratoga Slew
1972	Susan's Girl	1979	Davona Dale	1986	Tiffany Lass	1993	Hollywood Wildcat
1973	Desert Vixen	1980	Genuine Risk	1987	Sacahuista	1994	Heavenly Prize
1974	Chris Evert	1981	Wayward Lass	1988	Winning Colors	1995	Serena's Song
1975	Ruffian	1982	Christmas Past	1989	Open Mind	1996	Yanks Music
1976	Revidere	1983	Heartlight No. One	1990	Go for Wand	1997	Ajina
1977	Our Mims	1984	Life's Magic	1991	Dance Smartly	1998	Banshee Breeze

2-Year-Old Colt or Gelding

Year		Year		Year		Year	
1971	Riva Ridge	1978	Spectacular Bid	1985	Tasso	1992	Gilded Time
1972	Secretariat	1979	Rockhill Native	1986	Capote	1993	Dehere
1973	Protagonist	1980	Lord Avie	1987	Forty Niner	1994	Timber Country
1974	Foolish Pleasure	1981	Deputy Minister	1988	Easy Goer	1995	Maria's Mon
1975	Honest Pleasure	1982	Roving Boy	1989	Rhythm	1996	Boston Harbor
1976	Seattle Slew	1983	Devil's Bag	1990	Fly So Free	1997	Favorite Trick
1977	Affirmed	1984	Chief's Crown	1991	Arazi	1998	Answer Lively

2-Year-Old Filly

Year		Year		Year		Year	
1971	Numbered Account		& It's in the Air	1986	Brave Raj	1994	Flanders
1972	La Prevoyante	1979	Smart Angle	1987	Epitome	1995	Golden Attraction
1973	Talking Picture	1980	Heavenly Cause	1988	Open Mind	1996	Storm Song
1974	Ruffian	1981	Before Dawn	1989	Go for Wand	1997	Countess Diana
1975	Dearly Precious	1982	Landaluce	1990	Meadow Star	1998	Silverbulletday
1976	Sensational	1983	Althea	1991	Pleasant Stage		
1977	Lakeville Miss	1984	Outstandingly	1992	Eliza		
1978	(tie) Candy Eclair	1985	Family Style	1993	Phone Chatter		

Champion Turf Horse

Year		Year		Year		Year	
1971	Run the Gantlet (3)	1973	SECRETARIAT (3)	1975	Snow Knight (4)	1977	Johnny D (3)
1972	Cougar II (6)	1974	Dahlia (4)	1976	Youth (3)	1978	Mac Diarmida (3)

Champion Male Turf Horse

Year		Year		Year		Year	
1979	Bowl Game (5)	1984	John Henry (9)	1989	Steinlen (6)	1994	Paradise Creek (5)
1980	John Henry (5)	1985	Cozzene (4)	1990	Itsallgreektome (3)	1995	Northern Spur (4)
1981	John Henry (6)	1986	Manila (3)	1991	Tight Spot (4)	1996	Singspiel (4)
1982	Perrault (5)	1987	Theatrical (5)	1992	Sky Classic (5)	1997	Chief Bearhart (4)
1983	John Henry (8)	1988	Sunshine Forever (3)	1993	Kotashaan (5)	1998	Buck's Boy (5)

Champion Female Turf Horse

Year		Year		Year		Year	
1979	Trillion (5)	1984	Royal Heroine (4)	1989	Brown Bess (7)	1994	Hatoof (5)
1980	Just A Game II (4)	1985	Pebbles (4)	1990	Laugh and Be Merry (5)	1995	Possibly Perfect (5)
1981	De La Rose (3)	1986	Estrapade (6)	1991	Miss Alleged (4)	1996	Wandesta (5)
1982	April Run (4)	1987	Miesque (3)	1992	Flawlessly (4)	1997	Ryafan (3)
1983	All Along (4)	1988	Miesque (4)	1993	Flawlessly (5)	1998	Fiji (4)

Eclipse Awards (since 1971) (Cont.)
Sprinter

Year		Year		Year		Year	
1971	Ack Ack (5)	1978	(tie) Dr. Patches (4)	1984	Eillo (4)	1991	Housebuster (4)
1972	Chou Croute (4)		& J.O. Tobin (4)	1985	Precisionist (4)	1992	Rubiano (5)
1973	Shecky Greene (3)	1979	Star de Naskra (4)	1986	Smile (4)	1993	Cardmania (7)
1974	Forego (4)	1980	Plugged Nickle (3)	1987	Groovy (4)	1994	Cherokee Run (4)
1975	Gallant Bob (3)	1981	Guilty Conscience (5)	1988	Gulch (4)	1995	Not Surprising (4)
1976	My Juliet (4)	1982	Gold Beauty (3)	1989	Safely Kept (3)	1996	Lit de Justice (6)
1977	What a Summer (4)	1983	Chinook Pass (4)	1990	Housebuster (3)	1997	Smoke Glacken (3)
						1998	Reraise (3)

Steeplechase or Hurdle Horse

Year		Year		Year		Year	
1971	Shadow Brook (7)	1978	Cafe Prince (8)	1985	Flatterer (6)	1992	Lonesome Glory (4)
1972	Soothsayer (5)	1979	Martie's Anger (4)	1986	Flatterer (7)	1993	Lonesome Glory (5)
1973	Athenian Idol (5)	1980	Zaccio (4)	1987	Inlander (6)	1994	Warm Spell (6)
1974	Gran Kan (8)	1981	Zaccio (5)	1988	Jimmy Lorenzo (6)	1995	Lonesome Glory (7)
1975	Life's Illusion (4)	1982	Zaccio (6)	1989	Highland Bud (4)	1996	Correggio (5)
1976	Straight and True (6)	1983	Flatterer (4)	1990	Morley Street (6)	1997	Lonesome Glory (10)
1977	Cafe Prince (7)	1984	Flatterer (5)	1991	Morley Street (7)	1998	Flat Top (5)

Outstanding Jockey

Year		Year		Year		Year	
1971	Laffit Pincay Jr.	1978	Darrel McHargue	1985	Laffit Pincay Jr.	1992	Kent Desormeaux
1972	Braulio Baeza	1979	Laffit Pincay Jr.	1986	Pat Day	1993	Mike Smith
1973	Laffit Pincay Jr.	1980	Chris McCarron	1987	Pat Day	1994	Mike Smith
1974	Laffit Pincay Jr.	1981	Bill Shoemaker	1988	Jose Santos	1995	Jerry Bailey
1975	Braulio Baeza	1982	Angel Cordero Jr.	1989	Kent Desormeaux	1996	Jerry Bailey
1976	Sandy Hawley	1983	Angel Cordero Jr.	1990	Craig Perret	1997	Jerry Bailey
1977	Steve Cauthen	1984	Pat Day	1991	Pat Day	1998	Gary Stevens

Outstanding Apprentice Jockey

Year		Year		Year		Year	
1971	Gene St. Leon	1979	Cash Asmussen	1987	Kent Desormeaux	1995	Ramon B. Perez
1972	Thomas Wallis	1980	Frank Lovato Jr.	1988	Steve Capanas	1996	Neil Poznansky
1973	Steve Valdez	1981	Richard Migliore	1989	Michael Luzzi	1997	Roberto Rosado
1974	Chris McCarron	1982	Alberto Delgado	1990	Mark Johnston		& Philip Teator
1975	Jimmy Edwards	1983	Declan Murphy	1991	Mickey Walls	1998	Shaun Bridgmohan
1976	George Martens	1984	Wesley Ward	1992	Rosemary Homeister		
1977	Steve Cauthen	1985	Art Madrid Jr.	1993	Juan Umana		
1978	Ron Franklin	1986	Allen Stacy	1994	Dale Beckner		

Outstanding Trainer

Year		Year		Year		Year	
1971	Charlie Whittingham	1978	Laz Barrera	1985	D. Wayne Lukas	1992	Ron McAnally
1972	Lucien Laurin	1979	Laz Barrera	1986	D. Wayne Lukas	1993	Bobby Frankel
1973	H. Allen Jerkens	1980	Bud Delp	1987	D. Wayne Lukas	1994	D. Wayne Lukas
1974	Sherill Ward	1981	Ron McAnally	1988	Shug McGaughey	1995	Bill Mott
1975	Steve DiMauro	1982	Charlie Whittingham	1989	Charlie Whittingham	1996	Bill Mott
1976	Laz Barrera	1983	Woody Stephens	1990	Carl Nafzger	1997	Bob Baffert
1977	Laz Barrera	1984	Jack Van Berg	1991	Ron McAnally	1998	Bob Baffert

Outstanding Owner

Year		Year		Year		Year	
1971	Mr. & Mrs. E.E. Fogleson	1979	Harbor View Farm	1986	Mr. & Mrs. Gene Klein	1994	John Franks
1972-73	No award	1980	Mr. & Mrs. Bertram Firestone	1987	Mr. & Mrs. Gene Klein	1995	Allen Paulson
1974	Dan Lasater	1981	Dotsam Stable	1988	Ogden Phipps	1996	Allen Paulson
1975	Dan Lasater	1982	Viola Sommer	1989	Ogden Phipps	1997	Carolyn Hine
1976	Dan Lasater	1983	John Franks	1990	Frances Genter	1998	Frank Stronach
1977	Maxwell Gluck	1984	John Franks	1991	Sam-Son Farms		
1978	Harbor View Farm	1985	Mr. & Mrs. Gene Klein	1992	Juddmonta Farms		
				1993	John Franks		

Outstanding Breeder

Year		Year		Year		Year	
1971	Paul Mellon	1978	Harbor View Farm	1985	Nelson Bunker Hunt	1992	William S. Farish
1972	C.T. Chenery	1979	Claiborne Farm	1986	Paul Mellon	1993	Allan Paulson
1973	C.T. Chenery	1980	Mrs. Henry Paxson	1987	Nelson Bunker Hunt	1994	William T. Young
1974	John W. Galbreath	1981	Golden Chance Farm	1988	Ogden Phipps	1995	Juddmonte Farms
1975	Fred W. Hooper	1982	Fred W. Hooper	1989	North Ridge Farm	1996	Farnsworth Farms
1976	Nelson Bunker Hunt	1983	Edward P. Taylor	1990	Calumet Farm	1997	John & Betty Mabee
1977	Edward P. Taylor	1984	Claiborne Farm	1991	John & Betty Mabee	1998	John & Betty Mabee

Outstanding Achievement

Year		Year	
1971	Charles Engelhard*	1972	Arthur B. Hancock Jr.*

*Awarded posthumously.

Man of the Year

Year		Year	
1972	John W. Galbreath	1974	William L. McKnight
1973	Edward P. Taylor	1975	John A. Morris

Award of Merit

Year		Year		Year		Year	
1976	Jack J. Dreyfus	1981	Bill Shoemaker	1988	John Forsythe	1992	Joe Hirsch
1977	Steve Cauthen	1984	John Gaines	1989	Michael Sandler		& Robert P. Strub
1978	Dinny Phipps	1985	Keene Daingerfield	1990	Warner L. Jones	1995	James E. Bassett III
1979	Jimmy Kilroe	1986	Herman Cohen	1991	Fred W. Hooper	1997	Robert & Beverly
1980	John D. Shapiro	1987	J.B. Faulconer				Lewis

Special Award

Year		Year		Year		Year	
1971	Robert J. Kleberg	1980	John T. Landry	1985	Arlington Park	1989	Richard Duchossois
1974	Charles Hatton		& Pierre E. Bellocq	1987	Anheuser-Busch	1995	Russell Baze
1976	Bill Shoemaker	1984	C.V. Whitney	1988	Edward J. DeBartolo Sr.		

HARNESS RACING

Triple Crown Winners
PACERS

Eight 3-year-olds have won the Cane Pace, Little Brown Jug and Messenger Stakes in the same year since the Pacing Triple Crown was established in 1956. No trainer or driver has won it more than once.

Year		Driver	Trainer	Owner
1959	**Adios Butler**	Clint Hodgins	Paige West	Paige West & Angelo Pellillo
1965	**Bret Hanover**	Frank Ervin	Frank Ervin	Richard Downing
1966	**Romeo Hanover**	Bill Myer & George Sholty*	Jerry Silverman	Lucky Star Stables & Morton Finder
1968	**Rum Customer**	Billy Haughton	Billy Haughton	Kennilworth Farms & L.C. Mancuso
1970	**Most Happy Fella**	Stanley Dancer	Stanley Dancer	Egyptian Acres Stable
1980	**Niatross**	Clint Galbraith	Clint Galbraith	Niagara Acres, Niatross Stables & Clint Galbraith
1983	**Ralph Hanover**	Ron Waples	Stew Firlotte	Waples Stable, Pointsetta Stable, Grant's Direct Stable & P.J. Baugh
1997	**Western Dreamer**	Mike Lachance	Bill Robinson Stable	Matthew, Daniel and Patrick Daly

*Myer drove Romeo Hanover in the Cane, Sholty in the other two races.

TROTTERS

Six 3-year-olds have won the Yonkers Trot, Hambletonian and Kentucky Futurity in the same year since the Trotting Triple Crown was established in 1955. Stanley Dancer is the only driver/trainer to win it twice.

Year		Driver/Trainer	Owner
1955	**Scott Frost**	Joe O'Brien	S.A. Camp Farms
1963	**Speedy Scot**	Ralph Baldwin	Castleton Farms
1964	**Ayres**	John Simpson Sr.	Charlotte Sheppard
1968	**Nevele Pride**	Stanley Dancer	Nevele Acres & Lou Resnick
1969	**Lindy's Pride**	Howard Beissinger	Lindy Farms
1972	**Super Bowl**	Stanley Dancer	Rachel Dancer & Rose Hild Breeding Farm

Triple Crown Near Misses

PACERS

Nine horses have won the first two legs of the Triple Crown, but not the third. The Cane Pace (CP), Little Brown Jug (LBJ), and Messenger Stakes (MS) have not always been run in the same order so numbers after races won indicate sequence for that year.

Year		CP	LBJ	MS
1957	**Torpid**	won, 1	won, 2	DNF
1960	**Countess Adios**	won, 2	NE	won, 1
1971	**Albatross**	won, 2	2nd*	won, 1
1976	**Keystone Ore**	won, 1	won, 2	2nd*
1986	**Barberry Spur**	won, 1	won, 2	2nd*
1990	**Jake and Elwood**	won, 1	NE	won, 2
1992	**Western Hanover**	won, 1	2nd*	won, 2
1993	**Rijadh**	won, 1	2nd*	won, 2
1998	**Shady Character**	won, 1	won, 2	6th*

*Winning horses: Meadow Lands (1957), Nansemond (1971), Windshield Wiper (1976), Amity Chef (1986), Fake Left (1992), Life Sign (1993), Fit for Life (1998).
Note: Torpid (1957) scratched before the final heat; Countess Adios (1960) not eligible for Messenger; Jake and Elwood (1990) not eligible for Little Brown Jug.

TROTTERS

Eight horses have won the first two legs of the Triple Crown—the Yonkers Trot (YT) and the Hambletonian (Ham)—but not the third. The winner of the Ky. Futurity (KF) is listed.

Year		YT	Ham	KF
1962	**A.C.'s Viking**	won	won	Safe Mission
1976	**Steve Lobell**	won	won	Quick Pay
1977	**Green Speed**	won	won	Texas
1978	**Speedy Somolli**	won	won	Doublemint
1987	**Mack Lobell**	won	won	Napoletano
1993	**American Winner**	won	won	Pine Chip
1996	**Continentalvictory**	won	won	Running Sea
1998	**Muscles Yankee**	won	won	Trade Balance

Note: Green Speed (1977) not eligible for Ky. Futurity; Continentalvictory (1996) was withdrawn from the Ky. Futurity due to a leg injury.

The Hambletonian

For three-year-old trotters. Inaugurated in 1926 and has been held in Syracuse, N.Y.; Lexington, Ky.; Goshen, N.Y.; Yonkers, N.Y.; Du Quoin, Ill.; and since 1981 at The Meadowlands in East Rutherford, N.J.

Run at one mile since 1947. Winning horse must win two heats.

Drivers with most wins: John Campbell (5); Stanley Dancer, Billy Haughton and Ben White (4); Howard Beissinger, Del Cameron, Mike Lachance and Henry Thomas (3).

Year	Driver	Fastest Heat	Year	Driver	Fastest Heat
1926	**Guy McKinney**	Nat Ray	2:04¾	1964	**Ayres**	John Simpson Sr.	1:56⅘
1927	**Iosola's Worthy**	Marvin Childs	2:03¾	1965	**Egyptian Candor**	Del Cameron	2:03⅖
1928	**Spencer**	W.H. Lessee	2:02½	1966	**Kerry Way**	Frank Ervin	1:58⅘
1929	**Walter Dear**	Walter Cox	2:02¾	1967	**Speedy Streak**	Del Cameron	2:00
1930	**Hanover's Bertha**	Tom Berry	2:03	1968	**Nevele Pride**	Stanley Dancer	1:59⅖
1931	**Calumet Butler**	R.D. McMahon	2:03¼	1969	**Lindy's Pride**	Howard Beissinger	1:57⅗
1932	**The Marchioness**	Will Caton	2:01¼				
1933	**Mary Reynolds**	Ben White	2:03¾	1970	**Timothy T**	John Simpson Jr.	1:58⅖
1934	**Lord Jim**	Doc Parshall	2:02¾	1971	**Speedy Crown**	Howard Beissinger	1:57⅖
1935	**Greyhound**	Sep Palin	2:02¼	1972	**Super Bowl**	Stanley Dancer	1:56⅖
1936	**Rosalind**	Ben White	2:01¾	1973	**Flirth**	Ralph Baldwin	1:57⅕
1937	**Shirley Hanover**	Henry Thomas	2:01½	1974	**Christopher T**	Billy Haughton	1:58⅗
1938	**McLin Hanover**	Henry Tomas	2:02¼	1975	**Bonefish**	Stanley Dancer	1:59
1939	**Peter Astra**	Doc Parshall	2:04¼	1976	**Steve Lobell**	Billy Haughton	1:56⅖
				1977	**Green Speed**	Billy Haughton	1:55⅗
1940	**Spencer Scott**	Fred Egan	2:02	1978	**Speedy Somolli**	Howard Beissinger	1:55
1941	**Bill Gallon**	Lee Smith	2:05	1979	**Legend Hanover**	George Sholty	1:56⅕
1942	**The Ambassador**	Ben White	2:04				
1943	**Volo Song**	Ben White	2:02½	1980	**Burgomeister**	Billy Haughton	1:56⅗
1944	**Yankee Maid**	Henry Thomas	2:04	1981	**Shiaway St. Pat**	Ray Remmen	2:01⅕
1945	**Titan Hanover**	Harry Pownall Sr.	2:04	1982	**Speed Bowl**	Tommy Haughton	1:56⅘
1946	**Chestertown**	Thomas Berry	2:02½	1983	**Duenna**	Stanley Dancer	1:57⅖
1947	**Hoot Mon**	Sep Palin	2:00	1984	**Historic Freight**	Ben Webster	1:56⅖
1948	**Demon Hanover**	Harrison Hoyt	2:02	1985	**Prakas**	Bill O'Donnell	1:54⅗
1949	**Miss Tilly**	Fred Egan	2:01⅖	1986	**Nuclear Kosmos**	Ulf Thoresen	1:55⅖
				1987	**Mack Lobell**	John Campbell	1:53⅗
1950	**Lusty Song**	Del Miller	2:02	1988	**Armbro Goal**	John Campbell	1:54⅗
1951	**Mainliner**	Guy Crippen	2:02⅗	1989	**Park Avenue Joe**	Ron Waples	1:54⅗
1952	**Sharp Note**	Bion Shively	2:02⅗		& **Probe** *	Bill Fahy	
1953	**Helicopter**	Harry Harvey	2:01⅗				
1954	**Newport Dream**	Del Cameron	2:02⅘	1990	**Harmonious**	John Campbell	1:54⅕
1955	**Scott Frost**	Joe O'Brien	2:00⅗	1991	**Giant Victory**	Jack Moiseyev	1:54⅘
1956	**The Intruder**	Ned Bower	2:01⅖	1992	**Alf Palema**	Mickey McNichol	1:56⅖
1957	**Hickory Smoke**	John Simpson Sr.	2:00⅕	1993	**American Winner**	Ron Pierce	1:53⅕
1958	**Emily's Pride**	Flave Nipe	1:59⅘	1994	**Victory Dream**	Mike Lachance	1:54⅕
1959	**Diller Hanover**	Frank Ervin	2:01⅕	1995	**Tagliabue**	John Campbell	1:54⅘
				1996	**Continentalvictory**	Mike Lachance	1:52⅘
1960	**Blaze Hanover**	Joe O'Brien	1:59⅗	1997	**Malabar Man**	Mal Burroughs	1:55
1961	**Harlan Dean**	James Arthur	1:58⅘	1998	**Muscles Yankee**	John Campbell	1:52⅖
1962	**A.C.'s Viking**	Sanders Russell	1:59⅗	1999	**Self Possessed**	Mike Lachance	1:51⅗
1963	**Speedy Scot**	Ralph Baldwin	1:57⅗				

*In 1989, Park Avenue Joe and Probe finished in a dead heat in the race-off. They were later declared co-winners, but Park Avenue Joe was awarded 1st place money because his three-race summary (2-1-1) was better than Probe's (1-9-1).

The Little Brown Jug

Harness racing's most prestigious race for three-year-old pacers. Inaugurated in 1946 and held annually at the Delaware, Ohio County Fairgrounds. Winning horse must win two heats.

Drivers with most wins: Billy Haughton (5); Stanley Dancer and Mike Lachance (4); John Campbell, Frank Ervin and John Simpson Sr. (3); Adelbert Cameron, Herve Filion, Jack Moiseyev, Joe O'Brien, Bill O'Donnell, Ron Pierce, "Curly" Smart and Ron Waples (2).

Year		Driver	Fastest Heat	Year		Driver	Fastest Heat
1946	Ensign Hanover	"Curly" Smart	2:02	1973	Melvin's Woe	Joe O'Brien	1:57⅗
1947	Forbes Chief	Adelbert Cameron	2:05	1974	Armbro Omaha	Billy Haughton	1:57
1948	Knight Dream	Frank Safford	2:07	1975	Seatrain	Ben Webster	1:56⅘
1949	Good Time	Frank Ervin	2:03⅖	1976	Keystone Ore	Stanley Dancer	1:56⅘
1950	Dudley Hanover	Delvin Miller	2:02⅗	1977	Governor Skipper	John Chapman	1:56⅕
1951	Tar Heel	Adelbert Cameron	2:00	1978	Happy Escort	Bill Popfinger	1:55⅖
1952	Meadow Rice	"Curly" Smart	2:01⅗	1979	Hot Hitter	Herve Filion	1:55⅗
1953	Keystoner	Frank Ervin	2:02½	1980	Niatross	Clint Galbraith	1:54⅘
1954	Adios Harry	Morris MacDonald	2:02⅖	1981	Fan Hanover (f)	Glen Garnsey	1:56
1955	Quick Chief	Billy Haughton	2:00	1982	Merger	John Campbell	1:54⅗
1956	Noble Adios	John Simpson, Sr.	2:00⅘	1983	Ralph Hanover	Ron Waples	1:55⅗
1957	Torpid	John Simpson, Sr.	2:00⅘	1984	Colt Fortysix	Chris Boring	1:53⅗
1958	Shadow Wave	Joe O'Brien	2:01	1985	Nihilator	Bill O'Donnell	1:52⅕
1959	Adios Butler	Clint Hodgkins	1:59⅖	1986	Barberry Spur	Bill O'Donnell	1:52⅖
1960	Bullet Hanover	John Simpson, Sr.	1:58⅗	1987	Jaguar Spur	Dick Stillings	1:54
1961	Henry T. Adios	Stanley Dancer	1:58⅘	1988	B.J. Scoot	Mike Lachance	1:52⅗
1962	Lehigh Hanover	Stanley Dancer	1:58⅘	1989	Goalie Jeff	Mike Lachance	1:54½
1963	Overtrick	John Patterson, Sr.	1:57⅕	1990	Beach Towel	Ray Remmen	1:53⅗
1964	Vicar Hanover	Billy Haughton	2:00⅘	1991	Precious Bunny	Jack Moiseyev	1:53⅘
1965	Bret Hanover	Frank Ervin	1:57	1992	Fake Left	Ron Waples	1:53⅗
1966	Romeo Hanover	George Sholty	1:59⅗	1993	Life Sign	John Campbell	1:52
1967	Best Of All	Jim Hackett	1:59	1994	Magical Mike	Mike Lachance	1:52⅗
1968	Rum Customer	Billy Haughton	1:59⅗	1995	Nick's Fantasy	John Campbell	1:51⅖
1969	Laverne Hanover	Billy Haughton	2:00⅖	1996	Armbro Operative	Jack Moiseyev	1:52⅗
1970	Most Happy Fella	Stanley Dancer	1:57⅕	1997	Western Dreamer	Mike Lachance	1:51⅕
1971	Nansemond	Herve Filion	1:57⅖	1998	Shady Character	Ron Pierce	1:52⅘
1972	Strike Out	Keith Waples	1:56⅗	1999	Blissfull Hall	Ron Pierce	1:55⅗

All-Time Leaders

The all-time winning trotters, pacers and drivers through 1998, according to *The Trotting and Pacing Guide*. Purses for horses include races in foreign countries. Earnings and wins for drivers include only races held in North America.

Top 10 Horses — Money Won

		T/P	Sts	1st	Earnings
1	Peace Corps	T	42	35	$4,137,737
2	Ourasi (FRA)	T	N/A	32	4,010,105
3	Mack Lobell	T	86	65	3,917,594
4	Reve d'Udon	T	23	18	3,611,351
5	Zoogin	T	N/A	N/A	3,428,311
6	Nihilator	P	38	35	3,225,653
7	Sea Cove	T	N/A	N/A	3,138,986
8	Artsplace	P	49	37	3,085,083
9	Presidential Ball	P	38	26	3,021,363
10	Matt's Scooter	P	61	37	2,944,591

Top 10 Drivers — Races Won

		Yrs	1st	Earnings
1	Herve Filion	35	14,783	$85,044,653
2	Walter Case Jr.	21	8,291	32,655,632
3	Mike Lachance	31	8,288	110,326,519
4	Dave Magee	26	8,102	57,844,147
5	Cat Manzi	31	8,017	70,188,066
6	John Campbell	27	7,921	166,153,825
7	Jack Moiseyev	23	7,528	74,850,908
8	Carmine Abbatiello	42	7,170	50,323,136
9	Doug Brown	26	7,152	69,247,322
10	Eddie Davis	35	6,971	34,561,816

Annual Awards
Harness Horse of the Year

Selected since 1947 by U.S. Trotting Association and the U.S. Harness Writers Association; age of winning horse is noted; (t) indicates trotter and (p) indicates pacer. USTA added Trotter and Pacer of the Year awards in 1970.

Multiple winners: Bret Hanover and Nevele Pride (3); Adios Butler, Albatross, Cam Fella, Good Time, Mack Lobell, Niatross and Scott Frost (2).

Year		Year		Year		Year	
1947	Victory Song (4t)	1952	Good Time (6t)	1957	Torpid (3p)	1962	Su Mac Lad (8t)
1948	Rodney (4t)	1953	Hi Lo's Forbes (5p)	1958	Emily's Pride (3t)	1963	Speedy Scot (3t)
1949	Good Time (3p)	1954	Stenographer (3t)	1959	Bye Bye Byrd (4p)	1964	Bret Hanover (2p)
1950	Proximity (8t)	1955	Scott Frost (3t)	1960	Adios Butler (4p)	1965	Bret Hanover (3p)
1951	Pronto Don (6t)	1956	Scott Frost (4t)	1961	Adios Butler (5p)	1966	Bret Hanover (4p)

Year		Year		Year		Year	
1967	Nevele Pride (2t)	1975	Savoir (7t)	1983	Cam Fella (4p)	1991	Precious Bunny (3p)
1968	Nevele Pride (3t)	1976	Keystone Ore (3p)	1984	Fancy Crown (3t)	1992	Artsplace (4p)
1969	Nevele Pride (4t)	1977	Green Speed (3t)	1985	Nihilator (3p)	1993	Staying Together (4p)
1970	Fresh Yankee (7t)	1978	Abercrombie (3p)	1986	Forrest Skipper (4p)	1994	Cam's Card Shark (3p)
1971	Albatross (3p)	1979	Niatross (2p)	1987	Mack Lobell (3t)	1995	CR Kay Suzie (3t)
1972	Albatross (4p)	1980	Niatross (3p)	1988	Mack Lobell (4t)	1996	Continentalvictory (3t)
1973	Sir Dalrai (4p)	1981	Fan Hanover (3p)	1989	Matt's Scooter (4p)	1997	Malabar Man (3t)
1974	Delmonica Hanover (5t)	1982	Cam Fella (3p)	1990	Beach Towel (3p)	1998	Moni Maker (5t)

Driver of the Year

Determined by Universal Driving Rating System (UDR) and presented by the Harness Tracks of America since 1968. Eligible drivers must have at least 1,000 starts for the season.

Multiple winners: Herve Filion (10); John Campbell, Walter Case Jr. and Michel Lachance (3); Tony Morgan, Bill O'Donnell, Luc Ouellette and Ron Waples (2).

Year		Year		Year		Year	
1968	Stanley Dancer	1977	Donald Dancer	1985	Michel Lachance	1994	Dave Magee
1969	Herve Filion	1978	Carmine Abbatiello	1986	Michel Lachance	1995	Luc Ouellette
1970	Herve Filion		& Herve Filion	1987	Michel Lachance	1996	Tony Morgan
1971	Herve Filion	1979	Ron Waples	1988	John Campbell		& Luc Ouellette
1972	Herve Filion	1980	Ron Waples	1989	Herve Filion	1997	Tony Morgan
1973	Herve Filion	1981	Herve Filion	1990	John Campbell	1998	Walter Case Jr.
1974	Herve Filion	1982	Bill O'Donnell	1991	Walter Case Jr.		
1975	Joe O'Brien	1983	John Campbell	1992	Walter Case Jr.		
1976	Herve Filion	1984	Bill O'Donnell	1993	Jack Moiseyev		

STEEPLECHASE RACING

Champion Horses

Annual horse of the year since 1956 based on vote of the National Turf Writers Association and other selected media.

Multiple Winners: Flatterer and Lonesome Glory (4); Bon Nouvel and Zaccio (3); Café Prince, Morley Street and Neji (2).

Year		Year		Year		Year	
1956	Shipboard	1967	Quick Pitch	1977	Café Prince	1988	Jimmy Lorenzo
1957	Neji	1968	Bon Nouvel	1978	Café Prince	1989	Highland Bud
1958	Neji	1969	L'Escargot	1979	Martie's Anger	1990	Morley Street
1959	Ancestor	1970	Top Bid	1980	Zaccio	1991	Morley Street
1960	Benguala	1971	Shadow Brok	1981	Zaccio	1992	Lonesome Glory
1961	Peal	1972	Soothsayer	1982	Zaccio	1993	Lonesome Glory
1962	Barnaby's Bluff	1973	Athenian Idol	1983	Flatterer	1994	Warm Spell
1963	Amber Diver	1974	Gran Kan	1984	Flatterer	1995	Lonesome Glory
1964	Bon Nouvel	1975	Life's Illusion	1985	Flatterer	1996	Correggio
1965	Bon Nouvel	1976	Fire Control &	1986	Flatterer	1997	Lonesome Glory
1966	Tuscalee & Mako		Straight and True	1987	Inlander	1998	Flat Top

Champion Jockeys

Annual leading jockeys by races won since 1956, according to the National Steeplechase Association.

Multiple Winners: Joe Aitcheson Jr. (7); Jerry Fishback (5); John Cushman and Alfred P. Smithwick (4); Tom Skiffington and Jeff Teter (3); Ricky Hendriks, James Lawrence, Blythe Miller, Chip Miller and Thomas Walsh (2).

Year		Year		Year		Year	
1956	Alfred P. Smithwick	1967	Joe Aitcheson Jr.	1978	Tom Skiffington	1989	James Lawrence
1957	Alfred P. Smithwick	1968	Joe Aitcheson Jr.	1979	Tom Skiffington	1990	Jeff Teter
1958	Alfred P. Smithwick	1969	Joe Aitcheson Jr.	1980	John Cushman	1991	Jeff Teter
1959	James Murphy	1970	Joe Aitcheson Jr.	1981	John Cushman	1992	Craig Thornton
1960	Thomas Walsh	1971	Jerry Fishback	1982	John Cushman	1993	James Lawrence
1961	Joe Aitcheson Jr.	1972	Michael O'Brien	1983	John Cushman	1994	Blythe Miller
1962	Alfred P. Smithwick	1973	Jerry Fishback	1984	Jeff Teter	1995	Blythe Miller
1963	Joe Aitcheson Jr.	1974	Jerry Fishback	1985	Bernie Houghton	1996	Chip Miller
1964	Joe Aitcheson Jr.	1975	Jerry Fishback	1986	Ricky Hendriks	1997	Arch Kingsley Jr.
1965	Doug Small Jr.	1976	Tom Skiffington	1987	Ricky Hendriks		& Jonathan Kiser
1966	Thomas Walsh	1977	Jerry Fishback	1988	Jonathan Smart	1998	Chip Miller
							& Sean Clancy

Tennis

Andre Agassi registered an emotional, come-from-behind five-set victory over Andrei Medvedev in the finals of the French Open, then added a U.S. Open title for good measure.

AP/Wide World Photos

It's America's Game — Again

Andre Agassi leads the way with two Grand Slam titles in 1999.

by
Sal Paolantonio

Andre Agassi has been on top before. But it has never felt quite like this. His triumph at the 1999 U.S. Open completed his long journey back from tennis oblivion. In 1997 he was wandering around the satellite tournaments, trying to rediscover his signature baseball-swing forehand, the one that knocked the racquet from his opponents' hands.

"He was ranked 141 in the world at that time — 141!" said ESPN tennis analyst Luke Jensen. "It's like going back to play high school football, then playing your way back to the Super Bowl."

In 1999 Agassi also won the French Open, becoming only the fifth man in history to achieve the career Grand Slam — the Australian, the French, Wimbledon and the U.S. Open. He became the first player, man or woman, to do it on three different surfaces.

It was the first time in his career that Agassi won two Grand Slam tournaments in a single year. And thanks to Team Agassi, he seems to be getting better and stronger at age 29. The A-Team consists of Brad Gilbert, a former No. 4 in the world who helped Agassi develop a consistently accurate 115-mph serve, and Gil Reyes, a former migrant worker from New Mexico who, working as the strength and conditioning coach at the University of Nevada, Las Vegas, put Agassi in the best shape of his life.

"He came to me at my gym when he was 18 and asked what we did for the basketball players," said Reyes. "That's how it started." And now Agassi looks far from finished.

"I feel like I can play at this level for a very long time," said Agassi.

Sal Paolantonio covers tennis for ESPN.

AP/Wide World Photos

Americans **Lindsay Davenport** and **Pete Sampras** made it an all-American sweep at Wimbledon on July 4, 1999. It was Davenport's first Wimbledon title, while Sampras captured his sixth.

"I'm fit. I'm seeing the ball so well. The tennis court is my friend again."

From the beginning of the French Open in May until he won the U.S. Open, Agassi won 36 matches and lost only four, including three to Pete Sampras, who beat him in the finals at Wimbledon. That dream match was an encore for a rivalry that ruled the '90s. And the two great American sluggers, as they reach the age when most tennis players are hanging it up, seem poised to continue the hostilities into the next century.

Sampras' motivation is simple. Winning Wimbledon gave him 12 Grand Slam championships, tying him with Roy Emerson's long-standing career record. A herniated disc forced Sampras out of the U.S. Open, so he hopes to continue his chase of Emerson in 2000.

Several rivalries blossomed in the women's game in 1999 as well. Lindsay Davenport won Wimbledon, completing an all-American sweep at the All-England Club on a spectacular final Sunday on July 4th. But Davenport was denied back-to-back U.S. Open championships, losing to 17-year-old Serena Williams in the semifinals.

Williams and her sister Venus spent six months battling Davenport, Martina Hingis and each other during the long hardcourt and claycourt seasons. Hingis had won the Australian Open in January, then made another assault at the French, before succumbing to veteran Steffi Graf in three, tortuous sets. In the final set, Hingis imploded emotionally and had to be convinced by her mother to return to the court

AP/Wide World Photos

It was only a matter of time before one of the Williams sisters won a grand slam title. Seventeen-year-old **Serena** became the first one to accomplish the feat with a win over Martina Hingis at the U.S. Open.

after the match for the trophy presentations.

With Graf deciding to retire, Davenport, Hingis and the Williams sisters headed for a showdown at the U.S. Open. Venus, the older sister at 18, was getting all the press. But it was Serena who was compiling a nearly flawless record on hardcourts, losing only once since March 1. That one loss came at the hands of her sister Venus in the finals at Lipton.

In the semis at the Open, Serena, with a powerful serve and savvy backhand, dispatched Davenport. Venus, however, succumbed to cramps and Hingis' surgically accurate groundstrokes in three sets. Hingis has never beaten both sisters in the same tournament and this held true in the Open finals. Serena won in two sets, becoming the first African-American woman

to win the American championship in 31 years.

"To follow in Althea Gibson's footsteps and do it in the last major of the millennium is something great," said Williams. ∎

Sal Paolantonio's Top Ten Tennis Highlights of 1999

10. **Venus Williams beats Serena Williams** in the Lipton finals. The sisters have arrived.

9. **Pete Sampras suffers** a herniated disc, forcing him to drop out of the U.S. Open and preventing him from going for a record 13th major title.

8. **Jana Novotna retires,** finishing her career with one Grand Slam win — Wimbledon in 1998.

AP/Wide World Photos

Germany's **Steffi Graf** retired in 1999 with 22 career Grand Slam singles titles on her resume, the second-highest total of any player in history. Her final major came at the 1999 French Open at the expense of top seed Martina Hingis.

7. **Martina Hingis rolls** to a 6-2, 6-3 win over Amelie Mauresmo in the Australian Open, her only major win of the year.

6. **John McEnroe** is named captain of the United States Davis Cup team.

5. **One more for Steffi.** Graf wins the French Open title in three sets over Hingis, the last major of her career before announcing her retirement.

4. **Andre Agassi wins the French Open,** giving him the career Grand Slam. He is the first person in history to accomplish the feat on three different surfaces.

3. **Pete Sampras and Lindsay Davenport** make it an American sweep at Wimbledon, winning their titles on the same day — July 4th.

2. **Seventeen-year-old Serena Williams** upsets Martina Hingis to win the U.S. Open in straight sets.

1. **Andre Agassi wins** the U.S. Open in five sets over fellow countryman Todd Martin in the last major tournament of the century. ■

THE NUMBERS

INSIDE

QUEEN **STEFFI**

Over her illustrious 17-year career, Steffi Graf spent a grand total of 377 weeks as the top women's player in the world, including 186 weeks in a row from Aug. 17, 1987 to March 10, 1991. No current player is even close to that mark. Here is a look at the five women who have held the top spot for the most weeks since the computer ranking system began in 1975.

Player	Weeks
Steffi Graf	377
Martina Navratilova	331
Chris Evert	262
Monica Seles	178
Martina Hingis	103*

*as of Sept. 20, 1999

...AND PISTOL **PETE**

On August 2, 1999, Pete Sampras passed Ivan Lendl for the most total weeks at No. 1 since the inception of the ATP rankings in 1973. Here are the five men who have been ranked No. 1 longer than anyone.

Player	Weeks
Pete Sampras	276*
Ivan Lendl	270
Jimmy Connors	268
John McEnroe	170
Bjorn Borg	109

*as of Sept. 20, 1999

BABY BOOMERS

With her win in the U.S. Open in Sept. 1999, Serena Williams became just the eighth woman to win a Grand Slam event before her 18th birthday. All eight are listed below along with their age at the time of their earliest major win.

Player	Tournament	Age
C. Dod	1887 Wim.	15 yrs, 10 mos
M. Hingis	1997 Aus.	16 yrs, 3 mos
M. Seles	1990 French	16 yrs, 6 mos
T. Austin	1979 U.S.	16 yrs, 10 mos
A. Sanchez Vicario	1989 French	17 yrs, 5 mos
M. Court Smith	1960 Aus.	17 yrs, 6 mos
S. Graf	1987 French	17 yrs, 11 mos
S. Williams	1999 U.S.	17 yrs, 11 mos

ACE UP HIS SLEEVE

Goran Ivanisevic blasted 1,000 aces for the fourth time in his career in 1998. He has led the ATP Tour four out of the last five years and five of the last eight. Here are the ATP Tour's leaders in that category for the last five years.

Year	Player	Aces
1998	Goran Ivanisevic	1065
1997	Goran Ivanisevic	1048
1996	Goran Ivanisevic	1477
1995	Pete Sampras	974
1994	Goran Ivanisevic	1169

Source: ATP Tour

KEEPING BUSY

In four of the last five years, Russian Yevgeny Kafelnikov has led the ATP Tour in matches played. He led every year except 1997. No, he wasn't lazy. He missed three months after fracturing a finger but returned to form in 1998.

Year	Player	Matches
1998	Yevgeny Kafelnikov	150
1997	Jonas Bjorkman	158
1996	Yevgeny Kafelnikov	171
1995	Yevgeny Kafelnikov	167
1994	Yevgeny Kafelnikov	171

Source: ATP Tour ■

THE 2000 ESPN INFORMATION PLEASE SPORTS ALMANAC

T E N N I S
S T A T I S T I C S

THE SEASON IN REVIEW
1998-1999
MEN • WOMEN • LEADERS

SEC A

PAGE 817

Tournament Results

Winners of men's and women's pro singles championships from Oct. 31, 1998 through Sept. 26, 1999.

Men's ATP Tour

LATE 1998

Finals	Tournament	Winner	Earnings	Runner-Up	Score
Nov. 1	Eurocard Open (Stuttgart)	Richard Krajicek	$376,000	Y. Kafelnikov	64 63 63
Nov. 1	Mexican Open (Mexico City)	Jiri Novak	45,000	X. Malisse	64 63 63 63 63
Nov. 8	Paris Open	Greg Rusedski	393,000	P. Sampras	64 76 63
Nov. 8	Colombian Open (Bogota)	Mariano Zabaleta	45,000	R. Delgato	64 64
Nov. 15	Stockholm Open	Todd Martin	112,000	T. Johansson	63 64 64
Nov. 15	Kremlin Cup (Moscow)	Yevgeny Kafelnikov	157,400	G. Ivanisevic	76 76
Nov. 15	Chevrolet Cup (Santiago)	Francisco Clavet	45,000	Y. El Aynaoui	62 64
Nov. 22	ATP Doubles Champs. (Hartford)	Jacco Eltingh/ Paul Haarhuis	168,500	M. Knowles/ D. Nestor	64 62 75
Nov. 29	ATP World Championship (Hannover)	Alex Corretja	1,360,000	C. Moya	36 36 75 63 75

1999

Finals	Tournament	Winner	Earnings	Runner-Up	Score
Jan. 10	Australian Hardcourt Championships	Thomas Enqvist	$46,000	L. Hewitt	46 61 62
Jan. 10	Qatar Open (Doha)	Rainer Schuttler	137,000	T. Henman	64 57 61
Jan. 17	adidas International (Sydney)	Todd Martin	46,000	A. Corretja	63 76
Jan. 17	Heineken Open (Auckland)	Sjeng Schalken	46,000	T. Haas	64 64
Jan. 31	**Australian Open** (Melbourne)	Yevgeny Kafelnikov	458,975	T. Enqvist	46 60 63 76
Feb. 7	Marseille Open	Fabrice Santoro	72,000	A. Clement	63 46 64
Feb. 14	St. Petersburg Open (Russia)	Marc Rosset	46,000	D. Prinosil	63 64
Feb. 14	Dubai Open	Jerome Golmard	162,000	N. Kiefer	64 62
Feb. 14	Sybase Open (San Jose)	Mark Philippoussis	46,000	C. Mamiit	63 62
Feb. 21	ABN/Amro World Tennis Tournament (Rotterdam)	Yevgeny Kafelnikov	135,000	T. Henman	62 76
Feb. 21	Kroger/St.Jude International (Memphis)	Tommy Haas	120,000	J. Courier	64 61
Feb. 28	Guardian Direct Cup (London)	Richard Krajicek	128,000	G. Rusedski	76 67 75
Mar. 7	Franklin Templeton Classic (Scottsdale)	Jan-Michael Gambill	46,000	L. Hewitt	76 46 64
Mar. 7	Copenhagen Open	Magnus Gustafsson	30,400	F. Santoro	64 61
Mar. 14	Champions Cup (Indian Wells)	Mark Philippoussis	361,000	C. Moya	57 64 64 46 62
Mar. 28	Lipton Championships (Key Biscayne)	Richard Krajicek	360,000	S. Grosjean	46 61 62 75
Mar. 28	Grand Prix Hassan II (Casablanca)	Alberto Martin	30,400	F. Vicente	63 64
Apr. 11	Gold Flake Open (Chennai)	Byron Black	58,000	R. Schuttler	64 16 63
Apr. 11	Salem Open (Hong Kong)	Andre Agassi	46,000	B. Becker	67 64 64
Apr. 11	Estoril Open	Albert Costa	84,000	T. Martin	76 26 63
Apr. 18	Japan Open (Tokyo)	Nicolas Kiefer	99,000	W. Ferreira	76 75
Apr. 18	Open Seat Godo (Barcelona)	Felix Mantilla	135,000	K. Alami	76 63 63
Apr. 25	Monte Carlo Open	Gustavo Kuerten	361,000	M. Rios	64 21 (ret.)
Apr. 25	US Clay Court Champs. (Orlando)	Magnus Norman	37,500	G. Canas	60 63
May 2	BMW Open (Munich)	Franco Squillari	70,000	A. Pavel	64 63
May 2	AT&T Challenge (Atlanta)	Stefan Koubek	46,000	S. Grosjean	61 62
May 2	Skoda Czech Open (Prague)	Dominik Hrbaty	66,400	S. Dosedel	62 62
May 9	German Open (Hamburg)	Marcelo Rios	361,000	M. Zabaleta	67 75 57 76 62
May 9	Citrix Tennis Championships (Delray Beach)	Lleyton Hewitt	34,800	X. Malisse	64 67 61
May 16	Italian Open (Rome)	Gustavo Kuerten	350,000	P. Rafter	64 75 76
May 23	Raiffeisen Grand Prix (St. Polten)	Marcelo Rios	57,000	M. Zabaleta	44 (ret.)
May 23	ATP World Team Championships (Dusseldorf)	Australia	500,000	Sweden	2-1
June 6	**French Open** (Paris)	Andre Agassi	668,520	A. Medvedev	16 26 64 63 64
June 13	Stella Artois Grass Court (London)	Pete Sampras	122,000	T. Henman	67 64 76
June 13	Gerry Weber Open (Halle)	Nicolas Kiefer	85,000	N. Kulti	63 62

Tournament Results (Cont.)

Finals	Tournament	Winner	Earnings	Runner-Up	Score
June 13	Merano Open	Fernando Vicente	$46,000	H. Arazi	62 36 76
June 20	Nottingham Open	Cedric Pioline	46,000	K. Ullyett	63 75
June 20	Heineken Trophy ('s-Hertogenbosch)	Patrick Rafter	66,400	A. Pavel	36 76 64
July 4	**Wimbledon** (London)	Pete Sampras	724,133	A. Agassi	63 64 75
July 11	Hall of Fame Championships (Newport)	Chris Woodruff	41,800	K. Carlsen	67 64 64
July 11	Swedish Open (Bastad)	Juan Antonio Marin	46,000	A. Vinciguerra	63 76
July 11	Swiss Open (Gstaad)	Albert Costa	74,000	N. Lapentti	76 63 64
July 25	Mercedes Cup (Stuttgart)	Magnus Norman	157,000	T. Haas	67 46 76 60 63
Aug. 1	Generali Open (Kitzbühel)	Albert Costa	85,500	F. Vincente	75 62 67
Aug. 1	Croatian Championship (Umag)	Magnus Norman	54,000	J. Tarango	62 64
Aug. 1	Mercedes-Benz Cup (Los Angeles)	Pete Sampras	46,000	A. Agassi	76 76
Aug. 8	Grolsch Open (Amsterdam)	Younes El Aynaoui	66,400	M. Zabaleta	60 63
Aug. 8	du Maurier Open (Montreal)	Thomas Johansson	361,000	Y. Kafelnikov	16 63 63
Aug. 15	ATP Championship (Cincinnati)	Pete Sampras	361,000	P. Rafter	76 63
Aug. 15	Tennis International (San Marino)	Galo Blanco	39,000	A. Portas	46 64 63
Aug. 22	RCA/U.S. Hardcourts (Indianapolis)	Nicolas Lapentti	122,500	V. Spadea	46 64 64
Aug. 22	Legg Mason Classic (Washington D.C.)	Andre Agassi	99,000	Y. Kafelnikov	76 61
Aug. 29	Hamlet Cup (Long Island)	Magnus Norman	46,000	A. Corretja	76 46 63
Aug. 29	U.S. Pro Championships (Boston)	Marat Safin	46,000	G. Rusedski	64 76
Sept. 12	**U.S. Open** (New York)	Andre Agassi	750,000	T. Martin	64 67 67 63 62
Sept. 19	President's Cup (Tashkent)	Nicolas Kiefer	66,400	G. Bastl	64 62
Sept. 19	Mallorca Open	Juan Carlos Ferrero	66,400	A. Corretja	26 75 63
Sept. 20	Samsung Open (Bournemouth)	Adrian Voinea	375,000	S. Koubek	16 75 76

Women's WTA Tour
LATE 1998

Finals	Tournament	Winner	Earnings	Runner-Up	Score
Oct. 31	Seat Open (Luxembourg)	Mary Pierce	$27,000	S. Farina	60 20 (ret.)
Nov. 1	Bell Challenge	Tara Snyder	27,000	C. Rubin	46 64 76
Nov. 8	Sparkassen Cup	Steffi Graf	79,000	N. Tauziat	63 64
Nov. 15	Advanta Championships (Philadelphia)	Steffi Graf	79,000	L. Davenport	46 63 64
Nov. 22	Volvo Open (Pattaya)	Julie Halard-Decugis	17,700	F. Li	61 62
Nov. 22	WTA Tour Championship (New York)	Martina Hingis	500,000	L. Davenport	75 64 46 62

1999

Finals	Tournament	Winner	Earnings	Runner-Up	Score
Jan. 10	Australian Hardcourt Champs. (Gold Coast)	Patty Schnyder	$27,000	M. Pierce	46 76 62
Jan. 10	ASB Bank Classic (Auckland)	Julie Halard-Decugis	16,000	D. Van Roost	64 61
Jan. 17	adidas International (Sydney)	Lindsay Davenport	84,000	M. Hingis	64 63
Jan. 17	Tasmanian International (Hobart)	Chanda Rubin	16,000	R. Grande	62 63
Jan. 31	**Australian Open** (Melbourne)	Martina Hingis	369,950	A. Mauresmo	62 63
Feb. 7	Pan Pacific Open (Tokyo)	Martina Hingis	150,000	A. Coetzer	62 61
Feb. 14	Nokia Cup (Prostejov)	Henrieta Nagyova	112,500	S. Farina	76 64
Feb. 21	Faber Grand Prix (Hannover)	Jana Novotna	80,000	V. Williams	64 64
Feb. 21	Copa Colsanitas (Bogota)	Fabiola Zuluaga	22,000	C. Papadaki	61 63
Feb. 28	Open Gaz de France (Paris)	Serena Williams	80,000	A. Mauresmo	62 36 76
Feb. 28	IGA Classic (Oklahoma City)	Venus Williams	33,000	A. Coetzer	64 60
Mar. 13	Evert Cup (Indian Wells)	Serena Williams	200,000	S. Graf	63 36 75
Mar. 28	Lipton Championships (Key Biscayne)	Venus Williams	265,000	S. Williams	61 46 64
Apr. 4	Family Circle Cup (Hilton Head)	Martina Hingis	150,000	A. Kournikova	64 63
Apr. 11	Bausch & Lomb Champs. (Amelia Island)	Monica Seles	80,000	R. Dragomir	62 63
Apr. 11	Estoril Open	Katarina Srebotnik	22,000	R. Kuti Kis	63 61
Apr. 18	Japan Open (Tokyo)	Amy Frazier	27,000	A. Sugiyama	62 62
Apr. 25	Egypt Classic (Cairo)	Arantxa Sanchez Vicario	27,000	I. Spirlea	61 60
Apr. 25	Budapest Open	Sarah Pitkowski	22,000	C. Torrens-Valero	62 62
May 2	Betty Barclay Cup (Hamburg)	Venus Williams	80,000	M. Pierce	60 63
May 2	Croatian Bol Ladies Open	Corina Morariu	22,000	J. Halard-Decugis	62 60
May 9	Italian Open (Rome)	Venus Williams	150,000	M. Pierce	64 62
May 9	Warsaw Cup	Cristina Torrens-Valero	16,000	I. Gorrochategui	75 76
May 16	German Open (Berlin)	Martina Hingis	150,000	J. Halard-Decugis	60 61
May 16	Flanders Women's Open (Antwerp)	Justine Henin	16,000	S. Pitkowski	61 62
May 22	Internationaux de Strasbourg	Jennifer Capriati	27,500	E. Likhovtseva	61 63

Finals	Tournament	Winner	Earnings	Runner-Up	Score
May 22	Yellow Pages Open (Madrid)	Lindsay Davenport	$27,000	P. Suarez	61 63
June 6	**French Open** (Paris)	Steffi Graf	574,081	M. Hingis	46 75 62
June 13	DFS Classic (Birmingham)	Julie Halard-Decugis	27,000	N. Tauziat	62 36 64
June 13	Tashkent Open	Anna Smashnova	16,000	L. Courtois	63 63
June 20	Direct Line Insurance Int'l. (Eastbourne)	Natasha Zvereva	80,000	N. Tauziat	06 75 63
June 20	Heineken Trophy ('s-Hertogenbosch)	Kristina Brandi	27,000	S. Talaja	60 36 61
July 4	**Wimbledon** (London)	Lindsay Davenport	614,213	S. Graf	64 75
July 11	Egger Tennis Festival (Portschach)	Karina Habsudova	16,000	S. Talaja	26 64 64
July 18	International Tournament at Palermo	Anastasia Myskina	22,000	A. Montolio	36 76 62
July 18	Polish Open (Sopot)	Conchita Martinez	27,000	K. Habsudova	61 61
Aug. 1	Bank of the West Classic (Stanford)	Lindsay Davenport	80,000	V. Williams	76 62
Aug. 8	TIG Tennis Classic (San Diego)	Martina Hingis	80,000	V. Williams	64 60
Aug. 8	Sanex Trophy (Knokke-Zoute)	Maria Antonia Sanchez-Lorenzo	16,000	D. Chladkova	67 64 62
Aug. 15	Acura Classic (Los Angeles)	Serena Williams	80,000	J. Halard-Decugis	61 64
Aug. 22	du Maurier Open (Montreal)	Martina Hingis	150,000	M. Seles	64 64
Aug. 29	Pilot Pen International (New Haven)	Venus Williams	80,000	L. Davenport	62 75
Sept. 12	**U.S. Open** (Flushing)	Serena Williams	750,000	M. Hingis	63 76
Sept. 26	Princess Cup (Tokyo)	Lindsay Davenport	80,000	M. Seles	75 76
Sept. 26	Seat Open (Luxembourg)	Kim Clijsters	27,000	D. Van Roost	62 62

1999 Grand Slam Tournaments

Australian Open
MEN'S SINGLES

FINAL EIGHT— #7 Karol Kucera; #10 Yevgeny Kafelnikov; #15 Todd Martin; plus unseeded Thomas Enqvist, Tommy Haas, Nicolas Lapentti, Marc Rosset and Vincent Spadea.

Quarterfinals

Kafelnikov def. Martin	62 76(1) 62
Haas def. Spadea	76(5) 75 63
Enqvist def. Rosset	63 64 64
Lapentti def. Kucera	76(4) 67(6) 62 06 86

Semifinals

Kafelnikov def. Haas	63 64 75
Enqvist def. Lapentti	63 75 61

Final

Kafelnikov def. Enqvist	46 60 63 76(1)

WOMEN'S SINGLES

FINAL EIGHT— #1 Lindsay Davenport; #2 Martina Hingis; #5 Venus Williams; #6 Monica Seles; #7 Mary Pierce; #10 Steffi Graf; #11 Dominique Van Roost; plus unseeded Amelie Mauresmo.

Quarterfinals

Davenport def. Williams	64 60
Mauresmo def. Van Roost	63 76(3)
Seles def. Graf	75 61
Hingis def. Pierce	63 64

Semifinals

Mauresmo def. Davenport	46 75 75
Hingis def. Seles	62 64

Final

Hingis def. Mauresmo	62 63

DOUBLES FINALS

Men— #5 Jonas Bjorkman & Patrick Rafter def. #1 Mahesh Bhupathi & Leander Paes, 6-3, 4-6, 6-4, 6-7 (10-12), 6-4.

Women— #3 Martina Hingis & Anna Kournikova def. #1 Lindsay Davenport & Natasha Zvereva, 7-5, 6-3.

Mixed— David Adams & Mariaan De Swardt def. Max Mirnyi & Serena Williams, 6-4, 4-6, 7-6 (7-5).

French Open
MEN'S SINGLES

FINAL EIGHT— #6 Alex Corretja; #8 Gustavo Kuerten; #9 Marcelo Rios; #13 Andre Agassi; plus unseated Marcelo Filippini, Dominik Hrbaty, Andrei Medvedev and Fernando Meligeni.

Quarterfinals

Hrbaty def. Rios	76(4) 62 67(6) 63
Agassi def. Filippini	62 62 60
Meligeni def. Corretja	62 62 60
Medvedev def. Kuerten	75 64 64

Semifinals

Agassi def. Hrbaty	64 76(6) 36 64
Medvedev def. Meligeni	75 36 64 76(6)

Final

Agassi def. Medvedev	16 26 64 63 64

WOMEN'S SINGLES

FINAL EIGHT— #1 Martina Hingis; #2 Lindsay Davenport; #3 Monica Seles; #6 Steffi Graf; #7 Arantxa Sanchez Vicario; plus unseeded Conchita Martinez, Sylvia Plischke and Barbara Schwartz.

Quarterfinals

Hingis def. Schwartz	62 62
Sanchez Vicario def. Plischke	62 64
Seles def. Martinez	61 64
Graf def. Davenport	62 63

Semifinals

Hingis def. Sanchez Vicario	63 62
Graf def. Seles	67(2) 63 64

Final

Graf def. Hingis	46 75 62

DOUBLES FINALS

Men— #1 Mahesh Bhupathi & Leander Paes def. Goran Ivanisevic & Jeff Tarango, 6-2, 7-5.

Women—#9 Venus Williams & Serena Williams def. #2 Martina Hingis & Anna Kournikova 6-3, 6-7(2-7), 8-6.

Mixed— Katarina Srebotnik & Piet Norval def. #6 Larisa Neiland & Rick Leach 6-3, 3-6, 6-3.

Wimbledon
MEN'S SINGLES

FINAL EIGHT— #1 Pete Sampras; #2 Patrick Rafter; #4 Andre Agassi; #6 Tim Henman; Mark Philippoussis; #8 Todd Martin; #11 Gustavo Kuerten; plus unseeded Cedric Pioline.

Quarterfinals

Sampras def. Philippoussis	46 21 ret.
Henman def. Pioline	64 62 46 63
Agassi def. Kuerten	63 64 64
Rafter def. Martin	63 67(5) 76(5) 76(3)

Semifinals

Sampras def. Henman	36 64 63 64
Agassi def. Rafter	75 76(5) 62

Final

Sampras def. Agassi	63 64 75

WOMEN'S SINGLES

FINAL EIGHT— #2 Steffi Graf; #3 Lindsay Davenport; #5 Jana Novotna; #6 Venus Williams; #8 Nathalie Tauziat; plus unseeded Jelena Dokic, Mirjana Lucic and Alexandra Stevenson.

Quarterfinals

Stevenson def. Dokic	63 16 63
Davenport def. Novotna	63 64
Lucic def. Tauziat	46 64 75
Graf def. Williams	62 36 64

Semifinals

Davenport def. Stevenson	61 61
Graf def. Lucic	67(3) 64 63

Final

Davenport def. Graf	64 75

DOUBLES FINALS

Men— #1 Mahesh Bhupathi & Leander Paes def. #8 Paul Haarhuis & Jared Palmer 6-7 (10-12), 6-3, 6-4, 7-6 (7-4).

Women— #7 Lindsay Davenport & Corina Morariu def. #9 Mariaan de Swardt & Elena Tatarkova 6-4, 6-4.

Mixed— #1 Leander Paes & Lisa Raymond def. #3 Jonas Bjorkman & Anna Kournikova 6-4, 3-6, 6-3.

U.S. Open
MEN'S SINGLES

FINAL EIGHT— #2 Andre Agassi; #3 Yevgeny Kafelnikov; #5 Gustavo Kuerten; #7 Todd Martin; #12 Richard Krajicek; plus unseeded Slava Dosedel, Nicolas Escude and Cedric Pioline.

Quarterfinals

Martin def. Dosedel	63 57 64 64
Pioline def. Kuerten	46 76(6) 76(14) 76(8)
Kafelnikov def. Krajicek	76(0) 76(4) 36 76(8)
Agassi def. Escude	76(3) 63 64

Semifinals

Martin def. Pioline	64 61 62
Agassi def. Kafelnikov	16 63 63 63

Final

Agassi def. Martin	64 67(5) 67(2) 63 62

WOMEN'S SINGLES

FINAL EIGHT— #1 Martina Hingis; #2 Lindsay Davenport; #3 Venus Williams; #4 Monica Seles; #5 Mary Pierce; #7 Serena Williams; #12 Barbara Schett; plus unseeded Anke Huber.

Quarterfinals

Hingis def. Huber	62 60
V. Williams def. Schett	64 63
S. Williams def. Seles	46 63 62
Davenport def. Pierce	62 36 75

Semifinals

Hingis def. V. Williams	61 46 63
S. Williams def. Davenport	64 16 64

Final

S. Williams def. Hingis	63 76(4)

DOUBLES FINALS

Men— #11 Sebastien Lareau & Alex O'Brien def. #1 Mahesh Bhupathi & Leander Paes 7-6 (9-7), 6-4.

Women— #5 Venus Williams & Serena Williams def. Chanda Rubin & Sandrine Testud 4-6, 6-1, 6-4.

Mixed— #2 Ai Sugiyama & Mahesh Bhupathi def. Kimberly Po & Donald Johnson 6-4, 6-4.

1999 Fed Cup

Originally the Federation Cup and started in 1963 by the International Tennis Federation as the Davis Cup of women's tennis. Played by 32 teams over one week at one site through 1994. Tournament changed in 1995 to Davis Cup-style format of four rounds and home sides.

Quarterfinals
(April 16-18)

Winner	Loser
at United States 5	Croatia 0
at Russia 3	France 2
at Italy 3	Spain 0
Slovakia 5	at Switzerland 0

Russia 3, Slovakia 2
at Moscow, Russia (July 24-25)

Day One— Elena Likhovtseva (RUS) def. Ludmila Cervanova (SVK), 7-5, 6-7 (5-7), 6-3; Karina Habsudova (SVK) def. Tatyana Panova (RUS), 7-6 (7-5), 6-1.

Day Two— Likhovtseva (RUS) def. Habsudova (SVK), 3-6, 6-4, 6-2; Panova (RUS) def. Cervanova (SVK), 6-4, 6-4; Cervanova & Daniela Hantuchova (SVK) def. Elena Makarova & Elena Dementieva (RUS), 7-5, 7-6 (7-5).

Semifinals
United States 3, Italy 1
at Ancona, Italy (July 24-25)

Day One— Venus Williams (USA) def. Rita Grande (ITA), 6-2, 6-3; Silvia Farina (ITA) def. Monica Seles (USA), 6-4, 4-6, 6-4.

Day Two— V. Williams (USA) def. Farina (ITA), 6-1, 6-1; Serena Williams (USA)* def. Grande (ITA), 6-1, 6-1. V. Williams & S. Williams (USA) def. Adriana Serra-Zanetti & Tathiana Garbin (ITA), 6-2, 6-2.
*S. Williams was substituted for Seles who was injured before Sunday's match.

Finals
United States 4, Russia 1
at Palo Alto, Calif. (Sept. 18-19)

Day One— Venus Williams (USA) def. Elena Likhovtseva (RUS), 6-3, 6-4; Lindsay Davenport (USA) def. Elena Dementieva (RUS), 6-4, 6-0.

Day Two— Davenport (USA) def. Likhovtseva (RUS), 6-4, 6-4; Dementieva (RUS) def. V. Williams (USA), 1-6, 6-3, 7-6 (7-5); V. Williams & Serena Williams (USA) def. Dementieva & Elena Makarova (RUS), 6-2, 6-1.

Singles Leaders

Official Top 20 computer rankings and money leaders of men's and women's tours for 1998 and unofficial rankings and money leaders for 1999 (through Sept. 20), as compiled by the ATP Tour (Association of Tennis Professionals) and WTA (Women's Tennis Association). Note that money lists include doubles earnings.

Final 1998 Computer Rankings and Money Won

Listed are events won and times a finalist and semifinalist (Finish, 1-2-SF), match record (W-L), and earnings for the year.

MEN

		Finish 1-2-SF	W-L	Earnings
1	Pete Sampras	4-3-3	61-17	$3,931,497
2	Marcelo Rios	7-1-4	68-17	3,420,054
3	Alex Corretja	5-2-2	57-21	2,702,569
4	Patrick Rafter	6-0-2	60-21	2,867,017
5	Carlos Moya	2-2-4	49-28	2,572,553
6	Andre Agassi	5-5-2	68-18	1,836,233
7	Tim Henman	2-2-5	59-29	1,448,770
8	Karol Kucera	2-2-5	53-29	1,402,557
9	Greg Rusedski	2-3-3	53-22	1,860,437
10	Richard Krajicek	2-1-5	45-15	1,219,624
11	Yevgeny Kafelnikov	3-3-3	57-29	2,543,077
12	Goran Ivanisevic	1-4-1	44-28	1,541,177
13	Petr Korda	2-0-0	34-21	1,387,393
14	Albert Costa	2-2-0	47-25	1,013,446
15	Mark Philippoussis	1-1-1	33-20	1,272,620
16	Todd Martin	2-0-3	44-21	771,943
17	Thomas Johansson	0-2-6	45-31	667,858
18	Cedric Pioline	0-2-4	41-29	808,688
19	Jan Siemerink	2-0-3	41-25	638,990
20	Felix Mantilla	1-2-4	42-26	823,916

WOMEN

		Finish 1-2-SF	W-L	Earnings
1	Lindsay Davenport	6-4-5	69-15	$3,052,105
2	Martina Hingis	5-3-6	67-13	3,375,989
3	Jana Novotna	4-3-4	51-16	2,153,800
4	Arantxa Sanchez Vicario	2-3-4	48-20	1,596,154
5	Venus Williams	3-4-3	53-13	1,767,924
6	Monica Seles	2-2-5	46-13	1,054,130
7	Mary Pierce	4-1-0	35-12	703,692
8	Conchita Martinez	2-2-0	40-21	903,131
9	Steffi Graf	3-0-4	33-9	569,845
10	Nathalie Tauziat	0-2-6	42-24	1,038,310
11	Patty Schnyder	5-1-1	56-22	942,828
12	Dominique van Roost	1-4-2	47-26	483,601
13	Anna Kournikova	0-1-3	40-19	568,771
14	Sandrine Testud	1-1-4	52-27	499,940
15	Irina Spirlea	1-1-3	36-25	554,398
16	Natasha Zvereva	0-0-3	36-22	953,457
17	Amanda Coetzer	1-0-2	32-23	557,093
18	Ai Sugiyama	2-0-1	37-21	377,728
19	Silvia Farina	0-4-1	42-26	291,186
20	Serena Williams	0-0-1	29-11	310,211

1999 Computer Rankings (through Sept. 20)

Listed are tournaments won and times a finalist and semifinalist (Finish, 1-2-SF), match record (W-L), and computer points earned (Pts).

MEN

ATP Tour singles rankings based on total computer points from each player's 14 best tournaments covering the last 12 months. Tournaments, titles and match won-lost records, however, are for 1999 only.

Rank 99	(98)		Finish 1-2-SF	W-L	Pts
1	(6)	Andre Agassi	4-2-3	49-10	4470
2	(11)	Yevgeny Kafelnikov	2-2-4	49-22	3819
3	(1)	Pete Sampras	4-0-1	35-7	3544
4	(16)	Todd Martin	1-2-3	39-14	2969
5	(23)	Gustavo Kuerten	2-0-1	46-18	2207
6	(9)	Greg Rusedski	0-2-2	33-23	2336
7	(7)	Tim Henman	0-3-1	35-23	2300
8	(2)	Marcelo Rios	2-1-1	36-13	2276
9	(10)	Richard Krajicek	2-0-0	35-17	2243
10	(3)	Alex Corretja	0-3-2	32-18	2161
11	(34)	Tommy Haas	1-2-2	39-21	2097
12	(35)	Nicolas Kiefer	3-1-2	45-20	2064
13	(4)	Patrick Rafter	2-2-1	38-16	1939
14	(92)	Nicolas Lapentti	1-1-4	43-15	1866
15	(5)	Carlos Moya	0-1-3	38-23	1856
16	(18)	Cedric Pioline	1-0-3	37-24	1794
17	(22)	Thomas Enqvist	1-2-2	34-22	1774
18	(20)	Felix Mantilla	1-0-4	33-20	1536
19	(42)	Vince Spadea	0-1-0	30-20	1502
20	(8)	Karol Kucera	0-0-2	36-19	1496

WOMEN

Corel WTA Tour singles ranking system based on total Round and Quality Points for each tournament played during the last 12 months. Tournaments, titles and match won-lost records, however, are for 1999 only.

Rank 99	(98)		Finish 1-2-SF	W-L	Pts
1	(2)	Martina Hingis	6-3-3	57-9	5620
2	(1)	Lindsay Davenport	4-1-4	45-9	4697
3	(5)	Venus Williams	5-3-1	50-9	3991
4	(20)	Serena Williams	4-1-0	38-6	3144
5	(6)	Monica Seles	1-1-4	35-12	2976
6	(7)	Mary Pierce	0-3-1	33-14	2628
7	(23)	Barbara Schett	0-0-2	40-19	1918
8	(22)	Julie Halard-Decugis	2-3-0	41-13	1905
	(17)	Amanda Coetzer	0-2-3	35-19	1905
10	(10)	Nathalie Tauziat	0-2-0	21-20	1796
11	(4)	Arantxa Sanchez Vicario	1-0-3	24-15	1786
12	(14)	Sandrine Testud	0-0-2	26-18	1721
13	(12)	Dominique Van Roost	0-1-0	27-18	1718
14	(29)	Amelie Mauresmo	0-2-1	28-11	1699
15	(13)	Anna Kournikova	0-1-1	32-15	1619
16	(23)	Conchita Martinez	1-0-1	34-16	1541
17	(26)	Elena Likhovtseva	0-1-1	35-23	1449
18	(3)	Jana Novotna	1-0-2	26-13	1420
19	(15)	Irina Spirlea	0-1-1	17-19	1319
20	(21)	Anke Huber	0-0-0	24-18	1293

1999 Money Winners

Amounts include singles and doubles earnings through Sept. 20.

MEN

	Earnings			Earnings			Earnings
1 Andre Agassi	$2,251,128	10 Mark Philippoussis	$840,839	19 Felix Mantilla	$604,927
2 Yevgeny Kafelnikov	1,488,218	11 Nicolas Kiefer	784,918	20 Leander Paes	603,065
3 Pete Sampras	1,401,256	12 Carlos Moya	765,457	21 Dominik Hrbaty	554,972
4 Gustavo Kuerten	1,389,309	13 Jonas Bjorkman	714,735	22 Greg Rusedski	549,285
5 Patrick Rafter	1,254,574	14 Tommy Haas	690,318	23 Albert Costa	536,089
6 Marcelo Rios	917,447	15 Nicolas Lapentti	686,078	24 Fabrice Santoro	524,070
7 Todd Martin	901,124	16 Thomas Enqvist	665,256	25 Sandon Stolle	515,503
8 Tim Henman	886,694	17 Thomas Johansson	645,037		
9 Richard Krajicek	875,397	18 Cedric Pioline	626,788		

WOMEN

	Earnings			Earnings			Earnings
1 Martina Hingis	$2,204,180	10 Arantxa Sanchez Vicario	$496,221	19 Corina Morariu	$348,930
2 Serena Williams	1,664,171	11 Barbara Schett	430,385	20 Sandrine Testud	328,746
3 Lindsay Davenport	1,578,263	12 Elena Likhovtseva	411,707	21 Lisa Raymond	310,514
4 Venus Williams	1,428,082	13 Amelie Mauresmo	391,676	22 Ai Sugiyama	302,763
5 Steffi Graf	1,193,367	14 Natasha Zvereva	375,452	23 Chanda Rubin	277,396
6 Monica Seles	686,680	15 Julie Halard-Decugis	374,545	24 Patty Schnyder	277,259
7 Jana Novotna	604,854	16 Amanda Coetzer	369,970	25 Ruxandra Dragomir	271,872
8 Anna Kournikova	548,624	17 Conchita Martinez	353,542		
9 Mary Pierce	548,092	18 Nathalie Tauziat	350,582		

Davis Cup

Sweden captured its second straight Davis Cup title with a 4-1 decision over Italy in the 1998 Davis Cup Final. It was the Swedes' seventh title overall and their sixth in the last 14 years. Here is a recap of the 1998 final, plus a summary of the 1999 Davis Cup tournament through Sept. 26.

1998 Final

Sweden 4, Italy 1

at Milan, Italy (Dec. 4-6)

Day One— Magnus Norman (SWE) def. Andrea Gaudenzi (ITA), 6-7, 7-6, 4-6, 6-3, 6-6, ret; Magnus Gustafsson (SWE) def. Davide Sanguinetti (ITA) 6-1, 6-4, 6-0.

Day Two— Jonas Bjorkman & Nicklas Kulti (SWE) def. Sanguinetti/Diego Nargiso (ITA), 7-6 (7-1), 6-1, 6-3.

Day Three— Nargiso (ITA) def. Norman (SWE), 6-2, 6-3; Gustafsson (SWE) def. Gianluca Pozzi (ITA), 6-4, 6-2.

1999 Early Rounds

FIRST ROUND

(April 2-4)

Winner	Loser
United States 3	at Great Britain 2
Slovakia 3	at Sweden 2
Russia 3	at Germany 2
Australia 4	at Zimbabwe 1
at France 4	Netherlands 1
Brazil 3	at Spain 2
at Belgium 3	Czech Republic 1
at Switzerland 3	Italy 2

QUARTERFINALS

(July 16-18)

Winner	Loser
Australia 4	at United States 1
at Russia 3	Slovakia 2
at France 3	Brazil 2
at Belgium 3	Switzerland 2

SEMIFINALS

Australia 4, Russia 1

at Brisbane, Australia (Sept. 24-26)

Day One— Lleyton Hewitt (AUS) def. Marat Safin (RUS) 7-6 (7-0), 6-2, 6-6, 6-2; Wayne Arthurs (AUS) def. Yevgeny Kafelnikov (RUS) 6-7 (4-7), 6-2, 6-0.

Day Two— Kafelnikov & Andrei Olhovskiy (RUS) def. Mark Woodforde & Sandon Stolle (AUS) 6-1, 6-4, 4-6, 4-6, 8-6.

Day Three— Hewitt (AUS) def. Kafelnikov (RUS) 6-4, 7-5, 6-2; Arthurs (AUS) def. Safin (RUS) 6-3, 6-2.

France 4, Belgium 1

at Pau, France (Sept. 24-26)

Day One— Sebastien Grosjean (FRA) def. Xavier Malisse (BEL) 7-5, 6-2, 7-6 (7-3); Cedric Pioline (FRA) def. Filip Dewulf (BEL) 6-3, 5-7, 3-6, 6-3, 6-2.

Day Two— Olivier Delaitre & Fabrice Santoro (FRA) def. Malisse & Christophe Van Garsse (BEL) 6-3, 6-3, 6-3.

Day Three— Van Garsse (BEL) def. Pioline (FRA) 6-3, 6-4; Santoro def. Christophe Rochus (BEL) 7-5, 6-4.

FINAL

France will host Australia in the Davis Cup Final Dec. 3-5. It's the third time this decade France has made the finals. It won both previous appearances in 1991 and 1996. Australia is making its first trip to the finals in six years.

THE 2000
ESPN
INFORMATION PLEASE
SPORTS ALMANAC

T E N N I S
S T A T I S T I C S

THROUGH THE YEARS
1877-1999
MAJOR TITLES • LEADERS

SEC
B

PAGE
823

Grand Slam Championships
Australian Open
MEN

Became an Open Championship in 1969. Two tournaments were held in 1977; the first in January, the second in December. Tournament moved back to January in 1987, so no championship was decided in 1986.

Surface: Synpave Rebound Ace (hardcourt surface composed of polyurethane and synthetic rubber).

Multiple winners: Roy Emerson (6); Jack Crawford and Ken Rosewall (4); James Anderson, Rod Laver, Adrian Quist, Mats Wilander and Pat Wood (3); Boris Becker, Jack Bromwich, Ashley Cooper, Jim Courier, Stefan Edberg, Rodney Heath, Johan Kriek, Ivan Lendl, John Newcombe, Pete Sampras, Frank Sedgman, Guillermo Vilas and Tony Wilding (2).

Year	Winner	Loser	Score	Year	Winner	Loser	Score
1905	Rodney Heath	A. Curtis	46 63 64 64	1956	Lew Hoad	K. Rosewall	64 36 64 75
1906	Tony Wilding	H. Parker	60 64 64	1957	Ashley Cooper	N. Fraser	63 9-11 64 62
1907	Horace Rice	H. Parker	63 64 64	1958	Ashley Cooper	M. Anderson	75 63 64
1908	Fred Alexander	A. Dunlop	36 36 60 62 63	1959	Alex Olmedo	N. Fraser	61 62 36 63
1909	Tony Wilding	E. Parker	61 75 62				
				1960	Rod Laver	N. Fraser	57 36 63 86 86
1910	Rodney Heath	H. Rice	64 63 62	1961	Roy Emerson	R. Laver	16 63 75 64
1911	Norman Brookes	H. Rice	61 62 63	1962	Rod Laver	R. Emerson	86 06 64 64
1912	J. Cecil Parke	A. Beamish	36 63 16 61 75	1963	Roy Emerson	K. Fletcher	63 63 61
1913	Ernie Parker	H. Parker	26 61 62 63	1964	Roy Emerson	F. Stolle	63 64 62
1914	Pat Wood	G. Patterson	64 63 57 61	1965	Roy Emerson	F. Stolle	79 26 64 75 61
1915	Francis Lowe	H. Rice	46 61 61 64	1966	Roy Emerson	A. Ashe	64 68 62 63
1916-18	Not held	World War I		1967	Roy Emerson	A. Ashe	64 61 61
1919	A.R.F. Kingscote	E. Pockley	64 60 63	1968	Bill Bowrey	J. Gisbert	75 26 97 64
				1969	Rod Laver	A. Gimeno	63 64 75
1920	Pat Wood	R. Thomas	63 46 68 61 63				
1921	Rhys Gemmell	A. Hedeman	75 61 64	1970	Arthur Ashe	D. Crealy	64 97 62
1922	James Anderson	G. Patterson	60 36 63 63 62	1971	Ken Rosewall	A. Ashe	61 75 63
1923	Pat Wood	C.B. St. John	61 61 63	1972	Ken Rosewall	M. Anderson	76 63 75
1924	James Anderson	R. Schlesinger	63 64 36 57 63	1973	John Newcombe	O. Parun	63 67 75 61
1925	James Anderson	G. Patterson	11-9 26 62 63	1974	Jimmy Connors	P. Dent	76 64 46 63
1926	John Hawkes	J. Willard	61 63 61	1975	John Newcombe	J. Connors	75 36 64 75
1927	Gerald Patterson	J. Hawkes	36 64 36 18-16 63	1976	Mark Edmondson	J. Newcombe	67 63 76 61
1928	Jean Borotra	R.O. Cummings	64 61 46 57 63	1977	Roscoe Tanner	G. Vilas	63 63 63
1929	John Gregory	R. Schlesinger	62 62 57 75		Vitas Gerulaitis	J. Lloyd	63 76 57 36 62
				1978	Guillermo Vilas	J. Marks	64 64 36 63
1930	Gar Moon	H. Hopman	63 61 63	1979	Guillermo Vilas	J. Sadri	76 63 62
1931	Jack Crawford	H. Hopman	64 62 26 61				
1932	Jack Crawford	H. Hopman	46 63 36 63 61	1980	Brian Teacher	K. Warwick	75 76 63
1933	Jack Crawford	K. Gledhill	26 75 63 62	1981	Johan Kriek	S. Denton	62 76 67 64
1934	Fred Perry	J. Crawford	63 75 61	1982	Johan Kriek	S. Denton	63 63 62
1935	Jack Crawford	F. Perry	26 64 64 64	1983	Mats Wilander	I. Lendl	61 64 64
1936	Adrian Quist	J. Crawford	62 63 46 36 97	1984	Mats Wilander	K. Curren	67 64 76 62
1937	Viv McGrath	J. Bromwich	63 16 60 26 61	1985	Stefan Edberg	M. Wilander	64 63 63
1938	Don Budge	J. Bromwich	64 62 61	1986	Not held		
1939	Jack Bromwich	A. Quist	64 61 63	1987	Stefan Edberg	P. Cash	63 64 36 57 63
1940	Adrian Quist	J. Crawford	63 61 62	1988	Mats Wilander	P. Cash	63 67 36 61 86
1941-45	Not held	World War II		1989	Ivan Lendl	M. Mecir	62 62 62
1946	Jack Bromwich	D. Pails	57 63 75 36 62				
1947	Dinny Pails	J. Bromwich	46 64 36 75 86	1990	Ivan Lendl	S. Edberg	46 76 52 (ret.)
1948	Adrian Quist	J. Bromwich	64 36 63 26 63	1991	Boris Becker	I. Lendl	16 64 64 64
1949	Frank Sedgman	J. Bromwich	63 63 62	1992	Jim Courier	S. Edberg	63 36 64 62
				1993	Jim Courier	S. Edberg	62 61 26 75
1950	Frank Sedgman	K. McGregor	63 64 46 61	1994	Pete Sampras	T. Martin	76 64 64
1951	Dick Savitt	K. McGregor	63 26 63 61	1995	Andre Agassi	P. Sampras	46 61 76 64
1952	Ken McGregor	F. Sedgman	75 12-10 26 62	1996	Boris Becker	M. Chang	62 64 26 62
1953	Ken Rosewall	M. Rose	60 63 64	1997	Pete Sampras	C. Moya	62 63 63
1954	Mervyn Rose	R. Hartwig	62 06 64 62	1998	Petr Korda	M. Rios	62 62 62
1955	Ken Rosewall	L. Hoad	97 64 64	1999	Yevgeny Kafelnikov	T. Enqvist	46 60 63 76

WOMEN

Became an Open Championship in 1969. Two tournaments were held in 1977, the first in January, the second in December. Tournament moved back to January in 1987, so no championship was decided in 1986.

Multiple winners: Margaret Smith Court (11); Nancye Wynne Bolton (6); Daphne Akhurst (5); Evonne Goolagong Cawley, Steffi Graf and Monica Seles (4); Jean Hartigan, Martina Hingis and Martina Navratilova (3); Coral Buttsworth, Chris Evert Lloyd, Thelma Long, Hana Mandlikova, Mall Molesworth and Mary Carter Reitano (2).

Year	Winner	Loser	Score	Year	Winner	Loser	Score
1922	Mall Molesworth	E. Boyd	63 10-8	1964	Margaret Smith	L. Turner	63 62
1923	Mall Molesworth	E. Boyd	61 75	1965	Margaret Smith	M. Bueno	57 64 52 (ret)
1924	Sylvia Lance	E. Boyd	63 36 64	1966	Margaret Smith	N. Richey	walkover
1925	Daphne Akhurst	E. Boyd	16 86 64	1967	Nancy Richey	L. Turner	61 64
1926	Daphne Akhurst	E. Boyd	61 63	1968	Billie Jean King	M. Smith	61 62
1927	Esna Boyd	S. Harper	57 61 62	1969	Margaret Court	B.J. King	64 61
1928	Daphne Akhurst	E. Boyd	75 62	1970	Margaret Court	K. Melville	61 63
1929	Daphne Akhurst	L. Bickerton	61 57 62	1971	Margaret Court	E. Goolagong	26 76 75
1930	Daphne Akhurst	S. Harper	10-8 26 75	1972	Virginia Wade	E. Goolagong	64 64
1931	Coral Buttsworth	M. Crawford	16 63 64	1973	Margaret Court	E. Goolagong	64 75
1932	Coral Buttsworth	K. Le Messurier	97 64	1974	Evonne Goolagong	C. Evert	76 46 60
1933	Joan Hartigan	C. Buttsworth	64 63	1975	Evonne Goolagong	M. Navratilova	63 62
1934	Joan Hartigan	M. Molesworth	61 64	1976	Evonne Cawley	R. Tomanova	62 62
1935	Dorothy Round	N. Lyle	16 61 63	1977	Kerry Reid	D. Balestrat	75 62
1936	Joan Hartigan	N. Bolton	64 64		Evonne Cawley	H. Gourlay	63 60
1937	Nancye Wynne	E. Westacott	63 57 64	1978	Chris O'Neil	B. Nagelsen	63 76
1938	Dorothy Bundy	D. Stevenson	63 62	1979	Barbara Jordan	S. Walsh	63 63
1939	Emily Westacott	N. Hopman	61 62	1980	Hana Mandlikova	W. Turnbull	60 75
1940	Nancye Wynne	T. Coyne	57 64 60	1981	Martina Navratilova	C. Evert Lloyd	67 64 75
1941-45	Not held	World War II		1982	Chris Evert Lloyd	M. Navratilova	63 26 63
1946	Nancye Bolton	J. Fitch	64 64	1983	Martina Navratilova	K. Jordan	62 76
1947	Nancye Bolton	N. Hopman	63 62	1984	Chris Evert Lloyd	H. Sukova	67 61 63
1948	Nancye Bolton	M. Toomey	63 61	1985	Martina Navratilova	C. Evert Lloyd	62 46 62
1949	Doris Hart	N. Bolton	63 64	1986	Not held		
1950	Louise Brough	D. Hart	64 36 64	1987	Hana Mandlikova	M. Navratilova	75 76
1951	Nancye Bolton	T. Long	61 75	1988	Steffi Graf	C. Evert	61 76
1952	Thelma Long	H. Angwin	62 63	1989	Steffi Graf	H. Sukova	64 64
1953	Maureen Connolly	J. Sampson	63 62	1990	Steffi Graf	M.J. Fernandez	63 64
1954	Thelma Long	J. Staley	63 64	1991	Monica Seles	J. Novotna	57 63 61
1955	Beryl Penrose	T. Long	64 63	1992	Monica Seles	M.J. Fernandez	62 63
1956	Mary Carter	T. Long	36 62 97	1993	Monica Seles	S. Graf	46 63 62
1957	Shirley Fry	A. Gibson	63 64	1994	Steffi Graf	A.S. Vicario	60 62
1958	Angela Mortimer	L. Coghlan	63 64	1995	Mary Pierce	A.S. Vicario	63 62
1959	Mary Reitano	T. Schuurman	62 63	1996	Monica Seles	A. Huber	64 61
1960	Margaret Smith	J. Lehane	75 62	1997	Martina Hingis	M. Pierce	62 62
1961	Margaret Smith	J. Lehane	61 64	1998	Martina Hingis	C. Martinez	63 63
1962	Margaret Smith	J. Lehane	60 62	1999	Martina Hingis	A. Mauresmo	62 63
1963	Margaret Smith	J. Lehane	62 62				

French Open
MEN

Prior to 1925, entry was restricted to members of French clubs. Became an Open Championship in 1968, but closed to contract pros in 1972.

Surface: Red clay.

First year: 1891. **Most wins:** Max Decugis (8).

Multiple winners (since 1925): Bjorn Borg (6); Henri Cochet (4); Rene Lacoste, Ivan Lendl and Mats Wilander (3); Sergi Bruguera, Jim Courier, Jaroslav Drobny, Roy Emerson, Jan Kodes, Rod Laver, Frank Parker, Nicola Pietrangeli, Ken Rosewall, Manuel Santana, Tony Trabert and Gottfried von Cramm (2).

Year	Winner	Loser	Score	Year	Winner	Loser	Score
1925	Rene Lacoste	J. Borotra	75 61 64	1938	Don Budge	R. Menzel	63 62 64
1926	Henri Cochet	R. Lacoste	62 64 63	1939	Don McNeill	B. Riggs	75 60 63
1927	Rene Lacoste	B. Tilden	64 46 57 63 11-9	1941-45	Not held	World War II	
1928	Henri Cochet	R. Lacoste	57 63 61 63	1946	Marcel Bernard	J. Drobny	36 26 61 64 63
1929	Rene Lacoste	J. Borotra	63 26 60 26 86	1947	Joseph Asboth	E. Sturgess	86 75 64
1930	Henri Cochet	B. Tilden	36 86 63 61	1948	Frank Parker	J. Drobny	64 75 57 86
1931	Jean Borotra	C. Boussus	26 64 75 64	1949	Frank Parker	B. Patty	63 16 61 64
1932	Henri Cochet	G. de Stefani	60 64 46 63	1950	Budge Patty	J. Drobny	61 62 36 57 75
1933	Jack Crawford	H. Cochet	86 61 63	1951	Jaroslav Drobny	E. Sturgess	63 63 63
1934	Gottfried von Cramm	J. Crawford	64 79 36 75 63	1952	Jaroslav Drobny	F. Sedgman	62 60 36 64
1935	Fred Perry	G. von Cramm	63 36 61 63	1953	Ken Rosewall	V. Seixas	63 64 16 62
1936	Gottfried von Cramm	F. Perry	60 26 62 26 60	1954	Tony Trabert	A. Larsen	64 75 61
1937	Henner Henkel	H. Austin	61 64 63	1955	Tony Trabert	S. Davidson	26 61 64 62

Year	Winner	Loser	Score
1956	Lew Hoad	S. Davidson	64 86 63
1957	Sven Davidson	H. Flam	63 64 64
1958	Mervyn Rose	L. Ayala	63 64 64
1959	Nicola Pietrangeli	I. Vermaak	36 63 64 61
1960	Nicola Pietrangeli	L. Ayala	36 63 64 46 63
1961	Manuel Santana	N. Pietrangeli	46 61 36 60 62
1962	Rod Laver	R. Emerson	36 26 63 97 62
1963	Roy Emerson	P. Darmon	36 61 64 64
1964	Manuel Santana	N. Pietrangeli	63 61 46 75
1965	Fred Stolle	T. Roche	36 60 62 63
1966	Tony Roche	I. Gulyas	61 64 75
1967	Roy Emerson	T. Roche	61 64 26 62
1968	Ken Rosewall	R. Laver	63 61 26 62
1969	Rod Laver	K. Rosewall	64 63 64
1970	Jan Kodes	Z. Franulovic	62 64 60
1971	Jan Kodes	I. Nastase	86 62 26 75
1972	Andres Gimeno	P. Proisy	46 63 61 61
1973	Ilie Nastase	N. Pilic	63 63 60
1974	Bjorn Borg	M. Orantes	26 67 60 61 61
1975	Bjorn Borg	G. Vilas	62 63 64
1976	Adriano Panatta	H. Solomon	61 64 46 76
1977	Guillermo Vilas	B. Gottfried	60 63 60

Year	Winner	Loser	Score
1978	Bjorn Borg	G. Vilas	61 61 63
1979	Bjorn Borg	V. Pecci	63 61 67 64
1980	Bjorn Borg	V. Gerulaitis	64 61 62
1981	Bjorn Borg	I. Lendl	61 46 62 36 61
1982	Mats Wilander	G. Vilas	16 76 60 64
1983	Yannick Noah	M. Wilander	62 75 76
1984	Ivan Lendl	J. McEnroe	36 26 64 75 75
1985	Mats Wilander	I. Lendl	36 64 62 62
1986	Ivan Lendl	M. Pernfors	63 62 64
1987	Ivan Lendl	M. Wilander	75 62 36 76
1988	Mats Wilander	H. Leconte	75 62 61
1989	Michael Chang	S. Edberg	61 36 46 64 62
1990	Andres Gomez	A. Agassi	63 26 64 64
1991	Jim Courier	A. Agassi	36 64 26 61 64
1992	Jim Courier	P. Korda	75 62 61
1993	Sergi Bruguera	J. Courier	64 26 62 36 63
1994	Sergi Bruguera	A. Berasategui	63 75 26 61
1995	Thomas Muster	M. Chang	75 62 64
1996	Yevgeny Kafelnikov	M. Stich	76 75 76
1997	Gustavo Kuerten	S. Bruguera	63 64 62
1998	Carlos Moya	A. Corretja	63 75 63
1999	Andre Agassi	A. Medvedev	16 26 64 63 64

WOMEN

Prior to 1925, entry was restricted to members of French clubs. Became an Open Championship in 1968, but closed to contract pros in 1972.

First year: 1897. **Most wins:** Chris Evert Lloyd (7); Suzanne Lenglen and Steffi Graf (6).

Multiple winners (since 1925): Chris Evert Lloyd (7); Steffi Graf (6); Margaret Smith Court (5); Helen Wills Moody (4); Arantxa Sanchez Vicario, Monica Seles and Hilde Sperling (3); Maureen Connolly, Maureen Osborne duPont, Doris Hart, Ann Haydon Jones, Suzanne Lenglen, Simone Mathieu, Margaret Scriven, Martina Navratilova and Lesley Turner (2).

Year	Winner	Loser	Score
1925	Suzanne Lenglen	K. McKane	61 62
1926	Suzanne Lenglen	M. Browne	61 60
1927	Kea Bouman	I. Peacock	62 64
1928	Helen Wills	E. Bennett	61 62
1929	Helen Wills	S. Mathieu	63 64
1930	Helen Moody	H. Jacobs	62 61
1931	Cilly Aussem	B. Nuthall	86 61
1932	Helen Moody	S. Mathieu	75 61
1933	Margaret Scriven	S. Mathieu	62 46 64
1934	Margaret Scriven	H. Jacobs	75 46 61
1935	Hilde Sperling	S. Mathieu	62 61
1936	Hilde Sperling	S. Mathieu	63 64
1937	Hilde Sperling	S. Mathieu	62 64
1938	Simone Mathieu	N. Landry	60 63
1939	Simone Mathieu	J. Jedrzejowska	63 86
1940-45	Not held	World War II	
1946	Margaret Osborne	P. Betz	16 86 75
1947	Patricia Todd	D. Hart	63 36 64
1948	Nelly Landry	S. Fry	62 06 60
1949	Margaret duPont	N. Adamson	75 62
1950	Doris Hart	P. Todd	64 46 62
1951	Shirley Fry	D. Hart	63 36 63
1952	Doris Hart	S. Fry	64 64
1953	Maureen Connolly	D. Hart	62 64
1954	Maureen Connolly	G. Bucaille	64 61
1955	Angela Mortimer	D. Knode	26 75 10-8
1956	Althea Gibson	A. Mortimer	60 12-10
1957	Shirley Bloomer	D. Knode	61 63
1958	Susi Kormoczi	S. Bloomer	64 16 62
1959	Christine Truman	S. Kormoczi	64 75
1960	Darlene Hard	Y. Ramirez	63 64
1961	Ann Haydon	Y. Ramirez	62 61
1962	Margaret Smith	L. Turner	63 36 75
1963	Lesley Turner	A. Jones	26 63 75
1964	Margaret Smith	M. Bueno	57 61 62
1965	Lesley Turner	M. Smith	63 64

Year	Winner	Loser	Score
1966	Ann Jones	N. Richey	63 61
1967	Francoise Durr	L. Turner	46 63 64
1968	Nancy Richey	A. Jones	57 64 61
1969	Margaret Court	A. Jones	61 46 63
1970	Margaret Court	H. Niessen	62 64
1971	Evonne Goolagong	H. Gourlay	63 75
1972	Billie Jean King	E. Goolagong	63 63
1973	Margaret Court	C. Evert	67 76 64
1974	Chris Evert	O. Morozova	61 62
1975	Chris Evert	M. Navratilova	26 62 61
1976	Sue Barker	R. Tomanova	62 06 62
1977	Mima Jausovec	F. Mihai	62 67 61
1978	Virginia Ruzici	M. Jausovec	62 62
1979	Chris Evert Lloyd	W. Turnbull	62 60
1980	Chris Evert Lloyd	V. Ruzici	60 63
1981	Hana Mandlikova	S. Hanika	62 64
1982	Martina Navratilova	A. Jaeger	76 61
1983	Chris Evert Lloyd	M. Jausovec	61 62
1984	Martina Navratilova	C. Evert Lloyd	63 61
1985	Chris Evert Lloyd	M. Navratilova	63 67 75
1986	Chris Evert Lloyd	M. Navratilova	26 63 63
1987	Steffi Graf	M. Navratilova	64 46 86
1988	Steffi Graf	N. Zvereva	60 60
1989	A. Sanchez Vicario	S. Graf	76 36 75
1990	Monica Seles	S. Graf	76 64
1991	Monica Seles	A.S. Vicario	63 64
1992	Monica Seles	S. Graf	62 36 10-8
1993	Steffi Graf	M.J. Fernandez	46 62 64
1994	A. Sanchez Vicario	M. Pierce	64 64
1995	Steffi Graf	A.S. Vicario	76 46 60
1996	Steffi Graf	A.S. Vicario	63 61
1997	Iva Majoli	M. Hingis	64 62
1998	A. Sanchez Vicario	M. Seles	76 06 62
1999	Steffi Graf	M. Hingis	46 75 62

Wimbledon

MEN

Officially called "The Lawn Tennis Championships" at the All England Club, Wimbledon. Challenge round system (defending champion qualified for following year's final) used from 1877-1921. Became an Open Championship in 1968, but closed to contract pros in 1972.

Surface: Grass.

Multiple winners: Willie Renshaw (7); Pete Sampras (6); Bjorn Borg and Laurie Doherty (5); Reggie Doherty, Rod Laver and Tony Wilding (4); Wilfred Baddeley, Boris Becker, Arthur Gore, John McEnroe, John Newcombe, Fred Perry and Bill Tilden (3); Jean Borotra, Norman Brookes, Don Budge, Henri Cochet, Jimmy Connors, Stefan Edberg, Roy Emerson, John Hartley, Lew Hoad, Rene Lacoste, Gerald Patterson and Joshua Pim (2).

Year	Winner	Loser	Score	Year	Winner	Loser	Score
1877	Spencer Gore	W. Marshall	61 62 64	1938	Don Budge	H. Austin	61 60 63
1878	Frank Hadow	S. Gore	75 61 97	1939	Bobby Riggs	E. Cooke	26 86 36 63 62
1879	John Hartley	V. St. L. Gould	62 64 62	1940-45	Not held	World War II	
1880	John Hartley	H. Lawford	60 62 26 63	1946	Yvon Petra	G. Brown	62 64 79 57 64
1881	Willie Renshaw	J. Hartley	60 62 61	1947	Jack Kramer	T. Brown	61 63 62
1882	Willie Renshaw	E. Renshaw	61 26 46 62 62	1948	Bob Falkenburg	J. Bromwich	75 06 62 36 75
1883	Willie Renshaw	E. Renshaw	26 63 63 46 63	1949	Ted Schroeder	J. Drobny	36 60 63 46 64
1884	Willie Renshaw	H. Lawford	60 64 97	1950	Budge Patty	F. Sedgman	61 8-10 62 63
1885	Willie Renshaw	H. Lawford	75 62 46 75	1951	Dick Savitt	K. McGregor	64 64 64
1886	Willie Renshaw	H. Lawford	60 57 63 64	1952	Frank Sedgman	J. Drobny	46 62 63 62
1887	Herbert Lawford	E. Renshaw	16 63 36 64 64	1953	Vic Seixas	K. Nielsen	97 63 64
1888	Ernest Renshaw	H. Lawford	63 75 60	1954	Jaroslav Drobny	K. Rosewall	13-11 46 62 97
1889	Willie Renshaw	E. Renshaw	64 61 36 60	1955	Tony Trabert	K. Nielsen	63 75 61
1890	William Hamilton	W. Renshaw	68 62 36 61 61	1956	Lew Hoad	K. Rosewall	62 46 75 64
1891	Wilfred Baddeley	J. Pim	64 16 75 60	1957	Lew Hoad	A. Cooper	62 61 62
1892	Wilfred Baddeley	J. Pim	46 63 63 62	1958	Ashley Cooper	N. Fraser	36 63 64 13-11
1893	Joshua Pim	W. Baddeley	36 61 63 62	1959	Alex Olmedo	R. Laver	64 63 64
1894	Joshua Pim	W. Baddeley	10-8 62 86	1960	Neale Fraser	R. Laver	64 36 97 75
1895	Wilfred Baddeley	W. Eaves	46 26 86 62 63	1961	Rod Laver	C. McKinley	63 61 64
1896	Harold Mahony	W. Baddeley	62 68 57 86 63	1962	Rod Laver	M. Mulligan	62 62 61
1897	Reggie Doherty	H. Mahony	64 64 63	1963	Chuck McKinley	F. Stolle	97 61 64
1898	Reggie Doherty	L. Doherty	63 63 26 57 61	1964	Roy Emerson	F. Stolle	64 12-10 46 63
1899	Reggie Doherty	A. Gore	16 46 62 63 63	1965	Roy Emerson	F. Stolle	62 64 64
1900	Reggie Doherty	S. Smith	68 63 61 62	1966	Manuel Santana	D. Ralston	64 11-9 64
1901	Arthur Gore	R. Doherty	46 75 64 64	1967	John Newcombe	W. Bungert	63 61 61
1902	Laurie Doherty	A. Gore	64 63 36 60	1968	Rod Laver	T. Roche	63 64 62
1903	Laurie Doherty	F. Riseley	75 63 60	1969	Rod Laver	J. Newcombe	64 57 64 64
1904	Laurie Doherty	F. Riseley	61 75 86	1970	John Newcombe	K. Rosewall	57 63 62 36 61
1905	Laurie Doherty	N. Brookes	86 62 64	1971	John Newcombe	S. Smith	63 57 26 64 64
1906	Laurie Doherty	F. Riseley	64 46 62 63	1972	Stan Smith	I. Nastase	46 63 63 46 75
1907	Norman Brookes	A. Gore	64 62 62	1973	Jan Kodes	A. Metreveli	61 98 63
1908	Arthur Gore	R. Barrett	63 62 46 36 64	1974	Jimmy Connors	K. Rosewall	61 61 64
1909	Arthur Gore	M. Ritchie	68 16 62 62 62	1975	Arthur Ashe	J. Connors	61 61 57 64
1910	Tony Wilding	A. Gore	64 75 46 62	1976	Bjorn Borg	I. Nastase	64 62 97
1911	Tony Wilding	R. Barrett	64 46 26 62 (ret)	1977	Bjorn Borg	J. Connors	36 62 61 57 64
1912	Tony Wilding	A. Gore	64 64 46 64	1978	Bjorn Borg	J. Connors	62 62 63
1913	Tony Wilding	M. McLoughlin	86 63 10-8	1979	Bjorn Borg	R. Tanner	67 61 36 63 64
1914	Norman Brookes	T. Wilding	64 64 75	1980	Bjorn Borg	J. McEnroe	16 75 63 67 86
1915-18	Not held	World War I		1981	John McEnroe	B. Borg	46 76 76 64
1919	Gerald Patterson	N. Brookes	63 75 62	1982	Jimmy Connors	J. McEnroe	36 63 67 76 64
1920	Bill Tilden	G. Patterson	26 63 62 64	1983	John McEnroe	C. Lewis	62 62 62
1921	Bill Tilden	B. Norton	46 26 61 60 75	1984	John McEnroe	J. Connors	61 61 62
1922	Gerald Patterson	R. Lycett	63 64 62	1985	Boris Becker	K. Curren	63 67 76 64
1923	Bill Johnston	F. Hunter	60 63 61	1986	Boris Becker	I. Lendl	64 63 75
1924	Jean Borotra	R. Lacoste	61 36 61 36 64	1987	Pat Cash	I. Lendl	76 62 75
1925	Rene Lacoste	J. Borotra	63 63 46 86	1988	Stefan Edberg	B. Becker	46 76 64 62
1926	Jean Borotra	H. Kinsey	86 61 63	1989	Boris Becker	S. Edberg	60 76 64
1927	Henri Cochet	J. Borotra	46 46 63 64 75	1990	Stefan Edberg	B. Becker	62 62 36 36 64
1928	Rene Lacoste	H. Cochet	61 46 64 62	1991	Michael Stich	B. Becker	64 76 64
1929	Henri Cochet	J. Borotra	64 63 64	1992	Andre Agassi	G. Ivanisevic	67 64 64 16 64
1930	Bill Tilden	W. Allison	63 97 64	1993	Pete Sampras	J. Courier	76 76 36 63
1931	Sidney Wood	F. Shields	walkover	1994	Pete Sampras	G. Ivanisevic	76 76 60
1932	Ellsworth Vines	H. Austin	46 62 60	1995	Pete Sampras	B. Becker	67 62 64 62
1933	Jack Crawford	E. Vines	46 11-9 62 26 64	1996	Richard Krajicek	M. Washington	63 64 63
1934	Fred Perry	J. Crawford	63 60 75	1997	Pete Sampras	C. Pioline	64 62 64
1935	Fred Perry	G. von Cramm	62 64 64	1998	Pete Sampras	G. Ivanisevic	67 76 64 36 62
1936	Fred Perry	G. von Cramm	61 61 60	1999	Pete Sampras	A. Agassi	63 64 75
1937	Don Budge	G. von Cramm	63 64 62				

WOMEN

Officially called "The Lawn Tennis Championships" at the All England Club, Wimbledon. Challenge round system (defending champion qualified for following year's final) used from 1877-1921. Became an Open Championship in 1968, but closed to contract pros in 1972.

Multiple winners: Martina Navratilova (9); Helen Wills Moody (8); Dorothea Douglass Chambers and Steffi Graf (7); Blanche Bingley Hillyard, Billie Jean King and Suzanne Lenglen (6); Lottie Dod and Charlotte Cooper Sterry (5); Louise Brough (4); Maria Bueno, Maureen Connolly, Margaret Smith Court and Chris Evert Lloyd (3); Evonne Goolagong Cawley, Althea Gibson, Dorothy Round, May Sutton and Maud Watson (2).

Year	Winner	Loser	Score
1884	Maud Watson	L. Watson	68 63 63
1885	Maud Watson	B. Bingley	61 75
1886	Blanche Bingley	M. Watson	63 63
1887	Lottie Dod	B. Bingley	62 60
1888	Lottie Dod	B. Hillyard	63 63
1889	Blanche Hillyard	L. Rice	46 86 64
1890	Lena Rice	M. Jacks	64 61
1891	Lottie Dod	B. Hillyard	62 61
1892	Lottie Dod	B. Hillyard	61 61
1893	Lottie Dod	B. Hillyard	68 61 64
1894	Blanche Hillyard	E. Austin	61 61
1895	Charlotte Cooper	H. Jackson	75 86
1896	Charlotte Cooper	W. Pickering	62 63
1897	Blanche Hillyard	C. Cooper	57 75 62
1898	Charlotte Cooper	L. Martin	64 64
1899	Blanche Hillyard	C. Cooper	62 63
1900	Blanche Hillyard	C. Cooper	46 64 64
1901	Charlotte Sterry	B. Hillyard	62 62
1902	Muriel Robb	C. Sterry	75 61
1903	Dorothea Douglass	E. Thomson	46 64 62
1904	Dorothea Douglass	C. Sterry	60 63
1905	May Sutton	D. Douglass	63 64
1906	Dorothea Douglass	M. Sutton	63 97
1907	May Sutton	D. Chambers	61 64
1908	Charlotte Sterry	A. Morton	64 64
1909	Dora Boothby	A. Morton	64 46 86
1910	Dorothea Chambers	D. Boothby	62 62
1911	Dorothea Chambers	D. Boothby	60 60
1912	Ethel Larcombe	C. Sterry	63 61
1913	Dorothea Chambers	R. McNair	60 64
1914	Dorothea Chambers	E. Larcombe	75 64
1915-18	Not held	World War I	
1919	Suzanne Lenglen	D. Chambers	10-8 46 97
1920	Suzanne Lenglen	D. Chambers	63 60
1921	Suzanne Lenglen	E. Ryan	62 60
1922	Suzanne Lenglen	M. Mallory	62 60
1923	Suzanne Lenglen	K. McKane	62 62
1924	Kathleen McKane	H. Wills	46 64 64
1925	Suzanne Lenglen	J. Fry	62 60
1926	Kathleen Godfree	L. de Alvarez	62 46 63
1927	Helen Wills	L. de Alvarez	62 63
1928	Helen Wills	L. de Alvarez	62 63
1929	Helen Wills	H. Jacobs	61 62
1930	Helen Moody	E. Ryan	62 62
1931	Cilly Aussem	H. Kranwinkel	62 75
1932	Helen Moody	H. Jacobs	63 61
1933	Helen Moody	D. Round	64 68 63
1934	Dorothy Round	H. Jacobs	62 57 63
1935	Helen Moody	H. Jacobs	63 36 75
1936	Helen Jacobs	H.K. Sperling	62 46 75
1937	Dorothy Round	J. Jedrzejowska	62 26 75
1938	Helen Moody	H. Jacobs	64 60
1939	Alice Marble	K. Stammers	62 60
1940-45	Not held	World War II	
1946	Pauline Betz	L. Brough	62 64
1947	Margaret Osborne	D. Hart	62 64
1948	Louise Brough	D. Hart	63 86
1949	Louise Brough	M. duPont	10-8 16 10-8
1950	Louise Brough	M. duPont	61 36 61
1951	Doris Hart	S. Fry	61 60
1952	Maureen Connolly	L. Brough	75 63
1953	Maureen Connolly	D. Hart	86 75
1954	Maureen Connolly	L. Brough	62 75
1955	Louise Brough	B. Fleitz	75 86
1956	Shirley Fry	A. Buxton	63 61
1957	Althea Gibson	D. Hard	63 62
1958	Althea Gibson	A. Mortimer	86 62
1959	Maria Bueno	D. Hard	64 63
1960	Maria Bueno	S. Reynolds	86 60
1961	Angela Mortimer	C. Truman	46 64 75
1962	Karen Susman	V. Sukova	64 64
1963	Margaret Smith	B.J. Moffitt	63 64
1964	Maria Bueno	M. Smith	64 79 63
1965	Margaret Smith	M. Bueno	64 75
1966	Billie Jean King	M. Bueno	63 36 61
1967	Billie Jean King	A. Jones	63 64
1968	Billie Jean King	J. Tegart	97 75
1969	Ann Jones	B.J. King	36 63 62
1970	Margaret Court	B.J. King	14-12 11-9
1971	Evonne Goolagong	M. Court	64 61
1972	Billie Jean King	E. Goolagong	63 63
1973	Billie Jean King	C. Evert	60 75
1974	Chris Evert	O. Morozova	60 64
1975	Billie Jean King	E. Cawley	60 61
1976	Chris Evert	E. Cawley	63 46 86
1977	Virginia Wade	B. Stove	46 63 61
1978	Martina Navratilova	C. Evert	26 64 75
1979	Martina Navratilova	C. Evert Lloyd	64 64
1980	Evonne Cawley	C. Evert Lloyd	61 76
1981	Chris Evert Lloyd	H. Mandlikova	62 62
1982	Martina Navratilova	C. Evert Lloyd	61 36 62
1983	Martina Navratilova	A. Jaeger	60 63
1984	Martina Navratilova	C. Evert Lloyd	76 62
1985	Martina Navratilova	C. Evert Lloyd	46 63 62
1986	Martina Navratilova	H. Mandlikova	76 63
1987	Martina Navratilova	S. Graf	75 63
1988	Steffi Graf	M. Navratilova	57 62 61
1989	Steffi Graf	M. Navratilova	62 67 61
1990	Martina Navratilova	Z. Garrison	64 61
1991	Steffi Graf	G. Sabatini	64 36 86
1992	Steffi Graf	M. Seles	62 61
1993	Steffi Graf	J. Novotna	76 16 64
1994	Conchita Martinez	M. Navratilova	64 36 63
1995	Steffi Graf	A.S. Vicario	46 61 75
1996	Steffi Graf	A.S. Vicario	63 75
1997	Martina Hingis	J. Novotna	26 63 63
1998	Jana Novotna	N. Tauziat	64 76
1999	Lindsay Davenport	S. Graf	64 75

U.S. Open
MEN

Challenge round system (defending champion qualified for following year's final) used from 1884-1911. Known as the Patriotic Tournament in 1917 during World War I. Amateur and Open Championships held in 1968 and '69. Became an exclusively Open Championship in 1970.

Surface: Decoturf II (acrylic cement).

Multiple winners: Bill Larned, Richard Sears and Bill Tilden (7); Jimmy Connors (5); John McEnroe, Pete Sampras and Robert Wrenn (4); Oliver Campbell, Ivan Lendl, Fred Perry and Malcolm Whitman (3); Don Budge, Stefan Edberg, Roy Emerson, Neale Fraser, Pancho Gonzales, Bill Johnston, Jack Kramer, Rene Lacoste, Rod Laver, Maurice McLoughlin, Lindley Murray, John Newcombe, Frank Parker, Patrick Rafter, Bobby Riggs, Ken Rosewall, Frank Sedgman, Henry Slocum Jr., Tony Trabert, Ellsworth Vines and Dick Williams (2).

Year	Winner	Loser	Score	Year	Winner	Loser	Score
1881	Richard Sears	W. Glyn	60 63 62	1942	Fred Schroeder	F. Parker	86 75 36 46 62
1882	Richard Sears	C. Clark	61 64 60	1943	Joe Hunt	J. Kramer	63 68 10-8 60
1883	Richard Sears	J. Dwight	62 60 97	1944	Frank Parker	B. Talbert	64 36 63 63
1884	Richard Sears	H. Taylor	60 16 60 62	1945	Frank Parker	B. Talbert	14-12 61 62
1885	Richard Sears	G. Brinley	63 46 60 63	1946	Jack Kramer	T. Brown, Jr.	97 63 60
1886	Richard Sears	R. Beeckman	46 61 63 64	1947	Jack Kramer	F. Parker	46 26 61 60 63
1887	Richard Sears	H. Slocum Jr.	61 63 62	1948	Pancho Gonzales	E. Sturgess	62 63 14-12
1888	Henry Slocum Jr.	H. Taylor	64 61 60	1949	Pancho Gonzales	F. Schroeder	16-18 26 61 62 64
1889	Henry Slocum Jr.	Q. Shaw	63 61 46 62	1950	Arthur Larsen	H. Flam	63 46 57 64 63
1890	Oliver Campbell	H. Slocum Jr.	62 46 63 61	1951	Frank Sedgman	V. Seixas	64 61 61
1891	Oliver Campbell	C. Hobart	26 75 79 61 62	1952	Frank Sedgman	G. Mulloy	61 62 63
1892	Oliver Campbell	F. Hovey	75 36 63 75	1953	Tony Trabert	V. Seixas	63 62 63
1893	Robert Wrenn	F. Hovey	64 36 64 64	1954	Vic Seixas	R. Hartwig	36 62 64 64
1894	Robert Wrenn	M. Goodbody	68 61 64 64	1955	Tony Trabert	K. Rosewall	97 63 63
1895	Fred Hovey	R. Wrenn	63 62 64	1956	Ken Rosewall	L. Hoad	46 62 63 63
1896	Robert Wrenn	F. Hovey	75 36 60 16 61	1957	Mal Anderson	A. Cooper	10-8 75 64
1897	Robert Wrenn	W. Eaves	46 86 63 26 62	1958	Ashley Cooper	M. Anderson	62 36 46 10-8 86
1898	Malcolm Whitman	D. Davis	36 62 62 61	1959	Neale Fraser	A. Olmedo	63 57 62 64
1899	Malcolm Whitman	P. Paret	61 62 36 75	1960	Neale Fraser	R. Laver	64 64 97
1900	Malcolm Whitman	B. Larned	64 16 62 62	1961	Roy Emerson	R. Laver	75 63 62
1901	Bill Larned	B. Wright	62 68 64 64	1962	Rod Laver	R. Emerson	62 64 57 64
1902	Bill Larned	R. Doherty	46 62 64 86	1963	Rafael Osuna	F. Froehling	75 64 62
1903	Laurie Doherty	B. Larned	60 63 10-8	1964	Roy Emerson	F. Stolle	64 62 64
1904	Holcombe Ward	B. Clothier	10-8 64 97	1965	Manuel Santana	C. Drysdale	62 79 75 61
1905	Beals Wright	H. Ward	62 61 11-9	1966	Fred Stolle	J. Newcombe	46 12-10 63 64
1906	Bill Clothier	B. Wright	63 60 64	1967	John Newcombe	C. Graebner	64 64 86
1907	Bill Larned	R. LeRoy	62 62 64	1968	Am-Arthur Ashe	B. Lutz	46 63 8-10 60 64
1908	Bill Larned	B. Wright	61 62 86		Op-Arthur Ashe	T. Okker	14-12 57 63 33 61
1909	Bill Larned	B. Clothier	61 62 57 16 61	1969	Am-Stan Smith	B. Lutz	97 63 61
1910	Bill Larned	T. Bundy	61 57 60 68 61		Op-Rod Laver	T. Roche	79 61 63 62
1911	Bill Larned	M. McLoughlin	64 64 62	1970	Ken Rosewall	T. Roche	26 64 76 63
1912	Maurice McLoughlin	W.F. Johnson	36 26 62 64 62	1971	Stan Smith	J. Kodes	36 63 62 76
1913	Maurice McLoughlin	R. Williams	64 57 63 61	1972	Ilie Nastase	A. Ashe	36 63 67 64 63
1914	Dick Williams	M. McLoughlin	63 86 10-8	1973	John Newcombe	J. Kodes	64 16 46 62 63
1915	Bill Johnston	M. McLoughlin	16 60 75 10-8	1974	Jimmy Connors	K. Rosewall	61 60 61
1916	Dick Williams	B. Johnston	46 64 06 62 64	1975	Manuel Orantes	J. Connors	64 63 63
1917	Lindley Murray	N. Niles	57 86 63 63	1976	Jimmy Connors	B. Borg	64 36 76 64
1918	Lindley Murray	B. Tilden	63 61 75	1977	Guillermo Vilas	J. Connors	26 63 76 60
1919	Bill Johnston	B. Tilden	64 64 63	1978	Jimmy Connors	B. Borg	64 62 62
1920	Bill Tilden	B. Johnston	61 16 75 57 63	1979	John McEnroe	V. Gerulaitis	75 63 63
1921	Bill Tilden	W. Johnson	61 63 61	1980	John McEnroe	B. Borg	76 61 67 57 64
1922	Bill Tilden	B. Johnston	46 36 62 63 64	1981	John McEnroe	B. Borg	46 62 64 63
1923	Bill Tilden	B. Johnston	64 61 64	1982	Jimmy Connors	I. Lendl	63 62 46 64
1924	Bill Tilden	B. Johnston	61 97 62	1983	Jimmy Connors	I. Lendl	63 67 75 60
1925	Bill Tilden	B. Johnston	46 11-9 63 46 63	1984	John McEnroe	I. Lendl	63 64 61
1926	Rene Lacoste	J. Borotra	64 60 64	1985	Ivan Lendl	J. McEnroe	76 63 64
1927	Rene Lacoste	B. Tilden	11-9 63 11-9	1986	Ivan Lendl	M. Mecir	64 62 60
1928	Henri Cochet	F. Hunter	46 64 36 75 63	1987	Ivan Lendl	M. Wilander	67 60 76 64
1929	Bill Tilden	F. Hunter	36 63 46 62 64	1988	Mats Wilander	I. Lendl	64 46 63 57 64
1930	John Doeg	F. Shields	10-8 16 64 16-14	1989	Boris Becker	I. Lendl	76 16 63 76
1931	Ellsworth Vines	G. Lott Jr.	79 63 97 75	1990	Pete Sampras	A. Agassi	64 63 62
1932	Ellsworth Vines	H. Cochet	64 64 64	1991	Stefan Edberg	J. Courier	62 64 60
1933	Fred Perry	J. Crawford	63 11-13 46 60 61	1992	Stefan Edberg	P. Sampras	36 64 76 62
1934	Fred Perry	W. Allison	64 63 16 86	1993	Pete Sampras	C. Pioline	64 64 63
1935	Wilmer Allison	S. Wood	62 62 63	1994	Andre Agassi	M. Stich	61 76 75
1936	Fred Perry	D. Budge	26 62 86 16 10-8	1995	Pete Sampras	A. Agassi	64 63 46 75
1937	Don Budge	G. von Cramm	61 79 61 36 61	1996	Pete Sampras	M. Chang	61 64 76
1938	Don Budge	G. Mako	63 68 62 61	1997	Patrick Rafter	G. Rusedski	63 62 46 75
1939	Bobby Riggs	S.W. van Horn	64 62 64	1998	Patrick Rafter	M. Philippoussis	63 36 62 60
1940	Don McNeill	B. Riggs	46 68 63 63 75	1999	Andre Agassi	T. Martin	64 67 67 63 62
1941	Bobby Riggs	F. Kovacs	57 61 63 63				

WOMEN

Challenge round system used from 1887-1918. Five set final played from 1887-1901. Amateur and Open Championships held in 1968 and '69. Became an exclusively Open Championship in 1970.

Multiple winners: Molla Mallory Bjurstedt (8); Helen Wills Moody (7); Chris Evert Lloyd (6); Margaret Smith Court and Steffi Graf (5); Pauline Betz, Mario Bueno, Helen Jacobs, Billie Jean King, Alice Marble, Elisabeth Moore, Martina Navratilova and Hazel Hotchkiss Wightman (4); Juliette Atkinson, Mary Browne, Maureen Connolly and Margaret Osborne duPont (3); Tracy Austin, Mabel Cahill, Sarah Palfrey Cooke, Darlene Hard, Doris Hart, Althea Gibson, Monica Seles and Bertha Townsend (2).

Year	Winner	Loser	Score
1887	Ellen Hansell	L. Knight	61 60
1888	Bertha Townsend	E. Hansell	63 65
1889	Bertha Townsend	L. Voorhes	75 62
1890	Ellen Roosevelt	B. Townsend	62 62
1891	Mabel Cahill	E. Roosevelt	64 61 46 63
1892	Mabel Cahill	E. Moore	57 63 64 46 62
1893	Aline Terry	A. Schultz	61 63
1894	Helen Hellwig	A. Terry	75 36 60 36 63
1895	Juliette Atkinson	H. Hellwig	64 62 61
1896	Elisabeth Moore	J. Atkinson	64 46 62 62
1897	Juliette Atkinson	E. Moore	63 63 46 36 63
1898	Juliette Atkinson	M. Jones	63 57 64 26 75
1899	Marion Jones	M. Banks	61 61 75
1900	Myrtle McAteer	E. Parker	62 62 60
1901	Elizabeth Moore	M. McAteer	64 36 75 26 62
1902	Marion Jones	E. Moore	61 10(ret)
1903	Elizabeth Moore	M. Jones	75 86
1904	May Sutton	E. Moore	61 62
1905	Elizabeth Moore	H. Homans	64 57 61
1906	Helen Homans	M. Barger-Wallach	64 63
1907	Evelyn Sears	C. Neely	63 62
1908	Maud B. Wallach	Ev. Sears	63 16 63
1909	Hazel Hotchkiss	M. Wallach	60 61
1910	Hazel Hotchkiss	L. Hammond	64 62
1911	Hazel Hotchkiss	F. Sutton	8-10 61 97
1912	Mary Browne	E. Sears	64 62
1913	Mary Browne	D. Green	62 75
1914	Mary Browne	M. Wagner	62 16 61
1915	Molla Bjurstedt	H. Wightman	46 62 60
1916	Molla Bjurstedt	L. Raymond	60 61
1917	Molla Bjurstedt	M. Vanderhoef	46 60 62
1918	Molla Bjurstedt	E. Goss	64 63
1919	Hazel Wightman	M. Zinderstein	61 62
1920	Molla Mallory	M. Zinderstein	63 61
1921	Molla Mallory	M. Browne	46 64 62
1922	Molla Mallory	H. Wills	63 61
1923	Helen Wills	M. Mallory	62 61
1924	Helen Wills	M. Mallory	61 63
1925	Helen Wills	K. McKane	36 60 62
1926	Molla Mallory	E. Ryan	46 64 97
1927	Helen Wills	B. Nuthall	61 64
1928	Helen Wills	H. Jacobs	62 61
1929	Helen Wills	P. Watson	64 62
1930	Betty Nuthall	A. Harper	61 64
1931	Helen Moody	E. Whitingstall	64 61
1932	Helen Jacobs	C. Babcock	62 62
1933	Helen Jacobs	H. Moody	86 36 30(ret)
1934	Helen Jacobs	S. Palfrey	61 64
1935	Helen Jacobs	S. Fabyan	62 64
1936	Alice Marble	H. Jacobs	46 63 62
1937	Anita Lizana	J. Jedrzejowska	64 62
1938	Alice Marble	N. Wynne	60 63
1939	Alice Marble	H. Jacobs	60 8-10 64
1940	Alice Marble	H. Jacobs	62 63
1941	Sarah Cooke	P. Betz	75 62
1942	Pauline Betz	L. Brough	46 61 64
1943	Pauline Betz	L. Brough	63 57 63
1944	Pauline Betz	M. Osborne	63 86

Year	Winner	Loser	Score
1945	Sarah Cooke	P. Betz	36 86 64
1946	Pauline Betz	P. Canning	11-9 63
1947	Louise Brough	M. Osborne	86 46 61
1948	Margaret duPont	L. Brough	46 64 15-13
1949	Margaret duPont	D. Hart	64 61
1950	Margaret duPont	D. Hart	64 63
1951	Maureen Connolly	S. Fry	63 16 64
1952	Maureen Connolly	D. Hart	63 75
1953	Maureen Connolly	D. Hart	62 64
1954	Doris Hart	L. Brough	68 61 86
1955	Doris Hart	P. Ward	64 62
1956	Shirley Fry	A. Gibson	63 64
1957	Althea Gibson	L. Brough	63 62
1958	Althea Gibson	D. Hard	36 61 62
1959	Maria Bueno	C. Truman	61 64
1960	Darlene Hard	M. Bueno	64 10-12 64
1961	Darlene Hard	A. Haydon	63 64
1962	Margaret Smith	D. Hard	97 64
1963	Maria Bueno	M. Smith	75 64
1964	Maria Bueno	C. Graebner	61 60
1965	Margaret Smith	B.J. Moffitt	86 75
1966	Maria Bueno	N. Richey	63 61
1967	Billie Jean King	A. Jones	11-9 64
1968	Am-Margaret Court	M. Bueno	62 62
	Op-Virginia Wade	B.J. King	64 62
1969	Am-Margaret Court	V. Wade	46 63 60
	Op-Margaret Court	N. Richey	62 62
1970	Margaret Court	R. Casals	62 26 61
1971	Billie Jean King	R. Casals	64 76
1972	Billie Jean King	K. Melville	63 75
1973	Margaret Court	E. Goolagong	76 57 62
1974	Billie Jean King	E. Goolagong	36 63 75
1975	Chris Evert	E. Cawley	57 64 62
1976	Chris Evert	E. Cawley	63 60
1977	Chris Evert	W. Turnbull	76 62
1978	Chris Evert	P. Shriver	75 64
1979	Tracy Austin	C. Evert Lloyd	64 63
1980	Chris Evert Lloyd	H. Mandlikova	57 61 61
1981	Tracy Austin	M. Navratilova	16 76 76
1982	Chris Evert Lloyd	H. Mandlikova	63 61
1983	Martina Navratilova	C. Evert Lloyd	61 63
1984	Martina Navratilova	C. Evert Lloyd	46 64 64
1985	Hana Mandlikova	M. Navratilova	76 16 76
1986	Martina Navratilova	H. Sukova	63 62
1987	Martina Navratilova	S. Graf	76 61
1988	Steffi Graf	G. Sabatini	63 36 61
1989	Steffi Graf	M. Navratilova	36 75 61
1990	Gabriela Sabatini	S. Graf	62 76
1991	Monica Seles	M. Navratilova	76 61
1992	Monica Seles	A.S. Vicario	63 63
1993	Steffi Graf	H. Sukova	63 63
1994	A. Sanchez Vicario	S. Graf	16 76 64
1995	Steffi Graf	M. Seles	76 06 63
1996	Steffi Graf	M. Seles	75 64
1997	Martina Hingis	V. Williams	60 64
1998	Lindsay Davenport	M. Hingis	63 75
1999	Serena Williams	M. Hingis	63 76

Grand Slam Summary

Singles winners of the four Grand Slam tournaments–Australian, French, Wimbledon and United States–since the French was opened to all comers in 1925. Note that there were two Australian Opens in 1977 and none in 1986.

MEN

Three wins in one year: Jack Crawford (1933); Fred Perry (1934); Tony Trabert (1955); Lew Hoad (1956); Ashley Cooper (1958); Roy Emerson (1964); Jimmy Connors (1974); Mats Wilander (1988).

Two wins in one year: Roy Emerson and Pete Sampras (4 times); Bjorn Borg (3 times); Rene Lacoste, Ivan Lendl, John Newcombe and Fred Perry (twice); Andre Agassi, Boris Becker, Don Budge, Henri Cochet, Jimmy Connors, Jim Courier, Neale Fraser, Jack Kramer, John McEnroe, Alex Olmedo, Budge Patty, Bobby Riggs, Ken Rosewall, Dick Savitt, Frank Sedgman and Guillermo Vilas (once).

Year	Australian	French	Wimbledon	U.S.
1925	Anderson	Lacoste	Lacoste	Tilden
1926	Hawkes	Cochet	Borotra	Lacoste
1927	Patterson	Lacoste	Cochet	Lacoste
1928	Borotra	Cochet	Lacoste	Cochet
1929	Gregory	Lacoste	Cochet	Tilden
1930	Moon	Cochet	Tilden	Doeg
1931	Crawford	Borotra	Wood	Vines
1932	Crawford	Cochet	Vines	Vines
1933	Crawford	Crawford	Crawford	Perry
1934	Perry	von Cramm	Perry	Perry
1935	Crawford	Perry	Perry	Allison
1936	Quist	von Cramm	Perry	Perry
1937	McGrath	Henkel	Budge	Budge
1938	**Budge**	**Budge**	**Budge**	**Budge**
1939	Bromwich	McNeill	Riggs	Riggs
1940	Quist	—	—	McNeill
1941	—	—	—	Riggs
1942	—	—	—	Schroeder
1943	—	—	—	Hunt
1944	—	—	—	Parker
1945	—	—	-	Parker
1946	Bromwich	Bernard	Petra	Kramer
1947	Pails	Asboth	Kramer	Kramer
1948	Quist	Parker	Falkenburg	Gonzales
1949	Sedgman	Parker	Schroeder	Gonzales
1950	Sedgman	Patty	Patty	Larsen
1951	Savitt	Drobny	Savitt	Sedgman
1952	McGregor	Drobny	Sedgman	Sedgman
1953	Rosewall	Rosewall	Seixas	Trabert
1954	Rose	Trabert	Drobny	Seixas
1955	Rosewall	Trabert	Trabert	Trabert
1956	Hoad	Hoad	Hoad	Rosewall
1957	Cooper	Davidson	Hoad	Anderson
1958	Cooper	Rose	Cooper	Cooper
1959	Olmedo	Pietrangeli	Olmedo	Fraser
1960	Laver	Pietrangeli	Fraser	Fraser
1961	Emerson	Santana	Laver	Emerson
1962	**Laver**	**Laver**	**Laver**	**Laver**
1963	Emerson	Emerson	McKinley	Osuna

Year	Australian	French	Wimbledon	U.S.
1964	Emerson	Santana	Emerson	Emerson
1965	Emerson	Stolle	Emerson	Santana
1966	Emerson	Roche	Santana	Stolle
1967	Emerson	Emerson	Newcombe	Newcombe
1968	Bowrey	Rosewall	Laver	Ashe
1969	**Laver**	**Laver**	**Laver**	**Laver**
1970	Ashe	Kodes	Newcombe	Rosewall
1971	Rosewall	Kodes	Newcombe	Smith
1972	Rosewall	Gimeno	Smith	Nastase
1973	Newcombe	Nastase	Kodes	Newcombe
1974	Connors	Borg	Connors	Connors
1975	Newcombe	Borg	Ashe	Orantes
1976	Edmondson	Panatta	Borg	Connors
1977	Tanner & Gerulaitis	Vilas	Borg	Vilas
1978	Vilas	Borg	Borg	Connors
1979	Vilas	Borg	Borg	McEnroe
1980	Teacher	Borg	Borg	McEnroe
1981	Kriek	Borg	McEnroe	McEnroe
1982	Kriek	Wilander	Connors	Connors
1983	Wilander	Noah	McEnroe	Connors
1984	Wilander	Lendl	McEnroe	McEnroe
1985	Edberg	Wilander	Becker	Lendl
1986	–	Lendl	Becker	Lendl
1987	Edberg	Lendl	Cash	Lendl
1988	Wilander	Wilander	Edberg	Wilander
1989	Lendl	Chang	Becker	Becker
1990	Lendl	Gomez	Edberg	Sampras
1991	Becker	Courier	Stich	Edberg
1992	Courier	Courier	Agassi	Edberg
1993	Courier	Bruguera	Sampras	Sampras
1994	Sampras	Bruguera	Sampras	Agassi
1995	Agassi	Muster	Sampras	Sampras
1996	Becker	Kafelnikov	Krajicek	Sampras
1997	Sampras	Kuerten	Sampras	Rafter
1998	Korda	Moya	Sampras	Rafter
1999	Kafelnikov	Agassi	Sampras	Agassi

WOMEN

Three in one year: Helen Wills Moody (1928 and '29); Margaret Smith Court (1962, '65, '69 and '73); Billie Jean King (1972); Martina Navratilova (1983 and '84); Steffi Graf (1989, '93, '95 and '96); Monica Seles (1991 and '92); and Martina Hingis (1997).

Two in one year: Chris Evert Lloyd (5 times); Helen Wills Moody and Martina Navratilova (3 times); Maria Bueno, Maureen Connolly, Margaraet Smith Court, Althea Gibson, Billie Jean King (twice); Cilly Aussem, Pauleen Betz, Louise Brough, Evonne Goolagong Cawley, Shirley Fry, Darlene Hard, Margaret Osborne duPont, Suzanne Lenglen, Alice Marble and Arantxa Sanchez Vicario (once).

Year	Australian	French	Wimbledon	U.S.
1925	Akhurst	Lenglen	Lenglen	Wills
1926	Akhurst	Lenglen	Godfree	Mallory
1927	Boyd	Bouman	Wills	Wills
1928	Akhurst	Wills	Wills	Wills
1929	Akhurst	Wills	Wills	Wills
1930	Akhurst	Moody	Moody	Nuthall
1931	Buttsworth	Aussem	Aussem	Moody
1932	Buttsworth	Moody	Moody	Jacobs
1933	Hartigan	Scriven	Moody	Jacobs
1934	Hartigan	Scriven	Round	Jacobs

Year	Australian	French	Wimbledon	U.S.
1935	Round	Sperling	Moody	Jacobs
1936	Hartigan	Sperling	Jacobs	Marble
1937	Bolton	Sperling	Round	Lizana
1938	Bundy	Mathieu	Moody	Marble
1939	Westacott	Mathieu	Marble	Marble
1940	Bolton	—	—	Marble
1941	—	—	—	Cooke
1942	—	—	—	Betz
1943	—	—	—	Betz
1944	—	—	—	Betz

Year	Australian	French	Wimbledon	U.S.
1945	—	—	—	Cooke
1946	Bolton	Osborne	Betz	Betz
1947	Bolton	Todd	Osborne	Brough
1948	Bolton	Landry	Brough	du Pont
1949	Hart	du Pont	Brough	du Pont
1950	Brough	Hart	Brough	du Pont
1951	Bolton	Fry	Hart	Connolly
1952	Long	Hart	Connolly	Connolly
1953	**Connolly**	**Connolly**	**Connolly**	**Connolly**
1954	Long	Connolly	Connolly	Hart
1955	Penrose	Mortimer	Brough	Hart
1956	Carter	Gibson	Fry	Fry
1957	Fry	Bloomer	Gibson	Gibson
1958	Mortimer	Kormoczi	Gibson	Gibson
1959	Reitano	Truman	Bueno	Bueno
1960	Smith	Hard	Bueno	Hard
1961	Smith	Haydon	Mortimer	Hard
1962	Smith	Smith	Susman	Smith
1963	Smith	Turner	Smith	Bueno
1964	Smith	Smith	Bueno	Bueno
1965	Smith	Turner	Smith	Smith
1966	Smith	Jones	King	Bueno
1967	Richey	Durr	King	King
1968	King	Richey	King	Wade
1969	Court	Court	Jones	Court
1970	**Court**	**Court**	**Court**	**Court**
1971	Court	Goolagong	Goolagong	King
1972	Wade	King	King	King

Year	Australian	French	Wimbledon	U.S.
1973	Court	Court	King	Court
1974	Goolagong	Evert	Evert	King
1975	Goolagong	Evert	King	Evert
1976	Cawley	Barker	Evert	Evert
1977	Reid & Cawley	Jausovec	Wade	Evert
1978	O'Neil	Ruzici	Navratilova	Evert
1979	Jordan	Evert Lloyd	Navratilova	Austin
1980	Mandlikova	Evert Lloyd	Cawley	Evert Lloyd
1981	Navratilova	Mandlikova	Evert Lloyd	Austin
1982	Evert Lloyd	Navratilova	Navratilova	Evert Lloyd
1983	Navratilova	Evert Lloyd	Navratilova	Navratilova
1984	Evert Lloyd	Navratilova	Navratilova	Navratilova
1985	Navratilova	Evert Lloyd	Navratilova	Mandlikova
1986	—	Evert Lloyd	Navratilova	Navratilova
1987	Mandlikova	Graf	Navratilova	Navratilova
1988	**Graf**	**Graf**	**Graf**	**Graf**
1989	Graf	Vicario	Graf	Graf
1990	Graf	Seles	Navratilova	Sabatini
1991	Seles	Seles	Graf	Seles
1992	Seles	Seles	Graf	Seles
1993	Seles	Graf	Graf	Graf
1994	Graf	Vicario	Martinez	Vicario
1995	Pierce	Graf	Graf	Graf
1996	Seles	Graf	Graf	Graf
1997	Hingis	Majoli	Hingis	Hingis
1998	Hingis	Vicario	Novotna	Davenport
1999	Hingis	Graf	Davenport	S. Williams

Overall Leaders

All-Time Grand Slam titleists including all singles and doubles championships at the four major tournaments. Titles listed under each heading are singles, doubles and mixed doubles. Players active in 1999 are in **bold** type.

MEN

		Career	Australian	French	Wimbledon	U.S.	S-D-M	Total Titles
1	Roy Emerson	1959-71	6-3-0	2-6-0	2-3-0	2-4-0	12-16-0	28
2	John Newcombe	1965-76	2-5-0	0-3-0	3-6-0	2-3-1	7-17-1	25
3	Frank Sedgman	1949-52	2-2-2	0-2-2	1-3-2	2-2-2	5-9-8	22
4	Bill Tilden	1913-30	*	0-0-1	3-1-0	7-5-4	10-6-5	21
5	Rod Laver	1959-71	3-4-0	2-1-1	4-1-2	2-0-0	11-6-3	20
6	Jack Bromwich	1938-50	2-8-1	0-0-0	0-2-2	0-3-1	2-13-4	19
7	Ken Rosewall	1953-72	4-3-0	2-2-0	0-2-0	2-2-1	8-9-1	18
	Neale Fraser	1957-62	0-3-1	0-3-0	1-2-0	2-3-3	3-11-4	18
	Jean Borotra	1925-36	1-1-1	1-5-2	2-3-1	0-0-1	4-9-5	18
	Fred Stolle	1962-69	0-3-1	1-2-0	0-2-3	1-3-2	2-10-6	18
11	John McEnroe	1977-93	0-0-0	0-0-1	3-5-0	4-4-0	7-9-1	17
	Jack Crawford	1929-35	4-4-3	1-1-1	1-1-1	0-0-0	6-6-5	17
	Adrian Quist	1936-50	3-10-0	0-1-0	0-2-0	0-1-0	3-14-0	17
14	Laurie Doherty	1897-1906	*	*	5-8-0	1-2-0	6-10-0	16
15	Henri Cochet	1922-32	*	4-3-2	2-2-0	1-0-1	7-5-3	15
	Vic Seixas	1952-56	0-1-0	0-2-1	1-0-4	1-2-3	2-5-8	15
	Bob Hewitt	1961-79	0-2-1	0-1-2	0-5-2	0-1-1	0-9-6	15

WOMEN

		Career	Australian	French	Wimbledon	U.S.	S-D-M	Total Titles
1	Margaret Court Smith	1960-75	11-8-2	5-4-4	3-2-5	5-5-8	24-19-19	62
2	Martina Navratilova	1974-95	3-8-0	2-7-2	9-7-2	4-9-2	18-31-6	55
3	Billie Jean King	1961-81	1-0-1	1-1-2	6-10-4	4-5-4	12-16-11	39
4	Margaret du Pont	1941-60	*	2-3-0	1-5-1	3-13-9	6-21-10	37
5	Louise Brough	1942-57	1-1-0	0-3-0	4-5-4	1-12-4	6-21-8	35
	Doris Hart	1948-55	1-1-2	2-5-3	1-4-5	2-4-5	6-14-15	35
7	Helen Wills Moody	1923-38	*	4-2-0	8-3-1	7-4-2	19-9-3	31
8	Elizabeth Ryan	1914-34	*	0-4-0	0-12-7	0-1-2	0-17-9	26
9	Suzanne Lenglen	1919-26	*	6-2-2	6-6-3	0-0-0	12-8-5	25
10	**Steffi Graf**	1982-99	4-0-0	6-0-0	7-1-0	5-0-0	22-1-0	23
11	Pam Shriver	1981-97	0-7-0	0-4-1	0-5-0	0-5-0	0-21-1	22
12	Chris Evert	1974-89	2-0-0	7-2-0	3-1-0	6-0-0	18-3-0	21
	Darlene Hard	1958-69	*	1-3-2	0-4-3	2-6-0	3-13-5	21
14	**Natasha Zvereva**	1989—	0-3-2	0-6-0	0-5-0	0-4-0	0-18-2	20
	Nancye Wynne Bolton	1935-52	6-10-4	0-0-0	0-0-0	0-0-0	6-10-4	20

Men's, Women's & Mixed Doubles Grand Slam

The tennis Grand Slam has only been accomplished in doubles competition six times in the same calendar year. Here are the doubles teams to accomplish the feat. The two men and three women to win the tennis Grand Slam are noted in the Grand Slam Summary tables beginning on page 830.

Men's Doubles

1951 . . . . .Frank Sedgman, Australia
& Ken McGregor, Australia

Mixed Doubles

1963 . . . . .Ken Fletcher, Australia
& Margaret Smith, Australia
1967 . . . . .Owen Davidson and two partners*
*Davidson's partners: AUS—Lesley Turner; FR, WIM, U.S.—Billie Jean King.

Women's Doubles

1960 . . . . .Maria Bueno, Brazil & two partners†
1984 . . . . .Martina Navratilova, USA
& Pam Shriver, USA
1998 . . . .Martina Hingis, Switzerland & two partners#
† Bueno's partners: AUS—Christine Truman; FR, WIM, U.S.—Darlene Hard.
# Hingis's partners: AUS—Mirjana Lucic; FR, WIM, U.S.—Jana Novotna.

All-Time Grand Slam Singles Titles

Men and women with the most singles championships in the Australian, French, Wimbledon and U.S. championships, through 1999. Note that (*) indicates player never played in that particular Grand Slam event; and players active in singles play in 1999 are in **bold** type.

Top 15 Men

		Aus	Fre	Wim	US	Total
1	Roy Emerson	6	2	2	2	12
	Pete Sampras	2	0	6	4	12
3	Bjorn Borg	0	6	5	0	11
	Rod Laver	3	2	4	2	11
5	Bill Tilden	*	0	3	7	10
6	Jimmy Connors	1	0	2	5	8
	Ivan Lendl	2	3	0	3	8
	Fred Perry	1	1	3	3	8
	Ken Rosewall	4	2	0	2	8
10	Henri Cochet	*	4	2	1	7
	Rene Lacoste	*	3	2	2	7
	Bill Larned	*	*	0	7	7
	John McEnroe	0	0	3	4	7
	John Newcombe	2	0	3	2	7
	Willie Renshaw	*	*	7	*	7
	Dick Sears	*	*	0	7	7

Top 15 Women

		Aus	Fre	Wim	US	Total
1	Margaret Smith Court	11	5	3	5	24
2	**Steffi Graf**	4	6	7	5	22
3	Helen Wills Moody	*	4	8	7	19
4	Chris Evert	2	7	3	6	18
	Martina Navratilova	3	2	9	4	18
6	Billie Jean King	1	1	6	4	12
	Suzanne Lenglen	*	6	6	0	12
8	Maureen Connolly	1	2	3	3	9
	Monica Seles	4	3	0	2	9
10	Molla Bjurstedt Mallory	*	*	0	8	8
11	Maria Bueno	0	0	3	4	7
	Evonne Goolagong	4	1	2	0	7
	Dorothea D. Chambers	*	*	7	0	7
14	Nancy Bolton	6	0	0	0	6
	Louise Brough	1	0	4	1	6
	Margaret duPont	*	2	1	3	6
	Doris Hart	1	2	1	2	6
	Blanche Bingley Hillyard	*	*	6	*	6

Annual Number One Players

Unofficial world rankings for men and women determined by the *London Daily Telegraph* from 1914-72. Since then, official world rankings computed by men's and women's tours. Rankings included only amateur players from 1914 until the arrival of open (professional) tennis in 1968. No rankings were released during World Wars I and II.

MEN

Multiple winners: Pete Sampras and Bill Tilden (6); Jimmy Connors (5); Henri Cochet, Rod Laver, Ivan Lendl and John McEnroe (4); John Newcombe and Fred Perry (3); Bjorn Borg, Don Budge, Ashley Cooper, Stefan Edberg, Roy Emerson, Neale Fraser, Jack Kramer, Rene Lacoste, Ilie Nastase, Frank Sedgman and Tony Trabert (2).

Year		Year		Year		Year	
1914	Maurice McLoughlin	1937	Don Budge	1962	Rod Laver	1982	John McEnroe
1915-18	No rankings	1938	Don Budge	1963	Rafael Osuna	1983	John McEnroe
1919	Gerald Patterson	1939	Bobby Riggs	1964	Roy Emerson	1984	John McEnroe
1920	Bill Tilden	1940-45	No rankings	1965	Roy Emerson	1985	Ivan Lendl
1921	Bill Tilden	1946	Jack Kramer	1966	Manuel Santana	1986	Ivan Lendl
1922	Bill Tilden	1947	Jack Kramer	1967	John Newcombe	1987	Ivan Lendl
1923	Bill Tilden	1948	Frank Parker	1968	Rod Laver	1988	Mats Wilander
1924	Bill Tilden	1949	Pancho Gonzales	1969	Rod Laver	1989	Ivan Lendl
1925	Bill Tilden	1950	Budge Patty	1970	John Newcombe	1990	Stefan Edberg
1926	Rene Lacoste	1951	Frank Sedgman	1971	John Newcombe	1991	Stefan Edberg
1927	Rene Lacoste	1952	Frank Sedgman	1972	Ilie Nastase	1992	Jim Courier
1928	Henri Cochet	1953	Tony Trabert	1973	Ilie Nastase	1993	Pete Sampras
1929	Henri Cochet	1954	Jaroslav Drobny	1974	Jimmy Connors	1994	Pete Sampras
1930	Henri Cochet	1955	Tony Trabert	1975	Jimmy Connors	1995	Pete Sampras
1931	Henri Cochet	1956	Lew Hoad	1976	Jimmy Connors	1996	Pete Sampras
1932	Ellsworth Vines	1957	Ashley Cooper	1977	Jimmy Connors	1997	Pete Sampras
1933	Jack Crawford	1958	Ashley Cooper	1978	Jimmy Connors	1998	Pete Sampras
1934	Fred Perry	1959	Neale Fraser	1979	Bjorn Borg		
1935	Fred Perry	1960	Neale Fraser	1980	Bjorn Borg		
1936	Fred Perry	1961	Rod Laver	1981	John McEnroe		

WOMEN

Multiple winners: Helen Wills Moody (9); Steffi Graf (8); Margaret Smith Court and Martina Navratilova (7); Chris Evert Lloyd (5); Margaret Osborne duPont and Billie Jean King (4); Maureen Connolly and Monica Seles (3); Maria Bueno, Althea Gibson, Suzanne Lenglen (2).

Year		Year		Year		Year	
1925	Suzanne Lenglen	1948	Margaret duPont	1966	Billie Jean King	1984	Martina Navratilova
1926	Suzanne Lenglen	1949	Margaret duPont	1967	Billie Jean King	1985	Martina Navratilova
1927	Helen Wills	1950	Margaret duPont	1968	Billie Jean King	1986	Martina Navratilova
1928	Helen Wills	1951	Doris Hart	1969	Margaret Court	1987	Steffi Graf
1929	Helen Wills Moody	1952	Maureen Connolly	1970	Margaret Court	1988	Steffi Graf
1930	Helen Wills Moody	1953	Maureen Connolly	1971	Evonne Goolagong	1989	Steffi Graf
1931	Helen Wills Moody	1954	Maureen Connolly	1972	Billie Jean King	1990	Steffi Graf
1932	Helen Wills Moody	1955	Louise Brough	1973	Margaret Court	1991	Monica Seles
1933	Helen Wills Moody	1956	Shirley Fry	1974	Billie Jean King	1992	Monica Seles
1934	Dorothy Round	1957	Althea Gibson	1975	Chris Evert	1993	Steffi Graf
1935	Helen Wills Moody	1958	Althea Gibson	1976	Chris Evert	1994	Steffi Graf
1936	Helen Jacobs	1959	Maria Bueno	1977	Chris Evert	1995	Steffi Graf
1937	Anita Lizana	1960	Maria Bueno	1978	Martina Navratilova		& Monica Seles
1938	Helen Wills Moody	1961	Angela Mortimer	1979	Martina Navratilova	1996	Steffi Graf
1939	Alice Marble	1962	Margaret Smith	1980	Chris Evert Lloyd	1997	Martina Hingis
1940-45	No rankings	1963	Margaret Smith	1981	Chris Evert Lloyd	1998	Lindsay Davenport
1946	Pauline Betz	1964	Margaret Smith	1982	Martina Navratilova		
1947	Margaret Osborne	1965	Margaret Smith	1983	Martina Navratilova		

Annual Top 10 World Rankings (since 1968)

Year by year Top 10 world computer rankings for Men (ATP Tour) and Women (WTA Tour) since the arrival of open tennis in 1968. Rankings from 1968-72 made by Lance Tingay of the London Daily Telegraph. Since 1973, computerized rankings by ATP Tour (men) and WTA Tour (women).

MEN

1968
1. Rod Laver
2. Arthur Ashe
3. Ken Rosewall
4. Tom Okker
5. Tony Roche
6. John Newcombe
7. Clark Graebner
8. Dennis Ralston
9. Cliff Drysdale
10. Pancho Gonzales

1969
1. Rod Laver
2. Tony Roche
3. John Newcombe
4. Tom Okker
5. Ken Rosewall
6. Arthur Ashe
7. Cliff Drysdale
8. Pancho Gonzales
9. Andres Gimeno
10. Fred Stolle

1970
1. John Newcombe
2. Ken Rosewall
3. Tony Roche
4. Rod Laver
5. Arthur Ashe
6. Ilie Nastase
7. Tom Okker
8. Roger Taylor
9. Jan Kodes
10. Cliff Richey

1971
1. John Newcombe
2. Stan Smith
3. Rod Laver
4. Ken Rosewall
5. Jan Kodes
6. Arthur Ashe
7. Tom Okker
8. Marty Riessen
9. Cliff Drysdale
10. Ilie Nastase

1972
1. Stan Smith
2. Ken Rosewall
3. Ilie Nastase
4. Rod Laver
5. Arthur Ashe
6. John Newcombe
7. Bob Lutz
8. Tom Okker
9. Marty Riessen
10. Andres Gimeno

1973
1. Ilie Nastase
2. John Newcombe
3. Jimmy Connors
4. Tom Okker
5. Stan Smith
6. Ken Rosewall
7. Manuel Orantes
8. Rod Laver
9. Jan Kodes
10. Arthur Ashe

1974
1. Jimmy Connors
2. John Newcombe
3. Bjorn Borg
4. Rod Laver
5. Guillermo Vilas
6. Tom Okker
7. Arthur Ashe
8. Ken Rosewall
9. Stan Smith
10. Ilie Nastase

1975
1. Jimmy Connors
2. Guillermo Vilas
3. Bjorn Borg
4. Arthur Ashe
5. Manuel Orantes
6. Ken Rosewall
7. Ilie Nastase
8. John Alexander
9. Roscoe Tanner
10. Rod Laver

1976
1. Jimmy Connors
2. Bjorn Borg
3. Ilie Nastase
4. Manuel Orantes
5. Raul Ramirez
6. Guillermo Vilas
7. Adriano Panatta
8. Harold Solomon
9. Eddie Dibbs
10. Brian Gottfried

1977
1. Jimmy Connors
2. Guillermo Vilas
3. Bjorn Borg
4. Vitas Gerulaitis
5. Brian Gottfried
6. Eddie Dibbs
7. Manuel Orantes
8. Raul Ramirez
9. Ilie Nastase
10. Dick Stockton

1978
1. Jimmy Connors
2. Bjorn Borg
3. Guillermo Vilas
4. John McEnroe
5. Vitas Gerulaitis
6. Eddie Dibbs
7. Brian Gottfried
8. Raul Ramirez
9. Harold Solomon
10. Corrado Barazzutti

1979
1. Bjorn Borg
2. Jimmy Connors
3. John McEnroe
4. Vitas Gerulaitis
5. Roscoe Tanner
6. Guillermo Vilas
7. Arthur Ashe
8. Harold Solomon
9. Jose Higueras
10. Eddie Dibbs

Annual Top 10 World Rankings (since 1968) (Cont.)
MEN

1980
1 Bjorn Borg
2 John McEnroe
3 Jimmy Connors
4 Gene Mayer
5 Guillermo Vilas
6 Ivan Lendl
7 Harold Solomon
8 Jose-Luis Clerc
9 Vitas Gerulaitis
10 Eliot Teltscher

1981
1 John McEnroe
2 Ivan Lendl
3 Jimmy Connors
4 Bjorn Borg
5 Jose-Luis Clerc
6 Guillermo Vilas
7 Gene Mayer
8 Eliot Teltscher
9 Vitas Gerulaitis
10 Peter McNamara

1982
1 John McEnroe
2 Jimmy Connors
3 Ivan Lendl
4 Guillermo Vilas
5 Vitas Gerulaitis
6 Jose-Luis Clerc
7 Mats Wilander
8 Gene Mayer
9 Yannick Noah
10 Peter McNamara

1983
1 John McEnroe
2 Ivan Lendl
3 Jimmy Connors
4 Mats Wilander
5 Yannick Noah
6 Jimmy Arias
7 Jose Higueras
8 Jose-Luis Clerc
9 Kevin Curren
10 Gene Mayer

1984
1 John McEnroe
2 Jimmy Connors
3 Ivan Lendl
4 Mats Wilander
5 Andres Gomez
6 Anders Jarryd
7 Henrik Sundstrom
8 Pat Cash
9 Eliot Teltscher
10 Yannick Noah

1985
1 Ivan Lendl
2 John McEnroe
3 Mats Wilander
4 Jimmy Connors
5 Stefan Edberg
6 Boris Becker
7 Yannick Noah
8 Anders Jarryd
9 Miloslav Mecir
10 Kevin Curren

1986
1 Ivan Lendl
2 Boris Becker
3 Mats Wilander
4 Yannick Noah
5 Stefan Edberg
6 Henri Leconte
7 Joakim Nystrom
8 Jimmy Connors
9 Miloslav Mecir
10 Andres Gomez

1987
1 Ivan Lendl
2 Stefan Edberg
3 Mats Wilander
4 Jimmy Connors
5 Boris Becker
6 Miloslav Mecir
7 Pat Cash
8 Yannick Noah
9 Tim Mayotte
10 John McEnroe

1988
1 Mats Wilander
2 Ivan Lendl
3 Andre Agassi
4 Boris Becker
5 Stefan Edberg
6 Kent Carlsson
7 Jimmy Connors
8 Jakob Hlasek
9 Henri Leconte
10 Tim Mayotte

1989
1 Ivan Lendl
2 Boris Becker
3 Stefan Edberg
4 John McEnroe
5 Michael Chang
6 Brad Gilbert
7 Andre Agassi
8 Aaron Krickstein
9 Alberto Mancini
10 Jay Berger

1990
1 Stefan Edberg
2 Boris Becker
3 Ivan Lendl
4 Andre Agassi
5 Pete Sampras
6 Andres Gomez
7 Thomas Muster
8 Emilio Sanchez
9 Goran Ivanisevic
10 Brad Gilbert

1991
1 Stefan Edberg
2 Jim Courier
3 Boris Becker
4 Michael Stich
5 Ivan Lendl
6 Pete Sampras
7 Guy Forget
8 Karel Novacek
9 Petr Korda
10 Andre Agassi

1992
1 Jim Courier
2 Stefan Edberg
3 Pete Sampras
4 Goran Ivanisevic
5 Boris Becker
6 Michael Chang
7 Petr Korda
8 Ivan Lendl
9 Andre Agassi
10 Richard Krajicek

1993
1 Pete Sampras
2 Michael Stich
3 Jim Courier
4 Sergi Bruguera
5 Stefan Edberg
6 Andrei Medvedev
7 Goran Ivanisevic
8 Michael Chang
9 Thomas Muster
10 Cedric Pioline

1994
1 Pete Sampras
2 Andre Agassi
3 Boris Becker
4 Sergi Bruguera
5 Goran Ivanisevic
6 Michael Chang
7 Stefan Edberg
8 Alberto Berasategui
9 Michael Stich
10 Todd Martin

1995
1 Pete Sampras
2 Andre Agassi
3 Thomas Muster
4 Boris Becker
5 Michael Chang
6 Yevgeny Kafelnikov
7 Thomas Enqvist
8 Jim Courier
9 Wayne Ferreira
10 Goran Ivanisevic

1996
1 Pete Sampras
2 Michael Chang
3 Yevgeny Kafelnikov
4 Goran Ivanisevic
5 Thomas Muster
6 Boris Becker
7 Richard Krajicek
8 Andre Agassi
9 Thomas Enqvist
10 Wayne Ferreira

1997
1 Pete Sampras
2 Patrick Rafter
3 Michael Chang
4 Jonas Bjorkman
5 Yevgeny Kafelnikov
6 Greg Rusedski
7 Carlos Moya
8 Sergi Bruguera
9 Thomas Muster
10 Marcelo Rios

1998
1 Pete Sampras
2 Marcelo Rios
3 Alex Corretja
4 Patrick Rafter
5 Carlos Moya
6 Andre Agassi
7 Tim Henman
8 Karol Kucera
9 Greg Rusedski
10 Richard Krajicek

WOMEN

1968
1 Billie Jean King
2 Virginia Wade
3 Nancy Richey
4 Maria Bueno
5 Margaret Court
6 Ann Jones
7 Judy Tegart
8 Annette du Plooy
9 Leslie Bowrey
10 Rosie Casals

1969
1 Margaret Court
2 Ann Jones
3 Billie Jean King
4 Nancy Richey
5 Julie Heldman
6 Rosie Casals
7 Kerry Melville
8 Peaches Bartkowicz
9 Virginia Wade
10 Leslie Bowrey

1970
1 Margaret Court
2 Billie Jean King
3 Rosie Casals
4 Virginia Wade
5 Helga Niessen
6 Kerry Melville
7 Julie Heldman
8 Karen Krantczke
9 Francoise Durr
10 Nancy R. Gunter

1971
1 Evonne Goolagong
2 Billie Jean King
3 Margaret Court
4 Rosie Casals
5 Kerry Melville
6 Virginia Wade
7 Judy Tagert
8 Francoise Durr
9 Helga N. Masthoff
10 Chris Evert

1972
1 Billie Jean King
2 Evonne Goolagong
3 Chris Evert
4 Margaret Court
5 Kerry Melville
6 Virginia Wade
7 Rosie Casals
8 Nancy R. Gunter
9 Francoise Durr
10 Linda Tuero

1973
1 Margaret S. Court
2 Billie Jean King
3 Evonne G. Cawley
4 Chris Evert
5 Rosie Casals
6 Virginia Wade
7 Kerry Reid
8 Nancy Richey
9 Julie Heldman
10 Helga Masthoff

1974
1 Billie Jean King
2 Evonne G. Cawley
3 Chris Evert
4 Virginia Wade
5 Julie Heldman
6 Rosie Casals
7 Kerry Reid
8 Olga Morozova
9 Lesley Hunt
10 Francoise Durr

1975
1 Chris Evert
2 Billie Jean King
3 Evonne G. Cawley
4 Martina Navratilova
5 Virginia Wade
6 Margaret S. Court
7 Olga Morozova
8 Nancy Richey
9 Francoise Durr
10 Rosie Casals

1976
1 Chris Evert
2 Evonne G. Cawley
3 Virginia Wade
4 Martina Navratilova
5 Sue Barker
6 Betty Stove
7 Dianne Balestrat
8 Mima Jausovec
9 Rosie Casals
10 Francoise Durr

1977
1 Chris Evert
2 Billie Jean King
3 Martina Navratilova
4 Virginia Wade
5 Sue Barker
6 Rosie Casals
7 Betty Stove
8 Dianne Balestrat
9 Wendy Turnbull
10 Kerry Reid

1978
1 Martina Navratilova
2 Chris Evert Lloyd
3 Evonne G. Cawley
4 Virginia Wade
5 Billie Jean King
6 Tracy Austin
7 Wendy Turnbull
8 Kerry Reid
9 Betty Stove
10 Dianne Balestrat

1979
1 Martina Navratilova
2 Chris Evert Lloyd
3 Tracy Austin
4 Evonne G. Cawley
5 Billie Jean King
6 Dianne Balestrat
7 Wendy Turnbull
8 Virginia Wade
9 Kerry Reid
10 Sue Barker

1980
1 Chris Evert Lloyd
2 Tracy Austin
3 Martina Navratilova
4 Hana Mandlikova
5 Evonne G. Cawley
6 Billie Jean King
7 Andrea Jaeger
8 Wendy Turnbull
9 Pam Shriver
10 Greer Stevens

1981
1 Chris Evert Lloyd
2 Tracy Austin
3 Martina Navratilova
4 Andrea Jaeger
5 Hana Mandlikova
6 Sylvia Hanika
7 Pam Shriver
8 Wendy Turnbull
9 Bettina Bunge
10 Barbara Potter

1982
1 Martina Navratilova
2 Chris Evert Lloyd
3 Andrea Jaeger
4 Tracy Austin
5 Wendy Turnbull
6 Pam Shriver
7 Hana Mandlikova
8 Barbara Potter
9 Bettina Bunge
10 Sylvia Hanika

1983
1 Martina Navratilova
2 Chris Evert Lloyd
3 Andrea Jaeger
4 Pam Shriver
5 Sylvia Hanika
6 Jo Durie
7 Bettina Bunge
8 Wendy Turnbull
9 Tracy Austin
10 Zina Garrison

1984
1 Martina Navratilova
2 Chris Evert Lloyd
3 Hana Mandlikova
4 Pam Shriver
5 Wendy Turnbull
6 Manuela Maleeva
7 Helena Sukova
8 Claudia Kohde-Kilsch
9 Zina Garrison
10 Kathy Jordan

1985
1 Martina Navratilova
2 Chris Evert Lloyd
3 Hana Mandlikova
4 Pam Shriver
5 Claudia Kohde-Kilsch
6 Steffi Graf
7 Manuela Maleeva
8 Zina Garrison
9 Helena Sukova
10 Bonnie Gadusek

1986
1 Martina Navratilova
2 Chris Evert Lloyd
3 Steffi Graf
4 Hana Mandlikova
5 Helena Sukova
6 Pam Shriver
7 Claudia Kohde-Kilsch
8 M. Maleeva-Fragniere
9 Zina Garrison
10 Claudia Kohde-Kilsch

1987
1 Steffi Graf
2 Martina Navratilova
3 Chris Evert
4 Pam Shriver
5 Hana Mandlikova
6 Gabriela Sabatini
7 Helena Sukova
8 M. Maleeva-Fragniere
9 Zina Garrison
10 Claudia Kohde-Kilsch

1988
1 Steffi Graf
2 Martina Navratilova
3 Chris Evert
4 Gabriela Sabatini
5 Pam Shriver
6 M. Maleeva-Fragniere
7 Natalia Zvereva
8 Helena Sukova
9 Zina Garrison
10 Barbara Potter

1989
1 Steffi Graf
2 Martina Navratilova
3 Gabriela Sabatini
4 Z. Garrison-Jackson
5 A. Sanchez Vicario
6 Monica Seles
7 Conchita Martinez
8 Helena Sukova
9 M. Maleeva-Fragniere
10 Chris Evert

1990
1 Steffi Graf
2 Monica Seles
3 Martina Navratilova
4 Mary Joe Fernandez
5 Gabriela Sabatini
6 Katerina Maleeva
7 A. Sanchez Vicario
8 Jennifer Capriati
9 M. Maleeva-Fragniere
10 Z. Garrison-Jackson

1991
1 Monica Seles
2 Steffi Graf
3 Gabriela Sabatini
4 Martina Navratilova
5 A. Sanchez Vicario
6 Jennifer Capriati
7 Jana Novotna
8 Mary Joe Fernandez
9 Conchita Martinez
10 M. Maleeva-Fragniere

Annual Top 10 World Rankings (since 1968) (Cont.)
WOMEN

1992
1 Monica Seles
2 Steffi Graf
3 Gabriela Sabatini
4 A. Sanchez Vicario
5 Martina Navratilova
6 Mary Joe Fernandez
7 Jennifer Capriati
8 Conchita Martinez
9 M. Maleeva-Fragniere
10 Jana Novotna

1993
1 Steffi Graf
2 A. Sanchez Vicario
3 Martina Navratilova
4 Conchita Martinez
5 Gabriela Sabatini
6 Jana Novotna
7 Mary Joe Fernandez
8 Monica Seles
9 Jennifer Capriati
10 Anke Huber

1994
1 Steffi Graf
2 A. Sanchez Vicario
3 Conchita Martinez
4 Jana Novotna
5 Mary Pierce
6 Lindsay Davenport
7 Gabriela Sabatini
8 Martina Navratilova
9 Kimiko Date
10 Natasha Zvereva

1995
1 Steffi Graf
  Monica Seles
2 Conchita Martinez
3 A. Sanchez Vicario
4 Kimiko Date
5 Mary Pierce
6 Magdalena Maleeva
7 Gabriela Sabatini
8 Mary Joe Fernandez
9 Iva Majoli
10 Anke Huber

1996
1 Steffi Graf
2 Monica Seles
  A. Sanchez Vicario
3 Jana Novotna
4 Martina Hingis
5 Conchita Martinez
6 Anke Huber
7 Iva Majoli
8 Kimiko Date
9 Lindsay Davenport
10 Barbara Paulus

1997
1 Martina Hingis
2 Jana Novotna
3 Lindsay Davenport
4 Amanda Coetzer
5 Monica Seles
6 Iva Majoli
7 Mary Pierce
8 Irina Spirlea
9 A. Sanchez Vicario
10 Mary Joe Fernandez

1998
1 Lindsay Davenport
2 Martina Hingis
3 Jana Novotna
4 A. Sanchez Vicario
5 Venus Williams
6 Monica Seles
7 Mary Pierce
8 Conchita Martinez
9 Steffi Graf
10 Nathalie Tauziat

All-Time Singles Leaders
Tournaments Won

All-time tournament wins from the arrival of open tennis in 1968 through 1998. Men's totals include ATP Tour, Grand Prix and WCT tournaments. Players active in singles play in 1999 are in **bold** type.

MEN

		Total
1	Jimmy Connors	109
2	Ivan Lendl	94
3	John McEnroe	77
4	Bjorn Borg	62
	Guillermo Vilas	62
6	Ilie Nastase	57
7	**Pete Sampras**	56
8	**Boris Becker**	49
9	Rod Laver	47
10	**Thomas Muster**	44
11	Stefan Edberg	41
12	**Andre Agassi**	39
	Stan Smith	39
14	Arthur Ashe	33
	Michael Chang	33
	Mats Wilander	33
17	John Newcombe	32
	Manuel Orantes	32
	Ken Rosewall	32
20	Tom Okker	31
21	Vitas Gerulaitis	27
22	Jose-Luis Clerc	25
	Brian Gottfried	25
24	**Jim Courier**	23
	Yannick Noah	23
26	Eddie Dibbs	22
	Harold Solomon	22
28	Andres Gomez	21
	Goran Ivanisevic	21
30	Brad Gilbert	20

WOMEN

		Total
1	Martina Navratilova	167
2	Chris Evert	154
3	**Steffi Graf**	105
4	Margaret Court	92
5	Billie Jean King	67
6	E. Goolagong Cawley	65
7	Virginia Wade	55
8	**Monica Seles**	43
9	**Conchita Martinez**	30
10	Tracy Austin	29
11	Hana Mandlikova	27
	Gabriela Sabatini	27
13	**A. Sanchez Vicario**	26
14	Nancy Richey	25
15	**Jana Novotna**	23
16	Kerry Melville Reid	22
17	Pam Shriver	21
18	Julie Heldman	20
19	**Martina Hingis**	19
	M. Maleeva-Fragniere	19
21	**Lindsay Davenport**	18
22	Virginia Ruzici	17
	Regina Marsikova	17
24	Sue Barker	15
25	Peaches Bartkowicz	14
	Andrea Jaeger	14
	Sandra Cecchini	14
	Z. Garrison Jackson	14

Money Won

All-time money winners from the arrival of open tennis in 1968 through 1998. Totals include doubles earnings.

MEN

		Earnings			Earnings			Earnings
1	Pete Sampras	$35,992,155	11	Yevgeny Kafelnikov	$12,147,818	21	Wayne Ferreira	$6,474,974
2	Boris Becker	24,905,117	12	Thomas Muster	12,129,429	22	Paul Haarhuis	6,448,674
3	Ivan Lendl	21,262,417	13	Sergi Bruguera	11,252,155	23	Marcelo Rios	6,135,603
4	Stefan Edberg	20,630,941	14	Petr Korda	10,427,102	24	Jonas Bjorkman	6,134,727
5	Goran Ivanisevic	17,747,714	15	Jimmy Connors	8,641,040	25	Jakob Hlasek	5,784,225
6	Michael Chang	17,451,053	16	Richard Krajicek	8,054,963	26	Guy Forget	5,660,579
7	Andre Agassi	15,049,896	17	Mats Wilander	7,976,256	27	Todd Martin	5,596,692
8	Jim Courier	13,580,422	18	Mark Woodforde	7,463,551	28	Alex Corretja	5,547,784
9	Michael Stich	12,628,890	19	Patrick Rafter	7,382,729	29	Brad Gilbert	5,509,060
10	John McEnroe	12,539,622	20	Todd Woodbridge	6,865,044	30	Anders Jarryd	5,377,067

WOMEN

		Earnings			Earnings			Earnings
1	Steffi Graf	$20,646,410	11	Lindsay Davenport	$6,755,689	21	Lori McNeil	$3,399,932
2	Mart. Navratilova	20,344,061	12	Helena Sukova	6,391,245	22	Anke Huber	3,392,342
3	A. Sanchez Vicario	14,119,642	13	Pam Shriver	5,460,566	23	Hana Mandlikova	3,340,959
4	Monica Seles	10,928,640	14	Mary Joe Fernandez	4,993,771	24	M. Maleeva-Fragniere	3,244,811
5	Jana Novotna	10,507,680	15	Gigi Fernandez	4,681,906	25	Amanda Coetzer	3,172,951
6	Chris Evert	8,896,195	16	Z. Garrison Jackson	4,590,816	26	Wendy Turnbull	2,769,024
7	Gabriela Sabatini	8,785,850	17	Nathalie Tauziat	4,082,224	27	B. Schultz-McCarthy	2,552,518
8	Martina Hingis	8,331,496	18	Mary Pierce	3,965,201	28	Venus Williams	2,266,527
9	Conchita Martinez	7,780,941	19	Larisa Neiland	3,748,894	29	Irina Spirlea	2,260,666
10	Natasha Zvereva	7,036,143	20	Iva Majoli	3,464,778	30	Claudia Kohde-Klisch	2,227,116

Year-end Tournaments

MEN

Masters/ATP Tour World Championship

The year-end championship of the ATP men's tour since 1970. Contested by the year's top eight players. Originally a round-robin, the Masters was revised in 1972 to include a round-robin to decide the four semifinalists then a single elimination format after that. The tournament switched from December to January in 1977-78, then back to December in 1986. Held at Madison Square Garden in New York from 1978-89. Replaced by ATP Tour World Championship in 1990 and held in Frankfurt, Germany since then.

Multiple Winners: Ivan Lendl (5); Ilie Nastase and Pete Sampras (4); Boris Becker and John McEnroe (3); Bjorn Borg (2).

Year	Winner		Runner-Up		Year	Winner	Loser	Score
1970	Stan Smith (4-1)		Rod Laver (4-1)		1985	John McEnroe	I. Lendl	75 60 64
1971	Ilie Nastase (6-0)		Stan Smith (4-2)		1986	Ivan Lendl	B. Becker	62 76 63

Year	Winner	Loser	Score		Year	Winner	Loser	Score
1972	Ilie Nastase	S. Smith	63 62 36 26 63		1986	Ivan Lendl	B. Becker	64 64 64
1973	Ilie Nastase	T. Okker	63 75 46 63		1987	Ivan Lendl	M. Wilander	57 76 36 62 76
1974	Guillermo Vilas	I. Nastase	76 62 36 36 64		1988	Boris Becker	I. Lendl	57 76 36 62 76
1975	Ilie Nastase	B. Borg	62 62 61		1989	Stefan Edberg	B. Becker	46 76 63 61
1976	Manuel Orantes	W. Fibak	57 62 06 76 61		1990	Andre Agassi	S. Edberg	57 76 75 62
1978	Jimmy Connors	B. Borg	64 16 64		1991	Pete Sampras	J. Courier	36 76 63 64
1979	John McEnroe	A. Ashe	67 63 75		1992	Boris Becker	J. Courier	64 63 75
1980	Bjorn Borg	V. Gerulaitis	62 62		1993	Michael Stich	P. Sampras	76 26 76 62
1981	Bjorn Borg	I. Lendl	64 62 62		1994	Pete Sampras	B. Becker	46 63 75 64
1982	Ivan Lendl	V. Gerulaitis	67 26 76 62 64		1995	Boris Becker	M. Chang	76 60 76
1983	Ivan Lendl	J. McEnroe	64 64 62		1996	Pete Sampras	B. Becker	36 76 76 67 64
1984	John McEnroe	I. Lendl	63 64 64		1997	Pete Sampras	Y. Kafelnikov	63 62 62
					1998	Alex Corretja	C. Moya	36 36 75 63 75

Note: In 1970, Smith was declared the winner because he beat Laver in their round-robin match (4-6, 6-3, 6-4).

WCT Championship (1971-89)

World Championship Tennis was established in 1967 to promote professional tennis and led the way into the open era. It's major singles and doubles championships were held every May among the top eight regular season finishers on the circuit from 1971 until the WCT folded in 1989.

Multiple winners: John McEnroe (5), Jimmy Connors, Ivan Lendl and Ken Rosewall (2).

Year	Winner	Loser	Score		Year	Winner	Loser	Score
1971	Ken Rosewall	R. Laver	64 16 76 76		1974	John Newcombe	B. Borg	46 63 63 62
1972	Ken Rosewall	R. Laver	46 60 63 67 76		1975	Arthur Ashe	B. Borg	36 64 64 60
1973	Stan Smith	A. Ashe	63 63 46 64		1976	Bjorn Borg	G. Vilas	16 61 75 61

Year	Winner	Loser	Score	Year	Winner	Loser	Score
1977	Jimmy Connors	D. Stockton	67 61 64 63	1984	John McEnroe	J. Connors	61 62 63
1978	Vitas Gerulaitis	E. Dibbs	63 62 61	1985	Ivan Lendl	T. Mayotte	76 64 61
1979	John McEnroe	B. Borg	75 46 62 76	1986	Anders Jarryd	B. Becker	67 61 61 64
1980	Jimmy Connors	J. McEnroe	26 76 61 62	1987	Miloslav Mercir	J. McEnroe	60 36 62 62
1981	John McEnroe	J. Kriek	61 62 64	1988	Boris Becker	S. Edberg	64 16 75 62
1982	Ivan Lendl	J. McEnroe	62 36 63 63	1989	John McEnroe	B. Gilbert	63 63 76
1983	John McEnroe	I. Lendl	62 46 63 67 76				

WOMEN
WTA Tour Championship

Originally the Virginia Slims Championships from 1971-94. The WTA Tour's year-end tournament took place in March from 1972 until 1986 when the WTA decided to adopt a January-to-November playing season. Given the changeover, two championships were held in 1986. Held every year since 1979 at Madison Square Garden in New York.

Multiple winners: Martina Navratilova (8); Steffi Graf (5); Chris Evert (4); Monica Seles (3); Evonne Goolagong and Gabriela Sabatini (2).

Year	Winner	Loser	Score	Year	Winner	Loser	Score
1972	Chris Evert	K. Reid	75 64	1986	M. Navratilova	S. Graf	76 63 62
1973	Chris Evert	N. Richey	63 63	1987	Steffi Graf	G. Sabatini	46 64 60 64
1974	Evonne Goolagong	C. Evert	63 64	1988	Gabriela Sabatini	P. Shriver	75 62 62
1975	Chris Evert	M. Navratilova	64 62	1989	Steffi Graf	M. Navratilova	64 75 26 62
1976	Evonne Goolagong	C. Evert	63 57 63	1990	Monica Seles	G. Sabatini	64 57 36 64 62
1977	Chris Evert	S. Barker	26 61 61	1991	Monica Seles	M. Navratilova	64 36 75 60
1978	M. Navratilova	E. Goolagong	76 64	1992	Monica Seles	M. Navratilova	75 63 61
1979	M. Navratilova	T. Austin	63 36 62	1993	Steffi Graf	A. S. Vicario	61 64 36 61
1980	Tracy Austin	M. Navratilova	62 26 62	1994	Gabriela Sabatini	L. Davenport	63 62 64
1981	M. Navratilova	A. Jaeger	63 76	1995	Steffi Graf	A. Huber	61 26 61 46 63
1982	Sylvia Hanika	M. Navratilova	16 63 64	1996	Steffi Graf	M. Hingis	63 46 60 46 60
1983	M. Navratilova	C. Evert	62 60	1997	Jana Novotna	M. Pierce	76 62 63
1984	M. Navratilova	C. Evert	63 75 61	1998	Martina Hingis	L. Davenport	75 64 46 62
1985	M. Navratilova	H. Sukova	63 75 64				
1986	M. Navratilova	H. Mandlikova	62 60 36 61				

*Two tournaments in 1986 due to change in playing season.

Davis Cup

Established in 1900 as an annual international tournament by American player Dwight Davis. Originally called the International Lawn Tennis Challenge Trophy. Challenge round system until 1972. Since 1981, the top 16 nations in the world have played a straight knockout tournament over the course of a year. The format is a best-of-five match of two singles, one doubles and two singles over three days. Note that from 1900-24 Australia and New Zealand competed together as Australasia.

Multiple winners: USA (31); Australia (20); France (8); Sweden (7); Australasia (6); British Isles (5); Britain (4); Germany (3).

Challenge Rounds

Year	Winner	Loser	Score	Site	Year	Winner	Loser	Score	Site
1900	USA	British Isles	3-0	Boston	1930	France	USA	4-1	Paris
1901	Not held				1931	France	Britain	3-2	Paris
1902	USA	British Isles	3-2	New York	1932	France	USA	3-2	Paris
1903	British Isles	USA	4-1	Boston	1933	Britain	France	3-2	Paris
1904	British Isles	Belgium	5-0	Wimbledon	1934	Britain	USA	4-1	Wimbledon
1905	British Isles	USA	5-0	Wimbledon	1935	Britain	USA	5-0	Wimbledon
1906	British Isles	USA	5-0	Wimbledon	1936	Britain	Australia	3-2	Wimbledon
1907	Australasia	British Isles	3-2	Wimbledon	1937	USA	Britain	4-1	Wimbledon
1908	Australasia	USA	3-2	Melbourne	1938	USA	Australia	3-2	Philadelphia
1909	Australasia	USA	5-0	Sydney	1939	Australia	USA	3-2	Philadelphia
1910	Not held				1940-45	Not held	World War II		
1911	Australasia	USA	5-0	Christchurch, NZ	1946	USA	Australia	5-0	Melbourne
1912	British Isles	Australasia	3-2	Melbourne	1947	USA	Australia	4-1	New York
1913	USA	British Isles	3-2	Wimbledon	1948	USA	Australia	5-0	New York
1914	Australasia	USA	3-2	New York	1949	USA	Australia	4-1	New York
1915-18	Not held	World War I			1950	Australia	USA	4-1	New York
1919	Australasia	British Isles	4-1	Sydney	1951	Australia	USA	3-2	Sydney
1920	USA	Australasia	5-0	Auckland, NZ	1952	Australia	USA	4-1	Adelaide
1921	USA	Japan	5-0	New York	1953	Australia	USA	3-2	Melbourne
1922	USA	Australasia	4-1	New York	1954	USA	Australia	3-2	Sydney
1923	USA	Australasia	4-1	New York	1955	Australia	USA	5-0	New York
1924	USA	Australia	5-0	Philadelphia	1956	Australia	USA	5-0	Adelaide
1925	USA	France	5-0	Philadelphia	1957	Australia	USA	3-2	Melbourne
1926	USA	France	4-1	Philadelphia	1958	USA	Australia	3-2	Brisbane
1927	France	USA	3-2	Philadelphia	1959	Australia	USA	3-2	New York
1928	France	USA	4-1	Paris	1960	Australia	Italy	4-1	Sydney
1929	France	USA	3-2	Paris	1961	Australia	Italy	5-0	Melbourne

Year	Winner	Loser	Score	Site	Year	Winner	Loser	Score	Site
1962	Australia	Mexico	5-0	Brisbane	1965	Australia	Spain	4-1	Sydney
1963	USA	Australia	3-2	Adelaide	1966	Australia	India	4-1	Melbourne
1964	Australia	USA	3-2	Cleveland	1967	Australia	Spain	4-1	Brisbane

Final Rounds

Year	Winner	Loser	Score	Site	Year	Winner	Loser	Score	Site
1968	USA	Australia	4-1	Adelaide	1984	Sweden	USA	4-1	Göteborg
1969	USA	Romania	5-0	Cleveland	1985	Sweden	W. Germany	3-2	Munich
1970	USA	W. Germany	5-0	Cleveland	1986	Australia	Sweden	3-2	Melbourne
1971	USA	Romania	3-2	Charlotte	1987	Sweden	India	5-0	Göteborg
1972	USA	Romania	3-2	Bucharest	1988	W. Germany	Sweden	4-1	Göteborg
1973	Australia	USA	5-0	Cleveland	1989	W. Germany	Sweden	3-2	Stuttgart
1974	So. Africa	India	walkover	Not held					
1975	Sweden	Czech.	3-2	Stockholm	1990	USA	Australia	3-2	St. Petersburg
1976	Italy	Chile	4-1	Santiago	1991	France	USA	3-1	Lyon
1977	Australia	Italy	3-1	Sydney	1992	USA	Switzerland	3-1	Ft. Worth
1978	USA	Britain	4-1	Palm Springs	1993	Germany	Australia	4-1	Dusseldorf
1979	USA	Italy	5-0	San Francisco	1994	Sweden	Russia	4-1	Moscow
					1995	USA	Russia	3-2	Moscow
1980	Czech.	Italy	4-1	Prague	1996	France	Sweden	3-2	Malmo
1981	USA	Argentina	3-1	Cincinnati	1997	Sweden	USA	5-0	Göteborg
1982	USA	France	4-1	Grenoble	1998	Sweden	Italy	4-1	Milan
1983	Australia	Sweden	3-2	Melbourne					

Note: In 1974, India refused to play the final as a protest against the South African government's policies of apartheid.

Fed Cup

Originally the Federation Cup and started in 1963 by the International Tennis Federation as the Davis Cup of women's tennis. Played by 32 teams over one week at one site through 1994. Tournament changed in 1995 to Davis Cup-style format of four rounds and home site.

Multiple winners: USA (16); Australia (7); Czechoslovakia and Spain (5); Germany (2).

Year	Winner	Loser	Score	Site	Year	Winner	Loser	Score	Site
1963	USA	Australia	2-1	London	1982	USA	W. Germany	3-0	Santa Clara
1964	Australia	USA	2-1	Philadelphia	1983	Czech.	W. Germany	2-1	Zurich
1965	Australia	USA	2-1	Melbourne	1984	Czech.	Australia	2-1	Brazil
1966	USA	W. Germany	3-0	Italy	1985	Czech.	USA	2-1	Japan
1967	USA	Britain	2-0	W. Germany	1986	US	Czech.	3-0	Prague
1968	Australia	Holland	3-0	Paris	1987	W. Germany	USA	2-1	Vancouver
1969	USA	Australia	2-1	Athens	1988	Czech.	USSR	2-1	Melbourne
1970	Australia	Britain	3-0	W. Germany	1989	USA	Spain	3-0	Tokyo
1971	Australia	Britain	3-0	Perth	1990	USA	USSR	2-1	Atlanta
1972	So. Africa	Britain	2-1	Africa	1991	Spain	USA	2-1	Nottingham
1973	Australia	So. Africa	3-0	W. Germany	1992	Germany	Spain	2-1	Frankfurt
1974	Australia	USA	2-1	Italy	1993	Spain	Australia	3-0	Frankfurt
1975	Czech.	Australia	3-0	France	1994	Spain	USA	3-0	Frankfurt
1976	USA	Australia	2-1	Philadelphia	1995	Spain	USA	3-2	Valencia
1977	USA	Australia	2-1	Eastbourne	1996	USA	Spain	5-0	Atlantic City
1978	USA	Australia	2-1	Melbourne	1997	France	Netherlands	4-1	Nice, France
1979	USA	Australia	3-0	Spain	1998	Spain	Switzerland	3-2	Geneva
1980	USA	Australia	3-0	W. Germany	1999	USA	Russia	4-1	Palo Alto
1981	USA	Britain	3-0	Tokyo					

COLLEGES

NCAA team titles were not sanctioned until 1946. NCAA women's individual and team championships started in 1982.

Men's NCAA Individual Champions (1883-1945)

Multiple winners: Malcolm Chace and Pancho Segura (3); Edward Chandler, George Church, E.B. Dewhurst, Fred Hovey, Frank Guernsey, W.P. Knapp, Robert LeRoy, P.S. Sears, Cliff Sutter, Ernest Sutter and Richard Williams (2).

Year		Year		Year	
1883	J. Clark, Harvard (spring)	1891	Fred Hovey, Harvard	1900	Ray Little, Princeton
	H. Taylor, Harvard (fall)	1892	William Larned, Cornell	1901	Fred Alexander, Princeton
1884	W.P. Knapp, Yale	1893	Malcolm Chace, Brown	1902	William Clothier, Harvard
1885	W.P. Knapp, Yale	1894	Malcolm Chace, Yale	1903	E.B. Dewhurst, Penn
1886	G.M. Brinley, Trinity, CT	1895	Malcolm Chace, Yale	1904	Robert LeRoy, Columbia
1887	P.S. Sears, Harvard	1896	Malcolm Whitman, Harvard	1905	E.B. Dewhurst, Penn
1888	P.S. Sears, Harvard	1897	S.G. Thompson, Princeton	1906	Robert LeRoy, Columbia
1889	R.P. Huntington Jr, Yale	1898	Leo Ware, Harvard	1907	G.P. Gardner Jr, Harvard
1890	Fred Hovey, Harvard	1899	Dwight Davis, Harvard	1908	Nat Niles, Harvard

Year		Year		Year	
1909	Wallace Johnson, Penn	1922	Lucien Williams, Yale	1934	Gene Mako, USC
		1923	Carl Fischer, Phi. Osteo.	1935	Wilbur Hess, Rice
1910	R.A. Holden Jr, Yale	1924	Wallace Scott, Wash.	1936	Ernest Sutter, Tulane
1911	E.H. Whitney, Harvard	1925	Edward Chandler, Calif.	1937	Ernest Sutter, Tulane
1912	George Church, Princeton	1926	Edward Chandler, Calif.	1938	Frank Guernsey, Rice
1913	Richard Williams, Harv.	1927	Wilmer Allison, Texas	1939	Frank Guernsey, Rice
1914	George Church, Princeton	1928	Julius Seligson, Lehigh		
1915	Richard Williams, Harv.	1929	Berkeley Bell, Texas	1940	Don McNeill, Kenyon
1916	G.C. Caner, Harvard			1941	Joseph Hunt, Navy
1917-1918	Not held	1930	Cliff Sutter, Tulane	1942	Fred Schroeder, Stanford
1919	Charles Garland, Yale	1931	Keith Gledhill, Stanford	1943	Pancho Segura, Miami-FL
		1932	Cliff Sutter, Tulane	1944	Pancho Segura, Miami-FL
1920	Lascelles Banks, Yale	1933	Jack Tidball, UCLA	1945	Pancho Segura, Miami-FL
1921	Philip Neer, Stanford				

NCAA Men's Division I Champions

Multiple winners (Teams): Stanford (16); UCLA and USC (15); Georgia (3); William & Mary (2). (Players): Alex Olmedo, Mikael Pernfors, Dennis Ralston and Ham Richardson (2).

Year	Team winner	Individual Champion	Year	Team winner	Individual Champion
1946	USC	Bob Falkenburg, USC	1973	Stanford	Alex Mayer, Stanford
1947	Wm. & Mary	Garner Larned, Wm.& Mary	1974	Stanford	John Whitlinger, Stanford
1948	Wm. & Mary	Harry Likas, San Francisco	1975	UCLA	Bill Martin, UCLA
1949	San Francisco	Jack Tuero, Tulane	1976	USC & UCLA	Bill Scanlon, Trinity-TX
			1977	Stanford	Matt Mitchell, Stanford
1950	UCLA	Herbert Flam, UCLA	1978	Stanford	John McEnroe, Stanford
1951	USC	Tony Trabert, Cincinnati	1979	UCLA	Kevin Curren, Texas
1952	UCLA	Hugh Stewart, USC			
1953	UCLA	Ham Richardson, Tulane	1980	Stanford	Robert Van't Hof, USC
1954	UCLA	Ham Richardson, Tulane	1981	Stanford	Tim Mayotte, Stanford
1955	USC	Jose Aguero, Tulane	1982	UCLA	Mike Leach, Michigan
1956	UCLA	Alex Olmedo, USC	1983	Stanford	Greg Holmes, Utah
1957	Michigan	Barry MacKay, Michigan	1984	UCLA	Mikael Pernfors, Georgia
1958	USC	Alex Olmedo, USC	1985	Georgia	Mikael Pernfors, Georgia
1959	Tulane & Notre Dame	Whitney Reed, San Jose St.	1986	Stanford	Dan Goldie, Stanford
			1987	Georgia	Andrew Burrow, Miami-FL
1960	UCLA	Larry Nagler, UCLA	1988	Stanford	Robby Weiss, Pepperdine
1961	UCLA	Allen Fox, UCLA	1989	Stanford	Donni Leaycraft, LSU
1962	USC	Rafael Osuna, USC			
1963	USC	Dennis Ralston, USC	1990	Stanford	Steve Bryan, Texas
1964	USC	Dennis Ralston, USC	1991	USC	Jared Palmer, Stanford
1965	UCLA	Arthur Ashe, UCLA	1992	Stanford	Alex O'Brien Stanford
1966	USC	Charlie Pasarell, UCLA	1993	USC	Chris Woodruff, Tennessee
1967	USC	Bob Lutz, USC	1994	USC	Mark Merklein, Florida
1968	USC	Stan Smith, USC	1995	Stanford	Sargis Sargisian, Ariz. St.
1969	USC	Joaquin Loyo-Mayo, USC	1996	Stanford	Cecil Mamiit, USC
1970	UCLA	Jeff Borowiak, UCLA	1997	Stanford	Luke Smith, UNLV
1971	UCLA	Jimmy Connors, UCLA	1998	Stanford	Bob Bryan, Stanford
1972	Trinity-TX	Dick Stockton, Trinity-TX	1999	Georgia	Jeff Morrison, Florida

NCAA Women's Division I Champions

Multiple winners (Teams): Stanford (10); Florida (3); Texas and USC (2). (Players): Sandra Birch, Patty Fendick and Lisa Raymond (2).

Year	Team winner	Individual Champion	Year	Team winner	Individual Champion
1982	Stanford	Alycia Moulton, Stanford	1992	Florida	Lisa Raymond, Florida
1983	USC	Beth Herr, USC	1993	Texas	Lisa Raymond, Florida
1984	Stanford	Lisa Spain, Georgia	1994	Georgia	Angela Lettiere, Georgia
1985	USC	Linda Gates, Stanford	1995	Texas	Keri Phoebus, UCLA
1986	Stanford	Patty Fendick, Stanford	1996	Florida	Jill Craybas, Florida
1987	Stanford	Patty Fendick, Stanford	1997	Stanford	Lilia Osterloh, Stanford
1988	Stanford	Shaun Stafford, Florida	1998	Florida	Vanessa Webb, Duke
1989	Stanford	Sandra Birch, Stanford	1999	Stanford	Zuzana Lesenarova, S.
1990	Stanford	Debbie Graham, Stanford			Diego
1991	Stanford	Sandra Birch, Stanford			

Golf

Justin Leonard sparks a controversial premature celebration for the Americans after sinking a 40-foot birdie putt on 17 at The Country Club.

AP/Wide World Photos

America's Cup

The United States' comeback on Sunday at Brookline is a fitting end to one of the wilder years in golf.

by
Jimmy Roberts

Golf in 1999 was a lot like that old R.E.M. song: "It's the End of the World as We Know It." Three new world championship events was just the first step we were told. Golf was about to go global. What the PGA Tour fought tooth and nail just a few years ago when the idea was raised by a Greg Norman-fronted group...it now embraced.

If this was in fact the beginning of the end for the way things have been, remember what the song goes on to say: "I feel fine."

Who wouldn't? After all, a new television deal took total prize money for the year to more than $134 million. David Duval won the money title in 1998 with $2.5 million. In 1999, Tiger Woods roared past that number with three months yet to go in the season!

Even though some predicted 1999 would be not much more than a mer-

cenary bacchanalia, it instead turned out to be a season infused with great emotion, drama and significance.

Before spring's first azalea even bloomed, it looked like we might have the story of the year. It wasn't only that Duval won two of the year's first three events, or four of the first eight he entered, it was the way he got it done — typified by a final round 59 at the Bob Hope Chrysler Classic. But Duval's personal run ended the week before the Masters, and then as usual, the big four seized the spotlight.

In 1996, Greg Norman had frittered away a six-stroke final-day lead to Nick Faldo. The Shark's 78 on Sunday was one of the great final round collapses in sports history. Eventually he needed radical shoulder surgery. Former champion Jose Maria Olazabal (1994) wasn't even entered that year. A mysterious foot ailment had him bedridden. At the time, it was questionable as to whether or not he would ever play golf again. And yet

---

Jimmy Roberts covers golf for ESPN.

AP/Wide World Photos

"I just have a feeling about tomorrow," said American Ryder Cup captain **Ben Crenshaw** (center) on Saturday night with the Americans trailing 10-6. Nostradamus has nothing on Crenshaw as his squad crushed the Europeans 8½ to 3½ in singles matches on Sunday to bring the Cup back to the United States for the first time since they lost it in 1995.

here were these two golfing legends, risen from the ashes and playing together in Sunday's final group, battling back and forth until Olazabal finally prevailed.

At Pinehurst, Sunday's final pair also put an electric and emotional charge into the U.S. Open. Phil Mickelson had said he would pick up and go home, no matter what his position, if the beeper in his pocket went off. His wife was pregnant with the couple's first child, whose birth was imminent. A year earlier, Payne Stewart led all four rounds, only to miss a playoff when he couldn't convert a putt on the 72nd hole. This time, he made crucial putts on 16, 17 and 18 to collect his third major title. Mickelson was bitterly disappointed, until the next day when Amanda Brynn was

born at 6:11 p.m. It was the best Father's Day present he could have ever hoped for.

They hadn't played the British Open at Carnoustie in 24 years, and thus many expected a memorable event. What they got was a tournament dominated by high scores and player complaints of an unfair course ...until the last day. Frenchman Jean Van de Velde was cruising along with the title seemingly in hand. He stood on the 18th tee needing only a double-bogey six to claim the Claret Jug. But needlessly aggressive play resulted in a seven. Who will ever forget the sight of Van de Velde, pants rolled up, walking into the "Barry Burn" to consider hitting his fourth shot out of the water. Local hero Paul Lawrie, who started the final day 10 shots off the

AP/Wide World Photos

Spain's **Sergio Garcia** completely disregards the "keep your eye on the ball" rule as he blasts away on the 16th hole at the PGA Championship. The shot landed on the green and El Nino came away with a par for the hole as he finished runner-up to Tiger Woods at Medinah.

lead, went on to win in a playoff over Van de Velde and Justin Leonard.

The PGA at Medinah was simply Tiger's coronation. His dangerous downhill putt on the 71st hole was the crucial shot to hold off a hard charging Sergio Garcia, who had entirely seduced the crowd and given birth to a new phenomenon: American galleries rooting *against* Woods.

As good as the majors were, they were simply an opening act to the year's most dramatic and complicated event. The U.S. went into Sunday of the Ryder Cup trailing by four points. No team had ever rallied from that far back. But the Americans won eight of the 12 matches Sunday, and when Justin Leonard sank a 40-foot putt on 17, he not only secured the half point that won the cup, but set off a wild and premature celebration that became a

topic far beyond the boundaries of sport — an emphatic punctuation mark for a truly memorable year. ■

Jimmy Roberts' Top Ten Newsmakers of the Year in Golf

10. **Jim Awtrey.** The CEO of the PGA of America successfully navigated the Ryder Cup "pay for play" issue, a controversy which could have torn the team apart...and almost did.

9. **Bruce Fleisher.** He won the U.S. Amateur in 1968, and then his only PGA tour title 23 years later. He was a journeyman until he took life's mulligan: the Senior Tour, where he has been a dominating and somewhat surprising force.

8. **Carlos Franco.** Paraguay has a total of three golf courses. That didn't stop him from making it through Q-school (in the end, putting with his driver) or winning twice in 1999. Not bad for a guy who thinks practice is overrated.

7. **John Daly.** A talented and tragic figure who forfeited millions in endorsements saying he wanted to drink and gamble because, "It's in my blood."

6. **Justin Leonard.** He's won a U.S. Amateur, a Players Championship and a British Open, but what happened on the 17th green at Brookline has got to be the biggest thing that's ever happened in his golfing life.

5. **Jean Van de Velde.** His bizarre odyssey on the 72nd hole at Carnoustie and the good natured way in which he reacted leave him indelibly (and dubiously) seared in our memory.

4. **Sergio Garcia.** El Nino provided the year's charismatic spark. His shot from in back of a tree on the 16th hole at the PGA was one of the most remarkable shots in the history of major-tournament golf.

3. **David Duval.** A few years back, people wondered whether he would ever get over the hump and actually win a tournament. Better question through the first quarter of this year: If Duval's in the field, should anybody else have even bothered entering?

2. **Ben Crenshaw.** When he exited the media room Saturday night of the Ryder Cup by saying: "I just have a feeling about tomorrow," most of us thought it was simply

AP/Wide World Photos

Ouch! France's **Jean Van de Velde** can only smile as he stands in the burn that crosses the 18th fairway at Carnoustie. That little white thing under water would be his ball. Needing only a double-bogey on 18 to win the British Open, Van de Velde came away with a triple to force a three-way play-off, which he lost.

the captain trying to maintain a brave front. After all, no team in the 72-year history of the event had ever come back from this large a final-day deficit. Chances are, people will listen a lot more carefully when Crenshaw talks from now on...no matter what he says.

1. **Tiger Woods.** As if you could possibly finish anywhere else. A year after a one-win season in which people wondered whether or not he might be overrated, Woods answered with a dominating multi-win season, including a tenacious performance to win his second major at the PGA Championship. ∎

THE NUMBERS

INSIDE

	Rounds	Avg. drive (yds)
John Daly	55	305.6
Chris Couch	65	295.8
Tiger Woods	63	294.5
Rory Sabbatini	75	292.3
Harrison Frazar	89	290.5

OLD TIMERS, BIG EARNERS

While most guys their age are thinking about whether they can afford to retire a little early, some of the Senior PGA Tour players are making more money than ever, more in fact than the players that are supposed to be in their primes. Four times the Senior PGA Tour leader has outearned the PGA Tour leader. Here's a look at the Seniors to outearn their younger counterparts.

Yr.	Senior Leader	Total (000's)	PGA Leader	Total (000's)
90	L. Trevino	$1,191	G. Norman	$1,165
91	M. Hill	1,066	C. Pavin	979
97	H. Irwin	2,343	T. Woods	2,067
98	H. Irwin	2,862	D. Duval	2,591

SOFA WITH A SECRET

Everyone knows John Daly's reputation for being a big hitter. Tiger Woods is also famous for, among other things, his gargantuan blasts off the tee. But who in the wide, wide world of sports is Chris Couch? Couch, whose best PGA Tour finish so far was his tie for seventh at the 1999 Sony Open in Hawaii, is among golf's biggest hitters, even outdriving Woods.

THE BEST EVER?

David Duval tied the PGA Tour record when he carded an amazing 59 in the final round of the Bob Hope Chrysler Classic. Was it the best round of golf ever played? It's debatable considering it wasn't in a major tournament or on a notoriously challenging course like Johnny Miller's 63 in the 1973 U.S. Open or Ben Hogan's 67 in the 1951 U.S. Open. Here is a look at the lowest rounds in PGA Tour history.

Score	Round
59	Al Geiberger 2nd, 1977 Memphis Classic
59	Chip Beck 3rd, 1991 Las Vegas Invit.
59	David Duval 4th, 1999 Bob Hope Chrysler
60	Eleven tied

LONG ONE

Tyler Cundith, sports information director at Johnson County (Kan.) CC, knew he hit a good drive on the sixth hole at Oak County Golf Course in DeSoto, Kan. on July 20, 1999. He didn't know how good he hit the ball on the 488-yard dogleg par-5 until he found it—in the cup. The conditions were near perfect. The wind was at his back and the fairways were hard and dry from the summer sun. He played a slight hook over some trees and estimates he cut the distance to around 390 yards.

Yards	Dogleg Record	Date
496	Shaun Lynch, Teign Valley GC, Exeter, England	July 24, 1995
	Non-Dogleg Record	
447	Robert Mitera, Miracle Hills GC, Omaha, Neb.	Oct. 7, 1965

■

THE 2000 — ESPN INFORMATION PLEASE SPORTS ALMANAC

GOLF STATISTICS

SEC A

THE SEASON IN REVIEW
1998-1999
PGA • SENIORS • LPGA

PAGE 847

Tournament Results

Schedules and results of PGA, European PGA, PGA Seniors and LPGA tournaments in 1999.

PGA Tour

LATE 1998

Last Rd	Tournament	Winner	Earnings	Runner-Up
Nov. 1	The Tour Championship	Hal Sutton (274)*	$720,000	V. Singh (274)
Nov. 8	Sarazen World Open	Dudley Hart (272)	360,000	B. Tway (276)
Nov. 15	Shark Shootout	Steve Elkington/ Greg Norman (189)*	160,000 each	J. Cook/P. Jacobson (189)
Nov. 18	Grand Slam of Golf	Tiger Woods (2-up)	400,000	V. Singh
Nov. 29	The Skins Game	Mark O'Meara (8)	430,000	T. Lehman (7)
Dec. 6	JC Penney Classic	Meg Mallon/ Steve Pate (255)	218,750 each	R. Hetherington/R. Mediate (259)
Dec. 13	President's Cup	International Team (20½)	—	United States (11½)
Dec. 20	Wendy's Three-Tour Challenge	Senior PGA	100,000 each	PGA

*Playoffs: Tour Championship– Sutton won on 1st hole; **Shark–** Elkington/Norman won on the 3rd hole.

1999

Last Rd	Tournament	Winner	Earnings	Runner-Up
Jan. 10	Mercedes Championship	David Duval (266)	$468,000	M. O'Meara & B. Mayfair (275)
Jan. 17	Sony Open	Jeff Sluman (271)	468,000	5-way tie (273)
Jan. 24	Bob Hope Chrysler Classic	David Duval (334)	540,000	S. Pate (335)
Jan. 31	Phoenix Open	Rocco Mediate (273)	540,000	J. Leonard (275)
Feb. 7	AT&T Pebble Beach Pro-Am	Payne Stewart (206)#	504,000	F. Lickliter (207)
Feb. 14	Buick Invitational	Tiger Woods (266)	486,000	B. R. Brown (268)
Feb. 21	Nissan Open	Ernie Els (270)	504,000	3-way tie (272)
Feb. 28	Match Play Championship	Jeff Maggert (1-up)*	1,000,000	A. McGee
Feb. 28	Tucson Open	Gabriel Hjertstedt (276)*	495,000	T. Armour III (276)
Mar. 7	Doral-Ryder Open	Steve Elkington (275)	540,000	G. Kraft (276)
Mar. 14	Honda Classic	Vijay Singh (277)	468,000	P. Stewart (279)
Mar. 21	Bay Hill Invitational	Tim Herron (274)*	450,000	T. Lehman (274)
Mar. 28	The Players Championship	David Duval (285)	900,000	S. Gump (287)
Apr. 4	BellSouth Classic	David Duval (270)	450,000	S. Cink (272)
Apr. 11	**The Masters** (Augusta, Ga.)	Jose Maria Olazabal (280)	720,000	D. Love III (282)
Apr. 18	MCI Classic	Glen Day (274)*	450,000	J. Sluman & P. Stewart (274)
Apr. 25	Gr. Greensboro Chrysler Classic	Jesper Parnevik (265)	468,000	J. Furyk (267)
May 2	Shell Houston Open	Stuart Appleby (279)	450,000	J. Cook & H. Sutton (280)
May 9	Compaq Classic	Carlos Franco (269)	468,000	H. Frazar & S. Flesch (271)
May 16	GTE Byron Nelson Classic	Loren Roberts (262)*	540,000	S. Pate (262)
May 23	MasterCard Colonial	Olin Browne (272)	504,000	5-way tie (273)
May 30	Kemper Open	Rich Beem (274)	450,000	B. Glasson & B. Hughes (275)
June 6	Memorial Tournament	Tiger Woods (273)	459,000	V. Singh (275)
June 13	Fed Ex St. Jude Classic	Ted Tryba (265)	450,000	T. Herron & T. Lehman (267)
June 20	**U.S. Open** (Pinehurst, N.C.)	Payne Stewart (279)	625,000	P. Mickelson (280)
June 27	Buick Classic	Duffy Waldorf (276)*	450,000	D. Paulson (276)
July 4	Motorola Western Open	Tiger Woods (273)	450,000	M. Weir (276)
July 11	Greater Milwaukee Open	Carlos Franco (264)	414,000	T. Lehman (266)
July 18	**British Open** (Carnoustie)	Paul Lawrie (290)*	577,500	J. Leonard & J. Van de Velde (290)
July 25	John Deere Classic	J.L. Lewis (261)*	360,000	M. Brisky (261)
Aug. 1	Canon Greater Hartford Open	Brent Geiberger (262)	450,000	S. Kendall (265)
Aug. 8	Buick Open	Tom Pernice Jr. (270)	432,000	3-way tie (271)

Tournament Results (Cont.)

Last Rd	Tournament	Winner	Earnings	Runner-Up
Aug. 15	**PGA Championship** (Medinah, Ill.)	Tiger Woods (277)	630,000	S. Garcia (278)
Aug. 22	Sprint International†	David Toms (47)	468,000	D. Duval (44)
Aug. 29	NEC Invitational	Tiger Woods (270)	1,000,000	P. Mickelson (271)
Aug. 29	Reno-Tahoe Open	Notah Begay III (274)	495,000	C. Perry & D. Toms (277)
Sept. 5	Air Canada Championship	Mike Weir (266)	450,000	F. Funk (268)
Sept. 12	Bell Canadian Open	Hal Sutton (275)	450,000	D. Paulson (278)
Sept. 19	B.C. Open	Brad Faxon (273)*	288,000	F. Funk (273)
Sept. 26	Westin Texas Open	Duffy Waldorf (270)*	360,000	T. Tryba (270)
Sept. 26	**Ryder Cup** (Brookline, Mass.)	United States (14½)	—	Europe (13½)
Oct. 3	Buick Challenge	David Toms (271)	324,000	S. Appleby (274)
Oct. 10	Michelob Championship	Notah Begay III (274)*	450,000	T. Byrum (274)

#Weather-shortened.

†The scoring for the Sprint International was based on a modified Stableford system (8 points for a double eagle, 5 for an eagle, 2 for a birdie, 0 for a par, –1 for a bogey, –3 for double bogey or worse).

*Playoffs: Match Play Champs— Maggert won on 2nd hole; **Tucson—** Hjerstedt won on 1st hole; **Bay Hill—** Herron won on 2nd hole; **MCI—** Day one on 1st hole; **Byron Nelson—** Roberts won on 1st hole; **Buick—** Waldorf won on 1st hole; **British—** Lawrie won on 4th hole; **John Deere—** Lewis won on 5th hole; **B.C. Open—** Faxon won on 1st hole; **Texas—** Waldorf won on 1st hole; **Michelob—** Begay III won on 2nd hole.

Second place ties (3 players or more): 5-WAY—**Sony** (D. Love III, J. Maggert, L. Mattiace, C. Perry, T. Tolles); MasterCard (P. Goydos, J. Sluman, T. Herron, F. Funk, G. Kraft). 3-WAY—**Nissan** (D. Love III, T. Tryba, T. Woods); **Buick—** (T. Lehman, T. Tryba, B. Tway).

PGA Majors

The Masters

Edition: 63rd **Dates:** April 8–11
Site: Augusta National GC, Augusta, Ga.
Par: 36-36—72 (6925 yards) **Purse:** $4,000,000

		1	2	3	4	Tot	Earnings
1	Jose Maria Olazabal	70	66	73	71	280	$720,000
2	Davis Love III	69	72	70	71	282	432,000
3	Greg Norman	71	68	71	73	283	272,000
4	Bob Estes	71	72	69	72	284	176,000
	Steve Pate	71	75	65	73	284	176,000
6	David Duval	71	74	70	70	285	125,200
	Carlos Franco	72	72	68	73	285	125,200
	Phil Mickelson	74	69	71	71	285	125,200
	Nick Price	69	72	72	72	285	125,200
	Lee Westwood	75	71	68	71	285	125,200

Early round leaders: 1st— Brandel Chamblee, Love III, Scott McCarron, Price (69); 2nd— Olazabal (136); 3rd— Olazabal (209).

Top amateur: Sergio Garcia (295).

U.S. Open

Edition: 99th **Dates:** June 17–20
Site: Pinehurst Resort and Country Club (No. 2 course)
Par: 36-35—71 (7175 yards) **Purse:** $3,500,000

		1	2	3	4	Tot	Earnings
1	Payne Stewart	68	69	72	70	279	$625,000
2	Phil Mickelson	67	70	73	70	280	370,000
3	Tiger Woods	68	71	72	70	281	196,792
	Vijay Singh	69	70	73	69	281	196,792
5	Steve Stricker	70	73	69	73	285	130,655
6	Tim Herron	69	72	70	75	286	116,953
7	David Duval	67	70	75	75	287	96,260
	Jeff Maggert	71	69	74	73	287	96,260
	Hal Sutton	69	70	76	72	287	96,260
10	Darren Clarke	73	70	74	71	288	78,863
	Billy Mayfair	67	72	74	75	288	78,863

Early round leaders: 1st— Duval, Paul Goydos, Mayfair and Mickelson (67); 2nd— Duval and Mickelson (137); 3rd— Stewart (209).

Top amateur: Hank Kuehne (306).

British Open

Edition: 128th **Dates:** July 15–18
Site: Carnoustie Golf Club, Carnoustie, Scotland
Par: 71-71 (7316 yards) **Purse:** $2,900,000

		1	2	3	4	Tot	Earnings
1	Paul Lawrie*	73	74	76	67	290	$577,500
	Justin Leonard	73	74	71	72	290	305,250
	Jean Van de Velde	75	68	70	77	290	305,250
4	Angel Cabrera	75	69	77	70	291	165,000
	Craig Parry	76	75	67	73	291	165,000
6	Greg Norman	76	70	75	72	293	115,500
7	Tiger Woods	74	72	74	74	294	82,500
	Davis Love III	74	74	77	69	294	82,500
	David Frost	80	69	71	74	294	82,500
10	Scott Dunlap	72	77	76	70	295	57,420
	Jim Furyk	78	71	76	70	295	57,420
	Retief Goosen	76	75	73	71	295	57,420
	Jesper Parnevik	74	71	78	72	295	57,420
	Hal Sutton	73	78	72	72	295	57,420

*Lawrie won by three strokes in a four hole playoff.

Early round leaders: 1st— Rodney Pampling (71); 2nd— Van de Velde (143); 3rd— Van de Velde (213).

Top amateur: none.

PGA Championship

Edition: 81st **Dates:** Aug. 12–15
Site: Medinah Country Club, Medinah, Ill.
Par: 36-36—72 (7401 yards) **Purse:** $3,500,000

		1	2	3	4	Tot	Earnings
1	Tiger Woods	70	67	68	72	277	$630,000
2	Sergio Garcia	66	73	68	71	278	378,000
3	Stewart Cink	69	70	68	73	280	203,000
	Jay Haas	68	67	75	70	280	203,000
5	Nick Price	70	71	69	71	281	129,000
6	Bob Estes	71	70	72	69	282	112,000
	Colin Montgomerie	72	70	70	70	282	112,000
8	Steve Pate	72	70	73	69	284	96,500
	Jim Furyk	71	70	69	74	284	96,500
10	David Duval	70	71	72	72	285	72,167
	Corey Pavin	69	74	71	71	285	72,167
	Chris Perry	70	73	71	71	285	72,167
	Miguel A. Jimenez	70	70	75	70	285	72,167
	Jesper Parnevik	72	70	73	70	285	72,167
	Mike Weir	68	68	69	80	285	72,167

Early round leaders: 1st— Garcia (66); 2nd— Haas (135); 3rd— Woods and Weir (205).

Top amateur: none.

European PGA Tour

Official money won on the 1999 European Tour is presented in euro (E) with the conversion rate for the entire season fixed at the Jan. 14, 1999 exchange rate of £ = 1.4 euro.

LATE 1998

Last Rd	Tournament	Winner	Earnings	Runner-Up
Nov. 1	Volvo Masters	Darren Clarke (271)	£166,000	A. Coltart (273)
Nov. 8	Sarazen World Open	Dudley Hart (272)	$360,000	B. Tway (276)
Nov. 22	World Cup of Golf	ENG-David Carter/ Nick Faldo (568)	£119,402 each	ITA-C. Rocca/M. Florioli (570)

1999

Last Rd	Tournament	Winner	Earnings	Runner-Up
Jan. 17	Alfred Dunhill Championship	Ernie Els (273)	E83,564	R. Kaplan (277)
Jan. 24	South African Open	David Frost (279)	127,505	S. Dunlap & J.M. Singh (280)
Jan. 31	Heineken Classic	Jarrod Moseley (274)	152,447	3-way tie (275)
Feb. 7	Malaysian Open	Gerry Norquist (280)	103,223	A. Cejka & B. May (283)
Feb. 14	Dubai Desert Classic	David Howell (275)	198,324	L. Westwood (279)
Feb. 20	Qatar Masters	Paul Lawrie (268)	143,196	S. Kjeldsen & P. Price (275)
Mar. 7	Portuguese Open	Van Phillips (276)*	93,320	J. Bickerton (276)
Mar. 14	Turespana Masters	Miguel Angel Jiménez (264)	83,330	S. Webster (268)
Mar. 28	Madeira Island Open	Pedro Linhart (276)	81,660	M. James (277)
Apr. 18	Estoril Open	Jeff Remesy (286)	93,320	3-way (288)
Apr. 25	Spanish Open	Jarmo Sandelin (267)	140,000	3-way (271)
May 2	Italian Open	Dean Robertson (271)	166,660	P. Harrington (272)
May 9	French Open	Retief Goosen (272)*	141,660	G. Turner (272)
May 16	Benson & Hedges Intl. Open	Colin Montgomerie (273)	186,670	P. Johansson & A. Cabrera (276)
May 24	SAP Open	Tiger Woods (273)	280,000	R. Goosen (276)
May 31	Volvo PGA Championship	Colin Montgomerie (270)	303,350	M. James (275)
June 6	English Open	Darren Clarke (268)	166,660	J. Bickerton (270)
June 13	German Open	Jarno Sandelin (274)*	166,660	R. Goosen (274)
June 27	European Grand Prix	David Park (274)	151,660	D. Carter & R. Goosen (275)
July 4	Irish Open	Sergio Garcia (268)	233,320	A. Cabrera (271)
July 11	Loch Lomond World Invitational	Colin Montgomerie (268)	233,320	3-way tie (271)
July 18	**British Open** (Carnoustie)	Paul Lawrie (290)*	490,000	J. Leonard & J. Van de Velde (290)
July 25	Dutch Open	Lee Westwood (269)	186,660	G. Orr (270)
Aug. 2	European Open	Lee Westwood (271)	316,660	P. O'Malley & D. Clarke (274)
Aug. 8	Scandanavian Masters	Colin Montgomerie (268)	233,320	J. Parnevik (277)
Aug. 22	BMW International Open	Colin Montgomerie (268)	198,320	P. Harrington (271)
Aug. 29	NEC Invitational	Tiger Woods (270)	865,961	P. Mickelson (271)
Sept. 5	European Masters	Lee Westwood (270)	210,000	T. Björn (272)
Sept. 12	Victor Chandler British Masters	Bob May (269)	166,666	C. Montgomerie (270)
Sept. 19	Lancome Trophy	Pierre Fulke (270)	186,660	I. Garrido (271)
Oct. 3	German Masters	Sergio Garcia (277)*	291,700	I. Woosnam & P. Harrington (277)

#Weather-shortened

*Playoffs: **Portuguese—** Phillips won on 1st hole; **French–** Goosen won on 2nd hole; **German Open—** Sandelin won on 1st hole; **British—** Lawrie won on 4th hole; **German Masters—** Garcia won on 2nd hole.

Second place ties (3 players or more): 3-WAY **Heineken** (B. Langer, E. Els, P. Lonard); **Estoril** (M. Florioli, A. Coltart, D. Carter); **Spanish** (M.A. Jimenez, P. McGinley, I. Garrido); **Loch Lomond** (M. Jonzon, S. Garcia, M. Lanner).

The Official World Golf Ranking

Begun in 1986, the Official World Golf Ranking (formerly the Sony World Ranking) combines the best golfers on the five PGA men's tours (U.S., Europe, South Africa, Japan and Australasia). Rankings are based on a rolling two-year period and weighted in favor of more recent results. Points are awarded after each worldwide tournament according to finish. Final point averages are determined by dividing a player's total points by the number of tournaments played over that two-year period (through Oct. 3, 1999).

		Avg			Avg			Avg
1	Tiger Woods, USA	17.04	8	Payne Stewart, USA	7.89	15	Jesper Parnevik, Swe.	5.84
2	David Duval, USA	14.56	9	Nick Price, Zim.	7.80	16	John Huston, USA	5.63
3	Colin Montgomerie, Sco.	9.78	10	Mark O'Meara, USA	6.82	17	Sergio Garcia, Spa.	5.57
4	Davis Love III, USA	9.65	11	Phil Mickelson, USA	6.67	18	Jeff Maggert, USA	5.38
5	Lee Westwood, Eng.	9.19	12	Hal Sutton, USA	6.52	19	Jumbo Ozaki, Jpn.	5.35
6	Vijay Singh, Fij.	8.32	13	Justin Leonard, USA	6.36	20	Fred Couples, USA	5.22
7	Ernie Els, S. Afr.	8.12	14	Jim Furyk, USA	6.34			

Tournament Results (Cont.)
Senior PGA Tour
LATE 1998

Last Rd	Tournament	Winner	Earnings	Runner-Up
Nov. 1	Pacific Bell Classic	Joe Inman (202)	$165,000	L. Trevino (203)
Nov. 8	Senior Tour Championship	Hale Irwin (274)	347,000	G. Morgan (279)
Nov. 10@	Wendy's Three Tour Challenge	Senior PGA	100,000 each	PGA
Nov. 15	Senior Match Play Challenge	Hale Irwin (6&5)	240,000	G. Morgan

1999

Last Rd	Tournament	Winner	Earnings	Runner-Up
Jan. 24	MasterCard Championship	John Jacobs (203)	$185,000	J. Colbert & R. Floyd (206)
Jan. 31@	Senior Skins Game	Hale Irwin (7)	230,000	R. Floyd (4)
Feb. 7	Royal Caribbean Classic	Bruce Fleisher (205)	150,000	I. Aoki (207)
Feb. 14	American Express Invitational	Bruce Fleisher (203)	180,000	L. Nelson (206)
Feb. 21	GTE Classic	Larry Nelson (205)	180,000	B. Fleisher (207)
Feb. 28	ACE Group Championship	Allen Doyle (203)	180,000	V. Fernandez (208)
Mar. 3@	Senior Slam	Gil Morgan (132)	300,000	H. Irwin (134)
Mar. 14	Toshiba Senior Classic	Gary McCord (204)*	180,000	3-way tie (204)
Mar. 21@	Liberty Mutual Legends of Golf	Hubert Green/Gil Morgan (194)	316,000	J. Mahaffey/T. Wargo (197)
Mar. 28	Emerald Coast Classic	Bob Duval (200)	165,000	B. Fleisher (202)
Apr. 4	**The Tradition** (Scottsdale, Ariz.)	Graham Marsh (136)#	225,000	L. Nelson (139)
Apr. 18	**PGA Seniors' Championship** (Palm Beach Gardens, Fla.)	Allen Doyle (274)	315,000	V. Fernandez (276)
Apr. 25	Home Depot Invitational	Bruce Fleisher (205)	180,000	T. Dill & J. Holtgrieve (206)
May 2	Bruno's Memorial Classic	Larry Nelson (205)	180,000	D. Quigley (206)
May 9	Nationwide Championship	Hale Irwin (206)	210,000	B. Murphy (208)
May 16	Las Vegas Classic	Vicente Fernandez (274)	210,000	D. Eichelberger (276)
May 23	Bell Atlantic Classic	Tom Jenkins (205)*	165,000	J. Thorpe (206)
May 30	Boone Valley Classic	Hale Irwin (203)	210,000	A. Geiberger (205)
June 6	Cadillac NFL Golf Classic	Allen Doyle (204)*	165,000	J. Inman (204)
June 13	BellSouth Classic at Opryland	Bruce Fleisher (200)	210,000	A. Geiberger (201)
June 20	Southwestern Bell Dominion	John Mahaffey (204)*	165,000	J.M. Canizares & B. Fleisher (204)
June 27	**Senior Players Championship** (Dearborn, Mich.)	Hale Irwin (267)	300,000	G. Marsh (274)
July 4	State Farm Senior Classic	Christy O'Connor (198)	195,000	B. Fleisher (199)
July 11	**U.S. Senior Open** (Des Moines, Iowa)	Dave Eichelberger (281)	315,000	E. Dougherty (284)
July 18	Ameritech Senior Open	Hale Irwin (206)	195,000	3-way tie
July 25	Coldwell Banker Burnet Classic	Hale Irwin (201)	225,000	J. Dent & D. Douglass (203)
Aug. 1	Utah Showdown	Dave Eichelberger (197)*	202,500	D. Quigley (197)
Aug. 8	Lightpath Long Island Classic	Bruce Fleisher (206)	180,000	A. Doyle (208)
Aug. 15	Foremost Insurance Championship	Christy O'Connor (205)	150,000	3-way tie (209)
Aug. 22	BankBoston Classic	Tom McGinnis (205)*	180,000	H. Irwin (205)
Aug. 29	Canada Senior Open	Jim Ahern (272)*	202,500	H. Irwin (272)
Sept. 5	TD Waterhouse Champ.	Allen Doyle (198)	180,000	E. Dougherty (200)
Sept. 12	Comfort Classic	Gil Morgan (201)	180,000	E. Dougherty (203)
Sept. 19	Bank One Championship	Tom Watson (196)	195,000	B. Summerhays (201)
Sept. 26	Kroger Senior Classic	Gil Morgan (198)	210,000	E. Dougherty (200)
Oct. 3	Vantage Championship	Fred Gibson (195)	225,000	B. Fleisher (198)
Oct. 10	The Transamerica	Bruce Fleisher (199)	165,000	A. Doyle (200)

#Weather-shortened.

@ Unofficial Senior PGA Tour money event.

*Playoffs: **Toshiba**— McCord won on the 5th hole; **Bell Atlantic**— Jenkins won on 1st hole; **Cadillac NFL**— Doyle won on 4th hole; **Southwestern Bell**— Mahaffey won on 2nd hole; **Utah**— Eichelberger won on 1st hole; **BankBoston**— McGinnis won on 2nd hole; **Canada**— Ahern won on 2nd hole.

Second place ties (3 players or more): 3-WAY— **Toshiba** (A. Doyle, J. Jacobs, A. Geiberger); **Ameritech** (G. McCord, R. Floyd, B. Fleisher); **Foremost Insurance** (G. Archer, J. Jacobs, J. Thorpe).

Senior PGA Majors

The Tradition

Edition: 11th   **Dates:** April 1–2
Site: Desert Mt. Cochise Course, Scottsdale, Ariz.
Par: 36-36—72 (6967 yards)   **Purse:** $1,500,000

		1	2	Tot	Earnings
1	Graham Marsh	69-67		136	$225,000
2	Larry Nelson	73-66		139	132,000
3	Leonard Thompson	70-70		140	99,000
	Vicente Fernandez	70-70		140	99,000
5	Bob Duval	73-68		141	66,000
	Gary McCord	73-68		141	66,000
7	Jim Thorpe	73-69		142	51,000
	John D. Morgan	71-71		142	51,000
9	Brian Barnes	74-69		143	37,500
	Terry Dill	72-71		143	37,500
	John Bland	71-72		143	37,500
	Howard Twitty	69-74		143	37,500

Note: The final two rounds were cancelled due to snow.
Early round leaders: 1st— Marsh and Twitty (69).

PGA Seniors' Championship

Edition: 62nd   **Dates:** April 15–18
Site: PGA National GC, Palm Beach Gardens, Fla.
Par: 36-36—72 (6754 yards)   **Purse:** $1,750,000

		1	2	3	4	Tot	Earnings
1	Allen Doyle	71-71-68-64				274	$315,000
2	Vicente Fernandez	70-65-71-70				276	189,000
3	Bruce Fleisher	70-70-66-73				279	101,500
	Jose Maria Canizares	68-71-68-72				279	101,500
5	Dana Quigley	71-68-71-70				280	61,000
	Bruce Summerhays	66-70-74-70				280	61,000
7	Hugh Baiocchi	72-74-66-69				281	54,000
8	Larry Ziegler	70-70-72-70				282	47,000
	John Jacobs	69-70-72-71				282	47,000
	J.C. Snead	72-68-71-71				282	47,000

Early round leaders: 1st— Summerhays (66); 2nd— Fernandez (135); 3rd— Fernandez and Fleisher (206).

PGA Sr. Players Championship

Edition: 17th   **Dates:** June 24–27
Site: TPC of Michigan, Dearborn, Mich.
Par: 36-36—72 (6876 yards)   **Purse:** $2,100,000

		1	2	3	4	Tot	Earnings
1	Hale Irwin	67-71-64-65				267	$300,000
2	Graham Marsh	66-70-70-68				274	176,000
3	John Jacobs	71-69-68-67				275	144,000
4	Larry Nelson	66-72-69-69				276	120,000
5	Hubert Green	70-72-69-66				277	88,000
	Jose Maria Canizares	69-70-68-70				277	88,000
7	Gil Morgan	74-72-67-65				278	68,000
	Bruce Fleisher	72-68-68-70				278	68,000
9	Ray Floyd	73-69-70-67				279	52,000
	Bob Eastwood	71-69-70-67				279	52,000
	Kermit Zarley	68-72-69-70				279	52,000

Early round leaders: 1st— Marsh and Nelson (66); 2nd— Marsh (136); 3rd— Irwin (202).

U.S. Senior Open

Edition: 20th   **Dates:** July 8–11
Site: Des Moines Golf and Country Club, Des Moines, Iowa
Par: 36-36—72 (6888 yards)   **Purse:** $1,750,000

		1	2	3	4	Tot	Earnings
1	Dave Eichelberger	71-69-73-68				281	$315,000
2	Ed Dougherty	68-69-75-72				284	185,000
3	Joe Inman	72-71-72-71				286	89,903
	Gil Morgan	70-71-73-72				286	89,903
	Hale Irwin	71-72-70-73				286	89,903
6	Tom Wargo	73-70-75-69				287	59,680
7	Bruce Summerhays	70-73-70-75				288	53,602
8	Jim Dent	73-73-73-70				289	45,644
	Hugh Baiocchi	74-75-69-71				289	45,644
	Frank Conner	79-71-67-72				289	45,644

Early round leaders: 1st— Dougherty (68); 2nd— Dougherty (137); 3rd— Dougherty (212).

LPGA Tour

LATE 1998

Last Rd	Tournament	Winner	Earnings	Runner-Up
Nov. 1	Nichirei International	United States (24)	$25,000 each	Japan (12)
Nov. 8	Japan Classic	Hiromi Kobayashi (205)*	120,000	T. Barrett (205)
Nov. 22	PageNet Tour Championship	Laura Davies (277)	215,000	3-way tie (281)

*Playoffs: Japan Classic— Kobayashi won on 3rd hole.
Second-place ties: (3 players or more): **Tour Championship**— (B. Burton, P. Hurst, K. Webb).

1999

Last Rd	Tournament	Winner	Earnings	Runner-Up
Jan. 17	HealthSouth Inaugural	Kelly Robbins (205)	$82,500	T. Barrett & K. Webb (206)
Jan. 24	Naples LPGA Memorial	Meg Mallon (272)	112,500	H. Alfredsson & K. Robbins (273)
Jan. 30	The Office Depot	Karrie Webb (278)	101,250	D. Pepper & K. Tschetter (279)
Feb. 14	Valley of the Stars Championship	Catrin Nilsmark (204)*	97,500	A. Sorenstam (204)
Feb. 20	Hawaiian Ladies Open	Alison Nicholas (209)	97,500	A. Deluca & M. Dunn (210)
Feb. 28	Australian Ladies Masters	Karrie Webb (262)	112,500	J. Moodie (272)
Mar. 14	Welch's/Circle K Championship	Juli Inkster (273)	93,750	D. Pepper (274)
Mar. 21	Standard Register Ping	Karrie Webb (274)	127,500	L. Kane (278)
Mar. 28	**Nabisco Dinah Shore** (Rancho Mirage, Calif.)	Dottie Pepper (269)	150,000	M. Mallon (275)
Apr. 4	Longs Drugs Challenge	Juli Inkster (280)	90,000	S. Steinhauer (284)
Apr. 25	Chick-fil-A Charity Championship	Rachel Hetherington (204)*	120,000	L. Kane (205)
May 2	City of Hope Myrtle Beach Classic	Rachel Hetherington (137)#	101,250	3-way tie (138)
May 9	Titleholders Championship	Karrie Webb (271)	135,000	A. Sorenstam (274)
May 16	Sara Lee Classic	Meg Mallon (199)	112,500	A. Sorenstam & K. Tschetter (200)
May 23	The Philips Invitational	Akiko Fukushima (267)	120,000	C. Sorenstam (269)
May 30	Corning Classic	Kelli Kuehne (278)	112,500	R. Jones (279)

LPGA Tour (Cont.)

Last Rd	Tournament	Winner	Earnings	Runner-Up
June 6	**U.S. Women's Open** (West Point, Miss.)	Juli Inkster (272)	$315,000	S. Turner (277)
June 13	Wegmans Rochester International	Karrie Webb (280)	150,000	C. McCurdy (281)
June 20	ShopRite Classic	Se Ri Pak (198)	150,000	T. Johnson (200)
June 27	**McDonald's LPGA Championship** (Wilmington, Del.)	Juli Inkster (268)	210,000	L. Neumann (272)
July 4	Jamie Farr Kroger Classic	Se Ri Pak (276)*	135,000	5-way tie (276)
July 11	Michelob Light Classic	Annika Sorenstam (278)*	120,000	T. Barrett (278)
July 18	JAL Big Apple Classic	Sherri Steinhauer (273)*	127,500	L. Kane (273)
July 25	Giant Eagle LPGA Classic	J. Gallagher-Smith (199)	150,000	M. McGuire (202)
Aug. 1	**du Maurier Classic** (Calgary, Alberta)	Karrie Webb (277)	180,000	L. Davies (279)
Aug. 8	areaWEB.com Challenge	Mardi Lunn (275)	120,000	J. Stephenson (276)
Aug. 15	Weetabix Women's British Open	Sherri Steinhauer (283)	160,000	A. Sorenstam (284)
Aug. 22	Firstar Classic	Rosie Jones (207)*	97,500	B. Iverson & J. Stephenson (207)
Aug. 29	Oldsmobile Classic	Dottie Pepper (270)	105,000	K. Kuehne (272)
Sept. 6	State Farm Rail Classic	Mi Hyun Kim (204)	116,250	J. Moodie & P. Sinn (205)
Sept. 12	World Championship of Women's Golf	Se Ri Park (280)	150,000	K. Webb (281)
Sept. 19	Safeco Classic	Maria Hjorth (271)	97,500	C. Matthew (273)
Sept. 26	Safeway Championship	Juli Inkster (207)	120,000	T. Barrett & G. Park (213)
Oct. 3	New Albany Classic	Annika Sorenstam (269)	150,000	M. Lunn (272)

Weather-shortened

*Playoffs: Valley of the Stars— Nilsmark won on 1st hole; **Chick-fil-A Charity**— Hetherington won on 1st hole; **Jamie Farr**— Pak won on 1st hole; **Michelob Light**— Sorenstam won on 3rd hole; **Big Apple**— Steinhauer won on 5th hole; **Firstar**— Jones won on 4th hole.

Second place ties: (3 players or more): 5-WAY—**Jamie Farr** (K. Kuehne, C. Koch, M. Lunn, S. Steinhauer, K. Webb). 3-WAY—**Myrtle Beach** (H. Alfredsson, L. Lindley, K. Webb).

LPGA Majors

Dinah Shore

Edition: 28th   **Dates:** March 25–28
Site: Mission Hills CC, Rancho Mirage, Calif.
Par: 36-36—72 (6460 yards)   **Purse:** $1,000,000

		1 2 3 4	Tot	Earnings
1	Dottie Pepper	70-66-67-66—	269	$150,000
2	Meg Mallon	66-69-71-69—	275	93,093
3	Karrie Webb	73-71-70-66—	280	67,933
4	Kelly Robbins	69-73-67-72—	281	52,837
5	Charlotta Sorenstam	72-68-76-66—	282	42,772
6	Juli Inkster	72-66-71-74—	283	35,224
7	Catriona Matthew	72-73-69-70—	284	26,502
	Janice Moodie	69-68-75-72—	284	26,502
	Annika Sorenstam	70-73-71-70—	284	26,502
10	Helen Alfredsson	69-71-73-72—	285	19,289
	Maria Hjorth	77-68-68-72—	285	19,289
	Sherri Steinhauer	70-72-72-71—	285	19,289

Early round leaders: 1st— Mallon (66); 2nd— Mallon (135); 3rd— Pepper (203).
Top amateur: Grace Park (290).

LPGA Championship

Edition: 45th   **Dates:** June 24–27
Site: DuPont CC, Wilmington, Del.
Par: 35-36—71 (6386 yards)   **Purse:** $1,400,000

		1 2 3 4	Tot	Earnings
1	Juli Inkster	68-66-69-65—	268	$210,000
2	Liselotte Neumann	67-67-70-68—	272	130,330
3	Mardi Lunn	68-74-65-66—	273	84,538
	Nancy Scranton	69-68-66-70—	273	84,538
5	Rosie Jones	64-72-68-70—	274	54,596
	Cristie Kerr	70-64-69-71—	274	54,596
7	Laura Davies	65-71-71-68—	275	35,224
	Emilee Klein	72-68-67-68—	275	35,224
	Jill McGill	70-69-68-68—	275	35,224
	Se Ri Pak	68-69-67-71—	275	35,224

Early round leaders: 1st— Jones (64); 2nd— Jenny Liback, Kerr, Inkster and Neumann (134); 3rd— Scranton, Kerr and Inkster (203).

U.S. Women's Open

Edition: 54th   **Dates:** June 3–6
Site: Old Waverly Golf Club, West Point, Miss.
Par: 36-36—72 (6433 yards)   **Purse:** $1,750,000

		1 2 3 4	Tot	Earnings
1	Juli Inkster	65-69-67-71—	272	$315,000
2	Sherri Turner	69-69-68-71—	277	185,000
3	Kelli Kuehne	64-71-70-74—	279	118,227
4	Lorie Kane	70-64-71-75—	280	82,399
5	Meg Mallon	70-70-69-72—	281	62,938
	Carin Koch	72-69-68-72—	281	62,938
7	Karrie Webb	70-70-68-74—	282	53,132
8	Helen Dobson	71-70-73-69—	283	45,244
	Maria Hjorth	73-69-70-71—	283	45,244
	Catriona Matthew	69-68-74-72—	283	45,244
	Grace Park	70-67-73-73—	283	amateur

Early round leaders: 1st— Kuehne (64); 2nd— Inkster and Kane (134); 3rd— Inkster (201).
Top amateur: Park (283).

du Maurier Classic

Edition: 27th   **Dates:** July 29–Aug. 1
Site: Priddis Greens Golf & CC, Calgary, Alberta, Canada
Par: 36-36—72 (6415 yards)   **Purse:** $1,200,000

		1 2 3 4	Tot	Earnings
1	Karrie Webb	73-72-66-66—	277	$180,000
2	Laura Davies	72-66-69-72—	279	111,711
3	Juli Inkster	68-69-74-69—	280	81,519
4	Dawn Coe-Jones	72-65-72-74—	283	63,404
5	Catriona Matthew	68-70-72-74—	284	51,326
6	Maggie Will	74-69-74-68—	285	36,431
	Mi Hyun Kim	78-69-69-69—	285	36,431
	Lorie Kane	70-72-73-70—	285	36,431
9	Carin Koch	71-71-73-71—	286	24,486
	Sherri Turner	72-72-70-72—	286	24,486
	Jill McGill	72-71-71-72—	286	24,486
	Rosie Jones	67-74-72-73—	286	24,486

Early round leaders: 1st— Patti Rizzo and Jones (67); 2nd— Coe-Jones and Inkster (137); 3rd— Davies (207).
Top amateur: none.

A Pair of Aces

by Linda Cohn

In 1983, 23-year-old Juli Inkster burst onto the LPGA scene with the talent and passion for the sport that indicated she would dominate the Tour for years to come. While playing in just her fifth professional outing, she won the SAFECO Classic and later that season became the first rookie ever to win two major championships in one season (Dinah Shore and du Maurier).

But ten years later, the career that should have been was lost and Inkster's name rarely turned up on a leaderboard. Between 1990-96, in what should have been the prime of her career, she won just two events and the passion she showed a decade earlier was nowhere to be found.

Inkster was clearly feeling the pressure — but not only from the Tour. In 1990 she gave birth to daughter Hayley, and then to Hayley's sister Cori in 1994. While her colleagues were spending their downtime focusing on the next tournament, Inkster was changing diapers, driving to pre-school, reading bedtime stories and feeling the guilt that comes with being a loving mother who also feels a passion and devotion for her career.

"I really wanted to be there for them as a mom," said Inkster. "It was almost as if I felt a sense of guilt every time I was at a tournament and away from them. And my golf game suffered."

As a mother of two myself, I understand the conflicts of motherhood and career. However, by the time I began covering the LPGA in 1998, Inkster was already climbing back to the top of her game. The year before, she ranked sixth overall and in 1999 she won the LPGA Championship and became the first mom in history to win the U.S. Open. She also earned enough points, after winning the Safeway Championship in September, to be enshrined in the LPGA Hall of Fame.

Hayley and Cori now often travel with their mom, who seems to have struck a healthy balance between motherhood and being a professional golfer. On the Sunday of a tournament, for example, she cooks French toast for her girls before heading out to the tee. She's happy, driven, popular among players and fans, and her game shows it.

Inkster's performance this year has been surpassed only by that of 24-year-old Karrie Webb, whose six victories and 20 top-10 finishes (out of 23 tournaments) through September, have made her the top player on the tour and makes her look like Inkster did 15 years ago. Well, not exactly.

While Inkster has become one of the better liked players on the Tour, Webb has developed a reputation for being stoic and stand-offish. Perceptions that she is devoid of emotion have brought criticism from the press and other women on the Tour, including 12-year veteran Danielle Ammaccapane, who in early May blasted Webb and the younger generation of players for not doing enough to promote the LPGA.

"Everyone has their own opinion and Danielle is certainly entitled to hers," responded Webb. "I can't be someone I'm not. I'm not Nancy Lopez. My mom always told me to be myself and if people don't like you, that's too bad. I can't be a phony."

After meeting and speaking with Webb, I can tell you that while she is definitely serious, she is in no way dispassionate about her game. Try watching her on the 18th green when winning depends on whether or not she sinks a 20-foot putt and tell me she doesn't add excitement to the game.

No, we probably won't see Webb burst into tears and sprint around the green after a victory. It just isn't her, and who wants it to be? But with six victories and $1.5 million in earnings, it sure seems like she's smiling a lot more than before. ∎

Linda Cohn is a *SportsCenter* anchor and covers women's golf for ESPN.

1999 Ryder Cup

The 33rd Ryder Cup tournament, Sept. 24-26, at The Country Club, Brookline, Mass.

ROSTERS

The 1999 U.S. Ryder Cup Team was chosen on the basis of points compiled by the PGA of America, early 1998, through the 81st PGA Championship, Aug. 12-15, 1999. Points are awarded for top-10 finishes at PGA Tour co-sponsored or sanctioned events, with added emphasis on major championships and events played during the Ryder Cup year. The top 10 finishers on the points list automatically qualified for the 12-member team, and U.S. Captain Ben Crenshaw selected the final two players—Steve Pate and Hal Sutton.

The 1999 European Team Points Table began in September 1998, and concluded on August 22, 1999, after the BMW International Open. The top 10 players in the Points Table qualified automatically for the team, with European Captain Mark James selecting two additional players to complete the team—Andrew Coltart and Jesper Parnevik.

United States: Qualifiers— David Duval, Jim Furyk, Justin Leonard, Tom Lehman, Davis Love III, Jeff Maggert, Phil Mickelson, Mark O'Meara, Payne Stewart and Tiger Woods; Captain's Selections— Steve Pate and Hal Sutton.

Europe: Qualifiers— Darren Clarke (N. Ireland), Sergio Garcia (Spain), Padraig Harrington (Ireland), Miguel Angel Jimenez (Spain), Paul Lawrie (Scotland), Colin Montgomerie (Scotland), Jose Maria Olazabal (Spain), Jarmo Sandelin (Sweden), Jean Van de velde (France) and Lee Westwood (England); Captain's Selections— Andrew Coltart (Scotland) and Jesper Parnevik (Sweden).

First Day
Foursome Match Results

Winner	Score	Loser
Montgomery/Lawrie	3&2	Duval/Mickelson
Garcia/Parnevik	2&1	Lehman/Woods
Jimenez/Harrington	halved	Love III/Stewart
Maggert/Sutton	3&2	Clarke/Westwood

Europe wins morning, 2½-1½

Four-Ball Match Results

Winner	Score	Loser
Montgomery/Lawrie	halved	Love III/Leonard
Parnevik/Garcia	1-up	Mickelson/Furyk
Jimenez/Olazabal	2&1	Sutton/Maggert
Westwood/Clarke	1-up	Duval/Woods

Europe wins afternoon, 3½-½; (Europe leads, 6-2)

Second Day
Foursome Match Results

Winner	Score	Loser
Sutton/Maggert	1-up	Montgomerie/Lawrie
Clarke/Westwood	3&2	Furyk/O'Meara
Woods/Pate	1-up	Jimenez/Harrington
Parnevik/Garcia	3&2	Stewart/Leonard

Teams tie morning, 2-2; (Europe leads, 8-4)

Four-Ball Match Results

Winner	Score	Loser
Mickelson/Lehman	2&1	Clarke/Westwood
Parnevik/Garcia	halved	Love III/Duval
Jimenez/Olazabal	halved	Leonard/Sutton
Montgomerie/Lawrie	2&1	Pate/Woods

Teams tie afternoon, 2-2; (Europe leads, 10-6)

Third Day
Singles Match Results

Winner	Score	Loser
Lehman	3&2	Westwood
Sutton	4&2	Clarke
Mickelson	4&3	Sandelin
Love III	6&5	Van de Velde
Woods	3&2	Coltart
Duval	5&4	Parnevik
Harrington	1-up	O'Meara
Pate	2&1	Jimenez
Olazabal	halved	Leonard
Montgomerie	1-up	Stewart
Furyk	4&3	Garcia
Lawrie	4&3	Maggert

USA wins day, 8½-3½

USA wins Ryder Cup, 14½-13½

Overall Records

Team and Individual match play combined

United States	W-L-H		Europe	W-L-H
Hal Sutton	3-1-1		Sergio Garcia	3-1-1
Tom Lehman	2-1-0		Paul Lawrie	3-1-1
Steve Pate	2-1-0		Colin Montgomerie	3-1-1
Jeff Maggert	2-2-0		Jesper Parnevik	3-1-1
Phil Mickelson	2-2-0		Darren Clarke	2-3-0
Tiger Woods	2-3-0		Lee Westwood	2-3-1
Davis Love III	1-0-3		Jose Maria Olazabal	1-0-2
David Duval	1-2-1		Padraig Harrington	1-1-1
Jim Furyk	1-2-0		Miguel Angel Jimenez	1-2-2
Justin Leonard	0-1-3		Andrew Coltart	0-1-0
Payne Stewart	0-2-1		Jarmo Sandelin	0-1-0
Mark O'Meara	0-2-0		Jean Van de Velde	0-1-0

Showdown at Sherwood

Aug. 2 at Sherwood Country Club, Thousand Oaks, Calif.

This 18-hole match-play exhibition featured the world's top two golfers, Tiger Woods and David Duval, and was broadcast live during primetime on ABC. Duval won the first two holes, but Woods took control by winning five of the next 10. Woods closed out a 2&1 victory with a par on the par-3 17th. Each player donated $200,000 of their winnings to charity; **Purse:** $1.5 million ($1.1 million, $400,000); **Sponsored by:** Motorola; **TV Rating:** 6.9/12 (ABC).

SCORECARD

	Hole	1	2	3	4	5	6	7	8	9		
	Par	4	5	3	5	4	3	5	3	4	36	
	Yards	385	522	188	541	457	186	537	166	446	3428	
Woods		4	6	3	4	4	2	4	2	4	2-up	
Duval		3	5	4	5	4	x	4	3	4		

	Hole	10	11	12	13	14	15	16	17	18		
	Par	4	5	3	4	5	4	4	3	4	36	72
	Yards	341	531	202	459	534	425	449	232	424	3597	7025
Woods		4	5	2	5	5	4	3	3	x	even	2&1
Duval		4	5	3	4	4	4	5	3	x		

Money Leaders

Official money leaders of PGA, European PGA, Senior PGA and LPGA tours for 1998 and unofficial money leaders for 1999 (through Oct. 3, 1999), as compiled by the PGA, European PGA and LPGA. All European amounts in 1998 are in pound sterling (£), while 1999 amounts are in Euro dollars (€).

PGA

Arnold Palmer Award standings: listed are tournaments played (TP); cuts made (CM); 1st, 2nd and 3rd place finishes; and earnings for the year.

Final 1998

		TP	CM	Finish 1-2-3	Earnings
1	David Duval	23	19	4-1-1	$2,591,031
2	Vijay Singh	26	23	2-3-0	2,238,998
3	Jim Furyk	28	24	1-2-2	2,054,334
4	Tiger Woods	20	19	1-2-2	1,841,117
5	Hal Sutton	30	22	2-1-0	1,838,740
6	Phil Mickelson	24	19	2-2-1	1,837,246
7	Mark O'Meara	19	15	2-1-1	1,786,699
8	Justin Leonard	28	22	1-2-0	1,671,823
9	Fred Couples	17	16	2-2-1	1,650,389
10	John Huston	25	21	2-1-0	1,544,110

1999 (through Oct. 3)

		TP	CM	Finish 1-2-3	Earnings
1	Tiger Woods	18	18	5-1-2	$4,266,585
2	David Duval	19	18	4-1-1	3,471,206
3	Payne Stewart	19	16	2-2-0	2,077,950
4	Vijay Singh	25	22	1-1-1	1,961,750
5	Hal Sutton	21	18	1-1-0	1,906,511
6	Jeff Maggert	21	18	1-1-1	1,891,969
7	Davis Love III	21	19	0-3-2	1,865,328
8	Justin Leonard	25	23	0-2-2	1,773,491
9	David Toms	28	17	2-1-1	1,773,872
10	Carlos Franco	20	13	2-0-3	1,732,884

EUROPEAN PGA

Volvo Order of Merit standings: listed are tournaments played (TP); cuts made (CM); 1st, 2nd and 3rd place finishes; and earnings for the year.

Final 1998

		TP	CM	Finish 1-2-3	Earnings
1	Colin Montgomerie	17	15	3-1-1	£1,082,833
2	Darren Clarke	18	16	2-3-1	946,089
3	Lee Westwood	19	18	4-0-1	876,393
4	Miguel Angel Jimenez	24	19	2-1-0	632,573
5	Mark O'Meara	3	3	1-1-1	624,488
6	Ernie Els	9	9	1-3-2	574,619
7	Patrik Sjöland	23	19	1-3-1	570,812
8	Thomas Bjorn	20	16	2-0-1	504,817
9	Jose Maria Olazabal	20	18	1-2-1	503,206
10	Andrew Coltart	22	17	1-1-0	475,691

1999 (through Oct. 3)

		TP	CM	Finish 1-2-3	Earnings
1	Colin Montgomerie	18	18	5-1-1	€1,758,651
2	Sergio Garcia	13	13	2-2-0	1,147,982
3	Lee Westwood	17	17	3-1-0	1,147,272
4	Retief Goosen	25	25	1-3-0	854,886
5	Paul Lawrie	23	23	2-0-0	838,739
6	Padraig Harrington	23	23	0-4-0	718,608
7	Darren Clarke	18	18	1-1-0	645,344
8	Angel Cabrera	20	20	0-2-0	579,671
9	Miguel Angel Jimenez	20	20	1-1-0	574,613
10	Ernie Els	10	10	1-1-0	336,730

SENIOR PGA

Final 1998

		TP	CM	Finish 1-2-3	Earnings
1	Hale Irwin	22	22	7-6-2	$2,861,945
2	Gil Morgan	25	25	6-1-4	2,179,047
3	Larry Nelson	23	23	3-5-0	1,442,476
4	Jay Sigel	32	32	2-1-6	1,403,912
5	Hugh Baiocchi	35	35	2-1-2	1,183,959
6	Jim Colbert	32	32	1-2-1	1,122,413
7	Dana Quigley	38	38	2-1-0	1,103,882
8	Bruce Summerhays	37	37	1-3-2	1,098,942
9	Isao Aoki	22	22	1-2-3	1,042,200
10	Dave Stockton	27	27	0-2-2	1,040,524

1999 (through Oct. 3)

		TP	CM	Finish 1-2-3	Earnings
1	Bruce Fleisher	27	25	5-6-1	$1,949,630
2	Hale Irwin	22	22	5-2-2	1,919,732
3	Allen Doyle	26	26	4-2-0	1,596,388
4	Gil Morgan	25	24	2-0-6	1,442,082
5	Larry Nelson	26	25	2-2-1	1,321,572
6	Dana Quigley	33	33	0-2-3	1,321,572
7	Vicente Fernandez	26	24	1-2-1	1,056,911
8	Tom Jenkins	25	25	1-0-2	1,019,543
9	Graham Marsh	26	26	1-1-2	984,474
10	Jose Maria Canizares	28	28	0-1-3	955,301

LPGA

Final 1998

		TP	CM	Finish 1-2-3	Earnings
1	Annika Sorenstam	21	21	4-4-2	$1,092,748
2	Se Ri Pak	27	26	4-0-0	872,170
3	Donna Andrews	24	24	1-4-1	715,428
4	Karrie Webb	23	22	2-1-3	704,477
5	Liselotte Neumann	21	19	2-2-1	665,069
6	Juli Inkster	25	23	1-3-0	656,012
7	Brandie Burton	26	25	1-3-1	652,084
8	Pat Hurst	26	25	1-1-1	652,084
9	Meg Mallon	28	25	1-2-1	593,458
10	Dottie Pepper	25	23	0-3-2	539,792

1999 (through Oct. 3)

		TP	CM	Finish 1-2-3	Earnings
1	Karrie Webb	23	21	6-4-4	$1,426,584
2	Juli Inkster	22	21	5-0-3	1,263,703
3	Annika Sorenstam	20	19	2-4-3	840,406
4	Se Ri Pak	24	21	3-0-0	730,366
5	Lorie Kane	27	26	0-3-2	681,570
6	Meg Mallon	22	22	2-1-1	650,720
7	Sherri Steinhauer	27	24	2-2-0	626,706
8	Dottie Pepper	21	20	2-2-0	577,875
9	Rosie Jones	21	18	1-1-1	540,377
10	Rachel Hetherington	26	20	2-0-3	501,527

THE 2000 · ESPN INFORMATION PLEASE SPORTS ALMANAC

GOLF STATISTICS

THROUGH THE YEARS
1860-1999
MAJOR TITLES · LEADERS

SEC B

PAGE 856

Major Golf Championships
MEN
The Masters

The Masters has been played every year (except during World War II) since 1934 at the Augusta National Golf Club in Augusta, Ga. Both the course (6905 yards, par 72) and the tournament were created by Bobby Jones; (*) indicates playoff winner.

Multiple winners: Jack Nicklaus (6); Arnold Palmer (4); Jimmy Demaret, Nick Faldo, Gary Player and Sam Snead (3); Seve Ballesteros, Ben Hogan, Bernhard Langer, Byron Nelson, Jose Maria Olazabal, Horton Smith and Tom Watson (2).

Year	Winner	Score	Runner-up
1934	Horton Smith	284	Craig Wood (285)
1935	Gene Sarazen*	282	Craig Wood (282)
1936	Horton Smith	285	Harry Cooper (286)
1937	Byron Nelson	283	Ralph Guldahl (285)
1938	Henry Picard	285	Ralph Guldahl & Harry Cooper (287)
1939	Ralph Guldahl	279	Sam Snead (280)
1940	Jimmy Demaret	280	Lloyd Mangrum (284)
1941	Craig Wood	280	Byron Nelson (283)
1942	Byron Nelson*	280	Ben Hogan (280)
1943-45	Not held		World War II
1946	Herman Keiser	282	Ben Hogan (283)
1947	Jimmy Demaret	281	Frank Stranahan & Byron Nelson (283)
1948	Claude Harmon	279	Cary Middlecoff (284)
1949	Sam Snead	282	Lloyd Mangrum & Johnny Bulla (285)
1950	Jimmy Demaret	283	Jim Ferrier (285)
1951	Ben Hogan	280	Skee Riegel (282)
1952	Sam Snead	286	Jack Burke Jr. (290)
1953	Ben Hogan	274	Ed Oliver (279)
1954	Sam Snead*	289	Ben Hogan (289)
1955	Cary Middlecoff	279	Ben Hogan (286)
1956	Jack Burke Jr.	289	Ken Venturi (290)
1957	Doug Ford	283	Sam Snead (286)
1958	Arnold Palmer	284	Doug Ford & Fred Hawkins (285)
1959	Art Wall Jr.	284	Cary Middlecoff (285)
1960	Arnold Palmer	282	Ken Venturi (283)
1961	Gary Player	280	Arnold Palmer & Charles R. Coe (281)
1962	Arnold Palmer*	280	Dow Finsterwald & Gary Player (280)
1963	Jack Nicklaus	286	Tony Lema (287)
1964	Arnold Palmer	276	Jack Nicklaus & Dave Marr (282)
1965	Jack Nicklaus	271	Arnold Palmer & Gary Player (280)
1966	Jack Nicklaus*	288	Gay Brewer Jr. & Tommy Jacobs (288)
1967	Gay Brewer Jr.	280	Bobby Nichols (281)
1968	Bob Goalby	277	Roberto DeVicenzo (278)
1969	George Archer	281	Billy Casper, George Knudson & Tom Weiskopf (282)
1970	Billy Casper*	279	Gene Littler (279)
1971	Charles Coody	279	Jack Nicklaus & Johnny Miller (281)
1972	Jack Nicklaus	286	Bruce Crampton, Bobby Mitchell & Tom Weiskopf (289)
1973	Tommy Aaron	283	J.C. Snead (284)
1974	Gary Player	278	Tom Weiskopf, & Dave Stockton (280)
1975	Jack Nicklaus	276	Johnny Miller & Tom Weiskopf (277)
1976	Ray Floyd	271	Ben Crenshaw (279)
1977	Tom Watson	276	Jack Nicklaus (278)
1978	Gary Player	277	Hubert Green, Rod Funseth & Tom Watson (278)
1979	Fuzzy Zoeller*	280	Ed Sneed & Tom Watson (280)
1980	Seve Ballesteros	275	Gibby Gilbert & Jack Newton (279)
1981	Tom Watson	280	Jack Nicklaus & Johnny Miller (282)
1982	Craig Stadler*	284	Dan Pohl (284)
1983	Seve Ballesteros	280	Ben Crenshaw, & Tom Kite (284)
1984	Ben Crenshaw	277	Tom Watson (279)
1985	Bernhard Langer	282	Curtis Strange, Seve Ballesteros & Ray Floyd (284)
1986	Jack Nicklaus	279	Greg Norman & Tom Kite (280)
1987	Larry Mize*	285	Seve Ballesteros & Greg Norman (285)
1988	Sandy Lyle	281	Mark Calcavecchia (282)
1989	Nick Faldo*	283	Scott Hoch (283)
1990	Nick Faldo*	278	Ray Floyd (278)
1991	Ian Woosnam	277	J.M. Olazabal (278)
1992	Fred Couples	275	Ray Floyd (277)
1993	Bernhard Langer	277	Chip Beck (281)
1994	J.M. Olazabal	279	Tom Lehman (281)
1995	Ben Crenshaw	274	Davis Love III (275)
1996	Nick Faldo	276	Greg Norman (281)
1997	Tiger Woods	270	Tom Kite (282)
1998	Mark O'Meara	279	Fred Couples & David Duval (280)
1999	J.M. Olazabal	280	Davis Love III (282)

*PLAYOFFS:

1935: Gene Sarazen (144) def. Craig Wood (149) in 36 holes. **1942:** Byron Nelson (69) def. Ben Hogan (70) in 18 holes. **1954:** Sam Snead (70) def. Ben Hogan (71) in 18 holes. **1962:** Arnold Palmer (68) def. Gary Player (71) and Dow Finsterwald (77) in 18 holes. **1966:** Jack Nicklaus (70) def. Tommy Jacobs (72) and Gay Brewer Jr. (78) in 18 holes. **1970:** Billy Casper (69) def. Gene Littler (74) in 18 holes. **1979:** Fuzzy Zoeller (4-3) def. Ed Sneed (4-4) and Tom Watson (4-4) on 2nd hole of sudden death. **1982:** Craig Stadler (4) def. Dan Pohl (5) on 1st hole of sudden death. **1987:** Larry Mize (4-3) def. Greg Norman (4-4) and Seve Ballesteros (5) on 2nd hole of sudden death. **1989:** Nick Faldo (5-3) def. Scott Hoch (5-4) on 2nd hole of sudden death. **1990:** Nick Faldo (4-4) def. Raymond Floyd (4-x) on second hole of sudden death.

U.S. Open

Played at a different course each year, the U.S. Open was launched by the new U.S. Golf Association in 1895. The Open was a 36-hole event from 1895-97 and has been 72 holes since then. It switched from a 3-day, 36-hole Saturday finish to 4 days of play in 1965. Note that (*) indicates playoff winner and (a) indicates amateur winner.

Multiple winners: Willie Anderson, Ben Hogan, Bobby Jones and Jack Nicklaus (4); Hale Irwin (3); Julius Boros, Billy Casper, Ernie Els, Ralph Guldahl, Walter Hagen, Lee Janzen, John McDermott, Cary Middlecoff, Andy North, Gene Sarazen, Alex Smith, Payne Stewart, Curtis Strange and Lee Trevino (2).

Year	Winner	Score	Runner-up	Course	Location
1895	Horace Rawlins	173	Willie Dunn (175)	Newport GC	Newport, R.I.
1896	James Foulis	152	Horace Rawlins (155)	Shinnecock Hills GC	Southampton, N.Y.
1897	Joe Lloyd	162	Willie Anderson (163)	Chicago GC	Wheaton, Ill.
1898	Fred Herd	328	Alex Smith (335)	Myopia Hunt Club	Hamilton, Mass.
1899	Willie Smith	315	George Low, W.H. Way & Val Fitzjohn (326)	Baltimore CC	Baltimore
1900	Harry Vardon	313	J.H. Taylor (315)	Chicago GC	Wheaton, Ill.
1901	Willie Anderson*	331	Alex Smith (331)	Myopia Hunt Club	Hamilton, Mass.
1902	Laurie Auchterlonie	307	Stewart Gardner (313)	Garden City GC	Garden City, N.Y.
1903	Willie Anderson*	307	David Brown (307)	Baltusrol GC	Springfield, N.J.
1904	Willie Anderson	303	Gil Nicholls (308)	Glen View Club	Golf, Ill.
1905	Willie Anderson	314	Alex Smith (316)	Myopia Hunt Club	Hamilton, Mass.
1906	Alex Smith	295	Willie Smith (302)	Onwentsia Club	Lake Forest, Ill.
1907	Alec Ross	302	Gil Nicholls (304)	Phila. Cricket Club	Chestnut Hill, Pa.
1908	Fred McLeod*	322	Willie Smith (322)	Myopia Hunt Club	Hamilton, Mass.
1909	George Sargent	290	Tom McNamara (294)	Englewood GC	Englewood, N.J.
1910	Alex Smith*	298	Macdonald Smith & John McDermott (298)	Phila. Cricket Club	Chestnut Hill, Pa.
1911	John McDermott*	307	George Simpson & Mike Brady (307)	Chicago GC	Wheaton, Ill.
1912	John McDermott	294	Tom McNamara (296)	CC of Buffalo	Buffalo
1913	a-Francis Ouimet*	304	Harry Vardon & Ted Ray (304)	The Country Club	Brookline, Mass.
1914	Walter Hagen	290	a-Chick Evans (291)	Midlothian CC	Blue Island, Ill.
1915	a-John Travers	297	Tom McNamara (298)	Baltusrol GC	Springfield, N.J.
1916	a-Chick Evans	286	Jock Hutchinson (288)	Minikahda Club	Minneapolis
1917-18 Not held			World War I		
1919	Walter Hagen*	301	Mike Brady (301)	Brae Burn CC	West Newton, Mass.
1920	Ted Ray	295	Jock Hutchison, Jack Burke, Leo Diegel & Harry Vardon (296)	Inverness Club	Toledo, Ohio
1921	Jim Barnes	289	Walter Hagen & Fred McLeod (298)	Columbia CC	Chevy Chase, Md.
1922	Gene Sarazen	288	a-Bobby Jones & John Black (289)	Skokie CC	Glencoe, Ill.
1923	a-Bobby Jones*	296	Bobby Cruickshank (296)	Inwood CC	Inwood, N.Y.
1924	Cyril Walker	297	a-Bobby Jones (300)	Oakland Hills CC	Birmingham, Mich.
1925	Willie Macfarlane*	291	a-Bobby Jones (291)	Worcester CC	Worcester, Mass.
1926	a-Bobby Jones	293	Joe Turnesa (294)	Scioto CC	Columbus, Ohio
1927	Tommy Armour*	301	Harry Cooper (301)	Oakmont CC	Oakmont, Pa.
1928	Johnny Farrell*	294	a-Bobby Jones (294)	Olympia Fields CC	Matteson, Ill.
1929	a-Bobby Jones*	294	Al Espinosa (294)	Winged Foot CC	Mamaroneck, N.Y.
1930	a-Bobby Jones	287	Macdonald Smith (289)	Interlachen CC	Hopkins, Minn.
1931	Billy Burke*	292	George Von Elm (292)	Inverness Club	Toledo, Ohio
1932	Gene Sarazen	286	Bobby Cruickshank & Phil Perkins (289)	Fresh Meadow CC	Flushing, N.Y.
1933	a-Johnny Goodman	287	Ralph Guldahl (288)	North Shore GC	Glenview, Ill.
1934	Olin Dutra	293	Gene Sarazen (294)	Merion Cricket Club	Ardmore, Pa.
1935	Sam Parks Jr.	299	Jimmy Thomson (301)	Oakmont CC	Oakmont, Pa.
1936	Tony Manero	282	Harry E. Cooper (284)	Baltusrol GC	Springfield, N.J.
1937	Ralph Guldahl	281	Sam Snead (283)	Oakland Hills CC	Birmingham, Mich.
1938	Ralph Guldahl	284	Dick Metz (290)	Cherry Hills CC	Denver
1939	Byron Nelson*	284	Craig Wood & Denny Shute (284)	Philadelphia CC	Philadelphia

U.S. Open (Cont.)

Year	Winner	Score	Runner-up	Course	Location
1940	Lawson Little*	.287	Gene Sarazen (287)	Canterbury GC	Cleveland
1941	Craig Wood	.284	Denny Shute (287)	Colonial Club	Ft. Worth
1942-45	Not held		World War II		
1946	Lloyd Mangrum*	.284	Byron Nelson & Vic Ghezzi (284)	Canterbury GC	Cleveland
1947	Lew Worsham*	.282	Sam Snead (282)	St. Louis CC	Clayton, Mo.
1948	Ben Hogan	.276	Jimmy Demaret (278)	Riviera CC	Los Angeles
1949	Cary Middlecoff	.286	Clayton Heafner & Sam Snead (287)	Medinah CC	Medinah, Ill.
1950	Ben Hogan*	.287	Lloyd Mangrum & George Fazio (287)	Merion Golf Club	Ardmore, Pa.
1951	Ben Hogan	.287	Clayton Heafner (289)	Oakland Hills CC	Birmingham, Mich.
1952	Julius Boros	.281	Ed Oliver (285)	Northwood Club	Dallas
1953	Ben Hogan	.283	Sam Snead (289)	Oakmont CC	Oakmont, Pa.
1954	Ed Furgol	.284	Gene Littler (285)	Baltusrol GC	Springfield, N.J.
1955	Jack Fleck*	.287	Ben Hogan (287)	Olympic CC	San Francisco
1956	Cary Middlecoff	.281	Ben Hogan & Julius Boros (282)	Oak Hill CC	Rochester, N.Y.
1957	Dick Mayer*	.282	Cary Middlecoff (282)	Inverness Club	Toledo, Ohio
1958	Tommy Bolt	.283	Gary Player (287)	Southern Hills CC	Tulsa
1959	Billy Casper	.282	Bob Rosburg (283)	Winged Foot GC	Marmaroneck, N.Y.
1960	Arnold Palmer	.280	Jack Nicklaus (282)	Cherry Hills CC	Denver
1961	Gene Littler	.281	Doug Sanders & Bob Goalby (282)	Oakland Hills CC	Birmingham, Mich.
1962	Jack Nicklaus*	.283	Arnold Palmer (283)	Oakmont CC	Oakmont, Pa.
1963	Julius Boros*	.293	Arnold Palmer & Jacky Cupit (293)	The Country Club	Brookline, Mass.
1964	Ken Venturi	.278	Tommy Jacobs (282)	Congressional CC	Bethesda, Md.
1965	Gary Player*	.282	Kel Nagle (282)	Bellerive CC	St. Louis
1966	Billy Casper*	.278	Arnold Palmer (278)	Olympic CC	San Francisco
1967	Jack Nicklaus	.275	Arnold Palmer (279)	Baltusrol GC	Springfield, N.J.
1968	Lee Trevino	.275	Jack Nicklaus (279)	Oak Hill CC	Rochester, N.Y.
1969	Orville Moody	.281	Al Geiberger, Deane Beman & Bob Rosburg (282)	Champions GC	Houston
1970	Tony Jacklin	.281	Dave Hill (288)	Hazeltine National GC	Chaska, Minn.
1971	Lee Trevino*	.280	Jack Nicklaus (280)	Merion GC	Ardmore, Pa.
1972	Jack Nicklaus	.290	Bruce Crampton (293)	Pebble Beach GL	Pebble Beach, Calif.
1973	Johnny Miller	.279	John Schlee (280)	Oakmont CC	Oakmont, Pa.
1974	Hale Irwin	.287	Forest Fezler (289)	Winged Foot GC	Mamaroneck, N.Y.
1975	Lou Graham*	.287	John Mahaffey (287)	Medinah CC	Medinah, Ill.
1976	Jerry Pate	.277	Al Geiberger & Tom Weiskopf (279)	Atlanta AC	Duluth, Ga.
1977	Hubert Green	.278	Lou Graham (279)	Southern Hills CC	Tulsa
1978	Andy North	.285	Dave Stockton & J.C. Snead (286)	Cherry Hills CC	Denver
1979	Hale Irwin	.284	Gary Player & Jerry Pate (286)	Inverness Club	Toledo, Ohio
1980	Jack Nicklaus	.272	Isao Aoki (274)	Baltusrol GC	Springfield, N.J.
1981	David Graham	.273	George Burns & Bill Rogers (276)	Merion GC	Ardmore, Pa.
1982	Tom Watson	.282	Jack Nicklaus (284)	Pebble Beach GL	Pebble Beach, Calif.
1983	Larry Nelson	.280	Tom Watson (281)	Oakmont CC	Oakmont, Pa.
1984	Fuzzy Zoeller*	.276	Greg Norman (276)	Winged Foot GC	Mamaroneck, N.Y.
1985	Andy North	.279	Dave Barr, T.C. Chen & Denis Watson (280)	Oakland Hills CC	Birmingham, Mich.
1986	Ray Floyd	.279	Lanny Wadkins & Chip Beck (281)	Shinnecock Hills GC	Southampton, N.Y.
1987	Scott Simpson	.277	Tom Watson (278)	Olympic Club	San Francisco
1988	Curtis Strange*	.278	Nick Faldo (278)	The Country Club	Brookline, Mass.
1989	Curtis Strange	.278	Chip Beck, Ian Woosnam & Mark McCumber (279)	Oak Hill CC	Rochester, N.Y.
1990	Hale Irwin*	.280	Mike Donald (280)	Medinah CC	Medinah, Ill.
1991	Payne Stewart*	.282	Scott Simpson (282)	Hazeltine National GC	Chaska, Minn.
1992	Tom Kite	.285	Jeff Sluman (287)	Pebble Beach GL	Pebble Beach, Calif.
1993	Lee Janzen	.272	Payne Stewart (274)	Baltusrol GC	Springfield, N.J.

Year	Winner	Score	Runner-up	Course	Location
1994	Ernie Els*	279	Colin Montgomerie (279) & Loren Roberts (279)	Oakmont CC	Oakmont, Pa.
1995	Corey Pavin	280	Greg Norman (282)	Shinnecock Hills GC	Southampton, N.Y.
1996	Steve Jones	278	Davis Love III & Tom Lehman (279)	Oakland Hills CC	Bloomfield Hills, Mich.
1997	Ernie Els	276	Colin Montgomerie (277)	Congressional CC	Bethesda, Md.
1998	Lee Janzen	280	Payne Stewart (281)	Olympic Club	San Francisco
1999	Payne Stewart	279	Phil Mickelson (280)	Pinehurst CC	Pinehurst, N.C.

*PLAYOFFS:

1901: Willie Anderson (85) def. Alex Smith (86) in 18 holes. **1903:** Willie Anderson (82) def. David Brown (84) in 18 holes. **1908:** Fred McLeod (77) def. Willie Smith (83) in 18 holes. **1910:** Alex Smith (71) def. John McDermott (75) & Macdonald Smith (77) in 18 holes. **1911:** John McDermott (80) def. Mike Brady (82) & George Simpson (85) in 18 holes. **1913:** Francis Ouimet (72) def. Harry Vardon (77) & Edward Ray (78) in 18 holes. **1919:** Walter Hagen (77) def. Mike Brady (78) in 18 holes. **1923:** Bobby Jones (76) def. Bobby Cruickshank (78) in 18 holes. **1925:** Willie Macfarlane (75-72—147) def. Bobby Jones (75-73—148) in 36 holes. **1927:** Tommy Armour (76) def. Harry Cooper (79) in 18 holes. **1928:** Johnny Farrell (70-73—143) def. Bobby Jones (73-71—144) in 36 holes. **1929:** Bobby Jones (141) def. Al Espinosa (164) in 36 holes. **1931:** Billy Burke (149-148) def. George Von Elm (149-149) in 72 holes. **1939:** Byron Nelson (68-70) def. Craig Wood (68-73) and Denny Shute (76) in 36 holes. **1940:** Lawson Little (70) def. Gene Sarazen (73) in 18 holes. **1946:** Lloyd Mangrum (72-72—144) def. Byron Nelson (72-73—145) and Vic Ghezzi (72-73—145) in 36 holes. **1947:** Lew Worsham (69) def. Sam Snead (70) in 18 holes. **1950:** Ben Hogan (69) def. Llyod Mangrum (73) & George Fazio (75) in 18 holes. **1955:** Jack Fleck (69) def. Ben Hogan (72) in 18 holes. **1957:** Dick Mayer (72) def. Cary Middlecoff (79) in 18 holes. **1962:** Jack Nicklaus (71) def. Arnold Palmer (74) in 18 holes. **1963:** Julius Boros (70) def. Jacky Cupit (73) & Arnold Palmer (76) in 18 holes. **1965:** Gary Player (71) def. Kel Nagle (74) in 18 holes. **1966:** Billy Casper (69) def. Arnold Palmer (73) in 18 holes. **1971:** Lee Trevino (68) def. Jack Nicklaus (71) in 18 holes. **1975:** Lou Graham (71) def. John Mahaffey (73) in 18 holes. **1984:** Fuzzy Zoeller (67) def. Greg Norman (75) in 18 holes. **1988:** Curtis Strange (71) def. Nick Faldo (75) in 18 holes. **1990:** Hale Irwin (74-3) def. Mike Donald (74-4) on 1st hole of sudden death after 18 holes. **1991:** Payne Stewart (75) def. Scott Simpson (77) in 18 holes. **1994:** Ernie Els (74-4-4) def. Loren Roberts (74-4-5) and Colin Montgomerie (78-x-x) on 2nd hole of sudden death after 18 holes.

British Open

The oldest of the Majors, the Open began in 1860 to determine "the champion golfer of the world." While only professional golfers participated in the first year of the tournament, amateurs have been invited ever since. Competition was extended from 36 to 72 holes in 1892. Conducted by the Royal and Ancient Golf Club of St. Andrews, the Open is rotated among select golf courses in England and Scotland. Note that (*) indicates playoff winner and (a) indicates amateur winner.

Multiple winners: Harry Vardon (6); James Braid, J.H. Taylor, Peter Thomson and Tom Watson (5); Walter Hagen, Bobby Locke, Tom Morris Sr., Tom Morris Jr. and Willie Park (4); Jamie Anderson, Seve Ballesteros, Henry Cotton, Nick Faldo, Robert Ferguson, Bobby Jones, Jack Nicklaus and Gary Player (3); Harold Hilton, Bob Martin, Greg Norman, Arnold Palmer, Willie Park Jr. and Lee Trevino (2).

Year	Winner	Score	Runner-up	Course	Location
1860	Willie Park	174	Tom Morris Sr. (176)	Prestwick Club	Ayrshire, Scotland
1861	Tom Morris Sr.	163	Willie Park (167)	Prestwick Club	Ayrshire, Scotland
1862	Tom Morris Sr.	163	Willie Park (176)	Prestwick Club	Ayrshire, Scotland
1863	Willie Park	168	Tom Morris Sr. (170)	Prestwick Club	Ayrshire, Scotland
1864	Tom Morris Sr.	167	Andrew Strath (169)	Prestwick Club	Ayrshire, Scotland
1865	Andrew Strath	162	Willie Park (164)	Prestwick Club	Ayrshire, Scotland
1866	Willie Park	169	David Park (171)	Prestwick Club	Ayrshire, Scotland
1867	Tom Morris Sr.	170	Willie Park (172)	Prestwick Club	Ayrshire, Scotland
1868	Tom Morris Jr.	157	Robert Andrew (159)	Prestwick Club	Ayrshire, Scotland
1869	Tom Morris Jr.	154	Tom Morris Sr. (157)	Prestwick Club	Ayrshire, Scotland
1870	Tom Morris Jr.	149	Bob Kirk (161)	Prestwick Club	Ayrshire, Scotland
1871	Not held				
1872	Tom Morris Jr.	166	David Strath (169)	Prestwick Club	Ayrshire, Scotland
1873	Tom Kidd	179	Jamie Anderson (180)	St. Andrews	St. Andrews, Scotland
1874	Mungo Park	159	Tom Morris Jr. (161)	Musselburgh	Musselburgh, Scotland
1875	Willie Park	166	Bob Martin (168)	Prestwick Club	Ayrshire, Scotland
1876	Bob Martin*	176	David Strath (176)	St. Andrews	St. Andrews, Scotland
1877	Jamie Anderson	160	Bob Pringle (162)	Musselburgh	Musselburgh, Scotland
1878	Jamie Anderson	157	Bob Kirk (159)	Prestwick Club	Ayrshire, Scotland
1879	Jamie Anderson	169	Andrew Kirkaldy & James Allan (172)	St. Andrews	St. Andrews, Scotland
1880	Bob Ferguson	162	Peter Paxton (167)	Musselburgh	Musselburgh, Scotland
1881	Bob Ferguson	170	Jamie Anderson (173)	Prestwick Club	Ayrshire, Scotland
1882	Bob Ferguson	171	Willie Fernie (174)	St. Andrews	St. Andrews, Scotland
1883	Willie Fernie*	159	Bob Ferguson (159)	Musselburgh	Musselburgh, Scotland
1884	Jack Simpson	160	David Rollan & Willie Fernie (164)	Prestwick Club	Ayrshire, Scotland
1885	Bob Martin	171	Archie Simpson (172)	St. Andrews	St. Andrews, Scotland
1886	David Brown	157	Willie Campbell (159)	Musselburgh	Musselburgh, Scotland
1887	Willie Park Jr.	161	Bob Martin (162)	Prestwick Club	Ayrshire, Scotland
1888	Jack Burns	171	David Anderson & Ben Sayers (172)	St. Andrews	St. Andrews, Scotland
1889	Willie Park Jr.*	155	Andrew Kirkaldy (155)	Musselburgh	Musselburgh, Scotland

British Open (Cont.)

Year	Winner	Score	Runner-up	Course	Location
1890	a-John Ball	164	Willie Fernie (167) & A. Simpson (167)	Prestwick Club	Ayrshire, Scotland
1891	Hugh Kirkaldy	166	Andrew Kirkaldy & Willie Fernie (168)	St. Andrews	St. Andrews, Scotland
1892	a-Harold Hilton	305	John Ball, Sandy Herd & Hugh Kirkaldy (308)	Muirfield	Gullane, Scotland
1893	Willie Auchterlonie	322	Johnny Laidlay (324)	Prestwick Club	Ayrshire, Scotland
1894	J.H. Taylor	326	Douglas Rolland (331)	Royal St. George's	Sandwich, England
1895	J.H. Taylor	322	Sandy Herd (326)	St. Andrews	St. Andrews, Scotland
1896	Harry Vardon*	316	J.H. Taylor (316)	Muirfield	Gullane, Scotland
1897	a-Harold Hilton	314	James Braid (315)	Hoylake	Hoylake, England
1898	Harry Vardon	307	Willie Park Jr. (308)	Prestwick Club	Ayrshire, Scotland
1899	Harry Vardon	310	Jack White (315)	Royal St. George's	Sandwich, England
1900	J.H. Taylor	309	Harry Vardon (317)	St. Andrews	St. Andrews, Scotland
1901	James Braid	309	Harry Vardon (312)	Muirfield	Gullane, Scotland
1902	Sandy Herd	307	Harry Vardon (308)	Hoylake	Hoylake, England
1903	Harry Vardon	300	Tom Vardon (306)	Prestwick Club	Ayrshire, Scotland
1904	Jack White	296	James Braid (297)	Royal St. George's	Sandwich, England
1905	James Braid	318	J.H. Taylor (323) & Rolland Jones (323)	St. Andrews	St. Andrews, Scotland
1906	James Braid	300	J.H. Taylor (304)	Muirfield	Gullane, Scotland
1907	Arnaud Massy	312	J.H. Taylor (314)	Hoylake	Hoylake, England
1908	James Braid	291	Tom Ball (299)	Prestwick Club	Ayrshire, Scotland
1909	J.H. Taylor	295	James Braid (299)	Deal	Deal, England
1910	James Braid	299	Sandy Herd (303)	St. Andrews	St. Andrews, Scotland
1911	Harry Vardon*	303	Arnaud Massy (303)	Royal St. George's	Sandwich, England
1912	Ted Ray	295	Harry Vardon (299)	Muirfield	Gullane, Scotland
1913	J.H. Taylor	304	Ted Ray (312)	Hoylake	Hoylake, England
1914	Harry Vardon	306	J.H. Taylor (309)	Prestwick Club	Ayrshire, Scotland
1915-19 Not held			World War I		
1920	George Duncan	303	Sandy Herd (305)	Deal	Deal, England
1921	Jock Hutchison*	296	Roger Wethered (296)	St. Andrews	St. Andrews, Scotland
1922	Walter Hagen	300	George Duncan & Jim Barnes (301)	Royal St. George's	Sandwich, England
1923	Arthur Havers	295	Walter Hagen (296)	Royal Troon	Troon, Scotland
1924	Walter Hagen	301	Ernest Whitcombe (302)	Hoylake	Hoylake, England
1925	Jim Barnes	300	Archie Compston & Ted Ray (301)	Prestwick Club	Ayrshire, Scotland
1926	a-Bobby Jones	291	Al Watrous (293)	Royal Lytham	Lytham, England
1927	a-Bobby Jones	285	Aubrey Boomer (291)	St. Andrews	St. Andrews, Scotland
1928	Walter Hagen	292	Gene Sarazen (294)	Royal St. George's	Sandwich, England
1929	Walter Hagen	292	Johnny Farrell (298)	Muirfield	Gullane, Scotland
1930	a-Bobby Jones	291	Macdonald Smith & Leo Diegel (293)	Hoylake	Hoylake, England
1931	Tommy Armour	296	Jose Jurado (297)	Carnoustie	Carnoustie, Scotland
1932	Gene Sarazen*	283	Macdonald Smith (288)	Prince's	Prince's, England
1933	Denny Shute*	292	Craig Wood (292)	St. Andrews	St. Andrews, Scotland
1934	Henry Cotton	283	Sid Brews (288)	Royal St. George's	Sandwich, England
1935	Alf Perry	283	Alf Padgham (287)	Muirfield	Gullane, Scotland
1936	Alf Padgham	287	Jimmy Adams (288)	Hoylake	Hoylake, England
1937	Henry Cotton	290	Reg Whitcombe (292)	Carnoustie	Carnoustie, Scotland
1938	Reg Whitcombe	295	Jimmy Adams (297)	Royal St. George's	Sandwich, England
1939	Dick Burton	290	Johnny Bulla (292)	St. Andrews	St. Andrews, Scotland
1940-45 Not held			World War II		
1946	Sam Snead	290	Bobby Locke (294) & Johnny Bulla (294)	St. Andrews	St. Andrews, Scotland
1947	Fred Daly	293	Frank Stranahan & Reg Horne (294)	Hoylake	Hoylake, England
1948	Henry Cotton	284	Fred Daly (289)	Muirfield	Gullane, Scotland
1949	Bobby Locke*	283	Harry Bradshaw (283)	Royal St. George's	Sandwich, England
1950	Bobby Locke	279	Roberto de Vicenzo (281)	Royal Troon	Troon, Scotland
1951	Max Faulkner	285	Tony Cerda (287)	Royal Portrush	Portrush, Ireland
1952	Bobby Locke	287	Peter Thomson (288)	Royal Lytham	Lytham, England
1953	Ben Hogan	282	Frank Stranahan, Dai Rees, Tony Cerda & Peter Thomson (286)	Carnoustie	Carnoustie, Scotland

Year	Winner	Score	Runner-up	Course	Location
1954	Peter Thomson	283	Sid Scott, Dai Rees & Bobby Locke (284)	Royal Birkdale	Southport, England
1955	Peter Thomson	281	Johny Fallon (283)	St. Andrews	St. Andrews, Scotland
1956	Peter Thomson	286	Flory Van Donck (289)	Hoylake	Hoylake, England
1957	Bobby Locke	279	Peter Thomson (282)	St. Andrews	St. Andrews, Scotland
1958	Peter Thomson*	278	Dave Thomas (278)	Royal Lytham	Lytham, England
1959	Gary Player	284	Flory Van Donck & Fred Bullock (286)	Muirfield	Gullane, Scotland
1960	Kel Nagle	278	Arnold Palmer (279)	St. Andrews	St. Andrews, Scotland
1961	Arnold Palmer	284	Dai Rees (285)	Royal Birkdale	Southport, England
1962	Arnold Palmer	276	Kel Nagle (282)	Royal Troon	Troon, Scotland
1963	Bob Charles*	277	Phil Rodgers (277)	Royal Lytham	Lytham, England
1964	Tony Lema	279	Jack Nicklaus (284)	St. Andrews	St. Andrews, Scotland
1965	Peter Thomson	285	Christy O'Connor & Brian Huggett (287)	Royal Birkdale	Southport, England
1966	Jack Nicklaus	282	Doug Sanders & Dave Thomas (283)	Muirfield	Gullane, Scotland
1967	Roberto de Vicenzo	278	Jack Nicklaus (280)	Hoylake	Hoylake, England
1968	Gary Player	289	Jack Nicklaus & Bob Charles (291)	Carnoustie	Carnoustie, Scotland
1969	Tony Jacklin	280	Bob Charles (282)	Royal Lytham	Lytham, England
1970	Jack Nicklaus*	283	Doug Sanders (283)	St. Andrews	St. Andrews, Scotland
1971	Lee Trevino	278	Lu Liang Huan (279)	Royal Birkdale	Southport, England
1972	Lee Trevino	278	Jack Nicklaus (279)	Muirfield	Gullane, Scotland
1973	Tom Weiskopf	276	Johnny Miller & Neil Coles (279)	Royal Troon	Troon, Scotland
1974	Gary Player	282	Peter Oosterhuis (286)	Royal Lytham	Lytham, England
1975	Tom Watson*	279	Jack Newton (279)	Carnoustie	Carnoustie, Scotland
1976	Johnny Miller	279	Seve Ballesteros & Jack Nicklaus (285)	Royal Birkdale	Southport, England
1977	Tom Watson	268	Jack Nicklaus (269)	Turnberry	Turnberry, Scotland
1978	Jack Nicklaus	281	Tom Kite, Ray Floyd, Ben Crenshaw & Simon Owen (283)	St. Andrews	St. Andrews, Scotland
1979	Seve Ballesteros	283	Jack Nicklaus & Ben Crenshaw (286)	Royal Lytham	Lytham, England
1980	Tom Watson	271	Lee Trevino (275)	Muirfield	Gullane, Scotland
1981	Bill Rogers	276	Bernhard Langer (280)	Royal St. George's	Sandwich, England
1982	Tom Watson	284	Peter Oosterhuis & Nick Price (285)	Royal Troon	Troon, Scotland
1983	Tom Watson	275	Hale Irwin & Andy Bean (276)	Royal Birkdale	Southport, England
1984	Seve Ballesteros	276	Bernhard Langer & Tom Watson (278)	St. Andrews	St. Andrews, Scotland
1985	Sandy Lyle	282	Payne Stewart (283)	Royal St. George's	Sandwich, England
1986	Greg Norman	280	Gordon J. Brand (285)	Turnberry	Turnberry, Scotland
1987	Nick Faldo	279	Paul Azinger & Rodger Davis (280)	Muirfield	Gullane, Scotland
1988	Seve Ballesteros	273	Nick Price (275)	Royal Lytham	Lytham, England
1989	Mark Calcavecchia*	275	Greg Norman & Wayne Grady (275)	Royal Troon	Troon, Scotland
1990	Nick Faldo	270	Payne Stewart & Mark McNulty (275)	St. Andrews	St. Andrews, Scotland
1991	Ian Baker-Finch	272	Mike Harwood (274)	Royal Birkdale	Southport, England
1992	Nick Faldo	272	John Cook (273)	Muirfield	Gullane, Scotland
1993	Greg Norman	267	Nick Faldo (269)	Royal St. George's	Sandwich, England
1994	Nick Price	268	Jesper Parnevik (269)	Turnberry	Turnberry, Scotland
1995	John Daly*	282	Costantino Rocca (282)	St. Andrews	St. Andrews, Scotland
1996	Tom Lehman	271	Mark McCumber & Ernie Els (273)	Royal Lytham	Lytham, England
1997	Justin Leonard	272	Jesper Parnevik & Darren Clarke (275)	Royal Troon	Troon, Scotland
1998	Mark O'Meara*	280	Brian Watts (280)	Royal Birkdale	Southport, England
1998	Paul Lawrie*	290	Justin Leonard & Jean Van de Velde (290)	Carnoustie	Carnoustie, Scotland

*PLAYOFFS:

1876: Bob Martin awarded title when David Strath refused playoff. **1883:** Willie Fernie (158) def. Robert Ferguson (159) in 36 holes. **1889:** Willie Park Jr. (158) def. Andrew Kirkaldy (163) in 36 holes. **1896:** Harry Vardon (157) def. John H. Taylor *161) in 36 holes. **1911:** Harry Bardon won when Arnaud Massy conceded at 35th hole. **1921:** Jack Hutchison (150) def. Roger Wethered (159) in 36 holes. **1933:** Denny Shute (149) def. Craig Wood (154) in 36 holes. **1949:** Bobby Locke

(135) def. Harry Bradshaw (147) in 36 holes. **1958:** Peter Thomson (139) def. Dave Thomas (143) in 36 holes. **1963:** Bob Charles (140) def. Phil Rogers (148) in 36 holes. **1970:** Jack Nicklaus (72) def. Doug Sanders (73) in 18 holes. **1975:** Tom Watson (71) def. Jack Newton (72) in 18 holes. **1989:** Mark Calcavecchia (4-3-3-3 — 13) def. Wayne Grady (4-4-4-4 — 16) and Greg Norman (3-3-4-x) in 4 holes. **1995:** John Daly (3-4-4-4 — 15) def. Costantino Rocca (4-5-7-3 — 19) in 4 holes. **1998:** Mark O'Meara (4-4-5-4 — 17) def. Brian Watts (5-4-5-5 — 19) in 4 holes **1999:** Paul Lawrie (5-4-3-3 — 15) def. Justin Leonard (5-4-4-5 — 18) and Jean Van de Velde (6-4-3-5 — 18) in 4 holes.

PGA Championship

The PGA Championship began in 1916 as a professional golfers match play tournament, but switched to stroke play in 1958. Conducted by the PGA of America, the tournament is played on a different course each year.

Mulitple winners: Walter Hagen and Jack Nicklaus (5); Gene Sarazen and Sam Snead (3); Jim Barnes, Leo Diegel, Raymond Floyd, Ben Hogan, Byron Nelson, Larry Nelson, Gary Player, Paul Runyan, Denny Shute, Dave Stockton and Lee Trevino (2).

Year	Winner	Score	Runner-up	Course	Location
1916	Jim Barnes	1-up	Jock Hutchison	Siwanoy CC	Bronxville, N.Y.
1917-18	Not held		World War I		
1919	Jim Barnes	6 & 5	Fred McLeod	Engineers CC	Roslyn, N.Y.
1920	Jock Hutchison	1-up	J. Douglas Edgar	Flossmoor CC	Flossmoor, Ill.
1921	Walter Hagen	3 & 2	Jim Barnes	Inwood CC	Inwood, N.Y.
1922	Gene Sarazen	4 & 3	Emmet French	Oakmont CC	Oakmont, Pa.
1923	Gene Sarazen*	1-up/38	Walter Hagen	Pelham CC	Pelham, N.Y.
1924	Walter Hagen	2-up	Jim Barnes	French Lick CC	French Lick, Ind.
1925	Walter Hagen	6 & 5	Bill Mehlhorn	Olympia Fields CC	Matteson, Ill.
1926	Walter Hagen	5 & 3	Leo Diegel	Salisbury GC	Westbury, N.Y.
1927	Walter Hagen	1-up	Joe Turnesa	Cedar Crest CC	Dallas
1928	Leo Diegel	6 & 5	Al Espinosa	Five Farms CC	Baltimore
1929	Leo Diegel	6 & 4	John Farrell	Hillcrest CC	Los Angeles
1930	Tommy Armour	1-up	Gene Sarazen	Fresh Meadow CC	Flushing, N.Y.
1931	Tom Creavy	2 & 1	Denny Shute	Wannamoisett CC	Rumford, R.I.
1932	Olin Dutra	4 & 3	Frank Walsh	Keller GC	St. Paul, Minn.
1933	Gene Sarazen	5 & 4	Willie Goggin	Blue Mound CC	Milwaukee
1934	Paul Runyan*	1-up/38	Craig Wood	Park CC	Williamsville, N.Y.
1935	Johnny Revolta	5 & 4	Tommy Armour	Twin Hills CC	Oklahoma City
1936	Denny Shute	3 & 2	Jimmy Thomson	Pinehurst CC	Pinehurst, N.C.
1937	Denny Shute*	1-up/37	Harold McSpaden	Pittsburgh FC	Aspinwall, Pa.
1938	Paul Runyan	8 & 7	Sam Snead	Shawnee CC	Shawnee-on-Del, Pa.
1939	Henry Picard*	1-up/37	Byron Nelson	Pomonok CC	Flushing, N.Y.
1940	Byron Nelson*	1-up	Sam Snead	Hershey CC	Hershey, Pa.
1941	Vic Ghezzi*	1-up/38	Byron Nelson	Cherry Hills CC	Denver
1942	Sam Snead	2 & 1	Jim Turnesa	Seaview CC	Atlantic City, N.J.
1943	Not held		World War II		
1944	Bob Hamilton	1-up	Byron Nelson	Manito G & CC	Spokane, Wash.
1945	Byron Nelson	4 & 3	Sam Byrd	Morraine CC	Dayton, Ohio
1946	Ben Hogan	6 & 4	Porky Oliver	Portland GC	Portland, Ore.
1947	Jim Ferrier	2 & 1	Chick Harbert	Plum Hollow CC	Detroit
1948	Ben Hogan	7 & 6	Mike Turnesa	Norwood Hills CC	St. Louis
1949	Sam Snead	3 & 2	John Palmer	Hermitage CC	Richmond, Va.
1950	Chandler Harper	4 & 3	Henry Williams Jr.	Scioto CC	Columbus, Ohio
1951	Sam Snead	7 & 6	Walter Burkemo	Oakmont CC	Oakmont, Pa.
1952	Jim Turnesa	1-up	Chick Harbert	Big Spring CC	Louisville
1953	Walter Burkemo	2 & 1	Felice Torza	Birmingham CC	Birmingham, Mich.
1954	Chick Harbert	4 & 3	Walter Burkemo	Keller GC	St. Paul, Minn.
1955	Doug Ford	4 & 3	Cary Middlecoff	Meadowbrook CC	Detroit
1956	Jack Burke	3 & 2	Ted Kroll	Blue Hill CC	Boston
1957	Lionel Hebert	2 & 1	Dow Finsterwald	Miami Valley GC	Dayton, Ohio
1958	Dow Finsterwald	276	Billy Casper (278)	Llanerch CC	Havertown, Pa.
1959	Bob Rosburg	277	Jerry Barber & Doug Sanders (278)	Minneapolis GC	St. Louis Park, Minn.
1960	Jay Hebert	281	Jim Ferrier (282)	Firestone CC	Akron, Ohio
1961	Jerry Barber**	277	Don January (277)	Olympia Fields CC	Matteson, Ill.
1962	Gary Player	278	Bob Goalby (279)	Aronimink GC	Newtown Square, Pa.
1963	Jack Nicklaus	279	Dave Ragan (281)	Dallas AC	Dallas
1964	Bobby Nichols	271	Jack Nicklaus & Arnold Palmer (274)	Columbus CC	Columbus, Ohio
1965	Dave Marr	280	Jack Nicklaus & Billy Casper (282)	Laurel Valley GC	Ligonier, Pa.
1966	Al Geiberger	280	Dudley Wysong (284)	Firestone CC	Akron, Ohio
1967	Don January**	281	Don Massengale (281)	Columbine CC	Littleton, Colo.
1968	Julius Boros	281	Arnold Palmer & Bob Charles (282)	Pecan Valley CC	San Antonio
1969	Ray Floyd	276	Gary Player (277)	NCR GC	Dayton, Ohio

Year	Winner	Score	Runner-up	Course	Location
1970	Dave Stockton	279	Arnold Palmer & Bob Murphy (281)	Southern Hills CC	Tulsa
1971	Jack Nicklaus	281	Billy Casper (283)	PGA National GC	Palm Beach Gardens, Fla.
1972	Gary Player	281	Jim Jamieson & Tommy Aaron (283)	Oakland Hills GC	Birmingham, Mich.
1973	Jack Nicklaus	277	Bruce Crampton (281)	Canterbury GC	Cleveland
1974	Lee Trevino	276	Jack Nicklaus (277)	Tanglewood GC	Winston-Salem, N.C.
1975	Jack Nicklaus	276	Bruce Crampton (278)	Firestone CC	Akron, Ohio
1976	Dave Stockton	281	Don January & Ray Floyd (282)	Congressional CC	Bethesda, Md.
1977	Lanny Wadkins**	282	Gene Littler (282)	Pebble Beach GL	Pebble Beach, Calif.
1978	John Mahaffey**	276	Jerry Pate & Tom Watson (276)	Oakmont CC	Oakmont, Pa.
1979	David Graham**	272	Ben Crenshaw (272)	Oakland Hills CC	Birmingham, Mich.
1980	Jack Nicklaus	274	Andy Bean (281)	Oak Hill CC	Rochester, N.Y.
1981	Larry Nelson	273	Fuzzy Zoeller (277)	Atlanta AC	Duluth, Ga.
1982	Ray Floyd	272	Lanny Wadkins (275)	Southern Hills CC	Tulsa
1983	Hal Sutton	274	Jack Nicklaus (275)	Riviera CC	Los Angeles
1984	Lee Trevino	273	Lanny Wadkins & Gary Player (277)	Shoal Creek	Birmingham, Ala.
1985	Hubert Green	278	Lee Trevino (280)	Cherry Hills CC	Denver
1986	Bob Tway	276	Greg Norman (278)	Inverness Club	Toledo, Ohio
1987	Larry Nelson**	287	Lanny Wadkins (287)	PGA National	Palm Beach Gardens, Fla.
1988	Jeff Sluman	272	Paul Azinger 275)	Oak Tree GC	Edmond, Okla.
1989	Payne Stewart	276	Andy Bean, Mike Reid & Curtis Strange (277)	Kemper Lakes GC	Hawthorn Woods, Ill.
1990	Wayne Grady	282	Fred Couples (285)	Shoal Creek	Birmingham, Ala.
1991	John Daly	276	Bruce Lietzke (279)	Crooked Stick GC	Carmel, Ind.
1992	Nick Price	278	Nick Faldo, John Cook, Jim Gallagher & Gene Sauers (281)	Bellerive CC	St. Louis
1993	Paul Azinger**	272	Greg Norman (272)	Inverness Club	Toledo, Ohio
1994	Nick Price	269	Corey Pavin (275)	Southern Hills CC	Tulsa
1995	Steve Elkington**	267	Colin Montgomerie (267)	Riviera CC	Pacific Palisades, Calif.
1996	Mark Brooks**	277	Kenny Perry (277)	Valhalla GC	Louisville, Ky.
1997	Davis Love III	269	Justin Leonard (274)	Winged Foot GC	Mamaroneck, N.Y.
1998	Vijay Singh	271	Steve Stricker (273)	Sahalee CC	Redmond, Wash.
1999	Tiger Woods	277	Sergio Garcia (278)	Medinah CC	Medinah, Ill.

*While the PGA Championship was a match play tournament from 1916-57, the two finalists played 36 holes for the title. In the five years that a playoff was necessary, the match was decided on the 37th or 38th hole.

**PLAYOFFS:

1961: Jerry Barber (67) def. Don January (68) in 18 holes. **1967:** Don January (69) def. Don Massengale (71) in 18 holes. **1977:** Lanny Wadkins (4-4-4) def. Gene Littler (4-4-5) on 3rd hole of sudden death. **1978:** John Mahaffey (4-3) def. Jerry Pate (4-4) and Tom Watson (4-5) on 2nd hole of sudden death. **1979:** David Graham (4-4-2) def. Ben Crenshaw (4-4-4) on 3rd hole of sudden death. **1987:** Larry Nelson (4) def. Lanny Wadkins (5) on 1st hole of sudden death. **1993:** Paul Azinger (4-4) def. Greg Norman (4-5) on 2nd hole of sudden death. **1995:** Steve Elkington (3) def. Colin Montgomerie (4) on 1st hole of sudden death. **1996:** Mark Brooks (4) def. Kenny Perry (5) on 1st hole of sudden death.

Major Championship Leaders
Through 1999; active PGA players in bold type.

	US Open	British Open	PGA	Masters	US Am	British Am	Total
Jack Nicklaus	4	3	5	6	2	0	**20**
Bobby Jones	4	3	0	0	5	1	**13**
Walter Hagen	2	4	5	0	0	0	**11**
Ben Hogan	4	1	2	2	0	0	**9**
Gary Player	1	3	2	3	0	0	**9**
John Ball	0	1	0	0	0	8	**9**
Arnold Palmer	1	2	0	4	1	0	**8**
Tom Watson	1	5	0	2	0	0	**8**
Harold Hilton	0	2	0	0	1	4	**7**
Gene Sarazen	2	1	3	1	0	0	**7**
Sam Snead	0	1	3	3	0	0	**7**
Harry Vardon	1	6	0	0	0	0	**7**
Nick Faldo	0	3	0	3	0	0	**6**
Lee Trevino	2	2	2	0	0	0	**6**

Tournaments: U.S. Open, British Open, PGA Championship, Masters, U.S. Amateur and British Amateur.

Grand Slam Summary

The only golfer ever to win a recognized Grand Slam—four major championships in a single season—was Bobby Jones in 1930. That year, Jones won the U.S. and British Opens as well as the U.S. and British Amateurs.

The men's professional Grand Slam—the Masters, U.S. Open, British Open and PGA Championship—did not gain acceptance until 30 years later when Arnold Palmer won the 1960 Masters and U.S. Open. The media wrote that the popular Palmer was chasing the "new" Grand Slam and would have to win the British Open and the PGA to claim it. He did not, but then nobody has before or since.

Three wins in one year: Ben Hogan (1953). **Two wins in one year** (18): Jack Nicklaus (5 times); Ben Hogan, Arnold Palmer and Tom Watson (twice); Nick Faldo, Mark O'Meara, Gary Player, Nick Price, Sam Snead, Lee Trevino and Craig Wood (once).

Year	Masters	US Open	Brit. Open	PGA	Year	Masters	US Open	Brit. Open	PGA
1934	H. Smith	Dutra	Cotton	Runyan	1967	Brewer Jr.	Nicklaus	De Vicenzo	January
1935	Sarazen	Parks	Perry	Revolta	1968	Goalby	Trevino	Player	Boros
1936	H. Smith	Manero	Padgham	Shute	1969	Archer	Moody	Jacklin	Floyd
1937	B. Nelson	Guldahl	Cotton	Shute	1970	Casper	Jacklin	Nicklaus	Stockton
1938	Picard	Guldahl	Whitcombe	Runyan	1971	Coody	Trevino	Trevino	Nicklaus
1939	Guldahl	B. Nelson	Burton	Picard	1972	Nicklaus	Nicklaus	Trevino	Player
1940	Demaret	Little	—	B. Nelson	1973	Aaron	J. Miller	Weiskopf	Nicklaus
1941	Wood	Wood	—	Ghezzi	1974	Player	Irwin	Player	Trevino
1942	B. Nelson	—	—	Snead	1975	Nicklaus	L. Graham	T. Watson	Nicklaus
1943	—	—	—	—	1976	Floyd	J. Pate	Miller	Stockton
1944	—	—	—	Hamilton	1977	T. Watson	H. Green	T. Watson	L. Wadkins
1945	—	—	—	B. Nelson	1978	Player	North	Nicklaus	Mahaffey
1946	Keiser	Mangrum	Snead	Hogan	1979	Zoeller	Irwin	Ballesteros	D. Graham
1947	Demaret	Worsham	F. Daly	Ferrier	1980	Ballesteros	Nicklaus	T. Watson	Nicklaus
1948	Harmon	Hogan	Cotton	Hogan	1981	T. Watson	D. Graham	Rogers	L. Nelson
1949	Snead	Middlecoff	Locke	Snead	1982	Stadler	T. Watson	T. Watson	Floyd
1950	Demaret	Hogan	Locke	Harper	1983	Ballesteros	L. Nelson	T. Watson	Sutton
1951	Hogan	Hogan	Faulkner	Snead	1984	Crenshaw	Zoeller	Ballesteros	Trevino
1952	Snead	Boros	Locke	Turnesa	1985	Langer	North	Lyle	H. Green
1953	Hogan	Hogan	Hogan	Burkemo	1986	Nicklaus	Floyd	Norman	Tway
1954	Snead	Furgol	Thomson	Harbert	1987	Mize	S. Simpson	Faldo	L. Nelson
1955	Middlecoff	Fleck	Thomson	Ford	1988	Lyle	Strange	Ballesteros	Sluman
1956	Burke	Middlecoff	Thomson	Burke	1989	Faldo	Strange	Calcavecchia	Stewart
1957	Ford	Mayer	Locke	L. Hebert	1990	Faldo	Irwin	Faldo	Grady
1958	Palmer	Bolt	Thomson	Finsterwald	1991	Woosnam	Stewart	Baker-Finch	J. Daly
1959	Wall	Casper	Player	Rosburg	1992	Couples	Kite	Faldo	Price
1960	Palmer	Palmer	Nagle	J. Hebert	1993	Langer	Janzen	Norman	Azinger
1961	Player	Littler	Palmer	J. Barber	1994	Olazabal	Els	Price	Price
1962	Palmer	Nicklaus	Palmer	Player	1995	Crenshaw	Pavin	Daly	Elkington
1963	Nicklaus	Boros	Charles	Nicklaus	1996	Faldo	S. Jones	Lehman	Brooks
1964	Palmer	Venturi	Lema	Nichols	1997	Woods	Els	Leonard	Love
1965	Nicklaus	Player	Thomson	Marr	1998	O'Meara	Janzen	O'Meara	Singh
1966	Nicklaus	Casper	Nicklaus	Geiberger	1999	Olazabal	Stewart	Lawrie	Woods

Vardon Trophy

Awarded since 1937 by the PGA of America to the PGA Tour regular with the lowest adjusted scoring average. The award is named after Harry Vardon, the six-time British Open champion, who won the U.S. Open in 1900. A point system was used from 1937-41.

Multiple winners: Billy Casper and Lee Trevino (5); Arnold Palmer and Sam Snead (4); Ben Hogan, Greg Norman and Tom Watson (3); Fred Couples, Bruce Crampton, Tom Kite, Lloyd Mangrum and Nick Price (2).

Year		Pts
1937	Harry Cooper	.500
1938	Sam Snead	.520
1939	Byron Nelson	.473
1940	Ben Hogan	.423
1941	Ben Hogan	.494
1942-46	No award	

Year		Avg
1947	Jimmy Demaret	69.90
1948	Ben Hogan	69.30
1949	Sam Snead	69.37
1950	Sam Snead	69.23
1951	Lloyd Mangrum	70.05
1952	Jack Burke	70.54
1953	Lloyd Mangrum	70.22
1954	E.J. Harrison	70.41
1955	Sam Snead	69.86
1956	Cary Middlecoff	70.35
1957	Dow Finsterwald	70.30
1958	Bob Rosburg	70.11
1959	Art Wall	70.35

Year		Avg
1960	Billy Casper	69.95
1961	Arnold Palmer	69.85
1962	Arnold Palmer	70.27
1963	Billy Casper	70.58
1964	Arnold Palmer	70.01
1965	Billy Casper	70.85
1966	Billy Casper	70.27
1967	Arnold Palmer	70.18
1968	Billy Casper	69.82
1969	Dave Hill	70.34
1970	Lee Trevino	70.64
1971	Lee Trevino	70.27
1972	Lee Trevino	70.89
1973	Bruce Crampton	70.57
1974	Lee Trevino	70.53
1975	Bruce Crampton	70.51
1976	Don January	70.56
1977	Tom Watson	70.32
1978	Tom Watson	70.16
1979	Tom Watson	70.27

Year		Avg
1980	Lee Trevino	69.73
1981	Tom Kite	69.80
1982	Tom Kite	70.21
1983	Ray Floyd	70.61
1984	Calvin Peete	70.56
1985	Don Pooley	70.36
1986	Scott Hoch	70.08
1987	Dan Pohl	70.25
1988	Chip Beck	69.46
1989	Greg Norman	69.49
1990	Greg Norman	69.10
1991	Fred Couples	69.59
1992	Fred Couples	69.38
1993	Nick Price	69.11
1994	Greg Norman	68.81
1995	Steve Elkington	69.62
1996	Tom Lehman	69.32
1997	Nick Price	68.98
1998	David Duval	69.13

U.S. Amateur

Match play from 1895-64, stroke play from 1965-72, match play 1973-79, 36-hole stroke play qualifying before match play since 1979.

Multiple winners: Bobby Jones (5); Jerry Travers (4); Walter Travis and Tiger Woods (3); Deane Beman, Charles Coe, Gary Cowan, H. Chandler Egan, Chick Evans, Lawson Little, Jack Nicklaus, Francis Ouimet, Jay Sigel, William Turnesa, Bud Ward, Harvie Ward, and H.J. Whigham (2).

Year		Year		Year		Year	
1895	Charles Macdonald	1921	Jesse Guilford	1949	Charles Coe	1974	Jerry Pate
1896	H.J. Whigham	1922	Jess Sweetser			1975	Fred Ridley
1897	H.J. Whigham	1923	Max Marston	1950	Sam Urzetta	1976	Bill Sander
1898	Findlay Douglas	1924	Bobby Jones	1951	Billy Maxwell	1977	John Fought
1899	H.M. Harriman	1925	Bobby Jones	1952	Jack Westland	1978	John Cook
		1926	George Von Elm	1953	Gene Littler	1979	Mark O'Meara
1900	Walter Travis	1927	Bobby Jones	1954	Arnold Palmer		
1901	Walter Travis	1928	Bobby Jones	1955	Harvie Ward	1980	Hal Sutton
1902	Louis James	1929	Harrison Johnston	1956	Harvie Ward	1981	Nathaniel Crosby
1903	Walter Travis			1957	Hillman Robbins	1982	Jay Sigel
1904	H. Chandler Egan	1930	Bobby Jones	1958	Charles Coe	1983	Jay Sigel
1905	H. Chandler Egan	1931	Francis Ouimet	1959	Jack Nicklaus	1984	Scott Verplank
1906	Eben Byers	1932	Ross Somerville			1985	Sam Randolph
1907	Jerry Travers	1933	George Dunlap	1960	Deane Beman	1986	Buddy Alexander
1908	Jerry Travers	1934	Lawson Little	1961	Jack Nicklaus	1987	Billy Mayfair
1909	Robert Gardner	1935	Lawson Little	1962	Labron Harris	1988	Eric Meeks
		1936	John Fischer	1963	Deane Beman	1989	Chris Patton
1910	W.C. Fownes Jr.	1937	John Goodman	1964	Bill Campbell		
1911	Harold Hilton	1938	William Turnesa	1965	Bob Murphy	1990	Phil Mickelson
1912	Jerry Travers	1939	Bud Ward	1966	Gary Cowan	1991	Mitch Voges
1913	Jerry Travers			1967	Bob Dickson	1992	Justin Leonard
1914	Francis Ouimet	1940	Richard Chapman	1968	Bruce Fleisher	1993	John Harris
1915	Robert Gardner	1941	Bud Ward	1969	Steve Melnyk	1994	Tiger Woods
1916	Chick Evans	1942-45	Not held			1995	Tiger Woods
1917-18	Not held	1946	Ted Bishop	1970	Lanny Wadkins	1996	Tiger Woods
1919	Davidson Herron	1947	Skee Riegel	1971	Gary Cowan	1997	Matt Kuchar
		1948	William Turnesa	1972	Vinny Giles	1998	Hank Kuehne
1920	Chick Evans			1973	Craig Stadler	1999	David Gossett

British Amateur

Match play since 1885.

Multiple winners: John Ball (8); Michael Bonallack (5); Harold Hilton (4); Joe Carr (3); Horace Hutchinson, Ernest Holderness, Trevor Homer, Johnny Laidley, Lawson Little, Peter McEvoy, Dick Siderowf, Frank Stranahan, Freddie Tait and Cyril Tolley (2).

Year		Year		Year		Year	
1885	Allen MacFie	1912	John Ball	1948	Frank Stranahan	1975	Vinny Giles
1886	Horace Hutchinson	1913	Harold Hilton	1949	Samuel McCready	1976	Dick Siderowf
1887	Horace Hutchinson	1914	J.L.C. Jenkins			1977	Peter McEvoy
1888	John Ball	1915-19	Not held	1950	Frank Stranahan	1978	Peter McEvoy
1889	Johnny Laidley			1951	Richard Chapman	1979	Jay Sigel
		1920	Cyril Tolley	1952	Harvie Ward		
1890	John Ball	1921	William Hunter	1953	Joe Carr	1980	Duncan Evans
1891	Johnny Laidley	1922	Ernest Holderness	1954	Douglas Bachli	1981	Phillipe Ploujoux
1892	John Ball	1923	Roger Wethered	1955	Joe Conrad	1982	Martin Thompson
1893	Peter Anderson	1924	Ernest Holderness	1956	John Beharrell	1983	Philip Parkin
1894	John Ball	1925	Robert Harris	1957	Reid Jack	1984	Jose-Maria Olazabal
1895	Leslie Balfour-Melville	1926	Jesse Sweetser	1958	Joe Carr	1985	Garth McGimpsey
1896	Freddie Tait	1927	William Tweddell	1959	Deane Beman	1986	David Curry
1897	Jack Allan	1928	Thomas Perkins			1987	Paul Mayo
1898	Freddie Tait	1929	Cyril Tolley	1960	Joe Carr	1988	Christian Hardin
1899	John Ball			1961	Michael Bonallack	1989	Stephen Dodd
		1930	Bobby Jones	1962	Richard Davies		
1900	Harold Hilton	1931	Eric Smith	1963	Michael Lunt	1990	Rolf Muntz
1901	Harold Hilton	1932	John deForest	1964	Gordon Clark	1991	Gary Wolstenholme
1902	Charles Hutchings	1933	Michael Scott	1965	Michael Bonallack	1992	Stephen Dundas
1903	Robert Maxwell	1934	Lawson Little	1966	Bobby Cole	1993	Ian Pyman
1904	Walter Travis	1935	Lawson Little	1967	Bob Dickson	1994	Lee James
1905	Arthur Barry	1936	Hector Thomson	1968	Michael Bonallack	1995	Gordon Sherry
1906	James Robb	1937	Robert Sweeny Jr.	1969	Michael Bonallack	1996	Warren Bledon
1907	John Ball	1938	Charles Yates			1997	Craig Watson
1908	E.A. Lassen	1939	Alexander Kyle	1970	Michael Bonallack	1998	Sergio Garcia
1909	Robert Maxwell			1971	Steve Melnyk	1999	Graeme Storm
		1940-45	Not held	1972	Trevor Homer		
1910	John Ball	1946	James Bruen	1973	Dick Siderowf		
1911	Harold Hilton	1947	William Turnesa	1974	Trevor Homer		

WOMEN

The U.S. Women's Open began under the direction of the defunct Women's Professional Golfers Assn. in 1946, passed to the LPGA in 1949 and to the USGA in 1953. The tournament used a match play format its first year then switched to stroke play; (*) indicates playoff winner and (a) indicates amateur winner.

Multiple winners: Betsy Rawls and Mickey Wright (4); Susie Maxwell Berning, Hollis Stacy and Babe Zaharis (3); JoAnne Carner, Donna Caponi, Betsy King, Patty Sheehan, Annika Sorenstam and Louise Suggs (2).

U.S. Women's Open

Year		Year		Year		Year	
1946	Patty Berg	1960	Betsy Rawls	1974	Sandra Haynie	1988	Liselotte Neumann
1947	Betty Jameson	1961	Mickey Wright	1975	Sandra Palmer	1989	Betsy King
1948	Babe Zaharias	1962	Murle Lindstrom	1976	JoAnne Carner*		
1949	Louise Suggs	1963	Mary Mills	1977	Hollis Stacy	1990	Betsy King
		1964	Mickey Wright*	1978	Hollis Stacy	1991	Meg Mallon
1950	Babe Zaharias	1965	Carol Mann	1979	Jerilyn Britz	1992	Patty Sheehan*
1951	Betsy Rawls	1966	Sandra Spuzich			1993	Lauri Merten
1952	Louise Suggs	1967	a-Catherine Lacoste	1980	Amy Alcott	1994	Patty Sheehan
1953	Betsy Rawls*	1968	Susie M. Berning	1981	Pat Bradley	1995	Annika Sorenstam
1954	Babe Zaharias	1969	Donna Caponi	1982	Janet Anderson	1996	Annika Sorenstam
1955	Fay Crocker			1983	Jan Stephenson	1997	Alison Nicholas
1956	Kathy Cornelius*	1970	Donna Caponi	1984	Hollis Stacy	1998	Se Ri Pak*
1957	Betsy Rawls	1971	JoAnne Carner	1985	Kathy Baker	1999	Juli Inkster
1958	Mickey Wright	1972	Susie M. Berning	1986	Jane Geddes*		
1959	Mickey Wright	1973	Susie M. Berning	1987	Laura Davies*		

*PLAYOFFS:

1953: Betsy Rawls (71) def. Jackie Pung (77) in 18 holes. **1956:** Kathy Cornelius (75) def. Barbara McIntire (82) in 18 holes. **1964:** Mickey Wright (70) def. Ruth Jessen (72) in 18 holes. **1976:** JoAnne Carner (76) def. Sandra Palmer (78) in 18 holes. **1986:** Jane Geddes (71) def. Sally Little (73) in 18 holes. **1987:** Laura Davies (71) def. Ayako Okamoto (73) and JoAnne Carner (74) in 18 holes. **1992:** Patty Sheehan (72) def. Juli Inkster (74) in 18 holes. **1998:** Se Ri Pak def. Jenny Chuasiriporn on the second sudden death hole after both players were tied after an 18-hole playoff.

LPGA Championship

Officially the McDonald's LPGA Championship since 1994 (Mazda sponsored from 1987-93), the tournament began in 1955 and has had extended stays at the Stardust CC in Las Vegas (1961-66), Pleasant Valley CC in Sutton, Mass. (1967-68, 70-74), the Jack Nicklaus Sports Center at Kings Island, Ohio (1978-89) and Bethesda CC in Maryland (since 1990); (*) indicates playoff winner.

Multiple winners: Mickey Wright (4); Nancy Lopez, Patty Sheehan and Kathy Whitworth (3); Donna Caponi, Laura Davies, Sandra Haynie, Mary Mills and Betsy Rawls (2).

Year		Year		Year		Year	
1955	Beverly Hanson	1967	Kathy Whitworth	1979	Donna Caponi	1990	Beth Daniel
1956	Marlene Hagge*	1968	Sandra Post*	1980	Sally Little	1991	Meg Mallon
1957	Louise Suggs	1969	Betsy Rawls	1981	Donna Caponi	1992	Betsy King
1958	Mickey Wright			1982	Jan Stephenson	1993	Patty Sheehan
1959	Betsy Rawls	1970	Shirley Englehorn*	1983	Patty Sheehan	1994	Laura Davies
		1971	Kathy Whitworth	1984	Patty Sheehan	1995	Kelly Robbins
1960	Mickey Wright	1972	Kathy Ahern	1985	Nancy Lopez	1996	Laura Davies
1961	Mickey Wright	1973	Mary Mills	1986	Pat Bradley	1997	Chris Johnson*
1962	Judy Kimball	1974	Sandra Haynie	1987	Jane Geddes	1998	Se Ri Pak
1963	Mickey Wright	1975	Kathy Whitworth	1988	Sherri Turner	1999	Juli Inkster
1964	Mary Mills	1976	Betty Burfeindt	1989	Nancy Lopez		
1965	Sandra Haynie	1977	Chako Higuchi				
1966	Gloria Ehret	1978	Nancy Lopez				

*PLAYOFFS:

1956: Marlene Hagge def. Patti Berg in sudden death. **1968:** Sandra Post (68) def. Kathy Whitworth (75) in 18 holes. **1970:** Shirley Englehorn def. Kathy Whitworth in sudden death. **1997:** Chris Johnson def. Leta Lindley in sudden death.

Nabisco Dinah Shore

Formerly known as the Colgate Dinah Shore from 1972-81, the tournament become the LPGA's fourth designated major championship in 1983. Named after the entertainer, this tourney has been played at Mission Hills CC in Rancho Mirage, Calif., since it begin; (*) indicates playoff winner.

Multiple winners: (as a major): Amy Alcott and Betsy King (3); Juli Inkster and Dottie Pepper (2).

Year		Year		Year		Year	
1972	Jane Blalock	1979	Sandra Post	1986	Pat Bradley	1993	Helen Alfredsson
1973	Mickey Wright	1980	Donna Caponi	1987	Betsy King*	1994	Donna Andrews
1974	Jo Ann Prentice	1981	Nancy Lopez	1988	Amy Alcott	1995	Nanci Bowen
1975	Sandra Palmer	1982	Sally Little	1989	Juli Inkster	1996	Patty Sheehan
1976	Judy Rankin	1983	Amy Alcott	1990	Betsy King	1997	Betsy King
1977	Kathy Whitworth	1984	Juli Inkster*	1991	Amy Alcott	1998	Pat Hurst
1978	Sandra Post	1985	Alice Miller	1992	Dottie Pepper*	1999	Dottie Pepper

*PLAYOFFS:

1984: Juli Inkster def. Pat Bradley in sudden death. **1987:** Betsy King def. Patty Sheehan in sudden death. **1992:** Dottie Pepper def. Juli Inkster in sudden death.

du Maurier Classic

Formerly known as La Canadienne in 1973 and the Peter Jackson Classic from 1974-83, this Canadian stop on the LPGA Tour became the third designated major championship in 1979; (*) indicates playoff winner.

Multiple winners (as a major): Pat Bradley (3); Brandie Burton (2).

Year		Year		Year		Year	
1973	Jocelyne Bourassa	1980	Pat Bradley	1987	Jody Rosenthal	1994	Martha Nause
1974	Carole Jo Skala	1981	Jan Stephenson	1988	Sally Little	1995	Jenny Lidback
1975	JoAnne Carner	1982	Sandra Haynie	1989	Tammie Green	1996	Laura Davies
1976	Donna Caponi	1983	Hollis Stacy	1990	Cathy Johnston	1997	Colleen Walker
1977	Judy Rankin	1984	Juli Inkster	1991	Nancy Scranton	1998	Brandie Burton
1978	JoAnne Carner	1985	Pat Bradley	1992	Sherri Steinhaur	1999	Karrie Webb
1979	Amy Alcott	1986	Pat Bradley*	1993	Brandie Burton*		

*PLAYOFFS:

1986: Pat Bradley def. Ayako Okamoto in sudden death. **1993:** Brandie Burton def. Betsy King in sudden death.

Titleholders Championship (1937-72)

The Titleholders was considered a major title on the women's tour until it was discontinued after the 1972 tournament.

Multiple winners: Patty Berg (7); Louise Suggs (4); Babe Zaharias (3); Dorothy Kirby, Marilynn Smith, Kathy Whitworth and Mickey Wright (2).

Year		Year		Year		Year	
1937	Patty Berg	1947	Babe Zaharias	1955	Patty Berg	1963	Marilynn Smith
1938	Patty Berg	1948	Patty Berg	1956	Louise Suggs	1964	Marilynn Smith
1939	Patty Berg	1949	Peggy Kirk	1957	Patty Berg	1965	Kathy Whitworth
1940	Betty Hicks	1950	Babe Zaharias	1958	Beverly Hanson	1966	Kathy Whitworth
1941	Dorothy Kirby	1951	Pat O'Sullivan	1959	Louise Suggs	1967-71	Not held
1942	Dorothy Kirby	1952	Babe Zaharias	1960	Fay Crocker	1972	Sandra Palmer
1943-45	Not held	1953	Patty Berg	1961	Mickey Wright		
1946	Louise Suggs	1954	Louise Suggs	1962	Mickey Wright		

Western Open (1930-67)

The Western Open was considered a major title on the women's tour until it was discontinued after the 1967 tournament.

Multiple winners: Patty Berg (7); Louise Suggs and Babe Zaharias (4); Mickey Wright (3); June Beebe, Opal Hill, Betty Jameson and Betsy Rawls (2).

Year		Year		Year		Year	
1930	Mrs. Lee Mida	1940	Babe Zaharias	1950	Babe Zaharias	1960	Joyce Ziske
1931	June Beebe	1941	Patty Berg	1951	Patty Berg	1961	Mary Lena Faulk
1932	Jane Weiller	1942	Betty Jameson	1952	Betsy Rawls	1962	Mickey Wright
1933	June Beebe	1943	Patty Berg	1953	Louise Suggs	1963	Mickey Wright
1934	Marian McDougall	1944	Babe Zaharias	1954	Betty Jameson	1964	Carol Mann
1935	Opal Hill	1945	Babe Zaharias	1955	Patty Berg	1965	Susie Maxwell
1936	Opal Hill	1946	Louise Suggs	1956	Beverly Hanson	1966	Mickey Wright
1937	Betty Hicks	1947	Louise Suggs	1957	Patty Berg	1967	Kathy Whitworth
1938	Bea Barrett	1948	Patty Berg	1958	Patty Berg		
1939	Helen Dettweiler	1949	Louise Suggs	1959	Betsy Rawls		

Major Championship Leaders

Through 1999; active players in bold type.

	US Open	LPGA	duM	Dinah	Title	Western	US Am	Brit Am	Total
Patty Berg	1	0	0	0	7	7	1	0	16
Mickey Wright	4	4	0	0	2	3	0	0	13
Louise Suggs	2	1	0	0	4	4	1	1	13
Babe Zaharias	3	0	0	0	3	4	1	1	12
Juli Inkster	1	1	1	2	0	0	3	0	8
Betsy Rawls	4	2	0	0	0	2	0	0	8
JoAnne Carner	2	0	0	0	0	0	5	0	7
Kathy Whitworth	0	3	0	0	2	1	0	0	6
Pat Bradley	1	1	3	1	0	0	0	0	6
Betsy King	2	1	0	3	0	0	0	0	6
Patty Sheehan	2	3	0	1	0	0	0	0	6
Glenna C. Vare	0	0	0	0	0	0	6	0	6

Tournaments: U.S. Open, LPGA Championship, du Maurier Classic, Nabisco Dinah Shore, Titleholders (1930-72), Western Open (1937-67), U.S. Amateur, and British Amateur.

Grand Slam Summary

From 1955-66, the U.S. Open, LPGA Championship, Western Open and Titleholders tournaments served as the Women's Grand Slam. Since 1983, however, the U.S. Open, LPGA, du Maurier Classic in Canada and Nabisco Dinah Shore have been the major events. No one has won a four-event Grand Slam on the women's tour.

Three wins in one year (3): Babe Zaharias (1950), Mickey Wright (1961) and Pat Bradley (1986).

Two wins in one year (16): Patty Berg and Mickey Wright (3 times); Juli Inkster and Louise Suggs (twice); Laura Davies, Sandra Haynie, Betsy King, Meg Mallon, Se Ri Pak, Betsy Rawls and Kathy Whitworth (once).

Year	LPGA	US Open	T'holders	Western
1937	—	—	Berg	Hicks
1938	—	—	Berg	Barrett
1939	—	—	Berg	Dettweiler
1940	—	—	Hicks	Zaharias
1941	—	—	Kirby	Berg
1942	—	—	Kirby	Jameson
1943	—	—	—	Berg
1944	—	—	—	Zaharias
1945	—	—	—	Zaharias
1946	—	Berg	Suggs	Suggs
1947	—	Jameson	Zaharias	Suggs
1948	—	Zaharias	Berg	Suggs
1949	—	Suggs	Kirk	Suggs
1950	—	Zaharias	Zaharias	Zaharias
1951	—	Rawls	O'Sullivan	Berg
1952	—	Suggs	Zaharias	Rawls
1953	—	Rawls	Berg	Suggs
1954	—	Zaharias	Suggs	Jameson
1955	Hanson	Crocker	Berg	Berg
1956	Hagge	Cornelius	Suggs	Hanson
1957	Suggs	Rawls	Berg	Berg
1958	Wright	Wright	Hanson	Berg
1959	Rawls	Wright	Suggs	Rawls
1960	Wright	Rawls	Crocker	Ziske
1961	Wright	Wright	Wright	Faulk
1962	Kimball	Lindstrom	Wright	Wright
1963	Wright	Mills	M. Smith	Wright
1964	Mills	Wright	M. Smith	Mann
1965	Haynie	Mann	Whitworth	Maxwell
1966	Ehret	Spuzich	Whitworth	Wright
1967	Whitworth	a-LaCoste	—	Whitworth
1968	Post	Berning	—	—
1969	Rawls	Caponi	—	—

Year	LPGA	US Open	T'holders	Western
1970	Englehorn	Caponi	—	—
1971	Whitworth	Carner	—	—
1972	Ahern	Berning	Palmer	—
1973	Mills	Berning	—	—
1974	Haynie	Haynie	—	—
1975	Whitworth	Palmer	—	—
1976	Burfeindt	Carner	—	—
1977	Higuchi	Stacy	—	—
1978	Lopez	Stacy	—	—

Year	LPGA	US Open	duMaurier	D. Shore
1979	Caponi	Britz	Alcott	—
1980	Little	Alcott	Bradley	—
1981	Caponi	Bradley	Stephenson	—
1982	Stephenson	Anderson	Haynie	—
1983	Sheehan	Stephenson	Stacy	Alcott
1984	Sheehan	Stacy	Inkster	Inkster
1985	Lopez	Baker	Bradley	Miller
1986	Bradley	Geddes	Bradley	Bradley
1987	Geddes	Davies	Rosenthal	King
1988	Turner	Neumann	Little	Alcott
1989	Lopez	King	Green	Inkster
1990	Daniel	King	Johnston	King
1991	Mallon	Mallon	Scranton	Alcott
1992	King	Sheehan	Steinhaur	Pepper
1993	Sheehan	Merten	Burton	Alfredsson
1994	Davies	Sheehan	Nause	Andrews
1995	Robbins	Sorenstam	Lidback	Bowen
1996	Davies	Sorenstam	Davies	Sheehan
1997	Johnson	Nicholas	Walker	King
1998	Pak	Pak	Burton	Hurst
1999	Inkster	Inkster	Webb	Pepper

Vare Trophy

The Vare Trophy for best scoring average by a player on the LPGA Tour has been awarded since 1937 by the LPGA. The award is named after Glenna Collett Vare, winner of six U.S. women's amateur titles from 1922-35.

Multiple winners: Kathy Whitworth (7); JoAnne Carner and Mickey Wright (5); Patty Berg, Beth Daniel, Nancy Lopez, Judy Rankin and Annika Sorenstam (3); Pat Bradley and Betsy King (2).

Year		Avg	Year		Avg	Year		Avg
1953	Patty Berg	75.00	1969	Kathy Whitworth	72.38	1985	Nancy Lopez	70.73
1954	Babe Zaharias	75.48	1970	Kathy Whitworth	72.26	1986	Pat Bradley	71.10
1955	Patty Berg	74.47	1971	Kathy Whitworth	72.88	1987	Betsy King	71.14
1956	Patty Berg	74.57	1972	Kathy Whitworth	72.38	1988	Colleen Walker	71.26
1957	Louise Suggs	74.64	1973	Judy Rankin	73.08	1989	Beth Daniel	70.38
1958	Beverly Hanson	74.92	1974	JoAnne Carner	72.87			
1959	Betsy Rawls	74.03	1975	JoAnne Carner	72.40	1990	Beth Daniel	70.54
1960	Mickey Wright	73.25	1976	Judy Rankin	72.25	1991	Pat Bradley	70.66
1961	Mickey Wright	73.55	1977	Judy Rankin	72.16	1992	Dottie Pepper	70.80
1962	Mickey Wright	73.67	1978	Nancy Lopez	71.76	1993	Betsy King	70.85
1963	Mickey Wright	72.81	1979	Nancy Lopez	71.20	1994	Beth Daniel	70.90
1964	Mickey Wright	72.46	1980	Amy Alcott	71.51	1995	Annika Sorenstam	71.00
1965	Kathy Whitworth	72.61	1981	JoAnne Carner	71.75	1996	Annika Sorenstam	70.47
1966	Kathy Whitworth	72.60	1982	JoAnne Carner	71.49	1997	Karrie Webb	70.00
1967	Kathy Whitworth	72.74	1983	JoAnne Carner	71.41	1998	Annika Sorenstam	69.99
1968	Carol Mann	72.04	1984	Patty Sheehan	71.40			

U.S. Women's Amateur

Stroke play in 1895, match play since 1896.

Multiple winners: Glenna Collett Vare (6); JoAnne Gunderson Carner (5); Margaret Curtis, Beatrix Hoyt, Dorothy Campbell Hurd, Juli Inkster, Alexa Stirling, Virginia Van Wie, Anne Quast Decker Welts (3); Kay Cockerill, Beth Daniel, Vicki Goetze, Katherine Harley, Genevieve Hecker, Betty Jameson, Kelli Kuehne and Barbara McIntire (2).

Year		Year		Year		Year	
1895	Mrs. C.S. Brown	1922	Glenna Collett	1950	Beverly Hanson	1975	Beth Daniel
1896	Beatrix Hoyt	1923	Edith Cummings	1951	Dorothy Kirby	1976	Donna Horton
1897	Beatrix Hoyt	1924	Dorothy C. Hurd	1952	Jacqueline Pung	1977	Beth Daniel
1898	Beatrix Hoyt	1925	Glenna Collett	1953	Mary Lena Faulk	1978	Cathy Sherk
1899	Ruth Underhill	1926	Helen Stetson	1954	Barbara Romack	1979	Carolyn Hill
		1927	Miriam Burns Horn	1955	Patricia Lesser		
1900	Frances Griscom	1928	Glenna Collett	1956	Marlene Stewart	1980	Juli Inkster
1901	Genevieve Hecker	1929	Glenna Collett	1957	JoAnne Gunderson	1981	Juli Inkster
1902	Genevieve Hecker			1958	Anne Quast	1982	Juli Inkster
1903	Bessie Anthony	1930	Glenna Collett	1959	Barbara McIntire	1983	Joanne Pacillo
1904	Georgianna Bishop	1931	Helen Hicks			1984	Deb Richard
1905	Pauline Mackay	1932	Virginia Van Wie	1960	JoAnne Gunderson	1985	Michiko Hattori
1906	Harriot Curtis	1933	Virginia Van Wie	1961	Anne Quast Decker	1986	Kay Cockerill
1907	Margaret Curtis	1934	Virginia Van Wie	1962	JoAnne Gunderson	1987	Kay Cockerill
1908	Katherine Harley	1935	Glenna Collett Vare	1963	Anne Quast Welts	1988	Pearl Sinn
1909	Dorothy Campbell	1936	Pamela Barton	1964	Barbara McIntire	1989	Vicki Goetze
		1937	Estelle Lawson	1965	Jean Ashley		
1910	Dorothy Campbell	1938	Patty Berg	1966	JoAnne G. Carner	1990	Pat Hurst
1911	Margaret Curtis	1939	Betty Jameson	1967	Mary Lou Dill	1991	Amy Fruhwirth
1912	Margaret Curtis			1968	JoAnne G. Carner	1992	Vicki Goetze
1913	Gladys Ravenscroft	1940	Betty Jameson	1969	Catherine Lacoste	1993	Jill McGill
1914	Katherine Harley	1941	Elizabeth Hicks			1994	Wendy Ward
1915	Florence Vanderbeck	1942-45	Not held	1970	Martha Wilkinson	1995	Kelli Kuehne
1916	Alexa Stirling	1946	Babe D. Zaharias	1971	Laura Baugh	1996	Kelli Kuehne
1917-18	Not held	1947	Louise Suggs	1972	Mary Budke	1997	Silvia Cavalleri
1919	Alexa Stirling	1948	Grace Lenczyk	1973	Carol Semple	1998	Grace Park
		1949	Dorothy Porter	1974	Cynthia Hill	1999	Dorothy Delasin
1920	Alexa Stirling						
1921	Marion Hollins						

British Women's Amateur

Match play since 1893.

Multiple winners: Cecil Leitch and Joyce Wethered (4); May Hezlet, Lady Margaret Scott, Brigitte Varangot and Enid Wilson (3); Rhone Adair, Pam Barton, Dorothy Campbell, Elizabeth Chadwick, Helen Holm, Marley Spearman, Frances Stephens, Jessie Valentine and Michelle Walker (2).

Year		Year		Year		Year	
1893	Lady Margaret Scott	1922	Joyce Wethered	1952	Moira Paterson	1977	Angela Uzielli
1894	Lady Margaret Scott	1923	Doris Chambers	1953	Marlene Stewart	1978	Edwina Kennedy
1895	Lady Margaret Scott	1924	Joyce Wethered	1954	Frances Stephens	1979	Maureen Madill
1896	Amy Pascoe	1925	Joyce Wethered	1955	Jessie Valentine		
1897	Edith Orr	1926	Cecil Leitch	1956	Wiffi Smith	1980	Anne Quast Sander
1898	Lena Thomson	1927	Simone de la Chaume	1957	Philomena Garvey	1981	Belle Robertson
1899	May Hezlet	1928	Nanette le Blan	1958	Jessie Valentine	1982	Kitrina Douglas
		1929	Joyce Wethered	1959	Elizabeth Price	1983	Jill Thornhill
1900	Rhona Adair					1984	Jody Rosenthal
1901	Mary Graham	1930	Diana Fishwick	1960	Barbara McIntire	1985	Lillian Behan
1902	May Hezlet	1931	Enid Wilson	1961	Marley Spearman	1986	Marnie McGuire
1903	Rhona Adair	1932	Enid Wilson	1962	Marley Spearman	1987	Janet Collingham
1904	Lottie Dod	1933	Enid Wilson	1963	Brigitte Varangot	1988	Joanne Furby
1905	Bertha Thompson	1934	Helen Holm	1964	Carol Sorenson	1989	Helen Dobson
1906	Mrs. W. Kennion	1935	Wanda Morgan	1965	Brigitte Varangot		
1907	May Hezlet	1936	Pam Barton	1966	Elizabeth Chadwick	1990	Julie Wade Hall
1908	Maud Titterton	1937	Jessie Anderson	1967	Elizabeth Chadwick	1991	Valerie Michaud
1909	Dorothy Campbell	1938	Helen Holm	1968	Brigitte Varangot	1992	Bernille Pedersen
		1939	Pam Barton	1969	Catherine Lacoste	1993	Catriona Lambert
1910	Elsie Grant-Suttie					1994	Emma Duggleby
1911	Dorothy Campbell	1940-45	Not held	1970	Dinah Oxley	1995	Julie Wade Hall
1912	Gladys Ravenscroft	1946	Jean Hetherington	1971	Michelle Walker	1996	Kelli Kuehne
1913	Muriel Dodd	1947	Babe Zaharias	1972	Michelle Walker	1997	Alison Rose
1914	Cecil Leitch	1948	Louise Suggs	1973	Ann Irvin	1998	Kim Rostron
1915-19	Not held	1949	Frances Stephens	1974	Carol Semple	1999	Marine Monnet
				1975	Nancy Roth Syms		
1920	Cecil Leitch	1950	Lally de St. Sauveur	1976	Cathy Panton		
1921	Cecil Leitch	1951	Catherine MacCann				

Senior PGA
PGA Seniors' Championship

First played in 1937. Two championships played in 1979 and 1984.

Multiple winners: Sam Snead (6); Hale Irwin, Gary Player, Al Watrous and Eddie Williams (3); Julius Boros, Jock Hutchison, Don January, Arnold Palmer, Paul Runyan, Gene Sarazen and Lee Trevino (2).

Year		Year		Year		Year	
1937	Jock Hutchison	1954	Gene Sarazen	1970	Sam Snead	1984	Peter Thomson
1938	Fred McLeod*	1955	Mortie Dutra	1971	Julius Boros	1985	Not held
1939	Not held	1956	Pete Burke	1972	Sam Snead	1986	Gary Player
		1957	Al Watrous	1973	Sam Snead	1987	Chi Chi Rodriguez
1940	Otto Hackbarth*	1958	Gene Sarazen	1974	Roberto De Vicenzo	1988	Gary Player
1941	Jack Burke	1959	Willie Goggin	1975	Charlie Sifford*	1989	Larry Mowry
1942	Eddie Williams			1976	Pete Cooper		
1943-44	Not held	1960	Dick Metz	1977	Julius Boros	1990	Gary Player
1945	Eddie Williams	1961	Paul Runyan	1978	Joe Jiminez*	1991	Jack Nicklaus
1946	Eddie Williams*	1962	Paul Runyan	1979	Jack Fleck*	1992	Lee Trevino
1947	Jock Hutchison	1963	Herman Barron	1979	Don January	1993	Tom Wargo*
1948	Charles McKenna	1964	Sam Snead			1994	Lee Trevino
1949	Marshall Crichton	1965	Sam Snead	1980	Arnold Palmer*	1995	Ray Floyd
		1966	Fred Haas	1981	Miller Barber	1996	Hale Irwin
1950	Al Watrous	1967	Sam Snead	1982	Don January	1997	Hale Irwin
1951	Al Watrous*	1968	Chandler Harper	1983	Not held	1998	Hale Irwin
1952	Ernest Newnham	1969	Tommy Bolt	1984	Arnold Palmer	1999	Allen Doyle
1953	Harry Schwab						

*PLAYOFFS:

1938: Fred McLeod def. Otto Hackbarth in 18 holes. **1940:** Otto Hackbarth def. Jock Hutchison in 36 holes. **1946:** Eddie Williams def. Jock Hutchison in 18 holes. **1951:** Al Watrous def. Jock Hutchison in 18 holes. **1975:** Charlie Sifford def. Fred Wampler on 1st extra hole **1978:** Joe Jiminez def. Paul Harney on 1st extra hole. **1979:** Jack Fleck def. Bill Johnston on 1st extra hole. **1980:** Arnold Palmer def. Paul Harney on 1st extra hole. **1993:** Tom Wargo def. Bruce Crampton on 2nd extra hole.

U.S. Senior Open

Established in 1980 for senior players 55 years old and over, the minimum age was dropped to 50 (the PGA Seniors Tour entry age) in 1981. Arnold Palmer, Billy Casper, Hale Irwin, Orville Moody, Jack Nicklaus and Lee Trevino are the only golfers who have won both the U.S. Open and U.S. Senior Open.

Multiple winners: Miller Barber (3); Jack Nicklaus and Gary Player (2).

Year		Year		Year		Year	
1980	Roberto De Vicenzo	1985	Miller Barber	1990	Lee Trevino	1995	Tom Weiskopf
1981	Arnold Palmer*	1986	Dale Douglass	1991	Jack Nicklaus*	1996	Dave Stockton
1982	Miller Barber	1987	Gary Player	1992	Larry Laoretti	1997	Graham Marsh
1983	Bill Casper*	1988	Gary Player*	1993	Jack Nicklaus	1998	Hale Irwin
1984	Miller Barber	1989	Orville Moody	1994	Simon Hobday	1999	Dave Eichelberger

*PLAYOFFS:

1981: Arnold Palmer (70) def. Bob Stone (74) and Billy Casper (77) in 18 holes. **1983:** Tied at 75 after 18-hole playoff, Casper def. Rod Funseth with a birdie on the 1st extra hole. **1988:** Gary Player (68) def. Bob Charles (70) in 18 holes. **1991:** Jack Nicklaus (65) def. Chi Chi Rodriguez (69) in 18 holes.

Senior Players Championship

First played in 1983 and contested in Cleveland (1983-86), Ponte Vedra, Fla. (1987-89), and Dearborn, Mich. (since 1990).

Multiple winners: Arnold Palmer and Dave Stockton (2).

Year		Year		Year		Year	
1983	Miller Barber	1988	Billy Casper	1993	Jim Colbert	1998	Gil Morgan
1984	Arnold Palmer	1989	Orville Moody	1994	Dave Stockton	1999	Hale Irwin
1985	Arnold Palmer	1990	Jack Nicklaus	1995	J.C. Snead*		
1986	Chi Chi Rodriguez	1991	Jim Albus	1996	Ray Floyd		
1987	Gary Player	1992	Dave Stockton	1997	Larry Gilbert		

*PLAYOFF:

1995: J.C. Snead def. Jack Nicklaus on 1st extra hole.

The Tradition

First played in 1989 and played every year since at the Golf Club at Desert Mountain in Scottsdale, Ariz.

Multiple winners: Jack Nicklaus (4); Gil Morgan (2).

Year		Year		Year		Year	
1989	Don Bies	1992	Lee Trevino	1995	Jack Nicklaus*	1998	Gil Morgan
1990	Jack Nicklaus	1993	Tom Shaw	1996	Jack Nicklaus	1999	Graham Marsh
1991	Jack Nicklaus	1994	Ray Floyd*	1997	Gil Morgan		

*PLAYOFFS:

1994: Ray Floyd def. Dale Douglas on 1st extra hole. **1995:** Jack Nicklaus def. Isao Aoki on 3rd extra hole.

Major Senior Championship Leaders

Through 1999. All players are still active.

		PGA Sr.	US Open	Senior Players	Trad	Total			PGA Sr.	US Open	Senior Players	Trad	Total
1	Jack Nicklaus	1	2	1	4	8		Arnold Palmer	1	0	2	0	3
2	Gary Player	3	2	1	0	6	9	Billy Casper	0	1	1	0	2
3	Hale Irwin	3	1	1	0	5		Graham Marsh	0	1	0	1	2
4	Lee Trevino	2	1	0	1	4		Orville Moody	0	1	1	0	2
5	Miller Barber	0	2	1	0	3		Chi Chi Rodriguez	1	0	1	0	2
	Ray Floyd	1	0	1	1	3		Dave Stockton	0	0	2	0	2
	Gil Morgan	0	0	1	2	3							

Grand Slam Summary

The Senior Grand Slam has officially consisted of The Tradition, the PGA Senior Championship, the Senior Players Championship and the U.S. Senior Open since 1990. Jack Nicklaus won three of the four events in 1991, but no one has won all four in one season.

Three wins in one year: Jack Nicklaus (1991). **Two wins in one year:** Gary Player (twice); Hale Irwin, Gil Morgan, Orville Moody, Jack Nicklaus, Arnold Palmer and Lee Trevino (once).

Year	Tradition	PGA Sr.	Players	US Open	Year	Tradition	PGA Sr.	Players	US Open
1983	—	—	M. Barber	Casper	1992	Trevino	Trevino	Stockton	Laoretti
1984	—	Palmer	Palmer	M. Barber	1993	Shaw	Wargo	Colbert	Nicklaus
1985	—	Thomson	Palmer	M. Barber	1994	Floyd	Trevino	Stockton	Hobday
1986	—	Player	Rodriguez	Douglass	1995	Nicklaus	Floyd	Snead	Weiskopf
1987	—	Rodriguez	Player	Player	1996	Nicklaus	Irwin	Floyd	Stockton
1988	—	Player	Casper	Player	1997	Morgan	Irwin	Gilbert	Marsh
1989	Bies	Mowry	Moody	Moody	1998	Morgan	Irwin	Morgan	Irwin
1990	Nicklaus	Player	Nicklaus	Trevino	1999	Marsh	Doyle	Irwin	Eichelberger
1991	Nicklaus	Nicklaus	Albus	Nicklaus					

Annual Money Leaders

Official annual money leaders on the PGA, European PGA, Senior PGA and LPGA tours. European PGA earnings listed in pounds sterling (£).

PGA

Multiple leaders: Jack Nicklaus (8); Ben Hogan and Tom Watson (5); Arnold Palmer (4); Greg Norman, Sam Snead and Curtis Strange (3); Julius Boros, Billy Casper, Tom Kite, Byron Nelson and Nick Price (2).

Year		Earnings	Year		Earnings	Year		Earnings
1934	Paul Runyan	$6,767	1956	Ted Kroll	$72,836	1978	Tom Watson	$362,429
1935	Johnny Revolta	9,543	1957	Dick Mayer	65,835	1979	Tom Watson	462,636
1936	Horton Smith	7,682	1958	Arnold Palmer	42,608	1980	Tom Watson	530,808
1937	Harry Cooper	14,139	1959	Art Wall	53,168	1981	Tom Kite	375,699
1938	Sam Snead	19,534	1960	Arnold Palmer	75,263	1982	Craig Stadler	446,462
1939	Henry Picard	10,303	1961	Gary Player	64,540	1983	Hal Sutton	426,668
1940	Ben Hogan	10,655	1962	Arnold Palmer	81,448	1984	Tom Watson	476,260
1941	Ben Hogan	18,358	1963	Arnold Palmer	128,230	1985	Curtis Strange	542,321
1942	Ben Hogan	13,143	1964	Jack Nicklaus	113,285	1986	Greg Norman	653,296
1943	No records kept		1965	Jack Nicklaus	140,752	1987	Curtis Strange	925,941
1944	Byron Nelson	37,968	1966	Billy Casper	121,945	1988	Curtis Strange	1,147,644
1945	Byron Nelson	63,336	1967	Jack Nicklaus	188,998	1989	Tom Kite	1,395,278
1946	Ben Hogan	42,556	1968	Billy Casper	205,169	1990	Greg Norman	1,165,477
1947	Jimmy Demaret	27,937	1969	Frank Beard	164,707	1991	Corey Pavin	979,430
1948	Ben Hogan	32,112	1970	Lee Trevino	157,037	1992	Fred Couples	1,344,188
1949	Sam Snead	31,594	1971	Jack Nicklaus	244,491	1993	Nick Price	1,478,557
1950	Sam Snead	35,759	1972	Jack Nicklaus	320,542	1994	Nick Price	1,499,927
1951	Lloyd Mangrum	26,089	1973	Jack Nicklaus	308,362	1995	Greg Norman	1,654,959
1952	Julius Boros	37,033	1974	Johnny Miller	353,022	1996	Tom Lehman	1,780,159
1953	Lew Worsham	34,002	1975	Jack Nicklaus	298,149	1997	Tiger Woods	2,066,833
1954	Bob Toski	65,820	1976	Jack Nicklaus	266,439	1998	David Duval	2,591,031
1955	Julius Boros	63,122	1977	Tom Watson	310,653			

Note: In 1944-45, Nelson's winnings were in War Bonds.

Senior PGA

Multiple leaders: Don January (3); Miller Barber, Bob Charles, Jim Colbert, Hale Irwin, Dave Stockton and Lee Trevino (2).

Year		Earnings	Year		Earnings	Year		Earnings
1980	Don January	$44,100	1987	Chi Chi Rodriguez	$509,145	1994	Dave Stockton	$1,402,519
1981	Miller Barber	83,136	1988	Bob Charles	533,929	1995	Jim Colbert	1,444,386
1982	Miller Barber	106,890	1989	Bob Charles	725,887	1996	Jim Colbert	1,627,890
1983	Don January	237,571	1990	Lee Trevino	1,190,518	1997	Hale Irwin	2,343,364
1984	Don January	328,597	1991	Mike Hill	1,065,657	1998	Hale Irwin	2,861,945
1985	Peter Thomson	386,724	1992	Lee Trevino	1,027,002			
1986	Bruce Crampton	454,299	1993	Dave Stockton	1,175,944			

European PGA

Multiple leaders: Seve Ballesteros and Colin Montgomerie (6); Sandy Lyle (3); Gay Brewer Jr., Nick Faldo, Bernard Hunt, Bernard Langer, Peter Thomson and Ian Woosnam (2).

Year		Earnings	Year		Earnings	Year		Earnings
1961	Bernard Hunt	£4,492	1974	Peter Oosterhuis	£32,127	1987	Ian Woosnam	£439,075
1962	Peter Thomson	5,764	1975	Dale Hayes	20,507	1988	Seve Ballesteros	502,000
1963	Bernard Hunt	7,209	1976	Seve Ballesteros	39,504	1989	Ronan Rafferty	465,981
1964	Neil Coles	7,890	1977	Seve Ballesteros	46,436	1990	Ian Woosnam	737,977
1965	Peter Thomson	7,011	1978	Seve Ballesteros	54,348	1991	Seve Ballesteros	790,811
1966	Bruce Devlin	13,205	1979	Sandy Lyle	49,233	1992	Nick Faldo	1,220,540
1967	Gay Brewer Jr.	20,235	1980	Greg Norman	74,829	1993	Colin Montgomerie	798,145
1968	Gay Brewer Jr.	23,107	1981	Bernhard Langer	95,991	1994	Colin Montgomerie	920,647
1969	Billy Casper	23,483	1982	Sandy Lyle	86,141	1995	Colin Montgomerie	999,260
1970	Christy O'Connor	31,532	1983	Nick Faldo	140,761	1996	Colin Montgomerie	1,034,752
1971	Gary Player	11,281	1984	Bernhard Langer	160,883	1997	Colin Montgomerie	798,948
1972	Bob Charles	18,538	1985	Sandy Lyle	254,711	1998	Colin Montgomerie	1,082,833
1973	Tony Jacklin	24,839	1986	Seve Ballesteros	259,275			

LPGA

Multiple leaders: Kathy Whitworth (8); Mickey Wright (4); Patty Berg, JoAnne Carner, Beth Daniel, Betsy King, Nancy Lopez and Annika Sorenstam (3); Pat Bradley, Judy Rankin, Betsy Rawls, Louise Suggs and Babe Zaharias (2).

Year		Earnings	Year		Earnings	Year		Earnings
1950	Babe Zaharias	$14,800	1967	Kathy Whitworth	$32,937	1984	Betsy King	$266,771
1951	Babe Zaharias	15,087	1968	Kathy Whitworth	48,379	1985	Nancy Lopez	416,472
1952	Betsy Rawls	14,505	1969	Carol Mann	49,152	1986	Pat Bradley	492,021
1953	Louise Suggs	19,816	1970	Kathy Whitworth	30,235	1987	Ayako Okamoto	466,034
1954	Patty Berg	16,011	1971	Kathy Whitworth	41,181	1988	Sherri Turner	350,851
1955	Patty Berg	16,492	1972	Kathy Whitworth	65,063	1989	Betsy King	654,132
1956	Marlene Hagge	20,235	1973	Kathy Whitworth	82,864	1990	Beth Daniel	863,578
1957	Patty Berg	16,272	1974	JoAnne Carner	87,094	1991	Pat Bradley	763,118
1958	Beverly Hanson	12,639	1975	Sandra Palmer	76,374	1992	Dottie Pepper	693,335
1959	Betsy Rawls	26,774	1976	Judy Rankin	150,734	1993	Betsy King	595,992
1960	Louise Suggs	16,892	1977	Judy Rankin	122,890	1994	Laura Davies	687,201
1961	Mickey Wright	22,236	1978	Nancy Lopez	189,814	1995	Annika Sorenstam	666,533
1962	Mickey Wright	21,641	1979	Nancy Lopez	197,489	1996	Karrie Webb	1,002,000
1963	Mickey Wright	31,269	1980	Beth Daniel	231,000	1997	Annika Sorenstam	1,236,789
1964	Mickey Wright	29,800	1981	Beth Daniel	206,998	1998	Annika Sorenstam	1,092,748
1965	Kathy Whitworth	28,658	1982	JoAnne Carner	310,400			
1966	Kathy Whitworth	33,517	1983	JoAnne Carner	291,404			

All-Time Leaders

PGA, Senior PGA and LPGA leaders through 1998.

Tournaments Won

	PGA	No		Senior PGA	No		LPGA	No
1	Sam Snead	81	1	Lee Trevino	28	1	Kathy Whitworth	88
2	Jack Nicklaus	70	2	Miller Barber	24	2	Mickey Wright	82
3	Ben Hogan	63	3	Bob Charles	23	3	Patty Berg	57
4	Arnold Palmer	60	4	Don January	22	4	Betsy Rawls	53
5	Byron Nelson	52		Chi Chi Rodriguez	22	5	Louise Suggs	50
6	Billy Casper	51	6	Bruce Crampton	20	6	Nancy Lopez	48
7	Walter Hagen	40		Hale Irwin	20	7	JoAnne Carner	42
	Cary Middlecoff	40	8	Jim Colbert	19		Sandra Haynie	42
9	Gene Sarazen	38		Gary Player	19	9	Carol Mann	38
10	Lloyd Mangrum	36	10	Mike Hill	18	10	Patty Sheehan	35
11	Tom Watson	34		George Archer	18	11	Beth Daniel	32
12	Horton Smith	32	12	Dave Stockton	14	12	Pat Bradley	31
13	Harry Cooper	31	13	Raymond Floyd	13		Betsy King	31
	Jimmy Demaret	31		Gil Morgan	13		Babe Zaharias	31
15	Leo Diegel	30	15	Jim Dent	12	15	Amy Alcott	29
16	Gene Littler	29	16	Dale Douglass	11	16	Jane Blalock	26
	Paul Runyan	29		Orville Moody	11		Judy Rankin	26
18	Lee Trevino	27		Bob Murphy	11	18	Marlene Hagge	25
19	Henry Picard	26		Peter Thomson	11	19	Donna Caponi	24
20	Tommy Armour	24	20	Arnold Palmer	10	20	Marilynn Smith	21
	Macdonald Smith	24		Al Geiberger	10			
	Johnny Miller	24		Jack Nicklaus	10			

Note: Patty Berg's total includes 13 official pro wins prior to formation of LPGA in 1950.

Money Won
PGA

	Earnings			Earnings				Earnings
1 Greg Norman	...$11,936,443		10 Mark Calcavecchia	.$8,981,485			19 Phil Mickelson	....$6,964,977
2 Fred Couples	10,535,876		11 Corey Pavin	8,298,841			20 Jay Haas	6,906,099
3 Tom Kite	10,447,472		12 Paul Azinger	8,019,642			21 Tom Lehman	6,676,673
4 Mark O'Meara	...10,293,473		13 John Cook	7,254,627			22 Lee Janzen	6,493,245
5 Davis Love III	10,012,134		14 Curtis Strange	7,226,587			23 David Frost	6,475,440
6 Nick Price	9,813,834		15 Craig Stadler	7,220,968			24 David Duval	6,406,041
7 Payne Stewart	9,659,058		16 Ben Crenshaw	7,075,996			25 Jeff Sluman	6,293,739
8 Tom Watson	9,283,862		17 Steve Elkington	7,023,912				
9 Scott Hoch	9,136,303		18 Hal Sutton	6,972,978				

Senior PGA

	Earnings			Earnings				Earnings
1 Jim Colbert	.......$8,249,210		10 Isao Aoki	.........$6,172,337			19 Jim Albus	.........$4,487,178
2 Lee Trevino	8,165,927		11 Jim Dent	6,103,239			20 Al Geiberger	4,414,145
3 Dave Stockton	7,676,552		12 Dale Douglass	5,709,925			21 Tom Wargo	4,350,004
4 Bob Charles	7,646,958		13 Bob Murphy	5,188,326			22 Graham Marsh	4,159,051
5 Hale Irwin	7,620,253		14 Jay Sigel	4,995,067			23 Miller Barber	3,879,890
6 Mike Hill	6,611,263		15 Gary Player	4,933,813			24 Rocky Thompson	..3,802,281
7 George Archer	6,332,067		16 Bruce Crampton	...4,642,684			25 Gibby Gilbert	3,674,771
8 Ray Floyd	6,282,742		17 J.C. Snead	4,635,818				
9 Chi Chi Rodriguez	.6,184,587		18 Gil Morgan	4,496,948				

European PGA

	Earnings			Earnings				Earnings
1 Colin Montgomerie	.£7,862,030		10 Costantino Rocca	..£3,036,944			18 Sandy Lyle	........£2,558,178
2 Bernhard Langer	...6,397,661		11 Mark James	2,952,674			19 Fred Couples	2,537,911
3 Ian Woosnam	5,765,427		12 Darren Clarke	2,937,524			20 Frank Nobilo	2,453,968
4 Nick Faldo	5,491,860		13 Barry Lane	2,876,572			21 Vijay Singh	2,440,074
5 Seve Ballesteros	...4,593,503		14 Ronan Rafferty	2,690,927			22 Lee Westwood	2,269,055
6 Sam Torrance	4,453,563		15 Gordon Brand Jr.	...2,678,731			23 Eduardo Romero	...2,247,713
7 Jose Maria Olazabal	.4,056,786		16 Miguel Angel				24 Rodger Davis	2,135,267
8 Ernie Els	3,451,793		Jimenez	2,603,892			25 Per-Ulrik Johansson	.2,090,808
9 Mark McNulty	3,305,469		17 Anders Forsbrand	...2,575,086				

LPGA

	Earnings			Earnings				Earnings
1 Betsy King	.......$6,287,182		10 Rosie Jones	.......$3,672,074			19 Brandie Burton	...$2,796,570
2 Pat Bradley	5,591,035		11 Meg Mallon	3,640,049			20 Ayako Okamoto	...2,743,174
3 Patty Sheehan	5,454,161		12 Liselotte Neumann	.3,458,178			21 Colleen Walker	2,721,226
4 Beth Daniel	5,332,061		13 Jane Geddes	3,414,875			22 Karrie Webb	2,694,083
5 Nancy Lopez	5,159,690		14 Amy Alcott	3,320,754			23 Jan Stephenson	2,609,796
6 Dottie Pepper	4,517,561		15 Tammie Green	3,142,179			24 Michelle McGann	..2,514,377
7 Laura Davies	4,144,426		16 Kelly Robbins	3,131,879			25 Danielle	
8 Annika Sorenstam	.3,931,832		17 Chris Johnson	3,042,919			Ammaccapane	2,509,890
9 Juli Inkster	3,739,817		18 JoAnne Carner	2,921,687				

Annual Awards
PGA of America Player of the Year

Awarded by the PGA of America; based on points scale that weighs performance in major tournaments, regular events, money earned and scoring average.

Multiple winners: Tom Watson (6); Jack Nicklaus (5); Ben Hogan (4); Julius Boros, Billy Casper, Arnold Palmer and Nick Price (2).

Year		Year		Year		Year	
1948	Ben Hogan	1961	Jerry Barber	1974	Johnny Miller	1987	Paul Azinger
1949	Sam Snead	1962	Arnold Palmer	1975	Jack Nicklaus	1988	Curtis Strange
1950	Ben Hogan	1963	Julius Boros	1976	Jack Nicklaus	1989	Tom Kite
1951	Ben Hogan	1964	Ken Venturi	1977	Tom Watson	1990	Nick Faldo
1952	Julius Boros	1965	Dave Marr	1978	Tom Watson	1991	Corey Pavin
1953	Ben Hogan	1966	Billy Casper	1979	Tom Watson	1992	Fred Couples
1954	Ed Furgol	1967	Jack Nicklaus	1980	Tom Watson	1993	Nick Price
1955	Doug Ford	1968	No award	1981	Bill Rogers	1994	Nick Price
1956	Jack Burke	1969	Orville Moody	1982	Tom Watson	1995	Greg Norman
1957	Dick Mayer	1970	Billy Casper	1983	Hal Sutton	1996	Tom Lehman
1958	Dow Finsterwald	1971	Lee Trevino	1984	Tom Watson	1997	Tiger Woods
1959	Art Wall	1972	Jack Nicklaus	1985	Lanny Wadkins	1998	Mark O'Meara
1960	Arnold Palmer	1973	Jack Nicklaus	1986	Bob Tway		

Annual Awards (Cont.)
PGA Tour Player of the Year

Award by the PGA Tour starting in 1990. Winner voted on by tour members from list of nominees. Winner receives the Jack Nicklaus Trophy, which originated in 1997.

Multiple winners: Fred Couples and Nick Price (2).

Year		Year		Year	
1990	Wayne Levi	1993	Nick Price	1996	Tom Lehman
1991	Fred Couples	1994	Nick Price	1997	Tiger Woods
1992	Fred Couples	1995	Greg Norman	1998	Mark O'Meara

PGA Tour Rookie of the Year

Awarded by the PGA Tour in 1990. Winner voted on by tour members from list of first-year nominees.

Year		Year		Year	
1990	Robert Gamez	1993	Vijay Singh	1996	Tiger Woods
1991	John Daly	1994	Ernie Els	1997	Stewart Cink
1992	Mark Carnevale	1995	Woody Austin	1998	Steve Flesch

PGA Senior Player of the Year

Awarded by th PGA Seniors Tour starting in 1990. Winner voted on by tour members from list of nominees.

Multiple winner: Lee Trevino (3); Jim Colbert and Hale Irwin (2).

Year		Year		Year		Year	
1990	Lee Trevino	1992	Lee Trevino	1995	Jim Colbert	1997	Hale Irwin
1991	George Archer & Mike Hill	1993	Dave Stockton	1996	Jim Colbert	1998	Hale Irwin
		1994	Lee Trevino				

PGA Senior Tour Rookie of the Year

Awarded by th PGA Tour starting in 1990. Winner voted on by tour members from list of first-year nominees.

Year		Year		Year	
1990	Lee Trevino	1993	Bob Murphy	1996	John Bland
1991	Jim Colbert	1994	Jay Sigel	1997	Gil Morgan
1992	Dave Stockton	1995	Hale Irwin	1998	Joe Inman

European Golfer of the Year

Officially, the Johnnie Walker Trophy; voting done by panel of European golf writers and tour members.

Multiple winners: Seve Ballesteros, Nick Faldo and Colin Montgomerie (3); Bernhard Langer (2).

Year		Year		Year		Year	
1985	Bernhard Langer	1989	Nick Faldo	1993	Bernhard Langer	1997	Colin Montgomerie
1986	Seve Ballesteros	1990	Nick Faldo	1994	Ernie Els	1998	Lee Westwood
1987	Ian Woosnam	1991	Seve Ballesteros	1995	Colin Montgomerie		
1988	Seve Ballesteros	1992	Nick Faldo	1996	Colin Montgomerie		

LPGA Player of the Year

Awarded by the LPGA; based on performance points accumulated during the year.

Multiple winners: Kathy Whitworth (7); Nancy Lopez (4); JoAnne Carner, Beth Daniel, Betsy King and Annika Sorenstam (3); Pat Bradley and Judy Rankin (2).

Year		Year		Year		Year	
1966	Kathy Whitworth	1975	Sandra Palmer	1984	Betsy King	1993	Betsy King
1967	Kathy Whitworth	1976	Judy Rankin	1985	Nancy Lopez	1994	Beth Daniel
1968	Kathy Whitworth	1977	Judy Rankin	1986	Pat Bradley	1995	Annika Sorenstam
1969	Kathy Whitworth	1978	Nancy Lopez	1987	Ayako Okamoto	1996	Laura Davies
1970	Sandra Haynie	1979	Nancy Lopez	1988	Nancy Lopez	1997	Annika Sorenstam
1971	Kathy Whitworth	1980	Beth Daniel	1989	Betsy King	1998	Annika Sorenstam
1972	Kathy Whitworth	1981	JoAnne Carner	1990	Beth Daniel		
1973	Kathy Whitworth	1982	JoAnne Carner	1991	Pat Bradley		
1974	JoAnne Carner	1983	Patty Sheehan	1992	Dottie Mochrie		

Official World Rankings

Begun in 1986, the Official World Golf Ranking (formerly the Sony World Ranking) combines the best golfers on the five PGA men's tours throughout the world. Rankings are based on a rolling two-year period and weighed in favor of more recent results. While annual winners are not announced, certain players reaching No. 1 have dominated each year.

Multiple winners (at year's end): Greg Norman (6); Nick Faldo (3); Seve Ballesteros and Tiger Woods (2).

Year		Year		Year		Year	
1986	Seve Ballesteros	1990	Nick Faldo & Greg Norman	1993	Nick Faldo	1996	Greg Norman
1987	Greg Norman			1994	Nick Price	1997	Tiger Woods
1988	Greg Norman	1991	Ian Woosnam	1995	Greg Norman	1998	Tiger Woods
1989	Seve Ballesteros & Greg Norman	1992	Fred Couples & Nick Faldo				

National Team Competition
MEN
Ryder Cup

The Ryder Cup was presented by British seed merchant and businessman Samuel Ryder in 1927 for competition between professional golfers from Great Britain and the United States. The British team was expanded to include Irish players in 1973 and the rest of Europe in 1979. The United States leads the series 24-7-2 after 33 matches.

Year	Year	Year	Year
1927 USA, 9½-2½	1951 USA, 9½-2½	1969 Draw, 16-16	1987 Europe, 15-13
1929 Britain-Ireland, 7-5	1953 USA, 6½-5½	1971 USA, 18½-13½	1989 Draw, 14-14
1931 USA, 9-3	1955 USA, 8-4	1973 USA, 19-13	1991 USA, 14½-13½
1933 Great Britain, 6½-5½	1957 Britain-Ireland, 7½-4½	1975 USA, 21-11	1993 USA, 15-13
1935 USA, 9-3	1959 USA, 8½-3½	1977 USA, 12½-13½	1995 Europe, 14½-13½
1937 USA, 8-4	1961 USA, 14½-9½	1979 USA, 17-11	1997 Europe, 14½-13½
1939-45 Not held	1963 USA, 23-9	1981 USA, 18½-9½	1999 USA, 14½-13½
1947 USA, 11-1	1965 USA, 19½-12½	1983 USA, 14½-13½	
1949 USA, 7-5	1967 USA, 23½-8½	1985 Europe, 16½-11½	

Playing Sites

1927—Worcester CC (Mass.); **1929**—Moortown, England; **1931**—Scioto CC (Ohio); **1933**—Southport & Ainsdale, England; **1935**—Ridgewood CC (N.J.); **1937**—Southport & Ainsdale, England; **1939-45**—Not held. **1947**—Portland CC (Ore.); **1949**—Ganton GC, England; **1951**—Pinehurst CC (N.C.); **1953**—Wentworth, England; **1955**—Thunderbird Ranch &CC (Calif.); **1957**—Lindrick GC, England; **1959**—Eldorado CC (Calif.); **1961**—Royal Lytham & St. Annes, England; **1963**—East Lake CC (Ga.); **1965**—Royal Birkdale, England; **1967**—Champions GC (Tex.); **1969**—Royal Birkdale, England; **1971**—Old Warson CC (Mo.); **1973**—Muirfield, Scotland; **1975**—Laurel Valley GC (Pa.); **1977**—Royal Lytham & St. Annes, England; **1979**—The Greenbrier (W.Va.); **1981**—Walton Heath GC, England; **1983**—PGA National GC (Fla.); **1985**—The Belfry, England; **1987**—Muirfield Village GC (Ohio); **1989**—The Belfry, England; **1991**—Ocean Course (S.C.); **1993**—The Belfry, England; **1995**—Oak Hill CC (N.Y.); **1997**—Valderrama, Costa del Sol, Spain; **1999**—The Country Club (Mass.); **2001**— The Belfry, England; **2003**— Oakland Hills CC (Mich.).

Walker Cup

The Walker Cup was presented by American businessman George Herbert Walker in 1922 for competition between amateur golfers from Great Britain, Ireland and the United States. The U.S. leads the series against the combined Great Britain-Ireland team, 31-5-1, after 37 matches.

Year	Year	Year	Year
1922 USA, 8-4	1940-46 Not held	1965 Draw, 12-12	1985 USA, 13-11
1923 USA, 6½-5½	1947 USA, 8-4	1967 USA, 15-9	1987 USA, 16½-7½
1924 USA, 9-3	1949 USA, 10-2	1969 USA, 13-11	1989 Britain-Ireland,
1926 USA, 6½-5½	1951 USA, 7½-4½	1971 Britain-Ireland, 13-11	12½-11½
1928 USA, 11-1	1953 USA, 9-3	1973 USA, 14-10	1991 USA, 14-10
1930 USA, 10-2	1955 USA, 10-2	1975 USA, 15½-8½	1993 USA, 19-5
1932 USA, 9½-2½	1957 USA, 8½-3½	1977 USA, 16-8	1995 Britain-Ireland, 14-10
1934 USA, 9½-2½	1959 USA, 9-3	1979 USA, 15½-8½	1997 USA, 18-6
1936 USA, 10½-1½	1961 USA, 11-1	1981 USA, 15-9	1999 Britain-Ireland, 15-9
1938 Britain-Ireland, 7½-4½	1963 USA, 14-10	1983 USA, 13½-10½	

Presidents Cup

The Presidents Cup is a biennial event played in non-Ryder Cup years in which the world's best non-European players compete against players from the United States. The U.S. leads the series, 2-1.

Year	Year	Year
1994 USA, 20-12	1996 USA, 16½-15½	1998 International, 20½-11½

WOMEN
Solheim Cup

The Solheim Cup was presented by the Karsten Manufacturing Co. in 1990 for competition between women professional golfers from Europe and the United States. The U.S. leads the series, 4-1.

Year	Year	Year
1990 USA, 11½-4½	1994 USA, 13-7	1998 USA, 16-12
1992 Europe, 11½-6½	1996 USA, 17-11	

Curtis Cup

Named after British golfing sisters Harriot and Margaret Curtis, the Curtis Cup was first contested in 1932 between teams of women amateurs from the United States and the British Isles.

Competed for every other year since 1932 (except during WWII). The U.S. leads the series, 21-6-3, after 30 matches.

Year	Year	Year	Year
1932 USA, 5½-3½	1954 USA, 6-3	1970 USA, 11½-6½	1986 British Isles, 13-5
1934 USA, 6½-2½	1956 British Isles, 5-4	1972 USA, 10-8	1988 British Isles, 11-7
1936 Draw, 4½-4½	1958 Draw, 4½-4½	1974 USA, 13-5	1990 USA, 14-4
1938 USA, 5½-3½	1960 USA, 6½-2½	1976 USA, 11½-6½	1992 British Isles, 10-8
1940-46 Not held	1962 USA, 8-1	1978 USA, 12-6	1994 Draw, 9-9
1948 USA, 6½-2½	1964 USA, 10½-7½	1980 USA, 13-5	1996 British Isles, 11½-6½
1950 USA, 7½-1½	1966 USA, 13-5	1982 USA, 14½-3½	1998 USA, 10-8
1952 British Isles, 5-4	1968 USA, 10½-7½	1984 USA, 9½-8½	

COLLEGES

Men's NCAA Division I Champions

College championships decided by match play from 1897-1964 and stroke play since 1965.

Multiple winners (Teams): Yale (21); Houston (16); Oklahoma St. (8); Stanford (7); Harvard (6); LSU and North Texas (4); Florida and Wake Forest (3); Arizona St., Michigan, Ohio St. and Texas (2).

Multiple winners (Individuals): Ben Crenshaw and Phil Mickelson (3); Dick Crawford, Dexter Cummings, G.T. Dunlop, Fred Lamphrecht and Scott Simpson (2).

Year	Team winner	Individual champion	Year	Team winner	Individual champion
1897	Yale	Louis Bayard, Princeton	1949	North Texas	Harvie Ward, N.Carolina
1898	Harvard (spring)	John Reid, Yale	1950	North Texas	Fred Wampler, Purdue
1898	Yale (fall)	James Curtis, Harvard	1951	North Texas	Tom Nieporte, Ohio St.
1899	Harvard	Percy Pyne, Princeton	1952	North Texas	Jim Vichers, Oklahoma
1900	Not held		1953	Stanford	Earl Moeller, Oklahoma St.
1901	Harvard	H. Lindsley, Harvard	1954	SMU	Hillman Robbins, Memphis St.
1902	Yale (spring)	Chas. Hitchcock Jr., Yale	1955	LSU	Joe Campbell, Purdue
1902	Harvard (fall)	Chandler Egan, Harvard	1956	Houston	Rick Jones, Ohio St.
1903	Harvard	F.O. Reinhart, Princeton	1957	Houston	Rex Baxter Jr., Houston
1904	Harvard	A.L. White, Harvard	1958	Houston	Phil Rodgers, Houston
1905	Yale	Robert Abbott, Yale	1959	Houston	Dick Crawford, Houston
1906	Yale	W.E. Clow Jr., Yale	1960	Houston	Dick Crawford, Houston
1907	Yale	Ellis Knowles, Yale	1961	Purdue	Jack Nicklaus, Ohio St.
1908	Yale	H.H. Wilder, Harvard	1962	Houston	Kermit Zarley, Houston
1909	Yale	Albert Seckel, Princeton	1963	Oklahoma St.	R.H. Sikes, Arkansas
1910	Yale	Robert Hunter, Yale	1964	Houston	Terry Small, San Jose St.
1911	Yale	George Stanley, Yale	1965	Houston	Marty Fleckman, Houston
1912	Yale	F.C. Davison, Harvard	1966	Houston	Bob Murphy, Florida
1913	Yale	Nathaniel Wheeler, Yale	1967	Houston	Hale Irwin, Colorado
1914	Princeton	Edward Allis, Harvard	1968	Florida	Grier Jones, Oklahoma St.
1915	Yale	Francis Blossom, Yale	1969	Houston	Bob Clark, Cal St.-LA
1916	Princeton	J.W. Hubbell, Harvard	1970	Houston	John Mahaffey, Houston
1917-18	Not held		1971	Texas	Ben Crenshaw, Texas
1919	Princeton	A.L. Walker Jr., Columbia	1972	Texas	Ben Crenshaw, Texas
1920	Princeton	Jess Sweetster, Yale			& Tom Kite, Texas
1921	Dartmouth	Simpson Dean, Princeton	1973	Florida	Ben Crenshaw, Texas
1922	Princeton	Pollack Boyd, Dartmouth	1974	Wake Forest	Curtis Strange, W.Forest
1923	Princeton	Dexter Cummings, Yale	1975	Wake Forest	Jay Haas, Wake Forest
1924	Yale	Dexter Cummings, Yale	1976	Oklahoma St.	Scott Simpson, USC
1925	Yale	Fred Lamprecht, Tulane	1977	Houston	Scott Simpson, USC
1926	Yale	Fred Lamprecht, Tulane	1978	Oklahoma St.	David Edwards, Okla. St.
1927	Princeton	Watts Gunn, Georgia Tech	1979	Ohio St.	Gary Hallberg, Wake Forest
1928	Princeton	Maurice McCarthy, G'town	1980	Oklahoma St.	Jay Don Blake, Utah St.
1929	Princeton	Tom Aycock, Yale	1981	Brigham Young	Ron Commans, USC
1930	Princeton	G.T. Dunlap Jr., Princeton	1982	Houston	Billy Ray Brown, Houston
1931	Yale	G.T. Dunlap Jr., Princeton	1983	Oklahoma St.	Jim Carter, Arizona St.
1932	Yale	J.W. Fischer, Michigan	1984	Houston	John Inman, N.Carolina
1933	Yale	Walter Emery, Oklahoma	1985	Houston	Clark Burroughs, Ohio St.
1934	Michigan	Charles Yates, Ga.Tech	1986	Wake Forest	Scott Verplank, Okla. St.
1935	Michigan	Ed White, Texas	1987	Oklahoma St.	Brian Watts, Oklahoma St.
1936	Yale	Charles Kocsis, Michigan	1988	UCLA	E.J. Pfister, Oklahoma St.
1937	Princeton	Fred Haas Jr., LSU	1989	Oklahoma	Phil Mickelson, Ariz. St.
1938	Stanford	John Burke, Georgetown	1990	Arizona St.	Phil Mickelson, Ariz. St.
1939	Stanford	Vincent D'Antoni, Tulane	1991	Oklahoma St.	Warren Schuette, UNLV
1940	Princeton & LSU	Dixon Brooke, Virginia	1992	Arizona	Phil Mickelson, Ariz. St.
1941	Stanford	Earl Stewart, LSU	1993	Florida	Todd Demsey, Ariz. St.
1942	LSU & Stanford	Frank Tatum Jr., Stanford	1994	Stanford	Justin Leonard, Texas
1943	Yale	Wallace Ulrich, Carleton	1995	Oklahoma St.	Chip Spratlin, Auburn
1944	Notre Dame	Louis Lick, Minnesota	1996	Arizona St.	Tiger Woods, Stanford
1945	Ohio State	John Lorms, Ohio St.	1997	Pepperdine	Charles Warren, Clemson
1946	Stanford	George Hamer, Georgia	1998	UNLV	James McLean, Minnesota
1947	LSU	Dave Barclay, Michigan	1999	Georgia	Luke Donald, Northwestern
1948	San Jose St.	Bob Harris, San Jose St.			

Women's NCAA Division I Champions

College championships decided by stroke play since 1982.

Multiple winners (teams): Arizona St. (6); Florida, San Jose St. and Tulsa (2).

Year	Team winner	Individual champion	Year	Team winner	Individual champion
1982	Tulsa	Kathy Baker, Tulsa	1991	UCLA	Annika Sorenstam, Arizona
1983	TCU	Penny Hammel, Miami	1992	San Jose St.	Vicki Goetze, Georgia
1984	Miami-FL	Cindy Schreyer, Georgia	1993	Arizona St.	Charlotta Sorenstam, Ariz. St.
1985	Florida	Danielle Ammaccapane, Ariz.St.	1994	Arizona St.	Emilee Klein, Ariz. St.
1986	Florida	Page Dunlap, Florida	1995	Arizona St.	K. Mourgue d'Algue, Ariz. St.
1987	San Jose St.	Caroline Keggi, New Mexico	1996	Arizona	Marisa Baena, Arizona
1988	Tulsa	Melissa McNamara, Tulsa	1997	Arizona St.	Heather Bowie, Texas
1989	San Jose St.	Pat Hurst, San Jose St.	1998	Arizona St.	Jennifer Rosales, USC
1990	Arizona St.	Susan Slaughter, Arizona	1999	Duke	Grace Park, Arizona St.

Auto Racing

Jeff Gordon, right, and crew chief **Ray Evernham** teamed up for three Winston Cup championships in four years but parted ways in 1999.

AP/Wide World Photos

Triumph and Tragedy

The racing world saw its share of each in 1999. Dale Jarrett aimed for his first Winston Cup title while fatal crashes scarred both the CART and IRL circuits.

by
Rece Davis

Sitting in Dale Jarrett's motor home a couple of days before the season-opening Daytona 500, he and crew chief Todd Parrott mapped out how the race would go using Jarrett's son Zachary's Matchbox cars.

With a devilish grin, Jarrett playfully illustrated a scenario in which his 88 car would move from the back of the pack on the final laps, overturning all cars in his path. Jeff Gordon's 24 car and Dale Earnhardt's number 3 wound up on the floor beside Zachary's peanut butter and jelly sandwich.

In the real race, Gordon ended up winning, narrowly beating Earnhardt. And Jarrett was the one who wrecked.

That was about the last time things didn't go just the way Jarrett planned.

He finished second at Rockingham the next week, spawning a span of 21 races in which he'd finish no worse than 11th. Twenty times he came home in the top eight. Four times, he won. That's precisely the consistency you need to win a Winston Cup championship.

While Jarrett's front running was relentless, the year was hardly devoid of twists and turns. Rookie Tony Stewart burst onto the scene with undeniable talent and flair. He started on the front row at Daytona. He didn't finish there, but served notice that he'd be around for the long haul. In May, Stewart drove in the Indianapolis 500 and the Coca Cola 600 on the same day and notched top ten finishes

---

Rece Davis is the host of *RPM 2Night* on espn2.

Dale Jarrett (No. 88) passes **Jeff Gordon** late in the Pennsylvania 500 on July 25. The two competitors battled all season long and developed a friendly rivalry in the process. Well, most of the time it's friendly.

in both. He said he ran out of gas, figuratively, late in the Coca Cola 600 and cost his team a shot at winning. He ran out of gas, literally, a few weeks later in New Hampshire. The gaffe by his team two laps from the finish denied Stewart a certain victory. But nothing would stop "the Columbus Comet" at Richmond on Sept. 11 as he became the first rookie winner on the Winston Cup circuit since Davey Allison in 1987.

Gordon's dream of a Winston Cup three-peat fizzled amidst a run of mechanical failures and wrecks. His season received a stunning overhaul in September when he split with crew chief Ray Evernham. Though both men emphasized there was no rift, Evernham got out of his long-term contract with Hendrick Motorsports in late September to pursue his goal of owning his own team. ∎

CART

Alex Zanardi's departure to Formula One seemed to leave a gaping hole on the three-time reigning champion Target Chip Ganassi team. Enter rookie Juan Montoya. The 24-year-old Colombian twice threatened the CART record of four straight victories with a pair of three-race winning streaks.

In his quest for Target's unprecedented fourth straight championship, Montoya spent much of his time fighting off Dario Franchitti and Paul Tracy. That is, when Franchitti and Tracy weren't fighting off each other. Astonishingly they wrecked each other twice, but worked together well enough to come home 1-2 three times over the first 18 races.

Emergency personnel carry the body of one of the three spectators killed at Lowe's Motor Speedway in Charlotte on May 1, after driver Stan Wattles slammed into a retaining wall, sending debris hurtling into the stands. The race was subsequently canceled.

Sadly the season was marred by the death of rookie driver Gonzalo Rodriguez, who was killed during a practice crash at Laguna Seca. It was only the third on-track fatality for CART in 21 years. ■

IRL

Unfortunately, fatalities headlined the IRL season. Three spectators were killed in Charlotte when Stan Wattles car crashed into a wall, sending debris into the stands like missiles. The race was stopped and canceled. If there is a silver lining in a tragedy, the wreck prompted the IRL and CART to employ tethering devices to their cars to keep parts from flying into the stands after impact.

The IRL Championship went to 33-year-old Greg Ray, who held off defending champ Kenny Brack. Ray won three of the circuit's 10 races and clinched the title with a third-place showing in his backyard at the Texas Motor Speedway. ■

Formula One

When two-time champion Michael Schumacher broke his leg 30 seconds into the Grand Prix of Britain, Mika Hakkinen seemed to have a Sunday drive to his second straight driver's championship. But a few unforced errors by Hakkinen left the door open for Schumacher's Ferrari teammate Eddie Irvine. In the penultimate race, Irvine and Schumacher recorded a 1-2 finish in Malaysia but were subsequently disqualified for technical violations. Ferrari protested and actually won their appeal, setting up a final-race showdown between Hakkinen and Irvine.

AP/Wide World Photos

Take that too! As if beating Britain's **Ernie Irvine** at the Hungarian Grand Prix on Aug. 15 wasn't enough, **Mika Hakkinen** also seems to have gotten the better of this champagne fight after the race.

This is the same Irvine who proclaimed his goal for the season was to finish second in the standings. The idea then was to finish second to Schumacher, but you should be careful what you wish for. ■

Rece Davis' Top Ten Auto Racing Highlights of 1999

10. **Biffle's Dominance.** Last year's Craftsman Truck Rookie of the Year Greg Biffle wins the Orleans 250 in Las Vegas on Sept. 24 for his record ninth win of the year.

9. **CART-IRL talks fizzle.** Hope reigned that the silly split would come to an end. It actually seemed close for a while, but stubbornness, primarily from IRL czar Tony George, prevailed. Open wheel racing won't be what it could, or should be in America until the factions unite.

8. **Montoya breaks record.** The sensational Juan Montoya christens his team owner's new track in Chicago with a win. In the process, Montoya's sixth win breaks the legendary Nigel Mansell's record for wins by a rookie.

7. **Kenny Brack wins Indy.** One year after running out of gas likely cost him the race at Indy, Brack wins when Robby Gordon's tank comes up dry late in the race.

6. **Little E wrecks Matt Kenseth.** Dale Earnhardt Jr. spins his Busch series arch-rival and dominant race leader Matt Kenseth at Dover. He immediately takes the blame saying "friends aren't supposed to do that to each other."

5. **Earnhardt wrecks Terry Labonte.** Perhaps Little E learned from Dad. Claiming he only wanted to "rattle his cage," Earnhardt instead takes out the leader Labonte on the last lap and goes on to win at Bristol. Jimmy Spencer retaliates by trying to spin Earnhardt on his victory lap.

4. **Stewart's Double Dip.** Eleven hundred miles in one day. Two different cars. A helicopter ride. A jet ride. Top 10 finishes in the Indy 500 and Coca Cola 600. Studly.

3. **Force beats Top Fuel car.** John Force gives the funny cars bragging rights over the top fuel guys by beating Bob Vandergriff in the finals of the inaugural Winston Showdown. The real winner is the NHRA. Funny cars and top fuel dragsters head-to-head. Brilliant and entertaining.

2. **Gordon vs. Jarrett.** After an on-track incident in Loudon, Jarrett tells Gordon, "try that again and I'll knock that 'bleepety bleep' out of the race track." Our *RPM 2Night* cameras were rolling. It was the best TV argument this side of Jerry Springer. And it was real.

1. **Jeff Gordon-Ray Evernham Split.** Rival owner Felix Sabates once said, "Gordon would win nine races in a Jeep Wagoneer." Benny Parsons added, "Yeah, if Evernham had a week to work on it." Together, Gordon and Evernham were magic. They won 47 races and three championships, a dynasty that ended when Evernham left the team to pursue ownership opportunities. ■

THE NUMBERS

INSIDE

A DAY IN THE PASSING LANE

On July 11, Jeff Burton won the Jiffy Lube 300 in Loudon, N.H. from the 38th starting position. Only Johnny Mantz in 1950 recorded a bigger come-from-behind victory. Below are the lowest starting positions for race winners in Winston Cup history.

Pos.	Driver	Race
43	Johnny Mantz	1950 Southern 500
38	Jeff Burton	1999 Jiffy Lube 300
38	Bill Elliott	1988 Firecracker 400
37	Kyle Petty	1995 Miller 500

FAST TIMES FOR OLD-TIMERS

At 39, Scott Pruett is the elder statesman on the CART circuit. He needs 20 more years, however, if he wants to pass A.J. Foyt, who sits atop the list below of the oldest drivers ever to compete in a CART race. There is no truth to the rumor that Foyt mistakenly had his right turn signal on for his entire race.

Driver	Date	Age
A.J. Foyt	3/2/92	59 yrs, 2 mos, 6 days
Jim McElreath	8/14/83	55 yrs, 5 mos, 27 days
G. Bettenhausen	5/26/96	55 yrs, 5 mos, 26 days
Dick Simon	9/25/88	55 yrs, 4 days
Mario Andretti	10/9/94	54 yrs, 7 mos, 11 days

■

THE 2000

ESPN INFORMATION PLEASE **SPORTS ALMANAC**

AUTO RACING
S T A T I S T I C S

THE SEASON IN REVIEW
1998-1999
NASCAR • CART • IRL • F1

SEC A

PAGE 883

NASCAR RESULTS

Winston Cup Series
Winners of NASCAR Winston Cup races from Nov. 1, 1998 through Oct. 17, 1999.

LATE 1998

Date	Event	Location	Winner (Pos.)	Avg.mph	Earnings	Pole	Qual.mph
Nov. 1	AC-Delco 400	Rockingham	Jeff Gordon (9)	128.423	$111,575+	M. Martin	156.502
Nov. 8	NAPA 500	Atlanta	Jeff Gordon (21)	114.915	164,450+	K. Irwin	193.461

+Includes carryover Winston Cup leader bonus ($10,000 per race): **AC Delco 400**—Gordon ($20,000); **NAPA 500**—Gordon ($10,000).

Winning cars (for entire season): FORD THUNDERBIRD (16)— Martin (8), Jarrett (3), J. Burton (2), Mayfield, Rudd, Wallace; CHEVY MONTE CARLO (16)— Gordon (13), Earnhardt, Hamilton, T. Labonte; PONTIAC GRAND PRIX (2)— B. Labonte (2).

1999 SEASON

Date	Event	Location	Winner (Pos.)	Avg.mph	Earnings	Pole	Qual.mph
Feb. 7@	Bud Shootout	Daytona	Mark Martin (13)	181.745	$108,000	M. Skinner	179.140
Feb. 14	**Daytona 500**	Daytona	Jeff Gordon (1)	161.551	2,194,246+**	J. Gordon	195.067
Feb. 21	Big Kmart 400	Rockingham	Mark Martin (3)	120.750	104,635	R. Rudd	157.241
Mar. 7	Las Vegas 400	Las Vegas	Jeff Burton (19)	137.535	336,590	B. Labonte	170.643
Mar. 14	Cracker Barrel 500	Atlanta	Jeff Gordon (8)	143.296	117,650	B. Labonte	194.957
Mar. 21	TranSouth 400	Darlington	Jeff Burton (9)#	121.294	161,900+	J. Gordon	173.167
Mar. 28	Primestar 500	Ft. Worth	Terry Labonte (4)	144.276	376,840	K. Irwin	190.154
Apr. 11	Food City 500	Bristol	Rusty Wallace (1)	93.366	92,435	R. Wallace	125.142
Apr. 18	Goody's B.P. 500	Martinsville	John Andretti (21)	93.366	105,275	T. Stewart	95.275
Apr. 25	Sears DieHard 500	Talladega	Dale Earnhardt (17)	163.395	147,795	K. Schrader	197.765
May 2	California 500	Fontana	Jeff Gordon (5)	150.280	155,890	J. Burton	—*
May 15	Pontiac 400	Richmond	Dale Jarrett (21)	100.102	169,715+	J. Gordon	126.499
May 22@	The Winston	Concord	Terry Labonte (13)	183.495	207,500	B. Labonte	146.830
May 30	**Coca-Cola 600**	Concord	Jeff Burton (2)	151.367	1,212,500	B. Labonte	185.230
June 6	MBNA Platinum 400	Dover	Bobby Labonte (1)	120.603	144,820	B. Labonte	159.320
June 13	Kmart 400	Brooklyn	Dale Jarrett (6)	173.997	151,240+	J. Gordon	186.945
June 20	Pocono 500	Long Pond	Bobby Labonte (3)	118.198	151,110	S. Marlin	170.506
June 27	Save Mart/Kragen 350K	Sonoma	Jeff Gordon (1)	70.378	125,040	J. Gordon	98.519
July 3	Pepsi 400	Daytona	Dale Jarrett (12)	169.213	164,965+	J. Nemechek	194.860
July 11	Jiffy Lube 300	Loudon	Jeff Burton (38)	101.876	139,490	J. Gordon	131.171
July 25	Pennsylvania 500	Long Pond	Bobby Labonte (4)	116.982	139,385	M. Skinner	170.451
Aug. 7	Brickyard 400	Indianapolis	Dale Jarrett (4)	148.228	712,240+	J. Gordon	179.612
Aug. 15	Frontier at The Glen	Watkins Glen	Jeff Gordon (3)	87.772	119,860	R. Wallace	121.234
Aug. 22	Pepsi 400	Brooklyn	Bobby Labonte (19)	144.332	121,320	W. Burton	188.843
Aug. 28	Goody's 500	Bristol	Dale Earnhardt (26)	91.276	89,880	T. Stewart	124.589
Sept. 5	**Pepsi Southern 500**	Darlington	Jeff Burton (15)#	107.816	1,148,170**	K. Irwin	170.970
Sept. 11	Select Batteries 400	Richmond	Tony Stewart (2)	104.006	135,160	M. Skinner	125.465
Sept. 19	Dura Lube/Kmart 300	Loudon	Joe Nemechek (11)	100.673	157,625	R. Wallace	129.820
Sept. 26	MBNA Gold 400	Dover	Mark Martin (8)	127.434	115,710	R. Wallace	159.964
Oct. 3	NAPA AutoCare 500	Martinsville	Jeff Gordon (5)	72.624	110,090	J. Nemechek	95.223
Oct. 10	UAW-GM Quality 500	Charlotte	Jeff Gordon (22)	160.306	140,350	B. Labonte	185.682
Oct. 17	**Winston 500**	Talladega	Dale Earnhardt (27)	166.632	120,290	J. Nemechek	198.331

Note: Earnings include bonus money.
@ Non-points exhibition event
# Weather-shortened

+Includes carryover Winston Cup leader bonus ($10,000 per race): **Daytona 500**— Gordon ($10,000); **TransSouth 400**— Burton ($40,000); **Pontiac 400**— Jarrett ($60,000); **Kmart 400**— Jarrett ($30,000) **Pepsi 400**— Jarrett ($30,000); **Brickyard 400**— Jarrett ($30,000).

**Includes $1 million Winston "No Bull 5" bonus.

*Rain caused the cancellation of Bud Pole Qualifying. Positions 1-35 in the starting lineup were determined by the owner points standings. Positions 36-43 were determined by the postmarks on the drivers' entry blanks.

Winning Cars: CHEVY MONTE CARLO (12)— Gordon (7), Earnhardt (3), T. Labonte, Nemechek; FORD TAURUS (12)— Burton (5), Jarrett (4), Martin (2), Wallace; PONTIAC GRAND PRIX (6)— B. Labonte (4), Andretti, Stewart.

1999 Race Locations

February— DAYTONA 500 at Daytona International Speedway in Daytona Beach, Fla.; BIG KMART 400 at North Carolina Motor Speedway in Rockingham, N.C.

March— LAS VEGAS 400 at Las Vegas Motor Speedway; CRACKER BARREL 500 at Atlanta International Speedway in Atlanta, Ga.; TRANSOUTH FINANCIAL 400 at Darlington (S.C.) International Raceway; PRIMESTAR 500 at Texas Motor Speedway. **April**— FOOD CITY 500 at Bristol (Tenn.) Motor Speedway; GOODY'S BODY PAIN 500 at Martinsville (Va.) Speedway; SEARS DIEHARD 500 at Talladega (Ala.) Superspeedway.

May— CALIFORNIA 500 by NAPA at California Speedway in Fontana, Calif.; PONTIAC EXCITEMENT 400 at Richmond (Va.) International Speedway; COCA-COLA 600 at Lowe's Motor Speedway in Concord, N.C.

June— MBNA PLATINUM 400 at Dover Downs International Speedway; KMART 400 at Michigan Speedway in Brooklyn, Mich.; POCONO 500 at Pocono International Raceway in Long Pond, Pa.; SAVE MART/KRAGEN 350K at Sears Point International Raceway in Sonoma, Calif.

July— JIFFY LUBE 300 at New Hampshire International Speedway in Loudon, N.H.; PEPSI 400 at Daytona; PENNSYLVANIA 500 at Pocono.

August— BRICKYARD 400 at Indianapolis (Ind.) Motor Speedway; FRONTIER AT THE GLEN at Watkins Glen (N.Y.) International; PEPSI 400 at Michigan; GOODY'S HEADACHE POWDER 500 at Bristol.

September— PEPSI SOUTHERN 500 at Darlington; EXIDE NASCAR SELECT BATTERIES 400 at Richmond; DURA LUBE/KMART 300 at New Hampshire; MBNA GOLD 400 at Dover.

October— NAPA AUTOCARE 500 at Martinsville; UAW-GM QUALITY 500 at Lowe's; WINSTON 500 at Talladega; ROCKINGHAM 400 at North Carolina.

November— DURA-LUBE 500 at Phoenix (Ariz.) International Raceway; JIFFY LUBE MIAMI 400 at Miami-Dade Homestead Motorsports Complex in Homestead, Fla.; NAPA 500 at Atlanta.

1999 Daytona 500

Date— Sunday, Feb. 14 , 1999, at Daytona International Speedway. **Distance**— 500 miles; **Course**— 2.5 miles; **Field**— 43 cars; **Average speed**— 161.551 mph; **Margin of victory**— 0.128 seconds; **Time of race**— 3 hours, 5 minutes, 42 seconds; **Caution flags**— 4 for 20 laps; **Lead changes**— 14 among 7 drivers; **Lap leaders**— R. Wallace (104), M. Skinner (31); B. Labonte (20), J. Gordon (17); D. Jarrett (14), B. Elliot (7), J. Mayfield (7). **Pole sitter**— Jeff Gordon at 195.067; **Attendance**— 150,000 (estimated).

Driver (start pos.)	Team	Car	Laps	Ended	Earnings
1 Jeff Gordon (1)	DuPont	Chevrolet Monte Carlo	200	Running	$2,194,246
2 Dale Earnhardt (4)	GM Goodwrench	Chevrolet Monte Carlo	200	Running	613,659
3 Kenny Irwin (41)	Texaco/Havoline	Ford Taurus	200	Running	465,084
4 Mike Skinner (12)	Lowe's	Chevrolet Monte Carlo	200	Running	438,834
5 Michael Waltrip (13)	Philips/Klaussner	Chevrolet Monte Carlo	200	Running	290,596
6 Ken Schrader (7)	Skoal	Chevrolet Monte Carlo	200	Running	240,731
7 Kyle Petty (24)	Hot Wheels	Pontiac Grand Prix	200	Running	145,809
8 Rusty Wallace (10)	Miller Lite	Ford Taurus	200	Running	199,209
9 Chad Little (26)	John Deere	Ford Taurus	200	Running	142,884
10 Rick Mast (21)	Sonic	Ford Taurus	200	Running	164,096
11 Jerry Nadeau (25)	Cartoon Network	Ford Taurus	200	Running	144,206
12 Wally Dallenbach Jr. (34)	Budweiser	Chevrolet Monte Carlo	200	Running	128,156
13 Kevin Lepage (14)	PRIMESTAR	Ford Taurus	200	Running	129,009
14 Ernie Irvan (31)	M&M's	Pontiac Grand Prix	200	Running	146,084
15 Ted Musgrave (27)	Remington Arms	Ford Taurus	200	Running	116,571
16 Dave Marcis (35)	Realtree Camouflage	Chevrolet Monte Carlo	199	Running	127,809
17 Johnny Benson (39)	General Mills/Cheerios	Ford Taurus	199	Running	122,081
18 Derrike Cope (20)	Jimmy Dean	Pontiac Grand Prix	199	Running	133,859
19 Robert Pressley (15)	Jasper Engines/Federal-Mogul	Ford Taurus	199	Running	133,331
20 Jeremy Mayfield (6)	Mobil 1	Ford Taurus	199	Running	168,934
21 Darrell Waltrip (43)	Big Kmart	Ford Taurus	199	Running	104,946
22 Brett Bodine (40)	Paychex	Ford Taurus	199	Running	114,309
23 Mike Wallace (42)	Acu Turn/Kodiak	Ford Taurus	199	Running	111,806
24 Ward Burton (18)	Caterpillar	Pontiac Grand Prix	198	Running	138,679
25 Bobby Labonte (3)	Interstate	Pontiac Grand Prix	198	Running	191,951
26 Ricky Craven (28)	Hollywood Video	Ford Taurus	197	Running	123,004
27 Bill Elliot (37)	McDonald's	Ford Taurus	194	Running	128,451
28 Tony Stewart (2)	Home Depot	Pontiac Grand Prix	181	Running	102,204
29 Bobby Hamilton (16)	Kodak	Chevrolet Monte Carlo	173	Accident	135,679
30 Ricky Rudd (29)	Tide	Ford Taurus	168	Running	102,226
31 Mark Martin (9)	Valvoline	Ford Taurus	147	Handling	223,951
32 Sterling Marlin (17)	Coors Light	Chevrolet Monte Carlo	144	Handling	100,101
33 Rich Bickle (22)	10-10-345	Pontiac Grand Prix	142	Handling	92,504
34 Steve Park (23)	Pennzoil	Chevrolet Monte Carlo	139	Handling	119,751
35 Jeff Burton (5)	Exide	Ford Taurus	138	Handling	118,351
36 Joe Nemechek (32)	BellSouth	Chevrolet Monte Carlo	137	Accident	117,379
37 Dale Jarrett (8)	Quality Care/Food Credit	Ford Taurus	134	Accident	146,879
38 Terry Labonte (19)	Kellogg's	Chevrolet Monte Carlo	134	Accident	103,326
39 Geoffrey Bodine (30)	Power Team	Chevrolet Monte Carlo	134	Accident	106,154
40 Elliott Sadler (38)	Citgo	Ford Taurus	132	Accident	94,329
41 Jimmy Spencer (11)	Winston	Ford Taurus	121	Accident	110,701
42 Kenny Wallace (33)	Square D	Chevrolet Monte Carlo	92	Engine	105,626
43 John Andretti (36)	STP	Pontiac Grand Prix	25	Engine	91,751

Winston Cup Point Standings

Official Top 10 NASCAR Winston Cup point leaders and Top 15 money leaders for 1998 and unofficial Top 10 point leaders and Top 15 money leaders for 1999 (through Oct. 11). Points awarded for all qualifying drivers (winner receives 175) and lap leaders. Earnings include bonuses. Listed are starts (Sts), Top 5 finishes (1-2-3-4-5), poles won (PW) and points (Pts).

FINAL 1998

		Sts	Finishes 1-2-3-4-5	PW	Pts
1	Jeff Gordon	33	13-6-3-1-3	7	5328
2	Mark Martin	33	7-6-4-3-2	3	4964
3	Dale Jarrett	33	3-5-6-2-3	2	4619
4	Rusty Wallace	33	1-2-5-3-4	4	4501
5	Jeff Burton	33	2-4-2-5-5	0	4415
6	Bobby Labonte	33	2-3-2-4-0	3	4180
7	Jeremy Mayfield	33	1-1-3-2-5	1	4157
8	Dale Earnhardt	33	1-0-1-2-1	0	3928
9	Terry Labonte	33	1-1-2-1-0	0	3901
10	Bobby Hamilton	33	1-1-0-1-0	1	3786

1999 SEASON (through Oct. 11)

		Sts	Finishes 1-2-3-4-5	PW	Pts
1	Dale Jarrett	29	4-5-4-4-5	0	4427
2	Bobby Labonte	29	4-6-5-1-4	6	4205
3	Mark Martin	29	2-3-6-3-2	0	4165
4	Jeff Gordon	29	7-4-5-1-1	7	4031
5	Tony Stewart	29	1-2-1-4-3	2	4004
6	Jeff Burton	29	6-2-2-3-2	1	3921
7	Dale Earnhardt	29	3-3-0-0-1	0	3859
8	Rusty Wallace	29	1-0-1-3-1	4	3542
9	Mike Skinner	29	0-0-1-4-0	2	3362
10	Ward Burton	29	0-2-0-2-1	1	3347

Top 5 Finishing Order + Pole
1999 SEASON

No.	Event	Winner	2nd	3rd	4th	5th	Pole
1	Daytona 500	J. Gordon	D. Earnhardt	K. Irwin	M. Skinner	M. Waltrip	J. Gordon
2	Big Kmart 400	M. Martin	D. Jarrett	B. Labonte	J. Burton	J. Mayfield	R. Rudd
3	Las Vegas 400	J. Burton	W. Burton	J. Gordon	M. Skinner	B. Labonte	B. Labonte
4	Cracker Barrel 500	J. Gordon	B. Labonte	M. Martin	J. Burton	D. Jarrett	B. Labonte
5	TranSouth 400	J. Burton	J. Mayfield	J. Gordon	D. Jarrett	M. Martin	J. Gordon
6	Primestar 500	T. Labonte	D. Jarrett	B. Labonte	R. Wallace	J. Mayfield	K. Irwin
7	Food City 500	R. Wallace	M. Martin	D. Jarrett	J. Andretti	J. Burton	R. Wallace
8	Goody's B.P. 500	J. Andretti	J. Burton	J. Gordon	M. Skinner	M. Martin	T. Stewart
9	DieHard 500	D. Earnhardt	D. Jarrett	M. Martin	B. Labonte	T. Stewart	K. Schrader
10	California 500	J. Gordon	J. Burton	B. Labonte	T. Stewart	D. Jarrett	J. Burton
11	Pontiac 400	D. Jarrett	M. Martin	B. Labonte	B. Hamilton	R. Wallace	J. Gordon
12	Coca-Cola 600	J. Burton	B. Labonte	M. Martin	T. Stewart	D. Jarrett	B. Labonte
13	MBNA 400	B. Labonte	J. Gordon	M. Martin	T. Stewart	D. Jarrett	B. Labonte
14	Kmart 400	D. Jarrett	J. Gordon	J. Burton	W. Burton	B. Labonte	J. Gordon
15	Pocono 500	B. Labonte	J. Gordon	D. Jarrett	S. Marlin	T. Stewart	S. Marlin
16	Save Mart 350K	J. Gordon	M. Martin	J. Andretti	R. Wallace	J. Spencer	R. Wallace
17	Pepsi 400	D. Jarrett	D. Earnhardt	J. Burton	M. Skinner	B. Labonte	J. Nemechek
18	Jiffy Lube 300	J. Burton	K. Wallace	J. Gordon	D. Jarrett	B. Elliot	J. Nemechek
19	Pennsylvania 500	B. Labonte	D. Jarrett	M. Martin	T. Stewart	W. Dallenbach	M. Skinner
20	Brickyard 400	D. Jarrett	B. Labonte	J. Gordon	M. Martin	J. Burton	J. Gordon
21	Frontier at The Glen	J. Gordon	R. Fellows	R. Wallace	D. Jarrett	J. Nadeau	R. Wallace
22	Pepsi 400	B. Labonte	J. Gordon	T. Stewart	D. Jarrett	D. Earnhardt	W. Burton
23	Goody's 500	D. Earnhardt	J. Spencer	R. Rudd	J. Gordon	T. Stewart	T. Stewart
24	Pepsi Southern 500	J. Burton	W. Burton	J. Mayfield	M. Martin	K. Lepage	K. Irwin
25	Select 400	T. Stewart	B. Labonte	D. Jarrett	S. Marlin	K. Irwin	M. Skinner
26	Dura Lube/Kmart 300	J. Nemechek	T. Stewart	B. Labonte	J. Burton	J. Gordon	R. Wallace
27	MBNA Gold 400	M. Martin	T. Stewart	D. Jarrett	M. Kenseth	B. Labonte	R. Wallace
28	AutoCare 500	J. Gordon	D. Earnhardt	G. Bodine	R. Wallace	K. Wallace	J. Nemechek
29	Quality 500	J. Gordon	B. Labonte	M. Skinner	M. Martin	W. Burton	B. Labonte
30	Winston 500	D. Earnhardt	D. Jarrett	R. Rudd	W. Burton	K. Wallace	J. Nemechek

Money Leaders

FINAL 1998

		Earnings
1	Jeff Gordon	$6,175,867
2	Dale Jarrett	3,368,735
3	Mark Martin	3,279,370
4	Bobby Labonte	2,648,970
5	Dale Earnhardt	2,611,100
6	Rusty Wallace	2,133,435
7	Jeff Burton	2,114,597
8	Jeremy Mayfield	1,970,521
9	Terry Labonte	1,838,415
10	Bobby Hamilton	1,789,180
11	Ken Schrader	1,729,881
12	John Andretti	1,642,700
13	Jimmy Spencer	1,600,236
14	Ricky Rudd	1,564,145
15	Ernie Irvan	1,476,141

1999 SEASON (through Oct. 11)

		Earnings
1	Jeff Gordon	$4,946,491
2	Jeff Burton	4,725,226
3	Dale Jarrett	3,184,569
4	Bobby Labonte	2,906,166
5	Dale Earnhardt	2,377,549
6	Mark Martin	2,356,486
7	Terry Labonte	2,059,851
8	Tony Stewart	2,006,936
9	Mike Skinner	1,947,476
10	Rusty Wallace	1,898,474
11	Ward Burton	1,803,024
12	Kenny Irwin	1,766,301
13	Jeremy Mayfield	1,676,239
14	John Andretti	1,581,951
15	Bobby Hamilton	1,571,504

CART RESULTS

Winners of CART races from Oct. 18, 1998 through Oct. 17, 1999.

FedEx Championship Series
1999 SEASON

Date	Event	Location	Winner (Pos.)	Time	Avg.mph	Pole	Qual.mph
Mar. 21	GP of Miami	Homestead	Greg Moore (1)	1:38:54.535	136.671	G. Moore	217.279
Apr. 10	Firehawk 500	Motegi	Adrian Fernandez (4)	1:46:01.463	176.195	G. de Ferran	219.000
Apr. 18	GP of Long Beach	Long Beach	Juan Montoya (5)	1:45:48.688	87.915	T. Kanaan	107.454
May 2	Bosch GP	Nazareth	Juan Montoya (1)	1:46:13.527	120.225	J. Montoya	173.755
May 15	Rio 400	Rio de Janeiro	Juan Montoya (3)	1:36:32.233	125.120	C. Fittipaldi	174.002
May 29	Motorola 300	Madison	Michael Andretti (11)	2:25:35.829	123.513	J. Montoya	182.778
June 6	Miller Lite 200	West Allis	Paul Tracy (6)	1:48:49.169	128.029	H. Castro-Neves	169.404
June 20	Bud/G.I. Joe's 200	Portland	Gil de Ferran (8)	1:47:44.560	107.457	J. Montoya	121.808
June 27	GP of Cleveland	Cleveland	Juan Montoya (1)	2:01:04.277	93.931	J. Montoya	133.448
July 11	Texaco/Havoline 200	Elkhart Lake	Christian Fittipaldi (4)	1:37:00.799	137.697	M. Andretti	145.428
July 18	Molson Indy	Toronto	Dario Franchitti (2)	1:56:27.550	85.897	G. de Ferran	110.565
July 25	U.S. 500	Brooklyn	Tony Kanaan (11)	2:41:12.362	186.097	J. Vasser	229.606
Aug. 8	GP of Detroit	Detroit	Dario Franchitti (4)	2:02:24.662	81.643	J. Montoya	114.773
Aug. 15	Miller Lite 200	Lexington	Juan Montoya (8)	1:42:03.808	109.606	D. Franchitti	124.394
Aug. 22	Target GP	Cicero	Juan Montoya (10)	1:53:38.704	122.236	M. Papis	162.559
Sept. 5	Molson Indy	Vancouver	Juan Montoya (1)	2:01:08.183	65.279	J. Montoya	105.730
Sept. 12	Texaco/Havoline 300	Monterey	Bryan Herta (1)	1:49:20.898	101.924	B. Herta	117.903
Sept. 26	GP of Houston	Houston	Paul Tracy (3)	1:55:31.263	78.960	J. Montoya	93.651
Oct. 17	Honda Indy	Queensland	Dario Franchitti (1)	1:58:40.726	91.849	D. Franchitti	109.724

Note: CART does not release per race winnings.

Winning cars: REYNARD/MERCEDES-BENZ (1)— Moore; REYNARD/FORD (4)— Andretti, Fernandez, Fittipaldi, Herta; REYNARD/HONDA (14)— Montoya (7), Franchitti (3), Tracy (2), de Ferran, Kanaan.

1999 Race Locations

March— MARLBORO GRAND PRIX OF MIAMI Presented by Toyota at Miami-Dade Homestead Motorsports Complex at Homestead, Fla. **April**— FIREHAWK 500 at Twin Ring Motegi, Motegi, Japan; TOYOTA GP OF LONG BEACH at Long Beach, Calif. **May**— BOSCH SPARK PLUG GP Presented by Toyota at Nazareth (Pa.) Speedway; RIO 400 at Emerson Fittipaldi Speedway at Nelson Piquet International Raceway, Rio de Janeiro, Brazil; MOTOROLA 300 at Gateway International Raceway, Madison, Ill. **June**— MILLER LITE 200 at The Milwaukee Mile in West Allis, Wisc; BUDWEISER/G.I. JOE'S 200 Presented by Texaco/Havoline at Portland (Ore.) International Raceway; MEDIC DRUG GRAND PRIX OF CLEVELAND at Burke Lakefront Airport, Cleveland, Ohio. **July**— TEXACO/HAVOLINE 200 at Road America, Elkhart Lake, Wisc.; MOLSON INDY at Exhibition Place, Toronto, Ontario, Canada; U.S. 500 at Michigan International Speedway, Brooklyn, Mich. **August**— TENNECO AUTOMOTIVE GP OF DETROIT at The Raceway on Belle Isle, Detroit, Mich.; MILLER LITE 200 at Mid-Ohio Sports Car Course in Lexington, Ohio; TARGET GP at Chicago Motor Speedway, Cicero, Ill. **September**—MOLSON INDY VANCOUVER (B.C.) at Concord Pacific Place; GRAND PRIX OF MONTEREY Featuring the Texaco/Havoline 300 at Laguna Seca Raceway, Monterey, Calif.; TEXACO GRAND PRIX OF HOUSTON (Tex.). **October**— 1999 HONDA INDY at Gold Coast, Queensland, Australia; MARLBORO 500 Presented by Toyota at the California Speedway, Fontana, Calif.

1999 U.S. 500

Date— Sunday, July 25, 1999, at Michigan International Speedway. **Distance**— 500 miles; **Course**— 2 mile oval; **Field**—26 cars; **Winner's average speed**— 186.097 mph; **Margin of victory**— 0.032 seconds; **Time of race**— 2 hours, 41 minutes, 12.362 seconds; **Caution flags**— 4 for 29 laps; **Lead changes**— 29 by 7 drivers; **Lap leaders**— Papis (143), Andretti (65), Montoya (28), Kanaan (7), Franchitti (4), Tracy (2); Vasser (1); **Pole Sitter**— Jimmy Vasser at 229.606; **Attendance**— 55,000; Note that (r) indicates rookie driver.

Driver (start pos.)	Country	Car	Laps	Ended
1 Tony Kanaan (11)	Brazil	Reynard-Honda	250	Running
2 r-Juan Montoya (3)	Colombia	Reynard-Honda	250	Running
3 Paul Tracy (8)	Canada	Reynard-Honda	250	Running
4 Michael Andretti (4)	United States	Swift-Ford	250	Running
5 Dario Franchitti (9)	Scotland	Reynard-Honda	250	Running
6 Adrian Fernandez (2)	Mexico	Reynard-Ford	250	Running
7 Max Papis (6)	Italy	Reynard-Ford	250	Running
8 Christian Fittipaldi (16)	Brazil	Swift-Ford	250	Running
9 Jimmy Vasser (1)	United States	Reynard-Honda	249	Running
10 Patrick Carpentier (12)	Canada	Reynard-Mercedes	248	Running
11 Dennis Vitolo (23)	United States	Reynard-Ford	232	Running
12 Richie Hearn (20)	United States	Reynard-Toyota	207	Electrical
13 Al Unser Jr. (17)	United States	Penske-Mercedes	206	Engine
14 Scott Pruett (5)	United States	Reynard-Toyota	183	Contact
15 Gualter Salles (24)	Brazil	Eagle-Toyota	146	Engine
16 P.J. Jones	United States	Swift-Ford	132	Contact
17 r-Cristiano da Matta (10)	Brazil	Reynard-Toyota	126	Electrical
18 Alex Barron (18)	United States	Penske-Mercedes	120	Engine
19 Roberto Moreno (13)	Brazil	Reynard-Mercedes	113	Handling
20 Bryan Herta (7)	United States	Reynard-Ford	92	Suspension
21 Michel Jourdain Jr. (26)	Mexico	Lola-Ford	80	Drive Shaft
22 Mauricio Gugelmin (14)	Brazil	Reynard-Mercedes	64	Lost Power
23 Greg Moore (21)	Canada	Reynard-Mercedes	63	Transmission

Driver (start pos.)	Country	Car	Laps	Ended
24 Gil de Ferran (15)	Brazil	Reynard-Honda	59	Contact
25 Helio Castro-Neves (19)	Brazil	Lola-Mercedes	47	Electrical
26 Robby Gordon (25)	United States	Swift-Toyota	33	Handling

Note: CART does not release earnings on a per-race basis.

CART Point Standings

Official Top 10 PPG Cup point leaders and Top 15 money leaders for 1998 and unofficial Top 10 point leaders and Top 15 money leaders for 1999. Points awarded for places 1 to 12, fastest qualifier and overall lap leader. Listed are starts (Sts), Top 5 finishes, poles won (PW) and points (Pts).

FINAL 1998

		Sts	Finishes 1-2-3-4-5	PW	Pts
1	Alex Zanardi	19	7-5-3-1-0	0	285
2	Jimmy Vasser	19	3-1-1-2-1	2	169
3	Dario Franchitti	19	3-2-1-3-0	5	160
4	Adrian Fernandez......	19	2-1-1-1-2	1	154
5	Greg Moore...........	19	2-2-2-1-1	4	140
6	Scott Pruett...........	19	0-2-1-3-2	1	121
7	Michael Andretti	19	1-4-0-0-1	1	112
8	Bryan Herta...........	19	1-0-2-1-1	3	97
9	Tony Kanaan	19	0-0-2-2-1	0	92
10	Bobby Rahal	19	0-0-1-1-1	0	82

1999 SEASON (through Oct. 17)

		Sts	Finishes 1-2-3-4-5	PW	Pts
1	Dario Franchitti	19	3-3-4-0-1	2	209
2	Juan Montoya	19	7-2-0-0-0	7	200
3	Paul Tracy	18	1-3-2-2-1	0	161
4	Michael Andretti	19	1-2-1-2-2	1	151
5	Max Papis	19	0-1-1-2-5	1	133
6	Adrian Fernandez	15	1-0-2-2-3	0	120
7	Christian Fittipaldi......	14	1-0-3-0-1	1	107
8	Gil de Ferran	19	1-2-1-0-0	2	104
9	Greg Moore	19	1-1-1-2-0	1	97
10	Jimmy Vasser	19	0-0-2-3-1	1	94

Top 5 Finishing Order + Pole
1999 Season

No. Event	Winner	2nd	3rd	4th	5th	Pole
1 Miami GP	G. Moore	M. Andretti	D. Franchitti	J. Vasser	M. Papis	G. Moore
2 Firehawk 500	A. Fernandez	G. de Ferran	C. Fittipaldi	G. Moore	M. Andretti	G. de Ferran
3 Long Beach GP......	J. Montoya	D. Franchitti	B. Herta	A. Fernandez	C. Fittipaldi	T. Kanaan
4 Bosch GP...........	J. Montoya	P.J. Jones	P. Tracy	C. da Matta	A. Fernandez	J. Montoya
5 Rio 400	J. Montoya	D. Franchitti	C. Fittipaldi	M. Papis	T. Kanaan	C. Fittipaldi
6 Motorola 300.......	M. Andretti	H. Castro-Neves	D. Franchitti	R. Moreno	M. Papis	J. Montoya
7 Miller Lite 200	P. Tracy	G. Moore	G. de Ferran	J. Vasser	A. Fernandez	H. Castro-Neves
8 Bud/G.I. Joe's 200 ...	G. de Ferran	J. Montoya	D. Franchitti	A. Fernandez	P. Tracy	J. Montoya
9 Cleveland GP	J. Montoya	G. de Ferran	M. Andretti	P. Tracy	A. Unser Jr.	J. Montoya
10 Texaco 200........	C. Fittipaldi	M. Andretti	A. Fernandez	G. Moore	M. Papis	M. Andretti
11 Toronto...........	D. Franchitti	P. Tracy	C. Fittipaldi	R. Moreno	M. Papis	G. de Ferran
12 **U.S. 500**	T. Kanaan	J. Montoya	P. Tracy	M. Andretti	D. Franchitti	J. Vasser
13 GP of Detroit	D. Franchitti	P. Tracy	G. Moore	M. Andretti	J. Vasser	J. Montoya
14 Miller Lite 200	J. Montoya	P. Tracy	D. Franchitti	J. Vasser	M. Papis	D. Franchitti
15 Target GP	J. Montoya	D. Franchitti	J. Vasser	M. Papis	H. Castro-Neves	M. Papis
16 Vancouver.........	J. Montoya	P. Carpentier	J. Vasser	M. Gugelmin	C. da Matta	J. Montoya
17 Texaco 300........	B. Herta	R. Moreno	M. Papis	P. Tracy	A. Fernandez	B. Herta
18 Houston GP........	P. Tracy	D. Franchitti	M. Andretti	M. Papis	B. Herta	J. Montoya
19 Honda Indy........	D. Franchitti	M. Papis	A. Fernandez	B. Herta	M. Andretti	D. Franchitti

Money Leaders

FINAL 1998

		Earnings
1	Jimmy Vasser	$1,584,250
2	Alex Zanardi....................	1,219,250
3	Dario Franchitti.................	1,014,250
4	Adrian Fernandez...............	605,750
5	Greg Moore....................	599,250
6	Michael Andretti................	507,250
7	Scott Pruett....................	477,500
8	Bryan Herta	453,500
9	Tony Kanaan...................	366,500
10	Bobby Rahal..................	343,750
11	Gil de Ferran	318,250
12	Al Unser Jr....................	300,250
13	Mauricio Gugelmin.............	282,750
14	Christian Fittipaldi.............	269,750
15	Paul Tracy	259,500

Note: The 1998 totals don't include Performance Award earnings.

1999 SEASON (through Oct. 11)

		Earnings
1	Juan Montoya	$926,250
2	Dario Franchitti.................	740,250
3	Paul Tracy	644,750
4	Michael Andretti................	545,000
5	Gil de Ferran	446,750
6	Greg Moore	432,250
7	Christian Fittipaldi..............	431,750
8	Max Papis	415,000
9	Adrian Fernandez	406,750
10	Jimmy Vasser.................	371,250
11	Bryan Herta	329,750
12	Tony Kanaan..................	312,500
13	Roberto Moreno	277,750
14	Patrick Carpentier	274,250
15	P.J. Jones	239,000

INDY RACING LEAGUE RESULTS

Results of Indy Racing League events during the 1999 season.

1999 SEASON

Date	Event	Location	Winner (Pos.)	Time	Avg.mph	Pole	Qual.mph
Jan. 24	Indy 200 at WDW	Orlando	Eddie Cheever (13)	1:41:14.800	118.538	S. Sharp	171.371
Mar. 28	WorldCom 200	Phoenix	Scott Goodyear (3)	1:56:40.052	102.856	G. Ray	177.139
May 30	**Indianapolis 500**	Indianapolis	Kenny Brack (8)	3:15:51.182	153.176	A. Luyendyk	225.179
June 12	Longhorn 500	Fort Worth	Scott Goodyear (8)	2:00:06.816	151.177	M. Dismore	215.272
June 27	Radisson 200	Colorado Springs	Greg Ray (1)	1:29:28.676	134.111	G. Ray	176.005
July 17	Kobalt Tools 500	Atlanta	Scott Sharp (6)	2:12:15.235	141.546	B. Boat	215.251
Aug. 1	Mid-Atlantic 200	Dover	Greg Ray (3)	1:45:01.503	114.258	M. Dismore	182.639
Aug. 29	Colorado Indy 200	Colo. Springs	Greg Ray (1)	1:28:35.633	135.450	G. Ray	176.263
Sept. 26	Vegas.com 500	Las Vegas	Sam Schmidt (1)	2:29:50.204	124.936	S. Schmidt	209.465
Oct. 17	Mall.com 500	Fort Worth	Mark Dismore (2)	2:14:15.722	135.246	G. Ray	216.107

Note: The Visionaire 500K at Lowe's Motor Speedway in Charlotte, N.C. was cancelled after a crash on the 59th lap caused a tire to fly into the stands, killing three spectators.

Winning cars: DALLARA/OLDS AURORA (7)– Ray (3), Brack, Cheever, Dismore, Sharp; G-FORCE/OLDS AURORA (3)– Goodyear (2), Schmidt.

83rd Indianapolis 500

Date—Sunday, May 30, 1999, at Indianapolis Motor Speedway. **Distance**— 500 miles; **Course**— 2.5 mile oval; **Field**— 33 cars; **Winner's average speed**— 153.176 mph; **Margin of victory**— 6.557 seconds; **Time of race**— 3 hours, 15 minutes, 51.182 seconds; **Caution flags**— 8 for 42 laps; **Lead changes**— 18 by 7 drivers; **Lap leaders**— Brack (66), Luyendyk (63), Ray (32), Gordon (28), Cheever Jr. (4), Schmidt (4), Ward (3); **Pole Sitter**— Arie Luyendyk at 225.179; **Attendance**— 375,000 (est.); **TV Rating**— 5.0 (ABC). Note that (r) indicates rookie driver.

	Driver (start pos.)	Country	Car	Laps	Ended	Earnings
1	Kenny Brack (8)	Sweden	D/A/G	200	Running	$1,465,190
2	Jeff Ward (14)	United States	D/A/G	200	Running	583,150
3	Billy Boat (3)	United States	D/A/G	200	Running	435,200
4	Robby Gordon (4)	United States	D/A/F	200	Running	253,270
5	r-Robby McGehee (27)	United States	D/A/F	199	Running	247,750
6	Robbie Buhl (32)	United States	D/A/G	199	Running	257,500
7	Buddy Lazier (22)	United States	D/A/G	198	Running	285,100
8	Robby Unser (17)	United States	D/A/F	197	Running	195,500
9	Tony Stewart (24)	United States	D/A/G	196	Running	186,670
10	Hideshi Matsuda (10)	Japan	D/A/F	196	Running	186,000
11	Davey Hamilton (11)	United States	D/A/G	196	Running	220,500
12	Raul Boesel (33)	Brazil	R/A/G	195	Running	248,600
13	r-John Hollansworth Jr. (12)	United States	D/A/G	192	Running	265,400
14	Tyce Carlson (15)	United States	D/A/F	190	Running	247,000
15	r-Jeret Schroeder (21)	United States	G/I/F	175	Engine	176,250
16	Mark Dismore (5)	United States	D/A/G	168	Accident	235,300
17	Stan Wattles (20)	United States	D/A/G	147	Running	158,000
18	Eddie Cheever Jr. (16)	United States	D/I/G	139	Engine	246,800
19	Buzz Calkins (26)	United States	G/A/F	133	Running	228,000
20	Roberto Moreno (23)	Brazil	G/A/G	122	Transmission	225,670
21	Greg Ray (2)	United States	G/A/F	120	Accident pits	204,900
22	Arie Luyendyk (1)	Netherlands	G/A/F	117	Accident	382,350
23	r-Wim Eyckmans (29)	Belgium	D/A/G	113	Timing chain	145,250
24	Jimmy Kite (28)	United States	G/A/F	110	Engine	228,000
25	Roberto Guerrero (25)	United States	G/I/F	105	Engine	217,000
26	Steve Knapp (13)	United States	G/A/G	104	Handling	216,000
27	Scott Goodyear (9)	Canada	G/A/G	101	Engine	217,500
28	Scott Sharp (6)	United States	D/A/G	83	Transmission	221,500
29	Donnie Beechler (19)	United States	D/A/F	74	Engine	143,000
30	Sam Schmidt (7)	United States	G/A/F	62	Accident	213,800
31	Jack Miller (31)	United States	D/A/G	29	Clutch	146,000
32	Johnny Unser (30)	United States	D/A/G	10	Breaks	161,000
33	Eliseo Salazar (7)	Chile	G/A/F	7	Accident	141,000

Car Legend: Chassis/Engine/Tires. D—Dallara; G (chassis)—G Force; R—Riley & Scott; A—Oldsmobile Aurora V-8; I—Nissan Infiniti V-8; F—Firestone; G (tires)—Goodyear.

Indy Racing League Point Standings

FINAL 1998

		Sts	Finishes 1-2-3-4-5	PW	Pts
1	Kenny Brack	11	3-0-1-0-1	0	332
2	Davey Hamilton	11	0-1-1-3-1	0	292
3	Tony Stewart	11	2-1-1-0-1	4	289
4	Scott Sharp	11	2-0-1-0-1	0	272
5	Buddy Lazier	11	0-2-1-0-0	0	262
6	Jeff Ward	11	0-2-1-0-1	1	252
7	Scott Goodyear	11	0-1-1-2-0	0	244
8	Arie Luyendyk	11	1-0-0-1-1	0	227
9	Eddie Cheever Jr.	11	1-0-1-0-1	0	222
10	Marco Greco	11	0-0-1-0-1	0	219

FINAL 1999

		Sts	Finishes 1-2-3-4-5	PW	Pts
1	Greg Ray	10	3-1-1-0-0	4	293
2	Kenny Brack	10	1-1-2-0-0	0	256
3	Mark Dismore	10	1-0-1-0-0	2	240
4	Davey Hamilton	10	0-2-1-0-0	0	237
5	Sam Schmidt	10	1-1-1-0-2	1	233
6	Buddy Lazier	10	0-1-0-1-1	0	224
7	Eddie Cheever Jr.	10	1-0-0-2-0	0	222
8	Scott Sharp	10	1-0-0-2-0	0	220
9	Scott Goodyear	10	2-1-0-0-0	0	217
10	Robby Unser	10	0-1-0-0-0	0	209

Top 5 Finishing Order + Pole
1999 Season

No.	Event	Winner	2nd	3rd	4th	5th	Pole
1	Indy 200 at WDW	E. Cheever	S. Goodyear	J. Ward	S. Sharp	R. Boesel	S. Sharp
2	WorldCom 200	S. Goodyear	J. Ward	R. Buhl	B. Boat	S. Harrington	G. Ray
3	**Indianapolis 500**	K. Brack	J. Ward	B. Boat	R. Gordon	R. McGehee	A. Luyendyk
4	Longhorn 500	S. Goodyear	G. Ray	S. Schmidt	S. Gregoire	E. Salazar	M. Dinsmore
5	Radisson 200	G. Ray	S. Schmidt	D. Hamilton	E. Cheever Jr.	B. Lazier	G. Ray
6	Kobalt Tools 500	S. Sharp	R. Unser	K. Brack	E. Salazar	B. Calkins	B. Boat
7	Mid-Atlantic 200	G. Ray	B. Lazier	K. Brack	B. Boat	S. Schmidt	M. Dismore
8	Colorado Indy 200	G. Ray	D. Hamilton	M. Dismore	B. Lazier	S. Schmidt	G. Ray
9	Vegas.com 500	S. Schmidt	K. Brack	R. Buhl	S. Sharp	B. Calkins	S. Schmidt
10	Mall.com 500	M. Dismore	D. Hamilton	D. Ray	E. Cheever Jr.	J. Hollansworth	G. Ray

Money Leaders

FINAL 1998

		Earnings
1	Eddie Cheever Jr.	$1,811,200
2	Kenny Brack	1,096,700
3	Billy Boat	1,004,150
4	Tony Stewart	1,002,850
5	Buddy Lazier	984,850
6	Davey Hamilton	856,850
7	Jeff Ward	811,650
8	Scott Sharp	808,900
9	Scott Goodyear	761,450
10	Arie Luyendyk	746,100

FINAL 1999

		Earnings
1	Kenny Brack	$1,933,540
2	Greg Ray	986,800
3	Jeff Ward	981,850
4	Billy Boat	846,000
5	Scott Goodyear	800,450
6	Eddie Cheever Jr.	779,500
7	Mark Dismore	766,650
8	Sam Schmidt	750,900
9	Buddy Lazier	745,150
10	Scott Sharp	720,000

FORMULA ONE RESULTS

Results of Formula One Grand Prix races from Mar. 7 through Oct. 17, 1999.

1999 SEASON

Date	Grand Prix	Location	Winner (Pos.)	Time	Avg.mph	Pole	Qual.mph
Mar. 7	Australia	Melbourne	Eddie Irvine (6)	1:35:01.659	118.593	M. Hakkinen	131.107
Apr. 11	Brazilian	Sao Paulo	Mika Hakkinen (1)	1:36:03.785	119.656	M. Hakkinen	125.391
May 2	San Marino	Imola	Michael Schumacher (3)	1:33:44.792	121.198	M. Hakkinen	127.696
May 16	Monaco	Monte Carlo	Michael Schumacher (2)	1:49:31.812	89.412	M. Hakkinen	93.508
May 30	Spainish	Barcelona	Mika Hakkinen (1)	1:34:13.066	121.570	M. Hakkinen	128.840
June 13	Canadian	Montreal	Mika Hakkinen (1)	1:41:35.727	111.946	M. Schumacher	124.713
June 27	French	Magny Cours	Heinz-Harald Frentzen (5)	1:58:24.343	92.269	R. Barrichello	96.575
July 11	British	Silverstone	David Coulthard (3)	1:32:30.144	124.253	M. Hakkinen	135.581
July 25	Austrian	Zeltwig	Eddie Irvine (3)	1:28:12.438	125.152	M. Hakkinen	136.164
Aug. 1	German	Hockenheim	Eddie Irvine (5)	1:21:58.594	140.450	M. Hakkinen	148.253
Aug. 15	Hungarian	Budapest	Mika Hakkinen (1)	1:46:23.536	107.827	M. Hakkinen	113.684
Aug. 29	Belgian	Francorchamps	David Coulthard (2)	1:25:43.057	133.370	M. Hakkinen	141.277
Sept. 12	Italian	Monza	Heinz-Harald Frentzen (2)	1:17:02.923	146.232	M. Hakkinen	156.579
Sept. 26	European	Nurburg	Johnny Herbert (14)	1:41:54.314	100.004	H.H. Frentzen	127.537
Oct. 17	Malaysian	Kuala Lumpur	Mika Hakkinen (4)	1:46:48.237	119.550	M. Schumacher	124.084

Note: The Argentine Grand Prix scheduled for March 28, was canceled from the 1999 Formula One calendar due to a disagreement between the commercial rights holder and the local promoter.

Note: In the Malaysian GP, Eddie Irvine and Michael Schumacher finished first and second, but were disqualified by the International Automobile Federation because their cars' bodywork did not conform to technical regulations.

Winning Constructors: FERRARI (5)– Irvine (3), M. Schumacher (2); JORDAN-MUGEN HONDA (2)— Frentzen (2); McLAREN-MERCEDES (7)— Hakkinen (5), Coulthard (2); STEWART-FORD (1)— Herbert.

Formula One Point Standings

Official Top 10 Formula One World Championship point leaders for 1998 and unofficial Top 10 point leaders for 1999. Points awarded for places 1 through 6 only (i.e., 10-6-4-3-2-1). Listed are starts (Sts), Top 6 finishes, poles won (PW) and points (Pts). **Note:** Formula One does not keep Money Leader standings.

FINAL 1998

		Sts	Finishes 1-2-3-4-5-6	PW	Pts
1	Mika Hakkinen	14	8-2-1-1-0-1	9	100
2	Michael Schumacher	16	6-2-3-0-1-0	3	86
3	David Coulthard	16	1-6-2-0-0-2	3	56
4	Eddie Irvine	16	0-3-5-3-0-0	0	47
5	Jacques Villeneuve	16	0-0-2-2-2-2	0	21
6	Damon Hill	15	1-0-0-3-0-1	0	20
7	Heinz-Harald Frentzen	16	0-0-1-1-5-0	0	17
	Alexander Wurz	15	0-0-0-5-1-0	0	17
9	Giancarlo Fisichella	16	0-2-0-0-1-2	1	16
10	Ralf Schumacher	14	0-1-1-0-1-2	0	14

1999 SEASON (through Oct. 17)

		Sts	Finishes 1-2-3-4-5-6	PW	Pts
1	Mika Hakkinen	15	5-2-2-0-1-0	11	72
2	Eddie Irvine	15	3-2-2-2-1-2	0	60
3	Heinz-Harald Frentzen	15	2-1-3-5-0-0	1	53
4	David Coulthard	15	2-4-0-0-2-0	0	48
5	Ralf Schumacher	15	0-1-2-5-2-0	0	33
6	Michael Schumacher	9	2-1-1-0-1-0	2	32
7	Rubens Barrichello	15	0-0-4-1-2-0	1	23
8	Johnny Herbert	15	1-1-0-0-1-0	0	18
9	Giancarlo Fisichella	15	0-1-0-1-2-0	0	13
10	Mika Salo	9	0-1-1-0-0-0	0	10

Top 5 + Pole Finishing Order

No.	Event	Winner	2nd	3rd	4th	5th	Pole
1	Australian	E. Irvine	H.H. Frentzen	R. Schumacher	G. Fisichella	R. Barrichello	M. Hakkinen
2	Brazilian	M. Hakkinen	M. Schumacher	H.H. Frentzen	R. Schumacher	E. Irvine	M. Hakkinen
3	San Marino	M. Schumacher	D. Coulthard	R. Barrichello	D. Hill	G. Fisichella	M. Hakkinen
4	Monaco	M. Schumacher	E. Irvine	M. Hakkinen	H.H. Frentzen	G. Fisichella	M. Hakkinen
5	Spanish	M. Hakkinen	D. Coulthard	M. Schumacher	E. Irvine	R. Schumacher	M. Hakkinen
6	Canadian	M. Hakkinen	G. Fisichella	E. Irvine	R. Schumacher	J. Herbert	M. Schumacher
7	French	H.H. Frentzen	M. Hakkinen	R. Barrichello	R. Schumacher	M. Schumacher	R. Barrichello
8	British	D. Coulthard	E. Irvine	R. Schumacher	H.H. Frentzen	D. Hill	M. Hakkinen
9	Austrian	E. Irvine	D. Coulthard	M. Hakkinen	H.H. Frentzen	A. Wurz	M. Hakkinen
10	German	E. Irvine	M. Salo	H.H. Frentzen	R. Schumacher	D. Coulthard	M. Hakkinen
11	Hungarian	M. Hakkinen	D. Coulthard	E. Irvine	H.H. Frentzen	R. Barrichello	M. Hakkinen
12	Belgian	D. Coulthard	M. Hakkinen	H.H. Frentzen	E. Irvine	R. Schumacher	M. Hakkinen
13	Italian	H.H. Frentzen	R. Schumacher	M. Salo	R. Barrichello	D. Coulthard	M. Hakkinen
14	European	J. Herbert	J. Trulli	R. Barrichello	R. Schumacher	M. Hakkinen	H.H. Frentzen
15	Malaysian	M. Hakkinen	J. Herbert	R. Barrichello	H.H. Frentzen	J. Alesi	M. Schumacher

Major 1999 Endurance Races

24 Hours of Daytona
Jan. 30-31, at Daytona Beach, Fla.

Officially the Rolex 24 at Daytona and first held in 1962 (as a 3-hour race). An IMSA Camel GT race for exotic prototype sports cars and contested over a 3.56-mile road course at Daytona International Speedway. Listed are qualifying position, drivers, chassis, class and laps completed.

1 (5) Elliott Forbes-Robinson, Butch Leitzinger, Andy Wallace; RILEY & SCOTT-FORD; 708 laps (2,520.48 miles) at 104.957 mph; 2 laps, 115.6 seconds margin of victory.
2 (3) Max Angelelli, Didier de Radigues, Allan McNish and Wayne Taylor; FERRARI 333; SP; 706 laps.
3 (4) Stefan Johansson, Jim Matthews, Max Papis and Jimmy Vasser; FERRARI 333; SP; 694 laps.
4 (12) Lilian Bryner, Enzo Calderari, Carl Rosenglad and Angelo Zadra; FERRARI 333: SP; 679 laps.
5 (9) Henry Camferdam, Duncan Dayton, Eliseo Salazar and Scott Schubot; RILEY & SCOTT-FORD; 679 laps.
Fastest lap: Allan McNish (lap #39), FERRARI 333 SP; Can-Am.; 124.724 mph. **Top qualifier:** James Weaver (127.05 mph), 1:40.869.
Weather: Sunny then rainy. **Attendance:** 40,000 (est.).

24 Hours of Le Mans
June 12-13, at Le Mans, France

Officially the Le Mans Grand Prix d'Endurance and first held in 1923. Contested over the 8.451-mile Circuit de la Sarthe in Le Mans, France. Listed are qualifying position, drivers, car, and laps completed.

1 (6) Pierluigi Martini, Yannick Dalmas and Joachim Winkelhock; BMW V-12 LMR; 365 laps (3,086.615 miles) at 128.608 mph.
2 (8) Ukyo Katayama, Keiichi Tsuchiya and Toshio Suzuki; TOYOTA GT1; 364 laps.
3 (11) Frank Biela, Didier Theys and Emanuele Pirro; AUDI R8; 360 laps.
4 (9) Michele Alboreto, Laurent Aiello and Rinaldo Capello; AUDI R8; 346 laps.
5 (18) Thomas Bscher, Bill Auberlen and Steve Soper; BMW V-12; 345 laps.
Fastest lap: Ukyo Katayama; 141.66 mph. **Top qualifier:** Martin Brundle, Emmanuel Collard and Vincenzo Sospiri 144.970 mph (3:29.930).
Weather: Overcast. **Attendance:** 200,000 (est.).

NHRA RESULTS

Winners of National Hot Rod Association Drag Racing events in the Top Fuel, Funny Car and Pro Stock divisions through Oct. 10, 1999. All times are based on two cars racing head-to-head from a standing start over a straight line, quarter-mile course. Differences in reaction time account for apparently faster losing times.

1999 Season

Date	Event	Event	Winner	Time	MPH	2nd Place	Time	MPH
Feb. 7	Winternationals	Top Fuel	Mike Dunn	4.522	313.88	L. Dixon	13.595	60.85
		Funny Car	Tony Pedregon	4.970	311.49	G. Densham	5.047	282.13
		Pro Stock	Jeg Coughlin	6.969	198.52	T. Coughlin	11.667	76.64
Feb. 28	Kragen Nationals.........	Top Fuel	Joe Amato	4.565	320.66	K. Bernstein	4.649	316.75
		Funny Car	John Force	4.843	317.87	C. Pedregon	5.095	272.67
		Pro Stock	Kurt Johnson	6.970	197.97	T. Coughlin	8.095	120.38
Mar. 21	Gatornationals	Top Fuel	Mike Dunn	4.550	319.98	D. Herbert	4.563	318.62
		Funny Car	John Force	4.819	311.92	C. Lee	8.613	101.88
		Pro Stock	Warren Johnson	6.971	199.37	K. Johnson	7.250	167.07
Apr. 11	O'Reilly Nationals (TX)	Top Fuel	Doug Herbert	4.657	306.56	T. Schumacher	7.631	119.14
		Funny Car	John Force	4.878	307.02	T. Pedregon	13.630	69.25
		Pro Stock	Kurt Johnson	6.969	199.14	M. Edwards	7.009	197.77
Apr. 25	Castrol Nationals.........	Top Fuel	Gary Scelzi	4.563	319.60	D. Kalitta	4.588	318.02
		Funny Car	Tony Pedregon	4.982	309.70	D. Skuza	13.768	51.25
		Pro Stock	Warren Johnson	6.945	198.85	M. Edwards	7.002	196.72
May 2	Pennzoil Nationals (VA) ...	Top Fuel	Cory McClenathan	4.684	310.05	L. Dixon	5.383	223.99
		Funny Car	John Force	4.940	303.30	T. Pedregon	5.040	293.79
		Pro Stock	Allen Johnson	6.970	198.17	R. Stevens	6.960	198.20
May 16	Southern Nationals	Top Fuel	Gary Scelzi	4.698	307.23	D. Kalitta	4.771	291.01
		Funny Car	John Force	5.147	283.61	W. Bazemore	5.182	280.84
		Pro Stock	Warren Johnson	6.998	198.93	R. Stevens	7.023	196.93
May 23	Mopar Nationals	Top Fuel	Joe Amato	4.614	313.58	D. Hebert	11.958	89.51
		Funny Car	John Force	4.878	309.34	C. Pedregon	4.873	300.73
		Pro Stock	Richie Stevens	6.959	198.00	T. Martino	6.959	198.23
June 6	Fram Rte. 66 Nationals....	Top Fuel	Mike Dunn	4.702	316.67	K. Bernstein	11.542	79.18
		Funny Car	Tim Wilkerson	5.970	239.06	J. Force	7.358	178.87
		Pro Stock	Warren Johnson	6.987	198.06	T. Coughlin	7.110	196.19
June 13	Pontiac Nationals.........	Top Fuel	Doug Herbert	4.696	313.00	B. Vandergriff	4.763	282.84
		Funny Car	Phil Burkart	5.163	280.89	T. Wilkerson	8.707	98.79
		Pro Stock	Warren Johnson	7.008	197.57	J. Coughlin	7.061	197.97
June 27	Sears Craftsman Nat'ls.	Top Fuel	Gary Scelzi	4.602	312.13	T. Schumacher	8.029	105.94
		Funny Car	John Force	4.947	297.88	T. Pedregon	12.985	73.58
		Pro Stock	Jim Yates	7.018	195.85	A. Johnson	7.010	196.33
July 10	Winston Showdown	T.F./FC.*	John Force	5.470	262.18	B. Vandergriff	5.876	243.90
		Pro Stock	Jeg Coughlin	7.004	196.85	T. Coughlin	9.982	91.63
July 18	Mile-High Nationals	Top Fuel	Joe Amato	5.710	253.85	D. Kalitta	6.024	233.92
		Funny Car	Tony Pedregon	5.209	279.96	W. Bazemore	13.182	70.68
		Pro Stock	Jeg Coughlin	7.267	188.67	T. Coughlin	7.345	187.73
Aug. 1	Northwest Nationals	Top Fuel	Joe Amato	4.704	306.95	D. Katilla	4.697	307.58
		Funny Car	Del Worsham	5.283	279.67	W. Bazemore	7.302	163.67
		Pro Stock	Kurt Johnson	6.923	200.44	J. Yates	6.962	198.00
Aug. 8	Autolite Nationals	Top Fuel	Doug Kalitta	4.615	315.93	T. Schumacher	5.023	216.17
		Funny Car	Whit Bazemore	4.963	301.74	F. Pedregon	14.809	72.77
		Pro Stock	Jim Yates	6.982	197.48	K. Johnson	11.597	75.75
Aug. 22	Colonel's Nationals.......	Top Fuel	Larry Dixon	4.594	294.95	E. Hill	4.698	249.63
		Funny Car	John Force	4.929	313.80	W. Bazemore	5.000	305.77
		Pro Stock	Jeg Coughlin	7.063	194.60	W. Johnson	7.167	179.95
Sept. 6	U.S. Nationals	Top Fuel	Cory McClenathan	4.618	208.14	A. Cowin	4.829	292.71
		Funny Car	Frank Pedregon	5.086	284.33	J. Epler	8.027	101.78
		Pro Stock	Warren Johnson	6.944	198.61	G. Anderson	14.501	58.06
Sept. 19	Keystone Nationals	Top Fuel	Joe Amato	4.677	303.95	T. Schumacher	12.195	72.94
		Funny Car	Tommy Johnson Jr.	5.108	281.51	R. Capps	5.363	251.88
		Pro Stock	Jeg Coughlin	6.936	198.80	M. Pawuk	7.004	196.03

* At the Winston Showdown the Funny Car finalist competed against the Top Fuel finalist in one event.

Winston Point Standings

First place finishers in parentheses.

1999 SEASON (through Oct. 11)

Top Fuel	Pts	Funny Car	Pts	Pro Stock	Pts
1 Tony Schumacher	1221	1 John Force (9)	1739	1 Warren Johnson (6)	1512
2 Joe Amato (5)	1201	2 Tony Pedregon (3)	1444	2 Kurt Johnson (3)	1332
3 Gary Scelzi (3)	1155	3 Whit Bazemore (1)	1266	3 Jeg Coughlin (5)	1236
4 Doug Hebert (2)	1146	4 Frank Pedregon (1)	930	4 Jim Yates (2)	1087
5 Kenny Bernstein	1123	5 Dean Skuza	858	5 Richie Stevens	1004

AUTO RACING
STATISTICS

THROUGH THE YEARS

1911-1999

MAJOR RACES • LEADERS

SEC B

PAGE 892

THE 2000 SPORTS ALMANAC

NASCAR Circuit
The Crown Jewels

The four biggest races on the NASCAR (National Association for Stock Car Auto Racing) circuit are the Daytona 500, the Winston 500, the Coca-Cola 600 and the Pepsi Southern 500. The Winston Cup Media Guide lists them as the richest (Daytona), the fastest (Winston), the longest (Coca-Cola) and the oldest (Southern). The only drivers to win three of the races in a year are Lee Roy Yarbrough (1969), David Pearson (1976), Bill Elliott (1985) and Jeff Gordon (1997).

Daytona 500

Held early in the NASCAR season; 200 laps around a 2.5-mile high-banked oval at Daytona International Speedway in Daytona Beach, FL. First race in 1959, although stock car racing at Daytona dates back to 1936. Winning drivers who started from pole positions are in **bold** type.

Multiple winners: Richard Petty (7); Cale Yarborough (4); Bobby Allison (3); Bill Elliott, Jeff Gordon, Dale Jarrett and Sterling Marlin (2). **Multiple poles:** Buddy Baker and Cale Yarborough (4); Bill Elliott, Fireball Roberts and Ken Schrader (3); Donnie Allison (2).

Year	Winner	Car	Owner	MPH	Pole Sitter	MPH
1959	Lee Petty	Oldsmobile	Petty Enterprises	135.521	Bob Welborn	140.121
1960	Junior Johnson	Chevrolet	Ray Fox	124.740	Cotton Owens	149.892
1961	Marvin Panch	Pontiac	Smokey Yunick	149.601	Fireball Roberts	155.709
1962	**Fireball Roberts**	Pontiac	Smokey Yunick	152.529	Fireball Roberts	156.999
1963	Tiny Lund	Ford	Wood Brothers	151.566	Fireball Roberts	160.943
1964	Richard Petty	Plymouth	Petty Enterprises	154.334	Paul Goldsmith	174.910
1965-a	Fred Lorenzen	Ford	Holman-Moody	141.539	Darel Dieringer	171.151
1966-b	**Richard Petty**	Plymouth	Petty Enterprises	160.627	Richard Petty	175.165
1967	Mario Andretti	Ford	Holman-Moody	149.926	Curtis Turner	180.831
1968	**Cale Yarborough**	Mercury	Wood Brothers	143.251	Cale Yarborough	189.222
1969	Lee Roy Yarbrough	Ford	Junior Johnson	157.950	Buddy Baker	188.901
1970	Pete Hamilton	Plymouth	Petty Enterprises	149.601	Cale Yarborough	194.015
1971	Richard Petty	Plymouth	Petty Enterprises	144.462	A.J. Foyt	182.744
1972	A.J. Foyt	Mercury	Wood Brothers	161.550	Bobby Isaac	186.632
1973	Richard Petty	Dodge	Petty Enterprises	157.205	Buddy Baker	185.662
1974-c	Richard Petty	Dodge	Petty Enterprises	140.894	David Pearson	185.017
1975	Benny Parsons	Chevrolet	L.G. DeWitt	153.649	Donnie Allison	185.827
1976	David Pearson	Mercury	Wood Brothers	152.181	Ramo Stott	183.456
1977	Cale Yarborough	Chevrolet	Junior Johnson	153.218	Donnie Allison	188.048
1978	Bobby Allison	Ford	Bud Moore	159.730	Cale Yarborough	187.536
1979	Richard Petty	Oldsmobile	Petty Enterprises	143.977	Buddy Baker	196.049
1980	**Buddy Baker**	Oldsmobile	Ranier Racing	177.602*	Buddy Baker	194.099
1981	Richard Petty	Buick	Petty Enterprises	169.651	Bobby Allison	194.624
1982	Bobby Allison	Buick	DiGard Racing	153.991	Benny Parsons	196.317
1983	Cale Yarborough	Pontiac	Ranier Racing	155.979	Ricky Rudd	198.864
1984	**Cale Yarborough**	Chevrolet	Ranier Racing	150.994	Cale Yarborough	201.848
1985	**Bill Elliott**	Ford	Melling Racing	172.265	Bill Elliott	205.114
1986	Geoff Bodine	Chevrolet	Hendrick Motorsports	148.124	Bill Elliott	205.039
1987	**Bill Elliott**	Ford	Melling Racing	176.263	Bill Elliott	210.364†
1988	Bobby Allison	Buick	Stavola Brothers	137.531	Ken Schrader	198.823
1989	Darrell Waltrip	Chevrolet	Hendrick Motorsports	148.466	Ken Schrader	196.996
1990	Derrike Cope	Chevrolet	Bob Whitcomb	165.761	Ken Schrader	196.515
1991	Ernie Irvan	Chevrolet	Morgan-McClure	148.148	Davey Allison	195.955
1992	Davey Allison	Ford	Robert Yates	160.256	Sterling Martin	192.213
1993	Dale Jarrett	Chevrolet	Joe Gibbs Racing	154.972	Kyle Petty	189.426
1994	Sterling Marlin	Chevrolet	Morgan-McClure	156.931	Loy Allen	190.158
1995	Sterling Marlin	Chevrolet	Morgan-McClure	141.710	Dale Jarrett	193.498
1996	Dale Jarrett	Ford	Robert Yates	154.308	Dale Earnhardt	189.510
1997	Jeff Gordon	Chevrolet	Rick Hendrick	148.295	Mike Skinner	189.813
1998	Dale Earnhardt	Chevrolet	Richard Childress	172.712	Bobby Labonte	192.415
1999	**Jeff Gordon**	Chevrolet	Rick Hendrick	161.551	Jeff Gordon	195.067

*Track and race record for winning speed. †Track and race record for qualifying speed.
Notes: a–rain shortened 1965 to 332+ miles; b–rain shortened 1966 race to 495 miles; c–in 1974, race shortened 50 miles due to energy crisis. **Also:** Pole sitters determined by pole qualifying race (1959-65); by two-lap average (1966-68); by fastest single lap (since 1969).

Winston 500

Held at Talladega (Ala.) Superspeedway. **Multiple winners:** Bobby Allison, Davey Allison, Buddy Baker, Dale Earnhardt and David Pearson (3); Mark Martin, Darrell Waltrip and Cale Yarborough (2).

Year		Year		Year		Year	
1970	Pete Hamilton	1978	Cale Yarborough	1986	Bobby Allison	1994	Dale Earnhardt
1971	Donnie Allison	1979	Bobby Allison	1987	Davey Allison	1995	Mark Martin
1972	David Pearson	1980	Buddy Baker	1988	Phil Parsons	1996	Sterling Marlin
1973	David Pearson	1981	Bobby Allison	1989	Davey Allison	1997	Mark Martin
1974	David Pearson	1982	Darrell Waltrip	1990	Dale Earnhardt	1998	Dale Jarrett
1975	Buddy Baker	1983	Richard Petty	1991	Harry Gant	1999	Dale Earnhardt
1976	Buddy Baker	1984	Cale Yarborough	1992	Davey Allison		
1977	Darrell Waltrip	1985	Bill Elliott	1993	Ernie Irvan		

Coca-Cola 600

Held at Charlotte (N.C.) Motor Speedway. **Multiple winners:** Darrell Waltrip (5); Bobby Allison, Buddy Baker, Dale Earnhardt, Jeff Gordon and David Pearson (3); Neil Bonnett, Fred Lorenzen, Jim Paschal and Richard Petty (2).

Year		Year		Year		Year	
1960	Joe Lee Johnson	1970	Donnie Allison	1980	Benny Parsons	1990	Rusty Wallace
1961	David Pearson	1971	Bobby Allison	1981	Bobby Allison	1991	Davey Allison
1962	Nelson Stacy	1972	Buddy Baker	1982	Neil Bonnett	1992	Dale Earnhardt
1963	Fred Lorenzen	1973	Buddy Baker	1983	Neil Bonnett	1993	Dale Earnhardt
1964	Jim Paschal	1974	David Pearson	1984	Bobby Allison	1994	Jeff Gordon
1965	Fred Lorenzen	1975	Richard Petty	1985	Darrell Waltrip	1995	Bobby Labonte
1966	Marvin Panch	1976	David Pearson	1986	Dale Earnhardt	1996	Dale Jarrett
1967	Jim Paschal	1977	Richard Petty	1987	Kyle Petty	1997	Jeff Gordon
1968	Buddy Baker	1978	Darrell Waltrip	1988	Darrell Waltrip	1998	Jeff Gordon
1969	Lee Roy Yarbrough	1979	Darrell Waltrip	1989	Darrell Waltrip	1999	Jeff Burton

Southern 500

Held at Darlington (S.C.) International Raceway. **Multiple winners:** Cale Yarborough (5); Bobby Allison and Jeff Gordon (4); Buck Baker, Dale Earnhardt, Bill Elliott, David Pearson and Herb Thomas (3); Harry Gant and Fireball Roberts (2).

Year		Year		Year		Year	
1950	Johnny Mantz	1963	Fireball Roberts	1976	David Pearson	1989	Dale Earnhardt
1951	Herb Thomas	1964	Buck Baker	1977	David Pearson	1990	Dale Earnhardt
1952	Fonty Flock	1965	Ned Jarrett	1978	Cale Yarborough	1991	Harry Gant
1953	Buck Baker	1966	Darel Dieringer	1979	David Pearson	1992	Darrell Waltrip
1954	Herb Thomas	1967	Richard Petty	1980	Terry Labonte	1993	Mark Martin
1955	Herb Thomas	1968	Cale Yarborough	1981	Neil Bonnett	1994	Bill Elliott
1956	Curtis Turner	1969	Lee Roy Yarbrough	1982	Cale Yarborough	1995	Jeff Gordon
1957	Speedy Thompson	1970	Buddy Baker	1983	Bobby Allison	1996	Jeff Gordon
1958	Fireball Roberts	1971	Bobby Allison	1984	Harry Gant	1997	Jeff Gordon
1959	Jim Reed	1972	Bobby Allison	1985	Bill Elliott	1998	Jeff Gordon
1960	Buck Baker	1973	Cale Yarborough	1986	Tim Richmond	1999	Jeff Burton
1961	Nelson Stacy	1974	Cale Yarborough	1987	Dale Earnhardt		
1962	Larry Frank	1975	Bobby Allison	1988	Bill Elliott		

All-Time Leaders

NASCAR's all-time Top 20 drivers in victories, pole positions and earnings based on records through 1998. Drivers active in 1999 are in **bold** type.

Victories

1	Richard Petty	200
2	David Pearson	105
3	Bobby Allison	84
	Darrell Waltrip	84
5	Cale Yarborough	83
6	**Dale Earnhardt**	71
7	Lee Petty	55
8	Ned Jarrett	50
	Junior Johnson	50
10	Herb Thomas	48
	Rusty Wallace	48
12	Buck Baker	46
13	**Jeff Gordon**	42
14	**Bill Elliott**	40
	Tim Flock	40
16	Bobby Isaac	37
17	Fireball Roberts	32
18	**Mark Martin**	29
19	Fred Lorenzen	26
	Rex White	26

Pole Positions

1	Richard Petty	126
2	David Pearson	113
3	Cale Yarborough	70
4	**Darrell Waltrip**	59
5	Bobby Allison	57
6	Bobby Isaac	51
7	**Bill Elliott**	49
8	Junior Johnson	47
9	Buck Baker	44
10	Buddy Baker	40
11	Tim Flock	39
	Herb Thomas	39
13	**Mark Martin**	38
14	**Geoff Bodine**	37
15	Ned Jarrett	35
	Rex White	35
	Fireball Roberts	35
18	Fonty Flock	34
19	Fred Lorenzen	33
20	**Terry Labonte**	25

Earnings

1	**Dale Earnhardt**	$33,377,129
2	**Jeff Gordon**	26,009,046
3	**Bill Elliott**	19,483,233
4	**Terry Labonte**	18,809,710
5	**Rusty Wallace**	18,793,549
6	**Mark Martin**	18,759,698
7	**Darrell Waltrip**	17,197,205
8	**Dale Jarrett**	15,313,019
9	**Ricky Rudd**	15,015,215
10	**Geoff Bodine**	12,784,539
11	**Ken Schrader**	12,055,477
12	**Sterling Marlin**	11,592,188
13	**Ernie Irvan**	10,552,042
14	**Kyle Petty**	10,148,785
15	**Bobby Labonte**	9,041,244
16	Harry Gant	8,456,104
17	**Morgan Shepherd**	8,428,789
18	**Michael Waltrip**	8,024,951
19	Richard Petty	7,755,409
20	**Brett Bodine**	7,351,872

Richard Petty, in his infamous No. 43 car, waves to the crowd (ignoring the "both hands on the wheel" rule) after passing David Pearson at the Michigan Speedway on August 24, 1975. It is the 173rd of Petty's 200 NASCAR wins.

Winston Cup Champions

Originally the Grand National Championship, 1949-70, and based on official NASCAR records.

Multiple winners: Dale Earnhardt and Richard Petty (7); Jeff Gordon, David Pearson, Lee Petty, Darrell Waltrip and Cale Yarborough (3); Buck Baker, Tim Flock, Ned Jarrett, Terry Labonte, Herb Thomas and Joe Weatherly (2).

Year		Year		Year		Year	
1949	Red Byron	1962	Joe Weatherly	1975	Richard Petty	1988	Bill Elliott
1950	Bill Rexford	1963	Joe Weatherly	1976	Cale Yarborough	1989	Rusty Wallace
1951	Herb Thomas	1964	Richard Petty	1977	Cale Yarborough	1990	Dale Earnhardt
1952	Tim Flock	1965	Ned Jarrett	1978	Cale Yarborough	1991	Dale Earnhardt
1953	Herb Thomas	1966	David Pearson	1979	Richard Petty	1992	Alan Kulwicki
1954	Lee Petty	1967	Richard Petty	1980	Dale Earnhardt	1993	Dale Earnhardt
1955	Tim Flock	1968	David Pearson	1981	Darrell Waltrip	1994	Dale Earnhardt
1956	Buck Baker	1969	David Pearson	1982	Darrell Waltrip	1995	Jeff Gordon
1957	Buck Baker	1970	Bobby Isaac	1983	Bobby Allison	1996	Terry Labonte
1958	Lee Petty	1971	Richard Petty	1984	Terry Labonte	1997	Jeff Gordon
1959	Lee Petty	1972	Richard Petty	1985	Darrell Waltrip	1998	Jeff Gordon
1960	Rex White	1973	Benny Parsons	1986	Dale Earnhardt		
1961	Ned Jarrett	1974	Richard Petty	1987	Dale Earnhardt		

NASCAR Rookie of the Year

Award presented to rookie driver who accumulates the most Winston Cup points based on his best 15 finishes.

Year		Year		Year		Year	
1958	Shorty Rollins	1969	Dick Brooks	1980	Jody Ridley	1991	Bobby Hamilton
1959	Richard Petty	1970	Bill Dennis	1981	Ron Bouchard	1992	Jimmy Hensley
1960	David Pearson	1971	Walter Ballard	1982	Geoff Bodine	1993	Jeff Gordon
1961	Woodie Wilson	1972	Larry Smith	1983	Sterling Marlin	1994	Jeff Burton
1962	Tom Cox	1973	Lennie Pond	1984	Rusty Wallace	1995	Ricky Craven
1963	Billy Wade	1974	Earl Ross	1985	Ken Schrader	1996	Johnny Benson
1964	Doug Cooper	1975	Bruce Hill	1986	Alan Kulwicki	1997	Mike Skinner
1965	Sam McQuagg	1976	Skip Manning	1987	Davey Allison	1998	Kenny Irwin
1966	James Hylton	1977	Ricky Rudd	1988	Ken Bouchard		
1967	Donnie Allison	1978	Ronnie Thomas	1989	Dick Trickle		
1968	Pete Hamilton	1979	Dale Earnhardt	1990	Rob Moroso		

CART Circuit
PPG Cup Champions

Officially the PPG Indy Car World Series Championship since 1979 and based on official AAA (American Automobile Assn., 1909-55), USAC (U.S. Auto Club, 1956-78), and CART (Championship Auto Racing Teams, 1979-91). CART was renamed IndyCar in 1992 and then lost use of the name in 1997.

Multiple titles: A.J. Foyt (7); Mario Andretti (4); Jimmy Bryan, Earl Cooper, Ted Horn, Rick Mears, Louie Meyer, Bobby Rahal, Al Unser (3); Tony Bettenhausen, Ralph DePalma, Peter DePaolo, Joe Leonard, Rex Mays, Tommy Milton, Jimmy Murphy, Wilbur Shaw, Tom Sneva, Al Unser Jr., Bobby Unser, Rodger Ward and Alex Zanardi (2).

AAA

Year		Year		Year		Year	
1909	George Robertson	1920	Tommy Milton	1931	Louis Schneider	1942-45	No racing
1910	Ray Harroun	1921	Tommy Milton	1932	Bob Carey	1946	Ted Horn
1911	Ralph Mulford	1922	Jimmy Murphy	1933	Louie Meyer	1947	Ted Horn
1912	Ralph DePalma	1923	Eddie Hearne	1934	Bill Cummings	1948	Ted Horn
1913	Earl Cooper	1924	Jimmy Murphy	1935	Kelly Petillo	1949	Johnnie Parsons
1914	Ralph DePalma	1925	Peter DePaolo	1936	Mauri Rose	1950	Henry Banks
1915	Earl Cooper	1926	Harry Hartz	1937	Wilbur Shaw	1951	Tony Bettenhausen
1916	Dario Resta	1927	Peter DePaolo	1938	Floyd Roberts	1952	Chuck Stevenson
1917	Earl Cooper	1928	Louie Meyer	1939	Wilbur Shaw	1953	Sam Hanks
1918	Ralph Mulford	1929	Louie Meyer	1940	Rex Mays	1954	Jimmy Bryan
1919	Howard Wilcox	1930	Billy Arnold	1941	Rex Mays	1955	Bob Sweikert

USAC

Year		Year		Year		Year	
1956	Jimmy Bryan	1962	Rodger Ward	1968	Bobby Unser	1974	Bobby Unser
1957	Jimmy Bryan	1963	A.J. Foyt	1969	Mario Andretti	1975	A.J. Foyt
1958	Tony Bettenhausen	1964	A.J. Foyt	1970	Al Unser	1976	Gordon Johncock
1959	Rodger Ward	1965	Mario Andretti	1971	Joe Leonard	1977	Tom Sneva
1960	A.J. Foyt	1966	Mario Andretti	1972	Joe Leonard	1978	A.J. Foyt
1961	A.J. Foyt	1967	A.J. Foyt	1973	Roger McCluskey		

CART

Year		Year		Year		Year	
1979	Rick Mears	1984	Mario Andretti	1989	Emerson Fittipaldi	1994	Al Unser Jr.
1980	Johnny Rutherford	1985	Al Unser	1990	Al Unser Jr.	1995	Jacques Villeneuve
1981	Rick Mears	1986	Bobby Rahal	1991	Michael Andretti	1996	Jimmy Vasser
1982	Rick Mears	1987	Bobby Rahal	1992	Bobby Rahal	1997	Alex Zanardi
1983	Al Unser	1988	Danny Sullivan	1993	Nigel Mansell	1998	Alex Zanardi

All-Time CART Leaders

CART's all-time Top 20 drivers in victories, pole positions and earnings, based on records through 1998. Drivers active in 1999 are in **bold** type. Totals include victories, poles and earnings before CART was established in 1979.

Victories

1	A.J. Foyt	67
2	Mario Andretti	52
3	Al Unser	39
4	**Michael Andretti**	37
5	Bobby Unser	35
6	**Al Unser Jr.**	31
7	Rick Mears	29
8	Johnny Rutherford	27
9	Roger Ward	26
10	Gordon Johncock	25
11	Ralph DePalma	24
	Bobby Rahal	24
13	Tommy Milton	23
14	Tony Bettenhausen	22
	Emerson Fittipaldi	22
16	Earl Cooper	20
17	Jimmy Bryan	19
	Jimmy Murphy	19
19	Ralph Mulford	17
	Danny Sullivan	17

Pole Positions

1	Mario Andretti	67
2	A.J. Foyt	53
3	Bobby Unser	49
4	Rick Mears	40
5	**Michael Andretti**	31
6	Al Unser	27
7	Johnny Rutherford	23
8	Gordon Johncock	20
9	Rex Mays	19
	Danny Sullivan	19
11	Bobby Rahal	18
12	Emerson Fittipaldi	17
13	Tony Bettenhausen	14
	Don Branson	14
	Tom Sneva	14
16	Parnelli Jones	12
	Paul Tracy	12
18	Rodger Ward	11
	Danny Ongais	11
20	Johnny Thomson	10
	Dan Gurney	10
	Teo Fabi	10
	Nigel Mansell	10
	Alex Zanardi	10

Earnings

1	**Al Unser Jr.**	$18,652,406
2	Bobby Rahal	16,344,008
3	**Michael Andretti**	15,341,869
4	Emerson Fittipaldi	14,293,625
5	Mario Andretti	11,552,154
6	Rick Mears	11,050,807
7	Danny Sullivan	8,884,126
8	**Jimmy Vasser**	8,639,244
9	Arie Luyendyk*	7,732,188
10	Raul Boesel	6,971,887
11	Al Unser	6,740,843
12	**Paul Tracy**	6,227,520
13	Alex Zanardi	5,733,750
14	A.J. Foyt	5,357,589
15	**Scott Pruett**	5,229,144
16	Teo Fabi	5,045,081
17	Scott Brayton	4,807,274
18	Scott Goodyear*	4,579,451
19	Roberto Guerrero*	4,275,163
20	Johnny Rutherford	4,209,232

*Drivers active, but in IRL not CART.

CART Rookie of the Year

Award presented to rookie who accumulates the most PPG Cup points among first year drivers. Originally the CART Rookie of the Year; CART was renamed IndyCar in 1992 and then lost use of the name in 1997.

Year		Year		Year		Year	
1979	Bill Alsup	1984	Roberto Guerrero	1989	Bernard Jourdain	1994	Jacques Villeneuve
1980	Dennis Firestone	1985	Arie Luyendyk	1990	Eddie Cheever	1995	Gil de Ferran
1981	Bob Lazier	1986	Dominic Dobson	1991	Jeff Andretti	1996	Alex Zanardi
1982	Bobby Rahal	1987	Fabrizio Barbazza	1992	Stefan Johansson	1997	Patrick Carpentier
1983	Teo Fabi	1988	John Jones	1993	Nigel Mansell	1998	Tony Kanaan

Indy Racing League Circuit
Indianapolis 500

Held every Memorial Day weekend; 200 laps around a 2.5-mile oval at Indianapolis Motor Speedway. First race was held in 1911. The Indy Racing League began in 1996 and made the Indianapolis 500 its cornerstone event. Winning drivers are listed with starting positions. Winners who started from pole position are in **bold** type.

Multiple wins: A.J. Foyt, Rick Mears and Al Unser (4); Louis Meyer, Mauri Rose, Johnny Rutherford, Wilbur Shaw and Bobby Unser (3); Emerson Fittipaldi, Gordon Johncock, Arie Luyendyk, Tommy Milton, Al Unser Jr., Bill Vukovich and Rodger Ward (2).

Multiple poles: Rick Mears (6); Mario Andretti and A.J. Foyt (4); Arie Luyendyk, Rex Mays, Duke Nalon and Tom Sneva (3); Billy Arnold, Bill Cummings, Ralph DePalma, Leon Duray, Walt Faulkner, Parnelli Jones, Jack McGrath, Jimmy Murphy, Johnny Rutherford, Eddie Sachs and Jimmy Snyder (2).

Year	Winner (Pos.)	Car	MPH	Pole Sitter	MPH
1911	Ray Harroun (28)	Marmon Wasp	74.602	Lewis Strang	–
1912	Joe Dawson (7)	National	78.719	Gil Anderson	–
1913	Jules Goux (7)	Peugeot	75.933	Caleb Bragg	–
1914	Rene Thomas (15)	Delage	82.474	Jean Chassagne	–
1915	Ralph DePalma (2)	Mercedes	89.840	Howard Wilcox	98.90
1916-a	Dario Resta (4)	Peugeot	84.001	John Aitken	96.69
1917-18	Not held	World War I			
1919	Howdy Wilcox (2)	Peugeot	88.050	Rene Thomas	104.78
1920	Gaston Chevrolet (6)	Monroe	88.618	Ralph DePalma	99.15
1921	Tommy Milton (20)	Frontenac	89.621	Ralph DePalma	100.75
1922	**Jimmy Murphy** (1)	Murphy Special	94.484	Jimmy Murphy	100.50
1923	**Tommy Milton** (1)	H.C.S. Special	90.954	Tommy Milton	108.17
1924	L.L. Corum & Joe Boyer (21)	Duesenberg Special	98.234	Jimmy Murphy	108.037
1925	Peter DePaolo (2)	Duesenberg Special	101.127	Leon Duray	113.196
1926-b	Frank Lockhart (20)	Miller Special	95.904	Earl Cooper	111.735
1927	George Souders (22)	Duesenberg	97.545	Frank Lockhart	120.100
1928	Louie Meyer (13)	Miller Special	99.482	Leon Duray	122.391
1929	Ray Keech (6)	Simplex Piston Ring Special	97.585	Cliff Woodbury	120.599
1930	**Billy Arnold** (1)	Miller-Hartz Special	100.448	Billy Arnold	113.268
1931	Louis Schneider (13)	Bowes Seal Fast Special	96.629	Russ Snowberger	112.796
1932	Fred Frame (27)	Miller-Hartz Special	104.144	Lou Moore	117.363
1933	Louie Meyer (6)	Tydol Special	104.162	Bill Cummings	118.530
1934	Bill Cummings (10)	Boyle Products Special	104.863	Kelly Petillo	119.329
1935	Kelly Petillo (22)	Gilmore Speedway Special	106.240	Rex Mays	120.736
1936	Louie Meyer (28)	Ring Free Special	109.069	Rex Mays	119.644
1937	Wilbur Shaw (2)	Shaw-Gilmore Special	113.580	Bill Cummings	123.343
1938	**Floyd Roberts** (1)	Burd Piston Ring Special	117.200	Floyd Roberts	125.681
1939	Wilbur Shaw (3)	Boyle Special	115.035	Jimmy Snyder	130.138
1940	Wilbur Shaw (2)	Boyle Special	114.277	Rex Mays	127.850
1941	Floyd Davis & Mauri Rose (17)	Noc-Out Hose Clamp Special	115.117	Mauri Rose	128.691
1942-45	Not held	World War II			
1946	George Robson (15)	Thorne Engineering Special	114.820	Cliff Bergere	126.471
1947	Mauri Rose (3)	Blue Crown Spark Plug Special	116.338	Ted Horn	126.564
1948	Mauri Rose (3)	Blue Crown Spark Plug Special	119.814	Duke Nalon	131.603
1949	Bill Holland (4)	Blue Crown Spark Plug Special	121.327	Duke Nalon	132.939
1950-c	Johnnie Parsons (5)	Wynn's Friction Proofing	124.002	Walt Faulkner	134.343
1951	Lee Wallard (2)	Belanger Special	126.244	Duke Nalon	136.498
1952	Troy Ruttman (7)	Agajanian Special	128.922	Fred Agabashian	138.010
1953	**Bill Vukovich** (1)	Fuel Injection Special	128.740	Bill Vukovich	138.392
1954	Bill Vukovich (19)	Fuel Injection Special	130.840	Jack McGrath	141.033
1955	Bob Sweikert (14)	John Zink Special	128.213	Jerry Hoyt	140.045
1956	**Pat Flaherty** (1)	John Zink Special	128.490	Pat Flaherty	145.596
1957	Sam Hanks (13)	Belond Exhaust Special	135.601	Pat O'Connor	143.948
1958	Jimmy Bryan (7)	Belond AP Parts Special	133.791	Dick Rathmann	145.974
1959	Rodger Ward (6)	Leader Card 500 Roadster	135.857	Johnny Thomson	145.908
1960	Jim Rathmann (2)	Ken-Paul Special	138.767	Eddie Sachs	146.592

Year	Winner (Pos.)	Car	MPH	Pole Sitter	MPH
1961	A.J. Foyt (7)	Bowes Seal Fast Special	139.130	Eddie Sachs	147.481
1962	Rodger Ward (2)	Leader Card 500 Roadster	140.293	Parnelli Jones	150.370
1963	**Parnelli Jones** (1)	Agajanian-Willard Special	143.137	Parnelli Jones	151.153
1964	A.J. Foyt (5)	Sheraton-Thompson Special	147.350	Jim Clark	158.828
1965	Jim Clark (2)	Lotus Ford	150.686	A.J. Foyt	161.233
1966	Graham Hill (15)	American Red Ball Special	144.317	Mario Andretti	165.899
1967-**d**	A.J. Foyt (4)	Sheraton-Thompson Special	151.207	Mario Andretti	168.982
1968	Bobby Unser (3)	Rislone Special	152.882	Joe Leonard	171.559
1969	Mario Andretti (2)	STP Oil Treatment Special	156.867	A.J. Foyt	170.568
1970	**Al Unser** (1)	Johnny Lightning Special	155.749	Al Unser	170.221
1971	Al Unser (5)	Johnny Lightning Special	157.735	Peter Revson	178.696
1972	Mark Donohue (3)	Sunoco McLaren	162.962	Bobby Unser	195.940
1973-**e**	Gordon Johncock (11)	STP Double Oil Filters	159.036	Johnny Rutherford	198.413
1974	Johnny Rutherford (25)	McLaren	158.589	A.J. Foyt	191.632
1975-**f**	Bobby Unser (3)	Jorgensen Eagle	149.213	A.J. Foyt	193.976
1976-**g**	**Johnny Rutherford** (1)	Hy-Gain McLaren/Goodyear	148.725	Johnny Rutherford	188.957
1977	A.J. Foyt (4)	Gilmore Racing Team	161.331	Tom Sneva	198.884
1978	Al Unser (5)	FNCTC Chaparral Lola	161.363	Tom Sneva	202.156
1979	**Rick Mears** (1)	The Gould Charge	158.899	Rick Mears	193.736
1980	**Johnny Rutherford** (1)	Pennzoil Chaparral	142.862	Johnny Rutherford	192.256
1981-**h**	**Bobby Unser** (1)	Norton Spirit Penske PC-9B	139.084	Bobby Unser	200.546
1982	Gordon Johncock (5)	STP Oil Treatment	162.029	Rick Mears	207.004
1983	Tom Sneva (4)	Texaco Star	162.117	Teo Fabi	207.395
1984	Rick Mears (3)	Pennzoil Z-7	163.612	Tom Sneva	210.029
1985	Danny Sullivan (8)	Miller American Special	152.982	Pancho Carter	212.583
1986	Bobby Rahal (4)	Budweiser/Truesports/March	170.722	Rick Mears	216.828
1987	Al Unser (20)	Cummins Holset Turbo	162.175	Mario Andretti	215.390
1988	**Rick Mears** (1)	Pennzoil Z-7/Penske Chevy V-8	144.809	Rick Mears	219.198
1989	Emerson Fittipaldi (3)	Marlboro/Penske Chevy V-8	167.581	Rick Mears	223.885
1990	Arie Luyendyk (3)	Domino's Pizza Chevrolet	185.981*	Emerson Fittipaldi	225.301
1991	**Rick Mears** (1)	Marlboro Penske Chevy	176.457	Rick Mears	224.113
1992	Al Unser Jr. (12)	Valvoline Galmer '92	134.477	Roberto Guerrero	232.482
1993	Emerson Fittipaldi (9)	Marlboro Penske Chevy	157.207	Arie Luyendyk	223.967
1994	**Al Unser Jr.** (1)	Marlboro Penske Mercedes	160.872	Al Unser Jr.	228.011
1995	Jacques Villeneuve (5)	Player's Ltd. Reynard Ford	153.616	Scott Brayton	231.604
1996	Buddy Lazier (5)	Reynard Ford	147.956	Tony Stewart	233.100&
1997	**Arie Luyendyk** (1)	G-Force Olds Aurora	145.827	Arie Luyendyk	218.263
1998	Eddie Cheever Jr. (17)	Dallara Olds Aurora	145.155	Billy Boat	223.503
1999	Kenny Brack (8)	Dallara Olds Aurora	153.176	Arie Luyendyk	225.179

*Track record for winning time.
& Scott Brayton won the pole position with an avg. mph of 233.718 but was killed in a practice run. Stewart was given pole position with the next fastest speed.
Notes: a—1916 race scheduled for 300 miles; **b**—rain shortened 1926 race to 400 miles; **c**—rain shortened 1950 race to 345 miles; **d**—1967 race postponed due to rain after 18 laps (May 30), resumed next day (May 31); **e**—rain shortened 1973 race to 332.5 miles; **f**—rain shortened 1975 race to 435 miles; **g**—rain shortened 1976 race to 255 miles; **h**—in 1981, runner-up Mario Andretti was awarded 1st place when winner Bobby Unser was penalized a lap after the race was completed for passing cars illegally under the caution flag. Unser and car-owner Roger Penske appealed the race stewards' decision to the U.S. Auto Club. Four months later, USAC overturned the ruling, saying that the penalty was too harsh and Unser should be fined $40,000 rather than stripped of his championship.

Indy 500 Rookie of the Year

Voted on by a panel of auto racing media. Award does not necessarily go to highest-finishing first-year driver. Graham Hill won the race on his first try in 1966, but the rookie award went to Jackie Stewart, who led with 10 laps to go only to lose oil pressure and finish 6th.

Father and son winners: Mario and Michael Andretti (1965 and 1984); Bill and Billy Vukovich III (1968 and 1988).

Year		Year		Year		Year	
1952	Art Cross	1965	Mario Andretti	1978	Rick Mears	1989	Bernard Jourdain
1953	Jimmy Daywalt	1966	Jackie Stewart		& Larry Rice		& Scott Pruett
1954	Larry Crockett	1967	Denis Hulme	1979	Howdy Holmes	1990	Eddie Cheever
1955	Al Herman	1968	Bill Vukovich	1980	Tim Richmond	1991	Jeff Andretti
1956	Bob Veith	1969	Mark Donohue	1981	Josele Garza	1992	Lyn St. James
1957	Don Edmunds	1970	Donnie Allison	1982	Jim Hickman	1993	Nigel Mansell
1958	George Amick	1971	Denny Zimmerman	1983	Teo Fabi	1994	Jacques Villeneuve
1959	Bobby Grim	1972	Mike Hiss	1984	Michael Andretti	1995	Christian Fittipaldi
1960	Jim Hurtubise	1973	Graham McRae		& Roberto Guerrero	1996	Tony Stewart
1961	Parnelli Jones	1974	Pancho Carter	1985	Arie Luyendyk	1997	Jeff Ward
	& Bobby Marshman	1975	Bill Puterbaugh	1986	Randy Lanier	1998	Steve Knapp
1962	Jimmy McElreath	1976	Vern Schuppan	1987	Fabrizio Barbazza	1999	Robby McGehee
1963	Jim Clark	1977	Jerry Sneva	1988	Billy Vukovich III		
1964	Johnny White						

IRL Champions

Year		Year		Year		Year	
1996	Buzz Calkins & Scott Sharp	1997	Tony Stewart	1998	Kenny Brack	1999	Greg Ray

IRL Rookie of the Year

Officially the Sprint PCS Rookie of the Year. Award presented to rookie driver who accumulates the most points in the IRL standings.

Year		Year		Year		Year	
1996	None	1997	Jim Guthrie	1998	Robby Unser	1999	Scott Harrington

Formula One Circuit
United States Grand Prix

There have been 54 official Formula One races held in the United States since 1950, including the Indianapolis 500 from 1950-60. FISA sanctioned two annual U.S. Grand Prix–USA/East and USA/West–from 1976-80 and 1983. Phoenix was the site of the U.S. Grand Prix from 1989-91.

Indianapolis 500
Officially sanctioned as Grand Prix race from 1950-60 only. See IRL Circuit for details.

U.S. Grand Prix–East

Held from 1959-80 and 1981-88 at the following locations: Sebring, Fla. (1959); Riverside, Calif. (1960); Watkins Glen, N.Y. (1961-80); and Detroit (1982-88). There was no race in 1981. Race discontinued in 1989.

Multiple winners: Jim Clark, Graham Hill and Ayrton Senna (3); James Hunt, Carlos Reutemann and Jackie Stewart (2).

Year		Car	Year		Car
1959	Bruce McLaren, NZE	Cooper Climax	1974	Carlos Reutemann, ARG	Brabham Ford
1960	Stirling Moss, GBR	Lotus Climax	1975	Niki Lauda, AUT	Ferrari
1961	Innes Ireland, GBR	Lotus Climax	1976	James Hunt, GBR	McLaren Ford
1962	Jim Clark, GBR	Lotus Climax	1977	James Hunt, GBR	McLaren Ford
1963	Graham Hill, GBR	BRM	1978	Carlos Reutemann, ARG	Ferrari
1964	Graham Hill, GBR	BRM	1979	Gilles Villeneuve, CAN	Ferrari
1965	Graham Hill, GBR	BRM	1980	Alan Jones, AUS	Williams Ford
1966	Jim Clark, GBR	Lotus BRM	1981	Not held	
1967	Jim Clark, GBR	Lotus Ford	1982	John Watson, GBR	McLaren Ford
1968	Jackie Stewart, GBR	Matra Ford	1983	Michele Alboreto, ITA	Tyrrell Ford
1969	Jochen Rindt, AUT	Lotus Ford	1984	Nelson Piquet, BRA	Brabham BMW Turbo
1970	Emerson Fittipaldi, BRA	Lotus Ford	1985	Keke Rosberg, FIN	Williams Honda Turbo
1971	Francois Cevert, FRA	Tyrrell Ford	1986	Ayrton Senna, BRA	Lotus Renault Turbo
1972	Jackie Stewart, GBR	Tyrrell Ford	1987	Ayrton Senna, BRA	Lotus Honda Turbo
1973	Ronnie Peterson, SWE	Lotus Ford	1988	Ayrton Senna, BRA	McLaren Honda Turbo

U.S. Grand Prix–West

Held from 1976-83 at Long Beach, Calif. Races also held in Las Vegas (1981-82), Dallas (1984) and Phoenix (1989-91). Race discontinued in 1992.

Multiple winners: Alan Jones and Ayrton Senna (2).

Long Beach

Year		Car
1976	Clay Regazzoni, SWI	Ferrari
1977	Mario Andretti, USA	Lotus Ford
1978	Carlos Reutemann, ARG	Ferrari
1979	Gilles Villeneuve, CAN	Ferrari
1980	Nelson Piquet, BRA	Brabham Ford
1981	Alan Jones, AUS	Williams Ford
1982	Niki Lauda, AUT	McLaren Ford
1983	John Watson, GBR	McLaren Ford

Las Vegas

Year		Car
1981	Alan Jones, AUS	Williams Ford
1982	Michele Alboreto, ITA	Tyrrell Ford

Dallas

Year		Car
1984	Keke Rosberg, FIN	Williams Honda Turbo

Phoenix

Year		Car
1989	Alain Prost, FRA	McLaren Honda
1990	Ayrton Senna, BRA	McLaren Honda
1991	Ayrton Senna, BRA	McLaren Honda

All-Time Leaders

The all-time Top 15 Grand Prix winning drivers, based on records through 1998. Listed are starts (Sts), poles won (Pole), wins (1st), second place finishes (2nd), and third (3rd). Drivers active in 1999 and career victories in **bold** type.

		Sts	Pole	1st	2nd	3rd			Sts	Pole	1st	2nd	3rd
1	Alain Prost	199	33	**51**	35	20	9	Nelson Piquet	204	24	**23**	20	17
2	Ayrton Senna	161	65	**41**	23	16	10	**Damon Hill**	99	20	**22**	15	5
3	**M. Schumacher**	117	20	**33**	19	13	11	Stirling Moss	66	16	**16**	5	3
4	Nigel Mansell	187	32	**31**	17	11	12	Jack Brabham	126	13	**14**	10	7
5	Jackie Stewart	99	17	**27**	11	5		Emerson Fittipaldi	144	6	**14**	13	8
6	Jim Clark	72	33	**25**	1	6		Graham Hill	176	13	**14**	15	7
	Niki Lauda	171	24	**25**	20	9	15	Alberto Ascari	32	14	**13**	4	0
8	Juan-Manuel Fangio	51	28	**24**	1	1							

World Champions

Officially called the World Championship of Drivers and based on Formula One (Grand Prix) records through the 1998 racing season.

Multiple winners: Juan-Manuel Fangio (5); Alain Prost (4); Jack Brabham, Niki Lauda, Nelson Piquet, Ayrton Senna and Jackie Stewart (3); Alberto Ascari, Jim Clark, Emerson Fittipaldi, Graham Hill and Michael Schumacher (2).

Year		Car
1950	Guiseppe Farina, ITA	Alfa Romeo
1951	Juan-Manuel Fangio, ARG	Alfa Romeo
1952	Alberto Ascari, ITA	Ferrari
1953	Alberto Ascari, ITA	Ferrari
1954	Juan-Manuel Fangio, ARG	Maserati/Mercedes
1955	Juan-Manuel Fangio, ARG	Mercedes
1956	Juan-Manuel Fangio, ARG	Ferrari
1957	Juan-Manuel Fangio, ARG	Maserati
1958	Mike Hawthorn, GBR	Ferrari
1959	Jack Brabham, AUS	Cooper Climax
1960	Jack Brabham, AUS	Cooper Climax
1961	Phil Hill, USA	Ferrari
1962	Graham Hill, GBR	BRM
1963	Jim Clark, GBR	Lotus Climax
1964	John Surtees, GBR	Ferrari
1965	Jim Clark, GBR	Lotus Climax
1966	Jack Brabham, AUS	Brabham Repco
1967	Denis Hulme, NZE	Brabham Repco
1968	Graham Hill, GBR	Lotus Ford
1969	Jackie Stewart, GBR	Matra Ford
1970	Jochen Rindt, AUT	Lotus Ford
1971	Jackie Stewart, GBR	Tyrrell Ford
1972	Emerson Fittipaldi, BRA	Lotus Ford
1973	Jackie Stewart, GBR	Tyrrell Ford
1974	Emerson Fittipaldi, BRA	McLaren Ford
1975	Niki Lauda, AUT	Ferrari
1976	James Hunt, GBR	McLaren Ford
1977	Niki Lauda, AUT	Ferrari
1978	Mario Andretti, USA	Lotus Ford
1979	Jody Scheckter, SAF	Ferrari
1980	Alan Jones, AUS	Williams Ford
1981	Nelson Piquet, BRA	Brabham Ford
1982	Keke Rosberg, FIN	Williams Ford
1983	Nelson Piquet, BRA	Brabham BMW Turbo
1984	Niki Lauda, AUT	McL. TAG Porsche Turbo
1985	Alain Prost, FRA	McL. TAG Porsche Turbo
1986	Alain Prost, FRA	McL. TAG Porsche Turbo
1987	Nelson Piquet, BRA	Williams Honda Turbo
1988	Ayrton Senna, BRA	McLaren Honda Turbo
1989	Alain Prost, FRA	McLaren Honda
1990	Ayrton Senna, BRA	McLaren Honda
1991	Ayrton Senna, BRA	McLaren Honda
1992	Nigel Mansell, GBR	Williams-Renault
1993	Alain Prost, FRA	Williams-Renault
1994	Michael Schumacher, GER	Benetton Ford
1995	Michael Schumacher, GER	Benetton Renault
1996	Damon Hill, GBR	Williams-Renault
1997	Jacques Villeneuve, CAN	Williams-Renault
1998	Mika Hakkinen, FIN	McLaren-Mercedes

ENDURANCE RACES

The 24 Hours of Le Mans

Officially, the Le Mans Grand Prix d'Endurance. First run May 22-23, 1923, and won by Andre Lagache and Rene Leonard in a 3-litre Chenard & Walcker. All subsequent races have been held in June, except in 1956 (July) and 1968 (September). Originally contested over a 10.73-mile track, the circuit was shortened to its present 8.451-mile distance in 1932. The original start of Le Mans, where drivers raced across the track to their unstarted cars, was discontinued in 1970.

Multiple winners: Jacky Ickx (6); Derek Bell (5); Yannick Dalmas, Oliver Gendebien and Henri Pescarolo (4); Woolf Barnato, Luigi Chinetti, Hurley Haywood, Phil Hill, Al Holbert and Klaus Ludwig (3); Sir Henry Birkin, Ivoe Bueb, Ron Flockhart, Jean-Pierre Jaussaud, Gerard Larrousse, Andre Rossignol, Raymond Sommer, Hans Stuck, Gijs van Lennep and Jean-Pierre Wimille (2).

Year	Drivers	Car	MPH
1923	Andre Lagache & Rene Leonard	Chenard & Walcker	57.21
1924	John Duff & Francis Clement	Bentley	53.78
1925	Gerard de Courcelles & Andre Rossignol	La Lorraine	57.84
1926	Robert Bloch & Andre Rossignol	La Lorraine	66.08
1927	J.D. Benjafield & Sammy Davis	Bentley	61.35
1928	Woolf Barnato & Bernard Rubin	Bentley	69.11
1929	Woolf Barnato & Sir Henry Birkin	Bentley Speed 6	73.63
1930	Woolf Barnato & Glen Kidston	Bentley Speed 6	75.88
1931	Earl Howe & Sir Henry Birkin	Alfa Romeo	78.13
1932	Raymond Sommer & Luigi Chinetti	Alfa Romeo	76.48
1933	Raymond Sommer & Tazio Nuvolari	Alfa Romeo	81.40
1934	Luigi Chinetti & Philippe Etancelin	Alfa Romeo	74.74
1935	John Hindmarsh & Louis Fontes	Lagonda	77.85

Year	Drivers	Car	MPH
1936	Not held		
1937	Jean-Pierre Wimille & Robert Benoist	Bugatti 57G	85.13
1938	Eugene Chaboud & Jean Tremoulet	Delahaye	82.36
1939	Jean-Pierre Wimille & Pierre Veyron	Bugatti 57G	86.86
1940-48	Not held		
1949	Luigi Chinetti & Lord Selsdon	Ferrari	82.28
1950	Louis Rosier & Jean-Louis Rosier	Talbot-Lago	89.71
1951	Peter Walker & Peter Whitehead	Jaguar C	93.50
1952	Hermann Lang & Fritz Reiss	Mercedes-Benz	96.67
1953	Tony Rolt & Duncan Hamilton	Jaguar C	98.65
1954	Froilan Gonzalez & Maurice Trintignant	Ferrari 375	105.13
1955	Mike Hawthorn & Ivor Bueb	Jaguar D	107.05
1956	Ron Flockhart & Ninian Sanderson	Jaguar D	104.47
1957	Ron Flockhart & Ivor Bueb	Jaguar D	113.83

AP/Wide World Photos

French driver **Maurice Trintignant** rounds the track en route to a sixth-place finish at the 1953 Le Mans Grand Prix d'Endurance. A year later he teamed up with Froilan Gonzalez to win the race in a Ferrari 375.

Year	Drivers	Car	MPH
1958	Oliver Gendebien & Phil Hill	Ferrari 250	106.18
1959	Roy Salvadori & Carroll Shelby	Aston Martin	112.55
1960	Oliver Gendebien & Paul Frère	Ferrari 250	109.17
1961	Oliver Gendebien & Phil Hill	Ferrari 250	115.88
1962	Oliver Gendebien & Phil Hill	Ferrari 250	115.22
1963	Lodovico Scarfiotti & Lorenzo Bandini	Ferrari 250	118.08
1964	Jean Guichel & Nino Vaccarella	Ferrari 275	121.54
1965	Masten Gregory & Jochen Rindt	Ferrari 250	121.07
1966	Bruce McLaren & Chris Amon	Ford Mk. II	125.37
1967	A.J. Foyt & Dan Gurney	Ford Mk. IV	135.46
1968	Pedro Rodriguez & Lucien Bianchi	Ford GT40	115.27
1969	Jacky Ickx & Jackie Oliver	Ford GT40	129.38
1970	Hans Herrmann & Richard Attwood	Porsche 917	119.28
1971	Gijs van Lennep & Helmut Marko	Porsche 917	138.13
1972	Graham Hill & Henri Pescarolo	Matra-Simca	121.45
1973	Henri Pescarolo & Gerard Larrousse	Matra-Simca	125.67
1974	Henri Pescarolo & Gerard Larrousse	Matra-Simca	119.27
1975	Derek Bell & Jacky Ickx	Mirage-Ford	118.98
1976	Jacky Ickx & Gijs van Lennep	Porsche 936	123.49
1977	Jacky Ickx, Jurgen Barth & Hurley Haywood	Porsche 936	120.95
1978	Jean-Pierre Jaussaud & Didier Pironi	Renault-Alpine	130.60
1979	Klaus Ludwig, Bill Wittington & Don Whittington	Porsche 935	108.10
1980	Jean-Pierre Jaussaud & Jean Rondeau	Rondeau-Cosworth	119.23
1981	Jacky Ickx & Derek Bell	Porsche 936	124.94
1982	Jacky Ickx & Derek Bell	Porsche 956	126.85
1983	Vern Schuppan, Hurley Haywood & Al Holbert	Porsche 956	130.70
1984	Klaus Ludwig & Henri Pescarolo	Porsche 956	126.88
1985	Klaus Ludwig, Paolo Barilla & John Winter	Porsche 956	131.75
1986	Derek Bell, Hans Stuck & Al Holbert	Porsche 962	128.75
1987	Derek Bell, Hans Stuck & Al Holbert	Porsche 962	124.06
1988	Jan Lammers, Johnny Dumfries & Andy Wallace	Jaguar XJR	137.75
1989	Jochen Mass, Manuel Reuter & Stanley Dickens	Sauber-Mercedes	136.39
1990	John Nielsen, Price Cobb & Martin Brundle	Jaguar XJR-12	126.71
1991	Volker Weider, Johnny Herbert & Bertrand Gachof	Mazda 787B	127.31
1992	Derek Warwick, Yannick Dalmas & Mark Blundell	Peugeot 905B	123.89
1993	Geoff Brabham, Christophe Bouchut & Eric Helary	Peugeot 905	132.58
1994	Yannick Dalmas, Hurley Haywood & Mauro Baldi	Porsche 962LM	129.82
1995	Yannick Dalmas, J.J. Lehto & Masanori Sekiya	McLaren BMW	105.00
1996	Davy Jones, Manuel Reuter & Alexander Wurz	TWR Porsche	124.65
1997	Michele Alberto, Stefan Johansson & Tom Kristensen	TWR Porsche	126.88
1998	Laurent Aiello, Allan McNish & Stephane Ortelli	Porsche 911 GT1	123.86
1999	Yannick Dalmas, Joachim Winkelhock & Pierluigi Martini	BMW V-12 LMR	129.375

The 24 Hours of Daytona

Officially, the Rolex 24 at Daytona. First run in 1962 as a three-hour race and won by Dan Gurney in a Lotus 19 Ford. Contested over a 3.56-mile course at Daytona (Fla.) International Speedway. There have been several distance changes since 1962: the event was a three-hour race (1962-63); a 2,000-kilometer race (1964-65); a 24-hour race (1966-71); a six-hour race (1972) and a 24-hour race again since 1973. The race was canceled in 1974 due to a national energy crisis.

Multiple winners: Hurley Haywood (5); Peter Gregg, Pedro Rodriguez and Bob Wollek (4); Derek Bell, Butch Leitzinger and Rolf Stommelen (3); A.J. Foyt, Al Holbert, Ken Miles, Brian Redman, Elliott Forbes-Robinson, Lloyd Ruby, Al Unser Jr. and Andy Wallace (2).

Year	Drivers	Car	MPH
1962	Dan Gurney	Lotus 19 Ford	104.101
1963	Pedro Rodriguez	Ferrari GTO	102.074
1964	Pedro Rodriguez & Phil Hill	Ferrari GTO	98.230
1965	Ken Miles & Lloyd Ruby	Ford GT	99.944
1966	Ken Miles & Lloyd Ruby	Ford Mk. II	108.020
1967	Lorenzo Bandini & Chris Amon	Ferrari 330	105.688
1968	Vic Elford & Jochen Neerpasch	Porsche 907	106.697
1969	Mark Donohue & Chuck Parsons	Lola Chevrolet	99.268
1970	Pedro Rodriguez & Leo Kinnunen	Porsche 917	114.866
1971	Pedro Rodriguez & Jackie Oliver	Porsche 917K	109.203
1972	Mario Andretti & Jacky Ickx	Ferrari 312P	122.573
1973	Peter Gregg & Hurley Haywood	Porsche Carrera	106.225
1974	Not held		
1975	Peter Gregg & Hurley Haywood	Porsche Carrera	108.531
1976	Peter Gregg, Brian Redman & John Fitzpatrick	BMW CSL	104.040
1977	Hurley Haywood, John Graves & Dave Helmick	Porsche Carrera	108.801
1978	Peter Gregg, Rolf Stommelen & Antoine Hezemans	Porsche Turbo	108.743
1979	Hurley Haywood, Ted Field & Danny Ongais	Porsche Turbo	109.249
1980	Rolf Stommelen, Volkert Merl & Reinhold Joest	Porsche Turbo	114.303
1981	Bobby Rahal, Brian Redman & Bob Garretson	Porsche Turbo	113.153
1982	John Paul Sr., John Paul Jr. & Rolf Stommelen	Porsche Turbo	114.794
1983	A.J. Foyt, Preston Henn, Bob Wollek & Claude Ballot-Lena	Porsche Turbo	98.781
1984	Sarel van der Merwe, Tony Martin & Graham Duxbury	March Porsche	103.119
1985	A.J. Foyt, Bob Wollek, Al Unser Sr. & Thierry Boutsen	Porsche 962	104.162
1986	Al Holbert, Derek Bell & Al Unser Jr	Porsche 962	105.484
1987	Al Holbert, Derek Bell, Chip Robinson & Al Unser Jr	Porsche 962	111.599
1988	Raul Boesel, Martin Brundle & John Nielsen	Jaguar XJR-9	107.943
1989	John Andretti, Derek Bell & Bob Wollek	Porsche 962	92.009
1990	Davy Jones, Jan Lammers & Andy Wallace	Jaguar XJR-12	112.857
1991	Hurley Haywood, John Winter, Frank Jelinski, Henri Pescarolo & Bob Wollek	Porsche 962-C	106.633
1992	Masahiro Hasemi, Kazuyoshi Hoshino & Toshio Suzuki	Nissan R-91	112.897
1993	P.J. Jones, Mark Dismore & Rocky Moran	Toyota Eagle	103.537
1994	Paul Gentilozzi, Scott Pruett, Butch Leitzinger & Steve Millen	Nissan 300 ZXT	104.80
1995	Jurgen Lassig, Christophe Bouchut, Giovanni Lavaggi & Marco Werner	Porsche Spyder	102.280
1996	Wayne Taylor, Scott Sharp & Jim Pace	Oldsmobile Arness MK-III	103.32
1997	Rob Dyson, James Weaver, Butch Leitzinger, Andy Wallace, John Paul Jr. Eliot Forbes-Robinson & John Schneider	Ford R&S MK-III	102.29
1998	Mauro Baldi, Arie Luyendyk, Gianpiero Moretti & Didier Theys	Ferrari 333 SP	105.40
1999	Elliott Forbes-Robinson Butch Leitzinger & Andy Wallace	Riley & Scott Ford	104.957

NHRA Drag Racing
NHRA Winston Champions

Based on points earned during the NHRA Winston Drag Racing series. The series began for Top Fuel, Funny Car and Pro Stock in 1975.

Top Fuel

Multiple winners: Joe Amato (5); Don Garlits and Shirley Muldowney (3); Scott Kalitta and Gary Scelzi (2).

Year		Year		Year		Year	
1975	Don Garlits	1981	Jeb Allen	1987	Dick LaHaie	1993	Eddie Hill
1976	Richard Tharp	1982	Shirley Muldowney	1988	Joe Amato	1994	Scott Kalitta
1977	Shirley Muldowney	1983	Gary Beck	1989	Gary Ormsby	1995	Scott Kalitta
1978	Kelly Brown	1984	Joe Amato	1990	Joe Amato	1996	Kenny Bernstein
1979	Rob Bruins	1985	Don Garlits	1991	Joe Amato	1997	Gary Scelzi
1980	Shirley Muldowney	1986	Don Garlits	1992	Joe Amato	1998	Gary Scelzi

Funny Car

Multiple winners: John Force (8); Don Prudhomme, Kenny Bernstein (4); Raymond Beadle (3); Frank Hawley (2).

Year		Year		Year		Year	
1975	Don Prudhomme	1981	Raymond Beadle	1987	Kenny Bernstein	1993	John Force
1976	Don Prudhomme	1982	Frank Hawley	1988	Kenny Bernstein	1994	John Force
1977	Don Prudhomme	1983	Frank Hawley	1989	Bruce Larson	1995	John Force
1978	Don Prudhomme	1984	Mark Oswald	1990	John Force	1996	John Force
1979	Raymond Beadle	1985	Kenny Bernstein	1991	John Force	1997	John Force
1980	Raymond Beadle	1986	Kenny Bernstein	1992	Cruz Pedregon	1998	John Force

Pro Stock

Multiple winners: Bob Glidden (9); Lee Shepherd and Warren Johnson (4); Darrell Alderman and Jim Yates (2).

Year		Year		Year		Year	
1975	Bob Glidden	1981	Lee Shepherd	1987	Bob Glidden	1993	Warren Johnson
1976	Larry Lombardo	1982	Lee Shepherd	1988	Bob Glidden	1994	Darrell Alderman
1977	Don Nicholson	1983	Lee Shepherd	1989	Bob Glidden	1995	Warren Johnson
1978	Bob Glidden	1984	Lee Shepherd	1990	John Myers	1996	Jim Yates
1979	Bob Glidden	1985	Bob Glidden	1991	Darrell Alderman	1997	Jim Yates
1980	Bob Glidden	1986	Bob Glidden	1992	Warren Johnson	1998	Warren Johnson

All-Time Leaders
Career Victories

All-time leaders through 1998. Drivers active in 1999 are in **bold**.

Top Fuel		**Funny Car**		**Pro Stock**	
1	**Joe Amato** 45	1	**John Force** 70	1	Bob Glidden 85
2	Don Garlits............35	2	Don Prudhomme 35	2	**Warren Johnson** 72
3	**Cory McClenathan** ...22	3	**Kenny Bernstein** 30	3	**Darrell Alderman** 27
4	**Kenny Bernstein** 21	4	**Cruz Pedregon** 21	4	Lee Shepherd..........26
5	Gary Beck 19	5	Ed McCulloch 18	5	**Jim Yates**...............20
			Mark Oswald 18		

National-Event Victories (pro categories)

1	Bob Glidden 85	8	Don Garlits...............35	15	**Cruz Pedregon** 21
2	**Warren Johnson** 72	9	John Myers................33	16	**Matt Hines** 20
3	**John Force** 70	10	**Darrell Alderman**........27		Mark Oswald..............20
4	**Kenny Bernstein** 52	11	Lee Shepherd..............26		**Jim Yates**.................20
5	Don Prudhomme 49	12	Terry Vance................24	18	Gary Beck 19
6	**Joe Amato** 45	13	**Cory McClenathan**........22	20	Shirley Muldowney 18
7	**Dave Schultz** 42		Ed McCulloch...............22		Darrell Gwynn 18

Fastest Mile-Per-Hour Speeds

Fastest performances in NHRA major event history through 1998.

Top Fuel	**Funny Car**	**Pro Stock**
MPH	**MPH**	**MPH**
326.44.......Gary Scelzi, 11/1/98	323.89.......John Force, 5/17/98	201.34 .Warren Johnson, 10/24/98
324.32.......Gary Scelzi, 11/1/98	323.35.......John Force, 5/15/98	201.20...Warren Johnson, 3/14/98
323.85 .....Gary Scelzi, 11/13/98	322.81 ......John Force, 10/25/98	201.20 .Warren Johnson, 10/23/98
323.50.......Joe Amato, 5/17/98	321.35.......John Force, 5/17/98	201.11...Warren Johnson, 3/13/98
322.92 .Cory McClenathan, 2/22/98	321.27........John Force, 5/17/98	201.11...Warren Johnson, 3/22/98

Boxing

Lennox Lewis knows who deserved to win after his controversial 12-round world heavyweight championship bout at Madison Square Garden. Despite Lewis's confidence, the fight was ruled a draw. ——————

AP/Wide World Photos

Fuggeda-bout-it!

In a year marked by rising stars, boxing's brightest stars failed to create many decisive moments.

by
Al Bernstein

As boxing headed toward a new century it had an interesting, if not scintillating, transitional year that saw the emergence of several new stars, while several of the current ones still held onto the spotlight.

A quintet of young champions stayed undefeated in 1999 and gave evidence that the year 2000 might belong to them. Four of them are close enough in weight to possibly meet in the ring, while the other is smaller, but has his sights set on a Prince.

IBF Lightweight champ Shane Mosley saw the millions being made by Oscar De La Hoya, Felix Trinidad and Ike Quartey and decided he might like that too. So, after defending his 135-pound title twice, he jumped all the way up to 147 pounds, beat veteran welterweight Wilfredo Rivera and served notice he is after the big boys.

Al Bernstein has been ESPN's boxing analyst since 1980.

IBF Junior Middleweight titleholder Fernando Vargas defended his title twice and looked brilliant. In between winning fights and calling De La Hoya out for a match, he also ran afoul of the law when he was charged with assault. His legal problems aside, he looks to be racing straight toward a mega fight in the year 2000.

One of the men who could be Vargas' opponent in that big fight is fellow 1996 Olympian David Reid. He won the WBA version of the title at 154 pounds and has defended it twice, once against former champ Keith Mullings. He and Vargas may very well meet in what stands to be a terrific title unification match this coming year.

Floyd Mayweather Jr., yet another 1996 Olympian, defended his WBC super featherweight title three times, the last time with an absolutely brilliant performance against Carlos Gerena. He is poised to move up in weight next year, and eventually may

AP/Wide World Photos

Felix Trinidad scores a direct hit on **Oscar De La Hoya** in their Sept. 18 WBC/IBF Welterweight Championship bout. The judges thought that Trinidad scored enough to give him a majority decision.

even get to welterweight, where a fight with Mosley would be one of boxing's best.

Mexican hero Erik Morales easily defended his WBC super bantamweight title three times and looked devastating doing it each time. This 22-year old has power and boxing skills and as he headed into a late 1999 bout with ex-champ Wayne McCullough, he appeared set for a 2000 challenge to featherweight and box office champion Prince Naseem Hamed of Great Britain.

While these young men lived up to their billing, two mega fights did not. The March heavyweight title unification match between Lennox Lewis and Evander Holyfield was dominated by Lewis in a one sided and noncompetitive bout. Holyfield predicted a third round knockout win, and that was the only round in which he was

aggressive. Somehow the judges scored it a draw in one of the worst decisions in recent years.

"I'm really kind of ashamed something like that could happen in this country. It's embarrasing," said former heavyweight champ George Foreman, who doesn't shame or embarrass easily. "Lennox Lewis won the fight hands down."

Several investigations later, a rematch was set for Nov. 13, 1999 in Las Vegas.

While De La Hoya did participate in an excellent welterweight match with Quartey in February and had an exciting defense against a good challenger in Oba Carr, it will be his anxiously anticipated fight with Trinidad that defines his 1999 campaign. The Golden Boy lost a disputed majority decision to the IBF champ, when Trinidad made a big comeback in the last

AP/Wide World Photos

IBF judge **Eugenia Williams**, lower left, has a great view of the action during the Evander Holyfield/ Lennox Lewis bout at Madison Square Garden. Williams was the judge at the center of the considerable dispute surrounding the outcome of the world championship bout between Holyfield and Lewis. The fight, dominated by Lewis, was scored a draw after one judge scored it for Lewis, one scored it even and then Williams scored it 115-113 in favor of Holyfield.

three rounds to take the fight. Many thought De La Hoya had won the bout with his effective boxing from rounds three through nine, but Trinidad went back to his native Puerto Rico a winner, adding the WBC belt to his growing collection.

If the fight wasn't as thrilling in the ring as expected, Trinidad-De La Hoya was a winner financially. It broke the non-heavyweight record for pay-per-view sales with 1.25 million homes producing $64 million in revenue. Talk of a rematch was immediate.

Another current superstar, Roy Jones Jr., rolled along while waiting for an opponent, any opponent, to challenge him and help him produce a big revenue fight. He unified the light heavyweight title for the first time in years when he beat IBF champ Reggie Johnson on June 5 and he looked to be heading toward a late year confrontation with Germany's Graciano Rocchigiani. ∎

Al Bernstein's Ten Biggest Happenings of the Year

10. **Michael Carbajal's comeback.** After a two-year layoff former U.S. Olympian Michael Carbajal challenged Jorge Arce for the WBO junior flyweight title in Arce's home turf of Mexico, and came away with a stirring win. Carbajal won round one, lost the next nine and then in the 11th knocked Arce out to win the title.

AP/Wide World Photos

Paulie Ayala gives **Johnny Tapia** an up close look at his fist in their WBA bantamweight championship fight on June 26 in Las Vegas. Tapia lost a unanimous decision and his title belt in what was the fight of the year.

9. **Erik Morales emerges as a star.** With three defenses of his WBC super bantamweight title Erik Morales stamped himself as a budding superstar and the man most likely to silence the talkative Prince Naseem Hamed.

8. **David Reid wins world title.** In only his 11th professional fight, Olympic gold medalist David Reid won the WBA junior middleweight title. He became the third 1996 U.S. Olympian to win a major world title.

7. **Tyson beats Botha, goes to jail.** Mike Tyson's roller coaster year included a come from behind knockout win over Frans Botha, a return to jail for three months due to an altercation after a traffic ac-

cident, and then a fight later in the year with Orlin Norris.

6. **Mosley goes undefeated— becomes a welterweight.** After defending his lightweight title twice, Shane Mosley stepped up to welterweight to beat Wilfredo Rivera and challenge in boxing's most competitive division.

5. **De La Hoya beats Quartey.** In the first of two big welterweight bouts in 1999, Oscar De La Hoya edged Ike Quartey, winning a split decision by coming back with a furious rally in the last round.

4. **Jones unifies light heavyweight title.** By beating Reggie Johnson, Roy Jones Jr. did something very rare in boxing. He won three major titles in his weight division.

3. **Tapia/Ayala-Fight of the Year.** In a unanimous, but disputed, decision, Paulie Ayala upset Johnny Tapia to win the WBA bantamweight title. It was a thrilling and brilliantly fought match, that was unquestionably the best bout of 1999.

2. **Trinidad beats De La Hoya.** In a bout that didn't quite live up to expectations in the ring, Felix Trinidad used a late-fight rally to win a close and disputed majority decision over fellow welterweight champion Oscar De La Hoya. It was a huge financial success, breaking all non-heavyweight pay per view sales records.

1. **Lewis/Holyfield I is a draw.** In one of the most controversial decisions in boxing history, Evander Holyfield and Lennox Lewis fought to a draw in their mega fight at Madison Square Garden. Virtually every ringside observer had Lewis winning the bout. The hue and cry over this created a rematch that was set for Nov. 13, 1999. ∎

ONE-SIDED DRAW

The Evander Holyfield/Lennox Lewis heavyweight championship bout on Mar. 13 in New York was inexplicably ruled a draw. Ringside judge Stanley Christoudoulou of South Africa scored the fight 116-113 in favor of Lewis. Larry O'Connell of Great Britain had it 115-115 and Atlantic City's Eugenia Williams scored it 115-113 for Holyfield. What did Williams, and for that matter O'Connell, see that the rest of us didn't? Who knows, but here is a look at the punch statistics compiled by CompuBox Inc. to puzzle you further.

	Holyfield	Lewis
Total punches thrown	385	613
Total punches connected	130	348
Connect percentage	34	57
Jabs thrown	171	364
Jabs connected	52	187
Connect percentage	30	51
Power punches thrown	214	249
Power punches connected	78	161
Connect percentage	36	65
Knockdowns	0	0

TAPE MEASURING

Are today's heavyweights that much bigger and stronger than those of yesteryear? Well, yes they are. But a look at the tales of the tape for boxing's first heavyweight champ John L. Sullivan and today's top heavyweight Lennox Lewis may surprise you a little.

	Sullivan	Lewis
Height	5-10½	6-5
Weight	196	240
Reach	74	84
Chest/Norm	43	44
Chest/Expanded	48	46
Biceps	16¼	17
Neck	18	18
Fist	14	12

∎

THE **NUMBERS**

INSIDE

BOXING STATISTICS

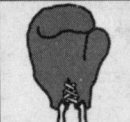

THE 2000 INFORMATION PLEASE SPORTS ALMANAC

SEC **A**

THE SEASON IN REVIEW

1998-1999

CHAMPIONS • TITLE BOUTS

PAGE 909

Current Champions
WBA, WBC and IBF Titleholders (through Oct. 18, 1999)

The champions of professional boxing's 17 principal weight divisions, as recognized by the Word Boxing Association (WBA), World Boxing Council (WBC) and International Boxing Federation (IBF).

	Weight Limit	WBA Champion	WBC Champion	IBF Champion
Heavyweight	—	Evander Holyfield 36-3-1, 25 KOs	Lennox Lewis 34-1-1, 27 KOs	Evander Holyfield 36-3-1, 25 KOs
Cruiserweight	190 lbs	Fabrice Tiozzo 40-1-0, 26 KOs	Juan Carlos Gomez 28-0-0, 23 KOs	Vassily Jirov 22-0-0, 20 KOs
Light Heavyweight	175 lbs	Roy Jones Jr.* 40-1-0, 33 KOs	Roy Jones Jr.* 40-1-0, 33 KOs	Roy Jones Jr. 40-1-0, 33 KOs
Super Middleweight	168 lbs	Byron Mitchell 20-0-0, 16 KOs	Richie Woodhall 25-1-0, 16 KOs	Sven Ottke 15-0-0, 2 KOs
Middleweight	160 lbs	William Joppy 28-1-1, 22 KOs	Keith Holmes 35-2-0, 23 KOs	Bernard Hopkins 35-2-1, 27 KOs
Jr. Middleweight	154 lbs	David Reid 14-0-0, 7 KOs	Javier Castillejo 45-4-0, 11 KOs	Fernando Vargas 17-0-0, 17 KOs
Welterweight	147 lbs	James Page 25-3-0, 19 KOs	Felix Trinidad 36-0-0, 30 KOs	Felix Trinidad 36-0-0, 30 KOs
Jr. Welterweight	140 lbs	Sharmba Mitchell 45-2-0, 29 KOs	Kostya Tszyu 22-1-1, 15 KOs	Terronn Millett* 22-1-1, 17 KOs
Lightweight	135 lbs	Stefano Zoff 28-6-2, 11 KOs	Stevie Johnson 28-1-0, 14 KOs	Paul Spadafora 27-0-0, 13 KOs
Jr. Lightweight	130 lbs	Lavka Sim* 10-1-0, 8 KOs	Floyd Mayweather 22-0-0, 17 KOs	Roberto Garcia 32-0-0, 24 KOs
Featherweight	126 lbs	Freddie Norwood 34-0-1, 20 KOs	Cesar Soto 53-7-0, 39 KOs	Manuel Medina 56-10-1, 25 KOs
Jr. Featherweight	122 lbs	Nestor Garza* 37-1-0, 29 KOs	Erik Morales 34-0-1, 28 KOs	Lehlohonolo Ledwaba 29-1-1, 19 KOs
Bantamweight	118 lbs	Paulie Ayala 28-1-0, 12 KOs	Veerapol Sahaprom 22-1-0, 16 KOs	Tim Austin 19-0-1, 18 KOs
Jr. Bantamweight	115 lbs	Hideki Todaka 15-2-1, 8 KOs	In-Joo Cho 16-0-0, 7 KOs	Mark Johnson 38-1-0, 26 KOs
Flyweight	112 lbs	Sornpichai Kratindaenggym 17-0-0, 14 KOs	Manny Pacquiao 26-1-0, 18 KOs	Irene Pacheco 24-0-0, 19 KOs
Jr. Flyweight	108 lbs	Phichitnoi C. Siriwat 21-1-0, 12 KOs	Choi Yo-sam 21-1-0, 10 KOs	Ricardo Lopez 48-0-1, 35 KOs
Minimumweight	105 lbs	Ricardo Lopez 48-0-1, 35 KOs	Ricardo Lopez 48-0-1, 35 KOs	Zolani Petelo 14-2-2, 8 KOs

Note: The following weight divisions are also known by these names—**Cruiserweight** as Jr. Heavyweight; **Jr. Middleweight** as Super Welterweight; **Jr. Welterweight** as Super Lightweight; **Jr. Lightweight** as Super Featherweight; **Jr. Featherweight** as Super Bantamweight; **Jr. Bantamweight** as Super Flyweight; **Jr. Flyweight** as Light Flyweight; and **Minimum** as Strawweight.

*Richard Hall (24-1-0, 23 KOs) is currently the interim WBA light heavyweight champion. Graciano Rocchigiani (40-4-1, 19 KOs) is currently the interim WBC light heavyweight champion. Zab Judah (21-0-0, 1 NC, 16 KOs) is currently the interim IBF junior welterweight champion. Joel Cassamayor (20-0-0, 12 KOs) currently is the WBA junior lightweight champion. Antonio Ceremeno (36-3, 23 KOs) is currently the interim WBA junior featherweight champion.

Major Bouts, 1998-99
Division by division, from Oct. 13, 1998 through Oct. 16, 1999.

WBA, WBC and IBF champions are listed in **bold** type. Note the following Result columm abbreviations (in alphabetical order): **Disq.** (won by disqualification); **KO** (knockout); **MDraw** (majority draw); **NC** (no contest); **SDraw** (split draw); **TDraw** (technical draw); **TKO** (technical knockout); **TWs** (won by technical split decision); **TWu** (won by technical unanimous decision); **Wm** (won by majority decision); **Ws** (won by split decision) and **Wu** (won by unanimous decision).

Heavyweights

Date	Winner	Loser	Result	Title	Site
Oct. 24	Vitali Klitschko	Mario Schiesser	KO 2	EBU	Hamburg, GER
Nov. 6	Brian Nielsen	Lionel Butler	KO 1	—	Copenhagen, DEN
Nov. 9	Jorge Luis Gonzalez	Josh Dempsey	KO 10	—	Bismarck, N.D.
Dec. 5	Vitali Klitschko	Francesco Spinelli	KO 1	EBU	Kiev, UKR
Dec. 8	Kirk Johnson	Al Cole	MDraw 10	—	New York City
Dec. 8	Jesse Ferguson	Obed Sullivan	Ws 10	—	New York City
Dec. 8	Shannon Briggs	Marcus Rhode	TKO 1	—	New York City
Dec. 19	David Tua	Hasim Rahman	TKO 10	USBA	Miami
Jan. 16	Mike Tyson	Frans Botha	KO 5	—	Las Vegas
Jan. 21	Razor Ruddock	Tony La Rosa	TKO 3	—	Marksville, La.
Jan. 30	Andrew Golota	Jesse Ferguson	Wu 10	—	Atlantic City
Jan. 30	Michael Grant	Ahmad Abdin	TKO 10	NABF	Atlantic City
Feb. 12	Brian Nielsen	Peter McNeeley	TKO 3	—	Copenhagen, DEN
Mar. 6	Henry Akinwande	Reynaldo Minus	TKO 2	—	Minneapolis, Minn.
Mar. 6	Lou Savarese	Lance Whitaker	Ws 10	—	Atlantic City
Mar. 7	James Toney	Terry Porter	TKO 8	—	Phoenix, Ariz.
Mar. 12	Hasim Rahman	Mike Rush	TKO 5	—	New York City
Mar. 13	**Lennox Lewis**	**Evander Holyfield**	Draw 12	**WBA/ WBC/IBF**	New York City
Mar. 13	John Ruiz	Mario Cawley	KO 4	—	New York City
Mar. 20	Ike Ibeabuchi	Chris Byrd	KO 5	—	Tacoma, Wash.
Mar. 20	Kirk Johnson	Al Cole	Wu 10	—	Washington, D.C.
Apr. 15	Hasim Rahman	David Weathers	KO 1	—	Miami
Apr. 16	Brian Nielsen	Tim Witherspoon	TKO 4	—	Copenhagen, DEN
May 8	Chris Byrd	John Sargent	TKO 2	—	Philadelphia
May 15	Henry Akinwande	Najee Shaheed	KO 9	—	Miami
June 3	Chris Byrd	Jose Ribalta	TKO 3	—	Mt. Pleasant, Mich.
June 5	Jorge Luis Gonzalez	Alex Stewart	TKO 3	—	Las Vegas
June 12	John Ruiz	Fernely Feliz	TKO 7	—	Worcester, Mass.
June 18	Larry Holmes	James Smith	TKO 8	—	Fayetteville, N.C.
June 18	Greg Page	Tim Witherspoon	TKO 7	—	Fayetteville, N.C.
June 19	Michael Grant	Lou Savarese	Wu 10	—	New York City
June 26	Vitali Klitschko	Herbie Hide	KO 2	WBO	London, ENG
June 26	Andrew Golota	Quinn Navarre	KO 6	—	Wroclaw, POL
July 17	David Tua	Gary Bell	TKO 1	USBA	Stateline, Nev.
July 17	Vitali Klitschko	Joseph Chinangu	TKO 5	WBO	Dusseldorf, GER
July 25	Jorge Luis Gonzalez	Tommy Martin	Ko 9	—	Kansas City, Mo.
Aug. 7	Frans Botha	Shannon Briggs	MDraw	—	Atlantic City
Sept. 25	Vladimir Klitschko	Axel Schulz	TKO 8	—	Cologne, GER
Oct. 9	Vitali Klitschko	Ed Mahone	KO 3	WBO	Oberhausen, GER

Cruiserweights (190 lbs)
(Jr. Heavyweights)

Date	Winner	Loser	Result	Title	Site
Oct. 30	Arthur Williams	**Imamu Mayfield**	KO 9	IBF	Biloxi, Miss.
Nov. 6	Thomas Hearns	Jay Snyder	TKO 1	—	Detroit, Mich.
Nov. 7	Virgil Hill	Jim Haynes	KO 1	—	Bismark, N.D.
Nov. 14	**Fabrice Tiozzo**	Ezequiel Paixao	KO 2	WBA	Paris
Dec. 5	Vassily Jirov	Alexander Vasilev	Wu 8	—	Kiev, UKR
Dec. 12	**Juan Carlos Gomez**	Rodney Gordon	TKO 2	WBC	Frankfurt, GER
Mar. 7	James Toney	Terry Porter	TKO 8	—	Phoenix, Ariz.
Mar. 13	**Juan Carlos Gomez**	Marcelo Dominguez	Wu 12	WBC	Lubeck, GER
Mar. 27	Johnny Nelson	Carl Thompson	TKO 5	WBO	Derby, ENG
Apr. 10	Thomas Hearns	Nate Miller	Wu 12	—	Manchester, ENG
Apr. 22	Vassily Jirov	Onebo Maxime	KO 5	—	Dallas, Tex.
May 9	Virgil Hill	Glen Thomas	Wu 12	—	Minot, N.D.
May 15	Johnny Nelson	Bruce Scott	Wu 12	WBO	Sheffield, ENG
May 28	Dale Brown	Sajad Abdukkah Aziz	Wu 12	—	Montreal, CAN
June 5	Vassily Jirov	**Arthur Williams**	TKO 7	IBF	Biloxi, Miss.
July 4	Robert Daniels	Derek Ames	KO 10	—	Ft. Lauderdale
July 4	Napoleon Tagoe	Ramon Garbey	Wm 10	—	Ft. Lauderdale
July 17	**Juan Carlos Gomez**	Bruce Scott	TKO 6	WBC	Dusseldorf, GER
July 30	James Toney	Adolpho Washington	TKO 10	—	Ledyard, Conn.

Date	Winner	Loser	Result	Title	Site
Aug. 7	Johnny Nelson	Willard Lewis	KO 5	WBO	Dagenham, ENG
Sept. 18	**Vassily Jirov**	Dale Brown	KO 10	IBF	Las Vegas
Sept. 18	Johnny Nelson	Sione Asipeli	Wu 12	WBO	Las Vegas

Light Heavyweights (175 lbs)

Date	Winner	Loser	Result	Title	Site
Nov. 6	Vinny Pazienza	Arthur Allen	Wu 10	—	Mashantucket, Conn.
Nov. 13	Eric Harding	Montell Griffin	Ws 12	NABF	Miami
Nov. 14	Roy Jones Jr.	Otis Grant	TKO 10	**WBA/WBC**	Mashantucket, Conn.
Dec. 5	Richard Hall	Anthony Bigeni	TKO 3	WBA*	Atlantic City
Dec. 12	D. Michalczewski.........	Drake Thadzi	TKO 9	WBO	Frankfurt, GER
Jan. 9	Roy Jones Jr.	Richard Frazier	TKO 2	**WBC/WBA**	Pensacola, Fla.
Feb. 5	Antonio Carver...........	John Williams	KO 4	—	Miami
Feb. 6	Derrick Harmon	Gilberto Brown	TKO 9	—	Washington, D.C.
Feb. 27	**Reggie Johnson**	Will Taylor	Wu 12	IBF	Miami
Apr. 3	D. Michalczewski.........	Muslim Biarslanov	TKO 7	WBO	Bremen, GER
May 9	Michael Nunn	William Guthrie	TKO 6	—	Minot, N.D.
June 5	Roy Jones Jr.	**Reggie Johnson**	Wu 12	**WBA/ WBC/IBF**	Biloxi, Miss.
June 23	Montell Griffin	Tim Cooper	KO 3	—	Chicago
July 23	David Telesco	Hector Sanjurjo	TKO 5	—	Des Moines, Iowa
Aug. 28	D. Michalczewski.........	Montell Griffin	KO 4	WBO	Bremen, GER

*Richard Hall won the vacant interim WBA title.

Super Middleweights (168 lbs)

Date	Winner	Loser	Result	Title	Site
Oct. 24	Sven Ottke	**Charles Brewer**	Ws 12	IBF	Dusseldorf, GER
Dec. 5	Glen Catley.............	Andy Flute	TKO 5	—	Bristol, ENG
Jan. 8	Vinny Pazienza	Undra White	TKO 9	—	Mashantucket, Conn.
Jan. 29	Dana Rosenblatt.........	Sam Calderon	Wu 10	—	Mashantucket, Conn.
Feb. 13	**Richie Woodhall**	Vincenzo Nardiello	TKO 6	**WBC**	Newcastle, ENG
Feb. 13	Joe Calzaghe	Robin Reid	Ws 12	WBO	Newcastle, ENG
Feb. 27	**Sven Ottke**	Giovanni Nardiello	KO 3	IBF	Berlin, GER
Mar. 6	Omar Gonzalez..........	Roberto Duran	Wu 10	—	Mar del Plata, ARG
Apr. 9	Vinny Pazienza	Joseph Kiwanuka	Wu 10	—	Mashantucket, Conn.
May 8	**Sven Ottke**	Gabriel Hernandez	Wu 12	IBF	Dusseldorf, GER
May 14	Omar Sheika	Demetrius Jenkins	KO 2	—	Pikesville, Md.
May 23	Randie Carver	William "Bo" James	Wu 12	—	Kansas City, Mo.
June 5	Joe Calzaghe	Rick Thornberry	Wu 12	WBO	Cardiff, WAL
June 12	Byron Mitchell...........	**Frankie Liles**	TKO 11	**WBA**	Wilmington, Mass.
June 25	Vinny Pazienza	Esteban Cervantes	Ws 10	—	Mashantucket, Conn.
July 16	James Butler	Merqui Sosa	KO 2	—	Hampton Beach, N.J.
Sept. 4	**Sven Ottke**	Thomas Tate	TWu 11	IBF	Magdeburg, GER

Middleweights (160 lbs)

Date	Winner	Loser	Result	Title	Site
Jan. 30	Bert Schenk..............	Freeman Barr	KO 4	WBO*	Cottbus, GER
Feb. 5	Andrew Council	Michael Ward	Wu 10	—	Pikesville, Md.
Feb. 6	**Bernard Hopkins**	Robert Allen	TKO 7	IBF	Washington, D.C.
Feb. 7	Keith Holmes.............	Alex Lubo	TKO 1	—	Bay St. Louis, Miss.
Feb. 20	Julio Cesar Green	Darren Obah	TKO 9	WBA†	New York City
Mar. 6	Robert McCracken........	Steve Fisher	TKO 9	—	Atlantic City
Apr. 24	Keith Holmes.............	**Hassine Cherifi**	TKO 7	**WBC**	Washington, D.C.
May 21	Dana Rosenblatt..........	Lloyd Bryan	Wu 10	—	Mashantucket, Conn.
May 22	Bert Schenk..............	Jose Ramon Medina-Padilla	Wu 12	WBO	Budapest, HUN
May 28	Davey Hilton Jr.	Stephane Ouellet	KO 3	—	Montreal, CAN
July 17	Jason Matthews	Ryan Rhodes	TKO 2	WBO‡	Doncaster, ENG
July 24	William Joppy	Napolean Pitt	KO 1	—	Las Vegas
Sept. 24	**William Joppy**	Julio Cesar Green	TKO 7	**WBA**	Washington, D.C.
Sept. 24	**Keith Holmes**	Andrew Council	Wu 12	**WBC**	Washington, D.C.

*Schenk won the vacant WBO title.

†Green won the vacant WBA interim title. Reigning WBA middleweight champ William Joppy suffered a broken neck in an automobile accident in Jan. 1999 so a bout for the interim belt was held. Joppy's WBA belt was not at risk for his July 24 fight with Napoleon Pitt.

‡Matthews won the vacant WBO interim title.

Junior Middleweights (154 lbs)
(Super Welterweights)

Date	Winner	Loser	Result	Title	Site
Oct. 24	David Reid	James Cooker	Wu 12	—	Atlantic City
Nov. 30	**Laurent Boudouani**	Terry Norris	TKO 9	**WBA**	Versailles, FRA

Date	Winner	Loser	Result	Title	Site
Dec. 12	Fernando Vargas	**Yori Boy Campas**	TKO 7*	IBF	Atlantic City
Jan. 29	Javier Castillejo	**Keith Mullings**	Wm 12	WBC	Leganes, SPA
Feb. 12	Bronco McKart	Rene Herrera	TKO 8	—	Las Vegas
Mar. 6	David Reid	**Laurent Boudouani**	Wu 12	WBA	Atlantic City
Mar. 13	**Fernando Vargas**	Howard Clarke	TKO 4	IBF	New York City
May 1	Harry Simon	Kevin Lueshing	TKO 3	WBO	London
May 15	**Javier Castillejo**	Humberto Aranda	TKO 4	WBC	Leganes, SPA
June 18	Hector Camacho	P.J. Goossen	Wu 10	—	Struthers, Ohio
June 26	Yori Boy Campas	Ron Weaver	Wu 10	—	Las Vegas
July 16	**David Reid**	Kevin Kelly	Wu 12	WBA	Atlantic City
July 17	**Fernando Vargas**	Raul Marquez	TKO 11	IBF	Stateline, Nev.
Aug. 28	**David Reid**	Keith Mullings	Wu 12	WBA	Las Vegas
Sept. 10	**Javier Castillejo**	Paolo Roberto	TKO 7	WBC	Leganes, SPA
Sept. 10	Bronco McKart	Jason Papillion	Wu 10	—	Mt. Pleasant, Mich.

*Campas quit prior to the seventh round.

Welterweights (147 lbs)

Date	Winner	Loser	Result	Title	Site
Nov. 20	Oba Carr	Verdell Smith	Wu 8	—	Las Vegas
Nov. 28	Ahmed Kotiev	Santos Cardona	Wu 12	WBO	Lubeck, GER
Dec. 5	**James Page**	Jose Luis Lopez	Wu 12	WBA	Atlantic City
Dec. 12	Vernon Forrest	Ed Griffin	TKO 2	—	Atlantic City
Feb. 13	Oba Carr	Frankie Randall	Wu 10	—	Las Vegas
Feb. 13	**Oscar De La Hoya**	Ike Quartey	Ws 12	WBC	Las Vegas
Feb. 20	**Felix Trinidad**	Pernell Whitaker	Wu 12	IBF	New York City
Feb. 20	Vernon Forrest	Mark Fernandez	TKO 2	—	New York City
Mar. 13	**James Page**	Sam Garr	Wu 12	WBA	New York City
Apr. 1	Julio Cesar Chavez	Verdell Smith	KO 4	—	El Paso, Tex.
Apr. 16	Vernon Forrest	Steve Martinez	KO 1	—	Tulsa, Miss.
Apr. 24	Ahmed Kotiev	Peter Malinga	TKO 3	WBO	Munich, GER
May 7	Kofil Jantuah	Daniel Santos	KO 5	—	Henderson, Nev.
May 8	Hector Camacho Jr.	Roberto Nunez	KO 1	—	Miami, Fla.
May 14	Michael Covington	Larry Marks	Wu 10	—	Pikesville, Md.
May 22	**Oscar De La Hoya**	Oba Carr	TKO 11	WBC	Las Vegas
May 29	**Felix Trinidad**	Hugo Pineda	KO 4	IBF	San Juan, P.R.
May 29	Michele Piccirillo	Juan Coggi	Wu 12	—	Barri, Italy
July 2	Willie Jorrin	Aristead Clayton	Wu 12	—	Sacramento, Calif.
July 10	Julio Cesar Chavez	Marty Jakubowski	TKO 4	—	Mexico
July 24	**James Page**	Freddie Pendelton	TKO 11	WBA	Las Vegas
Aug. 27	Vernon Forrest	Santiago Samaniego	KO 7	—	Augusta, Ga.
Sept. 18	**Felix Trinidad**	Oscar De La Hoya	Wm 12	WBC/IBF	Las Vegas
Sept. 25	Shane Mosley	Wilfredo Rivera	TKO 10	—	Temecula, Calif.
Sept. 25	David Kamau	Marco Antonio Lizarraga	Wu 12	—	Lake Tahoe, Nev.
Oct. 2	Willie Wise	Julio Cesar Chavez	Wu 10	—	Las Vegas

*Chavez failed to answer the bell at the start of round nine.
†Quartey vacated his WBA Welterweight title for a Nov. 21, 1998 fight against WBC champion Oscar De La Hoya.

Junior Welterweights (140 lbs)
(Super Lightweights)

Date	Winner	Loser	Result	Title	Site
Oct. 23	Paul Spadafora	Sam Girard	Wu 10	—	Chester, W.V.
Nov. 28	Kostya Tszyu	Diobelys Hurtado	TKO 5	WBC*	Indio, Calif.
Jan. 16	Zab Judah	Wilfredo Negron	KO 4	IBF†	Las Vegas
Jan. 22	Paul Spadafora	Rock Martinez	Wu 10	—	Chicago
Feb. 6	**Sharmba Mitchell**	Pedro Saiz	Wu 12	WBA	Washington, D.C.
Feb. 12	Antonio Diaz	Muro Lucero	TKO 4	—	Las Vegas
Feb. 20	Terronn Millett	**Vince Phillips**	TKO 5	IBF	New York City
Apr. 16	Zab Judah	Juan Torres	KO 1	IBF†	Tulsa, Miss.
Apr. 24	**Sharmba Mitchell**	Reggie Green	Wm 12	WBA	Washington, D.C.
May 4	Antonio Diaz	Marlon Thomas	Wu 12	—	Henderson, Nev.
May 15	Randall Bailey	Carlos Gonzalez	KO 1	WBO	Miami
May 15	Cosme Rivera	Hector Quiroz	Wu 12	—	Las Vegas
June 11	Cory Spinks	Rodolfo Gomez	Wu 8	—	Ft. Worth, Tex.
June 19	Diobelys Hurtado	Lonnie Smith	Wu 10	—	Miami
July 9	Zab Judah	David Sample	KO 1	IBF†	Hyannis, Mass.
July 10	Hector Camacho Jr.	Miguel Angel Ruiz	KO 9	—	Elgin, Ill.
July 16	Hector Camacho Jr.	Mike Cooley	KO 2	—	Atlantic City
July 16	Mickey Ward	Jermal Corbin	KO 5	—	Hampton Beach, N.J.
July 24	**Terronn Millett**	Virgil McClendon	TKO 12	IBF	Las Vegas
Aug. 8	Rafael Ruelas	Hicket Lau	Ws 10	—	Las Vegas
Aug. 21	Kostya Tszyu	Miguel Angel Gonzalez	TKO 10	WBC	Miami

Date	Winner	Loser	Result	Title	Site
Aug. 30	Hector Camacho Jr........	Simon Gonzalez	KO 1	—	Las Vegas
Sept. 3	Teddy Reid	Jose Aponte	TKO 1	—	Cherokee, N.C.
Sept. 16	Antonio Diaz	Emanuel Burton	Wu 12	—	Las Vegas
Oct. 1	Mickey Ward	Reggie Green	TKO 10	—	Salem, N.H.

*Tszyu won the vacant WBC interim title on Nov. 28, 1998 after Miguel Angel Gonzalez was sidelined with a rib injury. Tszyu then captured the regular belt (which was also vacant) on Aug. 21, 1999 in the fight that was suppossed to have happened in November.

†Judah won the vacant IBF interim title.

Lightweights (135 lbs)

Date	Winner	Loser	Result	Title	Site
Oct. 24	Artur Grigorian	Giorgio Campanella	TKO 10	WBO	Hamburg, GER
Oct. 24	John Brown	Gabriel Ruelas	TKO 8	—	Atlantic City
Oct. 30	**Cesar Bazan**...........	Mauro Lucero	Wm 12	**WBC**	Juarez, MEX
Nov. 14	**Shane Mosley**	Jesse James Leija	TKO 9*	**IBF**	Mashantucket, Conn.
Nov. 20	Stevie Johnston...........	Demtrio Ceballos	TKO 6	—	Las Vegas
Dec. 4	Paul Spadafora	Dezi Ford	TKO 10	—	Monroeville, PA
Dec. 12	Ivan Robinson...........	Arturo Gatti	Wu 10	—	Atlantic City
Jan. 8	**Shane Mosley**	Golden Johnson	KO 7	**IBF**	Pensacola, Fla.
Jan. 25	**Jean-Baptiste Mendy** ..	Alberto Sicurella	Wu 12	**WBA**	Versailles, FRA
Feb. 26	Israel Cardona	Joel Perez	TKO 7	—	Mashantucket, Conn.
Feb. 27	Stevie Johnston...........	**Cesar Bazan**	Ws 12	**WBC**	Miami
Mar. 3	Artur Grigorian	Oscar Garcia-Cano	Wu 12	WBO	Lubeck, GER
Mar. 3	Angel Manfredy..........	Ernesto Benitez	KO 3	—	Rosemont, Ill.
Apr. 10	Julien Lorcy	**Jean-Baptiste Mendy**	KO 6	**WBA**	Paris
Apr. 17	Angel Manfredy..........	Ivan Robinson	Wu 10	—	Indio, Calif.
Apr. 17	**Shane Mosley**	John Brown	KO 8	**IBF**	Indio, Calif.
June 4	Billy Irwin	John Lark	KO 2	—	Philadelphia
June 23	Angel Manfredy..........	Luis Lizarraga	KO 7	—	Chicago
June 26	**Stevie Johnston**........	Aldo Rios	Wu 12	**WBC**	Las Vegas
Aug. 7	Stefano Zoff	**Julien Lorcy**	Wu 12	**WBA**	Le Cannet, FRA
Aug. 14	**Stevie Johnston**........	Angel Manfredy	Wu 12	**WBC**	Mashantucket, Conn.
Aug. 20	Paul Spadafora	Israel Cardona	Wu 12	IBF†	Chester, W.V.
Sept. 3	Ivan Robinson...........	James Crayton	Wu 12	—	Cherokee, N.C.
Sept. 24	Billy Irwin	Larry O'Shields	KO 6	—	Philadelphia
Sept. 25	Cesar Bazan.............	Joseph Charles	Wu 12	—	Miami
Oct. 9	Artur Grigorian	Michael Clark	KO 5	WBO	Oberhausen, GER

*Leija's corner stopped the fight prior to the 10th round.

†Spadafora won the vacant IBF lightweight title.

Junior Lightweights (130 lbs)
(Super Featherweights)

Date	Winner	Loser	Result	Title	Site
Oct. 24	**Roberto Garcia**	Ramon Ledon	TKO 5	**IBF**	Atlantic City
Dec. 19	**Floyd Mayweather**	Angel Manfredy	TKO 2	**WBC**	Miami
Jan. 16	**Roberto Garcia**	Juan Molina	Wu 12	**IBF**	Las Vegas
Jan. 25	Anatoly Alexandrov.......	Arnulfo Castillo	TKO 8	WBO	Versailles, FRA
Feb. 13	**Takanori Hatakeyama**	Saul Duran	SDraw	**WBA**	Tokyo, JPN
Feb. 17	**Floyd Mayweather**	Carlos Rios	Wu 12	**WBC**	Grand Rapids, Mich.
Feb. 20	Antonio Hernandez.......	Justin Juuko	TKO 11	WBA*	Ft. Worth, Tex.
Mar. 14	Joel Casamayor	Russell Stoner Jones	Wu 10	—	Pueblo, Calif.
May 8	Augie Sanchez	Jorge Paez	KO 7	—	Las Vegas
May 10	Juan Manuel Marquez	Wilfredo Vargas	KO 2	—	Inglewood, Calif.
May 21	Edwin Santana...........	Richard Kiley	Draw	—	Mashantucket, Conn.
May 22	**Floyd Mayweather**	Justin Juuko	KO 9	**WBC**	Las Vegas
June 19	Joel Casamayor	Antonio Hernandez	Wu 12	WBA*	Miami
June 27	Lakva Sim	**Takanori Hatakeyama**	TKO 5	**WBA**	Tokyo
Aug. 7	Acelino Freitas	Anatoly Alexandrov	KO 1	WBO	Le Cannet, FRA
Aug. 7	Gabriel Ruelas	Jose Rodriguez	Wu 10	—	Miami
Aug. 14	Arturo Gatti	Reyes Munos	TKO 1	—	Mashantucket, Conn.
Sept. 11	**Floyd Mayweather**	Carlos Gerena	TKO 7	**WBC**	Las Vegas

*Hernandez won the interim WBA title and then lost it to Casamayor.

Featherweights (126 lbs)

Date	Winner	Loser	Result	Title	Site
Oct. 31	Naseem Hamed............	Wayne McCullough	Wu 12	WBO	Atlantic City
Nov. 28	**Luisito Espinosa**........	Kennedy McKinney	TKO 2	**WBC**	Indio, Calif.
Dec. 11	Richard DeJesus	Orlando Canizales	Wm 10	—	Philadelphia
Feb. 5	**Antonio Cermeno**......	Eddy Saenz	KO 2	**WBA**	Miami
Apr. 10	Naseem Hamed...........	Paul Ingle	TKO 11	WBO	Manchester, ENG

Date	Winner	Loser	Result	Title	Site
Apr. 16	**Manuel Medina**	Victor Polo	Ws 9*	IBF	Las Vegas
May 8	Kevin Kelley	Hector Velasquez	Wu 10	—	Las Vegas
May 10	Juan Manuel Marquez	Wilfredo Vargas	TKO 2	—	Los Angeles
May 15	Cesar Soto	**Luisito Espinosa**	Wu 12	**WBC**	El Paso, Tex.
May 29	Freddie Norwood	**Antonio Cermeno**	Ws 12	**WBA**	San Juan, P.R.
June 4	Orlando Canizales	Richard DeJesus	TKO 4	—	Philadelphia
Sept. 11	**Freddie Norwood**	Juan Manuel Marquez	Wu 12	**WBA**	Las Vegas
Sept. 18	Frankie Toledo	Orlando Canizales	Ws 10	—	Philadelphia
Sept. 25	Alejandro Gonzalez	Eduardo Barrios	TKO 8	—	Miami
Sept. 27	Antonio Diaz	Daniel Jimenez	Wu 10	—	E. St. Louis, Mo.

*The ringside physician stopped the fight in the ninth round after an accidental headbutt opened a deep cut in Medina's eyelid.

Junior Featherweights (122 lbs)
(Super Bantamweights)

Date	Winner	Loser	Result	Title	Site
Oct. 31	Marco Antonio Barrera	Richie Wenton	TKO 3*	WBO	Atlantic City
Oct. 31	**Vuyani Bungu**	Danny Romero	Wm 12	IBF	Atlantic City
Dec. 12	Nestor Garza	**Enrique Sanchez**	Wu 12	WBA	Indio, Calif.
Feb. 6	**Vuyani Bungu**	Victor Llerena	TKO 7	IBF	Hammanskraal, S.A.
Feb. 13	**Erik Morales**	Angel Chacon	KO 2	WBC	Las Vegas
Apr. 3	Marco Antonio Barrera	Paul Lloyd	TKO 2	WBO	London
May 8	**Erik Morales**	Juan Carlos Ramirez	TKO 9	WBC	Las Vegas
May 8	**Nestor Garza**	Carlos Barreto	TKO 8	WBA	Las Vegas
May 8	Danny Romero	David Vazquez	Wu 10	—	Las Vegas
May 29	Lehlohonolo Ledwaba	John Michael Johnson	Wu 12	IBF†	Hammanskraal, S.A.
June 11	Danny Romero	Erique Jupiter	Draw	—	Ft. Worth, Tex.
July 31	**Erik Morales**	Reynante Jamili	TKO 6	WBC	Tijuana, MEX
Aug. 7	Marco Antonio Barrera	Pastor Maurin	Wu 12	WBO	Atlantic City
Aug. 28	Kennedy McKinney	Mario Diaz	Wu 10	—	Tunica, Miss.
Aug. 30	Wayne McCullough	Len Martinez	Wu 10	—	Las Vegas
Sept. 25	**Lehlohonolo Ledwaba**	Edison Valencia	TKO 4	IBF	Temecula, Calif.

*Wenton didn't answer the bell for the fourth round.

†Ledwaba won the vacant jr. featherweight IBF title that Vuyani Bungu left behind when he moved up to the featherweight division.

Bantamweights (118 lbs)

Date	Winner	Loser	Result	Title	Site
Dec. 5	Johnny Tapia	"Nana" Yaw Konadu	Wm 12	WBA	Atlantic City
Dec. 29	Veerapol Sahaprom	**Joichiro Tatsuyoshi**	TKO 6	WBC	Osaka, JPN
Mar. 27	**Tim Austin**	Sergio Aguila	KO 9	IBF	Miami, Fla.
Mar. 27	Jorge Eliecer Julio	Julio Gamboa	Ws 12	WBO	Miami, Fla.
Apr. 24	Johnny Tapia	Alberto Martinez	Wu 10	—	Albuquerque, N.M.
May 21	**Veerapol Sahaprom**	Mauro Blanc	KO 5	WBC	Sara Buri, THAI
June 12	"Nana" Yaw Konadu	Hector Acero-Sanchez	Wu 10	—	Worcester, Mass.
June 26	Paulie Ayala	**Johnny Tapia**	Wu 12	WBA	Las Vegas
Aug. 14	Danny Romero	Leonardo Gutierrez	KO 6	—	Albuquerque, N.M.
Aug. 29	**Veerapol Sahaprom**	Joichiro Tatsuyoshi	TKO 7	WBC	Osaka, JPN

Junior Bantamweights (115 lbs)
(Super Flyweights)

Date	Winner	Loser	Result	Title	Site
Nov. 7	Victor Godoi	Pedro Morquecho	Ws 12	WBO	Chubut, ARG
Dec. 23	Jesus Rojas	**Satoshi Iida**	Wu 12	WBA	Nagoya, JPN
Jan. 10	**In-Joo Cho**	Joel Luna Zarate	Wm 12	WBC	Seoul, S. KOR
Mar. 28	**Jesus Rojas**	Hideki Todaka	TDraw 4*	WBA	Miyazaki, JPN
Apr. 10	Keiji Yamaguchi	Takayuki Akazawa	Wu 10	—	Ojayama, JPN
Apr. 24	Mark Johnson	**Rantanachai Vorapin**	Wu 12	IBF	Washington, D.C.
June 7	Diego Morales	Victor Godoi	TKO 11	WBO	Tijuana, MEX
June 13	**In-Joo Cho**	Pone Saengmorakot	KO 8	WBC	Seoul, S. KOR
July 31	Diego Morales	Ysaias Zamudio	TKO 8	WBO	Tijuana, MEX
July 31	Hideki Todaka	**Jesus Rojas**	Wu 12	WBA	Nagoya, JPN
Aug. 6	Eric Morel	Francisco Espitia	KO 1	—	Columbus, Ohio
Aug. 13	**Mark Johnson**	Jorge Lacierva	Wu 8	IBF	Mashantucket, Conn.
Sept. 5	**In-Joo Cho**	Keiji Yamaguchi	Wu 12	WBC	Tokyo
Sept. 18	Eric Morel	Miguel Angel Granados	Wu 10	—	Las Vegas

*The bout was stopped by the referee after Rojas was cut over the eye from a headbutt, despite the ringside physician's recommendation that it could continue.

Flyweights (112 lbs)

Date	Winner	Loser	Result	Title	Site
Dec. 4	Manny Pacquiao	**Chatchai Sasakul**	KO 8	WBC	Bangkok, THAI

Date	Winner	Loser	Result	Title	Site
Dec. 18	Ruben Sanchez-Leon	Salvatore Fanni	Wu 12	WBO	Sardinia, ITA
Mar. 5	Peter Culshaw	Zolile Mbityi	Ws 12	—	Liverpool, ENG
Mar. 13	Leo Gamez	**Hugo Soto**	TKO 3	**WBA**	New York City
Apr. 10	Irene Pacheco	Luis Cox	TKO 9	IBF*	Baranquilla, COL
Apr. 23	Jose Lopez Bueno	Ruben Sanchez-Leon	KO 3	WBO	Tijuana, MEX
Apr. 24	**Manny Pacquiao**	Gabriel Mira	KO 4	**WBC**	Quezon City, PHI
May 29	**Leo Gamez**	Jose Dickie Camacho	TKO 8	**WBA**	San Juan, P.R.
June 4	Jose Lopez Bueno	Igor Gerassimov	TKO 7	WBO	Malaga, SPA
Sept. 3	Sornpichai Kratindaenggym	**Leo Gamez**	KO 8	**WBA**	Mukdahan, THAI
Sept. 17	Medgoen Lukchaopormasak	**Manny Pacquiao**	TKO 3	**WBC**	Bangkok, THAI
Oct. 16	**Irene Pacheco**	Ferid Ben Jessou	TKO 4	IBF	Baranquilla, COL

*Pacheco won the IBF title left vacant by Mark Johnson when he moved up to junior bantamweight.

Junior Flyweights (108 lbs)
(Light Flyweights)

Date	Winner	Loser	Result	Title	Site
Nov. 26	**Saman Sor Jaturong**	Ladislao Vazquez	Wu 12	**WBC**	Pathum Thani, THAI
Dec. 5	Jorge Arce	Juan D. Cordoba	Wu 12	WBO	Tijuana, MEX
Dec. 18	Will Grigsby	Ratanpol Sow Voraphin	Wu 12	IBF*	Ft. Lauderdale, Fla.
Feb. 20	P. Chor Siriwat	Joma Gamboa	Wu 12	**WBA**	Koh Samui, THAI
Feb. 27	Michael Carbajal	Jose Luis De Jesus	KO 7	—	Tampa, Fla.
Mar. 6	**Will Grigsby**	Carmelo Caceres	Wu 12	IBF	Minneapolis, Minn.
Apr. 17	Jorge Arce	Salvatore Fanni	KO 6	WBO	Sassari, ITA
May 8	Michael Carbajal	Oscar Andrade	Wu 10	—	Miami, Fla.
July 2	Michael Carbajal	Oscar Calzada	KO 4	—	Tucson, Ariz.
July 31	Michael Carbajal	Jorge Arce	TKO 11	WBO	Tijuana, MEX
Oct. 2	Ricardo Lopez	**Will Grigsby**	Wu 12	IBF	Las Vegas
Oct. 16	Choi Yo-sam	**Saman Sor Jaturong**	Wu 12	**WBC**	Seoul, S. KOR

*Grigsby won the vacat IBF title that was forfeited by Mauricio Pastrana when he failed to make weight for his Aug. 29, 1998 title fight with Carlos Murillo.

Minimumweights (105 lbs)
(Strawweights or Mini-Flyweights)

Date	Winner	Loser	Result	Title	Site
Nov. 13	Ricardo Lopez	Rosendo Alvarez	Ws 12	**WBA***	Las Vegas
Jan. 30	Songkram Porpaoin	Ronnie Magramo	TWm 8†	WBA	Pattaya, THAI
Mar. 27	Kermin Guardia	Eric Jamili	Wu 12	WBO	Miami, Fla.
May 4	Wandee Chareon	Yasuo Tokimitsu	TKO 12	WBC‡	Kurashiki, JPN
May 29	**Zolani Petelo**	Eric Jamili	KO 1	IBF	Hammanskraal, S.A.

*Alvarez was stripped of his WBA title before the fight because he could not make the 105-pound weight limit. Lopez's WBC belt was therefore not at risk for this fight but Lopez did win the suddenly vacant WBA belt with his split decision over Alvarez.
†The bout went to the judges' score cards after Magramo threw Porpaoin to the mat in the eighth round. Porpaoin won the vacant WBA interim title on the technical majority decision.
‡Chareon won the interim WBC title.

Top Fighters Records

The career pro records of Welterweight Oscar De La Hoya, Light Heavyweight Roy Jones Jr. and Heavyweights Evander Holyfield, Lennox Lewis and Mike Tyson, as of Oct. 16, 1999.

Roy Jones Jr.

Born: Jan. 16, 1969 **Pro record:** 40-1-0, 33 KOs
Height: 5'11" **Weight:** 175
Olympic medal: 1988 Silver as a light middleweight.

No	Date	Opponent, location	Result
1	5/6/89	Ricky Randall, Pensacola, Fla.	KO 2
2	6/11/89	Stephan Johnson, Atlantic City	KO 8
3	9/3/89	Ron Amundsen, Pensacola, Fla.	KO 7
4	11/30/89	Dave McCluskey, Pensacola, Fla.	KO 3
5	1/8/90	Joe Edens, Mobile, Alabama	KO 2
6	2/28/90	Billy Mitchum, Pensacola, Fla.	TKO 2
7	3/28/90	Knox Brown, Pensacola, Fla.	KO 3
8	5/11/90	Ron Johnson, Pensacola, Fla.	KO 2
9	7/14/90	Tony Waddles, Pensacola, Fla.	KO 1
10	9/25/90	Rollin Williams, Pensacola, Fla.	KO 4
11	11/8/90	Reggie Miller, Pensacola, Fla.	KO 5
12	1/31/91	Ricky Stackhouse, Pensacola, Fla.	KO 1
13	4/13/91	Eddie Evans, Pensacola, Fla.	TKO 3
14	8/3/91	Kevin Daigle, Pensacola, Fla.	TKO 4
15	8/31/91	Lester Yarbrough, Pensacola, Fla.	KO 8
16	1/10/92	Jorge Vaca, New York City	KO 1
17	4/3/92	Art Serwano, Reno	KO 1
18	6/30/92	Jorge Castro, Pensacola, Fla.	Wu 12
19	8/18/92	Glenn Thomas, Pensacola, Fla.	KO 8
20	12/5/92	Percy Harris, Atlantic City	KO 4
21	2/13/93	Glenn Wolfe, Las Vegas	KO 1
22	5/22/93	Bernard Hopkins, Washington D.C.	Wu 12
		(won IBF middleweight title)	
23	8/14/93	Thulane Malinga, St. Louis Bay, Miss.	KO 6
24	11/30/93	Fermin Chirino, Pensacola, Fla.	W 10
25	3/22/94	Daniel Garcia, Pensacola, Fla.	KO 6
26	5/27/94	Thomas Tate, Las Vegas	KO 2
27	11/18/94	James Toney, Las Vegas	Wu 12
		(won IBF super middleweight title)	
28	3/18/95	Antoine Byrd, Pensacola, Fla.	TKO 1
29	6/24/95	Vinny Pazienza, Atlantic City	TKO 6
30	9/30/95	Tony Thornton, Pensacola, Fla.	TKO 2
31	1/12/96	Merqui Sosa, New York City	TKO 2
32	6/15/96	Eric Lucas, Jacksonville, Fla.	KO 11
33	8/4/96	Bryant Brannon, New York City	KO 2
34	11/22/96	Mike McCallum, Tampa, Fla.	Wu 12
		(won interim WBC light heavyweight title)	

No	Date	Opponent, location	Result
35	3/21/97	Montel Griffin, Atlantic City	L-DQ 9
		(lost WBC light heavyweight title)	
36	8/21/97	Montel Griffin, Mashantucket, Conn.	KO 1
		(won WBC light heavyweight title)	
37	4/25/98	Virgil Hill, Biloxi, Miss.	KO 4
38	7/18/98	Lou Del Valle, New York City	Wu 12
		(won WBA light heavyweight title)	

No	Date	Opponent, location	Result
39	11/14/98	Otis Grant, Mashantucket, Conn.	TKO 10
40	1/9/99	Richard Frazier, Pensacola, Fla.	TKO 2
41	6/5/99	Reggie Johnson, Biloxi, Miss.	Wu 12
		(won IBF light heavyweight title)	

Oscar De La Hoya

Born: Feb. 4, 1973   **Pro record:** 31-1, 25 KOs
Height: 5'10½"   **Weight:** 147
Olympic medal: 1992 Gold as a lightweight

No	Date	Opponent, location	Result
1	11/23/92	Lamar Williams, Inglewood, Calif.	KO 1
2	12/12/92	Cliff Hicks, Phoenix	KO 1
3	1/3/93	Paris Alexander, Hollywood	TKO 2
4	2/6/93	Curtis Strong, San Diego	TKO 4
5	3/13/93	Jeff Mayweather, Las Vegas	TKO 4
6	4/6/93	Mike Grable, Rochester, N.Y.	Wu 8
7	5/8/93	Frank Avelar, Lake Tahoe	TKO 4
8	6/7/93	Troy Dorsey, Las Vegas	TKO 1
9	8/14/93	Renaldo Carter, Bay St. Louis, Miss.	KO 6
10	8/27/93	Angelo Nunez, Beverly Hills	TKO 4
11	10/30/93	Narcisco Valenzuela, Phoenix	KO 1
12	3/5/94	Jimmi Bredahl, Los Angeles	TKO 10
13	5/27/94	Giogio Campenella, Las Vegas	KO 3
14	7/29/94	Jorge Paez, Las Vegas	KO 2
15	11/18/94	Carl Griffith, Las Vegas	KO 3
16	12/10/94	John Avila, Los Angeles	TKO 9
17	2/18/95	John John Molina, Las Vegas	Wu 12
18	5/6/95	Rafael Ruelas, Las Vegas	TKO 2

No	Date	Opponent, location	Result
		(won IBF lightweight title)	
19	9/9/95	Genaro Hernandez, Las Vegas	TKO 6
20	12/15/95	James Leija, New York City	TKO 2
21	2/9/96	Darryl Tyson, Las Vegas	KO 2
22	6/7/96	Julio Cesar Chavez, Las Vegas	TKO 4
		(won WBC super lightweight title)	
23	1/18/97	Miguel Angel Gonzalez, Las Vegas	Wu 12
24	4/12/97	Pernell Whitaker, Las Vegas	Wu 12
		(won WBC welterweight title)	
25	6/14/97	David Kamau, San Antonio	KO 2
26	9/13/97	Hector Camacho, Las Vegas	Wu 12
27	12/6/97	Wilfredo Rivera, Atlantic City	TKO 8
28	6/13/98	Patrick Charpentier, El Paso, Texas	TKO 3
29	9/18/98	Julio Cesar Chavez, Las Vegas	TKO 8
30	2/13/99	Ike Quartey, Las Vegas	Ws 12
31	5/22/99	Oba Carr, Las Vegas	TKO 11
32	9/18/99	Felix Trinidad, Las Vegas	Lm 12
		(lost WBC welterweight title)	

Evander Holyfield

Born: Oct. 19, 1962   **Pro record:** 36-3-1, 25 KOs
Height: 6' 2½"   **Weight:** 217
Olympic medal: 1984 Bronze as light heavyweight (disqualified for controversial late knockout punch in semifinal against Kevin Barry of New Zealand)

No	Date	Opponent, location	Result
1	11/15/84	Lionel Byarm, New York	Wu 6
2	1/20/85	Eric Winbush, Atlantic City	Wu 6
3	3/13/85	Freddie Brown, Norfolk	KO 1
4	4/20/85	Mark Rivera, Corpus Christi	KO 2
5	7/20/85	Tyrone Booze, Norfolk	Wu 8
6	8/29/85	Rick Myers, Atlanta	KO 1
7	10/30/85	Jeff Meachem, Atlantic City	KO 5
8	12/21/85	Anthony Davis, Virginia Beach	KO 4
9	3/1/86	Chisanda Mutti, Lancaster, Pa	KO 3
10	4/6/86	Jesse Shelby, Corpus Christi	KO 3
11	5/28/86	Terry Mims, Metairie, LA	KO 5
12	7/20/86	Dwight M. Qawi, Atlanta	Ws 15
		(won WBA cruiserweight title)	
13	12/8/86	Mike Brothers, Paris	KO 3
14	2/14/87	Henry Tillman, Reno	TKO 7
15	5/15/87	Rickey Parkey, Las Vegas	TKO 3
		(won IBF cruiserweight title)	
16	8/15/87	Ossie Ocasio, St.Topez, France	TKO 11
17	12/4/87	Dwight M. Qawi, Atlantic City	TKO 4
18	4/9/88	Carlos DeLeon, Las Vegas	KO 8
		(won WBC cruiserweight title)	
19	7/16/88	James Tillis, Lake Tahoe	KO 5
20	12/9/88	Pinklon Thomas, Atlantic City	TKO 7
21	3/11/89	Michael Dokes, Las Vegas	TKO 10
22	7/15/89	Adilson Rodrigues, Lake Tahoe	KO 2

No	Date	Opponent, location	Result
23	11/4/89	Alex Stewart, Atlantic City	TKO 8
24	6/1/90	Seamus McDonagh, Atlantic City	TKO 4
25	10/25/90	Buster Douglas, Las Vegas	KO 3
		(won undisputed heavyweight title)	
26	4/19/91	George Foreman, Atlantic City	Wu 12
27	11/23/91	Bert Cooper, Atlanta	TKO 7
28	6/19/92	Larry Holmes, Las Vegas	Wu 12
29	11/13/92	Riddick Bowe, Las Vegas	Lu 12
		(lost undisputed heavyweight title)	
30	6/26/93	Alex Stewart, Atlantic City	Wu 12
31	11/6/93	Riddick Bowe, Las Vegas	Wm 12
		(won IBF/WBA heavyweight titles)	
32	4/22/94	Michael Moorer, Las Vegas	Lm 12
		(lost IBF/WBA heavyweight titles)	
33	5/20/95	Ray Mercer, Atlantic City	Wu 10
34	11/4/95	Riddick Bowe, Las Vegas	TKO by 8
35	5/10/96	Bobby Czyz, New York	TKO 5
36	11/9/96	Mike Tyson, Las Vegas	TKO 11
		(won WBC heavyweight title)	
37	6/28/97	Mike Tyson, Las Vegas	W Disq. 3
38	11/8/97	Michael Moorer, Las Vegas	TKO 8
		(won IBF/WBA heavyweight titles)	
39	9/19/98	Vaughn Bean, Atlanta	Wu 12
40	3/13/99	Lennox Lewis, New York City	Draw 12

Lennox Lewis

Born: Sept. 9, 1965   **Pro record:** 34-1-1, 27 KOs
Height: 6' 5"   **Weight:** 246
Olympic medal: 1988 Gold as super heavyweight for Canada

No	Date	Opponent, location	Result
1	6/27/89	Al Malcolm, London	KO 2
2	7/21/89	Bruce Johnson, Atlantic City	TKO 2
3	9/25/89	Andy Gerrard, London	TKO 4
4	10/10/89	Stever Garber, Hull, ENG	KO 2
5	11/5/89	Melvin Epps, Kensington, ENG	W disq. 2
6	12/18/89	Greg Gorrell, Ontario	TKO 5
7	1/31/90	Noel Quarless, London	KO 2
8	3/22/90	Calvin Jones, Gateshead, ENG	KO 1
9	4/14/90	Mike Simuwelu, London	KO 1
10	5/9/90	Jorge Dascola, London	KO 1
11	5/20/90	Dan Murphy, Sheffield, ENG	TKO 6
12	6/27/90	Ossie Ocasio, Kensington, ENG	Wu 8
13	7/11/90	Mike Acey, Ontario	TKO 2
14	10/31/90	Jean Chanet, London	TKO 6
15	3/6/91	Gary Mason, London	TKO 6
16	7/12/91	Mike Weaver, Stateline, Nev.	KO 6
17	9/30/91	Glenn McCrory, Kensington, ENG	KO 2
18	11/23/91	Tyrell Biggs, Atlanta	TKO 3
19	2/1/92	Levi Billups, Las Vegas	Wu 10
20	4/30/92	Derek Williams, London	KO 3
21	8/11/92	Mike Dixon, Atlantic City	TKO 4
22	10/31/92	Razor Ruddock, London*	KO 2
23	5/8/93	Tony Tucker, Las Vegas	Wu 12
24	10/1/93	Frank Bruno, Cardiff, Wales	TKO 7
25	5/6/94	Phil Jackson, Atlantic City	KO 8
26	9/24/94	Oliver McCall, London	TKO by 2
		(lost WBC heavyweight title)	
27	5/13/95	Lionel Butler, Sacramento	KO 5
28	7/2/95	Justin Fortune, Dublin	TKO 4
29	10/7/95	Tommy Morrison, Atlantic City	TKO 6
30	5/10/96	Ray Mercer, New York City	Wu 12
31	2/7/97	Oliver McCall, London	W disq. 5†
		(won WBC heavyweight title)	
32	7/12/97	Henry Akinwande, Lake Tahoe	W disq. 5‡
33	10/4/97	Andrew Golota, Atlantic City	KO 1
34	3/28/98	Shannon Briggs, Atlantic City	TKO 5
35	9/26/98	Zeljko Mavrovic, Uncasville, Conn.	Wu 12
36	3/13/99	Evander Holyfield, New York City	Draw 12

*Lewis' bout with Ruddock was a title eliminator and Lewis was then awarded the belt when Riddick Bowe surrendered the title in December by dumping it in a London trash can.
†McCall was disqualified in the fifth round after he started crying and refused to put up a fight.
‡Akinwande was disqualified in the fifth round for excessive clutching and grabbing.

Mike Tyson

Born: June 30, 1966   **Pro record:** 45-3-0, 39 KOs
Height: 5'11"   **Weight:** 218

No	Date	Opponent, location	Result
1	3/6/85	Hector Mercedes, Albany, N.Y.	KO 1
2	4/10/85	Trent Singleton, Albany, N.Y.	TKO 1
3	5/23/85	Don Halpin, Albany, N.Y.	KO 4
4	6/20/85	Rick Spain, Atlantic City	KO 1
5	7/11/85	John Anderson, Atlantic City	TKO 2
6	7/19/85	Larry Sims, Poughkeepsie, N.Y.	KO 3
7	8/15/85	Lorenzo Canady, Atlantic City	TKO 1
8	9/5/85	Michael Johnson, Atlantic City	KO 1
9	10/9/85	Donnie Long, Atlantic City	KO 1
10	10/25/85	Robert Colay, Atlantic City	KO 1
11	11/1/85	Sterling Benjamin, Latham, N.Y.	TKO 1
12	11/13/85	Eddie Richardson, Houston	KO 1
13	11/22/85	Conroy Nelson, Latham, N.Y.	KO 2
14	12/6/85	Sammy Scaff, New York City	KO 1
15	12/27/85	Mark Young, Latham, N.Y.	KO 1
16	1/10/86	Dave Jaco, Albany, N.Y.	TKO 1
17	1/24/86	Mike Jameson, Atlantic City	TKO 5
18	2/16/86	Jesse Ferguson, Troy, N.Y.	TKO 6
19	3/10/86	Steve Zouski, Uniondale, N.Y.	KO 3
20	5/3/86	James Tillis, Glens Falls, N.Y.	Wu 10
21	5/20/86	Mitchell Green, New York City	Wu 10
22	6/13/86	Reggie Gross, New York City	TKO 1
23	6/28/86	William Hosea, Troy, N.Y.	KO 1
24	7/11/86	Lorenzo Boyd, Swan Lake, N.Y.	KO 2
25	7/26/86	Marvis Frazier, Glens Falls, N.Y.	KO 1
26	8/17/86	Jose Ribalta, Atlantic City	TKO 10
27	9/6/86	Alfonzo Ratliff, Las Vegas	KO 2
28	11/22/86	Trevor Berbick, Las Vegas	KO 2
		(won WBC heavyweight title)	
29	3/7/87	Bonecrusher Smith, Las Vegas	Wu 12
		(won WBA heavyweight title)	
30	5/30/87	Pinklon Thomas, Las Vegas	TKO 6
31	8/1/87	Tony Tucker, Las Vegas	Wu 12
		(won IBF heavyweight title)	
32	10/16/87	Tyrell Biggs, Atlantic City	TKO 7
33	1/22/88	Larry Holmes, Atlantic City	KO 4
34	3/21/88	Tony Tubbs, Tokyo	TKO 2
35	6/27/88	Michael Spinks, Atlantic City	KO 1
36	2/25/89	Frank Bruno, Las Vegas	TKO 5
37	7/21/89	Carl Williams, Atlantic City	TKO 1
38	2/10/90	Buster Douglas, Tokyo	KO by 10
		(lost world heavyweight title)	
39	6/16/90	Henry Tillman, Las Vegas	KO 1
40	12/8/90	Alex Stewart, Atlantic City	TKO 1
41	3/18/91	Razor Ruddock, Las Vegas	TKO 7
42	6/28/91	Razor Ruddock, Las Vegas	Wu 12
43	8/19/95	Peter McNeeley, Las Vegas	W disq. 1
		(first fight since release from prison)	
44	12/16/95	Buster Mathis Jr., Philadelphia	KO 3
45	3/16/96	Frank Bruno, Las Vegas	TKO 3
		(won WBC heavyweight title)	
46	9/7/96	Bruce Seldon, Las Vegas	TKO 1
		(won WBA heavyweight title)	
47	11/9/96	Evander Holyfield, Las Vegas	TKO by 11
		(lost WBA heavyweight title)	
48	6/28/97	Evander Holyfield, Las Vegas	L disq 3
		(disqualified for biting Holyfield's ears)	

THE 2000 ESPN INFORMATION PLEASE SPORTS ALMANAC

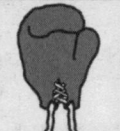

B O X I N G
S T A T I S T I C S

SEC B

THROUGH THE YEARS
1884-1999
WORLD CHAMPIONS

PAGE 918

World Heavyweight Championship Fights

Widely accepted world champions in **bold** type. Note following result abbreviations: KO (knockout), TKO (technical knock-out), Wu (unanimous decision), Wm (majority decision), Ws (split decision), Ref (referee's decision), ND (no decision), Disq. (won on disqualification).

Year	Date	Winner	Age	Wgt	Loser	Wgt	Result	Location
1892	Sept. 7	James J. Corbett	26	178	John L. Sullivan	212	KO 21	New Orleans
1894	Jan. 25	**James J. Corbett**	27	184	Charley Mitchell	158	KO 3	Jacksonville, Fla.
1897	Mar. 17	Bob Fitzsimmons	34	167	**James J. Corbett**	183	KO 14	Carson City, Nev.
1899	June 9	James J. Jeffries	24	206	**Bob Fitzsimmons**	167	KO 11	Coney Island, N.Y.
1899	Nov. 3	**James J. Jeffries**	24	215	Tom Sharkey	183	Ref 25	Coney Island, N.Y.
1900	Apr. 6	**James J. Jeffries**	24	NA	Jack Finnegan	NA	KO 1	Detroit
1900	May 11	**James J. Jeffries**	25	218	James J. Corbett	188	KO 23	Coney Island, N.Y.
1901	Nov. 15	**James J. Jeffries**	26	211	Gus Ruhlin	194	TKO 6	San Francisco
1902	July 25	**James J. Jeffries**	27	219	Bob Fitzsimmons	172	KO 8	San Francisco
1903	Aug. 14	**James J. Jeffries**	28	220	James J. Corbett	190	KO 10	San Francisco
1904	Aug. 25	**James J. Jeffries***	29	219	Jack Munroe	186	TKO 2	San Francisco
1905	July 3	Marvin Hart	28	190	Jack Root	171	KO 12	Reno, Nev.
1906	Feb. 23	Tommy Burns	24	180	**Marvin Hart**	188	Ref 20	Los Angeles
1906	Oct. 2	**Tommy Burns**	25	NA	Jim Flynn	NA	KO 15	Los Angeles
1906	Nov. 28	**Tommy Burns**	25	172	Phila. Jack O'Brien	163½	Draw 20	Los Angeles
1907	May 8	**Tommy Burns**	25	180	Phila. Jack O'Brien	167	Ref 20	Los Angeles
1907	July 4	**Tommy Burns**	26	181	Bill Squires	180	KO 1	Colma, Calif.
1907	Dec. 2	**Tommy Burns**	26	177	Gunner Moir	204	KO 10	London
1908	Feb. 10	**Tommy Burns**	26	NA	Jack Palmer	NA	KO 4	London
1908	Mar. 17	**Tommy Burns**	26	NA	Jem Roche	NA	KO 1	Dublin
1908	Apr. 18	**Tommy Burns**	26	NA	Jewey Smith	NA	KO 5	Paris
1908	June 13	**Tommy Burns**	26	184	Bill Squires	183	KO 8	Paris
1908	Aug. 24	**Tommy Burns**	27	181	Bill Squires	184	KO 13	Sydney
1908	Sept. 2	**Tommy Burns**	27	183	Bill Lang	187	KO 6	Melbourne
1908	Dec. 26	Jack Johnson	30	192	**Tommy Burns**	168	TKO 14	Sydney
1909	Mar. 10	**Jack Johnson**	30	NA	Victor McLaglen	NA	ND 6	Vancouver
1909	May 19	**Jack Johnson**	31	205	Phila. Jack O'Brien	161	ND 6	Philadelphia
1909	June 30	**Jack Johnson**	31	207	Tony Ross	214	ND 6	Pittsburgh
1909	Sept. 9	**Jack Johnson**	31	209	Al Kaufman	191	ND 10	San Francisco
1909	Oct. 16	**Jack Johnson**	31	205½	Stanley Ketchel	170¼	KO 12	Colma, Calif.
1910	July 4	**Jack Johnson**	32	208	James J. Jeffries	227	KO 15	Reno, Nev.
1912	July 4	**Jack Johnson**	34	195½	Jim Flynn	175	TKO 9	Las Vegas, Nev.
1913	Dec. 19	**Jack Johnson**	35	NA	Jim Johnson	NA	Draw 10	Paris
1914	June 27	**Jack Johnson**	36	221	Frank Moran	203	Ref 20	Paris
1915	Apr. 5	Jess Willard	33	230	**Jack Johnson**	205½	KO 26	Havana
1916	Mar. 25	**Jess Willard**	34	225	Frank Moran	203	ND 10	NYC (Mad.Sq. Garden)
1919	July 4	Jack Dempsey	24	187	**Jess Willard**	245	TKO 4	Toledo, Ohio
1920	Sept. 6	**Jack Dempsey**	25	185	Billy Miske	187	KO 3	Benton Harbor, Mich.
1920	Dec. 14	**Jack Dempsey**	25	188¼	Bill Brennan	197	KO 12	NYC (Mad. Sq. Garden)
1921	July 2	**Jack Dempsey**	26	188	Georges Carpentier	172	KO 4	Jersey City, N.J.
1923	July 4	**Jack Dempsey**	28	188	Tommy Gibbons	175½	Ref 15	Shelby, Mont.
1923	Sept. 14	**Jack Dempsey**	28	192½	Luis Firpo	216½	KO 2	NYC (Polo Grounds)
1926	Sept. 23	Gene Tunney	29	189½	**Jack Dempsey**	190	Wu 10	Philadelphia
1927	Sept. 22	**Gene Tunney**	30	189½	Jack Dempsey	192½	Wu 10	Chicago
1928	July 26	**Gene Tunney****	31	192	Tom Heeney	203	TKO 11	NYC (Yankee Stadium)

*James J. Jeffries retired as champion on May 13, 1905, then came out of retirement to fight Jack Johnson for the title in 1910.
**Gene Tunney retired as champion in 1928.

Year	Date	Winner	Age	Wgt	Loser	Wgt	Result	Location
1930	June 12	Max Schmeling	24	188	Jack Sharkey	197	Disq. 4	NYC (Yankee Stadium)
1931	July 3	**Max Schmeling**	25	189	Young Stribling	186½	TKO 15	Cleveland
1932	June 21	Jack Sharkey	29	205	**Max Schmeling**	188	Ws 15	Long Island City, N.Y.
1933	June 29	Primo Carnera	26	260½	**Jack Sharkey**	201	KO 6	Long Island City, N.Y.
1933	Oct. 22	**Primo Carnera**	26	259½	Paulino Uzcudun	229¼	Wu 15	Rome
1934	Mar. 1	**Primo Carnera**	27	270	Tommy Loughran	184	Wu 15	Miami
1934	June 14	Max Baer	25	209½	**Primo Carnera**	263¼	TKO 11	Long Island City, N.Y.
1935	June 13	James J. Braddock	29	193¾	**Max Baer**	209	Wu 15	Long Island City, N.Y.
1937	June 22	Joe Louis	23	197¼	**James J. Braddock**	197	KO 8	Chicago
1937	Aug. 30	**Joe Louis**	23	197	Tommy Farr	204¼	Wu 15	NYC (Yankee Stadium)
1938	Feb. 23	**Joe Louis**	23	200	Nathan Mann	193½	KO 3	NYC (Mad. Sq. Garden)
1938	Apr. 1	**Joe Louis**	23	202½	Harry Thomas	196	KO 5	Chicago
1938	June 22	**Joe Louis**	24	198¾	Max Schmeling	193	KO 1	NYC (Yankee Stadium)
1939	Jan. 25	**Joe Louis**	24	200¼	John Henry Lewis	180¾	KO 1	NYC (Mad. Sq. Garden)
1939	Apr. 17	**Joe Louis**	24	201¼	Jack Roper	204¾	KO 1	Los Angeles
1939	June 28	**Joe Louis**	25	200¾	Tony Galento	233¾	TKO 4	NYC (Yankee Stadium)
1939	Sept. 20	**Joe Louis**	25	200	Bob Pastor	183	KO 11	Detroit
1940	Feb. 9	**Joe Louis**	25	203	Arturo Godoy	202	Ws 15	NYC (Mad. Sq. Garden)
1940	Mar. 29	**Joe Louis**	25	201½	Johnny Paychek	187½	KO 2	NYC (Mad. Sq. Garden)
1940	June 20	**Joe Louis**	26	199	Arturo Godoy	201¼	TKO 8	NYC (Yankee Stadium)
1940	Dec. 16	**Joe Louis**	26	202¼	Al McCoy	180¾	TKO 6	Boston
1941	Jan. 31	**Joe Louis**	26	202½	Red Burman	188	KO 5	NYC (Mad. Sq. Garden)
1941	Feb. 17	**Joe Louis**	26	203½	Gus Dorazio	193½	KO 2	Philadelphia
1941	Mar. 21	**Joe Louis**	26	202	Abe Simon	254½	TKO 13	Detroit
1941	Apr. 8	**Joe Louis**	26	203½	Tony Musto	199½	TKO 9	St. Louis
1941	May 23	**Joe Louis**	27	201½	Buddy Baer	237½	Disq. 7	Washington, D.C.
1941	June 18	**Joe Louis**	27	199½	Billy Conn	174	KO 13	NYC (Polo Grounds)
1941	Sept. 29	**Joe Louis**	27	202¼	Lou Nova	202½	TKO 6	NYC (Polo Grounds)
1942	Jan. 9	**Joe Louis**	27	206¾	Buddy Baer	250	KO 1	NYC (Mad. Sq. Garden)
1942	Mar. 27	**Joe Louis**	27	207½	Abe Simon	255½	KO 6	NYC (Mad. Sq. Garden)

1942-45 World War II

Year	Date	Winner	Age	Wgt	Loser	Wgt	Result	Location
1946	June 9	**Joe Louis**	32	207	Billy Conn	187	KO 8	NYC (Yankee Stadium)
1946	Sept. 18	**Joe Louis**	32	211	Tami Mauriello	198½	KO 1	NYC (Yankee Stadium)
1947	Dec. 5	**Joe Louis**	33	211½	Jersey Joe Walcott	194½	Ws 15	NYC (Mad. Sq. Garden)
1948	June 25	**Joe Louis***	34	213½	Jersey Joe Walcott	194¾	KO 11	NYC (Yankee Stadium)
1949	June 22	**Ezzard Charles**	27	181¾	Jersey Joe Walcott	195½	Wu 15	Chicago
1949	Aug. 10	**Ezzard Charles**	28	180	Gus Lesnevich	182	TKO 8	NYC (Yankee Stadium)
1949	Oct. 14	**Ezzard Charles**	28	182	Pat Valentino	188½	KO 8	San Francisco
1950	Aug. 15	**Ezzard Charles**	29	183¼	Freddie Beshore	184½	TKO 14	Buffalo
1950	Sept. 27	**Ezzard Charles**	29	184½	Joe Louis	218	Wu 15	NYC (Yankee Stadium)
1950	Dec. 5	**Ezzard Charles**	29	185	Nick Barone	178½	KO 11	Cincinnati
1951	Jan. 12	**Ezzard Charles**	29	185	Lee Oma	193	TKO 10	NYC (Mad. Sq. Garden)
1951	Mar. 7	**Ezzard Charles**	29	186	Jersey Joe Walcott	193	Wu 15	Detroit
1951	May 30	**Ezzard Charles**	29	182	Joey Maxim	181½	Wu 15	Chicago
1951	July 18	Jersey Joe Walcott	37	194	**Ezzard Charles**	182	KO 7	Pittsburgh
1952	June 5	**Jersey Joe Walcott**	38	196	Ezzard Charles	191½	Wu 15	Philadelphia
1952	Sept. 23	Rocky Marciano	29	184	**Jersey Joe Walcott**	196	KO 13	Philadelphia
1953	May 15	**Rocky Marciano**	29	184½	Jersey Joe Walcott	197¾	KO 1	Chicago
1953	Sept. 24	**Rocky Marciano**	30	185	Roland LaStarza	184¾	TKO 11	NYC (Polo Grounds)
1954	June 17	**Rocky Marciano**	30	187½	Ezzard Charles	185½	Wu 15	NYC (Yankee Stadium)
1954	Sept. 17	**Rocky Marciano**	31	187	Ezzard Charles	192½	KO 8	NYC (Yankee Stadium)
1955	May 16	**Rocky Marciano**	31	189	Don Cockell	205	TKO 9	San Francisco
1955	Sept. 21	**Rocky Marciano****	32	188¼	Archie Moore	188	KO 9	NYC (Yankee Stadium)
1956	Nov. 30	Floyd Patterson	21	182¼	Archie Moore	187¾	KO 5	Chicago
1957	July 29	**Floyd Patterson**	22	184	Tommy Jackson	192½	TKO 10	NYC (Polo Grounds)
1957	Aug. 22	**Floyd Patterson**	22	187¼	Pete Rademacher	202	KO 6	Seattle
1958	Aug. 18	**Floyd Patterson**	23	184½	Roy Harris	194	TKO 13	Los Angeles
1959	May 1	**Floyd Patterson**	24	182½	Brian London	206	KO 11	Indianapolis
1959	June 26	Ingemar Johansson	26	196	**Floyd Patterson**	182	TKO 3	NYC (Yankee Stadium)

*Joe Louis retired as champion on Mar. 1, 1949, then came out of retirement to fight Ezzard Charles for the title in 1950.
**Rocky Marciano retired as undefeated champion on Apr. 27, 1956.

Year	Date	Winner	Age	Wgt	Loser	Wgt	Result	Location
1960	June 20	Floyd Patterson	25	190	**Ingemar Johansson**	194¾	KO 5	NYC (Polo Grounds)
1961	Mar. 13	**Floyd Patterson**	26	194¾	Ingemar Johansson	206½	KO 6	Miami Beach
1961	Dec. 4	**Floyd Patterson**	26	188½	Tom McNeeley	197	KO 4	Toronto
1962	Sept. 25	Sonny Liston	30	214	**Floyd Patterson**	189	KO 1	Chicago
1963	July 22	**Sonny Liston**	31	215	Floyd Patterson	194½	KO 1	Las Vegas
1964	Feb. 25	Cassius Clay**	22	210½	**Sonny Liston**	218	TKO 7	Miami Beach
1965	Mar. 5	Ernie Terrell WBA	25	199	Eddie Machen	192	Wu 15	Chicago
1965	May 25	**Muhammad Ali**	23	206	Sonny Liston	215¼	KO 1	Lewiston, Maine
1965	Nov. 1	Ernie Terrell WBA	26	206	George Chuvalo	209	Wu 15	Toronto
1965	Nov. 22	**Muhammad Ali**	23	210	Floyd Patterson	196¾	TKO 12	Las Vegas
1966	Mar. 29	**Muhammad Ali**	24	214½	George Chuvalo	216	Wu 15	Toronto
1966	May 21	**Muhammad Ali**	24	201½	Henry Cooper	188	TKO 6	London
1966	June 28	Ernie Terrell WBA	27	209½	Doug Jones	187½	Wu 15	Houston
1966	Aug. 6	**Muhammad Ali**	24	209½	Brian London	201½	KO 3	London
1966	Sept. 10	**Muhammad Ali**	24	203½	Karl Mildenberger	194¼	TKO 12	Frankfurt, W. Ger.
1966	Nov. 14	**Muhammad Ali**	24	212¾	Cleveland Williams	210½	TKO 3	Houston
1967	Feb. 6	**Muhammad Ali**	25	212¼	Ernie Terrell WBA	212¼	Wu 15	Houston
1967	Mar. 22	**Muhammad Ali**	25	211½	Zora Folley	202½	KO 7	NYC (Mad. Sq. Garden)
1968	Mar. 4	Joe Frazier	24	204½	Buster Mathis	243½	TKO 11	NYC (Mad. Sq. Garden)
1968	Apr. 27	Jimmy Ellis	28	197	Jerry Quarry	195	Wm 15	Oakland
1968	June 24	Joe Frazier NY	24	203½	Manuel Ramos	208	TKO 2	NYC (Mad. Sq. Garden)
1968	Aug. 14	Jimmy Ellis WBA	28	198	Floyd Patterson	188	Ref 15	Stockholm
1968	Dec. 10	Joe Frazier NY	24	203	Oscar Bonavena	207	Wu 15	Philadelphia
1969	Apr. 22	Joe Frazier NY	25	204½	Dave Zyglewicz	190½	KO 1	Houston
1969	June 23	Joe Frazier NY	25	203½	Jerry Quarry	198½	TKO 8	NYC (Mad. Sq. Garden)
1970	Feb. 16	Joe Frazier NY	26	205	Jimmy Ellis WBA	201	TKO 5	NYC (Mad. Sq. Garden)
1970	Nov. 18	**Joe Frazier**	26	209	Bob Foster	188	KO 2	Detroit
1971	Mar. 8	**Joe Frazier**	27	205½	Muhammad Ali	215	Wu 15	NYC (Mad. Sq. Garden)
1972	Jan. 15	**Joe Frazier**	28	215½	Terry Daniels	195	TKO 4	New Orleans
1972	May 26	**Joe Frazier**	28	217½	Ron Stander	218	TKO 5	Omaha, Neb.
1973	Jan. 22	George Foreman	24	217½	**Joe Frazier**	214	TKO 2	Kingston, Jamaica
1973	Sept. 1	**George Foreman**	24	219½	Jose (King) Roman	196½	KO 1	Tokyo
1974	Mar. 26	**George Foreman**	25	224¾	Ken Norton	212¾	TKO 2	Caracas, Venezuela
1974	Oct. 30	Muhammad Ali	32	216½	**George Foreman**	220	KO 8	Kinshasa, Zaire
1975	Mar. 24	**Muhammad Ali**	33	223½	Chuck Wepner	225	TKO 15	Cleveland
1975	May 16	**Muhammad Ali**	33	224½	Ron Lyle	219	TKO 11	Las Vegas
1975	July 1	**Muhammad Ali**	33	224½	Joe Bugner	230	Wu 15	Kuala Lumpur, Malaysia
1975	Oct. 1	**Muhammad Ali**	33	224½	Joe Frazier	215	TKO 14	Manila, Philippines
1976	Feb. 20	**Muhammad Ali**	34	226	Jean Pierre Coopman	206	KO 5	San Juan, P.R.
1976	Apr. 30	**Muhammad Ali**	34	230	Jimmy Young	209	Wu 15	Landover, Md.
1976	May 24	**Muhammad Ali**	34	220	Richard Dunn	206½	TKO 5	Munich, W. Ger.
1976	Sept. 28	**Muhammad Ali**	34	221	Ken Norton	217½	Wu 15	NYC (Yankee Stadium)
1977	May 16	**Muhammad Ali**	35	221¼	Alfredo Evangelista	209¼	Wu 15	Landover, Md.
1977	Sept. 29	**Muhammad Ali**	35	225	Earnie Shavers	211¼	Wu 15	NYC (Mad. Sq. Garden)
1978	Feb. 15	Leon Spinks	24	197¼	**Muhammad Ali**	224¼	Ws 15	Las Vegas
1978	June 9	Larry Holmes	28	209	Ken Norton WBC††	220	Ws 15	Las Vegas
1978	Sept. 15	Muhammad Ali†	36	221	**Leon Spinks**	201	Wu 15	New Orleans
1978	Nov. 10	Larry Holmes WBC	29	214	Alfredo Evangelista	208¼	KO 7	Las Vegas
1979	Mar. 23	Larry Holmes WBC	29	214	Osvaldo Ocasio	207	TKO 7	Las Vegas
1979	June 22	Larry Holmes WBC	29	215	Mike Weaver	202	TKO 12	NYC (Mad. Sq. Garden)
1979	Sept. 28	Larry Holmes WBC	29	210	Earnie Shavers	211	TKO 11	Las Vegas
1979	Oct. 20	John Tate	24	240	Gerrie Coetzee	222	Wu 15	Pretoria, S. Africa
1980	Feb. 3	Larry Holmes WBC	30	213½	Lorenzo Zanon	215	TKO 6	Las Vegas
1980	Mar. 31	Mike Weaver	27	232	John Tate WBA	232	KO 15	Knoxville, Tenn.
1980	Mar. 31	Larry Holmes WBC	30	211	Leroy Jones	254½	TKO 8	Las Vegas
1980	July 7	Larry Holmes WBC	30	214¼	Scott LeDoux	226	TKO 7	Minneapolis
1980	Oct. 2	Larry Holmes WBC	30	211½	Muhammad Ali	217½	TKO 11	Las Vegas
1980	Oct. 25	Mike Weaver WBA	28	210	Gerrie Coetzee	226½	KO 13	Sun City, S. Africa

**After defeating Liston, Cassius Clay announced that he had changed his name to Muhammad Ali. He was later stripped of his title by the WBA and most state boxing commissions after refusing induction into the U.S. Army on Apr. 28, 1967.

† Muhammad Ali retired as champion on June 27, 1979, then came out of retirement to fight Larry Holmes for the title in 1980.

†† WBC recognized Ken Norton as world champion when Leon Spinks refused to meet Norton before Spinks' rematch with Muhammad Ali. Norton had scored a 15-round split decision over Jimmy Young on Nov. 5, 1977 in Las Vegas.

Year	Date	Winner	Age	Wgt	Loser	Wgt	Result	Location
1981	Apr. 11	**Larry Holmes**	31	215	Trevor Berbick	215½	Wu 15	Las Vegas
1981	June 12	**Larry Holmes**	31	212½	Leon Spinks	200¼	TKO 3	Detroit
1981	Oct. 3	Mike Weaver WBA	29	215	James (Quick) Tillis	209	Wu 15	Rosemont, Ill.
1981	Nov. 6	**Larry Holmes**	32	213¼	Renaldo Snipes	215¾	TKO 11	Pittsburgh
1982	June 11	**Larry Holmes**	32	212½	Gerry Cooney	225½	TKO 13	Las Vegas
1982	Nov. 26	**Larry Holmes**	33	217½	Randall (Tex) Cobb	234¼	Wu 15	Houston
1982	Dec. 10	Michael Dokes	24	216	Mike Weaver WBA	209¾	TKO 1	Las Vegas
1983	Mar. 27	**Larry Holmes**	33	221	Lucien Rodriguez	209	Wu 12	Scranton, Pa.
1983	May 20	Michael Dokes WBA	24	223	Mike Weaver	218½	Draw 15	Las Vegas
1983	May 20	**Larry Holmes**	33	213	Tim Witherspoon	219½	Ws 12	Las Vegas
1983	Sept. 10	**Larry Holmes**	33	223	Scott Frank	211¼	TKO 5	Atlantic City
1983	Sept. 23	Gerrie Coetzee	28	215	Michael Dokes WBA	217	KO 10	Richfield, Ohio
1983	Nov. 25	**Larry Holmes**	34	219	Marvis Frazier	200	TKO 1	Las Vegas
1984	Mar. 9	Tim Witherspoon*	26	220¼	Greg Page	239½	Wm 12	Las Vegas
1984	Aug. 31	Pinklon Thomas	26	216	Tim Witherspoon WBC	217	Wm 12	Las Vegas
1984	Nov. 9	**Larry Holmes** IBF	35	221½	Bonecrusher Smith	227	TKO 12	Las Vegas
1984	Dec. 1	Greg Page	26	236½	Gerrie Coetzee WBA	218	KO 8	Sun City, S. Africa
1985	Mar. 15	**Larry Holmes** IBF	35	223½	David Bey	233¼	TKO 10	Las Vegas
1985	Apr. 29	Tony Tubbs	26	229	Greg Page WBA	239½	Wu 15	Buffalo
1985	May 20	**Larry Holmes** IBF	35	224¼	Carl Williams	215	Wu 15	Las Vegas
1985	June 15	Pinklon Thomas WBC	27	220¼	Mike Weaver	221¼	KO 8	Las Vegas
1985	Sept. 21	Michael Spinks	29	200	**Larry Holmes** IBF	221½	Wu 15	Las Vegas
1986	Jan. 17	Tim Witherspoon	28	227	Tony Tubbs WBA	229	Wm 15	Atlanta
1986	Mar. 22	Trevor Berbick	33	218½	Pinklon Thomas WBC	222¾	Wu 15	Las Vegas
1986	Apr. 19	**Michael Spinks** IBF	29	205	Larry Holmes	223	Ws 15	Las Vegas
1986	July 19	Tim Witherspoon WBA	28	234¾	Frank Bruno	228	TKO 11	Wembley, England
1986	Sept. 6	**Michael Spinks** IBF	30	201	Steffen Tangstad	214¾	TKO 4	Las Vegas
1986	Nov. 22	Mike Tyson	20	221¼	Trevor Berbick WBC	218½	TKO 2	Las Vegas
1986	Dec. 12	Bonecrusher Smith	33	228½	Tim Witherspoon WBA	233½	TKO 1	NYC (Mad. Sq. Garden)
1987	Mar. 7	Mike Tyson WBC	20	219	Bonecrusher Smith WBA	233	Wu 12	Las Vegas
1987	May 30	Mike Tyson	20	218¾	Pinklon Thomas	217¾	TKO 6	Las Vegas
1987	May 30	Tony Tucker**	28	222¼	Buster Douglas	227¼	TKO 10	Las Vegas
1987	June 15	**Michael Spinks**†	30	208¾	Gerry Cooney	238	TKO 5	Atlantic City
1987	Aug. 1	Mike Tyson	21	221	Tony Tucker IBF	221	Wu 12	Las Vegas
1987	Oct. 16	Mike Tyson	21	216	Tyrell Biggs	228¾	TKO 7	Atlantic City
1988	Jan. 22	Mike Tyson	21	215¾	Larry Holmes	225¾	TKO 4	Atlantic City
1988	Mar. 20	Mike Tyson	21	216¼	Tony Tubbs	238¼	KO 2	Tokyo
1988	June 27	Mike Tyson	21	218¼	**Michael Spinks**	212¼	KO 1	Atlantic City
1989	Feb. 25	**Mike Tyson**	22	218	Frank Bruno	228	TKO 5	Las Vegas
1989	July 21	**Mike Tyson**	23	219¼	Carl Williams	218	TKO 1	Atlantic City
1990	Feb. 11	Buster Douglas	29	231½	**Mike Tyson**	220½	KO 10	Tokyo
1990	Oct. 25	Evander Holyfield	28	208	**Buster Douglas**	246	KO 3	Las Vegas
1991	Apr. 19	**Evander Holyfield**	28	208	George Foreman	257	Wu 12	Atlantic City
1991	Nov. 23	**Evander Holyfield**	29	210	Bert Cooper	215	TKO 7	Atlanta
1992	June 19	**Evander Holyfield**	29	210	Larry Holmes	233	Wu 12	Las Vegas
1992	Nov. 13	Riddick Bowe	25	235	**Evander Holyfield**	205	Wu 12	Las Vegas
1993	Feb. 6	**Riddick Bowe**	25	243	Michael Dokes	244	TKO 1	NYC (Mad. Sq. Garden)
1993	May 8	Lennox Lewis WBC‡	27	235	Tony Tucker	235	Wu 12	Las Vegas
1993	May 22	**Riddick Bowe**	25	244	Jesse Ferguson	224	TKO 2	Washington, D.C.
1993	Oct. 1	Lennox Lewis WBC	28	233	Frank Bruno	238	TKO 7	Cardiff, Wales
1993	Nov. 6	Evander Holyfield	31	217	**Riddick Bowe** WBA/IBF	246	Wm 12	Las Vegas
1994	Apr. 22	Michael Moorer	26	214	**Evander Holyfield**	214	Wm 12	Las Vegas
1994	May 6	Lennox Lewis WBC	28	235	Phil Jackson	218	TKO 8	Atlantic City
1994	Sept. 25	Oliver McCall	29	231¼	**Lennox Lewis** WBC	238	TKO 2	London

*WBC recognized winner of Mar. 9, 1984 fight between Tim Witherspoon and Greg Page as world champion after Larry Holmes relinquished title in dispute. IBF then recognized Holmes.

**IBF recognized winner of May 30, 1987 fight between Tony Tucker and James (Buster) Douglas as world champion after Michael Spinks relinquished title in dispute.

†The July 15, 1987 Spinks-Cooney fight was not an official championship bout because it was not sanctioned by any boxing associations, councils or federations.

‡WBC recognized Lennox Lewis as world champion when Riddick Bowe gave up that portion of his title on Dec. 14, 1992, rather than fight Lewis, the WBC's mandatory challenger.

Year	Date	Winner	Age	Wgt	Loser	Wgt	Result	Location
1994	Nov. 5	George Foreman*	45	250	**Michael Moorer**	222	KO 10	Las Vegas
1995	Apr. 8	Oliver McCall WBC	29	231	Larry Holmes	236	Wu 12	Las Vegas
1995	Apr. 8	Bruce Seldon*	28	236	Tony Tucker	240	TKO 7	Las Vegas
1995	Apr. 22	**George Foreman***	46	256	Axel Schulz	221	Ws 12	Las Vegas
1995	Aug. 19	Bruce Seldon WBA	28	234	Joe Hipp	223	TKO 10	Las Vegas
1995	Sept. 2	Frank Bruno	33	248	Oliver McCall WBC	235	Wu 12	London
1995	Dec. 9	Frans Botha**	27	237	Axel Schulz	222	Wu 12	Stuttgart, GER
1996	Mar. 16	Mike Tyson	29	220	Frank Bruno WBC	247	TKO 3	Las Vegas
1996	June 22	Michael Moorer**	28	222	Axel Schulz	223	Ws 12	Dortmund, GER
1996	Sept. 7	Mike Tyson WBC†	30	219	Bruce Seldon WBA	229	TKO 1	Las Vegas
1996	Nov. 9	Evander Holyfield	34	215	**Mike Tyson** WBA	222	TKO 11	Las Vegas
1997	Feb. 7	Lennox Lewis†	31	251	Oliver McCall	237	TKO 5	Las Vegas
1997	Mar. 29	Michael Moorer IBF	29	212	Vaughn Bean	212	Wm 12	Las Vegas
1997	June 28	**Evander Holyfield** WBA‡	34	218	Mike Tyson	218	Disq. 3	Las Vegas
1997	July 12	Lennox Lewis WBC	31	242	Henry Akinwande	237½	Disq. 5	Stateline, Nev.
1997	Oct. 4	Lennox Lewis WBC	32	244	Andrew Golota	244	TKO 1	Atlantic City
1997	Nov. 8	Evander Holyfield WBA	35	214	Michael Moorer IBF	223	TKO 8	Las Vegas
1998	Mar. 28	Lennox Lewis WBC	32	243	Shannon Briggs	228	TKO 5	Atlantic City
1998	Sept. 19	**Evander Holyfield** WBA/IBF	35	217	Vaughn Bean	231	Wu 12	Atlanta
1998	Sept. 26	Lennox Lewis WBC	33	250	Zeljko Mavrovic	220	Wu 12	Uncasville, Conn.
1999	Mar. 13	Lennox Lewis WBC	33	246	**Evander Holyfield** WBA/IBF	215	Draw 12	NYC (Mad. Sq. Garden)

*George Foreman won WBA and IBF championships when he beat Michael Moorer on Nov. 5, 1994. He was stripped of WBA title on Mar. 4, 1995, when he refused to fight No. 1 contender Tony Tucker, and he relinquished IBF title on June 29, 1995, rather than give Axel Schulz a rematch. Tucker lost to Bruce Seldon in their April 8 fight for vacant WBA title.

**Frans Botha won the vacant IBF title with a controversial 12–round decision over Axel Schulz on Dec. 9, 1995, but after legal sparring, was eventually stripped of the IBF belt for using anabolic steroids. Moorer then claimed the revacated title with his June 22, 1996 win over Schulz.

†Mike Tyson won the WBC belt from Frank Bruno on Mar. 16, 1996 and still held it at the time of his Sept. 7, 1996 win over Bruce Seldon (although it was not at risk for that fight) but was forced to relinquish the title after the bout for not fighting mandatory challenge Lennox Lewis. Tyson also paid Lewis $4 million to step aside and allow the Tyson-Seldon bout to take place. Lewis then fought Oliver McCall for the vacant WBC belt. The fight was stopped 55 seconds into round 5 because, inexplicably, McCall was visibly distraught and stopped throwing punches.

‡Holyfield won the bout by disqualification and retained the WBA belt after Tyson spit out his mouthpiece and bit off a piece of Holyfield's ear. Tyson had received a two-point deduction from referee Mills Lane and after a stern warning and a short delay the fight was allowed to continue. Later in round 3, he bit Holyfield's other ear and Tyson was disqualified.

All-Time Heavyweight Upsets

Buster Douglas was a 42-1 underdog when he defeated previously-unbeaten heavyweight champion Mike Tyson on Feb. 10, 1990. That 10th-round knockout ranks as the biggest upset in boxing history. By comparison, 45-year-old George Foreman was only a 3-1 underdog before he unexpectedly won the title from Michael Moorer on Nov. 5, 1994.

Here are the best-known upsets in the annals of the heavyweight division. All fights were for the world championship except the Max Schmeling-Joe Louis bout.

Date	Winner	Loser	Result	KO Time	Location
9/7/1892	James J. Corbett	John L. Sullivan	KO 21	1:30	Olympic Club, New Orleans
4/5/1915	Jess Willard	Jack Johnson	KO 26	1:26	Mariano Race Track, Havana
9/23/26	Gene Tunney	Jack Dempsey	Wu 10	–	Sesquicentennial Stadium, Phila.
6/13/35	James J. Braddock	Max Baer	Wu 15	–	Mad.Sq.Garden Bowl, L.I. City
6/19/36	Max Schmeling	Joe Louis	KO 12	2:29	Yankee Stadium, New York
7/18/51	Jersey Joe Walcott	Ezzard Charles	KO 7	0:55	Forbes Field, Pittsburgh
6/26/59	Ingemar Johansson	Floyd Patterson	TKO 3	2:03	Yankee Stadium, New York
2/25/64	Cassius Clay	Sonny Liston	TKO 7	*	Convention Hall, Miami Beach
10/30/74	Muhammad Ali	George Foreman	KO 8	2:58	20th of May Stadium, Zaire
2/15/78	Leon Spinks	Muhammad Ali	Ws 15	–	Hilton Pavilion, Las Vegas
9/21/85	Michael Spinks	Larry Holmes	Wu 15	–	Riviera Hotel, Las Vegas
2/10/90	Buster Douglas	Mike Tyson	KO 10	1:23	Tokyo Dome, Tokyo
11/5/94	George Foreman	Michael Moorer	KO 10	2:03	MGM Grand, Las Vegas
11/9/96	Evander Holyfield	Mike Tyson	TKO 11	0:37	MGM Grand, Las Vegas

*Liston failed to answer bell for Round 7.

Muhammad Ali's Career Pro Record

Born Cassius Marcellus Clay, Jr. on Jan. 17, 1942, in Louisville; Amateur record of 100-5; won light-heavyweight gold medal at 1960 Olympic Games; Pro record of 56-5 with 37 KOs in 61 fights.

1960

Date	Opponent (location)	Result
Oct. 29	Tunney Hunsaker, Louisville	Wu 6
Dec. 27	Herb Siler, Miami Beach	TKO 4

1961

Date	Opponent (location)	Result
Jan. 17	Tony Esperti, Miami Beach	TKO 3
Feb. 7	Jim Robinson, Miami Beach	TKO 1
Feb. 21	Donnie Fleeman, Miami Beach	TKO 7
Apr. 19	Lamar Clark, Louisville	KO 2
June 26	Duke Sabedong, Las Vegas	Wu 10
July 22	Alonzo Johnson, Louisville	Wu 10
Oct. 7	Alex Miteff, Louisville	TKO 6
Nov. 29	Willi Besmanoff, Louisville	TKO 7

1962

Date	Opponent (location)	Result
Feb. 10	Sonny Banks, New York	TKO 4
Feb. 28	Don Warner, Miami Beach	TKO 4
Apr. 23	George Logan, Los Angeles	TKO 4
May 19	Billy Daniels, Los Angeles	TKO 7
July 20	Alejandro Lavorante, Los Angeles	KO 5
Nov. 15	Archie Moore, Los Angeles	KO 4

1963

Date	Opponent (location)	Result
Jan. 24	Charlie Powell, Pittsburgh	KO 3
Mar. 13	Doug Jones, New York	Wu 10
June 18	Henry Cooper, London	TKO 5

1964

Date	Opponent (location)	Result
Feb. 25	Sonny Liston, Miami Beach	TKO 7
	(won World Heavyweight title)	

After the fight, Clay announces he is a member of the Black Muslim religious sect and has changed his name to Muhammad Ali.

1965

Date	Opponent (location)	Result
May 25	Sonny Liston, Lewiston, Me	KO 1
Nov. 22	Floyd Patterson, Las Vegas	TKO 12

1966

Date	Opponent (location)	Result
Mar. 29	George Chuvalo, Toronto	Wu 15
May 21	Henry Cooper, London	TKO 6
Aug. 6	Brian London, London	KO 3
Sept. 10	Karl Mildenberger, Frankfurt	TKO 12
Nov. 12	Cleveland Williams, Houston	TKO 3

1967

Date	Opponent (location)	Result
Feb. 6	Ernie Terrell, Houston	Wu 15
Mar. 22	Zora Folley, New York	KO 7
Apr. 28	Refuses induction into U.S. Army and is stripped of world title by WBA and most state commissions the next day.	
June 20	Found guilty of draft evasion in Houston; fined $10,000 and sentenced to 5 years; remains free pending appeals, but is barred from the ring.	

1968-69 (Inactive)

1970

Date	Opponent (location)	Result
Feb. 3	Announces retirement.	
Oct. 26	Jerry Quarry, Atlanta	TKO 3
Dec. 7	Oscar Bonavena, New York	TKO 15

1971

Date	Opponent (location)	Result
Mar. 8	Joe Frazier, New York	Lu 15
	(for World Heavyweight title)	
June 28	U.S. Supreme Court reverses Ali's 1967 conviction saying he had been drafted improperly.	
July 26	Jimmy Ellis, Houston	TKO 12
	(won vacant NABF Heavyweight title)	
Nov. 17	Buster Mathis, Houston	Wu 12
Dec. 26	Jurgen Blin, Zurich	KO 7

1972

Date	Opponent (location)	Result
Apr. 1	Mac Foster, Tokyo	Wu 15
May 1	George Chuvalo, Vancouver	Wu 12
June 27	Jerry Quarry, Las Vegas	TKO 7
July 19	Al (Blue) Lewis, Dublin, Ire	TKO 11
Sept. 20	Floyd Patterson, New York	TKO 7
Nov. 21	Bob Foster, Stateline, Nev	TKO 8

1973

Date	Opponent (location)	Result
Feb. 14	Joe Bugner, Las Vegas	Wu 12
Mar. 31	Ken Norton, San Diego	Ls 12
	(lost NABF Heavyweight title)	
Sept. 10	Ken Norton, Inglewood, Calif	Ws 12
	(regained NABF Heavyweight title)	
Oct. 20	Rudi Lubbers, Jakarta, Indonesia	Wu 12

1974

Date	Opponent (location)	Result
Jan. 28	Joe Frazier, New York	Wu 12
Oct. 30	George Foreman, Kinshasa, Zaire	KO 8
	(regained World Heavyweight title)	

1975

Date	Opponent (location)	Result
Mar. 24	Chuck Wepner, Cleveland	TKO 15
May 16	Ron Lyle, Las Vegas	TKO 11
June 30	Joe Bugner, Kuala Lumpur, Malaysia	Wu 15
Oct. 1	Joe Frazier, Manila, Philippines	TKO 14

1976

Date	Opponent (location)	Result
Feb. 20	Jean-Pierre Coopman, San Juan	KO 5
Apr. 30	Jimmy Young, Landover, Md	Wu 15
May 24	Richard Dunn, Munich	TKO 5
Sept. 28	Ken Norton, New York	Wu 15

1977

Date	Opponent (location)	Result
May 16	Alfredo Evangelista, Landover	Wu 15
Sept. 29	Earnie Shavers, New York	Wu 15

1978

Date	Opponent (location)	Result
Feb. 15	Leon Spinks, Las Vegas	Ls 15
	(lost World Heavyweight title)	
Sept. 15	Leon Spinks, New Orleans	Wu 15
	(regained World Heavyweight title)	

1979

Date
June 27 Announces retirement.

1980

Date	Opponent (location)	Result
Oct. 2	Larry Holmes, Las Vegas	TKO by 11

1981

Date	Opponent (location)	Result
Dec. 11	Trevor Berbick, Nassau	Lu 10
	(retires after fight)	

Foreman and Frazier

The career pro records of George Foreman and Joe Frazier as of Oct. 1, 1999.

George Foreman

Born: Jan. 10, 1949 in Marshall, Tex.

Pro record: 75-5-0, 68 KOs

No	Date	Opponent, location	Result
1	6/23/69	Don Waldhelm, New York	KO 3
2	7/1/69	Fred Ashew, Houston	KO 1
3	7/14/69	Sylvester Dullaire, Wash., D.C.	KO 2
4	8/18/69	Chuck Wepner, New York	TKO 3
5	9/18/69	John Carroll, Seattle	KO 1
6	9/23/69	Cookie Wallace, Houston	KO 2
7	10/7/69	Vernon Clay, Houston	TKO 2
8	10/31/69	Roberto Davila, New York	Wu 8
9	11/5/69	Leo Peterson, Scranton	KO 4
10	11/18/69	Max Martinez, Houston	KO 2
11	12/6/69	Bob Hazelton, Las Vegas	KO 1
12	12/16/69	Levi Forte, Miami Beach	Wu 10
13	12/18/69	Gary Wilder, Seattle	TKO 1
14	1/6/70	Charley Polite, Houston	KO 4
15	1/26/70	Jack O'Halloran, New York	KO 5
16	2/16/70	Gregorio Peralta, New York	Wu 10
17	3/31/70	Rufus Brassell, Houston	KO 1
18	4/17/70	James J. Woody, New York	TKO 3
19	4/29/70	Aaron Easting, Cleveland	TKO 4
20	5/16/70	George Johnson, Inglewood	KO 7
21	7/20/70	Roger Russell, Philadelphia	TKO 1
22	8/4/70	George Chuvalo, New York	TKO 3
23	11/3/70	Lou Bailey, Oklahoma City	KO 3
24	11/18/70	Boone Kirkman, New York	TKO 2
25	12/19/70	Mel Turnbow, Seattle	TKO 1
26	2/8/71	Charlie Boston, St. Paul, Minn.	KO 1
27	4/3/71	Stanford Harris, Lake Geneva	KO 2
28	5/10/71	Gregorio Peralta, Oakland	TKO 10
29	9/14/91	Vic Scott, El Paso	KO 1
30	9/21/71	Leroy Caldwell, Beaumont, Tex.	KO 2
31	10/7/71	Ollie Wilson, San Antonio	TKO 2
32	10/29/71	Luis F. Pires, New York	KO 5
33	2/29/72	Murphy Goodwin, Austin, Tex.	KO 2
34	3/7/72	Clarence Boone, Beaumont, Tex.	TKO 2
35	4/10/72	Ted Gullick, Inglewood	KO 2
36	5/11/72	Miguel A. Paez, Oakland	KO 2
37	10/10/72	Terry Sorrels, Salt Lake City	KO 2
38	1/22/73	Joe Frazier, Kingston, Jamaica	TKO 2
		(won World Heavyweight title)	
39	9/1/73	Jose Roman, Tokyo	KO 1
40	3/26/74	Ken Norton, Caracus, Venezuela	TKO 2
41	10/30/74	Muhammad Ali, Kinshasa, Zaire	KO by 8
		(lost World Heavyweight title)	
42	1/24/76	Ron Lyle, Las Vegas	KO 5
43	6/15/76	Joe Frazier, Uniondale, N.Y.	TKO 5
44	8/14/76	Scott Le Doux, Utica, N.Y.	KO 3
45	10/15/76	Dino Denis, Hollywood, Fla.	TKO 4
46	1/22/77	Pedro Agosto, Pensacola, Fla.	TKO 4
47	3/17/77	Jimmy Young, Hato Rey, P.R.	Lu 12
		(retired after fight)	
48	3/9/87	Steve Zouski, Sacramento	TKO 4
		(first fight of comeback)	
49	7/9/87	Charles Hostetter, Oakland	KO 3
50	9/15/87	Bobby Crabree, Springfield, Mo.	TKO 6
51	11/21/87	Tim Anderson, Orlando	TKO 4
52	12/18/87	Rocky Sekorski, Las Vegas	TKO 3
53	1/23/88	Tom Trimm, Orlando	TKO 1
54	2/5/88	Guido Trane, Las Vegas	TKO 5
55	3/19/88	Dwight Qawi, Las Vegas	TKO 7
56	5/21/88	Frank Williams, Anchorage	KO 3
57	6/26/88	Carlos Hernandez, Atlantic City	TKO 4
58	8/25/88	Ladislao Mijangos, Ft. Myers	TKO 2
59	9/10/88	Bobby Hitz, Auburn Hills, Mich.	KO 1
60	10/27/88	Tony Fulilangi, Marshall, Tex.	TKO 2
61	12/28/88	David Jaco, Bakersfield, Calif.	KO 1

No	Date	Opponent, location	Result
62	1/26/89	Mark Young, Rochester, N.Y.	TKO 7
63	2/16/89	Manuel de Almeida, Orlando	TKO 3
64	4/30/89	J.B. Williamson, Galveston, Tex.	TKO 5
65	6/1/89	Bert Cooper, Phoenix	TKO 3
66	7/20/89	Everett Martin, Tucson	Wu 10
67	1/15/90	Gerry Cooney, Atlantic City	KO 2
68	4/17/90	Mike Jameson, Stateline, Nev.	TKO 4
69	6/16/90	Adilson Rodrigues, Las Vegas	KO 2
70	7/31/90	Ken Lakusta, Edmonton	KO 3
71	9/25/90	Terry Anderson, Millwall, England	KO 1
72	4/19/91	Evander Holyfield, Atlantic City	Lu 12
		(for World Heavyweight title)	
73	12/7/91	Jimmy Ellis, Reno, Nev.	TKO 3
74	4/11/92	Alex Stewart, Las Vegas	Wm 10
75	1/16/93	Pierre Coetzer, Reno, Nev.	TKO 8
76	6/7/93	Tommy Morrison, Las Vegas	Lu 12
77	11/5/94	Michael Moorer, Las Vegas	KO 10
		(won WBA/IBF Heavyweight titles)	
78	4/22/95	Axel Schulz, Las Vegas	Wm 12
79	11/3/96	Crawford Grimsley, Tokyo	Wu 12
80	11/22/97	Shannon Briggs, Atlantic City	Lm 12

Joe Frazier

Born: Jan. 12, 1944 in Beaufort, S.C.

Pro record: 32-4-1, 27 KOs

No	Date	Opponent	Result
1	8/16/65	Woody Gross	TKO 1
2	9/20/65	Michael Bruce	KO 3
3	9/28/65	Ray Staples	KO 2
4	11/11/65	Abe Davis	KO 1
5	1/17/66	Mel Turnbow	KO 1
6	3/4/66	Dick Wipperman	TKO 5
7	4/4/66	Charley Polite	TKO 2
8	4/28/66	Don Smith	KO 3
9	5/19/66	Chuck Leslie	KO 3
10	5/26/66	Memphis Jones	KO 1
11	7/25/66	Billy Daniels	TKO 6
12	9/21/66	Oscar Bonavena	Wu 10
13	11/21/66	Eddie Machen	TKO 10
14	2/21/67	Doug Jones	KO 6
15	4/11/67	Jeff Davis	KO 5
16	5/4/67	George Johnson	Wu 10
17	7/19/67	George Chuvalo	TKO 4
18	10/17/67	Tony Doyle	TKO 2
19	12/18/67	Marion Connors	KO 3
20	3/4/68	Buster Mathis	KO 11
21	6/24/68	Manuel Ramos	TKO 2
22	12/10/68	Oscar Bonavena	Wu 15
23	4/22/69	Dave Zyglewicz	KO 1
24	6/23/69	Jerry Quarry	TKO 7
25	2/16/70	Jimmy Ellis	TKO 5
		(won World Heavyweight title)	
26	11/18/70	Bob Foster	KO 2
27	3/8/71	Muhammad Ali	Wu 15
28	1/15/72	Terry Daniels	TKO 4
29	5/25/72	Ron Stander	TKO 5
30	1/22/73	George Foreman	TKO by 2
		(lost World Heavyweight title)	
31	7/2/73	Joe Bugner	Wu 12
32	1/28/74	Muhammad Ali	Lu 12
33	6/17/74	Jerry Quarry	TKO 5
34	4/1/75	Jimmy Ellis	TKO 9
35	10/1/75	Muhammad Ali	TKO by 14
		(for World Heavyweight title)	
36	6/15/76	George Foreman	KO by 5
37	3/12/81	Floyd Cummings	Draw 10

Major Titleholders

Note the following sanctioning body abbreviations: NBA (National Boxing Association), WBA (World Boxing Association), WBC (World Boxing Council), GBR (Great Britain), IBF (International Boxing Federation), plus other national and state commissions. Fighters who retired as champion are indicated by (*) and champions who abandoned or relinquished their titles are indicated by (†).

Heavyweights

Widely accepted champions in CAPITAL letters. Current champions in **bold** type (as of Oct. 11, 1999).

Note: Muhammad Ali was stripped of his world title in 1967 after refusing induction into the Army (see Muhammad Ali's Career Pro Record). George Foreman was stripped of his WBA and IBF titles in 1995, but remained active as linear champion (see Boxing: Major Bouts 1998-99).

Champion	Held Title
JOHN L. SULLIVAN	1885-92
JAMES J. CORBETT	1892-97
BOB FITZSIMMONS	1897-99
JAMES J. JEFFRIES	1899-1905*
MARVIN HART	1905-06
TOMMY BURNS	1906-08
JACK JOHNSON	1908-15
JESS WILLARD	1915-19
JACK DEMPSEY	1919-26
GENE TUNNEY	1926-28*
MAX SCHMELING	1930-32
JACK SHARKEY	1932-33
PRIMO CARNERA	1933-34
MAX BAER	1934-35
JAMES J. BRADDOCK	1935-37
JOE LOUIS	1937-49*
EZZARD CHARLES	1949-51
JERSEY JOE WALCOTT	1951-52
ROCKY MARCIANO	1952-56*
FLOYD PATTERSON	1956-59
INGEMAR JOHANSSON	1959-60
FLOYD PATTERSON	1960-62
SONNY LISTON	1962-64
CASSIUS CLAY (MUHAMMAD ALI)	1964-67
Ernie Terrell (WBA)	1965-67
Joe Frazier (NY)	1968-70
Jimmy Ellis (WBA)	1968-70
JOE FRAZIER	1970-73
GEORGE FOREMAN	1973-74
MUHAMMAD ALI	1974-78
LEON SPINKS	1978
Ken Norton (WBC)	1978
Larry Holmes (WBC)	1978-80

Champion	Held Title
MUHAMMAD ALI	1978-79*
John Tate (WBA)	1979-80
Mike Weaver (WBA)	1980-82
LARRY HOLMES	1980-85
Michael Dokes (WBA)	1982-83
Gerrie Coetzee (WBA)	1983-84
Tim Witherspoon (WBC)	1984
Pinklon Thomas (WBC)	1984-86
Greg Page (WBA)	1984-85
MICHAEL SPINKS	1985-87
Tim Witherspoon (WBA)	1986
Trevor Berbick (WBC)	1986
Mike Tyson (WBC)	1986-87
James (Bonecrusher) Smith (WBA)	1986-87
Tony Tucker (IBF)	1987
MIKE TYSON (WBC, WBA, IBF)	1987-90
BUSTER DOUGLAS (WBC, WBA, IBF)	1990
EVANDER HOLYFIELD (WBC, WBA, IBF)	1990-92
RIDDICK BOWE (WBA, IBF)	1992-93
Lennox Lewis (WBC)	1992-94
EVANDER HOLYFIELD (WBA, IBF)	1993-94
MICHAEL MOORER (WBA, IBF)	1994
Oliver McCall (WBC)	1994-95
GEORGE FOREMAN (WBA, IBF)	1994-95
Bruce Seldon (WBA)	1995-96
GEORGE FOREMAN	1995-96
Frank Bruno (WBC)	1995-96
Mike Tyson (WBC)	1996†
Mike Tyson (WBA)	1996
Michael Moorer (IBF)	1996-1997
Evander Holyfield (WBA, IBF)	1996—
Lennox Lewis (WBC)	1997—

Note: John L. Sullivan held the Bare Knuckle championship from 1882-85.

Light Heavyweights

Widely accepted champions in CAPITAL letters. Current champions in **bold** type.

Champion	Held Title
JACK ROOT	1903
GEORGE GARDNER	1903
BOB FITZSIMMONS	1903-05
PHILADELPHIA JACK O'BRIEN	1905-12*
JACK DILLON	1914-16
BATTLING LEVINSKY	1916-20
GEORGES CARPENTIER	1920-22
BATTLING SIKI	1922-23
MIKE McTIGUE	1923-25
PAUL BERLENBACH	1925-26
JACK DELANEY	1926-27†
Jimmy Slattery (NBA)	1927
TOMMY LOUGHRAN	1927-29
JIMMY SLATTERY	1930
MAXIE ROSENBLOOM	1930-34
George Nichols (NBA)	1932
Bob Godwin (NBA)	1933
BOB OLIN	1934-35
JOHN HENRY LEWIS	1935-38
MELIO BETTINA (NY)	1939
Len Harvey (GBR)	1939-42
BILLY CONN	1939-40†

Champion	Held Title
ANTON CHRISTOFORIDIS (NBA)	1941
GUS LESNEVICH	1941-48
Freddie Mills (GBR)	1942-46
FREDDIE MILLS	1948-50
JOEY MAXIM	1950-52
ARCHIE MOORE	1952-62
Harold Johnson (NBA)	1961
HAROLD JOHNSON	1962-63
WILLIE PASTRANO	1963-65
Eddie Cotton (Mich.)	1963-64
JOSE TORRES	1965-66
DICK TIGER	1966-68
BOB FOSTER	1968-74*
Vicente Rondon (WBA)	1971-72
John Conteh (WBC)	1974-77
Victor Galindez (WBA)	1974-78
Miguel A. Cuello (WBC)	1977-78
Mate Parlov (WBC)	1978
Mike Rossman (WBA)	1978-79
Marvin Johnson (WBC)	1978-79
Matthew (Franklin) Saad Muhammad (WBC)	1979-81
Marvin Johnson (WBA)	1979-80

Champion	Held Title
Eddie (Gregory)	
Mustapha Muhammad (WBA)	1980-81
Michael Spinks (WBA)	1981-83
Dwight (Braxton) Muhammad Qawi (WBC)	1981-83
MICHAEL SPINKS	1983-85†
J.B. Williamson (WBC)	1985-86
Slobodan Kacar (IBF)	1985-86
Marvin Johnson (WBA)	1986-87
Dennis Andries (WBC)	1986-87
Bobby Czyz (IBF)	1986-87
Leslie Stewart (WBA)	1987
Virgil Hill (WBA)	1987-91
Prince Charles Williams (IBF)	1987-93
Thomas Hearns (WBC)	1987
Donny Lalonde (WBC)	1987-88
Sugar Ray Leonard (WBC)	1988
Dennis Andries (WBC)	1989
Jeff Harding (WBC)	1989-90
Dennis Andries (WBC)	1990-91
Jeff Harding (WBC)	1991-94
Thomas Hearns (WBA)	1991-92
Iran Barkley (WBA)	1992†
Virgil Hill (WBA)	1992-97
Henry Maske (IBF)	1993-96
Virgil Hill (WBA/IBF)	1996-97
Mike McCallum (WBC)	1994-95
Fabrice Tiozzo (WBC)	1995-96
Roy Jones Jr. (WBC)	1996
Montell Griffin (WBC)	1996
D. Michaelczewski (WBA/IBF)	1997†
William Guthrie (IBF)	1997-98
Lou Del Valle (WBA)	1997-98
ROY JONES JR. (WBA/WBC)	1997—
Reggie Johnson (IBF)	1998-99
ROY JONES JR. (WBA/WBC/IBF)	1999—

Middleweights

Widely accepted champions in CAPITAL letters. Current champions in **bold** type.

Champion	Held Title
JACK (NONPAREIL) DEMPSEY	1884-91
BOB FITZSIMMONS	1891-97
CHARLES (KID) McCOY	1897-98
TOMMY RYAN	1898-1907
STANLEY KETCHEL	1908
BILLY PAPKE	1908
STANLEY KETCHEL	1908-10
FRANK KLAUS	1913
GEORGE CHIP	1913-14
AL McCOY	1914-17
Jeff Smith (AUS)	1914
Mick King (AUS)	1914
Jeff Smith (AUS)	1914-15
Lee Darcy (AUS)	1915-17
MIKE O'DOWD	1917-20
JOHNNY WILSON	1920-23
Wm. Bryan Downey (Ohio)	1921-22
Dave Rosenberg (NY)	1922
Jock Malone (Ohio)	1922-23
Mike O'Dowd (NY)	1922
Lou Bogash (NY)	1923
HARRY GREB	1923-26
TIGER FLOWERS	1926
MICKEY WALKER	1926-31†
GORILLA JONES	1931-32
MARCEL THIL	1932-37
Ben Jeby (NY)	1932-33
Lou Brouillard (NBA, NY)	1933
Vince Dundee (NBA, NY)	1933-34
Teddy Yarosz (NBA, NY)	1934-35
Babe Risko (NBA, NY)	1935-36
Freddie Steele (NBA, NY)	1936-38
FRED APOSTOLI	1937-39
Al Hostak (NBA)	1938
Solly Krieger (NBA)	1938-39
Al Hostak (NBA)	1939-40
CEFERINO GARCIA	1939-40
KEN OVERLIN	1940-41
Tony Zale (NBA)	1940-41
BILLY SOOSE	1941
TONY ZALE	1941-47
ROCKY GRAZIANO	1947-48
TONY ZALE	1948
MARCEL CERDAN	1948-49
JAKE La MOTTA	1949-51
SUGAR RAY ROBINSON	1951
RANDY TURPIN	1951
SUGAR RAY ROBINSON	1951-52*
CARL (BOBO) OLSON	1953-55
SUGAR RAY ROBINSON	1955-57
GENE FULLMER	1957
SUGAR RAY ROBINSON	1957
CARMEN BASILIO	1957-58
SUGAR RAY ROBINSON	1958-60
Gene Fullmer (NBA)	1959-62
PAUL PENDER	1960-61
TERRY DOWNES	1961-62
PAUL PENDER	1962-63
Dick Tiger (WBA)	1962-63
DICK TIGER	1963
JOEY GIARDELLO	1963-65
DICK TIGER	1965-66
EMILE GRIFFITH	1966-67
NINO BENVENUTI	1967
EMILE GRIFFITH	1967-68
NINO BENVENUTI	1968-70
CARLOS MONZON	1970-77*
Rodrigo Valdez (WBC)	1974-76
RODRIGO VALDEZ	1977-78
HUGO CORRO	1978-79
VITO ANTUOFERMO	1979-80
ALAN MINTER	1980
MARVELOUS MARVIN HAGLER	1980-87
SUGAR RAY LEONARD	1987
Frank Tate (IBF)	1987-88
Sumbu Kalambay (WBA)	1987-89
Thomas Hearns (WBC)	1987-88
Iran Barkley (WBC)	1988-89
Michael Nunn (IBF)	1988-91
Roberto Duran (WBC)	1989-90*
Mike McCallum (WBA)	1989-91
Julian Jackson (WBC)	1990-93
James Toney (IBF)	1991-93†
Reggie Johnson (WBA)	1992-93
Roy Jones Jr. (IBF)	1993-94†
Gerald McClellan (WBC)	1993-95†
John David Jackson (WBA)	1993-94
Jorge Castro (WBA)	1994-97
Julian Jackson (WBC)	1995
Bernard Hopkins (IBF)	1995—
Quincy Taylor (WBC)	1995-96
Shinji Takehara (WBA)	1995-96
William Joppy (WBA)	1996-97
Keith Holmes (WBC)	1996-98
Julio Cesar Green (WBA)	1997-98
William Joppy (WBA)	1998—
Hassine Cherifi (WBC)	1998-99
Keith Holmes (WBC)	1999—

Welterweights

Widely accepted champions in CAPITAL letters. Current champions in **bold** type.

Champion	Held Title	Champion	Held Title
PADDY DUFFY	1888-90	JOHNNY SAXTON	1956
MYSTERIOUS BILLY SMITH	1892-94	CARMEN BASILIO	1956-57†
TOMMY RYAN	1894-98	VIRGIL AKINS	1958
MYSTERIOUS BILLY SMITH	1898-1900	DON JORDAN	1958-60
MATTY MATTHEWS	1900	BENNY (KID) PARET	1960-61
EDDIE CONNOLLY	1900	EMILE GRIFFITH	1961
JAMES (RUBE) FERNS	1900	BENNY (KID) PARET	1961-62
MATTY MATHEWS	1900-01	EMILE GRIFFITH	1962-63
JAMES (RUBE) FERNS	1901	LUIS RODRIGUEZ	1963
JOE WALCOTT	1901-04	EMILE GRIFFITH	1963-66†
THE DIXIE KID	1904-05	Charlie Shipes (Calif.)	1966-67
HONEY MELLODY	1906-07	CURTIS COKES	1966-69
Mike (Twin) Sullivan	1907-08†	JOSE NAPOLES	1969-70
Harry Lewis	1908-11	BILLY BACKUS	1970-71
Jimmy Gardner	1908	JOSE NAPOLES	1971-75
Jimmy Clabby	1910-11	Hedgemon Lewis (NY)	1972-73
WALDEMAR HOLBERG	1914	Angel Espada (WBA)	1975-76
TOM McCORMICK	1914	JOHN H. STRACEY	1975-76
MATT WELLS	1914-15	CARLOS PALOMINO	1976-79
MIKE GLOVER	1915	Pipino Cuevas (WBA)	1976-80
JACK BRITTON	1915	WILFREDO BENITEZ	1979
TED (KID) LEWIS	1915-16	SUGAR RAY LEONARD	1979-80
JACK BRITTON	1916-17	ROBERTO DURAN	1980
TED (KID) LEWIS	1917-19	Thomas Hearns (WBA)	1980-81
JACK BRITTON	1919-22	SUGAR RAY LEONARD	1980-82
MICKEY WALKER	1922-26	Donald Curry (WBA)	1983-85
PETE LATZO	1926-27	Milton McCrory (WBC)	1983-85
JOE DUNDEE	1927-29	DONALD CURRY	1985-86
JACKIE FIELDS	1929-30	LLOYD HONEYGHAN	1986-87
YOUNG JACK THOMPSON	1930	JORGE VACA (WBC)	1987-88
TOMMY FREEMAN	1930-31	LLOYD HONEYGHAN (WBC)	1988-89
YOUNG JACK THOMPSON	1931	Mark Breland (WBA)	1987
LOU BROUILLARD	1931-32	Marlon Starling (WBA)	1987-88
JACKIE FIELDS	1932-33	Tomas Molinares (WBA)	1988-89
YOUNG CORBETT III	1933	Simon Brown (IBF)	1988-91
JIMMY McLARNIN	1933-34	Mark Breland (WBA)	1989-90
BARNEY ROSS	1934	MARLON STARLING (WBC)	1989-90
JIMMY McLARNIN	1934-35	Aaron Davis (WBA)	1990-91
BARNEY ROSS	1935-38	Maurice Blocker (WBC)	1990-91
HENRY ARMSTRONG	1938-40	Meldrick Taylor (WBA)	1991-92
FRITZIE ZIVIC	1940-41	Simon Brown (WBC)	1991
Izzy Jannazzo (Md.)	1940-41	Maurice Blocker (IBF)	1991-93
Freddie (Red) Cochrane	1941-46	Buddy McGirt (WBC)	1991-93
MARTY SERVO	1946*	Crisanto Espana (WBA)	1992-94
SUGAR RAY ROBINSON	1946-51†	Pernell Whitaker (WBC)	1993-97
Johnny Bratton	1951	**Felix Trinidad** (IBF)	1993—
KID GAVILAN	1951-54	Ike Quartey (WBA)	1994-98†
JOHNNY SAXTON	1954-55	**James Page** (WBA)	1998—
TONY DeMARCO	1955	Oscar De La Hoya (WBC)	1997-99
CARMEN BASILIO	1955-56	**Felix Trinidad** (WBC/IBF)	1999—

Lightweights

Widely accepted champions in CAPITAL letters. Current champions in **bold** type.

Champion	Held Title	Champion	Held Title
JACK McAULIFFE	1886-94	ROCKY KANSAS	1925-26
GEORGE (KID) LAVIGNE	1896-99	SAMMY MANDELL	1926-30
FRANK ERNE	1899-02	AL SINGER	1930
JOE GANS	1902-04	TONY CANZONERI	1930-33
JIMMY BRITT	1904-05	BARNEY ROSS	1933-35†
BATTLING NELSON	1905-06	TONY CANZONERI	1935-36
JOE GANS	1906-08	LOU AMBERS	1936-38
BATTLING NELSON	1908-10	HENRY ARMSTRONG	1938-39
AD WOLGAST	1910-12	LOU AMBERS	1939-40
WILLIE RITCHIE	1912-14	Sammy Angott (NBA)	1940-41
FREDDIE WELSH	1915-17	LEW JENKINS	1940-41
BENNY LEONARD	1917-25*	SAMMY ANGOTT	1941-42
JIMMY GOODRICH	1925	Beau Jack (NY)	1942-43

Champion	Held Title
Slugger White (Md.)	1943
Bob Montgomery (NY)	1943
Sammy Angott (NBA)	1943-44
Beau Jack (NY)	1943-44
Bob Montgomery (NY)	1944-47
Juan Zurita (NBA)	1944-45
IKE WILLIAMS	1947-51
JAMES CARTER	1951-52
LAURO SALAS	1952
JAMES CARTER	1952-54
PADDY DeMARCO	1954
JAMES CARTER	1954-55
WALLACE (BUD) SMITH	1955-56
JOE BROWN	1956-62
CARLOS ORTIZ	1962-65
Kenny Lane (Mich.)	1963-64
ISMAEL LAGUNA	1965
CARLOS ORTIZ	1965-68
CARLOS TEO CRUZ	1968-69
MANDO RAMOS	1969-70
ISMAEL LAGUNA	1970
KEN BUCHANAN	1970-72
Pedro Carrasco (WBC)	1971-72
Mando Ramos (WBC)	1972
ROBERTO DURAN	1972-79†
Chango Carmona (WBC)	1972
Rodolfo Gonzalez (WBC)	1972-74
Ishimatsu Suzuki (WBC)	1974-76
Esteban De Jesus (WBC)	1976-78
Jim Watt (WBC)	1979-81
Ernesto Espana (WBA)	1979-80
Hilmer Kenty (WBA)	1980-81
Sean O'Grady (WBA,WAA)	1981
Alexis Arguello (WBC)	1981-82
Claude Noel (WBA)	1981
Andrew Ganigan (WAA)	1981-82
Arturo Frias (WBA)	1981-82
Ray Mancini (WBA)	1982-84

Champion	Held Title
ALEXIS ARGUELLO	1982-83
Edwin Rosario (WBC)	1983-84
Choo Choo Brown (IBF)	1984
Livingstone Bramble (WBA)	1984-86
Harry Arroyo (IBF)	1984-85
Jose Luis Ramirez (WBC)	1984-85
Jimmy Paul (IBF)	1985-86
Hector Camacho (WBC)	1985-86
Edwin Rosario (WBA)	1986-87
Greg Haugen (IBF)	1986-87
Julio Cesar Chavez (WBA)	1987-88
Jose Luis Ramirez (WBC)	1987-88
JULIO CESAR CHAVEZ (WBC,WBA)	1988-89
Vinny Pazienza (IBF)	1987-88
Greg Haugen (IBF)	1988-89
Pernell Whitaker (IBF,WBC)	1989-90
Edwin Rosario (WBA)	1989-90
Juan Nazario (WBA)	1990
PERNELL WHITAKER (IBF, WBC, WBA)	1990-92†
Joey Gamache (WBA)	1992
Miguel A. Gonzalez (WBC)	1992-96
Tony Lopez (WBA)	1992-93
Dingaan Thobela (WBA)	1993
Fred Pendleton (IBF)	1993-94
Orzubek Nazarov (WBA)	1993-98
Rafael Ruelas (IBF)	1994-95
Oscar De La Hoya (IBF)	1995†
Phillip Holiday (IBF)	1995-97
Jean-Baptiste Mendy (WBC)	1996-97
Stevie Johnston (WBC)	1997-98
Shane Mosley (IBF)	1997-99†
Cesar Bazan (WBC)	1998-99
Jean-Baptiste Mendy (WBA)	1998-99
Julien Lorcy (WBA)	1999
Stevie Johnston (WBC)	1999—
Stefano Zoff (WBA)	1999—
Israel Cardona (IBF)	1999
Paul Spadafora (IBF)	1999—

Featherweights

Widely accepted champions in CAPITAL letters. Current champions in **bold** type.

Champion	Held Title
TORPEDO BILLY MURPHY	1890
YOUNG GRIFFO	1890-92
GEORGE DIXON	1892-97
SOLLY SMITH	1897-98
Ben Jordan (GBR)	1898-99
Eddie Santry (GBR)	1899-1900
DAVE SULLIVAN	1898
GEORGE DIXON	1898-1900
TERRY McGOVERN	1900-01
YOUNG CORBETT II	1901-04
JIMMY BRITT	1904
ABE ATTELL	1904
BROOKLYN TOMMY SULLIVAN	1904-05
ABE ATTELL	1906-12
JOHNNY KILBANE	1912-23
Jem Driscoll (GBR)	1912-13
EUGENE CRIQUI	1923
JOHNNY DUNDEE	1923-24†
LOUIS (KID) KAPLAN	1925-26†
Dick Finnegan (Mass.)	1926-27
BENNY BASS	1927-28
TONY CANZONERI	1928
ANDRE ROUTIS	1928-29
BATTLING BATTALINO	1929-32†
Tommy Paul (NBA)	1932-33
Kid Chocolate (NY)	1932-33
Freddie Miller (NBA)	1933-36
Baby Arizmendi (MEX)	1935-36

Champion	Held Title
Mike Belloise (NY)	1936-37
Petey Sarron (NBA)	1936-37
HENRY ARMSTRONG	1937-38†
Joey Archibald (NY)	1938-39
Leo Rodak (NBA)	1938-39
JOEY ARCHIBALD (NBA)	1939-40
Petey Scalzo (NBA)	1940-41
Jimmy Perrin (La.)	1940-41
HARRY JEFFRA	1940-41
JOEY ARCHIBALD	1941
Richie Lemos (NBA)	1941
CHALKY WRIGHT	1941-42
Jackie Wilson (NBA)	1941-43
WILLIE PEP	1942-48
Jackie Callura (NBA)	1943
Phil Terranova (NBA)	1943-44
Sal Bartolo (NBA)	1944-46
SANDY SADDLER	1948-49
WILLIE PEP	1949-50
SANDY SADDLER	1950-57*
HOGAN (KID) BASSEY	1957-59
DAVEY MOORE	1959-63
ULTIMINIO (SUGAR) RAMOS	1963-64
VICENTE SALDIVAR	1964-67*
Howard Winstone (GBR)	1968
Raul Rojas (WBA)	1968
Jose Legra (WBC)	1968-69
Shozo Saijyo (WBA)	1968-71

Champion	Held Title
JOHNNY FAMECHON (WBC)	1969-70
VICENTE SALDIVAR (WBC)	1970
KUNIAKI SHIBATA (WBC)	1970-72
Antonio Gomez (WBA)	1971-72
CLEMENTE SANCHEZ (WBC)	1972
Ernesto Marcel (WBA)	1972-74
JOSE LEGRA (WBC)	1972-73
EDER JOFRE (WBC)	1973-74
Ruben Olivares (WBA)	1974
Bobby Chacon (WBC)	1974-75
ALEXIS ARGUELLO (WBA)	1974-76†
Ruben Olivares (WBC)	1975
David (Poison) Kotey (WBC)	1975-76
DANNY (LITTLE RED) LOPEZ (WBC)	1976-80
Rafael Ortega (WBA)	1977
Cecilio Lastra (WBA)	1977-78
Eusebio Pedroza (WBA)	1978-85
SALVADOR SANCHEZ (WBC)	1980-82
Juan LaPorte (WBC)	1982-84
Wilfredo Gomez (WBC)	1984
Min-Keun Oh (IBF)	1984-85
Azumah Nelson (WBC)	1984-88
Barry McGuigan (WBA)	1985-86
Ki-Young Chung (IBF)	1985-86
Steve Cruz (WBA)	1986-87
Antonio Rivera (IBF)	1986-88

Champion	Held Title
Antonio Esparragoza (WBA)	1987-91
Calvin Grove (IBF)	1988
Jorge Paez (IBF)	1988-91†
Jeff Fenech (WBC)	1988-90†
Marcos Villasana (WBC)	1990-91
Yung-Kyun Park (WBA)	1991-93
Troy Dorsey (IBF)	1991
Manuel Medina (IBF)	1991-93
Paul Hodkinson (WBC)	1991-93
Tom Johnson (IBF)	1993-97
Goyo Vargas (WBC)	1993
Kevin Kelley (WBC)	1993-95
Eloy Rojas (WBA)	1993-96
Alejandro Gonzalez (WBC)	1995
Manuel Medina (WBC)	1995-96
Wilfredo Vasquez (WBA)	1996-98†
Luisito Espinosa (WBC)	1995-99
Naseem Hamed (IBF)	1997†
Hector Lizarraga (IBF)	1997-98
Freddie Norwood (WBA)	1998
Manuel Medina (IBF)	1998—
Antonio Cermeno (WBA)	1998-99
Cesar Soto (WBC)	1999—
Freddie Norwood (WBA)	1999—

Bantamweights

Widely accepted champions in CAPITAL letters. Current champions in **bold** type.

Champion	Held Title
TOMMY (SPIDER) KELLY	1887
HUGHEY BOYLE	1887-88
TOMMY (SPIDER) KELLY	1889
CHAPPIE MORAN	1889-90
Tommy (Spider) Kelly	1890-92
GEORGE DIXON	1890-91
Billy Plummer	1892-95
JIMMY BARRY	1894-99
Pedlar Palmer	1895-99
TERRY McGOVERN	1899-1900
HARRY HARRIS	1901-02
DANNY DOUGHERTY	1900-01
HARRY FORBES	1901-03
FRANKIE NEIL	1903-04
JOE BOWKER	1904-05
JIMMY WALSH	1905-06†
OWEN MORAN	1907-08
MONTE ATTELL	1909-10
FRANKIE CONLEY	1910-11
JOHNNY COULON	1911-14
Digger Stanley (GBR)	1910-12
Charles Ledoux (GBR)	1912-13
Eddie Campi (GBR)	1913-14
KID WILLIAMS	1914-17
Johnny Ertle	1915-18
PETE HERMAN	1917-20
Memphis Pal Moore	1918-19
JOE LYNCH	1920-21
PETE HERMAN	1921
JOHNNY BUFF	1921-22
JOE LYNCH	1922-24
ABE GOLDSTEIN	1924
CANNONBALL EDDIE MARTIN	1924-25
PHIL ROSENBERG	1925-27
Teddy Baldock (GBR)	1927
BUD TAYLOR (NBA)	1927-28†
Willie Smith (GBR)	1927-28
Bushy Graham (NY)	1928-29
PANAMA AL BROWN	1929-35
Sixto Escobar (NBA)	1934-35

Champion	Held Title
BALTAZAR SANGCHILLI	1935-36
Lou Salica (NBA)	1935
Sixto Escobar (NBA)	1935-36
TONY MARINO	1936
SIXTO ESCOBAR	1936-37
HARRY JEFFRA	1937-38
SIXTO ESCOBAR	1938-39*
Georgie Pace (NBA)	1939-40
LOU SALICA	1940-42
MANUEL ORTIZ	1942-47
HAROLD DADE	1947
MANUEL ORTIZ	1947-50
VIC TOWEEL	1950-52
JIMMY CARRUTHERS	1952-54*
ROBERT COHEN	1954-56
Raul Macias (NBA)	1955-57
MARIO D'AGATA	1956-57
ALPHONSE HALIMI	1957-59
JOE BECERRA	1959-60*
Johnny Caldwell (EBU)	1961-62
EDER JOFRE	1961-65
MASAHIKO FIGHTING HARADA	1965-68
LIONEL ROSE	1968-69
RUBEN OLIVARES	1969-70
CHUCHO CASTILLO	1970-71
RUBEN OLIVARES	1971-72
RAFAEL HERRERA	1972
ENRIQUE PINDER	1972-73
ROMEO ANAYA	1973
Rafael Herrera (WBC)	1973-74
ARNOLD TAYLOR	1973-74
SOO-HWAN HONG	1974-75
Rodolfo Martinez (WBC)	1974-76
ALFONSO ZAMORA	1975-77
Carlos Zarate (WBC)	1976-79
JORGE LUJAN	1977-80
Lupe Pintor (WBC)	1979-83
JULIAN SOLIS	1980
JEFF CHANDLER	1980-84
Albert Davila (WBC)	1983-85

Champion	Held Title
RICHARD SANDOVAL	1984-86
Satoshi Shingaki (IBF)	1984-85
Jeff Fenech (IBF)	1985
Daniel Zaragoza (WBC)	1985
Miguel (Happy) Lora (WBC)	1985-88
GABY CANIZALES	1986
BERNARDO PINANGO	1986-87
Wilfredo Vasquez (WBA)	1987-88
Kevin Seabrooks (IBF)	1987-88
Kaokor Galaxy (WBA)	1988
Moon Sung-Kil (WBA)	1988-89
Kaokor Galaxy (WBA)	1989
Raul Perez (WBC)	1988-91
Orlando Canizales (IBF)	1988-94†
Luisito Espinosa (WBA)	1989-91
Greg Richardson	1991
Joichiro Tatsuyoshi (WBC)	1991-92
Israel Contreras (WBA)	1991-92
Eddie Cook (WBA)	1992
Victor Rabanales (WBC)	1992-93
Jorge Julio (WBA)	1992-93
Jung-Il Byun (WBC)	1993
Junior Jones (WBA)	1993-94
Yasuei Yakushiji (WBC)	1993-95
John M. Johnson (WBA)	1994
Daorung Chuvatana (WBA)	1994-95
Harold Mestre (IBF)	1995
Mbulelo Botile (IBF)	1995-97
Wayne McCullough (WBC)	1995-96
Veeraphol Sahaprom (WBA)	1995-96
Nana Yaw Konadu (WBA)	1996
Daorung Chuvatana (WBA)	1996-97
Nana Yaw Konadu (WBA)	1997-98
Sirimongkol Singmanassak (WBC)	1996-97
Tim Austin (IBF)	1997—
Joichiro Tatsuyoshi (WBC)	1997-98
Johnny Tapia (WBA)	1998-99
Veerapol Sahaprom (WBC)	1998—
Paulie Ayala (WBA)	1999—

Flyweights

Widely accepted champions in CAPITAL letters. Current champions in **bold** type.

Champion	Held Title
Sid Smith (GBR)	1913
Bill Ladbury (GBR)	1913-14
Percy Jones (GBR)	1914
Joe Symonds (GBR)	1914-16
JIMMY WILDE	1916-23
PANCHO VILLA	1923-25
FIDEL LaBARBA	1925-27*
FRENCHY BELANGER (NBA,IBU)	1927-28
Izzy Schwartz (NY)	1927-29
Johnny McCoy (Calif.)	1927-28
Newsboy Brown (Calif.)	1928
FRANKIE GENARO (NBA,IBU)	1928-29
Johnny Hill (GBR)	1928-29
SPIDER PLADNER (NBA,IBU)	1929
FRANKIE GENARO (NBA,IBU)	1929-31
Willie LaMorte (NY)	1929-30
Midget Wolgast (NY)	1930-35
YOUNG PEREZ (NBA,IBU)	1931-32
JACKIE BROWN (NBA,IBU)	1932-35
BENNY LYNCH	1935-38†
Small Montana (NY,Calif.)	1935-37
PETER KANE	1938-43
Little Dado (NBA,Calif.)	1938-40
JACKIE PATERSON	1943-48
RINTY MONAGHAN	1948-50*
TERRY ALLEN	1950
SALVADOR (DADO) MARINO	1950-52
YOSHIO SHIRAI	1953-54
PASCUAL PEREZ	1954-60
PONE KINGPETCH	1960-62
MASAHIKO (FIGHTING) HARADA	1962-63
PONE KINGPETCH	1963
HIROYUKI EBIHARA	1963-64
PONE KINGPETCH	1964-65
SALVATORE BURRINI	1965-66
Horacio Accavallo (WBA)	1966-68
WALTER McGOWAN	1966
CHARTCHAI CHIONOI	1966-69
EFREN TORRES	1969-70
Hiroyuki Ebihara (WBA)	1969
Bernabe Villacampo (WBA)	1969-70
CHARTCHAI CHIONOI	1970
Berkrerk Chartvanchai (WBA)	1970
Masao Ohba (WBA)	1970-73
ERBITO SALAVARRIA	1970-73
Betulio Gonzalez (WBC)	1972
Venice Borkorsor (WBC)	1972-73
VENICE BORKORSOR	1973
Chartchai Chionoi (WBA)	1973-74
Betulio Gonzalez (WBA)	1973-74
Shoji Oguma (WBC)	1974-75
Susumu Hanagata (WBA)	1974-75
Miguel Canto (WBC)	1975-79
Erbito Salavarria (WBA)	1975-76
Alfonso Lopez (WBA)	1976
Guty Espadas (WBA)	1976-78
Betulio Gonzalez (WBA)	1978-79
Chan-Hee Park (WBC)	1979-80
Luis Ibarra (WBA)	1979-80
Tae-Shik Kim (WBA)	1980
Shoji Oguma (WBC)	1980-81
Peter Mathebula (WBA)	1980-81
Santos Laciar (WBA)	1981
Antonio Avelar (WBC)	1981-82
Luis Ibarra (WBA)	1981
Juan Herrera (WBA)	1981-82
Prudencio Cardona (WBC)	1982
Santos Laciar (WBA)	1982-85
Freddie Castillo (WBC)	1982
Eleoncio Mercedes (WBC)	1982-83
Charlie Magri (WBC)	1983
Frank Cedeno (WBC)	1983-84
Soon-Chun Kwon (IBF)	1983-85
Koji Kobayashi (WBC)	1984
Gabriel Bernal (WBC)	1984
Sot Chitalada (WBC)	1984-88
Hilario Zapate (WBA)	1985-87
Chong-Kwan Chung (IBF)	1985-86
Bi-Won Chung (IBF)	1986
Hi-Sup Shin (IBF)	1986-87
Dodie Penalosa (IBF)	1987
Fidel Bassa (WBA)	1987-89
Choi Chang-Ho (IBF)	1987-88
Rolando Bohol (IBF)	1988
Yong-Kang Kim (WBC)	1988-89
Duke McKenzie (IBF)	1988-89
Dave McAuley (IBF)	1989-92
Sot Chitalada (WBC)	1989-91
Jesus Rojas (WBA)	1989-90
Yul-Woo Lee (WBA)	1990
Leopard Tamakuma (WBA)	1990-91
Muangchai Kittikasem (WBC)	1991-92

Champion	Held Title
Yong-Kang Kim (WBA)	1991-92
Rodolfo Blanco (IBF)	1992
Yuri Arbachakov (WBC)	1992-97
Aquiles Guzman (WBA)	1992
Phichit Sithbangprachan (IBF)	1992-94†
David Griman (WBA)	1992-94
Saen Sor Ploenchit (WBA)	1994-96
Francisco Tejedor (IBF)	1995
Danny Romero (IBF)	1995-96

Champion	Held Title
Mark Johnson (IBF)	1996-99†
Jose Bonilla (WBA)	1996-97
Chatchai Sasakul (WBC)	1997-98
Hugo Soto (WBA)	1998-99
Manny Pacquiao (WBC)	1998—
Irene Pacheco (IBF)	1999—
Leo Gamez (WBA)	1999
Sornpichai Kratindaenggym (WBA)	1999—

Annual Awards
Ring Magazine Fight of the Year

First presented in 1945 by Nat Fleischer, who started *The Ring* magazine in 1922.

Multiple matchups: Muhammad Ali vs. Joe Frazier, Carmen Basilio vs. Sugar Ray Robinson and Rocky Graziano vs. Tony Zale (2).

Multiple fights: Muhammad Ali (6); Carmen Basilio (5); George Foreman and Joe Frazier (4); Rocky Graziano, Rocky Marciano and Tony Zale (3); Nino Benvenuti, Bobby Chacon, Ezzard Charles, Arturo Gatti, Marvin Hagler, Thomas Hearns, Evander Holyfield, Sugar Ray Leonard, Floyd Patterson, Sugar Ray Robinson and Jersey Joe Walcott (2).

Year	Winner	Loser	Result		Year	Winner	Loser	Result	
1945	Rocky Graziano	Red Cochrane	KO	10	1973	George Foreman	Joe Frazier	KO	2
1946	Tony Zale	Rocky Graziano	KO	6	1974	Muhammad Ali	George Foreman	KO	8
1947	Rocky Graziano	Tony Zale	KO	6	1975	Muhammad Ali	Joe Frazier	KO	14
1948	Marcel Cerdan	Tony Zale	KO	12	1976	George Foreman	Ron Lyle	KO	4
1949	Willie Pep	Sandy Saddler	W	15	1977	Jimmy Young	George Foreman	W	12
					1978	Leon Spinks	Muhammad Ali	W	15
1950	Jake LaMotta	Laurent Dauthuille	KO	15	1979	Danny Lopez	Mike Ayala	KO	15
1951	Jersey Joe Walcott	Ezzard Charles	KO	7					
1952	Rocky Marciano	Jersey Joe Walcott	KO	13	1980	Saad Muhammad	Yaqui Lopez	KO	14
1953	Rocky Marciano	Roland LaStarza	KO	11	1981	Sugar Ray Leonard	Thomas Hearns	KO	14
1954	Rocky Marciano	Ezzard Charles	KO	8	1982	Bobby Chacon	Rafael Limon	W	15
1955	Carmen Basilio	Tony DeMarco	KO	12	1983	Bobby Chacon	C. Boza-Edwards	W	12
1956	Carmen Basilio	Johnny Saxton	KO	9	1984	Jose Luis Ramirez	Edwin Rosario	KO	4
1957	Carmen Basilio	Sugar Ray Robinson	W	15	1985	Marvin Hagler	Thomas Hearns	KO	3
1958	Sugar Ray Robinson	Carmen Basilio	W	15	1986	Stevie Cruz	Barry McGuigan	W	15
1959	Gene Fullmer	Carmen Basilio	KO	14	1987	Sugar Ray Leonard	Marvin Hagler	W	12
					1988	Tony Lopez	Rocky Lockridge	W	12
1960	Floyd Patterson	Ingemar Johansson	KO	5	1989	Roberto Duran	Iran Barkley	W	12
1961	Joe Brown	Dave Charnley	W	15					
1962	Joey Giardello	Henry Hank	W	10	1990	Julio Cesar Chavez	Meldrick Taylor	KO	12
1963	Cassius Clay	Doug Jones	W	10	1991	Robert Quiroga	Akeem Anifowoshe	W	12
1964	Cassius Clay	Sonny Liston	KO	7	1992	Riddick Bowe	Evander Holyfield	W	12
1965	Floyd Patterson	George Chuvalo	W	12	1993	Michael Carbajal	Humberto Gonzalez	KO	7
1966	Jose Torres	Eddie Cotton	W	15	1994	Jorge Castro	John David Jackson	TKO	9
1967	Nino Benvenuti	Emile Griffith	W	15	1995	Saman Sorjaturong	Chiquita Gonzalez	KO	7
1968	Dick Tiger	Frank DePaula	W	10	1996	Evander Holyfield	Mike Tyson	TKO	11
1969	Joe Frazier	Jerry Quarry	KO	7	1997	Arturo Gatti	Gabriel Ruelas	KO	5
					1998	Ivan Robinson	Arturo Gatti	W	10
1970	Carlos Monzon	Nino Benvenuti	KO	12					
1971	Joe Frazier	Muhammad Ali	W	15					
1972	Bob Foster	Chris Finnegan	KO	14					

Ring Magazine Fighter of the Year

First presented in 1928 by Nat Fleischer, who started *The Ring* magazine in 1922.

Multiple winners: Muhammad Ali (5); Joe Louis (4); Joe Frazier, Evander Holyfield and Rocky Marciano (3); Ezzard Charles, George Foreman, Marvin Hagler, Thomas Hearns, Ingemar Johansson, Sugar Ray Leonard, Tommy Loughran, Floyd Patterson, Sugar Ray Robinson, Barney Ross, Dick Tiger and Mike Tyson (2)

Year		Year		Year		Year	
1928	Gene Tunney	1940	Billy Conn	1953	Carl (Bobo) Olson	1966	No award
1929	Tommy Loughran	1941	Joe Louis	1954	Rocky Marciano	1967	Joe Frazier
		1942	Sugar Ray Robinson	1955	Rocky Marciano	1968	Nino Benvenuti
1930	Max Schmeling	1943	Fred Apostoli	1956	Floyd Patterson	1969	Jose Napoles
1931	Tommy Loughran	1944	Beau Jack	1957	Carmen Basilio		
1932	Jack Sharkey	1945	Willie Pep	1958	Ingemar Johansson	1970	Joe Frazier
1933	No award	1946	Tony Zale	1959	Ingemar Johansson	1971	Joe Frazier
1934	Tony Canzoneri	1947	Gus Lesnevich			1972	Muhammad Ali
	& Barney Ross	1948	Ike Williams	1960	Floyd Patterson		& Carlos Monzon
1935	Barney Ross	1949	Ezzard Charles	1961	Joe Brown	1973	George Foreman
1936	Joe Louis			1962	Dick Tiger	1974	Muhammad Ali
1937	Henry Armstrong	1950	Ezzard Charles	1963	Cassius Clay	1975	Muhammad Ali
1938	Joe Louis	1951	Sugar Ray Robinson	1964	Emile Griffith	1976	George Foreman
1939	Joe Louis	1952	Rocky Marciano	1965	Dick Tiger	1977	Carlos Zarate

Year		Year		Year		Year	
1978	Muhammad Ali	1983	Marvin Hagler	1988	Mike Tyson	1994	Roy Jones Jr.
1979	Sugar Ray Leonard	1984	Thomas Hearns	1989	Pernell Whitaker	1995	Oscar De La Hoya
1980	Thomas Hearns	1985	Donald Curry	1990	Julio Cesar Chavez	1996	Evander Holyfield
1981	Sugar Ray Leonard		& Marvin Hagler	1991	James Toney	1997	Evander Holyfield
	& Salvador Sanchez	1986	Mike Tyson	1992	Riddick Bowe	1998	Floyd Mayweather
1982	Larry Holmes	1987	Evander Holyfield	1993	Michael Carbajal		

Note: Cassius Clay changed his name to Muhammad Ali after winning the heavyweight title in 1964.

All-Time Leaders

As compiled by *The Ring Record Book and Encyclopedia*.

Knockouts

		Division	Career	No
1	Archie Moore	Lt. Heavy	1936-63	130
2	Young Stribling	Heavy	1921-33	126
3	Billy Bird	Welter	1920-48	125
4	George Odwel	Welter	1930-45	114
5	Sugar Ray Robinson	Middle	1940-65	110
6	Sandy Saddler	Feather	1944-56	103
7	Sam Langford	Middle	1902-26	102
8	Henry Armstrong	Welter	1931-45	100
9	Jimmy Wilde	Fly	1911-23	98
10	Len Wickwar	Lt. Heavy	1928-47	93

Total Bouts

		Division	Career	No
1	Len Wickwar	Lt. Heavy	1928-47	463
2	Jack Britton	Welter	1905-30	350
3	Johnny Dundee	Feather	1910-32	333
4	Billy Bird	Welter	1920-48	318
5	George Marsden	n/a	1928-46	311
6	Maxie Rosenbloom	Lt. Heavy	1923-39	299
7	Harry Greb	Middle	1913-26	298
8	Young Stribling	Lt. Heavy	1921-33	286
9	Battling Levinsky	Lt. Heavy	1910-29	282
10	Ted (Kid) Lewis	Welter	1909-29	279

Former Champions Who Have Won Back Heavyweight Title

Only 10 times since 1892 has the heavyweight championship been lost by a fighter who was able to win it back. Eight men have done it and Muhammad Ali and Evander Holyfield have done it twice.

	Lost To	Won Back From		Lost To	Won Back From
Floyd Patterson	Johansson (1959)	Johansson (1960)	Mike Tyson	Douglas (1990)	Bruno (1996)
Muhammad Ali	Frazier (1971)	Foreman (1974)	Evander Holyfield	Moorer (1994)	Tyson (1996)
Muhammad Ali	L Spinks (1978)	L Spinks (1978)	Lennox Lewis	McCall (1994)	McCall (1997)
Tim Witherspoon	Thomas (1984)	Tubbs (1986)			
Evander Holyfield	Bowe (1992)	Bowe (1993)	*Moorer won the vacant IBF title in a fight with Germany's Axel Schulz		
George Foreman	Ali (1974)	Moorer (1994)			
Michael Moorer	Foreman (1994)	Schulz (1996)*			

Triple Champions

Fighters who have won widely-accepted world titles in more than two divisions. Henry Armstrong is the only fighter listed to hold three titles simultaneously. Note that (*) indicates title claimant.

Sugar Ray Leonard (5) WBC Welterweight (1979-80,82); WBA Jr. Middleweight (1981); WBC Middleweight (1987); WBC Super Middleweight (1988-90); WBC Light Heavyweight (1988).

Roberto Duran (4) Lightweight (1972-79); WBC Welterweight (1980); WBA Jr. Middleweight (1983-84); WBC Middleweight (1989-90).

Thomas Hearns (4) WBA Welterweight (1980-81); WBC Jr. Middleweight (1982-84); WBC Light Heavyweight (1987); WBA Light Heavyweight (1991); WBC Middleweight (1987-88).

Pernell Whitaker (4) IBF/WBC/WBA Lightweight (1989-92); IBF Jr. Welterweight (1992-93); WBC Welterweight (1993-97); WBC Jr. Middleweight (1995).

Alexis Arguello (3) WBA Featherweight (1974-77); WBC Jr. Lightweight (1978-80); WBC Lightweight (1981-83).

Henry Armstrong (3) Featherweight (1937-38); Welterweight (1938-40); Lightweight (1938-39).

Iran Barkley (3) WBC Middleweight (1988-89); IBF Super Middleweight (1992-93); WBA Light Heavyweight (1992).

Wilfredo Benitez (3) Jr. Welterweight (1976-79); Welterweight (1979); WBC Jr. Middleweight (1981-82).

Tony Canzoneri (3) Featherweight (1928); Lightweight (1930-33); Jr. Welterweight (1931-32,33).

Julio Cesar Chavez (3) WBC Jr. Lightweight (1984-87); WBA/WBC Lightweight (1987-89); WBC/IBF Jr. Welterweight (1989-91); WBC Jr. Welterweight (1991-94, 1994).

Oscar De La Hoya (3) IBF Lightweight (1995-96); WBC Super Lightweight (1996-97); WBC Welterweight (1997-99).

Jeff Fenech (3) IBF Bantamweight (1985); WBC Jr. Featherweight (1986-88); WBC Featherweight (1988-90).

Bob Fitzsimmons (3) Middleweight (1891-97); Light Heavyweight (1903-05); Heavyweight (1897-99).

Wilfredo Gomez (3) WBC Super Bantamweight (1977-83); WBC Featherweight (1984); WBA Jr. Lightweight (1985-86).

Leo Gamez (3) WBA Strawweight (1988-90); WBA Jr. Flyweight (1993-95); WBA Flyweight (1999).

Emile Griffith (3) Welterweight (1961,62-63,63-66); Jr. Middleweight (1962-63); Middleweight (1966-67,67-68).

Roy Jones Jr. (3) IBF Middleweight (1993-94); IBF Super Middleweight (1994-96); WBC Light Heavyweight (1996, 1997-); WBA Light Heavyweight (1998-); IBF Light Heavyweight (1999-).

Mike McCallum (3) WBA Jr. Middleweight (1984-88); WBA Middleweight (1989-91); WBC Light Heavyweight (1994-95).

Terry McGovern (3) Bantamweight (1889-1900); Featherweight (1900-01); Lightweight* (1900-01).

Barney Ross (3) Lightweight (1933-35); Jr. Welterweight (1933-35); Welterweight (1934, 35-38).

Wilfredo Vazquez (3) WBA Bantamweight (1987-88); WBA Jr. Featherweight (1992-95); WBA Featherweight (1996-98).

Miscellaneous Sports

Doug Swingley, of Lincoln, Mont., gets a lick from his lead dog **Elmer** after winning the 1999 Iditarod Trail Sled Dog Race that runs yearly from Anchorage to Nome, Alaska.

AP/Wide World Photos

CHESS

World Champions

Garry Kasparov became the youngest man to win the world chess championship when he beat fellow Russian Anatoly Karpov in 1985 at age 22. In 1993, Kasparov and then-No. 1 challenger Nigel Short of England broke away from the established International Chess Federation (FIDE) to form the PCA. FIDE retaliated by stripping Kasparov of their world title and arranging a playoff that was won by Karpov, the former title-holder. Karpov has since successfully defended the FIDE title several times.

In 1999 FIDE sponsored another World Championship tournament, this time at Caesar's Palace in Las Vegas from July 30-Aug. 29. Most of the greatest players in the world were there. However, both Kasparov and Karpov were not. Kasparov was off playing a game on the Internet against the world but Karpov was supposed to be in Las Vegas to defend his FIDE title. He did not show.

The 72 players in the tournament squared off in two- and four-game matches (extra games were held to break ties). The tournament was single elimination and in each round the field was cut in half. Alexander Khalifman was the sole survivor, beating Judith Polgar in the quarterfinals, then Liviu-Dieter Nisipeanu in the semis before facing Vladimir Akopian in the finals. Khalifman beat Akopian 3½-2½ to claim the $660,000 prize and become the new FIDE world champion.

Despite Khalifman's win in Las Vegas, Kasparov is still the world's top-ranked player and continues to be recognized as the world champion. Kasparov was scheduled to defended his crown against world #2 Viswanathan Anand in a 16-game match in late 1999.

Years		Years		Years	
1866-94	Wilhelm Steinitz, Austria	1948-57	Mikhail Botvinnik, USSR	1969-72	Boris Spassky, USSR
1894-1921	Emanuel Lasker, Germany	1957-58	Vassily Smyslov, USSR	1972-75	Bobby Fischer, USA*
1921-27	Jose Capablanca, Cuba	1958-59	Mikhail Botvinnik, USSR	1975-85	Anatoly Karpov, USSR
1927-35	Alexander Alekhine, France	1960-61	Mikhail Tal, USSR	1985—	Garry Kasparov, RUS
1935-37	Max Euwe, Holland	1961-63	Mikhail Botvinnik, USSR	*Fischer defaulted the championship
1937-46	Alexander Alekhine, France	1963-69	Tigran Petrosian, USSR	in 1975.

U.S. Champions

Boris Gulko beat Gregory Serper 2½-½ at the 1999 U.S. Chess Championships held Aug.22-Sept. 11 in Salt Lake City, Utah. Gulko took home $12,000 for winning the 16-player, round robin tournament.

Years		Years		Years	
1857-71	Paul Morphy	1954-57	Arthur Bisguier	1984-85	Lev Alburt
1871-76	George Mackenzie	1957-61	Bobby Fischer	1986	Yasser Seirawan
1876-80	James Mason	1961-62	Larry Evans	1987	Joel Benjamin
1880-89	George Mackenzie	1962-68	Bobby Fischer		& Nick DeFirmian
1889-90	Samuel Lipschutz	1968-69	Larry Evans	1988	Michael Wilder
1890	Jackson Showalter	1969-72	Samuel Reshevsky	1989	Roman Dzindzichashvili,
1890-91	Max Judd	1972-73	Robert Byrne		Stuart Rachels
1891-92	Jackson Showalter	1973-74	Lubomir Kavalek		& Yasser Seirawan
1892-94	Samuel Lipschutz		& John Grefe	1990	Lev Alburt
1894	Jackson Showalter	1974-77	Walter Browne	1991	Gata Kamsky
1894-95	Albert Hodges	1978-80	Lubomir Kabalek	1992	Patrick Wolff
1895-97	Jackson Showalter	1980-81	Larry Evans,	1993	Alexander Shabalov
1897-1906	Harry Pillsbury		Larry Christiansen		& Alex Yermolinsky
1906-09	Vacant		& Walter Browne	1994	Boris Gulko
1909-36	Frank Marshall	1981-83	Walter Browne	1995	Alexander Ivanov
1936-44	Samuel Reshevsky		& Yasser Seirawan	1996	Alexander Yermolinsky
1944-46	Arnold Denker	1983	Roman Dzindzichashvili,	1997	Joel Benjamin
1946-48	Samuel Reshevsky		Larry Christiansen	1998	Nick de Firmian
1948-51	Herman Steiner		& Walter Browne	1999	Boris Gulko
1951-54	Larry Evans				

DOGS

Iditarod Trail Sled Dog Race

Doug Swingley won his second Iditarod Trail Sled Dog Race in 1999, reaching the finish line on Front Street in Nome in nine days, 14 hours, 31 minutes and seven seconds. Swingley, of Lincoln, Mont., beat second place finisher and former champion Martin Buser by nearly nine hours, the widest margin since 1992 when Buser beat runner-up Susan Butcher by more than 10 hours.

Swingley overcame two broken sleds and earned $54,000 for the win, plus the keys to a new pickup truck and $9,000 in bonus money. Swingley's strategy was the same one he used in his first Iditarod victory back in 1995. Swingley's team, behind lead dog Elmer, jumped out ahead of the pack before taking the mandatory 24-hour rest and then held onto the lead. Other teams got stuck in bad weather and Swingley also benefited when Buser was forced to cut his team from 16 dogs down to 10 early on due to injuries.

In even-numbered years the trail follows the 1,151-mile Northern Route, while in odd-numbered years, it takes a slightly different 1,161-mile Southern Route.

Multiple winners: Rick Swenson (5); Susan Butcher (4); Martin Buser and Jeff King (3); Rick Mackey and Doug Swingley (2).

Year		Elapsed Time	Year		Elapsed Time
1973	Dick Wilmarth	20 days, 00:49:41	1977	Rick Swenson	16 days, 16:27:13
1974	Carl Huntington	20 days, 15:02:07	1978	Dick Mackey	14 days, 18:52:24
1975	Emmitt Peters	14 days, 14:43:45	1979	Rick Swenson	15 days, 10:37:47
1976	Gerald Riley	18 days, 22:58:17	1980	Joe May	14 days, 07:11:51

Year		Elapsed Time	Year		Elapsed Time
1981	Rick Swenson	12 days, 08:45:02	1991	Rick Swenson	12 days, 16:34:39
1982	Rick Swenson	16 days, 04:40:10	1992	Martin Buser	10 days, 19:17:00
1983	Rick Mackey	12 days, 14:10:44	1993	Jeff King	10 days, 15:38:15
1984	Dean Osmar	12 days, 15:07:33	1994	Martin Buser	10 days, 13:02:39
1985	Libby Riddles	18 days, 00:20:17	1995	Doug Swingley	9 days, 02:42:19*
1986	Susan Butcher	11 days, 15:06:00	1996	Jeff King	9 days, 05:43:13
1987	Susan Butcher	11 days, 02:05:13	1997	Martin Buser	9 days, 08:31:45
1988	Susan Butcher	11 days, 11:41:40	1998	Jeff King	9 days, 05:52:26
1989	Joe Runyan	11 days, 05:24:34	1999	Doug Swingley	9 days, 14:31:07
1990	Susan Butcher	11 days, 01:53:23	*Course record.		

Westminster Kennel Club
Best in Show

Ch. Loteki's Supernatural Being, a 6-pound male Papillon, won Best in Show at the 123rd annual Westminster Kennel Club show on Feb. 9 at Madison Square Garden in New York. The 8-year-old, who answers to the name Kirby, nearly won the competition in 1996. Kirby is owned by his handler John Oulton and was chosen from among 2,500 dogs from 152 breeds.

The Westminster show is the most prestigious dog show in the country, and one of America's oldest annual sporting events.

Multiple winners: Ch. Warren Remedy (3); Ch. Chinoe's Adamant James, Ch. Comejo Wycollar Boy, Ch. Flornell Spicy Piece of Halleston; Ch. Matford Vic, Ch. My Own Brucie, Ch. Pendley Calling of Blarney, Ch. Rancho Dobe's Storm (2).

Year	Breed		Year	Breed	
1907	Warren Remedy	Fox Terrier	1954	Carmor's Rise and Shine	Cocker Spaniel
1908	Warren Remedy	Fox Terrier	1955	Kippax Fearnought	Bulldog
1909	Warren Remedy	Fox Terrier	1956	Wilber White Swan	Toy Poodle
1910	Sabine Rarebit	Fox Terrier	1957	Shirkhan of Grandeur	Afghan Hound
1911	Tickle Em Jock	Scottish Terrier	1958	Puttencove Promise	Standard Poodle
1912	Kenmore Sorceress	Airedale	1959	Fontclair Festoon	Miniature Poodle
1913	Strathway Prince Albert	Bulldog	1960	Chick T'Sun of Caversham	Pekingese
1914	Brentwood Hero	Old English Sheepdog	1961	Cappoquin Little Sister	Toy Poodle
1915	Matford Vic	Old English Sheepdog	1962	Elfinbrook Simon	W. Highland Terrier
1916	Matford Vic	Old English Sheepdog	1963	Wakefield's Black Knight	English Springer Spaniel
1917	Comejo Wycollar Boy	Fox Terrier	1964	Courtenay Fleetfoot of Pennyworth	Whippet
1918	Haymarket Faultless	Bull Terrier	1965	Carmichaels Fanfare	Scottish Terrier
1919	Briergate Bright Beauty	Airedale	1966	Zeloy Mooremaides Magic	Fox Terrier
1920	Comejo Wycollar Boy	Fox Terrier	1967	Bardene Bingo	Scottish Terrier
1921	Midkiff Seductive	Cocker Spaniel	1968	Stingray of Derryabah	Lakeland Terrier
1922	Boxwood Barkentine	Airedale	1969	Glamoor Good News	Skye Terrier
1923	No best-in-show award		1970	Arriba's Prima Donna	Boxer
1924	Barberryhill Bootlegger	Sealyham	1971	Chinoe's Adamant James	E.S. Spaniel
1925	Governor Moscow	Pointer	1972	Chinoe's Adamant James	E.S. Spaniel
1926	Signal Circuit	Fox Terrier	1973	Acadia Command Performance	Standard Poodle
1927	Pinegrade Perfection	Sealyham	1974	Gretchenhof Columbia River	German SH Pointer
1928	Talavera Margaret	Fox Terrier	1975	Sir Lancelot of Barvan	Old Eng. Sheepdog
1929	Land Loyalty of Bellhaven	Collie	1976	Jo Ni's Red Baron of Crofton	Lakeland Terrier
1930	Pendley Calling of Blarney	Fox Terrier	1977	Dersade Bobby's Girl	Sealyham
1931	Pendley Calling of Blarney	Fox Terrier	1978	Cede Higgens	Yorkshire Terrier
1932	Nancolleth Markable	Pointer	1979	Oak Tree's Irishtocrat	Irish Water Spaniel
1933	Warland Protector of Shelterock	Airedale	1980	Sierra Cinnar	Siberian Husky
1934	Flornell Spicy Bit of Halleston	Fox Terrier	1981	Dhandy Favorite Woodchuck	Pug
1935	Nunsoe Duc de la Terrace of Blakeen	Stan. Poodle	1982	St. Aubrey Dragonora of Elsdon	Pekingese
1936	St. Margaret Magnificent of Clairedale	Sealyham	1983	Kabik's The Challenger	Afghan Hound
1937	Flornell Spicy Bit of Halleston	Fox Terrier	1984	Seaward's Blackbeard	Newfoundland
1938	Daro of Maridor	English Setter	1985	Braeburn's Close Encounter	Scottish Terrier
1939	Ferry v.Rauhfelsen of Giralda	Doberman	1986	Marjetta National Acclaim	Pointer
1940	My Own Brucie	Cocker Spaniel	1987	Covy Tucker Hill's Manhattan	German Shepherd
1941	My Own Brucie	Cocker Spaniel	1988	Great Elms Prince Charming II	Pomeranian
1942	Wolvey Pattern of Edgerstoune	W. Highland Terrier	1989	Royal Tudor's Wild As The Wind	Doberman
1943	Pitter Patter of Piperscroft	Miniature Poodle	1990	Wendessa Crown Prince	Pekingese
1944	Flornell Rarebit of Twin Ponds	Welsh Terrier	1991	Whisperwind on a Carousel	Stan. Poodle
1945	Shieling's Signature	Scottish Terrier	1992	Lonesome Dove	Fox Terrier
1946	Hetherington Model Rhythm	Fox Terrier	1993	Salilyn's Condor	E.S. Spaniel
1947	Warlord of Mazelaine	Boxer	1994	Chidley Willum	Norwich Terrier
1948	Rock Ridge Night Rocket	Bedling. Terrier	1995	Gaelforce Post Script	Scottish Terrier
1949	Mazelaine's Zazarac Brandy	Boxer	1996	Clussex Country Sunrise	Clumber Spaniel
1950	Walsing Winning Trick of Edgerstoune	Scot. Terrier	1997	Parsifal di Casa Netzer	Standard Schnauzer
1951	Bang Away of Sirrah Crest	Boxer	1998	Fairewood Frolic	Norwich Terrier
1952	Rancho Dobe's Storm	Doberman	1999	Loteki's Supernatural Being	Papillon
1953	Rancho Dobe's Storm	Doberman			

FISHING

IGFA All-Tackle World Records

All-tackle records are maintained for the heaviest fish of any species caught on any line up to 130-lb (60 kg) class and certified by the International Game Fish Association. Records logged through Aug. 26, 1999. **Address:** 300 Gulf Stream Way, Dania Beach, Fla. 33004. **Telephone:** 954-927-2628.

FRESHWATER FISH

Species	Lbs-Oz	Where Caught	Date	Angler
Barramundi	64-13	N. Queensland, Australia	Dec. 30, 1998	Alf Homewood
Bass, Guadalupe	3-11	Lake Travis, TX	Sept. 25, 1983	Allen Christenson Jr.
Bass, largemouth	22-4	Montgomery Lake, GA	June 2, 1932	George W. Perry
Bass, redeye	8-12	Apalachicola River, FL	Jan. 28, 1995	Carl W. Davis
Bass, Roanoke	1-5	Nottoway River, VA	Nov. 11, 1991	Tom Elkins
Bass, rock	3-0	York River, Ontario	Aug. 1, 1974	Peter Gulgin
Bass, smallmouth	10-14	Dale Hollow, TN	Apr. 24, 1969	John T. Gorman
Bass, spotted	9-9	Pine Flat Lake, CA	Oct. 12, 1996	Kirk Sakamoto
Bass, striped (landlocked)	67-8	O'Neill Forebay, San Luis, CA	May 7, 1992	Hank Ferguson
Bass, Suwannee	3-14	Suwannee River, FL	Mar. 2, 1985	Ronnie Everett
Bass, white	6-13	Lake Orange, VA	July 31, 1989	Ronald L. Sprouse
Bass, whiterock	27-5	Greers Ferry Lake, AR	Apr. 24, 1997	Jerald C. Shaum
Bass, yellow	2-9	Duck River, TN	Feb. 27, 1998	John T. Campbell
Bass, yellow (hybrid)	3-5	Big Cypress Bayou, TX	Mar. 27, 1991	Patrick Collin Myers
Bluegill	4-12	Ketona Lake, AL	Apr. 9, 1950	T.S. Hudson
Bowfin	21-8	Florence, SC	Jan. 29, 1980	Robert L. Harmon
Buffalo, bigmouth	70-5	Bussey Brake, Bastrop, LA	Apr. 21, 1980	Delbert Sisk
Buffalo, black	55-8	Cherokee Lake, TN	May 3, 1984	Edward H. McLain
Buffalo, smallmouth	82-3	Athens Lake, TX	June 6, 1993	Randy Collins
Bullhead, black	7-7	Mill Pond, NY	Aug. 25, 1993	Kevin Kelly
Bullhead, brown	6-1	Waterford, NY	Apr. 26, 1998	Bobby Triplett
Bullhead, yellow	4-4	Mormon Lake, AZ	May 11, 1984	Emily Williams
Burbot	18-11	Angenmanelren, Sweden	Oct. 22, 1996	Margit Agren
Carp	82-3	Lake Roduta, Romania	May 26, 1998	Christain Baldermair
Catfish, blue	111-0	Wheeler's Reservoir, TN	July 5, 1996	William McKinley
Catfish, channel	58-0	Santee-Cooper Res., SC	July 7, 1964	W.B. Whaley
Catfish, flathead	123-9	Elk City Reservoir, KS	Mar. 14, 1998	Ken Paulie
Catfish, flatwhiskered	9-4	Rio Paraquai, Brazil	Sept. 11, 1996	Cavour Pieranti
Catfish, gilded	85-8	Amazon River, Brazil	Nov. 15, 1986	Gilberto Fernandes
Catfish, redtail	97-7	Amazon River, Brazil	July 16, 1988	Gilberto Fernandes
Catfish, sharptoothed	79-5	Orange River, S. Africa	Dec. 5, 1992	Hennie Moller
Catfish, white	18-14	Inverness, FL	Sept. 21, 1991	Jim Miller
Char, Arctic	32-9	Tree River, Canada	July 30, 1981	Jeffery Ward
Crappie, black	4-8	Kerr Lake, VA	Mar. 1, 1981	L. Carl Herring Jr.
Crappie, white	5-3	Enid Dam, MS	July 31, 1957	Fred L. Bright
Dolly Varden	19-4	Unnamed River, AK	Sept. 4, 1998	Gary D. Ordway
Dorado	51-5	Corrientes, Argentina	Sept. 27, 1984	Armando Giudice
Drum, freshwater	54-8	Nickajack Lake, TN	Apr. 20, 1972	Benny E. Hull
Gar, alligator	279-0	Rio Grande, TX	Dec. 2, 1951	Bill Valverde
Gar, Florida	21-3	Boca Raton, FL	June 3, 1981	Jeff Sabol
Gar, longnose	50-5	Trinity River, TX	July 30, 1954	Townsend Miller
Gar, shortnose	5-12	Rend Lake, Ill.	July 16, 1995	Donna K. Willmart
Gar, spotted	9-12	Lake Mevia, TX	Apr. 7, 1994	Rick Rivard
Goldfish	6-10	Lake Hodges, CA	Apr. 17, 1996	Florentino M. Abena
Grayling, Arctic	5-15	Katseyedie River, N.W.T.	Aug. 16, 1967	Jeanne P. Branson
Inconnu	53-0	Pah River, AK	Aug. 20, 1986	Lawrence E. Hudnall
Kokanee	9-6	Okanagan Lake, Brit. Columbia	June 18, 1988	Norm Kuhn
Muskellunge	67-8	Hayward, WI	July 24, 1949	Cal Johnson
Muskellunge, tiger	51-3	Lac Vieux-Desert, WI-MI	July 16, 1919	John A. Knobla
Peacock, butterfly	10-8	Raraima, Brazil	Mar. 21, 1994	Larry Larsen
Peacock, speckled	27-0	Rio Negro, Brazil	Dec. 4, 1994	Gerald (Doc) Lawson
Perch, Nile	213-0	Lake Nasser, Egypt	Dec. 18, 1997	Adrian Brayshaw
Perch, white	4-12	Messalonskee Lake, ME	June 4, 1949	Mrs. Earl Small
Perch, yellow	4-3	Bordentown, NJ	May, 1865	Dr. C.C. Abbot
Pickerel, chain	9-6	Homerville, GA	Feb. 17, 1961	Baxley McQuaig Jr.
Pickerel, grass	1-0	Dewart Lake, IN	June 9, 1990	Mike Berg
Pickerel, redfin	2-4	St. Pauls, NC	June 27, 1997	Edward C. Davis
Pike, northern	55-1	Lake of Grefeern, Germany	Oct. 16, 1986	Lothar Louis
Redhorse, greater	9-3	Salmon River, Pulaski, NY	May 11, 1985	Jason Wilson
Redhorse, silver	11-7	Plum Creek, WI	May 29, 1985	Neal D.G. Long
Salmon, Atlantic	79-2	Tana River, Norway	1928	Henrik Henriksen
Salmon, chinook	97-4	Kenai River, AK	May 17, 1985	Les Anderson
Salmon, chum	35-0	Edye Pass, Brit. Columbia	July 11, 1995	Todd Johansson

Species	Lbs-Oz	Where Caught	Date	Angler
Salmon, coho	33-4	Salmon River, Pulaski, NY	Sept. 27, 1989	Jerry Lifton
Salmon, pink	13-1	St. Mary's River, Ontario	Sept. 23, 1992	Ray Higaki
Salmon, sockeye	15-3	Kenai River, AK	Aug. 9, 1987	Stan Roach
Sauger	8-12	Lake Sakakawea, ND	Oct. 6, 1971	Mike Fischer
Shad, American	11-4	Conn. River, S. Hadley, MA	May 19, 1986	Bob Thibodo
Shad, gizzard	4-6	Lake Michigan, IN	Mar. 2, 1996	Mike Berg
Sturgeon, lake	168-0	Georgian Bay, Canada	May 29, 1982	Edward Paszkowski
Sturgeon, white	468-0	Benicia, CA	July 9, 1983	Joey Pallotta 3rd
Tigerfish, giant	97-0	Zaire River, Kinshasa, Zaire	July 9, 1988	Raymond Houtmans
Tilapia	6-5	Lake Arsenal, Costa Rica	Feb. 10, 1995	Marvin C. Smith
Trout, Apache	5-3	White Mountain, AZ	May 29, 1991	John Baldwin
Trout, brook	14-8	Nipigon River, Ontario	July, 1916	Dr. W.J. Cook
Trout, brown	40-4	Little Red River, AR	May 9, 1992	Rip Collins
Trout, bull	32-0	Lake Pond Orielle, ID	Oct. 27, 1949	N.L. Higgins
Trout, cutthroat	41-0	Pyramid Lake, NV	Dec., 1925	John Skimmerhorn
Trout, golden	11-0	Cooks Lake, WY	Aug. 5, 1948	Charles S. Reed
Trout, lake	72-0	Great Bear Lake, N.W.T.	Aug. 19, 1995	Lloyd E. Bull
Trout, rainbow	42-2	Bell Island, AK	June 22, 1970	David Robert White
Trout, tiger	20-13	Lake Michigan, WI	Aug. 12, 1978	Peter M. Friedland
Walleye	25-0	Old Hickory Lake, TN	Aug. 2, 1960	Mabry Harper
Warmouth	2-7	Guess Lake, Holt, FL	Oct. 19, 1985	Tony D. Dempsey
Whitefish, lake	14-6	Meaford, Ontario	May 21, 1984	Dennis M. Laycock
Whitefish, mountain	5-8	Elbow River, Manitoba	Aug. 1, 1995	Randy G. Woo
Whitefish, round	6-0	Putahow River, Manitoba	June 14, 1984	Allan J. Ristori
Zander	25-2	Trosa, Sweden	June 12, 1986	Harry Lee Tennison

SALTWATER FISH

Species	Lbs-Oz	Where Caught	Date	Angler
Albacore	88-2	Gran Canaria, Canary Islands	Nov. 19, 1977	Siegfried Dickemann
Amberjack, greater	155-12	Challenger Bank, Bermuda	Aug. 16, 1992	Larry Trott
Amberjack, pacific	104-0	Baja Calif., Mexico	July 4, 1984	Richard Cresswell
Barracuda, great	85-0	Christmas Is., Rep. of Kiribati	Apr. 11, 1992	John W. Helfrich
Barracuda, Mexican	21-0	Phantom Island, Costa Rica	Mar. 27, 1987	E. Greg Kent
Barracuda, pickhandle	25-5	Scottburgh, South Africa	July 3, 1996	Demetrios Stamatis
Bass, barred sand	13-3	Huntington Beach, CA	Aug. 29, 1988	Robert Halal
Bass, black sea	9-8	Virginia Beach, VA	Jan. 9, 1987	Joe Mizelle Jr.
	9-8	Virginia Beach, VA	Dec. 22, 1990	Jack G. Stallings Jr.
Bass, European	20-11	Stes Maries de la Mer, France	May 6, 1986	Jean Baptiste Bayle
Bass, giant sea	563-8	Anacapa Island, CA	Aug. 20, 1968	J.D. McAdam Jr.
Bass, striped	78-8	Atlantic City, NJ	Sept. 21, 1982	Albert R. McReynolds
Bluefish	31-12	Hatteras, NC	Jan. 30, 1972	James M. Hussey
Bonefish	19-0	Zululand, South Africa	May 26, 1962	Brian W. Batchelor
Bonito, Atlantic	18-4	Faial Island, Azores	July 8, 1953	D. Gama Higgs
Bonito, Pacific	21-3	Malibu, CA	July 30, 1978	Gino M. Picciolo
Cabezon	23-0	Juan de Fuca Strait, WA	Aug. 4, 1990	Wesley Hunter
Cobia	135-9	Shark Bay, W. Australia	July 9, 1985	Peter W. Goulding
Cod, Atlantic	98-12	Isle of Shoals, NH	June 8, 1969	Alphonse Bielevich
Cod, Pacific	32-0	Unalaska Bay, AK	June 29, 1997	Donald Boston
Conger	133-4	South Devon, England	June 5, 1995	Vic Evans
Dolphinfish	88-0	Highbourne Cay, Bahamas	May 5, 1998	Richard D. Evans
Drum, black	113-1	Lewes, DE	Sept. 15, 1975	Gerald M. Townsend
Drum, red	94-2	Avon, NC	Nov. 7, 1984	David G. Deuel
Eel, American	9-4	Cape May, NJ	Nov. 9, 1995	Jeff Pennick
Eel, marbled	36-1	Durban, S. Africa	June 10, 1984	Ferdie van Nooten
Flounder, southern	20-9	Nassau Sound, FL	Dec. 23, 1983	Larenza Mungin
Flounder, summer	22-7	Montauk, NY	Sept. 15, 1975	Charles Nappi
Grouper, Warsaw	436-12	Gulf of Mexico, Destin, FL	Dec. 22, 1985	Steve Haeusler
Haddock	14-15	Saltraumen, Germany	Aug. 15, 1997	Heike Neblinger
Halibut, Atlantic	355-6	Valevag, Norway	Oct. 20, 1997	Odd Arve
Halibut, California	57-11	Santa Rosa Island, CA	June 6, 1999	William Akins
Halibut, Pacific	459-0	Dutch Harbor, AK	June 11, 1996	Jack Tragis
Jack, almaco (Pacific)	132-0	La Paz, Baja Calif., Mexico	July 21, 1964	Howard H. Hahn
Jack, crevalle	57-14	Southwest Pass, LA	Aug. 15, 1997	Leon D. Richard
Jack, horse-eye	29-8	Ascencion Island, South Atlantic	May 28, 1993	Mike Hanson
Jewfish	680-0	Fernandina Beach, FL	May 20, 1961	Lynn Joyner
Kawakawa	29-0	Clarion Island, Mexico	Dec. 17, 1986	Ronald Nakamura
Lingcod	69-0	Langara Is., Brit. Columbia	June 16, 1992	Murray M. Romer
Mackerel, cero	17-2	Islamorada, FL	Apr. 5, 1986	G. Michael Mills
Mackerel, king	93-0	San Juan, Puerto Rico	April 18, 1999	Steve Perez Graulau
Mackerel, Spanish	13-0	Ocracoke Inlet, NC	Nov. 4, 1987	Robert Cranton

Species	Lbs-Oz	Where Caught	Date	Angler
Marlin, Atlantic blue	1402-2	Vitoria, Brazil	Feb. 29, 1992	Paulo R.A. Amorim
Marlin, black	1560-0	Cabo Blanco, Peru	Aug. 4, 1953	A.C. Glassell Jr.
Marlin, Pacific blue	1376-0	Kaaiwi Point, Kona, HI	May 31, 1982	Jay W. deBeaubien
Marlin, striped	494-0	Tutakaka, New Zealand	Jan. 16, 1986	Bill Boniface
Marlin, white	181-14	Vitoria, Brazil	Dec. 8, 1979	Evandro Luiz Coser
Permit	56-2	Ft. Lauderdale, FL	June 30, 1997	Thomas Sebestyen
Pollack	27-6	Salcombe, Devon, England	Jan. 16, 1986	Robert S. Milkins
Pollock	50-0	Salstraumen, Norway	Nov. 30, 1996	Thor-Magnus Ukang
Pompano, African	50-8	Daytona Beach, FL	Apr. 21, 1990	Tom Sargent
Roosterfish	114-0	La Paz, Baja Calif., Mexico	June 1, 1960	Abe Sackheim
Runner, blue	11-2	Dauphin Island, AL	June 28, 1997	Stacey M. Moiren
Runner, rainbow	37-9	Clarion Island, Mexico	Nov. 21, 1991	Tom Pfleger
Sailfish, Atlantic	141-1	Luanda, Angola	Feb. 19, 1994	Alfredo de Sousa Neves
Sailfish, Pacific	221-0	Santa Cruz Is., Ecuador	Feb. 12, 1947	C.W. Stewart
Seabass, white	83-12	San Felipe, Mexico	Mar. 31, 1953	L.C. Baumgardner
Seatrout, spotted	17-7	Ft. Pierce, FL	May 11, 1995	Craig F. Carson
Shark, blue	454-0	Martha's Vineyard, MA	July 19, 1996	Pete Bergin
Shark, great white	2664-0	Ceduna, S. Australia	Apr. 21, 1959	Alfred Dean
Shark, Greenland	1708-9	Trondheimsfjord, Norway	Oct. 18, 1987	Terje Nordtvedt
Shark, hammerhead	991-0	Sarasota, FL	May 30, 1982	Allen Ogle
Shark, shortfin mako	1115-0	Black River, Mauritius	Nov. 16, 1988	Patrick Guillanton
Shark, porbeagle	507-0	Pentland Firth, Scotland	Mar. 9, 1993	Christopher Bennet
Shark, bigeye thresher	802-0	Tutukaka, New Zealand	Feb. 8, 1981	Dianne North
Shark, tiger	1780-0	Cherry Grove, SC	June 14, 1964	Walter Maxwell
Snapper, cubera	121-8	Cameron, LA	July 5, 1982	Mike Hebert
Snapper, red	50-4	Gulf of Mexico, LA	June 23, 1996	Capt. Doc Kennedy
Snook	53-10	Parismina Ranch, Costa Rica	Oct. 18, 1978	Gilbert Ponzi
Spearfish, Mediterranean	90-13	Madeira Island, Portugal	June 2, 1980	Joseph Larkin
Swordfish	1182-0	Iquique, Chile	May 7, 1953	L. Marron
Tarpon	283-4	Sherbro Is., Sierra Leone	Apr. 16, 1991	Yvon Victor Sebag
Tautog	25-0	Ocean City, NJ	Jan. 20, 1998	Anthony R. Monica
Tuna, Atlantic bigeye	392-6	Gran Canaria, Puerto Rico	July 25, 1996	Dieter Vogel
Tuna, blackfin	45-8	Key West, FL	May 4, 1996	Sam J. Burnett
Tuna, bluefin	1496-0	Aulds Cove, Nova Scotia	Oct. 26, 1979	Ken Fraser
Tuna, longtail	79-2	Montague Is., NSW, Australia	Apr. 12, 1982	Tim Simpson
Tuna, Pacific bigeye	435-0	Cabo Blanco, Peru	Apr. 17, 1957	Dr. Russell Lee
Tuna, skipjack	45-4	Flathead Bank, Mexico	Nov. 16, 1996	Brian Evans
Tuna, southern bluefin	348-5	Whakatane, New Zealand	Jan. 16, 1981	Rex Wood
Tuna, yellowfin	388-12	San Benedicto Island, Mexico	Apr. 1, 1977	Curt Wiesenhutter
Tunny, little	35-2	Cape de Garde, Algeria	Dec. 14, 1988	Jean Yves Chatard
Wahoo	158-8	Loreto, Baja Calif., Mexico	June 10, 1996	Keith Winter
Weakfish	19-2	Jones Beach, Long Island, NY	Oct. 11, 1984	Dennis R. Rooney
	19-2	Delaware Bay, DE	May 20, 1989	William E. Thomas

B.A.S.S. Masters Classic

Davy Hite, the 1997 B.A.S.S. Angler of the Year and 1996 B.A.S.S. Masters Classic runner-up, won the 29th annual B.A.S.S. Masters Classic Championship on the Louisiana Delta near New Orleans on July 31. His three-day total of 55 pounds, 10 ounces easily outdistanced runner-up and defending champion Denny Brauer (45-11). Over 23,000 fans turned out for the weigh-in at the Louisiana Superdome.

"I was fortunate to have a unique little area all to myself, which is a real luxury in a tournament like this," Hite said. "And I was able to catch a better stringer each day."

"This really makes up for finishing second (in the Classic) back in 1996. In that tournament, I thought I had it won and backed off of my fish late on the last day. But this time, I wasn't about to let that happen again. I fished hard until the end of the day."

Hite, a 34-year-old native of Prosperity, S.C., earned a winner's check for $101,000 using a junebug-colored 7-inch Gambler Bacon Rind, a strange-looking soft-plastic crawfish imitation rigged with a 3/8-ounce Florida Rig sinker, 5/0 Owner hook and 25-pound test Trilene line.

The B.A.S.S. Masters Classic is fishing's version of the Masters golf tournament. Invitees to the three-day event include the 25 top-ranked pros on the B.A.S.S. tour and the five top-ranked anglers from each BASSMASTER Invitational circuit. Anglers may weigh only seven bass per day and each bass must be at least 12 inches long. Competitors are allowed only seven rods and reels and are limited to the tackle they can pack into two tournament-approved tackleboxes. Only artificial lures are permitted. The first Classic, held at Lake Mead, Nev. in 1971, was a $10,000 winner-take-all event.

Multiple winners: Rick Clunn (4); George Cochran, Bobby Murray and Hank Parker (2).

Year		Weight	Year		Weight
1971	Bobby Murray, Hot Springs, Ark.	43-11	1978	Bobby Murray, Nashville, Tenn	37-9
1972	Don Butler, Tulsa, Okla	38-11	1979	Hank Parker, Clover, S.C	31-0
1973	Rayo Breckenridge, Paragould, Ark	52-8	1980	Bo Dowden, Natchitoches, La	54-10
1974	Tommy Martin, Hemphill, Tex	33-7	1981	Stanley Mitchell, Fitzgerald, Ga	35-2
1975	Jack Hains, Rayne, La	45-4	1982	Paul Elias, Laurel, Miss	32-8
1976	Rick Clunn, Montgomery, Tex	59-15	1983	Larry Nixon, Hemphill, Tex	18-1
1977	Rick Clunn, Montgomery, Tex	27-7	1984	Rick Clunn, Montgomery, Tex	75-9

Year		Weight	Year		Weight
1985	Jack Chancellor, Phenix City, Ala	45-0	1993	David Fritts, Lexington, N.C.	48-6
1986	Charlie Reed, Broken Bow, Okla.	23-9	1994	Bryan Kerchal, Newtown, Conn	36-7
1987	George Cochran, N. Little Rock, Ark	15-5	1995	Mark Davis, Mount Ida, Ark.	47-14
1988	Guido Hibdon, Gravois Mills, Mo.	28-8	1996	George Cochran, Hot Springs, Ark.	31-14
1989	Hank Parker, Denver, N.C.	31-6	1997	Dion Hibdon, Stover, Mo.	34-13
1990	Rick Clunn, Montgomery, Tex.	34-5	1998	Denny Brauer, Camdenton, Mo.	46-3
1991	Ken Cook, Meers, Okla	33-2	1999	Davy Hite, Prosperity, S.C.	55-10
1992	Robert Hamilton Jr., Brandon, Miss	59-6			

LITTLE LEAGUE BASEBALL

World Series

Played annually in late August in Williamsport, Pa. at Original Field in Williamsport, Pa. from 1947-1958 and at Howard J. Lamade Stadium since 1959.

Multiple winners: Taiwan (16); California (5); Connecticut, Japan, New Jersey and Pennsylvania (4); Mexico (3); New York, South Korea and Texas (2).

Year	Winner	Score	Loser	Year	Winner	Score	Loser
1947	Williamsport, PA	16-7	Lock Haven, PA	1974	Kao Hsiung, Taiwan	12-1	Red Bluff, CA
1948	Lock Haven, PA	6-5	St. Petersburg, FL	1975	Lakewood, NJ	4-3	*Tampa, FL
1949	Hammonton, NJ	5-0	Pensacola, FL	1976	Tokyo, Japan	10-3	Campbell, CA
1950	Houston, TX	2-1	Bridgeport, CT	1977	Li-Teh, Taiwan	7-2	El Cajon, CA
1951	Stamford, CT	3-0	Austin, TX	1978	Pin-Tung, Taiwan	11-1	Danville, CA
1952	Norwalk, CT	4-3	Monongahela, PA	1979	Hsien, Taiwan	2-1	Campbell, CA
1953	Birmingham, AL	1-0	Schenectady, NY	1980	Hua Lian, Taiwan	4-3	Tampa, FL
1954	Schenectady, NY	7-5	Colton, CA	1981	Tai-Chung, Taiwan	4-2	Tampa, FL
1955	Morrisville, PA	4-3	Merchantville, NJ	1982	Kirkland, WA	6-0	Hsien, Taiwan
1956	Roswell, NM	3-1	Merchantville, NJ	1983	Marietta, GA	3-1	Barahona, D. Rep.
1957	Monterrey, Mexico	4-0	La Mesa, CA	1984	Seoul, S. Korea	6-2	Altamonte, FL
1958	Monterrey, Mexico	10-1	Kankakee, IL	1985	Seoul, S. Korea	7-1	Mexicali, Mex.
1959	Hamtramck, MI	12-0	Auburn, CA	1986	Tainan Park, Taiwan	12-0	Tucson, AZ
1960	Levittown, PA	5-0	Ft. Worth, TX	1987	Hua Lian, Taiwan	21-1	Irvine, CA
1961	El Cajon, CA	4-2	El Campo, TX	1988	Tai Ping, Taiwan	10-0	Pearl City, HI
1962	San Jose, CA	3-0	Kankakee, IL	1989	Trumbull, CT	5-2	Kaohsiung, Taiwan
1963	Granada Hills, CA	2-1	Stratford, CT	1990	Taipei, Taiwan	9-0	Shippensburg, PA
1964	Staten Island, NY	4-0	Monterrey, Mex.	1991	Taichung, Taiwan	11-0	Danville, CA
1965	Windsor Locks, CT	3-1	Stoney Creek, Can.	1992	Long Beach, CA	6-0	Zamboanga, Phil.
1966	Houston, TX	8-2	W. New York, NJ	1993	Long Beach, CA	3-2	Panama
1967	West Tokyo, Japan	4-1	Chicago, IL	1994	Maracaibo, Venezuela	4-3	Northridge, CA
1968	Osaka, Japan	1-0	Richmond, VA	1995	Tainan, Taiwan	17-3	Spring, TX
1969	Taipei, Taiwan	5-0	Santa Clara, CA	1996	Taipei, Taiwan	13-3	Cranston, RI
1970	Wayne, NJ	2-0	Campbell, CA				(called after 5th inn.)
1971	Tainan, Taiwan	12-3	Gary, IN	1997	Guadalupe, Mexico	5-4	Mission Viejo, CA
1972	Taipei, Taiwan	6-0	Hammond, IN	1998	Toms River, NJ	12-9	Kashima, Japan
1973	Tainan City, Taiwan	12-0	Tucson, AZ	1999	Osaka, Japan	5-0	Phenix City, AL

*Foreign teams were banned from the tournament in 1975, but allowed back in the following year.

Note: In 1992, Zamboanga City of the Philippines beat Long Beach, 15-4, but was stripped of the title a month later when it was discovered that the team had used several players from outside the city limits. Long Beach was then awarded the title by forfeit, 6-0 (one run for each inning of the game).

POWER BOAT RACING

APBA Gold Cup

Chip Hanauer won the 96th edition of the APBA Gold Cup as he drove *Miss Pico* to victory July 11, 1999 on the Detroit River. Hanauer beat defending champ Dave Villwock in *Miss Budweiser* by three roostertails on the 2.5-mile course for his 11th career win in the race, becoming the first driver ever to break the 150 mph mark.

The American Power Boat Association Gold Cup for unlimited hydroplane racing is the oldest active motorsports trophy in North America. The first Gold Cup was competed for on the Hudson River in New York in June and September of 1904. Since then several cities have hosted the race, led by Detroit (30 times, including 1990) and Seattle (14). Note that (*) indicates driver was also owner of the winning boat.

Drivers with multiple wins: Chip Hanauer (11); Bill Muncey (8); Gar Wood (5); Dean Chenoweth (4); Caleb Bragg, Tom D'Eath, Lou Fageol, Ron Musson, George Reis, Dave Villwock and J.M. Wainwright (3); Danny Foster, George Henley, Vic Kliesrath, E.J. Schroeder, Bill Schumacher, Zalmon G. Simmons Jr., Joe Taggart, Mark Tate and George Townsend (2).

Year	Boat	Driver	Avg. MPH	Year	Boat	Driver	Avg. MPH
1904	*Standard* (June)	Carl Riotte*	23.160	1908	*Dixie II*	E.J. Schroeder*	29.938
1904	*Vingt-Et-Un II* (Sept.)	W. Sharpe Kilmer*	24.900	1909	*Dixie II*	E.J. Schroeder*	29.590
1905	*Chip I*	J.M. Wainwright*	15.000	1910	*Dixie III*	F.K. Burnham*	32.473
1906	*Chip II*	J.M. Wainwright*	25.000	1911	*MIT II*	J.H. Hayden*	37.000
1907	*Chip II*	J.M. Wainwright*	23.903	1912	*P.D.Q. II*	A.G. Miles*	39.462
				1913	*Ankle Deep*	C.S. Mankowski*	42.779

Year	Boat	Driver	Avg. MPH
1914	Baby Speed Demon II	Jim Blackton & Bob Edgren	48.458
1915	Miss Detroit	Johnny Milot & Jack Beebe	37.656
1916	Miss Minneapolis	Bernard Smith	48.860
1917	Miss Detroit II	Gar Wood*	54.410
1918	Miss Detroit II	Gar Wood	51.619
1919	Miss Detroit III	Gar Wood*	42.748
1920	Miss America I	Gar Wood*	62.022
1921	Miss America I	Gar Wood*	52.825
1922	Packard Chriscraft	J.G. Vincent*	40.253
1923	Packard Chriscraft	Caleb Bragg	43.867
1924	Baby Bootlegger	Caleb Bragg*	45.302
1925	Baby Bootlegger	Caleb Bragg*	47.240
1926	Greenwich Folly	George Townsend*	47.984
1927	Greenwich Folly	George Townsend*	47.662
1928	Not held		
1929	Imp	Richard Hoyt*	48.662
1930	Hotsy Totsy	Vic Kliesrath*	52.673
1931	Hotsy Totsy	Vic Kliesrath*	53.602
1932	Delphine IV	Bill Horn	57.775
1933	El Lagarto	George Reis*	56.260
1934	El Lagarto	George Reis*	55.000
1935	El Lagarto	George Reis*	55.056
1936	Impshi	Kaye Don	45.735
1937	Notre Dame	Clell Perry	63.675
1938	Alagi	Theo Rossi*	64.340
1939	My Sin	Z.G. Simmons Jr.*	66.133
1940	Hotsy Totsy III	Sidney Allen*	48.295
1941	My Sin	Z.G. Simmons Jr.*	52.509
1942-45	Not held		
1946	Tempo VI	Guy Lombardo*	68.132
1947	Miss Peps V	Danny Foster	57.000
1948	Miss Great Lakes	Danny Foster	46.845
1949	My Sweetie	Bill Cantrell	73.612
1950	Slo-Mo-Shun IV	Ted Jones	78.216
1951	Slo-Mo-Shun V	Lou Fageol	90.871
1952	Slo-Mo-Shun IV	Stan Dollar	79.923
1953	Slo-Mo-Shun IV	Joe Taggart & Lou Fageol	99.108
1954	Slo-Mo-Shun V	Lou Fageol	92.613
1955	Gale V	Lee Schoenith	99.552
1956	Miss Thirftway	Bill Muncey	96.552
1957	Miss Thriftway	Bill Muncey	101.787
1958	Hawaii Kai III	Jack Regas	103.000
1959	Maverick	Bill Stead	104.481
1960	Not held		
1961	Miss Century 21	Bill Muncey	99.678
1962	Miss Century 21	Bill Muncey	100.710
1963	Miss Bardahl	Ron Musson	105.124
1964	Miss Bardahl	Ron Musson	103.433
1965	Miss Bardahl	Ron Musson	103.132
1966	Tahoe Miss	Mira Slovak	93.019
1967	Miss Bardahl	Bill Shumacher	101.484
1968	Miss Bardahl	Bill Shumacher	108.173
1969	Miss Budweiser	Bill Sterett	98.504
1970	Miss Budweiser	Dean Chenoweth	99.562
1971	Miss Madison	Jim McCormick	98.043
1972	Atlas Van Lines	Bill Muncey	104.277
1973	Miss Budweiser	Dean Chenoweth	99.043
1974	Pay 'n Pak	George Henley	104.428
1975	Pay 'n Pak	George Henley	108.921
1976	Miss U.S.	Tom D'Eath	100.412
1977	Atlas Van Lines	Bill Muncey*	111.822
1978	Atlas Van Lines	Bill Muncey*	100.412
1979	Atlas Van Lines	Bill Muncey*	100.765
1980	Miss Budweiser	Dean Chenoweth	106.932
1981	Miss Budweiser	Dean Chenoweth	116.387
1982	Atlas Van Lines	Chip Hanauer	120.050
1983	Atlas Van Lines	Chip Hanauer	118.507
1984	Atlas Van Lines	Chip Hanauer	130.175
1985	Miller American	Chip Hanauer	120.643
1986	Miller American	Chip Hanauer	116.523
1987	Miller American	Chip Hanauer	127.620
1988	Miss Circus Circus	Chip Hanauer & Jim Prevost	123.756
1989	Miss Budweiser	Tom D'Eath	131.209
1990	Miss Budweiser	Tom D'Eath	143.176
1991	Winston Eagle	Mark Tate	137.771
1992	Miss Budweiser	Chip Hanauer	136.282
1993	Miss Budweiser	Chip Hanauer	141.296
1994	Smokin' Joe's	Mark Tate	145.532
1995	Miss Budweiser	Chip Hanauer	149.160
1996	Pico/American Dream	Dave Villwock	149.328
1997	Miss Budweiser	Dave Villwock	129.366
1998	Miss Budweiser	Dave Villwock	140.704
1999	Miss Pico	Chip Hanauer	152.591

PRO RODEO

All-Around Champion Cowboy

Ty Murray surpassed rodeo legends Tom Ferguson and Larry Mahan, winning his seventh all-around cowboy crown at the 40th Anniversary National Finals Rodeo held Dec. 4-13, 1998 in Las Vegas. Murray, winner of six straight All-Around titles from 1989-94 but had missed most of the last three seasons with shoulder and knee injuries, came back as good as ever in 1998 to win his record-setting championship. The 29-year-old also won his second Bull Riding World Championship at the NFR for the ninth gold buckle of his career.

The Professional Rodeo Cowboys Association (PRCA) title of All-Around World Champion Cowboy goes to the rodeo athlete who wins the most prize money in a single year in two or more events, earning a minimum of $2,000 in each event. Only prize money earned in sanctioned PRCA rodeos is counted. From 1929-44, All-Around champions were named by the Rodeo Association of America (earnings for those years is not available).

Multiple winners: Ty Murray (7); Tom Ferguson and Larry Mahan (6); Jim Shoulders (5); Lewis Feild and Dean Oliver (3); Joe Beaver, Everett Bowman, Louis Brooks, Clay Carr, Bill Linderman, Phil Lyne, Gerald Roberts, Casey Tibbs and Harry Tompkins (2).

Year		Year		Year		Year	
1929	Earl Thode	1933	Clay Carr	1937	Everett Bowman	1941	Homer Pettigrew
1930	Clay Carr	1934	Leonard Ward	1938	Burel Mulkey	1942	Gerald Roberts
1931	John Schneider	1935	Everett Bowman	1939	Paul Carney	1943	Louis Brooks
1932	Donald Nesbit	1936	John Bowman	1940	Fritz Truan	1944	Louis Brooks
						1945-46	No award

Year		Earnings	Year		Earnings	Year		Earnings
1947	Todd Whatley	$18,642	1965	Dean Oliver	$33,163	1983	Roy Cooper	$153,391
1948	Gerald Roberts	21,766	1966	Larry Mahan	40,358	1984	Dee Pickett	122,618
1949	Jim Shoulders	21,495	1967	Larry Mahan	51,996	1985	Lewis Feild	130,347
1950	Bill Linderman	30,715	1968	Larry Mahan	49,129	1986	Lewis Feild	166,042
1951	Casey Tibbs	29,104	1969	Larry Mahan	57,726	1987	Lewis Feild	144,335
1952	Harry Tompkins	30,934	1970	Larry Mahan	41,493	1988	Dave Appleton	121,546
1953	Bill Linderman	33,674	1971	Phil Lyne	49,245	1989	Ty Murray	134,806
1954	Buck Rutherford	40,404	1972	Phil Lyne	60,852	1990	Ty Murray	213,772
1955	Casey Tibbs	42,065	1973	Larry Mahan	64,447	1991	Ty Murray	244,231
1956	Jim Shoulders	43,381	1974	Tom Ferguson	66,929	1992	Ty Murray	225,992
1957	Jim Shoulders	33,299	1975	Tom Ferguson	50,300	1993	Ty Murray	297,896
1958	Jim Shoulders	32,212	1976	Tom Ferguson	87,908	1994	Ty Murray	246,170
1959	Jim Shoulders	32,905	1977	Tom Ferguson	65,981	1995	Joe Beaver	141,753
1960	Harry Tompkins	32,522	1978	Tom Ferguson	83,734	1996	Joe Beaver	166,103
1961	Benny Reynolds	31,309	1979	Tom Ferguson	96,272	1997	Dan Mortensen	184,559
1962	Tom Nesmith	32,611	1980	Paul Tierney	105,568	1998	Ty Murray	264,673
1963	Dean Oliver	31,329	1981	Jimmie Cooper	105,861			
1964	Dean Oliver	31,150	1982	Chris Lybbert	123,709			

RUGBY

World Cup

The inaugural Rugby World Cup was held in 1987. Like soccer's World Cup, it is held every four years. Sixteen national teams were assembled for the first three tournaments but, starting in 1999, 20 teams play for the William Webb Ellis Cup, named for the game's inventor. The Rugby World Cup is now billed as the world's third largest athletic event, behind the Olympics and the soccer World Cup.

The 1999 Rugby World Cup was scheduled for Oct. 1-Nov. 6. Although the host country for 1999 was Wales, games were to be held throughout the United Kingdom and France.

Year	Winner	Score	Runner up	Host Country
1987	New Zealand	29-9	France	Australia & New Zealand
1991	Australia	12-6	England	United Kingdom & France
1995	South Africa	15-12	New Zealand	South Africa

Five Nations Tournament

The annual Five Nations rugby tournament, a.k.a. the International Championship, was first contested in 1882 as a match between England and Wales. England, Ireland, Scotland and Wales competed in the early years. France made it five nations by joining the competition in 1910 and played until 1931 when they were expelled because of the sad state of French rugby. France rejoined the tournament in 1947. Each team plays each other once (two points are earned for a win and one for a tie) and the team with the most points is declared the winner. (*) indicates Grand Slam, meaning team won all four games.

The Five Nations will become the Six Nations in 2000 with the addition of Italy.

Multiple Winners: Wales (33); England (32); Scotland (21); France (19); Ireland (18).

Year		Year		Year	
1882	England	1909	Wales*	1940-46	Not held—WW II
1883	England	1910	England	1947	Wales & England
1884	England	1911	Wales*	1948	Ireland*
1885	Not completed	1912	England & Ireland	1949	Ireland
1886	England & Scotland	1913	England*	1950	Wales*
1887	Scotland	1914	England*	1951	Ireland
1888	Not completed	1915-19	Not held—WW I	1952	Wales*
1889	Not completed	1920	England, Scotland & Wales	1953	England
1890	England & Scotland	1921	England*	1954	England, France & Wales
1891	Scotland	1922	Wales	1955	France & Wales
1892	England	1923	England*	1956	Wales
1893	Wales	1924	England*	1957	England*
1894	Ireland	1925	Scotland*	1958	England
1895	Scotland	1926	Scotland & Ireland	1959	France
1896	Ireland	1927	Scotland & Ireland	1960	France & England
1897	Not completed	1928	England*	1961	France
1898	Not completed	1929	Scotland	1962	France
1899	Ireland	1930	England	1963	England
1900	Wales	1931	Wales	1964	Scotland & Wales
1901	Scotland	1932	England, Wales & Ireland	1965	Wales
1902	Wales	1933	Scotland	1966	Wales
1903	Scotland	1934	England	1967	France
1904	Scotland	1935	Ireland	1968	France*
1905	Wales	1936	Wales	1969	Wales
1906	Ireland & Wales	1937	England	1970	France & Wales
1907	Scotland	1938	Scotland	1971	Wales*
1908	Wales*	1939	England, Wales & Ireland	1972	Not completed

Year		Year		Year	
1973	Five way tie	1982	Ireland	1991	England*
1974	Ireland	1983	France & Ireland	1992	England*
1975	Wales	1984	Scotland*	1993	France
1976	Wales*	1985	Ireland	1994	Wales
1977	France*	1986	France & Scotland	1995	England*
1978	Wales*	1987	France*	1996	England
1979	Wales	1988	Wales & France	1997	France*
1980	England*	1989	France	1998	France*
1981	France*	1990	Scotland*	1999	Scotland

SOAP BOX DERBY

All-American Soap Box Derby

Fourteen-year-old Allan Endres, of Barberton, Ohio rode *Stardust* to a win in the Masters division at the 62nd All-American Soap Box Derby in Akron, Ohio on July 31, 1999. Endres, whose brother Joel was the 1994 Kit winner at the AASBD, posted a winning time of 28.60 seconds in the final heat. The local boy, the heaviest winner ever at 161 pounds, edged out Ashley Brand and A.J. Sanders in 97-degree heat during the championship run of a tournament that features more than 330 youngsters from around the world. Alisha Ebner of Salem, Ore., won the SuperStock title (28.79) and 12-year-old Justin Pillow beat out Sean Henderson and Lauren Demers for the Stock World Championship.

The All-American Soap Box Derby is a coasting race for small gravity-powered cars built by their drivers and assembled within strict guidelines on size, weight and cost. The Derby got its name in the 1930s when most cars were built from wooden soap boxes. Held every summer at Derby Downs in Akron, the Soap Box Derby is open to all boys and girls from 9 to 16 years old who qualify.

There are three competitive divisions: 1. Stock (ages 9-16)— made up of generic, prefab racers that come from Derby-approved kits, can be assembled in four hours and don't exceed 200 pounds when driver, car and wheels are weighed together; 2. Super Stock (ages 10-16)— the same as Stock only with a weight limit of 220 pounds; 3. Masters (ages 11-16)— made up of racers designed by the drivers, but constructed with Derby-approved hardware. The racing ramp at Derby Downs is 953.75 feet with an 11 percent grade.

One champion reigned at the All-American Soap Box Derby each year from 1934-75; Junior and Senior division champions from 1976-87; Kit and Masters champions from 1988-91; Stock, Kit and Masters champions from 1992-94; Stock, Super Stock and Masters champions starting in 1995.

Year		Hometown	Age	Year		Hometown	Age
1934	Robert Turner	Muncie, IN	11	1974	Curt Yarborough	Elk Grove, CA	11
1935	Maurice Bale Jr.	Anderson, IN	13	1975	Karren Stead	Lower Bucks, PA	11
1936	Herbert Muench Jr.	St. Louis	14	1976	JR: Phil Raber	Sugarcreek, OH	11
1937	Robert Ballard	White Plains, NY	12		SR: Joan Ferdinand	Canton, OH	14
1938	Robert Berger	Omaha, NE	14	1977	JR: Mark Ferdinand	Canton, OH	10
1939	Clifton Hardesty	White Plains, NY	11		SR: Steve Washburn	Bristol, CT	15
1940	Thomas Fisher	Detroit	12	1978	JR: Darren Hart	Salem, OR	11
1941	Claude Smith	Akron, OH	14		SR: Greg Cardinal	Flint, MI	13
1942-45	Not held			1979	JR: Russell Yurk	Flint, MI	10
1946	Gilbert Klecan	San Diego	14		SR: Craig Kitchen	Akron, OH	14
1947	Kenneth Holmboe	Charleston, WV	14	1980	JR: Chris Fulton	Indianapolis	11
1948	Donald Strub	Akron, OH	13		SR: Dan Porul	Sherman Oaks, CA	12
1949	Fred Derks	Akron, OH	15	1981	JR: Howie Fraley	Portsmouth, OH	11
1950	Harold Williamson	Charleston, WV	15		SR: Tonia Schlegel	Hamilton, OH	13
1951	Darwin Cooper	Williamsport, PA	15	1982	JR: Carol A. Sullivan	Rochester, NH	10
1952	Joe Lunn	Columbus, GA	11		SR: Matt Wolfgang	Lehigh Val., PA	12
1953	Fred Mohler	Muncie, IN	14	1983	JR: Tony Carlini	Del Mar, CA	10
1954	Richard Kemp	Los Angeles	14		SR: Mike Burdgick	Flint, MI	14
1955	Richard Rohrer	Rochester, NY	14	1984	JR: Chris Hess	Hamilton, OH	11
1956	Norman Westfall	Rochester, NY	14		SR: Anita Jackson	St. Louis	15
1957	Terry Townsend	Anderson, IN	14	1985	JR: Michael Gallo	Danbury, CT	12
1958	James Miley	Muncie, IN	15		SR: Matt Sheffer	York, PA	14
1959	Barney Townsend	Anderson, IN	13	1986	JR: Marc Behan	Dover, NH	9
1960	Fredric Lake	South Bend, IN	11		SR: Tami Jo Sullivan	Lancaster, OH	13
1961	Dick Dawson	Wichita, KS	13	1987	JR: Matt Margules	Danbury, CT	11
1962	David Mann	Gary, IN	14		SR: Brian Drinkwater	Bristol, CT	14
1963	Harold Conrad	Duluth, MN	12	1988	KIT: Jason Lamb	Des Moines, IA	10
1964	Gregory Schumacher	Tacoma, WA	14		MAS: David Duffield	Kansas City	13
1965	Robert Logan	Santa Ana, CA	12	1989	KIT: David Schiller	Dayton, OH	12
1966	David Krussow	Tacoma, WA	12		MAS: Faith Chavarria	Ventura, CA	12
1967	Kenneth Cline	Lincoln, NE	13	1990	MAS: Sami Jones	Salem, OR	13
1968	Branch Lew	Muncie, IN	11		KIT: Mark Mihal	Valparaiso, IN	12
1969	Steve Souter	Midland, TX	12	1991	MAS: Danny Garland	San Diego, CA	14
1970	Samuel Gupton	Durham, NC	13		KIT: Paul Greenwald	Saginaw, MI	13
1971	Larry Blair	Oroville, CA	13	1992	MAS: Bonnie Thornton	Redding, CA	12
1972	Robert Lange Jr.	Boulder, CO	14		KIT: Carolyn Fox	Sublimity, OR	11
1973	Bret Yarborough	Elk Grove, CA	11		STK: Loren Hurst	Hudson, OH	10

Year		Hometown	Age	Year		Hometown	Age
1993	MAS: Dean Lutton	Delta, OH	14	1997	MAS: Wade Wallace	Elk Hart, IN	11
	KIT: D.M. Del Ferraro	Stow, OH	12		SS: Dolline Vance	Salem, OR	13
	STK: Owen Yuda	Boiling Springs, PA	10		STK: Mark Stephens	Waynesboro, VA	13
1994	MAS: D.M. Del Ferraro	Akron, OH	13	1998	MAS: James Marsh	Cleveland, OH	12
	KIT: Joel Endres	Akron, OH	14		SS: Stacy Sharp	Kingman, AZ	14
	STK: Kristina Damond	Jamestown, NY	13		STK: Hailey Simpson	Salem, OR	10
1995	MAS: J. Fensterbush	Kingman, AZ	11	1999	MAS: Allan Endres	Barberton, OH	14
	SS: Darcie Davisson	Kingman, AZ	11		SS: Alisha Ebner	Salem, OR	15
	STK: Karen Thomas	Jamestown, NY	11		STK: Justin Pillow	Deland, FL	12
1996	MAS: Tim Scrofano	Conneaut, OH	12				
	SS: Jeremy Phillips	Charlestown, WV	14				
	STK: Matt Perez	No. Canton, OH	12				

SOFTBALL

Men's and women's national champions since 1933 in Major Fast Pitch, Major Slow Pitch and Super Slow Pitch (men only). Sanctioned by the Amateur Softball Association of America.

MEN

Major Fast Pitch

Multiple winners: Clearwater Bombers (10); Raybestos Cardinals (5); Sealmasters (4); Briggs Beautyware, Decatur Pride, Pay'n Pak and Zollner Pistons (3); Billard Barbell, Hammer Air Field, Kodak Park, National Health Care, Penn Corp and Peterbilt Western (2).

Year		
1933 J.L. Gill Boosters, Chicago	1958 Raybestos Cardinals	1981 Archer Daniels Midland,
1934 Ke-Nash-A, Kenosha, WI	1959 Sealmasters, Aurora, IL	Decatur, IL
1935 Crimson Coaches, Toledo, OH	1960 Clearwater Bombers	1982 Peterbilt Western
1936 Kodak Park, Rochester, NY	1961 Sealmasters	1983 Franklin Cardinals,
1937 Briggs Body Team, Detroit	1962 Clearwater Bombers	Stratford, CA
1938 The Pohlers, Cincinnati	1963 Clearwater Bombers	1984 California Kings, Merced, CA
1939 Carr's Boosters, Covington, KY	1964 Burch Tool, Detroit	1985 Pay'n Pak, Seattle
1940 Kodak Park	1965 Sealmasters	1986 Pay'n Pak
1941 Bendix Brakes, South Bend, IN	1966 Clearwater Bombers	1987 Pay'n Pak
1942 Deep Rock Oilers, Tulsa, OK	1967 Sealmasters	1988 TransAire, Elkhart, IN
1943 Hammer Air Field, Fresno, CA	1968 Clearwater Bombers	1989 Penn Corp, Sioux City, IA
1944 Hammer Air Field	1969 Raybestos Cardinals	1990 Penn Corp
1945 Zollner Pistons, Ft. Wayne, IN	1970 Raybestos Cardinals	1991 Gianella Bros., Rohnert Park, CA
1946 Zollner Pistons	1971 Welty Way, Cedar Rapids, IA	1992 National Health Care,
1947 Zollner Pistons	1972 Raybestos Cardinals	Sioux City, IA
1948 Briggs Beautyware, Detroit	1973 Clearwater Bombers	1993 National Health Care
1949 Tip Top Tailors, Toronto	1974 Gianella Bros., Santa Rosa, CA	1994 Decatur (IL) Pride
1950 Clearwater (FL) Bombers	1975 Rising Sun Hotel, Reading, PA	1995 Decatur Pride
1951 Dow Chemical, Midland, MI	1976 Raybestos Cardinals	1996 Green Bay All-Car,
1952 Briggs Beautyware	1977 Billard Barbell, Reading, PA	Green Bay, WI
1953 Briggs Beautyware	1978 Billard Barbell	1997 Tampa Bay Smokers,
1954 Clearwater Bombers	1979 McArdle Pontiac/Cadillac,	Tampa Bay, FL
1955 Raybestos Cardinals,	Midland, MI	1998 Meierhoffer-Fleeman, St. Joseph,
1956 Clearwater Bombers	1980 Peterbilt Western, Seattle	MO
1957 Clearwater Bombers		1999 Decatur Pride

Super Slow Pitch

Multiple winners: Ritch's/Superior (4); Howard's/Western Steer and Steele's Sports (3); Lighthouse/Worth (2).

Year		
1981 Howard's/Western Steer,	1987 Steele's Sports	1993 Ritch's/Superior
Denver, NC	1988 Starpath, Monticello, KY	1994 Bellcorp., Tampa
1982 Jerry's Catering, Miami	1989 Ritch's Salvage, Harrisburg, NC	1995 Lighthouse/Worth, Stone Mt., GA
1983 Howard's/Western Steer	1990 Steele's Silver Bullets	1996 Ritch's/Superior
1984 Howard's/Western Steer	1991 Sun Belt/Worth, Atlanta	1997 Ritch's/Superior
1985 Steele's Sports, Grafton, OH	1992 Ritch's/Superior,	1998 Lighthouse/Worth
1986 Steele's Sports	Windsor Locks, CT	1999 Team Easton, California

Major Slow Pitch

Multiple winners: Gatliff Auto Sales, Riverside Paving and Skip Hogan A.C. (3); Campbell Carpets, Hamilton Tailoring and Howard's Furniture (2).

Year		
1953 Shields Construction, Newport, KY	1957 Gatliff Auto Sales	1961 Hamilton Tailoring
1954 Waldneck's Tavern, Cincinnati	1958 East Side Sports, Detroit	1962 Skip Hogan A.C., Pittsburgh
1955 Lang Pet Shop, Covington, KY	1959 Yorkshire Restaurant, Newport, KY	1963 Gatliff Auto Sales
1956 Gatliff Auto Sales, Newport, KY	1960 Hamilton Tailoring, Cincinnati	1964 Skip Hogan A.C.

Year
1965 Skip Hogan A.C.
1966 Michael's Lounge, Detroit
1967 Jim's Sport Shop, Pittsburgh
1968 County Sports, Levittown, NY
1969 Copper Hearth, Milwaukee

1970 Little Caesar's, Southgate, MI
1971 Pile Drivers, Va. Beach, VA
1972 Jiffy Club, Louisville, KY
1973 Howard's Furniture, Denver, NC
1974 Howard's Furniture
1975 Pyramid Cafe, Lakewood, OH
1976 Warren Motors, J'ville, FL
1977 Nelson Painting, Okla. City

Year
1978 Campbell Carpets, Concord, CA
1979 Nelco Mfg. Co., Okla. City

1980 Campbell Carpets
1981 Elite Coating, Gordon, CA
1982 Triangle Sports, Minneapolis
1983 No.1 Electric & Heating,
     Gastonia, NC
1984 Lilly Air Systems, Chicago
1985 Blanton's Fayetteville, NC
1986 Non-Ferrous Metals, Cleveland
1987 Stapath, Monticello, KY
1988 Bell Corp/FAF, Tampa, FL
1989 Ritch's Salvage, Harrisburg, NC

Year
1990 New Construction,
     Shelbyville, IN
1991 Riverside Paving, Louisville
1992 Vernon's, Jacksonville, FL
1993 Back Porch/Destin (FL) Roofing
1994 Riverside Paving, Louisville
1995 Riverside Paving
1996 Bell II, Orlando, FL
1997 Long Haul TPS, Albertville, MN
1998 Chase Mortgage/Easton,
     Wilmington, NC
1999 Gasoline Heaven/Worth,
     Commack, NY

WOMEN
Major Fast Pitch

Multiple winners: Raybestos Brakettes (21); Orange Lionettes (9); Jax Maids (5); California Commotion (4); Arizona Ramblers and Redding Rebels (3); Hi-Ho Brakettes, J.J. Krieg's and National Screw & Manufacturing (2).

Year
1933 Great Northerns, Chicago
1934 Hart Motors, Chicago
1935 Bloomer Girls, Cleveland
1936 Nat'l Screw & Mfg., Cleveland
1937 Nat'l Screw & Mfg.
1938 J.J. Krieg's, Alameda, CA
1939 J.J. Krieg's

1940 Arizona Ramblers, Phoenix
1941 Higgins Midgets, Tulsa, OK
1942 Jax Maids, New Orleans
1943 Jax Maids
1944 Lind & Pomeroy, Portland, OR
1945 Jax Maids
1946 Jax Maids
1947 Jax Maids
1948 Arizona Ramblers
1949 Arizona Ramblers

1950 Orange (CA) Lionettes
1951 Orange Lionettes
1952 Orange Lionettes
1953 Betsy Ross Rockets, Fresno, CA
1954 Leach Motor Rockets, Fresno, CA
1955 Orange Lionettes
1956 Orange Lionettes

Year
1957 Hacienda Rockets, Fresno, CA
1958 Raybestos Brakettes,
     Stratford, CT
1959 Raybestos Brakettes

1960 Raybestos Brakettes
1961 Gold Sox, Whittier, CA
1962 Orange Lionettes
1963 Raybestos Brakettes
1964 Erv Lind Florists, Portland, OR
1965 Orange Lionettes
1966 Raybestos Brakettes
1967 Raybestos Brakettes
1968 Raybestos Brakettes
1969 Orange Lionettes

1970 Orange Lionettes
1971 Raybestos Brakettes
1972 Raybestos Brakettes
1973 Raybestos Brakettes
1974 Raybestos Brakettes
1975 Raybestos Brakettes
1976 Raybestos Brakettes
1977 Raybestos Brakettes
1978 Raybestos Brakettes
1979 Sun City (AZ) Saints

Year
1980 Raybestos Brakettes
1981 Orlando (FL) Rebels
1982 Raybestos Brakettes
1983 Raybestos Brakettes
1984 Los Angeles Diamonds
1985 Hi-Ho Brakettes, Stratford, CT
1986 So. California Invasion, LA
1987 Orange County Majestics,
     Anaheim, CA
1988 Hi-Ho Brakettes
1989 Whittier (CA) Raiders

1990 Raybestos Brakettes
1991 Raybestos Brakettes
1992 Raybestos Brakettes
1993 Redding (CA) Rebels
1994 Redding Rebels
1995 Redding Rebels
1996 California Commotion,
     Woodland Hills
1997 California Commotion
1998 California Commotion
1999 California Commotion

Other 1999 Champions

Slow Pitch
MEN
Class A—L&L Painting, Prattville, AL
Class B—Caraway Steel, Eufala, AL
Major Industrial—Action A's, Belden, MS
Class A Industrial—Toyota Power, Georgetown, KY
35-Over—Minnesota Merchants, Eden Prairie, MN
40-Over—Sun Devils, Orange, CA
45-Over—Maroadi Transfer, Pittsburgh, PA
50-Over Major—Dan Smith Softball, Spokane, WA
55-Over—Sawtre Texas, Garland, TX
60-Over—Florida Crush, Fort Myers, FL
Major Church—Rehobeth Presbyterian, Lilburn, GA
Class A Church—St. Mary's, Ponca City, OK

WOMEN
Class A—Macken/Budweiser, Rochester, MN
Church—New Testament, Columbus, GA

COED
Class A—War Ducks, Houston, TX

Fast Pitch
MEN
Class A—Texas Flyers, Houston, TX
Class B—Verner Contruction, Stockton, CA
Class C—Vanguard, Kearney, NJ
40-Over—Decatur Legends, Decatur, IL
45-Over—So. Cal. Eagles, El Cajon, CA
23-Under—Munger Bulldogs, Munger, MI

WOMEN
Class A—So. Cal. Legacy, Westminster, CA
Class B—Condors, Tujunga, CA
Class C—So Cal Jazz, Yorba Linda, CA

Modified Pitch
Women's Major—Stadium Sportswear, Spokane, WA
Men's Major—Texas Liquids/All Engery, New York, NY
Men's Class A—Budweiser, Greensboro, MD

Major Slow Pitch

Multiple winners: Spooks (5); Dana Gardens (4); Universal Plastics (3); Cannan's Illusions, Bob Hoffman's Dots and Marks Brothers Dots (2).

Year		
1959 Pearl Laundry, Richmond, VA	1974 Marks Brothers Dots, Miami	1986 Sur-Way Tomboys, Tifton, GA
1960 Carolina Rockets, High Pt., NC	1975 Marks Brothers Dots	1987 Key Ford Mustangs
1961 Dairy Cottage, Covington, KY	1976 Sorrento's Pizza, Cincinnati	1988 Spooks
1962 Dana Gardens, Cincinnati	1977 Fox Valley Lassies,	1989 Cannan's Illusions, Houston
1963 Dana Gardens	St. Charles, IL	1990 Spooks
1964 Dana Gardens	1978 Bob Hoffman's Dots, Miami	1991 Cannan's Illusions, San Antonio
1965 Art's Acres, Omaha, NE	1979 Bob Hoffman's Dots	1992 Universal Plastics, Cookeville, TN
1966 Dana Gardens	1980 Howard's Rubi-Otts,	1993 Universal Plastics
1967 Ridge Maintenance, Cleveland	Graham, NC	1994 Universal Plastics
1968 Escue Pontiac, Cincinnati	1981 Tifton (GA) Tomboys	1995 Armed Forces, Sacramento
1969 Converse Dots, Hialeah, FL	1982 Richmond (VA) Stompers	1996 Spooks
1970 Rutenschruder Floral, Cincinnati	1983 Spooks, Anoka, MN	1997 Taylor's, Glendale, MD
1971 Gators, Ft. Lauderdale, FL	1984 Spooks	1998 not held
1972 Riverside Ford, Cincinnati	1985 Key Ford Mustangs,	1999 Lakerettes, Conneaut Lake, PA
1973 Sweeney Chevrolet, Cincinnati	Pensacola, FL	

TRIATHLON

World Championship

Contested since 1989, the Triathlon World Championship consists of a 1.5-kilometer swim, a 40-kilometer bike ride and a 10-kilometer run. The 1999 championship took place on September 12 in Montreal, Canada

Multiple winners: MEN— Simon Lessing (4); Spencer Smith (2). WOMEN— Emma Carney, Michelle Jones and Karen Smyers (2).

MEN

Year		Time
1989	Mark Allen, United States	1:58:46
1990	Greg Welch, Australia	1:51:37
1991	Miles Stewart, Australia	1:48:20
1992	Simon Lessing, Great Britain	1:49:04
1993	Spencer Smith, Great Britain	1:51:20
1994	Spencer Smith, Great Britain	1:51:04
1995	Simon Lessing, Great Britain	1:48:29
1996	Simon Lessing, Great Britain	1:39:50
1997	Chris McCormack, Australia	1:48:29
1998	Simon Lessing, Great Britain	1:55:31
1999	Dimitry Gaag, Kazahkstan	1:45:25

WOMEN

Year		Time
1989	Erin Baker, New Zealand	2:10:01
1990	Karen Smyers, United States	2:03:33
1991	Joanne Ritchie, Canada	2:02:04
1992	Michellie Jones, Australia	2:02:08
1993	Michellie Jones, Australia	2:07:41
1994	Emma Carney, Australia	2:03:19
1995	Karen Smyers, USA	2:04:58
1996	Jackie Gallagher, Australia	1:50:52
1997	Emma Carney, Australia	1:59:22
1998	Joanne King, Australia	2:07:25
1999	Loretta Harrop, Australia	1:55:28

Ironman Championship

Contested in Hawaii since 1978, the Ironman Triathlon Championship consists of a 2.4-mile swim, a 112-mile bike ride and 26.2-mile run. The race begins at 7 a.m. and continues all day until the course is closed at midnight. The 1999 Ironman Championship was scheduled for Oct. 23.

MEN

Multiple winners: Mark Allen and Dave Scott (6); Scott Tinley (2).

Year	Date	Winner	Time	Runner-up	Margin	Start	Finish	Location
I	2/18/78	Gordon Haller	11:46	John Dunbar	34:00	15	12	Waikiki Beach
II	1/14/79	Tom Warren	11:15:56	John Dunbar	48:00	15	12	Waikiki Beach
III	1/10/80	Dave Scott	9:24:33	Chuck Neumann	1:08	108	95	Ala Moana Park
IV	2/14/81	John Howard	9:38:29	Tom Warren	26:00	326	299	Kailua-Kona
V	2/6/82	Scott Tinley	9:19:41	Dave Scott	17:16	580	541	Kailua-Kona
VI	10/9/82	Dave Scott	9:08:23	Scott Tinley	20:05	850	775	Kailua-Kona
VII	10/22/83	Dave Scott	9:05:57	Scott Tinley	0:33	964	835	Kailua-Kona
VIII	10/6/84	Dave Scott	8:54:20	Scott Tinley	24:25	1036	903	Kailua-Kona
IX	10/25/85	Scott Tinley	8:50:54	Chris Hinshaw	25:46	1018	965	Kailua-Kona
X	10/18/86	Dave Scott	8:28:37	Mark Allen	9:47	1039	951	Kailua-Kona
XI	10/10/87	Dave Scott	8:34:13	Mark Allen	11:06	1380	1284	Kailua-Kona
XII	10/22/88	Scott Molina	8:31:00	Mike Pigg	2:11	1277	1189	Kailua-Kona
XIII	10/15/89	Mark Allen	8:09:15	Dave Scott	0:58	1285	1231	Kailua-Kona
XIV	10/6/90	Mark Allen	8:28:17	Scott Tinley	9:23	1386	1255	Kailua-Kona
XV	10/19/91	Mark Allen	8:18:32	Greg Welch	6:01	1386	1235	Kailua-Kona
XVI	10/10/92	Mark Allen	8:09:08	Cristian Bustos	7:21	1364	1298	Kailua-Kona
XVII	10/30/93	Mark Allen	8:07:45	Paulli Kiuru	6:37	1438	1353	Kailua-Kona
XVIII	10/15/94	Greg Welch	8:20:27	Dave Scott	4:05	1405	1290	Kailua-Kona
XIX	10/7/95	Mark Allen	8:20:34	Thomas Hellriegel	2:25	1487	1323	Kailua-Kona
XX	10/26/96	Luc Van Lierde	8:04:08	Thomas Hellriegel	1:59	1420	1288	Kailua-Kona
XXI	10/18/97	Thomas Hellriegel	8:33:01	Jurgen Zack	6:17	1534	1365	Kailua-Kona
XXII	10/3/98	Peter Reid	8:24:20	Luc Van Lierde	7:37	1487	1379	Kailua-Kona

WOMEN

Multiple winners: Paula Newby-Fraser (8); Erin Baker and Sylviane Puntous (2).

Year	Winner	Time	Runner-up	Year	Winner	Time	Runner-up
1978	No finishers			1988	Paula Newby-Fraser	9:01:01	Erin Baker
1979	Lyn Lemaire	12:55.00	None	1989	Paula Newby-Fraser	9:00:56	Sylviane Puntous
1980	Robin Beck	11:21:24	Eve Anderson	1990	Erin Baker	9:13:42	P. Newby-Fraser
1981	Linda Sweeney	12:00:32	Sally Edwards	1991	Paula Newby-Fraser	9:07:52	Erin Baker
1982	Kathleen McCartney	11:09:40	Julie Moss	1992	Paula Newby-Fraser	8:55:28	Julie Anne White
1982	Julie Leach	10:54:08	Joann Dahlkoetter	1993	Paula Newby-Fraser	8:58:23	Erin Baker
1983	Sylviane Puntous	10:43:36	Patricia Puntous	1994	Paula Newby-Fraser	9:20:14	Karen Smyers
1984	Sylviane Puntous	10:25:13	Patricia Puntous	1995	Karen Smyers	9:16:46	Isabelle Mouthon
1985	Joanne Ernst	10:25:22	Liz Bulman	1996	Paula Newby-Fraser	9:06:49	Natascha Badmann
1986	Paula Newby-Fraser	9:49:14	Sylviane Puntous	1997	Heather Fuhr	9:31:43	Lori Bowden
1987	Erin Baker	9:35:25	Sylviane Puntous	1998	Natascha Badmann	9:24:16	Lori Bowden

Triathlon Added To Olympics

The triathlon will be held for the first time in an Olympic Games at Sydney in 2000. It was developed as a combination of the longest Olympic swimming distance, 1500 meters, the 40 kilometer cycling time trial, and the longest athletic track event of 10,000 meters. The triathlon will start and finish at the Sydney Opera House.

X GAMES

The ESPN Extreme Games, orginally envisioned as a biannual showcase for "alternative" sports, were first held June 24-July 1, 1995 in Newport and Providence, R.I. and Mt. Snow, Vt. The success of the inaugural event prompted organizers to make it an annual competition. Newport would again serve as host for the redubbed X Games in 1996 before they moved to San Diego for 1997 and 1998. The X Games has evolved rapidly since its inception. New sports and events are added while others are dropped.

In 1997, the first Winter X Games were held at Snow Summit Mountain Resort in Big Bear Lake, Calif. before moving to Crested Butte, Colo. in 1998.

The 1999 Summer X Games were held June 25-July 3 in San Francisco. The 1999 Winter X Games were again held in Crested Butte, Colo., January 14-17. The 2000 Winter X Games were scheduled for Feb. 3-6 at Mt. Snow, Vt.

Summer X Games

Bicycle Stunt

Year	Vert
1995	Matt Hoffman
1996	Matt Hoffman
1997	Dave Mirra
1998	Dave Mirra
1999	Dave Mirra

Year	Dirt
1995	Jay Miron
1996	Joey Garcia
1997	T.J. Lavin
1998	Brian Foster
1999	T.J. Lavin

Year	Street
1996	Dave Mirra
1997	Dave Mirra
1998	Dave Mirra
1999	Dave Mirra

Year	Flatland
1997	Trevor Meyer
1998	Trevor Meyer
1999	Trevor Meyer

Big-Air Snowboarding

Year	Men
1997	Peter Line
1998	Kevin Jones
1999	Peter Line

Year	Women
1997	Tina Dixon
1998	Janet Matthews
1999	Barrett Christy

Freestyle Motocross

Year	
1999	Travis Pastrana

Skysurfing

Year	
1995	Fradet/Zipser
1996	Furrer/Scmid
1997	Hartman/Pappadato
1998	Rozov/Burch
1999	Fradet/Iodice

Skateboard

Year	Vert Singles
1995	Tony Hawk
1996	Andy Macdonald
1997	Tony Hawk
1998	Andy Macdonald
1999	Bucky Lasek

Year	Vert Doubles
1997	Hawk/Macdonald
1998	Hawk/Macdonald
1999	Hawk/Macdonald

Year	Street
1995	Chris Senn
1996	Rodil de Araujo Jr.
1997	Chris Senn
1998	Rodil de Araujo Jr.
1999	Chris Senn

Bungee Jumping

Year	
1995	Doug Anderson
1996	Peter Bihun
1997	event discontinued

Street Luge

Year	Dual
1995	Bob Pereyra
1996	Shawn Goular
1997	Biker Sherlock
1998	Biker Sherlock
1999	Dennis Derammelaere

Year	Mass
1995	Shawn Gilbert
1996	Biker Sherlock
1997	Biker Sherlock
1998	Rat Sult
1999	not held

Year	Super Mass
1997	Biker Sherlock
1998	Rat Sult
1999	David Rogers

In-Line Skating

Year	Men's Vert
1995	Tom Fry
1996	Rene Hulgreen
1997	Tim Ward
1998	Cesar Mora
1999	Eito Yasutoko

Year	Women's Vert
1995	Tash Hodgeson
1996	Fabiola da Silva
1997	Fabiola da Silva
1998	Fabiola da Silva
1999	Ayumi Kawasaki

Year	Men's Street
1995	Matt Salerno
1996	Arlo Eisenberg
1997	Arron Feinberg
1998	Jonathan Bergeron
1999	Nicky Adams

Year	Women's Street
1997	Sayaka Yabe
1998	Jenny Curry
1999	Sayaka Yabe

Year	Vert Triples
1998	Malina/Fogarty/Popa
1999	Khris/Bujanda/Boekhorst

Year	Men's Downhill
1995	Derek Downing
1996	Dante Muse
1997	Derek Downing
1998	Patrick Naylor
1999	not held

Year	Women's Downhill
1995	Julie Brandt
1996	Gypsy Tidwell
1997	Gypsy Tidwell
1998	Julie Brandt
1999	not held

Sportclimbing

Year	Men's Difficulty
1995	Ian Vickers
1996	Arnaud Petit
1997	Francois Legrand
1998	Christian Core
1999	Chris Sharma

Year	Women's Difficulty
1995	Robyn Erbersfield
1996	Katie Brown
1997	Katie Brown
1998	Katie Brown
1999	Stephanie Bodet

Year	Men's Speed
1995	Hans Florine
1996	Hans Florine
1997	Hans Florine
1998	Vladimir Netsvetaev
1999	Aaron Shamy

Year	Women's Speed
1995	Elena Ovtchinnikova
1996	Cecile Le Flem
1997	Elena Ovtchinnikova
1998	Elena Ovtchinnikova
1999	Renata Piszczek

Watersports

Year	Barefoot Waterski Jumping
1995	Justin Seers
1996	Ron Scarpa
1997	Peter Fleck
1998	Peter Fleck
1999	not held

Year	Men's Wakeboarding
1996	Parks Bonifay
1997	Jeremy Kovak
1998	Darin Shapiro
1999	Parks Bonifay

Year	Women's Wakeboarding
1997	Tara Hamilton
1998	Andrea Gaytan
1999	Meaghan Major

X-Venture Race

Year	
1995	Team Threadbo*
1996	Team Kobeer
1997	Team Presidio
1998	event discontinued

*In 1995, Team Threadbo won the Eco-Challenge which was held in conjunction with the ESPN Extreme Games.

Winter X Games

CrossOver

Year	
1997	Brian Patch
1998	event discontinued

Free Skiing

Year	Men's Big Air
1999	J.F. Cusson

Year	Men's Skier X
1998	Dennis Rey
1999	Enak Gavaggio

Year	Women's Skier X
1999	Aleisha Cline

Ice Climbing

Year	Men's Difficulty
1997	Jaren Ogden
1998	Will Gadd
1999	Will Gadd

Year	Women's Difficulty
1997	Bird Lew
1998	Kim Csizmazia
1999	Kim Csizmazia

Year	Men's Speed
1997	Jared Ogden
1998	Will Gadd
1999	Event discontinued

Year	Women's Speed
1997	Bird Lew
1998	Kim Csizmazia
1999	Event discontinued

Skiboarding

Year	
1998	Mike Nick
1999	Chris Hawks

Snowboarding

Year	Men's Big Air
1997	Jimmy Halopoff
1998	Jason Borgstede
1999	Kevin Sansalone

Year	Women's Big Air
1997	Barrett Christy
1998	Tina Basich
1999	Barrett Christy

Year	Men's Boarder X
1997	Shaun Palmer
1998	Shaun Palmer
1999	Shaun Palmer

Year	Women's Boarder X
1997	Jennie Waara
1998	Tina Dixon
1999	Maelle Ricker

Year	Men's Halfpipe
1997	Todd Richards
1998	Ross Powers
1999	Jimi Scott

Year	Women's Halfpipe
1997	Shannon Dunn
1998	Cara-Beth Burnside
1999	Michele Taggart

Year	Men's Slopestyle
1997	Daniel Franck
1998	Ross Powers
1999	Peter Line

Year	Women's Slopestyle
1997	Barrett Christy
1998	Jennie Waara
1999	Tara Dakides

Super-modified Shovel Racing

Year	
1997	Don Adkins
1998	event discontinued

Snow Mountain Bike Racing

Year	Men's Downhill
1997	Shaun Palmer
1998	Andrew Shandro
1999	Event discontinued

Year	Women's Downhill
1997	Missy Giove
1998	Marla Streb
1999	Event discontinued

Year	Men's Speed
1997	Phil Tintsman
1998	Jurgen Beneke
1999	Event discontinued

Year	Women's Speed
1997	Cheri Elliott
1998	Elke Brutsaert
1999	Event discontinued

Year	Men's Biker X
1999	Steve Peat

Year	Women's Biker X
1999	Tara Llanes

Snocross

Year	
1998	Toni Haikonen
1999	Chris Vincent

YACHTING

The America's Cup

International yacht racing was launched in 1851 when England's Royal Yacht Squadron staged a 60-mile regatta around the Isle of Wight and offered a silver trophy to the winner. The 101-foot schooner *America*, sent over by the New York Yacht Club, won the race and the prize. Originally called the Hundred-Guinea Cup, the trophy was renamed The America's Cup after the winning boat's owners deeded it to the NYYC with instructions to defend it whenever challenged.

From 1870-1980, the NYYC successfully defended the Cup 25 straight times; first in large schooners and J-class boats that measured up to 140 feet in overall length, then in 12-meter boats. A foreign yacht finally won the Cup in 1983 when *Australia II* beat defender *Liberty* in the seventh and deciding race off Newport, R.I. Four years later, the San Diego Yacht Club's *Stars & Stripes* won the Cup back, sweeping the four races of the final series off Fremantle, Australia.

Then in 1988, New Zealand's Mercury Bay Boating Club, unwilling to wait the usual three- to four-year period between Cup defenses, challenged the SDYC to a match race, citing the Cup's 102-year-old Deed of Gift, which clearly stated that every challenge had to be honored. Mercury Bay announced it would race a 133-foot monohull. San Diego countered with a 60-foot catamaran. The resulting best-of-three series (Sept. 7-8) was a mismatch as the SDYC's catamaran *Stars & Stripes* won two straight by margins of better than 18 and 21 minutes. Mercury Bay syndicate leader Michael Fay protested the outcome and took the SDYC to court in New York State (where the Deed of Gift was first filed) claiming San Diego had violated the spirit of the deed by racing a catamaran instead of a monohull. N.Y. State Supreme Court judge Carmen Ciparick agreed and on March 28, 1989, ordered the SDYC to hand the Cup over to Mercury Bay. The SDYC refused, but did consent to the court's appointment of the New York Yacht Club as custodian of the Cup until an appeal was ruled on.

On Sept. 19, 1989, the Appellate Division of the N.Y. Supreme Court overturned Ciparick's decision and awarded the Cup back to the SDYC. An appeal by Mercury Bay was denied by the N.Y. Court of Appeals on April 26, 1990, ending three years of legal wrangling. To avoid the chaos of 1988-90, a new class of boat—75-foot monohulls with 110-foot masts—has been used by all competing countries since 1992.

The next America's Cup races will be held in New Zealand from Feb. 26-Mar. 11, 2000.

Note that (*) indicates skipper was also owner of the boat.

Schooners And J-Class Boats

Year	Winner	Skipper	Series	Loser	Skipper
1851	*America*	Richard Brown	—	—	—
1870	*Magic*	Andrew Comstock	1-0	*Cambria*, GBR	J. Tannock
1871	*Columbia* (2-1)	Nelson Comstock	4-0	*Livonia*, GBR	J.R. Woods
	& *Sappho* (2-0)	Sam Greenwood			
1876	*Madeleine*	Josephus Williams	2-0	*Countess of Dufferin*, CAN	J.E. Ellsworth
1881	*Mischief*	Nathanael Clock	2-0	*Atalanta*, CAN	Alexander Cuthbert*
1885	*Puritan*	Aubrey Crocker	2-0	*Genesta*, GBR	John Carter
1886	*Mayflower*	Martin Stone	2-0	*Galatea*, GBR	Dan Bradford
1887	*Volunteer*	Henry Haff	2-0	*Thistle*, GBR	John Barr
1893	*Vigilant*	William Hansen	3-0	*Valkyrie II*, GBR	Wm. Granfield
1895	*Defender*	Henry Haff	3-0	*Valkyrie III*, GBR	Wm. Granfield
1899	*Columbia*	Charles Barr	3-0	*Shamrock I*, GBR	Archie Hogarth
1901	*Columbia*	Charles Barr	3-0	*Shamrock II*, GBR	E.A. Sycamore
1903	*Reliance*	Charles Barr	3-0	*Shamrock III*, GBR	Bob Wringe
1920	*Resolute*	Charles F. Adams	3-2	*Shamrock IV*, GBR	William Burton
1930	*Enterprise*	Harold Vanderbilt*	4-0	*Shamrock V*, GBR	Ned Heard
1934	*Rainbow*	Harold Vanderbilt*	4-2	*Endeavour*, GBR	T.O.M. Sopwith
1937	*Ranger*	Harold Vanderbilt*	4-0	*Endeavour II*, GBR	T.O.M. Sopwith

12-METER BOATS

Year	Winner	Skipper	Series	Loser	Skipper
1958	*Columbia*	Briggs Cunningham	4-0	*Sceptre*, GBR	Graham Mann
1962	*Weatherly*	Bus Mosbacher	4-1	*Gretel*, AUS	Jock Sturrock
1964	*Constellation*	Bob Bavier & Eric Ridder	4-0	*Sovereign*, AUS	Peter Scott
1967	*Intrepid*	Bus Mosbacher	4-0	*Dame Pattie*, AUS	Jock Sturrock
1970	*Intrepid*	Bill Ficker	4-1	*Gretel II*, AUS	Jim Hardy
1974	*Courageous*	Ted Hood	4-0	*Southern Cross*, AUS	John Cuneo
1977	*Courageous*	Ted Turner	4-0	*Australia*	Noel Robins
1980	*Freedom*	Dennis Conner	4-1	*Australia*	Jim Hardy
1983	*Australia II*	John Bertrand	4-3	*Liberty*, USA	Dennis Conner
1987	*Stars & Stripes*	Dennis Conner	4-0	*Kookaburra III*, AUS	Iain Murray

60-FT CATAMARAN VS 133-FT MONOHULL

Year	Winner	Skipper	Series	Loser	Skipper
1988	*Stars & Stripes*	Dennis Conner	2-0	*New Zealand*, NZE	David Barnes

75-FT INTERNATIONAL AMERICA'S CUP CLASS

Year	Winner	Skipper	Series	Loser	Skipper
1992	*America[3]*	Bill Koch* & Buddy Melges	4-1	*Il Moro di Venezia*, ITA	Paul Cayard
1995	*Black Magic*, NZE	Russell Coutts	5-0	*Young America*, USA	Dennis Conner & Paul Cayard

Deaths

Where have you gone **Joe DiMaggio**? A nation turned its lonely eyes to the Yankees legend in March after he lost his long battle with lung cancer.

Northwestern Univ.

Ricky Byrdsong

AP/Wide World Photos

Catfish Hunter

AP/Wide World Photos

Kim Perrot

Joe Adcock, 71; power-hitting first baseman for the Milwaukee Braves who teamed up with Hank Aaron and Eddie Mathews in an extraordinarily powerful lineup of the 1950s; established the major-league record for total bases in a game (18) when he hit four home runs and a double against the Dodgers at Ebbets Field on July 31, 1954; notorious for ending Harvey Haddix's 12-inning perfect game with a home run in the 13th inning; hit 336 career home runs; batted .277 over 17 seasons with the Reds, Braves, Indians and Angels; managed Cleveland to an eighth-place finish in 1967; of natural causes (had Alzheimer's disease); in Coushatta, La., May 3.

Syl Apps, 83; a member of the Hockey Hall of Fame and winner of the first Calder Trophy in 1937 as the NHL's rookie of the year (although the NHL began recognizing a rookie of the year four years earlier); an exceptional athlete at McMaster University in Hamilton, Ontario, Apps captained the football team and won two individual pole vault titles; played seven seasons with the Toronto Maple Leafs of the NHL before enlisting in the Canadian Army; won the Lady Byng Trophy in 1942; twice named first-team and three times a second-team all-star, Apps won three Stanley Cup titles with Toronto; finished his career with 201 goals and 432 points; named Ontario Athletic Commissioner in 1946 and for 11 years (1963-74) was a Conservative member of the provincial parliament and served in Ontario's cabinet; cause of death not given; in Kingston, Ontario, Canada, Dec. 24, 1998.

Samuel Bartholomew, 81; blocking back who captained Tennessee's 1939 undefeated, unscored upon football team (reg. season); won trophy for outstanding blocker in the SEC in 1938 and 1939; three-year letterman in football and track; played one season of pro football in Philadelphia in 1941; earned the Purple Heart and Bronze Star while fighting with Gen. George Patton's 3rd Army in WWII; SEC football official for 15 years, retiring in 1967; worked as superintendent at Eastman Kodak Co. until his retirement in 1982; of pneumonia; in Johnson City, Tenn., Feb. 14.

Frank Brimsek, 83; NHL goalie dubbed "Mr. Zero" after shutting out the opposition in six of his first eight professional games; recorded 42 shutouts and won 252 games in his career with the Boston Bruins and Chicago Blackhawks; a member of both the U.S. and NHL halls of fame; cause of death not given; in Virginia, Minn., Nov. 11, 1998.

Brandon Burlsworth, 22; walk-on offensive lineman at the University of Arkansas who rose to become a starter before the 1996 season; earned All-SEC honors; was the first Arkansas player to earn a masters degree (business administration) before playing his last game; third-round draft pick of the Colts less than two weeks before his death; of injuries sustained in a car crash on U.S. 412; in Carrolton, Ark., Apr. 28.

Ricky Byrdsong, 43; former head basketball coach at Northwestern University; took Wildcats to their second postseason appearance in school history after the 1993-94 season; compiled 87-165 record as a head coach, including 34-78 in four seasons with Northwestern; fired with seven games left in the 1996-97 season; remembered for leaving the bench during a game in Minnesota (1993-94 season) and climbing up into the stands to chat with fans and exchange high-fives before taking a seat in the aisle; two members of his 1994-95 team were later convicted in a point-shaving scandal; played at Iowa St. and began his coaching career there as an assistant; had coaching stints at Arizona, Eastern Illinois, Western Michigan and Detroit Mercy; of gun shot wounds he received during a violent hate crime near Chicago in which a white supremacist apparently targeted minorities in a drive-by shooting spree; in Skokie, Ill., July 3.

Randie Carver, 24; North American Boxing Federation supermiddleweight champion; nicknamed "the Natural"; former Golden Gloves champion; professional record was 23-0-1 going into his final fight; lost consciousness in the 10th round of a title defense against Kabary Salem and underwent emergency brain surgery; in North Kansas City, Mo., Sept. 14.

Wilton Norman (Wilt) Chamberlain, 63; one of the 20th century's most recognized athletes, Chamberlain was a dominant basketball center who is best remembered for scoring a record 100 points in a game (3/2/62); nicknamed "Wilt the Stilt" and "The Big Dipper"; claimed by the Philadelphia (now Golden State) Warriors who used a special "territorial" draft pick to take the former Philadelphia high school star in 1959; played for the Harlem Globetrotters in 1958-59 after forgoing his senior year at the University of Kansas; his battles with Boston Celtics center Bill Russell entertained a generation of basketball fans and set the standard for all sports rivalries; the two met 142 times on the court, including twice in the NBA Finals, with Russell's Celtics winning both series; led NBA in scoring his first seven seasons and rebounding in 11 of his 14 pro seasons; only player to score 4,000 points in a season (1961-62), averaging 50.4 points a game; owned 20 of the 30 best regular-season scoring performances of all time at the time of his death; scored more than 50 points in a game 118 times; did not foul out of any of his more than 1,200 games; one of two players (Wes Unseld) to win NBA MVP and Rookie of the Year Award in the same year (1960); won NBA titles with Philadelphia in 1967 and Los Angeles in 1972; elected to Naismith Memorial Hall of Fame in 1978; named to NBA 50th Anniversary All-Time Team in 1996; of congestive heart failure; in Bel Air, Calif., Oct. 12.

Steve Chiasson, 32; Carolina Hurricanes defenseman who spent eight years in Detroit beginning in 1986; traded to Calgary in 1994 and what was then the Hartford Whalers in 1997; played in the NHL All-Star Game in 1993; in 1989-90 scored a career-high 14 goals and led all Detroit defensemen in scoring with 42 points; notched his 300th career point on Nov. 29, 1995; after a season-ending playoff loss, was involved in a one-car automobile crash in which his blood-alcohol level was more than three times the legal state limit; in Raleigh, N.C., May 3.

Joe DiMaggio, 84; one of the greatest players to ever play the game of baseball, DiMaggio reigned as the graceful king of the New York Yankees for more than 60 years; nicknamed "Joltin Joe" and "The Yankee Clipper," he hit successfully in 56 straight games in 1941, a baseball record most experts think won't be broken; born to Italian immigrants who moved to North Beach, the heavily Italian section near the San Francisco waterfront, the year Joe was born; began playing professionally with the San Francisco Seals of the Pacific Coast League at the age of 17; hit successfully in 61 straight games for the Seals in 1933; signed with the Yankees in 1936; roamed center field for the Bronx Bombers from 1936-51, missing three seasons (1943-45) to serve in WWII; won the American League MVP award in 1939, 1941 and 1947; his 369 career strikeouts (in 6,821 at bats) is a stunningly low total for a power hitter such as DiMaggio, who hit 361 career home runs; won back-to-back A.L. batting titles in 1939 and 1940 and finished his career with a lifetime .325 average; played in 11 All-Star Games; led the Yankees to 10 A.L. pennants and nine World Series championships; his rival, Red Sox legend Ted Williams, called him "the greatest baseball player of our time"; after divorcing his first wife in 1944, began dating actress Marilyn Monroe and married her in 1954; the relationship sparked a legion of new fans that helped turn him into one of the 20th century's most recognized personalities; after retirement he spent time as a broadcaster and spring training instructor with the Yankees, television spokesperson and coach with the Oakland Athletics; elected into the National Baseball Hall of Fame in his second year of eligibility, 1955; of lung cancer; in Hollywood, Fla., March 8.

Demetrius DuBose, 28; linebacker for Tampa Bay Buccaneers and team captain at Notre Dame; played for the Fighting Irish from 1989-92; second-round draft pick of Tampa Bay in 1993 and played four seasons with the team; signed with the Jets in 1997 but was released four months later; of gunshot wounds sustained after a struggle with police; in La Jolla, Calif., July 24.

Jimmy Dudley, 89; radio announcer for the Cleveland Indians from 1948-67; greeted fans with signature line "Hello, baseball fans everywhere," and when the count was full, he would say "the string is out"; also broadcast Browns, Baltimore Colts and Ohio State football games in the 1950s; inducted into the broadcasters' wing of the National Baseball Hall of Fame in 1997; of a stroke; in Tuscon, Ariz., Feb. 12.

Eddie Elias, 69; sports television pioneer and later a celebrity agent who established the Professional Bowlers Tour in 1958; also credited with helping turn bowling from a recreational sport to television's second-longest-running professional sport behind college football; was the first to organize corporate sponsorship of a nationally televised sporting event when he established the Firestone Tournament of Champions in 1958; founded Eddie Elias Enterprises, Inc., a sports marketing firm, which represents the pro golf tours and several celebrities; member of both the ABC and PBA Halls of Fame; in 1997 the PBA named the Ambassador of Bowling Award after him; of complications associated with pneumonia; in Akron, Ohio, Nov. 15, 1998.

E.W. (Skip) Etchells, 87; influential boat builder who won several U.S. and international yachting championships; designed the Etchells 22, a design now known as the International Etchells Class of sailboats; with his wife, Mary, as his crew, Etchells won the Star Class world championship in 1951; at the University of Michigan he won three consecutive Big Ten titles in the discus; retired in 1984; cause of death not given; in Easton, Md., Dec. 20, 1998.

Wilbur Charles (Weeb) Ewbank, 91; professional football coach with the N.Y. Jets and Baltimore Colts who won two of the sport's biggest games in history; led the Colts to a victory over the N.Y. Giants in the first ever sudden-death championship game in 1958 and pulled off the biggest upset in Super Bowl history when he guided the NY Jets past the Colts in 1968; he also won an NFL title in 1959 with the Colts; in 20 seasons was 134-130-7; while in the Navy served as an assistant coach to former college teammate at Miami University in Ohio—Paul Brown; coached under Brown again with the Cleveland Browns from 1949-53; elected to the Pro Football Hall of Fame in 1978 and the Indiana Sports Hall of Fame in 1974; of natural causes; in Oxford, Ohio, Nov. 18, 1998.

Bernie Faloney, 66; Canadian Football Hall of Fame quarterback who led the Hamilton Tiger-Cats to seven Grey Cup appearances and two titles in eight years beginning in 1957; named Most Outstanding Player after the 1961 season; won Grey Cup title his rookie season with Edmonton in 1954; left Hamilton in 1965 and played for Montreal and the B.C. Lions before retiring in 1967; of cancer; in Hamilton, Ontario, Canada, June 14.

Jaime Fields, 29; former member of the University of Washington's undefeated 1991 football team; fourth-round draft pick of the Kansas City Chiefs in 1993; retired in 1995; of injuries sustained in a hit-and-run accident; in Downey, Calif., Aug. 29.

Germain Glidden, 85; a national squash racquets champion in the 1930's and 1950s; founder of the National Art Museum of Sport, based in Indianapolis; cause of death not given; in Norwalk, Conn., Feb. 9.

Meredith Gourdine, 69; won the long jump silver medal at the 1952 Olympics in Helsinki; of a series of strokes; in Houston, Nov. 20, 1998.

M. Donald Grant, 94; former chairman of the board of the NY Mets from their inception in 1962 to 1978 when he was voted out by the team's eight-man board; won two pennants and one World Series with the Mets; infamous for trading fan-favorite Tom Seaver to Cincinnati in 1977; reportedly wouldn't allow the N.Y. Jets football team to play at Shea Stadium until after the baseball season, prompting the team's move to the Meadowlands before the 1984 season; was a director of the N.Y. Giants baseball team before moving to the Mets and was the lone vote in opposition to their move to San Francisco; of a long illness; in Hobe Sound, Fla., Nov. 28, 1998.

Howie Haak, 87; Pittsburgh Pirates scout who discovered future Hall-of-Famer Roberto Clemente and was instrumental in building Pirates teams that won three World Series and nine division titles; scouted extensively in Latin America for Pittsburgh from 1950-88, well before it became common practice in the major leagues; also discovered Pittsburgh greats Manny Sanguillen (Panama), Rennie Stennett (Dominican Republic) and Tony Pena (Puerto Rico); made headlines in 1982 by telling reporters that he heard fans were staying away from Three Rivers Stadium because the Pirates fielded an all-black team; left in 1988 after a confrontation with then-GM Syd Thrift and scouted for the Houston Astros for five years; of complications from a stroke; in Palm Springs, Calif., Feb. 22.

Anna McCune Harper, 99; replaced Helen Wills Moody as the top-ranked U.S. women's tennis player in 1930; won mixed doubles title at Wimbledon in 1931; called home in 1932 because of a family illness and never returned to pro tennis; member of the Cal Athletic Hall of Fame; cause of death not given; in Moraga, Calif., June 14.

Gene Hart, 68; Philadelphia radio and television broadcaster who announced hockey games for 28 years under the nickname "Voice of the Flyers"; called six Stanley Cup Finals, five NHL All-Star Games and two NHL-Soviet All-Star series; ended his broadcasts with "Good night, and good hockey"; relieved of his duties with the Flyers in 1995; elected to Flyers Hall of Fame in 1992 and the Hockey Hall of Fame in 1997; of an infection that developed following chemotherapy to treat a tumor; in Camden, N.J., July 14.

Matt Hartl, 23; fullback and key player on the 1995 Northwestern football team that returned to the Rose Bowl for the first time since 1949; of Hodgkin's disease; in Evanston, Ill., Aug. 30.

Jack Hartman, 73; former Kansas St. men's basketball coach who won more games than any other coach in school history; won National Coach of the Year Award from basketball writers after the 1980-81 season in which his team reached the NCAA regional finals and made the cover of *Sports Illustrated* with an upset of second-ranked Oregon St.; won three Big Eight titles; also coached a team led by Michael Jordan to a gold medal at the 1983 Pan-American Games, cause of death not given; in Santa Fe, N.M., Nov. 5, 1998.

Leon Hess, 85; owner of the New York Jets whose oil fortune made him one of the wealthiest owners in professional sports; his wish to see his team return to the Super Bowl for the first time since their 1969 title fell one game short in 1998; in March of 1963, a group including Hess and three partners purchased the American Football League's Jets, then known as the New York Titans, out of bankruptcy for $1 million; he eventually bought out his partners in 1977; angered the league when he moved the team from Shea Stadium to the Meadowlands in New Jersey for the 1984 season; saw the team through several recent coaching changes, including the hiring of Bill Parcells after the 1996-97 season; an oilman since the Depression, Hess turned a New Jersey refining company into the multi-billion dollar Amerada Hess Corp.; he resigned as chairman and CEO in 1995; of complications from blood disease; in New York City, May 7.

William (Flash) Hollett, 88; became the first NHL defenseman to score 20 goals in a season during the 1944-45 campaign with Detroit; record stood until Bobby Orr broke it by one goal 24 years later; played for Ottawa, Toronto, Boston and Detroit between 1933-46; nicknamed "Flash" because of his speed; cause of death not given; in Toronto, Apr. 20.

Kent Hollingsworth, 69; editor, then publisher of *The Blood-Horse* weekly magazine from 1963-86 who oversaw the publication's rise to become an authoritative source on thoroughbred racing and breeding; circulation increased from 6,800 to 21,700 during his 23-year tenure; wrote the magazine's "What's Going On Here" column; began as a news photographer and sports reporter for the *Lexington (Ky.) Leader* in 1954; authored two books; former president of the National Turf Writers, Thoroughbred Club of America and National Museum of Racing; former chairman of the Racing Hall of Fame Committee from 1982-86; practiced law after leaving the magazine and served as a Distinguished Lecturer in equine law in the Equine Industry Program at the University of Louisville; cause of death was not given; in Lexington, Ky., May 26.

William (Red) Holzman, 78; Hall of Fame coach who led the New York Knicks to their only two NBA championships in 1970 and 1973; in 18 years as an NBA coach Holzman posted a 696-604 record, placing him 11th on the all-time list at the time of his death; won 613 games as Knicks coach (that number hangs on the back of a jersey atop Madison Square Garden, paying tribute to the legendary coach); elected to NBA Hall of Fame in 1985; cause of death not given, but he was suffering from leukemia; in New Hyde Park, N.Y., Nov. 13, 1998.

Jim (Catfish) Hunter, 53; dominating right-handed pitcher of the early 1970s who was baseball's first big-money free agent; won five World Series rings with Oakland and the N.Y. Yankees; his 224 career wins includes five straight 20-victory seasons from 1971-75; pitched a perfect game against Minnesota May 8, 1968; won Cy Young Award in 1974; when A's owner Charles O. Finley failed to follow through on a payment to an insurance company, he became a free agent after the 1974 season and signed a five-year, $3.75 million contract with the Yankees; led A.L. with 30 complete games in 1975; eight-time All-Star; elected to the National Baseball Hall of Fame in 1987; his nickname was concocted by Finley and was based on a story he made up about Hunter returning from a fishing trip as a child with catfish slung over his shoulder, Hunter played along thinking it would never stick; diagnosed with Lou Gehrig's disease in September 1998; in Hertford, N.C., Sept. 9.

Lisa Hutchens, 37; Union University (Jackson, Tenn.) women's basketball co-coach whose team was ranked second in Division I NAIA at the time of her death; graduated from the school in 1983 and returned as an assistant in 1991; of self-inflicted gunshot wound; in Jackson, Tenn., Feb. 20.

Tommy Ivan, 88; Chicago Blackhawks vice president and former general manager; coached the Detroit Red Wings for seven seasons beginning in 1947 and led them to three Stanley Cup championships in 1950, 52 and 54; served as Chicago's GM for 25 years, bringing stars like Bobby Hull, Stan Mikita and Glenn Hall to the Blackhawks; inducted into Hockey Hall of Fame in 1974; won Lester Patrick Award for outstanding service to hockey in the United States in 1975; won King Clancy Memorial Award for long and continued service to hockey in 1994; cause of death not given; in Lake Forest, Ill., June 24.

Ben Jackson, 22; Valdosta State (Ga.) pitcher who was 13-8 during his three seasons with the team; was playing in a men's over-40 summer league when he was struck by lightning while on the mound and died an hour later; in Thomasville, Ga., Aug. 8.

Gene Jacobs, 86; thoroughbred horse trainer who retired in 1989 after a 45-year career; trained Shelia's Reward to the sprint championship in 1951 and 1952; brother of Hall of Fame trainer Hirsch Jacobs; of Parkinson's disease; in Queens, N.Y., May 20.

Lord Killanin, 84; sixth president of the International Olympic Committee who guided the organization through the turbulent tragedies of the 1970s between the reigns of Avery Brundage and Juan Antonio Samaranch; his eight-year term began in 1972, shortly after the massacre of Israeli athletes and coaches at the Munich Olympics; his moderate views on amateurism were a refreshing change from Brundage and led to eligibility reforms; began as Ireland's representative to the IOC in 1952 and moved up to senior vice president to Brundage in 1968; began his career as a journalist and political columnist in London from 1935-39; served in WWII and was discharged as a major in 1945; cause of death was not given; in Dublin, Apr. 25.

Baltimore Orioles

Cal Ripken Sr.

PGA Tour

Gene Sarazen

Dallas Cowboys

Mark Tuinei

Jim Kropfeld, 58; three-time national champion driver in unlimited hydroplane racing; piloted *Miss Budweiser* to national titles in 1984, 1986 and 1987; suffered a broken neck in 1988 during a crash in Miami; returned to racing briefly in 1989; his 22 career victories ranked fourth all-time at the time of his death; helped develop safety measures which became accepted practice, including fully enclosed cockpit canopies and onboard oxygen systems; inducted into the Unlimited Hydroplane Racing Association Hall of Fame in 1998; of cancer; in Cincinnati, Jan. 3.

Alvin John Krueger, 79; late 1930's college football star who guided USC to two straight Rose Bowl victories over undefeated, unscored-upon teams in 1939 and 1940; caught a 19-yard TD with 40 seconds left to upset Duke, 7-3, in 1939 and hauled in another touchdown pass a year later to help beat Tennessee 14-0; played professionally with Washington (1941-42) and Los Angeles (1946); served in the Navy from 1942-45; inducted into Rose Bowl Hall of Fame in 1995; of natural causes; in Lancaster, Calif., Feb. 20.

Steve Little, 43; University of Arkansas kicker who shares the NCAA record for longest field goal, a 67-yard boot against Texas in 1977; two-time All-American at Arkansas; held school record for career points (280) at the time of his death; chosen 15th overall at the 1978 March draft by the Cardinals who handed him the punting and kicking duties; released after six games in 1980, the same day (Oct. 16) he was in an automobile accident that left him paralyzed for life; cause of death not given; in Little Rock, Sept. 6.

Harry Litwack, 91; coached men's basketball team at Temple for 21 years, winning a NIT title in 1969 and earning two NCAA Final Four appearances (1956, 1958); nicknamed "The Chief," because it was a catch phrase he used when meeting new people; retired in 1973 with a 373-193 record; second all-time in school history at the time of his death; played guard for Temple from 1927-29; spent 20 years as freshman coach and an assistant before taking over head coaching duties; elected to Basketball Hall of Fame in 1975; of a stroke; in Huntingdon Valley, Penn., Aug. 7.

Dave Logan, 42; nose tackle with the Tampa Bay Buccaneers from 1979-86; finished his career ranked second on the team's all-time sack list and sixth in career tackles; named an All-Pro in 1994 and alternate three times in his career; played his final pro season in Green Bay in 1987; color-analyst on Tampa Bay radio broadcasts for the past eight seasons; of a heart attack; in Tampa, Fla., Jan. 12.

Gerald Martin, 55; well-respected reporter for *The News & Observer* in Raleigh, N.C. who covered stock car racing for three decades; praised by peers in the media as well as drivers and crews as one of the best ever to cover the NASCAR and Winston Cup circuit; graduated from Bluefield College in West Virginia and worked at newspapers in Martinsville and Roanoke, Va. before joining *The N&O* in 1969; served as president of the National Motorsports Press Association; of complications brought on by pancreatitis; in Raleigh, N.C., Jan. 3.

Mr. Prospector, 29; the nation's leading thoroughbred sire who was said to have sired a North American-record 1,014 foals and 162 stakes winners through the end of 1998; champion offspring included 1982 Horse of the Year Conquistador Cielo, Tank's Prospect, Seeking the Gold and grandsons Unbridled and Coronado's Quest; won seven races and $112,171 in his career between 1973-74; was euthanized after being diagnosed with acute inflammation of the membrane lining his stomach; in Lexington, Ky., June 1.

Wilmer Mizell, 68; former congressman and major league pitcher who went by the nickname "Vinegar Bend," which was the name of his hometown in Alabama; pitched for St. Louis, Pittsburgh and the N.Y. Mets from 1952-62; won a World Series title with the Pirates in 1960; won 90 career games and had a 3.85 career ERA; served from 1968-74 as the U.S. representative from North Carolina's 5th District; appointed Assistant Secretary of Commerce for Economic Development by President Ford in 1974 and Assistant Secretary of Agriculture for Governmental Affairs by President Reagan in 1982; cause of death not given; in Kerrville, Texas, Feb. 21.

Archie Moore, 84; prolific light heavyweight champion who set the record for knockouts in a career and was the only boxer to fight both Rocky Marciano and Muhammad Ali; nicknamed "Old Mongoose" and "Ancient Archie," he held the light heavyweight title for 11 of the 27 years he boxed; lost just four of 48 fights between 1935-38; won the light heavyweight title from Joey Maxim in 1952 at age 39; stripped of his title in 1962 due to inactivity; recorded 130 knockouts in his career, according to The Ring Record Book and Encyclopedia; retired in 1963 with a career record of 194-26-8; helped train George Foreman before his "Rumble in the Jungle" fight in 1974 and was assistant coach of the Nigerian boxing team at the 1976 Olympics; elected to International Boxing Hall of Fame in 1990; of a heart-related illness; in San Diego, Dec. 9, 1998.

Marion Motley, 79; explosive player who was one of pro football's best fullbacks, one of the NFL's first black players of the modern era and a Cleveland legend; discovered at McKinley High School in Canton, Ohio by future Browns founder and owner Paul Brown (who coached at the rival high school); played eight pro seasons with the Browns, half in the All-American Football Conference and half in the NFL, which absorbed the Browns in 1950; led the NFL in rushing that season, helping Cleveland win the NFL title; AAFC career rushing leader (3,024 yards); rushed for 4,720 yards and 31 touchdowns in his career on Brown's teams that emphasized the pass; knee troubles forced him to quit before the 1954 season; comeback with Pittsburgh as a linebacker failed a year later; a lack of opportunities for black coaches in the NFL relegated him to coaching a women's team in 1967 and scouting duties with the Browns; in 1968 became the second black player inducted into the Pro Football Hall of Fame; of prostate cancer; in Cleveland, June 27.

Chip Myers, 53; assistant coach of the Minnesota Vikings who was named offensive coordinator to replace Brian Billick who left to coach the Baltimore Ravens one month before his death; former Pro Bowl receiver with Cincinnati (1969-76); hired to coach Vikings' receivers in 1995 and switched to quarterbacks before the 1998 season; guided Randall Cunningham from his backup role to a Pro Bowl appearance in 1998; of a heart attack; in Long Lake, Minn., Feb. 23.

Hal Newhouser, 77; Detroit Tigers Hall of Fame left-hander who won back-to-back MVP awards in 1944 and 1945; a native of Detroit, Newhouser played for his hometown team from 1939-53; won Game 7 of the 1945 World Series; spent two seasons in Cleveland before retiring in 1955 after compiling a 207-150 record and a 3.02 ERA; elected to Baseball Hall of Fame in 1992 and five years later he became just the fourth player in Tigers history to have his number retired; he spent 20 years in banking before returning to baseball as a scout for the Astros; of a long illness; in Detroit, Nov. 10, 1998.

Tom Novak, 72; only four-time all-conference selection in Nebraska football history; played fullback and center and nicknamed "Train Wreck" for his hard hits; elected to Nebraska Football Hall of Fame in 1974; his #60 is the only Cornhuskers number permanently retired by the school; died of a series of long illnesses; in Lincoln, Neb., Nov. 1, 1998.

DeDe Owens, 53; teaching professional at Cog Hill Golf and Country Club in Lemont, Ill. and one of the country's most popular golf instructors; forced to leave LPGA Tour after a brief career due to Hodgkin's disease; joined LPGA Teaching and Club Professional Division in 1974 and began teaching at Cog Hill in 1977; two-time LPGA Teacher of the Year; author of several instructional books; was stricken by a heart attack on May 9 and remained in a coma until her death; in Palos Heights, Ill., May 16.

Kim Perrot, 32; electrifying Houston Comets point guard whose fiery determination led the team to the WNBA's first two league championship titles in 1997 and 1998; joined the Comets as an undrafted developmental player after a tryout for coach Van Chancellor; averaged 7.2 points, 4.0 assists and 2.6 steals a game over two WNBA seasons; defensive player of the year runner up in 1998; played four college seasons with the Ragin' Cajuns at Southwestern Louisiana; led the nation in scoring her senior year; posted six of USL's top seven scoring performances, including a 58-point game against SE Louisiana (2nd best in NCAA history); held 26 school records including career points, assists and steals at the time of her death; played for teams in Germany, Israel, France and Sweden (1990-97); U.S. national team member in 1989-90; of complications from lung cancer; in Houston, Aug. 19.

Herb Porter, 84; a mechanic whose engine work helped drivers like Bobby Unser, Johnny Rutherford and A.J. Foyt win Indianapolis 500 titles; along with partner Rick Long, owned Speedway Engine Development, Inc.; nicknamed "Herbie Horsepower"; died 27 days after suffering critical injuries in an auto accident on May 20, and 26 days after being inducted into the Indianapolis Motor Speedway Hall of Fame; of injuries related to an auto accident; in Indianapolis, June 16.

Harvey Postlethwaite, 55; Formula One car designer and engineer who started on the circuit in 1971; his Ferraris won the constructors title in 1982-83; of a heart attack; in Barcelona, Apr. 13.

Katrina Price, 23; Stephen F. Austin's all-time leading scorer with 2,278 career points and two-time Southland Conference player of the year; a third-team All-America selection her senior season (1997-98); Price averaged 22.1 points and 5.3 rebounds a game; seventh overall pick of the Long Beach StingRays in the 1998 ABL draft, but the team disbanded before she could play a game and was placed on the Philadelphia Rage roster in August; she was a reserve guard, playing in 12 of the Rage's 14 games before the league shut down in late December; of a self-inflicted shotgun wound to the head; in Nacogdoches, Texas, Jan. 18.

Jerry Quarry, 53; popular heavyweight boxer who fought former champions Floyd Patterson and Muhammad Ali; earned $2.1 million as a top contender in the 1960s and 70s; fought Ali when he returned from his banishment from boxing on Oct. 26, 1970; suffered from "dementia pugilistica," a type of brain damage that resembles Alzheimer's disease caused by repeated blows to the head; of cardiac arrest after his family directed doctors to remove him from life support; in Templeton, Calif., Jan. 3.

Joe Redington Sr., 82; founder of the Iditarod Trail Sled Dog Race in 1973; a musher in Alaska for the past 52 years; raced the Iditarod 19 times and finished in the top five as late as 1988, at the age of 71; in celebration of the U.S. bicentennial in 1976, organized the largest dog team on record: a 200-dog team which pulled a bus filled with tourists in Alaska; took a dog team to the summit of Mt. McKinley in 1979; credited with the growth of long distance mushing in South America and Europe; cause of death not given; in Knik, Alaska, June 24.

Pee Wee Reese, 81; Hall of Fame shortstop who was the undisputed leader of the "Boys of Summer," the Brooklyn Dodgers post-WWII teams; born Harold Henry Reese; stood 5-9, 140 pounds during his playing days; his nickname came from a common type of marble called a "pee-wee"; while in the minors was sold to the Dodgers by the Boston Red Sox for $40,000; became a Dodger starter in 1941 and helped the team win its first league title in 21 years; served in the Navy 1942-46; upon his return, teammates and fans became enveloped by his leadership which was exemplified best by his unbiased welcoming of Jackie Robinson, the major league's first black player; eight-time All-Star; won seven N.L. pennants and fielded the final out in Brooklyn's only World Series championship in 1955; retired after the 1957 season ranked No. 1 in Dodger history in runs scored (1,338) and No. 2 in at-bats (8,058) and hits (2,170); served as Dodger coach in 1959; did baseball telecasts for CBS and NBC; elected to National Baseball Hall of Fame in 1984; of lung cancer; in Louisville, Ky., Aug. 14.

Paul Reyna, 19; freshman lineman at Boise State who was injured when he hit his head on the artificial turf during the team's first scrimmage of fall practice; of a blood clot that developed from a torn vessel between his brain and skull; in Boise, Idaho, Aug. 23.

Rich Rice, 39; fastpitch softball player who was inducted into the Central Washington Men's Fastpitch Softball Hall of Fame the day of his death; collapsed during an all-star game following the induction ceremony; in Wenatchee, Wash., Sept. 5.

Cal Ripken Sr., 63; gritty manager, coach and player in the Baltimore Orioles family for 36 years; the only father to manage two sons simultaneously in the majors; began career as a catcher with the Orioles' Phoenix affiliate in 1957; his 13 years as a manager in the Baltimore farm system was the longest of any Orioles manager; managed his sons Cal Jr. and Billy during the 1987-88 season; fired as manager and replaced by Frank Robinson six games into the 1988 season, amidst the team's major league record 21-game losing streak to start the season; won 964 games in the minors and was 67-95 as the Orioles manager in 1987-88; returned to coach third base, retiring after the 1992 season; of lung cancer; in Baltimore, Mar. 25.

Riverman, 30; thoroughbred racehorse who had sired 127 stakes winners at the time of his death, placing him sixth on all-time list; through Aug. 8, 1999 sired 970 foals of racing age, 768 starters and 513 winners; with 10 percent stakes winners from foals accepted industry-wide as excellent, his 13 percent is remarkable; 23 of his 127 stakes winners (18 percent) won a Grade or Group 1 race; most famous sires included Triptych, Irish River and Detroit; euthanized because of complications from colic; in Lexington, Ky., July 31.

Ken Robinson, 29; Arizona Diamondbacks pitcher who missed all of 1998 because of shoulder surgery; appeared in major league games as a reliever with Toronto (1995,1997) and Kansas City (1996); had a major league record of 2-2 with a 3.91 ERA; waived by Toronto and signed by Arizona in February 1998; of injuries sustained in a car accident; in Tucson, Ariz., Feb. 28.

Lloyd (Shorty) Rollins, 69; won the first NASCAR Rookie of the Year Award in 1958; had one victory and 22 top-10 finishes that year; won the first stock car race at the Daytona International Speedway, a 100-lap preliminary run to the first Daytona 500 in 1959; left racing in 1960; in three seasons on the Grand National circuit made 43 starts and earned $17,019; of a brief illness; in Pensacola, Fla., Dec. 28, 1998.

Gene Sarazen, 97; one of the most influential professional golfers of the 20th century who helped establish the Masters as one of the world's greatest golf tournaments; eagled the par-5, 15th hole at Augusta National with a 4-wood from the fairway 235 yards away, earning him the 1935 Masters title and a spot in golfing legend; first golfer to win all four majors in a career; won seven majors in all, including both the U.S. and British Opens in 1932; won 38 PGA titles; led the PGA Tour in earnings in 1930 and 1932; named Associated Press Male Athlete of the Year in 1932; charter member of the World Golf Hall of Fame (1974); won PGA Tour's first Lifetime Achievement Award in 1996; from 1981-99 joined Byron Nelson and Sam Snead in hitting a ceremonial tee shot before each Masters tournament; credited with the invention of the sand wedge when he debuted the club at the British Open in 1932; from complications of pneumonia; in Naples, Fla., May 13.

Elizabeth (Betty) Robinson Schwartz, 87; became first woman to win an Olympic gold medal in track when she won the 100-meter dash in a then-world-record 12.2 seconds; injuries she sustained in a 1931 plane crash nearly ended her career; no longer able to crouch down for the sprint position, she switched to relays; won gold in 4x100m relay at 1936 games in Berlin; inducted into National Track & Field Hall of Fame in 1977; of cancer (had Alzheimer's disease); in Denver, Colo., May 18.

Eva Shain, 81; boxing judge who became the first woman to score a heavyweight championship fight at the Muhammad Ali–Earnie Shavers fight in 1977; earned professional license in 1975; judged more than 5,000 fights; retired in December of 1998; married to ring announcer Frank Shain; of cancer; in Englewood, N.J., Aug. 19.

Fritz Shurmur, 67; innovative and well-respected defensive coordinator for five NFL teams over two decades; instrumental in Green Bay's run to consecutive Super Bowls after the 1996 and 1997 seasons; began coaching in 1954 as a grad assistant at his alma mater Albion (Mich.) College; defensive coach at Univ. of Wyoming and later head coach from 1971-74; coached in the NFL at Detroit, New England, Los Angeles (Rams) and Phoenix before joining the Packers in 1994; followed Packers coach Mike Holmgren to Seattle in January of 1999; held a master's degree in education and wrote four books on defense; received an honorary doctorate from Albion in 1997; of cancer; in Green Bay, Wisc., Aug. 30.

Tody Smith, 50; defensive tackle who played for Dallas in the 1972 Super Bowl and younger brother of NFL star Bubba Smith; first-round pick of the Cowboys in 1971; his six-year career also included stints with Houston and Buffalo; played for USC from 1969-70 after transferring from Michigan St.; member of the "Wild Bunch," a defensive front that helped lead the Trojans to a 10-0-1 record and 10-3 victory over Michigan in the Rose Bowl in 1970; cause of death not given; in Los Angeles, July 18.

Eddie Stanky, 82; feisty second baseman who won N.L. pennants with Brooklyn, Boston and New York and later coached South Alabama to five NCAA Tournament appearances; nicknamed "The Brat "for his win-at-all-costs attitude on the field; batted .268 with 29 homers and 365 RBI in 11 major league seasons with five teams; led the N.L. in walks twice and runs scored once; managed the St. Louis Cardinals (1952-55) and Chicago White Sox (1966-68), plus the Texas Rangers for one game in 1977; a coach who preached the importance fundamentals, he often rewarded players with gifts such as suits and alligator-skin shoes for pitching a complete game or catching a pop fly with one's feet properly planted; South Alabama was ranked No. 1 in the nation twice and won two conference titles during his tenure; retired in 1983 with a 488-193 career collegiate coaching record; elected to Alabama Sports Hall of Fame in 1977; of a heart attack; in Fairhope, Ala., June 6.

(William) Payne Stewart, 42; PGA Tour golfer and defending U.S. Open champion who was killed when a plane on which he was flying crashed in South Dakota; a charismatic, free-spirit since he joined the Tour in 1981, Stewart could be recognized by his trademark knickers; won 11 career PGA Tour tournaments, including two U.S. Open titles (1991 and 1999) and a PGA Championship in 1989; compiled an 8-8-2 record in five Ryder Cup tournament appearances; won three consecutive Skins Games (1991-93); played 20 events in 1999 and was ranked eighth in the world; had two wins, two second-place finishes and was third on the 1999 money list; also third on the PGA Tour career earnings list with $11,737,008; in Mina, S.D., Oct. 25.

George (Birdie) Tebbetts, 86; a lifelong "baseball guy" who played catcher for Detroit and Boston, managed Cincinnati and Milwaukee and did both in Cleveland; batted .270 lifetime and played in 1,162 games, including four All-Star games; his record as a manager was 748-705; a heart attack in 1965 ended his career as a manager and moved him into scouting in 1968; was given his nickname by his grandmother who said of his high-pitched voice, "he chirps like a bird"; of congestive heart failure; in Bradenton, Fla., Mar. 24.

Dimitri Tertyshny, 22; rookie defenseman for the Philadelphia Flyers; scored two goals and had eight assists in 1998-99 season; drafted by the Flyers in the sixth round in 1995; bled to death after falling off a boat and being cut by the propeller; in Kelowna, British Columbia, Canada, July 23.

Bob Thurman, 81; former Negro League and major league outfielder in the 1940s and 50s; spent five seasons with the Cincinnati Reds; joined the Negro leagues in 1946 and played for the Homestead Grays and Kansas City Monarchs; played 11 seasons with the Santurce (Puerto Rico) Crabs and in 1992 was elected to the Puerto Rican Baseball Hall of Fame; cause of death not given; in Wichita, Kan., Nov. 4, 1998.

Whitney Tower, 75; longtime horse racing journalist and former chairman of the National Racing Museum and Hall of Fame; joined the staff of the *Cincinnati Enquirer* as a sports reporter in 1948, but left in 1954 to join a start-up called *Sports Illustrated* and held the position of turf editor for 22 years; left to become editor of *Classic* magazine; won NTRA award for magazine writing in 1967 and Eclipse Awards in 1976-77; was president of the National Museum of Racing for eight years; spent 10 more years as chairman, supervising its expansion to include the Hall of Fame; of complications from a stroke; in Saratoga Springs, N.Y., Feb. 11.

Mark Tuinei, 39; offensive lineman who helped the Dallas Cowboys win Super Bowls in 1993, 1994 and 1996; played 15 seasons in the NFL, including all but nine games between 1989-96; came to the Cowboys as an undrafted defensive lineman from Hawaii in 1983; moved to offensive line in 1985 and became a starter in 1987; played in two Pro Bowls (1994, 1995); teammates nicknamed him "Tui"; was released by the team in April 1998 after lingering knee injuries caught up to him after the 1997 season; from overdosing on a mix of heroin and a stimulant; in Plano, Texas, May 6.

Jim Turner, 95; longtime New York Yankees pitching coach who spent a record 51 consecutive years in professional baseball; played in or coached in 13 World Series; broke into the minor leagues in 1922 and 12 years later joined the major leagues as a pitcher for the Boston Bees; appeared as a player in the World Series with Cincinnati in 1940 and 1942 with the Yankees; had two coaching stints with the Yankees from 1949-59 and 1966-73; nicknamed "The Milkman" because of his off-season job delivering milk; of a long illness; in Nashville, Tenn., Nov. 29, 1998.

Elmer Vasko, 62; member of the last Chicago Blackhawks team to win a Stanley Cup in 1962; earned his nickname "Moose" from Chicago fans because of his 6-3, 220 pound-frame; as a defenseman from 1956-66, scored 32 goals and had 153 assists in 641 games; of cancer; in Chicago, Oct. 30. 1998.

Harry (The Hat) Walker, 80; left-handed outfielder who won the National League batting title in 1947 and had the deciding hit in the 1946 World Series; nicknamed "The Hat" for his habit of adjusting his cap between pitches; played 11 seasons in the majors including eight with the St. Louis Cardinals; hit a double to left center in the bottom of the eighth, scoring Enos Slaughter, giving the Cardinals the title over the Red Sox in 1946; appeared in three World Series and two All-Star Games; managed for 20 seasons with St. Louis, Pittsburgh and Houston; first head coach of University of Alabama-Birmingham baseball team; won two Sun Belt North Division titles and had an eight-year record of 211-175; of complications from a stroke; in Birmingham, Ala., Aug. 8.

Herman Wedemeyer, 74; an All-American running back at St. Mary's (Calif.) who later became a regular on TV's "Hawaii 5-0"; nicknamed "Squirmin' Herman" and "Hula-hipped Hawaiian"; Grantland Rice called him the most outstanding football player of 1945; first-round pick of the Los Angeles Dons of the All-America Football Conference, an injury cut short his career, returned to Hawaii where he later entered politics; elected to the Honolulu city council in 1968 and then the Hawaii House of Representatives in 1970 and again in 1972; played the role of Edward D. "Duke" Lukela on "Hawaii 5-0," appearing in more than 300 episodes; longtime volunteer with the Hawaiian Open golf tournament; cause of death was not given; in Honolulu, Jan. 25.

Charlie Whittingham, 86; three-time Eclipse Award winning trainer who at age 73 became the oldest to saddle a Kentucky Derby winner (Ferdinand 1986) and at 76 the oldest to saddle a Preakness winner (Sunday Silence 1989); prepared more than 2,500 winners during a career that spanned 62 years; more than 20 of the horses he trained topped $1 million in career earnings; held the national earnings title seven times (1970-73, 1975 and 1981-82); won Eclipse Awards as top trainer in 1971, 1982, 1989; inducted into horse racing's hall of fame in 1974; of leukemia; in Pasadena, Calif., Apr. 20.

Doug Wickenheiser, 37; St. Louis Blues center from 1983-87, best remembered for his overtime playoff goal in 1986 that became known as the "Monday Night Miracle"; on May 12, 1986 St. Louis rallied for three goals to force overtime against Calgary in Game 6 of the Campbell Conference Finals and Wickenheiser added the winner at 7:30 of the extra period; scored 111 goals and had 156 assists in 556 games over a 10-season career that also included stops with Montreal, Vancouver, the N.Y. Rangers and Washington from 1980-90; his battle with cancer and #14 jersey became an inspiration for the team during the two seasons prior to his death; of cancer; in St. Louis, Jan. 12.

Cleveland (Big Cat) Williams, 66; heavyweight boxer who overcame serious injuries to become a top contender in the 1960s; lost in the third round to Muhammad Ali in 1966; according to police, a state trooper's gun went off on the night of Nov. 29, 1964 after he and Williams started fighting during a traffic stop. The bullet left Williams with lifelong kidney problems; inducted into the World Boxing Hall of Fame in 1997; of injuries he suffered in an auto-pedestrian accident; in Houston, Sept. 10.

Whitlow Wyatt, 91; hard-throwing right-hander who won 22 games in 1941 and helped the Brooklyn Dodgers win their first league title in 21 years; won 70 games for Dodgers from 1940-43; broke in with the Tigers in 1929 but injuries held him to just 26 wins over nine seasons and three teams; retired in 1945 with a 106-95 career record; served as pitching coach for Philadelphia, Milwaukee and Atlanta and managed in the minor leagues; cause of death not given; in Carrollton, Ga., July 16.

Early Wynn, 79; Hall of Fame pitcher who recorded at least 20 victories in a season five times on his way to winning 300 career games; broke into the majors with the Washington Senators in 1939; went 23-11 in 1954 with the Cleveland Indians and won the A.L. pennant; won Cy Young Award in 1959 with the Chicago White Sox; returned to the Indians in 1963 at age 43 and won his 300th game on July 13; served as a pitching coach for Cleveland and Minnesota; inducted into the National Baseball Hall of Fame in 1972; cause of death not given; in Sarasota, Fla., Mar. 4.

Tiffany Young, 21; reserve guard on Purdue's 1999 NCAA national champion women's basketball team; averaged 3.3 points and 1.5 rebounds a game in her three-year career; started all 33 games during the Boilermakers' 1997-98 season; career highs: 16 points, seven rebounds; physical therapy major; named to the Academic All-Big 10 team during the 1998-99 season; of injuries sustained in a car accident caused by a drunk driver; in Gary, Ind., Aug. 1.

Norm Zauchin, 69; first baseman for Boston and Washington in six major league seasons; best known for driving in 10 runs with three home runs and a double in five innings during a 16-0 victory over Washington on May 27, 1955; finished third in A.L. Rookie of the Year voting in 1955; hit 35 home runs as a rookie in 1950 with the Birmingham Barons; of a long illness; in Birmingham, Ala., Jan. 31.

RESEARCH MATERIAL

Many sources were used in the gathering of information for this almanac. Day to day material was almost always found in copies of *USA Today*, *The Boston Globe*, and *The New York Times* or online at various world wide web addresses (see below).

Several weekly and bi-weekly periodicals were also used in the past year's pursuit of facts and figures, among them— *Baseball America*, *International Boxing Digest*, *ESPN the Magazine*, *FIFA News* (Soccer), *The Hockey News*, *The NCAA News*, *On Track*, *Soccer America*, *Sports Illustrated*, *The Sporting News*, *Track & Field News*, and *USA Today Baseball Weekly*.

In addition, the following books provided background material for one or more chapters of the almanac.

Arenas & Ballparks

The Ballparks, by Bill Shannon and George Kalinsky; Hawthorn Books, Inc. (1975); New York.

Diamonds, by Michael Gershman; Houghton Mifflin Co. (1993); Boston.

Green Cathedrals (Revised Edition), by Philip Lowry; Addison-Wesley Publishing Co. (1992); Reading, Mass.

The NFL's Encyclopedic History of Professional Football, Macmillan Publishing Co. (1977); New York.

Take Me Out to the Ballpark, by Lowell Reidenbaugh; The Sporting News Publishing Co. (1983); St. Louis.

24 Seconds to Shoot (An Informal History of the NBA), by Leonard Koppett; Macmillan Publishing Co. (1968); New York.

Plus many major league baseball, NBA, NFL, NHL league and team guides, and college football and basketball guides.

Auto Racing

Indy: 75 Years of Racing's Greatest Spectacle, by Rich Taylor; St. Martin's Press (1991); New York.

1999 CART FedEx Championship Series Media Guide; Championship Auto Racing Teams; Troy, Mich.

1999 Pep Boys Indy Racing League Media Guide, by IMS Publications; Indianapolis.

1999 Winston Cup Media Guide, compiled and edited by Sports Marketing Enterprises; NASCAR Winston Cup Series; Winston-Salem, N.C.

Marlboro Grand Prix Guide, 1950-98 (1999 Edition), compiled by Jacques Deschenaux and Claude Michele Deschenaux; Charles Stewart & Company Ltd; Brentford, England.

NASCAR Online, produced by Starwave Corp. and ESPN Inc.http://www.nascar.com

CART Online, maintained by CART and Quokkasports http://www.cart.com

Baseball

The All-Star Game (A Pictorial History, 1933 to Present), by Donald Honig; The Sporting News Publishing Co. (1987); St. Louis.

1999 American League Red Book, published by The Sporting News Publishing Co.; St. Louis.

The Baseball Chronology, edited by James Charlton; Macmillian Publishing Co. (1991); New York.

The Baseball Encyclopedia (Ninth Edition), editorial director, Rick Wolff; Macmillan Publishing Co. (1993); New York.

The Complete 1999 Baseball Record Book, edited by Craig Carter; The Sporting News Publishing Co.; St. Louis.

1999 National League Green Book, published by The Sporting News Publishing Co.; St. Louis.

The Scrapbook History of Baseball by Jordan Deutsch, Richard Cohen, Roland Johnson and David Neft; Bobbs-Merrill Company, Inc. (1975); Indianapolis/New York.

1999 Sporting News Official Baseball Guide, edited by Craig Carter and Dave Sloan; The Sporting News Publishing Co.; St. Louis.

1999 Sporting News Official Baseball Register, edited by Mark Bonavita and Brendan Roberts; The Sporting News Publishing Co.; St. Louis.

The Sports Encyclopedia: Baseball (1996 Edition), edited by David Neft and Richard Cohen; St. Martin's Press; New York.

Total Baseball (Fourth Edition), edited by John Thorn and Pete Palmer; HarperPerennial (1995); New York.

The Official Site of Major League Baseball, produced by Major League Baseball Properties, Inc. http://www.majorleaguebaseball.com

College Basketball

All the Moves (A History of College Basketball), by Neil D. Issacs; J.B. Lippincott Company (1975); New York.

College Basketball, U.S.A. (Since 1892), by John D. McCallum; Stein and Day (1978); New York.

Collegiate Basketball: Facts and Figures on the Cage Sport, by Edwin C. Caudle; The Paragon Press (1960); Montgomery, Ala.

The Encyclopedia of the NCAA Basketball Tournament, written and compiled by Jim Savage; Dell Publishing (1990); New York.

The Final Four (Reliving America's Basketball Classic), compiled by Billy Reed; Host Communications Inc. (1988); Lexington, Ky.

1997 NCAA Final Four Records Book, compiled by Gary Johnson; edited by Stephen R. Hagwell; NCAA Books; Overland Park, Kan.

The Modern Encyclopedia of Basketball (Second Revised Edition), edited by Zander Hollander; Dolphins Books (1979); Doubleday & Company, Inc.; Garden City, N.Y.

1999 NCAA Men's Records Book, compiled by Gary Johnson and Sean Straziscar; edited by Marty Benson; NCAA Books; Overland Park, Kan.

1999 NCAA Women's Records Book, compiled by Richard M. Campbell and Jenifer L. Scheibler; edited by Vanessa L. Abell; NCAA Books; Overland Park, Kan.

NCAA Online, produced by National Collegiate Athletic Association. http://www.ncaa.org

Plus many 1998-99 NCAA Division I conference guides from America East to the WAC.

Pro Basketball

The Official NBA Basketball Encyclopedia (Second Edition), edited by Alex Sachare; Villard Books (1994); New York.

1997-98 Sporting News Official NBA Guide, edited by Mark Broussard and Craig Carter; The Sporting News Publishing Co.; St. Louis.

1997-98 Sporting News Official NBA Register, edited by Mark Bonavita, Mark Broussard and Sean Stewart; The Sporting News Publishing Co.; St. Louis.

NBA Online, produced by Starwave Corp. http://www.nba.com

Bowling

1995 Bowlers Journal Annual & Almanac; Luby Publishing; Chicago.

1999 PWBA Guide, Professional Women's Bowling Association; Rockford, Ill.

1999 PBA Media Guide; Professional Bowlers Association; Akron, Ohio.

PBA Online, produced by the Pro Bowlers Association, http://www.pbatour.com

PWBA Online, produced by Professional Women's Bowling Association, http://www.pwba.com

Boxing

The Boxing Record Book (1996), edited by Phill Marder; Fight Fax Inc.; Sicklerville, N.J.

The Ring 1985 Record Book & Boxing Encyclopedia, edited by Herbert G. Goldman; The Ring Publishing Corp.; New York.

The Ring: Boxing, The 20th Century, Steven Farhood, editor-in-chief; BDD Illustrated Books (1993); New York.

College Sports

1994-95 National Collegiate Championships, edited by Ted Breidenthal; NCAA Books; Overland Park, Kan.

1996-97 NAIA Championships History and Records Book; National Assn. of Intercollegiate Athletics; Tulsa, Okla.

1996-97 National Directory of College Athletics, edited by Kevin Cleary; Collegiate Directories, Inc.; Cleveland.

NCAA Online, produced by National Collegiate Athletic Association. http://www.ncaa.org

College Football

Football: A College History, by Tom Perrin; McFarland & Company, Inc. (1987); Jefferson, N.C.

Football: Facts & Figures, by Dr. L.H. Baker; Farrar & Rinehart, Inc. (1945); New York.

Great College Football Coaches of the Twenties and Thirties, by Tim Cohane; Arlington House (1973); New Rochelle, N.Y.

1998 NCAA College Football Records Book, compiled by Richard Campbell, John Painter and Sean Straziscar; edited by Ted Breidenthal; NCAA Books; Overland Park, Kan.

Saturday Afternoon, by Richard Whittingham; Workman Publishing Co., Inc. (1985); New York.

Saturday's America, by Dan Jenkins; Sports Illustrated Books; Little, Brown & Company (1970); Boston.

Tournament of Roses, The First 100 Years, by Joe Hendrickson; Knapp Press (1989); Los Angeles.

NCAA Online, produced by National Collegiate Athletic Association. http://www.ncaa.org

Plus numerous college football team and conference guides, especially the 1998 guides compiled by the Atlantic Coast Conference, Big 12 and Southeastern Conference.

Pro Football

1998 Canadian Football League Guide, compiled by the CFL Communications Dept.; Toronto.

The Football Encyclopedia (The Complete History of NFL Football from 1892 to the Present), compiled by David Neft and Richard Cohen; St. Martin's Press (1994); New York.

The Official NFL Encyclopedia, by Beau Riffenburgh; New American Library (1986); New York.

Official NFL 1996 Record and Fact Book, compiled by the NFL Communications Dept. and Seymour Siwoff, Elias Sports Bureau; edited by Chris McCloskey and Chuck Garrity Jr.; produced by NFL Properties, Inc.; Los Angeles.

The Scrapbook History of Pro Football, by Richard Cohen, Jordan Deutsch, Roland Johnson and David Neft; Bobbs-Merrill Company, Inc. (1976); Indianapolis/New York.

1998 Sporting News Football Guide, edited by Craig Carter and Dave Sloan; The Sporting News Publishing Co.; St. Louis.

1998 Sporting News Football Register, edited Mark Bonavita and Sean Stewart; The Sporting News Publishing Co.; St. Louis.

1995 Sporting News Super Bowl Book, edited by Tom Dienhart, Joe Hoppel and Dave Sloan; The Sporting News Publishing Co.; St. Louis.

NFL.Com, produced by Starwave Corp. http://www.nfl.com

CFL Online, produced by SLAM! Sports. http://www.cfl.ca

Golf

The Encyclopedia of Golf (Revised Edition), compiled by Nevin H. Gibson; A.S. Barnes and Company (1964); New York.

Guinness Golf Records: Facts and Champions, by Donald Steel; Guinness Superlatives Ltd. (1987); Middlesex, England.

The History of the PGA Tour, by Al Barkow; Doubleday (1989); New York.

The Illustrated History of Women's Golf, by Rhonda Glenn, Taylor Publishing Co. (1991); Dallas.

1999 LPGA Player Guide, produced by LPGA Communications Dept.; Ladies Professional Golf Assn. Tour; Daytona Beach, Fla.

1999 PGA Tour Guide, written and edited by Chuck Adams, James Cramer, Lee Patterson, Dave Senko and Jamie Wiles; Professional Golfers Assn. Tour; Ponte Vedra, Fla.

Official Guide of the PGA Championships; Triumph Books (1994); Chicago.

The PGA World Golf Hall of Fame Book, by Gerald Astor, Prentice Hall Press (1991); New York.

1999 Senior PGA Tour Guide, written and edited by Dave Lancer, Dave Senko and Phil Stambaugh; Professional Golfers Assn. Tour; Ponte Vedra, Fla.

Pro-Golf 1999, PGA European Tour Media Guide, Virginia Water, Surrey, England.

The Random House International Encyclopedia of Golf, by Malcolm Campbell; Random House (1991); New York.

USGA Record Books (1895-1959, 1960-80 and 1981-90); U.S. Golf Association; Far Hills, N.J.

LPGA.com, produced by the LPGA and Black Dog Design Co., http://www.lpga.com

PGA.com, produced by the PGA of America, http://www.pgaonline.com

PGATour.com, produced by PGA Tour Inc., http://www.pgatour.com

Hockey

Canada Cup '87: The Official History, No.1 Publications Ltd.; Toronto.

The Complete Encyclopedia of Hockey; edited by Zander Hollander; Visible Ink Press (1993); Detroit.

The Hockey Encyclopedia, by Stan Fischler and Shirley Walton Fischler; research editor, Bob Duff; Macmillan Publishing Co. (1983); New York.

Hockey Hall of Fame (The Official History of the Game and Its Greatest Stars), by Dan Diamond and Joseph Romain; Doubleday (1988); New York.

The National Hockey League, by Edward F. Dolan Jr.; W H Smith Publishers Inc. (1986); New York.

The Official National Hockey League 75th Anniversary Commemorative Book, edited by Dan Diamond; McClelland & Stewart, Inc. (1991); Toronto.

1998-99 Official NHL Guide & Record Book, compiled by the NHL Public Relations Dept.; New York/Montreal/Toronto.

1997-98 Sporting News Hockey Guide, edited by Craig Carter; The Sporting News Publishing Co.; St. Louis.

1997-98 Sporting News Hockey Register, edited by Mark Bonavita and Sean Stewart; The Sporting News Publishing Co.; St. Louis.

The Stanley Cup, by Joseph Romain and James Duplacey; Gallery Books (1989); New York.

The Trail of the Stanley Cup (Volumns I-III), by Charles L. Coleman; Progressive Publications Inc. (1969); Sherbrooke, Quebec.

NHL.com, produced by the NHL Interactive Cyber Enterprises, http://www.nhl.com

Horse Racing

1999 NTRA Media Guide, compiled by the National Thoroughbred Racing Association; New York City

1997 American Racing Manual, compiled by the Daily Racing Form; Hightstown, N.J.

1997 Breeders' Cup Statistics; Breeders' Cup Limited; Lexington, Ky.

1996 Directory and Record Book, Thoroughbred Racing Associations of North America Inc.; Elkton, Md.

1996 Trotting and Pacing Guide, compiled and edited by John Pawlak; United States Trotting Association; Columbus, Ohio.

USTA online, produced by the USTA, http://www.ustrotting.com

NTRA online, hosted by Equibase, http://www.ntraracing.com

International Sports

Athletics: A History of Modern Track and Field (1860-1990, Men and Women), by Roberto Quercetani; Vallardi & Associati (1990); Milan, Italy.

1999 International Track & Field Annual, Association of Track & Field Statisticians; edited by Peter Matthews; SportsBooks Ltd.; Surrey, England.

Track & Field News' Little Blue Book; Metric conversion tables; From the editors of Track & Field News (1989); Los Altos, Calif.

US Ski Team online, produced by US Ski Team and SportsLine USA, http://www.usskiteam.com

Miscellaneous

The America's Cup 1851-1987 (Sailing for Supremacy), by Gary Lester and Richard Sleeman; Lester-Townsend Publishing (1986); Sydney, Australia.

The Encyclopedia of Sports (Fifth Revised Edition), by Frank G. Menke; revisions by Suzanne Treat; A.S. Barnes and Co., Inc. (1975); Cranbury, N.J.

The Great American Sports Book, by George Gipe; Doubleday & Company, Inc. (1978); Garden City, N.Y.

The 1999 Time/Information Please Almanac, edited by Borgna Brunner; Information Please, LLC; Boston.

1998 Official PRCA Media Guide, edited by Steve Fleming; Professional Rodeo Cowboys Association; Colorado Springs.

The Sail Magazine Book of Sailing, by Peter Johnson; Alfred A. Knopf (1989); New York.

Ten Years of the Ironman, Triathlete Magazine; October, 1988; Santa Monica, Calif.

The Ultimate Book of Sports Lists, by Mike Meserole; DK Publishing (1999); New York.

Iditarod online, produced by the Iditarod Trail Committtee and GCI, http://www.iditarod.com

PRCA online, produced by the Pro Rodeo Cowboys Association, http://www.prorodeo.com

Olympics

All That Glitters Is Not Gold (An Irreverent Look at the Olympic Games); by William O. Johnson, Jr.; G.P. Putnam's Sons (1972); New York.

Barcelona/Albertville 1992; edited by Lisa H. Albertson; for U.S. Olympic Committee by Commemorative Publications; Salt Lake City.

Chamonix to Lillehammer (The Glory of the Olympic Winter Games); edited by Lisa H. Albertson; for U.S. Olympic Committee by Commemorative Publication (1994); Salt Lake City.

The Complete Book of the Olympics (1992 Edition); by David Wallechinsky; Little, Brown and Co.; Boston.

The Games Must Go On (Avery Brundage and the Olympic Movement), by Allen Guttmann; Columbia University Press (1984); New York.

The Golden Book of the Olympic Games, edited by Erich Kamper and Bill Mallon; Vallardi & Associati (1992); Milan, Italy.

Hitler's Games (The 1936 Olympics), by Duff Hart-Davis; Harper & Row (1986); New York/London.

An Illustrated History of the Olympics (Third Edition); by Dick Schaap; Alfred A. Knopf (1975); New York.

The Nazi Olympics, by Richard D. Mandell; Souvenir Press (1972); London.

The Official USOC Book of the 1984 Olympic Games, by Dick Schaap; Random House/ABC Sports; New York.

The Olympics: A History of the Games, by William Oscar Johnson; Oxmoor House (1992); Birmingham, Ala.

Pursuit of Excellence (The Olympic Story), by The Associated Press and Grolier; Grolier Enterprises Inc. (1979); Danbury, Conn.

The Story of the Olympic Games (776 B.C. to 1948 A.D.), by John Kieran and Arthur Daley; J.B. Lippincott Company (1948); Philadelphia/New York.

United States Olympic Books (Seven Editions): 1936 and 1948-88; U.S. Olympic Association; New York.

The USA and the Olympic Movement, produced by the USOC Information Dept.; edited by Gayle Plant; U.S. Olympic Committee (1988); Colorado Springs.

Soccer

The American Encyclopedia of Soccer, edited by Zander Hollander; Everest House Publishers (1980); New York.

The European Football Yearbook (1994-95 Edition), edited by Mike Hammond; Sports Projects Ltd; West Midlands, England.

The Guinness Book of Soccer Facts & Feats, by Jack Rollin; Guinness Superlatives Ltd. (1978); Middlesex, England.

History of Soccer's World Cup, by Michael Archer; Chartwell Books, Inc. (1978); Secaucus, N.J.

The Simplest Game, by Paul Gardner; Collier Books (1994); New York.

The Story of the World Cup, by Brian Glanville; Faber and Faber Limited (1993); London/Boston.

1999 MLS Official Media Guide, edited by the MLS Communications staff; Los Angeles.

1991-92 MSL Official Guide, Major (Indoor) Soccer League; Overland Park, Kan.

FIFA online, produced by FIFA, http://www.fifa.com

MLSnet, produced by Major League Soccer, http://mlsnet.com

Tennis

Bud Collins' Modern Encyclopedia of Tennis, edited by Bud Collins and Zander Hollander; Visible Ink Press (1994); Detroit.

The Illustrated Encyclopedia of World Tennis, by John Haylett and Richard Evans; Exeter Books (1989); New York.

Official Encyclopedia of Tennis, edited by the staff of the U.S. Lawn Tennis Assn.; Harper & Row (1972); New York.

1999 ATP Tour Player Guide, edited by Greg Sharko; Association of Tennis Professionals Tour Publications; Ponte Vedra Beach, Fla.

1999 WTA Tour Media Guide, compiled by WTA Public Relations staff; edited by Jaye Cavallo and Toni Woods; St. Petersburg, Fla.

ATP Tour online, produced by ATP Tour, Inc., http://www.atptour.com

WTA Tour Site, produced by the WTA Tour, http://www.wtatour.com

Who's Who

The Guiness International Who's Who of Sport, edited by Peter Mathews, Ian Buchanan and Bill Mallon; Guiness Publishing (1993); Middlesex, England

101 Greatest Athletes of the Century, by Will Grimsley and the Associated Press Sports Staff; Bonanza Books (1987); Crown Publishers, Inc.; New York.

The New York Times Book of Sports Legends, edited by Joseph Vecchione; Simon & Schuster (1991); New York.

Superstars, by Frank Litsky; Vineyard Books, Inc. (1975); Secaucus, N.J.

A Who's Who of Sports Champions (Their Stories and Records), by Ralph Hickok, Houghton Mifflin Co. (1995); Boston.

Other Reference Books/Sites

Facts & Dates of American Sports, by Gorton Carruth & Eugene Ehrlich; Harper & Row, Publishers, Inc. (1988); New York.

Sports Market Place 1997 (January edition), edited by Kevin J. Myers; Franklin Quest Sports; Phoenix, Ariz.

The World Book Encyclopedia (1988 Edition); World Book, Inc.; Chicago.

The World Book Yearbook (Annual Supplements, 1954-95); World Book, Inc.; Chicago.

ESPN.com, produced by ESPN and Starwave Corp., http://ESPN.go.com

CBS SportsLine, produced by CBS and SportsLine USA, http://www.sportsline.com

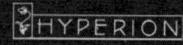